MAIN CITIES OF EUROPE

2004

Selection of hotels and restaurants

Sélection d'hôtels et de restaurants

Auswahl an Hotels und Restaurants

Selezione di alberghi e ristoranti

Selección de hoteles y restaurantes

Main Cities of Europe

Dear Reader

The Michelin Guide offers a selection of the best hotels and restaurants in many categories of comfort and price. It is compiled by a team of professionally trained inspectors who travel the country visiting new establishments as well as those already listed in the guide. Their mission is to check the quality and consistency of the amenities and service provided by the hotels and restaurants throughout the year. The inspectors are full-time Michelin employees and their assessments, made anonymously, are therefore completely impartial and independent.

The amenities found in each establishment are indicated by symbols, an international language which enables you to see at a glance whether a hotel has a car park or swimming pool. To take full advantage of the wealth of information contained in the guide, consult the introduction. A short descriptive text complements the symbols.

Entry in the Michelin Guide is completely free of charge and every year the proprietors of those establishments listed complete a questionnaire giving the opening times and prices for the coming year. Nearly 100,000 pieces of information are updated for each annual edition.

Our readers also contribute through the 45,000 letters and e-mails received annually commenting on hotels and restaurants throughout Europe.

Thank you for your support and please continue to send us your comments. We hope you enjoy travelling with the Michelin Guide 2004.

Contents

In addition to those situated in the main cities, restaurants renowned for their excellent cuisine will be found in the towns printed in light type in the list above.

How the Guide Works

With the aim of giving the maximum amount of information in a limited number of pages Michelin has adopted a system of symbols complemented by short descriptive texts, which is renowned the world over.
Without this system the present publication would run to several volumes.
Judge for yourselves by comparing the descriptive text below with the equivalent extract from the Guide.
In the following example prices are quoted in euro (€).

La Résidence (Paul) , 09 18 21 32 43, laresidence@wanadoo.fr
Fax 09 18 21 32 49, lake, ,
 - . BX **a**
March-November – **Meals** *(closed Sunday)* 53.50/99 – 11.60 – **25 rm** 76/122.
◆ A 19c villa on a hillside surrounded by woodland. Ornate panelled dining room overlooking gardens. Bedrooms all have antiques and private patios.
Spec. Goujonnettes de sole. Poulet aux écrevisses. Profiteroles.
Wines. Vouvray, Bourgueil.

This demonstration clearly shows that each entry contains a great deal of information. The symbols are easily learnt and knowing them will enable you to understand the Guide. The text provides a further summary, enabling you to choose which establishments meet your needs.

A very comfortable hotel where you will enjoy a pleasant stay and be tempted to prolong your visit. The excellence of the cuisine, which is personally supervised by the proprietor Mr Paul, is worth a detour on your journey. The hotel is in a quiet secluded setting, away from built-up areas.
To make a reservation phone 09 18 21 32 43 or e-mail laresidence@wanadoo.fr ; the Fax number is 09 18 21 32 49.
The hotel affords a fine view of the lake ; in good weather it is possible to eat outdoors.
The hotel has an indoor swimming pool and a private tennis court. Smoking is not allowed in certain areas of the hotel. Parking facilities, under cover, are available to hotel guests. The hotel accepts payment by MasterCard, American Express, and Japan Credit Bureau credit cards. Letters giving the location of the hotel on the town plan : BX **a**
The hotel is open from March to November but the restaurant closes every Sunday.
The set meal prices range from 53.50 € for the lowest to 99 € for the highest.
The cost of continental breakfast served in the bedroom is 11.60 €. 25 bedroomed hotel. The high season charges vary from 76 € for a single to 122 € for the best double or twin bedded room. Included for the gourmet are some culinary specialities, recommended by the hotelier : Strips of deep-fried sole fillets, Chicken with crayfish, Choux pastry balls filled with ice cream and covered with chocolate sauce. In addition to the best quality wines you will find many of the local wines worth sampling : Vouvray, Bourgueil.

Hotels, Restaurants

Categories, standard of comfort

	Luxury in the traditional style
	Top class comfort
	Very comfortable
	Comfortable
	Quite comfortable
	Other recommended accommodation
	Traditional pubs serving food
	Tapas bars
without rest	*The hotel has no restaurant*
with rm	*The restaurant also offers accommodation*
	The **"Bib Hotel"** *: Good accommodation at moderate prices*

Atmosphere and setting

...	*Pleasant hotels*
...	*Pleasant restaurants*
	Very quiet or quiet secluded hotel
	Quiet hotel
sea,	*Exceptional view, Panoramic view*
	Interesting or extensive view

Cuisine

	Exceptional cuisine in the country, worth a special journey
	Excellent cooking : worth a detour
	A very good restaurant in its category
Meals	*The* **"Bib Gourmand"** *: Good food at moderate prices*
	A particularly interesting wine list

Hotel facilities

30 rm	*Number of rooms*
	Lift (elevator) – Television in room
	Non-smoking areas
	Air conditioning
	Minitel – modem point in the bedrooms
	Tennis court(s) – Outdoor or indoor swimming pool
	Sauna – Exercise room – Wellness centre
	Garden – Park – Beach with bathing facilities
	Meals served in garden or on terrace
	Landing stage
P	*Valet parking – Garage – Car park, enclosed parking*
	Bedrooms accessible to people of restricted mobility
	Special facilities for children
150	*Equipped conference room : maximum capacity*
	Dogs are not allowed

Prices

These prices are given in the currency of the country in question. Valid for 2004 the rates shown should only vary if the cost of living changes to any great extent.

Meals

Meals 40/56	*Set meal prices*
Meals a la carte 48/64	*"a la carte" meal prices*
	Restaurants offering lower priced pre and/or post theatre menus
b.i.	*House wine included*
	Table wine available by the carafe
	Wine served by the glass

Hotels

30 rm 120/239	*Lowest price for a comfortable single and highest price for the best double room.*
30 rm 60/120 140/239	*In Germany and Austria the prices relate to the lowest/highest price for single rooms and the lowest/highest price for double rooms, breakfast included.*
30 rm 135/270	*Price includes breakfast*

Breakfast

16	*Price of breakfast*

Credit cards

MC AE GB JCB VISA	*Credit cards accepted*

Service and Taxes

Except in Greece, Hungary, Poland and Spain, prices shown are inclusive, that is to say service and V.A.T. included. In the U.K. and Ireland, s = service included. In Italy, when not included, a percentage for service is shown after the meal prices, eg. (16 %).

Town Plans

Main conventional signs

- Tourist Information Centre
- Hotel, restaurant – Reference letter on the town plan
- Place of interest and its main entrance } Reference letter on the town plan
- Interesting church or chapel } Reference letter on the town plan
- Thiers (R.) — Shopping street – Public car park – Park and Ride
- Tram
- Underground station
- One-way street
- Church or chapel
- Poste restante, telegraph – Telephone
- Public buildings located by letters :
- POL T M — Police (in large towns police headquaters) – Theatre – Museum
- Coach station – Airport – Hospital – Covered market
- Ruins – Monument, statue – Fountain
- Garden, park, wood – Cemetery, Jewish cemetery
- Outdoor or indoor swimming pool – Racecourse
- Golf course
- Cable-car – Funicular
- Sports ground, stadium – View – Panorama

Names shown on the street plans are in the language of the country to conform to local signposting.

Sights

- ★★★ Highly recommended
- ★★ Recommended
- ★ Interesting

Cher lecteur

Le Guide Michelin vous propose, dans chaque catégorie de confort et de prix, une sélection des meilleurs hôtels et restaurants. Cette sélection est effectuée par une équipe d'inspecteurs, professionnels de formation hôtelière, qui sillonnent le pays toute l'année pour visiter de nouveaux établissements et ceux déjà cités afin d'en vérifier la qualité et la régularité des prestations. Salariés Michelin, les inspecteurs travaillent en tout anonymat et en toute indépendance.

Les équipements et services sont signalés par des symboles, langage international qui vous permet de voir en un coup d'œil si un hôtel dispose, par exemple, d'un parking ou d'une piscine. Pour bien profiter de cette très riche source d'information, plongez-vous dans l'introduction. Un texte décrivant l'atmosphère de l'hôtel ou du restaurant complète ces renseignements.

L'inscription dans le guide est totalement gratuite. Chaque année, les hôteliers et restaurateurs cités remplissent le questionnaire qui leur est envoyé, nous fournissant les dates d'ouverture et les prix pour l'année à venir.

Près de 100 000 informations sont mises à jour pour chaque édition (nouveaux établissements, changements de tarif, dates d'ouverture).

Une grande aide vient aussi des commentaires des lecteurs avec près de 45 000 lettres et Email par an, pour toute l'Europe.

Merci d'avance pour votre participation et bon voyage avec le Guide Michelin 2004.

Hôtels, Restaurants

Classe et confort

XXXXX	*Grand luxe et tradition*
XXXX	*Grand confort*
XXX	*Très confortable*
XX	*Bon confort*
X	*Assez confortable*
	Autres formes d'hébergement conseillées
	Traditionnel "pub" anglais servant des repas
	Bars à tapas
without rest	*L'hôtel n'a pas de restaurant*
with rm	*Le restaurant possède des chambres*
	Le "Bib Hôtel" *: Bonnes nuits à petits prix*

L'agrément

...	*Hôtels agréables*
XXXXX ... X,	*Restaurants agréables*
	Hôtel très tranquille, ou isolé et tranquille
	Hôtel tranquille
sea,	*Vue exceptionnelle, panorama*
	Vue intéressante ou étendue

La table

✿✿✿	*Une des meilleures tables du pays, vaut le voyage*
✿✿	*Table excellente, mérite un détour*
✿	*Une très bonne table dans sa catégorie*
Meals	*Le* "Bib Gourmand" *: Repas soignés à prix modérés*
	Carte des vins offrant un choix particulièrement attractif

L'installation

30 rm	*Nombre de chambres*
	Ascenseur – Télévision dans la chambre
	Non-fumeurs
	Air conditionné
	Prise Modem – Minitel dans la chambre
	Tennis – Piscine : de plein air ou couverte
	Sauna – Salle de remise en forme – Wellness centre
	Jardin – Parc – Plage aménagée
	Repas servis au jardin ou en terrasse
	Ponton d'amarrage
	Voiturier – Garage – Parc à voitures, parking clos
	Chambres accessibles aux personnes à mobilité réduite
	Équipements d'accueil pour les enfants
150	*Salles de conférences : capacité maximum*
	Accès interdit aux chiens

Les prix

Les prix sont indiqués dans la monnaie du pays. Établis pour l'année 2004, ils ne doivent être modifiés que si le coût de la vie subit des variations importantes.

Au restaurant

Meals 40/56	*Prix des repas à prix fixes*
Meals à la carte 48/64	*Prix des repas à la carte*
	Restaurants proposant des menus à prix attractifs servis avant ou après le théâtre
b.i.	*Boisson comprise*
	Vin de table en carafe
	Vin servi au verre

A l'hôtel

30 rm 120/239	*Prix minimum pour une chambre d'une personne et maximum pour la plus belle chambre occupée par deux personnes*
30 rm 60/120 140/239	*En Allemagne et en Autriche, les prix indiqués correspondent au prix minimum/maximum des chambres pour une personne et au prix minimum/maximum des chambres pour deux personnes, petit déjeuner compris.*
30 rm 135/270	*Prix des chambres petit déjeuner compris*

Petit déjeuner

16	*Prix du petit déjeuner*

Cartes de paiement

AE JCB VISA	*Cartes de paiement acceptées*

Service et taxes

A l'exception de la Grèce, de la Hongrie, de la Pologne et de l'Espagne, les prix indiqués sont nets. Au Royaume Uni et en Irlande, s = service compris. En Italie, le service est parfois compté en supplément aux prix des repas. Ex. : (16 %).

Les Plans

Principaux signes conventionnels

Information touristique
Hôtel, restaurant – Lettre les repérant sur le plan
Monument intéressant et entrée principale } *Lettre les repérant sur le plan*
Église ou chapelle intéressante
Thiers (R.) *Rue commerçante – Parking – Parking Relais*
Tramway
Station de métro
Sens unique
Église ou chapelle
Poste restante, télégraphe – Téléphone
Édifices publics repérés par des lettres :
POL T M *Police (dans les grandes villes commissariat central) – Théâtre – Musée*
Gare routière – Aéroport – Hôpital – Marché couvert
Ruines – Monument, statue – Fontaine
Jardin, parc, bois – Cimetière, Cimetière israélite
Piscine de plein air, couverte – Hippodrome – Golf
Téléphérique – Funiculaire
Stade – Vue – Panorama

Les indications portées sur les plans sont dans la langue du pays, en conformité avec la dénomination locale.

Les curiosités

★★★ *Vaut le voyage*
★★ *Mérite un détour*
★ *Intéressante*

Lieber Leser

Der Michelin-Führer bietet Ihnen in jeder Komfort- und Preiskategorie eine Auswahl der besten Hotels und Restaurants. Diese Auswahl wird von einem Team von Inspektoren mit Ausbildung in der Hotellerie erstellt, die das Jahr hindurch das ganze Land bereisen. Ihre Aufgabe ist es, die Qualität und die Leistung der empfohlenen und der neu aufzunehmenden Hotels und Restaurants zu überprüfen. Als Angestellte bei Michelin arbeiten die Inspektoren anonym und völlig unabhängig.

Die Einrichtung und der gebotene Service der Betriebe wird durch Symbole gekennzeichnet- eine internationale Sprache, die auf einen Blick erkennen lässt, ob ein Hotel beispielsweise einen Parkplatz oder ein Schwimmbad besitzt. Um diese umfangreiche Information voll nutzen zu können, werfen Sie einen Blick in die Einleitung. Der Text, der die Atmosphäre eines Hotels oder Restaurants beschreibt, ergänzt die Symbole.

Die Empfehlung im Michelin-Führer ist absolut kostenlos. Alle empfohlenen Hotels und Restaurants füllen jedes Jahr einen Fragebogen aus, in dem uns die Schließungszeiten und die aktuellen Preise für das nächste Jahr genannt werden. Nahezu 100 000 Veränderungen für jede Ausgabe ergeben sich daraus (neue Betriebe, veränderte Preise und Schließungszeiten).

Eine sehr große Hilfe sind jedoch auch Sie, unsere Leser - mit beinahe 45 000 Briefen und E-Mails aus ganz Europa.

Wir bedanken uns im Voraus für Ihre Hilfe und wünschen Ihnen eine gute Reise mit dem Michelin-Führer 2004.

Hotels, Restaurants

Klasseneinteilung und Komfort

🏨🏨🏨🏨🏨	XXXXX	*Großer Luxus und Tradition*
🏨🏨🏨🏨	XXXX	*Großer Komfort*
🏨🏨🏨	XXX	*Sehr komfortabel*
🏨🏨	XX	*Mit gutem Komfort*
🏨	X	*Mit Standard-Komfort*
⌂		*Andere empfohlene Übernachtungsmöglichkeiten*
	🍺	*Traditionelle Pubs die Spsen anbieten*
	🍷	*Tapas bars*
	without rest	*Hotel ohne restaurant*
	with rm	*Restaurant vermietet auch Zimmer*
🛏		*Der* "**Bib Hotel**" *Hier übernachten Sie gut und Preiswert*

Annehmlichkeiten

🏨🏨🏨🏨🏨 ... 🏨	*Angenehme Hotels*
XXXXX ... X, 🍷	*Angenehme Restaurants*
🐴	*Sehr ruhiges oder abgelegenes und ruhiges Hotel*
🐴	*Ruhiges Hotel*
< sea, ✳	*Reizvolle Aussicht, Rundblick*
<	*Interessante oder weite Sicht*

Küche

✿✿✿	*Eine der besten Küchen des Landes : eine Reise wert*
✿✿	*Eine hervorragende Küche : verdient einen Umweg*
✿	*Eine sehr gute Küche : verdient Ihre besondere Beachtung*
🙂 **Meals**	*Der* "**Bib Gourmand**" *:* *Sorgfältig zubereitete preiswerte Mahlzeiten*
🍇	*Besonders interessante Weinkarte*

Einrichtung

30 rm	*Anzahl der Zimmer*
	Fahrstuhl – Fernsehen im Zimmer
	Nichtraucher – Klimaanlage
	Minitel Anschluß im Zimmer
	Tennis – Freibad – Hallenbad
	Sauna – Fitneßraum – Wellness centre
	Garten – Park – Strandbad
	Garten-, Terrassenrestaurant
	Bootssteg
	Wagenmeister – Garage – Parkplatz, gesicherter Parkplatz
	Für Körperbehinderte leicht zugängliche Zimmer
	Spezielle Einrichtungen/Angebote für Kinder
150	*Konferenzräume mit Höchstkapazität*
	Hunde sind unerwünscht

Die Preise

Die Preise sind in der jeweiligen Landeswährung angegeben. Sie gelten für das Jahr 2004 und ändern sich nur bei starken Veränderungen der Lebenshaltungskosten.

Im Restaurant

Meals 40/56	*Feste Menupreise*
Meals à la carte 48/64	*Mahlzeiten "a la carte"*
	Restaurants mit preiswerten Menus vor oder nach dem Theaterbesuch
b.i.	*Getränke inbegriffen*
	Preiswerter Wein in Karaffen
	Wein glasweise ausgeschenkt

Im Hotel

30 rm 120/239	*Mindestpreis für ein Einzelzimmer und Höchstpreis für das schönste Doppelzimmer für zwei Personen.*
30 rm 60/120 140/239	*In Deutschland und Österreich beziehen sich die Zimmer-Preise auf Einzelzimmer und Dpelzimmer jeweils Mindest- und Höchstpreis inclusive Frühstück.*
30 rm 135/270	*Zimmerpreis inkl. Frühstück*

Frühstück

16	*Preis des Frühstücks*

Kreditkarten

AE JCB VISA	*Akzeptierte Kreditkarten*

Bedienungsgeld und Gebühren

Mit Ausnahme von Griechenland, Ungarn, Polen und Spanien sind die angegebenen Preise Inklusivpreise. In den Kapiteln über Großbritannien und Irland bedeutet s = Bedienungsgeld inbegriffen. In Italien wird für die Bedienung gelegentlich ein Zuschlag zum Preis der Mahlzeit erhoben, zB (16 %).

Stadtpläne

Erklärung der wichtigsten Zeichen

Informationsstelle
Hotel, Restaurant – Referenzbuchstabe auf dem Plan
Sehenswertes Gebäude mit Haupteingang } *Referenzbuchstabe auf dem Plan*
Sehenswerte Kirche oder Kapelle
Thiers (R.) *Einkaufsstraße – Parkplatz, Parkhaus – Park-and-Ride-Plätze*
Straßenbahn
U-Bahnstation
Einbahnstraße
Kirche oder Kapelle
Postlagernde Sendungen, Telegraph – Telefon
Öffentliche Gebäude, durch Buchstaben gekennzeichnet :
POL T M *Polizei (in größeren Städten Polizeipräsidium) – Theater – Museum*
Autobusbahnhof – Flughafen
Krankenhaus – Markthalle
Ruine – Denkmal, Statue – Brunnen
Garten, Park, Wald – Friedhof, Jüd. Friedhof
Freibad – Hallenbad – Pferderennbahn
Golfplatz und Lochzahl
Seilschwebebahn – Standseilbahn
Sportplatz – Aussicht – Rundblick

Die Angaben auf den Stadtplänen erfolgen, übereinstimmend mit der örtlichen Beschilderung, in der Landessprache.

Sehenswürdigkeiten

★★★ *Eine Reise wert*
★★ *Verdient einen Umweg*
★ *Sehenswert*

Caro lettore

La Guida Michelin le propone, per ogni categoria di confort e di prezzo, una selezione dei migliori alberghi e ristoranti effettuata da un'équipe di professionisti del settore. Gli ispettori, dipendenti Michelin, attraversano il paese tutto l'anno per visitare nuovi esercizi e verificare la qualità e la regolarità delle prestazioni di quelli già citati, lavorando nel più stretto anonimato e in tutta autonomia.

Le attrezzature ed i servizi sono indicati da simboli, un immediato linguaggio internazionale che ti permetterà di capire in un attimo se, per esempio, un albergo dispone di parcheggio o di piscina. Per trarre il meglio da questa ricca fonte d'informazioni, le consigliamo di consultare l'introduzione. Le indicazioni sono poi completate da un testo che descrive l'atmosfera dell'albergo o del ristorante.

L'iscrizione nella guida è completamente gratuita. Ogni anno gli albergatori e i ristoratori citati compilano un questionario inviato loro per fornirci i periodi di apertura e i prezzi per l'anno a venire. Circa 100 000 dati sono aggiornati ad ogni edizione (nuovi esercizi, variazioni di tariffe, periodi di apertura).

Di grande aiuto sono anche i commenti dei lettori che ci inviano circa 45 000 lettere ed e-mail all'anno da tutta l'Europa.

Grazie sin d'ora per la sua partecipazione e buon viaggio con la Guida Michelin 2004.

Alberghi, Ristoranti

Categorie

🏨🏨🏨🏨🏨	XXXXX	*Gran lusso e tradizione*
🏨🏨🏨🏨	XXXX	*Gran confort*
🏨🏨🏨	XXX	*Molto confortevole*
🏨🏨	XX	*Di buon confort*
🏨	X	*Abbastanza confortevole*
⌂		*Forme alternative di ospitalità*
	🍺	*Pub con servizio cucina*
	🍷	*Tapas bars (in Spagna)*
	without rest	*L'albergo non ha ristorante*
	with rm	*Il ristorante dispone di camere*
Bib Hotel		*Il* "Bib Hotel" *: Buona sistemazione a prezzo contenuto*

Amenità e tranquillità

🏨🏨🏨🏨🏨 ... 🏨	*Alberghi ameni*
XXXXXX ... X, 🍷	*Ristoranti ameni*
🐦	*Albergo molto tranquillo, o isolato e tranquillo*
🐦	*Albergo tranquillo*
⋞ sea, ✳	*Vista eccezionale – vista panoramica*
⋞	*Vista interessante o estesa*

La Tavola

✿✿✿	*Una delle migliori tavole del Paese, vale il viaggio*
✿✿	*Tavola eccellente, merita una deviazione*
✿	*Un'ottima tavola nella sua categoria*
Bib Meals	*Il* "Bib Gourmand" *:*
	Pasti accurati a prezzi contenuti
🍇	*Carta dei vini con proposte particolarmente interessanti*

Installazioni

30 rm *Numero di camere*
Ascensore – Televisione in camera
Riservato ai non fumatori – Aria condizionata
Presa modem in camera
Tennis – Piscina: all'aperto, coperta
Sauna – Palestra – Wellness centre
Giardino – Parco – Spiaggia attrezzata
Pasti serviti in giardino o in terrazza – Pontile d'ormeggio
Posteggiatore – Garage – Parcheggio: all'aperto, chiuso
Camere accessibili a persone con difficoltà motoria
Attrezzaturaper accoglienza e ricreazione dei bambini
150 *Sale per conferenze: capienza massima*
Accesso vietato ai cani

I Prezzi

I prezzi sono indicati nella moneta del paese. Stabiliti par l'anno 2004, essi non dovranno essere modificati tranne il caso in cui avvengano variazioni importanti nel costo della vita.

Pasti

Meals 40/56 *Menu a prezzo fisso (minimo, massimo)*
Meals à la carte 48/64 *Pasto alla carta*
Ristoranti che offrono menù a prezzi ridotti prima e/o dopo gli spettacoli teatrali
b.i. *Bevanda compresa*
Vino sfuso – Vino servito a bicchiere

Camere

30 rm 120/239 *Prezzo per una camera singola e massimo per una camera per due persone in alta stagione.*
30 rm 60/120 140/239 *I prezzi riportati per la Germania e l'Austria si intendono rispettivamente riferiti al prezzo più basso e più alto sia per le camere singole che per le camere doppie, prima colazione inclusa.*
30 rm 135/270 *Prezzo della camera compresa la prima colazione*

Prima Colazione

16 *Prezzo della prima colazione*

Carte di credito

Carte di credito accettate dall'esercizio

Servizio e tasse

A eccezione della Grecia, dell'Ungheria, della Polonia e della Spagna, i prezzi indicati sono netti.
Nel Regno Unito e in Irlanda, s=servizio compreso.
In Italia il servizio è talvolta calcolato come supplemento al prezzo del pasto. Es.: (15 %).

Le Piante

Simboli vari

Ufficio informazioni turistiche
Albergo, Ristorante – Lettere di riferimento sulla pianta
Edificio interessante — *Lettere di riferimento sulla pianta*
Costruzione religiosa interessante B — *Lettere di riferimento sulla pianta*
Thiers (R.) *Via commerciale – Parcheggio*
Tram
Stazione della Metropolitana
Senso unico
Edificio religioso
Ufficio postale centrale – Telefono
Edificio pubblico indicato con lettera
POL T M *Polizia – Teatro – Museo*
Autostazione – Aeroporto
Ospedale – Mercato coperto
Ruderi – Monumento – Fontana
Giardino, parco, bosco – Cimitero, Cimitero israeliano
Piscina: all'aperto, coperto – Ippodromo
Golf
Teleferica – Funicolare
Stadio – Vista – Vista panoramica

Le indicazioni riportate sulle piante sono nella lingua del paese.

Curiosità

★★★ *Vale il viaggio*
★★ *Merita una deviazione*
★ *Interessante*

Amigo lector

La Guía Michelin le propone, para cada categoría de confort y de precio, una selección de los mejores hoteles y restaurantes. Esta selección la lleva a cabo un equipo de inspectores, todos ellos profesionales de la hostelería, que recorren el país durante todo el año para visitar nuevos establecimientos y verificar que las prestaciones de los que ya están citados siguen manteniendo la calidad y la regularidad. Los inspectores de Michelin trabajan siempre en el anonimato para guardar su independencia.

Las infraestructuras y servicios aparecen señalados por símbolos, un lenguaje internacional que le permitirá ver rápidamente si un hotel tiene aparcamiento o piscina. Para sacarle el mejor partido a toda esta información no deje de leer la introducción. Un pequeño texto describe las principales características de cada establecimiento.

La inscripción en la guía es totalmente gratuita. Todos los años, los hosteleros y restauradores mencionados rellenan un cuestionario en el que nos señalan sus fechas de apertura y precios para el año siguiente. En cada edición se actualizan alrededor de 100.000 datos (nuevos establecimientos, cambios de tarifas, fechas de apertura).

También nos resultan de una inestimable ayuda los casi 45.000 mails y cartas que recibimos cada año con los comentarios y sugerencias de nuestros lectores de toda Europa.

Le agradecemos de antemano su colaboración y sólo nos queda desearle un buen viaje con la Guía Michelin 2004.

Hoteles, Restaurantes

Categorías

🏨🏨🏨🏨🏨	XXXXX	*Gran lujo y tradición*
🏨🏨🏨🏨	XXXX	*Gran confort*
🏨🏨🏨	XXX	*Muy confortable*
🏨🏨	XX	*Confortable*
🏨	X	*Sencillo pero confortable*
⌂		*Otros tipos de alojamiento recomendados*
	🍺	*Pub tradicional inglés con servicio de comidas*
	🍷	*Bar de tapas*
	without rest	*El hotel no dispone de restaurante*
	with rm	*El restaurante tiene habitaciones*
Bib		*El* "Bib Hotel" *: Grato descanso a precio moderado*

Atractivo y tranquilidad

🏨🏨🏨🏨🏨 ... 🏨	*Hoteles agradables*
XXXXX ... X, 🍷	*Restaurantes agradables*
🐴	*Hotel muy tranquilo, o aislado y tranquilo*
🐴	*Hotel tranquilo*
< sea, ✳	*Vista excepcional*
<	*Vista interesante o extensa*

La Mesa

✿✿✿	*Una de las mejores mesas del país, justifica el viaje*
✿✿	*Mesa excelente, vale la pena desviarse*
✿	*Muy buena mesa en su categoría*
Bib Meals	*El* "Bib Gourmand" *: Buenas comidas a precios moderados*
🍇	*Carta de vinos que ofrece una seleccíon particularmente atractiva*

La instalación

30 rm	*Número de habitaciones*
	Ascensor – Televisión en la habitación
	No fumadores – Aire acondicionado
	Toma de Modem – Minitel en la habitación
	Tennis – Piscina: al aire libre o cubierta
	Sauna – Fitness – Wellness centre
	Jardin – Parque – Playa equipada
	Comidas servidas en el jardín o en la terraza
	Embarcadero
	Aparcacoches – Garaje – Aparcamiento exterior – Aparcamiento cerrado
	Habitaciones adaptadas para minusválidos
	Instalaciones infantiles
150	*Salas de conferencias : capacidad de las salas*
	Prohibidos los perros

Los precios

Los precios están expresados en la moneda del país. Las tarifas son válidas para 2004 salvo variaciones en el coste de bienes y servicios.

Comida

Meals 40/56	*Precios de las comidas a precio fijo*
Meals à la carte 48/64	*Precios de las comidas a la carta*
	Restaurantes con comidas a precios moderados servidas antes y después del espectáculo
b.i.	*Bebida incluida*
	Vino de mesa en jarra
	Vino servido por copas

Habitaciones

30 rm 120/239	*Precio mínimo de una habitacíon individual y precio máximo de la mejor habitacíon doble.*
30 rm 60/120 140/239	*Los precios indicados en Alemania y Austria corresponden al precio mínimo/máximo de una habitacíon individual y doble respectivamente, incluido desayuno.*
30 rm 135/270	*Precio de las habitaciones con desayuno incluido*

Desayuno

16	*Precio del desayuno*

Tarjetas de crédito

AE JCB VISA	*Tarjetas de crédito aceptadas*

Servicios e impuestos

A excepción de Grecia, Hungría, Polonia y España, los precios indicados son netos. En el Reino Unido e Irlanda, s = servicio incluido. En Italia, el servicio se añade a veces como suplemento a los precios de las comidas. Ej. : (16 %).

Los planos

Signos diversos

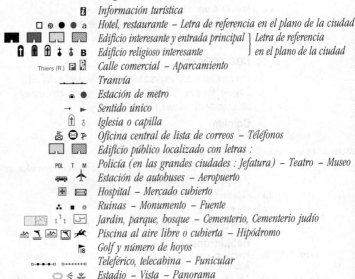

Información turística
Hotel, restaurante – Letra de referencia en el plano de la ciudad
Edificio interesante y entrada principal } *Letra de referencia en el plano de la ciudad*
Edificio religioso interesante
Thiers (R.) *Calle comercial – Aparcamiento*
Tranvía
Estación de metro
Sentido único
Iglesia o capilla
Oficina central de lista de correos – Teléfonos
Edificio público localizado con letras :
POL T M *Policía (en las grandes ciudades : Jefatura) – Teatro – Museo*
Estación de autobuses – Aeropuerto
Hospital – Mercado cubierto
Ruinas – Monumento – Fuente
Jardín, parque, bosque – Cementerio, Cementerio judío
Piscina al aire libre o cubierta – Hipódromo
18 *Golf y número de hoyos*
Teleférico, telecabina – Funicular
Estadio – Vista – Panorama

Las indicaciones de los planos están señaladas en el idioma del país de acuerdo con la denominación local.

Las curiosidades

★★★ *De interés excepcional*
★★ *Muy interesante*
★ *Interesante*

NEW YORK

UTC - 5
(Universal time co-ordinated/ Greenwich Mean Time)

DIRECT DAILY FLIGHTS
Total time of journey from city centre to city centre (in hours)

Amsterdam	9 1/4
Athens	12
Barcelona	9 1/4
Berlin	12 3/4
Brussels	10 3/4
Budapest	11
Copenhagen	9 3/4
Dublin	8 3/4
Düsseldorf	9 1/4
Frankfurt	9 3/4
Geneva	9 1/2
Glasgow	10
Hamburg	11
Helsinki	12
Lisbon	8 3/4
London	9 1/2
Luxembourg	11 1/2
Madrid	9 1/4
Milan	9 3/4
Munich	11 3/4
Oslo	9 1/2
Paris	9 3/4
Rome	10 1/2
Stockholm	11 1/2
Vienna	10 1/2
Warsaw	12 1/2
Zürich	9 3/4

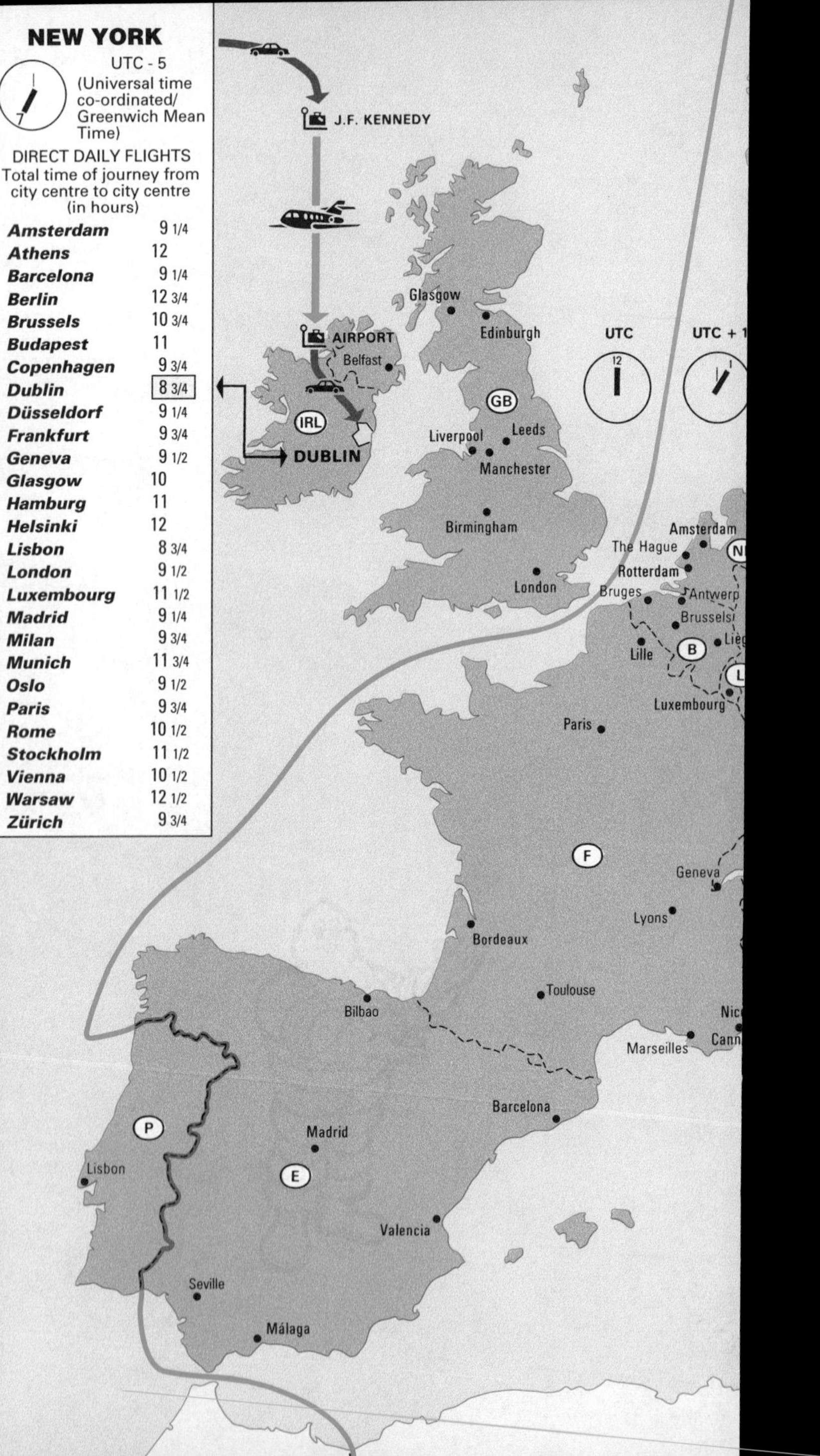

N
Oslo
S
Stockholm
FIN
Helsinki
UTC + 2
2
Gothenburg
DK
Copenhagen
Hamburg
Berlin
Warsaw
Hanover
PL
Leipzig
Dusseldorf
Dresden
Cologne
D
Prague
CZ
Frankfurt
Stuttgart
Vienna
Strasbourg
Munich
Salzburg
Budapest
A
Zürich
Innsbruck
H
CH
Basle
Berne
Venice
Milan
Turin
Florence
Monaco
I
Rome
Naples
GR
Athens
Palermo
Taormina
A Austria
B Belgium
CH Switzerland
CZ Czech Republic
D Germany
DK Denmark
E Spain
F France
FIN Finland
GB United Kingdom
GR Greece
H Hungary
I Italy
IRL Ireland
L Luxembourg
N Norway
NL Netherlands
PL Poland
P Portugal
S Sweden

DISTANCES BY ROAD

(in kilometres)

	Amsterdam	Athens	Barcelona	Berlin	Bern	Bordeaux	Brussels	Budapest	Cologne	Copenhagen	Dublin	Edinburgh	Frankfurt	Geneva	Hamburg	Helsinki	Lisbon	London	Luxembourg	Lyons	Madrid	Manchester	Marseilles	Milan	Munich	Oslo	Paris	Prague	Rome	Stockholm	Strasbourg	Stuttgart	Venice	Vienna	Warsaw
Athens	2849																																		
Barcelona	1506	2081																																	
Berlin	663	2274	1855																																
Bern	804	1557	931	914																															
Bordeaux	1088	2223	564	1633	850																														
Brussels	205	2092	1310	767	643	892																													
Budapest	1408	1480	1898	856	1111	1926	1369																												
Cologne	261	2599	1350	573	586	1067	210	1159																											
Copenhagen	783	2666	2088	388	1225	1795	913	1247	740																										
Dublin	949	2815	1863	1511	1366	1151	781	2151	992	750																									
Edinburgh	742	2971	2019	978	1522	1365	937	2307	1148	491	404																								
Frankfurt	433	2414	1318	544	422	1149	394	974	184	806	1177	1333																							
Geneva	920	1527	752	1070	159	692	719	1267	708	1382	1328	1484	578																						
Hamburg	471	2563	1776	285	913	1483	601	1145	428	324	1346	705	494	1069																					
Helsinki	1737	3123	3142	1286	2201	2917	1868	1656	1860	958	1260	1002	1832	2357	1278																				
Lisbon	2251	3251	1246	2796	2013	1160	2056	3067	2232	2960	2316	2530	2314	1922	2648	4084																			
London	486	2352	1400	1048	903	982	318	1688	529	1195	456	642	713	865	883	1324	2145																		
Luxembourg	415	1879	1148	766	430	926	215	1191	204	942	995	1151	238	507	629	2053	2090	532																	
Lyons	928	1624	636	1223	310	536	728	1370	716	1454	1325	1481	686	152	1142	2510	1700	862	515																
Madrid	1778	2678	615	2323	1527	686	1583	2494	1758	2486	1842	2056	1840	1348	2174	3610	630	1667	1618	1232															
Manchester	212	2688	1736	874	1239	1024	654	2024	865	552	203	360	1049	1201	682	1087	2188	329	867	1197	1715														
Marseilles	1240	1607	506	1534	575	647	1039	1423	1027	1766	1637	1793	997	430	1454	2821	1675	1173	826	314	1102	1510													
Milan	1045	1204	974	1030	349	996	883	938	827	1424	1607	1763	663	321	1111	2317	2144	1144	670	441	1571	1480	500												
Munich	832	2061	1353	587	424	1257	721	689	583	943	1528	1685	398	581	788	1875	2421	1065	508	731	1949	1401	986	490											
Oslo	1277	3115	2582	837	1731	2289	1407	1697	1234	611	790	532	1312	1888	819	798	3452	829	1436	1949	2979	591	2260	1833	1392										
Paris	506	2053	997	1051	586	579	311	1496	487	1215	865	1021	578	534	902	2339	1742	402	355	458	1269	738	769	848	821	1708									
Prague	874	1938	1698	337	757	1603	891	520	681	728	1634	1790	496	913	608	1519	2766	1171	727	1064	2293	1085	1376	862	381	1178	1032								
Rome	1617	759	1329	1496	921	1470	1455	1193	1399	1852	2179	2335	1235	857	1653	2783	2498	1716	1242	945	1925	2052	854	568	905	2301	1385	1290							
Stockholm	1451	3175	2756	898	1893	2463	1581	1757	1408	672	973	716	1474	2049	991	316	3626	1012	1610	2123	3153	775	2434	1894	1453	529	1881	1238	2361						
Strasbourg	596	1689	1123	755	239	1061	434	1018	361	1021	1196	1352	218	396	709	2042	2224	733	221	489	1719	1069	801	481	360	1527	490	598	1052	1689					
Stuttgart	617	2296	1215	633	286	1079	512	880	367	971	1319	1475	203	443	659	1921	2243	856	299	616	1812	1192	859	494	222	1477	613	476	1056	1639	149				
Venice	1214	1082	1228	1045	602	1256	1135	687	965	1401	1859	2015	801	581	1203	2246	2398	1396	922	701	1825	1732	754	269	454	1851	1109	805	524	1911	729	605			
Vienna	1149	1666	1788	620	852	1685	1110	248	900	1012	1893	2049	715	1008	909	1673	2849	1429	932	1159	2384	1765	1314	828	430	1461	1237	284	1083	1521	758	620	577		
Warsaw	1220	2157	2335	594	1394	2189	1324	677	1130	911	2069	1570	1067	1550	877	979	3352	1606	1289	1702	2879	1431	2013	1509	996	1360	1607	616	1773	413	1235	1114	1267	693	
Zurich	793	1490	1051	846	123	955	631	995	575	1177	1355	1511	411	279	865	2134	2119	892	418	429	1648	1228	695	282	308	1683	591	680	854	1845	225	211	534	735	1327

2042

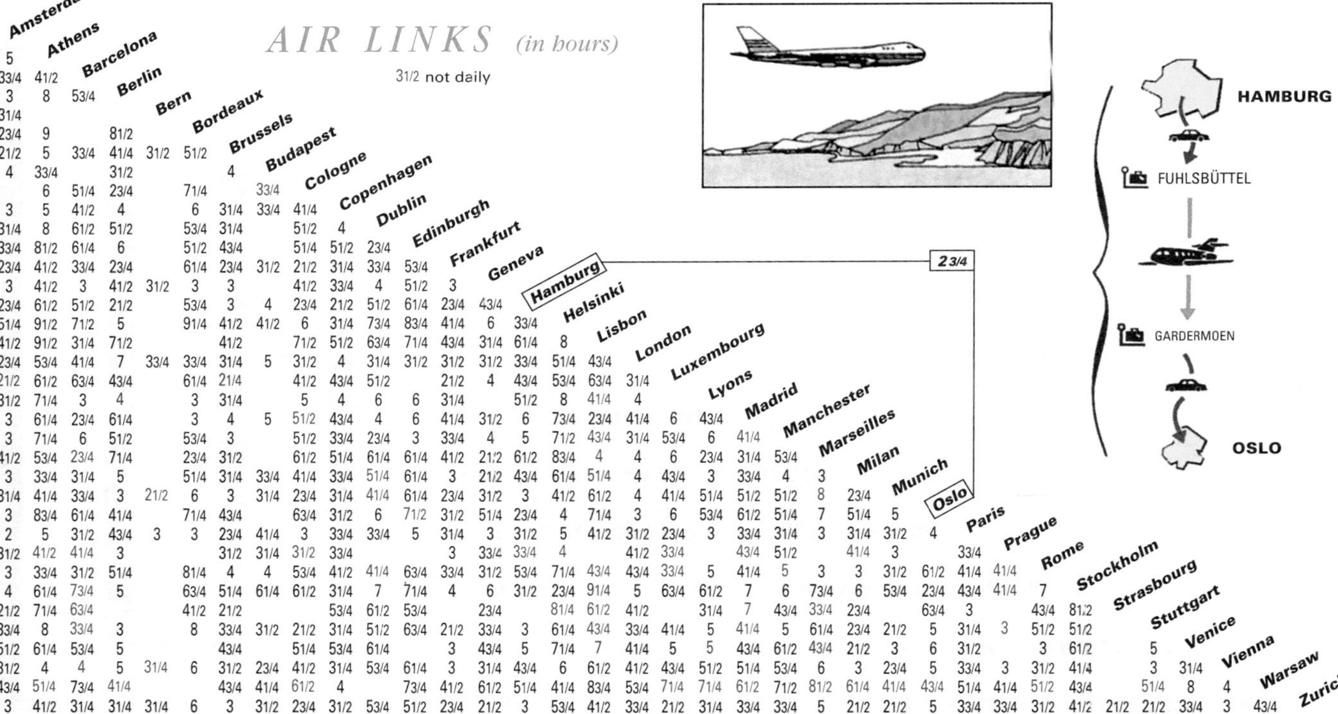

AIR LINKS (in hours)

3½ not daily

	Amsterdam	Athens	Barcelona	Berlin	Bern	Bordeaux	Brussels	Budapest	Cologne	Copenhagen	Dublin	Edinburgh	Frankfurt	Geneva	Hamburg	Helsinki	Lisbon	London	Luxembourg	Lyons	Madrid	Manchester	Marseilles	Milan	Munich	Oslo	Paris	Prague	Rome	Stockholm	Strasbourg	Stuttgart	Venice	Vienna	Warsaw
Athens	5																																		
Barcelona	3¾	4½																																	
Berlin	3	8	5¾																																
Bern	3¼																																		
Bordeaux	2¾	9		8½																															
Brussels	2½	5	3¾	4¼	3½	5½																													
Budapest	4	3¾		3½			4																												
Cologne		6	5¼	2¾		7¼		3¾																											
Copenhagen	3	5	4½	4		6	3¼	3¾	4¼																										
Dublin	3¼	8	6½	5½		5¾	3¼		5½	4																									
Edinburgh	3¾	8½	6¼	6		5½	4¾		5¼	5½	2¾																								
Frankfurt	2¾	4½	3¾	2¾		6¼	2¾	3½	2½	3¼	3¾	5¾																							
Geneva	3	4½	3	4½	3½	3	3		4½	3¾	4	5½	3																						
Hamburg	2¾	6½	5½	2½		5¾	3	4	2¾	2½	5½	6¼	2¾	4¾																					
Helsinki	5¼	9½	7½	5		9¼	4½	4½	6	3¼	7¾	8¾	4¼	6	3¾																				
Lisbon	4½	9½	3¼	7½			4½		7½	5½	6¾	7¼	4¾	3¼	6¼	8																			
London	2¾	5¾	4¼	7	3¾	3¾	3¼	5	3½	4	3¼	3½	3½	3½	3¾	5¼	4¾																		
Luxembourg	2½	6½	6¾	4¾		6¼	2¼		4½	4¾	5½		2½	4	4¾	5¾	6¾	3¼																	
Lyons	3½	7¼	3	4		3	3¼		5	4	6	6	3¼		5½	8	4¼	4																	
Madrid	3	6¼	2¾	6¼		3	4	5	5½	4¾	4	6	4¼	3½	6	7¾	2¾	4¼	6	4¾															
Manchester	3	7¼	6	5½		5¾	3		5½	3¾	2¾	3	3¾	4	5	7½	4¾	3¼	5¾	6	4¼														
Marseilles	4½	5¾	2¾	7¼		2¾	3½		6½	5¼	6¼	6¼	4½	2½	6½	8¾	4	4	6	2¾	3¼	5¾													
Milan	3	3¾	3¼	5		5¼	3¼	3¾	4¼	3¾	5¼	6¼	3	2½	4¾	6¼	5¼	4	4¾	3	3¾	4	3												
Munich	3¼	4¼	3¾	3	2½	6	3	3¼	2¾	3¼	4¼	6¼	2¾	3½	3	4½	6½	4	4¼	5¼	5½	5½	8	2¾											
Oslo	3	8¾	6¼	4¼		7¼	4¾		6¾	3½	6	7½	3½	5¼	2¾	4	7¼	3	6	5¾	6½	5¼	7	5¼	5										
Paris	2	5	3½	4¾	3	3	2¾	4¼	3	3¾	3¾	5	3¼	3	3½	5	4½	3½	2¾	3	3¾	3¼	3	3¼	3½	4									
Prague	3½	4½	4¼	3			3½	3¼	3½	3¾			3	3¾	3¾	4		4½	3¾		4¾	5½		4¼	3		3¾								
Rome	3	3¾	3½	5¼		8¼	4	4	5¾	4½	4¼	6¾	3¾	3½	5¾	7¼	4¾	4¾	3¾	5	4¼	5	3	3	3½	6½	4¼	4¼							
Stockholm	4	6¼	7¾	5		6¾	5¼	6¼	6½	3¼	7	7¼	4	6	3½	2¾	9¼	5	6¾	6½	7	6	7¾	6	5¾	2¾	4¾	4¼	7						
Strasbourg	2½	7¼	6¾			4½	2½			5¾	6½	5¾		2¾		8¼	6½	4½		3¼	7	4¾	3¾	2¾		6¾	3		4¾	8½					
Stuttgart	3¾	8	3¾	3		8	3¾	3½	2½	3¼	5½	6¾	2½	3¾	3	6¼	4¾	3¾	4¼	5	4¼	5	6¼	2¾	2½	5	3¼	3	5½	5½					
Venice	5½	6¼	5¾	5			4¾		5¼	5¾	6¼		3	4¾	5	7¼	7	4¼	5	5	4¾	6½	4¾	2½	3	6	3½		3	6½		5			
Vienna	3½	4	4	5	3¼	6	3½	2¾	4½	3¼	5¾	6¼	3	3¼	4¾	6	6½	4½	4¾	5½	5¼	5¾	6	3	2¾	5	3¾	3	3½	4¼		3	3¼		
Warsaw	4¾	5¼	7¾	4¼			4¾	4¼	6½	4		7¾	4½	6½	5¼	4¼	8¾	5¾	7¼	7¼	6½	7½	8½	6¼	4¼	4¾	5¼	4¼	5½	4¾		5¼	8	4	
Zurich	3	4½	3¼	3¼	3¼	6	3	3½	2¾	3½	5¾	5½	2¾	2½	3	5¾	4½	3¾	2½	3¼	3¾	3¾	5	2½	2½	5	3¾	3¾	3½	4½	2½	2½	3¾	3	4¾

Austria

Österreich

VIENNA

INNSBRUCK – SALZBURG

PRACTICAL INFORMATION

LOCAL CURRENCY

1 euro (€) = 1,20 USD ($) (Déc. 2003)

TOURIST INFORMATION

In Vienna: *Österreich-Information, 1040 Wien, Margaretenstr. 1, ✆ (01) 587 20 00, oewwien@austria.info.at, Fax (01) 588 66 48*
Niederösterreich Touristik-Information, 1010 Wien, Fischhof 3/3, ✆ (01) 53 61 00, tourismus@noe.co.at, Fax (01) 536 10 60 62

Austrian National Holiday: *26 October*

AIRLINES

Austrian-Airlines: *1010 Wien, Kärntner Ring 18, ✆ (05) 17 89, Fax (01) 1 76 61 76 99*

Air France: *1010 Wien, Kärntner Str. 49, ✆ (01) 5 02 22 24 00, Fax (01) 513 94 26*

British Airways: *1010 Wien, Kärntner Ring 10, ✆ (01) 5 06 60, Fax (01) 5 04 20 84*

Japan Airlines: *1010 Wien, Kärntner Str. 11, ✆ (01) 512 75 22, Fax (01) 512 75 54*

Lufthansa City Center: *1010 Wien, Wienerbergstr. 5, ✆ (01) 607 10 70*

FOREIGN EXCHANGE

Hotels, restaurants and shops do not always accept foreign currencies and it is wise, therefore, to change money and cheques at the banks and exchange offices which are found in the larger stations, airports and at the border.

SHOPPING and BANK HOURS

Shops are open from 9am to 6pm, but often close for a lunch break. They are closed Sunday and Bank Holidays (except the shops in railway stations).
Branch offices of banks are open from Monday to Friday between 8am and 12.30pm (in Salzburg 12am) and from 1.30pm to 3pm (in Salzburg 2pm to 4.30pm), Thursday to 5.30pm (only in Vienna).
In the index of street names, those printed in red are where the principal shops are found.

BREAKDOWN SERVICE

ÖAMTC: *See addresses in the text of each city.*

ARBÖ: *in Vienna: Mariahilfer Str. 180, ✆ (01) 89 12 10, Fax (01) 89 12 12 36 in Salzburg: Münchner Bundesstr. 9, ✆ (0662) 43 36 01, in Innsbruck: Stadlweg 7, ✆ (0512) 34 51 23*
In Austria the ÖAMTC (emergency number ✆ 120) and the ARBÖ (emergency number ✆ 123) make a special point of assisting foreign motorists. They have motor patrols covering main roads.

TIPPING

Service is generally included in hotel and restaurant bills. But in Austria, it is usual to give more than the expected tip in hotels, restaurants and cafés. Taxi-drivers, porters, barbers and theatre attendants also expect tips.

SPEED LIMITS

The speed limit in built up areas (indicated by place name signs at the beginning and end of such areas) is 50 km/h - 31 mph; on motorways 130 km/h - 80 mph and on all other roads 100 km/h - 62 mph. Driving on Austrian motorways is subject to the purchase of a road tax obtainable from border posts and ÖAMTC.

SEAT BELTS

The wearing of seat belts in Austria is compulsory for drivers and all passengers.

VIENNA
(WIEN)

Austria 730 V 4 – pop. 1 640 000 – alt. 156 m.

Budapest 208 ④ – München 435 ⑦ – Praha 292 ① – Salzburg 292 ⑦ – Zagreb 362 ⑥.

Tourist-information, Albertinaplatz, ✉ A-1010, ☎ (01) 245 55, info@info.wien.at, Fax (01) 24 55 56 66.
ÖAMTC, ✉ A-1010, Schubertring 1, ☎ (01) 71 19 90.

18 Freudenau 65a, ☎ (01) 728 95 64,
18 Weingartenallee 22, ☎ (01) 256 82 82
9 At Wienerberg ☎ (01) 661 23
✈ Wien-Schwechat by ③, ☎ (01) 7 00 70.
☎ (01) 58 00 29 89. – Exhibition Centre (Wiener Messe), Messestr. 1, ☎ (01) 727 20.

SIGHTS

THE HOFBURG★★★

Around the Hofburg JR: *St Michael's Square*★ – *St Michael's Gate*★ – *Swiss Gate*★ – *Josef's square*★ – *Heroe's Square*★ HJR
Souvenirs of the Habsburgs; Imperial Apartments★ – *Imperial porcelain and silver collection*★ ; *Milan centerpiece*★★ – *Imperial Treasury*★★★ ; *Rudolf Imperial Crown*★★★ ; *Insignia and regalia of the Holy Roman Germanic Empire*★★; *Imperial Crown*★★★ – *Holy Lance*★★ – *Spanish Riding School*★★ – *Austrian National Library*★ – *Albertina Collection of Graphic Art*★★ JR
Ephesos-Museum★★ *(Frieze from the Parthian momument*★★ *)*
Museum of Ancient Musical Instruments★★ – *Collection of Arms and Armour*★★ – *Ethnographic Museum*★ – *Papyrus Museum*★

SCHÖNBRUNN★★★

Palace of Schönbrunn AZ; *Tour of the Palace*★★ – *Great Gallery*★★★ – *Carriage Museum*★ – *Imperial Carriage*★★ – *Park*★★ ⩽★ *of the Gloriette*★★ – *Zoo*★ – *Palm House*★ – *Gloriette*★★

BUILDINGS AND MONUMENTS

St. Stephen's Cathedral★★★ KR – *Stephansplatz*★★
Church of the Capucins : Imperial Crypt of the Habsburg pantheon★★ JR *Lower Belvedere*★ CY *Museum of Austrian Medieval Art*★ – *Museum of Austrian Baroque Art*★★
Upper Belvedere★★ CY: *19C and 20C Austrian and International Art*★★ – *State Opera*★★ JS – *Church of Charles Borromero*★★ CY – *Burgtheater*★ HR – *St. Peter's Church*★ JR – *Church of the Jesuits*★ KLR – *Church Maria am Gestade*★ JP – *Abbey of the Scots*★, *Scotsaltar*★★ JPR – *City Palace of Prince Eugene of Savoy*★ KR

JUGENDSTIL AND SECESSION

Post Office Savings Bank★ KLR – *Wagner-Pavillons*★ JS – *Secession Pavilion*★★ JS – *Buildings*★ *by Wagner on Linke Wienzeile* – *Wagner Villas*★ *(in Penzing)*BYZ – *St. Leopold's Church in Penzing*★★ AY

STREETS, SQUARES AND PARKS

The Tour of the Ring★★ – *Graben*★ *(Plague Pillar*★★ *)*JR – *Donner's Fountain*★★ JR – *Volksgarten*★ HR – *Spittelberg Quarter*★ HS – *Prater*★ *(Giant Ferris Wheel*★★ *)* CY – *Zoo of Lainz*★ *West by* ⑦

MUSICAL VIENNA

Pasqualatihaus★ *(Beethoven)* HP **85** – *Figaro-Haus*★ *(Mozart)* KR *Schubert-Memorial*★ BY **M5** – *Haydn-Memorial*★ BYZ **M10** – *Johann-Strauß Memorial*★ LP – *House of Music*★★ KS

IMPORTANT MUSEUMS

Museum of Art History★★★ HS – *Quarter of Museums*★★ *(Leopold Museum*★ *)* HS – *Art Gallery of the Academy of Fine Arts*★★ JS – *Austrian Museum of Applied and Decorative Arts (MAK)*★★ LR – *Historical Museum of the City of Vienna*★ KS *Natural History Museum*★ HS – *City of Vienna Jewish Museum*★ JR – *Museum of Military History*★ CZ **M23** – *Treasure Chamber of the Grand Masters*★ KR – *Josephinum*★ BY – **M24** – *Sigmund Freud Museum*★ BY **M25** – *Tram Museum*★ CY **M3** – *Clock and Watch Museum*★ JR **M17** – *Technical Museum*★ AZ **M2** – *Imperial Furniture Depot*★ BY – *Cathedral Museum*★ KR **M19**

EXCURSIONS

UNO-City★ CY – *Danube Park*★ CX – *Danube Tower* ⩽★★ CX – *Kahlenberg*★ BX – *Leopoldsberg*★★ ⩽★★ BX – *Klosterneuburg Abbey*★ *(Altarpiece by Nicolas of Verdun*★★ *); Museum of the Abbey*★ – *Essl Collection*★ *North: 13km* – *Heiligenkreuz*★ *South-West: 32 km by* ⑥ – *Grinzing*★ BX – *Wienerwald*★ *South-West by* ⑥ – *Heiligenstadt*★ *(Karl-Marx-Hof*★ *)* BX.

STREET INDEX TO WIEN TOWN PLANS

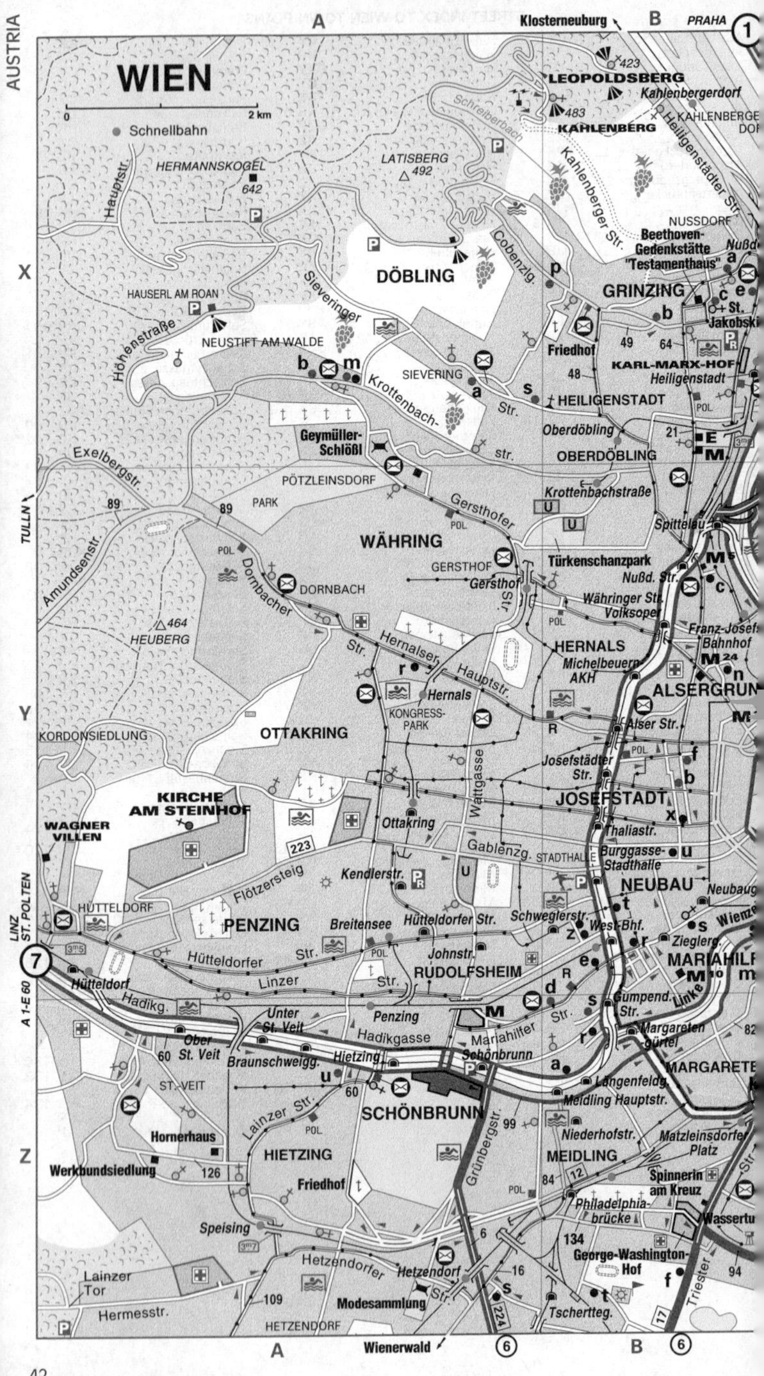
WIEN
0
2 km
Schnellbahn
Klosterneuburg
PRAHA
LEOPOLDSBERG
Kahlenbergerdorf
KAHLENBERG
HERMANNSKOGEL
642
LATISBERG
492
DÖBLING
GRINZING
Beethoven-Gedenkstätte "Testamenthaus"
NUSSDORF
HAUSERL AM ROAN
NEUSTIFT AM WALDE
SIEVERING
HEILIGENSTADT
KARL-MARX-HOF
Heiligenstadt
Geymüller-Schlößl
PÖTZLEINSDORF
OBERDÖBLING
Oberdöbling
Krottenbachstraße
Spittelau
WÄHRING
GERSTHOF
Gersthof
Türkenschanzpark
DORNBACH
HEUBERG
464
HERNALS
Hernals
Michelbeuern-AKH
ALSERGRUND
Alser Str.
Franz-Josefs-Bahnhof
OTTAKRING
Ottakring
KONGRESS-PARK
KORDONSIEDLUNG
KIRCHE AM STEINHOF
WAGNER VILLEN
JOSEFSTADT
Josefstädter Str.
Thaliastr.
Burggasse-Stadthalle
STADTHALLE
NEUBAU
Kendlerstr.
PENZING
Penzing
HÜTTELDORF
Hütteldorf
Breitensee
Hütteldorfer Str.
Schweglerstr.
West-Bhf.
RUDOLFSHEIM
Johnstr.
MARIAHILF
Zieglerg.
Gumpend. Str.
Margareten gürtel
MARGARETEN
Unter St. Veit
Ober St. Veit
ST. VEIT
Braunschweigg.
Hietzing
Schönbrunn
SCHÖNBRUNN
Längenfeldg.
Meidling Hauptstr.
Niederhofstr.
Matzleinsdorfer Platz
MEIDLING
HIETZING
Hornerhaus
Werkbundsiedlung
Friedhof
Speising
Philadelphia-brücke
Spinnerin am Kreuz
George-Washington-Hof
Hetzendorf
Modesammlung
Lainzer Tor
Hermesstr.
HETZENDORF
Tschertteg.
Wienerwald
TULLN
LINZ ST. PÖLTEN
A 1-E 60
A
B
X
Y
Z

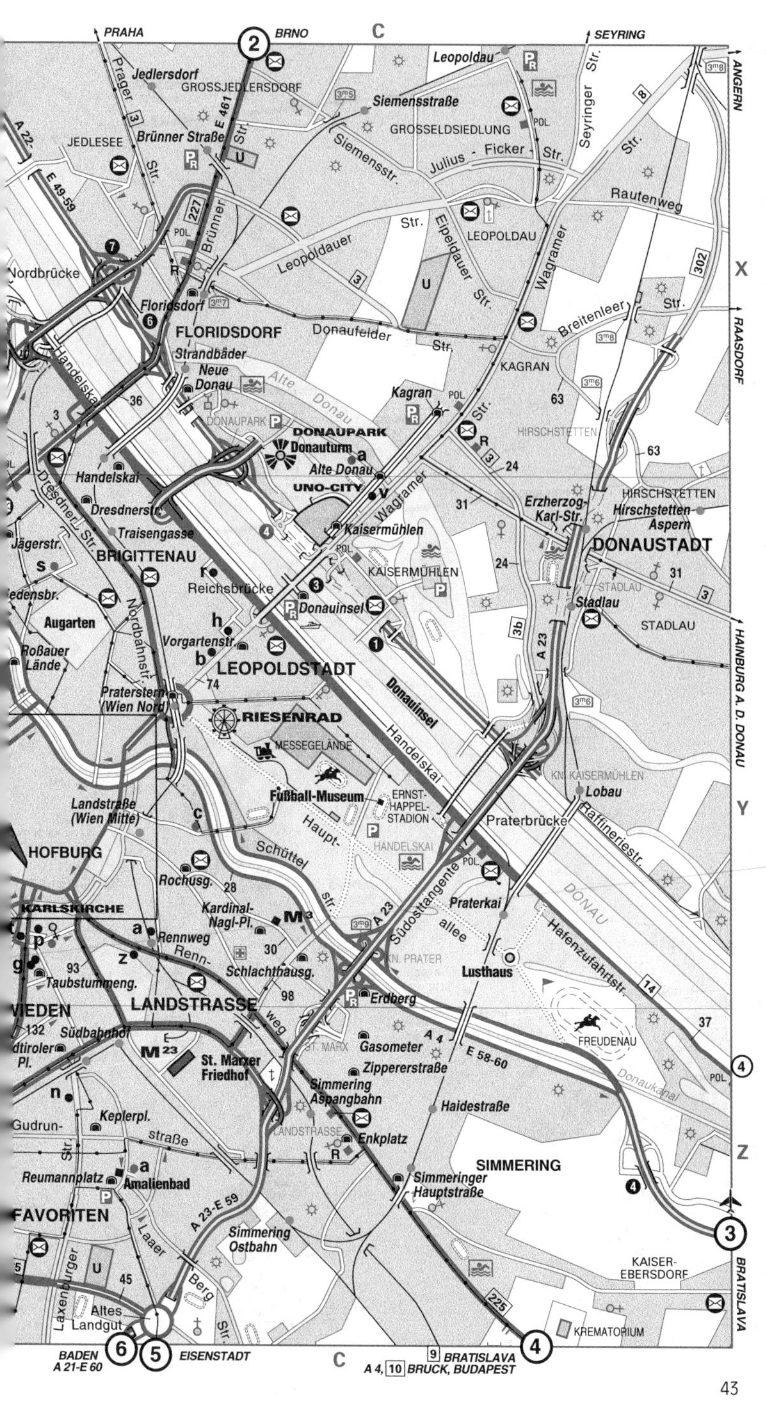
PRAHA
BRNO
SEYRING
ANGERN
RAASDORF
HAINBURG A. D. DONAU
BRATISLAVA
BADEN A 21-E 60
EISENSTADT
A 4, 10 BRUCK, BUDAPEST
9 BRATISLAVA
FLORIDSDORF
BRIGITTENAU
LEOPOLDSTADT
DONAUSTADT
LANDSTRASSE
SIMMERING
FAVORITEN
HOFBURG
KARLSKIRCHE
RIESENRAD
DONAUPARK
Donauturm
UNO-CITY
Donauinsel
Handelskai
Praterbrücke
Reichsbrücke
Nordbrücke
Fußball-Museum
ERNST-HAPPEL-STADION
MESSEGELÄNDE
Lusthaus
FREUDENAU
Donaukanal
DONAU
KAGRAN
LEOPOLDAU
GROSSJEDLERSDORF
JEDLESEE
GROSSELDSIEDLUNG
HIRSCHSTETTEN
STADLAU
KAISERMÜHLEN
KAISER-EBERSDORF
KREMATORIUM
St. Marxer Friedhof
Augarten
Südosttangente
Wagramer Str.
Prater Hauptallee
Schüttelstr.
Rennweg
Gasometer
Simmering
Erdberg
Praterstern (Wien Nord)
Landstraße (Wien Mitte)

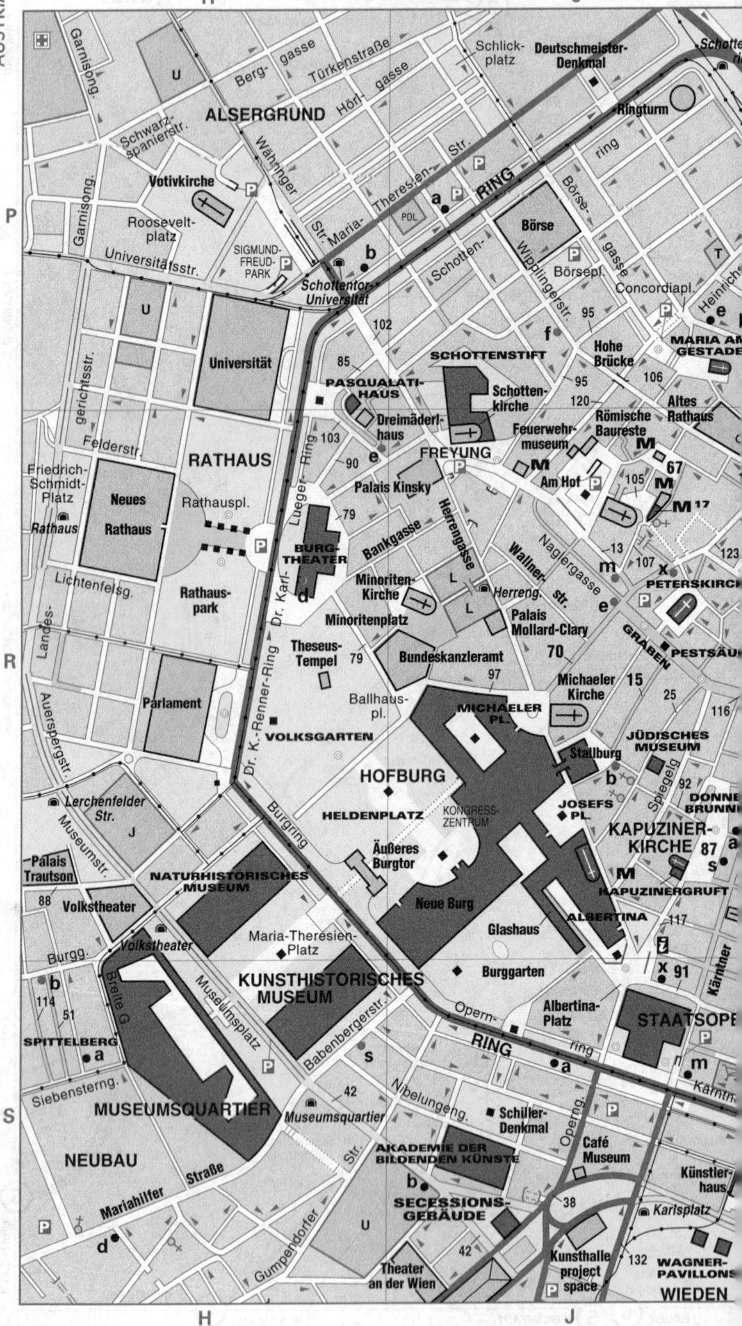
H
J
P
R
S
Garnisong.
U
Berg-
gasse
Türkenstraße
Hörl-
gasse
Schlick-
platz
Deutschmeister-
Denkmal
Schotte
ALSERGRUND
Schwarz-
spanierstr.
Ringturm
Währinger
Maria-
Theresien-
Str.
ring
Votivkirche
RING
Börse-
gasse
a
PÖL
Roosevelt-
platz
Garnisong.
Börse
Universitätsstr.
SIGMUND-
FREUD-
PARK
b
Schotten-
Wipplingerstr.
Börsepl.
T
Schottentor-
Universität
Concordiapl.
Heinrichs
U
Universität
102
95
e
f
MARIA AM
GESTADE
gerichtsstr.
85
SCHOTTENSTIFT
Hohe
Brücke
PASQUALATI-
HAUS
95
106
Schotten-
kirche
Dreimäderl-
haus
120
Altes
Rathaus
Römische
Baureste
Felderstr.
103
Feuerwehr-
museum
RATHAUS
90
e
FREYUNG
M
Friedrich-
Schmidt-
Platz
Neues
Rathaus
Rathauspl.
Palais Kinsky
Am Hof
105
67
Rathaus
79
Herrengasse
M 17
BURG-
THEATER
Bankgasse
Naglergasse
123
Lichtenfelsg.
Dr. Karl-
Lueger-
Ring
13
Wallner-
str.
107
x
Minoriten-
Kirche
m
PETERSKIRCHE
Rathaus-
park
L
Herreng.
d
L
e
Minoritenplatz
Palais
Mollard-Clary
GRABEN
PESTSÄULE
Landes-
Theseus-
Tempel
79
Bundeskanzleramt
70
Parlament
97
Michaeler
Kirche
15
25
Ballhaus-
pl.
Auerspergstr.
MICHAELER
PL.
116
Dr. K.-Renner-Ring
VOLKSGARTEN
JÜDISCHES
MUSEUM
Stallburg
HOFBURG
b
92
Lerchenfelder
Str.
Burgring
Spiegelg.
Museumstr.
J
HELDENPLATZ
KONGRESS-
ZENTRUM
JOSEFS
PL.
DONNER
BRUNNEN
KAPUZINER-
KIRCHE
Palais
Trautson
Äußeres
Burgtor
87
s
NATURHISTORISCHES
MUSEUM
M
KAPUZINERGRUFT
88
Volkstheater
Neue Burg
ALBERTINA
117
Maria-Theresien-
Platz
Glashaus
Burgg.
Volkstheater
Breite G.
KUNSTHISTORISCHES
MUSEUM
Burggarten
x
91
Kärntner
b
114
51
Museumsplatz
Babenbergerstr.
Opern-
Albertina-
Platz
STAATSOPER
SPITTELBERG
a
RING
ring
a
m
s
Siebensterng.
42
Nibelungeng.
Kärntner
MUSEUMSQUARTIER
Museumsquartier
Schiller-
Denkmal
Operng.
Café
Museum
NEUBAU
AKADEMIE DER
BILDENDEN KÜNSTE
Str.
Straße
Künstler-
haus
Mariahilfer
b
SECESSIONS-
GEBÄUDE
38
Karlsplatz
Gumpendorfer
U
d
42
Kunsthalle
project
space
132
WAGNER-
PAVILLONS
Theater
an der Wien
WIEDEN
H
J

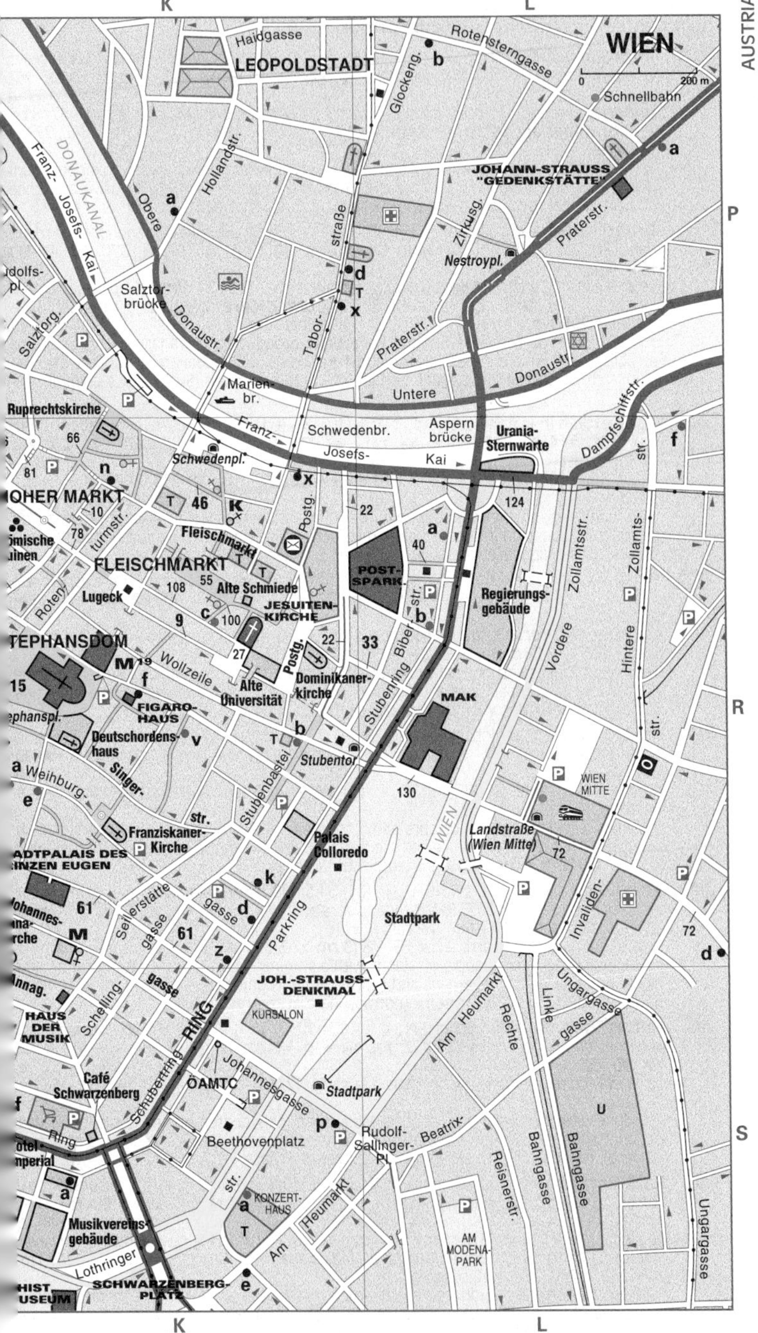

WIEN
0
200 m
Schnellbahn
LEOPOLDSTADT
Haidgasse
Rotensterngasse
Glockeng.
JOHANN-STRAUSS "GEDENKSTÄTTE"
Praterstr.
Nestroypl.
Zirkusg.
Hollandstr.
Obere
DONAUKANAL
Franz-Josefs-Kai
Salztorbrücke
Donaustr.
Taborstraße
Praterstr.
Donaustr.
Marienbr.
Untere
Ruprechtskirche
Schwedenbr.
Aspern brücke
Urania-Sternwarte
Dampfschiffstr.
Franz-Josefs-Kai
Schwedenpl.
HOHER MARKT
Fleischmarkt
FLEISCHMARKT
Postg.
POSTSPARK.
Regierungsgebäude
Zollamtsstr.
Zollamtsstr.
Vordere
Hintere
Lugeck
Alte Schmiede
JESUITENKIRCHE
Biberstr.
STEPHANSDOM
Wollzeile
Alte Universität
Dominikanerkirche
Stubenring
MAK
FIGARO-HAUS
Deutschordenshaus
Singerstr.
Weihburg-
Stubentor
Stubenbastei
WIEN MITTE
Franziskanerkirche
STADTPALAIS DES PRINZEN EUGEN
Palais Colloredo
Landstraße (Wien Mitte)
Seilerstätte
Parkring
Stadtpark
Invalidenstr.
Johannesgasse
JOH.-STRAUSS-DENKMAL
HAUS DER MUSIK
Schellinggasse
RING
KURSALON
Am Heumarkt
Rechte
Linke
Ungargasse
Café Schwarzenberg
Schubertring
ÖAMTC
Johannesgasse
Stadtpark
Rudolf-Sallinger-Pl.
Beatrixgasse
Hotel Imperial
Beethovenplatz
Bahngasse
Reisnerstr.
Bahngasse
Musikvereinsgebäude
KONZERTHAUS
Am Heumarkt
AM MODENA-PARK
Lothringer
SCHWARZENBERG-PLATZ
HIST. MUSEUM
Ungargasse
K
L
P
R
S

Town Centre, city districts (Stadtbezirke) 1 - 9 :

Imperial, Kärntner Ring 16, A-1015, (01) 50 11 00, *hotel.imperial@luxurycollection.com, Fax (01) 50110410*, – , rm, – 150. rest KS a
Imperial (booking essential) *(closed 3 weeks July)(dinner only)* **Meals** à la carte 47/81 – ***Café Imperial*** : **Meals** à la carte 30/45 – 31 – **138 rm** 455/771 – 546/771 – 30 suites.
◆ The Württemberg Palace is a jewel in Vienna's architectural crown. Lavish, luxurious room decor, plus fine antique furnishings breathing the spirit of the 19C. Exclusive ambience and traditional food in the Imperial. Delicious cakes in the Café Imperial.

Grand Hotel, Kärntner Ring 9, 1010, (01) 51 58 00, *sales@grandhotelwien.com, Fax (01) 5151312*, , – , rm, – 220. KS f
Le ciel *(closed Sunday)* **Meals** 39 (lunch) and à la carte 43/59 – ***Unkai*** (Japanese) *(closed Monday lunch)* **Meals** à la carte 18/56,50 – ***Grand Café*** : **Meals** à la carte 22/44 – 28 – **205 rm** 300/380 – 370/450 – 11 suites.
◆ The glories of the Belle Epoque have been brought to life again in this luxurious establishment whose superb décor and furnishings will appeal to all those with high standards of taste. The elegant Le Ciel above the rooftops. Sushi and sashimi in the Unkai.

Sacher, Philharmonikerstr. 4, 1010, (01) 51 45 60, *wien@sacher.com, Fax (01) 51456810* – , rm, – 100. rest JS x
Meals 35 *(lunch)* and à la carte 33/61,50 – 27 – **108 rm** 215/292 – 312/388 – 5 suites.
◆ This Vienna institution was opened in 1876. The establishment's atmosphere is enhanced by prize antiques and a famous painting collection. The classically elegant restaurant also serves typical Viennese fare such as Wiener Schnitzel and Sachertorte.

Bristol, Kärntner Ring 1, 1015, (01) 51 51 60, *hotel.bristol@westin.com, Fax (01) 51516550* – , rm, – 180. rest JS m
Meals see also ***Korso*** below – ***Sirk*** *(closed July 3 weeks for dinner)* **Meals** à la carte 35/61 – 28 – **140 rm** 393 – 602 – 10 suites.
◆ Choice antiques and original works of art decorate the rooms, which also feature fine plasterwork, ceiling paintings and period furniture. Exclusive tower rooms. The Rotisserie Sirk with tasteful décor of the utmost discretion. View of the Opera.

InterContinental, Johannesgasse 28, 1037, (01) 71 12 20, *vienna@intercont i.com, Fax (01) 7134489*, , – , rm, – 560. KS p
Meals à la carte 25,50/53,50 – 23 – **453 rm** 250/280 – 280/320 – 61 suites.
◆ Rooms with lovely warm colours and a touch of Mediterranean style. 10th-floor Club Lounge with exclusive ambience and spectacular city views. In the evening diners can enjoy Mediterranean cooking and a relaxed atmosphere.

Marriott, Parkring 12a, 1010, (01) 51 51 80, *vienna.marriott.info@marriotthotels.com, Fax (01) 515186736*, Massage, , , – , rm, – 300. rest KR d
Meals 26/45 and à la carte – 23 – **313 rm** 270/320 – 5 suites.
◆ The only hotel in the centre of Vienna with a swimming pool is known for comfort and highly professional management and service. Many rooms with a view of the City Park. Business floor. Classically welcoming atmosphere in the restaurant.

Hilton Vienna Plaza, Schottenring 11, 1010, (01) 31 39 00, *cb_vienna-plaza@hilton.com, Fax (01) 3139022422*, , – , rm, – 60. JP a
La Scala *(closed Sunday lunch)* **Meals** à la carte 42/65 – 24 – **218 rm** 324 – 364 – 20 suites.
◆ In love with Art Deco and classical Modernism, this contemporary grand hotel has designer rooms that impress with their cool luxuriousness. The Scala serves a stunning range of fine delicacies inspired by the cuisine of France.

Radisson SAS Palais, Parkring 16, 1010, (01) 51 51 70, *sales@radissonsas.com, Fax (01) 5122216*, , – , rm, – 240. rest KR z
Le siècle *(closed 10 to 18 April, mid July - mid August, Saturday, Sunday and Bank Holidays)* **Meals** à la carte 39/61 – ***Palais Café*** : **Meals** à la carte 17,50/32 – 23 – **247 rm** 240/245 – 240/265 – 42 suites.
◆ Stylish furnishings and discreetly patterned materials characterise the tasteful rooms in this pair of linked palaces opposite the City Park. The Le Siècle restaurant has an attractively traditional ambience. The Palais Café is a feature of the wintergarden.

Renaissance Penta, Ungargasse 60, ✉ 1030, ☎ (01) 71 17 50, *rhi.viese.sales@renaissancehotels.com, Fax (01) 711758146*, (former imperial riding school with modern hotel wing), Massage, rm, – 260. AE VISA JCB. rest CY a
Meals 27 *(buffet lunch)* and à la carte 23/34 – 17 – **340 rm** 150/165.
• You don't have to be an experienced equestrian to stay in this neo-Classical listed building that was once the Imperial military riding school. Bright, functional natural wood furnishings. Diners made welcome in the elegant Borromäus restaurant.

Hotel de France, Schottenring 3, ✉ 1010, ☎ (01) 31 36 80, *defrance@austria-hotels.at, Fax (01) 3195969*, – rm, – 80. AE VISA JCB HP b
Meals à la carte 34/44 – **212 rm** 240/260 – 295.
• A particularly lovely traditional city hotel. Guests are accommodated in well-presented rooms, mostly furnished with Viennese period pieces. Modern maisonettes on the top floor. Luxurious Bel Etage restaurant.

Ambassador, Kärntner Str. 22, ✉ 1010, ☎ (01) 96 16 10, *office@ambassador.at, Fax (01) 5132999* – – 50. AE VISA JCB. rest JR s
Meals see ***Mörwald im Ambassador*** below – 20 – **86 rm** 247/400 – 312/501.
• Tradition and Viennese charm in a pleasing symbiosis with Hi-Tech. Individual rooms with welcoming colours, elegant décor and classical comfort in the most modern style.

Das Triest, Wiedner Hauptstr. 12, ✉ 1040, ☎ (01) 58 91 80, *manager@dastriest.at, Fax (01) 5891818*, – rm, – 60. AE VISA CY t
Meals *(closed end July - early August, Saturday lunch and Sunday)* (Italian) 33/53 and à la carte 31/46 – **72 rm** 192 – 247 – 3 suites.
• The Terence Conran designed rooms with blue chairs and desks with modem links are functional and comfortable without being fussy. Contemporary ambience in the restaurant with lots of mirrors and attractive lighting effects.

Arcotel Wimberger, Neubaugürtel 34, ✉ 1070, ☎ (01) 52 16 50, *wimberger@arcotel.at, Fax (01) 52165811*, – rm, rm, – 650. AE VISA JCB. rest BY t
Meals 23 *(buffet lunch)* and à la carte 25/38 – 11 – **225 rm** 160 – 200 – 7 suites.
• Following fire damage to the old Hotel Wimberger, there are now modern rooms with natural wood furnishings devoted to the needs of business travellers. The Maskerade restaurant has been decorated with materials saved from the old ballroom.

NH Belvedere without rest, Rennweg 12a, ✉ 1030, ☎ (01) 2 06 11, *nhbelvedere@nh-hotels.com, Fax (01) 2061115*, – . AE VISA JCB CY z
13 – **114 rm** 155.
• Modern hotel occupying the neo-Classical building of the old State Printing Works. Attractive rooms, some with a view of the Botantical Gardens. Bistro with snacks.

Sofitel, Am Heumarkt 35, ✉ 1030, ☎ (01) 71 61 60, *h1276@accor-hotels.com, Fax (01) 71616844* – rm, – 120. AE VISA JCB. rest
Meals à la carte 23/38,50 – 17 – **211 rm** 150/178 – 170/198. KS e
• Art Nouveau features and Klimt reproductions give a welcoming feeling to these rooms with their timeless natural wood furnishings and modern technology. Central location. Restaurant with attractive place settings and Viennese specialities.

Kaiserhof without rest, Frankenberggasse 10, ✉ 1040, ☎ (01) 5 05 17 01, *info@hotel-kaiserhof.at, Fax (01) 505887588*, – . AE VISA JCB. CY p
74 rm 125/170 – 170/195.
• The Richard family have been looking after travellers since 1577. Built in 1896, the Kaiserhof is the ideal place for their talents, full of fine design and Viennese charm.

Dorint Biedermeier, Landstraßer Hauptstr. 28 (at Sünnhof), ✉ A-1030, ☎ (01) 71 67 10, *info.viebie@dorint.com, Fax (01) 71671503*, – rm, – 60. AE VISA JCB LR d
Meals à la carte 31/42 – 15 – **203 rm** 151/162 – 180 – 12 suites.
• All the rooms in this establishment have been provided with cherrywood Biedermeier-style furnishings and are welcoming and extremely comfortable. This is the place to experience Vienna's gastronomic diversity, whether in pub, wine cellar or terrace restaurant.

Kaiserin Elisabeth without rest, Weihburggasse 3, ✉ 1010, ☎ (01) 51 52 60, *info@kaiserinelisabeth.at, Fax (01) 515267* – . AE VISA JCB KR a
63 rm 115/160 – 200/220.
• Mozart and Wagner were regular guests in this hotel near the Cathedral. Elegant darkwood furnishings in turn-of-the-century style.

Altstadt Vienna without rest, Kirchengasse 41, ✉ 1070, ☎ (01) 5 26 33 99, *hotel@altstadt.at, Fax (01) 5234901* – . AE VISA BY u
36 rm 99/139 – 129/159 – 7 suites.
• Each of the rooms in this patrician mansion has its own distinctive character. Tasteful décor, with high ceilings, parquet floors and contemporary Italian furnishings.

König von Ungarn, Schulerstr. 10, ✉ 1010, ✆ (01) 51 58 40, *hotel@kvu.at, Fax (01) 515848* – |♦|, ▤ rm, TV – 15. AE MC VISA JCB KR f
Meals *(dinner only)* à la carte 29/58 – **33 rm** 133/153 – 153/188.
♦ This stylish décor of this traditional 16C hotel behind the Cathedral features warm colours. The courtyard is well worth a look. Follow in Mozart's footsteps ; the great composer once lived here.

K+K Hotel Maria Theresia without rest, Kirchberggasse 6, ✉ 1070, ✆ (01) 5 21 23, *kk.maria.theresia@kuk.at, Fax (01) 5212370,* – |♦|, rm, ▤ TV – 40. AE MC VISA JCB HS a
123 rm 160 – 210.
♦ A hotel in the idyllic artistic district of Spittelberg, with prettily decorated rooms, some with glass-topped work-desks. The rooms with a city view are particularly lovely.

K+K Palais Hotel without rest, Rudolfsplatz 11, ✉ 1010, ✆ (01) 5 33 13 53, *kk.palais.hotel@kuk.at, Fax (01) 533135370* – |♦| ▤ TV. AE MC VISA JCB JP h
66 rm 160/185 – 210.
♦ Anyone who likes the colour yellow will be pleased with this modern, comfortable hotel in the historic Stadtpalais. The Cathedral and Underground are close at hand.

Strudelhof without rest, Pasteurgasse 1, ✉ 1090, ✆ (01) 31 92 52 20, *seminarhotel@strudlhof.at, Fax (01) 319252210020,* – |♦| ▤ TV P – 240. AE MC VISA BY n
84 rm 121/153 – 164.
♦ This newly-constructed hotel offers its guests comfortable rooms with good technical facilities. The palace at the rear makes a stylish setting for business meetings.

Mercure Secession without rest, Getreidemarkt 5, ✉ 1060, ✆ (01) 5 88 38, *h3532@accor-hotels.com, Fax (01) 58838212* – |♦| TV – 30. AE MC VISA JCB JS b
68 rm 94/137 – 174.
♦ Thanks to its central location, this establishment is an excellent base for your exploration of the city. Homely, comfortable rooms plus apartments.

Opernring without rest, Opernring 11, ✉ 1010, ✆ (01) 5 87 55 18, *hotel@opernring.at, Fax (01) 587551829* – |♦| TV. AE MC VISA JCB JS a
35 rm 140/155 – 185/280.
♦ This establishment by the Opera has a lovely Art Nouveau facade. The spacious rooms combine liveability and comfort with the functionality of up-to-date accommodation.

Starlight Suiten Salzgries without rest, Salzgries 12, ✉ 1010, ✆ (01) 5 35 92 22, *reservation@starlighthotel.com, Fax (01) 535922211,* – |♦| ▤ TV. AE MC VISA JP e
12 – **49 suites** 138 – 198.
♦ If one room is not enough, stay in this modern hotel whose suites have an excellent combination of galley, natural wood furnishings, bright colours and up-to-date technology.

Cordial Theaterhotel without rest, Josefstädter Str. 22, ✉ 1080, ✆ (01) 4 05 36 48, *chwien@cordial.co.at, Fax (01) 4051406,* – |♦|, rm, TV – 30. AE MC VISA JCB BY x
54 rm 145 – 190.
♦ Right by the theatre in the Josephstadt district, this restored Art Nouveau building is a practical and well-presented place to stay. Small café-restaurant for hungry guests.

Arkadenhof without rest, Viriotgasse 5, ✉ 1090, ✆ (01) 3 10 08 37, *management@arkadenhof.com, Fax (01) 3107686* – |♦| ▤ TV – 20. MC VISA BY c
45 rm 115/137 – 151.
♦ Comfortable and homely, this is a well-presented and up-to-date place to stay for a while. Central location near the Franz-Josef railway station.

Lassalle without rest, Engerthstr. 173, ✉ 1020, ✆ (01) 21 31 50, *lassalle@austria.trend.at, Fax (01) 21315100,* – |♦| TV – 40. AE MC VISA JCB CY r
140 rm 116/135 – 155 – 4 suites.
♦ In a quiet but accessible location, this establishment has rooms with warm colours, tasteful furnishings and allergen-free carpets. Some rooms with connecting doors.

Erzherzog Rainer, Wiedner Hauptstr. 27, ✉ 1040, ✆ (01) 50 11 10, *rainer@schick-hotels.com, Fax (01) 50111350* – |♦|, rm, ▤ rest, TV – 30. AE MC VISA JCB CY g
Meals à la carte 19/33 – **84 rm** 134/169 – 179.
♦ This is an historic Vienna institution, with pleasant, traditionally furnished rooms, some with Art Nouveau pieces. Patronised in the past by figures such as Marie Curie. Attractive restaurant caters for the gastronomic needs of hotel guests.

Holiday Inn Vienna City, Margaretenstr. 53, ✉ 1050, ✆ (01) 5 88 50, *vienna.city@holiday-inn.at, Fax (01) 58850899,* – |♦|, rm, ▤ rest, TV – 40. AE MC VISA JCB. rest BY m
Meals à la carte 24/35 – 11 – **101 rm** 180 – 200.
♦ Cheerfully decorated and welcoming rooms not far from Opera, Cathedral and Ringstrasse. Excellent base for business or sightseeing. Restaurant in the style of Viennese Modernism. Attractive terrace to the rear.

Das Tyrol without rest, Mariahilfer Str. 15, ✉ 1060, ☎ (01) 5 87 54 15, *reception@das-tyrol.at, Fax (01) 58754159,* – |‡| ⇔ ▤ TV ☎. AE ⓓ ⓜ VISA HS d
30 rm ☕ 110/180 – 140/230.
◆ This lovingly restored corner building has rooms tastefully furnished with contemporary pieces. There is an excellent sauna in the basement.

Stefanie, Taborstr. 12, ✉ 1020, ☎ (01) 21 15 00, *stefanie@schick-hotels.com, Fax (01) 21150160,* – |‡| ⇔, ▤ rm, TV – 🏛 70. AE ⓓ ⓜ VISA JCB KLP d
Meals à la carte 27/43 – **126 rm** ☕ 125/189 – 162/199.
◆ Enjoy real Viennese atmosphere in this charming establishment. Furnishings in classic Vienna style give the hotel an attractively nostalgic feeling. A tree-shaded garden terrace complements the restaurant.

Mercure Wien City without rest, Hollandstr. 3, ✉ 1020, ☎ (01) 21 31 30, *h1568@accor-hotels.com, Fax (01) 21313230* – |‡|, ⇔ rm, ▤ TV ☎ ♿ – 🏛 40. AE ⓓ ⓜ VISA JCB KP a
☕ 13 – **123 rm** ☕ 125 – 145.
◆ Its ideal location makes this hotel an excellent venue for seminars and conferences. Some of the rooms were specifically designed with business travellers in mind.

Mercure Nestroy without rest, Rotensterngasse 12, ✉ 1020, ☎ (01) 2 11 40, *h1891@accor-hotels.com, Fax (01) 211407,* – |‡| ⇔ TV ☎ – 🏛 50. AE ⓓ ⓜ VISA JCB LP b
☕ 13 – **87 rm** 125/165 – 145/165 – 4 suites.
◆ This old butcher's shop has taken on a new lease of life as a hotel. Comfortable, modern rooms, some with parquet floors, mean that guests soon feel at home.

InterCityHotel, Mariahilferstr. 122, ✉ 1070, ☎ (01) 52 58 50, *wien@intercityhotel.at, Fax (01) 52585111,* – |‡|, ⇔ rm, TV ☎ ♿ – 🏛 60. AE ⓓ ⓜ VISA JCB
Meals 14 *(buffet lunch)* and à la carte 23/35 – ☕ 13 – **179 rm** 105 – 130 – 7 suites.
◆ Practical accommodation close to the West Station. Your room-card gives you great mobility, since use of local public transport is included in the room price. BY r

Amadeus without rest, Wildpretmarkt 5, ✉ 1010, ☎ (01) 5 33 87 38, *amadeus.vienna@aon.at, Fax (01) 533873838* – |‡| ▤ TV ☎. ⓓ ⓜ VISA. JR y
closed 20 to 26 December – **30 rm** ☕ 85/120 – 142/160.
◆ Contrasting with red carpets and fabrics, white-lacquered period furniture lends special allure to this welcoming, family-run establishment in the Wilpretmarkt art district.

City-Central without rest, Taborstr. 8, ✉ 1020, ☎ (01) 21 10 50, *city.central@schick-hotels.com, Fax (01) 21105140* – |‡| ⇔ ▤ TV ☎ ♿ P. AE ⓓ ⓜ VISA JCB KP x
58 rm ☕ 120/164 – 179.
◆ Behind the stylish façade of this historic building are rooms offering contemporary comforts in no way at the expense of typically Viennese atmosphere.

Am Parkring, Parkring 12, ✉ 1015, ☎ (01) 51 48 00, *parkring@schick-hotels.com, Fax (01) 5148040,* ≤ Vienna – |‡|, ⇔ rm, ▤ TV ☎ – 🏛 25. AE ⓓ ⓜ VISA JCB. rest KR k
Meals à la carte 32/58 – **64 rm** ☕ 149/205 – 219 – 8 suites.
◆ Great city views from the modern rooms of this hotel on the upper floors of the Parks Department skyscraper opposite the City Park. Ask for a room with a balcony. With skyline vistas, the Himmelstube (Bar of Heaven) restaurant lives up to its name.

Johann Strauss without rest, Favoritenstr. 12, ✉ A-1040, ☎ (01) 5 05 76 24, *info@hotel-johann-strauss.at, Fax (01) 5057628* – |‡| ⇔ ▤ TV ☎. AE ⓓ ⓜ VISA CY g
53 rm ☕ 116/130 – 159.
◆ The "uncrowned king" of the waltz gave this well-presented establishment its name. Behind the historic facade are comfortable and functional rooms with high ceilings.

Kummer, Mariahilfer Str. 71a, ✉ 1060, ☎ (01) 5 88 95, *kummer@austria-hotels.at, Fax (01) 5878133* – |‡|, ⇔ rm, TV ☎ – 🏛 20. AE ⓓ ⓜ VISA JCB BY s
Meals à la carte 22/37 – **99 rm** ☕ 160/215 – 230.
◆ In the centre of one's of Vienna's busiest shopping districts, this hotel with its neo-Classical façade from the turn of the century has spacious rooms with classic period furniture. Enjoy a break in the charming restaurant.

Mercure Wien Zentrum, Fleischmarkt 1a, ✉ 1010, ☎ (01) 53 46 00, *h0781@accor-hotels.com, Fax (01) 53460232* – |‡|, ⇔ rm, ▤ TV ☎ ♿. AE ⓓ ⓜ VISA JCB KR n
Meals à la carte 25/38,50 – ☕ 13 – **154 rm** 132/175 – 149/175.
◆ Right by the Cathedral in the historic heart of the city, this establishment offers practical rooms with fax and elegant modern wooden furnishings. Baby-sitting service. Recover from sightseeing in the modern, welcoming café-restaurant.

Capricorno without rest, Schwedenplatz 3, ✉ 1010, ☎ (01) 53 33 10 40, *capricorno@schick-hotels.com, Fax (01) 53376714* – |‡| ▤ TV ☎ P. AE ⓓ ⓜ VISA JCB KR x
46 rm ☕ 130 – 172.
◆ True Viennese atmosphere and Art Nouveau features throughout this establishment. The tasteful bedrooms are impressive as well, some of them with period furnishings.

Suitehotel Wien Messe without rest, Radingerstr. 2, ✉ 1020, ☎ (01) 24 58 80, *h3720@accor-hotels.com, Fax (01) 24588188,* – AE MC VISA JCB CY h
6 – **158 rm** 79.
• A novel concept ; guests are accommodated in spacious (30m2), colourfully decorated modern rooms featuring partitions which can be used to separate living and sleeping areas.

Europa, Kärntner Str. 18, ✉ 1010, ☎ (01) 51 59 40, *europa.wien@austria-trend.at, Fax (01) 51594888* – AE MC VISA JCB JR a
Meals à la carte 26/38,50 – **116 rm** 143/151 – 215.
• With its contemporary, colourfully decorated designer rooms, this is a good place to stay in the elegant Kärntner Strasse area. Ask for one of the spacious corner rooms. The stylish Wiener Café-Restaurant has been known for years for its fine cuisine.

Tourotel without rest, Mariahilferstr. 156, ✉ 1150, ☎ (01) 89 23 33 50, *hotel.maria hilf@tourotel.at, Fax (01) 8923335495* – P. AE MC VISA BY e
65 rm 119/139 – 149.
• Not far from the West Station, this modern-looking city building has good, functional and practically furnished rooms.

Ibis Messe, Lassallestr. 7a, ✉ 1020, ☎ (01) 21 77 00, *h2736@accor-hotels.com, Fax (01) 21770555* – rm, – 100. AE MC VISA CY b
Meals à la carte 16/25 – 9 – **166 rm** 62 – 77.
• This establishment close to the Prater has contemporary, brightly furnished and functional rooms, well-equipped with technical facilities and generous work-desks.

Steirereck, Rasumofskygasse 2/corner of Weißgerberlände, ✉ 1030, ☎ (01) 7 13 31 68, *wien@steirereck.at, Fax (01) 71351682* – AE MC VISA CY c
closed Christmas, Saturday, Sunday and Bank Holidays – **Meals** (booking essential) (tour of the wine-cellar possible) 35 *(lunch)*/70 and à la carte.
• The cuisine of the Steirereck is still among the best in Vienna. It is expected that the establishment will move in autumn 2004 to a new location in the City Park.
Spec. Bachforelle mit Avocado. Kaninchenrücken mit Zucchini und süßer Gemüseleber. Überbackene Birne auf Karamel.

Korso - Hotel Bristol, Kärntner Ring 1, ✉ 1010, ☎ (01) 51 51 65 46, *Fax (01) 51516575* – AE MC VISA JCB. JS m
closed 3 weeks August and Saturday lunch – **Meals** 38 *(lunch)* and à la carte 51/82.
• Reinhard Gerer's Viennese and French cuisine is served here in an atmosphere that manages to be festive without being over-formal, elegant but relaxed as well.
Spec. Riesling-Kalbsbeuscherl mit Briocheflan. Sautierte Kalbsnierenrose mit Rotweinzwiebeln. Geschmorte Kalbsbackerln mit Selleriepüree und Gemüse.

Mörwald im Ambassador, Kärntner Str. 22 (first floor), ✉ 1010, ☎ (01) 96 16 11 61, *ambassador@moerwald.at, Fax (01) 96161160* – AE MC VISA JCB JR s
closed Sunday and Bank Holidays – **Meals** (booking essential) 30 *(lunch)* and à la carte 35/64.
• In a neo-Classical building, an elegant first floor restaurant reached through a smart bar, setting the tone for the enjoyment of local cuisine and some creative specialities.
Spec. Vitello Tonnato aus dem rosa Kalbsrücken. Szegediner Hummerkrautfleisch. Souf-flierte Mannerschnitte.

Drei Husaren, Weihburggasse 4, ✉ 1010, ☎ (01) 51 21 09 20, *office@drei.husaren.at, Fax (01) 512109218* – AE MC VISA JCB KR u
Meals 33 *(lunch)*/68 and à la carte 38/75.
• In a side street close to the Cathedral, this is an historic gourmet restaurant with cheerful yellow-painted walls. A refined version of classic Viennese cuisine is served.

Niky's Kuchlmasterei, Obere Weissgerberstr. 6, ✉ 1030, ☎ (01) 7 12 90 00, *office@kuchlmasterei.at, Fax (01) 712900016,* – AE MC VISA LR f
closed Sunday and Bank Holidays (except December) – **Meals** à la carte 35/51.
• This opulent restaurant never fails to surprise. There are lots of Baroque features plus a lovely terrace and an enormous wine cellar.

Julius Meinl am Graben, Graben 19 (first floor), ✉ A-1010, ☎ (01) 5 32 33 34, *julius.meinl@restaurant.com, Fax (01) 532333423* – AE MC VISA JCB JR e
closed Sunday and Bank Holidays – **Meals** (booking essential) à la carte 41/53.
• A glass lift transports diners up through the famous delicatessen to this secret restaurant with its elegant ambience and refined Austrian cuisine.

Grotta Azzurra, Babenbergerstr. 5, ✉ 1010, ☎ (01) 5 86 10 44, *office@grotta-azzurra.at, Fax (01) 586104415* – AE MC VISA JCB HS s
Meals (Italian) à la carte 27/48.
• Vienna's oldest Italian establishment is lent its special character by wonderfully crafted Venetian glass and mosaics. Seasonal menu featuring Italian regional cuisine.

Steirer Stub'n, Wiedner Hauptstr. 111, ✉ 1050, ☎ (01) 5 44 43 49, *steirerstuben@chello.at, Fax (01) 5440888* – ▤. AE ⓓ ⓜⓒ VISA BZ k
closed Sunday and Bank Holidays – **Meals** (booking essential) 25 and à la carte 25/33 ♀.
◆ Typical Viennese dishes are proffered in an atmospheric setting, which the tastefully decorated, rustic dining rooms do much to enhance.

Selina, Laudongasse 13, ✉ 1080, ☎ (01) 4 05 64 04, *Fax (01) 4080459* – AE ⓓ ⓜⓒ VISA JCB BY f
closed Saturday lunch, Sunday and Bank Holidays – **Meals** à la carte 33/46,50 ♀.
◆ On the edge of the city centre, sophisticated cuisine served in an elegantly modern ambience accentuated by pictures and Classical features.

Walter Bauer, Sonnenfelsgasse 17, ✉ 1010, ☎ (01) 5 12 98 71, *Fax (01) 5129871* – AE ⓓ VISA KR c
closed 1 week Easter, 19 July - 13 August, Saturday - Monday lunch and Bank Holidays – **Meals** (booking essential) à la carte 34/51 ♀.
◆ This lovely vaulted restaurant is somewhat hidden away in a little alleyway not far from the Jesuits' Church - dating from the 14C, it was once a stables.
Spec. Klassisches Hummerkrautfleisch. Gansleberterrine mit Brioche. Variation von Sorbets und Früchten.

Ma'estro, Heumarkt 6 (at Wiener Konzerthaus), ✉ 1030, ☎ (01) 7 14 89 11, *maestro@gerstner.at, Fax (01) 24200721* – ▤. AE ⓓ ⓜⓒ VISA JCB KS a
closed July - August, Sunday – **Meals** *(dinner only)* (booking essential) à la carte 30/43 ♀.
◆ Owned by Gerstner's Imperial patisserie, this restaurant is in a wing of the Concert Hall. Plaster ceilings and crystal chandeliers lend it great atmosphere.

Fabios, Tuchlauben 6, ✉ 1010, ☎ (01) 5 32 22 22, *fabios@fabios.at, Fax (01) 5322225* – ▤. AE ⓓ ⓜⓒ VISA JR x
closed Sunday – **Meals** (Italian) (booking essential) à la carte 28,50/48,50 ♀.
◆ This fashionable Italian establishment offers not only fine cuisine but also sophisticated place settings and lovely, minimalist interior décor.

Vestibül, Dr. Karl-Lueger-Ring 2 (at Burgtheater), ✉ 1010, ☎ (01) 5 32 49 99, *restaurant@vestibuel.at, Fax (01) 532499910* – ♿. ⓜⓒ VISA HR d
closed Saturday lunch, Sunday and Bank Holidays – **Meals** à la carte 23/46 ♀.
◆ In a wing of the Burgtheater that was once the Emperor's private entrance, this stylish and elegant restaurant offers fine cuisine and classic Viennese specialities.

Novelli, Bräunerstr. 11, ✉ 1010, ☎ (01) 5 13 42 00, *novelli@haslauer.at, Fax (01) 512375250*, 🏠 – AE ⓓ ⓜⓒ VISA JR b
closed Sunday – **Meals** (Italian) (booking essential) à la carte 31/47 ♀.
◆ This is a place in which to enjoy a relaxed Italian atmosphere and appreciate classic food and drink from the shores of the Mediterranean.

Zum weißen Rauchfangkehrer, Weihburggasse 4, ✉ 1010, ☎ (01) 5 12 34 71, *rauchfangkehrer@utanet.at, Fax (01) 512347128* – ▤. ⓜⓒ VISA KR e
closed 4 to 15 January, 15 July - 25 August, 22 to 27 December, Sunday and Monday – **Meals** *(dinner only)* (booking essential) à la carte 35/48 ♀.
◆ One of Vienna's loveliest old restaurants. The décor guarantees good cheer, the menu features local delicacies. Ask how the place got its name ("The White Chimneysweep").

Indochine 21, Stubenring 18, ✉ 1010, ☎ (01) 5 13 76 60, *restaurant@indochine.at, Fax (01) 513766016*, 🏠 – ▤. AE ⓓ ⓜⓒ VISA JCB. ✂ LR b
Meals (Euro-Asian) à la carte 24,50/50 ♀.
◆ In an excellent city location this chic establishment brings a touch of old Indochina to Vienna. Fusion cuisine - French with an Asian touch - served to a very high standard.

Zum Schwarzen Kameel, Bognergasse 5, ✉ 1010, ☎ (01) 5 33 81 25, *info@kameel.at, Fax (01) 533812523*, 🏠 – ▤. AE ⓓ ⓜⓒ VISA JR m
closed Sunday and Bank Holidays – **Meals** (booking essential) à la carte 26,50/44 ♀.
◆ This fashionable and far from everyday restaurant is entered through a delicatessen. Lovely Art Nouveau style combines with Viennese charm to make it very special.

Schubertstüberln, Schreyvogelgasse 4, ✉ 1010, ☎ (01) 5 33 71 87, *schubertstueberln@i-one.at, Fax (01) 5353546*, 🏠 – AE ⓓ ⓜⓒ VISA JCB HR e
closed Saturday and Sunday – **Meals** à la carte 23/42.
◆ A series of dining rooms varying in style from rustic to traditional, and a choice of good solid dishes enlivened with Viennese delicacies and food from the Mediterranean.

Salut, Wildpretmarkt 3, ✉ 1010, ☎ (01) 5 33 13 22, *Fax (01) 5331322* – AE ⓓ ⓜⓒ VISA JR y
closed 3 weeks August, Sunday, Monday and Bank Holidays – **Meals** à la carte 30/38.
◆ This lovingly decorated restaurant is divided into a number of cosy, rustic dining rooms. As the name suggests, French dishes dominate the menu.

XX **Plachutta**, Wollzeile 38, ✉ 1010, ☎ (01) 5 12 15 77, *wollzeile@plachutta.at, Fax (01) 512157720*, – ▤. AE ◑ MC VISA KR b
Meals (booking essential) à la carte 32/43.
◆ The Plachutta family have long devoted themselves to traditional ways of preparing beef, which is served in all its variety in their green-panelled dining room.

XX **Gußhaus**, Gußhausstr. 23, ✉ 1040, ☎ (01) 5 04 47 50, *gusshaus@kainz-wexberg.at, Fax (01) 5059464*, . AE ◑ MC VISA CY p
closed Saturday lunch, Sunday and Bank Holidays – **Meals** 22 and à la carte 26/35 ♀.
◆ Still-life pictures decorate the warmly-painted walls of this bistro-style restaurant which owes its name ("casting house") to the adjacent Imperial foundry.

XX **Cantinetta Antinori**, Jasomirgottstrasse 3, ✉ 1010, ☎ (01) 5 33 77 22, *cantinetta.antinori@aon.at, Fax (01) 533772211* – ▤. AE ◑ MC VISA KR s
closed 1 to 10 August – **Meals** (Italian) (booking essential) à la carte 34/49 ♀.
◆ Savour classic Tuscan cuisine in a stylish bistro-type ambience with Italian décor. Excellent choice of fine Antinori wines, which are also served by the glass.

XX **Fadinger**, Wipplingerstr. 29, ✉ 1010, ☎ (01) 5 33 43 41, *restaurant@fadinger.at, Fax (01) 5324451* – JP f
closed Saturday, Sunday and Bank Holidays – **Meals** (booking essential) 18 *(lunch)* and à la carte 25,50/45 ♀.
◆ Attractive city centre establishment close to the stock exchange. Bright watercolours, cheerful atmosphere, and a mixture of local dishes and fine cuisine.

XX **Enoteca Frizzante**, Kumpfgasse 3, ✉ 1010, ☎ (01) 5 13 07 47, *Fax (01) 5133109*, – ▤. AE ◑ MC VISA KR v
closed 24 to 30 December, Sunday and Bank Holidays – **Meals** (Italian) à la carte 25/36 ♀.
◆ Not far from the Cathedral, this vaulted restaurant established in 1992 owes its appeal to its elegant cherrywood décor as well as to its classic range of dishes from Italy.

X **Tempel**, Praterstr. 56, ✉ 1020, ☎ (01) 2 14 01 79, *tempel@i-one.at, Fax (01) 2140179* – ◑ MC VISA LP a
closed 2 weeks August, 23 December - 7 January, Saturday lunch, Sunday and Monday – **Meals** 13 *(lunch)* and à la carte 23/38 ♀.
◆ This bistro-style little restaurant is tucked away in a courtyard. It serves local specialities as well as more refined dishes and is well worth looking for.

X **Schnattl**, Lange Gasse 40, ✉ 1080, ☎ (01) 4 05 34 00, *Fax (01) 4053400*, – AE ◑ BY b
closed 2 weeks April, 2 weeks end August, Saturday, Sunday and Bank Holidays – **Meals** à la carte 28,50/41.
◆ This well-run little restaurant with its simple but not unattractive interior is located on the edge of the city centre. It's very pleasant sitting out in the courtyard.

X **Zu ebener Erde und erster Stock**, Burggasse 13, ✉ 1070, ☎ (01) 5 23 62 54 – ▤. AE VISA HS b
closed 3 to 21 August, 1 to 8 January, Saturday lunch, Sunday, Monday and Bank Holidays – **Meals** à la carte 25/33,50 ♀.
◆ This Biedermeier-style establishment on the Spittelberg is a real bit of old Vienna. Simple fare on the ground floor, Austrian cuisine with a Mediterranean touch upstairs.

X **Hedrich**, Stubenring 2, ✉ A-1010, ☎ (01) 5 12 95 88 LR a
closed August, 24 December - 1 January, Saturday, Sunday and Bank Holidays – **Meals** à la carte 11/21 ♀.
◆ Even diners in a hurry can eat well here. Typical pub-type ambience and a menu full of tasty dishes ranging from local fare to more refined offerings.

City districts (Stadtbezirke) 10 - 15 :

Holiday Inn Vienna South, Triester Str. 72, ✉ 1100, ☎ (01) 6 05 30, *info@holiday-inn.co.at, Fax (01) 60530580*, , , – , rm, ▤ – 200. AE ◑ MC VISA JCB BZ f
Meals 26/30 *(buffet)* and à la carte 27,50/38 ♀ – 19 – **174 rm** 195 – 210 – 4 suites.
◆ This modern hotel with functional rooms is on the edge of town in a business park with a shopping centre. Rooms with fax and modem link. The high point of the Brasserie California restaurant is the vast hot and cold buffet.

Renaissance Wien, Ullmannstr. 71, ✉ 1150, ☎ (01) 89 10 20, *rhi.viehw@renaissancehotels.com, Fax (01) 89102300*, , – , rm, ▤ – 200. AE ◑ MC VISA JCB BZ a
Orangerie : **Meals** à la carte 32/43 – ***Allegro*** : **Meals** 31/38 (buffet only) – 20 – **309 rm** 222 – 245 – 3 suites.
◆ Guests are accommodated here in functional rooms with light-wood furnishings. There's more space in the Executive Rooms. City panorama from the covered pool. Columns add distinction to the elegant Orangerie. Excellent buffet in the Allegro.

Dorint Am Europaplatz, Felberstr. 4, ✉ 1150, ✆ (01) 98 11 10, *info.viebud@dorint.com, Fax (01) 98111930*, – |‡|, ⇹ rm, TV – 140. AE MC VISA. rest
Meals à la carte 18/33 – 15 – **253 rm** 145 – 165. BY z
• Pink on the outside, this corner building has a meticulously refurbished interior, with comfortable rooms offering all the facilities to be expected in a contemporary hotel. The Café-Restaurant Klimt is particularly inviting.

Landhaus Tschipan without rest, Friedhofstr. 12, ✉ 1100, ✆ (01) 6 89 40 11, *office@tschipan.at, Fax (01) 689401135* – |‡| TV P – 15. AE MC VISA.
closed 23 December - 7 January – **29 rm** 68 – 105. by Laaer Berg Straße CZ
• Attractive, well-run family establishment on the edge of town. Guests appreciate the well-kept, homely rooms with Italian period furnishings.

Gartenhotel Altmannsdorf, Hoffingergasse 26, ✉ 1120, ✆ (01) 8 01 23, *office@gartenhotel.com, Fax (01) 8012351*, Park, – |‡|, ⇹ rm, TV P – 60. AE MC VISA. rest AZ s
Meals à la carte 27/42 – **95 rm** 120/140 – 174.
• Behind the yellow facade are modern, functional rooms mostly used by conference delegates. Those with a view of the park are particularly pleasant. A former greenhouse makes an attractive wintergarden-like setting for the hotel restaurant.

Bosei, Gutheil-Schoder-Gasse 9, ✉ 1100, ✆ (01) 6 61 06, *bosei@austria-trend.at, Fax (01) 6610699* – |‡|, ⇹ rm, rest, TV P – 200. AE MC VISA JCB BZ t
Meals à la carte 22/32 – **193 rm** 112 – 138 – 8 suites.
• This modern hotel is located on the edge of a park with sport and recreational facilities (including golf and tennis). Functional rooms offering more than adequate space. Restaurant with a splendid view of the golf course through its glazed façade.

Stadthalle without rest, Hackengasse 20, ✉ 1150, ✆ (01) 9 82 42 72, *office@hotelstadthalle.at, Fax (01) 982723269* – |‡| ⇹ TV. MC VISA BY z
46 rm 73/83 – 109.
• Comfort together with colourful design and décor characterise this establishment close to the city centre. Breakfast is served in the attractively landscaped courtyard.

Favorita without rest, Laxenburger Str. 8, ✉ 1100, ✆ (01) 60 14 60, *favorita@austria-trend.at, Fax (01) 60146720*, – |‡| ⇹ TV – 150. AE MC VISA JCB
161 rm 112/132 – 138 – 3 suites. CZ n
• Behind the Art Nouveau façade of what were once working-class flats are functional rooms particularly suitable for the conference and business guest.

Reither without rest, Graumanngasse 16, ✉ 1150, ✆ (01) 8 93 68 41, *hotel.reither@aon.at, Fax (01) 8936835*, – |‡| ⇹ TV. AE MC VISA BZ r
closed 22 to 27 December – **50 rm** 92/108 – 130.
• This family establishment is known for typical Austrian hospitality. Practically furnished rooms with work-desks, some with balcony or terrace.

Altwienerhof with rm, Herklotzgasse 6, ✉ 1150, ✆ (01) 8 92 60 00, *office@altwienerhof.at, Fax (01) 89260008* – |‡| TV. AE MC VISA BZ s
Meals *(closed Saturday and Sunday)* à la carte 46/60 ♀, – **25 rm** 57 – 97.
• Visitors to this establishment are thoroughly pampered as they sit beneath panelled walls hung with tapestries. Wintergarden and courtyard.

Hietzinger Bräu, Auhofstr. 1, ✉ 1130, ✆ (01) 87 77 08 70, *hietzing@plachutta.at, Fax (01) 877708722*, – . AE MC VISA AZ u
closed 19 July - 14 August – **Meals** (mainly boiled beef dishes)(booking essential) à la carte 34/44 ♀.
• Behind the Art Nouveau façade is a temple devoted to the cult of beef. All kinds of famous Viennese beef specialities are served in this refined version of a typical pub.

Vikerl's Lokal, Würfelgasse 4, ✉ 1150, ✆ (01) 8 94 34 30, *Fax (01) 8924183* BYZ d
closed Sunday dinner and Monday – **Meals** *(weekdays dinner only)* (booking essential) 36 and à la carte 22/39 ♀.
• An enjoyable time is guaranteed at this family establishment, what with its rustic ambience and its hearty local dishes which vary according to the season.

Meixner's Gastwirtschaft, Buchengasse 64 / corner of Herndlgasse, ✉ 1100, ✆ (01) 6 04 27 10, *k.meixner@aon.at, Fax (01) 6063400*, – VISA CZ a
closed 8 to 29 August, Saturday - Sunday and Bank Holidays – **Meals** à la carte 18,50/32,50 ♀.
• Traditional inn with cheerful décor, where the landlady is known for her authentic and very tasty way with the local cuisine. Attractive pub garden to the rear.

City districts (Stadtbezirke) 16 - 19 :

Landhaus Fuhrgassl-Huber without rest, Rathstr. 24, ✉ 1190, ✆ (01) 4 40 30 33, *landhaus@fuhrgassl-huber.at, Fax (01) 4402714*, – |‡| TV. AE MC VISA AX m
closed 1 week early February – **38 rm** 70/77 – 107/115.
• A pleasant country-house atmosphere awaits guests to this family-run establishment with its comfortable and prettily decorated rooms. Excellent breakfast buffet.

Jäger without rest, Hernalser Hauptstr. 187, ✉ 1170, ☎ (01) 48 66 62 00, *hoteljaeger@aon.at, Fax (01) 48666208* – AE VISA AY r
17 rm 80/105 – 110/140.
◆ Attractive establishment with pretty front garden, family-owned for over 80 years, offering everything a visitor or business traveller could wish for. Good breakfast buffet.

Eckel, Sieveringer Str. 46, ✉ 1190, ☎ (01) 3 20 32 18, *restaurant.eckel@aon.at, Fax (01) 3206660,* – AE VISA AX s
closed 2 weeks August, 24 December - mid January, Sunday and Monday – **Meals** à la carte 22/58 ♀.
◆ This country house is partly traditional, partly bright and friendly. Regular visitors appreciate the lovely summer terrace as well as the local and classic cuisine.

Plachutta with rm, Heiligenstädter Str. 179, ✉ 1190, ☎ (01) 3 70 41 25, *nussdorf@plachutta.at, Fax (01) 370412520,* – . AE VISA BX e
closed 2 weeks July - August – **Meals** *(mainly boiled beef dishes)* à la carte 32/46 – 7 – **4 rm** 45 – 75.
◆ This friendly establishment has an amazing line in beef dishes such as hearty soups served from big copper cooking pots and filled with all kinds of delicious meaty morsels.

Mayer, Sieveringer Str. 137, ✉ 1190, ☎ (01) 9 46 41 30, *restaurant.mayer@chello.at* – VISA AX a
closed July – **Meals** *(weekdays dinner only)* 28 and à la carte 26/40 ♀.
◆ This attractive little restaurant occupies two floors. Interior with wood floor, plain wooden chairs, leather-covered benches and modern pictures.

City district (Stadtbezirk) 22 :

Crowne Plaza, Wagramer Str. 21, ✉ 1220, ☎ (01) 26 02 00, *crowneplazavienna@ichotelsgroup.com, Fax (01) 2602020,* – , rm, – 300. AE VISA JCB. rest CY v
Meals 27 *(buffet lunch)* and à la carte 23/34 – 18 – **252 rm** 190 – 250 – 3 suites.
◆ This establishment helps make life easy for the business traveller, what with a business centre, conference rooms with up-to-the-minute technology and functional rooms with work-desks and ISDN. In contemporary style, Stars Restaurant opens on to the foyer.

Mraz u. Sohn, Wallensteinstr. 59, ✉ 1200, ☎ (01) 3 30 45 94, *Fax (01) 3501536,* – VISA CY s
closed 3 weeks August, 2 weeks December, Saturday, Sunday and Bank Holidays – **Meals** (booking essential) 38 and à la carte 45/56 ♀.
◆ The outside gives no hint of what lies within - though the contemporary design and avant-garde place settings are more than matched by the exceptionally creative cooking.
Spec. Kletzengänseleber mit Brioche. Ochsenfilet mit Krautfleckerln. Schokoauflauf medium mit Chilischokolade.

Sichuan, Arbeiterstrandbadstr. 122, ✉ 1220, ☎ (01) 2 63 37 13, *info@sichuan.at, Fax (01) 2633714,* – VISA CX a
Meals (Chinese) 9 *(lunch)* and à la carte 21/27.
◆ Built in Chinese style, this establishment is surrounded by an astonishingly beautiful traditional garden. The restaurant's name indicates the nature of the regional cuisine.

Heurigen and Buschenschänken (wine gardens) – *(mostly self-service, hot and cold dishes from buffet, prices according to weight of chosen meals, therefore not shown below. Buschenschänken sell their own wines only) :*

Schübel-Auer, Kahlenberger Str. 22, ✉ 1190, ☎ (01) 3 70 22 22, *schuebel-auer@24on.cc, Fax (01) 3702222,* – AE VISA BX a
closed 22 December - 7 February, Sunday and Monday – **Meals** *(dinner only)* (buffet only) ♀.
◆ This old building was once a wine-grower's house with a mill and a run of millstones. It was carefully restored in 1972 and lovingly fitted out. Internal courtyard.

Feuerwehr-Wagner, Grinzingerstr. 53, ✉ 1190, ☎ (01) 3 20 24 42, *heuriger@feuerwehrwagner.at, Fax (01) 3209141* – AE VISA BX b
Meals *(dinner only)* (buffet only) ♀.
◆ This typical wine tavern with its cosy interior of dark wood and well-scrubbed tables is a great favourite with its regulars. The terraced garden is particularly attractive.

Mayer am Pfarrplatz, Pfarrplatz 2, ✉ 1190, ☎ (01) 3 70 33 61, *mayer@pfarrplaz.at, Fax (01) 3704714,* – VISA JCB BX c
closed 21 December - 15 January – **Meals** *(weekdays dinner only)* (buffet only) ♀.
◆ This is a wine tavern as it should be, with a rustic interior, a Viennese Schrammelmusik band, and a pretty courtyard. Another point of interest - Beethoven lived here !

Fuhrgassl Huber, Neustift am Walde 68, ✉ 1190, ☎ (01) 4 40 14 05, *weingut@fuhrgassl-huber.at, Fax (01) 4402730*, (wine-garden with Viennese Schrammelmusik), – AE MC VISA AX b

open from 2pm – **Meals** (buffet only) ♀.

◆ The little rooms of this establishment are an inviting place to taste your wine. Make sure you see the fireplace and gallery as well as the lovely courtyard. Schrammelmusik.

Wolff, Rathstr. 44, ✉ 1190, ☎ (01) 4 40 23 35, *wolff@wienerheuriger.at, Fax (01) 4401403* – DC MC VISA AX m

Meals (buffet) and à la carte 12,50/17 ♀.

◆ A glance at the 10 540 litre barrel will convince you that there's plenty of wine stored here. An earthy establishment with tasty morsels served at the tables. Pub garden.

Altes Preßhaus, Cobenzlgasse 15, ✉ 1190, ☎ (01) 3 20 02 03, *a.p.@aon.at, Fax (01) 320020323*, – AE DC MC VISA JCB BX p

closed January - February – **Meals** *(dinner only)* (buffet only) ♀.

◆ This is supposed to be the oldest wine tavern in Grinzing. It's virtually a museum, complete with Schrammelmusik. Make sure you see the cellar and the wine press.

at Auhof motorway station *West : 8 km by ⑦ :*

Novotel Wien-West, Am Auhof, ✉ 1140, ☎ (01) 97 92 54 20, *h0521@accor-hotels.com, Fax (01) 9794140*, , , – |‡|, ⇜ rm, ▤ TV ☎ ♿ P – 180. AE DC MC VISA JCB

Meals à la carte 15/31 – 11 – **111 rm** 88 – 96.

◆ This well-run establishment conveniently located near the access to the motorway running west from Vienna offers standard rooms and good service. The bistro-style Le Jardin restaurant serves meals until late.

at Vienna-Schwechat Airport *by ③ : 20 km :*

NH Vienna Airport, Hotelstr. 1 (at the airport), ✉ 1300, ☎ (01) 70 15 10, *nhviennaairport@nh-hotels.com, Fax (01) 7062828*, – |‡|, ⇜ rm, ▤ TV ☎ – 300. AE DC MC VISA JCB

Meals (Italian rest.) à la carte 29/47 ♀ – 16 – **358 rm** 200/280.

◆ This elegant establishment is a convenient resting place for birds of passage. Monitors in the foyer for flight information. The Don Giovanni restaurant offers a range of delicacies to assuage both hunger and fear of flying.

at Mayerling *Southwest : 20 km, by A23 and A21 CZ :*

Hanner with rm, Mayerling 1, ✉ 2534, ☎ (02258) 23 78, *hanner@hanner.cc, Fax (02258) 237841*, , , – |‡|, ⇜ rest, TV ☎ P – 25. AE DC MC VISA

see also ***Hanner*** *below* – ***Hanner léger :*** **Meals** à la carte 22/36 ♀ – **27 rm** 90/135 – 185.

◆ Run with great dedication, this hotel boasts impressive interior design : warm tones and natural materials reflect the surrounding countryside of the Vienna Woods. The 'Hanner leger' offers a new approach to bistro dining.

Restaurant Hanner - Hotel Hanner, Mayerling 1, ✉ 2534, ☎ (02258) 23 78, *hanner@hanner.cc, Fax (02258) 237841*, – P. AE DC MC VISA

Meals 59/80 and à la carte 52/69 ♀, .

◆ A modern, elegantly minimalist room in soft earth tones is the setting for Heinz Hanner's creative cuisine, served by an attentive, well-drilled team. Beautiful terrace.

Spec. Entenleber mit Marillentarte und Salzmandel. Bresse Taube mit Rosmarinpolenta und Artischocke. Gâteau au chocolat amer mit Kirschsorbet und Mandelemulsion.

INNSBRUCK *Austria* 730 *G 7 – pop. 120 000 – alt. 580 m – Wintersport : 580/2300 m* 3 *7.*

See : *Old Town*★ CDZ - *Maria-Theresien-Strasse* ★ CZ ≤ ★★ *on the Nordkette, Hungerburg* ★ AY, *Belfry (Stadtturm)* CZ **B** ✻ ★ *over the city – Little Golden Roof (Goldenes Dachl)* ★ CZ – *Helblinghaus* ★ CZ – *Dom (Inneres* ★, *Grabmal von Erzherzog Maximilian* ★) - *Hofburg* ★ *(Riesensaal* ★★) CZ – *Hofkirche* CZ *(Maximilian's Mausoleum* ★★, *Silver Chapel* ★★) – *Tyrol Museum of Popular Art (Tiroler Volkskunstmuseum)* ★★ CDZ – *"Ferdinandeum" Tyrol Museum (Tiroler Landesmuseum "Ferdinandeum")* ★ DZ**M2** – *Wilten Basilica* ★ AY.

Envir. : *Hafelekar* ✻ ★★ – *Schloss Ambras*★ *(Rüstkammern* ★, *Porträgalerie* ★, *Spanischer Saal* ★) – *Upland Tour (Mittelgebirge)* ★★ *(Hall in Tirol* ★, *St. Charles' Church at Volders* ★, *Swarowski Kristallwelten Wattens* ★, *Igls* ★, – *Ellbögen road* ★★, *Brenner road*★, *Bridge od Europe*★★) – *The Stubaital* ★★.

⛳9 *Innsbruck-Igls, Lans,* ☎ *(0512) 37 71 65 ;* ⛳18 *Innsbruck-Igls, Rinn,* ☎ *(05223) 7 81 77.*

ℹ *Innsbruck Information, Burggraben 3,* ✉ *A-6020,* ☎ *(0512) 53 56, Fax (0512) 535614.*

ÖAMTC, *Andechsstr. 81,* ☎ *(0512) 3 32 01 20, Fax (0512) 33206500.*

Wien 733 – München 140 – Salzburg 164.

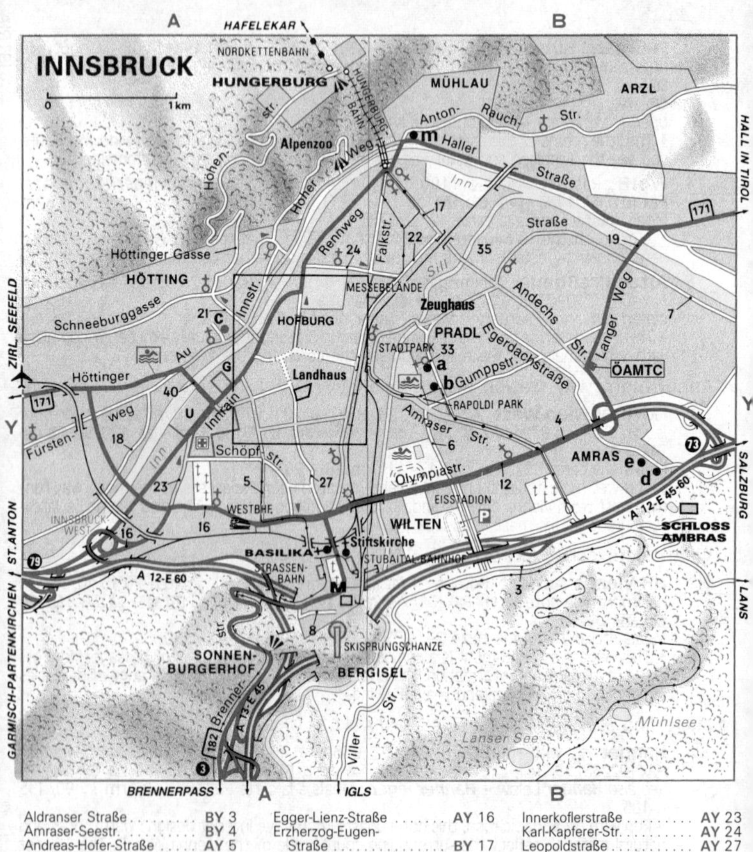

Aldranser Straße . . . . BY 3	Egger-Lienz-Straße . . . . . . AY 16	Innerkoflerstraße . . . . AY 23
Amraser-Seestr. . . . . BY 4	Erzherzog-Eugen-Straße . . . . BY 17	Karl-Kapferer-Str. . . . . AY 24
Andreas-Hofer-Straße . . . . AY 5	Fischnalerstraße . . . . AY 18	Leopoldstraße . . . . AY 27
Anton-Eder-Straße . . . . BY 6	Grenobler Brücke . . . . BY 19	Pradlerstraße . . . . BY 33
Archenweg . . . . BY 7	Höttinger Gasse . . . . AY 21	Prinz-Eugen-Straße . . . . . . BY 35
Bergiselweg . . . . AY 8	Ingenieur-Etzel-Straße . . . . . BY 22	Universitäts-Brücke . . . . AY 40
Burgenland-Straße . . . . BY 12		

Europa-Tyrol, Südtiroler Platz 2, ✉ 6020, ✆ (0512) 59 31, *hotel@europatyrol.com, Fax (0512) 587800*, ⇌ - 🛗, ⇍ rm, ▤ rest, 📺 📞 🚗 - 🏛 200. AE ⓓ ⓜ VISA. ⇍ rest — DZ a

Meals à la carte 26/44,50 - **122 rm** ☕ 130/180 - 280 - 6 suites.

◆ Patronised by many famous personalities, among them Queen Elizabeth II, this grand hotel of 1869 combines Tyrolean tradition with imperial flair. Splendid Baroque hall. Congenial, wood-panelled Europastüberl.

The Penz without rest, Adolf-Pichler-Platz 3, ✉ 6020, ✆ (0512) 5 75 65 70, *office@thepenz.com, Fax (0512) 5756579* - 🛗 ⇍ ▤ 📺 📞 ♿ - 🏛 120. AE ⓓ ⓜ VISA JCB — CZ z

96 rm ☕ 160 - 190.

◆ With its glazed façade, this is a particularly stylish hotel, close to the Old Town and linked to a new shopping gallery. Modern design in the interior as well.

Hilton, Salurner Str. 15, ✉ 6010, ✆ (0512) 5 93 50, *info-innsbruck@hilton.com, Fax (0512) 5935220*, ⇌ - 🛗, ⇍ rm, ▤ 📺 📞 - 🏛 250. AE ⓓ ⓜ VISA JCB. ⇍ rest — CDZ b

Guggeryllis : **Meals** à la carte 30/42,50 - ☕ 18 - **176 rm** 160 - 205 - 4 suites.

◆ Right in the centre of town, this establishment has functional rooms offering superb views of the Alps. Guests should try their luck in the Casino. With its palms and its attractively upholstered chairs, the Guggeryllis gets its name from a 16C court jester.

INNSBRUCK

Street	Grid	Street	Grid	Street	Grid
Adolf Pichler-Platz	CZ 2	Domplatz	CZ 15	Marktgraben	CZ
Anichstraße	CZ	Herzog-Friedrich-Straße	CZ 20	Meinhardstr.	DZ 28
Bozner Platz	DZ 10	Ingenieur-Etzel-Straße	DZ 22	Meraner Straße	CZ 30
Burggraben	CZ 14	Kiesbachgasse	CZ 25	Museumstraße	CDZ
		Landhausplatz	CZ 26	Pfarrgasse	CZ 32
		Leopoldstraße	CZ 27	Stiftgasse	CZ 37
		Maria-Theresien-Straße	CZ	Südbahnstraße	DZ 38

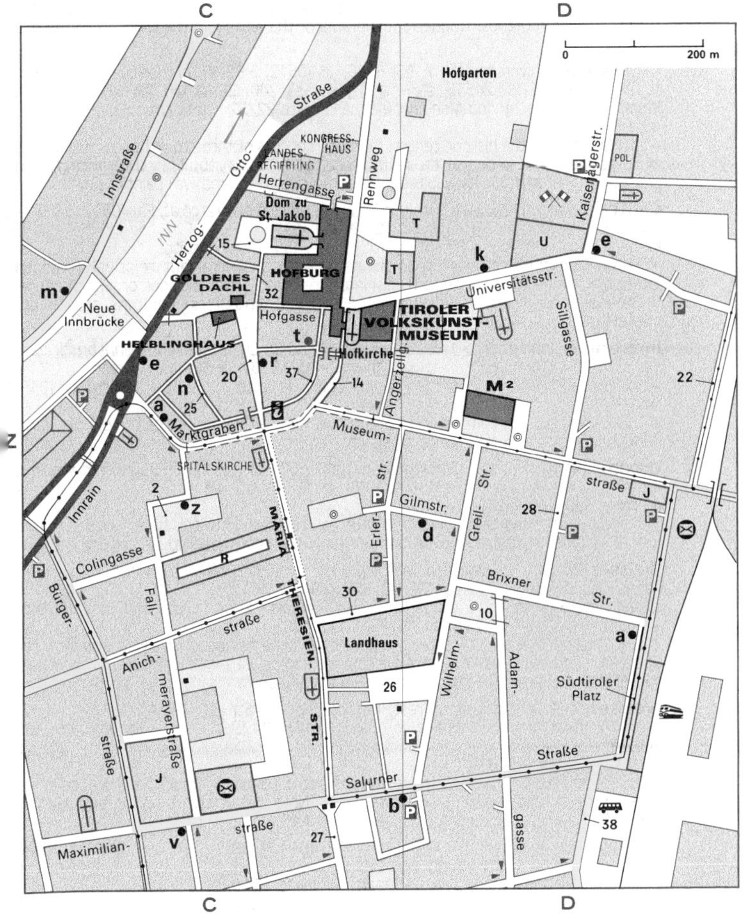

 **Romantik Hotel Schwarzer Adler**, Kaiserjägerstr. 2, ✉ A-6020, ☎ (0512) 58 71 09, *info@deradler.com, Fax (0512) 561697* – |‡|, ⇽ rm, ▤ TV ☎ – 🏛 40. AE ⓓ ⓜ VISA JCB. ⇽ rest DZ e

Meals *(closed Sunday and Bank Holidays)* à la carte 27/45 – **39 rm** ☐ 99/140 – 160/240 – 4 suites.

◆ Tradition and modernity go hand in hand here. The elegant, themed rooms are all different, some with designs by Versace and Swarovski, others in straightforward Tyrolean style. Guests dine in a cosy Tyrolean ambience beneath a splendid vault.

Neue Post, Maximilianstr. 15, ✉ 6020, ☎ (0512) 5 94 76, *innsbruck@hotel-neue-post.at, Fax (0512) 581818* – |‡|, ⇽ rm, TV ☎ P. AE ⓓ ⓜ VISA JCB. ⇽ CZ v

Meals *(closed Saturday lunch, Sunday and Bank Holidays)* à la carte 21/39 – **52 rm** ☐ 98/110 – 150.

◆ Built in 1902 in traditional style and a favourite with sportsmen and women, this hotel has transformed itself from simple inn to classically tasteful city hotel. Guests can dine in the winter garden or in the Japanese restaurant.

Sporthotel Penz, Fürstenweg 183, ✉ 6020, ☎ (0512) 2 25 14, *office@sporthotel-penz.at, Fax (0512) 22514124*, – | – 35. AE MC VISA. rest
Meals *(closed Sunday and Bank Holidays)* à la carte 25/33 – **77 rm** 77/93 – 118/133. by Fürstenweg AY

◆ Despite its name and its proximity to a recreation centre near the airport, this comfortable establishment is not just for sportspeople. Leisure centre and sauna high above the rooftops. Wonderful panorama of the Alps from the windows of the restaurant.

Grauer Bär, Universitätsstr. 7, ✉ 6020, ☎ (0512) 5 92 40, *grauer-baer@innsbruck-hotels.at, Fax (0512) 574535*, – – 240. AE MC VISA JCB DZ k
Meals *(closed Sunday and Monday lunch)* à la carte 22/52 – **194 rm** 95/120 – 185 – 11 suites.

◆ Just 200m from the historic centre, this hotel consists of three town houses with gables and balconies. Choose one of the refurbished rooms with natural wood furnishings. The restaurant features a lofty vaulted ceiling, massive pillars and wall-paintings.

Central, Gilmstr. 5, ✉ 6020, ☎ (0512) 59 20, *office@central.co.at, Fax (0512) 580310*, – , rm, – 30. AE MC VISA DZ d
Meals à la carte 15/33 – **85 rm** 105/115 – 130/150 – 9 suites.

◆ This establishment lives up to its name with a central but relatively tranquil location. Rooms with dark-wood furnishings. Breakfast buffet includes organic produce. Viennese coffeehouse tradition since 1875. Chandeliers, columns and lovely plasterwork.

Innsbruck, Innrain 3, ✉ 6020, ☎ (0512) 59 86 80, *office@hotelinnsbruck.com, Fax (0512) 572280*, – – 50. AE MC VISA. rest CZ e
Meals *(closed Sunday and Monday) (dinner only)* à la carte 22/36,50 – **113 rm** 101 – 142.

◆ This contemporary, comfortable hotel is built on the foundations of the old city walls. Functional rooms offering plenty of space.

Maximilian without rest, Marktgraben 7, ✉ 6020, ☎ (0512) 59 96 70, *hotel.maximilian@eunet.at, Fax (0512) 577450* – . AE MC VISA CZ a
35 rm 90/140 – 160.

◆ Everyday cares can be forgotten as soon as you check in to this hotel. Good standard rooms with oak furnishings. Breakfast served in the cosy, panelled Zirbelstube.

Weisses Rössl, Kiebachgasse 8, ✉ 6020, ☎ (0512) 58 30 57, *weisses@roessl.at, Fax (0512) 5830575*, – . MC VISA JCB CZ n
closed 2 weeks April and 2 weeks November – **Meals** *(closed Sunday and Bank Holidays)* à la carte 19,50/34 – **12 rm** 69/75 – 110/120.

◆ This little old building in Innsbruck's pedestrian zone has been receiving travellers for 600 years and could not be more welcoming. Rooms with light oak furnishings. Wood panelling and exposed beams give an attractively rustic ambience.

Weisses Kreuz without rest, Herzog-Friedrich-Str. 31, ✉ A-6020, ☎ (0512) 5 94 79, *hotel@weisseskreuz.at, Fax (0512) 5947990*, – . AE MC VISA CZ r
40 rm 61/94 – 108.

◆ Once patronised by Mozart, this establishment dates from the 15C and welcomes its guests with attractive and comfortable rooms. Note the wrought-iron inn sign and the oriel window with its frescoes. Tyrolean style restaurant.

Dengg, Riesengasse 13, ✉ 6020, ☎ (0512) 58 23 47, *dengg@chello.at, Fax (0512) 936088* – AE MC VISA JCB CZ t
closed Sunday and Bank Holidays – **Meals** à la carte 16,50/39.

◆ Restaurant occupying a venerable building in an Old Town alleyway. Three vaulted dining rooms with individual décor make an ideal setting for Cross-over cuisine.

at Innsbruck-Amras :

Kapeller, Philippine-Welser-Str. 96, ✉ 6020, ☎ (0512) 34 31 06, *office@kapeller.at, Fax (0512) 34310668*, – – 20. AE MC VISA BY e
closed July **Meals** *(closed Monday lunch, Sunday and Bank Holidays)* à la carte 20/40 – **36 rm** 55/80 – 138.

◆ Particularly convenient location on the edge of town near the motorway, but quiet. Comfortable rooms with practical wooden furnishings. Traditional hospitality in the dining rooms of the restaurant.

Bierwirt, Bichlweg 2, ✉ 6020, ☎ (0512) 34 21 43, *bierwirt@aon.at, Fax (0512) 3421435*, , – , rm, – 80. MC VISA BY d
Meals à la carte 20/33 – **60 rm** 69 – 105.

◆ This typical Alpine inn is one of the oldest and most historic of its kind in the area. Lovingly furnished, rustic bedrooms. Several small dining rooms in the local style.

at Innsbruck-Mariahilf :

Mondschein without rest, Mariahilfstr. 6, ✉ 6020, ✆ (0512) 2 27 84, *office@mondschein.at, Fax (0512) 2278490* – 30. CZ m
34 rm 87 – 119/145.
• Right by the Inn and classified as a historical monument, the city's oldest row of buildings includes this hotel. Distinctive, Italian-style rooms with PC and modem links.

Trattoria da Peppino, Kirschentalgasse 6, ✉ 6020, ✆ (0512) 27 56 99, *Fax (0512) 275699* – AY c
closed Sunday and Bank Holidays – **Meals** *(dinner only)* (Italian) à la carte 24/39.
• This little restaurant in contemporary trattoria style has been established in a dwelling-house. Italian cuisine based on first-rate, fresh produce.

at Innsbruck-Mühlau :

Dollinger, Haller Str. 7, ✉ 6020, ✆ (0512) 26 75 06, *hotel@dollinger.at, Fax (0512) 2675068*, – rm, BY m
Meals à la carte 12,50/27,50 – **59 rm** 55/70 – 85.
• This hotel is part of a family-run inn going back 150 years. The well-presented, functionally designed rooms are particularly appreciated by business travellers. Subdivided restaurant in contemporary Tyrolean style.

at Innsbruck-Pradl :

Parkhotel Leipzigerhof, Defreggerstr. 13, ✉ 6020, ✆ (0512) 34 35 25, *info@leipzigerhof.at, Fax (0512) 394357*, – rm, BY b
Meals *(closed Sunday and Bank Holidays)* à la carte 19/40,50 – **60 rm** 84/110 – 160.
• The Perger family's private hotel is located directly opposite the city park. Well-presented rooms in a variety of styles. Ask for one of the corner rooms. Nothing could be cosier than the Tyrolean-style restaurant with its niches and tiled stove.

Alpinpark, Pradlerstr. 28, ✉ 6020, ✆ (0512) 34 86 00, *Fax (0512) 364172*, – – 30. BY a
Meals à la carte 16/36 – **87 rm** 80/95 – 114/130.
• This yellow-coloured functional building on the edge of the city centre has solidly furnished rooms. In winter there is a shuttle service to the surrounding ski-slopes. Restaurant and rustic dining room.

at Igls *South : 4 km by Viller Straße AB :*

Schlosshotel, Viller Steig 2, ✉ 6080, ✆ (0512) 37 72 17, *hotel@schlosshotel-igls.com, Fax (0512) 377217198*, mountains, – – 15. rest
closed 3 weeks April, mid October - mid December – **Meals** à la carte 37/49 – **18 rm** 210/300 – 400 – 5 suites.
• In its garden, this refined establishment in the style of a nobleman's residence offers sheer luxury, with extremely elegant rooms and suites and first-class service. Tradition and elegance harmoniously combined in the mahogany-panelled restaurant.

Sporthotel Igls, Hilber Str. 17, ✉ 6080, ✆ (0512) 37 72 41, *hotel@sporthotel-igls.com, Fax (0512) 378679*, Massage, – – 50.
closed 1 October - 20 December – **Meals** à la carte 26/43 – **75 rm** 105/150 – 220 – 6 suites.
• This typically Alpine hotel makes a striking first impression with its spacious hall featuring an attractive open fireplace. Generously dimensioned, comfortable bedrooms. Cheerful, authentic atmosphere in the restaurant.

Batzenhäusl, Lanserstr. 12, ✉ 6080, ✆ (0512) 3 86 18, *hotel@batzenhaeusl.at, Fax (0512) 386187*, –
closed April and mid October - 1 December – **Meals** à la carte 22/42 – **30 rm** 66/104 – 122/136 – 4 suites.
• The chalet-style residence of the Arnold family enjoys an idyllic location on the edge of the forest. Guests are accommodated in attractive rooms, some with period furnishings. Spacious restaurant featuring mainly local dishes.

Römerhof, Römerstr. 62, ✉ 6080, ✆ (0512) 37 89 02, *roemerhof@netway.at, Fax (0512) 37890220*, – rest
closed 20 March - end April – **Meals** *(dinner only)* à la carte 20,50/34 – **18 rm** 70 – 110.
• This hotel right by the Olympic bob run has a striking mono-pitch roof. Tastefully furnished rooms complement the building's overall style. The modern restaurant has an almost Mediterranean feeling thanks to generous use of plants.

at Lans *Southeast : 6 km by Aldranser Straße* BY :

XX **Wilder Mann** with rm, Römerstr. 12, ✉ 6072, ✆ (0512) 37 96 96, *info.wildermann@chello.at, Fax (0512) 379139*, – P – 40. AE VISA
closed 7 to 11 January – **Meals** à la carte 20/39,50 – **14 rm** 62/87 – 134.
◆ This is one of the area's most popular establishments. Attractively subdivided, it has an exceptionally cheerful and welcoming atmosphere and the service is most friendly.

at Wattens *East : 16 km : by A 12* BY :

XX **Zum Schwan**, Swarovskistr. 2, ✉ 6112, ✆ (05224) 5 21 21, *Fax (05224) 55175*, – P
closed 23 December - 10 January, Saturday and Sunday – **Meals** à la carte 28/43.
◆ In his tiny kitchen, the owner prepares delicacies with great care and taste, which diners can then enjoy in the charming little rooms of his Tyrolean-style restaurant.

SALZBURG *Austria* 730 L 5 – *pop. 146 000 – alt. 425 m.*

See : *Old Town*★★ YZ - ≤ ★★ *over the town (from the Mönchsberg)* X *and* ≤★★ *(from Hettwer Bastei)*Y – *Hohensalzburg* ★★ X, Z : ≤★★ *(from the Kuenburg Bastion)*, ✱★★ *(from the Reck Tower), Museum (Burgmuseum)*★ – *St. Peter's Churchyard (Petersfriedhof)*★★ Z – *St. Peter's Church (Stiftskirche St. Peter)*★★ Z – *Residenz*★★ Z – *Natural History Museum (Haus der Natur)*★★ Y **M2** – *Franciscan's Church (Franziskanerkirche)*★ Z **A** – *Getreidegasse*★ Y – *Mirabell Garden (Mirabellgarten)*★ V *(Grand Staircase* ★★ *of the castle)* – *Baroque Museum* ★ V **M3** – *Cathedral (Dom)*★ Z.

Envir. : *Road to the Gaisberg (Gaisbergstraße)*★★ *(*≤★*) by* ① – *Untersberg*★ *by* ② *: 10 km (with* ⛡*)* – *Castle Hellbrunn (Schloß Hellbrunn)* ★ *(Volkskundemuseum* ★*) by Nonntaler Hauptstraße* X.

Salzburg-Wals, Schloß Klessheim, ✆ (0662) 85 08 51 ; Hof (by ① : 20 km), ✆ (06229) 23 90 ; St. Lorenz (by ① : 29 km), ✆ (06232) 3 83 50.

Innsbrucker Bundesstr. 95 (by ③), ✆ (0662) 8 58 00 - City Air Terminal (Autobus Station), Südtiroler Platz V.

Lastenstraße V.

Exhibition Centre (Messegelände), Linke Glanzeile 65, ✆ (0662) 2 40 40.

Salzburg-Information, Mozartplatz 5, ✉ 5020, ✆ (0662) 88 98 73 30, tourist@salzburginfo.at, Fax (0662) 8898732.

ÖAMTC, *Alpenstr. 102 (by ②).*

Wien 292 ① – Innsbruck 177 ③ – München 140 ③

Plans on following pages

Sacher, Schwarzstr. 5, ✉ 5020, ✆ (0662) 8 89 77, *salzburg@sacher.com, Fax (0662) 88977551*, , Massage, , – , rm, – 80. AE VISA JCB Y b
Zirbelstube : **Meals** à la carte 29/55 – ***Salzachgrill :*** **Meals** 13 and à la carte 17/33 – 26 – **118 rm** 219/285 – 329/549 – 3 suites.
◆ Built by Carl Freiherr von Schwarz, this historic grand hotel attracts guests from all over the world. Stylish elegance featuring every kind of luxury. Elegant, pine-panelled Alpine dining room. The Salzach Grill has a superb terrace overlooking the river.

Bristol, Makartplatz 4, ✉ 5020, ✆ (0662) 87 35 57, *hotel.bristol@salzburg.co.at, Fax (0662) 8735576* – , rm, – 60. AE VISA JCB Y a
closed 2 February - 2 April – ***Polo Lounge*** *(closed Sunday, except festival period)* **Meals** à la carte 37/54 – **60 rm** 207/266 – 313/392 – 9 suites.
◆ This stylish late-19C establishment stands in the heart of Mozart's home town. Individually decorated rooms, some with period furniture and unique city views. The Polo Lounge features mirrors, paintings, brass mouldings and immaculate place settings.

Altstadt Radisson SAS, Judengasse 15, ✉ 5020, ✆ (0662) 8 48 57 10, *radisson-altstadt@austria-trend.at, Fax (0662) 8485716*, – , rm, rm, – 40. AE VISA Y s
Meals *(closed 1 week February and Sunday, except festival period)* à la carte 35/42 – **62 rm** 149/265 – 220/390 – 13 suites.
◆ A jewel of a hotel dating from 1377. No one room resembles another ; they vary from romantic to imposing, some with ancient beams and ornamental stuccowork. The restaurant is one of Salzburg's most venerable dining establishments.

Crowne Plaza-Pitter, Rainerstr. 6, ✉ 5020, ✆ (0662) 88 97 80, *office@crowneplaza-salzburg.at, Fax (0662) 878893*, – , rm, – 160. AE VISA JCB V n
Meals à la carte 28/45 – 20 – **187 rm** 245/265 – 260/280 – 3 suites.
◆ This historic city centre establishment with its elegant and tasteful rooms dates from 1870. Spacious conference rooms with all facilities. Ballroom. The pine-panelled dining room has a cheerful and wonderfully authentic Austrian atmosphere.

SALZBURG

Auerspergstraße . . . . V 3
Bürglsteinstraße . . . . X 5
Erzabt-Klotz-Str. . . . . X 9
Gstättengasse . . . . X 12
Kaiserschützenstr. . . . . V 20
Lindhofstr. . . . . V 22
Mirabellplatz . . . . V 26
Nonntaler Hauptstr. . . . . . . X 29
Nußdorfer Straße . . . . X 31
Rainerstraße V
Schießstattstr. . . . . V 33
Schwarzstr. . . . . V 34
Späthgasse . . . . X 37

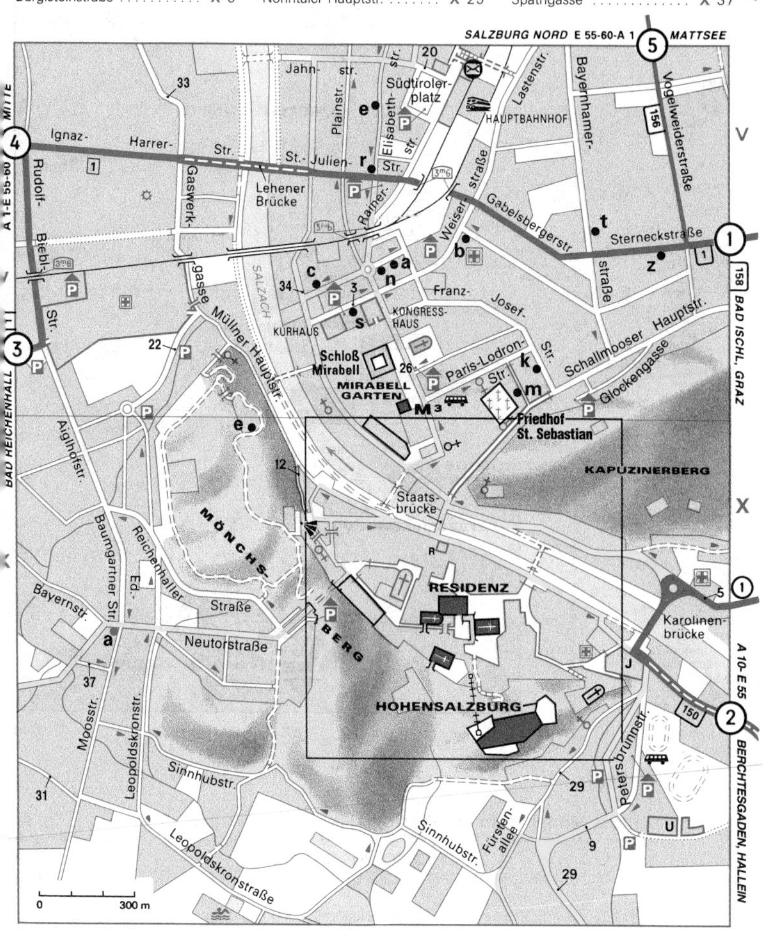

Sheraton, Auerspergstr. 4, ✉ 5020, ☎ (0662) 88 99 90, *sheraton.salzburg@sheraton.at, Fax (0662) 881776*, Massage, entrance to the spa facilities, – rm, – 50. AE VISA JCB V s

Mirabell : **Meals** à la carte 34/49 – 21 – **163 rm** 198/275 – 218/299 – 9 suites.

◆ The hotel has been sensitively inserted into the landscape of Kurpark and Mirabell Garden, and the harmony of form and function continues in the interior. Business facilities. The Mirabell has a classically tasteful ambience and a terrace overlooking the park.

Renaissance, Fanny-von-Lehnert-Str. 7, ✉ 5020, ☎ (0662) 4 68 80, *rhi.szgbr.business.center@renaissancehotels.com, Fax (0662) 4688298*, Massage, – rm, – 500. AE VISA JCB by Kaiserschützenstraße V

Meals à la carte 16/31 – **257 rm** 153/184 – 177/208.

◆ Close to the station, a spacious establishment with a tasteful and elegant atmosphere. Extensive conference facilities and the latest technology for successful business meetings.

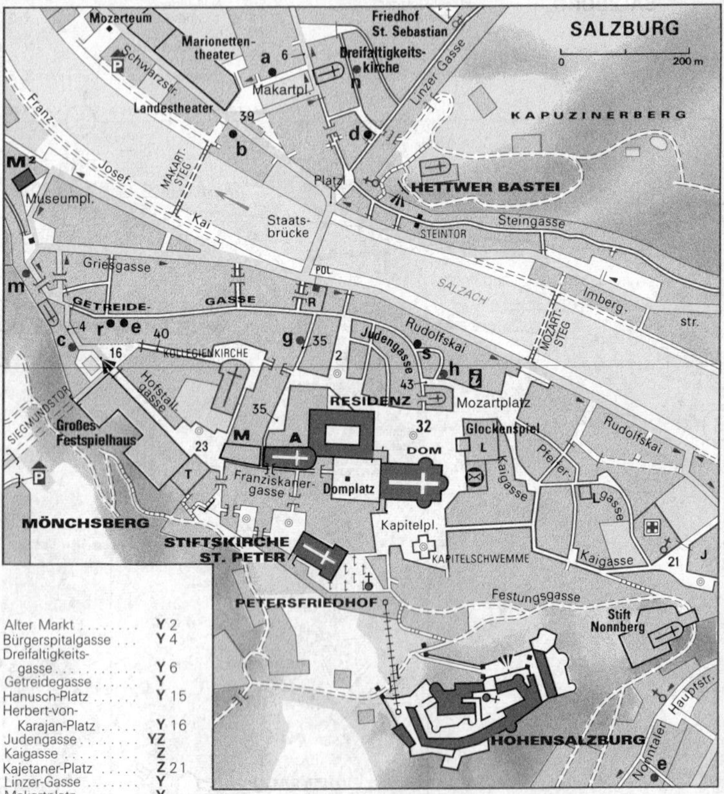

SALZBURG

Alter Markt	Y 2
Bürgerspitalgasse	Y 4
Dreifaltigkeitsgasse	Y 6
Getreidegasse	Y
Hanusch-Platz	Y 15
Herbert-von-Karajan-Platz	Y 16
Judengasse	YZ
Kaigasse	Z
Kajetaner-Platz	Z 21
Linzer-Gasse	Y
Makartplatz	Y
Max-Reinhardt-Platz	Z 23
Residenzplatz	Z 32
Sigmund-Haffner-Gasse	YZ 35
Theatergasse	Y 39
Universitätsplatz	Y 40
Waagplatz	Z 43

Schloss Mönchstein ⛰, Mönchsberg Park 26, ✉ 5020, ☎ (0662) 8 48 55 50, *salzburg@moenchstein.at, Fax (0662) 848559*, ≼ Salzburg and surroundings, 🍴, 🌳, 🎾 – 🛗 📺 📞 🚗 🅿 – 🎤 20. AE ⓓ ⓜ VISA JCB. ✗ rest X e

Meals 26,50 *(lunch)*/60 *(dinner)* and à la carte 42/55 🍷 – **24 rm** ☕ 268/348 – 335/435 – 5 suites.

◆ This charming little castle enjoys a parkland setting high above the city and charms its guests with its elegant, stylish rooms. There is a fascinating little wedding chapel and a classically tasteful first floor restaurant.

Goldener Hirsch, Getreidegasse 37, ✉ 5020, ☎ (0662) 8 08 40, *welcome@goldenerhorsch.com, Fax (0662) 843349* – 🛗, ✗ rm, ▤ 📺 📞 – 🎤 30. AE ⓓ ⓜ VISA JCB Y e

Meals à la carte 41/51,50 – ☕ 25 – **69 rm** 204/376 – 274/372 – 4 suites.

◆ The romantic charm of this 15C patrician residence has been perfectly preserved. Individual rooms with country-style appeal and originality, some with period furnishings. The restaurant has a lovely vault and an attractively rustic atmosphere.

Parkhotel Castellani, Alpenstr. 6, ✉ 5020, ☎ (0662) 20 60, *info@castellani-parkhotel.com, Fax (0662) 2060555*, 🍴, 🏋 – 🛗, ✗ rm, ▤ 📺 📞 🚗 🅿 – 🎤 100. AE ⓓ ⓜ VISA by ②

Salieri *(dinner only, except festival period)* **Meals** à la carte 30/45,50 – ***Eschenbach*** *(lunch only, except festival period)* **Meals** 18 (buffet lunch) and à la carte 25/35 – **153 rm** ☕ 110/130 – 140/160½ P 25.

◆ The modern hotel building is in fascinating contrast to the charming old patrician residence. Beyond the spacious foyer are tastefully decorated rooms. The Salieri in elegant contemporary style, the Eschenbach a mixture of modern and traditional

Dorint, Sternekstr. 20, ✉ 5020, ℘ (0662) 8 82 03 10, *info.szgsal@dorint.com, Fax (0662) 8820319*, – rm, – 140. AE MC VISA JCB. rest V z
Meals à la carte 23/32 – **139 rm** 108/190 – 133/215 – 4 suites.
◆ This hotel can be recommended for its central location, only ten minutes on foot from the Old Town. Functional rooms. Conference facilities and ISDN technology. Restaurant Amadeo with garden terrace.

Zum Hirschen, St.-Julien-Str. 21, ✉ 5020, ℘ (0662) 88 90 30, *zumhirschen@ains.at, Fax (0662) 8890358*, beer garden, Massage, – rm, – 30. AE MC VISA JCB. rm V r
Meals *(closed Sunday)* à la carte 17/30 – **64 rm** 88/111 – 121/132.
◆ Close to the station. The hotel offers traditional Salzburg hospitality in a tasteful setting with Italian period furnishings. Extensive roof-terrace sauna. Restaurant with five attractively decorated dining rooms.

NH Carlton without rest, Markus-Sittikus-Str. 3, ✉ 5020, ℘ (0662) 8 82 19 10, *nhcarlton@nh-hotels.com, Fax (0662) 88219188*, – AE MC VISA JCB V c
13 – **40 rm** 97/127 – 120/174 – 14 suites.
◆ A delightful city centre residence with all the charm of a comfortable private villa. Spacious rooms with high ceilings and elegant rustic furnishings.

NH Salzburg, Franz-Josef-Str. 26, ✉ 5020, ℘ (0662) 88 20 41, *nhsalzburg@nh-hotels.com, Fax (0662) 874240*, – rm, – 90. AE MC VISA JCB V k
Meals *(dinner only)* à la carte 17/34 – **140 rm** 108/138 – 131/186.
◆ Not far from the Mirabell Garden, this establishment offers business travellers solidly furnished, functional rooms with work-desks plus modem link on request.

CD Hotel, Am Messezentrum 2, ✉ 5020, ℘ (0662) 4 35 54 60, *salzburg@cdhotels.at, Fax (0662) 43951095*, – rm, – 300. AE MC VISA
Meals à la carte 17/24 – **120 rm** 98 – 137. by ④
◆ Close to the trade fair centre, this is a functional but comfortable place to stay for a while. Bedrooms with cherry-wood furnishings. Function rooms accommodating up to 300. Large, bistro-style dining hall.

Mercure, Bayerhamerstr. 14, ✉ 5020, ℘ (0662) 8 81 43 80, *h0984@accor-hotels.com, Fax (0662) 871111411*, – rm, – 100. AE MC VISA JCB V t
Meals à la carte 19,50/33 – 11 – **121 rm** 92/115 – 110/145.
◆ Modern hotel belonging to this well-known chain with standard, functionally furnished rooms. Located on the edge of the city centre.

Wolf-Dietrich, Wolf-Dietrich-Str. 7, ✉ 5020, ℘ (0662) 87 12 75, *office@salzburg-hotel.at, Fax (0662) 8712759*, – AE MC VISA JCB V m
Ährlich *(closed February - March, Sunday and Monday) (dinner only)* **Meals** à la carte 17/36 – **30 rm** 69/114 – 109/149.
◆ Tasteful, elegant old residence in a traffic-calmed part of town. Comfortable rooms, some offering perfect peace and quiet. Restaurant run on organic principles using only animal products raised in humane conditions.

arthotel Blaue Gans, Getreidegasse 41, ✉ 5020, ℘ (0662) 8 42 49 10, *office@blauegans.at, Fax (0662) 8424919* – AE MC VISA JCB Y r
Meals *(closed Tuesday, except festival period)* à la carte 24/41 – **40 rm** 99/109 – 129/169.
◆ One of Salzburg's oldest hotels, the "Inn at the sign of the Green Goose" was first mentioned in 1599. Today the venerable building has been harmoniously modernised and offers contemporary comfort. 500-year-old vaults in the historic Gasthaus.

Markus Sittikus without rest, Markus-Sittikus-Str. 20, ✉ 5020, ℘ (0662) 8 71 12 10, *info@markus-sittikus.at, Fax (0662) 87112158* – – 15. AE MC VISA JCB
39 rm 65/79 – 105/126. V a
◆ Prince Bishop Markus Sittikus von Hohenems - to whom the hotel owes its name - brought the Italian Baroque style to Salzburg. Ask for one of the refurbished rooms.

Hohenstauffen without rest, Elisabethstr. 19, ✉ 5020, ℘ (0662) 8 77 66 90, *hohenstauffen@aon.at, Fax (0662) 87219351* – AE MC VISA JCB V e
31 rm 72/95 – 109/145.
◆ Close to the station, this hotel has been in the same family ownership since 1906. Rooms individually furnished, some with a four-poster.

Lasserhof without rest, Lasserstr. 47, ✉ 5020, ℘ (0662) 87 33 88, *hotellasserhof@magnet.at, Fax (0662) 8733886* – AE MC VISA JCB V b
29 rm 55/70 – 85/105.
◆ This impeccably run hotel accommodates its guests in stylish and comfortable rooms.

Gablerbräu, Linzer Gasse 9, ✉ 5020, ℘ (0662) 8 89 65, *hotel@gablerbrau.com*, *Fax (0662) 8896555*, – AE VISA JCB 20. Y d
Meals *(closed 4 to 19 February)* à la carte 14/34 – **48 rm** 70/85 – 108/158.
♦ This centrally located, carefully restored 15C inn close to the Trinity Church offers comfortable, contemporary rooms. The restaurant is partly country-style - with old vaults - partly contemporary.

XX **Alt Salzburg**, Bürgerspitalgasse 2, ✉ 5020, ℘ (0662) 84 14 76, *altsalzburg@aon.at*, *Fax (0662) 8414764* – AE VISA JCB Y c
closed 1 week mid February, Sunday and Monday lunch, except festival period – **Meals** (booking essential for dinner) à la carte 24,50/43 ♀.
♦ Elegant country-style restaurant, fine for dining before or after visiting the opera. Local cuisine with an international touch.

XX **Gasthaus zu Schloss Hellbrunn**, Fürstenweg 37, ✉ 5020, ℘ (0662) 82 56 08, *office@taste-gassner.com*, *Fax (0662) 82560842*, – P. AE VISA by ②
closed February - March, dinner Sunday and Monday – **Meals** à la carte 34/54 ♀.
♦ In its setting of parkland and fountains, this Renaissance summer residence has fine interiors. Regional specialities at lunchtime, classic cuisine in the evening.

XX **Bei Bruno im Ratsherrnkeller**, Sigmund-Haffner-Gasse 4, ✉ 5020, ℘ (0662) 87 84 17, *bruno@restaurant-austria.net*, *Fax (0662) 8784174* – AE VISA JCB Y g
closed 2 weeks February, Sunday and Bank Holidays, except festival period – **Meals** à la carte 27,50/55 ♀.
♦ Leather upholstery, attractively laid tables, and walls in a warm shade of orange give this vaulted restaurant an attractive, almost Mediterranean atmosphere.

XX **Pan e Vin**, Gstättengasse 1 (1st floor), ✉ 5020, ℘ (0662) 84 46 66, *info@panevin.at*, *Fax (0662) 84466615* – AE VISA JCB Y m
closed Sunday, except festival period – **Meals** (Italian) à la carte 39/58 ♀ – ***Trattoria*** *(closed Sunday - Monday)* **Meals** à la carte 24,50/46.
♦ Well-chosen, discreet colours and decor lend a Mediterranean touch to the rooms in this 600-year old building. Relaxed atmosphere in the basement Trattoria.

XX **Riedenburg**, Neutorstr. 31, ✉ 5020, ℘ (0662) 83 08 15, *reservierung@riedenburg.at*, *Fax (0662) 843923*, – P. AE VISA X a
closed Sunday, except festival period – **Meals** à la carte 35/57.
♦ This establishment dishes up a choice of Austrian and international food. Country-style restaurant with a touch of elegance. Take a look at Salzburg's oldest garden pavilion.

XX **K+K Restaurant am Waagplatz**, Waagplatz 2 (1st floor), ✉ 5020, ℘ (0662) 84 21 56, *kk.restaurant@kuk.at*, *Fax (0662) 84215633*, – AE VISA JCB Z h
closed 3 February - 7 March – **Meals** (booking essential) à la carte 27/37,50 ♀.
♦ Listed building with an interior subdivided into a number of cosy little dining rooms. Guests are fed and entertained in medieval fashion in the vaulted cellars.

X **Perkeo**, Priesterhausgasse 20, ✉ 5020, ℘ (0662) 87 08 99, *Fax (0662) 870833*,
closed Saturday and Sunday, during festival period only Sunday – **Meals** (booking essential) à la carte 35/48 ♀. Y n
♦ Wooden benches and tables set the tone in this simple, attractive restaurant. Diners can take a look in the kitchen and browse among the books (on the theme of wine).
Spec. Eierschwammel-Parfait mit gebratenem Wolfsbarsch. Pochiertes Kalbsfilet mit Bohnen und Gnocchi. Crème Brûlée.

at Salzburg-Aigen *Southeast : 6 km, by Bürgelsteinstraße X :*

Rosenvilla without rest, Höfelgasse 4, ✉ 5020, ℘ (0662) 62 17 65, *hotel.rosenvilla@salzburg-online.at*, *Fax (0662) 6252308*, – P. AE VISA
14 rm 65/75 – 120/165.
♦ A feng-shui garden has been laid out in front of this villa not far from the city centre. Each room with individual décor, some with balcony. Internet access.

Doktorwirt, Glaser Str. 9, ✉ 5026, ℘ (0662) 6 22 97 30, *schnoell@doktorwirt.co.at*, *Fax (0662) 62171724*, , , (heated), – rest, P – 25. AE VISA JCB. rest
closed 2 weeks February and mid October - end November – **Meals** *(closed Monday, September - May Sunday dinner and Monday)* à la carte 14,50/33 ♀, – **39 rm** 64/90 – 105/160.
♦ This 12C building named after the doctor who bought it in 1670 is now a comfortable, country-style inn with a tasteful and welcoming ambience.The restaurant consists of two pine-panelled rooms from the eastern Tyrol.

Gasthof Schloss Aigen, Schwarzenbergpromenade 37, ✉ 5026, ☎ (0662) 62 12 84, *schloss-aigen@elsnet.at, Fax (0662) 6212844*, – P. AE ① MC VISA
closed 2 weeks mid February, Wednesday and Thursday lunch, except festival period – **Meals** 26 *(lunch)* à la carte 28/45 ♀.
◆ Once part of the castle estate, this rustic inn stands on the edge of the forest. Organic beef from the Pinzgau forms the basis of delicious dishes.

at Salzburg-Gnigl *East : 3,5 km, by ① :*

Pomodoro, Eichstr. 54, ✉ 5023, ☎ (0662) 64 04 38, – P. AE ① MC VISA
closed end July - end August, Monday and Tuesday – **Meals** (Italian) (booking essential) à la carte 24/37.
◆ This homely restaurant has been in the same ownership for over 20 years. Wooden panelling together with fish-nets spanning the ceiling contribute to the rustic atmosphere.

In Salzburg-Itzling *North : 1,5 km, by Kaiserschützenstraße V :*

Auerhahn, Bahnhofstr. 15, ✉ 5020, ☎ (0662) 45 10 52, *auerhahn@eunet.at, Fax (0662) 4510523*, – rest, TV P. AE ① MC VISA
closed 1 week February, 2 weeks July – **Meals** *(closed Sunday dinner and Monday, except August)* à la carte 18/36 ♀ – **13 rm** 43/46 – 72/81.
◆ This small hotel is in an old building close to the Salzburg-Itzling railway station. Contemporary rooms. The restaurant is a convivial, country-style place with a secluded garden beneath the chestnut trees.

at Salzburg-Liefering *Northwest : 4 km, by ④ :*

Brandstätter, Münchner Bundesstr. 69, ✉ 5020, ☎ (0662) 43 45 35, *info@hotel-brandstaetter.com, Fax (0662) 43453590*, , , , – TV P – 30. AE MC VISA. rest
closed 22 to 27 December – **Meals** *(closed 1 week early January and Sunday except in season)* (booking essential) à la carte 20,50/54 ♀ – **35 rm** 68/95 – 91/130.
◆ Personally run inn with lovingly decorated rooms and lots of local peasant furniture. Ask for one of the rooms with a balcony overlooking the garden. Cosy dining rooms where an exquisitely prepared array of local dishes is served.
Spec. Lauwarmer Kalbsbrust-Salat mit Gemüsevinaigrette. Hummergröstl mit Curry. Kalbs-Salonbeuschel mit Semmelknödel.

at Salzburg-Maria Plain *North : 3 km, by Plainstraße V :*

Maria Plain, Plainbergweg 41, ✉ 5101, ☎ (0662) 4 50 70 10, *info@mariaplain.com, Fax (0662) 45070119*, – , rest, TV P – 40. AE ① MC VISA
closed 1 week July – **Meals** *(closed Tuesday and Wednesday, except festival period)* à la carte 20/29 – **27 rm** 55/65 – 97/124 – 5 suites.
◆ This old 17C dairy was once used to accommodate the pilgrims to the nearby basilica. The rooms are furnished with period pieces. Convivial restaurant and romantic garden with chestnut trees.

at Salzburg-Nonntal :

Purzelbaum, Zugallistr. 7, ✉ 5020, ☎ (0662) 84 88 43, *info@purzelbaum.at, Fax (0662) 84888433*, – AE ① MC VISA Z e
closed Sunday and Monday lunch, except festival period – **Meals** à la carte 34/48 ♀.
◆ This venerable old city building houses a contemporary style restaurant offering French cuisine and friendly service.

on the Heuberg *Northeast : 3 km by ① – alt. 565 m*

Schöne Aussicht, Heuberg 3, ✉ 5023 *Salzburg*, ☎ (0662) 64 06 08, *hotel@salzburgpanorama.cc, Fax (0662) 6406082*, , , , , – TV P – 20. AE ① MC VISA
closed January and February – **Meals** à la carte 19/31 – **30 rm** 51/69 – 72/115.
◆ Around 300 years old, this farmstead stands on its own on the Heuberg hill and lives up to its name ("Beautiful View"). Ask for one of the rooms with a balcony. Country-style restaurant with a tiled stove, and a garden terrace for the view.

on the Gaisberg *East : 5 km, by ① :*

Vitalhotel Kobenzl, Am Gaisberg 11, *alt. 730 m*, ✉ 5020 *Salzburg*, ☎ (0662) 64 15 10, *info@kobenzl.at, Fax (0662) 642238*, , , Massage, , , – TV P – 40. AE ① MC VISA
closed 6 January - 6 March – **Meals** à la carte 37/51 – **40 rm** 120/142 – 142/233 – 4 suites.
◆ High above the city in lovely leafy surroundings, this elegant mountain hotel features lots of gilt and old wood. The visitors' book has been signed by many of the great (e.g. Richard Nixon) and good. Guests dine in a stylish setting.

Romantik Hotel Gersberg Alm, Gersberg 37, *alt. 800 m*, ✉ 5023 *Salzburg-Gnigl*, ☏ (0662) 64 12 57, *office@gersbergalm.at*, *Fax (0662) 644278*, – 80. AE MC VISA
Meals (booking essential) à la carte 24/38 – **45 rm** 87/129 – 158/270.
• Even in Mozart's time, the Gersberg Alpine meadow was a popular place for outings. The setting is tranquil, the view wonderful. Today's guests are accommodated in homely rooms, some with balcony. Restaurant with two cheerfully rustic dining rooms.

near Airport *Southwest : 5 km, by ③ :*

Airporthotel, Dr.-M.-Laireiter-Str. 9, ✉ A-5020 *Salzburg-Loig*, ☏ (0662) 85 00 20, *airporthotel@aon.at*, *Fax (0662) 85002044*, – rm, – 20. AE MC VISA JCB. rest
Meals (residents only) – **39 rm** 84/115 – 123/140.
• This airport hotel consists of a pair of linked country houses offering functional rooms, some with a balcony.

Ikarus, Wilhelm-Spazier-Str. 2 (Hangar-7, 1st floor), ✉ 5020, ☏ (662) 21 97, *office@hangar-7.com*, *Fax (0662) 21973709* – – 20. AE MC VISA JCB.
Meals (booking essential) 64/80 and à la carte.
• Built to shelter the Flying Bulls historic aircraft collection, Hangar 7 with its overarching, transparent canopy also sees guest chefs offering monthly themed menus.

at Anif *South : 7 km, by ② :*

Friesacher (with guest house Anifer Hof), Hellbrunner Str. 17, ✉ 5081, ☏ (06246) 89 77, *first@hotelfriesacher.com*, *Fax (06246) 897749*, Massage, – rm, – 25. AE MC VISA
closed June – **Meals** à la carte 15/34 – **70 rm** 59/88 – 93/120.
• This stylish, country-style house has been welcoming guests for 150 years. All rooms with balcony and ISDN. The restaurant is divided into a number of attractive little rooms.

Schlosswirt zu Anif (with guest house), Salzachtal Bundesstr. 22, ✉ 5081, ☏ (06246) 7 21 75, *info@schlosswirt-anif.com*, *Fax (06246) 721758*, – 50. AE MC VISA JCB
closed 2 weeks February and 3 weeks end October - early November – **Meals** *(closed Monday, except festival period)* 17,50 *(lunch)* à la carte 38/54 – **28 rm** 69 – 127.
• Like the neighbouring moated castle, this historic hotel dates back to 1350. It has been carefully restored and offers Biedermeier style rooms. The lord of the castle has had taverner's rights in the hotel restaurant since 1607.

at Bergheim *North : 7 km by Plainstrasse V :*

Gasthof Gmachl, Dorfstr. 35, ✉ 5101, ☏ (0662) 45 21 24, *info@gmachl.at*, *Fax (0662) 45212468*, (heated), – rm, – 40. AE MC VISA
Meals à la carte 18/33 – **72 rm** 78/96 – 136/164 – 7 suites.
• Historic, centrally located inn with cosy rooms and comfortable suites as well as an attractively laid out park with recreational facilities. Welcoming dining rooms in a variety of styles.

at Hallwang-Söllheim *Northeast : 7 km, by ① and Linzer Bundesstraße :*

Pfefferschiff (Fleischhaker), Söllheim 3, ✉ 5300, ☏ (0662) 66 12 42, *restaurant@pfefferschiff.at*, *Fax (0662) 661841*, – AE.
closed end June - mid July, 1 week September, Sunday and Monday, during festival period only Monday – **Meals** (booking essential) 30 *(lunch)*/61 *(dinner)* and à la carte 36/51.
• Step aboard a 350-year-old rectory anchored in a leafy setting. Individual, stylish interior. Navigate your way through a menu featuring the best of local cuisine.
Spec. Blunzengugelhupf mit Trüffel und Mangold. Lammkarree mit Porree und Kartoffelgratin. Rehrücken mit Ingwerkirschen und Petersilienpüree.

at Elixhausen *North : 11 km, by ⑤, direction Obertrum :*

Romantik Hotel Gmachl, Dorfstr. 14, ✉ 5161, ☏ (0662) 4 80 21 20, *romantikhotel@gmachl.com*, *Fax (0662) 48021272*, (heated), (indoor) – – 70. AE MC VISA
closed end June - mid July – **Meals** *(closed 21 to 27 December, Sunday dinner and Monday lunch, except festival period)* à la carte 21,50/44 – **49 rm** 73/109 – 116/169 – 3 suites.
• Once a tavern serving Benedictine monks, this lovely old inn of 1334 offers individually decorated, country-style bedrooms. Restaurant with a series of charming little dining rooms.

at Hof *East : 20 km, by ① and B 158 :*

Schloss Fuschl (with guest houses), Vorderelsenwang 19, ✉ 5322, ℘ (06229) 22 53 15 00, *schloss.fuschl@arabellasheraton.com, Fax (06229) 22531531,* ←, Massage, – ⊨ rm, – 100. AE VISA JCB. rest

Meals à la carte 42/58 ₹ – **84 rm** 150/440 – 180/470 – 3 suites.

◆ This former hunting lodge is idyllically sited on the Fuschlsee. Dating from the 15C, it has a Classical interior and in 1957 served as a setting for films about Empress Elizabeth. Dine like a king in the elegant restaurant !

ArabellaSheraton Hotel Jagdhof, Vorderelsenwang 29, ✉ 5322, ℘ (06229) 2 37 20, *jagdhof.fuschl@arabellasheraton.com, Fax (06229) 23722531,* ←, beer garden, – rm, – 280. AE VISA

Meals à la carte 30/44 – **143 rm** 99/270 – 136/290.

◆ This attractive establishment comprising an inn and two country-style buildings offers tasteful contemporary interiors as well as a spacious and well-equipped fitness area. Rustic restaurant with pleasant terrace.

at Fuschl am See *East : 26 km, by ① and B 158 :*

Ebner's Waldhof, Seestr. 30, ✉ 5330, ℘ (06226) 82 64, *info@ebners-waldhof.at, Fax (06226) 8644,* ←, Massage, – – 60. VISA. rest

closed 7 March - 3 April, November - 13 December – **Meals** (residents only) – ***Gütlstuben*** (booking essential) *(closed November - early May, Thursday and Friday lunch)* **Meals** à la carte 31/48 ₹ – **120 rm** 89/118 – 141/171 – 15 suites.

◆ This lakeside hotel in its picture-postcard setting offers comfortable rooms and a number of lavish suites - those facing the lake with balcony. The Gütlstuben in elegant Alpine style.

near the Mondsee *East : 28 km, by ⑤ (by motorway A 1, exit Mondsee, left lakeside, direction Attersee)*

Seehof, ✉ 5311 *Loibichl,* ℘ (06232) 50 31, *seehof@nextra.de, Fax (06232) 503151,* ←, Massage, – rest, VISA JCB

15 May - 13 September – **Meals** à la carte 33/48 ₹ – **30 rm** 250 – 290 – 4 suites.

◆ Tasteful, contemporary ambience and a touch of luxury characterise this parkland establishment of three individual buildings. Beauty Farm. Bright, elegant restaurant with lovely covered terrace.

Schloss Mondsee, Schlosshof 1a, ✉ 5310, ℘ (06232) 50 01, *office@schlossmondsee.at, Fax (06232) 500122,* Massage, – rm, rm, – 40. VISA.

Meals à la carte 23/38 – **68 rm** 91/121 – 140/180 – 6 suites.

◆ First mentioned in AD763, the castle is now a fascinating modern hotel, with rooms and maisonettes in an historic setting. Meals served among old vaults and exposed stonework.

Villa Wunderlich without rest, St. Lorenz, ✉ A-5310, ℘ (06232) 2 73 72, *info@villa-wunderlich.at, Fax (06232) 2737299,* – VISA.

7 rm 104 – 180.

◆ This villa in typical Salzkammergut style has been lovingly converted into a charming small hotel. Guests are accommodated in tasteful and individually decorated rooms.

Seegasthof Lackner with rm, Mondseestr. 1, ✉ 5310, ℘ (06232) 23 59, *office@seehotel-lackner.at, Fax (06232) 235950,* ← Mondsee and Alpes, – VISA

closed 13 November - 5 December and 16 February - 2 April – **Meals** *(closed Thursday)* à la carte 25/46 ₹, – **17 rm** 67/90 – 109/120½ P 20.

◆ This Inn on the banks of the Mondsee has contemporary interiors graced by modern works of art. Lovely terrace. Practical rooms.

at Golling *South : 25 km by ② and A 10 :*

Döllerer's Goldener Stern, Am Marktplatz 56, ✉ 5440, ℘ (06244) 4 22 00, *office@doellerer.at, Fax (06244) 691242,* – – 15. VISA

closed 2 weeks January and 1 week October – **Meals** *(closed September - July Sunday and Monday lunch)* 37/78 and à la carte 43/61 ₹, – ***Bürgerstube*** *(closed September - July Sunday and Monday lunch)* **Meals** à la carte 22,50/32,50 ₹ – **13 rm** 58 – 94.

◆ This historic 14C inn offers rooms overlooking park or castle, furnished with choice period pieces. Classic cuisine in the country-style restaurant, rustic flair in the Bürgerstube.

Spec. Gegrillter Hummer und gefüllter Schweinsfuß mit Basilikum-Linsen. Bresse-Taube mit Myrrhe parfümiert und Sellerie. Schokoladenzigarre mit Erdbeerragout und Balsamico.

at Werfen *South : 42 km by ② and A 10 :*

XXX ✿✿ **Karl-Rudolf Obauer** with rm, Markt 46, ✉ 5450, ☎ (06468) 5 21 20, *ok@obauer.com, Fax (06468) 521212,* – ▤ rest, TV P – 25. AE
Meals *(closed Monday - Tuesday, except season and festival period)* (booking essential) 35 *(lunch)*/68 *(dinner)* and à la carte 36/75 ♀ – **10 rm** ☐ 70/128 – 138/155.
◆ Gourmets come here to be treated to the very best in fine cuisine. The rustic ambience is coupled with a modern interior and international dishes with local fare.
Spec. Forellenstrudel mit Veltlinersauce und Pilzpüree. Wange und Filet vom Pinzgauer Rind mit Kürbiscanneloni. Grapefruitnocken mit Camparisorbet.

Benelux

Belgium

BRUSSELS – ANTWERP – BRUGES – LIÈGE

Grand Duchy of Luxembourg

LUXEMBOURG

Netherlands

AMSTERDAM – The HAGUE – ROTTERDAM

PRACTICAL INFORMATION

LOCAL CURRENCY

1 euro (€) = 1,20 USD ($) (Déc. 2003)

TOURIST INFORMATION

Telephone numbers and addresses of Tourist Offices are given in the text of each city under **ℹ**.

National Holiday: *Belgium: 21 July; Netherlands: 30 April; Luxembourg: 23 June.*

AIRPORTS

Brussels Airport at Zaventem, ☎ 0900 70000.

Schiphol Airport at Schiphol, ☎ 0900 724 47 465.

Luxembourg Airport, L-2987 Luxembourg, ☎ (00 352) 47 98 50 50.

FOREIGN EXCHANGE

In Belgium, *banks close at 4.30pm and weekends;*

in the Netherlands, *banks close at 5.00pm and weekends, Schiphol Airport exchange offices open daily from 6.30am to 11.30pm.*

TRANSPORT

Taxis: *may be hailed in the street, at taxi ranks or called by telephone.*

Bus, tramway: *practical for long and short distances and good for sightseeing.*

Brussels has a **Métro** *(subway) network. In each station complete information and plans will be found.*

POSTAL SERVICES – SHOPPING

Post offices open Monday to Friday from 9am to 5pm in Benelux.
Shops and boutiques are generally open from 9am to 7pm in Belgium and Luxembourg, and from 9am to 6pm in the Netherlands. The main shopping areas are:

in Brussels: *Rue Neuve, Porte de Namur, Avenue Louise, Avenue de la Toison d'Or, Boulevard de Waterloo, Rue de Namur - Also Brussels antique market on Saturday from 9am to 3pm, and Sunday from 9am to 1pm (around Place du Grand-Sablon) - Flower and Bird market (Grand-Place) on Sunday morning - Flea Market (Place du Jeu de Balles) – Shopping Centres: Basilix, Westland Shopping Center, Woluwé Shopping Center, City 2, Galerie Louise.*

in Luxembourg: *Grand'Rue and around Place d'Armes - Station Quarter.*

in Amsterdam: *Kalverstraat, Leidsestraat, Nieuwendijk, P.C. Hoofstraat, Beethovenstraat, Van Baerlestraat and Utrechtsestraat – Shopping Center, Magna Plaza – Second-hand goods and antiques (around Rijksmuseum and Spiegelgracht) – Flower Market – Amsterdam Flea Market (near Waterlooplein).*

BREAKDOWN SERVICE *24 hour assistance:*

Belgium: *TCB, Brussels ☎ 0 2 233 22 02 – VTB-VAB, Antwerp ☎ 0 3 253 63 63 – RACB, Brussels ☎ 0 2 287 09 11.*

Luxembourg: *ACL ☎ 45 00 451.*

Netherlands: *ANWB, The Hague ☎ (070) 314 71 47 – KNAC, The Hague ☎ (070) 383 16 12.*

TIPPING *In Benelux, prices include service and taxes.*

SPEED LIMITS – SEAT BELTS

In Belgium and Luxembourg, the maximum speed limits are 120 km/h-74 mph on motorways and dual carriageways, 90 km/h-56 mph on all other roads and 50 km/h-31 mph in built-up areas. In the Netherlands, 100/120 km/h-62/74 mph on motorways and "autowegen", 80 km/h-50 mph on other roads and 50 km/h-31 mph in built-up areas. In each country, the wearing of seat belts is compulsory for drivers and passengers.

BRUSSELS

(BRUXELLES/BRUSSEL)

1000 Région de Bruxelles-Capitale - Brussels Hoofdstedelijk Gewest 533 L 17 and 716 G 3 - Pop. 978 384.

Paris 308 - Amsterdam 204 - Düsseldorf 222 - Lille 116 - Luxembourg 219.

TOURIST OFFICES

TIB Hôtel de Ville, Grand'Place, ✉ 1000, ☎ 0 2 513 89 40, tourism.brussels@tib.be, Fax 0 2 514 45 38.
Office de Promotion du Tourisme (OPT), r. Marché-aux-Herbes 63, ✉ 1000, ☎ 0 2 504 02 00, info@opt.be, Fax 0 2 513 69 50.
Toerisme Vlaanderen, Grasmarkt 63, ✉ 1000, ☎ 0 2 504 03 90, info@toerismevlaanderen.be, Fax 0 2 504 02 70.

For more information on tourist attractions consult our Green Guide to Brussels and our Map N° 44.

BRUXELLES
BRUSSEL

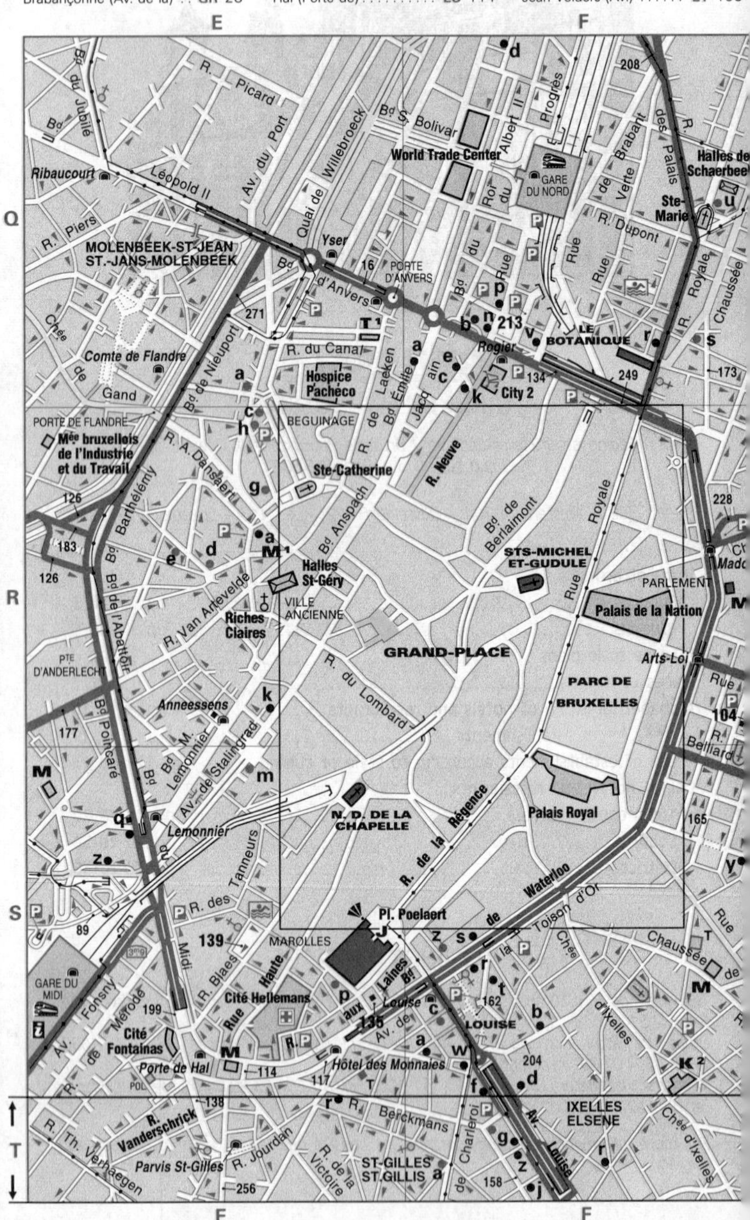

Jeu de Balle (Pl. du)	ES	139
Livourne (R. de)	FT	158
Louise (Galerie)	FS	161
Luxembourg (R. du)	FS	165
Marie-Louise (Sq.)	GR	171
Méridien (R. du)	FQ	173
Midi (Bd du)	ES	
Mons (Chée de)	ER	177
Nerviens (Av. des)	GS	181
Ninove (Chée de)	ER	183
Palmerston (Av.)	GR	187
Porte de Hal (Av. de la)	ES	199
Prince Royal (R. du)	FS	204
Reine (Av. de la)	FQ	208
Rogier (Pl. Charles)	FQ	213
Roi Vainqueur (Pl. du)	HS	216
Saint-Antoine (Pl.)	GT	220
Scailquin (R.)	FR	228
Victoria Regina (Av)	FQ	249
Waterloo (Chée de)	ET	256
9e de Ligne (Bd du)	EQ	271

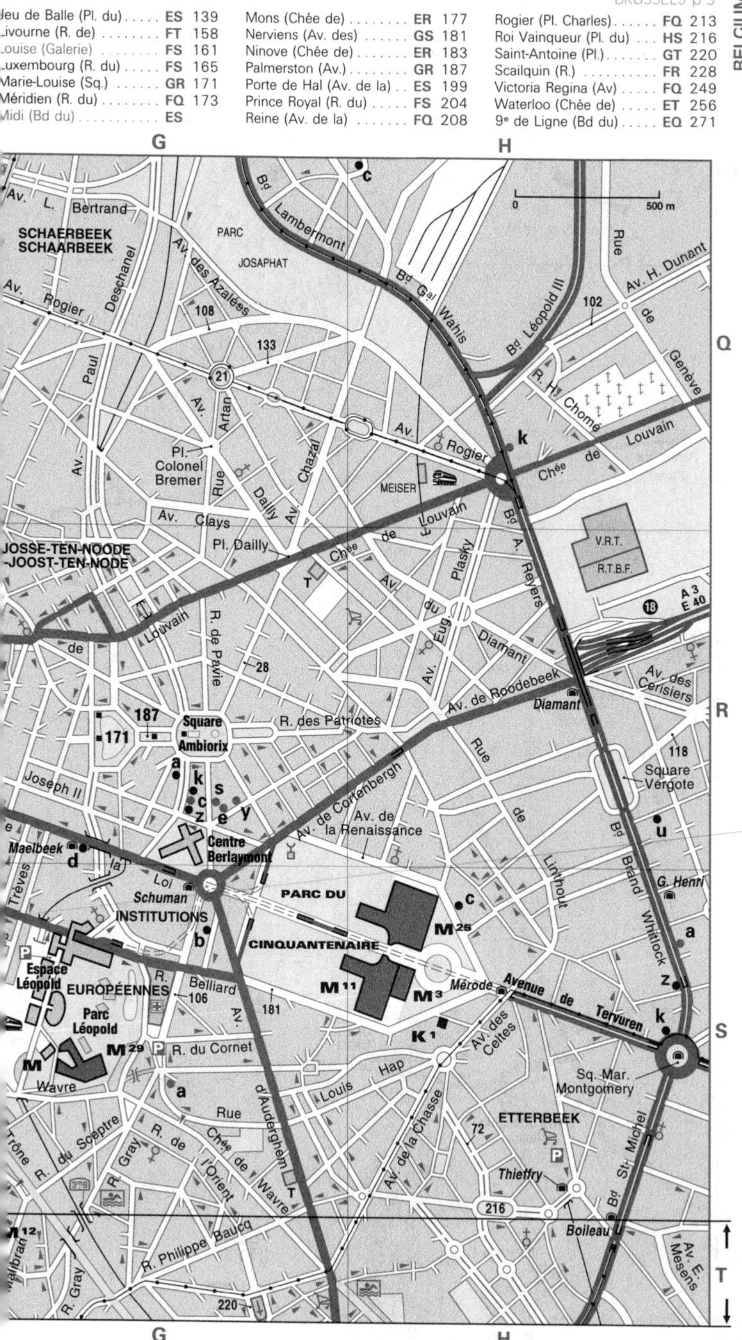

BRUXELLES BRUSSEL

Invalides (Bd des) .... HV 127
Jean Volders (Av.) .... ET 138
Joseph Stallaert (R.) ..... FV 141
Juliette Wytsman (R.) .... GU 145
Kamerdelle (Av.) .... EX 147
Legrand (Av.) .... FV 153
Livourne (R. de) .... FT 158
Louis Morichar (Pl.) ..... EU 160
Mutualité (R. de la) ..... EV 180
Nouvelle (Av.) .... GU 184
Paul Stroobant (Av.) ..... EX 193
Saint-Antoine (Pl.) .... GT 220
Saisons (Av. des) .... GV 223
Saturne (Av. de) .... FX 225
Savoie (R. de) .... EU 226
Tabellion (R. du) .... FU 234
Washington (R.) .... FU 253
Waterloo (Chée de) ..... ET 256
2e Rég. de Lanciers (Av. du) .... GHU 265
7 Bonniers (Av. des) .... EV 270

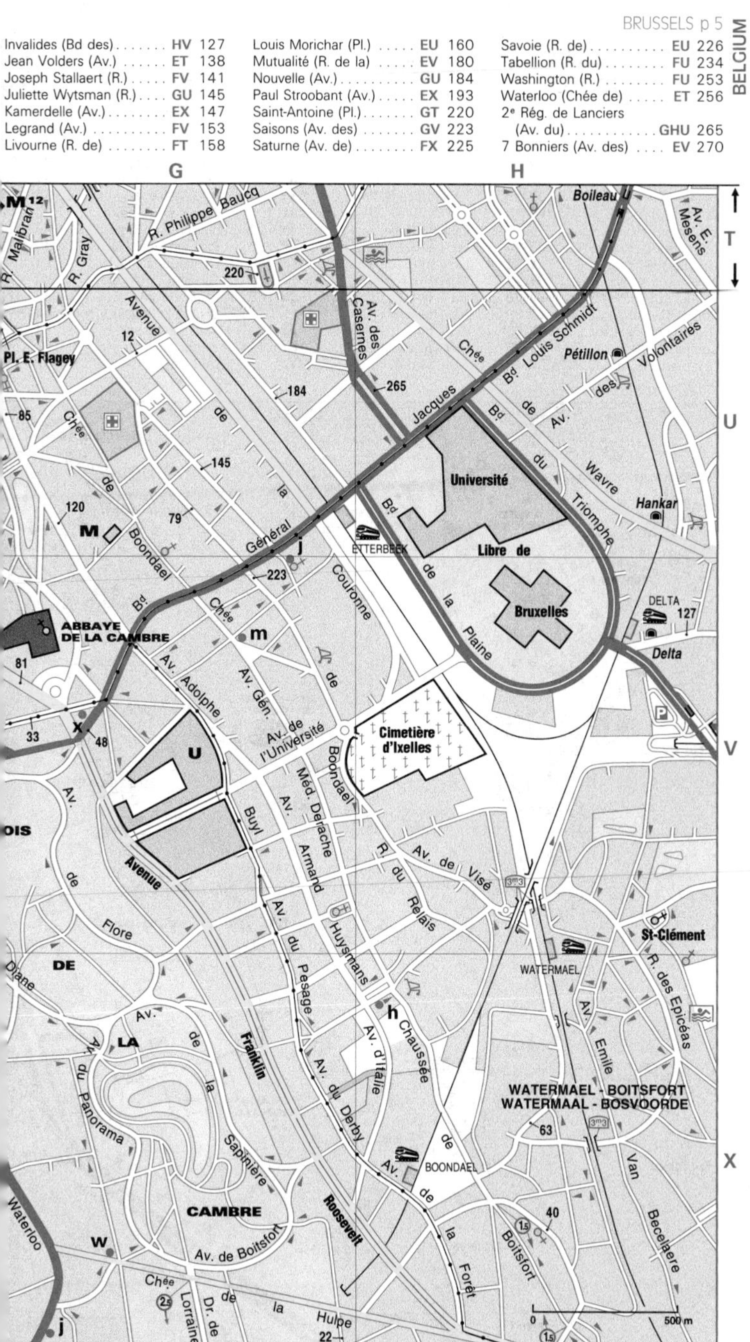

BRUXELLES BRUSSEL

Adolphe Max (Bd) . . . . . JY 3
Albertine (P. de l') . . . . . KZ 4
Anspach (Bd) . . . . JY
Assaut (R. d') . . . . KY 10
Baudet (R.) . . . . KZ 15
Beurre (Rue au) . . . . JY 19
Bortier (Galerie) . . . . JKZ 23
Bouchers (Petite rue des) . . . . . . JY 24
Bouchers (R. des) . . . . . . JY 25
Bourse (Pl. de la) . . . . . . JY 27
Briques (Quai aux) . . . . . JY 29
Chêne (R. du) . . . . JZ 39
Colonies (R. des) . . . . . . KY 43
Comédiens (R. des) . . . . KY 45
Commerce (R. du) . . . . . KZ 46
Croix-de-Fer (R. de la) . . . KY 52
Duquesnoy (Rue) . . . . . . JYZ 66
Ernest Allard (R.) . . . . JZ 86
Etuve (R. de l') . . . . JZ 87
Europe (Carr. de l') . . . . . KY 90
Fossé-aux-Loups (R. du) . . . . JKY 99
Fripiers (R. des) . . . . JY 105
Grand Sablon (Pl. du) . . . . KZ 112
Impératrice (Bd de l') . . . KY 124
Ixelles (Chée d') . . . . KZ 129
Laeken (R. de) . . . . JY 151
Lebeau (R.) . . . . JZ 152
Louvain (R. de) . . . . KY 163
Marché-aux-Herbes (R. du) . . . . JY 168
Marché-aux-Poulets (R. du) . . . . JY 169
Mercier (R. du Card.) . . . KY 172
Midi (R. du) . . . . JYZ
Montagne (Rue de la) . . . KY 178
Musée (Pl. du) . . . . KZ 179
Neuve (Rue) . . . . JY
Nord (Passage du) . . . . . . JY 182
Petit Sablon (Pl. du) . . . . . KZ 195
Presse (R. de la) . . . . KY 201
Princes (Galeries des) . . . . JY 205
Ravenstein (R.) . . . . KZ 207
Reine (Galerie de la) . . . . JY 210
Roi (Galerie du) . . . . KY 214
Rollebeek (R. de) . . . . JZ 217
Ruysbroeck (R. de) . . . . . . KZ 219
Ste-Catherine (Pl.) . . . . . . JY 221
Sainte-Gudule (Pl.) . . . . . . KY 222
Toison d'Or (Av. de la) . . . KZ 238
Trône (R. du) . . . . KZ 241
Ursulines (R. des) . . . . JZ 243
Waterloo (Bd de) . . . . KZ 255
6 Jeunes Hommes (R. des) . . . . KZ 268

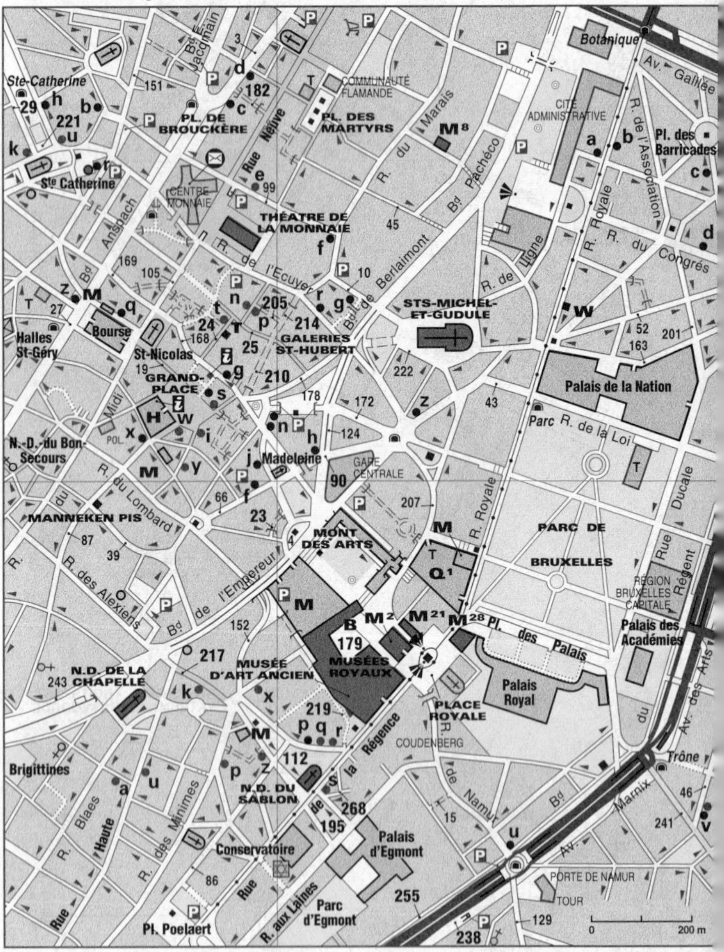

GOLF COURSES

18 9 Southeast : 14 km at Tervuren, Château de Ravenstein ☎ 0 2 767 58 01, Fax 0 2 767 28 41 – 18 Northeast : 14 km at Melsbroek, Steenwagenstraat 11 ☎ 0 2 751 82 05, Fax 0 2 751 84 25 – 18 at Anderlecht, Sports Area of la Pede, r. Scholle 1 ☎ 0 2 521 16 87, Fax 0 2 521 51 56 – 9 at Watermael-Boitsfort, chaussée de la Hulpe 53a ☎ 0 2 672 22 22, Fax 0 2 675 34 81 – 9 Southeast : 16 km at Overijse, Gemslaan 55 ☎ 0 2 687 50 30, Fax 0 2 687 37 68 – 9 West : 8 km at Itterbeek, J.M. Van Lierdelaan 24 ☎ 0 2 569 00 38, Fax 0 2 567 00 38 – 18 Northeast : 20 km at Kampenhout, Wildersedreef 56 ☎ 0 16 65 12 16, Fax 0 16 65 16 80 – 9 East : 18 km at Duisburg, Hertswegenstraat 59 ☎ 0 2 769 45 82, Fax 0 2 767 97 52.

PLACES OF INTEREST

BRUSSELS SEEN FROM ABOVE

Atomium★ – Basilica of the Sacred Heart★ – Arcades of the Royal Museum of the Army and Military History★ HS **M**[25].

FAMOUS VIEWS OF BRUSSELS

The Law Courts ES **J** – *Administrative sections of the City of Brussels* KY – *Place Royale★* KZ.

GREEN AREAS

Parks : Bruxelles, Wolvendael, Woluwé, Laeken, Cinquantenaire, Duden, Bois de la Cambre, Forêt de Soignes.

HISTORICAL MONUMENTS

Grand-Place★★★ JY – *Monnaie Theatre★* JY – *St Hubert Arcades★★* JKY – *Erasmus' House (Anderlecht)★★ – Castle and park (Gaasbeek)★★ (Southwest : 12 km) – Royal Greenhouses (Laeken)★★.*

CHURCHES

Sts-Michael's and Gudule's Cathedral★★ KY – *Church of N.-D. de la Chapelle★* JZ – *Church of N.-D. du Sablon★* KZ – *Abbey of la-Cambre (Ixelles)★★* FGV – *Church of Sts-Pierre and Guidon (Anderlecht)★.*

MUSEUMS

Museum of Ancient Art★★★ KZ – *Museum of the Cinquantenaire★★★* HS **M**[11] – *Museum of Modern Art★★* KZ **M**[2] – *Belgian Centre for Comic Strip Art★★* KY **M**[8] – *Autoworld★★* HS **M**[3] – *Natural Science Museum★★* GS **M**[29] – *Museum of Musical Instruments★★★* KZ **M**[21] – *Constantin Meunier Museum (Ixelles)★* FV **M**[13] – *Ixelles Community Museum (Ixelles)★★* GT **M**[12] – *Charlier Museum★* FR **M**[9] – *Bibliotheca Wittockiana (Woluwé-St-Pierre)★ – Royal Museum of Central Africa (Tervuren/district)★★ – Horta Museum (St-Gilles)★★* EFU **M**[20] – *Van Buuren Museum (Uccle)★* EFV **M**[6] – *Bellevue★* KZ **M**[28].

MODERN ARCHITECTURE

Atomium★ – Berlaymont Centre GR – *European Parliament* GS – *Arts Centre* KZ **Q**[1] – *Administrative sections of the City of Brussels* KY – *Garden-Cities Le Logis and Floréal (Watermael-Boitsfort) – Garden-Cities Kapelleveld (Woluwé-St-Lambert) – UCL Campus (Woluwé-St-Lambert) – Stoclet Palace (Tervuren/district)★ – Swift (La Hulpe/district) – Shop-front P. Hankar★* KY **W** – *Ixelles council building* FS **K**[2] – *Van Eetvelde Hotel★* GR 187 – *Old England★* KZ **N** – *Cauchie House (Etterbeek)★* HS **K**[1].

SCENIC AREAS

Grand-Place★★★ JY – *Grand and Petit Sablon★★* JZ – *St-Hubert Arcades★★* JKY – *Place du Musée* KZ – *Place Ste-Catherine* JY – *The Old Town (Halles St-Géry – vault of the Senne – Church of Riches Claires)* ER – *Rue des Bouchers★* JY – *Manneken Pis★★* JZ – *The Marolles District* JZ – *Galerie Bortier* JY.

Alphabetical listing of hotels and restaurants

Starred establishments

15 XXX **Comme Chez Soi**

✿✿

31	XXXXX	**Bijgaarden (De)**
34	XXXX	**Château du Mylord**
24	XXXX	**Bruneau**
15	XXXX	**Sea Grill (H. Radisson SAS)**
24	XXX	**Claude Dupont**

✿

32	XXXX	**Barbizon**
20	XXXX	**Maison du Bœuf** (H. Hilton)
21	XXXX	**Villa Lorraine**
29	XXX	**Vieux Boitsfort (Au)**
19	XXX	**Écailler du Palais Royal (L')**
32	XXX	**Michel**
33	XXX	**Orangeraie Roland Debuyst (L')**
23	XXX	**Saint Guidon**
24	XXX	**San Daniele**
21	XXX	**Truffe Noire (La)**
23	XX	**Brouette (La)**
30	XX	**Deux Maisons (les)**
29	XX	**Maurice à Olivier (de)**
28	X	**Bon-Bon**
25	X	**Marie**
29	X	**Passage (Le)**
27	X	**Senza Nome**

Establishments according to style of cuisine

Buffets

16 Atelier (L') *Q. de l'Europe*
20 Bistrol Stéphanie *Q. Louise*
19 Café d'Egmont (J. Hilton) *Q. Palais de Justice*
20 Café Wiltcher's (H. Conrad) *Q. Louise*
31 NH Brussels Airport *at Diegem*
22 Sheraton Towers *Q. Botanique, Gare du Nord*

Grill

24 Aub. de Boendael (L') *Ixelles Q. Boondael*
32 Aub. Napoleon *at Meise*
30 auberg'in (l') *Woluwé-St-Pierre*
26 French Kiss *Jette*
29 Grill (Le) *Watermael-Boitsfort*
26 Vieux Pannenhuis (Rôtiss. Le) *Jette*

Pub rest – Brasseries

23 Brasserie de la Gare (La) *Berchem-Ste-Agathe*
28 Brasseries Georges *Uccle*
23 Erasme *Anderlecht*
33 Istas *Env. at Overijse*
31 Kasteel Gravenhof *Env. at Dworp*
19 Lola *Q. des Sablons*
17 Matignon *Q. Grand'Place*
15 NH Grand Place Arenberg
22 Prince de Liège (Le) *Anderlecht*
25 Quincaillerie (La) *Ixelles Q. Bascule*
18 Roue d'Or (La) *Q. Grand'Place*
27 Saint-Germain (Le) Comfort Art H. Siru *St-Josse-Ten-Noode Q. Botanique*
32 Ster (De) *Env. at Itterbeek*
35 Stockmansmolen *Env. at Zaventem*
22 Ustel *Anderlecht*
26 Vigne... à l'Assiette (De la) *Ixelles Q. Louise*

Regional

15 In 't Spinnekopke
18 Kelderke ('t) *Q. Grand'Place*

Seafood – Oyster bar

18 Belle Maraîchère (La) *Q. Ste-Catherine*
18 Bistro M'Alain de la Mer *Q. Ste-Catherine*
28 Brasseries Georges *Uccle*
19 Écailler du Palais Royal (L') *Q. des Sablons*
18 François *Q. Ste-Catherine*
25 Quincaillerie (La) *Ixelles Q. Bascule*
15 Sea Grill (H. Radisson SAS)
34 Stoveke ('t) *Env. at Strombeek-Bever*
18 Truite d'Argent and H. Welcome (La) *Q. Ste-Catherine*
30 Vignoble de Margot (Le) *Woluwé-St-Pierre*

Chinese

22 Lychee *Q. Atomium*
22 Ming Dynasty *Q. Atomium*
23 New Asia *Auderghem*

Greek

19 Strofilia *Q. Ste-Catherine*

Indian

21 Porte des Indes (La) *Q. Louise*

Italian

28 Amici miei *Schaerbeek Q. Meiser*
17 Amigo *Q. Grand'Place*
33 Arlecchino (L') (H. Aub. de Waterloo) *Env. at Sint-Genesius-Rode*
21 Atelier de la Truffe Noir (L') *Q. Louise*
19 Castello Banfi *Q. des Sablons*
29 Da Mimmo *Woluwe-St-Lambert*
34 Il Brunello *Env. at Wemmel*
27 I Trulli *St-Gilles Q. Louise*
19 Jolly du Grand Sablon *Q. des Sablons*
16 Pappa e Citti *Q. de l'Europe*
29 Repos des Chasseurs (Au) *Watermael-Boitsfort*
24 San Daniele *Ganshoren*
27 Senza Nome *Schaerbeek*
25 Tutto Pepe *Ixelles Q. Louise*

Japanese

19 Herbe Rouge (L') *Q. des Sablons*
15 Samourai
21 Tagawa *Q. Louise*
16 Take Sushi *Q. de l'Europe*

Moroccan

Portuguese

Spanish

Thai

Vietnamese

BRUXELLES (BRUSSEL)

Radisson SAS, r. Fossé-aux-Loups 47, ✉ 1000, ☎ 0 2 219 28 28, *restaurant.brussels@radissonsas.com, Fax 0 2 219 62 62,* – – 25-450. AE VISA. rest KY f
Meals see ***Sea Grill*** below – ***Atrium*** *Lunch 26* – a la carte 40/51 ♀ – ☕ 25 – **271 rm** 235, – 10 suites.
◆ A luxury hotel whose atrium bears remnants of the city's 12C fortifications. High-tech rooms varying in layout. "Comic strip" bar. Large restaurant crowned by a high dome. Themed food weeks. Resident pianist.

Astoria, r. Royale 103, ✉ 1000, ☎ 0 2 227 05 05, *H1154@accor-hotels.com, Fax 0 2 217 11 50,* – – 25-210. AE VISA JCB. rest KY b
Meals ***Le Palais Royal*** *(closed 15 July-15 August and weekends)* *Lunch 40* – 25/40 ♀ – ☕ 25 – **104 rm** 180/335, – 14 suites.
◆ Churchill and Dali have both stayed at this elegant Belle Époque palace. Sumptuous lounges and bedrooms adorned with period furniture. Top-class service. Opulent restaurant with mirrors, a marble fireplace, frescoes, and moulded and gilt fixtures and fittings.

Le Plaza, bd. A. Max 118, ✉ 1000, ☎ 0 2 278 01 00, *reservations@leplaza-brussels.be, Fax 0 2 278 01 01* – – 25-800. AE VISA JCB FQ e
Meals *(closed Saturday lunch and Sunday dinner).* *Lunch 29* – a la carte 39/52 – ☕ 25 – **187 rm** 350/450, – 6 suites.
◆ Elegant rooms furnished with fine taste and a listed lounge-theatre are the main features of this 1930s hotel, whose plans were inspired by the Georges V in Paris. A wide cupola embellished with a celestial fresco adds a sense of space to the bar-restaurant.

Marriott, r. A. Orts 7 (opposite the Stock Exchange), ✉ 1000, ☎ 0 2 516 90 90 and 516 91 00 (rest), *mhrs.brudt.ays.mgr@marriotthotels.com, Fax 0 2 516 90 00,* – – 25-450. AE VISA JY z
Meals *(closed Sunday dinner).* *Lunch 12* – a la carte 22/36 ♀ – ☕ 24 – **212 rm** 210/230, – 6 suites.
◆ Situated in front of the Stock Exchange and with an imposing turn-of-the-century façade, the interior of this hotel is modern and very comfortable. Rotisserie and modern brasserie where the usual international fare is freshly prepared.

Métropole, pl. de Brouckère 31, ✉ 1000, ☎ 0 2 217 23 00 , *info@metropolehotel.be, Fax 0 2 218 02 20,* – – 25-500. AE VISA JCB JY c
Meals see ***L'Alban Chambon*** below – **291 rm** ☕ 279/429, – 14 suites.
◆ This late-19C palace extends along place de Brouckère, eulogised by Jacques Brel. Impressive entrance hall and sumptuous lounges. Pleasant bedrooms, varying in style.

NH Atlanta, bd A. Max 7, ✉ 1000, ☎ 0 2 217 01 20 , *nhatlanta@nh-hotels.be, Fax 0 2 217 37 58,* – – 25-160. AE VISA JY d
Meals. *Lunch 10 b.i.* – a la carte approx. 38 – ☕ 21 – **228 rm** 325/450, – 13 suites.
◆ Large-scale renovation work has given new life to this fine hotel built in the 1930s just a stone's throw from the nostalgic passage du Nord and place de Brouckère. The Atlanta's luxurious modern brasserie serves a range of French and Italian cuisine.

Bedford, r. Midi 135, ✉ 1000, ☎ 0 2 507 00 00, *info@hotelbedford.be, Fax 0 2 507 00 10,* – – 25-550. AE VISA JCB. ER k
Meals a la carte approx. 44 – **318 rm** ☕ 230/320, – 8 suites.
◆ Just a short walk from the Manneken Pis and 500m/550yd from the Grand-Place, this chain hotel has a dozen apartments, as well as over 300 well-appointed standard rooms. The emphasis on the menu and wine-list is firmly French.

President Centre without rest, r. Royale 160, ✉ 1000, ☎ 0 2 219 00 65 , *thierry.sluys@presidentcentre.be, Fax 0 2 218 09 10* – . AE VISA JCB. **73 rm** ☕ 170/245. KY a
◆ Morpheus extends his welcoming arms in the comfortable, soundproofed rooms of the Hotel President Centre. Invaluable car attendants, attentive service and a cosy bar.

Hesperia Grand'Place without rest, r. Colonies 10, ✉ 1000, ☎ 0 2 504 99 10, *regencypalace@skynet.be, Fax 0 2 503 14 51* – – 25. AE VISA KY z
47 rm ☕ 150/240.
◆ A new hotel with an ideal location between the Gare Centrale and Saints-Michel-et-Gudule Cathedral. Modern, comfortable rooms, plus a bright breakfast room.

Scandic Grand'Place, r. Arenberg 18, ✉ 1000, ☎ 0 2 548 18 11 , *grand.place@scandic-hotels.com, Fax 0 2 548 18 20,* – – 25-80. AE VISA JCB KY
Meals (dinner only weekends, Bank Holidays and school holidays). *Lunch 16* – a la carte 22/34 – **100 rm** ☕ 229/289.
◆ 250m/275yd from the Grand-Place, and accessible via the Galeries St-Hubert, this late 19C mansion has 100 small but charming rooms promising a good night's sleep. A soberly designed, yet welcoming modern brasserie.

NH Grand Place Arenberg, r. Assaut 15, ✉ 1000, ☎ 0 2 501 16 16, *nhgrandplace@nh-hotels.com, Fax 0 2 501 18 18* – AE VISA. KY g
Meals *(closed lunch Saturday, Sunday and Bank Holidays)* (pub rest). *Lunch 8* – 25 – 21 – **155 rm** 220/250.
◆ This chain hotel is well-placed for exploring the heart of the city. Modern, functional bedrooms with standard furnishings.

Agenda Midi without rest, bd Jamar 11, ✉ 1060, ☎ 0 2 520 00 10, *midi@hotel-agenda.com, Fax 0 2 520 00 20* – AE VISA JCB. ES z
35 rm 62/97.
◆ This renovated building on place Jamar is just a short distance from the Gare du Midi TGV railway station. Pleasant rooms and a brightly decorated breakfast room.

Chambord without rest, r. Namur 82, ✉ 1000, ☎ 0 2 548 99 10, *hotel-chambord@hotel-chambord.be, Fax 0 2 514 08 47* – AE VISA JCB. KZ u
69 rm 132/169.
◆ A 1960s-style hotel alongside the porte de Namur. Spacious, adequately furnished rooms, with those to the rear generally quieter. Public car park a few yards away.

Queen Anne without rest, bd E. Jacqmain 110, ✉ 1000, ☎ 0 2 217 16 00, *Fax 0 2 217 18 38* – AE VISA. EFQ a
60 rm 110/130.
◆ The Queen Anne is located on a major road linking the World Trade Center district and the old town. Plain, but carefully maintained bedrooms with double-glazing.

Sabina without rest, r. Nord 78, ✉ 1000, ☎ 0 2 218 26 37, *info@hotelsabina.be, Fax 0 2 219 32 39* – AE VISA. KY c
24 rm 75/90.
◆ A modest hotel with quiet, plain rooms that are gradually being refurbished, situated between the colonne du Congrès and the place des Barricades. Pleasant breakfast room.

Sea Grill - Hotel Radisson SAS, r. Fossé-aux-Loups 47, ✉ 1000, ☎ 0 2 227 31 20, *annick.colmant@radissonsas.com, Fax 0 2 227 31 05*, Seafood – AE VISA. KY f
closed 3 to 12 April, 21 July-15 August, Saturday, Sunday and Bank Holidays – **Meals** 49/110 b.i., – a la carte 83/140.
◆ A warm, Scandinavian-influenced ambience, ambitious fish-dominated menu, excellent wine cellar, plus a lounge offering a good choice of cigars. Friendly, impeccable service.
Spec. Tartare de thon rouge préparé à table. Bar entier cuit en croûte de sel. Manchons de crabe de la mer de Barents tiédis au beurre de persil plat.

L'Alban Chambon - Hotel Métropole, pl. de Brouckère 31, ✉ 1000, ☎ 0 2 217 23 00, *info@metropolehotel.be, Fax 0 2 218 02 20* – AE VISA JCB JY c
closed 19 July-15 August, Saturday, Sunday and Bank Holidays – **Meals**. *Lunch 35* – 55/90 b.i..
◆ The name of this restaurant pays homage to the Metropole's architect. Light, classic cuisine served in a former ballroom embellished with period furniture.

Comme Chez Soi (Wynants), pl. Rouppe 23, ✉ 1000, ☎ 0 2 512 29 21 , *info@commechezsoi.be, Fax 0 2 511 80 52* – AE VISA ES m
closed 1 May, 4 July-2 August, Christmas-New Year, Sunday and Monday – **Meals** (booking essential). *Lunch 64* – 112/152, – a la carte 64/214.
◆ Despite the slightly cramped feel, the Belle Époque atmosphere, recreated in this Horta-inspired decor, is the perfect foil for the superb cuisine and magnificent wine list.
Spec. Filets de sole, mousseline au Riesling et aux crevettes grises. Émincé de bœuf et pommes de terre charlottes grillées aux herbes de Provence, sauté d'asperges et pimientos. Damier de fraises de bois glacé de frangipane et mousse de fraises.

La Manufacture, r. Notre-Dame du Sommeil 12, ✉ 1000, ☎ 0 2 502 25 25, *info@manufacture.be, Fax 0 2 502 27 15*, Open until 11 p.m. – AE VISA ER e
closed Saturday lunch and Sunday – **Meals**. *Lunch 13* – a la carte 30/50.
◆ Metal, wood, leather and granite have all been used to decorate this trendy brasserie occupying the workshop of a renowned leather manufacturer. Contemporary cuisine.

Samourai, r. Fossé-aux-Loups 28, ✉ 1000, ☎ 0 2 217 56 39, *Fax 0 2 771 97 61*, Japanese cuisine – AE VISA JCB. JY e
closed 15 July-16 August, Tuesday and Sunday lunch – **Meals**. *Lunch 22* – a la carte 40/84.
◆ A Japanese restaurant near the Théâtre de la Monnaie with a menu offering a comprehensive choice. Fine selection of vintage Bordeaux wines. Minimalist atmosphere.

In 't Spinnekopke, pl. du Jardin aux Fleurs 1, ✉ 1000, ☎ 0 2 511 86 95, *info@spinnekopke.be, Fax 0 2 513 24 97*, Partly regional cuisine – AE VISA. ER d
closed Saturday lunch and Sunday – **Meals**. *Lunch 9* – a la carte 22/42.
◆ This charming, typical tavern serves a wide choice of bistro-style cuisine, accompanied by some good wines and local beers. Service with a smile.

Quartier de l'Europe

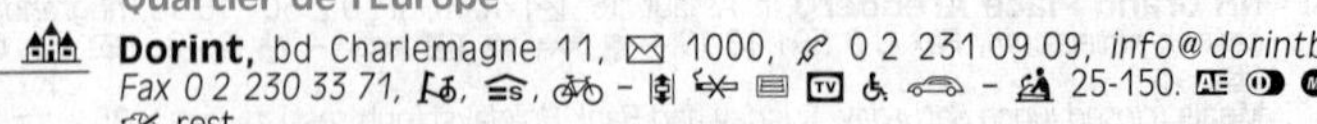

Dorint, bd Charlemagne 11, ✉ 1000, ☎ 0 2 231 09 09, *info@dorintbru.be, Fax 0 2 230 33 71,* – – 25-150. AE VISA. rest GR c
Meals ***L'Objectif*** *(closed lunch Saturday, Sunday and Bank Holidays) Lunch 24* – a la carte 45/54 – 24 – **210 rm** 260/290, – 2 suites.
◆ This newly built chain hotel with a designer appearance comprises two inter-connected buildings with spacious, striking rooms. The modernity of the dining room is in keeping with the innovative and attractive cuisine. Exhibition of contemporary photography.

Crowne Plaza Europa, r. Loi 107, ✉ 1040, ☎ 0 2 230 13 33, *brussels@ichotelsgroup.com, Fax 0 2 230 36 82,* – – 25-350. AE VISA JCB. GR d
Meals *(closed August)* (open until 11 p.m.). *Lunch 19* – a la carte 32/51 – **238 rm** 240/465, – 2 suites.
◆ The 1970s-built Europa, located a few steps from the main European institutions, has undergone large-scale renovation. Business centre and full conference facilities. Pleasant restaurant with buffet lunch options, eclectic à la carte menu and good wine-list.

Eurovillage, bd Charlemagne 80, ✉ 1000, ☎ 0 2 230 85 55, *Fax 0 2 230 56 35,* – – 25-130. AE VISA JCB GR a
Meals *(closed 1 to 25 August, Saturday and Sunday lunch). Lunch 22* – a la carte 27/44 – 16 – **103 rm** 200/250.
◆ A modern building alongside a verdant park with small but charming bedrooms, good seminar and business facilities, and spacious lounge areas. Plenty of menu choices, plus lunchtime buffets.

Holiday Inn Schuman, r. Breydel 20, ✉ 1040, ☎ 0 2 280 40 00, *hotel@holiday-inn-brussels-schuman.com, Fax 0 2 282 10 70,* – – 45. AE VISA JCB. GS b
Meals (residents only) – 20 – **53 rm** 225/245.
◆ A new hotel offering a high level of comfort with Picasso frescoes adorning some rooms and suites. On fine days, breakfast can be enjoyed outdoors.

New Hotel Charlemagne, bd Charlemagne 25, ✉ 1000, ☎ 0 2 230 21 35, *brusselscharlemagne@new-hotel.be, Fax 0 2 230 25 10,* – – 30-50. AE VISA JCB. rest GR k
Meals (residents only) – 18 – **66 rm** 210/230.
◆ This practical small hotel between Square Ambiorix and the Centre Berlaymont is popular with EU staff. Reception, lounge-bar and breakfast room on the same floor.

Pappa e Citti, r. Franklin 18, ✉ 1000, ☎ 0 2 732 61 10, *pappaecitti@skynet.be, Fax 0 2 732 57 40,* , Italian cuisine – AE VISA. GR e
closed August, 20 December-6 January, Saturday, Sunday and Bank Holidays – **Meals** *Lunch 27* – a la carte 34/89.
◆ Popular with European civil servants who head for this small, friendly Italian restaurant to enjoy Sardinian specialities and wines. Two lunch sittings. Veranda.

L'Atelier, r. Franklin 28, ✉ 1000, ☎ 0 2 734 91 40, *info@atelier-euro.be, Fax 0 2 735 35 98,* , Partly buffets – AE VISA GR y
closed August, weekends and Bank Holidays – **Meals**. *Lunch 18* – 22/28 b.i..
◆ The choice here includes menus and generous buffets. A respectable wine-list, reminding customers of the original vocation of this old warehouse. Collection of Khmer fabrics.

Take Sushi, bd Charlemagne 21, ✉ 1000, ☎ 0 2 230 56 27, *Fax 0 2 231 10 44,* , Japanese cuisine with Sushi-bar – AE VISA JCB GR z
closed Saturday and Sunday lunch – **Meals**. *Lunch 28* – a la carte 27/72.
◆ A corner of Japan at the heart of the city's European institutions district. Japanese décor, background music and small garden. Popular sushi bar. Kimono-clad waitresses.

Balthazar, r. Archimède 63, ✉ 1000, ☎ 0 2 742 06 00, *Fax 0 2 735 70 07,* – AE VISA GR s
closed 24 December-3 January, Saturday lunch and Sunday – **Meals**. *Lunch 10* – a la carte 29/46.
◆ A modern brasserie-style ambience where the focus is on Southern French and Italian dishes and wines from around the world. Multilingual service. Small garden.

Quartier Grand'Place (Ilot Sacré)

Royal Windsor, r. Duquesnoy 5, ✉ 1000, ☎ 0 2 505 55 55, *sales.royalwindsor@warwickhotels.com, Fax 0 2 505 55 00,* – – 25-350. AE VISA. JYZ f
Meals. *Lunch 13* – a la carte 30/43 – 21 – **248 rm** 400/525, – 17 suites.
◆ Luxury, comfort and refinement characterise this grand hotel in the historic centre. Quiet bedrooms with antique furniture, top-notch service and excellent facilities. Elegant gastronomic restaurant crowned by an impressive Art Deco dome.

Le Méridien, Carrefour de l'Europe 3, ✉ 1000, ☎ 0 2 548 42 11, *info@meridien.be, Fax 0 2 548 40 80*, ≤, – – 25-200. AE ⓓ MC VISA JCB.
Meals ***L'Épicerie*** *(closed 20 July-20 August and Saturday lunch)* Lunch 49 – a la carte 53/62 – ☕ 25 – **216 rm** 440/600, – 8 suites. KY h
◆ The hotel's majestic neo-Classical façade stands opposite the Gare Centrale. Gleaming interior décor, with elegant bedrooms boasting the very latest in facilities. An interesting restaurant menu is complemented by buffet lunches and a popular Sunday brunch.

Amigo, r. Amigo 1, ✉ 1000, ☎ 0 2 547 47 47, *sales@hotelamigo.com, Fax 0 2 513 52 77*, – – 25-200. AE ⓓ MC VISA JCB. JY x
Meals (Italian cuisne) a la carte 38/56 ♀ – ☕ 25 – **152 rm** 450/540, – 7 suites.
◆ This imposing building dating from 1958 shows Spanish Renaissance influence. Superior bedrooms with varied furnishings. Collection of works of art. The bright contemporary brasserie offers a traditional menu choice dedicated to typical Belgian dishes.

Le Dixseptième without rest, r. Madeleine 25, ✉ 1000, ☎ 0 2 502 17 17, *info@le dixseptieme.be, Fax 0 2 502 64 24* – – 25. AE ⓓ MC VISA. JY j
18 rm ☕ 200/250, – 6 suites.
◆ As its name indicates, this old town house dates from the 17C. Elegant lounges and large, homely bedrooms furnished with antiques from different periods.

Carrefour de l'Europe without rest, r. Marché-aux-Herbes 110, ✉ 1000, ☎ 0 2 504 94 00, *info@carrefoureurope.net, Fax 0 2 504 95 00* – – 25-200. AE ⓓ MC VISA JKY n
☕ 21 – **58 rm** 260/340, – 5 suites.
◆ This modern hotel just off the Grand-Place is in keeping with the harmony of the city's architecture. Bedrooms slightly on the drab side, but of a good standard nonetheless.

Novotel off Grand'Place, r. Marché-aux-Herbes 120, ✉ 1000, ☎ 0 2 514 33 33, *H1030@accor-hotels.com, Fax 0 2 511 77 23*, – – 25. AE ⓓ MC VISA JCB. rest JKY n
Meals a la carte 26/44 – ☕ 15 – **136 rm** 179/199.
◆ An ideal location just 200m/220yd from the Gare Centrale and Grand-Place. All the Novotel's bedrooms conform to the chain's latest quality standards.

Aris without rest, r. Marché-aux-Herbes 78, ✉ 1000, ☎ 0 2 514 43 00, *info@arishot el.be, Fax 0 2 514 01 19* – . ⓓ MC VISA JCB JY g
55 rm ☕ 210/235.
◆ This practical small hotel occupies a house close to the city's main square and the Galeries St-Hubert. 55 rooms offering modern comfort.

Matignon, r. Bourse 10, ✉ 1000, ☎ 0 2 511 08 88, *Fax 0 2 513 69 27*, – . AE ⓓ MC VISA JCB. rest JY q
Meals *(closed January-February and Monday)* (pub rest). Lunch 15 – a la carte 22/34 – **37 rm** ☕ 75/110.
◆ Half the cosy double-glazed rooms in this pleasant hotel offer attractive views over the Stock Exchange. Mainly frequented by tourists. The tavern-restaurant serves up a selection of well-presented bistro-style cuisine. Outdoor terrace in summer.

Floris without rest, r. Harengs 6, ✉ 1000, ☎ 0 2 514 07 60, *floris.grandplace@grou ptorus.com, Fax 0 2 548 90 39* – . AE ⓓ MC VISA JY s
12 rm ☕ 140/160.
◆ A pocket-sized hotel 50m/55yd from the Grand-Place with 11 reasonably spacious rooms with carpet or parquet flooring, all of which have just been completely renovated.

La Maison du Cygne, r. Charles Buls 2, ✉ 1000, ☎ 0 2 511 82 44, *lecygne@skynet.be, Fax 0 2 514 31 48*, With L'Ommegang on the ground floor – . AE ⓓ MC VISA. JY w
closed 31 July-30 August, 24 to 30 December, Saturday lunch, Sunday and Bank Holidays – **Meals**. Lunch 40 – a la carte 65/192 ♀.
◆ This 17C house on the Grand-Place was originally the headquarters of the Butchers' Guild. Panelled interior and themed lounges. Traditional cuisine with modern flourishes.

Aux Armes de Bruxelles, r. Bouchers 13, ✉ 1000, ☎ 0 2 511 55 98, *arbrux@b eon.be, Fax 0 2 514 33 81*, Open until 11 p.m. – . AE ⓓ MC VISA JY t
closed mid June-mid July and Monday – **Meals**. Lunch 23 b.i. – 30/45 b.i. ♀.
◆ A veritable Brussels institution at the heart of the historic centre, where the focus is resolutely Belgian. Three rooms in traditional, modern and brasserie style.

Le Cerf, Grand'Place 20, ✉ 1000, ☎ 0 2 511 47 91, *Fax 0 2 546 09 59*, Open until 11.30 p.m. – . AE ⓓ MC VISA JY s
closed 18 July-16 August, Saturday and Sunday – **Meals**. Lunch 22 b.i. – 46 b.i./54 b.i. ♀.
◆ Wood, stained-glass and warm fabrics dominate the décor of these early-18C houses. The rooms on the façade overlook the Grand-Place. Contemporary cuisine.

de l'Ogenblik, Galerie des Princes 1, ✉ 1000, ☎ 0 2 511 61 51, *ogenblik@tiscalinet.be, Fax 0 2 513 41 58*, , Open until midnight – AE ⓓ MC VISA JY p
closed Sunday – **Meals** – a la carte 47/64 ♀.
◆ This old café-style restaurant is known for its fine, classic cuisine, chef's suggestions and daily specials. Popular with the local business community.

La Roue d'Or, r. Chapeliers 26, ✉ 1000, ☎ 0 2 514 25 54, *Fax 0 2 512 30 81*, Open until midnight – AE ⓓ ⓜ VISA JY y
closed 18 July-16 August – **Meals**. *Lunch 10* – a la carte 26/45 ♀.
◆ A typical old café with a convivial atmosphere where the culinary emphasis is on staple Belgian brasserie fare. Surrealist wall paintings in the genre of Magritte.

Vincent, r. Dominicains 8, ✉ 1000, ☎ 0 2 511 26 07, *info@restaurantvincent.com, Fax 0 2 502 36 93*, 🍽, Open until 11.30 p.m. – ▤. AE ⓓ ⓜ VISA JCB JY n
closed first 2 weeks August and 2 to 12 January – **Meals**. *Lunch 18* – a la carte 27/63.
◆ Savour the typical Brussels atmosphere of this nostalgic rotisserie adorned with painted ceramic-tile frescoes. Local dishes to the fore, with meat and mussel specialities.

't Kelderke, Grand'Place 15, ✉ 1000, ☎ 0 2 513 73 44, *Fax 0 2 512 30 81*, Regional cooking, open until 2 a.m. – AE ⓓ ⓜ VISA JY i
closed 1 to 14 July – **Meals**. *Lunch 8* – a la carte 22/40.
◆ This quaint tavern-cum-restaurant occupies the vaulted cellar of a house on the Grand-Place. Copious cuisine with "local colour", plus an ambience to match.

Quartier Ste-Catherine (Marché-aux-Poissons)

Novotel Centre-Tour Noire, r. Vierge Noire 32, ✉ 1000, ☎ 0 2 505 50 50, *H2122@accor-hotels.com, Fax 0 2 505 50 00*, 🍽, 🏋 – 🛗 ⊁ ▤ 📺 – 🏛 25-350. AE ⓓ ⓜ VISA JY r
Meals – a la carte 24/41 – ☕ 15 – **217 rm** 165/180.
◆ Discreet elegance and functional modernity best describe this hotel, which owes it name to one of the towers that made up the city's first defensive walls.

Welcome, r. Peuplier 1, ✉ 1000, ☎ 0 2 219 95 46, *info@hotelwelcome.com, Fax 0 2 217 18 87*, 🍽 – 🛗, ▤ rest, 📺 🚗. ⓓ ⓜ VISA JY h
Meals ***La Truite d'Argent*** *(closed first 2 weeks August, first 2 weeks January, Saturday lunch and Sunday)* (seafood, open until 11.30 p.m.) 42/72 b.i. – ☕ 10 – **15 rm** 80/130.
◆ A friendly hotel occupying an attractive corner house, inside which the new décor of each room calls to mind a different country. Panelling, benches and chandeliers add a homely feel to the restaurant, where the menu shows a distinct seaward bias.

Atlas 🐴 without rest, r. Vieux Marché-aux-Grains 30, ✉ 1000, ☎ 0 2 502 60 06, *info@atlas.be, Fax 0 2 502 69 35* – 🛗 📺 ♿ 🚗 – 🏛 30. AE ⓓ ⓜ VISA. ⚔ ER a
88 rm ☕ 115/135.
◆ This 18C hotel stands on a small square in a well-to-do neighbourhood full of fashion boutiques. Most of the rooms look onto an inner courtyard.

Astrid Centre without rest, pl. du Samedi 11, ✉ 1000, ☎ 0 2 219 31 19, *info@astridhotel.be, Fax 0 2 219 31 70* – 🛗 ▤ 📺 ♿ 🚗 – 🏛 25-80. ⓓ ⓜ VISA JCB JY b
100 rm ☕ 175/200.
◆ A building of modern design between place Ste-Catherine and place de Brouckère. Facilities include standard, simply furnished rooms, a bar, lounge areas and conference rooms.

Bistro M'Alain de la Mer, pl. Ste-Catherine 15, ✉ 1000, ☎ 0 2 217 90 12, *alain.troubat@skynet.be, Fax 0 2 219 07 38*, 🍽, Seafood – AE ⓓ ⓜ VISA JY u
closed Sunday and Monday – **Meals**. *Lunch 25* – 38/53 b.i..
◆ As the name indicates, this new eatery near the church conjures up a bistro atmosphere with an emphasis on fish and seafood. Pleasant summer terrace.

François, quai aux Briques 2, ✉ 1000, ☎ 0 2 511 60 89, 🍽, Oyster bar, seafood – ▤ P. AE ⓓ ⓜ VISA JCB JY k
closed Sunday and Monday – **Meals**. *Lunch 25* – 32/37 ♀.
◆ Delicious fish and seafood, washed down with some great white wines, await customers at this in-vogue restaurant. The maritime interior is enlivened with nostalgic photos.

La Belle Maraîchère, pl. Ste-Catherine 11, ✉ 1000, ☎ 0 2 512 97 59, *Fax 0 2 513 76 91*, Seafood – ▤ P. AE ⓓ ⓜ VISA JY k
closed 2 weeks carnival, 3 weeks July, Wednesday and Thursday – **Meals** – 31/65 b.i. 🍇.
◆ Run by two brothers, the kitchen produces a consistently wide choice of dishes, with a preference for the sea. Enticing wine-list. Popular with business customers and locals.

Le Loup-Galant, quai aux Barques 4, ✉ 1000, ☎ 0 2 219 99 98, *loupgalant@swing.be, Fax 0 2 219 99 98* – AE ⓓ ⓜ VISA EQ a
closed 1 week Easter, first 2 weeks August, 1 week Christmas, Sunday and Monday – **Meals**. *Lunch 19* – 24/50 b.i..
◆ Make sure you hear the legend surrounding this old house at one end of the Vismet. Wide choice of cuisine and wine. Chimney and exposed beams in the dining room.

Bistro M'Alain Tradition, r. Flandre 6, ✉ 1000, ☎ 0 2 503 14 80, *alain.troubat@skynet.be, Fax 0 2 503 14 80* – AE ⓓ ⓜ VISA ER g
closed 1 week August, 1 week December, Sunday and Monday – **Meals**. *Lunch 23* – 30/45 b.i..
◆ This "new kid on the block" offers an interesting, well-balanced menu of delicious bistro-style and local dishes. A charming welcome and service.

Strofilia, r. Marché-aux-Porcs 11, 1000, 0 2 512 32 93, *strofilia@pi.be, Fax 0 2 512 09 94*, Greek cuisine, open until midnight – AE MC VISA. ER c
closed 24 December-3 January and Sunday – **Meals**. *Lunch 11* – a la carte 24/35.
• Named after a wine press, this much-improved Greek restaurant serves typical cuisine in its airy loft-style dining rooms showing touches of Byzantine decor. Good wine list.

Quartier des Sablons

Jolly du Grand Sablon, r. Bodenbroek 2, 1000, 0 2 518 11 00, *jollyhotelsablon@jollyhotels.be, Fax 0 2 512 67 66* – 25-150. AE MC VISA. rest KZ p

Meals *(closed 1 to 25 August and 20 December-5 January)* (Italian cuisine). *Lunch 18* – 22 – **192 rm** 315/375, – 1 suite.
• This Italian-owned hotel is located just a stone's throw from the city's prestigious royal museums. Well-appointed rooms, plus a conference centre with a range of tailor-made facilities. The restaurant offers Italian cuisine, buffets and daily specials.

L'Écailler du Palais Royal (Hahn), r. Bodenbroek 18, 1000, 0 2 512 87 51, *Fax 0 2 511 99 50*, Seafood – AE MC VISA. KZ r
closed August, Christmas-New Year, Sunday and Bank Holidays – **Meals** a la carte 58/107.
• The chef here successfully blends the flavours of the sea with beautiful presentation. Elegant grey décor and a choice of seating : benches, chairs or the bar-counter.
Spec. Moelleux de tourteau et croustillant de homard. Bouillabaisse de poisons de la mer du Nord. Mariage de turbot et sauté de homard, les deux sauces à l'estragon.

Trente rue de la Paille, r. Paille 30, 1000, 0 2 512 07 15, *info@resto-trenteruedelapaille.com, Fax 0 2 514 23 33* – AE MC VISA JZ x
closed mid July-mid August, Christmas-New Year, Saturday and Sunday – **Meals**. *Lunch 31* – a la carte 58/67.
• An open fire, exposed beams, brickwork, drapery, floral bouquets and assorted crockery characterise this warm and welcoming restaurant in the antiques district.

Castello Banfi, r. Bodenbroek 12, 1000, 0 2 512 87 94, *Fax 0 2 512 87 94*, Partly Italian cuisine – AE MC VISA KZ q
closed first week Easter, last 3 weeks August, late December, Sunday dinner and Monday – **Meals**. *Lunch 27* – a la carte 37/79.
• The menu at this gastronomic restaurant, hidden behind an 18C façade, encompasses specialities from both France and Italy. The name refers to a large Tuscan wine estate.

"Chez Marius" En Provence, pl. du Petit Sablon 1, 1000, 0 2 511 12 08, *chez.marius@skynet.be, Fax 0 2 512 27 89*, – AE MC VISA KZ s
closed 21 July-20 August, Saturday, Sunday and Bank Holidays – **Meals**. *Lunch 22* – 39/71 b.i..
• Memories of the south will come flooding back in this rustic-style restaurant, with its typically Provençal cuisine. In summer, why not enjoy a pastis on the terrace.

La Clef des Champs, r. Rollebeek 23, 1000, 0 2 512 11 93, *laclefdeschamps@resto.be, Fax 0 2 502 42 32*, – AE MC VISA JZ k
closed Saturday lunch, Sunday dinner and Monday – **Meals**. *Lunch 15* – 30/48 b.i..
• A recommended address with a light, bright feel, where the welcome is always cheerful. Cuisine from around France.

Lola, pl. du Grand Sablon 33, 1000, 0 2 514 24 60, *restaurant.lola@skynet.be, Fax 0 2 514 26 53*, Brasserie, open until 11.30 p.m. – AE MC VISA. JZ z
Meals a la carte 28/52.
• This convivial brasserie with its contemporary décor devotes its energies to the latest culinary trends. Choose between sitting on benches, chairs or at the bar.

L'Herbe Rouge, r. Minimes 34, 1000, 0 2 512 48 34, *Fax 0 2 511 62 88*, Japanese cuisine, open until 11 p.m. – AE MC VISA JZ p
closed Monday – **Meals**. *Lunch 15* – a la carte 26/48.
• A reasonably authentic and well-compiled Japanese menu is on offer in this simply furnished, contemporary-style restaurant ornamented with risqué Japanese prints.

Quartier Palais de Justice

Hilton, bd de Waterloo 38, 1000, 0 2 504 11 11 and 0 2 504 13 33 (rest), *bruhitwrm@hilton.com, Fax 0 2 504 21 11*, town, – 45-650. AE MC VISA JCB. FS s
Meals see ***Maison du Bœuf*** below – ***Café d'Egmont*** (partly buffets, open until midnight) *Lunch 35* – a la carte 39/58 – 32 – **420 rm** 450/480, – 13 suites.
• International business clientele will be well and truly pampered in this imposing Hilton built between the upper and lower towns. The hotel's Café d'Egmont offers buffets and themed food weeks beneath its Art Deco glass.

XXXX ✿ **Maison du Bœuf** - Hotel Hilton, 1st floor, bd de Waterloo 38, ✉ 1000, ☎ 0 2 504 13 34, *bruhitwrm@hilton.com, Fax 0 2 504 21 11*, ← - ▤ P. AE ⓓ ⓜⓒ VISA JCB. ✗ FS s
Meals. *Lunch 55* – 58/98 b.i., – a la carte 53/186 ♀.
◆ The Hilton's gastronomic restaurant proposes a resolutely traditional à la carte menu in keeping with its opulent décor. Extensive wine-list. Views over the Parc d'Egmont.
Spec. Côte de bœuf rôtie en croûte de sel. Bar rôti au thym frais, crème d'échalotes. Tartare maison au caviar.

XX **JB,** r. Grand Cerf 24, ✉ 1000, ☎ 0 2 512 04 84, *restaurantjb@vt4.net, Fax 0 2 511 79 30*, ☂ – ▤. AE ⓓ ⓜⓒ VISA FS z
closed Saturday lunch, Sunday and Bank Holidays – **Meals** – 20/40 b.i..
◆ A new address already attracting a steady flow of regulars just behind the affluent avenue Louise. Attractive à la carte and fixed-menu choices prepared with a modern eye.

X **L'Idiot du village,** r. Notre Seigneur 19, ✉ 1000, ☎ 0 2 502 55 82, Open until 11 p.m. – AE ⓓ ⓜⓒ VISA JZ a
closed 20 July-20 August, 23 December-2 January, Saturday and Sunday – **Meals**. *Lunch 15* – a la carte 39/49.
◆ An intelligently-run bistro despite the name ! A warm ambience, cuisine with an original modern touch, astute wine-list and friendly, smiling service.

X **Les Larmes du Tigre,** r. Wynants 21, ✉ 1000, ☎ 0 2 512 18 77, *Fax 0 2 502 10 03*, ☂, Thai cuisine – AE ⓓ ⓜⓒ VISA ES p
closed Tuesday and Saturday lunch – **Meals**. *Lunch 11* – a la carte 24/35.
◆ Thai cuisine is the focus in this mansion close to the Palais de Justice. An extensive range of traditional dishes, plus a buffet option on Sundays. Typical Thai décor.

Quartier Léopold *(see also at Ixelles)*

Stanhope, r. Commerce 9, ✉ 1000, ☎ 0 2 506 91 11, *reservations@stanhope.be, Fax 0 2 512 17 08*, Fö, ≘s – |‡| ▤ TV ⇔. AE ⓓ ⓜⓒ VISA. ✗ KZ v
Meals see ***Brighton*** below – ☕ 25 – **80 rm** 255/425, – 15 suites.
◆ This town house offers a welcome change from the city's larger hotels with its superb bedrooms - some split-level - fitted with computer equipment. Enclosed terrace.

XXX **Brighton** - Hotel Stanhope, r. Commerce 9, ✉ 1000, ☎ 0 2 506 95 55, *reservations@stanhope.be, Fax 0 2 512 17 08*, ☂ – ▤ P. AE ⓓ ⓜⓒ VISA. ✗ KZ v
closed Christmas-New Year, Saturday, Sunday and Bank Holidays – **Meals**. *Lunch 37* – a la carte 52/90.
◆ Period furniture, delicate frescoes, chandeliers, Oriental columns and shiny wood floors provide the décor for the Stanhope's elegant restaurant, with its à la mode menu.

Quartier Louise *(see also at Ixelles and at St-Gilles)*

Conrad, av. Louise 71, ✉ 1050, ☎ 0 2 542 42 42, *brusselsinfo@conradhotels.com, Fax 0 2 542 42 00*, ☂, ⊛, Fö, ≘s, ▣ – |‡| ⇹ ▤ TV ⇔ – 🔬 25-450. AE ⓓ ⓜⓒ VISA JCB FS f
Meals see ***La Maison de Maître*** below – ***Café Wiltcher's*** *Lunch 34* – a la carte 42/73 – ☕ 30 – **254 rm** 595/620, – 15 suites.
◆ An upmarket hotel brilliantly arranged inside a 1900s Brussels mansion. Spacious bedrooms with classic furnishings, a full range of seminar and leisure facilities, plus a chic, glass-crowned café. Lunch buffets and a splendid view from the terrace.

Bristol Stephanie, av. Louise 91, ✉ 1050, ☎ 0 2 543 33 11, *hotel_bristol@bristol.be, Fax 0 2 538 03 07*, Fö, ≘s, ▣ – |‡| ⇹ ▤ TV ⇔ – 🔬 25-400. AE ⓓ ⓜⓒ VISA JCB. ✗ FT g
Meals *(closed 17 July-22 August, 18 December-3 January and lunch Saturday and Sunday)* (partly buffets) a la carte 35/55 ♀ – ☕ 25 – **139 rm** 325/400, – 3 suites.
◆ This luxury property is spread across two interlinked buildings with large, elegant bedrooms. Typical Norwegian furniture adorns the hotel's suites. Contemporary dining in a Scandinavian-inspired ambience. Buffet options also available.

Le Châtelain ⛭, r. Châtelain 17, ✉ 1000, ☎ 0 2 646 00 55, *info@le-chatelain.net, Fax 0 2 646 00 88*, ☂, Fö – |‡| ⇹ ▤ TV ⇔ – 🔬 25-280. AE ⓓ ⓜⓒ VISA. ✗ FU t
Meals. *Lunch 17* – a la carte 39/48 – ☕ 25 – **106 rm** 310/430, – 2 suites.
◆ A new hotel with stylish, comfortable rooms featuring the very latest equipment and facilities. The restaurant offers a wide range of options with the emphasis on diversity.

Hyatt Regency, av. Louise 381, ✉ 1050, ☎ 0 2 649 98 00, *brussels@hyattintl.com, Fax 0 2 640 17 64* – |‡| ⇹ ▤ TV ⇔ – 🔬 25-50. AE ⓓ ⓜⓒ VISA JCB. ✗ FV a
Meals ***Barsey*** *(closed Sunday)* (open until midnight) *Lunch 19* – a la carte 37/50 – ☕ 22 – **96 rm** 345/380, – 3 suites.
◆ A characterful hotel near the Bois de la Cambre skilfully refurbished in Second Empire style. Elegant public areas and tasteful, well-appointed rooms. Personalised service.

Meliá Avenue Louise, r. Blanche 4, ✉ 1000, ☎ 0 2 535 95 00, *melia.avenue.louise@solmelia.com*, *Fax 0 2 535 96 00* – 35. AE VISA. FT z
Meals (residents only) – 22 – **80 rm** 230/320.
• The Avenue Louise enjoys a good location a few yards from place Stéphanie. Cosy, individually styled rooms with tasteful furnishings. Impressive lounge adorned with a chimney.

Floris Louise without rest, r. Concorde 59, ✉ 1000, ☎ 0 2 515 00 60, *florislouise@busmail.net*, *Fax 0 2 503 35 19* – . AE VISA FS d
36 rm 140/160.
• This hotel occupies two houses slightly set back from avenue Louise. Modern, well-appointed accommodation and a pleasant breakfast room.

Brussels without rest, av. Louise 315, ✉ 1050, ☎ 0 2 640 24 15, *brussels-hotel@skynet.be*, *Fax 0 2 647 34 63* – – 30. AE VISA JCB FU b
68 rm 195, – 1 suite.
• A "flat-hotel" offering two spacious standard room categories - normal or split-level with a kitchenette. All have been renovated and adequately soundproofed.

Agenda Louise without rest, r. Florence 6, ✉ 1000, ☎ 0 2 539 00 31, *louise@hotel-agenda.com*, *Fax 0 2 539 00 63* – . AE VISA JCB FT j
37 rm 104/116.
• Just 50m/55yd from the elegant avenue Louise, this completely renovated hotel offers guests a friendly welcome and well-appointed, reasonably-sized rooms.

La Maison de Maître - Hotel Conrad, av. Louise 77, ✉ 1050, ☎ 0 2 542 47 16, *brusselsinfo@conradhotels.com*, *Fax 0 2 542 42 00* – P. AE VISA JCB FS f
closed August, Saturday lunch, Sunday, Monday and Bank Holidays – **Meals**. Lunch 49 b.i. – a la carte 52/95 ♀.
• An elegant and refined gastronomic restaurant within the walls of the Hotel Conrad. Delicious, original cuisine that evolves with the seasons.

La Porte des Indes, av. Louise 455, ✉ 1050, ☎ 0 2 647 86 51, *brussels@laportedesindes*, *Fax 0 2 640 30 59*, Indian cuisine – . AE VISA. FV c
closed Sunday lunch – **Meals**. Lunch 20 – a la carte 23/59.
• If your taste-buds fancy a change, head for La Porte des Indes, with its exotic, deliciously flavoured cuisine. The restaurant interior is decorated with Indian antiques.

Tagawa, av. Louise 279, ✉ 1050, ☎ 0 2 640 50 95, *Fax 0 2 648 41 36*, Japanese cuisine – P. AE VISA JCB. FU e
closed 2 and 3 January, Saturday lunch, Sunday and Bank Holidays – **Meals**. Lunch 11 – a la carte 22/80.
• This simply furnished Japanese restaurant is worth tracking down inside one of the city's shopping galleries. Western and Oriental (tatamis) comfort, plus a sushi bar.

L'Atelier de la Truffe Noire, av. Louise 300, ✉ 1050, ☎ 0 2 640 54 55, *luigi.ciciriello@truffenoire.com*, *Fax 0 2 648 11 44*, Partly Italian cuisine, open until 11 p.m. – . AE VISA FU s
closed first 3 weeks August, first week January, Sunday and Monday lunch – **Meals** – a la carte 40/57 ♀.
• A "hip" brasserie whose originality and success lie in its fast service and truffle-based gastronomic menu. A well-thought-out and varied à la carte showing Italian influence.

Rouge Tomate, av. Louise 190, ✉ 1050, ☎ 0 2 647 70 44, *rougetomate@skynet.be*, *Fax 0 2 646 63 10*, , Open until 11.30 p.m. – AE VISA. FU c
Meals a la carte approx. 39.
• Behind the façade of this 19C house is a bright, designer dining room serving contemporary cuisine popular with a well-heeled clientele. Terrace to the rear.

Quartier Bois de la Cambre

Villa Lorraine (Vandecasserie), av. du Vivier d'Oie 75, ✉ 1000, ☎ 0 2 374 31 63, *info@villalorraine.be*, *Fax 0 2 372 01 95*, – P. AE VISA JCB GX w
closed last 3 weeks July and Sunday – **Meals**. Lunch 50 – 120 b.i., a la carte 68/172 ♀.
• A father and son man the kitchens of this top restaurant on the edge of a wood. Classic cuisine, matching décor and a prestigious wine cellar. Pleasant shady terrace.
Spec. Salade de crevettes géantes et copeaux de foie gras à l'huile de truffes. Sole à la normande. Tartare de bœuf aux truffes d'été.

La Truffe Noire, bd de la Cambre 12, ✉ 1000, ☎ 0 2 640 44 22, *luigi.ciciriello@truffenoire.com*, *Fax 0 2 647 97 04* – . AE VISA GV x
closed first 3 weeks August, Christmas-New Year, Saturday lunch and Sunday – **Meals**. Lunch 40 – 60/130 b.i., – a la carte 79/175 ♀.
• Truffle-lovers will feel well at home amid the foliage of the Cambre and the abbey of the same name. Elegant modern interior, refined cuisine and quality wines.
Spec. Carpaccio à la truffe. Saint-Pierre aux poireaux et truffes. Soufflé chaud aux noisettes grillées.

Quartier Botanique, Gare du Nord *(see also at St-Josse-ten-Noode)*

Sheraton Towers, pl. Rogier 3, ✉ 1210, ☎ 0 2 224 31 11, *reservations.brussels@sheraton.com, Fax 0 2 224 34 56,* – – 25-600. AE VISA. rest FQ n
Meals (partly buffets). *Lunch 31* – a la carte 41/50 – 25 – **467 rm** 335/410, – 44 suites.
♦ With its full range of facilities, the Sheraton is popular with business clientele. Spacious high-tech bedrooms, plus "smart rooms" combining a work environment with relaxation. Buffets, gastronomic theme weeks and attractive light cuisine in the restaurant.

President World Trade Center, bd du Roi Albert II 44, ✉ 1000, ☎ 0 2 203 20 20, *wtc.info@presidenthotels.be, Fax 0 2 203 24 40,* – – 25-350. AE VISA JCB. rest FQ d
Meals. *Lunch 27* – a la carte 45/66 – 19 – **286 rm** 248/348, – 16 suites.
♦ An imposing hotel offering high levels of comfort at one end of Brussels' "Manhattan", close to the Gare du Nord and the towers of the World Trade Center. The restaurant's classic menu includes several fixed options and good daily suggestions.

Tulip Inn Boulevard, av. du Boulevard 17, ✉ 1210, ☎ 0 2 205 15 11, *info.hotel@tulipinnbb.be, Fax 0 2 201 15 15,* – – 25-450. AE VISA JCB. FQ b
Meals (residents only) – **450 rm** 192/202, – 4 suites.
♦ This brand-new hotel is the second largest in the city in terms of capacity. Attractive, well-appointed small rooms with wood or carpeted floors.

Le Dome (annex Le Dome II), bd du Jardin Botanique 12, ✉ 1000, ☎ 0 2 218 06 80, *dome@skypro.be, Fax 0 2 218 41 12,* – , rm, – 25-80. AE VISA. FQ m
Meals. *Lunch 17* – a la carte 29/40 – **125 rm** 112/124.
♦ The dome crowning the 1900s-style façade overlooks the lively place Rogier. Fresh Art Nouveau tones in the hotel's public areas. Pleasant, spacious bedrooms. A modern brasserie with mezzanine serving a range of elaborate and more simple dishes.

President Nord without rest, bd A. Max 107, ✉ 1000, ☎ 0 2 219 00 60, *thierry.sluys@presidentnord.be, Fax 0 2 218 12 69* – . AE VISA JCB. FQ k
63 rm 145/195.
♦ A corner hotel just a couple of yards from the busy rue Neuve shopping street. The pleasant rooms have recently benefited from a major facelift.

Quartier Atomium (Centenaire - Trade Mart - Laeken)

Ming Dynasty, Parc des Expositions - av. de l'Esplanade BP 9, ✉ 1020, ☎ 0 2 475 23 45, *info@mingdynasty.be, Fax 0 2 475 23 50,* Chinese cuisine, open until 11 p.m. – . AE VISA
Meals. *Lunch 18* – a la carte 22/51.
♦ This Chinese restaurant opposite the parc des Expositions offers several fixed-menus, modern décor and appropriate background music. Respectable wine-list.

Lychee, r. De Wand 118, ✉ 1020, ☎ 0 2 268 19 14, Chinese cuisine, open until 11 p.m. – . AE VISA JCB
closed 15 to 30 July – **Meals**. *Lunch 8* – 22/33.
♦ A wide choice of Chinese dishes and a very reasonably-priced lunch are available at this long-established restaurant. Dining room with veranda.

La Balade Gourmande, av. Houba de Strooper 95, ✉ 1020, ☎ 0 2 478 94 34, *Fax 0 2 479 89 52,* – VISA
closed 2 weeks carnival, 15 August-early September, Sunday dinner and lunch Wednesday and Saturday – **Meals**. *Lunch 15* – 30.
♦ The à la carte and fixed-menu options at this local eatery cover a cross-section of traditional dishes prepared with a modern eye. Contemporary, attractive setting.

ANDERLECHT

Le Prince de Liège, chaussée de Ninove 664, ✉ 1070, ☎ 0 2 522 16 00, *reception.princedeliege@coditel.be, Fax 0 2 520 81 85* – , rm, – 25. AE VISA JCB
Meals (pub rest). *Lunch 14* – 22/38 – **32 rm** 59/93.
♦ The rooms at this family-run hotel located alongside a major road junction are functional, double-glazed and have recently been refurbished. Bar-restaurant serving classic à la carte choices, menus and seasonal suggestions.

Ustel, Square de l'Aviation 6, ✉ 1070, ☎ 0 2 520 60 53 and 0 2 522 30 25 (rest), *grand.ecluse@grouptorus, Fax 0 2 520 33 28,* – – 25-100. AE VISA. ES q
Meals *(closed mid July-mid August, Saturday and Sunday)* (brasserie) (lunch only). *Lunch 12* – a la carte 35/44 – **114 rm** 110/130.
♦ This hotel along the city's inner ring road has 94 simply furnished rooms of varying size, including twenty or so "apartments" with their own kitchenette. The machinery of an old lock provides an original backdrop to the hotel brasserie.

Erasme, rte de Lennik 790, ✉ 1070, ☎ 0 2 523 62 82, *comfort@skynet.be, Fax 0 2 523 62 83,* , – , rm, – 25-80. AE MC VISA JCB
Meals *(closed 24 December-2 January)* (pub rest) 17 – **73 rm** ☐ 75/129, – 1 suite.
◆ A chain hotel on the outskirts of the city, 1km/0.6mi beyond the ring road, with small but welcoming bedrooms with adequate soundproofing. Three seminar rooms. Varied international menu.

Saint Guidon 2nd floor, in the R.S.C. Anderlecht football stadium, av. Théo Verbeeck 2, ✉ 1070, ☎ 0 2 520 55 36, *saint-guidon@skynet.be, Fax 0 2 523 38 27* – – 25-500. MC VISA.
closed 20 June-21 July, Saturday, Sunday and first league match days – **Meals** (lunch only) 55 b.i. a la carte 55/75.
◆ This typical restaurant is situated on the second floor of Anderlecht's football stadium. Refined cuisine which evolves with the seasons. Car park.
Spec. Ravioles de homard aux truffes. Foie de veau poêlé au vinaigre balsamique et câpres. Côte à l'os Blanc Bleu Belge au gros sel.

Alain Cornelis, av. Paul Janson 82, ✉ 1070, ☎ 0 2 523 20 83, *alaincornelis@skynet.be, Fax 0 2 523 20 83,* – AE MC VISA
closed week before Easter, first 2 weeks August, Christmas-New Year, Wednesday dinner, Saturday lunch, Sunday and Bank Holidays – **Meals** – 29/59 b.i..
◆ A classically bourgeois restaurant with a traditional wine-list. The terrace to the rear is embellished with a small garden. Fixed-menus, à la carte and dishes of the month.

La Brouette, bd Prince de Liège 61, ✉ 1070, ☎ 0 2 522 51 69, *info@labrouette.be, Fax 0 2 522 51 69* – AE MC VISA
closed 15 to 21 March, 1 to 22 August, Saturday lunch, Sunday dinner and Monday – **Meals**. Lunch 20 – 33/65 b.i. ♀.
◆ La Brouette's steady flow of regulars appreciate the impeccable culinary skills of the kitchen as well as the harmony of the accompanying wine-list.
Spec. Petits-gris en raviolis à la nage de céleri. Tonnelet fumé au foie gras, légumes en tartare et jus de truffes. Blanc de cabillaud étuvé aux champignons, à la flamande.

AUDERGHEM (OUDERGEM)

La Grignotière, chaussée de Wavre 2041, ✉ 1160, ☎ 0 2 672 81 85, *Fax 0 2 672 81 85* – AE MC VISA
closed 1 to 20 August, Sunday and Monday – **Meals**. Lunch 35 – 46.
◆ On the edge of the Forêt de Soignes, with décor that varies from the simple and modern to the more measured and traditional. Multi-choice menus. Separate small lounge.

New Asia, chaussée de Wavre 1240, ✉ 1160, ☎ 0 2 660 62 06, *Fax 0 2 675 67 28,* , Chinese cuisine – . AE MC VISA. HU a
closed last 3 weeks August and Monday except Bank Holidays – **Meals**. Lunch 8 – 12/24.
◆ A relaxed ambience pervades this local restaurant created over 20 years ago. Traditional Chinese décor provides the backdrop for a huge choice of dishes and menus.

La Khaïma, chaussée de Wavre 1390, ✉ 1160, ☎ 0 2 675 00 04, *Fax 0 2 675 00 04,* Moroccan cuisine – . AE MC VISA.
closed August – **Meals** 27.
◆ Popular with aficionados of tagines and couscous, this small restaurant, with its typical pouffes, rugs and beaten copper, is housed beneath a Berber tent (khaïma).

BERCHEM-STE-AGATHE (SINT-AGATHA-BERCHEM)

La Brasserie de la Gare, chaussée de Gand 1430, ✉ 1082, ☎ 0 2 469 10 09, *Fax 0 2 469 10 09* – . AE MC VISA
closed Saturday lunch and Sunday – **Meals**. Lunch 12 – 26 ♀.
◆ This wood-panelled brasserie close to the station is known for its lively atmosphere, traditional cooking and enticing wine-list. Note the naïve fresco with a railway theme.

ETTERBEEK

Stirwen, chaussée St-Pierre 15, ✉ 1040, ☎ 0 2 640 85 41, *Fax 0 2 648 43 08* – AE MC VISA GS a
closed 2 weeks August, Saturday and Sunday – **Meals**. Lunch 25 – a la carte 37/55.
◆ "White Star" (stirwen) in Breton, this welcoming brasserie with its hints of Belle Époque architecture serves traditional dishes from around France.

Quartier Cinquantenaire (Montgomery)

Park without rest, av. de l'Yser 21, ✉ 1040, ☎ 0 2 735 74 00, *info@parkhotelbrussels.be, Fax 0 2 735 19 67,* , , – – 25-65. AE MC VISA JCB HS c
51 rm ☐ 250/350.
◆ An amalgam of two houses opposite the parc du Cinquantenaire, this hotel has 51 comfortable rooms, half of which are singles. The breakfast room looks onto a small garden.

EVERE

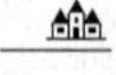

Belson without rest, chaussée de Louvain 805, ✉ 1140, ☎ 0 2 708 31 00, *resa@gresham-belsonhotel.com, Fax 0 2 708 31 66,* – |‡| ⇹ ▤ 📺 – 🅰 25. AE ⓓ ⓜ VISA. ✂
☕ 20 – **132 rm** 260/310, – 3 suites.
◆ This chain hotel provides easy access to both the city centre and airport (Zaventem). Two categories of rooms plus a fitness area.

Mercure, av. Jules Bordet 74, ✉ 1140, ☎ 0 2 726 73 35, *H0958@accor-hotels.com, Fax 0 2 726 82 95* – |‡| ⇹, ▤ rest, 📺 – 🅰 25-120. AE ⓓ ⓜ VISA JCB. ✂ rest
Meals *(closed mid July-mid August, Friday dinner, Saturday and Sunday lunch)*. Lunch 20 b.i. – a la carte 27/47 ♀ – ☕ 17 – **113 rm** 175/200, – 7 suites.
◆ A typical Accor chain hotel offering standard Mercure comfort, just a few yards from NATO and five minutes from Zaventem airport. Seminar rooms. Plainly decorated restaurant enlivened by cartoon-strip illustrations.

FOREST (VORST)

De Fierlant without rest, r. De Fierlant 67, ✉ 1190, ☎ 0 2 538 60 70, *de_fierlant@skynet.be, Fax 0 2 538 91 99* – |‡| 📺. AE ⓓ ⓜ VISA. ✂
40 rm ☕ 70/80.
◆ Conveniently located between the Gare du Midi and the Forest-National concert hall, this practical hotel occupies a small, modern building with standard, soundproofed rooms.

GANSHOREN

Bruneau, av. Broustin 75, ✉ 1083, ☎ 0 2 421 70 70, *Fax 0 2 425 97 26,* 🌳 – ▤ 🅿. AE ⓓ ⓜ VISA
closed 1 to 10 February, August, Bank Holiday Thursdays, Tuesday and Wednesday – **Meals**. Lunch 65 b.i. – 175 b.i., a la carte 73/227.
◆ This renowned restaurant has achieved a perfect creative balance while at the same time maintaining its commitment to local products. Prestigious wine-list. Summer terrace.
Spec. Rosace de homard à la truffe. Épigramme de bar aux girolles, beurre blanc au curry (July-October). Galette de pigeon de Vendée et ses cuisses caramélisées au soja.

Claude Dupont, av. Vital Riethuisen 46, ✉ 1083, ☎ 0 2 426 00 00, *claudedupont@resto.be, Fax 0 2 426 65 40* – AE ⓓ ⓜ VISA
closed July, Monday and Tuesday – **Meals**. Lunch 45 – 65/130 b.i., – a la carte 66/121 ♀.
◆ A master-class in culinary invention. The accolades and awards on display in the entrance hall are thoroughly deserved. Sumptuous cellar.
Spec. Coussinet de barbue soufflé au Champagne (October-late April). Écrevisses sautées à la bordelaise. Gibier en saison (September-February).

San Daniele (Spinelli), av. Charles-Quint 6, ✉ 1083, ☎ 0 2 426 79 23, *Fax 0 2 426 92 14,* Partly Italian cuisine – ▤. AE ⓓ ⓜ VISA
closed 15 July-15 August, 1 week April, Sunday and Monday – **Meals** – 50, a la carte 37/54 🍇.
◆ The warm, friendly welcome, extensive Italian menu and alluring choice of wines from across the Dolomites continue to attract a loyal following.
Spec. Calamaretti, gamberetti et scampis en friture. Ris de veau en crépinette de chou-vert aux truffes. Soufflé d'ananas glacé à l'orange sanguine.

Cambrils 1st floor, av. Charles-Quint 365, ✉ 1083, ☎ 0 2 465 50 70, *restaurant.cambrils@skynet.be, Fax 0 2 465 76 63,* 🌳 – ▤. AE ⓜ VISA
closed 12 July-2 August, Sunday and dinner Monday and Thursday – **Meals**. Lunch 22 – 30/55 b.i..
◆ The kitchens of this pleasant restaurant open out onto the dining room, which in turn looks onto avenue Charles-Quint. Traditional à la carte menu. Ground floor bar. Terrace.

IXELLES (ELSENE)

Le Yen, r. Lesbroussart 49, ✉ 1050, ☎ 0 2 649 07 47, 🌳, Vietnamese cuisine – AE ⓓ ⓜ VISA. ✂ FU f
closed Saturday lunch and Sunday – **Meals**. Lunch 9 – 18/23.
◆ Modern and simple Oriental décor provides the backdrop for this Vietnamese restaurant (yen translates as "the swallow") serving poetically named traditional dishes.

Quartier Boondael (University)

L'Aub. de Boendael, square du Vieux Tilleul 12, ✉ 1050, ☎ 0 2 672 70 55, *auberge-de-boendael@resto.be, Fax 0 2 660 75 82,* 🌳, Grill rest – 🅿. AE ⓓ ⓜ VISA HX h
closed 19 July-15 August, 24 December-1 January, Saturday, Sunday and Bank Holidays – **Meals** – 45 b.i..
◆ This rustic-style inn occupies a 17C house with a roaring fire in winter and a fine selection of grilled meats. Banquets at weekends.

La Pagode d'Or, chaussée de Boondael 332, ✉ 1050, ☎ 0 2 649 06 56, *Fax 0 2 649 09 00*, Vietnamese cuisine, open until 11 p.m. – AE ⓓ MC VISA. GV m
closed Monday – **Meals**. *Lunch 9* – 23/35.
◆ A fine ambassador for Vietnamese cuisine with its clear and consistent menu, "rice table" options, and an intimate dining room with discreet exotic touches.

Marie, r. Alphonse De Witte 40, ✉ 1050, ☎ 0 2 644 30 31, *Fax 0 2 644 27 37* – AE MC VISA. GU a
closed 18 July-17 August, 24 December-4 January, Saturday lunch, Sunday and Monday – **Meals**. *Lunch 16* – a la carte 46/60.
◆ Traditional cuisine peppered with southern influences and an attractive selection of wines are the hallmarks of this pleasant, pocket-sized gourmet bistro.
Spec. Brandade de morue à l'huile d'olives, concassée de tomates et coulis de poivrons. Tian d'épaule d'agneau braisée et aubergines rôties. Filet de daurade royale grillé au fenouil, jus de bouillabaisse au pistou.

Quartier Bascule, Châtelain, Ma Campagne

Maison Félix 1st floor, r. Washington 149 (square Henri Michaux), ✉ 1050, ☎ 0 2 345 66 93, *Fax 0 2 344 92 85* – AE ⓓ MC VISA. FV s
closed 1 to 23 August, 3 to 12 January, Sunday and Monday – **Meals**. *Lunch 35* – 38/60 b.i.
◆ Customers will need to pass through Monsieur Félix's delicatessen in order to reach the dining room on the first floor. A high standard of cuisine plus a superb wine-list.

O' comme 3 Pommes, pl. du Châtelain 40, ✉ 1050, ☎ 0 2 644 03 23, *resto@oc3pommes.be, Fax 0 2 644 03 23*, – AE ⓓ MC VISA FU q
closed Sunday and lunch Monday and Saturday – **Meals**. *Lunch 12* – 28/47.
◆ A fresh, modern restaurant with a slate menu teeming with stylish dishes enlivened with the occasional Asian touch.

La Quincaillerie, r. Page 45, ✉ 1050, ☎ 0 2 533 98 33, *info@quincaillerie.be, Fax 0 2 539 40 95*, Brasserie with oyster bar, open until midnight – P. AE ⓓ MC VISA JCB FU z
closed lunch Saturday, Sunday and Bank Holidays – **Meals**. *Lunch 13* – a la carte 36/73.
◆ A gleaming brasserie superbly laid out in this former Art Deco-style ironmonger's. Seafood bar and daily specials. Very professional service. Valet parking.

Les Perles de Pluie, r. Châtelain 25, ✉ 1050, ☎ 0 2 649 67 23, *info@lesperlesdepluie.be, Fax 0 2 644 07 60*, Thai cuisine, open until 11 p.m. – AE MC VISA FU n
closed Monday and Saturday lunch – **Meals**. *Lunch 15* – a la carte 24/52.
◆ This twin-roomed restaurant serves typical Thai cuisine. Typical interior décor embellished with traditional woodwork.

Tutto Pepe, r. Faider 123, ✉ 1050, ☎ 0 2 534 96 19, *tuttopepe@skynet.be, Fax 0 2 538 65 68*, Italian cuisine – AE ⓓ MC VISA. FU d
closed August, Saturday, Sunday and Bank Holidays – **Meals** a la carte 40/125.
◆ A tiny, authentic restaurant where the welcome is 100 % Italian and somewhat theatrical. The à la carte choices here are posted on menu boards.

Quartier Léopold *(see also at Bruxelles)*

Renaissance, r. Parnasse 19, ✉ 1050, ☎ 0 2 505 29 29, *renaissance.brussels@renaissancehotels.com, Fax 0 2 505 22 76*, – – 25-360. AE ⓓ MC VISA JCB. FS e
Meals ***Symphony*** *(closed Saturday and Sunday lunch) Lunch 19* – a la carte 42/65 – 23 – **256 rm** 269, – 6 suites.
◆ The Renaissance enjoys a good location on the edge of the European institutions district. Modern, well-appointed rooms, plus excellent business, conference and leisure facilities. The restaurant's focus is on contemporary cuisine, and includes a lunch menu.

Leopold, r. Luxembourg 35, ✉ 1050, ☎ 0 2 511 18 28, *reservations@hotel-leopold.be, Fax 0 2 514 19 39*, – – 25-80. AE ⓓ MC VISA. rest FS y
Meals ***Salon Les Anges*** *(closed Saturday lunch and Sunday)* (lunch only August) *Lunch 35* – a la carte 47/65 – 18 – **86 rm** 174/248.
◆ This continually expanding and improving hotel boasts smart, comfortable bedrooms, smart public areas, a winter garden on a shady inner courtyard, and a peaceful atmosphere, mirrored in the hushed restaurant, with its classic menu and interesting wine-list.

Quartier Louise *(see also at Bruxelles and at St-Gilles)*

Sofitel without rest, av. de la Toison d'Or 40, ✉ 1050, ☎ 0 2 514 22 00, *H1071@accor-hotels.com, Fax 0 2 514 57 44*, – – 25-120. AE ⓓ MC VISA JCB. FS r
23 – **166 rm** 330, – 4 suites.
◆ Discreet luxury and soft comfort characterise this renovated hotel popular with an international business clientele. Terrace and garden.

Four Points Sheraton, r. Paul Spaak 15, ✉ 1000, ☎ 0 2 645 61 11, *reservations.brussels@sheraton.com, Fax 0 2 646 63 44,* ≘, ⚘ - |≡| ⇹ ▤ TV ♿ ⇔ - 🏛 25-40. AE ⓓ ⓜ VISA JCB FU k
Meals (open until 11 p.m.). *Lunch 16* - a la carte approx. 37 ♀ - ⊡ 19 - **128 rm** 230.
• A large chain hotel close to avenue Louise. Spacious, slightly outdated bedrooms, but with good facilities. Sauna, jacuzzi and garden in which guests can unwind. The dining room menu shows a clear liking for beef, as well as Swiss delicacies.

Argus without rest, r. Capitaine Crespel 6, ✉ 1050, ☎ 0 2 514 07 70, *reception@hotel-argus.be, Fax 0 2 514 12 22* - |≡| TV. AE ⓓ ⓜ VISA FS t
42 rm ⊡ 100/120.
• The Argus has 41 standard, plainly furnished rooms with soundproofing. The breakfast room is decorated with Art Deco-style stained glass. Good value for money.

Beau-Site without rest, r. Longue Haie 76, ✉ 1000, ☎ 0 2 640 88 89, *beausite@coditel.net, Fax 0 2 640 16 11* - |≡| TV ⇔. AE ⓓ ⓜ VISA JCB FT r
38 rm ⊡ 97/157.
• 100m/110yd from the city's most elegant avenue. A small, attractive hotel where the welcome is friendly and the service attentive.

Beverly Hills ⚲ without rest, r. Prince Royal 71, ✉ 1050, ☎ 0 2 513 22 22, *beverlyhills@infonie.be, Fax 0 2 513 87 77,* Fō, ≘ - |≡| TV. AE ⓜ VISA FS b
⊡ 5 - **40 rm** 95/125.
• This hotel close to the avenue de la Toison d'Or offers rooms with comfortable facilities guaranteeing a good night's sleep. Fitness room and sauna.

De la Vigne... à l'Assiette, r. Longue Haie 51, ✉ 1000, ☎ 0 2 647 68 03, *Fax 0 2 647 68 03,* Bistro - AE ⓜ VISA FT k
closed 26 July-26 August, Saturday lunch, Sunday and Monday - **Meals**. *Lunch 13* - 20/32 ♀ ⚘.
• Wine-lovers will enjoy this restaurant, where the décor and ambience are plain and simple, the bistro-style menu well-balanced, and the advice from the wine-waiter invaluable.

JETTE

Rôtiss. Le Vieux Pannenhuis, r. Léopold Ier 317, ✉ 1090, ☎ 0 2 425 83 73, *levieuxpannenhuis@belgacom.net, Fax 0 2 420 21 20,* ⛱, Partly grill rest - ▤. AE ⓓ ⓜ VISA
closed July, Saturday lunch and Sunday - **Meals**. *Lunch 21* - 30/44 b.i..
• This attractively preserved coaching inn exuding rustic charm offers a wide-ranging choice of classic dishes including meat grilled on an open fire in the dining room.

French Kiss, r. Léopold Ier 470, ✉ 1090, ☎ 0 2 425 22 93, *Fax 0 2 428 68 24,* Partly grill rest - ▤. AE ⓓ ⓜ VISA
closed 19 July-16 August and Monday - **Meals**. *Lunch 17* - 27 ⚘.
• A pleasant brick-built restaurant-grill peppered with the occasional modern flourish. Large, varied menu accompanied by a well-compiled wine-list. Very popular with locals.

ST-GILLES (SINT-GILLIS)

Cascade without rest, r. Berckmans 128, ✉ 1060, ☎ 0 2 538 88 30, *info@cascadehotel.be, Fax 0 2 538 92 79* - |≡| ⇹ ▤ TV ⇔ - 🏛 25. AE ⓓ ⓜ VISA JCB. ⚘
80 rm ⊡ 215/280. ES r
• Built around a large inner courtyard, this modern building has 80 neat and well-appointed bedrooms with carpets and double-glazing.

Le Forcado, chaussée de Charleroi 192, ✉ 1060, ☎ 0 2 537 92 20, *Fax 0 2 537 92 20,* Portuguese cuisine - ▤. AE ⓓ ⓜ VISA FU a
closed carnival week, August, Sunday, Monday and Bank Holidays - **Meals** (dinner only) a la carte approx. 35.
• A corner of Portugal serving typical Portuguese cuisine including a wine-inclusive menu. Quiet dining room adorned with old lanterns and glazed tiles, plus a bright veranda.

Knhopff, r. St-Bernard 1, ✉ 1060, ☎ 0 2 534 20 04, *info@khnopff.be, Fax 0 2 534 34 95* - ▤. AE ⓓ ⓜ VISA FT a
closed Saturday lunch and Sunday - **Meals**. *Lunch 13* - 26/40 ♀.
• The 19C Belgian symbolist artist Fernand Khnopff painted several canvases here, hence the restaurant's name. Charming hosts, contemporary cuisine and a trendy atmosphere.

Quartier Louise *(see also at Bruxelles and at Ixelles)*

Manos Premier (annex Manos Stéphanie 50 rm - 5 suites), chaussée de Charleroi 102, ✉ 1060, ☎ 0 2 537 96 82 and 0 2 533 18 30 (rest), *manos@manoshotel.com, Fax 0 2 539 36 55,* ⛱, Fō, ≘, ⚘, 🚲 - |≡|, ▤ rm, TV ⇔ P - 🏛 25-100. AE ⓓ ⓜ VISA JCB. ⚘ rm FU w
Meals ***Kolya*** *(closed first 2 weeks August, 2 weeks December, Saturday lunch and Sunday)* (open until 11 p.m.) *Lunch 15* - 35 - **44 rm** ⊡ 285/310, - 5 suites.
• A graceful late-19C town house adorned with sumptuous Louis XV and Louis XVI furniture. Veranda breakfast room, ornamental garden and fitness equipment. Chic restaurant with a hushed lounge, in addition to an attractive terrace with a cool patio.

NH Brussels City Centre, chaussée de Charleroi 17, ✉ 1060, ☎ 0 2 539 01 60, *nhbrussels.city.centre@nh-hotels.com, Fax 0 2 537 90 11* – 🛗 ⇔ ▤ 📺 🚗 – 🎤 25-75. AE ⓓ MC VISA FS w
Meals *(closed lunch Saturday and Sunday)* – a la carte 22/35 – ☕ 19 – **246 rm** 175/215.
• This squat building perched in the upper section of the city has several room categories, including a dozen "executive" bedrooms. Dynamic staff. The new brasserie offers varied lunch and dinner choices.

NH Stéphanie without rest, r. Jean Stas 32, ✉ 1060, ☎ 0 2 537 42 50, *nhstephanie@nh-hotels.be, Fax 0 2 539 33 79* – 🛗 ⇔ 📺 🚗 – 🎤 30. AE ⓓ MC VISA FS a
68 rm ☕ 190/210.
• Set back slightly from the bustling place Stéphanie, this hotel of the same name boasts a number of bright, modern rooms. Public car park nearby.

I Trulli, r. Jourdan 18, ✉ 1060, ☎ 0 2 537 79 30, *Fax 0 2 538 98 20*, 🏡, Italian cuisine, open until 11 p.m. – ▤. AE ⓓ MC VISA JCB FS c
closed 11 to 31 July, 21 December-5 January and Sunday – **Meals**. Lunch 17 – a la carte 37/70.
• This traditional Italian restaurant - named after the typical houses from Puglia depicted on the wall frescoes - specialises in dishes from the region. Buffet of antipasti.

ST-JOSSE-TEN-NOODE (SINT-JOOST-TEN-NODE)

Quartier Botanique *(see also at Bruxelles)*

Gd H. Mercure Royal Crown, r. Royale 250, ✉ 1210, ☎ 0 2 220 66 11, *H1728@accor-hotels.com, Fax 0 2 217 84 44*, 🏋, ≘ – 🛗 ⇔ ▤ 📺 🚗 – 🎤 50-550. AE ⓓ MC VISA JCB. ✻ rest FQ r
Meals see ***Rue Royale*** below – ☕ 20 – **310 rm** 235, – 4 suites.
• A comfortable chain hotel located close to the Botanique cultural centre, with its terraced gardens. Numerous conference rooms. Parking, bellboy and room service available.

Crowne Plaza, r. Gineste 3, ✉ 1210, ☎ 0 2 203 62 00, *sales@crowneplaza.gth.be, Fax 0 2 203 55 55*, 🏡, 🏋 – 🛗 ⇔ ▤ 📺 – 🎤 25-500. AE ⓓ MC VISA. ✻ FQ v
Meals *(closed Saturday and Sunday lunch)*. Lunch 15 – 35 – ☕ 24 – **356 rm** 150/300, – 1 suite.
• A Belle Époque-style palace embellished with period furniture in which several rooms have preserved the spirit of the 1900s. Seminar and business centre. Large Art Deco brasserie attracting a well-heeled clientele.

Comfort Art H. Siru, pl. Rogier 1, ✉ 1210, ☎ 0 2 203 35 80, *art.hotel.siru@skynet.be, Fax 0 2 203 33 03* – 🛗 ⇔ 📺 – 🎤 25-80. AE ⓓ MC VISA JCB. ✻ rest FQ p
Meals *Le Saint-Germain* *(closed 15 July-15 August, Saturday, Sunday and Bank Holidays)* (brasserie) Lunch 14 – a la carte 30/46 🍷 – **101 rm** ☕ 130.
• Establishment situated in a 1920s building with modern decor and in the past frequented by such notables as the poets Paul Verlaine and Arthur Rimbaud. Enjoy a meal in the relaxed ambience of the Parisian-style brasserie.

Rue Royale - Gd H. Mercure Royal Crown, r. Royale 250, ✉ 1210, ☎ 0 2 220 66 11, *H1728@accor-hotels.com, Fax 0 2 217 84 44* – ▤ 🅿. AE ⓓ MC VISA JCB. ✻ FQ r
closed 18 July-15 August, Saturday, Sunday and Bank Holidays – **Meals**. Lunch 25 – a la carte 35/55.
• This hotel restaurant is known for its "70s"-style atmosphere, contemporary cuisine, a well-put-together lunch menu, and enticing Mercure chain wine-list.

Les Dames Tartine, chaussée de Haecht 58, ✉ 1210, ☎ 0 2 218 45 49, *Fax 0 2 218 45 49* – ⓓ MC VISA FQ s
closed first 3 weeks August, Saturday lunch, Sunday and Monday – **Meals**. Lunch 19 – 30/39.
• This small, intimate restaurant remains loyal to its past. Customers sit at sewing machine tables, surrounded by paintings of the owner's ancestors.

SCHAERBEEK (SCHAARBEEK)

Senza Nome (Bruno), r. Royale Ste-Marie 22, ✉ 1030, ☎ 0 2 223 16 17, *senzanome@skynet.be, Fax 0 2 223 16 17*, Italian cuisine – ▤. MC VISA. ✻ FQ u
closed August, 23 December-1 January, Saturday lunch and Sunday – **Meals** a la carte 38/47 🍷.
• Despite being established ten years ago, this small restaurant remains "nameless". A good range of Italian cuisine and wines, plus daily specials. Friendly, family atmosphere.
Spec. Vitello de Tonnato. Linguine Vongole. Panna Cotta.

Quartier Meiser

Lambermont without rest (annexes 61 rm 🔇 - jd), bd Lambermont 322, ✉ 1030, ☎ 0 2 242 55 95, *info@lambermont-hotel.com, Fax 0 2 215 36 13* – 🛗 ⇔ 📺. AE ⓓ MC VISA JCB GHQ c
45 rm ☕ 110/120.
• Despite being away from the centre, this comfortable hotel on a boulevard of the same name enjoys peace and quiet as well as easy access to the heart of the city.

Amici miei, bd Général Wahis 248, ✉ 1030, ☎ 0 2 705 49 80, *Fax 0 2 705 29 65,* , Italian cuisine – AE ⓓ MC VISA HQ k
closed Saturday lunch and Sunday – **Meals** a la carte 23/47.
◆ Judging by the décor, "My Friends" is also a pal of showbiz and sports personalities! As the name would suggest, the focus here is on Italian cuisine.

UCCLE (UKKEL)

County House, square des Héros 2, ✉ 1180, ☎ 0 2 375 44 20, *countyhouse@skynet.be, Fax 0 2 375 31 22* – , rest, – 25-150. AE ⓓ MC VISA. EX b
Meals a la carte 34/45 – **86 rm** 175, – 16 suites.
◆ This building on the northern edge of the Parc Wolvendael has 86 well-appointed rooms, all with a private terrace. Spacious restaurant, serving contemporary cuisine with special midweek menus.

Le Chalet de la Forêt, Drêve de Lorraine 43, ✉ 1180, ☎ 0 2 374 54 16, *chaletdelaforet@skynet.be, Fax 0 2 374 35 71,* – P – 30. AE ⓓ MC VISA
closed Saturday and Sunday – **Meals**. *Lunch 24* – a la carte 59/82.
◆ This former dairy on the edge of the Forêt de Soignes is now home to an attractive restaurant with modern decor, contemporary cuisine and a well-balanced wine list.

Les Frères Romano, av. de Fré 182, ✉ 1180, ☎ 0 2 374 70 98, *Fax 0 2 374 04 18* – P. AE ⓓ MC VISA FX d
closed 1 week Easter, last 2 weeks August and Sunday – **Meals**. *Lunch 35* – a la carte 40/64.
◆ Three brothers are in charge of this elegant restaurant housed in a villa dating from the 1900s. The menu here is traditional, occasionally enlightened by a modern flourish.

Villa d'Este, r. Etoile 142, ✉ 1180, ☎ 0 2 376 48 48, *Fax 0 2 376 48 48,* – P. AE ⓓ MC VISA
closed July, late December, Sunday dinner and Monday – **Meals** – 30/50.
◆ This impressive villa surrounded by vineyards offers two excellent multi-choice menus ("tradition" and "prestige") as well as two wine-lists.

Blue Elephant, chaussée de Waterloo 1120, ✉ 1180, ☎ 0 2 374 49 62, *brussels@blueelephant.com, Fax 0 2 375 44 68,* Thai cuisine – P. AE ⓓ MC VISA. GX j
closed Saturday lunch – **Meals**. *Lunch 12* – 45.
◆ Country antiques, cane furniture, floral arrangements and local colour combine to create an exotic atmosphere in this Thai restaurant.

Le Pain et le Vin, chaussée d'Alsemberg 812a, ✉ 1180, ☎ 0 2 332 37 74, *info@painvin.be, Fax 0 2 332 17 40,* – AE MC VISA
closed Easter, first week September, Christmas, New Year, Saturday lunch, Sunday and Monday – **Meals**. *Lunch 19* – a la carte 42/69.
◆ A modern, elegant restaurant concentrating on refined, seasonal dishes. Customers are spoilt for choice on the wine-list... with helpful advice from the sommelier.

Bon-Bon (Hardiquest), r. Carmélites 93, ✉ 1180, ☎ 0 2 346 66 15, *Fax 0 2 346 66 15* – AE ⓓ MC VISA. EV a
closed 21 July-15 August, 1 to 7 January, Saturday lunch, Sunday and Monday – **Meals**. *Lunch 25* – a la carte 49/71.
◆ Extravagant decor including a bar, wall panelling, mirrors, wood flooring, wrought-iron chairs and crystal chandeliers. Modern cuisine based on certified authentic products.
Spec. Brochette de ris de veau citronné aux langoustines. Volaille de l'Aisne et barigoule de violets. Gratin de fraises des bois.

Brasseries Georges, av. Winston Churchill 259, ✉ 1180, ☎ 0 2 347 21 00, *info@brasseriesgeorges.be, Fax 0 2 344 02 45,* , Oyster bar, open until midnight – P. AE ⓓ MC VISA FV n
Meals. *Lunch 20* – a la carte 26/46.
◆ One of the largest brasseries-seafood bars in the city. Parisian in style with an inexpensive lunchtime bar menu. Friendly service, plus useful valet parking.

Quartier St-Job

Les Menus Plaisirs, r. Basse 7, ✉ 1180, ☎ 0 2 374 69 36, *lesmenusplaisirs@belgacom.net, Fax 0 2 331 38 13,* – AE ⓓ MC VISA
closed 1 week carnival, 1 week Easter, first week September, Christmas-New Year, Saturday lunch, Sunday and Monday dinner – **Meals**. *Lunch 13* – 30.
◆ This small but stylish restaurant has developed a good local reputation for its personalised, modern cuisine. Pleasant garden for dining out in summer.

le pré en bulle, av. J. et P. Carsoel 5, ✉ 1180, ☎ 0 2 374 08 80, *Fax 0 2 372 93 67,* – P. AE MC VISA
closed Monday dinner and Tuesday – **Meals**. *Lunch 13* – 28/44 b.i.
◆ A small 17C farm with plain but attractive décor, a creative menu based on traditional dishes and several tempting menus. Pleasant terrace for the summer months.

Le Passage, av. J. et P. Carsoel 13, 1180, 0 2 374 66 94, *restaurant@lepassage.be, Fax 0 2 374 69 26,* – P. AE MC VISA
closed 3 weeks July, first week January, Saturday lunch, Sunday and Bank Holidays – **Meals**. *Lunch 19* – 36/46, – a la carte 40/68.
◆ An imaginative kitchen is behind the merited success of this pocket-sized restaurant, whose dining room is embellished with discreet Mediterranean touches.
Spec. Carpaccio de bœuf et foie d'oie aux brisures de truffes. Escalopines de ris de veau croustillantes, épinards et beurre au citron. Blanc de turbotin cuit au lait épicé, mousseline de crevettes grises.

WATERMAEL-BOITSFORT (WATERMAAL-BOSVOORDE)

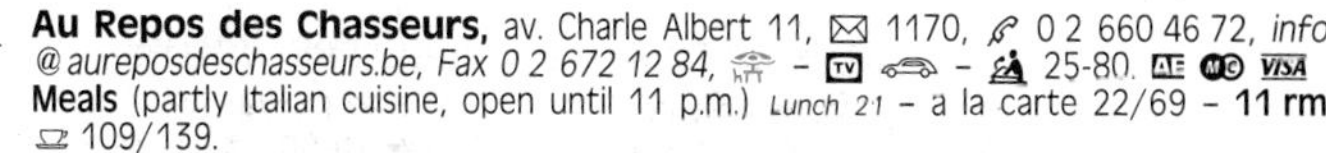

Au Repos des Chasseurs, av. Charle Albert 11, 1170, 0 2 660 46 72, *info@aureposdeschasseurs.be, Fax 0 2 672 12 84,* – TV – 25-80. AE MC VISA
Meals (partly Italian cuisine, open until 11 p.m.) *Lunch 21* – a la carte 22/69 – **11 rm** 109/139.
◆ Those in search of peace and quiet will undoubtedly find it at "Hunters' Rest", an old dairy on the edge of a wood with comfortably renovated rooms. A choice of classic French and Italian dishes dominates the restaurant menu. Large summer terrace.

Au Vieux Boitsfort (Gillet), pl. Bischoffsheim 9, 1170, 0 2 672 23 32, *Fax 0 2 660 22 94,* – AE MC VISA
closed first 3 weeks August, Saturday lunch and Sunday – **Meals** (booking essential) 40 b.i./85 b.i., – a la carte 57/70 ♀.
◆ This lauded corner restaurant has exchanged its original décor for a resolutely modern interior. Refined, traditional cuisine and a well-stocked cellar.
Spec. Escalope de foie d'oie poêlée et céleri confit. Risotto de Saint-Jacques au cresson et vieux parmesan. Noix de ris de veau à la crème d'artichauts en persillade d'échalotes.

Le Grill, r. Trois Tilleuls 1, 1170, 0 2 672 95 13, *Fax 0 2 660 22 94,* – AE MC VISA JCB
closed 2 weeks July, Saturday lunch and Sunday – **Meals** – 25.
◆ Le Grill offers a standard à la carte menu of grilled dishes on the edge of the Fôret de Soignes, in a dining room which has been pleasantly redesigned in contemporary style.

WOLUWE-ST-LAMBERT (SINT-LAMBRECHTS-WOLUWE)

Sodehotel La Woluwe, av. E. Mounier 5, 1200, 0 2 775 21 11, *sodehotel@sodehotel.be, Fax 0 2 770 47 80,* – TV P – 25-200. AE MC VISA. rest
Meals *Leonard* *Lunch 23* – a la carte 37/61 – 21 – **120 rm** 275/315, – 6 suites.
◆ Away from the centre, but with easy access, this chain hotel has 118 spacious rooms combining peace and quiet and modern comfort. Business and conference centre. Modern and refined restaurant with cuisine that matches the setting. Bright patio.

Monty without rest, bd Brand Whitlock 101, 1200, 0 2 734 56 36, *info@monty-hotel.be, Fax 0 2 734 50 05* – TV. AE MC VISA HS z
18 rm 100.
◆ This former private mansion has been skilfully renovated in modern style. The hotel's two main selling-points are its friendly staff and the designer fittings throughout.

Lambeau without rest, av. Lambeau 150, 1200, 0 2 732 51 70, *info@hotellambeau.com, Fax 0 2 732 54 90* – TV. AE MC VISA. HR u
16 rm 77/93.
◆ This small, family-run hotel is located in a residential district, just opposite a metro station. Compact, identically furnished modern rooms with plain furnishings.

Da Mimmo, av. du Roi Chevalier 24, 1200, 0 2 771 58 60, *mimmo1961@yahoo.it, Fax 0 2 771 58 60,* , Italian cuisine – . AE MC VISA.
closed 1 to 30 August, late December-early January, Saturday lunch and Sunday – **Meals**. *Lunch 25* – a la carte 43/67 ♀.
◆ Da Mimmo prides itself on its true Italian cuisine with no concessions to Belgian tastes. Pleasant, modern-style dining room. Good choice of wines shipped direct from Italy.

de Maurice à Olivier (Detombe) in the back room of a bookshop, chaussée de Roodebeek 246, 1200, 0 2 771 33 98 – . AE MC VISA
closed 15 to 31 July, Sunday and Monday dinner – **Meals**. *Lunch 20* – 40/50, – a la carte 44/61.
◆ A father and son are at the helm of this small brasserie with an unusual location behind the family bookshop. A bistro-style menu and a literary atmosphere.
Spec. Foie gras d'oie et canard en terrine. Noix de cochon de lait rôtie et jus aigre-doux au poivre Sichuan. Faux mille-feuille de chocolat noir amer et café blanc, crème d'œuf au Costa Rica.

La Table de Mamy, av. des Cerisiers 212, ✉ 1200, ☎ 0 2 779 00 96, – AE MC VISA
closed 3 weeks August, Saturday and Sunday – **Meals** – 25.
• Enjoy the traditional cuisine of yesteryear in this pleasant restaurant in which the nostalgic internal décor is a throwback to olden times.

Les Amis du Cep, r. Th. Decuyper 136, ✉ 1200, ☎ 0 2 762 62 95, *Fax 0 2 771 20 32*, – AE MC VISA JCB
closed 21 July-4 August, late December, Sunday and Monday – **Meals**. *Lunch 16* – a la carte approx. 46 ♀.
• This small villa which advertises itself as a gourmet bistro is known for its contemporary flair in the kitchen and a top-notch wine-list.

WOLUWE-ST-PIERRE (SINT-PIETERS-WOLUWE)

Montgomery, av. de Tervuren 134, ✉ 1150, ☎ 0 2 741 85 11, *banqueting@montgomery.be, Fax 0 2 741 85 00*, – – 35. AE MC VISA. HS k
Meals *(closed 17 to 25 July, 18 December-2 January, Saturday and Sunday)* 25 ♀ – 20 – **61 rm** 360/380, – 2 suites.
• The tasteful, individually furnished rooms in this small luxury hotel are inspired by colonial, British and "Ralph Lauren" styles. Lounge-library, fitness room and sauna. The cuisine in the snug restaurant will find favour with aficionados of modern cuisine.

Des 3 Couleurs, av. de Tervuren 453, ✉ 1150, ☎ 0 2 770 33 21, *Fax 0 2 770 80 45*, – AE MC VISA
closed 2 weeks Easter, last 2 weeks August, Saturday lunch, Sunday dinner and Monday – **Meals**. *Lunch 57 b.i.* – 52/99.
• White beams and furniture, allied with Burgundy stone, add cachet to the interior décor of this elegant villa with an attractive terrace. Traditional à la carte choices.

Le Vignoble de Margot, av. de Tervuren 368, ✉ 1150, ☎ 0 2 779 23 23, *Fax 0 2 779 05 45*, , Partly oyster bar – AE MC VISA.
closed Saturday lunch, Sunday and Bank Holidays – **Meals** a la carte 44/74.
• This former station-buffet encircled by its own "vineyard" enjoys views over a park and several ponds. Elaborate choice of classic dishes, plus a seafood bar. Banqueting room.

Les Deux Maisons (Demartin), Val des Seigneurs 81, ✉ 1150, ☎ 0 2 771 14 47, *les deuxmaisons@skynet.be, Fax 0 2 771 14 47*, – . AE MC VISA
closed first week Easter, first 3 weeks August, Christmas-New Year, Sunday and Monday – **Meals** – 33/82 b.i., – a la carte 45/93.
• A plain dining room with a contemporary look is the backdrop for refined cuisine with a modern touch enhanced by a superb wine-list. "Dégustation" and "Tradition" menus.
Spec. Bar en croûte de sel. Carpaccio de bonite au vinaigre d'abricot et gingembre confit. Blanquette de langues d'agneau à l'huile d'amandes.

Medicis, av. de l'Escrime 124, ✉ 1150, ☎ 0 2 779 07 00, *Fax 0 2 779 19 24*, – AE MC VISA.
closed Easter, Saturday lunch and Sunday – **Meals**. *Lunch 15* – 30/55.
• The Medicis occupies an Anglo-Norman-style villa where the modern menu is certain to sharpen your appetite. French-Italian wine-list and a fine selection of desserts.

l'auberg'in, r. au Bois 198, ✉ 1150, ☎ 0 2 770 68 85, *Fax 0 2 770 68 85*, , Grill rest – AE MC VISA
closed Saturday lunch, Sunday and Bank Holidays – **Meals** – 30.
• This small, Brabant-style 19C farm has been converted into a convivial restaurant with neo-rustic décor and a roaring fire. Grilled specialities cooked in the dining room.

La Tour d'Argent, av. Salomé 1, ✉ 1150, ☎ 0 2 762 99 80, Vietnamese cuisne – MC VISA
closed Wednesday and lunch Thursday and Saturday – **Meals**. *Lunch 11* – 24.
• A well-deserved name for this simple, family-run Vietnamese restaurant serving authentic dishes which will transport you to the Far East. Unfailingly friendly service.

BRUSSELS ENVIRONS

at Diegem *Brussels-Zaventem motorway A 201, Diegem exit C Machelen pop. 11 972 – ✉ 1831 Diegem :*

Crowne Plaza Airport, Da Vincilaan 4 ☎ 0 2 416 33 33, *cpbrusselsairport@ichotelsgroup.com, Fax 0 2 416 33 44*, – – 25-400. AE MC VISA. rest
Meals a la carte approx. 22 – 21 – **312 rm** 355/430, – 3 suites.
• Part of the Crowne Plaza chain, this new hotel is located in a business park close to the airport. Comfortable and spacious rooms as well as good conference facilities. The restaurant offers a choice of contemporary cuisine including a buffet lunch option.

Sofitel Airport, Bessenveldstraat 15 ✆ 0 2 713 66 66, *H0548@accor-hotels.com, Fax 0 2 721 43 45,* – rest
Meals *La Pléiade* *(closed lunch Saturday and Sunday)* Lunch 25 – a la carte 28/56 ♀ – ☕ 21 – **125 rm** 265/295.
◆ A top-of-the-range chain hotel alongside a motorway 4km/2.5mi from Zaventem airport with quiet, newly renovated rooms and full conference and leisure facilities. The pleasant restaurant serves a range of appetising modern dishes.

Holiday Inn Airport, Holidaystraat 7 ✆ 0 2 720 58 65, *hibrusselsairport@ichotelsgroup.com, Fax 0 2 720 41 45,* – 25-400. rest
Meals (open until 11 p.m.). Lunch 30 – a la carte 31/42 – ☕ 21 – **310 rm** 250/290.
◆ The Holiday Inn offers a range of facilities, such as conference and fitness rooms, sauna, hammam, solarium, pool and tennis court. Other advantages include proximity to the airport and quiet, restful rooms. Expansive restaurant menu with a few Tex-Mex dishes.

NH Brussels Airport, De Kleetlaan 14 ✆ 0 2 203 92 52, *nhbrusselsairport@nh-hotels.be, Fax 0 2 203 92 53,* – 25-80.
Meals *(closed Friday dinner, Saturday and Sunday)* (partly buffets). Lunch 30 – a la carte 29/50 – ☕ 21 – **234 rm** 275/300.
◆ A modern construction close to the airport with up-to-date, comfortable rooms with good soundproofing, in keeping with the standards expected of the NH chain. Contemporary tastes are well-catered for in the hotel restaurant.

Novotel Airport, Da Vincilaan 25 ✆ 0 2 725 30 50, *H0467@accor-hotels.com, Fax 0 2 721 39 58,* rest, – 25-100.
Meals. Lunch 35 b.i. – a la carte 27/44 ♀ – ☕ 15 – **207 rm** 165/200.
◆ Ideal for those with an early flight to catch. No surprises in the identical bedrooms, which conform to the Novotel's usual criteria. Seminar rooms and outdoor pool.

Rainbow Airport, Berkenlaan 4 ✆ 0 2 721 77 77, *info@rainbowhotel.be, Fax 0 2 721 55 96,* rest, – 25-100.
Meals *(closed lunch Saturday and Sunday)* a la carte approx. 38 ♀ – ☕ 16 – **76 rm** 189.
◆ Despite being on the small side, the rooms here are attractive, well-maintained and spotlessly clean. Modern decor in the restaurant, where the emphasis is on conventional dishes. A haven of peace of quiet for stopover or transit passengers.

at Dilbeek *West : 7 km – pop. 38 326 – ✉ 1700 Dilbeek :*

Relais Delbeccha, Bodegemstraat 158 ✆ 0 2 569 44 30, *relais.delbeccha@skynet.be, Fax 0 2 569 75 30,* – 25-100.
closed last 3 weeks July – **Meals** *(closed Sunday dinner)*. Lunch 25 – 31/64 b.i. – **12 rm** ☕ 93/120.
◆ A quiet hotel with just 14 rooms, where the welcome is warm and friendly. Pleasant interior, cosy lounge, comfortable rooms with classic furniture, meeting rooms and a garden. Reasonably stylish restaurant offering outdoor dining in the summer.

Host. d'Arconati with rm, d'Arconatistraat 77 ✆ 0 2 569 35 00, *arconati@hotmail.com, Fax 0 2 569 35 04,* – 40.
closed February and last week July – **Meals** *(closed Sunday dinner, Monday and Tuesday)* a la carte 43/52 – **4 rm** ☕ 87.
◆ A charming Art Deco villa with quaint rooms and a tree-shaded garden, ablaze with colour in summer, which provides the perfect setting in which to unwind.

De Kapblok, Ninoofsesteenweg 220 ✆ 0 2 569 31 23, *reservatie@dekapblok.be, Fax 0 2 569 67 23* –
closed 2 weeks Easter, late July-early August, late December-early January, Sunday and Monday – **Meals**. Lunch 35 – 45/75 b.i..
◆ The "Butcher's Block" is a small, local restaurant serving good quality traditional cuisine, appetising menus and a highly respectable choice of wines.

at Dworp *(Tourneppe) South : 16 km* C *Beersel pop. 23 043 – ✉ 1653 Dworp :*

Kasteel Gravenhof, Alsembergsesteenweg 676 ✆ 0 2 380 44 99, *info@gravenhof.be, Fax 0 2 380 40 60,* rm, – 25-120.
Meals (pub rest). Lunch 17 – a la carte 25/43 – ☕ 15 – **26 rm** 100/155.
◆ This impressive château is a 17C folly replete with old knick-knacks, period furniture, and spacious bedrooms overlooking a park with ornamental ponds. The charming tavern-restaurant is in the depths of the castle's old vaulted cellars.

at Grimbergen *North : 11 km – pop. 33 072 – ✉ 1850 Grimbergen :*

Abbey, Kerkeblokstraat 5 ✆ 0 2 270 08 88, *info@hotelabbey.be, Fax 0 2 270 81 88,* rest, – 30-200. rm
closed July – **Meals *'t Wit Paard*** *(closed Saturday and Sunday)* Lunch 32 – a la carte 48/64 – ☕ 15 – **28 rm** 125/150.
◆ The Abbey's imposing architecture is reminiscent of a Flemish farm. Quiet, spacious guest rooms, plus meeting halls, bar, fitness area and sauna. Traditional restaurant fare, log fires in winter and outdoor dining on the terrace in summer.

at Groot-Bijgaarden *Northwest : 7 km* *Dilbeek pop. 38 326 – ✉ 1702 Groot-Bijgaarden :*

Waerboom, Jozef Mertensstraat 140 ☎ 0 2 463 15 00, *info@waerboom.com, Fax 0 2 463 10 30,* – AE VISA. rm
closed mid July-mid August – **Meals** (residents only) – **35 rm** 97/165.
◆ This Flemish farm has been tastefully converted into an attractive, family-run hotel. Conventional rooms, indoor pool, sauna and well-tended garden. Banquets and seminars.

Gosset, Gossetlaan 52 ☎ 0 2 466 21 30, *info@gosset.be, Fax 0 2 466 18 50,* – 25-200. AE VISA.
closed 20 December-5 January – **Meals**. *Lunch 10* – a la carte 22/48 – **48 rm** 100/125.
◆ This comfortable modern hotel with adequately soundproofed rooms occupies a small building on an industrial estate near the ring road. Large, contemporary dining room crowned with a fresco depicting a celestial scene. Shuttle bus to the city centre.

De Bijgaarden, I. Van Beverenstraat 20 ☎ 0 2 466 44 85, *debijgaarden@skynet.be, Fax 0 2 463 08 11,* <, – AE VISA JCB
closed 5 to 12 April, 9 to 30 August, 2 to 5 January, Saturday lunch and Sunday – **Meals**. *Lunch 50* – 65/225 b.i., – a la carte 95/169
◆ An enchanting residence in a bucolic setting, with an elegant interior, fine, traditional cuisine, magnificent wine cellar, and Groot-Bijgaarden Castle as a backdrop.
Spec. Beignet de foie gras d'oie caramélisé au Porto. Homard norvégien rôti à la vanille. Ris de veau de lait au beurre truffé, champignons des bois en civet.

Michel (Van Landeghem), Gossetlaan 31 ☎ 0 2 466 65 91, *restaurant.michel@belgacom.net, Fax 0 2 466 90 07,* – AE VISA
closed 10 to 28 August, 18 December-1 January, Sunday and Monday – **Meals** – 46/80 b.i..
◆ The unassuming décor of this gastronomic restaurant is in sharp contrast to its refined cuisine, which follows classic lines. Good wine-list. Outdoor dining in summer.
Spec. Oeuf poché aux jets de houblon (mid February-mid April). Perdreau rôti à la feuille de vigne (October-November). Mijoté de homard aux champignons des bois et grenailles.

at Hoeilaart *Southeast : 13 km – pop. 9 939 – ✉ 1560 Hoeilaart :*

Aloyse Kloos, Terhulpsesteenweg 2 (at Groenendaal) ☎ 0 2 657 37 37, *Fax 0 2 657 37 37,* – VISA
closed August, Saturday lunch, Sunday dinner and Monday – **Meals**. *Lunch 25* – 47/70 b.i. .
◆ Classic cuisine and superb Luxembourg wines are the hallmarks of this villa on the edge of the massif de Soignes. Mushroom specialities, including truffles.

à Itterbeek *West : 8 km* *Dilbeek pop. 38 326 – ✉ 1701 Itterbeek :*

De Ster, Herdebeekstraat 169 (lieu-dit Sint-Anna-Pede) ☎ 0 2 569 78 08, *Fax 0 2 569 37 97,* , Pub – VISA
closed 2 weeks August, Monday, Tuesday and lunch Saturday and Sunday – **Meals**. *Lunch 16* – 35/45.
◆ Recognisable by its attractive half-timbered façade, this old inn on a main road has several dining rooms laid out on various levels, in addition to a pleasant summer terrace.

at Machelen *Northeast : 12 km – pop. 11 972 – ✉ 1830 Machelen :*

Pyramid, Heirbaan 210 ☎ 0 2 253 54 56, *rest.pyramid@skynet.be, Fax 0 2 253 47 65,* – AE VISA JCB
closed 18 July-9 August, Saturday and Sunday – **Meals**. *Lunch 36* – 70 .
◆ A tranquil setting with modern overtures, English garden, terrace and ornamental water feature. Contemporary cuisine.

at Meise *North : 14 km – pop. 18 471 – ✉ 1860 Meise :*

Aub. Napoléon, Bouchoutlaan 1 ☎ 0 2 269 30 78, *Fax 0 2 269 79 98,* Grill rest – AE VISA
closed August – **Meals**. *Lunch 36* – 56/74 b.i. .
◆ A small, welcoming inn on the approach to the town centre. Rustic-style interior décor based on the theme of Napoleon. Grilled specialities prepared in the dining room.

Koen Van Loven, Brusselsesteenweg 11 ☎ 0 2 270 05 77, *koen.van.loven@proximedia.be, Fax 0 2 270 05 46,* – 25-150. AE VISA.
closed carnival week, building workers holidays, Monday and Tuesday – **Meals** 30/73 b.i..
◆ This early-20C bourgeois residence is now home to a contemporary-style restaurant. Comprehensive cellar. Large room for banquets and seminars.

at Melsbroek *Northeast : 14 km* *Steenokkerzeel pop. 10 534 – ✉ 1820 Melsbroek :*

Boetfort, Sellaerstraat 42 ☎ 0 2 751 64 00, *boetfort@proximedia.be, Fax 0 2 751 62 00,* – – 25-50. AE VISA. DK p
closed carnival week, Wednesday dinner, Saturday lunch and Sunday – **Meals**. *Lunch 34* – 38/53.
◆ This 17C manor house with a park once hosted the Sun King himself. Much of the building's cachet lies in its strong historical links.

at Nossegem *East : 13 km* Ⓒ *Zaventem pop. 27 537 – ✉ 1930 Nossegem :*

XXX ✿ **L'Orangeraie Roland Debuyst,** Leuvensesteenweg 614 ☎ 0 2 757 05 59, *roland.debuyst@wanadoo.be, Fax 0 2 759 50 08,* ☂ – P – 🏠 35. AE ① MO VISA. ✂
closed 1 week Easter, first 2 weeks August, Saturday lunch, Sunday and Monday – **Meals**. *Lunch 41* – 60/96 b.i., – a la carte 64/92 ♀.
◆ Cuisine with a modern flair in a restaurant with soothing decorative tones. Summer dining under large sunshades. Business clientele.
Spec. Tarte fine aux pommes, boudin noir, foie d'oie rôti, tranche de lard paysan et éclats de truffes. Papillote de turbot aux asperges, morilles et jambon cru. Pigeonneau fumé et désossé à la rhubarbe et poivre vert.

at Overijse *Southeast : 16 km – pop. 23 864 – ✉ 3090 Overijse :*

🏨 **Soret** ⛔, Kapucijnendreef 1 (at Jezus-Eik) ☎ 0 2 657 37 82, *hotel.soret.bvba@pandora.be, Fax 0 2 657 72 66,* 🏋, ≘s, 🏊, 🚲 – 🛗 📺 P – 🏠 40. AE ① MO VISA. ✂
Meals see ***Istas*** below – **38 rm** ☕ 82, – 1 suite.
◆ A brand-new hotel situated on the edge of the Forêt de Soignes. Smartly decorated rooms of varying shapes but generally with plenty of space. Peace and quiet guaranteed.

XXXX ✿ **Barbizon** (Deluc), Welriekendedreef 95 (at Jezus-Eik) ☎ 0 2 657 04 62, *barbizon@euronet.be, Fax 0 2 657 40 66,* ☂ – P. AE MO VISA
closed 13 July-4 August, 6 to 28 January, Tuesday and Wednesday – **Meals**. *Lunch 36* – 46/100 b.i., – a la carte 78/108 🍇.
◆ This Norman-style villa bordering the forest is in harmony with its bucolic setting. Exquisite, classic cuisine. Terrace and a delightful garden for warm summer days.
Spec. Tournedos de langoustines juste raidi, compotée de tomates douces et roquette, crème au cresson. Barbue aux échalotes confites, coulis de côtes du Rhône à la carotte. Gibier (September-January).

XX **Lipsius,** Brusselsesteenweg 671 (at Jezus-Eik) ☎ 0 2 657 34 32, *Fax 0 2 657 31 47* – P. AE ① MO VISA
closed Easter holidays, 25 July-30 August, 20 December-3 January, Sunday lunch except 15 October-15 February, Saturday lunch, Sunday dinner and Monday – **Meals**. *Lunch 35* – a la carte 44/70.
◆ Exposed bricks and beams, "terracotta" walls and chasuble chairs make up the décor at this restaurant with its drinks-inclusive menus. Fine selection of wines.

X **Istas** - Hotel Soret, Brusselsesteenweg 652 (at Jezus-Eik) ☎ 0 2 657 05 11, ☂, Pub rest – P. MO VISA
closed 1 to 30 August, 24 to 31 December, Wednesday and Thursday – **Meals** – a la carte 22/43.
◆ A century-old tavern-cum-restaurant a stone's throw from the Forêt de Soignes. Traditional cuisine and colourful local dishes served in a convivial atmosphere.

at Sint-Genesius-Rode (Rhode-St-Genèse) *South : 13 km – pop. 17 830 – ✉ 1640 Sint-Genesius-Rode :*

🏨 **Aub. de Waterloo,** chaussée de Waterloo 212 ☎ 0 2 358 35 80, *aubergedewaterloo@skynet.be, Fax 0 2 358 38 06,* 🏋, ≘s – 🛗 ⇆ ▤ 📺 – 🏠 25-70. AE ① MO VISA
closed first 2 weeks August and late December – **Meals** see ***L'Arlecchino*** below – **87 rm** ☕ 129/191.
◆ This recently built hotel close to the site of Napoleon's downfall offers two categories of rooms, plus studios with Chinese or Syrian décor. Business clientele.

XX **L'Arlecchino** - Hotel Aub. de Waterloo, chaussée de Waterloo 212 ☎ 0 2 358 34 16, *Fax 0 2 358 28 96,* ☂, Italian cuisine, partly trattoria – ▤ P. AE ① MO VISA
closed August, Monday and Tuesday lunch – **Meals** – 33/41 b.i..
◆ The menu at this restaurant will delight lovers of all things Italian, as will the pizzas from the trattoria. Good choice of French and Italian wines. Buon appetito !

XX **Michel D,** r. Station 182 ☎ 0 2 381 20 66, *Fax 0 2 380 45 80,* ☂ – P. AE ① MO VISA
closed last 2 weeks July-first week August, Saturday lunch, Sunday and Monday – **Meals**. *Lunch 20* – 40/110 b.i. ♀.
◆ This restaurant adorned with rattan furniture is housed in a modern, comfortable setting. Comprehensive à la carte choices.

at Sint-Pieters-Leeuw *Southwest : 13 km – pop. 30 186 – ✉ 1600 Sint-Pieters-Leeuw :*

🏨 **Green Park** ⛔, V. Nonnemanstraat 15 ☎ 0 2 331 19 70, *greenparkhotel@belgacom.be, Fax 0 2 331 03 11,* ☂, 🏋, 🛶, 🚲 – 🛗 📺 🚗 P – 🏠 25-100. AE ① MO VISA
closed July – **Meals** (residents only) – **18 rm** ☕ 74/88.
◆ Green Park was built a few years ago in this verdant, peaceful setting by a lake. Small fitness centre. Popular with business customers.

at Strombeek-Bever *North : 9 km* © *Grimbergen pop. 33 072 – ✉ 1853 Strombeek-Bever :*

Rijckendael, J. Van Elewijckstraat 35 ✆ 0 2 267 41 24, *rijckendael@alfarijckendael.gth.be, Fax 0 2 267 94 01*, – 25-40. AE VISA
Meals. *Lunch 23* – 35/65 b.i. – 16 – **49 rm** 150.
◆ This hotel of modern design is located a short walk from the Atomium and Heysel stadium. Identical, well-appointed rooms. Private car park. Restaurant with a rustic feel laid out inside a small farm.

't Stoveke, Jetsestraat 52 ✆ 0 2 267 67 25, , Seafood – AE VISA.
closed 3 weeks June, Christmas-New Year, Sunday, Monday and Bank Holidays – **Meals**. *Lunch 31* – a la carte 56/71.
◆ A family-run restaurant where the emphasis is on fish and seafood. Tiny dining room with views of the kitchen, plus a small terrace open to the elements.

Val Joli, Leestbeekstraat 16 ✆ 0 2 460 65 43, *info@valjoli.be, Fax 0 2 460 04 00*, – P – 25-40. VISA
closed 2 weeks June, late October-early November, Monday, Tuesday and Wednesday lunch – **Meals**. *Lunch 10* – 28.
◆ A villa with a garden and terraces. From your table, you can watch the ducks frolicking on the lake. Varied cuisine.

at Vilvoorde *(Vilvorde) North : 17 km – pop. 35 567 – ✉ 1800 Vilvoorde :*

La Hacienda, Koningslosteenweg 34 ✆ 0 2 649 26 85, *lahacienda@lahacienda.be, Fax 0 2 647 43 50*, , Spanish cuisine – P – 25. AE VISA.
closed mid July-mid August, Sunday and Monday – **Meals**. *Lunch 24* – 39.
◆ This bright hacienda is tucked away in a cul-de-sac near the canal. Authentic Iberian cuisine with regional menus and grilled meats. Wide choice of Spanish wines.

de Rembrandt, Lange Molensstraat 60 ✆ 0 2 251 04 72, *vandaelejoris@hotmail.com* – AE VISA
closed mid July-mid August, Saturday and Sunday – **Meals** (dinner by arrangement). *Lunch 41* – a la carte 41/61.
◆ This family restaurant is overlooked by a 15C watchtower. Traditional cuisine, impressive wine-list, mezzanine, plus a sundry collection of paintings.

Rouge Glamour, Fr. Rooseveltlaan 18 ✆ 0 2 253 68 39, *rouge.glamour@advalvas.be, Fax 0 2 253 68 39* – VISA
closed last week October, Monday, Tuesday dinner and lunch Saturday and Sunday – **Meals**. *Lunch 20* – 30/69 b.i..
◆ Modern cuisine offered in a cabaret-style setting, with a plant-filled summer terrace at the back with dark wood furnishings.

at Wemmel *North : 12 km – pop. 14 256 – ✉ 1780 Wemmel :*

La Roseraie, Limburg Stirumlaan 213 ✆ 0 2 456 99 10 and 0 2 460 51 34 (rest), *hotel@laroseraie.be, Fax 0 2 460 83 20*, – P. AE VISA
Meals *(closed Saturday lunch, Sunday dinner and Monday)*. *Lunch 22* – a la carte 35/52 – **8 rm** 125/150.
◆ La Roseraie occupies a pretty villa with eight reasonably comfortable, individually furnished guest rooms with varying styles : African, Japanese, Roman etc. Friendly welcome. Traditionally furnished dining room serving cuisine with the occasional modern touch.

Le Gril aux herbes d'Evan, Brusselsesteenweg 21 ✆ 0 2 460 52 39, *Fax 0 2 461 19 12*, – P. AE VISA
closed 1 to 21 July, 24 to 31 December, Saturday lunch and Sunday – **Meals**. *Lunch 30* – 55/80 b.i. .
◆ The cuisine at this small villa with a large garden is based on high-quality, carefully selected products. The wine-list does justice to the reputation of French vineyards.

Parkhof, Parklaan 7 ✆ 0 2 460 42 89, *Fax 0 2 460 25 10*, – P. AE VISA
closed Sunday dinner and Monday – **Meals**. *Lunch 19* – 35/60 b.i..
◆ Located in a public park close to the Beverbos nature reserve, the Oliartes has a pleasant terrace for dining outdoors in summer.

Il Brunello, Vijverslaan 1 ✆ 0 2 460 55 64, *Fax 0 2 460 13 92*, , Italian cuisine, open until 11 p.m. – P. AE VISA
Meals. *Lunch 13* – a la carte 27/43.
◆ Il Brunello's extensive menu is mainly devoted to Italian cuisine. The contemporary interior is similarly influenced by Italy. Trattoria section, plus a summer restaurant.

at Zaventem *Brussels-Zaventem airport motorway A 201 – pop. 27 537 – ✉ 1930 Zaventem :*

Sheraton Airport, at airport ✆ 0 2 710 80 00, *reservations.brussels@sheraton.com, Fax 0 2 710 80 80*, – P – 25-600. AE VISA JCB
Meals ***Concorde*** *(closed Saturday lunch)* *Lunch 25* – a la carte 30/61 – 25 – **292 rm** 395/470, – 2 suites.
◆ The closest luxury hotel to the airport, the Sheraton is a popular choice with business customers from around the world. International à la carte menu and buffet lunches that are ideal for busy corporate travellers.

XX **Stockmansmolen** 1st floor, H. Henneaulaan 164 ☎ 0 2 725 34 34, *info@stockmansmolen.be*, *Fax 0 2 725 75 05*, Partly pub rest – P. AE VISA
closed last 2 weeks July-first week August, Christmas, New Year, Saturday and Sunday – **Meals**. Lunch 48 – 58/93 b.i..
◆ The brasserie and restaurant - the latter on the first floor - share the two parts of this 13C water mill, built using a combination of wood and stone.

ELLEZELLES (ELZELE) *7890 Hainaut* 533 H 18, 534 H 18 *and* 716 E 3 – *pop. 5 616 – 55 km.*

XXXX ✿✿ **Château du Mylord** (Thomaes brothers), r. St-Mortier 35 ☎ 0 68 54 26 02, *chateaudumylord@pi.be*, *Fax 0 68 54 29 33*, – P. AE VISA
closed 13 to 21 April, 16 to 30 August, 23 December-10 January, Monday lunch except Bank Holidays and dinner Sunday, Monday and Wednesday – **Meals**. Lunch 40 – 60/133 b.i., – a la carte 68/111.
◆ This splendid 19C manor house stands in the surroundings of a delightful park. Elegant décor, superb terrace, cuisine with modern nuances, and vintage wines. Exquisite !
Spec. Ravioli ouvert de foie gras et anguilles laquées. Morue confite, calmars fumés et jus de viande. Pavé de bar aux asperges de Malines et épinards aux coquillages (May-June).

ANTWERP (ANTWERPEN) *2000* 533 L 15 *and* 716 G 2 – *pop. 448 709.*

See : *Around the Market Square and the Cathedral★★★ : Market Square★ (Grote Markt), Vlaaikensgang★* FY, *Cathedral★★★ and its tower★★★* FY – *Butchers' House★ (Vleeshuis) : Musical instruments★* FY **D** – *Rubens' House ★★ (Rubenshuis)* GZ – *Interior★ of St. James' Church (St-Jacobskerk)* GY - *Hendrik Conscience Place★ – St. Charles Borromeo's Church★ (St-Carolus Borromeuskerk)* GY – *St. Paul's Church (St-Pauluskerk) : interior★★* FY – *Zoo★★ (Dierentuin)* DEU – *Zurenborg Quarter★★* EV – *The port (Haven)* FY.
Museums : Maritime "Steen"★ (Nationaal Scheepvaartmuseum Steen) FY – *Ethnographic Museum★* FY **M**[1] – *Plantin-Moretus★★★* FZ – *Mayer Van den Bergh★★ : Mad Meg★★ (Dulle Griet)* GZ – *Rockox House★ (Rockoxhuis)* GY **M**[4] – *Royal Art Gallery★★★ (Koninklijk Museum voor Schone Kunsten)* VC**M**[5] – *Museum of Photography★* CV **M**[6] – *Open-air Museum of Sculpture Middelheim★ (Openluchtmuseum voor Beeldhouwkunst) – Provincial Museum Sterckshof-Zilvercentrum★.*

18 9 *North : 15,5 km at Kapellen, G. Capiaulei 2 ☎ 0 3 666 84 56,* - 18 *South : 10 km at Aartselaar, Kasteel Cleydael, Cleydaellaan 36 ☎ 0 3 887 00 79* - 18 9 *East : 10 km at Wommelgem, Uilenbaan 15 ☎ 0 3 355 14 00* - 18 9 *East : 13 km at Broechem, Kasteel Bossenstein, Moor 16 0 3 485 64 46.*

Grote Markt 13 ☎ 0 3 232 01 03, visit@antwerpen.be, Fax 0 3 231 19 37 – Tourist association of the province, Koningin Elisabethlei 16, ✉ 2018, ☎ 0 3 240 63 73, info@tpa.be, Fax 0 3 240 63 83.

Brussels 48 – Amsterdam 159 – Luxembourg 261 – Rotterdam 103.

Plans on following pages

Old Antwerp

Hilton, Groenplaats ☎ 0 3 204 12 12, *marc.depunt@hilton.com*, *Fax 0 3 204 12 13*, – – 30-1000. AE VISA JCB FZ m
Meals see ***Het Vijfde Seizoen*** below – 25 – **199 rm** 300/375, – 12 suites.
◆ This luxury hotel occupies a fine early-20C building which started life as a large department store. Large, well-appointed rooms, plus a pleasant lounge and terrace-veranda.

De Witte Lelie without rest, Keizerstraat 16 ☎ 0 3 226 19 66, *hotel@dewittelelie.be*, *Fax 0 3 234 00 19* – . AE VISA JCB GY z
closed 28 December-10 January – **7 rm** 180/320, – 3 suites.
◆ Quiet and full of charm, this small "grand hotel" is spread across several 17C houses. Cosy, elegantly decorated rooms, in addition to an inviting patio.

Theater, Arenbergstraat 30 ☎ 0 3 203 54 10, *info@theater-hotel.be*, *Fax 0 3 233 88 58*, – – 25-50. AE VISA. GZ t
Meals *(closed 19 July-17 August, Saturday lunch, Sunday and Bank Holidays)*. Lunch 16 – a la carte 32/42 – 20 – **122 rm** 130/235, – 5 suites.
◆ A modern, comfortable hotel with an ideal location at the heart of the old city, just a short distance from the Bourla theatre and Rubens' house. Spacious bedrooms decorated in warm tones. The focus in the restaurant is on Franco-Mediterranean cuisine.

't Sandt, Het Zand 17 ☎ 0 3 232 93 90, *info@hotel-sandt.be*, *Fax 0 3 232 56 13* – – 25-150. AE VISA JCB. FZ w
Meals *de kleine Zavel* Lunch 20 – a la carte 29/50 – **29 rm** 130/235, – 1 suite.
◆ The fine Rococo façade of this impressive 19C residence contrasts vividly with the sober, contemporary décor of its interior. Delightful, Italianate winter garden, roomy, elegant guest accommodation, and good-quality bistro cuisine.

Rubens without rest, Oude Beurs 29 ☎ 0 3 222 48 48, *hotel.rubens@glo.be*, *Fax 0 3 225 19 40* – . AE VISA JCB. FY y
35 rm 170/230, – 1 suite.
◆ A quiet and friendly renovated hotel near the Grand-Place and cathedral. Some rooms overlook the inner courtyard, which is flower-decked in summer.

ANTWERPEN

Street	Grid	No.
van Aerdtstr.	DT	3
Amsterdamstr.	DT	4
Ankerrui	DT	6
Ballaerstr.	DV	12
Borsbeekbrug	EX	16
van Breestr.	DV	19
Brialmontlei	DV	21
Britselei	DV	22
Broederminstr.	CV	24
Brouwersvliet	DT	25
Brusselstr.	CV	27
Carnotstr.	EU	
Cassiersstr.	DT	31
Charlottalei	DV	33
Cockerillkaai	CV	36
Cogels-Osylei	EV	37
Cuperusstr.	EV	38
Dambruggestr.	ETU	39
Diksmuidelaan	EX	43
Emiel Banningstr.	CV	51
Emiel Vloorsstr.	CX	52
Erwtenstr.	ET	55
Falconplein	DT	58
Franklin Rooseveltpl.	DU	60
Gemeentestr.	DU	63
Gén. Armstrongweg	CX	64
Gén. van Merlenstraat	EV	65
Gérard Le Grellelaan	DX	66
de Gerlachekaai	CV	67
Gillisplaats	CV	69
Gitschotellei	EX	70
Graaf van Egmontstr.	CV	72
Haantjeslei	CDV	79
Halenstr.	ET	81
Hessenplein	DT	84
Jan de Voslei	CX	90
Jan van Gentstr.	CV	91
Jezusstr.	DU	96
Justitiestr.	DV	97
Kasteelpleinstr.	DV	102
de Keyserlei	DU	103
Kloosterstr.	CU	105
Kol. Silvertopstr.	CX	106
Koningin Astridplein	DEU	109
Koningin Elisabethlei	DX	110
Korte Winkelstr.	DTU	114
Lambertnontplaats	CV	116
Lange Winkelstr.	DT	118
Leopold de Waelplein	CV	120
Leopold de Waelstr.	CV	121
Leysstr.	DU	123
Londenstr.	DT	124
Maria-Henriettalei	DV	127
Marnixplaats	CV	129
Mercatorstr.	DEV	130
Namenstr.	CV	133
van den Nestlei	EV	135
Offerandestr.	EU	136
Ommeganckstr.	EU	138
Orteliuskaai	DT	141
Osystr.	DU	142
Oude Leeuwenrui	DT	148
Pelikaanstr.	DU	151
Plantinkaai	CU	153
Ploegstr.	EU	154
Posthofbrug	EX	157
Prins Albertlei	DX	159
Provinciestr.	EUV	162
Pyckestr.	CX	163
Quellinstr.	DU	165
Quinlen Matsijslei	DUV	166
Rolwagenstr.	EV	171
Schijnpoortweg	ET	174
van Schoonhovestr.	DEU	175
Simonsstr.	DEV	178
Sint-Bernardse steenweg	CX	180
Sint-Gummarusstr.	DT	181
Sint-Jansplein	DT	183
Sint-Jozefsstr.	DV	186
Sint-Michielskaai	CU	187
Turnhoutsebaan (BORGERHOUT)	EU	
Viaduct Dam	ET	202
Visestr.	ET	204
Volkstr.	CV	207
Vondelstr.	DT	208
Waterloostraat	EV	210

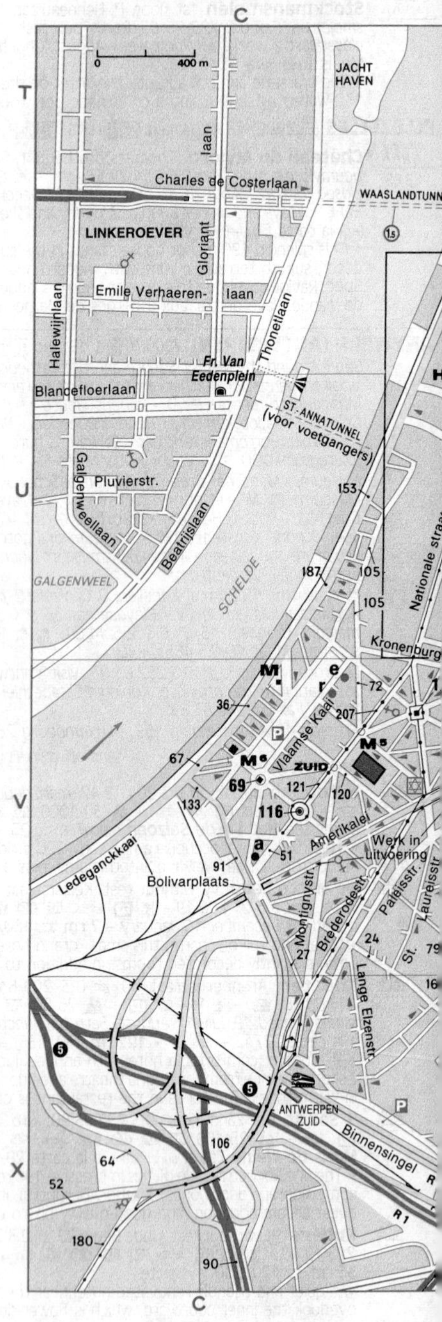

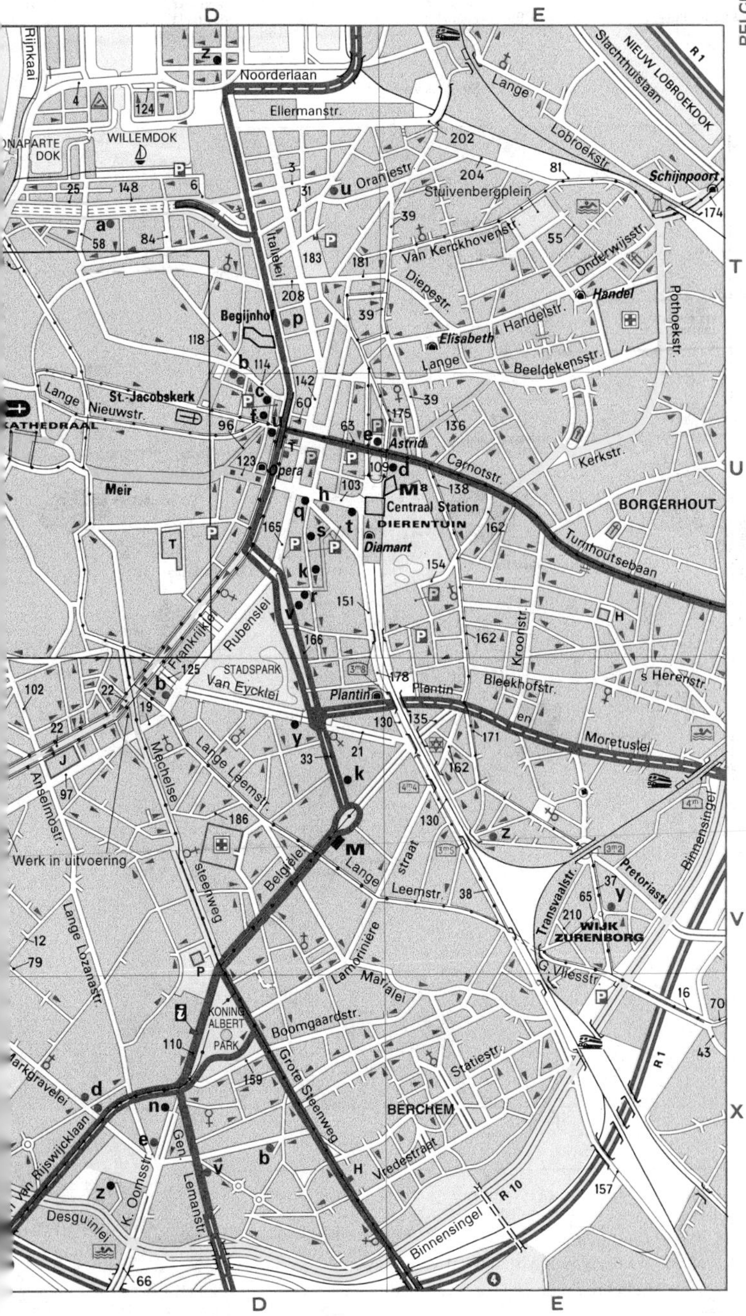

D
E
Rijnkaai
Noorderlaan
Ellermanstr.
WILLEMDOK
BONAPARTE DOK
Lange
Slachthuislaan
NIEUW LOBROEKDOK
R1
Lobroekstr.
202
204
81
Oranjestr.
Stuivenbergplein
Schijnpoort
174
Italiëlei
Van Kerckhovenstr.
Onderwijsstr.
Diepestr.
Handel
Handelstr.
Pothoekstr.
Begijnhof
Elisabeth
Lange Beeldekensstr.
St.-Jacobskerk
Lange Nieuwstr.
KATHEDRAAL
Astrid
Carnotstr.
Kerkstr.
Opera
Meir
Centraal Station
DIERENTUIN
Diamant
BORGERHOUT
Turnhoutsebaan
T
U
Rubenslei
Frankrijklei
STADSPARK
Van Eycklei
Plantin
Bleekhofstr.
Kroonstr.
s Herenstr.
Plantin en Moretuslei
Mechelse steenweg
Lange Leemstr.
Anselmostr.
Werk in uitvoering
Belgiëlei
Lange Leemstraat
Binnensingel
Pretoriastr.
Transvaalstr.
WIJK ZURENBORG
Lange Lozanastr.
Lamorinièrestr.
Maria lei
G. Vleesstr.
V
KONING ALBERT PARK
Boomgaardstr.
Grote Steenweg
Statiestr.
Markgravelei
BERCHEM
X
Van Rijswijcklaan
Gen. Lemanstr.
K. Oomsstr.
Vredestraat
Desguinlei
R 10
Binnensingel
R1
D
E

ANTWERPEN

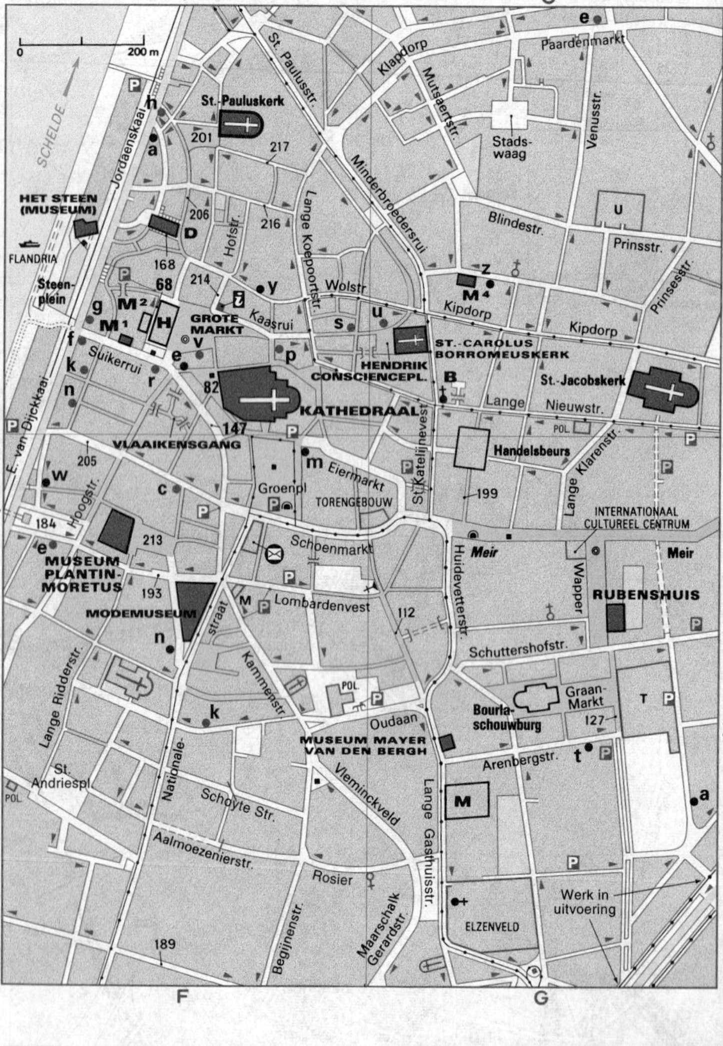

Pleasant hotels and restaurants are shown in the Guide by a **red sign**.

Please send us the names of any where you have enjoyed your stay.

Your **Michelin Guide** will be even better.

Villa Mozart, Handschoenmarkt 3 ☎ 0 3 231 30 31, *villa.mozart@wanadoo.be, Fax 0 3 231 56 85,* – AE VISA JCB FY e
Meals (pub rest, open until 11 p.m.). *Lunch 19* – a la carte 25/42 – 13 – **25 rm** 99/148.
• Superbly located in the bustling heart of Antwerp between the Grand-Place and the cathedral (visible from some rooms), this small hotel is a pleasant and highly practical option. The brasserie is decorated in modern style.

Antigone without rest, Jordaenskaai 11 ☎ 0 3 231 66 77, *info@antigonehotel.be, Fax 0 3 231 37 74* – 30. AE VISA JCB FY a
18 rm 75/95.
• A simple, but perfectly comfortable and adequate hotel housed in a bourgeois-style building near the Schelde River and Steen Museum. Individually decorated rooms.

't Fornuis (Segers), Reyndersstraat 24 ☎ 0 3 233 62 70, *Fax 0 3 233 99 03* – AE VISA. FZ c
closed August, Saturday and Sunday – **Meals** (booking essential) a la carte 64/85.
• This restaurant, occupying a fine 17C residence, offers an ambitious menu that is highly personalised and presented in theatrical fashion by the feisty chef! Rustic decor.
Spec. Aile de raie croustillante au beurre de moutarde en grains. Salade de poulet aux truffes. Sabayon au Champagne.

Huis De Colvenier, St-Antoniusstraat 8 ☎ 0 3 226 65 73, *info@colvenier.be, Fax 0 3 227 13 14,* – AE VISA FZ k
closed carnival week, August, Saturday lunch, Sunday and Monday – **Meals**. *Lunch 50* – a la carte 65/80.
• An elegant 19C townhouse embellished with wall frescoes and a winter garden. A good wine-list to accompany the appealing, "all-in" menus. Attentive service.

Het Vijfde Seizoen - Hotel Hilton, Groenplaats ☎ 0 3 204 12 12, *fb_antwerp@hilton.com, Fax 0 3 204 12 13* – AE VISA JCB FZ m
closed 25 Juuly-15 August, Sunday and Monday – **Meals**. *Lunch 39* – 69.
• This hotel-chain restaurant, with its extensive glass frontage, is a popular meeting-point for business clientele in the centre of the city.

La Rade 1st floor, E. Van Dijckkaai 8 ☎ 0 3 233 37 37, *larade@skynet.be, Fax 0 3 233 49 63* – AE VISA FY g
closed 12 to 17 April, 5 to 25 July, Saturday lunch, Sunday and Bank Holidays – **Meals** – a la carte 34/47.
• An unusual restaurant housed in a bourgeois 19C residence. The main features of interest here are the masonic enthronement seat, mosaic dome and oriental room.

De Kerselaar (Michiels), Grote Pieter Potstraat 22 ☎ 0 3 233 59 69, *dekerselaar@pandora.be, Fax 0 3 233 11 49* – AE VISA JCB FY n
closed 3 weeks July, Sunday and lunch Monday, Wednesday and Saturday – **Meals**. *Lunch 40* – a la carte 57/80.
• Food-lovers will feel pampered in this neatly decorated restaurant known for its creative French cuisine, well-designed menu, extensive cellar and stylish service.
Spec. Tartare de thon et crevettes à la tomate confite. Marbré au foie d'oie, patta negra et canard. La corne de glace au chocolat et fruits rouges.

't Silveren Claverblat, Grote Pieter Potstraat 16 ☎ 0 3 231 33 88, *Fax 0 3 231 31 46* – AE VISA. FY k
closed Tuesday, Wednesday and Saturday lunch – **Meals** 35/70 b.i..
• A pleasant, small building in the old town. Its emblem, a silver four-leafed clover, is said to bring good luck. Classic à la carte choices, a popular menu and daily specials.

De Gulden Beer, Grote Markt 14 ☎ 0 3 226 08 41, *Fax 0 3 232 52 09,* Partly Italian cuisine – AE VISA. FY v
Meals. *Lunch 25* – 37/75.
• This old house with its crow-step gables and attractive views stands on the Grand-Place. The focus here is on Franco-Italian cuisine, accompanied by a promising wine-list.

Het Nieuwe Palinghuis, Sint-Jansvliet 14 ☎ 0 3 231 74 45, *hetnieuwepalinghuis@resto.be, Fax 0 3 231 50 53,* Seafood – AE VISA. FZ e
closed 2 to 29 June, 24 December-13 January, Monday and Tuesday – **Meals** a la carte 39/75.
• Fish and seafood take pride of place in this restaurant, whose walls are adorned with nostalgic images of old Antwerp. Good choice of affordable wines.

P. Preud'Homme, Suikerrui 28 ☎ 0 3 233 42 00, *Fax 0 3 226 08 96,* Open until 11 p.m. – AE VISA JCB. FY r
closed 5 January-4 February – **Meals**. *Lunch 24* – a la carte 40/75.
• A bourgeois residence with sober, yet pleasant contemporary décor. Popular with tourists and locals alike. A complex menu, with plenty of mussel options in season.

Neuze Neuze 1st floor, Wijngaardstraat 19 ☎ 0 3 232 27 97, *neuzeneuze@pandora.be, Fax 0 3 225 27 38* – AE ⓓ ⓜ VISA JCB FY s
closed 5 to 25 August, 25 to 29 December, first week January, Saturday lunch and Sunday – **Meals**. *Lunch 25* – 50/76 b.i..
◆ An intimate setting where the clientele ranges from business people to romantic couples. Separate banqueting rooms. Copious cuisine and refined service.

Dock's Café, Jordaenskaai 7 ☎ 0 3 226 63 30, *info@docks.be, Fax 0 3 226 65 72*, Brasserie-Oyster bar, open until 11 p.m. – AE ⓜ VISA. ✻ FY h
closed Saturday lunch – **Meals** 28 ♀.
◆ A sense of travel pervades this seafood bar-cum-brasserie with its futurist, ship-based décor. Dining room with mezzanine and neo-Baroque staircase. Reservation recommended.

De Manie, H. Conscienceplein 3 ☎ 0 3 232 64 38, *restaurant.demanie@pi.be, Fax 0 3 232 64 38* – AE ⓓ ⓜ VISA JCB GY u
closed 15 August-2 September, Wednesday and Sunday dinner – **Meals**. *Lunch 25* – a la carte 42/60 ♀.
◆ On a pleasant square by the St-Charles-Borromée church, the De Manie's old façade is fronted by a summer terrace. Modern-rustic dining room serving contemporary cuisine.

De Reddende Engel, Torfbrug 3 ☎ 0 3 233 66 30, *Fax 0 3 233 73 79*, – AE ⓓ ⓜ VISA FY p
closed 22 February-4 March, 16 August-16 September, Tuesday, Wednesday and Saturday lunch – **Meals** – 24/31.
◆ This 17C house close to the cathedral is the rustic setting for this friendly restaurant whose menu covers the regions of France. Pleasant terrace in fine weather.

Maritime, Suikerrui 4 ☎ 0 3 233 07 58, *restaurant.maritime@pandora.be, Fax 0 3 233 18 87*, – AE ⓓ ⓜ VISA JCB FY f
closed June, Wednesday and Thursday – **Meals** – a la carte 35/78.
◆ As its name would suggest, fish and seafood reign supreme here with some of the city's best mussels and eel in season. A good choice of Burgundies and attentive service.

Town Centre, Station and Docks

Radisson SAS Park Lane, Van Eycklei 34, ✉ 2018, ☎ 0 3 285 85 85, *guest.antwerp@radissonsas.com, Fax 0 3 285 85 86*, – 25-600. AE ⓓ ⓜ VISA JCB. ✻ rest DV y
Meals *Longchamps* *(closed Sunday) Lunch 30* – a la carte 38/55 – ☐ 23 – **163 rm** 176/220, – 14 suites.
◆ This recently built luxury hotel is well-located on a main road away from the centre, opposite a public park. Full range of facilities and services for its mainly business clientele. The brasserie serves international cuisine and more inventive modern dishes.

Astrid Park Plaza, Koningin Astridplein 7, ✉ 2018, ☎ 0 3 203 12 34, *appres@parkplazahotels.be, Fax 0 3 203 12 51*, – 25-500. AE ⓓ ⓜ VISA JCB. ✻ rest DEU e
Meals *(closed Sunday)* a la carte 28/43 – ☐ 20 – **225 rm** 220/285, – 3 suites.
◆ This glamorous new hotel on a busy square near the central railway station occupies a prime location. Impeccable, spacious and well-appointed rooms. Bright restaurant where the emphasis is on innovative recipes.

Carlton, Quinten Matsijslei 25, ✉ 2018, ☎ 0 3 231 15 15, *info@carltonhotel-antwerp.com, Fax 0 3 225 30 90* – – 25-100. AE ⓓ ⓜ VISA. ✻ rest DU v
Meals *(closed 3 weeks August and Sunday dinner)* (dinner only) 42 – **127 rm** ☐ 189/320, – 1 suite.
◆ A comfortable hotel near the diamond centre and a municipal park. Most of the bedrooms have been renovated, with those on the higher floors offering pleasant views. Business centre. French cuisine tops the menu, in addition to a few Flemish-inspired dishes.

Alfa De Keyser without rest, De Keyserlei 66, ✉ 2018, ☎ 0 3 206 74 60, *Fax 0 3 232 39 70*, – 25-160. AE ⓓ ⓜ VISA DU t
☐ 20 – **120 rm** 130/180, – 3 suites.
◆ Easily accessible and advantageously located in the busy central district. Large, well-appointed rooms with good soundproofing. A popular business hotel, with a tavern-restaurant offering non-stop service from morning to night.

Hyllit without rest, De Keyserlei 28 (access by Appelmansstraat), ✉ 2018, ☎ 0 3 202 68 00, *info@hyllithotel.be, Fax 0 3 202 68 90*, – 25-120. AE ⓓ ⓜ VISA JCB. ✻ DU q
☐ 17 – **117 rm** 171/196, – 5 suites.
◆ This modern "apartment-hotel" popular with the business community enjoys an ideal location in the centre of the city. Comfortable rooms and junior suites.

Plaza without rest, Charlottalei 49, ✉ 2018, ☎ 0 3 287 28 70, *book@plaza.be, Fax 0 3 287 28 71* – |‡| ⇹ ▤ TV 🚗 – 🏃 25. AE ⓓ MC VISA. ✂ DV k
80 rm ☕ 150/175.
◆ A warm, friendly atmosphere is the hallmark of this old-style hotel on the edge of the city centre. Large, elegant rooms, a grand English-style lobby and Victorian bar.

Astoria without rest, Korte Herentalsestraat 5, ✉ 2018, ☎ 0 3 227 31 30, *info@carltonhotel-antwerp.com, Fax 0 3 227 31 39,* 🏋 – |‡| ⇹ ▤ TV. AE ⓓ MC VISA DU r
closed 2 weeks August and 2 weeks December – **66 rm** ☕ 140/175.
◆ Although slightly away from the action, the Astoria has a reasonable location near the diamond district and Stadtspark. Granite lobby and façade, and well-appointed rooms.

Antverpia without rest, Sint-Jacobsmarkt 85 ☎ 0 3 231 80 80, *antverpia@skynet.be, Fax 0 3 232 43 43* – |‡| TV 🚗. AE ⓓ MC VISA. ✂ DU f
closed 20 December-10 January – **18 rm** ☕ 97/175.
◆ A small, pleasant and splendidly-maintained city centre hotel occupying a narrow building near a major road junction. Attractive, spacious rooms with good-quality furnishings.

Alfa Empire without rest, Appelmansstraat 31, ✉ 2018, ☎ 0 3 203 54 00, *info@empirehotel.be, Fax 0 3 233 40 60* – |‡| ⇹ ▤ TV. AE ⓓ MC VISA DU s
☕ 15 – **70 rm** 135/155.
◆ Nestled at the heart of the diamond district, the Alfa Empire offers 70 large rooms, some recently refurbished. The hotel also has a locked and guarded garage.

NH Docklands Antwerp without rest, Kempisch Dok Westkaai 84 ☎ 0 3 231 07 26, *nhdocklandsantwerp@nh-hotels.be, Fax 0 3 231 57 49* – |‡| ⇹ TV – 🏃 25. AE ⓓ MC VISA. ✂ DT z
☕ 15 – **32 rm** 110/125.
◆ A new hotel with a glass/aluminium façade and designer entrance hall in front of the Kempisch Dock. Comfortable rooms with standard fittings and modern furnishings.

Colombus without rest, Frankrijklei 4 ☎ 0 3 233 03 90, *colombushotel@skynet.be, Fax 0 3 226 09 46,* 🏋, 🏊 – |‡| TV 🚗. AE ⓓ MC VISA. ✂ DU u
32 rm ☕ 90.
◆ Behind the hotel's classical façade are 32 rooms with good soundproofing and attractively decorated public areas. An excellent location just opposite the city's opera house.

Eden without rest, Lange Herentalsestraat 25, ✉ 2018, ☎ 0 3 233 06 08, *hotel.eden@skynet.be, Fax 0 3 233 12 28,* 🚲 – |‡| TV 🚗. AE ⓓ MC VISA JCB DU k
66 rm ☕ 100/110.
◆ A basic, but well-maintained hotel with a prime location in the middle of the diamond district, close to the railway station. The rooms here are gradually being refurbished.

De Barbarie, Van Breestraat 4, ✉ 2018, ☎ 0 3 232 81 98, *Fax 0 3 231 26 78,* ☂ – ▤. AE ⓓ MC VISA JCB DV b
closed Easter holidays, first 2 weeks September, Christmas holidays, Saturday lunch, Sunday and Monday – **Meals**. Lunch 40 – a la carte 59/120.
◆ The creative menu here includes several duck specialities, accompanied by a good choice of wines. The collection of silver tableware is particularly noteworthy.

La Luna, Italiëlei 177 ☎ 0 3 232 23 44, *info@laluna.be, Fax 0 3 232 24 41,* Multinational cuisines, open until 11 p.m. – ▤. AE ⓓ MC VISA DT p
closed 13 to 19 April, 3 to 24 August, Christmas-New Year, Saturday lunch, Sunday and Monday – **Meals** – 29 ♀.
◆ The American brasserie-style atmosphere and cosmopolitan menu are popular with the city's upwardly mobile clientele. A refined, reasonably priced menu and excellent wine list.

de nieuwe HARMONY, Mechelsesteenweg 169, ✉ 2018, ☎ 0 3 239 70 05, *acs.acs@tiscali.be, Fax 0 3 239 63 61* – ▤ P. AE ⓓ MC VISA DV n
closed 1 to 16 March, 19 July-10 August, Monday and Saturday lunch – **Meals**. Lunch 24 – 45/63 b.i. ♀.
◆ This new restaurant, housed in a renovated tavern, offers modern fare, including a midweek business menu. The ceiling is adorned with several attractive stained-glass windows.

De Lepeleer, Lange St-Annastraat 10 ☎ 0 3 225 19 31, *info@lepeleer.be, Fax 0 3 231 31 24,* ☂ – ▤ P – 🏃 25-50. AE ⓓ MC VISA DU b
closed 21 July-18 August, Saturday lunch, Sunday and Bank Holidays – **Meals**. Lunch 25 – 65/81 b.i..
◆ An attractive line of small maisonettes running along a paved cul-de-sac dating from the 16C. The menu favours traditional dishes, served in a cosy, rustic-style dining room.

't Peerd, Paardenmarkt 53 ☎ 0 3 231 98 25, *resto_t_peerd@yahoo.com, Fax 0 3 231 59 40,* ☂ – ▤. AE ⓓ MC VISA JCB GY e
closed 2 weeks Easter, 2 weeks October, Tuesday and Wednesday – **Meals**. Lunch 35 – a la carte 40/71.
◆ Halfway between the docks and the cathedral, this small restaurant full of character prides itself on its honest, traditional fare. Interesting wine-list.

XX **De Zeste,** Lange Dijkstraat 36, ✉ 2060, ☎ 0 3 233 45 49, *dezeste@xs4all.be, Fax 0 3 232 34 18* – ▤. AE ⓓ MC VISA DT u
closed 2 weeks July, Wednesday dinner and Sunday – **Meals**. *Lunch 60 b.i.* – a la carte 54/86.
◆ A welcoming address on the fringe of the city centre. The menu covers a range of traditional dishes prepared with an innovative touch. Good wine-list. Reservation recommended.

XX **Dôme,** Grote Hondstraat 2, ✉ 2018, ☎ 0 3 239 90 03, *Fax 0 3 239 93 90* – ▤. AE ⓓ MC VISA EV z
closed 23 December-2 January, Monday and lunch Tuesday and Saturday – **Meals**. *Lunch 28* – a la carte 49/66 ♀.
◆ This 19C house was formerly a café before its conversion into a contemporary restaurant crowned by a Baroque dome. Traditional cuisine.

X **Pazzo,** Oude Leeuwenrui 12 ☎ 0 3 232 86 82, *pazzo@skynet.be, Fax 0 3 232 79 34,* Open until 11 p.m. – ▤. AE ⓓ MC VISA DT a
closed 3 weeks August, Christmas-New Year, Saturday, Sunday and Bank Holidays – **Meals**. *Lunch 19* – a la carte 30/46 ♀.
◆ A lively restaurant occupying a former warehouse converted into a modern brasserie, where the emphasis is on contemporary dishes and wines chosen to complement the cuisine.

X **Yamayu Santatsu,** Ossenmarkt 19 ☎ 0 3 234 09 49, *Fax 0 3 234 09 49,* Japanese cuisine with Sushi-bar – ▤. AE ⓓ MC VISA JCB DTU b
closed 2 weeks August, 25 December-5 January, Sunday lunch and Monday – **Meals**. *Lunch 12* – a la carte 36/47.
◆ Halfway between the cathedral and the central rail terminal, this old house has been transformed into a pleasant, typically decorated Japanese restaurant and sushi bar.

South Quarter

Crowne Plaza, G. Legrellelaan 10, ✉ 2020, ☎ 0 3 259 75 00, *cpantwerp@ichotelsgroup.com, Fax 0 3 216 02 96,* – ▤ TV P – 25-600. AE ⓓ MC VISA JCB
Meals ***Plaza One for two*** *Lunch 30* – a la carte 35/51 – ☕ 21 – **256 rm** 245/280, – 6 suites.
◆ An international hotel near a motorway offering pleasantly decorated, well-appointed rooms. Good conference facilities and 24-hour service. Good buffet options at lunchtime.

Corinthia, Desguinlei 94, ✉ 2018, ☎ 0 3 244 82 11, *antwerp@corinthia.be, Fax 0 3 216 47 12,* – ▤ TV P – 25-590. AE ⓓ MC VISA. rest
Meals *(closed Saturday lunch and Sunday). Lunch 27* – a la carte 35/44 ♀ – ☕ 18 – **210 rm** 189/209, – 5 suites. DX z
◆ This chain hotel, with a diamond-like glass façade, is located close to the city's ring road and Midi station. Renovated rooms. The menu at the Tiffany's restaurant covers both traditional and international dishes, enhanced by the occasional local speciality.

Firean, Karel Oomsstraat 6, ✉ 2018, ☎ 0 3 237 02 60, *info@hotelfirean.com, Fax 0 3 238 11 68,* – ▤ TV. AE ⓓ MC VISA JCB DX n
closed 27 July-20 August – **Meals** see ***Minerva*** below – **15 rm** ☕ 131/205.
◆ A charming, quiet hotel with a patio occupying an Art Deco-style residence close to the Koning Albert Park. Rooms decorated with stylish antique furniture. Attentive service.

Industrie without rest, Emiel Banningstraat 52 ☎ 0 3 238 66 00, *hotelindustrie@pandora.be, Fax 0 3 238 86 88* – TV. AE ⓓ MC VISA. CV a
13 rm ☕ 75/87.
◆ A well-maintained small hotel occupying two mansions close to two of the city's best museums. Compact but well-appointed rooms with a touch of individuality.

XXX **Loncin,** Markgravelei 127, ✉ 2018, ☎ 0 3 248 29 89, *info@loncinrestaurant.be, Fax 0 3 248 38 66,* – ▤ P. AE ⓓ MC VISA DX d
closed Saturday lunch and Sunday – **Meals**. *Lunch 35* – a la carte 46/155.
◆ A discreetly elegant restaurant not far from the Koning Albert Park. Classic à la carte options plus menus and chef's suggestions. Game in season. Reservations required.

XX **Liang's Garden,** Markgravelei 141, ✉ 2018, ☎ 0 3 237 22 22, *Fax 0 3 248 38 34,* Chinese cuisine – ▤. AE ⓓ MC VISA DX d
closed mid July-mid August and Sunday – **Meals**. *Lunch 24* – a la carte 29/54.
◆ One of Antwerp's oldest Chinese restaurants, near the Koning Albert Park. Typical Oriental décor and a simple menu. Mainly business and local clientele.

XX **Minerva** - Hotel Firean, Karel Oomsstraat 36, ✉ 2018, ☎ 0 3 216 00 55, *restaurantminerva@skynet.be, Fax 0 3 216 00 55* – ▤. AE ⓓ MC VISA DX e
closed late July-20 August, 23 December-6 January, Sunday and Monday – **Meals** – a la carte 44/75.
◆ This modern, elegant restaurant has replaced the former garage that once stood here. Enticing traditional cuisine and seasonal suggestions. Easy parking in the evening.

Kommilfoo, Vlaamse Kaai 17 ☎ 0 3 237 30 00, *Fax 0 3 237 30 00* – ▤. AE ⓓ ⓜⓒ VISA. ✗ CV e
closed first 2 weeks July, Saturday lunch, Sunday and Monday – **Meals**. *Lunch 30* – 45/70 b.i..
• Located opposite a large, free car park a stone's throw from three museums, this former warehouse is sober yet modern in design, with a menu that is equally contemporary.

Suburbs

North – ✉ *2030* :

Novotel, Luithagen-haven 6 (Haven 200) ☎ 0 3 542 03 20, *H0465@accor-hotels.com, Fax 0 3 541 70 93,* – ▤ TV P – 25-180. AE ⓓ ⓜⓒ VISA
Meals. *Lunch 13* – a la carte 26/45 – ▭ 14 – **120 rm** 107.
• The renovated Novotel is situated to the northeast of the port area, close to a motorway junction and along a road that links it directly with the city centre.

at Berchem C *Antwerpen* – ✉ *2600 Berchem* :

De Tafeljoncker, Frederik de Merodestraat 13 ☎ 0 3 281 20 34, *restaurant.de-tafeljoncker@pandora.be, Fax 0 3 281 20 34,* – ▤. AE ⓓ ⓜⓒ VISA DX f
closed Easter week, first 2 weeks September, Sunday dinner, Monday and Tuesday – **Meals**. *Lunch 50* – 62/90 b.i..
• An attractive restaurant occupying a mansion with a small garden that is laid out in summer for al fresco dining. Although limited, the menu is both attractive and up-to-date.

Brasserie Marly, Generaal Lemanstraat 64 ☎ 0 3 281 23 23, *info@marly.be, Fax 0 3 281 33 10* – AE ⓓ ⓜⓒ VISA. ✗ DX c
closed 19 July-16 August, Saturday lunch and Sunday – **Meals** 25 b.i./43 ♀.
• A welcoming brasserie, located on the southern fringes of the city, with its own fish tanks, where fish, oysters and lobster take centre-stage. Valet parking.

De Troubadour, Driekoningenstraat 72 ☎ 0 3 239 39 16, *info@detroubadour.be, Fax 0 3 230 82 71* – ▤ P. AE ⓓ ⓜⓒ VISA DX a
closed Easter holidays, first 2 weeks August, Sunday and Monday – **Meals**. *Lunch 25* – 33 ♀.
• The imaginative, contemporary cuisine on offer in this warm and welcoming modern restaurant is ever-popular with regulars and the local business community.

at Borgerhout *East : 3 km* C *Antwerpen* – ✉ *2140 Borgerhout* :

Scandic, Luitenant Lippenslaan 66 ☎ 0 3 235 91 91, *info-antwerp@scandic-hotels.com, Fax 0 3 235 08 96,* – ▤ TV P – 25-230. AE ⓓ ⓜⓒ VISA JCB. ✗
Meals. *Lunch 25* – a la carte 37/63 ♀ – ▭ 17 – **201 rm** 185/236, – 3 suites.
• A renovated chain hotel with a good location along the ring road, close to Borgerhout railway station, the Sterchshof Museum (Zilvercentrum) and a golf course. Business centre. Modern-style brasserie with an international menu.

at Deurne *Northeast : 3 km* C *Antwerpen* – ✉ *2100 Deurne* :

De Violin, Bosuil 1 ☎ 0 3 324 34 04, *Fax 0 3 326 33 20,* – P. AE ⓓ ⓜⓒ VISA. ✗
closed Sunday and Monday dinner – **Meals**. *Lunch 41 b.i.* – a la carte 48/64.
• A charming restaurant occupying a small farm with painted shutters. Classic cuisine plus daily specials explained in person. Delightful Asia-inspired terrace in summer.

at Ekeren *North : 11 km* C *Antwerpen* – ✉ *2180 Ekeren* :

De Mangerie, Kapelsesteenweg 471 (par ②) ☎ 0 3 605 26 26, *Fax 0 3 605 24 16,* – P. AE ⓓ ⓜⓒ VISA
closed Saturday lunch – **Meals** – 29 ♀.
• An attractive, "Louisiana"-style façade, a maritime-inspired interior design and a choice of traditional and seasonal dishes. Mezzanine and terraces.

Environs

at Aartselaar *South : 10 km – pop. 14 378 – ✉ 2630 Aartselaar* :

Kasteel Solhof without rest, Baron Van Ertbornstraat 116 ☎ 0 3 877 30 00, *info@solhof.be, Fax 0 3 877 31 31,* – TV P – 25-50. AE ⓜⓒ VISA. ✗
closed Christmas-New Year – ▭ 20 – **24 rm** 149/225.
• This impressive mansion surrounded by water and greenery south of Antwerp has a number of outbuildings and a terrace overlooking a public park. Quiet, well-appointed rooms.

at Boechout *Southeast : 9 km – pop. 11 886 – ✉ 2530 Boechout* :

De Schone van Boskoop (Keersmaekers), Appelkantstraat 10 ☎ 0 3 454 19 31, *deschonevanboskoop@skynet.be, Fax 0 3 454 02 10,* – ▤ P. AE ⓓ ⓜⓒ VISA. ✗
closed Easter week, last 3 weeks August, Christmas-New Year, Sunday and Monday – **Meals**. *Lunch 45* – a la carte 70/132 ♀.
• A noteworthy restaurant with an artistic and contemporary interior design. Personalised menu with astute suggestions. Lake and statue-adorned terrace. Reservation essential.
Spec. Trois préparations de thon (Spring-Summer). Tête de veau tiède et sauce tartare. Ris de veau et son boudin truffé, sauce aux truffes.

at Edegem *Southeast : 5 km – pop. 22 024 – ✉ 2650 Edegem :*

Ter Elst, Terelststraat 310 (by Prins Boudewijnlaan) ☎ 0 3 450 90 00, *info@terelst.be, Fax 0 3 450 90 90*, ... 25-500. AE ① MC VISA.
Meals **Couvert Classique** *(closed July-14 August, 24, 25 and 31 December and 1 January)* Lunch 35 – a la carte 45/56 – ☕ 17 – **53 rm** *(closed 24, 25 and 31 December and 1 January)* 120/135.
◆ In a slightly isolated location to the south of the city, Ter Elst is a hotel of recent design linked to a sports centre. Modern auditorium and large, simply furnished rooms. Neo-rustic-style dining room serving traditional fare. Attractive wine-list.

XX ✿ **La Cabane** (Vandersteen), Mechelsesteenweg 11 ☎ 0 3 454 58 98, *restaurantlacabane@skynet.be, Fax 0 3 455 34 26* – AE ① MC VISA.
closed 1 week Easter, 19 July-8 August, 24 December-5 January, Saturday lunch, Sunday and Monday – **Meals**. Lunch 35 – 42/80 b.i., – a la carte 46/70 ♀.
◆ Modern interior décor, refined cuisine flirting with modern trends, a lunch menu with good choice and a well-stocked cellar. An upmarket address, despite the name !
Spec. Tempura d'anguille fumée, vinaigrette tiède verdurette (Summer). Ris de veau et concombre à l'aigre-doux, sauce au Madère. Baba au rhum, glace à la noix de coco.

at Kapellen *North : 15,5 km – pop. 25 612 – ✉ 2950 Kapellen :*

XXX ✿✿ **De Bellefleur** (Buytaert), Antwerpsesteenweg 253 ☎ 0 3 664 67 19, *Fax 0 3 665 02 01*, – P. AE ① MC VISA
closed July, Saturday lunch and Sunday – **Meals**. Lunch 55 b.i. – 90/110 b.i., – a la carte 107/210 ♀.
◆ This high-quality restaurant serves traditional cuisine prepared with a modern flourish. In summer, dine on the pretty veranda, surrounded by a flower-filled garden.
Spec. Navarin de sole aux chanterelles et truffes d'été (April-October). Cabillaud aux asperges et caviar. Grouse d'Écosse et gratin de figues, son jus au pur malt.

at Schoten *Northeast : 10 km – pop. 32 777 – ✉ 2900 Schoten :*

XXX **Kleine Barreel,** Bredabaan 1147 ☎ 0 3 645 85 84, *info@kleine-barreel.be, Fax 0 3 645 85 03* – P – 25-60. AE ① MC VISA JCB
Meals. Lunch 32 – 45/62 b.i. ♀.
◆ Known to everyone in the city, the Kleine Barreel attracts numerous business customers. The traditional menu, updated monthly, is enhanced by a good choice of seasonal dishes.

XX **Uilenspiegel,** Brechtsebaan 277 (3 km on N 115) ☎ 0 3 651 61 45, *Fax 0 3 652 08 08*, – P – 25. AE MC VISA.
closed 16 February-4 March, 12 to 29 July, Tuesday and Wednesday – **Meals**. Lunch 20 – 29/66 b.i. ♀.
◆ This charming, thatch-roofed villa with a garden and terrace is the setting for this well-maintained restaurant where the focus is on a varied selection of classic dishes.

at Wijnegem *East : 10 km – pop. 8 717 – ✉ 2110 Wijnegem :*

XXX **Ter Vennen,** Merksemsebaan 278 ☎ 0 3 326 20 60, *tervennen@skynet.be, Fax 0 3 326 38 47*, – P – 50. AE ① MC VISA JCB.
closed 13 to 18 April, 26 July-8 August, 2 to 7 November, Sunday dinner and Monday – **Meals**. Lunch 44 b.i. – 35/45 b.i..
◆ A lovely farm hidden beneath an abundance of foliage, with a terrace and garden is the backdrop for this charming restaurant. A la mode cuisine, plus a well-developed cellar.

Kruiningen *Zeeland (Netherlands)* C *Reimerswaal pop. 20 831* 532 J 14 *and* 715 D 7 – *56 km.*

Le Manoir , Zandweg 2 (West : 1 km), ✉ 4416 NA, ☎ (0 113) 38 17 53, *info@interscaldes.nl, Fax (0 113) 38 17 63*, ... – P. AE ① MC VISA JCB
closed 18 to 26 October and first 2 weeks January – **Meals** see **Inter Scaldes** below – ☕ 21 – **10 rm** 180/200, – 2 suites.
◆ This large, thatch-roofed villa stands on a polder dotted with lovingly-maintained orchards, hedges, rose gardens and fruit trees. Ten comfortable rooms.

XXXX ✿✿ Inter Scaldes (Brevet) - Hotel Le Manoir, Zandweg 2 (West : 1 km), ✉ 4416 NA, ☎ (0 113) 38 17 53, *info@interscaldes.nl, Fax (0 113) 38 17 63*, – P. AE ① MC VISA JCB
closed 18 to 26 October, first 2 weeks January, Monday and Tuesday.
◆ Following a serious fire, the Inter Scaldes is scheduled to re-open in the spring.

BRUGES (BRUGGE) *8000 West-Vlaanderen* 533 E 15 *and* 716 C 2 – *pop. 116 836.*

See : *Procession of the Holy Blood★★★ (De Heilig Bloedprocessie) – Historic centre and canals★★★ (Historisch centrum en grachten) – Market Square★★ (Markt)* AU, *Belfry and Halles★★★ (Belfort en Hallen) ≤★★ from the top* AU – *Market-town★★ (Burg)* AU – *Basilica of the Holy Blood★ (Basiliek van het Heilig Bloed) : low Chapel★ or St. Basiles Chapel (beneden- of Basiliuskapel)* AU **B** – *Chimney of the "Brugse Vrije"★ in the Palace of the "Brugse Vrije"* AU **S** – *Rosery quay (Rozenhoedkaai) ≤★★* AU **63** – *Dijver ≤★★* AU – *St. Boniface bridge (Bonifatiusbrug) : site★★* AU – *Beguinage★★ (Begijnhof)* AV – *Trips on the canals★★★ (Boottocht)* AU – *Church of Our Lady★ (O.-L.-Vrouwekerk) : tower★★, statue of the Madonna★★, tombstone★★ of Mary of Burgundy★★* AV **N.**

Museums : Groeninge★★★ (Stedelijk Museum voor Schone Kunsten) AU – *Memling★★★ (St. John's Hospital)* AV – *Gruuthuse★ : bust of Charles the Fifth★ (borstbeeld van Karel-V)* AU **M**[1] – *Arentshuis★* AU **M**[4] – *Folklore★ (Museum voor Volkskunde)* DY **M**[2].

Envir : *Southwest : 10,5 km at Zedelgem : baptismal font★ in the St. Lawrence's church – Northeast : 7 km : Damme★.*

18 *Northeast : 7 km at Sijsele, Doornstraat 16* ☎ *0 50 35 35 72, Fax 0 50 35 89 25.*

Burg 11 ☎ *0 50 44 86 86, toerisme@brugge.be, Fax 0 50 44 86 00 and at railway station, Stationsplein – Tourist association of the province, Koning Albert I-laan 120,* ☎ *0 50 30 55 00, info@westtoer.be,* Fax 0 50 30 55 90.

Brussels 96 – Ghent 45 – Lille 72 – Ostend 28.

Plans on following pages

Town Centre

Crowne Plaza ⛭, Burg 10 ☎ 0 50 44 68 44, *hotel@crowne-plaza-brugge.com, Fax 0 50 44 68 68,* ≤, 🍴, **Lo**, ≘s, ⊠ – |‡| ⇔ ▤ TV ♿ ⇔ P – 🏛 25-400. AE ⓪ ⓪ VISA JCB. ✻ AU a

Meals ***Het Kapittel*** *(closed Wednesday dinner, Saturday lunch and Sunday)* Lunch 20 – 31/67 b.i. – ***De Linde*** Lunch 9 – 22/32 b.i. – ☕ 19 – **93 rm** 226/270, – 3 suites.

◆ The Crowne Plaza offers a quiet base and high levels of comfort on Burg Square. The basement contains important vestiges and objects from medieval times. Gastronomic fare in the 't Kapittel restaurant. The De Linde doubles as a buffet-lunch venue and tea room.

de tuilerieën without rest, Dijver 7 ☎ 0 50 34 36 91, *info@hoteltuilerieen.com, Fax 0 50 34 04 00,* ≤, ≘s, ⊠, 🚲 – |‡| ▤ TV P – 🏛 25-45. AE ⓪ ⓪ VISA JCB AU c

☕ 24 – **43 rm** 286/390, – 2 suites.

◆ An elegant 17C residence lining one of the picturesque canals in the centre of Bruges is home to this refined hotel with its neat, well-appointed rooms.

Relais Oud Huis Amsterdam ⛭ without rest, Spiegelrei 3 ☎ 0 50 34 18 10, *info@oha.be, Fax 0 50 33 88 91,* ≤, 🌳 – |‡| ⇔ ▤ TV ⇔ – 🏛 25. AE ⓪ ⓪ VISA JCB

☕ 20 – **32 rm** 198/238, – 2 suites. AT d

◆ This former 17C Dutch trading centre along the banks of a canal has been transformed into a charming hotel with rooms offering pleasant views. Locked garage 300m/330yd away.

de orangerie ⛭ without rest, Kartuizerinnenstraat 10 ☎ 0 50 34 16 49, *info@hotelorangerie.com, Fax 0 50 33 30 16,* 🚲 – |‡| ▤ TV ♿ ⇔ P. AE ⓪ ⓪ VISA JCB AU e

☕ 24 – **19 rm** 233/312, – 1 suite.

◆ A quiet hotel in an old house bordering a delightful canal overlooked by four of the hotel's rooms. Period furniture, plus a charming patio and terrace by the water's edge.

Die Swaene ⛭, Steenhouwersdijk 1 ☎ 0 50 34 27 98, *info@dieswaene-hotel.com, Fax 0 50 33 66 74,* ≤, **Lo**, ≘s, ⊠ – |‡|, ▤ rm, TV P – 🏛 30. AE ⓪ ⓪ VISA JCB AU p

Meals *(closed 2 weeks July, 2 weeks January, Wednesday and Thursday lunch).* Lunch 40 – 55/99 b.i. 🍷 – ☕ 18 – **30 rm** 185/295, – 2 suites.

◆ Lovers of period furniture will enjoy staying at this peaceful hotel full of character with views of one of the city's canals. The 22 bedrooms, romantic to a fault, are all individually furnished. Cosy, intimate ambience in the gastronomic restaurant.

Sofitel, Boeveriestraat 2 ☎ 0 50 44 97 11, *H1278@accor-hotels.com, Fax 0 50 44 97 99,* **Lo**, ⊠, 🌳 – |‡| ⇔ ▤ TV – 🏛 25-150. AE ⓪ ⓪ VISA JCB CZ b

Meals ***Ter Boeverie*** Lunch 30 b.i. – 40 b.i./57 b.i. – ☕ 19 – **151 rm** 218.

◆ This attractive, centrally located hotel overlooks a large square. Spacious, pleasantly refurbished rooms furnished in a variety of styles. The restaurant's repertoire is extensive, covering standard fare, traditional dishes and a choice of vegetarian options.

Acacia ⛭ without rest, Korte Zilverstraat 3a ☎ 0 50 34 44 11, *info@hotel-acacia.com, Fax 0 50 33 88 17,* ≘s, ⊠ – |‡| ⇔ ▤ TV ⇔ P – 🏛 25-40. AE ⓪ ⓪ VISA JCB. ✻

closed 4 to 22 January – **46 rm** ☕ 130/190, – 2 suites. AU n

◆ Within a few yards of the Grand-Place, the Acacia is characterised by its impeccable appearance and the elegance of its furnishings. Spacious rooms, some split-level.

de' Medici ⛭, Potterierei 15 ☎ 0 50 33 98 33, *reservation@hoteldemedici.com, Fax 0 50 33 07 64,* **Lo**, ≘s, 🌳 – |‡| ⇔ ▤ TV ♿ ⇔ – 🏛 25-180. AE ⓪ ⓪ VISA JCB. ✻ CX g

Meals see rest ***Koto*** below – **81 rm** ☕ 174/209.

◆ A modern construction built away from the centre, facing a canal. A contemporary interior, with large, well-appointed rooms. Small Japanese garden.

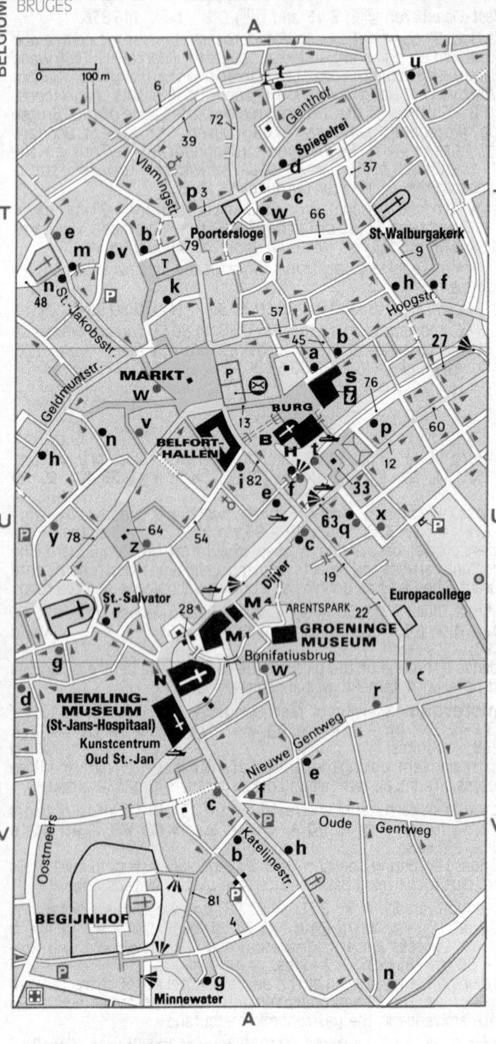

Street	Grid	No.	Street	Grid	No.
Academiestr.	AT	3	Mallebergpl.	ATU	45
Arsenaalstr.	AV	4	Moerstr.	CY, AT	48
Augustijnenrei	AT	6	Noordzandstr.	CY	49
Bloedput	BY	7	Noorweegsekaai	DX	51
Boomgaardstr.	AT	9	Oude Burg	AU	54
Braambergstr.	AU	12	Philipstockstr.	AT	57
Breidelstr.	AU	13	Predikherenstr.	AU	60
Eekhoutstr.	AU	19	Rolweg	DX	61
Garenmarkt	AU	22	Rozenhoedkaai	AU	63
Geldmunstr.	AU		Simon Stevinpl.	AU	64
Gistelsesteenweg	BZ	24	Sint-Jansstr.	AT	66
Gloribusstr.	CZ	25	Spanjaardstr.	AT	72
Groene Rei	ATU	27	Steenhouwersdijk	AU	76
Gruuthusestr.	AU	28	Steenstr.	AU	78
Huidenvetterspl.	AU	33	Vlamingstr.	AT	79
Koningstr.	AT	37	Wijngaardstr.	AV	81
Kortewinkel	AT	39	Wollestr.	AU	82
Maalse-steenweg	DY	43	Zuidzandstr.	CY	84
			Zwarte Leertouwersstr.	DY	85

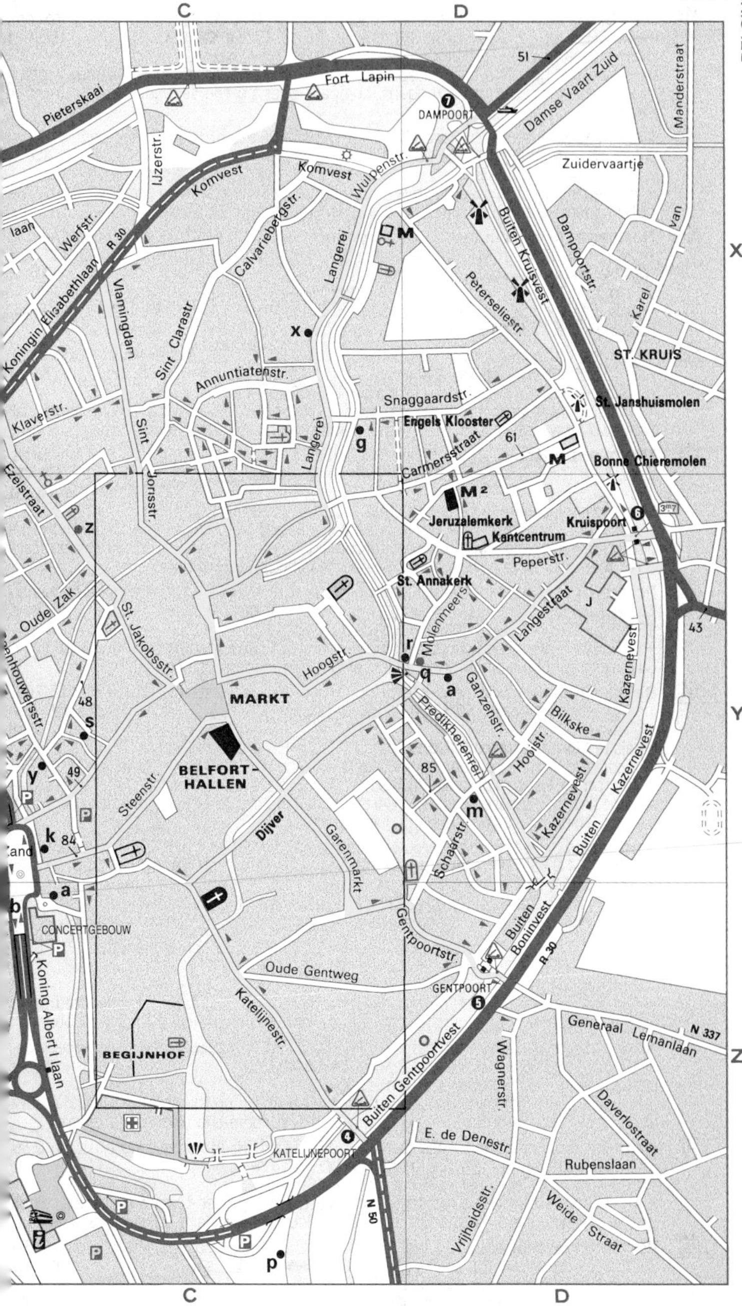

C D
X
Y
Z
Pieterskaai
Fort Lapin
DAMPOORT
Damse Vaart Zuid
Manderstraat
Zuidervaartje
Komvest
Wulpenstr.
IJzerstr.
Calvariebergstr.
Langerei
Buiten Kruisvest
Dampoortstr.
Van
Karel
Peterseliestr.
Werfstr.
R 30
Koningin Elisabethlaan
Vlamingdam
Sint Clarastr
Annuntiatenstr.
Snaggaardstr.
ST. KRUIS
St. Janshuismolen
Engels Klooster
Carmersstraat
Bonne Chieremolen
Klaverstr.
Sint Jorisstr.
M²
Jeruzalemkerk
Kruispoort
Kantcentrum
Peperstr.
Ezelstraat
St. Annakerk
Langestraat
Oude Zak
St. Jakobsstr.
Molenmeers
Hoogstr.
Kazernevest
MARKT
Ganzenstr.
Bilkske
Predikherenrei
Hooistr
BELFORT-HALLEN
Steenstr.
Dijver
Garenmarkt
Schaarstr.
Buiten Kazernevest
CONCERTGEBOUW
Gentpoortstr.
Buiten Boninvest
Koning Albert I laan
Oude Gentweg
GENTPOORT
Katelijnestr.
Generaal Lemanlaan
N 337
Buiten Gentpoortvest
Wagnerstr.
BEGIJNHOF
Daverlostraat
E. de Denestr.
KATELIJNEPOORT
Rubenslaan
N 50
Vrijheidsstr.
Weide Straat
C D

Jan Brito without rest, Freren Fonteinstraat 1 ☎ 0 50 33 06 01, *info@janbrito.com, Fax 0 50 33 06 52,* – – 25-40. AE VISA JCB AU j
19 rm 109/220, – 3 suites.
• Behind the hotel's typical façade are two floors - the larger, more luxurious rooms are on the first, the more modern, compact ones on the second. 16C-18C interior decor.

Pandhotel without rest, Pandreitje 16 ☎ 0 50 34 06 66, *info@pandhotel.com, Fax 0 50 34 05 56* – . AE VISA JCB AU q
20 – **24 rm** 135/230.
• An elegant hotel, spread out over three houses with character in the city centre. The hotel's rooms and junior suites have all been furnished with a keen, aesthetic eye.

Heritage without rest, N. Desparsstraat 11 ☎ 0 50 44 44 44, *info@hotel-heritage.com, Fax 0 50 44 44 40,* , , – . AE VISA JCB. AT k
24 rm 125/218.
• This majestic 19C residence between the Grand-Place and the theatre is now a comfortable hotel with a hushed ambience. Attractive 14C cellar with fitness facilities.

Walburg without rest, Boomgaardstraat 13 ☎ 0 50 34 94 14, *hotelwalburg@skynet.be, Fax 0 50 33 68 84* – – 30. AE VISA JCB. AT f
closed 5 January-5 February – **12 rm** 130/200, – 1 suite.
• Imposing neo-Classical architecture, with an old entrance leading to a monumental hall with two lofty galleries adorned with columns and balustrades. "King-size" rooms.

Novotel Centrum , Katelijnestraat 65b ☎ 0 50 33 75 33, *H1033@accor-hotels.com, Fax 0 50 33 65 56,* , , – – 50-400. AE VISA JCB AV h
Meals (dinner only) a la carte 27/36 – 14 – **126 rm** 122/139.
• A modern chain hotel near the Beguine convent and Memling Museum. Recently refurbished standard rooms with good soundproofing. Pleasant lobby-bar. The restaurant offers a full menu for dinner, with a much-restricted choice at lunchtime.

Prinsenhof without rest, Ontvangersstraat 9 ☎ 0 50 34 26 90, *info@prinsenhof.com, Fax 0 50 34 23 21* – . AE VISA JCB CY s
16 rm 128/278.
• This small, refined and welcoming hotel occupies a renovated mansion away from the busy centre. Rooms of differing styles, all offering modern comforts.

De Castillion (annex Het Gheestelic Hof - 14 rm), Heilige Geeststraat 1 ☎ 0 50 34 30 01, *info@castillion.be, Fax 0 50 33 94 75,* – rm, – 25-50. AE VISA JCB. rest AU r
Meals *le Manoir Quatre Saisons* *(closed 25 July-13 August and Sunday dinner and lunch Monday and Tuesday except Bank Holidays)* Lunch 35 – 45/87 b.i. – **20 rm** 150/325.
• The former bishop's palace (1743) is now home to this quite charming hotel with crow-step gables, personalised rooms, an Art Deco lounge and an attractive inner courtyard. Modern dining room, furnished in Louis XVI style.

Montanus without rest, Nieuwe Gentweg 78 ☎ 0 50 33 11 76, *info@montanus.be, Fax 0 50 34 09 38,* , – – 40. AE VISA JCB AV e
24 rm 120/235.
• A charming hotel recently established in a mansion to the south of the main sights of interest. Half of the stylish rooms overlook the garden and English-style pavilion.

Aragon without rest, Naaldenstraat 22 ☎ 0 50 33 35 33, *info@aragon.be, Fax 0 50 34 28 05* – – 25. AE VISA JCB. AT v
42 rm 120/172.
• A feeling of warmth pervades this hotel occupying two completely renovated town houses. Modern comforts in the cosy, soundproofed rooms. Pleasant bar and lounge.

Adornes without rest, St-Annarei 26 ☎ 0 50 34 13 36, *hotel.adornes@proximedia.be, Fax 0 50 34 20 85,* <, – . AE VISA AT u
closed January-12 February – **20 rm** 90/120.
• Four attractive adjoining houses with canal views make up this small, quiet and meticulous hotel. Good bedrooms, a welcoming breakfast room and old vaulted cellars.

Azalea without rest, Wulfhagestraat 43 ☎ 0 50 33 14 78, *info@azaleahotel.be, Fax 0 50 33 97 00,* – . AE VISA JCB CY y
closed 20 to 27 December – **25 rm** 122/160.
• An old house, formerly a brasserie, with an attractive garden-terrace that adds colour to the adjoining canal. Neat and tidy rooms, a lounge-library and a friendly ambience.

Portinari without rest, 't Zand 15 ☎ 0 50 34 10 34, *info@portinari.be, Fax 0 50 34 41 80* – – 25-80. AE VISA JCB CY k
closed 4 to 30 January – **40 rm** 120/150.
• The Potinari's functional rooms have been refurbished ; those to the rear are generally quieter. A large sheltered terrace looks out onto the 't Zand.

Navarra without rest, St-Jakobsstraat 41 ☎ 0 50 34 05 61, *reservations@hotelnavarra.com, Fax 0 50 33 67 90*, – 25-110. AE VISA JCB. AT n
87 rm 130/156.
◆ The spirit of the consul of Navarra - laid to rest in the nearby church - still haunts this hotel. Sober rooms, jazz bar, terrace and garden.

Parkhotel without rest, Vrijdagmarkt 5 ☎ 0 50 33 33 64, *info@parkhotel-brugge.be, Fax 0 50 33 47 63* – – 25-250. AE VISA CY j
86 rm 125/150.
◆ This popular group hotel has three categories of rooms, almost all of which have been refurbished. The breakfast room is crowned by a pyramidal glass roof.

Karos without rest, Hoefijzerlaan 37 ☎ 0 50 34 14 48, *hotel.karos@compaqnet.be, Fax 0 50 34 00 91*, – AE VISA BY f
closed 2 January-1 February – **54 rm** 65/125.
◆ A hotel with a half-timbered façade along the city's ring road. Indoor pool, plus a pleasant lounge decorated with birdcages. Sober rooms, with the better ones in the attic.

Ter Duinen without rest, Langerei 52 ☎ 0 50 33 04 37, *info@terduinenhotel.be, Fax 0 50 34 42 16*, – . AE VISA JCB. CX x
20 rm 98/149.
◆ By the Langerei canal, in a peaceful location away from the centre. A friendly welcome and rooms with a veranda or patio and views of the canal or garden. Good breakfast.

Flanders without rest, Langestraat 38 ☎ 0 50 33 88 89, *info@flandershotel.be, Fax 0 50 33 93 45*, – . AE VISA. DY a
closed 5 to 29 January – **39 rm** 115/175.
◆ A green façade is the main feature of this building dating from 1910. The renovated rooms, to the rear, are compact but quiet. Small inner courtyard with water feature.

Gd H. Oude Burg without rest, Oude Burg 5 ☎ 0 50 44 51 11, *grandhotel.oudeburg@skynet.be, Fax 0 50 44 51 00*, – – 25-160. AE VISA. AU i
138 rm 150/170.
◆ This modern building in the shadow of the belfry has 138 well-appointed, medium-sized rooms and good conference facilities. The versatile dining room covers a whole range of cuisine from French, Italian, Flemish and Dutch to Asian dishes.

Dante without rest, Coupure 30 ☎ 0 50 34 01 94, *info@hoteldante.be, Fax 0 50 34 35 39*, – . AE VISA. DY m
30 rm 116/131.
◆ The modern Dante stands along the banks of a canal, overlooking a lock. Functional rooms of similar design with a spacious feel and good soundproofing.

Academie without rest, Wijngaardstraat 7 ☎ 0 50 33 22 66, *info@hotelacademie.be, Fax 0 50 33 21 66* – . AE VISA AV b
74 rm 140/160.
◆ This practical option is close to the Lac d'Amour and the Begijnhof. A pleasant patio, new rooms with modern furniture and a lounge blending the classic and contemporary.

Hans Memling without rest, Kuipersstraat 18 ☎ 0 50 47 12 12, *hotel.memling@grouptorus.com, Fax 0 50 47 12 10* – – 25. AE VISA JCB. AT b
36 rm 161/173.
◆ A town mansion near the Grand-Place and theatre offering brightly decorated rooms of uniform comfort and varying size. Bar-lounge and a wall-enclosed terrace.

Ter Brughe without rest, Oost-Gistelhof 2 ☎ 0 50 34 03 24, *info@hotelterbrughe.com, Fax 0 50 33 88 73* – . AE VISA AT a
46 rm 100/175.
◆ A late-Gothic-style residence just a few yards from the Speelmansrei Canal. Plain, but individually furnished rooms. Breakfast served in the original vaulted cellars.

Bryghia without rest, Oosterlingenplein 4 ☎ 0 50 33 80 59, *info@bryghiahotel.be, Fax 0 50 34 14 30* – . AE VISA JCB. AT t
closed 19 December-17 February – **18 rm** 67/135.
◆ On a quiet square near a small bridge over the Speelmansrei Canal, this compact hotel has an attractive 15C façade and medium-sized rooms furnished in modern style.

Anselmus without rest, Ridderstraat 15 ☎ 0 50 34 13 74, *info@anselmus.be, Fax 0 50 34 19 16* – . AE VISA. AT h
closed January – **7 rm** 76/101.
◆ Close to the Markt and the Burg, the hotel's main entrance opens onto a quite charming lounge. Classically furnished bedrooms.

Relais Bourgondisch Cruyce without rest, Wollestraat 41 ☎ 0 50 33 79 26, *bour.cruyce@ssi.be, Fax 0 50 34 19 68*, canals and old Flemish houses – . AE VISA
16 rm 118/128. AU f
◆ The timber-framed façade provides a unique view of canals lined by old Flemish houses. Pleasant guest rooms.

Egmond without rest, Minnewater 15 (by Katelijnestraat) 0 50 34 14 45, *info@egmond.be, Fax 0 50 34 29 40,* ≤, – TV P. AV g
closed 4 January-15 February – **8 rm** 112/120.
◆ This charming early-20C residence near the Lac d'Amour was formerly the office of a notary public. The bedrooms overlook a peaceful garden. Access can be a problem.

Biskajer without rest, Biskajersplein 4 0 50 34 15 06, *info@hotelbiskajer.com, Fax 0 50 34 39 11* – TV. AE MC VISA AT w
17 rm 101/118.
◆ This small, well-kept hotel is situated along the Spiegelrei Canal, in a relatively quiet district just 5 minutes from the centre. Basic but perfectly comfortable rooms.

't Putje (annex - 13 rm), 't Zand 31 0 50 33 28 47, *hotelputje@pandora.be, Fax 0 50 34 14 23,* – TV. AE MC VISA CZ a
Meals (pub rest, open until 11 p.m.). Lunch 10 – 30/42 b.i. – **25 rm** 80/105.
◆ At the entrance to the old city, near the 't Zand. The hotel's rooms are welcoming and modern but with varying levels of soundproofing. Limited services. Public parking. Refined, contemporary tavern, plus a more intimate restaurant. Front terrace in summer.

ter Reien without rest, Langestraat 1 0 50 34 91 00, *hotel.ter.reien@online.be, Fax 0 50 34 40 48* – TV. AE MC VISA. DY r
closed January – **23 rm** 70/85.
◆ A waterfront hotel with smallish rooms, with the exception of the bridal suite. A dozen or so rooms enjoy views of the canal.

Bourgoensch Hof, Wollestraat 39 0 50 33 16 45, *info@bourgoensch-hof.be, Fax 0 50 34 63 78,* ≤ canals and old Flemish houses, – TV. MC VISA. rm
closed 6 January-15 February – **Meals** *(closed Thursday).* Lunch 25 – a la carte 28/36 – **23 rm** 117. AU f
◆ This old Flemish house overlooks one of Bruges' most beautiful canals, which is visible from some of the hotel's rooms. Reasonable comfort. Bistro-style restaurant serving a range of local specialities, plus a popular terrace during the summer months.

Gd H. du Sablon, Noordzandstraat 21 0 50 33 39 02, *info@sablon.be, Fax 0 50 33 39 08* – TV – 25-100. AE MC VISA. rest AU h
Meals (residents only) – **36 rm** 89/110.
◆ An old inn halfway between St-Sauveur Cathedral and the Grand-Place. The entrance hall, dating from 1900, is crowned by an Art Deco dome. Refurbished, soundproofed rooms.

De Barge, Bargeweg 15 0 50 38 51 50, *info@debargehotel.com, Fax 0 50 38 21 25,* – TV P. AE MC VISA. rm CZ p
Meals *(closed 19 December-10 February, 4 to 19 July, Sunday and Monday)* (dinner only) a la carte 32/80 – **22 rm** *(closed 19 December-10 February)* 92/140.
◆ This old barge moored on the canal linking Bruges with Ghent has been converted into a small floating hotel with guest "cabins" brightly decorated in nautical style. As you would expect, the cuisine at the captain's table is influenced by the sea.

Boterhuis, St-Jakobsstraat 38 0 50 34 15 11, *boterhuis@pandora.be, Fax 0 50 34 70 89* – TV. AE MC VISA JCB AT m
Meals *(closed Sunday dinner All Saints and Easter)* (open until 11 p.m.). Lunch 14 – a la carte 24/35 – **8 rm** 65/93.
◆ This old hotel within a few hundred yards of the Markt is crowned by a small tower which houses the hotel's best two rooms, accessible via a spiral staircase.

Malleberg without rest, Hoogstraat 7 0 50 34 41 11, *hotel@malleberg.be, Fax 0 50 34 67 69* – TV. AE MC VISA. ATU b
8 rm 70/94.
◆ The bedrooms of this small hotel just off the Place du Bourg are furnished in plain, modern style. The vaulted cellar now serves as the breakfast room.

De Karmeliet (Van Hecke), Langestraat 19 0 50 33 82 59, *Fax 0 50 33 10 11,* – P. AE MC VISA JCB. DY q
closed 17 June-15 July, 3 to 14 October, first 2 weeks January, Tuesday lunch and Sunday dinner October-May, Sunday lunch June-September and Monday – **Meals**. Lunch 50 – 90/220 b.i., – a la carte 97/160
◆ This temple of gastronomy is adorned with an enclosed internal terrace and numerous works of modern art. Stupendous cuisine that will satisfy the most demanding tastebuds.
Spec. Tuile sucrée-salée aux grosses langoustines rôties. Dos de gros turbot piqué au jambon, sabayon de pommes de terre aux crevettes de Zeebrugge (April-October). Ravioli à la vanille et pommes caramélisées en chaud-froid.

De Snippe with rm, Nieuwe Gentweg 53 0 50 33 70 70, *desnippe@pandora.be, Fax 0 50 33 76 62,* , – , rm, TV P. AE MC VISA AV r
Meals *(closed 18 January-12 February, Sunday and Monday lunch).* Lunch 38 – a la carte 51/104 – **9 rm** *(closed 18 January-12 February and Sunday November-April)* 145/275.
◆ An attractive 18C house is the setting for this highly rated restaurant with charming wall décor, innovative cuisine, superb wine-list, themed bedrooms and a shady terrace.

XXX **Den Braamberg,** Pandreitje 11 ☎ 0 50 33 73 70, *Fax 0 50 33 99 73* – AE ⓓ ⓜⓒ VISA AU q
closed 13 to 31 July, 1 to 10 January, Thursday and Sunday – **Meals**. *Lunch 31* – 45/89 b.i..
◆ A warm and friendly welcome is assured at this restaurant where the focus is on appetising traditional dishes. An antique four-poster bed serves as a "display table".

XXX **Den Gouden Harynck** (Serruys), Groeninge 25 ☎ 0 50 33 76 37, *goud.harynck@pandora.be, Fax 0 50 34 42 70* – P. AE ⓓ ⓜⓒ VISA AUV w
✿ *closed 1 week Easter, last 2 weeks July-first week August, last week December-first week January, Saturday lunch, Sunday and Monday* – **Meals**. *Lunch 50* – a la carte 67/91.
◆ The menu at this restaurant close to the city's main museums is both refined and inventive. Hushed atmosphere in the dining room. Pretty flower-decked courtyard in summer.
Spec. Langoustines braîsées au Vin Jaune et primeurs. Bar en croûte de sel parfumé de romarin. Pigeonneau à la fondue d'oignons et jus de truffes.

XXX **'t Pandreitje,** Pandreitje 6 ☎ 0 50 33 11 90, *info@pandreitje.be, Fax 0 50 34 00 70* – AE ⓓ ⓜⓒ VISA JCB AU x
closed 1 to 11 April, 4 to 21 July, 1 to 7 November, Wednesday and Sunday – **Meals**. *Lunch 40* – 55/110 b.i. ♀.
◆ The emphasis at this small restaurant housed in stylish, comfortable surroundings near the tourist centre is on luxury products and creative cuisine. Comprehensive wine-list.

XXX **Duc de Bourgogne** with rm, Huidenvettersplein 12 ☎ 0 50 33 20 38, *duc@ssi.be, Fax 0 50 34 40 37*, ≤ canals and typical houses – ▤ rest, TV. AE ⓓ ⓜⓒ VISA JCB AU t
closed 3 weeks July and January – **Meals** *(closed Monday and Tuesday lunch)*. *Lunch 36* – 58 ♀ – **10 rm** ☕ 110/150.
◆ At the junction of the city's most picturesque canals, this rustic-style restaurant serving traditional cuisine is decorated with late Middle Ages-style wall paintings.

XX **De Lotteburg,** Goezeputstraat 43 ☎ 0 50 33 75 35, *lotteburg@pi.be, Fax 0 50 33 04 04*, 🍽, Seafood – ▤. AE ⓓ ⓜⓒ VISA JCB. ✂ AV d
closed 28 July-12 August, 6 to 28 January, Monday, Tuesday and Saturday lunch – **Meals**. *Lunch 30* – 45/87 b.i. ♀.
◆ A delightful shady terrace adorned with teak furniture is hidden behind the restaurant's white façade and blue shutters. The culinary focus here is resolutely seaward.

XX **Patrick Devos,** Zilverstraat 41 ☎ 0 50 33 55 66, *info@patrickdevos.be, Fax 0 50 33 58 67*, 🍽 – P. AE ⓓ ⓜⓒ VISA JCB AU y
closed 18 July-9 August, 26 to 30 December, Saturday lunch, Sunday and Bank Holidays – **Meals**. *Lunch 37* – 55/66 ♀.
◆ Features of note in this restored old mansion include a Louis XVI lounge, Art Nouveau decor in the dining room and a pleasing patio. Contemporary cuisine.

XX **'t Stil Ende,** Scheepsdalelaan 12 ☎ 0 50 33 92 03, *stilende@skynet.be, Fax 0 50 33 26 22*, 🍽 – ▤. ⓜⓒ VISA BX a
closed carnival week, last 2 weeks July, All Saints, Saturday lunch, Sunday and Monday – **Meals** – 30/80 b.i..
◆ An address worth hunting down away from the main tourist haunts. Contemporary interior design, an extraordinary wine-cooling system, tasty menus and a summer terrace.

XX **Hermitage,** Ezelstraat 18 ☎ 0 50 34 41 73, *restaurant-hermitage@planetinternet.be, Fax 0 50 34 14 75* – AE ⓓ ⓜⓒ VISA JCB CY z
closed 1 week June, 1 week October, 1 week January, Sunday dinner and Monday – **Meals**. *Lunch 23* – a la carte 47/61.
◆ 1620 is the date embossed on the gable of this elegant, tastefully decorated restaurant, embellished with the odd antique. Standard à la carte choices with a modern flourish.

XX **De Florentijnen,** Academiestraat 1 ☎ 0 50 67 75 33, *info@deflorentijnen.be, Fax 0 50 67 75 33* – 25-60. AE ⓜⓒ VISA AT p
closed 18 July-4 August, 14 to 24 November, 1 to 15 January, Sunday except Bank Holidays and Monday – **Meals**. *Lunch 30* – 45/65 b.i..
◆ This spacious restaurant is housed in a former Florentine trading building, hence the name. The modern cuisine is matched by the contemporary-style interior design.

XX **Kardinaalshof,** St-Salvatorskerkhof 14 ☎ 0 50 34 16 91, *Fax 0 50 34 20 62* – AE ⓓ ⓜⓒ VISA AUV g
closed first 2 weeks July, Wednesday and Thursday lunch – **Meals** – 35/83 b.i..
◆ Fish and seafood are the prominent features within the walls of this building with its distinctive Baroque-style façade close to the Markt. Cosy ambience.

XX **Den Dijver,** Dijver 5 ✆ 0 50 33 60 69, *dijver@busmail.net, Fax 0 50 34 10 64,* 🏠, Beer cuisine – AE MC VISA AU c
closed Wednesday and Thursday lunch – **Meals**. *Lunch 30* – 39/67 b.i..
◆ A must for beer-lovers, where the cuisine is inspired by Belgium's favourite drink. A friendly ambience, in which each dish is best accompanied by a glass of the frothy stuff !

XX **Tanuki,** Oude Gentweg 1 ✆ 0 50 34 75 12, *Fax 0 50 33 82 42*, Japanese cuisine with Teppan-Yaki and Sushi-bar – ▤. AE MC VISA JCB AV f
closed 1 week carnival, 2 weeks July, 1 week All Saints, Monday and Tuesday – **Meals**. *Lunch 15* – 59.
◆ One of the few Japanese restaurants in Bruges. Authentic cuisine, including an impressive Teppan-Yaki menu and a sushi bar. Typical Oriental décor.

XX **Aneth,** Maria van Bourgondiëlaan 1 (behind the Graaf Visart park) ✆ 0 50 31 11 89, *info@aneth.be, Fax 0 50 32 36 46*, Seafood – AE ⓓ MC VISA JCB BY g
closed first 2 weeks January, Saturday lunch, Sunday and Monday – **Meals**. *Lunch 40* – 60/95 b.i. 𝕐.
◆ The Aneth occupies an early-20C villa opposite a canal and public park, where fish and seafood takes centre-stage. Easy parking.

XX **Spinola,** Spinolarei 1 ✆ 0 50 34 17 85, *spinola@pandora.be, Fax 0 50 34 13 71,* 🏠 – ▤. ⓓ MC VISA AT c
closed last week January-first week February, last week June-first week July, Sunday and Monday – **Meals**. *Lunch 38* – 46.
◆ A pleasant, rustic-style restaurant near the Spiegelrei Canal and statue of Jan Van Eyck. The mouth-watering choice of dishes is complemented by a comprehensive wine-list.

XX **'t Zwaantje,** Gentpoortvest 70 ✆ 0 50 34 38 85, *hetzwaantje@skynet.be, Fax 0 50 34 97 10,* 🏠 – MC VISA AV n
closed Wednesday, Thursday and lunch Friday and Saturday – **Meals** – 38 𝕐.
◆ Three small swans (zwaantjes) enliven the front of this charming restaurant with a veranda, rear terrace, romantic atmosphere and a menu inspired by current culinary trends.

X **Bhavani,** Simon Stevinplein 5 ✆ 0 50 33 90 25, *info@bhavani.be, Fax 0 50 34 89 52,* 🏠, Indian cuisine – AE ⓓ MC VISA. ✗ AU z
Meals. *Lunch 16* – a la carte 35/46.
◆ If you're tempted by some typical Indian cuisine while visiting the city, head for Place Simon Stevin, where the Bhavani offers a good choice, including vegetarian options.

X **Kurt's pan,** St-Jakobsstraat 58 ✆ 0 50 34 12 24, *kurt.vandaele@planetinternet.be, Fax 0 50 49 11 97* – ▤. AE MC VISA AT e
closed last week October and Monday – **Meals**. *Lunch 13* – 45 bc/60 b.i.
◆ A simply furnished, family-run restaurant with a rustic feel in a small Flemish-style house near St-Jacob's Church. A varied choice of typical dishes.

X **Koto** - Hotel de' Medici, Potterierei 15 ✆ 0 50 44 31 31, *koto@hoteldemedici.com, Fax 0 50 33 07 64*, Japanese cuisine with Teppan-Yaki – P. AE ⓓ MC VISA JCB. ✗ CX g
closed 3 to 18 January, Monday and lunch Tuesday and Wednesday – **Meals**. *Lunch 24* – 42/77 b.i. 𝕐.
◆ The Hotel de' Medici's Japanese restaurant has developed a loyal following for its Teppan-Yaki, sushi and sashimi. Modern décor showing Oriental influence.

X **Cafedraal,** Zilverstraat 38 ✆ 0 50 34 08 45, *Fax 0 50 33 52 41,* 🏠 – AE ⓓ MC VISA JCB AU s
closed Sunday and Monday – **Meals**. *Lunch 10* – a la carte 35/88.
◆ The engaging menu at this lively brasserie occupying a charming historic building is certain to satisfy its hungry customers. "Cuban" bar and an attractive interior terrace.

X **Huyze Die Maene,** Markt 17 ✆ 0 50 33 39 59, *huyzediemaene@pandora.be, Fax 0 50 33 44 60,* 🏠, Pub rest – ▤. AE ⓓ MC VISA AU w
closed February – **Meals**. *Lunch 13* – 22/31.
◆ The success of this tavern-restaurant is due to its fabulous location on the Markt, its attractive façade, brasserie atmosphere and appealing menu with daily specials.

Suburbs

Northwest : *5 km* – ✉ *8000* :

XXX **De gouden Korenhalm,** Oude Oostendsesteenweg 79a (Sint-Pieters) ✆ 0 50 31 33 93, *info@degoudenkorenhalm.be, Fax 0 50 31 18 96,* 🏠 – P. AE ⓓ MC VISA
closed late February-early March, late August-early September, Monday and Tuesday – **Meals**. *Lunch 31* – 40/71 b.i..
◆ This modern, Flemish-style building on the outskirts of the city has developed an enviable reputation for its varied menu of refined seasonal dishes. Quality French wine-list.

at Sint-Andries *Southwest : 4 km* 🄲 *Bruges* – ✉ *8200 Sint-Andries :*

Host. Pannenhuis ⛭, Zandstraat 2 ☎ 0 50 31 19 07, *hostellerie@pannenhuis.be, Fax 0 50 31 77 66,* – 🅿 – 25. AE MC VISA
Meals *(closed 1 to 22 July, 15 January-2 February, Tuesday dinner and Wednesday). Lunch 33* – 44/69 b.i. – **19 rm** *(closed 15 January-2 February)* 95/125.
◆ A quaint hostelry dating from the 1930s that has recently been refurbished. Quiet, spacious bedrooms. Relaxing summer terrace overlooking a delightful garden. The highly traditional menu includes several fish and lobster specialities.

Herborist (Hanbuckers) with rm, De Watermolen 15 (by ⑥ : 6 km, then on the right after E 40 - A 10) ☎ 0 50 38 76 00, *a.hanbuckers@aubergedeherborist.be, Fax 0 50 39 31 06,* – rest, 🅿 AE MC VISA.
closed 22 March-2 April, 21 June-2 July, 19 September-5 October, 19 to 31 December, Monday and dinner Thursday and Sunday – **Meals** (set menu only). *Lunch 49* – 68/107 b.i. – **4 rm** 93/140.
◆ Nestled in a rural setting, this inn has been restored with great taste. Original and promising à la carte and menu options, enhanced by a prestigious cellar.
Spec. Foie gras poêlé aux pommes de terre écrasées, vinaigrette de soja. Salade d'écrevisses, artichauts et vinaigrette à la tomate. Saint-Jacques et jambon de Parme au beurre de moules de bouchot (10 September-April).

at Sint-Kruis *East : 6 km* 🄲 *Bruges* – ✉ *8310 Sint-Kruis :*

Wilgenhof without rest, Polderstraat 151 ☎ 0 50 36 27 44, *info@hotel-wilgenhof.be, Fax 0 50 36 28 21,* – 🅿 AE MC VISA.
closed first 3 weeks January – **6 rm** 75/145.
◆ This charming small farm stands along the Damse Vaart canal, amid a landscape of open countryside and polders. Faultless rooms and a roaring log fire in the lounge in winter.

Ronnie Jonkman, Maalsesteenweg 438 (East : 2 km) ☎ 0 50 36 07 67, *Fax 0 50 35 76 96,* – 🅿 AE MC VISA JCB
closed 2 weeks May, 2 weeks October, Christmas-New Year, Sunday and Monday – **Meals** – 33/63 b.i..
◆ An attractive Flemish villa where the menu is contemporary, concise and based on the freshest products. Harmonious wine-list. Pleasant terraces with teak furniture.

at Sint-Michiels *South : 4 km* 🄲 *Bruges* – ✉ *8200 Sint-Michiels :*

Weinebrugge, Koning Albertlaan 242 ☎ 0 50 38 44 40, *weine-brugge@pi.be, Fax 0 50 39 35 63,* – 🅿 AE MC VISA.
closed last 2 weeks July and Tuesday – **Meals**. *Lunch 30* – 43.
◆ This comfortable restaurant, with a separate bar and lounge, occupies a Flemish villa on the edge of the Tillegem forest. Traditional cuisine with a modern flourish.

Casserole (Hotel school), Groene-Poortdreef 17 ☎ 0 50 40 30 30, *casserole@tergroenepoorte.be, Fax 0 50 40 30 35,* – 🅿 – 35. AE MC VISA
closed school holidays, Saturday and Sunday – **Meals** (lunch set menu only) 29/42 b.i..
◆ This restaurant is housed in a small farm in the middle of the country. Attractive country-style dining room, a menu that changes frequently and good, reasonably priced wines.

Environs

at Hertsberge *South by N 50 : 12,5 km* 🄲 *Oostkamp pop. 21 230* – ✉ *8020 Hertsberge :*

Manderley, Kruisstraat 13 ☎ 0 50 27 80 51, *manderley@pandora.be, Fax 0 50 27 80 51,* – 🅿 AE MC VISA
closed first 2 weeks October, 3 weeks January, Tuesday October-April, Sunday dinner and Monday – **Meals**. *Lunch 36* – 49/89 b.i.
◆ An old farm with a pleasant summer terrace overlooking a garden, a menu in tune with modern tastes and a large cellar. Roaring fires in winter.

at Varsenare *West : 6,5 km* 🄲 *Jabbeke pop. 13 692* – ✉ *8490 Varsenare :*

Manoir Stuivenberg (Scherrens brothers) with rm, Gistelsteenweg 27 ☎ 0 50 38 15 02, *info@manoirstuivenberg.be, Fax 0 50 38 28 92,* – rest, 🅿 – 25-300. AE MC VISA.
closed 19 July-5 August and 1 to 26 January – **Meals** *(closed Saturday lunch, Sunday dinner, Monday and Tuesday). Lunch 42* – 108 b.i., a la carte 76/102 – **8 rm** *(closed Sunday evening and Monday)* 124/162, – 1 suite.
◆ This chic manor house decorated with fine attention to detail is renowned for its modern take on traditional dishes and its attentive service.
Spec. Turbot braisé au citron et marmelade de tomates. Poitrine de pigeon en crapaudine. Gibier (in season).

at Waardamme *South by N 50 : 11 km* Ⓒ *Oostkamp pop. 21 230 – ✉ 8020 Waardamme :*

XX **Ter Talinge,** Rooiveldstraat 46 ✆ 0 50 27 90 61, *Fax 0 50 28 00 52,* 余 – P. AE MC VISA
closed 20 February-16 March, last week August-first week September, Wednesday, Thursday and dinner Monday and Tuesday – **Meals**. *Lunch 28* – a la carte 28/67 ♀.
◆ The teal (taling) has made its nest in this modern villa with a rustic-style interior and attractive terrace. Classic, traditional cuisine with a loyal band of regulars.

at Zedelgem *Southwest : 10,5 km – pop. 21 918 – ✉ 8210 Zedelgem :*

🏨 **Zuidwege,** Torhoutsesteenweg 128 ✆ 0 50 20 13 39, *angelo@zuidwege.be, Fax 0 50 20 17 39,* 余, 🚲 – ⇔, ▤ rm, TV P – 🏛 25. AE ⓓ MC VISA. ✂ rm
Meals *(closed first week July, Christmas holidays and Saturday)* (pub rest). *Lunch 10* – a la carte 22/41 – **20 rm** *(closed Christmas holidays)* ☕ 60/85.
◆ Located close to a main crossroads, the Zuidwege has 20 functional bedrooms with double-glazing. A well-maintained, modern hotel offering basic services. Buffet breakfast. Relaxed ambience in the restaurant.

XX **Ter Leepe,** Torhoutsesteenweg 168 ✆ 0 50 20 01 97, *Fax 0 50 20 88 54* – ▤ P – 🏛 220. AE ⓓ MC VISA
closed 20 July-4August, 15 to 25 January, Monday dinner, Wednesday and Sunday – **Meals**. *Lunch 38 b.i.* – 46/59 b.i..
◆ This villa is home to a restaurant with well-structured à la carte choices, a popular all-inclusive menu, and a selection of vintage wines. Banqueting room to the rear.

Kruishoutem *9770 Oost-Vlaanderen* 533 G 17 *and* 716 D 3 *– pop. 7 927 – 44 km.*

XXX ✿✿ **Hof van Cleve** (Goossens), Riemegemstraat 1 (near N 459, motorway E 17 - A 14, exit ⑥) ✆ 0 9 383 58 48, *vancleve@relaischateaux.com, Fax 0 9 383 77 25,* ≤, 余 – P. AE ⓓ MC VISA. ✂
closed 1 week Easter, 25 July-16 August, late December-early January, Sunday and Monday – **Meals**. *Lunch 60* – 95/185 b.i., – a la carte 96/189 ♀ 🍇.
◆ One of the musts of Belgian gastronomy with its inventive cuisine served in an elegant small farm with views overlooking a verdant valley.
Spec. Sot-l'y-laisse caramélisés et crevettes grises à la fondue de poireaux au gingembre et coulis de crustacés. Pigeonneau au lard croustillant, parmentière aux truffes et Banyuls. Crabe royal, caviar et mousseline de pommes de terre.

Waregem *8790 West-Vlaanderen* 533 F 17 *and* 716 D 3 *– pop. 35 954 – 47 km.*

XXXX ✿✿ **'t Oud Konijntje** (Mmes Desmedt), Bosstraat 53 (South : 2 km near E 17 - A 14) ✆ 0 56 60 19 37, *info@oudkonijntje.be, Fax 0 56 60 92 12,* 余 – ▤ P. AE ⓓ MC VISA
closed 1 week Easter, late July-early August, Christmas-New Year, Friday and dinner Thursday and Sunday – **Meals** – 75/145 b.i., – a la carte 79/140 ♀ 🍇.
◆ Pleasant interior décor, an enchanting terrace with a fountain, and a flower-filled garden in summer provide a scenic backdrop to this high-class starred restaurant.
Spec. Bouillon aux langoustines et morilles parfumé au basilic. Tronçon de turbot aux noisettes grillées et truffe (December-February). Pigeonneau rôti au romarin et mousseline de pommes de terre surprise.

Zeebrugge *West-Vlaanderen* Ⓒ *Brugge pop. 116 836* 533 E 14 *and* 716 C 1 *– ✉ 8380 Zeebrugge (Brugge) – 15 km.*

XX ✿✿ **'t Molentje** (Horseele), Baron de Maerelaan 211 (South : 2 km on N 31) ✆ 0 50 54 61 64, *molentje@pi.be, Fax 0 50 54 79 94,* 余 – P. AE MC VISA. ✂
closed 6 to 30 September, 1 to 19 January and Sunday except Easter – **Meals** (booking essential). *Lunch 42* – 130 b.i., a la carte 90/114.
◆ An isolated but attractive small farm accessible via the expressway to Bruges. Tastefully furnished, with cuisine that is both creative and refined. A formidable wine cellar.
Spec. Turbot au caviar d'Iran, sauce Champagne et ciboulette. Différentes préparations de coquilles Saint-Jacques. Gibier (in season).

Sluis *Zeeland (Netherlands)* 532 F 15 *and* 715 B 8 *– pop. 24 755 – 21 km.*

XXX ✿✿ **Oud Sluis** (Herman), Beestenmarkt 2, ✉ 4524 EA, ✆ (0 117) 46 12 69, *oudsluis@zeelandnet.nl, Fax (0 117) 46 30 05,* 余, Seafood – AE ⓓ MC VISA. ✂
closed first week April, 2 weeks June, 2 weeks October, last week December, Monday and Tuesday – **Meals**. *Lunch 45* – 63/85, – a la carte approx. 105 ♀ 🍇.
◆ This typical auberge fronting a lively small square is known for its refined, original cuisine where the emphasis is firmly on seafood. Efficient service.
Spec. 6 préparations d'huîtres de Zélande (September-April). Langoustines de trois façons (May-August). Filets de sole grillés et tempura d'anguilles régionales au jus de limon.

LIÈGE *4000* 533 S 19, 534 S 19 *and* 716 J 4 – *pop. 185 131.*

See : *Citadel* ≤ ★★ DW – *Cointe Park* ≤ ★ CX – *Old Town*★★ – *Palace of the Prince-Bishops*★ : *court of honour*★★ EY – *The Perron*★ *(market cross)* EY **A** – *Baptismal font*★★★ *of St. Bartholomew's church* FY – *Treasury*★★ *of St. Paul's Cathedral : reliquary of Charles the Bold*★★ EZ – *St. James church*★★ : *vaults of the nave*★★ EZ – *Altarpiece*★ *in the St. Denis church* EY – *Church of St. John : Wooden Calvary statues*★ EY – *Aquarium*★ FZ **D.**

Museums : Life in Wallonia★★ EY – *Religious and Roman Art Museum*★ FY **M**[5] – *Curtius and Glass Museum*★ : *evangelistary of Notger*★★★, *collection of glassware*★ FY **M**[1] – *Arms*★ FY **M**[3] – *Ansembourg*★ FY **M**[2] – *Modern Art and Contemporary Art*★ DX **M**[7].

Envir : *Northeast : 20 km : Blégny-Trembleur*★★ – *Southwest : 27 km : Baptismal font*★ *in the church*★ *of St. Severin – North : 17 km at Visé, Reliquary of St. Hadelin*★ *in the collegiate church.*

r. Bernalmont 2 ☎ *0 4 227 44 66, Fax 0 4 227 91 92* - *South : 8 km at Angleur, rte du Condroz 541* ☎ *0 4 366 20 21, Fax 0 4 337 20 26* - *Southeast : 18 km at Gomzé-Andoumont, Sur Counachamps, r. Gomzé 30* ☎ *0 4 360 92 07, Fax 0 4 360 92 06.*

☎ *0 4 342 52 14, Fax 0 4 229 27 33.*

En Féronstrée 92 ☎ *0 4 221 92 21, office.tourisme@liège.be, Fax 0 4 221 92 22 and Gare des Guillemins* ☎ *0 4 252 44 19 – Tourist association of the province, bd de la Sauvenière 77* ☎ *0 4 232 65 10, ftpl@ftpl.be, Fax 0 4 232 65 11.*

Brussels 97 – Amsterdam 242 – Antwerp 119 – Cologne 122 – Luxembourg 159 – Maastricht 32.

Plans on following pages

Bedford, quai St-Léonard 36 ☎ 0 4 228 81 11, *hotelbedfordlg@pophost.eunet.be, Fax 0 4 227 45 75,* – rm, – 25-240. AE MC VISA. DW **g**
Meals. *Lunch 25* – a la carte 23/39 – **147 rm** 210/235, – 2 suites.
◆ The Bedford occupies the site of a former convent on the banks of the Meuse. Pleasant, soundproofed rooms and an inner garden-terrace. The hotel dining room stands beneath an impressive 17C vaulted ceiling. Brasserie-style menu.

Jean-Marie Bouille, bd Frère Orban (Meuse-side setting) ☎ 0 4 252 13 21, *heliport_liege@msn.com, Fax 0 4 252 57 50,* ≤, – – 25 à 50. AE MC VISA CX **e**
closed 1 to 10 November, 1 to 12 January, Wednesday dinner, Saturday lunch and Sunday – **Meals**. *Lunch 35* – a la carte 50/74 ♀.
◆ A gastronomic restaurant along the river, near the Pont Albert 1er. Nautical ambience and an ambitious menu influenced by the sea. Sheltered terrace. Easy parking.

Old town

Mercure, bd de la Sauvenière 100 ☎ 0 4 221 77 11, *mercureliege@alliance-hospitality.com, Fax 0 4 221 77 01* – – 25-100. AE MC VISA EY **t**
Meals *(closed Saturday lunch and Sunday)* – a la carte 22/31 – **105 rm** 164/208.
◆ This recently renovated chain hotel enjoys a central location on one of the city's main boulevards, close to the lively "Le Carré". Quiet and comfortable rooms. The cuisine at the Bar à Thym brasserie shows a predilection for herbs and spices.

Au Vieux Liège, quai Goffe 41 ☎ 0 4 223 77 48, *Fax 0 4 223 78 60* – . AE MC VISA FY **a**
closed mid July-mid August, Wednesday dinner, Sunday and Bank Holidays – **Meals**. *Lunch 29* – 40/59 b.i..
◆ An attractive 16C residence with a rustic feel housing one of Liège's oldest restaurants. Conventional fare, occasionally enlivened by astute modern touches.

Max, pl. Verte 2 ☎ 0 4 222 08 59, *Fax 0 4 222 90 02,* , Seafood and oyster bar, open until 11 p.m. – – 25. AE MC VISA EY **a**
Meals. *Lunch 30* – a la carte 46/70.
◆ This elegant brasserie in the city centre has been decorated by Luc Genot. Its reputation is firmly rooted in its excellent fish and seafood. Oyster bar and heated terrace.

Folies Gourmandes, r. Clarisses 48 ☎ 0 4 223 16 44, – AE MC VISA EZ **q**
closed last 2 weeks April, Sunday dinner and Monday – **Meals** – 31/50 b.i. ♀.
◆ A small, family-run restaurant occupying an early-20C house with a garden terrace to the rear. Appetising fixed-menu choices and low-calorie options.

Septime, r. St-Paul 12 ☎ 0 4 221 03 06, *Fax 0 4 221 02 04,* Grill room – . AE MC VISA EZ **c**
Meals – a la carte 24/45.
◆ Along a busy pedestrianised street, overlooked by the cathedral. Interior décor of "raw concrete and mouse-colour velvet", a relaxed atmosphere and a meat-dominated menu.

L'Écailler, r. Dominicains 26 ☎ 0 4 222 17 49, *info@ecailler.be, Fax 0 4 387 63 74,* , Seafood – . AE MC VISA EY **n**
Meals. *Lunch 35* – a la carte 33/46.
◆ The brasserie's name (The Oyster Seller) is a clear indication of the culinary bias of this Parisian bistro-style brasserie with a nostalgic air on the edge of "Le Carré".

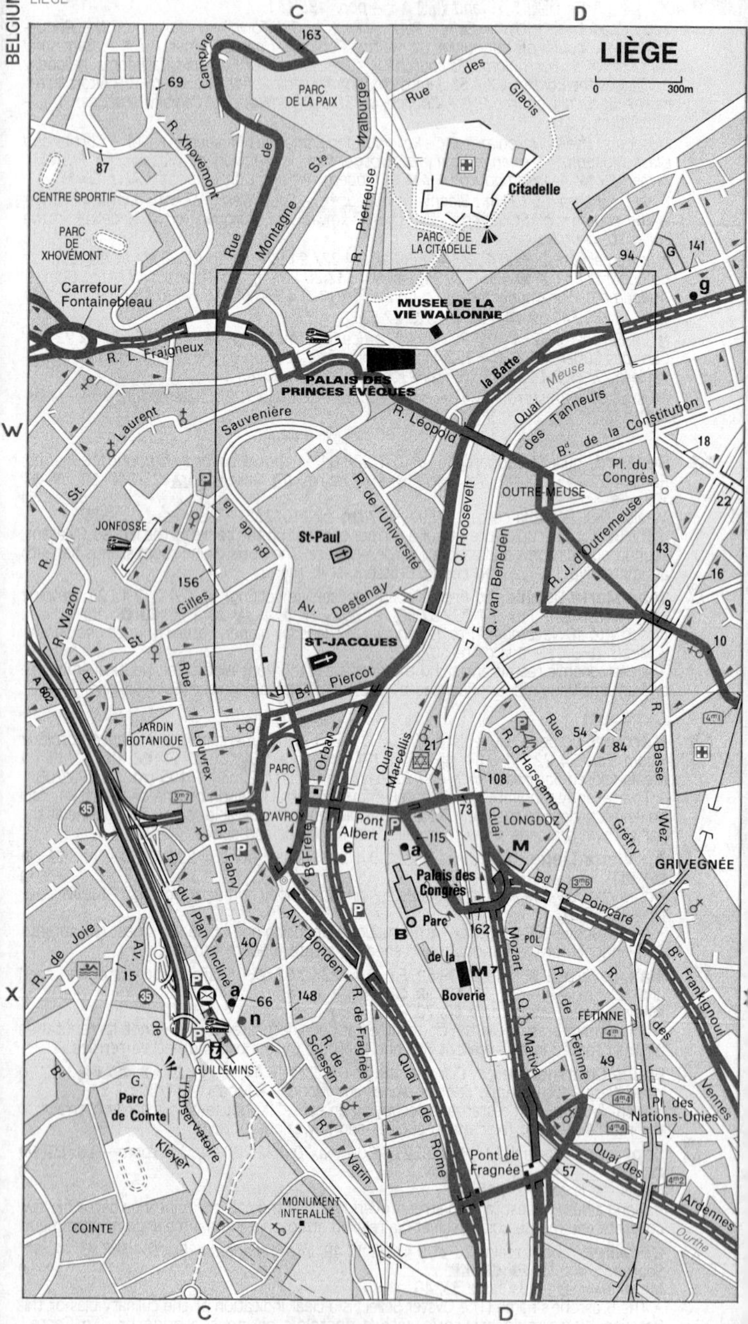

LIÈGE

0 300m

C D

Citadelle
PARC DE LA CITADELLE
Rue des Glacis
PARC DE LA PAIX
Rue de Campine
R. Xhovémont
Rue Montagne de Ste Walburge
R. Pierreuse
CENTRE SPORTIF
PARC DE XHOVÉMONT
Carrefour Fontainebleau
R. L. Fraigneux
MUSEE DE LA VIE WALLONNE
PALAIS DES PRINCES ÉVÊQUES
la Batte
Meuse
Quai des Tanneurs
Bd de la Constitution
Pl. du Congrès
R. Léopold
Sauvenière
St Laurent
OUTRE-MEUSE
R. J. d'Outremeuse
Q. Roosevelt
Q. van Beneden
Bd de la Sauvenière
R. de l'Université
St-Paul
Av. Destenay
JONFOSSE
R. St Gilles
R. Wazon
ST-JACQUES
Bd Piercot
Rue Louvrex
JARDIN BOTANIQUE
PARC D'AVROY
R. Orban
Quai Marcellis
Pont Albert Ier
R. d'Harscamp
Rue Basse Wez
Rue Grétry
LONGDOZ
Quai de Longdoz
Palais des Congrès
Parc de la Boverie
Bd Poincaré
GRIVEGNÉE
Bd Frère Orban
Av. Blonden
R. Fabry
R. du Plan Incliné
R. de Joie
Av. de l'Observatoire
R. de Fragnée
R. de Sclessin
Quai de Rome
Q. Mativa
R. Mozart
R. de Fétinne
FÉTINNE
Bd Frankignoul
R. des Vennes
Pl. des Nations-Unies
Quai des Ardennes
Ourthe
Pont de Fragnée
GUILLEMINS
Bd G. Kleyer
Parc de Cointe
COINTE
MONUMENT INTERALLIÉ
R. Varin
POL.
A 602

W X

C D

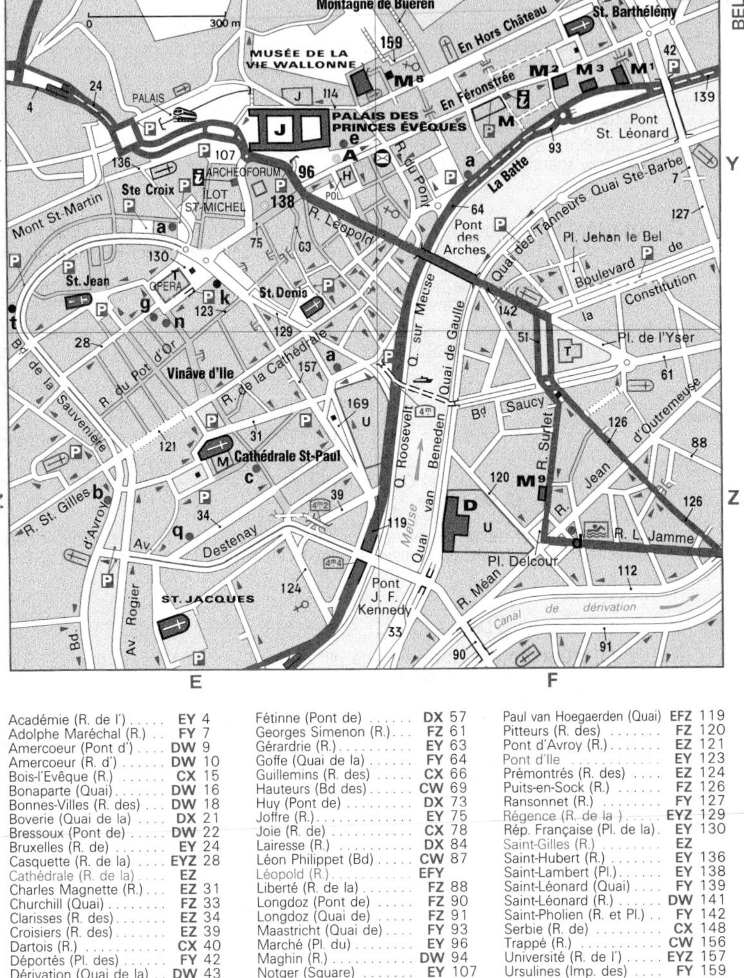

La Maison Blanche 1st floor, bd d'Avroy 18 ☎ 0 4 222 42 02, *Fax 0 4 221 48 88* – ▤. MC VISA EZ b
closed Saturday lunch and Sunday – **Meals**. *Lunch 24* – a la carte 46/58 ♀.
◆ This recommended restaurant is on the first floor of a former private mansion. References to U.S. presidents in the dining room, where the focus is on refined, modern dishes.

Enoteca, r. Casquette 5 ☎ 0 4 222 24 64, *Fax 0 4 222 24 64* – ▤. MC VISA EY g
closed Saturday lunch and Sunday – **Meals** – 18/48 b.i..
◆ This pleasant Italian restaurant is known for its authentic cuisine and wine-list. Contemporary interior with a kitchen visible from the dining room. Good-value lunch menu.

Le Bistrot d'en face, r. Goffe 8 ☎ 0 4 223 15 84, *Fax 0 4 223 15 86*, – AE MC VISA FY h

closed Monday and Saturday lunch – **Meals** – a la carte 31/39.

◆ This delightful Lyon-style bistro with a fine wooden façade and warm, friendly atmosphere is located behind the former meat market.

As Ouhès, pl. du Marché 19 ☎ 0 4 223 32 25, *as.ouhes@skynet.be, Fax 0 4 237 03 77*, , Brasserie, open until 11 p.m. – AE MC VISA EY e

Meals – a la carte 23/36.

◆ "The Birds" is a Liège institution with a classic, brasserie-style menu including local dishes and daily specials. A central location near Le Perron, the symbol of the city.

Guillemins

Comfort Inn without rest, r. Guillemins 116 ☎ 0 4 254 55 55, *comfort.inn.liege@skynet.be, Fax 0 4 254 55 00* – 25-60. AE MC VISA CX a

51 rm 64/99.

◆ This chain hotel near the Gare des Guillemins is a practical option for those with an early train to catch. Well-maintained rooms with good soundproofing.

Le Duc d'Anjou, r. Guillemins 127 ☎ 0 4 252 28 58, Mussels in season, open until 11.30 p.m. – AE MC VISA CX n

Meals – 21/31.

◆ Popular with passing trade and locals alike for its extensive and varied à la carte and menu options. Affordable wine-list and mussels aplenty in season.

Right banc (Outremeuse - Palais des Congrès)

Holiday Inn without rest, Esplanade de l'Europe 2, ✉ 4020, ☎ 0 4 349 20 00, *hiliege@alliance-hospitality.com, Fax 0 4 343 48 10*, – 40-70. AE MC VISA DX a

214 rm 184/214, – 5 suites.

◆ On the banks of the Meuse overlooking the conference centre and a large public park home to the city's modern art museum. Modern comforts for a mainly business clientele.

Suburbs

at Angleur *South : 4 km* Liège – ✉ *4031 Angleur* :

Le Val d'Ourthe without rest, rte de Tilff 412 ☎ 0 4 365 91 71, *Fax 0 4 365 62 89* – AE MC VISA. rest

9 – **12 rm** 82.

◆ Perched amid the greenery near a motorway junction, this small, pleasantly maintained hotel overlooks the Ourthe Valley between Angleur and Tilff. Spacious, modern rooms.

L'Orchidée Blanche, rte du Condroz 457 (N 680) ☎ 0 4 365 11 48, *Fax 0 4 367 09 16*, – AE MC VISA

closed 14 July-4 August, last week Janaury, Tuesday dinner and Wednesday – **Meals**. Lunch 27 – 39/57 b.i..

◆ A large, thatch-roofed villa on top of the Côte de Sart-Tilman. Refined cuisine with traditional influences. Open-air museum at the nearby university campus.

at Chênée *East : 7,5 km* Liège – ✉ *4032 Chênée* :

Le Gourmet, r. Large 91 ☎ 0 4 365 87 97, *info@legourmet.be, Fax 0 4 365 38 12*, – AE MC VISA

closed 2 weeks July, first 2 weeks January, Tuesday and Wednesday – **Meals**. Lunch 25 – 30/64 b.i..

◆ A pleasant restaurant with sophisticated décor and an attractive winter garden offering customers a classic, seasonally-orientated menu.

Le Vieux Chênée, r. Gravier 45 ☎ 0 4 367 00 92, *Fax 0 4 367 59 15*, Mussels in season – AE MC VISA

closed Thursday – **Meals**. Lunch 22 b.i. – 25/43 b.i..

◆ This old house with its typical Ardennes-style décor attracts a steady flow of locals and business customers. Conventional cuisine with mussels in season. Lobster tank.

at Rocourt *North : 4 km* Liège – ✉ *4000 Rocourt* :

La Petite Table (Gillard), pl. Reine Astrid 3 ☎ 0 4 239 19 00, *Fax 0 4 239 19 77* – MC VISA

closed 28 March-16 April, 1 to 20 August, 27 December-18 January, Monday, Tuesday and Saturday lunch – **Meals** (booking essential). Lunch 30 – a la carte 55/75.

◆ This small and charming family-run restaurant on a busy square makes up in quality what it lacks in size ! Kitchen open to the restaurant serving contemporary fare.

Spec. Marbré de foie d'oie et jambon de Parme aux pommes. Ravioles de Saint-Jacques au salpicon homard. Homard braisé au four, poireaux et jus crème.

Environs

at Ans *Northwest : 4 km – pop. 27 587 – ✉ 4430 Ans :*

XX **Le Marguerite,** r. Walthère Jamar 171 ☎ 0 4 226 43 46, *Fax 0 4 226 38 35,* – AE ⓓ MC VISA
closed Saturday lunch, Sunday and Monday dinner – **Meals**. *Lunch 28* – 35/62 b.i..
◆ Seasonal cuisine with a "menu du marché" and monthly festive menu. A welcoming restaurant which has just celebrated its quarter of a century with a facelift.

XX **La Fontaine de Jade,** r. Yser 321 ☎ 0 4 246 49 72, *la_fontaine@skynet.be, Fax 0 4 263 69 53,* Chinese cuisine, open until 11 p.m. – ▤. AE ⓓ MC VISA.
closed mid July-mid August and Tuesday – **Meals**. *Lunch 13* – 22/36 b.i. ♀.
◆ Chinese restaurants seem ten a penny on this busy road. This one stands out for its affluent, exotic appearance and extensive menu.

at Flémalle *Southwest : 16 km – pop. 25 501 – ✉ 4400 Flémalle :*

XXX **La Ciboulette,** chaussée de Chokier 96 ☎ 0 4 275 19 65, *la-ciboulette@teledisnet.be, Fax 0 4 275 05 81,* – ▤. AE MC VISA
closed 11 to 20 April, 25 July-8 August, 3 to 12 January, Monday, Saturday lunch and dinner Sunday and Wednesday – **Meals**. *Lunch 50 b.i.* – 24/100 b.i.
◆ An attractive group of well-kept Meuse-style houses is the setting for this restaurant offering a varied seasonal menu and wine-list. Patio with views over the garden-terrace.

XX **Le Gourmet Gourmand,** Grand-Route 411 ☎ 0 4 233 07 56, *Fax 0 4 233 19 21,* – ▤. AE ⓓ MC VISA
closed Monday and dinner Tuesday, Wednesday and Thursday – **Meals**. *Lunch 30* – 40/60 b.i..
◆ A small, traditional establishment where the menu changes with the seasons and includes a range of local dishes. Good wine cellar. Business clientele.

XX **Jacques Koulic,** chaussée de Chockier 82 ☎ 0 4 275 53 15, *jacques.koulic@cybernet.be,* – AE ⓓ MC VISA JCB.
closed 1 to 15 March, 1 to 15 September, Tuesday and Wednesday – **Meals** 31/90 b.i. ♀.
◆ An old house with a warm, rustic interior on the banks of the Meuse. Pleasantly modern cuisine, a diverse wine-list and wines by the glass. Terrace and enclosed garden.

at Herstal *Northeast : 6 km – pop. 36 359 – ✉ 4040 Herstal :*

XX **La Bergamote,** bd Ernest Solvay 72 (locality Coronmeuse) ☎ 0 4 342 29 47, *bergamote@sky.be, Fax 0 4 248 17 61,* – MC VISA
closed first week Easter holidays, 17 July-2 August, first week January, Sunday, Monday and Bank Holidays – **Meals** – 29/37.
◆ This esteemed restaurant in Coronmeuse is worth tracking down for its choice of menus, including a popular multi-choice option. A more intimate ambience on the first floor.

at Liers *North : 8 km* Ⓒ *Herstal pop. 36 359 – ✉ 4042 Liers :*

X **La Bartavelle,** r. Provinciale 138 ☎ 0 4 278 51 55, *info@labartavelle.be, Fax 0 4 278 51 57,* – P – 25 à 50. AE ⓓ MC VISA
closed carnival, 15 to 30 July and Saturday lunch – **Meals** (lunch only except weekends) 28/50 b.i..
◆ A convivial bistro-brasserie with an open fire serving Provençal-inspired cuisine, as the restaurant's name ("The Rock Partridge") would indicate. Charming terrace.

at Neuville-en-Condroz *South : 18 km* Ⓒ *Neupré pop. 9 696 – ✉ 4121 Neuville-en-Condroz :*

XXXX **Le Chêne Madame** (Mrs Tilkin), av. de la Chevauchée 70 (Southeast : 2 km in Rognacs wood) ☎ 0 4 371 41 27, *Fax 0 4 371 29 43,* – P. AE ⓓ MC VISA
✿ *closed August, Monday and dinner Thursday and Sunday* – **Meals** – 43/75, – a la carte 55/75.
◆ This elegant country inn is one of the temples of Liège gastronomy. A classic choice of seasonal dishes using the very finest ingredients.
Spec. Foie gras de canard poêlé aux pommes caramélisées, sauce au jus de truffes. Sandre farci en croûte et beurre blanc (June-February). Gibier (September-January).

at Tilleur *Southwest : 8 km* Ⓒ *St-Nicolas pop. 22 959 – ✉ 4420 Tilleur :*

X **Chez Massimo,** quai du Halage 78 ☎ 0 4 233 69 27, *Fax 0 4 234 00 31,* , Italian cuisine – MC VISA
closed Saturday lunch, Sunday and Monday – **Meals** – 28/37.
◆ This long-established Italian restaurant on the banks of the Meuse is renowned for its regional specialities and more run-of-the-mill national dishes.

LIÈGE

Maastricht *Limburg 532 T 17 and 715 I 9 – pop. 122 005 – 33 km.*

Right banc (Wyck - Station - MECC) :

XXXX ✿✿ **Beluga** (Van Wolde), Plein 1992 nr 12 (Centre Céramique), ✉ 6221 JP, ✆ (0 43) 321 33 64, *Fax (0 43) 326 03 56*, ≤ – ▤ P – 🏠 30. AE MC VISA JCB. ✂
closed Saturday lunch, Sunday and Monday – **Meals**. *Lunch 40* – 50/135 b.i., – a la carte 70/90 ♀.
◆ Space, light, elegant design and a view of the old tower and its barges all add to the gastronomic pleasures on offer here. Personalised cuisine by a highly talented chef.
Spec. Tajine de pigeon d'Anjou aux épices marocaines. Soufflé de langoustines et sauce curry vert. Rollmops de homard, thon rouge et truffes de saison.

Namur *5000 Namur 533 O 20, 534 O 20 and 716 H 4 – pop. 105 393 – 61 km.*

at Lives-sur-Meuse *East : 9 km* C *Namur* – ✉ *5101 Lives-sur-Meuse :*

XXXX ✿✿ **La Bergerie** (Lefevere) (hotel planned), r. Mosanville 100 ✆ 0 81 58 06 13, *marc@bergerielives.be*, *Fax 0 81 58 19 39* – ▤ P. AE ⓓ MC VISA
closed last 2 weeks February-early March, last 2 weeks August-early September, Sunday dinner, Monday and Tuesday – **Meals**. *Lunch 40* – 55/108 b.i., – a la carte 67/80 ♀ 🍇.
◆ This elegant, Namur-style residence in a luxuriant, waterside setting is one of the country's best tables. Outstanding classic cuisine accompanied by an extensive wine-list.
Spec. Truites de notre vivier. Agneau rôti "Bergerie". Le gâteau de crêpes soufflées.

Tongeren *3700 Limburg 533 R 18 and 716 J 3 – pop. 29 621 – 19 km.*

at Vliermaal *North : 5 km* C *Kortessem pop. 8 060* – ✉ *3724 Vliermaal :*

XXXXX ✿✿ **Clos St. Denis** (Denis), Grimmertingenstraat 24 ✆ 0 12 23 60 96, *info@closstdenis.be*, *Fax 0 12 26 32 07* – P. AE ⓓ MC VISA. ✂
closed 12 to 19 April, 13 to 28 July, 1 to 8 November, 28 December-10 January, Tuesday and Wednesday – **Meals**. *Lunch 55* – 99/185 b.i., – a la carte 82/155 🍇.
◆ Refined dining in a sumptuous 17C farm-château embellished with works of art. Charming terrace and adorable garden. A high-flying wine-list.
Spec. Gourmandise de homard, saumon mariné et raifort. Blanc de turbot, bintjes écrasées à l'huile d'olive, citron et câpres. Le grand dessert.

LUXEMBOURG – LËTZEBUERG

717 V 25 *and* 716 L 7 – *pop. 77 965.*

Amsterdam 391 – Bonn 190 – Brussels 219.

TOURIST OFFICE

Luxembourg City Tourist Office, pl. d'Armes, ✉ *2011,* ✆ *22 28 09, touristinfo@luxembourg_city.lu, Fax 46 70 70.*
Air Terminus, gare centrale ✉ *1010,* ✆ *42 82 82 20, info@ont.lu, Fax 42 82 82 30.*
Airport at Findel ✆ *42 82 82 21, info@ont.lu, Fax 42 82 82 30.*

GOLF COURSE

18 *Hoehenhof (Senningerberg) near Airport, r. de Trèves 1,* ✉ *2633,* ✆ *34 00 90, Fax 34 83 91.*

PLACES OF INTEREST

VIEWPOINTS

Place de la Constitution★★ F – *St-Esprit*★★ *Plateau* G – *Cliff Path*★★ G – *The Bock*★★ G – *Boulevard Victor Thorn*★ G 121 – *Three Acorns*★ DY.

MUSEUMS

National Museum of History and Art★ *: Gallo Roman section*★ *and Luxembourg Life section (decorative arts, folk art and traditions)*★★ G **M¹** – *Historical Museum of the City of Luxembourg*★ G **M³**.

OTHER THINGS TO SEE

Bock Casemates★★ G – *Grand Ducal Palace*★ G – *Cathedral of Our Lady*★ F – *Grand Duchess Charlotte Bridge*★ DY.

MODERN ARCHITECTURE

Plateau de Kirchberg : European Centre DEY.

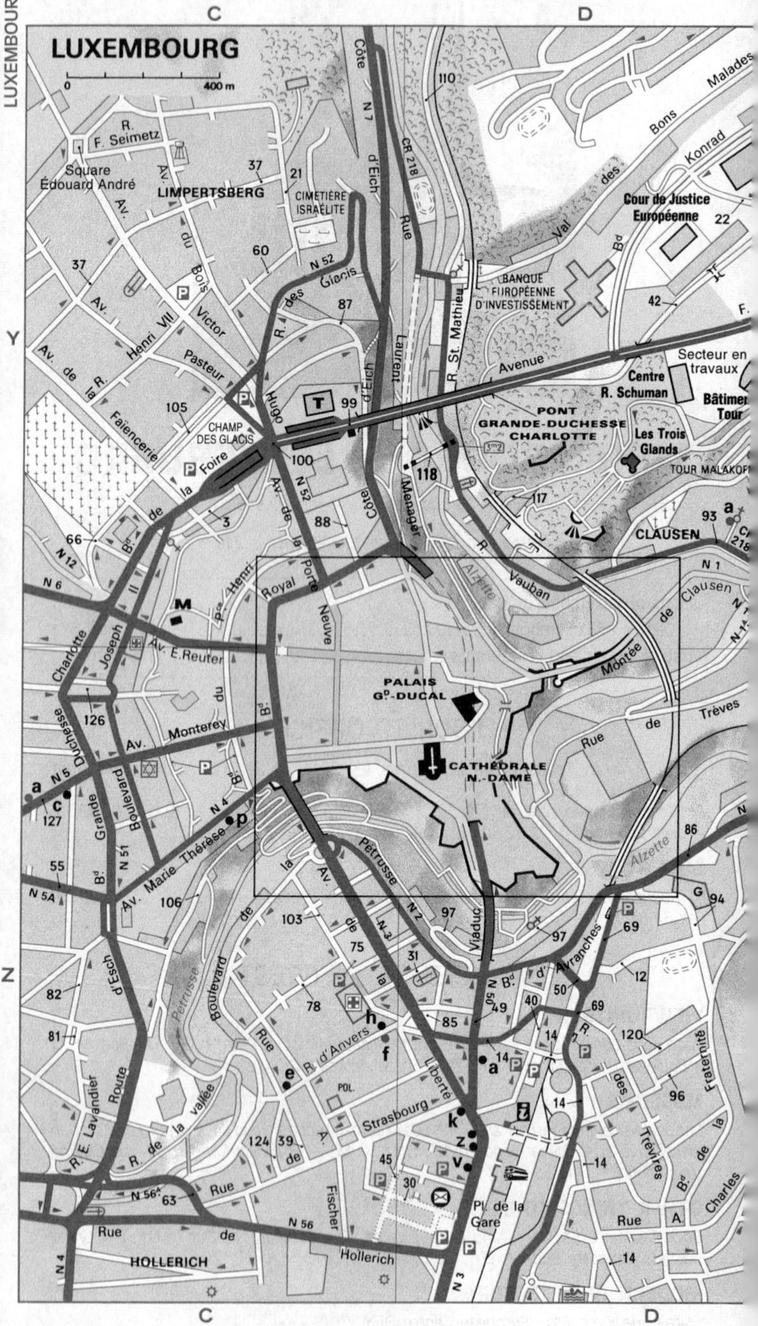

LUXEMBOURG

0 — 400 m

C
D
Y
Z

LIMPERTSBERG
Square Édouard André
R. F. Seimetz
Av. du Bois
Av. Victor Hugo
Av. Pasteur
Av. Henri VII
Av. de la Faïencerie
R. de la Foire
CIMETIÈRE ISRAÉLITE
R. des Glacis
CHAMP DES GLACIS
Côte d'Eich
Rue Laurent Ménager
R. St. Mathieu
BANQUE EUROPÉENNE D'INVESTISSEMENT
Val des Bons Malades
R. Konrad
Cour de Justice Européenne
Bd
Avenue
Secteur en travaux
Centre R. Schuman
Bâtiment Tour
PONT GRANDE-DUCHESSE CHARLOTTE
Les Trois Glands
TOUR MALAKOFF
CLAUSEN
R. Vauban
Alzette
Rue de Clausen
Montée de Clausen
Bd Royal
Av. de la Porte Neuve
Bd Joseph II
Bd Charlotte
Av. E. Reuter
Bd Prince Henri
Bd du Monterey
Av. Monterey
PALAIS Gᴰ-DUCAL
CATHÉDRALE N.-DAME
Rue de Trèves
Bd Grande Duchesse
Boulevard
Av. Marie Thérèse
Av. de la Pétrusse
Viaduc
Bd d'Avranches
Pétrusse
Boulevard de la Pétrusse
Route d'Esch
Av. de la Liberté
R. d'Anvers
Rue de Strasbourg
Rue de la Vallée
R. E. Lavandier
R. de la Vallée
Rue de Hollerich
HOLLERICH
Rue Fischer
Pl. de la Gare
R. des Trèves
Bd de la Fraternité
Bd Charles
Rue A.
POL.
N 7
CR 218
N 52
N 12
N 6
N 5
N 5A
N 4
N 51
N 3
N 2
N 50
N 56
N 56A
N 1
M
T
G
a c p e f h k z v
37 21 60 87 99 100 118 110 22 42 105 3 66 88 117 93 126 127 55 106 103 75 97 31 78 85 49 40 50 69 12 120 96 14 82 81 124 39 45 30 63 86 94

Rue		
Adames (R.)	CY	3
Albert Wehrer (R.)	EY	4
Alcide de Gasperi (R.)	EY	6
Aldringen (R.)	F	7
Athénée (R. de l'Ancien)	F	9
Auguste Lumière (R.)	DZ	12
Bains (R. des)	F	13
Bonnevoie (R. de)	DZ	14
Boucherie (R. de la)	G	15
Bruxelles (Pl. de)	F	16
Capucins (R. des)	F	
Cerisiers (R. des)	CY	21
Charles-Léon Hammes (R.)	DY	22
Chimay (R.)	F	24
Clairefontaine (Pl.)	FG	27
Clausen (R. de)	EY	28
Commerce (R. du)	CDZ	30
Curé (R. du)	F	
Dicks (R.)	CDZ	31
Eau (R. de l')	G	33
Ermesinde (R.)	CY	37
Etats-Unis (R. des)	CZ	39
Fort Neipperg (R. du)	DZ	40
Fort Niedergrünewald (R. du)	DY	42
Fort Thüngen (R. du)	EY	43
Fort Wedell (R. du)	CDZ	45
Fossé (R. du)	F	46
Franklin-Roosevelt (Bd)	F	48
Gare (Av. de la)	DZ	49
Gaulle (Av. du Gén.-de)	DZ	50
Grand-Rue	F	
Guillaume (Av.)	CZ	55
Guillaume Schneider (R.)	CY	60
Jean Baptiste Merkels (R.)	CZ	63
Jean Ulveling (Bd)	FG	64
J.P. Probst (R.)	CY	66
Jules Wilhem (R.)	EY	67
Laboratoire (R. du)	DZ	69
Léon Hengen (R.)	EY	70
Liberté (Av. de la)	CDZ	
Marché (Pl. du)	G	72
Marché aux Herbes (R. du)	FG	73
Martyrs (Pl. des)	CZ	75
Michel Rodange (R.)	CZ	78
Munster (R.)	G	79
Nancy (Pl. de)	CZ	81
Nassau (R. de)	CZ	82
Notre-Dame (R.)	F	84
Paris (Pl. de)	DZ	85
Patton (Bd du Général)	DZ	86
Paul Eyschen (R.)	CY	87
Pescatore (Av.)	CY	88
Pfaffenthal (Montée de)	FG	90
Philippe II (R.)	F	91
Pierre de Mansfeld (Allée)	DY	93
Pierre et Marie Curie (R.)	DZ	94
Pierre Hentges (R.)	DZ	96
Porte-Neuve (Av. de la)	CY	
Prague (R. de)	DZ	97
Robert Schuman (Bd)	CY	99
Robert Schuman (Rond-Point)	CY	100
Sainte-Zithe (R.)	CZ	103
Scheffer (Allée)	CY	105
Semois (R. de la)	CZ	106
Sigefroi (R.)	G	108
Sosthène Weis (R.)	G	109
Stavelot (R. de)	DY	110
Strasbourg (R. de)	CDZ	
Théâtre (Pl. du)	F	114
Tour Jacob (Av. de la)	EY	115
Trois Glands (R. des)	DY	117
Vauban (Pont)	DY	118
Verger (R. du)	DZ	120
Victor Thorn (Bd)	G	121
Willy Georgen (R.)	F	123
Wilson (R.)	CZ	124
Winston Churchill (Pl.)	CZ	126
10-Septembre (Av. du)	CZ	127

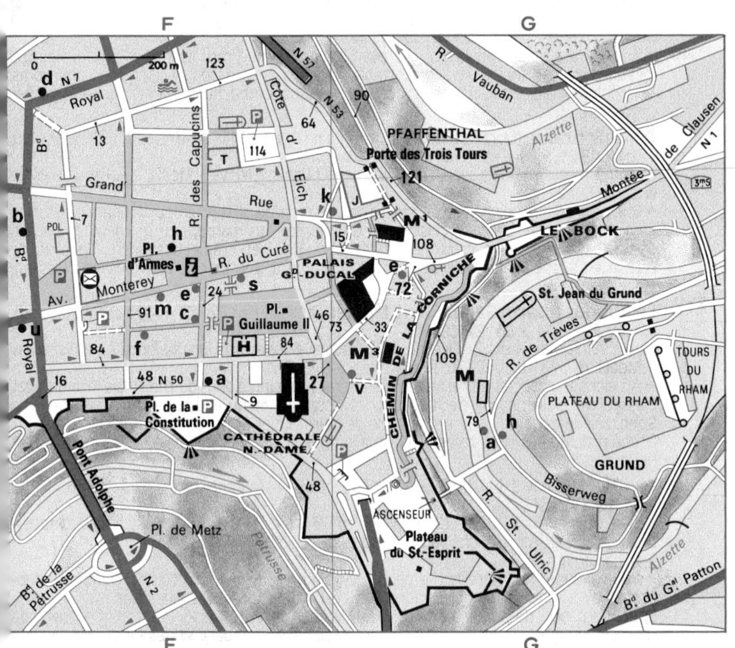

Luxembourg-Centre

Le Royal, bd Royal 12, ✉ 2449, ☎ 241 61 61, *reservations@hotelroyal.lu*, *Fax 22 59 48*, – 25-350. AE MC VISA F d
Meals see ***La Pomme Cannelle*** below – ***Le Jardin*** *Lunch 25* – a la carte 36/47 – 24 – **185 rm** 330/460, – 20 suites.
◆ A luxury hotel at the heart of Luxembourg's "Wall Street" with large, modern and superbly equipped bedrooms. Top-notch, personalised service around the clock. Business centre. Mediterranean-style brasserie. Buffet lunch served on Sundays.

Gd H. Cravat, bd Roosevelt 29, ✉ 2450, ☎ 22 19 75, *contact@hotelcravat.lu*, *Fax 22 67 11* – rest, – 25. AE MC VISA. rm F a
Meals *(closed August)* (pub rest). *Lunch 12* – 35/65 – **60 rm** 235/275.
◆ This small, classical palace stands in the shadow of the cathedral's spires, close to the city's pedestrianised area. Pleasant restaurant serving traditional fare on the first floor, in addition to a cosy tavern-restaurant on the ground floor.

Domus, av. Monterey 37, ✉ 2163, ☎ 467 87 81 and 467 87 88 (rest), *info@domus.lu*, *Fax 46 78 79*, – . AE MC VISA. F u
Meals ***le sot l'y laisse*** *(closed 3 weeks August, last 2 weeks December, Saturday, Sunday and Bank Holidays)* a la carte 24/41 – 11 – **38 rm** 115/131.
◆ A contemporary "flat-hotel" with spacious, modern rooms and fully equipped kitchenettes. The brasserie-restaurant and terrace, serving traditional cuisine, overlook a pleasant garden. Canvases by local artists are on display in the main dining room.

Rix without rest, bd Royal 20, ✉ 2449, ☎ 47 16 66, *rixhotel@vo.lu*, *Fax 22 75 35*, – . MC VISA. F b
closed 19 December-3 January – **21 rm** 152/175.
◆ The stylish, identical rooms in this pleasant family-run hotel all have their own balcony. Impressive breakfast room and priceless private parking.

Parc-Belle-Vue , av. Marie-Thérèse 5, ✉ 2132, ☎ 456 14 11, *bellevue@hpb.lu*, *Fax 456 14 12 22*, ≤, – – 25-350. AE MC VISA JCB CZ p
closed 20 December-1 January – **Meals** – 30/38 b.i. – **58 rm** 110/125.
◆ This hotel slightly away from the centre lives up to its name with its park and fine views. The bedrooms are well furnished with good soundproofing, while the welcoming panoramic terrace provides the perfect setting for dining during the summer months.

Français, pl. d'Armes 14, ✉ 1136, ☎ 47 45 34, *hfinfo@pt.lu*, *Fax 46 42 74*, – – 30. AE MC VISA F h
Meals. *Lunch 11* – 26 – **21 rm** 97/125.
◆ Run by the same family for the past 25 years, the Français enjoys a good central location, and offers guests comfortable, modern and reasonably spacious bedrooms. The hotel's traditional cuisine is certain to assuage the hunger of lunch and dinner customers.

Clairefontaine (Magnier), pl. de Clairefontaine 9, ✉ 1341, ☎ 46 22 11, *clairefo@pt.lu*, *Fax 47 08 21*, – . AE MC VISA G v
closed 3 weeks August, Saturday, Sunday and Bank Holidays – **Meals**. *Lunch 60 b.i.* – 67, a la carte 59/92 .
◆ The new kitchen team here perpetuates the tradition of this famous culinary institution known for its ever-evolving cuisine and the harmonious marriage of its menu and cellar.
Spec. Gambas géantes croustillantes au chou-fleur et crème citronnée. Poularde de Bresse en vessie Albufera. Mille-feuille à la crème anisée et céleri vert. **Wines** Riesling, Pinot blanc.

Le Bouquet Garni Salon Saint Michel (Duhr), r. Eau 32, ✉ 1449, ☎ 26 20 06 20, *Fax 26 20 09 11* – AE MC VISA G e
closed All Saints' week, 23 December-7 January, Sunday and lunch Monday and Saturday – **Meals**. *Lunch 38 b.i.* – 50/70, – a la carte 54/78 .
◆ An elegant, rustic-style restaurant in a street running alongside the Palais Grand-Ducal. Classic fare enlivened by elegant touches, a tasting menu and appealing desserts.
Spec. Salade tiède de pommes de terre de Noirmoutier et homard rôti. Gibier (in Season). Pêche rôtie au basilic et caramel, glace à la vanille (July-September). **Wines** Vin de la Barrique, Riesling.

Speltz, r. Chimay 8, ✉ 1333, ☎ 47 49 50, *info@restaurant-speltz.lu*, *Fax 47 46 77*, – AE MC VISA F c
closed 23 February, 3 to 12 April, 20 to 23 May, 14 to 30 August, 24 December-2 January, Saturday lunch, Sunday and Bank Holidays – **Meals**. *Lunch 40* – 49/99 b.i. – a la carte 51/70 .
◆ The refined décor here is the backdrop for delicious, modern cuisine, admirably supported by a wine cellar representing the best of the country's vineyards.
Spec. Carpaccio de homard et aïoli froid de courgettes. Gibier (in Season). Croquant de fraises au poivre noir et sorbet à la menthe (June-September). **Wines** Pinot gris, Riesling Koeppchen.

La Pomme Cannelle - Hotel Le Royal, bd Royal 12, ✉ 2449, ☎ 241 61 67 36, *reservations@hotelroyal.lu, Fax 22 59 48* – AE VISA. F d
closed Saturday lunch, Sunday and Bank Holidays – **Meals**. Lunch 45 – 65/120 b.i.
◆ The restaurant at Le Royal has adopted an original approach, in which New World spices take pride of place. The chic, yet welcoming interior calls to mind exotic locations.

Jan Schneidewind, r. Curé 20, ✉ 1368, ☎ 22 26 18, *info@schneidewind.lu, Fax 46 24 40,* – AE VISA F s
closed Monday and lunch Saturday and Sunday – **Meals**. Lunch 40 – 85.
◆ Customers can enjoy an appetising seasonal menu at this restaurant nestled between Place d'Armes and Place Guillaume II. The bare walls are enlivened with modern canvases.

La Lorraine 1st floor, pl. d'Armes 7, ✉ 1136, ☎ 47 14 36, *lorraine@pt.lu, Fax 47 09 64,* , Partly oyster bar and seafood – AE VISA F e
closed Sunday – **Meals** – a la carte 58/66.
◆ In a fine edifice on the place d'Armes, the Lorraine serves local cuisine, with oysters (in season) on the ground floor, and refined fare in an Art Deco room on the first.

L'Océan, r. Louvigny 7, ✉ 1946, ☎ 22 88 66, *braunpatrick@hotmail.com, Fax 22 88 67,* , Oyster bar and Seafood – AE VISA F f
closed 5 to 25 July, 26 December-11 January, Sunday dinner and Monday – **Meals** – 39.
◆ The name, plus the display of oysters at the entrance, says it all! A fine range of fish and seafood accompanied by a good choice of white wines.

la fourchette à droite, av. Monterey 5, ✉ 2163, ☎ 22 13 60, *Fax 22 24 95,* – AE VISA F m
closed Saturday lunch and Sunday – **Meals**. Lunch 19 – 26/46 b.i.
◆ An attractive, popular restaurant located in the heart of the city. The menu in the wood-adorned "brasserie"-style dining room includes a good-value lunch option.

Thai Céladon, r. Nord 1, ✉ 2229, ☎ 47 49 34, *Fax 47 49 34,* Thai cuisine – AE VISA. FG k
closed Saturday lunch and Sunday – **Meals**. Lunch 18 – 46.
◆ This central restaurant serves high-quality Thai cuisine and vegetarian dishes in an elegant and refined ambience. It takes its name from a glaze used by Oriental potters.

Luxembourg-Grund

Mosconi, r. Munster 13, ✉ 2160, ☎ 54 69 94, *Fax 54 00 43,* , Italian cuisine – AE VISA G a
closed 1 week Easter, 9 to 30 August, 24 December-3 January, Sunday, Monday and Bank Holidays – **Meals**. Lunch 34 – 40, a la carte 60/76.
◆ A bourgeois house on the River Alzette serving fine Italian cuisine. A welcoming setting where the emphasis is on discreet luxury. Attractive terrace by the water's edge.
Spec. Pâté de foie de poulet à la crème de truffes blanches. Risotto aux truffes blanches (October-December). Arista au Chianti (pork chop).

Kamakura, r. Münster 4, ✉ 2160, ☎ 47 06 04, *kamakura@pe.lu, Fax 46 73 30,* Japanese cuisine – AE VISA. G h
closed 3 weeks August, Sunday and lunch Saturday and Bank Holidays – **Meals**. Lunch 10 – 25/63 b.i..
◆ The Kamadura makes few concessions to the West with its minimalist ambience and design. Good sushi-bar and menus which remain loyal to Japanese customs. A firm favourite.

Luxembourg-Station

Gd H. Mercure Alfa, pl. de la Gare 16, ✉ 1616, ☎ 490 01 11, *H2058@accor-hotels.com, Fax 49 00 09* – – 25-80. AE VISA. rest DZ z
Meals (brasserie). Lunch 18 – a la carte 26/50 – 18 – **140 rm** 170/215, – 1 suite.
◆ This completely refurbished chain hotel is a useful address for rail travellers. Pleasant rooms where a good night's sleep is guaranteed. The Parisian-style brasserie floats amid the vast Art Deco restaurant. International menu and fresh seafood.

President without rest, pl. de la Gare 32, ✉ 1024, ☎ 48 61 61, *president@pt.lu, Fax 48 61 80* – – 30. AE VISA DZ v
42 rm 130/160.
◆ The rooms at this attractive, discreetly luxurious hotel in front of the station are comfortable and tastefully furnished.

City without rest, r. Strasbourg 1, ✉ 2561, ☎ 291 12 21, *mail@cityhotel.lu, Fax 29 11 33* – – 25-80. AE VISA DZ k
35 rm 110/154.
◆ This old building has a modern feel with spacious bedrooms equipped with every creature comfort and décor that bears the personal touch. Attentive service.

Christophe Colomb (annex Marco Polo - 18 rm) without rest, r. Anvers 10, ✉ 1130, ☎ 408 41 41, *mail@christophe-colomb.lu, Fax 40 84 08* – |₿| TV – 🏛 25. AE ⓓ MC VISA CZ h
24 rm ☐ 144/154.
• Just 500m/550yd from the station, this pleasant small hotel is ideal for those arriving in the city by train. Standard, reasonably spacious rooms with modern furnishings.

International, pl. de la Gare 20, ✉ 1616, ☎ 48 59 11, *info@hotelinter.lu, Fax 49 32 27* – |₿| ⇔, ▤ rest, TV – 🏛 25-50. AE ⓓ MC VISA DZ z
Meals *(closed 23 December-9 January and Saturday lunch)*. Lunch 18 – 26/40 b.i. – **67 rm** ☐ 112/137, – 1 suite.
• A recently renovated hotel facing the station, with comfortable, cosy rooms all with fax and modem connections. Internet room. The intimate restaurant is adorned with wood panelling. Inexpensive menu.

Le Châtelet (annex 🏠 - 9 rm) without rest, bd de la Pétrusse 2, ✉ 2320, ☎ 40 21 01, *contact@chatelet.lu, Fax 40 36 66* – |₿| TV. AE ⓓ MC VISA CZ e
36 rm ☐ 89/120.
• Overlooking the Pétrusse Valley, this hotel is an amalgam of several houses, one of which is crowned by an imposing turret. Pine furniture throughout and good soundproofing.

Nobilis, av. de la Gare 47, ✉ 1611, ☎ 49 49 71, *info@hotel-nobilis.com, Fax 40 31 01* – |₿| ▤ TV – 🏛 50. AE ⓓ MC VISA DZ a
Meals. Lunch 17 – a la carte approx. 22 – ☐ 15 – **46 rm** 115.
• This frequently renovated hotel stands halfway between the station and the viaduct leading to the old town. Functional bedrooms with the bonus of double-glazing.

Italia with rm, r. Anvers 15, ✉ 1130, ☎ 486 62 61, *italia@euro.lu, Fax 48 08 07*, 🏡, Partly Italian cuisine – TV. AE ⓓ MC VISA CZ f
Meals – a la carte 32/46 – **20 rm** ☐ 68/88.
• The menu here is strong on Italian cuisine. The mainly Franco-Italian cellar includes some Moselle wines. Candlelit dinners with music on Fridays from September-June.

Suburbs

Airport *Northeast : 8 km :*

Sheraton Aérogolf 🐦, rte de Trèves 1, ✉ 1019, ☎ 34 05 71, *Fax 34 02 17* – |₿| ⇔ ▤ TV P – 🏛 25-120. AE ⓓ MC VISA
Meals ***Le Montgolfier*** (open until midnight) Lunch 35 – a la carte 40/63 ♀ – ☐ 20 – **147 rm** 209/340, – 1 suite.
• A full range of creature comforts, sophisticated luxury, excellent soundproofing and impeccable service are the hallmarks of this top hotel...not forgetting the superb view of the slopes. The décor of the restaurant takes its inspiration from centuries past.

Ibis, rte de Trèves, ✉ 2632, ☎ 43 88 01, *H0974@accor-hotels.com, Fax 43 88 02*, ⋖, 🏡 – |₿| ▤ TV ♿ P – 🏛 25-80. AE ⓓ MC VISA
Meals. Lunch 10 – a la carte 22/41 – ☐ 10 – **120 rm** 80/90.
• A chain hotel with attractive lounge and dining areas plus a cheaper annexe for the budget-conscious. Despite limited space, the bedrooms offer the level of comfort you would expect from the Ibis name. A glass rotunda provides the backdrop for the restaurant.

Trust Inn without rest, r. Neudorf 679 (by rte de Trèves), ✉ 2220, ☎ 423 05 11, *trustinn@pt.lu, Fax 42 30 56*, 🚲 – ▤ TV P. AE ⓓ MC VISA
7 rm ☐ 62/72.
• Despite a compact feel, the rooms are pleasant and well-equipped. As the hotel does not have a restaurant, breakfast - the only service available - is brought to your room.

Le Grimpereau, r. Cents 140, ✉ 1319, ☎ 43 67 87, *bridard@pt.lu, Fax 42 60 26*, 🏡 – P. AE ⓓ MC VISA JCB
closed Easter, first 3 weeks August, Saturday lunch, Sunday dinner and Monday – **Meals** – 30/39.
• This neo-rustic restaurant in a foliage-adorned villa is named after the tree creepers that inhabit its walls. Popular with locals and airport staff. Excellent menu choice.

at Belair *West : 1,5 km* C *Luxembourg :*

Albert Premier 🐦 without rest, r. Albert Ier 2a, ✉ 1117, ☎ 442 44 21, *hotel-albert-premier@resto.lu, Fax 44 74 41*, 🏋, ≘ – |₿| TV 🚗. AE ⓓ MC VISA CZ c
☐ 13 – **14 rm** 220/240.
• A "chic" hotel on the city's outskirts. Warm, English-style décor created with great attention to detail, charming, well-appointed rooms, and friendly, attentive service.

Parc Belair, av. du X Septembre 111, ✉ 2551, ☎ 442 32 31, *paribel@hpb.lu, Fax 44 44 84*, <, 🌳, Fö, ≘s, 🚲 - |♦|, ⇔, ▤ rest, TV 🚗 - 🏛 25-260. AE ⓓ ⓜⓒ VISA
Meals ***Le Bistrot*** *(closed Bank Holidays and lunch Saturday and Sunday)* (open until 11 p.m.) a la carte 24/36 – **52 rm** ☐ 210/251.
◆ This luxury hotel on the edge of a park is appreciated by guests for its cosy feel. Modern bedrooms and excellent facilities for seminars. The extensive menu at the small bistro across the street will more than satisfy the needs of the hungriest of customers.

Astoria, av. du X Septembre 44, ✉ 2550, ☎ 44 62 23, *Fax 45 82 96* – ▤. AE ⓓ ⓜⓒ
closed 21 to 28 February, Saturday and dinner Sunday and Monday – **Meals**. Lunch 23 – a la carte 28/58. CZ a
◆ The Astoria is housed in an attractive bourgeois residence at the entrance to the city, its façade embellished with Art Deco features. A concise classic/traditional menu.

Thailand, av. Gaston Diderich 72, ✉ 1420, ☎ 44 27 66, Thai cuisine – AE ⓓ ⓜⓒ VISA. ✻
closed 15 August-15 September, Monday and Saturday lunch – **Meals** a la carte 36/54.
◆ At the heart of Belair, this exotic restaurant is known for its myriad Thai recipes and typical, relatively tasteful décor, including parasols adorning the ceiling.

at Clausen *(Klausen)* C *Luxembourg* :

les jardins du President ⛰, with rm pl. Ste-Cunégonde 2, ✉ 1367, ☎ 260 90 71, *jardins@president.lu, Fax 26 09 07 73*, 🌳, ☂ – |♦|, ▤ rm, TV P. AE ⓓ ⓜⓒ VISA DY a
Meals *(closed Saturday lunch and Sunday)*. Lunch 24 – a la carte 40/55 ♀ – **7 rm** ☐ 150/180.
◆ An elegant restaurant set amid an oasis of greenery producing dishes with a modern touch. The terrace overlooks a garden and waterfall. Individually designed bedrooms.

at Dommeldange *(Dummeldéng)* *North : 5,5 km* C *Luxembourg* :

Hilton ⛰, r. Jean Engling 12, ✉ 1466, ☎ 4 37 81, *hilton_luxembourg@hilton.com, Fax 43 60 95*, <, Fö, ≘s, 🏊, 🚲 – |♦| ⇔ ▤ TV 🚗 P – 🏛 25-360. AE ⓓ ⓜⓒ VISA JCB
Meals See ***Les Continents*** below – ***Café Stiffchen*** Lunch 30 – a la carte 34/55 ♀ – **298 rm** ☐ 298/358, – 39 suites.
◆ This luxury hotel hugs the side of the valley on the edge of the forest. Bedrooms with every creature comfort, attentive service and a full range of conference facilities. Brasserie-style restaurant, plus buffet lunches Monday-Friday in the Café Stiffchen.

Parc, rte d'Echternach 120, ✉ 1453, ☎ 435 64 30, *info@parc-hotel.lu, Fax 43 69 03*, 🌳, Fö, ≘s, 🏊, ☂, 🎾 – |♦|, ▤ rest, TV P – 🏛 25-1500. AE ⓓ ⓜⓒ VISA
Meals *(closed 24, 26 and 27 December)* – a la carte 26/49 – **217 rm** ☐ 115/140, – 3 suites.
◆ In a park surrounded by woodland, this family-run establishment has the feel of a chain hotel. The lobby areas and renovated bedrooms are generally spacious and pleasing to the eye. The veranda-restaurant overlooking the pool serves a choice of grilled meats.

Host. du Grünewald, rte d'Echternach 10, ✉ 1453, ☎ 43 18 82, *hostgrun@pt.lu, Fax 42 06 46*, ☂, 🚲 – |♦|, ▤ rest, TV P – 🏛 25-40. AE ⓓ ⓜⓒ VISA. ✻ rest
Meals *(closed 1 to 17 July, 1 to 20 January, Sunday and lunch Monday and Saturday)* 49/85 – **26 rm** ☐ 120/145, – 2 suites.
◆ A delightful, traditional-style hostelry with faded charm. Quaint bedrooms, all varying in shape and size. With its cosy feel, the overall atmosphere is quite romantic. A good classic menu and expansive wine list await guests in the restaurant.

Les Continents - Hotel Hilton, 1st floor, r. Jean Engling 12, ✉ 1466, ☎ 43 78 81 03, *hilton_luxembourg@hilton.com, Fax 43 60 95*, <, 🌳 – ▤ P. AE ⓓ ⓜⓒ VISA JCB
closed August, Saturday lunch, Sunday and Monday – **Meals**. Lunch 39 – a la carte 64/81 ♀.
◆ The success of the hotel's opulent restaurant is based on its excellent seasonal cuisine, its tempting menus and the harmonious marriage of its food and wine.

Upland of Kirchberg *(Kiirchbierg)* :

Sofitel ⛰, r. Fort Niedergrünewald 6 (European Centre), ✉ 2015, ☎ 43 77 61, *H1314@accor-hotels.com, Fax 42 50 91* – |♦| ⇔ ▤ TV ♿ 🚗 P – 🏛 25-75. AE ⓓ ⓜⓒ VISA EY a
Meals ***Oro e Argento*** *(closed August and Saturday)* à la carte approx. 50 – ☐ 20 – **100 rm** 295, – 4 suites.
◆ This bold, oval-shaped hotel with a central atrium is located at the heart of the European institutions district. Comfortable, spacious rooms with service to match. The intimate "d'or et d'argent" restaurant, with its hints of Venice, serves Italian cuisine.

LUXEMBOURG

Novotel, r. Fort Niedergrünewald 6 (European Centre), 2226, 429 84 81, *H1930@accor-hotels.com, Fax 43 86 58,* – – 25-300. AE MC VISA EY a
Meals (open until 11 p.m.). Lunch 22 – a la carte 19/38 – 15 – **206 rm** 155.
◆ The Novotel is run by the same group as its neighbour, the Sofitel, and offers business customers a full range of seminar facilities as well as large, pleasant bedrooms.

at Neudorf *(Neiduerf) Northeast : 4 km C Luxembourg :*

Ponte Vecchio without rest, r. Neudorf 271, 2221, 424 72 01, *vecchio@pt.lu, Fax 424 72 08 88* – AE MC VISA
46 rm 89/107.
◆ This old brewery has been redeveloped into impressive bedrooms (with and without kitchenettes) - including 9 split-level - and rooms adorned with charming Italianate frescoes.

at Rollingergrund *(Rolléngergronn) Northwest : 3 km C Luxembourg :*

Sieweburen, r. Septfontaines 36, 2534, 44 23 56, *Fax 44 23 53,* –
MC VISA
Meals *(closed 24 December-8 January and Wednesday)* (pub rest). Lunch 11 – a la carte 26/45 – **14 rm** 88/115.
◆ This half-timbered country house offers a choice of several sizes of bedroom, some of which are in the attic, all with adequate levels of comfort.

Environs

at Hesperange *(Hesper) Southeast : 5,5 km – pop. 10 519*

L'Agath (Steichen), rte de Thionville 274 (Howald), 5884, 48 86 87, *restaurant@agath.lu, Fax 48 55 05,* – – 60. AE MC VISA
closed 12 to 19 April, 31 May-7 June, 1 to 16 August, 1 to 9 January, Saturday lunch, Sunday and Monday – **Meals**. Lunch 58 – a la carte 62/75.
◆ The emphasis in this imposing villa set back from the road is on refined modern cuisine. A trompe-l'oeil decorates the cupola in the sumptuous dining room.
Spec. Carpaccio de bœuf à l'huile de truffes, copeaux de parmesean et foie gras. Daurade royale, légumes confits et coulis de poivrons doux. Carré d'agneau persillé et pommes Darphin aux herbes. **Wines** Riesling, Pinot gris.

at Strassen *(Strossen) West : 4 km – pop. 5 869*

L'Olivier with apartments, rte d'Arlon 140, 8008, 31 36 66, *olivier@mail.lu, Fax 31 36 27* – – 25-50. AE MC VISA JCB
Meals see ***La Cime*** below – **38 rm** 139/187, – 4 suites.
◆ This building 400m/440yd from the motorway offers modern comforts, double-glazing and some split- level rooms with kitchenette. The view to the rear is pleasantly rural.

La Cime - Hotel L'Olivier, rte d'Arlon 140a, 8008, 31 88 13, *olivier@mail.lu, Fax 31 36 27,* – AE MC VISA JCB
closed Saturday – **Meals**. Lunch 15 – 36/63 b.i.
◆ À la carte options at this hotel restaurant include traditional dishes, plus several menus offering a choice of meat, fish and vegetarian dishes. Large, modern dining room.

Le Nouveau Riquewihr, rte d'Arlon 373, 8011, 31 99 80, *leriquewihr@email.lu, Fax 31 97 05,* – AE MC VISA
closed 24 December-1 January and Sunday – **Meals**. Lunch 34 – a la carte 40/49.
◆ The uniqueness of the Riquewihr relates more to its décor - renovated in Italian Renaissance style - than to its cuisine, which remains resolutely traditional and copious.

at Walferdange *(Walfer) North : 5 km – pop. 6 451*

Moris, pl. des Martyrs, 7201, 330 10 51, *contact@morishotel.lu, Fax 33 30 70,* – , rest, – 50. AE MC VISA
Meals *(closed 2 to 22 August and 24 December-2 January)*. Lunch 35 – a la carte 34/49 – **24 rm** *(closed 24 December-2 January)* 85/110.
◆ An octagonal hotel located at a crossroads near the village church. Functional, reasonably spacious rooms, albeit lacking soundproofing. Private car park. The welcoming, harmonious restaurant serves classic dishes and regional specialities.

l'Etiquette, rte de Diekirch 50, 7220, 33 51 68, *Fax 33 51 69,* – AE MC VISA
closed 25 August-5 September, 27 December-5 January, Tuesday and Sunday dinner – **Meals**. Lunch 17 – 22/42.
◆ Originally a specialist wine store, which still exists to this day, l'Etiquette is now also known for its traditional cuisine and an exceptional cellar of regional wines.

Echternach *(Iechternach)* 717 X 24 *and* 716 M 6 *– pop. 4 555 – 36 km.*

at Geyershaff *(Geieschhaff) Southwest : 6,5 km by E 27* C *Bech pop. 943 :*

XXX **La Bergerie** (Phal), ✉ 6251, ☎ 79 04 64, *Fax 79 07 71,* ←, – P. AE ⓓ MC VISA

✿✿ *closed 2 January-12 February, Sunday dinner and Monday* – **Meals** (dinner only September-May) 99, a la carte 84/121.

◆ A charming restaurant known for its inventive cuisine nestled amid woods and fields. Cellar dominated by wines from Luxembourg and France. Delightful garden and veranda.

Spec. Foie gras aux cinq saveurs. Carré d'agneau de Sisteron grillé. Suprême de turbot, sauce au Champagne. **Wines** Pinot gris, Gewurztraminer.

Paliseul *6850 Luxembourg belge (Belgium)* 534 P 23 *and* 716 I 6 *– pop. 5 024 – 94 km.*

XXX **Au Gastronome** (Libotte) with rm, r. Bouillon 2 (Paliseul-Gare) ☎ 0 61 53 30 64, *Fax 0 61 53 38 91,* , – TV P. MC VISA

✿✿ *closed 29 June-9 July, 1 January-6 February, Sunday dinner, Monday and Tuesday* – **Meals**. *Lunch 52 b.i.* – 62/100, – a la carte 59/95 – ☕ 10 – **8 rm** 90/175.

◆ This elegant Ardennes hostelry is renowned for its skilful reworking of traditional dishes. Hushed and elegant dining room, cosy bedrooms, plus a swimming pool in the garden.

Spec. Le pied de porc farci de morilles et ris de veau, sauce diable. Grenouilles au jus de persil et aux croquettes d'ail. Carré de cochon de lait caramélisé, cuisse fumée en boudin, épaule farcie de poivre et pieds en Tatin.

AMSTERDAM

Noord-Holland 531 O 8 - ㉘ ㉙, 532 O 8 *and* 715 G 4 - ㉗ S *- pop. 735 526.*

Brussels 204 - Düsseldorf 227 - The Hague 60 - Luxembourg 419 - Rotterdam 76.

TOURIST OFFICE

VVV Amsterdam, Stationsplein 10, ✉ 1012 AB, ☎ (020) 201 88 00, info@amsterdam tourist.nl, Fax (0 20) 625 28 69.

For more information on tourist attractions consult our Green Guide to Amsterdam and our Map N° 36.

GOLF COURSES

18 West : 6 km at Halfweg, Machineweg 1b, ✉ 1165 NB, ☎ (0 23) 513 29 39, Fax (0 23) 513 29 35 - 9 South : 5 km at Duivendrecht, Zwarte Laantje 4, ✉ 1099 CE, ☎ (0 20) 694 36 50, Fax (0 20) 663 46 21 - 18 Buikslotermeerdijk 141, ✉ 1027 AC, ☎ (0 20) 632 56 50, Fax (0 20) 634 35 06 - 18 Southeast at Holendrecht, Abcouderstraatweg 46, ✉ 1105 AA, ☎ (0 294) 28 12 41, Fax (0 294) 28 63 47.

CASINO

Holland Casino KY, Max Euweplein 62, ✉ 1017 MB (near Leidseplein), ☎ (0 20) 521 11 11, Fax (0 20) 521 11 10.

PLACES OF INTEREST

VIEUWPOINTS

Keizersgracht★★ KVY – *from the sluice bridge on the Oudezijds Kolk and the Oudezijds Voorburgwal*★ LX.

HISTORICAL MONUMENTS

Dam : Royal Palace★ KX – *Beguine Convent*★★ KX – *Cromhout Houses*★ KY **A**[4] – *Westerkerk*★ KX – *Nieuwe Kerk*★★ KX – *Oude Kerk*★ LX.

HISTORICAL MUSEUMS

Amsterdam Historical Museum★★ KX – *Jewish Museum*★ LY – *Allard Pierson Museum*★ *: archeological finds* LXY – *the House of Anne Frank*★★ KX – *Netherlands Maritime History Museum*★★ MX – *Tropical Museum*★ – *Van Loon Museum*★ LY – *Willet-Holthuysen Museum*★ LY.

FAMOUS COLLECTIONS

Rijksmuseum★★★ KZ – *Van Gogh Museum*★★★ *(Rijksmuseum)* JZ – *Museum of Modern Art*★★★ JZ – *Amstelkring "Our Dear Lord in the Attic"*★ *(Museum Amstelkring Ons' Lieve Heer op Solder) : clandestine chapel* LX – *Rembrandt's House*★ *: works by the master* LX – *Cobra*★ *(Modern Art).*

MODERN ARCHITECTURE

Housing in the Jordaan district and around the Nieuwmarkt – Contemporary structures at Amsterdam Zuid-Oost (ING bank).

SCENIC AREAS AND PARKS

Old Amsterdam★★★ – *Herengracht*★★★ KVY – *Canals*★★★ *(Grachten) with hotel-boats (Amstel) – The Jordaan (Prinsengracht*★★*, Brouwersgracht*★*, Lijnbaansgracht, Looiersgracht, Egelantiersgracht*★*, Bloemgracht*★ *)* KX – JKY – *Reguliersgracht*★ LY – *Realeneiland – Dam*★ KX – *Thin Bridge*★ *(Magere Brug)* LY – *The Walletjes*★★ *(red light district)* LX – *Sarphatipark – Oosterpark – Vondelpark* JZ – *Artis*★ MY *(zoological park) – Singel*★★ KY.

J
K
V
X
Y
Z
Lindengracht
Noorderkerk
Noordermarkt
Brouwersgr.
Karthuizerhofje
Westerstraat
Marnixstr.
JORDAAN
Anjeliersstr.
Egelantiers
EGELANTIERSGR.
PRINSENGRACHT
KEIZERSGRACHT
HERENGRACHT
ANNE FRANK HUIS
Leliegracht
SINGEL
NIEUWE KERK
WESTERKERK
Raadhuisstr.
BLOEMGRACHT
Nieuwe Leliestr.
Rozengracht
Lauriergracht
Hartenstr.
KONINKLIJK PALEIS
AMSTERDAMS HISTORISCH MUSEUM
Wolvenstr.
BEGIJNHOF
Elandsgracht
Woonboot museum
Spui
CROMHOUTHUIZEN
Huis Marseille
Leidsegracht
BLOEMENMARKT
Leidsestraat
KEIZERSGR.
HERENGR.
PRINSENGR.
Kerkstr.
Voormalige NHM
LEIDSEPLEIN
CASINO
Paradiso
Weteringschans
Stadhouderskade
Vijzelgracht
RIJKSMUSEUM
Hooftstr.
P. C.
Paulus Potterstr.
MUSEUM PLEIN
STEDELIJK MUSEUM
VAN GOGH MUSEUM
VONDELPARK
OUD-ZUID
Vondelstraat
Huygensstr.
Overtoom
S 106
S 105
S 100
S 109
Kostverlorenvaart
Hendrikstraat
Nassau Kade
Singelgracht
Lijnbaansgracht
2e Hugo de Grootstr.
Fr.
de Clercqstr.
Da Costa gracht
Bilderdijk str.
Kinkerstr.
J.v. Lennep straat
Lennep Kanaal
Bosboom Toussaint str.
1e Constantijn
Marnixstraat
Looiersgr.
Weteringplantsoen
POL.

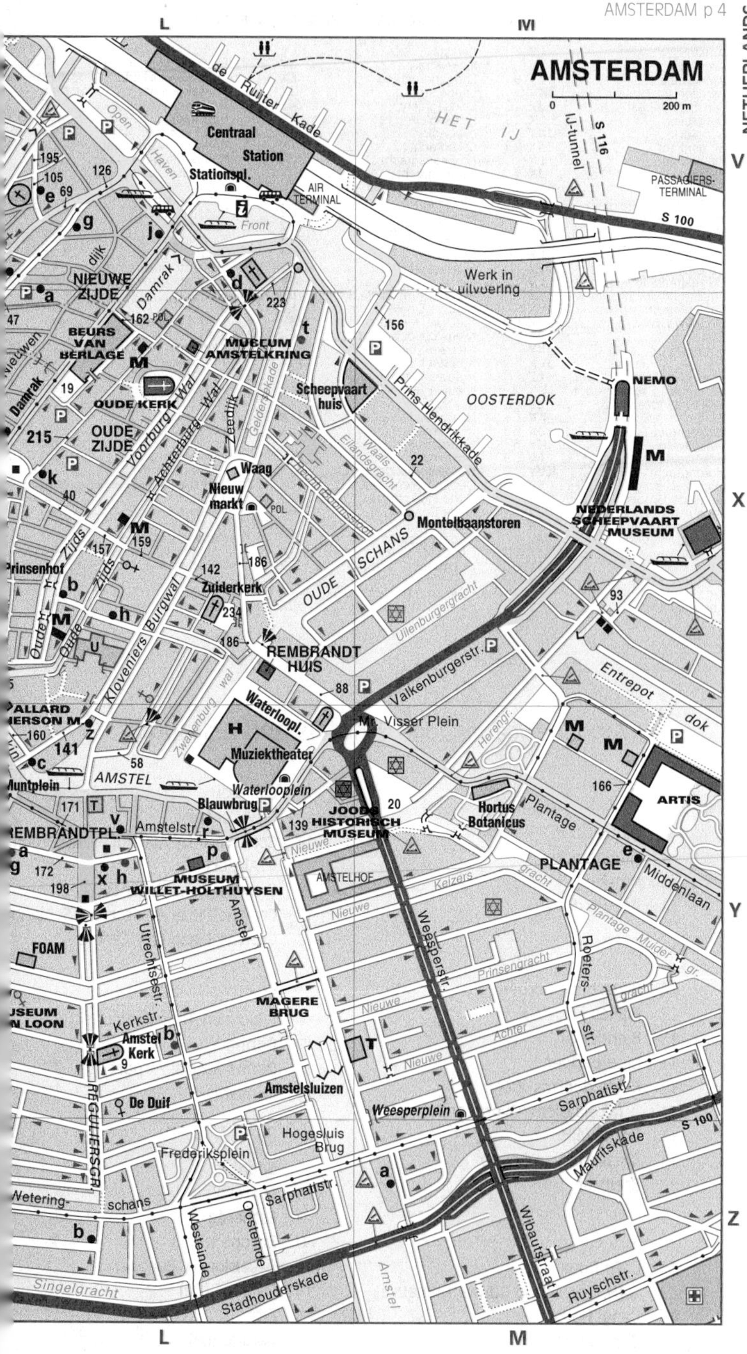

AMSTERDAM

STREET INDEX TO AMSTERDAM TOWN PLAN

Alphabetical listing of hotels and restaurants

Establishments according to style of cuisine

Buffets

18 Greenhouse (H. Hilton Schiphol) *Env. at Schiphol*

Pub rest – Brasseries

8 Amstel Bar and Brasserie (The) (H. Amstel) *Centre*
14 Brasserie Camelia (H. Okura) *South and West Q.*
8 Brasserie De Palmboom (H. Radisson SAS) *Centre*
14 Brasserie van Baerle *Rijksmuseum*
11 Café Roux (H. The Grand Sofitel Demeure) *Centre*
9 Crowne Plaza American *Centre*
10 Eden *Centre*
14 Garage (Le) *Rijksmuseum*
10 NH City Centre *Centre*
10 NH Schiller *Centre*
16 Novotel *Buitenveldert*
10 Port van Cleve (Die) *Centre*
10 NH Schiller *Centre*

Seafood – Oyster bar

12 Oesterbar *Centre*
12 Pêcheur (Le) *Centre*
15 Sirène (La) (H. Le Meridien Apollo) *South and West Q.*
15 visaandeschelde *South and West Q.*

American

16 *H. Holiday Inn Buitenveldert*

Asian

18 East West *(H. Hilton Schiphol) Env. at Schiphol*
9 Blakes *Centre*

Chinese

12 Sichuan Food *Centre*

Dutch regional

8 Dorrius (H. Crowne Plaza City Centre) *Centre*
11 Roode Leeuw (De) (H. Amsterdam) *Centre*

Indian

16 Pakistan *South and West Q.*

Indonesian

13 blue pepper *Centre*
11 Indrapura *Centre*
14 Radèn Mas *Rijksmuseum*

Italian

13 Bice (H. Golden Tulip Centre) *Rijksmuseum*
9 Caruso (H. Jolly Carlton) *Centre*
10 NH City Centre *Centre*
18 Radisson SAS Airport *Env. at Schiphol*
14 Roberto's (H. Hilton) *South and West Q.*
12 Segugio *Centre*
9 Swissôtel *Centre*

Japanese

12 Hosokawa *Centre*
14 Sazanka (H. Okura) *South and West Q.*
15 Yamazato (H. Okura) *South and West Q.*

Oriental

11 Dynasty *Centre*
12 Manchurian *Centre*

Vietnamese

13 Indochine (L') *Centre*

Centre

Amstel, Prof. Tulpplein 1, 1018 GX, (0 20) 622 60 60, *Fax (0 20) 622 58 08*, – – 25-180. AE VISA JCB. MZ a

Meals see ***La Rive*** below – ***The Amstel Bar and Brasserie*** (open until 11.30 p.m.) a la carte approx. 56 – 29 – **64 rm** 530/570, – 15 suites.

♦ This palace is a veritable haven of luxury and fine taste on the banks of the Amstel, its sumptuous rooms decorated with period furniture and magnificent detail. The cosy library-bar offers an appetising and cosmopolitan menu. Superb, attentive service.

The Grand Sofitel Demeure, O.Z. Voorburgwal 197, 1012 EX, (0 20) 555 31 11, *h2783@accor-hotels.com, Fax (0 20) 555 32 22*, – – 25-300. AE VISA JCB. LX b

Meals see ***Café Roux*** below – 25 – **270 rm** 380/465, – 12 suites.

♦ Authentic Art Nouveau lounges, exquisite bedrooms and an inner garden await guests behind the magnificent façade of this building, which in the 16C hosted Maria de' Medici.

NH Gd H. Krasnapolsky, Dam 9, 1012 JS, (0 20) 554 91 11, *reflet@nhkrasnapolsky.nh-hotels.nl, Fax (0 20) 622 86 07*, – – – 25-750. AE VISA JCB LX k

Meals ***Reflet*** *(closed Sunday)* (dinner only) 33 – 21 – **461 rm** 230/375, – 7 suites.

♦ This large hotel on the Dam offers a choice of "business" and "executive" rooms as well as apartments in modern or traditional style. The splendid Winter Garden dates from the 19C. The Reflet, created in 1883, has retained its original splendour and cosy feel.

de l'Europe, Nieuwe Doelenstraat 2, 1012 CP, (0 20) 531 17 77, *hotel@leurope.nl, Fax (0 20) 531 17 78*, – – 25-80. AE VISA JCB LY c

Meals see ***Excelsior*** and ***Le Relais*** below – 25 – **94 rm** 285/495, – 6 suites.

♦ A late-19C hotel-palace that combines both charm and tradition, with bedrooms decorated in fine taste. Collection of paintings by Dutch landscape artists. Attractive sea views.

NH Barbizon Palace, Prins Hendrikkade 59, 1012 AD, (0 20) 556 45 64, *info@nhbarbizon-palace.nh-hotels.nl, Fax (0 20) 624 33 53*, – – – 25-300. AE VISA JCB. LV d

Meals see ***Vermeer*** below – ***Hudson's Terrace and Restaurant*** (open until 11 p.m.) *Lunch 30* – a la carte approx. 47 – 20 – **272 rm** 240/390, – 3 suites.

♦ Near the railway station, the Barbizon Palace has recently undergone substantial renovation. The attic rooms are the most cosy, although the whole building has been restored with care. Fish, seafood and New World dishes take pride of place in the restaurant.

Radisson SAS, Rusland 17, 1012 CK, (0 20) 623 12 31, *reservations.amsterdam@radissonsas.com, Fax (0 20) 520 82 00*, – – – 25-180. AE VISA JCB. rest LX h

Meals ***Brasserie De Palmboom*** *Lunch 29* – a la carte 35/45 – 19 – **242 rm** 295, – 1 suite.

♦ A modern chain hotel with an 18C presbytery in the atrium. Comfortable rooms, decorated in Scandinavian, Dutch, Oriental and Art Deco styles. Mediterranean restaurant with an emphasis on Italian cuisine, plus a modern brasserie with a relaxed atmosphere.

Renaissance, Kattengat 1, 1012 SZ, (0 20) 621 22 23, *renaissance.amsterdam@renaissancehotels.com, Fax (0 20) 627 52 45*, – – – 25-400. AE VISA JCB. LV e

Meals (dinner only) a la carte 37/46 – 21 – **382 rm** 249/299, – 6 suites.

♦ Completely refurbished and equipped with superb conference facilities under the dome of a former church. Modern comfort in the bedrooms, junior suites and suites. Brasserie-restaurant serving a range of international cuisine.

Crowne Plaza City Centre, N.Z. Voorburgwal 5, 1012 RC, (0 20) 620 05 00, *info@crownplaza.nl, Fax (0 20) 620 11 73*, – – – 25-270. AE VISA JCB. LV g

Meals ***Dorrius*** *(closed Sunday)* (partly Dutch regional cooking, dinner only until 11 p.m.) a la carte 32/57 – 22 – **268 rm** 310/340, – 2 suites.

♦ Near the station, the Crowne Plaza offers the comfort expected of this chain. View of Amsterdam's rooftops from the "lounge club" on the top floor. Attractive panelled restaurant and authentic 19C café. Traditional menu choices plus a range of local dishes.

Pulitzer, Prinsengracht 323, 1016 GZ, (0 20) 523 52 35, *sales.amsterdam@starwoodhotels.com, Fax (0 20) 627 67 53*, – – – 25-150. AE VISA JCB KX m

Meals ***Pulitzers*** *Lunch 45* – a la carte approx. 53 – 25 – **227 rm** 450/515, – 3 suites.

♦ A group of 24 canal houses dating from the 17C and 18C, superbly converted into an exquisite hotel with new bedrooms designed to impeccable standards. A modern, original café-restaurant with humorous references to the painter Frans Hals.

Crowne Plaza American, Leidsekade 97, 1017 PN, (0 20) 556 30 00, *ameri can@ichotelsgroup.com, Fax (0 20) 556 30 01,* – rm, – 25-150. AE VISA. JY q
Meals (Art deco style pub rest, open until 11.30 p.m.). *Lunch 28* – a la carte 32/42 – 22 – **172 rm** 285/385, – 2 suites.
◆ Hidden behind the imposing historic façade is this pleasant hotel with rooms that, although identically furnished, vary in size. The sophisticated entrance hall, with its touches of Art Deco, is the setting for the hotel's tavern-restaurant.

Victoria, Damrak 1, 1012 LG, (0 20) 623 42 55, *vicres@parkplazahotels.nl, Fax (0 20) 625 29 97,* – – 30-150. AE VISA JCB. LV j
Meals. *Lunch 27* – a la carte 32/44 – 20 – **295 rm** 280/330, – 10 suites.
◆ This classical palace, embellished by a new wing, is in an ideal location for those arriving in the city by train. Four room categories. The entrance hall is crowned by an attractive glass roof. Modern cuisine.

Blakes, Keizersgracht 384, 1016 GB, (0 20) 530 20 10, *hotel@blakes.nl, Fax (0 20) 530 20 30,* – , rm, – 30. AE VISA. KX a
Meals *(closed Saturday lunch and Sunday)* (partly Asian cuisine). *Lunch 28* – a la carte 59/74 – 18 – **38 rm** 390/990, – 3 suites.
◆ Luxury and peace and quiet best describe this residence with its surprising Oriental-inspired décor. Highly individual rooms, and a restaurant with a rustic-modern feel where the emphasis is on the flavours of the East.

Jolly Carlton, Vijzelstraat 4, 1017 HK, (0 20) 622 22 66 and 623 83 20 (rest), *reservations@jollycarlton.nl, Fax (0 20) 626 61 83* – – 25-150. AE VISA. LY n
Meals ***Caruso*** *(closed 25 December)* (Italian cuisine, dinner only until 11 p.m.) a la carte 50/71 – **218 rm** 255/455.
◆ This chain hotel, housed in a building dating from the 1900s, is located close to Rembrandtplein. Standard rooms with Italian furnishings and good soundproofing. Elegant restaurant serving Italian cuisine, including well-balanced lunches and fixed menus.

Swissôtel, Damrak 96, 1012 LP, (0 20) 522 30 00, *emailus.amsterdam@swissotel.com, Fax (0 20) 522 32 23* – – 25-45. AE VISA JCB. LX s
Meals (partly Italian cuisine) 28 – 20 – **101 rm** 299/360, – 5 suites.
◆ The recently revamped rooms and junior suites in this hotel near the Dam are well-appointed and modern in feel. Business centre. Trendy brasserie-restaurant. "Mediterranean"-inspired cuisine, with an emphasis on Italian gastronomy.

Sofitel, N.Z. Voorburgwal 67, 1012 RE, (0 20) 627 59 00, *h1159@accor-hotels.com, Fax (0 20) 623 89 32,* – – 25-55. AE VISA JCB.
Meals a la carte 31/72 – 20 – **148 rm** 305. KX q
◆ This upmarket chain hotel, 500m/550yd from the main station, occupies an old mansion and an adjoining modern building. Recently refurbished façade and bedrooms. "Orient Express" atmosphere in the restaurant. Traditional menu.

Toren without rest, Keizersgracht 164, 1015 CZ, (0 20) 622 63 52, *info@hoteltoren.nl, Fax (0 20) 626 97 05,* – . AE VISA KV w
12 – **39 rm** 130/215, – 1 suite.
◆ Anne Frank's House is just 200m/220yd from this family-run hotel with its renovated, spotless and well-appointed rooms with good soundproofing.

NH Doelen without rest, Nieuwe Doelenstraat 24, 1012 CP, (0 20) 554 06 00, *nhdoelen@nh-hotels.nl, Fax (0 20) 622 94 10,* – – 25-100. AE VISA JCB. LY z
16 – **85 rm** 190/230.
◆ Built in 1856 on the banks of the Amstel, the Doelen is one of the oldest hotels in the city. English-style rooms with varying degrees of soundproofing.

Seven One Seven without rest, Prinsengracht 717, 1017 JW, (0 20) 427 07 17, *info@717hotel.nl, Fax (0 20) 423 07 17,* – . AE VISA KY c
8 rm 390/640.
◆ If you're looking for a quiet, intimate hotel, this elegant 18C residence could be just for you, with its exquisite, individually furnished and spacious bedrooms.

Ambassade without rest, Herengracht 341, 1016 AZ, (0 20) 555 02 22, *info@ambassade-hotel.nl, Fax (0 20) 555 02 77,* – . AE VISA KX x
16 – **51 rm** 165/195, – 8 suites.
◆ A group of typical 17C houses is the setting for this charming hotel bordered by two canals. Although varying in size, each bedroom is endowed with its own personal touch. Interesting library.

Estheréa without rest, Singel 305, 1012 WJ, (0 20) 624 51 46, *estherea@xs4all.nl, Fax (0 20) 623 90 01* – . AE VISA JCB. KX y
14 – **71 rm** 237/280.
◆ Set back from the hubbub of Amsterdam's central district, between the history museum and the Singel, this hotel is a complex of several adjoining houses with pleasant rooms.

Eden, Amstel 144, ✉ 1017 AE, ✆ (0 20) 530 78 78, *info.eden@edenhotelgroup.com, Fax (0 20) 623 32 67* – |♦| ⇔, ▤ rm, TV ♿. AE ◑ ◎ VISA JCB. ✂ LY r
Meals (pub rest, open until 11 p.m.). *Lunch 13* – 22/37 b.i. – ☕ 14 – **327 rm** 190/200.
• It's hard to believe that hidden behind the façade of these two narrow buildings along the banks of the Amstel is a hotel with over 300 rooms. Bar-restaurant with views of the river. Popular with both individual visitors and tour groups.

Amsterdam, Damrak 93, ✉ 1012 LP, ✆ (0 20) 555 06 66, *info@hotelamsterdam.nl, Fax (0 20) 620 47 16* – |♦| ⇔ ▤ TV. AE ◑ ◎ VISA JCB. ✂ rest LX s
Meals *De Roode Leeuw* (partly Dutch regional cooking) 30 – ☕ 17 – **79 rm** 240/310.
• This veteran Amsterdam hotel enjoys an unbeatable central location along the popular Damstraat. Rooms beyond reproach, with public parking nearby. The hotel brasserie serves a range of typically Dutch specialities.

NH Schiller, Rembrandtsplein 26, ✉ 1017 CV, ✆ (0 20) 554 07 00, *info@nhschiller.nh-hotels.nl, Fax (0 20) 626 68 31*, ☂ – |♦| ⇔ TV. AE ◑ ◎ VISA JCB. ✂ rm LY x
Meals (brasserie). *Lunch 20* – 30 – ☕ 16 – **91 rm** 190/230, – 1 suite.
• A 1900s-style building fronting a lively square adorned with a statue of Rembrandt. Adequately equipped rooms with quality furnishings. Pleasant lobby. In the Art Deco brasserie, make sure you try the Frisse Frits, the bar's home-brewed beer.

Albus Gd H. without rest, Vijzelstraat 49, ✉ 1017 HE, ✆ (0 20) 530 62 00, *sales@albusgrandhotel.com, Fax (0 20) 530 62 99* – |♦| ⇔ TV. AE ◎ VISA. ✂ LY g
☕ 13 – **74 rm** 160/205.
• A brand-new hotel within spitting distance of the flower market. Functional, identically furnished rooms of varying size with good soundproofing.

NH Caransa without rest, Rembrandtsplein 19, ✉ 1017 CT, ✆ (0 20) 554 08 00, *info@nhcaransa.nh-hotels.nl, Fax (0 20) 626 68 31* – |♦| ⇔ TV – 🎤 25-100. AE ◑ ◎ VISA. ✂ LY v
☕ 16 – **66 rm** 190/230.
• The Caransa's rooms are functional, well-maintained and reasonably sized. The warm furnishings add a cosy "British" feel. Four seminar rooms available for business meetings.

die Port van Cleve, N.Z. Voorburgwal 178, ✉ 1012 SJ, ✆ (0 20) 624 48 60, *sales-marketing@dieportvancleve.com, Fax (0 20) 622 02 40* – |♦| ⇔, ▤ rest, TV – 🎤 40. AE ◑ ◎ VISA JCB. ✂ KX w
Meals (brasserie). *Lunch 20* – a la carte 24/53 ♀ – ☕ 18 – **119 rm** 199/295, – 1 suite.
• The very first Dutch brewery group was established behind this imposing façade near the royal palace in the 19C. Noteworthy features today include the six junior suites and a charming Dutch-style bar. Grill-restaurant where steak holds pride of place.

Dikker and Thijs Fenice without rest, Prinsengracht 444, ✉ 1017 KE, ✆ (0 20) 620 12 12, *info@dtfh.nl, Fax (0 20) 625 89 86*, ⚓ – |♦| ⇔ TV. AE ◑ ◎ VISA JCB KY v
42 rm ☕ 145/345.
• This classical building is located 100m/110yd from the Leidseplein, opposite a small bridge spanning the Princes' Canal, which is visible from a few of the rooms.

NH City Centre, Spuistraat 288, ✉ 1012 VX, ✆ (0 20) 420 45 45, *nhcitycentre@nh-hotels.nl, Fax (0 20) 420 43 00*, ⋖, ⚓ – |♦| ⇔ TV ♿ 🚗. AE ◑ ◎ VISA JCB. ✂ KX g
Meals (pub rest, partly Italian cuisine). *Lunch 16* – a la carte 22/32 ♀ – ☕ 16 – **186 rm** 175.
• Nestled between the Singel and the Begijnhof, this chain hotel offers rooms of standard quality with sober furnishings. Large public areas but "minimalist" service.

Mercure Arthur Frommer without rest, Noorderstraat 46, ✉ 1017 TV, ✆ (0 20) 622 03 28, *h1032@accor-hotels.com, Fax (0 20) 620 32 08* – |♦| ⇔ ▤ TV 🚗 P. AE ◑ ◎ VISA JCB LYZ j
☕ 14 – **90 rm** 145/165.
• A series of houses lining a quiet street close to both the Rijksmuseum and the Museum Van Loon. Fairly standard rooms, basic levels of service, but a useful car park.

Canal House without rest, Keizersgracht 148, ✉ 1015 CX, ✆ (0 20) 622 51 82, *info@canalhouse.nl, Fax (0 20) 624 13 17* – |♦|. AE ◑ ◎ VISA JCB. ✂ KV k
26 rm ☕ 150/190.
• This 17C canal-front residence has preserved all its old charm. Individually styled rooms, with good views at the front and less noise at the rear. Eclectic mix of furniture.

Inntel without rest, Nieuwezijdskolk 19, ✉ 1012 PV, ✆ (0 20) 530 18 18, *infoamsterdam@hotelinntel.com, Fax (0 20) 422 19 19* – |♦| ⇔ ▤ TV ♿. AE ◑ ◎ VISA JCB LVX a
☕ 16 – **236 rm** 199/325.
• A modern hotel at the heart of the busy Nieuwe Zijde shopping district near the station. Rooms with double-glazing and soundproofed doors.

City Center without rest, N.Z. Voorburgwal 50, ✉ 1012 SC, ✆ (0 20) 422 00 11, *info@ams.nl, Fax (0 20) 420 03 57* – |♦| ⇔ TV ♿. AE ◑ ◎ VISA JCB. ✂ LV f
☕ 12 – **101 rm** 189.
• A modern building on the edge of the Nieuwe Zijde district, 400m/440yd from the main station. Basic, but well-maintained rooms. The underground car park is a major plus.

Wiechmann without rest, Prinsengracht 328, ✉ 1016 HX, ☎ (0 20) 626 33 21, *info@hotelwiechmann.nl, Fax (0 20) 626 89 62* – TV. MC VISA. KX d
37 rm ☕ 75/140.
◆ The Wiechmann occupies three small houses overlooking the Prinsengracht. The best, albeit slightly more rustic rooms are to be found on the corners of the building.

Lancaster without rest, Plantage Middenlaan 48, ✉ 1018 DH, ☎ (0 20) 535 68 88, *Fax (0 20) 535 68 89* – TV. AE MC VISA JCB. MY e
☕ 14 – **92 rm** 130/172.
◆ This completely renovated old residence stands opposite the zoo in a residential area away from the centre. Although differing in size, the rooms here are perfectly adequate.

La Rive - Hotel Amstel, Prof. Tulpplein 1, ✉ 1018 GX, ☎ (0 20) 520 32 64, *evert_groot@interconti.com, Fax (0 20) 520 32 66*, ≤, – P. AE MC VISA JCB. MZ a
closed 1 to 23 August, 31 December-12 January, Saturday lunch and Sunday – **Meals**. *Lunch 48 b.i.* – 85/98, – a la carte 69/94 ♀.
◆ Hushed tones, refined décor and incomparable comfort are the main features of the Amstel's gastronomic restaurant, from where guests can enjoy a superb view of the river.
Spec. Turbot et truffe enrobés de pommes de terre, blettes et jus de veau. Pigeonneau grillé et poivron rouge, sauce au maïs. Feuilleté aux pommes, cannelle, glace vanille et caramel au beurre salé.

Excelsior - Hotel de l'Europe, Nieuwe Doelenstraat 2, ✉ 1012 CP, ☎ (0 20) 531 17 05, *hotel@leurope.nl, Fax (0 20) 531 17 78*, ≤, , Open until 11 p.m., – P. AE MC VISA JCB LY c
closed 1 to 10 January and lunch Saturday and Sunday – **Meals**. *Lunch 45* – 65/95 b.i. ♀.
◆ This century-old palace provides a delightful backdrop to its pleasantly redecorated restaurant. Views of the Munttoren and the ever-busy Amstel River from the terrace.

Vermeer - Hotel NH Barbizon Palace, Prins Hendrikkade 59, ✉ 1012 AD, ☎ (0 20) 556 48 85, *vermeer@nh-hotels.nl, Fax (0 20) 556 48 58*, – P. AE MC VISA JCB.
closed 19 July-22 August, 24 December-9 January, Saturday lunch, Sunday and Bank Holidays – **Meals**. *Lunch 35* – 40/125, – a la carte 72/82 ♀. LV d
◆ Sadly, Vermeer never set up his easel at this restaurant which offers customers elegant, classically-based cuisine, enlivened by the occasional note of inventiveness.
Spec. Foie gras de canard fumé, confit d'oignons blancs. Ris de veau sauté et rognon rissolé, crème de chou-fleur mousseuse. Cinq petits desserts au chocolat.

Christophe (Royer), Leliegracht 46, ✉ 1015 DH, ☎ (0 20) 625 08 07, *info@christophe.nl, Fax (0 20) 638 91 32* – AE MC VISA KVX c
closed 27 December-5 January, Sunday and Monday – **Meals** (dinner only) 51/65, – a la carte 61/86 ♀.
◆ Ambitious cuisine peppered with Mediterranean touches served in a luxurious setting. Central location on the Leliegracht, near Anne Frank's House and the Jordaan district.
Spec. Lapin de 4 heures au foie gras et jus de cassis. Filet de bar poêlé et fenouil mariné, jus à l'ail fumé. Brochette d'agneau aux dattes fraîches, purée d'aubergine au curry.

Dynasty, Reguliersdwarsstraat 30, ✉ 1017 BM, ☎ (0 20) 626 84 00, *Fax (0 20) 622 30 38*, , Oriental cuisine – AE MC VISA. KY q
closed 27 December-27 January and Tuesday – **Meals** (dinner only) a la carte 32/50.
◆ Enjoy a wander through the flower market before sitting down to table at this Oriental restaurant with its refreshing, multi-coloured décor. Specialities from Southeast Asia.

d'Vijff Vlieghen, Spuistraat 294 (by Vlieghendesteeg), ✉ 1012 VX, ☎ (0 20) 530 40 60, *restaurant@vijffvlieghen.nl, Fax (0 20) 623 64 04*, , – AE MC VISA JCB. KX p
Meals (dinner only) 33 ♀.
◆ The "Five Flies" (Vijff Vlieghen) is a group of small 17C houses concealing a maze of charming, rustic-style rooms. Traditional à la carte choices and menus.

Café Roux - Hotel The Grand Sofitel Demeure, O.Z. Voorburgwal 197, ✉ 1012 EX, ☎ (0 20) 555 35 60, *h2783-fb@accor-hotels.com, Fax (0 20) 555 32 90*, – P. AE MC VISA JCB. LX b
Meals. *Lunch 29* – 34/48 b.i. ♀.
◆ The Sofitel Demeure's Art Deco brasserie is known for its inventive modern cuisine. A mural by K. Appel, a member of the Cobra artistic group, is visible near the entrance.

Het Tuynhuys, Reguliersdwarsstraat 28, ✉ 1017 BM, ☎ (0 20) 627 66 03, *Fax (0 20) 423 59 99*, – AE MC VISA JCB KY q
closed 31 December-1 January and lunch Saturday and Sunday – **Meals**. *Lunch 30* – a la carte 41/87.
◆ The menu is distinctly modern in this stylish split-level restaurant with an attractive garden terrace and contemporary dining room adorned with glazed ceramics.

Indrapura, Rembrandtplein 42, ✉ 1017 CV, ☎ (0 20) 623 73 29, *info@indrapura.nl, Fax (0 20) 624 90 78*, Indonesian cuisine – AE MC VISA LY h
closed 31 December – **Meals** (dinner only) 25/39.
◆ A good choice of Indonesian dishes, including the inevitable "rijsttafel" (rice table). A broad mix of customers, including tourists, locals and groups.

Sichuan Food, Reguliersdwarsstraat 35, ✉ 1017 BK, ☎ (0 20) 626 93 27, *Fax (0 20) 627 72 81*, Chinese cuisine – ▤. AE ⓓ MC VISA. ⚡ KY u
closed 31 December – **Meals** (dinner only, booking essential) 31/43, – a la carte 35/63.
◆ Hidden behind the ordinary façade is a temple of Asian gastronomy, where the flavours of Szechwan take pride of place. The décor is typical of any local Chinese restaurant.
Spec. Dim Sum. Canard laqué à la pékinoise. Huîtres sautées maison.

Hosokawa, Max Euweplein 22, ✉ 1017 MB, ☎ (0 20) 638 80 86, *info@hosokawa.nl*, *Fax (0 20) 638 22 19*, Japanese cuisine with Teppan-Yaki – AE ⓓ MC VISA JCB. ⚡ KY a
closed last week July-first 2 weeks August – **Meals** (dinner only) a la carte 24/77.
◆ A sober, modern Japanese restaurant with eight teppanyaki. Worth the trip just to admire the constant circulation of dishes in front of your eyes. Public car park.

Van Vlaanderen (Philippart), Weteringschans 175, ✉ 1017 XD, ☎ (0 20) 622 82 92, 🏕, ⚓ – ▤. AE MC VISA KZ k
closed mid July-first week August, last week December, Sunday and Monday – **Meals** (dinner only, booking essential) 40 a la carte 56/63 ♀.
◆ Modern and refined French cuisine, coupled with the occasional Belgian-inspired recipe, awaits customers at this recommended address near the Museum Van Loon and Rijksmuseum.
Spec. Émincé de cabillaud, homard et pommes de terre au coulis de crevettes. Caneton rôti, tarte tatin de figues et pommes sautées. Profiterolles au caramel de beurre salé et compote de coings.

Breitner, Amstel 212, ✉ 1017 AH, ☎ (0 20) 627 78 79, *Fax (0 20) 330 29 98* – AE ⓓ MC VISA JCB. ⚡ LY p
closed last 2 weeks July-early August, 25 December-1 January and Sunday – **Meals** (dinner only) a la carte 47/72 ♀.
◆ This restaurant takes its name from the Dutch impressionist artist. Modern cuisine, largely based on Mediterranean recipes. Wines from around the world. Views of the Amstel.

Takens, Runstraat 17d, ✉ 1016 GJ, ☎ (0 20) 627 06 18, *Fax (0 20) 624 28 61*, Open until 11 p.m. – AE ⓓ MC VISA KX s
closed Christmas-5 January – **Meals** (lunch by arrangement) a la carte 39/51 ♀.
◆ The culinary delights at this restaurant close to the Cromhouthuizen include reworked traditional dishes. A well-established wine cellar and a relaxed, friendly atmosphere.

Manchurian, Leidseplein 10a, ✉ 1017 PT, ☎ (0 20) 623 13 30, *info@manchurian.nl*, *Fax (0 20) 626 21 05*, Oriental cuisine – ▤. AE ⓓ MC VISA. ⚡ KY x
closed 30 April and 31 December – **Meals** 26/44 ♀.
◆ This Asian restaurant on the busy Leidseplein specialises in Thai cuisine as well as Chinese dishes from Canton, Shanghai and Szechwan.

Segugio, Utrechtsestraat 96, ✉ 1017 VS, ☎ (0 20) 330 15 03, *adriano@segugio.nl*, *Fax (0 20) 330 15 16*, Italian cuisine – ▤. AE ⓓ MC VISA. ⚡ LY b
closed 24 December-2 January and Sunday – **Meals** (dinner only until 11 p.m.) a la carte 45/58 ♀.
◆ A good sense of smell is all you need to locate this "ristorante" which takes its name from a breed of hunting dog also used as a truffle hound. Good choice of Italian wines.

Le Pêcheur, Reguliersdwarsstraat 32, ✉ 1017 BM, ☎ (0 20) 624 31 21, *Fax (0 20) 624 31 21*, 🏕, Seafood – AE ⓓ MC VISA JCB. ⚡ KY w
closed Sunday – **Meals**. Lunch 33 – a la carte 42/63.
◆ As its name (The Fisherman) would suggest, fish and seafood take pride of place in this restaurant alongside the flower market. Terrace to the rear and parking nearby.

d'theeboom, Singel 210, ✉ 1016 AB, ☎ (0 20) 623 84 20, *info@theeboom.nl*, *Fax (0 20) 421 25 12*, 🏕 – AE ⓓ MC VISA JCB KX b
closed 24 December-6 January and Sunday – **Meals** (dinner only) 33/43.
◆ Firmly established along the Singel, 200m/220yd from the Dam, "The Tea-Room" is anything but! It is in fact a restaurant with an interesting menu of inventive dishes.

Le Relais - Hotel de l'Europe, Nieuwe Doelenstraat 2, ✉ 1012 CP, ☎ (0 20) 531 17 77, *hotel@leurope.nl*, *Fax (0 20) 531 17 78*, Open until 11 p.m., ⚓ – ▤. AE ⓓ MC VISA JCB
Meals. Lunch 24 – 29 ♀. LY c
◆ A small, elegant restaurant within a large hotel where you immediately feel in good hands. Traditional choices on a menu without any particular culinary theme.

Oesterbar, Leidseplein 10, ✉ 1017 PT, ☎ (0 20) 623 29 88, *Fax (0 20) 623 21 99*, Seafood – ▤. AE ⓓ MC VISA. ⚡ KY x
closed 25, 26 et 31 December – **Meals** (dinner only until midnight) a la carte 44/158.
◆ A classical menu resolutely geared to the sea is on offer at this oyster bar occupying three floors of a building close to the Leidseplein theatre. Reservations recommended.

X **Bordewijk,** Noordermarkt 7, ✉ 1015 MV, ✆ (0 20) 624 38 99, *Fax (0 20) 420 66 03* – ▤. AE ⓓ ⓜ VISA. ✻ KV a
closed last week July-first 2 weeks August and Monday – **Meals** (dinner only) a la carte 52/60.
◆ One of the trendiest addresses in the Jordaan district with a lively dining room furnished in a sober, yet modern style. Appetising menu and good wine list.

X **Haesje Claes,** Spuistraat 275, ✉ 1012 VR, ✆ (0 20) 624 99 98, *info@haesjeclaes.nl, Fax (0 20) 627 48 17,* ☂ – ▤. AE ⓓ ⓜ VISA JCB. ✻ KX f
closed 30 April and 25, 26 and 31 December – **Meals** 19/29 ♀.
◆ With a real local atmosphere and a loyal local clientele, this welcoming restaurant serves true Flemish fare : unfussy, generous and satisfying. 100m from the History Museum.

X **Entresol,** Geldersekade 29, ✉ 1011 EJ, ✆ (0 20) 623 79 12, *entresol@chello.nl* – ▤. ⓜ VISA LX t
closed 3 weeks July, Monday and Tuesday – **Meals** (dinner only) a la carte approx. 40.
◆ This charming, small family restaurant near Amsterdam's Chinatown occupies a house over 300 years old. Dutch-style décor in the dining rooms spread over two floors.

X **blue pepper,** Nassaukade 366h, ✉ 1054 AB, ✆ (0 20) 489 70 39, *info@restaurantbluepepper.com,* Indonesian cuisine – AE ⓓ ⓜ VISA JCB. ✻ JY d
closed Sunday – **Meals** (dinner only) a la carte 33/43.
◆ Filtered light, monochrome blues and delicate floral touches provide the basis of Blue Pepper's tranquil decor. Refined Javanese cuisine served on attractive tableware.

X **L'Indochine,** Beulingstraat 9, ✉ 1017 BA, ✆ (0 20) 627 57 55, *kietle@wxs.nl,* Vietnamese cuisine – ▤. AE ⓓ ⓜ VISA JCB. ✻ KY b
closed Monday – **Meals** (dinner only) a la carte 34/47.
◆ Embark upon a gastronomic journey between the gulfs of Siam and Tonkin in this small, simply furnished restaurant with a "colonial" name. Choice of French wines.

Rijksmuseum (Vondelpark)

Marriott, Stadhouderskade 12, ✉ 1054 ES, ✆ (0 20) 607 55 55, *amsterdam@mariotthotels.com, Fax (0 20) 607 55 11,* ⚒, ≘s, ⚲ – |♦| ⇹ ▤ TV ♿ ⇔ – 🏛 25-450. AE ⓓ ⓜ VISA JCB. ✻ JY f
Meals (dinner only until midnight) a la carte 34/44 ♀ – ☕ 20 – **387 rm** 215, – 5 suites.
◆ Impressive American-style hotel on one of the city's main roads. Huge rooms with a full range of creature comforts. Business centre and conference facilities.

NH Amsterdam Centre, Stadhouderskade 7, ✉ 1054 ES, ✆ (0 20) 685 13 51, *nhamsterdamcentre@nh-hotels.nl, Fax (0 20) 685 16 11,* ⚒, ≘s – |♦| ⇹ ▤ TV ♿ – 🏛 25-200. AE ⓓ ⓜ VISA JCB. ✻ JY p
Meals a la carte 31/41 – ***Bice*** *(closed Sunday)* (Italian cuisine, dinner only) a la carte approx. 46 – ☕ 19 – **227 rm** 230/320, – 2 suites.
◆ This easily accessible, completely renovated chain hotel is located along the Singelgracht. Spacious, highly comfortable rooms with period furniture. Impressive restaurant serving Italian cuisine and a brasserie that stays open late.

The Gresham Memphis without rest, De Lairessestraat 87, ✉ 1071 NX, ✆ (0 20) 673 31 41, *info@gresham-memphishotel.nl, Fax (0 20) 673 73 12,* ⚒ – |♦| ⇹ TV – 🏛 40. AE ⓓ ⓜ VISA JCB. ✻
☕ 18 – **74 rm** 108/250.
◆ Pleasant rooms that are soundproofed and gradually being modernised. Attentive service. Tram number 16 runs from in front of the hotel to the centre of the city.

Jan Luyken without rest, Jan Luykenstraat 58, ✉ 1071 CS, ✆ (0 20) 573 07 30, *janluyken@bilderberg.nl, Fax (0 20) 676 38 41* – |♦| ⇹ ▤ TV. AE ⓓ ⓜ VISA JCB JZ m
☕ 16 – **62 rm** 200/258.
◆ An elegant hotel made up of three buildings dating from 1900 with modern interior decor. Large, well-appointed rooms and a good location at the heart of the museum district.

Toro ⛯ without rest, Koningslaan 64, ✉ 1075 AG, ✆ (0 20) 673 72 23, *toro@ams.nl, Fax (0 20) 675 00 31* – |♦| TV. AE ⓓ ⓜ VISA JCB. ✻
☕ 15 – **22 rm** 199/235.
◆ The interior of this quiet villa by the Vondelpark has been tastefully restored, while retaining its old charm. Individually designed rooms and a terrace overlooking a lake.

Vondel (annex) without rest, Vondelstraat 28, ✉ 1054 GE, ✆ (0 20) 612 01 20, *info@hotelvondel.nl, Fax (0 20) 685 43 21,* ⛟ – |♦| TV. AE ⓓ ⓜ VISA JCB JY m
70 rm ☕ 120/140.
◆ The Vondel occupies five houses dating from the late 19C. The building housing the reception has the best rooms, decorated in "boutique" style. Elegant lounges.

Lairesse without rest, De Lairessestraat 7, ✉ 1071 NR, ☎ (0 20) 671 95 96, *Fax (0 20) 671 17 56* – |₿| ⇎ TV. AE ⓓ MC VISA JCB. ⁂
☕ 15 – **29 rm** 235.
◆ Despite its plain façade, this hotel is well-maintained and enjoys a superb location close to three of the city's most important museums. Spacious rooms with modern furniture.

Fita without rest, Jan Luykenstraat 37, ✉ 1071 CL, ☎ (0 20) 679 09 76, *info@fita.nl, Fax (0 20) 664 39 69* – |₿| ⇎ TV. AE ⓓ MC VISA. ⁂ JZ s
closed 13 December-14 January – **16 rm** ☕ 110/140.
◆ A small hotel offering a perfect base for individual travellers with its three categories of functional bedrooms and great location close to Amsterdam's major museums.

De Filosoof without rest, Anna van den Vondelstraat 6, ✉ 1054 GZ, ☎ (0 20) 683 30 13, *reservations@hotelfilosoof.nl, Fax (0 20) 685 37 50* – |₿| TV – 25. AE MC VISA. ⁂
38 rm ☕ 108/122.
◆ The originality of this hotel on a one-way street skirting the Vondelpark lies in the decoration of its rooms, which is inspired by various cultural and philosophical themes.

Villa Borgmann without rest, Koningslaan 48, ✉ 1075 AE, ☎ (0 20) 673 52 52, *info@hotel-borgmann.nl, Fax (0 20) 676 25 80*, – |₿| TV. AE ⓓ MC VISA. ⁂
11 rm ☕ 98/155.
◆ This attractive, 1900s red-brick villa near the refreshing Vondelpark is family-run and offers a quiet alternative to the city centre. Large, modern rooms.

Radèn Mas, Stadhouderskade 6, ✉ 1054 ES, ☎ (0 20) 685 40 41, *Fax (0 20) 685 39 81*, Indonesian cuisine, open until 11 p.m. – ▤. AE ⓓ MC VISA JCB. ⁂ JY k
Meals. *Lunch 30* – a la carte 34/64.
◆ This Indonesian restaurant enjoys a flattering reputation for its embodiment of the culinary heritage of this former Dutch colony. Live pianist every evening except Tuesday.

Le Garage, Ruysdaelstraat 54, ✉ 1071 XE, ☎ (0 20) 679 71 76, *info@rest-legarage.nl, Fax (0 20) 662 22 49*, With streetfood in Le Garage en Pluche, open until 11 p.m. – ▤. AE ⓓ MC VISA
closed Easter, Whitsun, last 2 weeks July, Christmas, New Year and lunch Saturday and Sunday – **Meals**. *Lunch 30* – 33/49 ♀.
◆ A theatrical atmosphere and cosmopolitan exuberance pervade this modern brasserie whose menu is both varied and imaginative. Lively tapas bar-restaurant next door.

Spring, Willemsparkweg 177, ✉ 1071 GZ, ☎ (0 20) 675 44 21, *info@restaurantspring.nl, Fax (0 20) 676 94 14*, – ▤. AE ⓓ MC VISA
closed Saturday lunch, Sunday and Bank Holidays – **Meals**. *Lunch 30* – a la carte approx. 52 ♀.
◆ The front of this trendy eatery, with a long bench running across its centre, has neither a sign nor a menu - just two steles. Refined cuisine based on quality products.

Brasserie van Baerle, Van Baerlestraat 158, ✉ 1071 BG, ☎ (0 20) 679 15 32, *brasserie@hetnet.nl, Fax (0 20) 671 71 96*, , Open until 11 p.m. – AE ⓓ MC VISA. ⁂
closed 25 December-1 January and Saturday lunch – **Meals**. *Lunch 33* – 34 ♀.
◆ A typical restaurant popular with a loyal local clientele tempted by an attractive menu enhanced by a harmonious wine list. Sunday brunch.

South and West Quarters

Okura , Ferdinand Bolstraat 333, ✉ 1072 LH, ☎ (0 20) 678 71 11, *sales@okura.nl, Fax (0 20) 671 23 44*, , , , – |₿| ⇎ ▤ TV & P – 25-1200. AE ⓓ MC VISA JCB. ⁂
Meals see ***Ciel Bleu*** and ***Yamazato*** below – ***Sazanka*** (Japanese cuisine with Teppan-Yaki, dinner only) 49/67 ♀ – ***Brasserie Le Camelia*** (open until 11 p.m.) a la carte approx. 44 ♀ – ☕ 25 – **358 rm** 340/410, – 12 suites.
◆ This luxury Japanese-style international hotel overlooks the Noorder Amstel canal. Superb health centre and extensive conference facilities. Japanese restaurant with dishes cooked on typical hobs. The Camelia brasserie serves a variety of French cuisine.

Hilton, Apollolaan 138, ✉ 1077 BG, ☎ (0 20) 710 60 00, *info_amsterdam@hilton.com, Fax (0 20) 710 60 80*, <, , , , – |₿| ⇎ ▤ TV & P – 25-550. AE ⓓ MC VISA. ⁂ rest
Meals *Roberto's* (Italian cuisine with buffet) *Lunch 24* – a la carte 35/62 – ☕ 25 – **267 rm** 360/440, – 4 suites.
◆ Following a complete overhaul, the Hilton now offers smart new designer rooms, plus a canal-side garden and terraces. The pleasant Mediterranean-style Roberto's restaurant specialises in Italian cuisine with a choice of menus and antipasti buffets.

Bilderberg Garden, Dijsselhofplantsoen 7, ✉ 1077 BJ, ☎ (0 20) 570 56 00, *garden@bilderberg.nl, Fax (0 20) 570 56 54* – |₿| ⇎ ▤ TV P – 25-150. AE ⓓ MC VISA JCB
Meals see ***Mangerie De Kersentuin*** below – ☕ 20 – **120 rm** 165/350, – 2 suites.
◆ This small-sized "grand hotel" combines discreet luxury and charm. Rooms with everything you could possibly need, decorated with taste and a fine sense of detail.

Le Meridien Apollo, Apollolaan 2, ✉ 1077 BA, ☎ (0 20) 673 59 22, *info@apollo.com Fax (0 20) 570 57 44*, ≤, 🏖, Lδ, ⚓ - |‡| ⇔ ▤ 📺 🅿 - 🏊 25-200. AE ⓓ ⓜⓒ VISA JCB
Meals ***La Sirène*** (seafood) *Lunch 33* - a la carte 39/78 - ☕ 21 - **217 rm** 290/390, - 2 suites.

◆ Located away from the frenetic pace of the centre at the junction of five canals, the Meridien offers comfortable, recently renovated rooms and a full range of services.

Tulip Inn City West, Reimerswaalstraat 5, ✉ 1069 AE, ☎ (0 20) 410 80 00, *info@tiamsterdamcw.nl, Fax (0 20) 410 80 30* - |‡| ⇔ ▤ 📺 ♿ - 🏊 25-70. AE ⓓ ⓜⓒ VISA
Meals (dinner only) a la carte 22/34 - ☕ 14 - **162 rm** 135/175.

◆ This recently opened chain hotel is situated in a relatively quiet area of the city. Its main selling points are its spacious rooms and lounges, and the good parking facilities nearby. Although traditional, the restaurant menu shows contemporary influence.

Tulip Inn Art (annex Golden Tulip Art - 60 rm), Spaarndammerdijk 302 (Westerpark) ✉ 1013 ZX, ☎ (0 20) 410 96 70, *art@westlordhotels.nl, Fax (0 20) 681 08 02*, 🏖, 🚲 - |‡| ⇔ ▤ 📺 🚗 - 🏊 25. AE ⓓ ⓜⓒ VISA. ✂
Meals. *Lunch 18* - 25 - ☕ 15 - **130 rm** 170.

◆ A thoroughly modern hotel close to the ring-road with rooms designed with the modern business traveller in mind. Exhibition of paintings by contemporary artists. Trendy "brasserie"-style tavern-restaurant.

Ciel Bleu - Hotel Okura, 23rd floor, Ferdinand Bolstraat 333, ✉ 1072 LH, ☎ (0 20) 678 71 11, *sales@okura.nl, Fax (0 20) 671 23 44*, ≤ ville, ⚓ - |‡| ▤ 🅿. AE ⓓ ⓜⓒ VISA JCB. ✂
closed mis July-mid August and 28 December-4 January - **Meals** (dinner only) 73 ♀.

◆ This highly acclaimed restaurant, with its appetising and inventive menu, enjoys a superb view of the city's rooftops from the top of the Japanese-owned Okura Hotel.

Yamazato - Hotel Okura, Ferdinand Bolstraat 333, ✉ 1072 LH, ☎ (0 20) 678 83 51, *sales@okura.nl, Fax (0 20) 678 77 88*, Japanese cuisine, ⚓ - ▤ 🅿. AE ⓓ ⓜⓒ VISA JCB. ✂
Meals. *Lunch 39* - 50/90, - a la carte 39/68 ♀.

◆ A minimalist ambience pervades this restaurant serving a gamut of traditional Japanese dishes, under the watchful gaze of geisha girls. Small, private room also available.
Spec. Gyu Tohban-Yaki (beef). Kamakura (tuna, seawolf) (October-March). Ishikari-nabe (salmon).

visaandeschelde, Scheldeplein 4, ✉ 1078 GR, ☎ (0 20) 675 15 83, *info@visaandeschelde.nl, Fax (0 20) 471 46 53*, 🏖, Seafood, open until 11 p.m. - ▤. AE ⓓ ⓜⓒ VISA JCB ✂
closed 24 December-5 January and lunch Saturday and Sunday - **Meals**. *Lunch 29* - a la carte 42/65 ♀.

◆ The model of the boat in the window clearly demonstrates this restaurant's culinary intentions. A bright, somewhat spartan dining room in maritime blue and white.

Mangerie De Kersentuin - Hotel Bilderberg Garden, Dijsselhofplantsoen 7 ✉ 1077 BJ, ☎ (0 20) 570 56 00, *garden@bilderberg.nl, Fax (0 20) 570 56 54*, 🏖 - ▤ 🅿. AE ⓓ ⓜⓒ VISA JCB. ✂ rest
closed 31 December-1 January, Saturday lunch and Sunday - **Meals**. *Lunch 28* - 32 b.i./50 ♀

◆ A brasserie-style atmosphere pervades this "eatery", with its gleaming copper fittings and comfortable red benches. Inviting contemporary menu and welcoming summer terrace.

Blender, Van der Palmkade 16, ✉ 1051 RE, ☎ (0 20) 486 98 60, *info@blender2004.com, Fax (0 20) 486 98 51*, 🏖 - AE ⓓ ⓜⓒ VISA JV
Meals (dinner only until 11 p.m.) a la carte 37/45 ♀.

◆ Blender occupies the ground floor of a circular building where the atmosphere is distinctly young and trendy. A semi-circular counter and charming, attentive service.

Le Hollandais, Amsteldijk 41, ✉ 1074 HV, ☎ (0 20) 679 12 48, *lehollandais@planet.nl* - ▤. AE ⓜⓒ VISA JCB
closed Sunday - **Meals** (dinner only) a la carte approx. 46 ♀.

◆ An endearing local bistro-cum-restaurant attracting a professional/bohemian clientele. Modern cuisine in a plain, uncluttered setting.

Pakistan, Scheldestraat 100, ✉ 1078 GP, ☎ (0 20) 675 39 76, *Fax (0 20) 675 39 76*, Indian cuisine - AE ⓓ ⓜⓒ VISA
Meals (dinner only until 11 p.m.) 25/45.

◆ The popularity of this authentic Pakistani restaurant near the RAI remains high thanks to its range of copious menus. No pork on the menu, but plenty of beef.

East and Southeast Quarters

Mercure a/d Amstel, Joan Muyskenweg 10, ✉ 1096 CJ, ☎ (0 20) 665 81 81, *h1244@accor-hotels.com, Fax (0 20) 694 87 35*, Lδ, ♨, ⚓ - |‡| ⇔ ▤ 📺 ♿ 🅿 - 🏊 25-450. AE ⓓ ⓜⓒ VISA. ✂
Meals. *Lunch 21* - a la carte 37/48 ♀ - ☕ 17 - **368 rm** 210/250.

◆ This hotel on the fringes of the city boasts excellent seminar facilities and rooms that match the standards expected of this worldwide chain. The restaurant offers a range of international dishes plus the standard Mercure wine-list.

Voorbij het Einde, Sumatrakade 613, ✉ 1019 PS, ☏ (0 20) 419 11 43, *aperlot@wxs.nl, Fax (0 33) 479 31 92,* – VISA.
closed 12 July-2 August, 26 December-11 January, Sunday, Monday and Tuesday – **Meals** (lunch by arrangement) a la carte 42/50 ♀.
◆ A pleasant surprise behind a row of austere buildings. Interesting mix of design furniture, bright partitions, an open kitchen and modern windows looking onto a small park.

De Kas, Kamerlingh Onneslaan 3, ✉ 1097 DE, ☏ (0 20) 462 45 62, *info@restaurantdekas.nl, Fax (0 20) 462 45 63,* ≤, – AE VISA.
closed 24 December-3 January, Saturday lunch and Sunday – **Meals** (set menu only). Lunch 31 – 42.
◆ An unusual restaurant set out in an enormous greenhouse which produces a variety of market garden produce. The single menu, using the freshest of ingredients, changes daily.

VandeMarkt, Schollenbrugstraat 8, ✉ 1091 EZ, ☏ (0 20) 468 69 58, *bos.catering@wxs.nl, Fax (0 20) 463 04 54,* – AE VISA.
closed 2 weeks building workers holidays, 29 December-4 January, Sunday and Bank Holidays – **Meals** (dinner only) 36/45 ♀.
◆ A resolutely contemporary brasserie well worth tracking down in a line of somewhat austere buildings. Canal-side summer terrace.

Buitenveldert (RAI)

Holiday Inn, De Boelelaan 2, ✉ 1083 HJ, ☏ (0 20) 646 23 00, *reservations.amsnt@ichotelsgroup.nl, Fax (0 20) 517 27 64,* – TV P – 25-350. AE VISA
Meals (American cuisine) a la carte 31/48 ♀ – 20 – **254 rm** 295/425, – 2 suites.
◆ Located 800m/880yd from the RAI, this chain hotel offers guests a full range of services plus spacious, pleasant rooms. Friendly, attentive service, modern, American-inspired cuisine and an eclectic wine list.

Novotel, Europaboulevard 10, ✉ 1083 AD, ☏ (0 20) 541 11 23, *h0515@accor-hotels.com, Fax (0 20) 646 82 23,* – TV P – 25-225. AE VISA
Meals (pub rest, open until midnight). Lunch 20 – 22 ♀ – 17 – **611 rm** 195/260.
◆ This vast hotel is frequented by tour groups and business executives alike, with rooms of the standard you would expect from the Novotel name.

Rosarium, Amstelpark 1, ✉ 1083 HZ, ☏ (0 20) 644 40 85, *info@rosarium.net, Fax (0 20) 646 60 04,* ≤, – P – 25-250. AE VISA JCB
closed Saturday and Sunday – **Meals**. Lunch 30 – a la carte 44/52 ♀.
◆ This modern structure in the Amstelpark is home to a spacious modern restaurant, a wine-bar and eight meeting rooms. Polished designer decor.

by motorway The Hague (A 4 - E 19)

Mercure Airport, Oude Haagseweg 20 (exit ① Sloten), ✉ 1066 BW, ☏ (0 20) 617 90 05, *h1315-re@accor-hotels.com, Fax (0 20) 615 90 27* – TV P – 25-300. AE VISA JCB.
Meals. Lunch 20 – 30 b.i. ♀ – 17 – **152 rm** 190/210.
◆ A shuttle service covers the 3km/2mi between this hotel and Schiphol airport. Despite being on the motorway, the Mercure's large, comfortable rooms offer both peace and quiet.

Environs

at Amstelveen *South : 11 km – pop. 77 337.*

Thomas Cookstraat 1, ✉ 1181 ZS, ☏ (0 20) 441 55 45, info@vvvhollandsmidden.nl, Fax (0 20) 647 19 66

Grand Hotel, Bovenkerkerweg 81 (South : 2,5 km direction Uithoorn), ✉ 1187 XC, ☏ (0 20) 645 55 58, *info@grandhotelamstelveen.nl, Fax (0 20) 641 21 21,* – TV P AE VISA JCB.
Meals see ***Résidence Fontaine Royale*** below, shuttle service – **97 rm** 153/173, – 2 suites.
◆ Situated alongside a main road five minutes from the airport, the Grand Hotel's rooms are spacious and modern with adequate soundproofing.

De Jonge Dikkert, Amsterdamseweg 104a, ✉ 1182 HG, ☏ (0 20) 643 33 33, *Fax (0 20) 645 91 62,* – P AE VISA
closed lunch Saturday and Sunday – **Meals**. Lunch 31 – 32/45 ♀.
◆ Innovative, stylish cuisine in a picturesque setting. Behind the neat façade, the rustic dining room has incorporated the base of a 17C windmill. Highly original !

Résidence Fontaine Royale - Grand Hotel, Dr Willem Dreesweg 1 (South : 2 km, direction Uithoorn), ✉ 1185 VA, ☏ (0 20) 640 15 01, *reservering@fontaineroyale.nl, Fax (0 20) 640 16 61,* – P – 25-225. AE VISA JCB
closed Saturday lunch, Sunday and Monday dinner – **Meals**. Lunch 24 – a la carte 38/52 ♀.
◆ The Grand Hotel's restaurant occupies a separate building 150m/165yd away, where the trend is distinctly modern. Facilities for banquets and seminars.

at Badhoevedorp *Southwest : 15 km* [C] *Haarlemmermeer pop. 118 553 :*

Dorint, Sloterweg 299, ✉ 1171 VB, ☎ (0 20) 658 81 11, *Fax (0 20) 658 81 00*, – 25-150. rest
Meals. *Lunch 22* – a la carte 30/45 ♀ – 19 – **211 rm** 100, – 9 suites.
• This modern chain hotel to the southwest of the city near the airport (shuttle service) provides modern comforts in its 211 large, soundproofed rooms.

De Herbergh with rm, Sloterweg 259, ✉ 1171 CP, ☎ (0 20) 659 26 00, *info@herbergh.nl*, *Fax (0 20) 659 83 90*, – rest, – 35. rm
Meals *(closed Saturday lunch)*. *Lunch 23* – a la carte 37/51 ♀ – 11 – **24 rm** 111/120.

at Hoofddorp *by motorway A 4 - E 19* ④ - [C] *Haarlemmermeer pop. 118 553 – see also at Schiphol.*

Binnenweg 20, ✉ 2132 CT, ☎ (0 23) 563 33 90, hoofddorp@vvvhollandsmidden.nl, Fax (0 23) 562 77 59

Crowne Plaza Amsterdam-Schiphol, Planeetbaan 2, ✉ 2132 HZ, ☎ (0 23) 565 00 00, *sales.amsap@ichotelsgroup.com*, *Fax (0 23) 565 05 21*, – 25-350.
Meals. *Lunch 26* – a la carte 36/44 ♀ – 20 – **230 rm** 240/345, – 12 suites.
• A top-class hotel located between the centre of Hoofddorp and the motorway to Amsterdam-Schiphol airport. Rooms and suites with full amenities, plus a classic-contemporary restaurant serving innovative cuisine. Efficient service throughout.

Courtyard by Marriott - Amsterdam Airport, Kruisweg 1401, ✉ 2131 MD, ☎ (0 23) 556 90 00, *courtyard@claus.nl*, *Fax (0 23) 556 90 09*, – 25-160.
Meals. *Lunch 20* – 25 ♀ – 18 – **148 rm** 120/165.
• This modern hotel on the edge of a large park between Haarlem and the airport is geared towards business clientele. Spacious, modern rooms, plus a sauna and fitness room.

Schiphol A 4, Rijksweg A 4 nr 3 (Sud : 4 km, Den Ruygen Hoek), ✉ 2132 MA, ☎ (0 252) 67 53 35, *info@schiphol.valk.nl*, *Fax (0 252) 62 92 45*, – 25-1500.
Meals (open until 11 p.m.). *Lunch 15* – a la carte 28/56 ♀ – 15 – **430 ch** 85/100, – 2 suites.
• A practical option for those with a plane to catch. Numerous room categories and a huge conference capacity. Part of the Van der Valk group, with its colourful Toucan logo.

Marktzicht, Marktplein 31, ✉ 2132 DA, ☎ (0 23) 561 24 11, *info@restaurant-marktzicht.nl*, *Fax (0 23) 563 72 91*,
Meals. *Lunch 30* – a la carte approx. 44.
• This traditional "auberge" on the Markt dates from 1860 and was built during construction of the polder now home to Schiphol airport. Dutch dishes feature heavily on the menu.

at Ouderkerk aan de Amstel *South : 10 km* [C] *Amstelveen pop. 77 337 :*

't Jagershuis, Amstelzijde 2, ✉ 1184 VA, ☎ (0 20) 496 20 20, *info@jagershuis.com*, *Fax (0 20) 496 45 41*, – 30.
closed 29 December-2 January – **Meals** *(closed Saturday lunch)*. *Lunch 38* – a la carte 45/59 ♀ – **11 rm** 195.
• The summer terrace and cosy dining room of this auberge-cum-restaurant offer pleasant views of the Amstel. A substantial à la carte menu plus rooms with period furniture.

Ron Blaauw, Kerkstraat 56, ✉ 1191 JE, ☎ (0 20) 496 19 43, *info@ronblaauw.nl*, *Fax (0 20) 496 57 01*,
closed last week July-first week August, Saturday lunch, Sunday and Monday – **Meals**. *Lunch 38* – a la carte 49/58 ♀.
• On the village square, in front of the church. With its subtle Japanese undertones, the ambitious, regularly updated menu blends in well with the modern setting.
Spec. Filet de bar aux couteaux. Crevettes rouges au chutney. Cocktail d'orange et mandarines, glace au pain perdu.

Klein Paardenburg, Amstelzijde 59, ✉ 1184 TZ, ☎ (0 20) 496 13 35, *info@kleinpaardenburg.nl*, *Fax (0 20) 472 32 57*,
closed Saturday lunch – **Meals**. *Lunch 35* – 45/60 b.i. ♀.
• This small temple of gastronomy is situated in a highly sought-after location along the Amstel. Striking dining room-cum-veranda dominated by a mix of brick, leather and wood.

Lute, De Oude Molen 5, ✉ 1184 VW, ☎ (0 20) 472 24 62, *info@luterestaurant.nl*, *Fax (0 20) 472 24 63*,
closed 26 July-7 August, 27 December-9 January, Saturday lunch and Sunday – **Meals**. *Lunch 30* – a la carte 50/61 ♀.
• A contemporary, somewhat unexpected restaurant on the site of a former gunpowder factory. Loft-style, post-industrial architecture, plus a well-shaded glass conservatory.

at Schiphol *(international airport) Southwest : 15 km* ⓒ *Haarlemmermeer pop. 118 553 – see also at Hoofddorp – Casino, Schiphol airport - Terminal Centraal* ☎ *(0 23) 574 05 74, Fax (0 23) 574 05 77 :*

Sheraton Airport, Schiphol bd 101, ✉ 1118 BG, ☎ (0 20) 316 43 00, *sales.amsterdam@starwoodhotels.com, Fax (0 20) 316 43 99,* – 25-500. AE ⓓ ⓜⓒ VISA JCB.
Meals ***Voyager*** *Lunch 45* – a la carte 51/59 ♀ – ☕ 25 – **400 rm** 420/515, – 8 suites.
♦ The Schiphol Sheraton is designed predominantly for business clients, with six categories of rooms offering the latest in facilities. An attractive atrium, a comprehensive range of services, and a modern brasserie crowned by a blue cupola. Evening buffets.

Hilton Schiphol, Schiphol Bd 701, ✉ 1118 ZK, ☎ (0 20) 710 40 00, *fb_ap7-schiphil@hilton.nl, Fax (0 20) 710 40 80,* – 25-60. AE ⓓ ⓜⓒ VISA JCB. rest
Meals ***East West*** *(closed July, Saturday and Sunday)* (partly Asian cuisine, dinner only) a la carte 44/64 ♀ – ***Greenhouse*** *(open until 11 p.m.)* (buffets) a la carte 35/68 ♀ – ☕ 25 – **278 rm** 169/349, – 2 suites.
♦ Facilities at the airport Hilton include rooms with high levels of comfort, top-notch service, a business centre and seminar rooms. The East West restaurant is known for its fusion of Western and Asian flavours, as well as its Japanese options.

Dorint Schiphol Airport, Stationsplein Zuid-West 951 (Schiphol-Oost), ✉ 1117 CE, ☎ (0 20) 540 07 77, *info@dsaa.dorint.nl, Fax (0 20) 540 08 88,* – 25-640. AE ⓓ ⓜⓒ VISA JCB
Meals ***Nadar*** (lunch only) a la carte 26/39 – ☕ 19 – **393 rm** 325/470, – 4 suites.
♦ This modern hotel and conference centre between the airport and Amsterdamse Bos is arranged around a large patio. Numerous "executive" rooms, plus a 24-hour English-style pub. The Nadar restaurant is named after a famous 19C French balloonist.

Radisson SAS Airport, Boeing Avenue 2 (South : 4 km by N 201 at Rijk), ✉ 1119 PB, ☎ (0 20) 655 31 31, *reservations.amsterdam.airport@radissonsas.com, Fax (0 20) 655 31 00,* – 25-600. AE ⓓ ⓜⓒ VISA JCB.
Meals. *Lunch 20* – a la carte 27/42 ♀ – ☕ 19 – **277 rm** 255, – 2 suites.
♦ With its proximity to the airport and motorway, large, friendly feel and well-equipped, discreetly luxurious rooms, the Radisson is the perfect base for a business trip. The menu in the Mediterranean restaurant shows a distinct fondness for all things Italian !

De Oude Toren, Stationsplein Zuid-West 602 (Schiphol-Oost), ✉ 1117 CN, ☎ (0 20) 405 96 10, *info@deoudetoren-schiphol.nl, Fax (0 20) 405 96 11,* ≤, , Whith brasserie on the ground floor – – 55. AE ⓓ ⓜⓒ VISA.
closed Saturday lunch, Sunday and Bank Holidays – **Meals**. *Lunch 30* – a la carte 44/72 ♀.
♦ The airport's former control tower now houses a brasserie on the ground floor, a stylish restaurant on the third, and a lounge-bar on the fourth. Superb views of the runway.

Haarlem *Noord-Holland* 531 M 8, 532 M 8 *and* 715 E 4 – *pop. 147 831 – 20 km.*

at Overveen *West : 4 km* ⓒ *Bloemendaal pop. 17 097 :*

De Bokkedoorns, Zeeweg 53 (West : 2 km), ✉ 2051 EB, ☎ (0 23) 526 36 00, *bokkedoorns@alliance.nl, Fax (0 23) 527 31 43,* ≤ lake, – P. AE ⓓ ⓜⓒ VISA JCB.
closed 30 April, 5 and 24 December, 29 December-4 January, Monday and Saturday lunch – **Meals**. *Lunch 43* – 63/114 b.i., – a la carte 76/95 ♀.
♦ Modern architecture, interior design, wooded dunes and lake views from the terrace combine to create a magnificent setting for one of the best tables in North Holland.
Spec. Risotto au Parmesan et brunoise de queues de langoustines (May-September). Ris de veau aux petits pannequets et son rognon. Homard braisé à la badiane.

Zwolle *Overijssel* 531 V 7 *and* 715 J 4 – *pop. 109 000 – 111 km.*

De Librije (Boer), Broerenkerkplein 13, ✉ 8011 TW, ☎ (0 38) 421 20 83, *librije@alliance.nl, Fax (0 38) 423 23 29* – P. AE ⓜⓒ VISA.
closed 22 February-1 March, 18 July-9 August, Sunday, Monday and lunch Tuesday and Saturday – **Meals**. *Lunch 50* – 85/95, – a la carte 75/92 ♀.
♦ This celebrated restaurant in the wing of a 15C convent has been refurbished in modern style. Fine contemporary dining, where the emphasis is on flair and the personal touch.
Spec. 4 façons de manger le maquereau (September-January). Collier d'agneau aux zestes de limon (April-September). Dos de cabillaud à la pomme de terre aux truffes (October-February).

The HAGUE (Den HAAG or 's GRAVENHAGE) Zuid-Holland 532 K 10 and 715 D 5 – pop. 457 726.

See : Binnenhof★ : The Knight's Room★ (Ridderzaal) JY – Court pool (Hofvijver) ≤★ HJY – Lange Voorhout★ HJX – Madurodam★★ – Scheveningen★★.

Museums : Mauritshuis★★★ JY – Prince William V art gallery★ (Schilderijengalerij Prins Willem V) HY M² – Panorama Mesdag★ HX – Mesdag★ – Municipal★★ (Gemeentemuseum) – Bredius★ JY – The seaside sculpture museum★★ (Museum Beelden aan Zee) at Scheveningen.

18 Southeast : 5 km at Rijswijk, Delftweg 58, ✉ 2289 AL, ☎ (0 70) 319 24 24, Fax (0 70) 399 50 40 - 18 Northeast : 11 km at Wassenaar, Groot Haesebroekseweg 22, ✉ 2243 EC, ☎ (0 70) 517 96 07, Fax (0 70) 514 01 71 and 18 Dr Mansveltkade 15, ✉ 2242 TZ, ☎ (0 70) 517 88 99, Fax (0 70) 551 93 02.

✈ Amsterdam-Schiphol Northeast : 37 km ☎ (0 20) 601 91 11, Fax (0 20) 604 14 75 – Rotterdam-Zestienhoven Southeast : 17 km ☎ (0 10) 446 34 44, Fax (0 20) 446 34 99.

Kon. Julianaplein 30, ✉ 2595 AA, ☎ 0 900-340 35 05, info@denhaag.com, Fax (0 70) 347 21 02.

Amsterdam 55 – Brussels 182 – Rotterdam 27 – Delft 13.

Plan opposite

Centre

Des Indes, Lange Voorhout 54, ✉ 2514 EG, ☎ (0 70) 361 23 45, *info@desindes.com, Fax (0 70) 361 23 50* – TV P – 25-100. AE VISA JCB. rest JX s
Meals *Le Restaurant* *(closed Saturday lunch and Sunday)* Lunch 33 – 39/69 ♀ – 23 – **71 rm** 300/370, – 6 suites.
◆ This late-19C mansion fronts a shady square in the city's institutional district. Elegant, classical lounge, rooms with period furniture, and friendly staff and service. Opulent, classical-style dining room with continental cuisine in keeping with the period.

Crowne Plaza Promenade, van Stolkweg 1, ✉ 2585 JL, ☎ (0 70) 352 51 61, *info@crowneplazadenhaag.nl, Fax (0 70) 354 10 46,* ≤, , , , – TV P – 25-425. AE VISA JCB
Meals *Brasserie Promenade* Lunch 30 – 35/40 ♀ – ***Trattoria dell'Arte*** *(closed Saturday lunch)* (Italian cuisine, open until midnight and July-August dinner only) Lunch 29 – a la carte 40/49 – 23 – **93 rm** 295, – 1 suite.
◆ This large chain hotel alongside the inner ring road stands opposite a vast park. High levels of comfort, a collection of modern paintings and efficient service. A relaxed brasserie for those favouring a simple meal, plus a contemporary-style trattoria.

Dorint without rest, Johan de Wittlaan 42, ✉ 2517 JR, ☎ (0 70) 416 91 11, *info@dhd.dorint.nl, Fax (0 70) 416 91 00,* , , – TV – 25-2000. AE VISA. rest
18 – **214 rm** 370, – 2 suites.
◆ One of the pearls in the crown of the Dorint group : a strategic location "above" the city's conference centre, a modernist feel, spacious, bright rooms, and a huge infrastructure for seminars.

Carlton Ambassador , Sophialaan 2, ✉ 2514 JP, ☎ (0 70) 363 03 63, *info@ambassador.carlton.nl, Fax (0 70) 360 05 35,* – TV P – 25-150. AE VISA JCB. rm HX c
Meals *Henricus* (open until 11 p.m.) Lunch 29 – 33/51 ♀ – 21 – **77 rm** 290/330, – 1 suite.
◆ The rooms in this small palace in the Mesdag diplomatic quarter are either Dutch or English in style. Plenty of character, but varying levels of soundproofing. The relaxed, floral-inspired restaurant takes its influence from the shores of the Mediterranean.

Bel Air, Johan de Wittlaan 30, ✉ 2517 JR, ☎ (0 70) 352 53 54, *info@goldentulipbelairhotel.nl, Fax (0 70) 352 53 53,* , – TV P – 25-250. AE VISA JCB
Meals. Lunch 20 – a la carte 30/55 – 16 – **348 rm** 195.
◆ This huge hotel spread over nine floors has a total of 348 well-appointed rooms, in addition to impressively large public areas and lounges.

Sofitel, Koningin Julianaplein 35, ✉ 2595 AA, ☎ (0 70) 381 49 01, *h0755@accor-hotels.com, Fax (0 70) 382 59 27* – TV P – 25-150. AE VISA JCB
Meals *(closed lunch Saturday and Sunday).* Lunch 28 – 35 – 20 – **143 rm** 265/365, – 1 suite.
◆ A practical choice for rail travellers, the Sofitel offers the usual comforts associated with the chain in a modern building close to the station. The emphasis is on the contemporary in the restaurant, which recreates the atmosphere of an artist's studio.

Mercure Central without rest, Spui 180, ✉ 2511 BW, ☎ (0 70) 363 67 00, *h1317@accor-hotels.com, Fax (0 70) 363 93 98* – TV P – 25-135. AE VISA. JZ v
16 – **156 rm** 160/165, – 3 suites.
◆ Built in the 1980s, this centrally located hotel offers functional, well-maintained rooms with double-glazing. Mainly business clientele. "Minimalist" service.

DEN HAAG

Street	Grid	No.
Alexanderstr.	HX	
Amaliastr.	HX	3
Amsterdamse Veerkade	JZ	4
Annastr.	HY	7
Bleijenburg	JY	12
Boekhorststr.	HZ	
Breedstr.	HY	
Buitenhof	HY	
Denneweg	JX	
Drie Hoekjes	HY	22
Dunne Bierkade	JZ	
Fluwelen Burgwal	JY	24
Geest	HY	
Groene Wegje	JZ	31
Groenmarkt	HZ	
Grote Marktstr.	HJZ	
Herengracht	JY	
Heulstraat	HY	32
Hofweg	HJY	
Hogewal	HX	
Hoogstr.	HY	
Hooikade	JX	33
Huijgenspark	JZ	
Jan Hendrikstr.	HZ	
Kalvermarkt	JY	
Kazernestr.	HJ	
Kneuterdijk	HY	45
Korte Molenstr.	HY	52
Korte Poten	JY	54
Korte Vijverberg	JY	55
Korte Voorhout	JX	
Lange Houtstr.	JY	
Lange Poten	JY	
Lange Vijverberg	HJY	60
Lange Voorhout	JX	
Lutherse Burgwal	HZ	64
Mauritskade	HX	
Molenstr.	HY	70
Muzenstr.	JY	
Nieuwe Schoolstr.	HJX	75
Nieuwstr.	HZ	
Noordeinde	HXY	
Oranjestr.	HX	
Oude Molstraat	HY	80
Paleispromenade	HY	81
Paleisstr.	HXY	82
Papestr.	HY	84
Parkstr.	HX	
de Passage	HY	85
Paviljoensgracht	JZ	
Plaats	HY	
Plein	JY	
Plein 1813	HX	
Prinsegracht	HZ	
Prinsessegracht	JXY	
Prinsestr.	HY	
Scheveningseveer	HX	100
Sophialaan	HX	
Spui	JZ	
Spuiplein	JZ	
Spuistr.	JYZ	
Stille Veerkade	JZ	105
Torenstr.	HY	
Tournooiveld	JXY	108
Venestr.	HYZ	
Vlamingstr.	HZ	114
Vleerstr.	HZ	
Vos in Tuinstr.	JX	118
Wagenstr.	JZ	
Westeinde	HZ	
Willemstr.	HX	
Zeestr.	HX	
Zieken	JZ	

Parkhotel without rest, Molenstraat 53, ✉ 2513 BJ, ☎ (0 70) 362 43 71, *reserveringen@parkhoteldenhaag.nl, Fax (0 70) 361 45 25*, – |♦| TV – 25-200. AE MC VISA JCB. HY a
114 rm ☐ 140/240.
• This hotel was established in 1910 on the edge of the wooded park belonging to the Paleis Noordeinde. Cosy rooms, a third of which are singles.

Corona, Buitenhof 42, ✉ 2513 AH, ☎ (0 70) 363 79 30, *hotelcorona@planet.nl, Fax (0 70) 361 57 85* – |♦| TV – 25-100. AE MC VISA JCB HY v
Meals see rest ***Marc Smeets*** below – ☐ 15 – **35 rm** 155/175, – 1 suite.
• A small hotel occupying three houses on Buitenhof Square. Quaint rooms of varying sizes decorated in Louis XVI or Art Deco style. Popular with ministerial staff and diplomats.

Haagsche Suites without rest, Laan van Meerdervoort 155, ✉ 2517 AX, ☎ (0 70) 364 78 79, *info@haagschesuites.nl, Fax (0 70) 345 65 33*, – |♦| TV P. AE MC VISA
closed January – **1 rm** 340/425, – 3 suites.
• A sophisticated and exclusive small hotel with an intimate interior created with a discreet aesthetic eye. Designer garden. Private car park for guests.

Paleis without rest, Molenstraat 26, ✉ 2513 BL, ☎ (0 70) 362 46 21, *info@paleishotel.nl, Fax (0 70) 361 45 33* – |♦| TV. AE MC VISA JCB HY f
20 rm ☐ 150/160.
• A small luxury hotel fronted by an attractive salmon pink façade. Bright, lavishly decorated guest rooms with impressive retro-style bathrooms.

Novotel, Hofweg 5, ✉ 2511 AA, ☎ (0 70) 364 88 46, *h1180@accor-hotels.com, Fax (0 70) 356 28 89* – |♦| TV – 25-100. AE MC VISA HJY e
Meals (open until 11 p.m.) a la carte 22/33 – ☐ 15 – **106 rm** 155/160.
• The Novotel is located just opposite the Binnenhof in an old building with a shopping arcade. Levels of comfort and facilities in keeping with the standards of this chain.

Calla's (van der Kleijn), Laan van Roos en Doorn 51a, ✉ 2514 BC, ☎ (0 70) 345 58 66, *Fax (0 70) 345 57 10* – AE MC VISA. JX u
closed 25 July-16 August, 25 December-3 January, Saturday lunch, Sunday and Monday – **Meals**. Lunch 59 b.i. – 63/114 b.i., – a la carte 68/109.
• The design of this modern restaurant, originally a warehouse, is one of cream and coral tones with open views of the kitchens. Classic cuisine with a modern bent.
Spec. Brochette de Saint-Jacques à la réglisse et witlof (October-April). Turbot en soufflé de pommes de terre aillées (May-December). Crêpes farcies glacées et glace vanille.

Saur, Lange Voorhout 47, ✉ 2514 EC, ☎ (0 70) 346 25 65, *restaurant.saur@12move.nl, Fax (0 70) 362 13 13*, , Seafood – . AE MC VISA JCB JX h
closed Saturday lunch, Sunday and Bank Holidays – **Meals**. Lunch 33 – a la carte 46/113 ♀.
• This recently renovated restaurant and oyster bar is a safe bet for those looking for good fish and seafood.

Rousseau, Van Boetzelaerlaan 134, ✉ 2581 AX, ☎ (0 70) 355 47 43, – MC VISA
closed 21 to 29 February, 25 July-23 August, 24 December-3 January, Sunday and Monday – **Meals**. Lunch 25 – 30/50 ♀.
• The spirit of the 19C artist Jean Rousseau - the owner's namesake - lives on in this pleasant restaurant, adorned with a pleasant Rousseau-style fresco. Fortnightly menu.

Julien, Vos in Tuinstraat 2a, ✉ 2514 BX, ☎ (0 70) 365 86 02, *info@julien.nl, Fax (0 70) 365 31 47* – AE MC VISA JX s
closed Sunday – **Meals** – a la carte 45/62.
• The Julien will delight lovers of Art Nouveau with the décor of its restaurant and its sparkling 1900s-style mezzanine and bar. Traditional cuisine with seasonal influences.

The Raffles, Javastraat 63, ✉ 2585 AG, ☎ (0 70) 345 85 87, *Fax (0 70) 356 00 84*, Indonesian cuisine – . AE MC VISA JCB.
closed late July-early August, 1 week January and Sunday – **Meals** (dinner only) a la carte 31/52 ♀.
• Delicious and authentic Indonesian cuisine is served in this typically decorated restaurant along the appropriately named Javastraat.

Marc Smeets - Hotel Corona, Buitenhof 42, ✉ 2513 AH, ☎ (0 70) 363 79 30, *rest.marcsmeets@planet.nl, Fax (0 70) 361 57 85*, – . AE MC VISA JCB. HY v
closed Sunday dinner – **Meals**. Lunch 30 – a la carte 45/72.
• Named after the owner-chef, Marc Smeets, this restaurant with its new interior décor is on the ground floor of the Hotel Corona. Refined lunch and dinner menus.

Shirasagi, Spui 170 (relocation planned), ✉ 2511 BW, ☎ (0 70) 346 47 00, *shirasagi@planet.nl, Fax (0 70) 346 26 01*, Japanese cuisine with Teppan-Yaki – . AE MC VISA JCB. JZ v
closed 30 December-3 January and lunch Saturday, Sunday and Monday – **Meals**. Lunch 23 – 40/73.
• Part of the Mercure Central hotel, the Shirasagi's decor and cuisine is inspired by the land of the rising sun. Options here include fixed menus, à la carte, plus teppanyaki.

Koesveld, Maziestraat 10, ✉ 2514 GT, ☎ (0 70) 360 27 23, *Fax (0 70) 360 27 23*, - AE ⓓ MC VISA HX u
closed July, Sunday and Monday – **Meals** (dinner only until 11 p.m.) a la carte approx. 36 ♀.
◆ This small restaurant between the Panorama Mesdag and Paleis Noordeinde is known for its contemporary, well-presented cuisine.

Zilt, President Kennedylaan 1 (Statenkwartier), ✉ 2517 JK, ☎ (0 70) 338 76 22, *zilt@hetnet.nl, Fax (0 70) 338 77 28*, – P. MC VISA
closed Monday – **Meals**. *Lunch 29* – a la carte 32/43 ♀.
◆ Part of the municipal museum complex built according to plans by Berlage. Soberly decorated dining room, plus a summer terrace by the garden.

at Scheveningen *'s-Gravenhage – Seaside resort★★ – Casino, Kurhausweg 1, ✉ 2587 RT, ☎ (0 70) 306 77 77, Fax (0 70) 306 78 88.*

Gevers Deynootweg 1134, ✉ 2586 BX, ☎ 0-900-340 35 05, vvvscheveningen@spdh.net, Fax (0 70) 352 04 26

Kurhaus, Gevers Deynootplein 30, ✉ 2586 CK, ☎ (0 70) 416 26 36, *info@kurhaus.nl, Fax (0 70) 416 26 46*, ≤, - TV P – 35-600. AE ⓓ MC VISA JCB. rest
Meals ***Kandinsky*** *(closed Saturday lunch and Sunday)* (July-August dinner only) *Lunch 30* – 40/95 b.i. ♀ – ***Kurzaal*** (partly oyster bar) *Lunch 23* – 34 ♀ – 20 – **247 rm** 265/285, – 8 suites.
◆ A sumptuous palace by the beach with a remarkable late-19C concert room now converted into a restaurant. Elegant rooms with modern comforts. Impressive menu at the Kandinsky offering a modern take on classic fare. Oyster bar under the dome of the Kurzaal.

Europa, Zwolsestraat 2, ✉ 2587 VJ, ☎ (0 70) 416 95 95, *europa@bilderberg.nl, Fax (0 70) 416 95 55*, , , , – , rest, TV – 25-460. AE ⓓ MC VISA JCB. rest
Meals ***Oxo*** (dinner only until 11 p.m.) 30/53 b.i. ♀ – 17 – **174 rm** 177/216.
◆ Standing at a crossroads near the dam, the recently renovated Europa has modern, well-appointed rooms with balconies (some with sea views) and soundproofing. The décor in the restaurant provides a trendy backdrop for a cuisine that is decidedly cutting-edge.

Carlton Beach, Gevers Deynootweg 201, ✉ 2586 HZ, ☎ (0 70) 354 14 14, *info@beachcarlton.nl, Fax (0 70) 352 00 20*, ≤, , , , – TV P – 25-250. AE ⓓ MC VISA JCB
Meals – 35 – 20 – **183 rm** 225/235.
◆ This modern building at the end of the dam has 183 newly-decorated rooms and apartments with good soundproofing, some overlooking the beach. The restaurant, crowned by an attractive glass roof, offers good à la carte and menu options. Good sports facilities.

Badhotel, Gevers Deynootweg 15, ✉ 2586 BB, ☎ (0 70) 351 22 21, *info@badhotelscheveningen.nl, Fax (0 70) 355 58 70* – TV P – 25-100. AE ⓓ MC VISA JCB
Meals (dinner only) a la carte 33/49 – 15 – **90 rm** 110/158.
◆ This renovated hotel near the promenade, between the city centre and port, overlooks a busy street. Well-appointed rooms, with those at the back generally quieter.

Seinpost, Zeekant 60, ✉ 2586 AD, ☎ (0 70) 355 52 50, *mail@seinpost.nl, Fax (0 70) 355 50 93*, ≤, Seafood – . AE ⓓ MC VISA JCB
closed Saturday lunch, Sunday and Bank Holidays – **Meals**. *Lunch 38* – 48/93 b.i. ♀.
◆ The god Neptune dominates this round building, where the menu is awash with fish and seafood. Views of the sea from the comfortable, modern dining room.

Cap Ouest, Schokkerweg 37, ✉ 2583 BH, ☎ (0 70) 306 09 35, *info@capouest.nl, Fax (0 70) 350 84 54*, ≤, – . AE ⓓ MC VISA JCB
closed lunch Saturday and Sunday – **Meals**. *Lunch 23* – 25 ♀.
◆ Fish and seafood are the mainstays of this restaurant overlooking the port. The views from the modern dining room encompass the pleasure marina and fishing harbour.

Radèn Mas, Gevers Deynootplein 125, ✉ 2586 CR, ☎ (0 70) 354 54 32, *Fax (0 70) 350 60 42*, Partly Indonesian cuisine, open until 11 p.m. – . AE ⓓ MC VISA JCB.
Meals. *Lunch 30* – a la carte 34/62 ♀.
◆ The Far East takes pride of place on Scheveningen's main square, with Indonesian (including "rice tables") and Chinese dishes to the fore. "Javanese" ambience.

China Delight, Dr Lelykade 116, ✉ 2583 CN, ☎ (0 70) 355 54 50, *info@chinadelight.nl, Fax (0 70) 354 66 52*, Chinese cuisine, open until 11 p.m. – ⓓ MC VISA JCB
Meals (lunch by arrangement) a la carte approx. 28.
◆ This spacious Chinese restaurant is housed in an old warehouse alongside one of the town's docks. A respectable menu geared towards the cuisine of Beijing and Szechwan.

à Kijkduin *West : 4 km* 🄲 *'s-Gravenhage :*

Atlantic, Deltaplein 200, ✉ 2554 EJ, ☎ (0 70) 448 24 82, *info@atlantichotel.nl, Fax (0 70) 368 67 21,* ≤, 🏖, ≘s, 🏊, 🚲 - 🛗 ⇆ 📺 🅿 - 🏆 25-300. AE ⓓ ⓜⓒ VISA JCB. ⊁
Meals (buffet) a la carte approx. 35 – **152 rm** ☕ 158/260.
◆ Most of the rooms and studios at this hotel by the dam have views of the beach or dunes. Friendly staff and service. Swimming-pool and sauna. The sea-facing dining room offers a range of buffet options.

Environs

at Leidschendam *East : 6 km – pop. 43 185*

Green Park, Weigelia 22, ✉ 2262 AB, ☎ (0 70) 320 92 80, *info@greenpark.nl, Fax (0 70) 327 49 07,* ≤, 🏋, 🚲 - 🛗 📺 🅿 - 🏆 25-250. AE ⓓ ⓜⓒ VISA JCB
Meals see rest ***Chiparus*** below – **92 rm** ☕ 139/177, – 4 suites.
◆ This large chain hotel is built on piles on the edge of a lagoon. The bedrooms, laid out around a bright atrium, offer guests modern comfort. Pleasant service.

Villa Rozenrust, Veursestraatweg 104, ✉ 2265 CG, ☎ (0 70) 327 74 60, *villarozenrust@planet.nl, Fax (0 70) 327 50 62,* 🏖 - 🅿. AE ⓓ ⓜⓒ VISA. ⊁
closed Sunday – **Meals** (dinner only) a la carte 40/70.
◆ A completely renovated villa to the east of the Hague, with an attractive dining room and a charming terrace for the summer months. Contemporary cuisine.

Chiparus - Hotel Green Park, Weigelia 22, ✉ 2262 AB, ☎ (0 70) 320 92 80, *info@greenpark.nl, Fax (0 70) 327 49 07,* ≤ - ▤ 🅿. AE ⓓ ⓜⓒ VISA JCB
closed Sunday except Bank Holidays – **Meals**. Lunch 30 – a la carte 33/52 ♀.
◆ The early-20C Romanian sculptor Chiparus lent his name to this restaurant facing the sea. A fashionable menu, strongly influenced by the Mediterranean.

at Rijswijk South : 5 km – *pop. 54 690*

The Grand Winston (opening planned in Spring) Generaal Eisenhowerplein 1, ✉ 2288 AE, ☎ (0 70) 327 93 92, *info@grandwinston.nl* – 🛗 ⇆ ▤ 📺 🚗. ⊁
Meals see rest ***Imko's*** below – **252 rm.**
◆ The reception of this brand-new hotel by the railway station stands beneath the protective gaze of Winston Churchill. The guest rooms here are split between two modern towers. Contemporary-style brasserie.

Savarin, Laan van Hoornwijck 29, ✉ 2289 DG, ☎ (0 70) 307 20 50, *info@savarin.nl, Fax (0 70) 307 20 55,* 🏖 - 🅿 - 🏆 25-120. AE ⓓ ⓜⓒ VISA JCB
closed 27 December-5 January and lunch Saturday and Sunday – **Meals**. Lunch 30 – 35/45 ♀.
◆ This restaurant pays homage to the renowned 18C French gastronome with its modern cuisine inspired by France, Italy, the Netherlands and the New World.

Imko's (Binnerts) (opening planned in Spring), Generaal Eisenhowerplein 1, ✉ 2288 AE, ☎ (0 70) 327 93 92, *info@grandwinston.nl,* Seafood – ▤ 🅿. AE ⓓ ⓜⓒ VISA JCB. ⊁
closed Monday, Tuesday and Saturday lunch – **Meals**. Lunch 33 – 43/80 b.i., – a la carte 52/75 ♀.
◆ This highly recommended restaurant is high on design features, with a "suspended" dining room and high-tech lighting. Refined à la carte menu mainly based on fish and seafood.
Spec. Croquettes aux crevettes, mayonnaise au citron. Salade Niçoise maison. Turbot grillé et sa béarnaise.

't Ganzenest, Delftweg 58 (near A 13 - E 19, exit ⑧ Rijswijk-Zuid), ✉ 2289 AL, ☎ (0 70) 414 06 42, *ganzenest@wxs.nl, Fax (0 70) 414 07 05,* ≤, 🏖 - 🅿. AE ⓓ ⓜⓒ VISA. ⊁
closed 2 weeks building workers holidays, late December-early January, Sunday, Monday and lunch Tuesday and Saturday – **Meals**. Lunch 34 – 40/65 ♀.
◆ The welcoming "Goose Nest" (Ganzenest) occupies a small farmhouse on the edge of a golf course. Dashing interior décor, an enticing contemporary menu and a delightful terrace.

Paul van Waarden, Tollensstraat 10, ✉ 2282 BM, ☎ (0 70) 414 08 12, *info@paulvanwaarden.nl, Fax (0 70) 414 03 91,* 🏖 - AE ⓜⓒ VISA JCB
closed Saturday lunch, Sunday and Bank Holidays – **Meals**. Lunch 53 b.i. – 32/59 b.i., – a la carte 49/75 ♀.
◆ Paul van Waarden serves his inventive dishes in one of several adjoining rooms in this modern, brasserie-style restaurant with its wall-enclosed terrace.
Spec. Quatre préparations de quatre foies différents. Cabillaud croquant au potage de pois cassés et anguille fumée (21 September-21 March). Tatin à la rhubarbe (March-August).

at Voorburg *East : 5 km – pop. 43 185*

Mövenpick, Stationsplein 8, ✉ 2275 AZ, ☎ (0 70) 337 37 37, *hotel.den-haag@moevenpick.com, Fax (0 70) 337 37 00,* – 25-160.
Meals. *Lunch 16* – a la carte 22/41 – 14 – **125 rm** 114/149.
◆ A chain hotel built along modern lines with well-dimensioned, pleasantly furnished functional rooms with good soundproofing. Service with a smile. Excellent choice at lunch and dinner, with buffets, grilled meats and fish, and various wok dishes.

Savelberg with rm, Oosteinde 14, ✉ 2271 EH, ☎ (0 70) 387 20 81, *info@restauranthotelsavelberg.nl, Fax (0 70) 387 77 15,* – 35.
Meals *(closed Saturday lunch, Sunday and Monday). Lunch 43* – 60/120 b.i., – a la carte 67/91 – 16 – **14 rm** 138/195.
◆ This magnificent 17C residence offers a treat for the senses with its classical, yet innovative cuisine. 14 highly individual rooms, plus a summer terrace overlooking a park.
Spec. Salade de homard maison. Turbot façon saisonnier. Pigeon de Bresse rôti au four, artichaut violette, tomates séchées et jus d'olives vertes.

Brasserie Savelberg - De Koepel, Oosteinde 1, ✉ 2271 EA, ☎ (0 70) 369 35 72, *Fax (0 70) 360 32 14,* –
Meals (dinner only until 11 p.m.) 30.
◆ An opulent-looking brasserie in an impressive rotunda-shaped building crowned by an attractive cupola. Summer terrace, as well as a pleasant park for a post-prandial stroll.

Fouquet, Kerkstraat 52, ✉ 2271 CT, ☎ (0 70) 386 29 00, *Fax (0 70) 386 29 00,* –
closed Monday – **Meals** (dinner only) 30/40.
◆ A welcoming, modern brasserie-style eatery occupying two 19C listed houses, with red seats, yellow walls, tables laid out side-by-side and a number of mirrors.

Papermoon, Herenstraat 175, ✉ 2271 CE, ☎ (0 70) 387 31 61, *info@papermoon.nl, Fax (0 70) 387 75 20,* –
closed 31 December-1 January and Monday – **Meals** (dinner only) 28/51 b.i.
◆ This pleasant restaurant, with its hushed dining room ambience, offers a good choice of à la carte dishes and fixed menus.

at Wassenaar *Northeast : 11 km – pop. 25 801*

Aub. de Kieviet , Stoeplaan 27, ✉ 2243 CX, ☎ (0 70) 511 92 32, *receptie@dekieviet.nl, Fax (0 70) 511 09 69,* – 25-90.
Meals *(closed lunch Saturday and Sunday)* – a la carte 36/54 – 15 – **23 rm** 110/190, – 1 suite.
◆ Its worth tracking down this inn in a smart residential district. The redecorated rooms, some with a view of the flower-decked summer terrace, are pleasantly comfortable. Stylish cuisine, varied menus and good daily suggestions.

ROTTERDAM

Zuid-Holland 532 L 11 *and* 715 E 6 – *pop. 598 660 – Casino JY, Plaza-Complex, Weena 624 ✉ 3012 CN, ☎ (0 10) 206 82 06, Fax (0 10) 206 85 00.*

See : *Lijnbaan★ JY – St. Laurence Church (Grote- of St-Laurenskerk) : interior★ KY – Euromast★ (Tower) ★★, ★ JZ – The harbour★★ KZ – Willemsbrug★★ – Erasmusbrug★★ KZ – Delftse Poort (building)★ JY* **C** – *World Trade Center★ KY* **Y** – *The Netherlands architectural institute★ JZ* **W** – *Boompjes★ KZ – Willemswerf (building)★ KY.*
Museums : History Museum Het Schielandshuis★ KY **M**[4] – *Boijmans-van Beuningen★★★ JZ – History "De Dubbele Palmboom"★.*

Envir : *Southeast : 7 km, Kinderdijk Windmills★★.*

East : 8 km at Capelle aan den IJssel, 's Gravenweg 311, ✉ 2905 LB, ☎ (0 10) 442 21 09, Fax (0 10) 284 06 06 - Southwest : 11 km at Rhoon, Veerweg 2a, ✉ 3161 EX, ☎ (0 10) 501 80 58, Fax (0 10) 501 56 04 - Kralingseweg 200, ✉ 3062 CG, ☎ (0 10) 452 22 83.

Zestienhoven ☎ (0 10) 446 34 44, Fax (0 10) 446 34 99.

Europoort to Hull : P and O North Sea Ferries Ltd ☎ (0 181) 25 55 00 (information) and (0 181) 25 55 55 (reservations), Fax (0 181) 25 52 15.

Coolsingel 67, ✉ 3012 AC, ☎ 0 900-403 40 65, vvv.rotterdam@anwb.nl, Fax (0 10) 413 01 24.

Amsterdam 76 – The Hague 24 – Antwerp 103 – Brussels 148 – Utrecht 57.

Plans on following pages

Centre

The Westin, Weena 686, ✉ 3012 CN, ☎ (0 10) 430 20 00, *rotterdam.westin@westin.com, Fax (0 10) 430 20 01,* – 25-100. rest
Meals ***Lighthouse*** *(closed Sunday) Lunch 19* – a la carte 39/49 – 21 – **227 rm** 300/330, – 4 suites. JY z
◆ This new, futuristic skyscraper in front of the station has 227 spacious rooms offering a full range of creature comforts. Conference rooms and business centre. Modern cuisine in a resolutely contemporary setting.

ROTTERDAM

Street	Grid	No.
Adrianastr.	JY	4
Aert van Nesstr.	JY	5
Beursplein	KY	9
Binnenwegpl.	JY	10
Botersloot	KY	13
Coolsingel	JKY	
Delftsepl	JY	21
Delftsestr.	JY	22
Geldersekade	KY	24
Grotekerkpl.	KY	30
Haagseveer	KY	33
Jonker Fransstr.	KY	39
Karel Doormanstr.	JY	
Keizerstr.	KY	40
Korte Hoogstr.	KY	46
Korte Lijnbaan	JY	48
Kruiskade	JKY	51
Kruisplein	JY	52
Lijnbaan	JY	
Nieuwestr.	KY	70
van Oldenbarneveltplaats	JY	72
Pompenburg	JY	78
Posthoornstr.	KY	79
Regentessebrug	KY	82
Scheepstimmermanslaan	JZ	85
Schouwburgplein	JY	88
Spaansekade	KY	89
van Speykstr.	JY	91
Stadhuispl.	JY	93
Veerhaven	JKZ	102
Veerkade	JKZ	103
van Vollenhovenstr.	JZ	107
Westewagenstr.	KY	111
Wijnbrug	KY	112

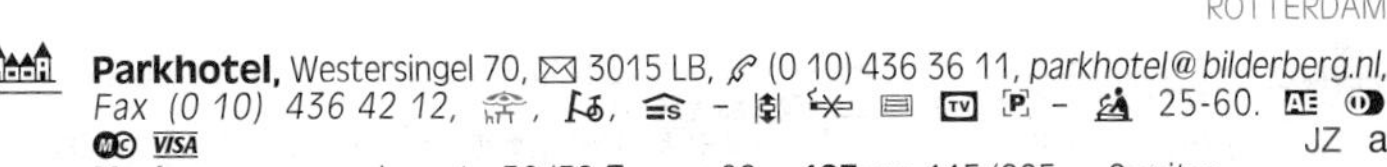

Parkhotel, Westersingel 70, ✉ 3015 LB, ✆ (0 10) 436 36 11, *parkhotel@bilderberg.nl, Fax (0 10) 436 42 12,* – – 25-60. AE VISA JZ a
Meals. *Lunch 21* – a la carte 36/50 – 20 – **187 rm** 115/295, – 2 suites.
◆ Six categories of rooms with the latest fixtures and fittings add a gloss to this silver-grey tower dominating the museum quarter, just a stone's throw from the Lijnbaan shopping area. Elegant, modern restaurant, plus a lounge-bar.

Hilton, Weena 10, ✉ 3012 CM, ✆ (0 10) 710 80 00, *sales-rotterdam@hilton.com, Fax (0 10) 710 80 80,* – – 25-250. AE VISA JCB JY s
Meals (open until 11 p.m.) a la carte 28/44 – 23 – **246 rm** 150/225, – 8 suites.
◆ A top chain hotel occupying a newish building near the World Trade Center. Large, soundproofed rooms with attractive décor. Small restaurant in the lounge. Original, "artist's palette" wine list.

NH Atlanta Rotterdam without rest, Aert van Nesstraat 4, ✉ 3012 CA, ✆ (0 10) 206 78 00, *info@nhatlanta-rotterdam.nh-hotels.nl, Fax (0 10) 413 53 20* – – 25-325. AE VISA JCB JY r
16 – **213 rm** 185, – 2 suites.
◆ Large-scale renovation work in this 1930s hotel-palace has resulted in the preservation of the Art Deco feel of the lobby, staircase, lounge, bar and breakfast room. Period dining room, with a Japanese-inspired menu including sushi and teppanyaki.

Holiday Inn City Centre, Schouwburgplein 1, ✉ 3012 CK, ✆ (0 10) 206 25 55, *hiccrotterdam@bilderberg.nl, Fax (0 10) 206 25 50* – – 25-300. AE VISA JCB. rest JY e
Meals (open until 11 p.m.). *Lunch 25* – a la carte 34/44 – 18 – **100 rm** 190/268.
◆ This centrally located modern hotel has benefited from a makeover by Adriaan Geuze. Contemporary furnishings and double-glazing in every room. Conference facilities. Traditional cuisine.

New York, Koninginnehoofd 1 (Wilhelminapier), ✉ 3072 AD, ✆ (0 10) 439 05 00, *info@hotelnewyork.nl, Fax (0 10) 484 27 01,* – – 25-800. AE VISA JCB. rest KZ m
Meals (open until midnight) a la carte 22/48 – 11 – **72 rm** 91/204.
◆ Once the headquarters of the Holland-America shipping line, this characterful building is now home to the New York Hotel. Individually and originally decorated rooms with views of the port, city and the river. Large dining room furnished in bistro style.

Inntel, Leuvehaven 80, ✉ 3011 EA, ✆ (0 10) 413 41 39, *info@hotelinntel.com, Fax (0 10) 413 32 22,* – – 25-250. AE VISA JCB. rest KZ d
Meals 23/55 – 19 – **148 rm** 130/230.
◆ A chain hotel alongside the Leuvehaven docks, just a few steps from the Erasmusbrug. Panoramic swimming-pool and bar on the top floor.

Savoy without rest, Hoogstraat 81, ✉ 3011 PJ, ✆ (0 10) 413 92 80, *info.savoy@edenhotelgroup.com, Fax (0 10) 404 57 12,* – – 25-60. AE VISA JCB. KY z
16 – **94 rm** 185/240.
◆ This pleasant hotel a short distance from the famous "cubic houses" designed by Blom has 94 modern rooms on seven floors. A nautical theme pervades the public areas.

Pax without rest, Schiekade 658, ✉ 3032 AK, ✆ (0 10) 466 33 44, *pax@bestwestern.nl, Fax (0 10) 467 52 78* – – 25 à 80. AE VISA JCB.
124 rm 125/165.
◆ With its location on a major highway, the Pax is a practical option for both road and rail users. Reasonably spacious accommodation with standard furnishings.

Tulip Inn, Willemsplein 1, ✉ 3016 DN, ✆ (0 10) 413 47 90, *reservations@tulipinnrotterdam.nl, Fax (0 10) 412 78 90,* – rest, – 25-60. AE VISA JCB. KZ s
closed 24 December-2 January – **Meals** a la carte approx. 41 – **108 rm** 109/119.
◆ Small, functional yet comfortable rooms in this hotel built alongside the Nieuwe Maas dock, in the shadow of the Erasmusbrug bridge.

Van Walsum, Mathenesserlaan 199, ✉ 3014 HC, ✆ (0 10) 436 32 75, *info@hotelvanwalsum.nl, Fax (0 10) 436 44 10* – AE VISA JCB. rest
closed 24 December-2 January – **Meals** (residents only) – **29 rm** 78/110.
◆ An imposing bourgeois residence with rooms of varying sizes, identical furnishings and double-glazing. The breakfast room opens onto the hotel terrace.

XXXX ✿✿✿ **Parkheuvel** (Helder), Heuvellaan 21, ⊠ 3016 GL, ✆ (0 10) 436 07 66, *Fax (0 10) 436 71 40*, ≤, 🏔 – 🅿. AE ⓓ MC VISA JCB JZ r
closed 19 July-7 August, 27 December-8 January, Saturday lunch and Sunday – **Meals**. *Lunch 48* – 65/148 b.i., – a la carte 70/99 ♀.
• Ingenious, creative cuisine is the order of the day in this modern, semi-circular building The tables by the terrace offer the best views of maritime life. A real treat!
Spec. Turbot grillé, crème d'anchois et champignons au basilic. Risotto au parmesan e ballottine de langoustines aux cèpes. Pot-au-feu de filet de bœuf à la truffe et au foi d'oie (April-September).

XXX **Old Dutch,** Rochussenstraat 20, ⊠ 3015 EK, ✆ (0 10) 436 03 44, *avdstel@hotmai com, Fax (0 10) 436 78 26*, 🏔 – 🅿. AE ⓓ MC VISA JZ
closed Saturday dinner July-August, Saturday lunch, Sunday and Bank Holidays – **Meals** *Lunch 33* – 58 ♀.
• A pleasant restaurant adorned with bourgeois furniture occupying an inn dating fron 1932. Traditional cuisine with several menu options. Wines from around the world.

XXX **Radèn Mas** 1st floor, Kruiskade 72, ⊠ 3012 EH, ✆ (0 10) 411 72 44, *Fax (0 10 411 97 11*, Indonesian cuisine – ▤. AE ⓓ MC VISA JCB. ⚘ JY a
Meals (dinner only until 11 p.m.) a la carte 34/65.
• This restaurant on the first floor of a new commercial building offers standard Indonesiar dishes, several menus, plus "rice tables" in a décor that is modern and exotic.

XX ✿ **La Vilette** (Mustert), Westblaak 160, ⊠ 3012 KM, ✆ (0 10) 414 86 92, *Fax (0 10 414 33 91* – ▤. AE ⓓ MC VISA JCB. ⚘ JY
closed 19 July-8 September, 24 December-2 January, Saturday lunch and Sunday – **Meals** *Lunch 29* – a la carte 39/52 ♀.
• A refined brasserie ambience permeates this pleasant restaurant with a restricted, yet appetising modern menu. Public car park nearby.
Spec. Ravioli de poussin et mousse de volaille. Canard laqué au lytchee. Crème brûlée e glace vanille bourbon.

XX **De Harmonie,** Westersingel 95, ⊠ 3015 LC, ✆ (0 10) 436 36 10, *Fax (0 10) 436 36 08* 🏔 – 🚣 25-60. AE ⓓ MC VISA JZ c
closed 26 December-2 January, Saturday lunch and Sunday – **Meals**. *Lunch 32* – a la carte 44/55 ♀.
• A pleasant restaurant by the Westersingel and Museumpark. Come the summer, the garden and terrace live up to the name. Enjoyable cuisine geared towards modern tastes

XX **ZeeZout,** Westerkade 11b, ⊠ 3016 CL, ✆ (0 10) 436 50 49, *Fax (0 10) 225 18 47*, 🏔 Seafood – ▤. AE ⓓ MC VISA JZ e
closed 25 and 26 December, 31 December dinner-1 January lunch, Saturday lunch, Sunday and Monday – **Meals**. *Lunch 28* – a la carte 44/61.
• The main attractions of this elegant brasserie are its fish and seafood recipes, hence its name (meaning "sea salt"), plus its terrace facing the Nieuwe Maas.

XX **Brancatelli,** Boompjes 264, ⊠ 3011 XD, ✆ (0 10) 411 41 51, *Fax (0 10) 404 57 34* Italian cuisine, open until 11 p.m. – ▤. AE ⓓ MC VISA KZ r
closed lunch Saturday and Sunday – **Meals**. *Lunch 32* – a la carte 35/56 ♀.
• This Italian restaurant on a lively quay offers a concise yet authentic choice of dishes accompanied by a good selection of wines received directly from Italy.

X **de Engel,** Eendrachtsweg 19, ⊠ 3012 LB, ✆ (0 10) 413 82 56, *engel@engelgroep.com Fax (0 10) 414 63 86* – ▤. AE ⓓ MC VISA JCB JZ z
closed 25, 26 and 31 December and Sunday – **Meals** (dinner only) a la carte approx. 57 ♀.
• One of Rotterdam's current "in" places. A relaxed atmosphere, a dining room adorned with period furniture, and meticulous, seasonal cuisine with a modern touch.

X ☺ **Foody's,** Nieuwe Binnenweg 151, ⊠ 3014 GK, ✆ (0 10) 436 51 63, *Fax (0 10) 436 54 42* 🏔 – ▤. AE MC VISA. ⚘ JZ k
closed 25 and 26 December and Monday – **Meals** (dinner only until midnight) 34/45 ♀ ✿
• A modern-style brasserie with "visible" kitchens where the focus is on "natural" modern cuisine using seasonal products. Wines served by the glass.

X ☺ **Rosso,** Van Vollenhovenstraat 15 (access by Westerlijk Handelsterrein), ⊠ 3016 BE ✆ (0 10) 225 07 05, *Fax (0 10) 436 95 04* – ▤. AE MC VISA. ⚘ JZ b
closed Sunday and Monday – **Meals** (dinner only until 11 p.m.) 33/40 ♀.
• Establishment situated in an old 19C warehouse which has been trendily remodernised With its fashionable clientele and atmosphere, this is THE place to be seen.

X **Anak Mas,** Meent 72a, ⊠ 3011 JN, ✆ (0 10) 414 84 87, *pturina@hotmail.com Fax (0 10) 412 44 74*, Indonesian cuisine – ▤. AE ⓓ MC VISA KY s
closed July and Sunday – **Meals** (dinner only) 22/57 b.i.
• This agreeable small Indonesian restaurant is hidden behind a somewhat dowdy façade. Typical wok-fried dishes and "rice tables" served to a backdrop of traditiona décor.

Suburbs

Airport *North : 2,5 km :*

Airport, Vliegveldweg 59, ✉ 3043 NT, ✆ (0 10) 462 55 66, *info@airporthotel.nl, Fax (0 10) 462 22 66,* – rest, – 25-425. AE VISA JCB.
Meals a la carte 27/38 – 16 – **96 rm** 165/193, – 2 suites.
◆ A modern hotel with good soundproofing. Smart, recently renovated and well-appointed rooms. The comfortable, contemporary dining room offers a range of classic cuisine. Shuttle service to the airport.

at Kralingen *East : 2 km Rotterdam :*

Novotel Brainpark, K.P. van der Mandelelaan 150 (near A 16), ✉ 3062 MB, ✆ (0 10) 253 25 32, *H1134@accor-hotels.com, Fax (0 10) 253 25 72,* – – 25-400. AE VISA
Meals – a la carte 32/40 – 15 – **202 rm** 125/135.
◆ The Novotel stands in a business park on the outskirts of the city. Every room has been upgraded to meet the chain's stringent standards. The brasserie-restaurant offers a selection of snacks in addition to a varied à la carte menu.

In den Rustwat, Honingerdijk 96, ✉ 3062 NX, ✆ (0 10) 413 41 10, *info@indenrustwat.nl, Fax (0 10) 404 85 40,* – . AE VISA JCB
closed last week July-first week August, late December-early January, Saturday lunch, Sunday and Monday – **Meals**. *Lunch 30* – a la carte 44/57 ♀.
◆ This charming, recently extended thatch-roofed inn built in 1597 is located alongside an arboretum. Inventive menu, plus a terrace and flower-decked summer garden.

Europoort zone *West : 25 km :*

De Beer Europoort, Europaweg 210 (N 15), ✉ 3198 LD, ✆ (0 181) 26 23 77, *bienvenue@hoteldebeer.nl, Fax (0 181) 26 29 23,* – – 25-180. AE VISA
Meals. *Lunch 19* – 34 – **78 rm** 86/101.
◆ Set back from the lively Europoort, this medium-sized hotel has 78 functional rooms, half with canal views. Good sports and seminar facilities. The dining room and terrace face out towards the Hartelkanaal.

Environs

at Capelle aan den IJssel *East : 8 km – pop. 65 226*

NH Capelle, Barbizonlaan 2 (near A 20), ✉ 2908 MA, ✆ (0 10) 456 44 55, *info@nhcapelle.nh-hotels.nl, Fax (0 10) 456 78 58,* – , rm, – 25-250. AE VISA JCB
Meals *(closed Sunday lunch). Lunch 19* – a la carte 34/43 ♀ – 16 – **100 rm** 190, – 1 suite.
◆ A contemporary building near a ring road exit just five minutes by car from the centre of Rotterdam. The spacious, renovated rooms here offer the usual modern comforts. In summer, tables are set on the terrace, with views of a nearby lake.

Rivium Royale, Rivium Boulevard 188, ✉ 2909 LK, ✆ (0 10) 202 56 33, *reserveren@riviumroyale.nl, Fax (0 10) 202 65 37,* – . VISA
closed 19 July-9 August, 24 December-3 January, Saturday and Sunday – **Meals**. *Lunch 28* – a la carte 43/67 ♀.
◆ An attractive circular building with a mezzanine-lounge beneath a contemporary dome, and a pleasant summer terrace overlooking the water.

at Rhoon *South : 10 km Albrandswaard pop. 18 092 :*

Het Kasteel van Rhoon, Dorpsdijk 63, ✉ 3161 KD, ✆ (0 10) 501 88 96, *info@hetkasteelvanrhoon.nl, Fax (0 10) 506 72 59,* – – 25-100. AE VISA.
closed Saturday lunch – **Meals**. *Lunch 28* – a la carte approx. 56 ♀.
◆ This comfortable, modern restaurant occupies the outbuildings of a château. Fairly refined cuisine based along classical lines, plus a good wine list. Banqueting rooms.

at Schiedam *West : 6 km – pop. 76 576.*

Buitenhavenweg 9, ✉ 3113 BC, ✆ (0 10) 473 30 00, vvv.schiedam@kabelfoon.nl, Fax (0 10) 473 66 95

Novotel, Hargalaan 2 (near A 20), ✉ 3118 JA, ✆ (0 10) 471 33 22, *H0517@accor-hotels.com, Fax (0 10) 470 06 56,* – – 25-200. AE VISA. rest
Meals. *Lunch 15* – a la carte 22/37 – 14 – **134 rm** 125/135.
◆ At a crossroads near the ring road. The soundproofed rooms have been given a facelift in line with the chain's new style. Pool-side terrace and well-tended garden.

Bistrot Hosman Frères, Korte Dam 10, ✉ 3111 BG, ✆ (0 10) 426 40 96, *Fax (0 10) 426 90 41* – . AE VISA JCB
closed 31 December-1 January, Monday and lunch Saturday and Sunday – **Meals** – 26/52 b.i. ♀.
◆ This charming inn, in a picturesque location near four old windmills in the old quarter, will delight customers with its "bistro-style" fare.

Czech Republic

Česká Republika

PRACTICAL INFORMATION

LOCAL CURRENCY

Crown : *100 CZK = 3,08 euro (€) (Dec. 2003)*

National Holiday in the Czech Republic : *1 May, 8 May, 28 October.*

PRICES

Prices may change if goods and service costs in the Czech Republic are revised and it is therefore always advisable to confirm rates with the hotelier when making a reservation.

FOREIGN EXCHANGE

It is strongly advised against changing money other than in banks, exchange offices or authorised offices such as large hotels, tourist offices, etc... Banks are usually open on weekdays from 9am to 5pm. Some exchange offices in the old city are open 24 hours a day.

HOTEL RESERVATIONS

In case of difficulties in finding a room through our hotel selection, it is always possible to apply to AVE Wilsonova 8, Prague 2, ☎ 224 223 521. CEDOK Na příkopě 18, Prague 1 ☎ 224 197 615.

POSTAL SERVICES

Post offices are open from 8am to 6pm on weekdays and 12 noon on Saturdays. The **General Post Office** *is open 7am to 8pm : Jindřišska 14, Prague 1, ☎ 221 131 445. There is a 24 hr postal service at Hybernská 13 ☎ 224 225 845.*

SHOPPING IN PRAGUE

In the index of street names, those printed in red are where the principal shops are found. Typical goods to be bought include embroidery, puppets, Bohemian glass, porcelain, ceramics, wooden toys... Shops are generally open from 9am to 7pm.

TIPPING

Hotel, restaurant and café bills include service in the total charge but it is up to you to tip the staff.

CAR HIRE

The international car hire companies have branches in Prague. Your hotel porter should be able to give details and help you with your arrangements.

BREAKDOWN SERVICE

A 24 hour breakdown service is operated by Autoklub, Opletalova 29, Prague 1. ☎ 224 221 820.

SPEED LIMITS - SEAT BELTS - MOTORWAYS TAX

The maximum permitted speed on motorways is 130 km/h - 80 mph, 90 km/h - 56 mph on other roads and 50 km/h - 31 mph in built up areas except where a lower speed limit is indicated.
The wearing of seat belts is compulsory for drivers and all passengers.
Driving on motorways is subject to the purchase of a single rate annual road tax obtainable from border posts and tourist offices.
In the Czech Republic, drivers must not drink alcoholic beverages at all.

PRAGUE

(PRAHA)

Česká Republika 731 F 3 – *Pop. 1 203 230*

Berlin 344 – Dresden 152 – Munich 384 – Nurnberg 287 – Wroclaw 272 – Vienna 291.

Prague Information Service : Na Příkope 20 (main office), Staroměstsk a radnice, and Main Railway Station ☎ 212 444

CEDOK : Na přikopě 18, Prague 1 ☎ 224 197 111, Fax 224 223 479.

Golf Club Praha, Motol-Praha 5, ☎ 257 216 584.

Ruzyně (Prague Airport) NW 20 km, by road nº 7 ☎ 220 113 314.

Bus to airport : Cedaz Bus at airlines Terminal Namesti Republicky ☎ 220 114 296.

CZECH AIRLINES (ČESKÉ AEROLINIE) V. Celnici 5, PRAGUE 1 ☎ 220 104 702.

See: *Castle District★★★ (Hradčany)* ABX : *Prague Castle★★★ (Pražský Hrad)* BX, *St Vitus' Cathedral★★★ (Chram sv. Víta)* BX, *Old Royal Palace★★ (Královský palác)* BX, *St George's Convent★★ (National Gallery's Early Bohemian Art★★) (Bazilika sv. Jiří/Jiřský Klašter)* BX, *Hradčany Square★★ (Hradčanské náměstí)* BX **37**, *Schwarzenberg Palace★ (Schwarzenberský Palác)* AX **R¹**, *Loretto Shrine★★★ (Loreta)* AX, *Strahov Abbey★★ (Strahovský Klášter)* AX – *Lesser Town★★★ (Malá Strana)* BX : *Charles Bridge★★★ (Karlův Most)* BCX, *Lesser Town Square★ (Malostranské náměstí)* BX, *St Nicholas Church★★★ (Sv. Mikuláše)* BX, *Neruda Street★★ (Nerudova)* BX, *Wallenstein Palace★★ (Valdštejnský Palác)* BX – *Old Town★★★ (Staré Město)* CX : *Old Town Square★★★ (Staroměstské náměstí)* CX, *Astronomical Clock★★★ (Orloj)* CX **R²**, *Old Town Hall★ – Extensive view★★ (Staroměstská radnice)* CX **R²**, *St Nicholas'★★ (Sv. Mikuláše)* CX, *Týn Church★★ (Týnský chrám)* CX, *Jewish Quarter★★★ (Josefov)* CX, *Old-New Synagogue★★★ (Staranová Synagóga)* CX, *Old Jewish Cemetery★★★ (Starý židovský hřbitov)* CX **R³**, *St Agnes Convent★★ (National Gallery's Collection of 19 C Czech Painting and Sculpture) (Anežský klášter)* CX, *Celetná Street★★ (Celetná)* CX, *Powder Tower★ (Prašná Brána)* DX, *House of the black Madonna★ (Dům u černe Matky boží)* CX **E**, *Municipal House★★★ (Obecní Dům)* DX **N²** – *New Town★ (Nové Město)* CDY : *Wenceslas Square★★★ (Václavské náměstí)* CDXY.

Museums: *National Gallery★★★ (Národní Galérie)* AX, *National Museum★ (Národní muzeum)* DY, *National Theatre★★ (Národní divadlo)* CY **T²**, *Decorative Arts Museum★ (Umělecko průmyslové muzeum)* CX **M⁶**, *City Museum★ (Prague model★★) (Muzeum hlavního města Prahy)* DX **M³**, *Vila America★ (Dvořák Museum)* DY.

Outskirts: *Karlštejn Castle SW : 30 km* ET – *Konopiště Castle SW : 40 km* FT.

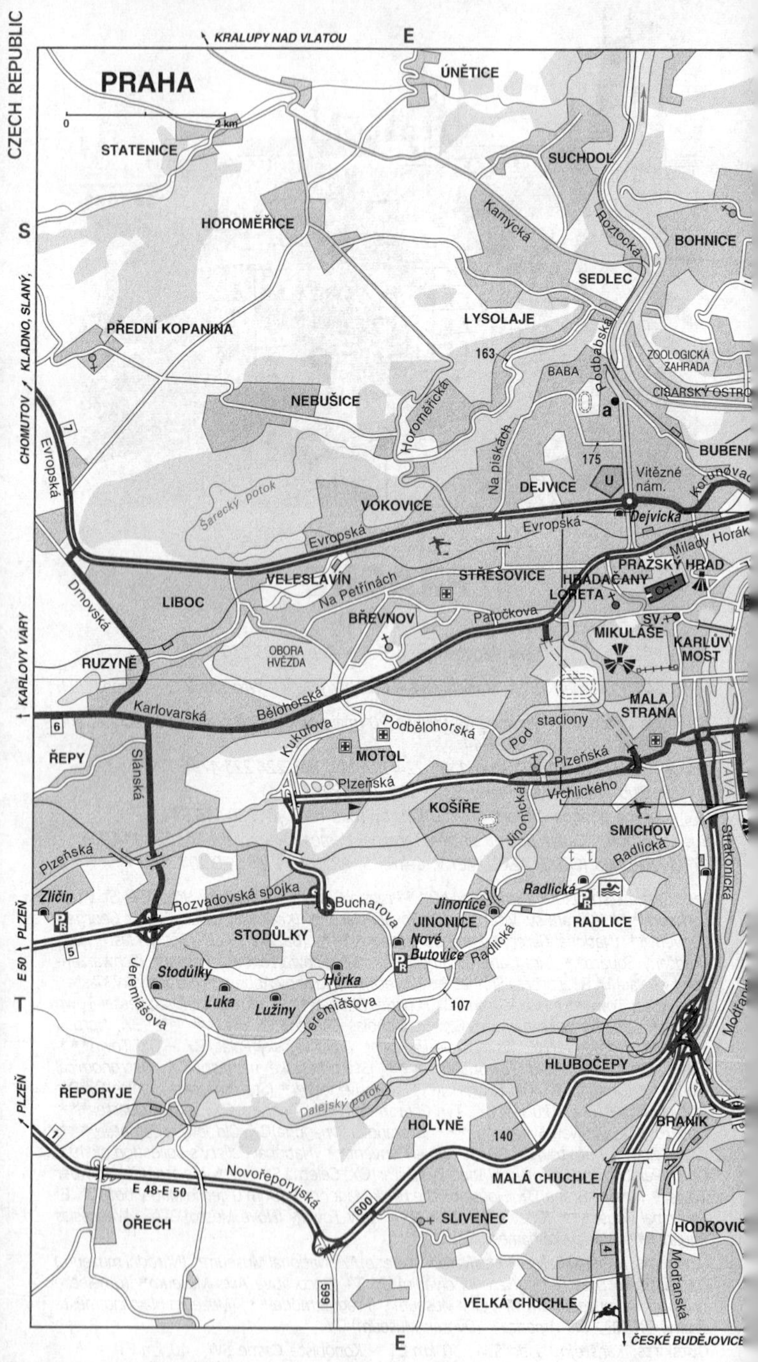
PRAHA
0
2 km
KRALUPY NAD VLATOU
ÚNĚTICE
STATENICE
SUCHDOL
HOROMĚŘICE
Kamýcká
Roztocká
BOHNICE
SEDLEC
LYSOLAJE
PŘEDNÍ KOPANINA
163
BABA
Podbabská
ZOOLOGICKÁ ZAHRADA
NEBUŠICE
Horoměřická
Na pískách
175
DEJVICE
Vítězné nám.
Šárecký potok
VOKOVICE
Dejvická
Evropská
Milady Horákové
VELESLAVÍN
Na Petřínách
STŘEŠOVICE
HRADČANY
PRAŽSKÝ HRAD
LORETA
LIBOC
Drnovská
BŘEVNOV
Patočkova
SV. MIKULÁŠE
KARLŮV MOST
OBORA HVĚZDA
RUZYNĚ
Bělohorská
Karlovarská
MALÁ STRANA
stadiony
Pod
Podbělohorská
Kukulova
ŘEPY
Slánská
MOTOL
Plzeňská
Vrchlického
VLTAVA
KOŠÍŘE
Jinonická
SMÍCHOV
Radlická
Strakonická
Plzeňská
Zličín
Rozvadovská spojka
Bucharova
Jinonice
Radlická
JINONICE
RADLICE
STODŮLKY
Nové Butovice
Stodůlky
Hůrka
Luka
Lužiny
Jeremiášova
107
HLUBOČEPY
ŘEPORYJE
Dalejský potok
HOLYNĚ
140
BRANÍK
E 48-E 50
Novořeporyjská
MALÁ CHUCHLE
600
SLIVENEC
OŘECH
599
VELKÁ CHUCHLE
Modřanská
HODKOVIČ
ČESKÉ BUDĚJOVICE
CHOMUTOV, KLADNO, SLANÝ,
KARLOVY VARY
E 50 PLZEŇ
PLZEŇ
E
S
T

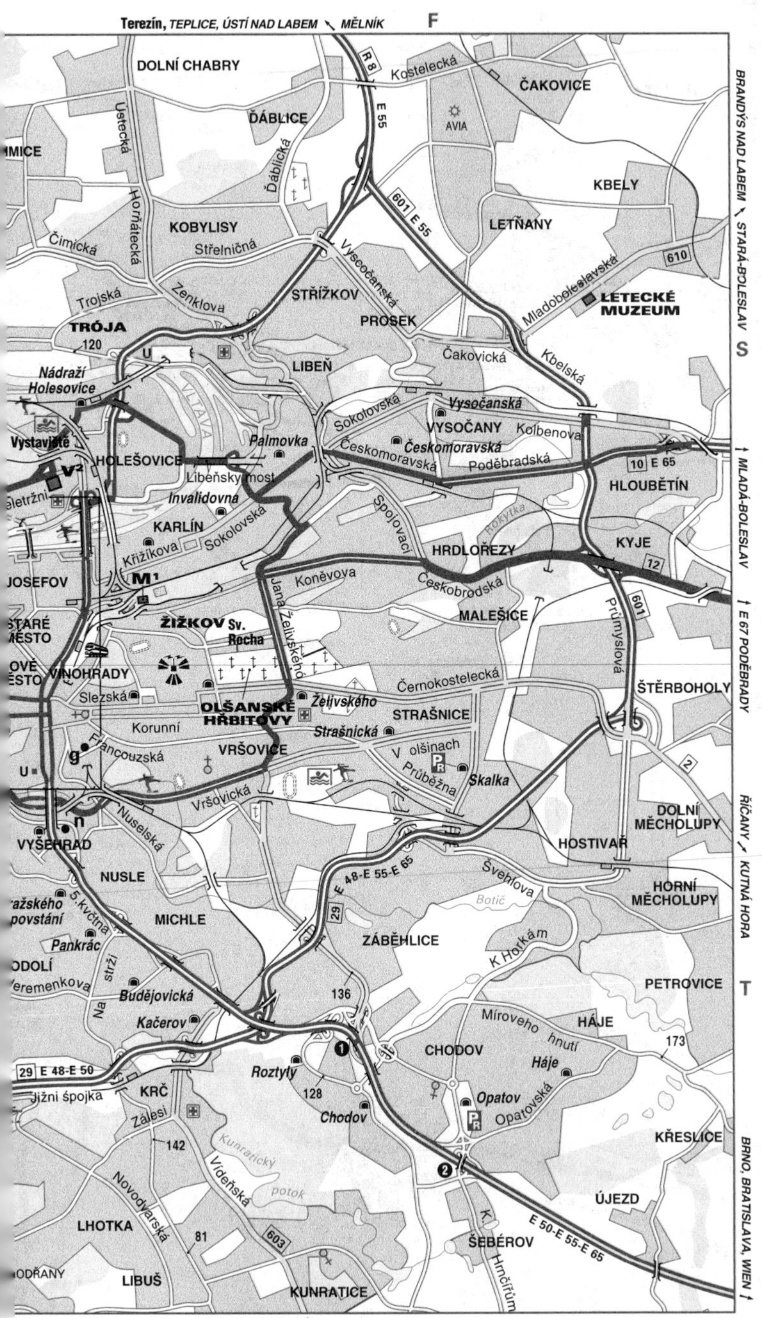
Terezín, TEPLICE, ÚSTÍ NAD LABEM
MĚLNÍK
F
DOLNÍ CHABRY
ČAKOVICE
ĎÁBLICE
AVIA
KBELY
KOBYLISY
LETŇANY
LETECKÉ MUZEUM
STŘÍŽKOV
PROSEK
TRÓJA
LIBEŇ
VYSOČANY
HOLEŠOVICE
HLOUBĚTÍN
KARLÍN
HRDLOŘEZY
KYJE
JOSEFOV
MALEŠICE
ŽIŽKOV
VINOHRADY
OLŠANSKÉ HŘBITOVY
STRAŠNICE
ŠTĚRBOHOLY
VRŠOVICE
VYŠEHRAD
HOSTIVAŘ
DOLNÍ MĚCHOLUPY
NUSLE
HORNÍ MĚCHOLUPY
MICHLE
ZÁBĚHLICE
PETROVICE
HÁJE
CHODOV
KRČ
KŘESLICE
ÚJEZD
LHOTKA
ŠEBÉROV
LIBUŠ
KUNRATICE
KAMENICE
BRANDÝS NAD LABEM
STARÁ BOLESLAV
MLADÁ-BOLESLAV
E 67 PODĚBRADY
ŘÍČANY
KUTNÁ HORA
BRNO, BRATISLAVA, WIEN
S
T
F

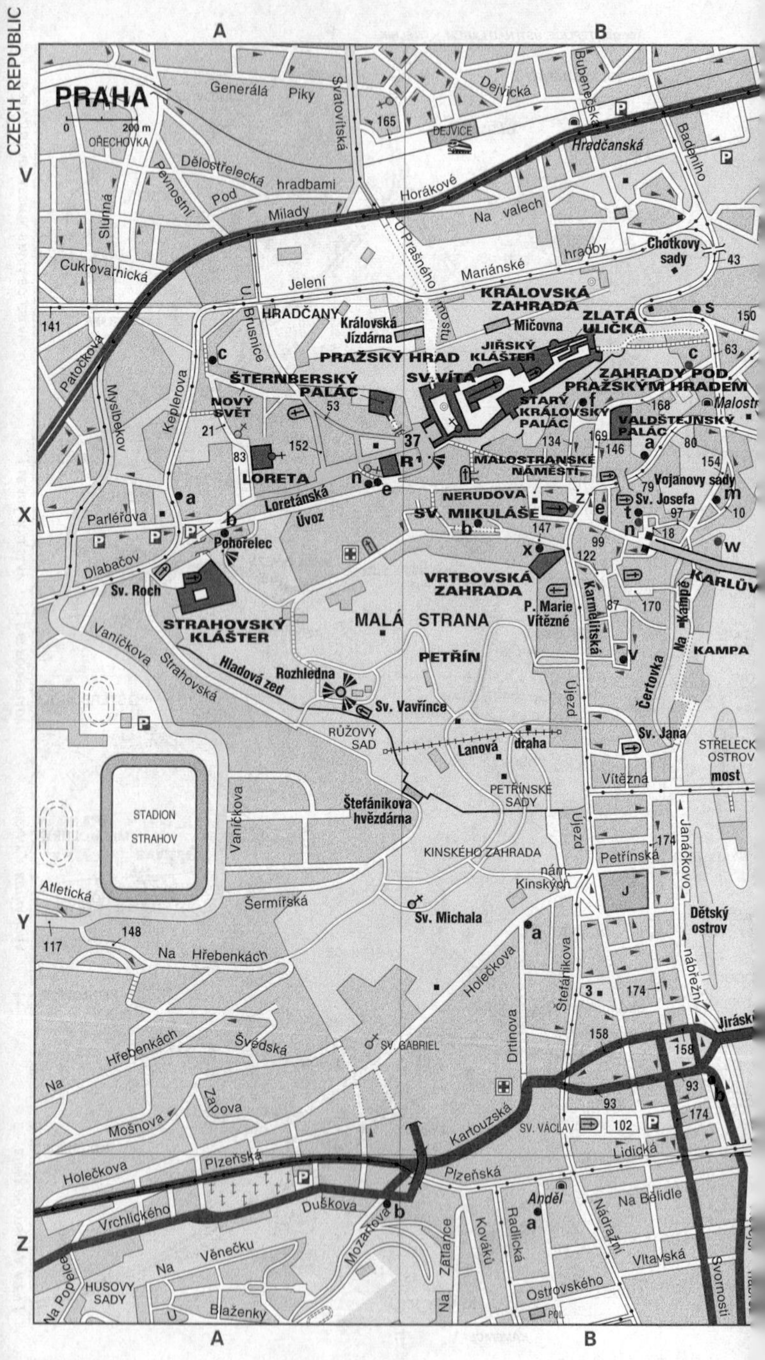
PRAHA
Generálá Piky
Svatovítská
Dejvická
Bubenečská
Hradčanská
Badeniho
DEJVICE
Dělostřelecká
Pevnostní
Pod hradbami
Milady Horákové
Na valech
Slunná
Cukrovarnická
U Prašného mostu
Jelení
Mariánské hradby
Chotkovy sady
KRÁLOVSKÁ ZAHRADA
HRADČANY
Královská Jízdárna
Míčovna
ZLATÁ ULIČKA
JIŘSKÝ KLÁŠTER
PRAŽSKÝ HRAD
ZAHRADY POD PRAŽSKÝM HRADEM
ŠTERNBERSKÝ PALÁC
SV. VÍTA
STARÝ KRÁLOVSKÝ PALÁC
VALDŠTEJNSKÝ PALÁC
NOVÝ SVĚT
LORETA
MALOSTRANSKÉ NÁMĚSTÍ
Vojanovy sady
Patočkova
Myslbekov
Keplerova
U Brusnice
Loretánská
Úvoz
NERUDOVA
SV. MIKULÁŠE
Sv. Josefa
Parléřova
Pohořelec
Dlabačov
Sv. Roch
STRAHOVSKÝ KLÁŠTER
VRTBOVSKÁ ZAHRADA
P. Marie Vítězné
Karmelitská
KARLŮV
Na Kampě
KAMPA
MALÁ STRANA
PETŘÍN
Vaníčkova
Strahovská
Hladová zeď
Rozhledna
Sv. Vavřince
Čertovka
Újezd
RŮŽOVÝ SAD
Lanová dráha
Sv. Jana
STŘELECKÝ OSTROV
Vítězná
most
PETŘÍNSKÉ SADY
Štefánikova hvězdárna
STADION STRAHOV
KINSKÉHO ZAHRADA
Petřínská
Janáčkovo nábřeží
nám. Kinských
Atletická
Šermířská
Sv. Michala
Dětský ostrov
Na Hřebenkách
Holečkova
Štefánikova
Drtinova
Švédská
SV. GABRIEL
Jiráskův
Zapova
Mošnova
Kartouzská
SV. VÁCLAV
Lidická
Plzeňská
Duškova
Vrchlického
Mozartova
Anděl
Na Bělidle
Nádražní
Radlická
Kováků
Zátlance
Na Věnečku
Vltavská
Svornosti
Na Popelce
HUSOVY SADY
U Blaženky
Ostrovského
POL
A
B
V
X
Y
Z
0 200 m
OŘECHOVKA

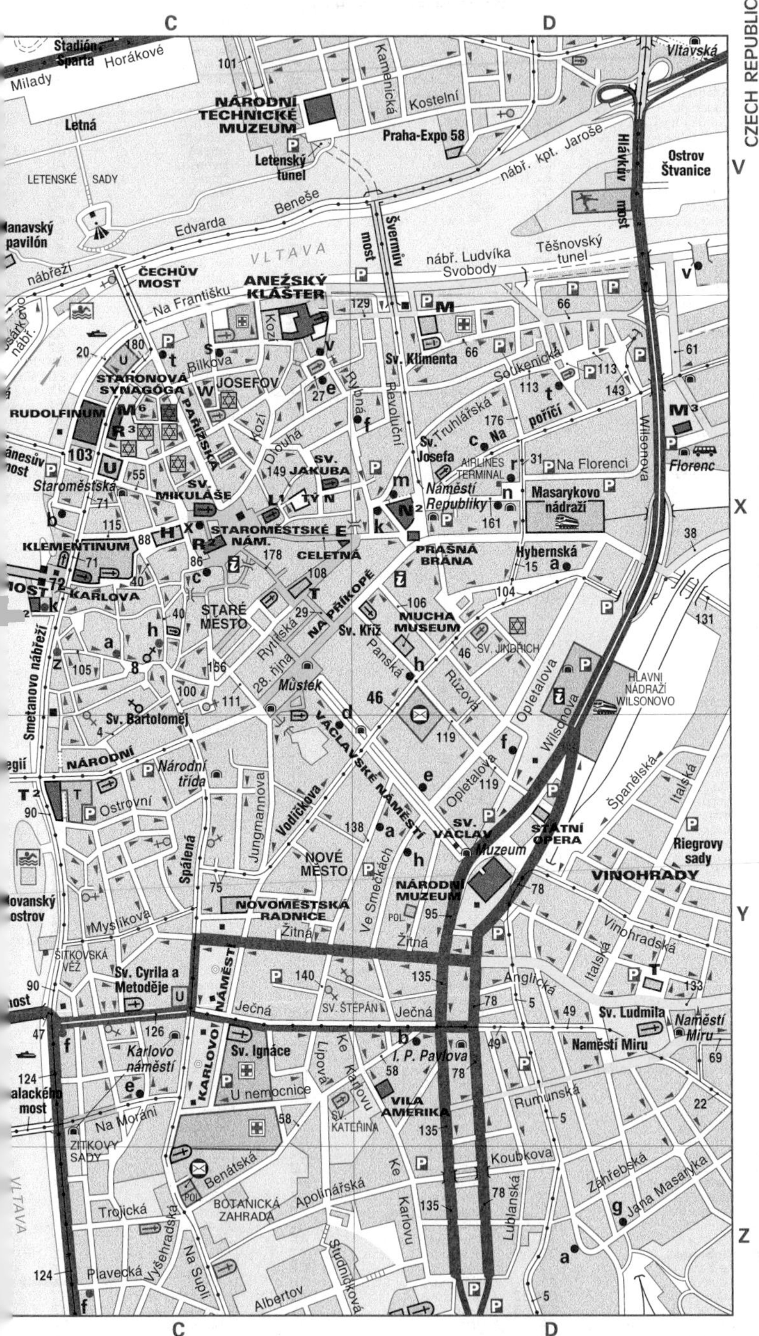
C
D
V
X
Y
Z
Stadión Sparta
Milady Horákové
Letná
LETENSKÉ SADY
NÁRODNÍ TECHNICKÉ MUZEUM
Letenský tunel
Kamenická
Kostelní
Praha-Expo 58
nábř. kpt. Jaroše
Hlávkův most
Ostrov Štvanice
Vltavská
Edvarda Beneše
Švermův most
VLTAVA
nábř. Ludvíka Svobody
Těšnovský tunel
nábřeží
ČECHŮV MOST
ANEŽSKÝ KLÁŠTER
Na Františku
Sv. Klimenta
Soukenická
Revoluční
Rybná
Bílkova
JOSEFOV
STARONOVÁ SYNAGOGA
RUDOLFINUM
PAŘÍŽSKÁ
Dlouhá
Kozí
SV. JAKUBA
TÝN
Truhlářská
Na poříčí
Sv. Josefa
AIRLINES TERMINAL
Na Florenci
Florenc
Wilsonova
Náměstí Republiky
Masarykovo nádraží
Mánesův most
Staroměstská
SV. MIKULÁŠE
STAROMĚSTSKÉ NÁM.
CELETNÁ
PRAŠNÁ BRÁNA
Hybernská
KLEMENTINUM
KARLOVA
STARÉ MĚSTO
Rytířská
NA PŘÍKOPĚ
Sv. Kříž
MUCHA MUSEUM
SV. JINDŘICH
Panská
Růžová
Opletalova
HLAVNÍ NÁDRAŽÍ WILSONOVO
Smetanovo nábřeží
28. října
Můstek
Sv. Bartoloměj
VÁCLAVSKÉ NÁMĚSTÍ
NÁRODNÍ
Národní třída
Ostrovní
Jungmannova
Vodičkova
Španělská
Italská
SV. VÁCLAV
Muzeum
STÁTNÍ OPERA
Riegrovy sady
VINOHRADY
NOVÉ MĚSTO
Ve Smečkách
NÁRODNÍ MUZEUM
Spálená
Slovanský ostrov
Myslíkova
NOVOMĚSTSKÁ RADNICE
Žitná
Vinohradská
ŠITKOVSKÁ VĚŽ
Sv. Cyrila a Metoděje
Anglická
Ječná
SV. ŠTĚPÁN
Sv. Ludmila
Náměstí Míru
KARLOVO NÁMĚSTÍ
Karlovo náměstí
Sv. Ignáce
I. P. Pavlova
U nemocnice
Lípová
Ke Karlovu
VILA AMERIKA
Palackého most
Na Moráni
SV. KATEŘINA
Rumunská
ZITKOVY SADY
Benátská
Koubkova
Trojická
BOTANICKÁ ZAHRADA
Apolinářská
Lublanská
Záhřebská
Jana Masaryka
Vyšehradská
Na Slupi
Plavecká
Albertov
Studničkova

STREET INDEX TO PRAHA TOWN PLAN

U Nikolajky . . . . . AZ
U Prašného mostu . . . . . BX
U Santošky . . . . . BZ
Uhelný trh . . . . . CX 156
Ujezd . . . . . BXY
Ústecká . . . . . FS
Úvoz . . . . . AX
V botanice . . . . . BY 158
V celnici . . . . . DX 161
V olšinach . . . . . FT
V sáreckém údolí . . . . . ES 163
Václavkova . . . . . AV 165
Václavské náměstí . . . . . CDY
Valdštejnská . . . . . BX 168
Valdštejnské náměstí . . . . . BX 169
Vaníčkova . . . . . AY
Ve Smečkách . . . . . DY
Veletržní . . . . . FS
Velkopřevorské náměstí . . . . . BX 170
Videňská . . . . . FT
Vinohradská . . . . . DY
Vlitavská . . . . . BZ
Vítězná . . . . . BY
Vítězné náměstí . . . . . ES
Vlašská . . . . . BX
Vnislavova . . . . . CZ 171
Vodičkova . . . . . CY
Vršovická . . . . . FT
Vratislavova . . . . . CZ
Vrchlického . . . . . AZ
Vyšehradská . . . . . CZ
Vyscočanská . . . . . FS
Výstavní . . . . . FT 173
Wilsonova . . . . . DXY
Xaveriova . . . . . AZ
Záhřebská . . . . . DZ
Zálesi . . . . . FT
Zapova . . . . . AY
Zborovská . . . . . BY 174
Zelená . . . . . ES 175
Zenklova . . . . . FS
Zlatnická . . . . . DX 176
Železná . . . . . CX 178
Žitná . . . . . CY
5. května . . . . . DZ
17.listopadu . . . . . CX 180
28.října CX

Four Seasons, Veleslavinova 2a, ✉ 110 00, ☎ 221 427 000, *prg.reservations@fourseasons.com, Fax 221 426 000,* – rm, – 120. MC AE VISA JCB CX b
Allegro : **Meals** - Italian - 1150 (lunch) and a la carte 1500/1830 – 825 – **141 rm** 8322/17280, 20 suites.
♦ Four houses - modern, neo-Classical, Baroque and neo-Renaissance - make up this elegant riverside hotel. Luxuriously appointed modern rooms ; state-of-the-art business facilities. Modern fine dining restaurant, softly lit and stylishly understated.

Inter-Continental, Nám. Curieových 43-45, ✉ 110 00, ☎ 296 631 111, *prague@interconti.com, Fax 296 631 282,* – rm, – 500. MC AE VISA JCB. CX t
Meals (see ***Zlatá Praha*** below) – 600 – **347 rm** 9287/12490, 25 suites.
♦ Prague's first luxury hotel provides all of the facilities expected of an international hotel. Elegant bedrooms, most enjoy views of the river or the old part of the city.

Carlo IV, Senovážné Nám. 13, ✉ 110 00, ☎ 224 593 111, *info@carloquarto.boscolo.com, Fax 224 593 000,* – rm, – 360. MC AE DC VISA JCB DX a
Box Block : **Meals** a la carte 1205/1710 – **152 rm** 11526/14568.
♦ 19C converted bank with marbled lobby and ornate ceiling. Contemporary pool and health centre. All bedrooms have stylish furniture and modern facilities. A stylish restaurant serving modern dishes with a strong Mediterranean influence.

Radisson SAS Alcron, Štěpánská 40, ✉ 110 00, ☎ 222 820 000, *sales.prague@radissonsas.com, Fax 222 820 120,* – – 150. MC AE VISA JCB. DY a
La Rotonde : **Meals** a la carte 920/1170 (see also ***Alcron*** below) – 544 – **205 rm** 6693/11495, 6 suites.
♦ Built in 1930's and recently refurbished to a very high standard. Original Art Deco theme carried through to include the spacious and extremely comfortable bedrooms. Immaculately laid out restaurant with a stylish Art Deco theme and an outdoor summer terrace.

Aria, Trziste 9, ✉ 118 00, ☎ 225 334 111, *stay@ariahotel.com, Fax 257 535 357,* – rm, – 30. MC AE DC VISA JCB BX x
Coda : **Meals** 795 (lunch) and a la carte 1145/1935 – **45 rm** 10406/12000, 7 suites.
♦ Stylish modern hotel in the castle district. Hi-tech bedrooms, each with its own musical theme from opera to jazz. Hotel has its own musical director. Choose from the stylish menu in intimate Coda or eat on the stunning roof top terrace.

Marriott, V Celnici 8, ✉ 110 00, ☎ 222 888 888, *prague.marriott@marriott.cz, Fax 222 888 889,* – rm, – 350. MC AE VISA JCB. rest DX n
Meals (buffet lunch) 420/595 and a la carte 530/865 – 595 – **258 rm** 6691/8291, 35 suites.
♦ International hotel, opened in 1999. First-class conference and leisure facilities. Committed service and modern, smart bedrooms with all the latest facilities. Brasserie offers a wide selection of cuisine from American, French to traditional Czech.

Hilton Prague, Pobřežní 1, ✉ 186 00, ☎ 222 841 111, *sales.prague@hilton.com, Fax 224 842 378,* squash – rm, P – 1500. MC AE VISA JCB. rest DV v
Citrus Restaurant : **Meals** (dinner only) a la carte 940/1110 – ***Café Bistro :*** **Meals** a la carte 810/960 – **765 rm** 8898/9760, 23 suites.
♦ Adjacent to the International Business Centre, glass building with a spectacular atrium - the largest hotel in the country. Impressive leisure facilities. Modern, Mediterranean repertoire at Citrus. Informal Café Bistro.

Renaissance, V Celnici 7, ✉ 111 21, ☎ 221 821 111, *renaissance.prague@renaissance.cz, Fax 221 822 200,* – rm, – 120. rest DX r
Seven :* Meals** a la carte approx. 1000 – ***U Korbele *(☎ 221 822 433)* **: Meals** a la carte 510/720 – 470 – **314 rm** 6049/7330.
◆ Luxury group hotel in the heart of the City. Geared to the modern corporate traveller ; well-equipped bedrooms, particularly those on the 'Renaissance Club' floor. Seven specialises in grills and seafood. Czech specialities in casual, relaxing U Korbele.

Palace, Panská 12, ✉ 111 21, ☎ 224 093 111, *palhoprg@palacehotel.cz, Fax 224 221 240,* – rm, – 50. rest
Meals a la carte approx 600 – ***Gourmet Club Restaurant :* Meals** 650 and a la carte 1065/1540 – **121 rm** 7651/10080, 3 suites. DX h
◆ Original façade dates back to 1906 and its Viennese Art Nouveau style. Elegant interior ; bedrooms combine period furniture with modern facilities and services. Brasserie and bar with all-day menu. Classic club ambience in the Gourmet Club Restaurant.

Savoy, Keplerova Ul. 6, ✉ 118 00, ☎ 224 302 430, *info@hotel-savoy.cz, Fax 224 302 128,* – rm, – 60. AX a
***Hradčany :* Meals** 590/980 and a la carte 1090/1350 – **60 rm** 7234/10178, 1 suite.
◆ Elegant lobby and relaxing library bar suggesting a bygone era. Up-to-date bedrooms with all mod cons and large, marbled bathrooms. Elegant pillared room with tall windows open on fine days. Uniformed staff and immaculate settings ; international ingredients.

Le Palais, U Zvonařky 1, ✉ 120 00, ☎ 234 634 111, *info@palaishotel.cz, Fax 234 634 635,* – rm, – 90. DZ a
Meals a la carte 960/1350 – **68 rm** 8642/9442, 4 suites.
◆ Elegant hotel in converted late 19C mansion in Belle Epoque style. Basement sauna, gym and treatment rooms. Luxurious bedrooms with modern comforts and equipment. Comfortable restaurant serving modern dishes and Czech specialities.

Corinthia Towers, Kongresová 1, ✉ 146 00, ☎ 261 191 111, *towers@corinthia.cz, Fax 261 225 011,* squash – rm, – 400. FT n
***Rickshaw :* Meals** - Asian - a la carte approx 900 – ***Toscana :* Meals** - Italian - a la carte approx 650 – **522 rm** 7364/8645, 22 suites.
◆ Modern corporate skyscraper, opposite the Congress Centre ; many rooms enjoy city views. Rickshaw serves a mix of Asian dishes. Toscana is a popular Italian restaurant.

Grand Hotel Bohemia, Králodvorská 4, ✉ 110 00, ☎ 234 608 111, *grand-hotel-bohemia@austria-hotels.icom.cz, Fax 222 329 545* – rm, – 140. rest DX k
Meals a la carte 550/800 – **78 rm** 7400/10800.
◆ Classic 1920's hotel, in an ideal location for tourists, with a splendid neo-Baroque ballroom. Comfortable bedrooms are generously proportioned and service professional. Restaurant with large windows which add to the feeling of light and space.

Hoffmeister, Pod Bruskou 7, ✉ 118 00, ☎ 251 017 111, *hotel@hoffmeister.cz, Fax 251 017 100,* – BX s
Meals a la carte 670/840 – **32 rm** 7044/9925, 4 suites.
◆ Charming residence at the foot of the Castle steps ; a 1920's feel and a huge collection of Adolf Hoffmeister art. Tasteful and comfortable. Elegant surroundings with original Adolf Hoffmeister cartoons. Attentive service ; French and Italian influenced cooking.

Andel's, Stroupeznického 21, ✉ 150 00, ☎ 296 889 688, *info@andelshotel.com, Fax 296 889 999,* – rm, – 350. BZ a
***Oscar's :* Meals** 149 (lunch) and a la carte approx 800 – ***Nagoya :* Meals** - Japanese - *(closed Tuesday)* 570/980 and a la carte approx 1000 – **235 rm** 7044/8003, 4 suites.
◆ Modern hotel in a large complex including a cinema. Conference and fitness centres. Stylish bedrooms decorated in muted tones, with hi-tech facilities. Dine informally from the fairly simple menu in Oscar's brasserie. Nagoya offers traditional Japanese dishes.

Mövenpick, Mozartova 261/1, ✉ 151 33, ☎ 257 151 111, *reservation@moevenpick.cz, Fax 257 153 002,* – rm, – 250. rest AZ b
***Il Giardino :* Meals** a la carte 680/1060 – ***Movenpick :* Meals** - Mediterranean - (buffet lunch) 680 (lunch) and a la carte 490/660 – **427 rm** 7203/8803, 7 suites.
◆ Unique two-part hotel. From the ground floor, a funicular railway climbs uphill to larger, better equipped, balconied rooms with panoramic views - superior in both senses. Modern brasserie on the ground floor. Mediterranean influences in Il Giardino.

Crowne Plaza, Koulova 15, ✉ 160 45, ☎ 296 537 111, *hotel@crowneplaza.cz, Fax 296 537 535,* – rm, – 250.
Meals a la carte approx 600 – 320 – **260 rm** 8964/10085, 4 suites. ES a
◆ An imposing example of Socialist Realism architecture. Softened interior retains a grandeur, with tapestries, stained glass and mosaics. Refurbished, well-equipped bedrooms. Ornate decoration lends a period feel to the restaurant.

Mercure, Na Poříčí 7, ✉ 110 00, ☎ 221 800 800, *h3440@accor-hotels.com, Fax 221 800 801,* – |♦|, ⇔ rm, ▤ TV ☎ ♿. MC AE VISA DX c
***Felice* : Meals** a la carte 735/830 – ☕ 450 – **173 rm** 4038/5169, 1 suite.
◆ Modern hotel behind ornate, period façade. Chapter Bar features works of famous Czech writers. Ask for a deluxe room ; more spacious. Booking advisable at this modern Parisien brasserie. Menus blend French and Czech classics.

Paříž, U obecního domu 1, ✉ 110 00, ☎ 222 195 195, *booking@hotel-pariz.cz, Fax 224 225 475,* – |♦|, ⇔ rm, ▤ TV ☎ – 55. MC AE VISA JCB. DX m
***Sarah Bernhardt* : Meals** 935 (lunch) and a la carte 1340/1465 ♀ – ***Café de Paris* : Meals** a la carte approx 450 – ☕ 650 – **85 rm** 10245, 1 suite.
◆ A city landmark ; famed for its neo-Gothic, Art Nouveau architecture. Original staircase with preserved window panels. Neat and clean bedrooms. Fine example of Art Nouveau in Sarah Bernhardt restaurant. Simple French fare in Café de Paris.

Riverside without rest., Janáčkovo nábřeži 15, ✉ 150 00, ☎ 225 994 611, *info@riversideprague.com, Fax 225 994 662,* ≤ – |♦|, ⇔ rm, ▤ TV ☎ ♿. MC AE VISA JCB BY b
☕ 480 **42 rm** 6403/8484, 3 suites.
◆ An early 20C façade facing the river conceals a modern sound-proofed hotel with bar and breakfast room. Stylish bedrooms with luxurious bathrooms ; many with views.

K + K Fenix, Ve Smečkách 30, ✉ 110 00, ☎ 233 092 222, *hotel.fenix@kkhotels.cz, Fax 222 212 141,* – |♦|, ⇔ rm, ▤ TV ☎ ♿ – 40. MC AE VISA JCB
Meals (in bar) a la carte 350/800 ♀ – **128 rm** ☕ 7302/7942. DY h
◆ Located in a quiet side street ; stylish and cosmopolitan interior behind a classic façade. Bedrooms vary in size and shape but all are smart, clean and comfortable. Open-plan café bar in the lobby ; tasty brasserie classics.

U Zlaté Studně, U Zlaté Studně 16614, Malá Strana, ✉ 118 00, ☎ 257 011 213, *hotel@zlatastudna.cz, Fax 257 533 320,* ≤ – |♦| ▤ TV ☎. MC AE VISA BX f
Meals (see ***U Zlaté Studně*** below) – **17 rm** ☕ 7900/9200, 3 suites.
◆ 16C Renaissance building in quiet spot between the castle and Ladeburg Gardens. Inviting rooms with contemporary and reproduction furniture : richly furnished but uncluttered.

Residence Nosticova, Nosticova 1, Malá Strana, ✉ 118 00, ☎ 257 312 513, *info@nosticova.com, Fax 257 312 517* – |♦| TV ☎ P. MC AE VISA JCB BX v
Alchymist (☎ *257 312 518*) **: Meals** 850 and a la carte 580/820 – ☕ 288 **5 rm** 6405/9642, **5 suites** 11293/16683.
◆ Tastefully refurbished 17C townhouse in a quiet, cobbled sidestreet. Stylish suites - all with their own kitchen - combine modern and antique furnishings and works of art.

Esplanade, Washingtonova 1600-19, ✉ 110 00, ☎ 224 501 111, *esplanade@esplanade.cz, Fax 224 229 306* – |♦|, ⇔ rm, ▤ rm, TV ☎ – 60. MC AE VISA JCB DY f
Meals 650 (lunch) and a la carte 465/819 ♀ – ☕ 224 – **74 rm** 4452/6407.
◆ Charming and atmospheric ; this Art Nouveau building is something of an architectural gem. Original features abound ; bedrooms enjoy style and a timeless elegance. Menu of traditional Czech and French specialities offered in friendly surroundings.

Josef without rest., Rybná 20, ✉ 110 00, ☎ 221 700 111, *reservations@hoteljosef.com, Fax 221 700 999,* – |♦|, ⇔ rm, ▤ TV ☎ ♿ – 90. MC AE VISA DX f
109 rm ☕ 6631/9485.
◆ Stylish designer hotel with light glass lobby, bar and breakfast room. Stylish bedrooms ; deluxe rooms have ultra modern bathrooms.

U Prince, Staroměstské Nám. 29, ✉ 110 00, ☎ 224 213 807, *reserve@hoteluprince.cz, Fax 224 213 807,* ≤ Prague, – |♦|, ⇔ rm, ▤ TV. MC AE VISA CX c
Meals a la carte 400/740 – **24 rm** ☕ 5990/10990.
◆ Restored 17C townhouse on main square with atmospheric rooms blending with mod cons and antique furnishings. Roof terrace with marvellous city views. Choose the half-panelled bar-restaurant for International cooking or the brick vaulted cellars for seafood.

Adria, Václavské Nám. 26, ✉ 110 00, ☎ 221 081 111, *mailbox@adria.cz, Fax 221 081 300* – |♦|, ⇔ rm, ▤ TV ☎ ♿ – 50. MC AE VISA JCB. CY d
***Triton* : Meals** (dinner booking essential) 690 and a la carte 640/840 – **82 rm** ☕ 5585/6825, 5 suites.
◆ Ornate façade hides a labyrinth inside that connects five separate houses. Combines the nostalgic charm of Old Prague with modern, recently refurbished bedrooms. Eye-catching Art Nouveau grotto. Savour international dishes in unique, candlelit surroundings.

Maximilian without rest., Haštalská 14, ✉ 110 00, ☎ 225 303 111, *maximilianhotel@hotmail.com, Fax 225 303 110* – |♦| ⇔ ▤ TV ♿ – 50. MC AE VISA JCB CX e
71 rm ☕ 6496/7744.
◆ Tall, converted terraced house in a quiet square. Immaculately kept, with elegant and understated bedrooms and a smart breakfast room. Welcoming and friendly service.

Kinsky Garden, Holečkova 7, 150 00, 257 311 173, *kinskygarden@vol.cz, Fax 257 211 184* – , rm, – 30. BY a
Meals 450 (lunch) and a la carte 610/760 – **60 rm** 4806/6088.
◆ Overlooking the Park, with an attractive period façade. Smart little lobby and bar, with lots of marble. Comfortable and spacious bedrooms in warm, neutral colours. International and Italian-influenced cooking.

Zlatá Hvězda, Nerudova 48, Malá Strana, 118 00, 257 532 867, *hvezda@ok.cz, Fax 257 533 624,* – . AX e
Meals a la carte approx 300 – **24 rm** 4806/5223, 2 suites.
◆ Imposing, part 18C burgher house in a delightful setting. Comfortable bedrooms and pleasant views of the town from the upper floors. Classic cooking from the traditional Czech repertory.

U Krále Karla, Uvoz 4, 118 00, 257 531 211, *ukrale@iol.cz, Fax 257 533 591* – , rm, . AX n
Meals 250 (lunch) and a la carte 600/830 – **19 rm** 5000/7900.
◆ Rebuilt in 1639 into a Baroque house from an original Gothic building of a Benedictine Order. Features stained glass windows and antique oak furnishings. Panelled dining room and an ambience of Old Prague complemented by the traditional menu.

U Modrého Klíče without rest., Letenská 14, 118 00, 257 534 361, *bluekey@mbox.vol.cz, Fax 257 534 372,* – . BX a
22 rm 4486/5447, 6 suites.
◆ 18C house in heart of old town. The smart modern rooms, facing the central courtyard, are decorated in forest green or blue and white ; some have kitchenettes.

Jalta, Václavské Nám. 45, 110 00, 222 822 111, *jalta@jalta.cz, Fax 224 213 866* – – 100. . rest DY e
Meals a la carte 355/555 – **89 rm** 3845/7690, 5 suites.
◆ Classic 1950's façade overlooking Wenceslas Square. Spacious feeling, extensive facilities and helpful staff. Good standard modern bedrooms. Elegant, sophisticated dining room with International and Czech dishes.

Novotel, Kateřinská 38, 120 00, 221 104 999, *h3194-re@accor-hotels.com, Fax 221 104 888,* , , , – , rm, – 120. DY b
Meals a la carte approx 750 – 345 – **145 rm** 3650/3890.
◆ 21C group hotel on the southern edge of the old town. Affordable accommodation, trim and practically designed, with spacious bedrooms. Modern restaurant with a neatly set terrace ; well-known international dishes.

U Páva, U Lužického Semináře 30, 118 00, 257 533 360, *hotelupava@iol.cz, Fax 257 530 919,* – . . rest BX m
Meals a la carte 520/890 – **15 rm** 5400/7000, 6 suites.
◆ Attractively located, converted 17C houses. Original stone columns in the hallways, nutwood furniture and ornately decorated rooms add to the character. Vaulted basement dining room has a warm and romantic feel. International menu with Czech specialities.

Questenberk without rest., Uvoz 15/155, 110 00, 220 407 600, *hotel@questenberk.cz, Fax 220 407 601,* – , rm, . AX b
30 rm 5383/7690.
◆ Converted 17C monastic hospital with ornate façade at the top of the Castle District. Arched corridors leading to sizable bedrooms with good facilities overlooking the city.

The Charles without rest., Josefská 1, 118 00, 257 532 913, *thecharles@bon.cz, Fax 257 532 910* – . . BX e
31 rm 5767/8648.
◆ Elegant and ideally situated little hotel. Spacious bedrooms decorated with stripped floorboards, hand painted ceilings and Baroque style furnishings.

U Raka without rest., Cerninská 10, 118 00, 220 511 100, *uraka@login.cz, Fax 233 358 041,* – . . AX c
6 rm 6900/7900.
◆ Two charming timbered cottages with flower-filled urns, troughs and millstones in a pretty rockery. Clean-lined, rustic rooms in warm brick and wood : cosy, inviting and romantic.

Casa Marcello , Rásnovka 783, 110 00, 222 311 230, *booking@casa-marcello.cz, Fax 222 313 323,* – rm, . CX v
Meals (dinner only October-March) a la carte 450/650 – **26 rm** 9000, 6 suites.
◆ Beside the 1000 year old St.Agnes Monastery ; bedrooms at this part 13C property were once the nuns' quarters. Several vaulted rooms with stately antique furniture. A traditional menu can be enjoyed on the secluded terrace or in the cosy panelled dining room.

Constans, Břetislavova 39, ✉ 118 00, ✆ 234 091 818, *hotel@hotelconstans.cz, Fax 234 091 860* – 🛗 📺 📞 🚗. MC AE DC VISA JCB BX b
Meals 385 and a la carte 280/452 – **32 rm** ☕ 4800/5850.
◆ Small hotel in narrow cobbled street in the Castle district. Good sized, light and airy bedrooms with locally made furniture. Simple café style restaurant-breakfast room-bar serving basic menu of international dishes.

Bellagio without rest., U Milosrdnâch 2, ✉ 110 00, ✆ 221 778 999, *bookings@bellagiohotel.cz, Fax 221 778 900* – 🛗, ⚭ rm, 📺 📞 ♿ – 🏛 30. MC AE DC VISA CX s
47 rm ☕ 4836/5413.
◆ Converted pink apartment block near the river. Brick-vaulted bar/breakfast room. Stylish bedrooms in warm colours with modern furniture, attractive tiled bathrooms.

Biskupský Dům, Dražického Nám. 6, ✉ 118 00, ✆ 257 532 320, *biskup@ok.cz, Fax 257 531 840* – 🛗 📺 ♿. MC AE VISA BX t
Meals 200 and a la carte approx 300 🍷 – **29 rm** ☕ 4804/5221.
◆ In a small square near the Charles Bridge, a renovated townhouse hotel on the site of the 13C bishop's court. Simple rooms furnished in dark wood. Familiar Czech and international dishes.

Ametyst, Jana Masaryka 11, ✉ 120 00, ✆ 222 921 947, *mailbox@hotelametyst.cz, Fax 222 921 999,* 🧖 – 🛗, ⚭ rm, ❄ rest, 📺 ♿. MC AE DC VISA JCB DZ g
Meals a la carte 645/885 🍷 – **84 rm** ☕ 4644/6246.
◆ Bright, white six-storey building with a neat, precise feel. Smart bedrooms with all modern facilities. Choose Austrian fare in the wine bar or typical Czech and International dishes in the more formal 'Galleria'.

Cerná Liška, Mikulášská 2, Staroměstské Nám., ✉ 110 00, ✆ 224 232 250, *hotel@cernaliska.cz, Fax 224 232 249,* 🌳 – 🛗 📺. MC DC VISA CX x
Meals a la carte approx 450 – **12 rm** ☕ 3971/5220.
◆ Delightful small hotel in the Old Town Square, a good base for exploring the city. All the bedrooms have character and charm. Simple ground floor café and 18C basement cellar restaurant with summer terrace ; vegetarian menu.

City H. Moran, Na Moráni 15, ✉ 120 00, ✆ 224 915 208, *bw-moran@login.cz, Fax 224 920 625* – 🛗, ⚭ rm, ❄ 📺. MC AE DC VISA CY e
Meals a la carte 295/456 🍷 – **57 rm** ☕ 5250/6250.
◆ Modern interior behind a characterful, period façade. Small, discreet marbled lobby leads up to clean, well-kept, functional bedrooms. Useful city centre accommodation. Simple restaurant for modern, International and Czech cooking.

Bílá Labuť, Biskupská 9, ✉ 110 00, ✆ 222 324 540, *cchotels@login.cz, Fax 222 322 905,* 🧖 – 🛗, ⚭ rm, 📺 ♿. MC AE DC VISA DX t
Meals a la carte approx. 450 🍷 – **55 rm** ☕ 4700/6000.
◆ Converted from a large office block. Now offers simple, clean and well maintained accommodation in a central location. Popular with the business community. Modern bar and restaurant for Czech and International cooking.

Zlatá Praha (at Inter-Continental H.), Nám. Curieových 43-45, ✉ 110 00, ✆ 296 630 914, *prague@interconti.com, Fax 296 631 282,* ≤ Prague, 🌳 – ❄. MC AE DC VISA JCB. ⚭ CX t
Meals 600/3600 and a la carte 1410/1720 🍷.
◆ Stunning views of the city skyline provide a backdrop to this elegant, formal room. Extensive menu at well-spaced tables. Grills, fish specials on the terrace in summer.

Flambée, Husova 5, ✉ 110 00, ✆ 224 248 512, *flambee@flambee.cz, Fax 224 248 513* – ❄. MC AE DC VISA JCB CX h
Meals 490/1769 and a la carte 1530/2090 🍇 – ***Cafe Flambée :*** **Meals** a la carte 340/680 🍷.
◆ Elegant fine dining in an established cellar restaurant : faultless, friendly service and well-judged classics - impressive selection of clarets. A little modern café-bistro open for coffees, desserts and brunch ; international dishes from the main kitchen.

Alcron (at Radisson SAS Alcron H.), Štěpánská 40, ✉ 110 00, ✆ 222 820 038, *sales.prague@radissonsas.com, Fax 222 820 100* – ❄ 🚗. MC AE VISA JCB. ⚭ DY a
closed Sunday – **Meals** - Seafood - (booking essential) (dinner only) a la carte 1390/1520 🍷.
◆ An Art Deco mural after de Lempicka dominates this intimate, semi-circular restaurant. Creative and classic seafood served by friendly, professional staff.

La Perle de Prague, Dancing House (7th floor), Rašínovo Nábřeží 80, ✉ 120 00, ✆ 221 984 160, *laperle@volny.cz, Fax 221 984 179,* ≤, 🌳 – 🛗 ❄. MC AE VISA CY f
closed Sunday and lunch Monday – **Meals** - French - 490/2500 and a la carte 990/1390 🍷.
◆ Eye-catching riverside building : free-form contours crowned by a mesh-metal onion dome. Superb terrace views and comfortable, strikingly modern decor. French-inspired menu.

XXX **Bellevue,** Smetanovo Nábřeží 18, ✉ 110 00, ✆ 222 221 443, *bellevue@pfd.cz, Fax 222 220 453*, ≤, 斎 – MC AE VISA CX z
closed 24 December – **Meals** 1190/1390 and a la carte 1110/1800 ♀.
◆ On the first floor of an elegant building, affording views of the river and bridge. Pleasant terrace, comfortable surroundings, knowledgeable staff, contemporary cuisine.

XXX **Vinárna V Zátiši,** Liliová 1, Betlémské Nám., ✉ 110 00, ✆ 222 221 155, *vzatisi@pfd.cz, Fax 222 220 629* – ⇔ rest, ▤. MC AE VISA. ✻ CX a
closed 24 December – **Meals** (dinner booking essential) 795/1175 and a la carte 1185/1385 ♀.
◆ Extensive menu includes traditional Czech flavours and more modern dishes. Friendly welcome. Divided into three rooms, each warmly decorated.

XXX **U Zlaté Studně** (at U Zlaté Studně H.), U Zlaté Studně 4, ✉ 118 00, ✆ 257 011 213, *zlata.studne@email.cz, Fax 257 533 320*, ≤ Prague, 斎 – ▤. MC AE VISA BX f
Meals a la carte 850/1140 ♀.
◆ Beautiful skyline views from a clean-lined top-floor restaurant and terrace, reached by its own lift. Affable staff ; full-flavoured modern dishes.

XXX **Mlynec,** Novotného Lávka 9, ✉ 110 00, ✆ 221 082 208, *mlynec@pfd.cz, Fax 221 082 391*, ≤ Charles Bridge, 斎 – MC AE VISA. ✻ CX k
closed 24 December – **Meals** 1390/1590 (dinner) and a la carte 735/1035 ♀.
◆ Spacious and contemporary : fine modern dishes combined with Czech classics - good Czech wines and terrace views of the Charles Bridge on fine summer evenings.

XXX **Pálffy Palác,** Valdstejnska 14, ✉ 118 00, ✆ 257 530 522, *palffy@palffy.cz, Fax 257 530 522*, 斎 – MC AE VISA BX c
closed 24 December – **Meals** 450/890 and a la carte 810/1085.
◆ First floor restaurant, a high ceilinged, ornate room in the 18C Prague Conservatory. A romantic setting in the evening ; delightful terrace in summer. Modern menu.

XXX **U Patrona,** Dražického Nám. 4, ✉ 118 00, ✆ 257 530 725, *upatrona@seznam.cz, Fax 257 530 723* – ⇔. MC AE DC VISA JCB BX n
Meals 290 (lunch) and a la carte 790/1090.
◆ Charming period house near Charles Bridge. Small ground floor restaurant or larger upstairs room with window into kitchen. French-influenced classics and Czech specialities.

X **Bistrot de Marlène,** Plavecká 4, ✉ 120 00, ✆ 224 921 853, *info@bistrotdemarlene.cz, Fax 224 920 743* – MC AE VISA CZ f
closed 1 week Christmas, Sunday and lunch Saturday – **Meals** - French - (booking essential at dinner) a la carte 1040/1200 ♀.
◆ Still smoothly run by the eponymous owner, a likeable little neighbourhood restaurant. Sound, well-judged and unpretentious authentic French cuisine in the best bistro tradition.

X **Cafe La Veranda,** Elišky Krásnohorské 2/10, ✉ 110 00, ✆ 224 814 733, *office@laveranda.cz* – ▤. MC AE DC VISA JCB CX w
Meals 540/1750 and a la carte 910/1145 ♀.
◆ Modern restaurant in the old Jewish district. Efficient service. Modern menu in keeping with the décor, fusing East and West to produce light dishes with interesting flavours.

X **Kampa Park,** Na Kampě 8b, ✉ 118 00, ✆ 257 532 685, *kontakt@kampapark.com, Fax 257 533 223*, ≤ Charles Bridge, 斎 – MC AE DC VISA BX w
Meals (dinner booking essential) 495 (lunch) and a la carte 1135/1475 ♀.
◆ Popular restaurant stunningly located by Charles Bridge. Lively modern designer main room, outside terrace or covered waterside terrace. Modern menu with global influences.

X **Square,** Malostranské Nám. 5/28, ✉ 118 00, ✆ 257 532 109, *kontakt@squarerestaurant.cz, Fax 257 532 107*, 斎 – MC AE DC VISA BX z
Meals 295 (lunch) and a la carte 505/805 ♀.
◆ Baroque building with contemporary décor and good view of square. Summer terrace and additional basement room. Modern menu with Mediterranean, mostly Italian, influence.

Denmark

Danmark

PRACTICAL INFORMATION

LOCAL CURRENCY

Danish Kroner: *100 DKK = 13,44 euro (€) (Dec. 2003)*

TOURIST INFORMATION

The telephone number and address of the Tourist Information office is given in the text under ℹ.

FOREIGN EXCHANGE

Banks are open between 9.30am and 4.00pm (6.00pm on Thursdays) on weekdays except Saturdays. The main banks in the centre of Copenhagen, the Central Station and the Airport have exchange facilities outside these hours.

AIRLINES

SAS/LUFTHANSA: *Hamerichsgade 1, ☏ 70 10 20 00*
AIR FRANCE: *Ved Versterpot 6, ☏ 33 12 76 76*
BRITISH AIRWAYS: *Rådhuspladsen 16, ☏ 33 14 60 00*

MEALS

At lunchtime, follow the custom of the country and try the typical buffets of Danish specialities (smørrebrød).
At dinner, the a la carte and set menus will offer you more conventional cooking.

SHOPPING IN COPENHAGEN

Strøget (Department stores, exclusive shops, boutiques).
Kompagnistræde (Antiques). Shops are generally open from 10am to 7pm (Saturday 9am to 4pm).
See also in the index of street names, those printed in red are where the principal shops are found.

THEATRE BOOKINGS

Your hotel porter will be able to make your arrangements or direct you to Theatre Booking Agents.

CAR HIRE

The international car hire companies have branches in Copenhagen. Your hotel porter should be able to give details and help you with your arrangements.

TIPPING

In Denmark, all hotels and restaurants include a service charge. As for the taxis, there is no extra charge to the amount shown on the meter.

SPEED LIMITS

The maximum permitted speed in cities is 50 km/h - 31 mph, outside cities 80 km/h - 50 mph and 110 km/h - 68 mph on motorways. Cars towing caravans 70 km/h – 44 mph and buses 80 km/h – 50 mph also on motorways.
Local signs may indicate lower or permit higher limits. On the whole, speed should always be adjusted to prevailing circumstances. In case of even minor speed limit offences, drivers will be liable to heavy fines to be paid on the spot. If payment cannot be made, the car may be impounded.

SEAT BELTS

The wearing of seat belts is compulsory for drivers and all passengers except children under the age of 3 and taxi passengers.

COPENHAGEN
(KØBENHAVN)

Danmark **711** Q 9 *– pop. 500 100, Greater Copenhagen 1 810 000.*

Berlin 385 – Hamburg 305 – Oslo 583 – Stockholm 630.

Copenhagen Tourist Information, Bernstorffsgade 1, ✉ *1577 V* ☎ *70 22 24 42, Fax 70 22 24 52.*

Dansk Golf Union 56 ☎ *43 45 55 55.*

Copenhagen/Kastrup SE : 10 km ☎ *32 31 32 31 – Air Terminal : main railway station* ☎ *33 14 17 01.*

Motorail for Southern Europe : ☎ *33 14 17 01.*

Further information from the D S B, main railway station or tourist information centre (see above).
Øresund Bridge-high speed road and rail link between Denmark and Sweden.

See : *Rosenborg Castle★★★ (Rosenborg Slot)* CX *– Amalienborg Palace★★ (Amalienborg)* DY *– Nyhavn★★★ (canal)* DY *– Tivoli★★ : May to mid September* BZ *– Christiansborg Palace★ (Christiansborg)* CZ *– Citadel★ (Kastellet)* DX *– Gråbrødretorv★* CY **28** *– Little Mermaid★★ (Den Lille Havfrue)* DX *– Marble Bridge★ (Marmorbroen)* CZ **50** *– Marble Church★ (Marmorkirke)* DY *– Kongens Nytorv★* DX *– Round Tower★ (Rundetårn)* CY **E** *– Stock Exchange★ (Børsen)* CDZ *– Strøget★* BCYZ *– Town Hall (Rådhuset)* BZ **H** *: Jens Olsen's astronomical clock★* BZ **H** *– Bibliothek★* CZ.

Museums : *National Museum★★★ (Nationalmuseet)* CZ *– Ny Carlsberg Glyptotek★★★: art collection* BZ *– National Fine Arts Museum★★ (Statens Museum for Kunst)* CX *– Thorvaldsen Museum★★ (Thorvaldsens Museum)* CZ **M¹** *– Den Hirschsprungske Samling★* CX *– Davids Samling★* CY.

Outskirts : *Ordrupgård★★: art collection (Ordrupgårdsamlingen) N : 10 km* CX *– Louisiana Museum of Modern Art★★★ (Museum for Moderne Kunst) N : 35 km* CX *– Arken Museum of Modern Art★★ SW : 17 km by 02 (BN) and 151 – Dragør★ SW : 13 km* CZ *– Rungstedlund★: Karen Blixen Museum N : 25 km* CX *– Open-Air Museum★ (Frilandsmuseet) NW : 12 km* AX.

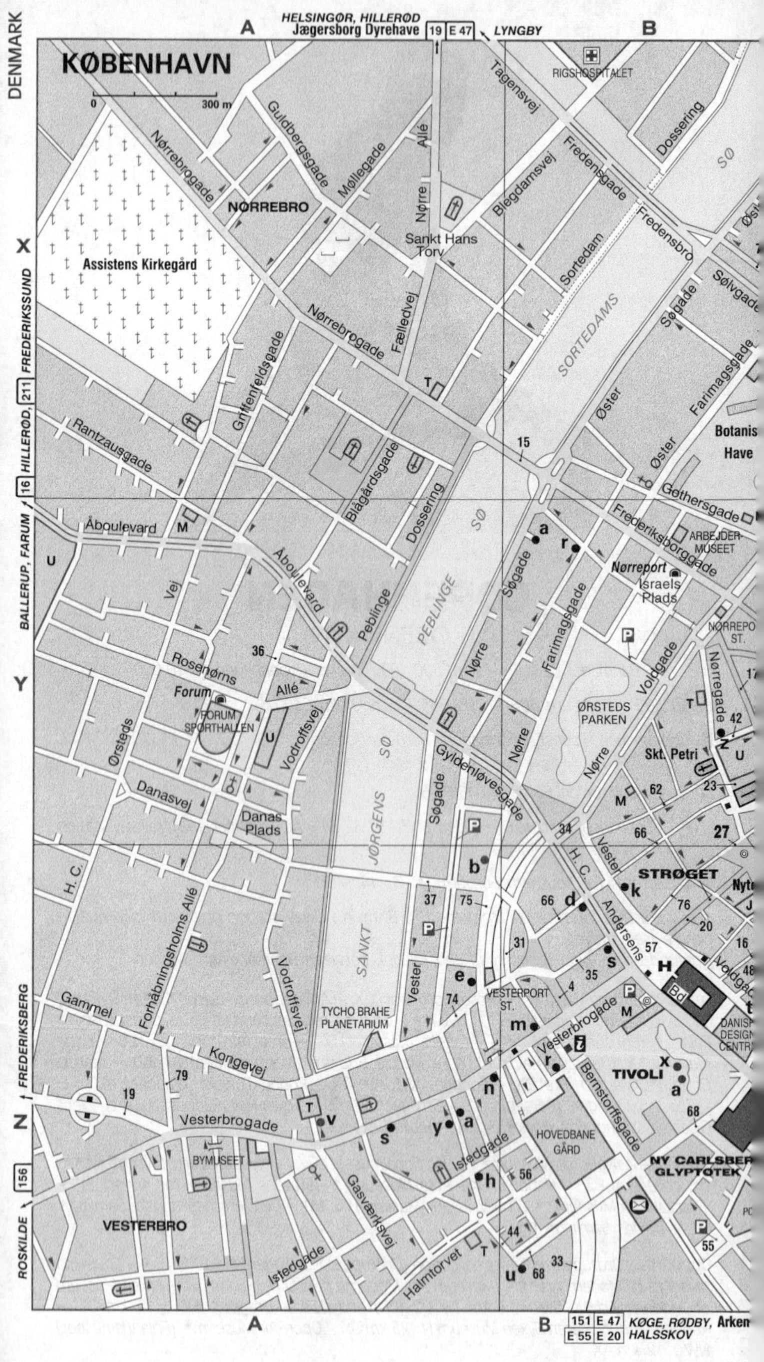
DENMARK
KØBENHAVN
0
300 m
A
B
X
Y
Z
HELSINGØR, HILLERØD
Jægersborg Dyrehave
19
E 47
LYNGBY
16
HILLERØD, 211 FREDERIKSSUND
BALLERUP, FARUM
FREDERIKSBERG
156
ROSKILDE
151
E 47
E 55
E 20
KØGE, RØDBY, Arken
HALSSKOV
RIGSHOSPITALET
NØRREBRO
Assistens Kirkegård
Nørrebrogade
Guldbergsgade
Møllegade
Nørre Allé
Tagensvej
Blegdamsvej
Fredensgade
Fredensbro
Dossering
SØ
Sankt Hans Torv
Fælledvej
Sortedam
SORTEDAMS
Søgade
Sølvgade
Farimagsgade
Øster
Botanisk Have
Griffenfeldsgade
Rantzausgade
Blågårdsgade
Åboulevard
PEBLINGE
Peblinge
Gothersgade
Frederiksborggade
ARBEJDERMUSEET
Nørreport
Israels Plads
NØRREPORT ST.
Voldgade
Farimagsgade
ØRSTEDS PARKEN
Nørre
Nørregade
Skt. Petri
Vej
Rosenørns Allé
Forum
FORUM SPORTHALLEN
Vodroffsvej
JØRGENS
Gyldenløvesgade
Ørsteds
Danasvej
Danas Plads
H. C.
Vester
H. C. Andersens
STRØGET
Nytorv
Forhåbningsholms Allé
SANKT
TYCHO BRAHE PLANETARIUM
VESTERPORT ST.
Vesterbrogade
TIVOLI
DANISH DESIGN CENTRE
Gammel Kongevej
Bernstorffsgade
HOVEDBANE GÅRD
Istedgade
NY CARLSBERG GLYPTOTEK
Gasværksvej
BYMUSEET
VESTERBRO
Halmtorvet

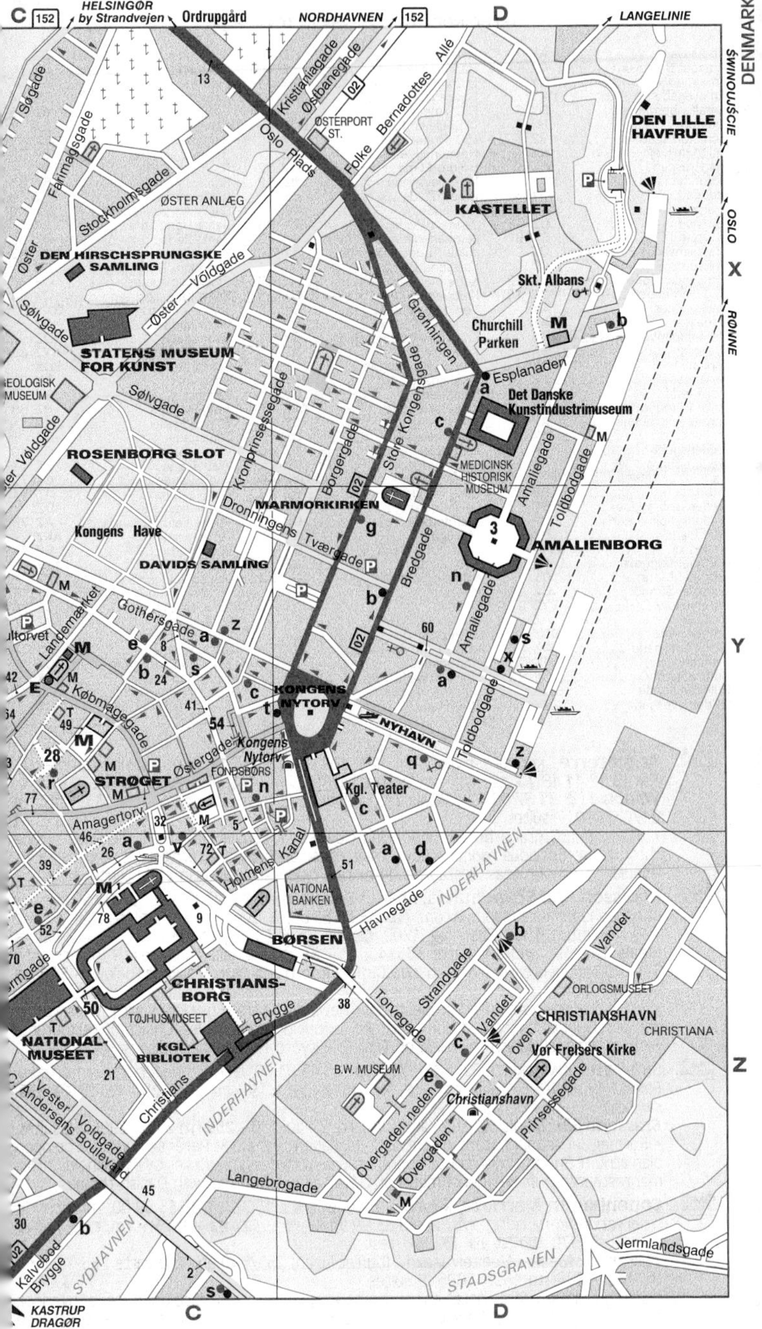

HELSINGØR by Strandvejen
Ordrupgård
NORDHAVNEN
LANGELINIE
DENMARK
ŚWINOUJŚCIE
OSLO
RØNNE
Søgade
Farimagsgade
Stockholmsgade
ØSTER ANLÆG
Kristianiagade
Østbanegade
ØSTERPORT ST.
Oslo Plads
Folke Bernadottes Allé
KASTELLET
DEN LILLE HAVFRUE
Skt. Albans
Churchill Parken
DEN HIRSCHSPRUNGSKE SAMLING
Øster Voldgade
Sølvgade
STATENS MUSEUM FOR KUNST
GEOLOGISK MUSEUM
Grønningen
Store Kongensgade
Esplanaden
Det Danske Kunstindustrimuseum
MEDICINSK HISTORISK MUSEUM
Amaliegade
Toldbodgade
ROSENBORG SLOT
Kronprinsessegade
Borgergade
MARMORKIRKEN
Dronningens Tværgade
Kongens Have
DAVIDS SAMLING
AMALIENBORG
Bredgade
Gothersgade
Landemærket
Købmagergade
KONGENS NYTORV
NYHAVN
Kongens Nytorv
FONDSBØRS
Østergade
STRØGET
Amagertorv
Kgl. Teater
Holmens Kanal
NATIONAL BANKEN
Havnegade
INDERHAVNEN
BØRSEN
CHRISTIANSBORG
TØJHUSMUSEET
KGL. BIBLIOTEK
NATIONALMUSEET
Christians Brygge
Torvegade
Strandgade
Vandet
ORLOGSMUSEET
CHRISTIANSHAVN
CHRISTIANA
Vor Frelsers Kirke
B.W. MUSEUM
Overgaden neden Vandet
Overgaden oven Vandet
Christianshavn
Prinsessegade
Vester Voldgade
H.C. Andersens Boulevard
Langebrogade
SYDHAVNEN
Kalvebod Brygge
STADSGRAVEN
Vermlandsgade
KASTRUP DRAGØR

STREET INDEX TO KØBENHAVN TOWN PLAN

Aboulevard AY
Amager Boulevard CZ 2
Amagertorv (Strøget) CY
Amaliegade DXY
Amalienborg Plads DY 3
Axeltorv BZ 4
Bernstorffsgade BZ
Blegdamsvej BX
Blågårdsgåde AX
Borgergade DXY
Bredgade DY
Bremerholm CY 5
Børsgade DZ 7
Christan IX's Gade CY 8
Christiansborg Slotsplads CZ 9
Christians Brygge CZ
Christmas Møllers Plads DZ 12
Dag Hammarskjölds Allé CX 13
Danas Plads AY
Danasvej AY
Dronningens Tværgade CDY
Dronning Louises Bro BX 15
Esplanaden DX
Farvergade BZ 16
Fiolstræde BY 17
Folke Bernadottes Allé DX
Forhåbningsholms Allé AZ
Fredensbro BX
Fredensgade BX
Frederiksberg Allé AZ 19
Frederiksberggade (Strøget) BZ 20
Frederiksborggade BY
Frederiksholms Kanal CZ 21
Frue Plads BY 23
Fælledvej AX
Gammel Kongevej AZ
Gammel Mønt CY 24
Gammel Strand CZ 26
Gammeltorv BYZ 27
Gasværksvej AZ
Gothersgade BCY
Griffenfeldsgade AX
Grønningen DX
Gråbrødretorv CY 28
Guldbergsgade AX
Gyldenløvesgade AY
Halmtorvet AZ
Hambrosgade CZ 30
Hammerichsgade BZ 31
Havnegade DZ
H.C. Andersens Boulevard BCZ
H.C. Ørsteds Vej AY
Holmens Kanal CDZ
Højbro Plads CY 32
Ingerslevsgade BZ 33
Israels Plads BY
Istedgade AZ
Jarmers Plads BY 34
Jernbanegade BZ 35
Julius Thomsens Gade AY 36
Kalvebod Brygge CZ
Kampmannsgade AZ 37
Knippelsbro DZ 38
Kompagnistræde CZ 39
Kongens Nytorv DY
Kristen Bernikows Gade CY 41
Kristianiagade DX
Kronprinsessegade CXY
Krystalgade BCY 42
Kultorvet CY
Kvægtorvsgade ABZ 44
Købmagergade CY
Landemaerket CY
Langebro CZ 45
Langebrogade CDZ
Læderstræde CYZ 46
Løngangstræde BZ 48
Løvstræde CY 49
Marmorbroen CZ 50
Møllegade AX
Niels Juels Gade DZ 51
Nybrogade CZ 52
Nygade (Strøget) CYZ 53
Nyhavn DY
Nytorv BZ
Nørre Allé AX
Nørrebrogade AX
Nørre Farimagsgade BY
Nørregade BY
Nørre Søgade ABY
Nørre Voldgade BY
Oslo Plads DX
Overgaden neden Vandet DZ
Overgaden oven Vandet DZ
Peblinge Dossering AY
Pistolstræde CY 54
Polititorvet BZ 55
Prinsessegade DZ
Rantzausgade AX
Reventlowsgade BZ 56
Rosenørns Allé AY
Rådhuspladsen BZ 57
Rådhusstræde CZ 59
Sankt Annæ Plads DY 60
Sankt Hans Torv AX
Sankt Peders Stræde BY 62
Skindergade CY 63
Sortedam Dossering BX
Stockholmsgade CX
Store Kannikestræde CY 64
Store Kongensgade DXY
Stormgade CZ
Strandgade DZ
Studiestræde BYZ 66
Sølvgade BCX
Sølvtorvet CX 67
Tagensvej BX
Tietgensgade BZ 68
Toldbodgade DXY
Torvegade DZ
Vandkunsten CZ 70
Webersgade BX 71
Ved Stranden CZ 72
Ved Vesterport AZ 74
Vermlandsgade DZ
Vester Farimagsgade AZ 75
Vesterbrogade ABZ
Vestergade BZ 76
Vester Søgade AYZ
Vester Voldgade BCZ
Vimmelskaftet (Strøget) CY 77
Vindebrogade CZ 78
Vodroffsvej AYZ
Værnedamsvej AZ 79
Østbanegade DX
Øster Farimagsgade BCX
Øster Søgade BCX
Øster Voldgade CX
Østergade (Strøget) CY

Angleterre, Kongens Nytorv 34, ✉ 1021 K, ☎ 33 12 00 95, *sales@remmen.dk, Fax 33 12 11 18*, ⛹, ≘s, ▢ - |♦|, ⇎ rm, ▤ TV ✆ ⇔ - ⛬ 400. MC AE ⓓ VISA JCB. ⊗
Wiinblad (☎ *33 37 06 45*) **: Meals** 225/325 and a la carte 371/722 ♀ - ☕ 135 - **116 rm** 2170/3470, 7 suites. CDY t
◆ Elegant 18C grand hotel overlooking New Royal Square. Luxury in lobby sets tone throughout. Spacious rooms enjoy classic décor and antique furniture. Grand ballroom. Popular afternoon teas. Restaurant in marine blue décor ; Danish and French dishes.

Radisson SAS Scandinavia, Amager Boulevard 70, ✉ 2300 S, ☎ 33 96 50 00, *guest.copenhagen@radissonsas.com, Fax 33 96 55 00*, ≤ Copenhagen, ⛹, ≘s, ▢, squash - |♦|, ⇎ rm, TV ✆ ♿ P - ⛬ 1200. MC AE ⓓ VISA JCB. ⊗ rest CZ s
Meals 195/395 and a la carte 335/455 ♀ - ***Kyoto* : Meals** - Japanese - (dinner only) 390/400 and a la carte (see also ***The Dining Room*** and ***Blue Elephant*** below) - **540 rm** 1830, 2 suites.
◆ Large modern hotel offering spectacular views of the city. Busy lobby with shops, casino and bar. Original bright bedrooms themed in four different styles. Choice of restaurants from traditional Danish to Italian or Thai. The Kyoto for Japanese dishes.

Skt.Petri, Krystalgade 22, ✉ 1172 K, ☎ 33 45 91 00, *reservation@hotelsktpetri.com, Fax 33 45 91 10*, 🏠, ⛹, ≘s - |♦|, ⇎ rm, ▤ TV ✆ ♿ ⇔ - ⛬ 250. MC AE ⓓ VISA. ⊗ rest BY z
***Brasserie Blu* : Meals** 325/615 and a la carte ♀ - ☕ 130 - **252 rm** 2095/2995, 18 suites.
◆ Former department store in central Copenhagen near old St Peter's Church. Large open plan atrium. Bright, stylish contemporary rooms with design features by Per Arnoldi. Informal restaurant ; international menu of classic brasserie disheswith Danish theme.

Copenhagen Marriott, Kalvebod Brygge 5, ✉ 1560, ☎ 88 33 99 00, *mhrs.cphdk.reservations@marriott.com, Fax 88 33 99 99*, ≤, 🏠, ⛹, ≘s - |♦|, ⇎ rm, ▤ TV ✆ ♿ ⇔ - ⛬ 570. MC AE ⓓ VISA. ⊗ rest CZ b
***Terraneo* : Meals** - Mediterranean - (buffet lunch) 255/340 and a la carte 265/405 ♀ - ☕ 145 - **386 rm** 1595/2095, 9 suites.
◆ Striking, glass-fronted hotel, its handsomely appointed rooms face the water or overlook the city and Tivoli. Top-floor executive rooms share a stylish private lounge. Lunchtime buffet and Mediterranean cuisine in the evening.

Radisson SAS Royal, Hammerichsgade 1, ✉ 1611 V, ✆ 33 42 60 00, *Fax 33 42 61 00,* ≤ Copenhagen, Lб, ≘s – |♦|, ⇔ rm, ▤ TV ✆ ♿ ⇐ P – 🧑 300. MC AE ⓞ VISA JCB *Alberto K :* Meals *(closed Sunday)* (dinner only) 455 ♀ – ***Café Royal :*** Meals (buffet lunch) 220 and a la carte 265/365 ♀ – ☕ 150 – **257 rm** 2290/2490, 3 suites. BZ m
◆ Large international hotel block dominating the skyline west of Tivoli and offering superb views. Scandinavian bedroom décor. Italian-influenced cuisine on 20th floor or simple ground floor brasserie.

Sofitel Plaza Copenhagen, Bernstorffsgade 4, ✉ 1577 V, ✆ 33 14 92 62, *reception plaza@accorhotel.dk, Fax 33 93 93 62* – |♦|, ⇔ rm, TV ✆ – 🧑 50. MC AE ⓞ VISA JCB. ✕ rest – ***Brasserie Flora Danica :*** Meals (dinner only) a la carte approx 330 ♀ – **87 rm** 1799/2199, 6 suites. BZ r
◆ Venerable hotel commissioned in the early 20C by King Frederik VIII and overlooking Tivoli Gardens. Classic style room décor and atmospheric library bar. Has both a modern, welcoming brasserie and a cosmopolitan fine dining restaurant.

Imperial, Vester Farimagsgade 9, ✉ 1606 V, ✆ 33 12 80 00, *imperial@imperialhotel.dk, Fax 33 93 80 31* – |♦|, ⇔ rm, ▤ rest, TV ♿ – 🧑 200. MC AE ⓞ VISA JCB. ✕ AZ e
Imperial Garden : Meals *(closed 21 December-8 January and Sunday)* (dinner only) 410/485 and a la carte 312/585 – ***Imperial Brasserie :*** Meals *(closed 24 and 31 December)* 156/332 and a la carte 156/318 ♀ – ☕ 95 – **163 rm** 1495/2750, 1 suite.
◆ Large mid 20C hotel located on a wide city thoroughfare. Well serviced rooms range in size and are richly furnished in 1950s Danish designer style. Fine dining in attractive indoor "winter garden". Less formal dining in ground floor brasserie.

Kong Frederik, Vester Voldgade 25, ✉ 1552 V, ✆ 33 12 59 02, *sales@remmen.dk, Fax 33 93 59 01* – |♦|, ⇔ rm, TV ✆ – 🧑 40. MC AE ⓞ VISA JCB. ✕ BZ k
Frederiks : Meals 325 and a la carte 278/374 ♀ – ☕ 125 – **108 rm** 1040/1840, 2 suites.
◆ Classic elegant old building in good location. Traditional style décor with dark wood panelling. Comfortable rooms with old-fashioned furniture. Atrium style banquet hall. Wood-panelled, atmospheric brasserie offering traditional Danish cooking.

Admiral, Toldbodgade 24-28, ✉ 1253, ✆ 33 74 14 14, *admiral@admiralhotel.dk, Fax 33 74 14 16,* ≤, ≘s – |♦|, ⇔ rm, TV P – 🧑 180. MC AE ⓞ VISA JCB. ✕ rest
Meals (see **Salt** below) – ☕ 105 – **366 rm** 1225/2110. DY s
◆ Converted 18C dockside warehouse. Maritime theme throughout. Bedrooms complement the rustic charm.

Kong Arthur, Nørre Søgade 11, ✉ 1370 K, ✆ 33 11 12 12, *hotel@kongarthur.dk, Fax 33 32 61 30,* ⛲, ≘s – |♦|, ⇔ rm, TV P – 🧑 50. MC AE ⓞ VISA JCB. ✕ BY a
Meals *(closed 24-26 December)* (dinner only) 285 and a la carte 273/343 – ***Sticks 'n' Sushi*** *(✆ 33 11 14 07) :* Meals - Japanese - *(closed 24-26 December and Bank Holidays)* (dinner only) 255/325 and a la carte – **107 rm** ☕ 1145/2900.
◆ Pleasant family run hotel on elegant late 19C residential avenue by Peblinge lake. Classic rooms furnished with antique furniture and equipped with modern facilities. Classical menu in the formal dining room. Sticks 'n' Sushi for Japanese dishes.

First H. Vesterbro, Vesterbrogade 23-29, ✉ 1620 V, ✆ 33 78 80 00, *reception.copenhagen@firsthotels.dk, Fax 33 78 80 80* – |♦| ⇔ ▤ TV ✆ ⇐. MC AE ⓞ VISA JCB
Restaurant : Meals *(closed Sunday)* a la carte approx 230 – ☕ 95 – **403 rm** 1799/2549.
◆ Large modern hotel with metal and glass façade on busy avenue. Rooms vary in size and fittings but offer same good modern facilities in a contemporary style. Chic dining room with open plan kitchen and simple menu. AZ s

Phoenix, Bredgade 37, ✉ 1260 K, ✆ 33 95 95 00, *phoenixcopenhagen@arp.hansen.dk, Fax 33 33 98 33* – |♦|, ⇔ rm, TV ⇐ – 🧑 100. MC AE ⓞ VISA. ✕ rest DY b
Von Plessen : Meals 295 (dinner) and a la carte approx 430 – ☕ 125 – **210 rm** 1490/2890, 3 suites.
◆ Parts of this elegant hotel, located in the lively modern art and antiques district, date from the 17C. It features a grand marbled lobby and comfortable high ceilinged rooms. Elegant basement dining room with discreet décor in neutral tones.

Radisson SAS Falconer, Falkoner Allé 9, ✉ 2000 Frederiksberg C, via Gammel Kongevej ✆ 38 15 80 01, *copenhagen@radissonsas.com, Fax 38 87 11 91,* ≤ Copenhagen, Lб, ≘s – |♦|, ⇔ rm, ▤ rm, TV ✆ ♿ ⇐ – 🧑 2000. MC AE ⓞ VISA. ✕
closed 20 December-5 January – ***Covent Garden :*** Meals 265 (dinner) and a la carte 244/413 ♀ – ☕ 120 – **166 rm** 1495/2195.
◆ Large hotel on busy shopping street in attractive suburb. Three sizes and styles of room : colonial, Art Deco and design. Good facilities. Caters well for conferences. Cheerful restaurant in atrium with palm trees, fountain and international menu.

71 Nyhavn, Nyhavn 71, ✉ 1051 K, ✆ 33 43 62 00, *71nyhavnhotel@arp-hansen.dk, Fax 33 43 62 01,* ≤ – |♦|, ⇔ rm, TV ✆. MC AE ⓞ VISA JCB. ✕ DY z
Pakhus Kaelder : Meals *(closed Sunday and Bank Holidays)* (bar lunch)/dinner 399 and a la carte approx 465 ♀ – ☕ 125 – **142 rm** 1390/2350, 8 suites.
◆ Charming converted warehouse by the canal. Interior features low ceilings with wooden beams throughout. Compact comfortable bedrooms, many with views of passing ships. Cellar restaurant with low wood-beamed ceiling. Interesting, seasonal menus.

Alexandra, H.C. Andersens Boulevard 8, ✉ 1553 V, ☎ 33 74 44 44, *reservations@hotel-alexandra.dk, Fax 33 74 44 88*, – |$|, ⇎ rm, TV. MC AE D VISA JCB. ⚹ rest closed 24-27 December – ***Muhlhausen*** **: Meals** *(closed Sunday lunch)* a la carte 200/335 ♀ – **61 rm** ☕ 1325/1525. BZ d

♦ Classic 19C hotel conveniently located for city centre. Brightly decorated rooms feature Danish style furniture and fittings and an original painting in each. Banquettes and crisp linen in a stylish brasserie with a Mediterranean tone.

Strand without rest., Havnegade 37, ✉ 1058 K, ☎ 33 48 99 00, *copenhagenstrand@arp-hansen.dk, Fax 33 48 99 01* – |$| ⇎ TV ☎. MC AE D VISA JCB DZ d
172 rm ☕ 1295/1595, 2 suites.

♦ Modern warehouse conversion on waterfront and a useful central location. Smart modern rooms with dark wood furniture and bright colours. Business centre.

DGI-byens, Tietgensgade 65, ✉ 1704 V, ☎ 33 29 80 50, *hotel@dgi-byen.dk, Fax 33 29 80 59*, , , – |$|, ⇎ rm, TV ☎ P – 🏛 60. MC AE D VISA. ⚹ BZ u
Vestauranten **: Meals** 295 (dinner) and a la carte approx 230 – **104 rm** ☕ 1295/1495.

♦ Turn of millennium hotel, part of huge, modern leisure complex with all the facilities. Large, well-equipped bedrooms with up to date facilities. Bright restaurant in original building offering a varied menu.

The Square without rest., Rådhuspladsen 14, ✉ 1550 K, ☎ 33 38 12 00, *thesquare@arp-hansen.dk, Fax 33 38 12 01* – |$| ⇎ ▤ TV ☎. MC AE D VISA BZ s
192 rm ☕ 1295/3195.

♦ Ideally located hotel in Town Hall Square. Breakfast room on 6th floor with view of city roofs. Good sized modern bedrooms with square theme in décor and fabrics.

City without rest., Peder Skrams Gade 24, ✉ 1054 K, ☎ 33 13 06 66, *hotelcity@hotelcity.dk, Fax 33 13 06 67* – |$| ⇎ TV. MC AE D VISA JCB DZ a
81 rm ☕ 995/1465.

♦ Well situated modern hotel between city centre and docks. Danish designer style interior décor. Modern décor and good technical facilities. Fifth floor rooms are superior.

The Mayfair without rest., Helgolandsgade 3, ✉ 1653 V, ☎ 33 31 48 01, *info@themayfairhotel.dk, Fax 33 23 96 86* – |$| ⇎ TV. MC AE D VISA JCB. ⚹ rest AZ a
closed 22 December-3 January – **102 rm** ☕ 1000/1500, 3 suites.

♦ Large well run hotel usefully located near station. Interior décor and furniture classic English in style. Good size rooms, well equipped with mod cons. Relaxing bar.

Grand, Vesterbrogade 9, ✉ 1620 V, ☎ 33 27 69 00, *grandhotel@arp-hansen.dk, Fax 33 27 69 01* – |$|, ⇎ rm, TV. MC AE VISA JCB. ⚹ rest AZ n
Frascati **: Meals** - Italian - a la carte approx 245 – **161 rm** ☕ 1325/3035.

♦ Classic 19C hotel well located near station and Tivoli Gardens. All rooms are a good size, with high ceilings and décor in keeping with period of hotel. Contemporary restaurant with extensive range of Italian and Mediterranean dishes.

Clarion H. Neptun, Sankt Annae Plads 18-20, ✉ 1250 K, ☎ 33 96 20 00, *info.neptun@clarion.choicehotels.dk, Fax 33 96 20 66* – |$|, ⇎ rm, TV – 🏛 40. MC AE D VISA. ⚹ DY a
Gendarmen *(☎ 33 96 20 39)* **: Meals** *(closed Sunday)* 345 (dinner) and a la carte 330/400 ♀ – **133 rm** ☕ 1375/1875.

♦ Converted from two characterful neighbouring houses in the popular Nyhavn district. Rooms are fitted with light wood furniture and offer good range of facilities. Rustic restaurant with wooden tables. French influenced, seasonal menu.

Sophie Amalie, Sankt Annae Plads 21, ✉ 1250 K, ☎ 33 13 34 00, *sales@remmen.dk, Fax 33 11 77 07*, ≤, – |$|, ⇎ rm, TV – 🏛 80. MC AE D VISA. ⚹ DY x
Sophie **: Meals** 295 and a la carte 328/378 – ☕ 115 – **122 rm** 875/1475, 12 suites.

♦ Plain modern hotel block on the quayside with clean-cut interior décor in pastel and neutral tones. Functional rooms vary in size. Most 6th floor rooms have balcony and view. Cosy, warm restaurant with polished wood décor. A menu for all tastes.

Ibsens, Vendersgade 23, ✉ 1363 K, ☎ 33 13 19 13, *hotel@ibsenshotel.dk, Fax 33 13 19 16*, – |$|, ⇎ rm, TV. MC AE D VISA JCB. ⚹ BY r
La Rocca **: Meals** - Italian - *(closed 24-26 December and Bank Holidays)* 285 (dinner) and a la carte 203/373 – **118 rm** ☕ 925/2100.

♦ Large characterful converted apartment block next to sister hotel Kong Arthur. Variety of rooms, all in cheerful colours with good facilities. Superior top floor bedrooms. Modern restaurant bringing the Mediterranean to Denmark.

Comfort H. Esplanaden without rest., Bredgade 78, ✉ 1260 K, ☎ 33 48 10 00, *info.esplanaden@comfort.choicehotels.dk, Fax 33 48 10 66* – |$| ⇎ TV. MC AE D VISA JCB
closed 22 December-3 January – **117 rm** ☕ 1225/1425. DX a

♦ Classic old corner building on wide avenue by park. Southfacing rooms overlook quieter courtyards. Range of room sizes, all with standard décor. Caters for groups.

Danmark without rest., Vester Voldgade 89, ✉ 1552 V, ☎ 33 11 48 06, *hotel@hotel-danmark.dk, Fax 33 14 36 30* – |$| ⇎ TV 🚗. MC AE D VISA JCB. ⚹ BZ t
88 rm ☕ 1025/1550.

♦ Centrally located close to Tivoli Gardens, this purpose built hotel offers well kept functional rooms with traditional Scandinavian style décor.

Absalon without rest., Helgolandsgade 15, ✉ 1653 V, ☎ 33 24 22 11, *info@absalon-hotel.dk, Fax 33 24 34 11* – 🛗 📺. MC AE Ⓓ VISA. ✂ AZ h
closed 19 December-2 January – **189 rm** ☕ 1000/1850.
◆ Period building located in no-frills, urban district. Rooms vary in size and overlook street or courtyard. Fifth floor rooms have most character. Popular with groups.

Top H. Hebron without rest., Helgolandsgade 4, ✉ 1653, ☎ 33 31 69 06, *tophotel@hebron.dk, Fax 33 31 90 67* – 🛗 ⇜ 📺 – 🏠 50. MC AE Ⓓ VISA. ✂ AZ y
closed 22 December-3 January – **93 rm** ☕ 850/1075, 6 suites.
◆ When it opened in 1900 it was one of the biggest hotels in the city and some of the original features remain. Bedrooms are surprisingly spacious for the price.

Kong Hans Kaelder, Vingårdsstraede 6, ✉ 1070 K, ☎ 33 11 68 68, *konghans@mail.tele.dk, Fax 33 32 67 68* – MC AE Ⓓ VISA JCB. ✂ CY n
closed 3 weeks in summer, 22-30 December, Monday June-August and Sunday – **Meals** (booking essential) (dinner only) a la carte 600/750 ♀.
◆ Discreetly located side street restaurant in vaulted Gothic cellar with wood flooring. Original, confidently prepared cuisine. Friendly and dedicated service.
Spec. Local pike perch with artichokes à la barigoule. Sautéed foie gras with fig 'carpaccio'. Variations of Valhrona chocolate.

Kommandanten, Ny Adelgade 7, ✉ 1104 K, ☎ 33 12 09 90, *kommandanten@kommandanten.com, Fax 33 93 12 23* – ⇜. MC AE Ⓓ VISA JCB. ✂ CY c
closed 18 August-1 September, 23 December-6 January, Sunday and Bank Holidays – **Meals** (booking essential) (dinner only) 690 and a la carte 560/720 ♀.
◆ Distinctive 18C townhouse : flowers, fine china, stylish contemporary décor and wrought-iron furniture. Exemplary service and original modern Danish and French cuisine.
Spec. Fried langoustines with sesame biscuit and aniseed. Chocolate desserts.

Pierre André (Houdet), Ny Østergade 21, ✉ 1101 K, ☎ 33 16 17 19, *Fax 33 16 17 72* – MC AE Ⓓ VISA. ✂ – *closed Easter, 3 weeks in summer, 24-27 December, 31 December-1 January, Sunday, Monday, lunch June-July, Saturday lunch and Bank Holidays* – **Meals** - French - (booking essential) 350/695 and a la carte 425/655 ♀. CY s
◆ Elegant, comfortable dining room with stylish décor in an attractive old building. Full-flavoured cuisine on a classical French base. Efficient and attentive service.
Spec. Foie gras "Emilia Romagna". Noisettes of spiced venison aux épices. Hot chocolate cake, Gianduja ice cream.

Restaurationen (Jacobsen), Møntergade 19, ✉ 1116 K, ☎ 33 14 94 95, *Fax 33 14 85 30* – MC AE Ⓓ VISA. ✂ CY e
closed Easter, 4 July-30 August, 21 December-4 January, Sunday, Monday and Bank Holidays – **Meals** (booking essential) (dinner only except December) (set menu only) 620 ♀.
◆ A stylish and personally run restaurant. Accomplished modern Danish cooking using well sourced ingrendients, accompanied by a comprehensive wine list.
Spec. Smoked eel and leek brawn. Roast tail of veal with foie gras and truffle sauce. Caramel ice cream with elderberry jelly.

Formel B (Jochumsen/Møller), Vesterbrogade 182, Frederiksberg, ✉ 1800 C, via Vesterbrogade ☎ 33 25 10 66, *info@formel-b.dk,* 🏖 – MC AE Ⓓ VISA JCB. ✂
closed Sunday – **Meals** (set menu only) (lunch by arrangement)/dinner 550 ♀.
◆ Chic restaurant on the ground floor of an attractive period house. Sleek interior with sandstone and granite. Set menu : precise cooking with well chosen accompanying wines.
Spec. Skate wing with prawns and butter sauce. Roast pigeon with wild mushroom tart and sweetcorn. Chocolate fondant, vanilla ice cream.

Era Ora, Overgaden neden Vandet 33B, ✉ 1414 K, ☎ 32 54 06 93, *era-ora@era-ora.dk, Fax 32 96 02 09,* 🏖 – MC AE Ⓓ VISA. ✂ – *closed 24-26 December and Sunday* – **Meals** - Italian - (booking essential) (set menu only) 280/890 ♀. DZ c
◆ Stylish, discreetly located canalside restaurant offers an excellent overview of the best of Italian cuisine, by offering diners large array of small dishes. Good wine list.
Spec. Halibut with barley and herb salad. Rabbit with spring beans, almond vinaigrette. Tagliarini with Swiss chard and anchovy.

Ensemble (Jensen/Maarbjerg), Tordenskjoldsgade 11, ✉ 1055 K, ☎ 33 11 33 52, *kontakt@restaurantensemble.dk* – MC AE Ⓓ VISA. ✂ – *closed Christmas, July, Sunday, Monday and Bank Holidays* – **Meals** (dinner only) (set menu only) 500 ♀. DY c
◆ Whites, greys and bright lighting add to the clean, fresh feel. Open-plan kitchen. Detailed and refined cooking from a set menu, with attentive and courteous service.
Spec. Pan-fried turbot with chestnuts and pig's trotter. Fallow deer with pepper sauce, foie gras and pear. Lemon tart with liquorice and lemon jam.

Il Grappolo Blu, Vester Farimagsgade 35, ✉ 1606 V, ☎ 33 11 57 20, *ilgrappoloblu@ilgrappoloblu.com, Fax 33 11 57 20* – MC AE Ⓓ VISA JCB. ✂ AZ b
closed Easter, July, 22 December-3 January and Sunday – **Meals** - Italian - (dinner only) (set menu only) 270/495.
◆ Behind the unpromising façade lies this friendly restaurant, personally run by the owner. Ornate wood panelling and carving. Authentic Italian dishes that just keep on coming.

Schiøtt's, Overgaden Neden Vandet 17, ✉ 1414, ☎ 32 54 54 08, *restaurant@schioetts.dk, Fax 32 54 54 08* – DZ e
closed Easter, Christmas, Sunday and Monday – **Meals** (set menu only) (dinner only) 315.
◆ Vaulted ceiling, tiled flooring and walls decorated with modern Danish artwork add to the informal style. Well sourced ingredients and some modern twists to the cooking.

Krogs, Gammel Strand 38, ✉ 1202 K, ☎ 33 15 89 15, *post@krogs.dk, Fax 33 15 83 19,* – CZ a
closed Easter, 22-26 December and Sunday – **Meals** - Seafood - (booking essential) 328 and a la carte 638/751 ♀.
◆ Characterful 18C house in pleasant canalside location. Spacious with high ceilings and well lit through large end window. Well-cooked seafood dishes attractively presented.

VB Square, Oster Sogade 114, ✉ 2100, via Oster Sogade at junction with Oslo Plads ☎ 35 42 22 77, *Fax 35 42 22 77* –
closed 22 December-9 January and Sunday lunch – **Meals** 245/375 and a la carte 285/415 ♀.
◆ Relatively compact restaurant with a genuine neighbourhood feel. Contemporary colour scheme of browns and pastels. Knowlegeable service and modern Danish cooking.

Castel, Gothersgade 35, ✉ 1123 K, ☎ 33 13 62 82, *admin@castel.dk, Fax 33 13 72 82* – CY a
closed 1 month in summer, 1 week Christmas and Sunday – **Meals** (dinner only) a la carte 270/350.
◆ Magnificent glass ceiling, original woodwork and contemporary art in a 19C apothecary's shop. Balanced, flavourful dishes from an open-plan kichen in the converted laboratory.

Gammel Mont, Gammel Mont 41, ✉ 1117 K, ☎ 33 15 10 60, *Fax 33 15 10 60* – CY b
closed 15 June-15 August, Sunday and Bank Holidays – **Meals** 225/550 and a la carte 335/525 ♀.
◆ Half-timbered house from 1732 with striking red façade in smart commercial district. Traditional cuisine with seasonal variations and interesting range of herring dishes.

The Dining Room (at Radisson SAS Scandinavia H.), 25th Floor, Amager Boulevard 70, ✉ 2300 S, ☎ 33 96 58 58, *info@thediningroom.dk,* ≤ Copenhagen – CZ s
closed Sunday and Bank Holidays – **Meals** - Mediterranean - (dinner only) 425/585 ♀.
◆ Situated on the 25th floor of the hotel, but run independently, and providing diners with wonderful panoramic views of the city. Strong Mediterranean influence to the menu.

Blue Elephant (at Radisson SAS Scandinavia H.), Amager Boulevard 70, ✉ 2300 S, ☎ 33 96 59 75, *copenhagen@blueelephant.com, Fax 33 96 59 71* –
closed 23-26 December – **Meals** - Thai - (dinner only) 300/600 and a la carte 290/545.
◆ One of a worldwide chain of Thai restaurants originally founded in Belgium by a collector of Oriental art. Beautiful carved wood setting and authentic cuisine. CZ s

Le Sommelier, Bredgade 63-65, ✉ 1260 K, ☎ 33 11 45 15, *mail@lesommelier.dk, Fax 33 11 59 79* – DX c
closed 22 December-2 January – **Meals** 245/315 and a la carte 303/435 ♀.
◆ Popular brasserie in the heart of the old town. The owners' passion for wine shows in posters, memorabilia and an excellent "by glass" list. Modern Danish cooking.

Salt (at Admiral H.), Toldbodgade 24-28, ✉ 1253, ☎ 33 74 14 48, *info@saltrestaurant.dk, Fax 33 74 14 16,* ≤, – DY s
Meals 315/345 and a la carte 320/400 ♀.
◆ Conran-designed restaurant in 18C warehouse ; outdoor summer tables. Only sea salt is used. Danish buffet and modern a la carte at midday ; more extensive modern dinner menu.

Godt (Rice), Gothersgade 38, ✉ 1123 K, ☎ 33 15 21 22, *restaurant.godt@get2net.dk* – CY z
closed 1 week February, Easter, July, 1 week October, 2 weeks Christmas-New Year, Sunday, Monday and Bank Holidays – **Meals** (booking essential) (dinner only) (set menu only) 480/600.
◆ Small stylish modern two floor restaurant with unusual grey painted décor, ceiling fans and old WWII shells as candle holders. Excellently conceived daily menu of modern fare.
Spec. Langoustine soup with monkfish cheeks. Turbot with beans, oyster beurre blanc. Fillet of hare, wild mushrooms and artichoke.

TyvenKokkenHansKoneOgHendesElsker, Magstraede 16, ✉ 1204 K, ☎ 33 16 12 92, *post@tyven.dk* – CZ e
closed Easter, 3 weeks July, 24 December-1 January and Sunday – **Meals** (dinner only) 565 and a la carte 465/575 ♀.
◆ 18C part timbered house in cobbled street. Named after the Peter Greenaway film. Set menu (5 courses) with small a la carte. Precise French based dishes with Danish influence.
Spec. Pike perch with lobster and braised endive. Lamb with ratatouille and new potatoes. Assiette of chocolate.

Kanalen, Christianshavn-Wilders Plads 2, ✉ 1403 K, ☎ 32 95 13 30, *info@restaurant-kanalen.dk, Fax 32 95 13 38,* ← – P. MC AE ① VISA JCB DZ b
closed 5-12 April, 24-30 December, Sunday and Bank Holidays – **Meals** (booking essential) (set menu only at dinner) 188/340 and lunch a la carte 340/406.
◆ Delightfully located former Harbour Police office on canalside. Simple elegant décor, informal yet personally run. Well balanced menu of modern Danish cooking.

Guldanden, Sortedam Dossering 103, ✉ 2100 K, via Oslo Plads at junction of Sortedam Dossering and Osterbrogade ☎ 35 42 66 06, *mail@guldanden.dk, Fax 35 42 66 05,* – ▤. MC ① VISA JCB.
closed 23-26 December and 1-5 January – **Meals** (set menu only at dinner) 245/325 and lunch a la carte approx 260 ♀.
◆ Glass-fronted restaurant with small summer terrace in residential district. Minimalist décor. Set menu with 3-7 course choice ; modern cooking with some unusual combinations.

Lumskebugten, Esplanaden 21, ✉ 1263 K, ☎ 33 15 60 29, *Fax 33 32 87 18,* – MC AE ① VISA JCB. DX b
closed 21 December-4 January, Sunday, Saturday lunch and Bank Holidays – **Meals** a la carte 328/875.
◆ Mid 19C café-pavilion near quayside and Little Mermaid. Interesting 19C maritime memorabilia and old paintings. Good traditional cuisine. Possibility of dining on boat.

M/S Amerika, Dampfaergevej 8 (Pakhus 12, Amerikakaj), ✉ 2100 K, via Folke Bernadettes Allée ☎ 35 26 90 30, *info@msamerika.dk, Fax 35 26 91 30,* – MC AE ① VISA JCB.
closed 24 December-2 January, Sunday and Bank Holidays – **Meals** (set menu only at dinner) 198/345 and lunch a la carte approx 345 ♀.
◆ Characterful 19C former warehouse in attractive quayside location, with popular terrace in the summer. Open plan kitchen provides fresh, appealing, modern Danish fare.

Fiasco, Gammel Kongevej 176, Frederiksberg, ✉ 1850 C, via Gammel Kongevej ☎ 33 31 74 87, *Fax 33 31 74 87* – MC AE ① VISA
closed Christmas-New Year – **Meals** - Italian - (set menu only at dinner) 168/245 and a la carte 245/335 ♀.
◆ Modern Italian restaurant to the west of the city centre. Bright room with fresh feel and large picture windows. Friendly young owners. Carefully prepared, authentic cuisine.

Passagens Spisehus, Vesterbrogade 42, ✉ 1620 V, ☎ 33 22 47 57, *info@passagens.dk, Fax 33 22 47 87,* – MC AE ① VISA JCB. AZ v
closed 21 December-7 January, Sunday and Monday – **Meals** (dinner only) 295/395 and a la carte 325/403 ♀.
◆ Appealing brasserie-style restaurant adjacent to theatre. Large counter bar, floor to ceiling windows and wood panelling. Simple well cooked modern seasonal fare.

Grabrodre Torv 21, Grabrodre Torv 21, ✉ 1154 K, ☎ 33 11 47 07, *info@graabroedre21.dk, Fax 33 12 60 19,* – MC AE ① VISA JCB. CY r
closed 22 December-5 January and Sunday lunch January-March – **Meals** 248/525 and a la carte 228/500 ♀.
◆ Pleasant little restaurant on corner of square. Light and airy décor with appealing terrace in the summer. Authentic rustic style traditional Danish specialities.

Den Sorte Ravn, Nyhavn 14, ✉ 1051 K, ☎ 33 13 12 33, *rest@sorteravn.dk, Fax 33 13 24 72* – ▤. MC AE ① VISA JCB. DY q
closed Easter, Whitsun, 2 weeks July, 24-27 December and 1-7 January – **Meals** 410/495 (dinner) and a la carte 293/552 ♀.
◆ Long-standing family run restaurant located down steps and well located in Nyhavn. Simple décor with open kitchen. Well balanced menu of interesting traditional fare.

in Tivoli : *Vesterbrogade 3 ✉ 1620 V (Entrance fee payable)*

The Paul (Cunningham), Vesterbrogade 3, ✉ 1630 K, ☎ 33 75 07 75, *paul@thepaul.dk, Fax 33 75 07 76,* – ▤. MC AE ① VISA. BZ x
9 April-19 September and dinner only Thursday-Saturday 18 November-19 December – **Meals** (set menu only) (restricted menus Sunday) 395/700 ♀.
◆ Elegant glass-domed 20C structure by the lake in Tivoli Gardens. Open-plan kitchen with chef's table. Set menu (3-7 courses) ; elaborate cooking using local produce.
Spec. Calamari with braised oxtail, truffle vinaigrette. Fillet of pork, brawn and horseradish foam. Green plums, lemon ice cream and chocolate mousse.

Divan 2, ☎ 33 75 07 50, *restaurant@divan2.dk, Fax 33 75 07 30,* – MC AE ① VISA JCB. BZ a
16 April-19 September and 18 November-21 December – **Meals** 195/595 and a la carte 385/755 ♀.
◆ Spacious elegant restaurant with lavish colourful floral decoration and welcoming terrace overlooking the gardens. Serves well cooked traditional Franco-Danish cuisine.

SMØRREBRØD

The following list of simpler restaurants and cafés/bars specialize in Danish open sandwiches and are generally open from 10.00am to 4.00pm.

Ida Davidsen, Store Kongensgade 70, ✉ 1264 K, ✆ 33 91 36 55, *ida.davidsen@circue.dk, Fax 33 11 36 55* – MC AE D VISA JCB DY g
closed Easter, July, Christmas-New Year, Saturday, Sunday and Bank Holidays – **Meals** (lunch only) a la carte 50/200.
◆ Family run for five generations, this open sandwich bar, on a busy city-centre street, is almost a household name in Denmark. Offers a full range of typical smørrebrød.

Amalie, Amaliegade 11, ✉ 1256, ✆ 33 12 88 10, 余 – MC AE D VISA DY n
closed 2 weeks July, Christmas-New Year and Sunday – **Meals** (booking essential) (lunch only) a la carte 60/212.
◆ Located in a pretty 18C townhouse. Wood panelled walls and a clean, uncluttered style. Helpful service and ideal for those looking for an authentic, traditional Danish lunch.

Slotskaelderen-Hos Gitte Kik, Fortunstraede 4, ✉ 1065 K, ✆ 33 11 15 37, *Fax 33 11 15 37* – MC AE D VISA JCB. ✻ CYZ v
closed Sunday, Monday and Bank Holidays – **Meals** (lunch only) a la carte 36/75.
◆ Welcoming family run enterprise in a semi-basement restaurant with pleasant traditional décor. Popular with local clientele. Interesting well prepared smørrebrød.

Sankt Annae, Sankt Annae Plads 12, ✉ 1250 K, ✆ 33 12 54 97, *Fax 33 15 16 61* – MC AE VISA. ✻ DY a
closed Sunday and Bank Holidays – **Meals** (lunch only) a la carte 39/125 ♀.
◆ Pretty terraced building in popular part of town. Simple décor with a rustic feel and counter next to kitchen. Typical menu of smørrebrød. Service prompt and efficient.

at Hellerup *North : 7 ½ km by Østbanegade* DX *and Road 2* – ✉ *2900 Hellerup :*

Hellerup Parkhotel, Strandvejen 203, ✉ 2900, ✆ 39 62 40 44, *info@helleruppar khotel.dk, Fax 39 45 15 90,* Fø, ≘s – |♦|, ⇔ rm, TV P – 🏃 150. MC AE D VISA JCB. ✻ rest
Via Appia :* Meals** - Italian - 295 (dinner) and a la carte 205/355 (see also ***Saison below) – **71 rm** ☐ 1225/2700.
◆ Attractive classic hotel located in affluent suburb north of the city. Rooms vary in size and colour décor but offer same good standard of facilities and level of comfort. Popular local Italian restaurant on side of hotel overlooking park.

Saison, Strandvejen 203, ✉ 2900, ✆ 39 62 48 42, *saison@saison.dk, Fax 39 62 20 30* – ▤ P. MC AE D VISA JCB. ✻
closed 3 weeks July, 25 December and Sunday – **Meals** 225/400 and a la carte 335/520 ♀.
◆ Run separately from the hotel in which it is located. Enjoys a bright and airy feel with high ceiling and large windows. Carefully prepared cooking using quality ingredients.

at Søllerød *North : 20 km by Tagensvej* BX *and Road 19* – ✉ *2840 Holte :*

Søllerød Kro, Søllerødvej 35, ✉ 2840 K, ✆ 45 80 25 05, *mail@soelleroed-kro.dk, Fax 45 80 22 70* – P. MC AE D VISA JCB. ✻
closed 3 weeks July, 2 weeks February, 24 December and 1 January – **Meals** 475/520 and a la carte 574/999 ♀.
◆ Characterful 17C thatched inn with attractive courtyard terrace and stylish Danish rustic-bourgeois décor. Classically based cooking with modern notes and excellent wine list.

at Kastrup Airport *Southeast : 10 km by Amager Boulevard* CZ – ✉ *2300 S :*

Hilton Copenhagen Airport, Ellehammersvej 20, Kastrup, ✉ 2770, ✆ 32 50 15 01, *rescopenhagen-airport@hilton.com, Fax 32 52 85 28,* ≤, Fø, ≘s, ☐ – |♦|, ⇔ rm, ▤ TV ✆ ♿, 🚗 – 🏃 450. MC AE D VISA JCB. ✻ rest
***Hamlet :* Meals** (dinner only) 420 and a la carte 357/525 ♀ – ***Horizon :* Meals** (buffet lunch) 209/219 ♀ – ☐ 140 – **382 rm** 2150.
◆ Glass walkway leads from arrivals to this smart business hotel. Bright bedrooms with light, contemporary Scandinavian furnishings and every modern facility. Open-plan formal restaurant or relaxed dining beneath the vast atrium.

Quality Airport H. Dan, Kastruplundgade 15, Kastrup, ✉ 2770, North : 2 ½ km by coastal rd ✆ 32 51 14 00, *info.airport.dan@quality.choicehotels.dk, Fax 32 51 37 01,* 余, Fø, ≘s – |♦|, ⇔ rm, ▤ rest, TV P – 🏃 80. MC AE D VISA JCB. ✻
closed 19 December-5 January – **Meals** (dinner buffet only) – **228 rm** ☐ 1195/1595.
◆ Airport hotel not far from beach and countryside, popular with business travellers. Three types of room, all with modern facilities. Some have views of canal. Traditional Danish cuisine in the restaurant.

Finland

Suomi

PRACTICAL INFORMATION

LOCAL CURRENCY

1 euro (€) = 1,20 USD ($) (Dec. 2003)

TOURIST INFORMATION

The Tourist Office is situated near the Market Square, Pohjoisesplanadi 19 ☎ (09) 169 3757. Open from 2 May to 30 September, Monday to Friday 9am - 8pm, Saturday and Sunday 9am - 6pm, and from 1 October to 30 April, Monday to Friday 9am - 6pm Saturday and Sunday from 10am to 4pm. Hotel bookings are possible from a reservation board situated in the airport arrival lounge and in the main railway station; information is also available free.

National Holiday in Finland: *6 December.*

FOREIGN EXCHANGE

Banks are open between 9.15am and 4.15pm on weekdays only. Exchange offices at Helsinki-Vantaa airport and Helsinki harbour open daily between 6.30am and 11pm and at the railway station between 7am and 10pm.

MEALS

At lunchtime, follow the custom of the country and try the typical buffets of Scandinavian specialities.

At dinner, the a la carte and set menus will offer you more conventional cooking. Booking is essential.

Many city centre restaurants are closed for a few days over the Midsummer Day period.

SHOPPING IN HELSINKI

Furs, jewellery, china, glass and ceramics, Finnish handicraft and wood.

In the index of street names, those printed in red are where the principal shops are found. Your hotel porter will be able to help you with information.

THEATRE BOOKINGS

The following agents sell tickets for opera, theatre, concerts, cinema and sports events: Lippupalvelu ☎ 0600 108 00, Lippupiste ☎ 0600 900 900, Tiketti ☎ 0600 116 16.

CAR HIRE

The international car hire companies have branches in Helsinki and at Vantaa airport. Your hotel porter should be able to help you with your arrangements.

TIPPING

Service is normally included in hotel and restaurant bills. Doormen, baggage porters etc. are generally given a gratuity; taxi drivers are not usually tipped.

SPEED LIMITS

The maximum permitted speed on motorways is 120 km/h - 74 mph (in winter 100 km/h - 62 mph), 80 km/h - 50 mph on other roads and 50 km/h - 31 mph in built-up areas.

SEAT BELTS

The wearing of seat belts in Finland is compulsory for drivers and all passengers.

HELSINKI

(HELSINGFORS)

Finland 711 L 21 – *Pop. 546 317.*

Lahti 103 – Tampere 176 – Turku 165.

City Tourist Office Pohjoisesplanadi 19 ☎ (09) 169 37 57, Fax (09) 169 38 39.

Helsingin golfklubi ☎ (09) 550 235.

Helsinki-Vantaa N : 19 km ☎ 0200 14636 (information) – Finnair Head Office, Tietotie 11 A – 01053 ☎ 818 8383 – Air Terminal : Scandic H. Continental, Mannerheimintie 46 – Finnair City Terminal : Asema – Aukio 3, ☎ 0203 140 160 (reservations).

To Sweden, Estonia and boat excursions : contact the City Tourist Office (see above) – Car Ferry: Silja Line ☎ 0203 74 552 – Viking Line ☎ 123577 – Eckerö Line ☎ 228 8544 – Nordic Jetline ☎ 681 770 – Tallink ☎ 2282 1277.

See: *Senate Square★★★ (Senaatintori)* DY **53** – *Market Square★★ (Kauppatori* DY **26** – *Esplanadi★★* CDY **8/43** – *Railway Station★★ (Rautatiesema)* CX – *Finlandia Hall★★ (Finlandia-talo)* BX – *National Opera House★★ (Kansallisoopera)* BX – *Church in the Rock★★ (Temppeliaukion kirkko)* BX – *Ateneum Art Museum★★ (Ateneum, Suomen Taiteen Museo)* CY **M¹** – *National Museum★★ (Kansallismuseo)* BX **M²** – *Lutheran Cathedral★★ (Tuomiokirkko)* DY – *Parliament House★ (Eduskuntatalo)* BX – *Amos Anderson Collection★ (Amos Andersinin taidemuseo)* BY **M⁴** – *Uspensky Cathedral★ (Uspenskin katedraali)* DY – *Cygnaeus home and collection★ (Cynaeuksen galleria)* DZ **B** – *Mannerheim home and collection★ (Mannerheim-museo)* DZ **M⁵** – *Olympic Stadium★ (Olympiastadion)* ✳★★ BX **21** – *Museum of Applied Arts★★ (Taideteollisuusmuseo)* CZ **M⁶** – *Sibelius Monument★ (Sibelius-monumentti)* AX **S** – *Ice-breaker fleet★* DX.

Outskirts: *Fortress of Suomenlinna★★ by boat* DZ – *Seurasaari Open-Air Museum★★* BX – *Urho Kekkonen Museum★ (Urho Kekkosen museo)* BX.

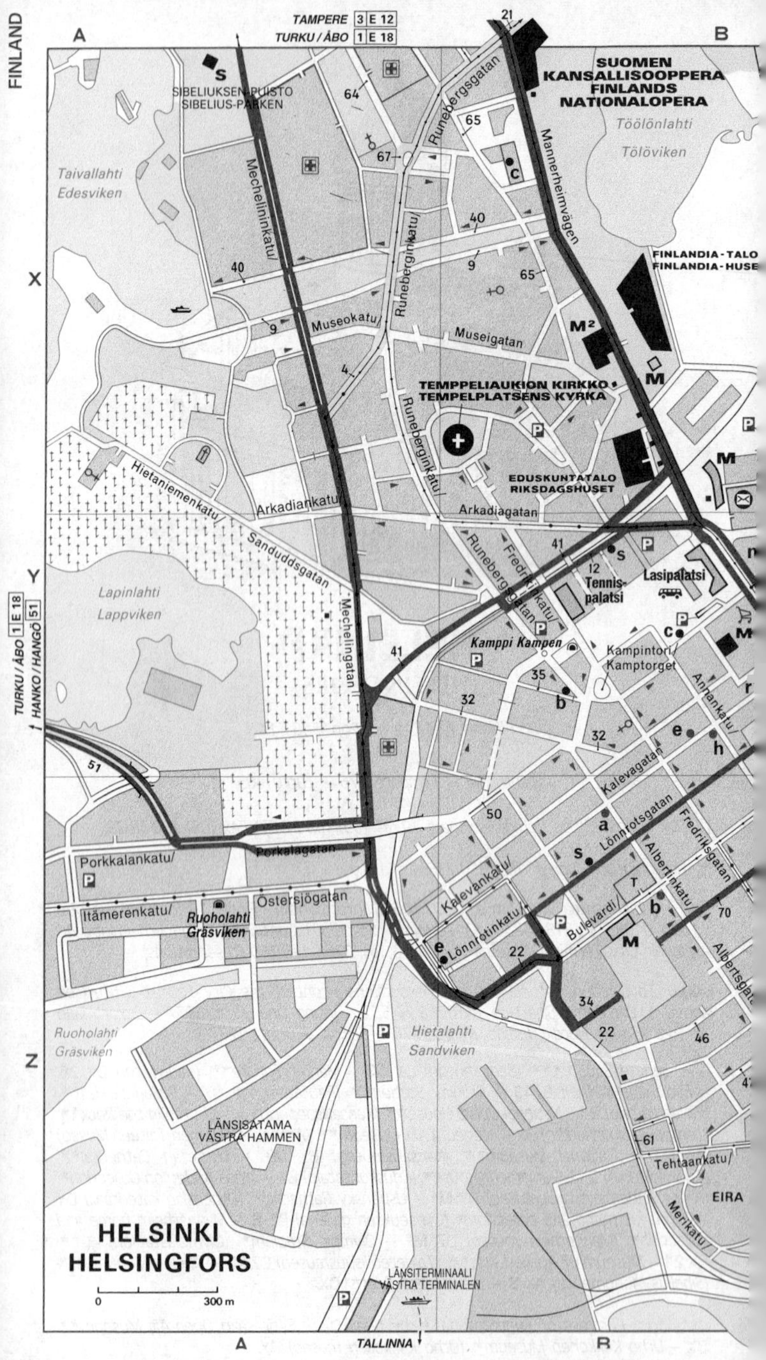
TAMPERE 3 E 12
TURKU / ÅBO 1 E 18
SIBELIUKSEN-PUISTO
SIBELIUS-PARKEN
SUOMEN KANSALLISOOPPERA
FINLANDS NATIONALOPERA
Töölönlahti
Tölöviken
Taivallahti
Edesviken
Mechelininkatu/
Runebergsgatan
Runeberginkatu/
Mannerheimvägen
FINLANDIA-TALO
FINLANDIA-HUSET
Museokatu/
Museigatan
TEMPPELIAUKION KIRKKO
TEMPELPLATSENS KYRKA
EDUSKUNTATALO
RIKSDAGSHUSET
Hietaniemenkatu/
Arkadiankatu/
Arkadiagatan
Sanduddsgatan
Fredrikinkatu/
Lasipalatsi
Tennis-palatsi
Lapinlahti
Lappviken
TURKU / ÅBO 1 E 18
HANKO / HANGÖ 51
Mechelingatan
Kamppi Kampen
Kampintori/
Kamptorget
Annankatu/
Kalevagatan
Lönnrotsgatan
Fredriksgatan
Albertinkatu/
Porkkalankatu/
Porkalagatan
Itämerenkatu/
Östersjögatan
Ruoholahti
Gräsviken
Kalevankatu/
Bulevardi/
Lönnrotinkatu/
Albertsgatan
Hietalahti
Sandviken
Ruoholahti
Gräsviken
LÄNSISATAMA
VÄSTRA HAMMEN
Tehtaankatu/
EIRA
Merikatu/
HELSINKI
HELSINGFORS
0
300 m
LÄNSITERMINAALI
VÄSTRA TERMINALEN
TALLINNA

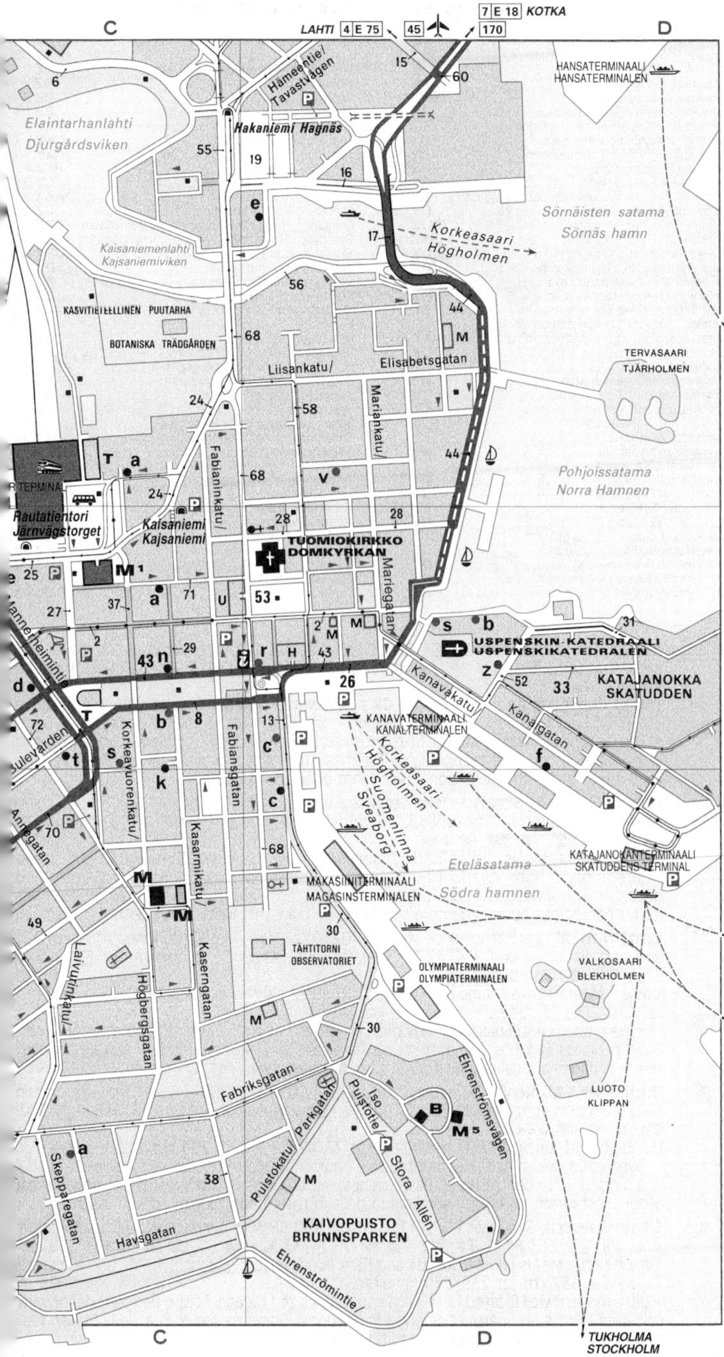

C
LAHTI 4 E 75
45
7 E 18 KOTKA
170
D
HANSATERMINAALI
HANSATERMINALEN
Hämeentie/
Tavastvägen
Elaintarhanlahti
Djurgårdsviken
Hakaniemi Hagnäs
Sörnäisten satama
Sörnäs hamn
Korkeasaari
Högholmen
Kaisaniemenlahti
Kajsaniemiviken
X
KASVITIETEELLINEN PUUTARHA
BOTANISKA TRÄDGÅRDEN
Liisankatu/
Elisabetsgatan
TERVASAARI
TJÄRHOLMEN
TRAVEMÜNDE
Mariankatu/
Fabianinkatu/
Pohjoissatama
Norra Hamnen
TERMINAL
Rautatientori
Järnvägstorget
Kaisaniemi
Kajsaniemi
TUOMIOKIRKKO
DOMKYRKAN
Mariegatan
USPENSKIN-KATEDRAALI
USPENSKIKATEDRALEN
Y
Mannerheimintie
KATAJANOKKA
SKATUDDEN
Kanavakatu
Kanalgatan
KANAVATERMINAALI
KANALTERMINALEN
Bulevarden
Korkeavuorenkatu/
Fabiansgatan
Korkeasaari
Högholmen
Suomenlinna
Sveaborg
Annegatan
Eteläsatama
Södra hamnen
KATAJANOKANTERMINAALI
SKATUDDENS TERMINAL
ROSTOCK
Kasarmikatu/
MAKASIINITERMINAALI
MAGASINSTERMINALEN
TÄHTITORNI
OBSERVATORIET
Kaserngatan
OLYMPIATERMINAALI
OLYMPIATERMINALEN
VALKOSAARI
BLEKHOLMEN
Laivurinkatu/
Högbergsgatan
TALLINNA
TALLINN
Fabriksgatan
Iso Puistotie/
Parkgatan
Ehrenströmsvägen
LUOTO
KLIPPAN
Skepparegatan
Puistokatu/
Stora Allén
Z
KAIVOPUISTO
BRUNNSPARKEN
Havsgatan
Ehrenströmintie/
C
D
TUKHOLMA
STOCKHOLM

STREET INDEX TO HELSINKI/HELSINGFORS TOWN PLAN

Albertinkatu/Albertsgatan . . . BZ
Aleksanterinkatu/Alexandersgatan . . . CDY 2
Annankatu/Annegatan . . . BCYZ
Arkadiankatu/Arkadiagatan . . . ABX
Bulevardi/Bulevarden . . . BCXY
Caloniuksenkatu/Caloniusgatan . . . AX 4
Ehrenströmintie/Ehrenströmsvägen . . . DZ
Eläintarhantie/Djurgårdsvägen . . . CX 6
Eteläesplanadi/Södra esplanaden . . . CY 8
Eteläinen Hesperiankatu/
Södra Hesperiagatan . . . ABX 9
Eteläinen Rautatiekatu/Södra Järnvägsgatan . . BY 12
Eteläranta/Södra kajen . . . DY 13
Fabianinkatu/Fabiansgatan . . . CXYZ
Fredrikinkatu/Fredriksgatan . . . BYZ
Haapaniemenkatu/Aspnäsgatan . . . DX 15
Hakaniemenranta/Hagnäskajen . . . DX 16
Hakaniemen silta/Hagnäs bro . . . DX 17
Hakaniemen tori/Hagnäs torg . . . DX 19
Helsinginkatu/Helsingegatan . . . BX 21
Hietalahdenranta/Sandvikskajen . . . BZ 22
Hietaniemenkatu/Sanduddsgatan . . . AXY
Hämeentie/Tavastvägen . . . DX
Iso Puistotie/Stora Allén . . . DZ
Itämerenkatu/Östersjögatan . . . AZ
Kaisaniemenkatu/Kajsaniemigatan . . . CX 24
Kaivokatu/Brunnsgatan . . . CY 25
Kalevankatu/Kalevagatan . . . BYZ
Kampintori/Kamptorget . . . BY
Kanavakatu/Kanalgatan . . . DXY
Kasarmikatu/Kaserngatan . . . CZ
Kauppatori/Salutorget . . . DY 26
Keskuskatu/Centralgatan . . . CY 27
Kirkkokatu/Kyrkogatan . . . DY 28
Kluuvikatu/Glogatan . . . CY 29
Korkeavuorenkatu/Högbergsgatan . . . CYZ
Laivasillankatu/Skeppsbrogatan . . . DZ 30
Laivastokatu/Maringatan . . . DY 31
Laivurinkatu/Skepparegatan . . . CZ
Lapinlahdenkatu/Lappviksgatan . . . BY 32
Liisankatu/Elisabetsgatan . . . DX
Luotsikatu/Lotsgatan . . . DY 33
Länsiväylä/Västerleden . . . AYZ
Lönnrotinkatu/Lönnrotsgatan . . . BZ
Mallaskatu/Maltgatan . . . BZ 34
Malminkatu/Malmgatan . . . BY 35
Mannerheimintie/Mannerheimvägen . . . BCXY
Mariankatu/Mariegatan . . . DXY
Mechelininkatu/Mechelingatan . . . AXY
Merikatu/Havsgatan . . . BCZ
Mikonkatu/Mikaelsgatan . . . CY 37
Museokatu/Museigatan . . . ABX
Neitsytpolku/Jungfrustigen . . . CZ 38
Pohjoinen Hesperiankatu/Norra Hesperiagatan . ABX 40
Pohjoinen Rautatiekatu/Norra Järnvägsgatan . ABY 41
Pohjoisesplanadi/Norra esplanaden . . . CDY 43
Pohjoisranta/Norra kajen . . . DX 44
Porkkalankatu/Porkalagatan . . . AZ
Puistokatu/Parkgatan . . . DZ
Punavuorenkatu/Rödbergsgatan . . . BZ 46
Pursimiehenkatu/Båtsmansgatan . . . BZ 47
Ratakatu/Bangatan . . . CZ 49
Rautatientori/Järnvägstorget . . . CY
Runeberginkatu/Runebergsgatan . . . ABXY
Ruoholahdenkatu/Gräsviksgatan . . . BZ 50
Satamakatu/Hamngatan . . . DY 52
Senaatintori/Senatstorget . . . DY 53
Siltasaarenkatu/Broholmsgatan . . . CX 55
Siltavuorenranta/Brobergskajen . . . DX 56
Snellmaninkatu/Snellmansgatan . . . DX 58
Sörnäisten rantatie/Sörnäs strandväg . . . DX 60
Tehtaankatu/Fabriksgatan . . . BCDZ
Telakkakatu/Docksgatan . . . BZ 61
Topeliuksenkatu/Topeliusgatan . . . AX 64
Töölönkatu/Tölögatan . . . BX 65
Töölöntori/Tölötorg . . . AX 67
Unioninkatu/Unionsgatan . . . DXYZ 68
Uudenmaankatu/Nylandsgatan . . . BCZ 70
Yliopistonkatu/Universitetsgatan . . . CY 71
Yrjönkatu/Georgsgatan . . . BCY 72

Kämp, Pohjoisesplanadi 29, ✉ 00100, ☎ (09) 576 111, *hotelkamp@luxurycollection.com, Fax (09) 576 1122,* – rm, – 120. MC AE D VISA JCB. CY n
closed Christmas and New Year – ***CK's Brasserie*** **: Meals** 35 and dinner a la carte 30.50/54.50 ♀ (see also ***est. 1887*** below) – ☕ 29 – **172 rm** 365, 7 suites.
◆ Top class historic hotel with de luxe British style décor. Rooms combine luxury and classic elegance with first rate technological facilities. Superb professional service. Sleek restaurant offering classic international fare from open plan kitchen.

Hilton Helsinki Strand, John Stenbergin Ranta 4, ✉ 00530, ☎ (09) 39 351, *helsinkistrand@hilton.com, Fax (09) 3935 3255,* – rm, – 300. MC AE D VISA. rest DX e
Atrium Plaza **: Meals** (buffet lunch) 38 and a la carte – ☕ 25 – **185 rm** 240/270, 7 suites.
◆ International hotel overlooking waterfront. Contemporary Finnish architecture and décor. Atrium style lobby. Comfortable spacious rooms with hi-tech facilities. Muted maritime themed restaurant, game a speciality, or main restaurant with central buffet.

Continental, Mannerheimintie 46, ✉ 00260, ☎ (09) 47 371, *continentalhelsinki@scandic-hotels.com, Fax (09) 4737 2255,* – rm, – 600. MC AE D VISA JCB. rest BX c
Olivo **: Meals** *(closed Sunday lunch)* 20/40 (lunch) and a la carte 26/39 ♀ – **500 rm** ☕ 170/260, 12 suites.
◆ Huge modern hotel block on busy main street with more welcoming local interior décor. Good business facilities. Third of rooms have lake view. Roomy modern restaurant with range of international cuisine focusing on Mediterranean and fish dishes.

Radisson SAS Royal, Runeberginkatu 2, ✉ 00100, ☎ (09) 69 580, *info.royal.helsinki@radissonsas.com, Fax (09) 6958 7100,* – rm, – 300. MC AE D VISA JCB. BY b
Meals (buffet lunch) 27/30 and a la carte 27/47 ♀ – ☕ 17 **254 rm** 212, 6 suites.
◆ Good-sized, well-maintained bedrooms - equipped with the business traveller in mind - in a modern, city centre hotel. Pasta dishes and a buffet of smörgasbord in an informal atrium restaurant or hearty steaks and grills in the clubby "Johan Ludvig" bistro.

Simonkenttä, Simonkatu 9, ✉ 00100, ☎ (09) 68 380, *simonkentta@scandic-hotels.com, Fax (09) 683 8111,* – – 80. MC AE D VISA JCB.
Simonkatu **: Meals** *(closed Sunday and Bank Holidays)* (buffet lunch) 18/38 and a la carte 22/31 ♀ – **357 rm** ☕ 235/270, 3 suites. BY c
◆ Ultra modern well located hotel with imposing glazed façade. Stylish designer décor with colourful fabrics and parquet flooring in all rooms. Some rooms with a view. Stylish restaurant offers range of popular traditional dishes.

Holiday Inn Helsinki City Centre, Elielinaukio 5, 00100, (09) 5425 5000, *helsinki.hihcc@restel.fi, Fax (09) 5425 5299,* - , rm, rest BX z
Verde : **Meals** *(closed lunch Saturday and Sunday)* a la carte 25/55 - 15 - **174 rm** 248/278.
• Modern city centre hotel near railway station, post office and all main shopping areas. Modern well-equipped bedrooms ; good city view from 8th floor. Open style dining room serving popular menu using Finnish produce ; lighter dishes available at lunch time.

Radisson SAS Seaside, Ruoholahdenranta 3, 00180, (09) 69 360, *sales.finland@radissonsas.com, Fax (09) 693 2123,* - , rm, - 150. ABZ e
Meals (buffet lunch) 27/35 and a la carte - 17 - **359 rm** 120/184, 5 suites.
• Large contemporary hotel overlooking harbour in peaceful area. Caters for groups but also for business people and individuals. Three room categories ; some with kitchenette. Brasserie style restaurant ; traditional Finnish and international fare.

Radisson SAS Plaza, Mikonkatu 23, 00100, (09) 77 590, *sales.finland@radissonsas.com, Fax (09) 7759 7100,* , - , rm, - 100. CX a
Meals a la carte 24/38 - 16 - **291 rm** 223, 6 suites.
• Near the station, this sizeable modern business hotel maintains the reputation of this international group. Well-equipped rooms, in "Nordic", "Classic" or "Italian" style. Modern informal brasserie ; striking, painted windows.

Holiday Inn Helsinki, Messuaukio 1, 00520, North : 4 km by Mannerheimintie, Nordenskiöldink, Savonkatu off Ratapihantie (09) 150 900, *holiday-inn@iaf.fi, Fax (09) 150 901,* , - , rm, - 1200. rest
Terra Nova : **Meals** (dinner only) a la carte 28.60/47.70 - **239 rm** 200/222, 5 suites.
• Modern hotel in same building as congress centre ; popular for conferences. Take breakfast in the winter garden style atrium. Spacious well equipped rooms with modern décor. Cheerful modern brasserie-style restaurant, popular international cooking.

Palace, Eteläranta 10, 00130, (09) 1345 6656, *reception@palacehotel.fi, Fax (09) 654 786,* , - - 350. rest
Meals (see ***Palace Gourmet*** and ***Palacenranta*** below) - **37 rm** 235/305, 2 suites.
• 1950s hotel by harbour, occupying upper floors of building with street level reception. Spacious comfortable rooms with tasteful décor and modern facilites. Some views. DZ c

Ramada H. Presidentti, Eteläinen Rautatiekatu 4, 00100, (09) 6911, *presidentti.ramada@restel.fi, Fax (09) 694 7886,* , - , rm, - 30
491 rm, 4 suites. BY s
• Imposing modern hotel block conveniently located for station. Rooms are functional and comfortable, some with city views. Lively and welcoming brasserie with colourful furnishings and wooden floor. Offers selection of traditional Finnish dishes.

Marski, Mannerheimintie 10, 00100, (09) 68 061, *marski@scandic-hotels.com, Fax (09) 642 377,* , - , rm, rest, - 30.
Marski : **Meals** *(closed Sunday, Saturday lunch and Bank Holidays)* (buffet lunch) 22/35 and dinner a la carte 16/58 - **283 rm** 240/275, 6 suites. CY d
• Large well run central hotel with imposing façade. Bright lobby with cosmopolitan coffee shop. Room styles are early and late 1990s and modern with good facilities. Welcoming bar and restaurant for traditional fare designed to appeal to all tastes.

Vaakuna, Asema-aukio 2, 00100, (09) 433 70, *sokos.hotels@sok.fi, Fax (09) 4337 7100,* , - , rm, rest BY n
closed Christmas - **Meals** a la carte 29/55 - **258 rm** 215/263, 12 suites.
• Modern accommodation, spacious, colourful and well-appointed, in this sizeable hotel, built for the 1952 Olympics. Convenient for the station. 10th-floor restaurant, with terrace for armchair dining. Lighter meals in coffee shop.

Grand Marina, Katajanokanlaitari 7, 00160, (09) 16 661, *grandmarina@scandic-hotels.com, Fax (09) 664 764,* , - , rm, - 600. rest DY f
Makasiim : **Meals** a la carte approx 35 - **442 rm** 162/192, 20 suites.
• Large harbourside hotel in converted warehouse opposite Marina Congress Centre. Modern rooms, functional fittings. Pub and coffee shop. Vast restaurant, modern Scandinavian décor. Extensive selection of international fare.

Klaus Kurki, Bulevardi 2, 00120, (09) 43 340, *respa.klauskurki@sok.fi, Fax (09) 4334 7100,* - , rm, . CY t
closed 25 December - ***Bulevardi Kaksi :*** **Meals** a la carte approx 35 - **136 rm** 176/270.
• Centrally located group run hotel in early 20C building. Welcoming coffee lounge. Compact rooms feature classic local décor and furniture. Modern bar and off-street deli. Cheerful restaurant ; unfussy menu featuring traditional local ingredients.

Pasila, Maistraatinportti 3, ✉ 00240, North : 4 km by Mannerheimintie, Nordenskiöldink off Vetuvitie ℘ (09) 433 50, *reception.pasila@sok.fi, Fax (09) 143 771,* squash – ‖, rm, ▤ TV ♿ P – 90. MC AE DC VISA. rest
closed Christmas – ***Sevilla*** **: Meals** a la carte 18.50/25.20 ♀ – **177 rm** 138/182, 1 suite.
◆ Large, modern business hotel in tranquil district out of town, a short tram ride from city centre. Rooms feature contemporary local décor and furnishings. Informal Mediterranean influenced restaurant ; popular menu.

Torni, Yrjönkatu 26, ✉ 00100, ℘ (09) 43 360, *reception.torni@sok.fi, Fax (09) 4336 7100,* – ‖, rm, TV – 35. MC AE DC VISA JCB. rest BY r
closed Christmas – ***Torni*** **: Meals** *(closed Sunday, Saturday lunch and Bank Holidays)* 21.50/31.50 and dinner a la carte 27/55 ♀ – **154 rm** 193/337.
◆ Traditional hotel in converted row of 1920s town houses in city centre. Rooms vary in size but all feature standard modern décor and facilities. Panoramic bar on 13th floor. Inviting restaurant overlooking street offering a traditional menu.

Helsinki, Kluuvikatu 8, ✉ 00100, ℘ (09) 43 320, *reception.sokoshotelhelsinki@sok.fi, Fax (09) 176 014,* – ‖, rm, ▤ TV ♿. MC AE DC VISA JCB. rest CY a
Fransmanni **: Meals** a la carte approx 25 ♀ – **202 rm** 153/177.
◆ A convenient base for tourists and shoppers alike. Unfussy, modern rooms ; quieter on higher floors. Lively nightclub a popular destination. Informal restaurant offering appealing French dishes, with specialities from Provence. 'Memphis' for grill favourites.

Rivoli Jardin without rest., Kasarmikatu 40, ✉ 00130, ℘ (09) 681 500, *rivoli.jardin@rivoli.fi, Fax (09) 656 988,* – ‖ TV ♿. MC AE DC VISA CYZ k
55 rm 199/325.
◆ Well run traditional hotel in a quiet location close to city centre. Rooms are functional and comfortable, two on top floor have terrace. Winter garden style breakfast area.

Seurahuone, Kaivokatu 12, ✉ 00100, ℘ (09) 69 141, *cumulus.seurahuone@restel.fi, Fax (09) 691 4010,* – ‖, rm, TV – 60. MC AE DC VISA. rest CY e
closed Easter and Christmas – **Meals** a la carte 24.50/40.60 ♀ – **118 rm** 195/220.
◆ Early 20C hotel, typical of its kind locally, opposite station. Décor and atmosphere reflect the charm of olden days. Rooms vary in size. Elegant restaurant retains a traditional charm. Offers menu featuring classic Finnish cuisine.

Lord , Lönnrotinkatu 29, ✉ 00180, ℘ (09) 615 815, *reception@lordhotel.fi, Fax (09) 680 1315,* – ‖, rm, TV ♿ – 200. MC AE DC VISA JCB.
closed 23-26 December – **Meals** *(closed Sunday and Bank Holidays)* 22/33 and dinner a la carte 33/45 ♀ – **47 rm** 145/175, 1 suite. BZ s
◆ Modern hotel adjoining Finnish Art Nouveau granite castle. Functional rooms with modern décor in fairly neutral tones and standard facilities. Appealing restaurant in the castle building offering a selection of traditional favourites.

est. 1887, Pohjoisesplanadi 29, ✉ 00100, ℘ (09) 5761 1204, *Fax (09) 5761 1209* – ▤. MC AE DC VISA JCB. CY n
closed Easter, Christmas, Sunday and Saturday lunch – **Meals** 25/86 and a la carte 40/71 ♀.
◆ Elegant restaurant with Corinthian columns and 19C oil paintings. Immaculate tables Interesting modern style dishes served by attentive and enthusiastic young team.

G.W. Sundmans, Eteläranta 16 (1st floor), ✉ 00130, ℘ (09) 622 6410, *maanti.palvelu@royalravintolat.com, Fax (09) 661 331,* – ▤ – 60. MC AE DC VISA. DY c
closed Easter, 2 weeks Christmas-New Year, lunch in July, Sunday and Saturday lunch – **Meals** 43/74 and a la carte 62/77 ♀ – ***Krog (ground floor)*** **: Meals** 40/45 and a la carte 35/50 ♀.
◆ 19C sea captain's Empire style mansion opposite harbour. Five classically decorated dining rooms with view. Elegant tables. Classically-based cuisine. Informal ground floor restaurant Menu features local seafood and international dishes.
Spec. Smoked salmon with white fish and langoustine. Fillet of deer with fried ceps. Mango soufflé, raspberry sorbet.

Nokka, Kanavaranta 7F, ✉ 00160, ℘ (09) 687 7330, *myyntipalvelu@royalravintolat.com, Fax (09) 6877 3330,* – ▤. MC AE DC VISA. DY b
closed 23 December-7 January, Sunday, Saturday lunch and Bank Holidays – **Meals** (booking essential) 27/44 (lunch) and dinner a la carte 34/60 ♀.
◆ Converted harbourside restaurant with nautical themed interior. Watch the chefs prepare appealing, modern Finnish cuisine. Bustling atmosphere.

Savoy, Eteläesplanadi 14 (8th floor), ✉ 00130, ℘ (09) 684 4020, *terhi.oksanen@royalravintolat.com, Fax (09) 628 715,* – ‖. MC AE DC VISA. CY b
closed Easter, 27 May, 24-27 June, 24 December-6 January, Saturday and Sunday – **Meals** 52/100 and dinner a la carte 55/87 ♀.
◆ Panoramic restaurant in city centre with typical Finnish design dating from 1937. Classic traditional menu of local specialities. Ask for a table in the conservatory.

XXX **Alexander Nevski,** Pohjoisesplanadi 17, ✉ 00170, ☎ (09) 686 9560, *myyntipalvelu@royalravintolat.com, Fax (09) 631 435* – ▤. MC AE ⓓ VISA. ⚘ DY r
closed 24-26 December and Sunday lunch – **Meals** - Russian - 32/56 and dinner a la carte 38/102 ♀.
◆ Well located restaurant in handsome old house. Elegant Russian style décor with columns and opulent drapes. Classic refined menu of Russian inspiration, with game in season.

XXX **Palace Gourmet** (at Palace H.), Eteläranta 10 (10th floor), ✉ 00130, ☎ (09) 1345 6787, *ilkka.rantanen@palaceravintolat.com, Fax (09) 657 474,* ≤ Helsinki and harbour – |‡| ▤. MC AE ⓓ VISA. ⚘ DZ c
closed Easter, July, Christmas, Saturday, Sunday and Bank Holidays – **Meals** 41/63 and dinner a la carte 63/83 ♀.
◆ Nicely situated restaurant with open view of harbour and sea. Local style décor and spacious layout. Serves traditional Finnish cuisine with hint of France.

XX ✿ **George** (Aremo), Kalevankatu 17, ✉ 00100, ☎ (09) 647 662, *george@george.fi, Fax (09) 647 110* – ▤. MC AE ⓓ VISA JCB. ⚘ BY e
closed 9-12 April, 26-27 June, 25 December, Sunday and Saturday lunch – **Meals** 19/79 and dinner a la carte 51/56 ♀.
◆ 19C town house in residential district. Chilled chocolate truffle cabinet in bar. Elegant tableware. Classically-based cooking, using local produce with seasonal interest.
Spec. Parma ham and mushroom risotto. Veal steak with stewed ceps. Cloudberries with liquorice mousse.

XX **Sipuli,** Kanavaranta 3 (2nd floor), ✉ 00160, ☎ (09) 622 9280, *myyntipalvelu@royalravintolat.com, Fax (09) 6229 2840,* ≤ – MC AE ⓓ VISA. ⚘ DY s
closed 8-12 April, 25 June-2 August, 22 December-9 January, Saturday and Sunday – **Meals** (booking essential) 28/61 and dinner a la carte 46.50/61 ♀.
◆ Old warehouse conversion next to Uspensky Orthodox cathedral, which it overlooks through a picture window. Serves selection of French inspired modern Finnish dishes.

XX **Havis Amanda,** Pohjoisesplanadi 17, ✉ 00170, ☎ (09) 6869 5660, *myyntipalvelu@royalravintolat.com, Fax (09) 631 435* – ▤. MC AE ⓓ VISA. ⚘ DY r
closed 8-12 April, 24-26 December and Sunday October-April – **Meals** - Seafood - (booking essential) 29/62 and a la carte 36/68 ♀.
◆ Cellar style restaurant with intimate atmosphere. Light modern décor and contemporary furniture. Interesting range of local seafood.

XX **Palacenranta** (at Palace H.), Eteläranta 10 (1st floor), ✉ 00130, ☎ (09) 1345 6749, *palacenranta@palacravintolat.com, Fax (09) 1345 6750,* ≤ Helsinki harbour – ▤. MC AE ⓓ VISA. ⚘ DZ c
closed July, Sunday, Saturday lunch and Bank Holidays – **Meals** 24.50/36 and a la carte 35.10/49.50 ♀.
◆ Stylish, modern restaurant with simple décor in neutral and dark tones and a wood panelled ceiling. Most tables have harbour views. Authentic Finnish cooking.

XX ✿✿ **Chez Dominique (Valimaki),** Ludviginkatu 3-5, ✉ 00130, ☎ (09) 612 7393, *info@chezdominique.fi, Fax (09) 6124 4220* – MC AE ⓓ VISA. ⚘ CY s
closed July, Sunday, Monday, Saturday lunch and Bank Holidays – **Meals** (booking essential) (set menu only Saturday) a la carte 74/90 ♀.
◆ Small well run restaurant in old district. Plain minimalist décor and tiled floor. Cosy layout and some banquette seating. Refined modern cuisine with attention to detail.
Spec. Terrine of foie gras, melon sorbet. Poached turbot with lobster agnolotti and apple sauce. Chocolate fondant, almond ice cream.

XX **Bellevue,** Rahapajankatu 3, ✉ 00160, ☎ (09) 179 560, *info@restaurantbellevue.com, Fax (09) 636 985* – ▤. MC AE ⓓ VISA DY z
closed 1 week December and lunch July, 6 December, 1 January, Saturday and Sunday – **Meals** - Russian - 25/52 and dinner a la carte 34.60/58.30 ♀.
◆ Near Orthodox cathedral, restaurant in old town house with fairly sombre traditional Russian décor and cosy intimate atmosphere. Menu features Russian delicacies.

XX **Rivoli,** Albertinkatu 38, ✉ 00180, ☎ (09) 643 455, *kala.cheri@rivoli.inet.fi, Fax (09) 647 780* – ⇔ ▤. MC AE ⓓ VISA JCB. ⚘ BZ a
closed 18-21 April, 24-26 December, Sunday, Saturday lunch and Bank Holidays – **Meals** 40/42 (dinner) and a la carte 26.70/65.20 ♀.
◆ Two different style dining rooms : smokers' is cosy with wood panelling ; non-smokers' is brasserie-style. Menu offers fusion of traditional, Finnish and French influences.

X ☺ **La Petite Maison,** Huvilakatu 28A, ✉ 00150, ☎ (09) 260 9680, *lapetite.maison@kolumbus.fi, Fax (09) 684 25 666* – MC AE ⓓ VISA. ⚘ CZ a
closed Easter, 23-26 June, Christmas and Sunday – **Meals** - French - (booking essential) (dinner only) 42/46 and a la carte 42.50/53.50 ♀.
◆ Cosy restaurant popular with local clientele in 1907 house not far from sea. Classic décor with strong French note. Good French-influenced classic fare.

Safka, Vironkatu 8, ✉ 00170, ℘ (09) 135 7287, *safka@safka.fi, Fax (09) 278 3178* – MC AE ⓓ VISA. ⌧ DX v
closed July, Christmas, Monday and lunch Saturday and Sunday – **Meals** (booking essential) 23/40 and a la carte 33.50/56 ♀.
◆ Modest local restaurant in converted shop near the cathedral in city centre. Cosy layout. Well run kitchen produces unfussy, fresh and seasonal, traditional Finnish food.

Serata, Bulevardi 32, ✉ 00120, ℘ (09) 680 1365, *serata@serata.net* – MC ⓓ VISA. ⌧
closed 4 days Easter, 24-27 June, 22 December-10 January, Monday dinner, Mondays in July, Saturday lunch, Sunday and Bank Holidays – **Meals** - Italian - (booking essential) 20/45 and a la carte 24.20/42.90 ♀. BZ b
◆ Converted shop in residential district. Open kitchen with some counter seating. Authentic Italian cooking with good value set menus including wine.

Lappi, Annankatu 22, ✉ 00100, ℘ (09) 645 550, *Fax (09) 645 551* – MC AE ⓓ VISA JCB. ⌧ BY h
closed Easter, midsummer and Christmas – **Meals** - Finnish - (booking essential) 26/45 (dinner) and a la carte 25.20/59.20 ♀.
◆ Small local restaurant with typical Lappish atmosphere created by dark rustic stone and wood décor with wood furniture. Traditional Lappish fare served in generous portions.

at Vantaa *North : 19 km by A 137 DX :*

Vantaa, Hertaksentie 2 (near Tikkurila Railway Station), ✉ 01300, ℘ (09) 857 851, *reception.vantaa@sok.fi, Fax (09) 8578 5555,* – , – |‡|, ⇎ rm, TV ♿ – P – 🎤 280. MC AE ⓓ VISA. ⌧ rest
closed Christmas – ***Sevilla*** **: Meals** a la carte approx 22.50 – **154 rm** ☐ 138/164, 8 suites.
◆ Beside the railway station and convenient for the airport ; a busy corporate hotel. Well equipped rooms in a modern Scandinavian style. Modern restaurant, Mediterranean influenced cooking.

Holiday Inn Garden Court Helsinki Airport, Rälssitie 2, ✉ 01510, ℘ (09) 870 900, *inn.holiday@tradeka.fi, Fax (09) 8709 0101,* – |‡|, ⇎ rm, TV ♿ P – 🎤 25. MC AE ⓓ VISA JCB. ⌧ rest
Meals - Bistro - *(closed Saturday and Sunday lunch)* a la carte approx 35 – **283 rm** ☐ 195/240.
◆ Modern international hotel which is well geared towards business people. Comfortable well equipped standard rooms with modern décor and fittings in local style. Friendly, modern restaurant serves a simple range of traditional International dishes.

France

PARIS AND ENVIRONS – BORDEAUX
CANNES – LILLE – LYONS
MARSEILLES – PRINCIPALITY OF MONACO
NICE – STRASBOURG
TOULOUSE

PRACTICAL INFORMATION

LOCAL CURRENCY

Euro : *1 euro (€) = 1,20 USD ($) (Dec 2003)*

TOURIST INFORMATION IN PARIS

Paris "Welcome" Office *(Office du Tourisme de Paris) : 25/27, rue des Pyramides 1st ✆ 08 92 68 30 00, 0,34 €/min*

American Express *9 rue Auber, 9th, ✆ 01 47 77 72 00, Fax 01 42 68 17 17*

National Holiday in France : *14 July*

AIRLINES

AMERICAN AIRLINES : *109 rue du faubourg St-Honoré, 8th, ✆ 08 10 87 28 72, Fax 01 42 99 99 95*

UNITED AIRLINES : *55 rue Raspail, Levallois-Perret, (92), ✆ 08 10 72 72 72*

DELTA AIRLINES : *106 bd Hausmann, 8th, ✆ 0800 35 40 80, Fax 01 55 69 55 35*

BRITISH AIRWAYS : *18 boulevard Malesherbes, 8th, ✆ 01 53 43 25 27, Fax 01 53 43 25 10*

AIR FRANCE : *119 avenue Champs-Élysées, 8th, ✆ 08 20 82 08 20, Fax 01 42 99 21 99*

FOREIGN EXCHANGE OFFICES

Banks : *close at 4.30pm and at weekends*

Orly Sud Airport : *daily 6.30am to 11pm*

Roissy-Charles-de-Gaulle Airport : *daily 6am to 11.30pm*

TRANSPORT IN PARIS

Taxis : *may be hailed in the street when showing the illuminated sign-available day and night at taxi ranks or called by telephone*

Bus-Métro (subway) : *for full details see the Michelin Plan de Paris n° 11. The metro is quicker but the bus is good for sightseeing and practical for short distances.*

POSTAL SERVICES

Local post offices : *open Mondays to Fridays 8am to 7pm ; Saturdays 8am to noon*

General Post Office : *52 rue du Louvre, 1st : open 24 hours, ✆ 01 40 28 76 00*

SHOPPING IN PARIS

Department stores : *boulevard Haussmann, rue de Rivoli and rue de Sèvres*

Exclusive shops and boutiques : *faubourg St-Honoré, rue de la Paix and rue Royale, avenue Montaigne.*

Antiques and second-hand goods : *Swiss Village (avenue de la Motte Picquet), Louvre des Antiquaires (place du Palais Royal), Flea Market (Porte Clignancourt).*

TIPPING

Service is generally included in hotel and restaurants bills but you may choose to leave more than the expected tip to the staff. Taxi-drivers, porters, barbers and theatre or cinema attendants also expect a small gratuity.

BREAKDOWN SERVICE

Some garages in central and outer Paris operate a 24 hour breakdown service. If you breakdown the police are usually able to help by indicating the nearest one.

SPEED LIMITS

The maximum permitted speed in built up areas is 50 km/h - 31 mph ; on motorways the speed limit is 130 km/h - 80 mph and 110 km/h - 68 mph on dual carriageways. On all other roads 90 km/h - 56 mph.

SEAT BELTS

The wearing of seat belts is compulsory for drivers and all passengers.

PARIS AND ENVIRONS

Maps: 54, 55, 56, 57 G. Paris.

Population : *Paris 2 147 857 ; Ile-de-France region : 10 952 011.*

Altitude : *Observatory : 60 m ; place Concorde : 34 m*

Air Terminals :

To ORLY

Orly Bus *(RATP) ☎ 08 36 68 77 14 from : place Denfert-Rochereau – 14th (exit RER)*

to ROISSY

Roissy Bus *(RATP) ☎ 08 36 68 77 14 from : Opéra, rue Scribe (angle rue Auber) 9th*

Orly *(Air France Bus) ☎ 01 41 56 89 00 from : Montparnasse, rue du Cdt-Mouchotte, Near SNCF station, 14th ; from : Invalides Aérogare, 2 rue Pelterie, 7th*

Roissy – CDG1 – CDG2 *(Air France Bus) from : Etoile, place Ch.-De-Gaulle, angle 1 avenue Carnot 17th, from : Porte Maillot, Palais des Congrès, near Méridien Hôtel, 17th*

Paris'Airports : *see Orly and Charles de Gaulle (Roissy)*

Railways, motorail : *information ☎ 01 53 90 20 20.*

ARRONDISSEMENTS

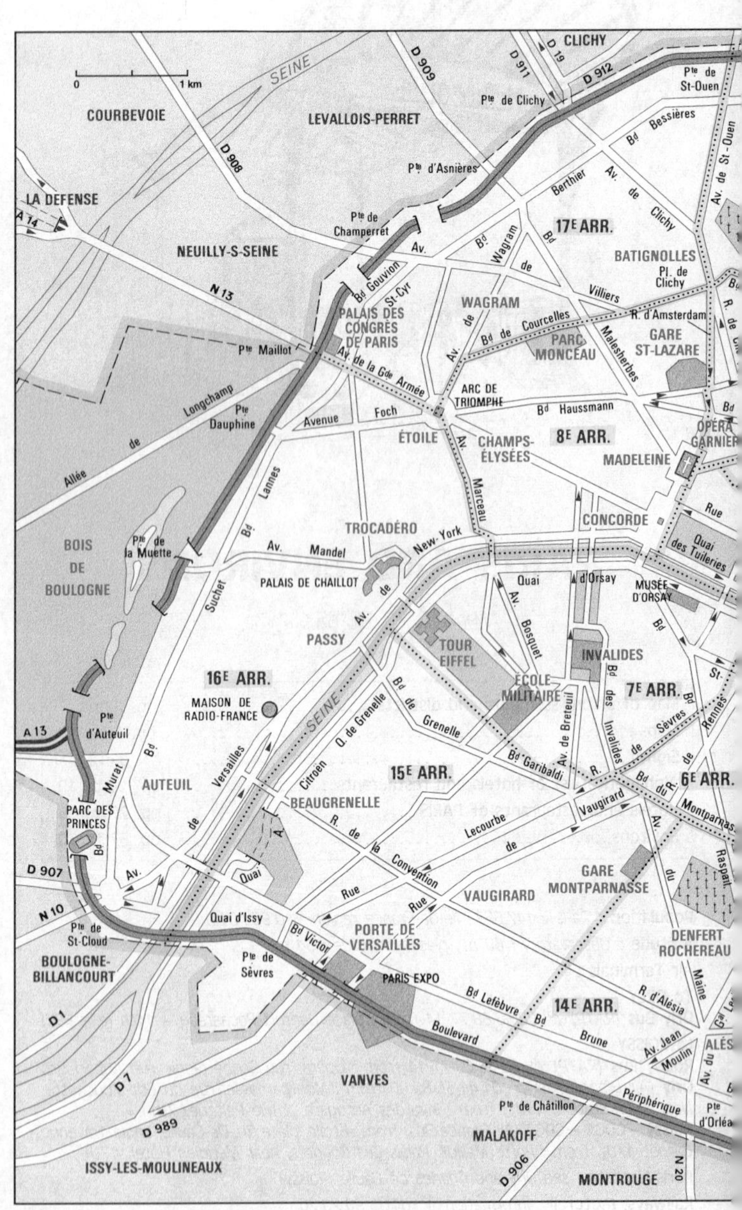

AND DISTRICTS

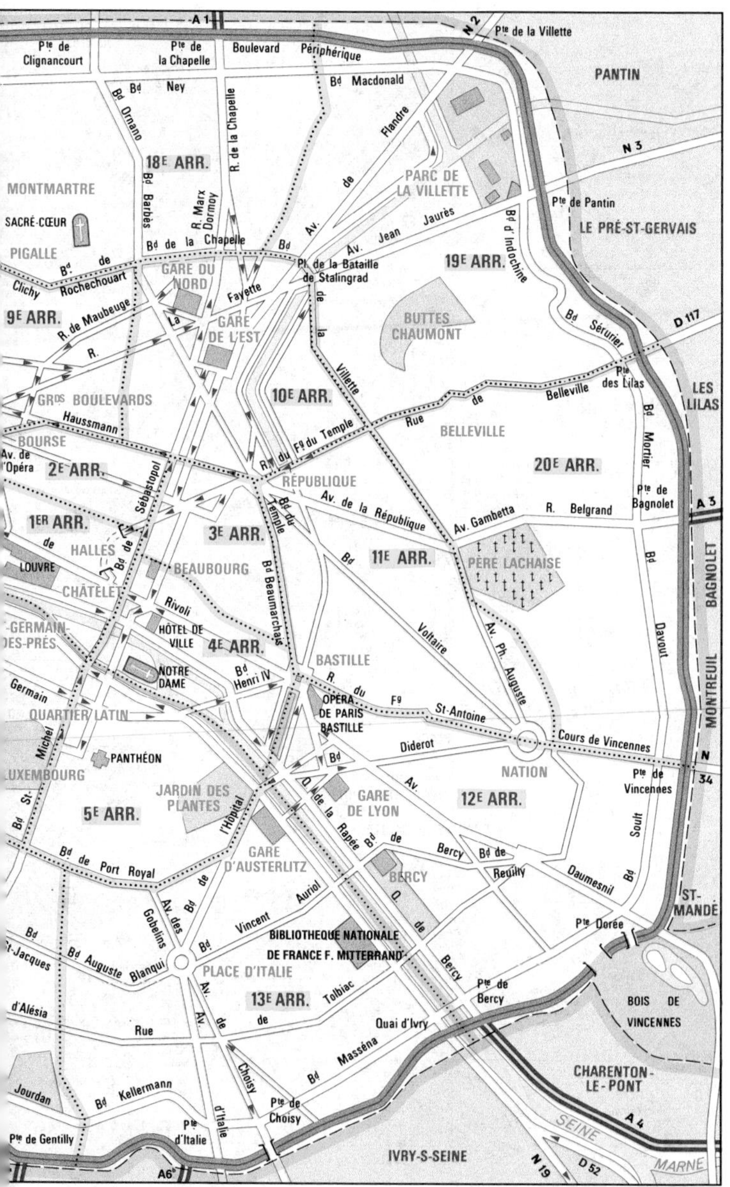

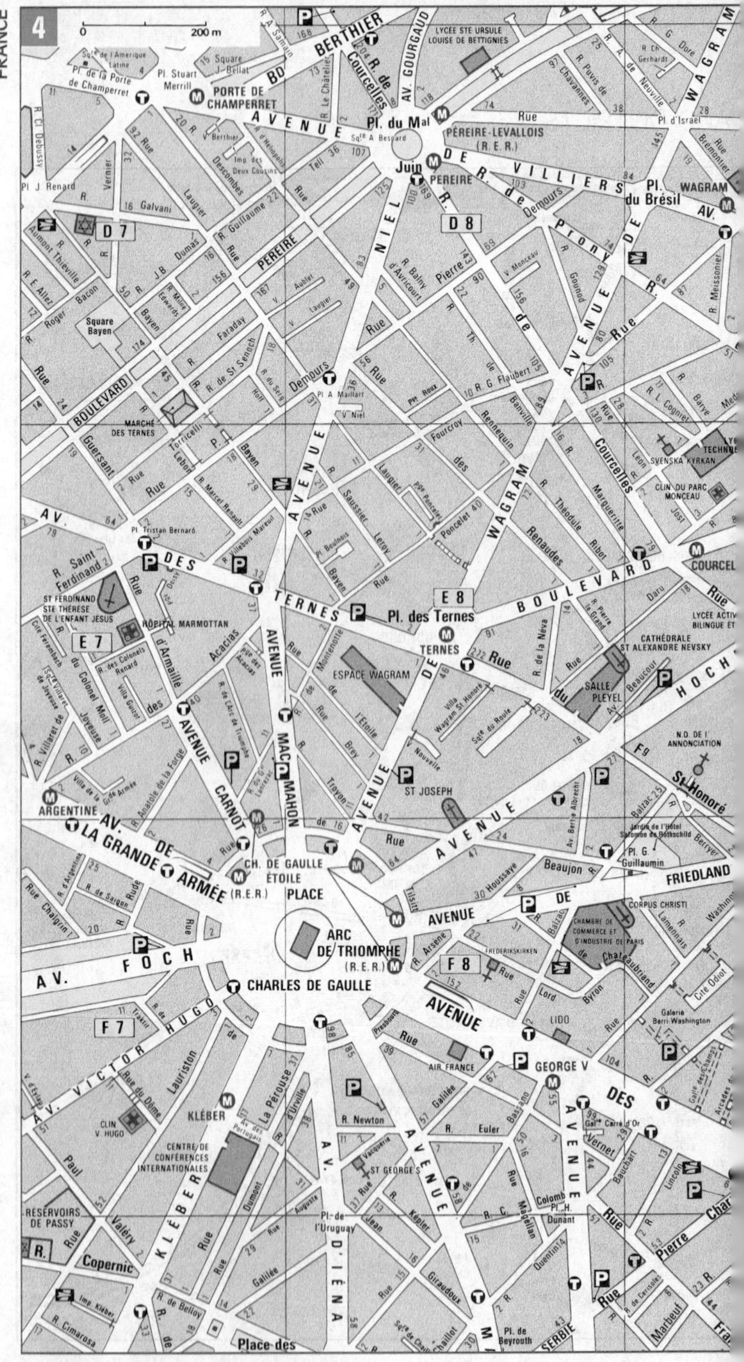
4
0
200 m
BD BERTHIER
PORTE DE CHAMPERRET
Pl. de la Porte de Champerret
Sq. de l'Amerique Latine
Square J. Bellat
Pl. Stuart Merrill
R. de Courcelles
AV. GOURGAUD
LYCÉE STE URSULE LOUISE DE BETTIGNIES
AVENUE
Pl. du Mal Juin
PEREIRE-LEVALLOIS (R.E.R.)
PEREIRE
R. DE VILLIERS
Pl. du Brésil
WAGRAM
AV. DE WAGRAM
R. de Prony
AVENUE DE VILLIERS
R. Ch. Gerhardt
R. A. de Neuville
R. Puvis de Chavannes
Pl. d'Israël
R. Brémontier
R. Meissonier
R. Cl. Debussy
Pl. J. Renard
R. Galvani
R. Laugier
R. Descombes
R. Guillaume Tell
Imp. des Deux Cousins
R. d'Héliopolis
R. V. Berthier
R. Vernier
D 7
D 8
R. Aumont Thiéville
R. E. Allez
R. Roger Bacon
Square Bayen
R. J.B. Dumas
R. Mille Edwards
R. Bayen
R. Faraday
R. de St Senoch
BOULEVARD PEREIRE
AVENUE NIEL
R. Balny d'Avricourt
R. Pierre Demours
R. Th. de Banville
R. G. Flaubert
R. Gounod
R. Médéric
R. L. Cogniet
R. Barye
Pl. A. Maillart
V. Niel
Pge Roux
R. Fourcroy
R. Rennequin
R. de Courcelles
R. Léon Jost
SVENSKA KYRKAN
CLIN. DU PARC MONCEAU
LYCÉE TECHNIQUE
MARCHÉ DES TERNES
R. Torricelli
R. Lebon
R. Poncelet
Pge Poncelet
R. Saussier Leroy
R. Laugier
Pl. Boulnois
AVENUE DE WAGRAM
R. Théodule Ribot
R. Marguerite
R. Renaudes
R. Guersant
R. Marcel Renault
R. Villebois Mareuil
Pl. Tristan Bernard
AV. DES TERNES
Pl. des Ternes
TERNES
BOULEVARD DE COURCELLES
COURCELLES
R. Pierre le Grand
R. de la Néva
R. Daru
LYCÉE ACTIV BILINGUE ÉT
CATHÉDRALE ST ALEXANDRE NEVSKY
SALLE PLEYEL
Av. Beaucour
AVENUE HOCHE
R. Saint Ferdinand
ST FERDINAND STE THÉRÈSE DE L'ENFANT JÉSUS
HÔPITAL MARMOTTAN
E 7
E 8
R. d'Armaillé
R. des Acacias
R. de l'Arc de Triomphe
AVENUE MAC MAHON
ESPACE WAGRAM
R. de l'Étoile
R. Brey
R. Troyon
Villa Wagram St Honoré
Sqe du Roule
V. Nouvelle
ST JOSEPH
Rue du Fg St Honoré
N.D. DE L'ANNONCIATION
Cité Ferembach
R. du Colonel Moll
R. Villaret de Joyeuse
R. des Colonels Renard
Villa Guizot
R. Anatole de la Forge
AVENUE CARNOT
ARGENTINE
AV. DE LA GRANDE ARMÉE
CH. DE GAULLE ÉTOILE (R.E.R.)
PLACE
ARC DE TRIOMPHE (R.E.R.)
CHARLES DE GAULLE
R. de Tilsitt
AVENUE DE FRIEDLAND
R. Beaujon
R. Arsène Houssaye
Av. Bertie Albrecht
R. Balzac
R. Berryer
Jardin de l'Hôtel Salomon de Rothschild
Pl. G. Guillaumin
CORPUS CHRISTI
CHAMBRE DE COMMERCE ET D'INDUSTRIE DE PARIS
R. de Chateaubriand
R. Lamennais
R. Washington
Cité Odiot
R. d'Argentine
R. de Saïgon
R. Rude
R. Chalgrin
AV. FOCH
F 7
F 8
FREDERIKSKIRKEN
R. Lord Byron
LIDO
Galerie Berri-Washington
AVENUE DES CHAMPS ÉLYSÉES
R. de Presbourg
R. Traktir
AV. VICTOR HUGO
R. Lauriston
R. du Dôme
CLIN. V. HUGO
KLÉBER
Av. des Portugais
R. La Pérouse
R. d'Urville
CENTRE DE CONFÉRENCES INTERNATIONALES
R. Paul Valéry
AV. KLÉBER
R. Dumont d'Urville
AV. D'IÉNA
R. Newton
R. Vacquerie
ST GEORGE'S
R. Galilée
R. Euler
R. Bassano
GEORGE V
AIR FRANCE
AVENUE MARCEAU
R. Jean Goujon
R. Magellan
Pl. H. Dunant
R. C. Colomb
AVENUE GEORGE V
R. Vernet
Galie Carré d'Or
R. Bauchart
R. Lincoln
R. Quentin Bauchart
R. Pierre Charron
Galie des Champs
Arcades des Champs
RÉSERVOIRS DE PASSY
R. Copernic
Imp. Kléber
R. Cimarosa
R. de Belloy
Rue Auguste Vacquerie
Pl. de l'Uruguay
R. Képler
R. Galilée
R. Jean Giraudoux
Sqe de Chaillot
R. de Chaillot
Pl. de Beyrouth
R. de Cérisoles
R. Marbeuf
R. François 1er
SERBIE
Place des

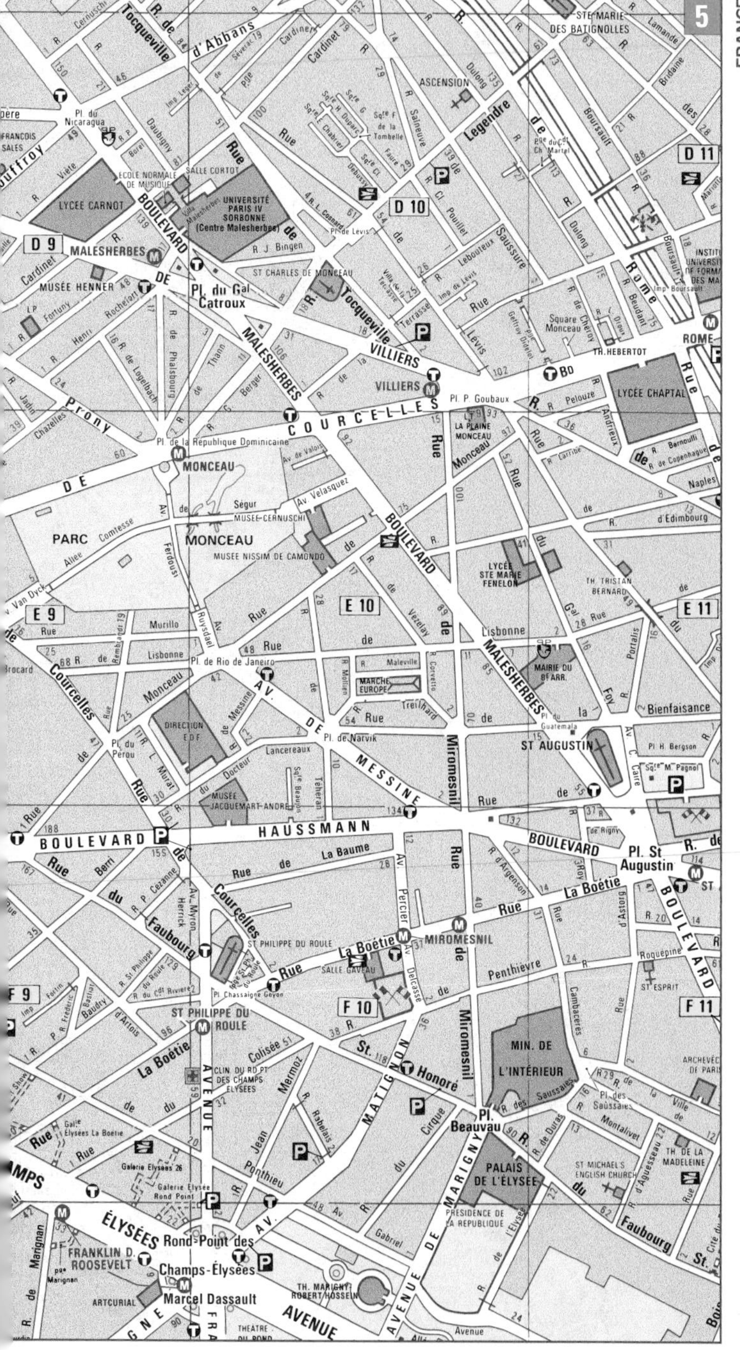
D 9
D 10
D 11
E 9
E 10
E 11
F 9
F 10
F 11
BOULEVARD DE MALESHERBES
BOULEVARD DE COURCELLES
BOULEVARD HAUSSMANN
AVENUE DE MESSINE
PARC MONCEAU
LYCEE CARNOT
UNIVERSITÉ PARIS IV SORBONNE (Centre Malesherbes)
ECOLE NORMALE DE MUSIQUE
SALLE CORTOT
MALESHERBES
MUSÉE HENNER
Pl. du Gal Catroux
ST CHARLES DE MONCEAU
ASCENSION
STE MARIE DES BATIGNOLLES
VILLIERS
Pl. de la République Dominicaine
MONCEAU
MUSEE CERNUSCHI
MUSEE NISSIM DE CAMONDO
LYCÉE CHAPTAL
LYCÉE STE MARIE FENELON
TH. TRISTAN BERNARD
TH. HEBERTOT
ROME
Square Monceau
Pl. de Rio de Janeiro
MARCHE EUROPE
MAIRIE DU 8E ARR.
DIRECTION E.D.F.
MUSÉE JACQUEMART-ANDRÉ
Pl. de Narvik
ST AUGUSTIN
Pl. St Augustin
ST PHILIPPE DU ROULE
SALLE GAVEAU
MIROMESNIL
MIN. DE L'INTÉRIEUR
PALAIS DE L'ÉLYSÉE
PRÉSIDENCE DE LA RÉPUBLIQUE
ST MICHAEL'S ENGLISH CHURCH
TH. DE LA MADELEINE
ST ESPRIT
CLIN. DU RD PT DES CHAMPS ÉLYSÉES
FRANKLIN D. ROOSEVELT
Rond-Point des Champs-Élysées
Marcel Dassault
ARTCURIAL
TH. MARIGNY ROBERT HOSSEIN
AVENUE DE MARIGNY
Rue du Faubourg St Honoré
Rue La Boétie
Rue de Miromesnil
Rue de Penthièvre
Rue de Lisbonne
Rue de Monceau
Rue de Prony
Rue de Rome
Rue Legendre
Rue de Tocqueville
Rue de Lévis
Rue de la Bienfaisance
Rue de Courcelles
ÉLYSÉES

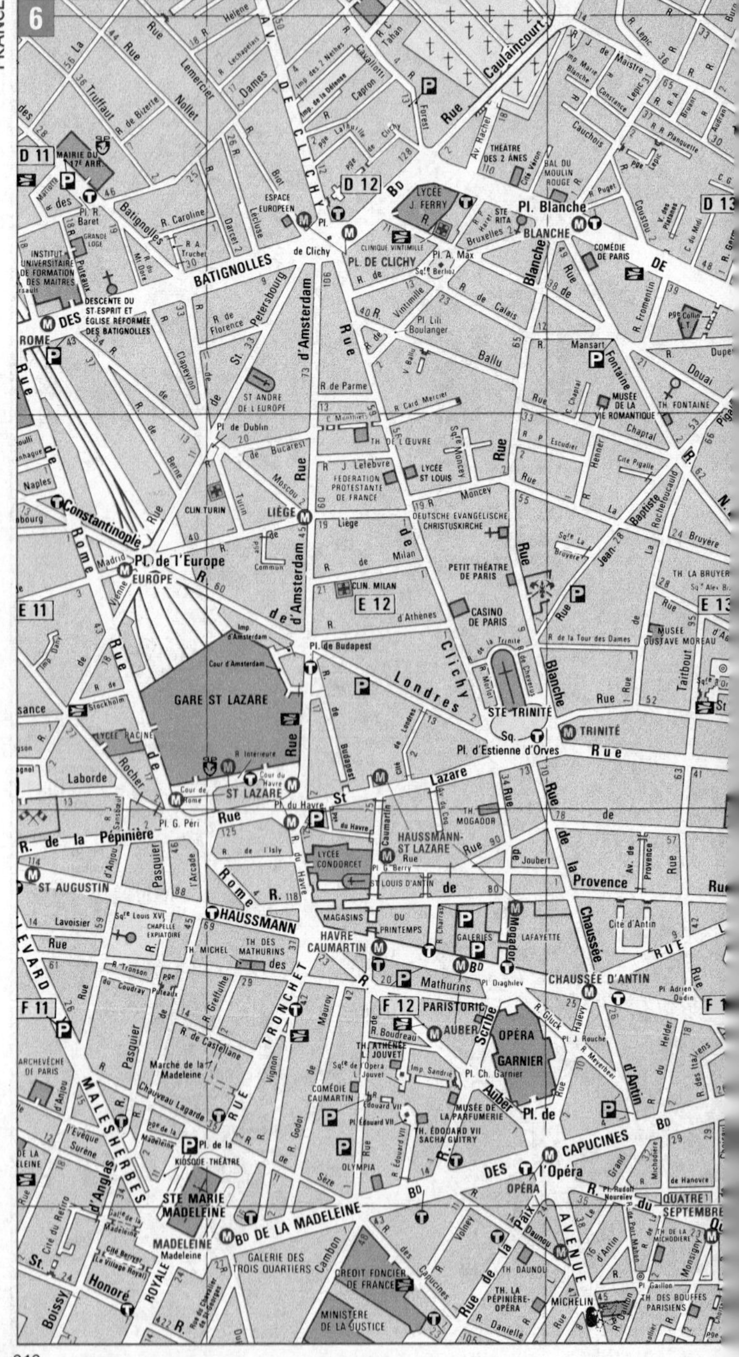
6
D 11
D 12
D 13
E 11
E 12
E 13
F 11
F 12
MAIRIE DU 17E ARR.
Rue Lemercier
Rue Nollet
Rue Truffaut
R. de Bizerte
Rue des Dames
AV. DE CLICHY
Rue Caulaincourt
THÉATRE DES 2 ANES
BAL DU MOULIN ROUGE
Pl. Blanche
BLANCHE
LYCÉE J. FERRY
ESPACE EUROPEEN
PL. DE CLICHY
CLINIQUE VINTIMILLE
BATIGNOLLES
R. Caroline
INSTITUT UNIVERSITAIRE DE FORMATION DES MAITRES
DESCENTE DU ST-ESPRIT ET ÉGLISE RÉFORMÉE DES BATIGNOLLES
ROME
COMÉDIE DE PARIS
R. de Calais
Rue Ballu
R. Fromentin
Rue de Douai
MUSÉE DE LA VIE ROMANTIQUE
TH. FONTAINE
Rue Fontaine
R. de Florence
Rue de St. Petersbourg
Rue d'Amsterdam
Rue de Clichy
ST ANDRE DE L'EUROPE
R. de Parme
TH. DE L'ŒUVRE
LYCÉE ST LOUIS
FEDERATION PROTESTANTE DE FRANCE
Rue Moncey
DEUTSCHE EVANGELISCHE CHRISTUSKIRCHE
Rue Chaptal
Rue de Bucarest
Rue de Moscou
Rue de Turin
CLIN. TURIN
LIÈGE
Rue de Liège
Rue de Milan
PETIT THÉATRE DE PARIS
Rue de Constantinople
Pl. de l'Europe
EUROPE
Rue de Rome
R. de Naples
R. de Madrid
R. de Vienne
CLIN. MILAN
CASINO DE PARIS
R. d'Athènes
Rue La Bruyère
Rue Jean-Baptiste Pigalle
TH. LA BRUYERE
MUSÉE GUSTAVE MOREAU
Rue Taitbout
R. de la Tour des Dames
Rue de la Rochefoucauld
GARE ST LAZARE
Cour d'Amsterdam
Pl. de Budapest
Rue de Londres
Rue de Budapest
STE TRINITÉ
TRINITÉ
Pl. d'Estienne d'Orves
Rue Blanche
Rue St Lazare
ST LAZARE
Cour de Rome
Cour du Havre
Pl. du Havre
LYCÉE RACINE
Rue Laborde
Rue du Rocher
R. de Stockholm
HAUSSMANN-ST LAZARE
TH. MOGADOR
Rue Joubert
Rue de Provence
Rue de la Chaussée d'Antin
Cité d'Antin
R. de la Pépinière
Pl. G. Péri
LYCÉE CONDORCET
ST LOUIS D'ANTIN
R. de l'Isly
Rue du Havre
Rue Caumartin
Rue Pasquier
Rue de l'Arcade
ST AUGUSTIN
Rue Lavoisier
Sq. Louis XVI
CHAPELLE EXPIATOIRE
HAUSSMANN
MAGASINS DU PRINTEMPS
GALERIES LAFAYETTE
Rue de Mogador
HAVRE CAUMARTIN
TH. DES MATHURINS
TH. MICHEL
Rue des Mathurins
CHAUSSÉE D'ANTIN
Pl. Diaghilev
PARISTORIC
AUBER
OPÉRA GARNIER
Pl. Ch. Garnier
Rue Scribe
Rue Auber
Rue Halévy
R. Meyerbeer
Rue du Helder
R. des Italiens
BOULEVARD MALESHERBES
ARCHEVÊCHÉ DE PARIS
Rue Tronchet
Rue Vignon
R. de Castellane
Marché de la Madeleine
Chauveau Lagarde
R. Godot de Mauroy
TH. ATHÉNÉE L. JOUVET
Sq. de l'Opéra L. Jouvet
COMÉDIE CAUMARTIN
MUSÉE DE LA PARFUMERIE
TH. ÉDOUARD VII SACHA GUITRY
Pl. Édouard VII
OLYMPIA
Rue de Sèze
Pl. de la Madeleine
KIOSQUE THÉATRE
STE MARIE MADELEINE
MADELEINE
BD DE LA MADELEINE
BD DES CAPUCINES
Pl. de l'Opéra
OPÉRA
AVENUE DE L'OPÉRA
QUATRE SEPTEMBRE
R. du Quatre Septembre
TH. DE LA MICHODIERE
R. de Hanovre
R. d'Antin
TH. DAUNOU
Rue Daunou
Rue de la Paix
TH. LA PÉPINIÈRE-OPÉRA
MICHELIN
TH. DES BOUFFES PARISIENS
Pl. Gaillon
Rue des Capucines
Rue Volney
R. Danielle Casanova
CREDIT FONCIER DE FRANCE
MINISTERE DE LA JUSTICE
GALERIE DES TROIS QUARTIERS
Rue Cambon
Rue Royale
Rue St. Honoré
Cité Berryer (Le Village Royal)
R. Boissy d'Anglas
R. de Surène
R. de l'Evêque
Cité du Retiro
R. d'Anjou

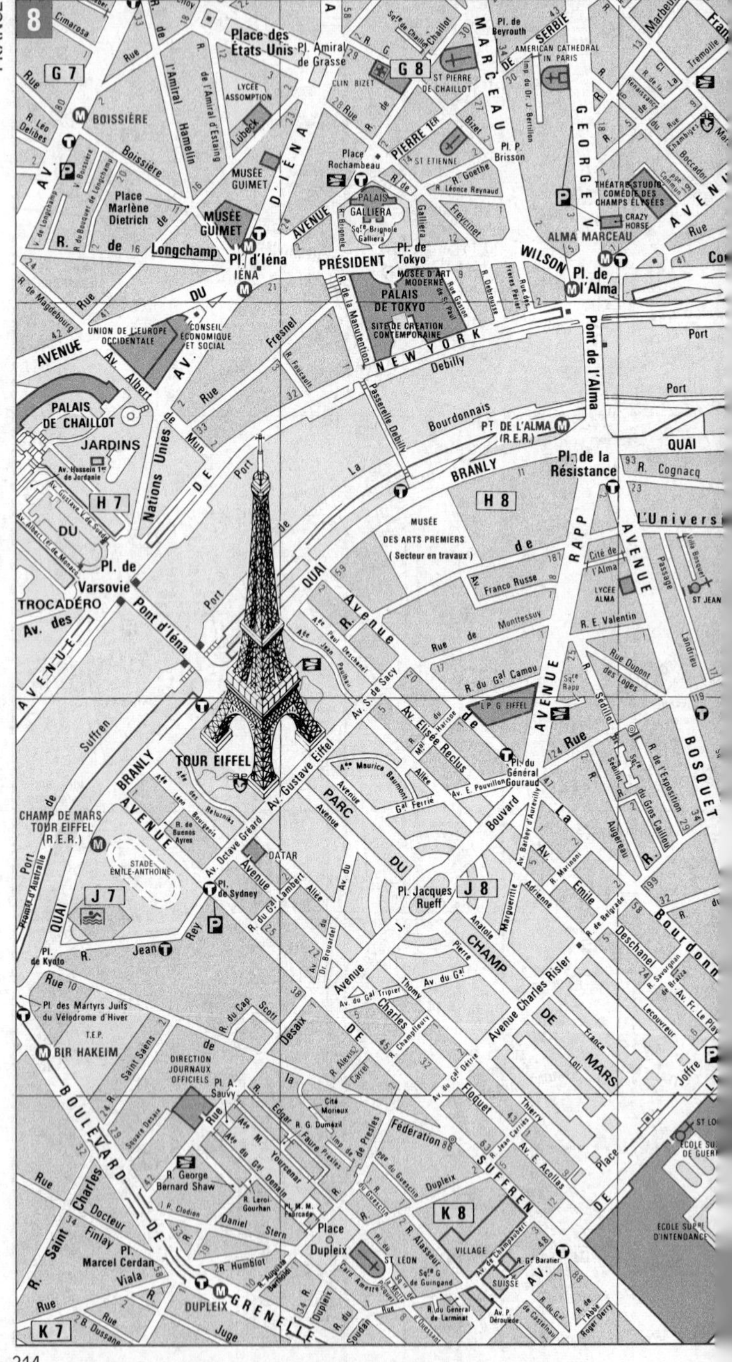
8
G 7
G 8
H 7
H 8
J 7
J 8
K 7
K 8
Cimarosa
BOISSIÈRE
R. Léo Delibes
Boissière
Place Marlène Dietrich
R. de Longchamp
l'Amiral Hamelin
R. de l'Amiral d'Estaing
Place des États Unis
Pl. Amiral de Grasse
LYCÉE ASSOMPTION
Lübeck
MUSÉE GUIMET
AVENUE D'IÉNA
Pl. d'Iéna
IÉNA
CLIN BIZET
ST PIERRE DE CHAILLOT
Place Rochambeau
PIERRE 1ER
ST ETIENNE
PALAIS GALLIERA
R. Galliera
R. Goethe
R. Léonce Reynaud
Freycinet
MARCEAU
Pl. de Beyrouth
SERBIE
AMERICAN CATHEDRAL IN PARIS
Imp. du Dr. J. Bertillon
Pl. P. Brisson
GEORGE V
THÉATRE STUDIO COMÉDIE DES CHAMPS ÉLYSÉES
CRAZY HORSE
ALMA MARCEAU
Marbeuf
Tremoille
Boccador
PRÉSIDENT WILSON
Pl. de Tokyo
MUSÉE D'ART MODERNE
PALAIS DE TOKYO
SITE DE CRÉATION CONTEMPORAINE
R. Gaston de St Paul
R. Debrousse
Rue des Frères Périer
Pl. de l'Alma
R. de la Manutention
Fresnel
R. Fouquet
NEW YORK
Debilly
Passerelle Debilly
Pont de l'Alma
Port
R. de Magdebourg
AVENUE DU
UNION DE L'EUROPE OCCIDENTALE
CONSEIL ÉCONOMIQUE ET SOCIAL
Av. Albert de Mun
PALAIS DE CHAILLOT
JARDINS
Av. Hussein 1er de Jordanie
Av. Gustave V de Suède
Av. Albert 1er de Monaco
Nations Unies
Port Bourdonnais
PT DE L'ALMA (R.E.R.)
BRANLY
Pl. de la Résistance
QUAI
R. Cognacq
L'Universi
MUSÉE DES ARTS PREMIERS (Secteur en travaux)
Franco Russe
Cité de l'Alma
LYCÉE ALMA
R. E. Valentin
RAPP
AVENUE
Passage Landrieu
Villa Bosquet
ST JEAN
Pl. de Varsovie
TROCADÉRO
Av. des
Pont d'Iéna
QUAI
Avenue
Allée Paul Deschanel
Allée Jean Paulhan
Rue de Monttessuy
R. du Gal Camou
LPG EIFFEL
Sq. Rapp
Rue Dupont des Loges
Sédillot
Av. S. de Sacy
Av. Élisée Reclus
R. du Mal Harispe
Pl. du Général Gouraud
BOSQUET
R. de l'Exposition
R. du Gros Caillou
Suffren
BRANLY
TOUR EIFFEL
Av. Gustave Eiffel
Allée Maurice Baumont
Allée des Refuzniks
Allée Léon Bourgeois
R. de Buenos Ayres
Av. E. Pouvillon
Gal Ferrié
CHAMP DE MARS TOUR EIFFEL (R.E.R.)
STADE ÉMILE-ANTHOINE
Av. Octave Gréard
DATAR
PARC DU CHAMP DE MARS
Bouvard
Av. Barbey d'Aurevilly
Av. de La Bourdonnais
Augereau
R. Marinoni
Adrienne
Marguerite
Av. Émile Deschanel
Pl. Jacques Rueff
Pl. de Sydney
R. de Belgrade
Bourdonnais
R. Savorgnan de Brazza
Av. Fr. Le Play
Port
Promd d'Australie
QUAI
Pl. de Kyoto
R. Jean Rey
Allée du Dr Brouardel
R. du Gal Lambert
Av. du
Anatole
Pierre
Allée Thomy Thierry
Av. du Gal Tripier
Av. du Gal
Avenue Charles Risler
CHAMP DE MARS
Lecouvreur
Rue
Pl. des Martyrs Juifs du Vélodrome d'Hiver
T.E.P.
BIR HAKEIM
R. du Cap. Scott
Desaix
Avenue Charles Floquet
R. Alexis Carrel
R. Champfleury
Av. du Gal Détrie
France
Loti
Joffre
DIRECTION JOURNAUX OFFICIELS
Pl. A. Sauvy
Rue de la Fédération
R. Edgar Faure
R. G. Dumézil
Cité Morieux
Imp. de Presles
R. Jean Carriès
Av. E. Acollas
Place
ST LO
ÉCOLE SUP. DE GUERRE
Saint Saens
Square Desaix
BOULEVARD DE GRENELLE
R. George Bernard Shaw
Allée M. Yourcenar
Allée du Gal Denain
R. Leroi-Gourhan
Pl. M. M. Fabrcade
Dupleix
Pge du Guesclin
R. du Guesclin
SUFFREN
ÉCOLE SUPre D'INTENDANCE
Rue Charles Docteur Finlay
R. Saint
Pl. Marcel Cerdan
Viala
R. Clodion
Daniel Stern
Place Dupleix
Pl. du ST LÉON
R. Alasseur
Sq. G. de Guingand
VILLAGE SUISSE
Av. de Champaubert
R. Gal Baratier
AV.
R. de l'Abbé Roger Derry
R. du Gal de Castelnau
R. Humblot
R. Auguste Bartholdi
Card Amette
Sq. de la Motte Picquet
R. du Général de Larminat
Av. P. Déroulède
R. Dupleix
DUPLEIX
GRENELLE
Juge
R. B. Dussane
Rue
R. du Soudan
Rue d'Ouessant

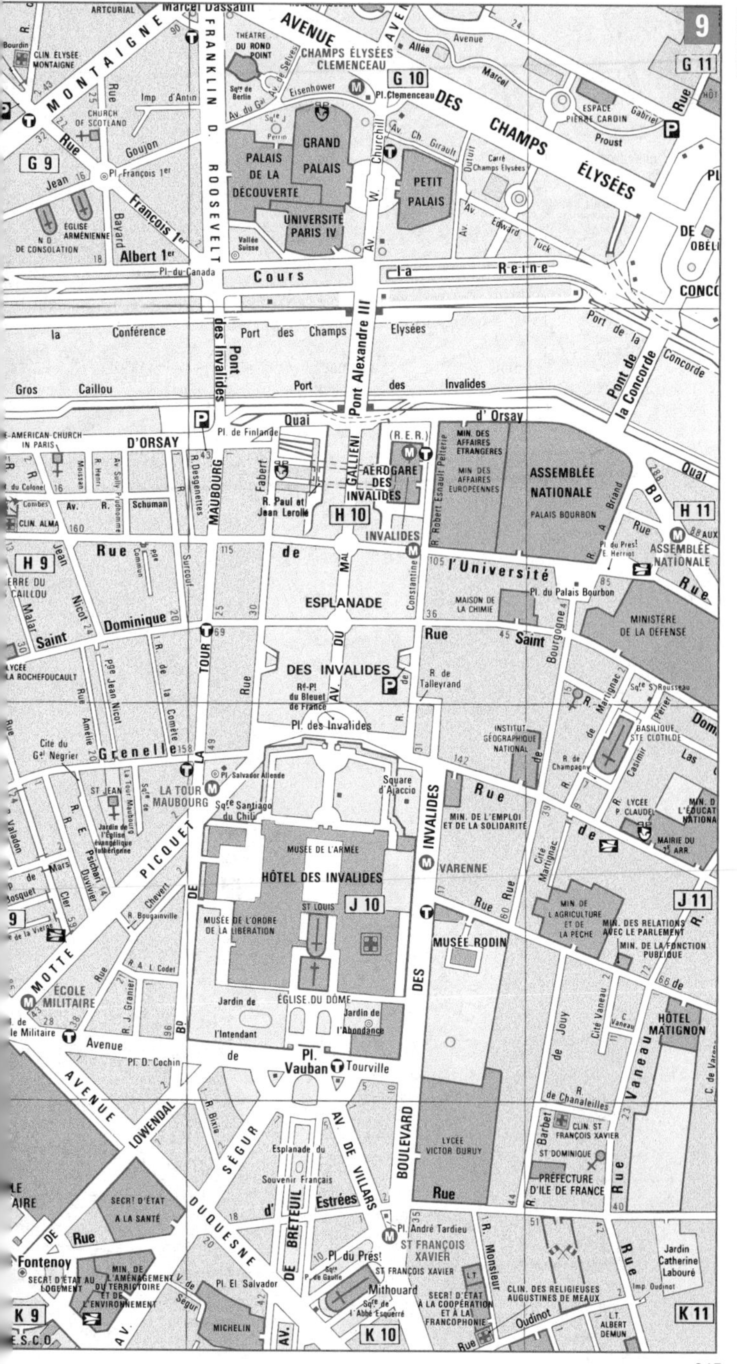
9
G 10
G 11
G 9
H 9
H 10
H 11
J 10
J 11
K 9
K 10
K 11
AVENUE DES CHAMPS ÉLYSÉES
Avenue Marcel
Allée Marcel Proust
ESPACE PIERRE CARDIN
Rue Gabriel
THEATRE DU ROND POINT
CHAMPS ÉLYSÉES CLEMENCEAU
Pl. Clemenceau
Eisenhower
Sq^re de Berlin
Av. de Selves
Av. du G^al
ARTCURIAL
Marcel Dassault
FRANKLIN D. ROOSEVELT
MONTAIGNE
CLIN. ELYSÉE MONTAIGNE
Bourdin
CHURCH OF SCOTLAND
Imp. d'Antin
Rue Goujon
Rue Jean
Pl. François 1er
François 1er
Bayard
Albert 1er
ÉGLISE ARMÉNIENNE
N.D. DE CONSOLATION
PALAIS DE LA DÉCOUVERTE
GRAND PALAIS
UNIVERSITÉ PARIS IV
PETIT PALAIS
Vallée Suisse
Av. W. Churchill
Av. Ch. Girault
Av. Dutuit
Carré Champs Elysées
Av. Edward Tuck
Pl. du Canada
Cours la Reine
CONC
DE OBÉL
Port de la Conférence
Port des Champs Elysées
Port du Gros Caillou
Port des Invalides
Pont des Invalides
Pont Alexandre III
Pont de la Concorde
Port de la Concorde
Quai d'Orsay
D'ORSAY
Pl. de Finlande
AMERICAN CHURCH IN PARIS
(R.E.R.)
AÉROGARE DES INVALIDES
GALLIENI
R. Paul et Jean Lerolle
Fabert
INVALIDES
MIN. DES AFFAIRES ÉTRANGÈRES
MIN. DES AFFAIRES EUROPÉENNES
ASSEMBLÉE NATIONALE
PALAIS BOURBON
R. Robert Esnault Pelterie
R. A. Briand
Quai
BD
Pl. du Pres! E. Herriot
ASSEMBLÉE NATIONALE
Rue Aux
R. Desgenettes
MAUBOURG
R. Moissan
R. Henri
Av. Sully Prudhomme
R. du Colonel
Combes
Av. R. Schuman
CLIN. ALMA
Rue de l'Université
Jean Nicot
Pge Commun
Surcouf
ESPLANADE DES INVALIDES
MAL
Constantine
MAISON DE LA CHIMIE
Pl. du Palais Bourbon
Bourgogne
MINISTÈRE DE LA DÉFENSE
Rue Saint Dominique
Malar
LYCÉE LA ROCHEFOUCAULT
Pge Jean Nicot
Rue Amélie
R. de la Comète
TOUR
R. de Talleyrand
Rd-Pt du Bleuet de France
Pl. des Invalides
Sq^re S. Rousseau
R. Martignac
Périer
BASILIQUE STE CLOTILDE
Las
Casimir
INSTITUT GÉOGRAPHIQUE NATIONAL
R. de Champagny
Cité du Gal Negrier
Rue de Grenelle
LA
Pl. Salvador Allende
ST JEAN
LA TOUR MAUBOURG
Sq^re Santiago du Chili
Square d'Ajaccio
Jardin de l'Église évangélique luthérienne
R. Psichari
R. Duvivier
R. Cler
Valadon
Mars
PICQUET
MUSÉE DE L'ARMÉE
HÔTEL DES INVALIDES
ST LOUIS
MUSÉE DE L'ORDRE DE LA LIBÉRATION
INVALIDES
VARENNE
Rue de Varenne
MIN. DE L'EMPLOI ET DE LA SOLIDARITÉ
R. LYCÉE P. CLAUDEL
MAIRIE DU 7e ARR.
Cité Martignac
MIN. DE L'AGRICULTURE ET DE LA PÊCHE
MIN. DES RELATIONS AVEC LE PARLEMENT
MIN. DE LA FONCTION PUBLIQUE
MUSÉE RODIN
R. Chevert
R. Bougainville
R. A. L. Codet
R. J. Granier
MOTTE
ÉCOLE MILITAIRE
Jardin de l'Intendant
ÉGLISE DU DÔME
Jardin de l'Abondance
DES
BD.
Avenue de Tourville
Pl. D. Cochin
Pl. Vauban
Cité Vaneau
C. Vaneau
Rue Vaneau
HÔTEL MATIGNON
C. de Varenne
Rue de Jouy
R. de Chanaleilles
AVENUE LOWENDAL
R. Bixio
SÉGUR
Esplanade du Souvenir Français
AV. DE VILLARS
BOULEVARD
LYCÉE VICTOR DURUY
Barbet
CLIN. ST FRANÇOIS XAVIER
ST DOMINIQUE
PRÉFECTURE D'ILE DE FRANCE
SECR^T D'ÉTAT À LA SANTÉ
DUQUESNE
Rue d'Estrées
DE BRETEUIL
Pl. André Tardieu
ST FRANÇOIS XAVIER
R. Monsieur
Rue de Fontenoy
SECR^T D'ÉTAT AU LOGEMENT
MIN. DE L'AMÉNAGEMENT DU TERRITOIRE ET DE L'ENVIRONNEMENT
Av. de Ségur
Pl. El Salvador
Pl. du Prés! Mithouard
Sq^re P. de Gaulle
Sq^re de l'Abbé Esquerré
SECR^T D'ÉTAT À LA COOPÉRATION ET À LA FRANCOPHONIE
CLIN. DES RELIGIEUSES AUGUSTINES DE MEAUX
Rue Oudinot
Imp. Oudinot
L.T. ALBERT DEMUN
Jardin Catherine Labouré
MICHELIN
AV.
E.S.C.O.

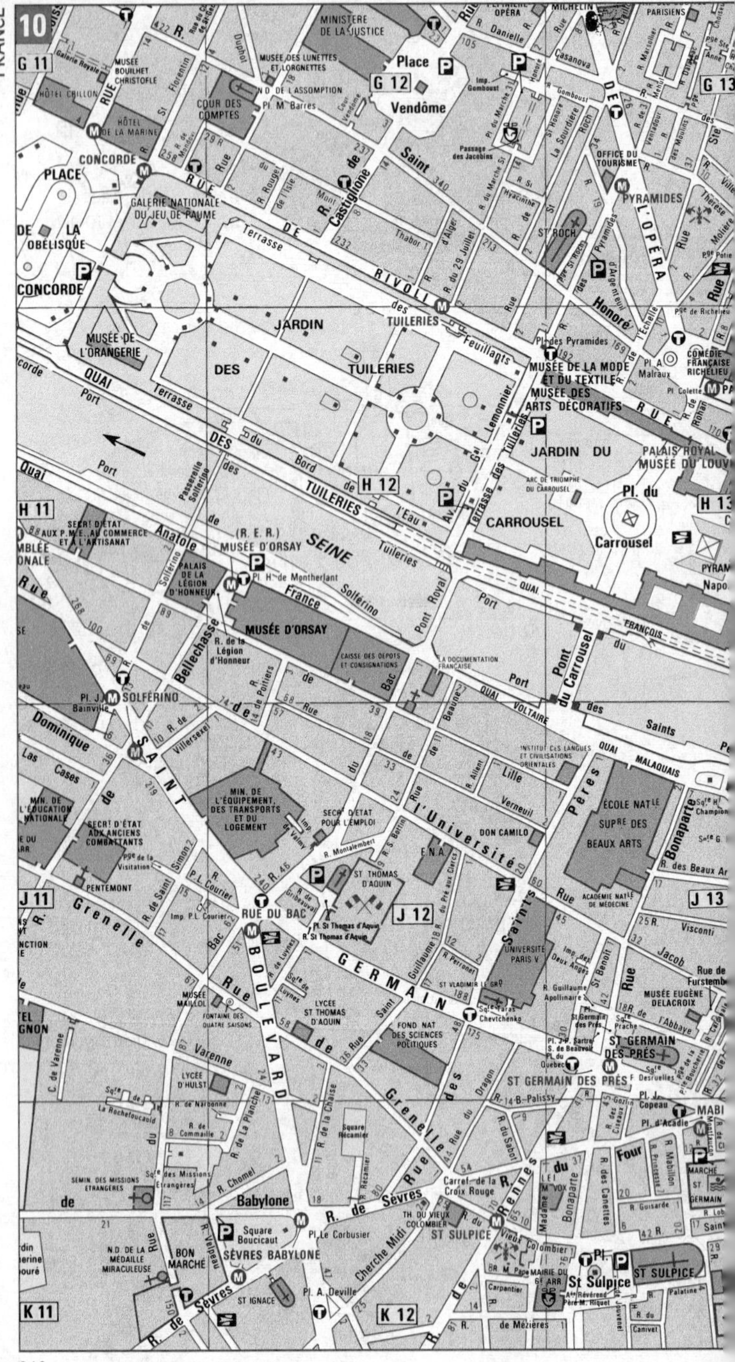
10
G 11
G 12
G 13
H 11
H 12
H 13
J 11
J 12
J 13
K 11
K 12
MINISTÈRE DE LA JUSTICE
MUSÉE DES LUNETTES ET LORGNETTES
N D DE L'ASSOMPTION
Pl. M. Barrès
Place Vendôme
MUSÉE BOUILHET CHRISTOFLE
Galerie Royale
HÔTEL CRILLON
HÔTEL DE LA MARINE
COUR DES COMPTES
CONCORDE
PLACE DE LA CONCORDE
OBÉLISQUE
GALERIE NATIONALE DU JEU DE PAUME
RUE DE RIVOLI
R. de Castiglione
Saint Honoré
Passage des Jacobins
ST ROCH
OFFICE DU TOURISME
PYRAMIDES
DE L'OPÉRA
Pl. des Pyramides
COMÉDIE FRANÇAISE RICHELIEU
Pl. A. Malraux
MUSÉE DE LA MODE ET DU TEXTILE
MUSÉE DES ARTS DÉCORATIFS
JARDIN DES TUILERIES
TUILERIES
MUSÉE DE L'ORANGERIE
QUAI DES TUILERIES
JARDIN DU CARROUSEL
ARC DE TRIOMPHE DU CARROUSEL
PALAIS ROYAL MUSÉE DU LOUVRE
Pl. du Carrousel
SEINE
Passerelle Solferino
Pont Royal
QUAI FRANÇOIS
Pont du Carrousel
Quai Anatole France
SECRt D'ETAT AUX P.M.E., AU COMMERCE ET À L'ARTISANAT
(R. E. R.) MUSÉE D'ORSAY
PALAIS DE LA LÉGION D'HONNEUR
Pl. H. de Montherlant
MUSÉE D'ORSAY
CAISSE DES DÉPOTS ET CONSIGNATIONS
LA DOCUMENTATION FRANÇAISE
QUAI VOLTAIRE
QUAI MALAQUAIS
INSTITUT DES LANGUES ET CIVILISATIONS ORIENTALES
SOLFÉRINO
Pl. J. Bainville
Rue de Bellechasse
R. de la Légion d'Honneur
Rue de Lille
Rue de Verneuil
Rue de l'Université
Rue Saint Dominique
Las Cases
BOULEVARD SAINT GERMAIN
MIN. DE L'ÉQUIPEMENT, DES TRANSPORTS ET DU LOGEMENT
SECRt D'ETAT POUR L'EMPLOI
MIN. DE L'ÉDUCATION NATIONALE
SECRt D'ÉTAT AUX ANCIENS COMBATTANTS
PENTEMONT
DON CAMILO
E.N.A.
ST THOMAS D'AQUIN
Pl. St Thomas d'Aquin
RUE DU BAC
ÉCOLE NATle SUPRe DES BEAUX ARTS
ACADÉMIE NATle DE MÉDECINE
Rue des Saints Pères
Rue Bonaparte
R. des Beaux Arts
R. Visconti
Rue Jacob
UNIVERSITÉ PARIS V
MUSÉE EUGÈNE DELACROIX
Rue de Grenelle
MUSÉE MAILLOL
FONTAINE DES QUATRE SAISONS
LYCÉE ST THOMAS D'AQUIN
FOND NAT DES SCIENCES POLITIQUES
ST GERMAIN DES PRÉS
Pl. du Québec
Rue de Varenne
LYCÉE D'HULST
Square Récamier
R. de Sèvres
Babylone
SEMIN. DES MISSIONS ÉTRANGÈRES
Carref. de la Croix Rouge
ST SULPICE
Square Boucicaut
Pl. Le Corbusier
SÈVRES BABYLONE
BON MARCHÉ
N.D. DE LA MÉDAILLE MIRACULEUSE
ST IGNACE
Pl. A. Deville
Cherche Midi
Rue de Rennes
Rue du Four
MAIRIE DU 6e ARR
St Sulpice
MARCHÉ ST GERMAIN
MABILLON

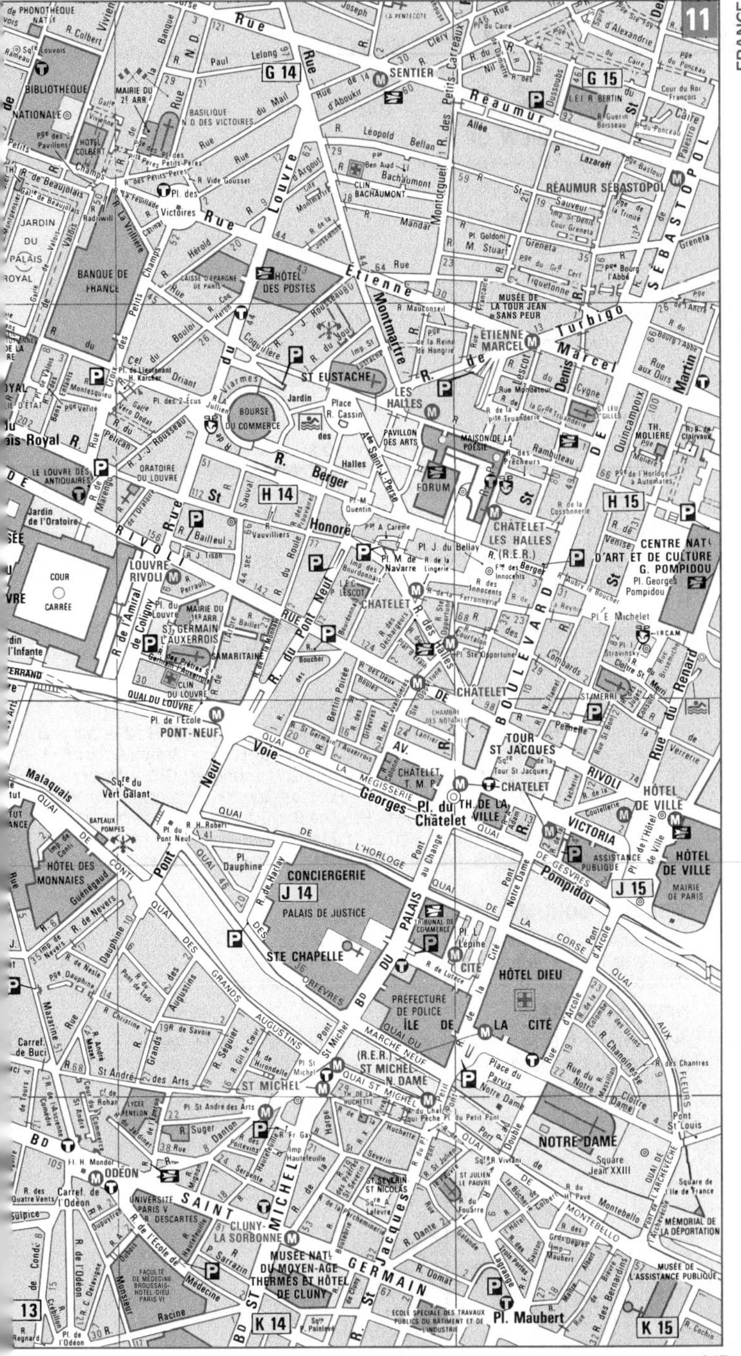
G 14
G 15
H 14
H 15
J 14
J 15
K 14
K 15
13
BIBLIOTHÈQUE NATIONALE
BANQUE DE FRANCE
JARDIN DU PALAIS ROYAL
BASILIQUE N.D. DES VICTOIRES
MAIRIE DU 2E ARR.
HÔTEL COLBERT
Pl. des Victoires
HÔTEL DES POSTES
CAISSE D'EPARGNE DE PARIS
SENTIER
Réaumur
RÉAUMUR SÉBASTOPOL
Rue Étienne Marcel
Montmartre
ÉTIENNE MARCEL
MUSÉE DE LA TOUR JEAN SANS PEUR
Turbigo
BOURSE DU COMMERCE
ST EUSTACHE
LES HALLES
PAVILLON DES ARTS
MAISON DE LA POÉSIE
FORUM
Rue Berger
Honoré
CHÂTELET LES HALLES (R.E.R.)
CENTRE NATL D'ART ET DE CULTURE G. POMPIDOU
Pl. Georges Pompidou
Rue Quincampoix
Rue Rambuteau
Boulevard de Sébastopol
Rue St Martin
Rue Rivoli
COUR CARRÉE
LOUVRE RIVOLI
MAIRIE DU 1ER ARR.
ST GERMAIN L'AUXERROIS
SAMARITAINE
ORATOIRE DU LOUVRE
LE LOUVRE DES ANTIQUAIRES
Rue du Pont Neuf
CHÂTELET
TOUR ST JACQUES
Sq. de la Tour St Jacques
CHAMBRE DES NOTAIRES
PONT-NEUF
QUAI DU LOUVRE
Sq. du Vert Galant
Quai de la Mégisserie
Voie Georges Pompidou
Pl. du Châtelet
CHÂTELET T.M.P.
TH. DE LA VILLE
HÔTEL DE VILLE
MAIRIE DE PARIS
ASSISTANCE PUBLIQUE
VICTORIA
HÔTEL DES MONNAIES
Quai de Conti
Pont Neuf
Pl. Dauphine
Quai de l'Horloge
CONCIERGERIE
PALAIS DE JUSTICE
STE CHAPELLE
TRIBUNAL DE COMMERCE
Pont au Change
Pont Notre Dame
Bd du Palais
CITÉ
HÔTEL DIEU
PRÉFECTURE DE POLICE
ÎLE DE LA CITÉ
Quai des Grands Augustins
Quai des Orfèvres
Quai de la Corse
Pont d'Arcole
Pont St Michel
Quai du Marché Neuf
ST MICHEL
(R.E.R.) ST MICHEL N. DAME
Quai St Michel
Place du Parvis Notre Dame
NOTRE DAME
Square Jean XXIII
Pont St Louis
Square de l'Île de France
MÉMORIAL DE LA DÉPORTATION
Quai aux Fleurs
Quai de l'Archevêché
Carref. de Buci
Rue St André des Arts
ODÉON
Carref. de l'Odéon
UNIVERSITÉ PARIS V R. DESCARTES
FACULTÉ DE MÉDECINE BROUSSAIS-HÔTEL-DIEU PARIS VI
Bd Saint Germain
Bd St Michel
CLUNY-LA SORBONNE
MUSÉE NATL DU MOYEN-AGE THERMES ET HÔTEL DE CLUNY
Rue St Jacques
ST SEVERIN ST NICOLAS
ST JULIEN LE PAUVRE
Sq. R. Viviani
Quai de Montebello
Pl. Maubert
ÉCOLE SPÉCIALE DES TRAVAUX PUBLICS DU BÂTIMENT ET DE L'INDUSTRIE
MUSÉE DE L'ASSISTANCE PUBLIQUE
R. des Bernardins

SIGHTS

How to make the most of a trip to Paris – some ideas :

A BIRD'S-EYE VIEW OF PARIS

★★★ *Eiffel Tower* J 7 – ★★★ *Montparnasse Tower* LM 11 – ★★★ *Notre-Dame Towers* K 15 – ★★★ *Sacré Cœur Dome* D 14 – ★★★ *Arc de Triomphe platform* F 8.

FAMOUS PARISIAN VISTAS

★★★ *Arc de Triomphe – Champs-Élysées – place de la Concorde : ⩽ from the rond point on the Champs-Élysées* G 10.

★★ *The Madeleine – place de la Concorde – Palais Bourbon (National Assembly) : ⩽ from the Obelisk in the middle of place de la Concorde* G 11.

★★★ *The Trocadéro – Eiffel Tower – Ecole Militaire : ⩽ from the terrace of the Palais de Chaillot* H 7.

★★ *The Invalides – Grand and Petit Palais : ⩽ from Pont Alexandre III* H 10.

MAIN MONUMENTS

The Louvre★★★ *(Cour Carrée, Perrault's Colonnade, Pyramid)* H 13 – *Eiffel Tower*★★★ J 7 – *Notre-Dame Cathedral*★★★ K 15 – *Sainte-Chapelle*★★★ J 14 – *Arc de Triomphe*★★★ F 8 – *The Invalides*★★★ *(Napoleon's Tomb)* J 10 – *Palais-Royal*★★ H 13 – *The Opéra*★★ F 12 – *The Conciergerie*★★ J 14 – *The Panthéon*★★ L 14 – *Luxembourg*★★ *(Palace and Gardens)* KL 13.

Churches : *Notre-Dame Cathedral*★★★ K 15 – *The Madeleine*★★ G 11 – *Sacré Cœur*★★ D 14 – *St-Germain-des-Prés*★★ J 13 – *St-Etienne-du-Mont*★★ – *St-Germain-l'Auxerrois*★★ H 14.

In the Marais : *place des Vosges*★★ – *Hôtel Lamoignon*★★ – *Hôtel Guénégaud*★★ *(Museum of the Chase and of Nature)* – *Hôtel de Soubise*★★ *(Historical Museum of France) by* HJ 15.

MAIN MUSEUMS

The Louvre★★★ H 13 – *Musée d'Orsay*★★★ *(mid-19C to early 20C)* H 12 – *National Museum of Modern Art*★★★ *(Centre Georges-Pompidou)* H 15 – *Army Museum*★★★ *(Invalides)* J 10 – *Guimet*★★★ *(musée national des arts asiatiques)* G 7 – *Museum of Decorative Arts*★★ *(107 rue de Rivoli)* H 13 – *Hôtel de Cluny*★★ *(Museum of the Middle Ages and Roman Baths)* K 14 – *Rodin*★★ *(Hôtel de Biron)* J 10 – *Carnavalet*★★ *(History of Paris)* J 17 – *Picasso*★★ H 17 – *Cité de la Science et de l'Industrie*★★★ *(La Villette)* – *Marmottan*★★ *(Impressionist artists)* – *Orangerie*★★ *(from the Impressionists until 1930)* H 11.

MODERN MONUMENTS

La Défense★★ *(CNIT, Grande Arche)* – *Centre Georges-Pompidou*★★★ H 15 – *Forum des Halles* H 14 – *Institut du Monde Arabe*★ – *Opéra Paris-Bastille*★ – *Bercy (Palais Omnisports, Ministry of Finance)* – *Bibliothèque Nationale de France.*

PRETTY AREAS

Montmartre★★★ D 14 – *Ile St-Louis*★★ J 14 J 15 – *the Quays*★★ *(between Pont des Arts and Pont de Sully)* J 14 J 15 – *St Séverin district*★★ K 14 – *the Marais*★★★.

K 14, G 10 *: Reference letters and numbers on the town plans.*

Use MICHELIN *Green Guide* Paris *for a well-informed visit.*

Alphabetical list (Hotels and restaurants)

C

D

E

F

G

H - I

J - K

L

P

Q

R

S

T

U - V

W - X

Y - Z

HOTELS, RESTAURANTS

Listed by districts and arrondissements

(List of Hotels and Restaurants in alphabetical order, see pp 13 to 21)

G 12: These reference letters and numbers correspond to the squares on the Michelin maps : plan Michelin Paris no 54. Paris avec répertoire no 55. Paris du Nord au Sud no 56 et Paris pa Arrondissement no 57.

Consult any of the above publications when looking for a car park nearest to a listed establishment.

Opéra, Palais-Royal, Halles, Bourse.

1st and 2nd arrondissements.

1st: ✉ 75001

2nd: ✉ 75002

Ritz, 15 pl. Vendôme (1st) Ⓜ *Opéra* ☎ 01 43 16 30 30, *resa@ritzparis.com Fax 01 43 16 36 68,* – ⎮ 30 - 80. AE ⓓ GB JCB.
see ***L'Espadon*** below - ***Ritz Club*** (dinner only) *(closed 26 July-31 August, Sunday an Monday)* **Meals** a la carte 80/120 – - ***Bar Vendôme*** (lunch only) **Meals** a la carte 80/10 ⅀ – 62 – **107 rm** 640/750, 55 suites. G 1
◆ It was in 1898 that César Ritz inaugurated the "perfect hotel" of his dreams. Valentino Proust, Hemingway and Coco Chanel have all stayed here. Matchless refinement. See an be seen in the Ritz Club. The Bar Vendôme has a delightful terrace.

Meurice, 228 r. Rivoli (1st) Ⓜ *Tuileries* ☎ 01 44 58 10 10, *reservations@meurice hot l.com, Fax 01 44 58 10 15,* rm, – 40 - 70. AE ⓓ GB JCB rest G 1
see ***Le Meurice*** below - ***Jardin d'Hiver*** ☎ 01 44 58 10 44 **Meals** 50 ⅀ – 45 – **121 rm** 650/800, 39 suites.
◆ One of the very first luxury hotels, founded in 1817 and turned into a palace in 190 Sumptuous rooms and a superb top-floor suite with a staggering view over the city. Lovel Art Nouveau glass canopy and innumerable exotic plants in the Jardin d'Hiver.

Inter-Continental, 3 r. Castiglione (1st) Ⓜ *Tuileries* ☎ 01 44 77 11 11, *paris@inte conti.com, Fax 01 44 77 14 60,* rm, – 15 - 350. AE ⓓ GB JCB. rest G 1
234 Rivoli ☎ 01 44 77 10 40 **Meals** 35 ⅀ – ***Terrasse Fleurie*** ☎ 01 44 77 10 40 *(Ma September)* **Meals** 35 ⅀ – 31 – **405 rm** 450/760, 33 suites.
◆ Splendid hotel of 1878 with rooms in all the styles of the 19C, some with a view of th Tuileries. Sumptuous Napoleon III-style lounges. Smart, convivial ambience at 234 Rivo Escape the clamour of the city in the Terrasse Fleurie facing the courtyard.

Costes, 239 r. St-Honoré (1st) Ⓜ *Concorde* ☎ 01 42 44 50 00, *Fax 01 42 44 50 01,* AE ⓓ GB JCB G 1
Meals a la carte 45/80 – 30 – **76 rm** 350/700, 3 suites, 3 duplex.
◆ Revived Napoleon III-style in the gilt and purple bedrooms, delightful Italian courtyar and splendid leisure centre in this sumptuous palace, a favourite with the jet-set. The hot restaurant is a stronghold of up-to-the-minute cuisine.

Vendôme without rest, 1 pl. Vendôme (1st) Ⓜ *Opéra* ☎ 01 55 04 55 00, *reservatic s@hoteldevendome.com, Fax 01 49 27 97 89* – AE ⓓ GB JCB.
35 – **19 rm** 460/580, 10 suites. G 1
◆ The Place Vendôme is a fine setting for this 18C town mansion with its antique fu nishings, marble, and up-to-the-minute facilities.

Park Hyatt, 5 r. Paix (2nd) *Opéra* 01 58 71 12 34, *vendome@paris.hyatt.com, Fax 01 58 71 12 35,* – rm, – 15 - 50.
Le Park 01 58 71 10 60 *(closed Saturday lunch, Sunday and Bank Holidays)* **Meals** a la carte 68/90 – 42 – **177 rm** 580/770, 10 suites. G 12
◆ With contemporary décor created by Ed Tuttle, modern art collection and hi-tech facilities, these five 19C buildings have metamorphosed into a designer palace. Contemporary cuisine and refined, sober and distinctive ambience in the Park restaurant.

Plaza Paris Vendôme, 4 r. Mont-Thabor (1st) *Tuileries* 01 40 20 20 00, *reservations@plazaparisvendome.com, Fax 01 40 20 20 01,* –
Meals see ***Pinxo*** below – 26 – **85 rm** 460/560, 12 suites.
◆ A 19C building transformed into a chic and refined modern hotel. Wood, beige and chocolate tones, and high-tech equipment in the bedrooms. Attractive Chinese bar.

Sofitel Castille, 37 r. Cambon (1st) *Madeleine* 01 44 58 44 58, *reservations@castille.com, Fax 01 44 58 44 00* – rm, – 30.
see ***Il Cortile*** below – 28 – **86 rm** 415/545, 7 suites, 14 duplex. G 12
◆ On the Opéra side, warm Italian Renaissance-style décor, smarter French ambience on the Rue de Rivoli side, enhanced by works by the famous 20C photographer Robert Doisneau.

Louvre, pl. A. Malraux (1st) *Palais Royal* 01 44 58 38 38, *hoteldulouvre@hoteldulouvre.com, Fax 01 44 58 38 01,* – rm, – 20 - 80. H 13
Brasserie Le Louvre 01 42 96 27 98 **Meals** 31 – 21 – **170 rm** 450/700, 7 suites.
◆ Picasso stayed here, in what was one of the city's first grand hotels. Unique view from some rooms of the Avenue de l'Opéra and the Palais Garnier. In the Brasserie Le Louvre, both the cuisine and the turn-of-the-century décor pay homage to tradition.

Westminster, 13 r. Paix (2nd) *Opéra* 01 42 61 57 46, *resa.westminster@warwickhotels.com, Fax 01 42 60 30 66,* – rm, – 15 - 40. G 12
see ***Céladon*** below - ***Petit Céladon*** (weekend only) *(closed August)* **Meals** 45 b.i. – 28 – **80 rm** 420/570, 22 suites.
◆ Once a convent, then a post hotel, this establishment took on the name of its celebrated ducal guest in 1846. Sumptuous bedrooms, luxurious apartments. At weekends, the Céladon becomes the Petit Céladon with a limited menu and informal service.

Lotti, 7 r. Castiglione (1st) *Tuileries* 01 42 60 37 34, *lotti.fr@jollyhotels.com, Fax 01 40 15 93 56* – rm, . G 12
Meals *(closed Sunday)* 36/46 (lunch) and a la carte 70/110 – 23 – **164 rm** 399/590, 5 suites.
◆ Close to the jewellery shops in Place Vendôme, this is a little gem of a hotel, with cosy rooms furnished in a variety of styles. Comfortable lounge beneath a glass roof.

Royal St-Honoré without rest, 221 r. St-Honoré (1st) *Tuileries* 01 42 60 32 79, *rsh@hroy.com, Fax 01 42 60 47 44* – – 15.
20 – **67 rm** 290/360, 5 suites. G 12
◆ This 19C edifice was built on the site of the old Hôtel de Noailles. Individual, very refined rooms. Louis XVI décor in the breakfast room.

Meliá Vendôme without rest, 8 r. Cambon (1st) *Concorde* 01 44 77 54 00, *melia.vendome@solmelia.com, Fax 01 44 77 54 01* – – 20. G 12
24 – **83 rm** 320/442.
◆ Opulent decor, stylish furniture and a hushed atmosphere dominate the recently refurbished rooms here. The elegant lounge is crowned by a Belle Époque glass roof.

Edouard VII without rest, 39 av. Opéra (2nd) *Pyramides* 01 42 61 56 90, *info@edouard7hotel.com, Fax 01 42 61 47 73* – – 15 - 25.
20 – **65 rm** 309/418, 4 suites. G 13
◆ This was where the future Edward VII stayed when still Prince of Wales. Spacious, luxurious rooms. Dark panelling and stained-glass in the bar.

Normandy without rest, 7 r. Échelle (1st) *Palais Royal* 01 42 60 30 21, *Fax 01 42 60 45 81* – rm, – 15 - 30. H 13
20 – **111 rm** 280/423, 4 suites.
◆ Just a step from the Louvre, the Normandy opened its doors in 1877 and was an immediate hit with English visitors. Spacious rooms with retro décor, many with period furnishings. The elegant Palazzo combines Baroque and designer styles. Italian cuisine.

Regina, 2 pl. Pyramides (1st) *Tuileries* 01 42 60 31 10, *reservation@regina-hotel.com, Fax 01 40 15 95 16,* – – 20 - 60. H 13
Meals *(closed August, Saturday, Sunday and Bank Holidays)* 31 and a la carte 55/70 – 26 – **120 rm** 323/535, 20 suites.
◆ Built in 1900, this hotel has kept its superb Art Nouveau foyer. Rooms filled with antique furnishings. Those on the patio side are quieter. Some with view of Eiffel Tower. Dining room with splendid fireplace, and a much appreciated courtyard in summer.

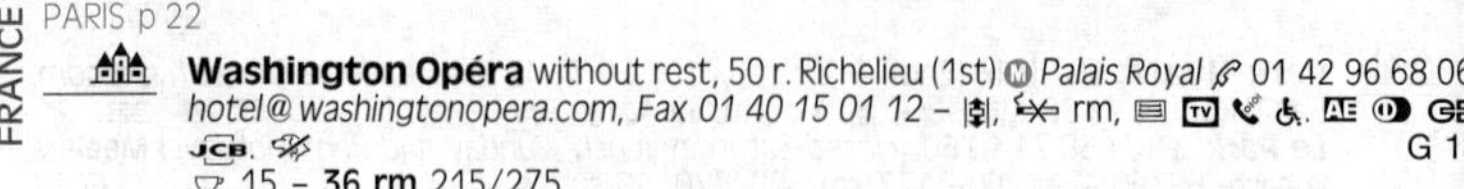

Washington Opéra without rest, 50 r. Richelieu (1st) Ⓜ *Palais Royal* ☎ 01 42 96 68 06, *hotel@washingtonopera.com, Fax 01 40 15 01 12* – ⎘, ⇔ rm, ▤ 📺 ☎ ♿. AE ⓓ GB JCB. ⅋ G 13
☐ 15 – **36 rm** 215/275.
◆ This old town mansion was once owned by Mme de Pompadour. Rooms with historic décor. Sixth-floor terrace with a lovely view over the garden of the Palais-Royal.

Stendhal without rest, 22 r. D. Casanova (2nd) Ⓜ *Opéra* ☎ 01 44 58 52 52, *h1610@accor-hotels.com, Fax 01 44 58 52 00* – ⎘ ▤ 📺 ☎. AE ⓓ GB JCB. ⅋ G 12
☐ 17 – **20 rm** 271/340.
◆ Follow in the footsteps of the famous writer and stay in the "Rouge et Noir" suite of this characterful establishment. The refined rooms are all decorated in two colours.

Mansart without rest, 5 r. Capucines (1st) Ⓜ *Opéra* ☎ 01 42 61 50 28, *hotel.mansart@esprit-de-france.com, Fax 01 49 27 97 44* – ⎘ 📺 ☎. AE ⓓ GB JCB. ⅋ G 12
☐ 10 – **57 rm** 108/295.
◆ This hotel has been renovated in a style that pays tribute to Louis XIV's architect, Mansart. The foyer has frescoes inspired by the gardens of Le Nôtre. Individual rooms.

L'Horset Opéra without rest, 18 r. d'Antin (2nd) Ⓜ *Opéra* ☎ 01 44 71 87 00, *lopera@paris-hotels-charm.com, Fax 01 42 66 55 54* – ⎘, ⇔ rm, ▤ 📺 ☎. AE ⓓ GB JCB G 13
54 rm ☐ 230/260.
◆ Warm colours and light-wood furnishings characterise the spacious rooms of this traditional hotel close to the Opéra. Cosy atmosphere in the lounge.

Novotel Les Halles, 8 pl. M.-de-Navarre (1st) Ⓜ *Châtelet* ☎ 01 42 21 31 31, *h0785@accor-hotels.com, Fax 01 40 26 05 79* – ⎘, ⇔ rm, ▤ 📺 ☎ ♿ – 🏛 15 - 20. AE ⓓ GB JCB H 14
Meals a la carte 28/36 ♀ – ☐ 14,50 – **285 rm** 276/465.
◆ Close to the Forum des Halles, this well-soundproofed hotel is up to the usual Novotel standards. Some rooms have been renovated and some have a view of the Church of St-Eustache. Palm-trees lend an exotic touch to the restaurant beneath its huge glass roof.

États-Unis Opéra without rest, 16 r. d'Antin (2nd) Ⓜ *Opéra* ☎ 01 42 65 05 05, *us opera@wanadoo.fr, Fax 01 42 65 93 70* – ⎘ ▤ 📺 ☎ – 🏛 25. AE ⓓ GB JCB. ⅋
☐ 10 – **45 rm** 125/195. G 13
◆ This hotel built in the 1930s offers a range of comfortable rooms renovated in modern style, some with period furniture.

Noailles without rest, 9 r. Michodière (2nd) Ⓜ *4 Septembre* ☎ 01 47 42 92 90, *goldentulip.denoailles@wanadoo.fr, Fax 01 49 24 92 71,* 🏋 – ⎘, ⇔ rm, ▤ 📺 ☎ ♿ – 🏛 20 AE ⓓ GB JCB G 13
☐ 15 – **61 rm** 250/270.
◆ Resolutely contemporary elegance behind a sober old façade. Japanese-style décor in the spacious rooms, most of which overlook an attractive patio.

Thérèse without rest, 5-7 r. Thérèse (1st) Ⓜ *Pyramides* ☎ 01 42 96 10 01, *hotelthérese@wanadoo.fr, Fax 01 42 96 15 22* – ⎘ ▤ 📺 ☎. AE ⓓ GB JCB. ⅋ G 13
☐ 12 – **43 rm** 130/250.
◆ Sober and refined decor in a modern style lightened with exotic touches, in this entirely renovated building. Charming rooms and breakfast room with vaulted ceiling.

Pavillon Louvre Rivoli without rest, 20 r. Molière (1st) Ⓜ *Pyramides* ☎ 01 42 60 31 20, *louvre@leshotelsdeparis.com, Fax 01 42 60 32 06* – ⎘ ▤ 📺 ☎ ♿. AE ⓓ GB JCB G 13
☐ 15 – **29 rm** 190/230.
◆ Well located between the Opéra and the Louvre, this comprehensively modernised hotel will please both art-lovers and shopaholics. Small but bright and colourful rooms.

L'Espadon - Hôtel Ritz, 15 pl. Vendôme (1st) Ⓜ *Opéra* ☎ 01 43 16 30 80, *food-bev@ritzparis.com, Fax 01 43 16 33 75,* 🏖 – ▤ 🚗. AE ⓓ GB JCB. ⅋ G 12
Meals 68 (lunch)/160 (dinner) and a la carte 125/170.
◆ A foyer drenched in gilt and drapes, dazzling décor celebrating many famous guests, an attractive terrace and well-planted garden, altogether a very ritzy establishment.
Spec. Homard bleu aux légumes, julienne de céleri en rémoulade truffée. Rosettes d'agneau sablées aux truffes. Millefeuille.

Le Meurice - Hôtel Meurice, 228 r. Rivoli (1st) Ⓜ *Tuileries* ☎ 01 44 58 10 55, *restauration@meuricehotel.com, Fax 01 44 58 10 15* – ▤ 🚗. AE ⓓ GB JCB. ⅋ G 12
closed 1 to 29 August, Saturday lunch and Sunday – **Meals** 60 (lunch)/150 and a la carte 110/170 ♀ 🍷.
◆ 18C-style dining room directly inspired by the Grands Appartements of the chateau of Versailles. Fine contemporary cuisine fit for a king!
Spec. Dos de saumon légèrement fumé en croûte de pommes de terre. Gibier (October-December). Dacquoise et ganache tendre au chocolat guanaja.

XXXX ✿✿✿ **Grand Vefour,** 17 r. Beaujolais (1st) Ⓜ *Palais Royal* ☎ 01 42 96 56 27, *grand.vefour@wanadoo.fr, Fax 01 42 86 80 71* – ▤ ⇌. AE ⊙ GB JCB. ⚹ G 13
closed 12 to 18 April, 1 to 30 August, 23 December-2 January, Friday dinner, Saturday and Sunday – **Meals** 75 (lunch)/240 and a la carte 150/220.
◆ In the Palais-Royal gardens, sumptuous late 18C interiors with splendid figures painted on glass pillars. Inspired, inventive cuisine worthy of a great historical monument.
Spec. Ravioles de foie gras à l'émulsion de crème truffée. Pigeon Prince Rainier III. Palet noisette et chocolat au lait.

XXXX ✿✿ **Carré des Feuillants** (Dutournier), 14 r. Castiglione (1st) Ⓜ *Tuileries* ☎ 01 42 86 82 82, *carre.des.feuillants@wanadoo.fr, Fax 01 42 86 07 71* – ▤ ⇌. AE ⊙ GB JCB G 12
closed August, Saturday and Sunday – **Meals** 58 (lunch)/138 and a la carte 115/145.
◆ This restaurant on the site of an old convent has a decidedly contemporary new look. Inventive cuisine with a Gascon touch. Impressive wine list.
Spec. Huîtres de Marennes, caviar d'Aquitaine et alges marines (November-April). Filets de perdreau gris poudrés de noisettes (October-November). Biscuit chaud fourré à la marmelade de mandarines (Winter).

XXXX ✿ **Drouant** see also ***Café Drouant***, pl. Gaillon (2nd) Ⓜ *4 Septembre* ☎ 01 42 65 15 16, *drouantrv@elior.com, Fax 01 49 24 02 15* – ▤ ⇌. AE ⊙ GB JCB G 13
closed August, Saturday and Sunday – **Meals** 56 (lunch)/104 (dinner) and a la carte 120/160 ♀.
◆ Little Art Deco interiors around a majestic staircase designed by Jacques-Emile Ruhlmann. The Prix Goncourt jury has met in the Louis XVI room since 1914.
Spec. Saint-Jacques aux truffes (season). Pigeon de Vendée rôti en feuilles de vigne. Feuilles de chocolat "hommage aux Goncourt".

XXXX ✿ **Gérard Besson,** 5 r. Coq Héron (1st) Ⓜ *Louvre-Rivoli* ☎ 01 42 33 14 74, *gerard.besson4@libertysurf.fr, Fax 01 42 33 85 71* – ▤. AE ⊙ GB JCB H 14
closed 2 to 24 August, Monday lunch except in July-August, Saturday except dinner from September-June and Sunday – **Meals** 48 (lunch)/100 (dinner) and a la carte 90/120 ♀.
◆ Just a step from Les Halles, an elegant and luxurious restaurant enhanced by a collection of precious ewers and faience cockerels. Classic cuisine with a contemporary touch.
Spec. Homard. Volaille de Bresse. Gibier (season).

XXXX ✿ **Goumard,** 9 r. Duphot (1st) Ⓜ *Madeleine* ☎ 01 42 60 36 07, *goumard.philippe@wanadoo.fr, Fax 01 42 60 04 54* – ⧉ ▤ ⇌. AE ⊙ GB JCB G 12
Meals - Seafood - 40 and a la carte 80/120 ♀.
◆ Intimate Art Deco interiors graced with seascape paintings. The original toilets designed by Louis Majorelle have survived and are well worth a look. Fine seafood.
Spec. Homard bleu, palmiste de l'île Maurice, curry et coriandre. Tronçon de gros turbot rôti, blettes et coques, jus iodé. Reine des reinettes mi-confite façon tatin, arlette aux épices.

XXX ✿ **Céladon** - Hôtel Westminster, 15 r. Daunou (2nd) Ⓜ *Opéra* ☎ 01 47 03 40 42, *christophemoisand@leceladon.com, Fax 01 42 61 33 78* – ▤ ⇌. AE ⊙ GB JCB G 12
closed August, Saturday, Sunday and Bank Holidays – **Meals** 48 b.i. (lunch)/62 (dinner) and a la carte 80/110.
◆ Superb dining rooms with a décor featuring early 18C furniture, willow-green ("céladon") walls, and a collection of Chinese porcelain. Contemporary cuisine.
Spec. Pâté de lapin de garenne (October-February). Saint-Pierre rôti à la crème d'andouille. Soufflé williamine, sorbet poire.

XXX **Macéo,** 15 r. Petits-Champs (1st) Ⓜ *Bourse* ☎ 01 42 97 53 85, *info@maceorestaurant.com, Fax 01 47 03 36 93* – ▤. GB. ⚹ G 13
closed 9 to 22 August, Saturday lunch and Sunday – **Meals** 29,50 (lunch)/36 and a la carte 36/62 ♀.
◆ Striking fusion of Second Empire décor and contemporary furnishings. Inventive cuisine, vegetarian specialities and wines from around the world. Convivial lounge/bar.

XXX ✿ **Il Cortile** - Hôtel Sofitel Castille, 37 r. Cambon (1st) Ⓜ *Madeleine* ☎ 01 44 58 45 67, *ilcortile@castille.com, Fax 01 44 58 45 69,* ⛱ – ▤ ⇌. AE ⊙ GB JCB G 12
closed Saturday, Sunday and Bank Holidays – **Meals** - Italian rest. - 85/120 b.i. and a la carte 65/85.
◆ A Villa d'Este of a dining room, a lively team around the piano, and a pretty tiled patio all make a fine setting for refined Italian cuisine.
Spec. Vitello tonnato. Osso buco gremolata, gnocchi "di patate" et cébettes. Tiramisu.

XXX **Fontaine Gaillon,** pl. Gaillon (2nd) Ⓜ *4 Septembre* ☎ 01 47 42 63 22, *Fax 01 47 42 82 84,* ⛱ – ▤ ⇌. AE ⊙ GB JCB G 13
closed August, Saturday and Sunday – **Meals** 36 and a la carte 45/65 ♀.
◆ Famous film stars Carole Bouquet and Gérard Depardieu are behind this elegant restaurant housed in a 17C private mansion, where the culinary emphasis is on fish and seafood.

XX **Pierre au Palais Royal,** 10 r. Richelieu (1st) Ⓜ *Palais Royal* ✆ 01 42 96 09 17, *pierreaupalaisroyal@wanadoo.fr, Fax 01 42 96 26 40* – ▤. AE ⓓ GB H 13
closed 8 to 23 August, Saturday lunch and Sunday – **Meals** 35 and a la carte 35/45.
◆ Aubergine tones, artwork featuring the nearby Palais-Royal and attractively laid tables make up the new decor of this fashionable restaurant serving seasonal cuisine.

XX **Palais Royal,** 110 Galerie de Valois - Jardin du Palais Royal (1st) Ⓜ *Bourse* ✆ 01 40 20 00 27, *palaisrest@aol.com, Fax 01 40 20 00 82,* ☂ – AE ⓓ GB G 13
closed 15 December-30 January, Saturday from October-May and Sunday – **Meals** a la carte 43/60 ♀.
◆ Beneath the windows of the flat where Colette once lived, a restaurant in Art Deco style with an idyllic terrace opening onto the gardens of the Palais-Royal.

XX **Chez Pauline,** 5 r. Villédo (1st) Ⓜ *Pyramides* ✆ 01 42 96 20 70, *chezpauline@wanadoo.fr, Fax 01 49 27 99 89* – ▤. AE GB G 13
closed Saturday except dinner in winter and Sunday – **Meals** 35 (lunch)/40 and a la carte 57/78 ♀.
◆ In a quiet little street, this comfortable establishment has the character of an early 20C bistro. The first floor room is more intimate. Classic cuisine.

XX **Café Drouant,** pl. Galion (2nd) Ⓜ *4 Septembre* ✆ 01 42 65 15 16, *Fax 01 49 24 02 15,* ☂ – ▤ ⇨♀. AE ⓓ GB JCB G 13
closed August, Saturday and Sunday – **Meals** 38 and a la carte 42/63 ♀.
◆ The little brother of the Restaurant Drouant offers seafood and "riff-raff" dishes beneath an unusual ceiling of silvered hair and plaster decorated with denizens of the deep.

XX **Cabaret,** 2 pl. Palais Royal (1st) Ⓜ *Palais Royal* ✆ 01 58 62 56 25, *Fax 01 58 62 56 40* – ▤. AE GB. ✂ H 13
closed 1 to 22 August and Sunday – **Meals** 68/78 and a la carte 40/60 ♀.
◆ The basement has unusual décor featuring Indian drapes and African bar. At half-past midnight the restaurant becomes a club, much favoured by the "beautiful people".

XX **Au Pied de Cochon** (24 hr service), 6 r. Coquillière (1st) Ⓜ *Châtelet-Les Halles* ✆ 01 40 13 77 00, *de.pied-de-cochon@blanc.net, Fax 01 40 13 77 09,* ☂ – |♦| ▤. AE ⓓ GB H 14
Meals 29 b.i. (lunch), 32 b.i./72 b.i. and a la carte 37/61.
◆ The "Pig's Trotter" has been famous ever since its opening in 1946, not least for catering for night-owls. Unusual frescoes and chandeliers with fruit motifs.

XX **Pays de Cocagne,** -Espace Tarn- 111 r. Réaumur (2nd) Ⓜ *Bourse* ✆ 01 40 13 81 81, *Fax 01 40 13 87 70* – ▤. AE ⓓ GB JCB G 14
closed 2 to 24 August, Saturday, Sunday and Bank Holidays – **Meals** -South West of France rest.- 27,50 b.i./29,90 and a la carte 36/50 ♀.
◆ On the upper floor of the Maison du Tarn, contemporary restaurant with pictures by regional artists. Cuisine from southwestern France and Gaillac wines.

XX ☺ **Gallopin,** 40 r. N.-D.-des Victoires (2nd) Ⓜ *Bourse* ✆ 01 42 36 45 38, *administration@brasseriegallopin.com, Fax 01 42 36 10 32* – ▤. AE ⓓ GB G 14
closed Sunday – **Meals** 28/33 b.i. and a la carte 30/50 ♀.
◆ Together with its elaborate Victorian décor, Arletty and Raimu have contributed to the fame of this brasserie opposite the Palais Brongniart. Lovely glass canopy to the rear.

X **Chez Georges,** 1 r. Mail (2nd) Ⓜ *Bourse* ✆ 01 42 60 07 11 – AE GB G 14
closed 29 July-19 August, Sunday and Bank Holidays – **Meals** a la carte 40/61.
◆ Full of the atmosphere of the Paris of 1900, this bistro is a local institution, with its traditional décor of zinc counter, benches, plasterwork and mirrors.

X **Pinxo** - Hôtel Plaza Paris Vendôme, 9 r. Alger (1st) Ⓜ *Tuileries* ✆ 01 40 20 72 00, *Fax 01 40 20 72 02* – ▤ ⇨♀. AE GB
closed August – **Meals** a la carte 35/60.
◆ Stylish furniture, a black and white colour scheme and an open-view kitchen provide a simple yet chic backdrop for Alain Dutournier's excellent tapas creations.

X ☺ **Aux Lyonnais,** 32 r. St-Marc (2nd) Ⓜ *Richelieu-Drouot* ✆ 01 42 96 65 04, *auxlyonnais@online.fr, Fax 01 42 97 42 95* – AE GB
closed 25 July-23 August, 24 December-3 January, Saturday lunch, Sunday and Monday – **Meals** (booking essential) 28 and a la carte 38/52.
◆ The bistro, founded in 1890, serves tasty Lyonnaise dishes which have a subtly modern touch, but still fit the delightfully retro style of the banquettes, mirrors and zinc bar.

X ☺ **Pierrot,** 18 r. Étienne Marcel (2nd) Ⓜ *Etienne Marcel* ✆ 01 45 08 00 10 – ▤. AE GB H 15
closed August, 1 to 7 January and Sunday – **Meals** a la carte 27/50 ♀.
◆ In the busy heart of the Sentier area, this cheerful bistro offers diners the authentic flavours of the Aveyron area. Small outdoor dining area in summer.

Bastille, République, Hôtel de Ville.

3rd, 4th and 11th arrondissements.
3rd: ✉ 75003
4th: ✉ 75004
11th: ✉ 75011

Pavillon de la Reine without rest, 28 pl. Vosges (3rd) Ⓜ *Bastille* ☎ 01 40 29 19 19, *contact@pavillon-de-la-reine.com, Fax 01 40 29 19 20* – 🛗 ▤ TV ☎ – 🏛 25. AE ⓓ GB JCB J17
☕ 25 – **31 rm** 385/410, 15 suites, 10 duplex.
◆ To the rear of one of the 36 brick mansions in the Place des Vosges, two buildings (one dating from the 17C) with refined rooms overlooking a courtyard or private garden.

Holiday Inn, 10 pl. République (11th) Ⓜ *République* ☎ 01 43 14 43 50, *holiday.inn.paris.republique@wanadoo.fr, Fax 01 47 00 32 34,* – 🛗, rm, ▤ TV ☎ ♿ – 🏛 25 - 150. AE ⓓ GB JCB. rest G 17
Meals 30 ♀ – ☕ 22 – **318 rm** 285/345.
◆ In this fine 19C building a listed wrought-iron staircase leads to functional rooms, the best of which overlook the Napoleon III-style inner courtyard. The convivial atmosphere at the Belle Époque-style restaurant is enhanced by the pleasant veranda-terrace.

Villa Beaumarchais without rest, 5 r. Arquebusiers (3rd) Ⓜ *Chemin Vert* ☎ 01 40 29 14 00, *beaumarchais@leshotelsdeparis.com, Fax 01 40 29 14 01* – 🛗, rm, ▤ TV ☎ ♿ – 🏛 15. AE ⓓ GB JCB H 17
☕ 26 – **50 rm** 480/880.
◆ Set well back from the bustle of the Boulevard Beaumarchais, this hotel has refined rooms with gilt furniture, all overlooking a pretty winter garden. Beneath its glass roof, the restaurant is drenched in greenery.

Bourg Tibourg without rest, 19 r. Bourg Tibourg (4th) Ⓜ *Hôtel de Ville* ☎ 01 42 78 47 39, *hotel.du.bourg.tibourg@wanadoo.fr, Fax 01 40 29 07 00* – 🛗 ▤ TV ☎ ♿. AE ⓓ GB JCB. – ☕ 12 – **31 rm** 150/250. J 16
◆ This charming hotel offers attractive refurbished rooms in a variety of styles - neo-Gothic, Baroque, or Oriental. A little gem in the heart of the Marais district.

Général without rest, 5 r. Rampon (11th) Ⓜ *République* ☎ 01 47 00 41 57, *info@legeneralhotel.com, Fax 01 47 00 21 56,* – 🛗 ▤ TV ☎ ♿. AE ⓓ GB JCB
☕ 12 – **47 rm** 140/250.
◆ Elegant decor and designer furniture add style to this exquisite hotel near place de la République. Wi-Fi technology, small business centre and pleasant fitness area.

Bretonnerie without rest, 22 r. Ste-Croix-de-la-Bretonnerie (4th) Ⓜ *Hôtel de Ville* ☎ 01 48 87 77 63, *hotel@bretonnerie.com, Fax 01 42 77 26 78* – 🛗 TV ☎. GB. J 16
☕ 9,50 – **22 rm** 110/145, 4 suites, 3 duplex.
◆ Some of the rooms in this elegant town mansion in the Marais district have canopied beds and exposed beams. Vaulted breakfast room.

Caron de Beaumarchais without rest, 12 r. Vieille-du-Temple (4th) Ⓜ *Hôtel de Ville* ☎ 01 42 72 34 12, *hotel@carondebeaumarchais.com, Fax 01 42 72 34 63* – 🛗 ▤ TV ☎. AE ⓓ GB. J 16
☕ 9,80 – **19 rm** 137/152.
◆ The creator of Figaro lived in this historic street in the Marais quarter, and the décor of this charming establishment pays homage to him. Comfortable little rooms.

Austin's without rest, 6 r. Montgolfier (3rd) Ⓜ *Arts et Métiers* ☎ 01 42 77 17 61, *austins.amhotel@wanadoo.fr, Fax 01 42 77 55 43* – 🛗. AE ⓓ GB JCB.
☕ 7 – **29 rm** 92/120.
◆ Situated in a quiet street opposite the Arts et Métiers museum. The rooms have been recently redecorated in a warm and bright style, some of them with original beams intact.

Marais Bastille without rest, 36 bd Richard Lenoir (11th) Ⓜ *Bréguet Sabin* ☎ 01 48 05 75 00, *maraisbastille@wanadoo.fr, Fax 01 43 57 42 85* – 🛗 TV ☎. AE ⓓ GB JCB – ☕ 10 – **36 rm** 130. J18
◆ The hotel faces onto the boulevard that has covered the Canal St-Martin since 1860. A renovated interior, with leather armchairs and oak furniture in the bedrooms.

Beaubourg without rest, 11 r. S. Le Franc (4th) Ⓜ *Rambuteau* ☎ 01 42 74 34 24, *htlbeaubourg@hotellerie.net, Fax 01 42 78 68 11* – 🛗 ▤ TV ☎. AE ⓓ GB JCB H 15
☕ 7 – **28 rm** 109/122.
◆ In a little street to the rear of the Pompidou Centre. Some of the welcoming and well-soundproofed rooms have exposed beams and stonework.

Lutèce without rest, 65 r. St-Louis-en-l'Ile (4th) Ⓜ *Pont Marie* ☎ 01 43 26 23 52, *hotel.lutece@free.fr, Fax 01 43 29 60 25* – 🛗 ▤ 📺 📞. AE GB. ⚔ K 16
☕ 11 – **23 rm** 158.
• The rustic charm of this hotel on the Ile-St-Louis is particularly appreciated by American visitors. Attractive, fairly quiet rooms. Fine antique wood panelling in the lounge.

Croix de Malte without rest, 5 r. Malte (11th) Ⓜ *Oberkampf* ☎ 01 48 05 09 36, *h2752-gm@accor-hotels.com, Fax 01 42 09 48 12* – 🛗, ⇆ rm, 📺. AE ⓓ GB JCB H 17
☕ 10 – **29 rm** 105/115.
• The tropical atmosphere in the Maltese Cross is provided by colourful furniture, a stuffed parrot and a breakfast room designed to resemble a winter garden.

Grand Hôtel Français without rest, 223 bd Voltaire (11th) Ⓜ *Nation* ☎ 01 43 71 27 57, *grand-hotel-francais@wanadoo.fr, Fax 01 43 48 40 05* – 🛗 📺 📞. AE ⓓ GB JCB K 20
☕ 10 – **36 rm** 95/120.
• This Haussmann-style corner building stands in a typically Parisian working class district. Recently renovated functional rooms, albeit lacking in finery. Good soundproofing.

Beaumarchais without rest, 3 r. Oberkampf (11th) Ⓜ *Oberkampf* ☎ 01 53 36 86 86, *reservation@hotelbeaumarchais.com, Fax 01 43 38 32 86* – 🛗 📺. AE GB JCB H 17
☕ 9 – **31 rm** 69/99.
• Despite their smallness, the brightly coloured rooms furnished with modern furniture have retained a certain charm. Leafy internal courtyard which is welcome in summer.

XXXX ✿✿✿ **L'Ambroisie** (Pacaud), 9 pl. des Vosges (4th) Ⓜ *St-Paul* ☎ 01 42 78 51 45 – ▤ 🚗. AE GB. ⚔ J 17
closed August, February Holidays, Sunday and Monday – **Meals** a la carte 181/246.
• Beneath the arcades of the Place des Vosges, princely décor and a subtle cuisine not far from perfection - was not Ambrosia the food of the gods ?
Spec. Feuillantine de langoustines aux graines de sésame. Foie gras de canard poêlé à l'aigre-doux, chutney de légumes. Tarte fine sablée au chocolat.

XXX ✿ **Hiramatsu,** 7 quai Bourbon (4th) Ⓜ *Pont Marie* ☎ 01 56 81 08 80, *paris@hiramatsu.co.jp, Fax 01 56 81 08 81* – ▤ 🚗 (dinner). AE ⓓ GB. ⚔ K 16
closed 1 to 8 August, 23 December-3 January, Sunday and Monday – **Meals** (booking essential) 95/130 and a la carte 105/130 🍇.
• Japanese refinement makes an excellent setting for fine French cuisine. Elegant small interior with beams, stonework and contemporary furnishings. Superb wine list.
Spec. Foie gras de canard aux choux frisés, sauce aux truffes. Pigeon rôti au miel, sauce vin rouge. Variation autour du chocolat.

XX **Ambassade d'Auvergne,** 22 r. Grenier St-Lazare (3rd) Ⓜ *Rambuteau* ☎ 01 42 72 31 22, *info@ambassade-auvergne.com, Fax 01 42 78 85 47* – ▤. GB JCB
Meals 27 and a la carte 32/52 🍷. H 15
• As good as its name, this establishment is an excellent ambassador for its province, with authentically Auverngat décor, furnishings, food and wine.

XX **Bofinger,** 5 r. Bastille (4th) Ⓜ *Bastille* ☎ 01 42 72 87 82, *Fax 01 42 72 97 68* – ▤. AE ⓓ GB JCB J 17
Meals 31,50 b.i. and a la carte 30/50.
• Illustrious guests and remarkable décor lend a special atmosphere to this brasserie founded in 1864. Delicate cupola, and, on the upper floor, an interior decorated by Hansi.

XX **L'Aiguière,** 37bis r. Montreuil (11th) Ⓜ *Faidherbe Chaligny* ☎ 01 43 72 42 32, *patrick-masbatin1@libertysurf.com, Fax 01 43 72 96 36* – ▤. AE ⓓ GB JCB K 20
closed Saturday lunch and Sunday – **Meals** 24 b.i./50 b.i. and a la carte 48/74 🍇.
• Shades of yellow and elegant fabrics provide the attractive decor for this restaurant with a collection of pitchers, hence the name. Seasonal cuisine plus a fine wine list.

XX ✿ **Benoît,** 20 r. St-Martin (4th) Ⓜ *Châtelet* ☎ 01 42 72 25 76, *Fax 01 42 72 45 68* – ▤. AE J 15
closed August – **Meals** 38 (lunch) and a la carte 55/81 🍷.
• Forget the fast-food joints all around ! Here is a smart and busy bistro run by the same family since 1912, who know all about serving up carefully prepared traditional food.
Spec. Cassoulet aux cocos de Paimpol. Saint-Jacques au naturel (season). Tête de veau sauce ravigote.

XX **Pamphlet,** 38 r. Debelleyme (3rd) Ⓜ *Filles du Calvaire* ☎ 01 42 72 39 24, *Fax 01 42 72 12 53* – ▤. GB H 17
closed 8 to 27 August, 1 to 15 January, Sunday, lunch Saturday and Monday – **Meals** 30/45 🍷.
• Attractive restaurant situated in the heart of the Marais. Rustic decor enlivened with bright paint and bullfighting posters. Traditional cuisine, with dishes from SW France.

XX **Vin et Marée,** 276 bd Voltaire (11th) Ⓜ *Nation* ☎ 01 43 72 31 23, *vin.maree@wanadoo.fr, Fax 01 40 24 00 23* – ▤ 🚗. AE GB K 21
Meals - Seafood - a la carte 33/52 🍷.
• Like its siblings elsewhere, pride of place on the menu is given to fish and seafood. The room to the rear, with its maritime décor, offers views of the kitchens.

Dôme du Marais, 53 bis r. Francs-Bourgeois (4th) Ⓜ *Rambuteau* ✆ 01 42 74 54 17, *Fax 01 42 77 78 17* – AE GB H16 J16
closed 8 to 30 August, Sunday and Monday – **Meals** 23 (lunch) and a la carte 32/61 ♀.
◆ The tables here are set out beneath the lovely dome above the hall of the old Crédit Municipal building as well as in an interior like a winter garden. Contemporary cuisine.

Mansouria, 11 r. Faidherbe (11th) Ⓜ *Faidherbe Chaligny* ✆ 01 43 71 00 16, *Fax 01 40 24 21 97* – ▤. GB. ✻ K 19
closed 9 to 15 August, Sunday, lunch Monday and Tuesday – **Meals** - Moroccan rest. - 29/44 b.i. and a la carte 31/43.
◆ Run by a former ethnologist who is now one of the city's leading names in Moroccan cuisine. The fragrant dishes are prepared by women and served amid typically Moorish décor.

Repaire de Cartouche, 99 r. Amelot (11th) Ⓜ *Sébastien Froissard* ✆ 01 47 00 25 86, *Fax 01 43 38 85 91* – GB H 17
closed August, Sunday and Monday – **Meals** 23 (lunch) and a la carte 31/42.
◆ The late-17C-early-18C bandit Cartouche took refuge nearby while undertaking his criminal activities : the frescoes retrace some of his exploits. Enticing wine-list.

Péché Mignon, 5 r. Guillaume Bertrand (11th) Ⓜ *St-Maur* ✆ 01 43 57 68 68, *Fax 01 49 83 91 62* – AE ⓓ GB H 19
closed August, Sunday dinner, Tuesday lunch and Monday – **Meals** 26.
◆ This restaurant could also be known as "The Two Brothers", as one prepares the modern and traditional cuisine, while the other takes care of the plainly furnished dining room.

Auberge Pyrénées Cévennes, 106 r. Folie-Méricourt (11th) Ⓜ *République* ✆ 01 43 57 33 78 – ▤. AE GB G 17
closed 29 July-22 August, 1 to 7 January, Saturday lunch and Sunday – **Meals** 26,50 and a la carte 27,90/53,50 ♀.
◆ Rows of hanging hams and sausages, chequered tablecloths and tables huddled close together characterise this friendly restaurant serving hearty, local cuisine.

Au Bascou, 38 r. Réaumur (3rd) Ⓜ *Arts et Métiers* ✆ 01 42 72 69 25, *Fax 01 42 72 69 25* – AE GB G 16
closed 1 to 29 August, 24 December-2 January, Saturday and Sunday – **Meals** a la carte 31,50/38 ♀.
◆ With its pleasingly textured walls, this is a place to come for the tasty cooking of the Basque country. Warm welcome plus freshly delivered produce from the region.

Astier, 44 r. J.-P. Timbaud (11th) Ⓜ *Parmentier* ✆ 01 43 57 16 35 – GB G 18
closed 17 to 25 April, August, 24 December-3 January, Saturday and Sunday – **Meals** (booking essential) 21 (lunch)/26.
◆ A pleasant ambience reigns in this typical bistro with its formica tables, busy staff and high noise levels. A seasonal range of dishes, plus an expansive wine-list.

L'Enoteca, 25 r. Charles V (4th) Ⓜ *St Paul* ✆ 01 42 78 91 44, *Fax 01 44 59 31 72* – GB
closed 13 to 18 August and lunch in August – **Meals** (booking essential) a la carte 27/40 ♀.
◆ The highlight of this lively restaurant within 16C walls is its superb wine list of some 500 exclusively Italian wines. A lively atmosphere to go with the Italian cuisine.

Quartier Latin, Luxembourg, Jardin des Plantes.

5th and 6th arrondissements.
5th: ✉ 75005
6th: ✉ 75006

Lutétia, 45 bd Raspail (6th) Ⓜ *Sèvres Babylone* ✆ 01 49 54 46 46, *lutetia-paris@lutetia-paris.com, Fax 01 49 54 46 00* – 🛗, ⇔ rm, ▤ TV ✆ – 🏛 300. AE ⓓ GB JCB K 12
see **Paris** below - ***Brasserie Lutétia*** ✆ 01 49 54 46 76 **Meals** 34 ♀ – ☕ 29 – **212 rm** 400/750, 26 suites.
◆ Built in 1907, this palatial Left Bank hotel has lost none of its glitter. Refined retro décor, Lalique chandeliers, fine sculpture. Refurbished rooms. Rendezvous of the Parisian elite. Splendid seafood menu in the Brasserie Lutétia.

Victoria Palace without rest, 6 r. Blaise-Desgoffe (6th) Ⓜ *St Placide* ☎ 01 45 49 70 00, *info@victoriapalace.com, Fax 01 45 49 23 75* – |♦|, ⇜ rm, ▤ TV ☎ ♿ 🚗 – 🏛 20. AE ⓓ GB JCB L 11
☕ 16 – **62 rm** 285/385.
♦ Small luxury establishment of undeniable charm. Bedrooms with choice fabrics, period furniture and marble bathrooms, lounges with pictures, porcelain and lots of red velvet.

d'Aubusson without rest, 33 r. Dauphine (6th) Ⓜ *Odéon* ☎ 01 43 29 43 43, *reservationmichael@hoteldaubusson.com, Fax 01 43 29 12 62* – |♦|, ⇜ rm, ▤ TV ☎ ♿ 🚗. AE ⓓ GB JCB BX 9
☕ 23 – **50 rm** 260/410, 3 studios.
♦ Refurbished 17C town mansion with individually decorated rooms, Versailles-style parquet floors, Aubusson tapestries, plus a bar that was once the city's first literary café.

Relais Christine 🐎 without rest, 3 r. Christine (6th) Ⓜ *St Michel* ☎ 01 40 51 60 80, *contact@relais-christine.com, Fax 01 40 51 60 81* – |♦|, ⇜ rm, ▤ TV ☎ 🚗 – 🏛 20. AE ⓓ GB JCB J 14
☕ 25 – **35 rm** 335/430, 16 duplex.
♦ Lovely town mansion built on the site of a 13C convent - guests breakfast in the old vaulted kitchens. Attractive individually decorated and well-presented rooms.

Bel Ami St-Germain-des-Prés without rest, 7-11 r. St-Benoit (6th) Ⓜ *St Germain des Prés* ☎ 01 42 61 53 53, *contact@hotel-bel-ami.com, Fax 01 49 27 09 33* – |♦| ▤ TV ☎ ♿. AE ⓓ GB JCB. ✂ J 13
☕ 20 – **115 rm** 290/410.
♦ Lovely 19C building next to the famous Flore and Deux Magots cafes. Resolutely contemporary décor with a touch of zen plus hi-tech facilities. A trendy establishment.

Buci without rest, 22 r. Buci (6th) Ⓜ *Mabillon* ☎ 01 55 42 74 74, *hotelbuci@wanadoo.fr, Fax 01 55 42 74 44* – |♦| ▤ TV ☎ ♿. AE ⓓ GB JCB. ✂ J 13
☕ 17 – **24 rm** 267/350.
♦ The hotel overlooks a picturesque street and its bustling market. Heavenly beds, English-style furniture. Refurbished, perfectly-soundproofed rooms. Piano bar.

L'Abbaye 🐎 without rest, 10 r. Cassette (6th) Ⓜ *St Sulpice* ☎ 01 45 44 38 11, *hotel.abbaye@wanadoo.fr, Fax 01 45 48 07 86* – |♦| ▤ TV ☎. AE GB. ✂ K 12
40 rm ☕ 206/305, 4 duplex.
♦ The charm of yesteryear, the comfort of today - what was once an 18C convent now has attractive rooms, some overlooking a patio. The duplex rooms have a terrace.

Littré without rest, 9 r. Littré (6th) Ⓜ *Montparnasse Bienvenue* ☎ 01 53 63 07 07, *hotellittre@hotellitreparis.com, Fax 01 45 44 88 13* – |♦|, ⇜ rm, ▤ TV ☎ – 🏛 20. AE ⓓ GB JCB. ✂ L 11
☕ 15 – **79 rm** 240/350, 11 suites.
♦ Halfway between Saint-Germain-des-Prés and Montparnasse, a classic building with reasonably spacious rooms, all attractively refurbished. Comfortable English bar.

L'Hôtel, 13 r. Beaux Arts (6th) Ⓜ *St Germain des Prés* ☎ 01 44 41 99 00, *reservation@l-hotel.com, Fax 01 43 25 64 81,* 🏋 – |♦| ▤ TV ☎. AE ⓓ GB JCB. ✂ J 13
Meals *(closed August, Sunday and Monday)* a la carte 50/68 🍷 – ☕ 16,80 – **16 rm** 272/625, 4 suites.
♦ Vertiginous light wells, exuberant half-Baroque/half Empire décor by Garcia ; the famous Hôtel is unique in its blend of joy and nostalgia. It was here that Oscar Wilde met his end. Green and gold tones and venerable lanterns in the restaurant.

Relais St-Germain without rest, 9 carrefour de l'Odéon (6th) Ⓜ *Odéon* ☎ 01 43 29 12 05, *hotelrsg@wanadoo.fr, Fax 01 46 33 45 30* – |♦| kitchenette ▤ TV ☎. AE ⓓ GB JCB K 13
22 rm ☕ 210/275.
♦ Three 17C buildings now house a refined hotel where old beams, lustrous fabrics and period furniture add an attractive touch to the bedrooms.

Madison without rest, 143 bd St-Germain (6th) Ⓜ *St Germain des Prés* ☎ 01 40 51 60 00, *resa@hotel-madison.com, Fax 01 40 51 60 01* – |♦| ▤ TV. AE ⓓ GB JCB J 13
54 rm ☕ 195/320.
♦ The writer Albert Camus was fond of this establishment, half of whose rooms have a view of the church of St-Germain-des-Prés. Elegant Louis-Philippe lounge.

Relais Médicis without rest, 23 r. Racine (6th) Ⓜ *Odéon* ☎ 01 43 26 00 60, *reservation@relaismedicis.com, Fax 01 40 46 83 39* – |♦| ▤ TV ☎. AE ⓓ GB JCB. ✂ K 13
16 rm ☕ 168/245.
♦ This hotel close to the Théatre de l'Odéon has rooms with a cheerful Provençal touch. Those facing the patio are quieter. Furniture picked up from antique dealers.

Villa Panthéon without rest, 41 r. Écoles (5th) Ⓜ *Maubert Mutualité* ☎ 01 53 10 95 95, *pantheon@leshotelsdeparis.com, Fax 01 53 10 95 96* – ⇜ rm, ▤ TV ☎ ♿. AE ⓓ GB JCB
☕ 25 – **59 rm** 280/496. K 14
♦ Parquet floors, brightly-coloured wall-hangings, exotic wood furniture and Liberty lamps lend foyer, rooms and bar of this hotel a distinctively British air.

Left Bank St-Germain without rest, 9 r. Ancienne Comédie (6th) Ⓜ *Odéon* ✆ 01 43 54 01 70, *lb@paris-hotels-charm.com, Fax 01 43 26 17 14* – AE GB JCB K 13
31 rm 200/240.
◆ Damask, Jouy fabrics, Louis XIII-style furniture and old timbers give this 17C building a distinctive character. Some of the rooms offer a glimpse of Notre-Dame.

Millésime Hôtel without rest, 15 r. Jacob (6th) Ⓜ *St Germain des Prés* ✆ 01 44 07 97 97, *reservation@millesimehotel.com, Fax 01 46 34 55 97* – AE GB JCB J 13
15 – **22 rm** 175/190.
◆ Sunny tones and elegant furniture and fabrics contribute to the warm feel in the delightful bedrooms of this renovated hotel. Impressive 17C staircase.

Résidence Henri IV without rest, 50 r. Bernardins (5th) Ⓜ *Maubert-Mutualité* ✆ 01 44 41 31 81, *reservation@residencehenri4.com, Fax 01 46 33 93 22* – kitchenette AE GB JCB K 15
9 – **8 rm** 155, 5 suites.
◆ Building dating from 1879 with refurbished rooms that have kept the charm of yesteryear, with mouldings, friezes and marble chimneypieces. Overlooks a leafy square.

Rives de Notre-Dame without rest, 15 quai St-Michel (5th) Ⓜ *St Michel* ✆ 01 43 54 81 16, *hotel@rivesdenotredame.com, Fax 01 43 26 27 09,* ← – AE GB JCB J 14
13,70 – **10 rm** 213/550.
◆ Beautifully preserved 16C building with spacious Provençal-style rooms overlooking the Seine and Notre-Dame. Penthouse on the top floor.

Au Manoir St-Germain-des-Prés without rest, 153 bd St-Germain (6th) Ⓜ *St Germain des Prés* ✆ 01 42 22 21 65, *msg@paris-hotels-charm.com, Fax 01 45 48 22 25* – AE GB JCB J 12
32 rm 168/240.
◆ Comfortably furnished rooms with Jouy fabrics and painted panelling. At the foot of the building are two of the city's most celebrated cafes, Le Flore and Les Deux Magots.

Ste-Beuve without rest, 9 r. Ste-Beuve (6th) Ⓜ *Notre Dame des Champs* ✆ 01 45 48 20 07, *saintebeuve@wanadoo.fr, Fax 01 45 48 67 52* – AE GB JCB L 12
14 – **22 rm** 130/272.
◆ With its intimate ambience, comfy sofas and open fires this establishment is more like a private residence than a hotel. Rooms a tasteful fusion of old and new.

Grands Hommes without rest, 17 pl. Panthéon (5th) Ⓜ *Luxembourg* ✆ 01 46 34 19 60, *reservation@hoteldesgrandshommes.com, Fax 01 43 26 67 32,* ← – – 20. AE GB JCB L 14
10 – **31 rm** 168/244.
◆ Facing the Panthéon, a pleasant hotel refurbished in late 18C style (mottled furniture). Most rooms look out over the last resting-place of France's great and good.

Jardins du Luxembourg without rest, 5 imp. Royer-Collard (5th) Ⓜ *Luxembourg* ✆ 01 40 46 08 88, *jardinslux@wanadoo.fr, Fax 01 40 46 02 28* – AE GB JCB. L 14
10 – **26 rm** 140/150.
◆ Sigmund Freud was once a guest in this hotel in a cul-de-sac in the Luxembourg quarter. Elegant, contemporary rooms. A brasserie counter of 1900 graces the reception.

Tour Notre-Dame without rest, 20 r. Sommerard (5th) Ⓜ *Cluny la Sorbonne* ✆ 01 43 54 47 60, *tour-notre-dame@magic.fr, Fax 01 43 26 42 34* – AE GB JCB K 14
12 – **48 rm** 155/229.
◆ This hotel has a wonderful location almost next to the Museé de Cluny. Refurbished rooms featuring famous Jouy fabrics. Ask for one of the quieter ones at the back.

Villa des Artistes without rest, 9 r. Grande Chaumière (6th) Ⓜ *Vavin* ✆ 01 43 26 60 86, *hotel@villa-artistes.com, Fax 01 43 54 73 70* – rm, AE GB JCB. L 12
12 – **59 rm** 173.
◆ The hotel's name pays homage to the artists who made Montparnasse what it is. Attractive rooms, many overlooking the courtyard. Glass-roofed breakfast room.

Relais St-Sulpice without rest, 3 r. Garancière (6th) Ⓜ *St Sulpice* ✆ 01 46 33 99 00, *relaisstsulpice@wanadoo.fr, Fax 01 46 33 00 10* – rm, AE GB JCB. K 13
12 – **26 rm** 165/200.
◆ The décor of this establishment with its 19C façade strikes an exotic note with its seductive mixture of African and Asian motifs.

Grand Hôtel St-Michel without rest, 19 r. Cujas (5th) Ⓜ *Luxembourg*
✆ 01 46 33 33 02, *grand.hotel.st.michel@wanadoo.fr, Fax 01 40 46 96 33* – AE Ⓓ GB JCB. K 14
12 – **40 rm** 150/220, 5 suites.
◆ A renovated Haussmann-style building with quiet rooms adorned with painted furniture. Architectural features include a Napoleon III-style lounge and vaulted breakfast room.

Fleurie without rest, 32 r. Grégoire de Tours (6th) Ⓜ *Odéon* ✆ 01 53 73 70 00, *bonjour@hotel-de-fleurie.tm.fr, Fax 01 53 73 70 20* – AE Ⓓ GB. K 13
10 – **29 rm** 145/265.
◆ Striking 18C façade enhanced by statues in niches. Pleasantly furnished rooms with soft colours and some attractive panelling. Welcoming family atmosphere.

St-Germain-des-Prés without rest, 36 r. Bonaparte (6th) Ⓜ *St Germain des Prés*
✆ 01 43 26 00 19, *hotel-saint-germain-des-pres@wanadoo.fr, Fax 01 40 46 83 63* – rm, AE GB J 13
8 – **30 rm** 160/255.
◆ Floral fabrics and exposed beams lend a cheerful note to most of the rooms. The quieter ones face the courtyard. Breakfast room overlooking a remarkable floral display.

Royal St-Michel without rest, 3 bd St-Michel (5th) Ⓜ *St Michel* ✆ 01 44 07 06 06, *hotel.royal.st.michel@wanadoo.fr, Fax 01 44 07 36 25* – rm, AE Ⓓ GB JCB K 14
15 – **39 rm** 200/230.
◆ Right by the fountain on the famous Boulevard-St-Michel, the doors of this establishment open directly onto the bustle of the Latin Quarter. Progressively refurbished rooms.

Notre Dame without rest, 1 quai St-Michel (5th) Ⓜ *St Michel* ✆ 01 43 54 20 43, *hotel.lenotredame@libertysurf.fr, Fax 01 43 26 61 75*, – rm, AE Ⓓ GB. K 14
7 – **22 rm** 150/244, 4 duplex.
◆ The comfortable little rooms of this hotel have all been refurbished and are air-conditioned and well-equipped. Most benefit from a view of Notre-Dame.

Relais St-Jacques without rest, 3 r. Abbé de l'Épée (5th) Ⓜ *Luxembourg*
✆ 01 53 73 26 00, *nevers.luxembourg@wanadoo.fr, Fax 01 43 26 17 81* – 20. AE Ⓓ GB JCB. L 14
14 – **23 rm** 255/280.
◆ Rooms in late 18C or Portuguese style, a breakfast room beneath a glass canopy, a Louis XV lounge and a 1920s bar - a random but very smart and successful fusion !

Jardin de l'Odéon without rest, 7 r. Casimir Delavigne (6th) Ⓜ *Odéon*
✆ 01 53 10 28 50, *hotel@jardindelodeon.com, Fax 01 43 25 28 12* – AE GB. K 13
10 – **41 rm** 135/300.
◆ The rooms at the front offer a glimpse of the Théatre de l'Odéon. Five of them have a terrace. Breakfast served on the patio in summer. Lovely Art Deco lounge.

Prince de Conti without rest, 8 r. Guénégaud (6th) Ⓜ *Odéon* ✆ 01 44 07 30 40, *princedeconti@wanadoo.fr, Fax 01 44 07 36 34* – rm, AE Ⓓ GB JCB. J 13
13 – **26 rm** 170/200.
◆ 18C building adjacent to the Hôtel de la Monnaie, ideal for anyone wanting to explore the famous art galleries of Montparnasse. Rooms and lounges with English-style décor.

Odéon Hôtel without rest, 3 r. Odéon (6th) Ⓜ *Odéon* ✆ 01 43 25 90 67, *odeon@odeonhotel.fr, Fax 01 43 25 55 98* – rm, AE Ⓓ GB JCB. K 13
10 – **33 rm** 130/270.
◆ As well as the façade, the exposed beams and stone walls of the rooms are evidence of the great age of this 17C building. Brightly tiled bathrooms.

Régent without rest, 61 r. Dauphine (6th) Ⓜ *Odéon* ✆ 01 46 34 59 80, *hotel.leregent@wanadoo.fr, Fax 01 40 51 05 07* – AE Ⓓ GB JCB. J 13
12 – **25 rm** 140/210.
◆ Long, low façade dating from 1769. Luxurious, well-equipped rooms. Basement breakfast room with exposed beams and stonework.

Select without rest, 1 pl. Sorbonne (5th) Ⓜ *Cluny la Sorbonne* ✆ 01 46 34 14 80, *info@selecthotel.fr, Fax 01 46 34 51 79* – AE Ⓓ GB JCB K 14
68 rm 139/165.
◆ Resolutely contemporary hotel in the heart of student Paris. Lounge embraces a leafy patio beneath a glass roof. Some of the rooms look out over the rooftops of the city.

d'Albe without rest, 1 r. Harpe (5th) Ⓜ *St Michel* ✆ 01 46 34 09 70, *albehotel@wanadoo.fr, Fax 01 40 46 85 70* – rm, AE Ⓓ GB JCB. K 14
11 – **45 rm** 115/160.
◆ Pleasant contemporary ambience in this hotel with somewhat small but bright and attractively decorated rooms. The Latin Quarter, the Ile de la Cité - Paris is at your feet !

Marronniers without rest, 21 r. Jacob (6th) Ⓜ *St Germain des Prés* ☎ 01 43 25 30 60, *Fax 01 40 46 83 56* – GB. J 13
12 – **37 rm** 155/210.
◆ Tucked away in a leafy courtyard off the lovely Rue Jacob, this hotel has delightful little rooms. Breakfast served in an attractive garden room.

Pas de Calais without rest, 59 r. Saints-Pères (6th) Ⓜ *St Germain des Prés* ☎ 01 45 48 78 74, *infos@hotelpasdecalais.com, Fax 01 45 44 94 57* – AE GB JCB
9 – **37 rm** 130/183.
◆ A discreet hotel fronting a busy street which has been well refurbished to include modern bedrooms and bathrooms, a new colour scheme and a welcoming breakfast room.

Pierre Nicole without rest, 39 r. Pierre Nicole (5th) Ⓜ *Port Royal* ☎ 01 43 54 76 86, *hotelpierre-nicole@voila.fr, Fax 01 43 54 22 45* – AE GB. M 13
6 – **33 rm** 65/85.
◆ The hotel is named after the famous 17C theologian of Port-Royal. Practical, reasonably spacious rooms. You can jog in the nearby gardens of the Observatory.

St-Jacques without rest, 35 r. Écoles (5th) Ⓜ *Maubert Mutualité* ☎ 01 44 07 45 45, *hotelsaintjacques@wanadoo.fr, Fax 01 43 25 65 50* – AE GB JCB. K 15
7,50 – **35 rm** 85/112.
◆ The hotel's rooms are being progressively refurbished without losing any of their character (mouldings, fireplaces and period furnishings). Breakfast room with a fine fresco.

Tour d'Argent (Terrail), 15 quai Tournelle (5th) Ⓜ *Maubert Mutualité* ☎ 01 43 54 23 31, *Fax 01 44 07 12 04*, ≤ Notre-Dame – AE GB JCB K 16
closed 2 to 23 August, Tuesday lunch and Monday – **Meals** 70 (lunch), 150/200 dinner and a la carte 150/220.
◆ Crowned (and other) heads have been wined and dined here since the 16C. Sixth floor dining room with unique views of Notre-Dame and the Seine. A legendary establishment.
Spec. Quenelles de brochet "André Terrail". Canard "Tour d'Argent". Poire "Vie parisienne".

Jacques Cagna, 14 r. Grands Augustins (6th) Ⓜ *St Michel* ☎ 01 43 26 49 39, *jacquescagna@hotmail.com, Fax 01 43 54 54 48* – AE GB JCB J 14
closed 31 July-25 August, Sunday, lunch Saturday and Monday – **Meals** 39 (lunch)/85 and a la carte 85/135.
◆ In one of the city's oldest buildings, this comfortable dining room has massive beams, 16C panelling and Flemish pictures. Refined cuisine.
Spec. Foie gras poêlé aux fruits de saison caramélisés. Noix de ris de veau en croûte de sel. Gibier (season).

Paris - Hôtel Lutétia, 45 bd Raspail (6th) Ⓜ *Sèvres Babylone* ☎ 01 49 54 46 90, *lutetia-paris@lutetia-paris.com, Fax 01 49 54 46 00* – AE GB JCB K 12
closed August, Saturday, Sunday and Bank Holidays – **Meals** 37 (lunch), 60/120 dinner and a la carte 75/100.
◆ Faithfully reflecting the style of the hotel, the Art Deco restaurant was designed by Sonia Rykiel to resemble a lounge of the liner Normandie. Talented contemporary cuisine.
Spec. Cannelloni de foie gras à la truffe. Turbot cuit sur sel de Guérande. Le "tout chocolat".

Relais Louis XIII (Martinez), 8 r. Grands Augustins (6th) Ⓜ *Odéon* ☎ 01 43 26 75 96, *rl13@free.fr, Fax 01 44 07 07 80* – (dinner). AE GB JCB. J 14
closed 8 to 31 August, Sunday and Monday – **Meals** 45 (lunch), 68/89 and a la carte 105/135.
◆ In a 16C building, three intimate interiors in Louis XIII style, with balustrades, striped fabrics and exposed stonework. Subtle cuisine of today.
Spec. Ravioli de homard, foie gras et crème de cèpes. Caneton challandais rôti aux épices, pommes de terre soufflées. Millefeuille à la vanille.

Hélène Darroze, 4 r. d'Assas (6th) Ⓜ *Sèvres Babylone* ☎ 01 42 22 00 11, *helene.darroze@wanadoo.fr, Fax 01 42 22 25 40* – AE GB K 12
closed Monday except dinner from mid-July-late August, Tuesday lunch and Sunday – **Meals** *(only dinner from 17 July-31 August)* 61 (lunch), 205 b.i. and a la carte 100/150 - ***Salon*** *(closed 17 July-23 August, Sunday and Monday)* **Meals** 33(lunch)b.i./95b.i.
◆ Near the Bon Marché department store, an establishment with bright, contemporary decor and delicious cuisine and wines from southwest France. Hélène Darroze holds court on the ground floor, dispensing tapas and snacks full of the flavour of the Landes.
Spec. Huîtres en gelée de pomme verte et caviar, crème glacée au foie gras (November-April). Oeuf coque, asperges, mousserons, foie gras, mouillettes à la truffe (Spring). Baba au vieil armagnac.

Procope, 13 r. Ancienne Comédie (6th) Ⓜ *Odéon* ☎ 01 40 46 79 00, *procope@blanc.net, Fax 01 40 46 79 09* – AE GB K 13
Meals 30 and a la carte 40/60.
◆ The distinctive interiors of this historic establishment, the city's oldest literary café, are still thronged with theatre folk, artists and tourists. Traditional dishes.

XXX **Lapérouse,** 51 quai Grands Augustins (6th) Ⓜ *St Michel* ✆ 01 43 26 68 04, *restaurantlaperouse@wanadoo.fr, Fax 01 43 26 99 39* – ▤ ⛶. AE ⓓ GB J 14
closed 25 July-20 August, Saturday lunch and Sunday – **Meals** 30 (lunch)/85 and a la carte 65/94.
◆ A smart city rendezvous since the late 19C and famous for its discreet and intimate interiors, this restaurant of 1766 has kept all its old spirit.

XX **Mavrommatis,** 42 r. Daubenton (5th) Ⓜ *Censier Daubenton* ✆ 01 43 31 17 17, *andreas@mavrommatis.fr, Fax 01 43 36 13 08* – ▤. AE GB JCB. ✗ M 15
closed Monday – **Meals** - Greek rest. - 29,80 and a la carte 40/55 ♀.
◆ This establishment provides Paris with the best of Greek cuisine. No folklore, but sobriety, elegance and comfort enhanced by subtle lighting. Attentive service. Terrace.

XX **La Truffière,** 4 r. Blainville (5th) Ⓜ *Place Monge* ✆ 01 46 33 29 82, *restaurant.latruffiere@wanadoo.fr, Fax 01 46 33 64 74* – ▤. AE ⓓ GB JCB
closed Monday – **Meals** 17 (lunch) and a la carte 62/87 ♀.
◆ This 17C house contains two rooms : one rustic in style with exosed beams, the other vaulted. Traditional cuisine rooted in SW France, plus an impressive wine list.

XX **Marty,** 20 av. Gobelins (5th) Ⓜ *Les Gobelins* ✆ 01 43 31 39 51, *restaurant.marty@wanadoo.fr, Fax 01 43 37 63 70* – ▤. AE ⓓ GB JCB M 15
Meals 36 and a la carte 38/62 ♀.
◆ At lunchtime this pleasant 1930s-style brasserie is the favoured haunt of international journalists based nearby. The menu here gives pride of place to fish and seafood.

XX **Ziryab,** 1 r. Fossés St-Bernard (5th) at Institut du Monde Arabe Ⓜ *Jussieu* ✆ 01 53 10 10 19, *ima@sodexho-prestige.fr, Fax 01 44 07 30 98,* ≤ Paris, 🏠 – ▤. AE ⓓ GB JCB. ✗ K 16
closed Sunday dinner and Monday – **Meals** Oriental rest. 26/34 and a la carte 40/50 ♀
◆ On the top floor of the Institut du Monde Arabe, this designer restaurant and its panoramic terrace offer a superb view of Notre-Dame and the Seine. Eastern cuisine.

XX **Yugaraj,** 14 r. Dauphine (6th) Ⓜ *Odéon* ✆ 01 43 26 44 91, *contact@yugaraj.com Fax 01 46 33 50 77* – ▤. AE ⓓ GB JCB J 14
closed August, Thursday lunch and Monday – **Meals** - Indian rest. - 31/39 and a la carte 50/65.
◆ Wainscoting, decorative panels, silk fabrics and venerable objets d'art lend this stronghold of Indian cuisine something of the air of a museum. Well-informed menu.

XX **Alcazar,** 62 r. Mazarine (6th) Ⓜ *Odéon* ✆ 01 53 10 19 99, *contact@alcazar.fr Fax 01 53 10 23 23* – ▤. AE ⓓ GB JCB J 13
Meals 26 b.i. (lunch) and a la carte 38/60.
◆ What was once a showy cabaret theatre has been converted into a vast and trendy restaurant with designer décor. Tables with view of what's cooking, contemporary cuisine.

XX **Chez Maître Paul,** 12 r. Monsieur-le-Prince (6th) Ⓜ *Odéon* ✆ 01 43 54 74 59, *chez.maitrepaul@aol.com, Fax 01 43 54 43 74* – ▤. AE ⓓ GB K 13
closed Sunday and Monday in July-August – **Meals** 28/33 b.i. and a la carte 34/60 ♀.
◆ Anodyne façade and an interior with particularly sober décor in a street full of the atmosphere of the Latin Quarter. Cuisine and wines from the Jura.

XX **Yen,** 22 r. St-Benoît (6th) Ⓜ *St Germain des Prés* ✆ 01 45 44 11 18, *restau-yen@wanadoo.fr, Fax 01 45 44 19 48* – ▤. AE ⓓ GB JCB J 13
closed 1 to 15 August and Sunday lunch – **Meals** - Japanese rest. - 40 and a la carte 36/54 ♀.
◆ Two dining rooms with minimalist Japanese décor, a little more cheerful on the first floor The menu makes the most of soba, the chef's speciality (buckwheat noodles).

X **Atelier Maître Albert,** 1 r. Maître Albert (5th) Ⓜ *Maubert Mutualité* ✆ 01 56 81 30 01 *ateliermaitrealbert@guysavoy.com, Fax 01 53 10 83 23* – ▤. AE ⓓ GB JCB K 15
closed Sunday – **Meals** (dinner only) a la carte 40/55.
◆ A new team has breathed fresh life into this renowned restaurant, adding a design feel alongside the medieval chimney and exposed beams. Refined cuisine and grilled meats.

X **L'Épi Dupin,** 11 r. Dupin (6th) Ⓜ *Sèvres Babylone* ✆ 01 42 22 64 56, *lepidupin@wanadoo.fr, Fax 01 42 22 30 42,* 🏠 – GB K 12
closed 31 July-26 August, Monday lunch, Saturday and Sunday – **Meals** (booking essential) 30.
◆ Beams and stonework for character, serried ranks of tables for conviviality, delicious dishes for your delight - this little restaurant has conquered the Bon Marché area.

X **Dominique,** 19 r. Bréa (6th) Ⓜ *Vavin* ✆ 01 43 27 08 80, *restaurant.dominique@mageos.com, Fax 01 43 27 03 76* – ▤. AE ⓓ GB JCB L 12
closed 25 July-24 August, Sunday and Monday – **Meals** - Russian rest. - (dinner only) 40/98 and a la carte 43/70.
◆ This stronghold of Russian cuisine is a vodka bar, grocery and restaurant all in one. Zakuski in the bistro, candlelit dining at the rear.

Brasserie Lipp, 151 bd St-Germain (6th) Ⓜ *St-Germain-des-Prés* ✆ 01 45 48 53 91, *lipp@magic.fr, Fax 01 45 44 33 20* – ▤. AE ⓓ GB J 13
Meals a la carte 33/52.
◆ Founded in 1880, this brasserie is one of the great institutions of St-Germain. Dine in the downstairs room with its ceramics, painted ceilings and celebrities.

Les Délices d'Aphrodite, 4 r. Candolle (5th) Ⓜ *Censier Daubenton* ✆ 01 43 31 40 39, *andreas@mavrommatis.fr, Fax 01 43 36 13 08* – ▤. AE GB JCB. M 15
closed Sunday – **Meals** - Greek rest. - a la carte 31/45.
◆ Tiny bistro with a holiday atmosphere - photos of Greek landscapes, bark-covered ceiling and cuisine redolent of the fruit of the olive tree.

Emporio Armani Caffé, 149 bd St-Germain (6th) Ⓜ *St Germain des Prés* ✆ 01 45 48 62 15, *Fax 01 45 48 53 17* – ▤. AE ⓓ GB JCB J 13
closed Sunday – **Meals** - Italian rest. - a la carte 30/55.
◆ On the first floor of the famous fashion shop a smart Italian café with sober and comfortable décor and a very Left Bank clientele. Italian cuisine.

Moissonnier, 28 r. Fossés-St-Bernard (5th) Ⓜ *Jussieu* ✆ 01 43 29 87 65, *Fax 01 43 29 87 65* – GB K 15
closed August, Sunday and Monday – **Meals** 23 (lunch) and a la carte 31/45 ♀.
◆ The typical bistro-style décor has remained unchanged for decades - gleaming zinc counter, old walls, benches... Cuisine from Lyon and jugs of Beaujolais.

Les Bouchons de François Clerc, 12 r. Hôtel Colbert (5th) Ⓜ *Maubert Mutualité* ✆ 01 43 54 15 34, *Fax 01 46 34 68 07* – AE GB JCB K 15
closed Saturday lunch and Sunday – **Meals** 41 ⚘.
◆ What it lacks in space this 17C Parisian house makes up for in charm, with features including a roasting spit in the main dining room. Impressive, reasonably priced wine list.

Ze Kitchen Galerie, 4 r. Grands Augustins (6th) Ⓜ *St Michel* ✆ 01 44 32 00 32, *zekitchen.galerie@wanadoo.fr, Fax 01 44 32 00 33* – ▤. AE ⓓ GB JCB J 14
closed Saturday lunch and Sunday – **Meals** 32 (lunch) and a la carte 43/55.
◆ Zis is ZE place to come on the Left Bank quayside. Cool interior enlivened by works of contemporary artists, design furniture and modish dishes prepared as you watch.

Faubourg-St-Germain, Invalides, École Militaire.

7th arrondissement.
7th: ✉ 75007

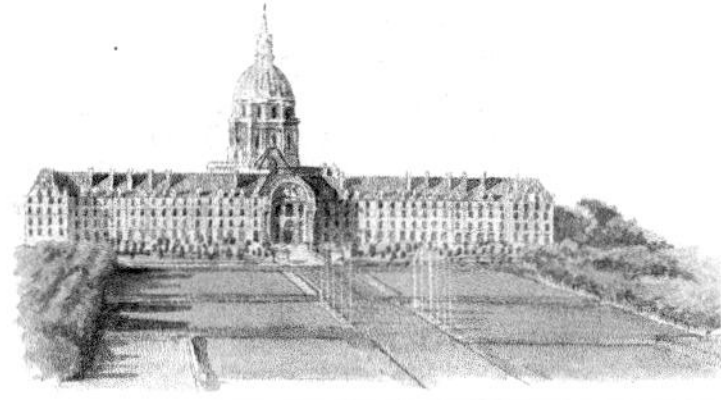

Pont Royal without rest, 7 r. Montalembert Ⓜ *Rue du Bac* ✆ 01 42 84 70 00, *hpr@hotel-pont-royal.com, Fax 01 42 84 71 00,* Fб – |♦|, ⇹ rm, ▤ TV ✆ ♿ – 🔬 35. AE ⓓ GB JCB
☕ 26 – **64 rm** 370/420, 11 suites.
◆ Bold colours and mahogany panelling in the rooms - Left Bank Bohemianism combined with the comfort of a refined "literary hotel".

Duc de Saint-Simon ⛵ without rest, 14 r. St-Simon Ⓜ *Rue du Bac* ✆ 01 44 39 20 20, *duc.de.saint.simon@wanadoo.fr, Fax 01 45 48 68 25* – |♦| TV ✆. AE ⓓ GB. ⚘ J 11
☕ 15 – **29 rm** 245/280, 5 suites.
◆ With bright colours, panelling, and antiques of various kinds, the atmosphere here is that of a fine residence of bygone days. Courteous reception plus tranquillity.

Montalembert, 3 r. Montalembert Ⓜ *Rue du Bac* ✆ 01 45 49 68 68, *welcome@montalembert.com, Fax 01 45 49 69 49,* 🏠 – |♦|, ⇹ rm, ▤ TV ✆ 🚗 – 🔬 20. AE ⓓ GB JCB J 12
Meals a la carte 50/69 ♀ – ☕ 20 – **48 rm** 340/430, 8 suites.
◆ Dark wood, leather, glass, steel, plus subtle shades of lilac, plum and tobacco, all the ingredients of contemporary style. Designer dining room, a terrace protected by a box hedge, and a two-stage cuisine to suit your appetite.

K+K Hotel Cayré without rest, 4 bd Raspail Ⓜ *Rue du Bac* ✆ 01 45 44 38 88, *reservations@kkhotels.fr, Fax 01 45 44 98 13* – |♦|, ⇹ rm, ▤ TV ✆ ♿. AE ⓓ GB JCB. ⚘ J 12
☕ 20 – **125 rm** 330/388.
◆ Ample space, good soundproofing and other facilities in this hotel located on a busy thoroughfare. Comfortable lounge with deep armchairs in raw silk covers.

Bourgogne et Montana without rest, 3 r. Bourgogne Ⓜ *Assemblée Nationale* ✆ 01 45 51 20 22, *bmontana@bourgogne-montana.com, Fax 01 45 56 11 98* – AE GB JCB H 11
28 rm 165/305, 4 suites.
◆ Beauty and refinement in every room of this discreet 18C establishment. The top floor rooms have a superb view of the Palais-Bourbon.

Tourville without rest, 16 av. Tourville Ⓜ *Ecole Militaire* ✆ 01 47 05 62 62, *hotel@tourville.com, Fax 01 47 05 43 90* – rm, AE GB JCB J 9
20 – **30 rm** 150/310.
◆ Refined rooms with a happy combination of modern and period furniture, pictures, and décor featuring acid colours. Lounge decorated by David Hicks. Attentive service.

Verneuil without rest, 8 r. Verneuil Ⓜ *Musée d'Orsay* ✆ 01 42 60 82 14, *hotelverneuil@wanadoo.fr, Fax 01 42 61 40 38* – AE GB. J 12
12 – **26 rm** 125/190.
◆ Old building in the "Left Bank Square" with décor like that of a private residence. Elegant rooms with engravings. A wall-plate at no 5bis indicates Serge Gainsbourg's home.

Lenox Saint-Germain without rest, 9 r. Université Ⓜ *St-Germain des Prés* ✆ 01 42 96 10 95, *hotel@lenoxsaintgermain.com, Fax 01 42 61 52 83* – AE GB JCB. J 12
12,50 – **29 rm** 120/160, 5 suites.
◆ Discreetly luxurious rooms, which are not particularly spacious but are attractively decorated. "Egyptian" frescoes adorn the breakfast room. Art Deco-style bar.

d'Orsay without rest, 93 r. Lille Ⓜ *Solférino* ✆ 01 47 05 85 54, *hotel.orsay@esprit-de-france.com, Fax 01 45 55 51 16* – AE GB JCB. H 11
9 – **41 rm** 118/165.
◆ The hotel occupies two lovely, recently refurbished buildings dating from the end of the 18C. Individually decorated rooms and attractive lounge with view of verdant patio.

Eiffel Park Hôtel without rest, 17bis r. Amélie Ⓜ *Latour Maubourg* ✆ 01 45 55 10 01, *reservation@eiffelpark.com, Fax 01 47 05 28 68* – AE GB. J 9
12 – **36 rm** 155/185.
◆ Old-style painted furniture and Chinese and Indian antiques transport guests into an exotic atmosphere. Top-floor terrace is very pleasant in summer.

Walt, 37 av. de La Motte Picquet Ⓜ *Ecole Militaire* ✆ 01 45 51 55 83, *lewalt@inwoodhotel.com, Fax 01 47 05 77 59*, – rm, AE GB JCB.
Meals 28 – 18 – **25 rm** 240/310.
◆ Imposing Renaissance portraits above the headboards and contemporary furniture are just some of the original features in the rooms of this new hotel near the École Militaire. Modern cuisine is served in the colourful dining room or on a small quiet terrace.

Les Jardins d'Eiffel without rest, 8 r. Amélie Ⓜ *Latour Maubourg* ✆ 01 47 05 46 21, *paris@hoteljardinseiffel.com, Fax 01 45 55 28 08* – rm, AE GB JCB. H 9
14 – **80 rm** 133/161.
◆ A recently enlarged establishment in a quiet street. The best rooms are the brightly decorated ones in the annexe, some of them overlooking an indoor garden.

Relais Bosquet without rest, 19 r. Champ-de-Mars Ⓜ *Ecole Militaire* ✆ 01 47 05 25 45, *hotel@relaisbosquet.com, Fax 01 45 55 08 24* – AE GB JCB J 9
10,50 – **40 rm** 130/165.
◆ Discreet outside, this hotel has an attractively furnished interior in late 18C style. Refurbished rooms, all decorated with the same attention to detail. Attentive service.

Timhôtel Invalides without rest, 35 bd La Tour Maubourg Ⓜ *Latour Maubourg* ✆ 01 45 56 10 78, *invalides@timhotel.fr, Fax 01 47 05 65 08* – rm, AE GB JCB H 10
10 – **30 rm** 185/265.
◆ The rooms in this 19C establishment feature red and white brick, Louis XVI-style furniture, and reproductions of Impressionist paintings.

Muguet without rest, 11 r. Chevert Ⓜ *Ecole Militaire* ✆ 01 47 05 05 93, *muguet@wanadoo.fr, Fax 01 45 50 25 37* – rm, AE GB. J 9
8 – **48 rm** 97/105.
◆ This small hotel on a quiet street has a modern lobby and rooms (three of which enjoy views of the Eiffel Tower and Les Invalides) adorned with Louis-Philippe-style furniture.

Londres Eiffel without rest, 1 r. Augereau Ⓜ *Ecole Militaire* ✆ 01 45 51 63 02, *info@londres-eiffel.com, Fax 01 47 05 28 96* – AE GB JCB. J 8
10 – **30 rm** 99/140.
◆ Close to the avenues of the Champ-de-Mars, this cosy hotel is decorated in bright colours. The second building beyond the little courtyard is quieter.

Cadran without rest, 10 r. Champ-de-Mars Ⓜ *Ecole Militaire* ✆ 01 40 62 67 00, *info@cadranhotel.com, Fax 01 40 62 67 13* – |♦|, ⇔ rm, ▤ TV ✆. AE ⓓ GB. ✻ J 9
☕ 10 – **42 rm** 152/165.
◆ Just a step from the busy market in the Rue Clerc. Modern rooms with a number of inspired Louis XVI touches. Leather-panelled lounge with 17C fireplace.

St-Germain without rest, 88 r. Bac Ⓜ *Rue du Bac* ✆ 01 49 54 70 00, *info@hotel-saint-germain.fr, Fax 01 45 48 26 89* – |♦| ▤ TV ✆. AE GB. ✻ J 11
☕ 12 – **29 rm** 180/200.
◆ This hotel owes its charm to its diversity, with Empire, Louis Philippe, and designer furniture, antiques, and contemporary paintings. Comfortable library, attractive patio.

Varenne without rest, 44 r. Bourgogne Ⓜ *Varenne* ✆ 01 45 51 45 55, *info@hoteldevarennecom, Fax 01 45 51 86 63* – |♦| ▤ TV ✆. AE GB
☕ 9 – **24 rm** 117/147.
◆ This relatively quiet hotel has been completely renovated and embellished with Empire and Louis XVI furniture. In summer, breakfast is served in a small leafy courtyard.

Champ-de-Mars without rest, 7 r. Champ-de-Mars Ⓜ *Ecole Militaire* ✆ 01 45 51 52 30, *stg@club-internet.fr, Fax 01 45 51 64 36* – |♦| TV ✆. GB. ✻ J 9
☕ 6,50 – **25 rm** 69/80.
◆ Between the Champ-de-Mars and the Invalides, small establishment with an English atmosphere. Green façade, cosy rooms, Liberty décor. Nowhere could be more snug.

Bersoly's without rest, 28 r. Lille Ⓜ *Musée d'Orsay* ✆ 01 42 60 73 79, *bersolys@wanadoo.fr, Fax 01 49 27 05 55* – |♦| ▤ TV ✆. AE ⓓ GB J 13
closed August – ☕ 10 – **16 rm** 100/130.
◆ Impressionist nights in a 17C building - each room pays homage to a painter (Renoir, Gauguin...) with works that can be seen at the neighbouring Musée d'Orsay.

XXXX ✿✿✿ **Arpège** (Passard), 84 r. Varenne Ⓜ *Varenne* ✆ 01 45 51 47 33, *arpege.passard@wanadoo.fr, Fax 01 44 18 98 39* – ▤. AE ⓓ GB JCB J 10
closed Saturday and Sunday – **Meals** 300 and a la carte 170/230.
◆ Contemporary elegance - precious woods and Lalique glass plus a masterchef's dazzling cuisine based on choice vegetables - the kitchen garden strikes back !
Spec. "Collection légumière". Dragée de pigeonneau à l'hydromel. Tomate confite farcie aux douze saveurs (dessert).

XXXX ✿✿ **Le Divellec,** 107 r. Université Ⓜ *Invalides* ✆ 01 45 51 91 96, *ledivellec@noos.fr, Fax 01 45 51 31 75* – ▤ ⇨. AE ⓓ GB JCB. ✻ H 10
closed 20 July-20 August, Saturday and Sunday – **Meals** - Seafood - 55 (lunch)/70 (lunch) and a la carte 115/200.
◆ Smart nautical décor, with lots of blue and white, wave motifs on frosted glass, and a lobster tank. Fine seafood freshly shipped in from the shores of the Atlantic.
Spec. Huîtres spéciales à la laitue de mer. Homard bleu à la presse avec son corail. Turbot rôti à l'arête.

XXX ✿ **Jules Verne,** Eiffel Tower : 2nd platform, lift in south leg Ⓜ *Bir Hakeim* ✆ 01 45 55 61 44, *Fax 01 47 05 29 41*, ← Paris – ▤ ⇨. AE ⓓ GB JCB. ✻ J 7
Meals 53 (lunch)/120 and a la carte 100/130.
◆ The hi-tech décor of this establishment in the sky can hardly compete with the fantastic spectacle of Paris itself. To make the most of the experience, reserve a window seat.
Spec. Persillé de langoustines, truffes et poireaux, foie gras. Saint-Jacques et fricassée de pigeon. Soufflé au praliné.

XXX ✿ **Violon d'Ingres** (Constant), 135 r. St-Dominique Ⓜ *Ecole Militaire* ✆ 01 45 55 15 05, *violondingres@wanadoo.fr, Fax 01 45 55 48 42* – ▤. AE GB JCB J 8
closed 31 July-23 August, Sunday and Monday – **Meals** 39 (lunch), 80/110 and a la carte 80/100.
◆ Wainscoting helps create a warm ambience in this gourmet rendezvous famed for its virtuoso cuisine and its piano-playing chef.
Spec. Foie gras de canard poêlé au pain d'épices. Suprême de bar croustillant aux amandes. Tatin de pied de porc caramélisée.

XXX ✿ **Pétrossian,** 144 r. Université Ⓜ *Invalides* ✆ 01 44 11 32 32, *Fax 01 44 11 32 35* – ▤ ⇨. AE ⓓ GB JCB H 10
closed 8 to 30 August, Sunday and Monday – **Meals** 38 (lunch), 48/150 and a la carte 90/140 ♀.
◆ The Pétrossian family have been treating Parisians to Caspian caviar since 1920. Elegant restaurant over the shop serving inventive cuisine.
Spec. Les "Coupes du Tsar". Tronçon de turbot, jus à l'arabica. Kyscielli (dessert).

XXX **Cantine des Gourmets,** 113 av. La Bourdonnais Ⓜ *Ecole Militaire* ✆ 01 47 05 47 96, *la.cantine@le-bourdonnais.com, Fax 01 45 51 09 29* – ▤. AE GB JCB J 9
Meals 40 (lunch), 52/80 and a la carte 80/110.
◆ Two luxurious interiors featuring straw tones, white flowers and ingeniously placed mirrors. Charming reception. Contemporary cuisine.

XX **Chamarré,** 13 bd La Tour-Maubourg Ⓜ *Invalides* ✆ 01 47 05 50 18, *chantallaval@wanadoo.fr, Fax 01 47 05 91 21* – ▤. AE GB JCB H 10
closed 9 to 22 August, Saturday lunch and Sunday – **Meals** 40 (lunch), 80/100 and a la carte 70/100.
◆ Smart, modern decor with exotic wood panelling, friendly service, and a chef who is a master at melding the flavours of France and Mauritius (from where the owner hails).
Spec. Bar en carpaccio, condiments mauriciens. Cochon de lait lardé au bois d'Inde, mousseline de banane plantain. Bringelles caramélisées au sucre "dark muscovado" de l'île Maurice.

XX **Bellecour** (Goutagny), 22 r. Surcouf Ⓜ *Latour Maubourg* ✆ 01 45 51 46 93, *Fax 01 45 50 30 11* – ▤. AE ⓓ GB H 9
closed August, Saturday lunch and Sunday – **Meals** 44.
◆ Specialities from Lyon on a menu redolent of that city and its region but nevertheless reflecting today's tastes. Sober, elegant décor, tables rather too close.
Spec. Quenelle de brochet au coulis de langoustines. Truffière de Saint-Jacques (15 December-15 April). Lièvre à la cuillère (15 October-15 December).

XX **Récamier,** 4 r. Récamier Ⓜ *Sèvres Babylone* ✆ 01 45 48 87 87, *Fax 01 45 48 87 87*, – ▤. AE GB K 12
closed Sunday – **Meals** a la carte 30/45 ♀.
◆ The menu at this "literary" address popular with authors and publishers offers a wide choice of savoury and sweet soufflés. Quiet, pleasant terrace on a traffic-free street.

XX **Vin sur Vin,** 20 r. de Monttessuy Ⓜ *Ecole Militaire* ✆ 01 47 05 14 20 – ▤. GB H 8
closed 1 to 26 August, 21 Dec.-6 January, Monday except dinner from September to Easter, Saturday lunch and Sunday – **Meals** (booking essential) a la carte 55/70.
◆ Friendly service, elegant decor, delicious traditional cuisine and a full wine list (600 appellations) - top marks for this restaurant situated close to the Eiffel Tower!
Spec. Galette de pieds de cochon. Agneau de Lozère. Millefeuille au chocolat.

XX **Claude Colliot,** 15 r. Babylone Ⓜ *Sèvres-Babylone* ✆ 01 45 49 14 40, *ccolliot@club-internet.fr, Fax 01 45 49 14 44* – ▤. GB. ✻ K 11
closed 10 to 20 August, 20 to 29 December, Saturday and Sunday – **Meals** 35 b.i./59 b.i. and a la carte 50/75.
◆ Pleasant establishment just a step from the Bon Marché. Sober contemporary decor of the dining rooms contrasts with tasty, creative cuisine. Attentive service.

XX **New Jawad,** 12 av. Rapp Ⓜ *Ecole Militaire* ✆ 01 47 05 91 37, *Fax 01 45 50 31 27* – ▤. AE ⓓ GB H 8
Meals Indian and Pakistani rest. 16/23 and a la carte 27/43 ♀.
◆ This restaurant near the Pont de l'Alma offers customers a luxurious ambience, attentive service and dishes from India and Pakistan.

XX **Beato,** 8 r. Malar Ⓜ *Invalides* ✆ 01 47 05 94 27, *beato.rest@wanadoo.fr, Fax 01 45 55 64 41* – ▤. AE GB JCB H 9
closed 18 July-15 August, 24 December-2 January, Saturday lunch and Sunday – **Meals** - Italian rest. - 25 (lunch) and a la carte 40/65 ♀.
◆ Frescoes and columns that could have come from Pompeii, and neo-Classical chairs - a version of Italian décor for a chic restaurant. Dishes from Milan, Rome and elsewhere.

XX **D'Chez Eux,** 2 av. Lowendal Ⓜ *Ecole Militaire* ✆ 01 47 05 52 55, *Fax 01 45 55 60 74* – ▤. AE ⓓ GB J 9
closed 1 to 27 August and Sunday – **Meals** 36 and a la carte 48/64.
◆ For over 40 years this restaurant has served copious portions inspired by the cuisine of Auvergne and southwest France. Provincial inn ambience and smock-coated staff.

X **Au Bon Accueil,** 14 r. Monttessuy Ⓜ *Alma Marceau* ✆ 01 47 05 46 11 – ▤. GB H 8
closed Saturday and Sunday – **Meals** 27 (lunch)/31 (dinner) and a la carte 45/62.
◆ In the shade of the Eiffel Tower, a modern interior or a small adjacent room with tasty food in contemporary style, well adapted to the season.

X **Les Olivades,** 41 av. Ségur Ⓜ *Ségur* ✆ 01 47 83 70 09, *Fax 01 42 73 04 75* – ▤. AE GB JCB K 9
closed 4 to 27 August, Sunday, lunch Saturday and Monday – **Meals** 32/55 and a la carte 51/65.
◆ An establishment fragrant with the scent of olive oil, offering an appetising version of Mediterranean cuisine. Bright and sunny ambience enlivened by motifs from Provence.

X **Clos des Gourmets,** 16 av. Rapp Ⓜ *Alma Marceau* ✆ 01 45 51 75 61, *Fax 01 47 05 74 20* – GB H 8
closed 10 to 25 August, Sunday and Monday – **Meals** 27 (lunch)/32.
◆ Recently redecorated in sunny colours, this modest place has its retinue of regulars who appreciate its appetising menu varied according to availability of fresh ingredients.

X **Maupertu,** 94 bd La Tour Maubourg Ⓜ *Ecole Militaire* ✆ 01 45 51 37 96, *info@restaurant-maupertu-paris.com, Fax 01 53 59 94 83* – GB J 10
closed Sunday dinner – **Meals** 28 ♀.
◆ The Invalides beckon whether you eat outside or in the veranda-like dining-room with its walls in sunny colours. Dishes inspired by the cuisine of Provence.

Florimond, 19 av. La Motte-Picquet Ⓜ *Ecole Militaire* ✆ 01 45 55 40 38, *Fax 01 45 55 40 38* – GB H 9
closed 31 July-22 August, 24 December-4 January, Saturday lunch and Sunday – **Meals** 18,50 (lunch)/31,50 and a la carte 38/51.
◆ Bearing the name of Monet's Giverny gardener, this tiny non-smoking establishment is decorated in bright colours and wood panelling. Dishes based on fresh market produce.

P'tit Troquet, 28 r. Exposition Ⓜ *Ecole Militaire* ✆ 01 47 05 80 39, *Fax 01 47 05 80 39* – GB. J 9
closed 1 to 23 August, Sunday, lunch Saturday and Monday – **Meals** (booking essential) 28 ♀.
◆ Small it may be, but the "little innkeeper" has a lot going for it including a cheerful atmosphere, old posters, and a tasty cuisine based on produce fresh from the market.

Champs-Élysées, St-Lazare, Madeleine.

8th arrondissement.
8th: ✉ 75008

Plaza Athénée, 25 av. Montaigne Ⓜ *Alma Marceau* ✆ 01 53 67 66 65, *reservation @plaza-athenee-paris.com, Fax 01 53 67 66 66*, – rm, – 20 - 60. AE GB JCB G 9
see ***Alain Ducasse au Plaza Athénée and Relais Plaza*** below ***La Cour Jardin*** (terrace) ✆ 01 53 67 66 02 *(mid-May-mid-September)* **Meals** a la carte 70/95 – ☕ 45 – **145 rm** 680/1010, 43 suites.
◆ With sumptuously refurbished rooms in classic or Art Deco style, musical teas in the Galerie des Gobelins, and a stunning designer bar, this is the epitome of the Parisian grand hotel. The Plaza's summer restaurant, the Cour Jardin, is a tranquil green oasis.

Four Seasons George V, 31 av. George V Ⓜ *George V* ✆ 01 49 52 70 00, *par.leci nq@fourseasons.com, Fax 01 49 52 70 10*, – rm, – 30 - 240. AE GB JCB F 8
see ***Le Cinq*** below - ***Galerie d'Été*** ✆ 01 49 52 70 06 **Meals** a la carte 100/120 ♀ – ☕ 30 – **184 rm** 565/890, 61 suites.
◆ Now completely refurbished in 18C style, this right royal hotel has luxurious and, by Parisian standards, huge rooms, wonderful art collections and a superb spa. The tables of the Galerie d'Été are set out in the delightful inner courtyard.

Bristol, 112 r. Fg St-Honoré Ⓜ *Miromesnil* ✆ 01 53 43 43 00, *resa@lebristolparis.com, Fax 01 53 43 43 01*, – rm, – 30 - 100. AE GB JCB. F 10
Meals see ***Bristol*** below – ☕ 46 – **143 rm** 620/730, 32 suites.
◆ Palatial 1925 grand hotel laid out around a magnificent garden. Luxurious rooms, mostly in Louis XV or XVI style and an exceptional boat-like pool on the top floor.

Crillon, 10 pl. Concorde Ⓜ *Concorde* ✆ 01 44 71 15 00, *crillon@crillon.com, Fax 01 44 71 15 02*, – rm, – 30 - 60. AE GB JCB G 11
see ***Les Ambassadeurs*** and ***L'Obélisque*** below – ☕ 45 – **103 rm** 665/865, 44 suites.
◆ The lounges of this private hotel dating from the 18C have kept their splendid ornamentation. The panelled bedrooms are magnificent. Palatial living, French style.

Royal Monceau, 37 av. Hoche Ⓜ *Ch. de Gaulle-Etoile* ✆ 01 42 99 88 00, *reservation s@royalmonceau.com, Fax 01 42 99 89 90*, – rm, – 25 - 100. AE GB JCB. E 8
see ***Le Jardin*** and ***Carpaccio*** below – ☕ 40 – **155 rm** 430/480, 47 suites.
◆ Marble, glass, a monumental staircase... The spacious foyer/lounge is the jewel in the crown of this 1920s grand hotel. Refined rooms. Well-equipped fitness centre. Squash.

Lancaster, 7 r. Berri Ⓜ *George V* ✆ 01 40 76 40 76, *reservations@hotel-lancaster.fr, Fax 01 40 76 40 00*, – rm, . AE GB. F 9
Meals (residents only) a la carte 55/80 – ☕ 28 – **45 rm** 470/520, 11 suites.
◆ B Pastoukhoff settled his bill here by painting pictures, thereby enriching the elegant décor of the venerable private hotel that was also a favourite of Marlene Dietrich.

Vernet, 25 r. Vernet Ⓜ *Ch. de Gaulle-Etoile* ✆ 01 44 31 98 00, *reservation@hotelvernet.com, Fax 01 44 31 85 69* – |≡|, ≡ TV ✆. AE ⓓ GB JCB. ✼ rest F 8
see ***Les Élysées*** below – ☕ 35 – **42 rm** 420/1200, 9 suites.
◆ Lovely 1920s stone building with wrought-iron balconies. Empire or Louis XVI-style rooms. Trendy grill-bar.

Sofitel Astor, 11 r. d'Astorg Ⓜ *Saint-Augustin* ✆ 01 53 05 05 05, *Fax 01 53 05 05 30,* Ⅰ6 – |≡|, ✕ rm, ≡ rm, TV ✆ ♿. AE ⓓ GB JCB. ✼ rest F 11
L'Astor ✆ 01 53 05 05 20 *(closed 31 July-29 August, Saturday, Sunday and Bank Holidays)* Meals 55/98 ♀ – ☕ 25 – **130 rm** 370/737, 4 suites.
◆ A successful fusion of Regency and Art Deco style in this cosy establishment much appreciated by a select circle of regular guests.

San Régis, 12 r. J. Goujon Ⓜ *Champs-Elysées-Clemenceau* ✆ 01 44 95 16 16, *message@hotel-sanregis.fr, Fax 01 45 61 05 48* – |≡| ≡ TV ✆. AE ⓓ GB JCB. ✼ G 9
Meals *(closed August)* a la carte 48/70 ♀ – ☕ 20 – **33 rm** 300/540, 11 suites.
◆ Newly refurbished town mansion of 1857 with delightful rooms graced here and there with mottled furniture. Haute couture boutiques nearby. The San Régis restaurant - a real little gem - is in an intimate and luxurious lounge-cum-library.

Le Faubourg Sofitel Demeure Hôtels, 15 r. Boissy d'Anglas Ⓜ *Concorde* ✆ 01 44 94 14 14, *h1295@accor-hotels.com, Fax 01 44 94 14 28,* Ⅰ6 – |≡|, ✕ rm, ≡ TV ✆ ♿ 🚗. AE ⓓ GB JCB. ✼ G 11
Café Faubourg ✆ 01 44 94 14 24 *(closed 1 to 15 August, Sunday lunch and Saturday)* Meals a la carte 60/75 – ☕ 27 – **174 rm** 525/600.
◆ The Faubourg-St-Honoré branch of Sofitel is housed in two 18C and 19C residences. Hi-tech rooms, 1930s-style bar and lounge beneath a glass roof. Up-to-the-minute décor, restful indoor garden and traditional cuisine at the Café Faubourg.

Sofitel Arc de Triomphe, 14 r. Beaujon Ⓜ *Ch. de Gaulle-Etoile* ✆ 01 53 89 50 50, *h1296@accor-hotels.com, Fax 01 53 89 50 51* – |≡|, ✕ rm, ≡ TV ✆ ♿ – 🏛 40. AE ⓓ GB JCB F 8
see ***Clovis*** below – ☕ 27 – **134 rm** 550/885.
◆ The building is from the Haussmann period, the decor inspired by the 18C, and the fixtures and fittings decidedly 21C. Elegant bedrooms, including the stunning "concept room".

Hyatt Regency, 24 bd Malhesherbes Ⓜ *Madeleine* ✆ 01 55 27 12 34, *madeleine@paris.hyatt.com, Fax 01 55 27 12 35,* Ⅰ6 – |≡|, ✕ rm, ≡ TV ✆ ♿ – 🏛 20. AE ⓓ GB JCB. ✼ rest F 11
Café M *(closed Sunday lunch and Saturday)* **Meals** a la carte 45/65 – ☕ 28 – **81 rm** 515/575, 4 suites.
◆ Close to the Madeleine, a discreet façade concealing a resolutely contemporary interior combining sobriety and warmth. The Café "M" has modern furnishings, soft upholstery, honey-coloured panelling and many other choice materials plus flavourful food.

de Vigny, 9 r. Balzac Ⓜ *Ch. de Gaulle-Etoile* ✆ 01 42 99 80 80, *reservation@hoteldevigny.com, Fax 01 42 99 80 40* – |≡|, ✕ rm, ≡ rm, TV ✆ 🚗. AE ⓓ GB JCB F 8
Baretto : **Meals** a la carte 47/66 ♀ – ☕ 25 – **26 rm** 395/540, 11 suites.
◆ A discreet, refined hotel with individual, cosy rooms close to the Champs-Élysées. The elegant, comfortable lounge is warmed by a blazing fire in winter. The Baretto restaurant combines Art Deco style with traditional cuisine and a smart, hushed ambience.

Concorde St-Lazare, 108 r. St-Lazare Ⓜ *St Lazare* ✆ 01 40 08 44 44, *stlazare@concordestlazare-paris.com, Fax 01 42 93 01 20* – |≡|, ✕ rm, ≡ TV ✆ – 🏛 250. AE ⓓ GB JCB E 12
Café Terminus ✆ 01 40 08 43 30 **Meals** 33/47b.i. 🌡 – ☕ 24 – **254 rm** 360/450, 12 suites.
◆ The monumental railway hotel of 1889 by the Gare St-Lazare has been completely refurbished. Its majestic foyer - a gem of 19C architecture and design - has been given a fresh new look. The Café Terminus has retro brasserie-style décor and bistro-type cuisine.

Marriott, 70 av. Champs-Élysées Ⓜ *Franklin-D.-Roosevelt* ✆ 01 53 93 55 00, *mhrs.pardt.ays@marriotthotels.com, Fax 01 53 93 55 01,* 🏨, Ⅰ6 – |≡|, ✕ rm, ≡ TV ✆ ♿ 🚗 – 🏛 15 - 165. AE ⓓ GB JCB. ✼ F 9
Pavillon ✆ 01 53 93 55 00 *(closed Saturday)* **Meals** 38 ♀ – ☕ 29 – **174 rm** 540/815, 18 suites.
◆ A combination of transatlantic efficiency and luxury in the rooms, some of which overlook the Champs Élysées. On the far side of the impressive atrium is the Pavillon, with a décor (lamps, frescoes) recalling a fondly imagined Paris of yesteryear.

Balzac, 6 r. Balzac Ⓜ *George V* ✆ 01 44 35 18 00, *reservation@hotelbalzac.com, Fax 01 44 35 18 05* – |≡|, ≡ rm, TV ✆. AE ⓓ GB JCB F 8
see ***Pierre Gagnaire*** below – ☕ 25 – **56 rm** 330/460, 14 suites.
◆ The hotel's name recalls the great 19C writer Honoré de Balzac who spent his last days at no 22 in this street. Elegant rooms, lounge with glass roof.

Warwick, 5 r. Berri *George V* 01 45 63 14 11, *resa.whparis@warwickhotels.com, Fax 01 43 59 00 98* – rm, – 30 - 110. AE GB JCB. rest F 9
see ***Le W*** below – 28 – **149 rm** 280/650.
◆ The recent refurbishment of this hotel, which first opened in 1981, has seen the introduction of warm materials, contemporary furniture and fabrics hanging from the walls.

Napoléon, 40 av. Friedland *Ch. de Gaulle-Etoile* 01 56 68 43 21, *napoleon@hotelnapoleonparis.com, Fax 01 56 68 44 40* – rm, – 15 - 80. AE GB JCB F 8
Meals *(closed August, dinner and weekends)* a la carte 40/57 – 26 – **75 rm** 250/580, 26 suites.
◆ Just a few steps from the Emperor's much-loved Étoile, this hotel evokes Napoleonic times with well-chosen pictures, figurines and autographs and with Directoire and Empire furniture. Luxurious, intimate bar/restaurant with limited menu and efficient service.

California, 16 r. Berri *George V* 01 43 59 93 00, *cal@hroy.com, Fax 01 45 61 03 62,* – rm, – 20 - 100. AE GB JCB. rest F 9
Meals *(closed August, Saturday and Sunday)* (lunch only) 35/43 – 27 – **158 rm** 380/430, 16 duplex.
◆ Art-lovers appreciate this 1920s grand hotel, whose walls are hung with thousands of pictures. Another attraction is the display of 200 brands of whisky in the piano bar. Restaurant extending onto a delightful patio with greenery, mosaics, and fountain.

Trémoille, 14 r. Trémoille *Alma Marceau* 01 56 52 14 00, *reservation@hotel-tremoille.com, Fax 01 40 70 01 08,* – rm, – 15. AE GB JCB G 9
Meals *(closed Sunday)* 36 (lunch)/55 – 22 – **88 rm** 399/570, 5 suites.
◆ This hotel has recently been brought up-to-date and successfully manages to combine antiques with modern design. Well-equipped marble bathrooms ; elegant dining room with genteel atmosphere and seasonal menu.

Mélia Royal Alma, 35 r. J. Goujon *Alma Marceau* 01 53 93 63 00, *melia.royal.alma@solmelia.com, Fax 01 53 93 63 01* – rm, – 15. AE GB JCB G 9
Meals *(closed August, Saturday, Sunday and Bank Holidays)* (lunch only) a la carte 29/51 – 24 – **64 rm** 320/503.
◆ Refined decor and Empire-style antique furniture in the recently renovated rooms. Panoramic views from the terrace on the top floor. Simple food and brunches on offer on the veranda with pretty little garden.

Bedford, 17 r. de l'Arcade *Madeleine* 01 44 94 77 77, *contact@hotel-bedford.com, Fax 01 44 94 77 97* – – 15 - 50. AE GB JCB. rest F 11
Meals *(closed 2 to 29 August, Saturday and Sunday)* (lunch only) 37/39 – 13 – **136 rm** 174/224, 10 suites.
◆ Built in 1860 in the elegant Madeleine district, the hotel has large, refurbished functional rooms. Ambience of 1900 with abundant decorative plasterwork and a lovely cupola in the restaurant, the Bedford's real jewel.

Montaigne without rest, 6 av. Montaigne *Alma Marceau* 01 47 20 30 50, *contact@hotel-montaigne.com, Fax 01 47 20 94 12* – . AE GB JCB G 9
19 – **29 rm** 340/430.
◆ Wrought-iron grilles, a fine flower-bedecked façade, and lovely décor make this a seductive place to stay. The avenue is a stronghold of the great couturiers.

Amarante Champs Élysées without rest, 19 r. Vernet *George V* 01 47 20 41 73, *amarante-champs-elysees@jjwhotels.com, Fax 01 47 23 32 15* – rm, – 30. AE GB JCB F 8
25 – **42 rm** 300/360.
◆ A pretty canopy graces the smart façade of this corner building. Period furniture in the rooms. Luxurious lounge with piano bar and fine fireplace.

François 1er without rest, 7 r. Magellan *George V* 01 47 23 44 04, *hotel@hotel-francois1er.fr, Fax 01 47 23 93 43* – rm, – 15. AE GB JCB F 8
21 – **40 rm** 290/460.
◆ Mexican marble, moulding, antique trinkets and furniture and numerous paintings contribute to the luxurious decor designed by Pierre-Yves Rochon. Substantial buffet breakfast.

Sofitel Champs-Élysées, 8 r. J. Goujon *Champs Elysées Clemenceau* 01 40 74 64 64, *h1184-re@accor-hotels.com, Fax 01 40 74 79 66,* – rm, – 15 - 150. AE GB JCB G 9
Les Signatures 01 40 74 64 94 *(lunch only) (closed 23/07-22/08, 24/12-03/01, Saturday and Sunday)* **Meals** 45 – 24 – **40 rm** 350/550.
◆ Private hotel from the time of Napoleon III in same building as the alumni association of the famous École Nationale. Refurbished contemporary rooms, latest facilities. Business centre. Les Signatures with cool décor, pretty terrace and journalistic clientele.

Radisson SAS Champs Élysées, 78 av. Marceau *Ch. de Gaulle-Etoile* *01 53 23 43 43, reservations.paris@radissonsas.com, Fax 01 53 23 43 44,* – , rm, . F 8
Meals *(closed Saturday, Sunday and Bank Holidays)* a la carte 59/77 – 27 – **46 rm** 315.
◆ A new hotel created in a building which once belonged to Louis Vuitton. Modern rooms, state-of-the-art equipment (plasma screen TVs) and efficient soundproofing. Dining by the bar or on the summer terrace. Concise à la carte menu showing Provençal influence.

Résidence du Roy without rest, 8 r. François 1er *Franklin D. Roosevelt* *01 42 89 59 59, rdr@residence-du-roy.com, Fax 01 40 74 07 92* – kitchenette – 25. G 9
19 – **12 rm** 290/330, 27 suites650.
◆ Up-to-date and quite spacious rooms, all with kitchenettes enabling visitors to stay in Paris while making themselves quite at home.

Pershing Hall, 49 r. P. Charon *George V* 01 58 36 58 00, *info@pershinghall.com, Fax 01 58 36 58 01* – – 60. G 9
Meals *(closed Sunday)* a la carte 40/82 – 34 – **20 rm** 390/720, 6 suites.
◆ Once the residence of US General Pershing, a veterans' club and now a charming hotel redesigned by Andrée Putmann. Smart interior and delightful vertical garden. Beyond the curtain of glass pearls a restaurant with up-to-the-minute ambience and trendy menu.

Chambiges Élysées without rest, 8 r. Chambiges *Alma Marceau* 01 44 31 83 83, *chamb@paris-hotels-charm.com, Fax 01 40 70 95 51* – , rm, . G 9
26 rm 245/330, 8 suites.
◆ Wood panelling, wall hangings, luxurious soft-furnishings and romantic atmosphere in this entirely renovated hotel. Quiet, cosy rooms and pretty little interior garden.

L'Arcade without rest, 7 et 9 r. Arcade *Madeleine* 01 53 30 60 00, *reservation@hotel-arcade.com, Fax 01 40 07 03 07* – – 25. F 11
9 – **37 rm** 140/215, 4 duplex.
◆ Marble and panelling in foyer and lounges, soft colours and choice furnishings in the bedrooms lend great charm to this discreet, elegant hotel near the Madeleine.

Monna Lisa, 97 r. La Boétie *St-Philippe du Roule* 01 56 43 38 38, *contact@hotelmonnalisa.com, Fax 01 45 62 39 90* – . F 9
Caffe Ristretto - Italian rest. *(closed Saturday and Sunday)* **Meals** a la carte 36/56 – 22 – **22 rm** 220/265.
◆ This attractive hotel housed in a building dating from 1860 is a shop window for bold and innovative Italian design. Enjoy a gastronomic journey around the Italian peninsula in the delightfully contemporary surroundings of the Caffe Ristretto.

Lavoisier without rest, 21 r. Lavoisier *St-Augustin* 01 53 30 06 06, *info@hotellavoisier.com, Fax 01 53 30 23 00* – . F 11
12 – **26 rm** 230/305, 4 suites.
◆ This hotel in the St-Augustin district has contemporary rooms, a small, cosy lounge-cum-library also serving as the bar, plus a vaulted breakfast room.

Queen Mary without rest, 9 r. Greffulhe *Madeleine* 01 42 66 40 50, *hotelqueenmary@wanadoo.fr, Fax 01 42 66 94 92* – . F 12
16 – **36 rm** 135/189.
◆ A refined hotel with a very British ambience and a welcome sherry on arrival. Attractive patio, pretty breakfast room and cosy bedrooms.

Vignon without rest, 23 r. Vignon *Madeleine* 01 47 42 93 00, *reservation@hotelvignon.com, Fax 01 47 42 04 60* – . F 12
15 – **30 rm** 275/340.
◆ Comfortable, contemporary rooms just a stone's throw from Place de la Madeleine ; those on the top floor have been refurbished and are light and airy. Elegant breakfast room.

Élysées Céramic without rest, 34 av. Wagram *Ternes* 01 42 27 20 30, *cerotel@aol.com, Fax 01 46 22 95 83* – . E 8
9,50 – **57 rm** 180/223.
◆ The stoneware Art Nouveau façade of 1904 is an architectural marvel, matched by the interior with furniture and décor inspired by the same style.

Pavillon Montaigne without rest, 34 r. J. Mermoz *Franklin D. Roosevelt* 01 53 89 95 00, *hotelpavillonmontaigne@wanadoo.fr, Fax 01 42 89 33 00* – . F 10
8,50 – **18 rm** 135/175.
◆ Two buildings linked by a breakfast room with a glass roof. Rooms, some with exposed beams, have a mixture of antique and contemporary furnishings.

Le "Cinq" - Hôtel Four Seasons George V, 31 av. George V Ⓜ *George V* ✆ 01 49 52 71 54, *par.lecinq@fourseasons.com, Fax 01 49 52 71 81,* – . AE GB JCB. F 8
Meals 80 (lunch), 120/200 and a la carte 120/200.
◆ Majestic interior evoking the glories of the Grand Trianon and opening on to a delightful internal garden. Refined ambience and talented, classic cuisine.
Spec. Poireau cuit à la ficelle aux saveurs d'automne et à la truffe (October-February). Homard en coque, fumé et rôti aux châtaignes (October-February). Fricassée de langoustines à la coriandre.

Les Ambassadeurs - Hôtel Crillon, 10 pl. Concorde Ⓜ *Concorde* ✆ 01 44 71 16 16, *restaurants@crillon.com, Fax 01 44 71 15 02* – . AE GB JCB. G 11
Meals 62 (lunch)/135 and a la carte 140/180.
◆ Once the ballroom of an 18C town mansion, this is a splendid interior, its gilt and marble décor reflected in huge mirrors. Refined cuisine.
Spec. Endives de pleine terre, jambon, comté, truffe noire (January-April). Caviar osciètre royal, réduction corsée, langoustines. Pigeonneau désossé, farci de foie gras, jus à l'olive.

Ledoyen, carré Champs-Élysées (1st floor) Ⓜ *Champs Elysées Clemenceau* ✆ 01 53 05 10 01, *ledoyen@ledoyen.com, Fax 01 47 42 55 01* – P. AE GB. G 10
closed 31 July-29 August, Monday lunch, Saturday, Sunday and Bank Holidays – **Meals** 73 (lunch), 168/244 b.i. and a la carte 135/180.
◆ Neo-Classical building erected in 1848 on the site of a Champs-Élysées dance-café. Napoleon III décor, garden views and fine cuisine featuring both meat and fish dishes.
Spec. Langoustines croustillantes, émulsion d'agrumes à l'huile d'olive. Blanc de turbot, pommes rattes truffées écrasées à la fourchette. Noix de ris de veau en brochette de bois de citronnelle.

Alain Ducasse au Plaza Athénée - Hôtel Plaza Athénée, 25 av. Montaigne Ⓜ *Alma Marceau* ✆ 01 53 67 65 00, *adpa@alain-ducasse.com, Fax 01 53 67 65 12* – . AE GB JCB. G 9
closed 16 July-23 August, 17 to 30 December, Saturday, Sunday, lunch Monday, Tuesday and Wednesday – **Meals** 190/280 and a la carte 200/275.
◆ The Plaza's sumptuous Regency decor has just been given a new fresh design look. Inventive dishes created by a team trained by Alain Ducasse. Comprehensive wine list.
Spec. Langoustines rafraîchies, nage réduite, caviar osciètre royal. Volaille de Bresse, sauce albuféra aux truffes d'Alba (15 October-31 December). Coupe glacée de saison.

Bristol - Hôtel Bristol, 112 r. Fg St-Honoré Ⓜ *Miromesnil* ✆ 01 53 43 43 40, *resa@lebristolparis.com, Fax 01 53 43 43 01,* – . AE GB JCB. F 10
Meals 70/150 and a la carte 125/175.
◆ With its oval shape and splendid panelling, the winter dining room resembles a little theatre. The summer dining room opens out on the hotel's magnificent garden.
Spec. Macaroni truffés farcis d'artichaut et foie gras de canard. Poularde de Bresse au château-chalon, cuite en vessie. Sabayon au chocolat noir.

Taillevent, 15 r. Lamennais Ⓜ *Ch. de Gaulle-Etoile* ✆ 01 44 95 15 01, *mail@taillevent.com, Fax 01 42 25 95 18* – . AE GB JCB. F 9
closed 24 July-23 August, Saturday, Sunday and Bank Holidays – **Meals** (booking essential) 70 (lunch), 130/180 and a la carte 110/140.
◆ The restaurant takes its name from a celebrated medieval master cook. Housed in a ducal town house, it has panelling, works of art, exquisite cuisine and a sumptuous cellar.
Spec. Epeautre en risotto truffé. Fricassée de ris et rognon de veau. Beignet au chocolat et à la liqueur de mandarine.

Lucas Carton (Senderens), 9 pl. Madeleine Ⓜ *Madeleine* ✆ 01 42 65 22 90, *lucas.carton@lucascarton.com, Fax 01 42 65 06 23* – . AE GB JCB. G 11
closed 1 to 24 August, 19 to 27 February, Sunday, lunch Monday and Saturday – **Meals** 76 (lunch)/300 and a la carte 150/230.
◆ Superb Art Nouveau panelling by Louis Majorelle in sycamore, maple and lemonwood enhanced by mirrors and exuberant floral ornamentation. Sublime synthesis of food and wine.
Spec. Entrée de homard et sa polenta crémeuse au corail. Bar de ligne au thym-citron. Canard croisé étouffé, rougail de poireaux, mangue et gingembre mariné au vieux xérès.

Lasserre, 17 av. F.-D.-Roosevelt Ⓜ *Franklin D. Roosevelt* ✆ 01 43 59 53 43, *lasserre@lasserre.fr, Fax 01 45 63 72 23* – . AE GB JCB. G 10
closed August, Sunday, lunch Saturday, Monday, Tuesday and Wednesday – **Meals** 110 (lunch)/185 and a la carte 120/170.
◆ One of the city's gastronomic institutions. The neo-Classical dining room is crowned by a stunning sunroof decorated with a troupe of dancers. Superb wine list.
Spec. Macaroni aux truffes et foie gras en léger gratin. Dos de bar de ligne clouté de citron confit, cuit en vapeur d'algues. Noix de ris de veau de lait en fine croûte blonde acidulée.

XXXXX ✿✿ **Laurent,** 41 av. Gabriel Ⓜ *Champs Elysées-Clemenceau* ✆ 01 42 25 00 39, *info@le-laurent.com, Fax 01 45 62 45 21,* 🏡 – AE ⓓ GB JCB. G 10
closed Saturday lunch, Sunday and Bank Holidays – **Meals** 65/140 and a la carte 120/185.
◆ Built by Jacques Hittorff, this antique-style pavilion with elegant leafy terraces and fine traditional cuisine is a little corner of paradise in the Champs-Élysées gardens.
Spec. Araignée de mer dans ses sucs en gelée, crème de fenouil. Grosses langoustines "tandoori" poêlées, copeaux d'avocat à l'huile d'amandes. Foie gras de canard poêlé, mangue rôtie au gingembre et citron vert.

XXXX ✿✿ **Les Élysées** - Hôtel Vernet, 25 r. Vernet Ⓜ *Ch. de Gaulle-Etoile* ✆ 01 44 31 98 98, *elysees@hotelvernet.com, Fax 01 44 31 85 69* – AE ⓓ GB JCB. F 8
closed 24 July-23 August, 18 to 26 December, Monday lunch, Saturday and Sunday – **Meals** 48 (lunch)/130 (dinner) and a la carte 105/145.
◆ Inventive, masterly and subtly flavoured cuisine beneath a superb Belle Epoque glass roof designed by Gustave Eiffel which fills the interior with soft light.
Spec. Pied de cochon en tartine, marinade acidulée aux raisins et champignons. Pithiviers de perdrix, poule faisane et grouse au genièvre, jus de presse (October-December). Citron de Menton confit en biscuit moelleux à la mélisse.

XXXX ✿✿✿ **Pierre Gagnaire** - Hôtel Balzac, 6 r. Balzac Ⓜ *George V* ✆ 01 58 36 12 50, *p.gagnaire@wanadoo.fr, Fax 01 58 36 12 51* – AE ⓓ GB F 8
closed 10-18/04, 15-31/07, 23/10-2/11, 19-27/02, Saturday, Bank Holidays, lunch August and Sunday – **Meals** 90 (lunch), 195/260 and a la carte 200/290.
◆ Smart, sober contemporary décor (pale panelling, modern works of art) can hardly compete with the spellbinding sounds of the resident jazzman.
Spec. Déclinaison de langoustines sur différentes cuissons. Bar de ligne cuit entier en papillote, pâte de piment nora. Canard rôti entier à la cannelle, peau laquée et cuisse confite.

XXXX ✿ **La Marée,** 1 r. Daru Ⓜ *Ternes* ✆ 01 43 80 20 00, *lamaree@wanadoo.fr, Fax 01 48 88 04 04* – AE ⓓ GB E 8
closed August, Saturday lunch and Sunday – **Meals** - Seafood - a la carte 75/125 ♀.
◆ A pretty half-timbered façade, stained-glass windows, Flemish paintings and warm panelling give this restaurant its refined character. Seafood specialities.
Spec. Pressé de jarret de veau aux langoustines. Fricassée de homard aux aromates. Mille-feuille chaud caramélisé aux amandes.

XXXX ✿ **Clovis** - Hôtel Sofitel Arc de Triomphe, 14 r. Beaujon Ⓜ *Ch. de Gaulle-Etoile* ✆ 01 53 89 50 53, *h1296@accor-hotels.com, Fax 01 53 89 50 51* – AE ⓓ GB JCB
closed 24 July-24 August, 24 December-2 January, Saturday, Sunday and Bank Holidays – **Meals** 49/98 and a la carte 70/90 ♀. F 8
◆ With its classic décor brought up to date (shades of beige and brown), attentive, smiling service and refined cuisine, this establishment is a rendezvous for local gourmets.
Spec. Duo de foie gras aux figues vigneronnes. Dos de bar rôti, cœur de fenouil fondant. Carré de veau à la mitonnée de girolles (Autumn-Winter).

XXX **Maison Blanche,** 15 av. Montaigne (6th floor) Ⓜ *Alma Marceau* ✆ 01 47 23 55 99, *margot-maisonblanche@wanadoo.fr, Fax 01 47 20 09 56,* ←, 🏡 – AE GB JCB
closed lunch Saturday and Sunday – **Meals** 75 (lunch) and a la carte 85/118 ♀. G 9
◆ On top of the Theatre des Champs-Élysées, a designer restaurant with an immense glass roof giving a view of the gilded dome of the Invalides. Languedoc influenced cuisine.

XXX ✿ **Jardin** - Hôtel Royal Monceau, 37 av. Hoche Ⓜ *Ch. de Gaulle-Etoile* ✆ 01 42 99 98 70, *Fax 01 42 99 89 94,* 🏡 – AE ⓓ GB JCB. E 8
closed August, Monday lunch, Saturday and Sunday – **Meals** 49 (lunch)/99 (dinner) and a la carte 90/130.
◆ Set in a pretty flower garden, the modern glass cupola houses an elegant interior where subtly-flavoured Mediterranean dishes are served.
Spec. Sandwich de foie gras de canard confit (Autumn). Sole de petite pêche laquée, jus au pimento de la Vera (Summer). Ris de veau de lait carmélisé aux fruits de la passion (Summer).

XXX **Fouquet's,** 99 av. Champs Élysées Ⓜ *George V* ✆ 01 47 23 50 00, *fouquets@lucienbarriere.com, Fax 01 47 23 50 55,* 🏡 – AE ⓓ GB JCB F 8
Meals 54 (lunch)/78 and a la carte 75/104.
◆ A select clientele has been frequenting Le Fouquet's since 1899. Highlights include the dining room refurbished by J. Garcia, a popular outdoor terrace and brasserie cuisine.

XXX ✿ **Le W** - Hôtel Warwick, 5 r. Berri Ⓜ *George V* ✆ 01 45 61 82 08, *lerestaurantw@warwickhotels.com, Fax 01 43 59 00 98* – AE ⓓ GB JCB. F 9
closed August, 27 December-3 January, Saturday and Sunday – **Meals** 40 (lunch)/65 (dinner) and a la carte 70/95.
◆ "W" stands for the Warwick hotel, in the heart of which this restaurant with its contemporary décor serves a lovely sun-kissed cuisine.
Spec. Persillé de sardines aux poireaux et tomates confites (Summer). Carpaccio de paleron aux truffes (Winter). Merlan argenté au beurre salé, pommes fondantes et girolles (Autumn).

XXX ✿ **Chiberta,** 3 r. Arsène-Houssaye Ⓜ *Ch. de Gaulle-Etoile* ✆ 01 53 53 42 00, *info@lechiberta.com, Fax 01 45 62 85 08* – ▤ ⇨. AE ⓓ GB F 8
closed August, Saturday lunch and Sunday – **Meals** 45 (lunch), 100/155 and a la carte 80/125.
◆ The spirit of the 1970s has been given new life by redecoration in Japanese style, but its intimacy has been preserved. Ideal for business meals, with contemporary cuisine.
Spec. Truffe noire de Provence cuite au champagne (15 November-15 February). Canette rôtie à la fleur de rose, sauce aigre-douce. Pavé de bar cuit à l'unilatéral, fumet truffé, purée de céleri.

XXX **L'Obélisque** - Hôtel Crillon, 6 r. Boissy d'Anglas Ⓜ *Concorde* ✆ 01 44 71 15 15, *restaurants@crillon.com, Fax 01 44 71 15 02* – ▤. AE ⓓ GB JCB G 11
closed 24 July-22 August and Bank Holidays – **Meals** 48 ♀.
◆ Interior featuring panelling, mirrors and decorative glass, plus diners packed tightly together. Never mind! The food is refined and tasty.

XXX **Marcande,** 52 r. Miromesnil Ⓜ *Miromesnil* ✆ 01 42 65 19 14, *info@marcande.com, Fax 01 42 65 76 85,* ☂ – ⇨. AE GB F 10
closed 9 to 22 August, 24 December-3 January, Saturday and Sunday – **Meals** 42/90 b.i. and a la carte 55/83.
◆ Modest establishment favoured by a business clientele. Contemporary interior giving onto an attractive patio that is very popular in summer.

XXX ✿ **Copenhague,** 142 av. Champs-Élysées (1st floor) Ⓜ *George V* ✆ 01 44 13 86 26, *floricadanica@wanadoo.fr, Fax 01 44 13 89 44,* ☂ – ▤ ⇨. AE ⓓ GB JCB F 8
closed 1 to 23 August, Saturday, Sunday and Bank Holidays – **Meals** - Danish rest. - 50 (lunch), 68/100 and a la carte 80/103 - ***Flora Danica :*** **Meals** 32 and a la carte 43/62 ♀.
◆ This restaurant in the Maison du Danemark features Scandinavian cuisine, elegant Danish design, a view of the Champs-Élysées and a terrace overlooking a charming garden. In Flora Danica, both shop and menu make the most of salmon-based products.
Spec. Blinis de saumon fumé sauvage de la Baltique (October-June). Tartare de Saint-Jacques au caviar oscietre (1 October-15 April). Noisettes de renne, jus acidulé aux cerises.

XXX ✿ **Bath's,** 9 r. La Trémoille Ⓜ *Alma Marceau* ✆ 01 40 70 01 09, *contact@baths.fr, Fax 01 40 70 01 22* – ▤ ⇨. AE GB G 9
closed August, 24 to 27 December, Saturday, Sunday and Bank Holidays – **Meals** 30 (lunch)/70 (dinner) and a la carte 70/95 ♀ ☘.
◆ This restaurant, decorated with paintings and sculptures by the owner, has a hushed, elegant ambience. The menu focuses on specialities from the Auvergne. Good wine list.
Spec. Tarte tiède de homard et légumes. Pigeon rôti, purée de pois. "Biscotin" à la vanille, glace basilic.

XX **Spoon,** 14 r. Marignan Ⓜ *Franklin D. Roosevelt* ✆ 01 40 76 34 44, *spoonfood@aol.com, Fax 01 40 76 34 37* – ▤ ⇨. AE ⓓ GB JCB. ✗ G 9
closed 24 July-24 August, 24 December-5 January, Saturday and Sunday – **Meals** 37 (lunch) and a la carte 53/80 ♀ ☘.
◆ Minimalist, contemporary interior with designer furniture, exotic wood and a view of the kitchens. Flexible menu featuring dishes from around the globe.

XX ✿ **Carpaccio** - Hôtel Royal Monceau, 37 av. Hoche Ⓜ *Ch. de Gaulle Etoile* ✆ 01 42 99 98 90, *reception@royalmonceau.com, Fax 01 42 99 89 94* – ⇨. AE ⓓ GB JCB E 8
closed 12 to 18 April, 26 July-23 August, 24 to 31 December, 16 to 22 February – **Meals** - Italian rest. - a la carte 68/80.
◆ Beyond the foyer of the Royal Monceau hotel is this attractive restaurant full of Venetian atmosphere. Murano glass chandeliers. Tasty Italian cuisine.
Spec. Filet de bar poêlé au fenouil. Spaghettis au homard. Carré de veau rôti aux légumes cuisinés à la méditerranéenne.

XX ✿ **Luna,** 69 r. Rocher Ⓜ *Villiers* ✆ 01 42 93 77 61, *mchoisnluna@noos.fr, Fax 01 40 08 02 44* – ▤. AE GB E 11
closed 4 to 25 August and Sunday – **Meals** - Seafood - a la carte 60/80 ♀.
◆ Sober Art Deco surroundings and cuisine based on daily deliveries of fine seafood from the shores of the Atlantic. Be sure to try the rum baba.
Spec. Salade de homard à l'huile de pistache. Daurade royale au gingembre en feuille de bananier. Baba au rhum de Zanzibar.

XX **Relais Plaza** - Hôtel Plaza Athénée, 25 av. Montaigne Ⓜ *Alma Marceau* ✆ 01 53 67 64 00, *reservation@plaza-athenee-paris.com, Fax 01 53 67 66 66* – ⇨. AE ⓓ GB JCB. ✗ G 9
closed 25 July-30 August – **Meals** 43 and a la carte 58/92.
◆ Chic, intimate rendezvous for people from the neighbouring fashion houses. Subtle renovation has restored the Art Deco interior to its original glory. Refined classic cuisine.

XX **Fermette Marbeuf 1900,** 5 r. Marbeuf Ⓜ *Alma Marceau* ✆ 01 53 23 08 00, *fermettemarbeuf@blanc.net, Fax 01 53 23 08 09* – ▤. AE ⓓ GB G 9
Meals 30 and a la carte 39/70 ♀.
◆ The extraordinary Art Nouveau decor of this glazed dining room dates from 1898 and was discovered only by chance in the course of restoration work. Traditional cuisine.

XX **Marius et Janette,** 4 av. George-V Ⓜ *Alma Marceau* ✆ 01 47 23 41 88, *Fax 01 47 23 07 19,* – ▤. AE ⓓ GB G 8
✿ **Meals** - Seafood - 60 b.i. (lunch) and a la carte 75/100.
◆ The restaurant's name evokes the Marseilles back country and the films of Robert Guédiguian. Nautical décor, attractive terrace, and a taste of the Mediterranean.
Spec. Carpaccio de thon (season). Petite friture. Loup grillé à l'écaille.

XX **Stella Maris,** 4 r. Arsène Houssaye Ⓜ *Ch. de Gaulle-Etoile* ✆ 01 42 89 16 22, *stella.maris.paris@wanadoo.fr, Fax 01 42 89 16 01* – ▤. AE ⓓ GB JCB. F 8
closed Sunday, lunch in August, Saturday and Monday – **Meals** 43 (lunch), 75/110 and a la carte 70/97.
◆ This restaurant near the Arc de Triomphe offers classic, modern cuisine attractively presented by the talented Japanese chef. Warm welcome and cool, minimalist decor.

XX **Les Bouchons de François Clerc "Étoile",** 6 r. Arsène Houssaye Ⓜ *Charles de Gaulle-Etoile* ✆ 01 42 89 15 51, *siegebouchons@wanadoo.fr, Fax 01 42 89 28 67* – ▤. AE GB JCB. F 8
closed Saturday lunch and Sunday – **Meals** - Seafood - 40 and a la carte approx. 55.
◆ The most recent of the François Clerc "Bouchon" restaurants, featuring fine seafood served in a setting evoking the oceans. Excellent choice of cost-price wines.

XX **Stresa,** 7 r. Chambiges Ⓜ *Alma-Marceau* ✆ 01 47 23 51 62 – ▤. AE ⓓ GB. G 9
closed August, 20 December-3 January, Saturday and Sunday – **Meals** - Italian rest. - (booking essential) a la carte 80/110.
◆ Set among the exclusive boutiques of the "Golden Triangle" this trattoria is favoured by artists and the jet-set and features works by the likes of Buffet and César.

XX **Bistrot du Sommelier,** 97 bd Haussmann Ⓜ *St-Augustin* ✆ 01 42 65 24 85, *bistrot-du-sommelier@noos.fr, Fax 01 53 75 23 23* – ▤. AE GB F 11
closed 31 July-22 August, 24 December-2 January, Saturday and Sunday – **Meals** 39 (lunch), 60 b.i./100 b.i. and a la carte 49/69 ♀.
◆ The bistro of Philippe Faure-Brac, recipient of the world's best sommelier award in 1992. A veritable temple of wine, with a quite outstanding cellar.

XX **Kinugawa,** 4 r. St-Philippe du Roule Ⓜ *St-Philippe du Roule* ✆ 01 45 63 08 07, *Fax 01 42 60 45 21* – ▤. AE ⓓ GB JCB. F 9
closed 24 December-6 January and Sunday – **Meals** - Japanese rest. - 54 (lunch), 72/108 and a la carte 40/71 ♀.
◆ Behind a modest façade close to the church of St-Philippe-du-Roule is a Japanese restaurant with a richly varied menu of specialities.

XX **L'Angle du Faubourg,** 195 r. Fg St-Honoré Ⓜ *Ternes* ✆ 01 40 74 20 20, *angledufaubourg@cavestaillevent.com, Fax 01 40 74 20 21* – ▤. AE ⓓ GB JCB E 9
✿ *closed 24 July-23 August, Saturday, Sunday and Bank Holidays* – **Meals** 35/60 and a la carte 48/64 ♀.
◆ On the corner of Rue Faubourg-St-Honoré and Rue Balzac this modern bistro with its cool interior offers classic cuisine brought up-to-date in a most acceptable manner.
Spec. Ravioles de champignons de Paris, sauce fleurette. Pigeonneau rôti pommes fondantes, sauce rouennaise. Savarin à l'ananas épicé.

XX **Les Bouchons de François Clerc,** 7 r. Boccador Ⓜ *Alma Marceau* ✆ 01 47 23 57 80, *jph21@wanadoo.fr, Fax 01 47 23 74 54* – AE GB JCB G 9
closed Saturday lunch and Sunday – **Meals** 41 ♀.
◆ The success of this famous restaurant stems from its cost-price wines, enabling customers to enjoy great vintages without breaking the bank. Chic, Belle Époque-style bistro.

XX **Al Ajami,** 58 r. François 1er Ⓜ *George V* ✆ 01 42 25 38 44, *ajami@free.fr, Fax 01 42 25 38 39* – ▤. AE ⓓ GB JCB. G 9
Meals - Lebanese rest - 22/37 and a la carte 30/45 ♀.
◆ The temple of Lebanese cuisine in the city, with recipes handed down from father to son since 1920. Oriental décor, friendly atmosphere and a faithful band of regulars.

XX **Village d'Ung et Li Lam,** 10 r. J. Mermoz Ⓜ *Franklin D. Roosevelt* ✆ 01 42 25 99 79, *Fax 01 42 25 12 06* – ▤ (dinner). AE ⓓ GB JCB F 10
closed lunch Saturday and Sunday – **Meals** - Chinese and Thai rest. - 19/29 and a la carte 36/43 ♀.
◆ Ung and Li welcome guests to this restaurant serving Thai and Chinese cuisine. Original Asian décor, with hanging aquariums and a molten glass floor with encrusted sand.

XX **Market,** 15 r. Matignon Ⓜ *Franklin-D.-Roosevelt* ✆ 01 56 43 40 90, *prmarketsa@aol.com, Fax 01 43 59 10 87* – ▤. AE GB F 10
Meals 32 (lunch)/40 (lunch) and a la carte 50/75.
◆ A trendy restaurant with an upmarket address. Wood and stone predominate, with African masks adorning wall niches. The menu covers a range of French, Italian and Asian dishes.

Café Lenôtre-Pavillon Elysée, 10 Champs-Elysées Ⓜ *Champs-Elysées-Clemenceau* ✆ 01 42 65 85 10, *Fax 01 42 65 76 23,* – ▤ P – 40. AE ⓓ GB JCB. **Meals** a la carte 40/70.
◆ Rejuvenated by a recent facelift, this elegant pavilion built for the 1900 World Exhibition is home to a cookery school and boutique, plus a resolutely modern restaurant.

Daru, 19 r. Daru Ⓜ *Courcelles* ✆ 01 42 27 23 60, *Fax 01 47 54 08 14* – ▤. AE GB *closed August, Saturday lunch, Sunday and Bank Holidays* – **Meals** - Russian rest. - 25 (lunch)/35 and a la carte 42/64. E 9
◆ Founded in 1918, Daru was the first Russian grocery store in Paris. Today, it continues to serve traditional zakouskis, blinis and caviar amid a décor of reds and black.

Boucoléon, 10 r. Constantinople Ⓜ *Europe* ✆ 01 42 93 73 33, *Fax 01 42 93 17 44* – GB *closed 6 to 30 August, Saturday lunch, Sunday and Bank Holidays* – **Meals** (booking essential) a la carte 27/40 ♀. E 11
◆ This pleasant, small bistro with its slate menu enjoys considerable success thanks to its well-prepared, moderately priced dishes based on the freshest of ingredients.

Opéra, Gare du Nord, Gare de l'Est, Grands Boulevards.

9th and 10th arrondissements.
9th: ✉ 75009
10th: ✉ 75010

Intercontinental Le Grand Hôtel, 2 r. Scribe (9th) Ⓜ *Opéra* ✆ 01 40 07 32 32, *legrand@interconti.com, Fax 01 42 66 12 51,* – rm, ▤ – 20 - 120. AE ⓓ GB JCB.
Meals see ***Café de la Paix*** below – ☕ 31 – **450 rm** 740/850, 28 suites.
◆ This famous palace dating from 1862 has just reopened after 18 months' renovation. The Second Empire feel has been maintained, and is now allied with more modern comforts.

Scribe, 1 r. Scribe (9th) Ⓜ *Opéra* ✆ 01 44 71 24 24, *h0663-re@accor-hotels.com, Fax 01 42 65 39 97* – rm, ▤ – 50. AE ⓓ GB JCB F 12
see ***Les Muses*** below - ***Jardin des Muses*** ✆ 01 44 71 24 19 **Meals** 31 – ☕ 27 – **206 rm** 440/600, 5 suites, 6 duplex.
◆ A discreetly luxurious hotel with English décor hidden behind the façade of a Haussmann-style building. It was here, in 1895, that the public were introduced to the film-making of the Lumière brothers. Brasserie menu at the Jardin des Muses in the basement.

Millennium Opéra, 12 bd Haussmann (9th) Ⓜ *Richelieu Drouot* ✆ 01 49 49 16 00, *opera@mill-cop.com, Fax 01 49 49 17 00,* – rm, ▤ rm, – 80. AE ⓓ GB JCB F 13
Brasserie Haussmann ✆ 01 49 49 16 64 **Meals** 26/36 ♀ – ☕ 25 – **150 rm** 400/700, 13 suites.
◆ This hotel dating from 1927 has lost little of its Roaring Twenties ambience, with tasteful bedrooms adorned with Art Deco furniture and modern comforts. A more trendy atmosphere reigns supreme in the Brasserie Haussmann, with its typical cuisine.

Ambassador, 16 bd Haussmann (9th) Ⓜ *Richelieu Drouot* ✆ 01 44 83 40 40, *ambass@concorde-hotels.com, Fax 01 42 46 19 84* – rm, ▤ – 110. AE ⓓ GB JCB
see ***16 Haussmann*** below – ☕ 22 – **292 rm** 360/495, 4 suites. F 13
◆ Painted wood panels, crystal chandeliers, antique furniture and objets d'art adorn this elegant 1920s hotel with spacious and comfortable bedrooms.

Villa Opéra Drouot without rest, 2 r. Geoffroy Marie (9th) Ⓜ *Grands Boulevards* ✆ 01 48 00 08 08, *drouot@leshotelsdeparis.com, Fax 01 48 00 80 60* – ▤ . AE ⓓ GB JCB F 14
☕ 20 – **29 rm** 217/298, 3 duplex.
◆ A subtle blend of Baroque décor and the latest in creature comforts await guests in rooms further embellished by drapes, velvet, silk and wood panelling.

Terminus Nord without rest, 12 bd Denain (10th) Ⓜ *Gare du Nord* ✆ 01 42 80 20 00, *h2761@accor-hotels.com, Fax 01 42 80 63 89* – rm, – 70. AE ⓓ GB JCB
☕ 14 – **236 rm** 217/275. E 16
◆ This hotel dating from 1865 has rediscovered its former glory following recent restoration. Art Nouveau glass, British decor and a cosy ambience add to the Victorian feel.

Holiday Inn Paris Opéra, 38 r. Échiquier (10th) Ⓜ *Bonne Nouvelle* ✆ 01 42 46 92 75, *information@hi-parisopera.com, Fax 01 42 47 03 97* – rm, – 45. F 15
Meals 35 b.i. – 19 – **92 rm** 228/273.
• A short walk from the city's major boulevards and their panoply of theatres and brasseries. Large rooms decorated in the spirit of the Belle Époque. The dining room is a jewel of the 1900s, with its mosaics, old glass, woodwork and fine Art Nouveau furniture.

Pavillon de Paris without rest, 7 r. Parme (9th) Ⓜ *Liège* ✆ 01 55 31 60 00, *mail@pavillondeparis.com, Fax 01 55 31 60 01* – D 12
15 – **30 rm** 230/285.
• Contemporary, minimalist décor and the latest in hotel technology (TV Internet access, fax and voice mail) are the key selling points of this sober, yet luxurious hotel.

Lafayette without rest, 49 r. Lafayette (9th) Ⓜ *Le Peletier* ✆ 01 42 85 05 44, *h2802-gm@accor-hotels.com, Fax 01 49 95 06 60* – kitchenette, rm, F 14
14 – **96 rm** 209/269, 7 suites.
• Elegant beige and wood furnishings in the lobby, plus bedrooms with a rustic, 18C feel and Liberty print fabrics. Winter garden atmosphere in the breakfast room.

St-Pétersbourg without rest, 33 r. Caumartin (9th) Ⓜ *Havre Caumartin* ✆ 01 42 66 60 38, *hotel.st-petersbourg@wanadoo.fr, Fax 01 42 66 53 54* – – 25. F 12
100 rm 165/206.
• Most of the hotel's rooms, furnished in Louis XVI style, are spacious and overlook the courtyard. The opulent lounge, with its wood panelling, coffered ceilings and armchairs, is lit via a colourful glass ceiling. Hushed restaurant with an 1890s counter.

Richmond Opéra without rest, 11 r. Helder (9th) Ⓜ *Chaussée d'Antin* ✆ 01 47 70 53 20, *paris@richmond-hotel.com, Fax 01 48 00 02 10* – F 13
11 – **59 rm** 167.
• Almost all the hotel's large and elegant bedrooms look onto the courtyard. The lounge is imposingly decorated in Empire style.

Carlton's Hôtel without rest, 55 bd Rochechouart (9th) Ⓜ *Anvers* ✆ 01 42 81 91 00, *carltons@club-internet.fr, Fax 01 42 81 97 04* – D 14
9 – **108 rm** 130/138.
• The Carlton's main features are its impressive location and rooftop terrace with views of the city. Comfortable rooms with good soundproofing in those facing the boulevard.

Villa Royale without rest, 2 r. Duperré (9th) Ⓜ *Pigalle* ✆ 01 55 31 78 78, *royale@leshotelsdeparis.com, Fax 01 55 31 78 70* – rm, D 13
20 – **31 rm** 250/410.
• Antique and modern furniture and artefacts set against a backdrop of shimmering colourful decor. Recently redecorated and featuring the latest modern equipment.

Albert 1er without rest, 162 r. Lafayette (10th) Ⓜ *Gare du Nord* ✆ 01 40 36 82 40, *paris@albert1erhotel.com, Fax 01 40 35 72 52* – E 16
11 – **55 rm** 97/113.
• A hotel with modern, well-appointed and constantly upgraded rooms with efficient double-glazing. Friendly atmosphere and service.

Opéra Cadet without rest, 24 r. Cadet (9th) Ⓜ *Cadet* ✆ 01 53 34 50 50, *infos@hotel-opera-cadet.fr, Fax 01 53 34 50 60* – – 50. F 14
12 – **82 rm** 172/190, 3 suites.
• Leave your car in the hotel garage, set up residence in this modern hotel, and take to the capital on foot. The rooms facing the garden are generally quieter.

Bergère Opéra without rest, 34 r. Bergère (9th) Ⓜ *Grands Boulevards* ✆ 01 47 70 34 34, *hotel.bergere@astotel.com, Fax 01 47 70 36 36* – – 40. F 14
14 – **134 rm** 167/182.
• A 19C building with a recently installed panoramic lift. The rooms, which have been renovated in stages, are pleasantly decorated, with some overlooking the garden-courtyard.

Franklin without rest, 19 r. Buffault (9th) Ⓜ *Cadet* ✆ 01 42 80 27 27, *h2779@accor-hotels.com, Fax 01 48 78 13 04* – rm, E 14
13 – **68 rm** 145/168.
• The elegant furnishings in the bedrooms are inspired by Napoleonic military campaigns. A good location in a quiet street plus an unusual naive trompe-l'oeil at reception.

Caumartin without rest, 27 r. Caumartin (9th) Ⓜ *Havre Caumartin* ✆ 01 47 42 95 95, *h2811@accor-hotels.com, Fax 01 47 42 88 19* – rm, F 12
14 – **40 rm** 171/181.
• Attractively decorated rooms with contemporary light-wood furniture, plus a pleasant breakfast room ornamented with brightly coloured paintings.

Blanche Fontaine without rest, 34 r. Fontaine (9th) *Blanche* 01 44 63 54 95, *tryp.blanchefontaine@solmelia.com, Fax 01 42 81 05 52* – rm, . AE GB JCB D 13
15 – **66 rm** 169/190, 4 suites.
• Tucked away from the hustle and bustle of the city, the Blanche Fontaine offers guests spacious, reasonably renovated rooms, in addition to an attractive breakfast room.

Anjou-Lafayette without rest, 4 r. Riboutté (9th) *Cadet* 01 42 46 83 44, *hotel.anjou.lafayette@wanadoo.fr, Fax 01 48 00 08 97* – . AE GB JCB E 14
11 – **39 rm** 120/155.
• A hotel with Second Empire-style ironwork close to the leafy Square Montholon. Comfortable, soundproofed rooms which have been completely renovated in modern style.

Paris-Est without rest, 4 r. 8 Mai 1945 (main courtyard East Railwaystation)(10th) *Gare de l'Est* 01 44 89 27 00, *hotelparisest-bestwestern@autogrill.fr, Fax 01 44 89 27 49* – . AE GB E 16
10 – **45 rm** 111/182.
• Although alongside a busy railway terminal, the hotel's renovated rooms face onto a quieter rear courtyard and have the benefit of efficient soundproofing.

Trois Poussins without rest, 15 r. Clauzel (9th) *St-Georges* 01 53 32 81 81, *h3p@les3poussins.com, Fax 01 53 32 81 82* – kitchenette, rm, . AE GB JCB E 13
10 – **40 rm** 130/180.
• Charming bedrooms offering several levels of comfort, with views of Paris from the upper floors. Attractively vaulted breakfast room and a small terrace-courtyard.

Pavillon République Les Halles without rest, 9 r. Pierre Chausson (10th) *Jacques Bonsergent* 01 40 18 11 00, *republique@leshotelsdeparis.com, Fax 01 40 18 11 06* – rm, . AE GB JCB F 16
11 – **58 rm** 140/160.
• Depending on your mood and taste, choose from one of the hotel's Art Deco rooms, or those with a more romantic ambience. Most rooms overlook the rear courtyard.

Mercure Monty without rest, 5 r. Montyon (9th) *Grands Boulevards* 01 47 70 26 10, *hotel@mercuremonty.com, Fax 01 42 46 55 10* – , rm, – 50. AE GB JCB F 14
12 – **70 rm** 164.
• A fine 1930s façade, Art Deco ambience in the lobby and standard Mercure chain furnishings are the predominant features of this hotel close to the Folies Bergères.

Corona without rest, 8 cité Bergère (9th) *Grands Boulevards* 01 47 70 52 96, *hotelcoronaopera@regetel.com, Fax 01 42 46 83 49* – . AE GB JCB F 14
12 – **56 rm** 150/196, 4 suites.
• The façade of this building in a quiet and picturesque passageway built in 1825 is adorned with an elegant canopy. Burr elm furniture in the bedrooms, plus a homely lounge.

Alba-Opéra without rest, 34 ter r. La Tour d'Auvergne (9th) *Pigalle* 01 48 78 80 22, *hotel-albaopera-residence@wanadoo.fr, Fax 01 42 85 23 13* – kitchenette . AE GB JCB. E 14
7 – **24 rm** 90/125.
• It was in this hotel, at the end of a cul-de-sac, that the trumpet player Louis Armstrong lived during the 1930s. Several room categories offering varying degrees of comfort.

Amiral Duperré without rest, 32 r. Duperré (9th) *Blanche* 01 42 81 55 33, *h2756@accor-hotels.com, Fax 01 44 63 04 73* – , rm, . AE GB JCB D 13
10 – **52 rm** 97/107.
• Trompe-l'œil paintings of naval battles and maritime prints adorn the walls of the hotel lobby. Art Deco furniture in bedrooms which verge on the smallish side.

Relais du Pré without rest, 16 r. P. Sémard (9th) *Poissonnière* 01 42 85 19 59, *relaisdupre@wanadoo.fr, Fax 01 42 85 70 59* – . AE GB E 15
10 – **34 rm** 82/102.
• Located close to its older siblings, this hotel offers the same refined levels of modern comfort in its guest rooms, in addition to a cosy and contemporary bar and lounge.

Ibis Gare de l'Est, 197 r. Lafayette (10th) *Château Landon* 01 44 65 70 00, *Fax 01 44 65 70 07* – , rm, rm, . AE GB E 17
Meals (dinner only) a la carte 17/20 – 6 – **165 rm** 74.
• Space and modern facilities are the main assets of this mid-range chain hotel. The bedrooms facing the street on the top floor enjoy views of the Sacré-Coeur. The restaurant, with its pleasant décor, offers bistrot-style cuisine.

XXXX **Les Muses** - Hôtel Scribe, 1 r. Scribe (9th) Ⓜ *Opéra* ✆ 01 44 71 24 26, *h0663-re@accor-hotels.com, Fax 01 44 71 24 64* – ▤ ⛍. AE ⓓ GB JCB F 12
closed August, 24 December-2 January, Saturday, Sunday and Bank Holidays – **Meals** 45 (lunch)/110 and a la carte 90/120 ♀.
♦ This restaurant housed in the hotel basement is adorned with a fresco and several canvases depicting the Opéra district in the 19C. Enticing à la carte menu.
Spec. Crème brûlée au foie gras, melba, fleur de sel et pralin. Turbot aux algues et consommé de crevettes grises à la citronnelle. Lièvre à la royale (season).

XXX **Café de la Paix** -Intercontinental Le Grand Hôtel, 12 bd Capucines (9th) Ⓜ *Opéra* ✆ 01 40 07 36 36, *Fax 01 40 07 36 33* – ▤ ⛍. AE ⓓ GB JCB.
Meals 37 and a la carte 45/70.
♦ An opulent and famous brasserie adorned with fine frescoes, gilded panelling and furniture inspired by the style of the Second Empire. Recently renovated and open 7am-midnight.

XX **Au Chateaubriant,** 23 r. Chabrol (10th) Ⓜ *Gare de l'Est* ✆ 01 48 24 58 94, *Fax 01 42 47 09 75* – ▤. AE GB JCB E 15
closed August, Sunday and Monday – **Meals** - Italian rest. - 28 and a la carte 36/65 ♀.
♦ A hushed ambience, attractively laid tables and a collection of modern paintings provide the setting for this restaurant where the cuisine is inspired by all things Italian.

XX **16 Haussmann** - Hôtel Ambassador, 16 bd Haussmann (9th) Ⓜ *Chaussée d'Antin* ✆ 01 44 83 40 40, *16haussmann@concorde-hotels.com, Fax 01 44 83 40 57* – ▤ ⛍. AE ⓓ GB F 13
closed Saturday lunch and Sunday – **Meals** 37 b.i. and a la carte 37/55.
♦ "Parisian" blues, golden yellows, sandy-coloured wood, red Starck-designed chairs and large bay windows looking onto the boulevard, the bustle of which adds to the ambience.

XX **Au Petit Riche,** 25 r. Le Peletier (9th) Ⓜ *Richelieu Drouot* ✆ 01 47 70 68 68, *aupetitriche@wanadoo.fr, Fax 01 48 24 10 79* – ▤ ⛍. AE ⓓ GB JCB F 13
closed Sunday – **Meals** 25,50 (lunch)/28,50 and a la carte 31/52 ♀.
♦ Graceful late-19C lounge/dining rooms embellished with mirrors. You might even end up sitting at the favourite table of Maurice Chevalier and other famous stars.

XX **Julien,** 16 r. Fg St-Denis (10th) Ⓜ *Strasbourg St Denis* ✆ 01 47 70 12 06, *Fax 01 42 47 00 65* – ▤ ⛍ (dinner). AE ⓓ GB F 15
Meals 33 and a la carte 35/45 ♀.
♦ This Belle Époque brasserie dating from 1903 offers a glorious array of Art Nouveau curves, counter-curves, floral motifs and allegorical figures made from molten glass.

XX **Brasserie Flo,** 7 cour Petites-Écuries (10th) Ⓜ *Château d'Eau* ✆ 01 47 70 13 59, *Fax 01 42 47 00 80* – ▤ ⛍ (dinner). AE ⓓ GB JCB F 15
Meals 22,90 b.i./32,90 b.i. and a la carte 30/50.
♦ At the heart of the picturesque cour des Petites-Écuries, the Flo's fine décor of plain wood, coloured glass and painted panels evokes Alsace at the beginning of the 20C.

XX **Terminus Nord,** 23 r. Dunkerque (10th) Ⓜ *Gare du Nord* ✆ 01 42 85 05 15, *Fax 01 40 16 13 98* – ▤. AE ⓓ GB JCB E 16
Meals 32,90 b.i. and a la carte 32/50.
♦ The high ceiling, frescoes, posters and sculptures reflect in the mirrors of this brasserie which successfully blends Art Deco and Art Nouveau styles. Cosmopolitan clientele.

X **Petite Sirène de Copenhague,** 47 r. N.-D. de Lorette (9th) Ⓜ *St Georges* ✆ 01 45 26 66 66 – GB E 13
closed August, 23 December-2 January, Saturday lunch, Sunday, Monday and Bank Holidays – **Meals** - Danish rest. - (booking essential) 24 (lunch)/29 and a la carte 50/60.
♦ This restaurant with a simple dining room decor of whitewashed walls and filtered lighting serves a range of typical Danish dishes. Excellent service.

X **L'Oenothèque,** 20 r. St-Lazare (9th) Ⓜ *Notre Dame de Lorette* ✆ 01 48 78 08 76, *loenotheque2@wanadoo.fr, Fax 01 40 16 10 27* – ▤. AE ⓓ GB JCB E 13
closed 1 to 11 May, 9 to 31 August, Saturday and Sunday – **Meals** 30 and a la carte 33/60.
♦ A simple restaurant-cum-wine merchant offering a fine selection of vintages to accompany specials written up on the daily menu.

X **I Golosi,** 6 r. Grange Batelière (9th) Ⓜ *Richelieu Drouot* ✆ 01 48 24 18 63, *i.golosi@wanadoo.fr, Fax 01 45 23 18 96* – ▤. GB F 14
closed 9 to 23 August, Saturday dinner and Sunday – **Meals** - Italian rest - a la carte 28/47 ♀.
♦ The minimalist feel of this first-floor Italian restaurant is compensated for by the jovial service. A café, shop and tasting section are all found on the ground floor.

X **Pré Cadet,** 10 r. Saulnier (9th) Ⓜ *Cadet* ✆ 01 48 24 99 64, *Fax 01 47 70 55 96* – ▤. AE ⓓ GB JCB F 14
closed 1 to 8 May, 4 to 24 August, Christmas-New Year, Saturday lunch and Sunday – **Meals** (booking essential) 30/50 and a la carte 38/52.
♦ The success of this small eatery near the "Folies" is based on a pleasant ambience and service, and good-value dishes such as "tête de veau", the house speciality.

Bastille, Gare de Lyon, Place d'Italie, Bois de Vincennes.

12th and 13th arrondissements.
12th: ✉ 75012
13th: ✉ 75013

Sofitel Paris Bercy, 1 r. Libourne (12th) Ⓜ *Cour St-Emilion* ✆ 01 44 67 34 00, *h2192@accor-hotels.com, Fax 01 44 67 34 01,* , – , rm, – 250. AE ⓓ GB JCB NP 20
Café Ké ✆ 01 44 67 34 71 *(closed 31 July-23 August, Saturday, Sunday and Bank Holidays)* **Meals** 31/49 ♀ – ☕ 24 – **376 rm** 365, 10 suites, 10 studios.
◆ An attractive glass façade, a modern interior in brown, beige and blue, plus the latest in facilities are the Sofitel's main features. Some rooms offer views of the city. The elegant Café Ké, with its refined cuisine, is a popular choice in the Bercy district.

Novotel Gare de Lyon, 2 r. Hector Malot (12th) Ⓜ *Gare de Lyon* ✆ 01 44 67 60 00, *h1735@accor-hotels.com, Fax 01 44 67 60 60,* , – , rm, – 75. AE ⓓ GB JCB L 18
Meals a la carte 22/35 ♀ – ☕ 13 – **253 rm** 180/201.
◆ This recently built hotel overlooks a quiet square. The functional bedrooms have a terrace on the 6th floor. 24-hour swimming pool with a well-equipped children's area. Contemporary, brasserie-style restaurant with benches, cubicles and bays. Traditional menu.

Holiday Inn Bastille without rest, 11 r. Lyon (12th) Ⓜ *Gare de Lyon* ✆ 01 53 02 20 00, *resa.hinn@guichard.fr, Fax 01 53 02 20 01* – , rm, – 75. AE ⓓ GB JCB L 18
☕ 14 – **125 rm** 198/229.
◆ The façade of this hotel dates from 1913. Bedrooms decked out in wood panelling, attractive fabrics and a mix of period and modern furniture. Elegant Baroque-style lounge.

Novotel Bercy (reopening in mid-march after works), 86 r. Bercy (12th) Ⓜ *Bercy* ✆ 01 43 42 30 00, *h0935@accor-hotels.com, Fax 01 43 45 30 60,* – , rm, – 80. AE ⓓ GB JCB M 19
Meals 22 and a la carte weekend 22/34 ♀ – ☕ 13,50 – **129 rm** 110/240.
◆ The Novotel's rooms have just had a facelift in line with the chain's new standards. Good location close to the Bercy indoor stadium. Veranda dining-room plus a popular terrace in fine weather. Classic Novotel à la carte menu.

Mercure Gare de Lyon without rest, 2 pl. Louis Armand (12th) Ⓜ *Gare de Lyon* ✆ 01 43 44 84 84, *h2217@accor-hotels.com, Fax 01 43 47 41 94* – , rm, – 15 - 90. AE ⓓ GB JCB L 18
☕ 13,50 – **315 rm** 170/180.
◆ A modern hotel overlooked by the tower of the Gare de Lyon, built in 1899. Refurbished bedrooms with ceruse wood furnishing and good soundproofing. Wine bar.

Holiday Inn Bibliothèque de France without rest, 21 r. Tolbiac (13th) Ⓜ *Bibliothèque F. Mitterand* ✆ 01 45 84 61 61, *tolbiac@club-internet.com, Fax 01 45 84 43 38* – , rm, – 25. AE ⓓ GB JCB P 18
☕ 13 – **71 rm** 160/190.
◆ Fronting a busy street, 20m from the nearest metro station, this hotel has well-maintained, comfortable rooms with double-glazing. Restaurant open in the evening for light meals.

Villa Lutèce Port Royal without rest, 52 r. Jenner (13th) Ⓜ *Campo-Formio* ✆ 01 53 61 90 90, *lutece@leshotelsdeparis.com, Fax 01 53 61 90 91* – rm, . AE ⓓ GB JCB N 16
☕ 20 – **39 rm** 310/480, 6 duplex.
◆ Interior with a literary theme, modern furniture, warm colours and cosy atmosphere : a successful marriage of contemporary decor and intimacy.

Paris Bastille without rest, 67 r. Lyon (12th) Ⓜ *Bastille* ✆ 01 40 01 07 17, *infos@hotelparisbastille.com, Fax 01 40 01 07 27* – – 25. AE ⓓ GB JCB
☕ 12 – **37 rm** 142/215. K 18
◆ Modern comfort, contemporary furniture and elegant fabrics characterise the rooms in this refurbished hotel opposite the Opéra ; those facing the courtyard are generally quieter.

Manufacture without rest, 8 r. Philippe de Champagne (13th) Ⓜ *Place d'Italie* ☎ 01 45 35 45 25, *lamanufacture.paris@wanadoo.fr, Fax 01 45 35 45 40* – AE GB JCB N 16
☕ 7,50 – **57 rm** 139/239.
◆ Cordial service and elegant décor are the prime assets of this well-maintained hotel with rooms that verge on the small side. Provençal atmosphere in the breakfast room.

Ibis Gare de Lyon Diderot without rest, 31bis bd Diderot (12th) Ⓜ *Gare de Lyon* ☎ 01 43 46 12 72, *h3211@accor-hotels.com, Fax 01 43 41 68 01* – rm, – 25. AE GB L 18
☕ 6 – **89 rm** 93.
◆ Located opposite the viaduc des Arts, with its artisans' workshops and boutiques, the Ibis has brand-new fixtures and fittings and excellent sound insulation.

Touring Hôtel Magendie without rest, 6 r. Corvisart (13th) Ⓜ *Corvisart* ☎ 01 43 36 13 61, *magendie@vvf-vacances.fr, Fax 01 43 36 47 48* – – 30. GB N 14
☕ 6,30 – **112 rm** 60/70.
◆ A hotel with small, soundproofed rooms furnished in laminated wood. Special efforts have been made here to accommodate guests with limited mobility.

Au Pressoir (Seguin), 257 av. Daumesnil (12th) Ⓜ *Michel Bizot* ☎ 01 43 44 38 21, *Fax 01 43 43 81 77* – GB JCB M 22
closed 1 to 29 August, Saturday and Sunday – **Meals** 72 and a la carte 72/100 ♀.
◆ A hushed ambience, attentive service and classic cuisine are the hallmarks of this restaurant full of provincial nostalgia, where the terrace fills up quickly at lunchtime.
Spec. Crème de chou-fleur à l'émincé de truffes blanches (October-November). Assiette de fruits de mer tiède (October-May). Lièvre à la royale (October-November).

Train Bleu, Gare de Lyon (12th) Ⓜ *Gare de Lyon* ☎ 01 43 43 09 06, *isabelle.car@compass-group.fr, Fax 01 43 43 97 96* – AE GB JCB L 18
Meals (1st floor) 42,50 and a la carte 49/80 ♀.
◆ This magnificent station buffet, opened in 1901, is adorned with gilding, stucco and frescoes recalling the famous PLM train line. Brasserie cuisine and classic French fare.

L'Oulette, 15 pl. Lachambeaudie (12th) Ⓜ *Cour St-Emilion* ☎ 01 40 02 02 12, *info@l-oulette.com, Fax 01 40 02 04 77,* – AE GB JCB N 20
closed Saturday and Sunday – **Meals** - South-West of France cuisine - 28 (lunch), 46 b.i./80 b.i. and a la carte 49/77.
◆ This contemporary restaurant in the new Bercy district serves up inventive cuisine influenced by SW France. Shady terrace behind the thuya trees.

Au Trou Gascon, 40 r. Taine (12th) Ⓜ *Daumesnil* ☎ 01 43 44 34 26, *Fax 01 43 07 80 55* – . AE GB JCB M 21
closed August, 25 December-2 January, Saturday and Sunday – **Meals** 36 (lunch) and a la carte 60/78.
◆ The decor of this old 1900s-style bistro blends period mouldings, design furniture and grey tones. The culinary emphasis here is on SW France. Wines from the same region.
Spec. Emincé de Saint-Jacques crues en galette de piquillos (October-April). Lièvre à la mode d'Aquitaine au fumet de madiran (November-December). Fraises des bois en feuilles croustillantes.

Petit Marguery, 9 bd Port-Royal (13th) Ⓜ *Gobelins* ☎ 01 43 31 58 59, *Fax 01 43 36 73 34* – AE GB
closed August, Sunday and Monday – **Meals** 25,20 (lunch)/33,60 ♀.
◆ A convivial atmosphere pervades the pleasant retro-style dining rooms of this restaurant serving typical "bistro" dishes to a numerous band of regular customers.

Janissaire, 22 allée Vivaldi (12th) Ⓜ *Daumesnil* ☎ 01 43 40 37 37, *Fax 01 43 40 38 39,* – AE GB M 20
closed Saturday lunch and Sunday – **Meals** Turkish rest. 13 (lunch)/23 and a la carte 24/44 ♀.
◆ The sign depicting an elite soldier from the Ottoman infantry hints at the typical Turkish atmosphere and cuisine inside.

Traversière, 40 r. Traversière (12th) Ⓜ *Ledru Rollin* ☎ 01 43 44 02 10, *Fax 01 43 44 64 20* – AE GB JCB K 18
closed 1 to 20 August, Sunday dinner and Monday – **Meals** 18 (lunch), 28/38,50 and a la carte 28/45 ♀.
◆ A restaurant with the friendly atmosphere of a country inn (façade, exposed beams), but furnished in contemporary style. Traditional cuisine ; game in season.

Jean-Pierre Frelet, 25 r. Montgallet (12th) Ⓜ *Montgallet* ☎ 01 43 43 76 65, *marie_rene.relet@club-internet.fr* – . GB L 20
closed August, February Holidays, Saturday lunch and Sunday – **Meals** 25 (dinner) and a la carte 34/44 ♀.
◆ Plain décor, tables set close together to create a convivial ambience, and generous helpings of seasonal dishes best describe this popular local eatery.

Anacréon, 53 bd St-Marcel (13th) *Les Gobelins* ☎ 01 43 31 71 18, *Fax 01 43 31 94 94* – ▤. AE ⓓ GB JCB M 16
closed 1 to 10 May, August, Wednesday lunch, Sunday and Monday – **Meals** 20 (lunch)/32.
◆ Named in honour of the Greek lyrical poet. Veranda-style dining room with paintings on the wall, friendly service and traditional cuisine with a touch of originality.

Quincy, 28 av. Ledru-Rollin (12th) *Gare de Lyon* ☎ 01 46 28 46 76, *Fax 01 46 28 46 76* – ▤ L 17
closed 10 August-10 September, Saturday, Sunday and Monday – **Meals** a la carte 42/70.
◆ A warm ambience reigns in this rustic bistro where the excellent cuisine, like the jovial owner "Bobosse", has plenty of character.

Biche au Bois, 45 av. Ledru-Rollin (12th) *Gare de Lyon* ☎ 01 43 43 34 38 – AE ⓓ GB K 18
closed 24 December-5 January and Monday lunch – **Meals** 22,30 and a la carte 22/35 ♀.
◆ Despite the noisy, smoky atmosphere and simple decoration, the service is attentive and the cuisine copious and traditional, including game in season.

L'Avant Goût, 26 r. Bobillot (13th) *Place d'Italie* ☎ 01 53 80 24 00, *Fax 01 53 80 00 77* – ▤. GB. ✻ P 15
closed 1 to 10 May, 14 August-6 September, 1 to 12 January, Saturday, Sunday and Monday – **Meals** (booking essential) 27 ♀.
◆ The Foretaste is a modern bistro that always seems to be full. The reasons behind its success stem from its tasty seasonal cuisine, quality wine list and relaxed atmosphere.

Auberge Etchegorry, 41 r. Croulebarbe (13th) *Les Gobelins* ☎ 01 44 08 83 51, *Fax 01 44 08 83 69* – AE ⓓ GB JCB N 15
closed 9 to 24 August, Sunday and Monday – **Meals** Basque cooking 24/30 and a la carte 35/47 ♀.
◆ A brochure recounts the history of this Basque restaurant and its district. Sausages, hams, Espelette peppers and garlic hanging from the ceiling set the culinary tone.

Sukhothaï, 12 r. Père Guérin (13th) *Place d'Italie* ☎ 01 45 81 55 88 – GB P 15
closed 2 to 22 August and Sunday – **Meals** Chinese and Thaï rest. 11,50 (lunch), 16/19 and a la carte 22/28.
◆ The former capital of a 13C-14C royal Thai kingdom has given its name to this restaurant serving both Thai and Chinese dishes under the watchful gaze of Buddha sculptures.

Vaugirard, Gare Montparnasse, Grenelle, Denfert-Rochereau.

14th and 15th arrondissements.
14th: ✉ 75014
15th: ✉ 75015

Méridien Montparnasse, 19 r. Cdt Mouchotte (14th) *Montparnasse Bienvenüe* ☎ 01 44 36 44 36, *meridien.montparnasse@lemeridien.com, Fax 01 44 36 49 00,* ←, – ▮, ⇆ rm, ▤ TV ☏ ♿ – 🏛 25 - 2 000. AE ⓓ GB JCB. ✻ rest M 11
see ***Montparnasse 25*** below - ***Justine*** ☎ 01 44 36 44 00 **Meals** a la carte 33/45 ♀ – ☕ 23 – **918 rm** 410/460, 35 suites.
◆ Most of the spacious, modern rooms in this glass and concrete building have been revamped, with superb views of the capital from the upper floors. Winter garden décor in the Justine restaurant with its leafy terrace. Buffet-style menu options.

Sofitel Porte de Sèvres, 8 r. L. Armand (15th) *Balard* ☎ 01 40 60 30 30, *h0572@accor-hotels.com, Fax 01 45 57 04 22,* ←, ♿, – ▮, ⇆ rm, ▤ rest, TV ☏ ♿ – 🏛 450. AE ⓓ GB JCB N 5
see ***Relais de Sèvres*** below - ***Brasserie*** ☎ 01 40 60 33 77 *(closed lunch Saturday and Sunday)* **Meals** a la carte approx. 40 – ☕ 22,50 – **620 rm** 360/405, 13 suites.
◆ This hotel opposite the heliport offers soundproofed rooms, partly refurbished in elegant, contemporary style. Views of the west of Paris from the higher floors. The Brasserie, with its mosaics, cupola, benches etc, evokes the ambience of the Roaring Twenties.

Novotel Tour Eiffel, 61 quai Grenelle (15th) Ⓜ *Charles Michels* ✆ 01 40 58 20 00, *h3546@accor-hotels.com, Fax 01 40 58 24 44,* ≤, ⅂, ☒ – |‡|, ⇍ rm, ▤ TV ✆ ♿ 🚗 – 🏛 500. AE ⓓ GB JCB

Café Lenôtre ✆ 01 40 58 20 75 **Meals** a la carte 42/58 ♀ – ☐ 20 – **752 rm** 350/440, 12 suites.

♦ An entirely renovated hotel with comfortable, modern rooms furnished with wood and bright colours, most with views of the Seine. The Café Lenôtre features pleasant, stylish decor, a contemporary à la carte menu and a delicatessen. High-tech conference centre.

Mercure Tour Eiffel Suffren, 20 r. Jean Rey (15th) Ⓜ *Bir Hakeim* ✆ 01 45 78 50 00, *h2175@accor-hotels.com, Fax 01 45 78 91 42,* ☂, ⅂ – |‡| ▤ TV ✆ – 🏛 30 - 100. AE ⓓ GB JCB J 7

Meals 35 ♀ – ☐ 20 – **394 rm** 215/265, 11 suites.

♦ With decor that takes nature for its inspiration, this soundproofed hotel has recently undergone careful restoration. Some rooms have views over the Eiffel tower. The large dining room opens onto a pleasant terrace surrounded by trees and greenery.

Novotel Vaugirard, 253 r. Vaugirard (15th) Ⓜ *Vaugirard* ✆ 01 40 45 10 00, *h1978 @accor-hotels.com, Fax 01 40 45 10 10,* ☂, ⅂ – |‡|, ⇍ rm, ▤ TV ✆ ♿ 🚗 – 🏛 25 - 300. AE ⓓ GB M 9

Transatlantique : Meals 35/40 ♁ – ☐ 13 – **187 rm** 215/230.

♦ A vast chain hotel at the heart of the 15th arrondissement with large, modern rooms fitted with double-glazing. The dining room of the Transatlantique recalls the days of the great steam liners via a series of models and paintings. Leafy summer terrace.

L'Aiglon without rest, 232 bd Raspail (14th) Ⓜ *Raspail* ✆ 01 43 20 82 42, *hotelaiglon @wanadoo.fr, Fax 01 43 20 98 72* – |‡| ▤ TV ✆. AE ⓓ GB JCB M 12

☐ 8 – **38 rm** 129/146, 8 suites.

♦ Hidden behind L'Aiglon's discreet façade is a fine, Empire-style interior with 34 pleasant rooms with efficient double-glazing. Some rooms are on the small side.

Mercure Tour Eiffel without rest, 64 bd Grenelle (15th) Ⓜ *Dupleix* ✆ 01 45 78 90 90, *hotel@mercuretoureiffel.com, Fax 01 45 78 95 55,* ⅂ – |‡|, ⇍ rm, ▤ TV ✆ ♿ 🚗 – 🏛 25 - 40. AE ⓓ GB JCB K 7

☐ 17 – **76 rm** 210/300.

♦ The rooms in the main building are furnished in line with the Mercure's normal standards ; those in the more recent wing offer superior comfort and numerous little extras.

Mercure Porte de Versailles without rest, 69 bd Victor (15th) Ⓜ *Porte de Versailles* ✆ 01 44 19 03 03, *h1131@accor-hotels.com, Fax 01 48 28 22 11* – |‡|, ⇍ rm, ▤ TV ✆ 🚗 – 🏛 50 - 250. AE ⓓ GB JCB N 7

☐ 14,50 – **91 rm** 250/295.

♦ This 1970s hotel is handily placed opposite the Parc des Expositions. The refurbished rooms are the best choice, as the others are fairly plain and functional.

Villa Royale Montsouris without rest, 144 r. Tombe-Issoire (14th) Ⓜ *Porte d'Orléans* ✆ 01 56 53 89 89, *montsouris@leshotelsdeparis.com, Fax 01 56 53 89 80* – |‡|, ⇍ rm, ▤ TV ✆ ♿. AE ⓓ GB JCB R 12

☐ 20 – **36 rm** 110/160.

♦ Beautiful hotel carefully decorated in Andalucian and Moorish styles. Small but cosy rooms, which are named after Moroccan cities.

Holiday Inn Paris Montparnasse without rest, 10 r. Gager Gabillot (15th) Ⓜ *Vaugirard* ✆ 01 44 19 29 29, *reservations@hiparis-montparnasse.com, Fax 01 44 19 29 39* – |‡| ▤ TV ✆ ♿ 🚗 – 🏛 30. AE ⓓ GB JCB. ⚘ M 9

closed 23 to 28 December – ☐ 13 – **60 rm** 165/175.

♦ A modern building in a quiet street, with a refurbished lobby and contemporary lounge crowned by a glass pyramid. The attractive, newly decorated rooms here are preferable.

Lenox Montparnasse without rest, 15 r. Delambre (14th) Ⓜ *Vavin* ✆ 01 43 35 34 50, *hotel@lenoxmontparnasse.com, Fax 01 43 20 46 64* – |‡| TV ✆. AE ⓓ GB JCB. ⚘

☐ 12 – **52 rm** 125/150.

♦ Popular with guests from the world of fashion. Stylish rooms with pleasant bathrooms, splendid suites on the 6th floor, and pleasant bar and lounges. M 12

Nouvel Orléans without rest, 25 av. Gén. Leclerc (14th) Ⓜ *Mouton Duvernet* ✆ 01 43 27 80 20, *nouvelorleans@aol.com, Fax 01 43 35 36 57* – |‡|, ⇍ rm, ▤ TV ✆. AE ⓓ GB JCB. ⚘ P 12

☐ 10 – **46 rm** 110/165.

♦ Named after the Porte d'Orléans, some 800m/880yd away, the hotel's 46 rooms are embellished with modern furniture and warm, colourful fabrics.

Delambre without rest, 35 r. Delambre (14th) Ⓜ *Edgar Quinet* ✆ 01 43 20 66 31, *delambre@club-internet.fr, Fax 01 45 38 91 76* – |‡| TV ✆ ♿. AE GB. ⚘ M 12

☐ 8 – **30 rm** 95.

♦ André Breton once stayed in this hotel on a quiet street near Montparnasse station. Contemporary decor, with plain, bright and for the most part spacious rooms.

Mercure Raspail Montparnasse without rest, 207 bd Raspail (14th) Ⓜ *Vavin* ✆ 01 43 20 62 94, *h0351@accor-hotels.com, Fax 01 43 27 39 69* – |♦|, ⇔ rm, ▤ TV ✆ ♿. AE ⓓ GB M 12
☕ 12,80 – **63 rm** 145/175.
◆ This Haussmann-style building enjoys an excellent location near the famous brasseries of the Montparnasse district. The hotel's rooms are modern with plain wood furnishings.

Apollinaire without rest, 39 r. Delambre (14th) Ⓜ *Edgar Quinet* ✆ 01 43 35 18 40, *infos@hotel.apollinaire.com, Fax 01 43 35 30 71* – |♦| ▤ TV ✆. AE ⓓ GB M 12
☕ 7 – **36 rm** 107/130.
◆ The name pays homage to this poet who used to meet fellow writers and artists in Montparnasse. Colourful, functional and well-maintained bedrooms, plus a comfortable lounge.

Mercure Paris XV without rest, 6 r. St-Lambert (15th) Ⓜ *Boucicaut* ✆ 01 45 58 61 00, *h0903@accor-hotels.com, Fax 01 45 54 10 43* – |♦|, ⇔ rm, ▤ TV ✆ ♿ 🚗 – 🏫 30. AE ⓓ GB M 7
☕ 11 – **56 rm** 133/139.
◆ 800m/880yd from the Porte de Versailles. The reception area and lounges are decorated in modern style, in keeping with the comfortable, well-maintained bedrooms.

Istria without rest, 29 r. Campagne Première (14th) Ⓜ *Raspail* ✆ 01 43 20 91 82, *hotelistria@wanadoo.fr, Fax 01 43 22 48 45* – |♦| TV ✆. AE GB. ✗ M 12
☕ 9 – **26 rm** 100/110.
◆ This hotel was immortalised by the French poet Aragon in "Il ne m'est Paris que d'Elsa". Small, basic rooms, a pleasant lounge, plus a breakfast room in the vaulted cellar.

Daguerre without rest, 94 r. Daguerre (14th) Ⓜ *Gaîté* ✆ 01 43 22 43 54, *hoteldaguerre@wanadoo.fr, Fax 01 43 20 66 84* – |♦| TV ✆ ♿. AE ⓓ GB JCB. ✗ N 11
☕ 11 – **30 rm** 75/110.
◆ An early-20C building with somewhat small, but well-furnished rooms. Attractive breakfast room with exposed stonework in the old cellar.

Apollon Montparnasse without rest, 91 r. Ouest (14th) Ⓜ *Pernety* ✆ 01 43 95 62 00, *apollonm@wanadoo.fr, Fax 01 43 95 62 10* – |♦| ▤ TV ✆. AE ⓓ GB JCB N 10-11
☕ 7 – **33 rm** 73/89.
◆ Courteous service, attractive rooms and proximity to Montparnasse and the Air France shuttle buses are the major plus-points of this hotel on a relatively quiet street.

Ibis Brancion without rest, 105 r. Brancion (15th) Ⓜ *Pte de Vanves* ✆ 01 56 56 62 30, *Fax 01 56 56 62 31* – |♦|, ⇔ rm, ▤ TV ✆ ♿. AE ⓓ GB. ✗ P 8-9
☕ 6 – **71 rm** 82.
◆ Close to the Parc Georges-Brassens and the rue Santos-Dumont, where the poet-cum-singer owned a house. Amusing entrance hall with décor based on the circus. Modern bedrooms.

Carladez Cambronne without rest, 3 pl. Gén. Beuret (15th) Ⓜ *Vaugirard* ✆ 01 47 34 07 12, *carladez@club-internet.fr, Fax 01 40 65 95 68* – |♦| TV ✆. AE ⓓ GB JCB M 9
☕ 7 – **28 rm** 75/79.
◆ A new blue, salmon and green colour scheme has spruced up the small yet well-maintained rooms in this hotel renowned for the friendliness of its staff.

Lilas Blanc without rest, 5 r. Avre (15th) Ⓜ *La Motte Picquet Grenelle* ✆ 01 45 75 30 07, *hotellilasblanc@minitel.net, Fax 01 45 78 66 65* – |♦| TV ✆. AE ⓓ GB K 8
closed 25 July-25 August and 19 to 25 December – ☕ 6 – **32 rm** 61/73.
◆ A compact hotel in a street that is generally quiet at night. Small, colourful rooms with basic laminated furnishings ; those on the ground floor are generally darker.

XXXX ✿ **Montparnasse 25** - Hôtel Méridien Montparnasse, 19 r. Cdt Mouchotte (14th) Ⓜ *Montparnasse Bienvenüe* ✆ 01 44 36 44 25, *meridien.montparnasse@lemeridien.com, Fax 01 44 36 49 03* – ▤ P. AE ⓓ GB JCB. ✗ M 11
closed 10 to 23 May, 12 July-29 August, 20 December-2 January, Saturday, Sunday and Bank Holidays – **Meals** 49 (lunch)/105 and a la carte 80/120 ♀ 🍇.
◆ The contemporary black-lacquer décor may come as a shock, yet the overall effect is warm and cosy. Cuisine to suit modern tastes, plus a superb cheese trolley.
Spec. Compression de poulet de Bresse. Saint-Pierre piqué aux anchois. Noix de ris de veau de lait rôtie.

XXXX ✿ **Relais de Sèvres** - Hôtel Sofitel Porte de Sèvres, 8 r. L. Armand (15th) Ⓜ *Balard* ✆ 01 40 60 33 66, *h0572@accor-hotels.com, Fax 01 40 60 30 00* – ▤ 🚗 P. AE ⓓ GB JCB N 5
closed 17 July-23 August, 18 December-3 January, Friday dinner, Saturday, Sunday and Bank Holidays – **Meals** 55/70 b.i. and a la carte 75/100 ♀.
◆ Elegant Sèvres blue decor acts as a backdrop to this impressive restaurant popular with gourmets and a business clientele. Traditional cuisine and an impressive wine list.
Spec. Emietté de tourteau au crèmeux de fenouil. Râble de lièvre aux deux pommes (season). Assiette de chocolats grands crus.

XXX **Ciel de Paris,** Maine Montparnasse Tower, at 56th floor (15th) Ⓜ *Montparnasse Bienvenüe* ☎ 01 40 64 77 64, *ciel-de-paris.rv@elior.com, Fax 01 43 21 48 37,* ≤ Paris – 🛗 ▤. AE ⓓ GB JCB. ✂ M 11
Meals 32 (lunch)/52 and a la carte 54/82 ♀.
◆ On clear days, the view from the pleasant modern dining room, looking out towards Les Invalides and the Eiffel Tower is hard to beat. A sky-high dining experience !

XXX ✿ **Le Duc,** 243 bd Raspail (14th) Ⓜ *Raspail* ☎ 01 43 20 96 30, *Fax 01 43 20 46 73* – ▤ ⛟. AE ⓓ GB JCB M 12
closed 31 July-23 August, 24 December-4 January, Saturday lunch, Sunday and Monday – **Meals** - Seafood - 46 (lunch) and a la carte 60/90.
◆ Le Duc serves simple but high-quality fish and seafood in a cosy yacht cabin-ambience based on mahogany panelling, maritime-inspired decoration and gleaming brass.
Spec. Tartare de bar et saumon. Saint-Pierre au beurre de vodka. Langoustines rôties au gingembre.

XXX **Benkay,** 61 quai Grenelle (4th floor)(15th) Ⓜ *Bir-Hakeim* ☎ 01 40 58 21 26, *h3546@accor-hotels.com, Fax 01 40 58 21 30,* ≤ – ▤ P. AE ⓓ GB JCB. ✂
Meals - Japanese rest. - 26 (lunch), 60/125 and a la carte 70/130.
◆ Situated on the top floor, this restaurant has beautiful views over the Seine. Abstemious decor (marble and wood) ; sushis and teppanyakis on the menu.

XXX **Le Dôme,** 108 bd Montparnasse (14th) Ⓜ *Vavin* ☎ 01 43 35 25 81, *Fax 01 42 79 01 19* – ▤. AE ⓓ GB JCB LM 12
closed Sunday and Monday in August – **Meals** - Seafood - a la carte 56/84.
◆ One of the haunts of bohemian writers and artists during the Roaring Twenties and now a chic restaurant which has preserved its Art Deco feel. Fish and seafood specialities.

XXX ✿ **Chen-Soleil d'Est,** 15 r. Théâtre (15th) Ⓜ *Charles Michels* ☎ 01 45 79 34 34, *Fax 01 45 79 07 53* – ▤. AE GB JCB K 6
closed August and Sunday – **Meals** - Chinese rest. - 40 (lunch)/75 and a la carte 80/100.
◆ Head away from the Seine to discover this authentic corner of Asia serving high-quality steamed and wok-based cuisine to a backdrop of furniture imported from China.
Spec. Fleurs de courgette au corps de tourteau. Demi-canard pékinois en trois services. Cocotte de chevreau au ginseng.

XX ✿ **Maison Courtine** (Charles), 157 av. Maine (14th) Ⓜ *Mouton Duvernet* ☎ 01 45 43 08 04, *Fax 01 45 45 91 35* – ▤. AE GB. ✂ N 11
closed 4 to 31 August, 25 December-4 January, Sunday, lunch Saturday and Monday – **Meals** 35 ♀.
◆ The menu here is a culinary Tour de France, served to a colourful, modern backdrop with Louis-Philippe-style furniture. Popular with a loyal group of aficionados.
Spec. Petites escalopes de foie gras poêlées aux raisins. Magret de canard cuit sur peau au sel de Guérande. Colvert rôti au miel du maquis (season).

XX **Pavillon Montsouris,** 20 r. Gazan (14th) Ⓜ *Cité Universitaire* ☎ 01 43 13 29 00, *Fax 01 43 13 29 02,* 🏡 – ⛟. AE GB
closed 15 February-2 March – **Meals** 49 ♀.
◆ This Belle Epoque building in the Parc Montsouris offers rural calm in the heart of Paris. Attractive glass, colonial-style decor and a terrace facing the park.

XX **La Coupole,** 102 bd Montparnasse (14th) Ⓜ *Vavin* ☎ 01 43 20 14 20, *cmonteiro@groupeflo.fr, Fax 01 43 35 46 14* – ▤. AE ⓓ GB L 12
Meals 32,90 b.i. and a la carte 34/62.
◆ The heart of old Montparnasse is still beating in this Art Deco brasserie with a lively ambience opened in 1927. 32 pillars decorated with works by artists from the period.

XX **Gauloise,** 59 av. La Motte-Picquet (15 th) Ⓜ *La Motte Picquet Grenelle* ☎ 01 47 34 11 64, *Fax 01 40 61 09 70,* 🏡 – AE GB K 8
Meals 26,50 and a la carte 35/60 ♀.
◆ Judging by the signed photos on the walls, this century-old brasserie has played host to huge numbers of celebrities over the years. Pleasant pavement terrace.

XX ☺ **Caroubier,** 82 bd Lefèbvre (15th) Ⓜ *Porte de Vanves* ☎ 01 40 43 16 12, *Fax 01 40 43 16 12* – ▤. AE GB N 11
closed 15 July-15 August and Monday – **Meals** - Morrocan rest. - 15/25 and a la carte 28/36 ♀.
◆ Contemporary decor enlivened by the occasional Oriental touch, a friendly, family atmosphere and generous Moroccan cuisine are the keys to the success of this restaurant.

XX **Fontanarosa,** 28 bd Garibaldi (15th) Ⓜ *Cambronne* ✆ 01 45 66 97 84, *Fax 01 47 83 96 30,* – ▤. AE GB JCB L 9
Meals - Italian rest. - 18,30 (lunch) and a la carte 46/80 ♀.
• Escape the bustle of the city and relax on the attractive patio-terrace of this delightful trattoria serving Sardinian cuisine. Good choice of Italian wines.

XX **L'Épopée,** 89 av. É. Zola (15th) Ⓜ *Charles Michels* ✆ 01 45 77 71 37, *Fax 01 45 77 71 37* – AE ⓓ GB JCB L 7
closed 28 July-28 August, 24 December-2 January, Saturday lunch and Sunday – **Meals** 32 ♀.
• A friendly and unpretentious small restaurant attracting a loyal following where the emphasis is on traditional cuisine. Impressive wine list.

X **Chez les Frères Gaudet,** 19 r. Duranton (15th) Ⓜ *Boucicaut* ✆ 01 45 58 43 17, *ff-gaudet@club-internet.fr, Fax 01 45 58 42 65* – AE ⓓ GB JCB M 6
closed 1 to 10 May, 1 to 29 August, Sunday, lunch Saturday and Monday – **Meals** 29/38.
• "Film-noir" blinds, period lamps and leatherette banquettes give this chic 50s-style restaurant the atmosphere of an Inspector Maigret mystery. Traditional menu.

X **Stéphane Martin,** 67 r. Entrepreneurs (15th) Ⓜ *Charles Michels* ✆ 01 45 79 03 31, *resto.stephanemartin@free.fr, Fax 01 45 79 44 69* – ▤. AE GB. L 7
closed 1 to 23 August, Sunday and Monday – **Meals** 25 b.i. (lunch), 32/40 and a la carte 34/42.
• A warm, friendly restaurant with a library-style decor (fresco depicting rows of books) serving seasonal, contemporary cuisine.

X **Bistro d'Hubert,** 41 bd Pasteur (15th) Ⓜ *Pasteur* ✆ 01 47 34 15 50, *message@bistrodhubert.com, Fax 01 45 67 03 09* – AE ⓓ GB JCB L 10
closed Saturday lunch – **Meals** 41 and a la carte 46/55 ♀.
• Jars and bottles on the shelves, chequered tablecloths, and views of the kitchen add to the charm of this restaurant decorated in the style of a farm in Les Landes.

X **Beurre Noisette,** 68 r. Vasco de Gama (15th) Ⓜ *Lourmel* ✆ 01 48 56 82 49, *Fax 01 48 56 82 49* – AE GB. N 6
closed 1 to 25 August, Sunday and Monday – **Meals** 20 (lunch)/29 ♀.
• Carefully prepared cuisine with a modern touch, plus seasonal suggestions on the specials board. Two plain yet contemporary dining rooms. Good choice of wine by the glass.

X **Régalade,** 49 av. J. Moulin (14th) Ⓜ *Porte d'Orléans* ✆ 01 45 45 68 58, *Fax 01 45 40 96 74* – ▤. GB R 11
closed August, Monday lunch, Saturday and Sunday – **Meals** (booking essential) 30.
• Smiling service and delicious country cooking are the main attributes of this small, simple but hugely popular bistro close to the Porte de Châtillon.

X **Troquet,** 21 r. F. Bonvin (15th) Ⓜ *Cambronne* ✆ 01 45 66 89 00, *Fax 01 45 66 89 83* – GB. L 9
closed August, 24 December-2 January, Sunday and Monday – **Meals** 24 (lunch), 29/31 ♀.
• This typical Parisian "troquet" (bar) offers a single menu advertised on a slate board. A retro-style dining room provides the setting for fine seasonal cuisine.

X **L'Os à Moelle,** 3 r. Vasco de Gama (15th) Ⓜ *Lourmel* ✆ 01 45 57 27 27, *Fax 01 45 57 27 27* – GB M 6
closed 3 to 25 August, Sunday and Monday – **Meals** 32.
• Customers can choose from the colourful decor and tasty seasonal menu in the bistro, or opt for a lighter meal in the friendly, rustic-style "Cave" opposite.

X **Cerisaie,** 70 bd E. Quinet (14th) Ⓜ *Edgar Quinet* ✆ 01 43 20 98 98, *Fax 01 43 20 98 98* – GB
closed 1 to 25 August, 19 December-2 January, Saturday lunch, Sunday and Bank Holidays – **Meals** (booking essential) 27,50/32,50.
• A tiny restaurant in the heart of the "breton" district : the owner - and chef - chalks up a daily-changing menu of carefully prepared south-western dishes on the blackboard.

X **A La Bonne Table,** 42 r. Friant (14th) Ⓜ *Porte d'Orléans* ✆ 01 45 39 74 91, *Fax 01 45 43 66 92* – AE ⓓ GB JCB
closed 11 July-1 August, 25 December-2 January, Saturday lunch and Sunday – **Meals** 25 and a la carte 34/55.
• Despite his Japanese origins, the chef prepares traditional French cuisine enhanced by his Oriental culinary expertise. A comfortable elongated dining room with a retro feel.

X **Severo,** 8 r. Plantes (14th) Ⓜ *Mouton Duvernet* ✆ 01 45 40 40 91 – GB N 11
closed 24 July-23 August, 19 December-3 January, Saturday dinner and Sunday – **Meals** a la carte 26/40 ♀.
• Meat delicacies from the Auvergne dominate the daily specials board in this friendly bistro with an eclectic, yet impressively comprehensive wine list.

Passy, Auteuil, Bois de Boulogne, Chaillot, Porte Maillot.

16th arrondissement.
16th: ✉ 75016 or 75116

Raphaël, 17 av. Kléber ✉ 75116 Ⓜ *Kléber* ☎ 01 53 64 32 00, *management@raphael-hotel.com, Fax 01 53 64 32 01,* , – , rm, – 50. AE GB JCB
Jardins Plein Ciel ☎ 01 53 64 32 30 (7th floor)-buffet *(May-October)* **Meals** 65(lunch)/80 – ***Salle à Manger*** ☎ 01 53 64 32 11 *(closed August, Saturday and Sunday)* **Meals** 50 b.i. (lunch) and a la carte 60/80 – 34 – **44 rm** 321/530, 25 suites.
◆ A superb wood-adorned gallery, elegant bedrooms, a panoramic rooftop terrace and an English bar are the treasures of the Raphaël, dating from 1925. 360ì view of Paris from the Jardins Plein Ciel and palatial-style décor in the attractive Salle à Manger. F 7

St-James Paris , 43 av. Bugeaud ✉ 75116 Ⓜ *Porte Dauphine* ☎ 01 44 05 81 81, *contact@saint-james-paris.com, Fax 01 44 05 81 82,* , , – – 25. AE GB JCB F 5
Meals *(closed weekends and Bank Holidays)* (residents only) 47 – 25 – **20 rm** 345/480, 28 suites580/730, 8 duplex.
◆ A fine mansion built by Madame Thiers in 1892 in the middle of a wooded garden. Majestic staircase, spacious bedrooms and a bar-library with the air of an English club.

Costes K. without rest, 81 av. Kléber ✉ 75116 Ⓜ *Trocadéro* ☎ 01 44 05 75 75, *costes.k@wanadoo.fr, Fax 01 44 05 74 74,* – , rm, . AE GB JCB G 7
20 – **83 rm** 300/550.
◆ This discreet, ultra-modern hotel designed by Ricardo Bofill offers a serene haven for guests in its large, refined rooms arranged around a pretty Japanese-style patio.

Sofitel Le Parc , 55 av. R. Poincaré ✉ 75116 Ⓜ *Victor Hugo* ☎ 01 44 05 66 66, *h2797@accor-hotels.com, Fax 01 44 05 66 00,* , – , rm, – 40 - 250. AE GB JCB G 6
Meals see ***59 Poincaré*** below – 26 – **95 rm** 410/590, 21 suites, 3 duplex.
◆ The Parc's charming "English"-style bedrooms are elegant and fitted with Wi-Fi technology. The open-air La Terrasse du Parc restaurant, on a pleasant inner courtyard, is popular with the city's smart set and serves a range of modern international cuisine.

Sofitel Baltimore, 88bis av. Kléber ✉ 75116 Ⓜ *Boissière* ☎ 01 44 34 54 54, *welcome@hotelblatimore.com, Fax 01 44 34 54 44,* – , rm, – 50. AE GB JCB G 7
see ***Table du Baltimore*** below – 26 – **103 rm** 580/750.
◆ Elegant furniture, "trendy" fabrics and old photos of the city of Baltimore contribute to the modern décor of the bedrooms, in contrast to the building's 19C architecture.

Square, 3 r. Boulainvilliers ✉ 75016 Ⓜ *Mirabeau* ☎ 01 44 14 91 90, *hotel.square@wanadoo.fr, Fax 01 44 14 91 99* – – 20. AE GB JCB. K 5
Zébra Square ☎ 01 44 14 91 91 **Meals** a la carte 38/60 – 20 – **20 rm** 255/330.
◆ This flagship of contemporary architecture opposite the Maison de la Radio is a hymn to modern design with its curves, colours, high-tech equipment and abstract canvases. Striped designer decor and a contemporary menu in the hotel's fashionable restaurant.

Trocadero Dokhan's without rest, 117 r. Lauriston ✉ 75116 Ⓜ *Trocadéro* ☎ 01 53 65 66 99, *welcome@dokhans.com, Fax 01 53 65 66 88* – , rm, . AE GB JCB. G 6
26 – **41 rm** 440/540, 4 suites.
◆ It is impossible not to be won over by this charming early-20C private mansion built in Palladian style with a neo-Classical interior and 18C celadon panelling in the lounge.

Villa Maillot without rest, 143 av. Malakoff ✉ 75116 Ⓜ *Porte Maillot* ☎ 01 53 64 52 52, *resa@lavillamaillot.fr, Fax 01 45 00 60 61* – , rm, – 25. AE GB JCB F 6
23 – **39 rm** 315/365, 3 suites.
◆ A stone's throw from Porte Maillot, this hotel offers comfortable rooms furnished in soft colours and with good soundproofing. Bright breakfast room overlooking greenery.

Élysées Régencia without rest, 41 av. Marceau ✉ 75116 Ⓜ *George V* ☎ 01 47 20 42 65, *info@regencia.com, Fax 01 49 52 03 42* – , rm, – 20. AE GB JCB. G 8
18 – **41 rm** 195/310.
◆ Three styles of bedrooms are on offer behind the hotel's gracious façade : Louis XVI, Napoleon "return from Egypt", and contemporary. Elegant lounge, bar and library.

Libertel Auteuil without rest, 8 r. F. David ✉ 75016 Ⓜ *Mirabeau* ☎ 01 40 50 57 57, *h2777@accor.hotels.com, Fax 01 40 50 57 50* – |‡|, ⇆ rm, ▤ TV ☎ ♿ 🚗 – 🏛 35. AE ⓓ GB K 5
☕ 14 – **94 rm** 175/255.
◆ A practically new building near the Maison de la Radio. Popular business choice, with bedrooms decorated in shades of beige. Piano in the modern, wicker-furnished lounge.

Pergolèse without rest, 3 r. Pergolèse ✉ 75116 Ⓜ *Argentine* ☎ 01 53 64 04 04, *hotel@pergolese.com, Fax 01 53 64 04 40* – |‡|, ⇆ rm, ▤ TV ☎. AE ⓓ GB JCB E 6
☕ 18 – **40 rm** 230/380.
◆ An understated 16C façade with an unusual blue door that sets the tone for the designer interior featuring mahogany, glass bricks, chromes and bright colours.

Argentine without rest, 1 r. Argentine ✉ 75116 Ⓜ *Argentine* ☎ 01 45 02 76 76, *h2757@accor-hotels.com, Fax 01 45 02 76 00* – |‡|, ⇆ rm, TV ☎ ♿. AE ⓓ GB JCB E 7
☕ 14 – **40 rm** 280/300.
◆ This bourgeois building in a quiet street is ornamented with a low relief offered by the Argentinian ambassador. Stylish, elegant rooms, and a cosy ambience in the lounge-bar.

Majestic without rest, 29 r. Dumont d'Urville ✉ 75116 Ⓜ *Kléber* ☎ 01 45 00 83 70, *management@majestic-hotel.com, Fax 01 45 00 29 48* – |‡|, ⇆ rm, ▤ TV ☎. AE ⓓ GB JCB F 7
☕ 15 – **27 rm** 240/335, 3 suites.
◆ A hotel with a discreet 1960s façade just a stone's throw from the Champs-Élysées. The guest rooms are spacious, quiet, traditionally furnished and impeccably maintained.

Élysées Union without rest, 44 r. Hamelin ✉ 75116 Ⓜ *Boissière* ☎ 01 45 53 14 95, *unionetoil@aol.com, Fax 01 47 55 94 79* – |‡| kitchenette TV ☎ ♿. AE ⓓ GB. ✗ G 7
☕ 9,50 – **50 rm** 115/145, 10 suites.
◆ Proust died on the fifth floor of this building on 18 November 1922. Directoire-style bedrooms, as well as apartments that are ideal for long stays. Small leafy courtyard.

Élysées Bassano without rest, 24 r. Bassano ✉ 75116 Ⓜ *George V* ☎ 01 47 20 49 03, *h2815-gm@accor-hotels.com, Fax 01 47 23 06 72* – |‡|, ⇆ rm, ▤ TV ☎. AE ⓓ GB JCB G 8
☕ 14 – **40 rm** 245/300.
◆ Attractive printed fabrics, old etchings and mahogany-coloured furniture are the main themes in the hotel's cosy rooms. Modern canvases adorn the walls of the breakfast room.

Résidence Bassano without rest, 15 r. Bassano ✉ 75116 Ⓜ *George V* ☎ 01 47 23 78 23, *info@hotel-bassano.com, Fax 01 47 20 41 22* – |‡|, ⇆ rm, ▤ TV ☎. AE ⓓ GB JCB. ✗ G 8
☕ 18 – **28 rm** 195/310, 3 suites.
◆ Although just a few hundred yards from the Champs-Élysées, the warm ambience, wrought-iron furniture and bright fabrics in this friendly hotel turn one's thoughts to Provence.

Etoile Residence Imperiale without rest, 155 av. de Malakoff ✉ 75116 Ⓜ *Porte Maillot* ☎ 01 45 00 23 45, *res.imperiale@wanadoo.fr, Fax 01 45 01 88 82* – |‡|, ⇆ rm, ▤ TV ☎ ♿. AE ⓓ GB JCB E 6
☕ 12 – **37 rm** 140/200.
◆ Significant renovation work has been carried out on this old hotel near Porte Maillot. Well-appointed, soundproofed rooms, with exposed beams in those on the top floor.

Passy Eiffel without rest, 10 r. Passy ✉ 75016 Ⓜ *Passy* ☎ 01 45 25 55 66, *passyeiffel@wanadoo.fr, Fax 01 42 88 89 88* – |‡| TV ☎. AE ⓓ GB JCB J 6
☕ 10 – **49 rm** 128/150.
◆ A family-run hotel in a busy street. Functional, well-maintained rooms, either facing the road (some with views of the Eiffel Tower) or overlooking a flower-decked courtyard.

Élysées Sablons without rest, 32 r. Greuze ✉ 75116 Ⓜ *Trocadéro* ☎ 01 47 27 10 00, *h2778-gm@accor-hotels.com, Fax 01 47 27 47 10* – |‡|, ⇆ rm, TV ☎ ♿. AE ⓓ GB JCB G 6
☕ 14 – **41 rm** 240/250.
◆ A modern hotel with rooms (a few with a mini-balcony) furnished in Art Deco style and an amusing breakfast room decorated to resemble the cabin of a boat.

Chambellan Morgane without rest, 6 r. Keppler ✉ 75116 Ⓜ *George V* ☎ 01 47 20 35 72, *chambellan-morgane@wanadoo.fr, Fax 01 47 20 95 69* – |‡| ▤ TV ☎ – 🏛 20. AE ⓓ GB JCB GF 8
☕ 12 – **20 rm** 150/165.
◆ A small, tranquil hotel full of character with rooms that proudly display the colours of Provence. Pleasant Louis XVI lounge decorated with painted woodwork.

Floride Étoile without rest, 14 r. St-Didier ✉ 75116 Ⓜ *Boissière* ☎ 01 47 27 23 36, *floride.etoile@wanadoo.fr, Fax 01 47 27 82 87* – |‡| ▤ TV ☎ – 🏛 30. AE ⓓ GB JCB. ✗ G 7
☕ 11,50 – **63 rm** 140/205.
◆ Close to Trocadéro. Ask for one of the large, modern and newly renovated rooms ; those by the courtyard are smaller but quieter. Tastefully decorated, flower-decked lounge.

Hameau de Passy without rest, 48 r. Passy ✉ 75016 Ⓜ *La Muette* ☎ 01 42 88 47 55, *hameau.passy@wanadoo.fr, Fax 01 42 30 83 72* – |‡| TV. AE ⓓ GB JCB J 5-6
32 rm ☕ 103/118.
◆ Tucked away in the 16th district, this discreet "hamlet" (hameau) with its pretty courtyard guarantees guests a good night's sleep. Small, modern and well-maintained rooms.

Bois without rest, 11 r. Dôme ✉ 75116 Ⓜ *Kléber* ☎ 01 45 00 31 96, *hoteldubois@wanadoo.fr, Fax 01 45 00 90 05* – TV. AE ⓓ GB JCB F 7
☕ 12 – **41 rm** 120/165.
◆ This cosy hotel stands in the 16C Montmartre street where Baudelaire breathed his last. Airy and stylish bedrooms, plus a Georgian-style lounge.

Palais de Chaillot without rest, 35 av. R. Poincaré ✉ 75116 Ⓜ *Trocadéro* ☎ 01 53 70 09 09, *palaisdechaillot-hotel@magic.fr, Fax 01 53 70 09 08* – |‡| TV ☎. AE ⓓ GB JCB. ⚘ G 6
☕ 8,50 – **28 rm** 105/135.
◆ This hotel decorated in the colours of Provence enjoys a good location near Trocadéro. Small, bright and functional bedrooms, with wicker furniture in the breakfast room.

Gavarni without rest, 5 r. Gavarni ✉ 75116 Ⓜ *Passy* ☎ 01 45 24 52 82, *reservation@gavarni.com, Fax 01 40 50 16 95* – |‡| ▤ TV ☎. AE ⓓ GB JCB. ⚘ J 6
☕ 12,50 – **25 rm** 99/200.
◆ This red-brick hotel offers guests compact, but well-equipped and stylish rooms ; those on the upper two floors are more elegant.

Longchamp without rest, 68 r. Longchamp ✉ 75116 Ⓜ *Trocadéro* ☎ 01 44 34 24 14, *hotelonch@wanadoo.fr, Fax 01 44 34 24 24* – |‡|, ⇔ rm, TV ☎. AE ⓓ GB G 6
☕ 10 – **23 rm** 105/145.
◆ A renovated façade and interior, smallish but soundproofed rooms, and a breakfast room in the style of a winter garden, mark out this hotel fronting a busy street.

XXX **59 Poincaré** - Hôtel Sofitel Le Parc, 59 av. R. Poincaré ✉ 75116 Ⓜ *Victor Hugo* ☎ 01 47 27 59 59, *le59poincare@tiscali.fr, Fax 01 47 27 59 00* – ▤ ⇔. AE ⓓ GB JCB. ⚘ G 6
closed 24 December-31 January, Saturday lunch, Sunday and Monday from October-April – **Meals** 49 (lunch), 90/115 and a la carte 65/90.
◆ An enchanting town house dating from the Belle Époque, with the design flourishes of P Jouin on the ground floor. Vegetables, lobster, beef and fruit dominate the themed menu.

XXX ✿✿ **Jamin** (Guichard), 32 r. Longchamp ✉ 75116 Ⓜ *léna* ☎ 01 45 53 00 07, *reservation@jamin.fr, Fax 01 45 53 00 15* – ▤. AE ⓓ GB. ⚘ G 7
closed 17 to 23 May, 30 July-23 August, 27 February-6 March, Saturday and Sunday – **Meals** 53 (lunch), 95/130 and a la carte 110/140.
◆ Behind this discreetly colourful façade, an elegant, simply decorated restaurant is the setting for an inventive menu that focuses on high-quality ingredients.
Spec. Cèpes grillés à la fleur de thym (Autumn). Fricassée de gros homard, jus relevé. Volaille de Bresse aux morilles (Spring).

XXX ✿✿ **Relais d'Auteuil** (Pignol), 31 bd Murat ✉ 75016 Ⓜ *Michel Ange Molitor* ☎ 01 46 51 09 54, *pignol-p@wanadoo.fr, Fax 01 40 71 05 03* – ▤ ⇔. AE ⓓ GB JCB L 3
closed 31 July-24 August, Sunday, lunch Saturday and Monday – **Meals** 48 (lunch), 105/135 and a la carte 100/135.
◆ Refined decor inspired by the Restoration and Louis-Philippe eras, with satin-covered seats and gondola chairs. Sophisticated cuisine high on virtuosity.
Spec. Petits chaussons de céleri-rave et truffes (November-February). Langoustines et topinambours infusés au bâton de citronnelle et marjolaine. Pigeon de Touraine désossé à la compotée de choux.

XXX ✿ **Seize au Seize,** 16 av. Bugeaud ✉ 75116 Ⓜ *Victor Hugo* ☎ 01 56 28 16 16, *Fax 01 56 28 16 78* – ▤ ⇔. AE ⓓ GB JCB F 6
closed August, Monday and Sunday – **Meals** a la carte 55/73 ♀.
◆ This excellent restaurant is well worth a visit for its inventive theme-based cuisine, outstanding wine list and elegant decor.
Spec. Pressé de foie gras. Côte de veau caramélisée. Soufflé chaud au baileys.

XXX ✿ **Pergolèse** (Corre), 40 r. Pergolèse ✉ 75116 Ⓜ *Porte Maillot* ☎ 01 45 00 21 40, *le-pergolese@wanadoo.fr, Fax 01 45 00 81 31* – ▤ ⇔. AE GB JCB F 6
closed 2 to 30 August, Saturday and Sunday – **Meals** 38/75 and a la carte 56/80 ♀.
◆ Yellow fabrics, light-coloured wood, mirrors and unusual sculptures combine to create this elegant setting a few yards from the select avenue Foch. Classic, refined cuisine.
Spec. Ravioli de langoustines à la duxelles de champignons. Saint-Jacques rôties en robe des champs (October-April). Légumière truffée de volaille en vinaigrette.

XXX ✿ **Table du Baltimore** - Hôtel Sofitel Baltimore, 1 r. Léo Delibes ✉ 75016 Ⓜ *Boissière* ✆ 01 44 34 54 34 – ▤ ⇨. AE ◐ GB JCB. ✂ G 7
closed 30 July-30 August, Saturday, Sunday and Bank Holidays – **Meals** 45 b.i./75 b.i. and a la carte 52/75.
◆ The decor here is a subtle mix of old wood panelling, contemporary furniture, warm colours and a collection of pictures on the walls. Fine cuisine to suit modern tastes.
Spec. Tourteau cuit dans une nage épicée. Pigeonneau rôti en casserole. Ananas en ravioli au parfum de passion.

XXX ✿ **Passiflore** (Durand), 33 r. Longchamp ✉ 75016 Ⓜ *Trocadéro* ✆ 01 47 04 96 81, *passiflore@club-internet.fr, Fax 01 47 04 32 27* – ▤. AE GB JCB G 7
closed 1 to 23 August, Saturday lunch and Sunday – **Meals** 35 (lunch), 54/85 and a la carte 75/95.
◆ Ethnically-inspired plain yet elegant décor provides the setting for this respected restaurant serving classical cuisine with a personal touch.
Spec. Ravioli de homard en mulligatony. Tournedos de pied de cochon. Les quatre sorbets verts pimentés.

XXX **Port Alma,** 10 av. New-York ✉ 75116 Ⓜ *Alma Marceau* ✆ 01 47 23 75 11, *Fax 01 47 20 42 92* – ▤. AE ◐ GB JCB H 8
closed August, 24 December-2 January, Sunday and Monday – **Meals** - Seafood - a la carte 54/70 ♀.
◆ This veranda dining room with blue beams on the banks of the Seine is a safe bet for excellent fish and seafood. The freshest of products and smiling service.

XX **Cristal Room Baccarat,** 11 pl. des Etats-Unis ✉ 75116 Ⓜ *Boissière* ✆ 01 40 22 11 10, *cristalroom@baccarat.fr, Fax 01 40 22 11 99* – ▤ ⇨. AE ◐ GB
closed Sunday – **Meals** (booking essential) a la carte 51/76 ♀.
◆ M.-L de Noailles' salons made her residence the talk of the town ; nowadays, with décor in Philippe Starck style, modern menus and VIP prices, it's still the place to be seen.

XX ✿ **Astrance** (Barbot), 4 r. Beethoven ✉ 75016 Ⓜ *Passy* ✆ 01 40 50 84 40 – AE ◐ GB. ✂ J 7
closed 1 to 7 May, 24 July-24 August, 6 to 14 November, February Holidays, Saturday and Sunday – **Meals** (booking essential) 35 (lunch), 90/115 and a la carte 80/105 🍇.
◆ The inventive cuisine, good wine list and contemporary decor at the Astrance (a flower, from the Latin aster, or star) have earned plaudits from across the city.
Spec. Chair de crabe à l'huile d'amande douce, fines lamelles d'avocat. Selle d'agneau grillée, aubergine laquée au miso. Café en granité, mousseux au lait.

XX **Fakhr el Dine,** 30 r. Longchamp ✉ 75016 Ⓜ *Trocadéro* ✆ 01 47 27 90 00, *resa@fakhreldine.com, Fax 01 53 70 01 81* – ▤ ⇨. AE ◐ GB. ✂ G 7
Meals - Lebanese rest. - 23/26 and a la carte 30/40.
◆ Mezzé, kafta and grilled meats all feature on the menu of this refined Lebanese restaurant worthy of Fakhr el Dine, one of the country's greatest princes.

XX ✿ **Tang,** 125 r. de la Tour ✉ 75116 Ⓜ *Rue de la Pompe* ✆ 01 45 04 35 35, *Fax 01 45 04 58 19* – ▤. AE GB. ✂ H 5
closed 1 to 23 August, 25 December-2 January, Sunday and Monday – **Meals** - Chinese and Thai rest. - 39 (lunch), 65/98 and a la carte 60/110.
◆ Behind the restaurant's wide bay windows is a high-ceilinged dining room with classical furnishings enlivened by the occasional oriental touch. Chinese and Thai specialities.
Spec. Salade d'hiver d'Enoki, soja, queues de langoustines et pâtes fraîches basmati aux truffes (November-February). Croustillants de langoustines en sauce caramélisée. Pigeonneau laqué épice aux cinq parfums.

XX **Paul Chêne,** 123 r. Lauriston ✉ 75116 Ⓜ *Trocadéro* ✆ 01 47 27 63 17, *Fax 01 47 27 53 18* – ▤ ⇨. AE ◐ GB. ✂ G 6
closed August, 23 December-1 January, Saturday lunch and Sunday – **Meals** 38/48 and a la carte 51/88.
◆ This restaurant has preserved its 1950s feel, with its old bar, comfortable benches, snug tables and lively atmosphere. Traditional dishes including the famous fried whiting.

XX **Vinci,** 23 r. P. Valéry ✉ 75116 Ⓜ *Victor Hugo* ✆ 01 45 01 68 18, *levinci@wanadoo.fr, Fax 01 45 01 60 37* – ▤. AE GB F 7
closed 1 to 22 August, Saturday and Sunday – **Meals** - Italian rest. - 31 and a la carte 45/64 ♀.
◆ Tasty Italian cuisine, a colourful interior and friendly service are the hallmarks of this small restaurant a short distance from the smart boutiques along avenue Victor-Hugo.

XX **Essaouira,** 135 r. Ranelagh ✉ 75016 Ⓜ *Ranelagh* ✆ 01 45 27 99 93, *Fax 01 45 27 56 36* – GB J 4
closed August, Monday lunch and Sunday – **Meals** North-African rest.- a la carte 39/57 ♀.
◆ The Moroccan city has lent its name to this restaurant serving couscous, tajines and mechoui. Typical décor, including a mosaic fountain, rugs and other craft objects.

XX **Chez Géraud,** 31 r. Vital ✉ 75016 Ⓜ *La Muette* ✆ 01 45 20 33 00, *Fax 01 45 20 46 60* – GB H 5
closed 31 July-31 August, Saturday and Sunday – **Meals** 30 and a la carte 55/65.
◆ The façade and interior fresco, both created from Longwy faience, add a decorative edge to this chic bistro where pride of place is given to game (in season).

XX **6 New-York,** 6 av. New-York ✉ 75016 Ⓜ *Alma Marceau* ✆ 01 40 70 03 30, *Fax 01 40 70 04 77* – AE GB JCB
closed 2 to 23 August, Saturday lunch and Sunday – **Meals** 35 and a la carte 48/60 ♀.
◆ A chic bistro with an eye-catching name, where the cuisine is in perfect harmony with the modern, refined setting.

X **Les Ormes** (Molé), 8 r. Chapu ✉ 75016 Ⓜ *Exelmans* ✆ 01 46 47 83 98, *Fax 01 46 47 83 98* – AE GB M 4
closed 1 to 21 August, 3 to 10 January, Sunday and Monday – **Meals** (booking essential) 32 (lunch)/40,50 and a la carte 48/56.
◆ Despite its small size and plain decor, the refurbished dining room behind the coloured glass façade is both warm and inviting. Contemporary à la carte offerings.
Spec. Coquilles Saint-Jacques (October-March). Lièvre à la royale (15 October-30 November). Foie gras de canard aux épices douces (October-April).

X **Natachef,** 9 r. Duban ✉ 75016 Ⓜ *La Muette* ✆ 01 42 88 10 15, *natachef@clubinternet.fr, Fax 01 45 25 74 71* – AE GB J 5
closed August, Saturday and Sunday – **Meals** 35 (lunch), 40/60 and a la carte 40/52.
◆ No problem if you've taken a liking to a glass, napkin or plate in this trendy Passy bistro, as everything's for sale here ! Mini-menu and cookery classes also available.

X **A et M Restaurant,** 136 bd Murat ✉ 75016 Ⓜ *Porte de St Cloud* ✆ 01 45 27 39 60, *am-bistrot-16@wanadoo.fr, Fax 01 45 27 69 71,* – AE GB JCB M 3
closed 1 to 20 August, Saturday lunch and Sunday – **Meals** 23/30 and a la carte 34/53.
◆ A trendy modern bistro close to the river, with sober decor in tones of cream and Havana brown, designer lighting and refined contemporary cuisine.

in the Bois de Boulogne :

XXXX **Pré Catelan,** rte Suresnes ✉ 75016 Ⓜ *Porte Dauphine* ✆ 01 44 14 41 14, *Fax 01 45 24 43 25,* – P. AE GB JCB H 2
closed 23 October-2 November, 13 February-7 March, Sunday except lunch in season and Monday – **Meals** 60 (lunch), 120/150 and a la carte 115/160.
◆ This elegant Napoleon III-style pavilion in the Bois de Boulogne has developed a worthy reputation for its inventive cuisine. Caran d'Ache décor, plus a delightful terrace.
Spec. Navet confit en croûte de sucre candi, sirop d'érable acidulé. Saint-Pierre cuit au plat, sauce mousseline aux zestes d'orange. Perdreau de chasse cuit à la broche, macaroni gratinés (Autumn).

XXXX **Grande Cascade,** allée de Longchamp (opposite the hippodrome) ✉ 75016 Ⓜ *Porte d'Auteuil* ✆ 01 45 27 33 51, *grandecascade@wanadoo.fr, Fax 01 42 88 99 06,* – P. AE GB JCB
closed 18 December-2 January and 19 February-5 March – **Meals** 59 (lunch)/165 and a la carte 130/165.
◆ One of the capital's famed addresses, at the foot of the Bois de Boulogne's Grande Cascade. Refined cuisine, served in the splendid 1850 pavilion or on the exquisite terrace.
Spec. Langoustines en beignets et chair de tourteau. Sole poêlée et beurre noisette aux artichauts poivrades. Porcelet en deux cuissons et lard paysan, crépine à la sarriette.

Clichy, Ternes, Wagram.

17th arrondissement.
17th: ✉ 75017

Meridien Étoile, 81 bd Gouvion St-Cyr Ⓜ *Neuilly-Porte Maillot* ✆ 01 40 68 34 34, *guest.etoile@lemeridien.com, Fax 01 40 68 31 31* – rm, rest, – 50 - 1 200. AE GB JCB. E 6
L'Orenoc ✆ 01 40 68 30 40 *(closed 25 July-25 August, Christmas Holidays, Sunday and Monday)* **Meals** 33/42 and a la carte 60/78 ♀ – ***Terrasse*** ✆ 01 40 68 30 85 *(closed Saturday)* **Meals** a la carte 40/63 ♀ – 24 – **1 008 rm** 540, 17 suites.
◆ This huge, completely renovated hotel opposite the Palais des Congrès also comprises a jazz club, bar and shops. Black granite and beige in the bedrooms, with tropical wood and trinkets from around the world in L'Orenoc. Simple à la carte menu at the Terrasse.

Concorde La Fayette, 3 pl. Gén. Koenig Ⓜ *Porte Maillot* ☎ 01 40 68 50 68, *info@concorde-lafayette.com, Fax 01 40 68 50 43,* ≤ – 🛗, ⇆ rm, ▤ TV ☎ ♿ – 🏛 40 - 2 000. AE ⓓ GB JCB E 6

La Fayette ☎ 01 40 68 51 19 **Meals** 32 ♀ – ☕ 22 – **917 rm** 290/490, 32 suites.

◆ This 33-storey tower within the Palais des Congrès complex offers guests unbeatable views of the city from most bedrooms (gradually undergoing refurbishment) and the panoramic bar. 70s-style coloured glass adds a decorative touch to La Fayette restaurant.

Splendid Étoile without rest, 1bis av. Carnot Ⓜ *Charles de Gaulle-Etoile* ☎ 01 45 72 72 00, *hotel@hsplendid.com, Fax 01 45 72 72 01* – 🛗 TV ☎ – 🏛 18. AE ⓓ GB F 7

☕ 22 – **57 rm** 255/285.

◆ A classical façade ornamented with elaborate balconies, behind which the 52 spacious rooms (some with views of the Arc de Triomphe) are furnished in Louis XV style.

Regent's Garden without rest, 6 r. P. Demours Ⓜ *Ternes* ☎ 01 45 74 07 30, *hotel.regents.garden@wanadoo.fr, Fax 01 40 55 01 42,* – 🛗, ⇆ rm, ▤ TV ☎. AE ⓓ GB JCB. ✻ E 7

☕ 11 – **39 rm** 163/276.

◆ This elegant mansion, built by Napoleon III for his private physician, has 39 large, stylish rooms, some of which overlook a garden which is particularly pleasant in summer.

Balmoral without rest, 6 r. Gén. Lanrezac Ⓜ *Charles de Gaulle-Etoile* ☎ 01 43 80 30 50, *balmoral@wanadoo.fr, Fax 01 43 80 51 56* – 🛗 ▤ TV ☎. AE ⓓ GB E 7

☕ 10 – **57 rm** 110/165.

◆ Personalised service and a calm ambience typify this old hotel (1911) a short distance from Étoile. Bright tones in the bedrooms and fine decorative woodwork in the lounge.

Ampère, 102 av. Villiers Ⓜ *Pereire* ☎ 01 44 29 17 17, *resa@hotelampere.com, Fax 01 44 29 16 50,* – 🛗 ▤ TV ☎ ♿ – 🏛 40 - 100. AE ⓓ GB D 8

Jardin d'Ampère ☎ *01 44 29 16 54 (closed 2 to 22 August and Sunday dinner)* **Meals** 31 and a la carte 40/65 ♀ – ☕ 15 – **100 rm** 190/315.

◆ A modern lobby, elegant piano-bar, high-tech web links and cosy rooms with a modern feel (some over the inner courtyard) are all features of this innovative hotel. Stylish décor and a pleasant terrace in the Jardin d'Ampère, with dinner concerts on fine days.

Novotel Porte d'Asnières, 34 av. Porte d'Asnières Ⓜ *Pereire* ☎ 01 44 40 52 52, *h4987@accorhotels.com, Fax 01 44 40 44 23* – 🛗, ⇆ rm, ▤ TV ☎ – 🏛 250. AE ⓓ GB JCB C 9

Meals 25 ♀ – ☕ 13 – **138 rm** 175/185.

◆ Situated in a modern building near the périphérique, but very well insulated from the traffic noise and with pleasant views from the rooms. Restaurant with contemporary decor offering popular grill fare.

Banville without rest, 166 bd Berthier Ⓜ *Porte de Champerret* ☎ 01 42 67 70 16, *hotelbanville@wanadoo.fr, Fax 01 44 40 42 77* – 🛗 ▤ TV ☎. AE ⓓ GB JCB D 8

☕ 13 – **38 rm** 140/200.

◆ This tastefully decorated building dating from 1926 has an inherent charm all of its own. Elegant lounges and stylish bedrooms with an individual touch.

Quality Pierre without rest, 25 r. Th.-de-Banville Ⓜ *Pereire* ☎ 01 47 63 76 69, *hotel@qualitypierre.com, Fax 01 43 80 63 96* – 🛗, ⇆ rm, ▤ TV ☎ ♿ – 🏛 30. AE ⓓ GB JCB D 8

☕ 20 – **50 rm** 190/280.

◆ Popular with business clients. The hotel's bedrooms have been refurbished in Directoire-style, with some overlooking the patio.

Villa Alessandra without rest, 9 pl. Boulnois Ⓜ *Ternes* ☎ 01 56 33 24 24, *alessandra@leshoteldeparis.com, Fax 01 56 33 24 30* – 🛗 ▤ TV ☎. AE ⓓ GB JCB E 8

☕ 20 – **49 rm** 274/291.

◆ This hotel on a charming small square is a quiet and popular option. Rooms decorated in Mediterranean style with wrought-iron beds and colourful wood furniture.

Villa Eugénie without rest, 167 r. Rome Ⓜ *Rome* ☎ 01 44 29 06 06, *eugenie@leshotelsdeparis.com, Fax 01 44 29 06 07* – 🛗, ⇆ rm, ▤ TV ☎ ♿ – 🏛 20. AE ⓓ GB JCB C 10

☕ 20 – **41 rm** 242/299.

◆ Empire furniture and toile de Jouy print wallpaper and fabrics combine to create a romantic atmosphere in the attractive bedrooms of this hotel. Cosy lounge.

Champerret Élysées without rest, 129 av. Villiers Ⓜ *Porte de Champerret* ☎ 01 47 64 44 00, *reservation@champerret-elysees.fr, Fax 01 47 63 10 58* – 🛗, ⇆ rm, ▤ TV ☎. AE ⓓ GB JCB. ✻ D 7

☕ 11 – **45 rm** 90/138.

◆ This "cyberhotel" with ADSL, Wi-Fi, two private telephone lines and fax facilities is bound to be popular with Internet-lovers. The quietest rooms overlook the courtyard.

Mercure Wagram Arc de Triomphe without rest, 3 r. Brey Ⓜ *Charles de Gaulle-Etoile* ✆ 01 56 68 00 01, *h2053@accor-hotels.com, Fax 01 56 68 00 02* – rm, AE GB JCB. E 8
14 – **43 rm** 205/215.
◆ This hotel between Étoile and Les Ternes has a welcoming lobby and small but stylish rooms decorated in light-coloured wood and sparkling fabrics on a nautical theme.

Villa des Ternes without rest, 97 av. Ternes Ⓜ *Neuilly-Porte Maillot* ✆ 01 53 81 94 94, *hotel@hotelternes.com, Fax 01 53 81 94 95* – AE GB JCB E 6
12 – **39 rm** 190/260.
◆ A recently built hotel next to the Palais des Congrès, and as such popular with business travellers. Warm tones in the bedrooms, equipped with modern bathrooms.

Magellan without rest, 17 r. J.B.-Dumas Ⓜ *Porte de Champerret* ✆ 01 45 72 44 51, *paris@hotelmagellan.com, Fax 01 40 68 90 36,* – AE GB. D 7
12 – **72 rm** 142.
◆ Functional and spacious bedrooms are a feature of this fine 1900s hotel with a small pavilion at the end of the small garden. The hotel lounge is furnished in Art Deco style.

Étoile St-Ferdinand without rest, 36 r. St-Ferdinand Ⓜ *Porte Maillot* ✆ 01 45 72 66 66, *ferdinand@paris-honotel.com, Fax 01 45 74 12 92* – AE GB JCB E 6-7
13 – **42 rm** 149/225.
◆ A classic Parisian building overlooking two relatively quiet streets near Porte Maillot. Pleasantly renovated rooms enlivened by bright and colourful décor.

Étoile Park Hôtel without rest, 10 av. Mac Mahon Ⓜ *Charles de Gaulle-Etoile* ✆ 01 42 67 69 63, *ephot@easynet.fr, Fax 01 43 80 18 99* – AE GB JCB E 8
12 – **28 rm** 95/150.
◆ Superbly located just a few yards from the Arc de Triomphe. Behind the stone façade is an attractive interior renovated in contemporary style. Pleasant breakfast room.

Star Hôtel Étoile without rest, 18 r. Arc de Triomphe Ⓜ *Charles de Gaulle-Etoile* ✆ 01 43 80 27 69, *star.etoile.hotel@wanadoo.fr, Fax 01 40 54 94 84* – 18. AE GB JCB E 7
12 – **62 rm** 145/150.
◆ Modern, medieval-inspired decor in the reception, lounge and breakfast room. Although the rooms are small, they are light, cheerful and relatively quiet.

Astrid without rest, 27 av. Carnot Ⓜ *Charles de Gaulle-Etoile* ✆ 01 44 09 26 00, *paris@hotel-astrid.com, Fax 01 44 09 26 01* – AE GB JCB E 7
10 – **41 rm** 125/137.
◆ Just 100m/110yd from the Arc de Triomphe, and run by the same family since 1936. Each room has a different style : Directoire, Tyrolian, Provençal etc.

Flaubert without rest, 19 r. Rennequin Ⓜ *Ternes* ✆ 01 46 22 44 35, *paris@hotelflaubert.com, Fax 01 43 80 32 34* – AE GB D 8
8 – **41 rm** 94/109.
◆ The major selling-point of this hotel with bright, modern decor is its peaceful and verdant patio, overlooked by a few rooms. Winter garden-style breakfast room.

Campanile, 4 bd Berthier Ⓜ *Porte de Clichy* ✆ 01 46 27 10 00, *resaind@campanile-berthier.com, Fax 01 46 27 00 57,* – rm, – 15 - 80. AE GB B 10
Meals 16,50/18,50 – 7 – **246 rm** 88.
◆ A functional, high-capacity hotel with rooms that conform to the Campanile's usual criteria. The chain's traditional buffet menus are served in the standardised restaurant as well as on the terrace.

Guy Savoy, 18 r. Troyon Ⓜ *Charles de Gaulle-Etoile* ✆ 01 43 80 40 61, *reserv@guysavoy.com, Fax 01 46 22 43 09* – AE GB JCB E 8
closed August, 23 December-3 January, Saturday lunch, Sunday and Monday – **Meals** 200/245 and a la carte 160/210.
◆ A décor of glass, leather, African wood and sculptures and works by leading names in modern art. Refined and inventive cuisine in this top, resolutely 21C restaurant.
Spec. Soupe d'artichaut à la truffe noire et brioche feuilletée aux champignons. Bar en écailles grillées aux épices douces. Agneau de lait "dans tous ses états".

Michel Rostang, 20 r. Rennequin Ⓜ *Ternes* ✆ 01 47 63 40 77, *rostang@relaischateaux.fr, Fax 01 47 63 82 75* – AE GB JCB D 8
closed 1 to 15 August, Sunday, lunch Monday and Saturday – **Meals** 65 (lunch), 175/230 and a la carte 130/180.
◆ An elegant and unusual setting in which decorative wood, Robj figurines, Lalique works and Art Deco stained-glass add to the luxurious decor. Excellent cuisine and wine list.
Spec. "Menu truffe" (15 December-15 March). Quenelle de brochet soufflée à la crème de homard. Foie chaud de canard rôti au sésame grillé.

Apicius (Vigato), 122 av. Villiers Ⓜ *Porte de Champerret* ✆ 01 43 80 19 66, *Fax 01 44 40 09 57* – AE GB JCB D 8
closed August, Saturday and Sunday – **Meals** 110 and a la carte 90/130.
◆ Pearl-grey walls, plain wood and paintings add a refined tone to this restaurant serving inventive cuisine that would surely have satisfied the Roman gastronome Apicius.
Spec. Foie gras de canard aux radis noirs confits. Milieu de très gros turbot rôti. Soufflé au chocolat.

Faucher, 123 av. Wagram Ⓜ *Wagram* ✆ 01 42 27 61 50, *Fax 01 46 22 25 72,* – AE GB D 8
closed Saturday and Sunday – **Meals** 50 (lunch)/95 and a la carte 70/100.
◆ Seasonal, personalised cuisine is the bedrock of this sober yet bright restaurant adorned with modern paintings. The tables by the rotunda are particularly pleasant.
Spec. Oeuf au plat, foie gras chaud et coppa grillée. Montgolfière de Saint-Jacques au velouté de cèpes (October-March). Ris de veau croustillants.

Sormani (Fayet), 4 r. Gén. Lanrezac Ⓜ *Ch. de Gaulle Etoile* ✆ 01 43 80 13 91, *Fax 01 40 55 07 37* – GB E 7
closed 1 to 24 August, 23 December-4 January, Saturday, Sunday and Bank Holidays – **Meals** - Italian rest. - 44 (lunch) and a la carte 55/125.
◆ A restaurant full of Latin charm and a "dolce vita" atmosphere near place de l'Étoile. Elegant Italian cuisine served to a backdrop of red decor, wood panelling and mirrors.
Spec. Chaud-froid de pâte à pain, artichaut et mozzarelle à la truffe blanche (October-December). Ravioli de tourteau et palourdes. Jarret de veau et gratin de macaroni au lard.

Pétrus, 12 pl. Mar. Juin Ⓜ *Pereire* ✆ 01 43 80 15 95, *Fax 01 47 66 49 86* – AE GB JCB D 8
closed 10 to 25 August – **Meals** - Seafood - 42 and a la carte 45/65 ♀.
◆ A profusion of excellent fresh fish and seafood is the order of the day in this pleasant, maritime-inspired restaurant.

Petit Colombier, 42 r. Acacias Ⓜ *Argentine* ✆ 01 43 80 28 54, *le.petit.colombier@wanadoo.fr, Fax 01 44 40 04 29* – AE GB E 7
closed 31 July-30 August, Saturday lunch and Sunday – **Meals** 35 and a la carte 55/77.
◆ The patina of age, antique clocks and Louis XV chairs add provincial charm to this restaurant which recalls the visits of the world's heads of state.

Les Béatilles (Bochaton), 11 bis r. Villebois-Mareuil Ⓜ *Ternes* ✆ 01 45 74 43 80, *Fax 01 45 74 43 81* – GB E 7
closed August, Christmas Holidays, Saturday and Sunday – **Meals** 40 (lunch), 45/70 and a la carte 68/92.
◆ Attentive service and imaginative and refined cuisine are the hallmarks of this restaurant with its simple and contemporary design.
Spec. Nems d'escargots et champignons des bois. Pastilla de pigeon et foie gras aux épices. La "Saint-Cochon" (November-March).

Dessirier, 9 pl. Mar. Juin Ⓜ *Pereire* ✆ 01 42 27 82 14, *dessirier@michelrostang.com, Fax 01 47 66 82 07* – AE GB JCB D 8
closed 11 to 17 August, Saturday and Sunday in July-August – **Meals** - Seafood - 45 and a la carte 51/83 ♀.
◆ A friendly brasserie-style restaurant where the armchairs, padded benches and fish- and seafood-inspired menu help to foster good humour and a convivial atmosphere.

Timgad, 21 r. Brunel ✆ 01 45 74 23 70, *Fax 01 40 68 76 46* – AE GB. E 7
Meals - Moroccan rest. - a la carte 40/60.
◆ The past splendour of the city of Timgad is revisited in this restaurant serving the perfumed cuisine of the Maghreb. Elegant, Moorish-inspired decor with Moroccan stucco.

Graindorge, 15 r. Arc de Triomphe Ⓜ *Charles de Gaulle-Etoile* ✆ 01 47 54 00 28, *Fax 01 47 54 00 28* – AE GB E 7
closed Saturday lunch and Sunday – **Meals** flemish rest. 28 (lunch)/32 and a la carte 42/64 ♀.
◆ Barley (orge) is the key ingredient in the beer which accompanies the delicious and copious Flemish dishes served in this Art Deco-style restaurant. Wine also available!

Braisière (Faussat), 54 r. Cardinet Ⓜ *Malesherbes* ✆ 01 47 63 40 37, *labraisiere@free.fr, Fax 01 47 63 04 76* – AE GB
closed August, Saturday lunch and Sunday – **Meals** 30 (lunch) and a la carte 43/59 ♀.
◆ Comfortable restaurant in gentle pastels. The imaginative chef draws inspiration from the traditions of the south-west and takes his cue from the day's market specials.
Spec. Terrine de lapin à la bohémienne. Pièce de bœuf "blonde d'Aquitaine". Cassonade crémeuse de noix.

Paolo Petrini, 6 r. Débarcadère Ⓜ *Porte Maillot* ✆ 01 45 74 25 95, *paolo.petrini@wanadoo.fr, Fax 01 45 74 12 95* – AE GB JCB. E 6
closed 1 to 21 August, Saturday lunch and Sunday – **Meals** - Italian rest. - 30/35 b.i. and a la carte 55/65 ♀.
◆ Forget pizza and macaroni, as this soberly decorated restaurant near Porte Maillot attracts discerning customers who come here to enjoy refined Italian cuisine.

XX **Ballon des Ternes,** 103 av. Ternes Ⓜ *Porte Maillot* ☎ 01 45 74 17 98, *leballondesternes@wanadoo.fr, Fax 01 45 72 18 84* – AE GB JCB E 6
closed 28 July-26 August – **Meals** a la carte 36/67 ♀.
◆ A pleasant brasserie with 1900s décor close to the Palais des Congrès. An emphasis on seafood and meat dishes, with attentive service.

XX **Taïra,** 10 r. Acacias Ⓜ *Argentine* ☎ 01 47 66 74 14, *Fax 01 47 66 74 14* – ▤. AE ⓓ GB E 7
closed 15 to 31 August, Saturday lunch and Sunday – **Meals** - Seafood - 34/64 and a la carte 44/66.
◆ The Japanese chef, whose first name is Taïra, prepares fish and seafood here with both finesse and simplicity, making the most of his Franco-Japanese culinary heritage.

XX **Chez Léon,** 32 r. Legendre Ⓜ *Villiers* ☎ 01 42 27 06 82, *Fax 01 46 22 63 67* – AE GB D 10
closed August, Christmas Holidays, Saturday, Sunday and Bank Holidays – **Meals** 24 b.i. and a la carte 33/43.
◆ Popular with a faithful band of locals over a number of years, "the" bistro in the Batignolles district is known for its refined, traditional cuisine served on two floors.

X **Soupière,** 154 av. Wagram Ⓜ *Wagram* ☎ 01 42 27 00 73, *Fax 01 46 22 27 09* – ▤. AE GB D 9
closed 4 to 24 August, Saturday lunch and Sunday – **Meals** 25/55 and a la carte 36/59.
◆ An amiable local restaurant with attentive service and a classic à la carte, including "mushroom" menus in season. Trompe-l'œil décor.

X **A et M Marée,** 105 r. Prony Ⓜ *Pereire* ☎ 01 44 40 05 88, *AM.Bistrot.17eme@wanadoo.fr, Fax 01 44 40 05 89,* 🏠 – ▤ ⇨. AE ⓓ GB D 8
closed August, Saturday lunch and Sunday – **Meals** 30 and a la carte 38/55.
◆ A trendy address with a bistro area and a large room decked out in grey and mauve and crowned by a glass dome. The sister restaurant in the 16th is of a similar standard.

X **Caves Petrissans,** 30 bis av. Niel Ⓜ *Pereire* ☎ 01 42 27 52 03, *cavespetrissans@noos.fr, Fax 01 40 54 87 56,* 🏠 – AE GB D 8
closed 23 July-22 August, Saturday and Sunday – **Meals** (booking essential) 33 and a la carte 38/70 🍇.
◆ This hundred-year-old-plus establishment, which doubles as a wine shop and restaurant, was frequented in bygone days by famous literary figures. Well-presented bistro cuisine.

X **Presqu'île,** 14 r. Saussier-Leroy Ⓜ *Ternes* ☎ 01 47 66 56 74, *Fax 01 40 54 83 86* – ▤. AE GB JCB E 8
closed August, Sunday, lunch Monday and Saturday – **Meals** - Seafood - 31 (lunch) and a la carte 40/60 - ***L'Huîtrier*** ☎ 01 40 54 83 44 *(closed July, August, Sunday in May-June and Monday from September-April)* **Meals** a la carte 31/73 ♀.
◆ The main selling-point of La Presqu'île is undoubtedly its superb à la carte fish menu, served on tightly spaced tables to a backdrop of wood panelling and marine decor. For oysters and seafood, head for l'Huîtrier, with its bistro-like atmosphere.

Montmartre, La Villette, Belleville.

18th, 19th and 20th arrondissements.
18th: ✉ 75018
19th: ✉ 75019
20th: ✉ 75020

Terrass'Hôtel, 12 r. J. de Maistre (18th) Ⓜ *Place de Clichy* ☎ 01 46 06 72 85, *reservation@terrass-hotel.com, Fax 01 42 52 29 11,* 🏠 – |♦|, ⇹ rm, ▤ TV ☏ – 🏛 25 - 100. AE ⓓ GB JCB C 13
Terrasse ☎ 01 44 92 34 00 **Meals** 21,50 b.i./28 and a la carte 32/50 – ☕ 14 – **87 rm** 204/270, 13 suites.
◆ At the foot of the Sacré-Cœur. An unbeatable view of Paris from the upper-floor rooms facing the street. A warm, stylish interior with an attractive chimney in the lounge. Cosy Provençal dining room with a rooftop "Terrasse" offering views of the capital.

Holiday Inn, 216 av. J. Jaurès (19th) Ⓜ *Porte de Pantin* ✆ 01 44 84 18 18, *hilavillet te@alliance-hospitality.com, Fax 01 44 84 18 20*, – rm, – 15 - 140. AE GB C 21
Meals *(closed Saturday and Sunday)* 28/58 ♀ – ☕ 15 – **182 rm** 270/345.
◆ A modern hotel opposite the Cité de la Musique and a few yards from the nearest métro stop. Spacious, soundproofed rooms with modern creature comforts. Sober brasserie-style dining room, plus a small terrace separated from the street by a curtain of greenery.

Mercure Montmartre without rest, 1 r. Caulaincourt (18th) Ⓜ *Place de Clichy* ✆ 01 44 69 70 70, *h0373@accor-hotels.com, Fax 01 44 69 70 71* – rm, – 20 - 70. AE GB D 12
☕ 13 – **305 rm** 174/184.
◆ All the usual facilities one would expect of the Mercure in this hotel at the heart of Paris nightlife, a short walk from the Moulin-Rouge. Pleasant mahogany-coloured bar.

Holiday Inn Garden Court Montmartre without rest, 23 r. Damrémont (18th) Ⓜ *Lamarck Caulaincourt* ✆ 01 44 92 33 40, *hiparmm@aol.com, Fax 01 44 92 09 30* – rm, – 20. AE GB JCB C 13
☕ 13 – **54 rm** 145/170.
◆ A fairly recent hotel on one of Montmartre's steep streets. Bright, functional rooms, plus a breakfast room decorated with an attractive trompe-l'œil.

Kyriad, 147 av. Flandres (19th) Ⓜ *Crimée* ✆ 01 44 72 46 46, *paris.lavillette@kyriad.fr, Fax 01 44 72 46 47* – rm, rest, – 70. AE GB JCB B 19
Meals 12/17 ♀ – ☕ 7 – **207 rm** 82.
◆ This modern hotel within spitting distance of the Cité des Sciences is a practical base with its proximity to bus and métro networks and ring road. Small, functional rooms. Basic food options (salads, grilled meats) available in the retro-style dining room.

Roma Sacré Cœur without rest, 101 r. Caulaincourt (18th) Ⓜ *Lamarck Caulaincourt* ✆ 01 42 62 02 02, *hotel.roma@wanadoo.fr, Fax 01 42 54 34 92* – . AE GB JCB C 14
☕ 7 – **57 rm** 85/160.
◆ The Roma displays the full charm of Montmartre with a garden to the front, steps to the side and the Sacré-Cœur above. Colourful, recently refurbished rooms.

Laumière without rest, 4 r. Petit (19th) Ⓜ *Laumière* ✆ 01 42 06 10 77, *le-laumiere@wanadoo.fr, Fax 01 42 06 72 50* – . GB D 19
☕ 7 – **54 rm** 49/65.
◆ If you're looking for some urban greenery, this recently renovated hotel could fit the bill, with its attractive small garden and proximity to the Parc des Buttes-Chaumont.

Damrémont without rest, 110 r. Damrémont (18th) Ⓜ *Jules Joffrin* ✆ 01 42 64 25 75, *hotel.damremont@wanadoo.fr, Fax 01 46 06 74 64* – rm, . GB JCB. B 13
☕ 7 – **35 rm** 75/100.
◆ This hotel near Montmartre offers modern, smallish but well-maintained rooms (those over the courtyard are quieter) with attractive mahogany-coloured furniture.

Crimée without rest, 188 r. Crimée (19th) Ⓜ *Crimée* ✆ 01 40 36 75 29, *hotelcrimee 19@wanadoo.fr, Fax 01 40 36 29 57* – . AE GB JCB C 18
☕ 6 – **31 rm** 57/65.
◆ This hotel is situated 300m/330yd from the Canal de l'Ourcq. Good soundproofing in the functional rooms, some of which open on to a small garden.

Beauvilliers, 52 r. Lamarck (18th) Ⓜ *Lamarck Caulaincourt* ✆ 01 42 54 54 42, *beauv illiers@club-internet.fr, Fax 01 42 62 70 30*, – . AE GB JCB C 14
closed Monday lunch, Sunday and Bank Holidays – **Meals** 30 (lunch), 45 b.i./61 b.i. and a la carte 65/100.
◆ This former bakery on Montmartre hill is now a charming restaurant. Magnificent Second Empire decor embellished with paintings and floral arrangements. Traditional cuisine.

Cottage Marcadet, 151 bis r. Marcadet (18th) Ⓜ *Lamarck Caulaincourt* ✆ 01 42 57 71 22, *Fax 01 42 57 71 22* – . GB. C 13
closed Easter Holidays, 31 July-30 August and Sunday – **Meals** 27/36,50 b.i. and a la carte 31/56.
◆ An intimate ambience awaits customers in this classical restaurant adorned with comfortable Louis XVI furniture. Refined, traditional cuisine.

Les Allobroges, 71 r. Grands-Champs (20th) Ⓜ *Maraîchers* ✆ 01 43 73 40 00, *Fax 01 40 09 23 22* – AE GB K 22
closed 18 to 26 April, August, 24 December-5 January, Sunday, Monday and Bank Holidays – **Meals** 20/33 and a la carte 34/48.
◆ Head off the beaten track to the Porte de Montreuil to discover this pleasant restaurant with its attractive but simple decor. Delicious contemporary cuisine.

XX **Relais des Buttes,** 86 r. Compans (19th) Ⓜ *Botzaris* ✆ 01 42 08 24 70, *Fax 01 42 03 20 44,* – GB E 20
closed August, 26 December-2 January, Saturday lunch and Sunday – **Meals** 31 and a la carte 40/58 ♀.
◆ A few yards from the Parc des Buttes-Chaumont. A warming fireplace in the modern dining room during the winter, plus a quiet courtyard terrace in summer. Traditional cuisine.

XX **Moulin de la Galette,** 83 r. Lepic (18th) Ⓜ *Abbesses* ✆ 01 46 06 84 77, *Fax 01 46 06 84 78,* – ▤. AE GB JCB
closed Sunday dinner and Monday – **Meals** 45 ♀.
◆ This windmill dating from 1622 was to become a well-known dance hall painted by Renoir and Toulouse-Lautrec. Today, it is a pleasant restaurant with a charming terrace.

XX **Au Clair de la Lune,** 9 r. Poulbot (18th) Ⓜ *Abbesses* ✆ 01 42 58 97 03, *Fax 01 42 55 64 74* – AE GB JCB D 14
closed 20 August-15 September, Monday lunch and Sunday – **Meals** 28 and a la carte 35/65.
◆ Pierrot will extend a warm welcome to his auberge located just behind the Place du Tertre. A friendly atmosphere, with the backdrop of frescoes depicting old Montmartre.

X **Poulbot Gourmet,** 39 r. Lamarck (18th) Ⓜ *Lamarck Caulaincourt* ✆ 01 46 06 86 00, *Fax 01 46 06 86 00* – GB C 14
closed 15 to 30 August and Sunday except lunch from October-May – **Meals** 34 and a la carte 35/55.
◆ This bistro will take you back to the time when street urchins (poulbots) were a common sight in Montmartre. Classic cuisine that will satisfy the most discerning gourmet.

X **L'Oriental,** 76 r. Martyrs (18th) Ⓜ *Pigalle* ✆ 01 42 64 39 80, *Fax 01 42 64 39 80* – AE GB. ✻ D 13-14
closed 22 July-28 August, Sunday and Monday – **Meals** - North-African rest. - 39 b.i. and a la carte 28/43.
◆ Smiling service and pleasing décor, including ornate mosaics and screens, typify this North African restaurant at the heart of cosmopolitan Pigalle.

X **Cave Gourmande,** 10 r. Gén. Brunet (19th) Ⓜ *Botzaris* ✆ 01 40 40 03 30, *la-cave-gourmande@wanadoo.fr, Fax 01 40 40 03 30* – ▤. GB E 20
closed August, February Holidays, Saturday and Sunday – **Meals** 32 and a la carte 32/38.
◆ Close to the Parc des Buttes-Chaumont, this friendly bistro is known for its varied range of daily specials. The decor here is a relaxed mix of wooden tables and bottle racks.

ENVIRONS

The outskirts of Paris up to 25Km

Cergy-Pontoise *95 Val-d'Oise* 305 D6 106 ⑤ 101 ②.
Paris 36.

at Cormeilles-en-Vexin – *pop. 863 alt. 111* – ✉ *95830* :

XXX ✿✿ **Relais Ste-Jeanne** (Cagna), on D 915 ✆ 01 34 66 61 56, *saintejeanne@hotmail.com, Fax 01 34 66 40 31,* – P. AE ① GB
closed 28 July-26 August, 22 to 29 December, Sunday dinner, Monday and Tuesday – **Meals** 60 b.i./110 b.i. and a la carte 90/112.
◆ Refined cuisine, a stylish dining room and fireplace, understated country décor and a pleasing terrace and garden are the hallmarks of this charming house northwest of Paris.
Spec. Escalopes de ris de veau poêlées, crème de volaille. Blanc de turbot rôti à l'huile d'olive, mirepoix de légumes. Adagio chocolat-pistache.

La Défense *92 Hauts-de-Seine* 311 J2 101 ⑭ – ✉ *92400 Courbevoie.*
See : *Quarter*★★ *: perspective*★ *from the parvis – Paris 8,5.*

Sofitel Grande Arche, 11 av. Arche, exit Défense 6 ✉ 92081 ✆ 01 47 17 50 00, *h3013@accor-hotels.com, Fax 01 47 17 55 66,* , – , rm, – 100. AE ① GB JCB. rest
Avant Seine ✆ 01 47 17 59 99 *(closed 11 to 24 August, Friday dinner, Saturday and Sunday)* **Meals** a la carte 45/50 – 23 – **368 rm** 395/445, 16 suites.
◆ Impressive ship prow architecture in glass and ochre-coloured stone. Spacious, elegant rooms, well-equipped lounges and auditorium (with interpreting booths). High-quality designer décor in the Avant Seine restaurant, where grilled meats are to the fore.

Renaissance, 60 Jardin de Valmy, by ring road, exit La Défense 7 ✉ 92918 *Puteaux* ✆ 01 41 97 50 50, *reservations@renaissancehotels.com, Fax 01 41 97 51 51,* – , rm, – 160. AE ① GB JCB.
Meals *(closed Sunday lunch and Saturday)* 26 ♀ – 23 – **324 rm** 239/540, 3 suites.
◆ At the foot of the Carrara-marbled Grande Arche, this large modern hotel offers guests well-appointed rooms decorated with refinement. Old brasserie atmosphere in the wood-clad restaurant offering views over the Valmy gardens. Full fitness facilities.

Hilton La Défense, 2 pl. Défense ✉ 92053 ✆ 01 46 92 10 10, *parlhicb@hilton.com, Fax 01 46 92 10 50,* – , rm, P – 5 - 60. AE ① GB JCB
Les Communautés ✆ 01 46 92 10 30 (lunch only) *(closed Saturday and Sunday)* **Meals** 56/100 ♀ – ***L'Échiquier*** ✆ 01 46 92 10 35 **Meals** a la carte 35/45 – 28 – **148 rm** 270/500, 6 suites.
◆ This refurbished hotel stands within the confines of the CNIT conference centre. Warm, designer-style rooms, some with facilities for the business traveller. Modern cuisine and good views from Les Communautés restaurant ; traditional cuisine in L'Échiquier.

Sofitel Centre, 34 cours Michelet by ring road, exit La Défense 4 ✉ 92060 *Puteaux* ✆ 01 47 76 44 43, *h0912@accor-hotels.com, Fax 01 47 76 72 10,* – , rm, – 100. AE ① GB. rest
Les 2 Arcs ✆ 01 47 76 72 30 *(closed 30 July-17 August, Friday dinner, Saturday, Sunday and Bank Holidays)* **Meals** 49/55 – ***Botanic*** ✆ 01 47 76 72 40 **Meals** a la carte approx. 40 ♀ – 24 – **151 rm** 395/445.
◆ A semi-circular building between the towers of La Défense. Large, well-equipped rooms, some of which have been refurbished. Hushed English-style bar, and contemporary decor and cuisine in Les 2 Arcs restaurant. Half-bar, half-brasserie ambience in Le Botanic.

Novotel La Défense, 2 bd Neuilly, exit Défense 1 ✆ 01 41 45 23 23, *h0747@accor-hotels.com, Fax 01 41 45 23 24* – , rm, – 130. AE ① GB JCB
Meals *(closed lunch Saturday and Sunday)* 21,90 ♀ – 13 – **280 rm** 220/275.
◆ La Défense district, with its impressive architecture and sculpture, stands at the foot of this hotel with its comfortable and functional rooms, some offering views of Paris. Contemporary décor in the trendy dining room, which features a buffet section.

Marne-la-Vallée *77206 S.-et-M.* 312 E2 101 ⑲.
18 *of Bussy-St-Georges (private)* ✆ *01 64 66 00 00 ;* 9 18 *of Disneyland Paris* ✆ *01 60 45 68 90.* – *Tourist Office pl. des passagers du vent - Disneyland Paris* ✆ *01 60 30 60 30.*
Paris 28.

at Disneyland Resort Paris *access by Highway A 4 and Disneyland exit.*
See : *Disneyland Resort Paris* ★★★*-Central reservation number for hotels :* ✆ *(00 33)01 60 30 60 30, Fax (00 33)01 64 74 57 50 – The rates for the hotels in Disneyland Resort Paris are based on a daily price that includes entrance to the Parks – As these rates vary according to the season, we suggest that you call the central reservation number for current information*

Orly (Paris Airports) *94396 Val-de-Marne* 312 D3 101 ㉖ – *pop. 21 646 alt. 89.*
✈ ✆ *01 49 75 15 15.*
Paris 15.

Hilton Orly, near airport station ✉ 94544 ✆ 01 45 12 45 12, *oryhitwrm@hilton.com, Fax 01 45 12 45 00,* – rm, – 280. AE GB JCB.
Meals (lunch buffet) 34 – 19 – **352 rm** 115/160.
• A 1960s hotel with subdued yet elegant rooms, and the latest high-tech equipment and facilities for business customers. Current décor, plus a choice of brasserie dishes, buffet options and a gastronomic à la carte menu in the restaurant.

Mercure, N 7, Z.I. Nord, Orlytech ✉ 94547 ✆ 01 49 75 15 50, *h1246@accor-hotels.com, Fax 01 49 75 15 51* – rm, – 40. AE GB JCB
Meals *(closed Sunday lunch and Saturday)* 23,50 – 12 – **192 rm** 128/152.
• A convenient stopover hotel, particularly for business travellers, with its good facilities and well-maintained rooms. Contemporary bistro atmosphere, brasserie-style dishes and the standard "Mercure" chain wine-list in the restaurant.

See also *Rungis*

Roissy-en-France (Paris Airports) *95700 Val-d'Oise* 305 G6 101 ⑧ – *pop. 2 367 alt. 85.*
✈ ✆ *01 48 62 22 80.*
Paris 26.

at Roissy-Town :

Millenium, allée du Verger ✆ 01 34 29 33 33, *resa.cdg@mill-cop.com, Fax 01 34 29 03 05,* – rm, – 150. AE GB JCB
Meals 28 b.i./40 b.i. – 19 – **239 rm** 250/310.
• The excellent facilities here include a bar, Irish pub, fitness centre, impressive pool, meeting rooms, and a floor specifically for business clientele. The brasserie concentrates on buffets and international cuisine, with lighter snacks available in the bar.

Courtyard Marriott, allée du Verger ✆ 01 34 38 53 53, *Fax 01 34 38 53 54,* – – 500. AE GB JCB.
Meals 26 and a la carte 36/55 – 17 – **296 rm** 169/300, 4 suites.
• The newest airport hotel offers modern facilities perfectly suited to business travellers in transit through Paris. The restaurant's classic cuisine is served to a backdrop of decor inspired by the City of Light's typical brasseries.

Country Inn and Suites, allée du Verger ✆ 01 30 18 21 00, *Fax 01 30 18 20 18,* – rm, – 15 - 95. AE GB JCB
Meals *(closed lunch Saturday, Sunday and Bank Holidays)* 27 – 11 – **174 rm** 195, 6 suites.
• This recently built hexagonal and somewhat plain hotel offers guests spacious rooms of varying sizes with modern attractive decor. The restaurant menu features a mixture of French cuisine and dishes from the other side of the Atlantic. English-style bar.

Mercure, allée des Vergers ✆ 01 34 29 40 00, *h1245@accor-hotels.com, Fax 01 34 29 00 18,* – rm, – 90. AE GB JCB
Meals 23 – 12 – **203 rm** 180/252.
• This chain hotel has had a recent facelift, with Provençal tones in the lobby, an old-style counter in the bar, and refurbished, soundproofed bedrooms offering plenty of space. The new-look dining room has been revamped with light-hearted bakery décor.

Ibis, av. Raperie ✆ 01 34 29 34 34, *h0815@accor-hotels.com, Fax 01 34 29 34 19* – rm, – 70. AE GB
Meals 15 – 8 – **304 rm** 70/125.
• An inexpensive stopover option for those on a budget, with bedrooms furnished in line with the chain's new design concept, and efficient soundproofing. Huge bistro-style dining room extended by a terrace arranged around a patio.

in Airport terminal nr 2 :

Sheraton ✆ 01 49 19 70 70, *Fax 01 49 19 70 71,* – rm, – 110. AE GB JCB
Les Étoiles *(closed 31/07-29/08, 20/12-3/01, Saturday, Sunday and Bank Holidays)* **Meals** 48,50(lunch)/55,50 – ***Les Saisons :*** **Meals** a la carte approx 42 – 25,50 – **254 rm** 395/650, 12 suites.
• Step off the plane and into this futuristic hotel with its original architecture. Décor by Andrée Putman, views of the runway, peace and quiet, and elegant bedrooms. A modern setting and cuisine in Les Étoiles, with brasserie dishes in Les Saisons.

at Roissypole :

Hilton, 01 49 19 77 77, *CDGHITWSAL@hilton.com, Fax 01 49 19 77 78*, – rm, – 500. rest
Gourmet *(closed July, August, Saturday and Sunday)* **Meals** 39/42 – ***Aviateurs*** - brasserie **Meals** 34 – **Oyster bar** - Seafood *(closed July, August, Saturday and Sunday)* **Meals** 38/55 – 24 – **379 rm** 495/564, 4 suites.
• Bold architecture, space and light are the key features of this upmarket chain hotel with all the latest facilities, making it an ideal base for work and relaxation. High gastronomy in Le Gourmet, plus a concise brasserie menu in the Aviateurs.

Sofitel, Zone centrale Ouest 01 49 19 29 29, *h0577@accor-hotels.com, Fax 01 49 19 29 00*, – rm, – 60. rest
brasserie ***L'Escale*** -Seafood **Meals** a la carte 40/50 – 20 – **342 rm** 370/551, 6 suites.
• The major selling-points of this Sofitel between the two terminals are its personalised service, quiet ambience, seminar rooms, elegant bar and refined guest rooms. Nautical décor and cuisine in the pleasant and aptly named "Escale" (Port of Call) restaurant.

Novotel, 01 49 19 27 27, *h1014@accor-hotels.com, Fax 01 49 19 27 99* – rm, – 60.
Meals 23 (dinner), 26/55 – 12 – **201 rm** 150.
• A mid-range chain hotel located opposite the airport's runways. The majority of its well-appointed rooms with double-glazing conform to the chain's new style. Restrained dining room designed with a brasserie feel, with modern furnishings and a simple layout.

Z.I. Paris Nord II – *95912 :*

Hyatt Regency, 351 av. Bois de la Pie 01 48 17 12 34, *cdg@paris.hyatt.com, Fax 01 48 17 17 17*, – rm, – 300. rest
Meals 53/81 – 22 – **383 rm** 385/460, 5 suites.
• Spectacular contemporary architecture marks out this hotel on the airport approach, with a vast atrium linking the two wings housing the hotel's 383 quiet rooms. Buffet and classic à la carte choices are available in the restaurant, crowned by a glass ceiling.

Rungis *94150 Val-de-Marne 312 D3 101 ㉖ – pop. 5 424 alt. 80. – Paris 14.*

at Pondorly : *Access : from Paris, Highway A 6 and take Orly Airport exit ; from outside of Paris, A 6 and Rungis exit :*

Holiday Inn, 4 av. Ch. Lindbergh 01 49 78 42 00, *hiorly.manager@alliance-hospitality.com, Fax 01 45 60 91 25* – rm, – 15 - 150. rest
Meals 25,70 – 15 – **168 rm** 160/191.
• A comfortable hotel alongside the motorway, with large, modern rooms fitted with double-glazing. The dining room has been recently renovated in contemporary style with the occasional discreet touch of Art Deco. Traditional cuisine.

Novotel, Zone du Delta, 1 r. Pont des Halles 01 45 12 44 12, *h1628@accor-hotels.com, Fax 01 45 12 44 13*, – rm, – 15 - 150.
Meals a la carte 22/29 – 12 – **181 rm** 137/159.
• The hotel's double-glazed bedrooms comply with the chain's normal standards. The bar is based on a comic strip theme ; the large restaurant on the city's wholesale markets.

Versailles *78000 Yvelines 311 I3 101 ㉓ – pop. 85 726 alt. 130.*

See : *Palace★★★ Y – Gardens★★★ (fountain display★★★ (grandes eaux) and illuminated night performances★★★ (fêtes de nuit) in summer) – Ecuries Royales★ Y – The Trianons★★ – Lambinet Museum★ Y* **M**.

of la Boulie (private) 01 39 50 59 41 by ③ : 2,5 km.

Tourist Office 2 bis av. Paris 01 39 24 88 88, Fax 01 39 24 88 89. – Paris 20 ①

Trianon Palace, 1 bd Reine **(r)** 01 30 84 50 00, *trian@westin.com, Fax 01 30 84 50 01*, <, – rm, rm, – 15 - 200. rest
see ***Les Trois Marches*** *below* - ***Café Trianon :*** **Meals** a la carte 52/70 – 30 – **166 rm** 286/616, 26 suites.
• The classic architecture of this luxury hotel on the edge of the park is a fine example of early-20C elegance. Excellent fitness centre. The Café Trianon, with its attractive glass ceiling, continues to enjoy local popularity for its refined modern cuisine.

Sofitel Château de Versailles, 2 bis av. Paris 01 39 07 46 46, *h1300@accor-hotels.com, Fax 01 39 07 46 47*, – rm, – 120. Y a
Meals *(closed 23 July-23 August, Friday and Saturday)* 30/50 b.i. – 20 – **146 rm** 380, 6 suites.
• Only the gate survives from the former artillery school here. Vast renovated rooms embellished with antique furniture and lithographs. The modern dining room, serving a range of French and international cuisine, is ornamented with Liberty print lambrequins.

VERSAILLES

Carnot (R.) . . . . Y
Chancellerie (R. de la) . Y 3
Clemenceau
(R. Georges) . . . . Y 7
Cotte (R. Robert-de) . . . Y 10
États-Généraux (R. des) . Z
Europe (Av. de l') . . . . . Y 14
Foch (R. du Mar.) . . . . . XY
Gambetta (Pl.) . . . . Y 17
Gaulle (Av. Gén.-de) . . . YZ 18
Hoche (R.) . . . . Y
Indép. Américaine
(R. de l') . . . . Y 20
Leclerc (R. du Gén.) . . . Z 24
Mermoz (R. Jean) . . . . . Z 27
Nolhac
(R. Pierre-de) . . . . Y 31
Orangerie (R. de l') . . . . YZ
Paroisse (R. de la) . . . . . Y
Porte de Buc (R. de la) . Z 34
Rockefeller (Av.) . . . . . . Y 37
Royale (R.) . . . . Z
Satory (R. de) . . . . YZ 42
Vieux-Versailles (R. du) . YZ 47

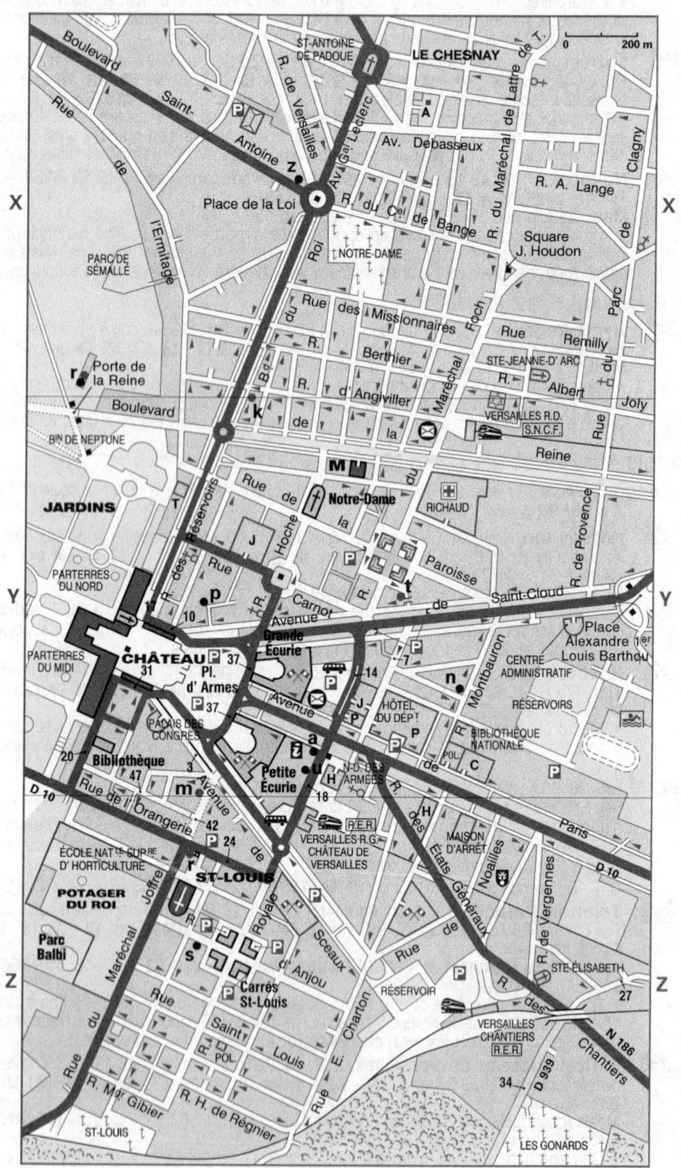

Versailles without rest, 7 r. Ste-Anne 01 39 50 64 65, *info@hotel-le-versailles.fr, Fax 01 39 02 37 85* – 25. AE GB JCB Y p
11 – **46 rm** 86/115.
◆ A combination of spacious rooms, Art Deco furniture, peace and quiet, a pretty terrace and attentive service explain the success of this pleasant and popular hotel.

Résidence du Berry without rest, 14 r. Anjou 01 39 49 07 07, *resa@hotel-berry.com, Fax 01 39 50 59 40* – rm, AE GB JCB Z s
12 – **39 rm** 115/140.
◆ Although small, the rooms in this 18C building between the Carrés St-Louis and the Potager du Roi are intimate and personalised. Cosy, elegant billiard bar.

Mercure without rest, 19 r. Ph. de Dangeau 01 39 50 44 10, *hotel@mercure-versailles.com, Fax 01 39 50 65 11* – 35. AE GB JCB Y n
8 – **60 rm** 91/99.
◆ This functional hotel situated in a quiet section of town has a well-furnished lobby which opens onto a pleasant breakfast room.

Ibis without rest, 4 av. Gén. de Gaulle 01 39 53 03 30, *Fax 01 39 50 06 31* – rm, AE GB Y u
6 – **85 rm** 82.
◆ The hotel shares the walls of this building with the Sofitel. None of its rooms (the best of which have been recently refurbished) directly overlook the street.

Les Trois Marches - Hôtel Trianon Palace, 1 bd Reine 01 39 50 13 21, *gerard.vie@westin.com, Fax 01 30 21 01 25*, – AE GB JCB X r
closed August, Sunday and Monday – **Meals** 58 (lunch), 145/200.
◆ The Trianon Palace's gastronomic restaurant is renowned for its refined cuisine, excellent wine list and elegant dining room overlooking the park and French gardens.
Spec. Foie gras de canard dans son consommée de cuisson en gelée. Saint-Pierre au lard caramélisé. Fondant de bœuf à la Rossini.

Marée de Versailles, 22 r. au Pain 01 30 21 73 73, *mareedeversailles@tiscali.fr, Fax 01 39 49 98 29*, – AE GB Y t
closed Sunday and Monday – **Meals** - Seafood - a la carte 38/54.
◆ A nautically themed restaurant where diners can sample a menu featuring a predominance of fish and seafood. Tightly packed tables, plus a busy terrace in summer.

Potager du Roy, 1 r. Mar.-Joffre 01 39 50 35 34, *Fax 01 30 21 69 30* – AE GB Z r
closed Sunday and Monday – **Meals** 32/47.
◆ A retro feel pervades this restaurant serving traditional cuisine with an emphasis on quality vegetables - perhaps understandable given its name (The King's Vegetable Garden) !

Étape Gourmande, 125 r. Yves Le Coz 01 30 21 01 63, – GB V n
closed August, 29 December-5 January, Wednesday, dinner Sunday and Tuesday – **Meals** (booking essential) 39.
◆ In winter, ask for a table by the fire in the rustic dining room ; in summer, enjoy the charming outdoor terrace. Personalised cuisine and good choice of Savennières wines.

Cuisine Bourgeoise, 10 bd Roi 01 39 53 11 38, *la.cuisine.bougeoise@wanadoo.fr, Fax 01 39 53 25 26* – GB XY k
closed Sunday, lunch Monday and Saturday – **Meals** 29,50 (lunch), 50/90 b.i.
◆ A pleasing decor of white walls adorned with paintings and wood panelling, orange fabrics and draped chairs. The cuisine in this Versailles restaurant is equally contemporary.

Le Falher, 22 r. Satory 01 39 50 57 43, *restaurant-le-falher@wanadoo.fr, Fax 01 39 49 04 66* – GB. Y m
closed Saturday lunch, Sunday and Monday – **Meals** 28/38.
◆ Coloured napkins, small table lamps and reproductions of paintings adorn the dining room of this simply styled rustic restaurant with friendly service.

at Le Chesnay – *pop. 28 530 alt. 120 – 78150 :*

Novotel Château de Versailles, 4 bd St-Antoine 01 39 54 96 96, *h1022@accor-hotels.com, Fax 01 39 54 94 40* – rm, – 90. AE GB X z
Meals 21 – 12 – **105 rm** 109/133.
◆ In this modern hotel, built alongside a roundabout, the leafy atrium-cum-lounge leads to renovated rooms that are functional and soundproofed. The modern bistro-style restaurant offers the usual Novotel chain à la carte choices and non-stop service.

Ibis without rest, av. Dutartre, Commercial Centre Parly II 01 39 63 37 93, *h0939@accor-hotels.com, Fax 01 39 55 18 66* – rm, AE GB JCB U n
6 – **72 rm** 75.
◆ Built within a large shopping mall, this Ibis has two types of rooms : those with the chain's new-style décor, and others with the traditional wall carpet and plastered look.

AND BEYOND.

Joigny *89300 Yonne 319 D4 – pop. 10 032 alt. 79.*
See : *Vierge au Sourire★ in St-Thibault's Church – Côte St-Jacques ≤★ 1,5 km by D 20.*
of Roncemay ☎ 03 86 73 50 50.
Tourist Office 4 quai H.-Ragobert ☎ 03 86 62 11 05, Fax 03 86 91 76 38, ot-joigny@wanadoo.fr.
Paris 147 – Auxerre 27 – Gien 75 – Montargis 59 – Sens 30 – Troyes 76.

Côte St-Jacques (Lorain), 14 fg Paris ☎ 03 86 62 09 70, *lorain@relaischateaux.com, Fax 03 86 91 49 70*, ≤, – rest, – 30. AE GB JCB
closed 3 January-3 February – **Meals** (Sunday booking essential) 72 b.i. (lunch), 140/160 and a la carte 119/166 – 27 – **27 rm** 135/330, 5 suites.
◆ Luxury establishment on the River Yonne, seemingly a universe away from the world and its cares. One of the great restaurants of France, with brilliant, inventive cuisine, plus a constantly renewed procession of great wines. Shop. Boat trips on the river.
Spec. Genèse d'un plat sur le thème de l'huître. Aile de raie en cuisson lente, tomates confites, infusion de lait de coco. Poularde de Bresse à la vapeur de champagne. **Wines** Bourgogne blanc, Irancy.

Rheims (Reims) *51100 Marne 306 G7 – pop. 187 206 alt. 85.*
See : *Cathedral★★★ – St-Remi Basilica★★ : interior★★★ – Palais du Tau★★ – Champagne cellars★★ – Place Royale★ – Porte Mars★ – Hôtel de la Salle★ – Foujita Chapel★ – Library★ of Ancien Collège des Jésuites – St-Remi Museum★★ – Hôtel le Vergeur Museum★ – Fine Arts Museum★.*
Envir. : *Fort de la Pompelle : German helmets★ 9 km to the SE by N 44.*
Rheims-Champagne ☎ 03 26 05 46 10 at Gueux ; to the NW by N 31-E 46 : 9,5 km.
Rheims-Champagne ☎ 03 26 07 15 15 : 6 km.
☎ 08 36 35 35 35.
Tourist Office 12 bd Gén.-Leclerc ☎ 03 26 77 45 00, Fax 03 26 77 45 19, TourismReims@netvia.com.
Paris 144 – Brussels 214 – Châlons-sur-Marne 48 – Lille 199 – Luxembourg 232.

Les Crayères, 64 bd Vasnier ☎ 03 26 82 80 80, *crayeres@relaischateaux.com, Fax 03 26 82 65 52*, ≤, – AE GB JCB
closed 20 December-11 January – **Meals** *(closed Monday and Tuesday)* (booking essential) 185 b.i./215 b.i. and a la carte 115/145 – 25 – **16 rm** 265/460, 3 suites.
◆ A fine noble residence in an English-style park close to the Gallo-Roman "crayères" (quarries) of the famous champagne houses. Luxurious bedrooms, sumptuous classical décor in the lounge, a terrace on the main courtyard, and cuisine of the highest quality.
Spec. Ile flottante à la truffe noire. Agneau de lait poêlé, enrubanné de pommes de terre croustillantes. Macaron, mousse de mascarpone, glace à l'huile d'olive. **Wines** Champagne.

Saulieu *21210 Côte-d'Or 320 F6 – pop. 2 837 alt. 535.*
See : *St-Andoche Basilica★ : capitals★★.*
Tourist Office 24 r. d'Argentine ☎ 03 80 64 00 21, Fax 03 80 64 21 96, Saulieu-tourisme@wanadoo.fr.
Paris 249 – Autun 41 – Avallon 38 – Beaune 64 – Clamecy 76 – Dijon 73.

Le Relais Bernard Loiseau, 2 r. Argentine ☎ 03 80 90 53 53, *loiseau@relaischateaux.com, Fax 03 80 64 08 92*, – rm, – 30. AE GB JCB
closed 3 to 25 January – **Meals** 92 b.i. (lunch), 120/172 and a la carte 118/196 – 28 – **22 rm** 195/330, 7 suites, 3 duplex.
◆ This luxury 18C hostelry is the emblem of this small Burgundian town renowned for centuries for its hospitality. Fine innovative cuisine by a master chef and elegant rooms opening on to an English-style garden.
Spec. Jambonnettes de grenouilles à la purée d'ail et au jus de persil. Sandre à la peau croustillante et fondue d'échalote, sauce au vin rouge. Blanc de volaille fermière, foie gras poêlé à la purée de pommes de terre truffée. **Wines** Meursault, Blagny.

Vézelay *89450 Yonne* 319 *F7 – pop. 492 alt. 285.*
Paris 221 – Auxerre 52 – Avallon 16 – Château-Chinon 58 – Clamecy 23.

at St-Père *South-East : 3 km by D 957 – pop. 385 alt. 148 – ✉ 89450.*

L'Espérance (Meneau) , ☎ 03 86 33 39 10, *Marc.Meneau@wanadoo.fr, Fax 03 86 33 26 15*, ←, , – ▤ rest, TV – 50. AE GB JCB
closed late January-early March – **Meals** *(closed Wednesday lunch and Tuesday)* (booking essential) 87 b.i. (lunch), 127/170 and a la carte 140/200 – 30 – **20 rm** 70/250, 6 suites.
◆ Traditional comfort in the main manor house, luxurious modernity in Le Pré des Marguerites, with more rusticity in Le Moulin. Conservatory-style restaurant with views of the delightful garden, and cuisine which blends the creative with the traditional.
Spec. Galets de pomme de terre, caviar. Turbot en pâte à sel, beurre de homard. Pigeon et homard en cocotte aux champignons sautés. **Wines** Bourgogne-Vézelay, Chablis.

BORDEAUX *33000 Gironde* 335 *H5 – pop. 215 363 alt. 4.*

See : *18C Bordeaux : façades along the quayside★★* EX, *Esplanade des Quinconces* DX, *Grand Théâtre★★* DX, *Notre-Dame Church★* DX, *Allées de Tourny* DX, *– Cours Clemenceau* DX, *Place Gambetta* DX, *Cours de l'Intendance* DX *– Old Bordeaux★★ : Place de la Bourse★★* EX, *Place du Parlement★* EX **109**, *St-Michel Basilica★* EY, *Great Bell★ (Grosse Cloche)* EY **D** *– Pey-Berland district : St-André Cathedral★* DY *(Pey-Berland Tower★ : ←★★* **E**) *– Mériadeck district* CY *– Battle-Cruiser Colbert★★ – Museums : Fine Arts★ (Beaux-Arts)* CDY **M**[1], *Decorative Arts★* DY **M**[2], *Aquitaine★★* DY **M**[4] *– Entrepôt Lainé★★ : Museum of Contemporary Art★.*

18 *Golf Bordelais* ☎ *05 56 28 56 04 by av. d'Eysines : 4 km ; of Bordeaux Lac* ☎ *05 56 50 92 72, to the N by D 209 : 10 km ; of Medoc at Louens* ☎ *05 56 70 11 90 to the NW by D 6 : 6 km ;* 27 *Internat. of Bordeaux-Pessac* ☎ *05 57 26 03 33 by N 250 ;* 18 *Bordeaux-Cameyrac* ☎ *05 56 72 96 79 by N 89 : 18 km.*

✈ *of Bordeaux-Mérignac :* ☎ *05 56 34 50 50 to the W : 11 km.*

☎ *08 36 35 35 35.*

ℹ *Tourist Office 12 cours 30 Juillet* ☎ *05 56 00 66 00, Fax 05 56 00 66 01, otb@bordeaux-tourisme.com.*

Paris 579 – Lyons 531 – Nantes 324 – Strasbourg 919 – Toulouse 245.

Burdigala, 115 r. G. Bonnac ☎ 05 56 90 16 16, *burdigala@burdigala.com, Fax 05 56 93 15 06* – , rm, ▤ TV – 25 - 100. AE GB JCB CX r
***Jardin de Burdigala* : Meals** 32 – 17 – **68 rm** 170/260, 8 suites, 7 duplex.
◆ Period or contemporary furnishings, choice materials, the very latest facilities... the well soundproofed rooms of this luxury hotel breathe elegance and serenity. The circular Jardin de Burdigala restaurant offers refinement, a fountain, and intimate lighting.

Mercure Cité Mondiale , 18 parvis des Chartrons ☎ 05 56 01 79 79, *h2877@accor.hotels.com, Fax 05 56 01 79 00*, – , rm, ▤ TV – 25 - 800. AE GB JCB. rest
closed 22 December-5 January – ***Le 20*** wine bar-rest. *(closed Friday dinner, Saturday and Sunday)* **Meals** a la carte approx. 25 ♀ – 12 – **96 rm** 104/135.
◆ Contemporary rooms, plus a panoramic terrace (where breakfast is served in summer) with a view over the whole of Bordeaux await guests inside the Cité Mondiale convention centre. Smart decor in the "20", with wine tasting and bistro-type fare.

Mercure Château Chartrons, 81 cours St-Louis ✉ 33300 ☎ 05 56 43 15 00, *h1810@accor-hotels.com, Fax 05 56 69 15 21*, – , rm, ▤ TV – 15 - 150. AE GB
Meals 18,50 ♀ – 12 – **144 rm** 99/160.
◆ Well-preserved, this lovely listed 18C structure was once a wine store. Spacious, comfortable rooms. The vines planted on the roof terrace are an amusing touch. Traditional menu served in a bistro-type ambience.

Mercure Mériadeck, 5 r.-Lateulade ☎ 05 56 56 43 43, *h1281@accor-hotels.com, Fax 05 56 96 50 59* – , rm, ▤ TV – 15 - 150. AE GB JCB CY v
Meals *(closed Saturday, Sunday and Bank Holidays)* 19 ♀ – 12 – **192 rm** 100/127.
◆ The décor of this establishment has a cinematic theme, with posters, photographs and other film memorabilia everywhere. Modern, welcoming rooms and excellent conference facilities. Le Festival pays homage to the silver screen, but local dishes are the stars.

Novotel Bordeaux-Centre, 45 cours Mar. Juin ☎ 05 56 51 46 46, *h1023@accor-hotels.com, Fax 05 56 98 25 56*, – , rm, ▤ TV – 80. AE GB JCB CY m
Meals 17 ♀ – 11,50 – **138 rm** 98/105.
◆ This Novotel has been carefully integrated into the Mériadeck district. The functional bedrooms are regularly refurbished and are well soundproofed. Soberly decorated dining room plus a terrace with a view of several typical old Bordeaux buildings.

C
D
X
Y
Z
Turenne
Barraud
R. Allo
R.
Dr. A.
Rue Turenne
R. du Palais
R. Fondaudège
139
Pl. de Tourny
Espl. des Quinconces
64
37
L
R. Huguerie
Clemenceau
A. ées de Tourny
MAISON DU VIN DE BORDEAUX
30
St-Seurin
R. Thiac
Abbé de l'Épée
POL.
Gallien
Pl. des Martyrs de la Résistance
Lachassaigne
75
Pl. du Chapelet
43
100
N.-DAME
133
GRAND THÉÂTRE
C rs de l'Intendance
R. de Grassi
21
Rue Judaïque
Pl. Gambetta
Pte Dijeaux
40
Bonnac
48
PEY BERLAND
R. des Remparts
V. Carles
VIEUX BORDEAUX
Centre Jean Moulin
3 Conils
Rue
Bonnier
R. C.
M
M3
M4
H
CATH. ST-ANDRÉ
130
Pl. Jullien
ST-BRUNO
HÔTEL DU DÉPT
MÉRIADECK
4m
Esplanade Ch. de Gaulle
d' Alsace
Ste Catherine
Hôtel de Région
Rue
57
ST-PAUL
PALAIS DES SPORTS
M1
ÉCOLE NATle DE LA MAGISTRATURE
R. Mal Joffre
d'Albret
Juin
Mal
63
POL.
Crs François de Sourdis
Pl. de la République
R. J. Burguet
R. de Cursol
Lande
Rue
Crs de la Libération
STE-EULALIE
Pasteur
Mouneyra
Belleville
R. L.
Pl. de Pressensé
Crs A. Briand
Porte d'Aquitaine
R. Ed. Costedoat
R. Villedieu
Tondu
Belfort
R. L. Mie
Rue
ST-VICTOR
du
R. F. Audeguil
Pessac
R. de Lamourous
St-Genès
Mazarin
Leberthon
Pl. de la Victoire
l'Argonne
Somme
Rue
de
R. P. Duhen
R. Cadroin
R. St-Nicolas
ST-NICOLAS
Crs de la
R. des Treuils
N.-D. DES ANGES
Rue
R. A. Baysselance
R. G. Rioux
Barrière de Pessac

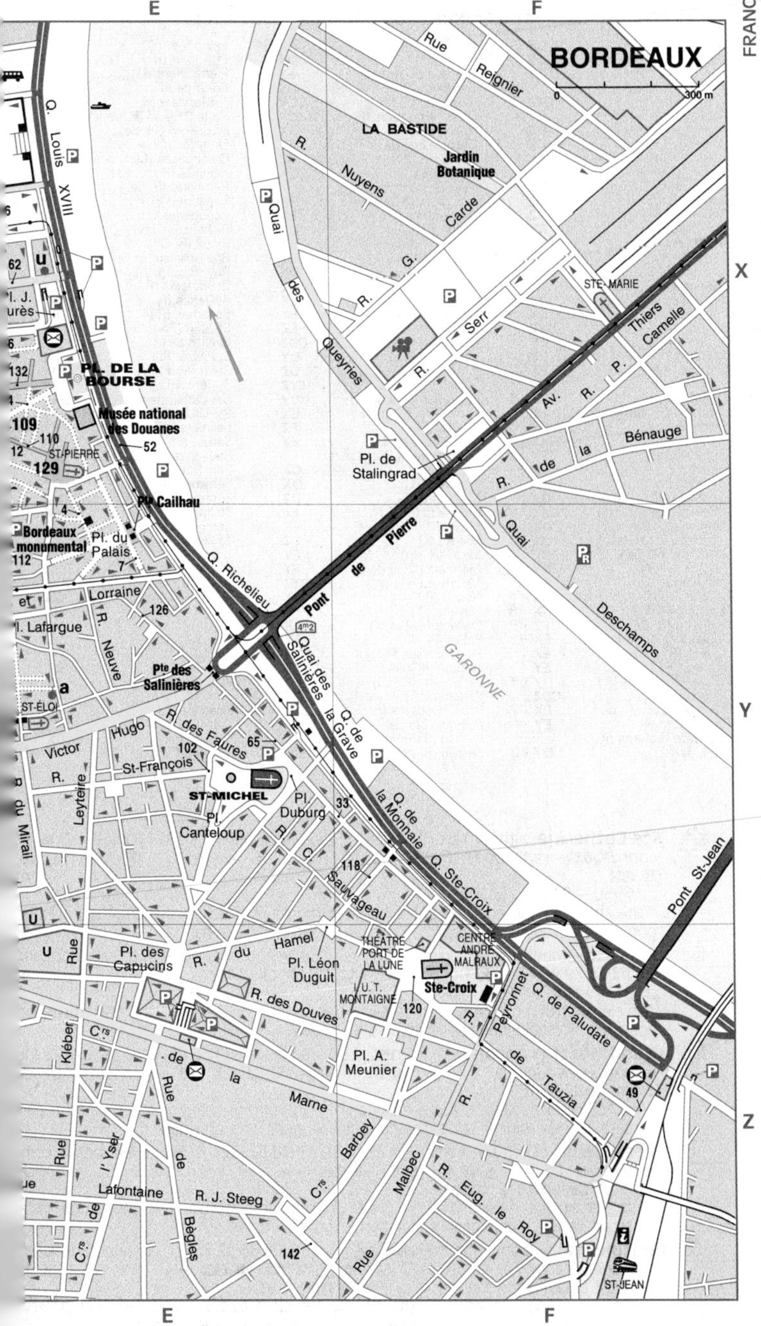

BORDEAUX

STREET INDEX TO BORDEAUX TOWN PLAN

Street	Grid	No.
Abbé de l'Epée (R.)	CX	
Albret (Crs d')	CY	
Allo (R. R.)	CX	
Alsace-Lorraine (Crs d')	DEZ	
Argentiers (R. des)	EY	4
Argonne (Crs de l')	DZ	
Audegil (R.F.)	CZ	
Ausone (R.)	EY	7
Barbey (Crs)	EFZ	
Baysselance (R. A.)	DZ	
Bègles (R. de)	EZ	
Belfort (R. de)	CYZ	
Belleville (R.)	CY	
Bénauge (R. de la)	FX	
Bir-Hakeim (Pl. de)	EY	
Bonnac (R. G.)	CXY	
Bonnier (R. C.)	CY	
Bordelaise (Galerie)	DX	21
Bourse (Pl. de la)	EX	
Briand (Crs A.)	DYZ	
Burguet (R. J.)	DY	
Cadroin (R.)	DZ	
Camelle (R.P.)	FX	
Canteloup (Pl.)	EY	
Capdeville (R.)	CX	30
Capucins (Pl. des)	EZ	
Carde (R. G.)	FX	
Carles (R. V.)	DXY	
Carpenteyre (R.)	EFY	33
Chapeau-Rouge (Crs)	EX	36
Chapelet (Pl. du)	DX	
Chartres (Allées de)	DX	37
Château-d'Eau (R. du)	CXY	40
Clemenceau (Crs G.)	DX	
Comédie (Pl. de la)	DX	43
Costedoat (R. Ed.)	DZ	
Cursol (R. de)	DY	
Deschamps (Quai)	FY	
Dr. Barraud (R. A.)	CX	
Dr. Nancel-Pénard (R.)	CX	48
Domercq (R. C.)	FZ	49
Douane (Quai de la)	EX	52
Douves (R. des)	EZ	
Duburg (Pl.)	EY	
Duffour-Dubergier (R.)	DY	57
Duhen (R. P.)	CDZ	
Esprit des Lois (R. de l')	EX	62
Faures (R. des)	EY	
Ferme de Richemont (Pl. de la)	DY	63
Foch (R. Mar.)	DX	64
Fondaudège (R.)	DX	
Fusterie (R. de la)	EY	65
Gambetta (Pl.)	DX	
Gaulle (Espl. Ch. de)	CY	
Grands-Hommes (Pl. des)	DX	75
Grassi (R. de)	DX	
Grave (Quai de)	EFY	
Hamel (R. du)	EZ	
Huguerie (R.)	DX	
Intendance (Crs de l')	DX	
Jean-Jaurès (Pl.)	EX	
Joffre (Crs Mar.)	DY	
Judaïque (R.)	CX	
Juin (Crs Mar.)	CY	
Jullian (Pl. C.)	DY	
Kléber (R.)	EZ	
Lachassaigne (R.)	CX	
Lafargue (Pl.)	EY	
Lafontaine (R.)	EZ	
Lamourous (R. de)	CDZ	
Lande (R. P. L.)	DY	
Leberthon (R.)	DZ	
Leyteire (R.)	EYZ	
Libération (Crs de la)	CDY	
Louis XVIII (Quai)	EX	
Malbec (R.)	FZ	
Marne (Crs de la)	EZ	
Martyrs de la Résistance (Pl. des)	CX	
Mautrec (R.)	DX	100
Mazarin (R.)	DZ	
Meuniers (Pl. A.)	FZ	
Meynard (Pl.)	EY	102
Mie (R. L.)	CZ	
Mirail (R. du)	EY	
Monnaie (Quai de la)	FY	
Mouneyra (R.)	CYZ	
Neuve (R.)	EY	
Nuyens (R.)	FX	
Orléans (Allées d')	EX	106
Palais (Pl. du)	EY	
Palais Gallien (R. du)	CX	
Paludate (Quai de)	FZ	
Parlement (Pl. du)	EX	109
Parlement St-Pierre (R. du)	EX	110
Pas-St-Georges (R. du)	EXY	112
Pasteur (Crs de)	DY	
Pessac (Barrière de)	CZ	
Pessac (R. de)	CZ	
Peyronnet (R.)	FZ	
Philippart (R. F.)	EX	114
Pierre (Pont de)	EFY	
Porte de la Monnaie (R.)	FY	118
Porte-Dijeaux (R. de la)	DX	
Pressensé (Pl. de)	DZ	
Queyries (Quai des)	EFX	
Quinconces (Espl. des)	DX	
Reignier (R.)	FX	
Remparts (R. des)	DXY	
Renaudel (Pl. P.)	FZ	
République (Pl. de la)	DY	
Richelieu (Quai)	EY	122
Rioux (R. G.)	DZ	
Rousselle (R. de la)	EY	126
Roy (R. Eug. le)	FZ	
St-François (R.)	EY	
St-Genès (R. de)	DZ	
St-James (R.)	EY	
St-Jean (Pont)	FY	
St-Nicolas (R.)	DZ	
St-Pierre (Pl.)	EX	129
St-Projet (Pl.)	DY	130
St-Rémi (R.)	EX	132
Ste-Catherine (R.)	DXY	
Ste-Croix (Quai)	FY	
Salinières (Quai des)	EY	
Sarget (Passage)	DX	133
Sauvageau (R. C.)	EFY	
Serr (R.)	FX	
Somme (Crs de la)	DZ	
Sourdis (R. F. de)	CYZ	
Stalingrad (Pl. de)	FX	
Steeg (R. J.)	EZ	
Tauzia (R. des)	FZ	
Thiac (R.)	CX	
Thiers (Av.)	EX	
Tondu (R. du)	CZ	
Tourny (Allées de)	DX	
Tourny (Pl. de)	DX	
Treuils (R. des)	CZ	
Turenne (R.)	CDX	
Verdun (Crs de)	DX	139
Victoire (Pl. de la)	DZ	
Victor-Hugo (Crs)	EY	
Vilaris (R.)	EZ	142
Villedieu (R.)	DZ	
Yser (Crs de l')	EZ	
Zola (R. E.)	CX	144
3 Conils (R. des)	DY	

Ste-Catherine without rest, 27 r. Parlement Ste-Catherine ✆ 05 56 81 95 12, *qualit y.bordeaux@wanadoo.fr, Fax 05 56 44 50 51* – |‡|, ⇔ rm, ▤ TV ✆ – 🏛 40. AE GB DX m
☕ 11,50 – **83 rm** 75/177.
◆ This charming 18C edifice is in the heart of the traffic-free city centre. Well-equipped rooms with colourful fabrics. A 17C well is a feature of the bar.

Majestic without rest, 2 r. Condé ✆ 05 56 52 60 44, *mail-majestic@hotel-majestic.com, Fax 05 56 79 26 70* – |‡|, ⇔ rm, ▤ TV ✆. AE ① GB JCB DX a
☕ 9 – **49 rm** 70/105.
◆ An elegant 18C hotel built in the typical style of the city. Plain but tastefully furnished rooms, comfortable lounge and attractive breakfast room.

Grand Hôtel Français without rest, 12 r. Temple ✆ 05 56 48 10 35, *infos@granc -hotel-français.com, Fax 05 56 81 76 18* – ⇔ rm, ✆. AE ① GB JCB DX v
35 rm ☕ 87/137.
◆ This 18C residence has a façade enhanced by wrought-iron balconies. Public rooms and staircase in their original state, the comfortable bedrooms are more modern.

Presse without rest, 6 r. Porte Dijeaux ✆ 05 56 48 53 88, *info@hoteldelapresse.com Fax 05 56 01 05 82* – |‡| ▤ TV ✆. AE ① GB JCB DX k
closed 25 December-2 January – ☕ 8 – **27 rm** 47/84.
◆ In the heart of the pedestrian area, this well-run and tastefully decorated hotel has a fine stone façade. Functional rooms. Controlled car access.

Continental without rest, 10 r. Montesquieu ✆ 05 56 52 66 00, *continental@hotel le-continental.com, Fax 05 56 52 77 97* – |‡| TV ✆. AE ① GB JCB DX b
closed 24 December-3 January – ☕ 7 – **50 rm** 54/93.
◆ Old town-mansion dating from the 18C located close to the Grands Hommes gallery. Pleasant rooms in bright colours. Comfortable, prettily furnished lounge.

Maison du Lierre without rest, 57 r. Huguerie ☏ 05 56 51 92 71, *infos@maisondulierre.com, Fax 05 56 79 15 16* – TV. ⚘
closed 17 December-23 January – ☕ 6 – **12 rm** 61/73.
◆ This pretty hotel takes its name from the ivy planted in the patio. Although small, the cosy rooms are furnished with antiques. Home-made breakfasts, A warm welcome assured.

Chapon Fin, 5 r. Montesquieu ☏ 05 56 79 10 10, *tmarx2@wanadoo.fr, Fax 05 56 79 09 10* – ▤. AE ⓞ GB JCB DX p
closed 1 to 23 August, Sunday and Monday – **Meals** 27 (lunch), 48/76 and a la carte 74/90 ♀.
◆ A real Bordeaux institution, famous and popular not only for its fine cuisine but also for the turn-of-the-century rocaille decor in the dining room.
Spec. Foie gras de canard confit. Bar aux noix de pécan (except winter). Canon d'agneau farci au beurre de sauge (except winter). **Wines** Graves blanc, Pauillac.

Pavillon des Boulevards (Franc), 120 r. Croix de Seguey ☏ 05 56 81 51 02, *pavillon.des.boulevards@wanadoo.fr, Fax 05 56 51 14 58,* ☂ – ▤. AE GB JCB
closed 9 to 30 August, 1 to 8 January, Sunday, lunch Monday and Saturday – **Meals** 58/80 and a la carte 70/90 ♀.
◆ Kitchen utensils adorn the walls of this unusual contemporary restaurant, whose dining room opens on to a lovely summer terrace. Innovative cuisine.
Spec. Foie gras de canard à la vanille. Liégeois de caviar d'Aquitaine, homard à la crème de chataîgnes. Côte de veau de Bazas rôtie. **Wines** Pessac-Léognan, Saint-Julien.

Jean Ramet, 7 pl. J. Jaurès ☏ 05 56 44 12 51, *jean.ramet@free.fr, Fax 05 56 52 19 80* – ▤. AE GB EX u
closed 7 to 30 August, 2 to 12 January, 11 to 19 April, Sunday and Monday – **Meals** 28 (lunch), 45/56 and a la carte 56/80 ♀.
◆ The traditional cuisine of this establishment on the banks of the Garonne is popular with locals. The cheerful decor is in harmony with the fine furnishings and wall-hangings.
Spec. Terrine de foie gras au pain d'épices. Poêlée de Saint-Jacques, sauce moussante au foie gras (November-February). "Tapas" de fruits rouges (May-October). **Wines** Graves, Saint-Estèphe.

Vieux Bordeaux, 27 r. Buhan ☏ 05 56 52 94 36, *Fax 05 56 44 25 11,* ☂ – ▤. AE ⓞ GB EY a
closed 2 to 23 August, 21 February-7 March, Sunday, Bank Holidays, lunch Monday and Saturday – **Meals** 27/47 and a la carte 50/70.
◆ The country-style decor of this two-roomed restaurant is enhanced by contemporary touches. One room opens onto an attractive patio. Generous traditional cuisine.

L'Alhambra, 111bis r. Judaïque ☏ 05 56 96 06 91, *Fax 05 56 98 00 52* – ▤. GB
closed 25 July-20 August, Sunday, Bank Holidays, lunch Monday and Saturday – **Meals** 18 (lunch), 27/37 and a la carte 40/53 ♀. CX e
◆ Attractive restaurant in the style of a winter garden with decor based on shades of green and comfortable cane furnishings. Traditional cuisine.

Les Cinq Sens, 26 r. Pas St-Georges ☏ 05 56 52 84 25, *Fax 05 56 51 93 25* – ▤. AE ⓞ GB JCB EX n
closed 10 to 24 August, Sunday, lunch Monday and Saturday – **Meals** (booking essential) 20 (lunch), 35/65 ♀.
◆ This old Bordeaux building houses a restaurant serving tempting, modern cuisine. The dining room is decorated in bright colours and adorned with contemporary objects.

Table Calvet, 81 cours Médoc ☏ 05 56 39 62 80, *latablecalvet@calvet.com, Fax 05 56 39 62 80,* ☂ – ▤. AE GB. ⚘
closed 1 to 22 August, 1 to 9 January, Saturday lunch, Monday dinner and Sunday – **Meals** 21 (lunch), 25/45 b.i. ♀.
◆ Created by the Maison Calvet wine company in an attractive former wine storehouse, this gourmet restaurant serves cuisine which is inspired by and evolves with the seasons.

Tupina, 6 r. Porte de la Monnaie ☏ 05 56 91 56 37, *latupina@latupina.com, Fax 05 56 31 92 11* – ⚐. AE ⓞ GB
Meals Typical South West rest. 32 b.i. (lunch)/48 ♀ ⚘.
◆ A relaxed atmosphere pervades this rustic restaurant specialising in dishes from SW France prepared over the stove or open fire as in bygone days. Comprehensive wine list.

Gravelier, 114 cours Verdun ☏ 05 56 48 17 15, *Fax 05 56 51 96 07* – ▤. AE ⓞ GB
closed 31 July-30 August, Saturday and Sunday – **Meals** 20 (lunch), 25/32 ♀.
◆ Refined teak and zinc fittings, warm colours (aubergine, aniseed green, orange), successfully creating a congenial, minimalist ambience. Fine, inventive cuisine.

Café du Théâtre, pl. Renaudel ✉ 33300 ☏ 05 57 95 77 20, *e.rene@jm-amat.com, Fax 05 57 95 65 91,* ☂ – AE GB FZ a
closed 25 July-17 August, Sunday and Monday – **Meals** 30 (lunch), 38/40 ♀.
◆ A trendy and attractive restaurant with contemporary, predominantly black decor, designer furniture, a long stone counter and small shady terrace. Concise regional menu.

L'Olivier du Clavel, 44 r. C. Domercq (face gare St-Jean) ✆ 05 57 95 09 50, *fgclavel@wanadoo.fr, Fax 05 56 92 15 28* – ▤. AE ◑ GB
closed August, 2 to 10 January, Saturday lunch, Sunday and Monday – **Meals** 19 (lunch)/28 ♀.
• The menu in this bistro is based on seasonal dishes prepared using different high-quality olive oils. Bright, spick-and-span decor and simply laid tables.

at Bordeaux-Lac *(Parc des Expositions) North of the town* – ✉ *33300 Bordeaux :*

Sofitel Aquitania, av. J. G. Domergue ✆ 05 56 69 66 66, *h0669@accor-hotels.com, Fax 05 56 69 66 00,* ⛱, ♨ – |♦|, ⇔ rm, ▤ TV ✆ P – 🏛 15 - 400. AE ◑ GB JCB
Flore : **Meals** 23/29 ♁ – ☕ 15 – **176 rm** 135/220, 7 suites.
• Hotel complex much favoured by business travellers thanks to its facilities for meetings and conferences. Spacious rooms, functional and well soundproofed. Neighbouring casino. There is a panoramic view of the lake from Le Flore and a terrace by the pool.

Novotel-Bordeaux Lac, av. J. G. Domergue ✆ 05 56 43 65 00, *h0403@accor-hotels.com, Fax 05 56 43 65 01,* ⛱, ♨, ⛲ – |♦|, ⇔ rm, ▤ TV ✆ ♿ P – 🏛 15 - 120. AE ◑ GB JCB
Meals a la carte 22/34 ♀ – ☕ 11,50 – **175 rm** 93/101.
• This 1970s hotel has the advantage of a location close to the exhibition grounds. Practical rooms, some with lake views. Garden with children's play facilities. Spacious dining room opening onto a terrace by the swimming-pool.

at Cenon *East, exit nr 25 – pop. 21 283 alt. 50 –* ✉ *33150 :*

La Cape (Magie), allée Morlette ✆ 05 57 80 24 25, *Fax 05 56 32 63 56,* ⛱ – GB
closed 1 to 23 August, Christmas Holidays, Saturday, Sunday and Bank Holidays – **Meals** 28 ♀.
• This discreet building housing two modern, colourful dining rooms is further enhanced by a pleasant terrace-garden. Fine, inventive cuisine and wines direct from the estate.
Spec. Galette de pieds de cochon. Filet de cabillaud et lomo Iberico poêlés. Roulé de brebis fumé à la confiture de cerises noires.

at Bouliac *SE : 8 km – pop. 3 248 alt. 74 –* ✉ *33270 :*

Hauterive et rest. St-James ⛰, pl. C. Hostein, near church ✆ 05 57 97 06 00, *reception@saint-james-bouliac.com, Fax 05 56 20 92 58,* ≤ Bordeaux, ⛱, ♨, ⛲ – |♦| ▤ rm, TV ✆ P – 🏛 15. AE ◑ GB JCB. ✗ rest
Meals *(closed January, Monday out of season and Sunday)* 50 and a la carte 75/100 ♀ – ***Le Bistroy*** ✆ 05 57 97 06 06 *(closed Sunday)* **Meals** 22 b.i. (lunch) and a la carte approx. 30 ♁ – ☕ 18 – **18 rm** 168/267.
• 17C wine-grower's house surrounded by buildings designed by J. Nouvel and inspired by tobacco-drying sheds. Zen-style designer rooms all with views of Bordeaux. Fine creative cuisine in the St-James ; local fare in the stripped-down bistro-style Bistroy.
Spec. Fricassée de petits gris à la fleurette d'ail (July-September). Pigeonneau en crapaudine (August-October). Mangue marinée et litchis, crème au gombavas. **Wines** Bordeaux blanc, Côtes de Blaye.

at Martillac *S : 9 km by exit nr 18 and N 113 – pop. 2 020 alt. 40 –* ✉ *33650 :*

Sources de Caudalie ⛰, chemin de Smith Haut-Lafitte ✆ 05 57 83 83 83, *sources@sources-caudalie.com, Fax 05 57 83 83 84,* ⛱, ⊛, Fø, ♨, ⛲ – |♦| ▤ TV ✆ P – 🏛 15 - 40. AE ◑ GB. ✗ rm
Meals ⚘ ***Grand'Vigne*** *(closed Monday and Tuesday)* **Meals** 57 – ***Table du Lavoir :*** **Meals** 32/52 b.i. ♀ – ☕ 20 – **43 rm** 215/450, 6 suites.
• Luxurious rejuvenation among the vineyards : this establishment advocates a regime based on the "French Paradox", with delicious food washed down with red wine. Inventive dishes served in the 18C orangery. "La Table" is situated in a restored wine storehouse.

to the W :

at the airport of Mérignac *11 km by A 630 : from the North, exit no 11=b, from the South exit no11 –* ✉ *33700 Mérignac :*

Mercure Aéroport, 1 av. Ch. Lindbergh ✆ 05 56 34 74 74, *H1508@accor-hotels.com, Fax 05 56 34 30 84,* ⛱, ♨ – |♦|, ⇔ rm, ▤ TV ✆ ♿ P – 🏛 15 - 110. AE ◑ GB
Meals *(closed weekends and Bank Holidays)* 20 ♀ – ☕ 12 – **148 rm** 108/118.
• This establishment was designed for a relaxing break between flights. Comfortable, well soundproofed rooms, attractive lounge/bar and meeting rooms with decor on the theme of travel. Traditional cuisine served in an elegant dining room facing the terrace.

Novotel Aéroport, av. J. F. Kennedy ✆ 05 57 53 13 30, *h0402@accor-hotels.com, Fax 05 56 55 99 64,* ⛱, ♨, ⛲ – |♦|, ⇔ rm, ▤ TV ✆ ♿ P – 🏛 20 - 70. AE ◑ GB JCB
Meals a la carte 25/35 ♀ – ☕ 11,50 – **137 rm** 99/107.
• Hotel separated from the airport by a pine wood. Rooms refurbished in Novotel's latest style. Good soundproofing. Outdoor children's play area. Restaurant with pleasant view of pool and garden and straightforward cuisine with emphasis on grills.

Eugénie-les-Bains *40320 Landes 335 I12 - pop. 507 alt. 65 - Spa (Feb.-Nov.).*
les Greens d'Eugénie ☎ 05.
Tourist Office 147 r. René Vielle (Feb.-Nov.) ☎ 05 58 51 13 16, Fax 05 58 51 12 02.
Bordeaux 151.

Les Prés d'Eugénie (Guérard), ☎ 05 58 05 06 07, *guerard@relaischateaux.fr, Fax 05 58 51 10 10,* - rm, - 40.
closed 29 November-17 December and 2 January-25 March - (low-calorie menu for residents only) - ***rest. Michel Guérard*** (booking essential) *(closed lunch weekdays except 19/07-24/08and Bank Holidays and Monday dinner)* **Meals** 130/180 and a la carte 115/135 - 28 - **22 rm** 315, 6 suites.
◆ This delightful 19C residence, incorporating a park and "farm" spa centre is a wonderful fusion of town and country. In his gastronomic restaurant Michel Guérard continues to win international acclaim for his elegant cuisine inspired by Mother Nature.
Spec. Salade de truffes de l'année aux pommes de terre nouvelles. Poitrine de volaille des Landes cuisinée au lard sur la braise. Tarte chaude aux fraises d'Eugénie (season). **Wines** Tursan blanc, Vin de Pays des Terroirs Landais.

Couvent des Herbes rest
closed 2 January-11 February - **Meals** see ***Les Prés d'Eugénie*** and ***Michel Guérard*** - 28 - **4 rm** 340/375, 4 suites470/500.
◆ Napoleon converted this pretty little 18C convent into a love-nest for his Eugénie. In a setting not unlike the Garden of Eden, its rooms will not fail to seduce you.

Maison Rose (see also ***rest. Michel Guérard***), ☎ 05 58 05 06 07, *guerard@relaischateaux.fr, Fax 05 58 51 10 10,* - kitchenette
closed 5 December-12 February - **Meals** (residents only) - 18 - **26 rm** 115/170, 5 studios.
◆ The "Pink House" blends restful pastel colours, white cane furniture, fresh-cut flowers, and a cosy lounge, creating an altogether welcoming ambience.

Ferme aux Grives with rm, ☎ 05 58 05 05 06, *guerard@relaischateaux.fr, Fax 05 58 51 10 10,*
closed 2 January-11 February - **Meals** *(closed Tuesday dinner and Wednesday except 13 July-24 August and Bank Holidays)* 40 - 25 - **1 rm** 340/375, 3 suites 470/500.
◆ Old village inn that has recaptured all the atmosphere of yesteryear. Cobblestones, kitchen garden, and old beams make a fine setting for a revived local cuisine.

Pauillac *33250 Gironde 335 G3 - pop. 5 175 alt. 20.*
Bordeaux 53.

Château Cordeillan Bages , to the S : 1 km by D 2 ☎ 05 56 59 24 24, *cordeillan@relaischateaux.fr, Fax 05 56 59 01 89,* - rm, rest
closed 10 December-15 February - **Meals** *(closed Monday, lunch Saturday and Tuesday)* 55 (lunch)/95 and a la carte 75/95 - 22 - **25 rm** 178/275, 4 suites.
◆ This 17C charterhouse in the heart of the vineyards is also the headquarters of the École du Bordeaux wine school. Cosy, elegant rooms opening on to the courtyard. Non-smoking restaurant and terrace overlooking the château's vineyards. Stunning modern cuisine.
Spec. Pressé d'anguille fumée "terre et estuaire". Tomate mi-cuite, caviar et huîtres prises dans leur jus. Agneau de lait en trois façons, légumes préparés en cocotte. **Wines** Moulis, Saint-Julien.

CANNES *06400 Alpes-Mar. 341 D6 - pop. 67 304 alt. 2 - Casinos Carlton Casino Club BYZ, Croisette BZ.*
See : *Site★★ - Seafront★★ : Boulevard★★ BCDZ and Pointe de la Croisette★ X - ≤★ from the Mont Chevalier Tower AZ* **V** *- The Castre Museum★ (Musée de la Castre) AZ - Tour into the Hills★ (Chemin des Collines) NE : 4 km V - The Croix des Gardes X* **E** *≤★ W : 5 km then 15 mn.*
of Cannes-Mougins ☎ 04 93 75 79 13 by ⑤ : 9 km ; of Cannes-Mandelieu ☎ 04 92 97 32 00 by ② ; Royal Mougins Golf Club at Mougins ☎ 04 92 92 49 69 by ④ : 10 km ; Riviera Golf Club at Mandelieu ☎ 04 92 97 49 49 by ② : 8 km.
Tourist Office "SEMEC", Palais des Festivals ☎ 04 93 39 24 53, Fax 04 92 99 84 23 and railway station, first floor ☎ 04 93 99 19 77, Fax 04 92 99 84 23, semoftou@semec.com.
Paris 903 ⑤ - Aix-en-Provence 146 ⑤ - Grenoble 312 ⑤ - Marseilles 159 ⑤ - Nice 32 ⑤ - Toulon 121 ⑤

Carlton Inter-Continental, 58 bd Croisette ☎ 04 93 06 40 06, *cannes@intercont i.com, Fax 04 93 06 40 25,* - rm, - 25 - 250. CZ e
Brasserie Carlton ☎ 04 93 06 40 21 **Meals** 36/42 - ***Plage*** ☎ 04 93 06 44 94 *(April-October)* **Meals** a la carte 70/105 - 32 - **298 rm** 620/905, 28 suites.
◆ Hitchcock filmed some of "To Catch a Thief" in this famous hotel with its two cupolas. Luxurious Art Deco interior, a prestigious history, a world in itself. Provençal cuisine in La Côte. Belle Epoque décor in the Brasserie Carlton with view of the Croisette.

CANNES

Albert-Édouard (Jetée) BZ
Alexandre-III (Bd) X 2
Alsace (Bd) BDY
Anc. Combattants d'Afrique du Nord (Av.) AYZ 4
André (R. du Cdt) CZ
Antibes (R. d') BCY
Bachaga Saïd Boualam (Av.) AY 5
Beauséjour (Av.) DYZ
Beau-Soleil (Bd) X 10
Belges (R. des) BZ 12
Blanc (R. Louis) AYZ
Broussailles (Av. des) V 16
Buttura (R.) BZ 17
Canada (R. du) DZ
Carnot (Bd) X
Carnot (Square) V 20
Castre (Pl. de la) AZ 21
Chabaud (R.) CY 22
Clemenceau (R. G.) AZ
Coteaux (Av. des) V
Croisette (Bd de la) BDZ
Croix-des-Gardes (Bd) VX 29
Delaup (Bd) AY 30
Dr-Pierre Gazagnaire (R.) AZ 32
Dr-R. Picaud (Av.) X
Dollfus (R. Jean) AZ 33
Etats-Unis (R. des) CZ 35
Faure (R. Félix) ABZ
Favorite (Av. de la) X 38
Félix-Faure (R.) ABZ
Ferrage (Bd de la) ABY 40
Fiesole (Av.) X 43
Foch (R. du Mar.) BY 44
Gallieni (R. du Mar.) BY 48
Gaulle (Pl. Gén.-de) BZ 51
Gazagnaire (Bd Eugène) X
Grasse (Av. de) VX 53
Guynemer (Bd) AY
Hespérides (Av. des) X 55
Hibert (Bd Jean) AZ
Hibert (R.) AZ
Isola-Bella (Av. d') X
Jaurès (R. Jean) BCY
Joffre (R. du Mar.) BY 60
Juin (Av. Mar.) DZ
Koenig (Av. Gén.) DY
Lacour (Bd Alexandre) X 62
Latour-Maubourg (R.) DZ
Lattre-de-T. (Av. de) AY 63
Laubeuf (Quai Max) AZ
Leader (Bd) VX 64
Lérins (Av. de) X 65
Lorraine (Bd. de) CDY
Macé (R.) CZ 66
Madrid (Av. de) DZ
Meynadier (R.) ABY
Midi (Bd du) X
Mimont (R. de) BY
Mont-Chevalier (R. du) AZ 72
Montfleury (Bd) CDY 74
Monti (R. Marius) AY 75
Noailles (Av. J.-de) X
Observatoire (Bd de l') X 84
Oxford (Bd d') V 87
Pantiero (la) ABZ
Paradis-Terrestre (Corniches du) V 88
Pasteur (R.) DZ
Pastour (R. Louis) AY 90
Perier (Bd du) V 91
Perrissol (R. Louis) AZ 92
Petit-Juas (Av. du) VX
Pins (Bd des) X 95
Pompidou (Espl. G.) BZ
Prince-de-Galles (Av. du) X 97
République (Bd de la) X
Riou (Bd du) VX
Riouffe (R. Jean de) BY 98
Roi-Albert 1er (Av.) X
Rouguière (R.) BY 100
St-Antoine (R.) AZ 102
St-Nicolas (Av.) BY 105
St-Pierre (Quai) AZ
Sardou (R. Léandre) X 108
Serbes (R. des) BZ 110
Source (Bd de la) X 112
Stanislas (Pl.) AY
Strasbourg (Bd de) CDY
Teisseire (R.) CY 114
Tuby (Bd Victor) AYZ 115
Vallauris (Av. de) VX 116
Vallombrosa (Bd) AY 118
Vautrin (Bd Gén.) DZ
Vidal (R. du Cdt) CY 120
Wemyss (Av. Amiral Wester) X 122

LE CANNET

Aubarède (Ch. de l') V 8
Bellevue (Pl.) V 13
Bréguières (Ch. de) V 14
Cannes (R. des) V 19
Carnot (Bd de) V
Cheval (Av. Maurice) V 23
Collines (Ch. des) V
Doumer (Bd Paul) V
Écoles (R. des) V 34
Four-à-Chaux (Bd du) V 45
Gambetta (Bd) V 50
Gaulle (Av. Gén.-de) V
Jeanpierre (Av. Maurice) V 58
Mermoz (Av. Jean) V 67
Monod (Bd Jacques) V 68
Mont-Joli (Av. du) V 73
N.-D.-des-Anges (Av.) V 79
Olivet (Ch. de l') V 85
Olivetum (Av. d') V 86
Paris (R. de) V 89
Pinède (Av. de la) V 94
Pompidou (Av. Georges) V 96
République (Bd de la) V
Roosevelt (Av. Franklin) V 99
St-Sauveur (R.) V 10
Victor-Hugo (R.) V 11
Victoria (Av.) V

VALLAURIS

Cannes (Av. de) V 18
Clemenceau (Av. G.) V 25
Golfe (Av. du) V 52
Isnard (Pl. Paul) V 56
Picasso (Av. P.) V 93
Rouvier (Bd Maurice) V 10
Tapis-Vert (Av. du) V 11

CANNES

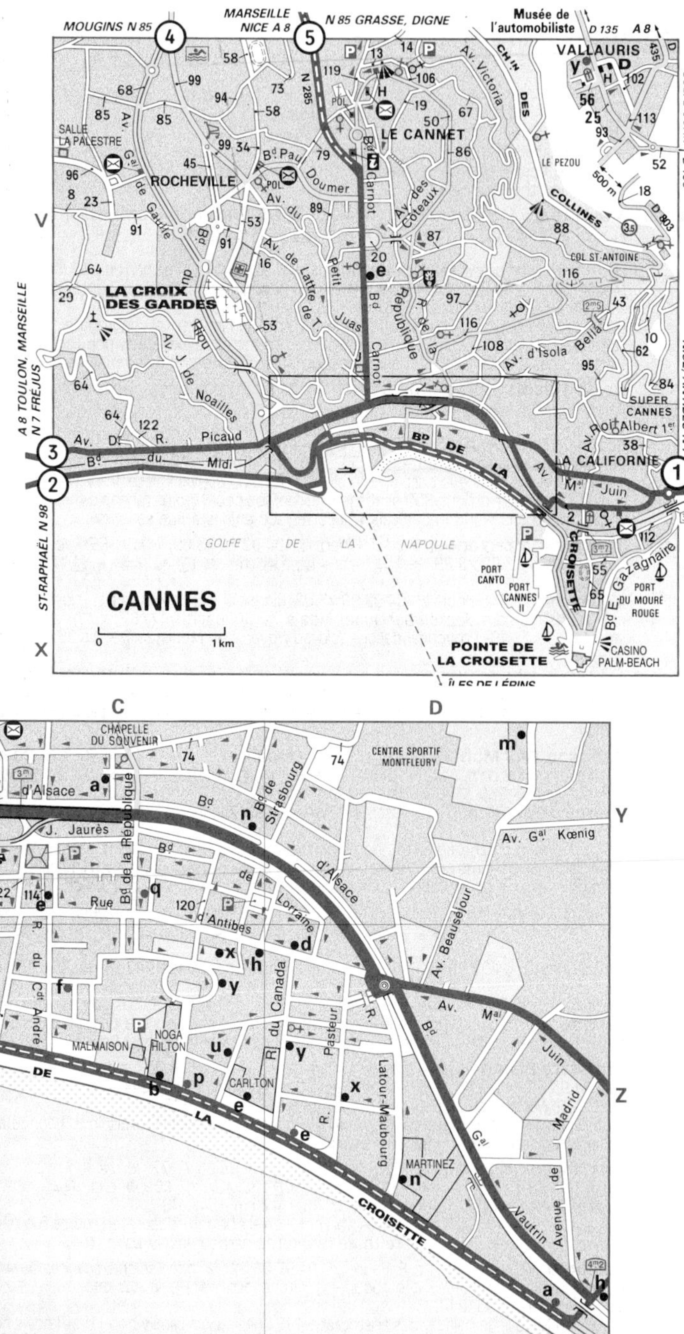
CANNES
MOUGINS N 85
MARSEILLE
NICE A 8
N 85 GRASSE, DIGNE
Musée de l'automobiliste
D 135
A 8
VALLAURIS
GOLFE-JUAN D 135
LE CANNET
ROCHEVILLE
SALLE LA PALESTRE
LA CROIX DES GARDES
LE PEZOU
COL ST-ANTOINE
SUPER CANNES
LA CALIFORNIE
NICE, ANTIBES N 7
A 8 TOULON, MARSEILLE N 7 FRÉJUS
ST-RAPHAËL N 98
GOLFE DE LA NAPOULE
PORT CANTO
PORT CANNES II
PORT DU MOURÉ ROUGE
POINTE DE LA CROISETTE
CASINO PALM-BEACH
ÎLES DE LÉRINS
Av. Victoria
CH. DES COLLINES
Bd Paul Doumer
Av. du Petit Juas
Bd Carnot
Av. des Coteaux
R. de la République
Av. de Lattre de T.
Bd du Riou
Av. J. de Noailles
Av. de Gaulle
Av. d'Isola Bella
Av. Roi Albert 1er
Av. Mal Juin
Bd de la Croisette
Bd E. Gazagnaire
Av. Dr R. Picaud
Bd du Midi
500 m
0
1 km
CHAPELLE DU SOUVENIR
CENTRE SPORTIF MONTFLEURY
d'Alsace
Bd de Strasbourg
J. Jaurès
Bd de Lorraine
Bd d'Alsace
Av. Gal Kœnig
Bd de la République
Rue d'Antibes
Av. Beauséjour
R. du Cdt André
R. du Canada
R. Pasteur
MALMAISON
NOGA HILTON
CARLTON
MARTINEZ
Latour-Maubourg
Av. Mal Juin
Bd Gal Vautrin
Avenue de Madrid
DE LA CROISETTE
Pointe de la Croisette

Majestic Barrière, 10 bd Croisette ✆ 04 92 98 77 00, *majestic@lucienbarriere.com, Fax 04 93 38 97 90*, ←, , , , – |♦|, ■ TV ✆ ♿ – 40 - 400. AE ◐ GB JCB BZ n
closed 15 November-30 December – see **Villa des Lys** below- ***Fouquet's*** ✆ 04 92 98 77 05 **Meals** 35/40b.i. ♀ – ***Plage*** ✆ 04 92 98 77 30 (lunch only) *(May-October)* **Meals** 35/40b.i. – ☐ 29 – **282 rm** 475/870, 23 suites.
◆ The immaculate, majestic façade dates from the 1920s. Luxury and refinement on every floor. The best rooms have sea views. Bright and inviting dining room with a veranda overlooking the Croisette.

Martinez, 73 bd Croisette ✆ 04 92 98 73 00, *martinez@concorde-hotels.com, Fax 04 93 39 67 82*, ←, , , , , – |♦| ■ TV ✆ ♿ – 40 - 600. AE ◐ GB JCB DZ n
see ***Palme d'Or*** below - ***Relais Martinez*** ✆ 04 92 98 74 12 *(dinner only in July-August)* **Meals** 31/55 – ***Plage*** ✆ 04 92 98 74 22 (lunch only) *(early April-late September)* **Meals** a la carte 50/75 – ☐ 30 – **386 rm** 830, 27 suites.
◆ This lovely Art Deco palace is where the stars of the film festival congregate. The luxury suites and attractive rooms with a view of the Croisette are extremely popular. The Relais Martinez has a smart, relaxed ambience, gourmet cuisine and a summer terrace.

Noga Hilton, 50 bd Croisette ✆ 04 92 99 70 00, *sales_cannes@hilton.com, Fax 04 92 99 70 11*, , , , – |♦|, ⇔ rm, ■ TV ✆ ♿ – 40 - 500. AE ◐ GB JCB CZ b
Scala : ✆ 04 92 99 70 93 **Meals** 38/50 – ***Plage*** ✆ 04 92 99 70 27 *(15 April-15 October)* **Meals** a la carte 45/65 – ☐ 25 – **186 rm** 349/799, 48 suites.
◆ This cube-like edifice is built on the site of the old Festival Palace. Very well-equipped rooms, remarkable atrium, 800-seat theatre, rooftop pool. Mediterranean dishes and wines from around the world in La Scala whose terrace enjoys a fine sea view.

Sofitel Méditerranée, 2 bd J. Hibert ✆ 04 92 99 73 00, *H0591-RE@accor-hotels.com, Fax 04 92 99 73 29*, ←, , – |♦|, ⇔ rm, ■ TV ✆ – 70. AE ◐ GB JCB AZ r
Méditerranée (7th floor) ✆ 04 92 99 73 02 (dinner only in July-August) *(closed Sunday and Monday from September-June)* **Meals** 37,50(lunch), 47/67 – ***Chez Panisse*** ✆ 04 92 99 73 10- Provencal decor - *(closed November)* **Meals** 29 ♀ – ☐ 25 – **149 rm** 175/337.
◆ 1930s hotel prettily decorated in Provençal style. Together with the rooftop pool most of the rooms have a splendid view over Cannes and its bay. Superb panorama from the tables of Le Méditerranée. The cuisine of Provence is celebrated in the Panisse.

Radisson SAS Montfleury , 25 av. Beauséjour ✆ 04 93 68 86 86, *info.montfleury@radissonsas.com, Fax 04 93 68 87 87*, ←, , , , – |♦|, ⇔ rm, ■ TV ✆ ♿ – 20 - 260. AE ◐ GB JCB. DY m
(swimming pool grill in July-August) - ***L'Olivier :*** **Meals** 25(lunch)37/47 ♀ – ☐ 20 – **181 rm** 380.
◆ This hotel is on the edge of the Californie area and its luxury villas. Modern rooms refurbished in maritime or Provençal style. Lovely terrace and pool beneath the palm trees. Attractive, sunny decor, open kitchen and Mediterranean cuisine in L'Olivier.

Gray d'Albion, 38 r. Serbes ✆ 04 92 99 79 79, *graydalbion@lucienbarriere.com, Fax 04 93 99 26 10*, – |♦|, ⇔ rm, ■ TV ✆ ♿ – 40 - 120. AE ◐ GB JCB BZ
Royal Gray ✆ 04 92 99 79 60 *(closed Sunday and Monday)* **Meals** 42 ♀ – ☐ 20 – **192 rm** 425, 8 suites.
◆ This 1970s building houses an arcade of luxury shops as well as cosy rooms which are regularly refurbished. Discotheque, piano bar, private beach on the Croisette. Mediterranean cuisine awaits diners in the warm surroundings of the Royal Gray.

Croisette Beach without rest, 13 r. Canada ✆ 04 92 18 88 00, *croisettebea@aws.fr, Fax 04 93 68 35 38*, – |♦|, ⇔ rm, ■ TV ✆ ♿ . AE ◐ GB JCB DZ
closed 22 November-27 December – ☐ 18 – **94 rm** 208/315.
◆ Spacious, well-soundproofed rooms with functional light-wood furnishings. Lounge and bar are regularly used for picture exhibitions.

Sun Riviera without rest, 138 r. d'Antibes ✆ 04 93 06 77 77, *info@sun-riviera.com, Fax 04 93 38 31 10*, , – |♦|, ⇔ rm, ■ TV ✆ ♿ . AE ◐ GB JCB CZ
closed 20 November-27 December – ☐ 15 – **42 rm** 154/240.
◆ In a street with lots of luxury shops, this hotel offers brightly decorated rooms furnished with period pieces. The best are those facing the garden (lovely palm tree).

Splendid without rest, 4 r. F. Faure ✆ 04 97 06 22 22, *hotel.splendid.cannes@wanadoo.fr, Fax 04 93 99 55 02*, ← harbour – |♦| kitchenette ■ TV ✆. AE GB BZ
☐ 16 – **62 rm** 103/214.
◆ Looking like a little palace, this aristocratic 19C building is a family hotel that knows how to pamper its guests. Some rooms have a view of the harbour and the Old Town.

Amarante, 78 bd Carnot 04 93 39 22 23, *amarante-cannes@jjwhotels.com, Fax 04 93 39 40 22,* – rm, – 25. AE GB JCB V e
Meals *(closed 28 November-23 December, weekends from October-March)* 32 – 15 – **71 rm** 230/260.
◆ Located on a busy boulevard. The décor of the well-soundproofed rooms features mahogany furnishings and Mediterranean colours. Dining room opening onto a terrace, with décor and food in Provençal style.

Cavendish without rest, 11 bd Carnot 04 97 06 26 00, *reservation@cavendish-cannes.com, Fax 04 97 06 26 01* – rm, . AE GB. BY t
18 – **34 rm** 150/240.
◆ Charming hotel in a residence dating from 1897. A delightful 1920s lift brings guests to carefully refurbished and cosy rooms. Pleasant lounge bar for relaxation.

Eden Hôtel without rest, 133 r. Antibes 04 93 68 78 00, *reception@eden-hotel-cannes.com, Fax 4 93 68 78 01* – rm, . AE GB DZ d
14 – **42 rm** 200/230.
◆ In the prestigious Rue d'Antibes, this hotel is ideally located for shopping. The refurbished rooms have parquet floors and are decorated with contemporary furniture.

America without rest, 13 r. St-Honoré 04 93 06 75 75, *info@hotel-america.com, Fax 04 93 68 04 58* – . AE GB JCB. BZ r
closed 26 November-26 December – 12 – **28 rm** 112/179.
◆ In a quiet street close to the Croisette. Bright, contemporary rooms, most of them spacious, all with good soundproofing.

California's without rest, 8 traverse Alexandre III 04 93 94 12 21, *nadia@californias-hotel.com, Fax 04 93 43 55 17,* – – 15. AE GB JCB DZ h
18 – **33 rm** 101/300.
◆ Two lovely buildings arranged around a pretty garden. Hand-crafted furniture, pastel shades and attractive fabrics adorn the rooms, some of which have balconies. Private boat.

Fouquet's without rest, 2 rd-pt Duboys d'Angers 04 92 59 25 00, *info@le-fouquets.com, Fax 04 92 98 03 39* – . AE GB CZ y
1 April-15 November – 12 – **10 rm** 170/230.
◆ On a not very busy roundabout, a hotel with spacious, well-equipped and individually decorated rooms. Pleasant small sitting area. Very well presented. Considerate service.

Mondial without rest, 1 r. Teisseire 04 93 68 70 00, *reservation@hotellemondial.com, Fax 04 93 99 39 11* – rm, . AE GB JCB CY e
12 – **39 rm** 110/180, 10 suites.
◆ The hotel has been refurbished in the spirit of Art Deco. Furnishings inspired by this period enhance the sprucely decorated rooms, some of them with balconies.

Cannes Riviera without rest, 16 bd Alsace 04 97 06 20 40, *reservation@cannesriviera.com, Fax 04 93 39 20 75,* – – 20. AE GB JCB. BY r
14 – **59 rm** 105/150.
◆ Hotel with recent Provençal-style make-over - pastel colours, and painted furniture. Soundproofed rooms. Rooftop pool and solarium overlooking Cannes.

Cézanne without rest, 40 bd Alsace 04 93 38 50 70, *contact@hotel-cezanne.com, Fax 04 92 99 20 99,* – – 40. AE GB JCB CY n
13 – **29 rm** 110/138.
◆ Delightful rooms with lustrous fabrics and reproduction pictures, pretty Mediterranean garden with a murmuring fountain - Cézanne's Provence barely 500m from the Croisette.

Paris without rest, 34 bd Alsace 04 97 06 98 40, *reservation@hotel-de-paris.com, Fax 04 93 39 04 61,* – – 25. AE GB JCB. CY a
closed 19 November-26 December – 13 – **47 rm** 135/150, 3 suites.
◆ Close to a busy main road, this private 19C establishment benefits from comprehensive soundproofing. Solid, somewhat old-fashioned rooms. Pool surrounded by palm trees.

Renoir without rest, 7 r. Edith Cavell 04 92 99 62 62, *contact@hotel-renoir-cannes.com, Fax 04 92 99 62 82* – kitchenette . AE GB JCB BY x
12 – **10 rm** 137/149, 17 suites.
◆ Painted furniture and colourful Provençal fabrics lend rooms an individual touch in this 1920s building overlooking the expressway. Breakfast served only in the rooms.

Villa de l'Olivier without rest, 5 r. Tambourinaires 04 93 39 53 28, *reception@hotelolivier.com, Fax 04 93 39 55 85,* – P. AE GB JCB. AZ e
closed 22 November-22 December – 10 – **24 rm** 91/125.
◆ Villa in the Old Town partly screened from the nearby main road by vegetation. Delightful soundproofed rooms with furnishings in various styles. Friendly reception.

Albert 1er without rest, 68 av. Grasse 04 93 39 24 04, *Fax 04 93 38 83 75* – P. GB AY d
closed 1-15 December – 6 - **11 rm** 60/70.
◆ Friendly atmosphere and warm welcome in this 1930s villa. Breakfast is taken on an attractive terrace redolent of the scents of Provence. Soberly decorated rooms.

XXXXX ✿✿ **Palme d'Or** - Hôtel Martinez, 73 bd Croisette ✆ 04 92 98 74 14, *martinez@concorde-hotels.com, Fax 04 93 39 03 38,* ←, – | ▤ ⇥ P. AE ◑ GB DZ n
closed 12 to 27 April, mid-November-mid-December, Sunday and Monday – **Meals** 55 b.i. (lunch), 70/140 and a la carte 105/160 ♀.
◆ Natural wood, elegant colours and photos of film stars adorn this restaurant, which opens out directly on to the Croisette. Lovely panoramic terrace. Mediterranean cuisine.
Spec. Gnocchi de jeunes carottes, melon, sucrine rôtie (Summer). Comme un stockfish, sardines en filets, chips de pérugine. Chocolat aux éclats de noisettes, gelée de roses. **Wines** Bellet, Vin de l'Ile Saint Honorat.

XXXXX ✿ **Villa des Lys** - Hôtel Majestic Barrière, 10 bd Croisette ✆ 04 92 98 77 41, *villadeslys@lucienbarriere.com, Fax 04 93 38 97 90* – ▤ ⇥. AE ◑ GB JCB BZ n
closed 14 November-30 December, Sunday and Monday – **Meals** *(dinner only)* 75/190 and a la carte 100/140.
◆ An elegant glass roof and Napoleon III-style decor provide the setting for the fine Mediterranean and Atlantic seafood served in this establishment.
Spec. Bocal de foie gras de canard. Canon d'agneau rôti au thym-citron. "Traou Mad" tiède à la vanille. **Wines** Côtes de Provence.

XXX **Mesclun,** 16 r. St-Antoine ✆ 04 93 99 45 19, *lemesclun@wanadoo.fr, Fax 04 93 47 68 29* – ▤. AE GB JCB AZ t
closed 20 November-20 December, 20 to 28 February and Wednesday – **Meals** (dinner only) 34 ♀.
◆ Luxurious ambience in this typical building of Old Cannes. Wainscoting, period furniture, pictures and discreet lighting form a lovely setting for intimate dinners.

XXX **Félix,** 63 bd Croisette ✆ 04 93 94 00 61, *Fax 04 93 94 06 90,* – ▤. AE GB DZ e
closed 20 November-20 December – **Meals** 42/45 and a la carte 45/77.
◆ Charles Trenet was a regular, and this elegant brasserie-style restaurant in a superb location on the Croisette also featured in the film La Bonne Année. Prestigious terrace.

XX **Festival,** 52 bd Croisette ✆ 04 93 38 04 81, *contact@lefestival.fr, Fax 04 93 38 13 82,* – ▤. AE ◑ GB JCB CZ p
closed 17 November-27 December – **Meals** 35/40 ♀ - ***Grill*** : **Meals** a la carte 33/49 ♁.
◆ Cut-away ship drawings enliven the pale panelling of this huge brasserie. See and be seen on the terrace facing the Croisette ! Cool modern decor, convivial ambience and terrace in the Grill. Plain cuisine, grills, salads, daily menu etc.

XX **Mantel,** 22 r. St-Antoine ✆ 04 93 39 13 10, *noel.mantel@wanadoo.fr, Fax 04 93 39 13 10* – ▤. GB
closed 25 June-10 July, 10 to 20 November, Thursday lunch and Wednesday – **Meals** 23 (lunch), 32/54 ♀.
◆ One of a number of restaurants along a picturesque street in the old town (Le Suquet). Renowned for its reliable cuisine combining Provençal recipes and Italian influences.

XX **Gaston et Gastounette,** 7 quai St-Pierre ✆ 04 93 39 47 92, *Fax 04 93 99 45 34,* – ▤. AE ◑ GB AZ v
closed 1 to 20 December – **Meals** 23 (lunch), 31/35 ♀.
◆ The light-wood panelling of the two dining rooms is enhanced by colourful representations of Côte d'Azur landscapes. Attractive terrace facing the port.

XX **Rest. Arménien,** 82 bd Croisette ✆ 04 93 94 00 58, *christian@lerestaurantarmenien.com, Fax 04 93 94 56 12* – ▤. ◑ GB DZ a
closed 15 to 30 December, lunch from Tuesday to Saturday and Monday – **Meals** - Armenian rest. - set menu only 40.
◆ A rather flashy dining room with stained-glass windows is the setting for this Armenian restaurant. No choice on the one set menu, but generous portions. Loyal clientele.

XX **3 Portes,** 16 r. Frères Pradignac ✆ 04 93 38 91 70, *Fax 04 93 94 13 57,* – ▤. AE GB JCB CZ f
closed 1 to 11 July, 15 to 25 December, lunch Monday, lunch Saturday and Sunday out of season – **Meals** 26 ♀.
◆ Fashion victims should feel at home here - contemporary Mediterranean-style cuisine, plus cool designer décor and trendy musical accompaniment.

X **Rendez-Vous,** 35 r. F. Faure ✆ 04 93 68 55 10, *Fax 04 93 38 96 21,* – ▤. AE GB AZ g
closed 6 to 17 January and 10 to 20 December – **Meals** 18,60/25,90 ♀.
◆ This smart establishment is a good place to meet after a highly perfumed morning spent in the neighbouring flower market. Traditional cuisine.

X **La Cave,** 9 bd République ✆ 04 93 99 79 87, *restaurantlacave@free.fr, Fax 04 93 46 15 12* – ▤. AE GB JCB CY c
closed Saturday lunch and Sunday – **Meals** 28 ♀ ♁.
◆ Mirrors, posters, leatherette banquettes and open kitchens - you eat tightly packed together in this cheerful contemporary bistro. A slate shows the dishes of the day.

Grasse 06130 Alpes-Mar. 341 C6 – pop. 43 874 alt. 250.
9 Victoria Golf Club ✆ 04 93 12 23 26 by D 4, D 3 and D 103 : 13 km ; 18 Grande Bastide at Opio ✆ 04 93 77 70 08, E : 6 km by D 7 ; 18 of St-Donat ✆ 04 93 09 76 60 : 5 km ; 18 Opio-Valbonne ✆ 04 93 12 00 08 by D 4 : 11 km ; 9 St-Philippe Golf Academy ✆ 04 93 00 00 57, E : 12 km.

Tourist Office 22 Crs H. Cresp ✆ 04 93 36 66 66, Fax 04 93 36 86 36, tourisme.grasse @wanadoo.fr.

Cannes 17.

Bastide St-Antoine (Chibois) with rm, 48 av. H. Dunant (quartier St-Antoine) by road of Cannes : 1,5 km ✆ 04 93 70 94 94, *info@jacques-chibois.com*, Fax 04 93 70 94 95, ←, – 20 - 80. AE GB JCB
Meals 53 (lunch), 130/170 and a la carte 98/134 – 23 – **11 rm** 290/318.
• This lovely 18C fortified house rises from a hill planted with ancient olive trees. Its tasty cuisine is a tribute to the capital of the perfume industry. Elegant rooms.
Spec. Homard en fraîcheur de glace de fromage blanc (spring-summer). Saint-Pierre en symphonie de pois gourmands et fenouil (spring-summer). Canette au jus de noix de Tonkin.
Wines Côtes de Provence, Bellet.

Juan-les-Pins 06160 Alpes-Mar. 341 D6 – alt. 2.
Tourist Office 51 bd Ch.-Guillaumont ✆ 04 92 90 53 05, Fax 04 93 61 55 13, acceuil@ antibes6juanlespins.com.

Cannes 8,5.

Juana , la Pinède, av. G. Gallice ✆ 04 93 61 08 70, *info@hotel-juana.com*, Fax 04 93 61 76 60, – 25. AE GB
closed mid-November-mid-December – ***Terrasse-Christian Morisset*** ✆ 04 93 61 20 37- (dinner only in July-August) *(closed mid-November-mid-December, Tuesday and Wednesday)* **Meals** 60(lunch), 92/135 and a la carte 105/160 – 23 – **35 rm** 320/635, 5 suites.
• Luxury 1930s hotel where guests are received like royalty. The elegant, well-equipped rooms have been refurbished in Art Deco style. Fine Mediterranean cuisine served beneath the palm trees in the delightful Terrasse. Cosy bar and smoking room.
Spec. Cannelloni de supions et palourdes à l'encre de seiche. Selle d'agneau de Pauillac cuite en terre d'argile de Vallauris. Millefeuille de fraises des bois à la crème de mascarpone (April-September). **Wines** Bellet, Côtes de Provence.

La Napoule 06210 Alpes-Mar. 341 C6.
9 18 of Mandelieu ✆ 04 92 97 32 00 ; 18 Riviera Golf Club ✆ 04 92 97 49 49.
Tourist Office av. H.Clews ✆ 04 93 49 95 31.

Cannes 9,5.

L'Oasis (Raimbault), r. J. H. Carle ✆ 04 93 49 95 52, *oasis@relaischateaux.com*, Fax 04 93 49 64 13, – AE GB
closed 12 December-14 January, Sunday dinner and Monday from November-March and Monday lunch from April-October – **Meals** 45 (lunch), 65/128 and a la carte 100/121.
• Lushly planted patio, elegant ambience, delicious Mediterranean cuisine with an oriental touch, a generous dessert trolley. No, it's not a mirage !
Spec. Soleil levant de poisson cru en salade d'orge perlée. Pavé de gros loup laqué et rôti à la braise. Selle de chevreuil en noisettes, sauce poivrade aux myrtilles (mid-October-early January). **Wines** Côtes de Provence, Coteaux d'Aix en Provence-les Baux.

LILLE 59000 Nord 302 G4 – pop. 184 657 alt. 10.
See : *Old Lille*★★ : *Old Stock Exchange*★★ *(Vieille Bourse)* EY, *Place du Général-de-Gaulle*★ EY **66**, *Hospice Comtesse*★ *(panelled timber vault*★★*)* EY, – *Rue de la Monnaie*★ EY **120** – *Vauban's Citadel*★ BV – *St-Sauveur district : Paris Gate*★ EFZ, ←★ *from the top of the belfry of the Hôtel de Ville* FZ – *Fine Arts Museum*★★★ *(Musée des Beaux-Arts)* EZ – *Général de Gaulle's Birthplace (Maison natale)* EY.

18 of Brigode at Villeneuve d'Ascq ✆ 03 20 91 17 86 : 9 km ; of Bondues ✆ 03 20 23 20 62 : 9,5 km ; 9 of Flandres ✆ 03 20 72 20 74 : 4,5 km ; 18 of Sart ✆ 03 20 72 02 51 : 7 km ; 18 Lille Métropole ✆ 03 20 47 42 42.

of Lille-Lesquin : ✆ 03 20 49 68 68 : 8 km.

✆ 08 36 35 35 35.

Tourist Office Palais Rihour ✆ 03 20 21 94 21, Fax 03 20 21 94 20, info@lilletourism.com.

L'Hermitage Gantois, 224 r. Paris ✆ 03 20 85 30 30, *contact@hotelhermitagegantois.com*, Fax 03 20 42 31 31 – – 20 - 60. AE GB JCB EZ b
Meals 34 - ***L'Estaminet*** : **Meals** 18 – 18 – **67 rm** 190/240.
• This listed 14C hospice is now a fine hotel teeming with character with original decor enhanced by modern touches. Most rooms look on to pleasant patios. Traditional dining under the restaurant's red and gold vaulted ceiling, Brasserie ambience in l'Estaminet.

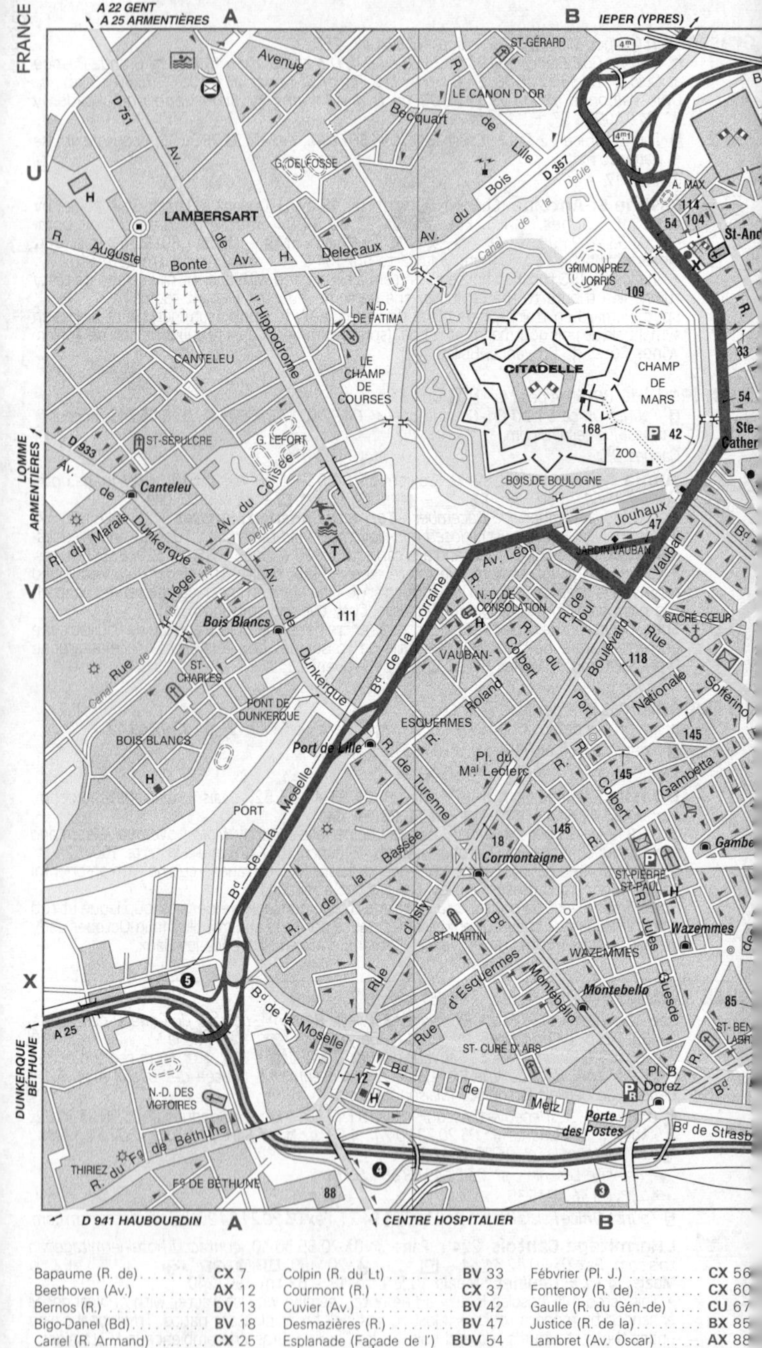
FRANCE
A 22 GENT
A 25 ARMENTIÈRES
A
B
IEPER (YPRES)
ST-GÉRARD
LE CANON D'OR
Avenue
R. Becquart de Lille
G. DELFOSSE
D 751
Av.
U
H
LAMBERSART
D 357
Av. du Bois
Canal de la Deûle
A. MAX
114
104
54
St-And
R. Auguste Bonte
Av. H. Delecaux
de l'Hippodrome
GRIMONPREZ JORRIS
109
N.-D. DE FATIMA
CANTELEU
LE CHAMP DE COURSES
CITADELLE
CHAMP DE MARS
33
54
Ste-Cather
LOMME ARMENTIÈRES
D 933
ST-SEPULCRE
G. LEFORT
168
42
ZOO
Av. de Canteleu
Av. du Colisée
BOIS DE BOULOGNE
Jouhaux
47
R. du Marais
Dunkerque
Deûle
T
JARDIN VAUBAN
Av. Léon
Vauban
V
R. Hegel
Av. de Dunkerque
111
N.-D. DE CONSOLATION
R. de Toul
SACRÉ CŒUR
Bois Blancs
H
Boulevard
Rue
Canal Rue de
ST-CHARLES
Bd de la Lorraine
VAUBAN-
R. Colbert
du Port
118
Solférino
Nationale
PONT DE DUNKERQUE
R. Roland
ESQUERMES
145
BOIS BLANCS
Port de Lille
R. de Turenne
Pl. du Mal Leclerc
R.
145
Gambetta
H
R. Colbert
L.
PORT
Bd de la Moselle
145
R.
Gambe
18
Cormontaigne
R. de la Bassée
ST-PIERRE ST-PAUL
H
R. Jules Guesde
Wazemmes
ST-MARTIN
Bd
d'Isly
Rue
WAZEMMES
X
Montebello
Montebello
d'Esquermes
85
Bd de la Moselle
Rue
ST-BEN LABR
A 25
ST- CURÉ D'ARS
DUNKERQUE BÉTHUNE
12
H
Bd de Metz
Pl. B. Dorez
N.-D. DES VICTOIRES
Porte des Postes
Bd de Strasb
R. du Fg de Béthune
THIRIEZ
Fg DE BÉTHUNE
88
D 941 HAUBOURDIN
A
CENTRE HOSPITALIER
B

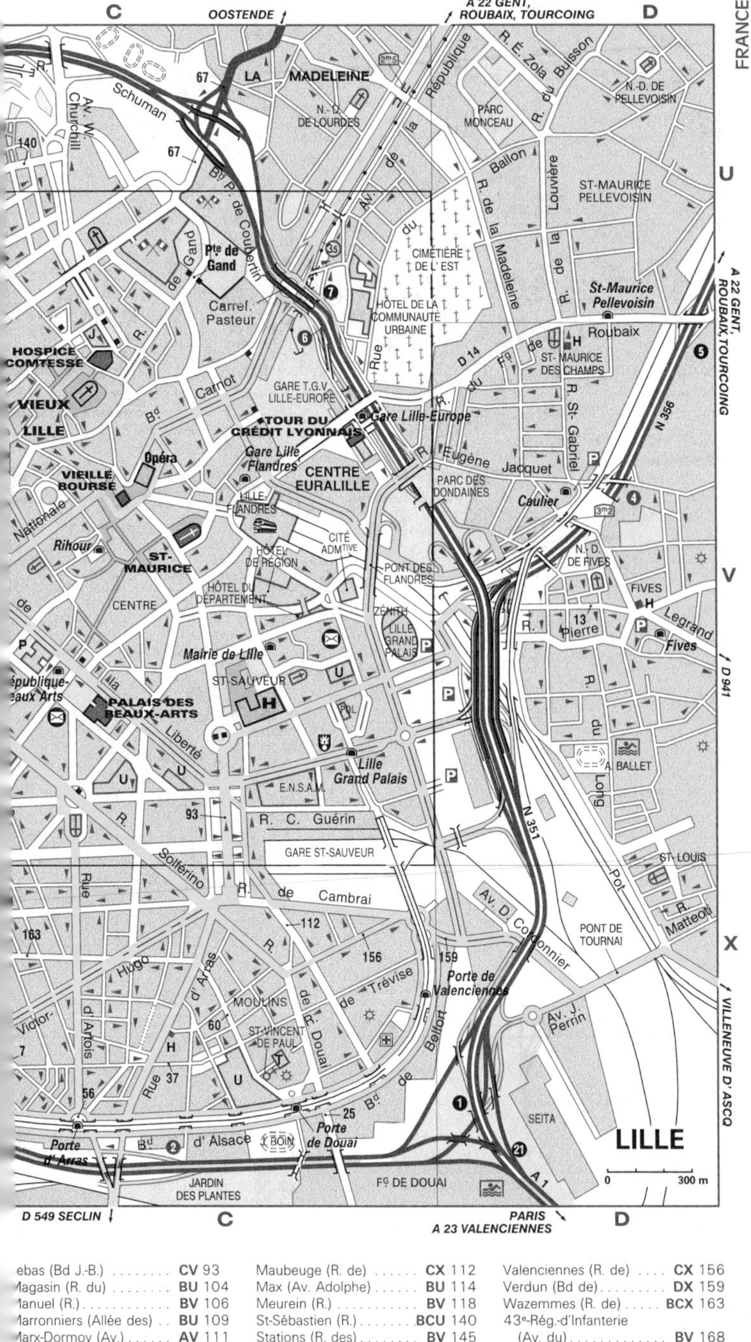
C
OOSTENDE
A 22 GENT, ROUBAIX, TOURCOING
D
LA MADELEINE
N.-D. DE LOURDES
R. de la République
R. É. Zola
R. du Buisson
N.-D. DE PELLEVOISIN
PARC MONCEAU
Schuman
Av. W. Churchill
140
67
Bd P. de Coubertin
Av. de la République
Ballon
R. de la Madeleine
Louvière
ST-MAURICE PELLEVOISIN
U
CIMETIÈRE DE L'EST
HÔTEL DE LA COMMUNAUTÉ URBAINE
Rue du
R. de la
St-Maurice Pellevoisin
A 22 GENT, ROUBAIX, TOURCOING
Pte de Gand
R. de Gand
Carref. Pasteur
7
6
D 14
R. du Fg de Roubaix
ST-MAURICE DES CHAMPS
5
HOSPICE COMTESSE
VIEUX LILLE
Bd Carnot
GARE T.G.V. LILLE-EUROPE
Gare Lille-Europe
TOUR DU CRÉDIT LYONNAIS
R. St-Gabriel
N 356
Opéra
Gare Lille Flandres
CENTRE EURALILLE
R. Eugène Jacquet
PARC DES DONDAINES
Caulier
VIEILLE BOURSE
Nationale
LILLE-FLANDRES
4
Rihour
ST-MAURICE
HÔTEL DE RÉGION
CITÉ ADMTIVE
PONT DES FLANDRES
N.-D. DE FIVES
V
HÔTEL DU DÉPARTEMENT
FIVES
CENTRE
ZÉNITH
LILLE GRAND PALAIS
R. Pierre
13
R. Legrand
Fives
Mairie de Lille
D 941
ST-SAUVEUR
République-Beaux Arts
PALAIS DES BEAUX-ARTS
R. de la Liberté
R. du Long Pot
Lille Grand Palais
A. BALLET
E.N.S.A.M.
93
R. C. Guérin
N 351
GARE ST-SAUVEUR
R. Solferino
ST-LOUIS
Rue
R. de Cambrai
Av. D. Cordonnier
R. Matteoti
163
112
156
159
PONT DE TOURNAI
X
Hugo
R. d'Arras
R. de Trévise
Porte de Valenciennes
VILLENEUVE D'ASCQ
Victor-
d'Artois
MOULINS
R. de Douai
Av. J. Perrin
60
ST-VINCENT DE PAUL
Bd de Belfort
7
37
Rue
56
25
1
SEITA
Porte d'Arras
Bd d'Alsace
2
BOIN
Porte de Douai
21
LILLE
JARDIN DES PLANTES
Fg DE DOUAI
A 1
0
300 m
D 549 SECLIN
C
PARIS
A 23 VALENCIENNES
D

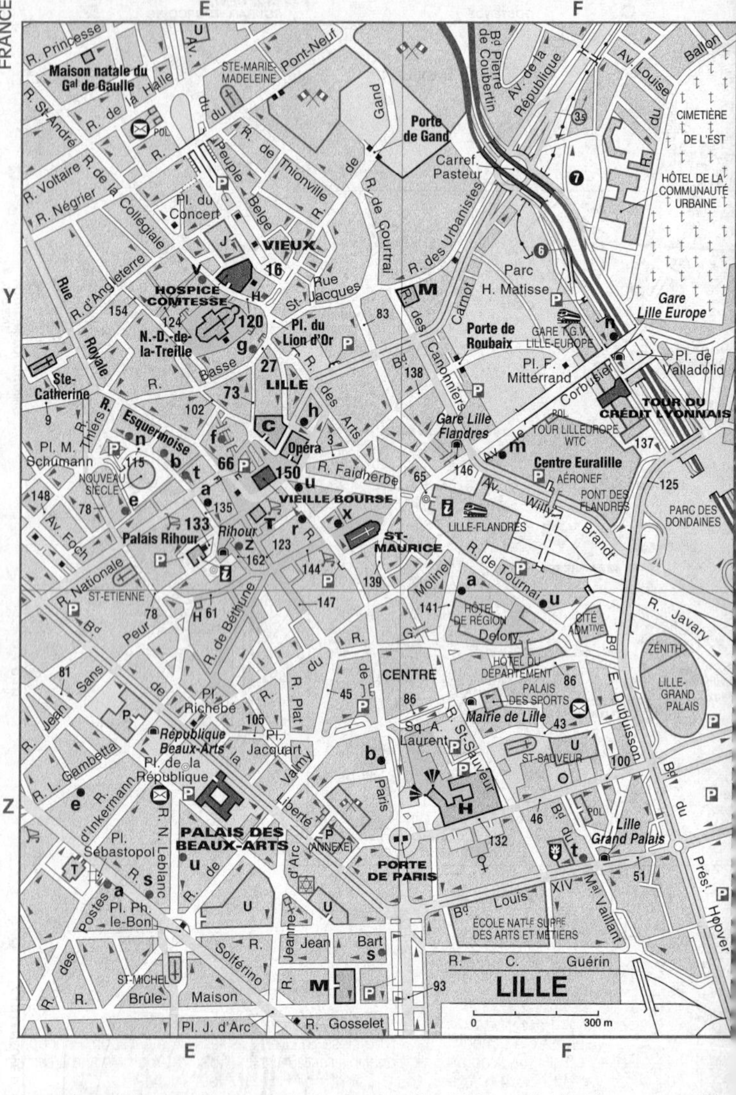

Anatole-France (R.)	EY	3	Gaulle (Pl. Gén.-de) (Gd Pl.)	EY	66	Réduit (R. du)	FZ	13
Barre (R. de la)	EY	9	Grande Chaussée (R. de la)	EY	73	Rihour (Pl.)	EY	13
Béthune (R. de)	EYZ		Hôpital-Militaire (R.)	EY	78	Roisin (R. Jean)	EY	13
Bettignies (Pl. L. de)	EY	16	Jacquemars-Giélée (R.)	EZ	81	Rotterdam (Parvis de)	FY	13
Chats-Bossus (R. des)	EY	27	Jardins (R. des)	EY	83	Roubaix (R. de)	EFY	13
Debierre (R. Ch.)	FZ	43	Kennedy (Av. Prés.)	FZ	86	St-Génois (R.)	EY	13
Delesalle (R. E.)	EZ	45	Lebas (Bd J.-B.)	FZ	93	St-Venant (Av. Ch.)	FYZ	14
Déportés (R. des)	FY	46	Lefèvre (R. G.)	FZ	100	Sec-Arembault (R. du)	EY	14
Dr.-Calmette (Bd)	FY	51	Lepelletier (R.)	EY	102	Suisses (Pl. des)	FY	14
Esquermoise (R.)	EY		Maillotte (R.)	EZ	105	Tanneurs (R. des)	EYZ	14
Faidherbe (R.)	EY		Mendès-France (Pl.)	EY	115	Tenremonde (R.)	EY	14
Faubourg de Roubaix	FY	55	Monnaie (R. de la)	EY	120	Théâtre (Pl. du)	EY	15
Fosses (R. des)	EYZ	61	Nationale (R.)	EYZ		Trois-Mollettes (R. des)	EY	15
Gambetta (R. Léon)	EZ		Neuve (R.)	EY	123	Vieille Comédie		
Gare (Pl. de la)	FY	65	Pasteur (Bd. L.)	FY	125	(R. de la)	EY	16

Crowne Plaza, 335 bd Leeds ☎ 03 20 42 46 46, *contact@lille-crowneplaza.com, Fax 03 20 40 13 14,* ≤, – |≡|, ⇔ rm, ▤ TV ✆ ♿ – 10 - 100. AE ⓓ GB JCB FY n
Meals 23 ♀ – ☐ 17 – **121 rm** 190.
◆ This cube-like building opposite the TGV station is home to a brand-new hotel with spacious, modern rooms that are minimalist yet fully equipped. Starck-inspired decor, including an attractive library. Modern à la carte and buffet dining in the restaurant.

Carlton without rest, 3 r. Paris ✉ 59800 ☎ 03 20 13 33 13, *carlton@carltonlille.com, Fax 03 20 51 48 17,* – |≡|, ⇔ rm, ▤ TV ✆ ♿ – 15 - 170. AE ⓓ GB JCB EY u
☐ 17 – **60 rm** 165/260.
◆ An early-20C town mansion located opposite the Old Bourse. Luxury suites and Louis XV- and Louis XVI-style rooms with tasteful decor. English-style bar.

Alliance , 17 quai du Wault ✉ 59800 ☎ 03 20 30 62 62, *alliancelille@alliance-hospitality.com, Fax 03 20 42 94 25* – |≡|, ⇔ rm, ▤ rm, TV ✆ ♿ P – 35 - 100. AE ⓓ GB JCB BV d
Meals *(closed Monday from 15 July-31 August)* 27/33 b.i. ♀ – ☐ 17 – **75 rm** 210, 8 suites.
◆ This 17C red-brick convent is halfway between Lille's historic centre and the Citadel. Rooms with contemporary décor around an indoor garden. A huge glass pyramid rises over the cloisters housing the restaurant. Piano bar.

Grand Hôtel Bellevue without rest, 5 r. J. Roisin ☎ 03 20 57 45 64, *grand.hotel.bellevue@wanadoo.fr, Fax 03 20 40 07 93* – |≡|, ⇔ rm, ▤ TV ✆ – 50 - 100. AE ⓓ GB JCB EY a
☐ 11 – **57 rm** 135.
◆ Beautiful stone building in the heart of the capital of French Flanders. Characterful rooms, attractively refurbished and with new furniture. Some overlook the Grand'Place.

Novotel Flandres, 49 r. Tournai ✉ 59800 ☎ 03 28 38 67 00, *H3165@accor-hotels.com, Fax 03 28 38 67 10,* – |≡|, ⇔ rm, ▤ TV ✆ ♿ – 80. AE ⓓ GB JCB FZ u
Meals a la carte 25/35 ♀ – ☐ 11 – **93 rm** 129/179, 5 suites.
◆ Next to Lille-Flandres railway station, this establishment conforms to the latest standards set by the Novotel chain. Huge foyer/lounge, modern, well-equipped rooms.

Mercure Le Royal without rest, 2 bd Carnot ✉ 59800 ☎ 03 20 14 71 47, *h0802@accor-hotels.com, Fax 03 20 14 71 48* – |≡|, ⇔ rm, ▤ TV ✆ – 25. AE ⓓ GB JCB EY h
☐ 11 – **99 rm** 136/190.
◆ Exposed beams and old brickwork lend charm to the foyer and lounge of this venerable stone-built establishment. Contemporary-style rooms, refurbished with care.

Paix without rest, 46 bis r. Paris ✉ 59000 ☎ 03 20 54 63 93, *hotelpaixlille@aol.com, Fax 03 20 63 98 97* – |≡| TV ✆. AE ⓓ GB JCB EY r
☐ 8,50 – **35 rm** 67/93.
◆ This hotel dates back to 1782. The owner is an enthusiastic art-lover who has filled the place with reproductions as well as painting the fresco adorning the breakfast room.

Express by Holiday Inn without rest, 75bis r. Gambetta ☎ 03 20 42 90 90, *expresslille@alliance-hospitality.com, Fax 03 20 57 14 24* – |≡|, ⇔ rm, TV ✆ ♿ – 15 - 160. AE ⓓ GB JCB EZ e
99 rm ☐ 95.
◆ The best things about this establishment are the reasonably quiet rooms facing the courtyard, the tasteful recent improvements, and a very convenient garage. Traditional and contemporary cuisine awaits diners in the restaurant.

Ibis Gare, 29 av. Ch. St-Venant ✉ 59800 ☎ 03 28 36 30 40, *h0901@accor-hotels.com, Fax 03 28 36 30 99,* – |≡| TV ✆ ♿ – 20 - 60. AE ⓓ GB FYZ a
Meals 20 and a la carte 16/30 – ☐ 6 – **151 rm** 80.
◆ Hotel complex in a modern structure close to Lille-Flandres railway station. Functional, carefully refurbished rooms. Traditional Ibis restaurant plus bistro-type fare and a certain number of dishes with a touch of the North of France about them.

Brueghel without rest, parvis St-Maurice ☎ 03 20 06 06 69, *hotel.brueghel@wanadoo.fr, Fax 03 20 63 25 27* – |≡| TV ✆. AE ⓓ GB EY x
☐ 7,50 – **60 rm** 64/88.
◆ Typical Flemish façade, retro charm in the foyer and lift, bright little rooms in pastel colours plus a central location make this a good choice as a place to stay.

✿ **A L'Huîtrière,** 3 r. Chats Bossus ✉ 59800 ☎ 03 20 55 43 41, *contact@huitriere.fr, Fax 03 20 55 23 10* – ▤. AE ⓓ GB JCB EY g
closed 22 July-24 August, dinner Sunday and Bank Holidays – **Meals** 43 (lunch)/110 and a la carte 75/110 ♀.
◆ The ceramics where the fish are displayed are well worth a look and will certainly whet your appetite. Beyond, three luxury dining rooms are a high point of local gastronomy.
Spec. Huîtres. Saint-Jacques au chou vert et à la truffe (October-May). Poêlée de homard aux pommes de terre et à l'estragon.

XXX ✿ **Sébastopol** (Germond), 1 pl. Sébastopol ✆ 03 20 57 05 05, *n.germond@restaurant-sebastopol.fr, Fax 03 20 40 11 31* – ▤. AE GB JCB EZ a
closed 8 to 30 August, Sunday dinner, lunch Saturday and Monday – **Meals** 28 (lunch)/44 and a la carte 60/75 ♀.
◆ The elegant façade is enhanced by the landscaping and unusual awning. Refurbished dining room with warm, contemporary decor. Classic fine cuisine and good wine list.
Spec. Crépinette de pieds de porc et foie gras aux cèpes (autumn). Filet de bœuf aux jets de houblon, jus à la bière (spring). Vaporeux glacé à la chicorée.

XXX ✿ **L'Esplanade** (Scherpereel), 84 façade Esplanade ✉ 59800 ✆ 03 20 06 58 58, *Fax 03 28 52 47 43* – ▤. AE ⓓ GB BV x
closed Saturday lunch and Bank Holidays – **Meals** 30 (lunch), 45/65 and a la carte 62/80 ♀.
◆ Brick building next door to the "Queen of Citadelles". Comfortable, contemporary first floor dining room. Up-to-date cuisine accompanied by a splendid wine list.
Spec. Langoustines rôties, chutney de pomme verte et raisin. Turbot sauvage meunière, panais, jus de volaille. Parfait glacé aux épices, spéculoos, sabayon vanille.

XX **Baan Thaï,** 22 bd J.-B. Lebas ✆ 03 20 86 06 01, *Fax 03 20 86 03 23* – ▤. AE GB EZ s
closed Sunday except lunch from October-March and Saturday lunch – **Meals** - Thai rest. - 39/45 ♀.
◆ This restaurant installed in a fine town house invites diners to take a trip to the Kingdom of Siam. Elegant exotic decor and traditional Thai cuisine.

XX **Clément Marot,** 16 r. Pas ✉ 59800 ✆ 03 20 57 01 10, *marot.clement4@wanadoo.fr, Fax 03 20 57 39 69* – ▤. AE ⓓ GB JCB EY n
closed Sunday except lunch out of season – **Meals** 22 (lunch), 31/45.
◆ Little brick-built establishment run by descendants of the Cahors poet Clément Marot. Modern setting, pictures on the walls and convivial atmosphere.

XX **Lanathaï,** 189 r. Solférino ✆ 03 20 57 20 20, 🏠 – AE GB. ✻ EZ s
closed Sunday – **Meals** - Thai rest. - 23/36.
◆ Elegant décor, with parquet floor, cane furniture, linen tablecloths, and an attractive teak terrace. Tasty, carefully prepared Thai cuisine.

XX **L'Écume des Mers,** 10 r. Pas ✉ 59800 ✆ 03 20 54 95 40, *aproye@nordnet.com, Fax 03 20 54 96 66* – ▤. AE ⓓ GB JCB EY n
closed Sunday dinner – **Meals** - Seafood - 20 and a la carte 28/45 ♀.
◆ The "Seaspray" is a vast and busy brasserie with a cheerful atmosphere, seafood menu changed daily, fine display of oysters plus some meat dishes for the really incorrigible.

XX **Brasserie de la Paix,** 25 pl. Rihour ✆ 03 20 54 70 41, *contact@brasserielapaix.com, Fax 03 20 40 15 52* – ▤. AE GB
Meals 16 (lunch)/24 ♀.
◆ With its ceramics, wainscoting, and ranks of tables and benches, this is an attractive brasserie only a few steps from the Tourist Office in the Palais Rihour.

X **Coquille,** 60 r. St-Étienne ✉ 59800 ✆ 03 20 54 29 82, *dadeleval@nordet.fr, Fax 03 20 54 29 82* – GB EY e
closed 1 to 15 August, Saturday lunch and Sunday – **Meals** (booking essential) 29 ♀.
◆ This 18C building has a striking brick façade. The interior is a harmonious combination of old beams, venerable walls and contemporary décor.

X **Alcide,** 5 r. Débris St-Étienne ✉ 59800 ✆ 03 20 12 06 95, *bigarade@easynet.fr, Fax 03 20 55 93 83* – ▤. AE ⓓ GB EY l
Meals 20/38.
◆ Founded in 1830 in a lane by the famous Grand'Place, this brasserie has kept its original atmosphere - benches, tight rows of tables, old panelling, and varied cuisine.

at Marcq-en-Barœul – *pop. 37 177 alt. 15* – ✉ *59700* :

🏨 **Sofitel,** av. Marne, by N 350 : 5 km ✆ 03 28 33 12 12, *h1099@accor-hotels.com, Fax 03 28 33 12 24* – ▮, ⇋ rm, ▤ TV ✆ P – 15 - 150. AE ⓓ GB
L'Europe ✆ 03 28 33 12 68 *(closed 17 July to 22 August, Saturday lunch and Sunday dinner)* **Meals** 22 ♀ – ☕ 18 – **125 rm** 189/199.
◆ Close to a motorway junction, this 1970s establishment is surrounded by greenery. Attractive refurbished rooms, comfortable lounge and pleasant piano bar. Brasserie Europe with a slate displaying dishes of the day, plus a traditional menu and oyster bar.

XXX **Septentrion,** parc du Château Vert Bois, by N 17 : 9 km ✆ 03 20 46 26 98, *leseptentrion@nordnet.fr, Fax 03 20 46 38 33,* 🏠, – P. AE GB
closed 19 July-14 August, 17 to 24 February, Monday, dinner Tuesday, Wednesday, and Thursday – **Meals** 23 b.i. (lunch), 30/60 and a la carte 48/64 ♀.
◆ Part of the Chateau du Vert-Bois and the Prouvost-Septentrion Foundation, this restaurant has a comfortable dining room with an attractive view over the park.

at Lille-Lesquin airport *by A 1 : 8 km – ✉ 59810 Lesquin :*

Mercure Aéroport, ✆ 03 20 87 46 46, *h1098@accor-hotels.com, Fax 03 20 87 46 47,* – rm, – 900. AE GB JCB
La Flamme **: Meals** 23b.i./36b.i. ♀ – ☕ 11 – **215 rm** 86/102.
◆ Imposing modern building opposite the airport. Spacious and very comfortable rooms, gradually being refurbished ; avoid those facing the motorway. Congenial atmosphere, traditional cuisine and excellent choice of meat dishes in the Flamme.

Suitehotel without rest, impasse Jean Jaurès ✆ 03 28 54 24 24, *h2855@accor-hotels.com, Fax 03 28 54 24 99,* – kitchenette, rm, AE GB HT u
☕ 12 – **73 rm** 77.
◆ One of a new generation of hotels with emphasis on space and autonomy : rooms (30 sq m) with an office/sitting area and kitchen ; business area and ready-made meals available.

Novotel Aéroport, 55 route de Douai ✆ 03 20 62 53 53, *h0427@accor-hotels.com, Fax 03 20 97 36 12,* – rm, – 25 - 200. AE GB JCB
Meals 24/29 ♀ – ☕ 11 – **92 rm** 91/93.
◆ This low structure was the first to be built (1967) by the company. Functional rooms refurbished in the style of more recent Novotels. Modern dining room with summer terrace overlooking the greenery. Usual Novotel menu.

Béthune *62400 P.-de-C.* 301 *I4 – pop. 27 808 alt. 34.*

Tourist Office Le Beffroi Gd Place ✆ 03 21 57 25 47, Fax 03 21 57 01 60.
Lille 39.

Meurin and Résidence Kitchener with rm, 15 pl. République ✆ 03 21 68 88 88, *marc.meurin@le-meurin.fr, Fax 03 21 68 88 89,* – kitchenette, rest, AE GB JCB
closed 12 to 18 April, 2 to 22 August, 2 to 10 January, Tuesday lunch, Sunday dinner and Monday – **Meals** 35 (lunch), 52/105 and a la carte 85/120 ♀ – ☕ 13 – **7 rm** 80/150.
◆ Lovely early 20C Flemish residence. Delightful dining rooms and terrace conservatory in Belle Epoque style. Inventive cuisine. Individually styled rooms.
Spec. Anguille sur toast au vert, beurre de krieck. Bar en salade de cèpes. Ris de veau, crème d'oignon brulé, rapures de truffe.

LYONS (LYON) *69000 Rhône* 327 *I5 – pop. 445 452 alt. 175.*

See : *Site★★★ (panorama★★ from Fourvière) – Fourvière hill : Notre-Dame Basilica* EX, *Museum of Gallo-Roman Civilization★★ (Claudian tablet★★★)* EY **M**[3], *Roman ruins* EY *– Old Lyons★★★ : Rue St-Jean★* FX, *St-Jean Cathedral★* FY, *Hôtel de Gadagne★ (Lyons Historical Museum★ and International Marionette Museum★)* EX **M**[1] *– Guignol de Lyon* FX **N** *– Central Lyons (Peninsula) : to the North, Place Bellecour* FY, *Hospital Museum (pharmacy★)* FY **M**[8], *Museum of Printing and Banking★★* FX **M**[6], *– Place des Terreaux* FX, *Hôtel de Ville* FX, *Palais St-Pierre, Fine Arts Museum (Beaux-Arts)★★* FX **M**[4] *– to the South, St-Martin-d'Ainay Basilica (capitals★)* FY, *Weaving and Textile Museum★★★* FY **M**[2], *Decorative Arts Museum★★* FY **M**[5] *– La Croix-Rousse : Silkweavers' House* FV **M**[11], *Trois Gaules Amphitheatre* FV **E** *– Tête d'Or Park★* GHV *– Guimet Museum of Natural History★★* GV **M**[7] *– Historical Information Centre on the Resistance and the Deportation★* FZ **M**[9].

Envir. : *Rochetaillée : Henri Malartre Car Museum★★, 12 km to the North.*

Verger-Lyon at St-Symphorien-d'Ozon ✆ 04 78 02 84 20, S : 14 km ; Lyon-Chassieu at Chassieu ✆ 04 78 90 84 77, E : 12 km by D 29 ; Salvagny (private) at the Tour of Salvagny ✆ 04 78 48 88 48 ; ; junction Lyon-Ouest : 8 km ; Golf Club of Lyon at Villette-d'Anthon ✆ 04 78 31 11 33.

of Lyon-Saint-Exupery ✆ 04 72 22 72 21 to the E : 27 km.

✆ 08 36 35 35 35.

Tourist Office pl. Bellecour ✆ 04 72 77 69 69, Fax 04 78 42 04 32, info@lyon-france.com.
Paris 462 – Geneva 151 – Grenoble 105 – Marseilles 313 – St-Étienne 60 – Turin 300.

Hotels

Town Centre (Bellecour-Terreaux) :

Sofitel, 20 quai Gailleton ✉ 69002 ✆ 04 72 41 20 20, *h0553@accor-hotels.com, Fax 04 72 40 05 50,* ← – rm, – 15 - 200. AE GB JCB FY p
Les Trois Dômes (8th floor) ✆ 04 72 41 20 97 *(closed 24 July to 23 August, 19 to 28 February, Sunday and Monday)* **Meals** 48(lunch), 63/114b.i. – ***Sofishop*** (ground floor) ✆ *04 72 41 20 80* **Meals** 29/41 b.i. ♀ – ☕ 24 – **137 rm** 277/310, 29 suites.
◆ The somewhat austere cubic exterior of this establishment contrasts with its luxurious interior. Ask for one of the refurbished rooms with their mahogany or light-wood furnishings. Panoramic view over the whole of Lyon from the Trois Dômes. Sofishop brasserie.

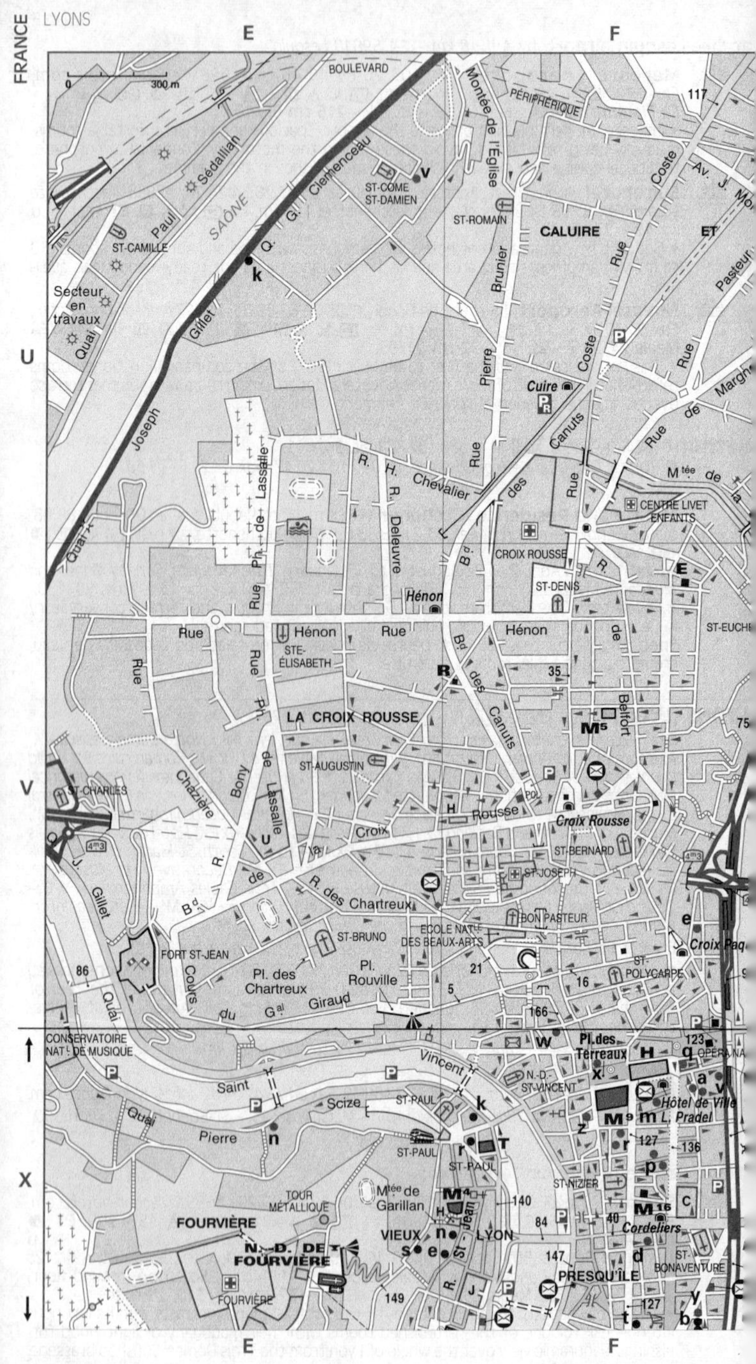
E
F
0
300 m
BOULEVARD
PÉRIPHÉRIQUE
Montée de l'Église
SAÔNE
Quai Paul Sédallian
Q. G. Clemenceau
ST-COME ST-DAMIEN
ST-ROMAIN
CALUIRE
ST-CAMILLE
Secteur en travaux
Quai Joseph Gillet
Rue Pierre Brunier
Rue Coste
Av. J. Monod
Rue Pasteur
Cuire
Rue des Canuts
Rue de Margnolles
CENTRE LIVET ENFANTS
R. H. Chevalier
R. Deleuvre
Rue Ph. de Lassalle
CROIX ROUSSE
ST-DENIS
Hénon
Rue Hénon
ST-ÉLISABETH
Bd des Canuts
R. de Belfort
ST-EUCHER
LA CROIX ROUSSE
ST-AUGUSTIN
Rue Chazière
R. Bony
ST-CHARLES
Croix Rousse
ST-BERNARD
ST-JOSEPH
R. des Chartreux
Bd de la Croix Rousse
BON PASTEUR
ÉCOLE NATLE DES BEAUX-ARTS
ST-BRUNO
FORT ST-JEAN
Pl. des Chartreux
Pl. Rouville
Cours du Gal Giraud
ST-POLYCARPE
Croix Paquet
CONSERVATOIRE NATL DE MUSIQUE
Quai Saint Vincent
Quai Pierre Scize
ST-PAUL
Pl. des Terreaux
OPÉRA NAT.
N.-D. ST-VINCENT
Hôtel de Ville L. Pradel
ST-NIZIER
TOUR MÉTALLIQUE
Mtée de Garillan
FOURVIÈRE
N.-D. DE FOURVIÈRE
VIEUX LYON
R. St-Jean
Cordeliers
PRESQU'ÎLE
ST-BONAVENTURE
U
V
X

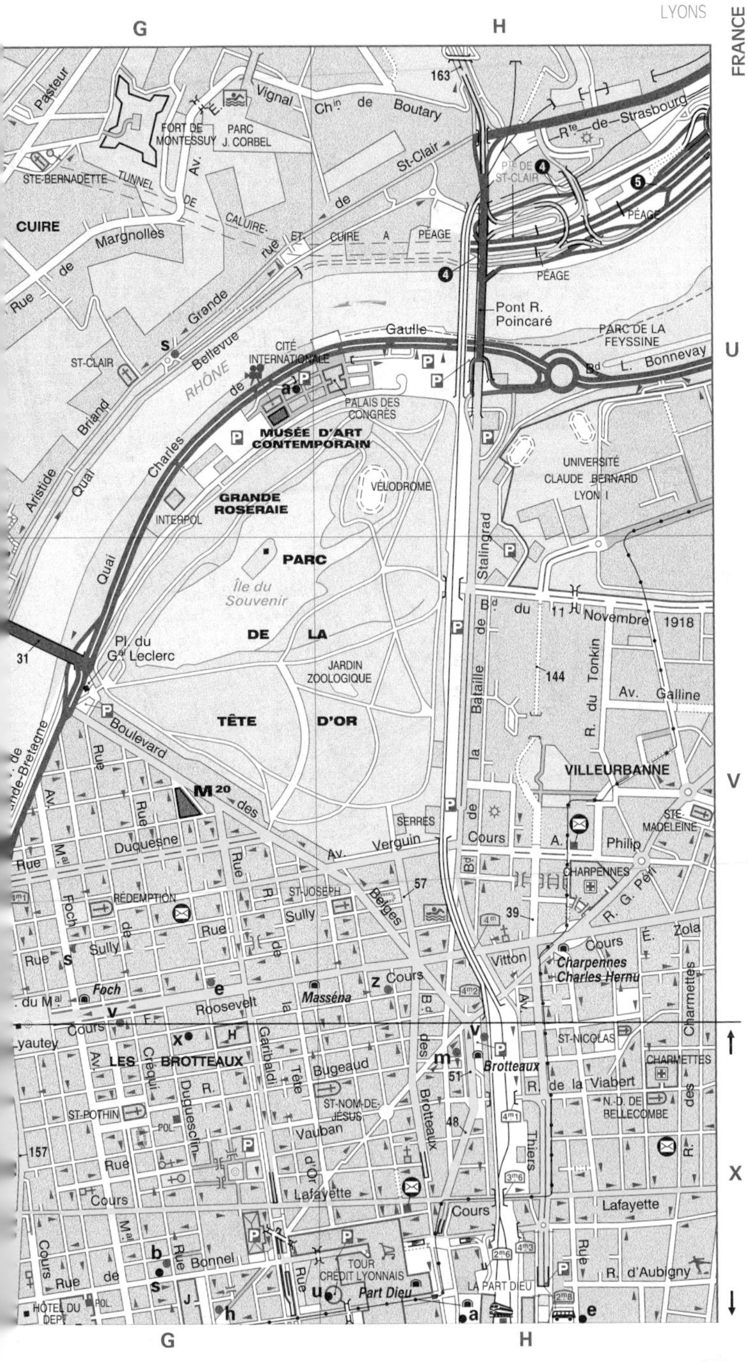
G
H
U
V
X
Pasteur
FORT DE MONTESSUY
PARC J. CORBEL
Vignal
Chin de Boutary
Rte de Strasbourg
CUIRE
STE-BERNADETTE
TUNNEL DE CALUIRE ET CUIRE A PÉAGE
Rue de Margnolles
Grande rue de St-Clair
PÉAGE
Pont R. Poincaré
PARC DE LA FEYSSINE
Bd L. Bonnevay
ST-CLAIR
RHÔNE
Quai Aristide Briand
Quai Charles de Gaulle
CITÉ INTERNATIONALE
PALAIS DES CONGRÈS
MUSÉE D'ART CONTEMPORAIN
VÉLODROME
UNIVERSITÉ CLAUDE BERNARD LYON I
GRANDE ROSERAIE
INTERPOL
PARC DE LA TÊTE D'OR
Île du Souvenir
Stalingrad
Bd du 11 Novembre 1918
Pl. du Gal Leclerc
JARDIN ZOOLOGIQUE
Bd de la Bataille de Stalingrad
R. du Tonkin
Av. Galline
VILLEURBANNE
Boulevard des Belges
SERRES
Av. Verguin
Cours A. Philip
CHARPENNES
R. G. Péri
Cours É. Zola
Cours Vitton
Charpennes Charles Hernu
Rue Duquesne
Rue Sully
RÉDEMPTION
ST-JOSEPH
Foch
Masséna
Cours Roosevelt
Cours Lyautey
LES BROTTEAUX
Av. Créqui
R. Duguesclin
Garibaldi
Rue Tête d'Or
Rue Bugeaud
Bd des Brotteaux
Brotteaux
ST-NICOLAS
CHARMETTES
R. de la Viabert
N.D. DE BELLECOMBE
R. des Charmettes
ST-POTHIN
ST-NOM-DE-JÉSUS
Vauban
Thiers
Cours Lafayette
Rue Bonnel
TOUR CRÉDIT LYONNAIS
Part Dieu
LA PART DIEU
R. d'Aubigny
HÔTEL DU DÉPT
Cours de la Liberté
Rue de

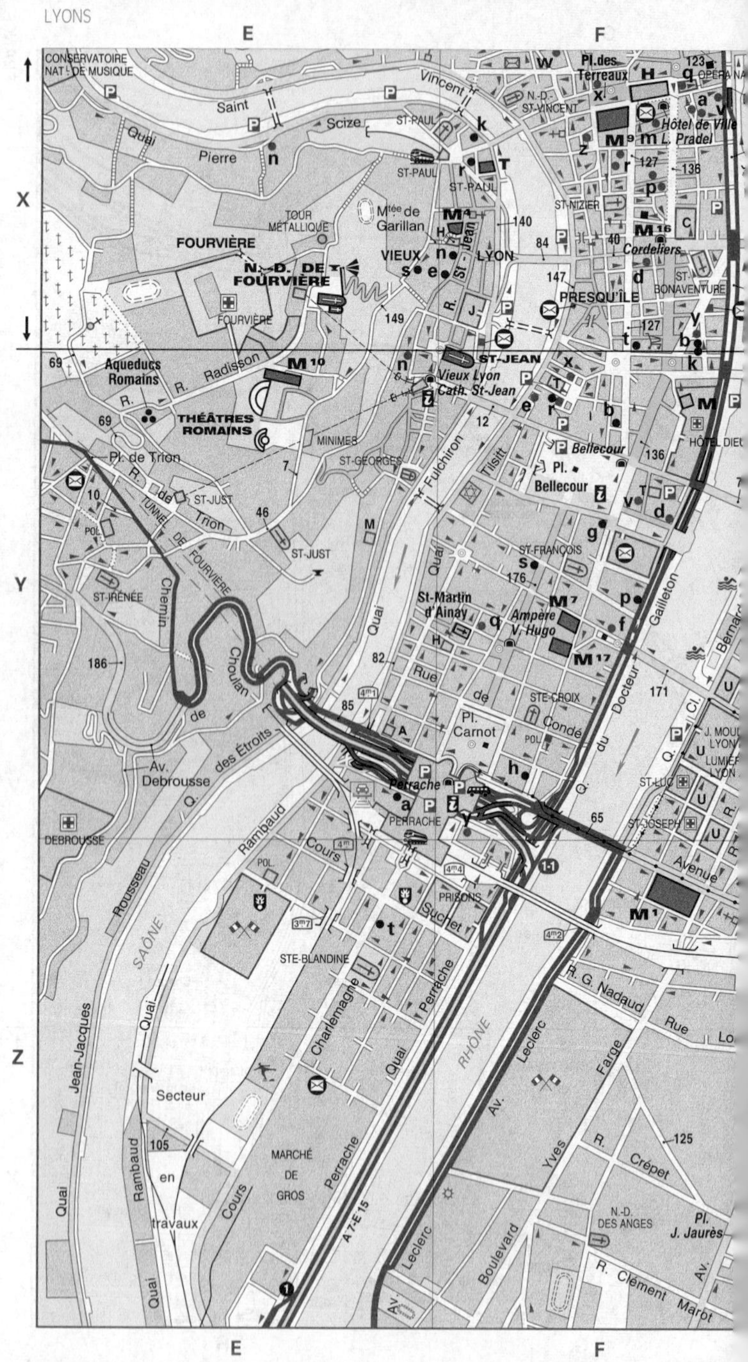

E
F
X
Y
Z
CONSERVATOIRE NATL DE MUSIQUE
Quai
Saint
Pierre
Scize
Vincent
ST-PAUL
N.-D. ST-VINCENT
Pl. des Terreaux
Hôtel de Ville
L. Pradel
OPÉRA
TOUR MÉTALLIQUE
Mtée de Garillan
FOURVIÈRE
N.-D. DE FOURVIÈRE
VIEUX LYON
R. St-Jean
ST-NIZIER
Cordeliers
PRESQU'ÎLE
ST-BONAVENTURE
ST-JEAN
Vieux Lyon Cath. St-Jean
Aqueducs Romains
R. Radisson
THÉÂTRES ROMAINS
MINIMES
ST-GEORGES
Pl. de Trion
R. de Trion
ST-JUST
TUNNEL DE FOURVIÈRE
Chemin de Choulan
ST-IRÉNÉE
Quai Fulchiron
Tilsitt
Bellecour
Pl. Bellecour
HÔTEL DIEU
ST-FRANÇOIS
St-Martin d'Ainay
Ampère V. Hugo
Rue de Condé
STE-CROIX
Pl. Carnot
Quai du Docteur Gailleton
J. MOULIN LYON
LUMIÈRE LYON
ST-LUC
ST-JOSEPH
Av. Debrousse
Q. des Étroits
Perrache
PERRACHE
DEBROUSSE
Rambaud
Cours Suchet
PRISONS
Avenue
STE-BLANDINE
Charlemagne
Quai Perrache
SAÔNE
RHÔNE
R. G. Nadaud
Rue
Quai Jean-Jacques Rousseau
Quai Rambaud
Secteur en travaux
MARCHÉ DE GROS
Cours
Perrache
A7-E15
Av. Leclerc
Yves Farge
R. Crépet
N.-D. DES ANGES
Pl. J. Jaurès
Boulevard
R. Clément Marot
Leclerc

STREET INDEX TO LYON TOWN PLAN

CALUIRE ET CUIRE

Boucle (Montée de la) FU
Boutary (Ch. de) HU
Briand (Cours A.) GUV
Brunier (R. P. FU
Canuts (Bd des) FUV
Chevalier (R. H.) EFU
Clemenceau (Quai G.) EU
Coste (Rue) FU
Église (Montée de l') FU
Margnolles (R. de) FGU
Monnet (Av. J.) FU
Pasteur (R.) FGU
Peissel (R. F.) FU 117
St-Clair (Grande R. de) GHU
Soldats (Montée des) HU 163
Strasbourg (Rte de) CP
Vignal (Av. E.) GU

LA MULATIÈRE

Rousseau (Quai J.-J.) ZE

LYON

Annonciade (R. de l') FV 5
Antiquaille (R. de l') EY 7
Aubigny (R. d') HX
Barret (R. Croix) GZ
Basses-Vercheres (R. des) EY 10
Bataille de Stalingrad (Bd de la) HUV
Béchevelin (R.) GY
Belfort (R. de) FV
Belges (Bd des) GHV
Bellecour (Place) FY
Bellevue (Quai) GU
Berliet (R. M.) HZ
Bernard (Quai Cl.) FY
Bert (R. P.) GHY
Berthelot (Av.) GHZ
Bloch (R. M.) GZ
Bonaparte (Pont) FY 12
Bonnel (R. de) GX
Bony (R.) EV
Boucle (Montée de la) FU
Brotteaux (Bd des) HVX
Bugeaud (R.) HX
Burdeau (Rue) FV 16
Canuts (Bd des) FUV
Carmélites (Montée des) FV 21
Carnot (Pl.) FY
Charlemagne (Cours) EZ
Charmettes (R. des) HVX
Chartreux (Pl. des) EV
Chartreux (R. des) EV
Chazière (Rue) EV
Chevalier (R. H.) EFU
Chevreul (Rue) GYZ
Choulans (Chin de) EY
Churchill (Pt W.) GV 31
Condé (R. de) FY
Courmont (Quai J.) FX 33
Crepet (Rue) FZ
Créqui (R. de) GVY
Croix-Rousse (Bd de la) EFV
Croix-Rousse (Grande R. de la) FV 35
Debrousse (Av.) EY
Deleuvre (R.) EUV
Dr-Gailleton (Quai) FY
Duguesclin (Rue) GVY
Duquesne (Rue) GV
Epargne (R. de l') HZ 41
Etroits (Quai des) EY
Farge (Bd Y.) FZ
Farges (R. des) EY 46
Faure (Av. F.) GHY
Favre (Bd J.) HX 48
Ferry (Pl. J.) HX 51
Flandin (R. M.) HXY
France (Bd A.) HV 57
Frères Lumière (Av. des) HZ
Fulchiron (Quai) EY
Gallieni (Pont) FY 65
Gambetta (Cours) GHY
Garibaldi (Rue) GVZ
Garillan (Montée de) EFX
Gaulle (Q. Ch. de) GHU
Gerland (R. de) GZ
Gerlier (R. Cardinal) EY 69
Gillet (Quai J.) EUV
Giraud (Cours Gén.) EV
Grande-Bretagne (Av. de) GV
Grenette (Rue) FX 71
Guillotière (Grande R. de la) GYZ
Guillotière (Pt de la) FY 73
Hénon (Rue) EFV
Herbouville (Cours d') FV 75
Jaurès (Av. J.) GY
Joffre (Quai Mar.) EY 82
Juin (Pt Alphonse) FX 84
Jutard (Pl. A.) GY
Koening (Pt Gén.) EV 86
La Fayette (Cours) GHX
La Fayette (Pont) GX 88
La Part Dieu HXY
Lassagne (Quai A.) FV 93
Lassalle (R. Ph. de) EUV
Lattre-de-Tassigny (Pt de) FV 94
Leclerc (Av.) EFZ
Leclerc (Pl. Gén.) GV
Liberté (Cours de la) GXY
Lortet (Rue) FZ
Lyautey (Pl. Mar.) GVX
Marchand (Pt Kitchener) EY 95
Marius Vivier Merle (Bd) HY 101
Marseille (R. de) GY
Montrochet (R. P.) EZ 105
Morand (Pont) FVX 107
Moulin (Quai J.) FX 109
Nadaud (R. G.) FZ
Perrache (Quai) EZ
Pompidou (Av. G.) HY
Pradel (Pl. L.) FX 123
Pré Gaudry (Rue) FZ 125
Prés. Herriot (R. du) FX 127
Radisson (R. R.) EY
Rambaud (Quai) EYZ
Repos (R. du) GZ 131
République (R. de la) FXY 136
Rolland (Quai R.) FX 140
Roosevelt (Cours F.) GVX
St-Antoine (Quai) FX 147
St-Barthélemy (Montée) EX 149
St-Jean (Rue) FX
St-Vincent (Quai) EFX
Sarrail (Quai Gén.) GX 157
Saxe (Av. Mar. de) GXY
Scize (Quai P.) EX
Sedallian (Quai P.) EU
Serbie (Quai de) GV
Servient (R.) GY
Stalingrad (Pl. de) GHY
Suchet (Cours) EFZ
Sully (Rue) GV
Tchécoslovaques (Bd des) HZ
Terme (Rue) FV 166
Terreaux (Pl. des) FX
Tête d'Or (Rue) GVX
Thiers (Av.) HVX
Tilsitt (Quai) FY
Trion (Pl. de) EY
Trion (R. de) EY
Université (Pont de l') FY 171
Université (R. de l') GY 172
Vauban (Rue) GHX
Verguin (Av.) HV
Viabert (R. de la) HX
Victor-Hugo (Rue) FY 176
Vienne (Rte de) GZ
Villette (R. de la) HY 178
Villon (Rue) HZ
Vitton (Cours) HV
Vivier (R. du) GZ 180
Wilson (Pont) FY 182
1re Div. Fr. Libre (Av.) EY 186

VILLEURBANNE

Bataille de Stalingrad (Bd de la) HUV
Bonnevay (Bd L.) HU
Charmettes (R. dezs) HVX
Dutrievoz (Av. A.) HV 39
Galline (Av.) HV
Péri (R. G.) HV
Philip (Cours A.) HV
Poincaré (Pt R.) HU
Rossellini (Av. R.) HV 144
Tonkin (R. du) HV
Zola (Crs É.) HV
11-Novembre-1918 (Bd du) HV

Sofitel Royal without rest, 20 pl. Bellecour ✉ 69002 ☎ 04 78 37 57 31, *h2952@accor-hotels.com, Fax 04 78 37 01 36* – |♦|, ⇹ rm, ▤ TV ✆. AE ⓞ GB JCB FY g
☕ 17 – **80 rm** 150/342.
• 19C building facing the most famous square in Lyon. Little "Clipper" rooms featuring brass and mahogany, larger rooms either functional or in Louis XV style.

Carlton without rest, 4 r. Jussieu ✉ 69002 ☎ 04 78 42 56 51, *h2950@accor-hotels.com, Fax 04 78 42 10 71* – |♦|, ⇹ rm, ▤ TV ✆. AE ⓞ GB JCB FX b
☕ 12 – **83 rm** 117/138.
• Purple and gold are a feature of this traditional hotel styled like a retro town mansion. The venerable lift cage has a certain charm too.

Mercure Plaza République without rest, 5 r. Stella ✉ 69002 ☎ 04 78 37 50 50, *h2951-gm@accor-hotels.com, Fax 04 78 42 33 34* – |♦|, ⇹ rm, ▤ TV ✆ ♿ – 🏛 20 - 35. AE ⓞ GB JCB FY k
☕ 12 – **78 rm** 123/148.
• A grotesque face sits atop each window of this 19C building whose external appearance is in surprising contrast to the resolutely contemporary interior.

Globe et Cécil without rest, 21 r. Gasparin 69002 04 78 42 58 95, *globe.et.cecil@wanadoo.fr, Fax 04 72 41 99 06* – 25. FY b
60 rm 115/135.
◆ The old 19C walls of this building conceal an establishment of great character. Individual rooms, furniture collected from antique dealers and a panelled breakfast room.

Beaux-Arts without rest, 75 r. Prés. E. Herriot 69002 04 78 38 09 50, *h2949@accor-hotels.com, Fax 04 78 42 19 19* – rm, – 15. FX t
12 – **75 rm** 135/142.
◆ Fine building of 1900 with rooms mostly furnished in Art Deco style, though four of them have been decorated by contemporary artists.

Grand Hôtel des Terreaux without rest, 16 r. Lanterne 69001 04 78 37 48 04, *ght@hotel-lyon.fr, Fax 04 78 37 79 75*, –
8,50 – **54 rm** 72,50/125.
◆ A dignified façade gives little hint of the recently refurbished interior, with its colourful fabrics and furniture in various styles. Covered pool for relaxation.

Résidence without rest, 18 r. V. Hugo 69002 04 78 42 63 28, *hotel-la-residence@wanadoo.fr, Fax 04 78 42 85 76* – FY s
6,50 - **67** rm 68.
◆ Establishment located in a traffic-free street close to Place Bellecour. Foyer and rooms in 1970s style, brighter, fresher decor in those recently refurbished.

Perrache :

Grand Hôtel Mercure Château Perrache, 12 cours Verdun 69002 04 72 77 15 00, *h1292@accor-hotels.com, Fax 04 78 37 06 56* – rm, – 20 - 200. EY a
Les Belles Saisons *(closed Saturday lunch)* **Meals** 23,50/33 and a la carte 38/43 –
13,50 – **111 rm** 96/188.
◆ The old PLM railway hotel has kept some of its Art Nouveau features, including the panelling in the foyer. Some rooms with original furnishings. Carved woodwork and frescoes in the superb Belles Saisons restaurant.

Charlemagne, 23 cours Charlemagne 69002 04 72 77 70 00, *charlemagne@hotel-lyon.fr, Fax 04 78 42 94 84*, – – 15 - 120. EZ t
Meals *(closed 2 to 24 August, 20 December-3 January, Saturday and Sunday)* 18 – 9 – **116 rm** 86/110.
◆ Two buildings separated by a courtyard. The rooms in the second building are more spacious and attractive. Breakfast room in the style of a winter garden. Modern décor in the restaurant, plus a pleasant terrace and traditional, unpretentious cuisine.

Ibis Perrache without rest, 28 cours de Verdun 69002 04 78 37 56 55, *h2751@accor-hotels.com, Fax 04 78 37 02 58* – rm, – 40.
6,50 – **121 rm** 70/85. FEY 20
◆ Recently refurbished 1920s edifice just a few steps from the historic centre of Lyon. A marble staircase lit by stained-glass windows leads to well-equipped rooms.

Vieux-Lyon :

Villa Florentine , 25 montée St-Barthélémy 69005 04 72 56 56 56, *florentine@relaischateaux.com, Fax 04 72 40 90 56*, Lyon, , , , – – 15. EFX s
Les Terrasses de Lyon (limited lunch menu, except Sunday) **Meals** 38(lunch), 70/110 and a la carte 85/145 – 30 – **20 rm** 335/500, 8 suites.
◆ This old hilltop convent with its Renaissance appearance is more than a match for the most sumptuous Tuscan villa. Refined, beautifully lit rooms. Idyllic surroundings, superb view of the city, plus contemporary cuisine in the Terrasses de Lyon.
Spec. Homard à la broche et nem de jarret de veau. Saint-Pierre entier cuit vapeur, jus de romarin. Couronne d'agneau clouté aux anchois marinés. **Wines** Vin du Bugey, Saint-Joseph.

Cour des Loges , 6 r. Boeuf 69005 04 72 77 44 44, *contact@courdesloges.com, Fax 04 72 40 93 61*, , – – 15 - 50. FX n
Les Loges : **Meals** 35 (lunch) and a la carte 50/64 – 22 – **52 rm** 220/460, 4 suites.
◆ Contemporary artists and designers have created the striking decor of this group of 15C and 17C buildings laid out around a superb galleried courtyard. Inventive, personalised cuisine in the Aux Loges restaurant.

Tour Rose , 22 r. Bœuf 69005 04 78 92 69 10, *latourrose@free.fr, Fax 04 78 42 26 02* – – 25. EFX e
Meals *(closed lunch in August and Sunday)* 53/106 – 18 – **12 rm** 250/355.
◆ A group of houses typical of Old Lyon, with stair tower and terraced gardens. Wonderful rooms decorated by the city's foremost silk specialists. Lovely glass roof at the foot of the pink tower and a luxurious dining room offering creative and spicy cuisine.

Phénix Hôtel without rest, 7 quai Bondy ✉ 69005 ☎ 04 78 28 24 24, *phenix-hotel@wanadoo.fr, Fax 04 78 28 62 86* – |♦|, ▤ TV ☎ ♿ 🚗 – 🧑‍🏫 30. AE ⓓ GB JCB FX k
☕ 10 – **36 rm** 125/155.
◆ Venerable edifice on the banks of the Saône. Spacious rooms with contemporary décor, some with open fireplace. Attractive breakfast room beneath a glass roof.

Collège without rest, 5 pl. St Paul ✉ 69005 ☎ 04 72 10 05 05, *contact@college-hotel.com, Fax 04 78 27 98 84* – |♦|, ⇔ rm, ▤ TV ☎ ♿ – 🧑‍🏫 20. AE ⓓ GB JCB
☕ 11 – **39 rm** 105/130.
◆ The Collège Hôtel is a quite extraordinary concept, with its school desks, pommel horse and geographical maps recreating the feel of schooling in bygone days.

La Croix-Rousse (bank of the River Saône) :

Lyon Métropole, 85 quai J. Gillet ✉ 69004 ☎ 04 72 10 44 44, *metropole@lyonmetropole_concorde.com, Fax 04 72 10 44 42,* ⛱, 🏊, 🎾 – |♦| ▤ TV ☎ ♿ 🚗 P – 🧑‍🏫 15 - 300. AE ⓓ GB JCB EU k
closed 24 December-3 January – ***Brasserie Lyon Plage :*** Meals 32 ♀ – ☕ 23 – **118 rm** 250.
◆ The yellow and white colour scheme of this 1980s establishment is reflected in the water of the Olympic pool. Sports hotel (tennis and squash courts) with refurbished rooms. Lyon Plage Brasserie with maritime decor and a terrace overlooking the water.

Les Brotteaux :

Hilton, 70 quai Ch. de Gaulle ✉ 69006 ☎ 04 78 17 50 50, *rm-lyon@hilton.com, Fax 04 78 17 52 52,* ⛱, 🏋 – |♦|, ⇔ rm, ▤ TV ☎ ♿ 🚗 – 🧑‍🏫 15 - 400. AE ⓓ GB JCB GU a
Blue Elephant ☎ 04 78 17 50 00 *(closed 20 July-20 August, Saturday lunch and Sunday)* Meals 27(lunch), 40/55 ♀ – ***Brasserie Belge*** ☎ 04 78 17 51 00 **Meals** 23b.i.(lunch) and a la carte 34/45 🍷 – ☕ 24 – **194 rm** 230/400, 5 suites.
◆ The Cité International includes this hotel as well as convention centre, casino, and modern art museum. Spacious rooms facing the Parc de la Tête d'Or or the Rhône. Thai cuisine in the Blue Elephant. Specialities from the Low Countries in the Brasserie Belge.

Roosevelt without rest, 48 r. Sèze ✉ 69006 ☎ 04 78 52 35 67, *hotel.roosevelt@wanadoo.fr, Fax 04 78 52 39 82* – |♦|, ⇔ rm, ▤ TV ☎ ♿ 🚗 P – 🧑‍🏫 15 - 40. AE ⓓ GB GX x
☕ 10 – **48 rm** 107/126.
◆ This establishment offers an attractive lounge/library as well as comfortable, contemporary style rooms - smaller at the front. Black and white photographs on the walls.

Patio Morand without rest, 99 r. Créqui ✉ 69006 ☎ 04 78 52 62 62, *accueil@hotel-morand.fr, Fax 04 78 24 87 88* – ⇔ rm, TV. AE ⓓ GB JCB GVX p
☕ 8,50 – **31 rm** 62/80.
◆ This small hotel close to the Opera offers rooms with varied decor. The quieter ones overlook the colourful, attractively planted patio where breakfast is served.

La Part-Dieu :

Méridien Part-Dieu 🐎, 129 r. Servient (32nd floor) ✉ 69003 ☎ 04 78 63 55 00, *info@lemeridien-lyon.com, Fax 04 78 63 55 20,* ≤ Lyons and Rhône Valley – |♦|, ⇔ rm, ▤ TV ☎ 🚗 – 🧑‍🏫 15 - 110. AE ⓓ GB JCB GX u
L'Arc-en-Ciel *(closed 15 July-25 August, Saturday lunch and Sunday)* **Meals** 36/53 b.i. 🏵 – ***Bistrot de la Tour*** (ground floor) *(closed Friday dinner, Sunday lunch and Saturday)* Meals 17,50/19 ♀ – ☕ 18 – **245 rm** 260/315.
◆ From the top (100m plus) of the tall tower known as "The Pencil" there is a panoramic view. Interior inspired by the traditional architecture of Lyon. Internal courtyard, galleries. From the Arc-en-Ciel on the 32nd floor the whole city is at your feet.

Novotel La Part-Dieu, 47 bd Vivier-Merle ✉ 69003 ☎ 04 72 13 51 51, *h0735@accor-hotels.com, Fax 04 72 13 51 99* – |♦|, ⇔ rm, ▤ TV ☎ ♿ 🚗 – 🧑‍🏫 15 - 70. AE ⓓ GB JCB HX a
Meals 19 ♀ – ☕ 11 – **124 rm** 117/139.
◆ Vast lounge/bar with internet facilities. Rooms are up to the Novotel group's current standards. Useful accommodation close to the station. The restaurant is popular with business people inbetween meetings or while awaiting a train.

Créqui Part-Dieu without rest, 37 r. Bonnel ✉ 69003 ☎ 04 78 60 20 47, *infosa@hotel-crequi.com, Fax 04 78 62 21 12* – |♦|, ⇔ rm, ▤ TV ☎ ♿ – 🧑‍🏫 30. AE ⓓ GB GX s
☕ 10 – **46 rm** 100/120, 3 suites.
◆ This establishment is located opposite the law courts. Room decor inspired by the fabrics and colours of Provence, though a new wing is in a more contemporary style.

Ibis La Part-Dieu Gare, pl. Renaudel ✉ 69003 ☎ 04 78 95 42 11, *h0618@accor-hotels.com, Fax 04 78 60 42 85,* ⛱ – |♦|, ⇔ rm, ▤ TV ☎ ♿ 🚗 – 🧑‍🏫 20. AE ⓓ GB HY k
Meals 17,80 ♀ – ☕ 6 – **144 rm** 82.
◆ Plain modern building close to the Part-Dieu railway station. Rooms in the current Ibis style with attractive pastel-coloured fabrics. Bistro-style dining room, conservatory and terrace to the rear overlooking a little square.

La Guillotière :

Libertel Wilson without rest, 6 r. Mazenod ✉ 69003 ☎ 04 78 60 94 94, *h2780@accor-hotels.com, Fax 04 78 62 72 01* – rm, AE GB JCB
12 – **54 rm** 111/130.
◆ Contemporary furnishings in Art Deco style and the bright fabrics to be expected in the capital of silk give the rooms of this recent riverside hotel their special character.

Gerland :

Novotel Gerland, 70 av. Leclerc ✉ 69007 ☎ 04 72 71 11 11, *h0736@accor-hotels.com, Fax 04 72 71 11 00,* – rm, – 90 - 150. AE GB
Meals 25 – 11 – **187 rm** 136/155.
◆ Modern building close to the Halle Tony-Garnier and the football stadium. Recently refurbished interior to current Novotel standards. The restaurant menu is in keeping with the chain's typical culinary format.

Montchat-Monplaisir :

Mercure Lumière, 69 cours A. Thomas ☎ 04 78 53 76 76, *h1535@accor-hotels.com, Fax 04 72 36 97 65* – rm, – 25 - 50. AE GB JCB
Meals *(closed Sunday lunch, Saturday and Bank Holidays)* 18/24 – 12 – **78 rm** 140/150.
◆ This hotel built where the Lumière brothers' invented cinematography more than 100 years ago celebrates their achievement with a contemporary-style restaurant adorned with images from the silver screen.

at Bron – *pop. 37 369 alt. 204* – ✉ *69500* :

Novotel Bron, av. J. Monnet ☎ 04 72 15 65 65, *h0436@accor-hotels.com, Fax 04 72 15 09 09,* – rm, – 15 - 500. AE GB
Meals 21,50 – 11 – **190 rm** 130/138.
◆ Between the A 43 motorway and the N 6 main road, a useful place to break your journey. Reasonably spacious rooms, good facilities for meetings, garden, pool. Restaurant up to the usual Novotel standard, conveniently located just outside Lyon.

Restaurants

Paul Bocuse, bridge of Collonges N : 12 km by the banks of River Saône (D 433, D 51 ✉ 69660 *Collonges-au-Mont-d'Or* ☎ 04 72 42 90 90, *paul.bocuse@bocuse.fr, Fax 04 72 27 85 87* – AE GB JCB
Meals 109/185 and a la carte 90/150.
◆ Anyone who is anyone patronises the palatial inn of "Monsieur Paul", one of the greatest of epicureans. Historic dishes plus a wall-painting of "great chefs" in the courtyard.
Spec. Soupe aux truffes. Loup en croûte feuilletée. Volaille de Bresse. **Wines** Saint-Véran, Brouilly.

Léon de Lyon (Lacombe), 1 r. Pleney ✉ 69001 ☎ 04 72 10 11 12, *leon@relaischateaux.fr, Fax 04 72 10 11 13* – AE GB JCB FX r
closed 1 to 23 August, Sunday and Monday – **Meals** 60 (lunch), 110/150 and a la carte 93/115.
◆ The great traditions of the cuisine of Lyon live on in the dining rooms of this establishment with its wood panelling and its pictures celebrating kitchen culture. Terrific !
Spec. Cochon fermier du Cantal, foie gras et oignons confits. Quenelles de brochet sauce Nantua. Cinq petits desserts à la praline de Saint-Genix. **Wines** Saint-Véran, Chiroubles.

Pierre Orsi, 3 pl. Kléber ✉ 69006 ☎ 04 78 89 57 68, *orsi@relaischateaux.com, Fax 04 72 44 93 34,* – AE GB JCB GV e
closed Sunday and Monday except Bank Holidays – **Meals** 43 (lunch), 77/107 and a la carte 75/100.
◆ This old building houses an elegant dining room and a terrace-cum-rose garden where fine Lyon cuisine is served. Splendid 200-year-old vaulted cellar.
Spec. Ravioles de foie gras au jus de porto et truffes. Homard en carapace. Pigeonneau en cocotte aux gousses d'ail confites. **Wines** Saint-Joseph, Mâcon-Villages.

Christian Têtedoie, 54 quai Pierre Scize ✉ 69005 ☎ 04 78 29 40 10, *restaurant@tetedoie.com, Fax 04 72 07 05 65* – AE GB EX n
closed 1 to 8 May, 1 to 23 August, 21 to 27 February, Saturday lunch and Sunday – **Meals** 36,50/54 and a la carte 56/76.
◆ Behind the dignified façade an interior delicately decorated in a range of yellows. Some tables with a view of the River Saône. Contemporary cuisine. Impressive wine cellar.
Spec. Marroné lyonnais et ailes de poule faisane à l'émulsion de cèpes et châtaignes (September-December). Filet de féra braisé à l'oseille. Tête de veau confite au vin de Cornas (September-April). **Wines** Saint-Péray, Coteaux du Tricastin.

XXX ✿ **L'Auberge de Fond Rose** (Vignat), 23 quai G. Clemenceau ✉ 69300 *Caluire-et-Cuire* ☏ 04 78 29 34 61, *contact@aubergedefondrose.com, Fax 04 72 00 28 67,* ☂, ☂ – ▤ P. AE ⓓ GB EU v
closed All Saints'Day Holidays, February Holidays, Sunday dinner and Monday – **Meals** 36/63 and a la carte 68/84 ♀.
◆ 1920s residence nestling in a lovely well-shaded garden. Refurbished dining room with open fireplace and an attractive terrace. Fine classic cuisine.
Spec. Rémoulade de grenouilles et fritot d'escargot (Spring-Summer). Féra du lac Léman à la peau argentée, mijotée de courgettes et tomates (mid May-mid September). Selle d'agneau farcie aux herbes, pommes Anna. **Wines** Gigondas, Fleurie.

XXX **Mère Brazier,** 12 r. Royale ✉ 69001 ☏ 04 78 28 15 49, *Fax 04 78 28 63 63* – AE ⓓ GB FV e
closed 23 July-25 August, Saturday lunch, Sunday, Tuesday and Bank Holidays – **Meals** 31 (lunch), 46/55 and a la carte 43/65.
◆ This restaurant is a stronghold of Lyon culinary tradition, honouring the memory of the legendary Mère Brazier. A menu set in stone for all time.

XXX **St-Alban,** 2 quai J. Moulin ✉ 69001 ☏ 04 78 30 14 89, *Fax 04 72 00 88 82* – ▤. AE ⓓ GB JCB FX v
closed 19 July-18 August, 1 to 6 January, Saturday lunch, Sunday and Bank Holidays – **Meals** 36/62 and a la carte 45/60 ♀.
◆ Designs in silk showing the sights of Lyon enliven the smart interior of this vaulted dining room close to the Opera. Classic cuisine brought up to date.

XX ✿✿ **Auberge de l'Ile** (Ansanay-Alex), sur l'Ile Barbe ✉ 69009 ☏ 04 78 83 99 49, *info@aubergedelile.com, Fax 04 78 47 80 46* – P. AE ⓓ GB JCB
closed 1 to 24 August, Sunday and Monday – **Meals** 75/95.
◆ This 17C establishment tucked away on an island in the River Saône has a characterful interior (non-smoking) and offers a subtle version of contemporary cuisine.
Spec. Cœur de thon rouge, caviar, vodka, betterave (September). Curry de Saint-Jacques et boudin noir (November). Glace réglisse, cornet de pain d'épices. **Wines** Condrieu, Côte-Rôtie.

XX ✿ **L'Alexandrin** (Alexanian), 83 r. Moncey ✉ 69003 ☏ 04 72 61 15 69, *Fax 04 78 62 75 57,* ☂ – ▤. AE GB GX h
closed 20 to 24 May, 11 to 14 July, 1 to 23 August, 11 to 15 November, 24 December-4 January – **Meals** *(closed Saturday lunch from May-August, Sunday, Monday and Bank Holidays)* 38 (lunch), 60/80 and a la carte 60/85 ✿.
◆ Contemporary decor, smiling service, good choice of Côtes-du-Rhône wines and innovative local cuisine, this establishment attracts the city's smart set.
Spec. Mousseline de brochet en quenelle et son crémeux d'écrevisses. Fricassée de volaille de Bresse au vinaigre. Madeleines guanaja et entremets chocolat amer, sorbet cacao. **Wines** Saint Péray, Crozes-Hermitage.

XX ✿ **Nicolas Le Bec,** 14 r. Grolée ✉ 69002 ☏ 04 78 42 15 00, *restaurant@nicolaslebec.com, Fax 04 72 40 98 97* – ▤ ⚐. AE ⓓ GB FX y
closed 1 to 16 August, Sunday and Monday – **Meals** 40 (lunch), 75/98 and a la carte 70/100 ♀.
◆ For lovers of all things Lyonnaise ! Smart, distinctly modern setting in beige and chocolate, subtly inventive cooking and a wine list which shows its true French colours.
Spec. Artichauts au bouillon d'eucalyptus, langoustines rôties. Filet de canard cuit sur l'os, jus de gentiane au navet. Riz crémeux, caramel mou, biscuits d'amande.

XX **Passage,** 8 r. Plâtre ✉ 69001 ☏ 04 78 28 11 16, *Fax 04 72 00 84 34* – ▤. AE GB JCB FX r
closed 8 to 23 August, Sunday, Monday and Bank Holidays – **Meals** 15 (lunch), 29/45 ♀.
◆ The bistro with cinema seating and a trompe l'oeil theatre curtain, the main dining room with club-type seats and luxurious decor - two seductive alternatives.

XX **Fleur de Sel,** 3 r. Remparts d'Ainay ✉ 69002 ☏ 04 78 37 40 37, *Fax 04 78 37 26 37* – GB FY q
closed August, Sunday and Monday – **Meals** 24 (lunch)/39 ♀.
◆ Green and yellow net curtains filter the light entering this vast dining room. Well-spaced tables and modern seats. Individual cuisine inspired by Provençal cooking.

XX ☺ **Chez Alex,** 40 r. Sergent Blandan ✉ 69001 ☏ 04 78 28 19 83, *Fax 04 78 29 42 32* – AE GB. ✗
closed 27 July-26 August, Tuesday lunch, Sunday dinner and Monday – **Meals** 15 (lunch), 20/38 ♀.
◆ Beyond the strikingly pretty façade is a bright half-panelled dining room with a library containing, among other volumes, early Michelin guides. Refined traditional cuisine.

XX **Jardin des Saveurs,** 95 cours Docteur Long ✉ 69003 *Montchat-Monplaisir* ☏ 04 78 53 27 05, *Fax 04 72 34 67 48* – ▤. ⓓ GB CQ a
closed 9 to 21 August and Sunday – **Meals** 27/50 ✿.
◆ A former bar transformed into a hugely popular restaurant. Its success is based on its well-prepared dishes, an astute wine list, attentive service and sensible prices.

Gourmet de Sèze (Mariller), 129 r. Sèze ✉ 69006 ☎ 04 78 24 23 42, *Fax 04 78 24 66 81* – ▤. AE GB HV z
closed 20 to 24 May, 24 July-23 August, 20 to 24 February, Sunday, Monday and Bank Holidays – **Meals** (booking essential) 31/52 b.i. ♀.
◆ Delightful little restaurant serving classic cuisine brought cleverly up to date. The gourmets of the Rue de Sèze are not alone in being seduced.
Spec. Croustillants de pieds de cochon. Saint-Jacques grillées à la crème de brocoli et jus de truffe (October-March). Le "Grand dessert". **Wines** Saint-Joseph blanc, Morgon.

Mathieu Viannay, 47 av. Foch ✉ 69006 ☎ 04 78 89 55 19, *Fax 04 78 89 08 39* – ▤. AE GB GV s
closed 2 to 23 August, 24 December-2 January, Saturday and Sunday – **Meals** 25/55 ♀.
◆ Recent, resolutely contemporary establishment with parquet floor, coloured seats, and unusual lighting - all in harmony with the contemporary cuisine on offer.

Maison Borie, 3 pl. Antonin Perrin ✉ 69007 *Gerland* ☎ 04 72 76 20 20, *Fax 04 37 37 10 00,* – ▤ P. GB BQ d
closed 10 to 24 August, 20 December-2 January and Sunday – **Meals** 25 (lunch), 45/80.
◆ Unusual contemporary decor, a trendy atmosphere and inventive cuisine are the main attractions inside this 19C house. More substantial dinner menu. Non-smoking dining rooms.

Chez Jean-François, 2 pl. Célestins ✉ 69002 ☎ 04 78 42 08 26, *Fax 04 72 40 04 51* – ▤. AE GB JCB FY x
closed 8 to 12 April, 23 July-23 August, Sunday, Monday and Bank Holidays – **Meals** 16,80/29,80 ♀.
◆ Decorated in contemporary style, this restaurant is often packed out with the crowd from the nearby Célestins Theatre. Generous local cuisine.

Tassée, 20 r. Charité ✉ 69002 ☎ 04 72 77 79 00, *jpborgeot@latassee.fr, Fax 04 72 40 05 91* – ▤. AE GB FY u
closed Sunday – **Meals** 26/46 ♀.
◆ Painted in the 1950s, the medieval-style Bacchanalian fresco lends special character to the bistro close to the Place Bellecour. Classic cuisine and local Lyon specialities.

Vivarais, 1 pl. Gailleton ✉ 69002 ☎ 04 78 37 85 15, *Fax 04 78 37 59 49* – ▤. AE ⓓ GB JCB FY f
closed 26 July-22 August, 25 December-2 January and Sunday – **Meals** 20 (lunch), 26/34 ♀.
◆ Wood panelling, old pictures... a fine setting in which to enjoy contemporary cuisine accompanied by a number of those tasty special delicacies from Lyon.

La Voûte - Chez Léa, 11 pl. A. Gourju ✉ 69002 ☎ 04 78 42 01 33, *Fax 04 78 37 36 41* – ▤. AE GB FY e
closed Sunday – **Meals** 16,50 (lunch), 25/35 ♀.
◆ The unchanging menu goes back to the time not so long ago when gastronomic life in Lyon was dominated by the famous "Mères". Retro decor downstairs, more refined upstairs.

Mère Vittet, 26 cours de Verdun ✉ 69002 ☎ 04 78 37 20 17, *merevittet@wanadoo.fr, Fax 04 78 42 40 70* – ▤. AE GB FY y
Meals 22/42 ♀.
◆ Next to Perrache station and open until 1am, this restaurant is much appreciated by night-owls for its traditional menu, oyster bar, and attractively provincial ambience.

Le Nord, 18 r. Neuve ✉ 69002 ☎ 04 72 10 69 69, *Fax 04 72 10 69 68,* – ▤. AE ⓓ GB JCB FX p
Meals brasserie 23 b.i./28 ♀.
◆ With its burgundy-coloured benches, mosaic floor, panelling and globe lighting, this establishment has all the atmosphere of a turn-of-the-century brasserie.

L'Est, Gare des Brotteaux, 14 pl. J. Ferry ✉ 69006 ☎ 04 37 24 25 26, *Fax 04 37 24 25 25,* – ▤. AE ⓓ GB JCB HX v
Meals brasserie 23 b.i./28 ♀.
◆ Old station converted into a trendy brasserie, featuring electric trains and cuisine from around the world ; all aboard, globe-trotting gourmets !

L'Ouest, 1 quai Commerce ✉ 69009 ☎ 04 37 64 64 64, *Fax 04 37 64 64 65,* – ▤. AE ⓓ GB JCB
Meals 23 b.i./28 ♀.
◆ Stunning modern brasserie combining wood, concrete and metal. Bar, giant screens, designer decor and a kitchen visible to all. A new addition to the Bocuse empire.

Le Sud, 11 pl. Antonin Poncet ✉ 69002 ☎ 04 72 77 80 00, *Fax 04 72 77 80 01,* – ▤. AE ⓓ GB JCB FY d
Meals 23 b.i./28 ♀.
◆ One of Paul Bocuse's "cardinal points" establishments in Lyon, this brasserie brings the Mediterranean to town, with bright yellow décor and sun-kissed cuisine.

Francotte, 8 pl. Célestins ✉ 69002 ✆ 04 78 37 38 64, *infos@francotte.fr, Fax 04 78 38 20 35* – ▤. AE GB FY r
closed Sunday and Monday – **Meals** 19 ♀.
◆ The ambience in this restaurant by the Célestins Theatre is part-traditional bouchon, part-bistro. Breakfast, afternoon tea and brasserie-style cuisine are served here.

Machonnerie, 36 r. Tramassac ✉ 69005 ✆ 04 78 42 24 62, *felix@lamachonnerie.com, Fax 04 72 40 23 32* – ▤. AE ⓓ GB EY n
closed Sunday and lunch except Saturday – **Meals** (booking essential) 18/40 b.i. ♀.
◆ Homely Lyon traditions are much in evidence in this restaurant, with its unpretentious service, convivial ambience and authentic cuisine.

Terrasse St-Clair, 2 Grande r. St-Clair ✉ 69300 *Caluire-et-Cuire* ✆ 04 72 27 37 37, *leon@relaischateaux.fr, Fax 04 72 27 37 38,* 🏠 – AE GB GU s
closed 21 December-11 January, dinner Monday and Sunday – **Meals** 22 ♀.
◆ This restaurant has tried to replicate the atmosphere of one of those old-fashioned, informal French cafés with a dance floor. Pleasant terrace shaded by plane trees.

Théodore, 34 cours Franklin Roosevelt ✉ 69006 ✆ 04 78 24 08 52, *Fax 04 72 74 41 21,* 🏠 – ▤. AE ⓓ GB JCB GVX v
closed 8 to 16 August, Sunday and Bank Holidays – **Meals** 17 (lunch), 19,50/42 ♀.
◆ Behind the modest painted façade is an establishment with a seductive bistro-type atmosphere and Belle Epoque décor. Attractive summer terrace. Traditional cuisine.

Les Muses de l'Opéra, pl. Comédie, 7th floor of the Opera ✉ 69001 ✆ 04 72 00 45 58, *Fax 04 78 29 34 01,* ≤ Fourvière, 🏠 – |$| ▤. AE GB FX q
Meals 24/29.
◆ Designed by Jean Nouvel, a determinedly contemporary panoramic restaurant atop the Opera. View of the backs of the statues of the eight Muses on the cornice.

L'Étage, 4 pl. Terreaux (2nd floor) ✉ 69001 ✆ 04 78 28 19 59, *Fax 04 78 28 19 59* – ▤. GB FX x
closed 26 July-23 August, 15 to 22 February, Sunday and Monday – **Meals** (booking essential) 18/26 ♀.
◆ This old silk workshop on the 2nd floor of a building without a lift is now a rather unusual, very contemporary place to dine, much in favour among local people.

Daniel et Denise, 156 r. Créqui ✉ 69003 ✆ 04 78 60 66 53, *Fax 04 78 60 66 53* – ▤. AE GB GX s
closed August, Saturday, Sunday and Bank Holidays – **Meals** a la carte 24/40.
◆ In the setting of an old charcuterie, this establishment is likely to become ever more popular as a place to wine and dine in.

Tablier de Sapeur, 16 r. Madeleine ✉ 69007 ✆ 04 78 72 22 40, *Fax 04 78 72 22 40* – ▤. AE ⓓ GB GY k
closed August, 25 December-2 January, Monday from October to June, Saturday from June to September and Sunday – **Meals** 20/35.
◆ Bright and welcoming family-run establishment offering refined traditional cuisine including local specialities like "tablier de sapeur" tripe and wines served in jugs.

BOUCHONS : *Regional specialities and wine tasting in a Lyonnaise atmosphere*

Garet, 7 r. Garet ✉ 69001 ✆ 04 78 28 16 94, *legaret@wanadoo.fr, Fax 04 72 00 06 84* – ▤. AE GB FX a
closed 24 July-22 August, 24 December-2 January, Saturday and Sunday – **Meals** (booking essential) 17 (lunch), 21/31 b.i. ♀.
◆ Shirt-sleeves, dungarees, business suits, all mingle here to savour traditional local delicacies prepared without regard to faddy ideas of what constitutes a healthy diet.

Chez Hugon, 12 rue Pizay ✉ 69001 ✆ 04 78 28 10 94, *Fax 04 78 28 10 94* – GB
closed August, Saturday and Sunday – **Meals** (booking essential) 22/30 ♀. FX m
◆ In full view of her faithful customers, the lady chef watches her pots in a convivial atmosphere calculated to warm the cockles of any diner's heart.

Au Petit Bouchon "Chez Georges", 8 r. Garet ✉ 69001 ✆ 04 78 28 30 46 – GB FX a
closed August, Saturday and Sunday – **Meals** 15,50/20,50 (lunch) and dinner a la carte.
◆ Eaten without ceremony, the specialities of this unpretentious establishment include tripe "tablier de sapeur", soufflé of quenelle, all washed down with jugs of Beaujolais.

Café des Fédérations, 8 r. Major Martin ✉ 69001 ✆ 04 78 28 26 00, *yr@lesfedeslyon.com, Fax 04 72 07 74 52* – ▤. GB JCB FX z
closed 24 July-22 August, Saturday and Sunday – **Meals** (booking essential) 19 (lunch)/23.
◆ Gingham tablecloths, diners cheek-by-jowl, giant sausages hanging from the ceiling, copious local cuisine - a real treat of a place !

Jura, 25 r. Tupin ✉ 69002 ℘ 04 78 42 20 57 – GB FX d
closed 21 July-21 August, Monday from September to April, Saturday from May to September and Sunday – **Meals** (booking essential) 18,50 ♀.
◆ Don't be put off by the sign, this is an authentic establishment that has kept its 1930s décor intact and provides diners with typical local treats.

Meunière, 11 r. Neuve ✉ 69001 ℘ 04 78 28 62 91 – GB FX p
closed 14 July-15 August, Sunday, Monday and Bank Holidays – **Meals** (booking essential) 17 (lunch), 20,50/27.
◆ The décor of this establishment in the Rue Neuve has remained unchanged since the 1920s. The appetising dishes often attract crowds of diners.

Environs

to the NE :

at Rillieux-la-Pape : *7 km by N 83 and N 84 – pop. 28 367 alt. 269 – ✉ 69140 :*

Larivoire (Constantin), chemin des Iles ℘ 04 78 88 50 92, *bernard.constantin@larivoire.com, Fax 04 78 88 35 22,* – P. AE GB
closed 16 to 28 August, 24 to 28 February, Tuesday, dinner Sunday and Monday – **Meals** 29/75 and a la carte 62/83.
◆ Pretty pink building housing an attractive modernised restaurant, with antique furnishings. Pleasant shaded terrace. Local cuisine with a contemporary touch.
Spec. Tourteau frais émietté servi comme un cocktail (May-September). Riz arborio en risotto crémeuse et écrevisses du Léman (May-September). Ris de veau pané en viennoise.
Wines Saint-Joseph blanc, Fleurie.

to the E :

at the Lyon St-Exupéry Airport *: 27 km by A 43 – ✉ 69125 Lyon St-Exupéry Airport :*

Sofitel Lyon Aéroport without rest, 3rd floor ℘ 04 72 23 38 00, *h0913@accor-hotels.com, Fax 04 72 23 98 00* – |$|, ⇔ rm, ▤ TV ℡. AE ⓓ GB JCB
☕ 18 – **120 rm** 198/249.
◆ In the main hall of the airport terminal, this chain hotel is a convenient place to stay, with functional rooms (some with a view of the runways) and a "tropical" bar.

Les Canuts, 1st floor in airport station ℘ 04 72 22 71 86, *Fax 04 72 22 71 72* – ▤. AE ⓓ GB
closed 2 to 22 August, Saturday and Sunday – **Meals** 30 and a la carte 30/38 ♀.
◆ The decor of this restaurant pays tribute to the famous silk-weavers of Lyon and their work. Cuisine based on contemporary recipes.

Bouchon, 1st floor in airport station ℘ 04 72 22 71 99, *Lyonaero@elior.com, Fax 04 72 22 71 72* – ▤. AE ⓓ GB JCB
Meals brasserie 15,50/25 ♀.
◆ In the style of a typical Lyon establishment, this unpretentious brasserie offers local dishes. Service is appropriately rapid.

to the W :

at Tour-de-Salvagny *11 km by N 7 – pop. 3 402 alt. 356 – ✉ 69890 :*

Rotonde, at Casino Le Lyon Vert ℘ 04 78 87 00 97, *restaurant-rotonde@g-partouche.fr, Fax 04 78 87 81 39* – ▤ 🅿. AE ⓓ GB JCB
closed 25 July-26 August, Sunday dinner, Tuesday lunch and Monday – **Meals** 38 (lunch), 75/115 and a la carte 90/120 ♀.
◆ Famous gourmet restaurant on the first floor of this celebrated casino established in 1882. The elegant Art Deco interior faces the abundant waters of a splendid fountain.
Spec. Quatre foies pressés et salade de fonds d'artichauts. Tajine de homard entier aux petits farcis. Cannelloni de chocolat amer à la glace de crème brûlée. **Wines** Condrieu, Côte-Rôtie.

to the NW :

at Ecully : *7 km by A6 exit n° 36 – pop. 18 011 alt. 240 – ✉ 69130 :*

Saisons, Château du Vivier, 8 chem. Trouillat ℘ 04 72 18 02 20, *Fax 04 78 43 33 51* – AE GB AP c
closed 9 to 22 August, 20 December-2 January, Wednesday dinner, Saturday, Sunday and Bank Holidays – **Meals** 24 (lunch), 29/35.
◆ This 19C château, now an international hotel school founded in 1990 by Paul Bocuse, stands in its own park. The cuisine and service are provided by the school's students.

Porte de Lyon - *motorway junction A6-N6 : 10 km – ✉ 69570 Dardilly :*

Novotel Lyon Nord, ✆ 04 72 17 29 29, *h0437@accor-hotels.com, Fax 04 78 35 08 45,* – rm, – 25 - 75. AE GB JCB
Meals 20,70 – 11 – **107 rm** 99/114.
◆ This 1970s Novotel is in the Dardilly business park. The rooms have been refurbished and brought up to the current Novotel standard. Bistro-style dining room overlooking a garden and serving traditional cuisine.

Ibis Lyon Nord, ✆ 04 78 66 02 20, *ibis.lyon.nord@wanadoo.fr, Fax 04 78 47 47 93,* – rm, – 20. AE GB
Meals 17,50/21,50 – 7 – **82 rm** 70/85.
◆ More individual and welcoming than the usual Ibis establishment thanks to the unusual design of the building and the restyled rooms. Lyon bistro-style décor in the restaurant and a terrace overlooking the swimming-pool.

Annecy *74000 H.-Savoie 328 J5 – pop. 50 348 alt. 448.*

See : *Old Annecy★★ : Descent from the Cross★ in church of St-Maurice, Palais de l'Isle★, rue Ste-Claire★, bridge over the Thiou ≤★ – Château★ – Jardins de l'Europe★.*

Envir. : *Tour of the lake★★★ 39 km (or 1 hour 30 min by boat).*

18 of the lac d'Annecy ✆ 04 50 60 12 89 : 10 km ; 9 18 of Giez ✆ 04 50 44 48 41 ; 9 of Belvédère at St-Martin-Bellevue ✆ 04 50 60 31 78.

of Annecy-Meythet ✆ 04 50 27 30 30 by N 508 and D 14 : 4 km.

Tourist Office Clos Bonlieu 1 r. J. Jaurès ✆ 04 50 45 00 33, Fax 04 50 51 87 20, ancytour@noos.fr.

Lyons 140.

at Veyrier-du-Lac *E : 5,5 km – pop. 2 063 alt. 504 – ✉ 74290*

La Maison de Marc Veyrat with rm, 13 Vieille rte des Pensières ✆ 04 50 60 24 00, *reservation@marcveyrat.fr, Fax 04 50 60 23 63,* ≤ lake, – AE GB
mid-May-mid-November and closed Tuesday except dinner in July-August, Monday and lunch except weekend – **Meals** 270/360 and a la carte 230/290 – 60 – **11 rm** 607/670.
◆ This enchanting blue house offers stunning cuisine using Alpine herbs and flowers, superb Savoy-style decor and a splendid terrace overlooking the lake.
Spec. Hostie virtuelle de crocus sauvage, bouillon de poule fumé. Cubisme de bar, caramel, fruits de la passion, verveine. Soufflé de semoule glacée au calament. **Wines** Roussette de Marestel, Mondeuse.

Le Bourget-du-Lac *73370 Savoie 333 I4 – pop. 3 945 alt. 240.*

Lyons 103.

Bateau Ivre - Hôtel Ombremont (Jacob), to the North, 2 km by N 504 ✆ 04 79 25 00 23, *ombremontbateauivre@wanadoo.fr, Fax 04 79 25 25 77,* ≤ lake and mountains, – AE GB JCB
mid-May-late October and closed Monday except dinner in July-August and lunch Tuesday and Thursday – **Meals** 52 (lunch), 75/145 and a la carte 93/127.
◆ Superb panorama of lake and Mont Revard from both the soberly elegant dining room and the attractive terrace. The cuisine of the "Drunken Boat" is far from abstemious.
Spec. Ecrevisses, chair d'araignée, miel et vinaigre de Xérès. Filet de perche poêlé et tombée de salades aux arachides grillées (June-September). Noisettes d'agneau rôties au lard, jus aux olives et anchois (May-September). **Wines** Chignin-Bergeron, Mondeuse d'Arbin.

Chagny *71150 S.-et-L. 320 I8 – pop. 5 591 alt. 215.*

Tourist Office 2 r. des Halles ✆ 03 85 87 25 95, Fax 03 85 87 14 44, ot.chagny-bourgogne@wanadoo.fr.

Lyons 145.

Lameloise, pl. d'Armes ✆ 03 85 87 65 65, *reception@lameloise.fr, Fax 03 85 87 03 57* – AE GB JCB
closed 22 December-27 January, Wednesday, lunch Thursday and Tuesday – **Meals** (booking essential) 85/120 and a la carte 80/110 – 20 – **16 rm** 125/275.
◆ The modest exterior of this old Burgundian house belies its refined interior. Spacious rooms. Rustic elegance, warm welcome, and traditional dishes that have made the dining room (non-smoking) a byword for fine cuisine. Shop.
Spec. Ravioli d'escargots de Bourgogne dans leur bouillon d'ail doux. Pigeonneau rôti à l'émietté de truffes. Griottines au chocolat noir sur une marmelade d'oranges amères. **Wines** Rully blanc, Chassagne-Montrachet rouge.

Megève *74120 H.-Savoie 328 M5 – pop. 4 509 alt. 1 113.*
Tourist Office Maison des Frères ✆ 04 50 21 27 28, Fax 04 50 93 03 09, megeve@megeve.com. – Lyons 182.

XXXX ✿✿✿ **La Ferme de mon Père** (Veyrat) with rm, 367 rte du Crêt ✆ 04 50 21 01 01, *reservation@marcveyrat.fr, Fax 04 50 21 43 43* – TV P. AE GB
mid-December-late April and closed Monday except hotel and lunch except weekends – **Meals** 270/360 and a la carte 230/290 – 60 – **6 rm** 550/915, 3 suites.
◆ A mountain farmstead featuring fine food flavoured with Alpine herbs and prepared by a chef ultra-conscious of the culinary heritage of Savoy. Superb rooms.
Spec. Soupe de courge au lard virtuel. Joue de porc aux agrumes, matafans savoyards. Bonbon de caviar, gelée de tussilage, pommes de terre râpées. **Wines** Chignin-Bergeron, Mondeuse.

Mionnay *01390 Ain 328 C5 – pop. 2 109 alt. 276. – Lyons 23.*

XXXX ✿✿ **Alain Chapel** with rm, ✆ 04 78 91 82 02, *chapel@relaischateaux.fr, Fax 04 78 91 82 37,* – TV P. AE GB JCB
closed January, Friday lunch, Monday and Tuesday – **Meals** 60 (lunch), 96/130 and a la carte 87/150 – 17 – **12 rm** 105/125.
◆ Master-chef Alain Chapel may have passed away, but his spirit lives on in this elegant establishment with its offerings to delight the epicurean. Lovely garden.
Spec. Salade de homard, gorges de pigeonneaux et pourpier aux truffes. Foie gras de canard poêlé en chapelure de pain d'épices (Spring-Summer). Poulette de Bresse en vessie, sauce légère au foie gras. **Wines** Mâcon-Clessé, Saint-Joseph.

Roanne *42300 Loire 327 D3 – pop. 38 896 alt. 265.*
of Champlong at Villerest ✆ 04 77 69 70 60.
Roanne-Renaison ✆ 04 77 66 85 77 by D 9.
Tourist Office 1 Crs République ✆ 04 77 71 51 77, Fax 04 77 71 07 11, contact@leroannais.com. – Lyons 87.

✿✿✿ **Troisgros,** pl. Gare ✆ 04 77 71 66 97, *troisgros@avo.fr, Fax 04 77 70 39 77,* – TV AE GB JCB
closed 3 to 18 August, 15 February-2 March, Tuesday and Wednesday – **Meals** (booking essential) 140/170 and a la carte 130/170 – 24 – **13 rm** 160/290, 5 suites.
◆ Charming bedrooms, a specialist gourmet library and collections of modern canvases are the hallmarks of this resolutely 21C station hotel. The holder of three stars since 1968, the Troisgros serves traditional cuisine with a modern twist. Excellent wine list.
Spec. Salade de noix de veau et caviar oscietre. Satay de cuisses de grenouilles. Soufflé aux groseilles aigrelettes (Spring-Summer). **Wines** Saint-Joseph blanc, Côte Rôtie.

St-Bonnet-le-Froid *43290 H.-Loire 331 I3 – pop. 194 alt. 1 126. – Lyons 101.*

XXX ✿✿ **Auberge et Clos des Cimes** (Marcon) with rm, ✆ 04 71 59 93 72, *contact@regismarcon.fr, Fax 04 71 59 93 40,* ←, – rm, rest, TV P AE GB
closed 19 December-19 March, Monday dinner (except June-October), Tuesday and Wednesday – **Meals** 80/130 and a la carte 86/108 – 17 – **12 rm** 155/215.
◆ A charming restaurant serving subtle cuisine that brings out the very best of the Auvergne. A compulsory stop on any culinary tour of the country. Twelve exquisite bedrooms.
Spec. Menu "champignons" (Spring and Autumn). Omble chevalier à l'huile de champignons grillés. Sandre piqué au saucisson de pays. **Wines** Saint-Joseph, Viognier de l'Ardèche.

Valence *26000 Drôme 332 C4 – pop. 64 260 alt. 126.*
See : *House of the Heads (Maison des Têtes)★ – Interior★ of the cathedral – Champ de Mars ←★ – Red chalk sketches by Hubert Robert★★ in the museum.*
of Chanalets ✆ 04 75 83 16 23 ; New Golf ✆ 04 75 59 48 18 at Montmeyran : 16 km by ③ ; of St-Didier ✆ 04 75 59 67 01, E : 14Km by D 119.
of Valence-Chabeuil ✆ 04 75 85 26 26.
Tourist Office Parvis de la Gare ✆ 04 75 44 90 40, Fax 04 75 44 90 41, info@tourisme-valence.com. – Lyons 101.

✿✿ **Pic,** 285 av. V. Hugo, Motorway exit signposted Valence-Sud ✆ 04 75 44 15 32, *pic@relaischateaux.com, Fax 04 75 40 96 03,* – TV P – 50. AE GB JCB
Meals *(closed 3 to 27 January, Tuesday from November-March, Sunday dinner and Monday)* (Sunday : booking essential) 50 (lunch), 115/135 and a la carte 110/170 – 30 – **12 rm** 165/280, 3 suites.
◆ A delightful, relaxed and friendly "auberge" with a Provençal air. The elegant dining rooms and charming garden-terrace provide the perfect backdrop for delicate cuisine with a Mediterranean flavour.
Spec. Ravioles de thon mariné aux épices douces, sorbet roquette (Summer). Turbot au beurre noisette, truffes, râpée d'asperges, jus au safran (Winter). Strate de filet de bœuf et foie gras, jus à l'Hermitage. **Wines** Saint-Péray, Hermitage.

Vienne *38200 Isère 333 C4 – pop. 29 975 alt. 160.*

See : *Site★ – St-Maurice cathedral★★ – Temple of Augustus and Livia★★ – Roman Theatre★ – Church★ and cloisters★ of St-André-le-Bas – Mont Pipet Esplanade ≤★ – Old church of St-Pierre★ : lapidary museum★ – Gallo-roman city★ of St-Romain-en-Gal – Sculpture group★ in the church of Ste-Colombe.*

Tourist Office 3 Crs Brillier ✆ 04 74 53 80 30, Fax 04 74 53 80 31, contact@vienne-tourisme.fr. – Lyons 31.

Pyramide (Henriroux), 14 bd F. Point ✆ 04 74 53 01 96, *pyramide.f.point@wanadoo.fr Fax 04 74 85 69 73*, – rm, – 25. AE GB JCB
closed February – **Meals** *(closed Sunday except Bank Holidays and Monday)* 50 b.i. (lunch), 85/130 and a la carte 110/150 – 19 – **21 rm** 190/230, 4 suites.
◆ This famous restaurant, founded by the late and great Fernand Point, one of the world's most renowned chefs, occupies an attractive house built in local style with stylish rooms and a pleasant garden. The inventive cuisine here is worthy of the master himself.
Spec. Le lapin en déclinaison. Grenouilles en tarte aux aromates, jus de poulet à l'ail du Lauragais. Piano au chocolat, sorbet cacao amer. **Wines** Condrieu, Côte-Rôtie.

Vonnas *01540 Ain 328 C3 – pop. 2 422 alt. 200.*
Lyons 63.

Georges Blanc, place du marché ✆ 04 74 50 90 90, *blanc@relaischateaux.com Fax 04 74 50 08 80*, – 80. AE GB JCB
closed January – **Meals** *(closed Wednesday lunch, Monday and Tuesday except Bank Holidays)* (booking essential) 98/220 and a la carte 110/155 – 23 – **35 rm** 150/400, 3 suites.
◆ Nestling in a flowery garden on the banks of the Veyle, this fine family-owned regional-style residence offers 32 spacious, personalised bedrooms. The superlative cuisine and magnificent wine cellar combine to create one of the jewels of French gastronomy.
Spec. Embrouillade de grenouilles aux épices. Poulet de Bresse aux gousses d'ail, sauce foie gras. Savarin chocolat à l'orange et cédrats confits. **Wines** Mâcon-Azé, Saint-Amour.

MARSEILLES (MARSEILLE) *13000 B.-du-R. 340 H6 – pop. 798 430.*

See : *Site★★★ – N.-D.-de-la-Garde Basilica ★★★ – Old Port★★ : Fish market (quai des Belges* ET **5***) – Palais Longchamp★* GS *: Fine Arts Museum★, Natural History Museum★ – St-Victor Basilica★ : crypt★★* DU *– Old Major Cathedral★* DS **N** *– Pharo Park ≤★* DU *– Hôtel du département et Dôme-Nouvel Alcazar★ – Vieille Charité★★ (Mediterranean archeology)* DS **R** *– Museums : Grobet-Labadié★★* GS **M'**, *Cantini★* FU **M⁵**, *Vieux Marseille★* DT **M²**, *History of Marseilles★* ET **M¹**.

Envir. : *Corniche road★★ of Callelongue S : 13 km along the sea front.*

Exc. : *Château d'If★★ (★★★) 1 h 30.*

18 of Marseilles-Aix ✆ 04 42 24 20 41 to the N : 22 km ; 9 of Allauch-Fonvieille (private) ✆ 04 91 05 09 69 ; junction Marseilles-East : 15 km, by D 2 and D 4=A ; 18 Country Club of la Salette ✆ 04 91 27 12 16 by A 50.

Marseilles-Provence : ✆ 04 42 14 14 14 to the N : 28 km.

✆ 08 36 35 35 35.

Tourist Office 4 Canebière, 13001 ✆ 04 91 13 89 00, Fax 04 91 13 89 20 and St-Charles railway station ✆ 04 91 50 59 18, info@marseille-tourisme.com.

Paris 772 – Lyons 312 – Nice 188 – Turin 407 – Toulon 64 – Toulouse 401.

Plans on following pages

Sofitel Palm Beach, 200 Corniche J.-F. Kennedy ✉ 13007 ✆ 04 91 16 19 00, *H3485@accor-hotels.com, Fax 04 91 16 19 39, ≤ baie du prado*, – rm, – 330. AE GB JCB
***Réserve* :** **Meals** a la carte 45/65 – 21 – **150 rm** 219/279, 10 suites.
◆ Squat rectangular building ideally located facing the famous Chateau d'If Island. Lovely interior refurbished in designer style. Up-to-the-minute ambience in La Réserve and contemporary cuisine based mainly on fish.

Sofitel Vieux Port, 36 bd Ch. Livon ✉ 13007 ✆ 04 91 15 59 00, *h0542@accor-hotels.com, Fax 04 91 15 59 50, ≤ old Port*, – rm, – 130. AE GB JCB DU r
Les Trois Forts ✆ 04 91 15 59 56 **Meals** 49/69 – 20 – **127 rm** 235/355, 3 suites.
◆ Dominating the Vieux Port and its historic forts, this luxury hotel offers guests spacious Provençal-style rooms and a nautical-themed bar. Superb view from the Trois Forts restaurant, which serves contemporary cuisine in a maritime decor.

Petit Nice (Passédat), anse de Maldormé (turn off when level with no 160 Corniche Kennedy) ✉ 13007 ☎ 04 91 59 25 92, *passedat@relaischateaux.com, Fax 04 91 59 28 08*, ≤ the sea, – ▤ TV P. AE ⓓ GB JCB
Meals *(closed Sunday and Monday except dinner from May-September)* 55 (lunch), 90/180 and a la carte 150/200 – ☕ 25 – **13 rm** 275/510, 3 suites.
◆ Overlooking the sea, these two villas dating from 1910 have been joined together and offer tastefully personalised rooms in an operetta-like setting. The restaurant's refined seafood has put this little corner of paradise on every celebrity's itinerary.
Spec. Menu "Découverte de la mer". Tronçon de loup de palangre "Lucie Passédat". Galinette de ligne en deux assiettes. **Wines** Côtes de Provence, Coteaux d'Aix en Provence.

Holiday Inn, 103 av. Prado ✉ 13008 ☎ 04 91 83 10 10, *himarseille@alliance-hospitality.com, Fax 04 91 79 84 12*, – ▤, rm, ▤ TV – 150. AE ⓓ GB JCB
Meals *(closed Bank Holidays)* 18/23 ♀ – ☕ 15 – **119 rm** 160/205, 4 suites.
◆ Near the convention centre and the city's legendary velodrome, this up-to-date hotel caters mainly for business travellers. Well-equipped rooms, all refurbished. Soberly decorated contemporary-style dining room and Mediterranean cuisine. Bar with armchairs.

Mercure Prado without rest, 11 av. Mazargues ✉ 13008 ☎ 04 96 20 37 37, *H3004@accor-hotels.com, Fax 04 96 20 37 99*, – ▤, rm, ▤ TV – 20. AE ⓓ GB BZ n
☕ 12 – **100 rm** 105/115.
◆ Dedicated Internet surfers will appreciate this "cyberhotel" that has been refurbished in designer style. Spacious rooms, three with panoramic terrace. Breakfast on the patio.

Mercure Euro-Centre, r. Neuve St-Martin ✉ 13001 ☎ 04 96 17 22 22, *h1148@accor-hotels.com, Fax 04 96 17 22 33* – ▤, rm, ▤ TV – 200. AE ⓓ GB EST g
Meals *(closed Sunday lunch)* 14/24 ♀ – ☕ 12 – **198 rm** 103/118.
◆ Big modern building by the Centre Bourse shopping centre and the Jardin des Vestiges. Spacious rooms. Cosy English-style bar. Brand-new business centre. Brasserie-style restaurant with Provençal decor. Lunchtime buffet and daily specials, limited dinner menu.

Novotel Vieux Port, 36 bd ch. Livon ✉ 13007 ☎ 04 96 11 42 11, *h0911@accor-hotels.com, Fax 04 96 11 42 20*, – ▤, rm, ▤ TV – 250. AE ⓓ GB JCB DU n
Meals 26/35 ♀ – ☕ 13 – **90 rm** 130/160.
◆ The spacious and comfortable rooms (many family-sized) of this establishment have all been recently refurbished. The best overlook the port or the Du Pharo park. Dining-room with veranda and attractive terrace with unrivalled view of the Vieux Port.

New Hôtel Bompard without rest, 2 r. Flots Bleus ✉ 13007 ☎ 04 91 99 22 22, *marseillebompard@new-hotel.com, Fax 04 91 31 02 14*, – ▤ kitchenette ▤ TV P – 25. AE ⓓ GB JCB
☕ 11 – **46 rm** 91/108.
◆ Quiet, comfortable hotel set back from the corniche road. Walls decorated with paintings donated by artists. Four new and elegant rooms (ask for the "mas").

Résidence du Vieux Port without rest, 18 quai du Port ✉ 13002 ☎ 04 91 91 91 22, *hotelresidence@wanadoo.fr, Fax 04 91 56 60 88*, ≤ old port – ▤, rm, ▤ TV – 30. AE ⓓ GB JCB
☕ 11 – **40 rm** 100,50/155,50.
◆ Rooms in traditional or Provençal style, with balconies overlooking the Vieux Port. An ideal location in which to make the most of a balmy evening in the city.

New Hôtel Vieux Port without rest, 3 bis r. Reine Élisabeth ✉ 13001 ☎ 04 91 99 23 23, *marseillevieux-port@new-hotel.com, Fax 04 91 90 76 24* – ▤ ▤ TV – 25. AE ⓓ GB JCB. ET u
☕ 11 – **42 rm** 135/200.
◆ This charming hotel with a touch of retro-style about it offers a number of rooms overlooking the boats anchored in the Vieux Port.

Alizé without rest, 35 quai Belges ✉ 13001 ☎ 04 91 33 66 97, *alize-hotel@wanadoo.fr, Fax 04 91 54 80 06*, ≤ – ▤ ▤ TV. AE ⓓ GB JCB ETU b
☕ 9,50 – **39 rm** 60/80.
◆ By the city's famous fish market, this is a functional establishment much appreciated by its business clientele. The best rooms, with a view of the port, are at the front.

Ibis Gare St-Charles, esplanade Gare St-Charles ✉ 13001 ☎ 04 91 95 62 09, *h1390@accor-hotels.com, Fax 04 91 50 68 42*, – ▤, rm, ▤ rm, TV – 40. AE ⓓ GB FS k
Meals 15 – ☕ 6 – **146 rm** 80, 26 suites.
◆ This vast hotel has been given a completely new look. Comfortable rooms with panoramic views of the city or of the railway tracks. Good soundproofing. Live display of train times. Spacious modern restaurant opening on to an attractive terrace.

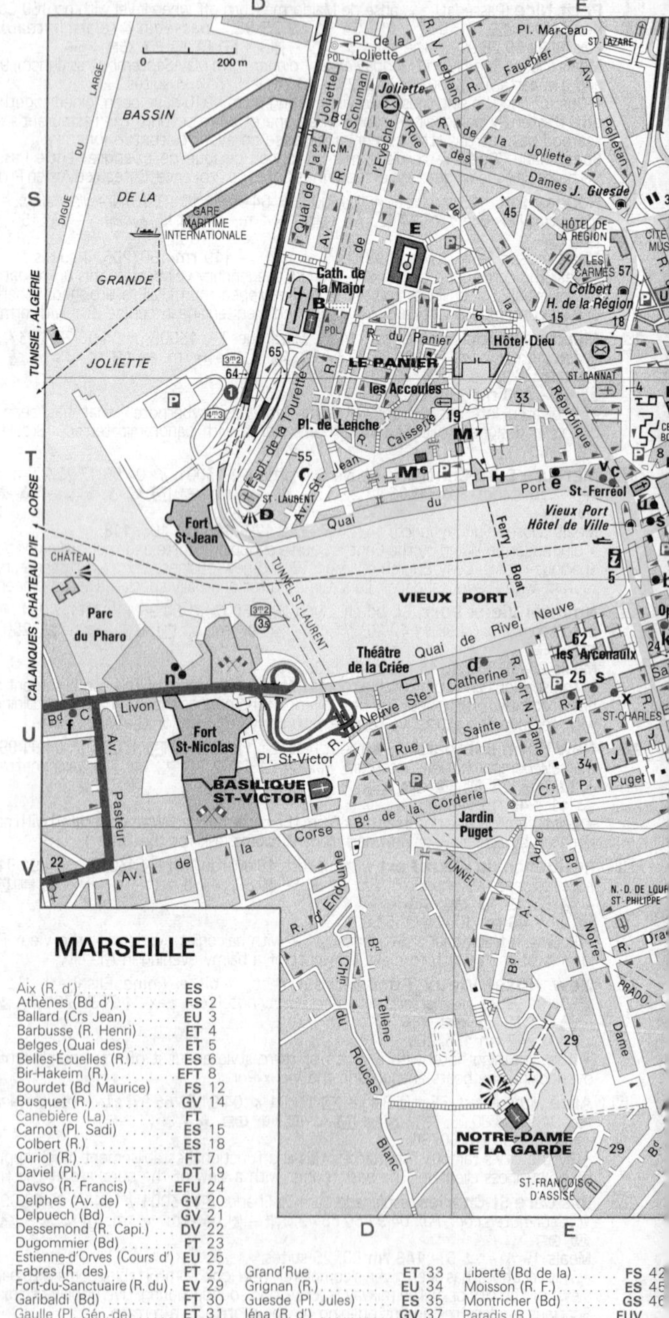

MARSEILLE

Aix (R. d') . . . . ES
Athènes (Bd d') . . . . FS 2
Ballard (Crs Jean) . . . . . . EU 3
Barbusse (R. Henri) . . . . . ET 4
Belges (Quai des) . . . . ET 5
Belles-Écuelles (R.) . . . . . . ES 6
Bir-Hakeim (R.) . . . . EFT 8
Bourdet (Bd Maurice) . . . FS 12
Busquet (R.) . . . . GV 14
Canebière (La) . . . . FT
Carnot (Pl. Sadi) . . . . ES 15
Colbert (R.) . . . . ES 18
Curiol (R.) . . . . FT 7
Daviel (Pl.) . . . . DT 19
Davso (R. Francis) . . . . . . EFU 24
Delphes (Av. de) . . . . GV 20
Delpuech (Bd) . . . . GV 21
Dessemond (R. Capi.) . . . DV 22
Dugommier (Bd) . . . . FT 23
Estienne-d'Orves (Cours d') EU 25
Fabres (R. des) . . . . FT 27
Fort-du-Sanctuaire (R. du) . EV 29
Garibaldi (Bd) . . . . FT 30
Gaulle (Pl. Gén.-de) . . . . . ET 31
Grand'Rue . . . . ET 33
Grignan (R.) . . . . EU 34
Guesde (Pl. Jules) . . . . . . ES 35
Iéna (R. d') . . . . GV 37
Liberté (Bd de la) . . . . . . FS 42
Moisson (R. F.) . . . . ES 45
Montricher (Bd) . . . . GS 46
Paradis (R.) . . . . FUV

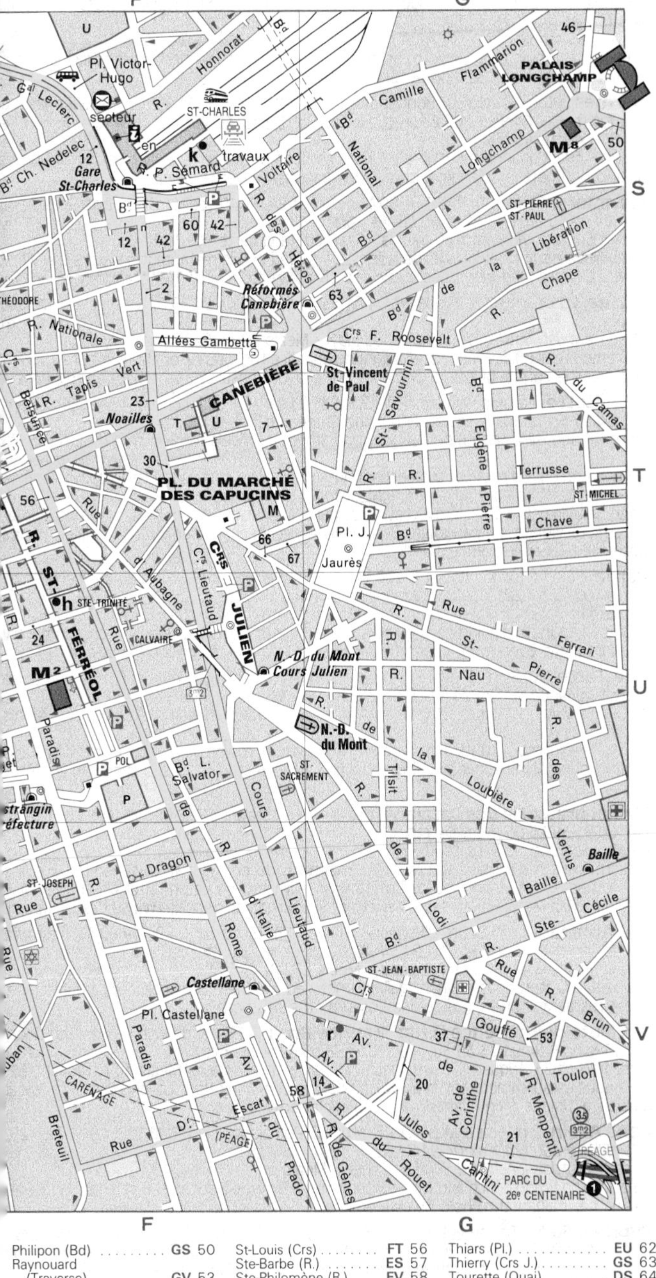
F
G
S
T
U
V
PALAIS LONGCHAMP
ST-CHARLES
CANEBIÈRE
PL. DU MARCHÉ DES CAPUCINS
Allées Gambetta
St-Vincent de Paul
N.-D. du Mont
Pl. Castellane
PARC DU 26e CENTENAIRE

Kyriad without rest, 31 r. Rouet ✉ 13006 ✆ 04 91 79 56 66, *kyriad.marseille@wanadoo.fr, Fax 04 91 78 33 85* – |‡|, ⇔ rm, ▤ TV ✆. AE GB
☕ 7 – **53 rm** 65/67.
• Recent establishment close to the busy Place Castellane. Identical, more or less spacious rooms. A very reasonable place for short stays.

Hermès without rest, 2 r. Bonneterie ✉ 13002 ✆ 04 96 11 63 63, *hotel.hermes@wanadoo.fr, Fax 04 96 11 63 64* – |‡|, ⇔ rm, ▤ TV ✆. AE ⊙ GB JCB ET e
☕ 8 – **28 rm** 45/76.
• Small, functional rooms, those on the 5th floor with a terrace overlooking the boats at anchor. Rooftop solarium with a lovely panorama over the city.

XXX **Miramar,** 12 quai Port ✉ 13002 ✆ 04 91 91 10 40, *contact@bouillabaisse.com, Fax 04 91 56 64 31,* 🏖 – ▤. AE ⊙ GB ET v
closed Sunday and Monday – **Meals** - Seafood - a la carte 60/80 ♀.
• Bouillabaisse and other fish specialities are served in this restaurant opposite the Vieux Port. The varnished wood decor and red chairs create a very 1960s ambience.

XXX **Ferme,** 23 r. Sainte ✉ 13001 ✆ 04 91 33 21 12, *Fax 04 91 33 81 21* – ▤. AE ⊙ GB JCB EU m
closed August, Saturday lunch and Sunday – **Meals** 38 and a la carte 45/55.
• Trompe l'oeil effects and careful lighting enhance the interior of this luxury restaurant close to the Cantini Museum. The cubicle-like layout ensures an intimate atmosphere.

XX ✿ **L'Épuisette,** Vallon des Auffes ✉ 13007 ✆ 04 91 52 17 82, *contact@l-epuisette.com, Fax 04 91 59 18 80,* ≤ îles du Frioul and Château d'If – ▤. AE GB
closed 7 August-7 September, Sunday and Monday – **Meals** 40/80 and a la carte 65/95 ♀.
• Anchored on the rocks of the enchanting Auffes valley, this glass vessel promises diners an exceptional culinary voyage. Bright decor in blue, white, and wood.
Spec. Supions et grosses crevettes roses panées, chutney de piquillos. Tajine de sole et artichauts violets en barigoule. Bouillabaisse des pêcheurs en deux services. **Wines** Coteaux-d'Aix-en-Provence, Bandol.

XX **Péron,** 56 corniche Kennedy ✉ 13007 ✆ 04 91 52 15 22, *info@restaurant-peron.com, Fax 04 91 52 17 29,* ≤ Frioul islands and Château d'If, 🏖 – AE ⊙ GB JCB AY a
Meals 41.
• This restaurant clinging to the rocks offers superb views plus elegant, contemporary interiors made even more appealing by the pictures painted by local artists.

XX **Une Table au Sud,** 2 quai Port (1st floor) ✉ 13002 ✆ 04 91 90 63 53, *unetableausud@wanadoo.fr, Fax 04 91 90 63 86,* ≤ – ▤. AE GB ET c
closed 31 July-23 August, 1 to 7 January, Saturday lunch, Sunday and Monday – **Meals** 39/65.
• This restaurant with its sunny decor offers diners a wonderful marriage of eye and palate : good Mediterranean cuisine and fine views of the forts and the "Bonne Mère" statue.

XX ✿ **Michel-Brasserie des Catalans** (Visciano), 6 r. Catalans ✉ 13007 ✆ 04 91 52 30 63, *Fax 04 91 59 23 05* – ▤. AE GB
Meals - Seafood - a la carte 40/77.
• Warm welcome in this establishment with retro decor and a sailor-suited Popeye. It's the "other" great stronghold of bouillabaisse, with today's catch on display in a boat.
Spec. Bouillabaisse. Supions sautés ail et persil. Bourride provençale. **Wines** Cassis, Bandol.

XX **Les Arcenaulx,** 25 cours d'Estienne d'Orves ✉ 13001 ✆ 04 91 59 80 30, *restaurant@les-arcenaulx.com, Fax 04 91 54 76 33,* 🏖 – ▤. AE ⊙ GB JCB EU s
closed 11 to 19 August and Sunday – **Meals** 27,50/49,50 ♀.
• In the 17C storehouses where galleys once tied up, there is a bookshop, a publisher's, and a restaurant offering a cuisine kissed by the southern sun.

XX **Les Mets de Provence "Chez Maurice Brun",** 18 quai de Rive Neuve (2nd floor) ✉ 13007 ✆ 04 91 33 35 38, *Fax 04 91 33 05 69* – ▤. GB EU d
closed 10 to 25 August, Sunday, lunch Monday and Saturday – **Meals** 36 b.i. (lunch)/52.
• Famous establishment set in an old convent in the Vieux Port. Lovely rustic Provençal ambience. Unique menu varied daily and explained verbally.

XX **René Alloin,** 9 pl. Amiral Muselier (by prom. G. Pompidou) ✉ 13008 ✆ 04 91 77 88 25, *allloinfilipe@aol.com, Fax 04 91 71 82 46,* 🏖 – ▤. GB
closed Saturday lunch and Sunday dinner – **Meals** 21 (lunch), 34/48.
• Facing the Prado beach and with contemporary Provençal decor, this stronghold of fine cuisine has managed to hold its own among the massed bars and pizzerias.

XX ☺ **Cyprien,** 56 av. Toulon ✉ 13006 ✆ 04 91 25 50 00, *Fax 04 91 25 50 00* – ▤. GB
closed 23 July-26 August and 24 December-6 January – **Meals** *(closed Monday dinner, Saturday except dinner from August-June, Sunday and Bank Holidays)* 23/60.
• Classic cuisine and decor. Not far from Place Castellane, this establishment is expert at providing fine food in a quiet setting with tasteful flower arrangements.

Côte de Bœuf, 35 cours d'Estienne d'Orves ✉ 13001 ✆ 04 91 54 89 08, *Fax 04 91 54 25 60* – ▤. AE GB JCB
closed 14 July-15 August, Sunday and Bank Holidays – **Meals** 29/32.
• In a venerable old shipping warehouse, this establishment features fine local cuisine, particularly meat dishes grilled on the spot, plus an exceptional selection of wines.

Chez Vincent, 25 r. Glandeves ✉ 13001 ✆ 04 91 33 96 78
closed August and Monday – **Meals** a la carte approx. 30.
• A modest façade, straightforward bistro-style décor, and a lady owner in charge since the 1940s - this is a Marseille institution providing generous portions of local cuisine.

Aix-en-Provence *13100 B.-du-R.* 340 *H4 – pop. 134 222 alt. 206.*

18 of Ste-Victoire ✆ 04 42 29 83 43 by N96 and D6 : 14 km ; 18 Set ✆ 04 42 29 63 69, O : 6 km by D17.

Tourist Office 2 pl. Gén.-de-Gaulle ✆ 04 42 16 11 61, Fax 04 42 16 11 62, info@aixenprovencetourism.com.

Marseilles 31.

Clos de la Violette (Banzo), 10 av. Violette ✆ 04 42 23 30 71, *restaurant@closdelaviolette.fr, Fax 04 42 21 93 03,* – ▤. AE GB.
closed 4 to 18 August, February Holidays, Monday except dinner from 1 June-30 September and Sunday – **Meals** (booking essential) 54 (lunch)/117 and a la carte 95/120.
• Away from the town's bustle, a lovely villa with garden invites diners to try the thousand and one delights of a characterful version of local cuisine. Elegant setting.
Spec. Grand menu de la truffe (20 December - 15 March). Poissons de Méditerranée. Poitrine de pigeon contisé au poivre de Penja. **Wines** Coteaux d'Aix en Provence.

Les Baux-de-Provence *13520 B.-du-R.* 340 *D3 – pop. 434 alt. 185.*

See : *Site★★★ – Château ★★ – Charloun Rieu monument ≤★ – Place St-Vincent★ – Rue du Trencat★ – Paravelle Tower ≤★ – Yves-Brayer museum★ (in Hôtel des Porcelet) – Shepherds' Festival★★ (Christmas midnight mass) – Cathédrale d'Images★ N : 1 km on the D 27 – ★★★ of the village N : 2,5 km on the D 27.*

9 of les Baux-de-Provence ✆ 04 90 54 40 20, S : 2 km.

Tourist Office Ilôt "Post Tenebras Lux" ✆ 04 90 54 34 39, Fax 04 90 54 51 15.

Marseilles 83.

in the Vallon :

Oustaù de Baumanière (Charial) with rm, ✆ 04 90 54 33 07, *baumaniere@relaischateaux.fr, Fax 04 90 54 40 46,* ≤, , , – ▤ TV P. AE GB JCB
closed 5/01-4/03, Wednesday lunch in October and in April, Thursday lunch and Wednesday from November-March – **Meals** 90/149 and a la carte 90/130 – 19,50 – **13 rm** 263/473.
• Venerable, vaulted 16C residence, a superb terrace with the Alpilles as a backdrop, this is a magical location. Fine cuisine redolent of the sun plus a sumptuous wine list.
Spec. Ravioli de truffes aux poireaux. Filets de rouget au basilic. Canon d'agneau en croûte. **Wines** Coteaux d'Aix-en-Provence-les Baux.

Manoir , ≤, , – ▤ rm, TV P. AE GB JCB
Meals see ***Oustaù de Baumanière*** – 19,50 – **7 rm** 263/284, 7 suites 425/457.
• The rooms of this elegant fortified house combine comfort, refinement and old-fashioned Provençal charm. Wooded park (with an ancient plane tree) and formal garden.

Lourmarin *84160 Vaucluse* 332 *F11 – pop. 1 119 alt. 224.*

Tourist Office 8 av. Ph.-de-Girard ✆ 04 90 68 10 77, Fax 04 90 68 10 77.

Marseilles 63.

Moulin de Lourmarin (Loubet) , r. Temple ✆ 04 90 68 06 69, *info@moulindelourmarin.com, Fax 04 90 68 31 76,* – ▤ TV . AE GB JCB
closed 15 November-15 December and 15 January-15 February – **Meals** *(closed Thursday lunch in season, Wednesday except dinner in season and Tuesday)* 91/152 and a la carte 120/200 – 19 – **19 rm** 190/490.
• Near the chateau, this charming 18C oil-mill has delightful rooms. Vaulted restaurant in the old press-house, a lovely terrace, and an inventive cuisine paying subtle homage to the flavours and colours of the Luberon.
Spec. Complicité de foie gras. Loup de ligne à l'unilatérale, infusion de sauge et orange. Carré d'agneau au serpolet, jus au thym citronné. **Wines** Côtes du Luberon.

Montpellier *34000 Hérault 339 I7 – pop. 225 392 alt. 27.*

of Coulondres ☎ 04 67 84 13 75, N : 12 km ; of Fontcaude at Juvignac ☎ 04 67 45 90 10, O : 9 km ; of Massane at Baillargues ☎ 04 67 87 87 89, E : 13 km.

of Montpellier-Méditerranée ☎ 04 67 20 85 85 te the SE :.

Tourist Office Triangle Comédie allée du Tourisme ☎ 04 67 60 60 60, Fax 04 67 60 60 61 and 78 av. du Pirée ☎ 04 67 22 06 16, contact@ot-montpellier.fr.

Marseilles 171.

XXXX ✿✿✿ **Jardin des Sens** (Jacques et Laurent Pourcel) with rm, 11 av. St-Lazare ☎ 04 99 58 38 38, *contact@jardindessens.com, Fax 04 99 58 38 39,* – – 25. AE GB

closed 2 to 9 January – **Meals** *(closed 2 to 16 January, Monday except dinner in 07/08, Tuesday lunch except 07/08, Wednesday lunch and Sunday)* (booking essential) 46 (lunch), 110/170 and a la carte 107/148 ♀ – 22 – **14 rm** 170/250.

◆ The tiered non-smoking dining-room in designer style opens on to a spiral garden. This is a place to tempt all five senses, in terms of both decor and cuisine. Smoking room.

Spec. Pressé de homard et légumes au jambon de canard. Filet de loup cuit au four, vinaigrette tiède au citron confit. Filets de pigeon rôtis au cacao. **Wines** Picpoul de Pinet, Coteaux du Languedoc.

MONACO (Principality of) (Principauté de) 341 F5 115 272 – *pop. 29 972 alt. 65 – Casino.*

Monaco *Capital of the Principality* 341 F5 – ✉ *98000.*

See : *Tropical Garden★★ (Jardin exotique) : ≤★ – Observatory Caves★ (Grotte de l'Observatoire) – St-Martin Gardens★ – Early paintings of the Nice School★★ in Cathedral – Recumbent Christ★ in the Misericord Chapel – Place du Palais★ – Prince's Palace★ – Museums : oceanographic★★★ (aquarium★★, ≤★★ from the terrace), Prehistoric Anthropology★, Napoleon and Monaco History★, Royal collection of vintage cars★.*

Urban racing circuit – A.C.M. 23 bd Albert-1er ☎ (00-377) 93 15 26 00, Fax (00-377) 93.

Paris 956 – Nice 21 – San Remo 44.

at Fontvieille

Columbus Hôtel, 23 av. Papalins ☎ (00-377) 92 05 90 00, *info@columbushotels.com, Fax (00-377) 92 05 91 67,* ≤, – , rm, – 25 - 80. AE GB JCB

Meals 20 (lunch)/30 ♀ – 25 – **153 rm** 290/330, 28 suites.

◆ A contemporary hotel combining elegant furniture and pleasing colours. Most bedrooms have balconies overlooking the port or park. Modern, Italian-style brasserie-restaurant, plus a pleasant terrace. Impressive auditorium.

Monte-Carlo *Fashionable resort of the Principality* 341 F5 – *Casinos Grand Casino, Monte-Carlo Sporting Club, Sun Casino.*

See : *Terrace★★ of the Grand Casino – Museum of Dolls and Automata★.*

Monte-Carlo ☎ 04 92 41 50 70 to the S by N 7 : 11 km.

Tourist Office 2A bd Moulins ☎ (00-377) 92 16 61 16, Fax (00-377) 92 16 60 00, dtc@monaco-tourisme.com.

Paris, pl. Casino ☎ (00-377) 92 16 30 00, *hp@sbm.mc, Fax (00-377) 92 16 38 50,* ≤, – , rm, – 70. AE GB JCB. rest

see ***Le Louis XV*** and ***Grill*** below - ***Salle Empire*** ☎ (00-377) 92 16 29 52 (dinner only) *(open July-August)* **Meals** a la carte 95/145 – ***Côté Jardin*** ☎ (00-377) 92 16 68 44 (lunch only) **Meals** 50 – 35 – **145 rm** 590/1150, 45 suites.

◆ An idyllic location, sumptuous furnishings, glittering past and long list of famous guests are the hallmarks of Monaco's most prestigious hotel, opened in 1864. Views of the rock from the Côté Jardin terrace. Majestic Salle Empire (gold, stucco and crystal).

Hermitage, square Beaumarchais ☎ (00-377) 92 16 40 00, *hh@sbm.mc, Fax (00-377) 92 16 38 52,* ≤, – – 80. AE GB JCB. rest

closed 29 December-2 January – see ***Vistamar*** below ***Limun Bar* : Meals** a la carte 45/60 – 32 – **213 rm** 750/900, 18 suites.

◆ Italian frescoes and loggias adorn the hotel's splendid façade facing the port. Inside, note the Eiffel-designed cast iron and glass cupola. Luxurious bedrooms. Refined, lemon-inspired decor and regional cuisine in the Limùn bar, which also acts as a tea-room.

Métropole (reopening in May after works), 4 av. Madone ☎ (00-377) 93 15 15 15, *metropole@metropole.mc, Fax (00-377) 93 25 24 44,* – – 60. AE GB JCB. rest

Meals a la carte 50/75 – 35 – **130 rm** 750, 15 suites.

◆ Built in 1889 and completely redesigned a century later, this palace is decorated in the spirit of the Belle Époque. Elegant bedrooms.

Méridien Beach Plaza, av. Princesse Grace, à la Plage du Larvotto (00-377) 93 30 98 80, *resa@lemeridien-montecarlo.com, Fax (00-377) 93 50 23 14,* rm, rm, 20 - 300. AE GB JCB. rm
Meals 32/42 – 31 – **338 rm** 380.
• The street-side façade gives little hint of the superb spa facilities that face out to sea. Modern, tastefully decorated bedrooms, plus a luxurious conference centre. Buffet-style dining, with recipes unsurprisingly inspired by the Mediterranean.

Port Palace, 7 av. J. F. Kennedy (00-377) 97 97 90 00, *ep@portpalace.com, Fax (00-377) 97 97 90 01,* Port et Rocher, AE GB JCB.
Grand Large : **Meals** (37) – 80 – 29 – **41 rm** 700/900, 9 suites.
• The latest in a line of palatial residences, this portside hotel is characterised by contemporary architecture and superbly appointed rooms with views of the Rock. Modern decor in the top-floor restaurant where the emphasis is on traditional dishes.

Monte-Carlo Grand Hôtel, 12 av. Spélugues (00 377) 93 50 65 00, *reservation @montecarlograndhotel.com, Fax (00-377) 93 30 01 57,* 1 500. AE GB JCB. rest
L'Argentin (dinner only) **Meals** a la carte 65/85 – ***Pistou*** *(15 March-1 December and closed Tuesday dinner from 23 September-1 December)* **Meals** a la carte 40/70 – 30 – **599 rm** 310/485, 20 suites.
• A vast hotel complex which includes a casino, cabaret, boutiques and conference centre. Mediterranean decor in the bedrooms, contrasting with the South American influence in L'Argentin. French and Italian cuisine in Le Pistou, with its sea-facing terrace.

Balmoral, 12 av. Costa (00-377) 93 50 62 37, *resa@hotel-balmoral.mc, Fax (00-377) 93 15 08 69,* rm, 20. AE GB JCB.
Meals coffee shop *(closed November, Sunday dinner and Monday)* (residents only) 25 – 15 – **58 rm** 200/220, 7 suites.
• Run by the same family since 1896, the main features of the Balmoral are its lounge furnished in Empire style and traditional bedrooms, half of which overlook the port. The food here is more snack-oriented.

Alexandra without rest, 35 bd Princesse Charlotte (00-377) 93 50 63 13, *hotelalexandra@imcn.net, Fax (00-377) 92 16 06 48* – AE GB JCB.
13 – **56 rm** 120/150.
• The richly ornamented façade bears witness to the ostentation of the Belle Époque. Breakfast is only served in guest bedrooms, which have a pleasantly old-fashioned feel.

Le Louis XV-Alain Ducasse - Hôtel de Paris, pl. Casino (00-377) 92 16 29 76, *lelouisxv@alain-ducasse.com, Fax (00-377) 92 16 69 21,* AE GB JCB.
closed 1 to 10 March, 30 November-29 December and 8 to 23 February – **Meals** *(closed lunch from 1 March-15 May except Saturday, Sunday, Wednesday except dinner from 23/06-25/08 and Tuesday)* 90 b.i. (lunch), 150/180 and a la carte 150/230.
• Sumptuous classical decor, sublime Mediterranean flavours, a truly outstanding wine cellar, plus a terrace overlooking the famous casino. A veritable feast for the senses!
Spec. Légumes des jardins de Provence à la truffe noire écrasée. Poitrine de pigeonneau, foie gras de canard sur la braise, polenta et jus aux abats (15 October-15 March). Le "Louis XV" au croustillant de pralin. **Wines** Côtes de Provence blanc, Bellet rouge.

Grill de l'Hôtel de Paris, pl. Casino (00-377) 92 16 29 66, *hp@sbm.mc, Fax (00-377) 92 16 38 40,* the Principality, AE GB JCB.
closed 5 to 22 January and lunch from 7 July-28 August – **Meals** a la carte 110/150.
• On the 8th floor of the hotel, offering spectacular views of the sea and principality, with a sunroof that opens out on to Monaco's azure skies.
Spec. Langoustines royales rôties, orge perlé et velours de potiron rouge. Carré d'agneau en croûte de pain d'épices. Poussin de nid rôti au thym frais. **Wines** Côtes de Provence.

Vistamar - Hôtel Hermitage, pl. Beaumarchais (00-377) 92 16 27 72, *hh@sbm.mc, Fax (00-377) 92 16 38 43,* Harbour and Principality, AE GB JCB
closed 29 December-2 January – **Meals** 59 and a la carte 94/137.
• Exquisite fish dishes and stunning sea views from the delightful panoramic terrace and bay-windowed dining room are the keys to the Vistamar's continued success.
Spec. Salade de homard. Loup grillé à la braise de feu de bois. Daurade en croûte de sel. **Wines** Bellet, Côtes de Provence.

Bar et Bœuf, av. Princesse Grace, au Sporting-Monte-Carlo (00-377) 92 16 60 60, *b.b@sbm.mc, Fax (00-377) 92 16 60 61,* AE GB JCB
14 May-18 September and closed Monday from 14 May to 21 June and from 30 August to 18 September – **Meals** (dinner only) a la carte 75/100.
• A Philippe Starck-designed restaurant whose menu favours sea bass (bar), beef (bœuf) and wines from around the world. A popular late-night haunt for serious gourmets.
Spec. "Tomate et tomates", sorbet tomate et bloody Mary. Cœur de filet de bar à la plancha, condiment goûteux à la sicilienne. Cheesecake, compotée de fruits rouges, sorbet fromage blanc. **Wines** Palette, Côtes de Provence.

XXX **Saint Benoit,** 10ter av. Costa ✆ (00-377) 93 25 02 34, *lesaintbenoit@montecarlo.mc, Fax (00-377) 93 30 52 64,* ≤ Harbour and Monaco, – ▤. AE ⓓ GB JCB
closed 20 December-4 January, Sunday dinner from November to March and Monday – **Meals** 28/38 and a la carte 42/80 ♀.
◆ Not the easiest place to find, but well worth the effort for the view from the terrace. Modern, spacious dining room.

XXX **L'Hirondelle,** 2 av. Monte-Carlo (aux Thermes Marins) ✆ (00-377) 92 16 49 30, *Fax (00-377) 92 16 49 02,* ≤ Harbour and rock, – ▤. AE ⓓ GB JCB.
closed 13 to 20 December – **Meals** (lunch only) 48 and a la carte 60/80 ♀.
◆ Part of the prestigious Thermes Marins, the bright dining room and terrace enjoy a fine view of the port and rock. A range of classic dishes and healthy cuisine.

XX **Café de Paris,** pl. Casino ✆ (00-377) 92 16 25 54, *cp@sbm.mc, Fax (00-377) 92 16 38 58,* – ▤. AE ⓓ GB JCB.
Meals a la carte 47/90 ♀.
◆ In 1897, Édouard Michelin made a notable entrance here... at the wheel of his motor car ! A Belle Époque-style brasserie with a lively outdoor terrace in summer.

XX **Zébra Square,** 10 av. Princesse Grace (Grimaldi Forum : 2nd floor by lift) ✆ (00-377) 99 99 25 50, *Fax (00-377) 99 99 25 60,* ≤, – ▤. AE ⓓ GB JCB
Meals a la carte 50/66 ♀.
◆ The same designer décor, trendy atmosphere and contemporary cuisine as its Paris sibling, with the bonus of a charming terrace with views of the Mediterranean.

XX **Maison du Caviar,** 1 av. St-Charles ✆ (00-377) 93 30 80 06, *Fax (00-377) 93 30 23 90,* – AE GB
closed August, Saturday lunch and Sunday – **Meals** 23 (lunch), 28/43 ♀.
◆ This discreet family-run restaurant popular with locals has been serving its traditional cuisine here since 1954 amid a decor of ironwork, bottle racks and rustic furniture.

X **Polpetta,** 2 r. Paradis ✆ (00-377) 93 50 67 84, *Fax (00-377) 93 50 67 84* – ▤. AE GB
closed 5 to 25 June, 1 to 15 November, Saturday lunch and Tuesday – **Meals** - Italian rest. - 23.
◆ This small Italian restaurant offers a choice of three dining options : the street-side veranda ; the rustic dining room ; or a more elegant and intimate room to the rear.

Roquebrune-Cap-Martin *06190 Alpes-Mar.* 341 F5 – *pop. 11 692 alt. 70.*

Monaco 9.

at Monte-Carlo-Beach *to the West by N 98 : 7 km* – ✉ *06190 Roquebrune-Cap-Martin :*

Monte-Carlo Beach Hôtel , av. Princesse Grace ✆ 04 93 28 66 66, *bh@sbm.mc, Fax 04 93 78 14 18,* ≤ sea and Monaco, , , , – ▤ ▤ ▣ ✆ ♿ P – 30. AE ⓓ GB JCB. rest
1 March-13 November – ***Salle à Manger :*** **Meals** a la carte 58/95 – ***Potinière*** ✆ 04 93 28 66 43 (lunch only) *(5 June-5 September)* **Meals** a la carte 60/80 – ***Vigie*** ✆ 04 93 28 66 44 *(26 June-29 August)* **Meals** 49(lunch)/58 – ***Rivage*** ✆ 04 93 28 66 42 (lunch only) *(10 April-10 October)* **Meals** a la carte 40/60 – ☕ 32 – **44 rm** 600, 3 suites.
◆ Created in 1929, this attractive, typically "monégasque" spa complex has welcomed stars such Nijinski, Cocteau etc. Italian-style bedrooms looking out on to the Rock and the open sea. Small but cosy fresco-adorned Salle à Manger. Open-air La Vigie restaurant.

NICE *06000 Alpes-Mar.* 341 E5 – *pop. 342 738 alt. 6 – Casino Ruhl* FZ.

See : *Site*★★ – *Promenade des Anglais*★★ EFZ – *Old Nice*★ : *Château* ≤★★ JZ, *Interior*★ *of church of St-Martin-St-Augustin* HY **D** – *Balustraded staircase*★ *of the Palais Lascaris* HZ **K**, *Interior*★ *of Ste-Réparate Cathedral* – HZ **L**, *St-Jacques Church*★ HZ **N**, *Decoration*★ *of St-Giaume's Chapel* HZ **R** – *Mosaic*★ *by Chagall in Law Faculty* DZ **U** – *Palais des Arts*★ HJY – *Miséricorde Chapel*★ HZ **S** – *Cimiez : Monastery*★ *(Masterpieces*★★ *of the early Nice School in the church)* HV **Q**, *Roman Ruins*★ HV – *Museums : Marc Chagall*★★ GX, *Matisse*★★ HV **M2**, *Fine Arts Museum*★★ DZ **M**, *Masséna*★ FZ **M1** – *Modern and Contemporary Art*★★ HY – *Parc Phoenix*★ – *Carnival*★★★ *(before Shrove Tuesday).*

Envir. : *St-Michel Plateau* ≤★★ *9,5 km.*

✈ *of Nice-Côte d'Azur* ✆ *04 93 21 30 30 : 7 km.*

🚗 ✆ *08 36 35 35 35.*

ℹ *Tourist Office 5 prom. des Anglais* ✆ *09 82 70 74 07, SNCF Station* ✆ *09 82 70 74 07, Nice-Ferber (Near the Airport)* ✆ *09 82 70 74 07 and Airport, Terminal 1* ✆ *09 82 70 74 07.*

Paris 932 – Cannes 32 – Genova 194 – Lyons 472 – Marseilles 188 – Turin 220.

Plans on following pages

Négresco, 37 promenade des Anglais ✆ 04 93 16 64 00, *direction@hotel-negresco.com, Fax 04 93 88 35 68,* ←, ⛱, 🏋 – |♦|, ▤ TV ✆ 🚗 – 🪑 30 - 200. AE ⓓ GB JCB FZ k
see **Chantecler** below - ***Rotonde*** : Meals 32 ♀ – ☕ 28 – **121 rm** 280/510, 12 suites.
◆ Built in 1913 by Henri Negresco, the son of a Romanian innkeeper, this majestic, almost mythical museum of a hotel is full of artworks and extravagant in every detail. The Rotonde is a striking brasserie with merry-go-round decor.

Palais Maeterlinck 🕊, 30 bd Maeterlinck, 6 km by Inferior Corniche ✉ 06300 ✆ 04 92 00 72 00, *info@palais-maeterlinck.com, Fax 04 92 04 18 10,* ← the coast, ⛱, 🏋, 🏊, 🎾, 🌳 – |♦| kitchenette ▤ TV ✆ 🚗 P – 🪑 25 - 80. AE ⓓ GB JCB. 🚫
Mélisande ✆ 04 92 00 72 01 *(closed Sunday dinner and Monday from November-February except Christmas Holidays)* **Meals** 43/73 ♀ – ☕ 28 – **16 rm** 300/720, 13 suites, 11 duplex.
◆ Once the home of a Flemish poet, this establishment is in a mixture of Baroque and Florentine neo-Classical styles. Garden and pool project over the sea. The Mélisande has a gallery of 19C Orientalist pictures and a terrace overlooking the city shoreline.

Méridien, 1 promenade des Anglais ✆ 04 97 03 44 44, *mail@lemeridien-nice.com, Fax 04 97 03 44 45,* ←, 🏋, 🏊 – |♦|, 🚭 rm, ▤ TV ✆ – 🪑 300. AE ⓓ GB JCB FZ d
Colonial Café ✆ 04 97 03 40 36 *(open dinner from 1 October-24 May)* **Meals** a la carte 40/55 ♀ – ***Terrasse du Colonial*** *(closed dinner from 1 October-24 May)* **Meals** a la carte 40/55 ♀ – ☕ 22 – **301 rm** 230/425, 17 suites.
◆ The highlight of this contemporary palace is its rooftop pool facing the Baie des Anges. Lovely rooms in Mediterranean colours, beauty salon, hi-tech business facilities. Ethnic décor and world cuisine in the Colonial Café. Sea views from the Terrasse.

Palais de la Méditerranée, 15 prom. Anglais ✆ 04 92 14 77 00, *reservation@lepalaisdelamediterranée.com, Fax 04 92 14 77 14,* ←, 🏊, 🏊 – |♦|, 🚭 rm, ▤ rm, TV ✆ ♿ 🚗 – 🪑 20 - 500. AE ⓓ GB. 🚫 rest FZ g
Padouk : Meals 60 ♀ – ***Pingala Bar*** : Meals a la carte 18/30 ♀ – ☕ 30 – **182 rm** 375/780, 6 suites.
◆ This legendary building with its listed Art Deco façade is now home to a brand-new hotel with modern, spacious rooms. Contemporary cuisine and warm decor in the Padouk restaurant, while the more modern Pingala Bar concentrates on cuisine from around the world.

Élysée Palace, 59, promenade des Anglais ✆ 04 93 97 90 90, *reservation@elyseepalace.com, Fax 04 93 44 50 40,* 🏊 – |♦|, 🚭 rm, ▤ TV ✆ ♿ 🚗 – 🪑 70 - 100. AE ⓓ GB JCB. 🚫 rest EZ d
Le Caprice : Meals 39/49 ♀ – ☕ 19 – **143 rm** 230/390.
◆ The most extraordinary feature of this futuristic building is the immense bronze Venus. Art Deco interiors, high level of comfort, exemplary soundproofing, rooftop pool. Attractive restaurant with panoramic summer terrace and cuisine with a local touch.

Sofitel, 2-4 parvis de l'Europe ✉ 06300 ✆ 04 92 00 80 00, *h1119@accor-hotels.com, Fax 04 93 26 27 00,* ⛱, 🏋, 🏊 – |♦|, 🚭 rm, ▤ TV ✆ ♿ 🚗 – 🪑 35 - 80. AE ⓓ GB JCB
L'Oliveraie *(closed 15 June-30 September)* **Meals** 27 ♀ – ***Sundeck*** *(15 June-30 September)* **Meals** 27 – ☕ 23 – **146 rm** 240/260, 6 suites. JX t
◆ On the site of Nice's acropolis, this hotel has been redesigned in contemporary style. Modern, well-presented rooms with good facilities. Lovely panoramic rooftop pool. Provençal décor in the Oliveraie. Grills and city and country views in the Sundeck.

Boscolo Hôtel Plaza, 12 av. Verdun ✆ 04 93 16 75 75, *saveurs-gourmandes@plaza-boscolo.com, Fax 04 93 88 61 11* – |♦| ▤ TV ✆ – 🪑 250 - 400. AE ⓓ GB JCB GZ u
Meals 32/40 ♀ – ☕ 16 – **182 rm** 401/530.
◆ Imposing hotel adjacent to the Jardin Albert 1er. Spacious rooms. Roof-terrace with lovely seaward views. Comprehensive meeting facilities. Dining room in warm colours and a generous panoramic terrace overlooking the city.

La Pérouse 🕊, 11 quai Rauba-Capéu ✉ 06300 ✆ 04 93 62 34 63, *lp@hroy.com, Fax 04 93 62 59 41,* ← Nice and Baie des Anges, ⛱, 🏋, 🏊, 🌳 – |♦|, ▤ rm, TV ✆ – 🪑 30. AE ⓓ GB JCB. 🚫 HZ k
Meals grill rest. *(mid-May-mid-September)* a la carte 32/51 ♀ – ☕ 17 – **58 rm** 220/405, 4 suites.
◆ This characterful hotel clinging to the castle rock offers refined, Provençal-style rooms and a delightful Mediterranean garden. The viewpoint was an inspiration for Dufy. In the restaurant-grill, enjoy your meal in perfect tranquillity under the lemon trees.

West End, 31 promenade des Anglais ✆ 04 92 14 44 00, *hotel-westend@hotel-westend.com, Fax 04 93 88 85 07,* ←, ⛱, 🎾 – |♦| ▤ TV ✆ – 🪑 100. AE ⓓ GB JCB FZ p
Le Siècle : Meals 28/39 ♀ – ☕ 17 – **116 rm** 220/315, 10 suites.
◆ Built in the early 19C, this listed hotel is in constant evolution. Ask for one of the rooms refurbished in English or Provençal style with a sea view. The smart Le Siècle brasserie is in Belle Epoque style and has two attractively planted terraces.

NICE

Alberti (R.) .... GHY 2
Alsace-Lorraine (Jardin) EZ 3
Armée-du-Rhin (Pl.) ... JX 5
Auriol (Pont V.) .... JV 7
Bellanda (Av.) .... HV 10
Berlioz (R.) .... FY 12
Bonaparte (R.) .... JY 13
Carnot (Bd) .... JZ 15
Desambrois (Av.) ..... GHX 18
Diables-Bleus (Av. des) .... JX 19
Europe (Parvis de l') .... JX 21
Félix-Faure (Av.) ...... GZ 22
France (R. de) .... DFZ
Gallieni (Av.) .... HJX 23
Gambetta (Bd) .... EXZ
Gautier (Pl. P.) .... HZ 25
Gioffredo (R.) .... HY
Hôtel-des-Postes (R.) .. HY 30
Ile-de-Beauté (Pl. de l') .... JZ 31
J.-Jaurès (Bd) .... HYZ 32
Liberté (R. de la) ...... GZ 35
Lunel (Quai) .... JZ 37
Masséna (Espace, Pl.) .... GZ
Masséna (R.) .... FGZ 43
Médecin (Av. J.) .... FGY 44
Meyerbeer (R.) .... FZ 45
Monastère (Av. et Pl. du) .... HV 46
Moulin (Pl. J.) .... HY 47
Paradis (R.) .... GZ 55
Passy (R. F.) .... EY 57
Pastorelli (R.) .... GY 58
Phocéens (Av. des) .... GZ 59
Ray (Av. du) .... FV 63

République (Av. de la) . . JXY 64	St-Jean Baptiste (Av.) . . . . HY 73	Verdun (Av.de) . . . . FGZ 89
Rivoli (R. de) . . . . FZ 65	Saleya (Cours) . . . . HZ 82	Walesa (Bd Lech) . . . . JYZ 91
St-François de Paule (R.) . . . . . . GHZ 72	Sauvan (R. H.) . . . . EZ 84	Wilson (Pl.) . . . . HY 92

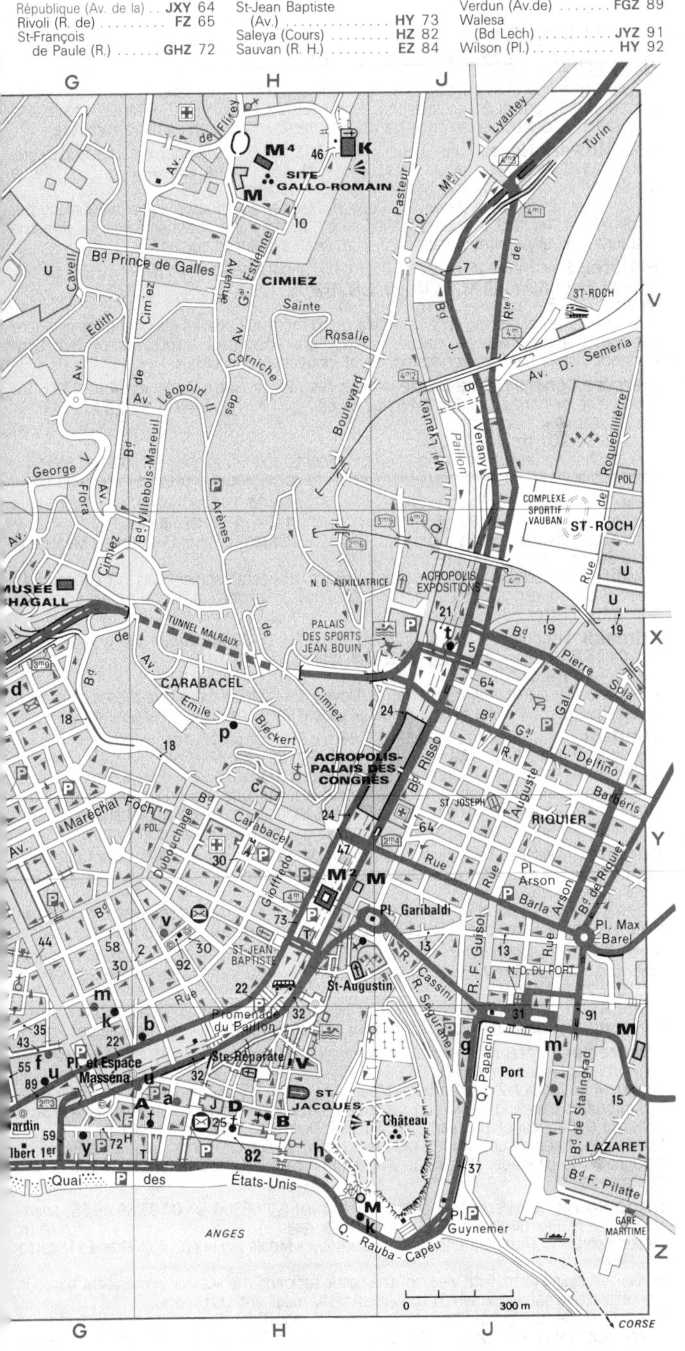

Holiday Inn, 20 bd V. Hugo ✆ 04 97 03 22 22, *reservations@holinice.com, Fax 04 93 03 22 23,* – rm, – 90. FY a
Meals 25 – 20 – **131 rm** 250/310.
◆ A concrete and glass building close to shops and traffic-free streets, with rooms decorated in different styles (colonial, maritime, taffeta etc). TV with internet access and Playstation. Spacious restaurant with colonial decor (plants and bamboo furniture).

Boscolo Park Hôtel, 6 av. Suède ✆ 04 97 03 19 00, *reservation@park.boscolo.com, Fax 04 93 82 29 27,* – – 150. FZ a
Meals *(dinner only)* a la carte 39/64 – 15 – **100 rm** 222/270.
◆ This hotel has rooms in classic, Art Deco, or Mediterranean style, some overlooking the Jardin Albert 1er and the sea. Brushed metal, mirrors and designer furniture give the restaurant a very contemporary ambience. Asian-influenced cuisine.

Hi Hôtel, 3 av. Fleurs ✆ 04 97 07 26 26, *hi@hi-hotel.net, Fax 04 97 07 26 27,* – rm,
Meals 25/30 – 18 – **38 rm** 150/360.
◆ A designer hotel bearing little resemblance to the traditional image of the term, where the use of space, materials, colour, furniture and equipment is totally innovative. Contemporary-style bar. Self-service choice of innovative cold dishes.

Mercure Centre Notre Dame without rest, 28 av. Notre-Dame ✆ 04 93 13 36 36, *h1291@accor-hotels.com, Fax 04 93 62 61 69,* – rm, – 90. FXY q
14,50 – **201 rm** 140/260.
◆ In addition to pretty, contemporary-style rooms, this completely refurbished Mercure hotel has a 2nd floor hanging garden, a beauty salon, and a rooftop terrace and pool.

Beau Rivage, 24 r. St-François-de-Paule ✉ 06300 ✆ 04 92 47 82 82, *info@nicebeaurivage.com, Fax 04 92 47 82 83,* – rm, – 50. GZ y
Bistrot du Rivage :* Meals** a la carte 30/45 – ***Plage *(16 April-15 October)* **Meals** a la carte 30/45 – 18 – **118 rm** 200/400.
◆ With its wonderful location and private beach, this establishment has lost count of its eminent past guests (Matisse, Nietzsche, Chekhov...). Spacious, practical rooms. Local cuisine in the Bistrot du Rivage. In summer, meals in La Plage right by the sea.

Grimaldi without rest, 15 r. Grimaldi ✆ 04 93 16 00 24, *zedde@le-grimaldi.com, Fax 04 93 87 00 24* – FY s
19 – **46 rm** 150/175.
◆ Provençal furnishings, wrought iron and lovely Souleûado fabrics give these rooms with little terraces on the top floor a personal touch. Very cosy foyer/bar/lounge.

Windsor, 11 r. Dalpozzo ✆ 04 93 88 59 35, *contact@hotelwindsornice.com, Fax 04 93 88 94 57,* – rest FZ f
Meals (coffee shop) *(closed lunch and Sunday)* a la carte approx. 31 – 8 – **57 rm** 105/155.
◆ This hotel has 20 fascinating "artists' rooms" including one bearing the signature of the local painter Ben. Exotic garden, leisure facilities including massage and a hammam. Meals at the bar in winter ; among the palms, bamboos and bougainvilleas in summer.

Durante without rest, 16 av. Durante ✆ 04 93 88 84 40, *info@hotel-durante.com, Fax 04 93 87 77 76,* – kitchenette
9 – **24 rm** 65/77.
◆ Newly renovated hotel with pretty bedrooms : the side road is so quiet that you can sleep with the windows open and let the scent of the orange trees waft in from the garden.

Petit Palais without rest, 17 av. E. Bieckert ✆ 04 93 62 19 11, *petitpalais@provence-riviera.com, Fax 04 93 62 53 60,* Nice and sea – rm, HX p
10 – **25 rm** 115/144.
◆ This villa of 1900 high up on the Cimiez hill was once lived in by Sacha Guitry. Most of the rooms look down over the rooftops of Nice's old town towards the Baie des Anges.

Chantecler - Hôtel Négresco, 37 promenade des Anglais ✆ 04 93 16 64 00, *direction@hotel-negresco.com, Fax 04 93 88 35 68* – FZ k
closed 14 November-21 December – **Meals** 45 (lunch), 90/130 and a la carte 95/140.
◆ Sumptuous panelling, Aubusson tapestries, Old Master paintings and damask curtains enhance the appeal of this early 18C interior. Delicious, highly individual cuisine.
Spec. Gelée tiède de coquillages, percebes, bulbe de fenouil, sorbet. Morue de Bilbao et bolognaise de pipérade. Mousseline d'agneau en tartelette sablée. **Wines** Bellet, Côtes-de-Provence.

L'Ane Rouge (Devillers), 7 quai Deux-Emmanuel ✉ 06300 ✆ 04 93 89 49 63, *anerouge@free.fr, Fax 04 93 89 49 63* – JZ m
closed February, Thursday lunch and Wednesday – **Meals** 26 (lunch), 45/60 and a la carte 51/72.
◆ Pleasant dining room with views of the castle rock and the activity in the yacht harbour - an attractive setting in which to savour tasty meat and fish dishes.
Spec. Fleur de courgette "Belle Niçoise" aux langoustines. Filet de loup rôti, barigoule d'artichaut. Tarte au chocolat. **Wines** Vin de pays de Saint-Jeannet, Côtes de Provence.

XXX **Don Camillo,** 5 r. Ponchettes ✉ 06300 ☎ 04 93 85 67 95, *vianostephane@wanadoo.fr, Fax 04 93 13 97 43* – ▤. AE ⓓ GB HZ h
closed 19 to 27 December, Sunday and Monday lunch – **Meals** - Niçoise and Italian specialities - 19 b.i. (lunch), 32/56 and a la carte 47/61 ♀.
◆ Harmonious décor, subtle colours and a welcoming atmosphere are the attractions of this restaurant in a quiet street. Local cuisine plus Italian specialities.

XXX **Les Viviers,** 22 r. A. Karr ☎ 04 93 16 00 48, *Fax 04 93 16 04 06* – ▤. AE GB FY k
closed August and Sunday – **Meals** 29/70 and a la carte 35/50 ♀.
◆ One dining room with elegant light-wood panelling, another with nautical decor - both serving identical food featuring fish, shellfish and daily specials.

XX ✿ **L'Univers-Christian Plumail,** 54 bd J. Jaurès ✉ 06300 ☎ 04 93 62 32 22, *plumailunivers@aol.com, Fax 04 93 62 55 69* – ▤. AE ⓓ GB HZ u
closed Sunday, lunch Saturday and Monday – **Meals** (booking essential) 38/65 and a la carte 51/70 ♀.
◆ The decor of this establishment is enhanced by pictures and modern sculpture. Individual local cuisine, which is very popular with locals.
Spec. Carpaccio de poulpes, vinaigrette de pistes. Loup de ligne piqué aux poivrons. Côtelettes de porcelet à la sauge et pied de porc farci. **Wines** Vin de Pays de Saint-Jeannet, Côtes de Provence.

XX **Boccaccio,** 7 r. Masséna ☎ 04 93 87 71 76, *infos@boccaccio-nice.com, Fax 04 93 82 09 06,* 🏠 – ▤. AE ⓓ GB JCB GZ f
Meals - Seafood - a la carte 39/69 ♀.
◆ In a busy traffic-free street, the Boccaccio has an imaginative interior on several levels designed to resemble an old ship. Mediterranean cuisine.

XX **Auberge de Théo,** 52 av. Cap de Croix ☎ 04 93 81 26 19, *aubergedetheo@wanadoo.fr, Fax 04 93 81 51 73* – ▤. GB BS u
closed 19 August-11 September, 23 December-3 January, Sunday dinner from September-April and Monday – **Meals** 19 (lunch)/29,50 ♀.
◆ On the city heights, this trattoria resembles nothing so much as Rome's famous Trastevere establishments. Rustic interior with beams and a real Neapolitan crib. Italian food.

XX **Brasserie Flo,** 4 r. S. Guitry ☎ 04 93 13 38 38, *Fax 04 93 13 38 39* – ▤. AE ⓓ GB GYZ m
Meals 29,90 b.i.
◆ In the style of a Paris brasserie, this establishment occupies an old theatre and presents a lively spectacle at all times, teeming with diners and hosts of serving staff.

XX **Les Épicuriens,** 6 pl. Wilson ☎ 04 93 80 85 00, *Fax 04 93 85 65 00,* 🏠 – ▤. AE GB HY v
closed 6 August-2 September, Saturday lunch and Sunday – **Meals** a la carte 33/52 ♀.
◆ Refined bistro-style decor, prettily planted terrace, up-to-the-minute cuisine with specials chalked up daily, much favoured by the business community.

XX **Les Pêcheurs,** 18 quai des Docks ☎ 04 93 89 59 61, *jbarbate@wanadoo.fr, Fax 04 93 55 47 50,* 🏠 – ▤. AE ⓓ GB JZ v
closed November-mid December, We., Th. lunch from May-October, Tu. dinner and We. from December-April – **Meals** - Seafood - 28 ♀.
◆ In the yacht harbour, this establishment seems to sum up the Cote d'Azur, with nautical décor, boats bobbing outside, and delicious seafood gracing your plate.

X **Mireille,** 19 bd Raimbaldi ☎ 04 93 85 27 23 – ▤. AE GB GX d
closed 7 June-1 July, 27 September-6 October, Monday and Tuesday – **Meals** - One dish only : paella - 20/27.
◆ Bang in the middle of Italian "Nizza", a restaurant with Hispanic décor and a real Provençal name. The only dish is paella, presented in a gleaming copper dish.

X **Merenda,** 4 r. Terrasse ✉ 06300 – ▤ HZ a
closed 26 April-2 May, 31 July-22 August, 29 November-12 December, 5 to 13 February, Saturday and Sunday – **Meals** - Niçoise specialities - (booking essential) a la carte 32/40 ♀.
◆ Uncomfortable stools, no credit cards accepted, payment in cash only... but it's worth it for the pleasure of savouring the real taste of Nice !

at the airport : *7 km* – ✉ *06200 Nice* :

🏨 **Novotel Arenas,** 455 promenade des Anglais ☎ 04 93 21 22 50, *h0478@accor-hotels.com, Fax 04 93 21 63 50* – 🛗, ⇔ rm, ▤ TV 📞 ♿ 🚗 – 🏛 25 - 150. AE ⓓ GB
Meals a la carte 23/35 – ☕ 12 – **131 rm** 115/130.
◆ With plenty of space, functional furnishings, good soundproofing and numerous meeting rooms, this well-presented Novotel is much appreciated by business travellers. More intimate atmosphere than usual in the restaurant. Provençal cuisine.

Èze *06360 Alpes-Mar.* 341 F5 – *pop. 2 509 alt. 390.*
Tourisme Office pl. de Gaulle ☎ 04 93 41 26 00, Fax 04 93 41 04 80, eze@webstore.fr.
Nice 12.

Château de la Chèvre d'Or, r. Barri (pedestrian access) ☎ 04 92 10 66 66, *reservation@chevredor.com, Fax 04 93 41 06 72,* ≤ coast and peninsula, – 20. AE GB JCB
5 March-early November – **Meals** *(closed Wednesday in March and November)* (booking essential) 60 (lunch)/130 and a la carte 130/170 – ☕ 35 – **27 rm** 500/750, 6 suites.
◆ With its hanging gardens high up on a rocky perch overlooking the Mediterranean, this enchanting establishment promises its guests an unforgettable experience. As well as delighting the eye, it's a treat for the taste-buds - a gastronomic paradise.
Spec. Les asperges "bourgeoises" (Spring). Filet mignon de veau rôti à l'infusion d'expresso torréfié (Summer). Perdreau "pattes grises", coffre rôti en feuille de vigne, jus pressé à la fine champagne (Autumn). **Wines** Côtes de Provence.

St-Martin-du-Var *06670 Alpes-Mar.* 341 E5 – *pop. 2 197 alt. 110.*
Nice 26.

Jean-François Issautier, on Nice road (N 202) 3 km ☎ 04 93 08 10 65, *jf.issautier@wanadoo.fr, Fax 04 93 29 19 73* – P. AE GB
closed 4 to 13 October, 3 January-3 February, Sunday dinner, Monday and Tuesday – **Meals** 47 b.i./92 and a la carte 85/115.
◆ This discreet restaurant, well-known to gourmets, is screened from the road by a conifer hedge. A fine classical repertoire favouring regional cuisine. Sophisticated setting.
Spec. Grosses crevettes poêlées en robe de pomme de terre. Pied de cochon croustillant. Cul d'agneau rôti rosé au jus de menthe. **Wines** Bellet, Côtes de Provence.

La Turbie *06320 Alpes-Mar.* 341 F5 – *pop. 3 021 alt. 495.* – *Nice 16.*

Hostellerie Jérôme (Cirino) with rm, 20 r. Comte de Cessole ☎ 04 92 41 51 51, *hostellerie.jerome@wanadoo.fr, Fax 04 92 41 51 50,* ≤, – rm, GB
closed 1 to 19 December, Monday and Tuesday except July-August – **Meals** (dinner only in July-August) 35 (lunch), 55/95 and a la carte 75/105 ♀ – ☕ 15 – **5 rm** 89/136.
◆ Handsome 13C building in a village better known for the Trophée des Alpes monument. Trim dining room with Italian décor and Mediterranean cuisine.
Spec. Tarte potagère aux gamberoni à l'huile d'olive. Foie gras de canard rôti aux agrumes de Menton (winter). Loup de mer à la compotée de fleurs et feuilles de courgettes. **Wines** Côtes de Provence, Bellet.

Vence *06140 Alpes-Mar.* 341 D5 – *pop. 16 982 alt. 325.*
Tourist Office, pl. Grand-Jardin ☎ 04 93 58 06 38, Fax 04 93 58 91 81, information@ville-vence.fr. – *Nice 23.*

Jacques Maximin, 689 chemin de La Gaude, by road of Cagnes : 3 km ☎ 04 93 58 90 75, *info@jacques-maximin.com, Fax 04 93 58 22 86,* – P. AE GB
closed mid Nov.-mid Dec., lunch in 07/08 except Sunday, Monday and Tuesday out of season except Bank Holidays – **Meals** (booking essential) 40 (lunch), 62/130 and a la carte 85/120.
◆ Surrounded by luxurious vegetation, this 19C house adorned with works of art created by renowned artists is the setting for cuisine that is as delicious as it is creative.
Spec. Filet de loup sauvage rôti à la niçoise. Canard du Lauragais rôti à l'ail doux. Sablé "biancospino" aux framboises de Vence (May-November). **Wines** Bellet, Vin de Pays des Alpes Maritimes.

STRASBOURG *67000 B.-Rhin* 315 K5 – *pop. 264 115 alt. 143.*
See : *Cathedral*** : Astronomical clock* – La Petite France** : rue du Bains-aux-Plantes** HJZ – Barrage Vauban ** – Ponts couverts* – Place de la Cathédrale* KZ* **26** *: Maison Kammerzell* KZ* **e** *– Mausoleum** in St-Thomas Church JZ – Place Kléber* – Hôtel de Ville* KY* **H** *– Orangery* – Palais de l'Europe* – Museum of Oeuvre N.-Dame** KZ* **M**[1] *– Boat trips on the Ill river and the canals* KZ – Museums** (decorative Arts, Fine Arts, Archeology) in the Palais Rohan* KZ – Alsatian Museum** KZ* **M**[2].
9 18 *at Illkirch-Graffenstaden (private) ☎ 03 88 66 17 22 ;* 18 *of the Wantzenau at Wantzenau (private) ☎ 03 88 96 37 73 ; N by D 468 : 12 km ;* 18 *of Kempferhof at Plobsheim ☎ 03 88 98 72 72, S by D 468 : 15 km.*
of Strasbourg International : ☎ 03 88 64 67 67 by D 392 : 12 km FR.
☎ 08 36 35 35 35.
Tourist Office 17 pl. de la Cathédrale ☎ 03 88 52 28 28, Fax 03 88 52 28 29, info@strasbourg.com, pl.gare ☎ 03 88 32 51 49, Pont de l'Europe ☎ 03 88 61 39 23.
Paris 490 – Basle 145 – Bonn 360 – Bordeaux 915 – Frankfurt 218 – Karlsruhe 81 – Lille 545 – Luxembourg 223 – Lyons 485 – Stuttgart 157.

Sofitel, pl. St-Pierre-le-Jeune ☎ 03 88 15 49 00, *h0568@accor-hotels.com, Fax 03 88 15 49 99,* – |‡|, ⇔ rm, ▤ TV ✆ – 🏛 100. AE ⓓ GB JCB JY s
L'Alsace Gourmande ☎ 03 88 15 49 10 **Meals** 29 ♀ – ☕ 20 – **155 rm** 195/230.
◆ The first Sofitel ever built in France (1964) is today a hotel allying modern comforts and excellent facilities. Stylish bedrooms, plus a lobby that opens onto a patio. The menu of l'Alsace Gourmande includes several local dishes, including sauerkraut.

Régent Petite France ⛵, 5 r. Moulins ☎ 03 88 76 43 43, *rpf@regent-hotels.com, Fax 03 88 76 43 76,* ≤, ☂, 🏋 – |‡|, ⇔ rm, ▤ TV ✆ ♿ – 🏛 30 - 80. AE ⓓ GB JCB JZ z
Meals *(closed Sunday from October-April and Monday from May-September)* 32/59 ♀ – ☕ 18,50 – **64 rm** 223/299, 4 suites, 4 duplex.
◆ Metal, glass, Starck furniture and high-tech gadgetry dominate this modern hotel in an old refrigeration plant on the banks of the Ill. A trendy interior and a pleasant view of the river and old town are the main attractions of the restaurant.

Hilton, av. Herrenschmidt ☎ 03 88 37 10 10, *sales_strasbourg@hilton.com, Fax 03 88 36 83 27,* ☂ – |‡|, ⇔ rm, ▤ TV ✆ ♿ – 🏛 25 - 350. AE ⓓ GB JCB
Table du Chef ☎ 03 88 37 41 42 (lunch only) *(closed 17 July-22 August, Saturday and Sunday)* **Meals** 38 – ***Jardin du Tivoli*** ☎ 03 88 35 72 61 **Meals** 30 ♀ – ☕ 21 – **243 rm** 210/290, 6 suites.
◆ The Hilton is a slender glass and steel building with refurbished rooms fitted with the latest in technology, shops, a multimedia centre and bars. Classic cuisine is served in the British ambience of La Table du Chef. Pleasant terrace at the Jardin du Tivoli.

Holiday Inn, 20 pl. Bordeaux ☎ 03 88 37 80 00, *histrasbourg@alliance-hospitality.com, Fax 03 88 37 07 04,* 🏋, 🏊 – |‡|, ⇔ rm, ▤ TV ✆ ♿ P – 🏛 300. AE ⓓ GB JCB. ✗ rest
Meals *(closed lunch Saturday and Sunday)* 25 ♀ – ☕ 15 – **171 rm** 195/275.
◆ An ideal business and seminar hotel with well-appointed rooms near the European courts and conference centre. Traditional cuisine with Provençal touches served amid "Louisiana"-style décor.

Régent Contades without rest, 8 av. Liberté ☎ 03 88 15 05 05, *rc@regent-hotels.com, Fax 03 88 15 05 15* – |‡|, ⇔ rm, ▤ TV ✆. AE ⓓ GB JCB LY f
☕ 16,50 – **47 rm** 165/325.
◆ A former 19C private mansion with an elegant décor of decorative panelling in the lounge and ubiquitous canvases. Pleasant view of the river from the breakfast room.

Beaucour without rest, 5 r. Bouchers ☎ 03 88 76 72 00, *beaucour@hotel-beaucour.com, Fax 03 88 76 72 60* – |‡| ▤ TV ✆ ♿ – 🏛 25. AE ⓓ GB JCB KZ k
☕ 11 – **49 rm** 126/169.
◆ These two 18C Alsatian houses are laid out around a flowery patio. Elegant furnishings with bedrooms that blend the rustic with the contemporary.

Maison Rouge without rest, 4 r. Francs-Bourgeois ☎ 03 88 32 08 60, *info@maison-rouge.com, Fax 03 88 22 43 73* – |‡| TV ✆ ♿ – 🏛 15 - 30. AE ⓓ GB JZ g
☕ 13 – **142 rm** 122/139.
◆ As the name would suggest, this refined hotel stands behind a red-stone façade. Personalised bedrooms, with each floor having its own superbly decorated lounge.

Europe without rest, 38 r. Fossé des Tanneurs ☎ 03 88 32 17 88, *info@hotel-europe.com, Fax 03 88 75 65 45* – |‡|, ⇔ rm, ▤ TV ✆ 🚗 – 🏛 30. AE ⓓ GB JCB JZ v
closed 23 to 29 December – ☕ 11 – **60 rm** 69/163.
◆ A half-timbered house with refurbished, spacious rooms and a hugely impressive 1 : 50 scale model of the cathedral on display in the lobby.

Monopole-Métropole without rest, 16 r. Kuhn ☎ 03 88 14 39 14, *infos@bw-monopole.com, Fax 03 88 32 82 55* – |‡|, ⇔ rm, TV ✆ 🚗 – 🏛 15. AE ⓓ GB JCB HY p
☕ 10 – **90 rm** 79/140.
◆ Close to the station, with two types of rooms : traditional, with period furniture ; and modern, featuring works by local artists. The lounges are museums in their own right.

Novotel Centre Halles, 4 quai Kléber ☎ 03 88 21 50 50, *h0439@accor-hotels.com, Fax 03 88 21 50 51* – |‡|, ⇔ rm, ▤ TV ✆ ♿ – 🏛 15 - 80. AE ⓓ GB JCB JY k
Meals a la carte 25/35 ♀ – ☕ 12 – **98 rm** 139/149.
◆ A completely overhauled hotel within Les Halles shopping centre. Functional, identical rooms, a bar decorated on the theme of the cinema, and an inviting restaurant with original décor which has moved away from the standard Novotel look.

Mercure Centre without rest, 25 r. Thomann ☎ 03 90 22 70 70, *h1106@accor-hotels.com, Fax 03 90 22 70 71* – |‡|, ⇔ rm, ▤ TV ✆ ♿ 🚗. AE ⓓ GB JCB JY q
☕ 12,50 – **98 rm** 129/139.
◆ This extensively renovated chain hotel occupies an excellent location in the city centre. The breakfast room on the 7th floor enjoys a panoramic view of Strasbourg's rooftops.

STRASBOURG

Abreuvoir (R. de l') ..... LZ 3
Arc-en-Ciel (R. de l') .... KLY 7
Austerlitz (R. d') .... KZ 10
Auvergne (Pont d') ...... LY 12
Bateliers (R. des) .... LZ 14
Bonnes-Gens (R. des) .... JY 19
Bouclier (R. du) .... JZ 20
Castelnau (R. Gén. de) ... KY 25
Cathédrale (Pl. de la) .... KZ 26
Chaudron (R. du) .... KY 28
Cheveux (R. des) .... JZ 29
Corbeau (Pl. du) .... KZ 31
Cordiers (R. des) .... KZ 32
Courtine (R. de la) .... LY 34
Dentelles (R. des) .... JZ 36
Division-Leclerc (R.) ..... JKZ
Écarlate (R. de l') .... JZ 43
Escarpée (R.) .... JZ 45
Étudiants (R. et Pl. des) ... KY 46
Faisan (Pont du) .... JZ 47
Fonderie (Pont de la) .... KY 52
Fossé-des-Tanneurs
(Rue du) .... JZ 57
Fossé-des-Treize (R. du) .. KY 58
Francs-Bourgeois
(R. des) .... JZ 60
Frey (Q. Charles) .... JZ 63
Grande-Boucherie
(Pl. de la) .... KZ 76
Gdes-Arcades (R. des) ... JKY
Gutenberg (R.) .... JKZ 7
Hallebardes (R. des) .... KZ 8
Haute-Montée (R.) ...... JY 8
Homme-de-Fer
(Pl. de l') .... JY 9
Hôpital-Militaire (R. de l'). LZ 9
Humann (R.) .... HZ 9
Ill (Quai de l') .... HZ 9
Kellermann (Quai) ...... JY 1
Kléber (Place) .... JY
Krutenau (Rue de la) .... LZ 1
Kuss (Pont) .... HY 1
Lamey (R. Auguste) .... LY 1
Lezay-Marnésia (Quai) ... LY 1
Luther (R. Martin) ...... JZ 1

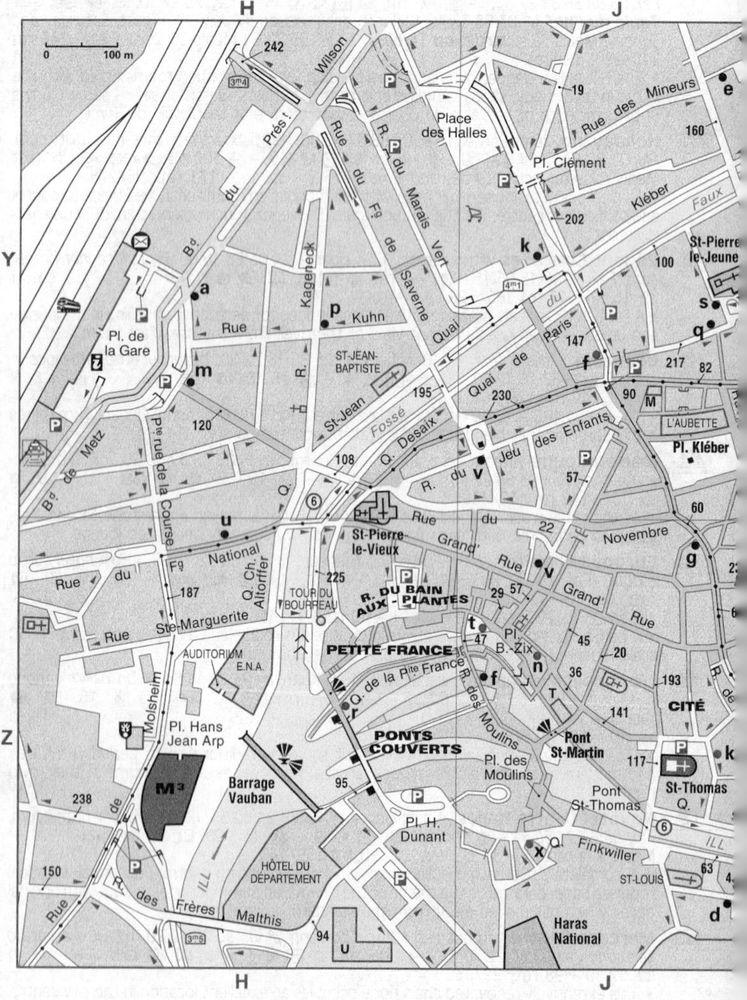

K
L
Y
Z
ST-PIERRE-LE-JEUNE
Palais du Rhin
Place de la République
BIBLIOTHÈQUE NATIONALE
ST-PAUL
Hôtel de Klinglin
HÔTEL D'ANDLAU
Hôtel des deux Ponts
ÉVÊCHÉ
Place Broglie
Pont Royal
Place St-Étienne
ST-ÉTIENNE
Pt. St-Guillaume
St-Guillaume
CATHÉDRALE NOTRE-DAME
Pl. du Château
PALAIS ROHAN
Pl. Gutenberg
Pl. du Pont aux Chats
Pl. de l'Université
Pl. du Foin
ANCIENNE
Anc^ne Douane
Pont du Corbeau
COUR DU CORBEAU
STE-MADELEINE
Pl. de Zurich
ST-NICOLAS
Pl. d'Austerlitz
Pl. de l'Hôpital
CITÉ ADMINISTRATIVE

France without rest, 20 r. Jeu des Enfants ☎ 03 88 32 37 12, *hotel.de.france.sa@wanadoo.fr, Fax 03 88 22 48 08* – rm, – 30. AE GB JY v
13 – **66 rm** 99/123.
◆ An ideal base from which to explore the old town on foot. Colourful, soundproofed rooms of a reasonable size, some with a balcony.

Gutenberg without rest, 31 r. Serruriers ☎ 03 88 32 17 15, *hotel.gutenberg@wanadoo.fr, Fax 03 88 75 76 67* – . GB. KZ m
closed 1 to 9 January – 7,30 – **42 rm** 57/89.
◆ The walls of this building dating from 1745 enclose 42 pleasant, well-appointed rooms ; those on the top floor are fitted with dormer windows. Glass roof in the breakfast room.

Diana-Dauphine without rest, 30 r. 1e Armée ☎ 03 88 36 26 61, *hotel.dianadauphine@wanadoo.fr, Fax 03 88 35 50 07* – . AE GB JCB
closed 24 December-1 January – 9 – **45 rm** 78/90.
◆ The tramway provides a rapid link between this hotel and the old town. Fine Louis XV and Louis XVI furniture in the bedrooms, enhanced by renovated bathrooms.

Dragon without rest, 2 r. Ecarlate ☎ 03 88 35 79 80, *hotel@dragon.fr, Fax 03 88 25 78 95* – rm, . AE GB. JZ d
10 – **32 rm** 69/112.
◆ Built around a charming small courtyard, this tranquil 17C residence has a resolutely modern feel with designer furniture and contemporary grey décor in its spotless rooms.

Cardinal de Rohan without rest, 17 r. Maroquin ☎ 03 88 32 85 11, *info@hotel-rohan.com, Fax 03 88 75 65 37* – rm, . AE GB JCB KZ u
10 – **36 rm** 63/122.
◆ In the heart of this tourist area, with rooms adorned with Louis XV-style furniture offering good levels of comfort and sound insulation. Elegant lounges.

Pax, 24 r. Fg National ☎ 03 88 32 14 54, *info@paxhotel.com, Fax 03 88 32 01 16,* – rm, – 15 - 60. AE GB JCB HYZ u
closed 24 December-2 January – **Meals** *(closed Sunday from November-February)* 15/23 – 7 – **106 rm** 68.
◆ The Pax stands along a road where the only traffic is the local tram. Bedrooms decorated in sober style. In fine weather, the tables in the restaurant, serving regional cuisine, are laid out on an attractive, vine-adorned patio-cum-terrace.

Couvent du Franciscain without rest, 18 r. Fg de Pierre ☎ 03 88 32 93 93, *info@hotel-franciscain.com, Fax 03 88 75 68 46* – – 15. AE GB JCB JY e
closed 24 December-9 January – 8 – **43 rm** 62/64.
◆ These two buildings at the end of a cul-de-sac are linked by a pleasant entrance hall. The rooms in the new wing are preferable. Breakfast room in the cellar.

Au Crocodile (Jung), 10 r. Outre ☎ 03 88 32 13 02, *info@au-crocodile.com, Fax 03 88 75 72 01* – . AE GB JCB. KY x
closed 11 July-2 August, 24 December-6 January, Sunday and Monday – **Meals** 54 (lunch), 79/122 and a la carte 91/121.
◆ With its splendid wood décor, canvases and the famous crocodile brought back from the Egyptian campaign by an Alsatian captain, the setting is as refined as the cuisine.
Spec. Cuisse de grenouilles et anguille au mille-choux. Foie de canard en croûte de sel, baeckeoffa de légumes truffé. Noisette de faon de biche à l'écorce d'orange (15 October-15 February). **Wines** Riesling, Tokay-Pinot gris.

Buerehiesel (Westermann), set in the Orangery Park ☎ 03 88 45 56 65, *westermann@buerehiesel.fr, Fax 03 88 61 32 00,* – . AE GB
closed 27 July-18 August, 31 December-20 January, Sunday dinner and Tuesday – **Meals** (dinner only Monday to Friday) 110/140 and a la carte 115/145.
◆ This authentic half-timbered farm rebuilt in 1904 and embellished with modern glass, is hidden amid the greenery of the Parc de l'Orangerie. A paradise of Alsatian gastronomy !
Spec. Foie gras d'oie frais truffé en croûte, gelée aux noix. Schniederspaetle et cuisses de grenouilles poêlées au cerfeuil. Ris de veau poêlé aux croûtons, oignons glacés et fricassée de légumes verts. **Wines** Sylvaner, Pinot noir.

Vieille Enseigne (Langs), 9 r. Tonneliers ☎ 03 88 32 58 50, *info@la-vieille-enseigne.com, Fax 03 88 75 63 80* – . AE GB JCB KZ f
closed Saturday lunch and Sunday – **Meals** 32 (lunch), 61/78 and a la carte 65/83.
◆ Refined, in-vogue cuisine, an extensive wine cellar, and a hushed, elegant setting characterise this restaurant housed within the walls of a fine 17C Alsatian mansion.
Spec. Grosses langoustines sur galette de pommes de terre. Pavé de sandre braisé au gewürztraminer. Pigeonneau des Vosges à l'huile de pistache. **Wines** Pinot blanc, Riesling.

Estaminet Schloegel, 19 r. Krütenau ☎ 03 88 36 21 98, *Fax 03 88 36 21 98* – . GB LZ q
closed August, Sunday, lunch Saturday and Monday – **Meals** 36/43 and a la carte 45/60.
◆ Set back from the historic centre, this former tavern is colourfully decorated with tasteful contemporary furnishings. A spiral wooden staircase adds further embellishment.

XXX **Maison des Tanneurs dite "Gerwerstub",** 42 r. Bain aux Plantes ✆ 03 88 32 79 70, *maison.des.tanneurs@wanadoo.fr, Fax 03 88 22 17 26* – AE ⓓ GB JZ t
closed 30 December-25 January, Sunday and Monday – **Meals** a la carte 40/66.
• Ideally situated on the banks of the Ill, this typical Alsatian house in the Petite France district is one of the best addresses in town for an authentic sauerkraut.

XXX **Maison Kammerzell and Hôtel Baumann** with rm, 16 pl. Cathédrale ✆ 03 88 32 42 14, *info@maison-kammerzell.com, Fax 03 88 23 03 92* – 80 - 100. AE ⓓ GB JCB KZ e
hotel : closed February – **Meals** 29/36 and a la carte 36/60 ♀ – ☐ 10 – **9 rm** 69/110.
• Wall paintings, stained-glass, wood sculptures and Gothic vaults provide a museum feel to this 16C Strasbourg institution serving typical Alsatian dishes.

XX ✿ **Julien,** 22 quai Bateliers ✆ 03 88 36 01 54, *restaurant.julien@wanadoo.fr, Fax 03 88 35 40 14* – ▤. AE ⓓ GB JCB KZ x
closed 4 to 12 April, 9 to 30 August, 2 to 10 January, Sunday and Monday – **Meals** 35 (lunch)/78 and a la carte 59/82 ♀.
• A fine 18C Alsatian house in which the décor of benches and glossy walls takes its inspiration from the bistros of the Belle Époque period. Cuisine with a personal touch.
Spec. Escalope de foie gras de canard. Filets de sole rôtis. Moelleux au chocolat guanaja.
Wines Riesling, Pinot auxerrois.

XX **Pont des Vosges,** 15 quai Koch ✆ 03 88 36 47 75, *pontdesvosges@noos.fr, Fax 03 88 25 16 85,* ☂ – AE GB LY h
closed Sunday – **Meals** a la carte 33/52 ♀.
• This brasserie-style restaurant on the ground floor of an old building, is arranged in a semi-circle. Retro decoration, plus a menu that includes a few regional specialities.

XX **S'Staefele,** 2 pl. St-Thomas ✆ 03 88 32 39 03, *Fax 03 88 21 90 80,* ☂ – AE GB JZ k
closed 16 to 31 August, 24 December-3 January, Sunday and Monday – **Meals** 25/33 ♀.
• Meat specialities served to order are the mainstays of the menu in the rustic dining room, with more simple fare in the bistro. The terrace overlooks a pretty, small square.

X **Au Rocher du Sapin,** 6 r. Noyer ✆ 03 88 32 39 65, *Fax 03 88 75 60 99,* ☂ – AE GB
closed Sunday – **Meals** 14,50/20,60 ♀. JY 20
• This venerable Alsatian brasserie in the department store district continues to be popular for its simple but copious local cuisine, served at tables in booths.

WINSTUBS : *Regional specialities and wine tasting in a typical Alsatian atmosphere :*

X **Ami Schutz,** 1 r. Ponts Couverts ✆ 03 88 32 76 98, *info@ami-schutz.com, Fax 03 88 32 38 40,* ☂ – AE ⓓ GB HZ r
closed Christmas Holidays – **Meals** 36,30 b.i./42,50 b.i.
• This beer tavern between the branches of the River Ill has a pleasant shaded terrace. The charming dining rooms have a warm atmosphere and superb antique wood panelling.

X **S'Muensterstuewel,** 8 pl. Marché aux Cochons de Lait ✆ 03 88 32 17 63, *munster stuewel@wanadoo.fr, Fax 03 88 21 96 02,* ☂ – ▤. AE ⓓ GB KZ y
closed 15 August-6 September, 6 to 20 February, Sunday and Monday – **Meals** 25 (lunch), 30/45.
• A former butcher's decorated in pure "winstub" style with pleasant rustic furniture. In summer, sit out on the terrace in front of a small square popular with tourists.

X **Le Clou,** 3 r. Chaudron ✆ 03 88 32 11 67, *Fax 03 88 75 72 83* – ▤. AE GB KY n
closed Wednesday lunch, Sunday and Bank Holidays – **Meals** a la carte 29/39 ♀.
• This typical Alsatian wine-bar near the cathedral is known for its traditional décor and convivial atmosphere. Popular with celebrities, as shown by the photos on the walls.

X **Au Pont du Corbeau,** 21 quai St-Nicolas ✆ 03 88 35 60 68, *corbeau@reperes.com, Fax 03 88 25 72 45* – ▤. GB KZ b
closed August, February Holidays, Sunday lunch and Saturday except December – **Meals** a la carte 23/32 ♀.
• On the banks of the river, next to the Musée Alsacien (popular art), this originally decorated restaurant is inspired by the Renaissance style of the area. Local specialities.

X **Zum Strissel,** 5 pl. Gde Boucherie ✆ 03 88 32 14 73, *Fax 03 88 32 70 24* – ▤. AE ⓓ GB KZ a
closed 3 July-2 August, 27 January-7 February, Sunday and Monday – **Meals** 10,30/22 ♀.
• This authentic "winstub" run by the same family since 1920 enjoys an attractive setting enhanced by works of wrought-iron and stained-glass showing Alsace's wine industry.

X **S'Burjerstuewel (Chez Yvonne),** 10 r. Sanglier ✆ 03 88 32 84 15, *info@chez-yvonne.com, Fax 03 88 23 00 18* – AE GB KYZ r
closed Sunday (except December) and Bank Holidays – **Meals** (booking essential) a la carte 30/40 ♁.
• The visit of Jacques Chirac and Helmut Kohl has placed this Strasbourg institution firmly in the limelight. Elbow-to-elbow dining, with a calmer ambience on the ground floor.

Fink'Stuebel, 26 r. Finkwiller ✆ 03 88 25 07 57, *Fax 03 88 36 48 82* – GB JZ x
closed 5 to 20 August, Sunday and Monday – **Meals** a la carte 26/41 ♀.
◆ Half-timbers, painted wood, local furniture and flowered tablecloths provide the décor in this typical "winstub". Regional cuisine, with pride of place given to foie gras.

Hailich Graab "Au St-Sépulcre", 15 r. Orfèvres ✆ 03 88 32 39 97, *Fax 03 88 32 39 97* – ▤. GB KZ d
closed 14 to 31 July, Sunday and Monday – **Meals** a la carte 17/22.
◆ An archetypal wine bar and restaurant that faithfully respects the traditions of Alsace in both its décor and cuisine. A friendly atmosphere guaranteed.

Environs

at La Wantzenau *NE by D 468 : 12 km – pop. 5 462 alt. 130 – ✉ 67610 :*

Relais de la Poste (Daull) with rm, 21 r. Gén. de Gaulle ✆ 03 88 59 24 80, *info@relais-poste.com, Fax 03 88 59 24 89,* – |‡|, ▤ rest, TV P – 15. AE GB JCB
closed 19 to 30 July and 2 to 22 January – **Meals** *(closed Saturday lunch, Sunday dinner and Monday)* 35 (lunch), 42/95 and a la carte 66/91 – ☕ 11 – **18 rm** 69/122.
◆ A typical Alsatian hostelry with elegant woodwork, frescoes and coffered ceilings. Personalised rooms, plus a veranda that looks out on to the countryside. Good wine list.
Spec. Foie gras frais à la gelée de muscat. Filet de sandre en paupiette, sauce riesling. Poussin grand'mère. **Wines** Riesling, Pinot noir.

Baerenthal *57 Moselle 307 Q5 – pop. 702 alt. 220 – ✉ 57230 Bitche.*
Strasbourg 64.

at Untermuhlthal *SE : 4 km by D 87 – ✉ 57230 Baerenthal :*

L'Arnsbourg (Klein), ✆ 03 87 06 50 85, *l.arnsbourg@wanadoo.fr, Fax 03 87 06 57 67,* – ▤ P. AE GB JCB
closed 20 to 28/04, 3 to 18/08, 16 to 24/11, 28/12-19/01, Monday dinner, Tuesday and Wednesday – **Meals** (weekends booking essential) 52 (lunch), 105/130 and a la carte 95/125.
◆ Right by the ruins of Arnsbourg castle, a lovely isolated house among the Vosges forests. Elegant dining room (non-smoking) above the Zinsel. Inventive, delicious cuisine.
Spec. Emulsion de pommes de terre et truffe (November-February). Aile de raie bouclée, écrasée de ratte, beurre noisette mousseux (June-October). Poitrine de pigeon relevé au wasabi. **Wines** Gewürztraminer, Muscat.

Illhaeusern *68970 H.-Rhin 315 I7 – pop. 646 alt. 173. – Strasbourg 60.*

Clairière without rest, rte Guémar ✆ 03 89 71 80 80, *hotel.la.clairiere@wanadoo.fr, Fax 03 89 71 86 22,* – |‡|, rm, TV P. GB
closed January and February – ☕ 13 – **25 rm** 77/202.
◆ On the edge of the Forêt de l'Ill, this huge building inspired by the architecture of Alsace has quiet and spacious rooms, all with distinctive décor and some with balconies.

Auberge de l'Ill (Haeberlin), 2 rue de Collonges ✆ 03 89 71 89 00, *auberge-de-l-ill@auberge-de-l-ill.com, Fax 03 89 71 82 83,* ≤ flowered gardens, – ▤ P. AE GB
closed 3 to 11 January, 2 February-8 March, Monday and Tuesday – **Meals** (booking essential) 90 (lunch), 108/131 and a la carte 90/140 ♀.
◆ The lovely landscaped banks of the River Ill provide a fine backdrop to the elegant dining room of this establishment. Traditional cuisine featuring sublime Alsatian dishes.
Spec. Mousseline de grenouilles " Paul Haeberlin". Volaille de Bresse rôtie à la broche, petit baeckoeffa aux truffes. Assiette "tout est bon dans le cochon". **Wines** Riesling, Pinot blanc.

Hôtel des Berges , ✆ 03 89 71 87 87, *hotel-des-berges@wanadoo.fr, Fax 03 89 71 87 88,* ≤, – |‡|, ▤ rm, TV – 15 - 25. AE GB
closed 3 to 11 January, 1 February-9 March and Tuesday – **Meals** see ***Auberge de l'Ill*** – ☕ 27 – **9 rm** 270/325, 4 suites.
◆ Attractively rebuilt tobacco-drying shed at the end of the garden belonging to the Auberge de l'Ill. Refined rooms, outdoor jacuzzi, and breakfast served on a boat !

Lembach *67510 B.-Rhin 315 K2 – pop. 1 689 alt. 190.*
Tourist Office 23 rte Bitche ✆ 03 88 94 43 16, Fax 03 88 94 20 04, info@ot-lembach.com. – Strasbourg 55.

Auberge du Cheval Blanc (Mischler) with rm, 4 rte Wissembourg ✆ 03 88 94 41 86, *info@au-cheval-blanc.fr, Fax 03 88 94 20 74,* – ▤ TV P – 25. AE GB
closed 5 to 23 July and 31 January-19 February – **Meals** *(closed Friday lunch, Monday and Tuesday)* 33/85,40 and a la carte 60/80 ♀ ***D'Rössel Stub*** *(closed 31 January-18 February, Wednesday and Thursday)* **Meals** a la carte approx. 30 ♀ – **3 rm** 107/138, 3 suites 199.
◆ A lovely paved courtyard leads to the huge dining room of this 18C stagecoach inn. Coffered ceiling, open fireplace, antique furniture and innovative Alsatian cuisine. The little bistro called D'Rössel Stub is in a tastefully restored old farmhouse.
Spec. Farandole de quatre foies d'oie chauds. Trilogie de grenouilles. Médaillons de chevreuil à la moutarde de fruits rouges (May-February). **Wines** Riesling, Pinot blanc.

Marlenheim *67520 B.-Rhin* 315 *I5 – pop. 3 365 alt. 195.*
Strasbourg 20.

Cerf (Husser), 30 rue du Général de Gaulle ☎ 03 88 87 73 73, *info@lecerf.com*, *Fax 03 88 87 68 08*, – TV P – 20. AE GB
closed 30 December-5 January, Tuesday and Wednesday – **Meals** 39 (lunch), 85/95 and a la carte 65/98 – 15 – **13 rm** 90/200.
◆ Old post hotel transformed into an elegant establishment consisting of several buildings around a prettily planted courtyard. Well-presented rooms. Restaurant with panelling and pictures from the regional school of painting. Fine Alsatian cuisine of today.
Spec. Tartare de daurade, garniture jardinière au raifort. Choucroute de cochon de lait au foie gras fumé. Soufflé au fromage blanc, soupe de fruits rouges (May-November).
Wines Riesling, Pinot noir.

TOULOUSE *31000 H.-Gar.* 343 *G3 – pop. 390 350 alt. 146.*
of Vieille-Toulouse ☎ 05 61 73 45 48 by D 4 : 8 km ; of Tournefeuille ☎ 05 61 07 09 09 by D 632 : 8 km ; of St-Gabriel at Montrabé ☎ 05 61 84 16 65 by 3 : 9 km.
of Toulouse-Blagnac ☎ 05 61 42 44 00.
☎ 08 36 35 35 35.
Tourist Office Donjon du Capitole ☎ 05 61 11 02 22, Fax 05 61 22 03 63, infos@ot.toulouse.fr.
Paris 699 – Bordeaux 248 – Lyons 536 – Marseilles 407 – Nantes 569.

Sofitel Centre, 84 allées J. Jaurès ☎ 05 61 10 23 10, *h1091@accor-hotels.com*, *Fax 05 61 10 23 20* – , rm, TV – 150. AE GB JCB, FX v
Meals ***L'Armagnac*** *(closed Sunday lunch and Saturday)* **Meals** 27 – 20 – **105 rm** 228/325, 14 suites.
◆ This hotel occupies eight floors of an imposing glass and red-brick building. Discreetly luxurious bedrooms with effective soundproofing. Business centre and attractive seminar room. The menu in the refined L'Armagnac restaurant highlights regional specialities.

Crowne Plaza, 7 pl. Capitole ☎ 05 61 61 19 19, *hicptoulouse@alliance-hospitality.com*, *Fax 05 61 23 79 96*, , – , rm, TV – 60. AE GB JCB EY t
Meals 23/54 – 22 – **159 rm** 290/305, 3 suites.
◆ This luxury hotel enjoys an excellent location on the famous Place du Capitole. Attractive, renovated rooms, some of which overlook the square. Intimate atmosphere in the restaurant, which opens on to a pleasant Florentine-style patio.

Grand Hôtel de l'Opéra without rest, 1 pl. Capitole ☎ 05 61 21 82 66, *contact@grand-hotel-opera.com*, *Fax 05 61 23 41 04*, – TV – 15 - 40. AE GB JCB EY a
20 – **57 rm** 130/259, 3 suites.
◆ Serenity and charm emanate from this hotel housed in a 17C convent. Attractive rooms adorned with wood panelling and red and yellow velvet. Pleasant lounge-bar.

Holiday Inn Centre, 13 pl. Wilson ☎ 05 61 10 70 70, *hi@capoul.com*, *Fax 05 61 21 96 70*, – , rm, TV – 50. AE GB JCB FY n
Meals ***Brasserie le Capoul*** ☎ 05 61 21 08 27 **Meals** a la carte 30/45 – 13 – **130 rm** 155/180.
◆ The main features of this long-established hotel on a lively square are its glass-crowned lobby and contemporary-style bedrooms with highly original bathrooms. At Le Capoul, the culinary focus is on seafood and regional specialities.

Brienne without rest, 20 bd Mar. Leclerc ☎ 05 61 23 60 60, *hoteldebrienne@wanadoo.fr*, *Fax 05 61 23 18 94* – TV P – 25. AE GB JCB DV n
9 – **71 rm** 73/85.
◆ The façade of this hotel, named after the nearby canal, is a blend of brick and glass. Clean, colourful, refurbished bedrooms, plus a verdant lobby opening on to a patio.

Mercure Atria, 8 espl. Compans Caffarelli ☎ 05 61 11 09 09, *h1585@accor-hotels.com*, *Fax 05 61 23 14 12*, – , rm, TV – 200. AE GB JCB DV k
Meals a la carte 26/34 – 11,50 – **136 rm** 109/114.
◆ With its direct link to the city's conference centre, this hotel with its modern, spacious and quiet bedrooms is a popular choice with business travellers. The restaurant affords pleasant views of the adjacent public park.

Novotel Centre , 5 pl. A. Jourdain ☎ 05 61 21 74 74, *h0906@accor-hotels.com*, *Fax 05 61 22 81 22*, , – , rm, TV – 100. AE GB JCB DV u
Meals a la carte 23/30 – 12 – **135 rm** 125.
◆ Designed in the style of the region, this hotel stands alongside a Japanese garden. Spacious bedrooms (currently being renovated), some with a terrace. A festival of colour in the dining room, with its leafy outlook and mix of traditional and local cuisine.

TOULOUSE

Alsace-Lorraine (R. d') ..... EXY
Arnaud-Bernard (R.) ..... EX 4
Astorg (R. d') ..... FY 5
Baronie (R.) ..... EY 9
Bilières (Av. E.) ..... DV 13
Bonrepos (Bd) ..... DV 16
Boulbonne (R.) ..... FY 18
Bouquières (R.) ..... FZ 19
Bourse (Pl. de la) ..... EY 20
Cantegril (R.) ..... FY 23
Capitole (Pl. du) ..... EY
Cartailhac (R. E.) ..... EX 26
Chaîne (R. de la) ..... EX 31
Cugnaux (R. de) ..... DV 35
Cujas (R.) ..... EY 36
Daurade (Quai de la) ..... EY 38
Demoiselles (Allées des) ..... DV 40
Esquirol (Pl.) ..... EY 54
Fonderie (R. de la) ..... EZ 60
Frères-Lion (R. des) ..... FY 62
Griffoul-Dorval (Bd) ..... DV 72
Henry-de-Gorsse (R.) ..... EZ 76
Jules-Chalande (R.) ..... EY 79
La Fayette (R.) ..... EY
Lapeyrouse (R.) ..... FY 85
Leclerc (Bd Mar.) ..... DV 87
Magre (R. Genty) ..... EY 91
Malcousinat (R.) ..... EY 92
Marchands (R. des) ..... EY 95
Mercié (R. A.) ..... EY 103
Metz (R. de) ..... EFY
Peyras (R.) ..... EY 113
Pleau (R. de la) ..... FZ 114
Poids-de-l'Huile (R.) ..... EY 115
Polinaires (R. des) ..... EZ 116
Pomme (R. de la) ..... EFY 117
Pompidou (Allée) ..... DV 118
Rémusat (R. de) ..... EX
République (R. de la) ..... DV 124
Riguepels (R.) ..... FY 127
Romiguières (R.) ..... EY 129
Roosevelt (Allées) ..... FXY 130
St-Antoine du T. (R.) ..... FY
St-Etienne (Port) ..... DV 133
St-Michel (Gde-Rue) ..... DV 134
Ste-Ursule (R.) ..... EY 137
St-Rome (R.) ..... EY
Sébastopol (R. de) ..... DV 139
Semard (Bd P.) ..... DV 142
Suau (R. J.) ..... EY 146
Temponières (R.) ..... EY 147
Trinité (R. de la) ..... EY 149
Vélane (R.) ..... FZ 158
Wilson (Pl. Prés) ..... FY
3-journées (R. des) ..... FY 162
3-Piliers (R. des) ..... EX 164

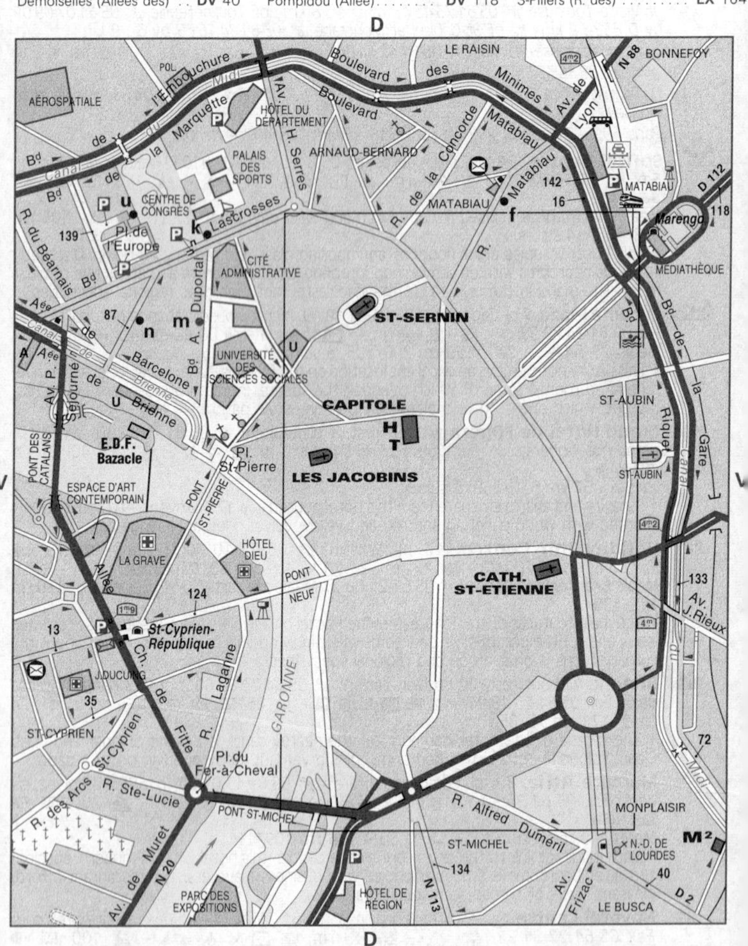

A good moderately priced meal : Repas 15/22

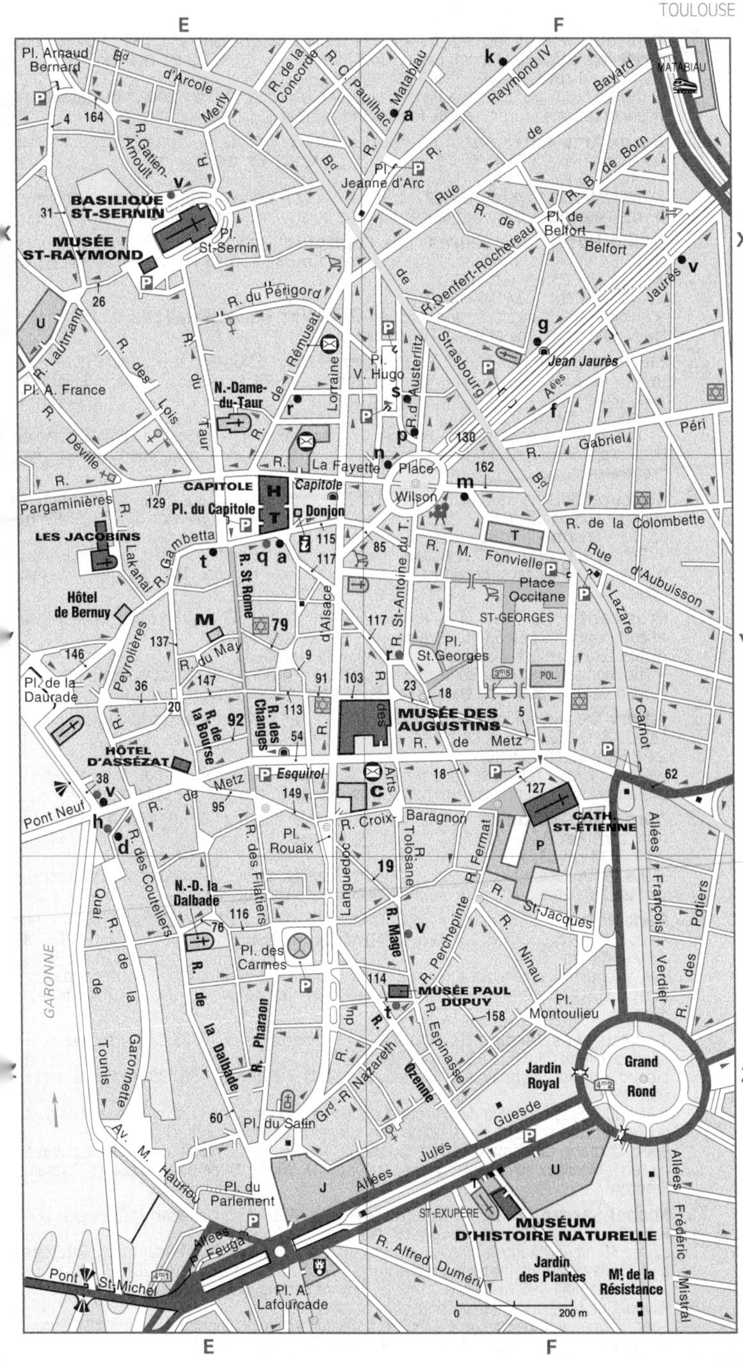

E
F
X
Y
Z
Pl. Arnaud Bernard
Bd d'Arcole
R. de la Concorde
R. C. Paulhac
Matabiau
Raymond IV
Bayard
MATABIAU
R. Gatien-Arnoult
Merly
R.
Pl. Jeanne d'Arc
Rue de
R. de Belfort
R. B. de Born
Pl. de Belfort
Belfort
BASILIQUE ST-SERNIN
MUSÉE ST-RAYMOND
Pl. St-Sernin
R. du Périgord
R. de Rémusat
R. Denfert-Rochereau
Bd de Strasbourg
Jaurès
R. Lautmann
R. des Lois
R. du Taur
N.-Dame-du-Taur
Lorraine
Pl. V. Hugo
R. d'Austerlitz
Jean Jaurès
Allées J.
Pl. A. France
R. Deville
R. La Fayette
Place Wilson
R. Gabriel Péri
Bd
R. Pargaminières
CAPITOLE
Pl. du Capitole
Capitole
Donjon
R. de la Colombette
LES JACOBINS
R. Lakanal
R. Gambetta
R. St Rome
R. d'Alsace
R. St-Antoine du T.
R. M. Fonvielle
Place Occitane
ST-GEORGES
Rue d'Aubuisson
Lazare
Hôtel de Bernuy
R. du May
Pl. St.Georges
POL
Pl. de la Daurade
Peyrolières
R. de la Bourse
R. des Changes
R. des
MUSÉE DES AUGUSTINS
R. de Metz
Carnot
HÔTEL D'ASSÉZAT
Esquirol
Arts
Pont Neuf
R. de Metz
R. Croix-Baragnon
CATH. ST-ÉTIENNE
R. des Couteliers
Pl. Rouaix
R. des Filatiers
Languedoc
R. Tolosane
R. Fermat
R. St-Jacques
Allées François Verdier
R. des Potiers
N.-D. la Dalbade
R. Mage
R. Perchepinte
R. Ninau
GARONNE
Quai de Tounis
R. de la Garonnette
Pl. des Carmes
R. de la Dalbade
R. Pharaon
MUSÉE PAUL DUPUY
Pl. Montoulieu
R. du
R. Ozenne
R. Espinasse
Jardin Royal
Grand Rond
Gd-R. Nazareth
Pl. du Salin
Guesde
Av. M. Hauriou
Allées Jules
Allées Frédéric Mistral
Pl. du Parlement
ST-EXUPÈRE
MUSÉUM D'HISTOIRE NATURELLE
Allées Feuga
R. Alfred Duméril
Jardin des Plantes
Mt de la Résistance
Pont St-Michel
Pl. A. Lafourcade
0
200 m

Capitouls without rest, 22 descente de la Halle aux Poissons ☎ 05 34 31 94 80, *contact@hoteldescapitouls.com, Fax 05 34 31 94 81* – . AE GB.
☕ 18 – **14 rm** 135/170.
◆ This old building in the city's historic quarter has a contemporary interior of stained oak flooring, designer furniture, silk fabrics and discreet Japanese touches.

Beaux Arts without rest, 1 pl. Pont-Neuf ☎ 05 34 45 42 42, *contact@hoteldesbeauxarts.com, Fax 05 34 45 42 43,* – . AE GB JCB. EY v
☕ 16 – **19 rm** 84/188.
◆ This tastefully transformed 18C house has 19 cosily elegant bedrooms, some with views of the Garonne. A charming insight into the colour and style of Occitania.

Grand Hôtel Jean Jaurès "Les Capitouls" without rest, 29 allées J. Jaurès ☎ 05 34 41 31 21, *info@hotel-capitouls.com, Fax 05 61 63 15 17* – , rm, – 20. AE GB JCB FX g
☕ 13 – **51 rm** 105/140.
◆ An old mansion by a busy and central metro station. Impressive red-brick vaulting in the lobby, and bedrooms offering TV Internet access.

Mermoz without rest, 50 r. Matabiau ☎ 05 61 63 04 04, *reservation@hotel-mermoz, Fax 05 61 63 15 64* – kitchenette – 30. AE GB JCB DV f
☕ 10,20 – **52 rm** 97.
◆ The hotel's décor recalls the heroic pilots of the Aéropostale airmail service. Bedrooms decorated in bright colours. Flowered veranda or shaded terrace for breakfasts.

Mercure Wilson without rest, 7 r. Labéda ☎ 05 34 45 40 60, *h1260@accor-hotels.com, Fax 05 34 45 40 61* – , rm, . AE GB JCB FY m
☕ 12 – **91 rm** 123/165, 4 suites.
◆ Behind the typically "toulousain" façade is a hotel with colourful, well-appointed rooms. On fine days breakfast is served on the terrace. The garage is a real bonus.

Président without rest, 43 r. Raymond IV ☎ 05 61 63 46 46, *contact@hotel-president.com, Fax 05 61 62 83 60* – . AE GB JCB. FX k
closed 28 December-4 January – ☕ 7,80 – **31 rm** 55/70.
◆ The rooms in this hotel, some of which are air-conditioned, are all attractively arranged around verdant patios on the ground floor. Contemporary decor.

Albert 1er without rest, 8 r. Rivals ☎ 05 61 21 17 91, *hotel.albert.1er@wanadoo.fr, Fax 05 61 21 09 64* – – 15. AE GB EX r
☕ 8,50 – **50 rm** 50/86.
◆ A good choice for those planning on exploring the "ville rose" on foot. Ask for one of the attractive, recently refurbished rooms - those to the rear are quieter.

Ours Blanc-Wilson without rest, 2 r. V. Hugo ☎ 05 61 21 62 40, *wilson@hotel-oursblanc.com, Fax 05 61 23 62 34* – . GB FX p
☕ 7 – **37 rm** 53/75.
◆ This 1930s hotel is located close to the city's busiest squares. Simple but spotless rooms, accessed via an old lift, with views from those on the top floor.

Park Hôtel without rest, 2 r. Porte Sardane ☎ 05 61 21 25 97, *contact@au-park-hotel.com, Fax 05 61 23 96 27,* – . AE GB FX s
☕ 7 – **44 rm** 59/64.
◆ A splendid position just a few yards from the city's main sights. Functional rooms, most of which have air-conditioning, efficient double-glazing and a small fitness room.

Toulousy-Les Jardins de l'Opéra, 1 pl. Capitole ☎ 05 61 23 07 76, *toulousy@wanadoo.fr, Fax 05 61 23 63 00* – . AE GB EY q
closed August, Sunday and Monday – **Meals** 40 (lunch), 66/90 and a la carte 90/115 ♀.
◆ Elegant, glass-canopied dining rooms decorated in Florentine style and separated by a pool dedicated to Neptune. A skilful interpretation of contemporary cuisine.
Spec. Carpacio de homard et foie gras à l'huile de truffes. Trilogie de bœuf et pomme de terre. Moelleux au chocolat guanaja et pistache. **Wines** Vin de pays du Comté Tolosan, Fronton.

Michel Sarran, 21 bd A. Duportal ☎ 05 61 12 32 32, *michelsarran@wanadoo.fr, Fax 05 61 12 32 33,* – . AE GB DV m
closed 30 July-30 August, 20 to 28 December, 1 to 4 January, Wednesday lunch, Saturday and Sunday – **Meals** (booking essential) 45 b.i./110 b.i. and a la carte 70/90.
◆ This charming 19C residence offers an elegant setting in which to enjoy the very best flavours of the south. Car parking valet at lunchtime.
Spec. Soupe tiède de foie gras à l'huître. Loup cuit et cru au chorizo. Allaiton de l'Aveyron à la tapenade de Lucques. **Wines** Côtes de Marmandais, Fronton.

XXX **Pastel** (Garrigues), 237 road of St-Simon, to the SW : 6 km ✉ 31100 ☎ 05 62 87 84 30, *lepastel@wanadoo.fr, Fax 05 61 44 29 22,* – P. AE GB.
closed 1 to 17 August, Sunday and Monday – **Meals** (booking essential) 38/78 and a la carte 65/85.
◆ This fine 19C building, with its pleasant garden-terrace, is the backdrop for a range of inventive cuisine and a full wine list featuring wines from the south of France.
Spec. Saint-Jacques "Jubilatoires" (10 October-10 April). Carré d'agneau de l'Aveyron aux pistaches (December-September). Râble de lièvre en saupiquet (October-December).

XX **7 Place St-Sernin,** 7 pl. St-Sernin ☎ 05 62 30 05 30, *Fax 05 62 30 04 06* –. AE GB EX v
closed Saturday lunch and Sunday – **Meals** 23/60 b.i.
◆ In a house built in typical Toulouse style, this flamboyantly decorated and elegantly furnished restaurant is adorned with modern canvases. Cuisine with a modern flourish.

XX **Brasserie Flo " Les Beaux Arts",** 1 quai Daurade ☎ 05 61 21 12 12, *Fax 05 61 21 14 80,* – AE GB JCB EY v
Meals 29,90 b.i.
◆ This brasserie on the banks of the Garonne, frequented in past years by Ingres, Matisse and Bourdelle, is a popular evening venue. Pleasant retro decor and a varied menu.

XX **Le 19,** 19 descente de la Halle aux Poissons ☎ 05 34 31 94 84, *contact@restaurant e 9.com, Fax 05 34 31 94 85* – AE GB.
closed 6 to 24 August, 25 December-3 January, Sunday, lunch Saturday and Monday – **Meals** 19 b.i. (lunch), 29/55.
◆ Welcoming dining rooms, including one beneath a superb 16C ribbed vault. The open wine cellar and smoking room adopt a resolutely modern style. International cuisine.

XX **Émile,** 13 pl. St-Georges ☎ 05 61 21 05 56, *restaurant-emile@wanadoo.fr, Fax 05 61 21 42 26,* –. AE GB FY r
closed 24 December-6 January, Monday (except dinner in summer) and Sunday – **Meals** 18 (lunch), 35/45.
◆ This popular restaurant created in the 1940s offers customers a range of local and fish dishes, plus an impressive wine-list. The outdoor terrace is always full in summer.

XX **Brasserie de l'Opéra,** 1 pl. Capitole ☎ 05 61 21 37 03, *Fax 05 62 27 16 49,* –. AE GB EY a
closed Sunday – **Meals** a la carte 25/40.
◆ A chic, 1930s-style brasserie frequented by the city's smart set and stars who have marked their presence with a signed photo. The veranda converts into a pleasant terrace.

X **Cosi Fan Tutte** (Donnay), 8 r. Mage ☎ 05 61 53 07 24, *Fax 05 61 52 27 92* – GB FZ v
closed 20 to 24 May, August, 19 December-4 January, Sunday and Monday – **Meals** - Italian rest. - (dinner only)(booking essential) 30/70 and a la carte 50/75.
◆ A small restaurant with red drapes, "leopard-skin" carpet and original paintings. Delicious seasonal cuisine prepared according to Italian traditions. Italian wines.
Spec. Saint-Jacques poêlées, crème de laitue et truffes (15 January-15 February). Pigeonneau au vino santo et polenta aux cèpes. Pain perdu à la banane.

X **Au Gré du Vin,** 10 r. Pléau ☎ 05 61 25 03 51, *Fax 05 61 25 03 51* – GB. FZ t
closed August, Christmas-New Year, Saturday, Sunday and Bank Holidays – **Meals** (booking essential) 16 (lunch), 27/40.
◆ This unassuming restaurant opposite the Musée Paul Dupuy has a rustic feel, red-brick walls, friendly ambience, simple and tasty cuisine and a choice of wines by the glass.

at Rouffiac-Tolosan *by ② : 12 km – pop. 1 404 alt. 210 – ✉ 31180 :*

XX **Ô Saveurs** (Biasibetti), 8 pl. Ormeaux (au village) ☎ 05 34 27 10 11, *o.saveurs@free.fr, Fax 05 62 79 33 84,* –. AE GB
closed 1 to 9 March, 11 to 31 August, Saturday lunch, Sunday dinner, and Monday – **Meals** 19 (lunch), 27/38 and a la carte 48/62.
◆ Set in a picturesque village, this delightful little house specialises in flavourful cooking with an up-to-date touch, served in welcoming dining rooms or on the terrace.
Spec. Millefeuille croustillant de crabe. Filet de rouget poêlé, piquillos farcis de brandade aux olives. Figues rôties au banyuls, crème d'amande.

at Colomiers *: 10 km by exit nr 4 and Cornebarieu – pop. 28 538 alt. 182 – ✉ 31770 :*

XXX **L'Amphitryon,** chemin de Gramont ☎ 05 61 15 55 55, *amphitryon@wanadoo.fr, Fax 05 61 15 42 30,* ←, – P. AE GB
Meals 30 (lunch), 45/90 and a la carte 75/105.
◆ This large modern building has a bright, welcoming feel and a terrace offering views of the local countryside. Fine innovative cuisine.
Spec. Sardine fraîche taillée au couteau, crème de morue et caviar de hareng. Rôtissot de lotte au lard grillé et piment d'Espelette. Pigeonneau à la truffe noire du Périgord. **Wines** Bergerac, Madiran.

at Blagnac *North-West : 7 km – pop. 20 586 alt. 135 – ✉ 31700 :*

Sofitel, 2 av. Didier Daurat, by road of airport, exit nr 3 ✆ 05 34 56 11 11, *h0565@accor-hotels.com, Fax 05 61 30 02 43,* – rm, – 90. AE GB JCB AS e
Caouec : Meals 23/32 ♀ – ☕ 19 – **100 rm** 205/230.
◆ A luxury chain hotel with a shuttle service to the airport. Elegant renovated bedrooms with yellow the dominant colour scheme. Pool and tennis court for those with time between flights. The sophisticated Le Caouec specialises in the cuisine of the southwest.

Holiday Inn Airport, pl. Révolution ✆ 05 34 36 00 20, *TLSAP@ichotelsgroup.com, Fax 05 34 36 00 30,* – rm, – 15 - 150. AE GB JCB AS h
Meals *(closed Friday dinner, Saturday and Sunday)* 20/33 – ☕ 17 – **150 rm** 195/245.
◆ The main features of the hotel's rooms are the warm, relaxing tones and contemporary furnishings. Pleasant brasserie-style restaurant decorated with frescoes paying homage to the olive tree. Fully equipped seminar area, plus an airport shuttle service.

Cercle d'Oc, 6 pl. M. Dassault ✆ 05 62 74 71 71, *cercledoc@wanadoo.fr, Fax 05 62 74 71 72,* – P. AE GB AS t
closed 1 to 9 May, 31 July-22 August, 20 December-4 January, Saturday and Sunday – **Meals** 30 b.i. (lunch)/43 ♀.
◆ This pretty 18C farm is a haven of greenery at the heart of a busy shopping area. The atmosphere of an English club in the lounge and elegant dining room. Charming terrace.

Pré Carré, Toulouse-Blagnac airport (2nd floor) ✆ 05 61 16 70 40, *Fax 05 61 16 70 50,* – AE GB JCB. AS n
closed 14 July-15 August, Sunday dinner and Saturday – **Meals** 27 b.i./46 ♀.
◆ On the second floor of the airport, overlooking the runway. Designer décor with the emphasis on wood and reddish tones. Traditional à la carte menu.

Bistrot Gourmand, 1 bd Firmin Pons ✆ 05 61 71 96 95, *bistrot-gourmand@bistrot-gourmand.com, Fax 05 61 15 68 21,* – AE GB AS v
closed 1 to 24 August, 31 December-3 January, Saturday lunch, Sunday and Monday – **Meals** 10,60/28.
◆ In the older part of Blagnac, with two rooms laid out on two floors. Pleasant terrace upstairs. The menu varies according to the season. Reasonable prices.

Laguiole *12210 Aveyron 338 J2 – pop. 1 248 alt. 1 004.*

Tourist Office pl. du Foirail ✆ 05 65 44 35 94, Fax 05 65 44 35 76, ot-laguiole@wanadoo.fr.
Toulouse 208.

to the East *6 km by road of Aubrac (D 15)*

Michel Bras , ✆ 05 65 51 18 20, *michel.bras@wanadoo.fr, Fax 05 65 48 47 02,* Landscapes of Aubrac – , rest, P. AE GB JCB.
April-October and closed Monday except July-August – **Meals** *(closed lunch Tuesday and Wednesday except July-August and Monday)* (booking essential) 50 (lunch), 90/146 and a la carte 110/150 – ☕ 22 – **15 rm** 197/333.
◆ This establishment looks like a spacecraft lost among the harsh landscapes of the Aubrac. Diners contemplate the scene while savouring an inspired version of local cuisine. Pure lines, bare rock, serene white surfaces, vast windows, plus designer cocktails.
Spec. "Gargouillou" de jeunes légumes. Pièce de bœuf Aubrac rôtie à la braise. Biscuit tiède de chocolat "coulant". **Wines** Gaillac, Marcillac.

Puymirol *47270 L.-et-G. 336 G4 – pop. 864 alt. 153.*

Toulouse 104.

Les Loges de l'Aubergade (Trama) , 52 r. Royale ✆ 05 53 95 31 46, *trama@aubergade.com, Fax 05 53 95 33 80,* – – 25. AE GB JCB
closed February Holidays, Monday except dinner in season, Sunday dinner, Tuesday lunch and Monday out of season – **Meals** 56 (lunch), 66/130 and a la carte 90/140 – ☕ 20 – **11 rm** 168/267.
◆ Contemporary interior design in two charming houses ; one dates from the 17C, the other is the 13C former seat of the counts of Toulouse. A breathtaking baroque room, delicious, imaginative cuisine and fine cigars complete a feast for the senses !
Spec. Papillote de pomme de terre en habit vert à la truffe. Hamburger de foie gras chaud aux cèpes, jus de canard corsé. Assiette des cinq sens. **Wines** Côtes de Duras, Buzet.

Germany

Deutschland

BERLIN – COLOGNE – DRESDEN

DÜSSELDORF – FRANKFURT ON MAIN

HAMBURG – HANOVER – LEIPZIG

MUNICH – STUTTGART

PRACTICAL INFORMATION

LOCAL CURRENCY

1 euro (€) = 1,20 USD ($) (Dec. 2003)

TOURIST INFORMATION

Deutsche Zentrale für Tourismus (DZT):
Beethovenstr. 69, 60325 Frankfurt, ✆ (069) 97 46 40, Fax (069) 75 19 03
National Holiday in Germany: *3 October.*

AIRLINES

DEUTSCHE LUFTHANSA AG: ✆ *(01803) 803803*
AIR CANADA: ✆ *(069) 27 11 51 11*
AIR FRANCE: ✆ *(0180) 5 83 08 30*
AMERICAN AIRLINES: ✆ *(01803) 242 324*
BRITISH AIRWAYS: ✆ *(01805) 26 65 22*
JAPAN AIRLINES: ✆ *(0180) 22 28 700*
AUSTRIAN AIRLINES: ✆ *(0180) 300 05 20*

FOREIGN EXCHANGE

In banks, savings banks and at exchange offices.
Hours of opening from Monday to Friday 8.30am to 12.30pm and 2.30pm to 4pm except Thursday 2.30pm to 6pm.

SHOPPING

In the index of street names, those printed in red are where the principal shops are found.

BREAKDOWN SERVICE

ADAC: *for the addresses see text of the towns mentioned*

AvD: *Lyoner Str. 16, 60528 Frankfurt-Niederrad, ✆ (069) 6 60 60, Fax (069) 660 67 89*
In Germany the ADAC (emergency number (01802) 22 22 22), and the AvD (emergency number (0800) 9 90 99 09), make a special point of assisting foreign motorists. They have motor patrols covering main roads.

TIPPING

In Germany, prices include service and taxes. You may choose to leave a tip if you wish but there is no obligation to do so.

SPEED LIMITS

The speed limit, generally, in built up areas is 50 km/h - 31 mph and on all other roads it is 100 km/h - 62mph. On motorways and dual carriageways, the recommended speed limit is 130 km/h - 80 mph.

SEAT BELTS

The wearing of seat belts is compulsory for drivers and all passengers.

BERLIN

L Berlin 542, I 24 - pop. 3 400 000 - alt. 40 m.

Frankfurt/Oder 105 - Hamburg 289 - Hannover 288 - Leipzig 183 - Rostock 222.

Berlin Tourismus Marketing, Am Karlsbad 11, ✉ 10785, ☏ (030) 25 00 25, information@btm.de
Tourist Info Center (at Brandenburger Tor), side-wing, Pariser Platz, ✉ 10787 Berlin
Tourist Info Café, Am Alexander Platz (at TV tower), Panoramastr. 1a, ✉ 10178 Berlin
Tourist Info Center (at Europa Center), Budapester Str. 45, ✉ 10787 Berlin-Charlottenburg

ADAC, Berlin-Wilmersdorf, Bundesallee 29.

18 9 Berlin-Wannsee, Golfweg 22, ☏ (030) 8 06 70 60 - 18 Berlin-Gatow, Kladower Damm 182, ☏ (030) 3 65 00 06 - 18 9 Gross Kienitz (South : 25 km), ☏ (033708) 5 37 70 - 18 9 Börnicke, Am Kallin 1 (North-West : 32 km), ☏ (033230) 89 40 - 9 Mahlow, Kiefernweg (South : 20 km), ☏ (033379) 37 05 95 - 18 18 Wildenbruch, Großer Seddiner See (South-West : 37 km), ☏ (033205) 73 20 - 18 Stolpe, Am Golfplatz 1 (North-West : 20 km), ☏ (03303) 54 92 14 - 9 Großbeeren, Am Golfplatz 1 (South 22 km), ☏ (033701) 3 28 90.

Berlin-Tegel EX, *☏ (0180) 5 00 01 86*
Berlin-Schönefeld (South : 25 km), ☏ (0180) 5 00 01 86
Berlin-Tempelhof GZ, *☏ (0180) 5 00 01 86*
Deutsche Lufthansa City Center, Kurfürstendamm 21, ☏ (030) 88 75 38 00.

Berlin-Wannsee, Reichsbahnstraße.
Exhibition Centre (Messegelände am Funkturm) BU, *☏ (030) 3 03 80, Fax (030) 30 38 23 25.*

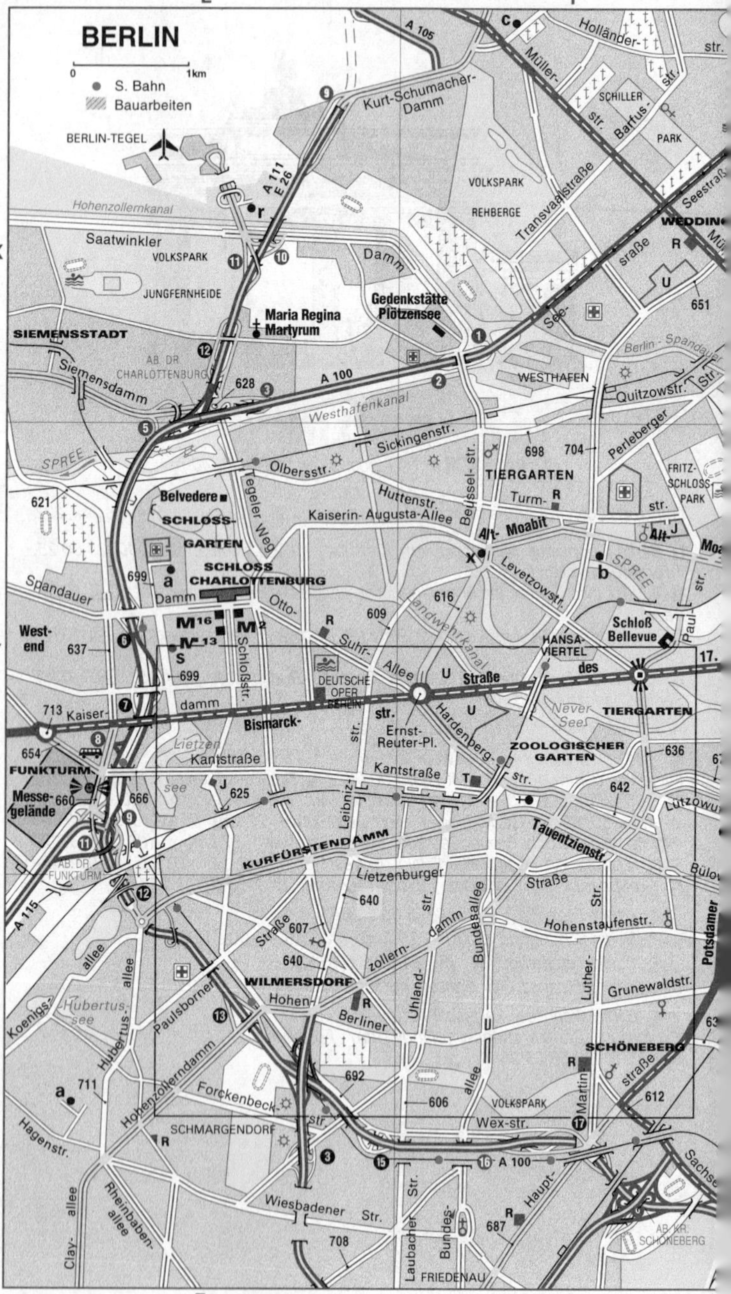

BERLIN

0 1km
S. Bahn
Bauarbeiten

E F
X Y Z

BERLIN-TEGEL
Hohenzollernkanal
Saatwinkler
VOLKSPARK
JUNGFERNHEIDE
SIEMENSSTADT
Siemensdamm
AB. DR CHARLOTTENBURG
A 111 E 26
A 105
Kurt-Schumacher-Damm
VOLKSPARK
REHBERGE
Damm
Gedenkstätte Plötzensee
Maria Regina Martyrum
A 100
628
Westhafenkanal
WESTHAFEN
Müller-
Holländer-
SCHILLER PARK
Barfus-str.
Transvaalstraße
Seestraße
WEDDING
See-straße
651
Berlin-Spandauer
Quitzowstr.
Perleberger str.
SPREE
Sickingenstr.
Olbersstr.
Tegeler Weg
Beussel-str.
698
704
TIERGARTEN
Turm-str.
FRITZ-SCHLOSS-PARK
621
Belvedere
SCHLOSS-GARTEN
Huttenstr.
Kaiserin-Augusta-Allee
Alt-Moabit
SCHLOSS CHARLOTTENBURG
699
Spandauer Damm
Levetzowstr.
SPREE
616
Landwehrkanal
609
Otto-Suhr-Allee
West-end
637
M16 M2 M13
Schloßstr.
699
Schloß Bellevue
HANSA-VIERTEL
Straße des 17.
713 Kaiser-damm
Bismarck-str.
DEUTSCHE OPER BERLIN
Ernst-Reuter-Pl.
Hardenberg-str.
Neuer See
TIERGARTEN
654
FUNKTURM
Messe-gelände
660
666
Lietzensee
Kantstraße
625
Leibniz-str.
Kantstraße
ZOOLOGISCHER GARTEN
636
642
Lützowu
Tauentzienstr.
KURFÜRSTENDAMM
Lietzenburger Straße
Bülow
AB. DR. FUNKTURM
A 115
640
Uhland-str.
Bundesallee
Hohenstaufenstr.
Potsdamer
Straße
607
640
zollern-damm
WILMERSDORF
Hohen-
Berliner
Grunewaldstr.
Luther-Str.
Koenigs-allee
Hubertussee
Hubertus-allee
Paulsborner
Hohenzollerndamm
SCHÖNEBERG
Martin-
straße
692
612
711
Forckenbeck-str.
606
VOLKSPARK
Wex-str.
SCHMARGENDORF
A 100
Haupt-
Sachse
Hagenstr.
Rheinbaben-allee
Clay-allee
Wiesbadener Str.
Laubacher Str.
Bundes-
687
AB. KR. SCHÖNEBERG
708
FRIEDENAU

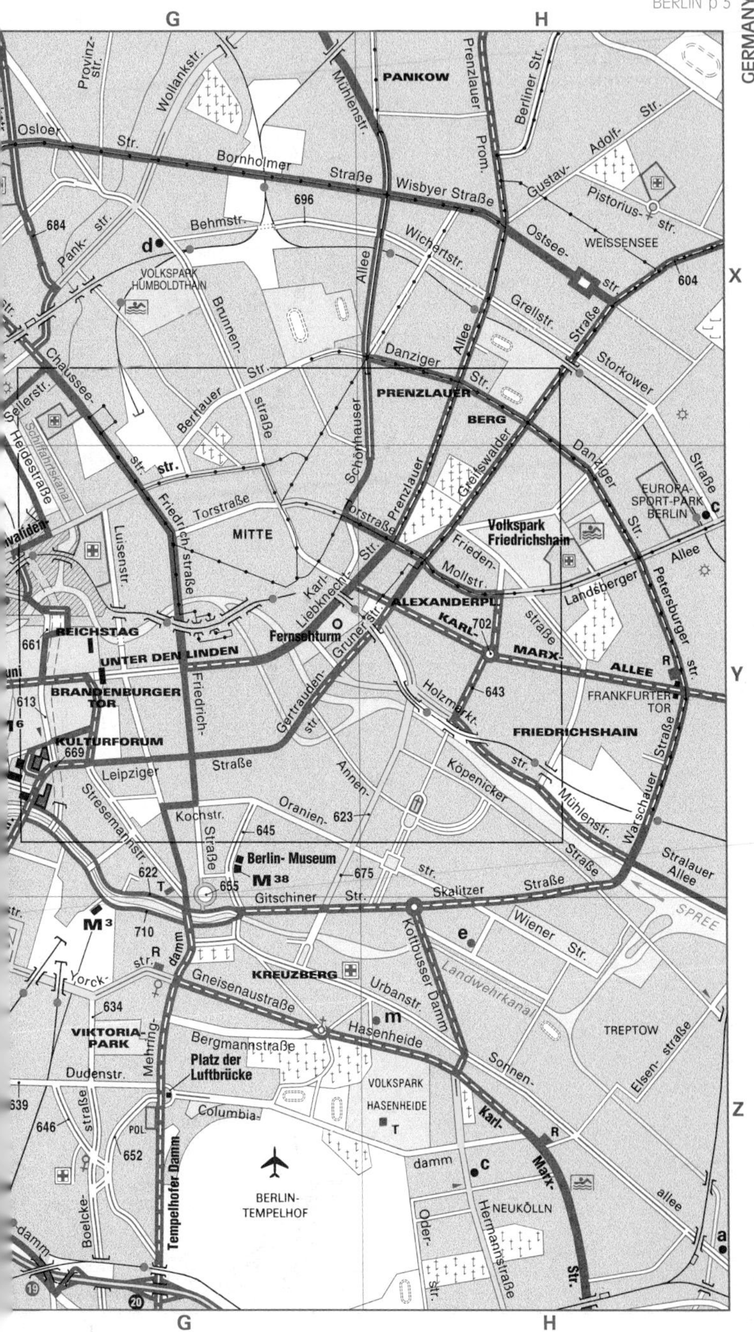
G
H
X
Y
Z
PANKOW
WEISSENSEE
PRENZLAUER BERG
MITTE
VOLKSPARK HUMBOLDTHAIN
Volkspark Friedrichshain
EUROPA-SPORT-PARK BERLIN
ALEXANDERPL.
Fernsehturm
REICHSTAG
UNTER DEN LINDEN
BRANDENBURGER TOR
KULTURFORUM
FRANKFURTER TOR
FRIEDRICHSHAIN
Berlin- Museum
KREUZBERG
VIKTORIA-PARK
Platz der Luftbrücke
VOLKSPARK HASENHEIDE
TREPTOW
NEUKÖLLN
BERLIN-TEMPELHOF
SPREE
Landwehrkanal
Schiffahrtskanal
Osloer Str.
Bornholmer Straße
Wisbyer Straße
Behmstr.
Wollankstr.
Provinz-str.
Pank-str.
Mühlenstr.
Schönhauser Allee
Prenzlauer Prom.
Berliner Str.
Gustav-Adolf-Str.
Pistorius-str.
Ostsee-str.
Wichertstr.
Grellstr.
Danziger Str.
Storkower Straße
Greifswalder Straße
Prenzlauer Allee
Brunnen-straße
Bernauer Str.
Chaussee-str.
Sellerstr.
Heidestraße
Invaliden-str.
Torstraße
Friedrichstraße
Luisenstr.
Karl-Liebknecht-Str.
Frieden-str.
Mollstr.
Landsberger Allee
Petersburger Str.
Karl-Marx-Allee
Gruner Str.
Gertrauden-str.
Holzmarkt-str.
Leipziger Straße
Stresemannstr.
Kochstr.
Friedrich-Straße
Annen-str.
Oranien-str.
Köpenicker Str.
Mühlenstr.
Warschauer Straße
Stralauer Allee
Skalitzer Straße
Gitschiner Str.
Wiener Str.
Kottbusser Damm
Yorck-str.
Mehring-damm
Gneisenaustraße
Urbanstr.
Hasenheide
Bergmannstraße
Dudenstr.
Columbia-damm
Sonnen-allee
Elsen-straße
Karl-Marx-Str.
Hermannstraße
Oder-str.
Tempelhofer Damm
Boelcke-straße
684
696
604
661
613
669
702
643
623
645
622
655
675
710
634
639
646
652
M 38
M 3
M 6
POL
d
c
e
m
a
R
T
19
20

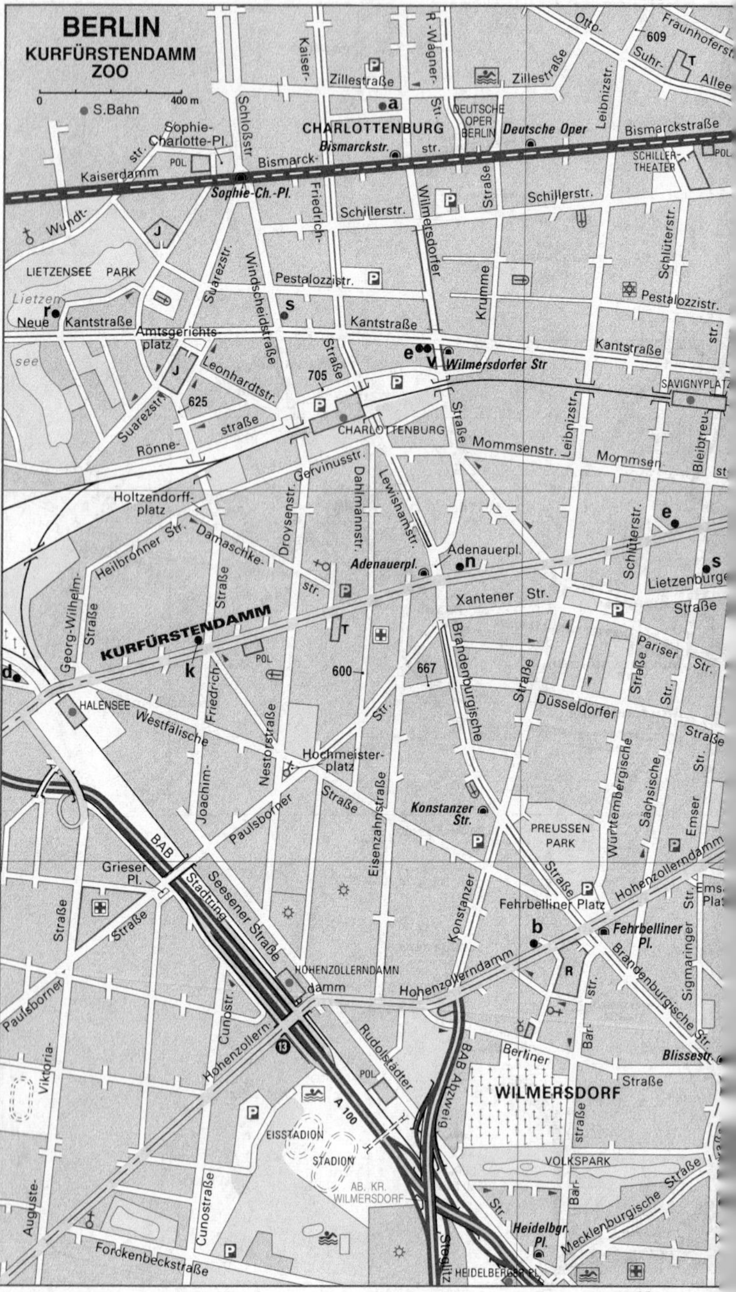
BERLIN
KURFÜRSTENDAMM
ZOO
0
400 m
S.Bahn
J
K
X
Y
Z
CHARLOTTENBURG
Bismarckstr.
Sophie-Ch.-Pl.
Sophie-Charlotte-Pl.
Kaiserdamm
Bismarckstraße
Zillestraße
DEUTSCHE OPER BERLIN
Deutsche Oper
SCHILLER-THEATER
Schillerstr.
Pestalozzistr.
Kantstraße
Wilmersdorfer Str
SAVIGNYPLATZ
LIETZENSEE PARK
Amtsgerichtsplatz
Leonhardtstr.
Suarezstr.
Windscheidstraße
Schloßstr.
Kaiser-Friedrich-Straße
Wilmersdorfer Straße
Leibnizstr.
Schlüterstr.
Mommsenstr.
Holtzendorffplatz
Damaschkestr.
Heilbronner Str.
Gervinusstr.
Droysenstr.
Dahlmannstr.
Lewishamstr.
Adenauerpl.
Xantener Str.
Lietzenburger Straße
KURFÜRSTENDAMM
Georg-Wilhelm-Straße
HALENSEE
Westfälische
Joachim-Friedrich-Straße
Nestorstraße
Hochmeisterplatz
Paulsborner Straße
Eisenzahnstraße
Brandenburgische
Düsseldorfer
Pariser Str.
Konstanzer Str.
PREUSSEN PARK
Württembergische
Sächsische Str.
Emser Str.
Fehrbelliner Platz
Fehrbelliner Pl.
Hohenzollerndamm
Brandenburgische Str.
Sigmaringer Str.
Blissestr.
Grieser Pl.
BAB
Stadtring
Seesener Straße
HOHENZOLLERNDAMM
Cunostr.
Rudolstädter
BAB Abzweig
Berliner Straße
WILMERSDORF
VOLKSPARK
A 100
EISSTADION
STADION
AB. KR. WILMERSDORF
Heidelbgr. Pl.
HEIDELBERGER PL.
Mecklenburgische Straße
Viktoria-
Auguste-
Cunostraße
Forckenbeckstraße
705
625
609
600
667
13

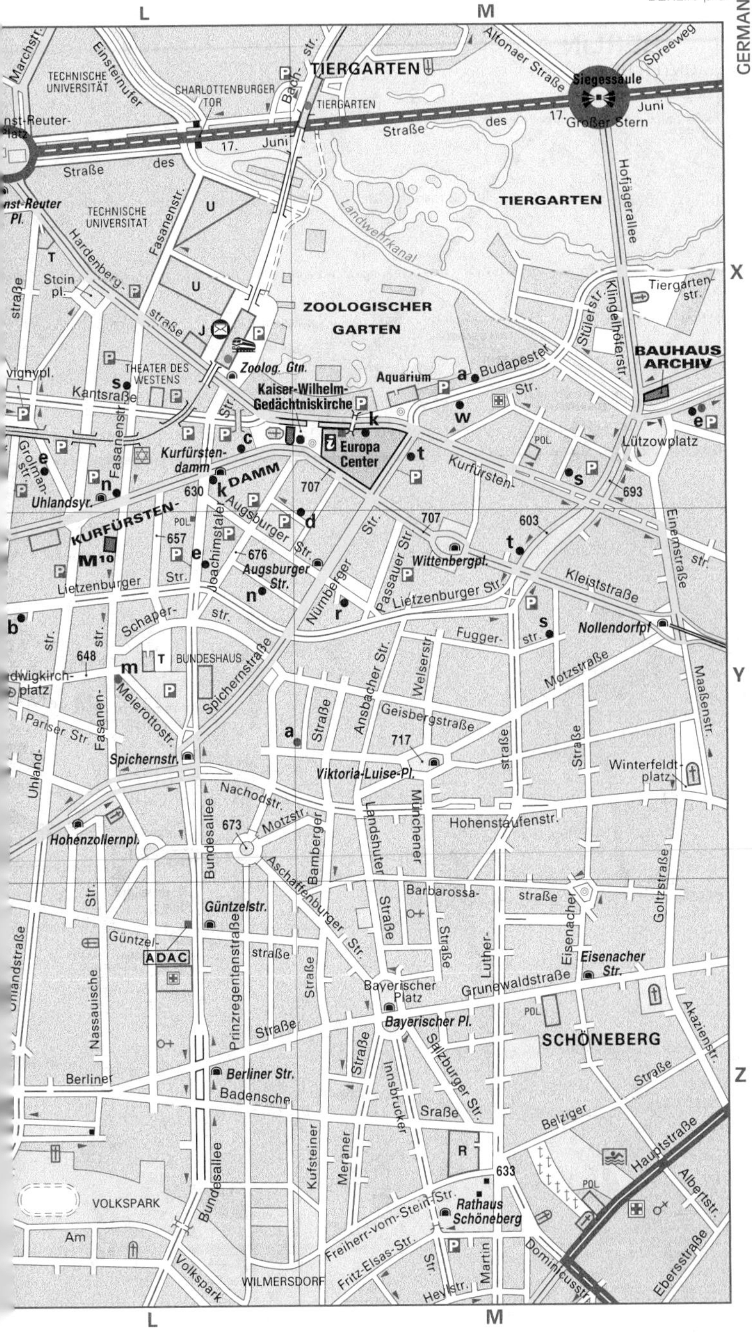

L M X Y Z

TIERGARTEN
Siegessäule
Altonaer Straße
Spreeweg
Juni
17. Großer Stern
Straße des 17. Juni
TECHNISCHE UNIVERSITÄT
CHARLOTTENBURGER TOR
Einsteinufer
Marchstr.
Ernst-Reuter-Platz
Ernst-Reuter Pl.
TECHNISCHE UNIVERSITAT
Fasanenstr.
Hardenberg-straße
Landwehrkanal
Hofjägerallee
Stein pl.
ZOOLOGISCHER GARTEN
Tiergarten-str.
Klingelhöferstr.
Stülerstr.
BAUHAUS ARCHIV
THEATER DES WESTENS
Zoolog. Gtn.
Aquarium
Budapester Str.
Kaiser-Wilhelm-Gedächtniskirche
Kantstraße
Savignypl.
Europa Center
Lützowplatz
Kurfürsten-damm
KURFÜRSTENDAMM
Kurfürstenstr.
Grolmanstr.
Uhlandstr.
Augsburger Str.
Joachimstaler Str.
Nürnberger Str.
Passauer Str.
Wittenbergpl.
Einemstraße
Kleiststraße
Lietzenburger Str.
Schaperstr.
Fuggerstr.
Nollendorfpl.
Ludwigkirchplatz
BUNDESHAUS
Spichernstraße
Meierottostr.
Motzstraße
Maaßenstr.
Pariser Str.
Fasanenstr.
Ansbacher Str.
Welserstr.
Geisbergstraße
Spichernstr.
Viktoria-Luise-Pl.
Winterfeldtplatz
Nachodstr.
Hohenstaufenstr.
Hohenzollernpl.
Bundesallee
Motzstr.
Landshuter Str.
Münchener Str.
Bamberger Str.
Aschaffenburger Str.
Barbarossastraße
Goltzstraße
Güntzelstr.
Güntzelstraße
ADAC
Prinzregentenstraße
Eisenacher Str.
Luther-str.
Grunewaldstraße
Bayerischer Platz
Bayerischer Pl.
Nassauische Str.
Uhlandstraße
Akazienstr.
SCHÖNEBERG
Salzburger Str.
Innsbrucker Str.
Berliner Str.
Badensche Str.
Belziger Straße
Hauptstraße
Kufsteiner Str.
Meraner Str.
Albertstr.
VOLKSPARK
Freiherr-vom-Stein-Str.
Rathaus Schöneberg
Am Volkspark
Fritz-Elsas-Str.
Martin-Luther-Str.
Dominicusstr.
Eberstraße
WILMERSDORF
Heylstr.

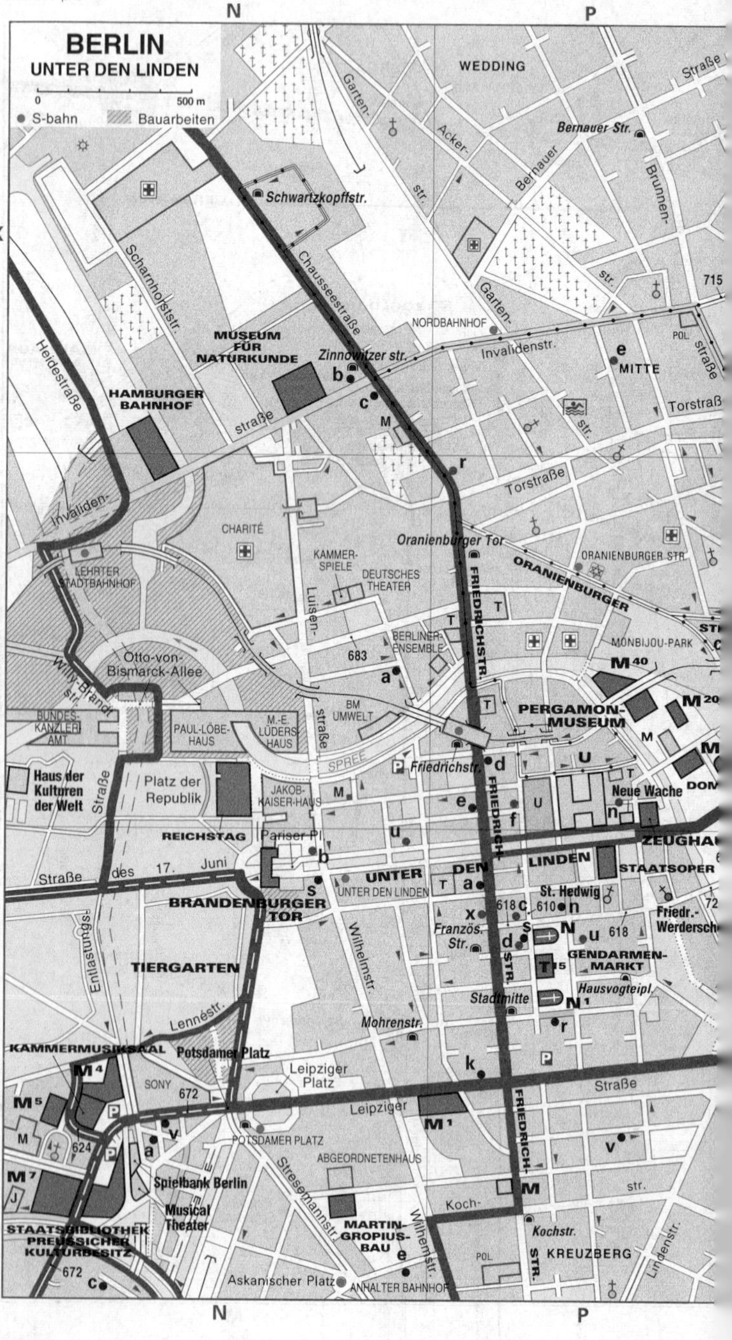

BERLIN
UNTER DEN LINDEN

0 500 m
S-bahn Bauarbeiten

N P
X Y Z

WEDDING
Garten-str.
Acker-str.
Bernauer Str.
Bernauer str.
Brunnen-str.
Schwartzkopffstr.
Scharnhorststr.
Chausseestraße
Heidestraße
MUSEUM FÜR NATURKUNDE
HAMBURGER BAHNHOF
Zinnowitzer str.
NORDBAHNHOF
Invalidenstr.
Invaliden-straße
MITTE
Torstraße
POL.
715
CHARITÉ
LEHRTER STADTBAHNHOF
KAMMER-SPIELE
DEUTSCHES THEATER
Oranienburger Tor
ORANIENBURGER STR.
FRIEDRICHSTR.
BERLINER-ENSEMBLE
MONBIJOU-PARK
Luisen-straße
683
Otto-von-Bismarck-Allee
Willy-Brandt-str.
BM UMWELT
PERGAMON-MUSEUM
BUNDES-KANZLERAMT
PAUL-LÖBE-HAUS
M.-E. LÜDERS HAUS
SPREE
Friedrichstr.
Haus der Kulturen der Welt
Platz der Republik
JAKOB-KAISER-HAUS
Neue Wache
DOM
REICHSTAG
Pariser Pl.
ZEUGHAUS
Straße des 17. Juni
UNTER DEN LINDEN
STAATSOPER
BRANDENBURGER TOR
St. Hedwig
618 610
Französ. Str.
Friedr.-Werdersche
GENDARMEN-MARKT
Wilhelmstr.
Entlastungs-str.
TIERGARTEN
Hausvogteipl.
Stadtmitte
Lennéstr.
Mohrenstr.
KAMMERMUSIKSAAL
Potsdamer Platz
Leipziger Platz
SONY
672
Leipziger Straße
POTSDAMER PLATZ
624
ABGEORDNETENHAUS
Spielbank Berlin
Stresemannstr.
Koch-str.
Musical Theater
STAATSBIBLIOTHEK PREUSSISCHER KULTURBESITZ
MARTIN-GROPIUS-BAU
Kochstr.
KREUZBERG
Lindenstr.
Askanischer Platz
ANHALTER BAHNHOF

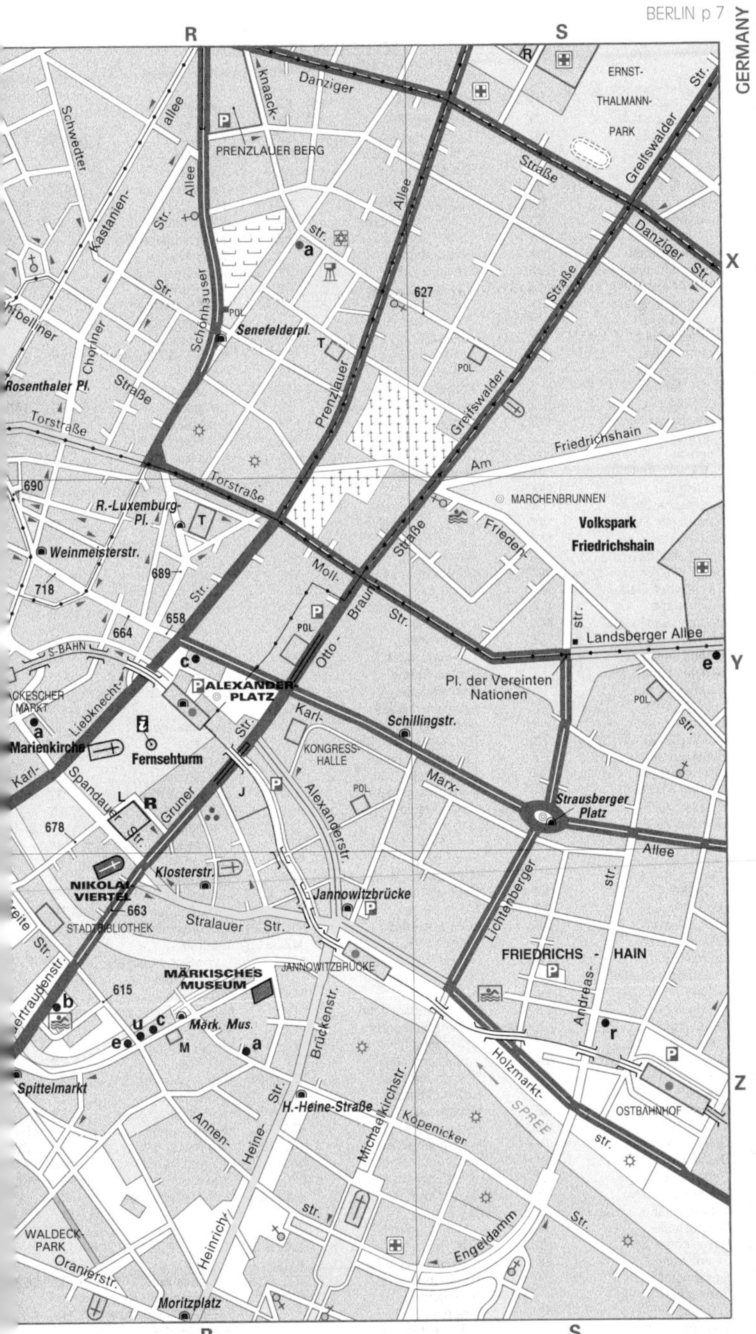
R
S
X
Y
Z
Danziger
Straße
Danziger Str.
ERNST-
THALMANN-
PARK
Greifswalder Str.
PRENZLAUER BERG
Schwedter
Kastanien-
allee
Schönhauser Allee
Senefelderpl.
Rosenthaler Pl.
Choriner Straße
Torstraße
Prenzlauer Allee
Greifswalder Straße
Am Friedrichshain
MARCHENBRUNNEN
Volkspark
Friedrichshain
R.-Luxemburg-Pl.
Weinmeisterstr.
Moll-Str.
Otto-Braun-Str.
Landsberger Allee
Pl. der Vereinten Nationen
ALEXANDER-PLATZ
Karl-Marx-Allee
Schillingstr.
KONGRESS-HALLE
Alexanderstr.
Marienkirche
Fernsehturm
Liebknecht-
Spandauer Str.
Gruner Str.
Strausberger Platz
Klosterstr.
NIKOLAI-VIERTEL
Jannowitzbrücke
Stralauer Str.
STADTBIBLIOTHEK
Lichtenberger
FRIEDRICHS - HAIN
Andreas-
MÄRKISCHES
MUSEUM
JANNOWITZBRÜCKE
Gertraudenstr.
Märk. Mus.
Spittelmarkt
Brückenstr.
Holzmarkt-str.
SPREE
OSTBAHNHOF
H.-Heine-Straße
Michaelkirchstr.
Köpenicker Str.
Annen-
Heine-Str.
Heinrich
Engeldamm
WALDECK-PARK
Oranienstr.
Moritzplatz
627
690
689
718
658
664
678
663
615

STREET INDEX TO BERLIN TOWN PLANS

STREET INDEX TO BERLIN TOWN PLANS (Concluded)

Müllerstraße p 2 **FX**
Münchener Straße p 5 **MY**
Münzstraße p 7 **RY** 664
Nachodstr. p 5 **LY**
Nassauische Straße p 5 **LZ**
Nestorstraße p 4 **JY**
Neue Kantstraße p 4 **EY** 666
Neue Königstr. p 7 **RY**
Nürnberger Str. p 5 **MY**
Oderstraße p 3 **HZ**
Olbersstraße p 2 **EY**
Oranienburger Str. (MITTE) p 6 **PY**
Oranienstraße p 7 **RZ**
Osloer Straße p 3 **GX**
Osteestraße p 3 **HX**
Otto-Braun-Str. **RY**
Otto-Suhr-Allee p 4 **KX**
Paderborner Str. p 4 **JY** 667
Pankstraße p 3 **GX**
Pariser Platz p 6 **NZ**
Pariser Straße p 4 **KY**
Passauer Straße p 5 **MY**
Paulsborner Straße p 4 **JZ**
Paulstraße p 2 **FY**
Perleberger Straße p 2 **FY**
Pestalozzistraße p 4 **JX**
Petersburger Str. p 3 **HY**
Platz der Republik p 6 **NY**
Platz der vereinten Nationen p 7 **SY**
Potsdamer Platz p 3 **GY** 669
Potsdamer Straße (SCHÖNEBERG) p 6 **NZ** 672
Prager Platz p 5 **LY** 673
Prenzlauer Allee p 7 **RX**
Prenzlauer Prom p 3 **HX**
Prinzenstraße p 3 **GY** 675
Prinzregentenstr. p 5 **LZ**
Provinzstraße p 3 **GX**
Quitzowstraße p 2 **FX**
Rankestraße p 5 **LY** 676
Rathausstraße p 7 **RY** 678
Rauchstraße p 5 **MX**
Reichpietschufer p 2 **FY** 679
Reinhardtstraße p 6 **NY** 683
Reinickendorfer Str. p 3 **GX** 684
Rheinbabenallee p 2 **EZ**
Rheinstraße p 2 **FZ** 687
Richard-Wagner-Str. p 4 **JX**
Rönnestraße p 4 **JX**
Rosa-Luxemburg-Str. p 7 **RY** 689
Rosenthaler Straße p 7 **RY** 690
Rudolstädter Str. p 2 **EZ** 692
Saatwinkler Damm p 2 **EX**
Sachsendamm p 2 **FZ**
Sächsische Straße p 4 **KY**
Salzburger Straße p 5 **MZ**
Savignyplatz p 5 **LX**
Schaperstraße p 5 **LY**
Scharnhorststr. p 6 **NX**
Schillerstraße p 4 **JX**
Schillstraße p 5 **MX** 693
Schivelbeiner Str. p 3 **GX** 696
Schloßstraße (CHARLOTTENBURG) p 4 **JX**
Schlüterstraße p 4 **KX**
Schönhauser Allee p 7 **RX**
Schwedter Str. p 7 **RX**
Seesener Straße p 4 **JY**
Seestraße p 2 **FX**
Sellerstraße p 3 **GX**
Sickingenstraße p 2 **FY**
Siemensdamm p 2 **EX**
Siemensstraße p 2 **FY** 698
Sigmaringer Straße p 4 **KZ**
Skalitzer Straße p 3 **HY**
Sonnenallee p 3 **HZ**
Sophie-Charlotten-Platz p 4 **JX**
Sophie-Charlotten-Str. p 2 **EY** 699
Spandauer Damm p 2 **EY**
Spandauer Str. p 7 **RY**
Spichernstraße p 5 **LY**
Spreeweg p 5 **MX**
Steinplatz p 5 **LX**
Storkower Straße p 3 **HX**
Stralauer Allee p 3 **HY**
Stralauer Straße p 7 **RZ**
Straße des 17 Juni p 5 **MX**
Strausberger Platz p 3 **HY** 702
Stresemannstraße p 6 **NZ**
Stromstraße p 2 **FY** 704
Stülerstraße p 5 **MX**
Stuttgarter Platz p 4 **JX** 705
Suarezstr. p 4 **JX**
Südwestkorso p 2 **EZ** 708
Tauentzienstraße p 5 **MX** 707
Tegeler Weg p 2
Tempelhofer Damm p 3 **GZ**
Tempelhofer Ufer p 3 **GZ** 710
Teplitzer Straße p 2 **EZ** 711
Theodor-Heuss-Platz p 2 **EY** 713
Tiergartenstraße p 5 **MX**
Torstraße p 6 **PX**
Transvallstraße p 2 **FX**
Turmstraße p 2 **FY**
Uhlandstraße p 5 **LZ**
Unter den Linden p 6 **NZ**
Urbanstraße p 3 **GZ**
Veteranenstraße p 6 **PX** 715
Viktoria-Luise-Platz p 5 **MY** 717
Warschauer Straße p 3 **HY**
Weinmeisterstraße p 7 **RY** 718
Welserstraße p 5 **MY**
Werderstraße p 6 **PZ** 720
Westfälische Str. p 4 **JY**
Wexstraße p 2 **FZ**
Wichertstraße p 3 **HX**
Wiener Straße p 3 **HZ**
Wiesbadener Str. p 2 **EZ**
Wilhelmstraße (MITTE) p 6 **NZ**
Wilmersdorfer Straße p 4 **JX**
Windscheidstraße p 4 **JX**
Winterfeldplatz p 5 **MY**
Wisbyer Straße p 3 **HX**
Wittenbergplatz p 5 **MY**
Wollankstraße p 3 **GX**
Württembergische Straße p 4 **KY**
Wundtstraße p 4 **JX**
Xantener Straße p 4 **JY**
Yorckstraße p 3 **GZ**
Zillestraße p 4 **JX**

SIGHTS

MUSEUMS, GALLERIES, COLLECTIONS

Museum Island (Museumsinsel)★★★ PY: *National Gallery (Alte Nationalgalerie)*★★★ **M**[20] *(Paintings of Caspar David Friedrich*★★★, *paintings of Adolph Menzel*★★★ *), Pergamon-Museum (Pergamonmuseum)*★★★, *Collection of Antiquities (Antikensammlung)*★★★ *: Altar of Pergamon (Pergamonaltar)*★★★; *Middle East Museum (Vorderasiatisches Museum)*★★; *Gate of Ishtar (Ischtartor)*★★★; *Museum of Islamic Art (Museum für Islamische Kunst)*★★, *Old Museum (Altes Museum)*★★ **M**[18] ; *Collection of Antiquities (Antikensammlung)*★★★: *Hildesheim silverware treasure (Hildesheimer Silberfund)*★★★ – *Forum of Culture (Kulturforum)*★★★ NZ: *Philharmonie and Chamber Music Hall (Kammermusiksaal)*★★★, *Musical Instruments Museum (Musikinstrumenten-Museum)*★ **M**[4], *Museum of Decorative Arts (Kunstgewerbemuseum)*★★, **M**[5] *Guelph Treasure (Welfenschatz)*★★★, *Lüneburg Treasure (Lüneburger Ratssilber)*★★★, *Gallery of Paintings (Gemäldegalerie)*★★★ **M**[6] *(Altars of Rogier van der Weyden)*★★★, *Collection of drawings (Kupferstichkabinett – Sammlung der Zeichnungen und Druckgraphik)*★, *New National Gallery (Neue Nationalgalerie)*★★ **M**[7], *Prussian State Library (Staatsbibliothek Preußischer Kulturbesitz)*★ – *Dahlem Museums (Museen Dahlem – Kunst und Kulturen der Welt)* BV: *Museum of Ethnography (Ethnologisches Museum)*★★★, *Division American archaeology (Abteilung Amerikanische Archäologie)*★★★: *Stone sculptures of Bilbao (Steinplastiken von Bilbao)*★★★, *Gold Room (Goldkammer)*★★★, *Museum of Indian Art (Museum für indische Kunst)*★★, *Collection of East Asian art (Museum für Ostasiatische Kunst*★, *European Culture Museum (Museum Europäischer Kulturen)*★ – *Charlottenburg Castle (Schloss Charlottenburg)*★★★ EY: *Old Castle (Altes Schloss)*★★, *New Wing (Neuer Flügel)*★★, *Gersaint's Shop Sign (Ladenschild des Kunsthändlers Gersaint)*★★★, *Embarcation for Cythera (Einschiffung nach Kythera)*★★★, *Museum of Pre- and Proto-History (Museum für Vor- und Frühgeschichte)*★, *Garden (Schlossgarten)*★★ *New Pavilion (Neuer Pavillon,*★, *Belvedere*★, *Mausoleum*★ *)* – *Egyptian Museum and Collection of Papyrus (Ägyptisches Museum und Papyrussammlung)*★★★ EY **M**[2], *Nefertiti (Nofretete)*★★★, *Amarna founds (Amarna-Funde)*★★★ – *Collection Berggruen – Picasso and his time (Sammlung Berggruen – Picasso und seine Zeit)*★★ EY **M**[16] – *Hamburg Station Museum (Hamburger Bahnhof – Museum für Gegenwart)*★★ NX – *German Museum of Technique (Deutsches Technikmuseum Berlin)*★★ GZ **M**[3] – *Jewish Museum (Jüdisches Museum)*★★ GZ **M**[38] – *Nature Museum (Museum für Naturkunde)*★★ NX – *March Museum (Märkisches Museum/Stadtmuseum Berlin)*★★ RZ – *Bröhan-Museum*★ EY **M**[13] – *Communications Museum (Museum für Kommunikation Berlin)*★★ PZ **M**[1] – *Friedrichswerder Church (Friedrichswerdersche Kirche)*★ PZ – *Museum of the artistic movement "Brücke" (Brücke-Museum)*★ *by Clay Allee* EZ **M**[36] – *Bauhaus Museum (Bauhaus-Archiv – Museum für Gestaltung)*★ MX – *Museum of Cinema (Filmmuseum) (at Sony Center)*★ NZ – *Botanical Museum (Botanisches Museum)*★ *by Rheinbabenallee* EZ

PARKS, GARDENS, LAKES

Zoological Garden (Zoologischer Garten)★★★ MX – *Tiergarten*★★ MX – *Victory Column (Siegessäule)*★ *Panorama (Aussicht)*★★ – *Grunewald*★★ *by Clay-Allee* EZ: *Hunting Lodge (Jagdschloss Grunewald)*★ **M**[28] – *Peacook Island (Pfaueninsel)*★★ *by Clay-Allee* EZ – *Park*★★, *Summer residence (Lustschloss)*★ – *Wannsee*★★ *by Clay-Allee* EZ – *Großer Müggelsee*★★ *by Stralauer Allee* HYZ – *Botanical Gardens (Botanischer Garten)*★★ *by Rheinbabenallee* EZ – *Viktoria-Park*★ GZ

HISTORIC BUILDINGS, STREETS, SQUARES

Potsdam Square (Potsdamer Platz)★★ NZ – *Quartier DaimlerChrysler*★ *(Sony Center)*★★ *(roof)*★★★ – *Martin-Gropius-Bau*★★ NZ – *Band des Bundes*★★ NY – *Chancellor's office (Bundeskanzleramt)*★★ – *Parliament (Reichstag)*★★ NY *(Panoramic platform (Panorama-Plattform))*★★ – *Brandenburg Gate (Brandenburger Tor)*★★ NZ – *Gendarmenmarkt*★★, PZ – *Schauspielhaus*★★, *French Cathedral (Französischer Dom)*★ *(Panorama Ausblick)*★★, *German Cathedral (Deutscher Dom)*★ – *Unter den Linden*★★ NPZ – *Administration building of DZ-Bank (Hauptverwaltung der DZ-Bank)*★★, *Prussian National Library (Staatsbibliothek-Preußischer Kulturbesitz)*★, *Monument of Frederick II (Reiterdenkmal Friedrichs II)*★, *Forum Fridericianum*★★ *(State Opera Unter den Linden Staatsoper Unter den Linden)*★, *Old Library (Alte Bibliothek)*★, *St-Hedwigs Cathedral (Sankt-Hedwigs-Kathedrale)*★, *New guardroom (Neue Wache)*★, *Arsenal (Zeughaus)*★★, *Crown Prince's Palace (Kronprinzenpalais)*★ – *Castle bridge (Schlossbrücke)*★ PYZ – *Cathedral (Berliner Dom)*★ PY – *Alexander Square (Alexanderplatz)*★ RY – *Television Tower (Fernsehturm)*★ *(view Aussicht)*★★★, *Red Town Hall (Rotes Rathaus)*★ – *Nicolai District (Nikolaiviertel)*★ RYZ – *Nicolai Church (Nikolaikirche)*★, *Knoblauchhaus Museum (Knoblauchhaus)*★, *Ephraim Palace (Ephraim-Palais)*★ – *Kurfürstendamm*★★ LXY – *Kaiser-Wilhelm Memorial Church (Kaiser-Wilhelm-Gedächtniskirche)*★★ – *KaDeWe Shopping Centre*★ MY – *Radio Tower (Funkturm)*★ *(Panorama (Aussicht))*★★★ EY – *Olympic Stadium (Olympiastadion)*★ *by Spandauer Damm* EY – *Citadel (Zitadelle Spandau)*★ *by Siemensdamm* EX – *St.-Nichola's Church Spandau (St-Nikolai-Kirche Spandau)*★ *by Siemensdamm* EX

Town Centre : Charlottenburg, Mitte, Schöneberg, Tiergarten, Wilmersdorf

Adlon, Unter den Linden 77, ✉ 10117, ☎ (030) 2 26 10, *adlon@kempinski.com, Fax (030) 22612222*, Massage, - rm, - 300. AE VISA JCB. rest NZ s

Meals see ***Lorenz Adlon*** below – ***Quarré*** **: Meals** à la carte 43/65 – ***Felix*** (Italian) *(closed Sunday) (dinner only)* **Meals** à la carte 30/50 – ***Adlon Stube*** *(closed July - August, Monday and Tuesday)* **Meals** à la carte 23/43 – 29 – **336 rm** 260/365 – 310/415 – 30 suites.

◆ A legend lives again ! The mother of all grand hotels has been rebuilt in its original palatial style. The Quarré is classically elegant and the Felix stylish. The Adlon Stube is in the style of an English gentleman's club.

Four Seasons, Charlottenstr. 49, ✉ 10117, ☎ (030) 2 03 38, *ber.guest@fourseasons.com, Fax (030) 20336119*, Massage, - rm, - 70. AE VISA JCB. rest PZ n

Seasons **: Meals** à la carte 50/73 – 27 – **204 rm** 265/325 – 300/360 – 29 suites.

◆ The ultimate in luxury. Beyond the stylish foyer are spacious and opulent rooms, all overlooking the Gendarmenmarkt or the hotel courtyard. Harmonious atmosphere and classical elegance in the restaurant with its lovely plasterwork and open fireplace.

Grand Hyatt, Marlene-Dietrich-Platz 2, ✉ 10785, ☎ (030) 25 53 12 34, *berlin@hyatt.de, Fax (030) 25531235*, Massage, - rm, - 320. AE VISA. NZ a

Vox **: Meals** à la carte 37/51 – 22 – **342 rm** 190 – 225 – 16 suites.

◆ Bold architectural forms on the rebuilt Potsdamer Platz. The contemporary architectural theme is carried through into the rooms with their authentic designer décor. The Vox has a subtly Asian atmosphere.

Grand Hotel Esplanade, Lützowufer 15, ✉ 10785, ☎ (030) 25 47 80, *info@esplanade.de, Fax (030) 254788222*, (conference boat with own landing stage), Massage, - rm, - 260. AE VISA JCB. rest MX e

Meals see ***Harlekin*** below – ***Eckkneipe*** **: Meals** à la carte 17/35 – 20 – **386 rm** 230/280 – 255/305 – 23 suites.

◆ This grand hotel with its contemporary design theme and paintings by the "Wild Berliners" fits in well with the surrounding cultural institutions. Solid Berlin specialities served at the wooden tables of the "Eckkneipe" corner pub.

Palace, Budapester Str. 45, ✉ 10787, ☎ (030) 2 50 20, *hotel@palace.de, Fax (030) 25021119*, Massage, - rm, - 300. AE VISA JCB MX k

Meals see ***First Floor*** below – 20 – **282 rm** 225/355 – 19 suites.

◆ Luxury with a personal touch on the famous Kurfürstendamm. Every room has an individual character ; some overlook the Memorial Church, others the Zoo.

Swissôtel, Augsburger Str. 44, ✉ 10789, ☎ (030) 22 01 00, *emailus.berlin@swissotel.com, Fax (030) 220102222*, - rm, - 220. AE VISA. rest LX k

44 **: Meals** à la carte 33/56 – 19 – **316 rm** 270.

◆ Berlin likes to think of itself as cosmopolitan and open to the world, and so does this newly built hotel in Postmodern style in the heart of the city. Cool elegance in the Restaurant 44.

Kempinski Hotel Bristol, Kurfürstendamm 27, ✉ 10719, ☎ (030) 88 43 40, *reservations.bristol@kempinski.com, Fax (030) 8836075*, Massage, - rm, - 280. AE VISA JCB. rest LX n

Kempinski Grill *(closed Sunday and Monday) (dinner only)* **Meals** à la carte 44/68 – ***Kempinski-Eck*** **: Meals** 14 (lunch) and à la carte 26/44 – 23 – **301 rm** 265/326 – 302/363 – 21 suites.

◆ A red carpet leads directly from the Kurfürstendamm into this elegant and luxurious 1950s establishment, a favourite with such guests as John F Kennedy and Sophia Loren. Legendary Kempinski Grill with exquisite décor. Brasserie-style Kempinski-Eck.

The Westin Grand, Friedrichstr. 158, ✉ 10117, ☎ (030) 2 02 70, *info@westin-grand.com, Fax (030) 20273362*, Massage, - rm, - 160. AE VISA JCB PZ a

Friedrichs **: Meals** à la carte 21/38,50 – ***Stammhaus*** **: Meals** à la carte 23/35 – 23 – **358 rm** 222/370 – 247/395 – 20 suites.

◆ In the very heart of old Berlin, the hotel's foyer has an imposing 30m-high glass roof. This is an establishment of great elegance and nostalgic charm. Traditional ambience in Friedrich's, Berlin specialities in the Stammhaus.

InterContinental, Budapester Str. 2, ✉ 10787, ☎ (030) 2 60 20, *berlin@intercont i.com, Fax (030) 26022600*, Massage, – rm, – 860. AE VISA JCB. rest MX a
Meals see ***Hugos*** below – ***L.A. Cafe :*** Meals à la carte 29/33 – 20 – **584 rm** 225/265 – 250/290 – 42 suites.
◆ From foyer to conference suite, this is a most impressive establishment. Tasteful, elegant rooms, those in the east wing in an attractively contemporary style. Splendidly equipped Vitality Club. American-style LA Café with lovely glass dome.

Hilton, Mohrenstr. 30, ✉ 10117, ☎ (030) 2 02 30, *info.berlin@hilton.com, Fax (030) 20234269*, Massage, – rm, – 300. AE VISA JCB PZ r
Fellini (Italian) *(closed mid July - mid August) (dinner only)* Meals à la carte 29/45 – ***Mark Brandenburg :*** Meals à la carte 30/41 – ***Trader Vic's*** *(dinner only)* Meals à la carte 31/50 – 20 – **575 rm** 150/255 – 150/275 – 14 suites.
◆ A splendid foyer welcomes guests to this prestigious establishment. All rooms facing the street overlook the Gendarmenmarkt. Lavish fitness facilities. Italian cuisine in Fellini, Mark Brandenburg with traditional décor.

Dorint Schweizerhof, Budapester Str. 25, ✉ 10787, ☎ (030) 2 69 60, *info.bersc h@dorint.com, Fax (030) 26961000*, Massage, – rm, – 460. AE VISA JCB MX w
Meals à la carte 26/36 – 19 – **384 rm** 195/220 – 220/245 – 10 suites.
◆ The ultra-modern foyer is glimpsed through the hotel's glass façade. Full range of business facilities. Wellness Centre with 25m pool. Warm colours and bold paintings in the Bistro-Restaurant.

Steigenberger, Los-Angeles-Platz 1, ✉ 10789, ☎ (030) 2 12 70, *berlin@steigenbe rger.de, Fax (030) 2127117*, Massage, – rm, – 300. AE VISA JCB. rest MY d
Louis *(closed 24 June - 7 August, Sunday and Monday) (dinner only)* Meals à la carte 38/49 – ***Berliner Stube :*** Meals à la carte 26/38 – 20 – **397 rm** 199/339 – 219/339 – 11 suites.
◆ A spacious foyer gives a foretaste of the standard of comfort of this old city establishment. Executive Floor with Club Lounge on the 6th floor. Varied bars. Restaurant Louis with refined atmosphere and creative cuisine. Cheerful "Berliner Stube" pub.

Brandenburger Hof, Eislebener Str. 14, ✉ 10789, ☎ (030) 21 40 50, *info@brand enburger-hof.com, Fax (030) 21405100*, Massage – rm, – 30. AE VISA JCB. rest LY n
Meals see ***Die Quadriga*** below – ***Der Wintergarten :*** Meals à la carte 34/44 – **82 rm** 165/245 – 240/280 – 4 suites.
◆ The contrast between the Classical façade and the Bauhaus-style interior of this sophisticated establishment is handled with great verve. The light and airy Wintergarten restaurant is laid out around a Japanese courtyard.

Maritim proArte, Friedrichstr. 151, ✉ 10117, ☎ (030) 2 03 35, *info.bpa@maritim.de, Fax (030) 20334209*, Massage, – rm, – 700. AE VISA JCB PY e
Atelier *(closed mid July - early August and Sunday) (dinner only)* Meals à la carte 36/46 – ***Bistro media*** *(lunch only)* Meals à la carte 22/30 – 18 – **403 rm** 149/265 – 168/278 – 29 suites.
◆ A stone's throw from the prestigious thoroughfare of Unter den Linden, this "designer hotel" is extremely stylish and full of avant-garde art. The Atelier has designer furniture and striking pictures, while the Bistro Media features items by Philippe Starck.

Jolly Hotel Vivaldi, Friedrichstr. 96, ✉ 10117, ☎ (030) 2 06 26 60, *vivaldi.jhb@jol lyhotels.de, Fax (030) 206266999*, – rm, – 50. AE VISA JCB PY d
Meals (Italian) à la carte 32/48 – 16 – **254 rm** 145/245 – 170/270.
◆ A spacious foyer welcomes guests to this modern, impeccably run hotel. Choice wood furnishings and attractive colours in the comfortable rooms. Bright open-plan restaurant.

Madison, Potsdamer Str. 3, ✉ 10785, ☎ (030) 5 90 05 00 00, *welcome@madison-b erlin.de, Fax (030) 590050500*, Massage, – rm, – 20. AE VISA. NZ v
Meals see ***Facil*** below – 20 – **167 rm** 130/230 – 155/270 – 17 suites.
◆ In the media district close to Sony, cinema and shopping mall. Apartment hotel with rooms with cooking facilities and shopping service.

Dorint am Gendarmenmarkt, Charlottenstr. 50, ✉ 10117, ☎ (030) 20 37 50, *inf o.bergen@dorint.com, Fax (030) 20375100*, – rm, – 80. AE VISA PZ s
Aigner : Meals 33 (dinner) and à la carte 21/40 – 22 – **92 rm** 215/270 – 245/300.
◆ Directly opposite the French Cathedral on the Gendarmenmarkt. Dating from GDR times but completely refurbished in straightforward contemporary style. The Aigner Restaurant has original features from a Viennese coffee-house.

Crowne Plaza, Nürnberger Str. 65, ✉ 10787, ☎ (030) 21 00 70, *info@cp-berlin.com, Fax (030) 2132009*, Massage, Fa, ≘s, ⊠ - |‡|, ⇆ rm, ▤ TV ✆ ♿ 🚗 P - 🏛 350. AE ⓓ MC VISA JCB. ✂ rest MX t

Meals *(closed Saturday lunch and Sunday dinner)* à la carte 24/39 – ☐ 17 – **423 rm** 170 – 205 – 10 suites.

◆ Well-located for a stroll along the Kurfuerstedamm or a visit to the KaDeWe department store. Distinctive but practical furnishings. Conference facilities including congress centre. Restaurant with wide range of international cuisine.

Sorat Hotel Spree-Bogen 🐎, Alt-Moabit 99, ✉ 10559, ☎ (030) 39 92 00, *spree-bogen@sorat-hotels.com, Fax (030) 39920999*, 🏖, ≘s - |‡|, ⇆ rm, ▤ TV ✆ 🚗 - 🏛 200. AE ⓓ MC VISA JCB. ✂ rest FY b

Meals *(lunch only)* à la carte 22/36 – **221 rm** ☐ 128/232 – 166/268.

◆ Perfect peace on the banks of the River Spree. Within the walls of an old dairy building is a series of surprisingly modern interiors. Private landing-stage. The restaurant combines old brick walls with the latest in design.

Savoy, Fasanenstr. 9, ✉ 10623, ☎ (030) 31 10 30, *info@hotel-savoy.com, Fax (030) 31103333*, 🏖, ≘s - |‡|, ⇆ rm, TV ✆ - 🏛 40. AE ⓓ MC VISA LX s

Meals *(closed Sunday)* à la carte 26/38 – **125 rm** ☐ 137/237 – 162/262 – 18 suites.

◆ Charming city hotel with 70 years of experience. Mentioned in his writings by Thomas Mann and still favoured by the celebrities of today. Cigar Lounge. Classic interiors including restaurant with easy chairs.

Mondial, Kurfürstendamm 47, ✉ 10707, ☎ (030) 88 41 10, *hotel-mondial@t-online.de, Fax (030) 88411150*, 🏖, ≘s, ⊠ - |‡|, ⇆ rm, TV ✆ ♿ 🚗 - 🏛 50. AE ⓓ MC VISA JCB. ✂ rest KY e

Meals à la carte 19/35 – **75 rm** ☐ 110/220 – 135/245.

◆ Right on the Ku'Damm and ideally placed for forays into its bustling shopping activity. Subsequent recovery aided by relaxation in your comfortable soundproofed rooms. Restaurant with timeless décor and buffet with vast choice.

Alexander Plaza, Rosenstr. 1, ✉ 10178, ☎ (030) 24 00 10, *info@hotel-alexander-plaza.de, Fax (030) 24001777*, 🏖, Fa, ≘s - |‡|, ⇆ rm, TV ✆ 🚗 - 🏛 70. AE ⓓ MC VISA JCB RY a

Meals *(closed Sunday)* à la carte 22/36 – ☐ 15 – **92 rm** 140/175 – 150/185.

◆ Very handy for the fashionable Hackesche Hoefe area, the hotel was built in 1897 for a dealer in furs. The mosaic floor in the hall is an unmissable feature. The restaurant is strikingly furnished with black leather sofas and red chairs.

NH Berlin-Mitte, Leipziger Str. 106, ✉ 10117, ☎ (030) 20 37 60, *nhberlinmitte@nh-hotels.com, Fax (030) 20376600*, Fa, ≘s - |‡|, ⇆ rm, ▤ TV ✆ ♿ 🚗 - 🏛 150. AE ⓓ MC VISA PZ k

Meals à la carte 23/48 – ☐ 15 – **392 rm** 129/189 – 149/209.

◆ Hotel with spacious foyer, modern, functional and comfortable rooms and an excellent central location. Leisure facilities on the 8th floor. Bistro-style restaurant opening on to the foyer.

Grosser Kurfürst, Neue Roßstr. 11, ✉ 10179, ☎ (030) 24 60 00, *grosserkurfuerst@deraghotels.de, Fax (030) 24600300*, Fa, ≘s - |‡|, ⇆ rm, ▤ TV ✆ ♿ - 🏛 20. AE ⓓ MC VISA JCB RZ e

Meals (Italian) à la carte 24/39 – **144 rm** ☐ 140/228 – 175/240 – 7 suites.

◆ Smart, well equipped modern rooms, some facing the Spree River, lead off from an impressive lobby beneath a landmark glass tower. Elegant Mediterranean restaurant with a menu to match.

Henriette, Neue Roßstr.13, ✉ 10179, ☎ (030) 24 60 09 00, *henriette@deraghotels.de, Fax (030) 24600940*, 🏖 - |‡|, ⇆ rm, TV ♿ - 🏛 50. AE ⓓ MC VISA RZ e

Meals (Indian) à la carte 14/20,50 – **53 rm** ☐ 135/190 – 165/215.

◆ Bedrooms and apartments are grouped around a four-storey light-well. Their décor makes use of fine materials to create a tasteful and comfortable atmosphere.

Alsterhof, Augsburger Str. 5, ✉ 10789, ☎ (030) 21 24 20, *info@alsterhof.com, Fax (030) 2183949*, beer garden, Massage, Fa, ≘s - |‡|, ⇆ rm, TV ✆ 🚗 - 🏛 120. AE ⓓ MC VISA JCB MY r

Meals *(closed Sunday dinner)* à la carte 21,50/31 – ***Zum Lit-Fass*** *(dinner only)* **Meals** à la carte 16/25 – ☐ 16 – **200 rm** 94/150 – 99/175.

◆ This corner building with a glazed roof-pavilion offers exceptionally comfortable rooms and a small but attractive 6th floor leisure area. Internet terminals. Basement hotel restaurant. The more informal Zum Lit-Fass with a leafy beer garden.

Seehof, Lietzensee-Ufer 11, ✉ 14057, ☎ (030) 32 00 20, *info@hotel-seehof-berlin.de, Fax (030) 32002251*, ≤, 🏖, ⊠ - |‡|, ⇆ rm, TV 🚗 - 🏛 30. AE MC VISA JX r

Meals *(closed 4 to 14 January)* à la carte 21/34 – **75 rm** ☐ 135/190 – 165/220.

◆ Well-run hotel on the leafy banks of the Lietzensee. Elegant, tasteful rooms, some with mahogany furniture, others with period pieces. Restaurant with classical ambience and lovely lakeside terrace.

President, An der Urania 16, ✉ 10787, ☎ (030) 21 90 30, *president@cca-hotels.de* *Fax (030) 2186120*, – rm, 70. MY
Meals à la carte 26/32 – 14 – **181 rm** 123 – 141.
◆ As well as functional Economy and Business rooms with pc connection the hotel has Club Rooms with extra-large desks and comfortable leather chairs. Redesigned restaurant with wicker furniture.

Art'otel Berlin Mitte, Wallstr. 70, ✉ 10179, ☎ (030) 24 06 20, *aobminfo@artotels.de*, *Fax (030) 24062222* – rm, rm, – 35. RZ
Meals *(closed Sunday)* à la carte 23/31 – **109 rm** 130/180 – 160/210.
◆ A wonderful synthesis of old patrician residence and ultramodern purpose-built hotel. Full-blooded designer interiors.

Hollywood Media Hotel without rest, Kurfürstendamm 202, ✉ 10719, ☎ (030) 88 91 00, *info@filmhotel.de*, *Fax (030) 88910280* – – 90. LY
185 rm 132/152 – 154/174 – 12 suites.
◆ Hollywood comes to Berlin in Artur Brauner's hotel, making every guest a star. Rooms evoke the world of film. Own cinema.

Domicil, Kantstr. 111a, ✉ 10627, ☎ (030) 32 90 30, *info@hotel-domicil-berlin.de* *Fax (030) 32903299*, – rm, – 50. JX
Meals à la carte 21/30 – **70 rm** 118/143 – 154/184 – 6 suites.
◆ A curving glass façade distinguishes this corner building. Elegant pine furnishings give the rooms a sunny, Italian atmosphere. Bright tiling and mosaic in the bathrooms. Rooftop restaurant with garden.

Hecker's Hotel, Grolmanstr. 35, ✉ 10623, ☎ (030) 8 89 00, *info@heckers-hotel.de* *Fax (030) 8890260* – rm, – 25. LX
Cassambalis *(closed Sunday)* **Meals** à la carte 30/42 – 15 – **69 rm** 110/170 – 130/180
◆ This establishment combines individuality and personal service. Some rooms are comfortably functional, others in contemporary designer style or with tasteful themed decor. Mediterranean cuisine served with flair in Cassamblis.

Bleibtreu, Bleibtreustr. 31, ✉ 10707, ☎ (030) 88 47 40, *info@bleibtreu.com* *Fax (030) 88474444*, – rm, KY
Meals à la carte 26,50/36 – 15 – **60 rm** 142/222 – 152/232.
◆ Restored city residence dating from the Kaiser's times. Contemporary furnishing throughout, specially designed for the hotel by German and Italian firms. Stylish bistro-type restaurant opening on to the foyer.

Ku'Damm 101 without rest, Kurfürstendamm 101, ✉ 10711, ☎ (030) 5 20 05 50, *info@kudamm101.com*, *Fax (030) 520055555*, – rm, – 65. JY
13 – **171 rm** 101/161 – 118/178.
◆ Uncompromising designer style throughout. Rooms in contemporary colours, with big windows and excellent technical facilities. 7th floor breakfast room with city views.

Luisenhof without rest, Köpenicker Str. 92, ✉ 10179, ☎ (030) 2 41 59 06, *info@luisenhof.de*, *Fax (030) 2792983* – – 30. RZ
27 rm 120/180 – 150/250.
◆ Fine old 1822 town house with a fascinating history, including period as a depot for horse tramway. Elegantly furnished with period items.

Novotel Berlin Mitte, Fischerinsel 12, ✉ 10179, ☎ (030) 20 67 40, *h3278@accor-hotels.com*, *Fax (030) 20674111*, – rm, – 220. rest RZ
Meals à la carte 18,50/34,50 – 13 – **238 rm** 139/189 – 154/214.
◆ This up-to-date establishment is located in a major building complex. Modern, functional rooms and a business centre on the top floor.

Dorint an der Charité, Invalidenstr. 38, ✉ 10115, ☎ (030) 30 82 60, *info.bercha@dorint.com*, *Fax (030) 30826100* – rm, – 100. NX
Meals à la carte 17,50/27,50 – 13 – **246 rm** 106/126 – 116/126.
◆ This modern hotel close to the natural history museum devotes itself wholeheartedly to business travellers. Rooms and corridors graced by enlargements of postcards.

Mercure am Checkpoint Charlie without rest, Schützenstr. 11, ✉ 10117, ☎ (030) 20 63 20, *h3120@accor-hotels.com*, *Fax (030) 20632111*, PZ
115 rm 158 – 186 – 28 suites.
◆ Successful combination of new design and typical Berlin sandstone architecture. Spacious, welcoming, contemporary rooms ; those facing the courtyard with balcony.

Art'otel Berlin City Center West, Lietzenburger Str. 85, ✉ 10719, ℘ (030) 8 87 77 70, *aobwinfo@artotels.de, Fax (030) 887777777* – rm, – 25. AE VISA JCB LY b
Meals à la carte 20,50/25 – **91 rm** 130/180 – 160/210.
◆ New, contemporary hotel. The Andy Warhols are set off by the colourful interiors, with bedrooms in lime green and violet and public spaces in shades of red. In very much the same spirit, the restaurant with its vast glazed façade.

Hamburg, Landgrafenstr. 4, ✉ 10787, ℘ (030) 26 47 70, *hoham@t-online.de, Fax (030) 2629394*, – – 50. AE VISA JCB. rest
Meals à la carte 26/37 – **191 rm** 115/134 – 146/200. MX s
◆ Just a short walk from the Tiergarten. Spacious foyer with open fireplace. Sailors will enjoy the atmosphere in the Hanse Bar. Restaurant with winter garden.

Die Zwölf Apostel, Hohenzollerndamm 33, ✉ 10713, ℘ (030) 86 88 90, *info@12-apostel.de, Fax (030) 86889103*, – , rm, KZ b
Meals (Italian) à la carte 19,50/39 – **36 rm** 93/99 – 117/130.
◆ Fiery red façade with attractive wall-paintings. Quiet rooms with period Italian furniture. Restaurant in the style of a superior trattoria, plus a sushi-bar.

Hackescher Markt without rest, Große Präsidentenstr. 8, ✉ 10178, ℘ (030) 28 00 30, *info@hackescher-markt.com, Fax (030) 28003111* – . AE VISA PY c
15 – **31 rm** 115/165 – 150/175.
◆ New establishment with a traditional façade in Berlin's trendiest district. Spacious rooms with natural wood furnishings. Courtyard terrace.

Kanthotel without rest, Kantstr. 111, ✉ 10627, ℘ (030) 32 30 20, *info@kanthotel.com, Fax (030) 3240952* – – 20. AE VISA JCB JX e
70 rm 135/185 – 145/185.
◆ This well-run hotel with its comfortable, functional rooms is located between the International Congress Centre and the Memorial Church.

Sorat Art'otel without rest, Joachimstaler Str. 29, ✉ 10719, ℘ (030) 88 44 70, *art-otel@sorat-hotels.com, Fax (030) 88447700* – – 25. AE VISA JCB LY e
133 rm 124 – 146.
◆ Good location in central western Berlin. The whole building has been designed in avant-guard style by Wolf Vostell. Contemporary pictures adorn the walls.

Adrema without rest, Gotzkowskystr. 20, ✉ 10555, ℘ (030) 20 21 34 00, *info@hewa-hotels.de, Fax (030) 20213444* – . AE VISA JCB FY x
53 rm 105/165 – 115/175.
◆ Crisp lines and functional fittings characterise the designer rooms of this establishment. Breakfast served at loft level with views of the River Spree.

Kronprinz without rest, Kronprinzendamm 1, ✉ 10711, ℘ (030) 89 60 30, *reception@kronprinz-hotel.de, Fax (030) 8931215* – – 25. AE VISA JCB
77 rm 115/130 – 145. JY d
◆ Well-known for its tosteful interior and situated on the western edge of town close to the International Congress Centre. Terrace beneath ancient chestnut trees.

Schlosspark-Hotel, Heubnerweg 2a, ✉ 14059, ℘ (030) 3 26 90 30, *schlossparkhotel@t-online.de, Fax (030) 326903600*, , – , rm, – 30. VISA EY a
Meals à la carte 20/27 – **39 rm** 92/150 – 112/170.
◆ Excellent starting point for visiting the nearby museums as well as the castle and its inviting park. It's a good idea to reserve a room facing the park. Restaurant-Café with rustic interior and conservatory.

Ramada, Chausseestr. 118, ✉ 10115, ℘ (030) 2 78 75 50, *berlin.mitte@ramada-treff.de, Fax (030) 278755550*, – , rm, – 20. AE VISA. rest NX c
Meals à la carte 25/35 – 15 – **145 rm** 85/175.
◆ Mainly catering for business travellers, this hotel has contemporary, functional rooms. Glass handbasins are an original touch.

Albrechtshof, Albrechtstr. 8, ✉ 10117, ℘ (030) 30 88 60, *albrechtshof-hotel@t-online.de, Fax (030) 30886100*, – , rm, – 45. AE VISA
Meals à la carte 26,50/35 – **100 rm** 118/169 – 148/199. NY a
◆ This comfortable establishment is one of the Christian Hotels chain. It has a chapel which can be used for weddings and christenings as well as for prayer and contemplation.

Park Inn, Alexanderplatz, ✉ 10178, ℘ (030) 2 38 90, *hotel@park-inn-alexanderplatz.de, Fax (030) 23894305*, – , rm, – 260. AE VISA JCB
Meals à la carte 17/28 – 15 – **1006 rm** 140/175 – 166/201. RY c
◆ A landmark on legendary Alexander-Platz, the Forum is one of the city's tallest buildings. Guests can try their luck in the Casino and dine in the Berlin-style Zille-Stube or in Humbolt's buffet.

Boulevard without rest, Kurfürstendamm 12, ✉ 10719, ☎ (030) 88 42 50, *info@hotel-boulevard.com, Fax (030) 88425450* – 15. AE MC VISA
57 rm 95 – 128. LX c
◆ The hotel takes its name from the cosmopolitan thoroughfare on which it is located. Roof terrace with café and fine views of city life.

Scandotel Castor without rest, Fuggerstr. 8, ✉ 10777, ☎ (030) 21 30 30, *scandotel@t-online.de, Fax (030) 21303160* – P. AE MC VISA JCB MY s
78 rm 95/120 – 107/148.
◆ Ku'Damm and KaDeWe, cinemas and cafes, are all close to this contemporary establishment with its functional and well-equipped rooms.

Kurfürstendamm am Adenauerplatz without rest, Kurfürstendamm 68, ✉ 10707, ☎ (030) 88 46 30, *info@hotel-kurfuerstendamm.de, Fax (030) 8825528* – P – 30. AE MC VISA JCB JY n
34 rm 90 – 140.
◆ Rooms identically furnished in cherrywood. The building also houses a catering college.

Fjord Hotel without rest, Bissingzeile 13, ✉ 10785, ☎ (030) 25 47 20, *fjordhotelberlin@t-online.de, Fax (030) 25472111* – P. AE MC VISA. NZ c
57 rm 85 – 100.
◆ Family-run hotel just a stone's throw from Potsdamer-Platz. Contemporary décor. Breakfast served on the roof terrace when it's fine.

Lorenz Adlon - Hotel Adlon, Unter den Linden 77, ✉ 10117, ☎ (030) 22 61 19 60, *adlon@kempinski.com, Fax (030) 22612222* – AE MC VISA JCB. NZ s
closed 2 weeks January, 4 weeks July - August, Sunday and Monday – **Meals** *(dinner only)* 95/150 and à la carte.
◆ Circular first-floor restaurant with view of the Brandenburg Gate. Stylishly elegant interior, impeccable service, lavish classic cuisine.
Spec. Kabeljau und Flusskrebse mit weißem Bohnencassoulet. Taubenbrust und Gänsestopfleber mit Perlgraupen. Komposition von Rhabarber und Himbeeren (season).

First Floor - Hotel Palace, Budapester Str. 45, ✉ 10787, ☎ (030) 25 02 10 20, *hotel@palace.de, Fax (030) 25021129* – AE MC VISA JCB. MX k
closed 19 July - 15 August and Saturday lunch – **Meals** 40 *(lunch)*/105 and à la carte 57/71.
◆ First class cuisine from the brilliant Matthias Buchholz, with silver service and a French menu varying with the seasons.
Spec. Gebratener Kabeljau unter der Kapernkruste mit Petersilienpüree. Pauillac-Lamm mit Aromaten gebraten und Bohnenmelange. Knusper vom Apfel.

Hugos - Hotel InterContinental, Budapester Str. 2, ✉ 10787, ☎ (030) 26 02 12 63, *mail@hugos-restaurant.de, Fax (030) 26021239*, Berlin – AE MC VISA JCB.
closed 2 weeks January, 4 weeks July - August and Sunday – **Meals** *(dinner only)* 74/127 and à la carte 64/75. MX a
◆ A wonderful combination of elegant modern design, fine settings, and the creative cuisine of Thomas Kammeier. Superb, roof-top dining !
Spec. Glasierte Gänsestopfleber mit Pattaya Mango. Kalbstafelspitz mit Trüffelbutter gratiniert. Variation von der Valrhona-Schokolade.

Margaux, Unter den Linden 78 (entrance Wilhelmstrasse), ✉ 10117, ☎ (030) 22 65 26 11, *hoffmann@margaux-berlin.de, Fax (030) 22652612*, – AE MC VISA NZ b
closed Sunday – **Meals** 35 *(lunch)* and à la carte 62/91.
◆ Dishes range from classic to avantgarde, served in a sumptuous setting of gilt, velvet, rosewood, honey-coloured onyx and black marble.
Spec. Taube mit Gewürzen. Boeuf à la mode. Schokoladencrème mit Olivenöl.

Facil - Hotel Madison, Potsdamer Str. 3 (5th floor), ✉ 10785, ☎ (030) 5 90 05 12 34, *welcome@facil-berlin.de, Fax (030) 590050500*, – AE MC VISA. NZ v
closed 1 to 25 January, 24 July - 8 August, Saturday - Sunday and Bank Holidays – **Meals** 33 *(lunch)*/145 and à la carte 62/82.
◆ A glass lift transports diners to this fully glazed restaurant on the 5th floor, characterised by its cool elegance and its leafy surroundings.
Spec. Bretonischer Hummer mit Bouillabaisse-Risotto und Venusmuscheln. Müritz-Lamm in Olivenknusperteig mit Bohnenkrautjus und Ofentomaten. Schokoladentarte mit Espressomousse.

Die Quadriga - Hotel Brandenburger Hof, Eislebener Str. 14, ✉ 10789, ☎ (030) 21 40 56 50, *info@brandenburger-hof.com, Fax (030) 21405100* – AE MC VISA JCB.
closed 1 to 11 January, 12 July - 15 August, Saturday and Sunday – **Meals** *(dinner only)* 70/90 and à la carte 52/72. LY r
◆ To the accompaniment of piano music, diners sit on Frank Lloyd Wright chairs and eat delightful delicacies off Berlin porcelain.
Spec. Gegrillte Jakobsmuscheln und Tatar vom Thunfisch. Lasagne vom geschmorten Ochsenschwanz und Rinderfilet mit Gänseleberschaum. Törtchen von Ananas und Schokolade mit gratiniertem Passionsfruchtparfait.

XXX **Harlekin** - Grand Hotel Esplanade, Lützowufer 15, ✉ 10785, ✆ (030) 2 54 78 86 30, *info@esplanade.de, Fax (030) 254788617,* – ▤. AE ⓓ ⓜ VISA JCB. ✈ MX e
closed 1 to 6 January, 20 to 28 April, Sunday and Monday – **Meals** *(dinner only)* 75 and à la carte 49/60 ♀.
◆ The restaurant is dominated by the cheeky harlequin figure sculpted by Markus Luepertz. Diners can get a close-up of the kitchen team working on their creative cuisine.

XX ✿ **VAU**, Jägerstr. 54, ✉ 10117, ✆ (030) 2 02 97 30, *restaurant@vau-berlin.de, Fax (030) 20297311,* – AE ⓓ ⓜ VISA. ✈ PZ u
closed Sunday – **Meals** 36 *(lunch)*/110 and à la carte 64/76 ♀.
◆ The architecture and design of this bistro-style establishment are as much a feast as its appetising cuisine.
Spec. Lauwarm marinierter Hummer mit Mango und Olive. Bresse-Taube mit Feigenchutney und gegrilltem Chicorée. Dreierlei vom Kalb mit Minzspinat und Flammkuchen.

XX **Ana e Bruno**, Sophie-Charlotten-Str. 101, ✉ 14059, ✆ (030) 3 25 71 10, *alexandra@ana-e-bruno.de, Fax (030) 3226895* – ▤. ✈ EY s
closed 2 weeks January - February, 2 weeks July - August, Sunday and Monday – **Meals** *(dinner only)* (Italian) à la carte 56/73, ⚘.
◆ Proprietor and chef Bruno Pellegrini explains to his guests how his menu has been composed and recommends appropriate wines. Elegant contemporary ambience.

XX **Alt Luxemburg**, Windscheidstr. 31, ✉ 10627, ✆ (030) 3 23 87 30, *info@altluxemburg.de, Fax (030) 3274003* – ▤. AE ⓓ ⓜ VISA JX s
closed Sunday – **Meals** *(dinner only)* (booking essential) 67/75 and à la carte 47/60.
◆ Pleasant late 19C ambience enhanced by fabrics by Josef Hoffmann, the great Viennese Art Nouveau designer. Classical cuisine served in an establishment of great individuality.

XX **Bocca di Bacco**, Friedrichstr. 167, ✉ 10117, ✆ (030) 20 67 28 28, *info@boccadibacco.de, Fax (030) 20672929* – AE ⓜ VISA. ✈ PZ x
closed Sunday lunch – **Meals** (Italian) 19,50 *(lunch)* and à la carte 30/41.
◆ "The Mouth of Bacchus" is a stylish modern restaurant offering friendly service and fine Italian food. Opulent paintings and smart bar.

XX **Kaiserstuben**, Am Festungsgraben 1, ✉ 10117, ✆ (030) 20 61 05 48, *info@kaiserstuben.de, Fax (030) 20610550* – AE ⓓ ⓜ VISA PY n
closed 3 weeks July - August, Sunday and Monday – **Meals** *(dinner only)* (booking essential) à la carte 46/56 – ***Die Möwe*** *(closed Sunday) (dinner only)* **Meals** à la carte 28/36.
◆ The Kaiserstuben have a new home ; on the first floor of this old aristocratic residence is the small, exquisitely decorated restaurant serving classic cuisine, while the Möwe has white tablecloths, a contemporary atmosphere and an international menu.

XX **Guy**, Jägerstr. 59 (courtyard), ✉ 10117, ✆ (030) 20 94 26 00, *info@guy-restaurant.de, Fax (030) 20942610,* – AE ⓜ VISA. ✈ PZ d
closed Saturday lunch and Sunday – **Meals** 20 *(lunch)* and à la carte 39/46 *(vegetarian menu available)* ♀.
◆ Charm abounds on all four levels of this stylish establishment, with its restaurant, imposing courtyard, wine cellar, bar and banqueting hall.

XX **Paris-Moskau**, Alt-Moabit 141, ✉ 10557, ✆ (030) 3 94 20 81, *Fax (030) 3942602,*
closed 2 weeks August – **Meals** *(dinner only)* (booking essential) à la carte 33/46 ♀.
◆ This old timber-framed building is close to where the Wall once ran. Timeless, tasteful ambience, and dishes imaginatively varied by season. GY s

X **Maothai**, Meierottostr. 1, ✉ 10719, ✆ (030) 8 83 28 23, *Fax (030) 88756558,* – AE ⓓ ⓜ VISA. ✈ LY m
Meals *(Monday - Friday dinner only)* (Thai) à la carte 20/42.
◆ This neo-Classical building with its elegant façade is just round the corner from the Fasanenplatz. Comprehensive menu and Thai music.

X **Rutz**, Chausseestr. 8, ✉ 10115, ✆ (030) 24 62 87 60, *info@rutz-weinbar.de, Fax (030) 24628761,* – AE ⓓ ⓜ VISA PY r
closed Sunday – **Meals** *(dinner only)* à la carte 37,50/48, ⚘.
◆ Laid out on two floors, the Rutz has achieved a coolly contemporary look. A highlight is the wine list with 1001 items.

X **Die Eselin von A.**, Kulmbacher Str. 15, ✉ 10777, ✆ (030) 2 14 12 84, *info@die-eselin-von-a.de, Fax (030) 21476948,* – ⓜ VISA MY a
closed 2 weeks early January, 2 weeks July – **Meals** *(dinner only)* à la carte 30/38 ♀.
◆ Bistro-style restaurant much appreciated by its many regulars for friendly service, relaxed atmosphere and contemporary international cuisine made from fresh ingredients.

X **Borchardt**, Französische Str. 47, ✉ 10117, ✆ (030) 20 38 71 10, *Fax (030) 20387150,* – AE ⓜ VISA PZ c
Meals à la carte 33/51.
◆ This is the place to see and be seen, in a fashionable setting enhanced by stucco ceilings and gilded capitals. Attractive courtyard.

Maxwell, Bergstr. 22 (entrance in courtyard), ✉ 10115, ☎ (030) 2 80 71 21, *maxwell.berlin@t-online.de, Fax (030) 28599848,* – AE ① MC VISA JCB PX e
Meals *(dinner only)* (booking essential) à la carte 28/40.
◆ This establishment occupies the courtyard of an old brewery. The building with its lovely neo-Gothic façade is worth a visit in itself. Attractive courtyard terrace.

Weinstein, Mittelstr. 1, ✉ 10117, ☎ (030) 20 64 96 69, *Fax (030) 20649699,* – AE ① MC VISA PY f
closed 2 weeks July, Saturday lunch, Sunday and Monday – **Meals** 29/41 and à la carte.
◆ The interior evokes the atmosphere of an exclusive Parisian bistro with an appealing touch of Art Deco. Ambitious cuisine with a Mediterranean flavour.

Lindenlife, Unter den Linden 44, ✉ 10117, ☎ (030) 2 06 29 03 33, *zinati@lindenlife.de, Fax (030) 206290335,* – AE ① MC VISA NZ u
Meals à la carte 26,50/33 – ***Weinlife :*** **Meals** à la carte 19,50/29.
◆ The Lindenlife is the MPs' restaurant - you could find yourself eating next to some prominent politician. "Weinlife" has a contemporary feel with lots of straight lines and right angles and wine conditioners set in the walls.

Lutter und Wegner, Charlottenstr. 56, ✉ 10117, ☎ (030) 2 02 95 40, *reservierung@lutter-wegner-gendarmenmarkt.de, Fax (030) 20295425,* – AE MC VISA PZ e
Meals 17 *(lunch)* and à la carte 27,50/42,50.
◆ The theme here is "wine, women and song", exemplified by the big columns painted by contemporary artists. Cheerful wine cellar.

at Berlin-Friedrichshain :

Inn Side Residence-Hotel, Lange Str. 31, ✉ 10243, ☎ (030) 29 30 30, *berlin@innside.de, Fax (030) 29303199,* – rm, – 35. AE ① MC VISA JCB. rest SZ
Meals à la carte 25/40 – 14 – **133 rm** 160/230 – 180/250.
◆ An amazing interaction of shapes and colours characterises the spacious interiors of this establishment, laid out over six floors laden with a variety of art objects. Basement restaurant with winter garden overlooking the courtyard.

NH Berlin-Alexanderplatz, Landsberger Allee 26, ✉ 10249, ☎ (030) 4 22 61 30, *nhberlinalexanderplatz@nh-hotels.com, Fax (030) 42261300,* – rm, – 160. AE ① MC VISA SY
Meals à la carte 23/36 – 13 – **225 rm** 100 – 115.
◆ Grandly-conceived reception area. Rooms identically furnished in pale natural woods and well fitted-out for the business traveller. Sophisticated bistro-style restaurant.

at Berlin-Grunewald :

The Regent Schlosshotel, Brahmsstr. 10, ✉ 14193, ☎ (030) 89 58 40, *schlosshotel@regenthotels.com, Fax (030) 89584800,* Massage, – rm, – 40. AE ① MC VISA JCB. rest EZ
Vivaldi *(closed 2 weeks January, 26 July - 15 August, Sunday and Monday)* **Meals** à la carte 67/93 – 23 – **54 rm** 280/390 – 310/430 – 12 suites.
◆ No, it's not a dream. Karl Lagerfeld was responsible for these amazing interiors. You can only stand and marvel. Alternatively, dine superlatively well among the chandeliers, stucco and gorgeous gilt of the Vivaldi restaurant.
Spec. Lauch-Canneloni gefüllt mit geeistem Taschenkrebs. Lauwarme Bouillon von Pfifferlingen und Sternanis mit Gänsestopfleber. Kross gebratener Wolfsbarsch mit weißer Gazpacho und kleinen Pimentos.

at Berlin-Kreuzberg :

relexa Hotel Stuttgarter Hof, Anhalter Str. 9, ✉ 10963, ☎ (030) 26 48 30, *berlin@relexa-hotel.de, Fax (030) 26483900,* – rm, – 160. AE ① MC VISA JCB NZ
Meals à la carte 25/31,50 – **207 rm** 120/195 – 150/225 – 10 suites.
◆ The Stuttgarter Hof was patronised by the prominent back in the Kaiser's day. Now has double the number of rooms as well as conference facilities.

Svevo, Lausitzer Str. 25, ✉ 10999, ☎ (030) 61 07 32 16, *Fax (030) 6107324*
closed August, Sunday and Monday – **Meals** *(dinner only)* à la carte 28,50/34. HZ
◆ This restaurant with its rather austere décor, wooden floor and furnishings is run by a young team. An unusual touch : the menu is displayed on punched cards in a little box.

Le Cochon Bourgeois, Fichtestr. 24, ✉ 10967, ☎ (030) 6 93 01 0…, *Fax (030) 6943480,* HZ
closed 1 to 12 January, 2 weeks July, Sunday and Monday – **Meals** *(dinner only)* à la carte 27/37.
◆ With a character all its own, this unique establishment successfully combines boldly rustic décor with fine French cuisine.

at Berlin-Lichtenberg *East : 5 km, by Karl-Marx-Allee* HY :

Abacus Tierpark Hotel, Franz-Mett-Str. 3, ✉ 10319, ☎ (030) 5 16 20, *info@abacus-hotel.de, Fax (030) 5162400*, – rm, – 250. AE MC VISA
Meals 15 *(lunch)*/24 *(buffet)* and à la carte – **278 rm** 99/145 – 125/200.
◆ Right by Europe's largest open-air animal park, this is an ideal place for animal-lovers to stay. Functional rooms ; informal bistro-cafeteria style restaurant.

at Berlin-Lichterfelde *Southwest : 7 km, by Boelcke Straße* GZ :

Villa Toscana without rest, Bahnhofstr. 19, ✉ 12207, ☎ (030) 7 68 92 70, *hotel@villa-toscana.de, Fax (030) 7734488*, – . AE MC VISA JCB.
16 rm 80/110 – 100/120.
◆ Turn-of-the-century villa with a distinctively Italian atmosphere, lacquer furniture and a Tuscan-style garden. Garden pool where koi carp perform their leisurely manoeuvres.

at Berlin-Mariendorf *South : 7 km, by Tempelhofer Damm* GZ :

Landhaus Alpinia, Säntisstr. 32, ✉ 12107, ☎ (030) 76 17 70 (hotel) 7 41 99 98 (rest.), *info@alpina-berlin.de, Fax (030) 7419835*, – rm, – 20. AE MC VISA
Villa Rossini (Italian) *(dinner only)* **Meals** à la carte 19/36 – **58 rm** 93/135 – 115/160.
◆ For anyone wanting to get away from the hectic atmosphere of the city centre and yet remain within easy reach, this establishment with its traditional, country-style interiors is ideal. Pale pine and rustic fittings in the restaurant.

at Berlin-Neukölln :

Estrel, Sonnenallee 225, ✉ 12057, ☎ (030) 6 83 10, *hotel@estrel.com, Fax (030) 68312345*, beer garden, Massage, – rm, – 2700. AE MC VISA JCB HZ a
Sans Souci *(dinner only)* **Meals** à la carte 22/39 – ***Portofino*** (Italian) **Meals** à la carte 21/43 – ***Estrel-Stube*** *(dinner only)* **Meals** à la carte 16/28 – 15 – **1125 rm** 123/235 – 134/246 – 60 suites.
◆ Germany's biggest hotel is a world in itself, with a glazed-over piazza, its own convention and festival centre, rail station and landing stage. International cuisine in the Sans Souci, pizza and pasta in the Portofino.

Mercure, Hermannstr. 214, ✉ 12049, ☎ (030) 62 78 00, *h1894@accor-hotels.com, Fax (030) 62780111*, – rm, – 250. AE MC VISA JCB HZ c
Meals à la carte 23/32 – 13 – **216 rm** 106/122 – 121/137.
◆ Particularly convenient for travellers using Tempelhof airport, this establishment incorporates a cinema, hairdresser and beauty salon, shopping mall and offices.

at Berlin Prenzlauer Berg :

Park Plaza, Storkower Str. 162, ✉ 10407, ☎ (030) 42 18 10, *ppbinfo@parkplazahotels.de, Fax (030) 42181111* – rm, – 50. AE MC VISA JCB. rest HY c
Meals *(closed Sunday dinner)* à la carte 22/31 – **155 rm** 100/120 – 120/140.
◆ This hotel and office complex is located directly opposite the Europa Sport Park, ideal for those following the 6-day race in the Velodrom.

Zander, Kollwitzstr. 50, ✉ 10405, ☎ (030) 44 05 76 79, *rolalbrecht@aol.com, Fax (030) 44057632*, – AE MC VISA RX a
closed Sunday – **Meals** 12 *(lunch)*/48 and à la carte 28/36.
◆ Straightforward restaurant laid out on two levels with bistro-type seating, freshly prepared international dishes and a menu changed weekly.

at Berlin-Reinickendorf :

Dorint Airport Hotel, Gotthardstr. 96, ✉ 13403, ☎ (030) 49 88 40, *info-berteg@dorint.com, Fax (030) 49884555* – rm, – 70. AE MC VISA JCB. rest FX c
Meals à la carte 20/35 – 12 – **303 rm** 68/129 – 71/141.
◆ The Tegel airport bus stops here and there are good public transport connections to the rest of the city. Italian-style interiors.

Rheinsberg am See, Finsterwalder Str. 64, ✉ 13435, ☎ (030) 4 02 10 02, *info@hotel-rheinsberg.com, Fax (030) 4035057*, Massage, – rm, – 30. AE MC VISA Northwest : 7 km, by Markstraße GX
Meals à la carte 25/45 – **81 rm** 94/99 – 109/125.
◆ This establishment in the north of the city has an attractive lakeshore location. Conference facilities in a splendidly converted old barn. Extensive fitness area. Open-plan restaurant with garden terrace.

at **Berlin-Siemensstadt** *Northwest : 12 km, by Siemensdamm* EX :

Holiday Inn Berlin-Esplanade, Rohrdamm 80, ✉ 13629, ☎ (030) 38 38 90, *info@hiberlin-esplanade.de, Fax (030) 38389900*, , , – |♦|, ⇔ rm, ▤ TV ☎ ♿ – 🏛 170. AE ⓓ MC VISA JCB. ⚘ rest
Meals *(closed Sunday dinner)* à la carte 23/32 – ☕ 16 – **336 rm** 133/199 – 158/224 – 4 suites.
♦ To enter the splendidly spacious foyer of this modern hotel is a wonderful relief after being cooped up in a plane or train. Bauhaus-style interiors throughout. Bright, contemporary restaurant.

Novotel, Ohmstr. 4, ✉ 13629, ☎ (030) 3 80 30, *h0483@accor-hotels.com Fax (030) 3819403*, – |♦|, ⇔ rm, TV ☎ ♿ – 🏛 200. AE ⓓ MC VISA
Meals à la carte 18/30 – ☕ 13 – **119 rm** 99 – 114.
♦ The impeccably run Novotel is right next to the Siemens complex. Rooms with generously dimensioned desks, inviting garden with pool.

at **Berlin-Steglitz** *Southwest : 5 km, by Hauptstr.* FZ :

Steglitz International, Albrechtstr. 2 (corner of Schloßstraße), ✉ 12165, ☎ (030) 79 00 50, *info@steglitz.bestwestern.de, Fax (030) 79005550* – |♦|, ⇔ rm, ▤ rest, TV ♿ – 🏛 270. AE ⓓ MC VISA. ⚘ rest
Meals à la carte 23/32 – **200 rm** ☕ 106 – 126 – 3 suites.
♦ Privileged location with city bustle to one side, the tamed Nature of the Botanical Gardens to the other. Meeting and events rooms.

Edogawa, Lepsiusstr. 36, ✉ 12063, ☎ (030) 79 70 62 40, *sino.com@t-online.de Fax (030) 79706240*, – AE ⓓ MC VISA
Meals *(Monday - Friday dinner only)* (Japanese) à la carte 15/31.
♦ Japanese minimalism creates this establishment's special allure, just the right setting in which to appreciate specialities from the land of the rising sun.

at **Berlin-Tegel** :

Sorat Hotel Humboldt-Mühle, An der Mühle 5, ✉ 13507, ☎ (030) 43 90 40, *humboldt-muehle@sorat-hotels.com, Fax (030) 43904444*, , , – |♦|, ⇔ rm, ▤ TV ☎ ♿ – 🏛 50. AE ⓓ MC VISA JCB Northwest : 13 km, by Müllerstraße FX
Meals à la carte 26/38 – **120 rm** ☕ 109/149 – 134/174.
♦ Its wheel may no longer turn, but Humbolt's Mill dates back to the 13C. Some rooms with views of millstream or Tegel harbour. Hotel has a private yacht. Restaurant reached via a slender bridge over a canal.

Novotel Berlin Airport, Kurt-Schumacher-Damm 202 (by airport approach) ✉ 13405, ☎ (030) 4 10 60, *h0791@accor-hotels.com, Fax (030) 4106700*, , , – |♦|, ⇔ rm, TV ☎ ♿ P – 🏛 150. AE ⓓ MC VISA EX
Meals à la carte 20/34 – ☕ 13 – **184 rm** 111 – 127.
♦ This Novotel is good at taking those tired of flying under its wing ; there's a reviving pool and a relaxing sauna.

COLOGNE (KÖLN) *Nordrhein-Westfalen* 543 N 4 – *pop.* 1 017 700 – *alt.* 65 *m.*

See : *Cathedral (Dom)*★★★ *(Magi's Shrine*★★★, *Gothic stained glass windows*★ *Cross of Gero (Gerokreuz)*★, *South chapel (Marienkapelle) : Patron Saints altar*★★★, *stalls*★, *treasury*★ GY *Roman-Germanic Museum (Römisch-Germanisches Museum)*★★ *(Dionysos Mosaic*★, *Roman glassware collection*★★*)* GY **M1** – *Wallraf-Richartz-Museum-Fondation Corboud*★★ GZ **M1** *Museum Ludwig*★★ FV **M2** – *Diocesan Museum (Diözesean Museum)*★ GY **M3** *Schnütgen-Museum*★★ GZ **M4** – *Museum of East-Asian Art (Museum für Ostasiatische Kunst)*★★ by *Hahnenstraße and Richard Wagner Straße* EV – *Museum for Applied Arts (Museum für Angewandte Kunst)*★ GYZ **M6** – *St. Maria Lyskirchen (frescoes*★★*)* FX – *St. Severin (interior*★*)* FX – *St. Pantaleon (rood screen*★*)* EX – *St. Kunibert (stained glass windows*★*)* FU – *St. Mary the Queen (St. Maria Königin) : wall of glass*★ *by Bonnerstraße* FX – *St. Aposteln (apse*★*)* EV K – *St. Ursula (treasury*★*)* FU – *St. Mary of the Capitol (St. Maria im Kapitol) (Romanesque wooden church door*★, *trefoil chancel*★*)* GZ – *Imhoff-Stollwerck-Museum*★ F – *Old Town Hall (Altes Rathaus)*★ GZ – *St. Gereon*★ *(Dekagon*★*)* EV.

Köln-Marienburg, Schillingsrotter Weg (South : 3 km), ☎ *(0221) 38 40 53 ;* *Köln-Rogendorf, Parallelweg 1 (by Erftstraße and A 57 : 16 km),* ☎ *(0221) 78 40 18 ;* *Bergisch Gladbach-Refrath, Golfplatz 2 (East : 17 km),* ☎ *(02204) 9 27 60 ;* *Pulheim Gut Lärchenhof, Hahnenstraße (Northwest : 19 km),* ☎ *(02238) 92 39 00.*

✈ *Köln-Bonn at Wahn (Southeast : 17 km)* ☎ *(02203) 4 00.*

Exhibition Centre (Messegelände) by Deutzer Brücke (FV), ☎ *(0221) 82 10, Fax (0221) 8212574.* – ℹ *Köln Tourismus, Unter Fettenhennen 19,* ✉ *50667,* ☎ *(0221) 22 13 04 0, koelntourismus@stadt-koeln.de,* Fax (0221) 22120410.

ADAC, *Luxemburger Str. 169.*

Berlin 566 – Düsseldorf 39 – Aachen 69 – Bonn 32 – Essen 68.

Plans on following pages

Excelsior Hotel Ernst, Domplatz, 50667, (0221) 27 01, *ehe@excelsiorhotel ernst.de, Fax (0221) 135150*, - rm, - 80. VISA JCB
Meals see ***Hanse-Stube*** and ***Taku*** below - **152 rm** 210/285 - 280/380 - 9 suites.
• The best address in Cologne, directly opposite the Cathedral and steeped in tradition. Stylish rooms. Lovely marble foyer. Piano bar. GY a

InterContinental, Pipinstr. 1, 50667, (0221) 2 80 60, *cologne@interconti.com, Fax (0221) 28061111* - rm, - 240. VISA JCB
Meals à la carte 32/46 - 20 - **262 rm** 230/280 - 9 suites. GZ d
• Modern design and harmonious colour schemes throughout, from the spacious foyer to the comfortable suites and rooms. Exclusive leisure area (fee). 1st floor Maulbeer restaurant with panoramic windows.

Im Wasserturm, Kaygasse 2, 50676, (0221) 2 00 80, *info@hotel-im-was serturm.de, Fax (0221) 2008888*, - rm, rest, - 120. VISA JCB. rest FX c
Meals see ***La Vision*** below - ***dΛblju, W'***: **Meals** à la carte 27/36,50 - 18 - **88 rm** 180/265 - 230/335 - 7 suites.
• Once Europe's tallest water-tower, this imposing brick edifice is now an elegant modern hotel. The 11m-high foyer is particularly striking. Designer style. Refined "W" bistro.

Dom Hotel, Domkloster 2a, 50667, (0221) 2 02 40, *sales@dom-hotel.com, Fax (0221) 2024444*, - rm, - 90. VISA JCB. rest
Meals à la carte 37/46 - 20 - **124 rm** 330/390 - 360/410 - 6 suites. GY d
• Tradition with perhaps a touch of nostalgia envelops residents in this stylish grand hotel dating from the Belle Epoque and located right by the Cathedral. Palm trees and cane furniture add to the Mediterranean atmosphere in the restaurant. Terrace with views.

Renaissance, Magnusstr. 20, 50672, (0221) 2 03 40, *sales.cologne@renaissan cehotels.com, Fax (0221) 2034777*, Massage, - rm, - 220. VISA JCB EV b
Raffael *(closed August)* **Meals** à la carte 25/36 - ***Valentino*** : **Meals** à la carte 21,50/29,50 - 17 - **236 rm** 175/355 - 205/395.
• A warmly coloured and intimate foyer greets guests on arrival. The beautiful rooms offer comfort, convenience and elegance. Refined atmosphere and lovely place settings characterise the Raffael. The Valentino has a bistro-like atmosphere.

Maritim, Heumarkt 20, 50667, (0221) 2 02 70, *info.kol@maritim.de, Fax (0221) 2027826*, Massage, - rm, - 1600. VISA JCB GZ m
Bellevue : **Meals** à la carte 40/52 - ***La Galerie*** *(closed 4 weeks July - August, Sunday and Monday) (dinner only)* **Meals** à la carte 23/34,50 - 15 - **454 rm** 169/199 - 189/219 - 28 suites.
• With its glass roof and granite floor the foyer is an architectural masterpiece. Enjoy a stroll through the hotel's more than ample public spaces. The Bellevue offers a view over the Rhine and Cologne's Old Town. La Galerie is in the foyer.

Jolly Hotel Media Park, Im Mediapark 8b, 50670, (0221) 2 71 50, *reservati on.jhk@jollyhotels.de, Fax (0221) 2715999*, - rm, - 200. VISA EU a
Meals (Italian) à la carte 27/41 - **214 rm** 135/170 - 160/195.
• A recent, centrally-located establishment with elegant rooms. Technical facilities are up-to-the-minute, with everything from fax to air conditioning and trouser-press. Restaurant opening onto the foyer with show kitchen and Italian atmosphere.

Dorint Kongress-Hotel, Helenenstr. 14, 50667, (0221) 27 50, *info.cgnchc@ dorint.com, Fax (0221) 2751301*, Massage, - rm, - 500. VISA JCB EV p
Meals 26 *(lunch)* and à la carte 31/40 - 16 - **284 rm** 165 - 171 - 12 suites.
• There is a striking view of the Cathedral from the hotel's 12th floor. Conferences and meetings can be held high over the city's rooftops, or you can dance to your heart's content in the hotel's own night-club. Classic restaurant.

Hilton, Marzellenstr. 13, 50668, (0221) 13 07 10, *info_cologne@hilton.com, Fax (0221) 1307120*, Massage, - - 310. VISA JCB GY h
Meals à la carte 23/35,50 - 19 - **296 rm** 175/430 - 200/455.
• This former post office building from the 1950s owes its special character as a hotel to the use of glass, steel and lovely wood veneers combined with subtle earth-colours. The Konrad and the trendy Ice Bar offer contrasting gastronomic experiences.

Savoy, Turiner Str. 9, 50668, (0221) 1 62 30, *office@hotelsavoy.de, Fax (0221) 1623200*, Massage, - rm, rm, - 70. VISA. rm FU s
Meals à la carte 26,50/39 - **97 rm** 135/155 - 165/187 - 3 suites.
• A successful combination of convenience and functionality characterise the rooms of this comfortable establishment. The lavish wellness area is a bonus. Diva's Bar and Restaurant is decorated in contemporary, welcoming style.

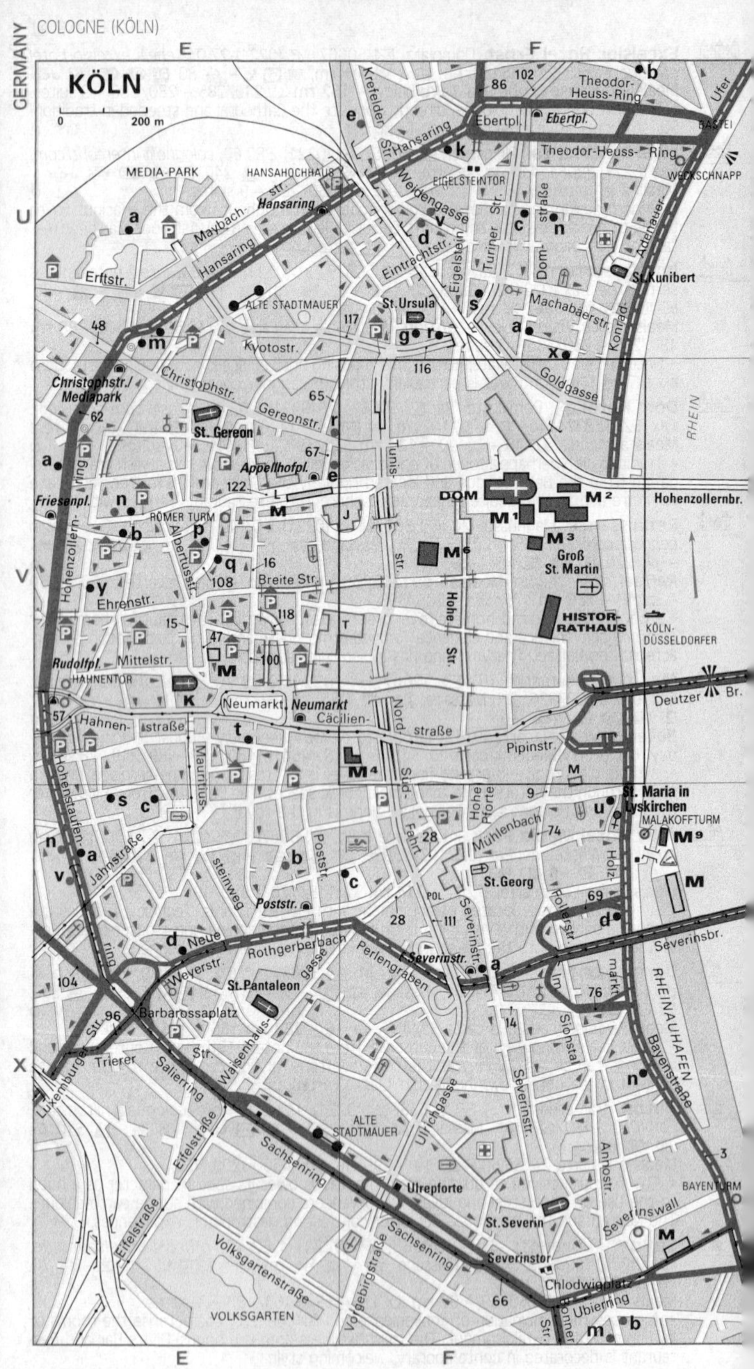
KÖLN
0
200 m
E
F
U
V
X
MEDIA-PARK
HANSAHOCHHAUS
Hansaring
Maybach-str.
Erftstr.
ALTE STADTMAUER
Kyotostr.
Christophstr./ Mediapark
Christophstr.
Gereonstr.
St. Gereon
Appellhofpl.
Friesenpl.
RÖMER TURM
Albertusstr.
Breite Str.
Ehrenstr.
Hohenzollern-ring
Mittelstr.
Rudolfpl.
HAHNENTOR
Neumarkt
Cäcilien-straße
Hahnen-straße
Mauritius
Hohenstaufen-ring
Jahnstraße
steinweg
Poststr.
Neue
Weyerstr.
Rothgerberbach
St.Pantaleon
Barbarossaplatz
Luxemburger Str.
Trierer Str.
Salierring
Waisenhaus-gasse
Eifelstraße
Sachsenring
ALTE STADTMAUER
Ulrepforte
Volksgartenstraße
VOLKSGARTEN
Vorgebirgstraße
Ulrichgasse
Krefelder Str.
Weidengasse
Ebertpl.
Theodor-Heuss-Ring
BASTEI
WECKSCHNAPP
Ufer
EIGELSTEINTOR
Eigelstein
Turiner Str.
Dom-straße
Eintrachtstr.
St.Ursula
Machabäerstr.
Konrad-Adenauer-
St.Kunibert
Goldgasse
RHEIN
Tunis-str.
DOM
Hohenzollernbr.
Groß St. Martin
Hohe Str.
HISTOR-RATHAUS
KÖLN-DÜSSELDORFER
Deutzer Br.
Nord-Süd-Fahrt
Pipinstr.
St. Maria in Lyskirchen
MALAKOFFTURM
Hohe Pforte
Mühlenbach
Holz-markt
St.Georg
POL.
Severinstr.
Perlengraben
Severinsbr.
Rolfer-str.
Im Sionstal
RHEINAUHAFEN
Bayenstraße
Annostr.
BAYENTURM
Severinswall
St.Severin
Severinstor
Chlodwigplatz
Ubierring
Bonner Str.

Am Bayenturm FX 3
Am Leystapel GZ 4
Am Malzbüchel GZ 5
An den Dominikanern GY 8
An der Malzmühle FX 9
An St-Katharinen FX 14
Apostelnstraße EV 15
Auf dem Berlich EV 16
Augustinerstraße GZ 19
Bechergasse GZ 22
Bischofsgarten-Straße GY 26
Blaubach FX 28
Breite Straße GZ
Brückenstraße GZ 32
Dompropst-Ketzer-Straße GY 38
Drususgasse GY 39
Ehrenstraße EV
Eigelstein FU
Gertrudenstraße EV 47
Gladbacher Straße EU 48
Glockengasse GZ 50
Große Budengasse GZ 52
Große Neugasse GY 54
Gürzenichstraße GZ 55
Habsburgerring EV 57
Hahnenstraße EV
Heinrich-Böll-Platz GY 58
Hohenstaufenring EX
Hohenzollernring EV
Hohe Straße GYZ
Kaiser-Wilhelm-Ring EV 62
Kardinal-Frings-Straße EV 65
Karolingerring FX 66
Kattenbug EV 67
Kleine Budengasse GZ 68
Kleine Witschgasse FX 69
Komödienstraße GY 71
Kurt-Hackenberg-Platz GY 72
Mathiasstraße FX 74
Mechtildisstraße FX 76
Minoritenstraße GZ 79
Mittelstraße EV
Neumarkt EV
Neusser Straße FU 86
Offenbachplatz GZ 90
Pfälzer Straße EX 96
Quatermarkt GZ 99
Richmodstraße EV 100
Riehler Straße FU 102
Roonstraße EX 104
Sankt-Apern-Straße EV 108

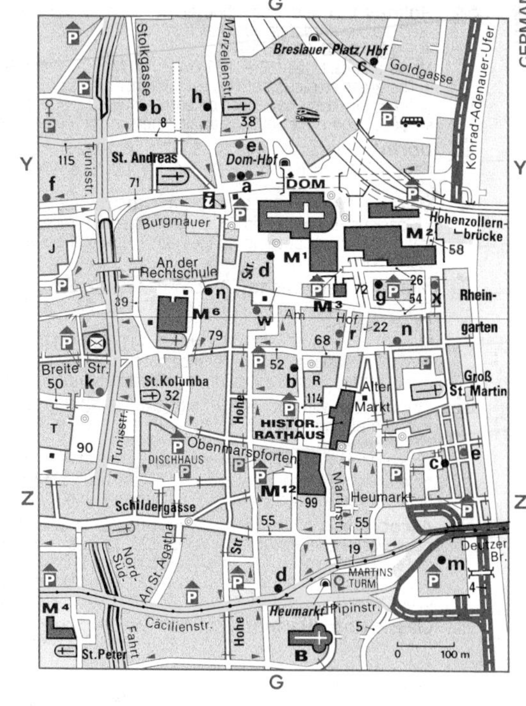

Schildergasse GZ
Severinstraße FX
Tel-Aviv-Straße FX 111
Unter Goldschmied GZ 114
Unter Sachsenhausen GY 115
Ursulastraße FU 116
Victoriastraße FU 117
Zeppelinstraße EV 118
Zeughausstraße EV 122

Crowne Plaza, Habsburgerring 9, ✉ 50674, ☎ (0221) 22 80, *info@crowneplaza-koeln.de, Fax (0221) 251206*, Massage, Fö, ≘s, ▭ - |♦|, ⇔ rm, ▤ TV ☏ ♿ ⇔ - 🏛 240. AE ⓪ ⓜⓒ VISA JCB. ✂ rest by Hahnenstraße EV

Meals à la carte 22/35 - ☐ 18 - **301 rm** 170/330 - 205/380.

◆ Rooms with contemporary décor and excellent access by public transport make this large hotel ideal for business travellers and conferences. Refined 1st-floor restaurant with floor-to-ceiling windows.

Lindner Dom Residence, An den Dominikanern 4a (entrance Stolkgasse), ✉ 50668, ☎ (0221) 1 64 40, *info.domresidence@lindner.de, Fax (0221) 1644440*, Fö, ≘s, ▭ - |♦|, ⇔ rm, ▤ TV ☏ ⇔ - 🏛 120. AE ⓪ ⓜⓒ VISA GY b

closed 22 December - 4 January – ***La Gazetta*** **: Meals** à la carte 24/36,50 - ☐ 16 - **129 rm** 122/252 - 142/252.

◆ Modern atrium building with balconies and plenty of glass. The 7th floor rooms have a terrace. Furnishings in functional style make this eminently suitable for business travellers. The glazed façade of La Gazetta allows a fine view of the courtyard.

Sofitel am Dom, Kurt-Hackenberg-Platz 1, ✉ 50667, ☎ (0221) 2 06 30, *h1306@accor-hotels.com, Fax (0221) 2063527*, ☂, Fö, ≘s - |♦|, ⇔ rm, ▤ TV ☏ ♿ ⇔ - 🏛 120. AE ⓪ ⓜⓒ VISA JCB GY g

Meals à la carte 29,50/35 - ☐ 17 - **207 rm** 170/189 - 190/209.

◆ Close to the Cathedral in an excellent central location, this hotel has modern, functional rooms with good technical facilities. Especially spacious suites and deluxe rooms. Contemporary style restaurant with tapas bar.

Holiday Inn (with guest house), Belfortstr. 9, ✉ 50668, ☎ (0221) 7 72 10, *hibelfortstrasse@eventhotels.com, Fax (0221) 7721259*, , , – , rm, , , – 70. AE VISA FU b
Meals à la carte 23/36 – **120 rm** 147/172 – 173/198.
◆ The great attraction of this establishment is its proximity to city centre and trade fair grounds. All rooms have been recently renovated with attractive modern furnishings. Classic décor and place settings await diners in the Restaurant Quirinal.

Dorint, Friesenstr. 44, ✉ 50670, ☎ (0221) 1 61 40, *info.cgncol@dorint.com, Fax (0221) 1614100*, – , rm, , – 160. AE VISA JCB. rest EV n
Meals à la carte 21,50/30 – 14 – **103 rm** 120/136 – 135/148.
◆ Spacious entrance and foyer with attentive reception. Refurbished, contemporary-style rooms. Adaptable spaces with up-to-the-minute meeting and conference facilities.

Mercure Severinshof, Severinstr. 199, ✉ 50676, ☎ (0221) 2 01 30, *h1206@accor-hotels.com, Fax (0221) 2013666*, , , – , rm, , – 250. AE VISA FX a
Meals à la carte 17/35 – **251 rm** 141/186 – 179/204 – 8 suites.
◆ Well-run business and conference hotel in central location. Standard, functional rooms, plus superior "Club Rooms" on the 4th and 5th floors. Spacious bar area.

Lyskirchen without rest, Filzengraben 26, ✉ 50676, ☎ (0221) 2 09 70, *lyskirchen@eventhotels.com, Fax (0221) 2097718*, , – , rest, . AE VISA FX u
closed 21 to 30 December – **103 rm** 118/175 – 150/225.
◆ Carefully refurbished establishment in the middle of the historic riverside district. Functional rooms with contemporary furnishings - mostly lightwood.

Ascot without rest, Hohenzollernring 95, ✉ 50672, ☎ (0221) 9 52 96 50, *info@ascot.bestwestern.de, Fax (0221) 952965100*, , – . AE VISA
closed 22 December - 1 January – **46 rm** 112/152 – 128/228. EV a
◆ This city centre hotel has retained its traditional façade, while its interior is in English country-house style. Cinemas, theatres and shops are right at hand.

Classic Hotel Harmonie without rest, Ursulaplatz 13, ✉ 50668, ☎ (0221) 1 65 70, *harmonie@classic-hotels.com, Fax (0221) 1657200* – . AE VISA JCB FU g
72 rm 95/110 – 120.
◆ This beautifully restored former monastery now offers guests a relaxing setting with an Italian flair. Contemporary furniture and warm Mediterranean colours set the tone.

Mauritius without rest, Mauritiuskirchplatz 3, ✉ 50676, ☎ (0221) 92 41 30, *info@mauritius-ht.de, Fax (0221) 92413333*, Massage, , , (heated), – . AE VISA EX c
59 rm 120/150 – 140/170.
◆ This quiet city centre establishment offers bright, contemporary and comfortable rooms. A special feature is the unusually extensive spa-area.

Viktoria without rest, Worringer Str. 23, ✉ 50668, ☎ (0221) 9 73 17 20, *hotel@hotelviktoria.com, Fax (0221) 727067* – . AE VISA.
closed Easter, 24 December - 1 January – **47 rm** 90 – 113.
◆ This hotel with individual rooms boasts a magnificent Art Nouveau façade and was originally a museum of musical history. Elegant atrium-style breakfast room.
by Konrad-Adenauer-Ufer FU

NH Köln, Holzmarkt 47, ✉ 50676, ☎ (0221) 2 72 28 80, *nhkoeln@nh-hotels.com, Fax (0221) 272288100*, – , rm, , – 130. AE VISA
Meals à la carte 21/30 – 14 – **205 rm** 125. FX
◆ This modern hotel by the Severin bridge over the Rhine was opened in 2002. The rooms offer cool lines, functional furnishings and marble-topped desks. The contemporary-style restaurant has a conservatory overlooking the courtyard.

Novotel City, Bayenstr. 51, ✉ 50678, ☎ (0221) 80 14 70, *h3127@accor-hotels.com, Fax (0221) 80147148*, , , – , rm, , – 150. AE VISA JCB FX r
Meals à la carte 21/29,50 – 13 – **222 rm** 130 – 150.
◆ Newly-built and up to the usual Novotel standard, with functional and contemporary rooms with natural lightwood furnishings.

Four Points Hotel Central, Breslauer Platz 2, ✉ 50668, ☎ (0221) 1 65 10, *fourpoints.koeln@arabellasheraton.de, Fax (0221) 1651333* – , rm, rest, – 30. AE VISA GY
Meals à la carte 16/26,50 – **116 rm** 150 – 170 – 5 suites.
◆ Only a few minutes' walk from the Cathedral and the lively city centre. The hotel's discreet elegance and high level of comfort are appreciated by business travellers.

Senats Hotel, Unter Goldschmied 9, 50667, (0221) 2 06 20, *info@senats-hotel.de, Fax (0221) 2062200* – rm, – 230. AE VISA JCB GZ b
closed 23 December - 1 January – ***Falstaff*** *(closed Saturday lunch, Sunday and Bank Holidays)* **Meals** à la carte 22/42 – **59 rm** 92 – 124.
• From the modern-style foyer a splendidly spacious - listed - staircase leads up to contemporary-style rooms. Aperitif and beer bar. Bright and welcoming restaurant with a touch of country style.

Cristall without rest, Ursulaplatz 9, 50668, (0221) 1 63 00, *info@hotelcristall.de, Fax (0221) 1630333* – . AE VISA JCB. FU r
closed 23 to 29 December – **84 rm** 72/102 – 95/133.
• This establishment has an extraordinarily varied décor. Fans of designer furniture will enjoy a stay here, especially if they try sitting in one of highly unusual sofas !

Coellner Hof, Hansaring 100, 50670, (0221) 1 66 60, *info@coellnerhof.de, Fax (0221) 1666166,* – rm, rest, – 30. AE VISA FU k
Meals *(closed Saturday and Sunday) (dinner only)* à la carte 17/38 – **70 rm** 70/95 – 90/105.
• What do you prefer Country-style or contemporary The individually furnished rooms give you the choice. Well-run establishment with a personal touch. Restaurant with tasteful wood décor.

Euro Garden Cologne without rest, Domstr. 10, 50668, (0221) 1 64 90, *info@eurotels.de, Fax (0221) 1649333,* – – 40. AE VISA
85 rm 75/115 – 105/145.
• Well-run establishment not far from the city centre. Solidly furnished, functional rooms and ample buffet in the stylish breakfast room. FU a

Königshof without rest, Richartzstr. 14, 50667, (0221) 2 57 87 71, *hotel@hotelkoenigshof.com, Fax (0221) 2578762* – . AE VISA JCB GY n
82 rm 80/115 – 110/166.
• This exceptionally well-run establishment is just a few steps from the Cathedral and the main shopping streets. Impeccable rooms with good facilities.

Esplanade without rest, Hohenstaufenring 56, 50674, (0221) 9 21 55 70, *info@hotelesplanade.de, Fax (0221) 216822* – . AE VISA JCB EX a
closed 22 December - 5 January – **32 rm** 90 – 116.
• Lavish décor in a cool, contemporary style. Some rooms have a balcony with a view of Cathedral or boulevard. Interesting glazed façade and splendid entrance area.

Antik Hotel Bristol without rest, Kaiser-Wilhelm-Ring 48, 50672, (0221) 13 98 50, *hotel@antik-hotel-bristol.de, Fax (0221) 131495* – . AE VISA EU m
closed 21 December - 2 January – **44 rm** 85 – 110.
• Ever dreamt of a night in a four-poster ? This attractive, well-run hotel is full of antique furniture in a variety of styles including Empire style.

Santo without rest, Dagobertstr. 22, 50668, (0221) 9 13 97 70, *info@hotelsanto.de, Fax (0221) 913977777* – . AE VISA JCB FU c
69 rm 128 – 149.
• This unusual establishment blends lovely wood veneers, natural floor materials and a specially designed lighting system into an avant-garde living concept of great comfort.

Hopper St. Antonius, Dagobertstr. 32, 50668, (0221) 1 66 00(hotel) 1 30 00 69 (rest.), *st.antonius@hopper.de, Fax (0221) 1660166,* – rm, – 15. AE VISA FU n
L. Fritz im Hopper *(closed lunch Saturday and Sunday)* **Meals** à la carte 24/31,50 – **54 rm** 110/130 – 140/210 – 5 suites.
• Urban heritage and contemporary design are perfectly blended here. The listed building has rooms with beautifully-styled modern teak furnishings. Dining is in an attractive, bistro-like setting.

Hopper, Brüsseler Str. 26, 50674, (0221) 92 44 00, *hotel@hopper.de, Fax (0221) 924406,* – rm, . AE VISA
closed Easter, Whit Sunday, Whit Monday and 20 December - 5 January – **Meals** *(closed Saturday lunch and Sunday dinner)* à la carte 25/30 – **49 rm** 90/100 – 120/130. by Hahnenstraße EV
• Outside, monastic charm ; inside, refined aesthetics and contemporary elegance. Unconventional accommodation with marble bathrooms and parquet floors. Sauna in vaulted cellars. A striking feature in the bistro-style restaurant is the impressive altar-painting.

Altera Pars, Thieboldsgasse 133, 50676, (0221) 27 23 30, *info@alterapars-koeln.de, Fax (0221) 2723366* – rm, . AE VISA EV t
Meals à la carte 18/25 – **13 rm** 77/112 – 113/201.
• This elegant and functional hotel welcomes its guests to rooms with contemporary basket-weave furnishings and attractive materials. Bistro-style restaurant.

CityClass Hotel Caprice without rest, Auf dem Rothenberg 7, ✉ 50667, ℘ (0221) 92 05 40, *caprice@cityclass.de, Fax (0221) 92054100,* – 🛗 ⇔ TV 📞 – 🏛 20. AE ⓓ MC VISA GZ c
53 rm ☕ 105/115 – 135.
◆ Centrally located in Cologne's Altstadt, this hotel is an ideal starting point for exploring the city. Contemporary rooms, good standard overall.

Ibis Barbarossaplatz without rest, Neue Weyerstr. 4, ✉ 50676, ℘ (0221) 2 09 60, *h1449@accor-hotels.com, Fax (0221) 2096199* – 🛗 ⇔ ▤ TV 📞 ♿ 🚗 – 🏛 25. AE ⓓ MC VISA EX d
☕ 9 – **208 rm** 59/71.
◆ Standard tour-group establishment with convenient, contemporary accommodation. Welcoming foyer and inviting bistro bar.

Metropol without rest, Hansaring 14, ✉ 50670, ℘ (0221) 13 33 77, *hotel-metropol@t-online.de, Fax (0221) 138307* – 🛗 TV. AE ⓓ MC VISA EU m
closed 22 December - 2 January – **26 rm** ☕ 64/85 – 95.
◆ This small city-hotel is easily reached from the motorway ring road and there is adjacent underground parking. Standard and well-cared for rooms.

XXXX **Hanse Stube** - Excelsior Hotel Ernst, Dompropst-Ketzer-Str. 2, ✉ 50667, ℘ (0221) 2 70 34 02, *ehe@excelsiorhotelernst.de, Fax (0221) 135150,* – ▤. AE ⓓ MC VISA JCB. GY e
Meals 31 *(lunch)* and à la carte 39,50/63 ♀.
◆ Stylish atmosphere in this elegant restaurant, where creative French cuisine is served to diners by the well-trained staff.

XXX ✿ **La Vision** - Hotel Im Wasserturm, Kaygasse 2, ✉ 50676, ℘ (0221) 2 00 80, *info@hotel-im-wasserturm.de, Fax (0221) 2008888* – 🛗 ▤. AE ⓓ MC VISA JCB. FX c
closed 2 to 27 January, end July - mid August, Sunday and Monday – **Meals** 48 and à la carte 52/60 ♀.
◆ Designer style restaurant on the 11th floor of a water-tower. Fantastic city views from the roof garden.
Spec. Terrine von Gänsestopflebermousse und Rehbockfilet mit Madeiragelée. Geschmortes und Rücken von Salzwiesenlamm mit confierten Gemüsen. Schokoladenparfait und Mousse mit Joghurt-Limonensorbet.

XXX ✿ **Börsen-Restaurant Maître** (Schäfer), Unter Sachsenhausen 10, ✉ 50667, ℘ (0221) 13 30 21, *Fax (0221) 133040* – ▤. AE ⓓ MC VISA. EV
closed 5 to 17 April, August, Saturday lunch, Sunday and Bank Holidays – **Meals** à la carte 49/67 ♀ – ***Börsen-Stube*** *(closed Saturday dinner, Sunday and Bank Holidays)* **Meals** à la carte 28/38 ♀.
◆ The IHK (Chamber of Commerce) has a stylish and elegant restaurant offering refined classic cuisine. The cellar Börsenstube is a more straightforward alternative.
Spec. Bretonische Felsen-Rotbarbe mit Aal und dicken Bohnen. Tournedos "Rossini" mit Périgord-Madeirajus und karamellisiertem Chicorée. Orangengratin mit Sauerrahmschaum und Roseneis.

XXX **Ambiance**, Komödienstr. 50, ✉ 50667, ℘ (0221) 9 22 76 52 – AE ⓓ MC VISA GY
closed mid August - early September, Saturday, Sunday and Bank Holidays – **Meals** 3 *(lunch)*/69 and à la carte 47/58.
◆ This fine old city building houses a classically elegant restaurant with lovely place settings, attentive service, and creative cooking.

XXX **Grande Milano**, Hohenstaufenring 29, ✉ 50674, ℘ (0221) 24 21 21, *grande-milano@ggd-net.de, Fax (0221) 244846,* – ▤. AE ⓓ MC VISA JCB EX
closed mid to end July, Saturday lunch and Sunday – **Meals** (Italian) à la carte 32/53 ♀
Pinot di Pinot : **Meals** 12,50 (lunch) and à la carte 15,50/32.
◆ Diners sit at beautifully presented tables in this elegant Italian restaurant. The cuisine is refined, specialising in dishes with truffles. A lighter, bistro-like ambience in the Pinot di Pinot.

XX **Domerie**, Buttermarkt 42, ✉ 50667, ℘ (0221) 2 57 40 44, *stefanruessel@netcologne.de, Fax (0221) 2574269,* – MC VISA. GZ
closed 1 to 15 January, carnival and Monday, except exhibitions – **Meals** à la carte 32/44,50.
◆ To dine in this 15C building among antique furnishings and beneath the beautiful ceiling is quite an experience. Summer terrace with Rhine views.

XX **Fischers**, Hohenstaufenring 53, ✉ 50674, ℘ (0221) 3 10 84 70, *info@fischers-wein.com, Fax (0221) 31084789,* – 🏛 40. ⓓ MC VISA EX
closed 27 December - 6 January, Saturday lunch, Sunday and Bank Holidays – **Meals** à la carte 29,50/42 ♀.
◆ With a list of over 500 wines, this establishment is particularly devoted to the grape, but good dining is taken care of too, with fusion cuisine.

Capricorn i Aries Restaurant, Alteburger Str. 34, ✉ 50678, ☎ (0221) 32 31 82, *Fax (0221) 323182* FX m
closed carnival, Easter, 2 weeks July, Monday and Tuesday – **Meals** *(dinner only)* (booking essential) 85 and à la carte 64/89 ♀.
• An air of refinement and elegance characterises this tiny little establishment where white is the dominant colour. Dishes from a creative kitchen presented on lovely crockery.
Spec. Variation von der Gänsestopfleber. Steinbutt mit Jakobsmuscheln und Gewürztraminersauce. Taube mit Trüffel-Kartoffelrosette.

Alfredo, Tunisstr. 3, ✉ 50667, ☎ (0221) 2 57 73 80, *info@ristorante-alfredo.com, Fax (0221) 2577380* – AE GZ k
closed 3 weeks July - August, 1 week December, Saturday lunch, Sunday and Bank Holidays – **Meals** (booking essential) à la carte 38/53 ♀.
• This elegant little Italian restaurant is something of a Cologne institution, where a second generation of owners treats guests to a refined, constantly changing menu.

Bizim, Weidengasse 47, ✉ 50668, ☎ (0221) 13 15 81, *Fax (0221) 131581* – MC VISA. ⚡
closed 2 weeks February, 3 weeks August - September, Saturday lunch, Sunday and Monday – **Meals** (Turkish) (booking essential for dinner) 29 *(lunch)* and à la carte 40/51,50.
• In the heart of the multicultural city centre, this Turkish restaurant serves typical dishes in a contemporary ambience. FU d

Em Krützche, Am Frankenturm 1, ✉ 50667, ☎ (0221) 2 58 08 39, *info@em-kruetzche.de, Fax (0221) 253417*, 🏠 – AE ⓓ MC VISA GY x
closed Holy week and Monday – **Meals** (booking essential for dinner) à la carte 28,50/40.
• Diners have been served in the nooks and crannies of this old city centre establishment for more than 400 years. Traditionally run family business.

Taku - Excelsior Hotel Ernst, Domplatz, ✉ 50667, ☎ (0221) 2 70 39 10, *Fax (0221) 135150* – ▤. AE ⓓ MC VISA. ⚡ rest GY a
closed mid July - mid August, Sunday and Monday – **Meals** à la carte 37/61 ♀.
• Asian delights served in a cool and elegant modern setting. A glass walkway and an aquarium set into the floor are among the unusual features of this establishment.

L'escalier, Brüsseler Str. 11, ✉ 50674, ☎ (0221) 2 05 39 98, *lescalier11@aol.com, Fax (02232) 419742* – MC VISA by Hahnenstr. EV
closed Saturday lunch, Sunday and Bank Holidays – **Meals** 29 *(lunch)* and à la carte 31/61 ♀.
• This restaurant is characterised by its cool, contemporary ambience and its no-frills classic cuisine based on fine ingredients.

Bosporus, Weidengasse 36, ✉ 50668, ☎ (0221) 12 52 65, *restaurant.bosporus@t-online.de, Fax (0221) 9123829*, 🏠 – AE ⓓ MC VISA FU v
closed Sunday lunch – **Meals** (Turkish) à la carte 24/37.
• Something of the atmosphere of A Thousand And One Nights pervades this classic interior, together with a hint of Turkish delights. The Bosporus links Cologne with the Orient.

Le Moissonnier, Krefelder Str. 25, ✉ 50670, ☎ (0221) 72 94 79, *Fax (0221) 7325461*, (typical French bistro) – MC VISA FU e
closed 1 week Easter, 3 weeks July - August, 24 December - 3 January, Sunday - Monday and Bank Holidays lunch – **Meals** (booking essential) à la carte 38,50/56,50 ♀.
• This highly original Art Nouveau bistro will transport you instantly to the heart of France with its creative offerings of refined French cuisine.
Spec. Foie gras Maison. Pigeonneau rôti. Crème brûlée glacée.

Capricorn i Aries Brasserie, Alteburgerstr. 31, ✉ 50678, ☎ (0221) 3 97 57 10, *Fax (0221) 323182* FX b
closed Carnival – **Meals** à la carte 23,50/34.
• Informal version of the establishment of the same name opposite. Elegant contemporary bistro atmosphere and polished service.

Daitokai, Kattenbug 2, ✉ 50667, ☎ (0221) 12 00 48, *kol@daitokai.de, Fax (0221) 137503* – ▤. AE ⓓ MC VISA JCB. ⚡ EV e
closed Monday and Tuesday lunch – **Meals** (Japanese) à la carte 36/48,50.
• The Daitokai, where chefs deploy their skills at the Teppan-Yaki and diners eat with chopsticks, brings an authentically Japanese atmosphere to the heart of the city.

Cologne brewery inns :

Peters Brauhaus, Mühlengasse 1, ✉ 50667, ☎ (0221) 2 57 39 50, *info@peters-brauhaus.de, Fax (0221) 2573962*, 🏠 – ⚡ GZ n
Meals à la carte 16/30.
• Rustic beer-hall in traditional style. Take a good look around, since each nook and cranny of the place has its own character. Tasty food to go with your glass of "Kölsch".

Brauhaus Sion, Unter Taschenmacher 5, ✉ 50667, ☎ (0221) 2 57 85 40, *Fax (0221) 2582081*, 🏠 – MC VISA GZ r
Meals à la carte 16/34.
• Spacious interiors, with barrel-staves and hop-sacks on the walls. A "Kölsch" or three taste all the better after a session on the skittle-alley.

Früh am Dom, Am Hof 12, ✉ 50667, ☎ (0221) 2 61 32 11, *gastronomie@frueh.de, Fax (0221) 2613299*, beer garden GY w
Meals à la carte 16,50/31,50.
◆ Traditional beer-hall from 1904, with larger-than-life waiters darting about as in the days of yore. The cellars where the beer was brewed have recently been opened up.

at Cologne-Braunsfeld *West : 5 km, by Rudolfplatz* EV *and Aachener Straße :*

Regent without rest, Melatengürtel 15, ✉ 50933, ☎ (0221) 5 49 90, *info@hotelregent.de, Fax (0221) 5499998*, – 80.
closed 24 December - 2 January – 14 – **120 rm** 93 – 113 – 5 suites.
◆ Located on one of Cologne's outer ring roads. Rooms with a high standard of contemporary décor, convenient and comfortable. 18 different sorts of jam at breakfast !

at Cologne-Deutz *East : 1 km, by Deutzer Brücke* FV :

Hyatt Regency, Kennedy-Ufer 2a, ✉ 50679, ☎ (0221) 8 28 12 34, *cologne@hyatt.de, Fax (0221) 8281370*, beer garden, Massage, rm, – 260.
Graugans (Euro-Asian) *(closed 2 weeks July - August, Saturday lunch and Sunday)* **Meals** 35 (lunch) and à la carte 45/64 – ***Glashaus*** (Italian) **Meals** 28 (lunch) and à la carte 38/56 – 19 – **288 rm** 160 – 185 – 17 suites.
◆ This late 1980s hotel stands directly on the Rhine. Beyond the impressively spacious foyer are comfortably furnished rooms. The Graugans restaurant is casually elegant, while the Glashaus has been designed like a gallery.

Radisson SAS, Messe Kreisel 3, ✉ 50679, ☎ (0221) 27 72 00, *info.cologne@radissonsas.com, Fax (0221) 2777010*, Massage, rm, – 250.
Meals à la carte 21,50/41 – 15 – **393 rm** 150.
◆ Convenient for the trade fairs, an extremely imposing and sophisticated establishment built on a V-shaped plan. Fascinating 15m high glass structure and luxuriously appointed modern rooms, buffet restaurant, Paparazzi with open pizza oven.

Dorint an der Messe, Deutz-Mülheimer-Str. 22, ✉ 50679, ☎ (0221) 80 19 00, *info.cgnmes@dorint.com, Fax (0221) 80190800*, Massage, rm – 350. rest
L'Adresse *(closed mid July - mid August, Sunday and Monday) (dinner only)* **Meals** 32/78 and à la carte – ***Bell Arte*** *(lunch only)* **Meals** à la carte 19,50/29,50 – 17 – **313 rm** 161/301 – 181/321 – 31 suites.
◆ Contemporary elegance and excellent technical facilities in the rooms of this new hotel directly opposite the entrance to the trade fair grounds. Lavish fitness area. Cool elegance in L'Adresse. Bright and welcoming Bell Arte.

fair more without rest, Adam-Stegerwald-Str. 9, ✉ 51063, ☎ (0221) 6 71 16 90, *info@fairandmore.com, Fax (0221) 67116910* –
closed 22 December - 1 January – **58 rm** 70/95 – 82/107.
◆ What was once a youth hostel and then an office building is now a modern, well-run business hotel with functional rooms, ideal for trade fair delegates.

Der Messeturm, Kennedy-Ufer (18th floor), ✉ 50679, ☎ (0221) 88 10 08, *Fax (0221) 818575*, Cologne – – 30.
closed 4 to 24 August, Wednesday and Saturday lunch – **Meals** 25 *(lunch)* and à la carte 31/44,50.
◆ Diners are taken by lift directly to the 16th floor, then there are two floors of stairs. The panoramic restaurant in the trade fair tower from 1928 offers wonderful views.

at Cologne-Ehrenfeld *West : 3 km, by Rudolfplatz* EV *and Aachener Straße :*

Holiday Inn City West, Innere Kanalstr. 15, ✉ 50823, ☎ (0221) 5 70 10, *city-west@eventhotels.com, Fax (0221) 5701999*, rm, – 180.
Meals à la carte 26/39 – **205 rm** 158/183 – 193/218.
◆ In an accessible location, modern glass building with functionally furnished and sensibly decorated rooms ideal for business travellers. Spacious restaurant with tall windows.

Imperial, Barthelstr. 93, ✉ 50823, ☎ (0221) 51 70 57, *hotel@hotel-imperial.de, Fax (0221) 520993*, rm, – 25. rest
Meals *(closed 23 December - 3 January, Friday to Sunday)* à la carte 19,50/36 – **35 rm** 102/144 – 153/230.
◆ Hotel in a residential area on the outer ring road with good access. Soberly decorated rooms, mostly with mahogany furnishings. Tasteful restaurant.

at Cologne-Holweide *Northeast : 10 km, by Konrad-Adenauer-Ufer* FU *and Mühlheimer Brücke :*

XXX **Isenburg**, Johann-Bensberg-Str. 49, ✉ 51067, ☎ (0221) 69 59 09, *info@isenburg.info, Fax (0221) 698703,* – P. MC VISA JCB
closed carnival, mid July - mid August, 20 to 31 October, Christmas, Saturday lunch, Sunday and Monday – **Meals** (booking essential) à la carte 29,50/48,50.
• The ivy-covered walls of this old moated castle are well worth a visit. The festive, medieval restaurant offers refined cuisine. Attractive outside terrace in summer.

at Cologne-Junkersdorf *West : 9 km, by Rudolfplatz* EV *and Aachener Straße :*

Brenner'scher Hof, Wilhelm-von-Capitaine-Str. 15, ✉ 50858, ☎ (0221) 9 48 60 00, *hotel@brennerscher-hof.de, Fax (0221) 94860010* – 25. AE MC VISA
Pino's Osteria (Italian) **Meals** à la carte 17/40,50 – ***Anno Pomm*** (only potato dishes) **Meals** à la carte 18/26 – **42 rm** 135 – 160 – 7 suites.
• An individual, attractive place, with estate buildings dating from 1754. Mediterranean flair, with Italian period furniture, terracotta floors and rooms with fireplaces. Pino's Osteria overlooks the lovely courtyard. Anno Pomm in rustic Mediterranean style.

Dorint, Aachener Str. 1059, ✉ 50858, ☎ (0221) 4 89 80, *info.cgnbud@dorint.com, Fax (0221) 48981000* – rm, – 80. AE MC VISA JCB. rest
Meals à la carte 20/30 – **145 rm** 97 – 118.
• Modern hotel in accessible location. Functional rooms. Soundproof windows guarantee a good night's rest.

at Cologne-Lindenthal *West : 4,5 km, by Rudolfplatz* EV *and B 264 :*

Holiday Inn Am Stadtwald, Dürener Str. 287, ✉ 50935, ☎ (0221) 4 67 60, *reservation-hi-cologne-amstadtwald@queensgruppe.de, Fax (0221) 433765,* beer garden – rm, rest, P – 250. AE MC VISA
Meals à la carte 19,50/34,50 – **150 rm** 165 – 200.
• This establishment is right on the lake in Cologne's city forest. Comfort is the hallmark of the interior. Business travellers will appreciate the functional room facilities.

XX **Osteria Toscana**, Dürener Str. 218, ✉ 50931, ☎ (0221) 40 80 22, *Fax (0221) 4009897* – AE MC VISA.
closed 2 weeks August and Monday, except exhibitions – **Meals** à la carte 24,50/34,50.
• The restaurant's name hints at the kind of food to be expected. Inside, the atmosphere is bright and elegant, light and welcoming.

at Cologne-Marienburg *South : 4 km, by Bonner Straße* FX *:*

Marienburger Bonotel, Bonner Str. 478, ✉ 50968, ☎ (0221) 3 70 20, *info@bonotel.de, Fax (0221) 3702132,* – rm, P – 40. AE MC VISA JCB
Meals à la carte 21,50/44,50 – **93 rm** 100 – 125.
• Conference and business establishment run to a high standard. Rooms furnished throughout with natural lightwood. Accessible location. Meals served in the Piano Lounge.

at Cologne-Marsdorf *West : 8 km, by Rudolfplatz* EV *and B 264 :*

Novotel Köln-West, Horbeller Str. 1, ✉ 50858, ☎ (02234) 51 40, *h0705@accor-hotels.com, Fax (02234) 514106,* beer garden, – rm, P – 120. AE MC VISA JCB
Meals à la carte 20,50/32 – 13 – **199 rm** 97 – 112.
• The hotel is just by the Frechen exit off the motorway. Newly refurbished rooms, convenient and functional. Garden swimming-pool with sun terrace.

at Cologne-Mülheim *North : 8 km, by Konrad-Adenauer-Ufer* FU *and Mühlheimer Brücke :*

Park Plaza, Clevischer Ring 121, ✉ 51063, ☎ (0221) 9 64 70, *ppcinfo@parkplazahotels.de, Fax (0221) 9647100,* – rm, rest, – 140. AE MC VISA JCB
Meals à la carte 16/39 – **188 rm** 115 – 155.
• The hotel's modern design is a harmonious blend of brick and glass. Very functional rooms suitable for ordinary travellers as well as business people. Contemporary restaurant opens onto the foyer.

at Cologne-Porz-Grengel *Southeast : 16 km, by Severin Brücke, follow signs to airport :*

Holiday Inn Aiport, Waldstr. 255 (near the airport), ✉ 51147, ☎ (02203) 56 10, *reservation.hi-cologne-bonn-airport@queensgruppe.de, Fax (02203) 5619,* beer garden – rm, P – 80. AE MC VISA JCB
Meals à la carte 24/41 – 15 – **177 rm** 129/149 – 164/184.
• Only 500m away from the airport and a good place for the airborne to land and refuel, not least because of the very liveable rooms and the atmospheric Münchhausen Bar.

at Köln - Porz-Langel *South : 17 km by Severinsbrücke FX and Siegburger Straße :*

Zur Tant (Hütter), Rheinbergstr. 49, ✉ 51143, ☎ (02203) 8 18 83, *Fax (02203) 87327*
<, – P. AE ⓓ ⓜ VISA
closed 16 to 24 February and Thursday – **Meals** à la carte 40/56 ♀ – ***Hütter's Piccolo*** *(closed Thursday)* **Meals** à la carte 25,50/33,50 ♀.
♦ This restaurant is housed in a pretty half-timbered building. The generous window-space gives a fine view of the Rhine. Hütter's Piccolo is a contemporary-style bistro - a few steps above the Zur Tant.
Spec. Das Beste vom Kalbskopf mit Wurzelgemüse. Taubenbrust mit Gänseleber und Balsamjus. Crépinette vom Lamm mit ligurischem Gemüse und Pesto.

at Cologne-Rodenkirchen *South : 8 km, by Bayernstraße FX and Agrippina Ufer :*

Atrium-Rheinhotel without rest (with guest house), Karlstr. 2, ✉ 50996, ☎ (0221) 93 57 20, *info@atrium-rheinhotel.de, Fax (0221) 93572222,* – – 15. AE ⓜ VISA
closed 24 December - 1 January – **68 rm** ☐ 85 – 120.
♦ The hotel stands in a quiet little lane close to the riverside in the old fishing village of Rodenkirchen. Choose between comfortable or more simply furnished rooms.

at Köln-Sürth : *Southeast : 10 km, by Bayenstraße FX via Rodenkirchen :*

Da Bruno, Sürther Hauptstr. 157, ✉ 50999, ☎ (02236) 6 93 85, *Fax (02236) 96125*
– AE ⓜ VISA.
closed mid July - early August and Monday – **Meals** *(dinner only)* (Italian) à la carte 39,50/66 ♀.
♦ Black and white floor tiles and modern pictures on the walls create an atmospheric ambience. The owner describes his Italian specialities verbally.
Spec. Mediterraner Kartoffelsalat mit Tagliata vom Thunfisch. Seeteufel mit Artischockenherzen. Spanferkelkotelett mit dicken Bohnen.

Bergisch Gladbach *Nordrhein-Westfalen 543 N 5 – pop. 104 000 – alt. 86 m.*

Köln 17.

Restaurant Dieter Müller - Schlosshotel Lerbach, Lerbacher Weg, ✉ 51465, ☎ (02202) 20 40, *info@schlosshotel-lerbach.com, Fax (02202) 204940* – P. AE ⓓ ⓜ VISA
closed 1 to 19 January, 3 weeks August, Sunday and Monday – **Meals** (booking essential) 62 *(lunch)*/130 and à la carte 72/104 ♀.
♦ Discreet elegance, attentive service and lavish table settings create an atmosphere of great refinement, which is matched by the excellent, classic cuisine.
Spec. Jakobsmuscheln in Kürbiskernkruste mit Piniensauce und Rahmpolenta. Rehrücken in der Brotkruste und geschmorte Schulter in Aprikosen-Chiboust. Soufflé von Guanaja Schokolade mit Passionsfrucht-Crémeux.

at Bergisch Gladbach-Bensberg :

Vendôme - Grandhotel Schloss Bensberg, Kadettenstraße, ✉ 51429, ☎ (02204) 42 19 41, *vendome@schlossbensberg.com, Fax (02204) 42985,* – P. AE ⓓ ⓜ VISA
closed 2 weeks carnival, 3 weeks July - August, Monday and Tuesday – **Meals** 5 *(lunch)*/125 and à la carte 76/102 ♀.
♦ Housed in a nobleman's residence, this gourmet restaurant provides attentive service and fine place settings. Well-chosen, classic dishes.
Spec. Feuilleté von roh marinierter Gänseleber mit Sommertrüffeln. In Limonen-Olivenöl pochierter Steinbutt mit geschmortem Fenchelgemüse. Perlhuhn mit Jahrgangsspeck auf Holzkohle gegrillt.

Neuenahr-Ahrweiler, Bad *Rheinland-Pfalz 543 O 5 – pop. 28 100 – alt. 92 m.*

Köln 63.

at Bad Neuenahr-Ahrweiler-Heppingen *East : 5 km :*

Steinheuers Restaurant Zur Alten Post with rm, Landskroner Str. 110 (entrance Konsumgasse), ✉ 53474, ☎ (02641) 9 48 60, *steinheuers.restaurant@t-online.de, Fax (02641) 948610,* – rest, P. AE ⓓ ⓜ VISA. rm
Meals *(closed 19 July - 12 August, Tuesday and Wednesday lunch)* 75/110 and à la carte 57/79, ♀ – ***Landgasthof Poststuben*** *(closed Tuesday and Wednesday lunch)* **Meals** à la carte 26,50/40,50 ♀ – **11 rm** ☐ 82/130 – 125/140.
♦ Taste, attention to detail, and a highly individual style characterise the seasonal repertoire, served in a discreetly elegant setting. Attractive rooms for an overnight stay. Refined local cuisine in the Poststuben in the style of a country inn.
Spec. Variation von der Gänsestopfleber. Steinbutt mit Trüffelkruste und Petersilienwurzel. Eifeler Reh.

Wittlich *Rheinland-Pfalz* 543 Q 4 – *pop. 18 000 – alt. 155 m.*
Köln 160.

at Dreis *Southwest : 8 km :*

Waldhotel Sonnora (Thieltges) with rm, Auf dem Eichelfeld, ✉ 54518, ✆ (06578) 9 82 20, *info@hotel-sonnora.de, Fax (06578) 1402,* ≤, – TV P. AE MC VISA. *closed January - early February, 2 weeks early July* – **Meals** *(closed Monday and Tuesday)* (booking essential) 95/115 and à la carte 65/82 – **20 rm** 70/120 – 100/170.
◆ An aura of classic elegance pervades the restaurant, where a master-chef displays his outstanding talents. There are also well-looked after rooms and a lovely garden.
Spec. Kleine Torte vom Rinderfilet-Tatar mit Imperial Kaviar und Kartoffelrösti. Bretonischer Steinbutt mit Basilikum-Tomaten und Spinat-Tortellini. Topfensoufflé mit geliertem Orangen-Physalis-Kompott.

Perl *Saarland* 543 R 3 – *pop. 6 500 – alt. 254 m.*
Köln 230.

at Perl-Nennig *North : 10 km by B 419 :*

Schloss Berg with rm, Schloßhof 7, ✉ 66706, ✆ (06866) 7 91 18, *info@schlossberg-nennig.de, Fax (06866) 79458,* ≤, – , rm, TV P. AE MC VISA
closed 3 weeks January, 3 weeks June - July – **Meals** *(closed Monday and Tuesday) (weekdays dinner only)* 118 and à la carte 64/81 – **17 rm** 130 – 160.
◆ Haute cuisine celebrated in an aristocratic setting. Treat yourself to one of the novel creations of chef Christian Bau, then spend the night in one of the stylish rooms.
Spec. Landaiser Gänseleber im Ganzen confiert mit Torcolatosauce. Sauté von Froschschenkeln und Sot-L'y-Laisse à la meunière. Steinbutt mit wilden Lorbeeraromaten gegart und zweierlei Sellerie.

DRESDEN L *Sachsen* 544 M 25 – *pop. 500 000 – alt. 105 m.*

See : *Zwinger★★★ (Picture Gallery Old Masters★★★ (Gemäldegalerie Alte Meister), Wallpavilion★★, Nymphs' Bath★★, Porcelain Collection★★, Mathematical-Physical Salon★★, Armoury★★)* AY – *Semper Opera★★* AY – *Former court church★★ (Hofkirche)* BY – *Palace (Schloss) : royal houses★ (Fürstenzug-Mosaik), Long Passage★ (Langer Gang)* BY – *Albertinum : Picture Gallery New Masters★★★ (Gemäldegalerie Neue Meister), Green Vault★★★ (Grünes Gewölbe)* BY – *Prager Straße★* ABZ – *Museum of History of Dresden★ (Museum für Geschichte der Stadt Dresden)* BY **L** – *Church of the Cross★ (Kreuzkirche)* BY – *Japanese Palace★ (Japanisches Palais)(garden ≤★)* ABX – *Museum of Saxonian Folk Art★ (Museum für Sächsische Volkskunst)* BX **M 2** – *Great Garden★ (Großer Garten)* CDZ – *Russian-Orthodox Church★ (Russisch-orthodoxe Kirche) (by Leningrader Str.* BZ *)* – *Brühl's Terrace ≤★ (Brühlsche Terrasse)* BY – *Equestrian statue of Augustus the Strong ★ (Reiterstandbild Augusts des Starken)* BX **E** – *Pfunds dairy (Pfunds Molkerei) (interior★) Bautzener Straße 97CX.*

Envir. : *Schloss (palace) Moritzburg★ (Northwest : 14 km by Hansastraße* BX*)* – *Schloss (palace) Pillnitz★ (Southeast : 15 km by Bautzner Straße* CX *)* – *Saxon Swiss★★★ (Sächsische Schweiz) : Bastei★★★ ≤★★, Bad Schandau★, Festung (fortress) Königstein★★ ≤★★, Großsedlitz : Baroque Garden★.*

Possendorf, Ferdinand-von-Schill-Str. 4 (South : 13 km), ✆ *(035206) 24 30 ; Ullersdorf, Am Golfplatz 1 (East : 8 km),* ✆ *(03528) 4 80 60.*

Dresden-Klotzsche (North : 13 km), ✆ *(0351) 8 81 33 60.*

Tourist-Information, Prager Str. 2a, ✉ *01069,* ✆ *(0351) 49 19 20, info@dresden-tourist.de,* Fax (0351) 49192116.

Tourist-Information, Schinkelwache, Theaterplatz, ✉ *01067,* ✆ *(0351) 49 19 20.*

ADAC, *Striesener Str. 37.*

Berlin 192 – Chemnitz 70 – Görlitz 98 – Leipzig 111 – Praha 152.

Plans on following pages

Kempinski Hotel Taschenbergpalais, Taschenberg 3, ✉ 01067, ✆ (0351) 4 91 20, *reservations.taschenbergpalais@kempinski.com, Fax (0351) 4912812,* , Massage, , , – , rm, TV – 320. AE MC VISA JCB
Meals à la carte 43/55 – 22 – **213 rm** 255/340 – 285/370 – 12 suites. BY a
◆ The guest is treated like a king in this restored Baroque palace. Elegant rooms and luxurious suites in beechwood with Baroque or designer furnishings. Coolly elegant atmosphere in the Intermezzo.

The Westin Bellevue, Große Meißner Str. 15, ✉ 01097, ✆ (0351) 80 50, *hotelinfo@westin-bellevue.com, Fax (0351) 8051609,* ≤, beer garden, , , – , rm, TV P – 440. AE MC VISA JCB. rest BX a
Meals à la carte 26/55 – **339 rm** 120/279 – 140/307 – 16 suites.
◆ Lovely garden location on the banks of the River Elbe with views of Semper Opera and Schloss. Beautiful, traditionally furnished rooms. A Canaletto is just one highlight of the elegant public interiors. Open-air and courtyard restaurants.

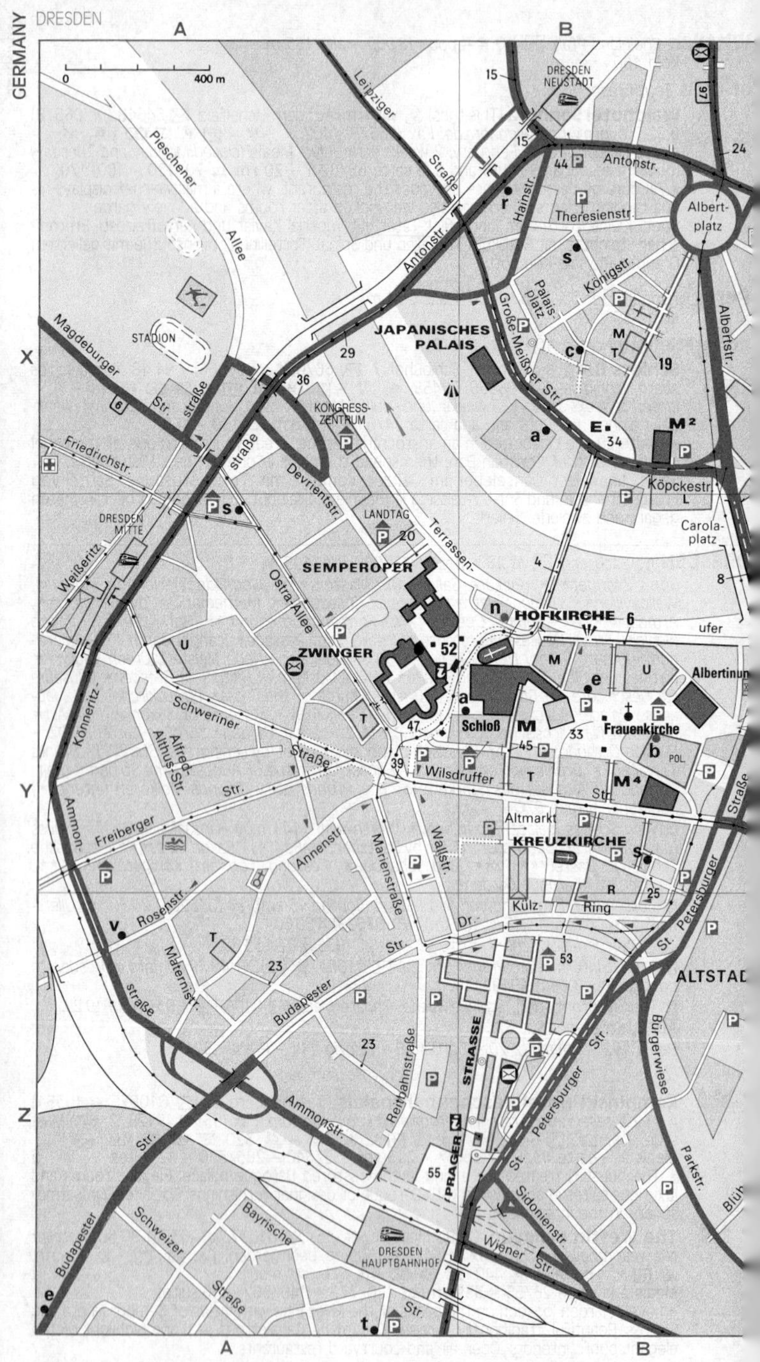
A
B
400 m
DRESDEN NEUSTADT
Leipziger Straße
Antonstr.
Hainstr.
Theresienstr.
Albertplatz
Königstr.
Palaisplatz
Große Meißner Str.
Albertstr.
Pieschener Allee
STADION
Magdeburger Str.
JAPANISCHES PALAIS
KONGRESS-ZENTRUM
Friedrichstr.
Devrientstr.
LANDTAG
Terrassen-ufer
Köpckestr.
Carolaplatz
DRESDEN MITTE
Weißeritz-
Ostra-Allee
SEMPEROPER
HOFKIRCHE
ZWINGER
Albertinum
Schloß
Frauenkirche
POL.
Schweriner Straße
Alfred-Althus-Str.
Wilsdruffer Str.
Könneritz-
Ammon-straße
Freiberger Str.
Altmarkt
KREUZKIRCHE
Annenstr.
Marienstraße
Wallstr.
Rosenstr.
Kulz-Ring
Dr.-
St. Petersburger Straße
ALTSTAD
Maternistr.
Budapester Str.
Reitbahnstraße
PRAGER STRASSE
Bürgerwiese
Ammonstr.
Parkstr.
Sidonienstr.
Bayrische Straße
Schweizer Str.
DRESDEN HAUPTBAHNHOF
Wiener Str.
X
Y
Z

DRESDEN

Street	Grid	No.
Albertbrücke	CX	2
Augustusbrücke	BY	4
Brühlsche Terrasse	BY	6
Carolabrücke	BY	8
Dr.-Külz-Ring	BYZ	
Hansastr	BX	15
Hauptstr.	BX	19
Holländische Str.	AY	20
Josephinenstr.	AZ	23
Königsbrücker Str.	BX	24
Königstr	BX	
Kreuzstr.	BYZ	25
Marienbrücke	AX	29
Neumarkt	BY	33
Neustädter-Markt	BX	34
Ostra-Ufer	AX	36
Postplatz	AY	39
Prager Str.	ABZ	
Reichpietschufer	CX	40
Rothenburger Straße	CX	42
Sachsenallee	CY	43
Schlesischer Pl.	BX	44
Schloßstr.	BY	45
Sophienstr	AY	47
Theaterplatz	BY	52
Waisenhausstr	BZ	53
Wiener Pl.	AZ	55
Wilsdruffer Str.	ABY	

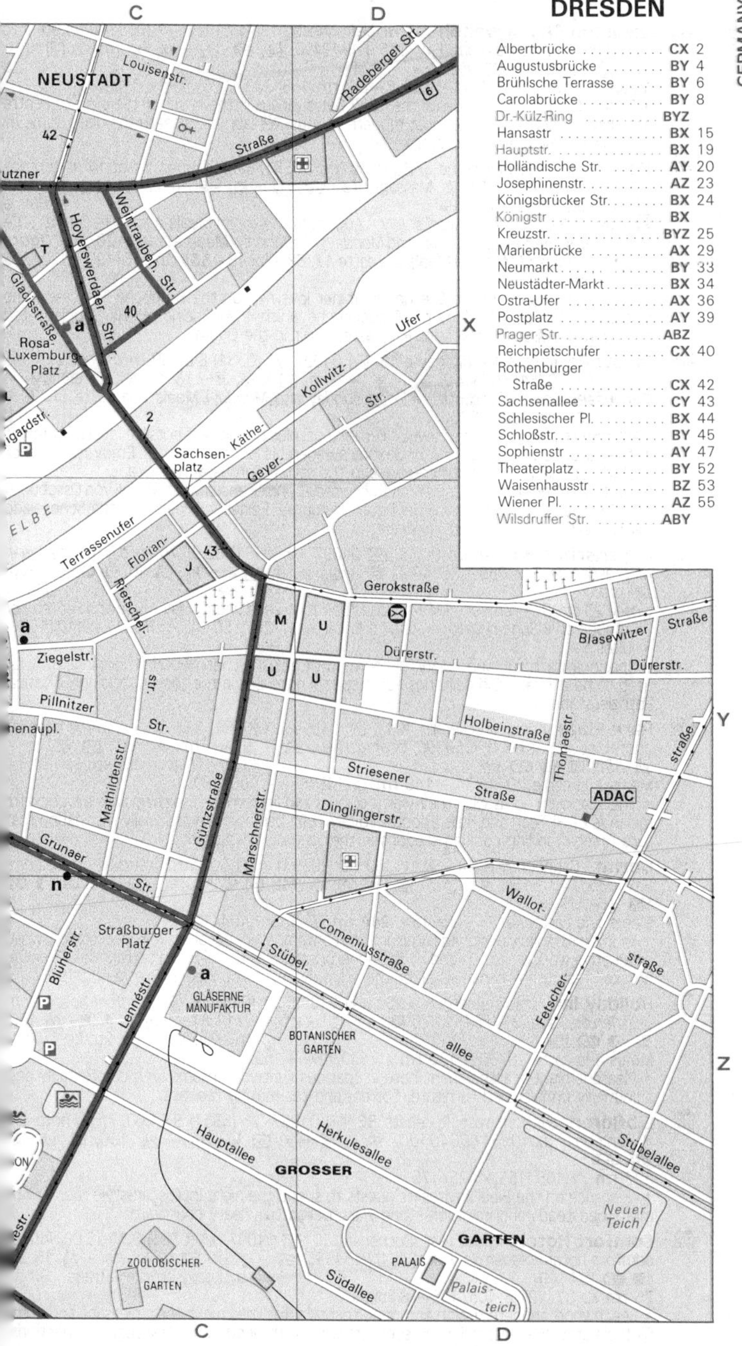

Radisson SAS Gewandhaus Hotel, Ringstr. 1, ✉ 01067, ✆ (0351) 4 94 90, *info.dresden@radissonsas.com, Fax (0351) 4949490*, Lδ, ≘s, ▢ - |ǂ|, ⇹ rm, ▤ TV ✆ ♿ P - 🏔 60. AE ⓓ ⓜⓒ VISA JCB BY s
Meals à la carte 27,50/42 - ☕ 16 - **97 rm** 135/200.
♦ Behind the historic façade of the 1525 Gewandhaus in the heart of the old city centre are elegant rooms with the most modern fittings. Restaurant beneath the glass dome of the lovely, airy central courtyard.

Hilton, An der Frauenkirche 5, ✉ 01067, ✆ (0351) 8 64 20, *info.dresden@hilton.com, Fax (0351) 8642725*, ☂, ⓦ, Massage, Lδ, ≘s, ▢ - |ǂ|, ⇹ rm, ▤ TV ✆ ♿ 🚗 P - 🏔 320. AE ⓓ ⓜⓒ VISA JCB BY e
Rossini (Italian) *(closed 2 weeks July - August)(dinner only)* **Meals** à la carte 34/48,50 - ***Wettiner Keller*** *(closed Sunday and Monday) (dinner only)* **Meals** à la carte 20/36 - ***Ogura*** (Japanese) *(closed Monday)* **Meals** à la carte 17/38 - ☕ 18 - **333 rm** 155/190 - 170/205 - 4 suites.
♦ The Hilton stands where Dresden is at her loveliest, on the Brühlsche Terrasse ("the balcony of Europe") right by the Frauenkirche which is now being rebuilt. Sophisticated cuisine in the first floor Rossini. Far Eastern flair in the Ogura.

Bülow Residenz, Rähnitzgasse 19, ✉ 01097, ✆ (0351) 8 00 30, *info@buelow-residenz.de, Fax (0351) 8003100*, ☂ - |ǂ|, ⇹ rm, TV ✆ ♿ P - 🏔 15. AE ⓓ ⓜⓒ VISA
✿ ***Caroussel*** (booking essential) *(closed Sunday and Monday)* **Meals** à la carte 58/70 - ☕ 17 - **30 rm** 180 - 220. BX c
♦ Rooms with gorgeous cherrywood furnishings, plus the highest possible level of comfort in the Baroque setting of one of Saxony's venerable princely palaces. Enjoy masterchef Stefan Herrmann's exquisite creations in the stylish Caroussel restaurant.
Spec. Gebratenes Rotbarbenfilet mit Ruccolasalat und Ofentomaten. Ravioli von Ossobucco und Gänsestopfleber mit zweierlei Petersilienpüree. Feines von der Valrhona-Schokolade mit glasierten Kirschen und Vanilleeis.

Bayerischer Hof, Antonstr. 33, ✉ 01097, ✆ (0351) 82 93 70, *info@bayerischer-hof-dresden.de, Fax (0351) 8014860*, ☂ - |ǂ|, ⇹ rm, TV 🚗 P - 🏔 40. ⓓ ⓜⓒ VISA JCB ⇹ rest BX r
closed 23 to 28 December - **Meals** *(closed Saturday and Sunday, May - June and September - October only Sunday) (dinner only)* à la carte 14/28 - **50 rm** ☕ 85/95 - 110/130 - 5 suites.
♦ Spacious, tasteful, and colourful rooms with elegant cherrywood furnishings in what used to be a library. Old paintings add a special note. Eat in the thoroughgoingly Classical Patrizierstube.

Park Plaza, Königsbrückerstr. 121a, ✉ 01099, ✆ (0351) 8 06 30, *ppdinfo@parkplazahotels.de, Fax (0351) 8063200*, beer garden, ≘s - |ǂ|, ⇹ rm, ▤ rest, TV ✆ 🚗 - 🏔 330. AE ⓓ ⓜⓒ VISA by Königsbrückerstraße BX
Meals à la carte 20,50/34 - **148 rm** ☕ 145/175 - 160/180.
♦ The spacious rooms with their warm colours and lightwood furnishings are a wonderful melange of Hi-Tech and Belle Epoque. Lovely 1891 ballroom. An especially fascinating feature : free-standing cooking stations in the Szenario restaurant.

Dorint, Grunaer Str. 14, ✉ 01069, ✆ (0351) 4 91 50, *info.drshdd@dorint.com, Fax (0351) 4915100*, ≘s, ▢ - |ǂ|, ⇹ rm, ▤ rest, TV ✆ ♿ 🚗 - 🏔 170. AE ⓓ ⓜⓒ VISA JCB CYZ r
Meals à la carte 24/35 - ☕ 15 - **244 rm** 99/136 - 104/141.
♦ Rooms with solidly designed furniture and contemporary décor make for relaxation, while productive work is encouraged by the generous desks with full technical facilities. The "Die Brücke" restaurant is named after the art movement founded in Dresden in 1905.

Holiday Inn, Stauffenbergallee 25a, ✉ 01099, ✆ (0351) 8 15 10, *info@holiday-inn-dresden.de, Fax (0351) 8151333*, Lδ, ≘s, ▢ - |ǂ|, ⇹ rm, ▤ rest, TV ✆ ♿ P - 🏔 100. AE ⓓ ⓜⓒ VISA by Königsbrücker Straße BX
Meals à la carte 20/30 - **120 rm** ☕ 130/160 - 148/175.
♦ Pleasant nights can be spent here in spacious lightwood rooms with comfortably and colourfully upholstered furniture. Coffee- and tea-making facilities.

Elbflorenz without rest, Rosenstr. 36, ✉ 01067, ✆ (0351) 8 64 00, *info@hotel-elbflorenz.de, Fax (0351) 8640100*, ≘s - |ǂ| ⇹, TV ✆ 🚗 - 🏔 150. AE ⓓ ⓜⓒ VISA JCB AZ v
227 rm ☕ 105/155 - 125/175.
♦ "Florence on the Elbe" invites its guests to spend the night in Tuscan-style rooms with metal bedsteads and imitation stone walls. Delightfully leafy courtyard.

Comfort Hotel without rest, Buchenstr. 10, ✉ 01097, ✆ (0351) 8 15 15 00, *info@comfort-hotel-dresden.de, Fax (0351) 8151555*, ≘s - |ǂ| ⇹ TV ✆ ♿ 🚗 - 🏔 15. AE ⓓ ⓜⓒ VISA JCB by Königsbrücker Straße BX
76 rm ☕ 87/120 - 103/135 - 8 Suites.
♦ Beechwood, modern design and good technical facilities make for a pleasant and comfortable stay. Well-located in Dresden-Neustadt with good public transport connections.

Art'otel, Ostra-Allee 33, ✉ 01067, ☎ (0351) 4 92 20, *aodrinfo@artotels.de, Fax (0351) 4922777*, – rm, – 300. AE ⓓ ⓜⓒ VISA
Meals *(closed Sunday lunch)* à la carte 26/31 – **174 rm** ☐ 160/180 – 175/195.
◆ Modern art enthusiasts will not be disappointed by the exuberant design of this establishment with its attached art gallery. Unusual rooms with fascinating features like a "magic window" to the bathroom. Restaurant combines art and contemporary fittings. AY s

Am Terrassenufer, Terrassenufer 12, ✉ 01069, ☎ (0351) 4 40 95 00, *hat@hotel-terrassenufer.de, Fax (0351) 4409600*, – rm, – 20. AE ⓓ ⓜⓒ VISA JCB CY a
Meals à la carte 15,50/26 – **196 rm** ☐ 100/148 – 110/172 – 6 suites.
◆ Spacious rooms with light furniture, generous working facilities and, thanks to location on the famous Brühlsche Terrasse, wonderful views of the Elbe, city centre, and Saxon Switzerland. Dine in the glazed Pavillon-Restaurant with its contemporary fittings.

Leonardo, Bamberger Str. 14, ✉ 01187, ☎ (0351) 4 66 00, *Info@leonardo.bestwestern.de, Fax (0351) 4660100*, – rm, – 35. AE ⓓ ⓜⓒ VISA JCB. rest by Budapester Str. AZ
Meals à la carte 16/30 – **92 rm** ☐ 96/116 – 126/150.
◆ Modern hotel with contemporary décor featuring attractive Mediterranean colours. Comfortable rooms with all technical facilities.Welcoming restaurant on two levels.

Martha Hospiz, Nieritzstr. 11, ✉ 01097, ☎ (0351) 8 17 60, *marthahospiz.dresden@t-online.de, Fax (0351) 8176222* – – 20. AE ⓜⓒ VISA JCB. rm
closed 22 to 27 December – ***Kartoffelkeller*** *(dinner only)* **Meals** à la carte 12/22,50 – **50 rm** ☐ 74/89 – 105/114. BX s
◆ Traditional establishment run by the Protestant Church. Rooms tastefully furnished, partly in Biedermeier style. Seven rooms with disabled facilities. Pleasant cellar restaurant.

Achat without rest, Budapester Str. 34, ✉ 01069, ☎ (0351) 47 38 00, *dresden@achat-hotel.de, Fax (0351) 47380999* – – 20. AE ⓓ ⓜⓒ VISA
158 rm ☐ 75/95 – 96/116. AZ e
◆ By the main railway station in the city centre, functional rooms with natural wood furnishings. Apartments with kitchenettes for longer term guests.

Privat, Forststr. 22, ✉ 01099, ☎ (0351) 81 17 70, *hotel-privat@t-online.de, Fax (0351) 8013953*, – – 25. AE ⓜⓒ VISA.
Meals à la carte 11/18 – **30 rm** ☐ 61 – 82/87. by Bautzener Str. DX
◆ Personally run, private hotel offering its guests functional rooms with all the amenities of contemporary accommodation. Bright restaurant with conservatory and attractive small terrace.

Kipping, Winckelmannstr. 6, ✉ 01069, ☎ (0351) 47 85 00, *reception@hotel-kipping.de, Fax (0351) 4785099*, – AE ⓜⓒ VISA JCB AZ t
Meals *(closed Sunday)* à la carte 14/23 – **20 rm** ☐ 70/95 – 85/115.
◆ This well-run, restored town house in a side street to the rear of the main station offers individually decorated, comfortable rooms.

Lesage, Lennéstr. 1, ✉ 01069, ☎ (0351) 4 20 42 50, *restaurant.lesage@kempinski.com, Fax (0351) 4204994*, – AE ⓓ ⓜⓒ VISA JCB CZ a
Meals à la carte 26/33 ♀.
◆ This restaurant has a unique location in the glass-walled Volkswagen works. Crisp design and elegant bistro style characterise the ambience.

Italienisches Dörfchen, Theaterplatz 3, ✉ 01067, ☎ (0351) 49 81 60, *gastro.theaterplatz@t-online.de, Fax (0351) 4981688*, beer garden – AE ⓓ ⓜⓒ VISA JCB
Bellotto (Italian) **Meals** à la carte 21/38,50 – ***Wein- und Kurfürstenzimmer*** : **Meals** à la carte 19/33. BY n
◆ The modern Bellotto restaurant is part of Dresden's "Italian Village", once home to the workmen who helped build the city. Elegant wine-cellar with fine plasterwork and warm red décor. Spectacular ceiling in the Kurfürstenzimmer.

Coselpalais, An der Frauenkirche 12, ✉ 01067, ☎ (0351) 4 96 24 44, *Fax (0351) 4962445*, – AE ⓓ ⓜⓒ VISA BY b
Meals à la carte 17/35.
◆ This restored palace dating from 1763 is a dream both inside and out. The interior has a coffee-house character which harmonises well with the building as a whole.

Am Glacis, Glacisstr. 8, ✉ 01099, ☎ (0351) 8 03 60 33, *restaurant@am-glacis.de, Fax (0351) 8036034*, – AE ⓓ ⓜⓒ VISA JCB CX a
closed 2 to 11 January and Sunday – **Meals** à la carte 25/41,50.
◆ This elegant contemporary restaurant is in the same building as the Mercure-Hotel Albertbrücke, and is guaranteed to take you on a fascinating gastronomic tour of France.

Alte Meister, Theaterplatz 1a, ✉ 01067, ☎ (0351) 4 81 04 26, *info@altemeister.net, Fax (0351) 4810479*, – AE ⓜⓒ VISA. AY e
Meals à la carte 20/28.
◆ Bright, high-ceilinged interiors and a vaulted ceiling with frescoes set the tone here. Splendid terrace with views of Opera and Theaterplatz.

Villandry, Jordanstr. 8, ✉ 01099, (0351) 8 99 67 24, *mail@villandry-restaurant.de, Fax (0351) 8996746*, – AE MC VISA by Königsbrücker Str. BX
closed 2 weeks February, 2 weeks August and Sunday – **Meals** *(dinner only)* (booking essential) à la carte 23/28.
◆ Mediterranean bistro-style ambience in this restaurant offering tasty international dishes as well as a relaxed atmosphere and live music.

at Dresden-Blasewitz *East : 5 km, by Blasewitzer Straße DY :*

Am Blauen Wunder, Loschwitzer Str. 48, ✉ 01309, (0351) 3 36 60, *dresden@hotel-am-blauen-wunder.de, Fax (0351) 3366299*, – – 20. AE MC VISA by Blasewitzer Straße DY
La Strada (Italian) *(closed Sunday) (dinner only)* **Meals** à la carte 19/37,50 – **39 rm** 95 – 120.
◆ By the famous "Blue Wonder" bridge over the Elbe, tasteful rooms in warm Mediterranean colours and all technical facilities. Completely refurbished La Strada in bistro-style.

at Dresden-Cotta *West : 5 km, by Magdeburger Straße (B 6) AX :*

Mercure Elbpromenade, Hamburger Str. 64 (B 6), ✉ 01157, (0351) 4 25 20, *h0479@t-online.de, Fax (0351) 4252420*, , – , rm, – 60. AE MC VISA JCB. rest
Meals *(closed Sunday lunch)* à la carte 16/44 – 13 – **103 rm** 59/80 – 72/87.
◆ Your residence in Dresden, the "Pearl of the North", is right on the Elbe. Spacious, bright rooms with furnishings in natural wood plus excellent working facilities.

Residenz Alt Dresden, Mobschatzer Str. 29, ✉ 01157, (0351) 4 28 10, *residenzaltdresden@ringhotels.de, Fax (0351) 4281988*, , , – , – 100. AE MC VISA JCB
Meals à la carte 20,50/38,50 – **124 rm** 90/114 – 107/140.
◆ Functional rooms with modern furnishings in a mixture of yellow and orange. Longer-term guests accommodated in the annexe. Breakfast in the winter garden. Straightforward, bistro-style restaurant.

In Dresden-Kemnitz *Northwest : 6 km, by Magdeburger Straße AX and Bremer Straße :*

Romantik Hotel Pattis, Merbitzer Str. 53, ✉ 01157, (0351) 4 25 50, *info@pattis.net, Fax (0351) 4255255*, , , Massage, , – , rm, rest, – 80. AE MC VISA
Gourmet-Restaurant *(closed 2 weeks February, 2 weeks August, Sunday and Monday) (dinner only)* **Meals** à la carte 55/65 – ***Vitalis :*** **Menu** à la carte 25/31 – **47 rm** 100/135 – 135/190 – 3 suites.
◆ A touch of luxury : extremely tastefully decorated rooms with Art Nouveau furnishings, plus a remarkable wellness area, and a small park. Gourmet restaurant with elegant interior. Vitalis restaurant has a pavilion-like character.

at Dresden-Klotzsche *Northeast : 9 km, by Königsbrücker Straße BX :*

Airport Hotel, Karl-Marx-Str. 25, ✉ 01109, (0351) 8 83 30, *bestwestern@airporthoteldresden.com, Fax (0351) 8833333*, , – , rm, rest, – 50. AE MC VISA JCB
Meals à la carte 19/29 – **100 rm** 97/108 – 114/128 – 7 suites.
◆ Happy landings in modern rooms arranged around an atrium and with solidly designed contemporary wooden furniture plus work desks with excellent facilities. Friendly restaurant with attractive room dividers.

at Dresden-Laubegast *East : 9 km by Striesener Straße DY :*

Ramada-Treff Resident Hotel, Brünner Str. 11, ✉ 01279, (0351) 2 56 20, *resident.dresden@ramada-treff.de, Fax (0351) 2562800* – , rm, – 45. AE MC VISA JCB. rest
Meals *(weekdays dinner only)* à la carte 17/30 – **122 rm** 70/90 – 86/102.
◆ Relax in cosy, pastel-coloured rooms, functionally designed and ideal for the business traveller.

at Dresden-Leubnitz-Neuostra *Southeast : 5,5 km, by Parkstraße BCZ and Teplitzer Straße*

Treff Hotel Dresden, Wilhelm-Franke-Str. 90, ✉ 01219, (0351) 4 78 20, *dresden@treff-hotels.de, Fax (0351) 4782550*, , , – , rm, – 350. AE MC VISA
Meals à la carte 24/33 – 13 – **262 rm** 88/98.
◆ Built in a semi-circle and close to the city centre, the Treff Hotel Dresden has comfortable rooms with tasteful furnishings in pale cherrywood. Large restaurant with sober contemporary décor.

at Dresden-Lockwitz *Southeast : 11 km, by Sankt Petersburger Str.* BZ *and B 172 :*

Landhaus Lockwitzgrund, Lockwitzgrund 100, ✉ 01257, ☎ (0351) 2 71 00 10, *tkaiser@landhaus-lockwitzgrund.de, Fax (0351) 27100130,* beer garden – rm, – 35. AE MC VISA
Meals *(closed January, Monday)* à la carte 16,50/30 – **12 rm** 50 – 65.
♦ This country-house hotel in the romantic Lockwitz valley makes a wonderful setting for relaxation. Comfortable rooms with many original details. Restaurant in the well-preserved vaulted stables.

at Dresden-Loschwitz *Northeast : 6 km, by Bautzner Straße* CDX *:*

Schloß Eckberg (with separate hotel wing), Bautzner Str. 134, ✉ 01099, ☎ (0351) 8 09 90, *email@hotel-schloss-eckberg.de, Fax (0351) 8099199,* Dresden and Elbe, , Massage, , , – , rm, – 70. AE MC VISA JCB. rest
Meals 20 *(lunch)* and à la carte 33/42 – **84 rm** 97/180 – 135/235.
♦ Consisting of a neo-Gothic castle and a modern gentleman's residence, this is a fascinating place to stay, set in an extensive park and with rooms furnished with fine antiques. The stylish, traditional restaurant fits in well with the historical surroundings.

at Dresden-Niedersedlitz *Southeast : 10 km by Parkstraße* BZ *and B 172, off Lockwitztalstraße :*

Ambiente , Meusegaster Str. 23, ✉ 01259, ☎ (0351) 20 78 80, *info@hotel-ambiente.de, Fax (0351) 2078836* – , rm, . MC VISA. rest
Meals *(closed Sunday) (dinner only)* (residents only) – **20 rm** 71/81 – 82/118.
♦ This personally run hotel has interiors of great sophistication and elegance. Rooms with cherrywood furniture, famously comfortable Treca beds, and tasteful fabrics.

at Dresden-Strehlen *South : 4 km, by Parkstraße* CZ *and B 172, off Caspar-David-Friedrich-Straße :*

Four Points Hotel Königshof, Kreischaer Str. 2 (Wasaplatz), ✉ 01219, ☎ (0351) 8 73 10, *fourpoints.koenigshof@arabellasheraton.com, Fax (0351) 8731499,* – , rm, – 180. AE MC VISA JCB
Meals à la carte 17,50/28 – 11 – **93 rm** 103 – 123 – 9 suites.
♦ In a listed building, this welcoming establishment has rooms with lovely beechwood furnishings and up-to-the-minute working facilities. Ask for a room with a four-poster. Cosy restaurant with bistro atmosphere.

at Dresden-Weixdorf *Northeast : 10 km, by Königsbrücker Str.* BX *:*

Quintessenz, Hohenbusch Markt 1, ✉ 01108, ☎ (0351) 88 24 40, *hotel.quintessenz@t-online.de, Fax (0351) 8824444,* – , rm, – 60. AE MC VISA
Meals *(closed Sunday) (dinner only)* à la carte 14/25 – **75** rm 69/84 – 87/99.
♦ On the edge of town on the way to the A3 autobahn, this good hotel in a modern shopping centre offers comfortable rooms. Pictures of Italian landscapes grace the walls of the little Toskana restaurant.

DÜSSELDORF

L *Nordrhein-Westfalen* 543 M 4 – *pop. 570 000 – alt. 40 m.*

See : *Königsallee★* EZ – *Hofgarten★* DEY *and Castle Jägerhof (Goethe-Museum★* EY **M1)** – *Hetjensmuseum★* DZ **M4** – *Museum of Art (museum kunst palast)★ (Glass Collection★★)* DY **M2** – *Collection of Art (Kunstsammlung NRW)★* DY **M3** – *Löbbecke-Museum and Aquazoo★ by Kaiserswerther Straße* AU – *Hetjens-Museum★* DZ **M4.**

Envir. : *Castle of Benrath (Schloß Benrath) (Parc★) South : 10 km by Siegburger Straße* CX.

Düsseldorf-Grafenberg, Rennbahnstr. 26, ☎ (0211) 9 64 49 50 ; *Gut Rommeljans, Rommeljansweg 12 (Northeast : 12 km), ☎ (02102) 8 10 92 ;* *Düsseldorf-Hubbelrath, Bergische Landstr. 700 (East : 12 km), ☎ (02104) 7 21 78 ;* *Düsseldorf-Hafen, Auf der Lausward 51, ☎ (0211) 41 05 29.*

Düsseldorf-Lohausen (North : 8 km), ☎ (0211) 42 10.

Hauptbahnhof.

Exhibition Centre (Messegelände), ☎ (0211) 45 60 01, Fax (0211) 4560668.

Tourist office, Immermannstr. 65b, ✉ 40210, ☎ (0211) 17 20 20, tourist@duesseldorf.de, Fax (0211) 161071.

ADAC, *Himmelgeister Str. 63.*

Berlin 552 – Amsterdam 225 – Essen 31 – Köln 40 – Rotterdam 237.

Plans on following pages

Steigenberger Parkhotel, Corneliusplatz 1, ✉ 40213, ☎ (0211) 1 38 10, *duesseldorf@steigenberger.de, Fax (0211) 1381592,* – , rm, – 110. AE MC VISA JCB. rest EY p
Menuett : **Meals** à la carte 37/63 – **133 rm** 195/320 – 260/380 – 6 suites.
♦ The first building on the square stands in a little city centre park. Beyond the classically beautiful façade is an elegant marble foyer and luxuriously appointed rooms. Dine in the stylish and comfortable setting of the Menuett.

A
B
U
V
X
GOLZHEIM
Reeser Pl.
Kaiserswerther Str.
Th.-Heuss-Brücke
THEODOR-HEUSS-BRÜCKE
Uerdinger Str.
ADAC
Cecilien
Kaiserswerther
Golzheimer Platz
KÖLN-DÜSSELDORFER
RHEIN-
PARK
Kennedydamm
Johannstr.
Roßstr.
Heinrich-Ehrhardt Str.
Ulmen-
Rather
Straße
Grashofstr.
Münsterstr.
Brehmstr.
DERENDORF
Collenbachstr.
Klever Straße
Straße
Gruner
Moltkestr.
Münsterstr.
S.-BAHN
Nordstr.
Prinz-
Georg-
Str.
Klever Str.
allee
Joseph-Beuys-Ufer
RHEIN
Duisburger
Str.
Kaiserstr.
Rethelstr.
D.-ZOO
Bagelstr.
Schinkel-
str.
Rethelstr.
Schumann
Adlerstr.
OBERKASSEL
Kaiser-
Friedrich-
Ring
Luegallee
Luegplatz
OBERKASSELER BRÜCKE
HOF-GARTEN
Jägerhofstr.
HOF-GARTEN
Grafenberg
D.-WEHRHAHN
Ackerstr.
Kölner
Kaiser-Wilhelm-Ring
Schlossturm
ALTSTADT
Königsallee
Allee
Worringer
str.
Str.
Rheinufertunnel
RHEINKNIEBRÜCKE
Berliner
Karl-
Handelszentrum
Hauptbahnhof
Stahlwerkstr.
LANDTAG
RHEINTURM
HAFEN
Stromstr.
Graf-
Adolf-
Str.
Eisenstr.
Hüttenstr.
Corneliusstr.
Ellerstr.
Oberbilker Markt
Lessingplatz
Reichsstr.
Fürstenwall
Str.
Kronprinzen-
str.
Elisabethstr.
Fürstenwall
Kruppstraße
D.-VÖLKLINGER STR.
Bilker
Allee
D.-FRIEDRICHSTADT
Oberbilker
Allee
Bachstr.
D.-VOLKSGARTEN
S.-BAHN
D.-BILK
S.-BAHN
VOLKSGARTEN
Str.
Volmerswerther
Straße
Merowingerstr.
Mecum-
Hennekamp
Aachener
Aurin
straße
Stoffeler Kapellenw
Völklinger
Südring
Südring
ADAC
A
B

STREET INDEX

Street	Square	No.
Aachener Straße	AX	
Achenbachstraße	BV	2
Ackerstraße	BV	
Adlerstraße	BV	
Am Wehrhahn	EY	3
Auf'm Hennekamp	BX	
Bachstraße	AX	
Bagelstraße	BV	
Bastionstraße	DZ	
Benrather Straße	DZ	
Benzenbergstraße	AX	5
Berger Allee	DZ	
Berliner Allee	EZ	
Bilker Allee	AX	
Bilker Straße	DZ	
Birkenstraße	CV	
Bismarckstraße	EZ	
Blumenstraße	EZ	7
Bolkerstraße	DY	8
Brehmplatz	BU	9
Brehmstraße	BU	
Breite Straße	EZ	
Brunnenstraße	BX	12
Burgplatz	DY	
Cecilienallee	AU	
Citadellstraße	DZ	13
Collenbachstraße	BU	
Corneliusstraße	EZ	15
Cranachstraße	CV	
Danziger Straße	AU	16
Dorotheenstraße	CV	
Duisburger Straße	EY	
Eisenstraße	BV	
Elberfelder Straße	EY	21
Elisabethstraße	DZ	
Ellerstraße	BX	
Erasmusstraße	BX	22
Erkrather Straße	CV	
Ernst-Reuter-Pl.	EZ	23
Eulerstraße	BU	24
Fischerstraße	EY	27
Flinger Straße	DY	28
Friedrich-Ebert-Straße	EZ	29
Friedrichstraße	EZ	
Fritz-Roeber-Straße	DY	
Fürstenplatz	BX	30
Fürstenwall	AX	
Gartenstraße	EY	
Gladbacher Straße	AX	31
Grabbeplatz	DY	32
Graf-Adolf-Platz	EZ	
Graf-Adolf-Straße	EZ	
Grafenberger Allee	BV	
Graf-Recke-Str.	CU	
Grashofstraße	BU	
Grunerstraße	BU	
Hans-Sachs-Straße	CV	39
Harkortstraße	BV	40
Haroldstraße	DZ	
Heinr.-Ehrhardt-Straße	BU	
Heinr.-Heine-Allee	EY	42
Heinrichstraße	CU	
Hellweg	CV	
Heresbachstraße	BX	43
Herzogstraße	BX	44
Höherweg	CV	
Hofgartenrampe	DY	45
Homberger Straße	AU	46
Hubertusstraße	DZ	
Hüttenstraße	BX	
Immermannstraße	EY	
Inselstraße	DY	
Jacobistraße	EY	
Jägerhofstraße	EY	
Jan-Wellem-Platz	EY	51
Johannstraße	AU	
Joseph-Beuys-Ufer	DY	
Jülicher Straße	BU	52
Jürgensplatz	AX	54
Kaiser-Friedrich-Ring	AU	
Kaiserstraße	EY	
Kaiserwerther Straße	AU	
Kaiser-Wilhelm-Ring	AV	
Karl-Geusen-Straße	CX	
Karlplatz	DZ	
Karlstraße	BV	
Kasernenstraße	DZ	
Kavalleriestraße	DZ	
Kennedydamm	AU	
Kettwiger Straße	CV	
Klever Straße	AU	
Klosterstraße	BV	56
Kölner Straße	BV	
Königsallee	EZ	
Königsberger Straße	CV	58
K.-Adenauer-Pl.	BV	59
Kopernikusstr.	AX	60
Kronprinzenstr.	AX	
Kruppstraße	BX	
Lenaustraße	CU	
Lessingplatz	BX	
Lichtstraße	CV	62
Lindemannstr.	CV	
Lorettostraße	AX	64
Luegallee	AV	
Luisenstraße	EZ	
Marktplatz	DY	68
Martin-Luther-Platz	EZ	69
Max.-Weyhe-Allee	EY	70
Mecumstraße	BX	
Merowingerstr.	AX	
Mintropstraße	BV	71
Mörsenbroicher Weg	CU	
Moltkestraße	BU	
Mühlenstraße	DY	73
Münsterstraße	BU	
Nördl.Zubringer	BU	77
Nordstraße	EY	
Oberbilker Allee	BX	
Oberbilker Markt	BX	80
Oberkasseler Br.	DY	
Oststraße	EZ	
Pempelforter Str.	BV	84
Plockstraße	AX	86
Poststraße	DZ	
Prinz-Georg-Str.	EY	
Rather Straße	BU	
Ratinger Straße	DY	88
Reichsstraße	AX	
Rethelstraße	BV	
Ronsdorfer Str.	CX	
Roßstraße	BU	
Schadowplatz	EY	90
Schadowstraße	EY	91
Scheurenstraße	BV	92
Schillerplatz	BV	93
Schinkelstraße	BV	
Schirmestraße	BV	94
Schneider-Wibbel-Gasse	DY	95
Schulstraße	DZ	96
Schumannstr.	BV	
Schwanenmarkt	DZ	97
Siegburger Straße	CX	
Simrockstraße	CU	98
Sonnenstraße	BX	99
Steinstraße	EZ	
Sternstraße	EY	
Stoffeler Kapellenweg	BX	
Stoffeler Straße	CX	100
Stresemannstr.	EZ	
Stromstraße	AV	
Südring	AX	
Th.-Heuss-Br.	AU	
Tiergartenstraße	CU	
Tonhallenstraße	EY	101
Uerdinger Straße	AU	
Ulmenstraße	BU	
Vagedesstraße	EY	104
Vautierstraße	CU	
Venloer Straße	EY	105
Victoriaplatz	DY	
Völklinger Str.	AX	
Volmerswerther Straße	AX	
Werdener Straße	CV	
Witzelstraße	BX	114
Worringer Platz	BV	115
Worringer Straße	BV	

DÜSSELDORF

Street	Grid	No.
Am Wehrhahn	EY	3
Berliner Allee	EZ	
Blumenstraße	EZ	7
Bolkerstraße	DY	8
Citadellstraße	DZ	13
Corneliusstraße	EZ	15
Elberfelder Str.	EY	21
Ernst-Reuter-Platz	EZ	23
Fischerstraße	EY	27
Flinger Str.	DY	28
Friedrich-Ebert-Straße	EZ	29
Grabbeplatz	DY	32
Graf-Adolf-Str.	EZ	
Heinrich-Heine-Allee	EY	42
Hofgartenrampe	DY	45
Jan-Wellem-Platz	EY	51
Königsallee	EZ	
Marktplatz	DY	68
Martin-Luther-Platz	EZ	69
Maximilian-Weyhe-Allee	EY	70
Mühlenstraße	DY	73
Ratinger Str.	DY	88
Schadowplatz	EY	90
Schadowstraße	EY	91
Schneider-Wibbel-Gasse	DY	95
Schulstraße	DZ	96
Schwanenmarkt	DZ	98
Tonhallenstraße	EY	101
Vagedesstraße	EY	104
Venloer Str.	EY	105

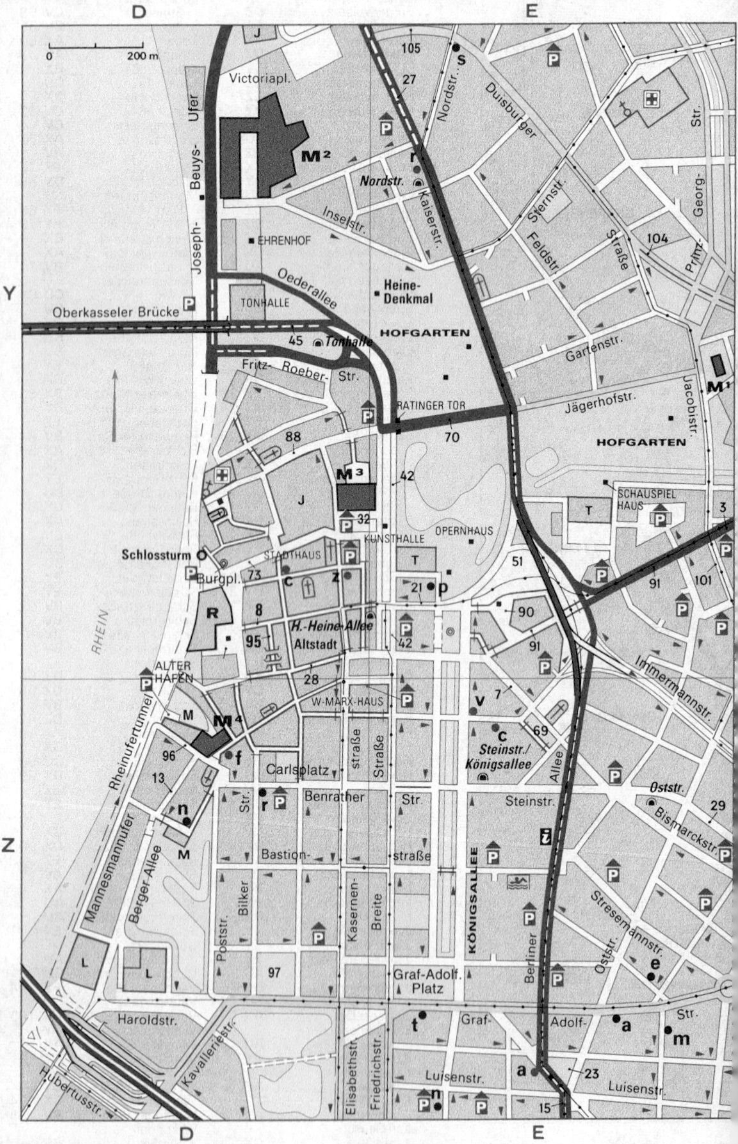

Nikko, Immermannstr. 41, ✉ 40210, ☎ (0211) 83 40, *info@nikko-hotel.de*, *Fax (0211) 161216*, – rm, – 270. AE VISA JCB. rest **Benkay** (Japanese) **Meals** à la carte 34/63 – ***Brasserie Nikkolette :*** **Meals** à la carte 25/42 – 17 – **301 rm** 198 – 225 – 6 suites. BV g
◆ The sushi-bar and a branch of the Mitsukoshi department store lend an exotically Oriental touch. Bird's-eye view over the city from swimming-pool and sauna. Experience the expertise of Japanese chefs in the Benkay restaurant.

Holiday Inn, Ludwig-Erhard-Allee 3, ✉ 40227, ☎ (0211) 7 77 10, *reservation.hi-duesseldorf@queensgruppe.de*, *Fax (0211) 7771888*, – rm, – 45. AE VISA JCB BV s
closed end December - early January – **Meals** à la carte 19/36 – 18 – **134 rm** 145/165 – 175/195 – 8 suites.
◆ Priding itself on its timeless elegance, this modern business hotel is well-located close to the central railway station. The lovely whirlpool bath is one of the highlights of the leisure area. You are invited to dine in the classical setting of Ludwig's.

Holiday Inn City Centre-Königsallee, Graf-Adolf-Platz 8, ✉ 40213, ☎ (0211) 3 84 80, *reservation.hiduesseldorf@queensgruppe.de*, *Fax (0211) 3848390*, – rm, rm, – 140. AE VISA JCB EZ t
Meals à la carte 26,50/44,50 – 18 – **253 rm** 195 – 225.
◆ Smart, functional establishment on the famous Königsallee with exemplary conference and meeting facilities. Finnish sauna ideal for relaxing after a busy day.

Majestic without rest, Cantadorstr. 4, ✉ 40211, ☎ (0211) 36 70 30, *info@majestic.bestwestern.de*, *Fax (0211) 3670399*, – – 30. AE VISA JCB. BV a
closed 23 December - 2 January – 14 – **52 rm** 139/157.
◆ City centre establishment with a secluded and comfortable atmosphere. Two allergen-free rooms. Düsseldorf's frenetic night-life just a short step away.

Günnewig Hotel Esplanade without rest, Fürstenplatz 17, ✉ 40215, ☎ (0211) 38 68 50, *hotel.esplanade@guennewig.de*, *Fax (0211) 38685555*, – – 60. AE VISA JCB BX s
80 rm 87/105 – 112.
◆ Business hotel in a tranquil but very central location on the Fürstenplatz, its spacious foyer much appreciated by its regular clientele.

Madison I, Graf-Adolf-Str. 94, ✉ 40210, ☎ (0211) 1 68 50, *reservierung@madison-hotels.de*, *Fax (0211) 1685328*, – rm, – 40. AE VISA BV n
Meals *(dinner only)* (residents only) – **100 rm** 110/130 – 130/160.
◆ The birthplace of the great actor Gustav Gründgens is nowadays much appreciated by travellers for its comfortable, country-style rooms.

Günnewig Hotel Uebachs without rest, Leopoldstr. 5, ✉ 40211, ☎ (0211) 17 37 10, *hotel.uebachs@guennewig.de*, *Fax (0211) 17371555* – – 25. AE VISA JCB BV r
82 rm 89/99 – 116.
◆ A quiet side-street location in central Düsseldorf makes this charming hotel an ideal base for exploring this fascinating city.

Stadt München without rest, Pionierstr. 6, ✉ 40215, ☎ (0211) 38 65 50, *info@hotel-stadt-muenchen.de*, *Fax (0211) 38655900*, – – 25. AE VISA EZ m
90 rm 65/100 – 100/140.
◆ Contemporary, functional rooms, impeccable service and a location just a few minutes walk from the Altstadt are the great advantages of this establishment.

Burns Art Hotel, Bahnstr. 76, ✉ 40210, ☎ (0211) 7 79 29 10, *info@hotel-burns.de*, *Fax (0211) 77929177* – rm, . AE VISA. rest EZ e
Sila Thai (Thai) **Meals** à la carte 23/41 – **35 rm** 125/175 – 145/185 – 3 suites.
◆ Behind the spruced-up 1898 façade pulses the life of a designer hotel which has successfully combined Italian charm and Asian minimalism. The ground floor Silai Thai restaurant adds to the fascinating mixture.

Madison II without rest, Graf-Adolf-Str. 47, ✉ 40210, ☎ (0211) 38 80 30, *c.bohacek@madison-hotels.de*, *Fax (0211) 3880388* – . AE VISA EZ a
closed 20 December - 3 January and July – **24 rm** 85/115 – 105/140.
◆ A comfortable, country-house atmosphere is created by lovely furniture in natural wood. Residents of both Madison hotels can test their fitness in the private sports-club.

Carat Hotel without rest, Benrather Str. 7a, ✉ 40213, ☎ (0211) 1 30 50, *info-d@carat-hotel.de*, *Fax (0211) 322214*, – rm, – 20. AE VISA
73 rm 120/130 – 145/150. DZ r
◆ Reliable, well looked-after accommodation in a city hotel. Good tramway connections. Secretarial and translations services available.

Antares without rest, Corneliusstr. 82, ✉ 40215, ☎ (0211) 38 65 60, *info@antares-duesseldorf.de, Fax (0211) 382050* – 🅿 – 20. AE VISA JCB BX s
48 rm ☕ 71/78 – 91/98.
◆ This solidly built city centre establishment offers modern, soundproofed rooms for a relaxed stay. Office facilities for business travellers.

Asahi without rest, Kurfürstenstr. 30, ✉ 40211, ☎ (0211) 3 61 20, *info@hotel-asahi.com, Fax (0211) 3612345*, – AE VISA JCB BV t
53 rm ☕ 123 – 141.
◆ Newspapers, breakfasts, special kinds of tea all proclaim this to be an authentically Japanese establishment. New sauna with the latest in showers, steam baths and solarium.

Astoria without rest, Jahnstr. 72, ✉ 40215, ☎ (0211) 38 51 30, *info@hotel-astoria-dus.de, Fax (0211) 372089* – 🅿. AE VISA JCB. BX b
closed 22 December - 8 January – **26 rm** ☕ 84/90 – 105/120 – 4 suites.
◆ Behind the venerable façade are welcoming, light and airy rooms. Relatively tranquil location. Impeccably run. Private parking.

Windsor without rest, Grafenberger Allee 36, ✉ 40237, ☎ (0211) 91 46 80, *dkiermeier@t-online.de, Fax (0211) 9140840*, – AE VISA BV c
closed 22 December - 2 January – **18 rm** ☕ 98 – 128.
◆ Fine Old-Town residence with a traditional sandstone façade. Period furniture harmonises with lovingly restored arched doorways and plaster ceilings.

Orangerie without rest, Bäckergasse 1, ✉ 40213, ☎ (0211) 86 68 00, *hotelorangerie@t-online.de, Fax (0211) 8668099* – – 30. AE VISA. DZ r
27 rm ☕ 100/116 – 126/180.
◆ In the very centre of the Old Town stands this neo-Classical edifice, framed by historic buildings like the Speesche Palais, the old Orangery, and the Maxkirche.

An der Kö without rest, Talstr. 9, ✉ 40217, ☎ (0211) 37 10 48, *hotelanderkoe@t-online.de, Fax (0211) 370835* – 🅿. AE VISA JCB EZ r
45 rm ☕ 87 – 123.
◆ Contemporary décor combined with professional office facilities, including dictation, typing, fax and translation. Private parking in the city centre an additional advantage.

Residenz without rest, Worringer Str. 88, ✉ 40211, ☎ (0211) 5 50 48 80, *info@residenzhotelduesseldorf.de, Fax (0211) 55048877* – . AE VISA BV z
34 rm ☕ 75 – 95.
◆ In the heart of Düsseldorf with direct bus and metro connections to airport and trade fair grounds. Functional rooms with cherrywood furniture. One non-smoking floor.

Victorian, Königstr. 3a (1st floor), ✉ 40212, ☎ (0211) 8 65 50 22, *Fax (0211) 8655013* – . AE VISA. EZ c
closed Sunday and Bank Holidays – **Meals** (booking essential) 32 *(lunch)* and à la carte 52/68 ☐, – ***Bistro im Victorian*** **:** **Meals** à la carte 23/37.
◆ Enjoy classic cooking in the elegant, English-style restaurant. Agreeable atmosphere created by chandeliers, mirrors, leather seats and benches. The bistro one floor lower down is no less stylish.
Spec. Spaghetti alla ghitarra mit Hummer und Estragon. Kross gebratener Seewolf mit Krustentierschaum und Fenchelpüree. Gefüllter Ochsenschwanz mit Kalbsbries.

Weinhaus Tante Anna, Andreasstr. 2, ✉ 40213, ☎ (0211) 13 11 63, *info@tante-anna.de, Fax (0211) 132974* – AE VISA JCB DY c
closed Sunday, except exhibitions – **Meals** *(dinner only)* (booking essential) à la carte 28,50/46.
◆ The 1593 chapel of a Jesuit monastery is now a cosy and characterful restaurant, with fine old paintings and antique furnishings.

La Terrazza, Königsallee 30 (3th floor), ✉ 40212, ☎ (0211) 32 75 40, *Fax (0211) 320975* – . AE VISA JCB EZ
closed Sunday and Bank Holidays, except exhibitions – **Meals** (booking essential) à la carte 41/58.
◆ With its glass walls, this is an excellent place to stop during your stroll round town. Mediterranean atmosphere and food with an Italian touch.

La Lampada, Hüttenstr. 9, ✉ 40215, ☎ (0211) 37 47 92, *info@lalampada.de, Fax (0211) 377799*, – AE VISA EZ
closed Saturday lunch and Sunday – **Meals** à la carte 24/37.
◆ Diners are cordially invited to take their places at attractively-laid tables in this restaurant's refined setting. Fresh produce is the basis of the Italian cuisine.

Nippon Kan, Immermannstr. 35, ✉ 40210, ☎ (0211) 17 34 70, *nippon-kan@dnk.jis.de, Fax (0211) 3613625* – AE VISA JCB. BV
closed Easter, Christmas - New Year and Sunday – **Meals** (Japanese) (booking essential) 36/92 and à la carte 19/53.
◆ This is the place for enjoying Japanese delicacies in a totally authentic setting - ikebana, decorated tatami rooms, rice matting, cushions and low-slung tables.

Daitokai, Mutter-Ey-Str. 1, ✉ 40213, ☎ (0211) 32 50 54, *dus@daitokai.de, Fax (0211) 325056* – AE VISA JCB. DY z
closed 22 July - 4 September, Sunday and Bank Holidays, except exhibitions – **Meals** *(dinner only)* (Japanese) à la carte 31/54.
• Gastronomy Japanese-style : you sit at Teppan-yaki tables and watch the sizzling delicacies being prepared before your very eyes. Alternatively, try the Otaru sushi-bar.

Brewery-inns :

Zum Schiffchen, Hafenstr. 5, ✉ 40213, ☎ (0211) 13 24 21, *info.schiffchen@stockheim.de, Fax (0211) 134596*, – AE VISA DZ f
closed 23 December - 1 January, Sunday and Bank Holidays, except exhibitions – **Meals** à la carte 23/37,50.
• 350-plus years old, this venerable beer-hall serves traditional Rhineland dishes at well-scrubbed tables as well as in the famous and attractive beer garden.

at Düsseldorf-Angermund *North : 15 km by Danziger Straße AU :*

Haus Litzbrück, Bahnhofstr. 33, ✉ 40489, ☎ (0203) 99 79 60, *info@hotel-litzbrueck.de, Fax (0203) 9979653*, , , , – TV P – 30. AE VISA
Meals *(closed Monday, except exhibitions)* à la carte 23/39,50 – **22 rm** 69/78 – 85/150.
• Litzbrück stands in its own park in the idyllic landscape of the Lower Rhine. Guests are accommodated in an aristocratic edifice dating from the 1930s. Classic restaurant in a refined setting, charming side rooms. Garden terrace.

at Düsseldorf-Derendorf :

Villa Viktoria without rest, Blumenthalstr. 12, ✉ 40476, ☎ (0211) 46 90 00, *info@villaviktoria.com, Fax (0211) 46900601*, , – TV – 15. AE VISA JCB BU c
closed 23 December - 4 January – 19 – **40 suites** 155/270.
• This architectural gem from 1914 offers tastefully decorated suites to discerning guests. Garden terrace with a garland of columns.

Lindner Hotel Rhein Residence, Kaiserswerther Str. 20, ✉ 40477, ☎ (0211) 4 99 90, *info.rheinresidence@lindner.de, Fax (0211) 4999499*, , Massage, , – , rm, TV – 20. AE VISA ABU f
Meals à la carte 22,50/34,50 – 15 – **126 rm** 140/165.
• Close to the Rhine promenade and the Königsallee and no distance from the trade fair grounds, this establishment provides relaxation on its garden terrace as well as in its fitness centre. Contemporary restaurant with international cuisine.

Gildors Hotel without rest (with guest house), Collenbachstr. 51, ✉ 40476, ☎ (0211) 5 15 85 00, *mail@gildors-hotel.de, Fax (0211) 51585050* – TV . AE VISA BU n
54 rm 90/133 – 155/180.
• Close to the centre, this establishment has a spacious breakfast room with views into the courtyard. Trade fair grounds, main station and airport only minutes away.

Cascade without rest, Kaiserswerther Str. 59, ✉ 40477, ☎ (0211) 49 22 00, *info@hotel-cascade.de, Fax (0211) 4922022* – TV . AE VISA JCB. AU c
closed Christmas - early January – **29 rm** 78/82 – 93/101.
• Functional rooms with good facilities. Central location on the edge of the Old Town ideal for business people and tourists alike.

at Düsseldorf-Düsseltal :

Haus am Zoo without rest (with guest house), Sybelstr. 21, ✉ 40239, ☎ (0211) 6 16 96 10, *leyh@hotel-haus-am-zoo.de, Fax (0211) 61696169*, , (heated), – TV . AE VISA BU h
22 rm 85/110 – 98/128.
• Leafy setting in the middle of town, the site of the city zoo a century ago. Now a family-run establishment with a garden and secluded guest house.

at Düsseldorf-Golzheim :

Hilton, Georg-Glock-Str. 20, ✉ 40474, ☎ (0211) 4 37 70, *info_duesseldorf@hilton.com, Fax (0211) 43772519*, , Massage, , , – , rm, TV P – 800. AE VISA JCB. rest AU r
Meals à la carte 35,50/52 – 20 – **375 rm** 115/495 – 135/515.
• Completely rebuilt in 2003, this exclusive establishment presents its glittering new face to the world. Warm colour schemes add a touch of luxury to the bedrooms. Elegant restaurant.

Radisson SAS Hotel, Karl-Arnold-Platz 5, ✉ 40474, ☎ (0211) 4 55 30, *info.duesseldorf@radissonsas.com, Fax (0211) 4553110*, , Massage, , , , – , rm, – 450. AE VISA JCB. rest AU q
Meals à la carte 31/45 – 18 – **309 rm** 169 – 12 suites.
◆ The hotel boasts a 10th floor conference centre with a fabulous view over the city. Guests can relax in the Pool-Club with whirlpool bath, fitness centre and massage. Light and airy atmosphere in Le Jardin restaurant.

Rosati, Felix-Klein-Str. 1, ✉ 40474, ☎ (0211) 4 36 05 03, *Fax (0211) 452963*, – . AE VISA JCB. AU s
closed Saturday lunch and Sunday, except exhibitions – **Meals** (Italian) (booking essential) à la carte 36/48,50 – ***Rosatidue :*** **Meals** à la carte 26,50/37.
◆ Renzo and Remo Rosati have been treating their guests to classic Italian dishes for decades. Informal but elegant bistro-style atmosphere, comfortable furnishings, and an open kitchen add to the Rosati experience.

at Düsseldorf-Kaiserswerth *North : 10 km, by Kaiserswerther Straße* AU :

Barbarossa without rest, Niederrheinstr. 365, ✉ 40489, ☎ (0211) 4 08 09 20, *info@hotel-barbarossa.com, Fax (0211) 40809270*, – – 50. AE VISA
50 rm 92 – 119.
◆ All the rooms in this refurbished hotel have been delightfully decorated and furnished in Italian country-house style. Some boast splendid brass bedsteads.

Im Schiffchen (Bourgueil), Kaiserswerther Markt 9 (1st floor), ✉ 40489, ☎ (0211) 40 10 50, *restaurant.imschiffchen@t-online.de, Fax (0211) 403667* – AE VISA.
closed Holy Week, 3 weeks July - August, Sunday and Monday – **Meals** *(dinner only)* (booking essential) à la carte 67/89 , .
◆ The classically elegant "Schiffchen" is on the first floor of an historic high-gabled house. Some of the country's finest French cuisine.
Spec. Brachfeldfrüchte im Knoblauchsud. Mit Kamillenblüten gedämpfter Hummer. Bastilla von der Taube mit Schnepfenjus.

Bistro Jean-Claude im Schiffchen, Kaiserswerther Markt 9 (ground floor), ✉ 40489, ☎ (0211) 40 10 50, *restaurant.imschiffchen@t-online.de, Fax (0211) 403667* –
closed Holy Week, 3 weeks July - August, Sunday and Monday – **Meals** *(dinner only)* (booking essential) à la carte 35/46.
◆ White predominates in this informal version of the highly rated Schiffchen restaurant, where Maître Bourgueil offers international, French-influenced dishes.

at Düsseldorf-Lörick *West : 6 km, by Luegallee* AV *and Arnulfstraße :*

Fischerhaus , Bonifatiusstr. 35, ✉ 40547, ☎ (0211) 59 79 79, *fischerhaus@aol.com, Fax (0211) 5979759* – rm, . AE VISA
closed 22 December - 4 January – **Meals** see ***Hummerstübchen*** below – 8 – **41 rm** 80 – 105.
◆ This brick-built hotel enjoys a central but tranquil location in a leafy setting. Footpaths and yacht harbour right by the door.

Hummerstübchen (Nöthel) - Hotel Fischerhaus, Bonifatiusstr. 35, ✉ 40547, ☎ (0211) 59 44 02, *fischerhaus@aol.com, Fax (0211) 5979759* – . AE VISA
closed 27 December - 3 January, 8 to 23 August and Sunday, except exhibitions – **Meals** *(dinner only)* (booking essential) 87/105 and à la carte 65/79 .
◆ The "Lobster Parlour" is as good as its name, though Peter Nöthel and his team offer a whole variety of tempting and expertly prepared dishes in this elegant setting.
Spec. Hummer-Menu. Hummersuppe mit Champagner. Loup de mer mit Gewürzkruste und Gazpacho.

at Düsseldorf-Lohausen *North : 8 km, by Danziger Straße* AU :

ArabellaSheraton Airport Hotel, at the airport, ✉ 40474, ☎ (0211) 4 17 30, *airporthotel.duesseldorf@arabellasheraton.com, Fax (0211) 4173707* – , rm, – 120. AE VISA JCB
Meals à la carte 31,50/47,50 – 18 – **200 rm** 185/240 – 210/265.
◆ Whether you want to get a taste of the big wide world or are just passing through, this airport hotel is conveniently connected with both the arrival and departure halls. Semi-circular restaurant on two floors with splendid panoramic windows.

at Düsseldorf-Mörsenbroich :

Renaissance, Nördlicher Zubringer 6, ✉ 40470, ☎ (0211) 6 21 60, *rhi.dusrn.dos@renaissancehotels.com, Fax (0211) 6216666*, , Massage, , – , rm, – 260. AE VISA JCB BU e
Meals à la carte 21,50/39 – 17 – **244 rm** 129 – 8 suites.
◆ Secluded, private atmosphere in the sixth-floor Club. Active relaxation in the penthouse swimming-pool with a view over Düsseldorf's rooftops. Also sauna, solarium and steam bath. The restaurant opens out into the bright and airy reception hall.

at **Düsseldorf-Oberbilk** :

NH Düsseldorf, Kölner Str. 186, ✉ 40227, ☎ (0211) 7 81 10, *nhduesseldorf@nh-hotels.com, Fax (0211) 7811800*, Fa, ≘s – |‡|, ⇔ rm, ▤ TV ✆ ♿ ⇔ – 🏛 90. AE ⓓ MC VISA JCB BV b
Meals à la carte 21/41 – ☕ 15 – **338 rm** 105/285 – 125/305.
◆ With its central and very accessible location, this imposing glass-fronted atrium hotel is ideal for business travellers. All rooms with PC facilities. The foyer restaurant is the place for a buffet lunch.

at **Düsseldorf-Oberkassel** *West : 5 km, by Luegallee AV :*

Lindner Congress Hotel, Emanuel-Leutze-Str. 17, ✉ 40547, ☎ (0211) 5 99 70, *info.congresshotel@lindner.de, Fax (0211) 59971111*, ≘s, ⊠ – |‡|, ⇔ rm, ▤ TV ✆ ⇔ P – 🏛 240. AE ⓓ MC VISA JCB. ⛌ rest
Meals 22 *(buffet lunch)* and à la carte 23/37 – ☕ 15 – **254 rm** 130/140 – 140/150.
◆ Up-to-the-minute business establishment. Functional rooms with fax, modem and internet connection, some with PC. Conference facilities with the latest technology. Contemporary décor gives the Belle Etoile restaurant a bistro-like character.

Inn Side Residence, Niederkasseler Lohweg 18a, ✉ 40547, ☎ (0211) 52 29 90, *duesseldorf@innside.de, Fax (0211) 52299522*, 🏠, Fa, ≘s – |‡|, ⇔ rm, ▤ rest, TV ✆ ⇔ P. AE ⓓ MC VISA
Meals *(closed Sunday)* à la carte 27/40 – **126 rm** ☕ 146 – 180 – 6 suites.
◆ The hotel has been completely restyled to offer a fascinating experience in modern living, with creative design and discreet elegance characterising everything, from reception area to your own room. Contemporary restaurant in the style of a dining room.

Mercure Seestern, Fritz-Vomfelde-Str.38, ✉ 40547, ☎ (0211) 53 07 60, *h2199@accor-hotels.com, Fax (0211) 53076444*, 🏠, Fa, ≘s – |‡|, ⇔ rm, ▤ TV ✆ ♿ ⇔ – 🏛 120. AE ⓓ MC VISA JCB. ⛌ rest
Meals (Italian) à la carte 17/36 – **160 rm** ☕ 139/152 – 169/175.
◆ The spacious reception area sets the tone for the contemporary style which pervades the whole hotel. Everything a guest could want is provided in a warm and friendly atmosphere. First-floor restaurant with cool, modern décor.

Courtyard by Marriott, Am Seestern 16, ✉ 40547, ☎ (0211) 59 59 59, *courtyard.duesseldorf@courtyard.com, Fax (0211) 593569*, 🏠, ≘s, ⊠ – |‡|, ⇔ rm, ▤ TV ✆ ⇔ – 🏛 120. AE ⓓ MC VISA JCB
Meals à la carte 21,50/35 – **217 rm** ☕ 113/123 – 127/137.
◆ Spacious rooms offer every comfort as well as all the facilities a business traveller could wish for. Five non-smoking floors. Contemporary restaurant with international cuisine.

Novotel-City-West, Niederkasseler Lohweg 179, ✉ 40547, ☎ (0211) 52 06 00, *h3279@accor-hotels.com, Fax (0211) 52060888*, Fa, ≘s – |‡|, ⇔ rm, ▤ TV ✆ ♿ ⇔ – 🏛 275. AE ⓓ MC VISA
Meals à la carte 20/37 – ☕ 15 – **232 rm** 124/139 – 139/154.
◆ Opened in 2001, this functional, modern establishment is perfectly attuned to the needs of business travellers and conference participants.

Hanseat without rest, Belsenstr. 6, ✉ 40545, ☎ (0211) 57 50 60, *info@hotel-hanseat.de, Fax (0211) 589662* – TV. AE ⓓ MC VISA
closed 24 December - 3 January – **37 rm** ☕ 85/95 – 105/130.
◆ A touch of elegance behind a lovely Art Nouveau façade, with antique furniture and individual details enhancing comfortable rooms and public spaces. Attractive garden terrace.

De' Medici, Amboßstr. 3, ✉ 40547, ☎ (0211) 59 41 51, *demedici@aol.com, Fax (0211) 592612* – AE ⓓ MC VISA
closed Saturday lunch, Sunday and Bank Holidays – **Meals** (Italian) (booking essential) à la carte 27/54.
◆ Well-run by the Pocaterra family for many years. Personal recommendations complement the classically Italian written menu.

at **Düsseldorf-Pempelfort** :

Rossini, Kaiserstr. 5, ✉ 40479, ☎ (0211) 49 49 94, *info@restaurant-rossini.de, Fax (0211) 4910819*, 🏠 – ▤. AE ⓓ MC VISA JCB. ⛌ EY r
closed Sunday and Bank Holidays, except exhibitions – **Meals** (Italian) à la carte 48/63 ♀.
◆ Much-favoured meeting place, with gourmet Italian cuisine and superb wine cellar. Elegant atmosphere with terracotta tiling in modern business premises.

at **Düsseldorf-Unterbilk** :

Courtyard by Marriott, Speditionstr. 11, ✉ 40221, ☎ (0211) 4 93 90, *cy.dushf.sales.mgr@courtyard.com, Fax (0211) 49392000*, 🏠, Massage, Fa, ≘s – |‡|, ⇔ rm, ▤ TV ✆ ♿ ⇔ P – 🏛 90. AE ⓓ MC VISA JCB by Gladbacherstraße AX
Meals à la carte 28/34 – ☕ 14 – **139 rm** 125/140 – 6 suites.
◆ Opened in 2001, this establishment has a homely atmosphere thanks to the contemporary furnishings and warm earth-colours of the décor in rooms and suites.

Sorat, Volmerswerther Str. 35, ✉ 40221, ☎ (0211) 3 02 20, *duesseldorf@sorat-hotels.com, Fax (0211) 3022555*, – ▮, ✗ rm, ▤ TV ☎ – P – 135. AE ⓓ ⓜⓒ VISA JCB AX c
Meals *(closed Sunday, except exhibitions)* à la carte 24,50/31 – **160 rm** 118 – 148.
◆ Comfortable rooms with warm colours and up-to-the-minute design features may tempt you to linger longer in what used to be the port area and is now the media and administrative district. Bistro-style modern restaurant.

Berens am Kai, Kaistr. 16, ✉ 40221, ☎ (0211) 3 00 67 50, *info@berensamkai.de, Fax (0211) 30067515*, – AE ⓜⓒ VISA AX d
closed 1 to 7 January, Saturday lunch, Sunday and Bank Holidays – **Meals** 42 and à la carte 55/65.
◆ Thanks to an imposing glass façade and a harbourside location, diners choosing this up-to-the-minute establishment will enjoy a lovely view of the Rhine.

Schorn with rm, Martinstr. 46a, ✉ 40223, ☎ (0211) 3 98 19 72, *Fax (0211) 8766195* – TV ☎. ⓜⓒ. ✗ rm AX s
closed 1 week Easter and 3 weeks July - August – **Meals** *(closed Sunday and Monday) (dinner only)* (booking essential) à la carte 41/61 ♀, – **4 rm** 105 – 150.
◆ Fine French-inspired cuisine is served in what was once a patisserie near St Martin's Church. Prettily decorated rooms available for overnight guests.

Rheinturm Top 180, Stromstr. 20, ✉ 40221, ☎ (0211) 8 48 58, *rheinturm@gunnewig.de, Fax (0211) 325619*, ✻ Düsseldorf and Rhein (▮, charge) – ▤ – 40. AE ⓓ ⓜⓒ VISA JCB. ✗ AV a
Meals à la carte 34/53.
◆ It takes less than 60 seconds to whizz up to the 172-metre-high restaurant, which slowly rotates around its axis, giving you a superb all-round panorama.

at Düsseldorf-Unterrath *North : 7 km, by Ulmenstraße* BU :

Lindner Hotel Airport, Unterrather Str. 108, ✉ 40468, ☎ (0211) 9 51 60, *info.airport@lindner.de, Fax (0211) 9516516*, – ▮, ✗ rm, ▤ TV ☎ P – 120. AE ⓓ ⓜⓒ VISA JCB
Meals à la carte 25/37,50 – 16 – **201 rm** 99/109.
◆ Weary travellers can wing their way here and refuel in the fitness centre, which also offers hydrojet massage and a relaxation programme specially designed for frequent flyers. The restaurant opening onto the hall is contemporary in style.

Avidon without rest, Unterrather Str. 42, ✉ 40468, ☎ (0211) 95 19 50, *hotel@avidon.de, Fax (0211) 95195333* – ▮ ✗ TV ☎ P – 15. AE ⓓ ⓜⓒ VISA JCB
closed Christmas to New Year – **33 rm** 89/129 – 99/139.
◆ Rooms with high-quality contemporary décor and ample work-desks, well-located in relation to airport, trade fair grounds and city centre. 24-hour bar.

at Meerbusch-Büderich *Northwest : 7 km, by Luegallee* AV *and Neusser Straße* :

Landhaus Mönchenwerth, Niederlörricker Str. 56 (at the boat landing stage), ✉ 40667, ☎ (02132) 75 76 50, *contact@moenchenwerth.de, Fax (02132) 757638*, <, , beer garden – P – 25. AE ⓓ ⓜⓒ VISA
closed Monday – **Meals** *(weekdays dinner only)* à la carte 43/58.
◆ This modernised country house stands right on the Rhine. Contemporary, welcoming restaurant with subtle decor. Classic dishes are the order of the day.

Lindenhof, Dorfstr. 48, ✉ 40667, ☎ (02132) 26 64, *service@lindenhof-restaurant.de, Fax (02132) 10196*, – AE ⓜⓒ VISA JCB
closed 27 December - 3 January and Monday – **Meals** (booking essential for dinner) à la carte 27,50/40,50.
◆ Brick-built establishment with country-style interior and changing picture collection. Local dishes, served in summer in a little beer garden.

at Meerbusch - Langst-Kirst *Northwest : 14 km by Luegallee* AV *and Neusser Straße* :

Rheinhotel Vier Jahreszeiten , Zur Rheinfähre 14, ✉ 40668, ☎ (02150) 91 40, *info@rheinhotel-meerbusch.de, Fax (02150) 914900*, , beer garden, – ▮, ✗ rm ▤ TV ☎ P – 120. AE ⓓ ⓜⓒ VISA JCB
Bellevue *(closed October - March Monday) (dinner only)* **Meals** à la carte 33/43,50 – ***Orangerie :*** **Meals** 24,50 (only buffet lunch) – ***Langster Fährhaus*** *(closed January - March, April - December Monday)* **Meals** à la carte 26,50/31 – **75 rm** 113/128 – 133/148 – 3 suites.
◆ This country hotel stands right by the landing-stage on the Rhine opposite airport and trade fair grounds. Rooms have all amenities. The bright and elegant Bellevue restaurant is in the villa, while the Langster Fährhaus has a more earthy character.

Dortmund *Nordrhein-Westfalen* 543 L 6 – *pop.* 598 000 – *alt.* 87 *m.*
Düsseldorf 78.

at Dortmund-Syburg *Southwest : 13 km :*

La Table, Hohensyburgstr. 200 (at the casino), ✉ 44265, ✆ (0231) 7 74 07 37, *latable@westspiel.de, Fax (0231) 774077,* – P. AE VISA JCB.
closed 1 to 10 January, 3 weeks July - August, Monday - Tuesday and Bank Holidays –
Meals *(dinner only)* 68/108 and à la carte 64/83 ♀.
◆ A careful combination of tradition and modernity gives this establishment its special quality. Exquisite French cuisine and attentive service.
Spec. Tandoori gewürztes Rotbarbenfilet mit Bouillabaisse. Soufflierter St. Pierre mit Gänsestopfleber und Champagnerschaum. Filet vom kanadischen Bison mit Sauce Foyot und Gemüsefondue.

Essen *Nordrhein-Westfalen* 543 L 5 – *pop.* 600 000 – *alt.* 120 *m.*
Düsseldorf 37.

at Essen-Kettwig *South : 11 km :*

Résidence (Bühler) with rm, Auf der Forst 1, ✉ 45219, ✆ (02054) 9 55 90, *info@hotel-residence.de, Fax (02054) 82501,* – TV P. AE VISA
closed 1 to 10 January and 3 weeks August – **Meals** *(closed Sunday and Monday) (dinner only)* (booking essential) 101 and à la carte 64/89 ♀, – 14 – **18 rm** 99 – 125.
◆ Master-chef Bühler lords it over this splendid Art Nouveau villa. His creations are matched by fine silver and porcelain, flowers, and exemplary service.
Spec. Mit Gänseleber und Trüffel gefüllter Schmorapfel. Geräucherte Roulade von Saibling und Jakobsmuschel. Atlantik-Hummer mit dicken Bohnen.

Grevenbroich *Nordrhein-Westfalen* 543 M 3 – *pop.* 62 000 – *alt.* 60 *m.*
Düsseldorf 28.

Zur Traube (Kaufmann) with rm, Bahnstr. 47, ✉ 41515, ✆ (02181) 6 87 67, *zurtraube-grevenbroich@t-online.de, Fax (02181) 61122* – TV P. VISA. rm
closed 5 to 19 April, 20 July - 10 August, 23 December - 13 January – **Meals** *(closed Sunday - Monday)* (booking essential) 48 *(lunch)*/108 and à la carte 61/80 ♀, – **6 rm** 118 – 148/190.
◆ You will appreciate the classically elegant ambience of this temple to fine dining. Expertly made from the finest ingredients, your meal is served with impeccable style.
Spec. Terrine von Wildlachs und Hummer. Birnenravioli mit warmer Gänseleber in Sauternes. Variation von der Ananas mit Rumeis.

FRANKFURT ON MAIN (FRANKFURT AM MAIN) *Hessen* 543 P 10 – *pop.* 650 000 – *alt.* 95 *m.*

See : *Zoo*★★ FX – *Goethe's House (Goethehaus)*★ GZ – *Cathedral (Dom)*★ *(Gothic Tower*★★, *Choir-stalls*★, *Museum*★*)* HZ – *Tropical Garden (Palmengarten)*★ CV – *Senckenberg-Museum*★ *(Department of Palaeontology*★★*)* CV **M9** – *Städel Museum (Städelsches Kunstinstitut und Städtische Galerie)* ★★ GZ – *Museum of Applied Arts (Museum für Angewandte Kunst)*★ HZ – *German Cinema Museum (Deutsches Filmmuseum)*★ GZ **M7** – *Museum of Modern Art (Museum für moderne Kunst)*★ HY **M10**.

Frankfurt-Niederrad, Golfstr. 41 (by Kennedy-Allee CDX*), ✆ (069) 6 66 23 17 ; Frankfurt-Niederrad, Schwarzwaldstr. 127 (by Kennedy-Allee* CDX*), ✆ (069)96 74 13 53 ; Hanau-Wilhelmsbad, Wilhelmsbader Allee 32 (East : 12 km by Hanauer Landstraße* FX*), ✆ (06181) 8 20 71 ; Dreieich, Hofgut Neuhof (South : 13 km by A 661 and exit Dreieich), ✆ (06102) 32 70 10.*

Rhein-Main (Southwest : 12 km), ✆ (069) 69 00.

at Neu-Isenburg, Kurt-Schumacher-Str., (South : 7 km).

*Exhibition Centre (Messegelände) (*CX*), ✆ (069) 7 57 50, Fax (069) 75756433.*

Tourist Information, Main Station (Hauptbahnhof), ✉ (069) 21 23 88 00, Fax (069) 21237880. – *Tourist Information, im Römer, ✉ 60311, ✆ (069) 21 23 88 00, info@tcf.frankfurt.de,* Fax (069) 21237880.

ADAC, *Schillerstr. 12. – Berlin 537 – Wiesbaden 41 – Bonn 178 – Nürnberg 226 – Stuttgart 204.*

Plans on following pages

Steigenberger Frankfurter Hof, Am Kaiserplatz, ✉ 60311, ✆ (069) 2 15 02, *frankfurter-hof@steigenberger.de, Fax (069) 215900,* , Massage, – , rm, TV – 250. AE VISA JCB GZ e
Meals see ***Français*** below – ***Oscar's*** *(closed Sunday lunch)* **Meals** à la carte 30,50/39 – ***Iroha*** *(closed Sunday and Bank Holidays)* **Meals** 32/87 and à la carte – 24 – **332 rm** 375/425 – 425/475 – 10 suites.
◆ A lavish refurbishment has restored the old Steigenberger headquarters, the grand hotel of 1876, to its original glory, visible throughout. Eat in Oscar's in bistro-style, or orientally in the Iroha.

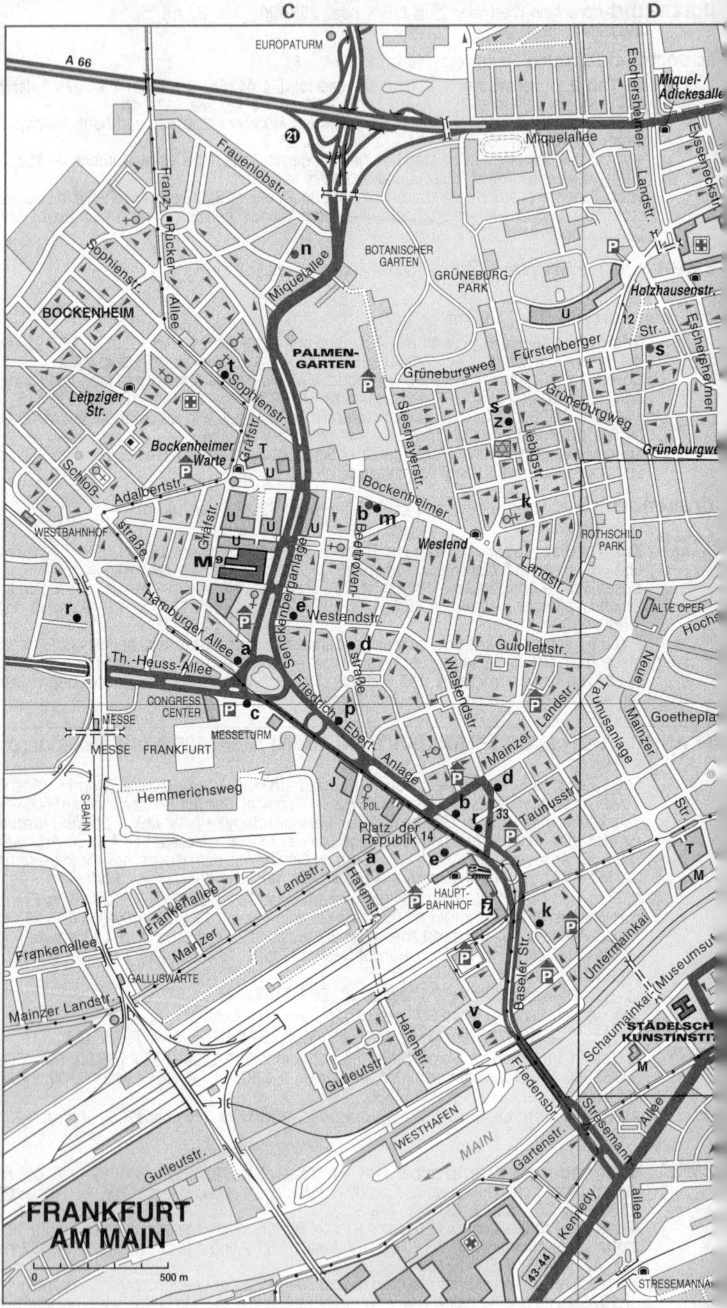

C
D
EUROPATURM
A 66
21
Miquel- / Adickesallee
Miquelallee
Eschersheimer Landstr.
Eysseneckstr.
Frauenlobstr.
Franz-Rücker-Allee
Sophienstr.
BOCKENHEIM
n
Miquelallee
BOTANISCHER GARTEN
GRÜNEBURG-PARK
Holzhausenstr.
12
Str.
s
Fürstenberger
Eschersheimer
V
PALMEN-GARTEN
Grüneburgweg
Grüneburgweg
Grüneburgweg
t
Sophienstr.
Leipziger Str.
Siesmayerstr.
s
z
Liebigstr.
Bockenheimer Warte
Gräfstr.
Schloß-straße
Adalbertstr.
WESTBAHNHOF
Gräfstr.
M[9]
Bockenheimer
b
m
Beethoven-straße
Westend
k
ROTHSCHILD PARK
Landstr.
r
Hamburger Allee
e
Westendstr.
Senckenberganlage
ALTE OPER
Hochs
a
d
Guiollettstr.
Th.-Heuss-Allee
Westendstr.
Neue Mainzer
Taunusanlage
CONGRESS CENTER
c
MESSE
Friedrich-Ebert-Anlage
p
Goethepla
Landstr.
MESSETURM
MESSE
FRANKFURT
Mainzer
J
d
Hemmerichsweg
S-BAHN
POL
b
r
33
Taunusstr.
Platz der Republik
14
Str.
a
e
T
Landstr.
Hafenstr.
M
Frankenallee
HAUPT-BAHNHOF
k
Frankenallee
Mainzer
Untermainkai
GALLUSWARTE
Baseler Str.
Museumsu
X
Mainzer Landstr.
v
Hafenstr.
Schaumainkai
STÄDELSCH KUNSTINSTI
M
Gutleutstr.
Friedensbr.
Stresemann-allee
WESTHAFEN
MAIN
Gutleutstr.
Gartenstr.
Kennedy
FRANKFURT AM MAIN
0
500 m
43-44
STRESEMANNA
C
D

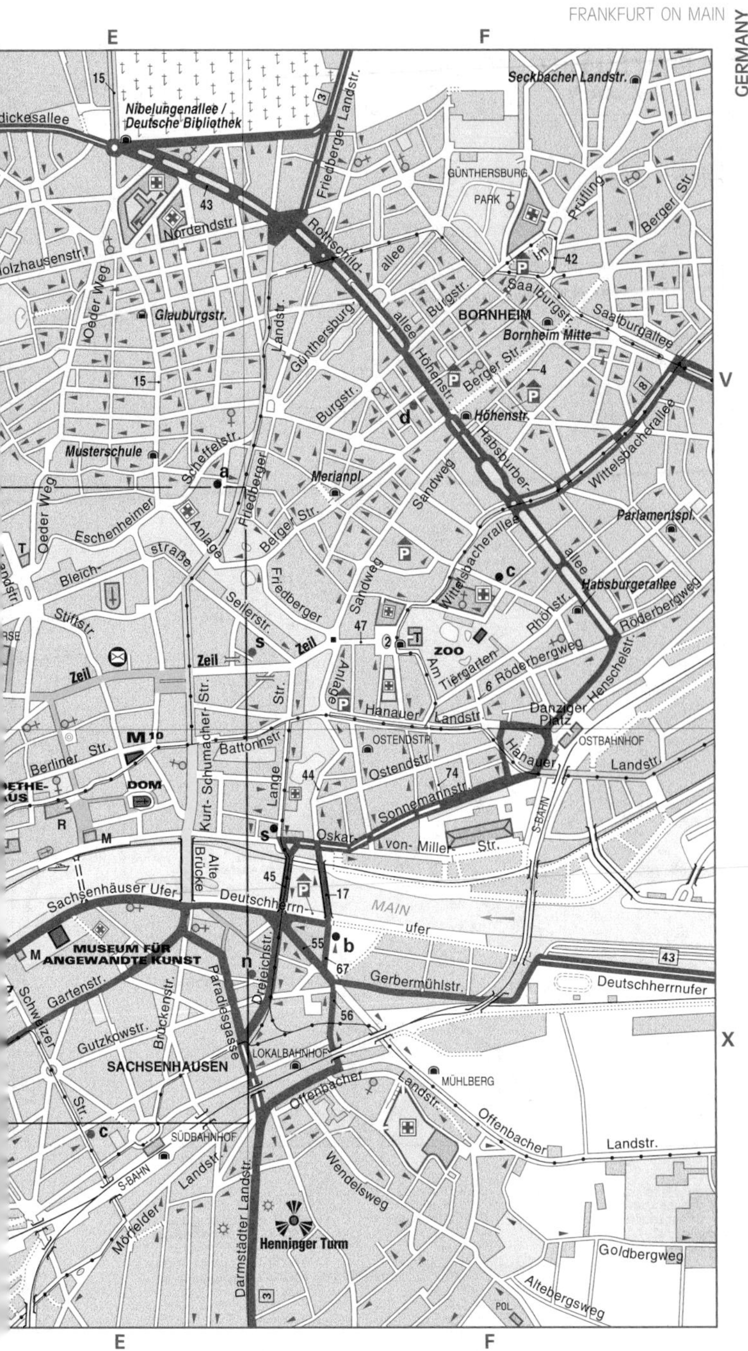
E
F
V
X
Nibelungenallee / Deutsche Bibliothek
Friedberger Landstr.
Seckbacher Landstr.
GÜNTHERSBURG PARK
Nordendstr.
Holzhausenstr.
Oeder Weg
Glauburgstr.
Rothschild-allee
Burgstr.
BORNHEIM
Bornheim Mitte
Saalburgallee
Berger Str.
Höhenstr.
Habsburgerallee
Wittelsbacherallee
Musterschule
Merianpl.
Sandweg
Parlamentspl.
Eschenheimer Anlage
Bleichstraße
Stiftstr.
Seilerstr.
Zeil
ZOO
Am Tiergarten
Röderbergweg
Hanauer Landstr.
Danziger Platz
OSTBAHNHOF
Henschelstr.
Berliner Str.
DOM
Kurt-Schumacher-Str.
Battonnstr.
Lange Str.
OSTENDSTR.
Ostendstr.
Sonnemannstr.
Oskar-von-Miller-Str.
Alte Brücke
MAIN
Sachsenhäuser Ufer
Deutschherrnufer
MUSEUM FÜR ANGEWANDTE KUNST
Gartenstr.
Brückenstr.
Paradiesgasse
Dreieichstr.
Gerbermühlstr.
Gutzkowstr.
SACHSENHAUSEN
LOKALBAHNHOF
Offenbacher Landstr.
MÜHLBERG
SÜDBAHNHOF
S-BAHN
Mörfelder Landstr.
Darmstädter Landstr.
Wendelsweg
Henninger Turm
Goldbergweg
Altebergsweg
POL.

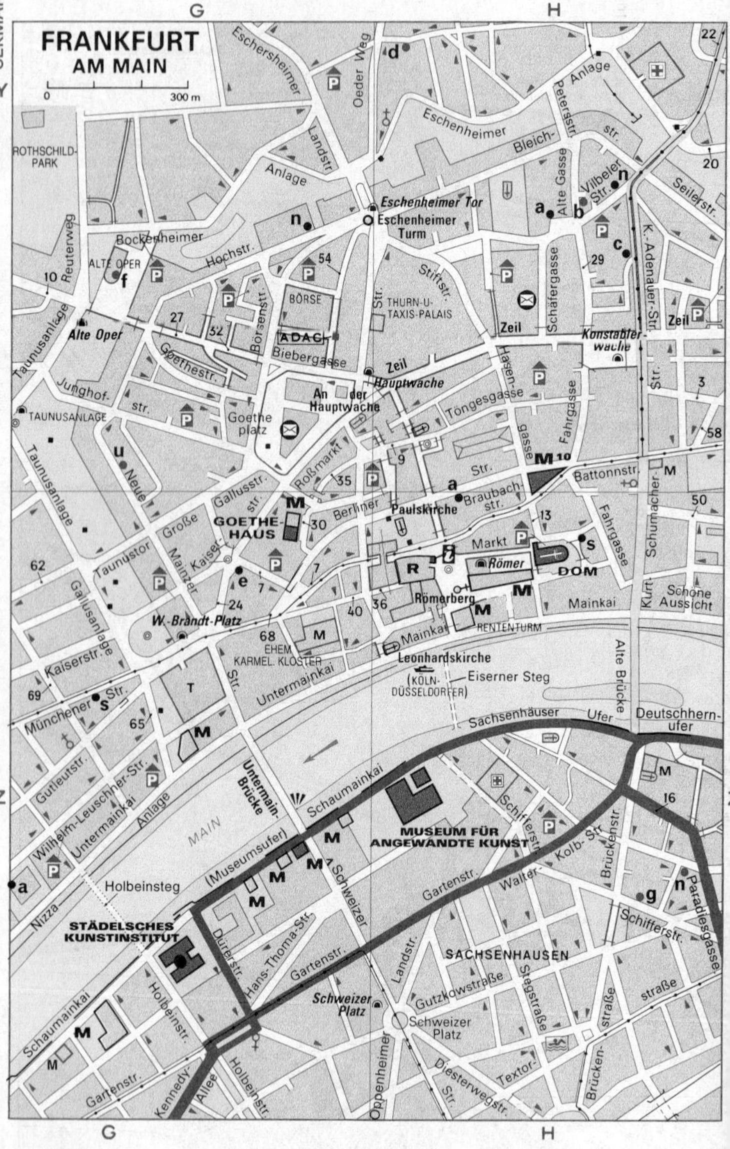
FRANKFURT
AM MAIN
0
300 m
G
H
Y
Z
ROTHSCHILD-PARK
Eschersheimer
Oeder Weg
Landstr.
Anlage
Eschenheimer
Bleich-
Anlage
Petersstr.
Str.
Alte Gasse
Vilbeler Str.
Seilerstr.
Eschenheimer Tor
Eschenheimer Turm
Bockenheimer
Hochstr.
ALTE OPER
Alte Oper
Reuterweg
Taunusanlage
BÖRSE
Börsenstr.
ADAC
Biebergasse
THURN-U-TAXIS-PALAIS
Stiftstr.
Zeil
Hauptwache
Schäfergasse
K. Adenauer-Str.
Konstabler-wache
Goethestr.
Junghof-str.
TAUNUSANLAGE
Goethe platz
An der Hauptwache
Töngesgasse
Hasen-gasse
Fahrgasse
Roßmarkt
Gallusstr.
Neue
Große
Mainzer
GOETHE-HAUS
Berliner
Paulskirche
Braubach-str.
Battonnstr.
Schumacher-
Kurt-
Markt
Römer
DOM
Römerberg
Mainkai
Schöne Aussicht
Taunustor
Kaiser-
Gallusanlage
W.-Brandt-Platz
EHEM KARMEL. KLOSTER
RENTENTURM
Mainkai
Leonhardskirche
(KÖLN-DÜSSELDORFER)
Eiserner Steg
Alte Brücke
Kaiserstr.
Münchener Str.
Untermainkai
Sachsenhäuser
Ufer
Deutschherrn-ufer
Gutleutstr.
Wilhelm-Leuschner-Str.
Untermainkai
Anlage
MAIN
Untermain-Brücke
Schaumainkai
(Museumsufer)
MUSEUM FÜR ANGEWANDTE KUNST
Schifferstr.
Kolb-Str.
Brückenstr.
Nizza
Holbeinsteg
STÄDELSCHES KUNSTINSTITUT
Dürerstr.
Hans-Thoma-Str.
Schweizer
Gartenstr.
Walter-
Schifferstr.
Paradiesgasse
SACHSENHAUSEN
Landstr.
Schweizer Platz
Gutzkowstraße
Stegstraße
straße
straße
Schaumainkai
Holbeinstr.
Schweizer Platz
Oppenheimer
Diesterwegstr.
Textor-
Brücken-
Gartenstr.
Kennedy-
Allee
Holbeinstr.
G
H

INDEX OF STREET NAMES IN FRANKFURT AM MAIN

Adalbertstr. .... **CV**
Adickesallee .... **EV**
Alfred-Brehm-Pl. .... **FV** 2
Allerheiligenstr. .... **HY** 3
Alte Brücke .... **HZ**
Alte Gasse .... **HY**
Altebergsweg .... **FX**
Am Tiergarten .... **FV**
An der Hauptwache .... **GHY**
Arnsburger Str. .... **FV** 4
Baseler Str. .... **CX**
Battonnstr. .... **HY**
Beethovenstr. .... **CV**
Berger Str. .... **FV**
Berliner Str. .... **GHZ**
Bethmannstr. .... **GZ** 7
Biebergasse .... **GY**
Bleichstr. .... **HY**
Bleidenstr. .... **HY** 9
Bockenheimer Anlage .... **GY**
Bockenheimer Landstr. .... **GY** 10
Braubachstr. .... **HZ**
Bremer Str. .... **DV** 12
Brückenstr. .... **HZ**
Burgstr. .... **FV**
Bärenstr. .... **FV** 6
Börsenstr. .... **GY**
Danziger Pl. .... **FV**
Darmstädter Landstr. .... **EFX**
Deutschherrnufer .... **HZ**
Diesterwegstr. .... **HZ**
Domstr. .... **HZ** 13
Dreieichstr. .... **FX**
Dürerstr. .... **GZ**
Düsseldorfer Str. .... **CX** 14
Eckenheimer Landstr. .... **EV** 15
Elisabethenstr. .... **HZ** 16
Eschenheimer Anlage .... **HY**
Eschersheimer Landstr. .... **GY**
Eysseneckstr. .... **DV**
Fahrgasse .... **HYZ**
Flößerbrücke .... **FX** 17
Frankenallee .... **CX**
Franz-Rücker-Allee .... **CV**
Frauenlobstr. .... **CV**
Friedberger Anlage .... **HY** 20
Friedberger Landstr. .... **HY** 22
Friedensbrücke .... **CX**
Friedensstr. .... **GZ** 24
Friedrich-Ebert-Anlage .... **CVX**
Fürstenberger Str. .... **CDV**
Gallusanlage .... **GZ**
Gartenstr. .... **GHZ**
Gerbermühlstr. .... **FX**
Goethepl. .... **GY**
Goethestr. .... **GY**
Goldbergweg .... **FX**
Gr. Bockenheimer Str. .... **GY** 27
Große Eschenheimer Str. .... **GY**
Große Friedbergerstr. .... **HY** 29
Große Gallusstr. .... **GYZ**
Großer Hirschgraben .... **GZ** 30
Gräfstr. .... **CV**
Grüneburgweg .... **CDV**
Guiollettstr. .... **CV**
Gunthersburgallee .... **FV**
Gutleutstr. .... **GZ**
Gutzkowstr. .... **HZ**
Habsburgerallee .... **FV**
Hafenstr. .... **CX**
Hamburger Allee .... **CV**
Hanauer Landstr. .... **FX**
Hans-Thoma-Str. .... **GZ**
Hasengasse .... **HY**
Hemmerichsweg .... **CX**
Henschelstr. .... **FV**
Hochstr. .... **GY**
Holbeinstr. .... **GZ**
Holzhausenstr. .... **EV**
Höhenstr. .... **FV**
Im Prüfling .... **FV**
Junghofstr. .... **GY**
Kaiserstr. .... **GZ**
Kalbächer Gasse .... **GY** 32
Karlstr. .... **CX** 33
Kennedy-Allee .... **GZ**
Kleiner Hirschgraben .... **GY** 35
Konrad-Adenauer-Str. .... **HY**
Kurt-Schumacher-Str. .... **HYZ**
Lange Str. .... **FX**
Leibigstr. .... **CV**
Limpurgergasse .... **HZ** 36
Mainkai .... **HZ**
Mainzer Landstr. .... **CVX**
Markt .... **HZ**
Miquelallee .... **CV**
Mörfelder Landstr. .... **EX**
Münchener Str. .... **GZ**
Münzgasse .... **GZ** 40
Neebstr. .... **FV** 42
Neue Mainzer Str. .... **GYZ**
Nibelungenallee .... **EFV** 43
Nizza Anlage .... **GZ**
Nordendstr. .... **EV**
Obermainanlage .... **FX** 44
Obermainbrücke .... **FX** 45
Oeder Weg .... **GY**
Offenbacher Landstr. .... **FX**
Oppenheimer Landstr. .... **HZ**
Oskar-von-Miller-Str. .... **FX**
Ostendstr. .... **FX**
Paradiesgasse .... **HZ**
Petersstr. .... **HY**
Pfingstweidstr. .... **FV** 47
Platz der Republik .... **CX**
Rechneigrabenstr. .... **HZ** 50
Reuterweg .... **GY**
Rhönstr. .... **FV**
Rothschildallee .... **FV**
Roßmarkt .... **GY**
Röderbergweg .... **FV**
Römerberg .... **HZ**
Saalburgallee .... **FV**
Saalburgstr. .... **FV**
Sachsenhäuser Ufer .... **HZ**
Sandweg .... **FV**
Schaumainkai .... **GHZ**
Scheffelstr. .... **FV**
Schifferstr. .... **HZ**
Schillerstr. .... **GY** 54
Schloßstr. .... **CV**
Schweizer Pl. .... **HZ**
Schweizer Str. .... **GHZ**
Schäfergasse .... **HY**
Schöne Aussicht .... **HZ**
Seehofstr. .... **FX** 55
Seilerstr. .... **HY**
Senckenberganlage .... **CV**
Siemensstr. .... **FX** 56
Siesmayerstr. .... **CV**
Sonnemannstr. .... **FX**
Sophienstr. .... **CV**
Stegstr. .... **HZ**
Stiffstr. .... **HY**
Stolzestr. .... **HY** 58
Stresemannallee .... **DX**
Taunusanlage .... **GY**
Taunusstr. .... **GZ** 62
Taunustor .... **GZ**
Textorstr. .... **HZ**
Theodor-Heuss-Allee .... **CV**
Töngesgasse .... **HY**
Untermainanlage .... **GZ** 65
Untermainbrücke .... **GZ**
Untermainkai .... **GZ**
Vilbeler Str. .... **HY**
Walter-Kolb-Str. .... **HZ**
Wasserweg .... **FX** 67
Weißfrauenstr. .... **GZ** 68
Wendelsweg .... **FX**
Weserstr. .... **GZ** 69
Westendstr. .... **CV**
Wilhelm-Leuschner-Str. .... **GZ**
Windeckstr. .... **FX** 74
Wittelsbacherallee .... **FV**
Zeil .... **HY**

Hessischer Hof, Friedrich-Ebert-Anlage 40, ✉ 60325, ☎ (069) 7 54 00, *info@hessischer-hof.com, Fax (069) 75402924* – lift, ✕ rm, ≡ TV ☎ ⇔ P – 🏛 110. AE ⓓ MC VISA JCB. ✕ rest CX p
Meals 26,50 *(lunch)*/46,50 and à la carte 42/52,50 – ☕ 19 – **117 rm** 213/263 – 258/331 – 3 suites.
• Exclusive antiques from the Prince of Hessen make a stay here a real experience. Contemporary rooms of great comfort and elegance will satisfy the most demanding guest. Sèvres porcelain and trompe l'oeil paintings lend the restaurant a special character.

ArabellaSheraton Grand Hotel, Konrad-Adenauer-Str. 7, ✉ 60313, ☎ (069) 2 98 10, *grandhotel.frankfurt@arabellasheraton.com, Fax (069) 2981810*, ⊛, Massage, Fö, ≘s, ⊡ – lift, ✕ rm, ≡ TV ☎ ⇔ – 🏛 280. AE ⓓ MC VISA. ✕ rest HY c
Meals à la carte 32/42 – ☕ 23 – **378 rm** 250/515 – 270/515 – 12 suites.
• Modern grand hotel with rooms and suites in decors ranging from Art Deco, Arabian and Asiatic to Bavarian. Roman "spa landscape" in the "Balneum Romanum". Giving onto the main hall, Atrium restaurant with open kitchen and food with a Mediterranean touch.

Hilton, Hochstr. 4, ✉ 60313, ☎ (069) 1 33 80 00, *sales_frankfurt@hilton.com, Fax (069) 13381338*, ⛱, Fö, ≘s, ⊡ – lift, ✕ rm, ≡ TV ☎ ♿ ⇔ – 🏛 300. AE ⓓ MC VISA JCB. ✕ GY n
Meals 28 *(buffet lunch)* and à la carte 32/43 – ☕ 24 – **342 rm** 299/374 – 3 suites.
• The fine old bathhouse in the ring of green around the city centre has been restored and integrated into this ultra-modern hotel, where it houses a unique fitness centre. "Fine American Style" is the motto of the Pacific Colours Restaurant.

Le Méridien Parkhotel, Wiesenhüttenplatz 28, ✉ 60329, ☎ (069) 2 69 70, *info.frankfurt@lemeridien.com, Fax (069) 2697884*, , Massage, Fá, ≘s – |‡|, ⇔ rm, ▤ TV ✆ ⇔ P – 🏛 180. AE ⓓ MC VISA JCB CX k
Meals à la carte 30/46 – ☐ 20 – **297 rm** 244/450.
◆ This hotel combines modernity and stylishness ; Business Class is functional and technologically perfect, while the rooms in the Art Nouveau Palais have been immaculately restored. Wide choice of dishes in the bistro-like Le Parc.

Marriott, Hamburger Allee 2, ✉ 60486, ☎ (069) 7 95 50, *info.frankfurt@marriotthotels.com, Fax (069) 79552374*, ≤ Frankfurt, Massage, Fá, ≘s – |‡|, ⇔ rm, ▤ TV ✆ ⇔ – 🏛 600. AE ⓓ MC VISA JCB. ⚘ rest CV a
Meals 21 *(buffet lunch)* and à la carte 24/48 – ☐ 20 – **588 rm** 145/235 – 10 suites.
◆ This skyscraper rises high into the clouds opposite the trade fair grounds. It features Frankfurt's biggest ballroom and bedrooms with broadband facilities. Enjoy specialities from the American South West in the Arizona restaurant.

Maritim, Theodor-Heuss-Allee 3, ✉ 60486, ☎ (069) 7 57 80, *info.fra@maritim.de, Fax (069) 75781000*, Massage, Fá, ≘s, ⊡ – |‡|, ⇔ rm, ▤ TV ✆ ♿ ⇔ – 🏛 210. AE ⓓ MC VISA JCB. ⚘ rest CVX c
Classico *(closed lunch Saturday and Sunday)* **Meals** à la carte 37/49 – ***SushiSho*** (Japanese) *(closed mid July - mid August)* **Meals** à la carte 25/45 – ☐ 20 – **543 rm** 250/440 – 295/485 – 24 suites.
◆ Standing among the skyscrapers of the city centre, this hotel offers fantastic views from its upper floors. Tall folk benefit from the extra long beds provided. International cuisine in the elegant Classico, seductive Oriental specialities in the SushiSho.

InterContinental, Wilhelm-Leuschner-Str. 43, ✉ 60329, ☎ (069) 2 60 50, *frankfurt@interconti.com, Fax (069) 252467*, Massage, Fá, ≘s, ⊡ – |‡|, ⇔ rm, ▤ TV ✆ ♿ – 🏛 400. AE ⓓ MC VISA JCB. ⚘ rest GZ a
Signatures : **Meals** à la carte 33/60 ♀ – ☐ 21 – **770 rm** 395/465 – 415/465 – 35 suites.
◆ Period furnishings, attractive colours and lovely materials give this hotel on the River Main its individual character. Wonderful city views from the 21st floor conference rooms. Signatures restaurant with warm and elegant decor. Smart conservatory.

Alexander am Zoo without rest, Waldschmidtstr. 59, ✉ 60316, ☎ (069) 94 96 00, *info@alexanderamzoo.de, Fax (069) 94960720*, ≘s – |‡| ⇔ TV ✆ ⇔ – 🏛 30. AE ⓓ MC VISA JCB FV c
59 rm ☐ 125 – 150 – 9 suites.
◆ Modern corner building with contemporary décor, not far from Frankfurt Zoo. During breaks from business meetings enjoy fine views of the city skyline from the hotel terraces.

An der Messe without rest, Westendstr. 104, ✉ 60325, ☎ (069) 74 79 79, *hotel.an.der.messe@web.de, Fax (069) 748349*, ⚘ – |‡| ▤ TV ✆ ⇔. AE ⓓ MC VISA JCB CV e
45 rm ☐ 123 – 149.
◆ Lacquered and gilded bedside tables, inlaid period furniture or gleaming modern veneers give each of the rooms in this establishment a highly individual character.

Palmenhof, Bockenheimer Landstr. 89, ✉ 60325, ☎ (069) 7 53 00 60, *info@palmenhof.com, Fax (069) 75300666* – |‡| TV ✆ P. AE ⓓ MC VISA JCB CV m
closed 24 December - 2 January – **Meals** see ***L'Artichoc*** below – ☐ 15 – **46 rm** 100/170 – 160/200.
◆ With a fascinating mixture of antique and modern furniture, each room here is unique. The rooms at the front have a fine view of old chestnut trees.

NH Frankfurt-City, Vilbelerstr. 2, ✉ 60313, ☎ (069) 9 28 85 90, *nhfrankfurtcity@nh-hotels.com, Fax (069) 928859100*, ≘s – |‡|, ⇔ rm, ▤ TV ✆ ♿ – 🏛 120. AE ⓓ MC VISA JCB. ⚘ rest HY n
Meals à la carte 22,50/37 – ☐ 17 – **256 rm** 130 – 8 suites.
◆ This well-run hotel is located in the city centre with the pedestrian zone just around the corner. Good technical facilities in the contemporary, comfortable rooms. First-floor restaurant with extensive buffet.

Villa Orange without rest, Hebelstr. 1, ✉ 60318, ☎ (069) 40 58 40, *contact@villa-orange.de, Fax (069) 40584100* – |‡| ⇔ TV ✆ – 🏛 25. AE ⓓ MC VISA EV a
38 rm ☐ 120/140 – 140/150.
◆ An establishment of real charm : behind the orange-coloured façade is a tasteful interior combining comfortable contemporary elegance with tradition.

Steigenberger MAXX Hotel, Lange Str. 5, ✉ 60311, ☎ (069) 21 93 00, *frankfurt@maxx-hotels.de, Fax (069) 21930599*, Fá – |‡|, ⇔ rm, ▤ TV ✆ ♿ ⇔ P – 🏛 120. AE ⓓ MC VISA JCB FX s
Meals à la carte 19/46 – ☐ 16 – **149 rm** 140/156 – 170/186.
◆ Opened in 2001, this hotel is particularly appreciated by business travellers. Tastefully decorated rooms with up-to-date technology, some with skyline views. Restaurant with open kitchen.

Imperial, Sophienstr. 40, ✉ 60487, ☎ (069) 7 93 00 30, *info@imperial.bestwestern.de, Fax (069) 79300388*, – ǀ, rm, P. AE VISA JCB CV t
closed Christmas - early January – **Meals** *(dinner only)* à la carte 18/28,50 – **60 rm** 120 – 149.
◆ Spacious air-conditioned rooms close to the Palmengarten park and only minutes on foot from the financial district, trade fair grounds, university and Metro. Shopping centre nearby. Cosy hotel restaurant with beer bar.

Mercure, Voltastr. 29, ✉ 60486, ☎ (069) 7 92 60, *h1204@accor-hotels.com, Fax (069) 79261606*, – rm, – 80. AE VISA JCB by Th.-Heuss-Allee CV
Meals à la carte 20/41 – **336 rm** 133/169 – 169/266 – 8 suites.
◆ Modern establishment facing the trade fair grounds. Spacious Club rooms on top floor. Long-term guests accommodated in the apartment block opposite.

Liebig-Hotel without rest, Liebigstr. 45, ✉ 60323, ☎ (069) 72 75 51, *hotelliebig@t-online.de, Fax (069) 727555* – . AE VISA. CV z
closed 22 December - 2 January – 12 – **20 rm** 103/152 – 128/179.
◆ Ask for a room on the second or third floor ; they have period English and Italian furniture as well as stylish traditional bathroom fittings.

Novotel Frankfurt City West, Lise-Meitner-Str. 2, ✉ 60486, ☎ (069) 79 30 30, *h1049@accor-hotels.com, Fax (069) 79303930*, – rm, P – 150. AE VISA JCB CV r
Meals à la carte 21/33 – 13 – **235 rm** 100/215 – 117/235.
◆ The functional rooms behind the modern façade of this corner hotel impress with their spacious and well-lit work facilities.

Bristol without rest, Ludwigstr. 15, ✉ 60327, ☎ (069) 24 23 90, *bristol-hotel@t-online.de, Fax (069) 251539* – – 20. AE VISA CX a
145 rm 55/65 – 70/85.
◆ Right by the main station and close to the city centre, this is an up-to-date establishment with modern rooms and all facilities for the business traveller.

InterCityHotel, Poststr. 8, ✉ 60329, ☎ (069) 27 39 10, *frankfurt@intercityhotel.de, Fax (069) 27391999* – rm, P – 80. AE VISA JCB CX e
Meals *(closed Saturday and Sunday lunch)* à la carte 17/26,50 – 13 – **384 rm** 110/197 – 134/244.
◆ With functionally designed interiors and bright, timeless furnishings, this hotel is located on the north side of Frankfurt's main station.

Plaza without rest, Esslinger Str. 8, ✉ 60329, ☎ (069) 2 71 37 80, *info@plaza-frankfurt.bestwestern.de, Fax (069) 237650* – P. AE VISA JCB CX v
closed Christmas - New Year – **45 rm** 105 – 148.
◆ What was once a social security centre now has a friendly and welcoming atmosphere with modern interiors in pale wood, well-crafted detailing and warmly coloured fabrics.

Atlantic without rest, Düsseldorfer Str. 20, ✉ 60329, ☎ (069) 27 21 20, *info@atlantic.pacat.com, Fax (069) 27212100* – . AE VISA JCB CX b
closed Easter and 19 December - 1 January – **60 rm** 80 – 100.
◆ Trendily designed reception area in sea-green. The theme is continued in the contemporary décor of the rooms with their brightly coloured bed-linen and pale green furniture.

Memphis without rest, Münchener Str. 15, ✉ 60329, ☎ (069) 2 42 60 90, *memphis-hotel@t-online.de, Fax (069) 24260999* – P. AE VISA GZ s
42 rm 90/110 – 110/130.
◆ In the middle of Frankfurt's trendy arts district, this designer hotel is a charming melange of forms and colours. The courtyard-facing rooms are very quiet.

Miramar without rest, Berliner Str. 31, ✉ 60311, ☎ (069) 9 20 39 70, *info@miramar-frankfurt.de, Fax (069) 92039769* – . AE VISA JCB HZ a
closed 23 December - 2 January – **39 rm** 90/120 – 120/140.
◆ Between the Römer and the Zeil shopping street, this hotel has well-kept, welcoming rooms with lovely dark furniture. Good technical features including internet connection.

Domicil without rest, Karlstr. 14, ✉ 60329, ☎ (069) 27 11 10, *info@domicil-frankfurt.bestwestern.de, Fax (069) 253266* – . AE VISA JCB CX d
closed Christmas - New Year – **67 rm** 105 – 142.
◆ Perfectly located for access to the airport by rail and underground and on foot to the trade fair grounds and main station.

Manhattan without rest, Düsseldorfer Str. 10, ✉ 60329, ☎ (069) 2 69 59 70, *manhattan-hotel@t-online.de, Fax (069) 269597777* – . AE VISA CX r
60 rm 85/110 – 100/130.
◆ Modern style throughout, from bright foyer with its parquet floor to smartly decorated rooms. Trade fair grounds, banks, cultural institutions all easily reached on foot.

Scala without rest, Schäfergasse 31, 60313, (069) 1 38 11 10, *info@scala.bestwestern.de, Fax (069) 284234* – HY a
40 rm 105 – 135.
◆ This is the place if you are looking for somewhere central to spend the night. Recently refurbished, the hotel has a contemporary look plus up-to-date technical facilities.

Atrium without rest, Beethovenstr. 30, 60325, (069) 97 56 70, *info@atrium.pacat.com, Fax (069) 97567100* – CV d
45 rm 99 – 129.
◆ Converted office building in a relatively quiet residential area, close to trade fair grounds, city centre and main station. Functional rooms with light-coloured furniture.

Am Dom without rest, Kannengießergasse 3, 60311, (069) 1 38 10 30, *info@hotelamdom.de, Fax (069) 283237* – HZ s
31 rm 85/95 – 110.
◆ Theatre people will find this city centre side street establishment very convenient. Ask for one of the rooms with a view of the Cathedral, the hotel's next-door neighbour.

Français - Hotel Steigenberger Frankfurter Hof, Am Kaiserplatz, 60311, (069) 21 51 18, *frankfurterhof@steigenberger.de, Fax (069) 215900* – GZ e
closed 7 weeks July - August, Sunday and Monday – **Meals** *(dinner only)* (booking essential) à la carte 49/61 ♀.
◆ The restaurant belonging to the imposing Frankfurter Hof grand hotel is a classically elegant institution, chandeliers and fine paintings giving it an aristocratic air.

Villa Merton, Am Leonhardsbrunnen 12, 60487, (069) 70 30 33, *jb@kofler-company.de, Fax (069) 7073820*, – CV n
closed 20 December - 15 January, Saturday, Sunday and Bank Holidays – **Meals** (booking essential) 28 *(lunch)*/72 and à la carte 49/68 ♀.
◆ Built in 1925 as an exclusive club for residents of the diplomatic quarter, this establishment is now a classically elegant restaurant for all to enjoy.
Spec. Marinierte Gänsestopfleber und gebackene Dörraprikosen-Knödel. Wolfsbarsch auf der Haut gebraten mit jungen Bohnenkernen. Knusprige Tarte von Zirusfrüchten mit Mangosorbet.

Tiger-Restaurant, Heiligkreuzgasse 20, 60313, (069) 92 00 22 25, *info@tigerpalast.com, Fax (069) 92002217*, (with variety-theatre) – FV s
closed 12 July - 25 August, Sunday and Monday – **Meals** *(dinner only)* (booking essential) à la carte 57,50/87,50 ♀ – ***Palast-Bistrot*** *(closed Monday) (dinner only)* **Meals** à la carte 33/42,50 ♀.
◆ This cellar bistro is a popular after-show rendezvous for theatre fans as well as for others who appreciate its artistic décor, creative cooking, and the cheerful atmosphere generated beneath its historic brick vaults.
Spec. Törtchen von Gänsestopfleber und Périgord-Trüffel mit glasierten Äpfeln. Gebratener Steinbutt mit Weinbergschnecken und jungem Lauch. Schokoladentarte mit Beeren.

Opéra, Opernplatz 1, 60313, (069) 1 34 02 15, *info@opera-restauration.de, Fax (069) 1340239*, – GY f
Meals à la carte 27/45 ♀.
◆ The old opera-house foyer with its parquet floor, plaster ceilings, wall decorations, and Art Nouveau chandeliers has been lavishly restored. Terrace with city views.

Aubergine, Alte Gasse 14, 60313, (069) 9 20 07 80, *Fax (069) 9200786* – HY b
closed 3 weeks July - August, Christmas - New Year, Saturday lunch, Sunday and Bank Holidays, except exhibitions – **Meals** (booking essential) 27 *(lunch)*/65 *(dinner)* and à la carte 45/54 ♀.
◆ This historic town mansion with its stained glass windows and modern art invites its guests to enjoy dishes with an Italian touch served on Versace tableware.

La Trattoria, Fürstenberger Str. 179, 60322, (069) 55 21 30, *info@latrattoria-ffm.de, Fax (069) 552130*, – DV s
closed 2 weeks mid June, 24 December - 4 January, Saturday and Sunday, except exhibitions – **Meals** (Italian) (booking essential) à la carte 49/59.
◆ Attractively-laid tables and competent service await diners in this Mediterranean-style restaurant in a corner building from the turn of the century.

L'Artichoc - Hotel Palmenhof, Bockenheimer Landstr. 91, 60325, (069) 90 74 87 71, *info@lartichoc.de, Fax (069) 90748772* – CV a
closed 24 December - 6 January, Saturday, Sunday and Bank Holidays – **Meals** 24 and à la carte 34/43 ♀.
◆ In the red-walled cellars of the Palmenhof Hotel, this restaurant serving fusion cuisine devotes itself to "Love of Kitchen and Cookery".

Main Tower Restaurant, Neue Mainzer Str. 52 (53th floor), ✉ 60311, ✆ (069) 36 50 47 77, *Fax (069) 36504871*, ≤ Frankfurt – |‡|. AE MC VISA. ⚘ GY u
closed Monday – **Meals** *(dinner only)* (booking essential) 49/90 and à la carte.
◆ High above the city roofs, diners eat in a cool contemporary setting, with floor-to-ceiling windows making the best of the views.

Gargantua, Liebigstr. 47, ✉ 60323, ✆ (069) 72 07 18, *gargantua@t-online.de, Fax (069) 71034695*, ☂ – AE ⓓ MC VISA CV s
closed 22 December - 8 January, Saturday lunch, Sunday and Bank Holidays – **Meals** (booking essential) 28 *(lunch)*/65 and à la carte 35/58.
◆ The small villa in the banking district houses an attractive restaurant with pretty table settings, wooden flooring and contemporary pictures. Cook-book collection on display.

Ernos Bistro, Liebigstr. 15, ✉ 60323, ✆ (069) 72 19 97, *Fax (069) 173838*, ☂ – AE MC VISA CV k
closed 3 weeks July - August, 20 December - 5 January, Saturday and Sunday – **Meals** (French) (booking essential) 31 *(lunch)* and à la carte 50/75 ♀.
◆ Bistro-style establishment with something of the countryside about it on the edge of Frankfurt's west end. Diners are treated to solid, tasty French cuisine.
Spec. Hausgemachte Gänsestopfleber "à la cuillère". Lammcarré mit Paprikaconfit und Tapenade. Gebratene Kirschen mit Pistazieneis und "Baba au Kirsch" (season).

Cyrano, Leibnizstr. 13, ✉ 60385, ✆ (069) 43 05 59 64, *info@cyrano-restaurant.de, Fax (069) 43055965*, ☂ – MC VISA. ⚘ FV d
Meals *(dinner only)* à la carte 34,50/44,50 ♀.
◆ Stone flooring, benches and chairs in dark wood and attractively laid tables create a pleasingly contemporary ambience, complemented by friendly and professional service.

Estragon, Jahnstr. 49, ✉ 60318, ✆ (069) 5 97 80 38, *Fax (069) 5978038* – AE MC VISA
closed end May - mid June and Sunday – **Meals** *(dinner only)* 28,50/45 and à la carte 32/39 ♀.
◆ This is an attractive and welcoming little bistro-style place, with warm colours and refined décor. Classic international dishes, some with a Mediterranean touch. HY d

Frankfurter Äppelwoilokale *(mainly light meals only)* :

Zum Rad, Leonhardsgasse 2 (Seckbach), ✉ 60389, ✆ (069) 47 91 28, *info@zum-rad.de, Fax (069) 47885057*, ☂ by Im Prüfling and Seckbacher Landstraße FV
closed 20 December - 15 January, Tuesday, November - March Monday - Tuesday – **Meals** *(weekdays open from 5.00 pm, Sunday and Bank Holidays from 3.00 pm)* à la carte 13/25.
◆ In the village of Seckbach, this 200-year old establishment boasts its own cider press, and guests can learn something of the secrets of Frankfurt's favourite tipple.

Klaane Sachsehäuser, Neuer Wall 11 (Sachsenhausen), ✉ 60594, ✆ (069) 61 59 83, *klaanesachse@web.de, Fax (069) 622141*, ☂ FX n
closed Sunday – **Meals** *(open from 4 pm)* à la carte 12/19.
◆ This earthy tavern has been making its own cider since 1876 and there's hearty Frankfurt food as well. You won't sit on your own here for very long !

Zum gemalten Haus, Schweizer Str. 67 (Sachsenhausen), ✉ 60594, ✆ (069) 61 45 59, *Fax (069) 6031457*, ☂ – VISA EX c
closed 2 weeks mid July, Monday and Tuesday, except exhibitions – **Meals** à la carte 10/19.
◆ In a setting of painted walls and ancient implements the drinkers down their mugs of cider which, miraculously, seem never to empty !

Fichtekränzi, Wallstr. 5 (Sachsenhausen), ✉ 60594, ✆ (069) 61 27 78, *Fax (069) 612778*, ☂ HZ n
Meals *(open from 5 pm)* à la carte 14/25.
◆ With its wooden benches and rustic décor this tavern has a particularly cheerful atmosphere. There are international dishes as well as cider and Frankfurt specialities.

at Frankfurt-Bergen-Enkheim *East : 8 km, by Wittelsbacherallee* FV :

Amadeus, Röntgenstr. 5, ✉ 60338, ✆ (06109) 37 00, *reservation@hotel-amadeus-frankfurt.de, Fax (06109) 370720*, ☂ – |‡|, ⇆ rm, ▤ TV ✆ ♿ ⇔ P – 🏛 100. AE MC VISA
Meals *(closed 22 December - 7 January)* à la carte 22/36 – ☕ 15 – **160 rm** 119/137 – 157.
◆ Modern, star-shaped conference hotel in the eastern part of the city with rooms in a contemporary version of Art Deco. Kitchenette apartments for longer stays.

at Frankfurt-Griesheim *West : 8 km, by Th.-Heuss-Allee* CV :

Courtyard by Marriott, Oeserstr. 180, ✉ 65933, ✆ (069) 3 90 50, *cy.fracv.sales@courtyard.com, Fax (069) 3808218*, ≘s, ▣ – |‡|, ⇆ rm, ▤ rest, TV ✆ P – 🏛 230. AE ⓓ MC VISA JCB
Meals à la carte 24,50/29 – ☕ 15 – **236 rm** 105/125.
◆ Well-located in the green belt between airport and city centre. The 12th floor has a fitness centre and terrace with superb views of the Frankfurt skyline.

at Frankfurt-Höchst *West : 10 km, by Mainzer Landstraße CX :*

Lindner Congress Hotel, Bolongarostr. 100, ✉ 65929, ☎ (069) 3 30 02 00, *info.frankfurt@lindner.de, Fax (069) 33002999*, rm, – 160. AE VISA JCB. rest
Meals à la carte 25/39 – 18 – **285 rm** 155 – 180.
◆ This hotel prides itself on its technical amenities and all its rooms are well-equipped with internet access and the very latest in on-line facilities.

at Frankfurt-Niederrad *Southwest : 6 km, by Kennedy-Allee CDX :*

ArabellaSheraton Congress Hotel, Lyoner Str. 44, ✉ 60528, ☎ (069) 6 63 30, *congress@arabellasheraton.com, Fax (069) 6633667*, rm, – 290. AE VISA JCB
Meals à la carte 21,50/41,50 – **396 rm** 205/345 – 240/370 – 4 suites.
◆ Optimal business location in the Niederrad office district, plus a combination of professional conference facilities and comfortable accommodation. Frankfurt's vast city-forest right at the door. Two restaurants serving à la carte international dishes.

Holiday Inn, Isenburger Schneise 40, ✉ 60528, ☎ (069) 6 78 40, *info.hi frankfurt-airportnorth@queensgruppe.de, Fax (069) 6784190*, beer garden, Massage, rm, – 250. AE VISA JCB
Meals à la carte 23/35,50 – 17 – **295 rm** 138/297 – 178/322.
◆ In a green setting in the middle of Germany's most extensive city-forest, this conference hotel has an enviable location midway between the airport and the centre of Frankfurt. Rooms with cherrywood furnishings, contemporary restaurant, and English-style bar.

Weidemann, Kelsterbacher Str. 66, ✉ 60528, ☎ (069) 67 59 96, *weidemann@t-online.de, Fax (069) 673928*, – AE VISA by Gartenstraße CX
closed Easter, Saturday lunch, Sunday and Bank Holidays – **Meals** (booking essential) 28 *(lunch)* and à la carte 40/59 ♀.
◆ Angelo Vega has realised his dream of his own restaurant and offers diners international fare prepared according to traditional recipes in a stylish and welcoming ambience.

at Frankfurt-Rödelheim : *Northwest : 10 km by Leipziger Straße CV and Rödelheimer Landstraße :*

Osteria Enoteca, Arnoldshainer Str. 2/corner of Lorscher Straße, ✉ 60489, ☎ (069) 7 89 22 16, *Fax (069) 7892216*, – AE VISA.
closed 22 December - 7 January, Saturday lunch, Sunday and Bank Holidays – **Meals** 50/65 and à la carte 47/69 ♀.
◆ Ring the bell to gain entry to this stylish establishment, sit yourself down, and let yourself be treated to expertly prepared Italian delicacies.
Spec. Conchiglie di S.Jacobo e Canneloni di salsiccia con Cipolle di Tropea. Paccheri di Gragnano alla Sorrentina. Rombo con pappa di sedano e fumet di pesce.

at Frankfurt-Sachsenhausen :

Main Plaza, Walther-von-Cronberg Platz 1, ✉ 60594, ☎ (069) 66 40 10, *info@main-plaza.com, Fax (069) 604014408*, Skyline, rm, – 50. AE VISA JCB. rest FX b
Meals see ***Brick Fine Dining*** below – ***Rivercafé*** **: Meals** à la carte 29/35 – 19 – **131 rm** 165/225 – 225/460.
◆ The silhouette of this red-brick skyscraper is reminiscent of 1930s New York. Inside are stylish and luxurious suites, all-embracing service, and a health club. Dine in the relaxed surroundings of the bistro-style River-Café on the banks of the Main.

Holiday Inn, Mailänder Str. 1, ✉ 60598, ☎ (069) 6 80 20, *info.hifrankfurt-citysouth@queensgruppe.de, Fax (069) 6802333*, rm, – 200. AE VISA JCB by Darmstädter Landstraße (B 3) FX
Meals à la carte 27/52 – 18 – **436 rm** 160/220 – 195/255.
◆ Bright rooms with cherrywood décor await guests opposite the Henninger office tower. There is a superb panorama of the city from the 25th floor. The elegant Le Chef restaurant offers international cuisine.

Brick Fine Dining - Hotel Main Plaza, Walther-von-Cronberg-Platz 1, ✉ 60594, ☎ (069) 66 40 10, *info@main-plaza.com, Fax (069) 664014408*, – AE VISA JCB. FX b
closed Saturday and Sunday – **Meals** *(dinner only)* 69/89 and à la carte ♀.
◆ This elegant, contemporary restaurant is to be found at basement level in the Main Plaza. The open kitchen gives diners an insight into the creative cooking practised here.
Spec. Marinierte Gänseleber mit karamellisierter Thai-Mango. Gebratener Wolfsbarsch mit Blumenkohl-Couscous und Blutwurst. Limousin-Lamm mit lauwarmen Antipasti-Gemüsen und kleiner Kartoffelpizza.

Maingaustuben, Schifferstr. 38, ✉ 60594, ☎ (069) 61 07 52, *maingau@t-online.de*, *Fax (069) 61995372* – AE ⓓ MC VISA JCB HZ g
closed end July - early August, Saturday lunch, Sunday dinner and Monday – **Meals** 11,50 *(lunch)* and à la carte 22/37 ♀.
◆ Enjoy tasty international delicacies in an elegant, contemporary setting, then stroll along the nearby Museum Embankment or visit Frankfurt's famous "cider district".

at Eschborn *Northwest : 12 km by A66* **CV** *:*

Mercure, Frankfurter Str. 71 (at industrial area south), ✉ 65760, ☎ (06196) 7 79 00, *h3128@accor-hotels.com, Fax (06196) 7790500* – rm, – 60. AE ⓓ MC VISA. rest
Meals à la carte 20,50/38,50 – 13 – **125 rm** 108/220 – 118/230.
◆ This modern, functional building with its domed atrium is located in a business area and provides impeccable service. The attractive bistro-style restaurant has a light and airy atmosphere.

Novotel, Helfmann-Park 10, ✉ 65760, ☎ (06196) 90 10, *h0491@accor-hotels.com, Fax (06196) 482114*, (heated), – rm, P – 200. AE ⓓ MC VISA
Meals à la carte 19/35 – 13 – **224 rm** 99/220 – 114/235.
◆ Spacious and functional rooms help guarantee a good night's rest. Families with children will appreciate the hotel's own pool, sunbathing lawn and play area.

Dorint, Philipp-Helfmannstr. 20, ✉ 65760, ☎ (06196) 9 69 70, *info.fraesc@dorint.de, Fax (06196) 9697100*, – rm, P – 100. AE ⓓ MC VISA
Meals 22 and à la carte 22/38 – 14 – **179 rm** 101/131 – 116/146.
◆ New, functional building and rooms with contemporary décor, particularly suitable for business travellers. Bistro-style Olive Tree restaurant with lavish buffet.

at Neu-Isenburg - Gravenbruch *Southeast : 11 km by Darmstädter Landstraße* **FX** *and B 459 :*

Kempinski Hotel Gravenbruch, An der Bundesstraße 459, ✉ 63263, ☎ (06102) 30 06 50, *reservations.gravenbruch@kempinski.com, Fax (06102) 30065199*, Massage, (heated), – rm, P – 350. AE ⓓ MC VISA JCB. rest
Meals 39/45 and à la carte ♀ – ***L'olivo*** (Italian) *(closed Saturday - Sunday) (dinner only)* **Meals** à la carte 24/33 – 22 – **283 rm** 285/425 – 365/450 – 15 suites.
◆ The winter garden overlooking the hotel's private lake is an experience in itself. This former country estate is still set in idyllic parkland and has spacious rooms and luxurious suites.

near Rhein-Main airport *Southwest : 12 km by Kennedy-Allee* **CX** *:*

Sheraton, Hugo-Eckener-Ring 15 (terminal 1), ✉ 60549 *Frankfurt*, ☎ (069) 6 97 70, *reservationsfrankfurt@sheraton.com, Fax (069) 69772209*, Massage, – rm, – 700. AE ⓓ MC VISA JCB. rest
Flavors : **Meals** à la carte 35/50 – ***Taverne*** *(closed Saturday and Sunday) (dinner only)* **Meals** à la carte 32/43 – **1006 rm** 310/575 – 345/610 – 28 suites.
◆ From table to plane or from jet to bed, this functional, soundproofed hotel is only separated by a glass bridge from the airport terminal. Varied international cuisine in Flavors. Grill and show-kitchens in the Taverne.

Steigenberger Esprix Hotel, Cargo City Süd, ✉ 60549 *Frankfurt*, ☎ (069) 69 70 99, *frankfurt@esprix-hotels.de, Fax (069) 69709444*, – rm, P – 100. AE ⓓ MC VISA JCB
Meals 22 *(buffet)* and à la carte 23/32 – 16 – **360 rm** 139/229 – 159/319.
◆ Cool, no frills design in soundproofed, spacious rooms whose functional décor does not prevent them from being comfortable and welcoming. The restaurant welcomes diners into its colourful, contemporary ambience.

Write to us...
If you have any comments on the contents of this Guide.
Your praise as well as your criticisms will receive careful consideration and, with your assistance, we will be able to add to our stock of information and, where necessary, amend our judgments.
Thank you in advance!

HAMBURG L *Stadtstaat Hamburg* 541 F 14 – *pop.* 1 700 000 – *alt.* 10 m.

See : *Jungfernstieg*★ GY – *Außenalster*★★★ GHXY – *Hagenbeck Zoo (Tierpark Hagenbeck)*★★ *by Schröderstiftstr.* EX – *Television Tower (Fernsehturm)*★ (✳★★) EX – *Fine Arts Museum (Kunsthalle)*★★ HY **M1** – *St. Michael's church (St. Michaelis)*★ *(tower* ✳★*)* EFZ – *Stintfang* (⩽★) EZ – *Port (Hafen)*★★ EZ – *Decorative Arts and Crafts Museum (Museum für Kunst und Gewerbe)*★ HY **M2** – *Historical Museum (Museum für Hamburgische Geschichte)*★ EYZ **M3** – *Communications Museum*★ FY **M4** – *Planten und Blomen Park*★ EFX – *Museum of Ethnography (Hamburgisches Museum für Völkerkunde)*★ *by Rothenbaumchaussee* FX.

Envir. : *Altona : Northern Germany Museum (Norddeutsches Landesmuseum)*★★ *by Reeperbahn* EZ – *Altona Balcony (Altonaer Balkon)* ⩽★ *by Reeperbahn* EZ – *Elbchaussee*★ *by Reeperbahn* EZ.

18 Hamburg-Blankenese, Falkenstein, In de Bargen 59 (West : 17 km), ☎ (040) 81 21 77 ; 18 Hamburg-Lehmsahl, Treudelberg, Lemsahler Landstr. 45 (North : 16 km), ☎ (040) 60 82 25 00 ; 27 Hamburg-Wendlohe, Oldesloer Str. 251 (North : 14 km), ☎ (040) 5 52 89 66 ; 18 Wentorf-Reinbek, Golfstr. 2 (Southeast : 20 km), ☎ (040) 72 97 80 68.

Hamburg-Fuhlsbüttel (North : 15 km), ☎ (040) 5 07 50.

Hamburg-Altona, Präsident-Krahn-Straße.

Exhibition Centre (Messegelände), St. Petersburger Str. 1 (EFX)*, ☎ (040) 3 56 90, Fax (040)35692180.*

Tourist-Information im Hauptbahnhof, ✉ 20099, ☎ (040) 30 05 13 00.

Tourist-Information am Hafen, Landungsbrücke 4-5, ✉ 20459, ☎ (040) 30 05 12 03, Fax (040) 313578.

ADAC, *Amsinckstr. 39.*

Berlin 284 – Bremen 120 – Hannover 151.

Plans on following pages

Town centre : Eimsbüttel, Harvestehude, Rotherbaum, Uhlenhorst

Vier Jahreszeiten, Neuer Jungfernstieg 9, ✉ 20354, ☎ (040) 3 49 40, *emailus.hvj@raffles.com, Fax (040) 34942600*, ⩽ Binnenalster, Massage, – 110. AE VISA JCB. GY v
Meals see ***Haerlin*** below – ***Doc Cheng's*** (Euro-Asian) *(closed Monday, lunch Saturday and Sunday)* **Meals** à la carte 35/47 – ***Jahreszeiten Grill* : Meals** à la carte 49/53 – 22 – **156 rm** 215/290 – 265/340 – 11 suites.
♦ On the banks of the Innenalster, this is one of the last truly grand Grand Hotels, where luxurious late 19C ambience blends with modern comfort. Doc Cheng's offers a wonderful combination of Eastern and Western cuisine, while the Grill is classically elegant.

Kempinski Hotel Atlantic, An der Alster 72, ✉ 20099, ☎ (040) 2 88 80, *hotel.atlantic@kempinski.com, Fax (040) 247129*, ⩽ Außenalster, , Massage, , – rm, – 220. AE VISA JCB. rest HY a
Meals *(closed Sunday lunch)* 29 (lunch) and à la carte 45/72 – 22 – **252 rm** 250/390 – 290/430 – 11 suites.
♦ The "White Giant" has been a rendezvous of city society since 1909. Rooms with stucco ceilings and period furnishings, some with a view of the Alster. Restaurant with tasteful, elegant ambience. Attractive courtyard terrace.

Park Hyatt, Bugenhagenstr. 8, ✉ 20095, ☎ (040) 33 32 12 34, *hamburg@hyatt.de, Fax (040) 33321235*, , , Massage, , , – rm, – 120. AE VISA JCB. HYZ t
Apples *(closed lunch Saturday and Sunday)* **Meals** à la carte 42/67 – 22 – **252 rm** 185 – 210 – 21 suites.
♦ The Hyatt occupies a classic Hamburg brick building. Inside is a coolly elegant world of precious fabrics, Canadian cherrywood, and bathrooms designed by Philippe Starck. Stylish modernity gives Apples its inimitable charms.

Le Royal Méridien, An der Alster 52, ✉ 20099, ☎ (040) 2 10 00, *info.lrmhamburg@lemeridien.com, Fax (040) 21001111*, Massage, , , – rm, – 200. AE VISA JCB. rest HY d
Meals 29/39 and à la carte 35/69 ♀ – 19 – **284 rm** 195/315 – 255/345 – 37 suites.
♦ Exclusive atmosphere throughout, from the spacious foyer to the tastefully decorated rooms combining hi-tech facilities and contemporary art. The 8th-floor Le Ciel restaurant offers fantastic views over the Außenalster lake.

Dorint, Alter Wall 40, ✉ 20457, ☎ (040) 36 95 00, *info.hamalt@dorint.com, Fax (040) 36951000*, , , Massage, , , – rm, – 350. AE VISA JCB. rest FZ g
Meals à la carte 35/48 – 19 – **241 rm** 175/240 – 205/250 – 16 Suites.
♦ Designer hotel in an old postal bank on a waterway. Interior a fascinating mixture of marble, exposed concrete, fine veneers and modern technology. Restaurant an example of "opulent Purism".

Steigenberger, Heiligengeistbrücke 4, ⊠ 20459, ☏ (040) 36 80 60, *hamburg@steigenberger.de, Fax (040) 36806777,* – |♦|, ⇹ rm, ▤ TV ☏ ♿ – 🧑‍🏫 180. AE ⓓ MC VISA JCB. ✗ rest FZ s

Calla *(closed 24 June - 4 August, 1 week early January, Monday, Sunday and Bank Holidays) (dinner only)* **Meals** à la carte 29/48 – ***Bistro am Fleet*** **: Meals** à la carte 21/33 – ☕ 18 – **234 rm** 175/220 – 201/246 – 4 suites.

• Dream location on the Alster Canal. Elegant establishment with a splendid red-brick façade. Conference rooms overlooking Hamburg's rooftops. Calla with a mix of European and Oriental flavours plus views of passing pleasure steamers. Bistro for those in a rush.

InterContinental, Fontenay 10, ⊠ 20354, ☏ (040) 4 14 20, *hamburg@interconti.com, Fax (040) 41422299,* ≤ Hamburg and Alster, Massage, – |♦|, ⇹ rm, ▤ TV P – 🧑‍🏫 300. AE ⓓ MC VISA JCB GX r

Windows *(closed Sunday) (dinner only)* **Meals** à la carte 51/75 ♀ – ***Signatures*** **: Meals** à la carte 21/37 – ☕ 19 – **281 rm** 180/250 – 12 suites.

• Beautifully located on the Alster, this hotel combines refined ambience with international flair and contemporary-style functional rooms. Wonderful panorama from the elegant Windows restaurant on the 9th floor. Bright and airy Signatures wintergarden.

Renaissance Hamburg Hotel, Große Bleichen, ⊠ 20354, ☏ (040) 34 91 80, *rhi.hamrn.doms@renaissancehotels.com, Fax (040) 34918919,* – |♦|, ⇹ rm, ▤ TV ☏ P – 🧑‍🏫 90. AE ⓓ MC VISA JCB. ✗ rest FY e

Meals à la carte 26/35 – ☕ 18 – **205 rm** 195/240.

• Tradition plus up-to-the-minute elegance. The old brick edifice with its wrought-iron balconies has spacious rooms with contemporary décor in warm shades of red, yellow, and orange. Restaurant with show-kitchen and bar area.

Elysée, Rothenbaumchaussee 10, ⊠ 20148, ☏ (040) 41 41 20, *info@elysee-hamburg.de, Fax (040) 41412733,* Massage, – |♦|, ⇹ rm, ▤ TV ☏ ♿ – 🧑‍🏫 325. AE ⓓ MC VISA JCB FX m

Piazza Romana (Italian) **Meals** à la carte 29/44 – ***Brasserie*** **: Meals** à la carte 20/31 – ☕ 15 – **305 rm** 138 – 158 – 4 suites.

• Sophisticated establishment with classic elegance and comfortable rooms. Library in the style of an English gentleman's club with international newspapers. The Italian restaurant serves fine cuisine in a Mediterranean atmosphere. Brasserie with Parisian flair.

SIDE, Drehbahn 49, ⊠ 20354, ☏ (040) 30 99 90, *info@side-hamburg.de, Fax (040) 30999399,* Massage, – |♦|, ⇹ rm, ▤ TV ☏ ♿ – 🧑‍🏫 160. AE ⓓ MC VISA FY h

Meals à la carte 29/44 – ☕ 19 – **178 rm** 180 – 205 – 10 suites.

• This is a newly built hotel with a far from everyday décor by Matteo Thun. Rooms and suites are spacious and have the latest technical facilities. Cool lines and minimalist décor set the tone in the Fusion restaurant.

Marriott, ABC-Str. 52, ⊠ 20354, ☏ (040) 3 50 50, *hamburg.marriott@marriotthotels.com, Fax (040) 35051777,* Massage, – |♦|, ⇹ rm, ▤ TV ☏ ♿ – 🧑‍🏫 150. AE ⓓ MC VISA FY b

Meals 17,50 *(buffet lunch)* and à la carte 25/46 – ☕ 18 – **277 rm** 179/217 – 5 suites.

• Right on Hamburg's Gänsemarkt (Goose Market), comfortable rooms brightly refurbished with colourful fabrics and Italian period furniture. Let yourself be tempted in the extraordinarily long American Place restaurant.

Europäischer Hof, Kirchenallee 45, ⊠ 20099, ☏ (040) 24 82 48, *info@europaeischer-hof.de, Fax (040) 24824799,* Massage, Squash – |♦|, ⇹ rm, ▤ rest, TV ☏ – 🧑‍🏫 200. AE ⓓ MC VISA. ✗ HY e

Meals *(closed Sunday - Monday) (Tuesday - Thursday dinner only)* à la carte 28/41 – ***Paulaner's*** **: Meals** à la carte 16/25 – **320 rm** ☕ 103/171 – 133/183.

• Luxurious rooms with warm colours and lovely veneers. The leisure area features a splendid six-storey high waterslide. Paulaners has a touch of country style.

Crowne Plaza, Graumannsweg 10, ⊠ 22087, ☏ (040) 22 80 60, *reservations.cphamburg@ichotelsgroup.com, Fax (040) 2208704,* – |♦|, ⇹ rm, ▤ TV ☏ ♿ – 🧑‍🏫 150. AE ⓓ MC VISA JCB by Lange Reihe HX

Meals à la carte 32/40 – ☕ 20 – **285 rm** 176/226.

• Daylight streams through the cupola into the atrium which is surrounded by elegant, English-style rooms in warm colours. Diners in the Blue Marlin restaurant enjoy a welcoming ambience.

Garden Hotel without rest (with guest houses), Magdalenenstr. 60, ⊠ 20148, ☏ (040) 41 40 40, *garden@garden-hotel.de, Fax (040) 4140420,* – |♦| ⇹ TV ☏ – 🧑‍🏫 15. AE ⓓ MC VISA by Mittelweg GX

☕ 12 – **59 rm** 125/145 – 145/185.

• The location is about as chic as they come here. Guests reside in three attractive houses, fascinating in themselves and with imaginatively decorated, elegantly modern rooms.

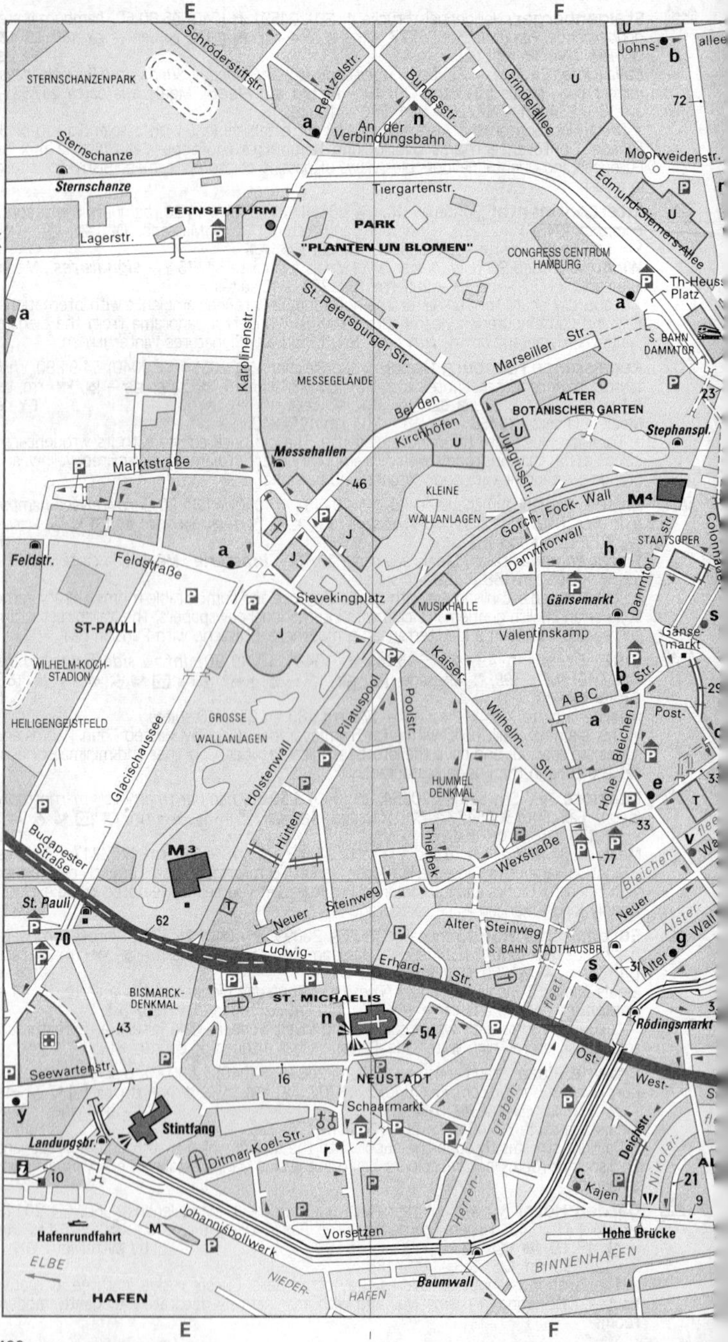

E F
STERNSCHANZENPARK
Schröderstiftstr.
Rentzelstr.
Bundesstr.
Grindelallee
U
Johns- b
allee
72
a
n
An der Verbindungsbahn
Sternschanze
Sternschanze
Moorweidenstr.
Edmund-Siemers-Allee
Tiergartenstr.
FERNSEHTURM
PARK
"PLANTEN UN BLOMEN"
X
Lagerstr.
CONGRESS CENTRUM HAMBURG
Th-Heuss Platz
a
St. Petersburger Str.
Karolinenstr.
S. BAHN DAMMTOR
Marseiller Str.
MESSEGELÄNDE
Bei den Kirchhöfen
ALTER BOTANISCHER GARTEN
23
Stephanspl.
Messehallen
Jungiusstr.
Marktstraße
46
KLEINE WALLANLAGEN
Gorch- Fock- Wall
M4
Colonnaden
Dammtorwall
STAATSOPER
h
Dammtorstr.
Feldstr.
Feldstraße
a
Gänsemarkt
Sievekingplatz
MUSIKHALLE
ST-PAULI
J
Valentinskamp
Gänsemarkt
Kaiser-Wilhelm-Str.
Y
WILHELM-KOCH-STADION
b Str.
29
ABC
HEILIGENGEISTFELD
GROSSE WALLANLAGEN
Pilatuspool
Poolstr.
Post-
Bleichen
Holstenwall
Glacischaussee
HUMMEL DENKMAL
Hohe
e
33
Hütten
Thielbek
33
Budapester Straße
M3
Wexstraße
77
Bleichen-fleet
Neuer Steinweg
Neuer
Alster-
St. Pauli
62
Alter Steinweg
S. BAHN STADTHAUSBR.
70
Ludwig-Erhard-Str.
Alter g Wall
31
s
BISMARCK-DENKMAL
ST. MICHAELIS
n
54
Rödingsmarkt
43
Ost-West-
16
NEUSTADT
Seewartenstr.
Z
y
Schaarmarkt
Herrengraben-fleet
Stintfang
Landungsbr.
Ditmar-Koel-Str.
r
Deichstr.
Nikolai-
c
Kajen
21
9
10
Hafenrundfahrt
M
Johannisbollwerk
Vorsetzen
Hohe Brücke
BINNENHAFEN
ELBE
NIEDER-HAFEN
Baumwall
HAFEN
E F

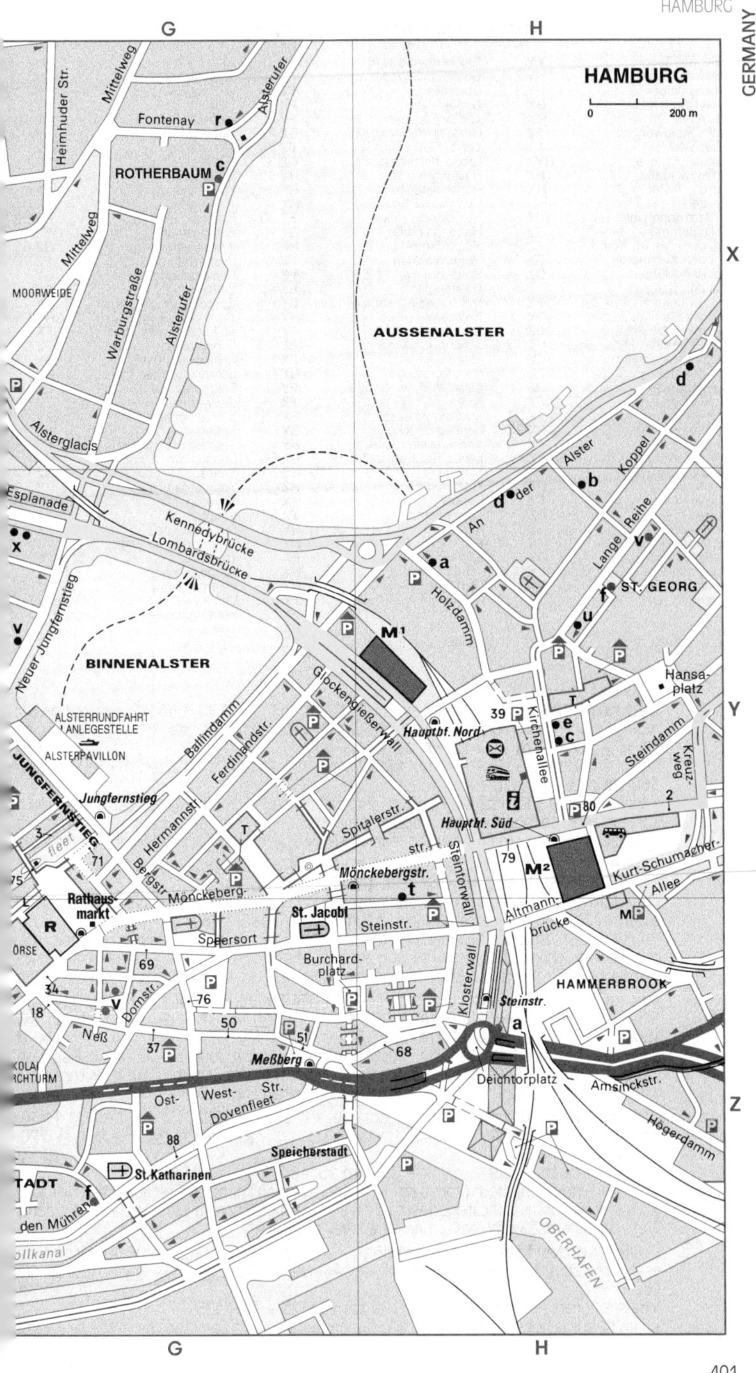
HAMBURG
0
200 m
G
H
X
Y
Z
AUSSENALSTER
BINNENALSTER
ROTHERBAUM
ST. GEORG
HAMMERBROOK
OBERHAFEN
Fontenay
Heimhuder Str.
Mittelweg
Alsterufer
Warburgstraße
MOORWEIDE
Alsterglacis
Esplanade
Kennedybrücke
Lombardsbrücke
Neuer Jungfernstieg
ALSTERRUNDFAHRT ANLEGESTELLE
ALSTERPAVILLON
JUNGFERNSTIEG
Jungfernstieg
Ballindamm
Ferdinandstr.
Hermannstr.
Bergstr.
Glockengießerwall
Hauptbf. Nord
Hauptbf. Süd
Holzdamm
An der Alster
Koppel
Lange Reihe
Hansaplatz
Kirchenallee
Steindamm
Kreuzweg
Spitalerstr.
Mönckebergstr.
Mönckeberg-
Steintorwall
Kurt-Schumacher-Allee
Altmannbrücke
Rathausmarkt
St. Jacobi
Steinstr.
Speersort
Burchardplatz
Domstr.
Neß
Klosterwall
Steinstr.
Meßberg
Deichtorplatz
Amsinckstr.
Högerdamm
West-
Ost-
Str.
Dovenfleet
Speicherstadt
St. Katharinen
den Mühren
fleet
M¹
M²
R
L
ÖRSE
KOLAI
RCHTURM
TADT
ollkanal
39
80
79
2
71
75
3
69
34
18
76
50
51
68
37
88

STREET INDEX TO HAMBURG TOWN PLAN

Radisson SAS Hotel, Marseiller Str. 2, ✉ 20355, ☎ (040) 3 50 20, *reservations.hamburg@radissonsas.com, Fax (040) 35023440*, ≤ Hamburg, – |‡|, ⇔ rm, – 🏃 400. AE ⓓ ⓜ VISA JCB FX a
Meals à la carte 25/36 – ***Trader Vic's*** *(dinner only)* **Meals** à la carte 24/45 – ☐ 15 – **560 rm** 145 – 20 suites.
◆ Skyscraper in the "Planten und Blomen" park, linked to the Congress Centre. Spacious interior and functional rooms. Popular top-floor Tower-Bar. Restaurant with attractive place settings and cream-coloured leather seats. South seas atmosphere in Trader Vic's.

Abtei 🐎, Abteistr. 14, ✉ 20149, ☎ (040) 44 29 05, *abtei@relaischateaux.com, Fax (040) 449820*, – rest, TV. AE ⓜ VISA. rest
closed 24 to 27 December – **Meals** *(closed Sunday and Monday) (dinner only)* (booking essential) 98 and à la carte 48/68 – **11 rm** ☐ 135/180 – 180/240.
◆ Well-chosen antiques complement the interior of this lovely, deliciously secluded villa, calculated to charm all comers, not only those in search of a nostalgic experience. Intimate restaurant with a refined, English-style atmosphere. by Rothenbaumchaussee FX

relexa Hotel Bellevue, An der Alster 14, ✉ 20099, ☎ (040) 28 44 40, *hamburg@relexa-hotel.de, Fax (040) 28444222* – |‡|, ⇔ rm, TV P – 🏃 40. AE ⓓ ⓜ VISA
Meals à la carte 22/32 – **92 rm** ☐ 100/120 – 145/185. HX d
◆ Traditional white hotel building. Mostly facing the Alster, rooms in the original section are especially attractive. Small but solid single rooms in the St Georg. Lunch with a view over the Alster, dine in the tasteful basement restaurant.

Hafen Hamburg (with Classic Residenz), Seewartenstr. 9, ✉ 20459, ☎ (040) 31 11 30, *info@hotel-hamburg.de, Fax (040) 31113755*, ≤, – |‡|, ⇔ rm, TV P – 🏃 220. AE ⓓ ⓜ VISA JCB EZ y
Meals à la carte 33/39 – ☐ 12 – **355 rm** 90/165.
◆ Overlooking the harbour from a lordly height, this is an impressive establishment. As well as functional rooms in 2 categories, there is also the modern, comfortable Classic Residenz. The spacious restaurant has a fine view over the port.

Dorint an der Messe, Schröderstiftstr. 3, ✉ 20146, ☎ (040) 45 06 90, *info.hammes@dorint.com, Fax (040) 450691000* – |‡|, ⇔ rm, TV – 🏃 70. AE ⓓ ⓜ VISA EX a
Meals à la carte 23/30 – ☐ 13 – **180 rm** 95/125 – 105/125.
◆ This business hotel right by the trade fair grounds is just a few steps from the television tower. Modern design, functional fittings.

Vorbach without rest, Johnsallee 63, ✉ 20146, ☎ (040) 44 18 20, *vorbach1@aol.com, Fax (040) 44182888* – 🛗 ⇔ 📺 📞 🚗 – 🏛 20. AE MC VISA FX b
116 rm ☕ 85/135 – 105/150.
◆ Classic turn-of-the-century town mansion with the spacious feel of the period. Comfortable rooms in the old part of the building, more functional rooms in the newer section.

Berlin, Borgfelder Str. 1, ✉ 20537, ☎ (040) 25 16 40, *hotelberlin.hamburg@t-online.de, Fax (040) 25164413*, 🌳 – 🛗 📺 🚗 P – 🏛 25. AE ⓓ MC VISA. ✂ rest
Meals à la carte 20/28 – **93 rm** ☕ 94 – 110. by Adenauerallee HY
◆ Even at first glance this star-shaped hotel makes a striking impression, and its original style is continued in the contemporary and colourful décor of the beautifully designed rooms. Restaurant and terrace are in equally good taste.

Senator without rest, Lange Reihe 18, ✉ 20099, ☎ (040) 24 12 03, *info@hotel-senator-hamburg.de, Fax (040) 2803717* – 🛗 ⇔ 📺 📞 🚗. AE ⓓ MC VISA JCB HY u
56 rm ☕ 99/149 – 119/175.
◆ Pale wood and lovely pastel-coloured fabrics give the interior décor of this establishment its harmonious character. Waterbeds in some rooms guarantee a good night's rest.

St. Raphael, Adenauerallee 41, ✉ 20097, ☎ (040) 24 82 00, *info@straphael-hamburg.bestwestern.de, Fax (040) 24820333*, ≘s – 🛗, ⇔ rm, 📺 📞 P – 🏛 30. AE ⓓ MC VISA JCB. ✂ rest by Adenauerallee HY
Meals *(closed Saturday lunch and Sunday dinner)* à la carte 16/26 – ☕ 11 – **125 rm** 104/124 – 121/141.
◆ Guests have a choice of functional rooms with varied decor. Some in colourful designer style, with motifs including "Nature", "Roses", and "Fishes". Restaurant with conservatory - self-service buffet in the evening.

Baseler Hof, Esplanade 11, ✉ 20354, ☎ (040) 35 90 60, *info@baselerhof.de, Fax (040) 35906918* – 🛗, ⇔ rm, 📺 📞 – 🏛 55. AE ⓓ MC VISA JCB. ✂ GY x
Kleinhuis *(closed 2 weeks July)* **Meals** 12,50 (lunch) and à la carte 26/33 – **153 rm** ☕ 79/99 – 109/119.
◆ This hotel midway between Aussenalster and Botanical Gardens forms part of the Christian Hotels chain. Well-kept rooms with varied furnishings - from mahogany to cane. The Kleinhuis is an attractive, bistro-style restaurant.

Arcadia, Spaldingstr. 70 (by Nordkanalstraße), ✉ 20097, ☎ (040) 23 65 04 00, *arcadiahotel@compuserve.com, Fax (040) 23650629*, ≘s – 🛗, ⇔ rm, ▤ 📺 📞 ♿ 🚗 P – 🏛 40. AE ⓓ MC VISA by Kurt-Schumacher-Straße HY *and Nagelsweg*
Meals *(closed Sunday)* à la carte 20/32 – **98 rm** ☕ 90 – 110.
◆ This former office building was converted into a hotel in 2000. Centrally located, it offers functional, well-equipped bedrooms. The Aquarius restaurant has a cool, contemporary look.

Novotel City Süd, Amsinckstr. 53, ✉ 20097, ☎ (040) 23 63 80, *h1163@accor-hotels.com, Fax (040) 234230*, ≘s – 🛗, ⇔ rm, 📺 📞 ♿ 🚗 P – 🏛 60. AE ⓓ MC VISA JCB by Amsinckstraße HZ
Meals à la carte 19/33 – **185 rm** ☕ 107/158 – 130/182.
◆ Bright, welcoming rooms offer plenty of space to relax and work in, and are especially suitable for business travellers. Restaurant with large show kitchen.

Wedina without rest (with guest houses), Gurlittstr. 23, ✉ 20099, ☎ (040) 2 80 89 00, *info@wedina.com, Fax (040) 2803894*, 🌳 – 📺 P. AE ⓓ MC VISA HY b
59 rm ☕ 85/120 – 105/145.
◆ Hotel consisting of several buildings, all in bright Bauhaus colours. Attractive interiors too, with much use of natural materials.

Ambassador, Heidenkampsweg 34, ✉ 20097, ☎ (040) 2 38 82 30, *mail@ambassador-hamburg.de, Fax (040) 230009*, 🏋, ≘s, 🏊 – 🛗, ⇔ rm, 📺 📞 🚗 P – 🏛 110. AE ⓓ MC VISA by Amsinckstraße HZ *and Süderstraße*
Meals à la carte 19/28 – **122 rm** ☕ 86/110 – 122/135.
◆ This city-centre hotel was completely renovated in 2000 and as well as a lovely reception area offers comfortable rooms in contemporary décor. Bistro-style restaurant.

Nippon, Hofweg 75, ✉ 22085, ☎ (040) 2 27 11 40, *reservations@nippon-hotel-hh.de, Fax (040) 22711490* – 🛗, ⇔ rm, 📺 📞 🚗 – 🏛 20. AE ⓓ MC VISA JCB. ✂
closed 23 December - 1 January – **Meals** *(closed Monday) (dinner only)* (Japanese) à la carte 24/40 – ☕ 10 – **42 rm** 95/118 – 113/146.
◆ Attractive, sober décor in this typically Japanese establishment, with lots of lightwood furnishings, pure colours, tatami floors, shoji partitions in front of the windows, and futons. The Way-Yo with its sushi-bar is a must for lovers of Japanese food.
by An der Alster HX *and Mundsburger Damm, off Papenhuder Str.*

Alster-Hof without rest, Esplanade 12, ✉ 20354, ☎ (040) 35 00 70, *info@alster-hof.de, Fax (040) 35007514* – 🛗 📺. AE ⓓ MC VISA JCB GY x
closed 23 December - 2 January – **118 rm** ☕ 70/96 – 99/114 – 3 suites.
◆ This city centre hotel close to the Alster offers its guests solidly furnished, functional rooms. Some have traditional furnishings, others have been renovated.

XXXXX ✿ **Haerlin** - Hotel Vier Jahreszeiten, Neuer Jungfernstieg 9, ✉ 20354, ✆ (040) 34 94 33 10, *emailus.hvj@raffles.com, Fax (040) 34942608*, ≤ Binnenalster – ▤. AE ⓓ MC VISA JCB. ✂ GY v
closed 14 to 22 March, 4 July - 2 August, 1 to 12 January, Sunday and Monday – **Meals** *(dinner only)* à la carte 56/73 ♀, ✿.
◆ Elegant, stylish setting, with attentive, highly professional service and outstanding classic cuisine. Fine view over the Binnenalster.
Spec. Feines von der Gänsestopfleber mit Apfelkompott. Kabeljau mit weißem Bohnenpüree und kleinen Tintenfischen. Warmer Haselnussauflauf mit eingelegten Zwergorangen.

XX **Sgroi**, Lange Reihe 40, ✉ 20099, ✆ (040) 28 00 39 30, *Fax (040) 28003931*, ☂ – MC VISA HY f
closed Sunday, lunch Saturday and Monday – **Meals** 50 and à la carte 39/45.
◆ Delightfully located on a little square, this restaurant has an attractive contemporary feel to it. Concise menu of Italian dishes made from fine ingredients.

XX **Tirol**, Milchstr. 19, ✉ 20148, ✆ (040) 44 60 82, *Fax (040) 44809327*, ☂ – AE MC VISA by Mittelweg GX
closed Sunday – **Meals** à la carte 29/44.
◆ The Alpine atmosphere of this establishment and the Austrian delicacies provided will quickly dispel any depression brought about by North German drizzle!

XX **Anna**, Bleichenbrücke 2, ✉ 20354, ✆ (040) 36 70 14, *Fax (040) 37500736*, ☂ – AE MC VISA. ✂ FY v
closed Sunday and Bank Holidays – **Meals** 20 *(lunch)* and à la carte 34/51.
◆ Tuscan flair rules here, with parquet floor, wicker seats and red-green fabrics, but the cuisine is more eclectic, ranging from borscht to sour-cream pancakes.

XX **Il Ristorante**, Große Bleichen 16 (1st floor), ✉ 20354, ✆ (040) 34 33 35, *Fax (040) 345748* – ▤. AE ⓓ MC FY c
Meals (Italian) à la carte 29/49.
◆ In an exclusive city-centre location, this welcoming place attracts a prestigious clientèle and features lavish floral designs. The chef specialises in classic Italian dishes.

XX **San Michele**, Englische Planke 8, ✉ 20459, ✆ (040) 37 11 27, *info@san-michele.de, Fax (040) 378121* – AE ⓓ MC VISA JCB EZ n
closed mid July - early August – **Meals** (Italian) 20,50 *(lunch)* and à la carte 34,50/49.
◆ Italianissimo! This most Italian of Italian restaurants directly opposite St Michael's Church serves classic Neapolitan cuisine in a bright and cheerful Mediterranean setting.

XX ☺ **Brook**, Bei den Mühren 91, ✉ 20457, ✆ (040) 37 50 31 28, *Fax (040) 37503127* – AE GZ f
closed Sunday – **Meals** 16 *(lunch)*/29 *(dinner)* and à la carte 31/45.
◆ Modern establishment with intentionally austere décor offering friendly service and a fine view of the spectacular warehouses of the floodlit Speicherstadt.

X **La Mirabelle**, Bundesstr. 15, ✉ 20146, ✆ (040) 4 10 75 85, *Fax (040) 4107585*. AE MC VISA FX n
closed 2 weeks July - August and Sunday – **Meals** *(dinner only)* à la carte 33/43.
◆ A likeable little place with a laid-back atmosphere and a touch of Gallic flair. The owner talks his guests through the daily specials with real enthusiasm!

X **Fischküche**, Kajen 12, ✉ 20459, ✆ (040) 36 56 31, *Fax (040) 36091153*, ☂ – AE ⓓ MC VISA FZ c
closed Saturday lunch, Sunday and Bank Holidays – **Meals** (booking essential) à la carte 27/50.
◆ With a contrasting combination of bright yellow walls and blue and white tiling, this unusual bistro by the harbourside has an open kitchen specialising in fish dishes.

X **Fischmarkt**, Ditmar-Koel-Str. 1, ✉ 20459, ✆ (040) 36 38 09, *Fax (040) 362191*, ☂ – AE MC VISA EZ r
closed Saturday lunch – **Meals** (booking essential) à la carte 25/55.
◆ The "Fish Market" grills and roasts, steams and poaches the bounty of river and ocean in a magical, Mediterranean setting.

X **Ilot**, ABC-Str. 46 (ABC-Forum), ✉ 20354, ✆ (040) 35 71 58 85, *Fax (040) 35715887*, ☂ – AE ⓓ MC VISA FY a
closed Sunday – **Meals** à la carte 16/32,50.
◆ This bistro-like establishment with its big windows is run by a Franco-German couple who give their guests a warm welcome and serve a variety of French-inspired dishes.

X ☺ **Le Plat du Jour**, Dornbusch 4, ✉ 20095, ✆ (040) 32 14 14, *jacqueslemercier@aol.com, Fax (040) 4105857* – AE ⓓ MC VISA GZ v
closed 23 December - 7 January, Sunday, July - August Saturday and Sunday – **Meals** (booking essential) 25,50 *(dinner)* and à la carte 24/34.
◆ Welcoming French bistro with wooden seats and red-and-white napkins. By Hamburg standards, the French dishes represent excellent value.

Casse-Croûte, Büschstr. 2, ✉ 20354, ☎ (040) 34 33 73, *info@casse-croute.de, Fax (040) 41283468* – AE MC VISA FY s
closed Sunday lunch – **Meals** 23,50 and à la carte 29/35.
◆ Attractive, bistro-style restaurant with open kitchen, contemporary ambience, and relaxed atmosphere.

Cox, Lange Reihe 68, ✉ 20099, ☎ (040) 24 94 22, *info@restaurant-cox.de, Fax (040) 28050902* – HY v
closed lunch Saturday and Sunday – **Meals** (booking essential for dinner) à la carte 26/35.
◆ Diners sit on striking red leather seats and are served creative international dishes in a welcoming atmosphere in this establishment close to Hamburg's principal theatre.

Matsumi, Colonnaden 96 (1st floor), ✉ 20354, ☎ (040) 34 31 25, *Fax (040) 344219* – AE DC MC VISA JCB FY r
closed 24 December - 4 January and Sunday – **Meals** (Japanese) à la carte 23/39.
◆ Diners can experience a wide range of authentic Japanese dishes here, magically created by Hideaki Morita to tempt connoisseurs and beginners alike.

Jena Paradies, Klosterwall 23, ✉ 20095, ☎ (040) 32 70 08, *jena-paradies@t-online.de, Fax (040) 327598* HZ a
closed 24 to 26 December – **Meals** à la carte 17,50/31 ♀.
◆ The lofty hall of the Academy of Arts is now a restaurant with Bauhaus-style décor serving international cuisine. Lunchtime menu featuring solid and inexpensive German dishes.

at Hamburg-Alsterdorf *North : 8 km, by Grindelallee FX and Breitenfelder Straße :*

Alsterkrug-Hotel, Alsterkrugchaussee 277, ✉ 22297, ☎ (040) 51 30 30, *rez@alsterkrug.bestwestern.de, Fax (040) 51303403*, – rm, – 50. AE DC MC VISA JCB
Meals à la carte 26/36 – ☕ 13 – **105 rm** 105/195 – 115/205.
◆ Let yourself be charmed by the Mediterranean flair of this establishment. Rooms in warm colours, with wickerwork chairs and abundant plants. Desks with fax and modem points. Warm colours too in the comfortable and welcoming restaurant.

at Hamburg-Altona *West : 5 km, by Reeperbahn EZ :*

Mercure Hotel Domicil without rest, Stresemannstr. 62, ✉ 22769, ☎ (040) 4 31 60 26, *h4995@accor-hotels.com, Fax (040) 4397579* – . AE DC MC VISA JCB by Budapester Straße EY
☕ 13 – **75 rm** 80/140 – 100/160.
◆ This hotel's rooms are decorated in lively colours, notably black and lilac ! Original details emphasise the individuality of the spacious rooms.

InterCityHotel, Paul-Nevermann-Platz 17, ✉ 22765, ☎ (040) 38 03 40, *hamburg@intercityhotel.de, Fax (040) 38034999* – , rm, – 60. AE DC MC VISA
Meals *(closed Sunday dinner)* à la carte 20/30 – ☕ 12 – **133 rm** 103/123 – 118/138.
◆ Right by the Altona main railway station, this establishment boasts contemporary rooms with lightwood furnishings. The room price includes use of the city public transport system. Hamburg specialities served in the cheerful winter garden restaurant.

Landhaus Scherrer, Elbchaussee 130, ✉ 22763, ☎ (040) 8 80 13 25, *info@landhausscherrer.de, Fax (040) 8806260* – AE DC MC VISA
closed Easter, Whit Sunday, Whit Monday and Sunday – **Meals** à la carte 42/72 ♀, –
Bistro : **Meals** 27,50 à la carte 34,50/40 ♀.
◆ Erotic paintings on walls contrast with the otherwise country-house style of this establishment. Both the orgiastic paintings of Bachmann and the French cuisine lead guests into temptation. Senses and taste-buds are further led astray in the elegant Bistro.
Spec. Gepökelter Kalbskopf mit Rosmarinsauce. Gebratenes Dorschmedaillon mit weißer Balsamico-Senfvinaigrette. Krosse Vierländer Ente (2 people).

Le Canard, Elbchaussee 139, ✉ 22763, ☎ (040) 8 80 50 57, *lecanard@viehhauser.de, Fax (040) 88913259*, – AE DC MC VISA.
closed Sunday – **Meals** (booking essential) 36 *(lunch)*/108 *(dinner)* and à la carte 52/67 ♀, .
◆ This stylised ship's hull stands by the Elbe. In it, fine French cuisine of a classic kind is served, perhaps best sampled at lunchtime when prices are lower.
Spec. Rahmsuppe vom Hummer. Krosse Vierländer Ente mit Bordeauxsauce. Topfensoufflé mit Champagnersabayon.

XXX **Fischereihafen-Restaurant**, Große Elbstr. 143, ✉ 22767, ☎ (040) 38 18 16, *info@fischereihafen-restaurant-hamburg.de, Fax (040) 3893021,* ≤, 余 – P. AE ⓓ MC VISA
Meals (seafood only) (booking essential) 17,50 *(lunch)* and à la carte 28/56.
• A favourite of celebrities, who appreciate its classical ambience and its offerings of sophisticated local specialities mostly featuring fish and various crustaceans.

XX **Au Quai**, Grosse Elbstr. 145 b-d, ✉ 22767, ☎ (040) 38 03 77 30, *info@au-quai.com, Fax (040) 38037732,* ≤, 余 – AE ⓓ MC VISA
closed lunch Saturday and Sunday – **Meals** à la carte 34/48.
• This trendy establishment with its waterside terrace is right on the harbour. Striking contemporary décor with designer items and holographic objects.

XX **IndoChine**, Neumühlen 11, ✉ 22763, ☎ (040) 39 80 78 80, *info@indochine.de, Fax (040) 39807882,* ≤, 余 – P. AE MC VISA JCB
Meals (Asian) à la carte 30/47.
• This contemporary, elegant restaurant is to be found on the 3rd and 4th floors of an office building. Traditional Asian cuisine enhanced by the fine views. Riverside terrace.

XX **Stocker**, Max-Brauer-Allee 80, ✉ 22765, ☎ (040) 38 61 50 56, *manfred.stocker@t-online.de, Fax (040) 38615058,* 余 – AE ⓓ MC VISA
closed 2 weeks January, Monday, lunch Saturday and Sunday – **Meals** 18 *(lunch)* and à la carte 28/43.
• Playful frescoes form an attractive pictorial background to the chef's innovative interpretation of classic Austrian dishes, cleverly enhanced with contemporary touches.

X **La Vela**, Große Elbstr. 27, ✉ 22767, ☎ (040) 38 69 93 93, *la-vela@t-online.de, Fax (040) 38086788,* ≤, 余 – AE MC VISA
Meals à la carte 30/36.
• Right next to the Fischmarkt, this recently opened bistro-style restaurant is known for its friendly service. Terrace overlooking the River Elbe.

X **Henssler Henssler**, Große Elbstr. 160, ✉ 22767, ☎ (040) 38 69 90 00, *Fax (040) 38699055,* 余 – AE
closed Sunday and Bank Holidays – **Meals** (Japanese) à la carte 25,50/39.
• Smart restaurant in what used to be a covered fish market. Japanese inspired black and white interior. Sushi bar and Japanese cuisine with a Californian touch.

X **Rive Bistro**, Van-der-Smissen-Str. 1 (Cruise-Centre), ✉ 22767, ☎ (040) 3 80 59 19, *info@rive.de, Fax (040) 3894775,* ≤, 余 – AE
Meals (booking essential) 18,50/24 and à la carte 22/44.
• This is the place to enjoy local seafood dishes, close to the fish market and with a harbour view. Unusual décor featuring metallic leaves. Fresh oysters at the bar.

X **Darling Harbour**, Neumühlen 17, ✉ 22763, ☎ (040) 3 80 89 00, *darling-harbour@t-online.de, Fax (040) 38089044,* ≤, 余 – 🚗. AE ⓓ MC VISA
closed Saturday lunch – **Meals** 37 and à la carte.
• Smart, trendy restaurant in a glazed office building close to the container terminal. Contemporary interior, imaginative cooking. Riverside terrace.

at Hamburg-Bahrenfeld *West : 7 km, by Budapester Straße* EY *and Stresemannstraße :*

Gastwerk, Beim Alten Gaswerk 3/corner of Daimlerstraße, ✉ 22761, ☎ (040) 89 06 20, *info@gastwerk-hotel.de, Fax (040) 8906220,* ≘s – |$|, ⇔ rm, TV ✆ P – 🏔 100. AE ⓓ MC VISA
Meals *(closed Saturday lunch and Sunday)* (Italian) à la carte 30/42 – ☕ 15 – **134 rm** 125/175 – 3 suites.
• The splendid old gasworks has become a loft-style designer hotel inviting you to stay in one of its spacious rooms. Natural materials and a host of lovely details. Relaxed atmosphere in the bistro-type restaurant with its red upholstered benches.

NH Hamburg-Altona, Stresemannstr. 363, ✉ 22761, ☎ (040) 4 21 06 00, *nhhamburgaltona@nh-hotels.com, Fax (040) 421060100,* ≘s – |$| ⇔ TV ✆ 🚗 – 🏔 150. AE ⓓ MC VISA JCB
Meals à la carte 22/41 – **232 rm** ☕ 105/142 – 121/155.
• Brick building opened in 2001, featuring standard rooms New hotel with brick façade and standard rooms with contemporary decor and good technical facilities. Modern restaurant with bountiful buffet.

XX **Tafelhaus** (Rach), Holstenkamp 71, ✉ 22525, ☎ (040) 89 27 60, *Fax (040) 8993324,* 余 – P. AE ⓓ MC VISA
closed 2 weeks early January, 1 week Easter, end July - mid August, Saturday lunch, Sunday and Monday – **Meals** (booking essential) 35 *(lunch)*/80 *(dinner)* and à la carte 46/53 ♀.
• Covered in plants, this dear little red building with its elegant interior and up-to-date facilities invites guests to indulge in chef Christian Rach's innovative cooking.
Spec. Saltinbocca vom Kaninchen mit Hummer und weißen Bohnen. Steinbutt mit Pfirsich und Pfifferlingen. Gebackene Zitronencreme mit Himbeeren und Kaffee-Eis.

Atlas, Schützenstr. 9a (Entrance Phoenixhof), ✉ 22761, ☎ (040) 8 51 78 10, *atlas@atlas.at, Fax (040) 8517811*, – P. AE MC VISA
Meals 15,50 *(lunch)*/25,50 *(dinner)* and à la carte 24/36 ♀.
◆ This old fish smokehouse is now a well-run restaurant in contemporary bistro style. Small, ivy-clad outdoor eating area to the rear.

at Hamburg-Barmbek *Northeast : 6 km, by An der Alster* HX *and Mundsburger Damm :*

Mercure Hotel Meridian without rest, Holsteinischer Kamp 59, ✉ 22081, ☎ (040) 2 91 80 40, *h4993@accor-hotels.com, Fax (040) 2983336*, , – , P – 25. AE MC VISA
13 – **67 rm** 85/115 – 95/125.
◆ Original colourful details and dark wood furniture give the décor here a special something. The spacious rooms have excellent working facilities.

at Hamburg-Billbrook *East : 8 km, by Amsinckstraße* HZ *and Billstraße :*

Böttcherhof, Wöhlerstr. 2, ✉ 22113, ☎ (040) 73 18 70, *info@boettcherhof.com, Fax (040) 73187899*, , – , rm, P – 150. AE MC VISA. rest
Meals à la carte 25/42 – 13 – **155 rm** 100/131 – 121/152.
◆ This modern, well-run establishment offers bright and tasteful rooms with colourful décor and solid cherrywood furnishings. Welcoming restaurant.

at Hamburg-Blankenese *West : 16 km, by Reeperbahn* EZ *and Elbchaussee :*

Süllberg - Seven Seas (Hauser) with rm, Süllbergsterrasse 12, ✉ 22587, ☎ (040) 8 66 25 20, *info@suellberg-hamburg.de, Fax (040) 866625213*, ≤, – – 100. AE MC VISA JCB
Meals *(closed 5 to 20 January, Monday and Tuesday) (dinner only)* 56/110 and à la carte 49/78 ♀, – ***Bistro* : Meals** à la carte 26/39 ♀ – 12 – **11 rm** 160 – 180.
◆ The luxurious Seven Seas fine dining restaurant is the centrepiece of the superbly renovated Süllberg complex. The ballroom, available for parties, reflects the glories of former times, while the bistro is light, modern and friendly.
Spec. Emincé von Flusskrebsen und Seezunge mit exotischen Gewürzen. Steinbutt auf der Haut gebraten mit Erbsen à la française. Topfensoufflé mit Apfelkompott und Sauerrahmeis.

at Hamburg-City Nord *North : 7,5 km, by Mittelweg* GX *and Hudtwalckerstraße :*

Queens Hotel, Mexikoring 1, ✉ 22297, ☎ (040) 63 29 40, *info.qhamburg@queensgruppe.de, Fax (040) 6322472*, , – , rm, rest, P – 120. AE MC VISA
Meals à la carte 25/40 – 14 – **182 rm** 117 – 140/172.
◆ Close to the city centre and only 10 minutes from the airport. Ask for one of the refurbished rooms with their bright and functional décor.

at Hamburg-Eppendorf *North : 5 km, by Grindelallee* FX *and Breitenfelder Straße :*

Piment (Nouri), Lehmweg 29, ✉ 20251, ☎ (040) 42 93 77 88, *Fax (040) 42937789*, – MC VISA
closed Easter, mid to end July and Sunday – **Meals** *(dinner only)* 48/65 and à la carte 44,50/58,50 ♀.
◆ This lovely Art Nouveau establishment has been immaculately restored by the couple who run it, and who serve classic dishes with a North African touch.
Spec. Weichgekochtes Gänsetopfleberei mit mit Topinambur-Carpaccio. Geschmorte Kalbsbäckchen mit Schalotten gratiniert und Kartoffelcreme. Topfenknödel mit glasierter Williamsbirne und Sauerrahmeis.

Poletto, Eppendorfer Landstr. 145, ✉ 20251, ☎ (040) 4 80 21 59, *Fax (040) 41406993*,
closed Saturday lunch, Sunday - Monday and Bank Holidays – **Meals** 39/59 and à la carte 43,50/61,50 ♀.
◆ Lovely place settings and unusual porcelain set the sophisticated tone in this establishment with its aristocratic yellow walls. Mediterranean dishes with an Italian touch.
Spec. Tramezzini mit gebratener Gänseleber und Gewürzapfel. Kartoffelagnolotti mit Trüffel. Dorade Royal in der Meersalzkruste mit Kirschtomaten-Fondue.

Sellmer, Ludolfstr. 50, ✉ 20249, ☎ (040) 47 30 57, *Fax (040) 4601569* – P. AE MC VISA
Meals (mainly seafood) à la carte 27/51.
◆ This traditional-style fish restaurant has been satisfying its regular customers for more than 20 years with its amazing range of seafood specialities.

at Hamburg-Flottbek *West : 9 km, by Budapester Straße* EY *and Stresemannstraße :*

Landhaus Flottbek, Baron-Voght-Str. 179, ✉ 22607, ☎ (040) 8 22 74 10, *info@landhaus-flottbeck.de, Fax (040) 82274151,* – 30. AE MC VISA JCB
Meals *(closed Sunday) (dinner only)* à la carte 26/39 – ***Club-House*** *(Monday - Thursday lunch only)* **Meals** à la carte 23/35 – **25 rm** 99/120 – 135/170.
◆ No ordinary hotel this, but a group of 18C farmhouses with a pretty garden and individual rooms lovingly decorated in country-house style. A characterful restaurant has been established in the old stables, and the Club-House Bistro is equally attractive.

at Hamburg-Fuhlsbüttel *North : 8 km, by Grindelallee* FX *and Breitenfelder Straße :*

Airport Hotel, Flughafenstr. 47 (at the airport), ✉ 22415, ☎ (040) 53 10 20, *service@airporthh.com, Fax (040) 53102222,* – rm, rest, – 140. AE MC VISA
Meals à la carte 27/40 – 15 – **159 rm** 140/210 – 165/235 – 11 suites.
◆ Only 500m from the runway, this charming country-style hotel offers harmonious, colourfully decorated and functional rooms. Wonderful trompe l'oeil murals in the swimming-pool. Tired flyers will enjoy recuperating in the hotel restaurant.

top air, Flughafenstr. 1 (at the airport, terminal 4, level 3), ✉ 22335, ☎ (040) 50 75 33 24, *top-air.hamburg@woellhaf-airport.de, Fax (040) 50751842* – AE MC VISA
closed 20 July - 10 August, 24 December - 10 January and Saturday – **Meals** 27 *(lunch)* and à la carte 30/51.
◆ Hungry travellers will appreciate being taken under the wing of this restaurant gracing the architecturally striking Terminal 4 building and serving international cuisine.

at Hamburg-Harburg *South : 15 km, by Amsinckstraße* HZ *and Wilhelmsburger Reichsstraße :*

Lindtner, Heimfelder Str. 123, ✉ 21075, ☎ (040) 79 00 90, *info@lindtner.com, Fax (040) 79009482,* – rm, rest, – 450. AE MC VISA JCB
Meals à la carte 33/45 – 13 – **115 rm** 120/145 – 145/175 – 7 suites.
◆ A spacious foyer greets guests to this cooly elegant modern hotel with its light interiors. Contemporay art collection. Restaurant partly with ceiling-high windows and show kitchen, partly with country-style ambience.

Panorama Harburg, Harburger Ring 8, ✉ 21073, ☎ (040) 76 69 50, *panoramaharburg@aol.com, Fax (040) 76695183* – rm, – 110. AE MC VISA JCB
Meals *(closed Sunday dinner)* à la carte 19/27 – **99 rm** 98/105 – 112.
◆ Business travellers will appreciate the functional accommodation here with its mahogany-coloured furniture and ample work space. The bright and welcoming restaurant has an attractive coffee-house atmosphere.

at Hamburg-Langenhorn *North : 8 km, by Grindelallee* FX *and Breitenfelder Straße :*

Dorint-Hotel-Airport, Langenhorner Chaussee 183, ✉ 22415, ☎ (040) 53 20 90, *info.hamburg@dorint.com, Fax (040) 53209600,* – rm, – 80. AE MC VISA JCB
Meals à la carte 25/44 – 16 – **146 rm** 133/188 – 155/210.
◆ Not far from the airport, this architecturally impressive edifice has glazed corridors and leafy courtyards. Guests are accommodated in functional, contemporary rooms.

Zum Wattkorn, Tangstedter Landstr. 230, ✉ 22417, ☎ (040) 5 20 37 97, *wattkorn@viehhauser.de, Fax (040) 5209044,* –
closed Monday and Tuesday – **Meals** à la carte 28,50/43.
◆ This charming country house with its thatched roof belongs to the Viehhauser family, one of whom is a famous chef. Regional cuisine with North Sea and Alpine specialities.

at Hamburg-Lemsahl-Mellingstedt *Northeast : 16 km, by An der Alster* HX *and B 4 :*

Marriott Hotel Treudelberg, Lemsahler Landstr. 45, ✉ 22397, ☎ (040) 60 82 20, *info@treudelberg.com, Fax (040) 60822444,* Massage, – rm, – 150. AE MC VISA JCB, rest
Meals à la carte 28/42 – 15 – **135 rm** 135.
◆ Fine views of the Alster valley are conducive to restful absorption in the historic atmosphere of Treudelberg. Elegant hotel with excellent recreational facilities. Relaxed atmosphere in the restaurant with its view of the hotel's golf course.

Stock's Fischrestaurant, An der Alsterschleife 3, ✉ 22399, ☎ (040) 6 02 00 43, *info@stocks.de, Fax (040) 6020028,* – AE MC VISA
closed Monday dinner and Saturday lunch – **Meals** (booking essential) à la carte 38/42,50.
◆ This thatched timber-framed building dating from the 18C has been restored to its original glory after a fire and provided with a conservatory.

at Hamburg-Niendorf : *North : 12 km, by Grindelallee* FX *and Garstedter Weg :*

Lutz und König, König-Heinrich-Weg 200, ✉ 22455, ☎ (040) 55 59 95 53, *Fax (040) 55599554*, – P. AE ① MC VISA JCB
closed 2 weeks early August, Monday and Saturday lunch – **Meals** (booking essential) à la carte 25/47.
◆ "Lutz" is your host, and you, the guest, are "König" (king), in this tastefully decorated country house, where he serves refined regional cuisine with a Mediterranean touch.

at Hamburg-Nienstedten *West : 13 km, by Reeperbahn* EZ *and Elbchaussee :*

Louis C. Jacob, Elbchaussee 401, ✉ 22609, ☎ (040) 82 25 50, *jacob@hotel-jacob.de*, *Fax (040) 82255444*, ≤ Harbour and Elbe, , – , rm, TV – 120. AE ① MC VISA JCB. rest
Meals (booking essential) 63 *(lunch)*/93 and à la carte 51/85 ♀ – ☕ 20 – **85 rm** 185 – 235/395 – 8 suites.
◆ Luxury establishment with restrained décor. Rooms are elegantly furnished with period pieces and all have individual colour schemes. Superb location overlooking the Elbe. Light, subtle tones and lovely table settings in the restaurant. Terrace with lime trees.
Spec. Sautierte Jakobsmuscheln mit Trüffelmayonnaise und Ofentomaten. Kalbskopfscheiben und Kalbsbäckchen mit Flusskrebsen. Milchlamm mit Salsa Verde gratiniert und Schmorjus.

at Hamburg-Rothenburgsort *Southwest : 3 km, by Amsinkstraße* HZ *:*

Holiday Inn, Billwerder Neuer Deich 14, ✉ 20539, ☎ (040) 7 88 40, *info@hi-hamburg.de*, *Fax (040) 78841000*, ≤, , , – TV P – 90. AE ① MC VISA. rest
Meals à la carte 28/37 – ☕ 14 – **385 rm** 115/135 – 135 – 12 suites.
◆ Right on the Elbe, the Holiday Inn is a good place to lay up at night. Ideal for business travellers looking for comfortable and well-equipped rooms with all facilities. Restaurant with terrace giving river views.

at Hamburg-St. Pauli :

NH Hamburg without rest, Feldstr. 53, ✉ 20357, ☎ (040) 43 23 20, *nhhamburg@nh.hotels.com*, *Fax (040) 43232300*, – TV – 10. AE ① MC VISA JCB EY a
☕ 14 – **119 rm** 98/168 – 98/181.
◆ All of the rooms in this hotel are arranged as apartments, with up-to-date facilities - kitchenette, dining and living areas. PC, fax and modem on request.

In Hamburg-Schnelsen :

Ökotel, Holsteiner Chaussee 347, ✉ 22457, ☎ (040) 5 59 73 00, *info@oekotel.de*, *Fax (040) 55973099* – TV – 15. AE VISA. R m
Meals *(closed Saturday and Sunday) (dinner only)* (residents only) – **23** rm ☕ 57/95 – 82/115 – 3 Suiten.
◆ A comfortable alternative for environmentally conscious travellers, this hotel is designed and run on ecological principles. Attractive rooms, some with balcony.

at Hamburg-Stellingen *Northwest : 7 km, by Schröderstiftstraße* FX *:*

Holiday Inn, Kieler Str. 333, ✉ 22525, ☎ (040) 54 74 00, *hihamburg-fo@ichotelsgroup.com*, *Fax (040) 54740100*, – , rm, TV P – 25. AE ① MC VISA JCB. rest
Meals à la carte 17,50/24,50 – **105 rm** ☕ 115/140 – 129/154.
◆ Plenty of space in these contemporary rooms, whose includes lightwood furniture and colourful modern pictures. Bus stop in front of the hotel. The restaurant also has a contemporary feel.

at Hamburg-Stillhorn *South : 11 km, by Amsinckstraße* HZ *and A 1 :*

Le Méridien, Stillhorner Weg 40, ✉ 21109, ☎ (040) 75 01 50, *gm1313@lemeridien.com*, *Fax (040) 75015501*, – , rm, rest, TV P – 120. AE ① MC VISA JCB
Meals à la carte 29/38 – ☕ 12 – **146 rm** 117/127 – 131/141.
◆ There is a feeling of being on safari in some of the rooms here, where boldly patterned bed-covers harmonise wonderfully well with solid furniture in dark red tones. The elegant restaurant enjoys lovely leafy views.

at Hamburg-Winterhude *North : 5 km, by Mittelweg* GX *:*

Allegria, Hudtwalckerstr. 13, ✉ 22299, ☎ (040) 46 07 28 28, *info@allegria-restaurant.de*, *Fax (040) 46072607*,
closed 2 weeks January, Monday and Saturday lunch – **Meals** à la carte 28/48.
◆ Right by the Fährhaus Theatre in the suburb of Winterhude, this modern, brightly-lit and colourful establishment offers refined international cuisine with an Austrian touch.

HANOVER (HANNOVER) Niedersachsen 541 I 13 – *pop. 530 000 – alt. 55 m.*

See : *Herrenhausen Gardens (Herrenhäuser Gärten)★★ (Großer Garten★★, Berggarten★)* CV – *Kestner-Museum★* DY **M1** – *Market Church (Marktkirche) (Altarpiece★★)* DY – *Museum of Lower Saxony (Niedersächsisches Landesmuseum) (Prehistorical department★)* EZ **M2** – *Sprengel-Museum★* EZ – *Historical Museum (Historisches Museum Hannover)★* DY.

Garbsen, Am Blauen See 120 (West : 14 km), (05137) 7 30 68 ; Isernhagen, Gut Lohne 22, (North : 14 km), (05139) 89 31 85 ; Langenhagen, Hainhaus 22 (North : 19 km), (0511) 73 68 32 ; Laatzen-Gleidingen, Am Golfplatz 1 (Southeast : 9 km), (05102) 30 55.

Hanover-Langenhagen (North : 11 km), (0511) 9 77 12 23.

Exhibition Centre (Messegelände) (by Bischofsholer Damm FY *and Messe Schnellweg), (0511) 8 90, Fax (0511) 8931216.*

Tourismus-Service, Ernst-August-Platz 2, 30159, (0511) 12 34 51 11, tourismus-service@hannover-stadt.de, Fax (0511) 12345112.

ADAC, *Nordmannpassage 4.*

Berlin 289 – Bremen 123 – Hamburg 151.

Plans on following pages

Kastens Hotel Luisenhof, Luisenstr. 1, 30159, (0511) 3 04 40, *info@kastens-luisenhof.de, Fax (0511) 3044807* – , rm, – 90. rest EX b
Meals *(closed Sunday July - August)* à la carte 31/56 – **152 rm** 139/325 – 178/380 – 7 suites.
◆ All-round comfort in Hanover's most venerable hotel, in family ownership since 1856. Elegant and highly individual décor. Tower Suite with city views. Modern conference and meeting facilities. A variety of eating-places cater for every requirement.

Maritim Grand Hotel, Friedrichswall 11, 30159, (0511) 3 67 70, *info.hgr@maritim.de, Fax (0511) 325195,* – , rm, – 250. rest *closed 21 to 28 December* – – ***L'Adresse - Brasserie :*** **Meals** à la carte 31/55 – ***Wilhelm-Busch-Stube*** *(closed Saturday and Sunday) (dinner only)* **Meals** à la carte 19/32 – 15 – **285 rm** 124 – 144 – 14 suites. DY a
◆ Central location, plus tasteful and elegant rooms, splendid public spaces for events of all kinds, and a tasteful lobby with open fire. L'Adresse restaurant is stylish, a lighter touch prevails in the Brasserie. Rustic setting in the Wilhelm-Busch-Stube.

Maritim Stadthotel, Hildesheimer Str. 34, 30169, (0511) 9 89 40, *info.hnn@maritim.de, Fax (0511) 9894900,* , , – , rm, – 250. rest EZ b
Meals à la carte 22/34 – 15 – **291 rm** 119 – 140.
◆ Living up to its name, the hotel greets you in classically maritime style at reception and bar. Rooms are functional and ideal for the business traveller. Traditional ambience in the restaurant.

Courtyard by Marriott, Arthur-Menge-Ufer 3, 30169, (0511) 36 60 00, *cy.hajcy.sales.mgr@courtyard.com, Fax (0511) 36600555,* , , – , rm, – 190. DZ b
Julian's : **Meals** à la carte 19/35 – ***Grand Café :*** **Meals** à la carte 14/22,50 – 14 – **149 rm** 111/127 – 5 suites.
◆ In this one-time casino, guests have the choice between comfortable functional rooms facing the Maschsee lake or the city centre. Fascinating pictures adorn the walls of Julian's restaurant.

Crowne Plaza Schweizerhof, Hinüberstr. 6, 30175, (0511) 3 49 50, *info@chhof.de, Fax (0511) 3495102* – , rm, – 220. rest
Gourmet's Buffet : **Meals** à la carte 28,50/39,50 – 16 – **201 rm** 127/175 – 4 suites.
◆ Close to the station, this contemporary atrium structure houses a comfortable hotel. Business rooms with combined fax-printer, TV with internet access and video games. Gourmet's Buffet : elegant Bistro. EX d

Congress Hotel am Stadtpark, Clausewitzstr. 6, 30175, (0511) 2 80 50, *info@congress-hotel-hannover.de, Fax (0511) 814652,* , Massage, , – , rm, – 1300. rest by Hans-Böckler Allee FY
Parkrestaurant Bristol : **Meals** à la carte 19/31 – **258 rm** 102/155 – 176 – 3 suites.
◆ Good standard of accommodation on 18 floors close to the congress centre. The rooms on the upper floors have panoramic views. Take a dip in the highest pool in town ! Then rendezvous in the Park restaurant.

Central-Hotel Kaiserhof, Ernst-August-Platz 4, 30159, (0511) 3 68 30, *mail@centralhotel.de, Fax (0511) 3683114,* – – 100. rm
Meals à la carte 28/50 – **78 rm** 116/145 – 145/155. EX a
◆ Classic, recently renovated hotel building diagonally opposite the station. Comfortable rooms, tastefully decorated in country-house style, with attractive bathrooms. Restaurant with open kitchen and Viennese café.

Grand Hotel Mussmann without rest, Ernst-August-Platz 7, ✉ 30159, ☎ (0511) 3 65 60, *grandhotel@hannover.de, Fax (0511) 3656145,* – 40. EX v
100 rm 92/132 – 142/162.
◆ Prettily-decorated, refurbished rooms giving onto the station square or onto a leafy courtyard. You have the choice between parquet floor and carpets.

Loccumer Hof, Kurt-Schumacher-Str. 16, ✉ 30159, ☎ (0511) 1 26 40, *office@loccumerhof.de, Fax (0511) 131192* – rm, – 35. DX s
Meals *(closed dinner Saturday and Sunday)* à la carte 20/31 – **87 rm** 87/95 – 114.
◆ This establishment forms part of Germany's most venerable hotel chain, the Christian Hotels Association. Well looked-after, family-run establishment with soundproofed windows. Subtle yellows and blues give the restaurant a welcoming atmosphere.

Concorde Hotel Berlin without rest, Königstr. 12, ✉ 30175, ☎ (0511) 4 10 28 00, *berlin@concorde-hotels.de, Fax (0511) 41028013* –
78 rm 100/110 – 120. EX e
◆ Hotel accommodation in upper section of city centre building, ideal for business travellers. Functional, contemporary rooms with cherrywood furnishings.

ANDOR Hotel Plaza, Fernroder Str. 9, ✉ 30161, ☎ (0511) 3 38 80, *mail@hotel-plaza-hannover.de, Fax (0511) 3388188* – rm, – 90. EX u
Meals à la carte 23/33 – **140 rm** 105/115 – 130.
◆ Just 100m from the station, this former department store has been converted into a contemporary, functional business hotel, with good technical facilities in the rooms. Esprit restaurant on the second floor.

Concorde Hotel am Leineschloss without rest, Am Markte 12, ✉ 30159, ☎ (0511) 35 79 10, *leineschloss@concorde-hotels.de, Fax (0511) 35791100* – DY e
81 rm 101 – 136.
◆ Well-run establishment with individual, comfortable and functional rooms. The 4th floor breakfast room offers a fine view of the Market Church.

Am Rathaus, Friedrichswall 21, ✉ 30159, ☎ (0511) 32 62 68, *info@hotelamrathaus.de, Fax (0511) 32626968* – rm, . rm EY y
Meals *(closed mid July - mid August, Saturday and Sunday) (dinner only)* à la carte 18/33 – **44 rm** 75/83 – 120/148.
◆ Run by the same family for three generations, this hotel opposite the lovely City Hall park has a homely atmosphere and practical, well-equipped rooms. Contemporary restaurant and separate, country-style bar.

Savoy, Schloßwender Str. 10, ✉ 30159, ☎ (0511) 1 67 48 70, *info@hotel-savoy.de, Fax (0511) 16748710,* – . rm CV e
Meals (residents only) – **18 rm** 89/99 – 114/125.
◆ City centre hotel successfully combining functionality with a touch of elegance. Business travellers will appreciate the up-to-the-minute technical facilities.

Landhaus Ammann with rm, Hildesheimer Str. 185, ✉ 30173, ☎ (0511) 83 08 18, *mail@landhaus-ammann.de, Fax (0511) 8437749,* – – 100. rest by Hildesheimer Straße EFZ
Meals 31 *(lunch)* and à la carte 44/64, – **16 rm** 120/170 – 140/195.
◆ A country house in the city ! Restaurant with elegant décor and fine French cuisine, plus a lovely open-air section.

Georgenhof-Stern's Restaurant, Herrenhäuser Kirchweg 20, ✉ 30167, ☎ (0511) 70 22 44, *georgenhof@gmx.de, Fax (0511) 708559,* –
Meals 19,50 *(lunch)* and à la carte 35/55, . by Engelbosteler Damm CV
◆ Close to the famous Herrenhausen gardens, this characterful country house offers a magical mixture of traditional taste and a touch of fantasy. Lovely garden terrace.

Clichy, Weißekreuzstr. 31, ✉ 30161, ☎ (0511) 31 24 47, *clichy@clichy.de, Fax (0511) 318283* – EV d
closed Saturday lunch and Sunday – **Meals** à la carte 33/47.
◆ "Luxury without frippery" could be the motto of this elegant Art Nouveau Paris-style bistro, where classical cuisine is given a contemporary touch.

Gattopardo, Hainhölzer Str. 1 / corner of Postkamp, ✉ 30159, ☎ (0511) 1 43 75, *clichy@clichy.de, Fax (0511) 14375,* – DV f
Meals *(dinner only)* (Italian) à la carte 30/37.
◆ Fans of all things Italian flock to this friendly ristorante with its relaxed, Mediterranean atmosphere and fine cuisine.

Le Monde, Marienstr. 116, ✉ 30171, ☎ (0511) 8 56 51 71, FY a
closed Sunday – **Meals** *(dinner only)* 19,50/31 and à la carte 22/34.
◆ Bright colours, modern pictures and windows giving onto a little park enhance the attractiveness of this bistro. Conscientiously prepared French cuisine.

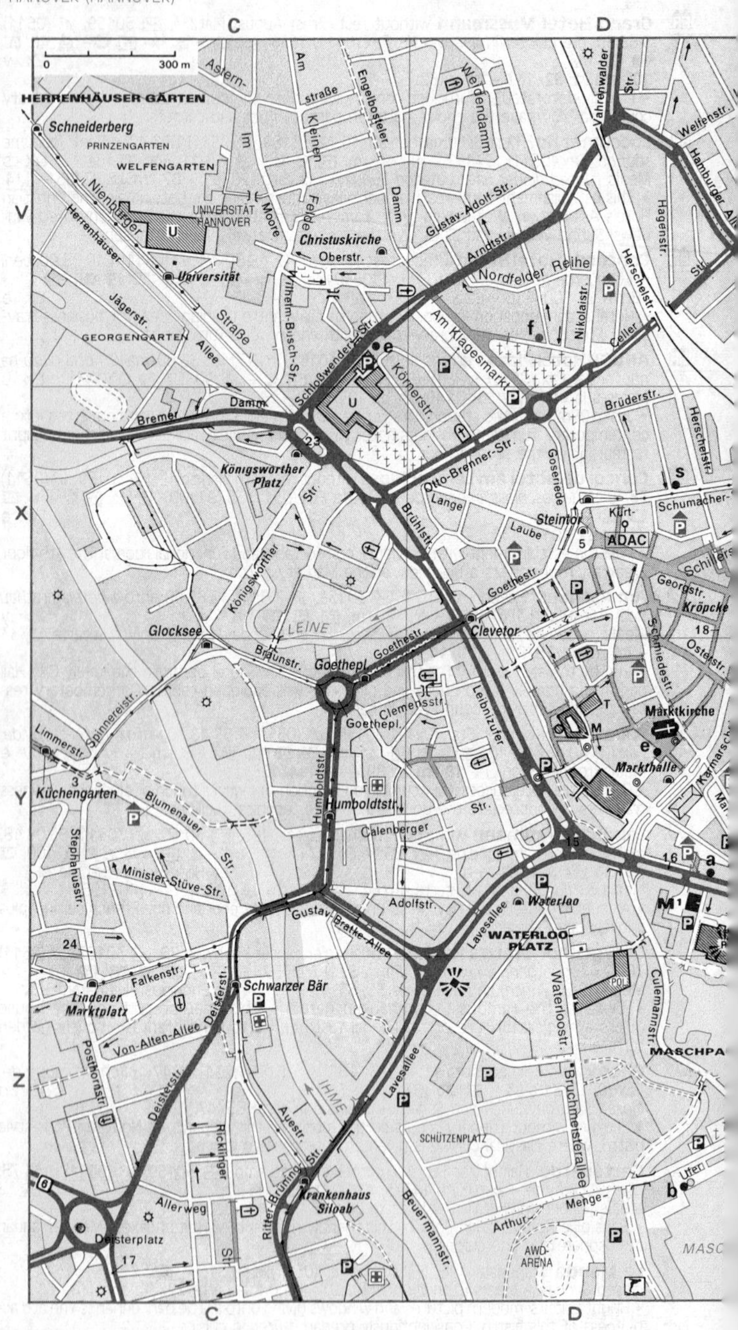
C
D
0
300 m
HERRENHÄUSER GÄRTEN
Schneiderberg
PRINZENGARTEN
WELFENGARTEN
UNIVERSITÄT HANNOVER
Universität
GEORGENGARTEN
Astern-
Am
straße
Kleinen
Engelbosteler
Im
Moore
Felde
Damm
Weidendamm
Christuskirche
Oberstr.
Wilhelm-Busch-Str.
Gustav-Adolf-Str.
Arndtstr.
Nordfelder Reihe
Vahrenwalder Str.
Hagenstr.
Welfenstr.
Hamburger Allee
Herschelstr.
Nikolaistr.
Celler
Am Klagesmarkt
Nienburger
Herrenhäuser
Jägerstr.
Straße
Allee
Bremer
Damm
Schloßwender Str.
Körnerstr.
Königsworther Platz
Brühlstr.
Otto-Brenner-Str.
Lange
Laube
Goseriede
Brüderstr.
Steintor
Kurt-
Schumacher-
ADAC
Schillerstr.
Georgstr.
Kröpcke
Königsworther Str.
Goethestr.
Clevetor
Glocksee
LEINE
Braunstr.
Goethepl.
Goethestr.
Clemensstr.
Goethepl.
Leibnizufer
Schmiedestr.
Osterstr.
Marktkirche
Markthalle
Karmarschstr.
Spinnereistr.
Limmerstr.
Küchengarten
Blumenauer
Str.
Humboldtstr.
Humboldtstr.
Calenberger
Str.
Stephanusstr.
Minister-Stüve-Str.
Gustav-Bratke-Allee
Adolfstr.
Lavesallee
Waterloo
WATERLOO-PLATZ
Falkenstr.
Schwarzer Bär
Lindener Marktplatz
Von-Alten-Allee
Deisterstr.
Posthornstr.
Waterloostr.
Culemannstr.
MASCHPA
Rickling
Auestr.
IHME
Lavesallee
Ritter-Brüning-Str.
Krankenhaus Siloah
Beuermannstr.
SCHÜTZENPLATZ
Bruchmeisterallee
Allerweg
Deisterplatz
Menge-
Arthur-
AWD-ARENA
Ufer
MASC
V
X
Y
Z
C
D

HANNOVER

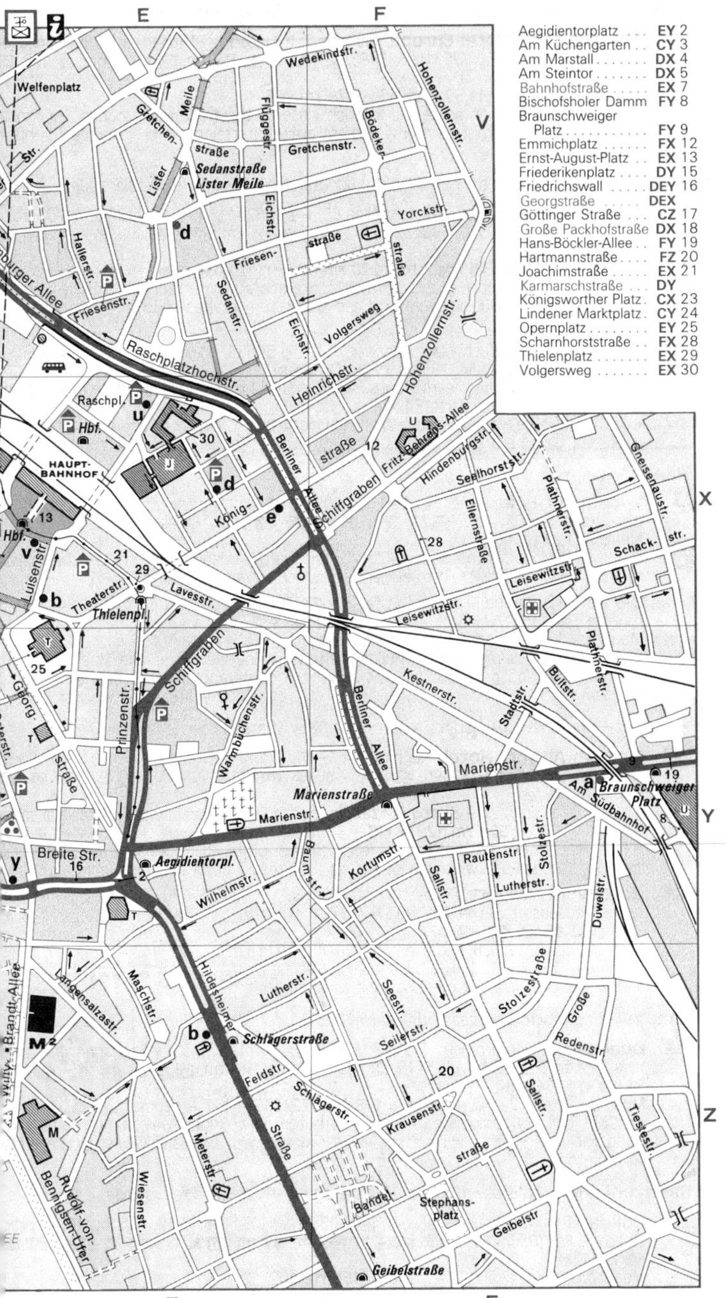
Aegidientorplatz . . . EY 2
Am Küchengarten . . CY 3
Am Marstall . . . . . . DX 4
Am Steintor . . . . . . DX 5
Bahnhofstraße . . . . EX 7
Bischofsholer Damm FY 8
Braunschweiger Platz . . . . FY 9
Emmichplatz . . . . . FX 12
Ernst-August-Platz . . EX 13
Friederikenplatz . . . . DY 15
Friedrichswall . . . . DEY 16
Georgstraße . . . . . DEX
Göttinger Straße . . . CZ 17
Große Packhofstraße DX 18
Hans-Böckler-Allee . . FY 19
Hartmannstraße . . . . FZ 20
Joachimstraße . . . . . EX 21
Karmarschstraße . . . DY
Königsworther Platz . CX 23
Lindener Marktplatz . CY 24
Opernplatz . . . . EY 25
Scharnhorststraße . . FX 28
Thielenplatz . . . . . . EX 29
Volgersweg . . . . . . EX 30
E
F
V
X
Y
Z
Welfenplatz
Wedekindstr.
Hohenzollernstr.
Meile
Flüggestr.
Bödeker
Gretchenstraße
Gretchenstr.
Lister
Sedanstraße Lister Meile
Eichstr.
Yorckstr.
Friesenstraße
Hallerstr.
Sedanstr.
Volgersweg
Friesenstr.
Raschplatzhochstr.
Heinrichstr.
Raschpl.
Hbf.
HAUPT-BAHNHOF
Berliner Allee
Fritz-Behrens-Allee
Hindenburgstr.
Seelhorststr.
Gneisenaustr.
Plathnerstr.
Ellernstraße
Schiffgraben
König-
Schackstr.
Luisenstr.
Theaterstr.
Thielenpl.
Lavesstr.
Leisewitzstr.
Kestnerstr.
Bultstr.
Stadtstr.
Prinzenstr.
Warmbüchenstr.
Marienstr.
Marienstraße
Braunschweiger Platz
Am Südbahnhof
Breite Str.
Aegidientorpl.
Wilhelmstr.
Baumstr.
Kortumstr.
Sallstr.
Rautenstr.
Lutherstr.
Stolzestr.
Düwelstr.
Langensalzastr.
Maschstr.
Hildesheimer Straße
Lutherstr.
Seestr.
Stolzestraße
Große Redenstr.
Willy-Brandt-Allee
Schlägerstraße
Seilerstr.
Feldstr.
Schlägerstr.
Krausenstr.
Tiestestr.
Meterstr.
Wiesenstr.
Rudolf-von-Bennigsen-Ufer
Bandel-straße
Stephansplatz
Geibelstr.
Geibelstraße
E
F

at Hannover-Bemerode *Southeast : 8 km, by Bischofsholer Damm* FY :

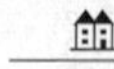

Ramada-Treff Hotel Europa, Bergstr. 2, ✉ 30539, ✆ (0511) 9 52 80, *hannover@ramada-treff.de, Fax (0511) 9528488,* – rm, – 180. AE VISA JCB
Meals à la carte 19/41,50 – 13 – **179 rm** 105.
• This hotel enjoys an accessible location close to the trade fair grounds. Functional but comfortably furnished rooms. Fitness area. Entertainment programme for hotel guests.

at Hanover-Buchholz *Northeast : 7 km, by Bödekerstraße* FV *and Podbielskistraße* :

Mercure Atrium, Karl-Wiechert-Allee 68, ✉ 30625, ✆ (0511) 5 40 70, *h1701@accor-hotels.com, Fax (0511) 5407826,* – rm, – 120. AE VISA JCB
Meals à la carte 28/46 – 14 – **220 rm** 107 – 117 – 6 suites.
• Glazed lifts transport guests to their contemporary-style rooms. Carefully planned conference area including secretarial and translation services and room with revolving stage.

Gallo Nero, Groß Buchholzer Kirchweg 72b, ✉ 30655, ✆ (0511) 5 46 34 34, *mail@gisyvino.de, Fax (0511) 548283,* – AE VISA
closed 3 weeks mid July - early August and Sunday – **Meals** (Italian) (booking essential for dinner) 25/52 and à la carte 34/47.
• 18C farmhouse with exposed beams and vinotheque. The mark of a fine wine, the black cockerel ("gallo nero") here stands for tasty cuisine. Permanent picture collection.

at Hanover-Döhren :

Wichmann, Hildesheimer Str. 230, ✉ 30519, ✆ (0511) 83 16 71, *gastw.wichmann@htp-tel.de, Fax (0511) 8379811,* – AE VISA by Hildesheimer Straße EFZ
Meals à la carte 37,50/60.
• This timber-framed house has a lovely courtyard garden. Diners choose among nine rooms - from country-style to elegant - in which to enjoy classic cuisine.

Die Insel, Rudolf-von-Bennigsen-Ufer 81, ✉ 30519, ✆ (0511) 83 12 14, *n.schu@t-online.de, Fax (0511) 831322,* – AE VISA
Meals (booking essential) 26 *(lunch)*/55 *(dinner)* and à la carte 30/52.
• This former swimming-pool building enjoys a fine view over the Maschsee lake. The long bar and generous windows give it a contemporary feel. Refined regional cuisine. by Rudolf-von Benningsen-Ufer EZ

at Hanover-Flughafen (Airport) *North : 11 km, by Vahrenwalder Straße* DV :

Maritim Airport Hotel, Flughafenstr. 5, ✉ 30669, ✆ (0511) 9 73 70, *info.hfl@maritim.de, Fax (0511) 9737590,* – rm, – 900. AE VISA JCB. rest
Meals (buffet only) 24 – ***Bistro Bottaccio*** *(closed Sunday and Monday)* **Meals** à la carte 27/41 – 15 – **528 rm** 128 – 143 – 30 suites.
• Built like a plane, this hotel looks ready to take off ! Elegant décor and high level of comfort. Club Lounge with view of runways. Tastefully decorated restaurant.

Holiday Inn Airport, Petzelstr. 60, ✉ 30662, ✆ (0511) 7 70 70, *reservation.hi-hannover@queensgruppe.de, Fax (0511) 737781,* – rm, – 150. AE VISA JCB
Meals 20 *(buffet lunch)* and à la carte 28/45 – **211 rm** 105/147 – 125/167.
• Right by the airport (shuttle-bus), this establishment offers tastefully refurbished rooms and modern facilities for meetings and conferences.

at Hanover-Kirchrode *Southeast : 8 km, by Hans-Böckler Allee* FY :

Queens, Tiergartenstr. 117, ✉ 30559, ✆ (0511) 5 10 30, *info.qhannover@queensgruppe.de, Fax (0511) 5103510,* – rm, – 150. AE VISA JCB
Meals à la carte 22/40 – 14 – **178 rm** 122/135 – 151 – 3 suites.
• 1960s building surrounded by the Tiergarten park. Bright, welcoming rooms with good facilities - some with balcony. Restaurant with pleasant views of the leafy surroundings.

at Hanover-Lahe *Northeast : 10 km, by Bödekerstraße* FV *and Podbielskistraße* :

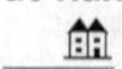

Holiday Inn, Oldenburger Allee 1, ✉ 30659, ✆ (0511) 6 15 50, *hannover@eventhotels.com, Fax (0511) 6155555,* – rm, rm, – 280. AE VISA
Meals à la carte 17,50/29 – 13 – **150 rm** 102/123.
• Accessible location in the northeastern part of town. Contemporary, functional rooms Executive rooms cater for the needs of business travellers.

at Hanover-List *Northeast : 5 km, by Bödekerstraße* FV :

ArabellaSheraton Pelikan, Podbielskistr. 145, ✉ 30177, ☎ (0511) 9 09 30, *pelikanhotel@arabellasheraton.com, Fax (0511) 9093555*, – rm, – 140. AE VISA JCB
5th Avenue : **Meals** à la carte 25/36 – 16 – **147 rm** 149 – 7 suites.
◆ Carefully converted factory building. Where once famous "Pelikan" pens were produced, guests now stay in an ambience enlivened with an array of amusing details. Cool design contributes to the restaurant's contemporary look.

Dorint, Podbielskistr. 21, ✉ 30163, ☎ (0511) 3 90 40, *info.hajhan@dorint.com, Fax (0511) 3904100*, – rm, rm, – 200. AE VISA JCB
Meals à la carte 22/36 – 16 – **206 rm** 122/151 – 131/161 – 4 suites.
◆ A famous biscuit factory once stood here. Nowadays there is an impressive combination of historical steam engines, avant-garde architecture and modern, comfortable rooms. Bright, elegant restaurant serving international dishes.

at Hanover-Messe (near Exhibition Centre) *Southeast : 9 km, by Hildesheimer Straße* EFZ :

Radisson SAS, Expo-Plaza 5 (at Exhibition Centre), ✉ 30539, ☎ (0511) 38 38 30, *info.hannover@radissonsas.com, Fax (0511) 383838000*, – rm, – 240. AE VISA JCB
Meals à la carte 23/37 – 15 – **250 rm** 110.
◆ This establishment offers guests a choice of contemporary themed rooms - Hi-Tech, Italian, Maritime, or Scandinavian. In the lobby, the restaurant is divided into a buffet and an à la carte area.

Parkhotel Kronsberg (with guest house), Gut Kronsberg 1 (at Exhibition Centre), ✉ 30539, ☎ (0511) 8 74 00, *parkh@kronsberg.bestwestern.de, Fax (0511) 867112*, – rm, rest, – 150. AE VISA JCB
Meals *(closed 27 December - 2 January)* à la carte 21/31 – **200 rm** 88/160 – 136/186.
◆ A lovely Mediterranean-style foyer with a glass dome welcomes guests to this comfortable establishment. Guests can check into a room chosen according to their star sign. A choice of restaurants and a garden terrace cater for every culinary aspiration.

at Hanover-Roderbruch *Northeast : 7 km, by Hans-Böckler Allee* FY *and Karl-Wiechert-Allee* :

Novotel, Feodor-Lynen-Str. 1, ✉ 30625, ☎ (0511) 9 56 60, *h1631@accor-hotels.com, Fax (0511) 9566333*, (heated) – rm, – 80. AE VISA
Meals à la carte 17,50/24 – 13 – **112 rm** 99 – 105.
◆ All rooms are brightly furnished and offer adequate space and work desks, making this a highly practical place to stay. Children have their very own play-area. Restaurant opening onto the lobby.

at Hanover-Vahrenwald *North : 4 km, by Vahrenwalder Straße* DV :

Fora, Großer Kolonnenweg 19, ✉ 30163, ☎ (0511) 6 70 60, *reservation.hannover@fora.de, Fax (0511) 6706111*, – rm, rest, – 100. AE VISA JCB
Meals à la carte 20/31 – **142 rm** 98/118 – 118/138.
◆ Functional accommodation for the business traveller, with generous work areas and your own fax to make things easy. Conference rooms are also provided, with modern facilities.

at Laatzen *South : 9 km, by Hildesheimer Straße* EFZ :

Copthorne, Würzburger Str. 21, ✉ 30880, ☎ (0511) 9 83 60, *sales.hannover@millcop.com, Fax (0511) 9836666*, – rm, rm, – 300. AE VISA JCB
Meals à la carte 22/40 – **222 rm** 150 – 190.
◆ A hotel only five minutes on foot from the trade fair grounds. Many prominent guests have already enjoyed the tasteful comforts of this modern establishment. The glass pyramid helps create the attractively bright ambience in Bentley's.

at Langenhagen *North : 10 km, by Vahrenwalder Straße* DV :

Allegro without rest, Walsroder Str. 105, ✉ 30853, ☎ (0511) 7 71 96 10, *hotel@hotel-allegro.de, Fax (0511) 77196196* – – 200. AE VISA
74 rm 85 – 105.
◆ The world in a room ! You have the freedom to decide whether to spend the night in English, Mexican, Moorish or Mediterranean style.

Ambiente, Walsroder Str. 70, ✉ 30853, ☎ (0511) 7 70 60, *hotel@ambiente.com, Fax (0511) 7706111* – rm, – 20. AE VISA
closed 24 December - 2 January – **Meals** *(closed lunch Saturday and Sunday)* à la carte 22/32 – **67 rm** 90 – 115.
◆ Modern, comfortable establishment with excellent technical facilities including internet connection and PC on demand. Tasteful ambience in the Kamin-Bar restaurant.

at Ronnenberg-Benthe *Southwest : 10 km, by Deisterplatz CZ Bornumer Straße and B 65 :*

Benther Berg, Vogelsangstr. 18, ✉ 30952, ℘ (05108) 6 40 60, *info@hotel-benther-berg.de, Fax (05108) 640650*, – rest, – 60. AE VISA
Meals à la carte 30/45 – **70 rm** 76/97 – 92/128.
◆ This idyllic establishment consists of three parts : you can choose from the homely Altes Haus (an 1894 manor house), the functional Neues Haus and the comfortable Landhaus. Elegant gastronomy with an international repertoire.

at Isernhagen *North : 14 km, by Podbielskistraße* B *and Sutelstr. :*

Engel without rest, Burgwedeler Str. 151 (HB), ✉ 30916, ℘ (0511) 97 25 60, *info@hotel-engel-isernhagen.de, Fax (0511) 9725646* – – 20. AE VISA
28 rm 46/97 – 72/112.
◆ This highly recommended country-house style establishment offers tasteful, comfortable bedrooms and an attractive room for your varied breakfast buffet.

at Garbsen-Frielingen *Northeast : 19 km, by Bremer Damm* CV *and Westschnellweg :*

Bullerdieck (mit Gästehaus), Bgm.-Wehrmann-Str. 21, ✉ 30826, ℘ (05131) 45 80, *info@bullerdieck.de, Fax (05131) 458222*, beer garden, Massage, – rm, – 35. AE VISA
Meals à la carte 18/36 – **56 rm** 65/75 – 90/100.
◆ This spacious establishment has been owned by the same family since 1869. Comfortable and individually decorated rooms. Beauty parlour with wide range of services. Relaxed atmosphere in the rustic restaurant.

Nenndorf, Bad Niedersachsen 541 I 12 – *pop. 10 700 – alt. 70 m.*
Hannover 33.

at Bad Nenndorf-Riepen *Northwest : 4,5 km by B 65 :*

XXX **La Forge** (Gehrke) - Schmiedegasthaus Gehrke, Riepener Str. 21, ✉ 31542, ℘ (05725) 9 44 10, *info@schmiedegasthaus.de, Fax (05725) 944141* – AE VISA.
closed 2 weeks January, 3 weeks July - August, Monday and Tuesday – **Meals** *(dinner only)* (booking essential) 42/90.
◆ Bright, friendly and elegant restaurant with lovely table settings, attentive service and classic French cuisine.
Spec. Jakobsmuscheln mit Sesam gebraten und Schnittlauchpüree. Soufflierte Taubenbrust mit Essig-Honigsauce und Gänseleber-Crêpes. Pfirsich und Orangen in Caipirinhagelée mit gratiniertem Limonenparfait.

LEIPZIG *Sachsen* 544 L 21 – *pop. 500 000 – alt. 118 m.*

See : *Old Town Hall★ (Altes Rathaus)* BY – *Old Stock Exchange★ (Alte Börse)* BY – *Museum of Fine Arts★★ (Museum der Bildenden Künste)* BZ – *St. Thomas' Church (Thomaskirche)★* BZ – *Grassi Museum (Museum of Fine Art★, Museum of Ethnography★, Musical Instrument Museum★)* CZ.

Leipzig-Seehausen, Bergweg 10 (North : 8 km by Eutritzscher Straße), ℘ *(034242) 5 21 74 42 ; Markleeberg, Mühlweg (South : 9 km by Harkortstraße and B 2),* ℘ *(0341) 3 58 26 86 ; Machern, Plagwitzer Weg 6d (East : 15 km by Dresdner Str. and B2)* ℘ *(034292) 6 80 32.*

Leipzig-Halle (Northwest : 15 km by Gerberstraße and Eutritzscher Straße BY*),* ℘ *(0341) 22 40.*

Exhibition Grounds (Neue Messe), Messe Allee 1 (by Eutritzscher Str BY*),* ✉ *04356,* ℘ *(0341) 67 80, Fax (0341) 6788762.*

Tourist-Service, Richard-Wagner Str. 1, ✉ *04109,* ℘ *(0341) 7 10 42 60, info@lts-leipzig.de,* Fax (0341) 7104271.

ADAC, *Augustusplatz 5/6.*

Berlin 180 – Dresden 109 – Erfurt 126.

Plans on following pages

Fürstenhof, Tröndlinring 8, ✉ 04105, ℘ (0341) 14 00, *fuerstenhof.leipzig@arabellasheraton.com, Fax (0341) 1403700*, Massage, – rm, – 65. AE VISA JCB. rest BY c
Meals *(closed Sunday) (dinner only)* à la carte 47/58 – 19 – **92 rm** 210/280 – 235/305 – 4 suites.
◆ Beyond the façade of this neo-Classical town mansion of 1770 is an interior of luxurious elegance and exquisite service. Luxury pool. Aristocratic décor and fine furniture in the restaurant.

Marriott, Am Hallischen Tor 1, ✉ 04109, ☎ (0341) 9 65 30, *leipzig.marriott@marriotthotels.com, Fax (0341) 9653999*, 🏋, ⛲, 🏊 - ⬍, ⇆ rm, ▤ TV ☎ ♿ 🚗 - 🏃 200. AE ⓓ MC VISA JCB BY n
Meals à la carte 24/32 - **231 rm** ☕ 119 - 135 - 11 suites.
• In the heart of the city, guests are accommodated in rooms lacking nothing in terms of comfort, convenience and technology ; all have internet access, modem point and answerphone. Allie's American Grill provides good food for every taste.

The Westin, Gerberstr. 15, ✉ 04105, ☎ (0341) 98 80, *info@westin-leipzig.com, Fax (0341) 9881229*, beer garden, Massage, 🏋, ⛲, 🏊 - ⬍, ⇆ rm, ▤ TV ☎ ♿ P - 🏃 360. AE ⓓ MC VISA JCB. ⇆ rest BY a
Meals *(closed Sunday lunch)* à la carte 30,50/42 – ***Yamato*** (Japanese) **Meals** 20/70 and à la carte - **447 rm** ☕ 162/192 - 177/207 - 21 suites.
• Overnight guests can arrive here by helicopter if they wish. Luxurious rooms. The Club rooms are particularly suitable for business travellers. Coolly elegant restaurant. Japanese delicacies in the Yamato.

Renaissance, Großer Brockhaus 3, ✉ 04103, ☎ (0341) 1 29 20, *renaissance.leipzig@renaissance.com, Fax (0341) 1292800*, 🏋, ⛲, 🏊 - ⬍, ⇆ rm, ▤ TV ☎ ♿ 🚗 - 🏃 350. AE ⓓ MC VISA JCB DY a
Meals 18 *(buffet lunch)* and à la carte 27/37 - **356 rm** ☕ 98/110 - 112/124.
• A superb, light and airy foyer greets guests to this impeccably run hotel. Bright, welcoming and comfortable rooms. International cuisine with an Oriental touch in the elegant Ambiente.

Victor's Residenz, Georgiring 13, ✉ 04103, ☎ (0341) 6 86 60, *info@victors-leipzig.bestwestern.de, Fax (0341) 6866899*, beer garden - ⬍, ⇆ rm, TV ☎ ♿ 🚗 P - 🏃 80. AE ⓓ MC VISA JCB CY e
Meals à la carte 21/39,50 - **101 rm** ☕ 90/120 - 105/135.
• Comfort and modernity make this historic building - plus a newly-built section - an attractive place to stay, meeting all contemporary needs. Chic restaurant in Paris bistro style.

Dorint, Stephanstr. 6, ✉ 04103, ☎ (0341) 9 77 90, *info.lejlei@dorint.com, Fax (0341) 9779100*, beer garden, ⛲ - ⬍, ⇆ rm, TV ☎ ♿ 🚗 - 🏃 150. AE ⓓ MC VISA JCB DZ n
Meals à la carte 25/36 - ☕ 14 - **174 rm** 90/108 - 93/113.
• Behind the striking, ultra-modern glazed exterior of this hotel are attractive, warmly coloured rooms with cherrywood furnishings and ample work facilities. The restaurant is only separated from the foyer by a glass wall.

Seaside Park Hotel, Richard-Wagner-Str. 7, ✉ 04109, ☎ (0341) 9 85 20, *info@parkhotelleipzig.de, Fax (0341) 9852750*, Massage, ⛲ - ⬍ ⇆, ▤ rest, TV ☎ ♿ 🚗 - 🏃 80. AE ⓓ MC VISA JCB CY s
Meals à la carte 18/36 - **288 rm** ☕ 105/125 - 126/140 - 5 suites.
• The individual Art Deco style rooms are fitted with the latest technology and are designed to function equally well as living and working space. The elegant Orient Express restaurant recreates the style of the golden age of rail travel.

Michaelis, Paul-Gruner-Str. 44, ✉ 04107, ☎ (0341) 2 67 80, *hotel.michaelis@t-online.de, Fax (0341) 2678100*, 🏖 - ⬍, ⇆ rm, TV ☎ ♿ 🚗 - 🏃 50. AE ⓓ MC VISA by Peterssteinweg BZ
Meals *(closed Saturday lunch and Sunday)* à la carte 31/53 - **59 rm** ☕ 75/85 - 100.
• This listed building dating from 1907 has been restored with loving attention to detail. The individually designed rooms are a harmonious combination of comfort and elegance. The restaurant is stylish and attractively modern.

Novotel, Goethestr. 11, ✉ 04109, ☎ (0341) 9 95 80, *h1784@accor-hotels.com, Fax (0341) 9958935*, 🏖, 🏋, ⛲ - ⬍, ⇆ rm, ▤ TV ☎ ♿ 🚗 - 🏃 90. AE ⓓ MC VISA CY n
Meals à la carte 19/37 - ☕ 13 - **200 rm** 90/127 - 105/142.
• The comfortable "Blue Harmonie" rooms with ample beds and up-to-the-minute technology are ideal for both relaxing and working.

Mercure Vier Jahreszeiten without rest, Kurt-Schumacher-Str. 23, ✉ 04105, ☎ (0341) 9 85 10, *h4997@accor-hotels.com, Fax (0341) 985122* - ⬍ ⇆ TV. AE ⓓ MC VISA JCB CY b
☕ 13 - **67 rm** 62/90 - 72/109.
• The rooms in this establishment are characterised by a harmonious combination of functionality, contemporary comfort, and carefully chosen colour schemes.

Leipziger Hof, Hedwigstr. 1, ✉ 04315, ☎ (0341) 6 97 40, *info@leipziger-hof.de, Fax (0341) 6974150*, beer garden, ⛲ - ⬍, ⇆ rm, TV ☎ P - 🏃 60. AE ⓓ MC VISA JCB. ⇆ rest by Eisenbahnstraße DY
Meals *(closed Sunday)* à la carte 21/44 - **72 rm** ☕ 73 - 85 - 4 suites.
• Guests spend the night in what amounts to an art gallery ; the whole establishment is hung with works by well-known Leipzig artists. Tasteful rooms match the quality of the art and the glittering décor of the restaurant is equally striking.

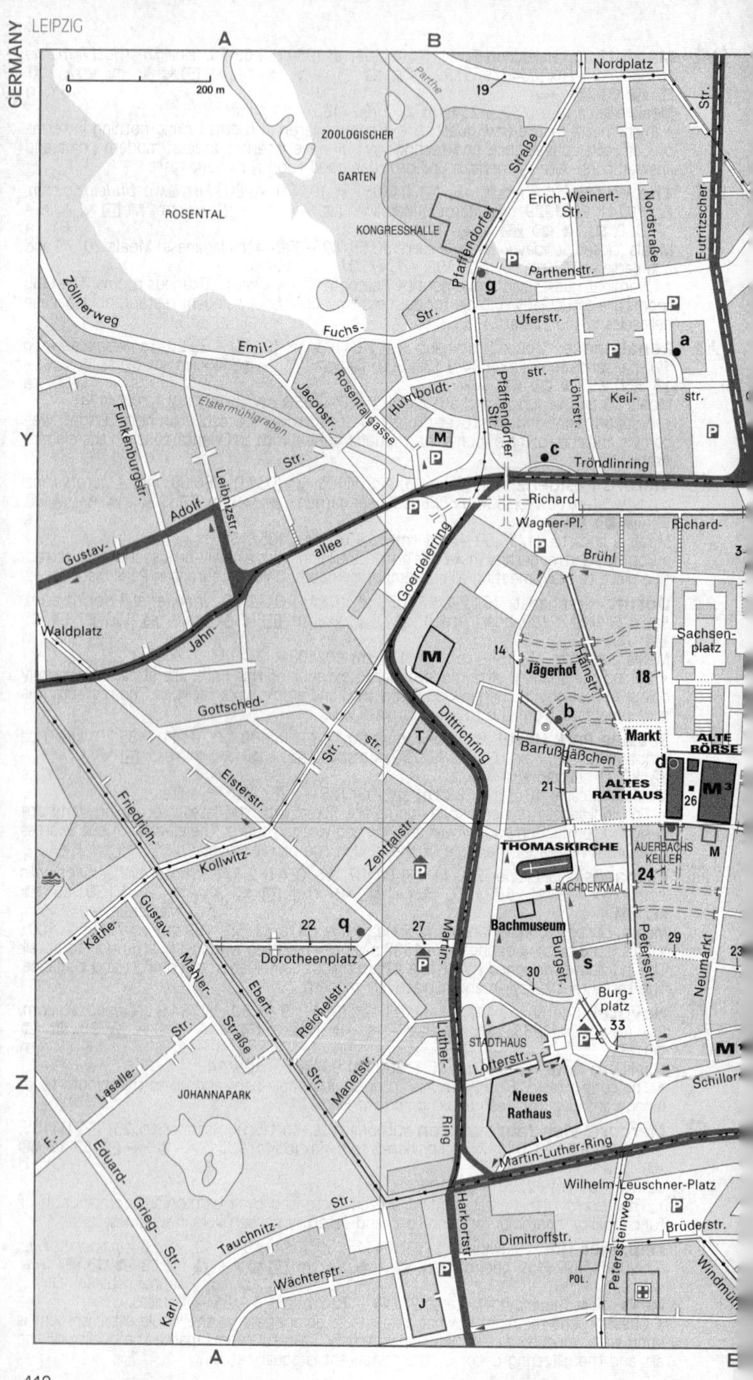

ZOOLOGISCHER GARTEN
ROSENTAL
KONGRESSHALLE
Nordplatz
Pfaffendorfer Straße
Erich-Weinert-Str.
Nordstraße
Eutritzscher Str.
Parthenstr.
Uferstr.
Löhrstr.
Keil-str.
Tröndlinring
Richard-Wagner-Pl.
Brühl
Emil-Fuchs-Str.
Zöllnerweg
Jacobstr.
Rosentalgasse
Humboldt-str.
Elstermühlgraben
Funkenburgstr.
Leibnizstr.
Gustav-Adolf-Str.
Jahn-allee
Goerdelerring
Waldplatz
Gottsched-str.
Dittrichring
Jägerhof
Hainstr.
Sachsenplatz
Markt
ALTE BÖRSE
Barfußgäßchen
ALTES RATHAUS
THOMASKIRCHE
AUERBACHS KELLER
BACHDENKMAL
Bachmuseum
Elsterstr.
Friedrich-Ebert-Str.
Kollwitz-
Käthe-
Zentralstr.
Dorotheenplatz
Martin-Luther-Ring
Burgstr.
Petersstr.
Neumarkt
Burgplatz
STADTHAUS
Lotterstr.
Neues Rathaus
Schillerstr.
Gustav-Mahler-Straße
Reichelstr.
Manetstr.
Lasalle-Str.
JOHANNAPARK
Eduard-Grieg-Str.
Karl-Tauchnitz-Str.
Wächterstr.
Harkortstr.
Wilhelm-Leuschner-Platz
Peterssteinweg
Brüderstr.
Dimitroffstr.
POL.
Windmühlen
Parthe
200 m

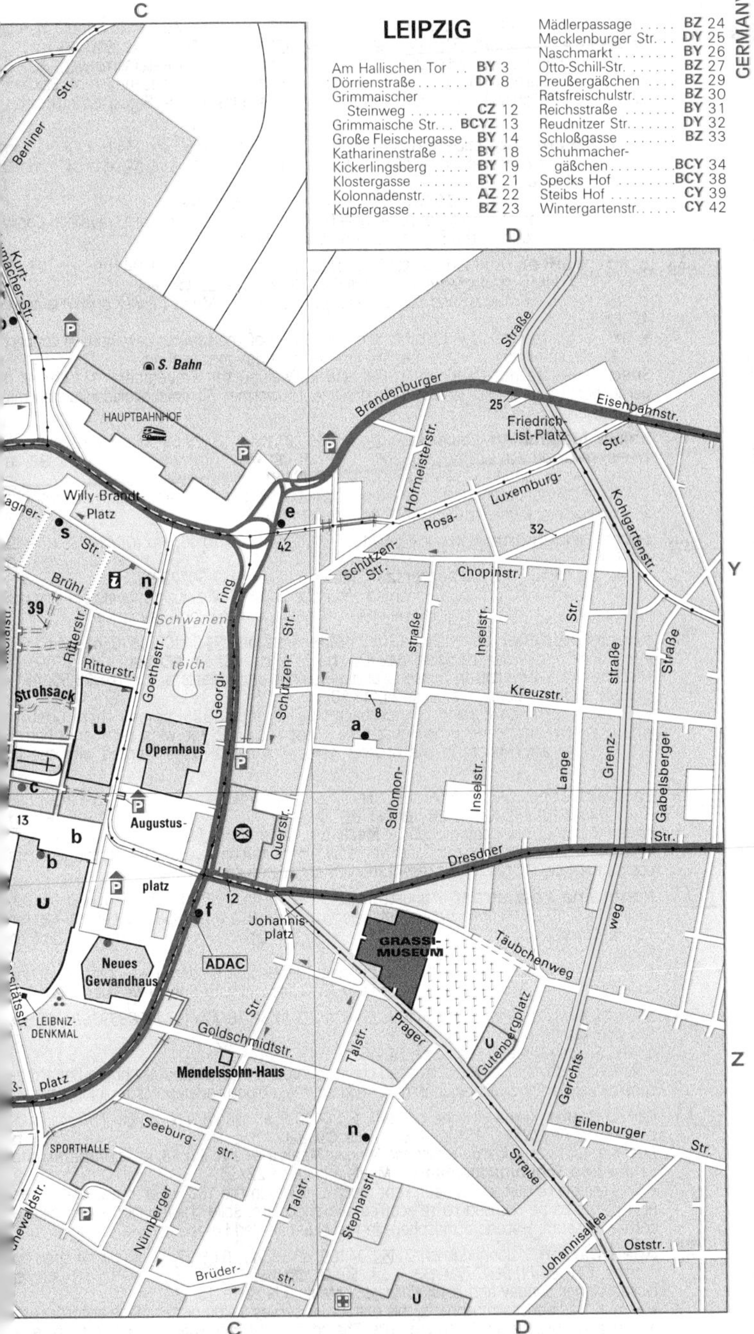
LEIPZIG
Am Hallischen Tor .. BY 3
Dörrienstraße .... DY 8
Grimmaischer Steinweg .... CZ 12
Grimmaische Str. .. BCYZ 13
Große Fleischergasse . BY 14
Katharinenstraße .... BY 18
Kickerlingsberg ..... BY 19
Klostergasse .... BY 21
Kolonnadenstr. ..... AZ 22
Kupfergasse .... BZ 23
Mädlerpassage ..... BZ 24
Mecklenburger Str. .. DY 25
Naschmarkt .... BY 26
Otto-Schill-Str. ...... BZ 27
Preußergäßchen .... BZ 29
Ratsfreischulstr. ..... BZ 30
Reichsstraße .... BY 31
Reudnitzer Str. ...... DY 32
Schloßgasse .... BZ 33
Schuhmachergäßchen .... BCY 34
Specks Hof .... BCY 38
Steibs Hof .... CY 39
Wintergartenstr. ..... CY 42
C
D
Y
Z
Berliner Str.
Kurt-Schumacher-Str.
S. Bahn
HAUPTBAHNHOF
Brandenburger
Straße
Eisenbahnstr.
Friedrich-List-Platz
Willy-Brandt-Platz
Hofmeisterstr.
Luxemburg-
Rosa-
Str.
Kohlgartenstr.
Schützen-Str.
Chopinstr.
Brühl
Ritterstr.
Goethestr.
Schwanenteich
Georgi-ring
Schützen-Str.
straße
Inselstr.
Str.
straße
Straße
Kreuzstr.
Strohsack
Opernhaus
Augustus-platz
Salomon-
Inselstr.
Lange
Grenz-
Gabelsberger Str.
Querstr.
Dresdner
Johannisplatz
GRASSI-MUSEUM
Täubchenweg
weg
ADAC
Neues Gewandhaus
LEIBNIZ-DENKMAL
Goldschmidtstr.
Mendelssohn-Haus
Talstr.
Prager
Gutenbergplatz
Gerichts-
Eilenburger Str.
Straße
Seeburg-str.
SPORTHALLE
Nürnberger
Talstr.
Stephanstr.
Johannisallee
Oststr.
Brüder-str.

Markgraf without rest, Körnerstr. 36, ✉ 04107, ✆ (0341) 30 30 30, *hotel@markgraf-leipzig.de, Fax (0341) 3030399,* – ✈ rm, TV ✆. AE ⓓ MC VISA JCB
9 – **54 rm** 65/90 – 75/125. by Peterssteinweg BZ
◆ Southern German hospitality from far-off Baden here in the heart of Saxony. Charming, comfortable and modern rooms in subtle shades of blue. Breakfast in the conservatory.

Mercure am Augustusplatz, Augustusplatz 5, ✉ 04109, ✆ (0341) 2 14 60, *mercure_leipzig@t-online.de, Fax (0341) 9604916* – ✈ rm, rest, TV P – 120. AE ⓓ MC VISA JCB CZ f
Meals à la carte 16/32 – **283 rm** 72/87 – 105 – 10 suites.
◆ Its central location makes this hotel ideal for both business and private travellers. Coolly elegant and functional rooms with pale grey furnishings.

Stadtpfeiffer, Augustusplatz 8 (at Neues Gewandhaus), ✉ 04109, ✆ (0341) 2 17 89 20, *info@stadtpfeiffer.de, Fax (0341) 1494470* – AE MC VISA CZ
closed 10 July - 8 August and Sunday, except December – **Meals** *(dinner only)* à la carte 49/63 ♀.
◆ This completely glazed-in restaurant occupies part of the famous Gewandhaus concert hall. Bright and friendly contemporary interior with designer seating.
Spec. Seezunge mit Périgord-Trüffel und Rotweinbutter (November - March). Mild geräucherte Taube mit Gänsestopflebersauce. Lauwarmer Bitterschokoladenkuchen mit Lavendeleis.

Kaiser Maximilian, Neumarkt 9, ✉ 04109, ✆ (0341) 9 98 69 00, *webmaster@kaiser-maximilian.de, Fax (0341) 9986901,* – AE MC VISA BZ a
closed 1 week January – **Meals** à la carte 30,50/39.
◆ With its contemporary décor the pillar room in the historic Städtisches Kaufhaus is bright and welcoming. Refined cuisine with an Italian touch.

Lotter Widemann, Markt 1, ✉ 04109, ✆ (0341) 2 25 10 45, *Fax (0341) 22510* – AE MC VISA BY d
Meals à la carte 39/57 – ***Lottersaal :*** **Meals** à la carte 17,50/28,50.
◆ This vaulted establishment is named after the builders of Leipzig's lovely old city hall in which it is located. The brasserie-style Lottersaal is a real local favourite.

Auerbachs Keller, Grimmaische Str. 2 (Mädler-Passage), ✉ 04109, ✆ (0341) 21 61 00, *info@auerbachs-keller-leipzig.de, Fax (0341) 2161011* – AE ⓓ MC VISA BYZ
Historische Weinstuben *(closed Sunday) (dinner only)* **Meals** à la carte 28,50/45 – ***Großer Keller :*** **Meals** à la carte 21/41,50.
◆ Diners have been coming to Auerbach's Cellar since 1525, among them Goethe, who set a famous scene in his Faust here. Faust rode into the wine cellar on a barrel. Art Nouveau atmosphere in the Grosser Keller. Traditional dishes served with special flair.

La Cachette, Pfaffendorfer Str. 26, ✉ 04105, ✆ (0341) 5 62 98 67, *Fax (0341) 5629869,* – AE ⓓ MC VISA. BY g
closed Sunday dinner and Monday – **Meals** à la carte 25/39,50 ♀.
◆ Wood fittings, warm colours and works by Alfons Mucha give this hospitable jewel its cosy ambience. Professional presentation of Mediterranean cuisine.

Panorama Restaurant, Augustusplatz 9 (29 th floor of MDR-Building), ✉ 04109, ✆ (0341) 7 10 05 90, *info@panorama-leipzig.de, Fax (0341) 7100589,* ≤ Leipzig – . AE ⓓ MC VISA CZ b
Meals à la carte 17/36,50.
◆ On the 29th floor of the MDR radio building, this elegant modern restaurant maintains an appropriately high standard. Floor-to-ceiling windows with fine views over the city.

Medici, Nikolaikirchhof 5, ✉ 04109, ✆ (0341) 2 11 38 78, *Fax (0341) 9839399* – AE ⓓ MC VISA JCB CY c
closed Sunday – **Meals** à la carte 34/46.
◆ Refined and creative Mediterranean cuisine served in a contemporary bistro-like atmosphere, next to the Nikolai Church. A striking steel structure supports a dining gallery.

Coffe Baum, Kleine Fleischergasse 4, ✉ 04109, ✆ (0341) 9 61 00 61, *coffebaum@t-online.de, Fax (0341) 9610030,* – AE MC VISA BY b
Lusatia (1st floor) *(closed August and Sunday)* **Meals** à la carte 31/38,50 – ***Lehmannsche Stube und Schuhmannzimmer :*** **Meals** à la carte 22/33.
◆ This temple to coffee has been kept much as it was in the 15C, when it was one of the first places to be licensed to sell coffee and chocolate. Solid traditional cooking, plus a coffee museum. Historic atmosphere in the blue-panelled Lusatia.

Apels Garten, Kolonnadenstr. 2, ✉ 04109, ✆ (0341) 9 60 77 77, *mueller@apels-garten.de, Fax (0341) 9607779,* – 30. AE MC VISA AZ q
closed dinner Sunday and Bank Holidays – **Meals** à la carte 15/26.
◆ Rich in traditional atmosphere, this restaurant serves Saxon dishes made according to historical recipes. Décor featuring dolls. The covered terrace is an attractive feature.

Thüringer Hof, Burgstr. 19, 04109, (0341) 9 94 49 99, *reservierung@thueringer-hof.de, Fax (0341) 9944933,* – BZ s
Meals à la carte 17,50/26.
• Dating from 1454, this is one of the oldest beer-halls in the city, offering tasty morsels such as famous Thuringian sausages. Modern section in the courtyard.

at Leipzig-Breitenfeld *Northwest : 8 km, by Euritzscher Straße* BX :

Breitenfelder Hof, Lindenallee 8, 04158, (0341) 4 65 10, *info@breitenfelderhof.de, Fax (0341) 4651133,* – rm, – 80.
***Gustav's :* Meals** à la carte 19/31 – 13 – **75 rm** 56/90.
• Stylish country hotel and separate villa in extensive parkland. Comprehensive leisure provision with hot-air balloon ascents, archery, badminton and competitive angling. The refurbished villa houses Gustav's restaurant.

at Leipzig-Connewitz *South : 2,5 km, by Harkort-Str.* BZ *and Richard-Lehmann-Str. :*

Leonardo Hotel und Residenz, Windscheidstr. 21, 04277, (0341) 3 03 30 (Hotel) 3 03 35 14 (Rest.), *info@hotel-leonardo.de, Fax (0341) 3033555,* , – , rm, rest, – 30. V v
Mona Lisa *(closed Saturday lunch and Sunday)* **Meals** à la carte 25/39,50 – **53 rm** 85/95 – 100 – 3 suites.
• With fine furnishings, king-size beds, generous desks with granite surfaces, and granite bath-tubs, this is a truly luxurious establishment. The Mona Lisa captivates with its sophisticated Italian atmosphere.

at Leipzig-Eutritzsch *by Eutritzscher Straße* BY :

Vivaldi without rest, Wittenberger Str. 87, 04129, (0341) 9 03 60, *info@hotel-vivaldi.de, Fax (0341) 9036234* – – 20.
107 rm 65/85 – 75/95.
• Everything about this establishment, from foyer to bedrooms, reflects contemporary design style with an Italian touch. City centre and new fair grounds within easy reach.

at Leipzig-Gohlis *North : 2,5 km, by Pfaffendorfer Straße* BY :

De Saxe, Gohliser Str. 25, 04155, (0341) 5 93 80, *hoteldesaxe@aol.com, Fax (0341) 5938299* –
Meals à la carte 12/21 – **33 rm** 50/56 – 60/67.
• Behind the sandstone facade of this city establishment are well-kept rooms, mostly furnished in honey-coloured cherrywood.

at Leipzig-Grosszschocher *Southwest : 7 km, by Käthe-Kollwitz-Straße* AZ *and Erich-Zeigner-Allee :*

Windorf, Ernst-Meier-Str. 1, 04249, (0341) 4 27 70, *info@windorf.bestwestern.de, Fax (0341) 4277222,* – , rm, – 55.
Meals à la carte 16/27,50 – **91 rm** 51 – 59/75.
• The bright and spacious rooms with natural wood furnishings throughout extend a friendly welcome. Ample work desks with state-of-the-art technology. The restaurant and winter garden stand ready with a selection of local and international dishes.

at Leipzig-Leutzsch *West : 5,5 km, by Friedrich-Ebert-Straße* AY :

Lindner Hotel, Hans-Driesch-Str. 27, 04179, (0341) 4 47 80, *info.leipzig@lindner.de, Fax (0341) 4478478,* , , – , rm, – 120.
Meals à la carte 29/36 – **200 rm** 97/110 – 117/130 – 7 suites.
• Modern establishment, recommended for conferences and meetings, and featuring beautiful rustic furnishings of superior quality. Excellent technical facilities. Striking use of glass in the foyer. Bright and cheerful bistro-style restaurant.

at Leipzig-Lindenau *West : 5 km, by Jahn-Allee* AY :

Lindenau, Georg-Schwarz-Str. 33, 04177, (0341) 4 48 03 10, *info@hotel-lindenau.de, Fax (0341) 4480300,* – , rm, – 20.
Meals *(closed Saturday and Sunday) (dinner only)* à la carte 14/23 – **52 rm** 56 – 70/76.
• With its lovely facade, this family-run hotel is in a vibrant city-centre location. Welcoming, functionally equipped rooms. Restaurant in subtle pastel tones.

at Leipzig-Paunsdorf *East : 5 km, by Dresdner Straße* DZ *and Wurzner Straße :*

Ramada Treff Hotel, Schongauer Str. 39, 04329, (0341) 25 40, *leipzig@ramada-treff.de, Fax (0341) 2541550,* , Massage, – , rm, – 630.
Meals à la carte 18,50/32,50 – 13 – **291 rm** 67/77.
• Light but solid contemporary furniture and little built-in sitting areas with red and blue striped fabrics. Tasteful rooms enhanced by up-to-the-minute technology.

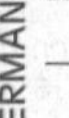

Artis Suite Hotel, Permoserstr. 50, 04328, (0341) 2 58 90, *leipzig@artis-hotels.de, Fax (0341) 2589444*, – rm, . AE MC VISA. rest
Meals *(closed Sunday dinner)* à la carte 15,50/28 – 8 – **82 rm** 65/75 – 75/85 – 70 suites.
◆ From the foyer to the comfortable apartments, the use of wood and cane furnishings together with harmonious and welcoming colours creates an attractive, slightly Tuscan atmosphere. Mediterranean-style restaurant.

at Leipzig-Portitz *Northeast : 10 km, by Berliner Straße CY :*

Accento, Tauchaer Str. 260, 04349, (0341) 9 26 20, *welcome@accento-hotel.de, Fax (0341) 9262100*, – rm, rest, – 80. AE MC VISA JCB
closed 21 December - 4 January – **Meals** à la carte 16,50/25,50 – 13 – **113 rm** 55/112.
◆ The living is stylish here, with many contemporary designer features including colourfully upholstered furniture. All rooms with modem and fax points. The bright and airy restaurant too is strikingly designed with strongly geometrical lines.

In Leipzig-Seehausen *North : 8 km, by Eutitzscher Straße BY and Theresienstraße :*

Im Sachsenpark, Walter-Köhn-Str. 3, 04356, (0341) 5 25 20, *info@sachsenparkhotel.de, Fax (0341) 5252528*, – rm, – 60. AE MC VISA.
Meals *(closed 24 December - 7 January and Sunday)* à la carte 19/28,50 – **112 rm** 76/82 – 86/96.
◆ Tempting location for trade fair visitors, only 100m from the Sachsenpark and 500m from the golf course. Reduced green fee for guests. Rooms with lightwood furnishings. Bright and airy restaurant with contemporary décor.

at Leipzig-Stötteritz *Southeast : 5 km, by Prager Straße DZ and Stötteritzer Straße :*

Balance Hotel Alte Messe, Breslauer Str. 33, 04299, (0341) 8 67 90, *info@balancehotel-leipzig.de, Fax (0341) 8679444*, – rm, rest, – 30. AE MC VISA
Meals à la carte 17/29 – 12 – **126 rm** 59/69 – 9 suites.
◆ Close to the centre, in a quiet 19C residential area close to the Battle of the Nations Memorial. Comfortable, spacious rooms and suites with lightwood furnishings.

at Leipzig-Wahren *Northwest : 5 km, by Eutritzscher Str. 35BY and B 6 :*

Amadeo without rest, Georg-Schumann-Str. 268 (B 6), 04159, (0341) 91 02 00, *amadeo-leipzig@t-online.de, Fax (0341) 9102091* – – 15. AE MC VISA.
34 rm 45/55 – 65/69.
◆ Contemporary furnishings in varieties of cane and wood characterise the comfortable rooms of this establishment. Buffet breakfast in attractive setting.

at Leipzig-Wiederitzsch *North : 7 km, by Eutritzscher Straße BY and Delitzscher Straße :*

NH Leipzig Messe, Fuggerstr. 2, 04448, (0341) 5 25 10, *nhleipzigmesse@nh-hotels.com, Fax (0341) 5251300*, – rm, – 220. AE MC VISA
Meals à la carte 19/33 – **308 rm** 89 – 100.
◆ This hotel is particularly devoted to the needs of business travellers. The functional rooms feature warm tones of orange and lightwood furnishings.

Hiemann, Delitzscher Landstr. 75, 04158, (0341) 5 25 30, *info@hotel-hiemann.de, Fax (0341) 5253154*, – rm, – 25. AE MC VISA
Meals à la carte 16/30 – **37** rm 59/69 – 77/88.
◆ Family run hotel offering attractive maisonettes with good work facilities, plus modern rooms, some with cane furniture and sculptures, some with lightwood furnishings. Contemporary restaurant with plenty of greenery and a light, airy ambience.

at Wachau *Southeast : 8 km, by Prager Straße DZ and Chemnitzer Straße :*

Atlanta Hotel, Südring 21, 04416, (034297) 8 40, *info@atlanta-hotel.de, Fax (034297) 84999*, – rm, – 250. AE MC VISA
Meals à la carte 18/27 – **196 rm** 55/65 – 70/85 – 6 suites.
◆ This establishment benefits from the nearby parklands such as the Agra Park. Rooms and suites in contemporary style with baths of Carrara marble. The restaurant too is stylishly contemporary.

Read the introduction with its explanatory pages to make the most of your ***Michelin Guide.***

MUNICH (MÜNCHEN) L *Bayern* 546 V 18 – *pop.* 1 300 000 – *alt.* 520 *m.*

See : *Old Town*★★ KYZ, *Marienplatz*★ KZ – *Church of Our Lady (Frauenkirche)*★, *(Memorial of Bavarian Emperor Ludwig*★, *tower* ✲★*)* KZ – *Schack-Galerie*★ P35LY – *German Museum (Deutsches Museum)*★★★ LZ – *Palace (Residenz)*★★ *(Treasury*★★, *Residenz Museum*★★, *Palace Theatre*★*)* KY – *Church of Asam Brothers (Asamkirche)*★ KZ – *Nymphenburg*★★ *(Castle*★, *Gallery of Beauties*★, *Parc*★, *Amalienburg*★★, *Botanical Garden (Botanischer Garten)*★★*)* by *Arnulfstr.* EV – *New Art Gallery (Neue Pinakothek)*★★ KY - *Old Art Gallery (Alte Pinakothek)*★★★ KY - *Gallery of Modern Art (Pinakothek der Moderne)*★★ KY – *City Historical Museum (Münchener Stadtmuseum)*★ *(Moorish Dancers*★★*)* KZ **M7** – *Villa Lenbach Collections (Städt. Galerie im Lenbachhaus)*★ JY **M4** – *Antique Collections (Staatliche Antikensammlungen)*★ JY **M3** – *Glyptothek*★ JY **M2** – *St Michael's Church (Michaelskirche)*★ KYZ – *Theatine Church (Theatinerkirche)*★ KY – *German Hunting and Fishing Museum (Deutsches Jagd- und Fischereimuseum)*★ KZ **M1** – *Olympic Park (Olympia-Park) (Olympic Tower* ✲★★★*)* by *Schleißheimer Straße* FU – *English Garden (Englischer Garten)*★ *(*≤ *from Monopteros Temple*★*)* LY - *Bavarian National Museum (Bayerisches Nationalmuseum)*★★ LY **M5** – *Hellabrunn Zoo (Tierpark Hellabrunn)*★ *by Lindwurmstraße (B 11)* EX.

9 *München-Riem, Graf-Lehndorff Str. 36, (East : 10 km),* ☎ *(089) 94 50 08 00 ;* 9 *München-Thalkirchen, Zentralländstr. 40, (South : 6 km),* ☎ *(089) 7 23 13 04 ;* 27 *Straßlach, Tölzerstr. 95 (South : 17 km),* ☎ *(08170) 9 29 18 11 ;* 18 *Eschenried, Kurfürstenweg 10 (Northwest : 16 km),* ☎ *(08131) 5 67 40.*

✈ *Flughafen Franz-Josef Strauß (Northeast : 29 km by Ungererstraße* HU*),* ☎ *(089) 9 75 00, City Air Terminal, Arnulfstraße (Main Station).*

🚘 *Ostbahnhof, Friedenstraße* (HX)*.*

Exhibition Centre (Messegelände) (by ③), ✉ *81823,* ☎ *(089) 9 49 01, Fax (089) 94920729.*

i *Tourist-Office, Bahnhofsplatz,* ✉ *80335,* ☎ *(089) 2 33 03 00, tourismus@ems.muenchen.de,* Fax (089) 23330233.

ADAC, *Sendlinger-Tor-Platz 9.*

Berlin 586 – Innsbruck 162 – Nürnberg 165 – Salzburg 140 – Stuttgart 222.

Plans on following pages

Bayerischer Hof, Promenadeplatz 2, ✉ 80333, ☎ (089) 2 12 00, *info@bayerischerhof.de, Fax (089) 2120906,* , Massage, , – |\$|, ⇎ rm, ▤ TV ☎ ♿ 🚗 – 🏛 850. AE ⓓ MC VISA JCB KY y

Garden-Restaurant (booking essential) **Meals** à la carte 40/57 – ***Trader Vic's*** (Polynesian) *(dinner only)* **Meals** à la carte 27,50/54 – ***Palais Keller*** (Bavarian beer inn) **Meals** à la carte 17/32 – ☕ 21 – **395 rm** 188/243 – 279/385 – 17 suites.

◆ Privately run grand hotel with a long history, combining personal charm and a high level of comfort in every room whether traditional, modern, or country-style. Elegant garden restaurant with classic cuisine. A touch of the south seas in Trader Vic's.

Mandarin Oriental, Neuturmstr. 1, ✉ 80331, ☎ (089) 29 09 80, *momuc-reservation@mohg.com, Fax (089) 222539,* (heated) – |\$| ▤ TV ☎ 🚗 – 🏛 50. AE ⓓ MC VISA JCB KZ s

Mark's (1st floor) *(closed Sunday and Monday) (dinner only)* **Meals** à la carte 45/70 ♀ – ***Mark's Corner*** *(lunch only Tuesday - Saturday)* **Meals** 28 (lunch) and à la carte 34,50/46 – ☕ 24 – **73 rm** 280/380 – 330/430 – 8 suites.

◆ The old ballroom has been transformed into a luxury hotel, losing none of its brilliance in the process. View of the Alps from the roof-terrace and pool. Marble staircase leads up to the stylishly elegant Mark's. Mark's Corner is the place to meet for lunch.

Königshof, Karlsplatz 25, ✉ 80335, ☎ (089) 55 13 60, *koenigshof@geisel-hotels.de, Fax (089) 55136113,* , – |\$|, ⇎ rm, ▤ TV ☎ 🚗 – 🏛 80. AE ⓓ MC VISA JCB JY s

✿

Meals *(closed 1 to 12 January, 25 July - 25 August, Sunday and Monday)* (booking essential) 35 *(lunch)*/118 and à la carte 48/69 ♀, – ☕ 20 – **87 rm** 215/260 – 260/350 – 10 suites.

◆ Grand hotel traditions are respected here, where classic elegance is combined with personal service. Enviable location right by the Stachus. Classic cuisine in the lovely restaurant with its round tables and immaculate place settings.

Spec. Variation von der Gänseleber. Gebratene Froschschenkel mit Schalottensauce und Petersilienpürée. Gratinierter Lammrücken mit Cremolatajus und Gewürztomaten.

Kempinski Hotel Vier Jahreszeiten, Maximilianstr. 17, ✉ 80539, ☎ (089) 2 12 50, *reservations.vierjahreszeiten@kempinski.com, Fax (089) 21252000,* Massage, , – |\$|, ⇎ rm, ▤ TV ☎ 🚗 – 🏛 220. AE ⓓ MC VISA JCB. ⇎ rest LZ a

Meals à la carte 40/57 – ☕ 25 – **316 rm** 300/450 – 345/495 – 51 suites.

◆ Travellers from all over the world have been enjoying the flair of this grand hotel since 1858. Rooms are a harmonious combination of traditional charm and contemporary comfort. Dine in the bistro-style restaurant with its view of the Maximilianstrasse.

STREET INDEX

Street	Grid	No.
Ackermannstraße	FU	
Adalbertstraße	GU	
Albrechtstraße	EU	
Alter Messeplatz	EX	3
Amalienstraße	KY	
Am Gasteig	LZ	4
Amiraplatz	KY	6
An der Hauptfeuerwache	JZ	7
Arcisstraße	JY	
Arnulfstraße	EV	
Asamstraße	GX	
Auenstraße	GX	
Auerfeldstraße	GX	
Augustenstraße	JY	
Aventinstraße	KZ	
Baaderstraße	KLZ	
Bahnhofplatz	JY	
Baldeplatz	GX	14
Barer Straße	JKY	
Baumgartnerstraße	EX	17
Bavariaring	EFX	
Bayerstraße	JY	
Beethovenplatz	JZ	
Beethovenstraße	JZ	20
Belgradstraße	GU	
Biedersteiner Straße	HU	25
Blumenstraße	KZ	
Blutenburgstraße	EV	
Bonner Platz	GU	
Bonner Straße	GU	26
Brienner Straße	JKY	
Burgstraße	KZ	30
Clemensstraße	GU	
Corneliusbrücke	KZ	
Corneliusstraße	KZ	
Dachauer Straße	JY	
Damenstiftstraße	JZ	32
Denninger Straße	HV	34
Dienerstraße	KZ	36
Dietlindenstraße	GHU	
Dom-Pedro-Straße	EU	
Eduard-Schmid-Str.	KLZ	
Ehrengutstraße	FX	
Einsteinstraße	HX	
Eisenmannstraße	KZ	39
Elisabethstraße	FGU	
Elisenstraße	JY	
Elsässer Straße	HX	42
Emil-Riedel-Straße	HV	45
Erhardtstraße	KLZ	
Feilitzschstraße	GU	
Flurstraße	HX	49
Franziskanerstraße	GX	
Franz-Joseph-Straße	GU	
Franz-Joseph-Strauß-Ring	LY	50
Frauenstraße	KZ	
Fraunhoferstraße	KZ	
Friedenstraße	HX	
Friedrichstraße	GU	52
Gabelsbergerstraße	JKY	
Gärtnerplatz	KZ	
Galileiplatz	HV	53
Ganghoferstraße	EX	
Gebsattelstraße	GX	55
Georgenstraße	FGU	59
Giselastraße	GU	60
Görresstraße	FU	
Goethestraße	JZ	
Gohrenstraße	GU	61
Grasserstraße	EV	63
Grillparzerstraße	HX	
Hackerbrücke	EV	65
Häberlstraße	JZ	
Hans-Sachs-Straße	KZ	

Continued on following pages

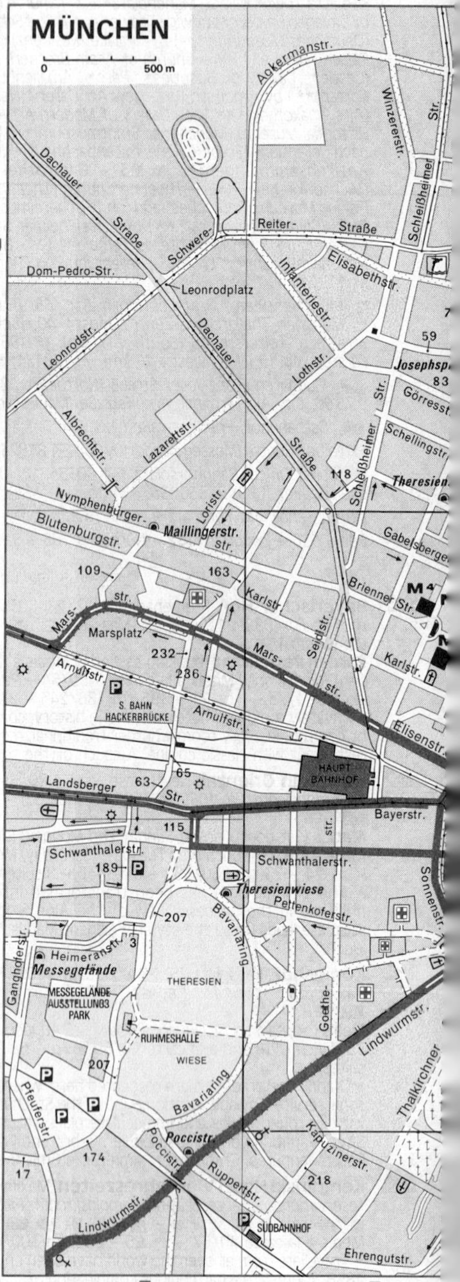

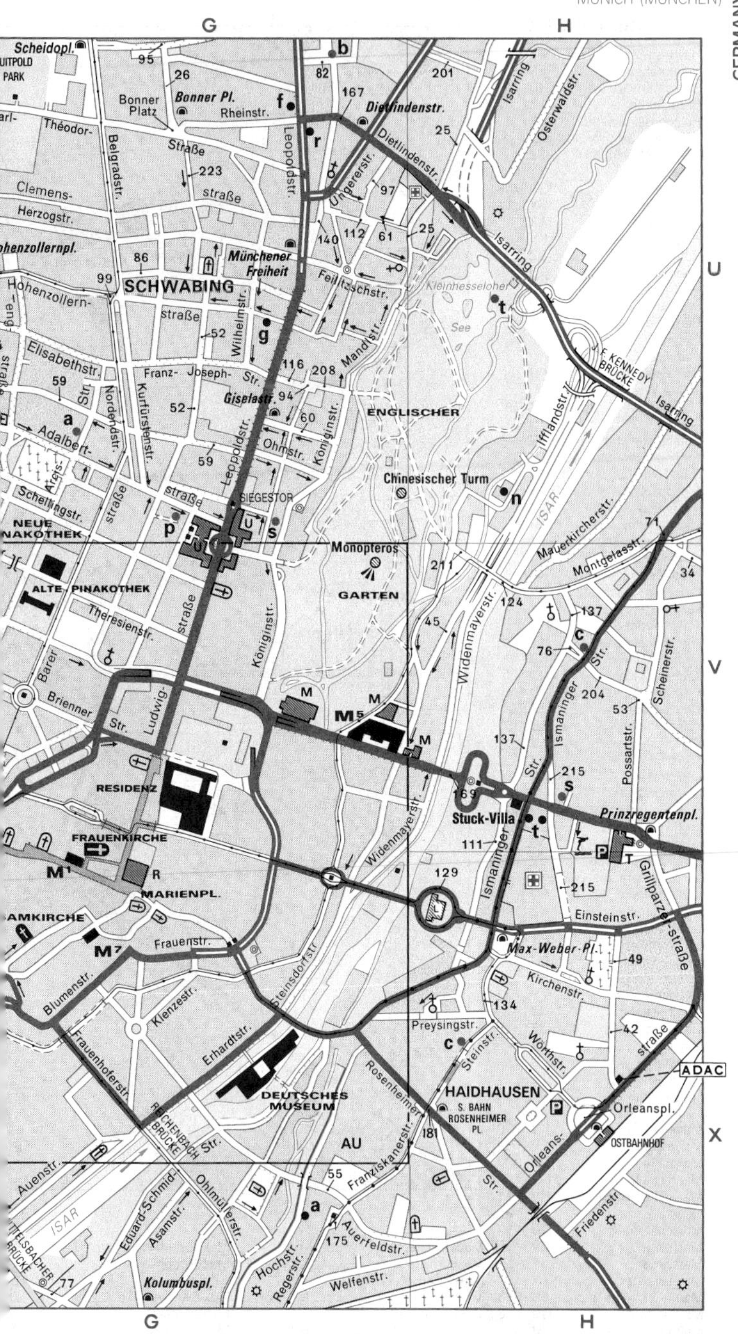
SCHWABING
ENGLISCHER
GARTEN
Chinesischer Turm
Monopteros
ALTE PINAKOTHEK
NEUE PINAKOTHEK
RESIDENZ
FRAUENKIRCHE
MARIENPL.
DEUTSCHES MUSEUM
HAIDHAUSEN
Stuck-Villa
Prinzregentenpl.
Max-Weber-Pl.
OSTBAHNHOF
ADAC
Kleinhesseloher See
J.-F.-KENNEDY-BRÜCKE
SIEGESTOR
AU
ISAR

STREET INDEX

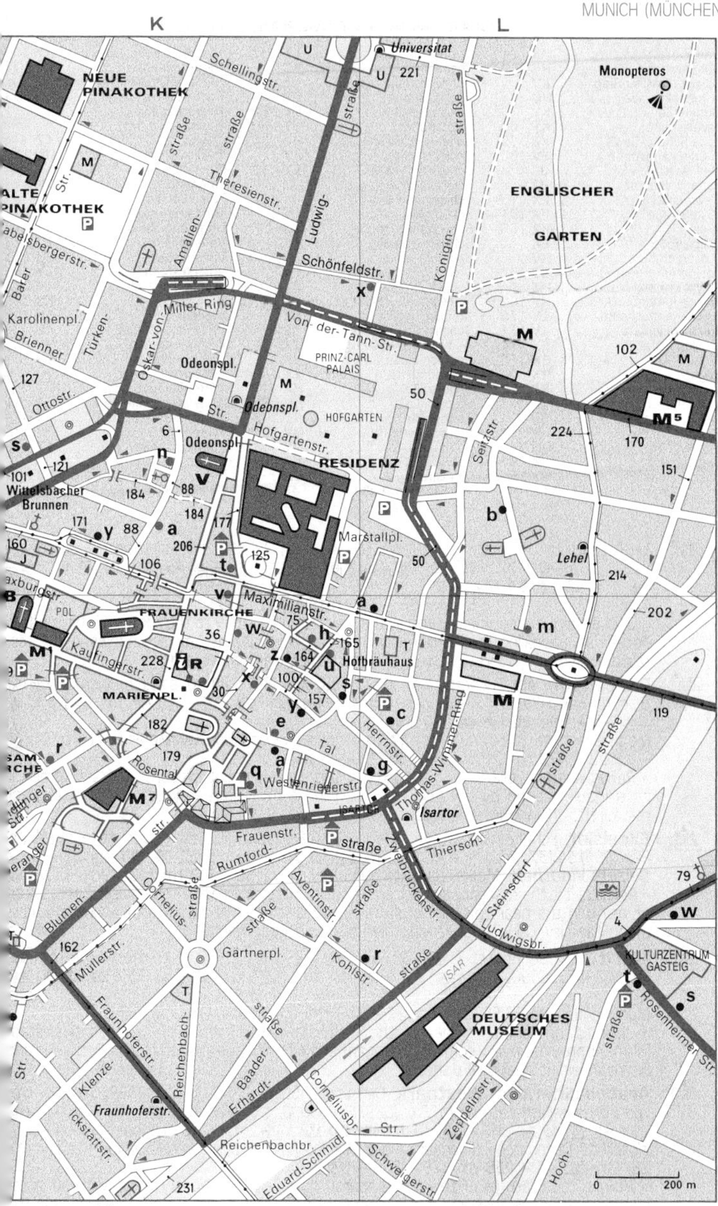

Continued on following page

STREET INDEX TO MÜNCHEN TOWN PLANS (Concluded)

Le Méridien, Bayerstr. 41, ✉ 80335, ☎ (089) 2 42 20, *info.muenchen@lemeridien.com, Fax (089) 24221111*, Massage, – rm, – 160. AE VISA JCB JZ w
Meals à la carte 34/56 – 20 – **381 rm** 245/375 – 9 suites.
• Cool elegance accompanies you all the way from the lobby to the rooms of this modern hotel with appealing lines and lovely materials throughout. Ample windows in the restaurant give a wonderful view of the attractive, leafy courtyard.

Park Hilton, Am Tucherpark 7, ✉ 80538, ☎ (089) 3 84 50, *sales_munich-park@hilton.com, Fax (089) 38452588*, beer garden, Massage, – rm, – 690. AE VISA JCB HU n
Meals à la carte 31,50/40 – ***Tse Yang*** (Chinese) *(closed Monday)* **Meals** à la carte 24/43 – 22 – **479 rm** 210/230 – 230/250 – 3 suites.
• Refurbished in 2000 regardless of cost, this establishment is appreciated above all for its tranquil location by the Englischer Garten, Munich's "green lung". Bistro-style Tivoli restaurant offering international cuisine as well as a buffet.

Excelsior, Schützenstr. 11, ✉ 80335, ☎ (089) 55 13 70, *excelsior@geisel-hotels.de, Fax (089) 55137121*, – rm, – 25. AE VISA JCB
Geisel's Vinothek : **Meals** à la carte 29/34,50 – 16 – **113 rm** 150/190 – 190/210
• Perhaps it is the rustically elegant ambience of foyer and rooms that give the impression of being in the heart of the countryside rather than in the middle of a bustling, cosmopolitan city. Country-style vinotheque with painted vaults. JY z

Maritim, Goethestr. 7, ✉ 80336, ☎ (089) 55 23 50, *info.mun@maritim.de Fax (089) 55235900*, – rm, – 250. AE VISA JCB JZ z
Meals à la carte 27,50/37 – 17 – **339 rm** 154/159 – 176 – 5 suites.
• Close to the Deutsches Theater, the Stachus and the Oktoberfest grounds, this establishment provides every comfort in elegant and tastefully decorated rooms. Rotisserie and bistro offer international dishes.

ArabellaSheraton Westpark, Garmischer Str. 2, ✉ 80339, ☎ (089) 5 19 60, *westpark@arabellasheraton.com, Fax (089) 51963000*, Massage, – rm rest, – 70. AE VISA JCB by Leopoldstraße GU
closed 19 December - 6 January – **Meals** *(closed 19 December - 12 January)* à la carte 28/39 – 16 – **258 rm** 175 – 200 – 6 suites.
• Among the features of this contemporary hotel are functional rooms with the latest communication facilities and a bright and cheerful leisure area. Elegant ambience in the restaurant.

Eden-Hotel-Wolff, Arnulfstr. 4, ✉ 80335, ☎ (089) 55 11 50, *sales@ehw.de Fax (089) 55115555* – rm, – 140. AE VISA JCB JY p
Meals à la carte 17,50/39,50 – **205 rm** 133/148 – 177/188.
• Reside in elegant surroundings, rich in tradition, right in the middle of Bavaria's capital city. Seven allergen-free rooms with parquet floors. Authentic Bavarian atmosphere in the Zirbelstube, with a choice of international cuisine or tasty local fare.

King's Hotel without rest, Dachauer Str. 13, ✉ 80335, ✆ (089) 55 18 70, *1stclass@kingshotels.de, Fax (089) 55187300* – 30. AE MC VISA JCB JY f
15 – **86 rm** 125/140.
• Wood, wherever you look! Its elegant Alpine style makes this a particularly welcoming hotel. And there's a four-poster in every room!

Exquisit without rest, Pettenkoferstr. 3, ✉ 80336, ✆ (089) 5 51 99 00, *info@hotel-exquisit.com, Fax (089) 55199499,* – – 25. AE MC VISA
50 rm 119/170 – 170/205 – 5 suites. JZ s
• In the very centre of town, this functional establishment has rooms with dark mahogany furniture. Marienplatz, Stachus and Oktoberfest grounds all within walking distance.

Anna, Schützenstr. 1, ✉ 80335, ✆ (089) 59 99 40, *info@annahotel.de, Fax (089) 59994333* – rm, . AE MC VISA JCB JYZ n
Meals à la carte 18,50/32 – **56 rm** 145 – 165.
• Right by the Stachus in Munich's Altstadt, this well-appointed hotel features contemporary design, attractive colour schemes and state-of-the-art technical facilities. Modern, bistro-type restaurant with sushi bar.

Platzl, Sparkassenstr. 10, ✉ 80331, ✆ (089) 23 70 30, *info@plazl.de, Fax (089) 23703800,* – rm, – 70. AE MC VISA
Pfistermühle *(closed Sunday)* **Meals** à la carte 22,50/40,50 – ***Ayingers*** **: Meals** à la carte 17/33 – **167 rm** 95/141 – 155/240. KZ z
• Comfortable rooms in traditional Bavarian style in the historic heart of the city. The rooms facing the courtyard enjoy peace and quiet. All the atmosphere of old Munich in the vaulted Pfistermühle. Ayingers with refined inn-type fare.

Drei Löwen without rest, Schillerstr. 8, ✉ 80336, ✆ (089) 55 10 40, *info@hotel3loewen.de, Fax (089) 55104905* – – 15. AE MC VISA JCB JZ m
96 rm 105/140 – 140/150 – 3 suites.
• In the city centre close to the main station, this hotel has comfortable modern rooms tastefully furnished in wood.

Stadthotel Asam without rest, Josephspitalstr. 3, ✉ 80331, ✆ (089) 2 30 97 00, *info@hotel-asam.de, Fax (089) 23097097* – . AE MC VISA JZ a
13 – **25 rm** 129/145 – 158/174 – 8 Suites.
• A small city centre hotel with more than a touch of luxury, offering rooms with many a stylish and tasteful detail.

Cortiina without rest, Ledererstr. 8, ✉ 80331, ✆ (089) 2 42 24 90, *info@cortiina.com, Fax (089) 242249100* – . AE MC VISA KZ y
33 rm 126/146 – 186.
• Cool furnishings and parquet floors in contemporary style rooms with state-of-the-art technical facilities. The attractive bar also serves light meals.

Torbräu, Tal 41, ✉ 80331, ✆ (089) 24 23 40(hotel) 22 80 75 23(rest.), *info@torbraeu.de, Fax (089) 24234235,* – rm, rm, – 30. AE MC VISA JCB LZ g
La Famiglia (Italian) **Meals** à la carte 32,50/40 – **92 rm** 130/155 – 165/220 – 3 suites.
• This historic 15C building is reputedly the city's oldest hotel. Well-kept rooms with ample space, all with air-conditioning. Tuscan flair and Italian cuisine in the La Famiglia restaurant with its terracotta tiled floor.

Mercure City, Senefelder Str. 9, ✉ 80336, ✆ (089) 55 13 20, *h0878@accor-hotels.com, Fax (089) 596444,* beer garden – rm, – 50. AE MC VISA JCB JZ v
Meals à la carte 19,50/32 – **167 rm** 133 – 166.
• Spacious, contemporary and functional rooms in this city centre establishment close to the main station.

Admiral without rest, Kohlstr. 9, ✉ 80469, ✆ (089) 21 63 50, *info@hotel-admiral.de, Fax (089) 293674* – . AE MC VISA JCB LZ r
33 rm 160 – 190.
• Just a short walk from the city centre, this hotel has functional rooms, some offering peace and quiet. Breakfast served in the little garden when fine.

King's Hotel Center without rest, Marsstr. 15, ✉ 80335, ✆ (089) 51 55 30, *center@kingshotels.de, Fax (089) 51553300* – . AE MC VISA JY b
12 – **90 rm** 98/120.
• A panelled foyer welcomes guests to this establishment close to the city centre. Comfortable rooms with elaborate four-posters.

NH Deutscher Kaiser without rest, Arnulfstr. 2, ✉ 80335, ✆ (089) 5 45 30, *nhdeutscherkaiser@nh-hotels.com, Fax (089) 54532255* – – 80. AE MC VISA JY r
15 – **174 rm** 124/135.
• Well-adapted to the requirements of business travellers, this hotel stands on the north side of the main station. Bright rooms with ample desks and comfortable chairs.

Drei Löwen Residenz without rest, Aldolf-Kolping-Str. 11, ✉ 80336, ☎ (089) 55 10 40, *info@hotel3loewen.de, Fax (089) 55104905* – |‡| ⇎ TV ☎. AE ⓓ MC VISA JCB JZ d
63 rm ☕ 90/115 – 125.
◆ A few steps away is a sister establishment of the same name. Welcoming, comfortable rooms ; those to the rear are very quiet.

Atrium without rest, Landwehrstr. 59, ✉ 80336, ☎ (089) 51 41 90, *info@atrium-hotel.de, Fax (089) 535066,* – |‡| ⇎ TV ☎ – 20. AE ⓓ MC VISA JCB JZ k
162 rm ☕ 139 – 169.
◆ Mirrors and marble distinguish the foyer of this elegant establishment. Rooms with natural wood furnishings and excellent technical facilities. Leafy little courtyard.

Tryp, Paul-Heyse-Str. 24, ✉ 80336, ☎ (089) 51 49 00, *reservation.trypmuenchen@solmelia.com, Fax (089) 51490701,* – |‡|, ⇎ rm, TV ☎ – 35. AE ⓓ MC VISA JZ c
Meals *(closed Saturday, Sunday and Bank Holidays)* à la carte 21/31 – **200 rm** ☕ 103/129 – 118/134.
◆ Contemporary hotel building close to the city centre. Functional rooms intended above all for the business traveller. Small restaurant with Spanish flavouring.

Domus without rest, St.-Anna-Str. 31, ✉ 80538, ☎ (089) 22 17 04, *Fax (089) 2285359* – |‡| ⇎ TV ☎. AE ⓓ MC VISA LY b
closed 23 to 27 December – **45 rm** ☕ 105 – 128.
◆ Between the Maximilianstrasse and the Prinzregentenstrasse, this tastefully decorated hotel couldn't be better placed for shops, art, and culture.

Carat-Hotel without rest, Lindwurmstr. 13, ✉ 80337, ☎ (089) 23 03 80, *info-m@carat-hotel.de, Fax (089) 23038199* – |‡| ⇎ TV ☎ – 15. AE ⓓ MC VISA JZ
70 rm ☕ 107/117 – 137/152.
◆ Contemporary, functional rooms, primarily intended for business travellers. Most with modem connection, some with air-conditioning.

Kraft without rest, Schillerstr. 49, ✉ 80336, ☎ (089) 59 48 23, *info@hotel-kraft.com, Fax (089) 5503856* – |‡| ⇎ TV ☎. AE ⓓ MC VISA JCB JZ
33 rm ☕ 80 – 95.
◆ Very liveable establishment, partly furnished with antique items. In the university clinic district, easy access to station, Oktoberfest, public transport and city centre.

Concorde without rest, Herrnstr. 38, ✉ 80539, ☎ (089) 22 45 15, *info@concorde-muenchen.de, Fax (089) 2283282* – |‡| ⇎ TV ☎. AE ⓓ MC VISA LZ
closed Christmas - early January – **71 rm** ☕ 98 – 128.
◆ This attentively run hotel in the Altstadt has well-kept practical rooms furnished in a variety of styles. Some face the quiet courtyard.

Cristal without rest, Schwanthalerstr. 36, ✉ 80336, ☎ (089) 55 11 10, *info@cristal.bestwestern.de, Fax (089) 55111992* – |‡| ⇎ TV ☎ – 90. AE ⓓ MC VISA JZ
100 rm ☕ 130/145 – 155.
◆ This modern hotel between the Oktoberfest grounds and the main station offers contemporary, functional rooms, some spacious and pleasantly quiet.

Apollo without rest, Mittererstr. 7, ✉ 80336, ☎ (089) 53 95 31, *info@apollohotel.de, Fax (089) 534033* – |‡| ⇎ TV ☎ P. AE ⓓ MC VISA JCB JZ
74 rm ☕ 82 – 99.
◆ This city centre hotel offers mahogany furnished rooms - spacious and comfortable. Ask for one facing the quiet courtyard.

Präsident without rest, Schwanthalerstr. 20, ✉ 80336, ☎ (089) 5 49 00 60, *hotel.praesident@t-online.de, Fax (089) 54900628* – |‡| ⇎ TV ☎ – 15. AE ⓓ MC VISA JCB JZ
42 rm ☕ 79/84 – 89.
◆ Ideal for theatre-goers, this completely rebuilt establishment is diagonally opposite Munich's Deutsches Theater. Contemporary rooms with bright natural wood furniture.

Schlicker without rest, Tal 8, ✉ 80331, ☎ (089) 2 42 88 70, *schlicker-munich@t-online.de, Fax (089) 296059* – |‡| TV ☎ P. AE ⓓ MC VISA KZ
closed 23 December - 7 January – **69 rm** ☕ 85/115 – 115/170.
◆ Within sight of City Hall with its world-famous glockenspiel, this venerable 16C building is now a modern hotel. Elegant or spacious rooms.

Olympic without rest, Hans-Sachs-Str. 4, ✉ 80469, ☎ (089) 23 18 90, *Fax (089) 23189199* – TV ☎. AE ⓓ MC VISA KZ
38 rm ☕ 90/120 – 130.
◆ Partly furnished in Biedermeier style, most of the rooms here overlook leafy and tranquil inner courtyards. Close to Marienplatz, Deutsches Museum and Metro station.

Meier without rest, Schützenstr. 12, ✉ 80335, ☎ (089) 5 49 03 40, *info@hotel-meier.de, Fax (089) 549034340* – AE VISA JCB JY x
closed 23 to 28 December – **50 rm** 90 – 110/130.
◆ Completely refurbished in the late 1990s, this upper-floor establishment now offers its guests standard, functional rooms.

Schuhbeck's in den Südtiroler Stuben, Platzl 6, ✉ 80331, ☎ (089) 2 16 69 00, *info@schuhbeck.de, Fax (089) 21669025* – AE VISA KZ u
closed 24 December - 15 January, Monday lunch, Sunday and Bank Holidays – **Meals** 42 *(lunch)*/92 *(dinner)* and à la carte.
◆ Elegance and country style happily combined. Wall panelling, plaster ceilings, and fine table settings make for a pleasant dining experience. Cooking school.
Spec. Gesulztes vom Saibling mit Meerrettichmousse und gebratener Jakobsmuschel. Wolfsbarsch mit Senfsauce und Kartoffel-Kräuterpüree. Rohrnudel mit Pralinensauce und Vanilleeis.

Boettner's, Pfisterstr. 9, ✉ 80331, ☎ (089) 22 12 10, *Fax (089) 29162024*, – AE VISA KZ h
closed Sunday, 15 April - 15 September Saturday and Sunday – **Meals** (booking essential) 31 *(lunch)* and à la carte 39/67 – ***Boettner's Atrium :*** **Meals** à la carte 20,50/27.
◆ Boettner's is a Munich institution. You dine in one of several rooms with elegant, traditional décor, some of them with venerable wooden panelling. Classic cuisine.

Halali, Schönfeldstr. 22, ✉ 80539, ☎ (089) 28 59 09, *halali-muenchen@t-online.de, Fax (089) 282786* – AE VISA JCB LY x
closed 3 weeks June, Saturday lunch, Sunday and Bank Holidays – **Meals** (booking essential) 21,50 *(lunch)* and à la carte 31/48.
◆ This historic, flower-bedecked 19C inn has a tasteful, rustic interior featuring plenty of wood panelling.

Ederer, Kardinal-Faulhaber-Str. 10, ✉ 80333, ☎ (089) 24 23 13 10, *Fax (089) 24231312*, – . AE VISA KY a
closed Sunday and Bank Holidays – **Meals** (booking essential) à la carte 35,50/58,50.
◆ Surrounded by exclusive shops and boutiques, this high-ceilinged establishment offers diners a smart, contemporary setting.

Hunsinger's Pacific, Maximiliansplatz 5 (entrance Max-Joseph-Straße), ✉ 80333, ☎ (089) 55 02 97 41, *Fax (089) 55029742* – . AE VISA JCB KY s
closed Saturday lunch and Sunday – **Meals** à la carte 23,50/44,50.
◆ What used to be the "Aubergine" has now been transported to the Pacific Rim, with trompe l'oeil paintings lit by chandeliers. International cuisine with an Asian touch.

Austernkeller, Stollbergstr. 11, ✉ 80539, ☎ (089) 29 87 87, *Fax (089) 223166* – AE VISA JCB LZ e
closed 23 to 26 December – **Meals** *(dinner only)* (booking essential) à la carte 26,50/47,50.
◆ This is the place to come for shellfish and other freshly caught denizens of the deep. With a décor of porcelain plates, these vaulted cellars are a listed historic monument.

Dallmayr, Dienerstr. 14 (1st floor), ✉ 80331, ☎ (089) 2 13 51 00, *gastro@dallmayr.de, Fax (089) 2135443* – . AE VISA JCB KZ w
closed Monday - Wednesday from 7 pm, Thursday and Friday from 8 pm, Saturday from 4 pm, Sunday and Bank Holidays – **Meals** à la carte 33,50/54.
◆ This is the restaurant of the famous delicatessen patronised by kings and emperors. The freshness and naturalness of its products have become a byword.

Nymphenburger Hof, Nymphenburger Str. 24, ✉ 80335, ☎ (089) 1 23 38 30, *Fax (089) 1233852*, – AE VISA. EV a
closed 23 December - 10 January, Saturday lunch, Sunday, Monday and Bank Holidays – **Meals** (booking essential) 18 *(lunch)* and à la carte 28/46,50.
◆ Bright and welcoming restaurant with a terrace. Pastel-coloured décor, plenty of flowers, and a refined cuisine with many local or Austrian-influenced specialities.

Lenbach, Ottostr. 6, ✉ 80333, ☎ (089) 5 49 13 00, *info@lenbach.de, Fax (089) 54913075*, – AE VISA JY c
closed Sunday and Bank Holidays – **Meals** à la carte 31,50/47.
◆ Part of the Lenbach Palace redesigned by Sir Terence Conran to house vast and fashionable dining-spaces including a sushi-bar and a contemporary restaurant.

Galleria, Sparkassenstr. 11 / corner of Ledererstraße, ✉ 80331, ☎ (089) 29 79 95, *info@ristorante-galleria.de, Fax (089) 2913653* – . AE VISA KZ x
closed 1 to 7 January, 2 weeks August and Sunday, except exhibitions and December – **Meals** (Italian) (booking essential) 27 *(lunch)* and à la carte 39/47.
◆ Intimate setting and wonderfully colourful décor. Changing selection of pictures. Cuisine based on classic Italian recipes.

Weinhaus Neuner, Herzogspitalstr. 8, ✉ 80331, ☎ (089) 2 60 39 54, *weinhaus-neuner@t-online.de, Fax (089) 266933* – AE MC VISA JCB JZ e
closed Sunday and Bank Holidays – **Meals** à la carte 24,50/36.
◆ This vaulted establishment of 1852 is claimed to be Munich's oldest wine restaurant. Splendid wall-paintings. Traditional and local dishes.

Dukatz, Salvatorplatz 1, ✉ 80333, ☎ (089) 2 91 96 00, *info@dukatz.de, Fax (089) 29196028* – KY n
closed Sunday – **Meals** (booking essential) à la carte 25,50/38,50.
◆ In the "Literature House", a former indoor market dating from 1870, a range of international dishes is served in lovely vaulted rooms on two levels.

Zum Alten Markt, Dreifaltigkeitsplatz 3, ✉ 80331, ☎ (089) 29 99 95, *lehner.gastr@zumaltenmarkt.de, Fax (089) 2285076,* KZ q
closed Sunday and Bank Holidays – **Meals** (booking essential for dinner) à la carte 23,50/34,50.
◆ With its homely Tyrolean atmosphere, this pub-type establishment on the Viktualienmarkt boasts lavish wood panelling, some of it authentic and more than 400 years old.

Brewery-inns :

Spatenhaus an der Oper, Residenzstr. 12, ✉ 80333, ☎ (089) 2 90 70 60, *spatenhaus@kuffler.de, Fax (089) 2913054,* – AE MC VISA KY t
Meals à la carte 23,50/41.
◆ This century-old town mansion has a number of cheerful first floor rooms with varying décor and a ground floor with an Alpine feel about it.

Weisses Bräuhaus, Tal 7, ✉ 80331, ☎ (089) 2 90 13 80, *info@weisses-brauhaus.de, Fax (089) 29013815,* – 30. MC VISA KZ e
Meals à la carte 15/31,50.
◆ Built around 1900, this establishment in the historic centre of town has a lovely façade. Inside, authentic local specialities served in a congenial atmosphere.

Augustiner Gaststätten, Neuhauser Str. 27, ✉ 80331, ☎ (089) 23 18 32 57, *augustinerstammhaus@yahoo.de, Fax (089) 2605379,* – AE MC VISA JCB JZ w
Meals à la carte 15,50/32.
◆ Beer was brewed here in the Augustiner headquarters right up to 1885. Arcade Garden and Shell Hall are among the great achievements of Munich Art Nouveau. Fine beer garden.

Altes Hackerhaus, Sendlinger Str. 14, ✉ 80331, ☎ (089) 2 60 50 26, *hackerhaus@aol.com, Fax (089) 2605027,* – AE MC VISA JCB KZ r
Meals à la carte 13,50/35.
◆ This establishment has many faces, including the lively beer garden, the romantic covered courtyard, the cheerful councillors' parlour, and the vaults of the Schäfflergewölbe

Zum Franziskaner, Residenzstr. 9/Perusastr. 5, ✉ 80333, ☎ (089) 2 31 81 20, *zum.franziskaner@t-online.de, Fax (089) 23181244,* – AE MC VISA KYZ v
Meals à la carte 18/31,50.
◆ Traditional hospitality in spacious surroundings close to the main post office. Bavarian delicacies ranging from famous "white sausage" to the produce of rivers and lakes.

Bratwurstherzl, Dreifaltigkeitsplatz 1 (at Viktualienmarkt), ✉ 80331, ☎ (089) 29 51 13, *mail@bratwurstherzl.de, Fax (089) 29163751,* beer garden – AE MC VISA
closed Sunday and Bank Holidays – **Meals** à la carte 12/23,50. KZ c
◆ The big draw here are the sausages you grill yourself. "Beginners" get six, "Advanced students" eight, and "Regulars" are served straightaway with a round dozen.

at Munich-Allach *Northwest : 12 km, by Arnulfstraße* EV *and Menzinger Straße :*

Lutter without rest, Eversbuschstr. 109, ✉ 80999, ☎ (089) 8 12 70 04, *hotel-lutter@t-online.de, Fax (089) 8129584* – MC VISA.
closed 20 December - 7 January – **27 rm** 70 – 77.
◆ Impeccably run establishment with functional rooms in the northwestern part of the city. Good value for the price.

at Munich-Bogenhausen :

ArabellaSheraton Grand Hotel, Arabellastr. 6, ✉ 81925, ☎ (089) 9 26 40, *grandhotel.muenchen@arabellasheraton.com, Fax (089) 92648009,* beer garden, Massage, – rm, – 650. AE MC VISA rest by Ismaninger Straße HVU
Die Ente vom Lehel *(closed August, Sunday and Monday) (dinner only)* **Meals** 39 and à la carte 46/61 – ***Paulaner's*** *(closed lunch Saturday, Sunday and Bank Holidays)* **Meals** à la carte 18,50/34,50 – 21 – **643 rm** 280/350 – 305/375 – 14 suites.
◆ Refurbished grand hotel with imposing foyer and beautifully decorated rooms. Opposite is the Arabellapark with its boutiques, bistros, cinemas and night-club. Opening onto the foyer, the Ente vom Lehel restaurant has a lively atmosphere.

Palace, Trogerstr. 21, ✉ 81675, ☎ (089) 41 97 10, *palace@kuffler.de, Fax (089) 41971819*, – rm, – 25. AE MC VISA HV t

Meals à la carte 31,50/43 – 15 – **72 rm** 155/200 – 220/230 – 3 suites.

◆ Elegant hotel with an exceptionally high standard of décor. All rooms with Louis XVI furniture, some with parquet floors. Roof-terrace and garden are well worth a visit when the sun shines. Elegant and stylish Palace Restaurant.

Prinzregent am Friedensengel without rest, Ismaninger Str. 42, ✉ 81675, ☎ (089) 41 60 50, *friedensengel@prinzregent.de, Fax (089) 41605466*, – – 35. AE MC VISA HV t

closed 23 December - 6 January – **66 rm** 169/215 – 200/245.

◆ This hotel is only five minutes from Munich's famous Englischer Garten. Attractive and comfortable, Alpine-style rooms. Lovely panelled breakfast room with conservatory.

Rothof without rest, Denninger Str. 114, ✉ 81925, ☎ (089) 9 10 09 50, *rothof@t-online.de, Fax (089) 915066*, – . AE MC VISA

closed 23 December - 6 January – **37 rm** 121/131 – 152/172.

◆ Well-run hotel offering bright, spacious and welcoming rooms with modern working facilties. Tennis courts under the same roof. by Ismaninger Straße HUV

Bogenhauser Hof, Ismaninger Str. 85, ✉ 81675, ☎ (089) 98 55 86, *bogenhause-hof@t-online.de, Fax (089) 9810221*, , (1825 former hunting lodge) – AE MC VISA HV c

closed 2 weeks Easter, 24 December - 8 January, Sunday and Bank Holidays – **Meals** (booking essential) à la carte 40/60.

◆ This hunting lodge dating from 1825 serves a refined version of classic Munich cuisine, which can also be savoured in the idyllic surroundings of the summer garden.

Acquarello, Mühlbaurstr. 36, ✉ 81677, ☎ (089) 4 70 48 48, *info@acquarello.com, Fax (089) 476464*, – AE MC. by Prinzregentenstraße HV

closed 1 to 4 January, lunch Saturday, Sunday and Bank Holidays – **Meals** (Italian) 27 *(lunch)*/77 and à la carte 37/57.

◆ The chef has succeeded in creating wonderfully contrasting variations on the theme of Italian cuisine. Walls painted in subtle colours enhance the Mediterranean ambience.

Spec. Ravioli mit Ricotta-Walnussfüllung auf zerlassener Butter und Radicchio. Taubenbrust mit schwarzer Nuss-Sauce und Petersilienmousse. Rinderschmorbraten mit Barolosauce und Selleriepüree.

Käfer Schänke, Prinzregentenstr. 73, ✉ 81675, ☎ (089) 4 16 82 47, *kaeferschaenke@feinkost-kaefer.de, Fax (089) 4168623*, – AE MC VISA JCB HV s

closed Sunday and Bank Holidays – **Meals** (booking essential) à la carte 34,50/55.

◆ Cheerful restaurant plus a whole series of differently decorated little parlours, like the "Meissenstube", where you eat surrounded by no fewer than 300 pieces of porcelain !

at Munich-Denning *East : 8 km, by Denninger Straße* HV :

Casale, Ostpreußenstr. 42, ✉ 81927, ☎ (089) 93 62 68, *Fax (089) 9306722*, – P. AE MC VISA

Meals (Italian) 41 and à la carte 35/40.

◆ Classic Italian cuisine awaits you in this bright and welcoming restaurant with its conservatory. Colourful pictures enhance the Mediterranean atmosphere.

at Munich-Haidhausen :

Hilton City, Rosenheimer Str. 15, ✉ 81667, ☎ (089) 4 80 40, *fom_munich-city@hilton.com, Fax (089) 48044804*, – rm, – 180. AE MC VISA JCB LZ s

Meals à la carte 21/36,50 – 22 – **481 rm** 280/339 – 300/359 – 4 suites.

◆ Close to the Philharmonic Hall and the Gasteig culture centre, this establishment has functional rooms intended above all for business travellers. Restaurant in Alpine style with a choice of local or international cuisine.

Preysing without rest, Preysingstr. 1, ✉ 81667, ☎ (089) 45 84 50, *Fax (089) 45845444*, – – 15. AE MC VISA JCB LZ w

closed 22 December - 6 January – **76 rm** 130/135 – 180 – 5 suites.

◆ Rooms with natural wood furnishings and exquisite attention to detail. The cares of the day can soon be dispersed in pool, jacuzzi or sauna.

Forum Hotel, Hochstr. 3, ✉ 81669, ☎ (089) 4 80 30, *muchb@ichotelsgroup.com, Fax (089) 4488277*, – rm, – 350. AE MC VISA. rest LZ t

Meals à la carte 22,50/37 – 18 – **580 rm** 170/190 – 12 suites.

◆ Modern conference hotel with spacious rooms, solid furnishings and lavish leisure provision. The vast new conference centre can accommodate 2000. Modern restaurant with a mixture of European and Oriental cuisine.

Vinaiolo, Steinstr. 42, ✉ 81667, ☎ (089) 48 95 03 56, *Fax (089) 48068011* – VISA HX c
closed Monday lunch – **Meals** (Italian) (booking essential for dinner) à la carte 33,50/41,50.
◆ The menu here is composed using fresh produce from the market, while the wines are displayed on the restored shelving of the old pharmacy that used to occupy the building.

at München-Laim *East : 4 km, by Landsberger Str.* EV *and Fürstenrieder Str. :*

Il Sorriso, Gotthartstr. 8, ✉ 80686, ☎ (089) 5 80 31 70, *restaurant.ilsorriso@epost.de, Fax (089) 51261812,* – AE VISA JCB
closed Sunday – **Meals** à la carte 23,50/36.
◆ Pleasant Italian establishment on the ground floor of a small high-rise not far from the Hirschgarten and Nymphenburg palace. Mediterranean atmosphere.

at Munich-Neu Perlach *Southeast : 10 km, by Rosenheimer Straße* HX *and Otto-Brunner-Straße :*

Mercure Orbis, Karl-Marx-Ring 87, ✉ 81735, ☎ (089) 6 32 70, *h1374@accor-hotels.com, Fax (089) 6327407,* – rm, – 120 AE VISA JCB
Meals à la carte 18/30 – **185 rm** 127 – 144 – 4 suites.
◆ Smart upkeep is the keynote here, from the elegant lobby to the well-furnished bedrooms, usefully equipped with technological mod cons.

Villa Waldperlach without rest, Putzbrunner Str. 250 (Waldperlach), ✉ 81739, ☎ (089) 6 60 03 00, *hotel@villa-waldperlach.de, Fax (089) 66003066* – AE VISA JCB
21 rm 80 – 95/100.
◆ All the rooms have contemporary oakwood furnishings, plus ample work-desks and excellent technical facilities. Exposed beams in some of the cosy top-floor rooms.

at München-Oberföhring *Northwest : 4 km, by Ismaninger Str.* HUV *:*

Freisinger Hof with rm, Oberföhringer Str. 189, ✉ 81925, ☎ (089) 95 23 02, *freisinger.hof@t-online.de, Fax (089) 9578516,* Biergarten – AE VISA
Meals à la carte 27/46,50 – **13 rm** 98/115 – 130/150.
◆ Despite modernisation, this 1875 inn has kept its charm and character. Local specialities served in a rustic setting. Warm country-style rooms.

at Munich-Pasing *West : 11 km, by Landsberger Straße* EV *:*

Zur Goldenen Gans, Planegger Str. 31, ✉ 81241, ☎ (089) 83 70 33, *Fax (089) 8204680,* – VISA JCB
closed Monday – **Meals** à la carte 26/38.
◆ Much appreciated by its many regular diners, this rural inn offers Bavarian specialities. Characterful country-style restaurant with warm colours and wood panelling.

at Munich-Schwabing :

Marriott, Berliner Str. 93, ✉ 80805, ☎ (089) 36 00 20, *muenchen.marriott@marriotthotels.com, Fax (089) 36002200,* Massage, – rm, – 300. AE VISA. rest by Ungererstraße (B 11) HU
Meals à la carte 26/38 – 18 – **348 rm** 159/199 – 13 suites.
◆ This grand-hotel style establishment boasts a conference floor with up-to-the-minute technical facilities. Attractively decorated rooms with floral fabrics. American-style restaurant with open kitchen and large and splendid buffet.

Holiday Inn City Nord, Leopoldstr. 194, ✉ 80804, ☎ (089) 38 17 90, *reservation.himuenchen@queengruppe.de, Fax (089) 38179888,* – rm, – 320. AE VISA JCB by Leopoldstraße GU
Meals à la carte 24,50/37,50 – 18 – **365 rm** 140/220.
◆ In Munich's arts and entertainment district, this modern business hotel has an array of amenities including Roman spa, sauna, solarium, massage, pool-side bar and sun terrace.

Renaissance Hotel, Theodor-Dombart-Str. 4 (corner of Berliner Straße), ✉ 80805, ☎ (089) 36 09 90, *rhi.mucbr.reservations@renaissancehotels.com, Fax (089) 360996900,* – rm, – 30. AE VISA JCB. rest
Meals à la carte 23/34,50 – 16 – **260 rm** 141 – 87 suites.
◆ Close to the Englischer Garten and the Olympic Stadium. Attractive rooms and elegant suites offer a high level of comfort. For relaxing there is the "recreational oasis". Mediterranean-style Bistro 46-47. by Ungererstraße (B 11) HU

Four Points Hotel München Olympiapark, Helene-Mayer-Ring 12, ✉ 80809, ☎ (089) 35 75 10, *fourpoints.olympiapark@arabellasheraton.com, Fax (089) 35751800,* – rm, – 30. AE VISA JCB
closed 22 December - 12 January – **Meals** *(closed Sunday and Bank Holidays)* à la carte 20/33 – 13 – **105 rm** 140/160. by Schleißheimer Straße FU
◆ Bang in the middle of the Olympia Park ! Elegant and functional rooms just a few steps away from the very best in sporting events and cultural highlights.

Cosmopolitan without rest, Hohenzollernstr. 5, ✉ 80801, ☎ (089) 38 38 10, *cosmo@cosmopolitan-hotel.de, Fax (089) 38381111* – . AE VISA JCB
71 rm 100 – 110. GU g
◆ In the heart of Schwabing, this hotel consists of two linked buildings offering modern rooms with designer furnishings and excellent technical facilities.

Mercure without rest, Leopoldstr. 120, ✉ 80802, ☎ (089) 3 89 99 30, *h1104@accor-hotels.com, Fax (089) 349344* – . AE VISA JCB GU r
65 rm 94/129 – 130/150.
◆ Not far from the Englischer Garten and close to Old Schwabing with its cabarets and pubs, functional rooms up to the usual standard of Mercure establishments.

Leopold, Leopoldstr. 119, ✉ 80804, ☎ (089) 36 04 30, *hotel-leopold@t-online.de, Fax (089) 36043150,* – rm, – 20. AE VISA JCB
closed 23 to 30 December – **Meals** à la carte 18,50/35,50 – **72 rm** 95/115 – 115/128.
◆ Charming hotel that has been in the same family for generations, located in the heart of the artistic district of Schwabing. Ask for a room with a view of the idyllic garden. GU f

Tantris, Johann-Fichte-Str. 7, ✉ 80805, ☎ (089) 3 61 95 90, *info@tantris.de, Fax (089) 3618469,* – AE VISA. GU b
closed 1 week January, Sunday - Monday and Bank Holidays – **Meals** (booking essential) 60 *(lunch)*/128 *(dinner)* and à la carte 56/88 .
◆ Number One on every Munich gourmet's list, and guarded by fabulous beasts, this black and orange temple to fine dining serves the magical dishes of an innovative chef.
Spec. Lauwarmer Lachs mit Tomaten und Buttermilchmarinade. Carré vom Lammrücken mit Auberginensauce und Artischockenragout. Gefülltes Sauerrahmsoufflé mit Wachauer Marillenkompott und Sauerrahmeis.

Seehaus, Kleinhesselohe 3, ✉ 80802, ☎ (089) 3 81 61 30, *seehaus@kuffler.de, Fax (089) 341803,* , beer garden – AE VISA HU t
Meals à la carte 23,50/42,50.
◆ In an idyllic setting on the Kleinhesseloher lake, this establishment dishes up both German and international cuisine. The delightful lakeside terrace is a great asset.

Spago, Neureutherstr. 15, ✉ 80799, ☎ (089) 2 71 24 06, *spago@spago.de, Fax (089) 2780448,* – AE VISA GU a
closed Sunday – **Meals** (Italian) à la carte 24/33.
◆ A favourite with artists and theatre people but also with ordinary folk, all of whom appreciate the Italian/Mediterranean style delicacies.

Bistro Terrine, Amalienstr. 89 (Amalien-Passage), ✉ 80799, ☎ (089) 28 17 80, *terrine.bistro@t-online.de, Fax (089) 2809316,* – AE VISA GU q
closed 1 to 6 January, Bank Holidays, Sunday, lunch Monday and Saturday – **Meals** (booking essential for dinner) 22,50 *(lunch)* and à la carte 30,50/42,50.
◆ This restaurant is full of French bistro-style flair, right down to the Art Nouveau lamps. Classic French cuisine prepared from the freshest of ingredients.

at Munich-Sendling *Southwest : 6 km, by Lindwurmstraße (B 11)* EX :

Holiday Inn München-Süd, Kistlerhofstr. 142, ✉ 81379, ☎ (089) 78 00 20, *sales@holiday-inn-muenchen-sued.de, Fax (089) 78002672,* – rm, – 90. AE VISA JCB
Meals à la carte 24/35 – 16 – **320 rm** 149/180 – 181/231.
◆ Modern business hotel with functional conference facilities. Business centre with internet provision, photocopier, PC and printer. Air-conditioned rooms with balconies.

K+K Hotel am Harras without rest, Albert-Rosshaupter-Str. 4, ✉ 81369, ☎ (089) 74 64 00, *info@kkhotels.de, Fax (089) 7212820* – . AE VISA JCB
106 rm 145 – 170.
◆ This establishment's many advantages include not only contemporary comforts and an attractive atmosphere but also a convenient location with good road and rail access.

at Munich-Untermenzing *Northwest : 12 km, by Dachauer Straße* EU *and Baldur Straße :*

Romantik Hotel Insel Mühle, Von-Kahr-Str. 87, ✉ 80999, ☎ (089) 8 10 10, *insel-muehle@t-online.de, Fax (089) 8120571,* , beer garden, – – 30. VISA JCB
Meals 18 *(lunch)* and à la carte 31/44 – **38 rm** 98/126 – 126/174.
◆ This restored 16C watermill houses comfortable, country-house style rooms featuring warm colours and natural wood furnishings. Pleasant restaurant with lovely terrace overlooking the River Würm.

at Unterhaching *South : 10 km, by Kapuzinerstraße GX and Tegernseer Landstraße :*

Holiday Inn, Inselkammer Str. 7, ✉ 82008, ☎ (089) 66 69 10, *info@holiday-inn-muenchen.de, Fax (089) 66691602,* beer garden, – rm, rest, – 220.
Meals à la carte 25/43 – ☕ 15 – **270 rm** 130/156 – 156/182 – 3 suites.
◆ Located in an industrial area, this large modern hotel offers contemporary, functional rooms and comfortable suites and maisonettes.

Schrenkhof without rest, Leonhardsweg 6, ✉ 82008, ☎ (089) 6 10 09 10, *hotel-schrenkhof@t-online.de, Fax (089) 61009150,* – – 30.
closed Easter and Christmas - early January – **25 rm** ☕ 119 – 154.
◆ This Alpine-style establishment offers tasteful, highly individual rooms, some with fine wood panelling, some with lovely four-posters.

NH Unterhaching without rest, Leipziger Str.1, ✉ 82008, ☎ (089) 66 55 20, *nhmuenchenunterhaching@nh-hotels.com, Fax (089) 66552200,* –
☕ 14 – **80 rm** 114 – 129.
◆ This foyer of this hotel is a bright and airy atrium. Functionally designed rooms, with living and sleeping areas separated by a sliding door.

at Aschheim *Northeast : 13 km, by Prinzregentenstraße HV and Riem :*

Schreiberhof, Erdinger Str. 2, ✉ 85609, ☎ (089) 90 00 60, *info@schreiberhof.de, Fax (089) 90006459,* – rm, – 90.
closed 23 December - 6 January – ***Alte Gaststube*** : **Meals** à la carte 29/38 – **87 rm** ☕ 116 – 156.
◆ The spacious, elegant and functional rooms are provided with splendid, natural stone bathrooms. The light and airy winter garden is ideal for that special meeting or conference. The cosy Alte Gaststube serves local and international cuisine.

at Aschheim-Dornach *Northeast : 12 km, by Prinzregentenstraße HV and Riem :*

Inn Side Residence-Hotel, Humboldtstr. 12 (Industrialpark-West), ✉ 85609, ☎ (089) 94 00 50, *muenchen@innside.de, Fax (089) 94005299,* – rm, rest, – 80.
closed 21 December - 1 January – **Meals** *(closed lunch Saturday and Sunday)* à la carte 23/42 – ☕ 14 – **134 rm** 149 – 183.
◆ Interesting rooms with some extraordinary design features, among others free-standing glazed showers. Allow yourself to be inspired by the highly original artworks on display. The Bistrorant Pappagallo has fusion cuisine with emphasis on Oriental dishes.

at Grünwald *South : 13 km by Wittelsbacher Brücke GX :*

Tannenhof without rest, Marktplatz 3, ✉ 82031, ☎ (089) 6 41 89 60, *info@tannenhof-gruenwald.de, Fax (089) 6415608* –
closed 20 December - 6 January – **21 rm** ☕ 82/100 – 105/120.
◆ The lady owner of this lovely, white, modernised villa has decorated it throughout with loving care in a style that harmonises beautifully with its Art Nouveau architecture.

at airport Franz-Josef-Strauß *Northeast : 37 km by A 9 and A 92 :*

Kempinski Airport München, Terminalstraße Mitte 20, ✉ 85356 *München,* ☎ (089) 9 78 20, *info@kempinski-airport.de, Fax (089) 97822610,* – rm, – 280. rest
Meals à la carte 25/43 – ☕ 23 – **389 rm** 181 – 195 – 40 suites.
◆ This outstanding example of the hotel architecture of today boasts a huge glazed atrium with 17m-high palm trees reaching upwards. The rooms are of an equivalent standard. Discreet elegance and contemporary style characterise the restaurant.

Aschau im Chiemgau *Bayern 546 W 20 – pop. 5200 – alt. 615 m.*

München 82.

Restaurant Heinz Winkler - Residenz Heinz Winkler, Kirchplatz 1, ✉ 83229, ☎ (08052) 1 79 91 52, *info@residenz-heinz-winkler.de, Fax (08052) 179966,* –
closed Monday lunch – **Meals** à la carte 50/86 ♀.
◆ The creative and highly individual use of seasonal specialities makes a visit to this superlative and very welcoming restaurant an experience to remember.
Spec. Roh marinierte Jakobsmuscheln mit Kaviar-Kartoffel. Lammrücken in Brotteig mit Kräuterjus. Schokoladentränen mit Kokosnusseis.

Wernberg-Köblitz *Bayern* 546 R 20 – *pop.* 5 000 – *alt.* 377 m.
München 193.

XXX ✿✿ **Kastell** - Hotel Burg Wernberg, Schloßberg 10, ✉ 92533, ☎ (09604) 93 90, *hotel@burg-wernberg.de, Fax (09604) 939139* – P. AE MC VISA. ✗
closed 2 to 29 January, Monday and Tuesday – **Meals** *(dinner only)* (booking essential) 85/105 and à la carte 54,50/77 ♀.
♦ It's a real treat to sample French seasonal cuisine in this elegant establishment with its whitewashed vaults and polished service.
Spec. Ragout vom Kalbschwanz in der Kiste. Canneloni von der Seezunge mit zweierlei Kaviar. Gebackene Feigen mit Rumsahne und Tonkabohneneis.

STUTTGART L *Baden-Württemberg* 545 T 11 – *pop.* 593 500 – *alt.* 245 m.

See : *Linden Museum* ★★ KY **M1** – *Park Wilhelma*★ HT *and Killesberg-Park*★ GT – *Television Tower (Fernsehturm)* ✻★ HX – *Stuttgart Gallery (Otto-Dix-Collection*★*)* LY **M4** – *Old Castle (Altes Schloss) (Renaissance courtyard*★*)* – *Württemberg Regional Museum*★ LY **M3** – *State Gallery*★★ *(Old Masters Collection*★★*)* LY **M2** – *Collegiate church (Stiftskirche) (Commemorative monuments of dukes*★*)* KY **A** – *State Museum of Natural History (Staatl. Museum für Naturkunde) (Löwentor Museum*★*)* HT **M5** – *Mercedes-Benz Museum*★ JV **M6** – *Porsche Museum*★ *by Heilbronner Straße* GT – *Castle Solitude*★ *by Rotenwaldstraße* FX.

Envir. : *Bad Cannstatt Spa Park (Kurpark)*★ *East : 4 km* JT.

18 Kornwestheim, Aldinger Str. 975 (North : 11 km), ☎ (07141) 87 13 19 ; 18 Schwieberdingen, Nippenburg 21 (North-West : 15 km), ☎ (07150) 3 95 30 ; 18 Mönsheim, Schlossfeld (North-West : 30 km by A 8), ☎ (07044) 9 11 04 10.

✈ *Stuttgart-Echterdingen, by Obere Weinsteige (B 27) GX, ☎ (0711) 94 80, City-Air-Terminal, Stuttgart, Lautenschlagerstr. 14 (LY).*

Exhibition Centre (Messegelände Killesberg) (GT), ☎ (0711) 2 58 90, Fax (0711) 2589440.

ℹ *Tourist-Info, Königstr. 1a, ✉ 70173, ☎ (0711) 2 22 82 40, info@stuttgart-tourist.de,* Fax (0711) 2228216.

ADAC, *Am Neckartor 2.*

Berlin 630 – Frankfurt am Main 204 – Karlsruhe 88 – München 222 – Strasbourg 156.

Plans on following pages

Steigenberger Graf Zeppelin, Arnulf-Klett-Platz 7, ✉ 70173, ☎ (0711) 2 04 80, *stuttgart@steigenberger.de, Fax (0711) 2048542,* ⊛, Massage, ≘s, ⊠ – |‡|, ⇆ rm, ▤ TV ☎ ♿ ⇔ – 🎓 300. AE ⊕ MC VISA JCB. ✗ rest LY v
Meals see ***Olivo*** below – ***Zeppelin Stüble*** *(closed Sunday dinner)* **Meals** à la carte 18,50/33 – ***Zeppelino's :*** **Meals** à la carte 24,50/37 – ☐ 17 – **177 rm** 195/205 – 220/240.
♦ A mixture of modernity and tradition is concealed behind this building's sober façade. Exclusive rooms in three varieties - classic, elegant or avantgarde. Eat informally in the cheerful Zeppelin-Stube.

Am Schlossgarten, Schillerstr. 23, ✉ 70173, ☎ (0711) 2 02 60, *info@hotelschlossgarten.com, Fax (0711) 2026888,* ☂ – |‡|, ⇆ rm, ▤ TV ☎ ⇔ – 🎓 100. AE ⊕ MC VISA. ✗ rest LY u
Meals see ***Zirbelstube*** below – ***Schlossgarten-Restaurant*** *(closed Friday and Saturday)* **Meals** à la carte 36/48 – ***Vinothek*** *(closed Sunday and Monday)* **Meals** 22,50 and à la carte 25/36 – ☐ 18 – **116 rm** 158/233 – 4 suites.
♦ Splendid location between shopping centre, state theatre and the lovely leafy Schlossgarten. Elegant, luxurious rooms with delightfully colourful fabrics. Restaurant with an elegant country-style ambience, plus a magnificent terrace overlooking the park.

Maritim, Seidenstr. 34, ✉ 70174, ☎ (0711) 94 20, *info.stu@maritim.de, Fax (0711) 9421000,* ☂, Massage, Fø, ≘s, ⊠ – |‡|, ⇆ rm, ▤ TV ☎ ♿ ⇔ – 🎓 400. AE ⊕ MC VISA JCB FV r
Meals *(August dinner only)* à la carte 19,50/39,50 – ☐ 15 – **555 rm** 157/167 – 180/190 – 12 suites.
♦ With space for 800, the late 19C Riding Hall attached to this establishment is ideal for conferences and banquets. The Piano Bar has become a favourite Stuttgart rendezvous. Something for every taste in the Rotisserie and the Bistro Reuchlin.

InterContinental, Willy-Brandt-Str. 30, ✉ 70173, ☎ (0711) 2 02 00, *stuttgart@interconti.com, Fax (0711) 20202020,* Massage, Fø, ≘s, ⊠ – |‡| ⇆ ▤ TV ☎ ⇔ – 🎓 300. AE ⊕ MC VISA JCB. ✗ rest HV t
Meals à la carte 29,50/45 – ☐ 17 – **276 rm** 175/300 – 28 suites.
♦ A modern grand hotel with tastefully decorated rooms, this establishment has been patronised by celebrities such as Placido Domingo and the Rolling Stones. The restaurant has a cheerful, pub-type character.

INDEX OF STREET NAMES IN STUTTGART

Albert-Schalfe-Str. .... HV 107
Alexanderstr. .... LZ HV
Am Kochenhof ..... FGU
Am Kräherwald ..... FUV
Arnulf-Klett-Pl. .... LY 6
Augsburger Str. ..... JTU
Augustenstr. .... KZ 7
Badstr. .... HJT
Bebelstr. .... FV
Benzstr. .... JU
Birkenwaldstr. ...... GU 114
Bismarckstr. .... FV
Blumenstr. .... LZ GV 10
Boheim Str. .... FX
Bolzstr. .... LY GV 15
Brückenstr. .... HT 69
Büchsenstr. .... KY
Calwer Str. .... KYZ 18
Cannstatter Str. ..... LY HU
Charlottenpl. .... LZ GV 20
Charlottenstr. .... LZ
Daimlestr. .... JTU
Danneckerstr. .... LZ
Dorotheenstr. .... LZ 24
Eberhardstr. .... KLZ GV 25
Feuerbach-Tal-Str. .... FTU
Filderstr. .... FG
Frauenkopstr. ...... HXJV
Friedrich-Ebert-Str. .... GTU 119
Friedrichspl. .... KY 27
Friedrichstr. .... KY GV
Fritz-Elsas-Str. .... KYZ GV 28
Gablenberger Haupstr. .... HV 105
Gaußstr. .... FV
Geißeichstr. .... FVX
Gerberstr. .... KZ
Gerokstr. .... HV
Haldenstr. .... HJT
Hauptstätter Str. .... KZ GV 30
Hegelpl. .... KY 32
Hegelstr. .... KY
Heilbronner Str. ...... LY GTV 34
Herdersstr. .... FV 112
Herdweg .... KY
Heusteigstr. .... KLZ
Hirschstr. .... KZ
Hohenheimer Str. ..... LZ GV
Holzgartenstr. .... KY
Holzstr. .... LZ GV 40
Immen hofer Str. .... GVX 117
Jägerstraße .... KY
Jahnstr. .... GHX
Johannesstr. .... FV 109
Karlspl. .... LY 43
Karlstr. .... LZ 44
Katharinenpl. .... LZ 45
Katharinenstr. .... LZ
Keplerstraße .... KY
Kirchstr. .... LZ 46
Königstr. .... KLYZ
Köning-Karl-Str. ...... JT 102
Konrad-Adenauer-Str. ...... LY 47
Kriegsbergstr. .... KY
Kronenstr. .... KLY 48
Kronprinzstr. .... KYZ 49
Landhausstr. ...... HUV HJV 103
Lange Str. .... KYZ
Lautenschlagerstr. .... LY
Lenbachstr. .... GTU
Lenzhalde .... FU
Leonhardspl. .... LZ 50
Libanonstr. .... HV 106
Löwentorstr. .... HT
Marienstr. .... KZ
Marktpl. .... KLZ 52
Marktstr. .... LZ 53
Mercedesstr. .... JU
Neckar-Str. .... HU
Neckartalstr. .... HJT
Neue Weinsteige ..... GX
Nordbahnhofstr. ...... HU
Olgastr. .... LYZ GVX
Österreichischer Pl. ... KZ 57
Panoramastr. .... KY
Parler Str. .... FGU
Paulinenstr. .... KZ
Pfarrstr. .... LZ 61
Pischekstr. .... HVX 108
Planckstr. .... HV
Planie .... GV 62
Pragstr. .... GHT
Reinsburgstr. .... KZ FGV
Rennweg .... JV
Robert-Mayer-Str. ..... GU 115
Rosenbergstr. .... FV
Rotebühlpl. .... KZ GV 66
Rotebühlstr. .... KZ 70
Rotenwaldstr. .... FVX
Schillerpl. .... KLY
Schillerstr. .... LY
Schloßpl. .... LY 72
Schloßstr. .... KY FGV
Schönestr. .... HT 42
Schulstr. .... KZ 75
Seestr. .... KY FGV
Siemensstr. .... GT
Silberburgstr. .... KZ 76
Sophienstr. .... KZ 78
Steiermärker Str. ..... FT
Stresemannstr. .... GT
Stuttgarter Str. (FEUERBACH) .... FT
Talstr. .... HJV
Taubenheim-Str. ..... JTU 118
Theodor-Heuss-Str. .. KYZ GV 80
Torstr. .... KZ 82
Tübinger Str. ...... KZ GVX 77
Tunnelstr. .... GT 84
Uferstr. .... HJV
Ulmer Str. .... JUV
Ulrichstr. .... KLY
Urbanstr. .... LY
Wagenburgstr. .... HV
Waiblinger Str. .... JT 55
Waldebene Ost ..... HXV
Wangener Str. .... JV 104
Weilimdorfer Str. ..... FT
Weinsteige .... GX 116
Weißenburgstr. .... KZ
Wilhelmspl. .... LZ 86
Wilhelmstr. .... LZ 88
Willi-Bleicher-Str. .... KY 91
Willy-Brandt-Str. ..... LY
Wolframstr. .... GU 68
Zeppelinstr. .... FV 113

Dorint City-Center, Heilbronner Str. 88, ✉ 70191, ✆ (0711) 25 55 80, *info.strbuc @dorint.com, Fax (0711) 25558100* – |‡|, ⇹ rm, ▤ TV ✆ ♿ 🚗 – 🏛 120. AE ⓓ ⓜ VISA JCB GU c
Meals à la carte 20/34,50 – ☕ 13 – **174 rm** 100/125 – 110/145.
◆ Bright and welcoming contemporary accommodation, particularly appreciated by business travellers - all rooms have ample work desks and PC and fax points. The Mediterranean-style restaurant brings a touch of the South to the establishment.

Royal, Sophienstr. 35, ✉ 70178, ✆ (0711) 6 25 05 00, *royalhotel@t-online.de, Fax (0711) 628809* – |‡|, ⇹ rm, ▤ TV 🚗 P – 🏛 60. AE ⓓ ⓜ VISA JCB KZ b
Meals *(closed 2 to 23 August, Sunday and Bank Holidays)* à la carte 21/47,50 – **100 rm** ☕ 96/120 – 125/145 – 3 suites.
◆ Well-run establishment with welcoming atmosphere. Tranquil, tasteful rooms, with integrated furnishings in either maple knotwood or cherrywood.

Wörtz zur Weinsteige, Hohenheimer Str. 28, ✉ 70184, ✆ (0711) 2 36 70 00, *info@hotel-woertz.de, Fax (0711) 2367007*, 🏛 – |‡|, ⇹ rm, TV ✆ ♿ 🚗 P. AE ⓓ ⓜ VISA JCB
Meals *(closed 3 weeks January, end July - mid August, Sunday, Monday and Bank Holidays,* à la carte 26/46 ♀, ⚘ – **33 rm** ☕ 76/120 – 85/200. LZ p
◆ The pride of this attentively run hotel is the Schloesschen, its elegant rooms featuring Italian furnishings. Comfortable, rustic rooms in the main building. Wood carving and wrought-iron lend the restaurant its distinctive character.

Kronen-Hotel 🐚 without rest, Kronenstr. 48, ✉ 70174, ✆ (0711) 2 25 10, *kronenhote @s.netic.de, Fax (0711) 2251404*, ≘s – |‡| ⇹ TV ✆ 🚗 – 🏛 20. AE ⓓ ⓜ VISA JCB closed 22 December - 7 January – **83 rm** ☕ 99/120 – 133/169. KY m
◆ Distinctively designed rooms, with lovely tiled bathrooms in pastel colours. From the non-smoking breakfast room there is a lovely view of the leafy surroundings.

Azenberg 🐚, Seestr. 114, ✉ 70174, ✆ (0711) 2 25 50 40, *info@hotelazenberg.de Fax (0711) 22550499*, ≘s, 🏊, 🌳 – |‡|, ⇹ rm, TV ✆ 🚗 P – 🏛 20. AE ⓓ ⓜ VISA JCB – **Meals** *(closed 13 to 16 April, 24 May - 5 June, 29 July - 11 September, 2 to 6 November, 22 December - 5 January, Saturday and Sunday) (dinner only)* (residents only) – **58 rm** ☕ 85/109 – 125/145. FU e
◆ On the slope of the Killesberg hill with a fantastic view over the city. Welcoming and convenient rooms. 24-hour room service at no extra charge.

STUTTGART

Street	Grid	No.
Arnulf-Klett-Platz	LY	6
Augustenstraße	KZ	7
Blumenstraße	LZ	10
Bolzstraße	LY	15
Calwer Str.	KYZ	18
Charlottenplatz	LZ	20
Dorotheenstraße	LZ	24
Eberhardstraße	KLZ	25
Friedrichsplatz	KY	27
Hauptstätter Str.	KZ	30
Hegelplatz	KY	32
Heilbronner Str.	LY	34
Holzstraße	LZ	40
Karlsplatz	LY	43
Karlstraße	LZ	44
Katharinenplatz	LZ	45
Kirchstraße	LZ	46
Königstraße	KLYZ	
Konrad-Adenauer- Str.	LY	47
Kronenstraße	KLY	48
Kronprinzstraße	KYZ	49
Leonhardsplatz	LZ	50
Marktplatz	KLZ	52
Marktstraße	LZ	53
Österreichischer Platz	KZ	57
Pfarrstraße	LZ	61
Rotebühlplatz	KZ	66
Rotebühlstraße	KZ	70
Schloßplatz	LY	72
Schulstraße	KZ	75
Silberburgstraße	KZ	76
Sophienstraße	KZ	78
Theodor- Heuss- Str.	KYZ	80
Torstraße	KZ	82
Wilhelmsplatz	LZ	86
Wilhelmstraße	LZ	88
Willi- Bleicher- Str.	KY	91

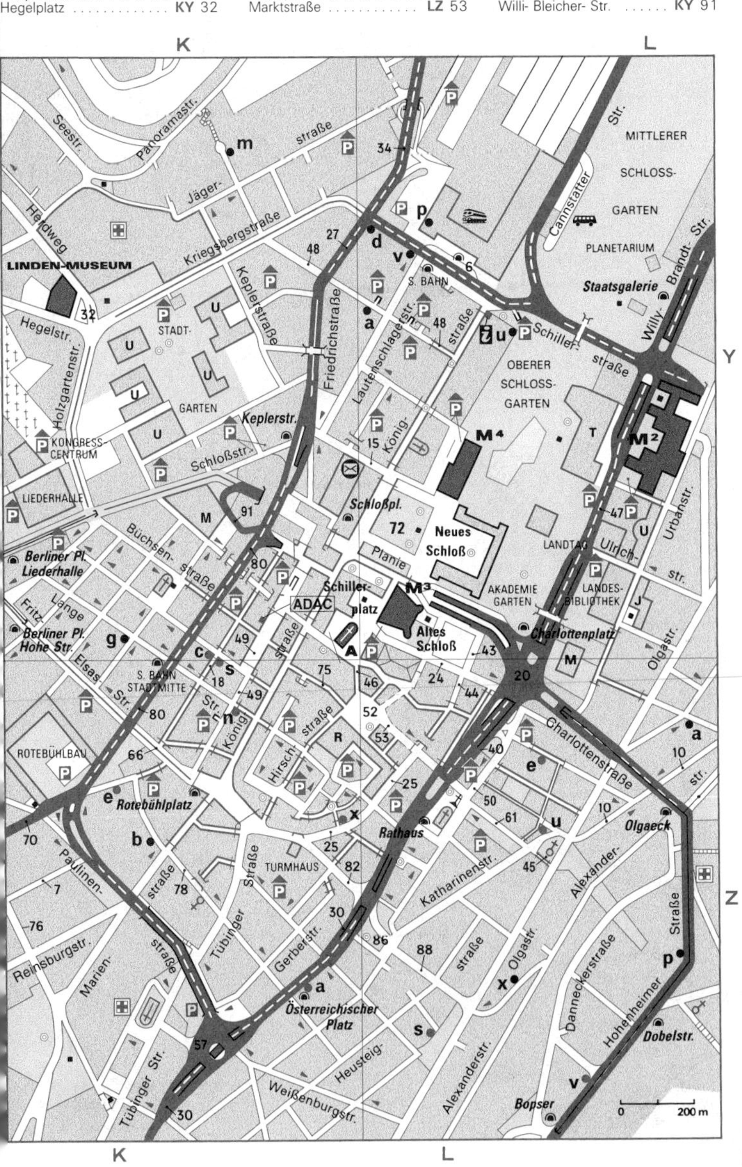

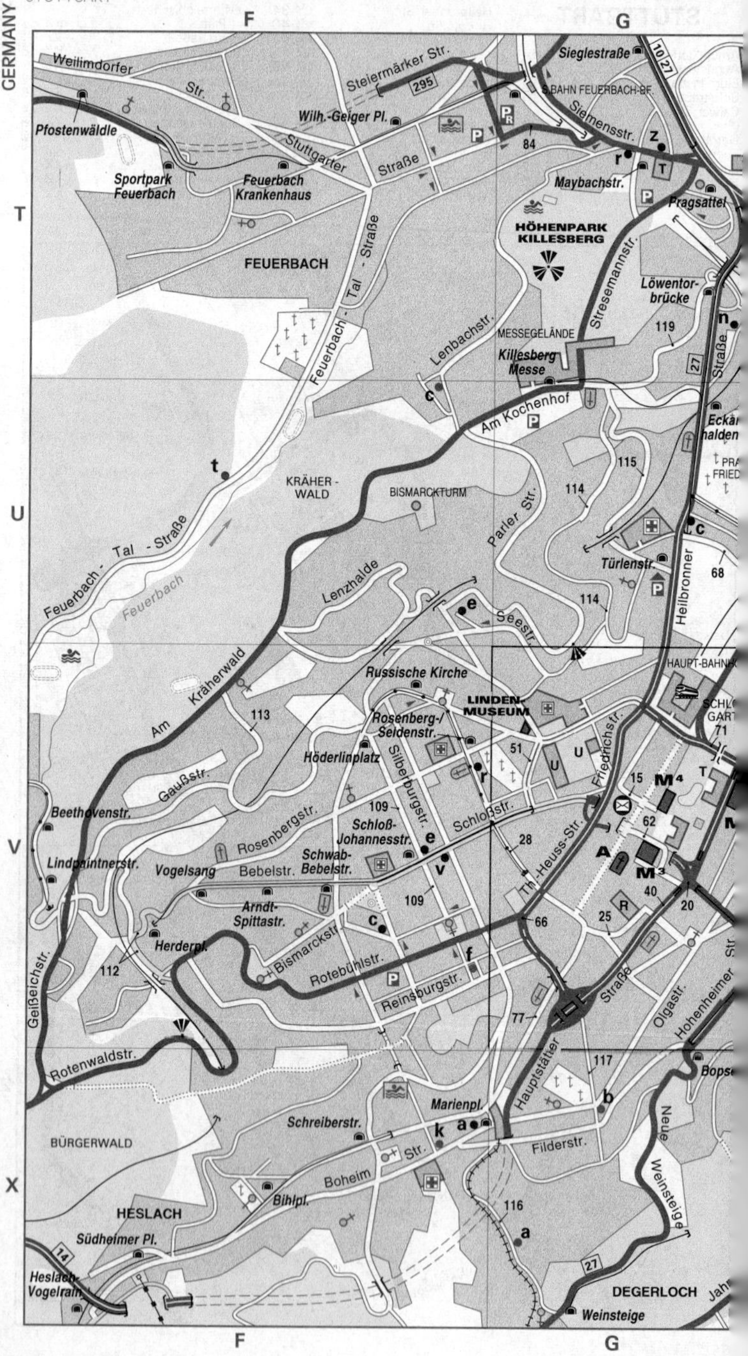

F
G
Weilimdorfer Str.
Steiermärker Str.
295
Sieglestraße
10 27
S-BAHN FEUERBACH-BF.
Siemensstr.
Pfostenwäldle
Wilh.-Geiger Pl.
Stuttgarter Straße
84
Z
r
Maybachstr.
Sportpark Feuerbach
Feuerbach Krankenhaus
Pragsattel
T
HÖHENPARK KILLESBERG
FEUERBACH
Stresemannstr.
Löwentorbrücke
Feuerbach - Tal - Straße
Lenbachstr.
MESSEGELÄNDE
119
n
Killesberg Messe
27
Straße
c
Am Kochenhof
Eckardtshalden
PRAG FRIEDHOF
t
KRÄHERWALD
BISMARCKTURM
115
114
U
Parler Str.
c
Feuerbach - Tal - Straße
Feuerbach
Lenzhalde
Türlenstr.
Heilbronner
68
e
Seestr.
114
Am Kräherwald
Russische Kirche
HAUPT-BAHNHOF
LINDEN-MUSEUM
SCHLOSSGARTEN
113
Rosenberg-/ Seidenstr.
71
Höderlinplatz
Silberburgstr.
51
U
U
T
Gaußstr.
r
Friedrichstr.
15
M4
Beethovenstr.
109
Schloßstr.
Rosenbergstr.
Schloß-Johannesstr.
e
62
M
V
Th.-Heuss-Str.
28
Lindpaintnerstr.
Vogelsang
Bebelstr.
Schwab-Bebelstr.
v
A
M3
109
40
20
Arndt-Spittastr.
R
c
66
25
Herderpl.
Bismarckstr.
f
112
Rotebühlstr.
Reinsburgstr.
Straße
Olgastr.
Hohenheimer Str.
Geißeichstr.
77
Hauptstätter
Rotenwaldstr.
117
Bopser
Marienpl.
b
Schreiberstr.
a
k
BÜRGERWALD
Boheim Str.
Filderstr.
Neue Weinsteige
X
Bihlpl.
116
HESLACH
a
Südheimer Pl.
14
27
Heslach-Vogelrain
DEGERLOCH
Jahn
Weinsteige
F
G

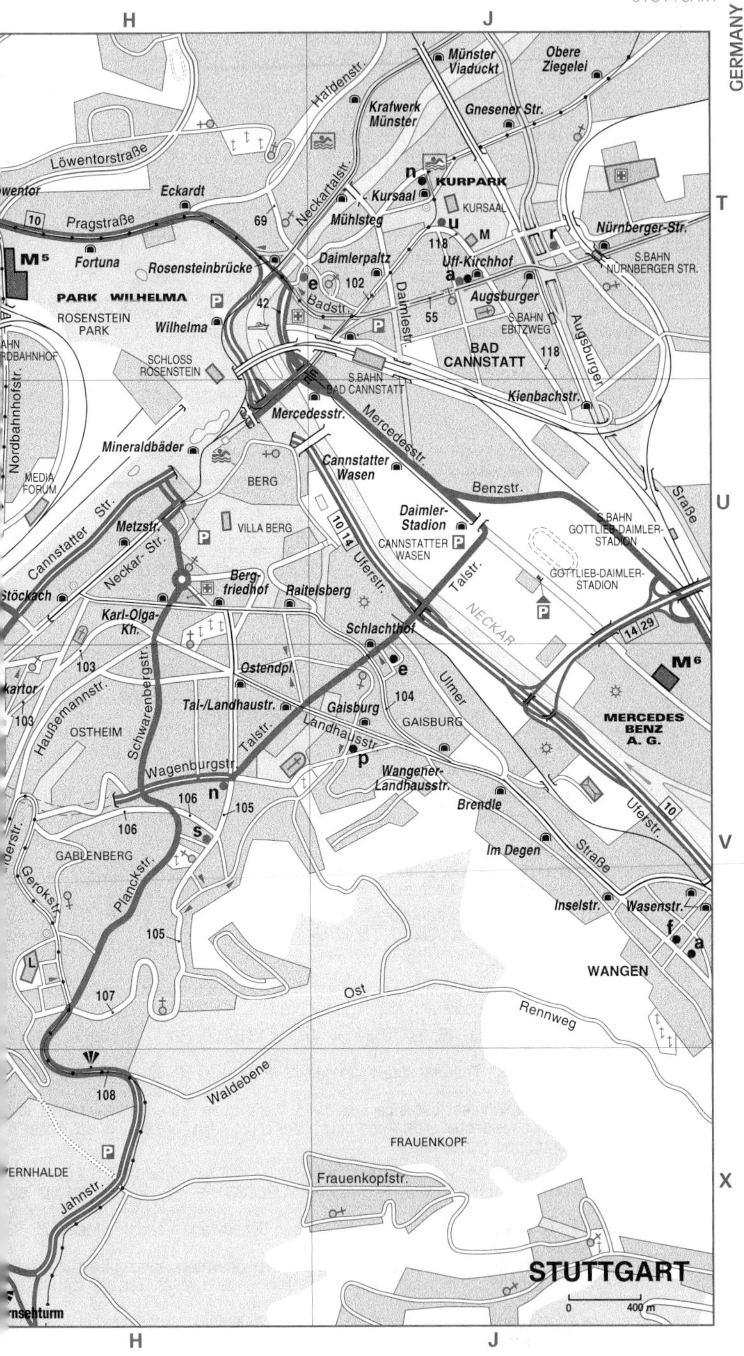
H
J
T
U
V
X
Münster Viaduckt
Obere Ziegelei
Haldenstr.
Krafwerk Münster
Gnesener Str.
Löwentorstraße
Eckardt
Neckartalstr.
KURPARK
Kursaal
KURSAAL
Mühlsteg
Pragstraße
Nürnberger-Str.
S.BAHN NÜRNBERGER STR.
Fortuna
Rosensteinbrücke
Daimlerpaltz
Uff-Kirchhof
PARK WILHELMA
Augsburger
Badstr.
Daimlerstr.
ROSENSTEIN PARK
Wilhelma
S.BAHN EBITZWEG
Augsburger
BAD CANNSTATT
SCHLOSS ROSENSTEIN
S.BAHN BAD CANNSTATT
Kienbachstr.
Nordbahnhofstr.
Mercedesstr.
Mercedesstr.
Mineralbäder
Cannstatter Wasen
MEDIA FORUM
BERG
Benzstr.
Straße
Cannstatter Str.
Metzstr.
VILLA BERG
Daimler-Stadion
S.BAHN GOTTLIEB-DAIMLER-STADION
CANNSTATTER WASEN
Neckar-Str.
Uferstr.
Talstr.
GOTTLIEB-DAIMLER-STADION
Stöckach
Berg-friedhof
Raitelsberg
Karl-Olga-Kh.
NECKAR
Schlachthof
Haußemannstr.
Ostendpl.
Schwarenbergstr.
Tal-/Landhaustr.
Gaisburg
GAISBURG
Ulmer
MERCEDES BENZ A. G.
OSTHEIM
Talstr.
Landhausstr.
Wagenburgstr.
Wangener-Landhausstr.
Brendle
Uferstr.
GABLENBERG
Gerokstr.
Planckstr.
Im Degen
Straße
Inselstr.
Wasenstr.
WANGEN
Ost
Rennweg
Waldebene
FRAUENKOPF
Frauenkopfstr.
Jahnstr.
STUTTGART
0
400 m

Unger without rest, Kronenstr. 17, ✉ 70173, ☎ (0711) 2 09 90, *info@hotel-unger.de, Fax (0711) 2099100* – 15. LY a
95 rm 102/128 – 143/158.
◆ Directly behind the pedestrian zone with contemporary comfort in every room. Despite the central location, quiet is guaranteed by the efficiently soundproofed windows.

InterCityHotel without rest, Arnulf-Klett-Platz 2, ✉ 70173, ☎ (0711) 2 25 00, *stuttgart@intercityhotel.de, Fax (0711) 2250499* – 25. LY p
112 rm 112/118 – 138/144.
◆ For travellers arriving by train it's just a short step to this establishment with its functional but very spacious rooms - it's located right by the station entrance.

Wartburg, Lange Str. 49, ✉ 70174, ☎ (0711) 2 04 50, *Fax (0711) 2045450* – rm, rest, – 40. rest KY g
closed Easter and 22 December - 6 January – **Meals** *(closed Saturday, Sunday and Bank Holidays) (lunch only)* à la carte 17/27 – **76 rm** 82/95 – 127/139.
◆ Well-run establishment. Choose between comfortable rooms with dark-stained furnishings or others in natural lightwood. Business people and bankers tend to gather here at lunchtime.

Abalon without rest, Zimmermannstr. 7 (approach by Olgastr. 79), ✉ 70182, ☎ (0711) 2 17 10, *info@abalon.de, Fax (0711) 2171217* – LZ x
42 rm 76/82 – 108/112.
◆ This modern building with its leafy roof terrace was built as a student hostel, hence its exceptional number of spacious rooms.

Central Classic without rest, Hasenbergstr. 49a, ✉ 70176, ☎ (0711) 6 15 50 50, *central-classic@gmx.de, Fax (0711) 61550530* – FV c
closed 22 December - 6 January – **34 rm** 65 – 79.
◆ This little hotel by the Feuersee lake is much appreciated by business people because of its individual work desks with fax and PC points as well as ISDN phone.

City-Hotel without rest, Uhlandstr. 18, ✉ 70182, ☎ (0711) 21 08 10, *info@cityhotel-suttgart.de, Fax (0711) 2369772* – LZ a
31 rm 79/85 – 95/115.
◆ Looking like a private house from the outside, this hotel has clean, well-presented rooms The breakfast room with its conservatory is a particularly attractive feature.

Rieker without rest, Friedrichstr. 3, ✉ 70174, ☎ (0711) 22 13 11, *info@hotel-rieker.de, Fax (0711) 293894* – LY d
66 rm 92/112 – 122/132.
◆ Located opposite the main station, this hotel has comfortably furnished rooms and offers its guests a cleaning and ironing service.

Ibis am Löwentor without rest, Presselstr. 15, ✉ 70191, ☎ (0711) 25 55 10, *h2202@accor-hotels.com, Fax (0711) 25551150* – GT n
9 – **132 rm** 66.
◆ Ideal location between city centre and motorway, this is a newly-built hotel with bright, well-presented rooms. 24-hour reception.

Ibis am Marienplatz without rest, Marienplatz 8, ✉ 70178, ☎ (0711) 12 06 40, *h3284@accor-hotels.com, Fax (0711) 12064160* – FX a
9 – **104 rm** 66/78.
◆ This city centre establishment is a practical choice especially for business travellers, since the rooms have work desks and all necessary points.

Bellevue, Schurwaldstr. 45, ✉ 70186, ☎ (0711) 48 07 60, *Fax (0711) 4807631* – JV p
Meals *(closed August, Tuesday and Wednesday)* à la carte 17,50/32 – **12 rm** 44/59 – 77.
◆ This family establishment dates back to 1913. Well-run and carefully maintained, it is located in a quiet residential area. A morning paper is provided for every guest. Cheerful and welcoming hotel restaurant.

Zirbelstube - Hotel Am Schlossgarten, Schillerstr. 23, ✉ 70173, ☎ (0711) 2 02 68 28 *info@hotelschlossgarten.com, Fax (0711) 2026888*, ←, – LY u
closed 1 to 12 January, 16 August - 6 September, Sunday and Monday – **Meals** 76/98 and à la carte 57/83 ♀.
◆ This is one of the top places to eat in Stuttgart. Gourmets appreciate the classic menu with a Mediterranean touch and the carefully chosen wines. Terrace with lovely view.
Spec. Variation von der Pelati-Tomate mit gebratenen Gambas. Jakobsmuscheln asiatisch mit Curry-Glasnudeln. Taubenkotelett gefüllt mit Trüffel und Gänsestopfleber.

XXX **Olivo** - Hotel Steigenberger Graf Zeppelin, Arnulf-Klett-Platz 7 (1st floor), ✉ 70173, ✆ (0711) 2 04 80, *stuttgart@steigenberger.de, Fax (0711) 2048542* – AE MC VISA JCB. LY v
closed August, Sunday and Monday – **Meals** (Italian) 64/104 and à la carte 42/59 ♀.
◆ Décor featuring soft colours gives this restaurant an elegantly Mediterranean character. Sophisticated presentation of Thomas Heilemann's fine Italian cuisine.
Spec. Salat von der Wachtel mit Sommertrüffel und Parmesan. Thunfischfilet im Ofen gebacken mit Backpflaumen und Zwiebellauch. Amaretti-Halbgefrorenes mit Orangenragout und Zabaione.

XX **Kern's Pastetchen**, Hohenheimer Str. 64, ✉ 70184, ✆ (0711) 48 48 55, *kerns.pastetchen@t-online.de, Fax (0711) 487565* LZ v
closed 24 to 28 February, 29 July - 14 August, Sunday and Monday – **Meals** *(dinner only)* 46/58 and à la carte 36,50/49.
◆ Elegant ambience with a touch of country style about it. International dishes influenced by the traditional cuisine of France and Austria.

XX **Délice** (Gutscher), Hauptstätter Str. 61, ✉ 70178, ✆ (0711) 6 40 32 22 – AE
closed 24 December - 6 January, Saturday, Sunday and Bank Holidays – **Meals** *(dinner only)* (booking essential) 70 and à la carte 44/56 ♀. KZ a
◆ This vaulted establishment with its open kitchen makes an elegant impression. The menu is introduced by the chef in person. Walls graced by contemporary art.
Spec. Marinierte Spaghettini mit Caviar. Filet vom St. Pierre mit Limonen-Kapernbutter und gestampften Kartoffeln. Graumohn-Auflauf mit Aprikosensauce und Rumeis.

XX **La Fenice**, Rotebühlplatz 29, ✉ 70178, ✆ (0711) 6 15 11 44, *g.vincenzo@t-online.de, Fax (0711) 6151146*, – AE MC VISA. KZ e
closed 2 weeks August, Monday, lunch Saturday and Sunday – **Meals** (Italian) à la carte 30,50/50.
◆ The Gorgoglione sisters have realised the dream of their own restaurant in this old post office building where Rosa serves excellent Italian dishes.

XX **Di Gennaro**, Kronprinzstr. 11, ✉ 70173, ✆ (0711) 22 29 60 51, *Fax (0211) 22296040* – AE MC VISA. KZ n
closed Sunday and Bank Holidays – **Meals** (Italian) à la carte 33/42.
◆ This modern city building with its glass façade is home to both an Italian restaurant and a delicatessen. Contemporary bistro-style interior.

XX **Da Franco**, Calwer Str. 23 (1st floor), ✉ 70173, ✆ (0711) 29 15 81, *info@dafrancostuttgart.de, Fax (0711) 294549* – AE MC VISA KYZ s
closed 4 weeks July - August and Monday – **Meals** (Italian) à la carte 29,50/51,50.
◆ First floor Italian establishment with a view down Stuttgart's main promenade. Unfussy, functional décor with lots of white plus contemporary art on the walls.

XX **La nuova Trattoria da Franco**, Calwer Str. 32, ✉ 70173, ✆ (0711) 29 47 44, *info@dafrancostuttgart.de, Fax (0711) 294549*, – AE MC VISA KYZ c
Meals (Italian) à la carte 24/37.
◆ See and be seen is the motto here. On two floors, with more refined Italian dishes available as well as the usual pasta and pizza.

XX **La Scala**, Friedrichstr. 41 (1st floor,), ✉ 70174, ✆ (0711) 29 06 07, *Fax (0711) 2991640* – AE MC VISA. KY e
closed Sunday and Bank Holidays lunch – **Meals** (Italian) 22/28 and à la carte 26/36.
◆ Classic first floor Italian establishment with typical cuisine plus a special something because of the panelled walls and direct view of the famous Friedrichsbau.

X **Der Zauberlehrling** with rm, Rosenstr. 38, ✉ 70182, ✆ (0711) 2 37 77 70, *kontakt@zauberlehrling.de, Fax (0711) 2377775* – rm, TV. LZ c
Meals *(closed lunch Saturday and Sunday)* à la carte 27/46 ♀ – **9 rm** 100/135 – 135/160.
◆ Refined country-style ambience. Diners sit at wooden tables and choose from a small but carefully composed menu of international dishes. Modern, designer rooms.

X **Vetter**, Bopserstr. 18, ✉ 70180, ✆ (0711) 24 19 16, *Fax (0711) 60189640*,
closed 3 weeks September - October, Sunday and Bank Holidays – **Meals** *(dinner only)* (booking essential) à la carte 19,50/36. LZ s
◆ This cheerful and well-run establishment in a city centre side street has contemporary décor and offers a choice of local and international specialities.

Swabian wine taverns (Weinstuben) *(mainly light meals only)* :

X **Weinstube Schellenturm**, Weberstr. 72, ✉ 70182, ✆ (0711) 2 36 48 88, *juergenwurst@t-online.de, Fax (0711) 2262699*, – AE LZ u
closed 24 December - 6 January, Sunday and Bank Holidays – **Meals** *(dinner only)* à la carte 19/39,50 ♀.
◆ This 16C fortified tower is the place to come and enjoy a typically Swabian atmosphere, with good wine and local specialities like Spätzle and Maultaschen.

Weinstube Klösterle, Marktstr. 71 (Bad Cannstatt), ✉ 70372, ☎ (0711) 56 89 62, Fax (0711) 558606, – Ⓜ HJT
closed Sunday and Bank Holidays – **Meals** (open from 5 pm) à la carte 16/26,50.
• The historic monastery building of 1463 is one of the oldest inhabited structures in Stuttgart, its rustic character enhanced by its décor.

Kachelofen, Eberhardstr. 10 (entrance Töpferstraße), ✉ 70173, ☎ (0711) 24 23 78, Fax (0711) 5299162, – Ⓜ VISA KZ
closed Sunday – **Meals** (open from 5 pm) à la carte 26/39.
• This wine tavern in the old Stadthaus has been a favourite celebrity rendezvous for years, a fact attested to by the photos and signatures on its walls.

Stuttgarter Stäffele, Buschlestr. 2a, ✉ 70178, ☎ (0711) 61 72 76, staeffele@aol.com, Fax (0711) 613535, – AE Ⓜ VISA FV
closed lunch Saturday, Sunday and Bank Holidays – **Meals** (booking essential) à la carte 15/36.
• With wood panelling and red-and-white striped curtains, this is an archetypal wine tavern. The menu features Swabian dishes and Württemberg wines.

Weinstube Klink, Epplestr. 1 (Degerloch), ✉ 70597, ☎ (0711) 7 65 32 05, Fax (0711) 760307, by Obere Weinsteige GX
closed mid August - early September, Saturday, Sunday and Bank Holidays – **Meals** (open from 5 pm) (booking essential) à la carte 25/40.
• You have to look carefully for the entrance to this establishment which is tucked away in a courtyard. An original feature is the daily menu, displayed on a blackboard.

Weinstube Träuble, Gablenberger Hauptstr. 66 (entrance Bussenstraße), ✉ 70186, ☎ (0711) 46 54 28, Fax (0711) 4207961, – HV
closed end August - mid September, 24 December - 6 January, Sunday and Bank Holidays – **Meals** (open from 5 pm) (only cold and warm light meals).
• This little place is 200 years old and looks a bit like a doll's house. It's great fun taking a glass or three next to the tiled stove in the cosy wood-panelled parlour.

Weinstube Kochenbas, Immenhofer Str. 33, ✉ 70180, ☎ (0711) 60 27 04, kochenbas@t-online.de, Fax (0711) 602704, GX
closed end August - mid September and Monday – **Meals** (booking essential) à la carte 15,50/22.
• Stuttgart's second oldest wine tavern is an appealing place, its rustic décor giving it a typical Swabian atmosphere. The kitchen conjures up tasty local specialities.

Weinhaus Stetter, Rosenstr. 32, ✉ 70182, ☎ (0711) 24 01 63, post@weinhaus-stetter.de, Fax (0711) 240193, LZ
closed 24 December - 8 January, Sunday and Bank Holidays – **Meals** (open Monday to Friday from 3 pm, Saturday 11 am to 3 pm) (only cold and warm light meals).
• You'd have to go a long way to find a longer list of wines - the choice here is enormous and includes excellent wines from abroad as well. You can buy as well as taste.

at Stuttgart-Büsnau West : 9 km, by Rotenwaldstraße FX :

relexa Waldhotel Schatten, Magstadter Straße 2 (Solitudering), ✉ 70569, ☎ (0711) 6 86 70, stuttgart@relexa-hotel.de, Fax (0711) 6867999, – rm, – 80. AE Ⓜ VISA JCB
La Fenêtre (closed Monday, Sunday and Bank Holidays) (dinner only) **Meals** à la carte 36/52 – **Kaminrestaurant :** **Meals** à la carte 22,50/37 – **136 rm** 105/194 – 139/21 – 8 suites.
• This 200-year-old establishment stands outside the gates of the town, and is a successful synthesis of old and new. Some of the rooms are graced with antique furniture. The La Fenêtre restaurant has an elegant touch, the Kaminrestaurant is more down to earth.

at Stuttgart-Bad Cannstatt :

Mercure, Teinacher Str. 20, ✉ 70372, ☎ (0711) 9 54 00, h1704@accor-hotels.com, Fax (0711) 9540630, – rm, – 100. AE Ⓜ VISA JT
Meals à la carte 23,50/43 – **156 rm** 120 – 153.
• This hotel offers comfortable, contemporary rooms. If you need extra space, ask for one of the very generously designed suites or apartments.

Krehl's Linde with rm, Obere Waiblinger Str. 113, ✉ 70374, ☎ (0711) 5 20 49 00, info@krehl-gastronomie.de, Fax (0711) 52049013, – 50. Ⓜ VISA JT
closed 3 weeks August - September – **Meals** (closed Sunday and Monday) 22,50 and à la carte 31/45 – **18 rm** 40/60 – 90.
• This traditional place has been in the same family since 1875. Stylish setting and a choice of local specialities or refined French delicacies. Solidly furnished rooms.

at Stuttgart-Degerloch :

XXX ✿ **Wielandshöhe** (Klink), Alte Weinsteige 71, ✉ 70597, ☎ (0711) 6 40 88 48, *Fax (0711) 6409408*, – AE VISA GX a
closed Sunday and Monday – **Meals** (booking essential) 64/98 *(dinner)* and à la carte 42/69.
◆ A famous chef is in charge here, a master of the classical repetoire with Mediterranean and local influences. Elegant ambience and wonderful view.
Spec. Ravioli von der Kalbshaxe mit Trüffelsauce. Loup de mer in der Salzkruste mit geschmortem Chicorée (2 people). Kotelett vom Schwäbisch Hallischen Jungschwein mit Pfefferjus.

XXX ✿ **Weber's Gourmet im Turm**, Jahnstr. 120, ✉ 70597, ☎ (0711) 24 89 96 10, *restaurant@fernsehturm-stgt.de, Fax (0711) 24899627*, ✳ Stuttgart and surroundings, (in TV-tower at 144 m,) – P. AE VISA. HX
closed 2 weeks January, 3 weeks February, Sunday - Monday – **Meals** *(dinner only)* (booking essential) à la carte 61/83.
◆ A lift propels diners to this restaurant, 144m up Stuttgart's famous TV tower. Creative cuisine, a remarkable wine list and a tasteful, stylish setting await at the top.
Spec. Schaumsüppchen von Palmenherzen und Zitronengras. Paella mit Hummer und Artischocken. Kalbskopf-Risotto mit Rote Bete und Trüffel.

XX **Das Fässle**, Löwenstr. 51, ✉ 70597, ☎ (0711) 76 01 00, *info@faessle.de, Fax (0711) 764432*, – – 20. AE VISA by Jahnstraße GX
closed Sunday and Monday lunch – **Meals** (booking essential) 30 and à la carte 27/41.
◆ This country-style restaurant provides versions of international and local cuisine. Cheerful atmosphere with lattice windows and lots of panelling.

at Stuttgart-Fasanenhof *South : 10 km, by Obere Weinsteige GX and B 27 :*

Fora Hotel, Vor dem Lauch 20, ✉ 70567, ☎ (0711) 7 25 50, *reservation.fasanenhof@fora.de, Fax (0711) 7255666*, , – , rm, – 55. AE VISA
Meals à la carte 22/33 – **101 rm** 115 – 131.
◆ Modern establishment right in the middle of Stuttgart's Businesspark catering almost exclusively for business travellers. Fax in room on request.

at Stuttgart-Feuerbach :

Messehotel Europe, Siemensstr. 33, ✉ 70469, ☎ (0711) 81 00 40 (hotel) 8 10 04 24 55 (rest.), *info.str@europe-hotels-int.de, Fax (0711) 810042555* – , rm, . AE VISA GT r
closed mid December - mid January and August – ***Landhausstuben*** *(dinner only)* **Meals** à la carte 17/24,50 – **114 rm** 102 – 128.
◆ The pride of this modern trade-fair hotel is the lobby with its glass-sided lifts and landscaped water feature. Comfortable, contemporary rooms. Country-style restaurant with welcoming atmosphere.

Kongresshotel Europe, Siemensstr. 26, ✉ 70469, ☎ (0711) 81 00 40, *info.str@europe-hotels-int.de, Fax (0711) 810041444*, , – , rm, – 120. AE VISA GT z
Meals *(closed lunch Saturday and Sunday)* à la carte 24/41,50 – **144 rm** 87/110 – 138 – 3 suites.
◆ Almost all the rooms have Spanish-style décor in warm colours. The rooms on the business floor have fax and modem points.

XX **Landgasthof im schönsten Wiesengrund** with rm, Feuerbacher-Tal-Str. 200, ✉ 70469, ☎ (0711) 1 35 37 20, *info@landgasthof-wiesengrund.de, Fax (0711) 13537210*, , beer garden – rm, P – 20. AE VISA JCB
Meals à la carte 25/44,50 – **14 rm** 65 – 105. FU t
◆ Traditional décor and a menu based on local dishes supplemented by seasonal specialities. Bright, modern guest rooms.

at Stuttgart-Flughafen (Airport) *South : 15 km by Obere Weinsteige GX and B 27 :*

Mövenpick-Hotel, Flughafenrandstr. 7, ✉ 70629, ☎ (0711) 7 90 70, *hotel.stuttgart-airport@moevenpick.com, Fax (0711) 793585*, , – , rm, P – 40. AE VISA JCB. rest
Meals à la carte 19,50/38 – 16 – **229 rm** 154/168 – 179/193.
◆ Conveniently located only 200m from the airport terminal. Comfortable rooms with optimal soundproofing. Close to the S-Bahn rapid transit station.

XXX ✿ **top air**, at the airport (terminal 1, level 4), ✉ 70629, ☎ (0711) 9 48 21 37, *top.air.stuttgart@woellhaf-airport.de, Fax (0711) 7979210* – P – 40. AE VISA
closed 2 weeks early January, August, 1 week end December, Saturday, Sunday and Bank Holidays – **Meals** 36 *(lunch)*/90 and à la carte.
◆ You can watch the planes taxiing past while being treated to the delightful French specialities of this uniquely located restaurant. Exquisite contemporary ambience.
Spec. Parfait von Kalbsbries mit Hummer und getrüffelten Bohnen. Bresse-Taube im Blätterteig mit geschmortem Chicorée. Topfen-Limonencrème mit Banyuls-Kirschen und Nougateis.

at Stuttgart-Hoheheim *South : 10 km, by Mittlere Filderstraße* HX :

Speisemeisterei (Öxle), Am Schloß Hohenheim, ✉ 70599, ☎ (0711) 4 56 00 37, *Fax (0711) 4560038* – 🅿.
closed 1 to 13 January, 26 July - 11 August, Monday and Tuesday – **Meals** *(weekdays dinner only)* (booking essential) 64/110 ♀, .
◆ Even the most jaded palate will be revived in the magnificent surroundings of Schloss Hohenheim, where the cuisine is as refined and aristocratic as the ambience.
Spec. Gänseleber und Perigord-Trüffel mit Ochsenschwanz-Madeiragelee. Steinbutt und Hummerschwanz im Gemüsemantel mit Kaviar-Nudeln. Schokoladen-Crêpes-Torte mit Vanillefeige.

at Stuttgart-Möhringen *Southwest : 8 km by Obere Weinsteige* GX *and B 27* :

Millennium Hotel and Resort (with **SI**), Plieninger Str. 100, ✉ 70567, ☎ (0711) 72 10, *sales.stuttgart@mill-cop.com, Fax (0711) 7212950,* , beer garden, direct entrance to the recreation centre Schwaben Quelle – , rm, – 650.
Meals (19 different restaurants, bars and cafes) à la carte 21/41 – 16 – **454 rm** 165/185 – 185/205.
◆ This modern high building stands opposite the Musical-Theaters. Elegant, tasteful rooms, and, a lavishly equipped leisure area. You can choose among 19 different themed restaurants and bars.

Gloria, Sigmaringer Str. 59, ✉ 70567, ☎ (0711) 7 18 50, *info@hotelgloria.de, Fax (0711) 7185121,* beer garden, – , rm, 🅿 – 50.
Möhringer Hexle : **Meals** à la carte 18/31 – **85 rm** 75/85 – 90/113.
◆ A lovely bright foyer welcomes guests to this family-run hotel, which offers a choice of rooms, contemporary-functional or traditional-comfortable. An attractive aspect of the traditional Möhringer Hexle restaurant is its winter garden.

Fora Hotel without rest, Filderbahnstr. 43, ✉ 70567, ☎ (0711) 71 60 80, *reservation.moehringen@fora.de, Fax (0711) 7160850* – .
closed 24 December - 6 January – **41 rm** 86 – 102.
◆ This hotel is set back from the main road. Guests stay in well-presented furnished rooms, their welcoming appearance enhanced by the use of bright colours.

Zur Linde, Sigmaringer Str. 49, ✉ 70567, ☎ (0711) 7 19 95 90, *info@gasthauszurlin.de, Fax (0711) 7199592,*
closed Saturday lunch – **Meals** à la carte 19/36 ♀.
◆ If you enjoy hearty food with a home-cooked flavour, the cheerful "Lime Tree" is the place for you. Tempting Swabian morsels lovingly prepared from traditional recipes.

at Stuttgart-Obertürkheim *East : 6 km, by Augsburger Straße* JU :

Brita Hotel, Augsburger Str. 671, ✉ 70329, ☎ (0711) 32 02 30, *info@brita-hotel.de, Fax (0711) 32023400* – , rm, – 80.
closed 20 December - 7 January – **Meals** *(closed 5 to 26 August, Saturday and Sunday) (dinner only)* à la carte 19,50/31 – **70 rm** 75/95 – 128.
◆ Friendly establishment with contemporary comforts. All rooms with soundproofed windows. Oversize beds on request. Good traditional cooking in the country-style Poststüble or the Kutscherstube.

at Stuttgart-Stammheim *North : 10 km, by Heilbronner Straße* GT :

Novotel-Nord, Korntaler Str. 207, ✉ 70439, ☎ (0711) 98 06 20, *h0501@accor-hotels.com, Fax (0711) 98062137,* , , (heated) – , rm, 🅿 – 130.
Meals à la carte 19/28 – 13 – **112 rm** 94 – 104.
◆ This hotel is well-located in relation to the motorway. Rooms to the usual Novotel standard, with bright and functional furniture.

at Stuttgart-Vaihingen *Southwest : 9,5 km, by Böblinger Straße* FX :

Dorint Fontana, Vollmoellerstr. 5, ✉ 70563, ☎ (0711) 73 00, *info.strfon@dorint.com, Fax (0711) 7302525,* , Massage, , , , – , rm, – 250.
 rest
Meals à la carte 24,50/41,50 – 16 – **252 rm** 162/192 – 177/207.
◆ Stylish rooms on 18 floors, tastefully and comprehensively furnished with work desks, little living areas, and exquisitely comfortable beds. Choose between the elegant and country-style sections of the restaurant.

at Stuttgart-Weilimdorf *Northwest : 12 km, by Steiermärker Straße* FT *and B 295* :

Holiday Inn, Mittlerer Pfad 25, ✉ 70499, ☎ (0711) 98 88 80, *holidayinn.stuttgart@t-online.de, Fax (0711) 988889,* beer garden, , – , rm, – 220.
Meals à la carte 21/39 – 16 – **321 rm** 150/166 – 7 suites.
◆ Standard rooms with comfortable, contemporary furnishings, all with tea- and coffee-making facilities. It's best to reserve a room in the main building.

at Stuttgart-Zuffenhausen *North : 8 km, by Heilbronner Straße* GT *and B 10 :*

Achat without rest, Wollinstr. 6, ✉ 70439, ☎ (0711) 82 00 80, *stuttgart@achat-hotel.de, Fax (0711) 82008999* – |♦|, ⇔ rm, TV ☎ 🚗. AE ⊕ ⊙ VISA. ✗ rest
☐ 11 – **104 rm** 74/89 – 74/99.
◆ This modern hotel was built in 1997. Attractive rooms with bright and welcoming décor, many with kitchenette.

at Fellbach *Northeast : 8 km, by Nürnberger Straße (B 14)* JT *:*

Classic Congress Hotel, Tainer Str. 7, ✉ 70734, ☎ (0711) 5 85 90, *info@cch-bw.de, Fax (0711) 5859304*, 🏋, ≘s – |♦|, ⇔ rm, TV ☎ 🚗 P – 🎤 55. AE ⊕ ⊙ VISA
closed 23 December - 6 January – **Meals** see also **Eduard M.** below – **149 rm** ☐ 145/149 – 168.
◆ The hotel is linked to the Schwabenlandhalle by an underground passageway. Recently refurbished rooms with bright and cheerful furniture.

Eduard M. - Classic Congress Hotel, Tainer Str. 7 (Schwabenlandhalle), ✉ 70734, ☎ (0711) 5 85 94 11, *restaurant@eduardm.de, Fax (0711) 5859427*, 🍽 – ▤. AE ⊕ ⊙ VISA
closed 27 to 30 December – **Meals** à la carte 27/46,50.
◆ The redesigned restaurant of the Classic Congress Hotel makes a attractive impression with its bright and welcoming décor and split levels.

Aldinger's Weinstube Germania, Schmerstr. 6, ✉ 70734, ☎ (0711) 58 20 37, *aldingers@t-online.de, Fax (0711) 582077*, 🍽 – ✗
closed 2 weeks February - March, 3 weeks August, Sunday and Monday – **Meals** (booking essential) à la carte 26/37 ♀.
◆ This wine tavern with a modern touch is run personally by the chef, an expert with local and seasonal dishes. Dining on the terrace when weather permits.

at Gerlingen *West : 12 km, by Rotenwaldstraße* FX *:*

Lamm, Leonberger Str. 2, ✉ 70839, ☎ (07156) 2 22 51, *Fax (07156) 48815*, 🍽 – ⊙ VISA
closed Tuesday and Saturday lunch – **Meals** à la carte 22,50/40.
◆ This partly panelled restaurant is divided up into friendly little niches. Traditional and local specialities suit the country-style atmosphere.

at Korntal-Münchingen *Northwest : 9 km, by Heilbronner Straße* GT *and B 10 :*

Mercure, Siemensstr. 50, ✉ 70825, ☎ (07150) 1 30, *h0685@accor-hotels.com, Fax (07150) 13266*, 🍽, beer garden, ≘s, 🏊 – |♦|, ⇔ rm, TV ☎ ♿ P – 🎤 180. AE ⊕ ⊙ VISA
Meals à la carte 28,50/38,50 – **200 rm** ☐ 108/138 – 132/162.
◆ Conference delegates appreciate this hotel's proximity to the motorway. Functional rooms all with work desks and some with living areas.

at Leinfelden-Echterdingen *South : 13 km, by Obere Weinsteige* GX *and B 27 :*

Am Park, Lessingstr. 4 (Leinfelden), ✉ 70771, ☎ (0711) 90 31 00, *info@hotelampark-leinfelden.de, Fax (0711) 9031099*, beer garden – |♦|, ⇔ rm, TV ☎ P – 🎤 15. AE ⊕ ⊙ VISA
Meals *(closed 24 December - 10 January, Saturday and Sunday)* à la carte 19/39 – **42 rm** ☐ 77 – 96.
◆ This welcoming establishment stands in a tranquil cul-de-sac surrounded by magnificent trees. Bright and attractively furnished rooms. Choose from the restaurant's range of well-prepared southern German specialities.

Filderland without rest, Tübinger Str. 16 (Echterdingen), ✉ 70771, ☎ (0711) 9 49 46, *hotel-filderland@t-online.de, Fax (0711) 9494888* – |♦| ⇔ TV ☎ 🚗 – 🎤 15. AE ⊕ ⊙ VISA. ✗
closed 23 December - 5 January – **48 rm** ☐ 63/76 – 83/91.
◆ Behind the attractive façade is a well-run hotel not far from the airport. Comfortable, contemporary interior.

Baiersbronn *Baden-Württemberg* 545 U 9 – *pop. 16 600 – alt. 550 m.*
Stuttgart 100.

Schwarzwaldstube - Hotel Traube Tonbach, Tonbachstr. 237, ✉ 72270, ☎ (07442) 49 26 65, *tischreservierung@traube-tonbach.de, Fax (07442) 492692*, ≤ – ▤ P. AE ⊕ ⊙ VISA. ✗
closed 7 to 30 January, 2 to 26 August, Monday and Tuesday – **Meals** (booking essential) 100/125 and à la carte 69/98 ♀, 🍷.
◆ The art of fine cuisine is practised here with supreme success. The exclusive interior complements the exquisite food, with solid wood furnishings and lovely fabrics.
Spec. Gebratene Jakobsmuscheln mit Ananas-Mangochutney und Thai-Currysauce. Polenta mit Gänseleber und einer Rosette von Perigord-Trüffeln. Dreierlei vom Michlkalb mit geschmortem Gemüse und Kartoffelmousseline.

XXXXX ✿✿ **Restaurant Bareiss** - Hotel Bareiss, Gärtenbühlweg 14, ✉ 72270, ✆ (07442) 4 70, *info@bareiss.com, Fax (07442) 47320,* ≤, - P. AE ⓓ ⓜ VISA.
closed 5 January - 6 February, 19 July - 20 August, Monday and Tuesday – **Meals** (booking essential) 98/118 and à la carte 63/96 ♀.
◆ Diners looking for something special will not be disappointed here, where the master-chef's creations are served in an elegant and tasteful setting.
Spec. Gänsestopflebertarte mit karamellisierter Apfelrosette. Crêpinette von der Bresse Taube mit Trüffelglace. Kreation von Mascarpone und Mandelkaramel.

Sulzburg *Baden-Württemberg* 545 W 7 – *pop. 2 600 – alt. 474 m.*
Stuttgart 229.

XXX ✿✿ **Hirschen** (Steiner) with rm, Hauptstr. 69, ✉ 79295, ✆ (07634) 82 08, *hirschen-sulzburg@t-online.de, Fax (07634) 6717,* (18 C inn)
closed 5 to 22 January and 26 July - 12 August – **Meals** *(closed Monday - Tuesday)* (booking essential) 35 *(lunch)* and à la carte 49/70,50 – **9 rm** ☕ 80 – 102.
◆ This 18C inn fits in unobtrusively into the street scene. Inside, there are fine antiques and period furniture, as well as a kitchen producing superlative fare.
Spec. Variation von der Gänseleber mit Brioche. Gratin von Krebsen mit Kalbskopf. Taubenbrust im Artischockenboden gegart mit Trüffelsauce.

Greece

Elláda

ATHENS

PRACTICAL INFORMATION

LOCAL CURRENCY

1 euro (€) = 1,20 USD ($) (Dec 2003)

TOURIST INFORMATION

National Tourist Organisation (EOT): *7, Tsoha str (Ampelokipi), info@gnto.gr, ✆ (210) 870 71 81. Hotel reservation: Hellenic Chamber of Hotels, 24 Stadiou, ✆ (210) 323 71 93, grhotels@otenet.gr. Fax (210) 322 54 49, also at Athens International Airport ✆ (210) 353 04 45 - Tourist Police: 4 Stadiou ✆ 171.*

National Holidays in Greece: *25 March and 28 October.*

FOREIGN EXCHANGE

Banks are usually open on weekdays from 8am to 2pm. A branch of the National Bank of Greece is open daily from 8am to 2pm (from 9am to 1pm at weekends) at 2 Karageorgi Servias (Sindagma).

AIRLINES

OLYMPIC AIRWAYS: *96 Singrou 117 41 Athens, ✆ (210) 926 73 33/926 91 11-3, 3 Kotopouli (Omonia), ✆ (210) 926 72 16-9, reservations only ✆ (210) 966 66 66.*
AIR FRANCE: *18 Vouliagmenis, Glyfada 166 75 Athens, ✆ (210) 960 11 00.*
BRITISH AIRWAYS: *1 Themistokleous Street 166 74 Glyfada ✆ (210) 890 6666.*
JAPAN AIRLINES: *22 Voulis 105 63 Athens, ✆ (210) 324 82 11.*
LUFTHANSA: *10 Ziridi St Maroussi ✆ (210) 617 52 00.*
SWISSAIR: *4 Othonos, (Ist floor) 105 57 Athens, ✆ (210) 353 03 82.*

TRANSPORT IN ATHENS

Taxis: *may be hailed in the street even when already engaged; it is always advisable to pay by the meter (double fare after midnight).*
Bus: *good for sightseeing and practical for short distances: 120 GRD.*
Metro: *Three lines cross the city from North east (Kifissia) to South west (Pireas) : from Northwest (Sepolia) to South (Dafni) and from Syntagma (Parliament Square) to Ethniki Amyna.*

POSTAL SERVICES

General Post Office: *100 Eolou (Omonia) with poste restante, and also at Sindagma.*
Telephone (OTE): *15 Stadiou and 85 Patission (all services).*

SHOPPING IN ATHENS

In summer, shops are usually open from 8am to 1.30pm, and 5.30 to 8.30pm. They close on Sunday, and at 2.30pm on Monday, Wednesday and Saturday. In winter they open from 9am to 5pm on Monday and Wednesday, from 10am to 7pm on Tuesday, Thursday and Friday, from 8.30am to 3.30pm on Saturday. Department Stores in Patission and Eolou are open fron 8.30 am to 8 pm on weekdays and 3 pm on Saturdays. The main shopping streets are to be found in Sindagma, Kolonaki, Monastiraki and Omonia areas. Flea Market (generally open on Sunday) and Greek Handicraft in Plaka and Monastiraki.

TIPPING

Service is generally included in the bills but it is usual to tip employees.

SPEED LIMITS

The speed limit in built up areas is 50 km/h (31 mph); on motorways the maximum permitted speed is 100 km/h (62 mph) and 80 km/h (50 mph) on others roads.

SEAT BELTS

The wearing of seat belts is compulsory for drivers and front seat passengers.

BREAKDOWN SERVICE

The ELPA (Automobile and Touring Club of Greece, ✆ (210) 60 68 800) operate a 24 hour breakdown service: phone 174 for tourist information, 104 for emergency road service.

ATHENS
(ATHÍNA)

Atikí 737 ㉚ *– Pop. 3 076 786 (Athens and Piraeus area).*

Igoumenítsa 581 – Pátra 215 – Thessaloníki 479.

Tourist Information (EOT), 7, Tsoha str. (Ampelokipi) ☎ (210) 870 71 81 info@gnto.gr
ELPA (Automobile and Touring Club of Greece), 395 Messogion ☎ (210) 606 88 00.
Glifáda ☎ (210) 894 68 20, Fax (210) 894 37 21.
E : 35 km, Athens International Airport ☎ (210) 369 83 00.
1 Karolou ☎ (210) 529 77 77.

SIGHTS

Views of Athens: Lycabettos (Likavitós) ☼★★★ DX – *Philopappos Hill (Lófos Filopápou)* ≤★★★ AY.

ANCIENT ATHENS

Acropolis★★★ (Akrópoli) ABY – *Theseion★★ (Thissío)* AY *and Agora★ (Arhéa Agorá)* AY – *Theatre of Dionysos★★ (Théatro Dionissou)* BY *and Odeon of Herod Atticus★ (Odío Iródou Atikoú)* AY – *Olympieion★★ (Naós Olimbíou Diós)* BY *and Hadrian's Arch★ (Píli Adrianoú)* BY – *Tower of the Winds★* BY **A** *in the Roman Forum (Romaïkí Agorá).*

OLD ATHENS AND THE TURKISH PERIOD

Pláka★★ : Old Metropolitan★★ BY **P**[1] – *Monastiráki★ (Old Bazaar) : Kapnikaréa (Church)* BY **K**, *Odós Pandróssou★* BY **29**, *Monastiráki Square★* BY.

MODERN ATHENS

Sindagma Square★ CY : *Greek guard on sentry duty – Academy, University and Library Buildings★ (Akadimía* CX, *Panepistímio* CX, *Ethnikí Vivliothíki* BX) – *National Garden★ (Ethnikós Kípos)* CY.

MUSEUMS

National Archaelogical Museum★★★ (Ethnikó Arheologikó Moussío) (Closed until Spring 2004) BX – *Acropolis Museum★★★* BY **M**[5] – *Museum of Cycladic and Ancient Greek Art★★* DY **M**[10] – *Byzantine Museum★★ (Vizandinó Moussío)* DY – *Benaki Museum★★ (Moussío Benáki, private collection of antiquities and traditional art)* CDY – *Museum of Traditional Greek Art★* BY **M**[7] – *National Historical Museum★* BY **M**[2] – *Jewish Museum of Greece★* BY **M**[3] – *National Gallery and Soutzos Museum★ (painting and sculpture)* DY **M**[1].

EXCURSIONS

Cape Sounion★★★ (Soúnio) SE : 71 km BY – *Kessariani Monastery★★, E : 9 km* DY – *Daphne Monastery★★ (Dafní) NW : 10 km* AX – *Aigina Island★ (Égina) : Temple of Aphaia★★, 3 hours return.*

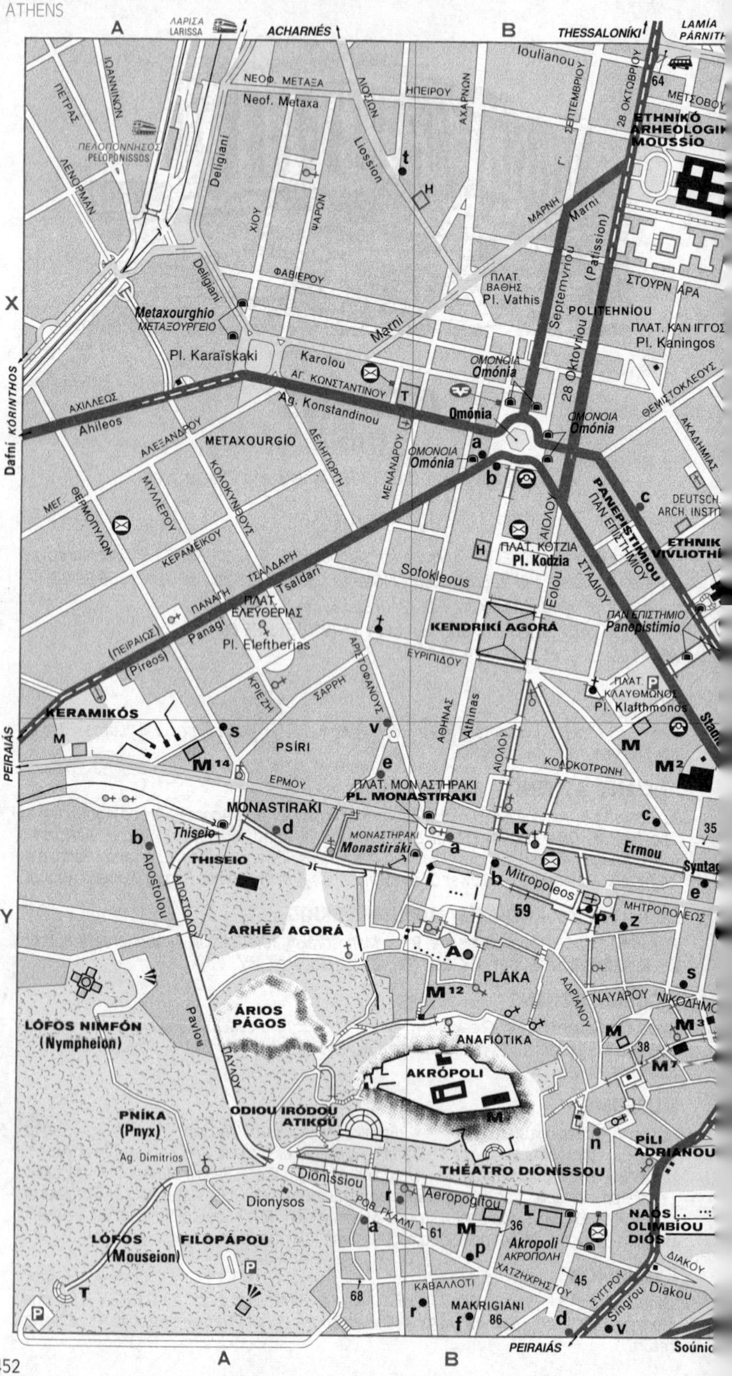

A
B
X
Y

ΛΑΡΙΣΑ LARISSA
ACHARNÉS
THESSALONÍKI
LAMÍA PÁRNITH
Dafní KÓRINTHOS
PEIRAIÁS
Soúnio

ΠΕΛΟΠΟΝΝΗΣΟΣ PELOPONISSOS
Metaxourghio ΜΕΤΑΞΟΥΡΓΕΙΟ
Pl. Karaïskaki
METAXOURGÍO
Neof. Metaxa
Liossion
ΠΛΑΤ. ΒΑΘΗΣ Pl. Vathis
POLITEHNÍOU
ΠΛΑΤ. ΚΑΝ ΙΓΓΟΣ Pl. Kaningos
ETHNIKÓ ARHEOLOGIK MOUSSÍO
Marni
Septemvriou
28 Oktovriou (Patission)
Karolou
Ag. Konstandinou
Ahileos
ΟΜΟΝΟΙΑ Omónia
Omónia
PANEPISTIMIOU
DEUTSCH. ARCH. INSTIT
ETHNIK VIVLIOTHI
ΠΛΑΤ. ΚΟΤΖΙΑ Pl. Kodzia
Sofokleous
Eolou
ΣΤΑΔΙΟΥ
ΠΑΝ ΕΠΙΣΤΗΜΙΟ Panepistimio
KENDRIKÍ AGORÁ
Tsaldari
ΠΛΑΤ. ΕΛΕΥΘΕΡΙΑΣ Pl. Eleftherias
Panagi
(ΠΕΙΡΑΙΩΣ) (Pireos)
Athinas
ΠΛΑΤ. ΚΛΑΥΘΜΩΝΟΣ Pl. Klafthmonos
Stadiou
KERAMIKÓS
PSÍRI
ΚΟΛΟΚΟΤΡΩΝΗ
ΕΡΜΟΥ
ΠΛΑΤ. ΜΟΝ ΑΣΤΗΡΑΚΙ PL. MONASTIRAKI
MONASTIRAKI
ΜΟΝΑΣΤΗΡΑΚΙ Monastiráki
Thiseio
THISEIO
Ermou
Syntag
Mitropoleos
ΜΗΤΡΟΠΟΛΕΩΣ
Apostolou
ARHÉA AGORÁ
PLÁKA
ΑΔΡΙΑΝΟΥ
ΝΑΥΑΡΟΥ ΝΙΚΟΔΗΜΟ
LÓFOS NIMFÓN (Nympheion)
ÁRIOS PÁGOS
ANAFIÓTIKA
AKRÓPOLI
Pavlou
ΠΑΥΛΟΥ
PNÍKA (Pnyx)
ODIOU IRÓDOU ATIKOÚ
Ag. Dimitrios
PÍLI ADRIANOU
THÉATRO DIONÍSSOU
Dionissiou
Aeropagitou
Dionysos
ΡΟΒ. ΓΚΑΛΛΙ
NAÓS OLIMBÍOU DIÓS
LÓFOS (Mouseion)
FILOPÁPOU
Akropoli ΑΚΡΟΠΟΛΗ
ΧΑΤΖΗΧΡΗΣΤΟΥ
ΣΥΓΓΡΟΥ Singrou
Diakou
ΔΙΑΚΟΥ
ΚΑΒΑΛΛΟΤΙ
MAKRIGIÁNI

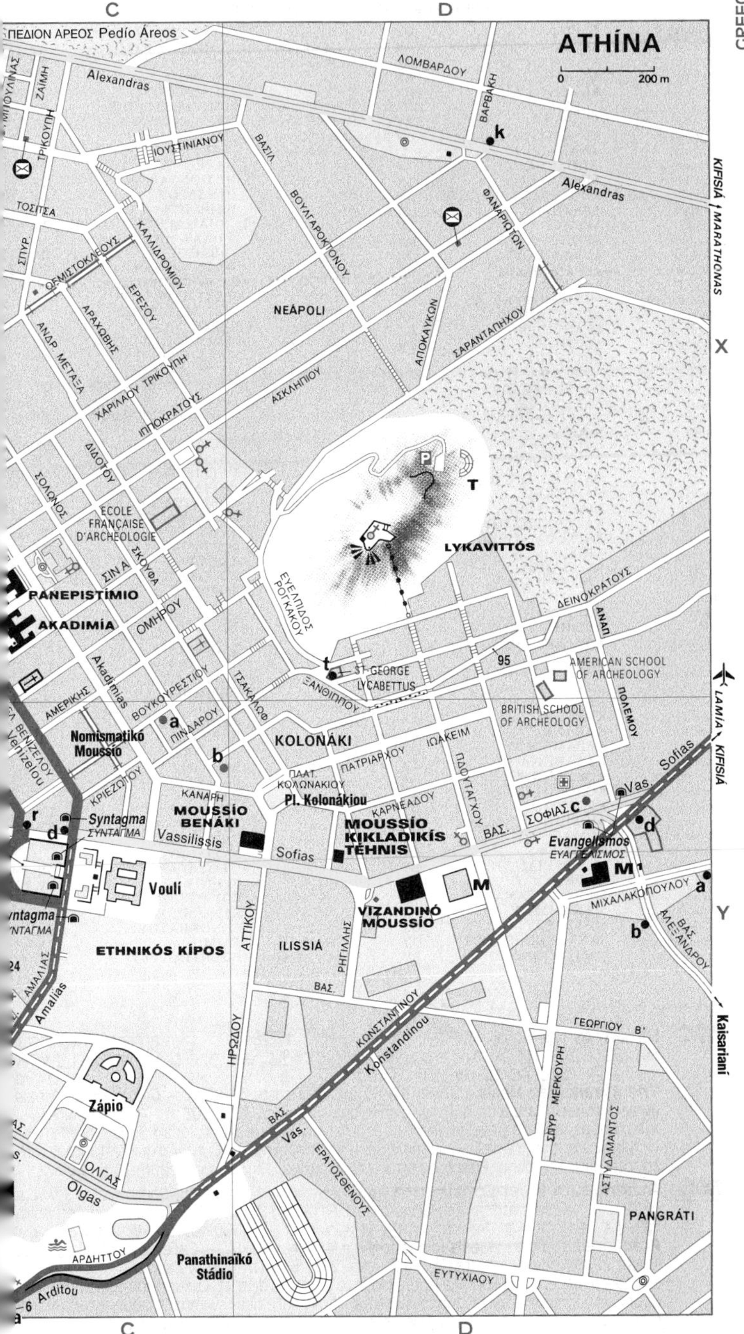
ATHÍNA
0 200 m
Alexandras
NEÁPOLI
LYKAVITTÓS
KOLONÁKI
Pl. Kolonákiou
MOUSSÍO BENÁKI
MOUSSÍO KIKLADIKÍS TÉHNIS
VIZANDINÓ MOUSSÍO
Voulí
ETHNIKÓS KÍPOS
ILISSIÁ
Zápio
Panathinaïkó Stádio
PANGRÁTI
PANEPISTÍMIO
AKADIMÍA
Nomismatikó Moussío
Syntagma
Evangelismos
AMERICAN SCHOOL OF ARCHEOLOGY
BRITISH SCHOOL OF ARCHEOLOGY
ECOLE FRANÇAISE D'ARCHEOLOGIE
ST-GEORGE LYCABETTUS
Pedío Áreos
Vassilissis Sofias
Vas. Konstandinou
Olgas
Arditou
Amalias
Akadimias
KIFISIÁ
MARATHONAS
LAMÍA
Kaisarianí

STREET INDEX TO ATHÍNA TOWN PLAN

Street	Greek	Grid	No.
Adrianou	ΑΔΡΙΑΝΟΥ	BY	
Ag. Konstandinou	ΑΓ. ΚΩΝΣΤΑΝΤΙΝΟΥ	AX	
Aharnon	ΑΧΑΡΝΩΝ	BX	
Ahilleos	ΑΧΙΛΛΕΩΣ	AX	
Akadimias	ΑΚΑΔΙΜΙΑΣ	BCX	
Alexandras	ΑΛΕΞΑΝΔΡΑΣ	CDX	
Amerikis	ΑΜΕΡΙΚΗΣ	CXY	
Anapavseos	ΑΝΑΠΑΥΣΕΩΣ	CY	3
Anapiron Polemou	ΑΝΑΠΗΡΩΝ ΠΟΛΕΜΟΥ	DXY	
Apokafkon	ΑΠΟΚΑΥΚΩΝ	DX	
Apostolou Pavlou	ΑΠΟΣΤΟΛΟΥ ΠΑΥΛΟΥ	AY	
Arahovis	ΑΡΑΧΩΒΗΣ	CX	
Arditou	ΑΡΔΗΤΤΟΥ	CY	
Aristofanous	ΑΡΙΣΤΟΦΑΝΟΥΣ	AX	
Asklipiou	ΑΣΚΛΗΠΙΟΥ	DX	
Ath. Diakou	ΑΘ. ΔΙΑΚΟΥ	BY	
Athinas	ΑΘΗΝΑΣ	BXY	
Bouboulinas	ΜΠΟΥΜΠΟΥΛΙΝΑΣ	CX	
Deligiani	ΔΕΛΗΓΙΑΝΝΗ	AX	
Deligiorgi	ΔΕΛΗΓΙΩΡΓΗ	AX	
Didotou	ΔΙΔΟΤΟΥ	CX	
Dionissiou Areopagitou	ΔΙΟΝΥΣΙΟΥ ΑΡΕΟΠΑΓΙΤΟΥ	ABY	
El. Venizelou	ΕΛ ΒΕΝΙΖΕΛΟΥ	CXY	
Eolou	ΑΙΟΛΟΥ	BXY	
Eratosthenous	ΕΡΑΤΟΣΘΕΝΟΥΣ	DY	
Ermou	ΕΡΜΟΥ	ABY	
Evelpidos Rongakou	ΕΥΕΛΠΙΔΟΣ ΡΟΓΚΑΚΟΥ	DX	
Fanarioton	ΘΑΝΑΡΙΩΤΩΝ	DX	
Favierou	ΘΑΒΙΕΡΟΥ	AX	
Filelinon	ΘΙΛΕΛΛΗΝΩΝ	BCY	8
Hadzihristou	ΧΑΤΖΗΧΡΗΣΤΟΥ	BY	
Harilaou Trikoupi	ΧΑΡΙΛΑΟΥ ΤΡΙΚΟΥΠΗ	CX	
Hiou	ΧΙΟΥ	AX	
Ioulianou	ΙΟΥΛΙΑΝΟΥ	AX	
Ioustinianou	ΙΟΥΣΤΙΝΙΑΝΟΥ	CX	
Ipirou	ΗΠΕΙΡΟΥ	ABX	
Ipokratous	ΙΠΠΟΚΡΑΤΟΥΣ	CX	
Irodou Atikou	ΗΡΩΔΟΥ ΑΤΤΙΚΟΥ	DY	
Kalidromiou	ΚΑΛΛΙΔΡΟΜΙΟΥ	CX	
Kanari	ΚΑΝΑΡΗ	CY	
Karageorgi Servias	ΚΑΡΑΓΙΩΡΓΗ ΣΕΡΒΙΑΣ	BY	13
Karneadou	ΚΑΡΝΕΑΔΟΥ	DY	
Karolou	ΚΑΡΟΛΟΥ	AX	
Kavaloti	ΚΑΒΑΛΛΟΤΙ	BY	
Keramikou	ΚΕΡΑΜΕΙΚΟΥ	AX	
Kidathineon	ΚΥΔΑΘΗΝΑΙΩΝ	BY	16
Kolokinthous	ΚΟΛΟΚΥΝΘΟΥΣ	AX	
Kolokotroni	ΚΟΛΟΚΟΤΡΩΝΗ	BY	
Kriezotou	ΚΡΙΕΖΩΤΟΥ	CY	
Liossion	ΛΙΟΣΙΩΝ	AX	
Lomvardou	ΛΟΜΒΑΡΔΟΥ	DX	
Makri	ΜΑΚΡΗ	BY	
Makrigiani	ΜΑΚΡΥΓΙΑΝΝΗ	BY	21
Marni	ΜΑΡΝΗ	ABX	
Meg. Alexandrou	ΜΕΓ. ΑΛΕΞΑΝΔΡΟΥ	AX	
Menandrou	ΜΕΝΑΝΔΡΟΥ	AX	
Metsovou	ΜΕΤΣΟΒΟΥ	BX	
Mihalakopoulou	ΜΙΧΑΛΑΚΟΠΟΥΛΟΥ	DY	
Mitropoleos	ΜΗΤΡΟΠΟΛΕΩΣ	BY	
Navarhou Nikodimou	ΝΑΥΑΡΧΟΥ ΝΙΚΟΔΗΜΟΥ	BY	
Neof. Metaxa	ΝΕΟΦ. ΜΕΤΑΞΑ	AX	
Omonia	ΟΜΟΝΟΙΑ	BX	
Pandrossou	ΠΑΝΔΡΟΣΟΥ	BY	29
Panepistimiou	ΠΑΝΕΜΙΣΤΗΜΙΟΥ	BX	
Parthenonos	ΠΑΡΘΕΝΩΝΟΣ	BY	30
Patission (28 Oktovriou)	ΠΑΤΗΣΙΩΝ (28 ΟΚΤΩΒΡΙΟΥ)	BX	
Patr. Ioakim	ΠΑΤΡ. ΙΩΑΚΕΙΜ	DY	
Pedío 'Areos	ΠΕΔΙΟΝ. ΑΡΕΟΣ	CX	
Pindarou	ΠΙΝΔΑΡΟΥ	CY	
Pireos (Panagi Tsaldari)	ΠΕΙΡΑΙΩΣ (ΠΑΝΑΓΗ ΤΣΑΛΔΑΡΗ)	AX	
Pl. Anexartissias (Vathis)	ΠΛΑΤ. ΑΝΕΞΑΡΤΗΣΙΑΣ (ΒΑΘΗΣ)	BX	
Pl. Egiptou	ΠΛΑΤ. ΑΙΓΥΠΤΟΥ	BX	33
Pl. Eleftherias	ΠΛΑΤ. ΕΛΕΥΘΕΡΙΑΣ	AX	
Pl. Eth. Andistasseos (Kodzia)	ΠΛΑΤ. ΕΘΝ. ΑΝΤΙΣΤΑΣΕΩΣ (ΚΟΤΖΙΑ)	BX	
Pl. Kaningos	ΠΛΑΤ. ΚΑΝΙΓΓΟΣ	BX	
Pl. Karaïskaki	ΠΛΑΤ. ΚΑΡΑΙΣΚΑΚΗ	AX	
Pl. Klafthmonos	ΠΛΑΤ. ΛΑΥΘΕΡΙΑΖ	BX	
Pl. Kolonakiou	ΠΛΑΤ. ΚΟΛΩΝΑΚΙΟΥ	DY	
Pl. Monastirakiou	ΠΛΑΤ. ΜΟΝΑΣΤΗΡΑΚΙΟΥ	ABY	
Ploutarhou	ΠΛΟΥΤΑΡΧΟΥ	DX	
Proklou	ΠΡΟΚΛΟΥ	DY	35
Psaron	ΨΑΡΩΝ	AX	
Radzieri	ΡΑΤΖΙΕΡΗ	AY	36
Rigilis	ΡΗΓΙΛΛΗΣ	DY	
Rovertou Gali	ΡΟΒΕΡΤΟΥ ΓΚΑΛΛΙ	AY	
Sarandapihou	ΣΑΡΑΝΤΑΠΗΧΟΥ	DX	
Sindagma	ΣΥΝΤΑΓΜΑ	CY	
Singrou	ΣΥΓΓΡΟΥ	BY	
Skoufa	ΣΚΟΥΦΑ	CX	
Sofokleous	ΣΟΦΟΚΛΕΟΥΣ	ABX	
Solonos	ΣΟΛΩΝΟΣ	CX	
Spir. Merkouri	ΣΗΥΡ. ΜΕΡΚΟΥΡΗ	DY	
Spir. Trikoupi	ΣΗΥΡ. ΤΡΙΚΟΥΠΗ	CX	
Stadiou	ΣΤΑΔΙΟΥ	BXY	
Stournara	ΣΤΟΥΡΝΑΡΑ	BX	
Syntagma	ΣΥΝΤΑΓΜΑ	CY	
Themistokleous	ΘΕΜΙΣΤΟΚΛΕΟΥΣ	BCX	
Thermopilon	ΘΕΡΜΟΠΥΛΩΝ	AX	
Tossitsa	ΤΟΣΙΤΖΑ	CX	
Tsakalof	ΤΣΑΚΑΛΩΦ	DXY	
Varvaki	ΒΑΡΒΑΚΗ	DX	
Vas. Alexandrou	ΒΑΣ. ΑΛΕΞΑΝΔΡΟΥ	DY	
Vas. Amalias	ΒΑΣ. ΑΜΑΛΙΑΣ	CY	
Vas. Georgiou B'	ΒΑΣ. ΓΕΩΡΓΙΟΥ Β	DY	
Vas. Konstandinou	ΒΑΣ. ΚΩΝΣΤΑΝΤΙΝΟΥ	DY	
Vas. Olgas	ΒΑΣ. ΟΛΓΑΣ	CY	
Vas. Sofias	ΒΑΣ. ΣΟΦΙΑΣ	CDY	
Vassiliou Voulgaroktonou	ΒΑΣΙΛΕΙΟΥ ΒΟΥΛΓΑΡΟΚΤΟΝΟΥ	DX	
Veïkou	ΒΕΙΚΟΥ	BY	39
Voukourestiou	ΒΟΥΚΟΥΡΕΣΤΙΟΥ	CXY	
Xanthipou	ΞΑΝΘΙΠΠΟΥ	DXY	
Xenokratous	ΞΕΝΟΚΠΑΤΟΥΣ	DX	41
Zaïmi	ΖΑΙΜΗ	CX	
3 Septemvriou	Γ'ΣΕΠΤΕΜΒΡΙΟΥ	BX	

Hilton, 46 Vas. Sofias Ave, ⊠ 115 28, ℘ (210) 7281 000, *sales-athens@hilton.com, Fax (021) 7281 111,* ≤ Athens and Acropolis, rm, – 2000. rest DY d
***The Byzantine* : Meals** (buffet) 32/35 and a la carte 36/86 – ***Galaxi BBQ* : Meals** *(May-October)* (barbecue buffet) (dinner only) 55 – 28 – **508 rm** 482, 19 suites.
• Luxurious modern hotel in the city centre near shops and Kolonaki Square. Bedrooms vary in size but all are well-equipped with every modern comfort. Informal restaurant with an international menu. Rooftop terrace and lounge/bar ; barbecuebuffet ; fine views.

Athenaeum Inter-Continental, 89-93 Singrou, ⊠ 117 45, Southwest : 2 ¾ km ℘ (210) 9206 000, *athens@interconti.com, Fax (210) 9206 500,* ≤ Athens and Acropolis, rm, – 2000.
Première (9th floor) **: Meals** (dinner only) a la carte 50/70 – ***Café Zoe* : Meals** (buffet lunch) 29/31 and a la carte 33/54 – 24 – **543 rm** 400, 60 suites.
• Modern, top class corporate hotel, close to business district. Luxuriously-appointed club floor rooms with exclusive lounge. Informal all-day café near swimming pool ; international menu, some Greek specialities. Roof-top gourmet restaurant ; splendid views.

Grande Bretagne, Constitution Sq, 105 64, (210) 3330 000, *info@grandebretagne.gr, Fax (210) 3228 034,* Athens, heated, - rm, - 380. VISA. CY d
GB Corner : Meals a la carte 50/68 – ***GB Rooftop :*** Meals (dinner only) a la carte 48/66 – **284 rm** 850, 37 suites.
◆ 19C hotel with classic, modernised interior overlooking Syntagma Square. Spa and pools. Luxuriously-appointed bedrooms and corner suites. GB Corner offers an international à la carte menu at lunch or dinner. GB Roof Top for authentic Greek dishes.

Ledra Marriott, 115 Singrou, 117 45, Southwest : 3 km (210) 9300 000, *athensledramarriott@marriotthotels.com, Fax (210) 9359 153,* Athens, - rm, - 500. VISA JCB.
Kona Kai : Meals - Polynesian and Japanese - *(closed 1 week August, 4 days Easter and Sunday)* (dinner only) 48/55 and a la carte 38.50/77 – ***Zephyros :*** Meals - Mediterranean and Greek - (buffet lunch) 18.50/35 and a la carte 24.50/35.50 – 19 – **258 rm** 440, 16 suites.
◆ Commercial hotel with panoramic views from rooftop terrace. Executive rooms have exclusive lounge and high-tech extras. Authentic Japanese dishes in Kona Kai basement restaurant. Zephyros on 1st floor for traditional and international buffet.

Metropolitan, 385 Singrou, 175 64, Southwest : 7 km (210) 9471 000, *metropolitan@chandris.gr, Fax (210) 9471 010,* - rm, - 450. VISA JCB.
Trocadero : Meals (buffet lunch Monday-Friday) 20 and a la carte 39/49 – 20 – **351 rm** 195/285, 10 suites.
◆ Striking, modern corporate hotel with easy access into and out of the city. Spacious, comfortable rooms with state-of-the-art facilities. Popular for business conventions. International or Italian fare can be taken overlooking the garden or beside the pool.

Divani Caravel, 2 Vas. Alexandrou, 161 21, (210) 7207 000, *divanis@divanicaravel.gr, Fax (210) 7253 770,* Athens, - rm, - 1000. VISA JCB. DY b
Brown's : Meals (dinner only) a la carte 47.50/66 – ***Café Constantinople :*** Meals (buffet lunch) 29/44 and a la carte 25/43 – 26 – **423 rm** 289, 48 suites.
◆ Modern hotel with spacious, marbled lobby. Conference facilities. Attractive roof garden with far-reaching views. Well-equipped rooms. Brown's for stylish dining and elegant cigar lounge. Café Constantinople open all-day for local and international dishes.

NJV Athens Plaza, 2 Vas. Georgiou A, Sindagma Sq, 105 64, (210) 3352 400, *salesnjv@grecotel.gr, Fax (210) 3235 856* – rm, - 250. VISA JCB. CY r
The Parliament : Meals a la carte 66/78 – 25 – **159 rm** 480/550, 23 suites.
◆ Modern hotel handy for the shopping and business districts. Local stone adorns the contemporary lobby and bar. Boldly decorated, hi-tech bedrooms and luxurious suites. Modern menu of international dishes on 1st floor, overlooking Syntagma Square.

Park H. Athens, 10 Alexandras Ave, 106 82, (210) 8894 500, *sales@athensparkhotel.gr, Fax (210) 8238 420,* Athens, - - 750. VISA JCB. BX c
Alexandras : Meals a la carte 30/50 – ***Park Café :*** Meals a la carte 27/30 – ***St'Astra :*** Meals *(closed Sunday)* (dinner only) 55/65 and a la carte 44/55 – 18 – **140 rm** 365/475, 10 suites.
◆ Modern, family owned hotel between the archeological museum and Pedio Areos Park. Smartly fitted rooms, suites with spa baths. Dine in Alexandra's with piano accompaniment. All-day Park Café for a light meal. Enjoy the view from Astra Café by the rooftop pool.

Divani Palace Acropolis, 19-25 Parthenonos, 117 42, (210) 9280 100, *divanis@divaniacropolis.gr, Fax (210) 9214 993,* - - 300. VISA JCB. BY r
Aspassia : Meals 35/60 and a la carte 35/60 – ***Roof Garden :*** Meals *(closed mid October-mid May and Tuesday)* (live music) (buffet dinner only) 45 – 26 – **242 rm** 230, 8 suites.
◆ Near the Parthenon yet fairly quiet with parts of Themistocles' wall in the basement. Particularly comfortable suites. Aspassia for formal meals. Roof Garden for barbecue buffet with live music.

Stratos Vassilikos, Michalakopoulou 114, 115 27, (210) 7706 611, *info@airotel.gr, Fax (210) 7708 137,* - - 150. VISA.
Meals a la carte 38/45 – **82 rm** 164, 6 suites.
◆ Elegant, modern hotel with coin-bar in reception. Spacious well-furnished bedrooms. Restaurant in the atrium for lunch or formal dinner.

St George Lycabettus, 2 Kleomenous, ✉ 106 75, ☎ (210) 7290 711, *info@sglyc abettus.gr, Fax (210) 7290 439,* ← Athens, – – 210. DX t
Le Grand Balcon : **Meals** *(closed Sunday-Monday)* (dinner only) a la carte 44.70/60 – ***Frame :*** **Meals** a la carte 28.70/38 – 26.12 – **152 rm** 357.50/455.46, 6 suites.
◆ Elevated position on Lycabettus Hill. Greek artwork and artifacts throughout. Roof-top pool. South rooms with balconies and view of the Acropoplis and Athens skyline. Le Grand Balcon roof-top restaurant for international menu. All-day Frame for Greek dishes.

Electra Palace, 18 Nikodimou St, ✉ 105 57, ☎ (210) 3370 000, *aelectrapalace@a th.forthnet.gr, Fax (210) 3241 875* – – 60.
Meals 19/22 and a la carte 21/31 – **95 rm** 200/240, 7 suites. BY s
◆ Modern interior behind a classical façade in Plaka. Ultra modern bedrooms and suites with classical décor ; some with view of the Acropolis. First-floor restaurant serving American buffet breakfast and a la carte lunch and dinner.

Zafolia, 87-89 Alexandras, ✉ 114 74, ☎ (210) 6449 002, *zafoliahotel@compulink.gr, Fax(210) 6442 042,* ← Athens, – – 180.
Meals 19/22 and a la carte 21/40 – **185 rm** 310/395, 7 suites. DX k
◆ Privately owned, commercial hotel on east side of city. Well-appointed bedrooms with good level of amenities. Rear rooms are quieter. Appealing terrace with city views. Modern first floor restaurant offering plenty of choice and a busy lunchtime buffet.

Holiday Inn, 50 Mihalakopoulou, ✉ 115 28, ☎ (210) 7278 000, *holinn@ath.forthnet.gr, Fax (210) 7278 600,* ←, – rm, – 650. DY a
Meals 29 and a la carte 29/45 – 29 – **192 rm** 205/335.
◆ Modern corporate hotel with state-of-the-art conference facilities. Rooftop terrace commands far-reaching city views. Executive rooms have ample work space. Restaurant offers international menu, with light meals on roof garden in summer.

Andromeda, 22 Timoleontos Vassou St, ✉ 115 21, via Vas. Sofias off Soutsou D. ☎ (210) 6415 000, *reservations@andromedaathens.gr, Fax (210) 6466 361* – rm, – 100.
Etrusco : **Meals** a la carte 42/80 – **18 rm** 450/475, 23 suites 500/650.
◆ Striking glass fronted 'boutique' hotel in a tranquil residential road. Blends contemporary style and traditional services. Individually designed rooms and annexe apartments. Modern restaurant with ornate décor and menu ranging from Asian to Italian.

Alexandros, 8 Timoleontos Vas., ✉ 115 21, via Vas. Sofias off Soutsou D. ☎ (210) 6430 464, *airotel@otenet.gr, Fax (210) 6441 084* – – 110.
Don Giovanni : **Meals** a la carte 25/80 – **90 rm** 132/170, 3 suites.
◆ A relaxed, contemporary hotel behind a church in quiet residential area. Boldly decorated, comfortably appointed rooms. Elegant little restaurant with marble floor and high vaulted ceiling. International and Mediterranean cuisine with some Greek specialities.

The Athenian Callirhoe, 52 Kallirrois Ave and Petmeza, ✉ 117 43, ☎ (210) 9215 353, *hotel@tac.gr, Fax (210) 9215 342,* ← Athens, – – 150. BY v
closed August – ***Chic :*** **Meals** a la carte 25/39 – **84 rm** 220/250.
◆ A bright, contemporary hotel with subtle Art Deco styling. City views from the rooftop terrace and balconies of the smartly fitted executive rooms. Equally individual restaurant ; the menu blends modern with rustic Greek.

Novotel, 4-6 Michail Voda, ✉ 104 39, ☎ (210) 8200 700, *h0866@accor-hotels.com, Fax (210) 8200 777,* Athens, – – 850. rest
Meals 21.50/33 and a la carte – 15 – **190 rm** 197/210, 5 suites. AX t
◆ Busy conference and family friendly hotel convenient for Larissa station and the National Museum. Bedrooms are clean and functional. Open-plan restaurant or lighter meals served on rooftop setting in summer.

Omonia Grand, 2 Pireos, Omonia Sq, ✉ 105 52, ☎ (210) 5235 230, *salesacr@grec otel.gr, Fax (210) 5231 361* – . rest BX a
closed August and 17-30 September – **Meals** 18/25 and a la carte 24/35 – **115 rm** 97/105.
◆ Beyond the bronze sculptured door and impressive marbled lobby is a bright and up-to-date hotel. Many of the interior-designed bedrooms overlook the bustling square. Appealing, modern first floor restaurant with international menu.

Athens Acropol, 1 Pireos, Omonia Sq, ✉ 105 52, ☎ (210) 5282 100, *salesacr@gr ecotel.gr, Fax (210) 5282 159* – – 350. rest BX b
closed August and 17-30 September – **Meals** 18/35 and a la carte 24/35 – **167 rm** 115/125, 2 suites.
◆ Sister hotel to Omonia, blending modern and classic styling. Soundproofed bedrooms offer sanctuary from the hustle and bustle of the city centre below. Spacious dining room with extensive international menu or lighter snacks in bar.

Herodion, 4 Rovertou Galli, 117 42, (210) 9236 832, *herodion@herodion.gr, Fax (210) 9211 650,* Acropolis – 50. VISA JCB. BY p
Meals 25/28 and a la carte 20/28 – **90 rm** 210/270.
• Privately owned and popular tourist hotel within a short walk of the Acropolis. Roof garden with panoramic views. Modern and well-equipped, rear rooms offer more seclusion. Pleasant conservatory-style restaurant with international menu.

Electra, 5 Ermou, 105 63, (210) 3378 000, *electrahotels@ath.forthnet.gr, Fax (210) 3220 310* – 70. VISA. BY e
Meals 25 (lunch) and a la carte 20/32 – **109 rm** 185/240.
• Popular tourist hotel within the lively pedestrianised shopping area. Soundproofed bedrooms are thoughtfully equipped and well maintained, some have spa baths. Restaurant on mezzanine level where lunch attracts a loyal local following.

Plaka without rest., 7 Kapnikareas and Mitropoleos St, 105 56, (210) 3222 096, *plaka@tourhotel.gr, Fax (210) 3222 412,* Athens – VISA.
67 rm 115/145. BY b
• Privately owned hotel among shops and tavernas, with a rooftop bar overlooking the old town. Spotless, sensibly priced modern rooms ; ask for one with a view of the Acropolis.

Hermes without rest., 19 Apollonos St, 105 57, (210) 3235 514, *hermes@tourhotel.gr, Fax (210) 3222 412* – VISA. BY z
45 rm 115/145.
• Small modern hotel in Plaka near the shops and the Acropolis. Spacious lobby and breakfast room. Bedrooms have balcony or terrace and all mod cons.

Jason Inn without rest., 12 Assomaton St Thission, 105 53, (210) 3251 106, *douros@otenet.gr, Fax (210) 3243 132* – VISA. AY s
57 rm 85/100.
• A busy, simple tourist hotel close to the Agora and a short distance from the flea market. Compact, yet well-equipped rooms ; outer rooms with balconies, quieter rooms at rear.

Achilleas without rest., 21 Lekka St, 105 62, (210) 3233 197, *achilleas@tourhotel.gr, Fax (210) 3222 412* – VISA. BY c
34 rm 115/145.
• A privately owned hotel close to Syntagma Square. Compact but usefully equipped bedrooms - quieter at the rear - represent good value : a popular tourist choice.

Philippos without rest., 3 Mitseon, 117 42, (210) 9223 611, *philippos@herodion.gr, Fax (210) 9223 615* – VISA. BY f
48 rm 152/205.
• Superior budget accommodation handy for the Acropolis, Pláka and the ancient theatre. Bedrooms in pastel colours with family rooms available. Ideal visiting base.

Museum without rest., 16 Bouboulinas St, 106 82, (210) 3805 611, *tsakiril@otenet.gr, Fax (210) 3800 507* – VISA. CX a
58 rm 150/190.
• Overlooking the National Archaeological Museum and offering comfortable accommodation. Bedrooms are a uniform size but all benefit from balconies and good facilities.

Spondi, 5 Pyronos, off Varnava Sq, 116 36, via Eratosthenous behind the Olympic Stadium (210) 7564 021, *info@spondi.gr, Fax (210) 7567 021,* – VISA JCB.
closed Easter and 1 week August – **Meals** (dinner only) 65/90 and a la carte 51.50/66.50.
• Its intimate atmosphere and courtyard terrace provide relaxing surroundings in which to enjoy this smoothly run restaurant. The menu is modern with a strong Gallic base.
Spec. Asparagus and artichoke with balsamic vinegar. Roast chicken breast, potato soufflé and mushrooms. Yoghurt mousse with caramel sauce.

Boschetto, Evangelismou, off Vas. Sofias, 116 76, (210) 7210 893, *Fax (210) 7223 598,* – VISA JCB. DY c
closed Easter, 25 December and Sunday – **Meals** - Italian influences - (dinner only) a la carte 54/76.
• Attractive summer house secluded within the neatly trimmed hedge of this small city park. Polished service of an elaborate international menu with strong Italian influences.

Symbosio, 46 Erehthiou, 117 42, (210) 9225 321, *sylector@otenet.gr, Fax (210) 9232 780,* – VISA. AY r
closed 1 week Easter, 4-27 August, 25 December and Sunday – **Meals** (booking essential) (dinner only) a la carte 46.20/65.50.
• Set discreetly in a smart residential road. In winter the charming terrace is enclosed in a spacious conservatory. Home grown produce and game specialities.

Edodi, 80 Veikou, 117 41, via Makrigiani (210) 9213 013, *Fax (210) 9213 013* – VISA.
closed Easter, 25 December, 1-2 January and Sunday – **Meals** (booking essential) (dinner only) 45/55 and a la carte 45/57.
• Restored 19C town house. Diners are presented with the day's specials instead of a menu from which to make their choice. Owners provide attentive and personal service.

XX **Kiku,** 12 Dimokritou St, ✉ 103 45, ☎ (210) 3647 033, *Fax (210) 3626 239* – ▤. MC AE ① VISA. ✈ CY a
closed August and Sunday – **Meals** - Japanese - (dinner only) 42/53 and a la carte 45/55 ♀.
• Stylish and authentic Japanese restaurant. Minimalist interior in shades of black and white with screens and soft lighting. Extensive selection of sushi and sashimi.

XX **Aristera-dexia,** 3 Andronikou and 140 Pireos St, ✉ 118 54, West : 1 km by Pireos St ☎ (210) 3422 380, *aristeradexia@hol.gr, Fax (210) 3411 559,* ☂ – ▤. MC AE ① VISA ✈
closed Sunday – **Meals** (dinner only) a la carte 25/38 ♀.
• Elegant modern restaurant with entrance café leading to dining room. The menu offers modern Greek cuisine.

X **Taverna Strofi,** 25 Rovertou Galli, ✉ 117 42, ☎ (210) 9214 130, ≤ Acropolis, ☂ – MC ① VISA. ✈ AY a
closed 24-26 and 31 December-2 January and Sunday – **Meals** (dinner only) a la carte 25/30.
• Personally run by the same owners since the 1970's, this taverna offers rustic and home-cooked Greek cooking. In summer, 2nd floor terrace has splendid Acropolis views.

X **Prytanio,** 7 Millioni St, Kolonaki, ✉ 106 73, ☎ (210) 3643 353, *info@prytaneion.gr Fax (210) 8074 319,* ☂ – ▤. MC AE ① VISA JCB. ✈ CY b
Meals a la carte 25/40.
• Watch the fashionable shoppers go by from a table on the terrace or choose the more rustic and intimate interior. Pleasant service and a modern Mediterranean-influenced menu.

X **Oraia Penteli,** Iroon Sq (Psiri), ✉ 105 54, ☎ (210) 3218 627, *Fax (210) 3218 627,* ☂ – MC VISA AXY v
Meals a la carte 16/26.70.
• Historic building in the centre of Psiri converted into café-restaurant preparing traditional Greek recipes ; live Greek music mid-week evenings and weekend afternoons.

X **Taverna Sigalas,** 2 Monastiraki Sq, ✉ 105 55, ☎ (210) 3213 036, *Fax (210) 3252 448* ☂ – MC AE ① VISA. ✈ BY a
Meals a la carte 12.10/14.70.
• Energetic service of robust local dishes and live music attract locals and tourists alike. Atmospheric taverna with walls hung with photographs of celebrities and statesmen.

X **To Kouti,** 23 Andrianou St, Thissio, ✉ 105 55, ☎ (210) 3213 229, *Fax (210) 3213 029* – ▤. MC AE VISA. ✈ AY c
closed Easter – **Meals** a la carte 26/35.
• Enjoys a popular local following, attracted by its slightly quirky décor and friendly, busy atmosphere. Menus written in children's books and offer simple, fresh dishes.

Environs

at Kifissia *Northeast : 15 km by Vas. Sofias* DY :

Pentelikon ⑤, 66 Diligianni, Kefalari, ✉ 145 62, off Harilaou Trikoupi, follow signs to Politia ☎ (210) 6230 650, *pentelik@otenet.gr, Fax (210) 8010 314,* ☂, ⛱, ☐ – |‡| ▤ TV P – 🔬 150. MC AE ① VISA. ✈
La Terrasse : **Meals** a la carte 28/54.30 ♀ (see also ***Vardis*** below) – ☕ 22 – **44 rm** 595/705, 6 suites.
• Imposing late 19C mansion in an affluent residential suburb. Opulence and antiques throughout. Most charming and peaceful rooms overlook the gardens. Traditional service. Conservatory restaurant with a Mediterranean theme offering full range of dishes.

The Kefalari Suites without rest., 1 Pentelis and Kolokotroni St, Kefalari, ✉ 145 62 ☎ (210) 6233 333, *info@kefalarisuites.gr, Fax (210) 6233 330* – |‡| ▤ TV ✆. MC AE ① VISA. ✈
12 suites ☕ 261/522.
• Early 20C villa set in a smart, quiet suburb ; stylish, airy, thoughtfully appointed rooms each on a subtle, imaginative theme, most with lounge and veranda. Rooftop spa bath.

XXXX ✿ **Vardis** (at Pentelikon H.), 66 Diligianni, Kefalari, ✉ 145 62, off Harilaou Trikoupi, follow signs to Politia ☎ (210) 6230 650, *Fax (210) 8010 314,* ☂ – ▤ P. MC AE ① VISA. ✈
closed 2 weeks August, 25 December, 1 January and Sunday – **Meals** - French - (dinner only) a la carte 54.50/85 ♀.
• Elegant pavilion behind the clubby bar, ornately decorated and sumptuous with fine table setting. Formal and polished service of elaborate classic French influenced cuisine.
Spec. Scallops with caviar and white wine cream sauce. Roast turbot with mashed potato and truffle oil. Pigeon with polenta and onion chutney.

at Athens International Airport *East : 35 km by Vas Sofias* DY :

Sofitel, ✉ 190 19, ☎ (210) 3544 000, *h3167@accor-hotels.com, Fax (210) 3544 444,* – rm, – 600. MC AE VISA JCB
***Karavi* : Meals** - French - (dinner only) a la carte 58/75 – ***Mesoghaia* : Meals** - Greek and Mediterranean - 31/33.50 and a la carte 32.50/50 – 22 – **332 rm** 250/276, 13 suites.
• Opened in 2001 ; the first hotel at the new airport. Modern and very well equipped from clubby library bar to exclusive leisure club. Spacious rooms and impressive bathrooms. Fine dining on the 9th floor. Informal brightly decorated ground floor restaurant.

at Lagonissi *Southeast : 40 km by Singrou* BY :

Grand Resort Lagonissi, Sounio Ave, ✉ 190 10, ☎ (22) 9107 6000, *lagonissi@lagonissiresort.gr, Fax (22) 9102 4514,* ≤ Saronic Gulf, heated, – – 180. MC AE VISA.
April-October – **Meals** - Mediterranean - a la carte 33/38 – ***Kohylia* : Meals** - Polynesian and Japanese - a la carte 67/95 – ***Captain's House* : Meals** - Italian - (dinner only and lunch Saturday and Sunday) a la carte 37/57 – ***Ouzeri* : Meals** - Greek - a la carte 34.50/50 – **155 rm** 800/971, 114 suites.
• Luxurious, stunning resort on a private peninsula. 16 beaches ; suites with private pools. Service to satisfy the most demanding. Mediterraneo for seafood. Polynesian and Japanese cuisine in Kohylia. Captain's House for Italian dishes. Greek cooking in Ouzeri.

at Pireas *Southwest : 10 km by Singrou* BY :

Varoulko (Lefteris), 14 Deligiorgi, off Omiridou Skilitsi, ✉ 185 33, ☎ (210) 4112 043, *Fax (210) 4221 283* – . MC AE VISA.
closed 24-26 and 31 December-2 January, Sunday and Monday – **Meals** - Seafood - (booking essential) (dinner only) a la carte 45/70.
• Difficult to find but well worth seeking out. Modern, informal restaurant with strong local following. Dégustation menu of finest local seafood. Friendly, knowledgeable staff.
Spec. Red mullet with beetroot and oregano sauce. Clams with cardamon sauce. Cuttlefish risotto.

at Vouliagmeni *South : 18 km by Singrou* BY :

Divani Apollon Palace, 10 Ag. Nicolaou and Iliou St (Kavouri), off Athinas, ✉ 166 71, ☎ (210) 8911 100, *divanis@divaniapollon.gr, Fax (210) 9658 010,* ≤ Saronic Gulf, – – 1200. MC AE VISA.
***Mythos* : Meals** *(closed Sunday)* (dinner only) a la carte 43/74 – ***Anemos* : Meals** 30/69 and a la carte 34/51 – **279 rm** 530/760, 7 suites.
• Modern hotel in fashionable resort. Poolside lounge. Spa and thalassotherapy centre. Executive bedrooms with balconies overlooking the Saronic Gulf. Small private beach. Dine in Mythos on the beach with local dishes.th global fare.

The Margi, 11 Litous St, off Athinas by Apollonos, ✉ 166 71, ☎ (210) 8962 061, *reservations@themargi.gr, Fax (210) 8960 229,* ≤, – – 500. MC AE VISA.
Meals a la carte 22/36 – **90 rm** 355/610.
• A stylish hotel that combines contemporary elegance with a colonial feel. Breakfast is taken on the poolside terrace. Bedrooms have antique pieces and smart marble bathrooms. Informal restaurant with its eclectic menu is popular with the 'in crowd'.

at Kalamaki *Southwest : 14 km by Singrou* BY :

Akrotiri, Agios Kosmas, ☎ (210) 9859 147, – . MC AE VISA.
Meals (dinner only) a la carte 47/62.
• A seaside restaurant combining simplicity and luxury. Candlelit dinners on the pool terrace ; DJ music. Menu of good quality international cuisine with French influence.

Hungary

Magyarország

BUDAPEST

PRACTICAL INFORMATION

LOCAL CURRENCY

Forint: *100 HUF = 0,31 euro (€) (Dec. 2003)*

National Holidays in Hungary: *15 March, 20 August, and 23 October.*

PRICES

Prices may change if goods and service costs in Hungary are revised and it is therefore always advisable to confirm rates with the hotelier when making a reservation.

FOREIGN EXCHANGE

It is strongly advised against changing money other than in banks, exchange offices or authorised offices such as large hotels, tourist offices, etc... Banks are usually open on weekdays from 8.30am to 4pm.

HOTEL RESERVATIONS

In case of difficulties in finding a room through our hotel selection, it is always possible to apply to the Tourist Information Offices (Liszt Ferenc square 11, ☎ 361 322 40 98, lisztiroda@budapestinfo.hu).

POSTAL SERVICES

Main post offices are open from 8am to 7pm on weekdays, and 8am to 1pm on Saturdays. Post offices with longer opening hours:
Teréz körút 51. (Mon-Sat: 7am-9pm; Sun: 8am-8pm)
Baross tér – Eastern Railway Station (Mon-Sat: 7am-9pm).

SHOPPING IN BUDAPEST

In the index of street names, those printed in red are where the principal shops are found. Typical goods to be bought include embroidery, lace, china, leather goods, paprika, salami, Tokay (Tokaij), palinka, foie-gras... Shops are generally open from 10am to 6pm on weekdays (7pm on Thursday) and 9am to 1pm on Saturday.

TIPPING

Hotel, restaurant and café bills often do not include service in the total charge. In these cases it is usual to leave the staff a gratuity which will vary depending upon the service given.

CAR HIRE

The international car hire companies have branches in Budapest. Your hotel porter should be able to give details and help you with your arrangements.

BREAKDOWN SERVICE

A breakdown service is operated by MAGYAR AUTÓKLUB ☎ 188.

SPEED LIMIT

On motorways, the maximum permitted speed is 130 km/h – 80 mph, 100 km/h – 62 mph on main roads, 90 km/h – 55 mph on others roads and 50 km/h – 31 mph in built up areas.

SEAT BELTS

In Hungary, the wearing of seat belts is compulsory for drivers and front seat passengers. On motorways : all passengers.

TRANSPORT

The three metro lines (yellow, red and blue) and the trams and buses make up an extensive public transport network. Tickets must be purchased in advance. Daily, weekly and monthly passes are available.
Airport buses : apply to your hotel porter.

TAXIS

Only use authorised taxis displaying clear signage and yellow number plates.

BUDAPEST

Hungary 732 D 8 – *Pop. 1 909 000.*

Munich 678 – Prague 533 – Venice 740 – Vienna 243 – Zagreb 350

Tourist Office of Budapest, Király Útca 93, ✉ *1077* ☏ *(01) 352 98 04, Fax (01) 352 14 33 – IBUSZ Head Office, Liszt Ferenc square 11,* ☏ *(01) 322 40 98 lisztiroda@budapestinfo.hu*

✈ *Ferihegy SE : 16 km by Üllol* DZ, ☏ *(01) 296 96 96 (information), Bus to airport : from International Bus station, Erzsébet tér, Station 6 Budapest 5th and Airport Minibus Service LRI – MALEV, Roosevelt tér 2, Budapest 5th* ☏ *(01) 296 85 55*

Views of Budapest

Citadel (Citadella)★★★ GX – *St. Gellert Monument (Szt. Gellért szobor)★★* GX – *Liberation Monument (Szabadság szobor)★★* GX – *Fishermen's Bastion (Halászbástya)* ≤★★ FU.

BUDA

Gellert Thermal Baths (Gellért Gyógyfürdő)★★★ GX – *Matthias Church★★ (Mátyástemplom)* FU – *Attractive Streets★★ (Tancsics Mihaly utca – Fortuna utca – Uri utca)* EFU – *Royal Palace★★★ (Budavári palota)* FV – *Hungarian National Gallery★★* – *Király Baths (Király Gyógyfürdő)★★* CY.

PEST

Parliament Building★★★ (Országház) GU – *Museum of Fine Arts★★★ (Szépművészeti Múzeum)* DY **M13** – *Hungarian National Museum★★ (Magyar Nemzeti Múzeum)* HVX – *Museum of Applied Arts★★ (Iparművészeti Múzeum)* CZ **M5** – *Széchenyi Thermal Baths★★★ (Széchenyi Gyógyfürdő)* DY **Q** – *Hungarian State Opera House★★ (Magyar Állami Operaház)* HU – *Chain Bridge (Széchenyi Lánchíd)★★* FGV – *Liberty Bridge (Szabadság híd)★★* GHX – *Ethnographical Museum (Néprajzi Múzeum)★★* GU – *Former Post Office Savings Bank (Posta Takarékpénztár)★★* GU – *Central Market Hall (Vásárcsarnok)★★* HX – *Dohány utca Synagogue (Dohány utcai zsinagóga)★★* HV – *Café New York★★* CZ **A**.

ADDITIONAL SIGHTS

Margaret Island★★ (Margit-sziget) CY – *Aquincum Museum★ (Aquincumi Muzéum) N : 12 km by Szentendrei út* CY – *St. Ann's Church★ (Szent Anna templom)* FU.

Envir.: *Szentendre★★ N : 20 km – Visegrád N : 42 km : Citadel, view★★★*

Kempinski H. Corvinus, Erzsébet tér 7-8, ✉ 1051, ✆ (01) 429 3777, *hotel.corvinus@kempinski.com, Fax (01) 429 4777,* , , , – , rm, – 450. rest GV a
closed 12-15 August – ***Ristorante Giardino :*** Meals - Italian - (dinner only) a la carte 7200/8900 ♀ – ***Bistro Jardin :*** Meals (buffet lunch) 10000 and a la carte 10000/12000 ♀ – 7015 – **335 rm** 75000/110000, 30 suites.
◆ Modern hotel in the heart of the city. Luxurious and spacious accommodation, providing top class comfort and facilities, with service to match. Mediterranean style Ristorante Giardino. Bistro Jardin buffet restaurant.

Corinthia Grand H. Royal, Erzsébet krt 43-49, ✉ 1073, ✆ (01) 479 4000, *royal@corinthia.hu, Fax (01) 479 4333* – , rm, . HU c
Brasserie Royale : Meals a la carte 4100/8500 ♀ – ***Rickshaw :*** Meals - Japanese - *(closed Sunday)* (dinner only) a la carte 4500/7700 – ***Bistro Royal :*** Meals a la carte 3500/7500 ♀ – 6250 – **389 rm** 60000/100000, 25 suites.
◆ Early 20C grand hotel with impressive reception. Well-appointed bedrooms - spacious or compact - with modern décor in warm colours. Brasserie Royale for formal dining. Rickshaw for Japanese dishes and sushi bar. Bistro Royale, an informal grill restaurant.

Hilton , Hess András tér 1-3, ✉ 1014, ✆ (01) 488 6600, *hiltonhu@hungary.net, Fax (01) 488 6644,* ← Danube and Pest, , – , rm, – 650. rest FU a
Dominican : Meals (dinner only) (pianist) a la carte 7600/10100 ♀ – ***Corvina :*** Meals (buffet lunch) 6000 and dinner a la carte 6100/7500 ♀ – ***Sushi Bar :*** Meals - Japanese - (dinner only) a la carte 6500/12000 – 5135 – **299 rm** 62500/87500, 23 suites.
◆ Large hotel in historic castle district with stunning views. Remains of 13C Dominican church and cellars. Spacious, well equipped rooms. Dominican, elegant dining room with superb views. Informal Corvina dining room. Sushi Bar with minimalist oriental décor.

Le Meridien, Erzsébet tér 9-10, ✉ 1051, ✆ (01) 429 5500, *info@le-meridien.hu, Fax (01) 429 5555,* , , , – , rm, – 200. rest GV c
Le Bourbon : Meals a la carte 4200/8050 ♀ – 5500 – **192 rm** 58750/106250, 26 suites.
◆ Top class hotel, ideally located for both business and leisure. Classically furnished, very comfortable bedrooms and particularly smart bathrooms. Atrium styled restaurant with Art Deco glass dome and wood panelling.

Sofitel Atrium, Roosevelt tér 2, ✉ 1051, ✆ (01) 266 1234, *h3229@accor-hotels.com, Fax (01) 266 9101,* ←, , , – , rm, – 400. rest GV e
Atrium Terrace : Meals (buffet lunch) 3900 and a la carte 4500/6400 ♀ – ***Focaccia :*** Meals - Mediterranean - a la carte 4000/6700 ♀ – 4500 – **328 rm** 62500/80000, 23 suites.
◆ Modern hotel near Chain Bridge. Impressive atrium with over 3000 plants and bi-plane suspended from roof. Comfortable, well equipped rooms. Stepped terrace leads up to elegant Atrium Terrace restaurant. Focaccia restaurant with Mediterranean menu and style.

Inter-Continental, Apáczai Csere János útca 12-14, ✉ 1368, ✆ (01) 327 6333, *budapest@interconti.com, Fax (01) 327 6357,* ← Danube and Buda, , , – , rm, – 900. rest GV n
Corso : Meals a la carte 5000/7900 ♀ – **383 rm** 83900/111000, 15 suites.
◆ Large hotel tower on river bank with good views from most rooms which have modern décor and all mod cons. Popular with business travellers. Viennese style coffee house. The Corso is restaurant, grill, café and bar all in one, with pleasant modern décor.

Marriott, Apáczai Csere János útca 4, ✉ 1052, ✆ (01) 266 7000, *marriott.budapest@pronet.hu, Fax (01) 266 5000,* ← Danube and Buda, , , squash – , rm, – 800. GV r
Duna Grill : Meals (buffet lunch) 3900/7500 and a la carte 3900/7500 ♀ – 4500 – **351 rm** 56500/84000, 11 suites.
◆ Huge American-style hotel on river bank where every room has a balcony. Late 20C style décor in lobby, bar and comfortable rooms. Informal Duna Grill, open all day, international menu.

Corinthia Aquincum, Árpád Fejedelem útca 94, ✉ 1036, ✆ (01) 436 4100, *cor.resv@aqu.hu, Fax (01) 436 4156,* ←, , , – , rm, – 260. rest HU c
Apicius : Meals (buffet lunch) 4900 and a la carte 6150/9120 – **302 rm** 57500/77500, 8 suites.
◆ Modern hotel on west bank north of centre with own comprehensive thermal spa and therapy centre. Open plan lobby. Rooms are comfortable and offer good facilities. Apicius restaurant with smart modern décor in warm tones and a pleasant atmosphere.

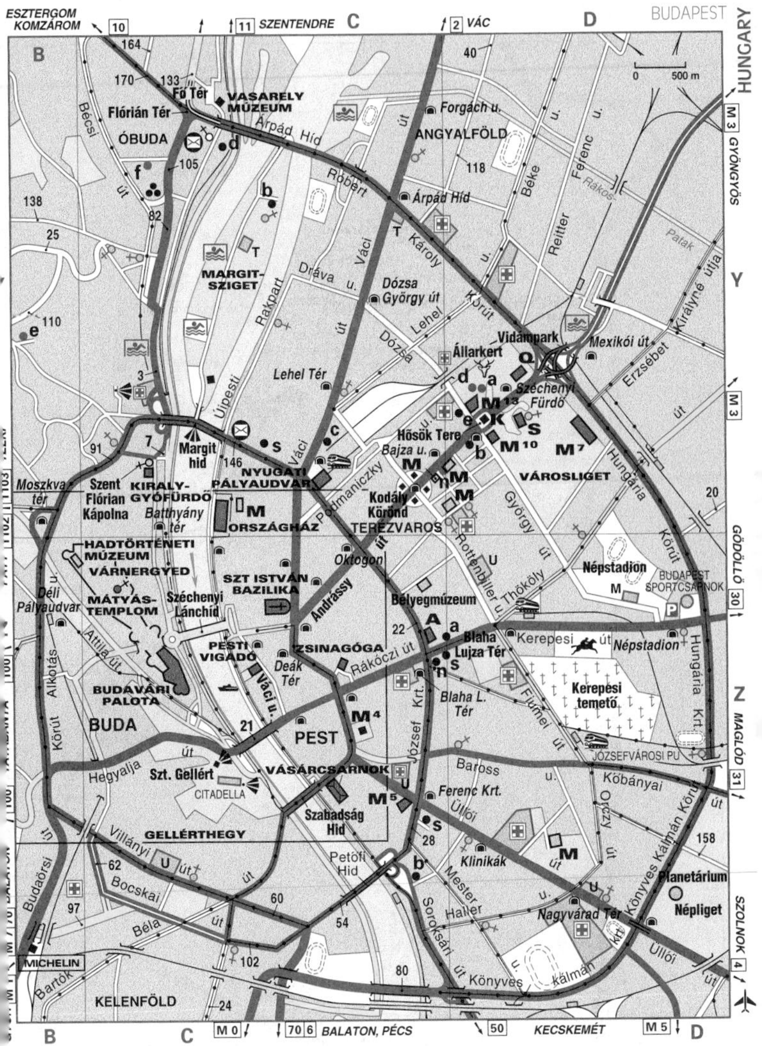

Danubius Thermal, Margitsziget, ✉ 1138, ✆ (01) 889 4700, *margotel@hungary.net, Fax (01) 889 4988*, 476, heated, rm, 350. rest CY b

***Platan* : Meals** (buffet lunch) 4250 and a la carte 4500/9100 – 4000 – **259 rm** 36000/57500, 8 suites.

◆ Concrete hotel set in island gardens in the Danube. Conference facilities. Huge thermal spa : heat, massage and water treatments. Modern bedrooms with a view. Buffet meals available at any time in Platan.

Hilton WestEnd, Váciútca 1-3, ✉ 1069, ✆ (01) 288 5500, *infobudapest-westend@hilton.com, Fax (01) 288 5588*, rm, 350.

***Arrabona* : Meals** (buffet lunch) 4900/7500 and a la carte 8200/9900 – 4500 – **230 rm** 40000/62000. CY c

◆ 21C hotel incorporated in large adjoining indoor shopping centre. Comprehensive business facilities, roof garden ; spacious bedrooms. A bright and contemporary dining room on the first floor of the hotel, with a Mediterranean theme.

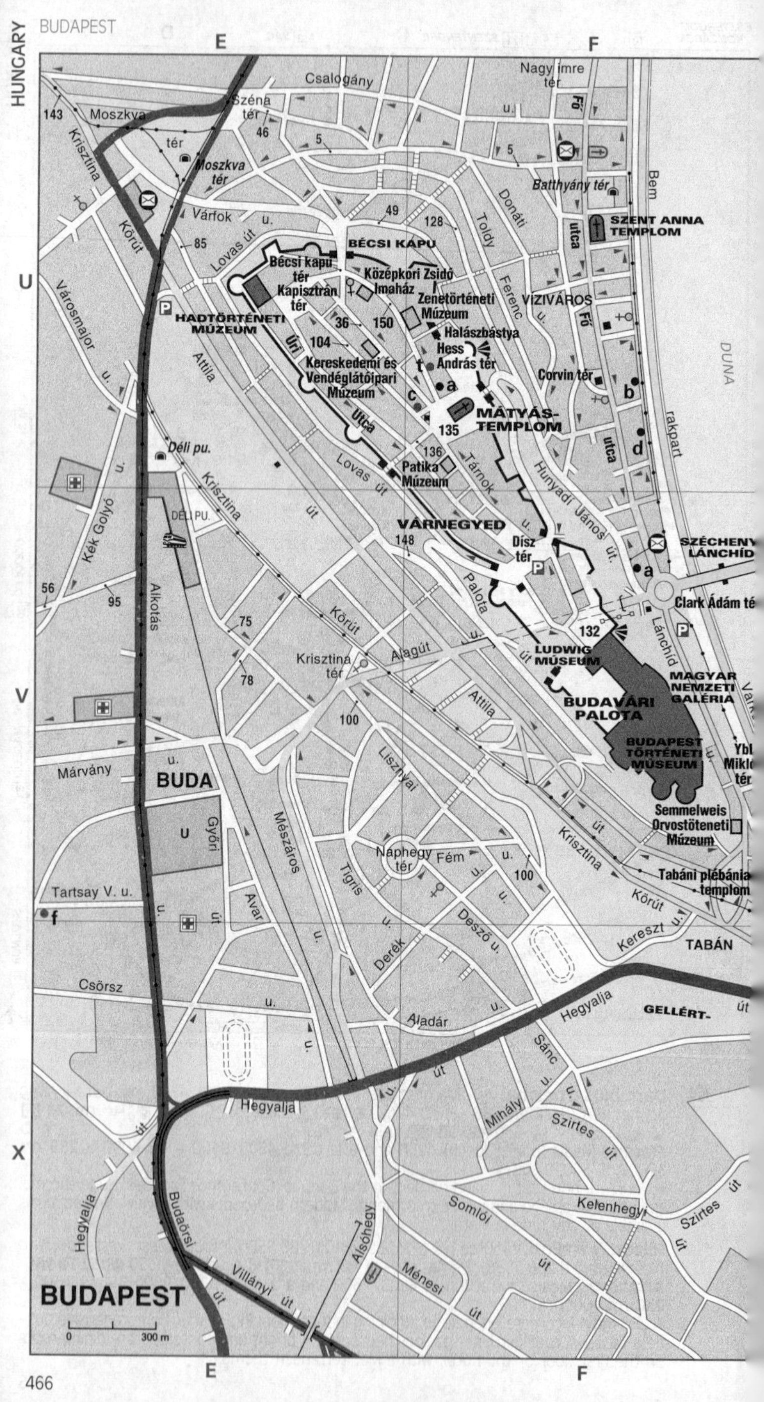
BUDAPEST
BUDA
BÉCSI KAPU
Bécsi kapu tér
Kapisztrán tér
Középkori Zsidó Imaház
Zenetörténeti Múzeum
HADTÖRTÉNETI MÚZEUM
Halászbástya
Hess András tér
Kereskedelmi és Vendéglátóipari Múzeum
MÁTYÁS-TEMPLOM
Patika Múzeum
VÁRNEGYED
Dísz tér
LUDWIG MÚZEUM
BUDAVÁRI PALOTA
MAGYAR NEMZETI GALÉRIA
BUDAPEST TÖRTÉNETI MÚZEUM
Semmelweis Orvostöténeti Múzeum
Tabáni plébánia templom
SZENT ANNA TEMPLOM
VÍZIVÁROS
Batthyány tér
Corvin tér
Clark Ádám tér
SZÉCHENYI LÁNCHÍD
Széna tér
Moszkva tér
Déli pu.
DÉLI PU.
Krisztina tér
Naphegy tér
TABÁN
GELLÉRT-
DUNA
Nagy Imre tér
Csalogány
Moszkva
Krisztina körút
Várfok u.
Lovas út
Városmajor u.
Attila út
Úri utca
Toldy Ferenc u.
Donáti
Fő utca
Bem rakpart
Tárnok u.
Hunyadi János út
Palota út
Lánchíd u.
Alagút
Kék Golyó u.
Alkotás u.
Márvány u.
Győri út
Mészáros u.
Tigris u.
Lisznyai
Fém u.
Desző u.
Derék u.
Avar u.
Tartsay V. u.
Csörsz u.
Aladár u.
Hegyalja út
Sánc u.
Mihály
Szirtes út
Kelenhegyi út
Somlói út
Ménesi út
Alsóhegy
Budaörsi út
Villányi út
Hegyalja
Kereszt u.
Ybl Miklós tér
0 300 m
E F U V X
143 46 5 49 128 85 36 150 104 135 136 148 132 56 95 75 78 100
a b c d f t

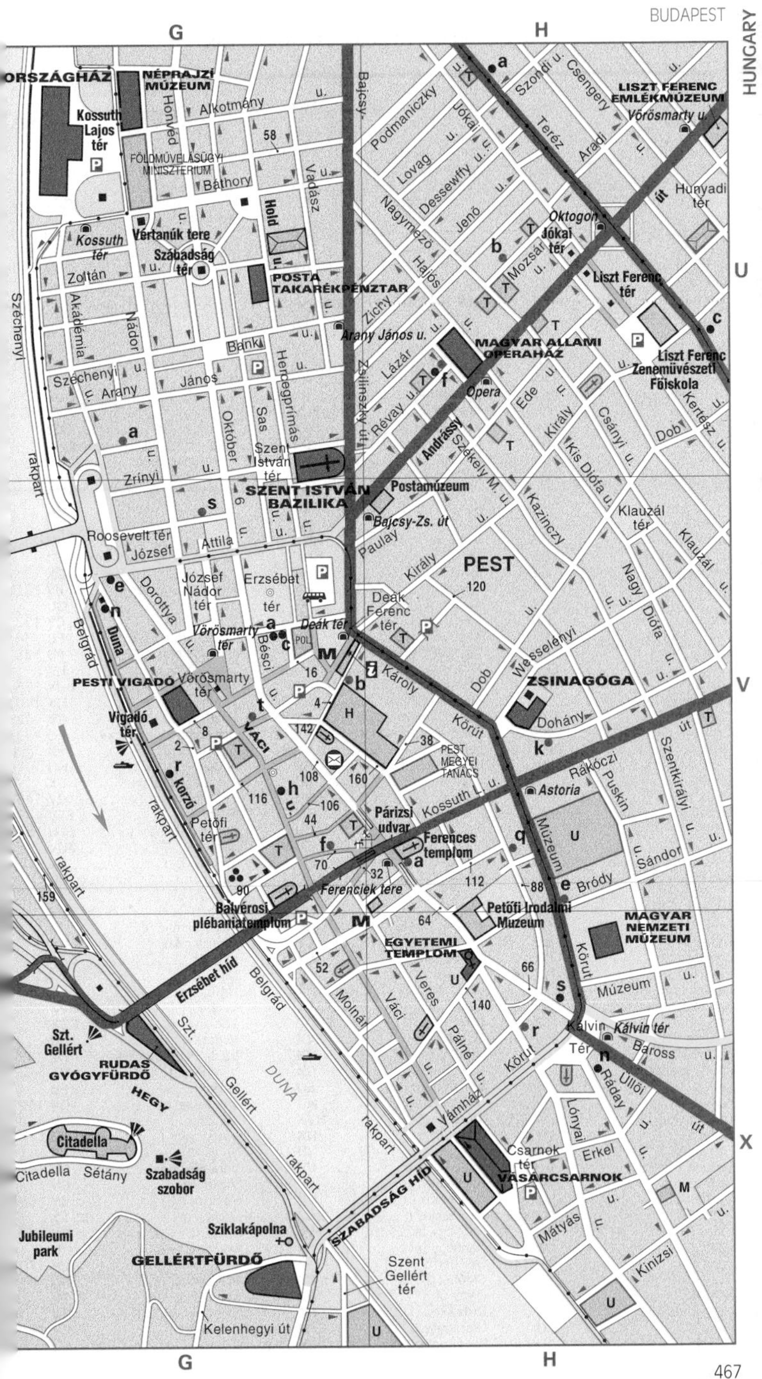
G
H
U
V
X
ORSZÁGHÁZ
NÉPRAJZI MÚZEUM
Kossuth Lajos tér
FÖLDMŰVELÉSÜGYI MINISZTERIUM
Vértanúk tere
Szabadság tér
POSTA TAKARÉKPÉNZTÁR
LISZT FERENC EMLÉKMÚZEUM
Oktogon
Jókai tér
Liszt Ferenc tér
MAGYAR ÁLLAMI OPERAHÁZ
Liszt Ferenc Zeneművészeti Főiskola
SZENT ISTVÁN BAZILIKA
Postamúzeum
Szent István tér
Roosevelt tér
József Nádor tér
Erzsébet tér
Vörösmarty tér
Deák tér
Deák Ferenc tér
PEST
ZSINAGÓGA
PESTI VIGADÓ
Vigadó tér
PEST MEGYEI TANÁCS
Astoria
Párizsi udvar
Ferences templom
Petőfi tér
Ferenciek tere
Belvárosi plébániatemplom
Petőfi Irodalmi Múzeum
MAGYAR NEMZETI MÚZEUM
EGYETEMI TEMPLOM
Erzsébet híd
Kálvin tér
Szt. Gellért
RUDAS GYÓGYFÜRDŐ
HEGY
Citadella
Citadella Sétány
Szabadság szobor
Jubileumi park
Sziklakápolna
GELLÉRTFÜRDŐ
SZABADSÁG HÍD
Szent Gellért tér
Csarnok tér
VÁSÁRCSARNOK
DUNA
Kelenhegyi út

STREET INDEX TO BUDAPEST TOWN PLAN

Art'otel, Bem Rakpart 16-19, ✉ 1011, ☎ (01) 487 9487, *budapest@artotel.hu, Fax (01) 487 9488,* ←, 🏠, Ⓕ, ⇋ - 🏢, ⇤ rm, ▤ TV ☎ ♿ 🚗 - 🏨 160. MC AE ◎ VISA. ✗ rest FU b

Chelsea : **Meals** a la carte 4400/5750 – **155 rm** ☕ 51084/56244, 9 suites.

◆ Half new building, half converted baroque houses. Stylish and original interior in cool shades and clean lines. Features over 600 pieces of original art by Donald Sultan. Bright dining room with vaulted ceiling topped with glass and modern artwork.

Danubius Grand H. 🍃, Margitsziget, ✉ 1138, ☎ (01) 889 4700, *sales.budapest-spa@danubiusgroup.com, Fax (01) 889 4988,* ←, 🏠 476, Ⓕ, ⇋, 🏊 - 🏢, ⇤ rm, ▤ TV ☎ ♿ 🚗 P - 🏨 120. MC AE ◎ VISA JCB. ✗ rest CY b

Széchenyi : **Meals** a la carte 4600/9200 🍷 – ☕ 4000 – **154 rm** 36000/39000, 10 suites.

◆ Grand 19C building pleasantly located on Margaret Island with direct access to thermal spa and therapy centre. All rooms have views and reflect the style of the house. Grand and formal restaurant with pleasant décor and very appealing terrace in summer.

Radisson SAS Béke, Teréz körút 43, ✉ 1067, ☎ (01) 301 1600, *sales.budapest@radissonsas.com, Fax (01) 301 1615,* ⇋, 🏊 - 🏢, ⇤ rm, ▤ TV ☎ ♿ 🚗 - 🏨 330. MC AE ◎ VISA JCB. ✗ rest HU a

Szondi Lugas : **Meals** (buffet lunch) 3500/3900 and dinner a la carte 5200/7400 – ☕ 4000 – **239 rm** 35000/42500, 8 suites.

◆ Classic façade with mosaic fronts large international hotel in busy shopping street. Rear bedrooms quieter. Tea salon is one of the best in the city. Spacious restaurant with classic modern décor and eye-catching murals.

N.H.Budapest, Vigszinház u. 3, ✉ 1137, ☎ (01) 814 0000, *nhbudapest@nh-hotels.com, Fax (01) 814 0100,* Ⓕ, ⇋ - 🏢, ⇤ rm, ▤ TV ☎ ♿ 🚗 - 🏨 100. MC AE VISA CY s

Meals (buffet lunch)/dinner 2000 and a la carte 3950/6750 – ☕ 4000 – **160 rm** 32500.

◆ Modern hotel in city suburbs. Conference facilities ; gym and sauna. Bright, modern, well-furnished rooms in bold colours with extra touches ; some with balconies. Simple restaurant ; dishes show Mediterranean influences.

K + K Opera 🍃, Révay útca 24, ✉ 1065, ☎ (01) 269 0222, *kk.hotel.opera@kkhotels.hu, Fax (01) 269 0230,* Ⓕ, ⇋ - 🏢, ⇤ rm, ▤ TV ☎ 🚗 - 🏨 80. MC AE ◎ VISA. ✗ HU f

Meals (light meals in bar) a la carte 4000/6900 🍷 – **203 rm** ☕ 41250/51250, 2 suites.

◆ Well run hotel in quiet street in business district near opera. Stylish modern interior design. Good size rooms smartly furnished and well equipped. Informal dining in bar with bright modern décor and pale wood furniture ; bistro style menu.

Andrássy, Andrássy útca 111, ✉ 1063, ☎ (01) 462 2100, *reservation@andrassyhotel.com, Fax (01) 4622 195,* 🏠, Ⓕ, ⇋ - 🏢, ⇤ rm, ▤ TV ☎ P. MC AE ◎ VISA. ✗ DY b

Mosaic Café : **Meals** 2600 (lunch) and a la carte 5250/8150 🍷 – ☕ 3750 – **62 rm** 28750/65000, 8 suites.

◆ A classical Bauhaus building converted into a hotel in 2001. Stylish lobby with marbled columns and large murals. Bright and contemporary bedrooms, most with balconies. Small, friendly and informal restaurant which doubles as a bar and café.

Mercure Korona, Kecskeméti útca 14, ✉ 1053, ☎ (01) 486 8800, *h1765@accor-hotels.com, Fax (01) 318 3867,* ⇋, 🏊 - 🏢 ⇤ ▤ TV ☎ ♿ 🚗 - 🏨 100. MC AE ◎ VISA. ✗ rest HX s

Meals a la carte 3650/7200 🍷 – ☕ 4000 – **413 rm** 32500, 11 suites.

◆ Well equipped quite modern business hotel close to Hungarian National Museum. Contemporary rooms with all mod cons. Cavernous lobby. Coffee bar on bridge spanning street. Large, fairly sombre restaurant above hotel lobby with tiled floor, columns and plants.

Novotel, Rákóczi út 43-45, ✉ 1088, ☎ (01) 477 5300, *h3560@accor-hotels.com, Fax (01) 477 5353,* Ⓕ, ⇋ - 🏢, ⇤ rm, ▤ TV ☎ ♿ 🚗 - 🏨 350. MC AE ◎ VISA JCB. ✗ CDZ s

Palace : **Meals** (buffet lunch)/dinner 5810 and a la carte 3300/6550 – ☕ 3900 – **227 rm** 25910.

◆ Early 20C Art Deco hotel with extensions, in the business district. Conference facilities ; basement leisure club. Spacious, well-fitted and modern bedrooms. The ornate, classic Palace restaurant serves an international menu.

Mercure Nemzeti, József Körút 4, ✉ 1088, ☎ (01) 477 2000, *h1686@accor-hotels.com, Fax (01) 477 2001* - 🏢, ⇤ rm, ▤ rm, TV ☎ - 🏨 60. MC AE ◎ VISA JCB. ✗ rest CZ n

Meals a la carte 3240/5670 🍷 – ☕ 3000 – **75 rm** 20850, 1 suite.

◆ Commercial hotel near city centre in elegant 19C building featuring impressive Art Nouveau décor. Bedrooms are modern and well equipped, offering most mod cons. Restaurant boasts elegant Art Nouveau décor and a particularly splendid coloured glass ceiling.

Taverna, Váciútca 20, ✉ 1052, ☎ (01) 485 3100, *hotel@hoteltaverna.hu, Fax (01) 485 3111,* – |‡|, ⇔ rm, ▤ TV – 🏆 100. MC AE ⓓ VISA JCB. ⚒ rest GV h

Gambrinus : Meals (dinner only) (gypsy music) a la carte 3690/8300 ♀ – ***Holsten Brasserie :*** Meals a la carte 2080/3750 ♀ – **223 rm** ☐ 31500/42500, 4 suites.

♦ Business and tourist hotel located on main pedestrianised shopping street. Extensive facilities offering something for everyone. Rooms are comfortable. Gambrinus restaurant with hunting scenes on walls. Convivial atmosphere at the Holsten Brasserie.

Mercure Metropol, Rákóczi útca 58, ✉ 1074, ☎ (01) 462 8100, *h2997@accor-hotels.com, Fax (01) 462 8181* – |‡|, ⇔ rm, ▤ TV ♿ – 🏆 50. MC AE ⓓ VISA JCB. ⚒ CDZ a

Meals a la carte 2340/4080 ♀ – ☐ 3000 – **130 rm** 20850.

♦ Opened in 2000, a newly constructed hotel lying in the heart of the business district. Bright bedrooms with fitted work desks and all the appropriate facilities. Small, simple restaurant behind the reception area with its own adjoining bar.

Uhu Villa 🔇, Keselyü I/a, ✉ 1025, Northwest : 8 km by Szilágyi Erzsébet fasor ☎ (01) 398 0570, *uhuvilla@uhuvilla.hu, Fax (01) 398 0571*, ≤, – ▤ TV P – 🏆 25. MC AE ⓓ VISA. ⚒

Meals *(closed Sunday)* a la carte 3850/7350 – ☐ 3750 – **11 rm** 32500/40000, 1 suite.

♦ Early 20C villa set in gardens in quiet location in the Buda Hills. Basement leisure centre with sauna and pool. Smart, contemporary bedrooms, with individual décor. Formal restaurant with terrace and view serving Italian influenced dishes.

Sissi without rest., Angyal útca 33, ✉ 1094, by TuzoltÉ Îtca ☎ (01) 215 0082, *hsissi@matavnet.hu, Fax (01) 216 6063,* – |‡| ⇔ TV ♿ – 🏆 25. MC AE ⓓ VISA

44 rm ☐ 25000/47250. CZ s

♦ Bedrooms are decorated in warm yellows and blues ; some have wooden floors and a Scandinavian feel. Breakfast served in a conservatory overlooking a small garden at the rear.

Victoria without rest., Bem Rakpart 11, ✉ 1011, ☎ (01) 457 8080, *victoria@victoria.hu, Fax (01) 457 8088,* ≤ Danube and Pest, – |‡| ▤ TV P. MC AE ⓓ VISA JCB FU d

27 rm ☐ 18500/25500.

♦ Family-run hotel, popular with tourists, in a row of town houses just below the castle. Rooms are spacious, equipped with good range of facilities and all offer fine views.

Carlton without rest., Apor Péter útca 3, ✉ 1011, ☎ (01) 224 0999, *carltonhotel@axelero.hu, Fax (01) 224 0990* – |‡| ⇔ ▤ TV – 🏆 25. MC AE ⓓ VISA FV a

95 rm ☐ 28250/34500.

♦ Usefully located hotel on Buda side of river, offering straightforward accommodation for the cost-conscious traveller. Rooms are functional and comfortable. Small bar.

Liget, Dózsa György útca 106, ✉ 1068, ☎ (01) 269 5300, *hotel@liget.hu, Fax (01) 269 5329,* – |‡|, ⇔ rm, ▤ TV P – 🏆 200. MC AE ⓓ VISA JCB. ⚒ DY e

Meals a la carte 2850/6150 – **139 rm** ☐ 19300/23200.

♦ Inexpensive modern hotel with salmon pink exterior and green roof near Heroes' Square. Bedrooms identical throughout, with modern functional décor and fittings. Small bar. Original paintings, all for sale to diners, brighten the simple, friendly restaurant.

Ibis Centrum without rest., Raday útca 6, ✉ 1092, ☎ (01) 215 8585, *ibiscentrum@pannoniahotels.hu, Fax (01) 215 8787* – ⇔ ▤ TV ♿. MC AE ⓓ VISA JCB HX n

☐ 2000 **126 rm** 14750/17250.

♦ Modern hotel well located for city and national museum. Good functional accommodation with all necessary facilities. Lounge, small bar, bright breakfast room, roof garden.

Mercure Relais Duna without rest., Soroksári út 12, ✉ 1095, ☎ (01) 455 8300, *h2025@accor-hotels.com, Fax (01) 455 8385* – |‡| ⇔ ▤ TV – 🏆 40. MC AE ⓓ VISA JCB CZ b

☐ 2750 – **124 rm** 16300/22500, 6 suites.

♦ Modern hotel catering well for business people and tourists, close to river and city. Fair sized bedrooms offer simple but modern comforts and reasonable level of mod cons.

Gundel, Állatkerti útca 2, ✉ 1146, ☎ (01) 468 4040, *info@gundel.hu, Fax (01) 363 1917,* – |‡| ▤ P – 🏆 200. MC AE ⓓ VISA JCB. ⚒ DY d

Meals (booking essential) 5900/9500 and a la carte 8910/13110 ♀ – ***1894 :*** Meals *(closed Sunday-Monday)* (dinner only) a la carte 3020/4820 ♀.

♦ Hungary's best known restaurant, an elegant classic. Spacious main room with walnut panelling and ornate ceiling. Traditional cuisine. Summer terrace. Live music at dinner.

Vadrózsa, Pentelei Molnár útca 15, ✉ 1025, via Rómer Flóris útca ☎ (01) 326 5817, *vadrozsa@hungary.net, Fax (01) 326 5809,* – ▤. MC AE ⓓ VISA JCB BY e

closed 24-26 December – **Meals** a la carte 5740/9680 ♀.

♦ Pleasant villa just out of town. Elegant dining room with wood panelling. Display of raw ingredients presented with the menu. Attractive summer terrace. Detailed service.

XXX **Alabárdos,** Országház útca 2, ✉ 1014, ☎ (01) 356 0851, *alabardos@axelero.hu, Fax (01) 214 3814,* – ▤. MC AE D VISA JCB. FU c
closed Sunday – **Meals** (booking essential) a la carte 8100/12700 ♀.
• Well run restaurant in vaulted Gothic interior of characterful 17C building with covered courtyard in castle square. Extensive menu of good traditional Hungarian classics.

XXX **Fortuna,** Hess András tér 4, ✉ 1014, ☎ (01) 355 7177, *fortuna@elender.hu, Fax (01) 375 6857,* – ▤. MC AE VISA. FU t
Meals a la carte 5200/9800 ♀.
• Attractive period building with Gothic style interior and 13C Champagne cellar. Good range of traditional dishes with some modern influence; medieval banquets a speciality.

XXX **Légrádi Antique,** Bárczy István útca 3-5 (first floor), ✉ 1052, ☎ (01) 266 4993 – MC AE D VISA GV b
closed 24 December, Saturday lunch and Sunday – **Meals** (booking essential) a la carte 8450/12500.
• Restaurant above small antiques shop has elegant décor, vaulted ceiling, marble balustrades and intimate ambience. Classic menu of robust traditional fare. Gypsy music.

XX **Fausto's,** Dohány útca 5, ✉ 1072, ☎ (01) 269 6806, *faustos@axelero.hu, Fax (01) 269 6806* – ▤. MC AE VISA. HV k
closed last 2 weeks July, first week January, 24-26 December, Easter Monday and Sunday – **Meals** - Italian - 3000 (lunch) and a la carte 6200/10800.
• Popular, personally run restaurant in tree-lined avenue next to impressive synagogue with smart décor and slick service. Attractive menu of Italian classics.

XX **Premier,** Andrássy út 101, ✉ 1062, ☎ (01) 342 1768, *premier-restaurant@axelero.hu, Fax (01) 322 1639,* – ▤. MC AE D VISA. CDY n
closed Sunday in winter – **Meals** a la carte 4050/6950 ♀.
• Early 20C Art nouveau villa with three basement rooms and a pleasant outdoor terrace. Attentive service. Menu of traditional and international dishes with weekly specials.

XX **Képiró,** Képiró u. 3, ✉ 1053, ☎ (01) 266 0430, *reservation@kepirorestaurant.com, Fax (01) 266 0425* – ▤. MC AE VISA HX r
closed Christmas and Sunday – **Meals** 2990 (lunch) and a la carte 3750/7300 ♀.
• Glass-fronted restaurant, in narrow street near city centre, divided by central bar. Approachable and friendly service. Modern style cooking with seasonal menus.

XX **Robinson,** Városligeti tó, ✉ 1146, ☎ (01) 422 0222, *robinson@axelero.hu, Fax (01) 422 0072,* – MC AE D VISA JCB. DY a
Meals a la carte 4650/7350 ♀.
• Pavilion on tiny island in park; fountains in lake. Spacious room with large picture windows; large terrace. Extensive menu of traditional fare. Guitar music at dinner.

XX **Bagolyvár,** Allatkertí ut 2, ✉ 1146, ☎ (01) 468 3110, *bagolyvar@gundel.hu, Fax (01) 363 1917,* – MC AE D VISA DY d
closed 25 December and dinner 24 December and 31 December – **Meals** 2500/3500 and a la carte 2780/9450 ♀.
• Unusual Austro-Hungarian castle style building next to its sister - Gundel. All female team serve home-style traditional fare prepared by all female kitchen.

XX **Kárpátia,** Ferenciek tere 7-8, ✉ 1053, ☎ (01) 317 3596, *restaurant@karpatia.hu, Fax (01) 318 0591* – . MC AE D VISA JCB HV a
Meals a la carte 5600/11600.
• One of the city's oldest restaurants with characterful vaulted Gothic style interior, beautifully painted walls and works of art. Extensive menu of good traditional cuisine.

XX **Lou Lou,** Vigyázó Ferenc útca 4, ✉ 1051, ☎ (01) 312 4505, *lou-lou.restaurant@axelero.hu, Fax (01) 472 0595* – ▤. MC AE VISA GU a
closed 24 December, Sunday and Saturday lunch – **Meals** a la carte 4500/7900.
• Divided into two rooms; one with walls covered with pictures, the other brighter and in terracotta colours. Well-judged service; modern cooking with strong presentation.

XX **Múzeum,** Múzeum körút 12, ✉ 1088, ☎ (01) 338 4221, *Fax (01) 338 4221* – ▤. MC AE D VISA. HV e
Meals a la carte 3200/9700.
• Founded in 1885, next to National Museum. High ceilings, tiled walls and large windows. Formally attired staff serve large portions of traditional Hungarian cooking.

XX **Cyrano,** Kristóf tér 7-8, ✉ 1052, ☎ (01) 266 3096, *Fax (01) 266 6818,* – ▤. MC AE D VISA. GV t
closed 24 December and dinner 31 December – **Meals** a la carte 4600/7600.
• Popular informal restaurant just off main shopping street with unusual dramatic modern designer style décor. Serves selection of good modern European and Hungarian food.

XX **Belcanto,** Dalszínház útca 8, ✉ 1061, ☎ (01) 269 2786, *restaurant@belcanto.hu, Fax (01) 311 9547* – ⇆ ▤. MC AE DC VISA JCB. ⅋ HU f
closed Christmas – **Meals** (booking essential) 1500 (lunch) and dinner a la carte 5190/13000.
◆ Next to the opera and famous for classical and operatic evening recitals, including impromptu performances by waiters ! Atmosphere is lively and enjoyable. Hungarian food.

X **Baraka,** Magyar útca 12-14, ✉ 1053, ☎ (01) 483 1355 – ▤. MC AE VISA. ⅋ HV q
closed Sunday – **Meals** (booking essential) (dinner only) a la carte 3650/7550 ♀.
◆ Small restaurant with simple décor and corner bar ; quieter tables on mezzanine floor. Modern, international dishes showing French and Asian influences ; blackboard specials.

X **Kisbuda Gyöngye,** Kenyeres útca 34, ✉ 1034, ☎ (01) 368 6402, *gyongye@remiz.hu, Fax (01) 368 9227,* – ▤. MC AE VISA CY f
closed 24-26 and 31 December, 1 January and Sunday – **Meals** (booking essential) a la carte 3420/7560 ♀.
◆ A genuine neighbourhood restaurant in a residential street. Wood panelling and murals. Attentive and very helpful service. Good value, carefully prepared and authentic food.

X **Krizia,** Mozsár útca 12, ✉ 1066, ☎ (01) 331 8711, *Fax (01) 331 8711* – ▤. MC VISA
closed 15 days July-August, 10 days January and Sunday – **Meals** - Italian - 2600 (lunch) and a la carte 3200/7700 ♀. HU b
◆ A pleasant intimate atmosphere, with candlelight and friendly service. Carefully prepared Italian cooking with the menu supplemented by regularly changing specials.

X **La Fontaine,** Mérleg útca 10, ✉ 1051, ☎ (01) 317 3715, *restaurant@lafontaine.hu, Fax (01) 318 8562* – MC AE VISA. ⅋ GV s
closed Saturday lunch and Sunday – **Meals** - French - a la carte 3870/8570 ♀.
◆ Authentic Gallic charm : even the tables are imported from France. High ceiling and tiled flooring adds to the airy feel. Traditional French menu with blackboard specials.

X **Náncsi Néni,** Ördögárok útca 80, Hüvösvölgy, ✉ 1029, Northwest : 10 km by Szilágyi Erzsébetfasor ☎ (01) 397 2742, *info@nancsineni.hu, Fax (01) 397 2742,* – MC VISA JCB
closed 24 December – **Meals** a la carte 2440/6520 ♀.
◆ Interior similar to a Swiss chalet, with gingham tablecloths, convivial atmosphere and large terrace. Well-priced home-style Hungarian cooking. Worth the drive from the city.

X **Arcade Bistro,** Kiss Janos Alt u. 38, ✉ 1126, ☎ (01) 225 1969, *Fax (01) 225 1968,* – ▤. MC VISA. ⅋ EV f
closed 2 weeks in summer and Sunday – **Meals** (booking essential) a la carte 3410/7770 ♀.
◆ Small local restaurant with central column water feature and colourful modern art décor. Seasonal menu of modern cuisine : daily specials and Mediterranean influences.

X **Remiz,** Budakeszi útca 5, ✉ 1021, Northwest : 5 km by Szilágyi Erzébet ☎ (01) 275 1396, *remiz@remiz.hu, Fax (01) 200 3843,* – MC AE VISA
closed 24 December – **Meals** a la carte 2120/6980 ♀.
◆ On the outskirts of town and popular with the locals. Dine in the conservatory or on the large summer terrace. Efficient service from large brigade. Classic Hungarian dishes.

X **Apostolok,** Kígyó útca 4, ✉ 1052, ☎ (01) 318 3559, *Fax (01) 318 3559* – ▤. MC AE DC VISA JCB. ⅋ GV f
Meals (booking essential) a la carte 3600/6650 ♀.
◆ Characterful chapel-style interior, designed in 1902, with stained glass and mosaics of the Twelve Apostles above each hand-crafted booth. Pleasant service, authentic menu.

Republic of Ireland

Eire

PRACTICAL INFORMATION

LOCAL CURRENCY

1 euro (€) = 1,20 USD ($) (Dec 2003)

TOURIST INFORMATION

The telephone number and address of the Tourist Information office is given in the text under ℹ.

National Holiday in the Republic of Ireland: *17 March.*

FOREIGN EXCHANGE

Banks are open between 10am and 4pm on weekdays only.

Banks in Dublin stay open to 5pm on Thursdays and banks at Dublin and Shannon airports are open on Saturdays and Sundays.

SHOPPING IN DUBLIN

In the index of street names, those printed in red are where the principal shops are found.

CAR HIRE

The international car hire companies have branches in each major city. Your hotel porter should be able to give details and help you with your arrangements.

TIPPING

Many hotels and restaurants include a service charge but where this is not the case an amount equivalent to between 10 and 15 per cent of the bill is customary. Additionally doormen, baggage porters and cloakroom attendants are generally given a gratuity.

Taxi drivers are tipped between 10 and 15 per cent of the amount shown on the meter in addition to the fare.

SPEED LIMITS

The maximum permitted speed in the Republic is 60 mph (97 km/h) except where a lower speed limit is indicated.

SEAT BELTS

The wearing of seat belts is compulsory if fitted for drivers and front seat passengers. Additionally, children under 12 are not allowed in front seats unless in a suitable safety restraint.

ANIMALS

It is forbidden to bring domestic animals (dogs, cats...) into the Republic of Ireland.

DUBLIN

(Baile Átha Cliath) *Dublin* 712 N 7 – *pop. 1 122 600.*

Belfast 103 – Cork 154 – Londonderry 146.

Bord Failte Offices, Baggot Street Bridge ☏ (01) 602 4000 ; information@dublin tourism.ie – Suffolk St – Arrivals Hall, Dublin Airport – The Square Shopping Centre, Tallaght.

18 Elm Park, Nutley House, Donnybrook ☏ (01) 269 3438 – 18 Milltown, Lower Churchtown Rd, ☏ (01) 497 6090, EV *– 18 Royal Dublin, North Bull Island, Dollymount, ☏ (01) 833 6346, NE : by R 105 – 18 Forrest Little, Cloghran ☏ (01) 840 1183 – 18 Lucan, Celbridge Rd, Lucan ☏ (01) 628 0246 – 18 Edmondstown, Rathfarnham ☏ (01) 493 2461 – 18 Coldwinters, Newtown House, St Margaret's ☏ (01) 864 0324.*

Dublin Airport ☏ (01) 814 1111, N : 5 ½ m. by N 1 – Terminal : Busaras (Central Bus Station) Store St

to Holyhead (Irish Ferries) 2 daily (3 h 15 mn) – to Holyhead (Stena Line) 1-2 daily (3 h 45 mn) – to the Isle of Man (Douglas) (Isle of Man Steam Packet Co Ltd.) (2 h 45 mn) – to Liverpool (Merchant Ferries Ltd) 2 daily (7 h 45 mn) – to Liverpool (P & O Irish Sea) (8 h).

SIGHTS

See: *City★★★ – Trinity College★★* JY *– Old Library★★★ (Treasury★★★, Long Room★★) – Dublin Castle★★ (Chester Beatty Library★★★)* HY *– Christ Church Cathedral★★* HY *– St Patrick's Cathedral★★* HZ *– Marsh's Library★★* HZ *– National Museum★★ (The Treasury★★)* KZ *– National Gallery★★* KZ *– Newman House★★* JZ *– Bank of Ireland★★* JY *– Custom House★★* KX *– Tailors' Hall★* HY *– City Hall★* HY *– Temple Bar★* HJY *– Liffey Bridge★* JY *– Merrion Square★* KZ *– Number Twenty-Nine★* KZ **D** *– Crafton Street★* JYZ *– Powerscourt Centre★* JY *– Rotunda Hospital Chapel★* JX *– O'Connell Street★* JX *– Hugh Lane Municipal Gallery of Modern Art★* JX **M⁴** *– Pro-Cathedral★* JX.

Envir.: *The Ben of Howth★ (≤★), NE: 6 m. by R 105* KX.

Exc.: *Powerscourt★★ (Waterfall★★* **AC***), S: 14 m. by N 11 and R 117* EV *– Russborough House★★★, SW: 22 m. by N 81* DV.

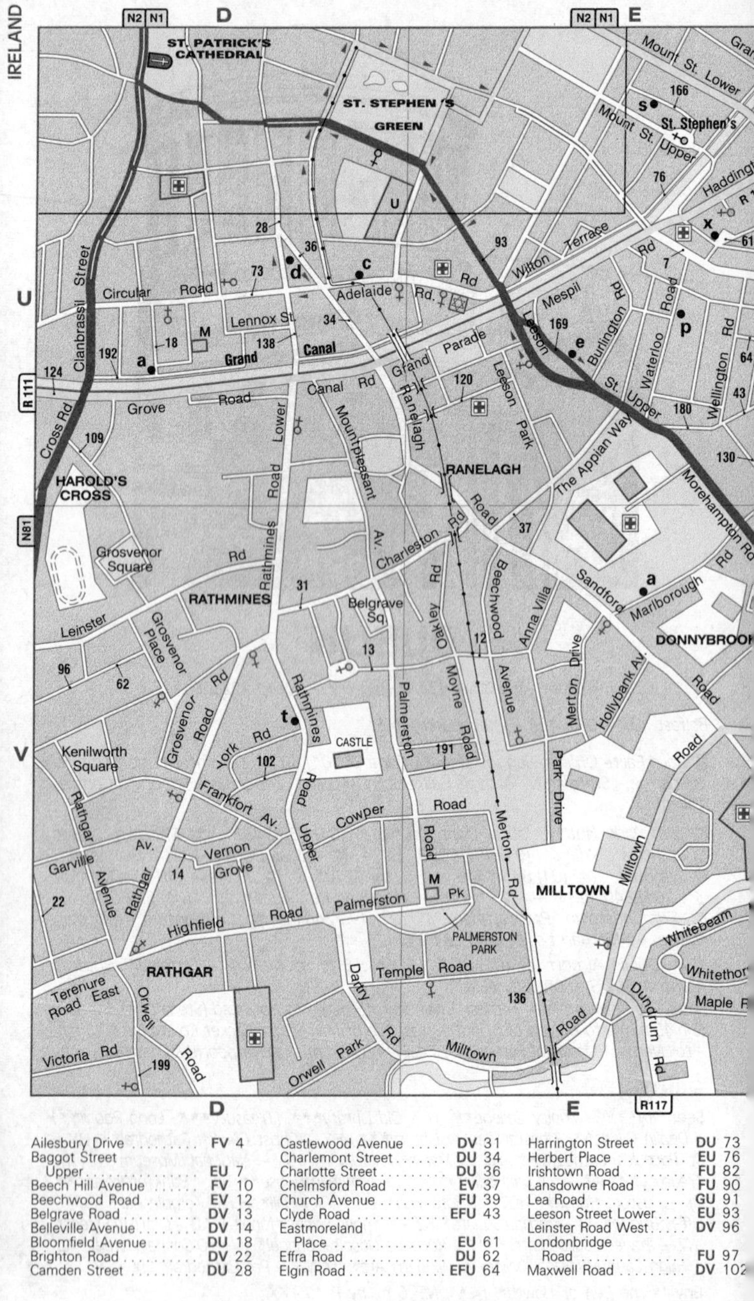

Ailesbury Drive	FV	4
Baggot Street Upper	EU	7
Beech Hill Avenue	FV	10
Beechwood Road	EV	12
Belgrave Road	DV	13
Belleville Avenue	DV	14
Bloomfield Avenue	DU	18
Brighton Road	DV	22
Camden Street	DU	28
Castlewood Avenue	DV	31
Charlemont Street	DU	34
Charlotte Street	DU	36
Chelmsford Road	EV	37
Church Avenue	FU	39
Clyde Road	EFU	43
Eastmoreland Place	EU	61
Effra Road	DU	62
Elgin Road	EFU	64
Harrington Street	DU	73
Herbert Place	EU	76
Irishtown Road	FU	82
Lansdowne Road	FU	90
Lea Road	GU	91
Leeson Street Lower	EU	93
Leinster Road West	DV	96
Londonbridge Road	FU	97
Maxwell Road	DV	102

Your recommendation is self-evident if you always walk into a hotel Guide in hand.

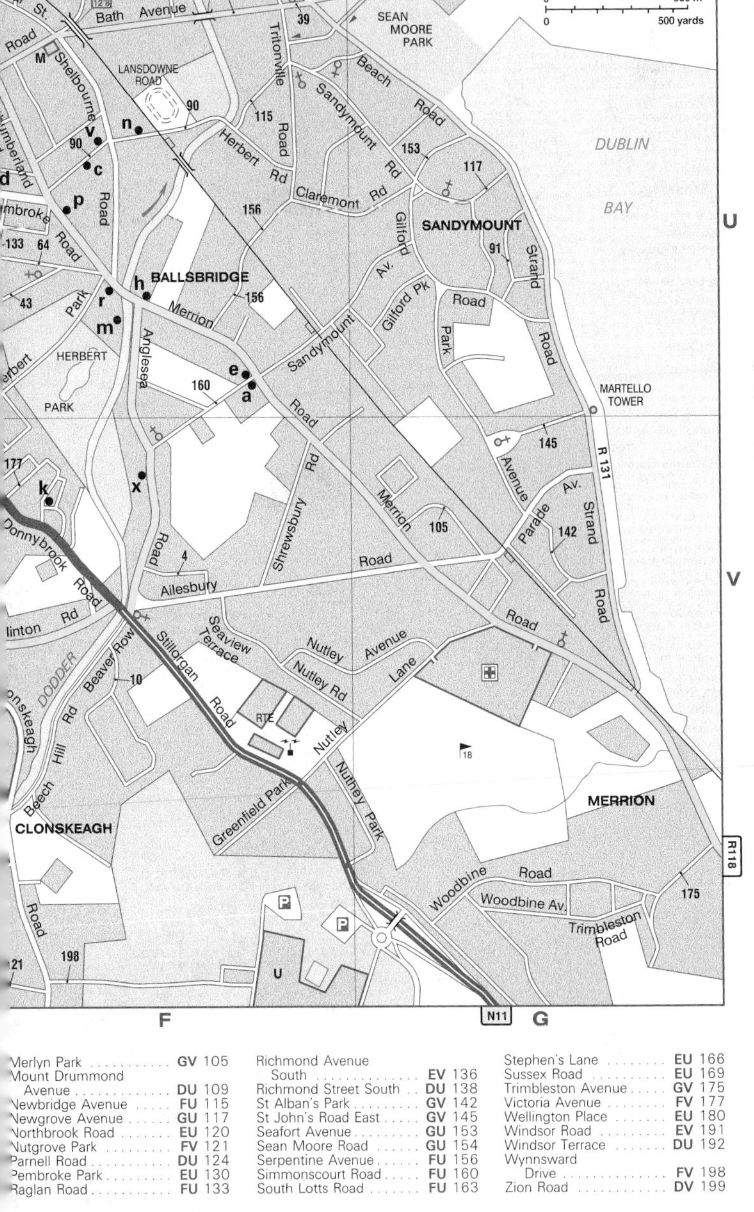

Merlyn Park . . . . **GV** 105
Mount Drummond
Avenue . . . . **DU** 109
Newbridge Avenue . . . . . **FU** 115
Newgrove Avenue . . . . . . **GU** 117
Northbrook Road . . . . **EU** 120
Nutgrove Park . . . . **FV** 121
Parnell Road . . . . **DU** 124
Pembroke Park . . . . **EU** 130
Raglan Road . . . . **FU** 133
Richmond Avenue
South . . . . **EV** 136
Richmond Street South . . **DU** 138
St Alban's Park . . . . **GV** 142
St John's Road East . . . . . **GV** 145
Seafort Avenue . . . . **GU** 153
Sean Moore Road . . . . **GU** 154
Serpentine Avenue . . . . . . **FU** 156
Simmonscourt Road . . . . . **FU** 160
South Lotts Road . . . . **FU** 163
Stephen's Lane . . . . **EU** 166
Sussex Road . . . . **EU** 169
Trimbleston Avenue . . . . . **GV** 175
Victoria Avenue . . . . **FV** 177
Wellington Place . . . . **EU** 180
Windsor Road . . . . **EV** 191
Windsor Terrace . . . . **DU** 192
Wynnsward
Drive . . . . **FV** 198
Zion Road . . . . **DV** 199

If you find you cannot take up a hotel booking you have made, please let the hotel know immediately.

DUBLIN

Street	Grid	No.
Anne Street South	JYZ	6
Brunswick Street North	HX	24
Buckingham Street	KX	25
Bull Alley	HZ	27
Chancery Street	HY	33
Clanbrassil Street	HZ	40
College Green	JY	45
College Street	JY	46
Cornmarket	HY	49
Dawson Street	JYZ	
D'Olier Street	JY	51
Dorset Street	HX	55
Duke Street	JY	58
Earlsfort Terrace	JZ	60
Essex Quay	HY	65
Essex Street	HY	66
Fishamble Street	HY	67
Fleet Street	JY	68
George's Quay	KY	69
Golden Lane	HZ	70
Grafton Street	JYZ	
Henrietta Street	HX	75
Henry Street	JX	
High Street	HY	78
Ilac Centre	HJX	
Irish Life Mall Centre	JKX	
Jervis Centre	HJX	
Kevin Street Upper	HZ	85
Kildare Street	JKZ	87
King Street South	JZ	88
Marlborough Street	JX	100
Merchants Quay	HY	103
Merrion Street	KZ	104
Montague Street	JZ	106
Mount Street Upper	KZ	112
Nicholas Street	HY	118
North Great Georges's Street	JX	119
O'Connell Street	JX	
Parnell Square East	JX	126
Parnell Square North	JX	127
Parnell Square West	HJX	129
St Mary's Abbey Street	HY	148
St Patrick Close	HZ	150
Stephen Street	HJY	165
Stephens Green	JZ	
Tara Street	KY	171
Wellington Quay	HJY	181
Werburgh Street	HY	183
Westland Row	KY	186
Westmoreland Street	JY	187
Wexford Street	HZ	189
Winetavern Street	HY	193
Wood Quay	HY	196

*Town plans:
roads most used by traffic
and those on which guide-
listed hotels and restaurants
stand are fully drawn;
the beginning only
of lesser roads is indicated.*

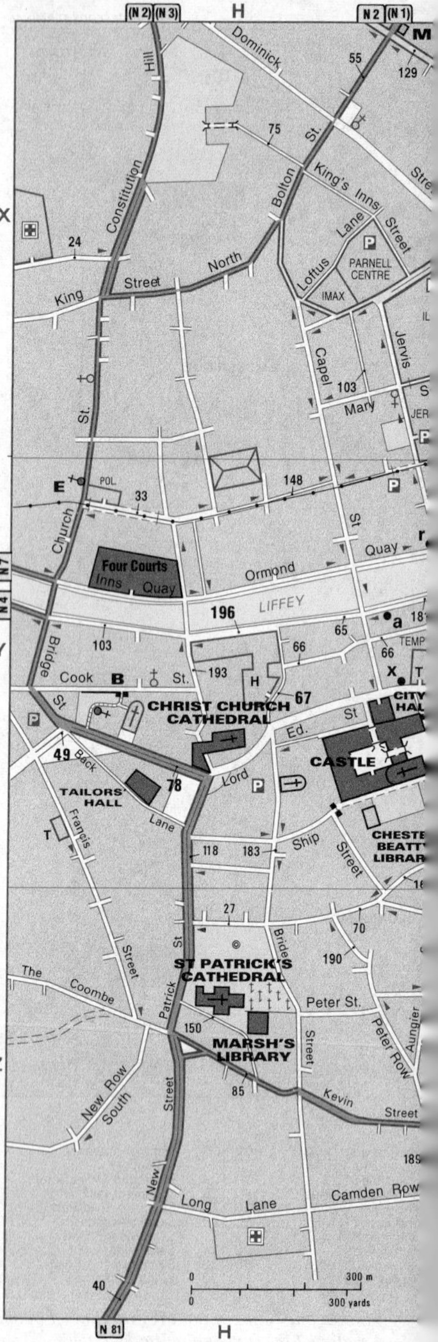

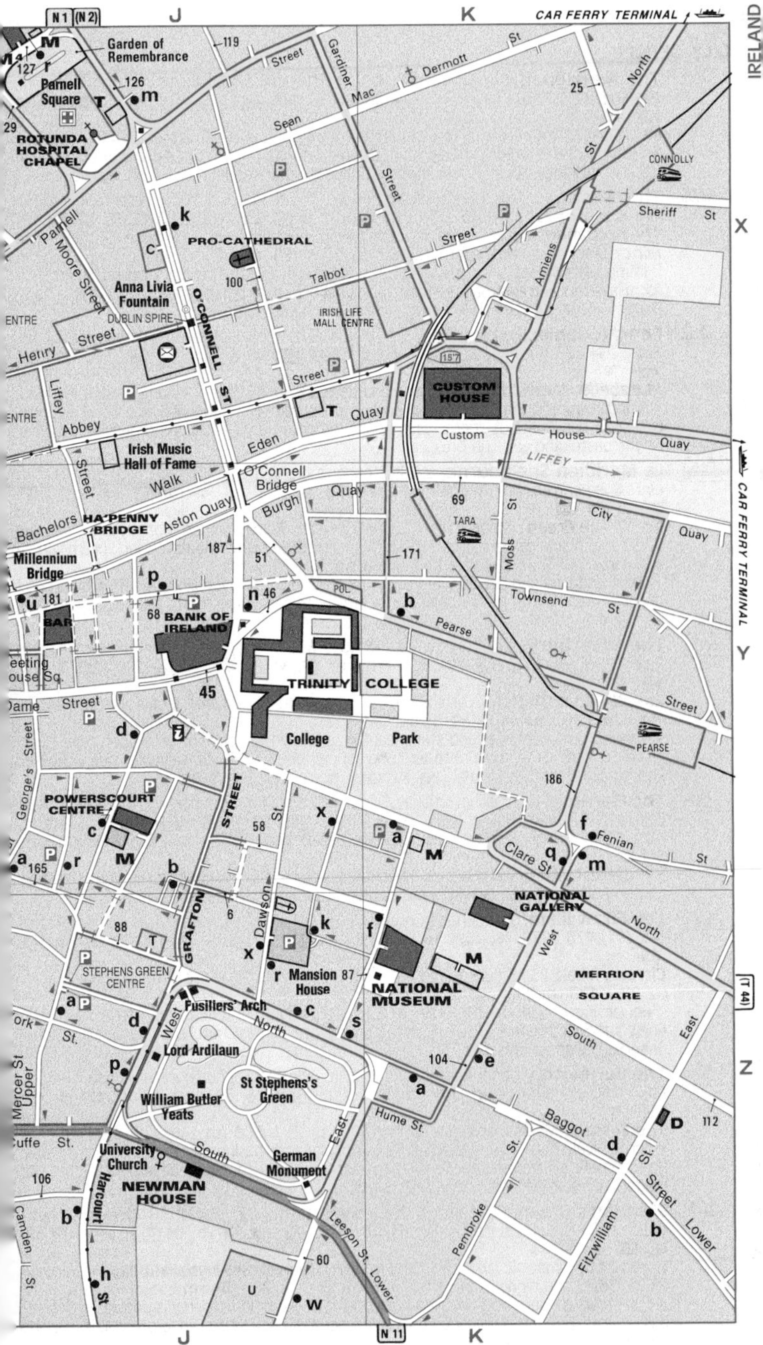

IRELAND
CAR FERRY TERMINAL
Garden of Remembrance
Parnell Square
ROTUNDA HOSPITAL CHAPEL
PRO-CATHEDRAL
Anna Livia Fountain
DUBLIN SPIRE
O'CONNELL ST
IRISH LIFE MALL CENTRE
CONNOLLY
CUSTOM HOUSE
Irish Music Hall of Fame
O'Connell Bridge
LIFFEY
HA'PENNY BRIDGE
Millennium Bridge
TARA
BANK OF IRELAND
TRINITY COLLEGE
College Park
PEARSE
POWERSCOURT CENTRE
GRAFTON STREET
NATIONAL GALLERY
STEPHENS GREEN CENTRE
Mansion House
NATIONAL MUSEUM
MERRION SQUARE
Fusiliers' Arch
Lord Ardilaun
William Butler Yeats
St Stephens's Green
University Church
NEWMAN HOUSE
German Monument

City Centre

The Merrion, Upper Merrion St, D2, ✆ (01) 603 0600, *info@merrionhotel.com, Fax (01) 603 0700,* – rm, – 50. MC AE VISA. KZ e
Meals (see ***The Cellar*** and ***The Cellar Bar*** below) – 26 – **135 rm** 320/435, 10 suites.
◆ Classic hotel in series of elegantly restored Georgian town houses; many of the individually designed grand rooms overlook pleasant gardens. Irish art in opulent lounges.

The Westin, College Green, Westmoreland St, ✆ (01) 645 1000, *reservations.dublin@westin.com, Fax (01) 645 1234* – rm, – 250. MC AE VISA.
The Exchange : **Meals** *(closed Saturday lunch)* 25.50 (lunch) and a la carte 42/53 – ***The Mint :*** **Meals** a la carte approx 20 – 25 – **150 rm** 410, 13 suites. JY n
◆ Immaculately kept and consummately run hotel in a useful central location. Smart, uniform interiors and an ornate period banking hall. Excellent bedrooms with marvellous beds. Formal, elegant 1920s-style dining in Art Deco surroundings.

Conrad Dublin, Earlsfort Terr, D2, ✆ (01) 676 5555, *dublininfo@conradhotels.com, Fax (01) 676 5424,* – rm, – 370. MC AE VISA. JZ w
Plurabelle : **Meals** 26.50/35.50 and a la carte 35.80/45.75 **s.** – 22 – **192 rm** 420.
◆ Smart, business oriented international hotel opposite the National Concert Hall. Popular, pub-style bar. Spacious rooms with bright, modern décor and comprehensive facilities. Bright pastel and well-run brasserie.

Le Meridien Shelbourne, 27 St Stephen's Green, D2, ✆ (01) 663 4500, *shelbourneinfo@lemeridien.com, Fax (01) 661 6006,* – rm, – 400. MC AE VISA JZ s
No.27 The Green : **Meals** *(closed Saturday lunch, Sunday dinner, Monday and Tuesday)* 33.50 (lunch) and dinner a la carte 37/61 – ***The Side Door :*** **Meals** *(closed Sunday lunch)* a la carte 26.50/43 – 21.50 – **168 rm** 361, 22 suites.
◆ Local landmark and byword for luxury. Take tea in Lord Mayor's lounge, or enjoy original décor of the Horseshoe Bar. Well-equipped leisure spa. Some rooms overlook the Green. Formal dining in No.27 The Green. Bright brasserie feel to The Side Door.

The Westbury, Grafton St, D2, ✆ (01) 679 1122, *westbury@jurysdoyle.com, Fax (01) 679 7078,* – rm, – 220. MC AE VISA. JY b
Russell Room : **Meals** a la carte approx 31.70 **s.** – ***The Sandbank :*** **Meals** a la carte 24/35 – 24 – **196 rm** 340/380, 8 suites.
◆ Imposing marble foyer and stairs leading to lounge famous for afternoon teas. Huge luxurious bedrooms, most with air-conditioning, offer every conceivable facility. Russell Room has distinctive, formal feel. Informal, bistro-style Sandbank.

The Clarence, 6-8 Wellington Quay, D2, ✆ (01) 407 0800, *reservations@theclarence.ie, Fax (01) 407 0820,* – – 60. MC AE VISA JCB. HY a
closed 24-26 December – **Meals** (see ***The Tea Room*** below) – 27.50 – **45 rm** 315, 5 suites.
◆ A discreet, stylish warehouse conversion in Temple Bar overlooking river and boasting contemporary interior design. Small panelled library. Modern, distinctive bedrooms.

The Fitzwilliam, St Stephen's Green, D2, ✆ (01) 478 7000, *enq@fitzwilliamhotel.com, Fax (01) 478 7878,* – rm, rest, – 70. MC AE VISA JCB. JZ d
Citron : **Meals** 23.75 (lunch) and a la carte 30/40.70 **s.** (see also ***Thornton's*** below) – 22 – **128 rm** 290/390, 2 suites.
◆ Rewardingly overlooks the Green and boasts a bright contemporary interior. Spacious, finely appointed rooms offer understated elegance. Largest hotel roof garden in Europe. Cheerful, informal brasserie.

The Burlington, Upper Leeson St, D4, ✆ (01) 660 5222, *burlington@jurysdoyle.com, Fax (01) 660 8496* – rm, rest, – 1500. MC AE VISA. EU e
The Sussex : **Meals** (bar lunch)/dinner 40 – 23 – **500 rm** 240/270, 6 suites.
◆ Large, lively hotel in a modern setting, popular with business clients and tour groups. Handsomely equipped bedrooms, gym for executive guests; basement nightclub. Large, charming Art Deco-styled dining room.

Stephen's Green, Cliffe St, off St Stephen's Green, D2, ✆ (01) 607 3600, *stephensgreenres@ocallaghanhotels.ie, Fax (01) 661 5663,* – rm, – 50. MC AE VISA. JZ f
closed 24 December-2 January – ***The Pie Dish :*** **Meals** *(closed lunch Saturday and Sunday)* 26.25/36.75 and dinner a la carte 29.25/38.55 – 20 – **64 rm** 295, 11 suites.
◆ This smart modern hotel housed in an originally Georgian property is popular with business clients. Bright, relatively compact bedrooms offer a good range of facilities. Bright and breezy bistro restaurant.

Brooks, 59-63 Drury St, D2, (01) 670 4000, *sales@brookshotel.ie, Fax (01) 670 4455,* – rm, – 30. AE VISA. JY r
closed 25 December and Good Friday – ***Francesca's* : Meals** (dinner only) 28.95/32.95 and a la carte 26.95/44.40 – 17.50 – **75 rm** 185/255.
◆ Commercial hotel in modern English town house style. Smart lounges and spacious rooms with tasteful feel and good facilities. Extras in top range rooms, at a supplement. Ground floor banquette restaurant with open kitchen for chef-watching.

The Alexander, Fienian St, Merrion Sq, D2, (01) 607 3700, *alexanderres@ocallaghanhotels.ie, Fax (01) 661 5663,* – rm, – 400. AE VISA. KY f
closed 24 December-2 January – ***Caravaggio's* : Meals** (bar lunch Saturday and Sunday) a la carte 43.50/46 – 20 – **98 rm** 295, 4 suites.
◆ This bright corporate hotel, well placed for museums and Trinity College, has a stylish contemporary interior. Spacious comfortable rooms and suites with good facilities. Stylish contemporary restaurant with wide-ranging menus.

The Davenport, Lower Merrion St, off Merrion Sq, D2, (01) 607 3500, *davenportres@ocallaghanhotels.ie, Fax (01) 661 5663,* – rm, – 275. AE VISA. KY m
***Lanyon* : Meals** *(closed lunch Saturday and Sunday)* a la carte 30.35/45.05 – 20 – **113 rm** 295, 2 suites.
◆ Sumptuous Victorian gospel hall façade heralds elegant hotel popular with business clientèle. Tastefully furnished, well-fitted rooms. Presidents bar honours past leaders. Dining room with formal, Georgian interior.

The Gresham, 23 Upper O'Connell St, D1, (01) 874 6881, *info@thegresham.com, Fax (01) 878 7175,* – – 400. AE VISA. JX k
***23* : Meals** (dinner only) 32/37 – ***The Aberdeen* : Meals** 21/37 and a la carte 33/52 – 19 – **282 rm** 310, 6 suites.
◆ Long established restored 19C property in a famous street offers elegance tinged with luxury. Some penthouse suites. Well-equipped business centre, lounge and Toddy's bar. The Aberdeen boasts formal ambience. 23 is named after available wines by glass.

Clarion H. Dublin IFSC, Excise Walk International Financial Services Centre, D1, (01) 433 8800, *info@clarionhotelifsc.com, Fax (01) 433 8811,* – rm, – 120. AE VISA. by Custom House Quay KX
closed 24-26 December – ***Sinergie* : Meals** *(closed Saturday lunch)* 28 and a la carte 27.75/36.95 – ***Kudos* : Meals** - Asian - a la carte 17.85/19.25 – **154 rm** 116/182, 8 suites.
◆ In the heart of a modern financial district, a swish hotel for the business person : smart gym and light, spacious, contemporary rooms, some with balconies. Busy bar leads to clean-lined restaurant with glass walls onto the kitchen.

Morrison, Lower Ormond Quay, D1, (01) 887 2400, *info@morrisonhotel.ie, Fax (01) 878 3185* – rm, AE VISA HY r
Meals (see ***Halo*** below) – 21.50 – **90 rm** 270, 4 suites.
◆ Modern riverside hotel with ultra-contemporary interior by acclaimed fashion designer John Rocha. Hi-tech amenities in rooms. "Lobo" late-night club and sushi bar.

brownes townhouse, 22 St Stephen's Green, D2, (01) 638 3939, *info@brownesdublin.com, Fax (01) 638 3900* – AE VISA. JZ c
closed 24 December-3 January – **Meals** (see ***brownes brasserie*** below) – **12 rm** 185/300.
◆ Restored Georgian town house with original fittings in situ. Combines traditional charm with modern comfort. Its dozen rooms are well-appointed and stylish, some with view.

La Stampa H., 35 Dawson St, D2, (01) 677 4444, *dine@lastampa.ie, Fax (01) 677 4411* – AE VISA. JZ x
closed 25 December – ***Tiger Becs* : Meals** - Thai - (dinner only) a la carte 33/46.50 (see also ***La Stampa*** below) – **24 rm** 100/210.
◆ A privately owned and discreetly stylish boutique hotel, close to St Stephen's Green. Individually appointed bedrooms with designer touches. Quieter rooms at rear.

The Morgan, 10 Fleet St, D2, (01) 679 3939, *reservations@themorgan.com, Fax (01) 679 3946* – rm, rest, AE JY p
closed 24-26 December – ***All Sports Cafe* : Meals** (grill rest.) a la carte 24/36 – 17.70 – **65 rm** 152/229, 1 suites.
◆ Discreet designer contemporary hotel in vibrant area emphasises style. Simple elegant foyer contrasts with large, busy bar. Sleek minimalist décor in well-equipped bedrooms. Café attracts vibrant crowd ; packed with sporting memorabilia.

Mont Clare, Lower Merrion St, off Merrion Sq, D2, ✆ (01) 607 3800, *montclareres@ocallaghanhotels.ie, Fax (01) 661 5663* – 120. *closed 24-26 December* – ***Goldsmiths :*** **Meals** 23.35 (lunch) and dinner a la carte 35.20/41.80 – 18 – **74 rm** 205. KY q

◆ Classic property with elegant panelled reception and tasteful comfortable rooms at heart of Georgian Dublin. Corporate suites available. Traditional pub style Gallery bar. Formal restaurant with tried-and-tested menus.

Chief O'Neills, Smithfield Village, Smithfield, D7, ✆ (01) 817 3838, *reservations@chiefoneills.com, Fax (01) 817 3839* – rm, – 240. by King St HX

closed 24-26 December – ***Kelly & Ping :*** **Meals** - Asian - *(closed Sunday and Bank Holidays)* 20/33 (dinner) and a la carte 20/29.20 – **73 rm** 180.

◆ Based in cultural hub. Interactive music centre celebrates traditional Irish music. Sleek modern rooms with hi-fi. Viewing tower with wonderful vistas of the surrounding city. Asian restaurant in sleek modish setting adjacent to Jameson distillery.

Cassidys, 6-8 Cavendish Row, Upper O'Connell St, D1, ✆ (01) 878 0555, *stay@cassidyshotel.com, Fax (01) 878 0687* – , rest, – 80. *closed 24-27 December* – ***Number Six :*** **Meals** (dinner only) 25 and a la carte 26.50/41 – **87 rm** 85/200, 1 suite. JX m

◆ Classic Georgian redbrick town house makes an elegant backdrop for modern comfort. Cheerful room décor. Limited on-street guest parking. Popular Groomes bar open to public. Bright, stylish dining room sports a homely ambience.

The Mercer, Mercer Street Lower, D2, ✆ (01) 478 2179, *stay@mercerhotel.ie, Fax (01) 478 0328* – , rm, – 100. JZ a

closed 23-28 December – ***Cusack's :*** **Meals** *(closed Sunday dinner)* 25/45 and a la carte 18.95/31.85 **s.** – 13.50 – **41 rm** 179/220.

◆ This modern boutique hotel, hidden away next to the Royal College of Surgeons, is pleasant and stylish. It offers comprehensive amenities including air conditioning. Smart yet relaxing restaurant.

Trinity Capital, Pearse St, D2, ✆ (01) 648 1000, *info@trinitycapital-hotel.com, Fax (01) 648 1010* – , rm, rest, – 40. KY b

closed 23-27 December – ***Siena :*** **Meals** *(closed Sunday)* (bar lunch)/dinner 25 and a la carte 25.90/42.50 **s.** – 14.50 – **82 rm** 165/192.

◆ Spacious lobby with striking modern furnishings leads off to stylish, soft-toned bedrooms, generously supplied with mod cons. A few minutes walk from Trinity College. Relaxed and fashionably styled dining room filled with natural light.

Buswells, Molesworth St, D2, ✆ (01) 614 6500, *buswells@quinn-hotels.com, Fax (01) 676 2090,* – , rm, rest, – 85. KZ f

closed 25-26 December – ***Brasserie :*** **Meals** (lunch only) 30 a la carte 28.80/38.73 – ***Trumans :*** **Meals** (dinner only) a la carte 31.90/40.95 **s.** – **67 rm** 146/222, 2 suites.

◆ Elegant little hotel in quiet central location offering modern amenities while retaining its Georgian charm. Relax in cushioned lounge or cosy, pleasingly furnished rooms. Light dining in elegant surroundings.

Camden Court, Camden St, D2, ✆ (01) 475 9666, *sales@camdencourthotel.com, Fax (01) 475 9677,* , , – , rest, – 125. DU d

closed 23-29 December – ***The Court :*** **Meals** (carving lunch)/dinner 22.50/30 and a la carte 28.20/34.65 – **246 rm** 210/280.

◆ A vaulted passageway leads to this smart, popular hotel in a thriving locality. Colourful soft furnishings in cosy, well-equipped rooms. Cheerful bar on an Irish myth theme. Open, informal restaurant with polished wood and popular menus.

Longfield's, 10 Lower Fitzwilliam St, D2, ✆ (01) 676 1367, *info@longfields.ie, Fax (01) 676 1542* – . KZ d

Meals (see ***Number Ten*** below) – **26 rm** 90/205.

◆ Classic Georgian town house on reputedly Europe's longest Georgian road. Spacious lounge ; stylish, individually furnished rooms of good size, all redolent of times gone by.

Harrington Hall without rest., 70 Harcourt St, D2, ✆ (01) 475 3497, *harringtonhall@eircom.net, Fax (01) 475 4544* – . JZ h

28 rm 138/215.

◆ Two usefully located mid-terrace Georgian town houses. Friendly and well-run. Bright, spacious bedrooms with soundproofing, ceiling fans, access to fax and internet.

Trinity Lodge without rest., 12 South Frederick St, D2, ✆ (01) 617 0900, *trinitylodge@eircom.net, Fax (01) 617 0999* – . JY x

closed 23-27 December – **16 rm** 95/190.

◆ Elegant Georgian town houses with local landmarks nearby. Spacious, well-furnished bedrooms with good level of comfort. Modern suites and de luxe rooms. Good value.

Eliza Lodge without rest., 23-24 Wellington Quay, D2, ☎ (01) 671 8044, *info@dublinlodge.com, Fax (01) 671 8362*, ← – |‡| ⇔ ▤ TV ☏. MC AE VISA. ✗ JY u
closed 22 December-2 January – **18 rm** ⊐ 76/152.
• Ideally placed for Temple Bar nightlife. Lounge with video facilities and internet access; comfortable, practical rooms: the balconied penthouse floor has fine river views. Glass-fronted restaurant facing the Liffey and Millennium Bridge.

Kilronan House without rest., 70 Adelaide Rd, D2, ☎ (01) 475 5266, *info@dublinn.com, Fax (01) 478 2841* – ⇔ TV. MC AE VISA. ✗ DU c
14 rm ⊐ 76/180.
• IIn the heart of Georgian Dublin, a good value, well-kept town house run by knowledgeable, friendly couple. Individually styled rooms; sustaining breakfasts.

XXXX ✿✿ **Patrick Guilbaud,** 21 Upper Merrion St, D2, ☎ (01) 676 4192, *restaurantpatrickguilbaud@eircom.net, Fax (01) 661 0052* – ▤. MC AE D VISA KZ e
closed 1 week Christmas, 17 March, Good Friday, Sunday and Monday – **Meals** 50 (lunch) and a la carte 80/113 ♀.
• Top class restaurant run by consummate professional offering accomplished Irish influenced dishes in elegant Georgian town house. Contemporary Irish art collection.
Spec. Lobster ravioli with coconut cream and almonds. Squab pigeon with foie gras and Savoy cabbage. Assiette of chocolate.

XXXX ✿✿ **Thornton's** (at The Fitzwilliam H.), 128 St Stephen's Green, D2, ☎ (01) 478 7008, *thorntonsrestaurant@eircom.net, Fax (01) 478 7009* – ▤ 🚗. MC AE D VISA JZ d
closed 1 week Christmas, Sunday and Monday – **Meals** 40/65 and a la carte 94/106 ♀.
• Stylish modern restaurant on second floor offers exciting culinary ideas drawing on Irish, French and Italian cuisine, and interesting views too. Good value lunch menus.
Spec. Sautéed prawns with prawn bisque, truffle sabayon. Fillet of sea bass with shrimps, baby spinach and squid ink sauce. Mango and passion fruit mousse, chocolate ice cream.

XXX **Shanahan's on the Green,** 119 St Stephen's Green, D2, ☎ (01) 407 0939, *info@shanahans.ie, Fax (01) 407 0940* – ⇔ ▤. MC AE D VISA JZ p
closed Christmas and Bank Holidays – **Meals** (booking essential) (dinner only and Friday lunch) a la carte 67.50/91.50 ♀.
• Sumptuous Georgian town house: upper floor window tables survey the Green. Supreme comfort enhances your enjoyment of strong seafood dishes and choice cuts of Irish beef.

XXX ✿ **L'Ecrivain** (Clarke), 109A Lower Baggot St, D2, ☎ (01) 661 1919, *enquiries@lecrivain.com, Fax (01) 661 0617*, 🏛 – ▤. MC AE VISA KZ b
closed 24 December-2 January, Saturday lunch, Sunday and Bank Holidays – **Meals** (booking essential) 35/57.50 and dinner a la carte 69.50/84.50 ♀.
• Soft piano notes add to the welcoming ambience. Robust, well prepared, modern Irish food with emphasis on fish and game. Private dining room has agreeable wine selection.
Spec. Seared loin of tuna, soya and honey glaze. Suprême of turbot with mushroom and foie gras tart, asparagus froth. A tasting of poussin.

XXX **Chapter One,** The Dublin Writers Museum, 18-19 Parnell Sq, D1, ☎ (01) 873 2266, *info@chapteronerestaurant.com, Fax (01) 873 2330* – ▤ P. MC AE D VISA JCB JX r
closed 2-18 August, 24 December-8 January, Sunday, Monday and Saturday lunch – **Meals** 29.50 (lunch) and dinner a la carte 39.50/45 🎭 ♀.
• In basement of historic building, once home to whiskey baron. Comfortable restaurant with Irish art on walls. Interesting menus focus on good hearty food: sample the oysters.

XX **The Tea Room** (at The Clarence H.), 6-8 Wellington Quay, D2, ☎ (01) 670 7766, *Fax (01) 670 7833* – MC AE D VISA HY a
closed Saturday lunch – **Meals** (booking essential) 25.20/55 ♀.
• Spacious elegant ground floor room with soaring coved ceiling and stylish contemporary décor offers interesting modern Irish dishes with hint of continental influence.

XX **Halo** (at Morrison H.), Ormond Quay, D1, ☎ (01) 887 2421, *Fax (01) 887 2499* – ▤. MC AE D VISA HY r
Meals 29/60 and dinner a la carte 40.50/64.50 ♀.
• Ultramodern, minimal, split level restaurant designed by John Rocha, offering talented Asian and French influenced cuisine featuring interesting and original dishes.

XX **brownes brasserie** (at brownes townhouse H.), 22 St Stephen's Green, D2, ☎ (01) 638 3939, *info@brownesdublin.ie, Fax (01) 638 3900* – ▤. MC AE D VISA JZ c
closed 24 December-3 January and Saturday lunch – **Meals** (booking essential) 20/25 (lunch) and a la carte 33.95/49.15 ♀.
• Smart, characterful, with a Belle Epoque feel. On the ground floor of the eponymous Georgian town house with interesting and appealing classic dishes. A good value location.

XX **The Cellar** (at The Merrion H.), Upper Merrion St, D2, ☎ (01) 603 0630, *Fax (01) 603 0700* – ▤ 🚗. MC AE D VISA JCB KZ e
closed Saturday lunch – **Meals** 22.95 (lunch) and dinner a la carte 24/47.50 ♀.
• Smart open-plan basement restaurant with informal ambience offering well prepared formal style fare crossing Irish with Mediterranean influences. Good value lunch menu.

XX **One Pico,** 5-6 Molesworth Pl, School House Lane, D2, ☎ (01) 676 0300, *eamonnoreill y@ireland.com, Fax (01) 676 0411* – ▤. MC AE ① VISA JZ k
closed 4-19 August, 25 December-7 January, Sunday and Bank Holidays – **Meals** 26 (lunch) and dinner a la carte 42/53 ♀.
◆ Wide-ranging cuisine, classic and traditional by turns, always with an elaborate, eclectic edge. Décor and service share a pleasant formality, crisp, modern and stylish.

XX **Les Frères Jacques,** 74 Dame St, D2, ☎ (01) 679 4555, *info@lesfreresjacques.com, Fax (01) 679 4725* – MC AE VISA HY x
closed 25 December-2 January, Saturday lunch and Sunday – **Meals** - French - 22/35 and dinner a la carte 45.50/58 ♀.
◆ Smart popular family-run bistro offering well prepared simple classic French cuisine with fresh fish and seafood a speciality, served by efficient team of French staff.

XX **Number Ten** (at Longfield's H.), 10 Lower Fitzwilliam St, D2, ☎ (01) 676 1367, *Fax (01) 676 1542* – MC AE ① VISA KZ d
closed Saturday lunch and Sunday – **Meals** 28/45 **s.** ♀.
◆ This bijou basement establishment with an atmosphere of understated elegance offers well cooked interesting menus combining traditional European cuisine with local flair.

XX **La Stampa** (at La Stampa H.), 35 Dawson St, D2, ☎ (01) 677 8611, *lastampa@eircom.net, Fax (01) 677 336* – MC AE ① VISA JZ x
Meals (booking essential) (dinner only) 41.50/58 and a la carte 41.50/130 ♀.
◆ 19C former ballroom retains its vast mirrors and superbly intricate mosaic ceiling. Flavourful modern Irish dishes. Fine collection of Graham Knuttel originals adorns the bar.

XX **Saagar,** 16 Harcourt St, D2, ☎ (01) 475 5060, *info@saagarindianrestaurants.com, Fax (01) 475 5741* – MC AE ① VISA JCB JZ b
closed 25 December, Saturday and Sunday lunch – **Meals** - Indian - a la carte 15.85/23.40.
◆ Well-run restaurant serving subtly toned, freshly prepared Indian fare in basement of Georgian terraced house. Main road setting. Ring bell at foot of stairs to enter.

XX **Locks,** 1 Windsor Terr, Portobello, D8, ☎ (01) 4543391, *Fax (01) 4538352* – MC AE ① VISA DU a
closed 1 week Christmas, Saturday lunch and Sunday – **Meals** 28.95/48.95 and a la carte 54.95/72.05.
◆ Street corner mainstay for 20 years ; watch the swans swimming by on adjacent canal. Offers wide range, from simple one course dishes to more elaborate classic French fare.

XX **Jacobs Ladder,** 4-5 Nassau St, D2, ☎ (01) 670 3865, *dining@jacobsladder.ie, Fax (01) 670 3868* – ⊁. MC AE ① VISA KY a
closed 2 weeks Christmas-New Year, 1 week August, 17 March, Sunday, Monday and Bank Holidays – **Meals** (booking essential) 31.75 (dinner) and a la carte 37.30/52.25 **s.** ♀.
◆ Up a narrow staircase, this popular small first floor restaurant with unfussy modern décor and a good view offers good value modern Irish fare and very personable service.

XX **Siam Thai,** 14-15 Andrew St, D2, ☎ (01) 677 3363, *siam@eircom.net, Fax (01) 670 7644* – ⊁. MC AE VISA JCB JY d
closed 25-26 December and Sunday – **Meals** 33 (dinner) and a la carte 26.50/37.
◆ Centrally located restaurant with a warm, homely feel, embodied by woven Thai prints. Basement room for parties. Daily specials ; Thai menus with choice and originality.

XX **Jaipur,** 41 South Great George's St, D2, ☎ (01) 677 0999, *dublin@jaipur.ie, Fax (01) 677 0979* – MC AE VISA JY a
closed 25-26 December – **Meals** - Indian - (dinner only) 30 and a la carte 29.50/39.50.
◆ Vivid modernity in the city centre ; run by knowledgable team. Immaculately laid, linen-clad tables. Interesting, freshly prepared Indian dishes using unique variations.

XX **Bang Café,** 11 Merrion Row, D2, ☎ (01) 676 0898, *Fax (01) 676 0899* – ▤. MC AE VISA KZ a
closed 25 December-2 January and Sunday – **Meals** (booking essential) a la carte 24.25/43.30.
◆ Stylish, mirror-lined lounge bar, closely set linen-topped tables and an open kitchen lend a lively, contemporary air. Flavourful menu balances the classical and the creative.

X **Bleu,** Joshua House, Dawson St, D2, ☎ (01) 676 7015, *Fax (01) 676 7027* – ▤. MC AE ① VISA JZ r
closed Bank Holidays – **Meals** a la carte 22/36.20 ♀.
◆ Distinctive modern interior serves as chic background to this friendly all-day diner. Appealing bistro fare, well executed and very tasty. Good selection of wines by glass.

X **Dobbin's,** 15 Stephen's Lane, off Lower Mount St, D2, ☎ (01) 676 4679, *dobbinswine bistro@eircom.net, Fax (01) 661 3331,* – ▤ P. MC AE ① VISA EU s
closed 1 week Christmas-New Year, Sunday, Monday dinner, Saturday lunch and Bank Holidays – **Meals** - Bistro - (booking essential) 23.50/30 and dinner a la carte 51.50/61 ♀.
◆ In the unlikely setting of a former Nissen hut in a residential part of town, this popular restaurant, something of a local landmark, offers good food to suit all tastes.

Bruno's, 21 Kildare St, D2, ☎ (01) 662 4724, *Fax (01) 662 3857* – ▤. MC AE ⓓ VISA JZ m
closed first 2 weeks August, Christmas-New Year, Sunday and Monday – **Meals** 19/22 (lunch) and dinner la carte 31/39.
• Narrow wrought iron stairs lead down to this basement cellar restaurant opposite the parliament which serves interesting, attractively presented modern Irish cuisine.

Pearl Brasserie, 20 Merrion St Upper, D2, ☎ (01) 661 3572, *info@pearl-brasserie.com, Fax (01) 661 3629* – ▤. MC AE VISA KZ n
closed lunch Saturday-Monday – **Meals** - French - a la carte 29/43.50 ♀.
• A metal staircase leads down to this intimate, vaulted cellar brasserie and oyster bar. Franco-Irish dishes served at granite-topped tables. Amiable and helpful service.

The Bistro, 4-5 Castlemarket, D2, ☎ (01) 671 5430, *Fax (01) 6703379,* 🏠 – MC AE VISA JY c
closed 25-26 December, 1 January and Good Friday – **Meals** a la carte 22/45 ♀.
• Friendly and buzzing in the heart of the city. Exposed floor boards, coir carpeting and vividly coloured walls. Additional terrace area. Interesting, modern dishes.

Eden, Meeting House Sq, Temple Bar, D2, ☎ (01) 670 5372, *Fax (01) 670 3330,* 🏠 – ▤. MC AE VISA HY e
closed 25-30 December and Bank Holidays – **Meals** 19/22 (lunch) and dinner a la carte 29.50/44.50 ♀.
• Modern minimalist restaurant with open plan kitchen serves good robust food. Terrace overlooks theatre square, at the heart of a busy arty district. Children welcome.

Mermaid Café, 69-70 Dame St, D2, ☎ (01) 670 8236, *info@mermaid.ie, Fax (01) 670 8205* – ▤. MC VISA HY d
closed 24-26 and 31 December, 1 January and Good Friday – **Meals** (booking essential) 22.95 (lunch) and a la carte 27.40/50.85.
• This small informal restaurant with unfussy décor and wood floors offers an interesting and well cooked selection of robust modern dishes. Good service.

Cafe Mao, 2-3 Chatham Row, D2, ☎ (01) 670 4899, *info@cafemao.com, Fax (01) 670 4893* – ▤. MC VISA JZ r
closed Good Friday and 25-26 December – **Meals** - South East Asian - (bookings not accepted) a la carte 25.85/31.20.
• Well run trendy modern restaurant serving authentic southeast Asian fusion cuisine in an informal setting buzzing with action and atmosphere. Tasty food at tasty prices.

La Maison des Gourmets, 15 Castlemarket, D2, ☎ (01) 672 7258, *lamaison@indigo.ie, Fax (01) 864 5672* – MC AE VISA JY c
closed 25-28 December, Sunday and Bank Holidays – **Meals** (lunch only) a la carte 21/29 **s.**
• Simple, snug restaurant on the first floor above an excellent bakery offering high quality breads and pastries. Extremely good value meals using fine local ingredients.

The Cellar Bar (at The Merrion H.), Upper Merrion St, D2, ☎ (01) 603 0631, *info@merrionhotel.com, Fax (01) 603 0700* – 🚗. MC AE ⓓ VISA KZ e
Meals (live music Sunday brunch) (lunch only) (carving lunch) a la carte 21.25/25.75 ♀.
• Characterful stone and brick bar-restaurant in the original vaulted cellars with large wood bar. Popular with Dublin's social set. Offers wholesome Irish pub lunch fare.

Ballsbridge

Dublin 4.

Four Seasons, Simmonscourt Rd, D4, ☎ (01) 665 4000, *sales.dublin@fourseasons.com, Fax (01) 665 4099,* 🏋, ♨, 🏊, 🌳 – 🛗, ⇔ rm, ▤ 📺 ☎ ♿ 🚗 🅿 – 🎤 800. MC AE ⓓ VISA FU e
Seasons : **Meals** 34/49 (dinner) and a la carte 53/66 – ***The Cafe :*** **Meals** a la carte 34/45 – ☕ 28 – **192 rm** 395/435, 67 suites 625/2200.
• Every inch the epitome of international style - supremely comfortable rooms with every facility ; richly furnished lounge ; a warm mix of antiques, oils and soft piano études. Dining in Seasons guarantees luxury ingredients. Informal comforts in The Café.

The Berkeley Court, Lansdowne Rd, D4, ☎ (01) 6653200, *berkeleycourt@jurysdoyle.com, Fax (01) 6617238,* 🏋 – 🛗, ⇔ rm, ▤ 📺 ☎ ♿ 🚗 🅿 – 🎤 450. MC AE ⓓ VISA. ✂ FU c
Berkeley Room : **Meals** 45 – ***Palm Court Café :*** **Meals** 30 – ☕ 24 – **182 rm** 325/365, 5 suites.
• Luxurious international hotel in former botanical gardens ; two minutes from the home of Irish rugby. Large amount of repeat business. Solidly formal feel throughout. Berkeley Room for elegant fine dining. Breakfast buffets a feature of Palm Court Café.

The Towers, Lansdowne Rd, D4, ☎ (01) 660 5000, *towers@jurysdoyle.com, Fax (01) 660 5540,* 🏋, ♨, 🏊 heated – 🛗 ⇔ ▤ 📺 ☎ ♿ 🅿. MC AE ⓓ VISA. ✂ FU p
Meals 50 – ☕ 20 – **100 rm** 325/365, 4 suites.
• Comfortable, unstintingly equipped bedrooms, in keeping with the discreet service and the air of pleasing exclusivity. Private cocktail lounge, and use of Jurys facilities. Classic formal dining room with rich elegant décor.

Jurys, Pembroke Rd, D4, ☎ (01) 660 5000, *ballsbridge@jurysdoyle.com, Fax (01) 660 5540*, heated – rm, rest, TV – 800. MC AE VISA. FU p
***Raglans* : Meals** (carvery lunch Sunday) 50 – 20 – **300** 260/295, 3 suites.
◆ Well located hotel popular with business people. Bustling glass roofed lobby. Large well appointed rooms. Long-running Irish cabaret. Relaxed Raglans proud of its real Irish dishes.

Herbert Park, D4, ☎ (01) 667 2200, *reservations@herbertparkhotel.ie, Fax (01) 667 2595*, – rm, TV – 100. MC AE VISA. FU m
***The Pavilion* : Meals** *(closed dinner Sunday and Monday)* 23.50/29.50 **s.** – 19 – **150 rm** 230/275, 3 suites.
◆ Stylish contemporary hotel. Spacious, open, modern lobby and lounges. Excellent, well-designed rooms with tasteful décor. Some offer views of park. Good business facilities. French-windowed restaurant with al fresco potential ; oyster/lobster specialities.

The Hibernian, Eastmoreland Pl, D4, ☎ (01) 668 7666, *info@hibernianhotel.com, Fax (01) 660 2655* – TV – 30. MC AE VISA JCB. EU x
closed 24-27 December – ***Patrick Kavanagh Room* : Meals** *(closed Saturday and Sunday lunch, Bank Holidays and Sunday dinner to non-residents)* 19.95 (lunch) and dinner a la carte 24.50/37.40 – **40 rm** 222/277.50.
◆ Stately Victorian red brick house in suburbs which prides itself on its hospitality. Traditional, comfortable rooms with warmly elegant fittings. Small sun lounge. Well-presented modern European and Irish cuisine in restaurant.

The Schoolhouse, 2-8 Northumberland Rd, D4, ☎ (01) 667 5014, *reservations@schoolhousehotel.com, Fax (01) 667 5015*, – rm, TV MC AE VISA.
closed 24-27 December – ***The Canteen* : Meals** (bar lunch Saturday) a la carte 21.90/34.90 – **31 rm** 159/199. EU a
◆ Spacious converted 19C schoolhouse, close to canal, boasts modernity and charm. Rooms contain locally crafted furniture. Inkwell bar has impressive split-level seating area. Old classroom now a large restaurant with beamed ceilings.

Ariel House without rest., 52 Lansdowne Rd, D4, ☎ (01) 668 5512, *reservations@ariel-house.net, Fax (01) 668 5845* – TV MC VISA. FU n
closed 22-27 December – **37 rm** 99/150.
◆ Restored, listed Victorian mansion in smart suburb houses personally run, traditional small hotel. Rooms feature period décor and original antiques ; some four poster beds.

Bewley's, Merrion Rd, D4, ☎ (01) 668 1111, *bb@bewleyshotels.com, Fax (01) 668 1999*, – rm, rest, TV – 30. MC AE VISA. FU a
closed 24-26 December – ***O'Connells*** *(☎ (01) 647 3400)* **: Meals** (carvery lunch)/dinner 25 and a la carte 30/55 **s.** – 9.90 – **220 rm** 99.
◆ Huge hotel offers stylish modern accommodation behind sumptuous Victorian façade of former Masonic school. Location, facilities and value for money make this a good choice. Informal modern O'Connells restaurant, cleverly constructed with terrace in stairwell.

Butlers Town House, 44 Lansdowne Rd, D4, ☎ (01) 667 4022, *info@butlers-hotel.com, Fax (01) 667 3960* – TV MC AE VISA. FU v
closed 23 December-5 January – **Meals** (room service only) – **20 rm** 140/215.
◆ Restored red brick town house in heart of embassy quarter. Individually styled rooms designed to recreate Victorian atmosphere while offering modern facilities and comfort.

Aberdeen Lodge, 53-55 Park Ave, D4, ☎ (01) 283 8155, *aberdeen@iol.ie, Fax (01) 283 7877*, – TV MC AE VISA JCB. GV e
Meals (light meals) (residents only) a la carte 22/32.50 – **17 rm** 90/140.
◆ Neat red brick house in smart residential suburb. Comfortable rooms with Edwardian style décor in neutral tones, wood furniture and modern facilities. Some garden views. Comfortable, traditionally decorated dining room.

Pembroke Townhouse without rest., 90 Pembroke Rd, D4, ☎ (01) 660 0277, *info@pembroketownhouse.ie, Fax (01) 660 0291* – TV MC AE VISA. FU d
closed 22 December-2 January – **48 rm** 165/210.
◆ Period-inspired décor adds to the appeal of a sensitively modernised, personally run Georgian terrace town house in the smart suburbs. Neat, up-to-date accommodation.

Waterloo House without rest., 8-10 Waterloo Rd, D4, ☎ (01) 660 1888, *waterloohouse@eircom.ie, Fax (01) 667 1955*, – TV MC VISA. EU p
closed 23-28 December – **17 rm** 59/165.
◆ Pair of imposing Georgian town houses. Elegant breakfast room with conservatory. Large comfortable rooms with coordinated heavy drapes and fabrics in warm modern colours.

Merrion Hall, 54-56 Merrion Rd, D4, ☎ (01) 668 1426, *merrionhall@iol.ie, Fax (01) 668 4280*, – TV – 40. MC AE VISA JCB. FU b
Meals (light meals) (residents only) a la carte 22/32.50 – **30 rm** 90/140, 4 suites.
◆ Red brick house on main road in suburbs. Welcoming lounge with open fires and homely ornaments. Well-equipped, pastel hued bedrooms with modern facilities. Charming bright and open hotel dining room overlooks well- tended gardens.

Glenogra House without rest., 64 Merrion Rd, D4, ✆ (01) 668 3661, *glenogra@indigo.ie, Fax (01) 668 3698* – ⇔ TV P. MC AE D VISA. ⚘ FU w
closed 20 December-20 January – **12 rm** ☕ 69/105.
◆ Neat and tidy bay windowed house in smart suburb. Personally run guesthouse with bedrooms attractively decorated in keeping with a period property. Modern facilities.

Cedar Lodge without rest., 98 Merrion Rd, D4, ✆ (01) 668 4410, *info@cedarlodge.ie, Fax (01) 668 4533,* ⚘ – ⇔ TV P. MC AE VISA. ⚘ FU g
closed 22 December-2 January – **16 rm** ☕ 75/150.
◆ Large ivy-clad red brick Edwardian house with modern extensions and garden to rear. Comfortable en suite guestrooms with tasteful modern décor and good range of facilities.

Anglesea Town House without rest., 63 Anglesea Rd, D4, ✆ (01) 668 3877, *Fax (01) 668 3461* – ⇔ TV. MC AE VISA. ⚘ FV x
closed 21 December-5 January – **7 rm** ☕ 70/140.
◆ Red brick Edwardian residence in smart suburb with many pieces of fine period furniture. Individually styled rooms with good facilities. Parking can be a challenge.

66 Townhouse without rest., 66 Northumberland Rd, D4, ✆ (01) 660 0333, *Fax (01) 660 1051* – ⇔ TV P. MC VISA. ⚘ FU z
closed 23 December-6 January – **8 rm** ☕ 70/120.
◆ Attractive Victorian red brick house with extension in smart suburb. Comfortable homely atmosphere. Good size rooms with tasteful décor and modern facilities.

Siam Thai, Sweepstake Centre, D4, ✆ (01) 660 1722, *siam@eircom.net* – ▤. MC AE VISA JCB FU h
closed 25-26 December, lunch Saturday and Sunday and Good Friday – **Meals** - Thai - 32/33 (dinner) and a la carte 28.50/35.50.
◆ Unerringly busy restaurant that combines comfort with liveliness. Smart waiters serve authentic Thai cuisine, prepared with skill and understanding. Good value lunches.

Roly's Bistro, 7 Ballsbridge Terrace, D4, ✆ (01) 668 2611, *ireland@rolysbistro.ie, Fax (01) 660 8535* – ▤. MC AE D VISA FU r
closed 25-27 December and Good Friday – **Meals** (booking essential) 17.95 (lunch) and a la carte 35.10/42.45 ♀.
◆ A Dublin institution : this roadside bistro is very busy and well run, with a buzzy, fun atmosphere. Its two floors offer modern Irish dishes and a very good value lunch.

Bella Cuba, 11 Ballsbridge Terrace, D4, ✆ (01) 660 5539, *info@bella-cuba.com, Fax (01) 660 5539* – MC AE VISA FU r
Meals - Cuban - (booking essential) (dinner only and lunch Wednesday-Friday) 20 (lunch) and a la carte 30.25/36.75 ♀.
◆ Family-owned restaurant with an intimate feel. Cuban memoirs on walls, fine choice of cigars. Authentic Cuban dishes, employing many of the island's culinary influences.

Donnybrook

Dublin 4.

Marble Hall without rest., 81 Marlborough Rd, D4, ✆ (01) 497 7350, *marblehall@eircom.net* – ⇔ TV P EV a
closed December – **3 rm** ☕ 55/100.
◆ Georgian townhouse with effusive welcome guaranteed. Individually styled throughout, with plenty of antiques and quality soft furnishings. Stylish, warmly decorated bedrooms.

Eglinton Manor without rest., 83 Eglinton Rd, D4, ✆ (01) 269 3273, *Fax (01) 269 7527,* ⚘ – ⇔ TV P. MC AE VISA EV c
8 rm ☕ 64/150.
◆ Elegant red brick early Victorian house in smart suburb. Rooms traditionally furnished with warm neutral walls and dark wood period style furniture. Comfortable guesthouse.

Ernie's, Mulberry Gdns, off Morehampton Rd, D4, ✆ (01) 269 3300, *Fax (01) 269 3260* – ▤. MC AE D VISA FV k
closed 1 week Christmas, Easter, Sunday and Monday – **Meals** 14.50/40 and a la carte 47/64 ♀.
◆ Discreet professionally run restaurant in tranquil location offering classic Irish fare. Bright room with garden aspect, modern feel and contemporary Irish art collection.

Rathgar

Dublin 6.

St Aiden's without rest., 32 Brighton Rd, D6, ✆ (01) 490 2011, *staidens@eircom.net, Fax (01) 492 0234* – TV P. MC VISA. ⚘ DV n
closed 22-31 December – **8 rm** ☕ 65/110.
◆ Friendly, family run guesthouse in early Victorian mid-terrace. Comfortable lounge with tea, coffee and books. Ample rooms with simple décor and furniture. Good facilities.

Rathmines

Dublin 6.

Uppercross House, 26-30 Upper Rathmines Rd, D6, ✆ (01) 4975486, *enquiries@uppercrosshousehotel.com, Fax (01) 4975361* – |‡|, ⇹ rm, TV ✆ P. MO AE ⓓ VISA DV d
closed 24-28 December – ***The Restaurant*** : **Meals** (dinner only and lunch Friday-Sunday) a la carte 18.75/35.25 **s.** ♀ – **49 rm** ⊐ 85/156.
◆ Privately run suburban hotel in three adjacent town houses with modern extension wing. Good size rooms and standard facilities. Live music midweek in traditional Irish bar. Restaurant offers a mellow and friendly setting with welcoming wood décor.

Zen, 89 Upper Rathmines Rd, D6, ✆ (01) 4979428 – ▤. MO AE ⓓ VISA DV t
closed 25-27 December – **Meals** - Chinese (Szechuan) - (dinner only and lunch Thursday, Friday and Sunday) 15/18 (lunch) and a la carte 24/42.
◆ Renowned Chinese restaurant in the unusual setting of an old church hall. Imaginative, authentic oriental cuisine with particular emphasis on spicy Szechuan dishes.

Terenure

Dublin 6.

Vermilion, 1st Floor above Terenure Inn, 94-96 Terenure Road North, D6, South : 6 m. by N 81 ✆ (01) 499 1400, *mail@vermilion.ie, Fax (01) 499 1300* – ⇹. MO AE ⓓ VISA
closed 25-26 December and Good Friday – **Meals** - Indian - (dinner only and Sunday lunch) a la carte 29.90/44.40 ♀.
◆ Smart restaurant above a busy pub in a residential part of town. Vividly coloured dining room and efficient service. Well-balanced, modern Indian food with a Keralan base.

at Dublin Airport *North : 6 ½ m. by N 1 DU and M 1 – ✉ Dublin*

Great Southern, ✆ (01) 844 6000, *res@dubairport-gsh.com, Fax (01) 844 6001* – |‡|, ⇹ rm, TV ✆ ♿ P – 🔒 450. MO AE ⓓ VISA. ✂
closed 24-26 December – ***Potters*** : **Meals** 20/35 and dinner a la carte approx 45 **s.** – ***O'Deas Bar*** : **Meals** (carvery lunch)/dinner a la carte 15/20 **s.** – ⊐ 17 – **227 rm** 250, 2 suites.
◆ Modern hotel catering for international and business travellers. Range of guest rooms, all spacious and smartly furnished with wood furniture and colourful fabrics. Potters has a spacious, formal feel. O'Deas Bar for intimate carvery menus.

Holiday Inn Dublin Airport, ✆ (01) 808 0500, *reservations-dublinairport@6c.com, Fax (01) 844 6002* – ⇹ rm, ▤ rest, TV ✆ ♿ P – 🔒 130. MO AE ⓓ VISA
closed 25 December – ***Bistro*** : **Meals** 15.65/27.95 and dinner a la carte 24.50/38 ♀ – ***Sampan's*** : **Meals** - Asian - *(closed Bank Holidays)* (dinner only) a la carte 14.20/25.45 ♀ – ⊐ 16.45 – **247 rm** 189.
◆ Modern commercial hotel offers standard or Millennium rooms, all with colourful feel and good facilities. Free use of leisure centre. Live music at weekends in Bodhran bar. Informal Bistro restaurant with monthly themed menus. Oriental specials at Sampan's.

at Clontarf *Northeast : 3 ½ m. by R 105 KX – ✉ Dublin*

Clontarf Castle, Castle Ave, D3, ✆ (01) 833 2321, *info@clontarfcastle.ie, Fax (01) 833 2279,* Lδ – |‡|, ⇹ rm, TV ✆ ♿ P – 🔒 500. MO AE ⓓ VISA. ✂
closed 25 December – ***Templars Bistro*** : **Meals** (carvery lunch Monday-Saturday)/dinner 25 and a la carte 28.35/35.50 ♀ – ⊐ 20 – **108 rm** 250/285, 3 suites.
◆ Set in an historic castle, partly dating back to 1172. Striking medieval style entrance lobby. Modern rooms and characterful luxury suites, all with cutting edge facilities. Restaurant with grand medieval style décor reminiscent of a knights' banqueting hall.

at Stillorgan *Southeast : 5 m. on N 11 GV – ✉ Dublin*

Radisson SAS St Helen's, Stillorgan Rd, D4, ✆ (01) 218 6000, *info.dublin@radissonsas.com, Fax (01) 218 6010,* Lδ, ⚘ – |‡| ⇹ ▤ TV ✆ ♿ P – 🔒 350. MO AE ⓓ VISA JCB. ✂
Le Panto : **Meals** *(closed Sunday-Tuesday)* (dinner only) a la carte 46.25/54.25 **s.** ♀ – ***Talavera*** : **Meals** - Italian - 31.50 (lunch) and a la carte 36/46 **s.** ♀ – ⊐ 21.50 – **130 rm** 140/350, 21 suites.
◆ Imposing part 18C mansion with substantial extensions and well laid out gardens. Well run with good level of services. Smart modern rooms with warm feel and all facilities. Elegant, intimate Le Panto. Delicious antipasti table at basement Tolavera.

Stillorgan Park, Stillorgan Rd, ✆ (01) 288 1621, *sales@stillorganpark.com, Fax (01) 283 1610* – |‡|, ⇹ rm, ▤ TV ♿ P – 🔒 600. MO AE ⓓ VISA. ✂
Purple Sage : **Meals** (carvery lunch)/dinner 36.50 and a la carte 29.50/41.50 **s.** – **125 rm** ⊐ 170/195.
◆ Modern commercial hotel in southside city suburb. Spacious rooms with modern facilities. Interesting horse theme décor in large stone floored bar with buffet. Purple Sage restaurant with mosaics, frescos and hidden alcoves.

at Monkstown *Southeast : 6 ½ m. by R 118 GV – ✉ Dublin*

XX **Siam Thai,** 8a The Crescent, ✆ (01) 284 3309, *Fax (01) 4935841* – MC AE ① VISA
closed 25-26 December and Good Friday – **Meals** - Thai - (dinner only) 29 and a la carte approx 31.
◆ Popular Thai restaurant on main street opposite a church. Cosy interior with dark glossy décor and friendly ambience. Full range of authentic and popular Thai cuisine.

at Foxrock *Southeast : 7 ½ m. by N 11 GV – ✉ Dublin*

XX **Bistro One,** 3 Brighton Rd, D18, ✆ (01) 289 7711, *bistroone@eircom.ie, Fax (01) 289 9858* – MC VISA
closed 25 December, 1 January, Sunday and Monday – **Meals** (booking essential) (dinner only) a la carte 24/42.
◆ Pleasantly set in residential area. Homely, with beams and walls of wine racks. Simple menu offers well-prepared classic Irish fare and Italian or Asian influenced dishes.

at Clondalkin *Southwest : 8 m. by N 7 HY on R 113 – ✉ Dublin*

Red Cow Moran, Naas Rd, D22, Southeast : 2 m. on N 7 at junction with M 50 ✆ (01) 459 3650, *info@morangroup.ie, Fax (01) 459 1588* – |♦|, ⅹ rm, ▤ TV ✆ ♿ P – 🏛 700. MC AE ① VISA. ✂
closed 24-26 December – ***The Winter Garden :*** **Meals** 27.50/40 and dinner a la carte 32.80/50.45 ♀ – **120 rm** ☕ 130/210, 3 suites.
◆ Splendid sweeping lobby staircase gives a foretaste of this smart commercial hotel's mix of traditional elegance and modern design. Landmark Red Cow inn and Diva nightclub. Large characterful Winter Garden restaurant with bare brick walls and warm wood floor.

Bewley's H. Newlands Cross, Newlands Cross, Naas Rd (N 7), D22, ✆ (01) 464 0140, *res@bewleyshotels.com, Fax (01) 464 0900* – |♦|, ⅹ rm, ▤ rest, TV ✆ ♿ P. MC AE ① VISA. ✂
closed 25-26 December – **Meals** (carving lunch)/dinner a la carte 24/33.45 **s.** – ☕ 6.75 – **258 rm** 79.
◆ Well run, busy, commercial hotel popular with business people. Spacious rooms with modern facilities can also accommodate families. Represents good value for money. Large, busy café-restaurant with traditional dark wood fittings and colourful décor.

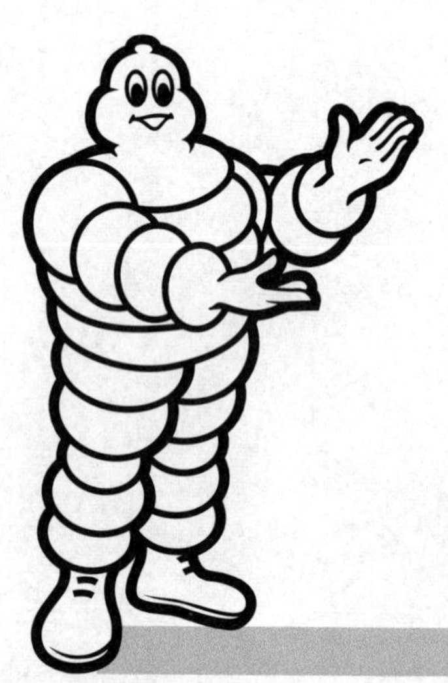

Italy

Italia

ROME – FLORENCE – MILAN – NAPLES
PALERMO – TAORMINA – TURIN – VENICE

PRACTICAL INFORMATION

LOCAL CURRENCY

1 euro (€) = 1,20 USD ($) (Dec 2003)

TOURIST INFORMATION

Welcome Office *(Azienda Promozione Turistica):*
– Via Parigi 5 - 00185 ROMA (closed Saturday afternoon and Sunday), ✆ 06 36 00 43 99, Fax 06 41 93 16
– Via Marconi 1 - 20123 MILANO, ✆ 02 72 52 43 01, Fax 02 72 52 43 50
See also telephone number and address of other Tourist Information offices in the text of the towns under 🅸*.*
American Express:
– Largo Caduti di El Alamein 9 - 00173 ROMA, ✆ 06 722801, Fax 06 72 22 30
– Via Larga 4 - 20122 MILANO, ✆ 02 72 10 41, Fax 02 89 00 990

National Holiday in Italy: *25 April.*

AIRLINES

ALITALIA: *Via Bissolati 13 - 00187 ROMA, ✆ 06 656 28 331, Fax 06 656 28 441*
Via Albricci 5 - 20122 MILANO, ✆ 02 24992700, Fax 02 805 67 57

AIR FRANCE: *Via Sardegna 40 - 00187 ROMA, ✆ 848884466, Fax 06 483803*
Piazza Cavour 2 - 20121 MILANO, ✆ 02 760731, Fax 02 760 73 355

DELTA AIRLINES: *via Malpensa 2000 - 20100 MILANO, ✆ 02 58 58 11 23, Fax 02 58 58 10 68*

FOREIGN EXCHANGE

Money can be changed at the Banca d'Italia, other banks and authorised exchange offices (Banks close at 1.30pm and at weekends).

POSTAL SERVICES

Local post offices: *open Monday to Friday 8.30am to 2.00pm (Saturday to noon)*

General Post Office *(open 24 hours only for telegrams):*
– Viale Europa 190 00144 ROMA – Piazza Cordusio 20123 MILANO

SHOPPING

In the index of street names, those printed in red are where the principal shops are found. In Rome, the main shopping streets are: Via del Babuino, Via Condotti, Via Frattina, Via Vittorio Veneto; in Milan: Via Dante, Via Manzoni, Via Monte Napoleone, Corso Vittorio Emanuele, Via della Spiga, Via Torino.

BREAKDOWN SERVICE

Certain garages in the centre and outskirts of towns operate a 24 hour breakdown service. If you break down the police are usually able to help by indicating the nearest one.

TIPPING

As well as the service charge, it is the custom to tip employees. The amount can vary depending upon the region and the service given.

SPEED LIMITS

On motorways, the maximum permitted speed is 130 km/h - 80 mph. On other roads, the speed limit is 90 km/h - 55 mph.

ROME

(ROMA)

00100 563 Q 19 38 *– Pop. 2 655 970 – alt. 20.*

Distances from Rome are indicated in the text of the other towns listed in this Guide.

via Parigi 5 ✉ 00185 ☎ 06 36 00 43 99, Fax 06 41 93 16 ;
Termini Station ☎ 06 47 82 51 94

A.C.I. *via Cristoforo Colombo 261 ✉ 00147 ☎ 06 514 971 and via Marsala 8 ✉ 00185 ☎ 06 49981, Fax 06 499 822 34.*

18 *and* 9 *Parco de' Medici (closed Tuesday) ✉ 00148 Roma SW : 4,5 km ☎ 06 655 34 77 – Fax 06 655 33 44.*

18 *Parco di Roma via Due Ponti 110 ✉ 00191 Roma N : 4,5 km. ☎ 06 33 65 33 96, Fax 06 33 66 09 31.*

18 *and* 9 *Marco Simone at Guidonia Montecelio ✉ 00012 Roma W : 7 km ☎ 0774 366 469, Fax 0774 366 476.*

18 *and* 9 *Arco di Costantino (closed Monday) ✉ 00188 Roma N : 15 km ☎ 06 33 62 44 40, Fax 06 33 61 29 19.*

18 *and* 9 *(closed Monday) at Olgiata ✉ 00123 Roma NW : 19 km ☎ 06 308 89 141, Fax 06 308 89 968.*

18 *Fioranello (closed Wednesday) at Santa Maria delle Mole ✉ 00040 Roma SE : 19 km ☎ 06 713 80 80, Fax 06 713 82 12.*

Ciampino SW : 15 km ☎ 794941.

Leonardo da Vinci di Fiumicino SE : 26 km ☎ 06 65631 – Alitalia, via Bissolati 20 ✉ 00187 ☎ 06 65621 and viale Alessandro Marchetti 111 ✉ 00148 ☎ 06 65643.

SIGHTS

How to make the most of a trip to Rome – some ideas :

Borghese Gallery★★★ *– Villa Giulia*★★★ DS *– Catacombs*★★★ *– Santa Sabina*★★ MZ *– Villa Borghese*★★ NOU *– Baths of Caracalla*★★★ ET *– St Lawrence Without the Walls*★★ FST **E** *– St Paul Without the Walls*★★ *– Old Appian Way*★★ *– National Gallery of Modern Art*★ DS **M**[7] *– Mausoleum of Caius Cestius*★ DT *– St Paul's Gate*★ DT **B** *– San'Agnese and Santa Costanza*★ FS **C** *– Santa Croce in Gerusalemme*★ FT **D** *– San Saba*★ ET *– E.U.R.*★ *– Museum of Roman Civilisation*★★.

ANCIENT ROME

Colosseum★★★ OYZ *– Roman Forum*★★★ NOY *– Basilica of Maxentius*★★★ OY **B** *– Imperial Fora*★★★ NY *– Trajan's Column*★★★ NY **C** *– Palatine Hill*★★★ NOYZ *– Pantheon*★★★ MVX *– Largo Argentina Sacred Precinct*★★ MY *– Altar of Augustus*★★ LU *– Temple of Apollo Sosianus*★★ MY **X** *– Theatre of Marcellus*★★ MY *– Tempio della Fortuna Virile*★ MZ **Y** *– Tempio di Vesta*★ MZ **Z** *– Isola Tiberina*★ MY.

CHRISTIAN ROME

Gesù Church★★★ MY – *St Mary Major*★★★ PX – *St John Lateran*★★★ FT – *Santa Maria d'Aracoeli*★★ NY **A** – *San Luigi dei Francesi*★★ LV – *Sant'Andrea al Quirinale*★★ OV **F** – *St Charles at the Four Fountains*★★ OV **K** – *St Clement's Basilica*★★ PZ – *Sant'Ignazio*★★ MV **L** – *Santa Maria degli Angeli*★★ PV **N** – *Santa Maria della Vittoria*★★ PV – *Santa Susanna*★★ OV – *Santa Maria in Cosmedin*★★ MNZ – *Basilica of St Mary in Trastevere*★★ KZ **S** – *Santa Maria sopra Minerva*★★ MX **V** – *Santa Maria del Popolo*★★ MU **D** – *New Church*★ KX – *Sant'Agostino*★ LV **G** – *St Peter in Chains*★ OY – *Santa Cecilia*★ MZ – *San Pietro in Montorio*★ JZ ≤★★★ – *Sant'Andrea della Valle*★★ LY **Q** – *Santa Maria della Pace*★ KV **R**.

PALACES AND MUSEUMS

Conservators' Palace★★★ MNY **M1** – *New Palace*★★★ *(Capitoline Museum*★★*)* NY **M1** – *Senate House*★★★ NY **H** – *Castel Sant'Angelo*★★★ JKV – *National Roman Museum*★★★ : *Aula Ottagona*★★★ PV **M9**, *Palazzo Massimo alle Terme* PV and *Altemps Palace*★★★ KLV – *Chancery Palace*★★ KX **A** – *Palazzo Farnese*★★ KY – *Quirinal Palace*★★ NOV – *Barberini Palace*★★ OV – *Villa Farnesina*★★ KY – *Palazzo Venezia*★ MY **M3** – *Palazzo Braschi*★ KX **M4** – *Palazzo Doria Pamphili*★ MX **M5** – *Palazzo Spada*★ KY – *Museo Napoleanico*★ KV.

THE VATICAN

St Peter's Square★★★ HV – *St Peter's Basilica*★★★ *(Dome* ≤★★★*)* GV – *Vatican Museums*★★★ *(Sistine Chapel*★★★*)* GHUV – *Vatican Gardens*★★★ GV.

PRETTY AREAS

Pincian Hill ≤★★★ MU – *Capitol Square*★★★ MNY – *Spanish Square*★★★ MNU – *Piazza Navona*★★★ LVX – *Fountain of the Rivers*★★★ LV **E** – *Trevi Fountain*★★★ NV – *Victor Emmanuel II Monument (Vittoriano)* ≤★★ MNY – *Quirinale Square*★★ NV – *Piazza del Popolo*★★ MU – *Gianicolo*★ JY – *Via dei Coronari*★ KV – *Ponte Sant'Angelo*★ JKV – *Piazza Bocca della Verità*★ MNZ – *Piazza Campo dei Fiori*★ KY **28** – *Piazza Colonna*★ MV **46** – *Porta Maggiore*★ FT – *Piazza Venezia*★ MNY.

STREET INDEX TO ROMA TOWN PLANS

Accaia (Via) .... **FT**
Adriana (Piazza) .... **JKV**
Albania (Piazza) .... **NZ**
Albenga (Via) .... **FT** 4
Alberteschi (Lungotevere) **MZ** 6
Aldrovandi (Via U.) .... **ES**
Altoviti (Lungotev. d.) .... **JV** 7
Amba Aradam (Via) ...... **PZ**
Angelico (Viale) .... **HU**
Anguillara
(Lungotereve d.) .... **LY** 9
Aosta (Via) .... **FT** 10
Arenula (Via) .... **LY**
Armi (Lungotev. d.) ...... **DS**
Augusta
(Lungotevere in) .... **LU**
Aurelia Antica (Via) ...... **GZ**
Aventino (Lungotevere) ... **MZ**
Aventino (Viale) .... **NZ**
Babuino (Via d.) .... **MU**
Bacelli (Viale) .... **ET** 12
Banchi Nuovi (Via d.) .... **KV** 13
Banchi Vecchi (Via d.) ... **KX** 15
Banco S. Spirito (Via d.) . **JV** 16
Barberini (Via) .... **OV**
Bari (Via) .... **FS**
Barletta (Via .... **HU**
Barrili (Via) .... **CT**
Bassi (Via U.) .... **JZ**
Battisti (Via C.) .... **NX** 19
Beccaria (Via C.) .... **LU**
Belle Arti (Viale d.) ...... **DS**
Belli (Piazza G. G.) .... **LYZ** 22
Bissolati (Via L.) .... **OU**
Bocca della Verità
(Piazza della) .... **NZ**
Boncompagni (Via) .... **OPU**
Bonghi (Via R.) .... **PY**
Botteghe Oscure (Via d.) . **MY** 22
Brasile (Piazzale) .... **OU**
Brescia (Lungotev. A. da) . **KU**
Britannia (Via) .... **FT** 24
Brofferio (Via A.) .... **JU**
Buozzi (Viale B.) .... **ES**
Busiri-Vici (Via A.) .... **HZ** 25
Cadiolo (Via A.) .... **CS**
Calabria (Via) .... **PU** 27
Campania (Via) .... **OPU**
Campidoglio (Pza d.) ..... **MY**
Campo dei Fiori (Piazza) . **KY** 28
Candia (Via) .... **GU**
Canonica (Vle P.) .... **NU**
Cappellari (Via d.) .... **KX** 30
Caravita (Via) .... **MV** 31
Carini (Via G.) .... **JZ**
Carso (Viale) .... **CS**
Casilina (Via) .... **FT** 33
Castello (Lungotev.) ...... **KV** 34
Castrense (Viale) .... **FT** 36
Castro Pretorio (Viale) .... **FS** 37
Catania (Via) .... **FS**
Cavalieri di Vittorio
Veneto (Viale d.) .... **CS** 39
Cavalli Marini (Vle d.) .... **ES** 40
Cavour (Piazza) .... **KV**
Cavour (Ponte) .... **KV**
Cavour (Via) .... **OY**
Cenci (Lungotev. d.) ...... **MY**
Cerchi (Via d.) .... **NZ**
Cesi (Via F.) .... **KU**
Cestio (Ponte) .... **MZ**
Chiana (Via) .... **FS**
Cicerone (Via) .... **KU**
Cinque Lune (Pza) .... **LV** 43
Cinquecento (Pza d.) ..... **PV**
Cipro (Via) .... **GU**
Circo Massimo (Via d.) ... **NZ**
Claudia (Via) .... **PZ**
Clementino (Via d.) ...... **MV** 45
Clodia
(Circonvallazione) ...... **CS**
Collina (Via) .... **PU**
Colonna (Piazza) .... **MV** 46
Colonna (Via M. A.) ...... **JKU**
Colonna (Via V.) .... **KV** 48
Conciliazione (V. d.) ..... **JV**
Condotti (Via d.) .... **MV**
Consolazione (V. d.) ..... **NY** 49
Conte Vezrde (Via) .... **FT** 51
Coronari (Via d.) .... **KV**
Corridoni (Via F.) .... **CS** 52
Corridori (Via d.) .... **HV** 54
Corso (Via d.) .... **MU**
Crescenzio (Via) .... **JU**
D'Annunzio (Vle G.) ...... **MU** 55
Damiata (Via) .... **JU**
Dandolo (Via) .... **KZ**
De Rossi (Via G. B.) ...... **FS**
Della Rovere (Pza) .... **JV** 57
Depretis (Via A.) .... **PV**
Dezza (Via G.) .... **HZ**
Dogana Vecchia
(V. della) .... **LV** 58
Domus Aurea (Via) .... **PY**
Doria (Via Andrea) .... **GU**
Druso (Via) .... **ET**
Due Macelli (Via) .... **NV**
Duilio (Via) .... **JU** 60
Einaudi (Viale L.) .... **PV** 61
Eleniana (Via) .... **FT** 63
Emo (Via A.) .... **GU**
Eroi (Piazzale d.) .... **GU**
Esquilino (Piazza di) ..... **PV**
Etruria (Via) .... **FT**

Fabricio (Ponte) MY 64
Farnesina (Lungotevere d.) KY
Fedro (Via) CS
Felice (Via C.) FT
Ferrari (Via G.) JU
Ferratella (Via d.) ET 67
Filiberto (Via E.) FT 69
Fiorentini (Lungotevere d.) JV 70
Fiume (Piazza) PU
Flaminia (Via) LU 73
Flaminnio (Lungotev.) DS
Florida (Via) MY
Fontanella Borghese (Via) MV 76
Fonteiana (Via) GZ
Fori Imperiali (Via d.) OY
Fornaci (Via d.) HYZ
Foro Olitorio (Via d.) MY 78
Franklin (Via B.) DT
Frattina (Via) MV
Gallia (Via) PZ
Galvani (Via) DT
Garibaldi (Ponte) LY 81
Garibaldi (Via) JY
Gelsomini (Viale) DT 82
Germanico (Via) JU
Gianicolense (Lungotevere) JX
Gianicolo (Passeggiata di) HY
Gianicolo (Via d.) HX 85
Giolitti (Via FT
Giotto (Viale) ET
Giovannelli (Via R.) ES 87
Giubbonari (Via d.) LY
Giulia (Via) KY
Giuliana (Via d.) GU
Giulio Cesare (Viale) JU
Glorioso (Viale) KZ
Gomenizza (Via) CS
Gorizia (Viale) FS
Governo Vecchio (Via d.) KV 88
Gracchi (Via d.) JU
Greca (Via d.) MZ 90
Gregorio VII (Viale) GY
Induno (Via G.) KZ
Ippocrate (Viale) FS
Ipponio (Via) PZ
Italia (Corso d') PU
Jugario (Vico) MY 91
La Malfa (Piazzale U.) NZ
La Spezia (Via) FT
Labicana (Via) PZ
Lanciani (Via R.) FS
Lanza (Via G.) PY
Lepanto (Via) JU
Libertà (Piazza d.) KU
Liegi (Viale) ES
Lucania (Via) PU 94
Lucce (Via d.) LZ
Ludovisi (Via) OU
Lungara (Via d.) JY
Lungaretta (Via d.) KZ 96
Magna Grecia (V.) FT
Magnolie (Vle d.) NU
Mameli (Via G.) KZ
Manara (Via L.) KZ
Manzoni (Viale) FT
Maresciallo Pilsudski (Viale) DS 102
Margutta (Via) MU
Marmorata (Via) DT
Marsala (Via) FT
Marzio (Lungotevere) LV
Mascherone (V. d.) KY 103
Massina (Via A.) JZ 105
Matteotti (Ponte G.) KU
Mazzini (Ponte) JY
Mazzini (Viale G.) DS
Mecenate (Via) PY
Medaglie d'Oro (V.) GU
Medici (Via G.) JZ
Mellini (Lungotev.) LU
Merulana (Via) PY
Michelangelo (Lungotevere) KU
Milano (Via) OX
Milizie (Viale d.) JU
Monserrato (Via) KY 106
Mte Brianzo (V.) LV 107
Montebello (Via) PU
Monza (Via) FT 108
Morgagni (Via) FS 109
Morosini (Via E.) KZ

Mura Aurelie (Vle) HY
Muro Torto (Vle) MU
Museo Borghese (Viale d.) OU
Navi (Lungotev. d.) DS
Navicella (Via d.) PZ
Navona (Piazza) LX
Nazionale (Via) OV
Nenni (Ponte P.) KU 111
Nizza (Via) PU
Nomentana (Via) FS
Oberdan (Lungotev.) DS
Oslavia (Via) CS
Ottaviano (Via) HU
Paglia (Via d.) KZ 114
Palatino (Ponte) MZ
Panama (Via) ES
Panisperna (Via) PX
Parioli (Viale d.) ES
Petroselli (Via) MZ
Piave (Via) PU
Piemonte (Via) OU
Pierleoni (Lungotevere) MZ 117
Pinciana (Via) OU
Pio (Borgo) JV
Piramide Cestia (Viale di) DT 118
Pisani (Via V.) GU
Platone (Viale) GU 120
Plebiscito (Via d.) MY 121
Po (Via) OU
Poerio (Via A.) CT
Policlinico (Via d.) FS 123
Pompeo Magno (Via) KU
Popolo (Piazza d.) MU
Pta Angelica (V.) HV 126
Pta Capena (Pza di) OZ
Pta Cavalleggeri (V.) GV
Pta Lavernale (V.) MZ 127
Porta Maggiore (Piazza di) FT
Porta Metronia (Piazza di) PZ
Porta Pinciana (V.) NU
Pta Portese (Pza) LZ
Porta Portese (Via) LZ 129
Portico d'Ottavia (V.) MY 130
Portuense (Via) KZ
Prati (Lungotevere) LV
Pretoriano (Viale) FT 133
Prince A. Savoia Aosta (Ponte) JV 135
Principe Amedeo (Galleria) HV
Principe Amedeo (Via) PVX
Province (Via d.) FS
Publicii (Clivo d.) NZ 136
Quattro Fontane (Via d.) OV
Quirinale (Pza d.) NV
Quirinale (Via d.) OV 138
Ravenna (Via) FS
Regina Elena (V.) FS
Regina Margherita (Ponte) KU 139
Regina Margherita (Viale) FS
Regolo (Via A.) JU 141
Repubblica (Piazza di) PV
Rienzo (Via Cola di) JU
Rinascimento (Corso d.) LX 142
Ripa (Lungotev.) MZ
Ripa Grande (Porto di) LMZ
Ripetta (Via di) MU
Risorgimento (Piazza) HU
Risorgimenta (Pte) DS 144
Rossetti (Via G.) JZ
Rotonda (Via) MX 147
Rovigo (Via FS 148
Saffi (Viale A.) KZ 150
Sallustiana (Via) PU
S. Alessio (Via) NZ
S. Angelo (Borgo) JV 151
S. Angelo (Ponte) KV
S. Chiara (Via) MX 153
S. Cosimato (Pza) KZ
S. Francesco d'Assisi (Piazza) LZ
S. Francisco a Ripa (Via di) KZ
S. Giovanni in Laterano (Via) PZ
S. Gregorio (Via) OZ
S. Ignazio (Piazza) MV 156

S. Marco (Via) MY 157
S. Maria del Pianto (Via) MY 159
S. Maria Maggiore (Via) PX 160
S. Pancrazio (Via) HZ
S. Pietro (Piazza) HV
S. Prisca (Via di) NZ 162
S. Sabina (Via di) MZ
S. Sonnino (Pza) LZ
S. Spirito (Borgo) JV
S. Stefano Rotondo (Via di) PZ
S. Teodoro (Via) NY
S. Uffizio (Via d.) HV 165
Sangallo (Lungotevere d.) JX
Sanzio (Lungotev.) LY
Sassia (Lungotev. in) JV
Savoia (Via F. di) LU 166
Savoia (Via L. di) LU
Scala (Via d.) KY
Scalo S. Lorenzo (Via) FT
Scipioni (Via d.) JU
Scrofa (Via d.) LV
Seminario (Via d.) MV 168
Sistina (Via) NV
Sisto (Ponte) KY
Spagna (Piazza di) NU
Sprovieri (Via F. S.) HZ 171
Statuto (Via d.) PY
Stelletta (Via d.) MV 174
Sublicio (Ponte) LZ
Tassoni (Largo) JV
Teatro di Marcello (Via d.) MY 175
Tebaldi (Lungotev. d.) KY
Terme Deciane (V.) NZ 177
Terme di Caracalla (Viale d.) OZ
Testaccio (Lungotev.) LZ 178
Teulada (Via) CS
Tevere (Via) PU
Tiziano (Viale) DS
Tomacelli (Via) MV
Tor di Nona (Lungotevere) KV
Torlonia (Via) FS
Torre Argentina (Via) MY 180
Traforo (Via d.) NV 181
Trastevere (Viale) KZ
Tre Madonne (V.) ES 183
Trieste (Corso) FS
Trinità dei Monti (Vle) NU
Trionfale (Circ.) GU
Tritone (Via d.) NV
Tuscolana (Via) FT 184
Uffici del Vicario (V.) MV 186
Umberto I (Ponte) KV
Università (Viale d.) FS
Vallati (Lungotev.) LY
Valle Giulia (Viale) ES 187
Valle Murcia (Via) NZ 189
Vascello (Via d.) HZ
Vaticano (Lungotev.) JV 190
Vaticano (Viale) GV
Venezia (Piazza) NY
Venezian (Via G.) KZ 192
Vercelli (Via) FT
Villa Massimo (Vle) FS 193
Villa Pamphili (Vle) HZ
Viminale (Via d.) PV
Virgilio (Via) JU
Vitellia (Via) GZ
Vittoria (Lungotevere d.) CS
Vittorio Emanuele II (Corso) KX
V. Emanuele II (Ponte) JV 195
V. Emanuele Orlando (Via) PV 196
Vittorio Veneto (Via) OU
Volturno (Via) PV 198
Zanardelli (Via) KV 199
4 Novembre (Via) NX 201
20 Settembre (V.) PU
24 Maggio (Via) NX
30 Aprile (Viale) JZ 202
XXI-Aprile (Viale FS

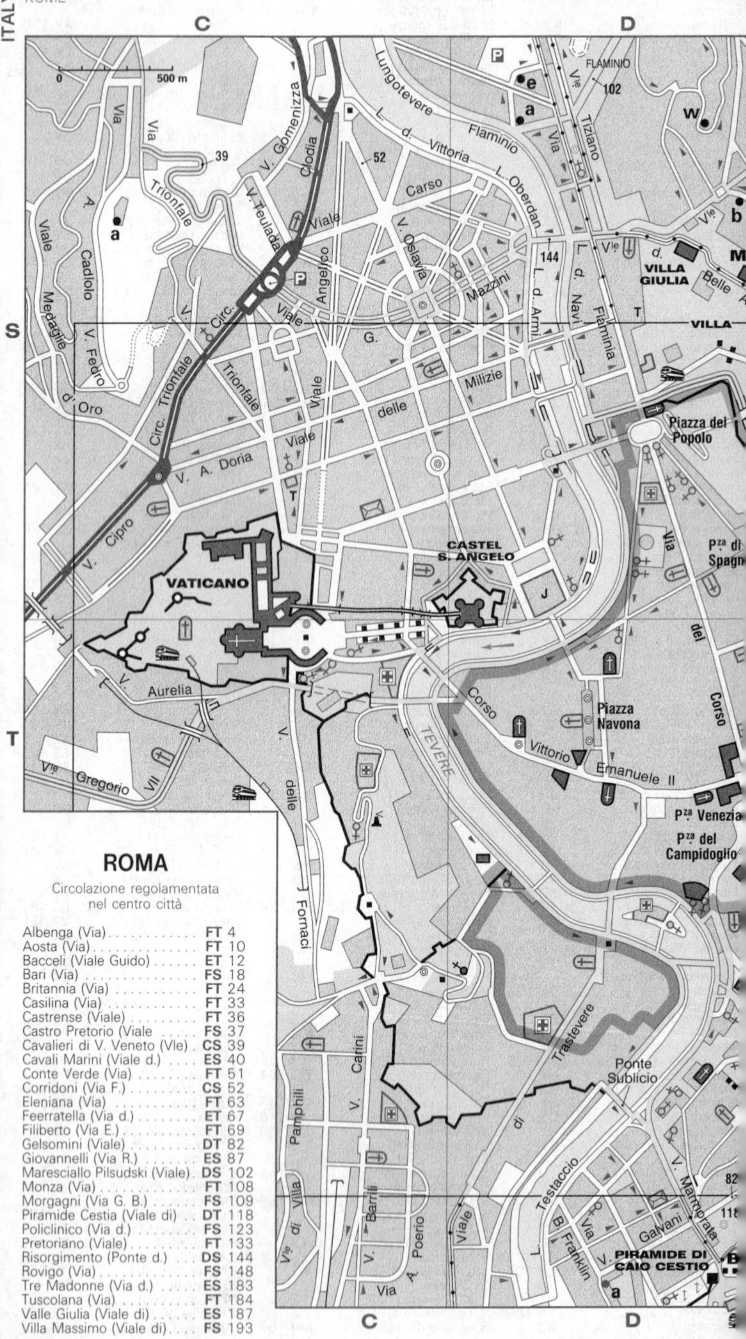
ROMA
Circolazione regolamentata
nel centro città
Albenga (Via) . . . . FT 4
Aosta (Via) . . . . FT 10
Bacceli (Viale Guido) . . . . . . ET 12
Bari (Via) . . . . FS 18
Britannia (Via) . . . . FT 24
Casilina (Via) . . . . FT 33
Castrense (Viale) . . . . FT 36
Castro Pretorio (Viale . . . . . . FS 37
Cavalieri di V. Veneto (Vle) . CS 39
Cavali Marini (Viale d.) . . . . ES 40
Conte Verde (Via) . . . . FT 51
Corridoni (Via F.) . . . . CS 52
Eleniana (Via) . . . . FT 63
Feerratella (Via d.) . . . . ET 67
Filiberto (Via E.) . . . . FT 69
Gelsomini (Viale) . . . . DT 82
Giovannelli (Via R.) . . . . ES 87
Maresciallo Pilsudski (Viale) . DS 102
Monza (Via) . . . . FT 108
Morgagni (Via G. B.) . . . . . . FS 109
Piramide Cestia (Viale di) . . DT 118
Policlinico (Via d.) . . . . FS 123
Pretoriano (Viale) . . . . FT 133
Risorgimento (Ponte d.) . . . DS 144
Rovigo (Via) . . . . FS 148
Tre Madonne (Via d.) . . . . . ES 183
Tuscolana (Via) . . . . FT 184
Valle Giulia (Viale di) . . . . . ES 187
Villa Massimo (Viale di) . . . FS 193
C
D
S
T
500 m
VATICANO
CASTEL S. ANGELO
Piazza del Popolo
Piazza Navona
P.za di Spagna
P.za Venezia
P.za del Campidoglio
VILLA GIULIA
TEVERE
Ponte Sublicio
PIRAMIDE DI CAIO CESTIO
FLAMINIO
Lungotevere Flaminio
Viale G. Cesare
V. A. Doria
V. Cipro
V. Aurelia
Corso Vittorio Emanuele II
Viale di Trastevere
Via delle Fornaci
V. Carini
Via Marmorata
Testaccio

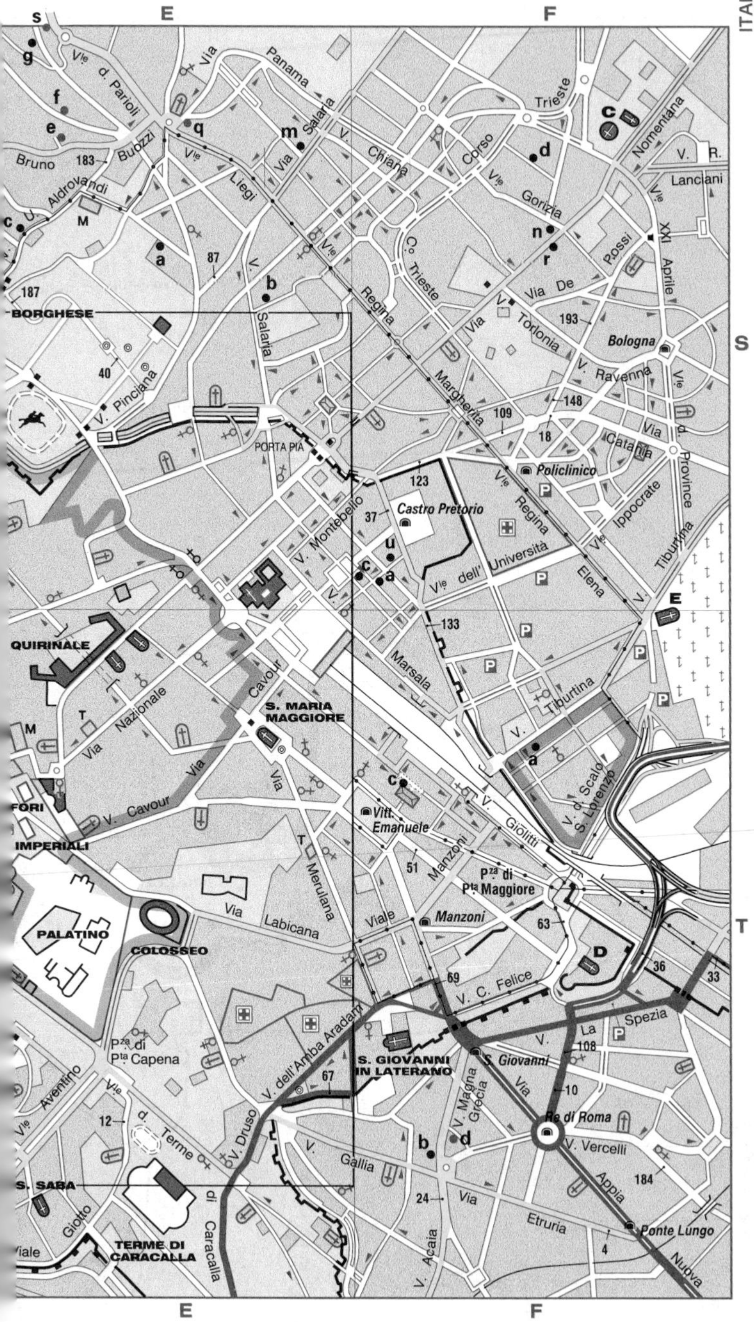

E
F
S
T
BORGHESE
V. Pinciana
PORTA PIA
Castro Pretorio
Policlinico
Bologna
QUIRINALE
S. MARIA MAGGIORE
FORI IMPERIALI
PALATINO
COLOSSEO
S. GIOVANNI IN LATERANO
S. SABA
TERME DI CARACALLA
Vittorio Emanuele
Manzoni
S. Giovanni
Re di Roma
Ponte Lungo
Vle d. Parioli
Via Panama
Via Salaria
V. Chiana
Corso Trieste
Trieste
Nomentana
Vle Gorizia
Vle Liegi
Vle Buozzi
Bruno
Aldrovandi
Vle Regina Margherita
Via De Possi
V. Torlonia
V. Ravenna
Vle XXI Aprile
V. R. Lanciani
Via Catania
Vle d. Province
Vle Ippocrate
Tiburtina
Vle Regina Elena
Vle dell' Università
V. Montebello
Marsala
Tiburtina
V. d. Scalo S. Lorenzo
V. Giolitti
Via Nazionale
Via Cavour
V. Cavour
Via Merulana
Via Labicana
Viale Manzoni
Pza di Pta Maggiore
V. C. Felice
V. La Spezia
Via Appia Nuova
V. Vercelli
V. Magna Grecia
V. dell'Amba Aradam
V. Druso
V. Gallia
Via Etruria
V. Acaia
Pza di Pta Capena
Vle Aventino
Vle d. Terme di Caracalla
Viale Giotto
183
187
87
40
193
148
109
18
123
37
133
51
63
36
33
69
108
10
67
12
184
24
4
a
b
c
d
e
f
g
m
n
q
r
s
u
C
D
E
M
T
P

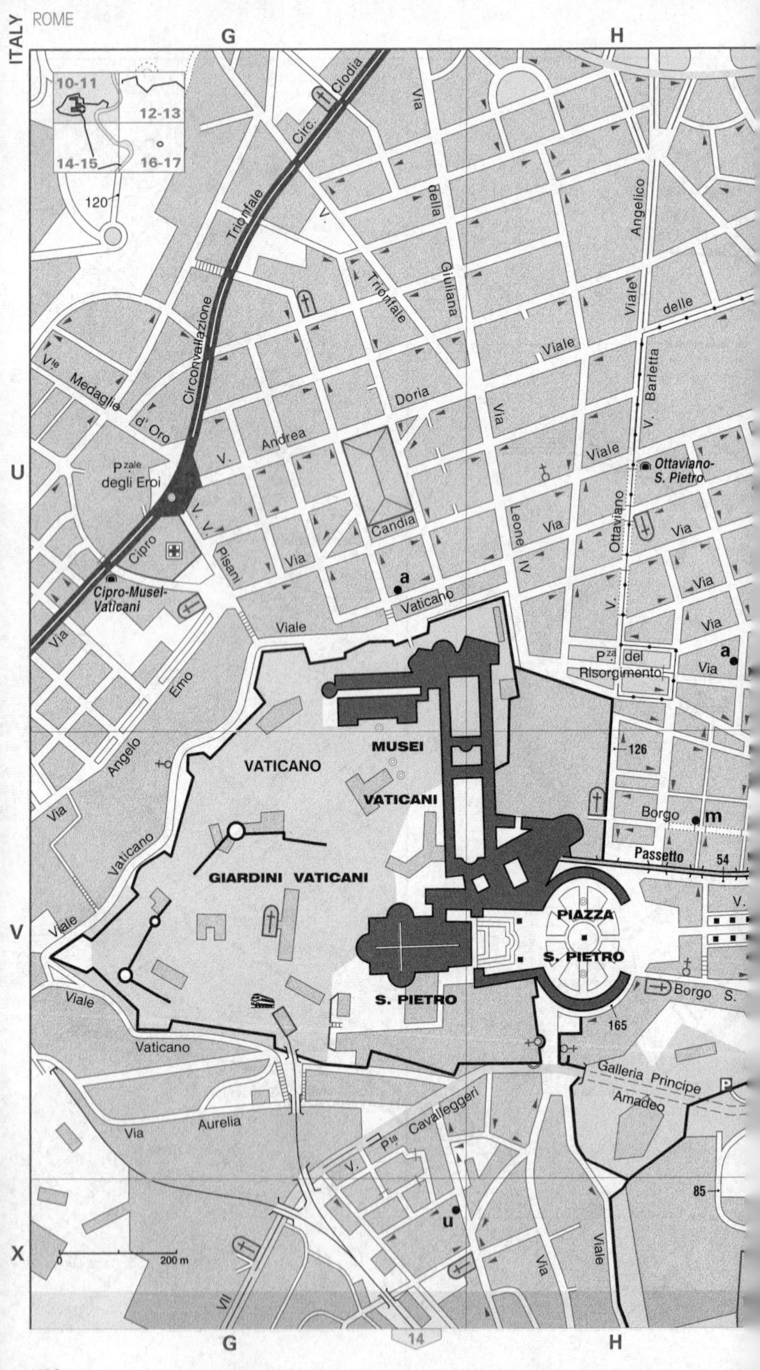
G
H
10-11
12-13
14-15
16-17
120
Clodia
Circ.
Via
Trionfale
Circonvallazione
V.
della
Giuliana
Trionfale
Angelico
Viale
delle
Viale
Barletta
V.
Vle
Medaglie
d' Oro
Andrea
Doria
Via
Viale
U
Pzale
degli Eroi
V.
V. V.
Candia
Leone IV
Via
Ottaviano
Ottaviano-
S. Pietro
Via
Cipro
Pisani
Via
a
Cipro-Musei-
Vaticani
Vaticano
Viale
V.
Via
Via
Via
Pza del
Risorgimento
Via
a
Emo
Angelo
126
VATICANO
MUSEI
VATICANI
Via
Vaticano
Borgo
m
Passetto
54
GIARDINI VATICANI
V.
V
Viale
PIAZZA
S. PIETRO
Viale
S. PIETRO
Borgo S.
165
Vaticano
Galleria Principe
Amadeo
Via
Aurelia
Pta
Cavalleggeri
V.
85
u
X
0
200 m
Viale
Via
VII
G
14
H

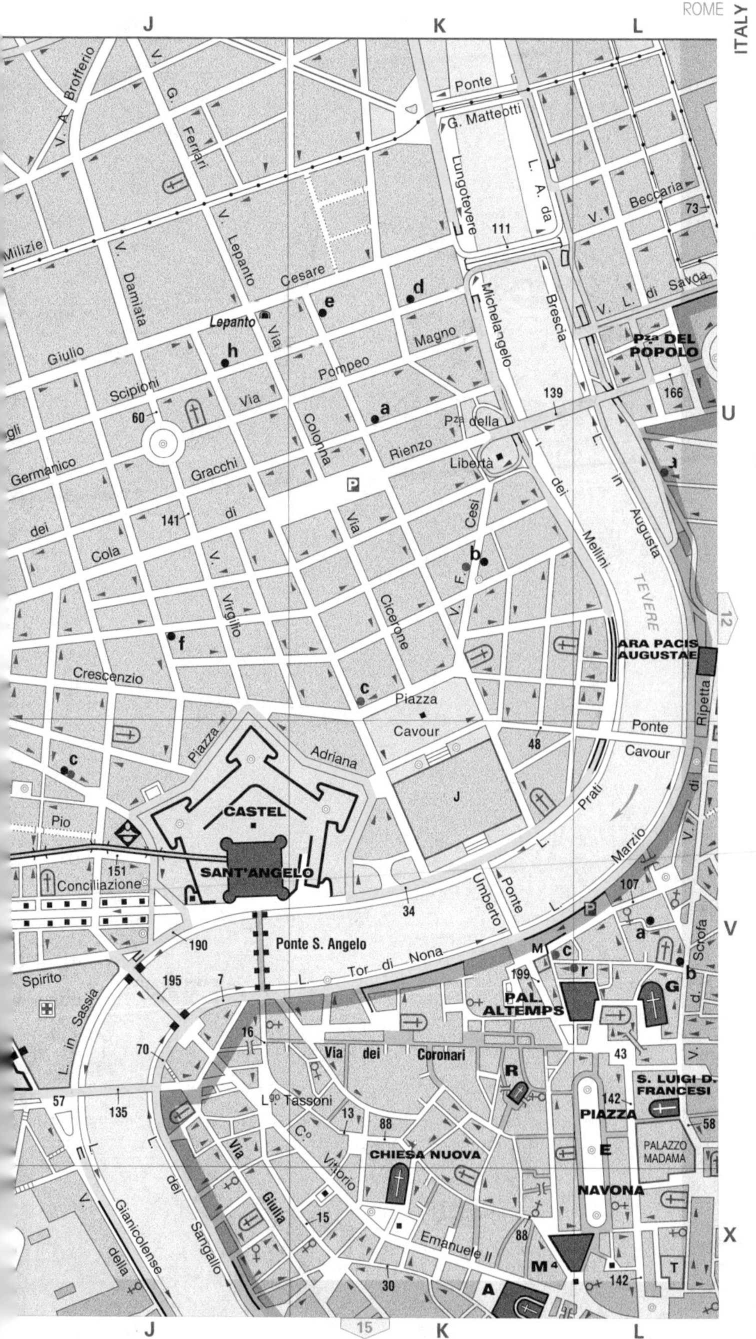
J
K
L
Ponte
G. Matteotti
Lungotevere
L. A. da
Beccaria
V.
73
111
V. A. Brofferio
V. G. Ferrari
Milizie
V. Damiata
V. Lepanto
Cesare
e
d
Lepanto
Via
V. L. di Savoia
Michelangelo
Brescia
Pza DEL POPOLO
Giulio
h
Magno
Pompeo
Scipioni
Via
Colonna
a
Pza della
Libertà
139
166
U
60
Germanico
Gracchi
Rienzo
141
di
dei
Cola
Via
Cesi
b
V. F.
V.
Virgilio
Cicerone
L. dei Mellini
L. in Augusta
TEVERE
12
f
ARA PACIS AUGUSTAE
Crescenzio
c
Piazza
Cavour
Ripetta
Ponte
Cavour
Piazza
Adriana
48
c
J
Prati
V. di
CASTEL
SANT'ANGELO
L.
Marzio
Pio
151
Conciliazione
34
Umberto I
Ponte
107
a
Scrofa
190
Ponte S. Angelo
V
M
c
r
b
Spirito
195
7
L. Tor di Nona
199
PAL. ALTEMPS
G
in Sassia
16
Via dei Coronari
43
70
R
S. LUIGI D. FRANCESI
57
135
Lgo Tassoni
13
88
142
PIAZZA
58
C.o Vittorio
CHIESA NUOVA
E
PALAZZO MADAMA
Via Giulia
NAVONA
L.
L. del Sangallo
15
88
Gianicolense
della
Emanuele II
M4
X
30
A
142
T
J
15
K
L

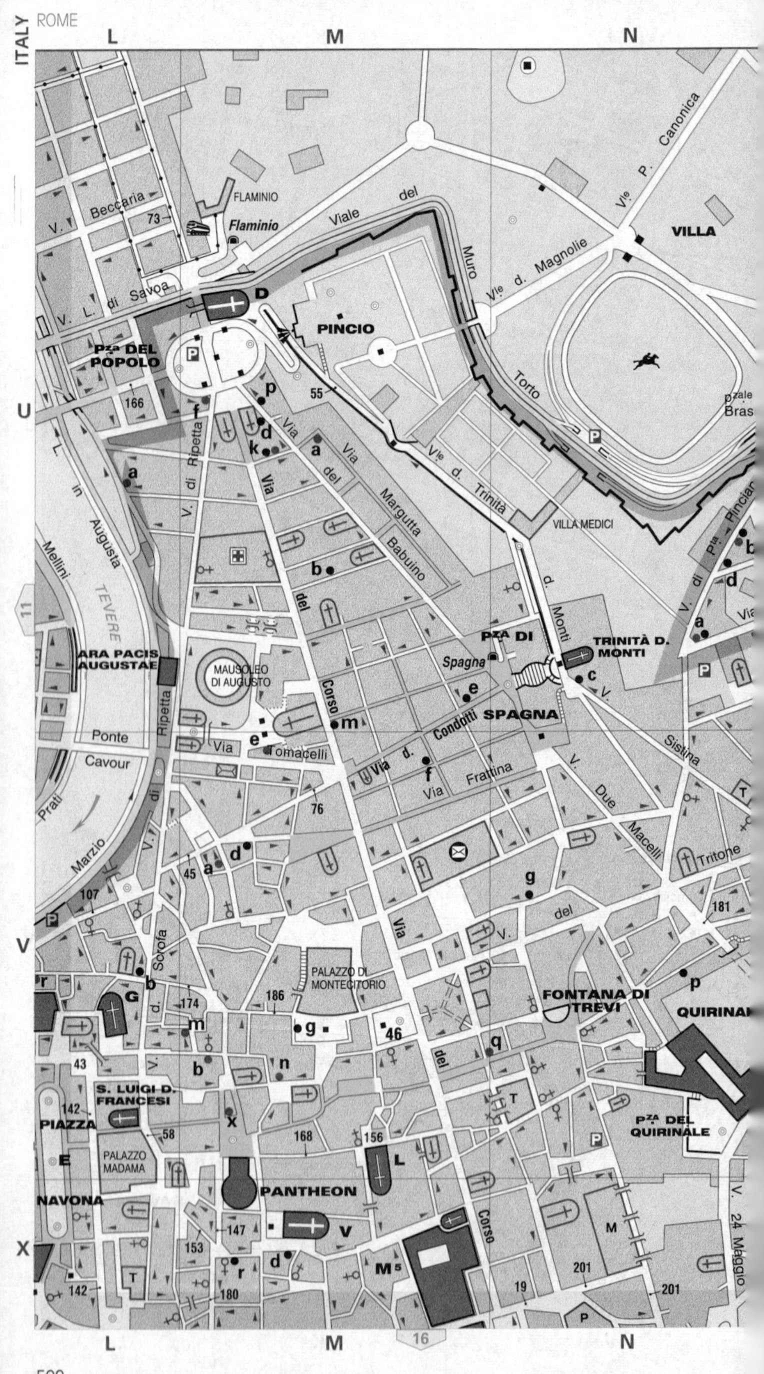
L
M
N
FLAMINIO
Flaminio
V. Beccaria
Viale del Muro Torto
V. L. di Savoia
D
PINCIO
Vle d. Magnolie
Vle P. Canonica
VILLA
Pza DEL POPOLO
Vle d. Trinità d. Monti
VILLA MEDICI
Via Margutta
Via del Babuino
V. di Ripetta
L. in Augusta
Mellini
TEVERE
ARA PACIS AUGUSTAE
MAUSOLEO DI AUGUSTO
Pza DI Spagna
TRINITÀ D. MONTI
SPAGNA
Via Condotti
Via Frattina
V. Sistina
V. Due Macelli
Via Tomacelli
Ponte Cavour
Prati
Marzio
Corso
Via del Corso
Tritone
V. di P.ta Pinciana
pzale Bras
PALAZZO DI MONTECITORIO
FONTANA DI TREVI
QUIRINALE
Pza DEL QUIRINALE
S. LUIGI D. FRANCESI
PIAZZA NAVONA
PALAZZO MADAMA
PANTHEON
V. d. Scrofa
V. 24 Maggio
U
V
X
16
11

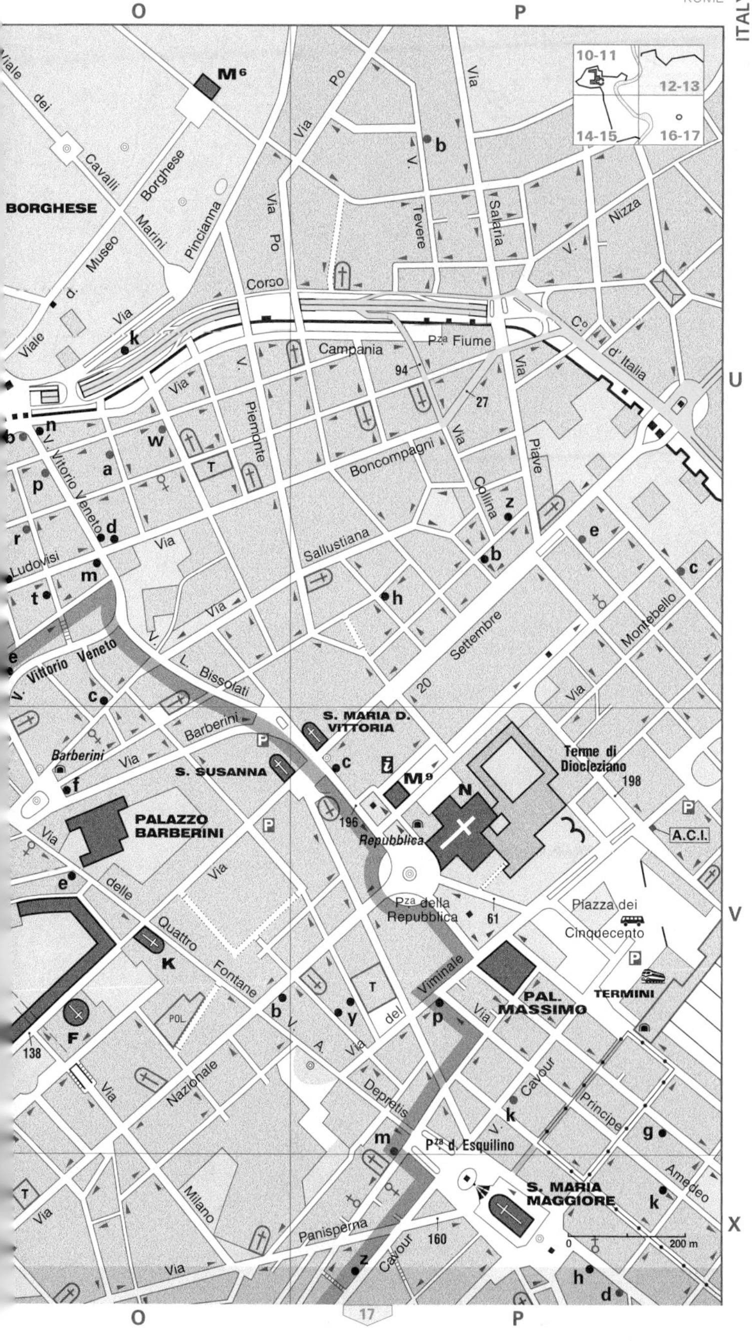

O P

BORGHESE
M6
Viale dei Cavalli Marini
Via Borghese
Viale d. Museo
Via Pinciana
Via Po
Via Po
V. Tevere
Via Salaria
V. Nizza
Corso d' Italia
Pza Fiume
Via Campania
V. Piemonte
Via Boncompagni
Via Collina
Via Piave
Via Sallustiana
Via Ludovisi
V. Vittorio Veneto
V. L. Bissolati
Via 20 Settembre
Via Montebello
S. MARIA D. VITTORIA
S. SUSANNA
Via Barberini
Barberini
PALAZZO BARBERINI
Terme di Diocleziano
M9
N
Repubblica
Pza della Repubblica
Piazza dei Cinquecento
A.C.I.
PAL. MASSIMO
TERMINI
Via delle Quattro Fontane
K
F
Via Nazionale
V. A. Depretis
Via del Viminale
Via Cavour
Via Principe Amedeo
Pza d. Esquilino
S. MARIA MAGGIORE
Via Milano
Via Panisperna
Via Cavour
Via
94 27 196 198 61 138 160
0 200 m
U V X

O P

17

G
10
H
X
Y
Z
0
200 m
85
u
Via
Viale
delle
Mura
Aurelie
Viale
Gregorio
VII
S. PIETRO
delle
Fornaci
di
Gianicolo
Passeggiata
Via
Aurelia
Antica
VILLA DORIA PAMPHILI
Pancrazio
di
S.
V.
V.
del
Vascello
V.le
di
Villa
Pamphili
Vitellia
Via
Fonteiana
Via
V.
Dezza
25
171
10-11
12-13
14-15
16-17
G
H

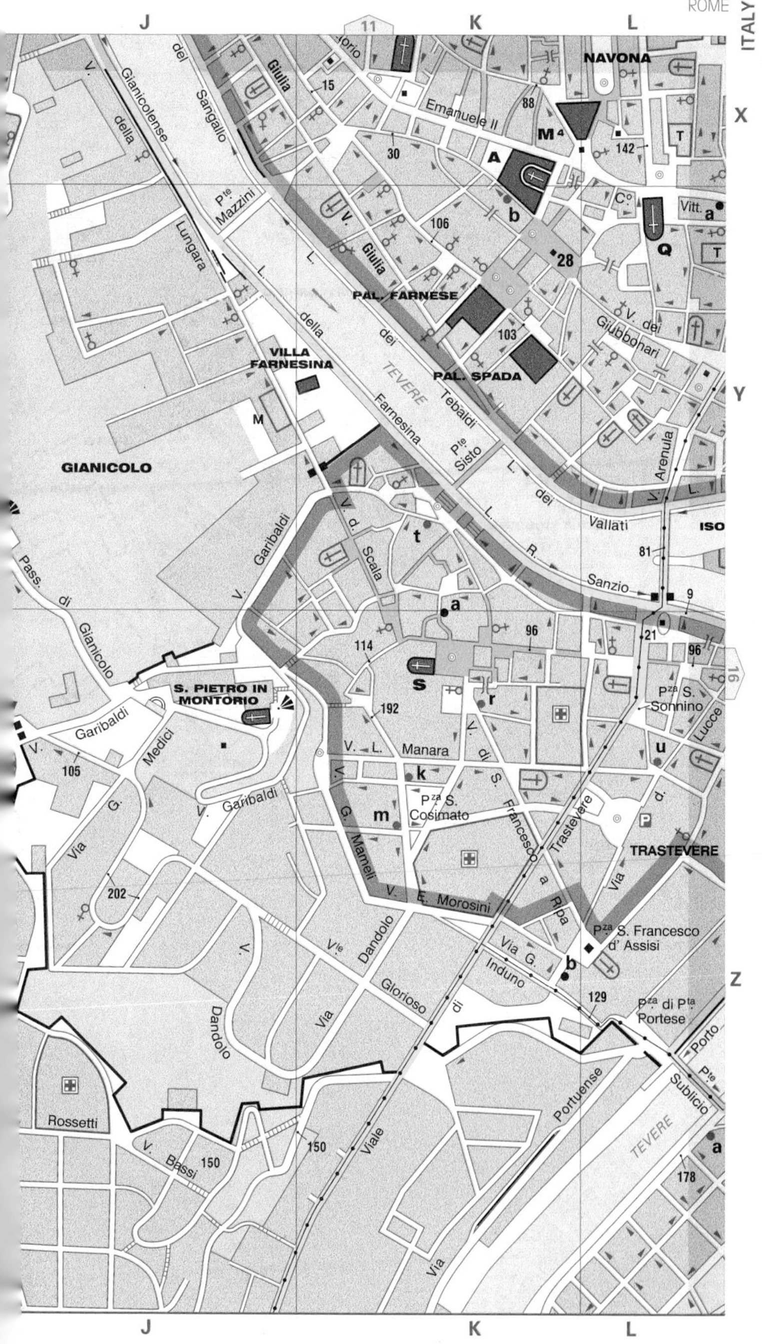
J
K
L
11
X
Y
Z
16
NAVONA
Giulia
Emanuele II
M4
A
b
Q
28
Vitt.
a
PAL. FARNESE
PAL. SPADA
V. dei Giubbonari
VILLA FARNESINA
TEVERE
GIANICOLO
Lungara
Gianicolense
del Sangallo
Pte Mazzini
L. della Farnesina
L. dei Tebaldi
Pte Sisto
L. dei Vallati
Arenula
L. R. Sanzio
ISO
V. d. Scala
V. Garibaldi
Pass. di Gianicolo
S. PIETRO IN MONTORIO
Garibaldi
Medici
V. L. Manara
Pza S. Cosimato
Pza S. Sonnino
Lucce
V. di S. Francesco a Ripa
Trastevere
TRASTEVERE
V. G. Mameli
V. E. Morosini
Pza S. Francesco d' Assisi
Via G. Induno
Pza di Pta Portese
Porto
Pte Sublicio
Vle Glorioso
Via Dandolo
Viale di Trastevere
Portuense
Rossetti
V. Bassi
M
t
a
s
r
u
k
m
b
P
15
30
88
142
106
103
81
9
21
96
114
192
105
202
129
150
178

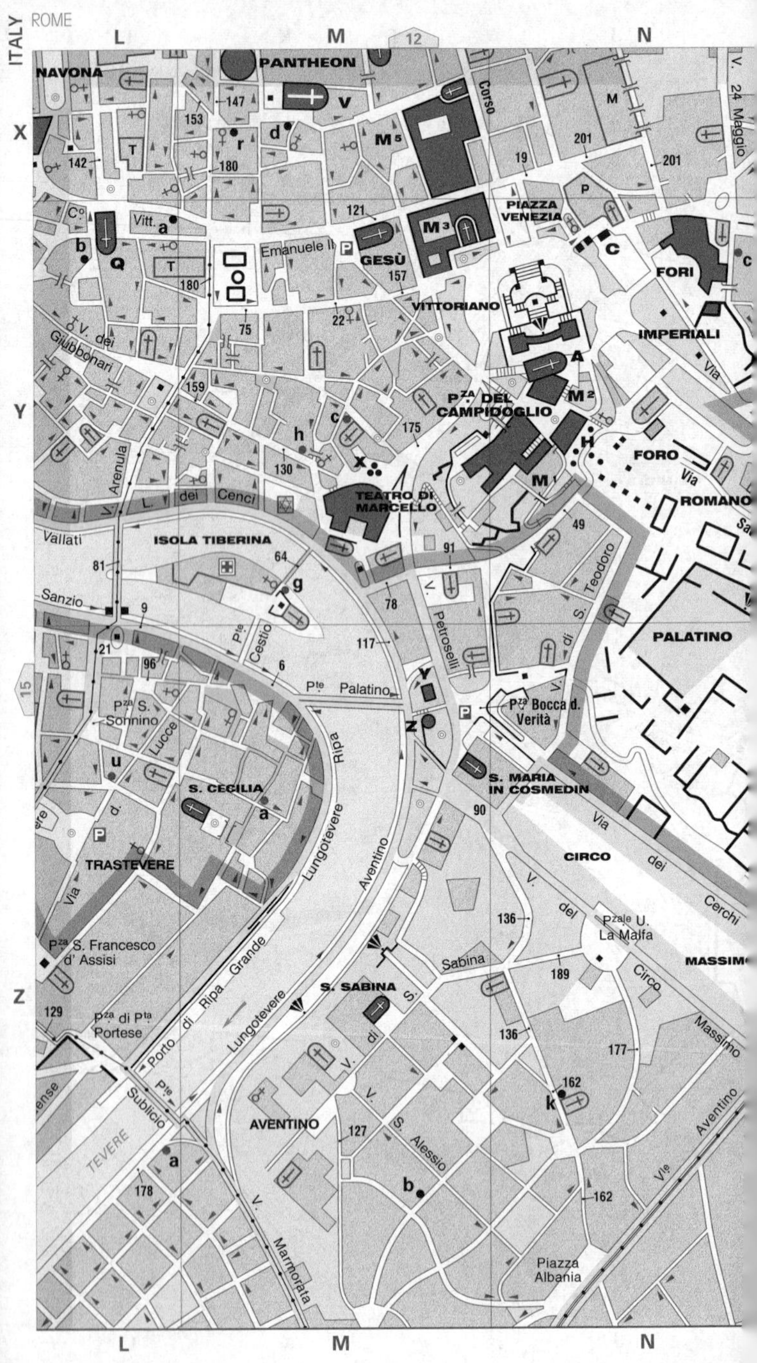

PANTHEON
NAVONA
PIAZZA VENEZIA
GESÙ
VITTORIANO
FORI
IMPERIALI
P.za DEL CAMPIDOGLIO
FORO
ROMANO
TEATRO DI MARCELLO
ISOLA TIBERINA
PALATINO
P.za Bocca d. Verità
S. MARIA IN COSMEDIN
CIRCO
MASSIMO
S. CECILIA
TRASTEVERE
P.za S. Sonnino
P.za S. Francesco d' Assisi
P.za di P.ta Portese
S. SABINA
AVENTINO
P.zale U. La Malfa
Piazza Albania
TEVERE
Corso
V. 24 Maggio
Vitt. Emanuele II
V. dei Giubbonari
Arenula
L. dei Cenci
Vallati
Sanzio
P.te Cestio
P.te Palatino
V. Petroselli
V. di S. Teodoro
Via dei Cerchi
V. del Circo Massimo
Lungotevere Ripa
Lungotevere Aventino
Porto di Ripa Grande
P.te Sublicio
V. Marmorata
V. di S. Sabina
V. S. Alessio
V.le Aventino

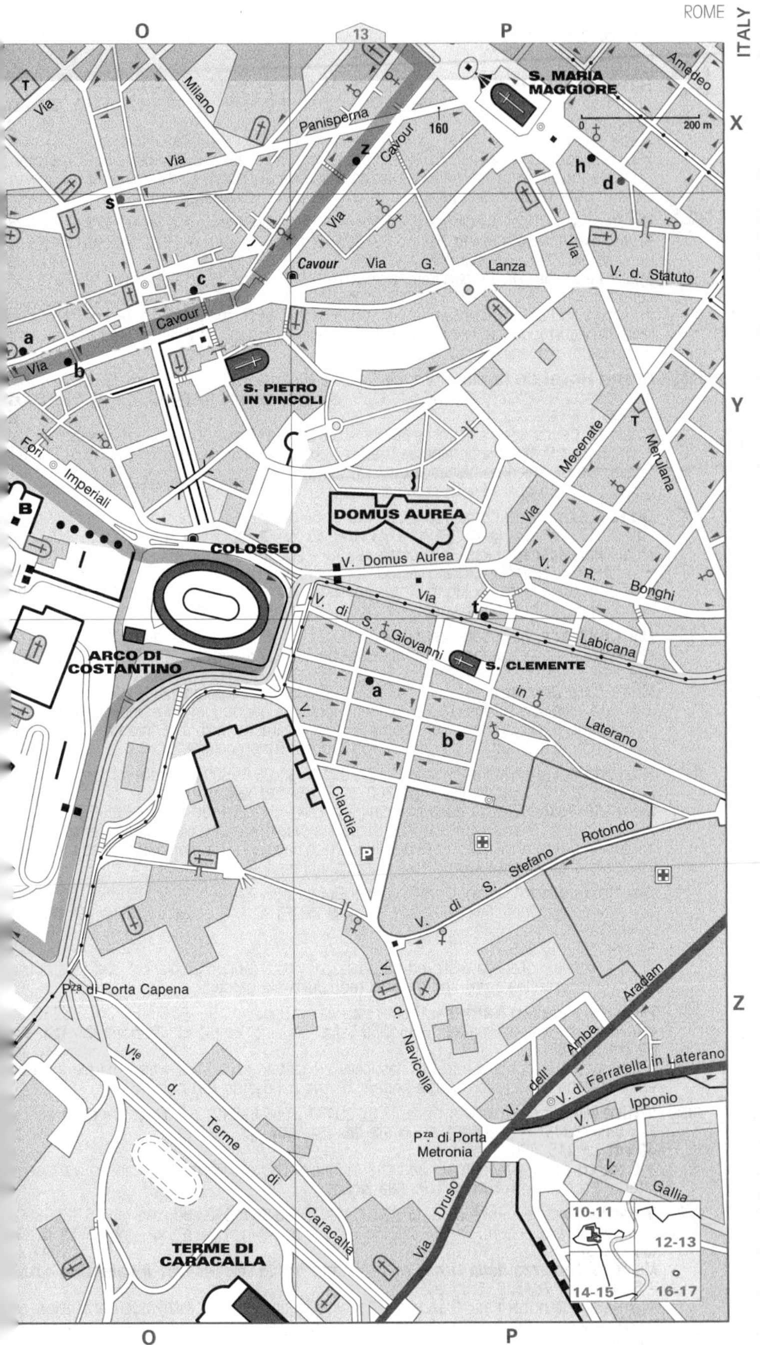
O
P
13
X
Y
Z
S. MARIA MAGGIORE
Amedeo
0
200 m
Via
Milano
Panisperna
Via
Cavour
160
Via
Cavour
Via G.
Lanza
Via
V. d. Statuto
Cavour
Via
S. PIETRO IN VINCOLI
Fori
Imperiali
DOMUS AUREA
Mecenate
Merulana
Via
COLOSSEO
V. Domus Aurea
V.
R.
Bonghi
Via
V. di
S.
Giovanni
Labicana
ARCO DI COSTANTINO
S. CLEMENTE
in
Laterano
V.
Claudia
Rotondo
Stefano
S.
di
V.
Aradam
Pza di Porta Capena
V.
d.
Navicella
Amba
dell'
V.
V. d. Ferratella in Laterano
Ipponio
V.
Vle
d.
Terme
di
Caracalla
Pza di Porta Metronia
Druso
Via
V.
Gallia
TERME DI CARACALLA
10-11
12-13
14-15
16-17

Historical Centre corso Vittorio Emanuele, piazza Venezia, Pantheon e Quirinale, piazza di Spagna, piazza Navona :

Hassler Villa Medici, piazza Trinità dei Monti 6 ✉ 00187 ☎ 06 699340, *booking@hotelhassler.it, Fax 06 6789991,* – – 100. AE VISA JCB. NU c
Meals a la carte 105/148 – ☕ 45 – **99 rm** 566/860, 13 suites.
◆ Looking onto the Spanish Steps, this is Rome's most luxurious hotel, where tradition, prestige and elegance merge to create an ambience of unparalleled pampering for guests. Dining in the rooftop restaurant is an unforgettable experience.

De Russie, via del Babuino 9 ✉ 00187 ☎ 06 328881 and rest. ☎ 06 32888870, *reservations@hotelderussie.it, Fax 06 32888888,* , , , – , rm, – 90. AE VISA JCB. MU p
Meals *Le Jardin du Russie* Rest. a la carte 60/79 – ☕ 25,30 – **125 rm** 450/810, 31 suites.
◆ Elegant and eclectic contemporary style in evidence in the pale coloured décor of this legendary cosmopolitan hotel, now with its "secret garden" by Valadier. Smart restaurant with windows opening onto terrace garden.

Grand Hotel de la Minerve, piazza della Minerva 69 ✉ 00186 ☎ 06 695201, *minerva@hotel-invest.com, Fax 06 6794165,* – , rm, – 120. AE VISA JCB. MX d
Meals *La Cesta* Rest. a la carte 60/81 – ☕ 27 – **116 rm** 360/550, 19 suites.
◆ The figure of Minerva dominates the Art Nouveau ceiling in the lobby of one of Rome's finest hotels, which combines luxury with every modern convenience. The restaurant offers cuisine prepared with creative panache, yet traditional in inspiration.

Gd H. Plaza, via del Corso 126 ✉ 00186 ☎ 06 69921111, *plaza@grandhotelplaza.com, Fax 06 69941575* – – 400. AE VISA JCB. MU m
Meals *Bar-Mascagni* Rest. a la carte 42/58 – **200 rm** ☕ 350/430, 15 suites.
◆ Dating from the mid-19C and remodelled in the Art Nouveau period, this charming hotel overlooks the Trinità dei Monti. The sumptuous lounge area has stucco decoration. The atmosphere of bygone splendour also pervades the charming restaurant.

D'Inghilterra, via Bocca di Leone 14 ✉ 00187 ☎ 06 699811 and rest. ☎ 06 69981500, *reservation.hir@royaldemeure.com, Fax 06 69922243* – . AE VISA JCB. MV t
Meals *Cafè Romano* Rest. a la carte 56/69 – ☕ 31 – **98 cam** 286/495, 8 suites.
◆ In a former royal lodge, this traditional hotel has period furniture and many pictures throughout its elegant interior ; rooms of great character with an English feel. The completely renovated restaurant serves international fusion cuisine.

Nazionale, piazza Montecitorio 131 ✉ 00186 ☎ 06 695001, *hotel@nazionaleroma.it, Fax 06 6786677* – – 800. AE VISA. rest MV g
Meals *Al Vicario* Rest. *(closed Monday)* a la carte 34/51 – **90 rm** ☕ 265/321, suite.
◆ Looking onto Piazza Montecitorio, there is a well-presented classical ambience to this hotel, composed of two separate buildings which have been harmoniously joined together. The comfortable restaurant offers a traditional menu.

Dei Borgognoni without rest., via del Bufalo 126 ✉ 00187 ☎ 06 69941505, *info@hotelborgognoni.it, Fax 06 69941501* – – 60. AE VISA JCB. NV g
54 rm ☕ 255/315.
◆ This genteel hotel is a restored 19C palazzo with a refined ambience ; spacious public areas, comfortable rooms and unexpected courtyard garden.

Piranesi-Palazzo Nainer without rest., via del Babuino 196 ✉ 00187 ☎ 06 328041 *info@hotelpiranesi.com, Fax 06 3610597,* , – . AE VISA. MU c
32 rm ☕ 263/310.
◆ This recently opened hotel is classically elegant in style. The white marble interior enhances the light, much to the benefit of the handsome furnishings.

White without rest., via in Arcione 77 ✉ 00187 ☎ 06 6991242, *white@travelroma.com Fax 06 6788451* – . AE VISA JCB. NV p
40 rm ☕ 215/400.
◆ Close to the Trevi fountain and the Quirinale, this comfortable hotel has a modern interior ; rooms with furniture in pale woods.

Valadier, via della Fontanella 15 ✉ 00187 ☎ 06 3611998 and rest. ☎ 06 3610880 *info@hotelvaladier.com, Fax 06 3201558,* – , rm, – 35. AE VISA JCB. MU k
Meals *La Terrazza della Luna* Rest. a la carte 36/46 see also rest. ***Il Valentino*** below – **55 rm** ☕ 270/370, 5 suites.
◆ An elegant hotel near Piazza del Popolo ; smart interior with much attention to detail as seen in the woodwork and mirrors which feature throughout. Panoramic roof garden.

The Inn at the Spanish Steps without rest., via dei Condotti 85 ✉ 00187 ℘ 06 69925657, *spanishstep@tin.it, Fax 06 6786470* – 🛗 ▤ 📺 📞. AE 💳 ⓞ MC VISA JCB. ✗ MU e
18 rm ☕ 385/550.
◆ In the same building as the famous Caffè Greco, this hotel fulfils the requirements of even the most romantic of visitors to the Eternal City.

Santa Chiara without rest., via Santa Chiara 21 ✉ 00186 ℘ 06 6872979, *stchiara@tin.it, Fax 06 6873144* – 🛗 ▤ 📺 📞 – 🏛 40. AE 💳 ⓞ MC VISA JCB. ✗ MX r
96 rm ☕ 170/256, 3 suites.
◆ Since 1830, an uninterrupted tradition of family hospitality has reigned in this now totally restored hotel near the Pantheon ; pleasing, classically elegant, ambience.

Della Torre Argentina without rest., corso Vittorio Emanuele 102 ✉ 00186 ℘ 06 6833886, *info@dellatorreargentina.com, Fax 06 68801641* – 🛗 ⇆ ▤ 📺 📞. AE 💳 ⓞ MC VISA JCB. ✗ LY a
52 rm ☕ 152/220, suite.
◆ Located between the old centre and the ancient sites, a refurbished hotel offering good facilities ; functional yet much attention to detail.

Portoghesi without rest., via dei Portoghesi 1 ✉ 00186 ℘ 06 6864231, *info@hotelportoghesiroma.com, Fax 06 6876976* – 🛗 ▤ 📺 📞. 💳 MC VISA JCB LV b
27 rm ☕ 145/185.
◆ Next to Sant'Antonio dei Portoghesi, a classically stylish hotel which, following its total refit combines modern comfort with a genteel ambience.

Mozart without rest., via dei Greci 23/b ✉ 00187 ℘ 06 36001915, *info@hotelmozart.com, Fax 06 36001735* – 🛗 ▤ 📺 📞. AE 💳 ⓞ MC VISA JCB. ✗ MU b
56 rm ☕ 165/225.
◆ Occupying a centrally-located 19C palazzo, this refurbished hotel has elegant period furnishings throughout ; attractive sun terrace.

Fontanella Borghese without rest., largo Fontanella Borghese 84 ✉ 00186 ℘ 06 68809504, *fontanellaborghese@interfree.it, Fax 06 6861295* – ▤ 📺 📞. AE 💳 ⓞ MC VISA JCB. ✗ MV d
24 rm ☕ 135/215.
◆ Peaceful yet centrally situated on the second and third floors of a historic building overlooking the Palazzo Borghese, this genteel and refined hotel is stylishly fitted out.

Hostaria dell'Orso, via dei Soldati 25/c ✉ 00186 ℘ 06 68301192, *hostaria@marchesi.it, Fax 06 68217063,* Elegant rest. – ▤. AE 💳 ⓞ MC VISA. ✗ KV c
closed August and Sunday – **Meals** (dinner only) (booking essential) 65/135 and a la carte 60/98 🍇.
◆ Revisit the bygone splendours of Roman high society in this elegant 15C building decorated in period style : restaurant, piano-bar and disco.

El Toulà, via della Lupa 29/b ✉ 00186 ℘ 06 6873498, *toula2@libero.it, Fax 06 6871115,* Elegant rest. – ▤. AE 💳 ⓞ MC VISA JCB. ✗ MV a
closed August, 24 to 26 December, Saturday lunch, Sunday and Monday – **Meals** (booking essential) a la carte 53/79 (15 %).
◆ In Rome's government district, a wonderful, long-established restaurant ; delightfully elegant with modern dishes on offer alongside more traditional Venetian fare.

Antico Bottaro, via Passeggiata di Ripetta 15 ✉ 00186 ℘ 06 3236763, *anticobottaro@anticobottaro.it, Fax 06 3236763* – ▤. AE 💳 ⓞ MC VISA JCB. ✗ LU a
closed 4 to 25 August and Monday – **Meals** a la carte 63/79.
◆ This 17C palazzo has terracotta floors and pink stucco walls. In business for around 130 years, the restaurant is under dynamic new management.

Il Convivio-Troiani, vicolo dei Soldati 31 ✉ 00186 ℘ 06 6869432, *info@ilconviviotroiani.com, Fax 06 6869432* – ▤. AE 💳 ⓞ MC VISA JCB. ✗ KLV r
closed 9 to 15 August, Sunday and Monday lunch – **Meals** (booking essential) a la carte 65/86 🍇.
◆ A modern creative slant to the meat and fish dishes served in the three elegant rooms of this restaurant, tucked away in an alley in the old centre.
Spec. Lasagnetta con crostacei, trippa di maiale, menta e pecorino. Trancio di spigola con salsa di yogurt e ostriche. Tartelletta di mele e amaretti con salsa di cannella e gelato al mandarino.

Enoteca Capranica, piazza Capranica 99/100 ✉ 00186 ℘ 06 69940992, *Fax 06 69940989* – ▤. AE 💳 ⓞ MC VISA JCB. ✗ MV n
closed Saturday lunch and Sunday ; in August open dinner only – **Meals** (booking essential for dinner) a la carte 44/64.
◆ Close to Montecitorio, this former wine bar has been transformed into an elegantly exclusive restaurant ; traditional Mediterranean dishes and an excellent wine list.

XXX **Il Valentino** - Hotel Valadier, via della Fontanella 14 ✉ 00187 ✆ 06 3610880, *Fax 06 3201558* – ▤. AE ⓢ ⓓ ⓜ VISA JCB. ✻ MU k
Meals a la carte 36/46.
◆ Pale woods and warm colours distinguish this refined restaurant. Its well-planned, creative menu is well suited to the elegant ambience ; good service.

XX ✿ **La Rosetta,** via della Rosetta 9 ✉ 00187 ✆ 06 6861002, *larosetta@tin.it, Fax 06 68215116* – ▤. AE ⓢ ⓓ VISA JCB. ✻ MV x
closed 10 to 18 August, Saturday lunch and Sunday – **Meals** (booking essential) seafood a la carte 53/103.
◆ The day's catch is displayed alluringly at the entrance of this restaurant ; luckily its popularity has not affected the quality of the cuisine or its pleasant ambience.
Spec. Antipasti di mare crudi e cotti. Strozzapreti con calamaretti e bottarga di muggine. Filetto di San Pietro con medaglioni di astice e sformato di zucchine.

XX **Dal Bolognese,** piazza del Popolo 1/2 ✉ 00187 ✆ 06 3611426, *Fax 06 3222799,* ☂ – ▤. AE ⓢ ⓓ ⓜ VISA JCB MU f
closed 5 to 25 August, Christmas, New Year and Monday – **Meals** a la carte 43/60.
◆ Taste the finest Emilian cuisine at this establishment, one of the most renowned restaurants in the city. Summer dining out in the piazza.

XX **Quirino,** via delle Muratte 84 ✉ 00187 ✆ 06 6794108, *eliquirino@libero.it, Fax 06 6791888,* ☂ – ⋟ ▤. AE ⓢ ⓜ VISA JCB. ✻ MNV c
closed August and Sunday – **Meals** Roman and sicilian rest. a la carte 35/40 (10 %).
◆ In a street near the Trevi fountain, this classically elegant restaurant offers traditiona Roman and fanciful Sicilian dishes.

XX ✿ **Quinzi Gabrieli,** via delle Coppelle 6 ✉ 00186 ✆ 06 6879389, *quinzigabrieli@tin.it Fax 06 6874940,* ☂ – ▤. AE ⓢ ⓓ ⓜ VISA. ✻ MV b
closed August, Christmas and Sunday – **Meals** (dinner only) (booking essential) seafood a la carte 88/110.
◆ All the fragrances and flavours of the sea in the middle of the city ; this quality restaurant is always busy and in vogue.
Spec. Selezione di frutti di mare (October-June). Paccheri di Gragnano con tartufi di mare e broccoletti siciliani. Nastri di seppie con carciofi croccanti (November-May).

XX **Il Margutta Vegetariani dal 1979,** via Margutta 118 ✉ 00187 ✆ 06 32650577 *staff@ilmargutta.it, Fax 06 36003287* – ⋟ ▤. AE ⓢ ⓓ ⓜ VISA JCB. ✻ MU a
Meals Vegetarian rest. a la carte 28/41.
◆ A marriage of strictly vegetarian cuisine and artwork in this modern restaurant, which hosts contemporary art exhibitions and has a varied and creative menu.

XX **Vecchia Roma,** via della Tribuna di Campitelli 18 ✉ 00186 ✆ 06 6864604 *Fax 06 6864604,* ☂ – ▤. AE ⓓ MY c
closed 10 to 25 August and Wednesday – **Meals** Roman and seafood rest. a la carte 40/56
◆ In the Campidoglio district, this traditional restaurant is made up of small, stylish, ye cosy rooms ; cuisine is seafood and Roman specialities.

XX **Reef,** piazza Augusto Imperatore 47 ✉ 00186 ✆ 06 68301430, *info@ristorantereef.it Fax 06 68217532,* ☂ – ▤ ♿. AE ⓢ ⓓ ⓜ VISA JCB. ✻ MV e
closed lunch except Saturday-Sunday – **Meals** seafood a la carte 58/75.
◆ Surprisingly innovative by the standards of the Eternal City, this contemporary res taurant also emphasises its modernity in its fish dishes.

X **Al Bric,** via del Pellegrino 51 ✉ 00186 ✆ 06 6879533, *Fax 06 6879533* – ▤. ⓢ ⓜ VISA KY b
closed lunch except Sunday from October to May – **Meals** a la carte 29/47 (10 %) ⚘.
◆ Terracotta floors and walls bearing the names of great wines and vineyards in an unusua restaurant offering creative modern cuisine.

X **Giggetto-al Portico d'Ottavia,** via del Portico d'Ottavia 21/a ✉ 0018 ✆ 06 6861105, *Fax 06 6832106,* ☂ – ⋟ ▤. AE ⓢ ⓓ ⓜ VISA. ✻ MY h
closed 14 to 27 July and Monday – **Meals** Roman and jewish specialities a la carte 28/44
◆ From its home made specialities to its atmosphere, everything is quintessentially Roma in this historic trattoria, near the Teatro di Marcello.

Termini Railway Station via Vittorio Veneto, via Nazionale, Viminale, Santa Mari Maggiore, Porta Pia :

🏛 **St. Regis Grand,** via Vittorio Emanuele Orlando 3 ✉ 00185 ✆ 06 47091 and res ✆ 06 47092736, *stregisgrandrome@stregis.com, Fax 06 4747307,* Ꝭ, ≘ – ▮ ▤ ▢ ✆ – 🏛 300. AE ⓢ ⓓ ⓜ VISA JCB. ✻ PV c
Meals ***Vivendo*** Rest. *(closed August and Sunday)* a la carte 50/90 ⚘ – ☕ 43 – **161 rn** 753,50/962,50, 8 suites.
◆ Frescoes, textiles and Empire furniture in the luxurious rooms and opulent public area of this hotel, which retains the splendour of its earliest days (opened in 1894). Gran atmosphere of bygone days in the restaurant.

The Westin Excelsior, via Vittorio Veneto 125 ✉ 00187 ☎ 06 47081, *excelsiorrome@westin.com, Fax 06 4826205,* – ⬍, ⇹ rm, ▤ TV ✆ – 🏢 600. AE ⊙ ⓞ MC VISA JCB. ✻ OU d
Meals a la carte 50/70 – ☕ 42 – **292 rm** 730/815, 24 suites.
◆ This large, prestigious hotel is run along traditional lines for a smart, discerning clientele. The sumptuous interior is well appointed with antique items ; Italy's largest suite is in this hotel. Brocades, velvet and chandeliers in the elegant restaurant.

Eden, via Ludovisi 49 ✉ 00187 ☎ 06 478121, *reservations@hotel-eden.it, Fax 06 4821584,* ≤, – ⬍ ⇹ ▤ TV ✆ – 🏢 80. AE ⊙ ⓞ MC VISA JCB. ✻ NU a
Meals (see rest. **La Terrazza** below) – ☕ 49,50 – **121 rm** 495/715, 13 suites.
◆ Stylish simplicity in this hotel where the elegant ambience does not dispel the warmth of the welcome. Service and accommodation to satisfy even the most demanding guest.

Sofitel, via Lombardia 47 ✉ 00187 ☎ 06 478021, *prenotazioni.sofitelroma@accor-hotels.it, Fax 06 4821019* – ⬍, ⇹ rm, ▤ TV ✆ – 🏢 45. AE ⊙ ⓞ MC VISA JCB. ✻ NU d
Meals a la carte 47/70 – **111 rm** ☕ 334/496.
◆ A historic building on the Via Veneto with a Neo-classical interior including an abundance of statues and busts. Fine view from the terrace. Elegant restaurant with vaulted ceilings in the old stable block.

Splendide Royal, porta Pinciana 14 ✉ 00187 ☎ 06 421689, *reservations@splendideroyal.com, Fax 06 42168800,* – ⬍ ▤ TV ✆ – 🏢 90. AE ⊙ ⓞ MC VISA. ✻ NU b
Meals (see rest. **Mirabelle** below) – **52 rm** ☕ 480/580, 8 suites.
◆ Gilding, damask and fine antique furniture grace the interior of this exclusive modern hotel, located in a former palazzo.

Aleph, via San Basilio 15 ✉ 00187 ☎ 06 422901, *boscolo.hotels@boscolo.com, Fax 06 42290777,* – ⇹ rm, ▤ TV ✆ ♿ P – 🏢 50. AE ⊙ ⓞ MC VISA JCB. ✻ OU c
Meals *Maremoto* Rest. a la carte 58/92 – ☕ 25 – **95 rm** 481/578, suite.
◆ A prestigious establishment in the design hotel mould ; unusual lobby with distinctive colour scheme. Innovatively styled rooms and good health spa. Modern cuisine and minimalist décor in the restaurant.

Regina Hotel Baglioni, via Vittorio Veneto 72 ✉ 00187 ☎ 06 421111, *regina.roma@baglionihotels.com, Fax 06 42012130* – ⬍, ⇹ rm, ▤ TV ✆ ♿ – 🏢 80. AE ⊙ ⓞ MC VISA JCB. ✻ OU m
Meals a la carte 65/80 (10 %) – ☕ 27,50 – **143 rm** 319/605, 6 suites.
◆ This hotel, occupying a restored Art Nouveau building, has a stylish ambience and top quality service ; the splendid rooms are elegant in their simplicity. A refined yet warm atmosphere in the restaurant, serving international cuisine.

Majestic, via Vittorio Veneto 50 ✉ 00187 ☎ 06 421441, *info@hotelmajestic.com, Fax 06 4880984* – ⬍ ▤ TV ✆ ♿ – 🏢 150. AE ⊙ ⓞ MC VISA JCB. ✻ OU e
Meals *La Veranda* Rest. *(closed August and Sunday)* a la carte 63/80 and ***La Ninfa*** Rest.-bistrot a la carte 50/70 – ☕ 40 – **78 rm** 460/610, 13 suites.
◆ Cosmopolitan luxury combines with Italian hospitality in the elegant atmosphere of this smart hotel, one of the capital's finest. Linen and silverware in the welcoming La Veranda restaurant.

Bernini Bristol, piazza Barberini 23 ✉ 00187 ☎ 06 488931 and rest. ☎ 06 488933288, *reservationsbb@sinahotels.it, Fax 06 4824266,* – ⬍, ⇹ rm, ▤ TV ✆ – 🏢 100. AE ⊙ ⓞ MC VISA JCB. ✻ OV f
Meals *L'Olimpo* Rest. a la carte 76/101 – ☕ 26 – **110 rm** 330/510,40, 10 suites.
◆ A perfect balance between bygone glories and modern comforts in one of Rome's most elegant hotels. Rooftop restaurant offers outside dining and fine views over the Eternal City.

Marriott Grand Hotel Flora, via Vittorio Veneto 191 ✉ 00187 ☎ 06 489929, *Fax 06 4820359,* – ⬍, ⇹ rm, ▤ TV ✆ ♿ – 🏢 150. AE ⊙ ⓞ MC VISA JCB. ✻ OU b
Meals only buffet lunch and a la carte 39/80 – ☕ 22 – **156 rm** 478, 7 suites.
◆ Following a complete refit, this hotel at the end of Via Veneto is a harmonious and functional combination of simple elegance and modern refinement. Parquet floors and other decorative features in wood lend an ambience of warmth to the restaurant.

Jolly Hotel Vittorio Veneto, corso d'Italia 1 ✉ 00198 ☎ 06 84951, *roma_vittorioveneto@jollyhotels.it, Fax 06 8841104* – ⬍, ⇹ rm, ▤ TV ♿ 🚗 – 🏢 380. AE ⊙ ⓞ MC VISA JCB. ✻ rest OU k
Meals (residents only) a la carte 39/53 – **200 rm** ☕ 232/341.
◆ A modern structure which benefits from its central location and every modern convenience ; large rooms, some with views over the Villa Borghese.

Empire Palace Hotel, via Aureliana 39 ✉ 00187 ☎ 06 421281, *gold@empirepalacehotel.com, Fax 06 42128400,* – ⬍, ⇹ rm, ▤ TV ✆ ♿ – 🏢 50. AE ⊙ ⓞ MC VISA JCB. ✻ PU h
Meals *(closed Sunday)* a la carte 38/62 – **113 rm** ☕ 275/396, 5 suites.
◆ A sophisticated hybrid of 19C building and contemporary design, with modern art displayed in the public areas ; simple elegance in the rooms. Cherry trees and red and blue chandeliers decorate the restaurant.

Rose Garden Palace without rest., via Boncompagni 19 ✉ 00187 ☎ 06 421741, *info@rosegardenpalace.com, Fax 06 4815608*, modern and minimalist design – 50. OU d
65 rm ☐ 248/374.
◆ Minimalist design has inspired the interiors of this new hotel, occupying an early 19C palazzo ; unusual.

Mecenate Palace Hotel without rest., via Carlo Alberto 3 ✉ 00185 ☎ 06 44702024, *info@mecenatepalace.com, Fax 06 4461354* – 45. PX h
62 rm ☐ 258/362, 3 suites.
◆ The elegant 19C-style interior makes for a welcoming ambience in this recently built hotel, with high standards of comfort and service.

Starhotel Metropole, via Principe Amedeo 3 ✉ 00185 ☎ 06 4774, *metropole.rm@starhotels.it, Fax 06 4740413* – 200. PV p
Meals a la carte 45/65 – **243 rm** ☐ 249/289, 8 suites.
◆ Located near the station, this recently built hotel is well appointed ; spacious public areas and good conference facilities. The modern restaurant offers an eclectic range of dishes.

Canada without rest., via Vicenza 58 ✉ 00185 ☎ 06 4457770, *info@hotelcanadaroma.com, Fax 06 4450749* – FS u
70 rm ☐ 132/155.
◆ In a period building near the station, this hotel has a simple elegance. Tastefully furnished, stylish rooms ; ask for one with a canopy bed.

Artemide, via Nazionale 22 ✉ 00184 ☎ 06 489911, *hotel.artemide@tiscalinet.it, Fax 06 48991700* – rm, – 120. OV b
Meals 30/47 – **85 rm** ☐ 237/325.
◆ Occupying an attractively restored Art Nouveau building, this classically stylish hotel offers all modern comforts ; good conference facilities.

Britannia without rest., via Napoli 64 ✉ 00184 ☎ 06 4883153, *info@hotelbritannia.it, Fax 06 4882343* – PV y
33 rm ☐ 210/290.
◆ Competent family management at this small hotel where much attention to detail is evident. Unusual rooms in eclectic style ; very comfortable.

Ambra Palace, via Principe Amedeo 257 ✉ 00185 ☎ 06 492330, *booking@ambrapalacehotel.com, Fax 06 49233100* – 40. rest FT c
Meals *(dinner only)* (residents only) a la carte 40/52 – **78 rm** ☐ 206/289.
◆ Occupying a mid-19C palazzo, this well-appointed hotel is especially popular with business people.

Barberini without rest., via Rasella 3 ✉ 00187 ☎ 06 4814993, *info@hotelbarberini.com, Fax 06 4815211* – OV e
☐ 20 – **35 rm** 226/298.
◆ Near the Barberini palace, this recently opened hotel is a restored historic building ; fine marble, opulent fabrics and decorative features in wood throughout.

The Bailey's Hotel without rest., via Flavia 39 ✉ 00187 ☎ 06 42020486, *info@hotelbailey.com, Fax 06 42020170* – PU b
29 rm ☐ 181/284.
◆ Rooms with fine furniture and marble baths ; a refined and tasteful look, and every modern convenience. Well-restored to high standards.

Royal Court without rest., via Marghera 51 ✉ 00185 ☎ 06 44340364, *theroyal@tin.it, Fax 06 4469121* – FS a
25 rm ☐ 130/165.
◆ Well-presented and stylish, this refurbished hotel has a friendly ambience and every modern comfort. Situated in a residential area close to the station.

Marcella Royal Hotel without rest., via Flavia 106 ✉ 00187 ☎ 06 42014591, *info@marcellaroyalhotel.com, Fax 06 4815832*, – PU z
75 rm ☐ 150/200.
◆ Close to the station and city centre, this hotel is comfortable and well-presented throughout ; breakfast served on the panoramic roof-garden terrace.

Astoria Garden, via Bachelet 8/10 ✉ 00185 ☎ 06 4469908, *astoria.garden@flashnet.it, Fax 06 4453329*, – FS c
Meals (residents only) 25/37 (10 %) – **34 rm** ☐ 130/150.
◆ This recently refurbished hotel near the station has a welcoming ambience and a large peaceful courtyard garden ; jacuzzi baths.

Ludovisi Palace without rest., via Ludovisi 43 ✉ 00187 ℘ 06 42020396, *info@ludovisipalacehotel.com, Fax 06 42020741* – AE VISA
57 rm 248/390. OU f
◆ Dedicated and experienced management at this hotel, where great attention to detail is evident throughout. A functional yet very comfortable establishment.

Ariston without rest., via Turati 16 ✉ 00185 ℘ 06 4465399, *hotelariston@hotelariston.it, Fax 06 4465396* – 100. AE VISA JCB. PV g
97 rm 170/235.
◆ Conveniently located near the station, a traditional family-run hotel ; well-appointed and offering high standards of service.

La Terrazza - Hotel Eden, via Ludovisi 49 ✉ 00187 ℘ 06 47812752, *reservations@hotel-eden.it, Fax 06 47812718* – AE VISA JCB. NU a
Meals (booking essential) a la carte 101/142.
◆ The focal point of this elegant, modern restaurant with roof garden is the panoramic view of Rome, an ideal backdrop against which to enjoy creative, high quality cuisine.
Spec. Spaghettoni con stinco d'agnello e bagoss. Coda di rospo avvolta in prosciutto di Parma croccante, olive taggiasche e finocchi. Tagliata di capriolo con polenta concia e salsa di Barolo.

Mirabelle - Hotel Splendide Royal, porta Pinciana 14 ✉ 00187 ℘ 06 42168838, – AE VISA. NU b
Meals (booking essential) a la carte 65/94.
◆ A luxurious and historic feel to this charming restaurant overlooking Rome ; dining outside in summer. Modern cuisine with Mediterranean roots.

Harry's Bar, via Vittorio Veneto 150 ✉ 00187 ℘ 06 484643, *info@harrysbar.it, Fax 06 4883117,* – – 40. AE VISA JCB. OU b
closed Sunday – **Meals** (booking essential) a la carte 60/112.
◆ Unchanging elegance, popularity and quality cuisine at this fashionable stalwart of the "dolce vita" ; excellent bar for evening drinks.

Agata e Romeo, via Carlo Alberto 45 ✉ 00185 ℘ 06 4466115, *ristorante@agataeromeo.it, Fax 06 4465842* – AE VISA JCB. PX d
closed 7 to 28 August, 1 to 13 January, Saturday and Sunday – **Meals** (booking essential) a la carte 57/78.
◆ This small restaurant, well-presented and elegant, draws together traditional cuisine and creativity. One of the finest wine-lists in Rome.
Spec. Sformato di formaggio di fossa con salsa di pere e miele (summer-winter). Vignarola (specialità romana a base di fave, piselli e carciofi ; spring). Baccalà islandese in quattro modi.

Asador Cafè Veneto, via Vittorio Veneto 116 ✉ 00187 ℘ 06 4827107, *cafeveneto@hotmail.com, Fax 06 42011240,* , Rest. cocktail bar – AE VISA JCB. OU p
closed 10 to 31 August and Monday – **Meals** Argentinian charbroiled specialities dinner and Sunday lunch a la carte 40/58.
◆ In the culinary hot-spot of the Via Veneto district, this stylish restaurant-cocktail bar serves classic dishes and Argentine specialities (beef direct from the Pampas).

Al Grappolo d'Oro, via Palestro 4/10 ✉ 00185 ℘ 06 4941441, *Fax 06 4452350* – AE VISA JCB. PU c
closed August, Saturday lunch and Sunday – **Meals** a la carte 32/46.
◆ Close to the Baths of Diocletian, this classic restaurant has been improved by recent refurbishment ; an extensive traditional menu.

Girarrosto Fiorentino, via Sicilia 46 ✉ 00187 ℘ 06 42880660, *girarrostofiorentino@yahoo.it, Fax 06 42010078* – AE VISA JCB. OU f
Meals a la carte 37/56.
◆ In the warm wood-panelled atmosphere of this restaurant, traditional Tuscan cuisine is offered (roast meats a speciality) alongside seafood dishes.

Monte Caruso Cicilardone, via Farini 12 ✉ 00185 ℘ 06 483549 – AE VISA. PV k
closed August, Sunday and Monday lunch – **Meals** Lucan rest. a la carte 33/51.
◆ The emphasis is on the flavours of the south in this warm and welcoming family-run restaurant ; menu based on Basilicatan dishes prepared authentically and simply.

Papà Baccus, via Toscana 32/36 ✉ 00187 ℘ 06 42742808, *papabaccus@papabaccus.com, Fax 06 42010005* – AE VISA JCB. OU w
Meals (booking essential) Tuscan rest. a la carte 45/69.
◆ Near Via Veneto, this popular traditional restaurant serves seafood and Tuscan specialities (best Chianina beef guaranteed).

Giovanni, via Marche 64 ✉ 00187 ℘ 06 4821834, *Fax 06 4817366* – AE VISA OU a
closed August, Friday dinner and Saturday – **Meals** a la carte 32/60.
◆ The tone of this establishment is unmistakably that of the Marche region, as indeed are its specialities. A friendly ambience with many regulars ; Roman cuisine also served.

Hostaria da Vincenzo, via Castelfidardo 6 ✉ 00185 ☎ 06 484596, *Fax 06 4870092* – ▤. AE ⊙ ⊕ ⊕ VISA JCB PU e
closed August and Sunday – **Meals** a la carte 25/37.
◆ A classic restaurant, in terms of atmosphere and cuisine, which takes in meat and seafood dishes. Pleasant friendly ambience ; many regulars and popular with business people.

Taverna Urbana, via Urbana 137 ✉ 00184 ☎ 06 4884439, *Fax 06 7010605* – ▤. AE ⊙ ⊕ ⊕ VISA JCB. ✻ PVX m
closed August and Monday – **Meals** seafood a la carte 24/40.
◆ Near the station, a traditional restaurant offering Lazio dishes and seafood specialities, all of which are prepared with the freshest ingredients.

Peppone, via Emilia 60 ✉ 00187 ☎ 06 483976, *Fax 06 483976*, Traditional rest. – ▤. AE ⊙ ⊕ ⊕ VISA JCB. ✻ OU r
closed Christmas, 15 August, Saturday and Sunday in August, only Sunday during other months – **Meals** a la carte 30/40 (15 %).
◆ Run by the same family since 1890, this is the quintessential place to savour traditional cuisine in an atmosphere of classic style.

Ancient Rome Colosseo, Fori Imperiali, Aventino, Terme di Caracalla, Porta San Paolo, Monte Testaccio :

Capo d'Africa without rest., via Capo d'Africa 54 ✉ 00184 ☎ 06 772801, *info@hotelcapodafrica.com, Fax 06 77280801*, ⅃₅ – |‡| ▤ TV ✆ ♿ – 🏛 70. AE ⊙ ⊕ ⊕ VISA JCB. ✻ PZ b
64 rm ☕ 290/320, suite.
◆ With a choice of larger or smaller rooms, this hotel is distinguished throughout by its fine furnishings and tasteful décor ; close to the Colosseum.

Forum, via Tor de' Conti 25 ✉ 00184 ☎ 06 6792446, *info@hotelforum.com, Fax 06 6786479* – |‡| ▤ TV – 🏛 100. AE ⊙ ⊕ ⊕ VISA JCB. ✻ OY a
Meals *(closed Sunday dinner)* a la carte 58/78 – **79 rm** ☕ 230/330.
◆ Enviably situated by the Fori Imperiali and not far from the Colosseum, this stylish hotel has elegant public areas and a fine terrace. Surrounded by the ruins of ancient Rome dining here is an unforgettable experience.

Borromeo without rest., via Cavour 117 ✉ 00184 ☎ 06 485856, *borromeo@travel.it, Fax 06 4882541* – |‡| ▤ TV ✆ ♿. AE ⊙ ⊕ ⊕ VISA JCB PX z
30 rm ☕ 230/260, 3 suites.
◆ Near Santa Maria Maggiore, this comfortable hotel has spacious well-appointed rooms with traditional furnishings, and a pleasant roof terrace.

Villa San Pio ⛭ without rest., via di Santa Melania 19 ✉ 00153 ☎ 06 5743547, *info@aventinohotels.com, Fax 06 5741112*, 🌳 – |‡| ▤ TV ♿ P – 🏛 25. AE ⊙ ⊕ ⊕ VISA JCB. ✻ MZ b
78 rm ☕ 199,10/216,70.
◆ Sharing a pleasant garden with two other establishments under the same management, this hotel has the feel of a genteel private home. A fine large lobby and modern rooms.

Duca d'Alba without rest., via Leonina 12/14 ✉ 00184 ☎ 06 484471, *info@hotelducadalba.com, Fax 06 4884840* – |‡| ▤ TV ✆. AE ⊙ ⊕ ⊕ VISA JCB OY c
☕ 8 – **27 rm** 130/185.
◆ In the picturesque quarter formerly known as the Suburra, this completely refurbished hotel has well-appointed rooms with classically elegant furnishings.

Celio without rest., via dei Santi Quattro 35/c ✉ 00184 ☎ 06 70495333, *info@hotelcelio.com, Fax 06 7096377* – ▤ TV. AE ⊙ ⊕ ⊕ VISA JCB PZ a
19 rm, ☕ 230/290.
◆ Combining refinement, comfort and atmosphere this welcoming hotel has elegant rooms of character ; well located for the Colosseum.

Domus Aventina ⛭ without rest., via Santa Prisca 11/b ✉ 00153 ☎ 06 5746135 *info@domus-aventina.com, Fax 06 57300044* – ▤ TV. AE ⊙ ⊕ ⊕ VISA JCB. ✻ NZ k
26 rm ☕ 125/205.
◆ Close to the Circus Maximus in the Aventino district, this hotel has large, modern rooms. Cramped but comfortable public areas.

Mercure Hotel Roma Delta Colosseo without rest., via Labicana 144 ✉ 00184 ☎ 06 770021, *mercure.romacolosseo@accor-hotels.it, Fax 06 7005781*, ⛱ – |‡| ▤ TV 🚗 – 🏛 60. AE ⊙ ⊕ ⊕ VISA. ✻ PYZ
160 rm ☕ 171/274.
◆ A curious contrast between the sites of ancient Rome and this contemporary-style hotel. The most striking feature is its swimming pool with terrace overlooking the Colosseum.

Cilicia without rest., via Cilicia 5/7 ✉ 00179 ☎ 06 7005554, *hotelcilicia@tin.it Fax 06 77250016* – |‡| ▤ TV ♿ P. AE ⊙ ⊕ ⊕ VISA. ✻
58 rm ☕ 103/150. by viale delle Terme di Caracalla OPZ
◆ Opened in 2000 after careful refurbishment, this comfortable establishment has handy parking ; the interior has fine wood-panelling and rooms with every modern convenience.

Piccadilly without rest., via Magna Grecia 122 ✉ 00183 ☎ 06 77207017, *piccadilly.rm@bestwestern.it, Fax 06 70476686* – AE VISA JCB. FT b
55 rm 112/165.
◆ A panoramic breakfast on the ninth floor of this functional hotel is the perfect start to the day ; well located for the metro, close to San Giovanni in Laterano.

Solis Invictus without rest., via Cavour 311 ✉ 00184 ☎ 06 69920587, *hotelsolis@tin.it, Fax 06 69923395* – TV. AE VISA. OY b
16 rm 170/225.
◆ This genteel, small hotel near the Colosseum now has a ground floor lobby ; well-proportioned rooms with good furnishings and every modern convenience.

Sant'Anselmo without rest., piazza Sant'Anselmo 2 ✉ 00153 ☎ 06 5748119, *info@aventinohotels.com, Fax 06 5783604,* – TV. AE VISA JCB. MZ m
45 rm 119,90/182,60.
◆ In the Aventino district, this Art Nouveau villa with courtyard garden is peaceful and genteel ; a charming turn of the century ambience.

Checchino dal 1887, via Monte Testaccio 30 ✉ 00153 ☎ 06 5746318, *checchino_roma@tin.it, Fax 06 5743816,* Historica building – . AE VISA JCB. DT a
closed August, 24 December-2 January, Sunday and Monday – **Meals** (booking essential) Roman rest. a la carte 35/59.
◆ Located in the distinctive Testaccio quarter, this is a historic backdrop against which to savour the largely meat- and offal-based specialities of Roman cuisine.

Maharajah, via dei Serpenti 124 ✉ 00184 ☎ 06 4747144, *maharajah@maharajah.it, Fax 06 47885393* – . AE VISA JCB. OY s
Meals Indian rest. a la carte 27/33 (10 %).
◆ Subdued lighting, rugs, and Indian prints and fabrics create the appropriate atmosphere in this restaurant ; authentic Indian dishes, rather than pale European imitations.

Papok, salita del Grillo 6/b ✉ 00184 ☎ 06 69922183, *papok@tiscali.it, Fax 06 69922183* – . AE VISA. NY c
closed 3 to 31 August and Monday – **Meals** a la carte 39/53.
◆ Near the Fori, this well-managed restaurant has a classic rustic ambience ; principally traditional seafood, but meat dishes also available.

Lo Scopettaro, lungotevere Testaccio 7 ✉ 00153 ☎ 06 5742408, *Fax 06 5757912* – . AE VISA JCB. LZ a
Meals Roman rest. a la carte 21/36.
◆ A friendly welcome and rustic atmosphere in this trattoria run by three generations of the same family ; good, homely Roman cuisine.

St. Peter's Basilica (Vatican City) Gianicolo, Monte Mario, Stadio Olimpico :

Cavalieri Hilton, via Cadlolo 101 ✉ 00136 ☎ 06 35091, *fom_rome@hilton.com, Fax 06 35092241,* ≤ city, , Private art collection, , , , , – , rm, TV P – 2000. AE VISA JCB. rest CS a
Meals *Il Giardino dell'Ulliveto* Rest. a la carte 79/144 see also rest. ***La Pergola*** below – 45 – **354 rm** 695/745, 17 suites.
◆ Fine views over the city, sun-terraces and pool with gardens ; these are some of the features of this great hotel which excels in every respect. An informal poolside restaurant offers dining with cabaret.

Jolly Hotel Villa Carpegna, via Pio IV 6 ✉ 00165 ☎ 06 393731, *roma_villacarpegna@jollyhotels.it, Fax 06 636856,* – , rm, TV P – 330. AE VISA JCB. rest by via Cipro CS
Meals (residents only) a la carte 29/51 – **201 rm** 220/250, 2 suites.
◆ The latest hotel in this chain's Roman contingent is a modern development with pool, parking and good conference facilities.

Visconti Palace without rest., via Federico Cesi 37 ✉ 00193 ☎ 06 3684, *viscontipalace@italyhotel.com, Fax 06 3200551* – , rm, TV – 150. AE VISA JCB. KU b
234 rm 270/300, 13 suites.
◆ A large 1970s building, this fully modernised, elegantly functional hotel appeals to business people and tourists alike ; large rooms with every modern convenience.

Jolly Leonardo da Vinci, via dei Gracchi 324 ✉ 00192 ☎ 06 328481, *roma_leonardodavinci@jollyhotels.it, Fax 06 3610138* – , rm, TV – 180. AE VISA. KU a
Meals (residents only) a la carte 31/46 – **239 rm** 209/268, 5 suites.
◆ A very comfortable hotel which is equally popular with business people and tourists. Lobby and much of the accommodation refurbished.

Atlante Star, via Vitelleschi 34 ✉ 00193 ✆ 06 6873233, *atlante.star@atlantehotels.com, Fax 06 6872300* – ▮ ▤ TV – 50. AE $ ⓓ MC VISA JCB JV c
Meals (see rest. ***Les Etoiles*** below) – **70 rm** ☕ 280/325, 3 suites.
◆ The dome of St Peter's seems almost within reach from the leafy roof-garden of this hotel, located between Castel Sant'Angelo and the Vatican ; well-presented, smart interiors.

Giulio Cesare without rest., via degli Scipioni 287 ✉ 00192 ✆ 06 3210751, *Fax 06 3211736,* – ▮ ▤ TV – 40. AE $ ⓓ MC VISA JCB. KU d
80 rm ☕ 250/300.
◆ An elegantly simple façade masks a welcoming interior at this former patrician villa with courtyard garden ; smart Louis XVI-style furniture.

Farnese without rest., via Alessandro Farnese 30 ✉ 00192 ✆ 06 3212553, *hotel.farnese@mclink.it, Fax 06 3215129* – ▮ ▤ TV P. AE $ ⓓ MC VISA. KU e
23 rm ☕ 180/248.
◆ In a restored patrician palace, this hotel is situated in the quiet Prati quarter, yet only 50m from the metro ; elegant and well-presented interior.

Starhotel Michelangelo, via Stazione di San Pietro 14 ✉ 00165 ✆ 06 398739, *michelangelo.rm@starhotels.it, Fax 06 632359* – ▮, rm, ▤ TV – 150. AE $ ⓓ MC VISA JCB. GX u
Meals a la carte 50/80 – **171 rm** ☕ 223/253, 8 suites.
◆ Close to St Peter's, this comfortable hotel conforms to the standards expected of its rating ; period furniture, both in the public areas and rooms. The restaurant also possesses an ambience of simple elegance.

Dei Consoli without rest., via Varrone 2/d ✉ 00193 ✆ 06 68892972, *info@hoteldeiconsoli.com, Fax 06 68212274* – ▮ ▤ TV. AE $ ⓓ MC VISA JCB. HU a
28 rm ☕ 200/290.
◆ Opened in 2000, this totally refurbished former palace is now a cosy hotel with much attention to detail in evidence, and a smart clientele ; elegant Empire-style rooms.

Sant'Anna without rest., borgo Pio 133 ✉ 00193 ✆ 06 68801602, *santanna@travel.it, Fax 06 68308717* – ▮ ▤ TV. AE $ ⓓ MC VISA JCB HV m
20 rm ☕ 150/200.
◆ Unusual trompe l'oeil décor and a charming inner courtyard at this small and welcoming hotel, occupying a 16C palace close to St Peter's.

Arcangelo without rest., via Boezio 15 ✉ 00192 ✆ 06 6874143, *hotel.arcangelo@travel.it, Fax 06 6893050,* ≤ St Peter's Basilica – ▮ ▤ TV. AE $ ⓓ MC VISA. JU f
33 rm ☕ 140/206.
◆ Tasteful decoration and attention to detail in the wood-panelled public areas of this 19C former palace ; sun terrace with view of St Peter's.

Gerber without rest., via degli Scipioni 241 ✉ 00192 ✆ 06 3216485, *info@hotelgerber.it, Fax 06 3217048* – ▮ ▤ TV. AE $ ⓓ MC VISA JCB. JU h
27 rm ☕ 100/135.
◆ This family-run traditional hotel is close to the metro ; pale wood in the pleasant public areas and the simple but appealing rooms.

Alimandi without rest., via Tunisi 8 ✉ 00192 ✆ 06 39723948, *alimandi@tin.it,* Fax 06 39723943, – ▤ TV. AE $ ⓓ MC VISA JCB. GU a
closed 8 January-10 February – **35 rm** ☕ 100/155.

La Pergola - Hotel Cavalieri Hilton, via Cadlolo 101 ✉ 00136 ✆ 06 35092152, *lapergola@hilton.com, Fax 06 35092165,* ≤ city, – ▤ P. AE $ ⓓ MC VISA JCB. CS a
closed 8 to 23 August, 1 to 26 January, Sunday and Monday – **Meals** (dinner only) (booking essential) 120/135 and a la carte 92/144.
◆ Luxurious yet refined elegance, impeccable service, and a delightful view of the Eternal City ; dinner at this rooftop restaurant is unforgettable.
Spec. Carpaccio di scampi con caviale ed erba cipollina. Tortellini di ricotta con pecorino e fave (spring). Crepinette di piccione e fegato grasso d'anatra.

Les Etoiles - Hotel Atlante Star, via dei Bastioni 1 ✉ 00193 ✆ 06 6893434, *les.etoiles@atlantehotels.com, Fax 06 6872300,* – ▤. AE $ ⓓ MC VISA JCB. JV c
Meals a la carte 79/117.
◆ Located near the Hotel Atlante Star, this restaurant has fine views over Rome's rooftops and St Peter's, especially from the summer roof-garden.

Il Simposio-di Costantini, piazza Cavour 16 ✉ 00193 ✆ 06 32111131 *Fax 06 3211502,* Wine bar and rest. – ▤. AE $ ⓓ MC VISA JCB. KU c
closed August, Saturday lunch and Sunday – **Meals** a la carte 39/54.
◆ This restaurant-wine bar offers the choice between a drink at the bar or dining in the elegant restaurant ; hot and cold dishes, and a good cheese selection.

XX **Antico Arco,** piazzale Aurelio 7 ✉ 00152 ☎ 06 5815274, *anticoarco@tiscali.it, Fax 06 5815274* – ▤. AE ⓢ ⓓ ⓜ VISA JZ a
closed 8 to 22 August and Sunday – **Meals** (booking essential) a la carte 38/55.
◆ Refurbished along minimalist lines, this is a popular spot which is always very busy. Just inside is the bar, while the restaurant is split over two levels ; good service.

XX **Taverna Angelica,** piazza Amerigo Capponi 6 ✉ 00193 ☎ 06 6874514, Post theatre restaurant, open until late – ▤. AE ⓢ ⓜ VISA. ✂ JV t
closed 10 to 20 August – **Meals** (dinner only) (booking essential) a la carte 28/48.
◆ Ideal for a romantic candlelit meal, perhaps after the theatre ; a friendly and intimate ambience with some imaginative interpretations of classic Italian dishes.

XX **L'Antico Porto,** via Federico Cesi 36 ✉ 00193 ☎ 06 3233661, *Fax 06 3203483* – ▤. ⓢ ⓓ ⓜ VISA JCB. ✂ KU b
closed August, Saturday lunch and Sunday – **Meals** a la carte 42/68.
◆ The reliably professional management here has focused on fish dishes with great success. Classical style and cosiness combined.

Parioli via Flaminia, Villa Borghese, Villa Glori, via Nomentana, via Salaria :

Grand Hotel Parco dei Principi, via Gerolamo Frescobaldi 5 ✉ 00198 ☎ 06 854421, *principi@parcodeiprincipi.com, Fax 06 8845104*, ≤, Fà, ⛱ heated – |♦| ▤ TV ☎ 🚗 – 🏛 600. AE ⓢ ⓓ ⓜ VISA. ✂ rest ES a
Meals ***Pauline Borghese*** Rest. a la carte 56/74 – **165 rm** ☕ 450/620, 20 suites.
◆ Overlooking the parkland of the Villa Borghese, this hotel is an oasis of verdant calm in the heart of Rome ; elegant warm interiors, with much attention to detail in evidence and excellent service. Exclusive restaurant offering well-presented eclectic cuisine.

Lord Byron ⊛, via De Notaris 5 ✉ 00197 ☎ 06 3220404, *info@lordbyronhotel.com, Fax 06 3220405* – |♦| ▤ TV ☎. AE ⓢ ⓓ ⓜ VISA JCB. ✂ DS b
Meals ***Sapori*** Rest. *(closed Sunday)* a la carte 50/66 – **27 rm** ☕ 363/445,50, 9 suites.
◆ Feeling more like an exclusive private residence than a hotel, this refined establishment has rooms combining luxury with modern comforts and faultless service. The smart dining room is equally suitable for intimate meals or meetings.

Aldrovandi Palace, via Ulisse Aldrovandi 15 ✉ 00197 ☎ 06 3223993, *hotel@aldrovandi.com, Fax 06 3221435*, Fà, ⛱ – |♦| ⇔ ▤ TV ☎ P – 🏛 300. AE ⓢ ⓓ ⓜ VISA JCB. ✂ ES c
Meals a la carte 105/130 – ☕ 27,50 – **122 rm** 500/600, 13 suites.
◆ Occupying an elegant late-19C palazzo with views of the Villa Borghese, this hotel has a small shaded park with pool, opulent interiors and genteel rooms.

The Duke Hotel, via Archimede 69 ✉ 00197 ☎ 06 367221, *theduke@thedukehotel.com, Fax 06 36004104* – |♦| ▤ TV ☎ ♿ 🚗 – 🏛 60. AE ⓢ ⓓ ⓜ VISA JCB. ✂ rest
Meals (residents only) a la carte 48/70 – **64 rm** ☕ 362/410, 14 suites. DS w
◆ The discreet, understated ambience of an English club is created in the stylish interiors of this well-appointed new hotel ; afternoon tea served in front of the fire.

Albani without rest., via Adda 45 ✉ 00198 ☎ 06 84991, *hotelalbani@flashnet.it, Fax 06 8499399* – |♦| ▤ TV 🚗 – 🏛 90. AE ⓢ ⓓ ⓜ VISA JCB. ✂ ES b
157 rm ☕ 186/270.
◆ Overlooking the parkland of the Villa Albani near the Via Veneto, this modern-style hotel has comfortable public areas, especially the fine and airy lobby.

Mercure Roma Corso Trieste without rest., via Gradisca 29 ✉ 00198 ☎ 06 852021, *mercure.romatrieste@accor-hotels.it, Fax 06 8412444* – |♦| ▤ TV ☎ ♿ 🚗 – 🏛 30. AE ⓢ ⓓ ⓜ VISA FS d
97 rm ☕ 180/200.
◆ Comfortable, spacious and modern rooms in this hotel, unusually situated in a residential quarter. Gym and sun deck on top floor.

Degli Aranci, via Oriani 11 ✉ 00197 ☎ 06 8070202, *hotel.degliaranci@flashnet.it, Fax 06 8070704*, 🏠 – |♦| ▤ TV – 🏛 40. AE ⓢ ⓓ ⓜ VISA JCB. ✂ ES g
Meals a la carte 25/75 – **54 rm** ☕ 135/240, 2 suites.
◆ Not far from Viale Parioli, this genteel hotel is situated in a quiet, leafy area ; pleasant, stylish public areas and very comfortable rooms. The restaurant looks out over the grounds.

Villa Grazioli without rest., via Salaria 241 ✉ 00199 ☎ 06 8416587, *info@villagrazioli.it, Fax 06 8413385* – |♦| ▤ TV. AE ⓢ ⓓ ⓜ VISA ES m
30 rm ☕ 140/180.
◆ Situated between the parks of Villa Ada and Villa Borghese, this new hotel has attractive public areas with coffered ceilings, and comfortable rooms.

Fenix, viale Gorizia 5 ✉ 00198 ☎ 06 8540741, *info@fenixhotel.it, Fax 06 8543632*, 🏠, 🌳 – |♦| ▤ TV 🚗. AE ⓢ ⓓ ⓜ VISA. ✂ FS n
Meals *(closed August, Saturday dinner and Sunday)* a la carte 24/40 – **76 rm** ☕ 130/200.
◆ Close to the parkland of Villa Torlonia, this establishment has smart well-presented public areas, and comfortable rooms which are tastefully furnished ; pleasant courtyard garden. Understated décor in the restaurant.

Hotel Astrid without rest., largo Antonio Sarti 4 ✉ 00196 ✆ 06 3236371, *info@otelastrid.com, Fax 06 3220806* – 🛗 ▤ 📺. AE 💲 ⓓ MC VISA JCB. ✂ DS
44 rm ☕ 100/140.
◆ Managed competently and cordially, this hotel offers refurbished accommodation wit every modern comfort, and serves a memorable breakfast on its panoramic terrace.

Villa del Parco withou rest., via Nomentana 110 ✉ 00161 ✆ 06 44237773, *info@hotelvilladelparco.it, Fax 06 44237572*, – 🛗 ▤ 📺 ♿. AE 💲 ⓓ MC VISA JCB. ✂ FS
29 rm ☕ 120/160.
◆ Occupying a charming late-19C villa with its own gardens, this welcoming family-run hot offers excellent levels of service.

Villa Glori without rest., via Celentano 11 ✉ 00196 ✆ 06 3227658, *Fax 06 321949* – 🛗 ▤ 📺. AE 💲 ⓓ MC VISA JCB. ✂ DS
58 rm ☕ 165/232,41.
◆ Well located close to the Tiber, this friendly and informal hotel benefits from a simp yet genteel interior, and well-appointed rooms.

Gallura, via Giovanni Antonelli 2 ✉ 00198 ✆ 06 8072971, *Fax 06 8078110*, – ▤ AE 💲 ⓓ MC VISA JCB. ✂ ES
closed 10 to 25 August, 1 to 10 January and Monday – **Meals** a la carte 61/87.
◆ Delightful summer dining outside at this well-located establishment, somewhat elevate from street level. Predominantly seafood cuisine.

Al Ceppo, via Panama 2 ✉ 00198 ✆ 06 8551379, *info@ristorantealceppo.i Fax 06 85301370* – ▤. AE 💲 ⓓ VISA. ✂ ES
closed 8 to 24 August and Monday – **Meals** (booking essential) a la carte 41/54.
◆ A rustic yet stylish feel to this restaurant, serving traditional cuisine and some mor modern dishes ; friendly atmosphere with many regulars.

La Scala, viale dei Parioli 79/d ✉ 00197 ✆ 06 8083978, *Fax 06 8084463*, – ▤ AE 💲 ⓓ MC VISA JCB. ✂ ES
closed 6 to 21 August and Wednesday – **Meals** Rest. and evening pizzeria a la carte 27/4
◆ Run by the same family for over 30 years, this classic restaurant offers traditional Itali fare ; pizzas also available in the evenings.

Ambasciata d'Abruzzo, via Pietro Tacchini 26 ✉ 00197 ✆ 06 8078256, *info@mbasciata-di-abruzzo.it, Fax 06 8074964*, – ▤. AE 💲 ⓓ MC VISA JCB ES
Meals a la carte 29/40.
◆ Specialising in the cuisine of the Abruzzo, but also serving Lazio dishes and seafood, th rustic and welcoming restaurant offers summer dining outside.

Al Fogher, via Tevere 13/b ✉ 00198 ✆ 06 8417032, *Fax 06 8558097* – ▤. AE 💲 ⓓ MC VISA JCB. ✂ PU
closed August, Saturday lunch and Sunday – **Meals** Venetian rest. a la carte 37/47.
◆ Located outside the old city walls, this pleasant establishment offers a wide variety Veneto cuisine including speciality pasta and rice dishes.

Coriolano, via Ancona 14 ✉ 00198 ✆ 06 44249863, *Fax 06 44249724*, Elegant tra toria – ▤. AE 💲 ⓓ MC VISA PU
closed 8 August-1 September – **Meals** (booking essential) a la carte 41/63.
◆ Named after its proprietor, who has recently celebrated 50 years in charge of th elegant trattoria, which has a friendly and courteous ambience.

Trastevere area (typical district) :

Santa Maria without rest., vicolo del Piede 2 ✉ 00153 ✆ 06 5894626, *hotel ntamaria@libero.it, Fax 06 5894815*, – ▤ 📺 ♿. AE 💲 ⓓ MC VISA JCB. ✂ KYZ
19 rm ☕ 155/207.
◆ Laid out around a courtyard garden, this peaceful new hotel occupies the site of a 1 cloister. Nearby is Santa Maria in Trastevere.

San Francesco without rest., via Jacopo de' Settesoli 7 ✉ 00153 ✆ 06 5830005 *hotelsanfrancesco@tin.it, Fax 06 85333413* – 🛗 ▤ 📺. AE 💲 MC VISA. ✂ KZ
24 rm ☕ 165/190.
◆ Formerly a hostel attached to the neighbouring church, the building has now been rebu as a hotel. Pleasant breakfast room, modern well-appointed accommodation.

Alberto Ciarla, piazza San Cosimato 40 ✉ 00153 ✆ 06 5818668, *alberto@alber ciarla.com, Fax 06 5884377*, – ▤. AE 💲 ⓓ MC VISA JCB. ✂ KZ
closed 1 week in August, 1 week in January and Sunday – **Meals** (dinner only) (bookir essential) seafood 47/80 and a la carte 50/63.
◆ Roman cuisine is offered alongside traditional seafood specialities in this elegant re taurant in the heart of the Trastevere district. Excellent wine-list.

Corsetti-il Galeone, piazza San Cosimato 27 ✉ 00153 ✆ 06 581631 *Fax 06 5896255*, – ▤. AE 💲 ⓓ MC VISA JCB. ✂ KZ
closed Wednesday lunch – **Meals** Roman and seafood rest. 27/32 b.i. and a la carte 29/5
◆ Set in an old galleon, this restaurant has a unique atmosphere. Run by the same fam since 1922 ; Roman cuisine and seafood specialities.

Sora Lella, via di Ponte Quattro Capi 16 (Isola Tiberina) ✉ 00186 ☎ 06 6861601, *Fax 06 6861601* – ▤. AE ⑤ ⓞ MC VISA JCB. ⚘ MY g
closed Easter, August, 24 to 26 December, New Year and Sunday – **Meals** Traditional Roman rest. a la carte 41/58.
◆ The son and grandchildren of the famous original proprietor maintain the traditions of a warm welcome and classic Roman cuisine at this restaurant.

Paris, piazza San Callisto 7/a ✉ 00153 ☎ 06 5815378, *Fax 06 5815378,* 余 – ▤. AE ⑤ ⓞ MC VISA JCB. ⚘ KZ r
closed August, Sunday dinner and Monday – **Meals** Roman rest. a la carte 30/55.
◆ In the heart of the Trastevere district, this cosy and genteel establishment offers polished interpretations of classic Roman cuisine. Very good wine-list.

Pastarellaro, via di San Crisogono 33 ✉ 00153 ☎ 06 5810871, *Fax 06 5810871*, Rest. wine bar with live piano music at dinner – ▤. AE ⑤ ⓞ MC VISA. ⚘ LZ u
Meals (dinner only except Sunday) Roman and seafood rest. a la carte 36/74 (10 %).
◆ This restaurant-wine bar has live music in the evening ; the menu offers flavoursome traditional Roman cuisine and fish dishes.

Asinocotto, via dei Vascellari 48 ✉ 00153 ☎ 06 5898985, *Fax 06 5898985* – ▤. AE ⑤ ⓞ MC VISA MZ a
closed 15 to 31 January and Monday – **Meals** (dinner only except Sunday) a la carte 42/64.
◆ Welcoming and well-run in its simplicity, this establishment offers creatively prepared traditional cuisine incorporating only the highest quality ingredients.

Checco er Carettiere, via Benedetta 10 ✉ 00153 ☎ 06 5817018, *osteria@tin.it, Fax 06 5884282,* 余 – ▤. AE ⑤ ⓞ MC VISA. ⚘ KY t
closed Sunday dinner also Monday lunch July-August – **Meals** Roman and seafood rest. a la carte 35/61.
◆ Situated in the picturesque Trastevere district, this classic trattoria serves seafood and Roman dishes ; pleasantly rustic ambience.

North-Western area via Flaminia, via Cassia, Balduina, Prima Valle, via Aurelia :

Colony without rest., via Monterosi 18 ✉ 00191 ☎ 06 36301843, *colony@iol.it, Fax 06 36309495,* – ▤ TV P – 🔬 90. AE ⑤ ⓞ MC VISA JCB
72 rm ☐ 130/150. by viale Maresciallo DS
◆ Not too far out of the centre, this hotel is popular with business people and tourists alike. Comfortable colonial-style rooms and good meeting rooms.

Sisto V without rest., via Lardaria 10 ✉ 00168 ☎ 06 35072185, *hotel.sistov@tiscali net.it, Fax 06 35072186* – ▤ TV. AE ⑤ ⓞ MC VISA. ⚘ by via Trionfale CS
22 rm ☐ 83/171.
◆ Close to the Policlinico Gemelli, this hotel was opened in 2000 ; garage parking and comfortable modern rooms ; standards in keeping with its category.

L'Ortica, via Flaminia Vecchia 573 ✉ 00191 ☎ 06 3338709, *Fax 06 3338709,* 余 – . AE ⑤ ⓞ MC VISA JCB by viale Maresciallo Pilsudski DS
closed 2 weeks in August and Sunday ; from October-April open Sunday lunch – **Meals** (dinner only) Neapolitan rest. a la carte 40/60.
◆ A good place to try Neapolitan dishes and other Campanian cuisine ; warm friendly ambience, decorated with unusual modern collectibles.

North-Eastern area via Salaria, via Nomentana, via Tiburtina :

Hotel la Giocca, via Salaria 1223 ✉ 00138 ☎ 06 8804411 and rest. ☎ 06 8804503, *hotel@lagiocca.it, Fax 06 8804495,* 余 – ▤ TV P – 🔬 180. AE ⑤ ⓞ MC VISA. ⚘ by via Salaria ES
Meals *Pappa Reale* Rest. Roman and seafood rest. a la carte 29/38 – **88 rm** ☐ 136,34/167,85, 3 suites.
◆ Modern efficiency and comfort in this recently refurbished hotel ; well-suited to business travellers. Classic style in the refitted rooms. Sizeable restaurant with pizzeria.

Carlo Magno without rest., via Sacco Pastore 13 ✉ 00141 ☎ 06 8603982, *desk@carlomagnohotel.com, Fax 06 8604355* – ▤ TV – 🔬 40. AE ⑤ ⓞ MC VISA JCB. ⚘ by via Salaria ES
60 rm ☐ 105/125.
◆ Well situated on Via Nomentana, this hotel has a smart and comfortable interior after a complete refit ; large top-floor terrace.

La Pergola without rest., via dei Prati Fiscali 55 ✉ 00141 ☎ 06 8107250, *info@hotellapergola.com, Fax 06 8124353,* – ▤ TV. AE ⑤ ⓞ MC VISA
96 rm ☐ 130/160. by via Salaria ES
◆ Family management makes for a homely atmosphere in this comfortable hotel near Via Salaria ; the well-presented pastel coloured rooms have modern furnishings.

Gabriele, via Ottoboni 74 ✉ 00159 ☎ 06 4393498, *ristorantegabriele@virgilio.it, Fax 06 43535366* – ▤. AE ⓢ ⓞ ⓜ VISA. ✻ by via Tiburtina FS
closed August, Saturday, Sunday and Bank Holidays – **Meals** (booking essential) a la carte 40/60.
◆ A classic restaurant with modern style ; under the same management for 40 years. Traditional Roman and other Italian dishes, both meat and seafood ; good wine-list.

Mamma Angelina, viale Arrigo Boito 65 ✉ 00199 ☎ 06 8608928, *mammangelina@libero.it* – ▤. AE ⓢ ⓞ ⓜ VISA. ✻ by via Salaria ES
closed August and Wednesday – **Meals** a la carte 30/48.
◆ Although the emphasis here is on fish, meat dishes are also available. Good value for money, classically stylish yet informal ambience.

South-Eastern area via Appia Antica, via Appia Nuova, via Tuscolana, via Casilina :

Appia Park Hotel without rest., via Appia Nuova 934 ✉ 00178 ☎ 06 716741, *info@appiaparkhotel.it, Fax 06 7182457,* – ▤ TV & – 90. AE ⓢ ⓞ ⓜ VISA. ✻
81 rm 130/160. by via Appia Nuova FT
◆ Set in its own gardens not far from the archaeological site of Appia Antica, ideal for those wanting a hotel out of the city centre. Classically stylish, comfortable rooms.

Rinaldo all'Acquedotto, via Appia Nuova 1267 ✉ 00178 ☎ 06 7183910, *Fax 06 7182968,* – ▤ P. AE ⓢ ⓞ ⓜ VISA. ✻ by via Appia Nuova FT
closed 16 to 24 August and Tuesday – **Meals** a la carte 31/51.
◆ A bright modern restaurant serving traditional cuisine and seafood ; the unusual veranda room has sliding doors and two trees growing through the roof.

Profumo di Mirto, viale Amelia 8/a ✉ 00181 ☎ 06 78395192 – ▤. AE ⓢ ⓜ VISA. ✻ by via Merulana PY
closed August and Monday – **Meals** Sardinian and seafood specialities a la carte 24/40.
◆ A modern restaurant with a family atmosphere, run by an enthusiastic and caring management ; seafood and Sardinian specialities.

Alfredo a via Gabi, via Gabi 36/38 ✉ 00183 ☎ 06 77206792, *Fax 06 77206792,* – ▤. AE ⓢ ⓞ ⓜ VISA FT d
closed August and Tuesday – **Meals** a la carte 26/35.
◆ This old-style trattoria, in the same hands since 1952, offers robust traditional Lazio and other Italian cuisine ; seafood and meat dishes.

South-Western area via Aurelia Antica, E.U.R., Città Giardino, via della Magliana, Portuense :

Sheraton Roma Hotel, viale del Pattinaggio 100 ✉ 00144 ☎ 06 54531, *res497.sheraton.roma@sheraton.com, Fax 06 5940689,* – rm, ▤ TV & P – 2000. AE ⓢ ⓞ ⓜ VISA JCB. ✻ by viale Aventino ES
Meals a la carte 75/112 – **634 rm** 317/508, 13 suites.
◆ This imposing modern development has well-appointed and varied accommodation ; adaptable meeting rooms well-suited to conferences. The elegant restaurant serves Italian and international cuisine.

Crowne Plaza Rome St. Peter's, via Aurelia Antica 415 ✉ 00165 ☎ 06 66420, *cpstpeter@hotel-invest.com, Fax 06 6637190,* – rm, ▤ TV & P – 260. AE ⓢ ⓞ ⓜ VISA JCB. ✻ by viale Gregorio VII CT
Meals ***Le Jardin d'Hiver*** Rest. international specialities a la carte 34/54 – 18 – **321 rm** 277/327.
◆ A large hotel with ample parking and peaceful gardens with pool, offering high standards of comfort both in its public areas and in its spacious rooms. The Jardin d'Hiver restaurant offers a varied menu.

Melià Roma Aurelia Antica, via degli Aldobrandeschi 223 ✉ 00163 ☎ 06 665441, *melia.roma@solmelia.com, Fax 06 66544467,* – ▤ TV & P – 750. AE ⓢ ⓞ ⓜ VISA. ✻ by viale Gregorio VII GY
Meals a la carte 28/50 – **270 rm** 309/325, suite.
◆ Despite having been constructed in record time, this hotel is extremely comfortable and well appointed ; very good conference facilities. The restaurant is of a high standard.

Villa Pamphili, via della Nocetta 105 ✉ 00164 ☎ 06 6602, *prenotazioni@hotelvillapamphili.com, Fax 06 66157747,* (covered in winter), – rm, ▤ TV & P – 500. AE ⓢ ⓞ ⓜ VISA JCB. ✻ by viale Gregorio VII CT
Meals a la carte 37/53 – **248 rm** 190/250, 10 suites.
◆ Peacefully-located adjacent to the parkland of Villa Doria Pamphili, this modern building has pleasant grounds ; shuttle service available to Piazza Risorgimento. The modern restaurant has two welcoming rooms.

Gd H. del Gianicolo without rest., viale Mura Gianicolensi 107 ✉ 00152 ☎ 06 58333405, *info@grandhotelgianicolo.it, Fax 06 58179434,* – ▤ TV – 120. AE ⓢ ⓞ ⓜ VISA JCB. ✻ JZ b
47 rm 160/230.
◆ Occupying an elegant small palazzo with well-kept garden and pool, this smart hotel offers comfortable, spacious accommodation and elegant public areas.

Shangri Là-Corsetti, viale Algeria 141 ✉ 00144 ☎ 06 5916441, *info@shangrilacorsetti.it, Fax 06 5413813,* – – 80. by viale Aventino ET
Meals (see rest. ***Shangri Là-Corsetti*** below) – **52 rm** 170/216.
♦ White domed ceilings, marble and sofas in the lobby of this 1960s hotel located in the EUR district, mainly used by business travellers ; attractive wooded gardens.

Dei Congressi, viale Shakespeare 29 ✉ 00144 ☎ 06 5926021, *info@hoteldeicongressiroma.com, Fax 06 5911903,* – – – 250.
closed 30 July-30 August – **Meals *La Glorietta*** Rest. *(closed 28 July-25 August and Saturday)* a la carte 30/49 – **105 rm** 135/200. by viale Aventino ET
♦ Close to the EUR palazzo dei Congressi, this functional hotel offers comfortable accommodation and numerous meeting rooms. The restaurant serves classic dishes and offers outdoor dining in summer.

Shangri-Là Corsetti, viale Algeria 141 ✉ 00144 ☎ 06 5918861, *Fax 06 5413813,* – by viale Aventino ET
closed 9 to 24 August – **Meals** Roman and seafood specialities a la carte 38/60.
♦ Laid out over three well-presented and comfortable rooms, with summer dining outside ; menu includes traditional fare, seafood and international cuisine.

Outskirts of Rome

Baschi *05023 Terni* 563 N 18 – *pop. 2670 alt. 165.*
Roma 118 – Orvieto 10 – Terni 70 – Viterbo 46.

Vissani, North : 12 km ✉ 05020 Civitella del Lago ☎ 0744 950206, *Fax 0744 950186* –
closed August, Sunday dinner, Wednesday and Thursday lunch – **Meals** (booking essential) a la carte 85/125 (15 %).
♦ Antiques and modern decorative items combine to provide an elegant and individualistic style throughout, with creative cuisine notable for its quality of ingredients.
Spec. Ravioli all'amatriciana, salsa di foiolo e maggiorana, carciofi in umido e animelle. Soufflé d'anatra ai pistacchi con rapette e patate all'olio d'oliva, burro d'ostriche ed olive nere. Zuppa di brasato con frappé di carote ghiacciato.

FLORENCE (FIRENZE)

See : *Cathedral★★★ (Duomo)* Y : *east end★★★, dome★★★ (✻★★) – Campanile★★★* Y **B** : *✻★★ – Baptistry★★★* Y **A** : *doors★★★, mosaics★★★ – Cathedral Museum★★* Y **M5** – *Piazza della Signoria★★* Z – *Loggia della Signoria★★* Z **K** : *Perseus★★★ by B. Cellini – Palazzo Vecchio★★★* Z **H** – *Uffizi Gallery★★★* EU **M** – *Bargello Palace and Museum★★★* EU **M** – *San Lorenzo★★★* DU **V** : *Church★★, Laurentian Library★★, Medici Tombs★★★ in Medicee Chapels★★ – Medici-Riccardi Palace★★* EU **S** : *Chapel★★★, Luca Giordano Gallery★★ – Church of Santa Maria Novella★★* DU **W** : *frescoes★★★ by Ghirlandaio – Ponte Vecchio★★* Z – *Pitti Palace★★* DV : *Palatine Gallery★★★, Silver Museum★★, Works★★ by Macchiaioli in Modern Art Gallery★ – Boboli Garden★* DV : *✻★ from the Citadel Belvedere – Porcelain Museum★* DV – *Monastery and Museum of St. Mark★★* ET : *works★★★ by Beato Angelico – Academy Gallery★★* ET : *Michelangelo gallery★★★ – Piazza della Santissima Annunziata★* ET **168** : *frescoes★ in the church, portico★★ with corners decorated with terracotta Medallions★★ in the Foundling Hospital★ – Church of Santa Croce★★* EU : *Pazzi Chapel★★ – Excursion to the hills★★ : ✻★★★ from Michelangelo Square* EFV, *Church of San Miniato al Monte★★* EFV– *Strozzi Palace★★* DU **S** – *Rucellai Palace★★* DU **S** – *Masaccio's frescoes★★★ in the Chapel Brancacci a Santa Maria del Carmine* DUV – *Last Supper of Fuligno★* DT, *Last Supper of San Salvi★* BS **G** – *Orsanmichele★* EU **R** : *tabernacle★★ by Orcagna – La Badia* EU **E** : *campanile★, delicate relief sculpture in marble★★, tombs★, Madonna appearing to St. Bernard★ by Filippino Lippi – Sassetti Chapel★★ and the Chapel of the Annunciation★ in the Holy Trinity Church* DU **X** – *Church of the Holy Spirit★* DUV – *Last Supper★ of Sant'Apollonia* ET – *All Saints' Church* DU : *Last Supper★ by Ghirlandaio – Davanzanti Palace★* Z **M** – *New Market Loggia★* Z **L** – *Museums : Archaeological★★ (Chimera from Arezzo★★, Françoise Vase★★)* ET, *Science★* EU **M** – *Marino Marini Museum★* Z **M** – *Bardini Museum★* EV – *La Specola Museum★* DV.

See also : *Casa Buonarroti★* EU **M** – *Semi-precious Stone Workshop★* ET **M** – *Crucifixion★ by Perugino* EU **C** – *Museo Horne★* EUV **M11**.

Envir. : *Medicee Villas★★ : villa della Petraia★, villa di Castello★, villa di Poggio a Caiano★★ by via P. Toselli* CT : *17 km – Galluzzo Carthusian Monastery★★ by via Senese* CV.

9 *Parco di Firenze ☎ 3480058590, Fax 055 785627, North : 4 km;*

18 *Dell'Ugolino (closed Monday March-September), to Grassina ✉ 50015 ☎ 055 2301009, Fax 055 2301141, South : 12 km* BS.

✈ *Amerigo Vespucci North-West : 4 km by via P. Toselli* **CT** *☎ 055 30615, Fax 055 2788400 – Alitalia, vicolo dell'Oro 1, ✉ 50123 ☎ 055 27881, Fax 055 2788400.*

via Cavour 1 r ✉ 50129 ☎ 055 290832, Fax 055 2760383 – piazza della Stazione 4 ✉ 50123 ☎ 055 212245, Fax 055 2381226 – **A.C.I.** *viale Amendola 36 ✉ 50121 ☎ 055 24861. – Roma 277 – Bologna 105 – Milano 298.*

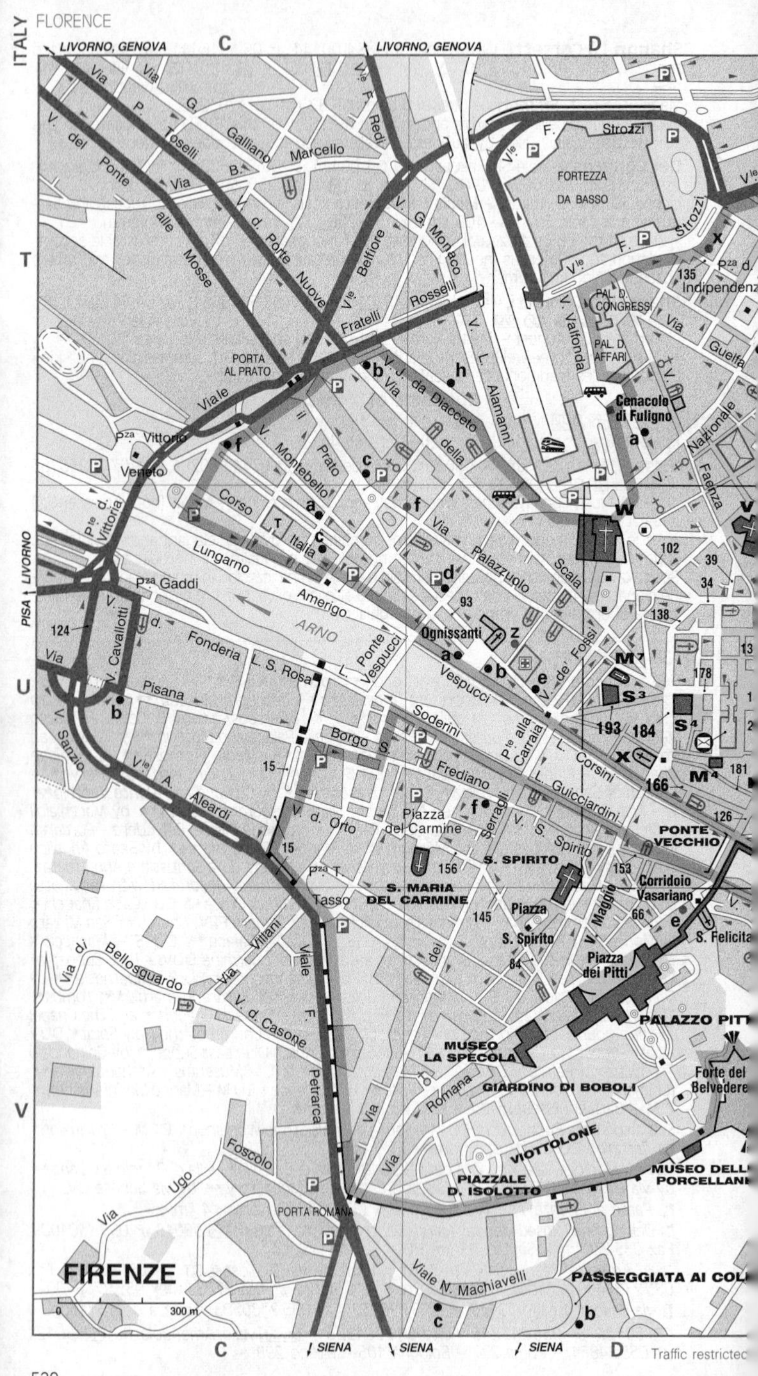
FIRENZE
C
D
T
U
V
LIVORNO, GENOVA
LIVORNO, GENOVA
PISA LIVORNO
SIENA
SIENA
SIENA
0
300 m
FORTEZZA
DA BASSO
PAL. D. CONGRESSI
PAL. D. AFFARI
Cenacolo di Fuligno
PORTA AL PRATO
Pza Vittorio Veneto
Pza Gaddi
ARNO
Ognissanti
PONTE VECCHIO
Corridoio Vasariano
S. SPIRITO
S. MARIA DEL CARMINE
Piazza del Carmine
Piazza S. Spirito
Piazza dei Pitti
PALAZZO PITTI
MUSEO LA SPECOLA
GIARDINO DI BOBOLI
Forte del Belvedere
VIOTTOLONE
PIAZZALE D. ISOLOTTO
MUSEO DELLE PORCELLANE
PORTA ROMANA
PASSEGGIATA AI COLLI
Pza T. Tasso
S. Felicita
Via G. Galliano
Via P. Toselli
V. del Ponte alle Mosse
Via B. Marcello
V. d. Porte Nuove
Vle F. Redi
Vle Belfiore
V. G. Monaco
Vle Fratelli Rosselli
Vle F. Strozzi
V. Valfonda
V. L. Alamanni
Via J. da Diacceto
Via della Scala
Viale
V. Montebello
Via il Prato
Corso Italia
Via Palazzuolo
Lungarno Amerigo Vespucci
Ponte Vespucci
Pte alla Carraia
L. Corsini
L. Guicciardini
V. Fonderia
L. S. Rosa
Via Pisana
V. Cavallotti
V. Sanzio
Vle A. Aleardi
Borgo S. Frediano
V. d. Orto
Serragli
V. S. Spirito
V. Maggio
Via dei
Via di Bellosguardo
Via Villani
V. d. Casone
Viale F. Petrarca
Via Romana
Via Foscolo
Via Ugo
Viale N. Machiavelli
Pte d. Vittoria
Pza d. Indipendenza
Via Guelfa
V. Nazionale
V. Faenza
V. de' Fossi
124
102
39
34
138
93
178
193
184
181
166
126
153
66
156
145
84
135
15
M7
S3
S4
M4
W
X
T

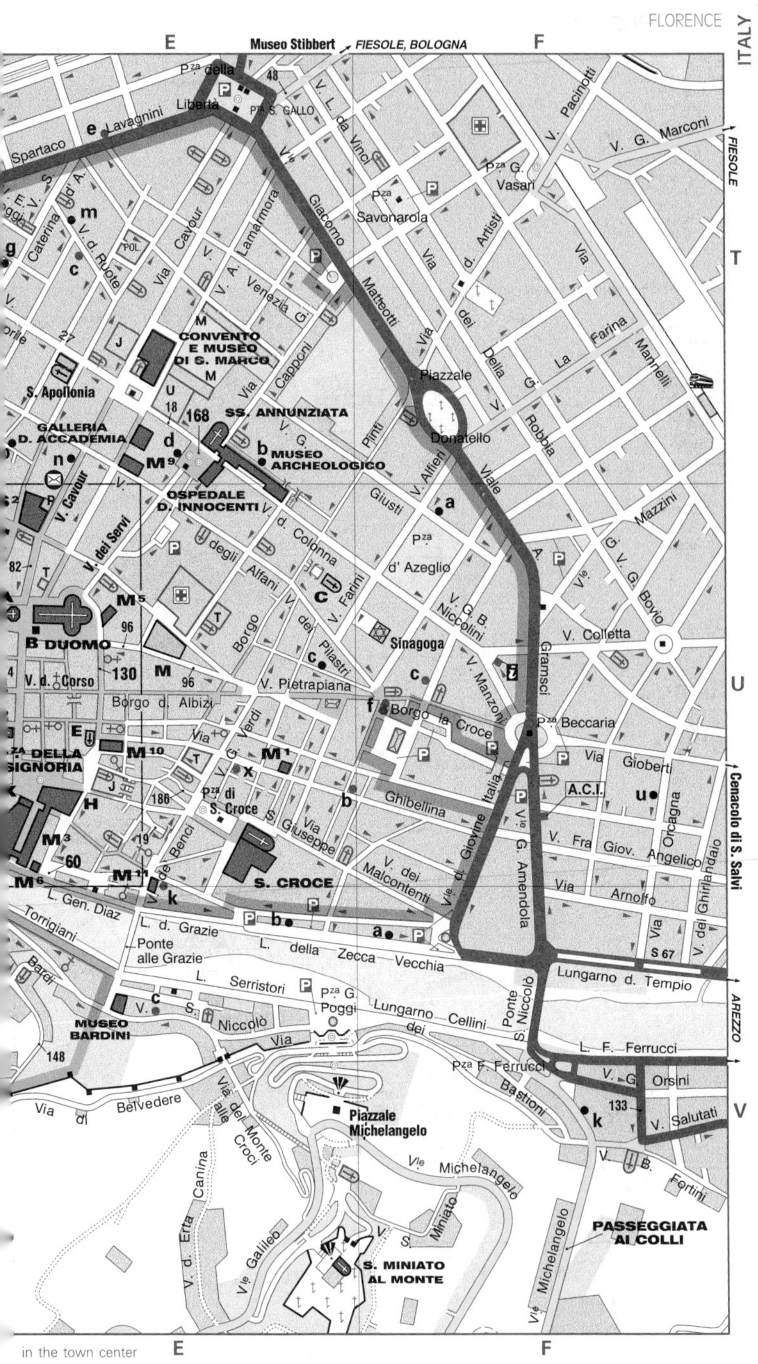

in the town center

FIRENZE

- Agli (Via degli) .... Y 3
- Antinori (Piazza degli) ... Y 10
- Archibusieri (Lungarno) .... Z 12
- Avelli (Via degli) .... Y 16
- Brunelleschi (Via de) .... YZ 22
- Calimala .... Z 24
- Calzaiuoli (Via dei) .... YZ
- Canto de' Nelli (Via del) .. T 27
- Castellani (Via de') ...... Z 31
- Dante Alighieri (Via)..... Z 42
- Davanzati (Piazza) ...... Z 43
- Fiordalisa (Via del) ...... Z 52
- Gondi (Via dei) .... Z 61
- Lambertesca (Via) ...... Z 69
- Leoni (Via dei) .... Z 70
- Madonna degli Aldobrandini (Piazza di) .... Y 75
- Magazzini (Via dei) ...... Z 76
- Melarancio (Via del)...... Y 85
- Monalda (Via) .... Z 88
- Oriuolo (Via d.) .... Y 96
- Orsanmichele (Via)...... Z 99
- Parte Guelfa (Piazza di) .. Z 106
- Pelliccena (Via) .... Z 109
- Pescioni (Via de') ...... YZ 111
- Por S. Maria (Via) ...... Z 126
- Porta Rossa (Via) ...... Z
- Roma (Via) .... YZ
- Rondinelli (Via de') ..... Y 138
- S. Giovanni (Piazza) .... Y 150
- S. Jacopo (Borgo)...... Z
- S. Trinita (Piazza) ...... Z 163
- Sassetti (Via de') ...... Z 171
- Spada (Via della) ...... Z 173
- Speziali (Via degli) ..... Z 174
- Strozzi (Piazza) .... Z 177
- Strozzi (Via degli) ...... Z
- Tavolini (Via dei) 180
- Terme (Via delle) 181
- Tornabuoni (Via) ...... Z
- Trebbio (Via del) ...... Y 187
- Uffizi (Piazzale degli).... Z 188
- Vacchereccia (Via) ..... Z 189
- Vecchio (Ponte) .... Z

Traffic restricted in the town centre

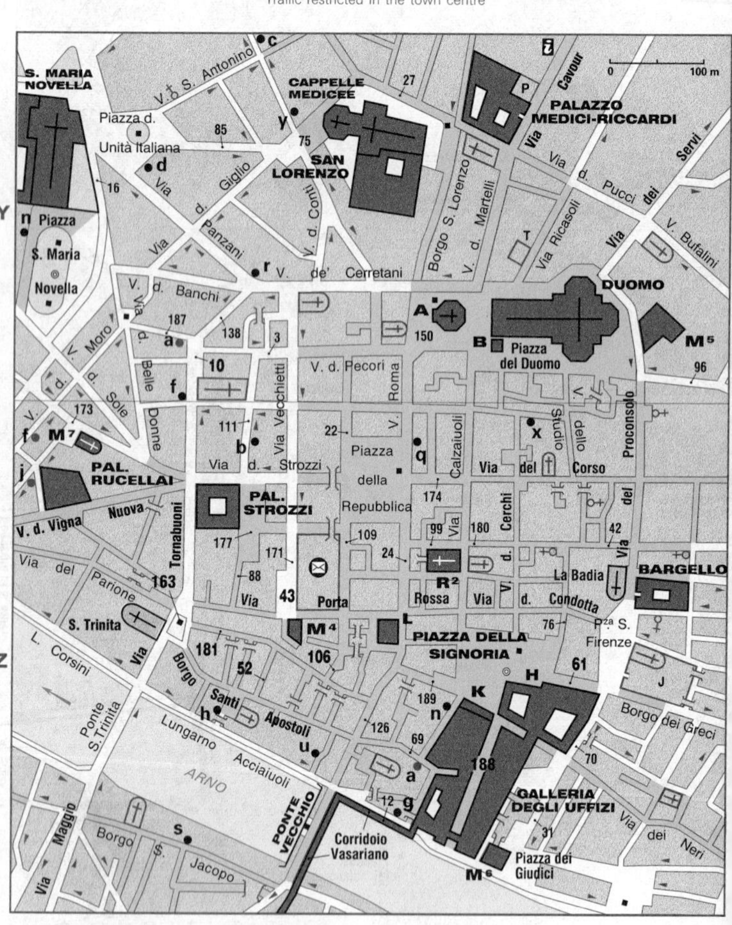

Send us your comments on the restaurants we recommend
and your opinion on the specialities
and local wines they offer.

STREET INDEX TO FIRENZE TOWN PLAN

The Westin Excelsior, piazza Ognissanti 3 ✉ 50123 ℘ 055 264201, *excelsiorflorence.res043@starwoodhotel.com, Fax 055 210278* – rm, – 180. DU b
Meals *Il Cestello* Rest. a la carte 49/65 – 47 – **149 rm** 591/710, 11 suites.
◆ Sumptuous interiors within this former aristocratic residence on the banks of the Arno, where tradition and the most modern comforts meet to create an exclusive and dignified hotel. A regal atmosphere to the dining room.

Grand Hotel, piazza Ognissanti 1 ✉ 50123 ℘ 055 288781, *res045grandhotelflorence@luxurycollection.com, Fax 055 217400,* – rm, . DU a
Meals *Incanto Cafè Restaurant* Rest. a la carte 50/68 – 47 – **96 rm** 546/737, 7 suites.
◆ The atmosphere of Renaissance Florence combines with 21C comfort in the elegant surroundings of this prestigious titan of the hotel world. The sophisticated restaurant adjoins the hall with its terrace onto the piazza and on-show kitchen.

Grand Hotel Villa Medici, via Il Prato 42 ✉ 50123 ℘ 055 277171, *villa.medici@sinahotels.it, Fax 055 2381336,* – – 90. CT c
Meals a la carte 60/71 – 33 – **103 rm** 539, 14 suites.
◆ Situated in a garden oasis (with swimming pool) in the centre of Florence, this traditional hotel is in an 18C palazzo with impressive, well-maintained interiors. A stylish dining room, with the option of eating outside in summer.

Regency, piazza Massimo D'Azeglio 3 ✉ 50121 ℘ 055 245247, *info@regency-hotel.com, Fax 055 2346735,* – . rest FU a
Meals *Relais le Jardin* Rest. (booking essential) a la carte 40/66 – **33 rm** 363/605, 2 suites.
◆ An atmosphere of charm and comfort offering respite from the tourist trail. Guests can relax in the pampered environment of the elegant lounge or the hidden calm of the garden, which may be seen from the more informal of the two dining rooms.

Albani, via Fiume 12 ✉ 50123 ℘ 055 26030, *hotel.albani@firenzealbergo.it, Fax 055 211045* – rm, – 300. rest DT a
Meals a la carte 34/45 – **98 rm** 335/350, 4 suites.
◆ Close to the station, in a prestigious early 20C building, a refined Neo-classical style permeates throughout this charming hotel. Polychrome panels decorate the walls of the elegant dining room.

Helvetia e Bristol, via dei Pescioni 2 ✉ 50123 ℘ 055 26651, *reservation.hbf@royaldemeure.com, Fax 055 288353* – . Z b
Meals *Il Giardino d'Inverno* Rest. (dinner only) (booking essential) a la carte 42/66 – 29,70 – **45 rm** 297/550, 13 suites.
◆ The elegant allure of days gone by in an imposing 19C building, furnished with authentic antiques and 17C Florentine pictures. Chairs upholstered in red velvet and impressive drapery in the dining room. Very near Palazzo Strozzi.

Plaza Hotel Lucchesi, lungarno della Zecca Vecchia 38 ✉ 50122 ℘ 055 26236, *phl@plazalucchesi.it, Fax 055 2480921,* – – 160. rest EV b
Meals (residents only) 21/33 – **97 rm** 237/387.
◆ This elegant riverside hotel has been restored in keeping with the building which it occupies. Many rooms look onto the river and Santa Croce.

Savoy, piazza della Repubblica 7 ✉ 50123 ℘ 055 27351, *reservations@hotelsavoy.it, Fax 055 2735888,* – – 80. Z q
Meals *L'Incontro* Rest. a la carte 45/70 – 26,40 – **98 rm** 407/803, 9 suites.
◆ After total refurbishment, this great hotel (founded 1893) has been revitalised, offering a mix of elegance, comfort and high-tech gadgetry. The brasserie style restaurant opens stylishly onto the piazza in summer.

Gd H. Minerva, piazza Santa Maria Novella 16 ✉ 50123 ℘ 055 27230, *info@grandhotelminerva.com, Fax 055 268281,* – rm, – 80. rest Y n
Meals a la carte 43/68 – **98 rm** 270/370, 5 suites.
◆ Next to the church of Santa Maria Novella, a very comfortable modern hotel, with well-proportioned public areas. Lovely view from the terrace with pool. A huge window looks onto the internal garden from the larger of the dining rooms.

Grand Hotel Baglioni, piazza Unità Italiana 6 ✉ 50123 ℘ 055 23580, *info@hotelbaglioni.it, Fax 055 23588895* – – 200. Y d
Meals a la carte 37/55 – **190 rm** 277/329, 3 suites.
◆ Genteel hospitality and stylish interiors set in an elegant historic building ; of world renown and only a stone's throw from the station. Fine views over Florence from the roof-garden restaurant.

Lungarno, borgo Sant'Jacopo 14 ✉ 50125 ✆ 055 27261, *lungarno@lungarnohotels.com, Fax 055 268437,* ← – |‡|, ⇔ rm, ▤ TV ✆ – 🏛 25. AE ⓢ ⓞ ⓜ VISA JCB. ✂ rest
Meals *(closed August and Sunday)* (dinner only) a la carte 54/64 – **60 rm** ☕ 363/407, 13 suites. Z s
◆ Rooms with priceless views in a hotel on the very banks of the Arno, where the management's attention to detail is evident throughout. Fine collection of modern pictures. Restaurant also overlooks the river.

Sofitel Firenze, via de' Cerretani 10 ✉ 50123 ✆ 055 2381301, *sofitel.firenze@accor-hotels.it, Fax 055 2381312* – |‡|, ⇔ rm, ▤ TV ✆ ♿. AE ⓢ ⓞ ⓜ VISA JCB. ✂ Y r
Meals *Il Patio* Rest. a la carte 32/42 – **83 rm** ☕ 380/420, suite.
◆ A 17C patrician palace, now restored to offer all mod cons including very effective soundproofing, a real benefit given the central location ; the elegant restaurant is set in a glass-roofed terrace.

Starhotel Michelangelo, viale Fratelli Rosselli 2 ✉ 50123 ✆ 055 2784, *michelangelo.fi@starhotels.it, Fax 055 2382232* – |‡|, ⇔ rm, ▤ TV ✆ ♿ 🏛 250. AE ⓢ ⓞ ⓜ VISA JCB. ✂ CT f
Meals *Il David* Rest. a la carte 40/60 – **119 rm** ☕ 259/289.
◆ After a total refit this is effectively a brand new hotel, with accommodation boasting every comfort (even TV in the bathrooms) ; well-equipped conference rooms. An atmosphere of refinement in the dining room.

De la Ville without rest., piazza Antinori 1 ✉ 50123 ✆ 055 2381805, *delaville@firenze.net, Fax 055 2381809* – |‡| ▤ TV ✆ – 🏛 60. AE ⓢ ⓞ ⓜ VISA JCB Y f
71 rm ☕ 240/500, 4 suites.
◆ Situated in the most exclusive shopping district, this hotel of distinction has been refitted. Offers spacious and stylish accommodation with modern bathrooms.

Palazzo Magnani Feroni without rest., borgo San Frediano 5 ✉ 50124 ✆ 055 2399544, *info@florencepalace.it, Fax 055 2608908,* 🏋 – ▤ TV ✆. AE ⓢ ⓞ ⓜ VISA JCB. ✂ DU f
12 suites ☕ 320/590.
◆ Occupying a 16C patrician palazzo with a small courtyard in the Oltrarno quarter, this hotel offers fine all round views of the city from its terraces.

Gallery Hotel Art, vicolo dell'Oro 5 ✉ 50123 ✆ 055 27263 and rest. ✆ 055 27266987, *gallery@lungarnohotels.com, Fax 055 268557* – |‡|, ⇔ rm, ▤ TV ✆ ♿. AE ⓢ ⓞ ⓜ VISA JCB. ✂ rest Z u
Meals *The Fusion Bar-Shozan Gallery* Rest. *(closed Monday)* a la carte 26/43 – **65 rm** ☕ 330/363, suite.
◆ Contemporary design by a leading architect and cosmopolitan artwork displayed along art gallery lines are the ingredients making this truly modern hotel so unusual. A sophisticated, trendy restaurant with fusion cuisine.

Degli Orafi without rest., lungarno Archibusieri 4 ✉ 50122 ✆ 055 26622, *info@hoteldegliorafi.it, Fax 055 2662111* – |‡| ▤ TV ✆ ♿. AE ⓢ ⓞ ⓜ VISA JCB. ✂ Z g
42 rm ☕ 240/380.
◆ This elegant and historic establishment is close to the Ponte Vecchio and the Uffizi. The ideal place to stay for those in quest of charm.

Anglo American Hotel, via Garibaldi 9 ✉ 50123 ✆ 055 282114, *reservation.ghr@framon-hotels.it, Fax 055 268513* – ⇔ ▤ ✆ ♿ – 🏛 90. AE ⓢ ⓞ ⓜ VISA JCB CU a
Meals a la carte 38/54 – ☕ 16,50 – **82 rm** 308/352, 15 suites.
◆ Central but surprisingly tranquil, close to the Lungarno. A cosy, welcoming atmosphere, with an unusual glass gallery lounge area. Evocations of days gone by in the dining room.

Brunelleschi, piazza Santa Elisabetta 3 ✉ 50122 ✆ 055 27370, *info@hotelbrunelleschi.it, Fax 055 219653,* ← – |‡|, ⇔ rm, ▤ TV ✆ – 🏛 100. AE ⓢ ⓞ ⓜ VISA JCB. ✂ rest Z c
Meals *(closed Sunday)* (residents only) a la carte 35/40 – **87 rm** ☕ 235/340, 7 suites.
◆ It seems possible to touch Brunelleschi's dome from some of the rooms in this elegant, unusual hotel. The tower dating to Byzantine times houses its own small museum.

Londra, via Jacopo da Diacceto 18 ✉ 50123 ✆ 055 27390, *info@hotellondra.com, Fax 055 210682,* 🏋, ≘s – |‡|, ⇔ rm, ▤ TV 🚗 – 🏛 200. AE ⓢ ⓞ ⓜ VISA JCB. ✂ rest
Meals a la carte 45/60 – **166 rm** ☕ 250/335. DT h
◆ Located near the station, this comfortable and functional modern hotel has spacious public areas, a business centre and conference rooms. A contemporary-style dining room, with an adjoining terrace offering a more romantic setting.

J and J without rest., via di Mezzo 20 ✉ 50121 ✆ 055 26312, *reservation@jandj.it, Fax 055 240282* – ▤ TV ✆. AE ⓢ ⓞ ⓜ VISA JCB. ✂ EU c
15 rm ☕ 315, 5 suites.
◆ An eclectic feel pervades throughout this atmospheric and original hotel, which was once a 16C convent.

UNA Hotel Vittoria, via Pisana 59 50143 055 22771, *una.vittoria@unahotels.it, Fax 055 22772* – rm, – 100. rest
Meals a la carte 26/39 – **84 rm** 461. CU b
◆ An unusual techno-hotel combining comfort with innovation. The imaginative design brief has created a charming and unique ambience. Original dining room with refectory table.

Pierre without rest., via De' Lamberti 5 50123 055 216218, *pierre@remarhotels.com, Fax 055 2396573* – . Z t
44 rm 265/370.
◆ A centrally located and comfortable hotel ; behind its historic façade is a renovated interior. Rooms with furnishings along traditional Florentine or Venetian lines.

Grand Hotel Adriatico, via Maso Finiguerra 9 50123 055 27931 and rest. 055 294447, *info@hoteladriatico.it, Fax 055 289661* – – 150. DU d
Meals 20/35 and ***La Vela*** Rest. a la carte 33/41 – **119 rm** 240/290, 3 suites.
◆ This recently refitted hotel benefits from a very central location, private parking, and a spacious, comfortable interior ; rooms in both modern and antique style. An attractive classical-style feel to the La Vela restaurant.

Berchielli without rest., lungarno Acciaiuoli 14 50123 055 264061, *info@berchielli.it, Fax 055 218636,* – – 80. . Z h
76 rm 300/335.
◆ To not only be in the heart of Florence, but also on the Arno with a view of the Ponte Vecchio ; such is the enviable location of this comfortable hotel of distinction.

Rivoli without rest., via della Scala 33 50123 055 278601, *info@hotelrivoli.it, Fax 055 294041,* – – 100. . DU m
69 rm 210/300.
◆ Near Santa Maria Novella, this hotel has spacious rooms, large public areas and an attractive atrium with whirlpool bath.

Ville sull'Arno, lungarno Colombo 3 50136 055 670971, *info@hotelvillesullarno.com, Fax 055 678244,* , , – – 25. . rest by lungarno del Tempio FV
Meals (residents only) a la carte 31/39 – **47 cam** 143/220.
◆ On the banks of the Arno, this hotel is laid out around a central building with two wings ; modern furnishings and a small garden with swimming pool.

Il Guelfo Bianco without rest., via Cavour 29 50129 055 288330, *info@ilguelfobianco.it, Fax 055 295203* – . . ET n
30 rm 135/210.
◆ This small but distinguished hotel is close to the Duomo, housed in a restored 16C palazzo ; fine rooms, some with coffered ceilings.

Botticelli without rest., via Taddea 8 50123 055 290905, *info@hotelbotticelli.it, Fax 055 294322* – . ET p
34 rm 135/220.
◆ Near San Lorenzo market, in a 16C palazzo, a charming hotel with frescoed vaulting in its public areas and a small covered terrace ; rooms with modern furnishings

Palazzo Benci without rest., piazza Madonna degli Aldobrandini 3 50123 055 213848, *palazzobenci@iol.it, Fax 055 288308,* – – 30. . Y y
35 rm 140/192.
◆ Next to San Lorenzo ; traces of the original 16C structure can still be seen in the public areas of this hotel which has a charming inner courtyard and comfortable rooms.

De Rose Palace Hotel without rest., via Solferino 5 50123 055 2396818, *firenze@hotelderose.it, Fax 055 268249* – . CU c
18 rm 135/210.
◆ In a restored 19C palace, an elegant hotel with period furnishings and some fine Venetian lamps ; relaxing family atmosphere.

Loggiato dei Serviti without rest., piazza SS. Annunziata 3 50122 055 289592, *info@loggiatodeiservitihotel.it, Fax 055 289595* – . ET d
38 rm 140/205, 4 suites.
◆ Occupying the 16C twin of Brunelleschi's foundling hospital, this hotel has preserved its historic charm throughout.

Morandi alla Crocetta without rest., via Laura 50 50121 055 2344747, *welcome@hotelmorandi.it, Fax 055 2480954* – . ET b
11 – **10 rm** 115/175.
◆ The cosy atmosphere of a grand private house pervades this stylishly furnished hotel with many period details ; in the centre near the Museo Archeologico.

River without rest., lungarno della Zecca Vecchia 18 ✉ 50122 ✆ 055 2343529, *hotelriver@hotelriver.com, Fax 055 2343531,* ← – AE VISA JCB. FV a
closed 15 to 27 December – **38 rm** 190.
◆ Well located in a 19C palazzo on the Arno. The top floor rooms overlooking the river benefit from a delightful terrace. Attractively restored.

Malaspina without rest., piazza dell'Indipendenza 24 ✉ 50129 ✆ 055 489869, *info@malaspinahotel.it, Fax 055 474809* – AE VISA. ET g
31 rm 130/199.
◆ An attractive hotel founded ten years ago after the reconstruction of an old palazzo ; welcoming public areas and stylish rooms.

Benivieni without rest., via delle Oche 5 ✉ 50122 ✆ 055 2382133, *info@hotelbenivieni.it, Fax 055 2398248* – AE VISA JCB Z x
15 rm 160/220.
◆ In a 15C palazzo close to the Duomo, which in the late 18C housed a Jewish religious school. Small covered garden in the courtyard.

Royal without rest., via delle Ruote 52 ✉ 50129 ✆ 055 483287, *info@hotelroyalfirenze.it, Fax 055 490976,* – AE VISA JCB ET m
39 rm 120/200.
◆ This former aristocratic residence with its fine garden and handy parking is pleasantly tranquil despite its central location ; comfortable rooms.

Villa Azalee without rest., viale Fratelli Rosselli 44 ✉ 50123 ✆ 055 214242, *villaazalee@fi.flashnet.it, Fax 055 268264,* – AE VISA CT b
25 rm 158,64/170.
◆ 19C villa situated on one of the main thoroughfares into the city. Charming garden.

Galileo without rest., via Nazionale 22/a ✉ 50123 ✆ 055 496645, *hgalileo@dada.it, Fax 055 496447* – AE VISA DT b
15 – **31 rm** 175/230.
◆ This recently refurbished hotel now incorporates a lounge which has enhanced the small reception area. Comfortable rooms with antique furniture.

Rosary Garden without rest., via di Ripoli 169 ✉ 50126 ✆ 055 6800136, *info@rosarygarden.it, Fax 055 6800458* – AE VISA by via Salutati FV
13 rm 98/200.
◆ "Feel at home in your hotel" is the slogan of this delightful English-style hotel ; cherry-wood furniture and prints in the rooms. Do not miss afternoon tea.

Goldoni without rest., via Borgo Ognissanti 8 ✉ 50123 ✆ 055 284080, *info@hotelgoldoni.com, Fax 055 282576* – AE VISA DU e
20 rm 135/185.
◆ Situated in an 18C palazzo close to the Ponte Vecchio, with views of the Arno, this pleasant hotel has recently been refitted.

Enoteca Pinchiorri, via Ghibellina 87 ✉ 50122 ✆ 055 242777, *ristorante@enoteca.pinchiorri.com, Fax 055 244983,* – AE VISA JCB EU x
closed August, December, Sunday, Monday and Tuesday-Wednesday lunch – **Meals** (booking essential) a la carte 165/235.
◆ Impeccable food, service and atmosphere ; summer dining outside. Sublime cuisine and a famously peerless wine list.
Spec. Gamberoni in tre versioni. Ravioli di ricotta e bietola con lingua stufata, arachidi, carote novelle e lamelle di ricotta salata. Composizione di coniglio all'aglio con fagiolini rifatti alla fiorentina e crostone di fegatini.

Cibreo, via A. Del Verrocchio 8/r ✉ 50122 ✆ 055 2341100, *cibreo.fi@tin.it, Fax 055 244966* – AE VISA JCB FU f
closed 26 July-6 September, 31 December-6 January, Sunday and Monday – **Meals** (booking essential) a la carte 64/74 see also rest. ***Trattoria Cibrèo-Cibreino.***
◆ Perennially fashionable restaurant popular for its informal elegance ; young, relaxed staff and a dedicated, imaginative culinary style.

Don Chisciotte, via Ridolfi 4 r ✉ 50129 ✆ 055 475430, *Fax 055 485305* – AE VISA JCB. DT x
closed August, Sunday and Monday lunch – **Meals** (booking essential) a la carte 41/56.
◆ Close to the Fortezza da basso, an elegant atmosphere pervades in what is one of the city's finest restaurants ; creative modern twists to classic dishes.

Taverna del Bronzino, via delle Ruote 25/27 r ✉ 50129 ✆ 055 495220, *tavernadelbronzino@rabottiumberto.191.it, Fax 055 4620076* – AE VISA ET c
closed Easter, August, Christmas and Sunday – **Meals** (booking essential) a la carte 58/72.
◆ In a 15C palazzo, courteous hospitality and the historic setting set the tone for fine traditional cuisine.

Alle Murate, via Ghibellina 52 r ✉ 50122 ✆ 055 240618, *Fax 055 288950* – ▤. ᴀᴇ 𝕤 ⦿ ⓜⓒ VISA JCB. ✻ EU
closed 7 to 28 December and Monday – **Meals** (dinner only) (booking essential) 52/6 (15 %).
◆ An intimate restaurant with some elegant touches, soft lights and a cosy ambience. Th ideal place for a candlelit dinner ; Tuscan cuisine.

Targa Bistrot Fiorentino, lungarno Colombo 7 ✉ 50136 ✆ 055 677377, *info@targ bistrot.net, Fax 055 676493* – ▤. ᴀᴇ 𝕤 ⦿ ⓜⓒ VISA by lungarno del Tempio FV
closed Sunday – **Meals** (booking essential) a la carte 35/50.
◆ Located on the banks of the Arno, this atmospheric restaurant overlooks the rive through large windows ; informal yet efficient service.

Osteria n. 1, via del Moro 18/22 r ✉ 50123 ✆ 055 284897, *Fax 055 294318* – ▤ ᴀᴇ 𝕤 ⦿ ⓜⓒ VISA JCB Z
closed 3 to 26 August, Sunday and Monday lunch – **Meals** a la carte 34/5 (10 %).
◆ An elegant atmosphere with subdued lighting and stylish furnishings distin guish this restaurant ; the cuisine provides interesting variations to tradition dishes.

Osteria Farniente, via della Mattonaia 19 r ✉ 50121 ✆ 055 2466473, *info@ost riafarniente.it, Fax 055 2009294,* ☂ – ▤. ᴀᴇ 𝕤 ⓜⓒ VISA FU
closed August and Sunday – **Meals** (dinner only) a la carte 29/38.
◆ Laid out over two floors of a former artisans' workshop. Large windows and a long ba downstairs, while the first floor wine bar has bench seating.

Buca Lapi, via del Trebbio 1 r ✉ 50123 ✆ 055 213768, *Fax 055 284862* – ▤. ᴀᴇ ⦿ ⓜⓒ VISA JCB Y
closed August and Sunday – **Meals** (dinner only) (booking essential for dinner) a la cart 48/65 (10 %).
◆ In the ancient cellars of the palazzo Antinori, with well-presented typical Tuscan dishe Very atmospheric.

Enoteca Pane e Vino, via di San Niccolò 70 a/r ✉ 50125 ✆ 055 2476956, *pan evino@yahoo.it, Fax 055 2476956* – ▤. 𝕤 ⦿ ⓜⓒ VISA. ✻ EV
closed 7 to 21 August and Sunday – **Meals** (dinner only) a la carte 31/39.
◆ Stylish yet rustic establishment over the Arno, ideal for candlelit dining. Traditional cuisin with an imaginative twist.

Il Cavaliere, viale Lavagnini 20/A ✉ 50129 ✆ 055 471914, *Fax 055 471914,* ☂ – ▤ ᴀᴇ 𝕤 ⦿ ⓜⓒ VISA JCB. ✻ ET
closed Wednesday – **Meals** (booking essential) a la carte 22/27.
◆ Small restaurant with stylish touches ; courtyard garden ideal for summer dining. Goo value for money.

Antico Fattore, via Lambertesca 1/3 r ✉ 50122 ✆ 055 288975, *Fax 055 28334* – ▤. ᴀᴇ 𝕤 ⦿ ⓜⓒ VISA Z
closed 15 July-15 August and Sunday – **Meals** a la carte 25/36 (12 %).
◆ This trattoria close to the Uffizi has two well-presented traditional dining rooms ; Tusca dishes predominate.

La Carabaccia, via Palazzuolo 190 r ✉ 50123 ✆ 055 214782, *Fax 055 213203* – ▤ ᴀᴇ 𝕤 ⦿ ⓜⓒ VISA JCB CDU
closed Sunday and Monday lunch – **Meals** (booking essential) a la carte 30/47.
◆ An informal atmosphere pervades in this rustic establishment, specialising in the fragrar flavours of genuine Tuscan cuisine.

Del Fagioli, corso Tintori 47 r ✉ 50122 ✆ 055 244285, *Fax 055 244285*, Typical Tus can trattoria – ▤. ✻ EV
closed August, Saturday and Sunday – **Meals** (booking essential) a la carte 22 29.
◆ A genuine welcome at this classic, family-run Tuscan trattoria offering traditional Flo rentine dishes.

Trattoria Cibrèo-Cibreino, via dei Macci 122/r ✉ 50122 ✆ 055 2341100, *cibre .fi@tin.it* – ▤. ᴀᴇ 𝕤 ⦿ ⓜⓒ VISA JCB FU
closed 26 July-6 September, 31 December-6 January, Sunday and Monday **Meals** (few tables available ; no booking) a la carte 23/33 see also res ***Cibreo.***
◆ An offshoot of Cibreo ; an informal atmosphere where, having successfully negotiate the queue, diners are served imaginative dishes at intimate tables.

Il Latini, via dei Palchetti 6 r ✉ 50123 ✆ 055 210916, *torlatin@tin.it, Fax 055 28979* Typical trattoria – ᴀᴇ 𝕤 ⦿ ⓜⓒ VISA JCB. ✻ Z
closed 24 December-5 January and Monday – **Meals** a la carte 30/40.
◆ The quintessential Florentine trattoria, not only because of its cuisine, but also o account of its cheerful, friendly service and informal atmosphere.

on the hills *South : 3 km :*

Gd H. Villa Cora , viale Machiavelli 18 ✉ 50125 ☎ 055 2298451, *reservations@villacora.it, Fax 055 229086*, , Shuttle service to city centre, – | – 50. AE VISA JCB. rest DV b
Meals ***Taverna Machiavelli*** Rest. a la carte 71/99 – **48 rm** 430/450, 9 suites.
◆ This 19C Neo-renaissance hotel is a succession of frescoed rooms with marble, stucco work and statues. Situated in its own parkland with swimming pool. The restaurant has a sophisticated menu ; outside dining on the veranda in summer.

Villa Belvedere without rest., via Benedetto Castelli 3 ✉ 50124 ☎ 055 222501, *reception@villa-belvedere.com, Fax 055 223163*, ≤ town and hills, , , – | . AE VISA JCB. by via Senese CV
March-20 November – **23 rm** 165/207, 3 suites.
◆ This 1930s villa with extensive gardens, swimming pool and fine views, offers tranquillity in a stylish and friendly atmosphere.

Classic without rest., viale Machiavelli 25 ✉ 50125 ☎ 055 229351, *info@classichotel.it, Fax 055 229353*, – | . AE VISA DV c
8 – **19 rm** 110/150.
◆ Along the passeggiata ai colli ; a 19C villa with gardens, transformed ten years ago into a welcoming hotel ; charming, well-appointed rooms.

at Arcetri *South : 5 km*

Villa Montartino, via Silvani 151 ☎ 055 223520, *info@montartino.com, Fax 055 223495*, ≤ the hills, countryside and the Certosa, , heated, – – 35. AE VISA. by viale Michelangelo FV
Meals (residents only) (booking essential) 40/75 – **7 rm** 235/285.
◆ This elegant historic villa in the hills is furnished with some fine antiques creating the atmosphere of a grand private house. Sensitively restored to its former glory.

Colle di Val d'Elsa *53034 Siena 563 L 15 G. Toscana – pop. 19 292 alt. 223.*

via Campana 43 ☎ 0577 922791, Fax 0577 922621.
Roma 255 – Arezzo 88 – Firenze 50 – Pisa 87 – Siena 24.

Arnolfo with rm, via XX Settembre 52 ☎ 0577 920549, *arnolfo@arnolfo.it, Fax 0577 920549* – . AE VISA.
closed 27 July-11 August and 13 January-11 February – **Meals** *(closed Tuesday, Wednesday, Christmas dinner and New Year lunch)* (booking essential) a la carte 74/100 – **4 rm** 130/160.
◆ An impressive and self-confident style of cuisine mixing traditional with contemporary ; set in a 16C building with two elegant dining rooms and a terrace for summer evenings.
Spec. Pici con ragù di capretto, fave e pecorino di Pienza (summer). Variazione di agnello alle olive taggiasche con tortino di melanzane e zucchine (summer). Torta con crema bianca alle arance, gelato di cioccolato amaro e mousse al latte (autumn-winter).

San Casciano in Val di Pesa *50026 Firenze 563, 430 L 15 G. Toscana – pop. 16 284 alt. 306.*

Roma 283 – Firenze 17 – Livorno 84 – Siena 53.

a Cerbaia *North-West : 6 km – ✉ 50020 :*

La Tenda Rossa, piazza del Monumento 9/14 ☎ 055 826132, *latendarossa@tin.it, Fax 055 825210* – . AE VISA JCB.
closed August, Christmas, Sunday and Monday lunch – **Meals** (booking essential) a la carte 66/96.
◆ Several very organised members of the same family run this well known establishment ; an elegant ambience in which to enjoy gastronomic cuisine.
Spec. Astice al sale e spezzatino di ostriche allo zafferano in vellutata di carciofi (September-April). Raviolini d'anatra con sfoglia alle olive nere, zabaglione al pecorino (autumn-winter). Piccione farcito di fegato grasso con salsa al Porto.

San Vincenzo *57027 Livorno 563 M 13 G. Toscana – pop. 6 837 – High Season : 15 June-15 September.*

via Beatrice Alliata 2 ☎ 0565 701533, apt7sanvincenzo@livorno.turismo.toscano.it, Fax 0565 706914.
Roma 260 – Firenze 146 – Grosseto 73 – Livorno 60 – Piombino 21 – Siena 109.

Gambero Rosso, piazza della Vittoria 13 ☎ 0565 701021, *Fax 0565 704542*, ≤ – . AE VISA
closed 27 October-10 January, Monday and Tuesday – **Meals** (booking essential) a la carte 90/125.
◆ Occupying a historic building, this elegant restaurant on the quayside of San Vincenzo has a refined menu which successfully balances creativity with practicality.
Spec. Sandwich di spigola. Penne al salmone. Muflone ai profumi di Maremma.

ITALY

MILAN (MILANO) *20100* P 561 F 9, 46 *G. Italy – pop. 1 301 551 alt. 122.*

See : *Cathedral★★★ (Duomo)* MZ – *Cathedral Museum★★* MZ **M** – *Via and Piazza Mercanti★* MZ **155** – *La Scala Opera House★★* MZ – *Manzoni House★* MZ **M** – *Brera Art Gallery★★★* KV – *Castle of the Sforza★★★* JV – *Ambrosian Pinacoteca★★* MZ : *Raphael's cartoons★★★ and Basket of fruit★★★ by Caravaggio – Poldi-Pezzoli Museum★★* KV **M** : *portrait of woman★★★ (in profile) by Pollaiolo – Palazzo Bagatti Valsecchi★★* KV **L** – *Natural Histor Museum★* LV **M** – *Leonardo da Vinci Museum of Science and Technology★* HX **M** – *Churc of St. Mary of Grace★* HX : *Leonardo da Vinci's Last Supper★★★ – Basilica of St. Ambrose★★* HJX : *altar front★★ – Church of St. Eustorgius★* JY : *Portinari Chapel★★ – Genera Hospital★* KXY **U** – *Church of St. Satiro★ : dome★* MZ – *Church of St. Maurice★★* JX – *Church of St. Lawrence Major★* JY.

Envir. : *Chiaravalle Abbey★ South-East : 7 km by corso Lodi* FGS – *Motor-Racing circu at Monza Park North : 20 km ☏ 039 24821.*

27 (closed Monday) at Monza Park ✉ 20052 Monza ☏ 039 303081, Fax 039 30442 North : 20 km;

18 Molinetto (closed Monday) at Cernusco sul Naviglio ✉ 20063 ☏ 02 92105128, Fa 02 92106635, North-East : 14 km;

18 Barlassina (closed Monday) via Privata Golf 42 ✉ 20030 Birago diCamnagc ☏ 0362 560621, Fax 0362 560934, North : 26 km;

18 (closed Monday) at Zoate di Tribiano ✉ 20067 ☏ 02 90632183, Fax 02 9063186 South-East : 20 km;

18 Le Rovedine (closed Monday) at Noverasco di Opera ✉ 20090 ☏ 02 57606420, Fa 02 57606405, by via Ripamonti FS.

Forlanini of Linate East : 8 km ☏ 02 74852200.

Malpensa North-West : 45 km ☏ 02 74852200 – Alitalia Sede ☏ 02 24991, cors Como 15 ✉ 20154 ☏ 02 24992500, Fax 02 24992525 and via Albricci 5 ✉ 2012 ☏ 02 24992700, Fax 02 8056757.

via Marconi 1 ✉ 20123 ☏ 02 72524301, Fax 02 72524350 – Central Station ✉ 2012 ☏ 02 72524360.

A.C.I. *corso Venezia 43 ✉ 20121 ☏ 02 77451.*

Roma 572 – Genève 323 – Genova 142 – Torino 140.

Plans on following pages

Historical centre – Duomo, Scala, Sforza Castle, corso Magenta, via Torino, cors Vittorio Emanuele, via Manzoni

Four Seasons, via Gesù 8 ✉ 20121 ☏ 02 77088, *milano@fourseasons.com Fax 02 77085000,* – 280. AE VISA JCB.
Meals ***La Veranda*** Rest. a la carte 64/94 see also rest. ***Il Teatro*** below – 26,50 – **77 rm** 627/737, 25 suites 1100/4675. KV
◆ Within Milan's golden triangle, this former 15C convent retains some of its original fea tures, and is the most exclusive and elegant hotel in the city. Its refined restaurant over looks a courtyard garden.

Grand Hotel et de Milan, via Manzoni 29 ✉ 20121 ☏ 02 723141, *infos@gran hoteletdemilan.it, Fax 02 86460861,* – 50. AE VISA JCB
Meals ***Caruso*** Rest. *(closed dinner)* a la carte 42/59 see also rest ***Don Carlos*** below 31,82 – **95 rm** 517/605, 8 suites. KV
◆ The spirit of Verdi, who lived here, still lingers within this prestigious hotel's sumptuou late-19C interiors. Well-presented rooms with fine antique furniture. Well-lit restauran dedicated to the maestro.

Carlton Hotel Baglioni, via Senato 5 ✉ 20121 ☏ 02 77077, *carlton.milano@ba ionihotels.com, Fax 02 783300,* – rm, – 80. AE VISA JCB. KV
Meals ***Il Baretto al Baglioni*** Rest. a la carte 65/90 – 23 – **84 rm** 451/605, 8 suite
◆ Careful details, from the period furnishings to the fine tapestries, give warmth to th public areas and rooms of this elegant jewel in the heart of fashionable Milan. The elegar yet cosy rooms of the restaurant have wood panelled walls.

Grand Hotel Duomo, via San Raffaele 1 ✉ 20121 ☏ 02 8833, *bookings@grand otelduomo.com, Fax 02 86462027,* ≤ Duomo, – rm, – 100. VISA JCB MZ
Meals a la carte 50/63 – **141 rm** 320/430, 21 suites.
◆ A 1950s feel to the interior of this elegant hotel, situated next to the Duomo ; its spire seem almost within reach from the terrace and many of the rooms. The smart dining roor has an aura of exclusivity, and overlooks Piazza Duomo.

Starhotel Rosa, via Pattari 5 ✉ 20122 ☏ 02 8831, *rosa.mi@starhotels.i Fax 02 8057964* – rm, – 130. AE VISA JCB. NZ
Meals a la carte 46/56 – **246 rm** 299/359, 2 suites.
◆ Situated close to the Duomo, this recently refurbished establishment has large an elegant public areas with much marble and stucco work, and comfortable rooms. We equipped conference centre. The restaurant offers a traditional dining experience.

MILANO

Street	Grid	No.
Albricci (V.A.)	MZ	3
Arcivescovado (V.)	MNZ	10
Augusto (Largo)	NZ	12
Baracchini (V.)	MZ	17
Bergamini (V.)	NZ	27
Borgogna (V.)	NZ	36
Cantu (V.C.)	MZ	48
Cordusio (Pza)	MZ	73
Edison (Pza)	MZ	83
Festa del Perdono (V.)	NZ	93
Gonzaga (V.)	MZ	104
Laghetto (V.)	NZ	120
Manzoni (V.A.)	MZ	140
Marçoni (V.)	MZ	144
Manno (Pza)	MZ	147
Mengoni (V.)	MZ	153
Mercanti (Pza)	MZ	155
Mercanti (V.)	MZ	156
Misson (Pza)	MZ	162
Monforte (Cso)	NZ	168
Monte Napoleone (V.)	NZ	171
Morone (V.)	MNZ	176
Orefici (V.)	MZ	188
Pattan (V.)	NZ	197
S. Clemente (NZ)	NZ	231
S. Radegonda (V.)	MZ	237
S. Stefano (Pza)	NZ	240
Sforza (V.F.)	NZ	248
Unione (V.)	MZ	264
Verdi (V.)	MZ	269
Verziere (V.)	NZ	270
Visconti di Modrone (V.)	NZ	275
Vittorio Emanuele II (Cso)	NZ	

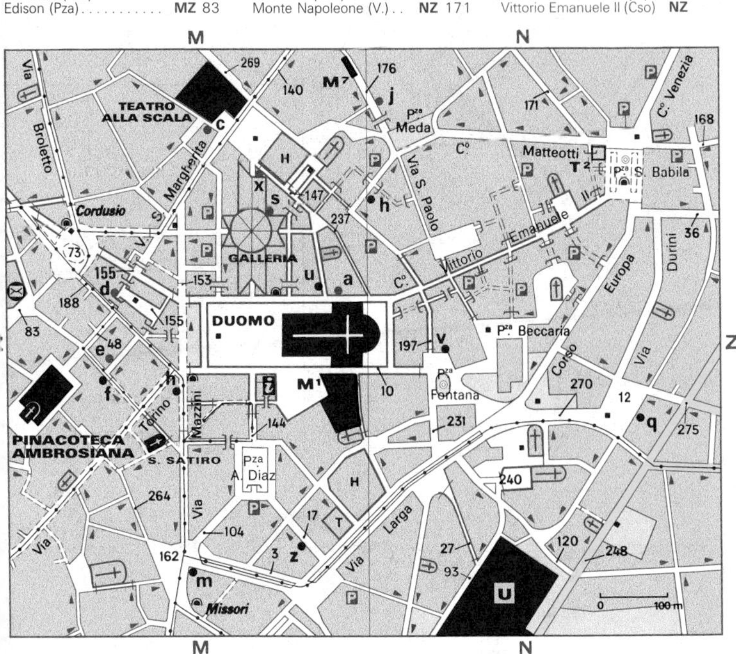

Jolly Hotel President, largo Augusto 10 ✉ 20122 ☎ 02 77461, *milano_president@jollyhotels.it, Fax 02 783449* – lift, no smoking rm, air-conditioning TV – conference 100. AE DC MC VISA JCB. no smoking rest NZ q

Meals *Il Verziere* Rest. a la carte 37/54 – **241 rm** 268/327, 16 suite.

◆ In a central location, this large international hotel has conference rooms, and spacious public areas. Every convenience to be expected in a hotel of this category is apparent. Elegantly genteel restaurant.

Brunelleschi, via Baracchini 12 ✉ 20123 ☎ 02 88431, *Fax 02 804924* – lift, air-conditioning TV, disabled access. AE DC MC VISA JCB. no smoking rest MZ z

closed 4 to 26 August – **Meals** a la carte 37/68 – **123 rm** 240/310, 5 suites.

◆ Black and white marble gives an air of rigorous austerity to the well-lit lobby of this Neo-classically-inspired modern hotel ; a softer look in evidence in the comfortably elegant rooms. Columns, glass and mirrors in the smart restaurant downstairs.

UNA Hotel Cusani, via Cusani 13 ✉ 20121 ☎ 02 85601, *una.cusani@unahotels.it, Fax 02 8693601* – lift, air-conditioning TV, garage. AE DC MC VISA JCB. no smoking JV a

Meals a la carte 34/54 – **87 rm** 381/447, 5 suites.

◆ Occupying a fine position opposite the Castello Sforzesco, this comfortable hotel has large rooms with mahogany furnishings and decorated with pastels. The small restaurant is light and stylish.

De la Ville, via Hoepli 6 ✉ 20121 ☎ 02 8791311 and rest. ☎ 02 8051231, *reservationsdlv@sinahotels.it, Fax 02 866609*, gym, sauna, pool – lift, no smoking rm, air-conditioning TV, disabled access – conference 60. AE DC MC VISA JCB. no smoking NZ h

Meals *L'Opera* Rest. *(closed Sunday)* a la carte 39/51 – **105 rm** 306,90/356,40, suite.

◆ A warm English drawing room feel with panelling, velvet and wood floors in evidence. This very central hotel has well-appointed rooms and a smart restaurant.

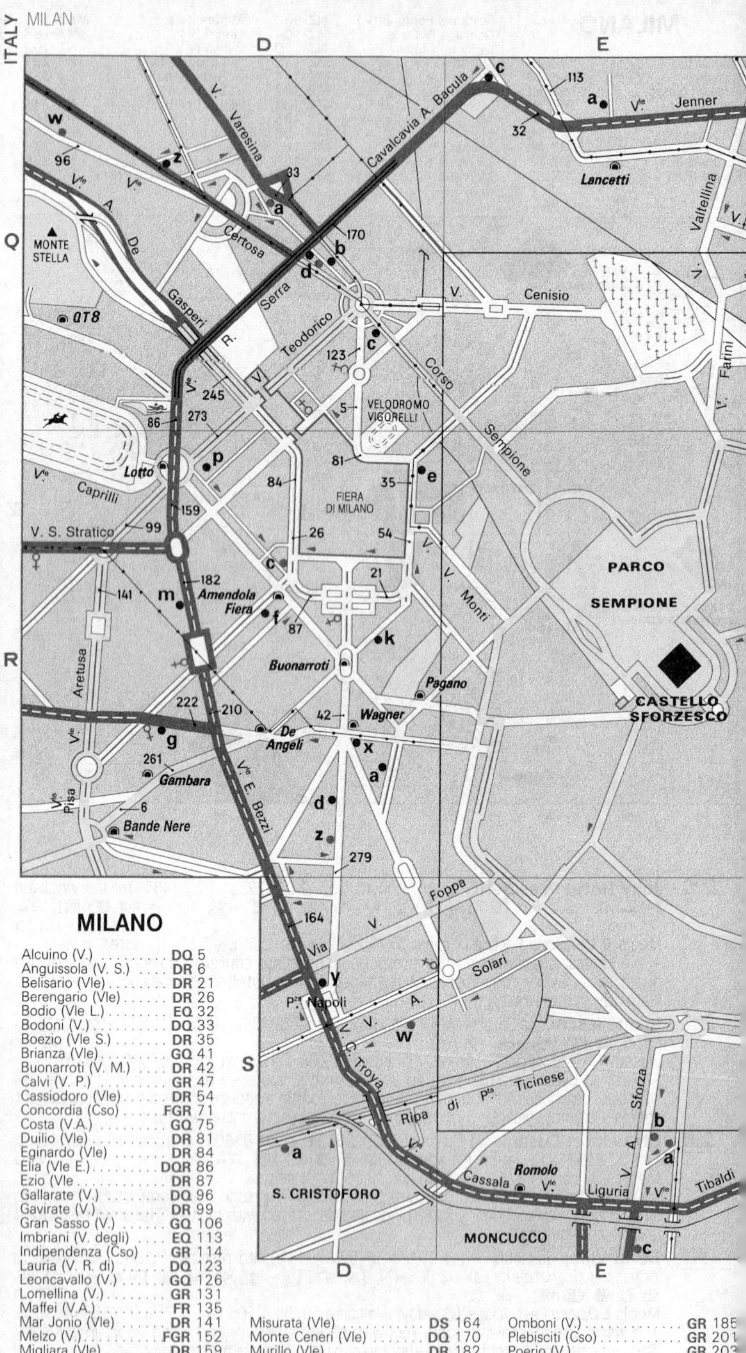

MILANO

Alcuino (V.) . . . . **DQ** 5
Anguissola (V. S.) . . . . **DR** 6
Belisario (Vle) . . . . **DR** 21
Berengario (Vle) . . . . . . **DR** 26
Bodio (Vle L.) . . . . **EQ** 32
Bodoni (V.) . . . . **DQ** 33
Boezio (Vle S.) . . . . **DR** 35
Brianza (Vle) . . . . **GQ** 41
Buonarroti (V. M.) . . . . **DR** 42
Calvi (V. P.) . . . . **GR** 47
Cassiodoro (Vle) . . . . . . **DR** 54
Concordia (Cso) . . . . . **FGR** 71
Costa (V.A.) . . . . **GQ** 75
Duilio (Vle) . . . . **DR** 81
Eginardo (Vle) . . . . **DR** 84
Elia (Vle E.) . . . . **DQR** 86
Ezio (Vle . . . . **DR** 87
Gallarate (V.) . . . . **DQ** 96
Gavirate (V.) . . . . **DR** 99
Gran Sasso (V.) . . . . . . **GQ** 106
Imbriani (V. degli) . . . . **EQ** 113
Indipendenza (Cso) . . . **GR** 114
Lauria (V. R. di) . . . . . . **DQ** 123
Leoncavallo (V.) . . . . . . **GQ** 126
Lomellina (V.) . . . . **GR** 131
Maffei (V.A.) . . . . **FR** 135
Mar Jonio (Vle) . . . . **DR** 141
Melzo (V.) . . . . **FGR** 152
Migliara (Vle) . . . . **DR** 159
Misurata (Vle) . . . . **DS** 164
Monte Ceneri (Vle) . . . . . **DQ** 170
Murillo (Vle) . . . . **DR** 182
Omboni (V.) . . . . **GR** 185
Plebisciti (Cso) . . . . **GR** 201
Poerio (V.) . . . . **GR** 203

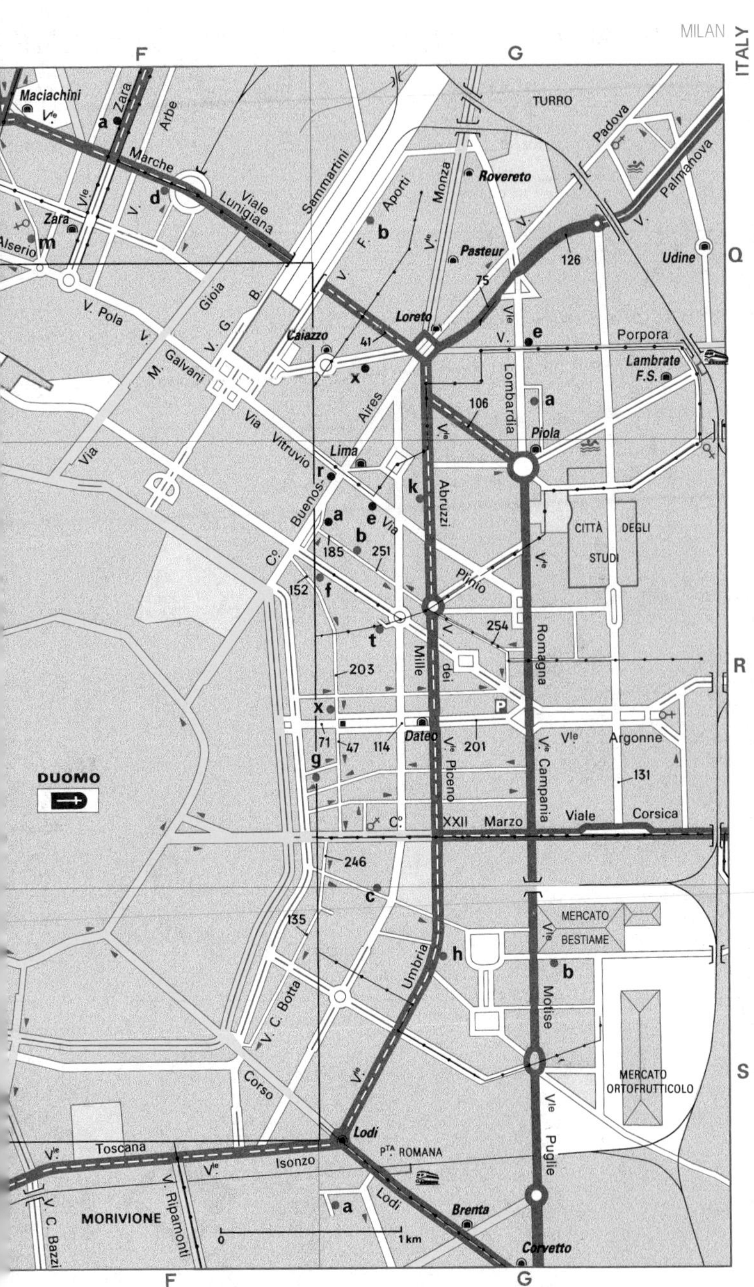
F
G
Q
R
S
Maciachini
Zara
Arbe
Marche
Viale Lunigiana
Sammartini
Aporti
Monza
Rovereto
TURRO
Padova
Palmanova
Pasteur
Udine
126
75
Loreto
Caiazzo
41
V. Pola
Gioia
V. G. B.
M. Galvani
Via Vitruvio
Aires
Lima
Buenos-
106
Lombardia
Porpora
Lambrate F.S.
Piola
Abruzzi
CITTÀ DEGLI STUDI
185
251
152
Plinio
254
Romagna
Mille
dei
203
Dateo
114
47
71
201
Argonne
Campania
131
Piceno
DUOMO
XXII Marzo
Viale Corsica
246
135
MERCATO BESTIAME
Umbria
Molise
V. C. Botta
Corso
MERCATO ORTOFRUTTICOLO
Lodi
Toscana
Isonzo
Pta ROMANA
Puglie
Brenta
MORIVIONE
V. Ripamonti
V. C. Bazzi
Corvetto
0
1 km

MILANO

Within the green shaded area, the city is divided into zones wich are signposted all the way round. Once entered, it is not possible to drive from one zone into another.

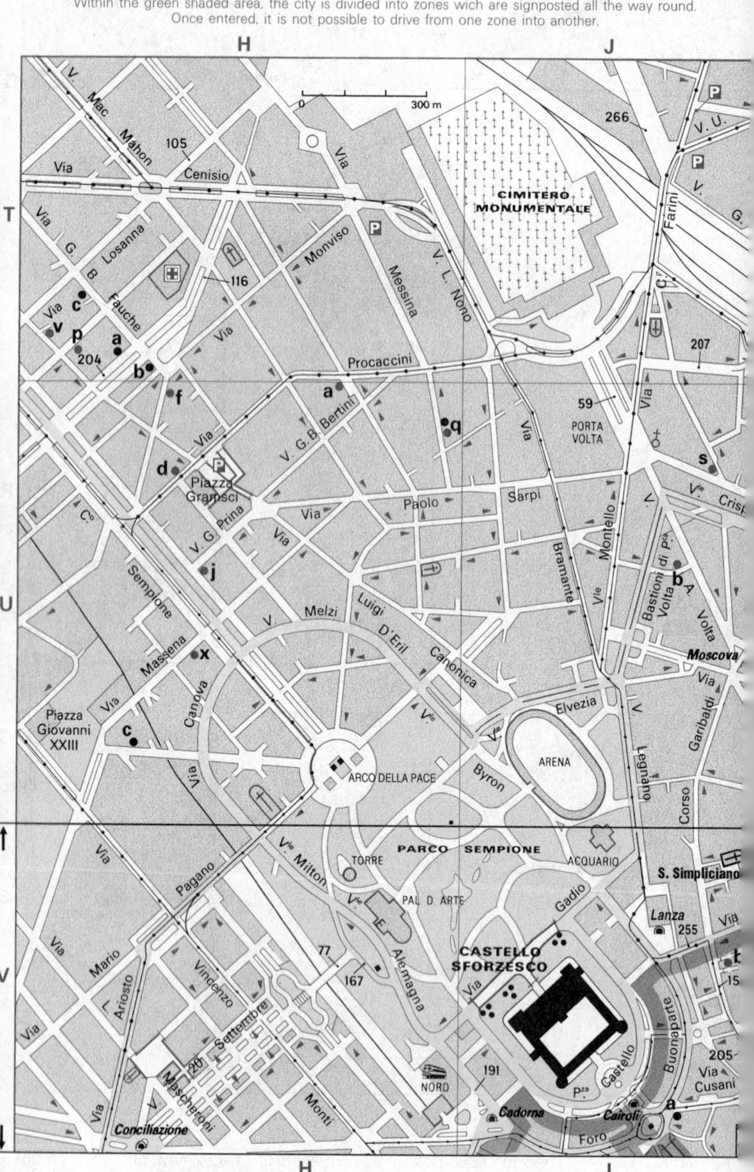

Gran S. Bernardo (V.) . . . **HT** 105
Guastalla (V.) . . . **KX** 110
Induno (V. Fratelli) . . . **HT** 116
Lambertenghi (V.P.) . . . **KT** 122
Lepetit (V.) . . . **LTU** 128
Maffei (V. A.) . . . **LY** 135
Manzoni (V. A.) . . . **KV**
Melzö (V.) . . . **LU** 152
Mercato (V.) . . . **JV** 158
Modestino (V.) . . . **HY** 165
Molière (Vie E.) . . . **HV** 167
Monte Napoleone (V.) . . . **KV**
Muraton (V.L.) . . . **LY** 180
Oggiono (V. M. d') . . . **HJY** 183
Orseolo (V.) . . . **HY** 189
Paleocapa (V.) . . . **JV** 191
Pastrengo (V.) . . . **KT** 195
Perasto (V.) . . . **KT** 198
Poliziano (V.) . . . **HTU** 204
Ponte Vetero (V.) . . . **JY** 205
Quadrio (V.M.) . . . **JT** 207
Restelli (Vie F.) . . . **KT** 214
Ruffini (V. Fratelli) . . . **HX** 225
S. Babila (Pza) . . . **KX** 228
S. Calimero (V.) . . . **KY** 230
Savoia (Vie F. di) . . . **KU** 243
Spiga (V. della) . . . **KV**
Tivoli (V.) . . . **HV** 255
Torchio (V.) . . . **JX** 257
Tornani (V.N.) . . . **LU** 258
Trau (V.) . . . **KT** 260
Valtellina (V.) . . . **JT** 266
Vercelli (Cso) . . . **HX** 267
Verdi (V.) . . . **KV** 269
Vittono Veneto (Vie) . . . **KLU** 278
Zezon (V.) . . . **LU** 281

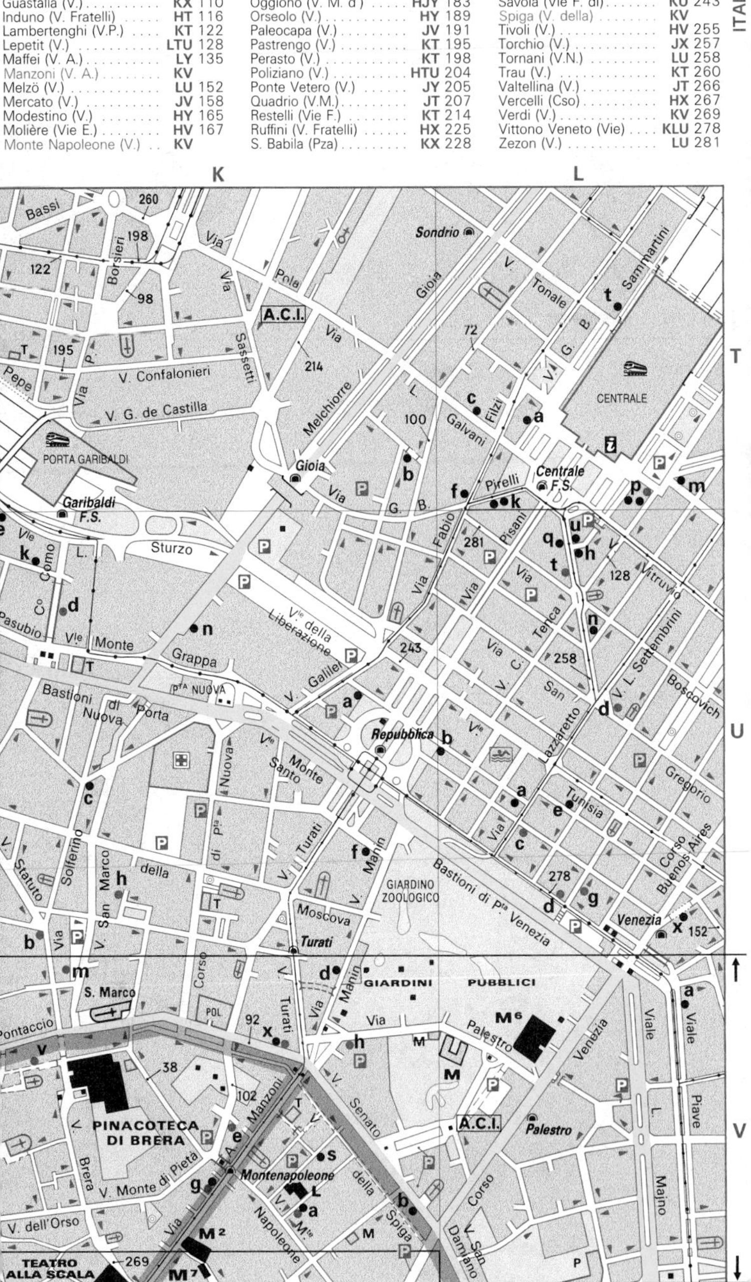

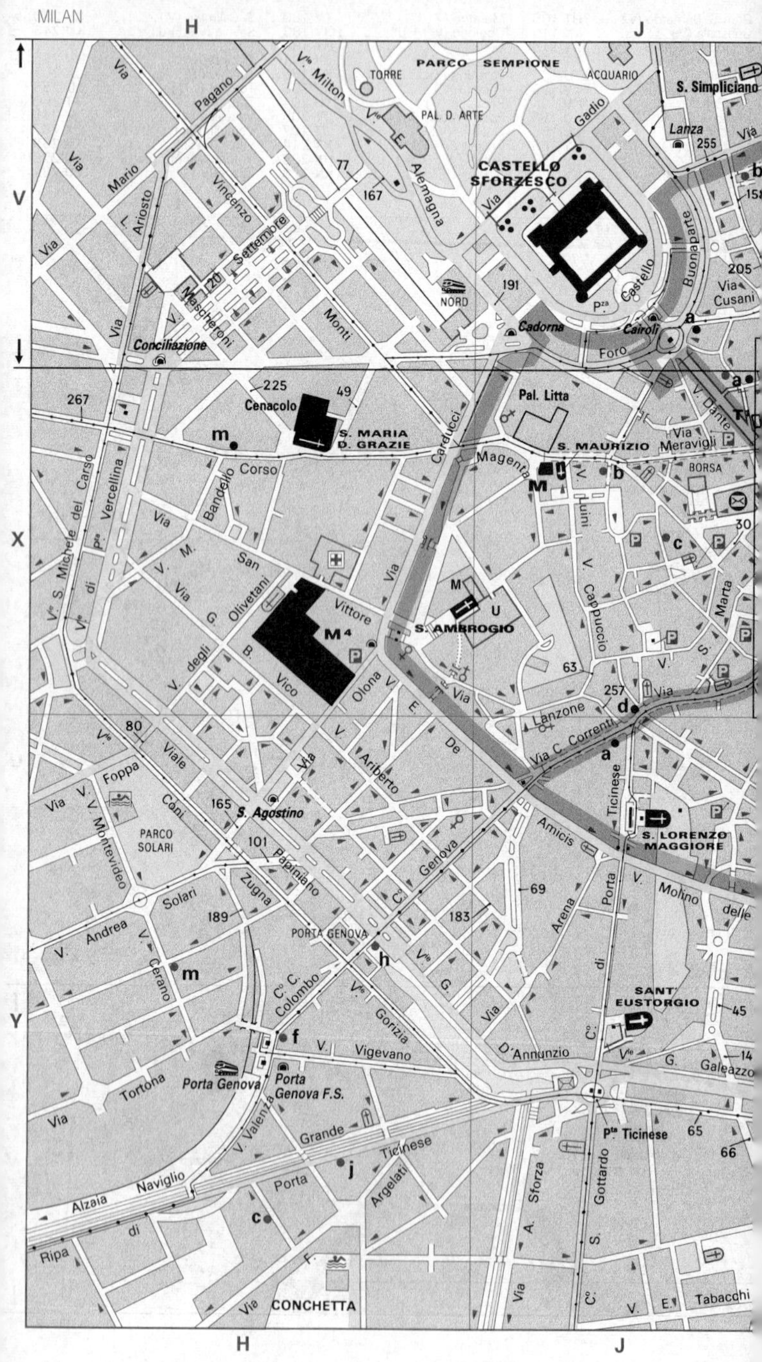

PARCO SEMPIONE
CASTELLO SFORZESCO
S. MARIA D. GRAZIE
Cenacolo
S. MAURIZIO
Pal. Litta
S. AMBROGIO
S. LORENZO MAGGIORE
SANT' EUSTORGIO
S. Simpliciano
BORSA
PARCO SOLARI
CONCHETTA
Cadorna
Cairoli
Conciliazione
S. Agostino
Porta Genova
Porta Genova F.S.
Pta Ticinese
PORTA GENOVA
NORD
Lanza
TORRE
ACQUARIO
PAL. D. ARTE

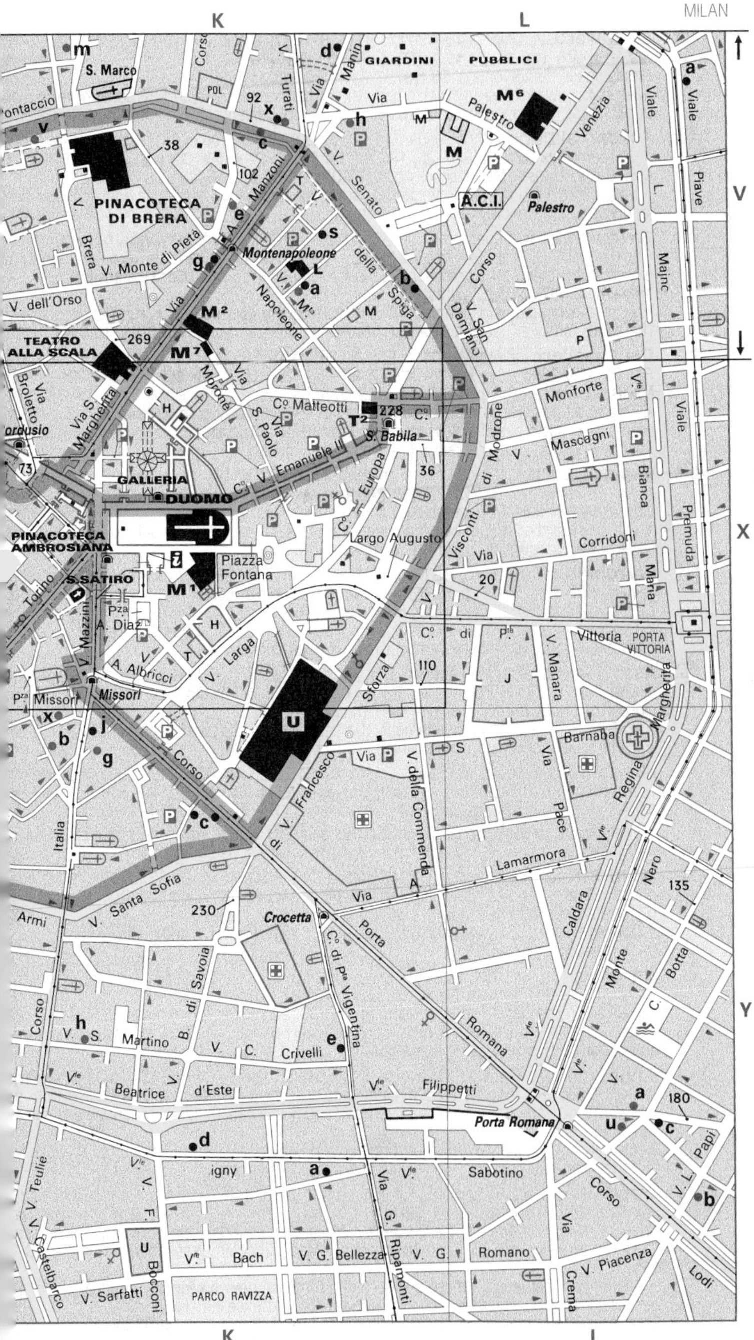

Sir Edward, via Mazzini 4 20123 02 877877, *siredward@libero.it, Fax 02 877844*, – rm, . MZ h
Meals snack dinner only – **38 rm** 210/262.
• A relaxing water-feature welcomes visitors to this exclusive and personal hotel ; small public areas, but good-sized rooms with every convenience for the business traveller.

Spadari al Duomo, via Spadari 11 20123 02 72002371, *reservation@spadarihotel.com, Fax 02 861184* – rm, . MZ f
closed Christmas – **Meals** snacks only – **40 rm** 238/268, suite.
• Italy's first art hotel is ten years old ; small, elegant and exclusive, it houses a fine collection of contemporary art and design.

Cavour, via Fatebenefratelli 21 20121 02 620001, *booking@hotelcavour.it, Fax 02 6592263* – rm, – 80. KV x
closed August and 24 December-6 January – **Meals** (see rest. ***Conte Camillo*** below) – **113 rm** 205/235, 5 suites.
• A large colonnaded lobby introduces visitors to this establishment, run for decades by the same family of leading Milanese hoteliers. Excellent recently refitted rooms.

Dei Cavalieri, piazza Missori 1 20123 02 88571, *hc@hoteldeicavalieri.com, Fax 02 72021683* – rm, – 250.
Meals a la carte 46/71 – **177 rm** 282/366, 3 suites. MZ m
• This hotel celebrated its fiftieth birthday in 1999. Slightly cramped public areas, but a recent refit has created a pleasant space in which to entertain, and there is a fine terrace. The well-proportioned restaurant is traditionally stylish.

Regina without rest., via Cesare Correnti 13 20123 02 58106913, *info@hotelregina.it, Fax 02 58107033* – – 40. JY a
closed August and 23 December-7 January – **43 rm** 185/250.
• The courtyard of an 18C building covered by a glass pyramid is the lobby of this modern-style hotel ; parquet floors in the well-presented rooms.

Carrobbio without rest., via Medici 3 20123 02 89010740, *info@hotelcarrobbio.it, Fax 02 8053334* – – 30. JX d
closed August and 22 December-6 January – **56 rm** 180/256.
• Central, but in a secluded location, this good quality, if functional, hotel has recently been renovated. Well-appointed rooms with good furnishings.

Ascot without rest., via Lentasio 3/5 20122 02 58303300, *info@hotelascotmilano.it, Fax 02 58303203* – – 75. KY c
closed 23 December-6 January – **64 rm** 235/350.
• Under competent new management, this central hotel has comfortable public areas and small but well-appointed rooms which are nicely furnished.

Manzoni without rest., via Santo Spirito 20 20121 02 76005700, *info@hotelmanzoni.com, Fax 02 784212* – . KV s
closed August and 24 December-4 January – 15 – **49 rm** 120/163, 3 suites.
• Friendly welcome from reception and management at this well-run hotel located near via Montenapoleone. Handy private garage ; classically-styled guest rooms.

Lloyd without rest., corso di Porta Romana 48 20122 02 58303332, *info@lloydhotelmilano.it, Fax 02 58303365* – – 100.
closed 22 December-6 January – **56 rm** 235/350, suite. KY c
• Opposite San Nazaro Maggiore, this recently refitted hotel is comfortably functional ; small meeting rooms.

Zurigo without rest., corso Italia 11/a 20122 02 72022260, *zurigo@brerahotels.it, Fax 02 72000013* – . KY j
closed 20 December-7 January – **39 rm** 140/200.
• Near Piazza Missori, a historic building completely refurbished inside, with well-appointed quiet rooms ; courtesy bikes available.

Savini, galleria Vittorio Emanuele II 20121 02 72003433, *savini@thi.it, Fax 02 72022888*, Elegant traditional decor – . MZ s
closed 6 to 27 August, 1 to 6 January and Sunday – **Meals** (booking essential) a la carte 53/75 (12 %).
• A traditional hotel in a historic setting in the prestigious Galleria. Redolent of the luxury of times gone by, with red velvet, crystal lamps and mirrors.

Cracco-Peck, via Victor Hugo 4 20123 02 876774, *cracco-peck@peck.it, Fax 02 876774* – . MZ e
closed 3 weeks in August, 22 December-10 January, Sunday and Saturday lunch, also Saturday dinner from 15 June to August – **Meals** (booking essential) a la carte 69/115.
• A legendary name in Milanese cuisine and a famous chef ; a winning combination for a new restaurant. Classic elegance, perfect service and excellent food.
Spec. Musetto di maiale con scampi e pomodori verdi. Risotto allo zafferano con midollo. Vitello impanato alla milanese con pomodoro e zucchine.

XXXX **Il Teatro** - Hotel Four Seasons, via Gesù 8 ✉ 20121 ☎ 02 77088, *milano@fourseasons.com* – ▤. AE ⊙ ⊙ MC VISA JCB. ⚡ KV a
closed August and Sunday – **Meals** (dinner only) (booking essential) a la carte 56/90.
◆ A very elegant and exclusive ambience in this restaurant among the stunning surroundings of the Four Seasons hotel. Creatively prepared cuisine.

XXX **Don Carlos** - Grand Hotel et de Milan, via Manzoni 29 ✉ 20121 ☎ 02 72314640, *banqueting@grandhoteletdemilan.it, Fax 02 86460861*, Late night dinners – ▤. AE ⊙ ⊙ MC VISA JCB KV g
closed August – **Meals** (dinner only) (booking essential) a la carte 74/99.
◆ An atmosphere of snug luxury with panelling, red lamps, and drawings and photos of the Verdi era ; varied, creative cuisine including seasonal dishes and Milanese favourites.

XXX **Conte Camillo** - Hotel Cavour, via Fatebenefratelli 21 (galleria di Piazza Cavour) ✉ 20121 ☎ 02 6570516, *booking@hotelcavour.it, Fax 02 6592263* – ▤. AE ⊙ ⊙ MC VISA JCB. ⚡ KV x
closed August, 24 December-6 January and Sunday – **Meals** a la carte 37/49.
◆ Attentive service and elegant surroundings, together with an intimate welcoming atmosphere ; traditional cuisine with a modern twist, with themed menus available.

XXX **Marino alla Scala**, piazza della Scala 5 (Trussardi palace) ✉ 20121 ☎ 02 80688201, *ristorante@marinoallascala.it, Fax 02 80688287* – |♦| ▤. AE ⊙ ⊙ MC VISA MZ c
closed 2 weeks in August, 25 December-6 January, Saturday lunch and Sunday – **Meals** (booking essential) a la carte 34/83.
◆ Tradition and innovation meet in the cuisine of this design-conscious establishment ; a stylish restaurant close by Milan's famous opera house.

XXX **Antico Ristorante Boeucc**, piazza Belgioioso 2 ✉ 20121 ☎ 02 76020224, *Fax 02 796173* – ▤. AE. ⚡ NZ j
closed 13 to 17 April, August, 24 December-2 January, Saturday and Sunday lunch – **Meals** (booking essential) a la carte 50/66.
◆ In the stable block of the 18C Palazzo Belgioioso, an elegant and historic establishment ; the choice of Milan's elite for 300 years ; traditional cuisine.

XX **Armani/Nobu**, via Pisoni 1 ✉ 20121 ☎ 02 62312645, *Fax 02 62312674* – ⚡ ▤. AE ⊙ ⊙ MC VISA JCB. ⚡ KV e
closed August, 25 December-7 January, Sunday and Monday lunch – **Meals** (booking essential) Japanese rest. with South American influences a la carte 48/76 (10 %).
◆ An exotic marriage of fashion with gastronomy ; Japanese fusion cuisine with South American influences, served in stylishly simple surroundings inspired by Japanese design.

XX **Bistrot Duomo**, via San Raffaele 2 (Rinascente Duomo 7th floor) ✉ 20121 ☎ 02 877120, *bistrotduomo@gmristorazione.it, Fax 02 877035*, ⛱ – |♦| ▤. AE ⊙ ⊙ MC VISA JCB MZ a
closed 5 to 25 August, Sunday and Monday lunch – **Meals** (booking essential) a la carte 44/60.
◆ Charming establishment overlooked by the Gothic spires of the Duomo, which may be admired either from inside or from the fine terrace ; balanced cuisine with a modern slant.

XX **Nabucco**, via Fiori Chiari 10 ✉ 20121 ☎ 02 860663, *info@nabucco.it, Fax 02 8361014* – ▤. AE ⊙ ⊙ MC VISA JCB KV v
Meals (booking essential) a la carte 42/61 (10 %).
◆ In one of the Brera district's characteristic alleyways, this restaurant offers some interesting and unusual dishes ; candlelit dining in the evenings.

XX **Tandur**, via Maddalena 3/5 ✉ 20122 ☎ 02 8056192, *Fax 02 89010737* – ▤. AE ⊙ ⊙ MC VISA KY g
closed Sunday lunch and Monday – **Meals** (booking essential) Indian rest. a la carte 26/37.
◆ Authentic Indian dishes and a genteel atmosphere in this restaurant, opened a couple of years ago by Indian management to offer a true flavour of the subcontinent.

XX **L'Assassino**, via Amedei 8, angolo via Cornaggia ✉ 20123 ☎ 02 8056144, *Fax 02 86467374* – ▤. AE ⊙ MC VISA KY x
closed 23 December-2 January, Friday dinner and Saturday July-August, Monday in other months – **Meals** (booking essential) a la carte 34/47.
◆ Situated in the palazzo Recalcati, this classic venue is always very popular. Traditional cuisine ; the fresh, home made pasta is especially good.

XX **La Felicità**, via Rovello 3 ✉ 20121 ☎ 02 865235, *Fax 02 865235* – ▤. AE ⊙ ⊙ MC VISA JCB. ⚡ JX a
Meals Chinese rest. 15/20 and a la carte 19/26.
◆ Cantonese cuisine and a wide variety of other South East Asian dishes in this smart oriental restaurant ; the mezzanine floor offers the cosiest and most romantic ambience.

Alla Collina Pistoiese, via Amedei 1 ✉ 20123 ☎ 02 877248, *Fax 02 877248* – ▤. AE VISA KY b
closed Easter, 10 to 20 August, 24 December-2 January, Friday and Saturday lunch – **Meals** a la carte 36/57.
◆ The spirit of old Milan in a historic setting, run by the same family since 1938 ; the menu shows all aspects of Italy's cuisine but specialises in Tuscan and Milanese dishes.

Al Mercante, piazza Mercanti 17 ✉ 20123 ☎ 02 8052198, *Fax 02 86465250,* – ▤. AE VISA MZ d
closed 1 to 27 August, 1 to 7 January and Sunday – **Meals** a la carte 36/43.
◆ A lively establishment charmingly situated in a medieval square offering summer dining outside ; country cuisine and a fine buffet of antipasti.

Hostaria Borromei, via Borromei 4 ✉ 20123 ☎ 02 86453760, *Fax 02 86452178,* – AE VISA. JX c
closed 8 August-1 September, 24 December-7 January, Saturday lunch and Sunday – **Meals** (booking essential) Mantuan specialities a la carte 29/40.
◆ Delightful summer dining in the courtyard of a historic building in the centre ; seasonal Lombard cuisine with an emphasis on the Mantova region.

La Brisa, via Brisa 15 ✉ 20123 ☎ 02 86450521, *Fax 02 86450521* – AE VISA. JX b
closed 8 August-8 September, 23 December-3 January, Saturday and Sunday lunch – **Meals** a la carte 40/48.
◆ Opposite a Roman archaeological site, a modern-style trattoria which also offers traditional dishes ; veranda and garden for summer dining.

Trattoria Torre di Pisa, via Fiori Chiari 21/5 ✉ 20121 ☎ 02 874877, *Fax 02 804483* – ▤. AE VISA. JV b
closed Saturday lunch and Sunday – **Meals** Tuscan rest. a la carte 35/41.
◆ A family-run Tuscan trattoria in the heart of the historic Brera district. A flavour of Dante country at reasonable prices.

Papà Francesco, via Marino 7 angolo piazza della Scala ✉ 20121 ☎ 02 862177, *papafrancesco@tiscalinet.it, Fax 02 45409112,* – ▤. VISA JCB. MZ x
closed 1 to 20 January, Monday and Tuesday lunch – **Meals** a la carte 35/70.
◆ A long-established restaurant near Piazza della Scala ; well-lit dining room decorated with photos of famous customers. Ideal for post-theatre meals.

Directional centre – via della Moscova, via Solferino, via Melchiorre Gioia, viale Zara, via Carlo Farini

Grand Hotel Verdi, via Melchiorre Gioia 6 ✉ 20124 ☎ 02 62371, *mail@grandhotelverdi.com, Fax 02 6237050* – – 25. AE VISA JCB KU n
closed 11 to 24 August – **Meals** a la carte 45/61 – **96 rm** 299/316, 3 suites.
◆ A recently built and well-appointed hotel. Deep red predominates in the modern interior which also evokes the decoration inside La Scala. Good quality cuisine in the elegant restaurant which has a smart red and white colour scheme.

Executive, viale Luigi Sturzo 45 ✉ 20154 ☎ 02 62942807, *prenotazioni@hotel-executive.com, Fax 02 62942713* – rm, – 800. AE VISA JCB. KU e
Meals a la carte 38/59 – **414 rm** 264/304, 6 suites.
◆ Opposite the stazione Garibaldi, a large 1970s hotel with excellent conference facilities (18 meeting rooms) ; pleasant well-lit rooms, many of which have been refitted. Elegant modern restaurant.

Una Hotel Tocq, via A. de Tocqueville 7/D ✉ 20154 ☎ 02 62071, *una.tocq@unahotels.it, Fax 02 6570780* – – 110. AE VISA JCB. KU k
Meals a la carte 33/43 – **122 rm** 323/380, suite.
◆ Sophisticated design and modern technology are the central themes of this minimalist-style hotel with a strong contemporary feel. The main area of the restaurant is brightly decorated with a parquet floor in natural Danish oak.

Four Points Sheraton Milan Center, via Cardano 1 ✉ 20124 ☎ 02 667461, *bookin@fourpointsmilano.it, Fax 02 6703024,* – rm, – 180. AE VISA JCB. rest KT b
Meals a la carte 32/54 – 15 – **195 rm** 250/310, 10 suites.
◆ Inside this modern building is an elegantly decorated interior with restful public areas ; good comfortable rooms, all recently refurbished. Large windows give plenty of light in the tastefully decorated dining room.

Sunflower without rest., piazzale Lugano 10 ✉ 20158 ☎ 02 39314071, *sunflower.hotel@tiscalinet.it, Fax 02 39320377* – – 100. AE VISA JCB. EQ c
closed 5 to 27 August and 24 December-6 January – 10,33 – **55 rm** 123,95/175,60.
◆ Recently opened, this large hotel offers comfortable, functional accommodation ; rooms have wooden furnishings and ceramic floors.

XXX **Santini,** via San Marco 3 20121 ☎ 02 6555587, *info@ristorantesantini.it, Fax 02 6592589* – ▤ ⇔. AE ⑤ ⓓ MC VISA JCB KV m
closed 9 to 25 August, Saturday lunch and Sunday – **Meals** 30 b.i (lunch only) and a la carte 63/78.
◆ An elegant establishment with modern overtones, but also offering two lounge areas more classically traditional in feel ; imaginatively fused flavours distinguish the cuisine.

XX **Casa Fontana-23 Risotti,** piazza Carbonari 5 ✉ 20125 ☎ 02 6704710, *trattoria@23risotti.it, Fax 02 66800465* – ▤. AE ⑤ ⓓ MC VISA. ✻ FQ d
closed Easter, August, Christmas, 1 to 6 January, Monday, Saturday lunch and Saturday dinner-Sunday in July – **Meals** (booking essential) risotto specialities a la carte 31/41.
◆ Worth seeking out is this small friendly restaurant slightly away from the centre ; the ritual 25-minute wait is necessary for preparation of one of their trademark risottos.

XX **Alla Cucina delle Langhe,** corso Como 6 ✉ 20154 ☎ 02 6554279, *Fax 02 29006859* – ⊁ ▤. AE ⑤ ⓓ MC VISA JCB. ✻ KU d
closed August, Sunday also Saturday in July – **Meals** Lombardy and Piedmontese specialities a la carte 41/51.
◆ Classic trattoria in terms of both ambience and menu ; excellent traditional cuisine with speciality Lombard and Piedmontese dishes.

XX **Antica Osteria il Calessino,** via Thaon de Revel 9 ✉ 20159 ☎ 02 6684935, *Fax 02 6684935*, ⛱, Live music and cabaret – ▤. AE ⑤ ⓓ MC VISA FQ m
closed 1 to 10 January and Monday – **Meals** (dinner only) a la carte 48/67.
◆ A rustic atmosphere with raftered ceilings and live music and cabaret in the evenings ; dining outside in the courtyard during the summer. Classic Lombard cuisine.

XX **Rigolo,** largo Treves ang. via Solferino 11 ✉ 20121 ☎ 02 86463220, *ristorante.rigolo@tiscalinet.it, Fax 02 86463220* – ⊁ ▤. AE ⑤ ⓓ MC VISA. ✻ KU b
closed August and Monday – **Meals** a la carte 29/42.
◆ Run by the same family for over 40 years, this recently refurbished restaurant in a fashionable district has many regulars, and serves meat and fish dishes.

XX **Antica Trattoria della Pesa,** viale Pasubio 10 ✉ 20154 ☎ 02 6555741, *Fax 02 29006859*, Typical trattoria old Milan – ▤. AE ⑤ ⓓ MC VISA JCB. ✻ JU s
closed Sunday – **Meals** Lombardy rest. a la carte 48/64.
◆ A pleasantly dated ambience in this old Milanese trattoria so typical of bygone Italy, serving dishes native to the city and Lombardy.

XX **Serendib,** via Pontida 2 ✉ 20121 ☎ 02 6592139, *Fax 02 6592139* – ▤. ⑤ MC VISA
closed 10 to 20 August – **Meals** (dinner only) (booking essential) Indian and Sinhalese rest. 13/18 and a la carte 24/27. JU b
◆ Singhalese and Indian cuisine authentically prepared and décor to match in this pleasant restaurant, which bears the ancient name of Sri Lanka.

Central Station – corso Buenos Aires, via Vittor Pisani, piazza della Repubblica

Principe di Savoia, piazza della Repubblica 17 ✉ 20124 ☎ 02 62301, *principe@hotelprincipedisavoia.com, Fax 02 6595838*, Ⓕ, ≘s, ⊡ – |♦| ⊁ ▤ TV – 🔬 700. AE ⑤ ⓓ MC VISA JCB. ✻ KU a
Meals ***Galleria*** Rest. a la carte 76/99 – ☐ 46 – **404 rm** 651/814, 63 suites.
◆ Opulence on a grand scale throughout this showcase hotel, with its fine furnishings and unparalleled attention to tasteful detail ; regal suites with own pool. Magnificent restaurant with beautiful furniture and period features.

The Westin Palace, piazza della Repubblica 20 ✉ 20124 ☎ 02 63361, *westin.palacemilan@westin.com, Fax 02 654485*, Ⓕ – |♦|, ⊁ rm, ▤ TV ☎ ♿ ⇔ P – 🔬 250. AE ⑤ ⓓ MC VISA JCB. ✻ rest LU b
Meals ***Casanova Grill*** Rest. *(closed August)* (booking essential) a la carte 68/82 – ☐ 39 – **228 rm** 443/594, 7 suites.
◆ Modern skyscraper with sumptuous interior of brocades, gilding, panelling and fine details ; all the grandeur of a hotel of the highest quality. Well-spaced tables, comfortable seating and soft tones make for a pampered ambience in the restaurant.

Excelsior Gallia, piazza Duca d'Aosta 9 ✉ 20124 ☎ 02 67851, *sales@excelsiorgallia.it, Fax 02 66713239*, Ⓕ, ≘s – |♦|, ⊁ rm, ▤ TV ☎ – 🔬 700. AE ⑤ ⓓ MC VISA JCB. ✻ rest
Meals 49 – ☐ 33 – **237 rm** 445/545, 13 suites. LT a
◆ Next to the railway station, this giant of the Milanese hotel scene has been a byword for discreet hospitality, uncompromising luxury, and a prestigious clientele since opening in 1932. The sophisticated restaurant is located on the top floor.

Hilton Milan, via Galvani 12 ✉ 20124 ☎ 02 69831, *sales.milan@hilton.com, Fax 02 66710810* – |♦|, ⊁ rm, ▤ TV ☎ ♿ – 🔬 180. AE ⑤ ⓓ MC VISA JCB. ✻
Meals a la carte 46/58 – ☐ 26 – **319 rm** 455/475. LT c
◆ Following a recent refit, this modern hotel is well appointed and extremely comfortable, both in its public areas and in its rooms ; a new conference centre has also been added. The restaurant is contemporary in style.

Starhotel Ritz, via Spallanzani 40 ✉ 20129 ✆ 02 2055, *ritz.mi@starhotels.it, Fax 02 29518679* – |‡|, ⇆ rm, ▤ TV ✆ – 🏛 180. AE $ ◑ MC VISA JCB. ✻ GR a

Meals ***La Loggia*** Rest. a la carte 55/65 – **195 rm** ☐ 259/319, 6 suites.

◆ Central but quiet, this modern hotel has been refurbished and offers high levels of comfort and attention to detail throughout.

UNA Hotel Century, via Fabio Filzi 25/b ✉ 20124 ✆ 02 675041, *una.century@unahotels.it, Fax 02 66980602,* Fб – |‡|, ⇆ rm, ▤ TV ✆ – 🏛 80. AE $ ◑ MC VISA JCB. ✻ LT f

Meals a la carte 31/49 – **144 suites** ☐ 315/370.

◆ This 17-storey modern hotel is very well appointed ; the rooms, all en-suite, can be divided to provide separate day areas. A relaxing atmosphere in the elegant dining room.

Michelangelo, via Scarlatti 33 ang. piazza Luigi di Savoia ✉ 20124 ✆ 02 67551, *michelangelo@milanhotel.it, Fax 02 6694232* – |‡|, ⇆ rm, ▤ TV ✆ ♿ 🚗 – 🏛 500. AE $ ◑ MC VISA JCB. ✻ rest LT s

Meals a la carte 47/58 – **303 rm** ☐ 280/330, 10 suites.

◆ An unprepossessing façade to a hotel with spacious rooms of a sober elegance offering every modern convenience ; excellent well-equipped conference centre. A sophisticated ambience to the dining room.

Jolly Hotel Touring, via Tarchetti 2 ✉ 20121 ✆ 02 6335, *milano_touring@jollyhotels.it, Fax 02 6592209* – |‡|, ⇆ rm, ▤ TV ✆ ♿ – 🏛 120. AE $ ◑ MC VISA. ✻ KU f

Meals ***Amadeus*** Rest. a la carte 34/48 – **282 rm** ☐ 250/310, 7 suites.

◆ Between Piazza della Republica and the Via Palestro gardens, this quality hotel is well suited to conferences ; fine rooms, most of which have been recently refurbished. A stylish yet cosy atmosphere to the restaurant, with round tables and fitted carpets.

Sheraton Diana Majestic, viale Piave 42 ✉ 20129 ✆ 02 20581 and rest. ✆ 02 20582033, *sheraton.diana.majestic@starwood.com, Fax 02 20582058,* 🍴, Fб, 🌳 – |‡|, ⇆ rm, ▤ TV ✆ P – 🏛 180. AE $ ◑ MC VISA JCB. ✻ LV a

Meals ***Il Milanese Curioso*** Rest. a la carte 39/72 – ☐ 36 – **107 rm** 388/450, suite.

◆ An early 20C feel and all modern comforts combine in this historic hotel, which has recently been well restored ; fine shaded garden. An elegant restaurant offering outdoor dining in the summer.

Jolly Hotel Machiavelli, via Lazzaretto 5 ✉ 20124 ✆ 02 631141 and rest ✆ 02 63114921, *machiavelli@jollyhotels.it, Fax 02 6599800* – |‡|, ⇆ rm, ▤ TV ✆ ♿ – 🏛 80. AE $ ◑ MC VISA JCB LU a

Meals ***Caffè Niccolò*** Rest. a la carte 37/52 – **103 rm** ☐ 216/256.

◆ An airy and harmonious design taking in all the public areas of this modern hotel lends it a contemporary and comfortable style. The rooms are attractively furnished. Smart bistro-style restaurant which also has a wine bar.

Doria Grand Hotel, viale Andrea Doria 22 ✉ 20124 ✆ 02 67411411, *info@doriagrandhotel.it, Fax 02 6696669* – |‡|, ⇆ rm, ▤ TV ✆ ♿ – 🏛 120. AE $ ◑ MC VISA JCB. ✻ GQ x

Meals *(closed 27 July-23 August and 24 December-6 January)* a la carte 40/67 – **118 rm** ☐ 305/400, 2 suites.

◆ A caring management at this comfortable new hotel ; public areas decorated in an early-20C style, while a warmer, softer look is used in the rooms. Pale wood panelling and mirrors in the stylish restaurant.

Manin, via Manin 7 ✉ 20121 ✆ 02 6596511, *info@hotelmanin.it, Fax 02 6552160,* 🌳 – |‡| ▤ TV ✆ – 🏛 100. AE $ ◑ MC VISA JCB. ✻ rest KV d

closed 6 to 29 August – **Meals *Il Bettolino*** Rest. *(closed Saturday)* a la carte 32/46 – **112 rm** ☐ 175/230, 6 suites.

◆ A garden complete with plane trees is an unexpected pleasure at this hotel, soon to celebrate its centenary and recently refurbished ; stylish, well-appointed rooms. A smart yet cosy atmosphere in the excellent restaurant.

Bristol without rest., via Scarlatti 32 ✉ 20124 ✆ 02 6694141, *hotel.bristol@comm2000.it, Fax 02 6702942* – |‡| ▤ TV ✆ – 🏛 60. AE $ ◑ MC VISA. ✻ LT m

closed August and 24 December-2 January – **68 rm** ☐ 150/200.

◆ Welcoming public areas tastefully furnished with antiques and rooms of classic style offering every modern convenience in this hotel near the station.

Sanpi without rest., via Lazzaro Palazzi 18 ✉ 20124 ✆ 02 29513341, *info@hotelsanpimilano.it, Fax 02 29402451,* 🌳 – |‡|, ⇆ rm, ▤ TV ♿ 🚗 – 🏛 30. AE $ ◑ MC VISA JCB. ✻ LU e

closed 9 to 25 August and 24 December-2 January – **79 rm** ☐ 235/295.

◆ Fine attention to detail in the public areas and a charming garden. A pleasant modern hotel with soft pastel rooms.

Auriga without rest., via Pirelli 7 ✉ 20124 ☎ 02 66985851, *auriga@auriga-milano.com, Fax 02 66980698* – |♦|, ⇔ rm, ▤ TV ☎ – 🏛 25. AE $ ◐ MC VISA JCB. ✗ LTU k
closed August and 24 December-2 January – **52 rm** ☐ 190/250.
◆ An interesting mixture of colours and styles in this hotel, from its striking façade through to its extravagant interiors and more classically styled rooms.

Mediolanum without rest., via Mauro Macchi 1 ✉ 20124 ☎ 02 6705312, *info@mediolanumhotel.com, Fax 02 66981921* – |♦| ▤ TV ☎. AE $ ◐ MC VISA JCB. ✗ LU n
51 rm ☐ 225/285, suite.
◆ A warm welcome at this comfortable well-run hotel, managed by the owner himself ; recently refurbished, it has presentable functional rooms with modern furnishings.

Augustus without rest., via Napo Torriani 29 ✉ 20124 ☎ 02 66988271, *info@augustushotel.it, Fax 02 6703096* – |♦| ▤ TV. AE $ ◐ MC VISA JCB LU q
closed 1 to 18 August and 23 to 28 December – **56 rm** ☐ 165/215.
◆ Among many other hotels near the station, this establishment has comfortable public areas and peaceful, welcoming rooms, decorated in soft tones.

Atlantic without rest., via Napo Torriani 24 ✉ 20124 ☎ 02 6691941, *booking@atlantichotel.it, Fax 02 6706533* – |♦| ▤ TV ☎ 🚗 – 🏛 25. AE $ ◐ MC VISA JCB. ✗ LU h
62 rm ☐ 160/250.
◆ Near the main station, a classic, comfortably functional hotel ; fairly quiet well-proportioned rooms with every modern convenience.

Grand Hotel Puccini without rest., corso Buenos Aires 33, galleria Puccini ✉ 20124 ☎ 02 29521344, *reservation@grandhotelpuccini.it, Fax 02 2047825* – |♦|, ⇔ rm, ▤ TV ☎ ♿. AE $ ◐ MC VISA JCB GR r
65 rm ☐ 135/186.
◆ An elegant and atmospheric hotel which has recently been refurbished ; each floor has its own colour scheme and is named after a Puccini opera.

Fenice without rest., corso Buenos Aires 2 ✉ 20124 ☎ 02 29525541, *fenice@hotelfenice.it, Fax 02 29523942* – |♦| ▤ TV. AE $ ◐ MC VISA. ✗ LU x
closed 6 to 28 August – **46 rm** ☐ 114/166.
◆ In a cosmopolitan area, this recently opened hotel is elegant and welcoming ; functional, well-appointed rooms.

Albert without rest., via Tonale 2 ang. via Sammartini ✉ 20125 ☎ 02 66985446, *albert hotel@libero.it, Fax 02 66985624* – |♦| ▤ TV ♿ – 🏛 35. AE $ ◐ MC VISA. ✗ LT t
closed two weeks in August and two weeks at Christmas – **62 rm** ☐ 128/178.
◆ Next to the station, this relaunched historic hotel is a comfortable establishment with genteel, well-presented rooms.

Demidoff without rest., via Plinio 2 ✉ 20129 ☎ 02 29513889, *demidoff@milanohotels.com, Fax 02 29405816* – |♦| ▤ TV ☎. AE $ ◐ MC VISA GR e
closed August – **40 rm** ☐ 115/150.
◆ Well placed for the metro, this hotel has limited but nicely furnished public areas ; the comfortable rooms are practical and functional.

Mini Hotel Aosta without rest., piazza Duca d'Aosta 16 ✉ 20124 ☎ 02 6691951, *aosta@minihotel.it, Fax 02 6696215* – |♦| ▤ TV. AE $ ◐ MC VISA. ✗ LT p
63 rm ☐ 115/175.
◆ This hotel facing the main station may be slightly dated inside but it is still comfortable ; many rooms recently redecorated and breakfast room with a fine view.

New York without rest., via Pirelli 5 ✉ 20124 ☎ 02 66985551, *info@hotelnewyorkspa.com, Fax 02 6697267* – |♦| ▤ TV. AE $ ◐ MC VISA. ✗ LTU k
closed 1 to 28 August and 24 December-5 January – **69 rm** ☐ 115/179.
◆ Situated among many other hotels, this establishment is comfortable throughout ; a modern look to the rooms. Those which face inwards are quieter.

San Carlo without rest., via Napo Torriani 28 ✉ 20124 ☎ 02 6693236, *sancarlo@sancarlo-hotel.it, Fax 02 6703116* – |♦| ▤ TV – 🏛 40. AE $ ◐ MC VISA JCB. ✗ LU u
75 rm ☐ 180/220.
◆ Well located near the main station, this practical hotel is popular with business travellers ; refurbished rooms with every modern convenience.

Florida without rest., via Lepetit 33 ✉ 20124 ☎ 02 6705921, *info@hotelfloridamilan.com, Fax 02 6692867* – |♦| ▤ TV. AE $ ◐ MC VISA LT p
55 rm ☐ 113/160, suite.
◆ In a quiet street near the main station, this comfortable hotel appeals to business travellers. Modern furnishings throughout.

XXX **La Terrazza di Via Palestro,** via Palestro 2 ✉ 20121 ☎ 02 76002186, *terrazzapalestro@gmristorazione.it, Fax 02 76003328,* <, 🏠 – ▤ – 🧑 200. AE ⓢ ⓞ ⓜⓒ VISA JCB
closed 10 August-2 September, 23 December-8 January, Saturday and Sunday – **Meals** (booking essential) a la carte 46/66. KV h
◆ Refined modern elegance with dining on the terrace in summer ; Among its innovative dishes, do not miss the Mediterranean sushi, an Italian spin on the Japanese classic.

XX **Piccolo Sogno,** via Stoppani 5 angolo via Zambelletti ✉ 20129 ☎ 02 2046003 – ▤. AE ⓢ ⓞ ⓜⓒ VISA JCB. ✗ GR b
closed 20 days in August, 1 to 10 January, Saturday lunch and Sunday – **Meals** (booking essential) a la carte 42/64.
◆ A recent change of management and name at this well-presented restaurant ; a warm welcome and traditional cuisine.

XX **Mediterranea,** piazza Cincinnato 4 ✉ 20124 ☎ 02 29522076, *Fax 02 201156* – ▤. AE ⓢ ⓞ ⓜⓒ VISA JCB. ✗ LU d
closed 5 to 25 August, 1 to 10 January, Sunday and Monday lunch – **Meals** seafood a la carte 41/61 🍇.
◆ A maritime feel here thanks to the blue glass throughout and the shellfish tanks ; simple flavoursome seafood.

XX ✿ **Joia,** via Panfilo Castaldi 18 ✉ 20124 ☎ 02 29522124, *Fax 02 2049244* – ✗ ▤ P. AE ⓢ ⓞ ⓜⓒ VISA JCB LU c
closed 4 to 25 August, Saturday lunch and Sunday – **Meals** (booking essential) Vegetarian and seafood rest. a la carte 43/73 🍇.
◆ Dark wood floors and skylights in the non-smoking main area ; creative seafood and conceptual vegetarian cuisine which looks and tastes great.
Spec. Elogio alla Sicilia. Grande raviolo rinascimentale. Riso basmati e melanzane in cinque gusti (spring-summer).

XX **Torriani 25,** via Napo Torriani 25 ✉ 20124 ☎ 02 67479548, *torriani25@tiscali.it, Fax 02 67077890* – AE ⓢ ⓞ ⓜⓒ VISA JCB. ✗ LU t
closed 1 to 25 August, 25 December-1 January, Saturday lunch and Sunday – **Meals** (booking essential) seafood a la carte 34/54.
◆ A spacious modern restaurant with an open kitchen and a buffet just inside, to whet the appetite of arriving diners in search of the elaborate cuisine on offer.

XX **I Malavoglia,** via Lecco 4 ✉ 20124 ☎ 02 29531387 – ▤. AE ⓢ ⓞ ⓜⓒ VISA JCB. ✗
closed Easter, 1 May, August, 24 December-4 January and Sunday – **Meals** (dinner only) (booking essential) Sicilian and seafood rest. a la carte 45/56. LU g
◆ Run by the same husband and wife team since 1973, this pleasant, smart and tastefully presented restaurant specialises in Sicilian dishes and seafood with a modern twist.

XX **Da Ilia,** via Lecco 1 ✉ 20124 ☎ 02 29521895, *ristdailia@tin.it, Fax 02 29409165,* 🏠 – AE ⓢ ⓞ ⓜⓒ VISA JCB LU d
closed Easter, August, 26 December-5 January, Friday and Saturday lunch – **Meals** a la carte 30/35.
◆ An informal atmosphere to this family-run restaurant, serving classic dishes with a strong Milanese influence.

XX **Giglio Rosso,** piazza Luigi di Savoia 2 ✉ 20124 ☎ 02 6696659, *Fax 02 6694174,* 🏠 – ▤. AE ⓢ ⓞ ⓜⓒ VISA LT p
closed August, 24 December-6 January, Saturday and Sunday lunch – **Meals** a la carte 28/39 (12 %).
◆ This friendly traditional restaurant is surrounded by hotels and thus always busy ; a wide ranging menu of both meat and seafood dishes.

X ☺ **Da Giannino-L'Angolo d'Abruzzo,** via Pilo 20 ✉ 20129 ☎ 02 29406526, *Fax 02 29406526* – ▤. AE ⓢ ⓞ ⓜⓒ VISA JCB. ✗ GR t
Meals (booking essential for dinner) Abruzzi specialities a la carte 23/30.
◆ This family-run restaurant, in the same hands for 45 years, has a welcoming, light and airy ambience ; authentic Abruzzo cuisine at modest prices.

X **La Cantina di Manuela,** via Poerio 3 ✉ 20129 ☎ 02 76318892, *la_cantina_di_manuela4@tin.it, Fax 02 76312971,* 🏠, Rest. wine-bar – AE ⓢ ⓜⓒ VISA GR x
closed Sunday – **Meals** a la carte 25/32 🍇.
◆ Quality ingredients and interesting choices in a relaxed ambience ; all dishes on the traditional menu are very gratifying, from meats through to cheeses

Romana-Vittoria – corso Porta Romana, corso Lodi, corso XXII Marzo, corso Porta Vittoria

🏨 **UNA Hotel Mediterraneo,** via Muratori 14 ✉ 20135 ☎ 02 550071, *una.mediterraneo@unahotel.it, Fax 02 550072217* – |♦|, ✗ rm, ▤ TV ☎ – 🧑 75. AE ⓢ ⓞ ⓜⓒ VISA JCB. ✗ LY c
Meals a la carte 31/43 – **93 rm** ☕ 245/288.
◆ In the Porta Romana district near the metro a completely refurbished hotel with a comfortable modern feel throughout ; quiet and relaxing rooms.

Da Giacomo, via B. Cellini angolo via Sottocorno 6 ✉ 20129 ℘ 02 76023313, *Fax 02 76024305* – ▤. AE ⓢ ⓞ ⓜⓒ VISA. ✻ FGR g
closed August, 23 December-7 January, Monday and Tuesday lunch – **Meals** seafood a la carte 42/57.
◆ Well-presented family-run trattoria with closely spaced tables ; fish dominates the varied menu but meat dishes are also available.

Isola dei Sapori, via Anfossi 10 ✉ 20135 ℘ 02 54100708, *Fax 02 54100708* – ▤. AE ⓢ ⓜⓒ VISA. ✻ GS c
closed August, 26 December-4 January, Sunday and Monday lunch – **Meals** (booking essential for dinner) a la carte 33/46.
◆ A welcome newcomer to the Milan scene, opened two years ago by three young Sardinians, specialising in seafood ; modern decoration.

Masuelli San Marco, viale Umbria 80 ✉ 20135 ℘ 02 55184138, *masuelli.trattoria @tin.it, Fax 02 54124512*, Typical trattoria – ▤. AE ⓢ ⓞ ⓜⓒ VISA JCB GS h
closed 16 August-10 September, 25 December-6 January, Sunday and Monday lunch – **Meals** (booking essential for dinner) Lombardy-Piedmontese rest. a la carte 36/45.
◆ A genteel rustic atmosphere in this traditional trattoria, in the same hands since 1921 ; cuisine in the Lombard-Piedmontese tradition.

Dongiò, via Corio 3 ✉ 20135 ℘ 02 5511372, *Fax 02 5401869* – ⋟ ▤. AE ⓢ ⓞ ⓜⓒ VISA LY u
closed August, Saturday lunch and Sunday – **Meals** (booking essential for dinner) a la carte 25/37.
◆ One of the last authentic trattorias, unfussy and family-run ; the specialities are fresh pasta, meat dishes and Calabrian cuisine.

Al Merluzzo Felice, via Lazzaro Papi 6 ✉ 20135 ℘ 02 5454711 – AE ⓢ ⓞ ⓜⓒ VISA JCB. ✻ LY b
closed 7 to 31 August, Sunday and Monday lunch – **Meals** (booking essential) Sicilian rest. a la carte 28/45.
◆ This little piece of Sicily is tiny but warm and welcoming ; a simple, family atmosphere in which to savour the rich and flavoursome Sicilian menu.

Giulio Pane e Ojo, via Muratori 10 ✉ 20135 ℘ 02 5456189, *info@giuliopaneojo.com, Fax 02 45494646*, 🏕 – ▤. AE ⓢ ⓞ ⓜⓒ VISA JCB LY a
closed 10 to 17 August and Sunday – **Meals** (booking essential) Roman rest. a la carte 26/32.
◆ A small, informal etablishment run by young management offering typical Roman cuisine at competitive prices. Deservedly popular, booking is essential in the evenings.

Navigli – via Solari, Ripa di Porta Ticinese, viale Bligny, piazza XXIV Maggio

D'Este without rest., viale Bligny 23 ✉ 20136 ℘ 02 58321001, *reception@hoteldes temilano.it, Fax 02 58321136* – |‡| ⋟ ▤ TV ☏ – 🏛 80. AE ⓢ ⓞ ⓜⓒ VISA. ✻ KY d
79 rm ☕ 150/220.
◆ A well-lit, 1980s-style lobby and spacious public areas in this hotel ; rooms decorated in a variety of styles, but all are equally comfortable and quiet.

Crivi's without rest., corso Porta Vigentina 46 ✉ 20122 ℘ 02 582891, *crivis@tin.it, Fax 02 58318182* – |‡| ▤ TV ☏ 🚗 – 🏛 120. AE ⓢ ⓞ ⓜⓒ VISA JCB KY e
closed August – **86 rm** ☕ 170/240, 3 suites.
◆ Centrally located and near the metro station, an agreeable hotel with pleasant public areas ; modern furnishings in the rooms, which are reasonably spacious and comfortable.

Liberty without rest., viale Bligny 56 ✉ 20136 ℘ 02 58318562, *reserve@hotelliber ty-milano.com, Fax 02 58319061* – |‡| ▤ TV. AE ⓢ ⓞ ⓜⓒ VISA. ✻ KY a
closed 1 to 24 August – ☕ 10,33 – **52 rm** 131,70/232,40.
◆ The public areas of this elegant hotel, near the Bocconi university, are Art Nouveau in style with antique furniture ; many rooms with jacuzzi baths.

Des Etrangers without rest., via Sirte 9 ✉ 20146 ℘ 02 48955325, *info@hoteldes etrangers.it, Fax 02 48955325* – ▤ TV 🚗. AE ⓢ ⓞ ⓜⓒ VISA DS y
96 rm ☕ 95/150.
◆ Access down a flight of steps to this totally renovated establishment on a quiet street ; practicality and comfort in evidence throughout.

Sadler, via Ettore Troilo 14 angolo via Conchetta ✉ 20136 ℘ 02 58104451, *sadler @sadler.it, Fax 02 58112343*, 🏕 – ▤. ⓢ ⓞ ⓜⓒ VISA JCB. ✻ ES a
closed 8 August-2 September, 1 to 12 January and Sunday – **Meals** (dinner only) (booking essential) a la carte 66/114 🍇.
◆ Stylish both in design and cuisine, this elegant modern restaurant is a famous name among its Milanese peers ; a creative menu.
Spec. Filetti di alici dorate in crosta di patate all'aceto di lamponi e salsa verde (spring-summer). Ravioli di coniglio e borragine, tartufo nero e asparagi (spring). Crostatina di pomodori verdi con gelato di yogurt e barbabietole (summer).

XX **Al Porto,** piazzale Generale Cantore ✉ 20123 ✆ 02 89407425, *alportodimilano@a ena.it, Fax 02 8321481* – ▤. AE ⓢ ⓞ ⓜⓒ VISA JCB. ✻ HY
closed August, 24 December-3 January, Sunday and Monday lunch – **Meals** (booking essential) seafood a la carte 42/65.
◆ In the old 19C customs house of Porta Genova. This rustic, exclusively seafood, restaurant is a city favourite.

XX **Osteria di Porta Cicca,** ripa di Porta Ticinese 51 ✉ 20143 ✆ 02 8372763 *Fax 02 8372763* – ▤. AE ⓢ ⓞ ⓜⓒ VISA JCB. ✻ HY
closed Saturday lunch and Sunday – **Meals** (booking essential) a la carte 36/51.
◆ Opened in 1995, this smart and welcoming restaurant run by young management offers a modern spin to traditional cuisine.

XX **Tano Passami l'Olio,** via Vigevano 32/a ✉ 20144 ✆ 02 8394139, *info@tanopas amilolio.it, Fax 02 83240104* – ▤. AE ⓢ ⓞ ⓜⓒ VISA. ✻ HY
closed August, 24 December-6 January and Sunday – **Meals** (dinner only) (booking essential) a la carte 57/80.
◆ Soft lighting and a romantic atmosphere in this cosy restaurant, with a menu of light meat and fish dishes using extra virgin olive oil.

XX **Il Torchietto,** via Ascanio Sforza 47 ✉ 20136 ✆ 02 8372910, *info@il.torchietto.com Fax 02 8372000* – ▤. AE ⓢ ⓞ ⓜⓒ VISA. ✻ ES
closed August, 26 December-3 January, Saturady lunch and Monday – **Meals** Mantuan rest a la carte 34/45.
◆ Elegant and spacious trattoria on the Naviglio Pavese which has been recently refurbished ; menu offers seasonal dishes and regional (especially Mantuan) specialities.

XX **Il Navigante,** via Magolfa 14 ✉ 20143 ✆ 02 89406320, *info@navigante.it Fax 02 89420897* – ▤ P. AE ⓢ ⓞ ⓜⓒ VISA JCB JY
closed August, Sunday lunch and Monday – **Meals** a la carte 38/61.
◆ Close to the Naviglio, this restaurant has live music every night. Run by a former ship's cook, there is an unusual underfloor aquarium and plenty of seafood.

XX **Le Buone Cose,** via San Martino 8 ✉ 20122 ✆ 02 58310589, *lebuonecose@hotmail.com, Fax 02 58310589* – ▤. ⓢ ⓞ ⓜⓒ VISA. ✻ KY
closed August, Saturday lunch and Sunday – **Meals** (booking essential) seafood a la carte 30/50.
◆ Small, elegant and welcoming, this informal establishment has many regulars ; traditional but flavoursome seafood.

X **Trattoria Trinacria,** via Savona 57 ✉ 20144 ✆ 02 4238250, *trattoria.trinacria@libero.it* – ▤. ⓢ ⓞ ⓜⓒ VISA. ✻ DS
closed Sunday – **Meals** (dinner only) (booking essential) Sicilian rest. a la carte 35/43.
◆ This recently opened Sicilian restaurant is pleasingly simple and modern ; the menu is in dialect with Italian subtitles.

X **Trattoria Aurora,** via Savona 23 ✉ 20144 ✆ 02 8323144, *trattoriaurora@libero.it, Fax 02 89404978,* ☂ – AE ⓢ ⓜⓒ VISA HY
closed Monday – **Meals** Piedmontese rest. 15 (lunch only) 35 b.i. (dinner only).
◆ An atmospheric restaurant which in summer opens onto a fine garden to provide outdoor dining ; many regulars, drawn by the classic Piedmontese cuisine.

X **Shri Ganesh,** via Lombardini 8 ✉ 20143 ✆ 02 58110933, *shriganesh@virgilio.it, Fax 02 58110949* – ▤. ⓢ ⓞ ⓜⓒ VISA JCB HY
closed 14 to 18 August and Sunday July-August – **Meals** (dinner only) Indian rest. a la carte 20/30.
◆ Named after the Hindu elephant god associated with good fortune, this atmospheric oriental restaurant offers authentic Indian food and drink.

Fiera-Sempione – corso Sempione, piazzale Carlo Magno, via Monte Rosa, via Washington

Hermitage, via Messina 10 ✉ 20154 ✆ 02 318170, *hermitage.res@monrifhotels.it, Fax 02 33107399,* Fǻ – |\$|, ⇔ rm, ▤ TV ✆ ♿ 🚗 – 🏛 200. AE ⓢ ⓞ ⓜⓒ VISA JCB. ✻ HU
closed August – **Meals** (see rest. ***Il Sambuco*** below) – **119 rm** ☕ 247/314, 12 suites.
◆ Refinement and comfort are the key words at this hotel which combines a classically stylish interior with every modern convenience ; popular with models and VIPs.

Melià Milano, via Masaccio 19 ✉ 20149 ✆ 02 44406, *melia.milano@solmelia.com, Fax 02 44406600* – ⇔ rm, ▤ TV ✆ ♿ – 🏛 500. AE ⓢ ⓞ ⓜⓒ VISA JCB. ✻ DR
Meals *Alacena* Rest. *(closed Easter, August, Christmas, New Year and Sunday)* Spanish rest. a la carte 39/66 and ***Il Patio*** Rest. (lunch only) a la carte 38/48 – ☕ 26 – **288 rm** 350, 6 suites.
◆ A prestigious modern hotel ; marble, crystal chandeliers and antique tapestries in the lobby, and imposing but very comfortable rooms ; excellent-quality Spanish cuisine in the smart "Alacena" restaurant.

Milan Marriott Hotel, via Washington 66 ✉ 20146 ☎ 02 48521 and rest ☎ 02 48522834, *marriott@tin.it, Fax 02 4818925,* – rm, – 1300. DR d
Meals ***La Brasserie de Milan*** Rest. a la carte 40/66 – 18 – **322 rm** 425/690, suite.
◆ An unusual contrast between the modern façade and the classically elegant interiors in this hotel, which hosts many corporate events. Well-presented functional rooms. Traditional-style dining room with open kitchen.

UNA Hotel Scandinavia, via Fauchè 15 ✉ 20154 ☎ 02 336391, *una.scandinavia@unahotels.it, Fax 02 33104510,* – rm, – 170. HT c
Meals ***Una Restaurant*** Rest. a la carte 32/42 – **153 rm** 310/364.
◆ An elegant hotel near the Fiera which offers stylish accommodation and well equipped conference facilities. The smart dining room features marble and mahogany, and overlooks the courtyard garden.

Gd H. Fieramilano, viale Boezio 20 ✉ 20145 ☎ 02 336221, *prenotazioni@grandhotelfieramilano.com, Fax 02 314119* – – 220. rest DR e
closed August – **Meals *Ambrosiano*** Rest. (dinner only) a la carte 40/60 – **238 rm** 235/295.
◆ Opposite the Fiera, this recently refitted hotel has every modern convenience and a high level of comfort ; in summer breakfast is served in the gazebo outside. Quiet, elegant dining room.

Enterprise Hotel, corso Sempione 91 ✉ 20154 ☎ 02 318181 and rest ☎ 02 31818855, *info@enterprisehotel.com, Fax 02 31818811* – – 350. DQ c
Meals ***Sophia's*** Rest. *(closed August)* a la carte 40/70 – **109 rm** 390, 2 suites.
◆ A marble and granite exterior, coupled with made-to-measure furnishings give a strong geometrical theme to this elegant hotel where the emphasis is on design and detail. An unusual yet pleasant ambience for lunch or dinner.

Capitol Millennium, via Cimarosa 6 ✉ 20144 ☎ 02 438591, *info@capitolmillennium.com, Fax 02 4694724,* – – 70. DR a
Meals (residents only) a la carte 37/50 – 18 – **66 rm** 245/365, 5 suites.
◆ Rising from the ashes of its predecessor, this small elegant hotel is a modern jewel. Excellent attention to detail throughout.

Regency without rest., via Arimondi 12 ✉ 20155 ☎ 02 39216021, *regency@regency-milano.com, Fax 02 39217734* – – 50. DQ b
closed 5 to 25 August and 24 December-7 January – **71 rm** 180/230.
◆ This late-19C aristocratic residence with its genteel courtyard is charming and very tastefully decorated throughout ; it has a particularly pleasant lounge with roaring fire.

Poliziano Fiera without rest., via Poliziano 11 ✉ 20154 ☎ 02 3191911, *info@hotelpolizianofiera.it, Fax 02 3191931* – rm, – 90. HT a
closed 25 July-25 August and 18 December-7 January – **98 rm** 333/377, 2 suites.
◆ This small, modern hotel has been totally refurbished ; polite and attentive management ; well-proportioned, pleasantly decorated rooms.

Domenichino without rest., via Domenichino 41 ✉ 20149 ☎ 02 48009692, *hd@hoteldomenichino.it, Fax 02 48003953* – – 50. DR f
closed 6 to 22 August and 23 December-6 January – **77 rm** 130/185, 2 suites.
◆ On a tree-lined road close to the Fiera, this elegant hotel has high standards of service ; confined public areas but comfortable rooms with modern furnishings.

Mozart without rest., piazza Gerusalemme 6 ✉ 20154 ☎ 02 33104215, *info@hotelmozartmilano.it, Fax 02 33103231* – – 35. HT b
closed 31 July-22 August and 24 December-2 January – **119 rm** 195/248, 3 suites.
◆ Classical elegance and attentive service at this recently refurbished hotel near the Fiera ; modern furniture in the well-appointed rooms.

Metrò without rest., corso Vercelli 61 ✉ 20144 ☎ 02 4987897, *hotelmetro@tin.it, Fax 02 48010295* – – 35. DR x
40 rm 115/150.
◆ This family-run establishment is well placed for shopping ; pleasant public areas and elegant well-appointed rooms.

Astoria without rest., viale Murillo 9 ✉ 20149 ℘ 02 40090095, *info@astoriahotelmilano.com, Fax 02 40074642* – 30. AE VISA DR m
closed 28 July-28 August – **68 rm** 130/210, suite.
◆ Situated on a busy road, this recently refitted hotel is popular with tourists and business people alike ; modern rooms with excellent soundproofing.

Mini Hotel Tiziano without rest., via Tiziano 6 ✉ 20145 ℘ 02 4699035, *tiziano@minihotel.it, Fax 02 4812153* – AE VISA. DR k
54 rm 140/195.
◆ Near the Fiera but in a quiet location, this hotel has the advantage of its own gardens to the rear ; comfortable rooms.

Berlino without rest., via Plana 33 ✉ 20155 ℘ 02 324141, *hotelberlino@traveleurope.it, Fax 02 39210611* – AE VISA DQ d
47 rm 135/225.
◆ Popular with business travellers, this comfortable hotel near the Fiera has traditionally-stylish public areas, with its (largely refurbished) rooms along more modern lines.

Lancaster without rest., via Abbondio Sangiorgio 16 ✉ 20145 ℘ 02 344705, *h.lancaster@tin.it, Fax 02 344649* – rm, AE VISA JCB HU c
closed August, Christmas and New Year – **30 rm** 109/170.
◆ This 19C building is in a quiet residential district ; a pleasant hotel with welcoming, if cramped, public areas and well-maintained, smart rooms.

Antica Locanda Leonardo without rest., corso Magenta 78 ✉ 20123 ℘ 02 48014197, *desk@leoloc.com, Fax 02 48019012* – AE VISA JCB. HX m
closed 5 to 25 August and 31 December-6 January – **20 rm** 165/190.
◆ A combination of genteel surroundings and warm welcome at this hotel, which looks onto a small courtyard ; close by is Leonardo's Last Supper.

Il Sambuco - Hotel Hermitage, via Messina 10 ✉ 20154 ℘ 02 33610333, *info@ilsambuco.it, Fax 02 33611850* – AE VISA JCB HU q
closed 1 to 20 August, 25 December-3 January, Saturday lunch and Sunday – **Meals** seafood a la carte 43/85.
◆ Like the hotel in which it is located, this restaurant is elegant and has high service standards ; renowned for its seafood cuisine, both traditional and modern.

Montecristo, corso Sempione angolo via Prina ✉ 20154 ℘ 02 3495049, *Fax 02 312760* – AE VISA. HT j
closed August, 25 December-2 January, Tuesday and Saturady lunch – **Meals** seafood a la carte 40/59.
◆ A choice of dining on the ground floor with fish tanks, or in the more intimate basement taverna, at this restaurant serving traditional flavoursome seafood.

Arrow's, via Mantegna 17/19 ✉ 20154 ℘ 02 341533, *Fax 02 33106496,* – AE VISA. HU f
closed August, Sunday and Monday lunch – **Meals** (booking essential) seafood a la carte 36/61.
◆ Packed at lunchtime, largely with business diners, but more intimate during the evenings, this restaurant near Corso Sempione specialises in traditional seafood.

Sadler Wine e Food, via Monte Bianco 2/A ✉ 20149 ℘ 02 4814677, *winefood@cri.fostwebnet.it,* Rest. and wine bar – AE VISA JCB DR c
closed 1 to 26 August and Sunday – **Meals** (booking essential) a la carte 30/40.
◆ A trendy atmosphere in this modern restaurant with wine bar ; efficient service combined with quality cuisine, from simple to gastronomic.

El Crespin, via Castelvetro 18 ✉ 20154 ℘ 02 33103004, *Fax 02 33103004* – AE VISA. HT p
closed August, 26 December-7 January, Saturday lunch and Sunday – **Meals** (booking essential) a la carte 37/57.
◆ Old photos decorate the entrance area of this tastefully presented restaurant, where the menu is dictated by the changing seasons.

Da Stefano il Marchigiano, via Arimondi 1 angolo via Plana ✉ 20155 ℘ 02 33001863 – AE VISA JCB. DQ d
closed August, Friday dinner and Saturday – **Meals** a la carte 31/57.
◆ For over twenty years this restaurant has been a favourite for lovers of good traditional cuisine ; meat and seafood dishes using quality ingredients.

Osteria del Borgo Antico, via Piero della Francesca 40 ✉ 20154 ℘ 02 3313641, *osteria@borgoantico.net* – AE VISA. HT v
closed August, Saturday lunch and Sunday – **Meals** seafood a la carte 41/54.
◆ Opened a couple of years ago, this small well-run restaurant is nicely decorated and has a friendly atmosphere ; especially good seafood.

Montina, via Procaccini 54 ✉ 20154 ☎ 02 3490498, – ▤. AE ⓢ ⓓ ⓜ VISA HU d
closed 8 August-1 September, 30 December-9 January, Sunday and Monday lunch – **Meals** a la carte 24/39.
◆ Pleasant bistro atmosphere with closely spaced tables and soft lighting in this restaurant run by twin brothers ; seasonal cuisine which is mainly Milanese.

Quadrifoglio, via Procaccini 21 angolo via Aleardi ✉ 20154 ☎ 02 341758 – ▤. ⓢ ⓓ ⓜ VISA. HU a
closed 5 to 28 August, 24 December-5 January, Tuesday and Wednesday lunch – **Meals** (booking essential) a la carte 34/54.
◆ Original décor (painted ceramics and pictures) lends this trattoria-style restaurant its personal character ; very good single course meals.

Pace, via Washington 74 ✉ 20146 ☎ 02 43983058, *Fax 02 468567*, – ▤. AE ⓢ ⓓ ⓜ VISA. DR z
closed Easter, 1 to 24 August, 24 December-5 January, Saturday lunch and Wednesday – **Meals** a la carte 25/37.
◆ This family-run trattoria, simple yet well presented, has been offering diners a warm welcome for over 30 years ; traditional meat and fish dishes.

Outskirts of Milan

North-Western area – viale Fulvio Testi, Niguarda, viale Fermi, viale Certosa, San Siro, via Novara

Grand Hotel Brun, via Caldera 21 ✉ 20153 ☎ 02 452711, *brun.res@monrifhotels.it*, *Fax 02 48204746* – |‡|, ⇔ rm, ▤ TV ☎ – 🚶 500. AE ⓢ ⓓ ⓜ VISA.
closed 23 December-4 January – **Meals *Don Giovanni*** Rest. *(closed Saturday and Sunday)* (dinner only) a la carte 50/75 and ***La Terrazza Rest.*** a la carte 30/40 – **309 rm** ☕ 250/320, 6 suites. by via S. Stratico DR
◆ In a peaceful location away from the centre, this hotel with its spacious public areas, functional rooms and well-proportioned meeting rooms, is ideal for business people. The pastel coloured dining room is decorated with trompe l'oeil scenes.

Rubens, via Rubens 21 ✉ 20148 ☎ 02 40302, *rubens@antareshotels.com*, *Fax 02 48193114* – |‡|, ⇔ rm, ▤ TV ☎ P – 🚶 35. AE ⓢ ⓓ ⓜ VISA JCB. rest DR g
Meals (residents only) 30/40 – **87 rm** ☕ 210/265.
◆ Contemporary artwork on the walls in the public areas and rooms of this elegant, functional hotel ; much attention to detail in evidence throughout.

Blaise e Francis, via Butti 9 ✉ 20158 ☎ 02 66802366, *info@blaiseefrancis.it*, *Fax 02 66802909* – |‡|, ⇔ rm, ▤ TV ☎ ♿ – 🚶 200. AE ⓢ ⓓ ⓜ VISA JCB. rest
Meals (dinner only) (residents only) a la carte 32/45 – **110 rm** ☕ 260/295. EQ a
◆ Located away from the centre, the top floors of this relatively new 14-storey hotel have fine views over the city ; comfortable rooms.

Mirage without rest., via Casella 61 angolo viale Certosa ✉ 20156 ☎ 02 39210471, *mirage@gruppomirage.it*, *Fax 02 39210589* – |‡| ▤ TV ☎ – 🚶 50. AE ⓢ ⓓ ⓜ VISA JCB. DQ z
closed 1 to 24 August – **86 rm** ☕ 160/220.
◆ Out of town but not far from the Fiera, ideal for the business traveller ; currently being extended, this hotel has modern public areas and comfortable rooms.

Valganna without rest., via Varè 32 ✉ 20158 ☎ 02 39310089, *info@hotelvalganna.it*, *Fax 02 39312566* – |‡| ▤ TV ☎. AE ⓢ ⓓ ⓜ VISA JCB by via degli Imbriani EQ
36 rm ☕ 113/165.
◆ Near the new Bovisa campus and one stop from the airport on the Malpensa Express, this comfortable family-run hotel offers good value for money.

Affori, via Astesani ang. via Novaro ✉ 20161 ☎ 02 66208629, *tolesavi@jumpy.it*, *Fax 02 66280414* – ▤ P. AE ⓢ ⓓ ⓜ VISA JCB by via Degli Imbriani EQ
closed 4 to 25 August and Monday – **Meals** (booking essential) a la carte 27/41.
◆ Dynamic young management serving modern Mediterranean cuisine in an elegant restaurant ; slightly out of town but well worth the trip.

Innocenti Evasioni, via privata della Bindellina ✉ 20155 ☎ 02 33001882, *ristorante@innocentievasioni.com*, *Fax 02 33001882*, – ▤. AE ⓢ ⓓ ⓜ VISA JCB DQ a
closed August, 3 to 9 January, Sunday and Monday – **Meals** (dinner only) (booking essential) a la carte 35/44.
◆ An unpromising exterior hides a pleasant modern restaurant, with soft lighting and windows onto a small garden ; whimsical creative cuisine.

La Pobbia, via Gallarate 92 ✉ 20151 ☎ 02 38006641, *lapobbia@tiscali.it*, *Fax 02 38000724*, , Ancient Milanese rest. – ▤ – 🚶 30. AE ⓢ ⓜ VISA. DQ w
closed August and Sunday – **Meals** a la carte 42/55.
◆ Well-established urbane restaurant (opened in 1920), with an elegant rustic ambience and al fresco dining in summer. Lombard and international cuisine.

North-Eastern area – viale Monza, via Padova, via Porpora, viale Romagna, viale Argonne, viale Forlanini

Concorde, viale Monza 132 ✉ 20125 ℘ 02 26112020, *concorde@antareshotels.com, Fax 02 26147879* – |‡|, ▤ TV ☎ – 🚗 – 🎤 160. AE ⓢ ⓞ ⓜⓒ VISA JCB. ✻
Meals (residents only) a la carte 42/65 – **120 rm** ☕ 208/260. by viale Monza GQ
♦ This comfortable out-of-town hotel is ideal for business people and corporate events ; recently refurbished rooms and versatile meeting rooms.

Starhotel Tourist, viale Fulvio Testi 300 ✉ 20126 ℘ 02 6437777, *tourist.mi@starhotels.it, Fax 02 6472516,* Fб – |‡|, ⇆ rm, ▤ TV 🚗 P – 🎤 150. AE ⓢ ⓞ ⓜⓒ VISA JCB. ✻ by viale Zara FQ
Meals a la carte 40/50 – **140 rm** ☕ 215/255.
♦ Away from the centre, but well placed for motorway access, this hotel conforms to its group's standards ; a spacious refitted ground floor with well-appointed meeting rooms. Smart restaurant with bar.

Lombardia, viale Lombardia 74 ✉ 20131 ℘ 02 2824938, *hotelomb@tin.it, Fax 02 2893430* – |‡|, ⇆ rm, ▤ TV ☎ 🚗 – 🎤 100. AE ⓢ ⓞ ⓜⓒ VISA JCB. ✻ rest
closed 4 to 19 August – **Meals** *(closed Saturday and Sunday)* (dinner only) (residents only) 22/32 – **80 rm** ☕ 105/180. GQ e
♦ This well-presented hotel in the Piazzale Loreto district has a light spacious lobby and quiet, inner-facing rooms with modern furnishings.

Tre Pini, via Tullo Morgagni 19 ✉ 20125 ℘ 02 66805413, *Fax 02 66801346,* 🍴 – ▤. AE ⓢ ⓞ ⓜⓒ VISA by via Arbe FQ
closed 9 to 22 August and Saturday – **Meals** (booking essential) char-grilled specialities a la carte 39/48.
♦ Completely refurbished, this spacious restaurant has doors opening out onto a terrace for summer dining ; roast meats a speciality, prepared in an open kitchen.

Centro Ittico, via Ferrante Aporti 35 ✉ 20125 ℘ 02 26823449, *Fax 02 26143774* – ▤. ⓢ ⓞ ⓜⓒ VISA. ✻ GQ b
closed August, 25 December-7 January, Sunday and Monday lunch – **Meals** (booking essential for dinner) seafood a la carte 34/70.
♦ Beneath the platforms of the main station, this former fish market is unfussy in presentation and serves fresh seafood cuisine at its best.

Charmant, via G. Colombo 42 ✉ 20133 ℘ 02 70100136 – ▤. AE ⓢ ⓞ ⓜⓒ VISA. ✻
closed Sunday – **Meals** (booking essential) seafood a la carte 39/55. GR k
♦ In the Citta Studi district, this elegant restaurant specialises in seafood along classic Mediterranean lines.

Baia Chia, via Bazzini 37 ✉ 20131 ℘ 02 2361131, 🍴 – ▤. ⓢ ⓜⓒ VISA. ✻ GQ a
closed Easter, 3 weeks in August, 24 December-2 January, Sunday and Monday lunch – **Meals** (booking essential) Sardinian and seafood rest. a la carte 26/36.
♦ Newly extended giving additional space, this pleasant family-run restaurant offers fine seafood and Sardinian specialities.

South-Eastern area – viale Molise, corso Lodi, via Ripamonti, corso San Gottardo

Quark, via Lampedusa 11/a ✉ 20141 ℘ 02 84431, *commerciale@quarkhotel.com, Fax 02 8464190,* Fб, 🏊 – |‡|, ⇆ rm, ▤ TV 🚗 P – 🎤 1000. AE ⓢ ⓞ ⓜⓒ VISA JCB. ✻ by via C. Bazzi FS
closed 1 to 8 January – **Meals** a la carte 40/50 – **190 rm** ☕ 189/233, 92 suites 199/243.
♦ A large recently built hotel, originally conceived as flats and thus offering spacious rooms and many suites ; it has one of the city's largest conference centres. Large windows and pastel décor in the restaurant.

Starhotel Business Palace, via Gaggia 3 ✉ 20139 ℘ 02 53545, *business.mi@starhotels.it, Fax 02 57307550,* Fб – |‡| ▤ TV ☎ 🚗 – 🎤 200. AE ⓢ ⓞ ⓜⓒ VISA JCB. ✻ by corso Lodi FGS
Meals (residents only) a la carte 35/50 – **248 rm** ☕ 229/259, 33 suites.
♦ Well placed for road and metro links, a fine example of a formal industrial building converted for hotel use. Spacious public areas and good conference facilities.

Novotel Milano Est Aeroporto, via Mecenate 121 ✉ 20138 ℘ 02 507261, *novotel.milanoest@accor-hotels.it, Fax 02 58011086,* 🏊 – |‡| ⇆ ▤ TV ☎ ♿ P – 🎤 350. AE ⓢ ⓞ ⓜⓒ VISA. ✻ rest by viale Corsica GR
Meals a la carte 28/50 – **206 rm** ☕ 225/269.
♦ Popular with business travellers and corporate clients on account of its proximity to Linate airport and road links ; levels of comfort in keeping with group standards. Open-air pool and modern restaurant offering Italian and international cuisine.

La Plancia, via Cassinis 13 ✉ 20139 ℘ 02 5390558, *info@laplancia.it, Fax 02 5390558* – ▤. AE ⓢ ⓞ ⓜⓒ VISA JCB by corso Lodi FGS
closed August, 1 to 6 January and Sunday – **Meals** seafood and pizzeria a la carte 28/41.
♦ This bright modern pizzeria-style restaurant, with fish tank displays, offers the choice of pizzas or seafood ; also open for lunch.

Nuovo Macello, via Cesare Lombroso 20 ✉ 20137 ☎ 02 59902122, *Fax 02 59902122* – ▤ GS b
closed Saturday lunch and Sunday – **Meals** (booking essential) a la carte 41/47.
◆ This local trattoria has been in business since 1940 ; it was fully refurbished in 1998 and offers a friendly ambience with creative cuisine rooted in rural tradition.

Taverna Calabiana, via Calabiana 3 ✉ 20139 ☎ 02 55213075 – ▤. AE ⓢ ⓓ VISA. ✂ GS a
closed Easter, August, 24 December-5 January, Sunday and Monday – **Meals** Rest. and pizzeria a la carte 24/32.
◆ A welcoming rustic atmosphere with heavy wooden tables ; seasonal cuisine from various regions and authentic pizzas.

South-Western area – viale Famagosta, viale Liguria, via Lorenteggio, viale Forze Armate, via Novara

Holiday Inn, via Lorenteggio 278 ✉ 20152 ☎ 02 413111, *sales@holidayinn-milano.it, Fax 02 413113,* – ▤ TV – 85. AE ⓢ ⓓ MC VISA. ✂ by via Foppa DES
Meals ***Il Molinetto*** Rest. a la carte 29/45 – ☕ 20 – **119 rm** 302/334.
◆ A recent glass and concrete structure along American lines, offering a comfortable ambience in keeping with the group's standards ; well-appointed rooms. Italian and international cuisine in the welcoming dining room.

Il Luogo di Aimo e Nadia, via Montecuccoli 6 ✉ 20147 ☎ 02 416886, *info@aimoenadia.com, Fax 02 48302005* – ▤. AE ⓢ ⓓ MC VISA. ✂ by via Foppa DES
closed August, 1 to 8 January, Saturday lunch and Sunday – **Meals** (booking essential) 33 (lunch) 77 and a la carte 67/131.
◆ A leading light of the city's culinary scene, this restaurant, with an impressive display of modern works of art, has cuisine memorable for its creativity.
Spec. Tagliolini di pasta fresca con pesce di scoglio e verdure al basilico. Scamone di vitello piemontese sanato farcito di prosciutto di cinta senese e fegato d'oca. Sformato caldo di cioccolato venezuelano all'olio extravergine con granita di caffé.

L'Ape Piera, via Lodovico il Moro 11 ✉ 20143 ☎ 02 89126060, *info@ape-piera.com* – ▤. AE ⓢ ⓓ MC VISA DS a
closed 3 August-3 September and Sunday – **Meals** (dinner only) (booking essential) a la carte 45/73.
◆ In a historic setting redolent of old Milan, this recent gastronomic novelty has established itself as a leading restaurant.

on national road 35-Milanofiori *by via Ascanio* ES *: 10 km :*

Royal Garden Hotel, via Di Vittorio ✉ 20090 Assago ☎ 02 457811, *garden.res@monrifhotels.it, Fax 02 45702901,* – ▤ TV P – 180. AE ⓢ ⓓ MC VISA. ✂
closed August and 24 December-5 January – **Meals** a la carte 40/62 – **121 rm** ☕ 207/298, 33 suites.
◆ The unusual style of this hotel is evident on entering the 25m-high lobby with its fountain and escalators ; innovation and comfort in tandem. The restaurant also has a quirky modernist ambience.

Jolly Hotel Milanofiori, Strada 2 ✉ 20090 Assago ☎ 02 82221, *milanofiori@jollyhotels.it, Fax 02 89200946,* – ▤ TV P – 110. AE ⓢ ⓓ MC VISA. ✂ rest
closed August and 24 December-6 January – **Meals** a la carte 38/49 – **255 rm** ☕ 198/288.
◆ This recently built hotel is plain and functional, and caters mainly for business travellers and corporate events ; attached to the Milanofiori conference centre. Comfortable rooms with modern furnishings, and a large restaurant along contemporary lines.

Abbiategrasso *20081 Milano 561 F 8 – pop. 28079 alt. 120.*
Roma 590 – Alessandria 80 – Milano 24 – Novara 29 – Pavia 33.

at Cassinetta di Lugagnano *North : 3 km – ✉ 20081 :*

Antica Osteria del Ponte, piazza G. Negri 9 ☎ 02 9420034, *Fax 02 9420610,* – ▤. AE ⓢ ⓓ MC VISA. ✂
closed August, 25 December-12 January, Sunday and Monday – **Meals** (booking essential) a la carte 90/149.
◆ This 16C bridge over the Naviglio now houses a gourmet's paradise ; wonderful creative cuisine and a stylish welcome in historic surroundings with exposed beams.
Spec. Gamberi di San Remo marinati con cipollotto fresco e caviale oscietra. Risotto con zucchine in fiore e zafferano in fili (June-October). Guanciale di vitello brasato al vino amarone, cardamono e zenzero (October-March).

Bergamo *24100* P 561 E 11 *G. Italy – pop. 117 415 alt. 249.*

parco dei Colli ✆ 035 250033, Fax 035 4326540;

Bergamo L'Albenza (closed Monday) at Almenno San Bartolomeo ✉ 24030 ✆ 035 640028, Fax 035 643066;

La Rossera (closed Tuesday) at Chiuduno ✉ 24060 ✆ 035 838600, Fax 035 4427047.

Orio al Serio ✆ 035 326111, Fax 035 326339.

viale Vittorio Emanuele II 20 ✉ 24121 ✆ 035 210204, aptbg@apt.bergamo.it, Fax 035 230184.

A.C.I. *via Angelo Maj 16 ✉ 24121 ✆ 035 285985.*

Roma 601 – Brescia 52 – Milano 47.

XXX ✿✿ **Da Vittorio,** viale Papa Giovanni XXIII 21 ✉ 24121 ✆ 035 213266, *info@davittorio.com, Fax 035 210805* – ▤. AE ⑤ ⓓ ⓜⓒ VISA
closed August and Wednesday – **Meals** (booking essential) a la carte 76/141.
◆ Named after its enthusiastic proprietor who passionately escorts his clients on a creative journey through the highlights of Italian cuisine.
Spec. Scamponi croccanti con salsa di patate e funghi prataioli. Baccalà con fagioli, pomodori canditi e salsa alle cipolle (spring-summer). Filetto di manzo bollito, in brodo speziato e salsa verde (autumn-winter).

Canneto sull'Oglio *46013 Mantova* 561 G 13 *– pop. 4 569 alt. 35.*
Roma 493 – Brescia 51 – Cremona 32 – Mantova 38 – Milano 123 – Parma 44.

towards Carzaghetto *North-West : 3 km :*

XXXX ✿✿✿ **Dal Pescatore,** ✉ 46013 ✆ 0376 723001, *santini@dalpescatore.com, Fax 0376 70304,* , Elegant installation, – ▤ P. AE ⑤ ⓓ ⓜⓒ VISA JCB. ✂
closed 9 August-5 September, 1 to 21 January, Monday, Tuesday and Wednesday lunch – **Meals** (booking essential) a la carte 96/146.
◆ A Lombard farm with authentic homely cuisine ; an elegant mix of warm welcome and sophistication makes for an unforgettable experience ; garden dining in summer.
Spec. Terrina di salmone, astice e caviale asetra malossol. Risotto con pistilli di zafferano e carciofi fritti (October-May). Maialino di razza cinta senese al forno con pepe nero di Szechuan.

Concesio *25062 Brescia* 561 F 12 *– pop. 12 793 alt. 218.*
Roma 544 – Bergamo 50 – Brescia 10 – Milano 91.

XXX ✿✿ **Miramonti l'Altro,** via Crosette 34, località Costorio ✆ 030 2751063, *info@miramontialtro.it, Fax 030 2753189* – ▤ P. ⑤ ⓓ ⓜⓒ VISA. ✂
closed 5 to 20 August and Monday – **Meals** (booking essential) a la carte 52/84.
◆ Against a modern, Neo-classical-style backdrop, tradition and innovation combine to provide a memorable gastronomic experience.
Spec. Sfogliatina di lumache e funghi alla curcuma (spring). Risotto ai formmaggi dolci di montagna. Crescendo di agnello con finale di suo carré .

Erbusco *25030 Brescia* 561 F 11 *– pop. 6 927 alt. 251.*
Roma 578 – Bergamo 35 – Brescia 22 – Milano 69.

XXXX ✿✿ **Gualtiero Marchesi,** via Vittorio Emanuele 11 (North : 1,5 km) ✆ 030 7760562, *ristorante@marchesi.it, Fax 030 7760379,* ← lake and mountains, Elegant installation – ▤ P. AE ⑤ ⓓ ⓜⓒ VISA JCB. ✂
closed 7 January-10 February, Sunday dinner and Monday – **Meals** (booking essential) a la carte 69/123.
◆ A temple to Italian gastronomy, this place is a joy to behold in all its refined simplicity. Mouthwatering menu.
Spec. Insalata di capesante allo zenzero. Raviolo aperto. Filetto di vitello alla Rossini secondo Gualtiero Marchesi.

Soriso *28018 Novara* 561 E 7, 219 ⑯ *– pop. 770 alt. 452.*
Roma 654 – Arona 20 – Milano 78 – Novara 40 – Stresa 35 – Torino 114 – Varese 46.

XXXX ✿✿✿ **Al Sorriso** with rm, via Roma 18 ✆ 0322 983228, *sorriso@alsorriso.com, Fax 0322 983328* – ✂, ▤ rest, TV. AE ⑤ ⓓ ⓜⓒ VISA JCB. ✂
closed 3 to 28 August and 7 to 28 January – **Meals** *(closed Monday and Tuesday)* (booking essential) a la carte 98/138 – **8 rm** 120/190.
◆ Culinary artistry in this temple to gastronomy ; peerless imaginative cuisine in a beautifully presented ambience of refined elegance. An unforgettable experience.
Spec. Gamberi di fiume con gelé di pomodoro e cocomero agli agrumi (February-November). Zuppetta di melanzane al timo con seppioline croccanti (spring-summer). Lasagnetta di patate con cardi gobbi, fonduta di Bettelmat al tartufo d'Alba (autumn-winter).

NAPLES (NAPOLI) *80100* P 564 E 24 *G. Italy – pop. 1 000 470 – High Season : April-October.*

See : *National Archaeological Museum★★★* KY – *New Castle★★* KZ – *Port of Santa Lucia★★* BU : ≤★★ *of Vesuvius and bay* – ≤★★★ *at night from via Partenope of the Vomero and Posillipo* FX – *San Carlo Theatre★* KZ **T** – *Piazza del Plebiscito★* JKZ – *Royal Palace★* KZ – *Carthusian Monastery of St. Martin★★* JZ.

Spaccanapoli and Decumano Maggiore★★ KLY – *Tomb★★ of King Robert the Wise and Cloisters★★ in Church of Santa Chiara★* KY – *Cathedral★ (Duomo)* LY – *Sculptures★ in Chapel Sansevero* KY – *Arch★, Tomb★ of Catherine of Austria, apse★ in Church of St. Lawrence Major* LY – *Capodimonte Palace and National Gallery★★.*

Mergellina★ : ≤★★ *of the bay* – *Villa Floridiana★* EVX : ≤★ – *Catacombs of St. Gennaro★★* – *Church of Santa Maria Donnaregina★* LY – *Church of St. Giovanni a Carbonara★* LY – *Capuan Gate★* LMY – *Cuomo Palace★* LY – *Sculptures★ in the Church of St. Anne of the Lombards* KYZ – *Posillipo★* – *Marechiaro★* – ≤★★ *of the bay from Virgiliano Park (or Rimembranza Park).*

Exc. : *Bay of Naples★★★* – *Campi Flegrei★★* – *Sorrento Penisula★★ Island of Capri★★★ Island of Ischia★★★.*

(closed Tuesday) at Arco Felice ✉ *80078* ☎ *081 412881, Fax 081 2520438, West : 19 km.*

Ugo Niutta of Capodichino North-East : 6 km ☎ *081 7805697 – Alitalia, viale Ruffo di Calabria* ✉ *80144* ☎ *081 7899150, Fax 081 7899150.*

to Capri (1 h 15 mn), Ischia (1 h 25 mn) e Procida (1 h), daily – Caremar-Travel and Holidays, molo Beverello ✉ *80133* ☎ *081 5513882, Fax 081 5522011; to Cagliari 19 June-14 July Thursday and Saturday, 15 July-11 September Thursday and Tuesday (15 h 45 mn) and Palermo daily (11 h) – Tirrenia Navigazione, Stazione Marittima, molo Angioino* ✉ *80133* ☎ *081 2514740, Fax 081 2514767 ; to Ischia daily (1 h 20 mn) – Linee Lauro, molo Beverello* ✉ *80133* ☎ *081 5522838, Fax 081 5513236; to Aeolian Island Wednesday and Friday, 15 June-15 September Monday, Tuesday, Thursday, Friday, Saturday and Sunday (14 h) – Siremar-Genovese Agency, via De Petris 78* ✉ *80133* ☎ *081 5512112, Fax 081 5512114.*

to Capri (45 mn), Ischia (45 mn) and Procida (35 mn), daily – Caremar-Travel and Holidays, molo Beverello ✉ *80133* ☎ *081 5513882, Fax 081 5522011; to Ischia (30 mn) and Capri (40 mn), daily – Alilauro, via Caracciolo 11* ✉ *80122* ☎ *081 7611004, Fax 081 7614250 and Linee Lauro, molo Beverello* ✉ *80133* ☎ *081 5522838, Fax 081 5513236; to Capri daily (40 mn) – Navigazione Libera del Golfo, molo Beverello* ✉ *80133* ☎ *081 5520763, Fax 081 5525589; to Capri (45 mn), to Aeolian Island June-September (4 h) and Procida-Ischia daily (35 mn) – Aliscafi SNAV, via Caracciolo 10* ✉ *80122* ☎ *081 7612348, Fax 081 7612141.*

via San Carlo 9 ✉ *80132* ☎ *081 402394 – Central Station* ✉ *80142* ☎ *081 268779 – piazza del Gesù Nuovo 7* ✉ *80135* ☎ *081 5523328 - Stazione Mergellina* ✉ *80122* ☎ *081 7612102.*

A.C.I. *piazzale Tecchio 49/d* ✉ *80125* ☎ *081 7253811.*

Roma 219 – Bari 261

Plans on following pages

Grand Hotel Vesuvio, via Partenope 45 ✉ 80121 ☎ 081 7640044, *info@vesuvio.it, Fax 081 7644483,* ≤ gulf and Castel dell'Ovo, – rm, – 400. AE VISA. FX n
Meals (see rest. ***Caruso*** below) – **146 rm** 320/400, 17 suites.
◆ The timeless charm of bygone splendour in this elegant setting, which has been a byword for Neapolitan hospitality since 1882 ; views over the sea and Castel dell'Ovo.

Excelsior, via Partenope 48 ✉ 80121 ☎ 081 7640111, *info@excelsior.it, Fax 081 7649743* – rm, AE VISA JCB. rest GX w
Meals ***La Terrazza*** Rest. *(closed Sunday)* a la carte 48/66 – **109 rm** 270/330, 12 suites.
◆ Echoes of elegant days gone by throughout in this jewel among Naples hotels, which has preserved an ambience of long-forgotten opulence. Luxurious rooms and a breathtaking view of the sea and Castel dell'Ovo from the rooftop restaurant.

Gd H. Parker's, corso Vittorio Emanuele 135 ✉ 80121 ☎ 081 7612474, *info@grandhotelparkers.it, Fax 081 663527* – rm, – 250. AE VISA JCB. EX r
Meals ***George's*** Rest. a la carte 45/71 – **73 rm** 260/350, 10 suites.
◆ A harmonious marriage of modern comfort and classical elegance in this traditional hotel which underwent a total refit in 1990 ; each floor is furnished in a different style. Amazing views over the sea from the fine restaurant.

Gd H. Santa Lucia, via Partenope 46 ✉ 80121 ☎ 081 7640666, *reservations@santalucia.it, Fax 081 7648580,* ≤ gulf and Castel dell'Ovo – rm, – 100. AE VISA. GX c
Meals (see rest. ***Megaris*** below) – **88 rm** 382/392, 8 suites.
◆ Splendid views over the sea and Castel dell'Ovo and a refined and stylish ambience to this late 19C hotel ; attentive service and excellent rooms.

NAPOLI

Arcoleo (Via G.) . . . . **FX** 5
Arena della Sanità (Via) . . **GU** 6
Artisti (Piazza degli) . . . . . . **EV** 9
Bernini (Via G. L.) . . . . **EV** 12
Bonito (Via G.) . . . . **FV** 13
Carducci (Via G.) . . . . **FX** 20
Chiatamone (Via) . . . . **FX** 25
Cirillo (Via D.) . . . . **GU** 27
Colonna (Via Vittoria) . . . . . **FX** 29
Crocelle ai Vergini (Via) . . . **GU** 35
D'Auria (Via G.) . . . . **FV** 40
Ferraris (Via Galileo) . . . . . . **HV** 54
Gaetani (Via) . . . . **FX** 61
Gen. Pignatelli (Via) . . . . **HU** 63
Giordano (Via L.) . . . . **EV** 64
Martini (Via Simone) . . . . . . **EV** 75
Mazzocchi (Via Alessio) . . . **HU** 76
Menzinger (Via G.) . . . . **EV** 77

Traffic restricted in the town centre

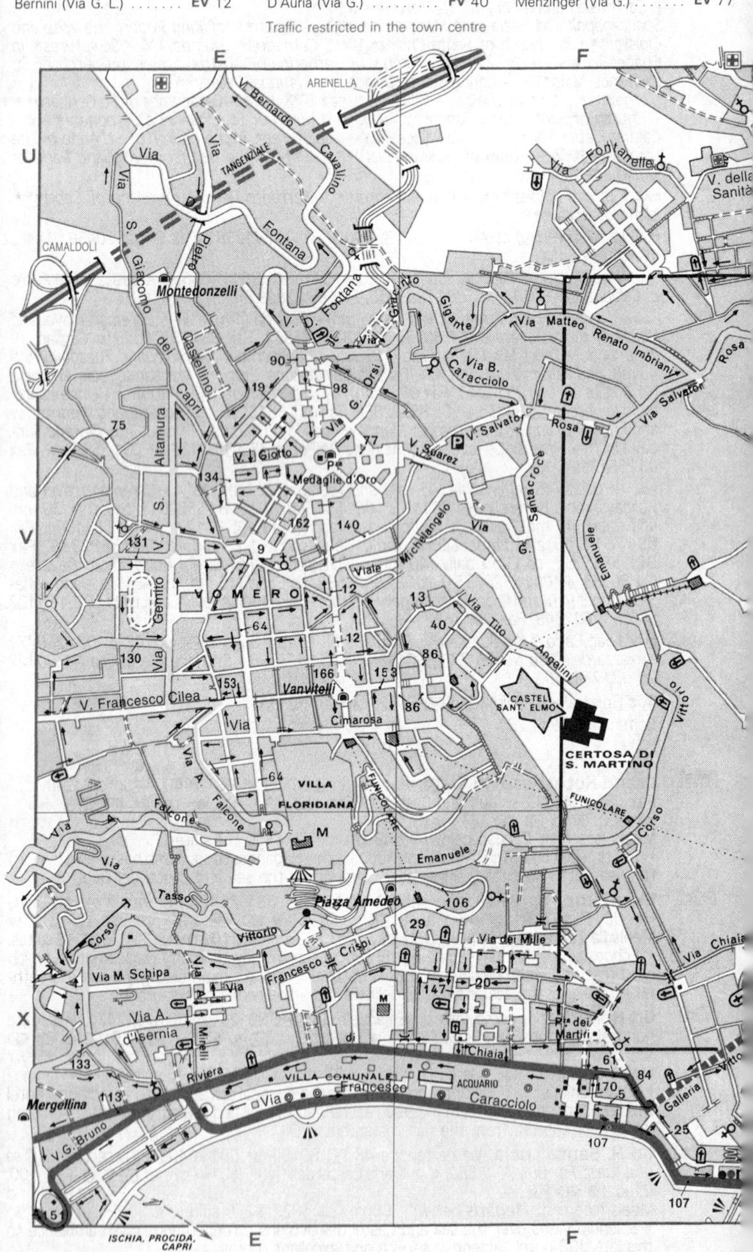

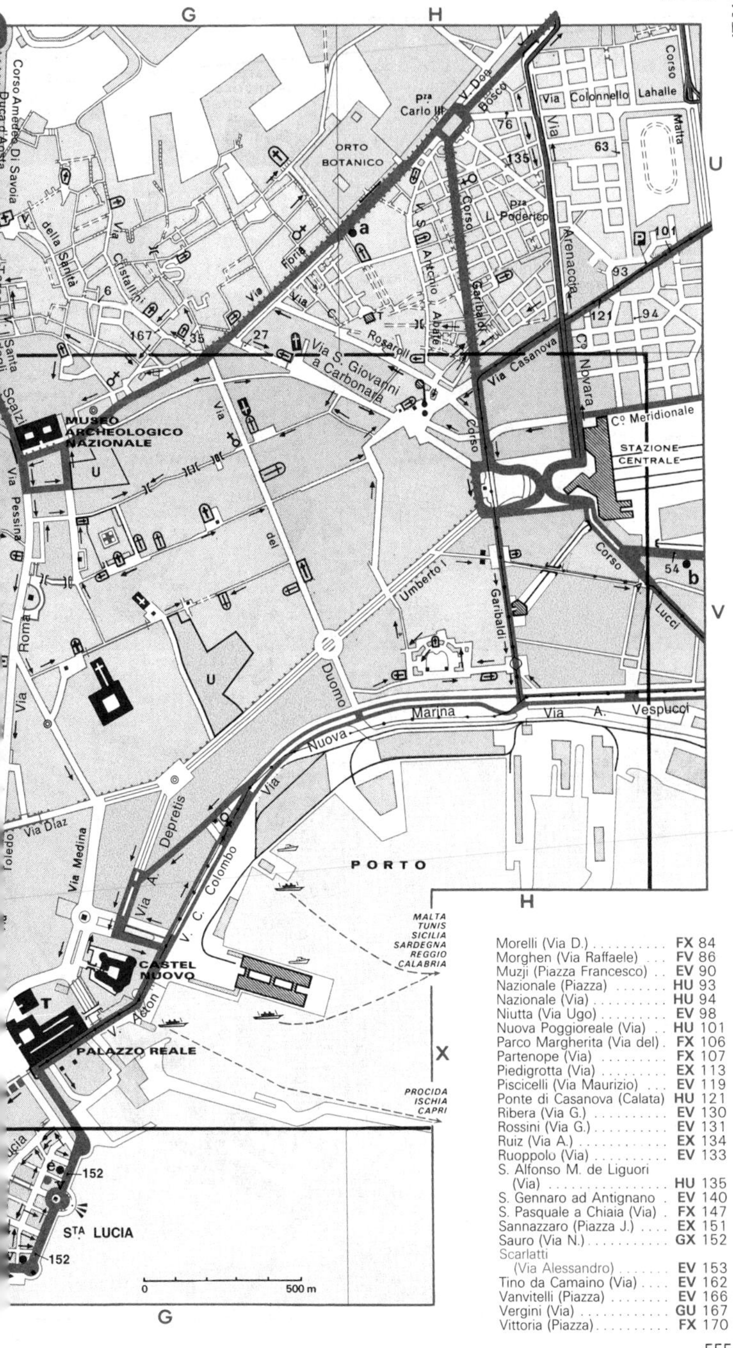

Morelli (Via D.)	FX	84
Morghen (Via Raffaele)	FV	86
Muzji (Piazza Francesco)	EV	90
Nazionale (Piazza)	HU	93
Nazionale (Via)	HU	94
Niutta (Via Ugo)	EV	98
Nuova Poggioreale (Via)	HU	101
Parco Margherita (Via del)	FX	106
Partenope (Via)	FX	107
Piedigrotta (Via)	EX	113
Piscicelli (Via Maurizio)	EV	119
Ponte di Casanova (Calata)	HU	121
Ribera (Via G.)	EV	130
Rossini (Via G.)	EV	131
Ruiz (Via A.)	EX	134
Ruoppolo (Via)	EV	133
S. Alfonso M. de Liguori (Via)	HU	135
S. Gennaro ad Antignano	EV	140
S. Pasquale a Chiaia (Via)	FX	147
Sannazzaro (Piazza J.)	EX	151
Sauro (Via N.)	GX	152
Scarlatti (Via Alessandro)	EV	153
Tino da Camaino (Via)	EV	162
Vanvitelli (Piazza)	EV	166
Vergini (Via)	GU	167
Vittoria (Piazza)	FX	170

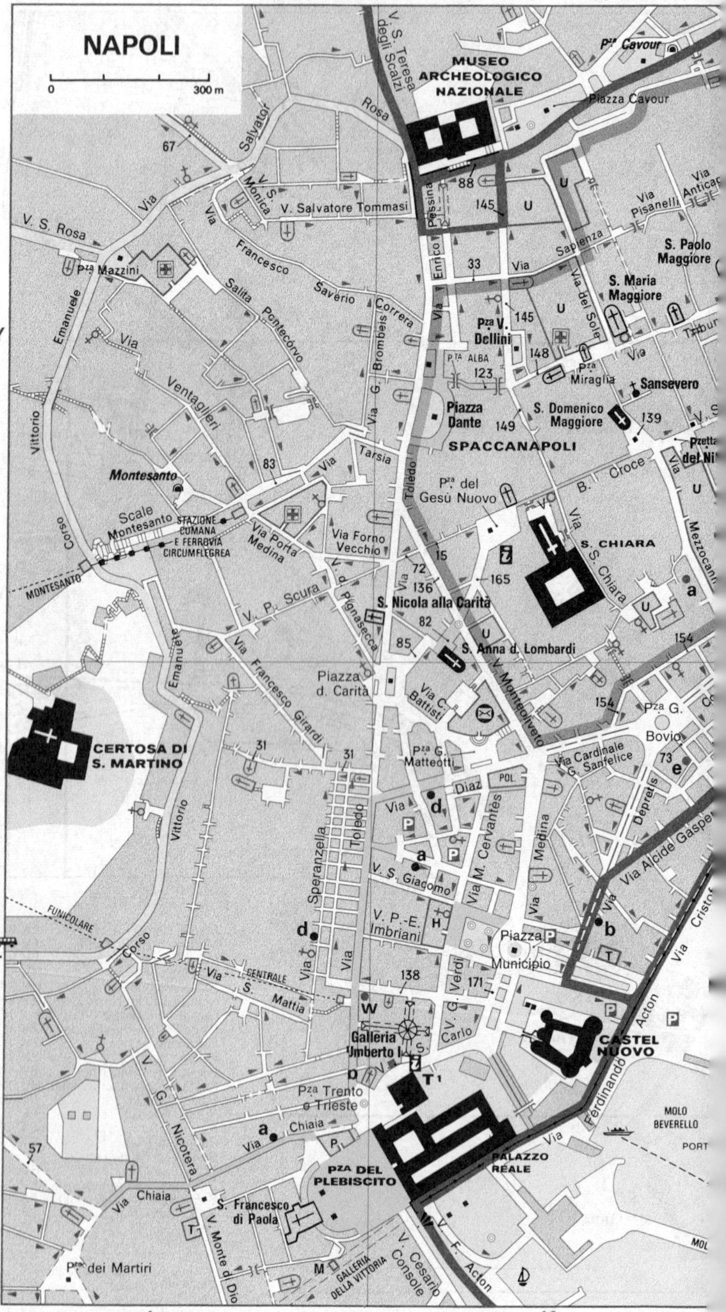

NAPOLI

0 300 m

J K

MUSEO ARCHEOLOGICO NAZIONALE
P^za Cavour
Piazza Cavour
V. S. Teresa degli Scalzi
Rosa
Salvator Rosa
Via
V. S. Rosa
P^za Mazzini
V. S. Monica
V. Salvatore Tommasi
Via Francesco Saverio Correra
Salita Pontecorvo
Via Ventaglieri
Via Pessina
Enrico
Via Sapienza
Via Pisanelli
Via Anticaglia
S. Paolo Maggiore
S. Maria Maggiore
Via del Sole
P^za V. Bellini
P.^TA ALBA
P^za Miraglia
Sansevero
Piazza Dante
S. Domenico Maggiore
SPACCANAPOLI
Corso Vittorio Emanuele
Montesanto
Scale Montesanto
STAZIONE CUMANA E FERROVIA CIRCUMFLEGREA
MONTESANTO
Via Tarsia
Via G. Brombeis
Via Porta Medina
Via Forno Vecchio
V. P. Scura
V. d. Pignasecca
Via Toledo
P^za del Gesù Nuovo
V. B. Croce
S. CHIARA
Via S. Chiara
Via Mezzocannone
P^zetta del Nilo
S. Nicola alla Carità
S. Anna d. Lombardi
Via Francesco Girardi
Piazza d. Carità
Via C. Battisti
V. Monteoliveto
P^za G. Bovio
Via Cardinale G. Sanfelice
Via Depretis
P^za G. Matteotti
Via Diaz
POL.
CERTOSA DI S. MARTINO
Via M. Cervantes
Via Medina
Via Alcide Gasperi
V. S. Giacomo
V. P.-E. Imbriani
Piazza Municipio
Via Speranzella
FUNICOLARE
CENTRALE
Corso
Via S. Mattia
V. G. Verdi
V. S. Carlo
Galleria Umberto I
CASTEL NUOVO
Via Ferdinando Acton
Via Cristoforo Colombo
P^za Trento e Trieste
Via Chiaia
P^ZA DEL PLEBISCITO
PALAZZO REALE
MOLO BEVERELLO
PORT
V. G. Nicotera
S. Francesco di Paola
V. Monte di Dio
GALLERIA DELLA VITTORIA
V. Cesario Console
V. F. Acton
P^za dei Martiri

J K

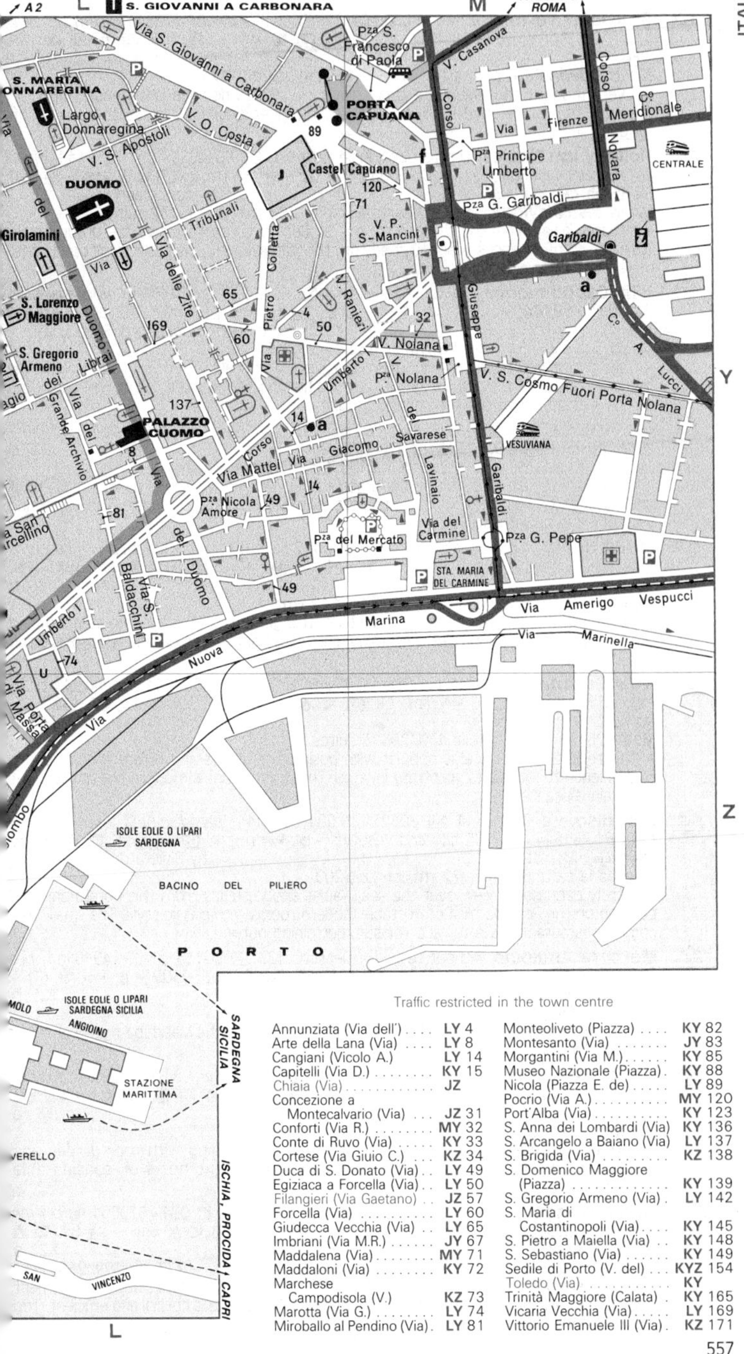

Traffic restricted in the town centre

Annunziata (Via dell')	LY 4	Monteoliveto (Piazza)	KY 82
Arte della Lana (Via)	LY 8	Montesanto (Via)	JY 83
Cangiani (Vicolo A.)	LY 14	Morgantini (Via M.)	KY 85
Capitelli (Via D.)	KY 15	Museo Nazionale (Piazza)	KY 88
Chiaia (Via)	JZ	Nicola (Piazza E. de)	LY 89
Concezione a Montecalvario (Via)	JZ 31	Pocrio (Via A.)	MY 120
Conforti (Via R.)	MY 32	Port'Alba (Via)	KY 123
Conte di Ruvo (Via)	KY 33	S. Anna dei Lombardi (Via)	KY 136
Cortese (Via Giuio C.)	KZ 34	S. Arcangelo a Baiano (Via)	LY 137
Duca di S. Donato (Via)	LY 49	S. Brigida (Via)	KZ 138
Egiziaca a Forcella (Via)	LY 50	S. Domenico Maggiore (Piazza)	KY 139
Filangieri (Via Gaetano)	JZ 57	S. Gregorio Armeno (Via)	LY 142
Forcella (Via)	LY 60	S. Maria di Costantinopoli (Via)	KY 145
Giudecca Vecchia (Via)	LY 65	S. Pietro a Maiella (Via)	KY 148
Imbriani (Via M.R.)	JY 67	S. Sebastiano (Via)	KY 149
Maddalena (Via)	MY 71	Sedile di Porto (V. del)	KYZ 154
Maddaloni (Via)	KY 72	Toledo (Via)	KY
Marchese Campodisola (V.)	KZ 73	Trinità Maggiore (Calata)	KY 165
Marotta (Via G.)	LY 74	Vicaria Vecchia (Via)	LY 169
Miroballo al Pendino (Via)	LY 81	Vittorio Emanuele III (Via)	KZ 171

Starhotel Terminus, piazza Garibaldi 91 ✉ 80142 ☎ 081 7793111, *terminus.na@starhotels.it, Fax 081 206689* – 🛗 ⇔ ▤ TV ☎ – 🅰 300. AE ⑤ ⓪ MC VISA JCB. ✻ MY a
Meals ***Odeon*** Rest. a la carte 35/45 – **168 rm** ☕ 159/179.
◆ Every modern convenience and classically elegant furnishings in this hotel opposite the station ; conference facilities, a charming inner courtyard and panoramic roof-garden.

Holiday Inn Naples, centro direzionale Isola E/6 ✉ 80143 ☎ 081 2250111, *hinapl es@hotel-invest.com, Fax 081 2250683,* Ⓕ, ≘s – 🛗, ⇔ rm, ▤ TV ☎ ♿ – 🅰 320. AE ⑤ ⓪ MC VISA JCB. ✻ by corso Meridionale MY
Meals ***Bistrot Victor*** Rest. a la carte 31/42 – **298 rm** ☕ 195, 32 suites.
◆ Situated away from the city centre, this 22-floor hotel conforms to the group's standards of comfort and is well equipped for corporate events. The restaurant opens onto a pleasant inner courtyard.

Villa Capodimonte 🏞, via Moiariello 66 ✉ 80131 ☎ 081 459000, *villacap@tin.it, Fax 081 299344,* ←, 🌳, 🌳, 🎾 – 🛗 ▤ TV ☎ P – 🅰 130. AE ⑤ ⓪ MC VISA. ✻ by corso Amedeo di Savoia GU
Meals a la carte 31/44 – **56 rm** ☕ 154,25/207,46.
◆ Taking its name from the hill on which it sits, this hotel in its own grounds with fine sea views has everything one might expect in a historic villa ; elegant, large, well-appointed rooms. Restaurant offers the chance to dine outside in summer.

Oriente, via Diaz 44 ✉ 80134 ☎ 081 5512133, *ghorient@tin.it, Fax 081 5514915* – 🛗 ▤ TV ☎ – 🅰 300. AE ⑤ ⓪ MC VISA. ✻ KZ d
Meals a la carte 38/49 – **129 rm** ☕ 155/220, 2 suites.
◆ In the city centre, this refurbished hotel has elegant and spacious public areas and is well suited to hosting conferences ; simple, classic furnishings in the rooms. The welcoming restaurant is similarly stylish.

Majestic, largo Vasto a Chiaia 68 ✉ 80121 ☎ 081 416500, *info@majestic.it, Fax 081 410145* – 🛗, ⇔ rm, ▤ TV – 🅰 120. AE ⑤ ⓪ MC VISA JCB. ✻ rest FX b
Meals *(closed Sunday)* a la carte 43/59 – **112 rm** ☕ 160/200, 6 suites.
◆ Very centrally-located close to Via dei Mille, this genteel hotel has completely refitted rooms which are functional yet welcoming. The restaurant has a pleasant atmosphere and good service.

New Europe, via Galileo Ferraris 40 ✉ 80142 ☎ 081 3602111, *nehotel@tin.it, Fax 081 200758* – 🛗, ⇔ rm, ▤ TV ☎ ♿ – 🅰 800. AE ⑤ ⓪ MC VISA JCB. ✻ rest HV b
Meals 25/35 – **156 rm** ☕ 170/205, 3 suites.
◆ This recently built hotel is popular with business travellers and offers every modern convenience to its guests ; centrally located. The dining room is modern but not without a certain elegance.

Paradiso, via Catullo 11 ✉ 80122 ☎ 081 2475111, *paradiso.na@bestwestern.it, Fax 081 7613449,* ← gulf, city and Vesuvius – 🛗, ⇔ rm, ▤ TV – 🅰 80. AE ⑤ ⓪ MC VISA JCB. ✻ rest by Riviera di Chiaia EFX
Meals a la carte 35/44 – **72 rm** ☕ 120/200.
◆ A truly paradisaical view over the sea, Naples and Vesuvius from this hotel's enviable position on the Posillipo hill. Comfortable modern rooms with classic style. The small, welcoming restaurant has a terrace for summer dining outside.

Mercure Angioino without rest., via Depretis 123 ✉ 80133 ☎ 081 4910111, *pre notazioni.mercurenapoliangioino@accor-hotels.it, Fax 081 5529509* – 🛗 ⇔ ▤ TV – 🅰 30. AE ⑤ ⓪ MC VISA JCB KZ b
85 rm ☕ 152/180.
◆ This functional new hotel, run by friendly young staff, is in the Maschio Angioini district ; comfortable rooms and a splendid breakfast buffet.

Miramare without rest., via Nazario Sauro 24 ✉ 80132 ☎ 081 7647589, *info@hot elmiramare.com, Fax 081 7640775,* ← gulf and Vesuvius – 🛗 ▤ TV. AE ⑤ ⓪ MC VISA JCB. ✻ GX e
30 rm ☕ 190/299.
◆ Formerly an aristocratic residence, this early 20C building with roof garden and fine views towards the sea and Vesuvius, is an elegant hotel of considerable character.

Mediterraneo, via Nuovo Ponte di Tappia 25 ✉ 80133 ☎ 081 7970001, *info@me diterraneonapoli.com, Fax 081 2520079* – 🛗, ⇔ rm, ▤ TV ☎ ♿ – 🅰 81. AE ⑤ ⓪ MC VISA. ✻ KZ a
Meals *(closed August and Sunday)* a la carte 28/48 – ☕ 20 – **277 rm** 199/259.
◆ Public areas dotted over several floors represent one of the dynamic new management innovations. All rooms are recently refurbished and the service is cordial and efficient. Top floor restaurant offering panoramic views.

Montespina Park Hotel, via San Gennaro 2 ✉ 80125 ☎ 081 7629687, *info@montespina.it*, *Fax 081 5702962*, – |‡| ▤ TV ☏ ♿ P – 🏛 100. AE MC VISA. ✗
Meals a la carte 27/51 (10 %) – **43 rm** ☐ 160/220. by Riviera di Chiaia EFX
◆ An oasis in the traffic-bound city, this hotel with pool is set in its own gardens on a small hill, near the Terme di Agnano ; well-presented rooms. A smart dining room, and room for functions.

Hotel del Real Orto Botanico, via Foria 192 ✉ 80139 ☎ 081 4421528, *hoteldelreal@hotmail.com*, *Fax 081 4421346*, – |‡| ▤ TV ♿. AE MC VISA JCB. ✗ HU a
Meals (dinner only) (residents only) a la carte 28/49 – **32 rm** ☐ 99/162, 4 suites.
◆ Formerly an aristocratic palazzo, this hotel has elegant rooms in a variety of styles, and a fine dining room.

Chiaia Hotel de Charme without rest., via Chiaia 216 ✉ 80121 ☎ 081 415555, *info@hotelchiaia.it*, *Fax 081 422344* – ▤ TV ☏. AE MC VISA JCB. ✗ JZ a
27 rm ☐ 95/175.
◆ Situated on the first floor in a charming part of the city, this hotel's reputation is built on the personal touch, so much so that it feels more like a large, beautiful home.

Suite Esedra without rest., via Cantani 12 ✉ 80133 ☎ 081 287451, *Fax 081 287451*, – |‡| ▤ TV ☏. AE MC VISA JCB. ✗ LY a
17 rm ☐ 114/140, suite.
◆ A library, breakfast served round a large 19C table, rooms named after signs of the zodiac ; all this and more at this new jewel of the local hotel scene.

Il Convento without rest., via Speranzella 137/a ✉ 80132 ☎ 081 403977, *info@hotelilconvento.com*, *Fax 081 400332* – |‡| ▤ TV ♿. AE MC VISA JCB. ✗ JZ d
14 rm ☐ 114/150.
◆ In the evocative Spanish quarter, close to the busy Via Toledo, this small hotel is extremely popular ; breakfast served in delightful surroundings.

Caruso - Hotel Grand Hotel Vesuvio, via Partenope 45 ✉ 80121 ☎ 081 76400044, *info@vesuvio.it*, *Fax 081 7644483*, ≤ gulf and Castel dell'Ovo, – AE MC VISA. ✗ FX n
closed 5 to 25 August and Monday – **Meals** a la carte 42/78.
◆ Named after the great tenor who frequented the Grand Hotel Vesuvio, this stylish rooftop restaurant serves fine Neapolitan and Italian cuisine.

Megaris - Hotel Gd H. Santa Lucia, via Santa Lucia 175 ✉ 80121 ☎ 081 7640511, *megaris@santalucia.it*, *Fax 081 7648580* – ▤. AE MC VISA JCB. ✗ GX c
closed August and Sunday – **Meals** a la carte 36/50.
◆ Named after the island on which is perched Castel dell'Ovo, visible from the windows of this well-run and elegant restaurant ; esteemed dishes, both meat and fish.

La Cantinella, via Cuma 42 ✉ 80132 ☎ 081 7648684, *la.cantinella@lacantinella.it*, *Fax 081 7648769* – ▤. AE MC VISA JCB. ✗ GX v
closed 12 to 27 August, 24-25 December and Sunday (except November-May) – **Meals** (booking essential for dinner) a la carte 39/61.
◆ Much bamboo furniture in evidence at this elegant restaurant, situated on one of the world's most beautiful shorelines ; good wine-list, meat and seafood dishes.

'A Fenestella, via Calata del Ponticello a Marechiaro 23 ✉ 80123 ☎ 081 7690020, *afenestella@tin.it*, *Fax 081 5750686*, ≤ sea and gulf, – P. AE MC VISA JCB. ✗ by via V. G. Bruno EX
closed 14 to 16 August, Sunday dinner and Wednesday lunch, closed Sunday July-August ; dinner only in August – **Meals** a la carte 29/43 (15 %).
◆ Taking its name from a popular song by Salvatore Di Giacomo, this spectacularly located restaurant offers fine sea views. Dining on the terrace in summer ; local cuisine.

Giuseppone a Mare, via Ferdinando Russo 13-Capo Posillipo ✉ 80123 ☎ 081 5756002, *Fax 081 5756002*, ≤ city and gulf – ▤ P. AE MC VISA JCB. ✗ by via Caracciolo FX
closed 18 August-4 September, 24-25 December, Sunday dinner and Monday – **Meals** a la carte 23/45.
◆ Well located in the smartest part of Naples. Panoramic views through large windows overlooking the city and the sea ; seafood cuisine.

Mimì alla Ferrovia, via Alfonso d'Aragona 21 ✉ 80139 ☎ 081 5538525, *info@mimiallaferrovia.it*, *Fax 081 289004* – ▤. AE MC VISA JCB MY f
closed 13 to 22 August and Sunday – **Meals** a la carte 27/35 (15 %).
◆ Close to the station, this lively and elegant restaurant is popular with showbusiness people and has been restored recently. Traditional fish and local dishes.

Don Salvatore, strada Mergellina 4 A ✉ 80122 ☎ 081 681817, *donsalvatore@virgilio.it*, *Fax 081 661241* – ▤. AE MC VISA JCB by Riviera di Chiaia EFX
closed Wednesday – **Meals** Rest. and pizzeria a la carte 34/47.
◆ A long-established family-run concern, this modern restaurant offers classic fare ; a buffet of antipasti, plus pizzas and very fresh fish.

XX **Rosolino-Il Posto Accanto,** via Nazario Sauro 2/7 ✉ 80132 ✆ 081 7649873, *info@rosolino.it, Fax 081 7649870* – ▤ – 🅿 70. AE 💳 ⓓ MC VISA JCB. ✂ GX a
closed Sunday dinner – **Meals** Rest. and pizzeria a la carte 24/45.
◆ This versatile pizzeria-restaurant has rooms large and small, offering a variety of ambiences in which to eat ; a good choice of seafood and Neapolitan dishes.

XX **Ciro a Santa Brigida,** via Santa Brigida 73 ✉ 80132 ✆ 081 5524072, *Fax 081 5528992* – ▤. AE 💳 ⓓ MC VISA JCB. ✂ JZ w
closed 7 to 25 August and Sunday (except December) – **Meals** Rest. and pizzeria a la carte 28/34.
◆ In the heart of old Naples, this animated pizzeria-restaurant is a city institution, modern in style but rooted in tradition ; meat and seafood dishes.

XX **Transatlantico,** via Luculliana-borgo Marinari ✉ 80132 ✆ 081 7648842, *Fax 081 7649201*, 🏖 – AE 💳 ⓓ MC VISA. ✂ by via Nazario Sauro GX
closed 21 January-4 February and Tuesday – **Meals** a la carte 23/28.
◆ Overlooked by Castel dell'Ovo, this charming establishment is classically elegant ; outside dining in summer on the quayside of Santa Lucia. Traditional cuisine.

X **Taverna dell'Arte,** rampe San Giovanni Maggiore 1/A ✉ 80134 ✆ 081 5527558, *Fax 081 5527558* – ▤. 💳 MC VISA KY a
closed 4 to 25 August and Sunday – **Meals** (booking essential) a la carte 20/35.
◆ By the university, an authentic taverna in the tradition of its Aragonese antecedents of the 17C ; the convivial atmosphere and timeless flavours of old Naples.

X **L'Europeo di Mattozzi,** via Campodisola 4/6/8 ✉ 80133 ✆ 081 5521323, *Fax 081 5521323* – ⊁ ▤. AE 💳 ⓓ MC VISA JCB. ✂ KZ e
closed 15 to 31 August, Saturday dinner and Sunday 1 July-15 August, Monday, Tuesday and Wednesday dinner in other months – **Meals** Rest. and pizzeria a la carte 35/50 (12 %).
◆ Regulars and first-timers alike receive the same red carpet treatment from the owner of this busy, simple pizzeria, run by the same family for decades ; local cuisine.

Island of Capri *80073 Napoli* 564 F 24 *G. Italy – pop. 13 189 alt. – High Season : Easter and June-September.*

The limitation of motor-vehicles' access is regulated by legislative rules.

Gd H. Quisisana, via Camerelle 2 ✆ 081 8370788, *info@quisi.com, Fax 081 8376080*, ≤ sea and Certosa, 🏖, 🏋, ≘s, 🏊, 🏊, 🌳, 🎾 – |‡| ▤ TV ✆ – 🅿 550. AE 💳 ⓓ MC VISA. ✂
March-October – **Meals *La Colombaia*** Rest. and pizzeria *(25 March-2 November ; closed dinner except 15 April to September)* a la carte 40/55 ⊛ see also rest. ***Quisi*** – **149 rm** ☕ 490, 6 suites.
◆ A historic and luxurious window on the world, this hotel is a byword for the highest standards of comfort ; garden with pool. An elegant atmosphere in the candle-lit La Colombaia restaurant ; Mediterranean cuisine.

Casa Morgano 🐦 without rest., via Tragara 6 ✆ 081 8370158, *info@casamorgano.com, Fax 081 8370681*, ≤ sea and Certosa, 🏊 heated – |‡| ▤ TV. AE 💳 ⓓ MC VISA JCB. ✂
28 rm ☕ 450.
◆ Among the best features of this elegant establishment are the terrace among pines, fine views of the sea and the Certosa, and rooms offering excellent levels of comfort.

Punta Tragara 🐦, via Tragara 57 ✆ 081 8370844, *hotel.tragara@capri.it, Fax 081 8377790*, ≤ Faraglioni and coast, 🏖, 🏊 heated – |‡| ▤ TV. AE 💳 ⓓ MC VISA JCB. ✂
8 April-17 October – **Meals** 46 – **43 rm** ☕ 350/450, 8 suites.
◆ This Le Corbusier-designed hotel is the quintessence of Capri refinement. Lunch can be outside on the poolside terrace, followed by dinner in the well-presented dining room.

Scalinatella 🐦 without rest., via Tragara 8 ✆ 081 8370633, *Fax 081 8378291*, ≤ sea and Certosa, 🏊 heated – |‡| ▤ TV. AE 💳 MC VISA. ✂
15 March-5 November – **30 rm** ☕ 400/560.
◆ The flagship of a family-run group, this hotel with its exclusive reputation nestles in the hillside ; luxurious rooms.

Luna 🐦, viale Matteotti 3 ✆ 081 8370433, *luna@capri.it, Fax 081 8377459*, ≤ mare, Faraglaioni e Certosa, 🏖, 🏊, 🌳 – |‡| ▤ TV. AE 💳 ⓓ MC VISA JCB. ✂
Easter-October – **Meals** (residents only) 34/41 – **50 rm** ☕ 155/365, 4 suites.
◆ Perched high on the cliffs, the hotel has a large garden and terrace from which to admire the sea, the Faraglioni and the Certosa ; ask for a room with a view.

Villa Brunella , via Tragara 24 ℘ 081 8370122, *villabrunella@capri.it, Fax 081 8370430*, ≤ sea and coast, , heated – . AE VISA.
19 March-5 November – **Meals *Brunella Terrace*** Rest. (booking essential) a la carte 38/56 (12 %) – **20 rm** 230/265.
◆ A succession of planted terraces descend towards the sea ; a heated pool, enchanting panoramic views and well-appointed rooms. The elegant restaurant has a veranda offering a view of the sea and the island.

Canasta without rest., via Campo di Teste 6 ℘ 081 8370561, *canasta@capri.it, Fax 081 8376675* – . AE VISA.
closed 15 January-15 March – **17 rm** 110/220.
◆ A charming family-run establishment near the Certosa di San Giacomo ; an elegant reception area and bright, simple rooms with good quality tasteful furnishings.

Syrene, via Camerelle 51 ℘ 081 8370102, *syrene@capri.it, Fax 081 8370957*, ≤, , , – . AE VISA JCB.
April-October – **Meals** *(closed Tuesday except June to September)* a la carte 35/43 – **32 rm** 252/346.
◆ Located on one of Capri's main shopping streets, this comfortable hotel has generously proportioned public areas ; the rooms vary from classical to modern in style. The fine garden has a pool and lemon trees. Imposing columns in the dining room.

Villa Krupp without rest., via Matteotti 12 ℘ 081 8370362, *Fax 081 8376489*, ≤ Faraglioni and coast – VISA.
April-October – **12 rm** 85/150.
◆ Maxim Gorky once lived in this villa, now converted into a hotel ; simply furnished but charmingly situated with panoramic views.

Quisi - Gd H. Quisisana**,** via Camerelle 2 ℘ 081 8370788, *info@quisi.com, Fax 081 8376080*, – . AE VISA JCB.
March-October ; closed lunch and Sunday June-September – **Meals** a la carte 62/82.
◆ Comfortable seats, candles, all-encompassing attention to detail and an elegant ambience in this evenings only restaurant. High quality international cuisine.

La Capannina, via Le Botteghe 12 bis/14 ℘ 081 8370732, *capannina@capri.it, Fax 081 8376990* – . AE VISA.
10 March-10 November ; closed Wednesday except June to September – **Meals** (booking essential for dinner) a la carte 43/59 (15 %).
◆ This establishment, founded in the 1930s, remains perennially fashionable ; a wide variety of local dishes, somewhat refined to appeal to the international clientele.

Aurora, via Fuorlovado 18 ℘ 081 8370181, *aurora@capri.it, Fax 081 8376533*, – . AE VISA.
closed January-March – **Meals** Rest. and pizzeria a la carte 37/62 (15 %).
◆ A table outside is much in demand here, a long-established family-run restaurant of considerable charm. Seafood, meat dishes and pizzas.

Da Tonino, via Dentecala 12 ℘ 081 8376718, – AE VISA.
closed 10 January-14 March – **Meals** a la carte 30/39.
◆ In a rural setting towards the Arco Naturale with an airy terrace in summer ; creative dishes and fine selection of wines from the rock-hewn cellar.

at Anacapri *alt. 275* – ✉ *80071* :

Capri Palace Hotel, via Capodimonte 2 ℘ 081 9780111, *info@capri-palace.com, Fax 081 8373191*, ≤, , Rooms with small private swimming pools, , , heated, – – 200. AE VISA JCB.
March-November – **Meals *L'Olivo*** Rest. a la carte 75/95 – **82 rm** 520/595, 7 suites.
◆ A symphony of soft, creamy tones throughout ; overlooking planted terraces and swimming pool. White is predominant in the elegant dining room ; delightful outside in summer.

Caesar Augustus , via Orlandi 4 ℘ 081 8373395, *info@caesar-augustus.com, Fax 081 8371444*, – . AE VISA JCB
April-October – **Meals** a la carte 40/80 – 15 – **52 rm** 310/385, 5 suites.
◆ This hotel terrace, perched above the waves, offers breathtaking views and evokes a desire to take to the skies ; the refitted rooms are pleasant and comfortable.

La Rondinella, via Orlandi 245 ℘ 081 8371223, *Fax 081 8373222*, – AE VISA
closed January and February – **Meals** Rest. and evening pizzeria a la carte 34/45 (10 %).
◆ Attentive service at this restaurant offering a rustic ambience in winter, and an attractive planted summer terrace ; seafood, Caprese dishes and also pizzas in the evening.

at Marina Grande – ✉ **80073** :

Da Paolino, via Palazzo a Mare 11 ℘ 081 8376102, *dapaolino@iol.it, Fax 081 8375611*, , – AE VISA JCB
Easter-October ; closed lunch June to September – **Meals** a la carte 40/51 (10 %).
◆ A bright, rustic feel to this pleasantly spacious family-run establishment ; in summer diners eat among lush lemon trees. Country cuisine.

Sant'Agata sui due Golfi *80064 Napoli 564 F 25 G. Italy – alt. 391 – High Season : April-September.*
Roma 266 – Castellammare di Stabia 28 – Napoli 55 – Salerno 56 – Sorrento 9.

XXX ✿✿ **Don Alfonso 1890** with rm, corso Sant'Agata 11 ☏ 081 8780026, *donalfonso@sy rene.it, Fax 081 5330226,* – , rest, . AE VISA JCB.
closed 7 January-10 March and 24-25 December – **Meals** *(closed Monday and Tuesday lunch June-September, Monday and Tuesday in other months)* (booking essential) a la carte 74/99 – 5 suites 195.
◆ This hospitable establishment serves imaginatively prepared cuisine making the most of local ingredients. Interesting and robust dishes.
Spec. Ravioli di caciotta fresca con maggiorana e pomodorini del Vesuvio. Casseruola di pesce di scoglio, crostacei e frutti di mare. Capretto lucano alle erbe fresche mediterranee.

For business or tourist interest:
MICHELIN Guide: EUROPE.

PALERMO (Sicily) *90100* P *565 M 22 G. Italy – pop. 679 290.*

See : *Palace of the Normans★★ : the palatine Chapel★★★, mosaics★★★, Ancient Royal Apartments★★* AZ *– Oratory of St Dominic's Rosary★★★* BY **N** *– Oratory of St Cita★★★* BY **N** *– Church of St. John of the Hermits★★ : cloister★* AZ *– Piazza Pretoria★★* BY *– Piazza Bellini★* BY *: Martorana Church★★, Church of St. Cataldo★★ – Abatellis Palace★ : Regional Gallery of Sicily★★* CY **G** *– Magnolia fig trees★★ in Garibaldi Gardens* CY *– International Museum of Marionettes★★* CY **M** *– Archaeological Museum★ : metopes from the temples at Selinus★★, the Ram★★* BY **M** *– Villa Malfitano★★ – Botanical garden★ : magnolia fig trees★★* CDZ *– Capuchin Catacombs★★ – Villa Bonanno★* AZ *– Cathedral★* AYZ *– Quattro Canti★* BY *– Gancia, interior★* CY *– Magione : facade★* CZ *– St Francis of Assisi★* CY *– Mirto Palace★* CY *– Chiaramonte Palace★* CY *– St Mary of the chain★* CY **S** *– Gallery of Modern Art E. Restivo★* AX *– Villino Florio★ – St John of the Lepers★ – Zisa★ – Cuba★.*
Envir. : *Monreale★★★ by Corso Calatafimi : 8 km* AZ *– Addura's Caves★ North-East.*

Falcone-Borsellino East : 30 km ☏ 091 7020111, Fax 091 7020394 – Alitalia, via Mazzini 59 ✉ 90139 ☏ 091 6019111, Fax 091 6019346.

to Genova daily except Sunday (20 h) and to Livorno Tuesday, Thursday and Saturday (17 h) – Grimaldi-Grandi Navi Veloci, calata Marinai d'Italia ✉ 90133 ☏ 091 587404, Fax 091 6110088; to Napoli daily (11 h), to Genova Monday, Wednesday and Friday and Sunday 18 June-31 December (24 h) and Cagliari Saturday (13 h 30 mn) – Tirrenia Navigazione, calata Marinai d'Italia ✉ 90133 ☏ 1478 99000, Fax 091 6021221.

to Aeolian Island June-September daily (1 h 50 mn) – SNAV Barbaro Agency, piazza Principe di Belmonte 51/55 ✉ 90139 ☏ 091 586533, Fax 091 584830.

piazza Castelnuovo 34 ✉ 90141 ☏ 091 583847, info@palermotourism.com, Fax 091 586338 *– Falcone-Borsellino Airport at Cinisi ☏ 091 591698 – piazza Giulio Cesare (Central Station) ✉ 90127 ☏ 091 6165914 – salita Belmonte 1 (Villa Igea) ☏ 091 6398011, info@aziendaturismopalermomonreale.it,* Fax 091 6375400.

A.C.I. *via delle Alpi 6 ✉ 90144 ☏ 091 305227.*
Messina 235.

Plans on following pages

Villa Igiea Gd H., salita Belmonte 43 ✉ 90142 ☏ 091 6312111, *villa-igiea@thi.it, Fax 091 547654,* ←, , , , – , rm, – 400. AE VISA JCB.
by via Crispi BX
Meals a la carte 62/101 – **108 rm** 211/374, 6 suites.
◆ Bygone splendour abounds in this Art Nouveau villa with planted terraces running down towards the sea ; this hotel is a refined environment offering all the comforts of modern hospitality. The restaurant is equally elegant and impressive.

Astoria Palace Hotel, via Montepellegrino 62 ✉ 90142 ☏ 091 6281111 and rest. ☏ 091 6280194, *astoria@ghshotels.it, Fax 091 6371227* – , rm, – 750. AE VISA.
by via Crispi BX
Meals ***Il Cedro*** Rest. 25/40 – **301 rm** 140/173, 14 suites.
◆ Friendly, cheerful staff and high standards at this modern hotel, with large and pleasant public areas ; state-of-the-art conference facilities. An air of elegant modernity in the "Il Cedro" restaurant.

Centrale Palace Hotel, corso Vittorio Emanuele 327 ✉ 90134 ☏ 091 336666, *info@centralepalacehotel.it, Fax 091 334881,* – – 120. AE VISA.
BY b
Meals a la carte 33/60 – **103 rm** 157/260, 9 suites.
◆ The sumptuous surroundings of an 18C aristocratic residence mask the presence of every modern convenience in this sensitively restored hotel. Delightful dining on the terrace in summer, with splendid views.

San Paolo Palace, via Messina Marine 91 ✉ 90123 ☎ 091 6211112, *hotel@sanpaolopalace.it, Fax 091 6215300,* – 1600. by via Ponte di Mare DZ
Meals a la carte 23/33 – **234 rm** 110/135, 10 suites.
◆ A panoramic lift gives access to a wonderful roof-garden with pool at this modern hotel, located a little way from the city centre with fine views over the sea. Roof-garden dining in summer.

Principe di Villafranca, via G. Turrisi Colonna 4 ✉ 90141 ☎ 091 6118523, *info@principedivillafranca.it, Fax 091 588705,* – rm, – 100. AX d
Meals *(closed August)* a la carte 35/48 – **34 rm** 130/185.
◆ Rising from the ashes of a previous hotel on this site, this new establishment was opened in 1998. Classically stylish throughout with period furnishings in abundance. The restaurant shares the same elegant atmosphere.

Vecchio Borgo without rest., via Quintino Sella 1/7 ✉ 90139 ☎ 091 6111446, *hotelvecchioborgo@classicahotel.com* – rm, BX b
34 rm 140/180.
◆ An intimately proportioned establishment offering good service ; elegant lobby, breakfast room and accommodation with much attention to detail in evidence.

Massimo Plaza Hotel without rest., via Maqueda 437 ✉ 90133 ☎ 091 325657, *booking@massimoplazahotel.com, Fax 091 325711* – BY e
15 rm 130/185.
◆ Occupying a palazzo in the centre opposite the Teatro Massimo, this smart modern hotel is well-presented and elegant throughout.

Tonic without rest., via Mariano Stabile 126 ✉ 90139 ☎ 091 581754, *hoteltonic@hoteltonic.com, Fax 091 585560* – AXY g
44 rm 75/95.
◆ This stylish modern hotel occupies a historic palazzo in the heart of the city ; recently refitted, it has impeccably presented interiors with furniture in dark woods.

Holiday Inn Palermo, viale Regione Siciliana 2620 ✉ 90145 ☎ 091 6983111, *holidayinn.palermo@alliancealberghi.com, Fax 091 408198,* – – 90. rest by via della Libertà AX
Meals a la carte 19/35 – **95 rm** 171,60/204,46.
◆ Conveniently located for road links, this traditional hotel has been recently refitted and offers comfortable accommodation ; modern furnishings and fitted carpets in the rooms. The restaurant has a rustic decorative theme.

Villa d'Amato, via Messina Marine 180 ✉ 90123 ☎ 091 6212767, *villadamato@jumpy.it, Fax 091 6212767,* – – 150. rest by via Ponte di Mare DZ
Meals *(closed Sunday lunch)* a la carte 18/25 – **38 rm** 85/115.
◆ Well located on the city outskirts between the sea and the Messina road, this comfortable hotel has a large garden ; bright rooms with modern furnishings. Relaxing restaurant.

La Scuderia, viale del Fante 9 ✉ 90146 ☎ 091 520323, *la.scuderia@tiscalinet.it, Fax 091 520467,* – by via C.A. Dalla Chiesa AX
closed 13 to 30 August and Sunday – **Meals** a la carte 32/54.
◆ Located in the Parco della Favorita, the spacious and stylish interior of this historic restaurant is adorned with columns and large windows ; traditional cuisine.

Friend's Bar, via Brunelleschi 138 ✉ 90145 ☎ 091 201401, *catering@friendsbarsrl.com, Fax 091 201066,* – by via della Libertà AX
closed 10 to 31 August and Monday – **Meals** (booking essential) a la carte 29/38.
◆ This modern restaurant on the outskirts has an elegant ambience ; well-presented cuisine which imaginatively interprets traditional dishes.

Lo Scudiero, via Turati 7 ✉ 90139 ☎ 091 581628, *Fax 091 581628* – AX c
closed 10 to 20 August and Sunday – **Meals** a la carte 24/43.
◆ An elegant environment with beamed ceilings opposite the Teatro Politeama ; excellently run with good courteous service and traditional cuisine.

Il Ristorantino, piazza De Gasperi 19 ✉ 90146 ☎ 091 512861, *Fax 091 6702999,* – by via C.A. Dalla Chiesa AX
closed 10 to 30 August, 1 to 9 January and Monday – **Meals** a la carte 35/46.
◆ This youthful yet elegant establishment, close to Parco della Favorita, offers a varied menu ranging from traditional dishes to modern cuisine.

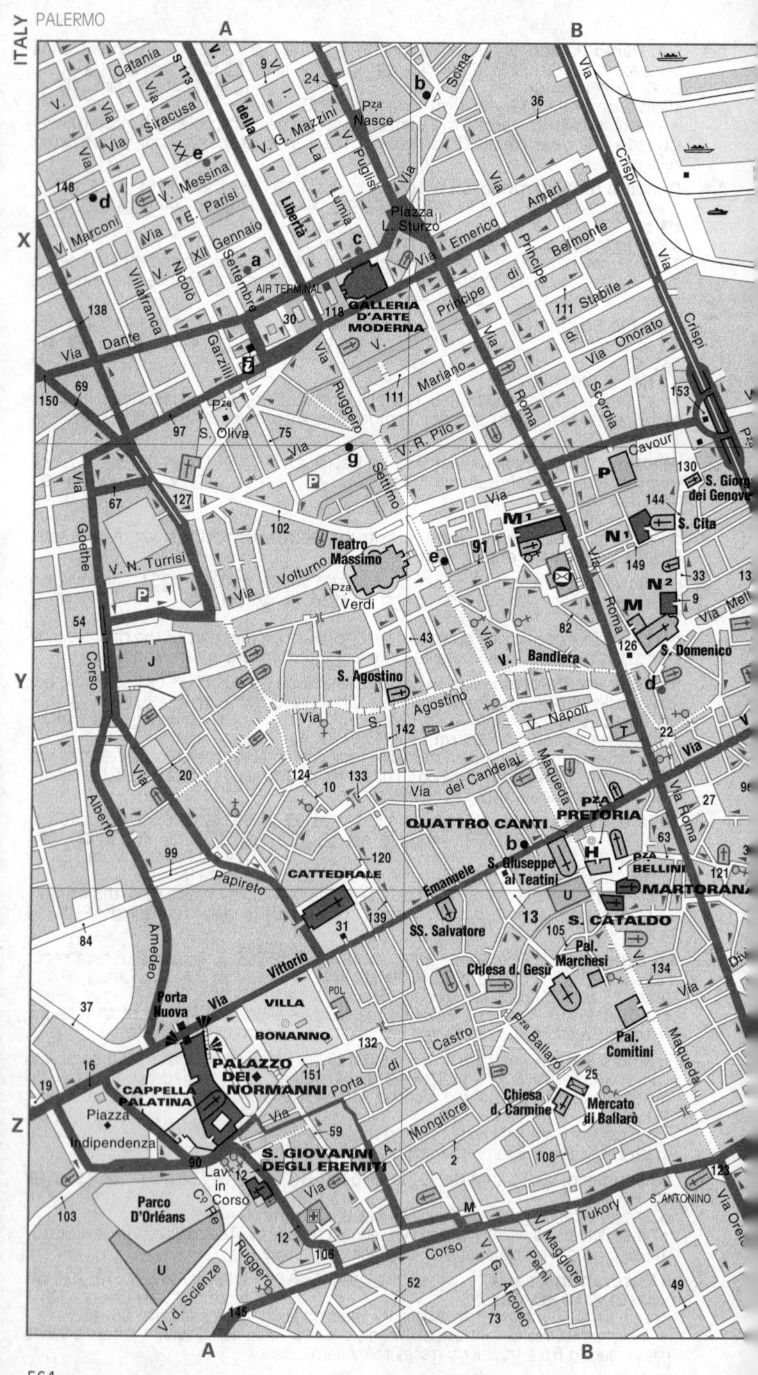

A
B
X
Y
Z
GALLERIA D'ARTE MODERNA
AIR TERMINAL
Piazza L. Sturzo
Teatro Massimo
Pza Verdi
S. Agostino
QUATTRO CANTI
Pza PRETORIA
Pza BELLINI
MARTORANA
S. CATALDO
S. Giuseppe ai Teatini
CATTEDRALE
SS. Salvatore
Chiesa d. Gesù
Pal. Marchesi
Pal. Comitini
Chiesa d. Carmine
Mercato di Ballarò
Pza Ballarò
Porta Nuova
VILLA BONANNO
PALAZZO DEI NORMANNI
CAPPELLA PALATINA
Piazza Indipendenza
S. GIOVANNI DEGLI EREMITI
Parco D'Orléans
S. Domenico
S. Cita
S. Giorg dei Genove
S. ANTONINO
Via Dante
Via Libertà
Via Roma
Via Maqueda
Via Vittorio Emanuele
Corso Alberto Amedeo
Via Crispi
Via Cavour
Via Volturno
V. N. Turrisi
Via Goethe
Via Papireto
Via dei Candelai
V. Bandiera
V. Napoli
Via S. Agostino
Via Ruggero Settimo
V. R. Pilo
Via Mariano Stabile
Via Principe di Belmonte
Via Emerico Amari
V. G. Mazzini
Via Villafranca
V. Nicolò Garzilli
Via XII Gennaio
Via E. Parisi
V. Messina
Via Siracusa
V. Catania
V. Marconi
Via Onorato
Via Scordia
Pza Nasce
Pza S. Oliva
Via Porta di Castro
Via A. Mongitore
Corso Tukory
V. Maggiore Perni
V. G. Arcoleo
V. d. Scienze
Cº Re Ruggero
Lav in Corso
POL

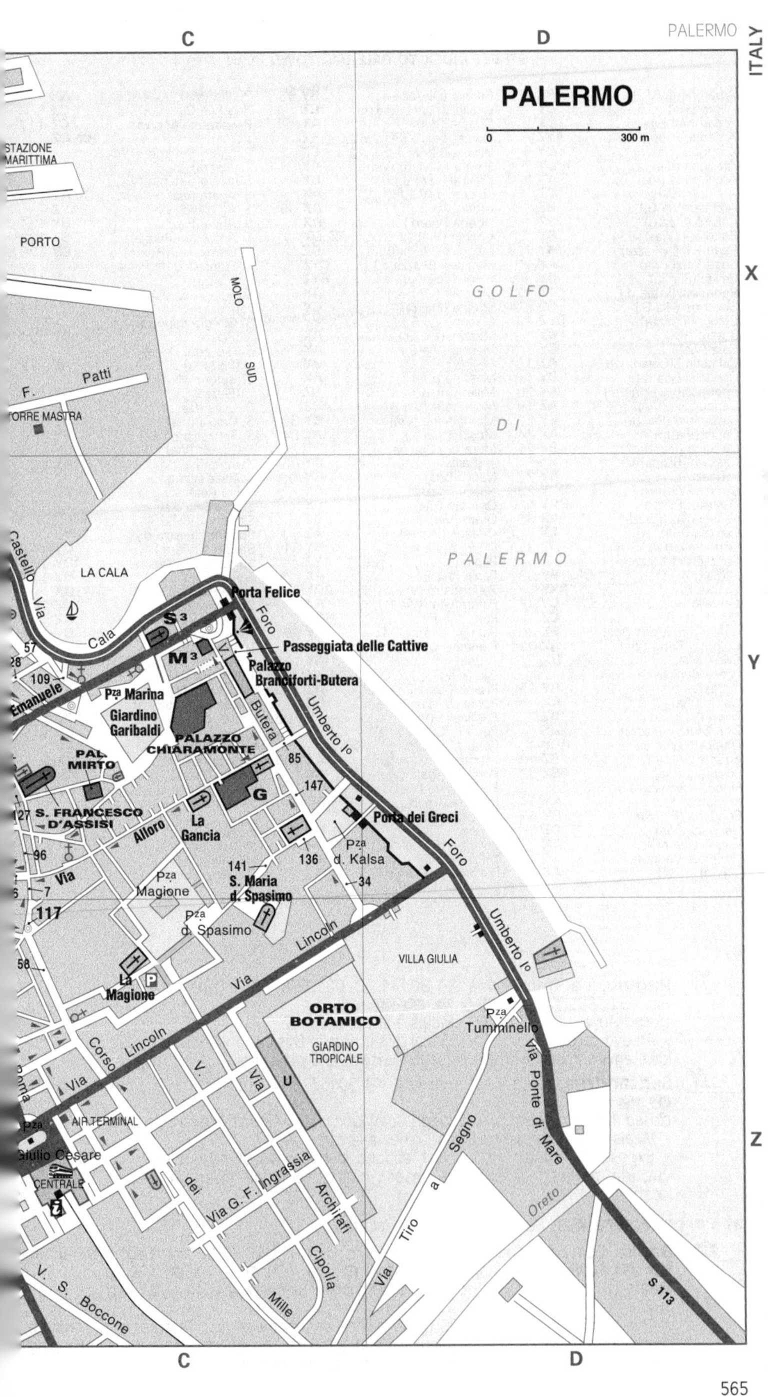
PALERMO
0
300 m
C
D
X
Y
Z
STAZIONE MARITTIMA
PORTO
MOLO SUD
GOLFO DI PALERMO
F. Patti
TORRE MASTRA
LA CALA
Via Castello
Cala
Porta Felice
Foro Umberto I°
Passeggiata delle Cattive
Palazzo Branciforti-Butera
S3
M3
Emanuele
Pza Marina
Giardino Garibaldi
PALAZZO CHIARAMONTE
PAL. MIRTO
S. FRANCESCO D'ASSISI
Butera
Alloro
La Gancia
G
Porta dei Greci
Pza d. Kalsa
Pza Magione
S. Maria d. Spasimo
Pza d. Spasimo
La Magione
Via Lincoln
Corso Via Lincoln
VILLA GIULIA
ORTO BOTANICO
GIARDINO TROPICALE
Pza Tumminello
Via Ponte di Mare
Via Tiro a Segno
Oreto
S 113
AIR TERMINAL
Pza Giulio Cesare
CENTRALE
Via G. F. Ingrassia
V. dei Mille
Archirafi
Cipolla
V. S. Boccone
U
57
28
109
127
96
7
117
58
85
147
136
141
34

STREET INDEX TO PALERMO TOWN PLAN

Street	Grid	No.
Albergheria (Via)	BZ	2
Alloro (Via)	CY	
Amari (Via E.)	BX	
Amedeo (Corso A.)	AYZ	
Aragona (Piazza)	CY	6
Aragona (Via)	CY	7
Archimede (Via)	AX	9
Archirafi (Via)	CZ	
Arcoleo (Via G.)	BZ	
Ballarò (Piazza)	BZ	
Bandiera (Via)	BY	
Beati Paoli (Piazza)	AY	124
Beati Paoli (Via)	AY	10
Bellini (Piazza)	BY	
Benedettini (Via d.)	AZ	12
Boccone (Via S.)	CZ	
Bologni (Piazza)	BYZ	13
Butera (Via)	CY	
Cala (Via)	CY	
Calatafimi (Corso)	AZ	16
Candelai (Via d.)	BY	
Cappuccinelle (Via d.)	AY	20
Cappuccini (Via)	AZ	19
Caracciolo (Piazza)	BY	22
Carini (Via I.)	AX	24
Carmine (Piazza d.)	BZ	25
Cassa di Risparmio (Piazza)	BY	27
Cassari (Via)	BCY	28
Castello (Piazza)	BCY	
Castelnuovo (Piazza)	AX	30
Catania (Via)	AX	
Cattedrale (Piazza d.)	AZ	31
Cavalieri di Malta (Largo)	BY	33
Cavour (Via)	BXY	
Cervello (Via)	CY	34
Cipolla (Via)	CZ	
Collegio di Maria (Via)	BX	36
Colonna Rotta (Via)	AZ	37
Crispi (Via)	BX	
Croce dei Vespri (Piazza d.)	BY	39
Dante (Via)	AX	
Divisi (Via)	BZ	
Don Sturzo (Piazza)	ABX	
Donizetti (Via G.)	ABY	43
Errante (Via V.)	BZ	49
Filiciuzza (Via)	ABZ	52
Finocchiaro Aprile (Corso)	AY	54
Fonderia (Piazza)	CY	57
Garibaldi (Via)	CZ	58
Garzilli (Via N.)	AX	
Generale Cadorna (Via)	AZ	59
Giudici (Discesa d.)	BY	63
Giullio Cesare (Piazza)	CZ	
Goethe (Via)	AY	
Indipendenza (Piazza)	AZ	
Ingrassia (Via G. F.)	CZ	
Juvara Cluviero (Via)	AY	67
Kalsa (Piazza d.)	CY	
La Lumia (Via I.)	AX	
Latini (Via B.)	AX	69
Libertà (Via d.)	AX	
Lincoln (Via)	CZ, DY	
Maggiore Perni (Via)	BZ	
Magione (Piazza d.)	CYZ	
Maqueda (Via)	BYZ	
Marconi (Via)	AX	
Marina (Piazza)	CY	
Marino (Via S.)	BZ	73
Mazzini (Via G.)	AX	
Meccio (Via S.)	AX	75
Meli (Via)	BY	
Messina (Via)	AX	
Mille (Corso d.)	CZ	
Mongitore (Via A.)	ABZ	
Monteleone (Via)	BY	82
Mosca (Via G.)	AZ	84
Mura del Cattive (Salita)	CY	85
Napoli (Via)	BY	
Nasce (Piazza)	AX	
Onorato (Via)	BX	
Oreto (Via)	BZ	
Orleans (Piazza)	AZ	90
Orlogio (Via d.)	BY	91
Papireto (Via)	AYZ	
Parisi (Via E.)	AX	
Paternostro (Via A.)	BCY	96
Paternostro (Via P.)	AX	97
Patti (Via F.)	BCX	
Peranni (Piazza D.)	AY	99
Pignatelli d'Aragona (Via)	AY	102
Pilo (Via R.)	BXY	
Pisani (Corso P.)	AZ	103
Ponte di Mare (Via)	DZ	
Ponticello (Via)	BZ	105
Porta di Castro (Via)	ABZ	
Porta Montalto (Piazza)	AZ	106
Porta S. Agata (Via)	BZ	108
Porto Salvo (Via)	CY	109
Pretoria (Piazza)	BY	
Principe di Belmonte (Via)	BX	
Principe di Scordia (Via)	BX	
Principe Granatelli (Via)	ABX	111
Puglisi (Via)	AX	
Rao (Via C.)	CZ	
Rivoluzione (Piazza)	CZ	117
Roma (Via)	BX, CZ	
Ruggero Settimo (Piazza)	AX	118
Ruggero Settimo (Via)	AXY	
S. Agata (Via)	AY	120
S. Agostino (Via)	AYZ	
S. Anna (Piazza)	BY	121
S. Antonino (Piazza)	BZ	123
S. Domenico (Piazza)	BY	126
S. Francesco da Paola (Piazza)	AY	127
S. Francesco d'Assisi (Piazza)	CY	129
S. Giorgio dei Genovesi (Piazza)	BY	130
S. Giovanni Decollato (Piazetta)	AZ	132
S. Isidoro alla Guilla (Piazza)	AY	133
S. Oliva (Piazza)	AX	
S. Orsola (Via)	BZ	134
S. Sebastiano (Via)	BY	135
S. Teresa (Via)	CY	136
Sammartino (Via)	AX	138
Scienze (Via d.)	AZ	
Scina (Via)	BX	
Scuole (Via d.)	AZ	139
Siracusa (Via)	AX	
Spasimo (Piazza d.)	CYZ	
Spasimo (Via d.)	CY	141
Spirito Santo (Via d.)	ABY	142
Squarcialupo (Via)	BY	144
Stabile (Via M.)	AY, BX	
Stazzone (Piazza)	AZ	145
Tiro a Segno (Via)	DZ	
Torremuzza (Via)	CY	147
Tumminello (Piazza)	DZ	
Tukory (Corso)	ABZ	
Turrisi (Via N.)	AY	
Turrisi Colonna (Via)	AX	148
Umberto I (Foro)	CY, DZ	
Valverde (Via)	BY	149
Verdi (Piazza)	ABY	
Villafranca (Via)	AX	
Virgilio (Piazza)	AX	150
Vittoria (Piazza d.)	AZ	151
Vittorio Emanuele (Via)	AZ, CY	
Volturno (Via)	AY	
XII Gennaio (Via)	AX	
XIII Vittime (Piazza)	BX	153
XX Settembre (Via)	AX	

XX **Regine,** via Trapani 4/a ✉ 90141 ℘ 091 586566, *regine@ristoranteregine.it*, *Fax 091 586566* – ▤. AE ⓢ ⓓ MC VISA JCB. ✻ AX e
closed August and Sunday – **Meals** a la carte 35/42.
• An eye catching seafood and starters buffet in this elegantly modern restaurant ; the ideal environment in which to savour Sicilian and other Italian dishes.

XX **Santandrea,** piazza Sant'Andrea 4 ✉ 90133 ℘ 091 334999, ☂ – ▤. AE ⓢ ⓓ MC VISA BY d
closed January, Tuesday and Wednesday lunch, July-August closed Sunday and Monday – **Meals** (booking essential) local dishes a la carte 29/47.
• Exposed beams and woodwork abound in this oasis of hospitality in the midst of Vucciria market's picturesque chaos ; hearty regional cuisine in keeping with the location.

at Borgo Molara *West : 8 km* – ✉ *90126 Palermo* :

Baglio Conca d'Oro, via Aquino 19/d ℘ 091 6406286, *hotelbaglio@libero.it*, *Fax 091 6408742*, ☂ – |♦| ⇔ ▤ TV ♿ P – 🏛 400. AE ⓢ ⓓ MC VISA. ✻
Meals *(closed Sunday)* (booking essential) a la carte 24/41 – **27 rm** ☐ 116/162.
• This sensitively restored 18C paper-mill retains many original features and is now a charming hotel offering style, elegance and comfort. The smart restaurant is in keeping with the refined interiors of the rest of the establishment.

at Sferracavallo *North-West : 12 km – ✉ 90148 Palermo :*

Il Delfino, via Torretta 80 ☎ 091 530282, *trattorialdelfino@virgilio.it, Fax 091 6914256* – ▤. AE ⓢ ⓞ ⓜ VISA JCB. ✂
closed November and Monday – **Meals** seafood 21.
◆ Always busy, this simple restaurant spares customers the trouble of choosing for themselves ; a fine set-menu of exclusively fish dishes.

Villafrati *90030 Palermo 565 N 22 – pop. 3 394 alt. 450.*
Palermo 36 – Agrigento 87 – Caltanissetta 100.

Mulinazzo, strada statale 121, località Bolognetta North : 9 Km ☎ 091 8724870, *mulinazzo@libero.it, Fax 091 8737533* – ⇔ ▤ P. AE ⓢ ⓞ ⓜ VISA
closed 3 weeks July, 15 days January, Monday and dinners Sunday, Easter, Christmas and New Year – **Meals** a la carte 33/66.
◆ This country villa has a pleasantly elegant ambience ; the menu is rooted in country cuisine, creatively interpreted by the chef.
Spec. Mosaico di tonno, salsa alle olive e capperi (May-October). Minestra di aragosta con spaghetti spezzati. Involtino di mupa (pesce bianco) su caponata croccante al miele di zagara.

TAORMINA **(Sicily)** *98039 Messina 565 N 27 G. Italy – pop. 10 697 alt. 250.*
See : *Site★★★ – Greek Theatre★★★ : ≤★★★ BZ – Public garden★★ BZ – ✳★★ from the Square 9 Aprile AZ – Corso Umberto★ ABZ – Castle : ≤★★ AZ.*
Exc. : *Etna★★★ South-West : for Linguaglossa Mola Castle★ North-West : 5 km Alcantara Gorge★.*
18 Picciolo (closed Tuesday) via Picciolo 1 ✉ 95030 Castiglione di Sicilia ☎ 0942 986252, Fax 0942 986252, West : 25 km.
ℹ piazza Santa Caterina (Corvaja palace) ☎ 0942 23243, info@gate2taormina.com, Fax 0942 24941.
Catania 52 ② – Enna 135 ② – Messina 52 ① – Palermo 255 ② – Siracusa 111 ② – Trapani 359 ②

Plans on following pages

Gd H. Timeo Villa Flora ⛭, via Teatro Greco 59 ☎ 0942 23801, *reservation.tim@framon-hotels.it, Fax 0942 628501,* ≤ sea, coast and Etna, 🏛, ⛱ – 🛗 ▤ TV P – 🏟 200. AE ⓢ ⓞ ⓜ VISA JCB BZ x
Meals *Il Dito e La Luna* Rest. a la carte 49/73 – ☕ 22 – **73 rm** 277,20/389,40, 12 suites.
◆ Fine gardens and planted terraces surround this hotel, synonymous with Sicily's famed hospitality ; a magical splendour pervades the superbly comfortable interiors. The restaurant looks onto the Greek theatre, affording diners one of the world's finest views.

San Domenico Palace ⛭, piazza San Domenico 5 ☎ 0942 613111, *san-domenico@thi.it, Fax 0942 625506,* 🏛, Fð, ⛱ heated, 🌳 – 🛗 ▤ TV ♿ P – 🏟 400. AE ⓢ ⓞ ⓜ VISA JCB. ✂ AZ m
Meals a la carte 54/75 – **108 rm** ☕ 250/509, 7 suites.
◆ It is difficult to describe this marvellous hotel, a former convent dating from the 15C set in beautiful gardens with exceptional views of Mount Etna and the sea. The restaurant is outstanding and has a charming terrace.

Villa Diodoro, via Bagnoli Croci 75 ☎ 0942 23312, *diodoro@gaishotels.com, Fax 0942 23391,* ≤ sea, coast and Etna, ⛱, 🌳 – 🛗 ▤ TV ♿ P – 🏟 400. AE ⓢ ⓞ ⓜ VISA. ✂ BZ q
Meals a la carte 35/48 – **95 rm** ☕ 189/264, 4 suites.
◆ A large pool dominates the marvellous terrace, which appears to stretch far out towards Mount Etna. This well-restored hotel has many fine features, and a charming restaurant.

Gd H. Miramare, via Guardiola Vecchia 27 ☎ 0942 23401, *ghmiramare@tiscali.it, Fax 0942 626223,* ≤ sea and coast, 🏛, ⛱, 🌳, 🎾 – 🛗 ▤ TV P. AE ⓢ ⓞ ⓜ VISA. ✂
March-October – **Meals** 35 – **66 rm** ☕ 170/210, 2 suites. CZ c
◆ This imposing structure, pleasantly located in parkland, has particularly appealing public areas adorned with Empire-style furniture. Large restaurant and well-kept grounds.

Villa Fabbiano, via Pirandello 81 ☎ 0942 626058, *info@villafabbiano.com, Fax 0942 23732,* ≤ sea and coast, ⛱, 🌳 – 🛗 ▤ TV 📞 P. ⓢ ⓜ VISA. ✂ CZ a
March-October – **Meals** (lunch only) (residents only) 25/40 – **26 rm** ☕ 150/205, 4 suites.
◆ An early 20C aristocratic residence stylishly decorated and passionately run ; all rooms offer fine views, as does the attractively planted terrace.

Villa Ducale ⛭ without rest., via Leonardo da Vinci 60 ☎ 0942 28153, *villaducale@tao.it, Fax 0942 28710,* ≤ sea, coast and Etna – ▤ TV P. AE ⓢ ⓞ ⓜ VISA JCB AZ p
closed until 24 February – **13 rm** ☕ 196/240.
◆ In a delightful situation, this charming hotel, formerly a family villa, has atmosphere and great character ; well run by an enterprising young couple.

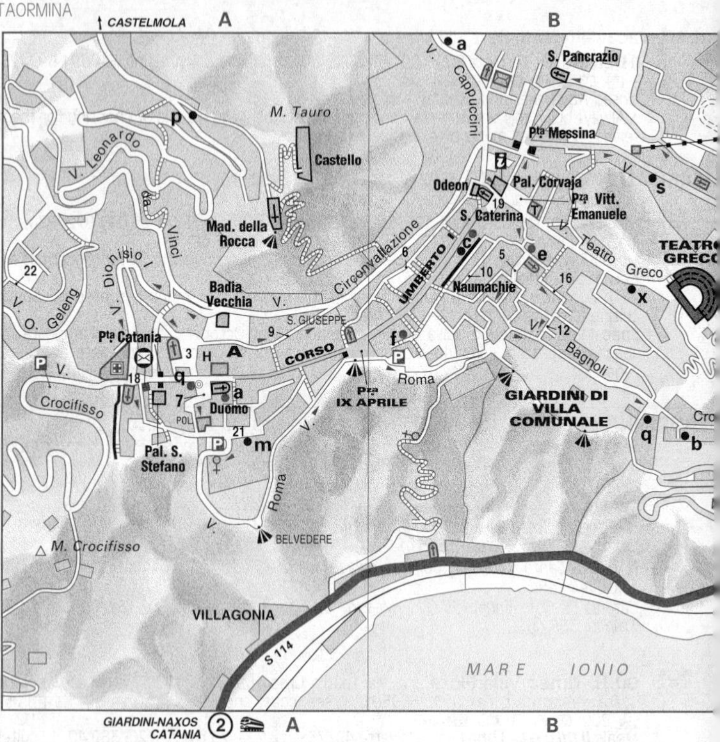

CASTELMOLA A B
S. Pancrazio
M. Tauro
Castello
Pta Messina
V. Leonardo da Vinci
Odeon
Pal. Corvaja
Pza Vitt. Emanuele
S. Caterina
Mad. della Rocca
V. Cappuccini
Circonvallazione
UMBERTO I
Naumachie
V. Teatro Greco
TEATRO GRECO
V. Dionisio I
Badia Vecchia
V. S. GIUSEPPE
V. O. Geleng
Pta Catania
CORSO
V. Bagnoli
V. Crocifisso
Duomo
Pza IX APRILE
Roma
GIARDINI DI VILLA COMUNALE
Pal. S. Stefano
V. Roma
BELVEDERE
M. Crocifisso
VILLAGONIA
S 114
MARE IONIO
GIARDINI-NAXOS CATANIA 2 A B

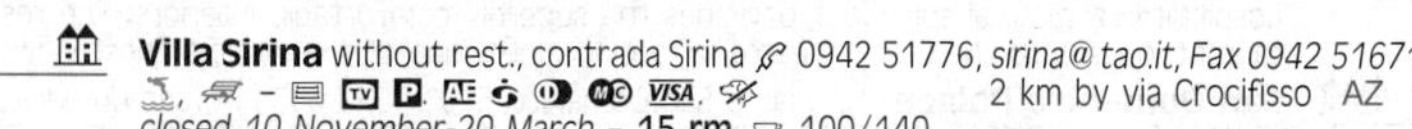

Villa Sirina without rest., contrada Sirina ☏ 0942 51776, *sirina@tao.it, Fax 0942 51671*, ⛱, ⛱ – ▤ TV P. AE ⓢ ⓓ MC VISA. ✗ 2 km by via Crocifisso AZ
closed 10 November-20 March – **15 rm** ☕ 100/140.
◆ In the lower part of the town, near the entrance to the public gardens, this restored villa offers comfortable accommodation. Furnished in keeping with the local style.

Villa Belvedere, via Bagnoli Croci 79 ☏ 0942 23791, *info@villabelvedere.it, Fax 0942 625830*, ≤ gardens, sea and Etna, ⛱, ⛱ – ▤ ▤ TV P. ⓢ MC VISA. ✗ rest BZ b
10 March-26 November – **Meals** *(10 April-October ; closed dinner)* (residents only) – **49 rm** ☕ 120/198, suite.
◆ Well-designed public areas and simple yet presentable rooms ; breathtaking views, grounds planted with palms, and a pool are further features of this hotel.

Andromaco ⛰ without rest., via Fontana Vecchia ☏ 0942 23834, *info@andromaco.it, Fax 0942 24985*, ≤, ⛱ – ▤ TV P. AE ⓢ MC VISA by via Cappuccini BZ
20 rm ☕ 90/120.
◆ This informal hotel is situated in a quiet residential area with fine views. The well-appointed interiors make good use of space ; efficient and friendly management.

La Giara, vico La Floresta 1 ☏ 0942 23360, *Fax 0942 23233*, ⛱ ≤, Rest. and piano bar – ▤. AE ⓢ ⓓ MC VISA. ✗ BZ f
closed March (except Friday-Saturday) November, February, Monday and lunch (except July-September) – **Meals** (booking essential) a la carte 44/57.
◆ Undoubtedly the town's most fashionable restaurant with soft lights, good service, and views over rooftops and terraces. Popular piano-bar in the evenings ; stylish clientele.

Casa Grugno, via Santa Maria de' Greci ☏ 0942 21208, *info@casagrugno.it*, ⛱ – ▤ AE ⓢ ⓓ MC VISA. ✗ AZ a
closed 1 to 20 December, February, Sunday lunch and Wednesday (except April-September) – **Meals** a la carte 44/58 ☙.
◆ This recently opened restaurant prides itself on its creative seafood cuisine, offering interesting flavour combinations. A refined atmosphere ; located in the town centre.

TAORMINA

Traffic restricted
in the town centre

Carmine (Piazza d.)	AZ 3
Don Bosco (Via)	BZ 6
Duomo (Piazza d.)	AZ 7
Fazzello (Via)	AZ 9
Giardinazzo (Via)	BZ 10
Ginnasio (Via d.)	BZ 12
Giovanni (Via d.)	BZ 13
Guardjola Vecchia (Via)	BCZ 15
Jallia Bassia (Via)	BZ 16
S. Antonio (Piazza)	AZ 18
S. Caterina (Largo)	BZ 19
S. Domenico (Piazzale)	AZ 21
Umberto (Corso)	ABZ
Von Gloeden (Via VV.)	AZ 22

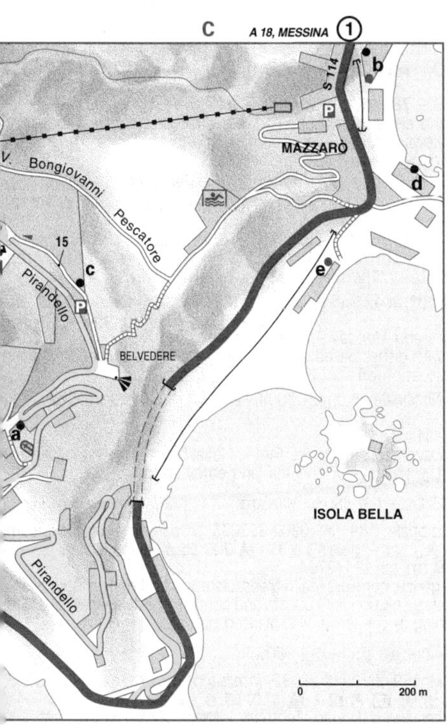

Al Duomo, vico Ebrei 11 0942 625656, *info@ristorantealduomo.it,* – . AZ q
closed November, January and Monday – **Meals** (booking essential) Sicilian rest. a la carte 34/52.
◆ After approaching along an alley and entering this restaurant, customers find themselves in smart surroundings overlooking the Piazza del Duomo. Summer dining on the terrace.

La Griglia, corso Umberto 54 0942 23980 – . BZ c
closed 20 November-20 December and Tuesday – **Meals** a la carte 21/36.
◆ Situated on the town's main street, this classic restaurant is generously strewn with plants. Traditional cuisine along seasonal lines.

Il Baccanale, piazzetta Filea 1 0942 625390, *Fax 0942 625390,* – . BZ e
closed Thursday except April-September – **Meals** a la carte 22/37.
◆ The option to dine outside in the square or indoors at closely-spaced tables in this simple establishment, which has an atmosphere of genuine rusticity. Popular with tourists.

at Capotaormina *South : 4 km – 98030 Mazzarò :*

Grande Albergo Capotaormina , via Nazionale 105 0942 572111, *prenotazione@capotaorminahotel.com, Fax 0942 625467,* , , sea water – , rm, – 450.
April-October – **Meals** a la carte 37/56 – **194 rm** 293/430, 4 suites.
◆ A splendid clifftop location makes for some of the finest views in the area. Among the many natural beauties is the beach with an unusual cave. The restaurant serves meals on the delightful terrace overlooking the sea.

at Mazzarò *East : 5,5 km CZ – 98030 :*

Grand Hotel Mazzarò Sea Palace, via Nazionale 147 0942 612111, *info@mazzaroseapalace.it, Fax 0942 626237,* small bay, , , , – , rm, – 100. CZ b
March-November – **Meals** a la carte 39/88 – **88 rm** 230/402, 9 suites.
◆ Elegant interiors, luxurious furnishings, numerous terraces, and a pool with fine views are some of the ingredients which make such a harmonious whole at this fine hotel. Smart restaurant with terrace for candlelit dining.

Atlantis Bay, via Nazionale 161 ☎ 0942 618011, *info@atlantisbay.it, Fax 0942 23194*, – 200.
March-November – **Meals** 49 – **78 rm** 350/420, 7 suites.
◆ This recently opened hotel is elegant and sophisticated, with sumptuous interiors and spacious rooms, all with sea views, offering every comfort. Splendid pool with terrace and private beach. Attention to detail evident in the excellent restaurant.

Villa Sant'Andrea, via Nazionale 137 ☎ 0942 23125, *reservation.vsa@framon-hotels.it, Fax 0942 24838*, ≤ small bay, – 150. CZ d
April-8 November – **Meals** a la carte 46/67 – 16,50 – **77 rm** 232,10/326,70, 2 suites.
◆ Wonderfully located on the beachfront, this traditional hotel occupies a recently renovated 19C villa ; stylish hospitality. The restaurant has delightful views.

Da Giovanni, via Nazionale ☎ 0942 23531, ≤ sea and Isolabella –
closed 7 January-10 February and Monday – **Meals** a la carte 31/46.
◆ Classic seaside restaurant with dishes based on fresh locally caught fish prepared along traditional lines. Panoramic situation offering fine views of Isola Bella.

Il Delfino-da Angelo, via Nazionale ☎ 0942 23004, *Fax 0942 23004*, ≤ small bay, –
15 March-October – **Meals** a la carte 26/40.
◆ Located between an attractive garden and the famous local beach, this establishment is the ideal place to savour the flavours of the sea, and enjoy a dip.

at Lido di Spisone *North-East : 1,5 km – ✉ 98030 Mazzarò :*

Hotel Caparena, via Nazionale 189 ☎ 0942 652033, *caparena@gaishotels.com, Fax 0942 36913*, ≤, – 200.
Meals a la carte 35/48 – **88 rm** 194/270.
◆ The seaside at its best ; elegance, comfort, palm trees, clear water, fine furnishings and a pleasant atmosphere. The ideal solution for tourists and conference delegates alike. The restaurant offers outside dining in the large, well-planted gardens.

at Castelmola *North-West : 5 km AZ – alt. 550 – ✉ 98030 :*

Villa Sonia, via Porta Mola 9 ☎ 0942 28082, *intelisano@tao.it, Fax 0942 28083*, ≤ Etna, – 110.
closed November-20 December and 6 January-February – **Meals** ***Parco Reale*** Rest. a la carte 52/62 – 15 – **37 rm** 120/170, 3 suites.
◆ Occupying a restored historic villa on the way into a pretty little town, this hotel's interior is adorned with antiques and Sicilian craftware. The soberly smart restaurant is also furnished with period items.

TURIN (TORINO) *10100* **P** **561** G 5 *G. Italy – pop. 900 987 alt. 239.*

See : *Piazza San Carlo★★ CXY – Egyptian Museum★★★, Sabauda Gallery★★ in Academy of Science* CX **M1** – *Cathedral★ VX : relic of the Holy Shroud★★★ – Mole Antonelliana★ ★★ DX – Madama Palace★ : museum of Ancient Art★ CX* **A** – *Royal Palace★ : Royal Armoury★ CDVX – Risorgimento Museum★ in Carignano Palace★★ CX* **M2** – *Carlo Biscaretti di Ruffia Motor Museum★★ – Model medieval village★ in the Valentino Park CDZ.*

Envir. : *Basilica of Superga★ : ≤★★★ – Sacra di San Michele ★★★ – Tour to the pass, Colle della Maddalena★ : ≤★★ of the city from the route Superga-Pino Torinese, ≤★ of the city from the route Colle della Maddalena-Cavoretto _ Palazzina di Caccia di Stupinigi ★*

27, I Roveri (March-November ; closed Monday) at La Mandria ✉ 10070 Fiano Torinese ☎ 011 9235719, Fax 011 9235669, North : 18 km;

18, 18 Torino (closed Monday, January and February), at Fiano Torinese ✉ 10070 ☎ 011 9235440, Fax 011 9235886, North : 20 km;

18 Le Fronde (closed Tuesday, January and February) at Avigliana ✉ 1005[illegible] ☎ 011 9328053, Fax 011 9320928, West : 24 km;

9 Stupinigi (closed Monday), corso Unione Sovietica 506/a ✉ 10135 Torino ☎ 011 3472640, Fax 011 3978038.

Turin Airport of Caselle North : 15 km ☎ 011 5676361 – Alitalia, via Cernaia 18 ✉ 10122 ☎ 011 57691, Fax 011 5769220.

piazza Castello 161 ✉ 10122 ☎ 011 535181, Fax 011 530070 – Porta Nuova Railway Station ✉ 10125 ☎ 011 531327, Fax 011 5617095 – Turin Airport of Caselle ✉ 1012[illegible] ☎ 011 5678124.

A.C.I. *via Giovanni Giolitti 15 ✉ 10123 ☎ 011 57791.*

Roma 669 – Briançon 108 – Chambéry 209 – Genève 252 – Genova 170 – Grenoble 22[illegible] – Milano 140 – Nice 220.

Plans on following pages

Turin Palace Hotel, via Sacchi 8 10128 011 5625511, *palace@thi.it, Fax 011 5612187* – 200. . CY u
Meals *Vigna Reale* Rest. *(closed August, Saturday and Sunday lunch)* a la carte 28/44 – **120 rm** 225/277, suite.
◆ Style and tradition abound in this classic grand hotel which has been part of the city's life for more than a century ; a warm atmosphere and simple period elegance throughout. A cosier ambience in the genteel and welcoming restaurant ; excellent service.

Le Meridien Lingotto, via Nizza 262 10126 011 6642000, *reservations@lemeridien-lingotto.it, Fax 011 6642001,* , – , rm, – 67. . by via Nizza CZ
closed 10 to 26 August – **Meals *Torpedo*** Rest. *(closed Monday)* a la carte 41/55 – **226 rm** 290, 14 suites.
◆ This hotel, carved out of the Lingotto industrial complex, has its own tropical garden ; luxurious rooms with design features. Comfortable seating in the bright and elegant restaurant serving first class cuisine.

Gd H. Sitea, via Carlo Alberto 35 10123 011 5170171, *sitea@thi.it, Fax 011 548090* – – 100. . rest CY t
Meals *Carignano* Rest. *(closed Saturday lunch)* a la carte 42/53 – **114 rm** 190/255, 2 suites.
◆ Hospitality, atmosphere, antique furniture ; a harmonious refinement is evident throughout at this traditional grand hotel (opened 1925) which has been recently renovated. Pleasant views from the subtly elegant restaurant.

Starhotel Majestic, corso Vittorio Emanuele II 54 10123 011 539153, *majestic.to@starhotels.it, Fax 011 534963* – , rm, – 500. . CY e
Meals *le Regine* Rest. a la carte 43/65 – **162 rm** 239, 2 suites.
◆ Spacious and comfortable throughout, this centrally-located elegant hotel has been recently refitted. A large dome of coloured glass dominates the attractive dining room ; international cuisine.

Jolly Hotel Ambasciatori, corso Vittorio Emanuele II 104 10121 011 5752, *torino-ambasciatori@jollyhotels.it, Fax 011 544978* – , rm, – 400. . rest BX a
Meals *Il Diplomatico* Rest. a la carte 39/63 – **199 rm** 195/225, 4 suites.
◆ Occupying an angular modern building, this hotel is continuously updated to meet the requirements of its corporate-function clientele ; comfortable rooms, in keeping with the group's standards. Bright restaurant with a stylish atmosphere.

Jolly Hotel Ligure, piazza Carlo Felice 85 10123 011 55641, *torino_ligure@jollyhotels.it, Fax 011 535438* – , rm, – 200. . rest CY b
Meals a la carte 31/45 – **167 rm** 196/229, 2 suites.
◆ A long-established hotel occupying a 19C palazzo ; recent refitting has created an interior which is modern and functional throughout. Low vaulted ceilings in the restaurant offering varied Italian cuisine.

Villa Sassi , strada al Traforo del Pino 47 10132 011 8980556, *info@villassassi.com, Fax 011 8980095,* – – 200. . rest by corso Casale DY
closed August – **Meals** *(closed Sunday)* a la carte 49/67 – **16 rm** 185/240.
◆ Set in relaxing parkland surroundings, this former 17C aristocratic residence offers a genteel atmosphere and fine function rooms. Summer dining outside on a pleasant terrace, which is well suited to banquet events.

Concord, via Lagrange 47 10123 011 5176756, *prenotazioni@hotelconcord.com, Fax 011 5176305* – – 200. . rest CY s
Meals a la carte 32/48 – **135 rm** 230/280, 4 suites.
◆ Centrally located near Porta Nuova, this comfortable establishment with its spacious interior is well suited to corporate events. Classic restaurant with an elegant ambience, plus an American-style bar.

Boston without rest., via Massena 70 10128 011 500359, *direzione@hotelbostontorino.it, Fax 011 599358,* – , rm, – 50. BZ c
82 rm 120/160, 5 suites.
◆ Restoration has combined high standards of comfort with tasteful decoration in this hotel ; Oriental-style furnishings in the new rooms. Caring hospitality.

Victoria without rest., via Nino Costa 4 10123 011 5611909, *reservation@hotelvictoria-torino.com, Fax 011 5611806* – . . CY v
103 rm 130/173.
◆ Antique furniture, a harmonious colour scheme and canopy beds ; much attention to detail in evidence at this elegant hotel which oozes atmosphere and charm.

TORINO

Traffic restricted in the town centre

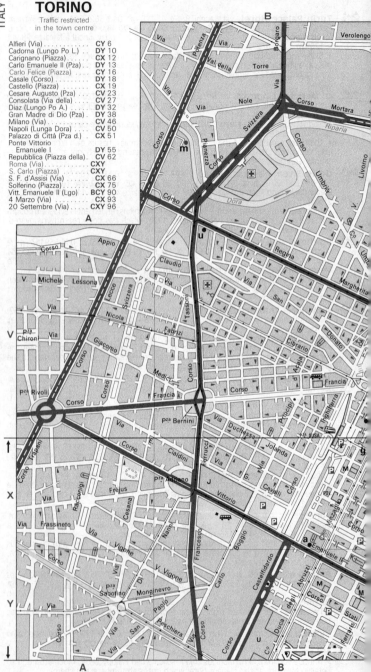

Street	Grid ref.
Alfieri (Via)	CY 6
Cadorna (Lungo Po L.)	DY 10
Carignano (Piazza)	CX 12
Carlo Emanuele II (Pza)	DY 13
Carlo Felice (Piazza)	CY 16
Casale (Corso)	DY 18
Castello (Piazza)	CX 19
Cesare Augusto (Pza)	CV 23
Consolata (Via della)	CV 27
Diaz (Lungo Po A.)	DY 32
Gran Madre di Dio (Pza)	DY 38
Milano (Via)	CV 46
Napoli (Lunga Dora)	CV 50
Palazzo di Città (Pza d.)	CX 51
Ponte Vittorio Emanuele I	DY 55
Repubblica (Piazza della)	CV 62
Roma (Via)	CXY
S. Carlo (Piazza)	CXY
S. F. d'Assisi (Via)	CX 66
Solferino (Piazza)	CX 75
Vitt. Emanuele II (Lgo)	BCY 90
4 Marzo (Via)	CX 93
20 Settembre (Via)	CXY 96

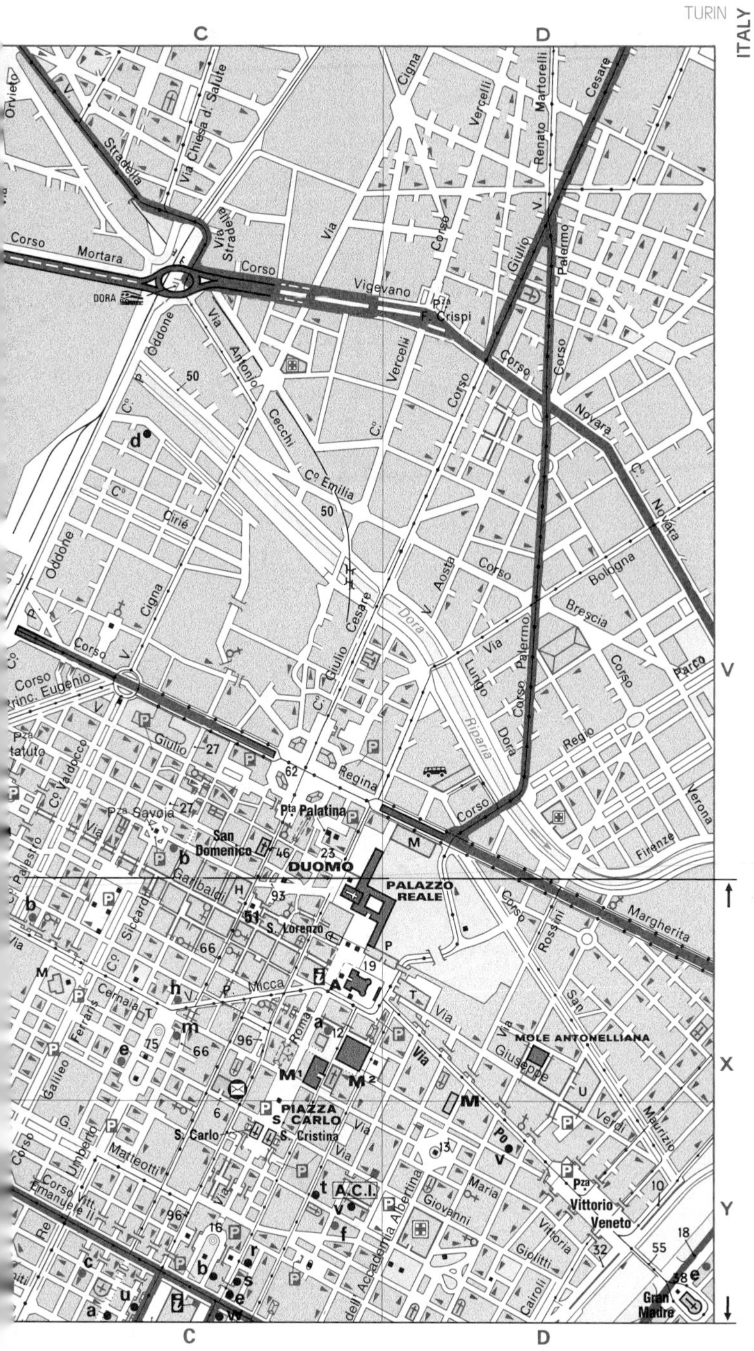
C
D
Corso Mortara
DORA
Via Stradella
Via Chiesa d. Salute
Corso Vigevano
Pza F. Crispi
Via Cigna
Corso Vercelli
Renato Martorelli
Cesare
Giulio
Corso Palermo
Corso Novara
Cº Novara
Via Antonio Cecchi
Cº Emilia
Cº Oddone
Cº Ciriè
Corso Bologna
Corso Brescia
Corso Aosta
Dora
Lungo Dora
Riparia
Corso Parco
Corso Regio
Corso Verona
Corso Firenze
Corso Princ. Eugenio
Pza Statuto
Cº Valdocco
Pza Savoia
Pta Palatina
San Domenico
DUOMO
PALAZZO REALE
Corso Regina
Garibaldi
S. Lorenzo
Corso Margherita
Corso Rossini
Cº Siccardi
Cernaia
P. Micca
Roma
Via San
MOLE ANTONELLIANA
Via Giuseppe Verdi
Maurizio
PIAZZA S. CARLO
S. Carlo
S. Cristina
A.C.I.
dell' Accademia Albertina
Maria
Giovanni
Pza Vittorio Veneto
Vittoria
Giolitti
Cairoli
Gran Madre
Galileo Ferraris
G. Umberto
Matteotti
Corso Vitt. Emanuele II
Corso Re
Palestro
V
X
Y
50
27
62
46
23
93
51
66
19
12
75
96
6
13
10
16
32
55
18
38

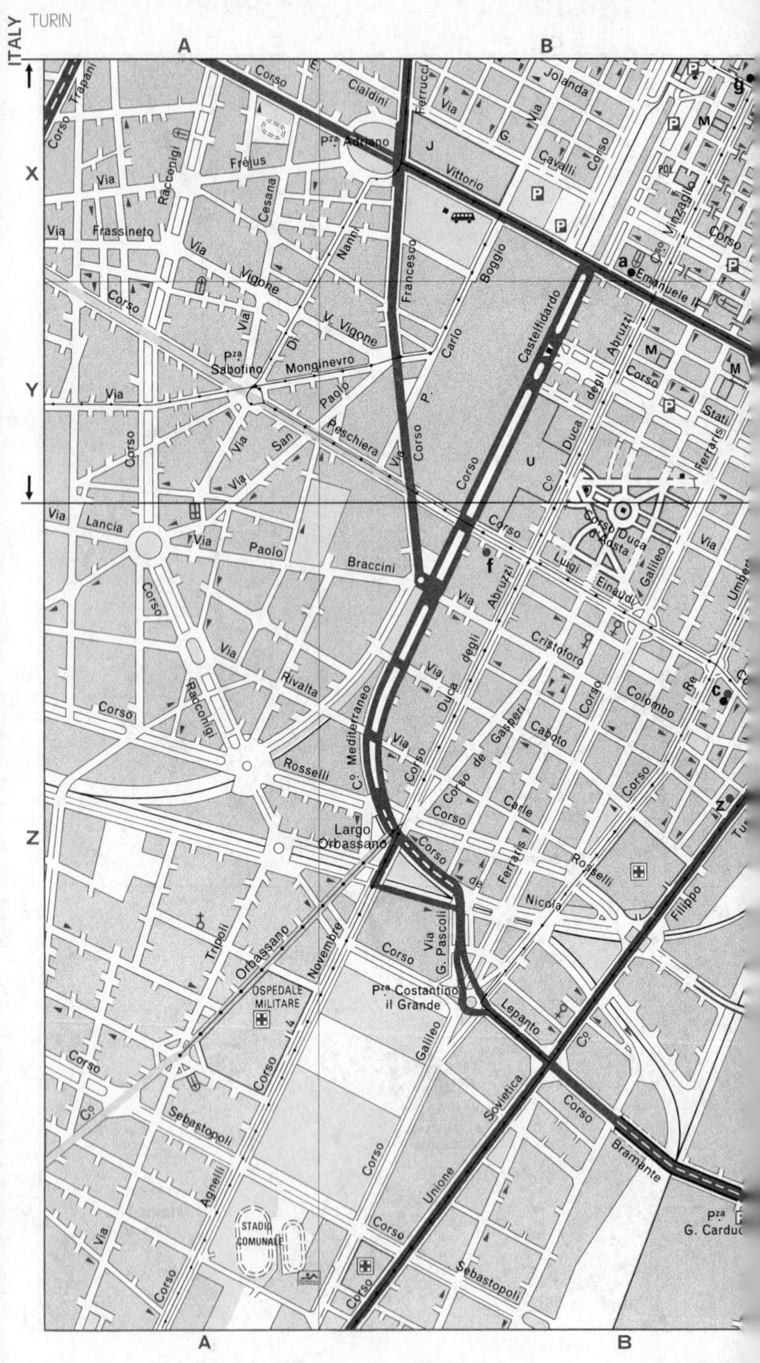

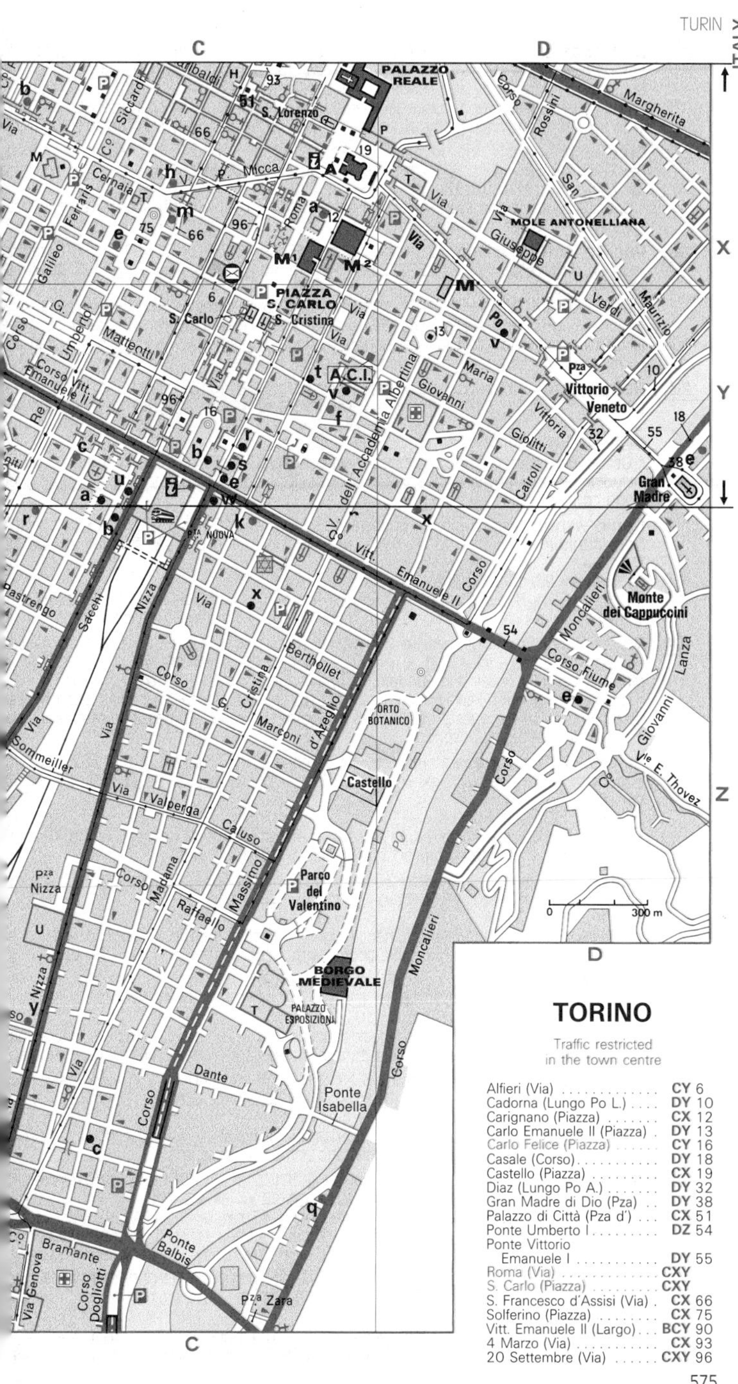
C
D
X
Y
Z
PALAZZO REALE
S. Lorenzo
MOLE ANTONELLIANA
PIAZZA S. CARLO
S. Carlo
S. Cristina
A.C.I.
Vittorio Veneto
Gran Madre
Monte dei Cappuccini
P^TA NUOVA
ORTO BOTANICO
Castello
Parco del Valentino
BORGO MEDIEVALE
PALAZZO ESPOSIZIONI
Ponte Isabella
Ponte Balbis
P^za Zara
P^za Nizza
PO
Corso Vitt. Emanuele II
Corso Moncalieri
Corso Fiume
V^le E. Thovez
Corso Massimo d'Azeglio
Via Nizza
Corso Dante
Corso Bramante
Via Genova
Corso Dogliotti
Via Madama Cristina
Via Berthollet
Corso G. Marconi
Via Valperga Caluso
Corso Raffaello
Via Sommeiller
Via Pastrengo
Via Sacchi
Corso Re Umberto
Via Matteotti
Corso Galileo Ferraris
Via Cernaia
Via Micca
Via Roma
Via Po
Via Giuseppe Verdi
Via Maria Vittoria
Via Giovanni Giolitti
Via Cairoli
Via dell' Accademia Albertina
Corso San Maurizio
Corso Margherita
Via Rossini
Corso Lanza
Corso Giovanni Lanza
0 300 m
TORINO
Traffic restricted in the town centre
Alfieri (Via) . . . . CY 6
Cadorna (Lungo Po L.) . . . . DY 10
Carignano (Piazza) . . . . CX 12
Carlo Emanuele II (Piazza) . DY 13
Carlo Felice (Piazza) . . . . . . CY 16
Casale (Corso) . . . . DY 18
Castello (Piazza) . . . . CX 19
Diaz (Lungo Po A.) . . . . DY 32
Gran Madre di Dio (Pza) . . DY 38
Palazzo di Città (Pza d') . . . CX 51
Ponte Umberto I . . . . DZ 54
Ponte Vittorio Emanuele I . . . . DY 55
Roma (Via) . . . . CXY
S. Carlo (Piazza) . . . . CXY
S. Francesco d'Assisi (Via) . CX 66
Solferino (Piazza) . . . . CX 75
Vitt. Emanuele II (Largo) . . . BCY 90
4 Marzo (Via) . . . . CX 93
20 Settembre (Via) . . . . . . CXY 96

Diplomatic, via Cernaia 42 ✉ 10122 ☎ 011 5612444, *info@hotel-diplomatic.it, Fax 011 540472* – |‡|, ⇹ rm, ▤ TV ☎ – 🏛 180. AE ⚲ ⓓ ⓜⓒ VISA. ⚹ rest BX g
Meals *(closed Saturday and Sunday)* (residents only) – **123 rm** ☕ 200/260, 3 suites.
◆ Near Porta Susa station, concealed behind the 19C porticoes so characteristic of Turin, is the modern entrance lobby of this new hotel ; small but very comfortable rooms.

City without rest., via Juvarra 25 ✉ 10122 ☎ 011 540546, *cityhotel@iol.it, Fax 011 548188* – |‡| ▤ TV 🚗 – 🏛 60. AE ⚲ ⓓ ⓜⓒ VISA JCB. ⚹ BV e
☕ 7,75 – **57 rm** 180/232.
◆ Unusual contemporary style gives character to this conveniently located hotel near Porta Susa station ; quiet, well-appointed rooms.

Pacific Hotel Fortino, strada del Fortino 36 ✉ 10152 ☎ 011 5217757, *hotelfortino@pacifichotels.it, Fax 011 5217749* – ⇹ rm, ▤ TV ☎ ♿ 🚗 – 🏛 450. AE ⚲ ⓓ ⓜⓒ VISA JCB. ⚹ CV c
Meals a la carte 37/49 – ☕ 13 – **92 rm** 168/222, 8 suites.
◆ Modern hotel designed to meet the needs of the business traveller. Several suites available fitted with the latest in Information Technology gadgetry. The spacious restaurant forms part of the hotel's dedicated conference facilities.

Holiday Inn Turin City Centre, via Assietta 3 ✉ 10128 ☎ 011 5167111, *hi.tort@libero.it, Fax 011 5167699* – |‡|, ⇹ rm, ▤ TV ☎ ♿ 🚗 – 🏛 40. AE ⚲ ⓓ ⓜⓒ VISA JCB. ⚹ rest CY a
Meals (dinner only) 20 – **57 rm** ☕ 160/212.
◆ Occupying a restored 19C palazzo, this well-situated hotel offers every modern comfort including jacuzzis, power showers and saunas in its rooms. The restaurant is also designed along contemporary lines.

Genio without rest., corso Vittorio Emanuele II 47 ✉ 10125 ☎ 011 6505771, *info@hotelgenio.it, Fax 011 6508264* – |‡|, ⇹ rm, ▤ TV – 🏛 25. AE ⚲ ⓓ ⓜⓒ VISA JCB CYZ w
117 rm ☕ 98/134, 3 suites.
◆ Close to Porta Nuova station, this recently enlarged and refurbished hotel has an elegant ambience ; well-presented rooms with much attention to detail in evidence.

Royal, corso Regina Margherita 249 ✉ 10144 ☎ 011 4376777, *info@hotelroyal.to, Fax 011 4376393* – |‡| ▤ TV ♿ 🚗 P – 🏛 600. AE ⚲ ⓓ ⓜⓒ VISA JCB. ⚹ BV u
Meals *(closed Saturday and Sunday lunch)* a la carte 29/39 – **75 rm** ☕ 110/150.
◆ Despite being slightly away from the centre, this pleasant hotel, which has recently been restored, appeals to guests of all types ; good conference facilities. The restaurant has a classically refined atmosphere.

Genova e Stazione without rest., via Sacchi 14/b ✉ 10128 ☎ 011 5629400, *hotel.genova@hotelres.it, Fax 011 5629896* – |‡| ▤ TV ♿ – 🏛 70. AE ⚲ ⓓ ⓜⓒ VISA CZ b
78 rm ☕ 98/135, 2 suites.
◆ A genteel hotel near Porta Nuova ; recently refitted to provide its clientele with the ideal balance between modern comfort and a classic, stylish interior.

Giotto without rest., via Giotto 27 ✉ 10126 ☎ 011 6637172, *giottohotel@libero.it, Fax 011 6637173* – |‡| ▤ TV. AE ⚲ ⓓ ⓜⓒ VISA JCB. ⚹ CZ
50 rm ☕ 115/148.
◆ Close to Lingotto and Valentino, hence slightly out of town, this modern hotel has been refurbished to provide comfortable rooms with jacuzzi baths or power showers.

Lancaster without rest., corso Filippo Turati 8 ✉ 10128 ☎ 011 5681982, *hotel@lancaster.it, Fax 011 5683019* – |‡| ▤ TV ♿ – 🏛 40. AE ⚲ ⓓ ⓜⓒ VISA BZ
closed 5 to 20 August – **75 rm** ☕ 103/136.
◆ Situated a little out of town in a residential district, this genteel establishment is comfortable and well presented, both in its public areas and in its above-average rooms.

Crimea without rest., via Mentana 3 ✉ 10133 ☎ 011 6604700, *hotel.crimea@hotelres.it, Fax 011 6604912* – |‡| ▤ TV ☎ – 🏛 35. AE ⚲ ⓓ ⓜⓒ VISA DZ
49 rm ☕ 98/140, suite.
◆ Pleasantly understated and elegant interiors in this hotel, quietly located in a residential district away from the centre ; modern and comfortable rooms.

Gran Mogol without rest., via Guarini 2 ✉ 10123 ☎ 011 5612120, *info@hotelgranmogol.it, Fax 011 5623160* – |‡|, ⇹ rm, ▤ TV. AE ⚲ ⓓ ⓜⓒ VISA CY
closed 1 to 22 August and 24 to 31 December – **45 rm** ☕ 98/134.
◆ Near the Museo Egizio, this very central hotel has been refitted ; a genteel ambience appealing to business travellers and tourists alike. The rooms are very comfortable.

Piemontese without rest., via Berthollet 21 ✉ 10125 ☎ 011 6698101, *info@hotelpiemontese.it, Fax 011 6690571* – |‡| ⇹ ▤ TV P. AE ⚲ ⓓ ⓜⓒ VISA CZ
39 rm ☕ 124/134.
◆ Ongoing renovation of this hotel's accommodation continues (many rooms now with jacuzzi or sauna-shower) ; between Porta nuova and the Po. Colourful décor in the public areas

Amadeus without rest., via Principe Amedeo 41 bis ✉ 10123 ☎ 011 8174951, *Fax 011 8174953* – DY v
closed August – **26 rm** 90/115, 2 suites.
◆ Close to the Mole Antonelliana, this hotel has modern rooms, some with self-catering facilities ; pleasant breakfast room with winter-garden theme.

Cairo without rest., via La Loggia 6 ✉ 10134 ☎ 011 3171555, *hcairo@ipsnet.it*, *Fax 011 3172027* – by corso Unione Sovietica BZ
closed 1 to 28 August – **50 rm** 100/140.
◆ Situated out of town and offering parking, this family-run hotel has a welcoming ambience ; the newer rooms in the annexe are the most comfortable.

Del Cambio, piazza Carignano 2 ✉ 10123 ☎ 011 543760, *cambio@thi.it*, *Fax 011 535282*, Historic traditional restaurant – CX a
closed 12 to 18 August, 1 to 7 January and Sunday – **Meals** (booking essential) 64 and a la carte 50/64 (15 %).
◆ Turin's regal past and the spirit of Cavour are in evidence throughout the rich 19C interiors of this historic establishment with a fine culinary tradition.

Vintage 1997, piazza Solferino 16/h ✉ 10121 ☎ 011 535948, *info@vintage1997.com*, *Fax 011 535948* – CX e
closed 6 to 31 August, 1 to 7 January, Saturday lunch and Sunday – **Meals** (booking essential) a la carte 40/58.
◆ Deep red fabrics and wood-panelled walls in this atmospheric restaurant in the city centre ; caring personal service and creative cuisine.
Spec. Acciughe al verde su patate di Entracque. Agnolotti del plin con sugo d'arrosto e rosmarino. Code di scampi con costolette di coniglio su crema di scalogno.

Casa Vicina, via Massena 66 ✉ 10128 ☎ 011 590949, *casavicina@libero.it*, – BZ c
closed 1 to 15 August, Sunday dinner and Monday – **Meals** (dinner only) a la carte 40/55.
◆ Formerly at the Canavese, the solid family management team here have preserved the name, style and traditional Piedmontese cuisine.

Norman, via Pietro Micca 22 ✉ 10122 ☎ 011 540854, *norman@norman.it*, *Fax 011 5113838* – CX h
Meals a la carte 37/55.
◆ An elegant feel to both the café on the ground floor and the restaurant upstairs, overlooking Piazza Solferino ; modern cuisine. Reduced menu at lunchtime.

La Cloche, strada al Traforo del Pino 106 ✉ 10132 ☎ 011 8992851, *lacloche@tiscalinet.it*, *Fax 011 8981522*, – – 100.
closed 1 week in August, Sunday dinner, Monday and lunch in August – **Meals** a la carte 43/69. by corso Moncalieri CDZ
◆ A rural setting in the foothills for this warm and elegant restaurant ; good banqueting room. Piedmontese cuisine following seasonal lines.

Marco Polo, via Marco Polo 38 ✉ 10129 ☎ 011 599900, *ristorantemarcopolo@libero.it*, *Fax 011 50842266* – BZ f
Meals (booking essential) seafood a la carte 42/85.
◆ A number of different rooms make up this restaurant, each offering specific cuisine ; thus seafood in one room, and meat dishes in another. Elegant surroundings upstairs.

La Barrique, corso Dante 53 ✉ 10126 ☎ 011 657900, *Fax 011 657995* – CZ y
closed 2 weeks in August, Monday, Saturday and Sunday lunch – **Meals** (booking essential) a la carte 30/63.
◆ A small and friendly oasis of peace and elegance in a somewhat busy district ; good service and imaginative cuisine using quality ingredients.

Moreno La Prima dal 1979, corso Unione Sovietica 244 ✉ 10134 ☎ 011 3179191, *laprimamoreno@libero.it*, *Fax 011 3143423* – GU c
closed 20 days in August – **Meals** (booking essential) a la carte 45/65.
◆ From the ring road an unexpected lane leads to this well-presented and elegant establishment. The tables overlooking the gardens are especially pleasant ; traditional cuisine.

Al Garamond, via Pomba 14 ✉ 10123 ☎ 011 8122781 – CY f
closed Saturday lunch and Sunday – **Meals** (booking essential) 40 and a la carte 40/62.
◆ Named after an officer of Napoleon's army, this establishment, run by a youthful but professional staff, serves imaginative modern dishes.

Locanda Mongreno, strada Mongreno 50 ✉ 10132 ☎ 011 8980417, *pikuz@libero.it*, *Fax 011 8227345*, – by corso Moncalieri DZ
closed 25 August-10 September, 26 December-10 January, Monday and lunch (except Sunday) – **Meals** (booking essential) a la carte 48/55.
◆ A passionate young management has transformed this former rustic establishment into a stylish restaurant, serving innovative seasonal cuisine.

XX **Al Gatto Nero,** corso Filippo Turati 14 ✉ 10128 ☎ 011 590414, *info@gattonero.it* *Fax 011 502245* – ▤. AE ⓢ ⓓ MC VISA. ✂ BZ z
closed August and Sunday – **Meals** a la carte 38/50.
◆ Cats of all kinds gaze from the periphery of this perennially popular restaurant with many celebrity regulars ; traditional Tuscan cuisine.

XX **Ij Brandè,** via Massena 5 ✉ 10128 ☎ 011 537279, *Fax 011 5180668* – ▤. AE ⓢ ⓓ MC VISA CY c
closed Sunday and Monday lunch – **Meals** (booking essential for dinner) a la carte 31/51
◆ A warm, friendly restaurant with real fire in the Porta Nuova district ; traditional dishes interpreted with imagination and style.

XX **Savoia,** via Corte d'Appello 13 ✉ 10122 ☎ 011 4362288, *r.savoia97@libero.it* *Fax 011 4362288* – ▤. AE ⓢ ⓓ MC VISA. ✂ CV b
closed Saturday lunch and Sunday – **Meals** a la carte 31/51.
◆ Fanciful and surprising modern dishes at this long established restaurant. Elegantly furnished, good service and atmosphere.

XX **Galante,** corso Palestro 15 ✉ 10122 ☎ 011 537757, *011 32163* – ▤. AE ⓢ ⓓ MC VISA JCB CX b
closed August, Saturday lunch and Sunday – **Meals** a la carte 30/50.
◆ Pale colours and upholstered seating in this small Neo-classical jewel ; many roast specialities, both meat and fish, on the menu.

XX **Porta Rossa,** via Passalacqua 3/b ✉ 10122 ☎ 011 530816, *Fax 011 530816* – ▤. AE ⓢ ⓓ MC VISA. ✂ CV a
closed August, 26 December-6 January, Saturday lunch and Sunday – **Meals** (booking essential) seafood 38/48 and a la carte 32/67.
◆ Near Piazza Statuto, this animated modern restaurant has closely-spaced tables and a wide selection of wonderfully-fresh fish dishes.

XX **Al Bue Rosso,** corso Casale 10 ✉ 10131 ☎ 011 8191393, *Fax 011 8191393* – ▤. AE ⓢ MC VISA. ✂ DY e
closed August, Saturday lunch and Monday – **Meals** a la carte 34/45 (10 %).
◆ In the same competent hands for over 30 years, this classically elegant restaurant near the Gran Madre church is on the banks of the Po ; rustic cuisine.

XX **Perbacco,** via Mazzini 31 ✉ 10123 ☎ 011 882110 – ▤. AE ⓢ ⓓ MC VISA DZ x
closed August and Sunday – **Meals** (dinner only) 28.
◆ Centrally located, pleasant restaurant (evenings only) with an elegant modern atmosphere ; à la carte menu of seasonal Piedmontese cuisine.

XX **Il 58,** via San Secondo 58 ✉ 10128 ☎ 011 505566, *ristoranteil58@libero.it* *Fax 011 505566* – ▤. ⓢ ⓓ MC VISA JCB CZ a
closed September and Monday – **Meals** seafood a la carte 28/37.
◆ Genteel restaurant with two elegant and welcoming rooms ; good service and excellent ingredients evident in the generously portioned cuisine (mainly seafood).

X **Taverna delle Rose,** via Massena 24 ✉ 10128 ☎ 011 538345, *Fax 011 538345* – ▤. AE ⓢ ⓓ MC VISA JCB. ✂ CZ
closed August, Saturday lunch and Sunday – **Meals** a la carte 31/40.
◆ An enchanting ambience in this restaurant offering a wide range of traditional dishes for evening dining choose the romantic room with exposed brickwork and soft lights.

X **Ristorantino Tefy,** corso Belgio 26 ✉ 10153 ☎ 011 837332, *Fax 011 837332* – ▤ AE ⓢ MC VISA JCB by corso Novara DV
closed August, 15 to 30 January and Sunday – **Meals** (booking essential) Umbrian rest 25/28 and a la carte 25/31.
◆ Passion and devotion are evident in the management of this welcoming establishment ask the owner for his recommendations (Umbrian dishes a speciality).

X **C'era una Volta,** corso Vittorio Emanuele II 41 ✉ 10125 ☎ 011 6504589 *Fax 011 6505774* – ▤. AE ⓢ ⓓ MC VISA CZ k
closed August and Sunday – **Meals** (dinner only) Piedmontese rest. a la carte 25/34.
◆ Situated on the first floor of a building near Porta Nuova, this classic restaurant has been in business for over 20 years ; Piedmontese dishes are the house speciality.

X **Da Toci,** corso Moncalieri 190 ✉ 10133 ☎ 011 6614809, ♧ – ▤. ⓢ MC VISA JCB CZ c
closed 16 August-5 September, Sunday and Monday lunch – **Meals** seafood a la carte 23/40.
◆ The new owner of this simple, well-presented restaurant has introduced some Tuscan dishes, but seafood is still the mainstay of the menu here.

X **Anaconda,** via Angiolino 16 (corso Potenza) ✉ 10143 ☎ 011 752903, *Fax 011 752903* ♧, Rustic trattoria – P. AE ⓢ ⓓ MC VISA JCB BV n
closed August, Friday dinner and Saturday – **Meals** 25/30.
◆ Robust Piedmontese cuisine served in a rustic setting with ample parking and outside dining in summer ; a slice of rural life on the outskirts of town.

Le Maschere, via Fidia 28 ang. via Vandalino ✉ 10141 ☎ 011 728928, *lemaschere@libero.it* – ▤. AE ⓢ ⓓ ⓜⓒ VISA by corso Francia ABV
closed Sunday and Wednesday dinner – **Meals** (booking essential) a la carte 20/34.
◆ All manner of masks decorate this out-of-town restaurant ; family-run with a bright minimalist ambience. Homely cuisine with Piedmontese and seasonal dishes.

Torre Pellice *10066 Torino 561 H 3 – pop. 4 606 alt. 516.*

Roma 708 – Cuneo 64 – Milano 201 – Sestriere 71 – Torino 58.

XXX ✿✿ **Flipot** with rm, corso Gramsci 17 ☎ 0121 953465, *flipot@flipot.com, Fax 0121 91236* – TV. AE ⓢ ⓓ ⓜⓒ VISA.
closed 10 to 30 June and 24 December-10 January – **Meals** *(closed Monday and Tuesday, only Tuesday July-August)* a la carte 58/79 – **7 rm** ☕ 65/80.
◆ Deep in the Valli Valdesi, this establishment seems lost in bygone times ; a welcoming family environment with creative dishes drawing on timeless flavours.
Spec. Salmerino di torrente cotto su pietra di Luserna, spuma di petto d'anatra affumicato. Agnoli di lumache al profumo di erba ruta. Filetto di cervo in salsa di pino mugo, pera allo zafferano e polenta di farina di mandorle.

When looking for a quiet hotel
use the maps in the introduction
or look for establishments with the sign

In this guide
a symbol or a character,
printed in ***red*** *or* ***black****, in light or* ***bold*** *type,*
does not have the same meaning.
Pay particular attention to the explanatory pages.

VENICE (VENEZIA) *30100* P 562 F 19 *G. Venice – pop. 275 368.*

See : *St. Marks Square★★★* KZ : *Basilica★★★* LZ – *Doges Palace★★★* LZ – *Campanile★★* : ※★★ KLZ **Q** – *Correr Museum★★* KZ **M** – *Bridge of Sighs★★* LZ.
Santa Maria della Salute★★ DV – *St. Giorgio Maggiore★* : ※★★★ *from campanile* FV – *St. Zanipolo★★* LX – *Santa Maria Gloriosa dei Frari★★★* BTU – *St. Zaccaria★★* LZ – *Interior decoration★★ by Veronese in the Church of St. Sebastiano* BV – *Ceiling★ of the Church of St. Pantaleone* BU – *Santa Maria dei Miracoli★* KLX – *St. Francesco della Vigna★* FT – *Ghetto★★* BT.
Scuola di St. Rocco★★★ BU – *Scuola di St. Giorgio degli Schiavoni★★★* FU – *Scuola dei Carmini★* BV – *Scuola di St. Marco★* LX – *Palazzo Labia★★* BT – *Murano★★ : Glass Museum★, Church of Santi Maria e Donato★★ – Burano★★ – Torcello★★ : mosaics★★ in the basilica of Santa Maria Assunta.*
Grand Canal★★★ : Rialto Bridge★★ KY – *Ca' d'Oro★★★* JX – *Academy of Fine Arts★★★* BV – *Ca' Rezzonico★★* BV – *Ca' Dario★* DV – *Grassi Palace★* BV – *Peggy Guggenheim Collection★★ in Palace Venier dei Leoni* DV – *Ca' Pesaro★* JX.

18 *(closed Monday) at Lido Alberoni ✉ 30011 ☎ 041 731333, Fax 041 731339, 15 mn by boat and 9 km;*

18 *et* 9 *Cà della Nave (closed Tuesday) at Martellago ✉ 30030 ☎ 041 5401555, Fax 041 5401926, North-West : 12 km;*

27 *Villa Condulmer (closed Monday), at Mogliano Veneto ✉ 30020 ☎ 041 457062, Fax 041 457062, North : 17 km.*

✈ *Marco Polo of Tessera, North-East : 13 km ☎ 041 2606111 – Alitalia, via Sansovino 3 Mestre-Venezia ✉ 30175 ☎ 041 2581111, Fax 041 2581246.*

⛴ *to Lido San Nicolò from piazzale Roma (Tronchetto) daily (30 mn); to isola di Pellestrina-Santa Maria del Mare from Lido Alberoni daily (10 mn).*

⛴ *to Punta Sabbioni from Riva degli Schiavoni daily (40 mn) ; to islands of Burano (30 mn), Torcello (40 mn), Murano (1 h 10 mn) from Punta Sabbioni daily; to islands of Murano (10 mn), Burano (45 mn), Torcello (50 mn) from Fondamenta Nuove dailyto Treporti di Cavallino from Fondamenta Nuove daily (1 h); to Venezia-Fondamenta Nuove from Treporti di Cavallino daily (1 h) to islands of Murano (50 mn), Burano (15 mn), Torcello (5 mn) daily – Information : Actv, Cannaregio 3935 ✉ 30131 ☎ 041 2722111, Fax 041 5207135.*

ℹ *calle Ascensione-San Marco 71/f ✉ 30124 ☎ 041 5297811, Fax 041 5230399 – Santa Lucia Railway station ✉ 30121 ☎ 041 5298727, Fax 041 5281246 – Marco Polo Airport ☎ 041 5298711.*

Roma 528 ① – Bologna 152 ① – Milano 267 ① – Trieste 158 ①

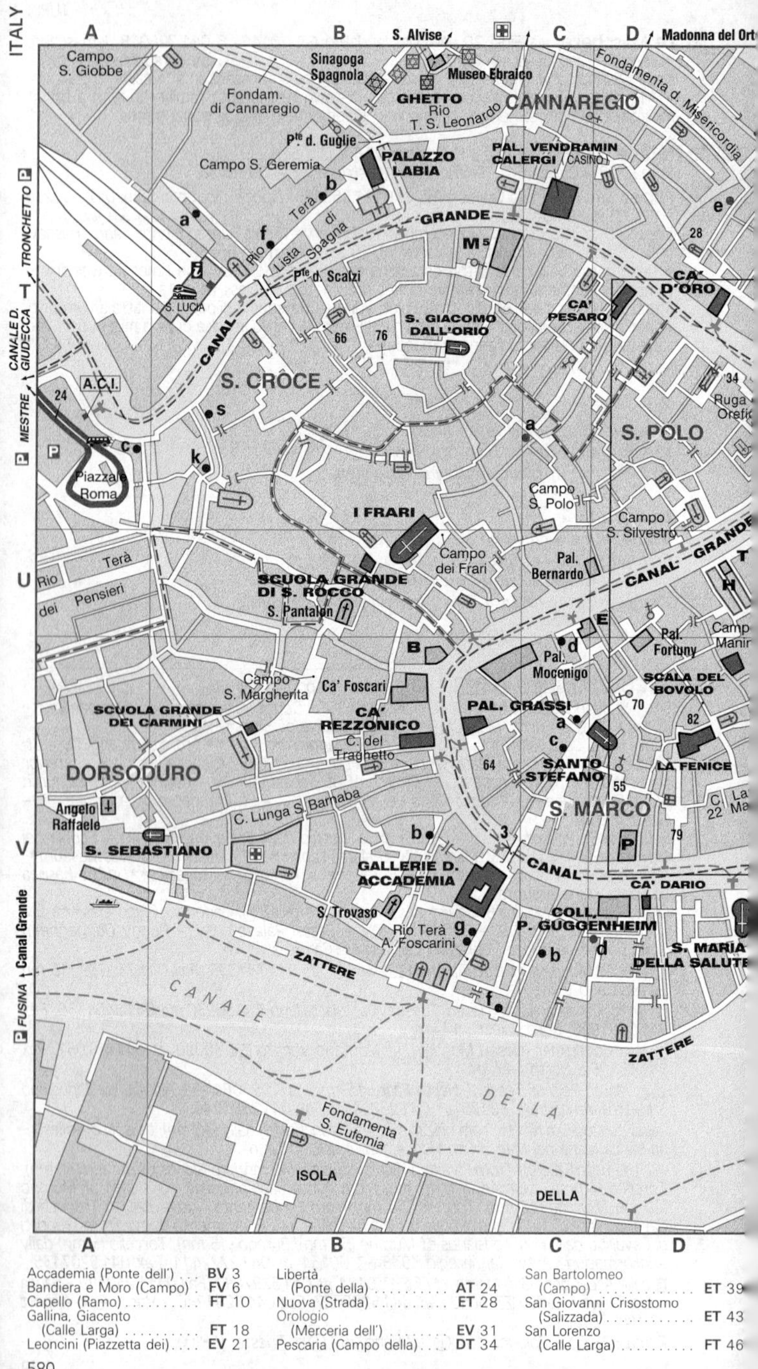

Accademia (Ponte dell')	**BV** 3	Libertà (Ponte della)	**AT** 24	San Bartolomeo (Campo)	**ET** 39
Bandiera e Moro (Campo)	**FV** 6	Nuova (Strada)	**ET** 28	San Giovanni Crisostomo (Salizzada)	**ET** 43
Capello (Ramo)	**FT** 10	Orologio (Merceria dell')	**EV** 31	San Lorenzo (Calle Larga)	**FT** 46
Gallina, Giacento (Calle Larga)	**FT** 18	Pescaria (Campo della)	**DT** 34		
Leoncini (Piazzetta dei)	**EV** 21				

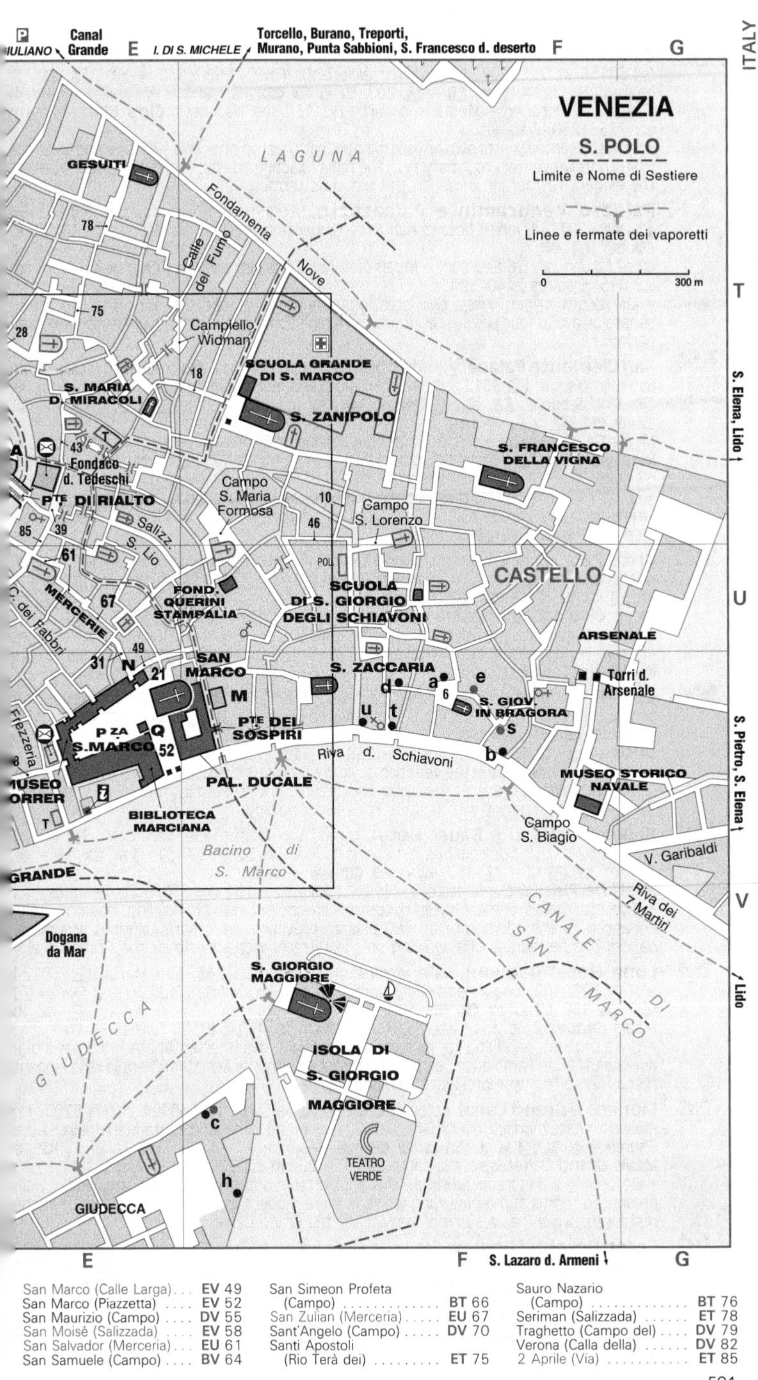

VENEZIA
S. POLO
Limite e Nome di Sestiere
Linee e fermate dei vaporetti
0
300 m
Canal Grande
I. DI S. MICHELE
Torcello, Burano, Treporti, Murano, Punta Sabbioni, S. Francesco d. deserto
LAGUNA
GESUITI
Fondamenta Nove
Calle del Fumo
Campiello Widman
SCUOLA GRANDE DI S. MARCO
S. ZANIPOLO
S. MARIA D. MIRACOLI
Fondaco d. Tedeschi
Pte DI RIALTO
Campo S. Maria Formosa
Campo S. Lorenzo
Salizz. S. Lio
MERCERIE
C. dei Fabbri
FOND. QUERINI STAMPALIA
SCUOLA DI S. GIORGIO DEGLI SCHIAVONI
CASTELLO
S. FRANCESCO DELLA VIGNA
ARSENALE
Torri d. Arsenale
S. ZACCARIA
S. GIOV. IN BRAGORA
SAN MARCO
Pte DEL SOSPIRI
P ZA S.MARCO
Frezzeria
MUSEO CORRER
PAL. DUCALE
BIBLIOTECA MARCIANA
Riva d. Schiavoni
MUSEO STORICO NAVALE
Campo S. Biagio
V. Garibaldi
Riva dei 7 Martiri
Bacino di S. Marco
GRANDE
Dogana da Mar
CANALE DI SAN MARCO
S. GIORGIO MAGGIORE
ISOLA DI S. GIORGIO MAGGIORE
TEATRO VERDE
GIUDECCA
S. Elena, Lido
S. Pietro, S. Elena
Lido
S. Lazaro d. Armeni
E
F
G
T
U
V

Cipriani, isola della Giudecca 10, 5 minutes by private shuttle from San Marco's pier ✉ 30133 ☎ 041 5207744, *info@hotelcipriani.it, Fax 041 5203930*, ≤, heated, – 200. AE VISA. FV h
2 April-24 October – **Meals** a la carte 86/130 see also rest. ***Cip's Club*** – **70 rm** 775/1250, 7 suites.
◆ Situated serenely in its own private gardens with heated pool, this exclusive and luxurious grand hotel never fails to satisfy even the most exacting guests. Two dining options ; either the elegant restaurant inside, or the romantic terrace.

Palazzo Vendramin e Palazzetto, isola della Giudecca 10 ✉ 30133 ☎ 041 5207744, *info@hotelcipriani.it*, ≤ Giudecca canal and San Marco – . AE VISA. FV c
closed 4 January-26 February – **Meals** (see hotel **Cipriani** and **Cip's Club** below) – **10 rm** 815, 5 suites 2440/3945.
◆ Of recent origin, these two prestigious annexes of the Cipriani offer the atmosphere of a luxurious private residence, with high staffing levels to ensure maximum pampering.

San Clemente Palace, isola di San Clemente 1, 10 minutes by private shuttle from San Marco's pier ✉ 30124 ☎ 041 2445001, *sanclemente@thi.it, Fax 041 2445800*, ≤, Golf 3 buche, heated, rm, – 450. AE VISA JCB. rest
Meals ***Ca' del Frati*** Rest. *(closed Monday)* (dinner only) a la carte 88/113 ***Le Maschere*** Rest. a la carte 76/98 and ***Gli Arazzi*** Rest. a la carte 70/92 – **205 rm** 467,50/480, 32 suites.
◆ Luxury and the highest standards of comfort pervade throughout this charming establishment, located on an island 15 minutes by boat from Piazza San Marco. Splendid view from the Cà dei Frati restaurant.

Gritti Palace, campo Santa Maria del Giglio 2467, San Marco ✉ 30124 ☎ 041 794611, *grittipalace@luxurycollection.com, Fax 041 5200942*, ≤ Grand Canal, – rm, . AE VISA JCB. JZ a
Meals ***Club del Doge*** Rest. a la carte 110/160 – 50 – **82 rm** 819, 9 suites.
◆ The exclusive charm of bygone days in this delightful jewel of the Venetian hotel scene ; effusive yet discreet in its hospitality and luxury. Fine fabrics, marble and wooden ceilings in the very elegant restaurant.

Danieli, riva degli Schiavoni 4196, Castello ✉ 30122 ☎ 041 5226480, *danieli@luxurycollection.com, Fax 041 5200208*, ≤ San Marco Canal, – – 150. AE VISA JCB. LZ a
Meals a la carte 100/135 – 50 – **233 rm** 438/712, 12 suites.
◆ The sumptuous lobby in the Venetian-style covered courtyard, once a market for oriental spices and textiles, prepares the visitor for this unique and charming hotel. Fine views from the rooftop restaurant with terrace for summer dining.

Bauer Il Palazzo e Bauer Hotel, campo San Moisè 1459, San Marco ✉ 30124 ☎ 041 5207022, *booking@bauervenezia.it, Fax 041 5207557*, – rm, – 150. AE VISA JCB. KZ h
Meals ***De Pisis*** Rest. a la carte 81/111 – 41,80 – **191 rm** 500/600, 49 suites.
◆ The prestigious original hotel, occupying an opulent historic building, has now been enhanced by the addition of an 18C palazzo providing even more luxurious accommodation. The restaurant offers dining on the terrace, with views over the Grand Canal.

Luna Hotel Baglioni, calle larga dell'Ascensione 1243, San Marco ✉ 30124 ☎ 041 5289840, *luna.venezia@baglionihotels.com, Fax 041 5287160*, – – 150. AE VISA JCB. KZ p
Meals ***Canova*** Rest. a la carte 65/87 – **109 rm** 490/520, 20 suites.
◆ Once probably a lodging for pilgrims and templars, this unostentatious hotel has a dignified and refined ambience ; early-18C frescoed ceiling by School of Tiepolo. The elegant restaurant offers well presented eclectic cuisine.

Monaco e Grand Canal, calle Vallaresso 1332, San Marco ✉ 30124 ☎ 041 5200211, *malibox@hotelmonaco.it, Fax 041 5200501*, ≤ Grand Canal and Santa Maria della Salute Church – . AE VISA JCB. KZ e
Meals ***Grand Canal*** Rest. a la carte 57/78 – **99 rm** 304/532, 8 suites.
◆ Occupying a panoramic position, this comfortable hotel has a refined ambience ; well-presented rooms and a new wing which is more modern in style. Simple elegance in the restaurant which has a summer terrace on the Grand Canal.

Grand Hotel dei Dogi, Fondamenta Madonna dell'Orto 3500, Cannaregio ✉ 30121 ☎ 041 2208111, *reservation@deidogi.boscolo.com, Fax 041 722278*, – – 50. AE VISA JCB by Madonna dell'Orto DT
Meals ***Il Giardino di Luca*** Rest. a la carte 69/87 – **68 rm** 522/627, 2 suites.
◆ Off the tourist trail, this 17C palazzo set in its own grounds overlooking the lagoon is now a fine hotel with elegant airy interiors. A simple yet stylish look in the restaurant, with exposed beams and stone floors.

VENEZIA

Avvocati (Calle degli) ..... JZ 4	Pio X (Salizzada) .... KY 37	San Maurizio (Campo) .... JZ 55
Beccarie (Campo delle) ... JX 7	Rialto (Ponte di) .... KY	San Moisé (Salizzada) .... KZ 58
Canonica (Calle di) .... LZ 9	San Bartolomeo (Campo) .... KY 39	San Salvador (Merceria) ... KY 61
Franceschi (Rio Terà dei) .. KX 13	San Giovanni (Ruga Vecchia) .... JX 42	San Zulian (Merceria) ..... KY 67
Frezzeria .... KZ 15	San Giovanni Crisostomo (Salizzada) .... KX 43	Santa Maria Formosa (Calle Lunga) .... LY 72
Frezzeria (Piscina di) ...... KZ 16	San Lorenzo (Calle Larga) .... LY 46	Santa Maria Formosa (Ruga Giuffa) .... LY 73
Gallina, Giacento (Calle Larga) .... LX 18	San Marco (Calle Larga) ... LYZ 49	Traghetto (Campo del) .... JZ 79
Leoncini (Piazzetta dei) .... LZ 21	San Marco (Piazza) .... KZ	Verona (Calle della) ...... JZ 82
Mazzini (Calle Larga) ..... KY 25	San Marco (Piazzetta) .... LZ 52	2 Aprile (Via) .... KY 85
Orefici (Ruga degli) .... KX 30		22 Marzo (Calle Larga) ... JZ
Orologio (Merceria dell') ... KY 31		
Pescaria (Campo della) .... JX 34		

Metropole, riva degli Schiavoni 4149, Castello ✉ 30122 ✆ 041 5205044, *venice@hotelmetropole.com, Fax 041 5223679,* ≤ San Marco Canal, 🏛, 🏛, ⚓ – |‡| ▤ TV ✆ – ♿ 100. AE 💳 ⓓ MC VISA JCB. ✗ rest FV t

Meals *Met* Rest. a la carte 65/80 – **66 rm** ☕ 390/475, 4 suites.

◆ A prestigious location for this smart hotel on the lagoon, which has an unusual collection of antique objects (crucifixes, clocks, armour). Restaurant with pleasant atmosphere and eclectic menu.

Londra Palace, riva degli Schiavoni 4171 ✉ 30122 ☎ 041 5200533, *info@hotelondra.it, Fax 041 5225032,* ≤ San Marco Canal, – . AE VISA JCB. LZ t
Meals ***Do Leoni*** Rest *(closed January)* (booking essential) a la carte 54/84 – **53 rm** ☕ 585.
◆ An abundance of charm and fine detail in this recently refurbished Neo-classical-style hotel, which prides itself on having 100 windows overlooking the lagoon. Restaurant with panoramic summer dining terrace on the lagoon.

The Westin Europa e Regina, corte Barozzi 2159, San Marco ✉ 30124 ☎ 041 2400001, *RES075.europaregina@westin.com, Fax 041 5231533,* ≤ Grand Canal, – – 120. AE VISA JCB. rest KZ d
Meals ***La Cusina*** Rest. a la carte 90/130 – ☕ 52 – **175 rm** 405/899, 10 suites.
◆ Marble, damask, glass and stucco work adorn the opulent, spacious interiors of this hotel on the Grand Canal, which, following refitting, offers high standards of comfort throughout. Open kitchen off the richly decorated restaurant ; canalside summer terrace.

Sofitel, Fondamenta Condulmer 245, Santa Croce ✉ 30135 ☎ 041 710400, *sofitel.venezia@accor-hotels.it, Fax 041 710394,* – rm, – 50. AE VISA JCB. BT k
Meals a la carte 46/62 – **97 rm** ☕ 400/490.
◆ Near Piazzale Roma, this smart hotel has classic style and every modern convenience throughout. The charming restaurant, which has cork trees and plants, makes for an unexpected feature.

Ca' Pisani, rio terà Foscarini 979/a, Dorsoduro ✉ 30123 ☎ 041 2401411 and rest ☎ 041 2401425, *info@capisanihotel.it, Fax 041 2771061,* , roof-terrace solarium – rm, . AE VISA JCB. BV g
Meals ***La Rivista*** Rest. *(closed Monday)* a la carte 43/58 – **29 rm** ☕ 297/342.
◆ Occupying a 14C building, the ambience inside is that of the 1930s, with futurist artwork on the walls ; a bold and unusual combination at this design hotel. Polychrome marble, bamboo and red leather in the "wine and cheese bar".

Palazzo Sant'Angelo Sul Canal Grande without rest., San Marco 3488 ✉ 30124 ☎ 041 2411452, *palazzosantangelo@sinahotels.it, Fax 041 2411557,* – . AE VISA JCB CUV d
4 rm ☕ 423,50/484, 10 suites 594/627.
◆ In a small palazzo on the Grand Canal, this charming establishment has an intimate and understated ambience.

Colombina without rest., calle del Remedio 4416, Castello ✉ 30122 ☎ 041 2770525, *info@hotelcolombina.com, Fax 041 2776044,* – – 20. AE VISA JCB LY d
32 rm ☕ 360/395.
◆ Looking onto the Bridge of Sighs canal, this smart hotel offers all modern comforts and elegant Venetian décor ; ask for a room with a view of the bridge.

Locanda Vivaldi without rest., riva degli Schiavoni 4150/52, Castello ✉ 30122 ☎ 041 2770477, *info@locandavivaldi.it, Fax 041 2770489,* ≤ San Giorgio Island and lagoon, – – 50. AE VISA FV u
27 rm ☕ 310/440, suite.
◆ Next to the church of the Pieta, this building where Vivaldi once studied is now a genteel hotel with large rooms decorated in period style ; small panoramic terrace.

Concordia, calle larga San Marco 367 ✉ 30124 ☎ 041 5206866, *venezia@hotelconcordia.it, Fax 041 5206775,* ≤ San Marco Square – rm, . AE VISA. rest LZ r
Meals a la carte 39/64 – **56 rm** ☕ 326/345.
◆ Offering a unique view of the Basilica of St Mark from its windows, this refurbished hotel has elegant 18C Venetian-style rooms. The new restaurant looks onto Piazzetta dei Leoncini.

Giorgione, calle Larga dei Proverbi 4587, Cannaregio ✉ 30131 ☎ 041 5225810 and rest. ☎ 041 5221725, *giorgione@hotelgiorgione.com, Fax 041 5239092* – . AE VISA JCB. KX b
Meals ***Osteria Giorgione*** Rest. *(closed 1 to 15 July and Wednesday)* a la carte 30/49 – **76 rm** ☕ 105/360, 2 suites.
◆ Near the Ca' d'Oro, this smart hotel has a pleasant courtyard garden ; elegant antique furniture in both the public areas and the rooms.

Bellini without rest., lista di Spagna 116, Cannaregio ✉ 30121 ☎ 041 5242488, *reservation@bellini.boscolo.com, Fax 041 715193* – . AE VISA JCB. BT t
97 rm ☕ 400/450.
◆ This refined hotel near the station has high standards of service ; rooms ranging from simple to sumptuous, some with views of the Grand Canal.

Saturnia e International, calle larga 22 Marzo 2398, San Marco ✉ 30124 ✆ 041 5208377, *info@hotelsaturnia.it, Fax 041 5207131,* – rm, – 60. AE VISA JCB JZ n
Meals (see rest. **La Caravella** below) – **91 rm** 280/450.
◆ This delightful hotel, occupying a 14C patrician palace, has been run by the same family since 1908 ; period furnishings in the rooms and a sun deck with fine views.

Bisanzio without rest., calle della Pietà 3651, Castello ✉ 30122 ✆ 041 5203100, *email@bisanzio.com, Fax 041 5204114,* – . AE VISA JCB FV d
44 rm 250/290.
◆ In a quiet alley, this recently restored hotel is a successful fusion of ancient and modern ; smart interiors and welcoming rooms.

Savoia e Jolanda, riva degli Schiavoni 4187, Castello ✉ 30122 ✆ 041 5206644, *info@hotelsavoiajolanda.com, Fax 041 5207494,* ≤ San Marco Canal, – . AE VISA JCB. LZ x
Meals a la carte 33/64 (12 %) – **51 rm** 358/398, suite.
◆ Fine views over the Canale di San Marco and the island of San Giorgio from this attractively renovated hotel, occupying an 18C building ; richly elegant rooms. The fine restaurant also has a pleasant terrace.

Kette without rest., piscina San Moisè 2053, San Marco ✉ 30124 ✆ 041 5207766, *info@hotelkette.com, Fax 041 5228964,* – . AE VISA. JZ s
61 rm 330/350, 2 suites.
◆ Close to La Fenice, this completely restored hotel overlooks a canal ; furnished to a high standard throughout.

Rialto, riva del Ferro 5149, San Marco ✉ 30124 ✆ 041 5209166, *info@rialtohotel.com, Fax 041 5238958,* ≤ Rialto bridge, – . AE VISA JCB. KY v
Meals *(April-October)* a la carte 35/53 (12 %) – **79 rm** 206/232.
◆ A memorable view of the Rialto bridge from the windows of this elegant hotel with high service standards ; rooms in classic Venetian style. Modern restaurant and terrace looking onto the Grand Canal.

Gabrielli Sandwirth, riva degli Schiavoni 4110, Castello ✉ 30122 ✆ 041 5231580, *hotelgabrielli@libero.it, Fax 041 5209455,* , , – . AE VISA JCB. rest FV b
closed until 12 February – **Meals** 29/44 – **100 rm** 250/440.
◆ This genteel hotel in a historic palazzo on the lagoon has a terrace overlooking the Canale di San Marco, and a small courtyard garden, where meals are served during the summer.

Amadeus, lista di Spagna 227, Cannaregio ✉ 30121 ✆ 041 2206000 and rest ✆ 041 2206517, *htlamadeus@gardenahotels.it, Fax 041 2206020,* – , rest, – 120. AE VISA JCB. BT b
Meals ***Mirai*** Rest. *(closed Monday)* (dinner only) Japanese rest. a la carte 35/50 – **63 rm** 335.
◆ Located close to Santa Lucia station, this smart hotel has a garden and function room ; 18C Venetian-style furnishings in the rooms. Highly regarded and popular Japanese restaurant.

Montecarlo, calle dei Specchieri 463, San Marco ✉ 30124 ✆ 041 5207144, *mail@venicehotelmontecarlo.com, Fax 041 5207789* – . AE VISA JCB LY c
Meals (see rest. **Antico Pignolo** below) – **48 rm** 210/290.
◆ Near Piazza San Marco, this hotel offers excellent service ; after a refit the rooms are of a good standard and tastefully decorated in traditional Venetian style.

Cà dei Conti without rest., fondamenta Remedio 4429, Castello ✉ 30122 ✆ 041 2770500, *info@cadeiconti.com, Fax 041 2770727,* – . AE VISA JCB LY a
15 rm 350/413.
◆ Near San Marco, this charming canalside hotel offers very comfortable accommodation furnished in 18C Venetian style.

Al Ponte dei Sospiri without rest., calle larga San Marco 381 ✉ 30124 ✆ 041 2411160, *info@alpontedeisospiri.com, Fax 041 2410268* – . AE VISA JCB LZ e
8 rm 320/460.
◆ This newly opened hotel is in a 17C palazzo in a delightful position ; rooms with space to relax in, and rich fabrics and antique furniture.

Abbazia without rest., calle Priuli dei Cavalletti 68, Cannaregio ✉ 30121 ✆ 041 717333, *abbazia@iol.it, Fax 041 717949,* – . AE VISA JCB. BT a
39 rm 225/250.
◆ Occupying a restored Carmelite Friary, this charming hotel has a simple style, as evident in its bar, formerly a refectory with choir stalls and pulpit.

Ala without rest., campo Santa Maria del Giglio 2494, San Marco ✉ 30124 ☎ 041 5208333, *info@hotelala.it, Fax 041 5206390,* – AE MC VISA JCB. JZ e
closed 6 to 21 January – **85 rm** 170/320.
◆ Situated in a little square not far from San Marco, this recently refurbished hotel has comfortable rooms and a small collection of arms and armour.

San Zulian without rest., campo de la Guerra 527, San Marco ✉ 30124 ☎ 041 5225872, *h.sanzulian@iol.it, Fax 041 5232265* – AE MC VISA JCB KY h
22 rm 205/230.
◆ A warm, welcoming hotel in the heart of the city which has recently been well refurbished ; good service and spacious well-equipped rooms with typical Venetian furnishings.

Panada without rest., calle dei Specchieri 646, San Marco ✉ 30124 ☎ 041 5209088, *info@hotelpanada.com, Fax 041 5209619* – AE MC VISA JCB LY v
48 rm 200/250.
◆ A very central, charming hotel with attractive public areas such as its characteristic bar with wood panelling and antique mirrors ; welcoming period-style rooms.

Santa Chiara without rest., fondamenta Santa Chiara 548, Santa Croce ✉ 30125 ☎ 041 5206955, *conalve@doge.it, Fax 041 5228799* – AE MC VISA. AT c
40 rm 137/220.
◆ Unique in Venice, this hotel is accessible by car and overlooks the Grand Canal. Welcoming rooms with classical furnishings ; newer, more spacious accommodation in the annexe.

Gardena without rest., fondamenta dei Tolentini 239, Santa Croce ✉ 30135 ☎ 041 2205000, *info@gardenahotels.it, Fax 041 2205020,* – AE MC VISA JCB. BT s
22 rm 175/268.
◆ Bright contemporary wall paintings decorate the public areas and rooms of this recently refurbished establishment, occupying a historic canalside building.

Pensione Accademia-Villa Maravage without rest., fondamenta Bollani 1058, Dorsoduro ✉ 30123 ☎ 041 5237846, *info@pensioneaccademia.it, Fax 041 5239152,* – AE MC VISA JCB. BV b
27 rm 125/233.
◆ Situated in a pretty garden among the alleys and canals of old Venice, this 17C villa has a charm all of its own ; spacious well-presented interior decorated in period style.

American without rest., fondamenta Bragadin 628, Dorsoduro ✉ 30123 ☎ 041 5204733, *reception@hotelamerican.com, Fax 041 5204048,* – AE MC VISA. CV b
30 rm 220/250.
◆ A quiet canalside setting, smart public areas with wood panels and classical furnishings and rooms in traditional Venetian style ; many with balconies overlooking the water.

Belle Arti without rest., rio terà Foscarini 912/A, Dorsoduro ✉ 30123 ☎ 041 5226230 *info@hotelbellearti.com, Fax 041 5280043,* – AE MC VISA. BV g
65 rm 145/205.
◆ Near the Accademia, this comfortable modern hotel has a pleasant garden and a spacious interior ; the rooms offer every modern comfort.

Tre Archi without rest., fondamenta di Cannaregio 923, Cannaregio ✉ 30121 ☎ 041 5244356, *info@hoteltrearchi.com, Fax 041 5244356,* – AE MC VISA JCB BT
24 rm 210/240.
◆ In Cannaregio where tourists are fewer and the ambience is authentically Venetian this recently opened hotel has a courtyard garden, period furnishings and comfortable rooms.

La Calcina, fondamenta zattere ai Gesuati 780, Dorsoduro ✉ 30123 ☎ 041 5206466 *la.calcina@libero.it, Fax 041 5227045,* ≤ canal and Giudecca island, – AE MC VISA JCB. BV
Meals *(closed Monday)* a la carte 40/46 – **29 rm** 106/182, 4 suites.
◆ The relaxed atmosphere of old Venice pervades this charming hotel offering subtly understated hospitality ; bar with fine terrace on the Giudecca and a small, pleasant restaurant with canal views.

Santo Stefano without rest., campo Santo Stefano 2957, San Marco ✉ 30124 ☎ 041 5200166, *info@hotelsantostefanovenezia.com, Fax 041 5224460* – AE MC VISA CV
11 rm 220/280.
◆ Occupying a 15C tower in Campo Santo Stefano, this atmospheric hotel has very smart rooms with painted furniture and Murano glass lamps.

Canaletto without rest., calle de la Malvasia 5487, Castello ✉ 30122 ✆ 041 5220518, *info@hotelcanaletto.com, Fax 041 5229023* – ▤ TV. AE ⊕ ⓓ ⓜ VISA KY b
38 rm ☕ 220/240.
◆ A comfortable hotel named after the famous artist who once lived here ; located between the Rialto and Piazza San Marco, the refurbished accommodation has period furnishings.

Locanda la Corte without rest., calle Bressana 6317, Castello ✉ 30122 ✆ 041 2411300, *info@locandalacorte.it, Fax 041 2415982* – ⇎ ▤ TV ✆ ♿. ⊕ ⓜ VISA
18 rm ☕ 120/176.
◆ Takes its name from its picturesque courtyard, where breakfast is served in summer, rooms decorated in classic Venetian style. LY p

Campiello without rest., calle del Vin 4647, Castello ✉ 30122 ✆ 041 5239682, *campiello@hcampiello.it*, Fax 041 5205798 – ▤ ▤ TV. AE ⊕ ⓓ ⓜ VISA. ✗ LZ b
15 rm ☕ 130/190.
◆ Close to Piazza San Marco and San Zaccaria, this small genteel hotel is run by a polite and efficient management ; limited public areas and well-presented rooms.

Caffè Quadri, piazza San Marco 120 ✉ 30124 ✆ 041 5222105, *quadri@quadriveni ce.com, Fax 041 5208041,* ≤ – ⇎ ▤. AE ⊕ ⓓ ⓜ VISA. ✗ KZ y
closed Monday November-March – **Meals** (booking essential) a la carte 75/110.
◆ Situated in the smartest part of the city, this historic establishment boasts a wealth of stucco work, Murano glass and fine fabrics ; fine Venetian and other Italian cuisine.

Osteria da Fiore, calle del Scaleter 2202/A, San Polo ✉ 30125 ✆ 041 721308, *Fax 041 721343* – ▤. AE ⊕ ⓓ ⓜ VISA JCB CT a
closed August, 25 December-15 January, Sunday and Monday – **Meals** (booking essential) seafood a la carte 76/112.
◆ Perennially fashionable and popular with locals and tourists alike, this welcoming modern restaurant serves original interpretations of traditional seafood dishes.
Spec. Triglie con fichi e menta (spring-summer). Spaghettoni pugliesi con mazzancolle e uva fragola. Moeche cotte a vapore.

La Caravella - Hotel Saturnia e International, calle Larga 22 Marzo 2397, San Marco ✉ 30124 ✆ 041 5208901, *caravella@hotelsaturnia.it, Fax 041 5205858,* 🏠, Typical rest. – ▤. AE ⊕ ⓓ ⓜ VISA JCB. ✗ JZ n
Meals (booking essential) a la carte 62/83.
◆ The interior of this establishment is reminiscent of a galleon's lower decks with wood panelling everywhere ; meals also served on the outside terrace. Traditional dishes.

La Colomba, piscina di Frezzeria 1665, San Marco ✉ 30124 ✆ 041 5221175, *colomba@sanmarcohotels.com, Fax 041 5221468,* 🏠 – ⇎ ▤ – 🏛 60. AE ⊕ ⓓ ⓜ VISA JCB. ✗ KZ m
closed Wednesday and Thursday lunch except May-Ocotber – **Meals** a la carte 62/98 (15 %).
◆ Creative interpretations of traditional fare in this contemporary atmosphere ; walls hung with biennale artwork.

Antico Pignolo, calle dei Specchieri 451, San Marco ✉ 30124 ✆ 041 5228123, *anticopignolo@libero.it, Fax 041 5209007,* 🏠, ⚓ – ⇎ ▤. AE ⊕ ⓓ ⓜ VISA JCB. ✗
Meals a la carte 63/99 (12 %). LY v
◆ A classically elegant restaurant at its best in the evenings ; traditional Venetian cuisine along seasonal lines. Good wine-list.

Fiaschetteria Toscana, San Giovanni Grisostomo 5719, Cannaregio ✉ 30121 ✆ 041 5285281, *Fax 041 5285521,* 🏠 – ▤. AE ⊕ ⓓ ⓜ VISA JCB. ✗ KX p
closed 24 July-13 August, Monday lunch and Tuesday – **Meals** a la carte 43/60 🍇.
◆ Good service and a lively ambience in this restaurant, which has nothing to do with Tuscany, serving robust meat and fish dishes. Outside dining in summer.

Do Forni, calle dei Specchieri 457/468, San Marco ✉ 30124 ✆ 041 5237729, *info@doforni.it, Fax 041 5288132* – ⇎ ▤. AE ⊕ ⓓ ⓜ VISA JCB LY c
Meals (booking essential) a la carte 50/75 (12 %) 🍇.
◆ This long established restaurant is popular with tourists and office workers alike ; a choice of rooms and ambiences, from intimate to spacious. Traditional local cuisine.

Cip's Club - Hotel Cipriani, fondamenta de le Zitelle 10, Giudecca ✉ 30133 ✆ 041 5207744, *info@hotelcipriani.it, Fax 041 2408519,* 🏠 – ▤. AE ⊕ ⓓ ⓜ VISA. ✗
closed 4 January-26 February – **Meals** a la carte 85/106. FV c
◆ This restaurant has an informal yet elegant atmosphere and in summer offers dining outside on the Giudecca. Traditional meat and fish dishes, with Venetian specialities.

Hostaria da Franz, fondamenta San Giuseppe 754, Castello ✉ 30122 ✆ 041 5220861, *Fax 041 2419278,* 🏠 – ▤. AE ⊕ ⓜ VISA. ✗
closed 11 November-24 December and 11 January-11 February – **Meals** seafood a la carte 47/68. by riva dei 7 Martiri
◆ Situated away from the tourist trail in the Castello district, this recently reopened family-run restaurant has a rustic ambience ; seafood cuisine.

XX **Al Covo,** campiello della Pescaria 3968, Castello ✉ 30122 ☎ 041 5223812, *Fax 041 5223812,* – ■. FV s
closed 15 December-15 January, Wednesday and Thursday – **Meals** a la carte 55/75.
◆ Close to Riva degli Schiavoni, this elegantly rustic establishment is very much in vogue and popular with tourists ; light lunchtime dishes and richer cuisine in the evening.

XX **Al Graspo de Ua,** calle dei Bombaseri 5094/A, San Marco ✉ 30124 ☎ 041 5200150, *graspo.deua@flashnet.it, Fax 041 5209389* – ■. AE VISA JCB. KY d
closed Monday – **Meals** (booking essential) a la carte 69/83 (12 %).
◆ A historic Venetian restaurant being restored to its former glory by an enthusiastic and competent new management ; meat and fish dishes.

XX **Le Bistrot de Venise,** calle dei Fabbri 4685, San Marco ✉ 30124 ☎ 041 5236651, *info@bistrotdevenise.com, Fax 041 5202244,* – ■. VISA KY e
Meals a la carte 40/64 (15 %).
◆ A cosy ambience and closely spaced tables in this restaurant of character ; traditional cuisine and a tempting wine list (some available by the glass).

XX **Ai Mercanti,** corte Coppo 4346/A, San Marco ✉ 30124 ☎ 041 5238269, *info_aimercanti@libero.it, Fax 041 5238269,* – ■. VISA. KZ u
closed Sunday and Monday lunch – **Meals** a la carte 43/64.
◆ Centrally-located in a small and peaceful courtyard a little away from the main tourist trail, this smart, unostentatious restaurant mainly serves seafood.

XX **Ai Gondolieri,** fondamenta de l'Ospedaleto 366, Dorsoduro ✉ 30123 ☎ 041 5286396, *aigond@gpnet.it, Fax 041 5210075* – . AE VISA JCB. DV d
closed Tuesday – **Meals** (dinner only July-August) (booking essential for dinner) beef dishes only a la carte 50/69.
◆ Next to the Guggenheim, this rustic establishment with wood-panelled walls concentrates on serving classic meat dishes from the Veneto region.

X **L'Osteria di Santa Marina,** campo Santa Marina 5911, Castello ✉ 30122 ☎ 041 5285239, *ostsmarina@libero.it, Fax 041 5285239,* – ■. VISA. LY m
closed 18 August-4 September, 7 to 25 January, Sunday and Monday lunch – **Meals** seafood a la carte 41/62.
◆ A dedicated young management run this restaurant which, despite its no frills appearance, serves good, imaginative seafood alongside more traditional fare.

X **Vini da Gigio,** fondamenta San Felice 3628/a, Cannaregio ✉ 30131 ☎ 041 5285140, *info@vinidagigio.com, Fax 041 5228597,* Inn serving food – ■. AE VISA DT e
closed 15 to 31 August, 15 to 31 January and Monday – **Meals** (booking essential) a la carte 36/54.
◆ Located in the Cannaregio district, this simple restaurant has an informal rustic atmosphere with open kitchen serving meat and seafood ; good wine-list.

X **Trattoria alla Madonna,** calle della Madonna 594, San Polo ✉ 30125 ☎ 041 5223824, *Fax 041 5210167,* Venetian trattoria – AE VISA JCB. JY e
closed 4 to 17 August, 24 December-January and Wednesday – **Meals** a la carte 29/40 (12 %).
◆ Near the Rialto, this traditional Venetian trattoria is always busy ; a simple yet animated environment in which to savour typical local dishes.

X **Anice Stellato,** fondamenta della Sensa 3272, Cannaregio ✉ 30121 ☎ 041 720744 – ■. VISA by fondamenta della Misericordia CDT
closed 3 weeks in August, 24 to 31 January, Monday and Tuesday – **Meals** (booking essential) a la carte 35/50.
◆ Off the beaten track, this restaurant is popular with Venetians, offering authentic seafood cuisine. Informal ambience and service ; friendly and efficient family management.

X **Alle Testiere,** calle del Mondo Novo 5801, Castello ✉ 30122 ☎ 041 5227220, *Fax 041 5227220,* Inn serving food – ■. VISA. LY g
closed 25 July-25 August, 24 December-12 January, Sunday and Monday – **Meals** (booking essential) seafood a la carte 46/61.
◆ This refined "bacaro" has simple wooden tables and a pleasant, informal atmosphere ; seafood only, prepared with care and imagination.

X **Osteria al Bacco,** fondamenta Capuzine 3054, Cannaregio ✉ 30121 ☎ 041 721415, *Fax 041 717493,* *Inn serving food* – AE VISA JCB.
closed 10 to 25 August, 10 to 25 January and Monday – **Meals** (booking essential) a la carte 30/42. by via Fondamenta della Misericordia CDT
◆ Away from the tourist trail in the unspoilt Cannaregio district, this restaurant retains its original early 20C fittings ; Venetian seafood dishes.

in Lido : *15 mn by boat from San Marco KZ – ✉ 30126 Venezia Lido. Car access throughout the year from Tronchetto.*
(June-September) Gran Viale S. M. Elisabetta 6 ☎ 041 5298711 :

The Westin Excelsior, lungomare Marconi 41 ☎ 041 5260201, *Fax 041 5267276*, ←, rm, – 600. AE VISA JCB
15 March-20 November – **Meals** a la carte 75/110 – **196 rm** 675/846, 19 suites.
◆ In a beachfront location, this crenellated, vaguely Moorish style edifice has opulent charm and has been fashionable since opening in 1908. The elegant restaurant is in keeping with the splendour of the entire hotel.

Villa Mabapa, riviera San Nicolò 16 ☎ 041 5260590, *info@villamabapa.com, Fax 041 5269441*, – – 60. AE VISA JCB. rest
Meals *(closed lunch except 15 June-October)* a la carte 43/59 – **70 rm** 195/305, suite.
◆ This genteel and spacious hotel occupies a 1930s villa and is directly managed by the proprietors ; tastefully furnished rooms. Classically elegant restaurant ; summer dining outside.

Quattro Fontane, via 4 Fontane 16 ☎ 041 5260227, *Info@quattrofontane.com, Fax 041 5260726*, – – 40. AE VISA. rest
April-14 November – **Meals** a la carte 71/93 – **59 rm** 380/400.
◆ The evidence of over 60 years of collecting and travelling by its owners is on show throughout this hotel. A large and pleasant garden where guests may dine in summer.

Hungaria Palace Hotel, Gran Viale S.M. Elisabetta 28 ☎ 041 2420060, *info@hungaria.it, Fax 041 5264111*, – rm, – 60. AE VISA JCB. rest
Meals (dinner only) a la carte 38/90 (15 %) – **79 rm** 290/330, 3 suites.
◆ One of the great names of the Lido, this establishment has, after a period of closure and extensive refurbishment, returned to centre stage of the Venetian hotel scene ; lots of charm and atmosphere. Elegant restaurant with classic dishes and plenty of seafood.

Le Boulevard without rest., Gran Viale S. M. Elisabetta 41 ☎ 041 5261990, *boulevard@leboulevard.com, Fax 041 5261917*, – . AE VISA JCB
45 rm 230/360.
◆ Occupying a period building, this centrally located hotel has undergone recent refitting ; elegant public areas and functional rooms.

Ca' del Borgo without rest., piazza delle Erbe 8, località Malamocco South : 6 km ☎ 041 770749, *Fax 041 770744*, ←, – . AE VISA JCB
15 February-15 November – **7 rm** 259.
◆ The cosy charm of a private residence pervades this hotel, formerly a 16C aristocratic villa ; furnished with antiques and fine fabrics throughout.

Villa Tiziana without rest., via Andrea Gritti 3 ☎ 041 5261152, *info@hoteltiziana.com, Fax 041 5262145* – . AE VISA.
16 rm 215/260.
◆ This peaceful hotel in a refitted modern building has superior standards of comfort throughout (full courtesy pack, including bathrobes).

Trattoria Favorita, via Francesco Duodo 33 ☎ 041 5261626, *Fax 041 5261626*, – . AE VISA JCB
closed 15 January-15 February, Monday and Tuesday lunch – **Meals** seafood a la carte 40/53.
◆ This family-run rustic trattoria has two welcoming rooms and space outside for summer dining ; seafood cuisine and Venetian specialities.

Al Vecio Cantier, via della Droma 76, località Alberoni South : 10 km ✉ 30011 Alberoni ☎ 041 5268130, *Fax 041 5268130*, – AE VISA JCB.
closed November, January, Monday and Tuesday, June-September open Tuesday dinner- **Meals** (booking essential) seafood a la carte 32/66.
◆ A friendly welcome and informal ambience at this trattoria with nautical-themed décor ; extremely fresh good quality ingredients evident in its seafood dishes.

in Murano *10 mn by boat from Fondamenta Nuove* EFT *and 1 h 10 mn by boat from Punta Sabbioni – ✉ 30141 :*

Busa-alla Torre, piazza Santo Stefano 3 ☎ 041 739662, *Fax 041 739662*, – AE VISA JCB
Meals (lunch only) a la carte 30/46 (12 %).
◆ This appealingly rustic trattoria has lots of outdoor dining space in a charming little square with a well at its centre ; seafood and Venetian specialities.

Ai Frati, Fondamenta Venier 4 ☎ 041 736694, *Fax 041 739346*, – VISA
closed 15 days July, 15 days February and Thursday – **Meals** a la carte 40/50 (12 %).
◆ In business as a bar since the mid-19C and serving food for half a century, this seafood trattoria is an important feature of Murano life ; summer dining on the canal terrace.

in Burano *50 mn by boat from Fondamenta Nuove* EFT *and 32 mn by boat from Punta Sabbioni – ✉ 30012 :*

✗ **Da Romano,** via Galuppi 221 ☎ 041 730030, *info@daromano, Fax 041 735217,* – AE VISA JCB
closed 15 December-5 February, Sunday dinner and Tuesday – **Meals** a la carte 40/56.
◆ Famed for its lace, the island of Burano has enjoyed this restaurant's cuisine for over 100 years. Contemporary art on the walls and flavoursome seafood.

✗ **Al Gatto Nero-da Ruggero,** Fondamenta della Giudecca 88 ☎ 041 730120, *Fax 041 735570,* , Typical trattoria – AE VISA
closed 15 to 30 November, 15 to 31 January and Monday – **Meals** a la carte 36/56.
◆ An informal and relaxed atmosphere in this classic trattoria with pleasant terrace ; Venetian dishes and seafood using only the finest ingredients.

in Torcello *45 mn by boat from Fondamenta Nuove* EFT *and 37 mn by boat from Punta Sabbioni – ✉ 30012 Burano :*

✗✗ **Locanda Cipriani,** piazza Santa Fosca 29 ☎ 041 730150, *info@locandacipriani.com, Fax 041 735433,* , – . AE VISA
closed January-15 February and Tuesday – **Meals** 41/75 and a la carte 60/75.
◆ This trattoria has a charming, old-fashioned ambience and a refined, traditional menu ; dining in the garden in summer is a delightful experience.

Isola Rizza *37050 Verona 562 G 15 – pop. 2 799.*

Roma 487 – Ferrara 91 – Mantova 55 – Padova 84 – Verona 27.

✗✗✗ ✿✿ **Perbellini,** via Muselle 11, exit highway 434 to Legnano ☎ 045 7135352, *ristorante@perbellini.com, Fax 045 7135899* – P. VISA
closed 8 to 31 August, 10 days January, Sunday dinner, Monday and Tuesday lunch ; July-August also Sunday lunch – **Meals** (booking essential) 55 (lunch only except Bank Holidays) 105 and a la carte 83/116.
◆ Creative seafood drawing on the quality local produce ; a gourmet's delight, particularly given its unlikely industrial location.
Spec. Colori e sapori del mare. Wafer al sesamo con tartare di branzino e caprino all'erba cipollina, senzazioni di liquirizia. Filetto rosa di manzo bollito al sale grosso e puré al limone.

Rubano *35030 562 F 17 – pop. 13 611 alt. 18.*

Roma 490 – Padova 8 – Venezia 49 – Verona 72 – Vicenza 27.

✗✗✗ ✿✿✿ **Le Calandre,** strada statale 11, località Sarmeola ☎ 049 630303, *alajmo@calandre.com, Fax 049 633000* – P. AE VISA.
closed 7 to 30 August, 1 to 21 January, Sunday and Monday – **Meals** (booking essential) a la carte 70/110.
◆ A classically modern, bright environment, this restaurant is renowned for its attention to detail in the preparation of imaginative and interesting cuisine.
Spec. Cappuccino di seppie al nero. Risotto bianco con polvere di caffè e capperi di Pantelleria. Cannelloni croccanti di ricotta e mozzarella di bufala con passata di pomodoro.

Verona *37100 P 562 F 14 G. Italy – pop. 257 477 alt. 59.*

18 Verona (closed Tuesday) at Sommacampagna ✉ 37066 ☎ 045 510060, Fax 045 510242, West : 13 km.

of Villafranca South-East : 14 km ☎ 045 8095666, Fax 045 8095706.

via degli Alpini 9 ☎ 045 8068680, iatbra@tiscalinet.it, Fax 045 8003638 – *Porta Nuova Railway station ☎ 045 8000861, iatfs@tiscalinet.it – Villafranca Airport ☎ 045 8619163, iataeroporto@tiscalinet.it, Fax 045 8619163.*

A.C.I. *via della Valverde 34 ✉ 37122 ☎ 045 595003.*

Roma 503 – Milano 157 – Venezia 114.

✗✗✗ ✿✿ **Il Desco,** via Dietro San Sebastiano 7 ✉ 37121 ☎ 045 595358, *Fax 045 590236* – . VISA JCB.
closed Easter, 15 to 30 June, 25 December-10 January, Sunday and Monday, open Monday dinner in July-August and December – **Meals** (booking essential) a la carte 76/106.
◆ One of the brightest stars in Italy's gastronomic firmament, this restaurant succeeds in combining an elegant, period atmosphere with creative and imaginative cuisine.
Spec. Insalata tiepida di tonno fresco e fagioli con erbe aromatiche e flan di cipolle. Zuppa di porri e patate con nervetti all'aglio. Filetto di branzino con animelle, salsa d'ostriche e tartufo nero.

Norway

Norge

OSLO

PRACTICAL INFORMATION

LOCAL CURRENCY

Norwegian Kroner: *100 NOK = 12,35 euro (€) (Dec. 2003)*

TOURIST INFORMATION

The telephone number and address of the Tourist Information office is given in the text under **i**.

National Holiday in Norway: *17 May.*

FOREIGN EXCHANGE

In the Oslo area banks are usually open between 8.15am and 3.30pm but in summertime, 15/5 - 31/8, they close at 3pm. Saturdays and Sundays closed.
Most large hotels, main airports and Tourist information office have exchange facilities. At Oslo Airport the bank is open from 6.30am to 8pm (weekdays), 6.30am to 6pm (Saturday), 7am to 8pm (Sunday), all year round.

MEALS

At lunchtime, follow the custom of the country and try the typical buffets of Scandinavian specialities.
At dinner, the a la carte and set menus will offer you more conventional cooking.

SHOPPING IN OSLO

Knitware, silverware, pewter and glassware.

Your hotel porter should be able to help you with information.

CAR HIRE

The international car hire companies have branches in each major city. Your hotel porter should be able to give details and help you with your arrangements. Cars can also be hired from the Tourist Information Office.

TIPPING IN NORWAY

A service charge is included in hotel and restaurant bills and it is up to the customer to give something in addition if he wants to.
The cloakroom is sometimes included in the bill, sometimes an extra charge is made.
Taxi drivers don't expect to be tipped. It is up to you if you want to give a gratuity.

SPEED LIMITS

The maximum permitted speed within built-up areas is 50 km/h - 31mph. Outside these areas it is 80 km/h - 50mph. Where there are other speed limits (lower or higher) they are signposted.

SEAT BELTS

The wearing of seat belts in Norway is compulsory for drivers and all passengers.

OSLO

Norge 711 M 7 – pop. 507 467.

Hamburg 888 – København 583 – Stockholm 522.

i The Tourist Information Centre in Oslo, Fridtj of Nansens plass 5 0160 ☎ 24 14 77 00, Fax 22 42 92 22 – KNA (Kongelig Norsk Automobilklub) Royal Norwegian Automobile Club, Cort Adelers gt 16 ☎ 21 60 49 00 – NAF (Norges Automobil Forbund), Storg. 2 ☎ 22 34 14 00.

18 Oslo Golfklubb ☎ 22 51 05 60.

✈ Oslo-Gardermden NE: 45 km ☎ 64 81 20 00 – SAS Booking Office: ☎ 815 20 400 – Air Terminal: Galleri Oslo, Schweigaards gate 6.

⛴ Copenhagen, Frederikshavn, Kiel, Hirtshals : contact tourist information centre (see above).

See: Bygdøy ABZ Viking Ship Museum★★★ (Vikingskipshuset) ; Folk Museum★★★ (Norsk Folkemuseum) ; Fram Museum★★ (Frammuseet) ; Kon-Tiki Museum★★ (Kon-Tiki Museet) ; Maritime Museum★★ (Norsk Sjøfartsmuseum) – Munch Museum★★ (Munch-Museet) DY – National Gallery★★★ (Nasjonalgalleriet) CY **M¹** – Vigelandsanlegget★ (Vigeland sculptures and museum) AX – Akershus Castle★ (Akershus Festning : Resistance Museum★) CZ **M²** – Oslo Cathedral (Domkirke: views★★ from steeple) CY – Ibsen-museet★ BY **M⁴**.

Outskirts: Holmenkollen★ (NW: 10 km): view from ski-jump tower and ski museum BX – Sonia Henie-Onstad Art Centre★★ (Sonia Henie-Onstad Kunstsenter) (W: 12 km) AY.

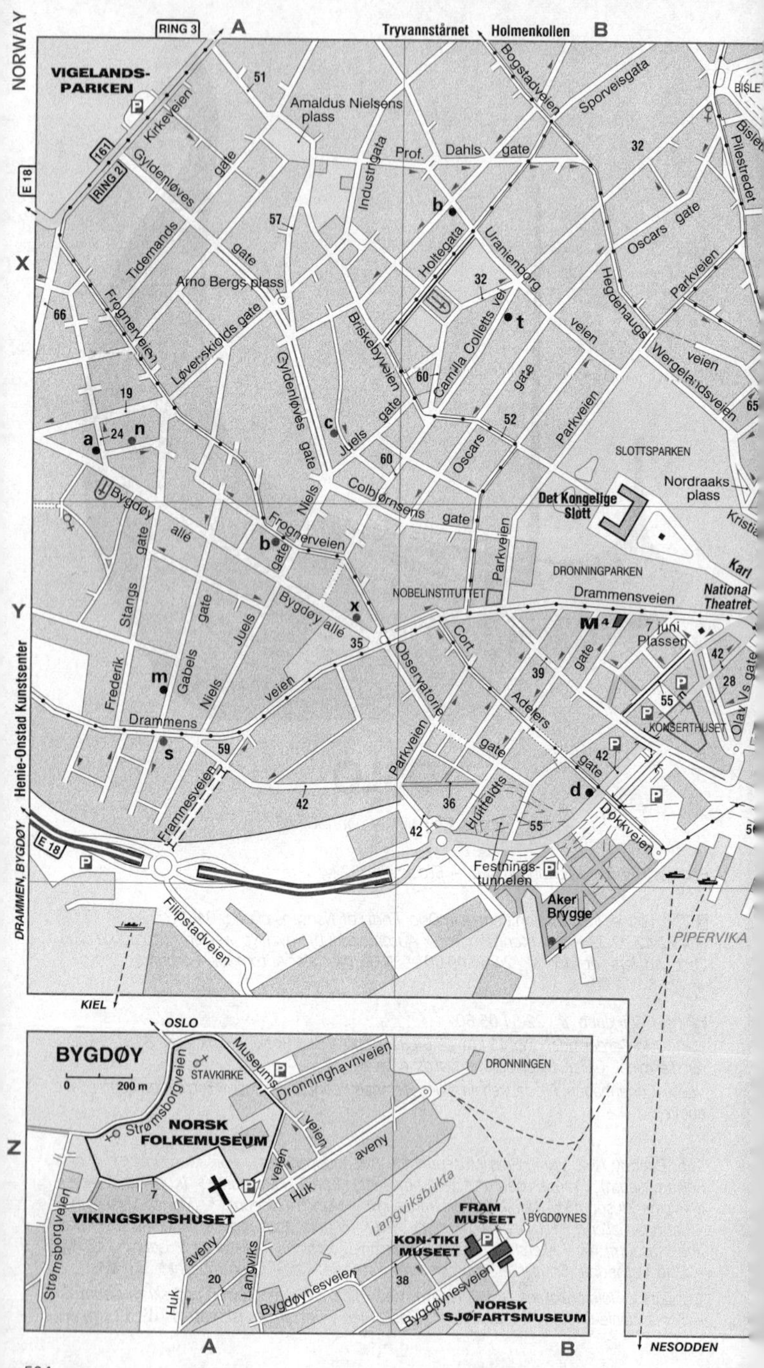

RING 3
Tryvannstårnet
Holmenkollen
VIGELANDS-PARKEN
Amaldus Nielsens plass
Prof. Dahls gate
Bogstadveien
Sporveisgata
BISLET
Pilestredet
Kirkeveien
Gyldenløves gate
Industrigata
Holtegata
Uranienborg veien
Oscars gate
Hegdehaugs veien
Parkveien
Wergelandsveien
Tidemands gate
Arno Bergs plass
Frognerveien
Løvenskiolds gate
Briskebyveien
Camilla Colletts vei
Gyldenløves gate
Juels gate
Niels Juels gate
Colbjørnsens gate
SLOTTSPARKEN
Nordraaks plass
Det Kongelige Slott
Bygdøy allé
Stangs gate
Gabels gate
Frognerveien
Parkveien
DRONNINGPARKEN
Karl
National Theatret
NOBELINSTITUTTET
Drammensveien
7 juni Plassen
Observatorie gate
Cort Adelers gate
Olav Vs gate
KONSERTHUSET
Frederik Stangs gate
Drammens veien
Henie-Onstad Kunstsenter
Framnesveien
Parkveien
Huitfeldts gate
Dokkveien
Festnings-tunnelen
Aker Brygge
PIPERVIKA
DRAMMEN, BYGDØY
Filipstadveien
KIEL
OSLO
BYGDØY
0 200 m
STAVKIRKE
Museumsveien
Dronninghavnveien
DRONNINGEN
Strømsborgveien
NORSK FOLKEMUSEUM
Huk aveny
Langviksbukta
VIKINGSKIPSHUSET
FRAM MUSEET
BYGDØYNES
KON-TIKI MUSEET
Langviksveien
Bygdøynesveien
NORSK SJØFARTSMUSEUM
NESODDEN

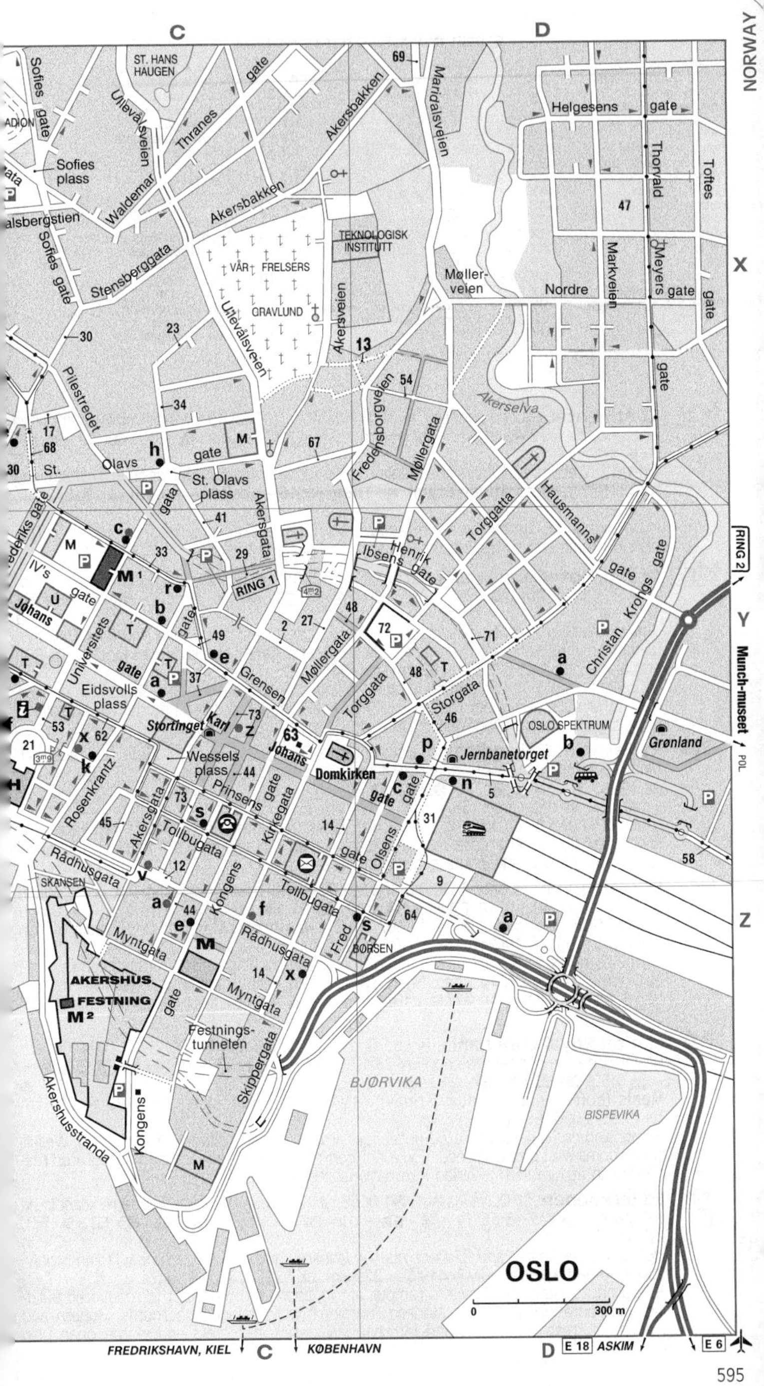
OSLO
ST. HANS HAUGEN
VÅR FRELSERS GRAVLUND
TEKNOLOGISK INSTITUTT
Sofies plass
St. Olavs plass
Eidsvolls plass
Wessels plass
Stortinget
Domkirken
Jernbanetorget
OSLO SPEKTRUM
Grønland
BØRSEN
AKERSHUS FESTNING
Festnings-tunnelen
SKANSEN
BJØRVIKA
BISPEVIKA
Akerselva
RING 1
RING 2
Munch-museet
FREDRIKSHAVN, KIEL
KØBENHAVN
E 18 ASKIM
E 6
300 m

STREET INDEX TO OSLO TOWN PLAN

Apotekergata . . . . CY 2
Biskop Gunnerus' gate . . . . DY 5
Bygdøy kappellvei . . . . . . AZ 7
Christian Frederiks plass . . . DY 9
Christiania torv . . . . CY 12
Damstredet . . . . CDX 13
Dronningens gate . . . . CYZ 14
Dronning Mauds gate . . . . BY 16
Edvard Storms gate . . . . . CX 17
Elisenbergveien . . . . AX 19
Fredriksborgveien . . . . AZ 20
Fridtjof Nansens plass . . . . CY 21
Frimanns gate . . . . CX 23
Gimleveien . . . . AX 24
Grensen . . . . CY
Grubbegata . . . . CY 27
Haakon VII's gate . . . . BY 28
Hammersborgtunnelen . . . . CY 29
Holbergs gate . . . . CX 30
Jernbanetorget . . . . DY 31
Josefines gate . . . . ABX 32
Karl Johans gate . . . . BCDY
Kristian Augusts gate . . . . BCY 33
Langés gate . . . . CX 34
Lapsetorvet . . . . AY 35
Lassons gate . . . . BY 36
Lille Grensen . . . . CY 37
Løchenveien . . . . ABZ 38
Løkkeveien . . . . BY 39
Munchs gate . . . . CXY 41
Munkedamsveien . . . . ABY 42
Nedre Slottsgate . . . . CYZ 44
Nedre Vollgate . . . . CY 45
Nygata . . . . DY 46
Olaf Ryes plass . . . . DX 47
Pløens gate . . . . DY 48
Professor Aschehougs pl. . . . . CY 49
Professor Dahls gate . . . . . AX 51
Riddervolds gate . . . . BX 52
Roald Amundsens gate . . . CY 53
Rosteds gate . . . . DX 54
Ruseløkkveien . . . . ABY 55
Rådhusplassen . . . . BCY 56
Schives gate . . . . AX 57
Schweigaards gate . . . . DY 58
Skillebekk . . . . AY 59
Skovveien . . . . ABX 60
Stortingsgata . . . . CY 62
Stortorvet . . . . CY 63
Strandgata . . . . DZ 64
Sven Bruns gate . . . . BX 65
Thomas Heftyes gate . . . . . AX 66
Thor Olsens gate . . . . CX 67
Torggata . . . . CDY
Tullins gate . . . . CX 68
Uelands gate . . . . DX 69
Vaterlandtunnelen . . . . DY 71
Youngstorget . . . . DY 72
Øvre Slottsgate . . . . CY 73

Continental, Stortingsgaten 24-26, ✉ 0117, ☎ 22 82 40 00, *booking@hotel-continental.no, Fax 22 42 96 89* – |♦|, ⇋ rm, ▤ TV ☎ ⇔ – 🅰 200. MC AE ⊙ VISA JCB. ⊘ CY n

closed 23 December-2 January – **Meals** *(closed Sunday-Monday)* (dinner only) 570/890 and a la carte ♀ (see also ***Annen Etage*** and ***Theatercaféen*** below) – **146 rm** ☐ 1930/2750, 8 suites.

♦ De luxe hotel, run by the same family for 100 years. Comfortable, spacious, richly furnished rooms and suites.Elegant banquet facilities and selection of restaurants.

Grand Hotel, Karl Johans Gate 31, ✉ 0101, ☎ 23 21 20 00, *grand@rica.no, Fax 23 21 21 00,* ⌂s, ⊡ – |♦|, ⇋ rm, ▤ TV ⇔ – 🅰 300. MC AE ⊙ VISA JCB. ⊘ CY a

Julius Fritzner : **Meals** *(closed July, 23 December-4 January, Sunday and Bank Holidays)* (dinner only) 525 and a la carte 515/600 ♀ – ***Grand Café :*** **Meals** (buffet lunch) 245/600 and a la carte 370/575 ♀ – **282 rm** ☐ 1845/2495, 7 suites.

♦ Opulent 1874 hotel, in prime location. De luxe well furnished rooms. Swimming pool on roof. Informal meals under the glass roof of the Palm Court. Julius Fritzner for fine dining in traditional surroundings. Informal brasserie-style in Grand Café.

Radisson SAS Scandinavia, Holbergsgate 30, ✉ 0166, ☎ 23 29 30 00, *sales.scandinavia@radissonsas.com, Fax 23 29 30 01,* ≤ Oslo and Fjord, ℔, ⌂s, ⊡ – |♦|, ⇋ rm, ▤ TV ☎ ♿ ⇔ – 🅰 720. MC AE ⊙ VISA JCB. ⊘ CX e

Enzo : **Meals** a la carte 235/450 ♀ – **476 rm** ☐ 1650/2130, 12 suites.

♦ Modern hotel block offering spectacular views. Vast international lobby with variety of shops, and good conference facilities. Spacious comfortable rooms. Panoramic bar. Small and simple Enzo offers popular international dishes.

Bristol, Kristian IV's Gate 7, ✉ 0164, ☎ 22 82 60 00, *post@bristol.no, Fax 22 82 60 01,* ℔, ⌂s – |♦|, ⇋ rm, ▤ TV ☎ – 🅰 500. MC AE ⊙ VISA JCB. ⊘ rest CY b

Bristol Grill : **Meals** (dinner only) 350/450 ♀ – ***Hambro's :*** **Meals** *(closed Sunday)* (lunch only) 195/295 ♀ – **243 rm** ☐ 1730/2030, 9 suites.

♦ 1920's hotel with original elegant décor and furnishings. Tasteful and comfortable bedrooms with good facilities. Bristol Grill, 1920s restaurant with extensive international menu. Hambro's, simple café-bar for club sandwiches, cakes and some hot dishes.

Clarion Royal Christiania, Biskop Gunnerus' Gate 3, ✉ 0106, ☎ 23 10 80 00, *christiania@clarion.choicehotels.no, Fax 23 10 82 82,* ℔, ⌂s, ⊡ – |♦| ⇋ ▤ TV ☎ ♿ ⇔ – 🅰 450. MC AE ⊙ VISA JCB. ⊘ DY p

Meals (buffet lunch Monday-Friday) 185/325 and a la carte 395/495 – **435 rm** ☐ 1195/2095, 68 suites.

♦ Imposing conveniently located hotel built around a vast atrium. Spacious lobby. Well lit large rooms with pleasant décor. Excellent conference facilities. Pleasantly decorated restaurant in atrium with a varied international menu.

Edderkoppen, St Olavs Plass 1, ✉ 0165, ☎ 23 15 56 00, *edderkoppen@scandic-hotels.com, Fax 23 15 56 11,* ℔, ⌂s – ⇋ ▤ ☎ ⇔ – 🅰 100. MC AE ⊙ VISA. ⊘ rest CX h

closed 1 week Easter and 22 December-2 January – **Meals** *(closed Sunday)* (dinner only) 250/450 and a la carte 277/419 ♀ – **229 rm** ☐ 1215/1415, 6 suites.

♦ 550 photographs of Norway's famous actors adorn the walls of this renovated building, incorporating a theatre. Modern functional well-equipped bedrooms. Modern and traditional fresh Norwegian and international dishes in Jesters and in the open plan bar.

Radisson SAS Plaza, Sonja Henies Plass 3, ✉ 0134, ☎ 22 05 80 00, *sales.plaza.oslo@radisson.sas.com, Fax 22 05 80 30,* ≤ Oslo and Fjord, – 950. rest DY b
Meals (light lunch)/dinner 395/475 and a la carte 415/545 – **655 rm** 1825/2225, 19 suites.
◆ Business-oriented hotel block, the tallest in Norway, with footbridge link to congress centre. Well furnished modern rooms. Superb views from top of tower. Panoramic bar. First floor restaurant and bar offering a modern menu of Mediterranean dishes.

Opera, Christian Frederiks plass 5, ✉ 0103, ☎ 24 10 30 00, *opera@rainbow-hotels.no, Fax 24 10 30 10,* ≤, – rm, – 240.
Meals (buffet lunch) 235/425 and dinner a la carte 380/490 – **432 rm** 1020/1890, 2 suites. DZ a
◆ A recent arrival in town, located next to the railway station and overlooking the harbour. Large modern building with functional yet contemporary furnishings and décor. Restaurant with huge windows affording panoramic views. Elaborate traditional cooking.

Rica Oslo, Europarådets Plass 1, ✉ 0154, ☎ 23 10 42 00, *rica.oslo.hotel@rica.no, Fax 23 10 42 10,* – rm, – 100. rest
***Bjørvigen* : Meals** *(closed Sunday and Bank Holidays)* (buffet lunch) 225/350 and dinner a la carte 319/423 – **173 rm** 1295/1495, 2 suites. DY c
◆ Modern hotel in three connected buildings close to station. Sound-proofed bedrooms have charming décor and paintings by local artists on walls. Cosy English style bar. Wood furnished restaurant offering a concise selection of traditional Norwegian dishes.

Rica Victoria, Rosenkrantzgate 13, ✉ 0121, ☎ 24 14 70 00, *rica.victoria.hotel.oslo@rica.no, Fax 24 14 70 01* – rm, – 50. rest
closed 22 December-3 January – **Meals** *(closed Sunday)* (lunch only) (buffet only) 155/200 – **194 rm** 1295/1495, 5 suites. CY k
◆ Large modern hotel popular with business people, built around glazed-in atrium. Spacious comfortable rooms with sound-proofing, good quality fittings and modern facilities. Offers a simple menu of traditional cuisine on the enclosed patio.

Noble House without rest., Kongens Gate 5, ✉ 0153, ☎ 23 10 72 00, *noble.house@firsthotels.no, Fax 23 10 72 10,* – .
53 rm 1399/1799, 16 suites. CZ e
◆ Charming hotel in good location. Spacious rooms with parquet floors, top quality furniture and modern facilities. All rooms equipped with kitchenette. Pleasant roof terrace.

Bastion without rest., Skippergaten 7, ✉ 0152, ☎ 22 47 77 00, *booking@hotelbastion.no, Fax 22 33 11 80,* – – 50.
closed Christmas and New Year – **93 rm** 1200/1500, 6 suites. CZ x
◆ Comfortable modern hotel handily placed for motorway. Welcoming rooms with good comforts and facilities. Furniture and paintings in part reminiscent of English style.

Rica H. Bygdø y Allé without rest., Bygdø y Allé 53, ✉ 0207, ☎ 23 08 58 00, *rica.hotel.bygdoey.alle@rica.no, Fax 23 08 58 08* – – 40.
closed 2-13 April and 19 December-5 January – **57 rm** 1130/1695. AX a
◆ Neo-Gothic hotel (1890's) with elegant façade and period character in residential area. Period paintings in lounge and lobby. Beautifully decorated rooms with personal touch.

Stefan, Rosenkrantzgate 1, ✉ 0159, ☎ 23 31 55 00, *stefan@rainbow-hotels.no, Fax 23 31 55 55* – – 50. CY r
closed 23 December-3 January – **Meals** *(closed Sunday)* (buffet lunch only) 195/345 – **139 rm** 1215/1515.
◆ Modern hotel on convenient corner site. Rooms are well equipped with functional furniture and good facilties. Good variety of room types. Families and groups catered for. Eighth floor restaurant with small terrace. Popular buffets.

Gabelshus without rest., Gabelsgate 16, ✉ 0272, ☎ 23 27 65 00, *reception@gabelshus.no, Fax 23 27 65 60* – – 60. AY m
closed Easter – **43 rm** 1295/1495.
◆ Attractive early 20C vine-clad hotel in quiet district. Charming, homely lounge with antiques. Large well-fitted bedrooms ; some on front with balconies, quieter at the rear.

Ambassadeur without rest., Camilla Colletts Vei 15, ✉ 0258, ☎ 23 27 23 00, *post@hotelambassadeur.no, Fax 22 44 47 91,* – – 30.
33 rm 1210/1415, 8 suites. BX t
◆ Hotel with pastel painted façade and window boxes in residential street. Rooms are individually decorated by theme and offer a good level of comfort and facilities.

Millennium, Tollbugaten 25, ✉ 0157, ☎ 21 02 28 00, *millennium@firsthotels.no, Fax 21 02 28 30* – rm, . rest CY s
Meals *(closed Sunday)* (dinner only) (coffee shop) a la carte 330/520 – **102 rm** 1299/1499, 10 suites.
◆ Functional modern hotel near harbour and restaurants. Internet access. Spacious well equipped rooms ; top floor with balconies ; quietest on inside although overlooked. Grill type kitchen open to room offers simple range of international bar snacks.

Børsparken without rest., Tollbugaten 4, ✉ 0152, ✆ 22 47 17 17, *booking.boersparken@comfort.choicehotels.no, Fax 22 47 17 18* – 75. VISA. CDZ s
closed Easter and Christmas – **198 rm** 975.
◆ Modern functional chain hotel on corner site in city centre. Pleasant lobby opening onto tree-lined square. Compact practical rooms, well equipped for business clientele.

Byporten without rest., Jernbanetorget 6, ✉ 0154, ✆ 23 15 55 00, *byporten@scandic-hotels.com, Fax 23 15 55 11* – VISA. DY n
236 rm 1375/1575, 4 suites.
◆ Modern hotel in vast office/commercial centre block by station. Functional soundproofed rooms with environmentally friendly decor. Breakfast in nearby public restaurant.

Savoy, Universitetsgata 11, ✉ 0164, ✆ 23 35 42 00, *savoy@quality-choicehotels.no, Fax 23 35 42 01* – VISA. CY c
Meals (see **restauranteik** below) – **80 rm** 1195/1395.
◆ Classic early 20C hotel in the city centre behind the museum. Stylish public areas. Spacious well-kept bedrooms with good facilities.

Norlandia Saga without rest., Eilert Sundtsgt. 39, ✉ 0259, ✆ 22 43 04 85, *saga@norlandia.no, Fax 22 44 08 63* – 25. VISA JCB BX b
closed Christmas-New Year – **37 rm** 975/1175.
◆ Family-run hotel in quiet area. Cosy winter lounge with fire. Well lit rooms with classic furnishings and facilities; rear rooms are quietest. Complimentary mid-week supper.

Spectrum without rest., Brugata 7, ✉ 0133, ✆ 23 36 27 00, *spectrum@rainbow-hotels.no, Fax 23 36 27 50* – VISA. DY a
closed 17 December-2 January – **151 rm** 1075/1915.
◆ Conveniently located hotel in pedestrian street not far from station. Two styles of room: "old" are fairly functional; "new" have more interesting décor and furniture.

Vika Atrium, Munkedamsveien 45, ✉ 0121, ✆ 22 83 33 00, *vika.atrium@rainbow-hotels.no, Fax 22 83 09 57,* – rm, – 240. VISA. rest BY d
Meals *(closed weekends and Bank Holidays)* (buffet lunch) 150/300 and a la carte 180/430 – **91 rm** 1255/1755.
◆ Located in large office block built around an atrium. Comfortable lobby lounge. Well serviced rooms with functional modern fittings. Good conference facilities.

Norrøna, Grensen 19, ✉ 0159, ✆ 23 31 80 00, *norrona@rainbow-hotels.no, Fax 23 31 80 01* – rm, – 120. VISA JCB. CY e
closed 4-13 April and 23 December-3 January – **Meals** *(closed Sunday)* (buffet rest.) (lunch only) 50/150 and a la carte – **93 rm** 1060/1310.
◆ Located right in the city centre, ideal for shopping and exploring on foot. Comfortable functional hotel with pleasant Scandinavian décor. Conference facilities. Busy coffee-shop popular with locals, offering selection of traditional local fare and soups.

Annen Etage (at Continental H.), Stortingsgaten 24-26, ✉ 0117, ✆ 22 82 40 70, *annen.etageàhotel-continental.no, Fax 22 42 09 89* – VISA JCB. CY n
closed Easter, 5 July-5 August, 22 December-5 January and Sunday – **Meals** (dinner only) 570/665 and a la carte 585/855.
◆ Elegant formal dining room decorated in early 1920s style in a comfortable setting. Gourmet menu offers interesting range of attractively presented contemporary cuisine.
Spec. Scallops with cauliflower and truffle purée. Pan-fried turbot with lobster, mussels and saffron. Vanilla and strawberry tart, vanilla ice cream.

Bagatelle (Hellstrøm), Bygdøy Allé 3, ✉ 0257, ✆ 22 12 14 40, *bagatelle@bagatelle.no, Fax 22 43 64 20* – VISA JCB. AY x
closed 1 week Easter, 18 July-10 August, 1 week Christmas and Sunday – **Meals** (booking essential) (dinner only) 650/750 and a la carte 670/880.
◆ Highly reputed classic restaurant with colourful contemporary décor and numerous paintings on walls. Excellent traditional cuisine. Wine cellar may be viewed by diners.
Spec. Crustaceans panaché. Grilled turbot with anchovy butter. Game in season.

Statholdergaarden (Stiansen), Rådhusgate 11, (entrance by Kirkegate) 1st floor, ✉ 0151, ✆ 22 41 88 00, *post@statholdergaarden.no, Fax 22 41 22 24* – VISA. CZ f
closed 5-12 April, 12 July-2 August, 22 December-4 January and Sunday – **Meals** (booking essential) (dinner only) 750/950 and a la carte 550/670 – ***Statholderens Krostue*** : **Meals** *(closed Sunday-Monday)* 205/490 and a la carte 400/460.
◆ Fine 17C house offers elegant 1st floor dining room with original décor beneath beautiful period stucco ceilings, whose motifs reappear on the china. High quality cuisine. Three cosy vaulted basement rooms constitute the bistro-style alternative.
Spec. Trout and scallops with spring onions and soya sauce. Fillet of lamb with sweetbread and mushroom sausage. Cloudberry and chocolate soufflé, Lakka sauce.

XXX ✿ **Le Canard,** President Harbitz Gate 4, ✉ 0259, ☎ 22 54 34 00, *lecanard@lecanard.no, Fax 22 54 34 10,* 🏠 – ▤. MC AE D VISA. ✂ AX c
closed Easter, Christmas and Sunday – **Meals** (dinner only) 565 and a la carte 568/845 ♀.
◆ Tastefully decorated 1900 villa in residential district. Elegant dining room has beautiful antiques, a wall fresco and Baroque décor. Cuisine for the discerning gourmet.
Spec. Grilled scallops with foie gras and orange syrup. Roast duck in two servings. Game and fowl in season.

XXX ✿ **Spisestedet Feinschmecker,** Balchensgate 5, ✉ 0265, ☎ 22 12 93 80, *kontakt@feinschmecker.no, Fax 22 12 93 88* – ▤. MC AE D VISA. ✂ AX n
closed 1 week Easter, 3 weeks in summer and Sunday – **Meals** (booking essential) (dinner only) 525/695 and a la carte 650/740 ♀.
◆ Busy restaurant in residential building with inviting façade and tasteful colourful décor. Spacious dining room has warm, cosy atmosphere. Expertly cooked contemporary fare.
Spec. Terrine of foie gras. Roast scallops and crawfish. Rack of lamb.

XXX ✿ **Oro** (Ness), Tordenskioldsgate 6A, ✉ 0160, ☎ 23 01 02 40, *post@restaurantoro.no, Fax 23 01 02 48* – ▤. MC AE D VISA JCB. ✂ CY x
closed 8-12 April, 22 December-4 January and Sunday – **Meals** (booking essential) (dinner only except December) 595/955 and a la carte 645/795 ♀ – ***Plata*** **: Meals** - Tapas - 25/85 and a la carte 165/255 ♀.
◆ Elegant, modern designer décor in muted tones with an informal atmosphere. Open-plan kitchen offers inventive cuisine with a Mediterranean influence. Booking a must. Plata, the adjoining tapas bar with a large counter displaying cold and some warm dishes.
Spec. Scallops with baked shallots and truffles. Glazed pigeon with pan-fried foie gras. Chocolate Oro-Manjari.

XX **Det Gamle Raadhus,** Nedre Slottsgate 1, ✉ 0157, ☎ 22 42 01 07, *gamle.raadhus@gamle-raadhus.no, Fax 22 42 04 90,* 🏠 – MC AE D VISA JCB. ✂ CZ a
closed 1 week Easter, 3 weeks July, 1 week Christmas and Sunday – **Meals** (dinner only) 395/455 and a la carte 381/540 ♀.
◆ Well run restaurant operating for over a century located in Oslo's original City Hall, dating from 1641. Elegant rustic interior décor and English style atmosphere in bar.

XX **restauranteik,** Universitetsgata 11, ✉ 0164, ☎ 22 36 07 10, *eikefjord@restauranteik.no, Fax 22 36 07 11* – ▤. MC AE D VISA. ✂ CY c
closed 1 week Easter, 1 week Christmas, 4 weeks summer, Sunday and Monday – **Meals** (set menu only) 315/435.
◆ Restaurant in striking minimalist style ; open plan kitchen with chef's table. Good value set menu of 3 or 5 courses of interesting dishes.

XX **Theatercaféen** (at Continental H.), Stortingsgaten 24-26, ✉ 0117, ☎ 22 82 40 50, *theatercafeen@hotel-continental.no, Fax 22 41 20 94* – MC AE D VISA JCB. ✂ CY n
closed Sunday lunch – **Meals** (light lunch) 475/750 (dinner) and a la carte 420/670 ♀.
◆ An institution in the city and the place to see and be seen. Elaborate lunchtime sandwiches make way for afternoon/evening brasserie specials.

XX **Mares,** Frognesveien 12B, ✉ 0263, ☎ 22 54 89 80, *mares@mares.no, Fax 22 54 89 85* – MC AE D VISA JCB. ✂ AY b
closed Easter, July and Christmas – **Meals** - Seafood - (booking essential) (dinner only) 395/595 and a la carte 360/495 ♀.
◆ Fish restaurant in traditional house in residential area. Well lit pleasant interior with modern designer décor, black and white photos on walls and local atmosphere.

X **Brasserie Hansken,** Akersgata 2, ✉ 0158, ☎ 22 42 60 88, *Fax 22 42 24 03* – ▤. MC AE D VISA JCB. ✂ CY v
closed 1 week Easter, 1 week Christmas and Sunday – **Meals** (booking essential) 275/595 and a la carte 415/603 ♀.
◆ Busy restaurant in lively district with strictly contemporary bistro-style décor and dark wood fittings. Good quality brasserie fare. Terrace bar on the square in summer.

X **A Touch of France,** Øvre Slottsgate 16, ✉ 0157, ☎ 23 10 01 65, *dartagnan@dartagnan.no, Fax 23 10 01 61,* 🏠 – ▤. MC AE D VISA JCB CY z
closed 1 week Easter, 1 week Christmas-New Year and Sunday – **Meals** (dinner only except Saturday and in summer) 299 and a la carte 335/475 ♀.
◆ French brasserie style dining room at D'Artagnan ; entrance from pedestrian street. Wall benches, bistro chairs and open kitchen at end of room. Interesting French dishes.

X **Lofoten Fiskerestaurant,** Stranden 75, ✉ 0250, ☎ 22 83 08 08, *lofoten@fiskerestaurant.no, Fax 22 83 68 66,* ≤ – MC AE D VISA JCB. ✂ BZ r
closed 25 December – **Meals** - Seafood - 250/450 and a la carte 400/525 ♀.
◆ A firm favourite with locals ; attractive, modern fjord-side restaurant at Aker Brygge. Chef patron offers a tempting array of seafood and shellfish.

Hos Thea, Gabelsgate 11, 0272, 22 44 68 74, *Fax 22 44 68 74* – AE VISA JCB. AY s
closed 25 December and 1 January – **Meals** (dinner only) 430 and a la carte 329/495.
◆ Discreet black façade in residential area conceals this typical little restaurant fitted out with simple Scandinavian style décor. Family atmosphere. Appealing menu.

at Lillestrøm *Northeast : 18 km by E 6 DZ :*

Arena, Nesgata 1, 2004, Northeast : 18 km by E6 66 93 60 00, *arena@rainbow-hotels.no, Fax 66 93 63 00,* – – 1000. AE VISA JCB.
closed Easter and 19 December-2 January – ***Madame Thrane :*** **Meals** (dinner only) a la carte 362/505 – ***Amfi :*** **Meals** (buffet lunch)/dinner 415/595 – **274 rm** 1445/1745, 4 suites.
◆ Large modern hotel in trade fair centre with direct train access to airport and city centre. Spacious, contemporary rooms with every possible facility ; a few singles. Madame Thrane for interesting contemporary dishes. Buffet style service at the informal Amfi.

at Holmenkollen *Northwest : 10 km by Bogstadveien* BX *Sørkedalsveien and Holmenkollveien :*

Holmenkollen Park, Kongeveien 26, 0787, 22 92 20 00, *holmenkollen.park.hotel.rica@rica.no, Fax 22 14 61 92,* Oslo and Fjord, – – 500. AE VISA JCB. rest
closed Christmas-New Year – ***De Fem Stuer :*** **Meals** (buffet lunch)/dinner 425/595 and a la carte 500/720 – ***Galleriet :*** **Meals** (buffet lunch) 225/535 and dinner a la carte 285/375 – **210 rm** 1295/1995, 11 suites.
◆ Smart hotel near Olympic ski jump ; superb views. Part built (1894) in old Norwegian "dragon style" decorated wood. Chalet style rooms, some with balconies or views or saunas. International cuisine in De Fem Stuer. Informal Galleriet for a more popular menu.

at Oslo Airport *Northeast : 45 km by E 6 DZ at Gardermoen :*

Radisson SAS Airport, 2061, 63 93 30 00, *sales.airport.oslo@radissonsas.com, Fax 63 93 30 30,* – rm, – 220. AE VISA JCB. rest
Meals 425 (dinner) and a la carte 380/555 – **348 rm** 1550/1750, 2 suites.
◆ Ultra-contemporary business hotel on a semi-circular plan overlooking runway, but well sound-proofed. Rooms are a good size, well equipped and have varied décor. Modern restaurant offering a variety of international dishes to appeal to all comers.

Clarion Oslo Airport, West : 6 km, 2060, 63 94 94 94, *oslo.airport@clarion.choicehotels.no, Fax 63 94 94 95,* – rm, – 450. AE VISA JCB. rest
Meals (buffet lunch) 250 and dinner a la carte approx. 400 – **357 rm** 1395/1495, 1 suite.
◆ Modern Norwegian design hotel in wood and red tiles on star plan. Compact functional rooms with good modern facilities. Well equipped for conferences. Families at weekend. Vast restaurant offers a standard range of international dishes to cater for all tastes.

Trugstad Gård, Trugstadveien 10, 2034 Holter, Southwest : 10 km by Road 120 63 99 58 90, *restaurant@trugstad.no, Fax 63 99 50 87* – AE VISA JCB.
closed July, Christmas and Sunday – **Meals** (booking essential) 250/750 and a la carte 495/625.
◆ Attractive and lovingly restored farmhouse yet only a short distance from the airport. Attentive and friendly service of modern set menu using the finest local ingredients.

Poland

Polska

Warsaw

PRACTICAL INFORMATION

LOCAL CURRENCY

Zloty : *100 PLN = 21,57 euro (€) (Dec. 2003)*

National Holidays in Poland: *1 and 3 May, 15 August, 1 and 11 November.*

PRICES

Prices may change if goods and service costs in Poland are revised and it is therefore always advisable to confirm rates with the hotelier when making a reservation.

FOREIGN EXCHANGE

It is strongly advised against changing money other than in banks, exchange offices or authorised offices such as large hotels and Kantor. Banks are usually open on weekdays from 8am to 6pm.

HOTEL RESERVATIONS

In case of difficulties in finding a room through our hotel selection, it is always possible to apply to the Tourist Office, ☎ (022) 94 31, Fax (022) 524 11 43, open on weekdays from 8am to 7pm.

POSTAL SERVICES

Post offices are open from 8am to 8pm on weekdays.

The **General Post Office** *is open 7 days a week and 24 hours a day : Poczta Glówna, Świetokrzyska 31/33.*

SHOPPING IN WARSAW

In the index of street names, those printed in red are where the principal shops are found. They are generally open from 10am to 7pm on weekdays and 9am to 3pm on Saturday.

THEATRE BOOKING

Your hotel porter will be able to make your arrangements or direct you to a theatre booking office: Kasy ZASP, Al Jerozolimskie 25 ☎ (022) 621 93 83, open from 11am to 2pm and 2.30pm to 6pm.

TIPPING

Hotel, restaurant and café bills often do not include service in the total charge. In these cases it is usual to leave the staff a gratuity which will vary depending upon the service given.

CAR HIRE

The international car hire companies have branches in Warsaw. Your hotel porter should be able to give details and help you with your arrangements.

BREAKDOWN SERVICE

A 24 hour breakdown service is operated calling ☎ 981.

SPEED LIMIT

On motorways, the maximum permitted speed is 110 km/h – 68 mph, 90 km/h – 56 mph on other roads and 60 km/h – 37 mph in built up areas. In Warsaw the maximum speed limit is 31 mph, 50 km/h.

SEAT BELTS

In Poland, the wearing of seat belts is compulsory for drivers and all passengers.

WARSAW

(WARSAWA)

Polska 720 E 13 – *Pop. 1 900 000.*

Berlin 591 – Budapest 670 – Gdansk 345 – Kiev 795 – Moscow 1253 – Zagreb 993.

Warsaw Tourist Information Centre, Krakowskie Przedmieście 89, ☎ (022) 94-31, Fax (022) 524 11 43, Al. Jerozolimskie 54 (in railway station) ☎ (022) 94-31, Warsaw Airport (Arrivals Hall).

18 First Warsaw Golf Club and Country Club, Rajszew 70, 05-110 Jabłonna ☎ (022) 782 45 55. Fax (022) 782 41 63

Okęcie (Warsaw Airport) SW 10 km, by Żwirki i Wigury ☎ 0801 300 952 or 953.
Bus to airport: from major hotels in the town centre (ask the reception).
Polish Airlines (LOT) Al Jerozolmiskie 65/79, Warsaw ☎ (022) 577 99 52.

SIGHTS

OLD TOWN★★★ (STARE MIASTO) BX

Castle Square★ (Plac Zamkowy) BX **33** – *Royal Palace★★ (Zamek Królewski)* BX – *Beer Street (Ulica Piwna)* BX – *Ulica Świętojańska* BX **57** – *St John's Cathedral★ (Katedra Św. Jana)* BX – *Old Town Marketplace★★★ (Rynek Starego Miasta)* BX **54** – *Warsaw History Museum★ (Muzeum Historyczne Warsawy)* BX **M¹** – *Barbakan* BX **A**.

NEW TOWN★ (NOWE MIASTO) ABX

New Town Marketplace (Rynek Nowego Miasta) ABX **36** – *Memorial to the Warsaw Uprising (Pomnik Powstania Warzszawskiego)* AX **D**.

ROYAL WAY★ (TRAKT KRÓLEWSKI)

St Anne's Church (Kościół Św. Anny) BX – *Krakow's District Street (Krakowskie Przedmieście)* BXY – *New World Street (Nowy Świat)* BYZ – *Holy Cross Church (Św. Krzyża)* BY – *National Museum★★ (Muzeum Narodowe)* CZ.

LAZIENKI PARK★★★ (PARK ŁAZIENKOWSKI) FUV

Chopin Memorial (Pomnik Chopina) – Palace-on-the-Water★★ (Pałac na Wodzie) – Belvedere Palace (Belweder).

WILANÓW★★★ GV

ADDITIONAL SIGHTS

John Paul II Collection★★ (Muzeum Kolekcji im. Jana Pawła II) AY – *Palace of Culture and Science (Pałac Kultury i Nauki): view★★ from panoramic gallery* AZ.

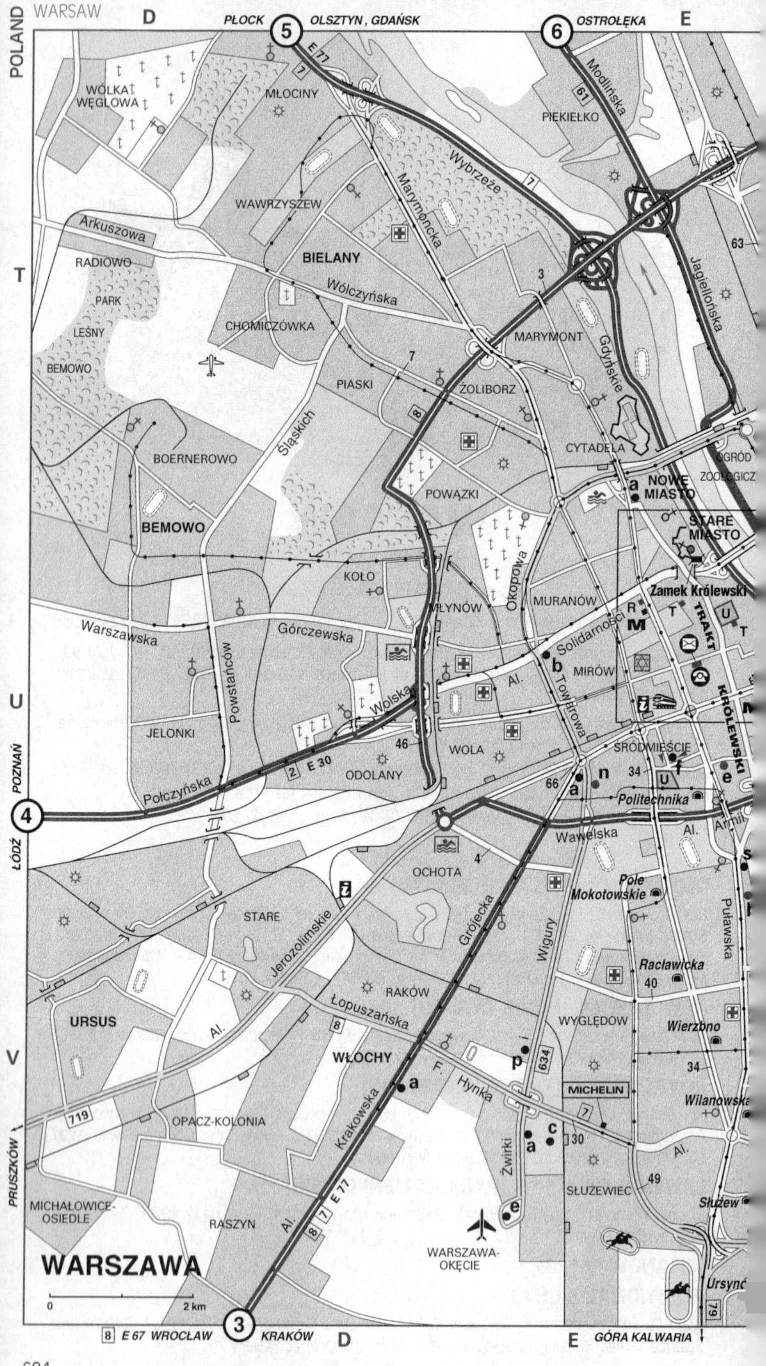

PŁOCK
OLSZTYN, GDAŃSK
OSTROŁĘKA
WÓLKA WĘGLOWA
MŁOCINY
PIEKIEŁKO
Modlińska
Wybrzeże
Marymoncka
WAWRZYSZEW
Arkuszowa
RADIOWO
BIELANY
Wólczyńska
PARK
LEŚNY
BEMOWO
CHOMICZÓWKA
MARYMONT
Gdyńskie
Jagiellońska
PIASKI
ŻOLIBORZ
BOERNEROWO
Śląskich
CYTADELA
OGRÓD ZOOLOGICZ
POWĄZKI
NOWE MIASTO
STARE MIASTO
BEMOWO
KOŁO
Okopowa
Zamek Królewski
MŁYNÓW
MURANÓW
Solidarności
TRAKT
KRÓLEWSKI
Warszawska
Górczewska
MIRÓW
Powstańców
Al.
Towarowa
Wolska
JELONKI
WOLA
ŚRÓDMIEŚCIE
POZNAŃ
Połczyńska
E 30
ODOLANY
Politechnika
ŁÓDŹ
Wawelska
Al. Armii
OCHOTA
Pole Mokotowskie
STARE
Jerozolimskie
Grójecka
Wigury
Puławska
Racławicka
RAKÓW
Łopuszańska
URSUS
Al.
WYGLĘDÓW
Wierzbno
WŁOCHY
F. Hynka
MICHELIN
Wilanowska
PRUSZKÓW
OPACZ-KOLONIA
Krakowska
Żwirki
Al.
SŁUŻEWIEC
Służew
MICHAŁOWICE-OSIEDLE
RASZYN
Al.
E 77
WARSZAWA-OKĘCIE
Ursynó
WARSZAWA
0
2 km
E 67 WROCŁAW
KRAKÓW
GÓRA KALWARIA

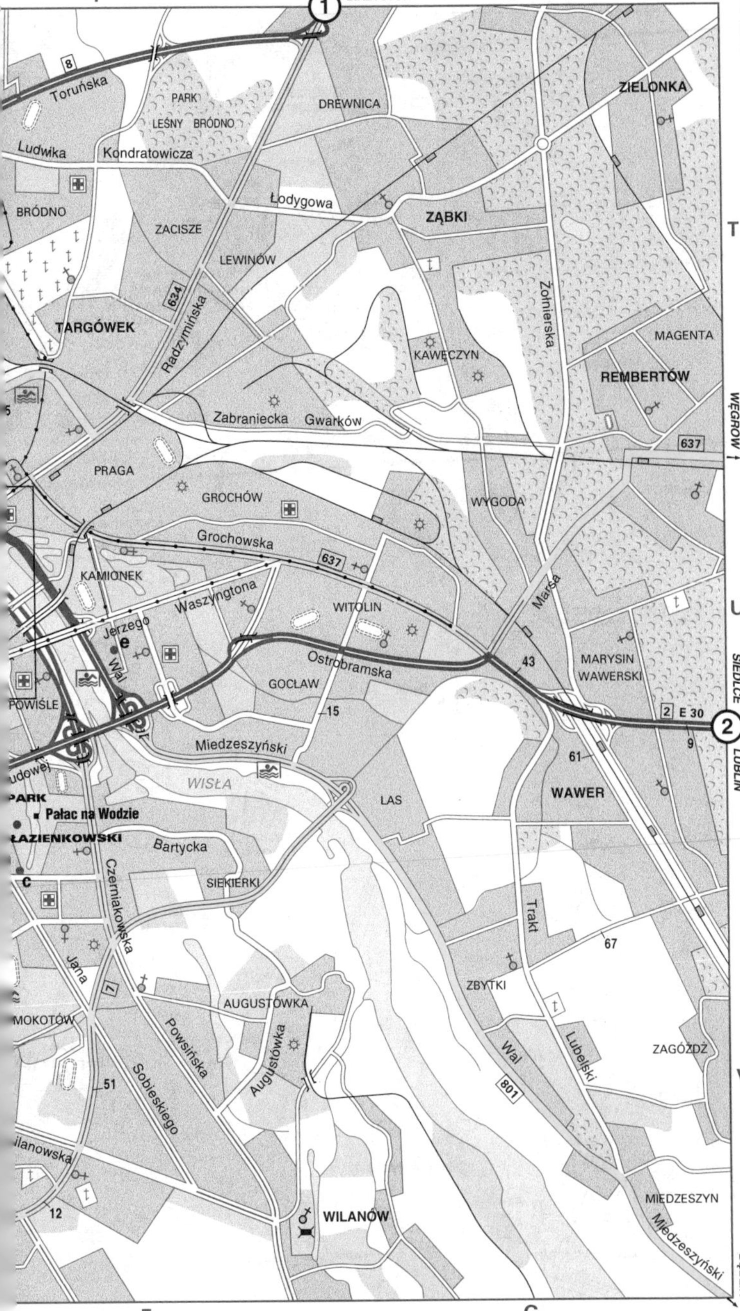

F
G
T
U
V
1 BIAŁYSTOK
2 E 30
WĘGRÓW
SIEDLCE
LUBLIN
DĘBLIN
ZIELONKA
DREWNICA
PARK LEŚNY BRÓDNO
Toruńska
Ludwika
Kondratowicza
Łodygowa
ZĄBKI
BRÓDNO
ZACISZE
LEWINÓW
Radzymińska
634
TARGÓWEK
Żołnierska
MAGENTA
KAWĘCZYN
REMBERTÓW
Zabraniecka
Gwarków
637
PRAGA
GROCHÓW
WYGODA
Grochowska
KAMIONEK
Waszyngtona
WITOLIN
Marsa
Jerzego
Wał
Ostrobramska
43
MARYSIN WAWERSKI
POWIŚLE
GOCŁAW
15
Miedzeszyński
61
9
WISŁA
LAS
WAWER
PARK
Pałac na Wodzie
ŁAZIENKOWSKI
Bartycka
SIEKIERKI
Czerniakowska
Trakt
67
Jana
7
ZBYTKI
AUGUSTÓWKA
MOKOTÓW
Powsińska
Augustówka
Lubelski
Wał
801
ZAGÓŹDŹ
51
Sobieskiego
Wilanowska
12
WILANÓW
MIEDZESZYN
Miedzeszyński
8

A B

NOWE MIASTO
Nawiedzenia Maryi Panny
Kościół Sakramentek
36
Freta
52
Św. Jacka
6
T
M
Sapieżyńska
Franciszkańska
Ciasna
Generała Władysława Andersa
Wałowa
Bonifraterska
Świętojerska
Św. Ducha
Pałac Raczyńskich
37
33
Syrena
STARE MIASTO
54
n
Kościół Jezuitów
ŚW. JANA
57
19
13
ZAMEK KRÓLEWSKI
Piwna
Podwale
64
Pałac Pod Blachą
Most Śląsko
Wybrzeże Gdańskie
724
X
24
D
Długa
PAŁAC KRASIŃSKICH
OGRÓD KRASIŃSKICH
PAŁAC POD CZTEREMA WIATRAMI
Miodowa
Nowolipki
MUZEUM ARCHEOLOGICZNE
Długa
Al. Solidarności
PAŁAC PRYMASOWSKI
Św. Anny
MARIENSZTAT
Dobra
Wybrzeże
Bednarska
Krakowskie
MURANÓW
Bielańska
Moliera
Kościół Karmelitów
Furmańska
Senatorska
58
TEATR WIELKI
a
Pałac Potockich
Pałac Radziwiłłów
Solidarności
R
Pl. Bankowy
Al.
Wierzbowa
MUZEUM KOLEKCJI IM. JANA PAWŁA II
n
TRAKT
28
Kościół Wizytek
Przechodnia
Elektoralna
Ptasia
Ogród Saski
42
Królewska
Przedmieście
U
Y
Pl. Mirowski
d
R. Traugutta
39
Św. Krzyża
MIRÓW
25
31
22
Królewska
Muzeum Etnograficzne
10
Al. Jana Pawła II
Grzybowska
a
f
g
Pl. Grzybowski
Świętokrzyska
Nowy Świat
T
Twarda
Marszałkowska
Jasna
45
Warecka
Ordynacka
KRÓLEWSKI
22
Świętokrzyska
Rondo Onz
FILHARMONIA
Pl. Defilad
JUNIOR
Górskiego
Chmielna
Prosta
a
Emilii Plater
Złota
SAWA
Zgoda
Pałac Branickich
n
Z
Twarda
Sienna
e
WARS
Krucza
16
Al. Jana Pawła II
Złota
Pałac Kultury i Nauki
Bracka
Chmielna
Al. Jerozolimskie
h
Nowogrodzka
Żurawia
Krucza
WARSZAWA CENTRALNA
Nowogrodzka
b
ŚRÓDMIEŚCIE

A B

STREET INDEX TO WARSZAWA TOWN PLANS

For maximum information from town plans: consult the conventional signs key.

Le Royal Meridien Bristol, Krakowskie Przedmieście 42-44, ✉ 00 325, ☎ (022) 551 10 00, *bristol@lemeridien.com.pl, Fax (022) 625 25 77,* – rm, – 130. rest BY n
Marconi : **Meals** - Mediterranean - (buffet lunch) 107/149 and a la carte 112/214 (see also ***Malinowa*** below) – 103 – **175 rm** 1675/2140, 30 suites.
◆ Imposing late 19C façade, partly decorated in Art Nouveau style fronts classic hotel, a byword for luxury and meeting place for Warsaw High Society. Spacious elegant rooms. Fairly informal restaurant with terrace offers a varied menu of Mediterranean fare.

Intercontinental, Emilii Plater 49, ✉ 00 125, ☎ (022) 328 88 88, *rsvn@icwarsaw.it.pl, Fax (022) 328 88 89,* – rm, – 490. rest AZ a
Frida : **Meals** *(closed Sunday and lunch Saturday)* a la carte 68/102 – ***Downtown :*** **Meals** (buffet lunch) 36/85 and lunch a la carte 63/85 – ***Hemisphere :*** **Meals** *(closed Monday)* (dinner only) a la carte 54/90 – 108 – **301 rm** 1155, 25 suites.
◆ Stunning skyscraper with modern facilities and leisure centre. Large, well-equipped bedrooms with contemporary décor. Frida for Mexican dishes from open plan kitchen. Downtown for an eclectic mix of styles. Informal Hemisphere with live contemporary music.

Hyatt Regency, Belwederska Ave 23, ✉ 00 761, ☎ (022) 558 12 34, *warsaw.reservations@hyattintl.com, Fax (022) 558 12 35,* – rm, – 120. FV a
Venti Tre : **Meals** - Italian - 65/75 (lunch) and a la carte 78/174 – 100 – **231 rm** 675/815, 19 suites.
◆ Striking glass fronted and ultra modern corporate hotel beside Lazienki Park. Capacious bedrooms with every conceivable facility and comfort. Enjoy contemporary Italian fare in relaxed surroundings. Central open kitchen with wood fired specialities.

The Westin, Aleja Jana Pawla II 21, ✉ 00 133, ☎ (022) 450 86 00, *warsaw@westin.com, Fax (022) 450 81 11,* – rm, – 560. rest AYZ g
Fusion : **Meals** (buffet lunch) 44/65 and a la carte 75/193 – 107 – **346 rm** 1111/2227, 15 suites.
◆ Modern hotel in the business district with glass lift shaft. Splendid glass atrium and spacious public areas. 'Heavenly beds' and modern facilities in comfortable bedrooms. Contemporary Fusion offers culinary delights with an Asian influence.

Sheraton, Ul. B. Prusa 2, ✉ 00 493, ☎ (022) 450 61 00, *warsaw@sheraton.com, Fax (022) 450 62 00,* – rm, – 350. rest CZ c
The Oriental : **Meals** - Oriental - a la carte 100/193 – ***Lalka :*** **Meals** (buffet lunch) 90/182 and a la carte 88/179 – 103 – **331 rm** 1111/1669, 19 suites.
◆ Luxurious business hotel in well situated imposing modern building. Spacious modern rooms with the latest hi-tech facilities. Authentic Asian fare in ornately decorated Oriental. All-day bistro with city view ; Mediterranean and traditional Polish dishes.

Marriott, Al. Jerozolimskie 65-79, ✉ 00 697, ☎ (022) 630 63 06, *marriott@it.com.pl, Fax (022) 830 03 11,* City, – – 700. rest AZ b
Parmizzano's : **Meals** - Italian - 93/209 and a la carte – ***Lila Weneda :*** **Meals** (buffet lunch) 84/163 and a la carte – 93 – **497 rm** 651/744, 25 suites.
◆ Modern high-rise business hotel near station. Extremely well equipped business centre. Excellent rooms with all mod-cons and every comfort. Relaxed Parmizzano's offers Italian fare. Classic Polish cooking in Lila Weneda.

Sofitel Victoria, Ul. Krølewska 11, ✉ 00 065, ☎ (022) 657 80 11, *sof.victoria@orbis.pl, Fax (022) 657 57 64,* – rm, – 400. rest BY d
Canaletto : **Meals** - Italian - 121/186 and a la carte – **329 rm** 1092, 12 suites.
◆ Large central modern hotel overlooking vast square. Rooms are well equipped and comfortable with muted classic modern décor. Good business facilities available. Gourmet Italian restaurant.

Radisson SAS Centrum, Grzybowska 24, ✉ 00 132, ☎ (022) 321 88 88, *info.warsaw@radissonsas.com, Fax (022) 321 88 89,* – rm, – 160. AY a
Latino Brasserie at Ferdy's : **Meals** - Argentinian - 50/65 (lunch) and a la carte 88/130 – 84 – **292 rm** 839/932, 19 suites.
◆ State of the art meeting facilities and well-equipped bedrooms make this a popular corporate hotel. Equallly impressive leisure. Elegant brasserie offers authentic Argentine and Latin American specialities.

Jan III Sobieski, Plac Artura Zawiszy 1, 02 025, (022) 579 10 00, *hotel@sobieski.com.pl, Fax (022) 659 88 28,* – rm, – 80. rest EU a
Meals a la carte 84/182 – **392 rm** 904/1326, 35 suites.
• Stylish modern city centre hotel popular with business clientele. Lobby leads to shops and atrium. Spacious well equipped modern rooms. Good conference facilities. Restaurant offers classic menu of traditional local fare with international overtones.

Holiday Inn, Ul. Złota 48-54, 00 120, (022) 697 39 99, *holiday@orbis.pl, Fax (022) 697 38 99,* – rm, – 200. rest AZ e
***Symfonia* : Meals** a la carte 83/228 – ***Brasserie* : Meals** (buffet only) 89 – 75 – **326 rm** 769/908, 10 suites.
• Modern corporate hotel near business district. Well furnished pleasant modern bedrooms with good level of comfort and facilities. Gourmet style restaurant for International cuisine and live music. Light and spacious brasserie.

Mercure Fryderyk Chopin, Al. Jana Pawła II 22, 00 133, (022) 620 02 01, *mercure@perytnet.pl, Fax (022) 620 87 79,* – rm, – 250 AY f
***Balzac* : Meals** – ***Stanislas* : Meals 242 rm**, 8 suites.
• Modern hotel located in business district, catering well for business clientele. Practically appointed rooms. Formal dining room offers good selection of French cuisine. Brasserie-style restaurant for traditional Polish and European dishes.

Novotel Centrum, Ul. Nowogrodzka 24-26, 00 511, (022) 621 02 71, *nov.warszawa@orbis.pl, Fax (022) 625 04 76* – rm, – 250. rest BZ h
Meals (buffet lunch) 40/140 and a la carte 40/70 – **723 rm** 630/699, 10 suites.
• 1970s style hotel tower block. Spacious well serviced rooms, with a mix of contemporary and original décor. Ask for a refurbished room with city views. Rotisserie restaurant for International cuisine.

Rialto, Wilcza 73, 00 670, (022) 584 87 00, *info@hotelrialto.com.pl, Fax (022) 584 87 01,* – – 25. rest EU f
***Kurt Scheller's* : Meals** 160 (dinner) and a la carte 80/218 – **33 rm** 895/1125, 11 suites.
• Modern hotel in converted 1906 building with super Art Deco features. Cosy smoking room and library. Individually decorated bedrooms with the latest in comfortand facilities. Modern and traditional dishes among the Art Deco posters in the restaurant.

Belwederski, Ul. Sulkiewicza 11, 00 758, (022) 840 40 11, *info@hotelbelwederski.pl, Fax (022) 840 08 47* – – 80. rest FU d
Meals 60/100 and a la carte 46/111 – **42 rm** 300/360, 8 suites.
• Comfortable hotel near park with functional lobby. Rooms are well equipped and well maintained. Singles are particularly pleasant. Fairly compact restaurant with peaceful atmosphere. Menu offers standard variety of traditional Polish cuisine.

Hetman, Klopotowskiego 36, 03 717, (022) 511 98 00, *hetman@hotelhetman.pl, Fax (022) 618 51 39* – rm, – 110. rest CX a
Meals (buffet lunch) 25/80 and a la carte 43/80 – **68 rm** 300/360.
• Modern hotel in a converted 19C apartment block, short walk over the river from the Old Town and city centre. Jacuzzi suite open to residents. Large modern bedrooms. Traditional dishes in Hetman.

Reytan, Ul. Rejtana 6, 02 516, (022) 646 31 66, *hotel@reytan.pl, Fax (022) 646 29 89* – rm, – 30. rest EU s
Meals 54/100 and a la carte 40/100 – **86 rm** 360/430.
• Plain modern hotel façade on quiet street. Rooms located in main building and rear annexe across car park. Modern décor and good functional fittings and facilities. Menu specialises in Polish and eastern borderland cooking ; vegetarian dishes also available.

Ibis Stare Miasto, Ul. Muranowska 2, 00 209, (022) 310 10 00, *h3714@accor-hotels.com, Fax (022) 310 10 10* – rm, rest, – 45. rest ET a
***l'Estaminet* : Meals** 51 and a la carte 61/68 – 26 – **333 rm** 340.
• Modern hotel close to the Old Town with 24-hour bar and business centre. Spacious, comfortable bedrooms with en suite shower ; larger rooms on 6th floor with balconies. Bistro-style restaurant providing simple traditional European dishes.

Ibis Centrum, Al. Solidarności 165, 00 876, (022) 520 30 00, *h2894@accor-hotels.com, Fax (022) 520 30 30* – rm, – 40. EU b
Meals 51 and a la carte 60/80 – 26 – **190 rm** 340.
• Located at intersection of two main roads by Warsaw Trade Tower. Good size rooms are light and airy, well sound-proofed, with modern functional fittings. Bistro-style restaurant on ground floor offers unfussy International, essentially Franco-Polish, cuisine.

Malinowa (at Le Royal Meridien Bristol H.), Krakowskie Przedmieście 42-44, ✉ 00 325, ✆ (022) 551 18 33, *Fax (022) 625 25 77* – ▤. AE VISA JCB. BY n
Meals - French - (dinner only) 163/479 and a la carte 168/480.
◆ Spacious formal dining room with classic elegant décor and chandeliers adding opulence. Elaborate gourmet menu offers international cuisine with a strong French influence.

Dom Polski, Ul. Francuska 11, ✉ 03 906, ✆ (022) 616 24 32, *restauracjadompolski@wp.pl, Fax (022) 616 24 88,* – ▤. AE VISA JCB. FU e
closed 24 and 31 December – **Meals** 26/93 and a la carte 58/101 ♀.
◆ Elegant house in city suburb with pleasant terrace-garden. Comfortable dining rooms on two floors with welcoming ambience. Interesting well presented traditional cuisine.

Belvedere, Ul. Agrykoli 1 (entry from Parkowa St), ✉ 00 460, ✆ (022) 841 22 50, *restauracja@belvedere.com.pl, Fax (022) 841 71 35,* – P. AE VISA JCB
closed 24 December-2 January – **Meals** a la carte 92/347 ♀.
◆ Elegant restaurant occupying late 19C orangery in Lazienkowski park. Dining room filled with statuesque plants. French-influenced International and Polish cuisine. FU d

Villa Foksal, Ul. Foksal 3-5, ✉ 00 924, ✆ (022) 827 87 16, *info@restauracjavillafoksal.pl, Fax (022) 826 53 37* – ▤ – 100. AE VISA JCB. CZ a
closed Spring Bank Holiday, 25 December and Sunday July-August – **Meals** (booking essential) a la carte 80/177 ♀.
◆ Restored villa restaurant tucked away in a quiet street. Book a table on the pretty terrace in summer. Modern cooking makes this a busy spot and a fashionable destination.

Restauracja Polska "Tradycja", Belwederska Ave 18A, ✉ 00 762, ✆ (022) 840 09 01, *restpolska@poczla.com.pl, Fax (022) 840 09 50,* – ▤ P. AE VISA JCB. FV c
closed 24 and 31 December – **Meals** (booking essential) a la carte 54.50/115.
◆ Five small dining rooms in a suburban house with garden terrace : 1920's décor, live piano music, candles and lace tablecloths. Well prepared traditional Polish cooking.

Casa Valdemar, Ul. Piekna 7-9, ✉ 00 539, ✆ (022) 628 81 40, *Fax (022) 622 88 96,* – ▤ EU e
◆ Elegant Spanish style installation inside and out with pleasant wooden terrace to front. Authentic Spanish cooking ; try the meat and fish from the clay oven.

La Bohème, Plac Teatralny 1, ✉ 00 950, ✆ (022) 692 06 81, *mail.restauracja.laboheme@laboheme.com.pl, Fax (022) 692 06 84,* – ▤. AE VISA BY a
closed 25 December-1 January – **Meals** 18/110 and a la carte 75/211 ♀.
◆ Beyond the bustling café you'll find a cosy and elegant restaurant. Menu offers an interesting mix of French and Italian specialities. Basement popular at dinner.

Flik, Ul. Puławska 43, ✉ 02 508, ✆ (022) 849 44 34, *restauracja@flik.com.pl, Fax (022) 849 44 06,* – ▤. AE VISA JCB EV h
Meals (buffet lunch) 48.50 and a la carte 51.50/102 ♀.
◆ Welcoming restaurant with good reputation overlooking square. Two contemporary style dining rooms with collection of paintings. Good quality well prepared traditional fare.

Restauracja Polska, Ul. Nowy Świat 21 (in the basement of the Polish Sculptors Union's Gallery), ✉ 00 029, ✆ (022) 826 38 77, *Fax (022) 828 31 32* – ▤ P. AE VISA JCB. BZ n
closed 24 and 31 December – **Meals** a la carte 54.50/115.
◆ Spacious dining room with local style décor, colourful table linen and subdued lighting augmented by candles. Menu offers variety of elaborate traditional cuisine.

U Fukiera, Rynek Starego Miasta 27, ✉ 00 272, ✆ (022) 831 10 13, *ufukiera@ufukiera.pl, Fax (022) 831 58 08,* –. AE VISA JCB. BX n
closed 24, 25 and 31 December – **Meals** a la carte 78/214.
◆ On central historic city square, stylish well run restaurant with traditional Polish décor and pleasant patio terrace to rear. Serves very sound traditional cuisine.

Swiętoszek, Ul. Jezuicka 6-8, ✉ 00 281, ✆ (022) 831 56 34, *rest.swietoszek@interia.pl, Fax (022) 635 59 47* – AE VISA. BX r
Meals 44/49 (lunch) and a la carte 67/152 ♀.
◆ Characterful restaurant in charming vaulted cellar in historic district. Rustic furniture, spot lights and candles add to ambience. Serves tasty traditional specialities.

Montmartre, Ul. Nowy Świat 7, ✉ 00 496, ✆ (022) 628 63 15, *poczta@restauracjamontmartre.com, Fax (022) 816 13 28* – P. AE VISA JCB BZ x
Meals a la carte 72/154 ♀.
◆ Well run traditional restaurant with old fashioned décor and tables arranged around serving bar. Cuisine is French influenced but essentially international in scope.

Inaba, Ul. Nowogrodzka 84-86, ✉ 02 018, (in the basement) ✆ (022) 622 59 55, *inaba@inaba.com.pl, Fax (022) 622 59 56* – ▤. AE VISA JCB. EU n
closed Easter, Christmas and lunch Saturday and Sunday – **Meals** - Japanese - 26/190 and a la carte 65/87.
◆ Choose from the lively sushi-bar or the relaxed restaurant in this discreetly located basement restaurant. Authentic Japanese cuisine prepared with skill and precision.

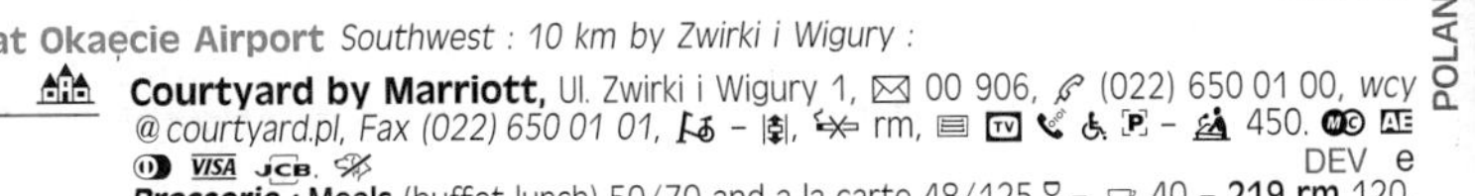

at Okęcie Airport *Southwest : 10 km by Zwirki i Wigury :*

Courtyard by Marriott, Ul. Zwirki i Wigury 1, ✉ 00 906, ☎ (022) 650 01 00, *wcy@courtyard.pl, Fax (022) 650 01 01,* – |⇕|, ⇍ rm, ▤ TV ✆ ♿ P – 🏛 450. MC AE ⓓ VISA JCB. ✗ DEV e
***Brasserie* : Meals** (buffet lunch) 50/70 and a la carte 48/125 ♀ – ▭ 40 – **219 rm** 120, 7 suites.
◆ Modern hotel opposite the airport entrance. Bar and cyber café with internet access ; conference facilities. Well-equipped modern bedrooms with effective sound proofing. Mezzanine brasserie offering an eclectic range of international dishes.

Airport Okęcie, Ul. 17 Stycznia 24, ✉ 02 146, ☎ (022) 456 80 00, *rezerwacja@airporthotel.pl, Fax (022) 456 80 29,* – |⇕|, ⇍ rm, ▤ TV ✆ ♿ P – 🏛 60. MC AE ⓓ VISA JCB. ✗ rest EV c
***Club* : Meals** a la carte 63/128 – ***Mirage* : Meals** (buffet only) 50/110 and a la carte 62/98 ♀ – **173 rm** ▭ 532/649, 7 suites.
◆ Bright and modern corporate hotel 800 metres from the airport. Spacious meeting and bedrooms have both the international traveller and conference delegate in mind. Elegant and intimate 'Club'. Lively and popular 'Mirage' with open plan kitchen and buffet.

Lord, Al. Krakowska 218, ✉ 02 219, ☎ (022) 574 20 20, *okecie@hotellord.com.pl, Fax (022) 574 20 01,* – |⇕| ▤ TV ✆ ♿ P – 🏛 60. MC AE ⓓ VISA JCB. ✗ rest
Meals a la carte approx 85 – **92 rm** ▭ 310/350, 4 suites. DV a
◆ Bright and modern corporate hotel convenient for Frederic Chopin International Airport. Well kept and functional bedrooms. 6th floor café bar with terrace and city views. Elegant dining room offers classic Polish cooking.

Novotel Airport, Ul. Sierpnia 1, ✉ 02 134, ☎ (022) 575 60 00, *nov.airport@orbis.pl, Fax (022) 575 69 99,* – |⇕|, ⇍ rm, ▤ TV ✆ ♿ P – 🏛 300. MC AE ⓓ VISA JCB. ✗ rest EV p
Meals and a la carte 76/112 ♀ – **270 rm** ▭ 596/652.
◆ Modern functional hotel not far from airport, which caters well for families and business people. Rooms are of adequate size, practical and well maintained. Private garden. Bright and modern restaurant specialises in international cuisine to suit all tastes.

Gromada, Ul. Stycznia 32, ✉ 02 148, ☎ (022) 576 46 50, *airport@gromada.pl, Fax (022) 846 71 01* – |⇕|, ⇍ rm, TV P – 🏛 1200. MC AE ⓓ VISA JCB EV a
Meals a la carte approx 70 ♀ – **323 rm** ▭ 499/610, 29 suites.
◆ Practical hotel in vicinity of airport ; and one of the city's largest conference venues. Try and reserve a bedroom in the more recent extension. Functional restaurant to cater to international tastes. Menu offers selection of traditional Polish dishes.

Portugal

LISBON

PRACTICAL INFORMATION

LOCAL CURRENCY

1 euro (€) = 1,20 USD ($) (Dec 2003)

National Holiday in Portugal: *10 June.*

FOREIGN EXCHANGE

Hotels, restaurants and shops do not always accept foreign currencies and the tourist is therefore advised to change cheques and currency at banks, saving banks and exchange offices. The general opening times are as follows: banks 8.30am to 3pm (closed on Saturdays, Sundays, and Bank Holidays), money changers 9.30am to 6pm (usually closed on Sundays and Bank Holidays).

TRANSPORT

Taxis may be hailed when showing the green light or "Livre" sign on the windscreen. Metro (subway) network. In each station complete information and plans will be found.

SHOPPING IN LISBON

Shops and boutiques are generally open from 9am to 7pm. In Lisbon, the main shopping streets are: Rua Augusta, Rua do Carmo, Rua Garrett (Chiado), Rua do Ouro, Rua da Prata, Av. de Roma, Av. da Liberdade, Shopping Center Amoreiras, Shopping Center Colombo.

TIPPING

Hotels, restaurants and café bills always include service in the total charge. Nevertheless it is usual to leave the staff a small gratuity which may vary depending upon the district and the service given. Doormen, porters and taxi-drivers are used to being tipped.

SPEED LIMITS

The maximum permitted speed on motorways is 120 km/h - 74 mph, on other roads 90 km/h -56 mph and in built up areas 50 km/h - 37 mph.

SEAT BELTS

The wearing of seat belts is compulsory for drivers and all passengers.

THE FADO

The Lisbon Fado (songs) can be heard in restaurants in old parts of the town such as the Alfama, the Bairro Alto and the Mouraria. A selection of fado cabarets will be found at the end of the Lisbon restaurant list.

LISBON

(LISBOA)

(LISBOA) P 733 P 2 – *Pop. 662 782 – alt. 111.*

Paris 1785 – Madrid 624 – Bilbao 902 – Porto 310 – Sevilla 402.

Palácio Foz, Praça dos Restaudores ✉ 1250-187 ☎ 21 346 33 14, Fax 21 346 87 72 – Santa Apolónia Station (International Arrivals), ✉ 1100-105, ☎ 21 882 16 04, and airport ✉ 1700-111, ☎ 21 845 06 60, Fax 21 845 06 58 – A.C.P. Rua Rosa Araújo 49, ✉ 1250-195, ☎ 21 318 01 10, Fax 21 318 02 27.

18, 9 *Estoril* **W** *: 25 km ☎ 21 468 01 76, Fax 21 468 27 96 –* 18 *Lisbon Sports Club* **NW** *: 20 km ☎ 21 431 00 77 –* 18 *Club de Campo da Aroeira* **S** *: 15 km ☎ 21 297 91 10 Aroeira, Charneca da Caparica.*

Lisbon Airport **N** *: 8 km from city centre ☎ 21 841 35 00 – T.A.P., Av. de Berlim (Orient Station Building), ✉ 1800-033, ☎ 21 317 91 00 – Portugalia, Rua C – Edifício 70, Lisbon airport ✉ 1749-078, ☎ 21 842 55 00 and airport ☎ 21 841 50 00.*

Santa Apolónia ☎ 21 881 61 21 MX.

SIGHTS

VIEWS OVER LISBON

<★★ from the Suspension Bridge (Ponte 25 de Abril★) **S**: *by Av. da Ponte* EU – *✳★★ from Christ in Majesty (Cristo Rei)* **S**: *by Av. da Ponte* EU – *St. Georges Castle★★ (Castelo de São Jorge: <★★★)* LX – *Santa Luzia Belvedere★ (Miradouro de Santa Luzia): <★★* LY **L¹** – *Santa Justa Lift★ (Elevador de Santa Justa): <★* KY – *São Pedro de Alcântara Belvedere★ (Miradouro de São Pedro de Alcâtara): <★★* JX **L²** – *Alto de Santa Catarina Belvedere★* JZ **A¹** – *Senhora do Monte Belvedere (Miradouro da Senhora do Monte): ✳★★★* LV – *Largo das Portas do Sol★: <★★* LY – *Church & Convent of Our Lady of Grace Belvedere (Igreja e Convento de Nossa Senhora da Graça, Miradouro★)* LX

MUSEUMS

Museum of Ancient Art★★★ (Museum Nacional de Arte Antiga; polyptych da Adoração de São Vicente★★★, Tentação de Santo Antão★★★, Japanese folding screens★★, Twelve' Apostles★, Anunciação★, Chapel★) EU **M¹⁶** – *Gulbenkian Foundation (Calouste Gulbenkian Museum★★★* FR, *Modern Art Centre★* FR **M²**) – *Maritime Museum★★ (Museu de Marinha: model boats★★★)* **W**: *by Av. 24 de Julho* EU – *Azulejo Museum★★ (Madre de Deus Convent: Church★★, chapter house★)* **NE**: *by Av. Infante D. Henrique* MX – *Water Museum EPAL★ (Museu da Água da EPAL)* HT **M⁵** – *Costume Museum★ (Museu Nacional do Traje)* **N**: *by Av. da República* GR – *Theatre Museum★ (Museu Nacional do Teatro)* **N**: *by Av. da República* GR – *Military Museum (Museu Militar; cellings★)* MY **M¹⁵** – *Museum of Decorative Arts★★ (Museu de Artes Decorativas: Fundação Ricardo do Espírito Santo Silva)* LY **M¹³** – *Archaeological Museum (Igreja do Carmo★)* KY **M⁴** – *São Roque Arte Sacra Museum★ (vestments★)* JKX **M¹¹** – *Chiado Museum★ (Museu Nacional do Chiado)* KZ **M¹⁸** – *Music Museum★ (Museu da Música)* **N**: *by Av. da República* GR – *Rafael Bordalo Pinheiro Museum (ceramics★)* **N**: *by Av. da Republica* GR.

CHURCHES AND MONASTERIES

Cathedral★★ (Sé: gothic tombs★, grille★, tresor★) LY – *Hieronymite Monastery★★★ (Monasteiro dos Jerónimos): Santa Maria Church★★★ (vaulting★★, cloister★★★; Archaeological Museum: treasury★)* **W**: *by Av. 24 de Julho* EU – *São Roque Church★ (São João Baptista Chapel★★, interior★)* JX – *São Vicente de Fora Church (azulejos★)* MX – *Our Lady of Fátima Church (Igreja de Nossa Senhora de Fátima: windows★)* FR **D²** – *Estrela Basilica★ (garden★)* EU **A²** – *Old Conception Church (Igreja da Conceição Velha: south front★)* LZ **D¹** – *Santa Engrácia Church★* MX.

HISTORIC QUARTERS

Belém★★ (Culture Centre★) **W**: *by Av. 24 de Julho* EU – *The Baixa★★* JKXYZ – *Alfama★★* LY – *Chiado and Bairro Alto★* JKY.

PLACES OF INTEREST

Praça do Comércio★★ (or Terreiro do Paço) KZ – *Belém Tower★★★ (Torre de Belém)* **W**: *by Av. 24 de Julho* EU – *Marquis Fronteira Palace★★ (Palácio dos Marqueses de Fronteira: azulejos★★)* ER – *Rossio★ (station: neo-manuelina façade★)* KX – *Do Carmo st. and Garrett st. (Rua do Carmo and Rua Garrett)* KY – *Liberdade Ave★ (Avenida da Liberdade)* JV – *Edward VII Park★ (Parque Eduardo VII: <★, greenhouse★)* FS – *Zoological Garden★★ (Jardin Zoológico)* ER – *Águas Livres Aqueduct★ (Aqueduto das Águas Livres)* ES – *Botanic Garden★ (Jardim Botánico)* JV – *Monsanto Park★ Belvedere (Parque Florestal de Monsanto: Miradouro: ✳★)* ER – *Campo de Santa Clara★* MX – *Santo Estêvão stairway and terrace★ (<★)* MY – *Ajuda Palace★ (Palacio da Ajuda)* **W**: *by Av. 24 de Julho* EU – *Arpad Szenes-Vieira da Silva Foundation★* EFS – *Boat trip on the river Tagus★ (<★★)* – *Vasco da Gama bridge★★* **NE**: *by Av. Infante D. Henrique* MX – *Lisbon oceanarium★★* **NE**: *by Av. Infante D. Henrique* MX – *East Station★ (Estação de Oriente)* **NE**: *by Av. Infante D. Henrique* MX.

STREET INDEX TO LISBOA TOWN PLANS

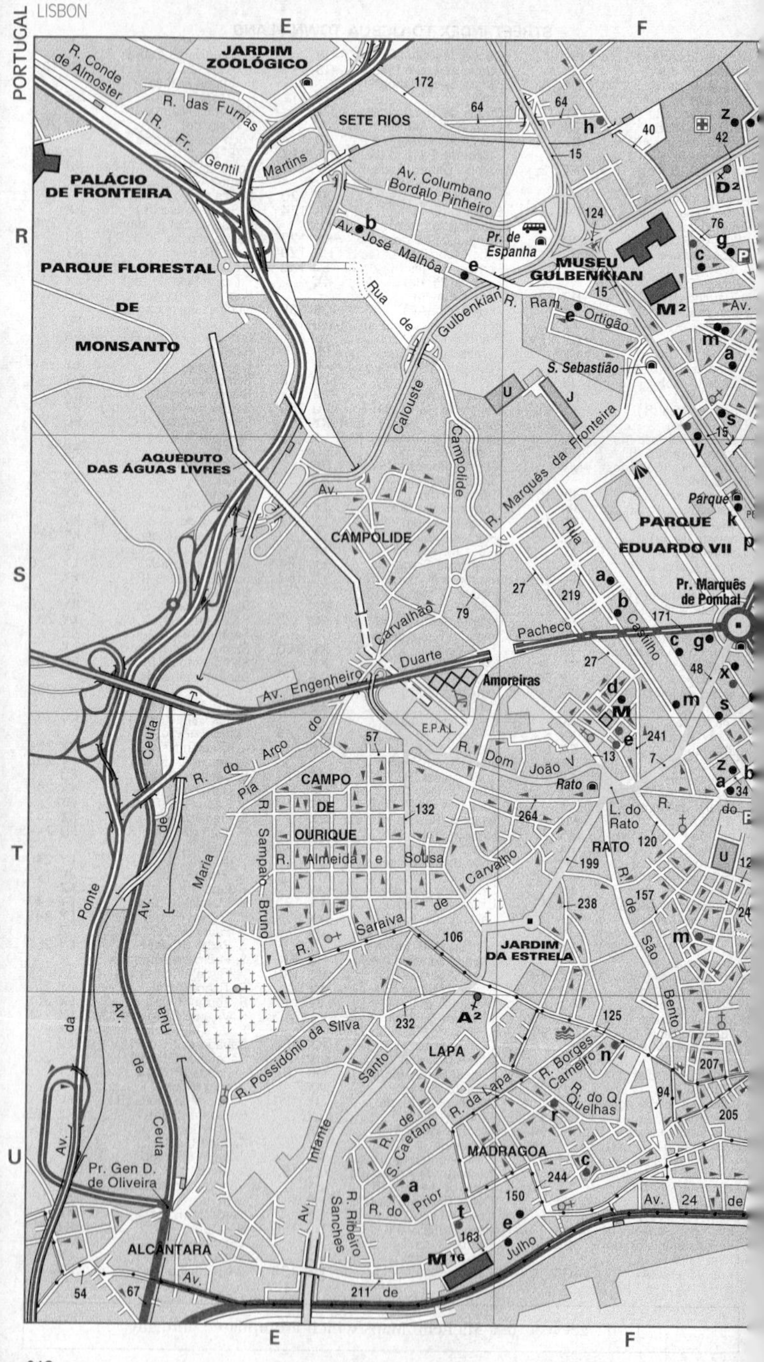
JARDIM ZOOLÓGICO
SETE RIOS
PALÁCIO DE FRONTEIRA
PARQUE FLORESTAL DE MONSANTO
AQUEDUTO DAS ÁGUAS LIVRES
CAMPOLIDE
MUSEU GULBENKIAN
S. Sebastião
Pr. de Espanha
PARQUE EDUARDO VII
Pr. Marquês de Pombal
Amoreiras
E.P.A.L.
CAMPO DE OURIQUE
Rato
L. do Rato
RATO
JARDIM DA ESTRELA
LAPA
MADRAGOA
ALCÂNTARA
Pr. Gen D. de Oliveira
R. Conde de Almoster
R. das Furnas
R. Fr. Gentil Martins
Av. Columbano Bordalo Pinheiro
Av. José Malhôa
Rua de
Calouste Gulbenkian
R. Ram. Ortigão
Campolide
R. Marquês da Fronteira
Rua
Castilho
Pacheco
Carvalhão
Av. Engenheiro Duarte
R. Dom João V
R. do Arco do
Pia
R. Sampaio Bruno
R. Almeida e Sousa
Carvalho
R. Saraiva de
R. de São Bento
R. Possidónio da Silva
Santo
Infante
Av.
R. Ribeiro Sanches
R. de S. Caetano
R. da Lapa
R. Borges Carneiro
R. do Q. Quelhas
R. do Prior
Julho
Av. 24 de
Av. de Ceuta
Rua de Ceuta
Av. da Ponte
Maria
Av.
Av. 211 de
M16
A2
M2
D2
U
J
M

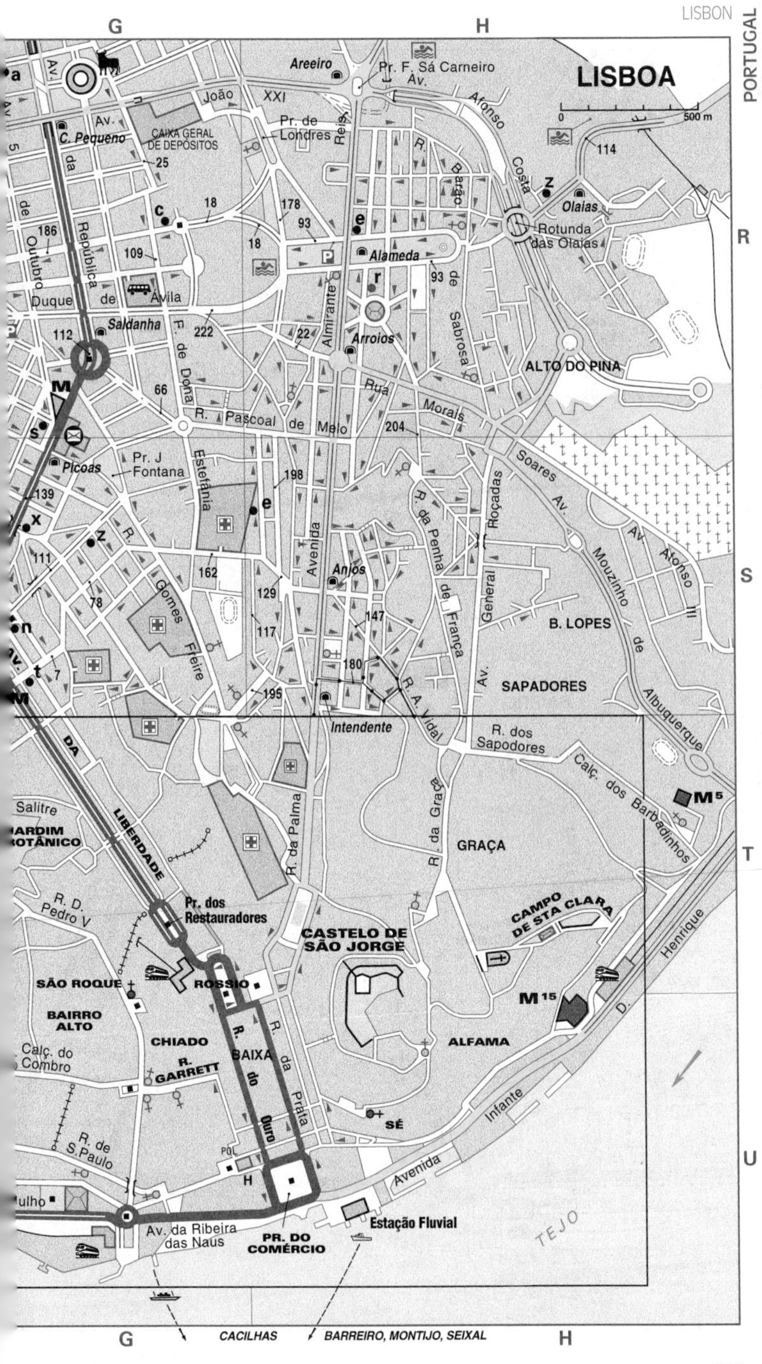
LISBOA
G
H
R
S
T
U
Areeiro
Pr. F. Sá Carneiro
Av. João XXI
Pr. de Londres
Av. Afonso Costa
Reis
0
500 m
114
CAIXA GERAL DE DEPÓSITOS
C. Pequeno
Av. da República
Av. 5 de Outubro
R. Barão de Sabrosa
Olaias
Rotunda das Olaias
Alameda
Arroios
Saldanha
Duque de Ávila
Av. Almirante Reis
ALTO DO PINA
Picoas
Pr. J Fontana
R. Pascoal de Melo
Rua Morais Soares
R. Estefânia
F. de Dona
R. Gomes Freire
Avenida
Anjos
R. da Penha de França
General Roçadas
Av. Afonso III
Av. Mouzinho de Albuquerque
B. LOPES
SAPADORES
Intendente
R. A. Vidal
R. dos Sapadores
Calç. dos Barbadinhos
Salitre
JARDIM BOTÂNICO
DA LIBERDADE
R. da Palma
R. da Graça
GRAÇA
R. D. Pedro V
Pr. dos Restauradores
CASTELO DE SÃO JORGE
CAMPO DE STA CLARA
SÃO ROQUE
ROSSIO
BAIRRO ALTO
CHIADO
R. GARRETT
BAIXA
R. do Ouro
R. da Prata
ALFAMA
Calç. do Combro
SÉ
Infante D. Henrique
R. de S.Paulo
Avenida
Estação Fluvial
Av. da Ribeira das Naus
PR. DO COMÉRCIO
TEJO
CACILHAS
BARREIRO, MONTIJO, SEIXAL

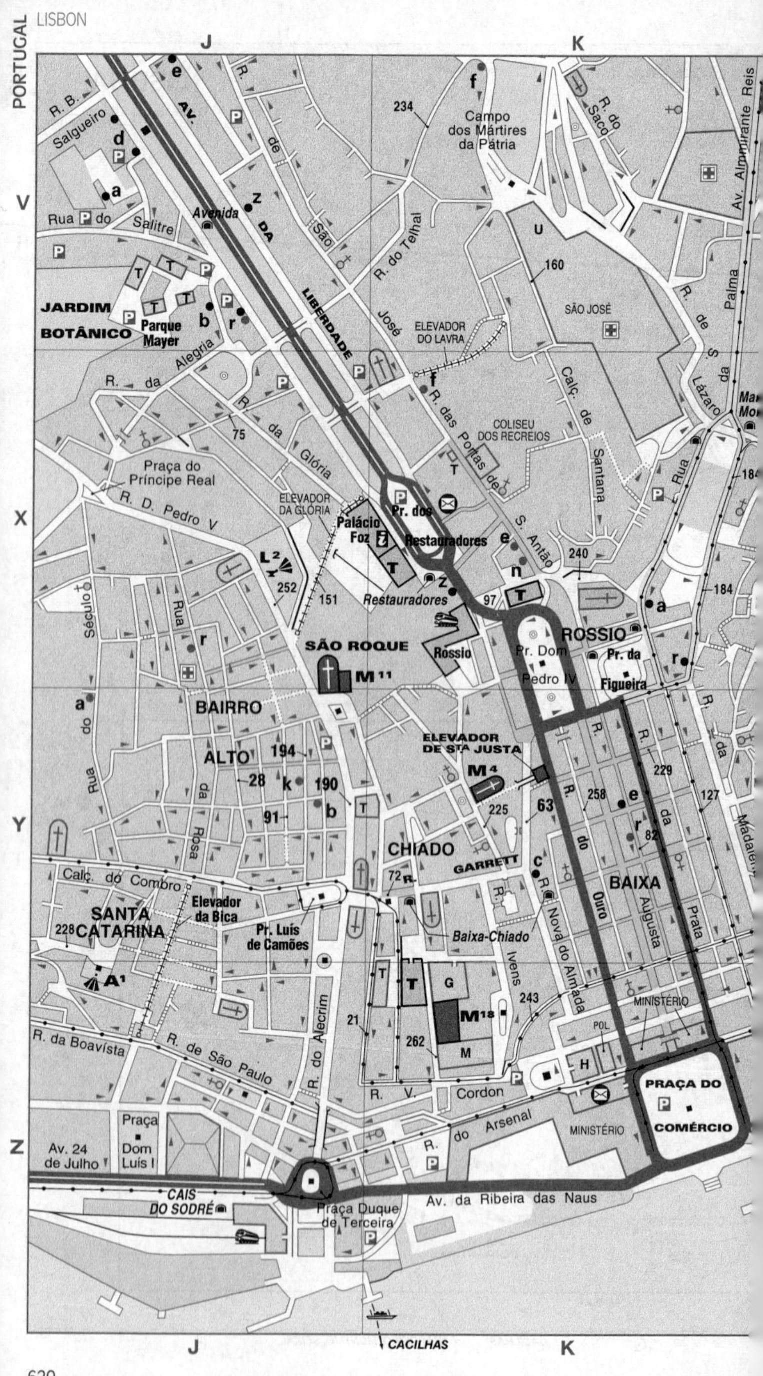

Campo dos Mártires da Pátria
JARDIM BOTÂNICO
Parque Mayer
Rua do Salitre
R. B. Salgueiro
Avenida
AV. DA LIBERDADE
R. de São José
R. do Telhal
ELEVADOR DO LAVRA
R. do Saco
Av. Almirante Reis
SÃO JOSÉ
R. de S. Lázaro
R. da Palma
Calç. de Santana
R. das Portas de S. Antão
COLISEU DOS RECREIOS
R. da Alegria
R. da Glória
Praça do Príncipe Real
R. D. Pedro V
ELEVADOR DA GLÓRIA
Palácio Foz
Pr. dos Restauradores
Restauradores
Rossio
ROSSIO
Pr. Dom Pedro IV
Pr. da Figueira
SÃO ROQUE
BAIRRO ALTO
Rua da Rosa
Rua do Século
ELEVADOR DE STA JUSTA
CHIADO
GARRETT
BAIXA
R. do Ouro
R. Augusta
R. da Prata
R. da Madalena
R. Nova do Almada
R. Ivens
Baixa-Chiado
Calç. do Combro
Elevador da Bica
SANTA CATARINA
Pr. Luís de Camões
R. do Alecrim
R. da Boavista
R. de São Paulo
R. V. Cordon
R. do Arsenal
MINISTÉRIO
POL
PRAÇA DO COMÉRCIO
Praça Dom Luís I
Av. 24 de Julho
CAIS DO SODRÉ
Praça Duque de Terceira
Av. da Ribeira das Naus
CACILHAS

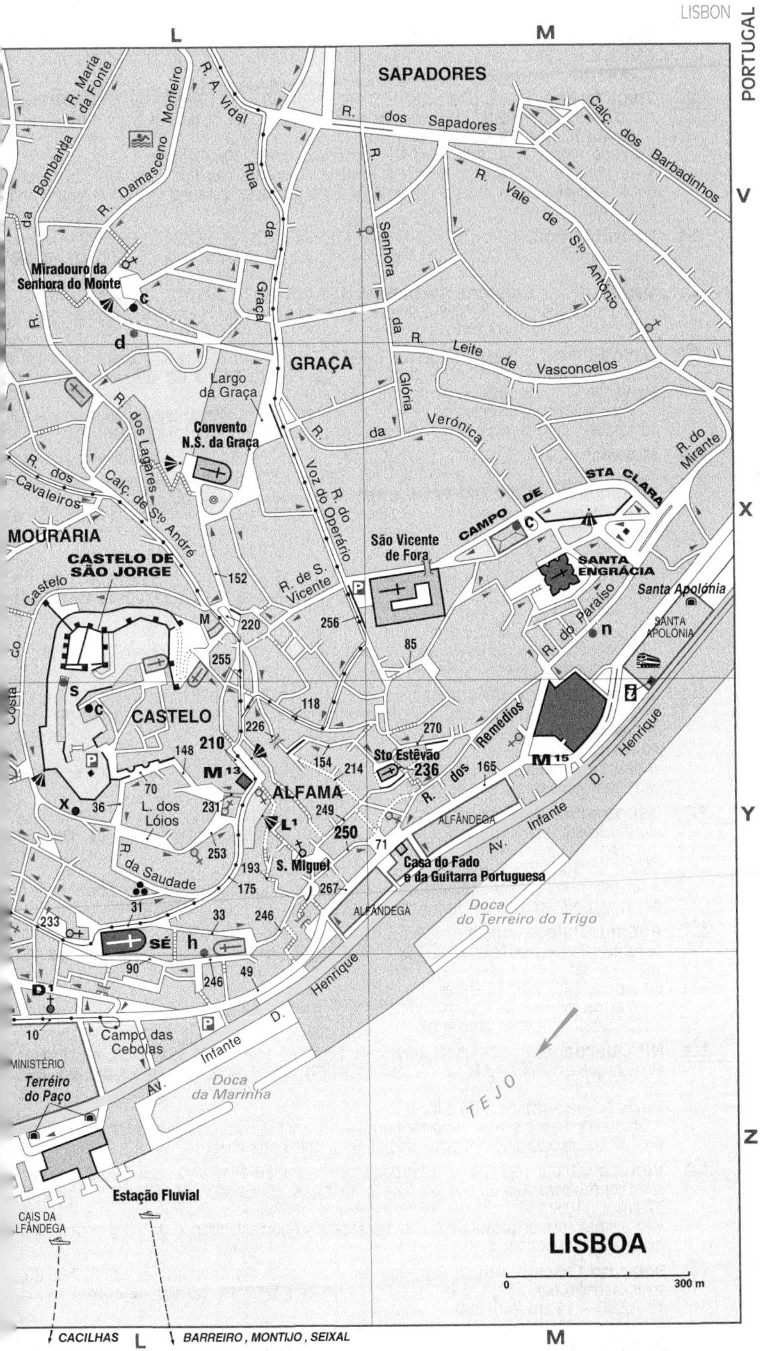
LISBOA
SAPADORES
GRAÇA
MOURARIA
CASTELO DE SÃO JORGE
CASTELO
ALFAMA
Miradouro da Senhora do Monte
Convento N.S. da Graça
Largo da Graça
São Vicente de Fora
CAMPO DE STA CLARA
SANTA ENGRÁCIA
Santa Apolónia
Sto Estêvão
S. Miguel
Casa do Fado e da Guitarra Portuguesa
SÉ
Terréiro do Paço
Estação Fluvial
Doca do Terreiro do Trigo
Doca da Marinha
TEJO
CAIS DA ALFÂNDEGA
CACILHAS
BARREIRO, MONTIJO, SEIXAL
R. dos Sapadores
Calç. dos Barbadinhos
R. Vale de Sto António
R. Leite de Vasconcelos
R. da Verónica
R. do Mirante
R. Senhora da Glória
Rua da Graça
R. A. Vidal
R. Damasceno Monteiro
R. Maria da Fonte
R. da Bombarda
R. dos Lagares
Calç. de Sto André
R. dos Cavaleiros
Costa do Castelo
R. de S. Vicente
R. do Voz do Operário
R. do Paraíso
R. dos Remédios
R. da Saudade
L. dos Lóios
Av. Infante D. Henrique
Campo das Cebolas
MINISTÉRIO
ALFÂNDEGA
300 m

Centre : Av. da Liberdade, Praça dos Restauradores, Praça Dom Pedro IV (Rossio), Praça do Comércio, Rua Dom Pedro V, Rua de Santa Catarina, Campo de Santa Clara, Rua dos Sapadores

Tivoli Lisboa, Av. da Liberdade 185, ✉ 1269-050, ☎ 21 319 89 00, *htlisboa@mail.telepac.pt, Fax 21 319 89 50,* ≤ city from the terrace, , heated – 25 40/200. AE VISA JCB. JV d
Terraço : **Meals** a la carte 44/74 – **300 rm** 250/270, 29 suites.
• Elegant, comfortable and with fine views from the top floor. Pleasant, tastefully decorated and well-equipped bedrooms. The Terraço restaurant is both smart and traditional.

Sofitel Lisboa, Av. da Liberdade 127, ✉ 1269-038, ☎ 21 322 83 00, *h1319@accor-hotels.com, Fax 21 322 83 60* – rm, – 25/300. AE VISA JCB JV r
Meals (see rest. ***Brasserie Avenue*** below) – **165 rm** 205/225, 5 suites.
• A friendly welcome, comfortable and with a contemporary classic feel. Enjoy a pleasant stay in agreeable surroundings.

Lisboa Plaza, Travessa do Salitre 7, ✉ 1269-066, ☎ 21 321 82 18, *plaza.hotels@heritage.pt, Fax 21 347 16 30* – – 25/140. AE VISA JCB. JV b
Meals 22,50 – 12,50 – **94 rm** 210/230, 12 suites.
• Near the famous Avenida da Liberdade. Very traditional with distinguished and tasteful atmosphere and classic décor. A large buffet is available in the dining room.

Mundial, Rua D. Duarte 4, ✉ 1100-198, ☎ 21 884 20 00, *info@hotel-mundial.pt, Fax 21 884 21 10,* ≤ – – 25/120. AE VISA JCB. KX a
- ***Varanda de Lisboa :*** **Meals** a la carte 27/44 – **262 rm** 147/152.
• Refurbished with all mod cons. Pleasant, well-appointed bedrooms in the heart of the Baixa Pombalina area. There are splendid views from the Varanda restaurant on the 8th floor.

Tivoli Jardim, Rua Julio Cesar Machado 7, ✉ 1250-135, ☎ 21 359 10 00, *htjardim@mail.telepac.pt, Fax 21 359 12 45,* – – 25/40. AE VISA JCB. JV a
Meals a la carte 22/25,50 – **119 rm** 170/185.
• Modern efficiency for the business traveller. A large foyer, conference rooms and pleasantly decorated bedrooms. The brightly-lit dining room offers traditional dishes.

Lisboa Regency Chiado without rest, Rua Nova do Almada 114, ✉ 1200-290, ☎ 21 325 61 00, *regencychiado@madeiraregency.pt, Fax 21 325 61 61* – . AE VISA. KY c
40 rm 185/195.
• Pleasantly situated in a building in the old part of the city. Friendly, professional service, with bedrooms decorated in oriental style.

Lisboa coffee shop only, Rua Barata Salgueiro 5, ✉ 1166-069, ☎ 21 350 00 00, *reservas-hotlis@netcabo.pt, Fax 21 355 41 39* – . AE VISA JCB. JV e
55 rm 300/400, 6 suites.
• An ideal hotel for the business traveller in an important business district. Comfort, tradition and efficiency in a small, former palace. Well-equipped bedrooms.

Avenida Palace without rest, Rua 1º de Dezembro 123, ✉ 1200-359, ☎ 21 321 81 00, *hotel.av.palace@mail.telepac.pt, Fax 21 342 28 84* – – 25/100. AE VISA JCB. KX z
64 rm 135/165, 18 suites.
• An attractive and well-run hotel in the cultural and commercial quarter. Service, quality and a classic old-world ambience.

NH Liberdade, Av. da Liberdade 180-B, ✉ 1250-146, ☎ 21 351 40 60, *nhliberdade@nh-hotels.es, Fax 21 314 36 74,* – – 25/35. AE VISA JCB. JV z
Meals 30 – **83 rm** 226/240.
• Situated in Lisbon's most important business district. A comfortable and functional hotel with all the quality and characteristic style of this hotel chain.

Veneza without rest, Av. da Liberdade 189, ✉ 1250-141, ☎ 21 352 26 18, *comercial@3khoteis.com, Fax 21 352 66 78* – . AE VISA JCB. JV d
37 rm 105/130.
• In a small former palace with a lovely façade. A perfect balance of old grandeur and modern day functionality.

Solar do Castelo without rest, Rua das Cozinhas 2, ✉ 1100-181, ☎ 21 887 09 09, *solar.castelo@heritage.pt, Fax 21 887 09 07* – . AE VISA JCB. LY c
12,50 – **14 rm** 245/280.
• A small 18C palace in an area with lots of historic monuments. A comfortable and completely renovated interior. Modern bedrooms with attractive design details.

Solar dos Mouros without rest, Rua do Milagre de Santo Antonio 6, ✉ 1100-351, ☎ 218 85 49 40, *reservation@solardosmouros.pt, Fax 218 85 49 45,* ≤ - ▤ TV. AE ① MC VISA JCB LY x
8 rm ☕ 175/240.
◆ A typical house which has been modernised and furnished with personal touches, including four paintings by the owner himself. Colourful bedrooms, some with excellent views.

Albergaria Senhora do Monte without rest, Calçada do Monte 39, ✉ 1170-250, ☎ 21 886 60 02, *senhoradomonte@hotmail.com, Fax 21 887 77 83,* ≤ São Jorge castle, town and river Tagus - |‡| ▤ TV. AE ① MC VISA. ✻ LV c
28 rm ☕ 99/126.
◆ Quiet accommodation in the residential district of Graça. A small, attractive and well-run hotel. Pleasant bedrooms with classic décor, some with balcony.

Lisboa Tejo without rest, Poço do Borratém 4, ✉ 1100-408, ☎ 21 886 61 82, *hotellisboatejo.reservas@evidenciagrupo.com, Fax 21 886 51 63* - |‡| ▤ TV. AE ① MC VISA JCB. ✻ KX r
58 rm ☕ 100/110.
◆ Moderate prices and pleasant, well-appointed bedrooms in the Baixa Pombalina district. A modern, refurbished and central hotel with a traditional atmosphere and elegant décor.

Insulana without rest, Rua da Assunção 52, ✉ 1100-044, ☎ 21 342 76 25, *insulana@netc.pt, Fax 21 342 89 24* - |‡| ▤ TV. AE ① MC VISA. ✻ KY e
32 rm ☕ 50/60.
◆ In the heart of the Baixa Pombalina district with reasonable prices. A pleasant, comfortable and well-situated hotel with adequate facilities.

XXXX **Clara,** Campo dos Mártires da Pátria 49, ✉ 1150-225, ☎ 21 885 30 53, *clararestaurant@mail.telepac.pt, Fax 21 885 20 82,* 🏖 - ▤. AE ① MC VISA JCB. ✻ KV f
closed 1 to 15 August, Saturday lunch and Sunday - **Meals** a la carte 25/29,50.
◆ In the city centre and with a beautiful terrace-garden and attractive décor. An elegant, friendly and very comfortable restaurant in a pleasant setting.

XXX **Gambrinus,** Rua das Portas de Santo Antão 25, ✉ 1150-264, ☎ 21 342 14 66, *Fax 21 346 50 32* - ▤. AE MC VISA. ✻ KX n
Meals a la carte 72/86.
◆ In the historic centre of the city near the Rossio district. A restaurant with a well-established reputation backed up by fine cuisine and an excellent wine list.

XXX **Brasserie Avenue** - *Hotel Sofitel Lisboa* with buffet, Av. da Liberdade 127 A/B, ✉ 1269-038, ☎ 21 322 83 50, *h1319-fb@accor-hotels.com, Fax 21 322 83 60,* 🏖 - ▤ 🚗. AE ① MC VISA JCB. ✻ JV r
Meals 26,20 and a la carte 27/36.
◆ In the elegant Hotel Sofitel. A pleasant restaurant offering fine cooking in a distinguished setting. Both à la carte and buffet.

XXX **Consenso,** Rua da Académia das Ciências 1-A, ✉ 1200-003, ☎ 21 343 13 13, *reservas@restauranteconsenso.com, Fax 21 343 13 12* - ▤. AE ① MC VISA JCB JY a
Meals - dinner only - a la carte 18,40/37,80.
◆ Good modern Portuguese cuisine. A pleasant dining room with modern décor and a relaxed atmosphere.

XXX **Escorial,** Rua das Portas de Santo Antão 47, ✉ 1150-160, ☎ 21 346 44 29, *Fax 21 346 37 58,* 🏖 - ▤. AE ① MC VISA JCB. ✻ KX e
Meals a la carte 25/42.
◆ Near the Rossio district. A well-established and well-run restaurant with pleasant décor and furnishings. Attentive and friendly service.

XXX **Casa do Leão,** Castelo de São Jorge, ✉ 1100-129, ☎ 21 887 59 62, *guest@pousadas.pt, Fax 21 887 63 29,* ≤, 🏖 - ▤. AE ① MC VISA JCB. ✻ LXY s
Meals a la carte approx. 40.
◆ Situated in the walls of the castle of Sao Jorge. An elegant restaurant in traditional Portuguese-style with an exclusive ambience.

XX **Via Graça,** Rua Damasceno Monteiro 9-B, ✉ 1170-108, ☎ 21 887 08 30, *restauranteviagraca@hotmail.com, Fax 21 887 03 05,* ≤ São Jorge castle, town and river Tagus - ▤. AE ① MC VISA JCB. ✻ LV d
closed Sunday - **Meals** a la carte 27/39.
◆ On the outskirts of Alfama with a magnificent panorama. Excellent cuisine in a busy, friendly and comfortable restaurant.

XX **O Faz Figura,** Rua do Paraíso 15-B, ✉ 1100-396, ☎ 21 886 89 81, *faz.figura@mail.telepac.pt, Fax 21 882 21 03,* ≤, 🏖 - ▤. AE ① MC VISA. ✻ MX n
closed Saturday lunch and Sunday - **Meals** a la carte 24,50/37,50.
◆ Beside the church of Santa Engrácia on the outskirts of Alfama. A well-run establishment in a traditional and elegant setting.

XX **Solar dos Presuntos,** Rua das Portas de Santo Antão 150, ✉ 1150-269, ☎ 21 342 42 53, *restaurante@solardospresuntos.com, Fax 21 346 84 68* – ▤. AE ⓓ MC VISA JCB. ✂ KX b
closed August, Sunday and Bank Holidays – **Meals** a la carte approx. 39.
• A locally-run, comfortable restaurant with a wide selection of well-prepared traditional dishes and some specialities from Minho.

X **O Múni,** Rua dos Correeiros 115, ✉ 1100-163, ☎ 21 342 89 82 – ▤. AE MC VISA. ✂
closed September, Saturday, Sunday and Bank Holidays – **Meals** a la carte approx. 29,72.
• A small and friendly restaurant in the centre of Baixa Pombalina. A relaxed and pleasant atmosphere with pleasant décor and furnishings. KY r

X **Mercado de Santa Clara,** Campo de Santa Clara (at market), ✉ 1170, ☎ 21 887 39 86, *Fax 21 887 39 86* – ▤. AE ⓓ MC VISA. ✂ MX c
closed 15 August-15 September, Sunday dinner, Monday and Bank Holidays – **Meals** a la carte 21,50/30.
• Near the Campo de Santa Clara. A comfortable restaurant with a relaxed atmosphere, an old-fashioned feel and subtle charm.

East : Praça Marquês de Pombal, Av. da Liberdade, Av. Almirante Reis, Av. João XXI, Av. da República, Av. Estados Unidos de América, Av. de Berlim

Tivoli Tejo, Av. D. João II (Parque das Nações), ✉ 1990-083, ☎ 21 891 51 00, *httejo@tivoli.pt, Fax 21 891 53 45,* ←, Fö, ⛱ – |♦| ▤ TV ♿ 🚗 – 🏛 25/250. AE ⓓ MC VISA JCB. ✂ North-East : by Av. Infante D. Henrique MX
A VIII Colina **Meals** a la carte 30/38 - ***O Ardina*** *(lunch only)* **Meals** a la carte 25,50/30 – **262 rm** ☕ 170/190, 17 suites.
• Facing the Tajo estuary. Modern bedrooms and small bathrooms. Smallish, but pleasantly decorated public rooms. Fine views from the A VIII Colina restaurant.

Altis Park H., Av. Engenheiro Arantes e Oliveira 9, ✉ 1900-221, ☎ 21 843 42 00, *reservations@altisparkhotel.com, Fax 21 846 08 38* – |♦| ▤ TV ♿ 🚗 – 🏛 25/600. AE ⓓ MC VISA. ✂ rest HR z
Meals 19 – **285 rm** ☕ 200/250, 15 suites – PA 37.
• In a main business district. Modern, very well-run hotel with excellent facilities. Ideal for conferences and business meetings. Fine cuisine in the Navegadores restaurant.

Barcelo Lisboa, Av. Duque de Loulé 45, ✉ 1050-086, ☎ 21 351 04 80, *lisboa.com@barcelo.com.pt, Fax 21 353 18 65,* ⛱ – |♦| ▤ TV ♿ 🚗 – 🏛 25/50. AE ⓓ MC VISA JCB. ✂ GS z
Meals *(closed Sunday)* a la carte 18/31,50 – **80 rm** ☕ 190/210, 4 suites.
• Central location near the famous Praça Marquês de Pombal square. All the comfort and characteristic style of the Meliá chain in large, quiet and functional bedrooms.

Holiday Inn Lisbon, Av. António José de Almeida 28-A, ✉ 1000-044, ☎ 21 004 40 00, *hil@grupo-continental.com, Fax 21 793 66 72,* Fö – |♦| ▤ TV ♿ 🚗 – 🏛 25/300. AE ⓓ MC VISA JCB. ✂ GR c
Meals 24 – ☕ 10 – **161 rm** 170/185, 8 suites.
• Centrally located : ideal for the business or leisure traveller. Few public rooms but comfortable bedrooms. A pleasant dining room with wickerwork furniture and a buffet.

AC Palacio Sottomayor, Av. Fontes Pereira de Melo 16, ✉ 1050-121, ☎ 210 05 09 30, *acpsottomayor@ac-hotels.com, Fax 210 05 09 31,* Fö – |♦| ▤ TV ♿ – 🏛 25/60. AE ⓓ MC VISA. ✂ GS x
Meals - dinner only - 30 – **81 rm** ☕ 168, 2 suites.
• Located in the rear part of the palace, this hotel has a modern façade and a reception area that is typical of the AC chain. Pleasant lounge and meeting areas, plus modern, well-appointed bedrooms. An attractive, albeit soberly decorated restaurant.

Roma, Av. de Roma 33, ✉ 1749-074, ☎ 21 796 77 61, *info@hotelroma.pt, Fax 21 793 29 81,* ←, Fö, ⛱ – |♦| ▤ TV ♿ – 🏛 25/230. AE ⓓ MC VISA JCB. ✂
Meals 17,50 – **263 rm** ☕ 90/120. North : by Av. Almirante Reis HR
• On a major avenue. A modern hotel with large, comfortable rooms that promise a restful stay. Sixty executive bedrooms.

Dom Carlos coffee shop only, Av. Duque de Loulé 121, ✉ 1050-089, ☎ 21 351 25 90, *hdcarlos@mail.telepac.pt, Fax 21 352 07 28* – |♦| ▤ TV – 🏛 25/40. AE ⓓ MC VISA JCB. ✂ GS n
76 rm ☕ 98/118.
• Traditional and elegant hotel in a very good location with restful ambience. Pleasant rooms with bathrooms decorated in marble and a small sitting area.

Presidente without rest, Rua Alexandre Herculano 13, ✉ 1150-005, ☎ 21 317 35 70, *hpresidente@mail.telepac.pt, Fax 21 352 02 72* – |♦| ▤ TV – 🏛 25/40. AE ⓓ MC VISA JCB. ✂ GS t
59 rm ☕ 92/106.
• Situated between Baixa and Praça Marquês de Pombal. A pleasant and functional hotel where guests receive a warm welcome. Comfort and good service.

A.S. Lisboa without rest, Av. Almirante Reis 188, ✉ 1000-055, ☎ 21 842 93 60, *info@hotel-aslisboa.com, Fax 21 842 93 74* – 🛗 ▤ 📺 – 🚶 25/80. AE ⓓ MC VISA. ✻ HR e
75 rm ☕ 62,35/72,33.
◆ In an interesting and lively area of the city. Comfort, a pleasant atmosphere and attentive, friendly service in a modern, functional style hotel.

Dom João without rest, Rua José Estêvão 43, ✉ 1150-200, ☎ 21 314 41 71, *Fax 21 352 45 69* – 🛗 ▤ 📺. AE ⓓ MC VISA. ✻ HS e
18 rm ☕ 40/45.
◆ A small hotel with a friendly and pleasant traditional atmosphere. The majority of rooms have bathrooms fitted with showers.

D'Avis, Rua do Grilo 98, ✉ 1900-707, ☎ 21 868 13 54, *Fax 21 868 13 54* – ▤. AE MC VISA. ✻ East : by Av. Infante D. Henrique MX
closed Sunday – **Meals** - Alentejo rest - a la carte 18,40/20,90.
◆ A small but well-run traditional restaurant. Interesting cooking at good prices, served in pleasant surroundings with décor in the style of the beautiful Alentejo region.

West : Av. da Liberdade, Av. 24 de Julho, Av. da India, Largo de Alcântara, Av. da India, Av. Infante Santo, Praça Marquês de Pombal, Av. António Augusto de Aguiar, Av. de Berna, Praça de Espahna

Four Seasons H. The Ritz Lisbon, Rua Rodrigo da Fonseca 88, ✉ 1099-039, ☎ 21 381 14 00, *ritzfourseasons@mail.telepac.pt, Fax 21 383 17 83,* ←, 🏛, 🏋 – 🛗 ▤ 📺 ♿ 🚗 🅿 – 🚶 25/500. AE ⓓ MC VISA JCB. ✻ FS b
Meals 45 - ***Varanda*** : **Meals** a la carte 55/71 – ☕ 24,50 – **262 rm** 378/404, 20 suites.
◆ Luxury is the keynote in these exquisite bedrooms, more than matched by the superb public rooms. The exclusive restaurant in classic style serves sophisticated, immaculately presented cuisine.

Sheraton Lisboa H. & Towers, Rua Latino Coelho 1, ✉ 1069-025, ☎ 21 312 00 00, *sheraton.lisboa@sheraton.com, Fax 21 354 71 64,* ←, 🏋, 🏊 heated – 🛗 ▤ 📺 ♿ 🚗 – 🚶 25/550. AE ⓓ MC VISA. ✻ GR s
Panorama *(dinner only)* **Meals** a la carte 47/62 - ***Caravela*** *(lunch only)* **Meals** a la carte 32/47 – **374 rm** ☕ 300/320, 7 suites.
◆ Business travellers should ask for the wonderful, fully equipped executive bedrooms. Conferences, receptions and dinners catered for. The Panorama restaurant is a very pleasant setting in which to sample finely prepared dishes.

Lapa Palace 🔇, Rua do Pau de Bandeira 4, ✉ 1249-021, ☎ 21 394 94 94, *info@lapa-palace.com, Fax 21 395 06 65,* ←, 🏛, 🏋, 🏊, 🏊, 🌳 – 🛗 ▤ 📺 ♿ 🚗 🅿 – 🚶 25/250. AE ⓓ MC VISA. ✻ EU a
Hotel Cipriani *(Italian rest)* **Meals** a la carte 45/57,50 – **92 rm** ☕ 450, 9 suites.
◆ Classic splendour on a hill with the river Tajo in the distance. A restored 19C palace, with secluded corners and evocative gardens with a waterfall among the trees. The restaurant offers very carefully prepared Italian cuisine in a refined ambience.

Carlton Palace H. 🔇, Rua Jau 54, ✉ 1300-314, ☎ 21 361 56 00, *carlton.palace@pestana.com, Fax 21 361 56 01,* 🏋, 🏊, 🏊, 🌳 – 🛗 ▤ 📺 ♿ 🚗 – 🚶 25/520. AE ⓓ MC VISA JCB. ✻ West : by Av. 24 de Julho EU
Valle Flor : **Meals** a la carte 37/58 – ☕ 19 – **173 rm** 330/350, 17 suites.
◆ A beautiful 19C palace, restored and decorated in period style with grand public rooms and bedrooms with careful detail. A restaurant which is magnificent as much for its cuisine as for the luxury of its dining rooms.

Le Meridien Park Atlantic Lisboa, Rua Castilho 149, ✉ 1099-034, ☎ 21 381 87 00, *reservas.lisboa@lemeridien.pt, Fax 21 389 05 05,* ← – 🛗, 🚭 rm, ▤ 📺 ♿ 🚗 – 🚶 25/550. AE ⓓ MC VISA JCB. ✻ rest FS a
Meals 16,82 - ***L'Appart*** : **Meals** a la carte 40/47 – ☕ 20 – **313 rm** 550, 17 suites.
◆ A full range of facilities and professional service in the comfort of modern bedrooms and suites. Bathrooms fitted with marble and high quality furnishings. A pleasantly decorated restaurant offering à la carte, buffet or dish of the day.

Altis, Rua Castilho 11, ✉ 1269-072, ☎ 21 310 60 00, *reservations@hotel-altis.pt, Fax 21 310 62 62,* 🏋, 🏊 – 🛗 ▤ 📺 ♿ 🚗 – 🚶 25/700. AE ⓓ MC VISA JCB. ✻
Girassol *(lunch only except Sunday)* **Meals** a la carte 36/45 - ***Grill Dom Fernando*** *(closed Sunday)* **Meals** a la carte 49/61 – **290 rm** ☕ 350/450, 53 suites. FT z
◆ A long-established hotel situated near to the Praça Marquês de Pombal square. Very classic rooms in pleasant modern style. In the Girassol restaurant guests help themselves to a large buffet.

Holiday Inn Lisbon Continental, Rua Laura Alves 9, ✉ 1069-169, ☎ 21 004 60 00, *hic@grupo-continental.com, Fax 21 797 36 69* – 🛗 ▤ 📺 ♿ 🚗 – 🚶 25/180. AE ⓓ MC VISA JCB. ✻ FR q
Meals a la carte approx. 30,20 – **210 rm** ☕ 135/145, 10 suites.
◆ A hotel with a modern exterior that is very popular for business meetings. Pleasant, well-appointed bedrooms and adequate public areas. The dining room is not up to the standards of the rest of the hotel.

Real Parque, Av. Luís Bivar 67, ✉ 1069-146, ☎ 21 319 90 00, *info@hoteisreal.com* *Fax 21 357 07 50* – 🛗 ▤ 📺 ♿ 🚗 – 🧑‍🏫 25/100. AE ⓓ ⓜⓒ VISA JCB. ✂ FR
Cozinha do Real : **Meals** a la carte 22,45/42,40 – **147 rm** ☕ 150/170, 6 suites.
◆ Ideal for meetings, business and leisure travel. Elegant furnishings, quality and good taste everywhere. A modern exterior, classic contemporary décor and a charming lounge area. Good food served in a pleasant dining room.

Real Palacio, Rua Tomás Ribeiro, ✉ 1050-228, ☎ 213 19 95 00, *info@hoteisreal.com* *Fax 213 19 95 01,* Fitness – 🛗, ⇸ rm, ▤ 📺 ♿ 🚗 – 🧑‍🏫 25/230. AE ⓓ ⓜⓒ VISA JCB. ✂
Meals a la carte 25,50/35 – **143 rm** ☕ 180/200, 4 suites. FR
◆ The Real Palacio is a mix of the modern and traditional with its stylish marble and elegant woodwork. Panelled meeting rooms and fully-equipped bedrooms. Options in the restaurant include the à la carte menu and an extensive buffet.

Villa Rica, Av. 5 de Outubro 295, ✉ 1600-035, ☎ 21 004 30 00, *Fax 21 004 34 99,* Fitness, – 🛗 ▤ 📺 ♿ 🚗 – 🧑‍🏫 25/500. AE ⓓ ⓜⓒ VISA JCB. ✂ North : by Av. da República GR
Ouro Preto **Meals** a la carte 45/61 – **166 rm** ☕ 126/142, 5 suites.
◆ An original hotel both architecturally and for the modern design of its furnishings and décor. Well-lit public areas. The Ouro Preto restaurant offers a choice of high quality dishes

Lisbon Marriott H., Av. dos Combatentes 45, ✉ 1600-042, ☎ 21 723 54 00, *lisbom@marriotthotels.com, Fax 21 726 42 81,* ←, garden, Fitness, pool, – 🛗 ▤ 📺 ♿ 🚗 🅿 – 🧑‍🏫 25/600. AE ⓓ ⓜⓒ VISA. ✂ North : by Av. António Augusto de Aguiar FR
Citrus : **Meals** a la carte 18/32 – ☕ 16 – **577 rm** 250, 12 suites.
◆ Since this hotel joined the Marriott group there has been a noticeable improvement in the standard of facilities. Spacious bedrooms and large garden areas. The restaurant specialises in Mediterranean cuisine.

Metropolitan Lisboa H., Rua Soeiro Pereira Gomes-parcela 2, ✉ 1600-198 ☎ 21 798 25 00, *comer@metropolitan-lisboa-hotel.pt, Fax 21 795 08 64* – 🛗 ▤ 📺 ♿ 🚗 – 🧑‍🏫 25/250. AE ⓓ ⓜⓒ VISA JCB. ✂ North : by Av. da República GR
Meals 16 – **315 rm** ☕ 131/157.
◆ Modern efficiency for the business traveller. A large foyer, well-equipped conference rooms and pleasantly decorated modern bedrooms.

Fénix, Praça Marquês de Pombal 8, ✉ 1269-133, ☎ 21 386 21 21, *h.fenix@ip.pt* *Fax 21 386 01 31* – 🛗 ▤ 📺 ♿ – 🧑‍🏫 25/100. AE ⓓ ⓜⓒ VISA JCB. ✂ FS
Bodegón : **Meals** a la carte 20/31 – **119 rm** ☕ 220/240, 4 suites.
◆ A classic hotel right on the Praça Marquês de Pombal square. The pleasant public rooms are matched by the well-appointed comfort of the hotel in general. A restaurant with elegant details and décor of soft colours.

Marquês de Pombal coffee shop only, Av. da Liberdade 243, ✉ 1250-143 ☎ 21 319 79 00, *info@hotel-marquesdepombal.pt, Fax 21 319 79 90* – 🛗 ▤ 📺 ♿ 🚗 – 🧑‍🏫 25/120. AE ⓓ ⓜⓒ VISA JCB. ✂ FS
123 rm ☕ 156/168.
◆ A recently built hotel. Conferences and business meetings in an atmosphere of modern efficiency. Elegantly furnished with up-to-date technology and conference hall.

Sana Classic Reno H. without rest, Av. Duque d'Ávila 195-197, ✉ 1050-082 ☎ 21 313 50 00, *sanaclassic-reno@sanchotels.com, Fax 21 313 50 01,* pool – 🛗 ▤ 📺 ♿ 🚗 – 🧑‍🏫 25/115. AE ⓓ ⓜⓒ VISA. ✂ FR
89 rm ☕ 120/130, 3 suites.
◆ Professional service on the edge of the Eduardo VII park. Refurbished and extended in 1998, with an elegant foyer and comfortably functional bedrooms.

Diplomático, Rua Castilho 74, ✉ 1250-071, ☎ 21 383 90 20, *reservas@hotel-diplomatico.mailpac.pt, Fax 21 386 21 55* – 🛗 ▤ 📺 🅿 – 🧑‍🏫 25/80. AE ⓓ ⓜⓒ VISA JCB. ✂
Meals 20 – **90 rm** ☕ 85,50/92. FS
◆ A wise choice in the centre of Lisbon for business meetings, conferences or leisure travel. Refurbished with pleasant public areas and comfortable bedrooms. Good service in the restaurant, and décor with touches of classical elegance.

Barcelona without rest, Rua Laura Alves 10, ✉ 1050-138, ☎ 21 795 42 73, *reservas@3khoteis.com, Fax 21 795 42 81* – 🛗 ▤ 📺 ♿ 🚗 – 🧑‍🏫 25/230. AE ⓓ ⓜⓒ VISA JCB. ✂ FR
120 rm ☕ 125/150, 5 suites.
◆ An up-to-date hotel in the financial district of the city. Modern surroundings with avant-garde touches. Cheerful colourist décor and good level of comfort.

Mercure Lisboa Malhoa, Av. José Malhoa-lote 1684, ✉ 1099-051, ☎ 21 720 80 00 *h3346@accor-hotels.com, Fax 21 720 80 89,* outdoor pool, indoor pool – 🛗, ⇸ rm, ▤ 📺 ♿ 🚗 – 🧑‍🏫 25/200. AE ⓜⓒ VISA. ✂ ER
Meals a la carte approx. 25 – ☕ 7,70 – **103 rm** 94/100, 1 suite.
◆ Bedrooms with avant-garde design combining pleasant surroundings and optimum comfort. Panoramic views from the attractive swimming-pool. Dining room with an informal feel and a choice of à la carte or buffet.

Quality H., Campo Grande 7, ✉ 1700-087, ℘ 21 791 76 00, *quality.lisboa@mail.telepac.pt*, *Fax 21 795 75 00*, – 25/70. AE VISA JCB.
Meals 19 – **80 rm** 250/280, 2 suites. North : by Av. da República GR
◆ A functional-style hotel with well-equipped bedrooms. A modern and practical atmosphere ; popular for large business meetings.

Amazónia Jamor, Av. Tomás Ribeiro 129 Queijas, ✉ 2795-891 Linda-A-Pastora, ℘ 21 417 56 38, *reservas@amazoniahoteis.com*, *Fax 21 417 56 30*, – – 25/200. AE VISA JCB.
West : 10 km by Av. Engenheiro Duarte Pacheco ES
Meals a la carte 21/29,50 – **93 rm** 135/170, 4 suites.
◆ Spacious rooms in a modern style, the best with Jacuzzi. Good facilities. Conferences, meetings, dinners and receptions catered for.

Flórida without rest, Rua Duque de Palmela 34, ✉ 1250-098, ℘ 21 357 61 45, *sales@hotel-florida.pt*, *Fax 21 314 13 47* – 25/100. AE VISA JCB.
72 rm 120/135. FS x
◆ A traditional hotel recently refurbished. The bedroom furniture is a bit outdated, although, in compensation, the bathrooms have marble fittings. A bright breakfast room.

Amazónia Lisboa without rest, Travessa Fábrica dos Pentes 12, ✉ 1250-106, ℘ 21 387 70 06, *reservas@amazoniahoteis.com*, *Fax 21 387 90 90*, heated – – 25/200. AE VISA JCB. FS d
192 rm 125/150.
◆ Near the Praça Marquês de Pombal square. Modern suites and functional-style bedrooms, the best with balconies. Professionally managed.

Clarión Suites coffee shop only, Rua Rodrigo da Fonseca 44, ✉ 1250-193, ℘ 21 004 66 00, *clarion.suites@grulo-continental.com*, *Fax 21 386 30 00*, – . AE VISA JCB. FS m
8 – **57 suites** 145/166.
◆ Limited space in the hotel's lounge and reception areas, although the suites on offer here are comfortable and functional, with contemporary decor and furnishings.

York House, Rua das Janelas Verdes 32, ✉ 1200-691, ℘ 21 396 25 44, *reservations@yorkhouselisboa.com*, *Fax 21 397 27 93*, – rm, – 25/90. AE VISA JCB. FU e
Meals a la carte 33/37 – 14 – **32 rm** 170/190.
◆ In a 16C convent. The rooms have period furniture and individual décor with a Portuguese feel. Charm, modern comfort and distinguished elegance. There is a quiet and pleasant dining terrace shaded by trees.

Novotel Lisboa, Av. José Malhoa 1642, ✉ 1099-051, ℘ 21 724 48 00, *Ho784@accor-hotels.com*, *Fax 21 724 48 01*, – , rm, – 25/300. AE VISA. rest ER e
Meals 18,46 – 7 – **246 rm** 130/150.
◆ Functional décor. Adequate facilities, modern service and well-appointed rooms. Conferences, dinners and receptions catered for. A large buffet is available in the dining room.

Sana Classic Executive H. without rest, Av. Conde Valbom 56, ✉ 1050-069, ℘ 21 795 11 57, *sana-classic.executive@sanahotels.com*, *Fax 21 795 11 66* – – 25/55. AE VISA. FR g
72 rm 110/120.
◆ Good location and ideal for the business traveller. Practical and functional. A modern foyer-reception, comfortable, well-equipped rooms and bathrooms with marble fittings.

Miraparque, Av. Sidónio Pais 12, ✉ 1050-214, ℘ 21 352 42 86, *hotel@miraparque.com*, *Fax 21 357 89 20* – . AE VISA. FS k
Meals 16,50 – **101 rm** 90/100.
◆ In spite of this hotel's outdated style, its atmosphere has a pleasant, friendly and timeless feel. The façade has been redecorated and the rooms are of a reasonable standard.

Eduardo VII, Av. Fontes Pereira de Melo 5, ✉ 1069-114, ℘ 21 356 88 22, *sales@hoteleduardovii.pt*, *Fax 21 356 88 33*, – – 25/100. AE VISA. FS p
***Varanda* : Meals** a la carte 22/38 – 6 – **137 rm** 85/97, 1 suite.
◆ Beside the Eduardo VII park. This hotel surprises with its classic, pleasant style. Smallish rooms which, nevertheless, offer high standards of comfort and careful décor. There are spectacular panoramic views over the city from the Varanda restaurant.

Marquês de Sá, Av. Miguel Bombarda 130, ✉ 1050-167, ℘ 21 791 10 14, *hotelmarquesdesa@hotelmarquesdesa.pt*, *Fax 21 793 69 86* – – 25/150. AE VISA JCB. FR c
Meals 15,50 – **164 rm** 139/167.
◆ Beside the Gulbenkian Foundation. Business and pleasure in a pleasant atmosphere of quality. Friendly service and well-appointed rooms. Well-lit dining room with décor in blue tones and a large foyer.

As Janelas Verdes without rest, Rua das Janelas Verdes 47, ✉ 1200-690, ☎ 21 396 81 43, *jverdes@heritage.pt*, *Fax 21 396 81 44* – AE VISA JCB. FU e
12,50 – **29 rm** 245/280.
◆ A late-18C mansion house with a beautiful patio and a charming function room. Traditional, romantic atmosphere.

Nacional without rest, Rua Castilho 34, ✉ 1250-070, ☎ 21 355 44 33, *hotelnacional@mail.telepac.pt*, *Fax 21 356 11 22* – AE VISA. FST s
59 rm 80/92, 2 suites.
◆ Up-to-date in style with professional management and friendly service. Bedrooms a little on the small side but modern and well equipped.

Sana Classic Rex H., Rua Castilho 169, ✉ 1070-050, ☎ 21 388 21 61, *sanaclassic.rex@sanahotels.com*, *Fax 21 388 75 81* – 25/50. AE VISA. FS a
Meals 9,50 – **68 rm** 120/130.
◆ Refurbished in 1996. A modern and friendly hotel right in the city centre. A pleasant atmosphere, a charming reception area and well-appointed rooms. Dining room with a rustic feel and décor in wood where you can combine à la carte and buffet.

Da Torre, Rua dos Jerónimos 8, ✉ 1400-211, ☎ 21 361 69 40, *hoteldatorre.belem@mail.telepac.pt*, *Fax 21 361 69 46* – 25/50. AE VISA JCB. West : by Av. 24 de Julho EU
Meals (see rest. ***São Jerónimo*** below) – **59 rm** 75,52/90,09.
◆ In Belém near the los Jerónimos monastery. Attractive lounge area in classic Portuguese-style and small but very adequate rooms with beautiful wood and tile décor.

Berna without rest, Av. António Serpa 13, ✉ 1069-199, ☎ 21 781 43 00, *hotelberna@viphotels.com*, *Fax 21 793 62 78* – 25/180. AE VISA. GR a
5,50 – **240 rm** 59.
◆ A hotel for either business or pleasure in the city centre. Small but well-equipped rooms, bathrooms a little reduced in size and adequate public areas.

Real Residência, Rua Ramalho Ortigão 41, ✉ 1070-228, ☎ 21 382 29 00, *info@hoteisreal.com*, *Fax 21 382 29 30* – 25/70. AE VISA JCB. FR e
Meals 17,50 – 5 – **24 suites** 140/175.
◆ Quality, comfort and elegance. Large, well-equipped apartments : bathrooms fitted with marble, traditional décor of good quality furnishings and fittings. The smallish dining room is pleasant and combines modern elements with attractive rustic details.

Ibis Lisboa Liberdade without rest, Rua Barata Salgueiro 53, ✉ 1250-043, ☎ 21 330 06 30, *h3137@accor-hotels.com*, *Fax 21 330 06 31* – rm, AE VISA FT a
4 – **70 rm** 59.
◆ All the true style of this hotel chain in the heart of the city. A small lounge and a functional dining room for breakfast and bedrooms equipped with the basics.

Nazareth without rest, Av. António Augusto de Aguiar 25-4º, ✉ 1050-012, ☎ 21 354 20 16, *reservas@residencianazareth.com*, *Fax 21 356 08 36* – AE VISA. FRS y
32 rm 48/53.
◆ This hotel has a welcoming feel with pleasant, well-appointed bedrooms and fully-equipped bathrooms. A friendly atmosphere in the centre of Lisbon.

Casa da Comida, Travessa das Amoreiras 1, ✉ 1250-025, ☎ 21 388 53 76, *reservas@casadacomida.pt*, *Fax 21 387 51 32* – AE VISA JCB. FT e
closed Saturday lunch, Sunday and Monday lunch – **Meals** a la carte 45/70.
◆ Don't miss out on this gem of a restaurant ! Refined and imaginative cuisine with professional service and a beautiful plant-filled patio. Elegant and welcoming.

Pabe, Rua Duque de Palmela 27-A, ✉ 1250-097, ☎ 21 353 74 84, *Fax 21 353 64 37* – AE VISA. FS x
Meals a la carte 31/46.
◆ An attractive English pub in a welcoming rustic style which has three comfortable and pleasant public areas. The best is the bar area. Great ambience !

Conventual, Praça das Flores 45, ✉ 1200-192, ☎ 21 390 91 96, *Fax 21 390 91 96* – AE VISA FT m
closed August, Saturday lunch, Sunday and Monday lunch – **Meals** a la carte 29/40.
◆ Don't leave Lisbon without trying this elegant and well-established restaurant. Pleasant furnishings and décor, an exclusive atmosphere and a good menu.

São Jerónimo - *Hotel Da Torre*, Rua dos Jerónimos 12, ✉ 1400-211, ☎ 21 364 87 97, *Fax 21 363 26 92* – AE VISA JCB. West : by Av. 24 de Julho EU
closed Saturday lunch and Sunday – **Meals** a la carte 24,50/36,50.
◆ This restaurant belongs to the Hotel Da Torre. A spacious bar and waiting area and welcoming décor with modern decoration. Carefully prepared dishes and professional service.

XL, Calçada da Estrela 57, 1200-661, 21 395 61 18, *Fax 21 395 85 12* – . AE MC VISA. FU n
closed 1 to 21 August and Sunday – **Meals** - dinner only, booking essential - a la carte approx. 34.
◆ For lovers of good cuisine. A good list of Spanish wines and delicious young lamb. A rather labyrinthine layout but a charming colonial atmosphere.

Saraiva's, Rua Engenheiro Canto Resende 3, 1050-104, 21 354 06 09, *Fax 21 353 19 87* – . AE MC VISA JCB. FR v
closed Saturday – **Meals** a la carte 21,25/28,75.
◆ Carpeted floors and elegant modern-style furnishings. Very professional service, a well-heeled clientele and a lively ambience.

Estufa Real, Jardim Botânico da Ajuda - Calçada do Galvão, 1400, 21 361 94 00, *estufa.real@clix.pt, Fax 21 361 90 18* – P. AE MC VISA.
closed Saturday – **Meals** - lunch only - a la carte 28,50/39.
◆ A relaxing location in the Jardim Botânico da Ajuda. A lovely glassed-in conservatory with attractive modern design details. West : by Av. 24 de Julho EU

Adega Tia Matilde, Rua da Beneficéncia 77, 1600-017, 21 797 21 72, *Fax 21 797 21 72* – . AE MC VISA. FR h
closed Saturday dinner and Sunday – **Meals** a la carte 22,50/25.
◆ A popular establishment, friendly and professional. Portuguese specialities. Classic-modern style with plants and fresh flowers on the tables.

Varanda da União, Rua Castilho 14 C-7º, 1250-069, 21 314 10 45, *Fax 21 314 10 46,* – . AE MC VISA JCB. FT b
closed Saturday lunch, Sunday and Bank Holidays lunch – **Meals** a la carte 22/35.
◆ A fine panorama of Lisbon rooftops from the 7th floor of a residential building. A large number of waiting staff and success based on the quality of the cuisine.

O Polícia, Rua Marquês Sá da Bandeira 112, 1050-150, 21 796 35 05, *Fax 21 796 97 91* – . AE MC VISA. FR c
closed Saturday dinner, Sunday and Bank Holidays – **Meals** a la carte 21/30.
◆ Renowned for fish. Well-decorated establishment, with large dining room, friendly service and a busy atmosphere. Reservation recommended.

Sua Excelência, Rua do Conde 34, 1200-367, 21 390 36 14, *sua xcelencia@mail.telepac.pt, Fax 21 396 75 85,* – . AE MC VISA JCB EU t
closed September and Wednesday – **Meals** a la carte 26,50/40,50.
◆ Simple and pleasant. Comfortable and friendly, offering cooking with an individual touch. Patio with a canopy.

A Travessa, Travessa do Convento das Bernardas 12, 1200-638, 21 390 20 34, *Fax 21 394 08 39* – . AE MC VISA FU c
closed Sunday – **Meals** - French rest - a la carte 26/29.
◆ A change of location has resulted in significant improvements in terms of space and comfort. A range of Portuguese and French dishes served in simple, friendly surroundings.

Caseiro, Rua de Belém 35, 1300-354, 21 363 88 03, *Fax 21 364 23 39* – . AE MC VISA JCB. West : by Av. 24 de Julho EU
closed August and Sunday – **Meals** a la carte 26,44/32,29.
◆ Traditional establishment serving delicious, simply prepared dishes which have made this restaurant well known in the locality.

The fado restaurants :

Clube de Fado, São João da Praça 94, 1100-521, 21 885 27 04, *info@clube-de-fado.com, Fax 21 888 26 94* – . AE MC VISA JCB. LYZ h
Meals - dinner only - a la carte 37/51.
◆ A restaurant with a well-cared for appearance, a pleasant ambience and a bar with a friendly atmosphere. Simple décor.

Sr. Vinho, Rua do Meio-à-Lapa 18, 1200-723, 21 397 26 81, *restsrvinho@telepac.pt, Fax 21 395 20 72* – . AE MC VISA JCB. FU r
Meals - dinner only - a la carte 45/55.
◆ Traditional cuisine of the region to the classic Lisbon sound of fado in a pleasant and welcoming setting. The dining room is a little crowded but the menu is good.

A Severa, Rua das Gáveas 51, 1200-206, 21 342 83 14, *Fax 21 346 40 06* – . AE MC VISA. JY b
closed Thursday – **Meals** a la carte 34/50.
◆ A traditional fado restaurant run by a large family who base their success on good cuisine. Comfortable and with classic Portuguese décor.

Adega Machado, Rua do Norte 91, 1200-284, 21 322 46 40, *Fax 21 346 75 07* – . AE MC VISA. JY k
closed Monday – **Meals** - dinner only - a la carte 37,70/43,25.
◆ Pleasant décor in a typical restaurant of the region where the singing of fado tends to predominate over the cuisine. Rather small tables.

Spain

España

MADRID – BARCELONA – BILBAO
MÁLAGA – SEVILLE – VALÈNCIA

PRACTICAL INFORMATION

LOCAL CURRENCY

1 euro (€) = 1,20 USD ($) (Dec 2003)

National Holiday in Spain: *12 October*

TOURIST INFORMATION

The telephone number and address of the Tourist Information offices is given in the text of the towns under ℹ.

FOREIGN EXCHANGE

Banks are usually open fron 8.30am to 2pm (closed on Saturdays and Sundays in summer).

Exchange offices in Sevilla and Valencia airports open from 9am to 2pm, in Barcelona airport from 9am to 2pm and 7 to 11pm. In Madrid and Málaga airports, offices operate a 24-hour service.

TRANSPORT

Taxis may be hailed when showing the green light or "Libre" sign on the windscreen. Madrid, Barcelona, Bilbao and Valencia have a Metro (subway) network. In each station complete information and plans will be found.

SHOPPING

In the index of street names, those printed in red are where the principal shops are found.

The big stores are easy to find in town centres; they are open from 10am to 9.30pm. Exclusive shops and boutiques are open from 10am to 2pm and 5 to 8pm. In Madrid they will be found in Serrano, Princesa and the Centre; in Barcelona, Passeig de Gràcia, Diagonal and the Rambla de Catalunya.

Second-hand goods and antiques: El Rastro (Flea Market), Las Cortes, Serrano in Madrid; in Barcelona, Les Encantes (Flea Market), Gothic Quarter.

TIPPING

Hotel, restaurant and café bills always include service in the total charge. Nevertheless it is usual to leave the staff a small gratuity which may vary depending upon the district and the service given. Doormen, porters and taxi-drivers are used to being tipped.

SPEED LIMITS

The maximum permitted speed on motorways is 120 km/h - 74 mph, and 90 km/h - 56 mph on other roads.

SEAT BELTS

The wearing of seat belts is compulsory for drivers and all passengers.

"TAPAS"

Bars serving "tapas" (typical Spanish food to be eaten with a glass of wine or an aperitif) will usually be found in central, busy or old quarters of the following selected cities.

MADRID

Madrid 28000 P 576 K 19, 575 K 19 and 121 H 7 – Pop. 2 957 058 – alt. 646.

Paris (by Irún) 1276 – Barcelona 617 – Bilbao 395 – A Coruña/La Coruña 684 – Lisboa 625 – Málaga 494 – Porto 609 – Sevilla 531 – València 352 – Zaragoza 322.

Duque de Medinaceli 2, ✉ 28014, ☎ 902 100 007, turismo@orgmadrid.org, Fax 91 429 37 05, Pl. Mayor 3, ✉ 28012, ☎ 91 588 16 36, inforturismo@munimadrid.es, Fax 91 366 54 77, Puerta de Toledo Market, ✉ 28005, ☎ 902 100 007, turismo@orgmadrid.org, Fax 91 364 24 32, Atocha Station, ✉ 28007, ☎ 902 100 007, turismo@orgmadrid.org, Fax 91 530 79 55 Chamartín Station, ✉ 28036, ☎ 902 100 007 turismo@orgmadrid.org, Fax 91 323 79 51 and Madrid-Barajas airport ✉ 28042, ☎ 902 100 007, turismo@orgmadrid.org, Fax 91 305 41 95 – R.A.C.E. Isaac Newton – Parque Technológico de Madrid (PTM), ✉ 28760 Tres Cantos (Madrid), ☎ 91 594 74 00, Fax 91 594 72 49.

18 18 9 Club de Campo-Villa de Madrid, North-west by Av. de la Victoria ☎ 91 550 20 10 DU
18 18 La Moraleja, North : 11 km by Pas. de la Castellana ☎ 91 650 07 00 GR– 9 Club Barberán, South-west : 10 km by Av. de Portugal ☎ 91 509 11 40 DX
18 9 Las Lomas – El Bosque, South-west : 18 km by Av. de Portugal and detour to Boadilla del Monte ☎ 91 616 75 00 DX
18 Real Automóvil Club de España, North : 28 km by Pas. de la Castellana ☎ 91 657 00 11 GR
18 Nuevo Club de Madrid, Las Matas, West : 26 km by Av. de la Victoria ☎ 91 630 08 20 DU
9 Somosaguas, West : 10 km by Puente del Rey ☎ 91 352 16 47 DX
9 18 Club Olivar de la Hinojosa, North-east by Av. de América and detour to M 40 ☎ 91 721 18 89 JT
18 La Dehesa, Villanueva de la Cañada, West : 28 km by Av. de la Victoria and detour to El Escorial ☎ 91 815 70 22 DU
18 18 Real Sociedad Hipica Española Club de Campo, North : 28 km by Pas. de la Castellana ☎ 91 657 10 18 GR.

Madrid-Barajas E : 12 km ☎ 902 353 570 – Iberia : Velázquez 130, ✉ 28006, ☎ 91 587 87 87 HUV, Santa Cruz de Marcenado 2, ✉ 28015, ☎ 902 400 500 EV and at airport, ✉ 28042, ☎ 91 587 87 87.
Chamartín ☎ 902 24 02 02 HR.

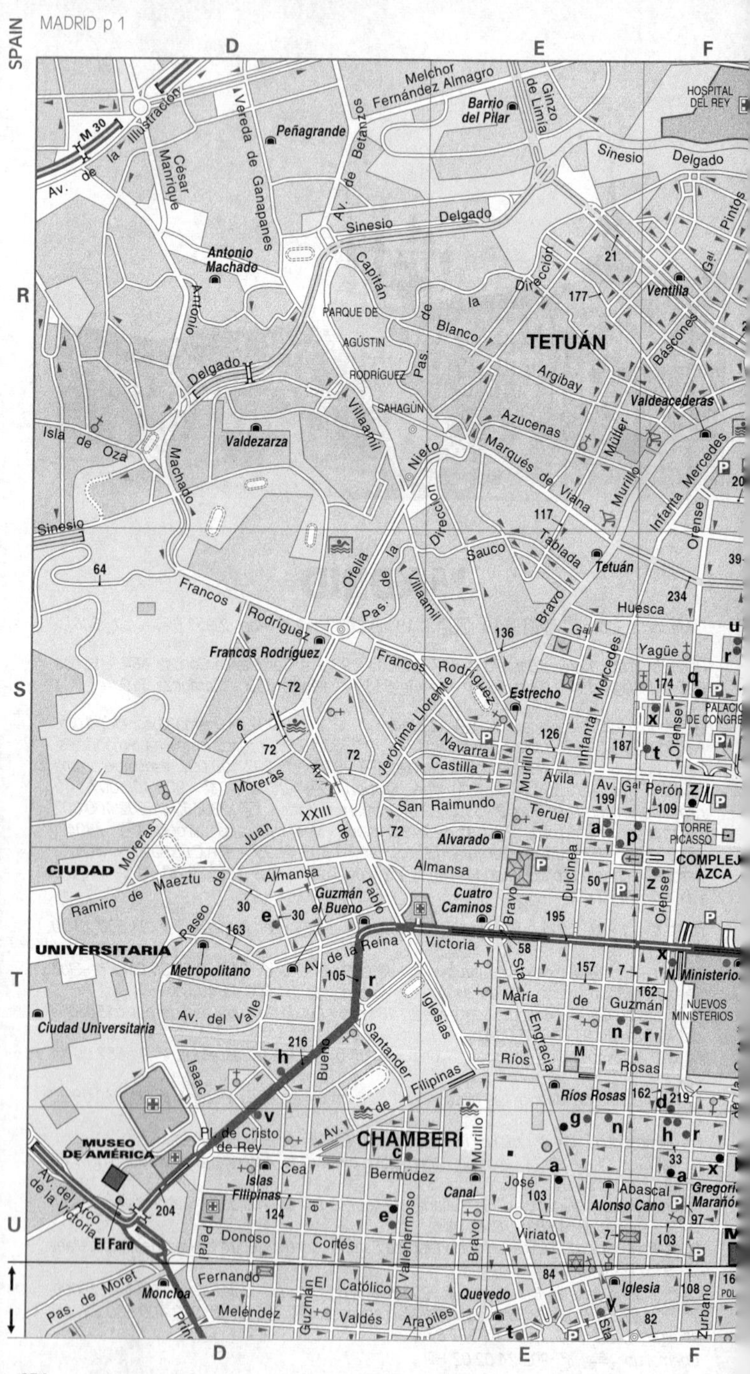
TETUÁN
CHAMBERÍ
CIUDAD UNIVERSITARIA
MUSEO DE AMÉRICA
PARQUE DE AGÚSTIN RODRÍGUEZ SAHAGÚN
HOSPITAL DEL REY
PALACIO DE CONGRESOS
TORRE PICASSO
COMPLEJO AZCA
NUEVOS MINISTERIOS
Peñagrande
Barrio del Pilar
Antonio Machado
Valdezarza
Ventilla
Valdeacederas
Tetuán
Francos Rodríguez
Estrecho
Alvarado
Guzmán el Bueno
Cuatro Caminos
Metropolitano
Ciudad Universitaria
Ríos Rosas
Islas Filipinas
Canal
Alonso Cano
Gregorio Marañón
Nuevos Ministerios
Moncloa
El Faro
Quevedo
Iglesia
Av. de la Ilustración
Melchor Fernández Almagro
Sinesio Delgado
Vereda de Ganapanes
César Manrique
Av. de Betanzos
Ginzo de Limía
Capitán Blanco Argibay
Pas. de la Dirección
Antonio Machado
Isla de Oza
Villaamil
Nieto
Azucenas
Marqués de Viana
Müller
Murillo
Infanta Mercedes
Bascones
Pintor
Gal.
Tablada
Sauco
Bravo Murillo
Huesca
Ofelia
Pas. de la Villaamil
Francos Rodríguez
Jerónima Llorente
Navarra
Castilla
Ávila
Moreras
Av. de Juan XXIII
San Raimundo
Teruel
Av. Gal. Perón
Orense
Dulcinea
Yagüe
Almansa
Ramiro de Maeztu
Paseo de Moreras
Pablo Iglesias
Av. de la Reina Victoria
Sta. María de Guzmán
Santa Engracia
Ríos Rosas
Av. del Valle
Isaac Peral
Bueno
Santander
Av. de Filipinas
Pl. de Cristo de Rey
Cea Bermúdez
José Abascal
Viriato
Donoso Cortés
Vallehermoso
Fernando el Católico
Meléndez Valdés
Arapiles
Guzmán el Bueno
Av. del Arco de la Victoria
Pas. de Moret
Princesa
Zurbano
M 30
D
E
F
R
S
T
U

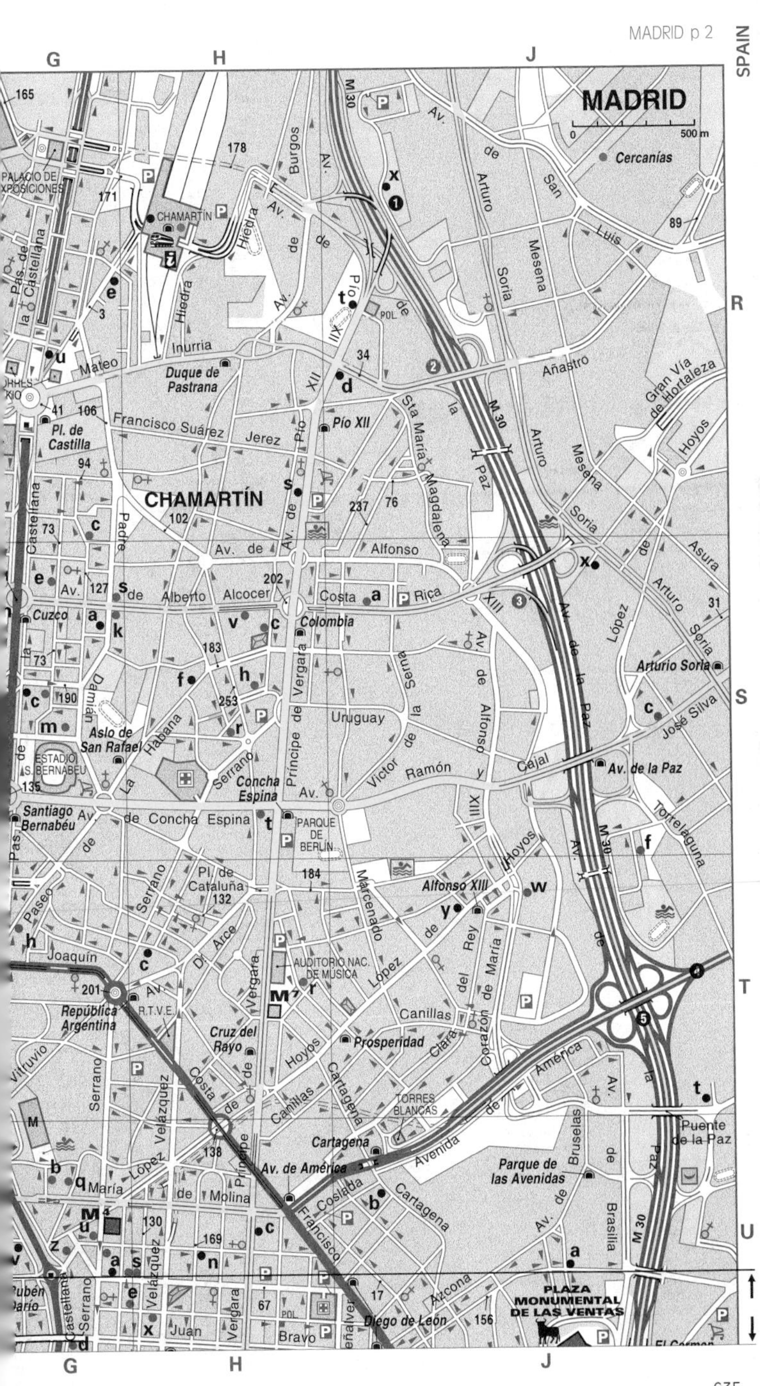
MADRID
0
500 m
G
H
J
R
S
T
U
CHAMARTÍN
PLAZA MONUMENTAL DE LAS VENTAS

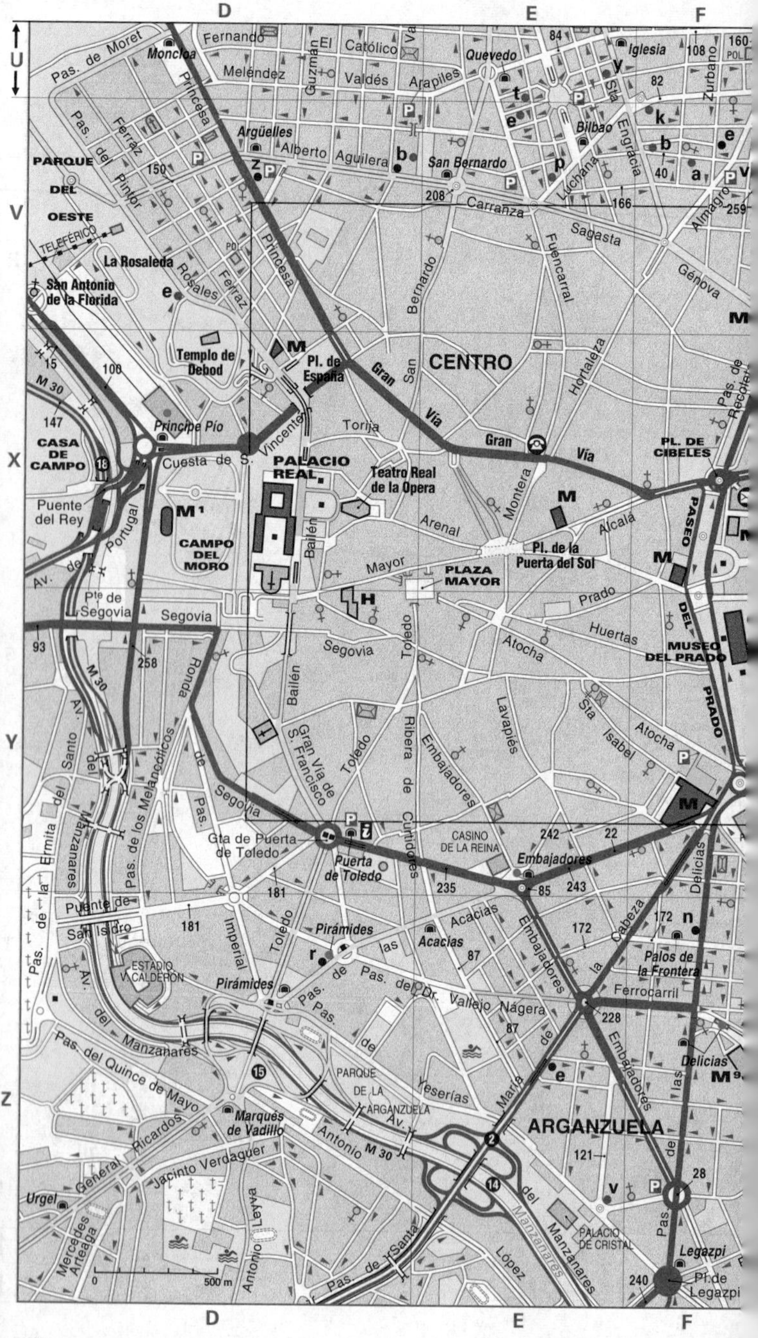
D
E
F
U
V
X
Y
Z
Pas. de Moret
Moncloa
Fernando
El
Católico
Meléndez
Valdés
Arapiles
Guzmán
Quevedo
Iglesia
Zurbano
Princesa
Argüelles
Alberto Aguilera
San Bernardo
Bilbao
Sta Engracia
Luchana
Almagro
Pas. del Pintor
Ferraz
PARQUE DEL OESTE
TELEFÉRICO
La Rosaleda
Rosales
San Antonio de la Florida
Carranza
Sagasta
Génova
Fuencarral
Bernardo
San
Templo de Debod
Pl. de España
Gran Vía
CENTRO
Hortaleza
Pas. de Recoletos
Principe Pío
Cuesta de S. Vicente
Torija
PALACIO REAL
Teatro Real de la Opera
Montera
PL. DE CIBELES
M 30
CASA DE CAMPO
Puente del Rey
Portugal
CAMPO DEL MORO
Arenal
Alcalá
Pl. de la Puerta del Sol
PASEO DEL PRADO
Av. de Portugal
Mayor
PLAZA MAYOR
Bailén
Pte de Segovia
Segovia
Prado
Huertas
Atocha
MUSEO DEL PRADO
Toledo
Ronda de Segovia
Lavapiés
Sta Isabel
Av. del Manzanares
Ermita del Santo
Pas. de los Melancólicos
Gran Vía de S. Francisco
Ribera de Curtidores
Embajadores
Gta de Puerta de Toledo
Puerta de Toledo
CASINO DE LA REINA
Delicias
Puente de San Isidro
Imperial
Pirámides
Acacias
la Cabeza
Palos de la Frontera
ESTADIO V. CALDERÓN
Pas. de la Ermita
Pas. del Dr. Vallejo Nágera
Ferrocarril
Pas. del Quince de Mayo
PARQUE DE LA ARGANZUELA
Yeserías
María de Molina
ARGANZUELA
Marqués de Vadillo
General Ricardos
Av. Antonio M 30
Jacinto Verdaguer
Urgel
Mercedes Arteaga
Antonio Leyva
Pas. de Santa María
del Manzanares
López
PALACIO DE CRISTAL
Legazpi
Pl. de Legazpi
Pas. de las Delicias
500 m

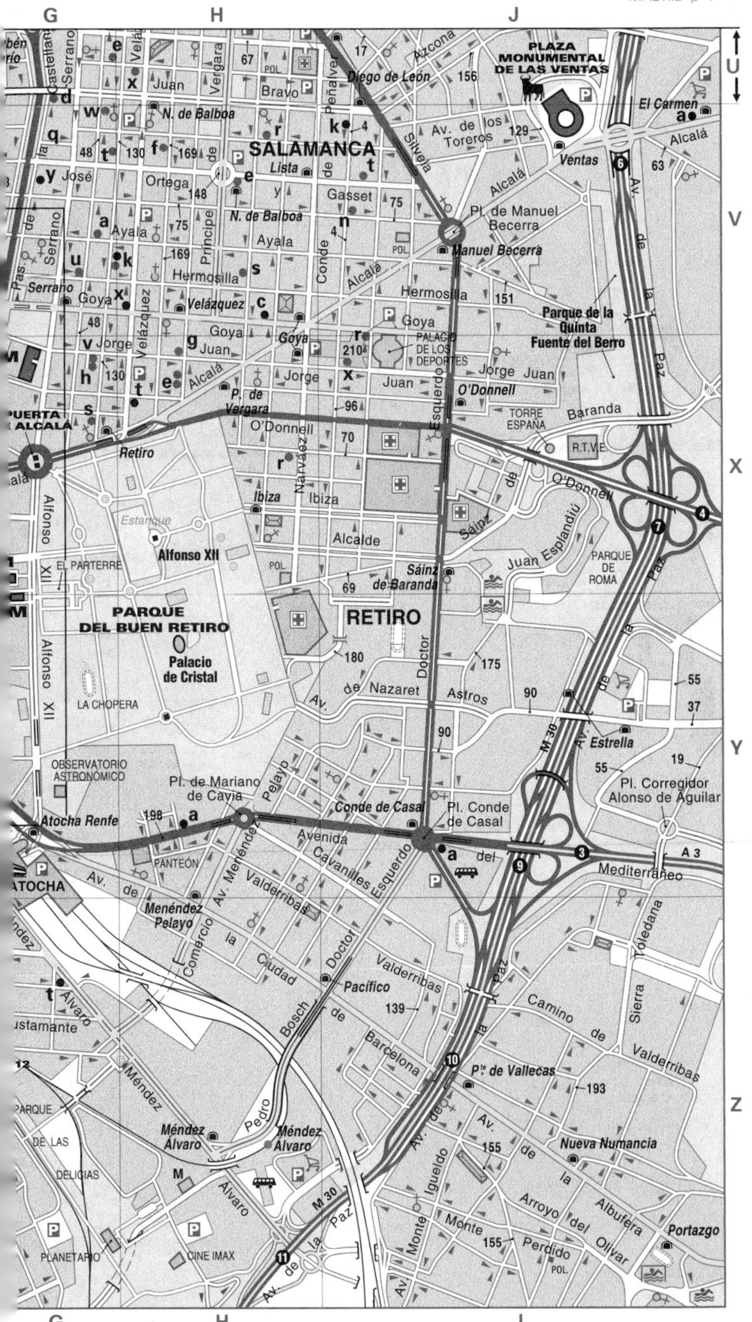
G
H
J
U
V
X
Y
Z
PLAZA MONUMENTAL DE LAS VENTAS
SALAMANCA
RETIRO
PARQUE DEL BUEN RETIRO
Palacio de Cristal
Alfonso XII
Estanque
EL PARTERRE
LA CHOPERA
OBSERVATORIO ASTRONÓMICO
PANTEÓN
PUERTA DE ALCALÁ
ATOCHA
Atocha Renfe
PARQUE DE LAS DELICIAS
PLANETARIO
CINE IMAX
Parque de la Quinta Fuente del Berro
PARQUE DE ROMA
TORRE ESPAÑA
R.T.V.E.
PALACIO DE LOS DEPORTES
Diego de León
Núñez de Balboa
Lista
Velázquez
Goya
Serrano
Príncipe de Vergara
Retiro
Ibiza
Sáinz de Baranda
O'Donnell
Manuel Becerra
Pl. de Manuel Becerra
Ventas
El Carmen
Estrella
Conde de Casal
Pl. Conde de Casal
Pl. de Mariano de Cavia
Pl. Corregidor Alonso de Aguilar
Menéndez Pelayo
Pacífico
Pte. de Vallecas
Nueva Numancia
Portazgo
Méndez Álvaro
Av. de Menéndez Pelayo
Av. Ciudad de Barcelona
Av. Doctor Esquerdo
Av. de la Paz
Av. del Mediterráneo
Av. de la Albufera
Av. de Nazaret
Camino de Valderribas
Arroyo del Olivar
Monte Perdido
Monte Igueldo
Doctor Esquerdo
Alcalá
Hermosilla
Ayala
Ortega y Gasset
Juan Bravo
Jorge Juan
Alcalde Sáinz de Baranda
Juan Esplandiú
Conde de Peñalver
Narváez
Castellana
Alfonso XII
Pedro Bosch
Sierra Toledana
Av. de los Toreros
Azcona
Baranda
Astros
Cavanilles
Valderribas
Comercio
Álvaro Bustamante
M 30
A 3
POL.

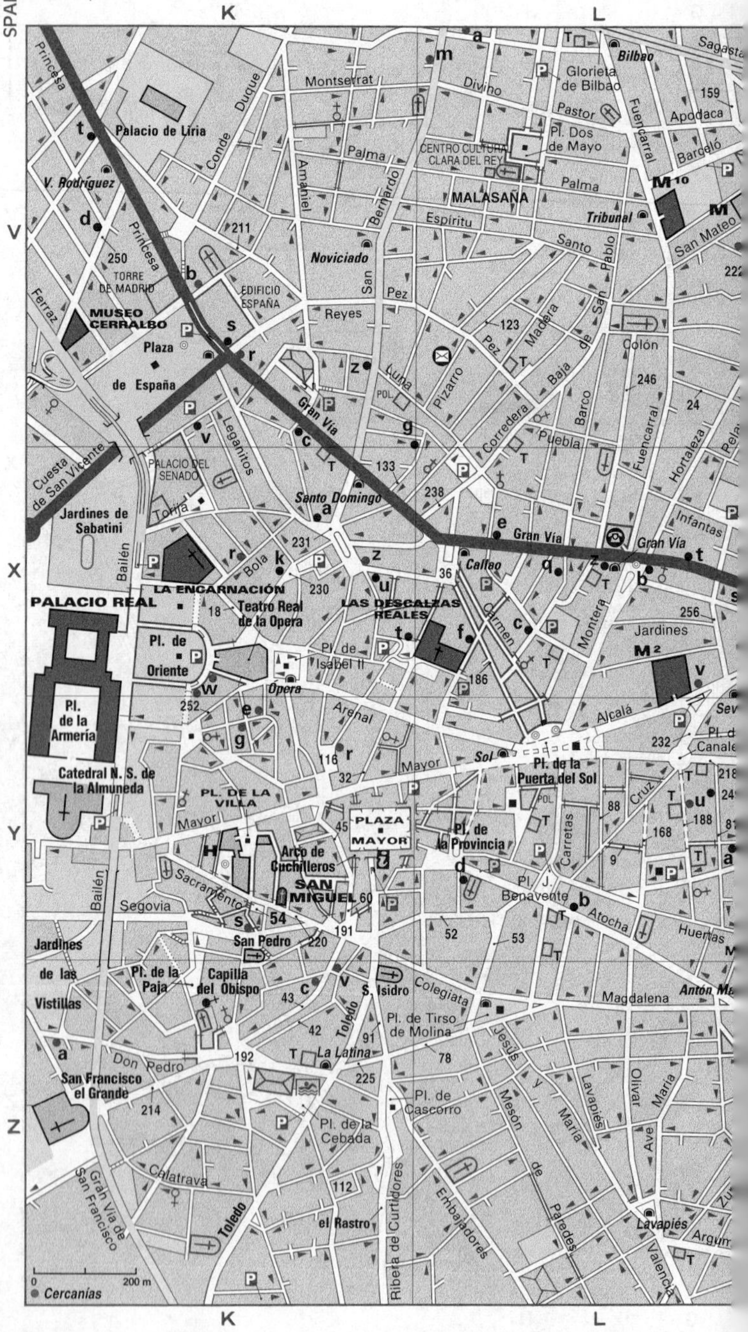

K L

V X Y Z

Princesa
Palacio de Liria
V. Rodríguez
Conde Duque
Montserrat
Amaniel
San Bernardo
Palma
Divino Pastor
Glorieta de Bilbao
Bilbao
Sagasta
Apodaca
Barceló
Fuencarral
Pl. Dos de Mayo
CENTRO CULTURAL CLARA DEL REY
MALASAÑA
Espíritu Santo
Tribunal
San Mateo
Noviciado
San Pablo
Torre de Madrid
Edificio España
Ferraz
MUSEO CERRALBO
Plaza de España
Reyes
Pez
Madera
Baja de San Pablo
Colón
Luna
Pizarro
Corredera
Barco
Puebla
Hortaleza
Infantas
Gran Vía
Cuesta de San Vicente
Palacio del Senado
Leganitos
Santo Domingo
Jardines de Sabatini
Torija
Bailén
Bola
Callao
LA ENCARNACIÓN
PALACIO REAL
Teatro Real de la Opera
LAS DESCALZAS REALES
Carmen
Montera
Jardines
Pl. de Oriente
Pl. de Isabel II
Opera
Arenal
Alcalá
Pl. de la Armería
Catedral N. S. de la Almuneda
PL. DE LA VILLA
Mayor
Sol
Pl. de la Puerta del Sol
Cruz
Carretas
PLAZA MAYOR
Pl. de la Provincia
Arco de Cuchilleros
SAN MIGUEL
Sacramento
Segovia
San Pedro
Pl. J. Benavente
Atocha
Huertas
Jardines de las Vistillas
Pl. de la Paja
Capilla del Obispo
S. Isidro
Colegiata
Magdalena
Antón Ma
Toledo
Pl. de Tirso de Molina
La Latina
Don Pedro
San Francisco el Grande
Pl. de Cascorro
Jesús y María
Mesón de Paredes
Lavapiés
Olivar
Ave María
Pl. de la Cebada
Calatrava
Gran Vía de San Francisco
el Rastro
Ribera de Curtidores
Embajadores
Valencia
Argum
0 200 m
Cercanías

MADRID

Street	Grid	No.
Alcalá	MX	
Álvarez Gato	LY	9
Arenal	KY	
Arrieta	KX	18
Augusto Figueroa	MV	24
Ayala	NV	25
Bárbara de Braganza	NV	27
Bordadores	KY	32
Callao (Pl. del)	LX	36
Carmen	LX	
Cava Alta	KZ	42
Cava Baja	KZ	43
Cava de San Miguel	KY	45
Ciudad de Barcelona (Av. de la)	NZ	46
Colón (Pl. de)	NV	49
Concepción Jerónima	LY	52
Conde de Romanones	LY	53
Cordón (Pl. del)	KY	54
Cortes (Pl. de las)	MY	57
Cuchilleros	KY	60
Duque de Alba	LZ	78
Duque de Medinaceli	MY	79
Echegaray	LY	81
Espoz y Mina	LY	88
Estudios	KZ	91
Felipe IV	NY	
Fernando el Santo	NV	99
Fuencarral	LV	
General Vara del Rey (Pl. del)	KZ	112
Goya	NV	114
Gran Vía	LX	
Herradores (Pl. de los)	KY	116
Hortaleza	LX	
Independencia (Pl. de la)	NX	118
Infanta Isabel (Pas. de la)	NZ	119
Jesús del Valle	LV	123
Libreros	KX	133
Madrazo	MY	141
Marqués de Cubas	MY	145
Mayor	KY	
Mayor (Pl.)	KY	
Mejía Lequerica	LMV	159
Montera	LX	
Núñez de Arce	LY	168
Preciados	LX	186
Príncipe	LY	188
Puerta Cerrada (Pl. de)	KY	191
Puerta de Moros (Pl. de)	KZ	192
Puerta del Sol (Pl. de la)	LY	
Recoletos	NX	196
San Bernardino	KV	211
San Francisco (Carrera de)	KZ	214
San Jerónimo (Carrera de)	LMY	218
San Justo	KY	220
San Lorenzo	LV	222
San Millán	KZ	225
Santa Engracia	MV	226
Santo Domingo (Cuesta)	KX	230
Santo Domingo (Pl. de)	KX	231
Sevilla	LY	232
Tudescos	LX	238
Valverde	LV	246
Ventura de la Vega	LY	249
Ventura Rodríguez	KV	250
Vergara	KY	252
Villa de París (Pl. de la)	NV	255
Virgen de los Peligros	LX	256

Michelin
pone sus mapas constantemente al día.
Llévelos en su coche y no tendrà Vd. sorpresas desagradables en caretera.

STREET INDEX TO

Acacias (Pas. de las) p. 3 **EZ**
Agustín de Foxá p. 2 **GR** 3
Alberto Aguilera p. 3 **DV**
Alberto Alcocer (Av. de) p. 2 **HS**
Albufera (Av. de la) p. 4 **JZ**
Alcalá p. 6 **MX**
Alcalde Sáinz de Baranda p. 4 **JX**
Alcántara p. 4 **JV** 4
Alfonso XI p. 6 **NX**
Alfonso XII p. 6 **NX**
Alfonso XIII (Av. de) p. 2 **JS**
Almagro p. 3 **FV**
Almansa p. 1 **DT**
Almirante p. 6 **MV**
Almirante Francisco Moreno p. 1 **DS** 6
Alonso Cano p. 1 **ET** 7
Alonso Martínez (Pl. de) p. 6 **MV**
Álvarez Gato p. 5 **LY** 9
Amaniel p. 5 **KV**
América (Av. de) p. 2 **JT**
Áncora p. 4 **GZ** 10
Aniceto Marinas p. 3 **DX** 15
Antonio Leyva p. 3 **DZ**
Antonio López p. 3 **DZ**
Antonio Machado p. 1 **DR**
Antonio Maura p. 6 **NY**
Añastro p. 2 **JR**
Apodaca p. 5 **LV**
Arapiles p. 1 **EU**
Arco de la Victoria (Av. de la) p. 1 **DU**
Ardemans p. 2 **JU** 17
Arenal p. 5 **KY**
Argensola p. 6 **MV**
Argumosa p. 5 **LZ**
Arrieta p. 5 **KX** 18
Arroyo de la Media Legua p. 4 **JY** 19
Arroyo del Olivar p. 4 **JZ**
Arturo Soria p. 2 **JRS**
Astros p. 4 **JY**
Asturias (Av. de) p. 1 **ER** 21
Asura p. 2 **JS**
Atocha p. 5 **LY**
Atocha (Ronda de) p. 3 **EY** 22
Augusto Figueroa p. 6 **MV** 24
Ave María p. 5 **LZ**
Ávila p. 1 **ES**
Ayala p. 6 **NV** 25
Azcona p. 2 **JU**
Azucenas p. 1 **ER**
Bailén p. 5 **KY**
Bárbara de Braganza p. 6 **NV** 27
Barceló p. 5 **LV**
Barco p. 5 **LV**
Barquillo p. 6 **MX**
Báscones p. 1 **FR**
Beata María Ana de Jesús (Pl. de la) p. 3 **FZ** 28
Beatriz de Bobadilla p. 1 **DT** 30
Belisana p. 2 **JS** 31
Betanzos (Av. de) p. 1 **DR**
Bilbao (Glta de) p. 5 **LV**
Bola p. 5 **KX**
Bolívar p. 4 **GZ**
Bordadores p. 5 **KY** 32
Brasilia (Av. de) p. 2 **JU**
Bravo Murillo p. 1 **EU**
Bretón de los Herreros p. 1 **FU** 33
Bruselas (Av. de) p. 2 **JU**
Burgos (Av. de) p. 2 **HR**
Bustamante p. 4 **GZ**
Caídos de la División Azul p. 2 **JR** 34
Calatrava p. 5 **KZ**
Callao (Pl. del) p. 5 **LX** 36
Camino de los Vinateros p. 4 **JY** 37
Canalejas (Pl. de) p. 5 **LY**
Canillas p. 2 **JT**
Cánovas del Castillo (Pl. de) p. 6 **MY**
Capitán Blanco Argibay p. 1 **ER**
Capitán Haya p. 1 **FS** 39

Caracas p. 3 **FV** 40
Carmen p. 5 **LX**
Carranza p. 3 **EV**
Carretas p. 5 **LY**
Cartagena p. 2 **JU**
Cascorro (Pl. de) p. 5 **LZ**
Castellana (Pas. de la) p. 6 **NV**
Castilla p. 1 **ES**
Castilla (Pl. de) p. 2 **GR** 41
Cataluña (Pl. de) p. 2 **HT**
Cava Alta p. 3 **KZ** 42
Cava Baja p. 3 **KZ** 43
Cava de San Miguel p. 5 **KY** 45
Cavanilles p. 4 **JY**
Cea Bermúdez p. 1 **DU**
Cebada (Pl. de la) p. 5 **KZ**
César Manrique p. 1 **DR**
Cibeles (Pl. de) p. 6 **MX**
Ciudad de Barcelona (Av. de la) p. 6 **NZ** 46
Clara del Rey p. 2 **JT**
Claudio Coello p. 4 **GV** 48
Claudio Moyano p. 6 **NZ**
Colegiata p. 5 **LZ**
Colón p. 5 **LV**
Colón (Pl. de) p. 6 **NV** 49
Comandante Zorita p. 1 **ET** 50
Comercio p. 4 **HZ**
Concepción Jerónima p. 5 **LY** 52
Concha Espina (Av. de) p. 2 **HS**
Conde de Casal (Pl. del) p. 4 **JY**
Conde de Peñalver p. 2 **JU**
Conde de Romanones p. 5 **LY** 53
Conde Duque p. 5 **KV**
Corazón de María p. 2 **JT**
Cordón (Pl. del) p. 5 **KY** 54
Corredera Baja de San Pablo p. 5 **LV**
Corregidor Alonso de Aguilar (Pl. del) p. 4 **JY**
Corregidor Diego Cabeza de Vaca p. 4 **JY** 55
Cortes (Pl. de las) p. 6 **MY** 57
Coslada p. 2 **JU**
Costa Rica p. 2 **JS**
Cristo Rey (Pl. de) p. 1 **DU**
Cruz p. 5 **LY**
Cuatro Caminos (Glta de) p. 1 **ET** 58
Cuchilleros p. 5 **KY** 60
Cuzco (Pl. de) p. 2 **GS** 61
Daroca (Av. de) p. 4 **JV** 63
Dehesa de la Villa (Carret. de la) p. 1 **DS** 64
Delicias (Pas. de las) p. 3 **FYZ**
Diego de León p. 2 **HU** 67
Dirección (Pas. de la) p. 1 **ER**
Divino Pastor p. 5 **LV**
Doce de Octubre p. 4 **JX** 69
Doctor Arce (Av. del) p. 2 **HT**
Doctor Castelo p. 4 **JX** 70
Doctor Esquerdo p. 4 **JY**
Doctor Federico Rubio y Galí (Av. del) p. 1 **DS** 72
Doctor Fléming p. 2 **GS** 73
Doctor Vallejo Nájera (Pas. del) p. 3 **EZ**
Don Pedro p. 5 **KZ**
Don Ramón de la Cruz p. 4 **HV** 75
Donoso Cortés p. 1 **DU**
Dos de Mayo (Pl. del) p. 5 **LV**
Drácena p. 2 **JR** 76
Dulcinea p. 1 **ET**
Duque de Alba p. 5 **LZ** 78
Duque de Medinaceli p. 6 **MY** 79
Echegaray p. 5 **LY** 81
Eduardo Dato (Pas. de) p. 1 **FU** 82
Eloy Gonzalo p. 1 **EU** 84
Embajadores p. 5 **LZ**
Embajadores (Glta de) p. 3 **EY** 85
Emperador Carlos V (Pl. del) p. 6 **NZ**
Ermita del Santo (Pas. de la) p. 3 **DY**
Espalter p. 6 **NZ**
España (Pl. de) p. 5 **KV**

Esperanza (Pas. de la) p. 3 **EZ** 87
Espíritu Santo p. 5 **LV**
Espoz y Mina p. 5 **LY** 88
Estación de Hortaleza (Carret. a la) p. 2 **JR** 89
Estrella Polar p. 4 **JY** 90
Estudios p. 5 **KZ** 91
Extremadura (Pas. de) p. 3 **DY** 93
Felipe IV p. 6 **NY**
Félix Boix p. 2 **GR** 94
Fernán González p. 4 **JX** 96
Fernández de la Hoz p. 1 **FU** 97
Fernando VI p. 6 **MV**
Fernando El Católico p. 1 **DU**
Fernando el Santo p. 6 **NV** 99
Ferraz p. 3 **DV**
Ferrocarril p. 3 **FZ**
Filipinas (Av. de) p. 1 **ET**
Florida (Pas. de la) p. 3 **DX** 100
Francisco Silvela p. 2 **HU**
Francisco Suárez p. 2 **HR**
Francos Rodríguez p. 1 **DS**
Fray Bernardino Sahagún p. 2 **HR** 102
Fúcar p. 6 **MZ**
Fuencarral p. 5 **LV**
Ganapanes (Vereda de) p. 1 **DR**
García de Paredes p. 1 **EU** 103
General Ibáñez de Ibero p. 1 **DT** 105
General López Pozas p. 2 **GR** 106
General Martínez Campos (Pas. del) p. 1 **FU** 108
General Moscardó p. 1 **FS** 109
General Perón (Av. del) p. 1 **FS**
General Pintos p. 1 **FR**
General Ricardos p. 3 **DZ**
General Vara del Rey (Pl. del) p. 5 **KZ** 112
General Yagüe p. 1 **FS**
Génova p. 6 **NV**
Ginzo de Limía p. 1 **ER**
Goya p. 6 **NV** 114
Gran Vía p. 5 **LX**
Gravina p. 6 **MV**
Guzmán El Bueno p. 1 **DU**
La Habana (Pas. de) p. 2 **HS**
Hermosilla p. 4 **HV**
Herradores (Pl. de los) p. 5 **KY** 116
Hiedra p. 2 **HR**
Hierbabuena p. 1 **ER** 117
Hortaleza p. 5 **LX**
Hortaleza (Gran Via de) p. 2 **JR**
Huertas p. 5 **LY**
Huesca p. 1 **ES**
Ibiza p. 4 **JX**
Illustración (Av. de la) p. 1 **DR**
Imperial (Pas.) p. 3 **DZ**
Independencia (Pl. de la) p. 6 **NX** 118
Infanta Isabel (Pas. de la) p. 6 **NZ** 119
Infanta Mercedes p. 1 **ES**
Infantas p. 5 **LX**
Isaac Peral p. 1 **DT**
Isabel II (Pl. de) p. 5 **KX**
Isla de Oza p. 1 **DR**
Jacinto Benavente (Pl. de) p. 5 **LY**
Jacinto Verdaguer p. 3 **DZ**
Jaime El Conquistador p. 3 **EZ** 121
Jardines p. 5 **LX**
Jerez p. 2 **HR**
Jerónima Llorente p. 1 **DS**
Jesús p. 6 **MY**
Jesús del Valle p. 5 **LV** 123
Jesús y María p. 5 **LZ**
Joaquín Costa p. 2 **GT**
Joaquín María López p. 1 **DU** 124
Jorge Juan p. 4 **HX**
José Abascal p. 1 **EU**
José Ortega y Gasset p. 4 **HV**
José Silva p. 2 **JS**

MADRID TOWN PLAN

Street	Page	Grid	No.
Juan XXIII (Pas. de)	p. 1	**DS**	
Juan Bravo	p. 2	**HU**	
Juan de Olías	p. 1	**ES**	126
Juan Esplandiú	p. 4	**JX**	
Juan Ramón Jiménez	p. 2	**GS**	127
Julio Camba	p. 4	**JV**	129
Lagasca	p. 4	**HV**	130
Lavapiés	p. 5	**LZ**	
Lealtad (Pl. de la)	p. 6	**NY**	
Leganitos	p. 5	**KX**	
Legazpi (Pl. de)	p. 3	**FZ**	
Leizarán	p. 2	**HT**	132
Libreros	p. 5	**KX**	133
Lima (Pl. de)	p. 2	**GS**	135
Lope de Haro	p. 1	**ES**	136
López de Hoyos	p. 2	**JT**	
López de Hoyos (Glta de)	p. 2	**HU**	138
Luchana	p. 3	**EV**	
Luis Mitjans	p. 4	**JZ**	139
Luna	p. 5	**KV**	
Madera	p. 5	**LV**	
Madrazo	p. 6	**MY**	141
Magdalena	p. 5	**LZ**	
Manuel Becerra (Pl. de)	p. 4	**JV**	
Manzanares (Av. del)	p. 3	**DEYZ**	
Marcenado	p. 2	**JT**	
María de Guzmán	p. 1	**ET**	
María de Molina	p. 2	**HU**	
Mariano de Cavia (Pl. de)	p. 4	**HY**	
Marqués de Cubas	p. 6	**MY**	145
Marqués de Monistrol (Pas. del)	p. 3	**DX**	147
Marqués de Salamanca (Pl. del)	p. 4	**HV**	148
Marqués de Urquijo	p. 3	**DV**	150
Marqués de Viana	p. 1	**ER**	
Marqués de Zafra (Pas. del)	p. 4	**JV**	151
Marqués del Riscal	p. 4	**GV**	153
Martínez de la Riva	p. 4	**JZ**	155
Martínez Izquierdo	p. 2	**JU**	156
Mateo Inurria	p. 2	**HR**	
Maudes	p. 1	**ET**	157
Mayor	p. 5	**KY**	
Mayor (Pl.)	p. 5	**KY**	
Mediterráneo (Av. del)	p. 4	**JY**	
Mejía Lequerica	p. 5	**LV**	159
Melancólicos (Pas. de los)	p. 3	**DY**	
Melchor Fernández Almagro	p. 1	**DR**	
Meléndez Valdés	p. 1	**DU**	
Méndez Álvaro	p. 4	**HZ**	
Menéndez Pelayo (Av. de)	p. 4	**HX**	
Mercedes Arteaga	p. 3	**DZ**	
Mesena	p. 2	**JR**	
Mesón de Paredes	p. 5	**LZ**	
Miguel Ángel	p. 1	**FU**	160
Modesto Lafuente	p. 1	**FT**	162
Moncloa (Av. de la)	p. 1	**DT**	163
Monforte de Lemos (Av. de)	p. 2	**GR**	165
Montalbán	p. 6	**NX**	
Monte Igueldo (Av. del)	p. 4	**JZ**	
Monte Perdido	p. 4	**JZ**	
Montera	p. 5	**LX**	
Montserrat	p. 5	**KV**	
Moratín	p. 6	**MZ**	
Moreras	p. 1	**DS**	
Moret (Pas. de)	p. 1	**DU**	
Moreto	p. 6	**NY**	
Müller	p. 1	**ER**	
Murillo (Pl. de)	p. 6	**NZ**	
Narváez	p. 4	**HX**	
Navarra	p. 1	**ES**	
Nazaret (Av. de)	p. 4	**JY**	
Nicasio Gallego	p. 3	**EV**	166
Núñez de Arce	p. 5	**LY**	168
Núñez de Balboa	p. 4	**HV**	169
O'Donnell	p. 4	**JX**	
Ofelia Nieto	p. 1	**DS**	
Olivar	p. 5	**LZ**	
Orense	p. 1	**FS**	
Oriente (Pl. de)	p. 5	**KX**	
Pablo Iglesias (Av. de)	p. 1	**DT**	
Padre Damián	p. 2	**GS**	
Padre Francisco Palau y Quer	p. 2	**GR**	171
Paja (Pl. de la)	p. 5	**KZ**	
Palma	p. 5	**LV**	
Palos de la Frontera	p. 3	**FZ**	172
Paz (Av. de la)	p. 4	**JV**	
Paz (Pte de la)	p. 2	**JU**	
Pedro Bosch	p. 4	**HZ**	
Pedro Teixeira	p. 1	**FS**	174
Pelayo	p. 6	**MV**	
Pez	p. 5	**LV**	
Pez Volador	p. 4	**JY**	175
Pinos Alta	p. 1	**ER**	177
Pintor Rosales (Pas. del)	p. 3	**DV**	
Pío XII (Av. de)	p. 2	**HR**	
Pío XII (Túnel de)	p. 2	**HR**	178
Pío Baroja	p. 4	**JY**	180
Pizarro	p. 5	**LV**	
Pontones (Pas. de los)	p. 3	**DZ**	181
Portugal (Av. de)	p. 3	**DX**	
Potosí	p. 2	**HS**	183
Pradillo	p. 2	**HT**	184
Prado	p. 6	**MY**	
Prado (Pas. del)	p. 6	**NZ**	
Preciados	p. 5	**LX**	186
Presidente Carmona (Av. del)	p. 1	**ES**	187
Prim	p. 6	**NV**	
Princesa	p. 5	**KV**	
Príncipe	p. 5	**LY**	
Príncipe de Vergara	p. 2	**HS**	
Profesor Waksman	p. 2	**GS**	190
Provincia (Pl. de la)	p. 5	**LY**	
Puebla	p. 5	**LV**	
Puerta Cerrada (Pl. de)	p. 5	**KY**	191
Puerta de Moros (Pl. de)	p. 5	**KZ**	192
Puerta de Toledo (Glta de)	p. 3	**DY**	
Puerta del Sol (Pl. de la)	p. 5	**LY**	
Puerto de Canfranc	p. 4	**JZ**	193
Quince de Mayo (Pas. del)	p. 3	**DZ**	
Raimundo Fernández Villaverde	p. 1	**ET**	195
Ramiro de Maeztu	p. 1	**DT**	
Ramón y Cajal (Av. de)	p. 2	**JS**	
Recoletos	p. 6	**NX**	196
Recoletos (Pas. de)	p. 6	**NV**	
Reina Cristina (Pas. de la)	p. 4	**HY**	198
Reina Mercedes	p. 1	**ES**	199
Reina Victoria (Av. de la)	p. 1	**DET**	
República Argentina (Pl. de la)	p. 1	**GT**	201
República Dominicana (Pl. de la)	p. 2	**HS**	202
Rey (Pte del)	p. 3	**DX**	
Reyes	p. 5	**KV**	
Reyes Católicos (Av. de los)	p. 1	**DU**	204
Ribera de Curtidores	p. 5	**KZ**	
Río	p. 5	**KV**	
Ríos Rosas	p. 1	**ET**	
Rosario Pino	p. 1	**FR**	207
Ruiz Jiménez (Glta de)	p. 3	**EV**	208
Sacramento	p. 5	**KY**	
Sagasta	p. 5	**LV**	
Salvador Dalí (Pl. de)	p. 4	**JX**	210
San Bernardino	p. 5	**KV**	211
San Bernardo	p. 5	**KV**	
San Francisco (Carrera de)	p. 5	**KZ**	214
San Francisco (Gran Vía de)	p. 5	**KZ**	
San Francisco de Sales (Pas. de)	p. 1	**DT**	216
San Isidro (Pte de)	p. 3	**DZ**	
San Jerónimo (Carrera de)	p. 5	**LY**	218
San Juan de la Cruz (Pl. de)	p. 1	**FT**	219
San Justo	p. 5	**KY**	220
San Lorenzo	p. 5	**LV**	222
San Luis (Av. de)	p. 2	**JR**	
San Marcos	p. 6	**MX**	
San Mateo	p. 5	**LV**	
San Millán	p. 5	**KZ**	225
San Raimundo	p. 1	**ES**	
San Vicente (Cuesta de)	p. 3	**DX**	
Santa Bárbara (Pl. de)	p. 6	**MV**	
Santa Engracia	p. 6	**MV**	226
Santa Isabel	p. 6	**MZ**	
Santa María de la Cabeza (Glta de)	p. 3	**EZ**	228
Santa María de la Cabeza	p. 3	**DFZ**	
Santa María Magdalena	p. 2	**JR**	
Santander	p. 1	**DT**	
Santo Domingo (Cuesta)	p. 5	**KX**	230
Santo Domingo (Pl. de)	p. 5	**KX**	231
Sauco	p. 1	**ES**	
Segovia	p. 3	**DY**	
Segovia (Pte de)	p. 3	**DY**	
Segovia (Ronda de)	p. 3	**DY**	
Serrano	p. 6	**NV**	
Sevilla	p. 5	**LY**	232
Sierra Toledana	p. 4	**JZ**	
Sinesio Delgado	p. 1	**DR**	
Sor Ángela de la Cruz	p. 1	**FS**	234
Tablada	p. 1	**ES**	
Teruel	p. 1	**ES**	
Tirso de Molina (Pl. de)	p. 5	**LZ**	
Toledo	p. 5	**KZ**	
Toledo (Ronda de)	p. 3	**EY**	235
Toreros (Av. de los)	p. 4	**JV**	
Torija	p. 5	**KX**	
Torpedero Tucumán	p. 2	**JR**	237
Torrelaguna	p. 2	**JS**	
Tudescos	p. 5	**LX**	238
Uruguay	p. 2	**JS**	
Vado de Santa Catalina	p. 3	**FZ**	240
Valderribas	p. 4	**JZ**	
Valderribas (Camino de)	p. 4	**JZ**	
Valencia	p. 3	**EY**	242
Valencia (Ronda de)	p. 3	**EY**	243
Valle (Av. del)	p. 1	**DT**	
Vallehermoso	p. 1	**DU**	
Valverde	p. 5	**LV**	246
Velázquez	p. 2	**HU**	
Ventura de la Vega	p. 5	**LY**	249
Ventura Rodríguez	p. 5	**KV**	250
Vergara	p. 5	**KY**	252
Victor Andrés Belaunde	p. 2	**HS**	253
Victor de la Serna	p. 2	**JS**	
Villa (Pl. de la)	p. 5	**KY**	
Villa de París (Pl. de la)	p. 6	**NV**	255
Villaamil	p. 1	**DR**	
Villanueva	p. 6	**NV**	
Virgen de los Peligros	p. 5	**LX**	256
Virgen del Puerto (Pas. de la)	p. 3	**DY**	258
Viriato	p. 1	**EU**	
Vitruvio	p. 2	**GT**	
Yeserías (Pas. de)	p. 3	**EZ**	
Zurbano	p. 1	**FU**	
Zurbarán	p. 3	**FV**	259
Zurita	p. 5	**LZ**	

SIGHTS

VIEW OVER MADRID

Moncloa Beacon (Faro de Madrid): ✳★★ DU.

MUSEUMS

Prado-Museum★★★ NY – *Thyssen Bornemisza Museum*★★★ MY **M**[6] – *Royal Palace*★★ *(Palacio Real)* KXY *(Palace*★*: Throne Room*★*, Royal Armoury*★★*, Royal Carriage Museum*★ DX **M**[1]*)* – *National Archaeological Museum*★★ *(Dama de Elche*★★★*)* NV – *Lázaro Galdiano Museum*★★ *(collection of enamels and ivories*★★★*)* GU **M**[4] – *Casón del Buen Retiro*★ *(annexe to the Prado)* NY – *Reina Sofia Art Museum*★ *(Picasso's Guernica*★★★*)* MZ – *Army Museum*★ *(Museo del Ejército)* NY – *Museum of the Americas*★ *(Museo de América; Treasure of Los Quimbayas*★*, Cortesano Manuscript*★★★*)*, DU – *San Fernando Royal Fine Arts Academy*★ *(Real Academia de Bellas Artes de San Fernando)* LX **M**[2] – *Cerralbo Museum*★ KV – *Sorolla Museum*★ FU **M**[5] – *City Museum (Museo de la Ciudad : models*★*)* HT **M**[7] – *Naval Museum (ship models*★*, map of Juan de la Cosa*★★*)* NXY **M**[3] – *National Museum of Decorative Arts (embossed leather*★*)* NX **M**[8] – *Municipal Museum (facade*★★*, model of Madrid*★*)* LV **M**[10] – *National Museum of Science and Technology (ballestilla*★★*)* FZ **M**[9].

CHURCHES AND MONASTERIES

Descalzas Reales Monastery★★ KLX – *San Francisco el Grande Church (stall*★ *in chancel and sacristy)* KZ – *Royal Convent of the Incarnation*★ *(Real Monasterio de la Encarnación)* KX – *San Antonio de la Florida Chapel*★ *(frescoes*★★*)* DV – *Saint Michael Church*★ KY

THE OLD TOWN

Eastern Quarter★★ *(Barrio de Oriente)* KVXY – *Bourbon Madrid*★★ MNXYZ – *Old Madrid*★ KYZ

PLACES OF INTEREST

Plaza Mayor★★ KY – *Buen Retiro Park*★★ HY – *Zoo-Aquarium*★★ *West : by Casa de Campo Park*★ DX – *Plaza de la Villa*★ KY – *Vistillas Gardens (*✳★*)* KYZ – *Campo del Moro Winter Garden*★ DX – *University City*★ *(Ciudad Universitaria)* DT – *Casa de Campo (Park)*★ DX – *Plaza de Cibeles*★ MNX – *Paseo del Prado*★ MNXYZ – *Alcalá Arch*★ *(Puerta de Alcalá)* NX – *Bullring*★ *(Plaza Monumental de las Ventas)* JUV – *West Park*★ *(Parque del Oeste)* DV

Centre : Paseo del Prado, Puerta del Sol, Gran Vía, Alcalá, Paseo de Recoletos, Plaza Mayor

The Westin Palace, pl. de las Cortes 7, ✉ 28014, ☎ 91 360 80 00, *reservation.palacemadrid@westin.com, Fax 91 360 81 00,* – rm, – 25/500. AE VISA JCB. MY e

Meals a la carte 45/54 – 25 – **417 rm** 389/498, 48 suites.

◆ An elegant historic building in front of the Congreso de Diputados with a lovely patio in the middle and a Modernist-style glass dome. A harmonious blend of tradition and luxury.

Villa Real, pl. de las Cortes 10, ✉ 28014, ☎ 91 420 37 67, *villareal@derbyhotels.es, Fax 91 420 25 47,* – – 35/220. AE VISA JCB. rest MY c

Europa **: Meals** a la carte 29/41 – 18 – **96 rm** 301/337, 19 suites.

◆ This hotel has a valuable collection of Greek and Roman art on display in its public areas. The comfortable bedrooms have attractive decorative details and mahogany furnishings. A pleasant restaurant with contemporary lithographs.

Crowne Plaza Madrid City Centre, pl. de España, ✉ 28013, ☎ 91 454 85 00, *reservas@crowneplazamadrid.com, Fax 91 548 13 20,* – – 25/220. AE VISA JCB. KV s

Meals a la carte approx. 39,41 – 19 – **295 rm** 270/294, 11 suites.

◆ A traditional-style hotel in a cultural quarter of the city. Comfortable and well-appointed bedrooms and several lounges. A very good restaurant with beautiful views.

Tryp Ambassador, Cuesta de Santo Domingo 5, ✉ 28013, ☎ 91 541 67 00, *ambasador@trypnet.com, Fax 91 559 10 40* – – 25/300. AE VISA KX k

Meals a la carte approx. 35 – 17 – **159 rm** 187/235, 24 suites.

◆ A rather grand hotel in keeping with the tone of this area of the city. A beautiful covered interior patio and comfortable rooms with elegant and high-quality furnishings. With its glass roof, the restaurant has the feel of a winter garden.

NH Nacional, paseo del Prado 48, ✉ 28014, ☎ 91 429 66 29, *nhnacional@nh-hotels.com, Fax 91 369 15 64* – – 25/150. AE VISA JCB. rest NZ r

Meals *(closed August)* a la carte 25,80/39,80 – 16 – **213 rm** 171/205, 1 suite.

◆ A hotel with an attractive façade and a privileged location. A large foyer-reception and welcoming rooms with light toned décor and modern comfort.

Liabeny, Salud 3, ✉ 28013, ☎ 91 531 90 00, *liabeny@apunte.es, Fax 91 532 74 21* – – 25/125. AE VISA. LX c

Meals 20 – 13 – **222 rm** 107/144 – PA 43.

◆ A hotel in a busy commercial area. The old-fashioned English-style bar lends a touch of class to the public areas. Comfortable rooms with classic functional décor and furnishings. The restaurant has an intimate ambience.

Santo Domingo, pl. de Santo Domingo 13, ✉ 28013, ☎ 91 547 98 00, *reserva@hotelsantodomingo.com, Fax 91 547 59 95* – – 25/200. AE VISA. KX a

Meals 30,25 – 11,25 – **120 rm** 160/213.

◆ Numerous works of art decorate the walls of this hotel. Comfortable rooms with modern bathrooms, some with hydro-massage baths.

Palacio San Martín, pl. San Martín 5, ✉ 28013, ☎ 91 701 50 00, *sanmartin@intur.com, Fax 91 701 50 10,* – – 25. AE VISA. KX t

Meals a la carte approx. 36 – 15 – **93 rm** 154/192, 1 suite.

◆ A historic building which in the 1950s was the United States Embassy. A patio with a glass roof serves as a lounge area. Traditional-style bedrooms, plus a panoramic restaurant on the top floor.

H10 Villa de la Reina, Gran Vía 22, ✉ 28013, ☎ 91 523 91 01, *villadelareina@h10.es, Fax 91 521 75 22* – – 25/40. AE VISA. LX t

Meals a la carte approx. 26,80 – 14 – **73 rm** 175/190, 1 suite.

◆ An attractive building dating from the early 20C with an elegant foyer-reception decked in marble and fine wood. All the charm of former times and comfortable rooms.

Preciados, Preciados 37, ✉ 28013, ☎ 91 454 44 00, *preciadoshotel@preciadoshotel.com, Fax 91 454 44 01* – – 25/100. AE VISA JCB. KX u

Meals 18 – 12,02 – **68 rm** 174,29, 5 suites.

◆ The severe 19C Classicism of this hotel's architecture is in complete contrast to its modern and well-appointed facilities. A small but pleasant lounge.

Arosa coffee shop only, Salud 21, ✉ 28013, ☎ 91 532 16 00, *arosa@hotelarosa.com, Fax 91 531 31 27* – – 25/45. AE VISA JCB LX q

13 – **134 rm** 127,60/195,80.

◆ A wide range of cultural and leisure activities on your doorstep. The rooms have been modernised to improve comfort and décor.

Mayorazgo, Flor Baja 3, ✉ 28013, ✆ 91 547 26 00, *comercial@hotelmayorazgo.com, Fax 91 541 24 85* – 🛗 ▤ TV 🚗 – 🎓 25/250. AE ⓓ MC VISA JCB. ✂ KV c
Meals 26 – ☕ 13 – **200 rm** 140/175.
◆ Close to the Plaza de España with a classic foyer, elegant rooms and pleasant décor. Facilities include a shop, boutique and a hairdressing salon. An intimate and elegant dining room with both a buffet and à la carte dishes.

A. Gaudí, Gran Vía 9, ✉ 28013, ✆ 91 531 22 22, *gaudi@hoteles-catalonia.es, Fax 91 531 54 69,* 🏋 – 🛗 ▤ TV ♿ – 🎓 25/120. AE ⓓ MC VISA. ✂ LX s
Meals 13 – ☕ 12 – **185 rm** 166/198.
◆ Right in the centre of Madrid with an attractive early 20C façade behind which is a lively and modern interior. Well-lit, comfortable and modern rooms.

Senator Gran Vía, Gran Vía 21, ✉ 28013, ✆ 91 531 41 51, *senator.granvia@playasenator.com, Fax 91 524 07 99,* 🏊 – 🛗 ▤ TV ♿ – 🎓 25. AE ⓓ MC VISA. ✂ LX b
Meals 17 – ☕ 12 – **136 rm** 165/195 – PA 41.
◆ Behind the Senator's distinctive classical façade is an interior with the latest in modern comforts, including avant-garde bedrooms. Dining options include a simply styled restaurant offering à la carte and buffet dining, and a spacious cafeteria.

Lope de Vega without rest, Lope de Vega 49, ✉ 28014, ✆ 91 360 00 11, *lopedevega@hotellopedevega.com, Fax 91 429 23 91* – 🛗 ▤ TV 🚗 – 🎓 25/50. AE ⓓ MC VISA JCB. ✂ MY c
☕ 11 – **59 rm** 150/165.
◆ A modern hotel with a marble foyer-reception and an adjoining convention centre. Contemporary-style bedrooms with written references to the playwright and 17C Madrid.

Suecia, Marqués de Casa Riera 4, ✉ 28014, ✆ 91 531 69 00, *bookings@hotelsuecia.com, Fax 91 521 71 41* – 🛗 ▤ TV – 🎓 25/150. AE ⓓ MC VISA JCB. ✂ MX
Meals 23 – ☕ 14 – **119 rm** 142/178, 9 suites – PA 60.
◆ Opened in 1956, the Suecia has welcomed many famous guests, including Ernest Hemingway. The hotel's rooms are a successful mix of antique furniture and modern touches. The welcoming restaurant is part of the spacious, multi-purpose entrance hall-cum reception.

Catalonia Moratín, Atocha 23, ✉ 28012, ✆ 91 369 71 71, *moratin@hoteles-catalonia.es, Fax 91 360 12 31* – 🛗 ▤ TV ♿ – 🎓 25/30. AE ⓓ MC VISA JCB. ✂ LY b
Meals 13 – ☕ 12 – **59 rm** 166/198, 4 suites.
◆ This 18C building combines original features, such as the staircase, with others of a more modern, practical design, including the stylish bedrooms. Attractive inner patio, as well as a pleasant restaurant in the basement serving refined cuisine.

Tryp Atocha without rest, Atocha 83, ✉ 28012, ✆ 91 330 05 00, *tryp.atocha@solmelia.com, Fax 91 420 15 60* – 🛗 ▤ TV – 🎓 25/210. AE ⓓ MC VISA JCB. ✂ MZ
☕ 13 – **150 rm** 173/217.
◆ This small palace dating from 1913 offers guests modern, functional facilities. The spacious lounge areas include the glass-adorned "salón de actos" and a superb staircase.

Atlántico without rest, Gran Vía 38, ✉ 28013, ✆ 91 522 64 80, *informacion@hotelatlantico.es, Fax 91 531 02 10* – 🛗 ▤ TV. AE ⓓ MC VISA JCB. ✂ LX
78 rm ☕ 112/150.
◆ The comfort in this centrally located mansion has increased following a recent expansion. Harmonious decor in the bedrooms with matching wallpaper and curtains.

Casón del Tormes without rest, Río 7, ✉ 28013, ✆ 91 541 97 46, *hotormes@infonegocio.com, Fax 91 541 18 52* – 🛗 ▤ TV. AE ⓓ MC VISA. ✂ KV
☕ 6,50 – **63 rm** 79/97.
◆ Large, bright and well-renovated public areas. Although lacking the best decor, the hotel bedrooms have modern bathrooms and facilities expected of this category.

El Prado without rest, Prado 11, ✉ 28014, ✆ 91 369 02 34, *hotelprado@pradohotel.com, Fax 91 429 28 29* – 🛗 ▤ TV – 🎓 25/35. AE ⓓ MC VISA. ✂ LY
☕ 5,30 – **47 rm** 93,45/113,40.
◆ Modern and central and in an area which is lively at night. Rooms functional but equipped in keeping with their category. Coffee shop with a separate entrance.

Tryp Gran Vía without rest, Gran Vía 25, ✉ 28013, ✆ 91 522 11 21, *tryp.gran.via@solmelia.com, Fax 91 521 24 24* – 🛗 ▤ TV ♿ – 🎓 25/50. AE ⓓ MC VISA JCB. ✂ LX
☕ 11 – **175 rm** 132/165.
◆ A landmark hotel frequented by Ernest Hemingway. Facilities here include a small foyer, a good breakfast room and pleasant bedrooms with marble bathrooms.

Carlos V without rest, Maestro Vitoria 5, ✉ 28013, ✆ 91 531 41 00, *recepcion@hotelcarlosv.com, Fax 91 531 37 61* – 🛗 ▤ TV. AE ⓓ MC VISA JCB. ✂ LX
67 rm ☕ 98,50/124.
◆ The classic decor in the hotel lounge creates an atmosphere that is both warm and welcoming. The bedrooms here are pleasant, albeit on the functional side.

Los Condes without rest, Los Libreros 7, ✉ 28004, ☎ 91 521 54 55, *info@hotel-loscondes.com, Fax 91 521 78 82* – |‡| ▤ TV. AE ⓓ MC VISA JCB. ✂ KLV g
68 rm ☕ 86,92/135,50.
◆ Los Condes has a small reception area, pleasant lounge and a functional cafeteria for breakfast, along with bedrooms furnished and decorated in simple style.

Alexandra without rest, San Bernardo 29, ✉ 28015, ☎ 91 542 04 00, *alexhot@teleline.es, Fax 91 559 28 25* – |‡| ▤ TV – 🏛 25/90. AE ⓓ MC VISA JCB. ✂ KV z
☕ 7,50 – **68 rm** 73/92.
◆ This hotel is discreetly run by friendly staff. The bedrooms have somewhat functional decor with standard furnishings and modern bathrooms.

La Terraza del Casino, Alcalá 15-3°, ✉ 28014, ☎ 91 521 87 00, *laterraza@casinodemadrid.es, Fax 91 523 44 36,* ☂ – |‡| ▤. AE ⓓ MC VISA JCB. ✂ LX v
closed August, Saturday lunch, Sunday and Bank Holidays – **Meals** 90 and a la carte 62/70,10.
◆ In the 19C Madrid Casino building. The lounges have a classy feel and the very attractive terrace is a delightful setting in which to eat.
Spec. Cigala con sésamo y aire de té verde. Canelón de piel de leche con foie-gras y trufa. Pez de San Pedro con puré de limón y huevas de bacalao.

Paradis Madrid, Marqués de Cubas 14, ✉ 28014, ☎ 91 429 73 03, *paradis_madrid@paradis.es, Fax 91 429 32 95* – ▤. AE ⓓ MC VISA. ✂ MY v
closed Saturday lunch, Sunday and Bank Holidays – **Meals** a la carte 35/45.
◆ Located next to the Palacio de Congresos, this modern restaurant with one large dining room and two private dining rooms beyond is accessed via a delicatessen shop.

Café de Oriente, pl. de Oriente 2, ✉ 28013, ☎ 91 541 39 74, *cafeoriente@grupolezama.com, Fax 91 547 77 07* – ▤. AE ⓓ MC VISA JCB. ✂ KXY w
Meals a la carte 37,50/49,50.
◆ In front of the Palacio Real and with a luxury café and an attractive wine cellar-style dining room. International menu with a modern twist.

Moaña, Hileras 4, ✉ 28013, ☎ 91 548 29 14, *Fax 91 541 65 98* – |‡| ▤ 🚗. AE ⓓ MC VISA JCB. ✂ KY r
closed Sunday dinner – **Meals** - Galician rest - a la carte 25,07/39,76.
◆ A comfortable, elegant restaurant in a central and historic area. A busy, popular bar, various private rooms and a large fish-tank containing a tempting selection of seafood.

Bajamar, Gran Vía 78, ✉ 28013, ☎ 91 548 48 18, *rtebajamar@jazzfree.com, Fax 91 559 13 26* – ▤. AE ⓓ MC VISA JCB. ✂ KV r
Meals - Seafood - a la carte 32/46.
◆ Beside the Plaza de España and with fish and seafood on display in the window. Very popular with foreign tourists. Very good fish and seafood dishes.

Errota-Zar, Jovellanos 3-1°, ✉ 28014, ☎ 91 531 25 64, *errota@errota-zar.com, Fax 91 531 25 64* – ▤. AE ⓓ MC VISA. ✂ MY s
closed Holy Week, 3 weeks in August and Sunday – **Meals** - Basque rest - a la carte 33,73/43,24.
◆ In front of the Zarzuela theatre. The sober but elegant dining room serves Basque cuisine accompanied by an extensive wine and cigar list. One private room is also available.

El Asador de Aranda, Preciados 44, ✉ 28013, ☎ 91 547 21 56, *Fax 91 556 62 02* – ▤. AE ⓓ MC VISA. ✂ KX z
closed 15 July-8 August and Monday dinner – **Meals** - Roast lamb - a la carte approx. 22,90.
◆ An attractive Castilian restaurant with beautiful wood ceilings. Traditional dishes and roast meats cooked in a wood fired oven a speciality.

Arce, Augusto Figueroa 32, ✉ 28004, ☎ 91 522 04 40, *restarce@yahoo.es, Fax 91 522 59 13* – ▤. AE ⓓ MC VISA JCB. ✂ MV c
closed Holy Week, 16 to 31 August, Saturday lunch and Sunday – **Meals** a la carte 40/60.
◆ Small but with great atmosphere and with décor that combines modernity with traditional and rustic details. Good innovative cooking.

Casa Matías, San Leonardo 12, ✉ 28015, ☎ 91 541 76 83, *Fax 91 541 93 70* – ▤. AE ⓓ MC VISA. ✂ KV b
closed Sunday dinner – **Meals** - Braised meat specialities - a la carte 35/42.
◆ This Basque-style cider-house, adorned with large casks of its trademark brew for customers to taste, has two spacious rustic-modern rooms, one with an open grill.

Julián de Tolosa, Cava Baja 18, ✉ 28005, ☎ 91 365 82 10, *Fax 91 366 33 08* – ▤. AE ⓓ MC VISA JCB. ✂ KZ c
Meals - Braised meat specialities - a la carte approx. 32,50.
◆ A pleasant restaurant in neo-rustic style offering the best T-bone steaks in the city. The limited menu is more than compensated for by the quality of the food.

XX **La Ópera de Madrid,** Amnistía 5, ✉ 28013, ✆ 91 559 50 92, *Fax 91 559 50 92* – ▤ AE ⓓ ⓜⓒ VISA. ✗ KY g
closed August and Sunday – **Meals** a la carte 25,20/30.
◆ A good place to start an evening out or to discuss a play seen in the nearby theatre while enjoying something delicious. Elegant décor and a well-balanced menu.

XX **Pinocchio Bel Canto,** Sánchez Bustillo 5, ✉ 28012, ✆ 91 468 73 73, *restaurante@pinocchio.es, Fax 91 662 18 65,* Lively evening meals – ▤. AE ⓓ ⓜⓒ VISA. ✗ NZ
closed August, Saturday lunch and Sunday – **Meals** a la carte 22/28,55.
◆ A very good location in front of the Centro de Arte Reina Sofía. Classic-modern décor and Italian influenced cuisine to the sound of bel canto.

XX **El Mentidero de la Villa,** Santo Tomé 6, ✉ 28004, ✆ 91 308 12 85 – ▤. AE ⓓ ⓜⓒ VISA. ✗ MV b
closed August, Saturday lunch, Sunday and Bank Holidays – **Meals** a la carte 29,40/39,40
◆ A friendly, intimate restaurant with original and tasteful decor. Very carefully prepared and bold international cuisine.

XX **El Landó,** pl. Gabriel Miró 8, ✉ 28005, ✆ 91 366 76 81, *ellandomadrid@hotmail.com, Fax 91 366 25 56* – ▤. AE ⓓ ⓜⓒ VISA. ✗ KZ
closed Holy Week, August and Sunday – **Meals** a la carte 31,26/41,47.
◆ Near to the Basilica de San Francisco el Grande, this restaurant has a bar, dining room in the basement, and private room, all classically furnished with a profusion of wood.

XX **El Rincón de Esteban,** Santa Catalina 3, ✉ 28014, ✆ 91 429 92 89, *Fax 91 365 87 7* – ▤. AE ⓓ ⓜⓒ VISA. ✗ MY
closed August and Sunday – **Meals** a la carte 40/48.
◆ Frequented by politicians because of its proximity to the Palacio de Congresos. Intimat and elegant and offering traditional-style dishes.

XX **La Cava del Faraón,** Segovia 8, ✉ 28005, ✆ 91 542 52 54, *Fax 91 457 45 30* – ▤ AE ⓓ ⓜⓒ VISA. ✗ KY
closed Monday – **Meals** - Egyptian rest, dinner only - a la carte 28,75/31,80.
◆ A typical Egyptian setting, with a tea-room, domed ceilings and a dining room wher you can sample the cuisine of the country and enjoy a belly-dancing performance.

X **La Barraca,** Reina 29, ✉ 28004, ✆ 91 532 71 54, *Fax 91 523 82 73* – ▤. AE ⓓ ⓜ VISA JCB. ✗ LX
Meals - Rice dishes - a la carte 25,05/40,65.
◆ Popular with tourists because of its renown and its location. Traditional Valencian décc with lots of ceramic tiles. Rice dishes a speciality.

X **La Vaca Verónica,** Moratín 38, ✉ 28014, ✆ 91 429 78 27 – ▤. AE ⓓ ⓜⓒ VISA JC MZ
closed Saturday lunch – **Meals** a la carte 23,50/28.
◆ This delightfully intimate and friendly restaurant is decorated in original style with colou ful paintings, mirrored ceilings and candles on every table.

X **Casa Vallejo,** San Lorenzo 9, ✉ 28004, ✆ 91 308 61 58 – ▤. ⓜⓒ VISA JCB. ✗ LV
closed Holy Week, August, Sunday, Monday dinner and Bank Holidays – **Meals** a la car 21/29,10.
◆ A charming and friendly restaurant near the Municipal Museum. A good traditional men in addition to a varied selection of daily specials.

X **La Bola,** Bola 5, ✉ 28013, ✆ 91 547 69 30, *Fax 91 541 71 64* – ▤. ✗ KX
closed Saturday dinner, Sunday in July-August and Sunday dinner the rest of the year
Meals - Madrid style stew - a la carte 22/30.
◆ A long-established Madrid tavern with the flavour of old Madrid. Traditional stewed dish a speciality. Try the meat and chickpea stew.

X **La Esquina del Real,** Amnistía 2, ✉ 28013, ✆ 91 559 43 09, *jedine1@mi.madritel.* – ▤. AE ⓜⓒ VISA. ✗ KY
closed 15 August-15 September, Saturday lunch and Sunday – **Meals** a la car 34,50/41,80.
◆ An intimate and pleasant rustic-style restaurant with stone and brick walls. Frienc service and French dishes.

X **Taberna Carmencita,** Libertad 16, ✉ 28004, ✆ 91 531 66 12, *carmencita@im blue.com, Fax 91 522 48 38* – ▤. AE ⓓ ⓜⓒ VISA JCB. ✗ MX
closed August, Saturday lunch and Sunday – **Meals** a la carte 19,21/31,26.
◆ A small restaurant founded in 1850 with dining areas on two levels. A traditional me and some Basque specialities. Good ambience.

🍷 **La Botillería,** pl. de Oriente 4, ✉ 28013, ✆ 91 548 46 20, *cafeoriente@grupoleza a.com, Fax 91 547 77 07,* 🏛 – ▤. AE ⓓ ⓜⓒ VISA. ✗ KX
Tapa 3,25 – **Ración** approx. 10,10.
◆ In an area that is very lively at night. Traditional Viennese café-style décor and a wi variety of canapes accompanied by good wines served by the glass.

Prada a Tope, Príncipe 11, ✉ 28012, ☎ 91 429 59 21 – ▤. VISA. 🚭 LY u
closed August and Monday – **Tapa** 5 – **Ración** - Dishes from El Bierzo - approx. 8,50.
◆ A traditional establishment with a bar and rustic-style tables. Wood décor, photos on the walls and the opportunity to buy various products.

Taberna de San Bernardo, San Bernardo 85, ✉ 28015, ☎ 91 445 41 70 – ▤. AE MC VISA. 🚭 LV m
Tapa 1,60 – **Ración** approx. 5,50.
◆ An informal, rustic tavern with three separate sections. Popular house specialities include two vegetarian dishes - papas con huevo and fritura de verduras.

Bocaito, Libertad 6, ✉ 28004, ☎ 91 532 12 19, *bocaito@bocaito.com, Fax 91 522 56 29* – ▤. D MC VISA. 🚭 MX b
closed August, Saturday lunch and Sunday – **Tapa** 2,10 – **Ración** approx. 9.
◆ A bull fighting atmosphere and décor. Ideal for sampling tapas either at the splendid bar or at a table. Deep fried and egg-based tapas are specialities.

Typical atmosphere :

Posada de la Villa, Cava Baja 9, ✉ 28005, ☎ 91 366 18 60, *povisa@posadadelavilla.com, Fax 91 366 18 80* – ▤. AE D MC VISA JCB. 🚭 KZ v
closed August and Sunday dinner except May – **Meals** a la carte 23/37,70.
◆ An old inn with a friendly ambience and Castilian décor. Regional menu and traditional roasts cooked in a wood fired oven. Madrid-style chickpea stew a speciality.

Botín, Cuchilleros 17, ✉ 28005, ☎ 91 366 42 17, *Fax 91 366 84 94* – ▤. AE D MC VISA JCB. 🚭 KY n
Meals a la carte 26,20/43,75.
◆ Founded in 1725 and said to be the oldest restaurant in the world. The old-style décor, traditional wine-cellar and wood fired oven all convey a strong feeling of the past.

Zerain, Quevedo 3, ✉ 28014, ☎ 91 429 79 09, *Fax 91 429 17 20*, Basque cider press – ▤. AE D MC VISA JCB. 🚭 MY x
closed Holy Week, August and Sunday – **Meals** a la carte 25,50/31.
◆ A Basque cider house with huge barrels. Friendly atmosphere and attractive décor with pictures of the Basque Country. Traditional cider house menu at reasonable prices.

Retiro, Salamanca, Ciudad Lineal : Paseo de la Castellana, Velázquez, Serrano, Goya, Príncipe de Vergara, Narváez, Don Ramón de la Cruz

Ritz, pl. de la Lealtad 5, ✉ 28014, ☎ 91 701 67 67, *leroyalmeridianritz@.com, Fax 91 701 67 76*, 🏞, Fб – 🛗 ▤ TV ♿ – 🎤 25/250. AE D MC VISA JCB. 🚭 rest NY k
Meals a la carte 62/79 – ☕ 30 – **137 rm** 560, 30 suites.
◆ A hotel of international renown in a former 19C palace which had diplomatic connections. Sumptuous décor in the bedrooms and beautiful public areas. The well-known restaurant has attractive lounges and a pleasant terrace.

Villa Magna, paseo de la Castellana 22, ✉ 28046, ☎ 91 587 12 34, *hotel@villamagna.es, Fax 91 431 22 86*, 🏞, Fб – 🛗 ▤ TV 🚗 – 🎤 25/400. AE D MC VISA GV y
Meals 39,50 - ***Le Divellec*** *(closed August and Sunday)* **Meals** a la carte 36,25/55,25 - ***Tsé Yang*** *(Chinese rest)* **Meals** a la carte 33/49 – ☕ 26 – **164 rm** 310/360, 18 suites.
◆ Luxury, elegance and décor in the style of the time of Charles IV. Spacious rooms. Le Divellec restaurant is tasteful and has fine wood furnishings.

Wellington, Velázquez 8, ✉ 28001, ☎ 91 575 44 00, *wellington@hotel-wellington.com, Fax 91 576 41 64*, 🏊 – 🛗 ▤ TV 🚗 – 🎤 25/200. AE D MC VISA JCB. 🚭 HX t
Meals - see rest. ***Goizeko Wellington*** below – ☕ 18 – **259 rm** 175/300, 25 suites.
◆ In an elegant area of Madrid close to the Retiro. Classic style which has been updated in public rooms and bedrooms. Bullfighting aficionados meet here regularly.

Gran Meliá Fénix, Hermosilla 2, ✉ 28001, ☎ 91 431 67 00, *gran.melia.fenix@solmelia.com, Fax 91 576 06 61* – 🛗 ▤ TV ♿ 🚗 – 🎤 25/100. AE D MC VISA JCB. 🚭 NV c
Meals a la carte 39,20/52,60 – ☕ 19 – **204 rm** 300/359, 13 suites.
◆ A distinguished hotel. Large public areas such as the elegant foyer with its cupola. Rooms comfortably furnished.

Meliá Galgos, Claudio Coello 139, ✉ 28006, ☎ 91 562 66 00, *melia.galgos@solmelia.es, Fax 91 561 76 62*, Fб – 🛗 ▤ TV 🚗 – 🎤 25/300. AE D MC VISA JCB. 🚭 GU a
Diábolo : **Meals** a la carte 32/47 – ☕ 18 – **350 rm** 144,50/353, 6 suites.
◆ Modern but traditional in style and frequented by business travellers and executives. Large and attractive public areas and bedrooms refurbished to a high level of comfort. Pleasant décor in the restaurant and excellent service.

Foxá M-30, Serrano Galvache 14, ✉ 28033, ☎ 91 384 04 00, *foxam30@foxa.com, Fax 91 384 04 02,* – rm, – 25/650. AE VISA. rest JR x

Meals a la carte 31/35 – 10 – **73 rm** 175, 2 suites.

◆ A magnificent hotel with works of art and antique furnishings. A grand staircase in the foyer and light and airy rooms, individually decorated. The elegant dining room offers traditional specialities and international dishes.

Adler, Velázquez 33, ✉ 28001, ☎ 91 426 32 20, *hoteladler@iova-sa.com, Fax 91 426 32 21* – AE VISA. HV x

Meals a la carte 51/56 – 22 – **45 rm** 295/365.

◆ An exclusive hotel with an elegant décor. High-quality furnishings and comfortable and very well-appointed rooms. A pleasant restaurant with a friendly atmosphere.

Puerta Madrid, Juan Rizi 5, ✉ 28027, ☎ 91 743 83 00, *booking.puertamadrid@hoteles-silken.com, Fax 91 743 83 01* – – 25/350. AE VISA. East : by Av. de América JT

Meals a la carte approx. 45 – 15 – **188 rm** 228,38/270,46, 6 suites.

◆ A recently constructed hotel. Large public areas with concrete pillars and walls and modern and functional rooms with excellent bathrooms. Contemporary-style restaurant

Sofitel Madrid Airport, av. de la Capital de España Madrid 10, ✉ 28042, ☎ 91 721 00 70, *h1606@accor-hotels.com, Fax 91 721 05 15,* – rm, – 50/120. AE VISA. rest North-East : by Av. de América JT

Meals 30 - ***Mare Nostrum* :** **Meals** a la carte 45/50 – 22 – **176 rm** 252/272, 3 suites.

◆ Near the Recinto Ferial. Fine hall, well-fitted rooms and an attractive dining room styled like a southern patio. Inventive à la carte in the stylish Mare Nostrum restaurant.

NH Príncipe de Vergara, Príncipe de Vergara 92, ✉ 28006, ☎ 91 563 26 95, *nhprincipedevergara@nh-hotels.com, Fax 91 563 72 53,* – – 25/300 AE VISA. HU c

Meals a la carte 27/35 – 16,50 – **170 rm** 175/208, 3 suites.

◆ A hotel in an area well-served by public transport and with all the facilities and style of the NH chain. Practical, functional and with well-lit bedrooms.

NH Sanvy, Goya 3, ✉ 28001, ☎ 91 576 08 00, *nhsanvy@nh-hotels.com Fax 91 575 24 43* – – 25/160. AE VISA JCB. NV

Meals (see rest. ***Sorolla*** below) – 17 – **139 rm** 210/284, 10 suites.

◆ A functional though comfortable building and with attractive modern décor. Professiona management and good service.

Bauzá, Goya 79, ✉ 28001, ☎ 91 435 75 45, *info@hotelbauza.com, Fax 91 431 09 43* – – 25/425. AE VISA. HV

Meals a la carte approx. 32 – 12 – **169 rm** 174/251, 8 suites – PA 52,70.

◆ This is the refurbished former Hotel Pintor Goya. Modern facilities and elegant comfort A beautiful lounge/library with a fireplace and a light and airy modern dining room.

Quinta de los Cedros, Allendesalazar 4, ✉ 28043, ☎ 91 515 22 00, *reservas@quintadeloscedros.com, Fax 91 415 20 50,* – – 25/40. AE VISA. JS

Los Cedros *(closed Sunday dinner)* **Meals** a la carte 30,50/43,50 – 9 – **32 r** 152,90/191,40.

◆ This modern building, in the style of a Tuscan villa, is surrounded by lawns an adorned with attractive decorative features. An extensive main floor, with persona lised, fully equipped bedrooms. The classical-style restaurant comprises three separat rooms.

Agumar coffee shop only, paseo Reina Cristina 7, ✉ 28014, ☎ 91 552 69 00, *hotagumar@h-santos.es, Fax 91 433 60 95* – – 25/250. AE VIS JCB. HY

Meals 22,50 – 16,05 – **239 rm** 171,20/214, 6 suites.

◆ Pleasant public areas and a renovated cafeteria, albeit soberly furnished. Well-equippe bedrooms and marble bathrooms. Classic dining room offering menus and à la carte.

Novotel Madrid Puente de La Paz, Albacete 1, ✉ 28027, ☎ 91 724 76 00, *h084@accor-hotels.com, Fax 91 724 76 10,* – rm, – 25/25 AE VISA JT

***Claravía* :** **Meals** a la carte 20,75/27 – 13 – **240 rm** 137.

◆ A functional-style hotel with a modern façade and welcoming rooms with simple deco The comfortable dining room has a terrace for the summer months.

NH Parque Avenidas, Biarritz 2, ✉ 28028, ☎ 91 361 02 88, *nhparque@nh-hote.com, Fax 91 361 21 38,* – – 25/500. AE VISA JC rest JU

Meals a la carte 24/39 – 13,90 – **198 rm** 184, 1 suite.

◆ Near the bullring, with all the functionality and comfort you would expect from the N chain. Well-maintained, with an abundance of wood decor.

Zenit Conde de Orgaz, Moscatelar 24, ✉ 28043, ☎ 91 748 97 60, *condeorgaz@zenithoteles.com, Fax 91 388 00 09* – rest North-East : by José Silva JS
Meals 24 - ***Bouquet :*** **Meals** a la carte approx. 27,60 – 9,90 – **90 rm** 144/170.
• A cheerful, welcoming hotel in a residential district with good communications to the airport. Functional bedrooms, plus several private rooms for business meetings. A glass-topped terrace provides the setting for the modern dining room.

Rafael H. Ventas, Alcalá 269, ✉ 28027, ☎ 91 326 16 20, *ventas@rafaelhoteles.com, Fax 91 326 18 19* – 25/165. JV a
Meals 15 – 10,50 – **110 rm** 130/154, 1 suite – PA 40,50.
• Modern in both facilities and decoration. The comfortable bedrooms have recently been refurbished with the emphasis on wood. A large traditional dining room with attractive oil paintings on the walls.

AC Avenida de América coffee shop dinner only, Cartagena 83, ✉ 28028, ☎ 91 724 42 40, *acamerica@ac-hoteles.com, Fax 91 724 42 41* – 25/50. JU b
11 – **145 rm** 168.
• Ideal for business executives and with good communications. Modern and functional and with a coffee shop that is also a bar depending on the time of day.

Jardín de Recoletos, Gil de Santivañes 4, ✉ 28001, ☎ 91 781 16 40, *Fax 91 781 16 41*. NV p
Meals 22,60 – **43 rm** 177,10/184,05 – PA 56,59.
• A hotel with an attractive façade embellished with balustraded balconies. An elegant glass-crowned foyer-reception area, large studio-type bedrooms and an attractive patio-terrace. The walls of the pleasant dining room are adorned with landscape murals.

NH Lagasca, Lagasca 64, ✉ 28001, ☎ 91 575 46 06, *nhlagasca@nh-hotels.com, Fax 91 575 16 94* – 25/60. GHV k
Meals *(closed August, Saturday and Sunday)* a la carte approx. 24 – 13,90 – **100 rm** 192/220.
• Good and comfortable rooms in a functional hotel where great thought is given to the needs and comfort of guests. Professional management.

Novotel Madrid Campo de las Naciones, Amsterdan 3, ✉ 28042, ☎ 91 721 18 18, *h1636@accor-hotels.com, Fax 91 721 11 22*, – rm, – 25/200. rest
Claravía : **Meals** a la carte 21,10/32,60 – 13 – **240 rm** 145/155, 6 suites.
• A classic-modern hotel near the Parque Ferial. Sufficiently large public rooms and comfortable bedrooms with functional furniture. A bright dining room with a summer terrace. North-East : by Av. de América JT

NH Balboa, Núñez de Balboa 112, ✉ 28006, ☎ 91 563 03 24, *nhbalboa@nh-hotels.com, Fax 91 562 69 80* – 25/60. HU n
Meals *(closed August, Saturday and Sunday)* a la carte approx. 30 – 13 – **120 rm** 146/156.
• Great comfort in a hotel with very professional staff. Design and functionality along with cheerful décor.

Zenit Abeba, Alcántara 63, ✉ 28006, ☎ 91 401 16 50, *abeba@zenithoteles.com, Fax 91 402 75 91*. JV k
Meals a la carte approx. 30 – 10 – **90 rm** 140/187.
• In the Salamanca district of Madrid. A functional and modern hotel with refurbished rooms, contemporary furniture and up-to-date bathrooms.

NH Sur without rest, paseo Infanta Isabel 9, ✉ 28014, ☎ 91 539 94 00, *nhsur@nh-hotels.com, Fax 91 467 09 96* – 25/30. NZ a
12 – **68 rm** 134/168.
• A hotel with décor in keeping with modern hotel standards and the small lounge is complemented by a breakfast room. Comfortable bedrooms.

Club 31, Alcalá 58, ✉ 28014, ☎ 91 531 00 92, *club31@club31.net, Fax 91 531 00 92*. NX e
closed August – **Meals** a la carte 36,70/51,75.
• A well-established restaurant with 40-or-so years of tradition. Traditional décor with wood-clad walls. International cooking and an excellent wine-list.

El Amparo, Puigcerdá 8, ✉ 28001, ☎ 91 431 64 56, *rte.elamparo@terra.es, Fax 91 575 54 91*. GX h
closed Holy Week, Saturday lunch and Sunday – **Meals** a la carte 60/67.
• A distinguished restaurant with neo-rustic décor and dining areas on different levels and skylights in the roof. Good wine-list and attentive staff.

Combarro, José Ortega y Gasset 40, ✉ 28006, ☎ 91 577 82 72, *combarro@combarro.com, Fax 91 435 95 12*. HV e
closed Holy Week, August and Sunday dinner – **Meals** - Seafood - a la carte 43,64/57,40.
• Large and rather magnificent restaurant with a fish-tank and granite and wood décor.

XXX **Pedro Larumbe,** Serrano 61-2nd floor, ✉ 28006, ☎ 91 575 11 12, *info@larumbe.com, Fax 91 576 60 19* – ⇕ ▤. AE ⓓ ⓜⓒ VISA. ✗ GV r
closed 15 days in August, Saturday lunch, Sunday and Bank Holidays – **Meals** a la carte 35,81/56,91.
♦ In an elegant palace with three grand dining rooms, each individually decorated with great taste. Interesting menu of dishes elaborated with a creative touch.

XXX **Goizeko Wellington** - *Hotel Wellington*, Villanueva 34, ✉ 28001, ☎ 91 577 01 38, *goizeko@goizekowellington.com, Fax 91 555 16 66* – ▤. AE ⓓ ⓜⓒ VISA. ✗ HX t
closed Saturday lunch in summer and Sunday – **Meals** a la carte 60/75.
♦ A modern restaurant with a minimalist design run separately from the hotel. Well-prepared traditional dishes in addition to more innovative specialities.

XXX **Sorolla** - *Hotel NH Sanvy*, Hermosilla 4, ✉ 28001, ☎ 91 431 27 15, *Fax 91 431 83 75* – ▤. AE ⓓ ⓜⓒ VISA JCB. ✗ NV r
closed August – **Meals** a la carte 34,50/47.
♦ Excellent, traditional-style restaurant with four private rooms. International cuisine plus dishes prepared on a charcoal grill. A fine selection of coffees, teas and cigars.

XXX **Suntory,** paseo de la Castellana 36, ✉ 28046, ☎ 91 577 37 34, *rsmad@nova.es, Fax 91 577 44 55* – ▤ 🚗. AE ⓓ ⓜⓒ VISA JCB. ✗ GU d
closed Sunday and Bank Holidays – **Meals** - Japanese rest - a la carte 44,50/53.
♦ Japanese specialities and elegant traditional atmosphere in a large restaurant. Dishes prepared in front of the diner.

XXX **Balzac,** Moreto 7, ✉ 28014, ☎ 91 420 01 77, *restaurantebalzac@yahoo.es, Fax 91 429 83 70* – ▤. AE ⓓ ⓜⓒ VISA. ✗ NY a
closed 1 to 15 August, Saturday lunch and Sunday – **Meals** a la carte approx. 60.
♦ An ideal place to rest after visiting the nearby museums. Classic comfortable style with modern and innovative cuisine.

XXX **Ponteareas,** Claudio Coello 96, ✉ 28006, ☎ 91 575 58 73, *Fax 91 431 99 57* – ▤ 🚗. AE ⓓ ⓜⓒ VISA JCB. ✗ GV w
closed 20 days in August and Sunday – **Meals** - Galician rest - a la carte 32/46,28.
♦ Traditional Galician dishes in large traditional dining rooms with wood décor and chandeliers. Private bar at the front of the restaurant. Many regular customers.

XXX **Paradis Casa América,** paseo de Recoletos 2, ✉ 28001, ☎ 91 575 45 40, *casa-america@paradis.es, Fax 91 576 02 15,* 🏛 – ▤. AE ⓓ ⓜⓒ VISA. ✗ NX r
closed Saturday lunch, Sunday and Bank Holidays – **Meals** a la carte 33,66/46,12.
♦ A particularly attractive restaurant with elegant decor inside the Palacio de Linares. A wide-ranging international menu, plus excellent cod and rice dishes.

XXX **Castelló 9,** Castelló 9, ✉ 28001, ☎ 91 435 00 67, *castello9@castello9.com, Fax 91 435 91 34* – ▤. AE ⓓ ⓜⓒ VISA. ✗ HX e
closed Holy Week, August and Sunday – **Meals** a la carte 32,85/42,80.
♦ Classic elegance in the Salamanca district. Intimate dining rooms offering an international à la carte choice plus a tasting menu featuring a variety of shared dishes.

XX **La Paloma,** Jorge Juan 39, ✉ 28001, ☎ 91 576 86 92, *Fax 91 575 51 41* – ▤. AE ⓓ ⓜⓒ VISA. ✗ HX g
closed Christmas, Holy Week, August, Sunday and Bank Holidays – **Meals** a la carte 37,50/46,75.
♦ A well-established and successful restaurant with a dining room on two levels and excellent service. An interesting menu and good wine-list.

XX **Viridiana,** Juan de Mena 14, ✉ 28014, ☎ 91 523 44 78, *viridiana@restauranteviridiana.com, Fax 91 532 42 74* – ▤. ⓜⓒ VISA. ✗ NY
closed Sunday – **Meals** a la carte 57/85.
♦ Allusions to Buñuel's films in the décor, highly creative dishes and international specialities. A good choice for those who are looking for something really different.

XX **La Torcaz,** Lagasca 81, ✉ 28006, ☎ 91 575 41 30, *Fax 91 431 83 88* – ▤. AE ⓓ ⓜⓒ VISA. ✗ GHV
closed Holy Week, August and Sunday – **Meals** a la carte 33,40/42,75.
♦ A friendly restaurant with a display of different wines near the entrance, a dining room divided into two areas and mirrors on the walls. Excellent service.

XX **Montana,** Lagasca 5, ✉ 28001, ☎ 91 435 99 01, *restaurantemontana@hotmail.com, Fax 91 426 04 18* – ▤. AE ⓓ ⓜⓒ VISA. ✗ GX
closed 9 to 23 August and Sunday – **Meals** a la carte 22,15/35,95.
♦ The Retiro's atmosphere is best defined by its wood flooring and minimalist decor. A modern take on traditional cuisine, with an emphasis on presentation and natural products.

XX **Al Mounia,** Recoletos 5, ✉ 28001, ☎ 91 435 08 28, *Fax 91 575 01 73* – ▤. AE ⓓ ⓜⓒ VISA. ✗ NV u
closed Holy Week, August, Sunday and Monday – **Meals** - North African rest - a la carte 24,10/34,92.
◆ An exotic restaurant near the National Archaeological Museum. Moroccan décor with carved wood, plaster work and low tables. Traditional Arab dishes.

XX **Teatriz,** Hermosilla 15, ✉ 28001, ☎ 91 577 53 79, *Fax 91 431 69 10* – ▤. AE ⓓ ⓜⓒ VISA. ✗ GV u
Meals a la carte 24,90/35,80.
◆ In the stalls of the former Teatro Beatriz. A tapas bar near the entrance and a dining area and a bar on the stage, all with attractive Modernist décor.

XX **La Miel,** Maldonado 14, ✉ 28006, ☎ 91 435 50 45, *manuelcoto@restaurantelamiel.com* – ▤. AE ⓓ ⓜⓒ VISA. ✗ HU x
closed Holy Week, 8 to 30 August and Sunday – **Meals** a la carte 31/40.
◆ A traditional, comfortable restaurant run by the proprietors. Attentive service, a good menu of international dishes and an impressive wine cellar.

XX **El Chiscón de Castelló,** Castelló 3, ✉ 28001, ☎ 91 575 56 62, *Fax 91 575 56 05* – ▤. AE ⓓ ⓜⓒ VISA. ✗ HX e
closed August, Sunday and Bank Holidays – **Meals** a la carte 25,10/32,10.
◆ Hidden behind the typical façade is a warmly decorated interior that gives it the feel of a private house, particularly on the first floor. Well-priced traditional cuisine.

XX **El Asador de Aranda,** Diego de León 9, ✉ 28006, ☎ 91 563 02 46, *Fax 91 556 62 02* – ▤. AE ⓓ ⓜⓒ VISA. ✗ HU s
closed August and Sunday dinner – **Meals** - Roast lamb - a la carte approx. 22,90.
◆ Classic Castilian décor and a wood fired oven for roasting meat. The main dining room, with stained-glass windows, is on the 1st floor.

XX **Nicolás,** Villalar 4, ✉ 28001, ☎ 91 431 77 37, *jam@mail.ddnet.es, Fax 91 577 86 65* – ▤. AE ⓓ ⓜⓒ VISA. ✗ NX t
closed Holy Week, August, Sunday and Monday – **Meals** a la carte 26,85/35,35.
◆ A restaurant with minimalist décor. The traditional menu does not have many dishes but the quality of the food more than compensates for this.

XX **Guisando,** Núñez de Balboa 75, ✉ 28006, ☎ 91 575 10 10, *Fax 91 575 09 00* – ▤. AE ⓓ ⓜⓒ VISA. ✗ HV f
closed holy Week, August and Sunday dinner – **Meals** a la carte approx. 30.
◆ Very popular with a younger clientele and very good prices. Bar near the entrance and also a spacious and light dining room. Different dishes available on a daily basis.

X ✿ **Casa d'a Troya,** Emiliano Barral 14, ✉ 28043, ☎ 91 416 44 55, *Fax 91 416 42 80* – ▤. ⓓ ⓜⓒ VISA. ✗ JS f
closed 24 December-2 January, 15 July-1 September, Sunday and Bank Holidays – **Meals** - Galician rest, Seafood - a la carte 28/38.
◆ A family-run restaurant offering excellent Galician food prepared in a traditionally simple way. A bar-entrance area and traditional furnishings in the dining room.
Spec. Pulpo a la gallega. Merluza a la gallega. Tarta de Santiago.

X **Asador Velate,** Jorge Juan 91, ✉ 28009, ☎ 91 435 10 24, *catering@asadorvelate.com, Fax 91 576 12 40* – ▤. AE ⓓ ⓜⓒ VISA JCB. ✗ JX x
closed August and Sunday – **Meals** - Basque rest - a la carte 33,80/40,35.
◆ A traditional Basque-Navarrese grill-restaurant specialising in grilled hake and T-bone steaks. Dining areas with décor resembling a farmhouse of the region. Traditional menu.

X **Pelotari,** Recoletos 3, ✉ 28001, ☎ 91 578 24 97, *informacion@asador-pelotari.com, Fax 91 431 60 04* – ▤. AE ⓓ ⓜⓒ VISA. ✗ NV u
closed 15 days in August and Sunday – **Meals** a la carte 29,72/43,70.
◆ A traditional Basque grill-restaurant which has improved both its service and its décor which is in the classic style of the Basque region.

X **La Trainera,** Lagasca 60, ✉ 28001, ☎ 91 576 05 75, *Fax 91 575 06 31* – ▤. AE ⓓ ⓜⓒ VISA JCB. ✗ GHV k
closed August and Sunday – **Meals** - Seafood - a la carte 29,80/41,50.
◆ A fish restaurant which is just about comfortable enough. Simple dining rooms with décor with a maritime feel which offer very high quality food. No tablecloths.

X **El Pescador,** José Ortega y Gasset 75, ✉ 28006, ☎ 91 402 12 90, *Fax 91 401 30 26* – ▤. ⓜⓒ VISA. ✗ JV t
closed Holy Week, August and Sunday – **Meals** - Seafood - a la carte 43,40/55,30.
◆ A modest restaurant with simple décor with a maritime feel which looks a little outdated. Excellent fish and seafood.

X **La Castela,** Doctor Castelo 22, ✉ 28009, ☎ 91 574 00 15 – ▤. AE ⓓ ⓜⓒ VISA JCB. ✗
closed August and Sunday – **Meals** a la carte approx. 30. HX r
◆ An establishment in the tradition of Madrid taverns with a tapas bar and a simple traditional dining room offering traditional dishes.

José Luis, General Oráa 5, ✉ 28006, ☎ 91 561 64 13, *joseluis@nexo.es,* – AE MC VISA. GU z
Tapa 1,40 – **Ración** approx. 15.
◆ A well-known establishment with a wide range of canapés, Basque-style tapas and servings of different dishes in elegant surroundings with traditional décor.

Mesón Cinco Jotas, Callejón de Puigcerdá, ✉ 28001, ☎ 91 575 41 25, *m5jjorgejuan@osborne.es, Fax 91 575 56 35,* – AE MC VISA. GX v
Tapa 2,50 – **Ración** - Ham specialities - approx. 10.
◆ Well-known for the high quality of its hams and other fine pork products. A wonderful terrace where you can enjoy well-made and appetising tapas.

Tasca La Farmacia, Diego de León 9, ✉ 28006, ☎ 91 564 86 52, *Fax 91 556 62 02* – AE MC VISA. GHU s
closed 15 August-8 September and Sunday – **Tapa** 2,50 – **Ración** - Cod specialities - approx. 5,50.
◆ A traditional establishment with a beautiful tiled bar. Don't miss the opportunity to try the tapas or larger servings of salt-cod dishes.

Mesón Cinco Jotas, Serrano 118, ✉ 28006, ☎ 91 563 27 10, *m5jserrano@osborne.es, Fax 91 561 32 84,* – AE MC VISA. GU a
Tapa 2,50 – **Ración** - Ham specialities - approx. 10.
◆ Good service in a modern establishment with a variety of tapas and larger portions of different dishes. The hams and fine pork products are very good.

El Barril, Goya 86, ✉ 28009, ☎ 91 578 39 98 – AE MC VISA JCB. JVX r
closed Sunday dinner – **Tapa** 3 – **Ración** - Shellfish specialities - approx. 15.
◆ A good fish restaurant with a bar with a wide display of fish and seafood. Eat at the bar or enjoy the food in greater comfort in the dining room.

José Luis, Serrano 89, ✉ 28006, ☎ 91 563 09 58, *joseluis@nexo.es, Fax 91 563 31 02,* – AE MC VISA. GU u
Tapa 1,40 – **Ración** approx. 15.
◆ This was the first bar opened in Madrid by this chain and it is in a very good location. A wide variety of Basque and traditional-style tapas.

Taberna de la Daniela, General Pardiñas 21, ✉ 28001, ☎ 91 575 23 29, *Fax 91 409 07 11* – AE MC VISA. HV s
Tapa 2 – **Ración** approx. 5.
◆ Behind the tiled façade of this typical Madrid tavern are a number of dining rooms where you can enjoy a range of creative tapas, raciones, stews and fish dishes.

El Barril, Don Ramón de la Cruz 91, ✉ 28006, ☎ 91 401 33 05 – AE MC VISA.
Tapa 6 – **Ración** - Shellfish - approx. 12. JV n
◆ A fish restaurant which is both well-known and popular as much for the service as for the quality of the food. A bar specialising in different beers near the entrance.

Jurucha, Ayala 19, ✉ 28001, ☎ 91 575 00 98 – GV a
closed August, Sunday and Bank Holidays – **Tapa** 1,20 – **Ración** approx. 4.
◆ Delicious Basque-style tapas along with the Spanish omelette and croquettes have made this bar very popular with anybody enjoying an evening of tapas in Madrid.

Arganzuela, Carabanchel, Villaverde : Antonio López, Paseo de Las Delicias, Paseo Santa María de la Cabeza

Rafael H. Atocha, Méndez Álvaro 30, ✉ 28045, ☎ 91 468 81 00, *atocha@rafaelhoteles.com, Fax 91 468 81 20* – – 25/450. AE MC VISA.
Meals 19 – 10 – **245 rm** 165/200. GZ t
◆ A modern hotel with elegant décor, good furnishings and tasteful paintings. Very good service and rooms with every mod con.

Rafael H. Pirámides, paseo de las Acacias 40, ✉ 28005, ☎ 91 517 18 28, *piramides@rafaelhoteles.com, Fax 91 517 00 90* – – 25/80. AE MC VISA. DZ r
Meals 16,50 – 10,40 – **84 rm** 130/164, 9 suites.
◆ A hotel with exposed brickwork and sufficient public areas and a light and airy foyer-reception. Refurbished rooms with attractive curtains and wooden bathroom floors.

Carlton, paseo de las Delicias 26, ✉ 28045, ☎ 91 539 71 00, *carlton@hotelcarlton.com, Fax 91 527 85 10* – – 25/200. AE MC VISA JCB. FZ n
Meals 25,50 – 12,40 – **105 rm** 153/191, 7 suites.
◆ A 1970s hotel with a traditional atmosphere and modernised, carpeted rooms with contemporary furnishings and welcoming lounges. It has an elegant restaurant.

Aramo, paseo de Santa María de la Cabeza 73, ✉ 28045, ☎ 91 473 91 11, *reservas-aramo@abbahoteles.com, Fax 91 473 92 14* – – 25/200. AE MC VISA. EZ e
Meals 12,60 – 10,50 – **108 rm** 92/104.
◆ Refurbished rooms with carpets and wallpaper. The bathrooms are a little small. Well-equipped conference rooms and a modern restaurant with a wooden floor.

Hontoria, pl. del General Maroto 2, ✉ 28045, ☎ 91 473 04 25 – ▤. AE ◑ MC VISA. ✂ EZ v
closed Holy Week, August, Sunday and Bank Holidays – **Meals** a la carte 24,19/34,69.
• A restaurant well-run by its chef-owner. A small traditional-style dining room. Lots of regular customers.

Moncloa : Princesa, Paseo del Pintor Rosales, Paseo de la Florida, Casa de Campo

Husa Princesa, Princesa 40, ✉ 28008, ☎ 91 542 21 00, *husaprincesa@husa.es, Fax 91 542 73 28,* Fá, ⛱ – |‡| ▤ TV ♿ 🚗 – 🎤 25/500. AE ◑ MC VISA JCB. ✂ rest DV z
Meals *(closed 1 to 15 August, Sunday and Monday dinner)* a la carte 31,30/36,40 – ☕ 21 – **263 rm** 275/302, 12 suites.
• A magnificent hotel situated on one of the principal arteries of the city, with expansive lounge areas and spacious rooms offering high levels of comfort. An intimate, modern dining room offering a choice of traditional and international cuisine.

Meliá Madrid Princesa, Princesa 27, ✉ 28008, ☎ 91 541 82 00, *melia.madrid.princesa@solmelia.com, Fax 91 541 19 88,* Fá – |‡| ▤ TV ♿ – 🎤 25/350 KV t
253 rm, 23 suites.
• This hotel's location and facilities make it ideal for conferences and other group functions. Politicians, business executives and artists frequent this modern and refurbished hotel. There is a very good restaurant where you can enjoy fine cuisine.

Sofitel Madrid Plaza de España without rest, Tutor 1, ✉ 28008, ☎ 91 541 98 80, *h1320@accor-hotels.com, Fax 91 542 57 36* – |‡|, ⇹ rm, ▤ TV ♿. AE ◑ MC VISA JCB
☕ 22 – **97 rm** 258/277.
• Well refurbished with high-quality furnishings in the bedrooms and marble fittings in the bathrooms. A perfect balance of elegance and comfort. KV d

Monte Real 🐦, Arroyofresno 17, ✉ 28035, ☎ 91 316 21 40, *montereal@hotelmontereal.com, Fax 91 316 39 34,* ⛱ – |‡| ▤ TV 🚗 P – 🎤 25/250. AE ◑ MC VISA. ✂ North-West : by Av. de la Victoria DU
Meals 27,05 – ☕ 15,50 – **76 rm** 130/160, 4 suites.
• A hotel with a refreshing swimming pool surrounded by lawns. Refurbishment of the bedrooms, lounges and reception have made it much more comfortable. The pleasant and well-lit dining room is in traditional style and has decor in shades of vanilla.

Sal Gorda, Beatriz de Bobadilla 9, ✉ 28040, ☎ 91 553 95 06 – ▤. AE ◑ MC VISA. ✂ DT e
closed August and Sunday – **Meals** a la carte 25,60/27,60.
• What a find ! Well-known professionals run this friendly and attractive restaurant. Traditional décor and good furnishings and an interesting menu at reasonable prices.

El Molino de los Porches, paseo Pintor Rosales 1, ✉ 28008, ☎ 91 548 13 36, *Fax 91 547 97 61,* 🍽 – ▤. AE ◑ MC VISA. ✂ DV e
Meals - Roast specialities - a la carte 41,50/51,50.
• A hotel located in the Parque del Oeste with several lounges and a pleasant glazed-in terrace. The meat produced from the wood fired oven and charcoal grill is delicious.

Currito, av. de las Provincias - Casa de Campo, ✉ 28011, ☎ 91 464 57 04, *curritomadrid@telefonica.net, Fax 91 479 72 54,* 🍽 – ▤ P. AE ◑ MC VISA. ✂ West : by Av. de Portugal DX
closed Sunday dinner – **Meals** - Basque rest - a la carte 32,81/40,81.
• A spacious and well-known restaurant located in the Vizcaya Pavilion of the Casa de Campo. Traditional Basque cuisine. A pleasant terrace and a public bar at the entrance.

Chamberí : San Bernardo, Fuencarral, Alberto Aguilera, Santa Engracia

AC Santo Mauro, Zurbano 36, ✉ 28010, ☎ 91 319 69 00, *santo-mauro@ac-hotels.com, Fax 91 308 54 77,* 🍽, Fá, ⛱ – |‡| ▤ TV ♿ 🚗 – 🎤 25/50. AE ◑ MC VISA JCB. ✂ rest FV e
Santo Mauro **: Meals** a la carte 44,62/52,40 – ☕ 20 – **43 rm** 280/338, 8 suites.
• A hotel in a beautiful French-style palace with garden situated in a classy district of Madrid. Elegant and with touches of luxury in the rooms. The restaurant is in a beautiful library-room which lends distinction to the food.

Miguel Ángel, Miguel Ángel 31, ✉ 28010, ☎ 91 442 00 22, *comercial.hma@oh-es.com, Fax 91 442 53 20,* 🍽, Fá, ⛱ – |‡| ▤ TV ♿ 🚗 – 🎤 25/200. AE ◑ MC VISA JCB. ✂ FU c
Arco **: Meals** a la carte 31,50/40 – ☕ 21 – **243 rm** 325/375, 20 suites.
• A prestigious and up-to-date hotel located in the Castellana district of Madrid. Well-appointed rooms and large public areas with classically elegant decor. Superb restaurant with a terrace for the summer months.

Intercontinental Castellana, paseo de la Castellana 49, ✉ 28046, ☎ 91 700 73 00, *madrid@interconti.com, Fax 91 308 54 23,* – – AE VISA JCB. GU v
Meals a la carte 30/45 – 24 – **270 rm** 335/365, 27 suites.
◆ Right in the heart of the banking and financial district. Totally refurbished and offering a high level of comfort and elegant décor.

Hesperia Madrid, paseo de la Castellana 57, ✉ 28046, ☎ 91 210 88 00, *hotel@hesperia-madrid.com, Fax 91 210 88 99* – – 25/300. AE VISA JCB. rest FU b
Meals - see also rest. ***Santceloni*** below - 35 – 22 – **139 rm** 310/340, 32 suites.
◆ A hotel with modern décor and attractive design. A large lounge and light and airy foyer and reception area and a patio in the middle. Traditional bedrooms. A good dining room with many very tasteful details of décor.

Orfila, Orfila 6, ✉ 28010, ☎ 91 702 77 70, *inforeservas@hotelorfila.com, Fax 91 702 77 72,* – – 25/80. AE VISA JCB. NV d
Meals 46 – 25 – **28 rm** 297/365, 4 suites.
◆ A hotel in a late 19C palace situated in an exclusive residential zone. A grand atmosphere and rooms with traditional and elegant furnishings. A welcoming dining room and interior garden where you can enjoy the à la carte menu.

NH Abascal, José Abascal 47, ✉ 28003, ☎ 91 441 00 15, *nhabascal@nh-hotels.com, Fax 91 442 22 11,* – – 25/150. AE VISA JCB. rest FU a
Meals *(closed August)* a la carte 38/50 – 17 – **180 rm** 163/180, 3 suites.
◆ An elegant and traditional building with an attractive façade. An excellent foyer with marble columns. The social areas are limited to one lounge bar.

NH Zurbano, Zurbano 79-81, ✉ 28003, ☎ 91 441 45 00, *nhzurbano@nh-hotels.com, Fax 91 441 32 24* – – 25/180. AE VISA. FU x
Meals 22 – 14 – **255 rm** 173/234, 11 suites.
◆ A hotel divided into two buildings each with its own facilities. Tasteful décor in a functional style. Regular guests are business travellers and well-known sports teams.

NH Embajada, Santa Engracia 5, ✉ 28010, ☎ 91 594 02 13, *nhembajada@nh-hotels.com, Fax 91 447 33 12* – – 25/60. AE VISA. MV r
Meals *(closed August)* a la carte approx. 22 – 12,50 – **101 rm** 206.
◆ A hotel with a refurbished interior that leans towards the avant-garde in contrast to the very traditional façade. Contemporary and practical feel.

NH Alberto Aguilera, Alberto Aguilera 18, ✉ 28015, ☎ 91 446 09 00, *nhalbertoaguilera@-hotels.com, Fax 91 446 09 04* – – 25/100. AE VISA JCB. DV b
Meals *(closed July, August, Saturday and Sunday)* a la carte approx. 32 – 13,50 – **148 rm** 147/172, 5 suites.
◆ Modern and welcoming although the public areas are limited to a lounge-coffee shop and the dining room. Comfort and well-equipped rooms are the hallmarks of this chain.

NH Prisma, Santa Engracia 120, ✉ 28003, ☎ 91 441 93 77, *nhprisma@nh-hotels.com, Fax 91 442 58 51* – – 25/70. AE VISA JCB. EU g
Meals *(closed August, Saturday and Sunday)* a la carte approx. 31,45 – 12,50 – **103 suites** 184, 7 hab.
◆ In three separate buildings with the reception and lounge-coffee shop in the main one The majority of the rooms are apartments with a sitting room.

Tryp Alondras coffee shop only, José Abascal 8, ✉ 28003, ☎ 91 447 40 00, *trypalondras@solmelia.com, Fax 91 593 88 00* – . AE VISA JCB. EU a
11,50 – **72 rm** 167/177.
◆ A traditional-style hotel with spacious, bright rooms which have all been refurbished A good foyer-reception with a coffee shop on one side offering a limited menu.

Santceloni - *Hotel Hesperia Madrid,* paseo de la Castellana 57, ✉ 28046 ☎ 91 210 88 40, *santceloni@hesperia-madrid.com, Fax 91 210 88 99* – . AE VISA. FU b
closed August, Saturday lunch, Sunday and Bank Holidays – **Meals** 90 and a la carte 76/81
◆ A restaurant with a modern façade and neo-rustic beams in the entrance. A spacious room with décor in minimalist style and designer tableware. Quite a culinary experience
Spec. Huevo poché con caviar y coliflor. Langosta con emulsión de yema al lémon grase Pato de sangre asado en la auténtica broche.

La Broche, Miguel Ángel 29, ✉ 28010, ☎ 91 399 34 37, *info@labroche.com Fax 91 399 37 78* – . AE VISA JCB. FU c
closed Holy Week, August, Saturday and Sunday – **Meals** 75 and a la carte 65/81,02.
◆ A spacious restaurant with bare white walls which allow all attention to be focused on the very innovative cuisine.
Spec. Lascas de foie, carabineros y zamburiñas con all i oli ahumado. Lomo de mero asado con un salteado de patatas y cebolla. Coca de hígado de pato y verduras asadas al horno

XXXX **Las Cuatro Estaciones,** General Ibáñez de Íbero 5, ✉ 28003, ☎ 91 553 63 05, *Fax 91 535 05 23* – ▤. AE ⓓ MC VISA JCB. ⊁ DT r
closed Holy Week, August, Saturday lunch and Sunday – **Meals** a la carte 42,99/64,98.
• A classic-style restaurant with a carpeted floor and fibre-optic lighting. The exclusive bar and waiting area lead into a pleasant and intimate dining room.

XXX **Il Gusto,** Espronceda 27, ✉ 28003, ☎ 91 535 39 02, *Fax 91 535 08 61* – ▤. AE ⓓ MC VISA. ⊁ FTU d
closed 9 to 24 August – **Meals** - Italian rest - a la carte 30/36.
• Discover the delicious nuances of Italian cuisine in this modern restaurant with an entrance hall and elegant restaurant, where the decor is a combination of wood and marble.

XXX **Annapurna,** Zurbano 5, ✉ 28010, ☎ 91 319 87 16, *annapurna@inicia.es, Fax 91 308 32 49* – ▤. AE ⓓ MC VISA JCB. ⊁ MV w
closed 15 to 31 August, Saturday lunch, Sunday and Bank Holidays – **Meals** - Indian rest - a la carte 24/30.
• A spacious restaurant with a private garden. Traditional Hindu decorative motifs and some colourful dishes with all the aromas and sensuousness of India.

XXX **Lur Maitea,** Fernando el Santo 4, ✉ 28010, ☎ 91 308 03 50, *restaurante@lurmaitea.com, Fax 91 308 62 25* – ▤. AE ⓓ MC VISA. ⊁ MV u
closed August, Saturday lunch, Sunday and Bank Holidays – **Meals** - Basque rest - a la carte 37,40/44,70.
• A carriage entrance is the way in to one of the best known places to try Basque cuisine. Traditional, with a large menu and a delicatessen.

XXX **Soroa,** Modesto Lafuente 88, ✉ 28003, ☎ 91 553 17 95, *soroa@restaurantesoroa.com, Fax 91 553 17 98* – ▤. AE ⓓ MC VISA JCB. ⊁ FT x
closed Sunday – **Meals** a la carte 40,50/47.
• An interesting menu of innovative dishes. Modern décor with a spacious dining room in light shades and a private dining area with wine-cellar décor in the basement.

XX **La Cava Real,** Espronceda 34, ✉ 28003, ☎ 91 442 54 32, *cavareal@restaurante.net, Fax 91 442 34 04*, Wine-cellar – ▤. AE ⓓ MC VISA JCB. ⊁ FU h
closed August, Sunday and Bank Holidays – **Meals** a la carte 30,10/43,75.
• Restaurant and wine-cellar with traditional décor with dining rooms on two levels and an entrance area. A good menu and wine available by the glass. Very welcoming.

XX **Escolástico,** Santa Engracia 24, ✉ 28010, ☎ 91 594 04 67 – ▤. AE MC VISA. ⊁ FV b
closed August, Sunday and Monday dinner – **Meals** a la carte 30/41.
• A restaurant with a modern exterior and opaque windows and a bar near the entrance. A pleasant dining room with traditional dishes.

XX **La Vendimia,** pl. del Conde del Valle de Suchil 7, ✉ 28015, ☎ 91 445 73 77, *Fax 91 448 86 72* – ▤. AE ⓓ MC VISA. ⊁ DV b
closed August and Sunday – **Meals** a la carte 31,50/41,21.
• A menu offering traditional and Basque dishes in a classic contemporary restaurant. Good service. Regular customers from nearby offices.

XX **El Fogón de Zein,** Cardenal Cisneros 49, ✉ 28010, ☎ 91 593 33 20, *info@elfogondezein.com, Fax 91 591 00 34* – ▤. AE ⓓ MC VISA. ⊁ EU t
closed Holy Week, 11 to 17 August and Sunday – **Meals** a la carte 27,30/34,10.
• A highly professional restaurant with a bar near the entrance leading to a small private room and the redecorated dining room, hung with contemporary paintings.

XX **Odriozola,** Zurbano 13, ✉ 28010, ☎ 91 319 31 50, *Fax 91 319 12 93* – ▤. AE ⓓ MC VISA JCB MV d
closed Holy Week, 15 to 31 August, Saturday lunch and Sunday – **Meals** - Basque rest - a la carte 40/48.
• A restaurant with a bar and a pleasant but small dining area. Traditional furnishings, slate floor and a private dining area on the mezzanine.

XX **Gala,** Espronceda 14, ✉ 28003, ☎ 91 442 22 44 – ▤. AE ⓓ MC VISA. ⊁ EU n
closed 10 to 25 August and Sunday – **Meals** a la carte 31/38.
• A pleasant modern restaurant with avant-garde décor which is in contrast to the wine-cellar-style private dining area. Very popular with a younger clientele.

XX **Tsunami,** Caracas 10, ✉ 28010, ☎ 91 308 05 69, *tsunamicaracas@telefonica.net, Fax 91 308 05 69* – ▤. AE MC VISA. ⊁ FV a
closed Saturday lunch, Sunday and Bank Holidays – **Meals** - Japanese rest - a la carte 33,97/37,59.
• A western-style bar near the entrance, modern dining rooms with designer furniture and a back bar where sushi is prepared in front of the customer.

XX **Alborán,** Ponzano 39-41, ✉ 28003, ☎ 91 399 21 50, *alboran@alboran-rest.com, Fax 91 399 21 50* – ▤. AE ⓓ MC VISA. ⊁ EU g
closed Sunday dinner – **Meals** a la carte 38/40.
• A coffee shop with tapas near the entrance and two dining areas with high-quality furnishings. Decor on a maritime theme with wooden floors and walls.

La Plaza de Chamberí, pl. de Chamberí 10, ✉ 28010, ✆ 91 446 06 97, *Fax 91 594 21 20* – ▤. AE ⓓ MC VISA JCB. ✻ FV k
closed Holy Week and Sunday – **Meals** a la carte 28,10/35,60.
◆ A restaurant which deserves the success it now has. A private bar and a pleasant dining room on two levels. A select menu of traditional dishes.

Villa de Foz, Gonzálo de Córdoba 10, ✉ 28010, ✆ 91 446 89 93, *285711@terra.es* – ▤. AE MC VISA. ✻ EV e
closed August and Sunday – **Meals** - Galician rest - a la carte 26/32,50.
◆ Good traditional Galician cuisine in a modern dining room. The menu is limited but the food is of very high quality.

Enzo, Orfila 2, ✉ 28010, ✆ 91 308 16 47, *restaurante@pinocchio.es, Fax 91 662 18 65* – ▤. AE ⓓ MC VISA. ✻ NV d
closed August, Saturday lunch and Sunday – **Meals** - Italian rest - a la carte 25/29,50.
◆ An intimate and welcoming Italian restaurant with an attractive menu. Decorative features include exposed brickwork, wood flooring and modern furniture.

Balear, Sagunto 18, ✉ 28010, ✆ 91 447 91 15, *Fax 91 445 19 97* – ▤. AE MC VISA. ✻ EU y
Meals - Rice dishes - a la carte 27/45.
◆ Here you enter directly into a room in the style of an old fashioned café. A private dining room in the basement. A Balearic menu with rice dishes a speciality.

La Despensa, Cardenal Cisneros 6, ✉ 28010, ✆ 91 446 17 94 – ▤. AE ⓓ MC VISA. ✻ EV p
closed 15 August-15 September, Sunday dinner and Monday – **Meals** a la carte approx. 21,05.
◆ A pleasant and friendly restaurant offering simple home cooking at reasonable prices. An intimate setting, functionally refurbished in classical style.

Mesón Cinco Jotas, paseo de San Francisco de Sales 27, ✉ 28003, ✆ 91 544 01 89, *m5jsfsales@osborne.es, Fax 91 549 06 51*, 龠 – ▤. AE ⓓ MC VISA. ✻ DT h
Tapa 2,50 – **Ración** - Ham specialities - approx. 10.
◆ In the style of this chain with two areas where you can have a single dish or eat à la carte. Also a variety of tapas, fine hams and pork products.

José Luis, paseo de San Francisco de Sales 14, ✉ 28003, ✆ 91 441 20 43, *joseluis@nexo.es*, 龠 – ▤. AE ⓓ MC VISA. ✻ DU v
Tapa 1,40 – **Ración** approx. 15.
◆ One of the more simple establishments in this well-known chain. A variety of Basque-style tapas and larger portions of dishes. Also a terrace.

Asturianos, Vallehermoso 94, ✉ 28003, ✆ 91 533 59 47, *Fax 91 533 59 47*, 龠 – ▤. AE ⓓ MC VISA. ✻ DU c
Tapa 3 – **Ración** approx. 7,50.
◆ A small tavern with exposed wood and brickwork. A great variety of tapas and larger portions of Asturian dishes. Good wines by the glass.

Zubia, Espronceda 28, ✉ 28003, ✆ 91 441 04 32, *info@restaurantezubia.com, Fax 91 441 10 43* – ▤. AE ⓓ MC VISA. ✻ FU h
closed Holy Week, 12 August-12 September, Saturday lunch and Sunday – **Tapa** 1,35 – **Ración** approx. 6.
◆ This professionally run bar is known for its high-quality Basque-style tapas and raciones The reasonable menu on offer here is served in two small dining rooms.

La Taberna de Don Alonso, Alonso Cano 64, ✉ 28003, ✆ 91 533 52 49 – ▤. ✻
closed Holy Week, August and Sunday dinner – **Tapa** 1,80 – **Ración** approx. 11.
◆ A tavern with a selection of Basque-style tapas and a blackboard listing tapas prepared to order and larger servings of dishes available. Wine by the glass. EFT r

Taberna El Maño, Vallehermoso 59, ✉ 28015, ✆ 91 448 40 35, 龠, Bullfighting theme – MC VISA DU e
closed Sunday dinner and Monday – **Tapa** 3 – **Ración** approx. 10.
◆ A popular bar with a taurine atmosphere with lots of tapas and larger servings of dishes Good seafood and ham. Relaxed atmosphere.

Chamartín, Tetuán : Paseo de la Castellana, Capitán Haya, Orense, Alberto Alcocer Paseo de la Habana

Meliá Castilla, Capitán Haya 43, ✉ 28020, ✆ 91 567 50 00, *melia.castilla@solmelia.com, Fax 91 567 50 51*, ⛱ – 🛗 ▤ TV ♿ 🚗 – 🎤 25/800. AE ⓓ MC VISA JCB. ✻ FR c
Meals (see rest. ***L'Albufera*** and rest. ***La Fragata*** below) – ☕ 19 – **904 rm** 253/262 12 suites.
◆ An entrance with lots of plants and large and attractive rooms. A large hotel popular for social functions and conventions.

NH Eurobuilding, Padre Damián 23, ✉ 28036, ℘ 91 353 73 00, *nheurobuilding@nh-hoteles.es, Fax 91 345 45 76,* Fa, ⛱, – lift, rm, TV ♿ – 25/900. AE ⓓ MC VISA. GS a
Magerit *(closed August and Sunday)* **Meals** a la carte 34/45 – ☕ 19 – **421 rm** 246, 39 suites.
◆ Recently refurbished in keeping with this chain's usual standards of comfort. Spacious, modern and well-appointed bedrooms plus a variety of meeting areas. An attractive, high-quality restaurant in welcoming surroundings.

Holiday Inn Madrid, pl. Carlos Trías Beltrán 4 (entrance by Orense 22-24), ✉ 28020, ℘ 91 456 80 00, *Fax 91 456 80 01,* Fa, ⛱ – lift TV ♿ – 25/400. AE ⓓ MC VISA JCB. FS z
Big Blue : **Meals** a la carte 19,40/37,35 – ☕ 18 – **282 rm** 283/300, 31 suites.
◆ A good location near the Azca Complex with its many offices and leisure facilities. A classic foyer, shops and Internet facilities. The Big Blue restaurant has unusual modern décor and a good menu.

AC Aitana, paseo de la Castellana 152, ✉ 28046, ℘ 91 458 49 70, *aitana@ac-hotels.com, Fax 91 458 49 71,* Fa – lift TV ♿. AE ⓓ MC VISA JCB. GS c
Meals 20 – ☕ 13 – **109 rm** 186/209, 2 suites.
◆ Completely refurbished and with the latest mod cons. The décor and furnishings are very modern in style and with wood decoration.

NH La Habana, paseo de La Habana 73, ✉ 28036, ℘ 91 443 07 20, *nhhabana@nh-hotels.es, Fax 91 457 75 79* – lift, rm, TV – 25/250. AE ⓓ MC VISA JCB. HS f
Meals *(closed August)* 25 – ☕ 13,90 – **155 rm** 159/190, 1 suite.
◆ A modern hotel with an excellent reception and very comfortable rooms, although they are a little on the small side. A regular clientele of business travellers.

Confortel Pío XII, av. Pío XII-77, ✉ 28016, ℘ 91 387 62 00, *com.confortel@once.es, Fax 91 302 65 22* – lift TV ♿ – 25/350. AE ⓓ MC VISA JCB. JR t
Meals 18 – ☕ 13 – **214 rm** 178.
◆ Comfortable rooms decorated in soft tones with modern furnishings and wooden floors. Well-adapted for handicapped guests. A good restaurant with minimal decoration.

Orense, Pedro Teixeira 5, ✉ 28020, ℘ 91 597 15 68, *reservas@hotelorense.com, Fax 91 597 12 95* – lift TV – 25/50. AE ⓓ MC VISA JCB. FS q
Meals a la carte 29/32,50 – ☕ 12 – **140 rm** 193/225.
◆ A modern hotel featuring comfortable well-appointed rooms with attractive decor. Small lounge area but a good range of meeting rooms.

Confortel Suites Madrid, López de Hoyos 143, ✉ 28002, ℘ 91 744 50 00, *info@confortelsuitesmadrid.com, Fax 91 415 30 73* – lift TV ♿ – 25/350. AE ⓓ MC VISA JCB. JT y
Meals *(closed August, Saturday and Sunday)* 15 – ☕ 12 – **120 suites** 170/195.
◆ A modern but not very luxurious hotel with good facilities which has a regular clientele of business customers. Suite-type rooms, but not very large.

Don Pío without rest, av. Pío XII-25, ✉ 28016, ℘ 91 353 07 80, *hoteldonpio@hoteldonpio.com, Fax 91 353 07 81* – lift TV P. AE MC VISA. HR s
☕ 13 – **40 rm** 130/145.
◆ An attractive patio foyer with a classic-modern skylight which runs through the building. The bedrooms are quite large and have facilities such as hydro-massage.

Cuzco coffee shop only, paseo de la Castellana 133, ✉ 28046, ℘ 91 556 06 00, *hotelcuzco@mundivia.es, Fax 91 556 03 72,* Fa – lift TV ♿ P – 25/450. AE ⓓ MC VISA. FS a
☕ 11,25 – **322 rm** 162/203, 8 suites.
◆ A traditional hotel a few metres from the Palacio de Congresos. Spacious, well-maintained bedrooms with somewhat old-fashioned decor. Popular with business travellers.

Castilla Plaza, paseo de la Castellana 220, ✉ 28046, ℘ 91 567 43 00, *castilla-plaza@abbahoteles.com, Fax 91 315 54 06* – lift TV – 25/150. AE ⓓ MC VISA JCB. GR u
Meals 19 – ☕ 14,50 – **139 rm** 139 – PA 52.
◆ A beautiful glass building which is part of the Puerta de Europa complex. Comfortable and very much in accord with modern tastes. An attractive restaurant specialising in traditional cuisine.

Foxá 32, Agustín de Foxá 32, ✉ 28036, ℘ 91 733 10 60, *foxa32@foxa.com, Fax 91 314 11 65* – lift TV – 25/250. AE ⓓ MC VISA. GR e
Meals 10,50 – ☕ 10,50 – **63 rm** 174/195, 98 suites.
◆ Although the foyer-reception is on the small side, the hotel's apartment-type rooms are elegantly decorated and furnished with high-quality antiques. The restaurant has an attractive covered terrace.

Chamartín, Agustín de Foxá, ✉ 28036, ☎ 91 334 49 00, *chamartin@husa.es, Fax 91 733 02 14* – |‡| ▤ TV – 25/500. AE ⓓ ⓜ VISA JCB. ✻ HR
Meals (see rest. ***Cota 13*** below) – ☕ 11,11 – **360 rm** 148/175, 18 suites.
◆ Situated at Chamartín train station and with a very busy foyer. Functional bedrooms and some lounges which are used for more than one purpose.

La Residencia de El Viso, Nervión 8, ✉ 28002, ☎ 91 564 03 70, *reservas@residenciadelviso.com, Fax 91 564 19 65,* – |‡| ▤ TV. AE ⓓ ⓜ VISA. ✻ HT c
Meals *(closed Sunday dinner)* a la carte 30,80/56,40 – ☕ 9 – **12 rm** 76/127.
◆ A charming little hotel with a lounge that encompasses the bar and reception. Cheerful rooms and a garden which offers peace and tranquillity in the middle of the city. The dining room is in a glass pavilion beside an interior terrace which is used in summer.

Aristos, av. Pío XII-34, ✉ 28016, ☎ 91 345 04 50, *hotelaristos@elchaflan.com, Fax 91 345 10 23* – |‡| ▤ TV. AE ⓓ ⓜ VISA. ✻ JR d
Meals (see rest. ***El Chaflán*** below) – ☕ 12,17 – **22 rm** 120,18/163,39, 1 suite.
◆ A functional hotel with very well-equipped rooms and décor reminiscent of the 1980s. Good management and service.

Zalacain, Álvarez de Baena 4, ✉ 28006, ☎ 91 561 48 40, *Fax 91 561 47 32* – ▤. AE ⓓ ⓜ VISA JCB. ✻ GU b
closed Holy Week, August, Saturday lunch, Sunday and Bank Holidays – **Meals** 82 and a la carte 53/72.
◆ A refined restaurant with traditional and intimate dining rooms and highly-trained staff. An elegant atmosphere enhanced by decor showing fine attention to detail.
Spec. Bogavante y gambas en gelatina con gazpacho al estilo Zalacain. Merluza a la plancha con vinagreta de cítricos. Pato asado al Chartreuse verde con rollitos de berza rellenos de hígado de oca.

Príncipe de Viana, Manuel de Falla 5, ✉ 28036, ☎ 91 457 15 49, *principeviana@ya.com, Fax 91 457 52 83* – ▤. AE ⓓ ⓜ VISA. ✻ GS c
closed August, Saturady lunch, Sunday and Bank Holidays – **Meals** - Basque rest - a la carte 52/60,50.
◆ Well-known restaurant serving Basque-Navarrese inspired cooking. Traditional dining areas and excellent service.

El Bodegón, Pinar 15, ✉ 28006, ☎ 91 562 88 44, *Fax 91 562 97 25* – ▤. AE ⓓ ⓜ VISA. ✻ GU c
closed August, Saturday lunch, Sunday and Bank Holidays – **Meals** a la carte 43/65.
◆ A rather grand and elegant restaurant with a private bar and a dining room on various levels with windows overlooking a pleasant garden.

L'Albufera - *Hotel Meliá Castilla,* Capitán Haya 45, ✉ 28020, ☎ 91 567 51 97 *Fax 91 567 50 51* – ▤ 🚗. AE ⓓ ⓜ VISA JCB FR c
Meals - Rice dishes - a la carte 34,60/46,65.
◆ A restaurant with three attractive dining rooms and another in a conservatory in a central patio with numerous plants.

Combarro, Reina Mercedes 12, ✉ 28020, ☎ 91 554 77 84, *combarro@combarro.com Fax 91 534 25 01* – ▤. AE ⓓ ⓜ VISA JCB. ✻ ES a
closed Holy Week, August and Sunday dinner – **Meals** - Seafood - a la carte 43,64/57,40.
◆ Galician cuisine based on good quality seafood and fish. Public bar, dining room on the 1st floor and two more rooms in the basement all in distinguished traditional style.

El Chaflán - *Hotel Aristos,* av. Pío XII-34, ✉ 28016, ☎ 91 350 61 93, *restaurante@elchaflan.com, Fax 91 345 10 23,* – ▤. AE ⓓ ⓜ VISA. ✻ JR c
closed 15 days in August, Saturday lunch and Sunday – **Meals** 60 and a la carte 54,15/64,80.
◆ A restaurant in minimalist style which prides itself on its service. An olive tree has pride of place in the centre of the room. Interesting and innovative cuisine.
Spec. Espárragos blancos fritos con mahonesa tibia. Pollo de campo asado a la forma tradicional, en tartar y polenta. Lomo de atún rojo, torta suspendida cremosa y tomate raff.

La Fragata - *Hotel Meliá Castilla,* Capitán Haya 45, ✉ 28020, ☎ 91 567 51 96 *Fax 91 567 50 51* – ▤ 🚗. AE ⓓ ⓜ VISA. ✻ FR
closed August and Bank Holidays – **Meals** a la carte approx. 45.
◆ A separate entrance and an elegant private bar. The dining area surrounds a central patio with lots of plants. A good traditional menu.

Aldaba, av. de Alberto Alcocer 5, ✉ 28036, ☎ 91 345 21 93, *Fax 91 345 21 93* – ▤ AE ⓓ ⓜ VISA. ✻ GS
closed August, Saturday lunch and Sunday – **Meals** a la carte 30,81/51,41.
◆ A bar near the entrance from which follows a pleasant dining room in classic-modern style. There are also private rooms. Excellent wine-list.

XXX **José Luis,** Rafael Salgado 11, ✉ 28036, ✆ 91 457 50 36, *joseluis@nexo.es, Fax 91 344 10 46* – ▤. AE ⓓ ⓜ VISA. ✂ GS m
closed August and Sunday – **Meals** a la carte approx. 45.
◆ A well-known restaurant in front of the Santiago Bernabeu Stadium. A pleasant dining room with a tapas bar and two glass covered terraces. International and Basque dishes.

XXX ✿ **Goizeko Kabi,** Comandante Zorita 37, ✉ 28020, ✆ 91 533 01 85, *Fax 91 533 02 14* – ▤. AE ⓓ ⓜ VISA. ✂ ES a
closed Sunday – **Meals** - Basque rest - 80 and a la carte 60/80.
◆ A Basque restaurant with prestige in the city. Elegant and comfortable although the tables are a little close together.
Spec. Tártaro de atún con vinagreta de mango. Rodaballo salvaje en su caldo corto. Costillar de lechal churro asado al momento.

XXX **El Olivo,** General Gallegos 1, ✉ 28036, ✆ 91 359 15 35, *bistrotelolivosl@retemail.es, Fax 91 345 91 83* – ▤. AE ⓓ ⓜ VISA JCB. ✂ GR c
closed 15 to 31 August, Sunday and Monday – **Meals** a la carte 39/58.
◆ Modern décor in shades of green and attractive decorative details alluding to olive oil. Carefully prepared cosmopolitan and Mediterranean dishes.

XXX **El Foque,** Suero de Quiñones 22, ✉ 28002, ✆ 91 519 25 72, *Fax 91 561 07 99* – ▤. AE ⓓ ⓜ VISA. ✂ HT r
closed Sunday – **Meals** - Cod dishes specialities - a la carte 33,81/38,61.
◆ An intimate restaurant near the Auditorio Nacional de Música. A dining room on two levels decorated in maritime style. An interesting menu which specialises in cod dishes.

XXX **Castelló 9,** Corazón de María 78, ✉ 28002, ✆ 91 519 34 15, *castello9@castello9.com, Fax 91 519 37 23* – ▤. AE ⓓ ⓜ VISA. ✂ JT w
closed August and Sunday – **Meals** a la carte 30,90/45.
◆ Modern traditional décor and furnishings in a very professionally run restaurant. Good and unpretentious international cuisine.

XX **De Vinis,** paseo de la Castellana 123, ✉ 28046, ✆ 91 556 40 33, *vic.vino@teleline.es, Fax 91 556 08 58* – ▤. AE ⓓ ⓜ VISA. ✂ GS h
closed August, Saturday lunch, Sunday and Bank Holidays – **Meals** a la carte 41,62/55,10.
◆ Modern and intimate dining areas and excellent service. An innovative menu and a wide selection of wines served by the glass.

XX **La Tahona,** Capitán Haya 21 (side), ✉ 28020, ✆ 91 555 04 41, *Fax 91 556 62 02* – ▤. AE ⓓ ⓜ VISA. ✂ FS u
closed 1 to 15 August and Sunday dinner – **Meals** - Roast lamb - a la carte approx. 25.
◆ A bar near the entrance with a wood fired oven and wood ceiling from which lead off several dining areas. Traditional roast meat accompanied by the house rosé is delicious.

XX **O'Pazo,** Reina Mercedes 20, ✉ 28020, ✆ 91 553 23 33, *Fax 91 554 90 72* – ▤. ⓜ VISA. ✂ EFS p
closed Holy Week, August and Sunday – **Meals** - Seafood - a la carte 45/56.
◆ Although the decor is a little out of date, O'Pazo has a large dining room and a library-lounge for private meetings. A good choice of fish and seafood always on display here.

XX **Pedralbes,** Basílica 15, ✉ 28020, ✆ 91 555 30 27, *Fax 91 570 95 30*, ⛱ – ▤. AE ⓓ ⓜ VISA. ✂ FT z
closed Sunday dinner – **Meals** - Catalonian rest - a la carte 30/35.
◆ Restaurant with Mediterranean feel with lots of plants and pictures, evoking the palace after which it is named. Dining areas on three levels and traditional Catalan cuisine.

XX **Rianxo,** Oruro 11, ✉ 28016, ✆ 91 457 10 06, *Fax 91 457 22 04* – ▤. AE ⓓ ⓜ VISA. ✂ HS h
closed 14 August-14 September – **Meals** - Galician rest - a la carte 35/48.
◆ Galician cuisine prepared in the classic way and based more on the quality of ingredients than elaborate preparation. A bar and attractive traditional dining room.

XX **Carta Marina,** Padre Damián 40, ✉ 28036, ✆ 91 458 68 26, *Fax 91 458 68 26* – ▤. AE ⓓ ⓜ VISA. ✂ GS k
closed August and Sunday – **Meals** - Galician rest - a la carte 41/54.
◆ A restaurant with wood decor and an attractive private bar. Pleasant dining rooms with terrace. Traditional Galician cooking.

XX **Gaztelupe,** Comandante Zorita 32, ✉ 28020, ✆ 91 534 90 28, *Fax 91 554 65 66* – ▤. AE ⓓ ⓜ VISA. ✂ ES p
closed Sunday in July-August and Sunday dinner the rest of the year – **Meals** - Basque rest - a la carte 40/55.
◆ A bar at the entrance, refurbished dining areas with decor in regional style, and two private rooms in the basement. An extensive menu of traditional Basque dishes.

XX **El Comité,** pl. de San Amaro 8, ✉ 28020, ✆ 91 571 87 11, *Fax 91 435 43 27*, Bistrot – ▤. AE ⓓ ⓜ VISA. ✂ FS x
closed Holy Week, 15 days in August, Saturday lunch and Sunday – **Meals** a la carte approx. 35,50.
◆ Restaurant in a welcoming bistro-style, with café-type furniture and lots of old photos on the walls. French cuisine.

XX **Cota 13** - *Hotel Chamartín*, Chamartín railway station, ✉ 28036, ✆ 91 334 49 00, *cha martin@husa.es, Fax 91 733 02 14* – ▤. AE ⓓ ⓜ VISA JCB. ✂ HR
closed August – **Meals** a la carte 25,50/34.
◆ A dining room with a ceiling like the roof of an old railway station. Décor in the style of a restaurant-car, circa 1900. Simple international cuisine and fixed-price menu.

XX **Sayat Nova,** Costa Rica 13, ✉ 28016, ✆ 91 350 87 55 – ▤. AE ⓓ ⓜ VISA. ✂ JS a
closed 8 to 22 August and Sunday dinner – **Meals** - Armenian rest - a la carte 23,75/35.
◆ A good address to discover the gastronomics merits of Armenian cuisine. Two rooms with parquet flooring and decor alluding to the minstrel who gives the restaurant its name.

X **Kabuki,** av. Presidente Carmona 2, ✉ 28020, ✆ 91 417 64 15, *Fax 91 556 02 32*, ☂ – ▤. AE ⓓ ⓜ VISA JCB. ✂ FS t
closed Holy Week, 1 to 23 August, Saturday lunch, Sunday and Bank Holidays – **Meals** - Japanese rest - a la carte 26,96/36,59.
◆ An intimate Japanese restaurant with tasteful, minimalist decor. A modern terrace, in addition to a bar/kitchen serving popular dishes such as sushi.

X **Fass,** Rodríguez Marín 84, ✉ 28002, ✆ 91 563 74 47, *info@fassgrill.com, Fax 91 563 74 53* – ▤. AE ⓓ ⓜ VISA. ✂ HS t
Meals - German rest - a la carte 19,45/32,70.
◆ A bar at the front but a separate entrance for the restaurant. Rustic décor with lots of wood in pure Bavarian style. German cuisine.

X **El Asador de Aranda,** pl. de Castilla 3, ✉ 28046, ✆ 91 733 87 02, *Fax 91 556 62 02* – ▤. AE ⓓ ⓜ VISA. ✂ GR b
closed 15 August-7 September and Sunday dinner – **Meals** - Roast lamb - a la carte approx. 28,95.
◆ A restaurant in a good location near the Kio towers. Typical Castilian charm with sober yet elegant decor. The suckling pig is one of several house specialities.

Y/ **Tasca La Farmacia,** Capitán Haya 19, ✉ 28020, ✆ 91 555 81 46, *Fax 91 556 62 02* – ▤. AE ⓓ ⓜ VISA. ✂ FS r
closed 15 to 30 August and Sunday – **Tapa** 2,50 – **Ración** - Cod specialities - approx. 5,90.
◆ A beautiful restaurant with décor of exposed brickwork, tiles, wood and wonderful stained glass. A wide selection of tapas although cod dishes are the house speciality.

Y/ **Mesón Cinco Jotas,** Padre Damián 42, ✉ 28036, ✆ 91 350 31 73, *m5jpdamian@osborne.es, Fax 91 345 79 51*, ☂ – ▤. AE ⓓ ⓜ VISA. ✂ GS s
Tapa 2,50 – **Ración** - Ham specialities - approx. 10.
◆ This establishment belongs to a chain specialising in ham and other pork products. Two attractive eating areas plus a limited choice of set menus.

Y/ **José Luis,** paseo de La Habana 4, ✉ 28036, ✆ 91 562 75 96, *joseluis@nexo.es, Fax 91 562 31 18* – ▤. AE ⓓ ⓜ VISA. ✂ GT h
Tapa 1,40 – **Ración** approx. 15.
◆ Well-known to lovers of tapas. A relaxed and youthful ambience and a good selection of various dishes served in an adjoining room.

Environs

by motorway N II :

Meliá Barajas, av. de Logroño 305 - N II and detour to Barajas city : 15 km, ✉ 28042 ✆ 91 747 77 00, *reservas.tryp.barajas@solmelia.com, Fax 91 747 87 17*, ☂, Fö, ⛱, ✿ – |‡| ▤ TV ♿ P – 🏛 25/675. AE ⓓ ⓜ VISA JCB. ✂
Meals 23,74 – ☕ 16 – **220 rm** 169/211, 9 suites.
◆ Comfortable and traditional with extremely well-equipped rooms and refurbished bathrooms. A number of conference/meeting rooms around the swimming pool and garden. One dining room serves à la carte cuisine, the other food prepared on a charcoal grill.

Tryp Alameda Aeropuerto, av. de Logroño 100 - N II and detour to Barajas city 15 km, ✉ 28042, ✆ 91 747 48 00, *tryp.alameda.aeropuerto@solmelia.com Fax 91 747 89 28*, ⛱ – |‡| ▤ TV P – 🏛 25/280. AE ⓓ ⓜ VISA JCB. ✂
Meals 24,50 – ☕ 14 – **145 rm** 164/196, 3 suites.
◆ Bright and comfortable guest rooms furnished in modern style with cherry tones and well-equipped bathrooms. The hotel's lounges and meeting areas are in the process of being refurbished.

Aparthotel Convención Barajas without rest, no ☕, Noray 10 - N II, detour to Barajas city and Industrial Zone : 10 km, ✉ 28042, ☎ 91 371 74 10, *aparthotel@hotel-convencion.com, Fax 91 371 79 01* – 25. AE VISA JCB.
95 suites 135/170.
• Two towers with few areas in common although they have spacious apartment-type bedrooms with a small sitting room and kitchen.

NH Barajas without rest, Catamarán 1 - N II, detour to Barajas city and Industrial Zone : 10 km, ✉ 28042, ☎ 91 742 02 00, *exbarajas@nh-hoteles.es, Fax 91 741 11 00* – TV. AE VISA.
☕ 8 – **173 rm** 91/128.
• This budget hotel, part of the NH chain, offers reasonable comfort and value for money, although its lounges and public areas are somewhat on the small side.

by motorway N VI :

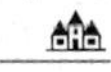

AC Forum Aravaca, Camino de la Zarzuela 23 - Aravaca : 10,2 km - exit 10 motorway, ✉ 28023, ☎ 91 740 07 10, *forum@ac-hotels.com, Fax 91 740 07 11* – TV – 30/210. AE VISA JCB.
Meals a la carte approx. 30 – ☕ 11 – **78 rm** 142.
• Functionality, design and good décor and furnishings in this hotel with comfortable bedrooms with wooden floors and modern bathrooms. A pleasant lounge area.

AC Aravaca coffe shop dinner only, Camino de la Zarzuela 3 - Aravaca : 10,2 km - exit 10 motorway, ✉ 28023, ☎ 91 740 06 80, *acaravaca@ac-hotels.com, Fax 91 740 06 81*, – rm, TV – 25/35. AE VISA.
☕ 10 – **110 rm** 135,10.
• Modern facilities with well-appointed bedrooms. Social areas in the lounge-reception area with a multi-use area where breakfast is served.

Los Remos, Sopelana 3 - La Florida : 13 km - exit 12 motorway, ✉ 28023, ☎ 91 307 72 30, *Fax 91 372 84 35* – P. AE VISA.
Meals - Seafood - a la carte approx. 45.
• A bar with a maritime feel with fish-tank and a glazed-in dining room. Fish and seafood a speciality.

Gaztelubide, Sopelana 13 - La Florida : 12,8 km - exit 12 motorway, ✉ 28023, ☎ 91 372 85 44, *gaztelubide@teleline.es, Fax 91 372 84 19*, – P. AE VISA.
closed Sunday dinner – **Meals** - Basque rest - a la carte 35,82/39,33.
• A rustic-style restaurant with one à la carte dining room and one private room. Simpler set-menu options on the first floor. A glass-covered terrace, plus banqueting suites.

by motorway N I *North : 13 km :*

La Moraleja coffee shop only, av. de Europa 17 - Parque Empresarial La Moraleja, ✉ 28108, ☎ 91 661 80 55, *info@hotellamoraleja.com, Fax 91 661 21 88*, – TV P – 25. AE VISA
☕ 17 – **37 suites** 180.
• This hotel's location in a business district and excellent facilities make it an ideal choice for the business traveller. Magnificent suite-type rooms.

Moralzarzal 28411 *Madrid* 444 *J 18. pop. 2 248 alt. 979.*

Madrid 44.

El Cenador de Salvador with rm, av. de España 30 ☎ 91 857 77 22, *cenador@infonegocio.com, Fax 91 857 77 80*, – TV P. AE VISA.
Meals *(closed Sunday dinner and Monday)* 72 and a la carte 50/58 – ☕ 15,03 – **7 rm** 150,25.
• An elegant villa with dining rooms on two levels with classic furnishings and excellent service. Garden-terrace and charming rooms.
Spec. Pipirrana de congrio con vinagreta de almendras tiernas. Góndola de cigalas en panetone con salsa de especias. Brownie con mousse de los tres chocolates.

Write to us...
If you have any comments on the contents of this Guide. Your praise as well as your criticisms will receive careful consideration and, with your assistance, we will be able to add to our stock of information and, where necessary, amend our judgments. Thank you in advance!

BARCELONA *08000* P 574 H 36 122 D 8. *pop. 1 505 325.*

See : *Gothic Quarter★★ (Barri Gòtic : Ardiaca House★* MX**A**, *Cathedral★* MX, *No 10 Carrer Paradis (Roman columns★)* MX**133**, *Plaça del Rei★★* MX**150**, *Museum of the City's History★★ (The Roman City★★★)* MX**M1**, *Santa Ágata Chapel★★ (Altarpiece of the Constable★★)* MX**F**, *Rei Martí Belvedere ≤★★* MX**K** *– Frederic Marès Museum★* MX**M2**, *La Rambla★★ : Barcelona Contemporary Art Museum★★ (MACBA) (building★★)* HX**M10**, *Barcelona Contemporary Culture Centre (CCCB) : patio★* HX**R**, *(Former) Hospital of Santa Creu (Gothic patio★)* LY, *Santa Maria del Pi Church★* LX, *Virreina Palace★* LX, *Güell Palace★★* LY, *Plaça Reial★★* MY *– The Sea Front★ : Shipyards (Drassanes) and Maritime Museum★★* MY, *Old Harbour★ (Port Vell) : Aquarium★* NY, *Mercè Basilica★* NY, *La Llotja★ (Gothic Hall★★)* NX, *França Station★* NVX, *Ciutadella Park★* NV, KX *(Waterfall★, Three Dragons Pavilion★★* NV**M7**, *Zoology Museum★* NV**M7**, *Zoo★* KX*) – La Barceloneta★* KXY, *Museum of the Catalonian History★* KY**M9**, *Vila Olímpica★ (marina★★, twin towers ✻★★★) East : by Av. d'Icària* KX, *Carrer de Montcada★★ : Picasso Museum★* NV, *Santa Maria del Mar Church★★ (rose window★)* NX *– Montjüic★ (≤★ from castle terraces) South : by Av. de la Reina María Cristina* GY *: Mies van der Rohe Pavilion★★, National Museum of Catalonian Art★★★, Spanish Village★ (Poble Espanyol), Anella Olímpica★ (Olympic Stadium★, Sant Jordi Sports Centre★★) – Joan Miró Foundation★★★, Greek Theatre★, Archaeological Museum★ – Eixample District★★ : La Sagrada Familia Church★★★ (East or Nativity Façade★★, ≤★★ from east spire)* JU, *Hospital Sant Pau★ North : by Padilla* JU, *Passeig de Gràcia★★* HV *(Lleó Morera House★* HV**Y**, *Amatller House★* HV**Y**, *Batlló House★★* HV**Y**, *La Pedrera or Milà House★★★* HV**P***) – Terrades House (les Punxes★)* HV**Q**, *Güell Park★★ (rolling bench★★, Gaudí House-Museum★) North : by Padilla* JU *– Catalonian Concert Hall★★ (Palau de la Mùsica Catalana : façade★, inverted cupola★★)* MV - *Antoni Tàpies Foundation★★* HV**S**.

Additional sights : *Santa Maria de Pedralbes Monastery★★ (Church★, Cloister★, Sant Miquel Chapel frescoes★★★ – Pedralbes Palace (Decorative Arst Museum★* EX, *Güell Stables★ (Pabellones)* EX, *Sant Pau del Camp Church (Cloister★)* LY.

Sant Cugat, North-West : 20 km ☎ 93 674 39 08.

of El Prat - Barcelona, South-West : 18 km ☎ 93 401 33 93 Fax 93 401 33 62 – Iberia : Diputació 258, ✉ 08007, ☎ 902 400 500 HV.

Sants ☎ 902 240 202.

. to the Balearic Islands : Cía. Trasmediterránea, Moll de Sant Beltrà - Estació Marítima, ✉ 08039, ☎ 93 295 91 00, Fax 93 295 91 34.

pl. de Catalunya 17-S ✉ 08002 ☎ 906 301 282 teltur@barcelonaturisme.com Fax *93 304 31 55 passeig de Gràcia 107 (Palau Robert) ✉ 08008 ☎ 93 238 40 00* Fax *93 238 40 10, Sants Estació ✉ 08014 ☎ 906 30 12 82 teltur@barcelonaturisme.com and at Airport ☎ 93 478 47 04 (Terminal A) and ☎ 93 478 05 65 (Terminal B) – R.A.C.E. Muntaner 81-bajo, ✉ 08011 ☎ 93 451 15 51 Fax 93 451 22 57.*

Madrid 627 – Bilbao 607 – Lleida/Lérida 169 – Perpignan 187 – Tarragona 109 – Toulouse 388 – València 361 – Zaragoza 307.

Plans on following pages

Old Town and the Gothic Quarter : Ramblas, Pl. de Catalunya, Via Laietana, Pl. St. Jaume, Passeig de Colom, Passeig de Joan Borbó Comte de Barcelona

Le Méridien Barcelona, La Rambla 111, ✉ 08002, ☎ 93 318 62 00, *lemeridien@meridienbarcelona.com, Fax 93 301 77 76* – rm, – 25/200. AE VISA. rest LX b
Meals a la carte 35/40 – 19 – **197 rm** 330/360, 7 suites.
◆ A hotel with local flavour and modern cosmopolitanism that has an excellent location right on the Ramblas. A very elegant and traditional atmosphere. The patio restaurant offers both à la carte and a buffet.

Colón, av. de la Catedral 7, ✉ 08002, ☎ 93 301 14 04, *info@hotelcolon.es, Fax 93 317 29 15* – – 25/120. AE VISA JCB MV e
Meals 28 – 14,50 – **138 rm** 155/220, 9 suites.
◆ The gothic quarter on your doorstep. A magnificent traditional-style hotel with well-appointed rooms. The dining room has a welcoming and intimate feel.

Rivoli Rambla, La Rambla 128, ✉ 08002, ☎ 93 481 76 76, *reservas@rivolihotels.com, Fax 93 317 50 53,* – – 25/180. AE VISA. LX r
Meals a la carte 28/41,50 – 18 – **81 rm** 205/246, 9 suites.
◆ A historic building with an avant-garde interior with Art Deco details. Elegant bedrooms and a terrace from which there are panoramic views. The restaurant offers imaginative cuisine.

Royal coffee shop only, La Rambla 117, ✉ 08002, ☎ 93 301 94 00, *hotelroyal@hroyal.com, Fax 93 317 31 79* – – 25/100. AE VISA JCB. LX e
13 – **108 rm** 175/215.
◆ Located in the most lively part of the city. A pleasant hotel with classic style, attentive service and high levels of comfort.

Catalonia Duques de Bergara, Bergara 11, ✉ 08002, ☎ 93 301 51 51, *duques@hoteles-catalonia.es, Fax 93 317 34 42,* – ♿ – 25/400. AE VISA. LV f
Meals 19 – ☕ 12 – **148 rm** 210/242.
• Very close to the Plaça Catalunya square. An attractive Modernist building with an interior that combines a sense of the past with present-day comfort. The restaurant offers delicious Catalan dishes.

Montecarlo without rest, La Rambla 124, ✉ 08002, ☎ 93 412 04 04, *hotel@montecarlobcn.com, Fax 93 318 73 23* – AE VISA. LX r
☕ 13 – **55 rm** 120/176, 1 suites.
• Situated on the famous Ramblas, near where the bird and flower sellers have their stalls. A perfect combination of tradition and modernity which creates a pleasant atmosphere.

G.H. Barcino without rest, Jaume I-6, ✉ 08002, ☎ 93 302 20 12, *reserve@gargallo-hotels.com, Fax 93 301 42 42* – ♿. AE VISA JCB MX r
☕ 14 – **53 rm** 175,20/212.
• Right in the heart of the Gothic Quarter and surrounded by beautiful historic monuments. Comfortable and well-equipped rooms, some in the third floor attic.

Inglaterra coffee shop only, Pelai 14, ✉ 08001, ☎ 93 505 11 00, *recepcion@hotel-inglaterra.com, Fax 93 505 11 09* – ♿. AE VISA JCB. HX c
☕ 13 – **55 rm** 175/200.
• A small and modern hotel with a beautiful traditional façade situated in a lively part of the city. Comfortable rooms and beds with large wooden headboards.

Tryp Apolo coffee shop only, av. del Paral.lel 57-59, ✉ 08004, ☎ 93 343 30 00, *tryp.apolo@solmelia.com, Fax 93 443 00 59* – ♿ – 25/500. AE VISA JCB. LY e
☕ 13,50 – **314 rm** 162/194.
• Friendly and functional and ideal for the business traveller. Lounges fitted with marble and bedrooms that have recently been refurbished.

Barcelona Universal, av. del Paral.lel 76-78, ✉ 08001, ☎ 93 567 74 47, *bcnuniversal@nnhotels.es, Fax 93 567 74 40,* – ♿ – 25/100. AE VISA JCB. LY a
Meals a la carte 25/37 – ☕ 13 – **164 rm** 175/190, 3 suites.
• A newly built hotel in a modern style with large well-appointed bedrooms with wooden floors and well-equipped bathrooms.

Laietana Palace without rest, Via Laietana 17, ✉ 08003, ☎ 93 268 79 40, *info@hotellaietanapalace.com, Fax 93 319 02 45* – ♿. AE VISA. MX g
☕ 10,52 – **62 rm** 211/235,94.
• A hotel in a former, completely refurbished neo-classical palace. A welcoming foyer area and comfortable bedrooms with hydro-massage baths.

Montblanc, Via Laietana 61, ✉ 08003, ☎ 93 343 55 55, *montblanc@hcchotels.es, Fax 93 343 55 58* – ♿ – 25/300. AE VISA JCB. LV c
Meals 21,63 – ☕ 14 – **157 rm** 165/206 – PA 57.
• A hotel in contemporary style with well-equipped rooms. Modern, good-sized bedrooms, pleasantly furnished and with bathrooms fitted with marble.

Catalonia Albinoni without rest, av. Portal de l'Àngel 17, ✉ 08002, ☎ 93 318 41 41, *albinoni@hoteles-catalonia.es, Fax 93 301 26 31* – ♿. AE VISA. LV a
☕ 12 – **74 rm** 160/172.
• In the former Rocamora Palace and near the Gothic Quarter. The foyer area has original decorative details and bedrooms in the style of the period.

Reding, Gravina 5-7, ✉ 08001, ☎ 93 412 10 97, *reding@occidental-hotels.com, Fax 93 268 34 82* – ♿. AE VISA JCB. HX d
Meals *(closed Sunday and Bank Holidays)* a la carte 17/29 – ☕ 10,50 – **44 rm** 160/180.
• Close to the Plaza Catalunya square. Comfortable and well-equipped rooms. Efficiently managed.

Lleó coffee shop only, Pelai 22, ✉ 08001, ☎ 93 318 13 12, *reservas@hotel-lleo.es, Fax 93 412 26 57* – ♿ – 25/150. AE VISA JCB HX a
☕ 9 – **89 rm** 115/145.
• Modern hotel with an elegant façade. Adequately comfortable rooms. The lounge area has recently been enlarged.

Regina coffee shop only, Bergara 2, ✉ 08002, ☎ 93 301 32 32, *reservas@reginahotel.com, Fax 93 318 23 26* – AE VISA JCB. LV r
☕ 15 – **99 rm** 180/215.
• Good location for the Ramblas and Gothic Quarter. Pleasant large and comfortable rooms.

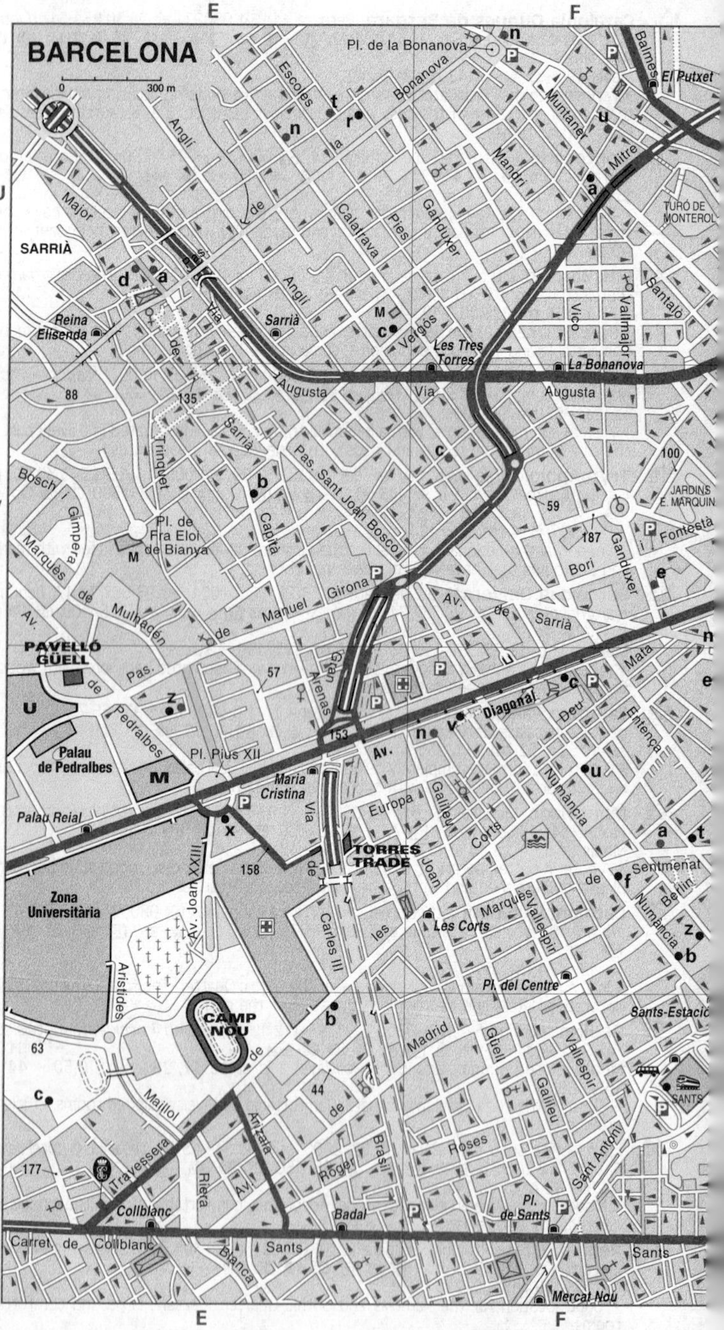

BARCELONA

0 300 m

E F

U V X Y

Pl. de la Bonanova
Bonanova
Balmes
El Putxet
Escoles
Pies
la
de
Calatrava
Muntaner
Mandri
Mitre
Ganduxer
Anglí
Major
SARRIÀ
TURÓ DE MONTEROLS
Via Augusta
Sarrià
Vergós
Les Tres Torres
La Bonanova
Augusta
Vico
Valmajor
Santaló
Reina Elisenda
de
Sarrià
Trinquet
88
135
Pas. Sant Joan Bosco
Capità
100
JARDINS E. MARQUINA
59
187
Bosch i Gimpera
Marquès de Mulhacén
Pl. de Fra Eloi de Bianya
Bori
Fontestà
Ganduxer
Girona
Manuel
de
Av. de Sarrià
Av.
PAVELLÓ GÜELL
Pas. de Pedralbes
57
Gran Arenas
Mata
Diagonal
Deu
Entença
Palau de Pedralbes
Pl. Pius XII
153
Av.
Maria Cristina
Europa
Galileu
Numància
Palau Reial
Via de Carles III
TORRES TRADE
Joan
Corts
158
Sentmenat
de
Berlín
Zona Universitària
Av. Joan XXIII
les
Marquès
Vallespir
Les Corts
Numància
Aristides
Pl. del Centre
CAMP NOU
Sants-Estació
63
de
Madrid
Güell
Vallespir
Galileu
44
SANTS
Maillol
Travessera
Arizala
de
Brasil
Roses
Sant Antoni
177
Riera
Av.
Roger
Collblanc
Badal
Pl. de Sants
Carret. de Collblanc
Blanca
Sants
Sants
Mercat Nou

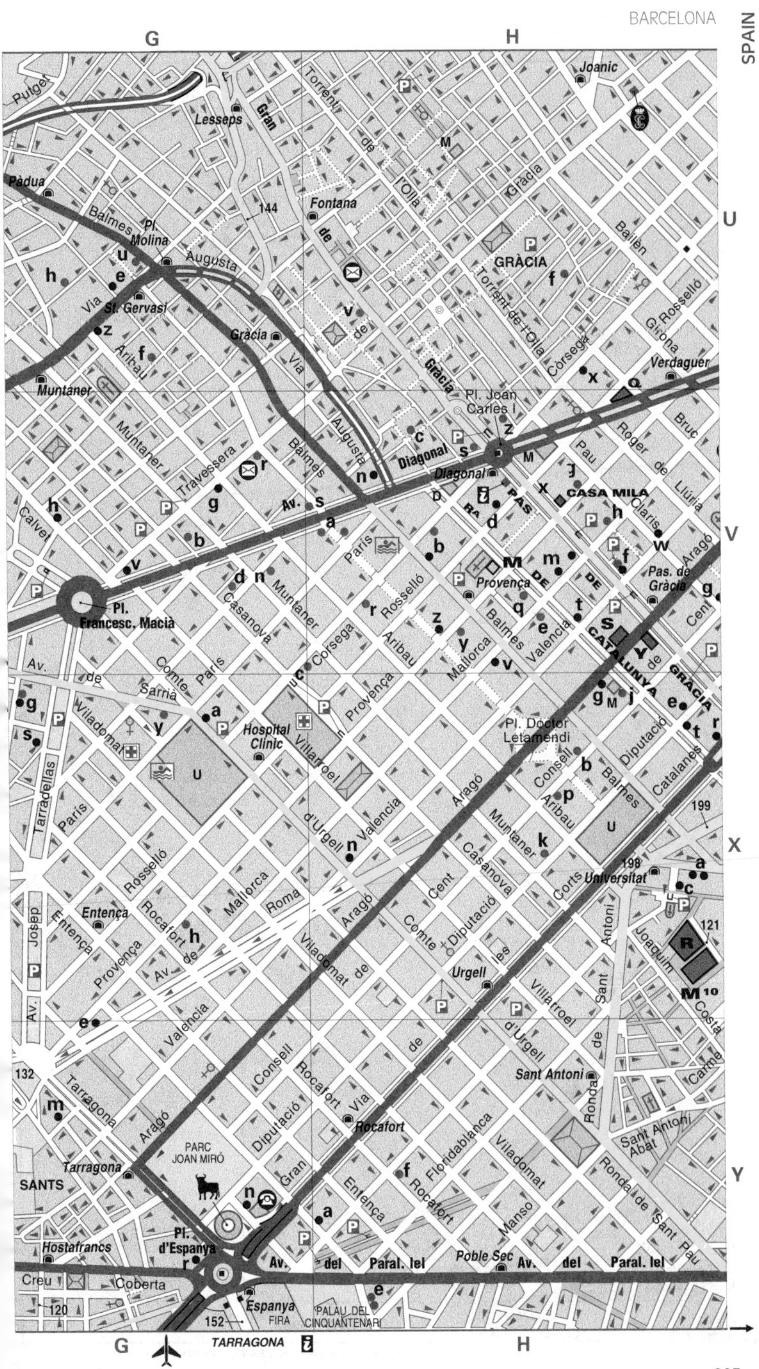
G
H
U
V
X
Y
Lesseps
Gran
Torrent de l'Olla
Joanic
Pàdua
Fontana
Balmes
Pl. Molina
Augusta
Via
St. Gervasi
Gràcia
GRÀCIA
Bailèn
Rosselló
Girona
Verdaguer
Còrsega
Muntaner
Aribau
Pl. Joan Carles I
Diagonal
Travessera
Roger de Llúria
Bruc
Pau Claris
CASA MILA
Calvet
Av.
París
Rosselló
Provença
Aragó
Pl. Francesc. Macià
Casanova
Còrsega
Mallorca
Valencia
CATALUNYA
GRÀCIA
Comte
Sarrià
Viladomat
Hospital Clínic
Villarroel
Pl. Doctor Letamendi
Consell
Diputació
Catalanes
Tarradellas
Josep
Entença
Rocafort
d'Urgell
Cent
Corts
Universitat
Antoni
Joaquim Costa
Roma
Urgell
Sant Antoni
Ronda de Sant Antoni
Sant Antoni Abat
Carme
132
Tarragona
Rocafort
Floridablanca
Manso
Ronda de Sant Pau
PARC JOAN MIRÓ
SANTS
Pl. d'Espanya
Hostafrancs
Creu
Coberta
Poble Sec
Av. del Paral. lel
Espanya
FIRA
PALAU DEL CINQUANTENARI
TARRAGONA
120
152
144
198
199
121
M 10

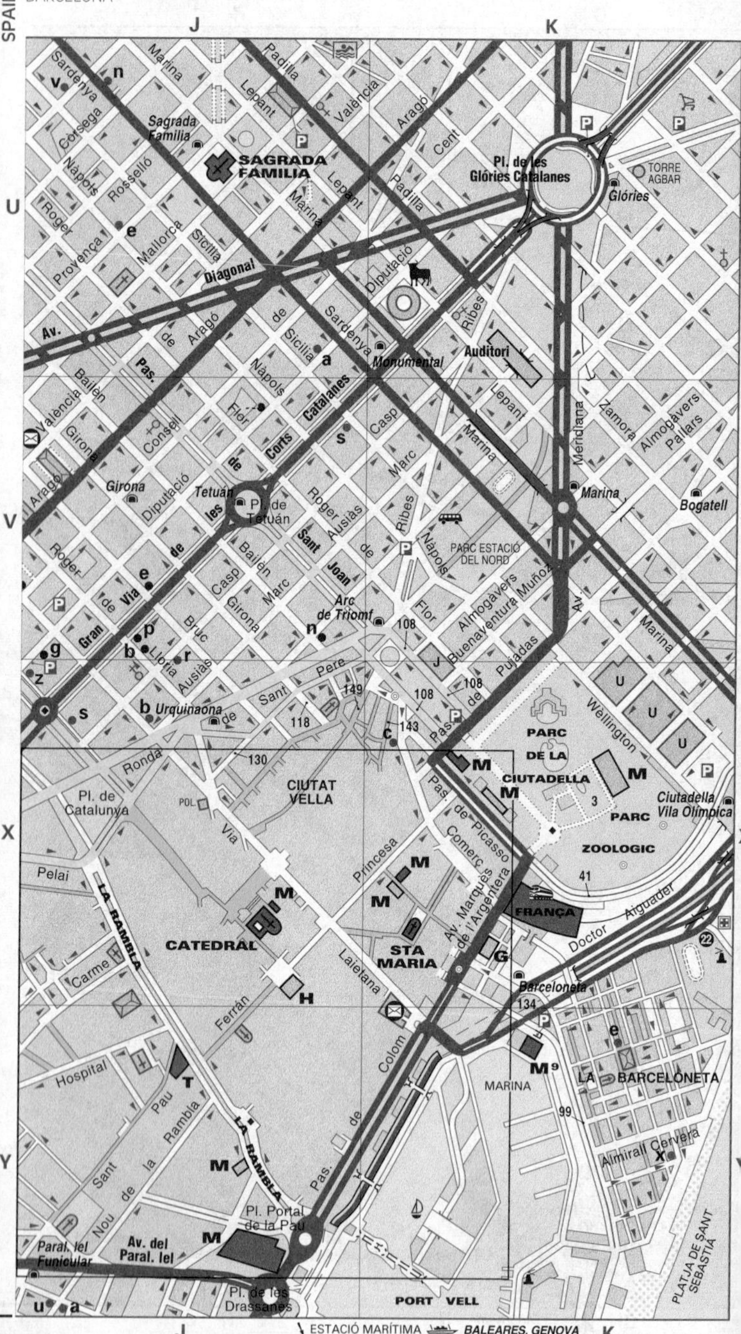
J
K
U
V
X
Y
Sardenya
Marina
Padilla
Lepant
València
Aragó
Cent
Sagrada Família
SAGRADA FAMILIA
Pl. de les Glòries Catalanes
TORRE AGBAR
Glòries
Còrsega
Nàpols
Rosselló
Roger
Provença
Mallorca
Sicília
Diagonal
Diputació
Ribes
Av.
Pas. de Aragó
de Sicília
Monumental
Auditori
Bailèn
València
Girona
Consell
Flor
Corts Catalanes
Casp
Zamora
Almogàvers
Pallars
Meridiana
Marc
Girona
Diputació
Tetuán
Pl. de Tetuán
les
de
Gran Via de les Corts Catalanes
Sant Joan
Ausiàs
Roger de
Ribes
Nàpols
Marina
Bogatell
PARC ESTACIÓ DEL NORD
Almogàvers
Buenaventura Muñoz
Av.
Marina
Bruc
Girona
Marc
Arc de Triomf
108
Llòria
Ausiàs
Sant Pere
149
118
Urquinaona
Ronda
143
108
108
Pujadas
Pas. de
Wellington
PARC DE LA CIUTADELLA
Ciutadella Vila Olímpica
PARC ZOOLOGIC
3
130
CIUTAT VELLA
Pl. de Catalunya
POL.
Via
Pas. de Picasso
Comerç
Princesa
Pelai
LA RAMBLA
CATEDRAL
Av. Marquès de l'Argentera
FRANÇA
41
Doctor Aiguader
STA MARIA
Laietana
Barceloneta
Carme
Ferran
134
Colom
Hospital
Pau
Rambla
MARINA
LA BARCELONETA
99
LA RAMBLA
Sant
Nou de la Rambla
Pas. de
Almirall Cervera
Pl. Portal de la Pau
Paral. lel Funicular
Av. del Paral. lel
Pl. de les Drassanes
PORT VELL
PLATJA DE SANT SEBASTIÀ
ESTACIÓ MARÍTIMA BALEARES, GENOVA

STREET INDEX TO BARCELONA TOWN PLAN

In addition to establishments indicated by XXXXX ... X, many hotels possess good class restaurants.

BARCELONA

Bacardí (Pas.) . . . . **MY** 5
Banys Nous . . . . **MX** 7
Bergara . . . . **LV** 10
Bisbe . . . . **MX** 15
Bòria . . . . **MV** 18
Born (Pas. del) . . . . **NX** 20
Boters . . . . **MX** 23
Canaletes
(Rambla de) . . . . **LV** 27
Canonge Colom (Pl.) . . . . . **LY** 28
Canvis Vells . . . . **NX** 32
Caputxins
(Rambla dels) . . . . **MY** 35
Cardenal Casañas . . . . **LX** 36
Catalunya (Pl. de) . . . . **LV**
Catedral (Av.) . . . . **MV** 40
Ciutat . . . . **MX** 43
Comercial (Pl.) . . . . **NV** 45
Cucurella . . . . **LX** 55
Doctor Joaquim Pou . . . . . **MV** 61
Escudellers . . . . **MY**
Estudis (Rambla dels) . . . . . **LX**
Francesc Cambó (Av.) . . . . **MV** 79
Garriga i Bachs (Pl.) . . . . . . **MX** 83
Isabel II (Pas. d') . . . . **NX** 98
Montcada . . . . **NX** 122
Montjuïc del Bisbe . . . . **MX** 123
Nou de Sant Francesc . . . . **MY** 126
Nova (Pl.) . . . . **MX** 128
Paradís . . . . **MX** 133
Pi (Pl. del) . . . . **LX** 137
Pintor Fortuny . . . . **LX** 140
Portal Santa
Madrona . . . . **MY** 142
Ramon Berenguer
el Gran (Pl. de) . . . . **MX** 148
Rei (Plaça del) . . . . **MX** 150
Sant Felip Neri (Pl.) . . . . . . **MX** 163
Sant Josep (Rambla de) . . . **LX** 168
Sant Josep Oriol . . . . **LX** 171
Sant Iu (Pl. de) . . . . **MX** 172
Sant Miquel (Pl. de) . . . . . . **MX** 173
Sant Sever . . . . **MX** 181
Santa Maria (Pl.) . . . . **NX** 189
Santa Mònica
(Rambla de) . . . . **MY**
Seu (Pl. de la) . . . . **MX** 192
Tapineria . . . . **MX** 193
Universitat
(Ronda de la) . . . . **LV** 199

We suggest:

For a successful tour, that you prepare it in advance. ***Michelin maps*** *and* ***guides*** *will give you much useful information on route planning, places of interest, accommodation, prices, etc.*

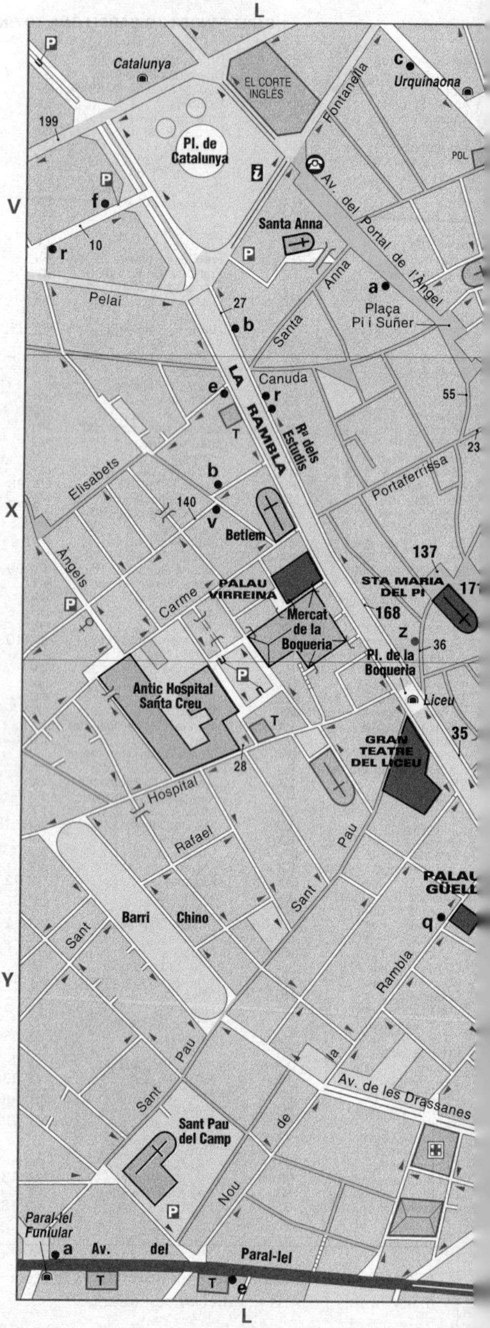

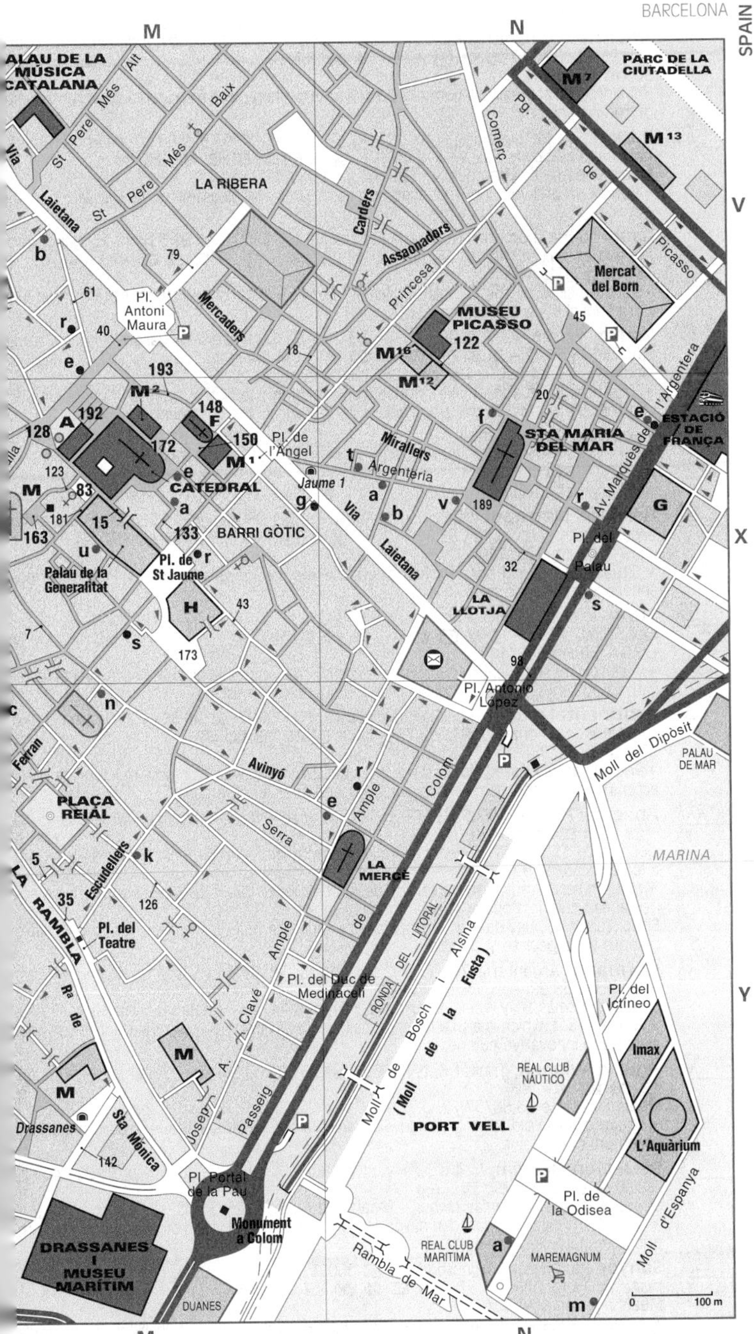
M
N
PALAU DE LA MÚSICA CATALANA
PARC DE LA CIUTADELLA
LA RIBERA
Mercat del Born
MUSEU PICASSO
Pl. Antoni Maura
STA MARIA DEL MAR
ESTACIÓ DE FRANÇA
Pl. de l'Àngel
Jaume 1
CATEDRAL
BARRI GÒTIC
Pl. de St Jaume
Palau de la Generalitat
Pl. del Palau
LA LLOTJA
Pl. Antonio López
Moll del Dipòsit
PALAU DE MAR
MARINA
PLAÇA REIAL
LA MERCÈ
LA RAMBLA
Pl. del Teatre
Pl. del Duc de Medinaceli
RONDA DEL LITORAL
Moll de Bosch i Alsina (Moll de la Fusta)
Pl. del Ictíneo
Imax
REAL CLUB NÀUTICO
PORT VELL
L'Aquàrium
Pl. Portal de la Pau
Monument a Colom
Pl. de la Odisea
Moll d'Espanya
REAL CLUB MARITIMA
MAREMAGNUM
Rambla de Mar
DRASSANES I MUSEU MARÍTIM
DUANES
Drassanes
Sta Mònica
Passeig Josep A. Clavé
Escudellers
Avinyó
Serra
Ample
Colom
Ferran
Laietana
Via Laietana
Mercaders
Carders
Assaonadors
Princesa
Miralles
Argenteria
Av. Marquès de l'Argentera
Pg. de Picasso
Comerç
St Pere Més Alt
St Pere Més Baix
V
X
Y
0
100 m

Atlantis without rest, Pelai 20, ✉ 08001, ☎ 93 318 90 12, *inf@hotelatlantis-bcn.com, Fax 93 412 09 14* – AE VISA. HX a
50 rm 120/150.
◆ A hotel to feel really at home in. Friendly atmosphere, well managed and with the best of the city nearby.

Park H., av. Marquès de l'Argentera 11, ✉ 08003, ☎ 93 319 60 00, *parkhotel@parkhotelbarcelona.com, Fax 93 319 45 19* – AE VISA. NX e
Meals - see rest. **Àbac** below – **91 rm** 110/145.
◆ Functional and very well-managed hotel with large and pleasant rooms. Bar with a modern feel.

Gaudí coffee shop only, Nou de la Rambla 12, ✉ 08001, ☎ 93 317 90 32, *gaudi@hotelgaudi.es, Fax 93 412 26 36,* – – 25. AE VISA JCB LY q
73 rm 120/160.
◆ Located close to the Ramblas. Spacious, well-equipped rooms, a new fitness suite and a traditional-style coffee bar.

Rialto, Ferran 42, ✉ 08002, ☎ 93 318 52 12, *reserve@gargallo-hotels.com, Fax 93 318 53 12* – AE VISA JCB. rest MX s
Meals 15 – 11,90 – **197 rm** 105/126,50, 1 suite.
◆ This hotel's situation makes it ideal for exploring the Gothic Quarter. Functional but comfortable rooms. There is a spacious restaurant in the basement.

Regencia Colón without rest, Sagristans 13, ✉ 08002, ☎ 93 318 98 58, *info@hotelregenciacolon.com, Fax 93 317 28 22* – AE VISA JCB MV r
9,50 – **51 rm** 148.
◆ A very well-equipped hotel in one of the prettiest and most typical areas of the city.

Hesperia Metropol without rest, Ample 31, ✉ 08002, ☎ 93 310 51 00, *hotel@hesperia-metropol.com, Fax 93 319 12 76* – – 25. AE VISA. NY r
9 – **68 rm** 125/140.
◆ Situated in the old town with comfortable and well-decorated rooms. Friendly atmosphere and pleasant staff.

Turín without rest, Pintor Fortuny 9, ✉ 08001, ☎ 93 302 48 12, *hotelturin@teleline.es, Fax 93 302 10 05* – AE VISA. LX v
9 – **60 rm** 100/142.
◆ A hotel which is ideal for getting a taste of the ambience of the city. A simple hotel with good rooms of a reasonable size and standard furnishings.

Continental without rest, Rambles 138-2º, ✉ 08002, ☎ 93 301 25 70, *ramblas@hotelcontinental.com, Fax 93 302 73 60* – AE VISA LV b
35 rm 85/95.
◆ Friendly hotel located close to the Plaza Catalunya square which gets much of its character from the bedrooms which are furnished in an English style.

Àbac, Rec 79-89, ✉ 08003, ☎ 93 319 66 00, *abac12@telefonica.net, Fax 93 319 45 19* – AE VISA. NX e
closed 6 to 13 January, 3 weeks in August, Sunday and Monday lunch – **Meals** 75,13 and a la carte 50/70,92.
◆ Modern restaurant with minimalist design details. Excellent service and creative Mediterranean cuisine. Popular with a young clientele.
Spec. Tartar de buey de mar, champiñones y aguacate. Foie-gras al vapor de bambú. Sablé caliente de chocolate y su polo.

Hofmann, Argenteria 74-78 (1º), ✉ 08003, ☎ 93 319 58 89, *hofmann@ysi.es, Fax 93 319 58 89* – AE VISA. NX v
closed Christmas, Holy Week, August, Saturday and Sunday – **Meals** a la carte 39,90/59,45.
◆ A restaurant, which is also a catering college, in a historic building. Pleasant décor with plants and innovative cuisine.

Agut d'Avignon, Trinitat 3, ✉ 08002, ☎ 93 302 60 34, *Fax 93 302 53 18* – AE VISA JCB. MY n
Meals a la carte 23,56/37,72.
◆ Situated in the old town area and with dining areas on different levels. Delicious dishes based on local cuisine.

Reial Club Marítim, Moll d'Espanya, ✉ 08039, ☎ 93 221 71 43, *Fax 93 221 44 12,* – AE VISA JCB. NY a
closed August and Sunday dinner – **Meals** a la carte 25,25/36,05.
◆ A large and pleasant glazed-in dining room with wonderful views of the marina. Medium priced menu of local dishes.

Senyor Parellada, Argenteria 37, ✉ 08003, ☎ 93 310 50 94, *fondaparellada@hotmail.com, Fax 93 268 31 57* – AE VISA JCB. NX t
Meals a la carte 14,20/20,50.
◆ A spacious restaurant with classic-contemporary décor, bar and pleasant dining areas. Varied menu.

XX **7 Portes,** passeig d'Isabel II-14, ✉ 08003, ☎ 93 319 30 33, *reservas@7portes.com, Fax 93 319 30 46* – ▤. AE ⓓ ⓜ VISA JCB. ✻ NX s
Meals a la carte 22,15/29,80.
◆ A venerable Barcelona institution dating back to 1836. Dining areas with a pleasant old-fashioned feel and carefully prepared dishes.

XX **La Nau,** Manresa 4-6, ✉ 08003, ☎ 93 268 77 47, *artpoldplus.sl@passadis.com, Fax 93 310 15 66* – ▤. AE ⓓ ⓜ VISA. ✻ NX b
closed 3 weeks in August and Sunday – **Meals** a la carte 35/50.
◆ Situated in a former factory with a cocktail bar near the entrance and two traditional-style dining areas.

XX **L'Elx al Moll,** Moll d'Espanya-Maremagnun, Local 9, ✉ 08039, ☎ 93 225 81 17, *Fax 93 225 81 20*, ←, 🏠 – ▤. AE ⓜ VISA NY m
Meals - Rice dishes - a la carte 17,40/28,30.
◆ Pleasant restaurant specialising in rice dishes with a terrace dining area. Good views of the marina.

X **Can Ramonet,** Maquinista 17, ✉ 08003, ☎ 93 319 30 64, *canramonet@hotmail.com, Fax 93 319 70 14*, 🏠 – ▤. AE ⓓ ⓜ VISA JCB. ✻ KY e
closed 14 to 30 January, 17 to 31 August and Sunday dinner – **Meals** - Seafood - a la carte 25,63/40,81.
◆ Friendly restaurant with a bar near the entrance and traditional-style dining areas. Cuisine based on well-chosen ingredients.

X **Pitarra,** Avinyó 56, ✉ 08002, ☎ 93 301 16 47, *Fax 93 301 85 62* – ▤. AE ⓓ ⓜ VISA JCB NY e
closed August, Sunday and Bank Holidays dinner – **Meals** a la carte 18/35.
◆ A pleasant and welcoming interior with objects connected with the poet Pitarra. Good service and friendly staff.

X **Can Majó,** Almirall Aixada 23, ✉ 08003, ☎ 93 221 54 55, *canmajo@terra.es, Fax 93 221 54 55*, 🏠 – ▤. AE ⓓ ⓜ VISA JCB. ✻ KY x
closed Sunday dinner and Monday – **Meals** - Seafood - a la carte 27,20/45,08.
◆ Situated in the Barceloneta area. Well-known restaurant with friendly service and a good menu. Seafood and fish a speciality.

🍷 Estrella de Plata, pl. del Palau 13, ✉ 08003, ☎ 93 268 06 35, *tapas@estrella-de-plata.es, Fax 93 310 38 50* – ▤ NX r
◆ A well-known restaurant managed by very professional, young staff. Excellent service and delicious haute cuisine tapas and a variety of other dishes.

🍷 **Sagardi,** Argenteria 62, ✉ 08003, ☎ 93 319 99 93, *sagardi@sagardi.es, Fax 93 268 48 86*, Basque cider press – ▤. AE ⓓ ⓜ VISA JCB. ✻ NX a
Tapa 1,50 - Basque tapas.
◆ A Basque cider house situated near the historic church of Santa María del Mar. A very wide range of Basque-style tapas and dining room with cider barrels and charcoal grill.

🍷 **Irati,** Cardenal Casanyes 17, ✉ 08002, ☎ 93 302 30 84, *sagardi@sagardi.es, Fax 93 412 73 76* – ▤. AE ⓓ ⓜ VISA JCB. ✻ LX z
Tapa 1,10 - Basque tapas.
◆ Traditional-style Basque bar and grill- restaurant near to the Liceo theatre with a simple menu.

🍷 **El Xampanyet,** Montcada 22, ✉ 08003, ☎ 93 319 70 03 – ⓜ VISA NX f
closed Holy Week, August, Sunday dinner, Monday and Bank Holidays dinner – **Tapa** 3 – **Ración** - Preserves and salted foods - approx. 6.
◆ Friendly, well-established and family-run bar with a good range of tapas.

South of Av. Diagonal : Gran Via de les Corts Catalanes, Passeig de Gràcia, Balmes, Muntaner, Aragó

🏨 **Arts** ⛰, Marina 19, ✉ 08005, ☎ 93 221 10 00, *info@harts.es, Fax 93 221 10 70*, ←, 🏠, Ⅎ6, ☼ – |♦| ▤ 📺 ♿ 🚗 – 🏛 25/900. AE ⓓ ⓜ VISA. ✻ rest
Meals a la carte 60/75 - ***Arola*** *(closed Monday and Tuesday)* a la carte approx. 55 – ☕ 25 – **397 rm** 450, 86 suites. East : by Av. d'Icària KX
◆ A good situation in the Olympic Port with views of Barcelona and surrounding areas. Very well-equipped rooms with designer furnishings. The Arola restaurant successfully combines fine attention to detail and innovative cuisine.

🏨 **Rey Juan Carlos I** ⛰, av. Diagonal 661, ✉ 08028, ☎ 93 364 40 40, *hotel@hrjuancarlos.com, Fax 93 364 42 32*, ← city, 🏠, Ⅎ6, ☼, ☼, 🌳 – |♦| ▤ 📺 ♿ 🚗 🅿 – 🏛 25/1000. AE ⓓ ⓜ VISA. ✻ West : by Av. Diagonal EX
Chez Vous *(closed 27 December-7 January, Saturday lunch and Sunday)* **Meals** a la carte 39/48,50 - ***Café Polo*** *(buffet)* **Meals** a la carte 29/35 – ☕ 19 – **375 rm** 315/420, 37 suites.
◆ A hotel with wonderful modern facilities surrounded by an area of park with a pond and swimming-pool. An exclusive atmosphere and very tasteful décor. The Chez Vous à la carte restaurant has a distinguished ambience.

Eurostar Grand Marina H., Moll de Barcelona (World Trade Center), ✉ 08039, ☎ 93 603 90 00, *info@grandmarinahotel.com, Fax 93 603 90 90,* ☀, ₺, ⛱ - 🛗 ▤ TV ♿ 🚗 - 🏛 25/500. AE ⓓ MC VISA JCB. ✕ rest East : by Av. d'Icària KX
Meals 60 - ☕ 19 - **258 rm** 240/325, 15 suites.
◆ A circular building in a very modern style with a patio in the middle. Rooms with a high level of comfort, attractive design details and original works of art. A well-lit restaurant with good service.

Ritz, Gran Via de les Corts Catalanes 668, ✉ 08010, ☎ 93 510 11 30, *ritz@ritzbcn.com, Fax 93 318 01 48* - 🛗 ▤ TV - 🏛 25/280. AE ⓓ MC VISA JCB. ✕ JV p
Diana *(closed August and Sunday)* **Meals** a la carte 46,10/72 - ☕ 20 - **119 rm** 355/380, 6 suites.
◆ A famous and distinguished hotel set in a beautiful building surrounded by wide boulevards and theatres. Luxury, elegance and traditional, exquisite taste with a restaurant to match.

Claris ⛫, Pau Claris 150, ✉ 08009, ☎ 93 487 62 62, *claris@derbyhotels.es, Fax 93 215 79 70,* ₺, ⛱ - 🛗 ▤ TV 🚗 - 🏛 25/120. AE ⓓ MC VISA. ✕ rest HV w
***East 47* : Meals** a la carte approx. 37,50 - ☕ 19 - **80 rm** 319/354, 40 suites.
◆ An elegant hotel with a rather aristocratic feel in the former Vedruna palace where tradition and modernity meet in harmony. The hotel houses an important archaeological collection and has a restaurant with a distinguished ambience.

Majestic, passeig de Gràcia 68, ✉ 08007, ☎ 93 488 17 17, *recepcion@hotelmajestic.es, Fax 93 488 18 80,* ₺, ⛱ - 🛗 ▤ TV ♿ 🚗 - 🏛 25/400. AE ⓓ MC VISA. ✕
Meals - see rest. ***Drolma*** below - 28 - ☕ 20 - **273 rm** 330, 30 suites. HV f
◆ A well-established and modern hotel on the Paseo de Gràcia. Good facilities for business meetings and conferences. Attractive, spacious and well-equipped rooms. Functional dining room with both an à la carte menu and a buffet.

Fira Palace, av. Rius i Taulet 1, ✉ 08004, ☎ 93 426 22 23, *sales@fira-palace.com, Fax 93 424 86 79,* ₺, 🏊 - 🛗 ▤ TV ♿ 🚗 - 🏛 25/1300. AE ⓓ MC VISA. ✕
Meals 22,25 - ***El Mall* : Meals** a la carte 26/34,50 - ☕ 13,50 - **258 rm** 227/264, 18 suites.
◆ Close to the exhibition and trade fair sector. Modern-style hotel with very well-equipped rooms. Ideal for conventions, conferences and social functions. Restaurant with a rustic feel, exposed brickwork and pleasant furnishings. South : by Lleida HY

G.H. Havana, Gran Via de les Corts Catalanes 647, ✉ 08010, ☎ 93 412 11 15, *hotelhavana@hoteles-silken.com, Fax 93 412 26 11* - 🛗 ▤ TV ♿ 🚗 - 🏛 25/150. AE ⓓ MC VISA. ✕ rest JV e
Meals 25 - ***Grand Place* : Meals** a la carte 25,40/42 - ☕ 16 - **141 rm** 280/310, 4 suites.
◆ A luxurious and centrally located hotel in a historic building with large rooms for social functions. An elegant setting, great comfort and a pleasant restaurant.

Meliá Barcelona, av. de Sarrià 50, ✉ 08029, ☎ 93 410 60 60, *melia.barcelona@solmelia.com, Fax 93 410 77 44,* ≤, ₺ - 🛗 ▤ TV 🚗 - 🏛 25/500. AE ⓓ MC VISA. ✕
Meals a la carte 31,75/40 - ☕ 18 - **299 rm** 210/235, 15 suites.
◆ A traditional-style hotel in the most modern area of the city. Large and very well-equipped rooms and spa facilities available. A spacious and welcoming restaurant. FV n

Princesa Sofía Inter-Continental, pl. Pius XII-4, ✉ 08028, ☎ 93 508 10 00, *barcelona@interconti.com, Fax 93 508 10 01,* ≤, ₺, 🏊, 🌳 - 🛗 ▤ TV ♿ 🚗 - 🏛 25/1200. AE ⓓ MC VISA JCB. ✕ EX x
Meals 22 - ☕ 20 - **475 rm** 390, 25 suites.
◆ In the business and commercial district. Excellent facilities, luxurious lounges and comfortable rooms. Ideal for business trips and conventions. A modern-style restaurant with both à la carte menu and a buffet.

Hilton Barcelona, av. Diagonal 589, ✉ 08014, ☎ 93 495 77 77, *barcelona@hilton.com, Fax 93 495 77 00,* ☀, ₺ - 🛗 ▤ TV ♿ 🚗 P - 🏛 25/600. AE ⓓ MC VISA JCB. ✕ FX v
Meals a la carte 34,50/43 - ☕ 20 - **287 rm** 305/335, 2 suites.
◆ Situated on one of the main arteries of the city. Spacious and well-furnished bedrooms, bathrooms fitted with marble and elegant public areas. The restaurant offers both a varied buffet and an à la carte menu of Mediterranean cuisine.

AC Diplomatic, Pau Claris 122, ✉ 08009, ☎ 93 272 38 10, *Fax 93 272 38 11,* ₺ - 🛗 ▤ TV ♿ 🚗 - 🏛 25/70. AE ⓓ MC VISA JCB. ✕ HV g
Meals a la carte approx. 30 - ☕ 15 - **209 rm** 242, 2 suites.
◆ A hotel situated right in the middle of the Ensanche area. Comfortable, with very good facilities and with modern bedrooms and bathrooms.

NH Calderón, Rambla de Catalunya 26, ✉ 08007, ☎ 93 301 00 00, *nhcalderon@nh-hoteles.es, Fax 93 412 41 93,* ₺, ⛱, 🏊 - 🛗 ▤ TV 🚗 - 🏛 25/200. AE ⓓ MC VISA JCB. ✕ HX t
Meals a la carte approx. 30,50 - ☕ 17,50 - **224 rm** 220, 29 suites.
◆ This hotel's location in the business district of the city makes it ideal for the business traveller. Excellent facilities and high levels of comfort.

Catalonia Barcelona Plaza, pl. d'Espanya 6, ✉ 08014, ☎ 93 426 26 00, *plaza@hoteles-catalonia.es, Fax 93 426 04 00,* heated – AE VISA. GY r
Gourmet Plaza : **Meals** a la carte approx. 28 – 12 – **338 rm** 210/242, 9 suites.
• A modern hotel just opposite the site used for exhibitions and trade fairs. The excellent facilities make it ideal for the business traveller. A restaurant with a pleasant atmosphere and décor.

Barceló H. Sants, pl. dels Paûsos Catalans, ✉ 08014, ☎ 93 503 53 00, *sants@bchoteles.com, Fax 93 490 60 45,* – – 25/1500. AE VISA JCB. FY
Meals *(closed Sunday)* a la carte approx. 44,36 – 13 – **364 rm** 180, 13 suites.
• A hotel located at Sants train station that has views of the city and its surroundings. Classic style, very good facilities and a spacious foyer area. A well-lit dining room with two areas, one offering à la carte dishes the other a buffet.

Condes de Barcelona (Monument and Centre), passeig de Gràcia 75, ✉ 08008, ☎ 93 467 47 80, *reservas@condesdebarcelona.com, Fax 93 467 47 85* – – 25/200. AE VISA JCB. rest HV m
Thalassa : **Meals** a la carte 32,50/45,50 – 15,75 – **181 rm** 290, 2 suites.
• A hotel set in two well-known and emblematic Barcelona buildings, the Casa Batlló and the Casa Durella. The rooms are comfortable and the décor has many period details. A charming restaurant with a wide variety of dishes.

G.H. Catalonia, Balmes 142, ✉ 08008, ☎ 93 415 90 90, *grancatalonia@hoteles-catalonia.es, Fax 93 415 22 09* – – 50/230. AE VISA JCB.
Meals 17 – 12 – **84 rm** 210/242. HV b
• A hotel in the heart of the Ensanche area with modern facilities and comfortable and well-appointed bedrooms and bathrooms with marble fittings.

Avenida Palace, Gran Via de les Corts Catalanes 605, ✉ 08007, ☎ 93 301 96 00, *avpalace@husa.es, Fax 93 318 12 34* – – 25/350. AE VISA JCB. HX r
Meals 25 – 18 – **146 rm** 198/235, 14 suites.
• A hotel located close to the famous Paseo de Gràcia with elegant style and very comfortable rooms. The restaurant has a distinguished atmosphere, pleasant furnishings and very good service.

L'Illa, av. Diagonal 555, ✉ 08029, ☎ 93 410 33 00, *hotelilla@husa.es, Fax 93 410 88 92* – – 25/100. AE VISA. FX c
Meals *(closed Saturday and Sunday lunch)* 15 – 13 – **93 rm** 155/180, 10 suites.
• A hotel situated on the Diagonal with a distinguished ambience and spacious and well-lit rooms. There is a pleasant public area on the first floor and a traditional-style restaurant.

Abba Sants, Numància 32, ✉ 08029, ☎ 93 600 31 00, *abba-sants@abbahoteles.com, Fax 93 600 31 01* – – 25/200. AE VISA. FX b
Amalur : **Meals** a la carte 26,30/42,10 – 13,88 – **140 rm** 134,10/153,90.
• A newly constructed hotel of modern design. Adequate public areas and bedrooms, which are smallish but comfortable. Pleasant dining room with a menu based on Basque cuisine.

Ritz Barcelona Roger de Llúria, Roger de Llúria 28, ✉ 08010, ☎ 93 343 60 80, *ritz@rogerdelluria.com, Fax 93 343 60 81* – – 25/60. AE VISA.
Meals *(closed Sunday)* a la carte approx. 40 – 15,50 – **46 rm** 210/235, 2 suites.
• A hotel with a welcoming and intimate feel. A small foyer but large, very comfortable and well-appointed bedrooms. A spacious restaurant with a stately ambience. JV b

Rafael H. Diagonal Port, Lope de Vega 4, ✉ 08005, ☎ 93 230 20 00, *diagonalport@rafaelhoteles.com, Fax 93 230 20 10* – – 25/175. AE VISA. East : by Av. d'Icària KX
Meals 15 – 10,50 – **115 rm** 150/172.
• A modern and functional hotel with comfortable and quiet bedrooms with carpeted floors and bathrooms fitted with marble. Sufficient public areas.

AC Front Marítim, passeig García Faria 69, ✉ 08019, ☎ 93 303 44 40, *acfmaritim@ac-hotels.com, Fax 93 303 44 41,* – – 25/160. AE VISA JCB. East : by Av. d'Icària KX
Meals - dinner only, residents only - 14 – 11 – **177 rm** 158/170.
• A hotel in contemporary style with functional bedrooms which are well-furnished. Modern bathrooms, most of which have showers. Dinner is available to guests of the hotel.

Gallery H., Rosselló 249, ✉ 08008, ☎ 93 415 99 11, *email@galleryhotel.com, Fax 93 415 91 84,* – – 25/200. AE VISA JCB.
Meals 20 – 14 – **108 rm** 232/264, 5 suites. HV d
• Situated near to the Plaza Joan Carles I square. Good, modern facilities and comfortable and well-appointed bedrooms. The restaurant specialises in Catalan cuisine and has a pleasant terrace.

St. Moritz, Diputació 264, 08007, 93 412 15 00, *s.armengol@hocchotels.com, Fax 93 412 12 36* – – 25/200. JV g
Meals 21 – 17 – **91 rm** 206/247.
• A hotel with a traditional façade with well-appointed rooms and spacious public areas which are suitable for any type of social function. Efficiently managed.

Gran Derby without rest, Loreto 28, 08029, 93 322 20 62, *info@derbyhotels.es, Fax 93 419 68 20,* – – 25/100. GX g
14 – **29 rm** 195/215, 12 suites.
• A small and traditional-style hotel with a welcoming atmosphere and spacious and well-lit bedrooms.

City Park H., Nicaragua 47, 08029, 93 363 74 74, *j.reservas@cityparkhoteles.com, Fax 93 419 71 63* – – 25/75. rest FX z
Meals 15,18 – 14 – **80 rm** 223/270.
• Close to Sants train station. Very comfortable and with avant-garde, Barcelona New Design décor. The restaurant has a separate entrance and designer furnishings.

NH Podium, Bailén 4, 08010, 93 265 02 02, *nhpodium@nh-hoteles.es, Fax 93 265 05 06,* – – 25/240. rest JV n
***Corella* : Meals** a la carte 26,90/35,70 – 15,50 – **140 rm** 155/201, 5 suites.
• In the Modernist part of the Ensanche area. A traditional façade with a modern interior with avant-garde design details. Welcoming and well-lit rooms. Intimate restaurant with pleasant décor and contemporary paintings.

Balmes, Mallorca 216, 08008, 93 451 19 14, *balmes@derbyhotels.es, Fax 93 451 00 49,* – – 25/30. HV v
Meals 12 – 13 – **93 rm** 175/195, 8 suites.
• A modern-style hotel with large bedrooms with wooden floors and marble fittings in the bathrooms. There is a pleasant terrace area with a swimming-pool.

Derby coffee shop only, Loreto 21, 08029, 93 322 32 15, *info@derbyhotels.es, Fax 93 410 08 62* – – 25/60. FX e
14 – **107 rm** 210,50/240,50, 4 suites.
• A classic hotel in the business district of the city. Spacious public areas and a coffee shop with a separate entrance, an English-style bar and comfortable rooms.

Hesperia del Mar, Espronceda 6, 08005, 93 502 97 00, *hotel@hesperia-delmar.com, Fax 93 502 97 01,* – – 25/175.
Meals 15 – 12 – **78 rm** 165/175, 6 suites. East : by Av. d'Icària KX
• This hotel is located close to the sea in an area in the process of redevelopment. Facilities here include spacious lounge areas, well-equipped guest rooms with modern, practical furnishings, and a bright, airy restaurant.

Vincci Marítimo, Llull 340, 08019, 93 356 26 00, *maritimo@vinccihoteles.com, Fax 93 356 06 69,* – – 25/250.
Meals 11 – 6 – **144 rm** 156/180. East : by Av. d'Icària KX
• A good level of general comfort, although the hotel's outstanding feature is its designer decor, with original avant-garde features in the bathrooms and on the bed headboards. The restaurant is bright and simply designed.

AC Vilamarí, Vilamarí 34-36, 08015, 93 289 09 09, *acvilamari@ac-hotels.com, Fax 93 289 05 01,* – – 25/35. HY a
Meals a la carte approx. 28 – 11 – **90 rm** 170.
• Meticulous in style, this hotel is successfully combines functionality with the world of design. Comfortable bedrooms, half of which have bathtubs, the remainder showers. The subtly lit restaurant is modern yet intimate.

Alexandra, Mallorca 251, 08008, 93 467 71 66, *informacion@hotel-alexandra.com, Fax 93 488 02 58* – – 25/100. HV v
Meals 19,83 – 17 – **95 rm** 260/300, 5 suites.
• A modern and welcoming hotel with spacious, well-equipped rooms, pleasant furnishings, carpeted floors and bathrooms with marble fittings. Pleasant public areas.

NH Master, València 105, 08011, 93 323 62 15, *nhmaster@nh-hotels.com, Fax 93 323 43 89* – – 25/100. rest HX n
Meals *(closed 23 to 27 December, 30 December-2 January, August, Saturday and Sunday)* 13 – 12,90 – **80 rm** 137/165, 1 suite.
• Both central and modern, with the characteristic style of this hotel chain. Pleasantly decorated and functional bedrooms which are ideal for business travellers.

Cristal Palace, Diputació 257, 08007, 93 487 87 78, *reservas@hotelcristalpalace.com, Fax 93 487 90 30* – – 25/100. rest
Meals 16,83 – 10,84 – **147 rm** 212/243, 1 suite. HX e
• A modern-style hotel with well-equipped rooms of a high standard of comfort. Efficiently-managed and friendly staff.

NH Numància, Numància 74, ✉ 08029, ☏ 93 322 44 51, *nhnumancia@nh-hotels.com, Fax 93 410 76 42* – |♦| ▤ TV 🚗 – 🏛 25/70. AE ⦿ MC VISA. ✻ FX f
Meals 20 – ☕ 12,90 – **140 rm** 123/170.
◆ Close to Sants train station. Pleasant public areas and comfortable bedrooms with modern décor and furnishings.

América without rest, Provença 195, ✉ 08008, ☏ 93 487 62 92, *america@hotel-america-barcelona.com, Fax 93 487 25 18,* Lō, 🏊 – |♦| ▤ TV ♿ – 🏛 25/125. AE ⦿ MC VISA JCB. ✻ HV z
☕ 13,25 – **60 rm** 189/222.
◆ A modern and spacious hotel with a combined reception and public areas. Comfortable bedrooms with minimalist décor and personalised service.

Núñez Urgell without rest, Comte d'Urgell 232, ✉ 08036, ☏ 93 322 41 53, *nunezurgell@nnhotels.es, Fax 93 419 01 06* – |♦| ▤ TV 🚗 – 🏛 25/150. AE ⦿ MC VISA JCB. ✻ GX a
☕ 12 – **106 rm** 160/175, 2 suites.
◆ A hotel with a welcoming foyer, coffee shop and bedrooms with a high level of comfort, modern furnishings and bathrooms with marble fittings.

Barcelona Mar, Provençals 10, ✉ 08019, ☏ 93 266 52 00, *barcelonamar@husa.es, Fax 93 266 52 07,* 🏊 – |♦| ▤ TV ♿ 🚗. AE ⦿ MC VISA JCB. ✻
Meals *(closed Saturday and Sunday)* 11 – ☕ 11 – **75 rm** 140/175.
◆ Close to the beach and with a large entrance and reception area and well-lit rooms with light-coloured wood décor. Friendly service. East : by Av. d'Icària KX

Senator Barcelona, Cardenal Reig 11, ✉ 08028, ☏ 93 260 99 00, *senator.bcn@senatorhoteles.com, Fax 93 449 30 30,* Lō, 🏊 – |♦| ▤ TV ♿ 🚗 – 🏛 25/600. AE ⦿ MC VISA. ✻ EY c
Meals - dinner only - 18 – ☕ 12 – **213 rm** 165/195.
◆ A hotel with spacious, quiet and well-appointed rooms and a fitness and beauty centre. A varied buffet is available in the dining room.

Capital, Arquitectura 1, ✉ 08908 L'Hospitalet de Llobregat, ☏ 93 298 05 30, *info@hotel-capita.com, Fax 93 298 05 31* – |♦| ▤ TV ♿ 🚗 – 🏛 26/60. AE ⦿ MC VISA. ✻ South : by Gran Via de les Corts Catalanes GY
Meals 18 – ☕ 9 – **103 rm** 151/161.
◆ A hotel with rooms decorated in tones of beige and grey, standard furnishings and modern bathrooms. There are panoramic views from the lifts.

Expo H. Barcelona, Mallorca 1, ✉ 08014, ☏ 93 600 30 20, *comercialbcn@expogrupo.com, Fax 93 292 79 60,* 🏊 – |♦| ▤ TV 🚗 – 🏛 25/300. AE ⦿ MC VISA. ✻ GY m
Meals 12 – **435 rm** ☕ 163/181.
◆ Close to Sants train station and with welcoming public areas and well-equipped but simply decorated bedrooms. The well-lit dining room is on the first floor.

Regente without rest, Rambla de Catalunya 76, ✉ 08008, ☏ 93 487 59 89, *regente@hcchotels.es, Fax 93 487 32 27,* 🏊 – |♦| ▤ TV – 🏛 25/120. AE ⦿ MC VISA JCB. ✻ HV t
☕ 16,50 – **79 rm** 191/232.
◆ Centrally located hotel with a Modernist façade. A small foyer and bedrooms that are sufficiently comfortable, with modern furnishings and bathrooms with marble fittings.

Hesperia Carlit without rest, Diputació 383, ✉ 08013, ☏ 93 505 26 00, *hotel@hesperia-carlit.com, Fax 93 505 26 10* – |♦| ▤ TV ♿. AE ⦿ MC VISA. ✻ JV x
☕ 9 – **38 rm** 96/140.
◆ Despite lacking overall space, this hotel is both functional and modern in style. Well-appointed guest rooms, most of which come with a shower rather than a bath.

NH Forum, Ecuador 20, ✉ 08029, ☏ 93 419 36 36, *nhforum@nh-hotels.com, Fax 93 419 89 10* – |♦| ▤ TV 🚗 – 🏛 25/50. AE ⦿ MC VISA JCB. ✻ rest FX t
Meals *(closed Christmas, August, Saturday, Sunday and Bank Holidays)* 25 – ☕ 12,50 – **47 rm** 165, 1 suite – PA 56,50.
◆ A modern hotel with the characteristic style of the NH chain. Pleasant and well-equipped rooms.

NH Rallye, Travessera de les Corts 150, ✉ 08028, ☏ 93 339 90 50, *nhrallye@nh-hotels.com, Fax 93 411 07 90,* Lō, 🏊 – |♦| ▤ TV ♿ 🚗 – 🏛 25/300. AE ⦿ MC VISA JCB. ✻ EY b
Meals a la carte 20,95/35 – ☕ 12,90 – **105 rm** 129/170, 1 suite.
◆ A modern and functional hotel with the characteristic style of the NH chain and situated near to the Camp Nou football ground. Spacious, well-equipped and comfortable rooms.

NH Les Corts coffee shop dinner only, Travessera de les Corts 292, ✉ 08029, ☏ 93 322 08 11, *nhcorts@nh-hoteles.es, Fax 93 322 09 08* – |♦| ▤ TV ♿ 🚗 – 🏛 25/80. AE ⦿ MC VISA JCB. ✻ FX u
☕ 12,50 – **80 rm** 119/165, 1 suite.
◆ Pleasant rooms with brightly coloured modern décor and multi-functional social areas. Efficient management and friendly staff.

Onix Fira without rest, Llançà 30, ✉ 08015, ☎ 93 426 00 87, *reservas.hotelsonix@icyesa.es, Fax 93 426 19 81,* – ▤ ▤ TV & – 25/70. AE VISA. ☕ 9 – **80 rm** 120/150. GY n

◆ Close to the old bullring. An intimate and comfortable hotel with a large coffee shop and functional rooms. Décor with an attractive use of marble.

Abbot without rest, av. de Roma 23, ✉ 08029, ☎ 93 430 04 05, *informacion@hotel-abbot.com, Fax 93 419 57 41* – ▤ ▤ TV & – 25/80. AE VISA JCB. ☕ 11 – **35 rm** 123/153, 4 suites. GXY e

◆ Modern, comfortable rooms and with adequate facilities for the category of the hotel. A pleasant place for business meetings or work-related trips.

XXXX **La Dama,** av. Diagonal 423, ✉ 08036, ☎ 93 202 06 86, *reservas@ladama-restaurant.com, Fax 93 200 72 99* – ▤. AE VISA JCB. HV a

Meals a la carte 41/57,50.

◆ An elegant restaurant with Modernist decorative details both inside and on the façade. Professional staff.

XXXX **Drolma** - *Hotel Majestic,* passeig de Gràcia 68, ✉ 08007, ☎ 93 496 77 10, *drolma@hotelmajestic.es, Fax 93 488 18 80* – ▤ ▤. AE VISA JCB. HV f

closed Sunday – **Meals** a la carte 78/107.

◆ Traditional style, predominantly wood, décor creating an elegant and refined atmosphere. Professional staff.

Spec. Puré de patata, zabaione y tuber magnatum (October-December). Canelones de faisana con trufa negra (December-15 March). Cabrito embarrado a la cuchara.

XXXX **Beltxenea,** Mallorca 275, ✉ 08008, ☎ 93 215 30 24, *Fax 93 487 00 81,* – ▤. AE VISA. HV h

cerrado Christmas, August, Saturday lunch and Sunday – **Meals** a la carte 47/58.

◆ An elegant restaurant in a historic building with an atmosphere of the past. A dining room with views of the garden and an attractive, carved wooden fireplace.

XXX **Casa Calvet,** Casp 48, ✉ 08010, ☎ 93 412 40 12, *restaurant@casacalvet.es, Fax 93 412 43 36* – ▤. AE VISA JCB. JVX r

closed Holy Week, Sunday and Bank Holidays – **Meals** a la carte 39,50/49,80.

◆ A restaurant in an attractive building designed by Gaudí. The dining room is welcoming and there is an excellent à la carte menu.

XXX **Jaume de Provença,** Provença 88, ✉ 08029, ☎ 93 430 00 29, *Fax 93 439 29 50* – ▤. AE VISA JCB. GX h

closed Holy Week, August, Sunday dinner and Monday – **Meals** a la carte 40,50/46.

◆ A classic-style restaurant with a small bar from which you enter a spacious dining room with an intimate ambience. The service is very good.

XXX **Windsor,** Còrsega 286, ✉ 08008, ☎ 93 415 84 83, *windsor@minorisa.es, Fax 93 238 66 08* – ▤. AE VISA JCB. HV b

closed Holy Week, August, Saturday lunch and Sunday – **Meals** a la carte 29/43.

◆ An elegant restaurant with a beautiful interior patio, several dining areas and a private bar. An interesting menu and a good wine-list.

XXX **Oliver y Hardy,** av. Diagonal 593, ✉ 08014, ☎ 93 419 31 81, *oliveryhardy@husa.es, Fax 93 419 18 99,* – ▤. AE VISA. FX n

closed Saturday lunch and Sunday – **Meals** a la carte 31,50/42,50.

◆ A pleasant, modern restaurant serving traditional dishes of the region with, additionally, an elegant bar/night-club where diners may continue their evening.

XXX **Talaia Mar,** Marina 16, ✉ 08005, ☎ 93 221 90 90, *talaia@talaia-mar.es, Fax 93 221 89 89,* ← – ▤. AE VISA. East : by Av. d'Icària KX

closed Monday – **Meals** a la carte 32/42.

◆ In the Olympic Village. An original circular and glazed-in dining area. Creative cuisine.

XXX **Maria Cristina,** Provença 271, ✉ 08008, ☎ 93 215 32 37, *Fax 93 215 83 23* – ▤. AE VISA. HV g

closed Sunday – **Meals** a la carte 31,45/43,15.

◆ A modern-style restaurant a few metres from Gaudí's famous La Pedrera. A pleasant dining room with an interesting à la carte menu.

XXX **Gargantua i Pantagruel,** Còrsega 200, ✉ 08036, ☎ 93 453 20 20, *gipa@gargantuaipantagruel.com, Fax 93 419 29 22* – ▤ GHV c

Meals a la carte 31/43.

◆ Since its relocation the restaurant has expanded in size, and now offers customers classic surroundings and modern decor. The menu includes a selection of dishes from Lérida.

XX **Orotava,** Consell de Cent 335, ✉ 08007, ☎ 93 487 73 74, *nuriaposo@terra.es, Fax 93 488 26 50* – ▤. AE VISA JCB HX j

closed Sunday – **Meals** a la carte 32/49.

◆ A classic-style restaurant close to the Fundació Tàpies with contemporary paintings hanging on the walls and a cosmopolitan menu.

XX **Els Pescadors,** pl. Prim 1, ✉ 08005, ☎ 93 225 20 18, *contacte@elspescadors.com, Fax 93 224 00 04,* – ▤. AE ⓓ ⓜ VISA JCB East : by Av. d'Icària KX
closed Holy Week – **Meals** a la carte 29,95/42,40.
◆ This restaurant has one dining room in the style of an early 20C café-bar and two more with more modern décor. A varied menu of fish and seafood.

XX **El Asador de Aranda,** Londres 94, ✉ 08036, ☎ 93 414 67 90, *Fax 93 414 67 90* – ▤. AE ⓓ ⓜ VISA. GV n
closed Sunday dinner – **Meals** - Roast lamb - a la carte approx. 30.
◆ In a street off the Avenida Diagonal. A spacious restaurant with traditional Castilian-style décor, bar and a wood fired oven for roasting suckling pig and lamb.

XX **Boix de la Cerdanya,** Consell de Cent 303, ✉ 08007, ☎ 93 451 50 75, *Fax 93 451 50 75* – ▤ P. AE ⓓ ⓜ VISA JCB. HX b
closed Sunday – **Meals** a la carte 25,65/31,05.
◆ A bright and airy restaurant with an unusual décor in the style of an industrial building offering Catalan cuisine with a modern twist.

XX **Comerç 24,** Comerç 24, ✉ 08003, ☎ 93 319 21 02, *comerc24@telefonica.net, Fax 93 268 39 57* – AE ⓜ VISA. KX c
closed 2 weeks in December, 2 weeks in August, Sunday and Monday – **Meals** a la carte 18,50/42,50.
◆ A modern restaurant with avant-garde décor offering different menus of creative cuisine. Popular with a younger clientele.

XX **Rías de Galicia,** Lleida 7, ✉ 08004, ☎ 93 424 81 52, *info@riasdegalicia.com, Fax 93 426 13 07* – ▤. AE ⓓ ⓜ VISA JCB. HY e
Meals - Seafood - a la carte 32,71/48,64.
◆ Close to the site used for exhibitions and trade fairs. This restaurant has a bar open to the public with seafood and dining areas on two levels. Good service.

XX **La Provença,** Provença 242, ✉ 08008, ☎ 93 323 23 67, *restofi@terra.es, Fax 93 451 23 89* – ▤. AE ⓓ ⓜ VISA HV y
Meals a la carte 19,70/25.
◆ A modern restaurant near to the famous Paseo de Gràcia. Comfortable and with cheerful décor. Generous cooking at reasonable prices.

XX **El Asador de Aranda,** Pau Claris 70, ✉ 08010, ☎ 93 342 55 78, *asador@asadoraranda.com, Fax 93 342 55 78* – ▤. AE ⓓ ⓜ VISA. JX b
closed Sunday dinner – **Meals** - Roast lamb - a la carte approx. 30.
◆ The standard features of this chain are evident here, with a bar at the entrance, a roasting oven in open view, and two inviting dining rooms with elegant Castilian decor.

XX **Vinya Rosa-Magí,** av. de Sarrià 17, ✉ 08029, ☎ 93 430 00 03, *info@vinyarosamagi.com, Fax 93 430 00 41* – ▤. AE ⓓ ⓜ VISA GX y
closed Saturday lunch and Sunday – **Meals** a la carte 33,97/52,41.
◆ This small restaurant has an intimate and welcoming atmosphere and attractive décor details. Cosmopolitan cuisine.

XX **Gorría,** Diputació 421, ✉ 08013, ☎ 93 245 11 64, *Fax 93 232 78 57* – ▤. AE ⓓ ⓜ VISA JCB. JU a
closed Holy Week, August, Sunday and Bank Holidays dinner – **Meals** - Basque rest - a la carte 34/42.
◆ A well-established and pleasant restaurant with good service. Very good menu and cuisine.

XX **La Llotja,** Aribau 55, ✉ 08011, ☎ 93 453 89 58, *llotja@hotmail.com, Fax 93 453 34 13* – ▤. AE ⓓ ⓜ VISA JCB. HX u
closed Sunday dinner – **Meals** - Meat, braised fish and cod specialities - a la carte 25/30.
◆ A modern restaurant with objects and photos connected with Barcelona's football team. A wide range of dishes and a number of specialities.

XX **Casa Darío,** Consell de Cent 256, ✉ 08011, ☎ 93 453 31 35, *casadario@casadario.com, Fax 93 451 33 95* – ▤. AE ⓓ ⓜ VISA JCB. HX p
closed August and Sunday – **Meals** a la carte 33,40/59,45.
◆ A classic-style restaurant with a bar near the entrance which leads onto three pleasantly-furnished dining areas. Cuisine based on careful choice of quality ingredients.

XX **Anfiteatro,** av. Litoral (Parc del Port Olímpic), ✉ 08005, ☎ 659 69 53 45, *anfiteatrobcn@terra.es, Fax 93 457 14 19,* – ▤. AE ⓜ VISA.
closed 12 to 19 January, Holy Week, 15 to 25 November, Sunday dinner and Monday – **Meals** a la carte 38,10/51,40. East : by Av. d'Icària KX
◆ A modern restaurant with a friendly atmosphere, an abundance of natural light and careful attention to detail. A large fountain adds to the overall charm.

XX **El Túnel del Port,** Moll de Gregal 12 (Port Olímpic), ✉ 08005, ☎ 93 221 03 21, *info@eltuneldelport.com, Fax 93 221 35 86,* ←, – ▤. AE ⓓ ⓜ VISA. East : by Av. d'Icària KX
closed Sunday dinner and Monday – **Meals** a la carte 26,50/32,90.
◆ A traditional restaurant with a pleasant terrace and service in keeping with its category.

XX **Saüc,** passatge Lluís Pellicer 12, ✉ 08036, ℘ 93 321 01 89, *sauc@saucrestaurant.com* – ▤. MC VISA. ✗ GV d
closed 7 days in January, 15 days in August, Sunday, Monday and Bank Holidays – **Meals** a la carte 32,95/43,80.
◆ The couple who run this restaurant, functional in style but with the occasional avant-garde touch, offer a personal slant on regional cuisine based on high-quality products.

X **Nervión,** Còrsega 232, ✉ 08036, ℘ 93 218 06 27 – ▤. AE ⓓ MC VISA JCB. ✗ HV r
closed Holy Week, August, Sunday and Bank Holidays – **Meals** - Basque rest - a la carte 21/43,05.
◆ A small and well-managed restaurant. Delicious traditional Basque dishes and friendly service.

X **Elche,** Vila i Vilà 71, ✉ 08004, ℘ 93 441 30 89, *Fax 93 329 40 12* – ▤. AE MC VISA. ✗
Meals - Rice dishes - a la carte 18,60/26,80. JY a
◆ A welcoming restaurant with service in keeping with its category. Traditional Catalan dishes and a good range of rice dishes.

X **Cañota,** Lleida 7, ✉ 08004, ℘ 93 325 91 71, *info@riasdegalicia.com, Fax 93 426 13 07,* 🏖 – ▤. AE ⓓ MC VISA. ✗ HY e
Meals - Braised meat specialities - a la carte 19,72/27,05.
◆ A well-lit and functional-style restaurant with a charcoal grill offering very good meat dishes at reasonable prices.

𝕐/ **Mesón Cinco Jotas,** Rambla de Catalunya 91-93, ✉ 08008, ℘ 93 487 89 42, *m5jrambla@osborne.es, Fax 93 487 91 21,* 🏖 – AE ⓓ MC VISA. ✗ HV q
Tapa 2,50 – **Ración** - Ham specialities - approx. 10.
◆ A spacious bar with traditional wood décor where customers can sample a good selection of fine hams and other pork products. Beyond the bar there is a dining room.

𝕐/ **ba-ba-reeba,** passeig de Gràcia 28, ✉ 08007, ℘ 93 301 43 02, *btap01@retemail.es, Fax 93 342 55 39,* 🏖 – ▤. AE ⓓ MC VISA. ✗ JX z
Tapa 3,50 – **Ración** approx. 8.
◆ In one of the tourist areas of Barcelona near the Plaza Catalunya square. A good range of tapas and a variety of other dishes. Popular with a younger clientele.

𝕐/ **El Trobador,** Enric Granados 122, ✉ 08008, ℘ 93 416 00 57, *Fax 93 238 61 45* – ▤. AE ⓓ MC VISA HV a
Tapa 3,25 – **Ración** approx. 20.
◆ A spacious and comfortable restaurant with tasteful décor and the kitchen in full view. A great variety of delicious tapas.

𝕐/ **Txapela,** passeig de Gràcia 8-10, ✉ 08007, ℘ 93 412 02 89, *Fax 93 412 24 78,* 🏖 – ▤. AE ⓓ MC VISA JCB JV s
Tapa 1,50 - Basque tapas.
◆ A Basque-style bar and restaurant situated on the Paseo de Gràcia. Spacious and with a pleasant terrace.

𝕐/ **Cervecería Catalana,** Mallorca 236, ✉ 08008, ℘ 93 216 03 68, *jahumada@62online.com, Fax 93 488 17 97,* 🏖 – ▤. AE ⓓ MC VISA JCB. ✗ HV e
Tapa 3 – **Ración** approx. 5.
◆ A bar specialising in different beers with wood décor and a wide range of well-presented tapas made from carefully selected ingredients.

North of Av. Diagonal : Via Augusta, Capità Arenas, Ronda General Mitre, Passeig de la Bonanova, Av. de Pedralbes

🏨 **G.H.La Florida** 🐌, carret. Vallvidrera al Tibidabo 83-93, ✉ 08035, ℘ 93 259 30 00, *reservas@hotellaflorida.com, Fax 93 259 30 01,* ≤ city and El Vallès, 🏖, Fб, 🏊, 🏊, 🌳 – 🛗, ✗ rm, ▤ 📺 🚗 – 🏛 25/80. AE ⓓ MC VISA. ✗ rest North-West : by Via Augusta EU
L'Orangerie : **Meals** a la carte 45,50/54,50 – ☕ 25 – **55 rm** 310, 19 suites.
◆ This deluxe hotel on top of Mount Tibidabo carries the signature of the world's leading interior designers, as witnessed in the subtle combination of elegance, the avant-garde, and high levels of comfort. Superb views from the attractively laid-out restaurant.

🏨 **Sansi Pedralbes,** av. Pearson 1-3, ✉ 08034, ℘ 93 206 38 80, *sansihotels@iws.es, Fax 93 206 38 81* – 🛗 ▤ 📺 🚗 – 🏛 25/60. AE ⓓ MC VISA. ✗ rest
Meals *(closed Saturday and Sunday)* a la carte 31/52,48 – ☕ 14 – **70 rm** 146/166.
◆ A high-quality and modern hotel close to the famous monastery of Pedralbes. Excellent bedrooms with good furnishings and baths fitted with blue granite. The restaurant offers a good menu of carefully prepared dishes. West : by Av. de Pedralbes EV

🏨 **Hesperia Sarrià,** Vergós 20, ✉ 08017, ℘ 93 204 55 51, *hotel@hesperia-sarria.com, Fax 93 204 43 92* – 🛗 ▤ 📺 🚗 – 🏛 25/300. AE ⓓ MC VISA. ✗ EU c
Meals 19 – ☕ 13 – **134 rm** 168/198.
◆ A modern hotel with a spacious foyer and reception area and comfortable and very well-appointed bedrooms. Large meeting rooms.

Catalonia Córcega, Còrsega 368, ✉ 08037, ☎ 93 208 19 19, *corcega@hoteles-catalonia.es, Fax 93 208 08 57* – ▮ ▤ TV ♿. AE ◑ MC VISA JCB. ✈ HU x
Meals 13 – ☕ 12 – **77 rm** 160/172, 2 suites.
• A modern hotel with pleasant and welcoming rooms with contemporary-style furniture and bathrooms fitted with marble. A rather small lounge.

Balmoral coffee shop only, Via Augusta 5, ✉ 08006, ☎ 93 217 87 00, *info@hotelbalmoral.com, Fax 93 415 14 21* – ▮ ▤ TV 🚗 – 🎓 25/200. AE ◑ MC VISA. ✈ HV n
☕ 11,70 – **106 rm** 175/245.
• A comfortable hotel with professional staff in a traditional style. Well-appointed bedrooms and large function rooms.

Catalonia Suite, Muntaner 505, ✉ 08022, ☎ 93 212 80 12, *suite@hoteles-catalonia.es, Fax 93 211 23 17* – ▮ ▤ TV 🚗 – 🎓 25/90. AE ◑ MC VISA. ✈ FU a
Meals 14 – ☕ 12 – **117 rm** 160/172.
• In a main residential and business district. Functional and elegantly decorated rooms and a restful atmosphere.

AC Irla, Calvet 40-42, ✉ 08021, ☎ 93 241 62 10, *acirla@ac-hotels.com, Fax 93 241 62 11,* 🏋 – ▮ ▤ TV – 🎓 25/30. AE ◑ MC VISA. ✈ GV h
Meals a la carte approx. 28 – ☕ 13 – **36 rm** 154.
• Quality materials, design features and a sense of the functional add to the overall charm of this welcoming hotel. Spacious bathrooms with showers rather than baths.

Turó de Vilana coffee shop lunch only, Vilana 7, ✉ 08017, ☎ 93 434 03 63, *hotel@turodevilana.com, Fax 93 418 89 03* – ▮ ▤ TV 🚗 – 🎓 25/40. AE ◑ MC VISA EU r
☕ 10 – **20 rm** 140/160.
• A charming hotel in a residential area. Good spacious public areas and well-equipped rooms with attractive design details.

NH Cóndor, Via Augusta 127, ✉ 08006, ☎ 93 209 45 11, *nhcondor@nh-hoteles.es, Fax 93 202 27 13* – ▮ ▤ TV – 🎓 25/50. AE ◑ MC VISA. ✈ GU z
Meals *(closed August, Saturday and Sunday)* a la carte approx. 27,50 – ☕ 12,90 – **66 rm** 141/170, 12 suites.
• A functional and comfortable hotel with all the characteristic style of this hotel chain. Modern furnishings and wood décor creating an intimate atmosphere.

St. Gervasi, Sant Gervasi de Cassoles 26, ✉ 08022, ☎ 93 253 17 40, *stgervasi.booking@hoteles-silken.com, Fax 93 253 17 41* – ▮ ▤ TV ♿ 🚗 – 🎓 25/50. AE ◑ MC VISA. ✈ GU e
Meals 13,82 – ☕ 10 – **51 rm** 150/180.
• A comfortable and well-managed hotel with carpeted bedrooms, functional furniture in light tones and fully-fitted bathrooms.

Husa Pedralbes coffee shop dinner only, Fontcuberta 4, ✉ 08034, ☎ 93 203 71 12, *nhpedralbes@nh-hoteles.es, Fax 93 205 70 65* – ▮ ▤ TV. AE ◑ MC VISA JCB. ✈ EV b
☕ 11 – **30 rm** 130/160.
• A hotel with all the characteristic style of this hotel chain situated in a residential area. Functional, modern, light and airy rooms with pleasant décor.

Victoria H. Suites, Beltran i Rózpide 7-9, ✉ 08034, ☎ 93 206 99 00, *victoria@hotelvictoriabarcelona.com, Fax 93 280 52 67,* 🏊 – ▮ ▤ TV 🚗. AE ◑ MC VISA. ✈ EX z
Meals 20 – ☕ 12 – **67 rm** 145/170, 7 suites.
• A classic-style hotel with a welcoming atmosphere and comfortable well-furnished bedrooms and bathrooms fitted with marble. A pleasant restaurant with attractive décor.

Covadonga without rest, av. Diagonal 596, ✉ 08021, ☎ 93 209 55 11, *covadonga@hcchotels.com, Fax 93 209 58 33* – ▮ ▤ TV. AE ◑ MC VISA. ✈ GV v
☕ 14,40 – **101 rm** 160/200.
• A hotel in a classic early-20C building. Comfortable and with an intimate atmosphere and light and airy bedrooms.

Condado without rest, Aribau 201, ✉ 08021, ☎ 93 200 23 11, *hotel@condadohotel.com, Fax 93 200 25 86* – ▮ ▤ TV ♿. AE ◑ MC VISA. ✈ GV g
☕ 10 – **81 rm** 105/130.
• In the central business district of the city, with a luxurious marble-fitted entrance and functional rooms with little details that make your stay that bit more pleasant.

Catalonia Albéniz coffee shop dinner only, Aragó 591, ✉ 08026, ☎ 93 265 26 26, *albeniz@hoteles-catalonia.es, Fax 93 265 40 07* – ▮ ▤ TV ♿ – 🎓 25/40. AE ◑ MC VISA. ✈ North-East : by Gran Via de les Corts Catalanes HX
☕ 9 – **47 rm** 122/140.
• Very close to the Sagrada Familia church. Pleasant social areas and modern bedrooms with standard furniture in the characteristic style of this hotel chain.

Colors without rest, Campoamor 79, ✉ 08031, ☎ 93 274 99 20, *gruptravi@hotelcolors.com, Fax 93 427 42 20* – |♦| ▤ TV. AE ⓓ ⓜ VISA. ✻ North : by Padilla JU
25 rm ☐ 78/104.
♦ An intimate little hotel in the Horta area. Basic but pleasant with simple décor which changes in colour from floor to floor. Friendly service.

Neichel, Beltran i Rózpide 1, ✉ 08034, ☎ 93 203 84 08, *neichel@relaischateaux.com, Fax 93 205 63 69* – ▤. AE ⓓ ⓜ VISA JCB. ✻ EX z
closed August, Sunday and Monday – **Meals** 54 and a la carte 49/62.
♦ Creative and innovative cuisine to satisfy even the most demanding palate. An elegant and pleasant restaurant with a garden.
Spec. Las tres pequeñas ensaladas mediterráneas, mar, montaña y huerto. Cuscus de pisto y salvia, gambas salteadas, jugo de ave al Forum. Strudel crujiente de higos a la canela y Streusel, compota de ruibarbo Sechuan.

Via Veneto, Ganduxer 10, ✉ 08021, ☎ 93 200 72 44, *pmonje@adam.es, Fax 93 201 60 95* – ▤. AE ⓓ ⓜ VISA. ✻ FV e
closed 1 to 20 August, Saturday lunch and Sunday – **Meals** 58 and a la carte 46,01/55,21.
♦ A restaurant with elegant Belle Epoque décor and impeccable service with an interesting menu. A highly professional staff.
Spec. Huevos escalfados con caviar sobre crema de patatas al azafrán. Lomo de rape dorado al horno con arroz negro y calamares. Crujiente de oliva arbequina con muselina de chocolate blanco y helado de vino dulce.

Jean Luc Figueras, Santa Teresa 10, ✉ 08012, ☎ 93 415 28 77, *jlfigueras@infonegocio.com, Fax 93 218 92 62* – ▤. AE ⓓ ⓜ VISA JCB. ✻ HV z
closed Sunday – **Meals** 67 and a la carte 48/68.
♦ A very pleasant setting in which to enjoy creative and innovative dishes. Several elegant dining areas and décor with exquisitely tasteful design details.
Spec. Coca de caballa, foie ahumado, mango y salsa de coco al curry. Múrgulas a la crema con foie (spring). Lubina de playa, crujiente de butifarra negra, erizos de mar y salsa de pan tostado.

Reno, Tuset 27, ✉ 08006, ☎ 93 200 91 29, *reno@restaurantreno.com, Fax 93 414 41 14* – ▤. AE ⓓ ⓜ VISA. ✻ GV r
closed August, Saturday lunch and Sunday – **Meals** a la carte 44/58,10.
♦ A traditional-style restaurant with a welcoming atmosphere and a menu firmly rooted in the gastronomic culture of the region but with a modern twist. A very good wine-list.

Gaig, passeig de Maragall 402, ✉ 08031, ☎ 93 429 10 17, *RTGAIG@teleline.es, Fax 93 429 70 02,* ☂ – ▤. AE ⓓ ⓜ VISA JCB. ✻
closed Christmas, Holy Week, 3 weeks in August, Monday and Bank Holidays dinner – **Meals** 67,31 and a la carte 38,88/58,80. North : by Travessera de Gràcia HU
♦ Modern style décor incorporating lots of wood and excellent service. Very creative cuisine.
Spec. Gambas de Palamós escalfadas con lasaña de judías verdes y jamón ibérico. Cochinillo lechal crujiente y alubias blancas del Ganxet. La innovación de la crema catalana.

Botafumeiro, Gran de Gràcia 81, ✉ 08012, ☎ 93 218 42 30, *info@botafumeiro.es, Fax 93 415 58 48* – ▤. AE ⓓ ⓜ VISA JCB. ✻ HU v
Meals - Seafood - a la carte 34,75/50.
♦ A well-known restaurant in the Gràcia district of the city with a maritime feel to it and a menu to match.

El Racó d'en Freixa, Sant Elíes 22, ✉ 08006, ☎ 93 209 75 59, *freixa@chi.es, Fax 93 209 79 18* – ▤. AE ⓓ ⓜ VISA. ✻ GU h
closed Holy Week, August, Monday and Bank Holidays dinner – **Meals** 60,70 and a la carte 48,50/57,50.
♦ An intimate and welcoming restaurant with a neo-rustic feel. Family run and with a creative menu.
Spec. Sobre una tostada de pan con tomate, conejo sofrito y hierbas grasas. Liebre a la royal (winter). Sopa instant de frutas con nata y especias (spring-summer).

El Trapío, Esperanza 25, ✉ 08017, ☎ 93 211 58 17, *Fax 93 417 10 37,* ☂ – ▤. AE ⓓ ⓜ VISA. ✻ EU t
closed Sunday dinner – **Meals** a la carte 19/27,19.
♦ A restaurant in a house with a rather aristocratic feel to it. An attractive dining room, a spacious function room and a pleasant terrace.

Can Cortada, av. de l'Estatut de Catalunya, ✉ 08035, ☎ 93 427 23 15, *gruptravi@cancortada.com, Fax 93 427 02 94,* ☂ – |♦| ▤ P. AE ⓓ ⓜ VISA. ✻
Meals a la carte approx. 26,23. North : by Padilla JU
♦ A restaurant in an old Catalan farmhouse with stone walls and wooden beams. A pleasant atmosphere and good regional cooking.

XX **El Asador de Aranda,** av. del Tibidabo 31, ✉ 08022, ☎ 93 417 01 15, *Fax 93 212 24 82,* – ▤ P. AE ⓓ MC VISA. North-West : by Balmes FU
closed Sunday dinner – **Meals** - Roast lamb - a la carte approx. 30.
♦ A wonderful setting in the Modernist Casa Roviralta. Traditional Castilian cooking with very good suckling pig and young lamb.

XX **Roig Robí,** Sèneca 20, ✉ 08006, ☎ 93 218 92 22, *roigrobi@roigrobi.com, Fax 93 415 78 42,* – ▤. AE ⓓ MC VISA JCB. HV c
closed 3 weeks in August, Saturday lunch and Sunday – **Meals** a la carte 43/65.
♦ A modern restaurant in a splendid setting with a pleasant garden-terrace. A very varied and original menu.

XX **Tram-Tram,** Major de Sarrià 121, ✉ 08017, ☎ 93 204 85 18, – ▤. AE ⓓ MC VISA. EU d
closed 23 to 31 December, Holy Week, 15 days in August, Sunday and Monday – **Meals** a la carte 43/53.
♦ An intimate and welcoming restaurant in a historic residential building in an uptown area of the city. Creative and innovative contemporary cuisine.

XX **St. Rémy,** Iradier 12, ✉ 08017, ☎ 93 418 75 04, *Fax 93 434 04 34* – ▤. AE ⓓ MC VISA JCB EU n
closed Sunday dinner – **Meals** a la carte 17,75/29,31.
♦ A restaurant on two levels with two spacious and well-lit dining rooms and wicker furniture. Catalan dishes at reasonable prices.

XX **Hisop,** passatge de Marimon 9, ✉ 08021, ☎ 93 241 32 33, *hisop@hisop.com* – ▤. AE ⓓ MC VISA GV b
closed 9 to 23 August, Saturday lunch and Sunday – **Meals** a la carte 39/63.
♦ A popular restaurant of the district. Minimalist décor with bare walls, good service and very creative cuisine.

XX **Laurak,** La Granada del Penedès 14-16, ✉ 08006, ☎ 93 218 71 65, *Fax 93 218 98 67* – ▤. AE ⓓ MC VISA. HV e
closed 22 December-2 January and Sunday – **Meals** - Basque rest - a la carte 40/44.
♦ A modern restaurant with wood-clad walls and designer lamps. Traditional Basque cuisine. Friendly staff.

XX **Le Quattro Stagioni,** Dr. Roux 37, ✉ 08017, ☎ 93 205 22 79, *restaurante@4stagioni.com, Fax 93 205 78 65,* – ▤. AE ⓓ MC VISA JCB. FV c
closed Holy Week, Sunday and Monday (July-10 September), Sunday dinner and Monday the rest of the year – **Meals** - Italian rest - a la carte 23,60/29,80.
♦ A well-run restaurant with comfortable dining areas with modern décor and a pleasant patio-terrace. Cuisine in the Italian tradition.

XX **La Petite Marmite,** Madrazo 68, ✉ 08006, ☎ 93 201 48 79, *Fax 93 202 23 43* – ▤. AE ⓓ MC VISA. GU f
closed Holy Week, August, Sunday and Bank Holidays – **Meals** a la carte 19,20/30.
♦ A traditional-style restaurant situated in a central business district. A cosmopolitan menu with subtle twists.

X **Vivanda,** Major de Sarrià 134, ✉ 08017, ☎ 93 205 47 17, *vivanda1@yahoo.es, Fax 93 212 48 85,* – ▤. ⓓ MC VISA. EU a
closed Sunday and Monday lunch – **Meals** a la carte 26,50/30.
♦ A restaurant situated in the residential area of Sarrià with a modern dining room, wicker furniture and adequate service. An interesting menu at reasonable prices.

X **OT,** Torres 25, ✉ 08012, ☎ 93 284 77 52, *otrestaurant@hotmail.com, Fax 93 284 77 52* – ▤. MC VISA. HU f
closed Christmas, 3 weeks in August, Saturday lunch and Sunday – **Meals** - Set monthly menu - a la carte 29,45/45.
♦ An intimate and welcoming restaurant behind an unpromising façade. The menu is changed on a monthly basis and offers creative and innovative cuisine.

X **La Venta,** pl. Dr. Andreu, ✉ 08035, ☎ 93 212 64 55, *Fax 93 212 51 44,* – ▤. AE ⓓ MC VISA North-West : by Balmes FU
closed Sunday – **Meals** a la carte 24,50/32,46.
♦ A traditional establishment in a former café-bar. A pleasant terrace beyond which are two dining areas with an old-fashioned feel.

X **La Taula,** Sant Màrius 8-12, ✉ 08022, ☎ 93 417 28 48, *Fax 93 434 01 27* – ▤. AE ⓓ MC VISA JCB. FU u
closed August, Saturday lunch, Sunday and Bank Holidays – **Meals** a la carte 16,66/27,25.
♦ A small, popular and welcoming restaurant with a lively ambience. Unpretentious cuisine at good prices.

X **La Yaya Amelia,** Sardenya 364, ✉ 08025, ☎ 93 456 45 73 – ▤. AE ⓓ MC VISA JCB JU n
Meals - Basque rest - a la carte 20,50/30.
♦ Just a stone's throw from the Sagrada Familia. A basic and friendly restaurant serving traditional Basque cuisine. A good wine-list.

José Luis, av. Diagonal 520, ✉ 08006, ✆ 93 200 83 12, *joseluis@nexo.es, Fax 93 200 83 12,* – ▤. AE ⓓ ⓜⓒ VISA. ✂ HV s
Tapa 1,40 – **Ración** approx. 15.
◆ On the city's main artery. A tapas bar with tables and on the first floor two pleasant dining areas.

Casa Pepe, pl. de la Bonanova 4 ✆ 93 418 00 87, *Fax 93 418 95 53* – ▤. VISA. ✂ FU n
closed 3 weeks in August and Monday – **Tapa** 8,50 – **Ración** approx. 16.
◆ An unusual meeting place where you can enjoy tapas and servings of a variety of dishes or buy gourmet food products in a relaxed and cheerful atmosphere.

Casa Pepe, Balmes 377, ✉ 08022, ✆ 93 417 11 76, *Fax 93 418 95 53* – ▤. VISA. ✂ GU u
closed 16 to 23 August and Monday – **Tapa** 8,50 – **Ración** approx. 16.
◆ A central and friendly tapas bar where you can buy some fine food products. A well-run establishment.

Typical atmosphere :

La Bona Cuina, Pietat 12, ✉ 08002, ✆ 93 268 23 94, *lacuineta@sp-editores.es, Fax 93 315 08 12* – ▤. AE ⓓ ⓜⓒ VISA. ✂ MX e
Meals a la carte 27,65/45.
◆ Friendly and elegant restaurant close to the cathedral. Traditional Catalan cuisine.

Can Culleretes, Quintana 5, ✉ 08002, ✆ 93 317 64 85, *Fax 93 412 59 92* – ▤. ⓜⓒ VISA JCB. ✂ MY c
closed 5 to 30 July, Sunday dinner and Monday – **Meals** a la carte 14/23.
◆ A family-run restaurant going back to 1786. Traditional décor with beams and lots of paintings, creating a welcoming atmosphere.

Los Caracoles, Escudellers 14, ✉ 08002, ✆ 93 302 31 85, *caracoles@versin.com, Fax 93 302 07 43* – ▤. AE ⓓ ⓜⓒ VISA JCB. ✂ MY k
Meals a la carte 27,60/41.
◆ A well-established and very popular restaurant situated in the old town area. Traditional rustic décor with a flavour of the past. Good menu.

Environs

at Esplugues de Llobregat *West : 5 km :*

La Masía, av. Paüsos Catalans 58-60, ✉ 08950 Esplugues de Llobregat, ✆ 93 371 00 09, *lamasia@lamasia-rte.com, Fax 93 372 84 00,* – ▤ P. AE ⓓ ⓜⓒ VISA JCB. ✂
closed Sunday dinner – **Meals** a la carte 25,50/38,25.
◆ This restaurant has traditional furnishings and impeccable service. There are large function rooms and a pleasant terrace shaded by pine trees.

at Sant Just Desvern *West : 6 km :*

Hesperia Sant Just, Frederic Mompou 1, ✉ 08960 Sant Just Desvern, ✆ 93 473 25 17, *hotel@hesperia-santjust.com, Fax 93 473 24 50,* ≤, Fá – |≡| ▤ TV – 🏎 25/450. AE ⓓ ⓜⓒ VISA. ✂
Alambí : **Meals** a la carte 28/34 – ☕ 12 – **144 rm** 170/210, 6 suites.
◆ A hotel in an industrial area on the outskirts of Barcelona. Large social areas and comfortable rooms in a classic modern style. The Alambí restaurant has a good reputation for roast meats which are prepared in a wood fired oven.

El Mirador de Sant Just, av. Indústria 12, ✉ 08960 Sant Just Desvern, ✆ 93 499 03 42, *elmirador@elmirador.org, Fax 93 499 03 42,* ≤ – ▤. AE ⓓ ⓜⓒ VISA
closed 15 to 31 August and Sunday dinner – **Meals** a la carte 28,30/37,95.
◆ A very unusual restaurant housed in a former factory, featuring a spacious and circular dining room with panoramic views.

at Sant Joan Despí *West : 7 km :*

Novotel Barcelona Sant Joan Despí, de la TV3-2, ✉ 08970 Sant Joan Despí, ✆ 93 475 58 00, *H3289@accor-hotels.com, Fax 93 373 52 13,* , ⛱ – |≡|, ⇆ rm, ▤ TV ♿ – 🏎 25/300. AE ⓓ ⓜⓒ VISA
Meals 26 – ☕ 13,91 – **161 rm** 115.
◆ A modern and functional hotel with warm toned décor which creates a welcoming feel. Large function rooms.

Hesperia Sant Joan coffee shop only, Josep Trueta 2, ✉ 08970 Sant Joan Despí, ✆ 93 477 30 03, *hotel@hesperia-santjoansuites.com, Fax 93 477 33 88,* Fá, ⛱ – |≡| ▤ TV ♿ – 🏎 25/90. AE ⓓ ⓜⓒ VISA. ✂
☕ 9,50 – **128 rm** 150/175.
◆ A modern-style hotel with spacious studio-type rooms each with a small kitchen.

at Sant Cugat del Vallès *North-West : 18 km :*

Novotel Barcelona Sant Cugat, pl. Xavier Cugat, ✉ 08190, ☎ 93 589 41 41, *h1167@accor-hotels.com, Fax 93 589 30 31*, ≤, 🏖, 🏊 – |♿|, ⇆ rm, ▤ 📺 ♿ 🚗 – 🏛 25/300. AE ⓪ MC VISA
Meals 22,25 – ☕ 13 – **146 rm** 125, 4 suites.
◆ In a business district with several rooms for conventions and conferences as well as leisure facilities. Comfortable bedrooms but bathrooms rather small. Well-lit dining room with plants.

Girona or **Gerona** *17000 Girona* 574 G 38 122 G 5. *pop. 75 256 alt. 70.*
See : *The Old town (Força Vella)★★ – Cathedral★ (nave★★, main altar★, Tresor★★ : Beatus★★, Tapestry of the Creation★★★, Cloister★) – Museum of Art★★ : Beam Cruilles★, Púbol Altar★, Sant Miquel of Cruilles alatar★★ – Collegiate Church of Sant Feliu★ : tomb★ – Sant Pere of Galligants Monastery★ : Archaeological Museum (Season'stomb)★ – Moorish Baths★.*
Envir. : *Pùbol (Castell Gala Dalí House Museum★) East : 16 km by C 255.*
Girona, Sant Julià de Ramis - North : 4 km ☎ 972 17 16 41 Fax 972 17 16 82.
of Girona, by ② : 13 km ☎ 972 18 66 00. – Rambla de la Llibertat 1 ✉ 17004 ☎ 972 22 65 75 oficinadeturismo@ajgirona.org Fax 972 22 66 12 – R.A.C.C. carret. de Barcelona 22 ✉ 17002 ☎ 972 22 36 62 Fax 972 22 15 57. – Madrid 708 – Barcelona 97.

XXX ✿✿ **El Celler de Can Roca,** carret. Taialà 40, ✉ 17007, ☎ 972 22 21 57, *Fax 972 48 52 59* – ▤ P. AE ⓪ MC VISA. ✂
closed 24 December-20 January, 1 to 15 July, Sunday and Monday – **Meals** a la carte 39,65/62,20.
◆ A well-known restaurant with classic-modern design and stucco walls which is run with great professionalism by three members of one family. Comfortable furnishings.
Spec. Timbal de manzana y foie-gras con aceite de vainilla. Cochinillo confitado con cebolletas caramelizadas con naranja y clavo. Soufflé coulant de chocolate y helado de jengibre.

Roses or **Rosas** *17480 Girona* 574 F 39 122 J 3. *pop. 13 594 – Seaside resort.*
See : *City★ – Ciudadela★.*
Av. de Rhode 101 ☎ 972 25 73 31 otroses@ddgi.es Fax 972 15 11 50.
Madrid 763 – Barcelona 153 – Girona/Gerona 56.

at Cala Montjoi *South-East : 7 km :*

XXX ✿✿✿ **El Bulli,** ✉ 17480 apartado 30 Roses, ☎ 972 15 04 57, *bulli@elbulli.com, Fax 972 15 07 17*, ≤, 🏖 – ▤ P. AE ⓪ MC VISA JCB
April-October – **Meals** *(closed Monday and Tuesday except July-September)* - dinner only - 145 and a la carte 65/82.
◆ A gastronomic mecca in a hidden cove. Rustic and with a beautiful terrace. Highly professional staff and an abundance of imagination.
Spec. Cinta ibérica con buey de mar. Civet de conejo con gelatina caliente de manzanas. Encerrado de chocolate con pimienta de Jamaica.

Sant Celoni *08470 Barcelona* 574 G 37 122 E 6. *pop. 11 937 alt. 152.*
Envir. : *North-West : Sierra de Montseny★ : itinerary★★ from Sant Celoni to Santa Fé del Montseny – Road★ from Sant Celoni to Vic by Montseny.*
Madrid 662 – Barcelona 51 – Girona/Gerona 54.

XXXX ✿✿✿ **Can Fabes** with rm, Sant Joan 6 ☎ 93 867 28 51, *canfabes@canfabes.com, Fax 93 867 38 61* – |♿| ▤ 📺 ♿ 🚗. AE ⓪ MC VISA JCB. ✂ rm
Meals *(closed 1 to 15 February, 27 June-11 July, Sunday dinner and Monday)* 140 and a la carte 88/102 – ☕ 30 – **5 rm** 180/280.
◆ A stone house with an interior where rusticity and elegance alternate. Delicious and imaginative food.
Spec. Cocotte de crustáceos con verduras. Pintada ahumada con frutas a la sartén. Timbal de fresas con sorbete de citronela (spring).

Sant Pol de Mar *08395 Barcelona* 574 H 37 122 F 7. *pop. 2 383 – Seaside resort.*
Madrid 679 – Barcelona 46 – Girona/Gerona 53.

XXXX ✿✿ **Sant Pau,** Nou 10 ☎ 93 760 06 62, *santpau@ruscalleda.com, Fax 93 760 09 50* – ▤ P. AE ⓪ MC VISA. ✂
closed 3 to 23 May, 1 to 21 November, Sunday dinner, Monday and Thursday lunch – **Meals** 89 and a la carte 82/92.
◆ This restaurant's impeccable dining rooms are the ideal place to enjoy the creative and carefully-prepared dishes it offers which are based on local traditional cuisine.
Spec. Sepia hecha justo al punto, almendras tiernas, cacao, judías verdes finas y tacita de caldo aparte (June-August). Merluza de palangre, pan con tomate, crema ligera de ajo y Jerez seco. Postres temáticos en dos servicios.

BILBAO 48000 P Bizkaia 573 C 20. pop. 353 943.

See : Guggenheim Bilbao Museum★★★ DX – Fine Arts Museum★ (Museo de Bellas Artes : Antique Art Collection★★) DYM.

Laukariz, urb. Monte Berriaga-carret de Munguía, North-East by railway BI 631 FYZ 94 674 08 58 Fax 94 674 08 62.

de Bilbao, Sondica, North-East : 11 km by railway BI 631 94 486 96 64 – Iberia : Ercilla 20 48009 902 400 500 DY.

Abando 902 24 02 02.

. Vapores Suardiaz. Bilbao, Colón de Larreátegui 30 48009 94 423 43 00 Telex 32056 Fax 94 424 74 59 EY.

Rodriguez Arias 3 48008 94 479 57 60 bit@ayto.bilbao.net Fax 94 479 57 61 and av. de Abandoibarra 2 48001 94 479 57 60 bit@ayto.bilbao.net Fax 94 479 57 61 – R.A.C.V.N. (R.A.C. Vasco Navarro) Rodríguez Arias 59 bis 48013 94 442 58 08 Fax 94 442 52 56.

Madrid 393 – Barcelona 613 – A Coruña/La Coruña 567 – Lisboa 899 – Donostia-San Sebastián 102 – Santander 103 – Toulouse 449 – València 600 – Zaragoza 305.

Plans on following pages

López de Haro, Obispo Orueta 2, 48009, 94 423 55 00, lh@hotellopezdeharo.com, Fax 94 423 45 00 – – 25/40. AE VISA JCB. EY r
Club Náutico (closed 1 to 15 August, Saturday lunch and Sunday) **Meals** a la carte 34,12/48,64 – 11,50 – **49 rm** 150/197,65, 4 suites.
• An exclusive hotel in a quiet area of Bilbao with elegant décor. Excellent restaurant where the very good service raises Basque cuisine to an art form.

G.H. Domine Bilbao, Alameda Mazarredo 61, 48009, 94 425 33 00, reservas@granhoteldominebilbao.com, Fax 94 425 33 01, – – 25/300. AE VISA JCB. DX a
Beltz The Black (closed 1 to 15 August and Sunday dinner) **Meals** a la carte 38/46,75 – 18 – **139 rm** 215/240, 6 suites.
• This hotel shows the characteristic hallmarks of the designer Javier Mariscal. Modern design details throughout, particularly in the magnificent bedrooms, many with views of the Guggenheim. The restaurant combines subtle decor with contemporary cuisine.

Carlton, pl. de Federico Moyúa 2, 48009, 94 416 22 00, carlton@aranzazu-hoteles.com, Fax 94 416 46 28 – – 25/200. AE VISA JCB. DY x
Meals a la carte 38/46 – 15 – **141 rm** 148/185, 7 suites.
• A historic hotel with a warm welcome and traditional and spacious rooms. Famous guests have included Federico García Lorca, Einstein and King Alfonso XIII. A small but elegant dining room, although its location could be better.

Indautxu, pl. Bombero Etxaniz, 48010, 94 421 11 98, reservas@hotelindautxu.com, Fax 94 422 13 31 – – 25/400. AE VISA JCB. DZ b
Meals (see rest. ***Etxaniz*** below) – 12 – **181 rm** 150/175, 3 suites.
• A modern, functional hotel in a busy shopping district. Well-equipped, pleasant rooms offering high levels of comfort, with one floor reserved for business travellers.

Ercilla, Ercilla 37, 48011, 94 470 57 00, ercilla@hotelercilla.es, Fax 94 443 93 35 – – 25/400. AE VISA JCB DY a
Meals (see rest. ***Bermeo*** below) – 11,50 – **335 rm** 109/137,15, 10 suites.
• In the social, economic and cultural centre of the city. A very well-managed hotel which is ideal for conferences and business meetings.

NH Villa de Bilbao, Gran Vía de Don Diego López de Haro 87, 48011, 94 441 60 00, nhvilladebilbao@nh-hotels.com, Fax 94 441 65 29 – – 25/250. AE VISA JCB. CY n
- *La Pérgola* (closed Sunday in August) **Meals** a la carte 24,70/30,20 – 12 – **139 rm** 148, 3 suites.
• The Villa de Bilbao benefits from all the qualities and facilities associated with this hotel chain. Pleasant, well-appointed rooms with good attention to detail.

Abando, Colón de Larreátegui 9, 48001, 94 423 62 00, abando@aranzazu-hoteles.com, Fax 94 424 55 26 – – 25/150. AE VISA JCB. EY b
Meals (closed Sunday and Bank Holidays) a la carte 30/42 – 10,50 – **142 rm** 82,60/139, 3 suites.
• A functional hotel with good facilities and a pleasant atmosphere in the business and economic area of the city. Traditional, well-appointed rooms, some of which have been refurbished. An à la carte dining room with an intimate atmosphere.

Hesperia Zubialde, Camino de la Ventosa 34, 48013, 94 400 81 00, hotel@hesperia-zubialde.com, Fax 94 400 81 10 – P – 25/300. AE VISA JCB. West : by Juan Antonio Zunzunegui CY
El Botxo : **Meals** a la carte 25,70/40,73 – 10,80 – **82 rm** 128.
• A former school with modern facilities. The restaurant offers both à la carte and fixed price menus. Good views of the estuary.

Barceló H. Avenida, av. Zumalacárregui 40, ✉ 48006, ☎ 94 412 43 00, *avenida@bchoteles.com, Fax 94 411 46 17* – 🅿 – 25/800. AE VISA.
Meals 17 – 12 – **140 rm** 116/145, 3 suites. FZ a
◆ A hotel with a sizeable foyer and a pleasant piano-bar. The bedrooms, along with their highly original bathrooms, combine modern comfort with functional furnishings. A pleasant restaurant with a buffet and cosmopolitan à la carte menu.

Barceló H. Nervión, paseo Campo de Volantín 11, ✉ 48007, ☎ 94 445 47 00, *hotelbcnervion@barceloclavel.com, Fax 94 445 56 08* – – 25/350. AE VISA. EY a
Meals *(closed Sunday)* 16,53 – 12 – **326 rm** 113/166, 22 suites.
◆ A refurbished, classic-style hotel, efficiently managed by friendly staff and mainly geared towards business travellers. A large foyer area and comfortable facilities. A restaurant on more than one level with a large buffet and an à la carte menu.

Jardines de Albia, San Vicente 6, ✉ 48001, ☎ 94 435 41 40, *jardinesalbia@husa.es, Fax 94 435 41 42,* – – 25/100. AE VISA. EY p
Meals (see rest. ***Zuria*** below) – 12 – **136 rm** 130/165, 2 suites.
◆ A functional hotel but one which is very up-to-date both in the level of comfort and the décor. Facilities include a gym and fitness centre.

Abba Parque without rest, Rodríguez Arias 66, ✉ 48013, ☎ 94 441 31 00, *parque@abbahoteles.com, Fax 94 442 21 97,* – – 25/225. AE VISA
10,60 – **171 rm** 96,88, 5 suites. CY w
◆ The hotel's main feature is the attractive minimalism of the reception, piano-bar and lounge areas. Some rooms are traditional in style, while others have a more modern feel.

Tryp Arenal, Fueros 2, ✉ 48005, ☎ 94 415 31 00, *tryp.arenal@solmelia.com, Fax 94 415 63 95* – – 25/65. AE VISA JCB. EYZ m
Meals 10,25 – 10,50 – **40 rm** 112,50/142,50.
◆ This chain hotel is located in Bilbao's old quarter. All the bedrooms have modern bathrooms, although the lounge areas and function rooms are limited in terms of space. The restaurant menu is resolutely based on Basque cuisine.

Miró without rest, Alameda Mazarredo 77, ✉ 48009, ☎ 94 661 18 80, *reservas@mirohotelbilbao.com, Fax 94 425 51 82,* – – 25/50. AE VISA JCB.
12 – **50 rm** 120/170. DX b
◆ Everything here is in keeping with the modern decor, by the Catalan designer Gabriel Miró. A successful combination of comfort and practicality, particularly in the bathrooms.

Petit Palace Arana without rest, Bidebarrieta 2, ✉ 48005, ☎ 94 415 64 11, *petit.palace.arana@hthotels.com, Fax 94 416 12 05* – . AE VISA. EZ b
10 – **64 rm** 85/90.
◆ An old building with vestiges of its past, including exposed beams and the staircase, which combine harmoniously with its unusual minamalist style. Limited communal areas.

Iturrienea without rest, Santa María 14, ✉ 48005, ☎ 94 416 15 00, *Fax 94 415 89 29* – . VISA. EZ e
4,28 – **21** rm 48,23/57.88.
◆ A friendly hotel right in the heart of the old town. The social areas are not very large although the bedrooms are well-appointed and with pleasant décor.

Vista Alegre without rest, Pablo Picasso 13, ✉ 48012, ☎ 94 443 14 50, *info@hotelvistaalegre.com, Fax 94 443 14 54* – . VISA. DZ t
4,50 – **35 rm** 52/62.
◆ A well-managed hotel with functional rooms and standard furnishings. The pleasant, friendly ambience makes this hotel popular with a regular clientele of business travellers.

Zabálburu without rest, Pedro Martínez Artola 8, ✉ 48012, ☎ 94 443 71 00, *reservas@hotelzabalburu.com, Fax 94 410 00 73* – . AE VISA. DZ d
6 – **38 rm** 47/61.
◆ A small, comfortable and friendly hotel with adequate facilities, rooms of varying sizes and a renovated lounge area.

Zortziko, Alameda de Mazarredo 17, ✉ 48001, ☎ 94 423 97 43, *zortziko@zortziko.es, Fax 94 423 56 87* – . AE VISA. EY e
closed Holy Week, 23 August-15 September, Sunday and Monday dinner – **Meals** 60 and a la carte 33,62/49,70.
◆ This centrally located, traditional and elegant restaurant has two dining rooms each with its own ambience. Pleasant décor and furnishings.
Spec. Quinoa y bogavante en risotto con verduras y pequeños mariscos. Bacalao llauna a la plancha servido sobre un pil-pil de hongos, quenefa de puré de patata. Presa de cerdo ibérico asada a baja temperatura con sorbete de melón.

Bermeo - *Hotel Ercilla*, Ercilla 37, ✉ 48011, ☎ 94 470 57 00, *ercilla@hotelercilla.es, Fax 94 443 93 35* – . AE VISA JCB. DY a
closed 1 to 15 August, saturday lunch and sunday dinner – **Meals** a la carte 35,90/52.
◆ An excellent and very well-known restaurant with its own individual style. The décor has a maritime feel and the menu features traditional dishes of the region.

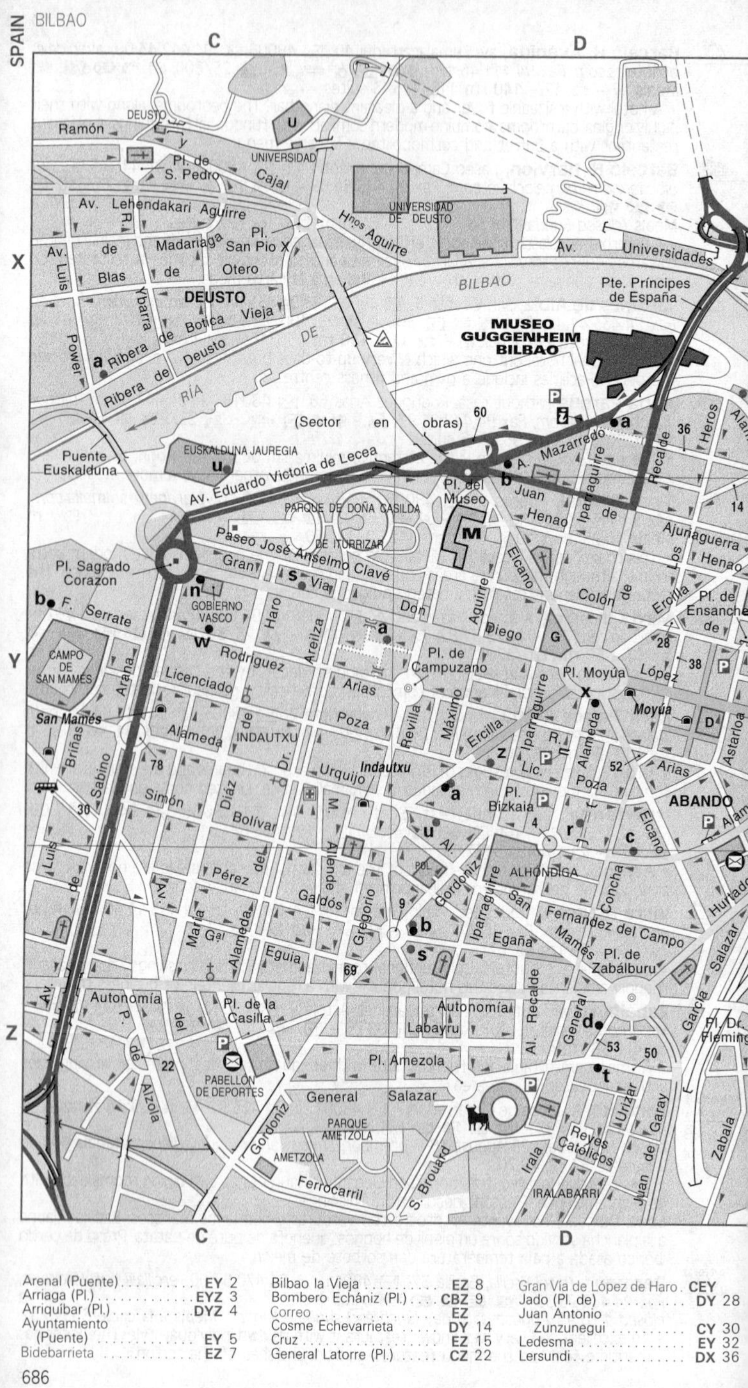
C
D
X
Y
Z
DEUSTO
Ramón
Pl. de S. Pedro
UNIVERSIDAD
Cajal
UNIVERSIDAD DE DEUSTO
Hnos Aguirre
Av. Lehendakari Aguirre
Pl. San Pio X
Av. Luis Power
R. de Blas Ybarra
Madariaga
de Otero
Av. Universidades
BILBAO
Pte. Príncipes de España
DEUSTO
Botica Vieja
Ribera de Deusto
RÍA DE BILBAO
MUSEO GUGGENHEIM BILBAO
(Sector en obras)
Puente Euskalduna
EUSKALDUNA JAUREGIA
Av. Eduardo Victoria de Lecea
Mazarredo
Pl. del Museo
Juan de Ajuriaguerra
Henao
Iparraguirre
Recalde
Heros
Alameda
Los
PARQUE DE DOÑA CASILDA DE ITURRIZAR
Paseo José Anselmo Clavé
Pl. Sagrado Corazon
Gran Vía
GOBIERNO VASCO
F. Serrate
Don Diego
Elcano
Colón
Ercilla
Pl. de Ensanche
CAMPO DE SAN MAMÉS
Rodriguez
Licenciado Arias Poza
Areilza
Haro
Pl. de Campuzano
Pl. Moyúa
López
Moyúa
San Mamés
Alameda
INDAUTXU
Revilla
Máximo
Arana
Briñas
Sabino
Simón
Bolívar
Urquijo
Indautxu
Dr.
Díaz
Pl. Bizkaia
Lic. Poza
Arias
ABANDO
Astarloa
Alameda
POL.
ALHONDIGA
Concha
Hurtado
Luis de
Pérez Galdós
Allende
M.
Av. María
Gal Eguia
Alameda
Gregorio
Gordoniz
San Mamés
Egaña
Fernandez del Campo
Pl. de Zabálburu
Salazar
Garcia
Pl. Dr. Fleming
Autonomía
Pl. de la Casilla
Labayru
Al. Recalde
General
PABELLÓN DE DEPORTES
P. de Alzola
Pl. Amezola
General Salazar
PARQUE AMETZOLA
AMETZOLA
Ferrocarril
S. Brouard
Irala
Reyes Católicos
Urizar
Juan de Garay
Zabala
IRALABARRI

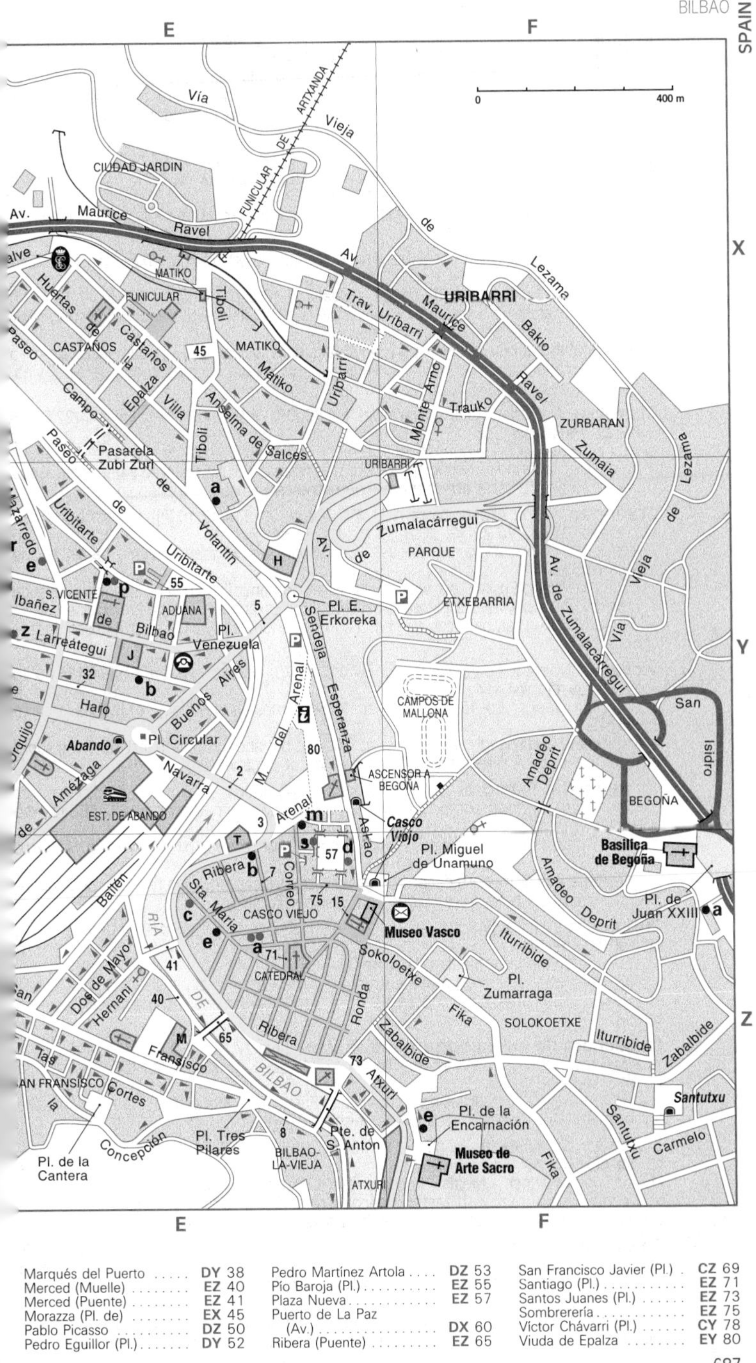

Marqués del Puerto	DY 38		Pedro Martínez Artola	DZ 53		San Francisco Javier (Pl.)	CZ 69
Merced (Muelle)	EZ 40		Pío Baroja (Pl.)	EZ 55		Santiago (Pl.)	EZ 71
Merced (Puente)	EZ 41		Plaza Nueva	EZ 57		Santos Juanes (Pl.)	EZ 73
Morazza (Pl. de)	EX 45		Puerto de La Paz (Av.)	DX 60		Sombrerería	EZ 75
Pablo Picasso	DZ 50		Ribera (Puente)	EZ 65		Víctor Chávarri (Pl.)	CY 78
Pedro Eguillor (Pl.)	DY 52					Viuda de Epalza	EY 80

XXX **Etxaniz** - *Hotel Indautxu,* Gordoniz 15, ✉ 48010, ☎ 94 421 11 98, *reservas@hotelindautxu.com, Fax 94 422 13 31* – ▤. AE ⓓ ⓜ VISA JCB. ✻ DZ b
closed Holy Week, 1 to 15 August and Sunday – **Meals** a la carte 24,81/34,62.
◆ A tastefully furnished restaurant with wooden flooring, where the colour scheme is based on reds and blues. The menu here is a good mix of traditional and innovative cuisine.

XXX **Guria,** Gran Vía de Don Diego López de Haro 66, ✉ 48011, ☎ 94 441 57 80, *guria@restauranteguria.com, Fax 94 441 85 64* – ▤. AE ⓓ ⓜ VISA. ✻ CY s
closed Sunday dinner – **Meals** a la carte 45,75/56,75.
◆ Close to the San Mamés football stadium. A pleasant restaurant with classic elegance and leather covered armchairs.

XXX ✿ **Goizeko Kabi,** Particular de Estraunza 4, ✉ 48011, ☎ 94 442 11 29, *gkabi.bi@telefonica.net, Fax 94 441 50 04* – ▤. AE ⓓ ⓜ VISA. ✻ CDY a
closed 31 July-15 August and Sunday – **Meals** 36,10 and a la carte 38,35/47,45.
◆ Centrally located in a lively area of the city. A comfortable restaurant with friendly staff and decor of the region. Basque cuisine.
Spec. Rodaballo al txakoli con espárrago silvestre y espinaca tostada. Jamoncito de gallo de corral lacado con bizcocho de mollejas y pasta fresca. Requesón con peras al vino, espuma de yogur y jalea de pétalos de rosa.

XXX **Gorrotxa,** Alameda Urquijo 30 (arcade), ✉ 48008, ☎ 94 443 49 37, *Fax 94 422 05 35* – ▤. AE ⓓ ⓜ VISA. ✻ DY r
closed 8 to 12 April, 22 August-6 September and Sunday – **Meals** a la carte 38/49.
◆ An elegant setting for classic cuisine created from carefully selected ingredients. Good service in a comfortable atmosphere. The entrance is through a shopping centre.

XXX ✿ **Etxanobe,** av. de Abandoibarra 4-3º, ✉ 48009, ☎ 94 442 10 71, *etxanobe@abaforum.es, Fax 94 442 10 23,* ≤, 斋 – |‡| ▤. AE ⓓ ⓜ VISA. ✻ CXY u
closed 8 to 15 April, 21 days in August, Sunday and Bank Holidays dinner – **Meals** 39 and a la carte 35/44.
◆ Inside the Palacio Euskalduna, with access via a panoramic lift. The fine interior, furnished in modern style, provides a pleasant backdrop for Etxanobe's innovative cuisine.
Spec. Verduras en tempura con gambas. Lenguado asado con su pil-pil. La mousse de tres chocolates.

XX **Víctor,** pl. Nueva 2-1º, ✉ 48005, ☎ 94 415 16 78, *victor@cyl.com, Fax 94 415 06 16* – ▤. AE ⓓ ⓜ VISA. ✻ EZ s
closed Holy Week, 1 to 15 August, 1 to 15 September and Sunday – **Meals** a la carte 31,43/43.
◆ An intimate and friendly restaurant with a tapas bar and a traditional-style dining room on the first floor. A wine-list with a good range of Rioja wines.

XX **Guggenheim Bilbao,** av. de Abandoibarra 2, ✉ 48001, ☎ 94 423 93 33, *info@restauranteguggenheim.com, Fax 94 424 25 60,* Modern decor – ▤. AE ⓓ ⓜ VISA. ✻ DX
closed 15 days in January, Sunday dinner, Monday and Tuesday dinner – **Meals** a la carte 44,60/52,70.
◆ A restaurant with modern décor in keeping with its location within the famous Guggenheim Museum. Contemporary cuisine and designer furnishings.

XX **Zuria,** Uribitarte 7, ✉ 48001, ☎ 94 424 60 80, *zuria@zuria.biz, Fax 94 435 50 27* – ▤. AE ⓓ ⓜ VISA. ✻ EY p
closed Sunday dinner – **Meals** a la carte 26/32,30.
◆ This restaurant has a separate entrance to the Hotel Jardines de Alba. A spacious split-level dining room with modern décor, a wooden floor and many attractive design details.

XX **La Cuchara de Euskalduna,** Ribera de Botica Vieja 27, ✉ 48014, ☎ 94 448 01 24, *joseba@restaurantelacuchara.com, Fax 94 476 15 59* – ▤. AE ⓓ ⓜ VISA. ✻ CX a
Meals a la carte 45/55.
◆ A busy and lively restaurant near the Palacio Euskalduna. Modern decor, a comfortable atmosphere, with dishes rooted in the cuisine of northern Spain.

XX **El Asador de Aranda,** Egaña 27, ✉ 48010, ☎ 94 443 06 64, *Fax 94 443 06 64* – ▤. AE ⓓ ⓜ VISA. ✻ DZ s
closed Sunday dinner – **Meals** - Roast lamb - a la carte 22,90/30.
◆ A central restaurant with tasteful décor. Three dining rooms with beautiful wooden ceilings and another private room. Delicious roast meats.

XX **Baita Gaminiz,** Alameda Mazarredo 20, ✉ 48009, ☎ 94 424 22 67, *Fax 94 431 81 92,* 斋 – ▤. AE ⓜ VISA JCB. ✻ DX c
closed Holy Week, 1 to 14 September, Sunday and Monday dinner – **Meals** - Cod specialities - a la carte 32,85/40.
◆ A bar for guests at the entrance, a glass-adorned dining room serving traditional cuisine, including cod specialities, and a terrace overlooking the estuary. Small wine shop.

Rogelio, carret. de Basurto a Castrejana 7, ✉ 48002, ☎ 94 427 30 21, *Fax 94 427 17 78* – ▤. **VISA**. ✻ West : by Av. Autonomía CZ
closed 25 July-August and Sunday – **Meals** a la carte 25/30.
◆ A renowned local restaurant accessed through a rustic-style public bar, with a dining room of similar style on the first floor. Simple cuisine based on quality products.

Serantes, Licenciado Poza 16, ✉ 48011, ☎ 94 421 21 29, *restauranteserantes@telefonica.net, Fax 94 444 59 79* – ▤. AE **VISA**. ✻ DY z
closed 26 August-17 September – **Meals** - Seafood - a la carte 39,43/48,85.
◆ Centrally located and with an entrance through a public bar. Attentive service and cuisine based on carefully selected fish and seafood.

Colmado Ibérico, Alameda de Urquijo 20, ✉ 48008, ☎ 94 443 60 01, *colmado@colmadoiberico.com, Fax 94 470 30 39* – ▤. AE **VISA**. ✻ DYZ c
closed Sunday – **Tapa** 1,30 – **Ración** - Ham specialities - approx. 8,50.
◆ A spacious establishment with a bar with a wide range of Basque-style tapas. There is also a dining area with a menu of selected hams and other fine pork products.

Gatz, Santa María 10, ✉ 48005, ☎ 94 415 48 61 – ▤. ✻ EZ c
closed 15 to 30 September, Sunday dinner and Bank Holidays – **Tapa** 1,40 – **Ración** approx. 9.
◆ In the heart of the old town. Excellent management and professional staff. Carefully prepared and well-presented food make this a pleasant meeting place.

Xukela, El Perro 2, ✉ 48005, ☎ 94 415 97 72 – ▤. **VISA**. ✻ EZ a
Tapa 1,25 – **Ración** - Cheeses and patés - approx. 7.
◆ A well-run establishment and a pleasant place to sample tapas. Good atmosphere.

Víctor Montes, pl. Nueva 8, ✉ 48005, ☎ 94 415 70 67, *victormontes.sl@terra.es, Fax 94 415 95 10,* – ▤. AE **VISA**. ✻ EZ d
closed Sunday except December and August – **Tapa** 1,50 – **Ración** approx. 9.
◆ Over a hundred years old, charming and with a Modernist façade and a bistro-like interior. In addition to the bar there is a small dining room on the first floor.

Rio-Oja, El Perro 4, ✉ 48005, ☎ 94 415 08 71 – ▤. **VISA**. ✻ EZ a
closed 12 to 18 April, 24 days in September and Monday – **Tapa** 4,50 – **Ración** approx. 6.
◆ In the old-town area of the city. A recently refurbished establishment which is run professionally and offers good service. Delicious food in a friendly atmosphere.

Donostia-San Sebastián

20000 **P** *Gipuzkoa* 573 C 24. *pop. 181 064 – Seaside resort.*
See : *Location and bay★★★ – Monte Igueldo ≤★★★ – Monte Urgull ≤★★ – Aquarium-Palacio del Mar★.*
Envir. : *Monte Ulía ≤★ North-East : 7 km by N I.*
18 of San Sebastián Jaizkíbel, East : 14 km by N I ☎ 943 61 68 45.
of San Sebastián, Fuenterrabía, North-East : 20 km ☎ 943 66 85 00 – Iberia : Bengoetxea 3 ✉ 20004 ☎ 902 400 500 and airport ☎ 943 66 85 19.
Erregina Erregentearen 3 ✉ 20003 ☎ 943 48 11 66 cat@donostia.org Fax 943 48 11 72 – R.A.C.V.N. (R.A.C. Vasco Navarro) Foruen pasealekua 4 ✉ 20005 ☎ 943 43 08 00 Fax 943 42 91 50.
Madrid 453 – Bayonne 54 – Bilbao 102 – Pamplona 79 – Vitoria-Gasteiz 95.

María Cristina, Okendo 1, ✉ 20004, ☎ 943 43 76 00, *hmc@westin.com, Fax 943 43 76 76,* ≤ – ▤ – 25/300. AE **VISA** JCB. ✻ rest
Easo : **Meals** a la carte 36/56,20 – 21 – **108 rm** 264/481, 28 suites.
◆ San Sebastián's flagship hotel. An early 20C building with a very elegant interior. Magnificent and very well-equipped rooms. A distinguished restaurant with a glazed-in terrace.

Arzak, alto de Miracruz 21, ✉ 20015, ☎ 943 27 84 65, *restaurante@arzak.es, Fax 943 27 27 53* – ▤ P. AE **VISA** JCB. ✻
closed 13 to 30 June, 7 to 30 November, Tuesday except July-December, Sunday dinner and Monday – **Meals** 99 and a la carte 84/96.
◆ Elegant and traditional with a friendly atmosphere. Creative cooking with Basque roots. A treat for all the senses.
Spec. Sopa de marisco en directo. Bonito con ajedrea y espina mentolada (July-October). Tarta de manzana con tapenade de aceitunas.

Akelaŕe, paseo del Padre Orcolaga 56 (barrio de Igueldo) : 7,5 km, ✉ 20008, ☎ 943 31 12 09, *restaurante@akelarre.net, Fax 943 21 92 68,* ≤ – ▤ P. AE **VISA**. ✻
closed February, 1 to 15 October, Tuesday except July-December, Sunday dinner and Monday except Bank Holidays weekends – **Meals** 95 and a la carte 60,50/80.
◆ A house on a hillside with views of the sea. Great professionalism, creative cuisine and very good service.
Spec. Burbujas de moluscos al vapor con salicornia, sandwich frío de foie-gras y su vasito caliente con sopako. Rape mechado de verduras, cintas y glace de las mismas. Pechuga de pichón sangrante con pipas de melón.

Ganbara, San Jerónimo 21, ✉ 20003, ✆ 943 42 25 75, *Fax 943 42 25 75* – ▤. AE ⓞ ⓜ VISA. ✗
closed 15 to 30 June, 15 to 30 November, Sunday dinner and Monday – **Tapa** 1,80 – **Ración** approx. 11,80.
◆ The efficient staff and the quality of the tapas have made this establishment extremely successful. There is a pleasant and intimate dining room in the basement.

Martínez, Abutzuaren 31-13, ✉ 20003, ✆ 943 42 49 65 – ▤. ✗
closed 15 to 31 January, 15 to 30 June, Thursday and Friday lunch – **Tapa** 1,55 – **Ración** approx. 7,80.
◆ This pleasant family-run bar in the city's old quarter has been serving tapas of the highest quality for several generations. One of the city's best-known landmarks.

Txepetxa, Arrandegui 5, ✉ 20003, ✆ 943 42 22 27, *txepetxa1@clientes.euskaltel.es* – ▤
closed 15 days in June, 15 days in October and Monday – **Tapa** 1,60 – **Ración** approx. 6.
◆ A well-established bar renowned for its superb anchovies and other delicious tapas. A relaxed, friendly atmosphere.

Tamboril, Arrandegui 2, ✉ 20003, ✆ 943 42 35 07, *tamboril@teleline.es, Fax 943 43 17 63,* ⛱ – ▤. VISA. ✗
closed 15 days in April, 1 to 21 November, Monday and Tuesday lunch – **Tapa** 1,50 – **Ración** approx. 6.
◆ A selection of quality tapas in a small, friendly and well-maintained bar.

Aloña Berri, Bermingham 24 (Gros), ✉ 20001, ✆ 943 29 08 18 – ▤. ⓜ VISA. ✗
closed 15 days in April and 1 to 15 November – **Tapa** 1,80 – **Ración** approx. 6.
◆ This stylish bar offers a wide selection of Basque-style tapas, including a tasting menu featuring 12 different hot and cold specialities.

Bergara, General Arteche 8 (Gros), ✉ 20002, ✆ 943 27 50 26, *tapasbarbergara@eresmas.com* – ▤. ✗
closed 15 to 31 October – **Tapa** 1,80 – **Ración** approx. 7,20.
◆ This excellent bar prides itself on the high quality of its tapas, which can be enjoyed at the bar or at one of a number of tables.

Lasarte-Oria *20160 Gipuzkoa* 573 C 23. *pop. 18 165 alt. 42.*

Madrid 491 – Bilbao 98 – Donostia-San Sebastián 8.

XXXX ✿✿✿ **Martín Berasategui,** Loidi 4 ✆ 943 36 64 71, *martin@martinberasategui.com, Fax 943 36 61 07,* ≤, ⛱ – ▤ P. AE ⓞ ⓜ VISA. ✗
closed 15 December-15 January, Saturday lunch, Sunday dinner, Monday and Tuesday – **Meals** 97 and a la carte 69/81.
◆ A restaurant in a modern version of the Basque type farmhouse. A large entrance area from which follows an elegant and spacious glazed-in room with pleasant décor.
Spec. Vieiras y ostras en láminas con licuado gelatinizado de su coral. Germinado de cebolleta dulce y anchoa con emulsión de pimiento, patata y tomate. Carrillera confitada con ñoquis cremosos, aceite de oliva negra y crujiente de patata.

Oiartzun or Oyarzun *20180 Gipuzkoa* 573 C 24. *pop. 8 393 alt. 81.*

Madrid 481 – Bilbao 113 – Donostia-San Sebastián 11.

XXX ✿✿ **Zuberoa,** pl. Bekosoro 1 (barrio Iturriotz) - 2,2 km ✆ 943 49 12 28, *Fax 943 49 26 79,* ⛱ – ▤ P. AE ⓞ ⓜ VISA. ✗
closed 1 to 15 January, 12 to 19 April, 15 to 30 October, Sunday and Wednesday – **Meals** 89 and a la carte 60,10/68,25.
◆ A very well-known restaurant with very professional staff. In a 15C farmhouse with a pleasant terrace and elegant rustic dining room.
Spec. Tartaleta de alcachofas y vieiras al aroma de trufa (November-May). Arroz cremoso de bogavante y azafrán. Morros de ternera guisados y asados.

In this guide
a symbol or a character,
*printed in red or **black**, in light or **bold** type,*
does not have the same meaning.
Pay particular attention to the explanatory pages.

MÁLAGA *29000* 578 V 16 124 H 5. *pop. 534 207 – Seaside resort.*

See : *Gibralfaro : ≤★★ EY – Alcazaba★★ ≤★ (Archaeological Museum★) EY – Cathedral★ DY – El Sagrario Church (marienista altarpiece★) DYF – Sanctuary of the Virgin of Victory★ North : by Victoria st. EY.*

Envir. : *Finca de la Concepción★ North : 7 km – The Retiro★ West : 15 km by Av. de Andalucía CZ.*

Málaga, South-West : 9 km ☎ 95 237 66 77 Fax 95 237 66 12 – El Candado, East : 5 km ☎ 95 229 93 40 Fax 95 229 48 12.

Málaga, South-West : 9 km ☎ 95 204 88 44 – Iberia : Molina Larios 13, ✉ 29015, ☎ 95 212 01 97 CY and airport ☎ 902 400 500.

☎ 902 240 202.

to Melilla : Cía Trasmediterránea, Estación Marítima, Local E-1 ✉ 29016 CZ, ☎ 95 206 12 06 Fax 95 206 12 21.

Pasaje de Chinitas 4 ✉ 29015 ☎ 95 221 34 45 otmalaga@andalucia.org Fax 95 222 94 21 and av. Cervantes 1 ✉ 29016 ☎ 95 213 47 30 info@malagaturismo.com Fax 95 221 41 20 – R.A.C.E. Córdoba 17 (bajo) ✉ 29001 ☎ 95 222 98 36 Fax 95 260 83 83.

Madrid 494 – Algeciras 133 – Córdoba 175 – Sevilla 217 – València 651.

Plans on following pages

Parador de Málaga-Gibralfaro, Castillo de Gibralfaro, ✉ 29016, ☎ 95 222 19 02, *Fax 95 222 19 04*, ≤ Málaga and sea, – – 25/60. AE VISA JCB. FY a
Meals 25,30 – 9,70 – **38 rm** 123.
◆ Overlooking the bay and the city lying at the foot of the Alcazaba. An elegant compromise between tradition and modernity in the well-equipped rooms. The restaurant has attractive décor and a refined atmosphere.

AC Málaga Palacio, Cortina del Muelle 1, ✉ 29015, ☎ 95 221 51 85, *mpalacio@achoteles.com, Fax 95 222 51 00*, ≤, – – 25/60. AE VISA JCB. DZ n
Meals 23 – 12 – **197 rm** 135, 17 suites.
◆ Large rooms and good service. A spacious social area and bedrooms which have pleasant modern furnishings. The dining room has a welcoming atmosphere and attentive service and offers a fixed price menu.

NH Málaga, av. Río Guadalmedina, ✉ 29007, ☎ 95 207 13 23, *nhmalaga@nhhoteles.es, Fax 95 239 38 62*, – – 25/900. AE VISA JCB. CZ y
Meals 35 – 12 – **129 rm** 150/175, 4 suites.
◆ Minimalist décor, good furnishings and modern facilities. A spacious foyer-reception and quiet bedrooms.

Tryp Alameda without rest, av. de la Aurora (C.C. Larios), ✉ 29002, ☎ 95 236 80 20, *alameda@trypnet.com, Fax 95 236 81 28* – . AE VISA JCB.
12 – **130 rm** 126/156,50, 2 suites. West : by Av. de Andalucía CZ
◆ A traditional city-hotel, modern and well-equipped with large bedrooms, pleasant furnishings and modern bathrooms. A good breakfast room.

Larios, Marqués de Larios 2, ✉ 29005, ☎ 95 222 22 00, *info@hotel-larios.com, Fax 95 222 24 07* – – 25/150. AE VISA. DY s
Meals *(closed Sunday)* 27 – **40 rm** 115/153.
◆ Elegance and comfort in the heart of the city. Bedrooms have light coloured lacquered furniture and well-equipped bathrooms fitted with marble.

Don Curro coffee shop only, Sancha de Lara 7, ✉ 29015, ☎ 95 222 72 00, *reservas@hoteldoncurro.com, Fax 95 221 59 46* – – 25/60. AE VISA JCB. DZ e
5,50 – **118 rm** 71/103.
◆ A very traditional hotel with a refined elegance. Bedrooms with wood décor and some have been refurbished and are more modern in style.

Los Naranjos without rest, paseo de Sancha 35, ✉ 29016, ☎ 95 222 43 19, *reser@hotel-losnaranjos.com, Fax 95 222 59 75* – . AE VISA.
6,25 – **40 rm** 67,50/98,50, 1 suite. East : by Paseo de Reding FY
◆ Friendly service in this pleasant and well-managed hotel. Attractively maintained and well-appointed bedrooms with marble fitted bathrooms.

California without rest, paseo de Sancha 17, ✉ 29016, ☎ 95 221 51 64, *hcalifornia@spa.es, Fax 95 222 68 86* – . AE VISA.
5,95 – **25 rm** 54,02/78,27. East : by Paseo de Reding FY
◆ In a modernised old house. Small lounges with an old fashioned feel and pleasant rooms. A professionally-run family business.

Don Paco without rest, Salitre 53, ✉ 29002, ☎ 95 231 90 08, *recepcion@hotel-donpaco.com, Fax 95 231 90 62* – . AE VISA.
3,20 – **25 rm** 60,10/90,10. South-West : by Av. Manuel Agustín Heredia DZ
◆ A friendly and well-managed hotel with functional rooms and modern bathrooms around an internal patio.

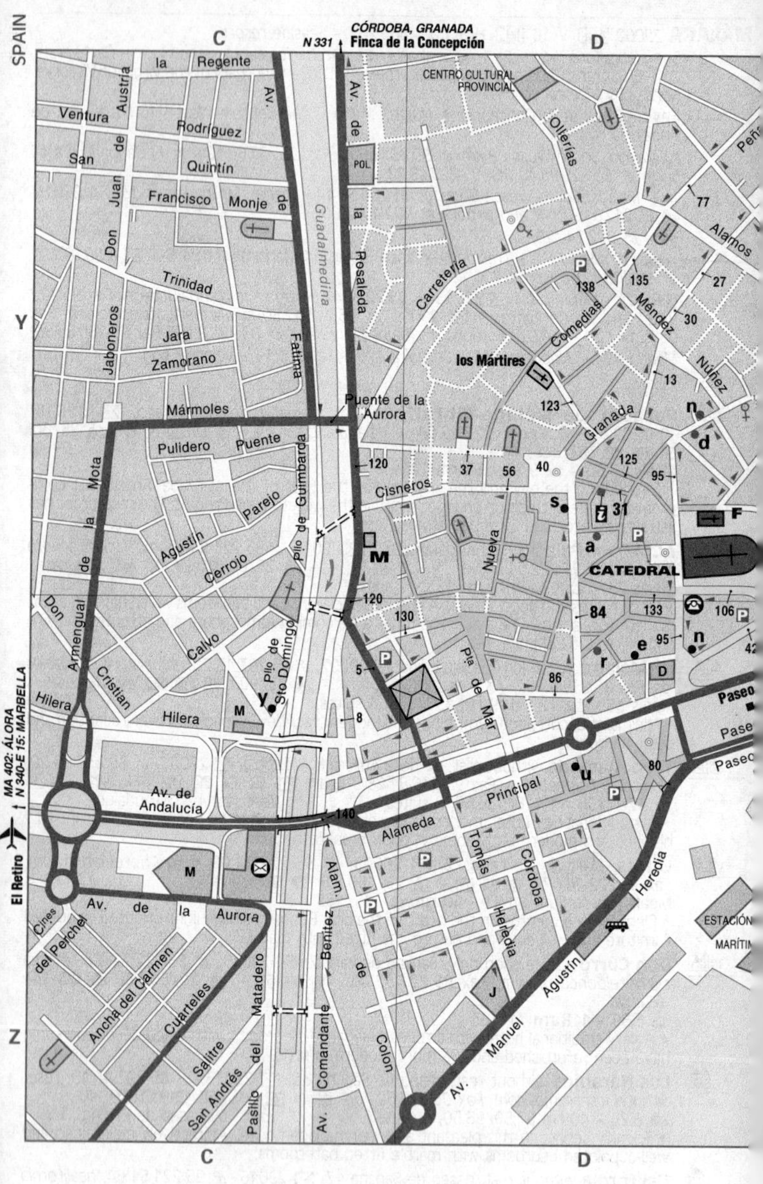

Aduana (Pl. de la) .... DY 2
Arriola (Pl. de la) .... CZ 5
Atocha (Pasillo) .... CZ 8
Calderería .... DY 13
Cánovas del Castillo (Paseo) .... FZ 18
Cárcer .... DY 27
Casapalma .... DY 30
Chinitas (Pasaje) .... DY 31
Colón (Alameda de) .... CZ 32
Compañía .... DY 37
Constitución .... DY 40
Cortina del Muelle .... DZ 42
Especerías .... DY 56
Frailes .... EY 61
Granada .... DEY
Huerto del Conde .... EY 67

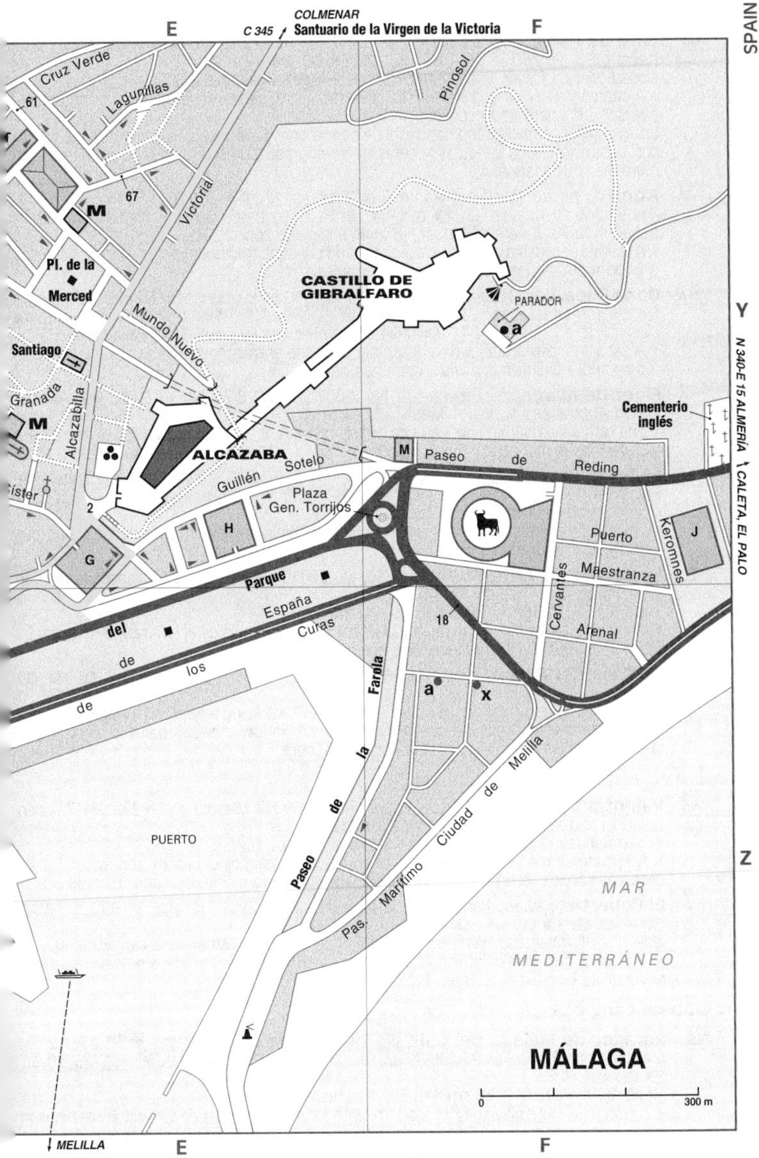

COLMENAR
C 345 Santuario de la Virgen de la Victoria

E F

Cruz Verde
Lagunillas
61
67
M
Victoria
Pinosol
Pl. de la Merced
CASTILLO DE GIBRALFARO
PARADOR
a
Y
N 340-E 15 ALMERÍA
Mundo Nuevo
Santiago
Granada
M
Alcazabilla
ALCAZABA
Cementerio inglés
M
Paseo de Reding
Císter
2
Guillén Sotelo
Plaza Gen. Torrijos
H
G
Puerto
Keromnes
J
CALETA, EL PALO
Maestranza
Parque del España
Cervantes
18
Arenal
de los Curas
de
Farola
a
x
Melilla
de la
de
Ciudad
PUERTO
Paseo
Marítimo
Z
Pas.
MAR
MEDITERRÁNEO

MÁLAGA

0 300 m

MELILLA

E F

Café de París, Vélez Málaga 8, ✉ 29016, ✆ 95 222 50 43, *cafedeparis@rcafedeparis.com, Fax 95 260 38 64* – ▤ . AE ⓓ ⓜ VISA JCB. ✂ FZ x
closed 15 to 31 July, Sunday and Monday – **Meals** a la carte 42/53.
• A charming friendly and well-run establishment with pleasantly elegant décor and attentive service. Imaginative cooking.
Spec. Ajoblanco malagueño con sushi de boquerones y salsa de soja. Carpaccio de gamba con caramelo salado de curry y setas de temporada. Lomo de cochinillo confitado con mermelada de mango.

Adolfo, paseo Marítimo Pablo Ruiz Picasso 12, ✉ 29016, ✆ 95 260 19 14, *Fax 95 260 19 14* – ▤. AE ⓓ ⓜ VISA. ✂ East : by Paseo Cánovas del Castillo FZ
closed 1 to 23 June and Sunday – **Meals** a la carte approx. 30.
• A restaurant with a relaxed atmosphere and pleasant traditional décor with rustic detail. A good menu and a select and regular clientele.

Doña Pepa, Vélez Málaga 6, ✉ 29016, ✆ 95 260 34 89, *donapepa@infhosteleria.com, Fax 95 260 34 89* – ▤. AE ⓓ ⓜ VISA. ✂ FZ a
closed 5 to 11 January, 24 August-24 September and Sunday – **Meals** a la carte 23/32.
• A pleasant restaurant, with a public bar near the entrance, which has several function rooms and a dining room with restrained décor.

Figón de Juan, pasaje Esperanto 1, ✉ 29007, ✆ 95 228 75 47 – ▤. AE ⓜ VISA JCB. ✂
closed August and Sunday – **Meals** a la carte 20,40/28,20.
• The rather unassuming appearance of this restaurant is compensated for by the attentive service. A mid-priced menu of quality dishes. West : by Av. de Andalucía CZ

El Trillo, Don Juan Díaz 4, ✉ 29015, ✆ 95 260 39 20, *chaportorre@hotmail.com, Fax 952 60 23 82,* 🏠 – ▤. AE ⓜ VISA. ✂ DZ r
closed Sunday – **Tapa** 1,80 – **Ración** approx. 8.
• An establishment with a tapas bar and a pleasant dining area with rustic décor. Numerous waiting staff and good service.

La Posada de Antonio, Granada 33, ✉ 29015, ✆ 95 221 70 69, *laposadadeantonio@hotmail.com* – ▤. AE ⓓ VISA. ✂ DY n
Tapa 1,35 – **Ración** - Meat specialities - approx. 5.
• A friendly tapas bar with traditional décor where you can sample a range of delicious foods in a youthful and relaxed ambience. Pleasant staff.

La Casa del Piyayo, Granada 36, ✉ 29015, ✆ 95 222 00 96 – ▤. AE ⓓ ⓜ VISA. ✂ DY d
closed Monday except Bank Holidays – **Tapa** 1,50 – **Ración** - Seafood - approx. 4.
• The same ownership as La Posada and specialising in fish and seafood which is displayed in an original way in a boat. A pleasant atmosphere.

at El Palo *East : 6 km by Paseo Cánovas del Castillo :*

Valentín V., av. Juan Sebastián Elcano 44, ✉ 29017 Málaga, ✆ 95 229 55 17, *valentinv@infhosteleria.com,* 🏠 – ▤. AE ⓓ ⓜ VISA. ✂
closed Sunday dinner and Monday – **Meals** a la carte 26/30.
• A terrace at the entrance with an open grill. The main dining room, renowned for its excellent service, is on the ground floor, with a second dining area one floor up.

El Cobertizo, av. Pío Baroja 25 (urb. Echeverría), ✉ 29017 Málaga, ✆ 95 229 59 39, 🏠 – ▤. AE ⓓ ⓜ VISA. ✂
closed September and Wednesday except Bank Holidays – **Meals** a la carte 23/30.
• This small but well-maintained family-run establishment has a fine wine-cellar to complement its interesting cuisine. Typical decor and furnishings.

at Club de Campo *South-West : 9 km :*

Parador de Málaga del Golf, ✉ 29080 apartado 324 Málaga, ✆ 95 238 12 55, *malaga@parador.es, Fax 95 238 89 63,* ≤, 🏠, ⛱, 🎾, 18 – ▤ TV ♿ P – 🏃 25/70. AE ⓓ ⓜ VISA. ✂
Meals 24 – ☕ 9,70 – **56 rm** 113,30, 4 suites.
• A hotel ideal for playing golf. Modern, with large rooms with décor and furnishings in wood, leather and wicker. Close to the airport. A spacious and airy dining room with large windows and views of the swimming-pool.

at Urbanización Mijas Golf *South-West : 30 km by N 340 :*

Byblos Andaluz 🛇, ✉ 29640, ✆ 95 247 30 50, *comercial@byblos-andaluz.com, Fax 95 247 67 83,* ≤ golf course and mountains, 🏠, Thalassotherapy facilities, 🏋, ⛱, ⛱, 🎾, 18 18 – 🛗 ▤ TV P – 🏃 20/170. AE ⓓ ⓜ VISA. ✂
Le Nailhac *(dinner only, closed 7 to 31 January and Wednesday)* **Meals** a la carte 42/50
- *Byblos Andaluz* *(dinner only)* **Meals** a la carte 36/45 – **108 rm** ☕ 254/312, 36 suites.
• A luxurious Andalusian-style hotel complex situated between two golf courses. Large, comfortable rooms plus a wide variety of facilities and services. The Nailhac restaurant is both pleasant and elegant and has a poolside terrace.

Marbella *29600 Málaga* 578 W 15 124 E 6. *pop.* 84 410 – *Seaside resort.*
See : *City★★ – The Old Town★ – Naranjos Square★ – Contemporary Spain Print Museum★.*
Envir. : *Puerto Banús (Pleasure harbour★★) by ② : 8 km.*
Río Real, by ① : 5 km ☎ 95 276 57 33 Fax 95 277 21 40 – Los Naranjos, by ② : 7 km ☎ 95 281 24 28 Fax 95 281 14 28 – Aloha, urb. Aloha by ② : 8 km ☎ 95 281 23 88 Fax 95 281 23 89 – Las Brisas, Nueva Andalucía by ② : 11 km, ☎ 95 281 08 75 Fax 95 281 55 18.
Glorieta de la Fontanilla ☎ 95 277 14 42 info@turismomarbella.com Fax 95 277 94 57 and Pl. de los Naranjos ☎ 95 282 35 50 info@turismomarbella.com Fax 95 277 36 21.
Madrid 602 ① – Málaga 59 ①

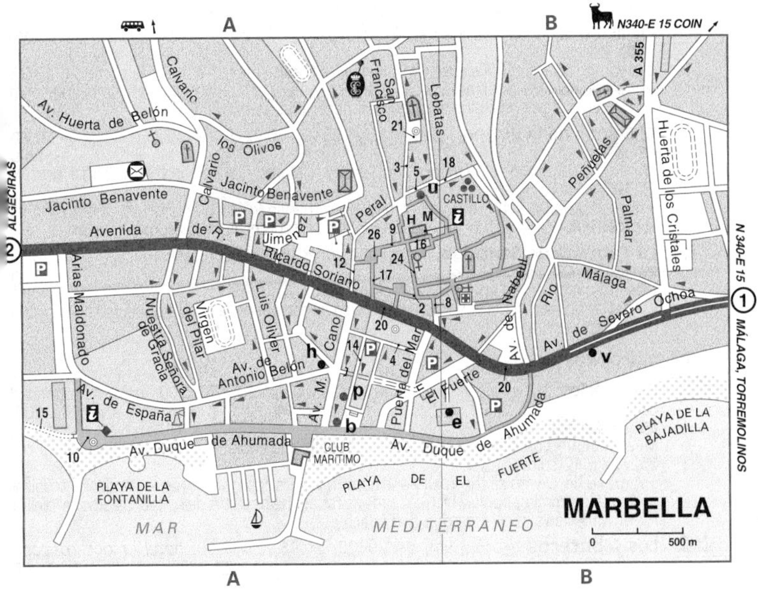

Street	Square	No.
Alameda	A	2
Ancha	A	3
Carlos Mackintosch	A	4
Chorrón	A	5
Enrique del Castillo	AB	8
Estación	A	9
Fontanilla (Glorieta de la)	A	10
Huerta Chica	A	12
Mar (Av. del)	A	14
Marítimo (Pas.)	A	15
Naranjos (Pl. de los)	A	16
Pedraza	A	17
Portada	B	18
Ramón y Cajal (Av.)	AB	20
Santo Cristo (Pl. de)	A	21
Valdés	A	24
Victoria (Pl. de la)	A	26

Gran Meliá Don Pepe, José Meliá ☎ 95 277 03 00, *gran.melia.don.pepe@solmelia.es, Fax 95 277 99 54,* ≤ sea and mountains, – 🅿 – 25/300. AE VISA. by ②
Meals 50 - ***Grill La Farola* : Meals** a la carte 48/59 – 21 – **184 rm** 266/340, 17 suites.
◆ An oasis of peace and beauty beside the sea, surrounded by a carefully tended sub-tropical garden. Excellent, comfortable and well-appointed rooms. The Grill La Farola offers interesting dishes in an elegant ambience.

El Fuerte, av. El Fuerte ☎ 95 286 15 00, *elfuerte@fuertehoteles.com, Fax 95 282 44 11,* ≤, – TV 🅿 – 25/400. AE VISA. B e
Meals - dinner only except July and August - a la carte 32/41 - ***Beach Club*** *(closed January)* **Meals** a la carte 20,75/38 – **261 rm** 116/166, 2 suites.
◆ Pleasant rooms with harmonious décor and social areas designed for relaxation. A good location beside the beach with areas of garden and palm trees. The Beach Club restaurant has a balcony overlooking the sea.

Fuerte Miramar, pl. José Luque Manzano ☎ 95 276 84 00, *miramarspa@fuertehoteles.com, Fax 95 276 84 14,* ≤, Therapeutic facilities, – TV – 25/320. AE VISA. B v
Meals - buffet dinner only except July and August - 31 – **201 rm** 116/166, 25 suites.
◆ Near to the city centre but away from its hustle and bustle. Modern and very comfortable, with a small swimming-pool beside the beach and well-equipped bedrooms. Dining room with buffet service.

Lima without rest, av. Antonio Belón 2 ☎ 95 277 05 00, *LIMAHOTEL@terra.es, Fax 95 286 30 91* – |\$| ▤ TV. AE ⓓ ⓜⓒ VISA. ✂ A h
☕ 5 – **64 rm** 76/99.
◆ A centrally located hotel with a good level of comfort for its category. The small social area is compensated for by the refurbished rooms with rustic décor.

Santiago, av. Duque de Ahumada 5 ☎ 95 277 43 39, *reservas@restaurantesantiago.com, Fax 95 282 45 03,* 🏖 – ▤. AE ⓓ ⓜⓒ VISA JCB. ✂ A b
closed November – **Meals** - Seafood - a la carte 34/42.
◆ This is considered to be one of the best restaurants in the city. Good management and attentive staff. Fish and seafood a speciality. An impressive wine-list.

Cenicienta, av. Cánovas del Castillo 52 (bypass) ☎ 95 277 43 18, *Fax 95 277 43 18,* 🏖 – ⓜⓒ VISA by ②
closed 15 January-15 February and Sunday – **Meals** - dinner only - a la carte 31/48,50.
◆ A small villa with a terrace by the entrance. A very attractive and well-run dining room with beautiful lace curtains and regional decorative details.

El Balcón de la Virgen, Remedios 2 ☎ 95 277 60 92, *Fax 95 277 60 92,* 🏖 – AE ⓓ ⓜⓒ VISA A u
closed 20 December-20 January and Sunday – **Meals** - dinner only - a la carte approx. 27,40.
◆ A restaurant in a 16C building named after the Virgin Mary, an altar to whom is on its façade. Simple and rustic. The secret of this restaurant is its reasonable prices.

La Taberna de Santiago, av. del Mar 20 ☎ 95 277 00 78, *Fax 95 282 45 03,* 🏖 – ▤. AE ⓓ ⓜⓒ VISA JCB. ✂ A p
closed November – **Tapa** 1,50 – **Ración** approx. 6.
◆ A tapas bar with a tile covered façade, a small bar where tapas are displayed and several marble topped tables.

by the motorway to Málaga ① :

Don Carlos 🐌, exit Elviria : 10 km, ✉ 29600, ☎ 95 276 88 00, *info@hoteldoncarlos.com, Fax 95 283 34 29,* <, 🏖, Fö, ⛱ heated, 🌳, 🎾 – |\$| ▤ TV ♿ P – 🏛 25/1200. AE ⓓ ⓜⓒ VISA. ✂
Meals 43,50 - ***Los Naranjos*** *(dinner only)* **Meals** a la carte 39/52 – ☕ 18,60 – **229 rm** 232/271, 12 suites.
◆ A grand hotel with all the luxury and comfort of its category. It has a wonderful tropical area with swimming-pools which extends as far as the beach. A delightful traditional dining room with views of the garden and beach.

Los Monteros 🐌, 5,5 km, ✉ 29600, ☎ 95 277 17 00, *hotel@monteros.com, Fax 95 282 58 46,* <, 🏖, Fö, ⛱, 🎾, 🌳, 🎾 – |\$| ▤ TV ♿ P – 🏛 25/400. AE ⓓ ⓜⓒ VISA JCB. ✂
Meals 42 - ***El Corzo*** *(dinner only)* **Meals** a la carte 48/65 – ☕ 19 – **33 rm** 330, 149 suites.
◆ A tourist complex with a beautiful subtropical garden and elegant social and leisure areas. Good rooms with a high level of comfort. The El Corzo restaurant has a traditional and refined atmosphere.

Río Real 🐌, urb. Río Real - exit Torre Real : 3,5 km and detour 1,5 km, ✉ 29600, ☎ 95 276 57 32, *comercial@rioreal.com, Fax 95 277 21 40,* <, ⛱, 18 – |\$| ▤ TV 🚗 P. AE ⓓ ⓜⓒ VISA. ✂
Meals a la carte 32/42 – **30 rm** ☕ 209/258, 2 suites.
◆ A modern hotel beside a golf course with comfortable rooms and décor by the well known interior designer Pascua Ortega. A pleasant restaurant in minimalist style.

Artola without rest, 12,5 km, ✉ 29600, ☎ 95 283 13 90, *hotelartola@inves.es, Fax 95 283 04 50,* <, ⛱, 🌳, 9 – |\$| TV 🚗 P. AE ⓜⓒ VISA
31 rm ☕ 73/116, 2 suites.
◆ This hotel in a former inn is situated on a golf course and retains its regional characteristics. Good comfort and facilities. Various sports facilities available.

La Hacienda, exit Las Chapas : 11,5 km and detour 1,5 km, ✉ 29600, ☎ 95 283 12 67, *info@restaurantelahacienda.com, Fax 95 283 33 28,* 🏖 – P. AE ⓓ ⓜⓒ VISA
closed 15 November-20 December, Tuesday (except July) and Monday – **Meals** - dinner only in July and August - a la carte 42/55.
◆ A rustic villa which retains all the charm and tradition of another era along with very good and attentive service. Terrace-patio with an arcade.

El Lago, av. Las Cumbres - urb. Elviria Hills - exit Elviria : 10 km and detour 2 km, ✉ 29600, ☎ 95 283 23 71, *ellago@restauranteellago.com, Fax 95 283 90 82,* 🏖 – ▤ P. AE ⓜⓒ VISA. ✂
closed 9 to 23 December and Monday except August – **Meals** - dinner only - a la carte 39,50/43.
◆ In an attractive location on a golf course beside an artificial lake. Attractive dining rooms and interesting cuisine.

Las Banderas, urb. El Lido-Las Chapas : 9,5 km and detour 0,5 km, ✉ 29600, ✆ 95 283 18 19, – P. AE MC VISA.
closed Wednesday – **Meals** a la carte 27/40.
◆ The awkward location of this restaurant is compensated for by its pleasant setting in an attractive house with a terrace and lawn. Good menu.

by the motorway to Cádiz ② :

Marbella Club, Bulevar Príncipe Alfonso von Hohenlohe : 3 km, ✉ 29600, ✆ 95 282 22 11, *hotel@marbellaclub.com, Fax 95 282 98 84*, heated, – TV P – 25/120. AE MC VISA.
Meals a la carte 58/69 – 28 – **84 rm** 370/425, 53 suites.
◆ A classic and very elegant hotel with Andalusian charm, great comfort and attractive beachside areas. The sophisticated dining room has a pleasant terrace.

Puente Romano, 3,5 km, ✉ 29600, ✆ 95 282 09 00, *reservas@puenteromano.com, Fax 95 277 57 66*, heated, – TV P – 25/160. AE MC VISA JCB. rest
Roberto *(dinner only)* **Meals** a la carte 42/53 – 20 – **175 rm** 324/406, 99 suites.
◆ An elegant Andalusian-style complex in a magnificent subtropical garden which lends it a certain intimacy. Bungalow-type rooms that are spacious and very comfortable. The Roberto restaurant with wood décor offers Italian dishes.

G.H. Guadalpín, Boulevard Príncipe Alfonso Von Hohenlohe : 2 km, ✉ 29600, ✆ 95 289 94 00, *info@granhotelguadalpin.com, Fax 95 289 94 01*, – TV – 25/200. AE MC VISA.
Meals - see rest. ***Mesana*** below – 15 – **30 rm** 240/300, 97 suites.
◆ The hotel's pleasant entrance hall leads to an attractive lobby bar to the rear. All the guest rooms are embellished with high-quality, classic furnishings, as well as a terrace. The restaurant offers a varied and cosmopolitan à la carte menu.

Coral Beach, 5 km, ✉ 29600, ✆ 95 282 45 00, *reservas.coral@oh-es.com, Fax 95 282 62 57*, – TV P – 25/200. AE MC VISA.
15 March-October - ***Florencia*** *(dinner only)* **Meals** a la carte approx. 40 – 18 – **148 rm** 235,40/267,50, 22 suites.
◆ A complex designed in modern-Mediterranean style surrounding a central swimming-pool. Comfortable and spacious rooms each with its own balcony and beautiful sea views. The Florencia restaurant boasts an Arab-style watercourse with plants.

Mesana - Hotel G.H. Guadalpín, Boulevard Príncipe Alfonso Von Hohenlohe : 2 km, ✉ 29600, ✆ 95 289 94 00, *info@granhotelguadalpin.com, Fax 95 289 94 01* – . AE MC VISA.
closed Sunday – **Meals** - dinner only - a la carte 47/76.
◆ This fine restaurant has an entrance separate from the hotel. The refined classical-cum-modern style here is matched by the inventive menu created by the renowned chef.

La Meridiana, camino de la Cruz : 3,5 km, ✉ 29600, ✆ 95 277 61 90, *Fax 95 282 60 24*, – P. AE MC VISA
closed 6 January-12 February – **Meals** - dinner only - a la carte 41/60.
◆ A pleasant hotel with elegant décor, attractive conservatory-type lounges and a pleasant terrace with palm trees and ponds.

Villa Tiberio, 2,5 km, ✉ 29600, ✆ 95 277 17 99, *Fax 95 282 47 72*, – P. AE MC VISA.
closed Sunday – **Meals** - dinner only - a la carte 43,40/50,40.
◆ An Italian-style restaurant with an attractive garden-terrace. A traditional dining room with comfortable furnishings and decorative details in refined taste.

El Portalón, 3 km, ✉ 29600, ✆ 95 282 78 80, *restaurante@elportalonmarbella.com, Fax 95 277 71 04* – P. AE MC VISA.
closed Sunday – **Meals** a la carte 42/60.
◆ Restaurant with wood décor in an attractive rustic cabin-style house. A good menu with traditional Castilian roast meats and creative touches.

at Puerto Banús *West : 8 km* :

Cipriano, av. Playas del Duque - edificio Sevilla, ✉ 29660 Nueva Andalucía, ✆ 95 281 10 77, *rtecipriano@infonegocio.com, Fax 95 281 10 77*, – P. AE MC VISA.
closed 6 January-6 February – **Meals** a la carte 37/51.
◆ Magnificent traditional-style restaurant with décor incorporating high quality wood and elegant details. A good bar and a spacious dining room on two levels.

SEVILLE (SEVILLA) *41000* P 578 T 11 y 12. *pop.* 702 520 *alt.* 12.

See : *La Giralda★★★ (✱★★)* BX – *Cathedral★★★ (Capilla Mayor altarpiece★★★, Capilla Real★★)* BX – *Real Alcázar★★★* BXY *(Admiral Apartment : Virgin of the Mareantes altarpiece★ ; Pedro el Cruel Palace★★★ : Ambassadors room vault★★★ ; Carlos V Palace : tapestries★★, gardens★ : grutesco gallery★)* – *Santa Cruz Quarter★★★* BCX *(Venerables Hospital★)* – *Fine Arts Museum★★★ (room V★★★, room X★★)* AV – *Pilate's House★★ (Azulejos★★, staircase★★ : dome★)* CX – *Maria Luisa Park★★ (España Square★, Archaelogical Museum★ : Carambolo tresor★, roman collection★)* South : by *Paseo de las Delicias* BY.

Other curiosities : *Charity Hospital★ (church★★)* BY - *Santa Paula Convent★* CV *(front★ church)* – *Salvador Church★* BX *(baroque altarpieces★★, Lebrija Countess Palace★* BV) – *San José Chappel★* BX – *Town Hall (Ayuntamiento) : east front★* BX – *Santa María la Blanca Church★* CX - *Isla Mágica★ North : by Torneo* AV - *San Luis de los Franceses Church★ (inside★★)* North : by *Bustos Tavera* CV.

18 Pineda, South-East : 3 km ☎ 95 461 14 00.

✈ Sevilla-San Pablo, North-East : 14 km ☎ 95 444 90 00 – Iberia : Av. de la Buhaira 8, (edificio Cecofar) ✉ 41018, ☎ 95 498 82 08.

🚗 Santa Justa ☎ 902 240 202.

i Av. de la Constitución 21-B ✉ 41004 ☎ 95 422 14 04 otsevilla@andalucia.org Fax 95 422 97 53, Paseo de las Delicias 9 ✉ 41013 ☎ 95 423 44 65 Fax 95 422 95 66, Santa Justa station ✉ 41018 ☎ 95 453 76 26 and airport ☎ 95 444 91 28 – R.A.C.E. Av. Eduardo Dato 22, ✉ 41018 ☎ 95 463 13 50, Fax 95 465 96 04.

Madrid 531 – A Coruña/La Coruña 917 – Lisboa 410 – Málaga 211 – València 659.

Plans on following pages

Alfonso XIII, San Fernando 2, ✉ 41004, ☎ 95 491 70 00, *Fax 95 491 70 99*, ⛱, 🏊, – |‡| ▤ TV 🚗 – 🏃 25/500. AE ⓓ ⓜⓒ VISA JCB. ✂ BY c
San Fernando* : Meals** à la carte 36/51 - ***Kaede *(Japanese rest)* **Meals** à la carte 28/63 – ☕ 20 – **127 rm** 347/455, 19 suites.
◆ A majestic Andalusian-style building with a grand and exquisitely tasteful interior with arches, mosaics and arabesques. The effect is imposing and elegant. The San Fernando restaurant has sumptuous décor with a marble floor and attractive glass lamps.

Meliá Colón, Canalejas 1, ✉ 41001, ☎ 95 450 55 99, *melia.colon@solmelia.com, Fax 95 422 09 38* – |‡| ▤ TV ♿ 🚗 – 🏃 25/200. AE ⓓ ⓜⓒ VISA JCB. ✂ AX s
Meals (see rest. ***El Burladero*** below) – ☕ 17 – **204 rm** 194/270, 14 suites.
◆ All the advantages of a central location. Very professional management and service and excellent bedrooms.

Hesperia Sevilla, av. Eduardo Dato 49, ✉ 41018, ☎ 95 454 83 00, *hotel@hesperia-sevilla.com, Fax 95 453 23 42*, 🏊 – |‡| ▤ TV ♿ P – 🏃 25/600. AE ⓓ ⓜⓒ VISA JCB. ✂
Meals *(closed August and Sunday dinner)* à la carte 29,71/45,44 – ☕ 13 – **242 rm** 140/171, 2 suites. East : by Demetrio de los Ríos CXY
◆ In an important commercial and residential district. A pleasant social area, modern meeting room and very well-equipped rooms. Pleasant dining room with light toned décor.

Meliá Sevilla, Doctor Pedro de Castro 1, ✉ 41004, ☎ 95 442 15 11, *melia.sevilla@solmelia.es, Fax 95 442 16 08*, 🏋, 🏊 – |‡| ▤ TV ♿ 🚗 – 🏃 25/1000. AE ⓓ ⓜⓒ VISA JCB. ✂
closed July-August - ***La Albufera* : Meals** à la carte 24,50/39,50 – ☕ 16 – **359 rm** 234/266, 5 suites. South-East : by Av. de Portugal CY
◆ A large and very well-managed hotel which is ideal for conventions and conferences. Comfortable and functional rooms. A pleasant restaurant with a restful atmosphere and subtle décor.

Meliá Lebreros, Luis Morales 2, ✉ 41018, ☎ 95 457 94 00, *melia.lebreros@solmelia.es, Fax 95 458 23 09*, 🏊 – |‡| ▤ TV ♿ 🚗 – 🏃 25/600. AE ⓓ ⓜⓒ VISA. ✂ East : by La Florida CX
Meals (see rest. ***La Dehesa*** below) – ☕ 16 – **431 rm** 234/266, 6 suites.
◆ Well-situated in a popular business district, this chain hotel has excellent facilities which include a floor reserved for business executives with a separate reception.

Tryp Macarena, San Juan de Ribera 2, ✉ 41009, ☎ 95 437 58 00, *melia.confort.macarena@solmelia.es, Fax 95 438 18 03*, 🏊 – |‡| ▤ TV ♿ – 🏃 25/700. AE ⓓ ⓜⓒ VISA. ✂ North : by María Auxiliadora CV
Meals 21 – ☕ 13 – **321 rm** 135/152, 10 suites.
◆ Traditional and spacious public rooms in a hotel with rooms which although not very big are pleasant. Bathrooms fitted with marble. An elegant dining room with classic mouldings on the ceiling, attractive lamps and beautiful soft furnishings.

Occidental Sevilla coffee shop only, av. Kansas City, ✉ 41018, ☎ 95 491 97 97, *reservas-sevilla@occidental-hoteles.com, Fax 95 458 46 15*, 🏊 – |‡| ▤ TV ♿ – 🏃 25/450. AE ⓓ ⓜⓒ VISA JCB. ✂ East : by La Florida CX
☕ 12 – **228 rm** 220, 13 suites.
◆ In a busy commercial district. Very good meeting rooms and large function rooms. Well-appointed and comfortable bedrooms with marble-fitted bathrooms.

Inglaterra, pl. Nueva 7, ✉ 41001, ☎ 95 422 49 70, *hotin@hotelinglaterra.es, Fax 95 456 13 36* – 25. AE VISA JCB. AX r
Meals 30 – 10 – **105 rm** 125,38/156,83, 4 suites.
• A long-established and centrally located hotel with traditional furniture and pleasant bedrooms each with different coloured soft furnishings. The intimate restaurant has subtle décor.

AC Ciudad de Sevilla, av. Manuel Siurot 25, ✉ 41013, ☎ 95 423 05 05, *csevilla@ac-hotels.com, Fax 95 423 85 39,* – 25/150. AE VISA. South-East : by Paseo de las Delicias BY
Meals 25 – 13 – **91 rm** 160, 3 suites.
• A surprising contrast between the grand, historic looking façade and the very modern and functional interior. Quality furnishings in the bedrooms and marble-fitted bathrooms.

NH Viapol, Balbino Marrón, ✉ 41018, ☎ 95 464 52 54, *nhviapol@nh-hoteles.es, Fax 95 464 66 68* – 25/250. AE VISA.
Meals 24 – 12 – **90 rm** 221/243, 6 suites. East : by Av. de Carlos V CY
• A classic NH hotel close to the Santa Cruz district. Good furnishings and excellent facilities. Well-managed by a young, professional and pleasant staff.

NH Plaza de Armas, av. Marqués de Paradas, ✉ 41001, ☎ 95 490 19 92, *nhplaza@nh-hoteles.es, Fax 95 490 12 32,* – 25/250. AE VISA JCB. AV c
Meals 18 – 11,50 – **260 rm** 122, 2 suites.
• A modern hotel situated in the city centre and ideal for business travellers. Very attractive décor. A functional and cheerful dining room decorated with a colourful collage.

Casa Imperial without rest, Imperial 29, ✉ 41003, ☎ 95 450 03 00, *info@casaimperial.com, Fax 95 450 03 30* – AE VISA JCB. CX r
18 rm 220/305, 8 suites.
• A delight. A former palace, now carefully restored with beautiful Andalusian-style patios. Well-appointed rooms.

Bécquer coffee shop only, Reyes Católicos 4, ✉ 41001, ☎ 95 422 89 00, *becquer@hotelbecquer.com, Fax 95 421 44 00* – 25/45. AE VISA.
10 – **137 rm** 165, 2 suites. AX v
• Comfort and tradition in a good location. Carpeted floors and good quality furnishings in large bedrooms with marble-fitted bathrooms. Very professional service from staff.

AC Santa Justa, Luis Fuentes Bejarano 15, ✉ 41020, ☎ 95 426 06 90, *acsantajusta@ac-hotels.com, Fax 95 426 06 91,* – 25/500. AE VISA. East : by La Florida CX
Meals - dinner only - a la carte approx. 26 – 9 – **144 rm** 118.
• The bedrooms, adorned with furniture in cherry tones, are further embellished with green marble bathrooms. The entrance hall and bright lounges provide access to the patio.

Novotel Sevilla Marqués del Nervión, av. Eduardo Dato 71, ✉ 41005, ☎ 95 455 82 00, *h3210@accor-hotels.com, Fax 95 453 42 33,* – rm, – 25/160. AE VISA. rest East : by Demetrio de los Ríos CXY
Meals a la carte 21/31 – 13 – **169 rm** 139/159, 2 suites.
• The Novotel's trademark modern, bright and functional facilities include rooms which all feature a double bed and sofa-bed. Panoramic swimming pool on the top floor.

Las Casas del Rey de Baeza, Santiago (pl. Jesús de la Redención 2), ✉ 41003, ☎ 95 456 14 96, *lascasasdelreydebaeza@hospes.es, Fax 95 456 14 41,* – AE VISA. CV s
Meals *(closed Sunday and Monday lunch)* a la carte approx. 25,70 – 12 – **41 rm** 140/170.
• In a historic building in the city centre. The architecture of the hotel is traditional and the furnishings of good quality. Very pleasant rooms with slate floors.

Las Casas de los Mercaderes without rest, Álvarez Quintero 9, ✉ 41004, ☎ 95 422 58 58, *mercaderes@casasypalacios.com, Fax 95 422 98 84* – AE VISA. BX e
12 – **47 rm** 88/128.
• In the heart of the commercial centre of the city with a pleasant covered patio and bedrooms which are adequately equipped. Those on the 1st floor are particularly large.

G.H. Lar, pl. Carmen Benítez 3, ✉ 41003, ☎ 95 441 03 61, *larhotel@vianwe.com, Fax 95 441 04 52* – 25/300. AE VISA JCB. CX f
Meals 19 – 7,90 – **129 rm** 86,50/120, 8 suites.
• Although the décor is a little dated the level of comfort in this hotel is good and it is well managed. Traditional functionality throughout. A spacious restaurant.

Zenit Sevilla, Pagés del Corro 90, ✉ 41010, ☎ 95 434 74 34, *sevilla@zenithoteles.com, Fax 95 434 27 07* – 25/220. AE VISA JCB. AY a
Meals a la carte 24/37 – 11 – **112 rm** 225/235, 16 suites.
• A modern hotel with rustic furniture. The public areas are adequate and the bedrooms functional and there are three well-equipped function rooms. Good management. The charming traditional restaurant offers interesting cuisine.

SEVILLA

Street	Grid	No.
Agua (Callejón del)	CY	4
Alemanes	BX	12
Alfaro (Pl. de)	CXY	15
Alianza (Pl. de la)	BX	19
Almirante Apodaca	CV	20
Almirante Lobo	BY	21
Álvarez Quintero	BX	22
Amador de los Ríos	CVX	23
Antillano Campos	AX	26
Aposentadores	BV	29
Arco de la Juderia	BY	30
Argote de Molina	BX	31
Banderas (Patio de)	BXY	35
Capitán Vigueras	CY	42
Cardenal Spínola	AV	47
Castelar	AX	55
Chapina (Puente)	AX	59
Doña Elvira (Pl. de)	BX	95
Doña Guiomar	AX	97
Escuelas Pías	CV	112
Farmacéutico E. Murillo Herrera	AY	115
Feria	BV	123
Francisco Carrión Mejías	CV	126
Francos	BX	
Fray Ceferino González	BX	127
García de Vinuesa	BX	130
General Polavieja	BX	135
Gloria	BXY	137
Gonzalo Bílbao	CV	138
Jesús de la Vera Cruz	AV	147
José María Martínez Sánchez Arjona	AY	150
Julio César	AX	152
Júpiter	CV	153
Luis Montoto	CX	160
Marcelino Champagnat	AY	172
Marqués de Paradas	AX, AV	185
Martín Villa	BV	190
Mateos Gago	BX	192
Mesón del Moro	BX	197
Murillo	AV	202
Museo (Pl.)	AV	205
Navarros	CVX	207
O'Donnell	BV	210
Pascual de Gayangos	AV	220
Pastor y Landero	AX	222
Pedro del Toro	AV	227
Pimienta o Susona	BCY	228
Ponce de León (Pl.)	CV	234
Puente y Pellón	BV	242
Puerta de Jerez	BY	243
República Argentina (Av.)	AY	255
Reyes Católicos	AX	260
Rodrigo Caro (Callejón de)	BX	261
Romero Morube	BX	264
San Gregorio	BY	272
San Juan de la Palma	BV	277
San Pedro (Pl.)	BV	286
San Sebastián (Pl.)	CY	287
Santa Isabel (Pl. de)	CV	296
Santa María la Blanca	CX	297
Santa Marta (Pl. de)	BX	298
Santa Teresa	CX	299
Santander	BY	300
Saturno	CV	302
Sierpes	BVX	
Temprado	BY	304
Tetuán	BX	
Tres Cruces (Pl. de las)	CX	306
Triunfo (Pl.)	BX	307
Velázquez	BV	310
Venerables (Pl. de los)	BCX	312
Virgen de los Reyes (Pl. de la)	BX	324
Viriato	BV	329

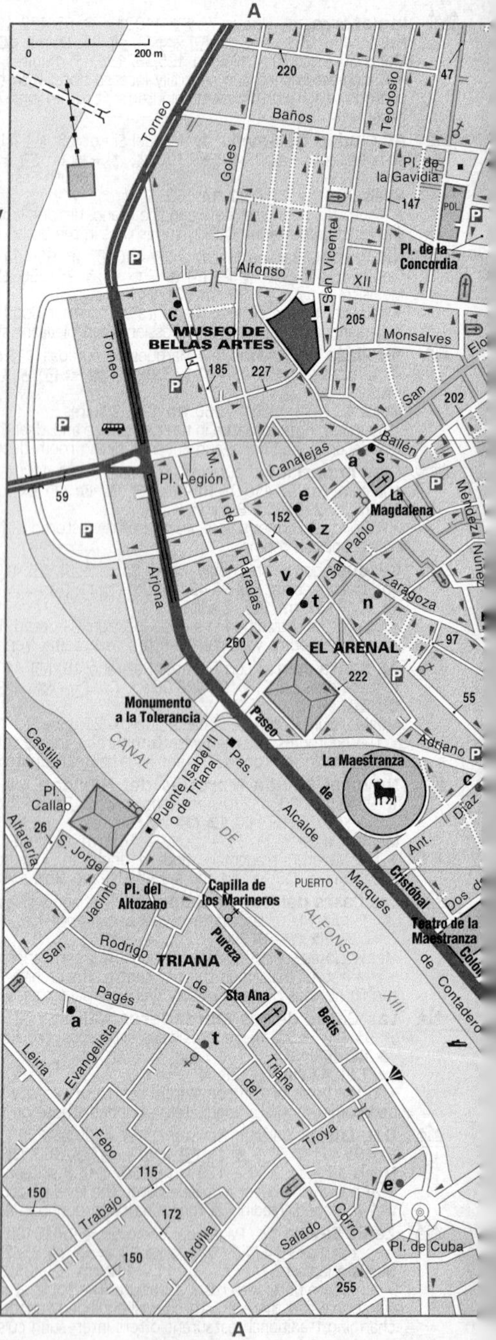

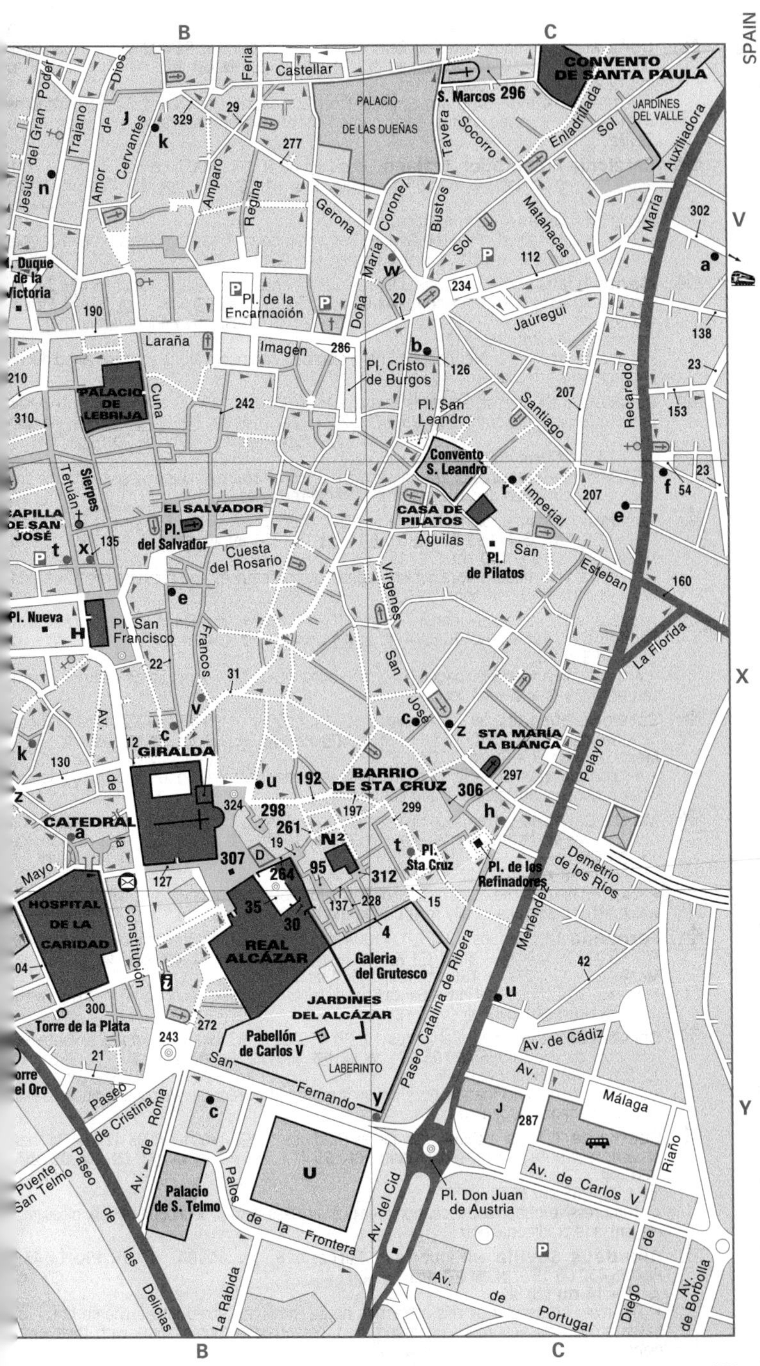

B
C
CONVENTO DE SANTA PAULA
PALACIO DE LAS DUEÑAS
S. Marcos
296
JARDINES DEL VALLE
Castellar
Feria
329
29
277
Jesús del Gran Poder
Trajano
Amor de Dios
Cervantes
Amparo
Regina
Gerona
Doña María Coronel
Bustos
Tavera
Socorro
Enladrillada
Sol
Auxiliadora
Matahacas
María
302
V
Duque de la Victoria
190
Pl. de la Encarnación
20
234
112
Jáuregui
138
Laraña
Imagen
286
Pl. Cristo de Burgos
126
23
210
PALACIO DE LEBRIJA
Cuna
242
Pl. San Leandro
Santiago
207
Recaredo
153
310
Convento S. Leandro
Imperial
23
54
Tetuán
Sierpes
EL SALVADOR
Pl. del Salvador
CASA DE PILATOS
Águilas
207
CAPILLA DE SAN JOSÉ
135
Cuesta del Rosario
Pl. de Pilatos
San Esteban
160
Pl. Nueva
Pl. San Francisco
Vírgenes
La Florida
22
Francos
31
San José
X
Av.
12
GIRALDA
STA MARÍA LA BLANCA
Pelayo
130
192
BARRIO DE STA CRUZ
306
297
324
298
197
299
CATEDRAL
261
19
Pl. Sta Cruz
Pl. de los Refinadores
Demetrio de los Ríos
Mayo
307
264
95
312
127
137
228
15
HOSPITAL DE LA CARIDAD
35
30
4
Constitución
REAL ALCÁZAR
Galeria del Grutesco
Menéndez
Paseo Catalina de Ribera
42
JARDINES DEL ALCÁZAR
300
Torre de la Plata
272
Pabellón de Carlos V
243
Av. de Cádiz
21
San Fernando
LABERINTO
Av.
Torre del Oro
Paseo de Cristina
Y
287
Málaga
Av. de Roma
Puente San Telmo
Paseo de las Delicias
Palacio de S. Telmo
Palos de la Frontera
Av. del Cid
Pl. Don Juan de Austria
Av. de Carlos V
Riaño
La Rábida
Av. de Portugal
Diego de
Av. de Borbolla
C

Doña María without rest, Don Remondo 19, ✉ 41004, ☎ 95 422 49 90, *reservas@hdmaria.com, Fax 95 421 95 46*, ← , – . AE (D) MC VISA. BX u
breakfast 12 – **66 rm** 100/190, 2 suites.
• A traditional hotel with a magnificent terrace facing the Giralda. Grand bedrooms with décor in varied styles each named after a different famous woman from Seville.

Catalonia Emperador Trajano, José Laguillo 8, ✉ 41003, ☎ 95 441 11 11, *trajano@hoteles-catalonia.es, Fax 95 453 57 02* – – 🍽 25/150. AE (D) MC VISA. CV a
Meals 14 – breakfast 9 – **76 rm** 170/195.
• The hotel is named after the famous Roman emperor Trajan who was born in Seville. The bedrooms are functional, well-equipped and comfortable.

Monte Triana coffee shop only, Clara de Jesús Montero 24, ✉ 41010, ☎ 95 434 31 11, *montetriana@hotelesmonte.com, Fax 95 434 33 28* – – 🍽 25/40. AE (D) MC VISA. West : by Puente Isabel II AX
breakfast 8,50 – **117 rm** 107/117.
• A good choice in the ever popular Triana district. Good public areas and restrained décor in an elegant atmosphere.

Pasarela without rest, av. de la Borbolla 11, ✉ 41004, ☎ 95 441 55 11, *hotelpasarela@hotelpasarela.com, Fax 95 442 07 27*, – – 🍽 25. AE (D) MC VISA. South-East : by Av. de Portugal CY
breakfast 10,40 – **77 rm** 108,18/198,33, 5 suites.
• Situated in a quiet area of the city and full of comfortable, traditional style. Rooms are adequately equipped and the décor is to modern tastes.

Catalonia Giralda, Sierra Nevada 3, ✉ 41003, ☎ 95 441 66 61, *giralda@hoteles-catalonia.es, Fax 95 441 93 52* – – 🍽 25/250. AE (D) MC VISA JCB. CX e
Meals 12 – breakfast 9 – **110 rm** 170/195.
• A central and modern hotel which is ideal for conferences and business meetings and has well-appointed bedrooms.

Alcázar without rest, Menéndez Pelayo 10, ✉ 41004, ☎ 95 441 20 11, *hotelalcazar@retemail.es, Fax 95 442 16 59* – . AE (D) MC VISA. CY u
breakfast 8 – **93 rm** 82/103.
• A traditional and well-managed hotel with adequate public rooms. Large bedrooms with carpeted floors and very good service.

Catalonia Hispalis, av. de Andalucía 52, ✉ 41006, ☎ 95 452 94 33, *hispalis@hoteles-catalonia.es, Fax 95 467 53 13* – – 🍽 25/50. AE (D) MC VISA. East : by La Florida CX
Meals 12 – breakfast 9 – **99 rm** 170/195.
• A name evocative of ancient Roman Seville. A modern hotel and good furnishings. Somewhat functional but pleasant and comfortable.

Monte Carmelo coffee shop only, Virgen de la Victoria 7, ✉ 41011, ☎ 95 427 90 00, *montecarmelo@hotelesmonte.com, Fax 95 427 10 04* – – 🍽 25/35. AE (D) MC VISA. South : by Pl. de Cuba AY
breakfast 8,50 – **68 rm** 107/117.
• A restful hotel in the quiet district of Los Remedios. Modern bedrooms with bathrooms which after being beautifully refurbished merit a special mention.

Fernando III, San José 21, ✉ 41004, ☎ 95 421 77 08, *fernandoiii@altur.com, Fax 95 422 02 46*, – – 🍽 25/250. AE (D) MC VISA. CX z
Meals 16 – breakfast 10,80 – **156 rm** 162/180, 1 suite.
• A traditional-style hotel in the Santa Cruz district. Restrained décor and furnishings with good facilities and level of comfort.

Cervantes without rest, Cervantes 10, ✉ 41003, ☎ 95 490 02 80, *hotelcervantes@infonegocio.com, Fax 95 490 05 36* – . AE (D) MC VISA. BV k
breakfast 8,10 – **48 rm** 78/111.
• A small, central and friendly hotel which is managed with pride. Welcoming public areas and comfortable, large bedrooms.

Puerta de Triana without rest, Reyes Católicos 5, ✉ 41001, ☎ 95 421 54 04, *reservashotel@hotelpuertadetriana.com, Fax 95 421 54 01* – . AE (D) MC VISA JCB. AX t
breakfast 1,75 – **65 rm** 65/85.
• An impressive lounge and reception area but with less striking bedrooms. A very pleasant, elegant and traditional hotel.

Amadeus Sevilla without rest, Farnesio 6, ✉ 41004, ☎ 95 450 14 43, *Fax 95 450 00 19* – . VISA CX c
breakfast 7 – **14 rm** 63/88.
• The main philosophy of this attractive house, now converted into a theme hotel, is based around classical music. Soundproofed, personalised rooms, some with their own piano.

Montecarlo (annexe), Gravina 51, ✉ 41001, ☎ 95 421 75 03, *hotel@hotelmontecarlosevilla.com, Fax 95 421 68 25* – AE VISA. AX e
Meals *(closed January)* 17,25 – 9 – **51 rm** 94,50/126.
• Two buildings with one reception area. Very comfortable bedrooms ; those of the annex are more modern than those of the older building.

La Casa del Maestro without rest, Almudena 5, ✉ 41003, ☎ 95 450 00 07, *reservas@lacasadelmaestro.com, Fax 95 450 00 06* – AE VISA. CV b
closed August – **11 rm** 107/134.
• The famous flamenco guitarist Niño Ricardo was born and grew up in this small house, which is nowadays a hotel with individually furnished bedrooms with plush decor.

Reyes Católicos without rest, no, Gravina 57, ✉ 41001, ☎ 95 421 12 00, *hotel@hotelreyescatolicos.info, Fax 95 421 63 12* – AE VISA. AX z
27 rm 94,50/126.
• A charming little hotel with a friendly atmosphere and good management and service. Well-appointed rooms with fully equipped bathrooms.

Egaña Oriza, San Fernando 41, ✉ 41004, ☎ 95 422 72 54, *oriza@jet.es, Fax 95 450 27 27* – AE VISA JCB. CY y
closed August, Saturday lunch and Sunday – **Meals** a la carte 39,44/51,67.
• A distinguished restaurant beside the old city walls with very good food. An attractive conservatory-style dining room with a wooden floor.

Taberna del Alabardero with rm, Zaragoza 20, ✉ 41001, ☎ 95 450 27 21, *rest.alabardero@esh.es, Fax 95 456 36 66* – AE VISA. AX n
closed August – **Meals** a la carte approx. 47 – **7 rm** 195/235.
• Do try this beautiful restaurant in a former palace, now restored. Fine cuisine, exquisitely tasteful décor and very good and attentive service.

El Burladero - *Hotel Melia Colón*, Canalejas 1, ✉ 41001, ☎ 95 450 55 99, *melia.colon@solmelia.com, Fax 95 422 09 38* – AE VISA. AX a
closed 15 July-August – **Meals** a la carte 33,54/42,81.
• A good choice. A restaurant with its own identity despite being part of the Hotel Meliá Colón. A pleasant bull fighting atmosphere and regional décor and cuisine.

La Dehesa - *Hotel Meliá Lebreros*, Luis Morales 2, ✉ 41018, ☎ 95 457 62 04, *melia.lebreros@solmelia.es, Fax 95 458 23 09* – AE VISA.
Meals - Braised meat specialities - a la carte 33/42. East : by La Florida CX
• Traditional Andalusian décor and a pleasant atmosphere. Wooden ceilings and white walls and a small tapas bar. Grilled meat a speciality.

Marea Grande, Diego Angulo Íñiguez 16 - edificio Alcázar, ✉ 41018, ☎ 95 453 80 00, *Fax 95 453 80 00* – AE VISA. East : by Demetrio de los Ríos CXY
closed 15 to 31 August and Sunday – **Meals** - Seafood - a la carte 27/35,10.
• A tapas bar and comfortable dining room with interesting cuisine. Elegant furniture and very good service.

Al-Mutamid, Alfonso XI-1, ✉ 41005, ☎ 95 492 55 04, *modesto@andalunet.com, Fax 95 492 25 02* – AE VISA. East : by Demetrio de los Ríos CXY
closed 15 to 31 August – **Meals** a la carte 22,50/31,40.
• Good food which combines international cuisine with regional dishes. A pleasant restaurant although the tables are a little close together. Very good management.

La Albahaca, pl. Santa Cruz 12, ✉ 41004, ☎ 95 422 07 14, *la-albahaca@terra.es, Fax 95 456 12 04,* – AE VISA JCB. CX t
closed Sunday – **Meals** a la carte 29/34.
• The flavour of good regional ingredients. A fine old house situated in the old part of Seville with a bar and three well-furnished dining areas.

La Isla, Arfe 25, ✉ 41001, ☎ 95 421 26 31, *laisla@restaurantelaisla.com, Fax 95 456 22 19* – AE VISA. BX a
closed August – **Meals** a la carte 31,78/47,53.
• The entrance is through a bar with a refrigerated cabinet displaying seafood. Well-cooked fish, professional service and a pleasant atmosphere.

El Asador de Aranda, Luis Montoto 150, ✉ 41005, ☎ 95 457 81 41, *Fax 95 457 81 41,* – P. AE VISA. East : by La Florida CX
closed August and Sunday dinner – **Meals** - Roast lamb - a la carte 20,30/25,25.
• A restaurant in an old and well-restored Castilian-style palace, with décor that has touches of local tradition. Well-prepared traditional food.

Az-Zait, pl. San Lorenzo 1, ✉ 41002, ☎ 95 490 64 75, *Fax 95 423 36 71* – AE VISA. North : by Torneo AV
closed August and Sunday dinner – **Meals** a la carte 18,15/27,75.
• The Az-Zait's owner-chef has succeeded in endowing this restaurant, spread over several rooms, with characteristic Andalucian style. Impeccable and attentive service.

Casa Robles, Álvarez Quintero 58, ✉ 41004, ✆ 95 456 32 72, *info@roblesrestaurantes.com, Fax 95 456 44 79* – ▤. AE ⓓ ⓜ VISA JCB. ✻ BX c
Meals a la carte approx. 35,50.
◆ A well-known and long established restaurant, popular with tourists. Access to the dining room through a bar. Traditional décor. There is an annex for social functions.

Horacio, Antonia Díaz 9, ✉ 41001, ✆ 95 422 53 85, *horacio@andalunet.com, Fax 95 421 79 27* – ▤. AE ⓓ ⓜ VISA JCB. ✻ AX c
closed 15 August-2 September – **Meals** a la carte 21,35/25,80.
◆ A simple, friendly and well-managed establishment with a public bar and two dining rooms on different levels with wicker furniture.

El Rinconcillo, Gerona 40, ✉ 41003, ✆ 95 422 31 83, *yojamarc@telefonica.net* – ▤. AE ⓓ ⓜ VISA. ✻ CV w
closed 17 July-2 August – **Tapa** 1,50 – **Ración** approx. 3,80.
◆ Professionally run and in the oldest tavern in the city. A pleasant ambience, regional décor and home cooking.

Mesón Cinco Jotas, Albareda 15, ✉ 41001, ✆ 95 421 05 21, *m5jalbareda@osborne.es, Fax 95 456 41 44* – ▤. AE ⓓ ⓜ VISA. ✻ BX t
Tapa 2,50 – **Ración** - Ham specialities - approx. 10.
◆ Centrally located and with a wide variety of tapas and tables to sit at. There is also small dining room.

Modesto, Cano y Cueto 5, ✉ 41004, ✆ 95 441 68 11, *modesto@andalunet.com, Fax 95 492 25 02,* ☂ – ▤. AE ⓓ ⓜ VISA. ✻ CX h
Tapa 1,90 – **Ración** - Seafood - approx. 9,25.
◆ Situated in the Santa Cruz district. Delicious tapas and servings of a variety of fish and shellfish. A public bar and a dining area on the 1st floor.

España, San Fernando 41, ✉ 41004, ✆ 95 422 72 11, *oriza@jet.es, Fax 95 450 27 27,* ☂ – ▤. AE ⓓ ⓜ VISA JCB. ✻ CY y
closed August and Sunday (15 june-15 September) – **Tapa** 1,80 – **Ración** approx. 6.
◆ The tapas bar for the restaurant Egaña Oriza. A large bar filled with a wide range of tapas. A pleasant atmosphere and an attractive terrace beside the old city walls.

José Luis, pl. de Cuba 3, ✉ 41011, ✆ 95 427 20 17, *joseluis@nexo.es, Fax 95 427 64 80,* ☂ – ▤. AE ⓓ ⓜ VISA. ✻ AY e
Tapa 2 – **Ración** approx. 12,02.
◆ An establishment in classic José Luis chain style. A variety of tapas and servings of other dishes or if you prefer choose from the menu offered in the dining room.

Bodeguita Romero, Harinas 10, ✉ 41001, ✆ 95 421 41 78, *sabenye@hotmail.com* – ▤. AE ⓜ VISA. ✻ BX k
closed 15 to 31 August and Monday – **Tapa** 1,80 – **Ración** approx. 15,03.
◆ Well-known and well-established with a large variety of delicious tapas. Very good management in a very pleasant bar.

Albahaca, Pagés del Corro 119, ✉ 41010, ✆ 95 427 41 63, *Fax 95 427 41 63,* ☂ – ▤. ⓜ VISA. ✻ AY t
closed 14 to 31 August and Sunday – **Tapa** 1,80 – **Ración** approx. 7,50.
◆ In the ever popular Triana district. Entrance is through the bar to a large dining room with a welcoming atmosphere where good tapas and other dishes are served.

Casa La Viuda, Albareda 2, ✉ 41001, ✆ 95 421 54 20, *hostelse@eresmas.com, Fax 95 422 38 00,* ☂ – ▤. ⓜ VISA. ✻ BX x
Tapa 1,65 – **Ración** approx. 8.
◆ A centrally located bar with all the atmosphere of a good tapas bar. A wide choice of well made tapas. A lively and youthful ambience.

Mesón Cinco Jotas, Castelar 1, ✉ 41001, ✆ 95 421 58 62, *m5jarfe@osborne.es, Fax 95 421 27 86,* ☂ – ▤. AE ⓓ ⓜ VISA. ✻ BX z
Tapa 2,50 – **Ración** - Ham specialities - approx. 10.
◆ Delicious tapas to be sampled at the bar, on the pleasant terrace or in one of the two dining rooms. A good selection of fine hams and pork products.

Robles Placentines, Placentines 2, ✉ 41004, ✆ 95 456 32 72, *info@roblesrestaurantes.com, Fax 95 456 44 79,* ☂ – ▤. AE ⓓ ⓜ VISA JCB. ✻ BX v
Tapa 1,95 – **Ración** approx. 5,90.
◆ A tapas bar in the style of an old inn. Very good management and a varied choice of tapas and small portions of various dishes.

at Castilleja de la Cuesta *West : 7 km :*

Hacienda San Ygnacio, Real 190 ✆ 95 416 92 90, *reservas@haciendasanygnacio.com, Fax 95 416 14 37,* ☂, ⛱, 🐎 – ▤ TV P – 🎤 25/200. AE ⓓ ⓜ VISA JCB. ✻
Almazara : **Meals** a la carte 29,50/34,50 – **16 rm** ☕ 105/140.
◆ A typical hacienda-style building with a whitewashed façade. Comfortable rooms with wooden floors, well-equipped bathrooms and rustic decoration details. The restaurant is in what was once an olive mill.

at Sanlúcar la Mayor *West : 18 km :*

Hacienda Benazuza , Virgen de las Nieves ☎ 95 570 33 44, *hbenazuza@elbullihotel.com, Fax 95 570 34 10*, ≤, , , – | | – 25/400. AE VISA. closed 7 to 22 January – **Meals - *La Alquería*** *(dinner only, closed Sunday and Monday)* **Meals** a la carte 63,50/77,50 – 25 – **26 rm** 390, 18 suites.
• A magnificent hotel in a 10C farmhouse. Spacious rooms luxuriously decorated in exquisite taste which are filled with the scent of flowers. The welcoming restaurant has wooden floors and beams.
Spec. Gazpacho de bogavante perfumado a la albahaca (summer). Salmonetes Gaudí. Chocolate en texturas.

VALÈNCIA *46000* P 577 N 28 y 29. *pop. 746 612 alt. 13.*

See : *The Old Town★ : Cathedral★ (El Miguelete★, Capilla del Santo Cáliz★) EX – Palacio de la Generalidad★ (golden room : ceiling★) EXD – Lonja★ (silkhall★★) DY – City of Arts and Sciences★ by Av. Jacinto Benavente FZ.*

Other curiosities : *Ceramic Museum★★ (Palacio del Marqués de Dos Aguas★★)* EYM1 - *Fine Arts San Pío V Museum★ (Valencian primitifs★★) FX – Patriarch College or of the Corpus Christi★ (Passion triptych★) EY* N – *Serranos Towers★ EX.*

Club de Golf Manises, East : 12 km, ☎ 96 153 40 69 – Club Escorpión, North-West : 19 km by road to Liria ☎ 96 160 12 11 – El Saler-Parador de El Saler, South-East : 19 km ☎ 96 161 03 84.

Valencia-Manises, East : 11 km ☎ 96 159 85 00 – Iberia : Paz 14, ✉ 46003, ☎ 902 400 500 EFY.

To the Balearic Islands : Cía Trasmediterránea, Muelle de Poniente ✉ 46024 ☎ 96 316 48 59 Fax 96 316 48 55 by Av. Regne de València FZ.

Pl. del Ayuntamiento 1, ✉ 46002 ☎ 96 351 04 17 touristinfo.aytovalencia@turisme.m400.gva.es Fax 96 352 58 12, Paz 48 ✉ 46003 ☎ 96 398 64 22 touristinfo.valencia@turisme.m400.gva.es Fax 96 398 64 21 Xàtiva 24 (North Station) ✉ 46007 ☎ 96 352 85 73 touristinfo.renfe@turisme.m400.gva.es Fax 96 352 85 73 and Poeta Querol ✉ 46002 ☎ 96 351 49 07 touristinfo.dipuvalencia@turisme.m400.gva.es Fax 96 351 99 27 – R.A.C.E. (R.A.C. de València) Gran Vía Marqués del Turia 79, ✉ 46005, ☎ 96 334 39 89 Fax 96 334 39 89.

Madrid 352 – Albacete 183 – Alacant/Alicante (by coast) 174 – Barcelona 355 – Bilbao 600 – Castelló de la Plana/Castellón de la Plana 75 – Málaga 608 – Sevilla 659 – Zaragoza 318.

Plans on following pages

Meliá Valencia Palace, paseo de la Alameda 32, ✉ 46023, ☎ 96 337 50 37, *melia.valencia.palace@solmelia.com, Fax 96 337 55 32*, ≤, , – | & – 25/800. AE VISA JCB. East : by Puente de Aragón FZ
Meals 25 – 12 – **243 rm** 160/195, 5 suites.
• A hotel in the 18C palace of The Dukes of Cardona. Extremely comfortable and with traditional details of décor. A spectacular entrance hall. The restaurant is in classic modern-style with minimalist details of décor.

Astoria Palace, pl. Rodrigo Botet 5, ✉ 46002, ☎ 96 398 10 00, *info@hotel-astoria-palace.com, Fax 96 398 10 10*, – | & – 25/500. AE VISA JCB.
Meals - see rest. ***Vinatea*** below – 11,70 – **196 rm** 173,30/218,50, 8 suites.
• An unforgettable stay in a very modern and luxurious hotel. An elegant lounge, excellent bedrooms and a fitness centre. EY p

Meliá Rey Don Jaime, av. Baleares 2, ✉ 46023, ☎ 96 337 50 30, *hotel.melia.rey.don.jaime@solmelia.es, Fax 96 337 15 72*, – | & – 25/250. AE VISA. East : by Puente de Aragón FZ
Meals a la carte approx. 28 – 11,77 – **317 rm** 144/177,75, 1 suite.
• A grand hotel in traditional style which has been slowly refurbished to provide facilities of the highest standard. Enjoy all the comfort of the magnificent rooms. The dining room is good although a little on the small side for the category of the hotel.

NH Las Artes I, av. Instituto Obrero 28, ✉ 46013, ☎ 96 335 13 10, *nhlasartes@nh-hotels.com, Fax 96 374 86 22*, , – | – 25/250. AE VISA JCB.
Meals 25 – 12 – **172 rm** 156, 2 suites. South : by Av. Regne de València FZ
• Excellent facilities and high level of comfort come together in this modern hotel. Well-appointed bedrooms and a range of extra facilities. A multi-use restaurant.

Hesperia Parque Central, pl. Manuel Sanchís Guarner, ✉ 46006, ☎ 96 303 91 00, *hotel@hesperia-parquecentral.com, Fax 96 303 91 30*, – | – 25/250. AE VISA. South : by Alicante EZ
Meals 17,12 – 9 – **178 rm** 130/165, 14 suites.
• A classic modern city hotel. Large, comfortable and well-equipped rooms. Several lounges.

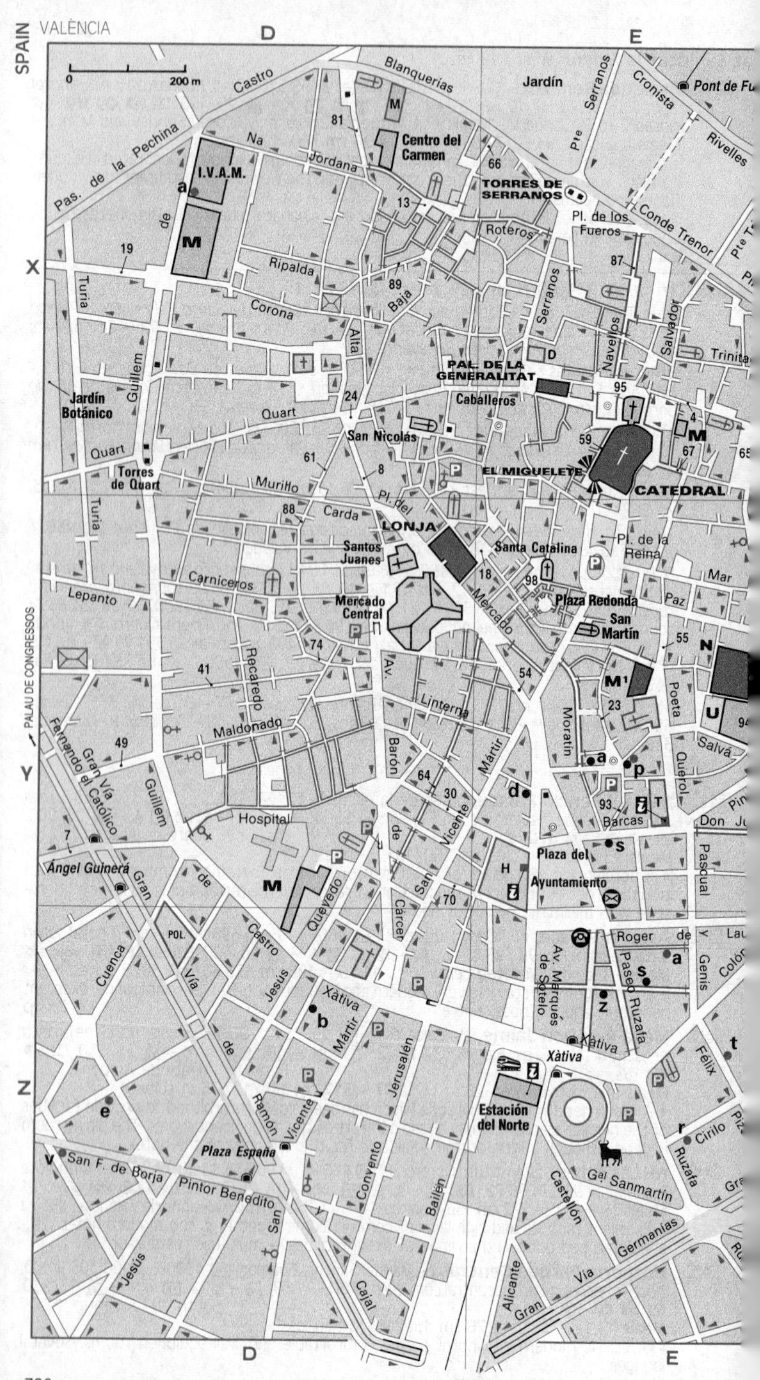
D
E
X
Y
Z
0
200 m
Castro
Blanquerías
Jardín
Serranos
Pte
Cronista
Pont de Fu
Rivelles
Pas. de la Pechina
Na
Jordana
I.V.A.M.
Centro del Carmen
M
81
66
TORRES DE SERRANOS
13
Conde Trenor
Pl. de los Fueros
Roteros
de
Ripalda
19
87
89
Baja
Corona
Turia
Alta
Serranos
Navellos
Salvador
Trinitat
Guillem
PAL. DE LA GENERALITAT
D
Jardín Botánico
24
Caballeros
95
Quart
San Nicolás
59
4
67
65
Quart
Torres de Quart
61
8
P
EL MIGUELETE
CATEDRAL
Murillo
Pl. del
88
Carda
LONJA
Turia
Santos Juanes
Santa Catalina
Pl. de la Reina
Carniceros
18
98
Mar
Lepanto
Mercado Central
Mercado
Plaza Redonda
Paz
San Martín
74
55
N
Recaredo
41
54
M¹
Poeta
Av.
Linterna
23
U
Moratín
Maldonado
Mártir
Salvá
PALAU DE CONGRESSOS
49
Fernando el Católico
Gran Vía
Barón
a
p
Querol
Guillem
64
30
d
Hospital
Vicente
93
T
Barcas
Don Ju
7
s
Ángel Guinerá
de
San
Plaza del Ayuntamiento
H
Gran
M
Quevedo
Cárcel
70
Pascual
POL.
Castro
Roger de Lau
Cuenca
Vía
Av. Marqués de Sotelo
Paseo Ruzafa
a
Genís
Colón
s
Jesús
Xàtiva
z
b
Mártir
Xàtiva
de
Jerusalén
Xàtiva
Félix
t
Estación del Norte
Z
e
Ramón
Vicente
Cirilo
r
Convento
Ruzafa
v
San F. de Borja
Plaza España
Pintor Benedito
Bailén
Gal Sanmartín
Castellón
San
Germanías
Jesús
Cajal
Alicante
Vía
Gran
D
E

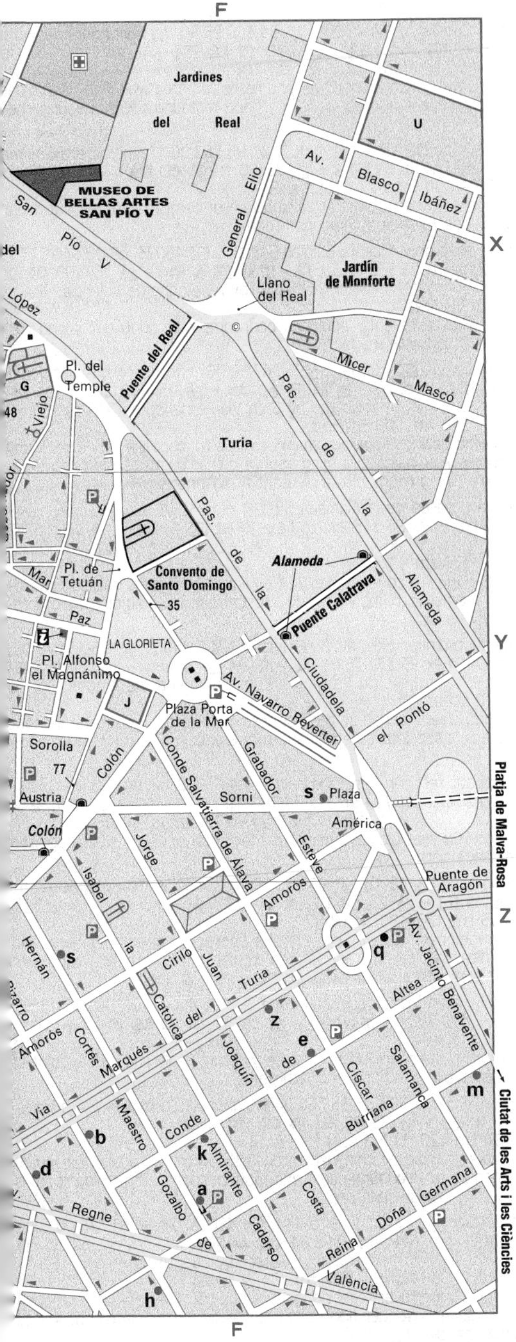

VALÈNCIA

Street	Ref.
Almirante	EX 3
Almudin	EX 4
Ángel Guimerá	DY 7
Ayuntamiento (Pl. del)	EY
Bolsería	DX 8
Carmen (Pl. del)	DX 13
Dr. Collado (Pl.)	EY 18
Dr. Sanchís Bergón	DX 19
Embajador Vich	EY 23
Esparto (Pl. del)	DX 24
Garrigues	DY 30
General Palanca	FY 35
Guillém Sorolla	DY 41
Maestres	FX 48
Maestro Palau	DY 49
María Cristina (Av.)	EY 54
Marqués de Dos Aguas	EY 55
Marqués de Sotelo (Av.)	EZ
Micalet	EX 59
Moro Zeit	DX 61
Músico Peydro	DY 64
Nápoles y Sicilia (Pl.)	EX 65
Padre Huérfanos	EX 66
Palau	EX 67
Pascual y Genís	EYZ
Paz	EFY
Periodista Azzati	DY 70
Pie de la Cruz	DY 74
Poeta Quintana	FY 77
Salvador Giner	DX 81
San Vicente Ferrer (Pl.)	EY 83
San Vicente Mártir	DY
Santa Ana (Muro)	EX 87
Santa Teresa	DY 88
Santo Tomás	DX 89
Transits	EY 93
Universidad	EY 94
Virgen (Pl. de la)	EX 95
Virgen de la Paz (Pl.)	EY 98

We suggest:
For a successful tour, that you prepare it in advance.
Michelin maps *and* ***guides*** *will give you much useful information on route planning, places of interest, accommodation, prices, etc.*

Vincci Lys, Martínez Cubells 5, ✉ 46002, ☎ 96 350 95 50, *lys@vinccihoteles.com, Fax 96 350 95 52* – |‡| ▤ TV – 25/70. AE VISA JCB. EZ s
Meals 15 – ☕ 10,50 – **95 rm** 195/237, 5 suites.
◆ Elegant and traditional with a spacious foyer and reception area which also serves as lounge and bar area. Magnificent bedrooms. A very good restaurant with a young chef in charge.

Meliá Plaza, pl. del Ayuntamiento 4, ✉ 46002, ☎ 96 352 06 12, *melia.plaza@solmelia.com, Fax 96 352 04 26,* – |‡| ▤ TV ♿ – 25/80. AE VISA JCB. EY d
Meals 17,50 – ☕ 9,50 – **100 rm** 140/176, 1 suite.
◆ A hotel which has been slowly refurbished to a high level of comfort with elegant décor and well-chosen furnishings. Excellently equipped rooms.

Abba Acteón coffee shop only, Vicente Beltrán Grimal 2, ✉ 46023, ☎ 96 331 07 07, *acteon@abbahoteles.com, Fax 96 330 22 30,* – |‡| ▤ TV ♿ – 25/400. AE VISA. East : by Av. Regne de València FZ
☕ 11,50 – **182 rm** 90, 5 suites.
◆ Quality and design. Large, excellently equipped bedrooms with good décor and furnishings and bathrooms fitted with marble.

NH Center, Ricardo Micó 1, ✉ 46009, ☎ 96 347 50 00, *nhcenter@nh-hotels.com, Fax 96 347 62 52,* heated, – |‡| ▤ TV ♿ – 25/400. AE VISA JCB. North : by Gran Vía Fernando el Católico DY
Meals 23 – ☕ 11,50 – **190 rm** 113, 3 suites.
◆ A classic chain hotel which is above average thanks to little touches like bathrobes being provided in the bathrooms. A covered swimming-pool which can be made open air in summer. A spacious and airy dining room with a pleasant atmosphere.

Holiday Inn Valencia, paseo de la Alameda 38, ✉ 46023, ☎ 96 303 21 00, *reservas@holidayinnvalencia.com, Fax 96 303 21 26,* – |‡| ▤ TV ♿ – 25/55. AE VISA JCB East : by Puente de Aragón FZ
Meals 12,50 – ☕ 12 – **200 rm** 97/110.
◆ A hotel of modern design with comfortable, well-equipped bedrooms geared towards business travellers. Terrace-bar with fine views and a restaurant which adjoins the coffee-shop in the foyer.

AC València coffee shop dinner only, av. de Francia 67, ✉ 46023, ☎ 96 331 70 00, *acvalencia@ac-hotels.com, Fax 96 331 70 01,* – |‡| ▤ TV ♿ – 25/100. AE VISA. East : by Puente de Aragón FZ
☕ 10 – **181 rm** 130, 2 suites.
◆ Modern, functional and clearly aimed at the business market, this hotel has pleasant lounge and meeting areas, a spacious cafeteria and rooms with the usual creature comforts.

Jardín Botánico without rest, Dr. Peset Cervera 6, ✉ 46008, ☎ 96 315 40 12, *infreservas@hoteljardinbotanico.com, Fax 96 315 34 08* – |‡| ▤ TV. AE VISA.
☕ 9 – **16 rm** 220. West : by Gran Vía Fernando el Católico DY
◆ A very well-refurbished 100-year-old building with modern interior décor. Well-appointed rooms with hydro-massage baths.

Conqueridor, Cervantes 9, ✉ 46007, ☎ 96 352 29 10, *hconquer@infonegocio.com, Fax 96 352 28 83* – |‡| ▤ TV – 25/80. AE VISA JCB. DZ b
Meals 20 – ☕ 10 – **55 rm** 120/180, 4 suites.
◆ A centrally located traditional hotel with comfortable bedrooms, good furnishings and modern bathrooms. A pleasant foyer reception area with a coffee shop. A dining room with harmonious décor and with a lot of wood on the walls and floors.

Dimar coffee shop only, Gran Vía Marqués del Turia 80, ✉ 46005, ☎ 96 395 10 30, *hdimar@terra.es, Fax 96 395 19 26* – |‡| ▤ TV – 25/50. AE VISA JCB.
☕ 10 – **103 rm** 73/127, 1 suite. FZ q
◆ A traditional hotel right in the heart of the city. Very comfortable and well-appointed rooms with pleasant décor and well-equipped bathrooms.

Reina Victoria, Barcas 4, ✉ 46002, ☎ 96 352 04 87, *hreinavictoriavalencia@husa.es, Fax 96 352 27 21* – |‡| ▤ TV – 25/75. AE VISA. EY s
Meals 15 – ☕ 10 – **94 rm** 120/170, 3 suites – PA 34.
◆ A beautiful façade and a splendid location just a stone's throw from the principal museums. Elegant and with an attractive lounge area and modern rooms. The dining room is on the 1st floor beside the English-style bar.

NH Ciudad de Valencia , av. del Puerto 214, ✉ 46023, ☎ 96 330 75 00, *nhciudaddevalencia@nh-hotels.com, Fax 96 330 98 64* – |‡| ▤ TV – 30/80. AE VISA. East : by Puente de Aragón FZ
Meals *(closed Christmas)* 15,03 – ☕ 9 – **147 rm** 131, 2 suites.
◆ A classic NH chain hotel. A large foyer-reception and lounge-bar. The very well-equipped rooms have design details such as wooden floors and triple glazing. The dining room is large and with pleasant functional décor.

Catalonia Excelsior without rest, Barcelonina 5, ✉ 46002, ☎ 96 351 46 12, *excelsior@hoteles-catalonia.es, Fax 96 352 34 78* – 🛗 ▤ 📺 ♿. AE ⓓ VISA. ✗ EY a
☕ 9 – **81 rm** 128/160.
◆ The best thing about this totally refurbished hotel is its central location. Few social areas and rather small but very well-equipped bedrooms.

Turia, Profesor Beltrán Baguena 2, ✉ 46009, ☎ 96 347 00 00, *reservas@hotelturia.es, Fax 96 347 32 44* – 🛗 ▤ 📺 🚗 – 🎤 25/300. AE MC VISA. ✗
Meals - dinner only - 18 – **160 rm** ☕ 88, 10 suites.
◆ A modern hotel beside the bus station with well-equipped rooms with hydro-massage baths. The foyer-lounge area has restrained décor.

North-West : by Gran Vía Fernando el Católico DY

Cónsul del Mar, av. del Puerto 39, ✉ 46021, ☎ 96 362 54 32, *reservas@hotelconsuldelmar.com, Fax 96 362 16 25,* 🏋, 🏊 – 🛗 ▤ 📺 🅿 – 🎤 25/50. AE MC VISA East : by Puente de Aragón FZ
Meals 10 – ☕ 6 – **45 rm** 93,72/100.
◆ The grand style of 1900 has been preserved in this hotel. Well-appointed bedrooms and bathrooms. Those on the 3rd floor have attic roofs. The dining room is pleasant.

NH Abashiri, av. de Ausias March 59, ✉ 46013, ☎ 96 373 28 52, *nhabashiri@nh-hotels.es, Fax 96 373 49 66* – 🛗 ▤ 📺 🚗 – 🎤 30/250. AE MC VISA JCB. ✗
Meals 17 – ☕ 10 – **168 rm** 94/113 – PA 39.
◆ Now in two buildings after further extension. All the practicality of this chain. Small lounges and intimate bedrooms. The dining room has lots of natural light.

South : by Av. Regne de València FZ

NH Villacarlos without rest, av. del Puerto 60, ✉ 46023, ☎ 96 337 50 25, *nhvillacarlos@nh-hotels.com, Fax 96 337 50 74* – 🛗 ▤ 📺. AE ⓓ MC VISA. ✗
☕ 9,50 – **51 rm** 131. East : by Puente de Aragón FZ
◆ Comfortable despite being a small and functional hotel. Traditional bedrooms, some rather small and only with a shower.

Ad-Hoc, Boix 4, ✉ 46003, ☎ 96 391 91 40, *adhoc@adhochoteles.com, Fax 96 391 36 67* – 🛗 ▤ 📺. AE ⓓ MC VISA. ✗ rest FX a
Meals *(closed Saturday lunch and Sunday)* 32 – ☕ 9 – **28 rm** 132/163.
◆ In an attractive 19C building. An intimate lounge and rooms with restrained neo-rustic décor of exposed brickwork, wooden beams and clay tiles.

NH Las Artes II without rest, av. Instituto Obrero 26, ✉ 46013, ☎ 96 335 60 62, *exlasartes@nh-hotels.com, Fax 96 333 46 83* – 🛗 ▤ 📺 🚗. AE ⓓ MC VISA JCB. ✗
☕ 9 – **121 rm** 85. South : by Av. Regne de València FZ
◆ A functional-style hotel with good facilities. The lounge is small and the basic rooms have cheerful decor.

Renasa coffee shop only, av. de Cataluña 5, ✉ 46010, ☎ 96 369 24 50, *reservas@hotel-renasa.com, Fax 96 393 18 24* – 🛗 ▤ 📺 – 🎤 25/75. AE ⓓ MC VISA. ✗
69 rm ☕ 66/90, 4 suites. East : by Puente del Real FX
◆ A functional hotel that has raised its standards by refurbishing its rooms to provide great comfort, traditional furnishings, thoughtful lighting and fully-equipped bathrooms.

Sorolla without rest, Convento de Santa Clara 5, ✉ 46002, ☎ 96 352 33 92, *reservasorolla@infonegocio.com, Fax 96 352 14 65* – 🛗 ▤ 📺. AE ⓓ MC VISA JCB. ✗ EZ z
☕ 7,50 – **58 rm** 79/115.
◆ Totally refurbished to provide adequate, functional comfort. The lounge area is small but the bedrooms are well-equipped.

Rías Gallegas, Cirilo Amorós 4, ✉ 46004, ☎ 96 352 51 11, *Fax 96 351 99 10* – ▤ 🅿. AE ⓓ MC VISA EZ r
closed August and Sunday – **Meals** a la carte 40,22/51,06.
◆ Faultless ! Traditional Galician cooking with a mid-priced menu of fish and seafood. An elegant dining room on two levels with excellent service.

Eladio, Chiva 40, ✉ 46018, ☎ 96 384 22 44, *michel@resteladio.com, Fax 96 384 64 21* – ▤. AE ⓓ MC VISA. ✗ West : by Ángel Guimerá DY
closed August and Sunday – **Meals** a la carte approx. 39,75.
◆ Elegant, traditional restaurant with a private bar and a menu of dishes with Galician roots. Efficient management and professional staff.

Torrijos, Dr. Sumsi 4, ✉ 46005, ☎ 96 373 29 49, *rte.torrijos@terra.es, Fax 96 316 24 86* – ▤. AE ⓓ MC VISA. ✗ FZ h
closed 15 days in January, Holy Week, 25 August-15 September, Saturday lunch and Sunday in summer, Sunday dinner and Monday the rest of the year – **Meals** 45 and a la carte 40/51.
◆ An elegant restaurant with good furnishings and excellent service run by the chef-owner and his son-in-law. A menu of carefully prepared dishes.
Spec. Tartar de atún con ajo blanco de piñones e higos (May-August). Pulpo con galleta de sobrasada, piña y emulsión de María Luisa. Arroz meloso con ventresca de congrio y oreja crujiente.

XXX **Albacar,** Sorní 35, ✉ 46004, ☎ 96 395 10 05, *Fax 96 395 60 55* – ▤. AE ⓓ ⓜ VISA. ✂ FY s
closed Holy Week, 8 August-8 September, Saturday lunch and Sunday – **Meals** a la carte 34/39.
◆ This restaurant enjoys a certain amount of prestige within Valencia. Classic modern style and innovative and creative cooking. Many satisfied customers.

XXX **La Sucursal,** Guillém de Castro 118, ✉ 46003, ☎ 96 374 66 65, *Fax 96 392 41 54* – ▤. ⓓ ⓜ VISA. ✂ DX a
closed 15 to 31 August, Saturday lunch and Sunday – **Meals** a la carte approx. 35/45.
◆ Part of the same building as the IVAM, with a cafeteria on the ground floor and a minimalist dining room on the first offering a fusion of the innovative and the traditional.

XXX **Vinatea** - *Hotel Astoria Palace,* Vilaragut 4, ✉ 46002, ☎ 96 398 10 00, *Fax 96 398 10 10* – ▤. AE ⓓ ⓜ VISA JCB. ✂ EY p
Meals a la carte 21/34.
◆ An excellent restaurant with a separate entrance where there is high quality food. Elegant traditional décor with good furnishings.

XXX **Riff,** Conde de Altea 18, ✉ 46005, ☎ 96 333 53 53, *restaurante@restaurante-riff.com* – ▤. AE ⓓ ⓜ VISA. ✂ FZ k
closed Holy Week, August, Sunday and Monday – **Meals** a la carte 35/55.
◆ This establishment follows the current trends in restaurant cooking and provides creative cuisine in a setting that is minimalist in design. Efficient staff.

XX **Kailuze,** Gregorio Mayáns 5, ✉ 46005, ☎ 96 335 45 39, *Fax 96 335 48 93* – ▤. AE ⓓ ⓜ VISA. ✂ FZ d
closed Holy Week, August, Saturday lunch and Sunday – **Meals** - Basque rest - a la carte 50/60.
◆ Pleasant design and excellent service in an establishment with an entrance hall and a charming lounge. Good, traditional Basque-Navarrese cuisine.

XX **El Gastrónomo,** av. Primado Reig 149, ✉ 46020, ☎ 96 369 70 36 – ▤ 🚗. AE ⓜ VISA. ✂ North-East : by Puente del Real FX
closed 30 December-7 January, Holy Week, August, Sunday, Monday dinner and Bank Holidays – **Meals** a la carte 29,25/36,50.
◆ A restaurant that is old fashioned both in how it is run and in its wide gastronomic offerings. Pleasant and adequately-equipped dining room.

XX **El Ángel Azul,** Conde de Altea 33, ✉ 46005, ☎ 96 374 56 56, *restauranteelangelazul@yahoo.es, Fax 96 374 56 56* – ▤. AE ⓓ ⓜ VISA JCB. ✂ FZ e
closed 15 August-15 September, Sunday and Monday – **Meals** a la carte 37,60/43,93.
◆ The owner of this restaurant, formerly its chef, is continuing the good work with an interesting menu of creative dishes. Modern traditional decor.

XX **Joaquín Schmidt,** Visitación 7, ✉ 46009, ☎ 96 340 17 10, *info@joaquinschmidt.com, Fax 96 340 17 10,* 🏠 – ▤. ⓜ VISA. ✂ North : by Cronista Rivelles EX
closed 15 days in Holy Week, 15 to 31 August, Sunday and Monday lunch – **Meals** a la carte 35/56.
◆ A welcoming restaurant, in an old house with a patio, that enjoys great prestige in the city. Good décor in its dining rooms and attentive service.

XX **Civera,** Lérida 11, ✉ 46009, ☎ 96 347 59 17, *civera@ole.com, Fax 96 346 50 50* – ▤. AE ⓓ ⓜ VISA JCB. ✂ North : by Cronista Rivelles EX
closed Holy Week, August, Sunday dinner and Monday – **Meals** - Seafood - a la carte 28,30/40,87.
◆ A well-known fish and seafood restaurant with a lively bar from which follow several dining areas in traditional regional style. A large menu of quality fish and seafood.

XX **Civera Centro,** Mosén Femades 10, ✉ 46002, ☎ 96 352 97 64, *civera@ole.com Fax 96 346 50 50,* 🏠 – ▤. AE ⓓ ⓜ VISA JCB. ✂ EZ a
closed Holy Week and July – **Meals** - Seafood - a la carte 28,30/40,87.
◆ A popular and well-known restaurant. Friendly staff and attentive service and good food.

XX ✿ **Ca'Sento,** Méndez Núñez 17, ✉ 46024, ☎ 96 330 17 75 – ▤. AE VISA. ✂
closed Holy Week, August, Sunday and Monday dinner – **Meals** - booking essential - 60 and a la carte 39/51. East : by Puente de Aragón FZ
◆ A family-run restaurant. Good fish and seafood dishes. Creative cuisine influenced by contemporary restaurant cooking.
Spec. Gambas de Dénia asadas sobre un caldo de crustáceos y menestra de hierbas. Cochinillo asado con salsa de naranja y clavo. Sopa de Campari con helado de fresones, chocolate blanco en crema y aceite de oliva y sal.

XX **Alejandro,** Amadeo de Saboya 15, ✉ 46010, ☎ 96 393 40 46, *Fax 96 393 40 46* – ▤ AE ⓜ VISA. ✂ East : by Puente de Aragón FZ
closed Sunday – **Meals** a la carte approx. 36.
◆ A restaurant with future promise run by its talented chef-proprietor. A pleasant traditional-style dining room with minimalist design details.

XX **El Gourmet,** Martí 3, ✉ 46005, ☎ 96 395 25 09, *Fax 96 333 84 35* – ▤. AE ⓓ ⓜ VISA. ✂ FZ b
closed Holy Week, August and Sunday – **Meals** a la carte approx. 28,60.
• Two traditional dining rooms, which are now a little old-fashioned in style, preceded by a bar. Good management and service and a very good menu.

XX **Chust Godoy,** Boix 6, ✉ 46003, ☎ 96 391 38 15, *Fax 96 391 38 15* – ▤. AE ⓓ ⓜ VISA. ✂ FX a
closed Holy Week, August, Saturday lunch and Sunday – **Meals** a la carte 35/44.
• Personal attention from the chef who runs this restaurant with his wife. A neo-rustic dining room with exposed brickwork and wooden beams and excellent service.

XX **El Cabanyal,** Reina 128, ✉ 46011, ☎ 96 356 15 03, *Fax 96 355 29 00* – ▤. AE ⓓ ⓜ VISA. ✂ East : by Puente de Aragón FZ
closed 15 August-15 September and Sunday – **Meals** a la carte approx. 36,50.
• A restaurant in an old house with a perfect façade near to the Playa de Levante. A pleasant traditional dining room with good gastronomic choice.

X **Montes,** pl. Obispo Amigó 5, ✉ 46007, ☎ 96 385 50 25 – ▤. AE ⓓ ⓜ VISA. ✂ DZ v
closed Holy Week, August, Sunday dinner and Monday – **Meals** a la carte 22/30.
• A restaurant with a main dining room with pleasant décor and better than average service. Enter through an entrance hall area and bar which lead into a long dining room.

X **Mey Mey,** Historiador Diago 19, ✉ 46007, ☎ 96 384 07 47 – ▤. AE ⓓ ⓜ VISA. ✂
closed Holy Week and the last 3 weeks in August – **Meals** - Chinese rest - a la carte 18,90/25,30. DZ e
• Good and traditional Chinese restaurant décor. It has a circular fountain with gold fish, an extensive menu and a youthful ambience.

X **Eguzki,** av. Baleares 1, ✉ 46023, ☎ 96 337 50 33, *Fax 96 337 50 33* – ▤. ⓓ ⓜ VISA. ✂ East : by Puente de Aragón FZ
closed August and Sunday – **Meals** - Basque rest - a la carte 26,40/35,65.
• A Basque restaurant run with friendly enthusiasm and with a lovely stone façade. There is a bar and the pleasant dining room is on the 1st floor.

X **Palace Fesol,** Hernán Cortés 7, ✉ 46004, ☎ 96 352 93 23, *palacefesol@hotmail.com, Fax 96 352 93 23*, Regional decor – ▤. AE ⓓ ⓜ VISA. ✂ FZ s
Meals a la carte 23/29.
• A fairly basic and long-established restaurant. A public bar near the entrance and a dining room with simple décor in regional style. An unpretentious menu.

X **Bazterretxe,** Maestro Gozalbo 25, ✉ 46005, ☎ 96 395 18 94 – ▤. VISA. ✂ FZ a
closed August and Sunday dinner – **Meals** - Basque rest - a la carte 18,21/22,83.
• A pleasant restaurant offering a fairly simple menu of traditional Basque cuisine. A large bar and a dining room with rather small tables.

X **El Romeral,** Gran Vía Marqués del Turia 62, ✉ 46005, ☎ 96 395 15 17 – ▤. AE ⓓ ⓜ VISA. ✂ FZ z
closed 12 to 18 April, August, Sunday dinner and Monday – **Meals** a la carte 19,87/27,99.
• A city institution ! Old fashioned décor in the two dining rooms and a mid-priced menu offering simple dishes made from good ingredients.

by road C 234 *North-West : 8,5 km :*

NH Jardines del Turia, Pintor Velázquez, ✉ 46100 Burjassot, ☎ 96 390 54 60, *nhjardinesdelturia@nh-hotels.com, Fax 96 364 63 61* – |♦| ▤ TV ⇔ – 🏟 25/100. AE ⓓ ⓜ VISA JCB. ✂ North-West : by Gran Vía Fernando el Católico DY
Meals 22 – ☐ 10 – **97 suites** 90/120, 15 rm.
• Pleasant and functional in the style of the chain. The apartment-type rooms have a kitchen and a sitting room. Lifts from which there are views of the beautiful interior patio. A pleasant and well-lit dining room.

at Alboraia *North-East : 8 km :*

Olympia, Maestro Serrano 5, ✉ 46120 Alboraia, ☎ 902 30 01 32, *reservas@olympiagrupo.com, Fax 902 30 01 42*, Thermal spa, Fø, ⛆ – |♦| ▤ TV ⇔ – 🏟 25/600. AE ⓓ ⓜ VISA. ✂
Meals 16,25 – ☐ 9 – **164 rm** 70/90, 3 suites.
• Wonderful facilities which include a gym and thermal baths. An attractive terrace beneath a coloured glass dome. A classic modern-style restaurant offering rice dishes of the region.

at Almàssera *North-East : 9 km :*

XX **Lluna de València,** Camí del Mar 56, ✉ 46132 Almàssera, ☎ 96 185 10 86, *Fax 96 185 10 06* – ▤ P. AE ⓓ ⓜ VISA. ✂ by Puente del Real FX
closed Holy Week, Saturday lunch and Sunday – **Meals** a la carte 23,70/29,20.
• A thousand-year-old olive tree presides over the entrance to this restaurant, a former farmhouse. Attractive dining rooms ; the main one has a pleasant rustic atmosphere.

at El Saler *South : 12 km :*

Sidi Saler, beach - 3 km, 46012 València, 96 161 04 11, *reservas@saler.hotelessidi.es, Fax 96 161 08 38*, – 25/300.

Meals 28,50 - ***Les Dunes*** *(dinner only)* **Meals** a la carte 34,50/57,25 - ***Brasserie Le Jardin*** *(lunch only)* **Meals** a la carte 34,50/57,25 – 14 – **260 rm** 198/236, 16 suites.

◆ An attractive hotel complex beside the beach with excellent social areas. The bedrooms, all of which have sea views, are spacious and well equipped. Les Dunes restaurant is elegant and has live music.

Parador de El Saler, av. Pinares 151 - 7 km, 46012 València, 96 161 11 86, *saler@parador.es, Fax 96 162 70 16*, – 25/200.

Meals 25,30 – 9,70 – **58 rm** 126,20.

◆ A hotel situated on a golf course with the sea in the background. The splendid facilities invite you to relax and the attractive bedrooms have all mod cons. The Pleasant dining room offers cuisine anchored in tradition.

at Manises *on the airport road - East : 10 km :*

Tryp Azafata, autopista del aeropuerto 15, 96 154 61 00, *tryp.azafata@solmelia.com, Fax 96 153 20 19*, – 25/300. rest

Meals 19,25 – 10 – **124 rm** 122,25/147,25, 4 suites.

◆ A traditional-style hotel close to the airport. Good social areas and rooms of adequate comfort.

at Puçol *North : 23 km by motorway A 7 :*

Monte Picayo, urb. Monte Picayo, 96 142 01 00, *Fax 96 142 21 68*, – 25/500.

Meals a la carte 40/48 – 11,72 – **79 rm** 125/150, 3 suites.

◆ On a mountainside with magnificent vistas over the Valencian fertile plain. Spacious rooms such as the elegant lounge. A traditional restaurant with faultless service.

Sweden

Sverige

STOCKHOLM – GOTHENBURG

PRACTICAL INFORMATION

LOCAL CURRENCY

Swedish Kronor: *100 SEK = 11,15 euro (€) (Dec. 2003)*

TOURIST INFORMATION

In Stockholm, the Tourist Centre is situated in Sweden House, entrance from Kungsträdgården at Hamngatan. Open Mon-Fri 9am-6pm. Sat. and Sun. 9am-3pm. Telephone weekdays (08) 789 24 00, weekends to Excursion Shop and Tourist Centre (08) 789 24 90. For Gothenburg, see information in the text of the town under ℹ.

National Holiday in Sweden: *6 June.*

FOREIGN EXCHANGE

Banks are open between 10am and 3pm on weekdays only. Most large hotels and the Tourist Centre have exchange facilities. Arlanda airport has banking facilities between 7am to 10pm seven days a week.

SHOPPING

In the index of street names, those printed in red are where the principal shops are found.
The main shopping streets in the centre of Stockholm are: Hamngatan, Biblioteksgatan, Drottninggatan, Sturegallerian.
In the Old Town mainly Västerlånggatan.

THEATRE BOOKINGS

Your hotel porter will be able to make your arrangements or direct you to Theatre Booking Agents.

CAR HIRE

The international car hire companies have branches in Stockholm, Gothenburg, Arlanda and Landvetter airports. Your hotel porter should be able to give details and help you with your arrangements.

TIPPING

Hotels and restaurants normally include a service charge of 15 per cent. Additionally cloakroom attendants are normally tipped 10 SEK. Doormen, baggage porters etc. are generally given a gratuity.
Taxis include 10 % tip in the amount shown on the meter.

SPEED LIMITS - SEAT BELTS

The maximum permitted speed on motorways and dual carriageways is 110 km/h - 68 mph, 90 km/h - 56 mph on other roads except where a lower speed limit is indicated and in built up areas 50 km/h - 31 mph.
The wearing of seat belts is compulsory for drivers and all passengers.
In Sweden, drivers must not drink alcoholic beverages at all.

BREAKDOWN SERVICE

A 24 hour breakdown service is operated ☎ 112.

STOCKHOLM

Sverige 711 M 15 – *pop. 674 459 Greater Stockholm 1 491 726.*

Hamburg 935 – Copenhagen 630 – Oslo 522.

Stockholm Visitors Board, Tourist Centre, Sverigehuset, Hamngatan 27 ☎ (08) 789 24 00.

Svenska Golfförbundet (Swedish Golf Federation) ☎ (08) 622 15 00.

Stockholm-Arlanda NW : 40 km ☎ (08) 797 61 00 – SAS : Reservations (020) 727 727 – Air-Terminal : opposite main railway station – Arlanda Express rail link : departs Central Station every 15 mins – journey time 20 mins.

Motorail for Southern Europe : Ticket Travel-Agency, Sturegatan ☎ (08) 400 51 00.

To Finland : contact Silja Line ☎ (08) 22 21 40 or Viking Line ☎ (08) 452 40 00 – Excursions by boat : contact Stockholm Visitors Board (see below).

See: *Old Town★★★ (Gamla Stan)* AZ – *Vasa Museum★★★ (Vasamuseet)* DY – *Skansen Open-Air Museum★★★* DY.
Royal Palace★★ (Kungliga Slottet) AZ ; *Royal Apartments★★ ; Royal Armoury★ ; Royal Treasury★★ – Stockholm Cathedral★★ (Storkyrkan)* AZ – *City Hall★★ (Stadhuset) : Blue Hall★★★, Golden Hall★★★ ; ※★★★* BY **H** – *Prins Eugens Waldemarsudde★★ (house and gallery)* DY – *Thiel Gallery★★ (Thielska Galleriet)* DZ.
House of the Nobility★ (Riddarhuset) AZ **R** – *Riddarholmen Church★ (Riddarholmskyrkan)* AZ **K**[1] – *Österlånggatan★* AZ.
Kaknäs TV Tower (Kaknästornet) ※★★★ DY – *Stigberget : Fjällgatan ※★* DZ – *Skinnerviksberget : ※★* BZ.

Museums: *National Art Gallery★★ (Nationalmuseum)* DY **M**[5] – *Nordic Museum★★ (Nordiska Museet)* DY – *Museum of National Antiquities★★ (Historiska Museet)* DY – *Museum of Medieval Stockholm★★ (Stockholms Medeltidsmuseet)* CY **M**[1] – *Museum of Far Eastern Antiquities★ (Östasiatiska Museet)* DY **M**[6] – *Hallwyl Collection★ (Hallwylska Museet)* CY **M**[3] – *Museum of Modern Art (Moderna Museet) (collections★★)* DY **M**[4] – *Strindberg Museum★ (Strindbergsmuseet)* BX **M**[2] – *Junibacken★* DY.

Outskirts : *Drottningholm Palace★★★ (Drottningholm Slott) W : 12 km* BY – *Stockholm Archipelago★★★ – Millesgården★★ (house and gallery) E : 4 km* BX – *Skogskyrkogården (UNESCO World Heritage Site).*

Excursions : *Gripsholms Slott★★ – Skokloster★★ – Ulriksdal★ – Birka★ – Strängnas★ – Sigtuna★ – Uppsala★★.*

STOCKHOLM

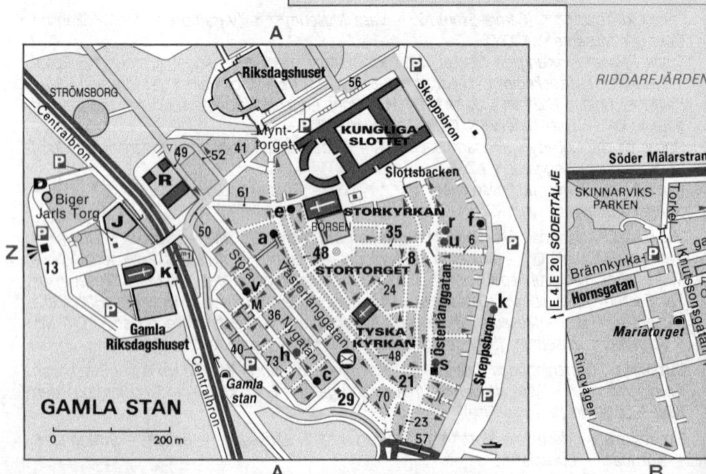

GAMLA STAN
0
200 m
Riksdagshuset
KUNGLIGA SLOTTET
Slottsbacken
Mynttorget
STRÖMSBORG
Centralbron
Skeppsbron
Biger Jarls Torg
STORKYRKAN
BÖRSEN
STORTORGET
TYSKA KYRKAN
Gamla Riksdagshuset
Västerlånggatan
Österlånggatan
Stora Nygatan
Gamla stan
RIDDARFJÄRDEN
Söder Mälarstrand
SKINNARVIKS-PARKEN
Brännkyrka-
Hornsgatan
Mariatorget
Ringvägen
Torkel
Knutssonsgatan
SÖDERTÄLJE
E 4 E 20
A
B
Z

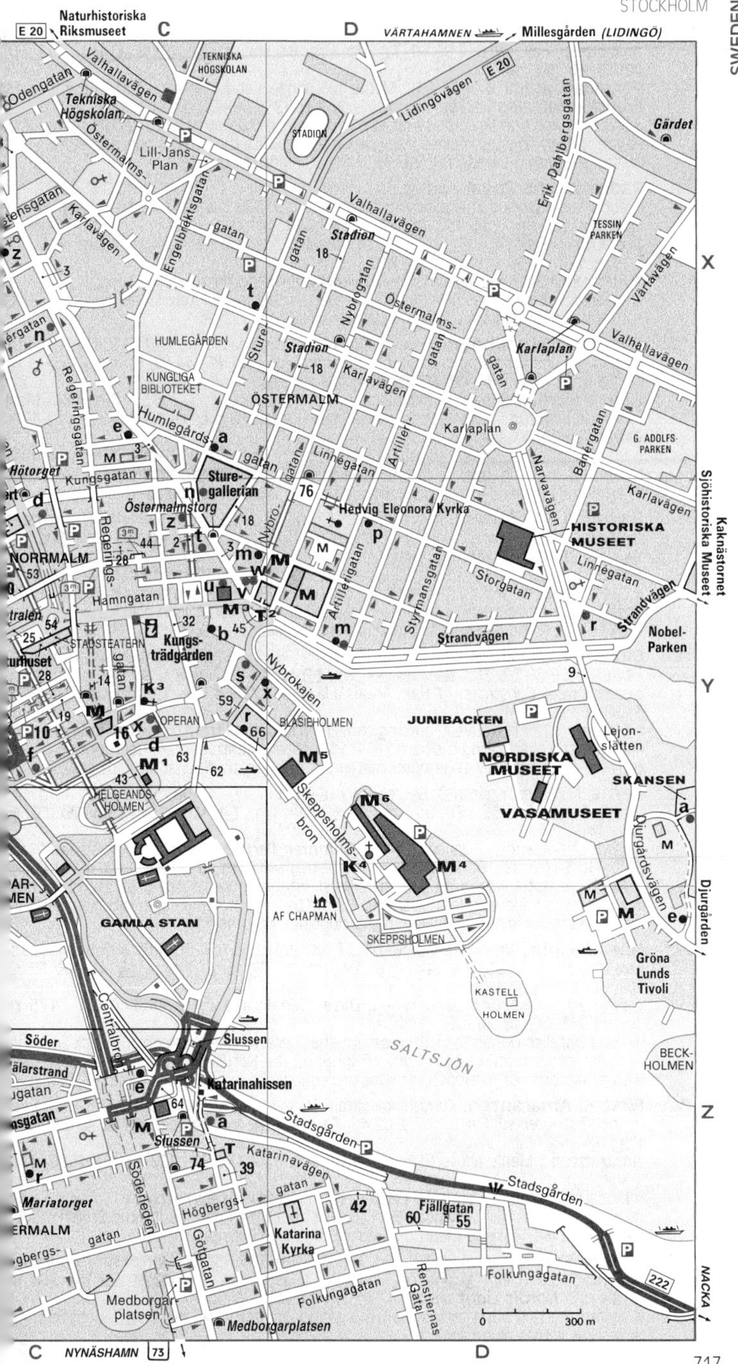
Naturhistoriska Riksmuseet
E 20
C
D
VÄRTAHAMNEN
Millesgården (LIDINGÖ)
TEKNISKA HÖGSKOLAN
STADION
Lidingövägen
Valhallavägen
Tekniska Högskolan
Östermalms-
Lill-Jans Plan
Engelbrektsgatan
Erik Dahlbergsgatan
Gärdet
Karlavägen
Valhallavägen
Stadion
TESSIN PARKEN
Värtavägen
X
Nybrogatan
Östermalms-gatan
HUMLEGÅRDEN
Sture-
Stadion
Karlaplan
KUNGLIGA BIBLIOTEKET
ÖSTERMALM
Karlavägen
Regeringsgatan
Humlegårds-gatan
Linnégatan
Artilleri-
Karlaplan
Banérgatan
G. ADOLFS-PARKEN
Hötorget
Kungsgatan
Sture-gallerian
Östermalmstorg
Hedvig Eleonora Kyrka
Narvavägen
Karlavägen
Sjöhistoriska Museet
Kaknästornet
HISTORISKA MUSEET
NORRMALM
Hamngatan
Artillerigatan
Styrmansgatan
Storgatan
Linnégatan
Strandvägen
STADSTEATERN
Kungs-trädgården
Strandvägen
Nobel-Parken
Nybrokajen
Y
OPERAN
BLASIEHOLMEN
JUNIBACKEN
Lejon-slätten
NORDISKA MUSEET
SKANSEN
HELGEANDS-HOLMEN
Skeppsholms-bron
VASAMUSEET
Djurgårdsvägen
AF CHAPMAN
GAMLA STAN
SKEPPSHOLMEN
Djurgården
Gröna Lunds Tivoli
KASTELL HOLMEN
SALTSJÖN
Söder
Centralbron
Slussen
BECK-HOLMEN
Katarinahissen
Z
Stadsgården
Slussen
Katarinavägen
Mariatorget
Söderleden
Högbergs-gatan
Fjällgatan
Stadsgården
Katarina Kyrka
Götgatan
Folkungagatan
Renstiernas Gata
Medborgar-platsen
Medborgarplatsen
0
300 m
222
NACKA
C
NYNÄSHAMN
73
D

Grand Hôtel, Södra Blasieholmshamnen 8, S-111 47, (08) 679 35 00, *info@g andhotel.se, Fax (08) 611 86 86,* – rm, rest, – 600. CY
Verandan *(* *(08) 679 35 86)* **: Meals** 425 (dinner) and a la carte 310/545 (see als ***Franska Matsalen*** below) – 195 – **289 rm** 2300/4400, 21 suites.
◆ Sweden's top hotel occupies a late 19C mansion on the waterfront overlooking the Roya Palace and Old Town. Combines traditional elegance with the latest modern facilities. Classi restaurant with a wonderful outlook. Famous Smörgåsbord.

Radisson SAS Royal Viking, Vasagatan 1, S-101 24, (08) 506 540 00, *rese rvations.royal.stockholm@radissonsas.com, Fax (08) 506 540 01,* – rm – 130. rest BY
Stockholm Fisk *((08) 506 541 02)* **: Meals** - Seafood - 320 and a la carte 273/73 – 125 – **456 rm** 2195/2395, 3 suites.
◆ Panoramic Sky Bar with impressive views over Stockholm, at the top of 9 floors o comfortable bedrooms. In busy part of the city but completely sound-proofed. Stylis contemporary restaurant offers an array of seafood dishes.

Sheraton Stockholm H. and Towers, Tegelbacken 6, S-101 23, (08 412 34 00, *sheraton.stockholm@sheraton.com, Fax (08) 412 34 09,* – rm – 380. rest CY
Liberty Kitchen **: Meals** (buffet lunch) 170 and a la carte 170/295 – ***Die Ecke*** **: Meal** - German Bierstub - *(closed Sunday and Bank Holidays)* a la carte 170/295 – 170 **449 rm** 2900, 13 suites.
◆ International hotel popular with business people, overlooking Gamla Stan and offerin the largest rooms in town. Comprehensive guest facilities. Open plan all-day restaurant wit international dishes. Authentic German dishes in classic wood panelled 'bierstube.

Radisson SAS Strand, Nybrokajen 9, S-103 27, (08) 506 640 00, *sales.stra d.stockholm@radissonsas.com, Fax (08) 506 640 01,* – rm, 100. CDY
Strand **: Meals** 280 (lunch) and a la carte – 180 – **132 rm** 1990/2380, 20 suite
◆ Characterful old world architecture in red brick overlooking the harbour. Rooms featur classic elegant décor with traditional Swedish style furniture. Open plan lobby restaura with accomplished Swedish and international cooking.

Diplomat, Strandvägen 7c, S-104 40, (08) 459 68 02, *info@diplomathotel.co Fax (08) 459 68 20,* – rm, DY
closed 1 week Christmas – ***T Bar*** **: Meals** a la carte 273/638 – **125 rm** 1995/279 3 suites.
◆ Elegant 1911 Art Nouveau building converted into hotel from diplomatic lodgings plea antly located overlooking the harbour. Traditional and contemporary bedrooms. A popul terrace, contemporary style hotel restaurant offering traditional Swedish cooking.

Berns, Näckströmsgatan 8, Berzelii Park, S-111 47, (08) 566 322 00, *info@be ns.se, Fax (08) 566 322 01,* – rm, – 180. CY
closed 17 December-7 January – ***The Summer Terrace*** **: Meals** (grill rest.) a la car 305/610 (see also ***Berns Restaurant*** below) – **61 rm** 2150/4000, 4 suites.
◆ Boutique hotel with a modern minimalist interior décor verging on trendy ; detai in cherry wood and marble. Modern facilities in bedrooms, some have balconies. The Sun mer Terrace for dinner, drinking, night clubbing and breakfast.

Nordic Light, Vasaplan, S-101 37, (08) 505 630 00, *info@nordichotels.s Fax (08) 505 630 90,* – rm, – 40. BY
closed 20 December-3 January – ***L Dine*** **: Meals** a la carte 265/465 – **175 r** 2500/3600, 15 suites.
◆ Sister hotel to Nordic Sea with most facilities here. Modern harmonious black and whi designer décor features symphony of lights on the Nordic Lights theme. Modern me with a backdrop of kaleidoscopic light projections.

First H. Amaranten, Kungsholmsgatan 31, S-104 20, (08) 692 52 00, *ama nten@firsthotels.se, Fax (08) 652 62 48,* – rest, rest BY
Amaranten **: Meals** *(closed Sunday)* a la carte 310/438 – **422 rm** 1999/224 1 suite.
◆ Modernised, commercial hotel conveniently located with easy access to subway. Stylis quiet public areas with American Bar ; compact but up-to-date bedrooms. Stylish mode eating area with a large menu of modern Swedish cooking.

Nordic Sea, Vasaplan, S-101 37, (08) 505 630 00, *info@nordichotels.s Fax (08) 505 630 90* – rm, – 100.
Meals (see ***Nordic Light*** above) – **367 rm** 2000/3600. BY
◆ Stylish modern hotel with sea theme. Unique Ice Bar is a "must see". Contempora bedrooms with a blue theme.

Birger Jarl, Tulegatan 8, ✉ S-104 32, ☎ (08) 674 18 00, *info@birgerjarl.se, Fax (08) 673 73 66,* – rest, ☎ – 150. CX z
Meals *(closed lunch Saturday and Sunday)* a la carte 218/332 – **230 rm** 1645/2450, 5 suites.
◆ Modern hotel building in quieter part of city. Lobby features many art and sculpture displays. Some rooms decorated by local artists of international reputation. Simple and stylish restaurant with unfussy Swedish cooking.

Scandic H. Park, Karlavägen 43, ✉ S-102 46, ☎ (08) 517 348 00, *park@scandic-hotels.com, Fax (08) 517 348 11,* – 60. rest CX t
Park Village : **Meals** 360 (dinner) and a la carte approx 400 – **196 rm** 2030/2630, 3 suites.
◆ Convenient location by one of the city's prettiest parks (view from suites). All rooms are a good size, modern and comfortable with good range of facilities and comforts. Modern restaurant with small summer terrace ; traditional Swedish and international fare.

Elite H. Stockholm Plaza, Birger Jarlsgatan 29, ✉ S-103 95, ☎ (08) 566 220 00, *info.stoplaza@elite.se, Fax (08) 566 220 20,* – rm, – 50. CX e
closed 23-27 December – **Meals** (see ***Vassa Eggen*** below) – **147 rm** 1845/2395, 4 suites.
◆ Well preserved 1884 building with up-to-date comforts. Compact well run commercial hotel with conference rooms, basement sauna and high percentage of single rooms.

Lydmar, Sturegatan 10, ✉ S-114 36, ☎ (08) 566 113 00, *info@lydmar.se, Fax (08) 566 113 01* – rm, rest CX a
The Dining Room : **Meals** a la carte 265/435 – **61 rm** 1950/2600, 1 suite.
◆ Well located in the shopping and night life area, this boutique hotel overlooking the park offers style : bar with regular light music ; individually furnished bedrooms. Stylish, informal dining with original, modern cooking with eclectic influences.

Rica City H. Stockholm, Slöjdgatan 7, ✉ S-111 57, ☎ (08) 723 72 00, *info.stockholm@rica.se, Fax (08) 723 72 09,* – 70.
closed 23-27 December – ***Oasen :*** **Meals** 77/300 and lunch a la carte 189/260 – **292 rm** 1650/2220. CY c
◆ Conveniently located at heart of shopping district so popular with tourists. Rooms distributed around Atrium, beneath which is a winter garden. Stylish modern bedrooms. Eclectic range of international dishes in restaurant overlooking the street.

Comfort Hotel Wellington without rest., Storgatan 6, ✉ S-114 51, ☎ (08) 667 09 10, *info.wellington@comfort.choicehotels.se, Fax (08) 667 12 54,* – DY p
restricted opening Christmas and New Year – **58 rm** 1845/2245, 2 suites.
◆ Apartment block converted into hotel in late 1960s, well placed for shopping and night life. Compact but well-equipped bedrooms ; city views from upper floor balconies.

Hotel Riddargatan without rest., Riddargatan 14, ✉ S-114 35, ☎ (08) 555 730 00, *reservation@hotelriddargatan.com, Fax (08) 555 730 11* –
56 rm 1595/1795, 2 suites. CY m
◆ Modern style hotel in quiet location behind the Royal Dramatik Theatre, near shops and restaurants. Swedish design bedrooms with good internet facilities.

Freys, Bryggargatan 12, ✉ S-101 31, ☎ (08) 50 62 13 00, *freys@freyshotels.com, Fax (08) 50 62 13 13,* – rm, – 50. rest BY u
closed Christmas – ***Hörnans Kok :*** **Meals** *(closed lunch Saturday and Sunday)* (light lunch)/dinner a la carte 286/348 – **117 rm** 1595/2200, 1 suite.
◆ Well located near central station. Paintings by local artists for sale. First-floor terrace. Fairly compact bedrooms with informal furnishings, superior rooms with balconies. Short, exclusive menu offers traditional fare and also some Belgian specialities.

Operakällaren, Operahuset, Karl XII's Torg, ✉ S-111 86, ☎ (08) 676 58 01, *info@operakallaren.se, Fax (08) 676 58 72,* – . CY d
closed mid July-mid August and 24 December-6 January – **Meals** (dinner only) 550/1350 and a la carte 660/900.
◆ Magnificent dining room with original 19C carved wood décor and fresco paintings situated in the historic Opera House. Extensive menu of well prepared gourmet dishes.
Spec. Fillet of tuna, chard salad, caper sauce. Pigeon with hazelnuts and dried fruit salad, chocolate flavoured gravy. Vanilla raviolo, sorbet of sweet pepper and raspberry.

Franska Matsalen (at Grand Hôtel), Södra Blasieholmshamnen 8, ✉ S-103 27, ☎ (08) 679 35 84, *franska@mbox301.swipnet.se, Fax (08) 611 86 86,* Royal Palace and Old Town – . CY r
closed Christmas and Sunday – **Meals** (dinner only and Saturday lunch) a la carte 730/1465.
◆ Classic comfortable restaurant which is part elegant historic dining room with mahogany and crystal decor, part window terrace overlooking Royal Palace and Old Town.

XXX **Bon Lloc** (Dahlgren), Regeringsgatan 111, ✉ S-111 39, ✆ (08) 660 60 60, *bonlloc@telia.com, Fax (08) 10 76 35* – ▤. MC AE ① VISA. ✂ CX n
✿ *closed 5 July-2 August, Christmas-New Year and Sunday* – **Meals** (booking essential) (dinner only) 710/765 and a la carte 535/745 ♀.
◆ Highly regarded, innovative restaurant where the owner draws inspiration from French, Italian and Spanish cuisines. Exacting service, relaxed surroundings. Booking a must.
Spec. Terrine of crab, avocado, tomato vinaigrette. Barbecue of free range pork. Double espresso soufflé with milk sorbet.

XXX **Vassa Eggen** (at Elite H. Stockholm Plaza), Birger Jarlsgatan 29, ✉ S-114 25, ✆ (08) 21 61 69, *info@vassaeggen.com, Fax (08) 20 34 46*, 🏠 – ✂. MC AE ① VISA. ✂ CX e
closed Saturday and Sunday lunch – **Meals** 625 ♀.
◆ Refined restaurant popular with those in the know. Modern style reflected in both the décor and the cuisine, which is original and innovative.

XX **Fredsgatan 12** (Andersson), Fredsgatan 12, ✉ S-111 52, ✆ (08) 24 80 52, *info@fredsgatan12.com, Fax (08) 23 76 05* – ▤. MC AE ① VISA JCB. ✂ CY f
✿ *closed July, Christmas-New Year, Saturday and Sunday* – **Meals** (booking essential) 295/795 and a la carte 295/795 ♀.
◆ Stylish retro interior design with predominant 1920's theme in a wing of the Academy of Arts. Good value business lunch offered. Creative and original modern cuisine.
Spec. Carpaccio of beef with foie gras and figs. Bleak roe 'Taco'. Scallops with carrot, ginger and lime.

XX **Paul and Norbert,** Strandvägen 9, ✉ S-114 56, ✆ (08) 663 81 83, *restaurang.paul.norbert@telia.se, Fax (08) 661 72 36* – MC AE ① VISA. ✂ DY m
closed Christmas, New Year, Sunday, Monday lunch and Bank Holidays – **Meals** (booking essential) 180/350 (lunch) and dinner a la carte approx 630 ♀.
◆ Small sophisticated well run restaurant on harbour with stylish modern décor and art work. Some tables in booths. Numerous menus featuring seasonal produce.

XX **Berns Restaurant** (at Berns H.), Berzelii Park, ✉ S-111 47, ✆ (08) 566 322 22, *Fax (08) 566 323 23* – MC AE ① VISA. ✂ CY b
closed late June-mid August, 17 December-7 January, lunch Saturday and Sunday and Monday dinner – **Meals** 375 (dinner) and a la carte 285/595 ♀.
◆ A stunningly restored 19C rococo ballroom with galleries overlooking the dining room. Modern international cuisine. Live music. The place to be seen in.

XX **Wedholms Fisk,** Nybrokajen 17, ✉ S-111 48, ✆ (08) 611 78 74, *info@wedholmsfisk.se, Fax (08) 678 60 11*, 🏠 – ▤. MC AE ① VISA JCB. ✂ CY s
✿ *closed Sunday and Bank Holidays* – **Meals** - Seafood - a la carte 495/855 ♀.
◆ Classic 19-20C building near harbour. Classic style restaurant serving superb quality fresh fish and shellfish, simply but accurately prepared ; similar dishes in the bar.
Spec. Fricassée of sole, turbot, lobster and scallops with Champagne sauce. Boiled turbot with butter and horseradish. Swedish shellfish and seafood.

XX **Café Opera,** Operahuset, Karl XII's Torg, ✉ S-111 86, ✆ (08) 676 58 07, *info@cafeopera.se, Fax (08) 676 58 71*, 🏠 – ▤. MC AE ① VISA JCB. ✂ CY x
closed 24 December – **Meals** (booking essential) (dinner only) (music and dancing after 12pm) a la carte 355/505 ♀.
◆ Characterful rotunda style historic restaurant with ceiling painted in 1895, Corinthian pillars, fine mouldings and covered terrace. Swedish-influenced, international menu.

XX **Teatergrillen,** Nybrogatan 3, ✉ S-111 48, ✆ (08) 545 035 62, *riche@riche.se, Fax (08) 545 035 69* – ▤. MC AE ① VISA. ✂ CY v
closed July, Sunday and Bank Holidays – **Meals** a la carte 225/494 ♀.
◆ Most pleasant in the evening and with an intimate, traditional atmosphere - an institution in the city. Same menu as Riche ; traditional cooking of Scandinavian classics.

XX **Clas På Hörnet** with rm, Surbrunnsgatan 20, ✉ S-113 48, ✆ (08) 16 51 30, *hotel@claspahornet.com, Fax (08) 612 53 15*, 🏠 – |‡| ✂, ▤ rm, TV ✆. MC AE ① VISA JCB. ✂
Meals 95/245 and a la carte approx 296 ♀ – **10 rm** ☕ 1345/1745. CX
◆ Well established and busy restaurant in part-18C inn with character. Simple traditional rustic cooking using good quality local produce. Cosy, well-equipped bedrooms.

X **Restaurangen,** Oxtorgsgatan 14, ✉ S-111 57, ✆ (08) 22 09 52, *restaurangen.tm@telia.com, Fax (08) 22 09 54*, 🏠 – MC AE ① VISA. ✂ CY
closed July, Saturday lunch and Sunday – **Meals** (booking essential) (light lunch)/dinner 35… and a la carte approx 350 ♀.
◆ Contemporary interior with clean-cut minimalist décor and modern furnishings. Unusu… menu concept based on a tasting of several small dishes.

X **Halv Trappa Plus Gård,** Lästmakargatan 3, ✉ 111 36, ✆ (08) 678 10 50, *info@alvtrappaplusgard.se, Fax (08) 678 10 51* – MC AE ① VISA JCB CY
closed 22 December-6 January, Sunday and Monday – **Meals** - Chinese-Szechuan - (booking essential) (dinner only) 375/395 and a la carte 500/520 ♀.
◆ Busy basement restaurant without external sign or menu. Authentic Chinese cooking from Szechuan : hot and spicy. Well presented balanced set menus or individual dishe…

BRASSERIES AND BISTRO

KB, Smålandsgatan 7, ✉ S-111 46, ☎ (08) 679 60 32, *konstbaren@telia.com, Fax (08) 611 82 83* – MC AE ⓓ VISA. ✻ CY u
closed July, Christmas and Sunday – **Meals** 295/570 and a la carte 277/590 ♀.
• 19C building with impressive façade and original wall frescoes in bar - a home of Swedish artists with interesting modern art on the walls. Traditional Swedish cooking.

Prinsen, Mäster Samuelsgatan 4, ✉ S-111 44, ☎ (08) 611 13 31, *kontoret@restaurangprinsen.se, Fax (08) 611 70 79,* – MC AE ⓓ VISA JCB. ✻ CY t
closed 24-25 and 31 December, 25 June and Sunday lunch – **Meals** (booking essential) a la carte 370/490 ♀.
• Long standing and classic, busy but well-run brasserie with literary associations. Exhibition of graphic art renewed monthly in basement room. Classic Swedish cooking.

Sturehof, Stureplan 2-4, ✉ S-114 46, ☎ (08) 440 57 30, *info@sturehof.com, Fax (08) 678 11 01,* – MC AE ⓓ VISA JCB. ✻ CY n
Meals - Seafood - a la carte 305/545 ♀.
• Very popular classic café-brasserie with closely packed tables and a busy atmosphere due to the steady stream of local business clientele. Good choice of seafood dishes.

Eriks Bakficka, Fredrikshovsgatan 4, ✉ S-115 23, ☎ (08) 660 15 99, *info.bakfickan@eriks.se, Fax (08) 663 25 67,* – MC AE ⓓ VISA JCB. ✻ DY r
closed 23-25 December, 1 January and lunch Saturday and Sunday – **Meals** a la carte 270/405 ♀.
• Quiet residential situation, offering small terrace, bistro, bar-counter and more conventional dining room. Interesting choice of traditional Swedish dishes.

Riche, Birger Jarlsgatan 4, ✉ S-114 53, ☎ (08) 545 035 60, *riche@riche.se, Fax (08) 545 035 69* – ▤. MC AE ⓓ VISA. ✻ CY v
closed 24-26 December, 1 and 6 January, 21 April, 9 and 21 June and Sunday – **Meals** a la carte 225/494 ♀.
• The lively bar and bustling restaurant, very different from but with same menu as its sister Teatergrillen. Serves classic Scandinavian as well as international dishes.

at Gamla Stan (Old Stockholm) :

First H. Reisen, Skeppsbron 12, ✉ S-111 30, ☎ (08) 22 32 60, *reisen@firsthotels.se, Fax (08) 20 15 59,* ≤, ≘s – |‡|, ✻ rm, TV ☏ ♿. MC AE ⓓ VISA. ✻ AZ f
closed 24-26 December – ***The Dining Room*** : **Meals** (dinner only) a la carte 358/565 ♀ – **137 rm** ☐ 1899/3199, 7 suites.
• 19C hotel on waterfront with original maritime décor. Popular piano bar. Sauna in 17C vault. Deluxe and superior rooms offer qyayside view and small balconies. Maritime interior and a warm and welcoming atmosphere. Traditional Swedish and international menu.

Victory, Lilla Nygatan 5, ✉ S-111 28, ☎ (08) 506 400 00, *info@victory-hotel.se, Fax (08) 506 400 10,* ≘s – |‡|, ✻ rm, TV ☏ P – 🔬 80. MC AE ⓓ VISA JCB. ✻ AZ v
Meals (see ***Leijontornet*** below) – **42 rm** ☐ 2190/3590, 3 suites.
• Pleasant 17C hotel with Swedish rural furnishings and maritime antiques. Rooms named after sea captains with individually styled fittings, mixing modern and antique.

Rica City H. Gamla Stan without rest., Lilla Nygatan 25, ✉ S-111 28, ☎ (08) 723 72 50, *info.gamlastan@rica.se, Fax (08) 723 72 59* – |‡| ✻ TV ☏. MC AE ⓓ VISA JCB AZ c
closed Christmas – **50 rm** ☐ 1695/1945, 1 suite.
• Conveniently located 17C house with welcoming style. Well-furnished rooms with traditional décor and antique style furniture. Pleasant top-floor terrace with rooftop outlook.

Lady Hamilton without rest., Storkyrkobrinken 5, ✉ S-111 28, ☎ (08) 506 401 00, *info@lady-hamilton.se, Fax (08) 506 401 10,* ≘s – |‡| ✻ TV. MC AE ⓓ VISA. ✻ AZ e
closed 20 December-7 January – **34 rm** ☐ 1990/2690.
• 15C houses of character full of fine Swedish rural furnishings. Rooms boast antique pieces and modern facilities. Sauna and 14C well plunge pool in basement.

Lord Nelson without rest., Västerlånggatan 22, ✉ S-111 29, ☎ (08) 506 401 20, *info@lord-nelson.se, Fax (08) 506 401 30,* ≘s – |‡| ✻ TV ☏. MC AE ⓓ VISA JCB. ✻ AZ a
closed 19 December-7 January – **29 rm** ☐ 1790/2090.
• Charming late 17C house located in lively Old Town, with ship style interior and maritime antiques. Small cabin style rooms with good level of comfort and compact bathrooms.

Pontus in the Green House, Österlånggatan 17, ✉ S-111 31, ☎ (08) 545 273 00, *info@pontusfrithiof.com, Fax (08) 796 60 69* – MC AE DC VISA AZ u
closed 15 June-15 August, Saturday, Sunday and Bank Holidays – **Meals** (booking essential) a la carte 640/870 ♀.
◆ Restaurant with charm and style in 15C house. Classic décor and some booths in more formal upstairs room. Modern innovative or 'classic rustique' menu ; accomplished cuisine.

Leijontornet (at Victory H.), Lilla Nygatan 5, ✉ S-111 28, ☎ (08) 506 400 80, *info@leijontornet.se, Fax (08) 506 400 85* – ⇔. MC AE DC VISA JCB. ✗ AZ v
closed Christmas-New Year and Sunday – **Meals** (booking essential) 265/750 and a la carte 475/575 ♀.
◆ Characterful dining room features remains of a 14C fortified tower and a glass fronted wine cellar sunk into floor. Main menu offers good range of original modern dishes.

Mistral (Andersson), Lilla Nygatan 21, ✉ S-111 28, ☎ (08) 10 12 24, *rest.mistral@telia.com* – MC AE DC VISA. ✗ AZ h
restricted opening in July and closed 19 December-6 January, Sunday, Monday and Bank Holidays – **Meals** (dinner only) 515/710 and a la carte 450/540 ♀.
◆ Small personally-run restaurant with modern décor. Open plan kitchen preparing original and creative dishes ; three choices per course and a degustation menu of 8 courses.
Spec. Smelt with cauliflower cream, oyster sauce. Crispy pig's cheek with quinoa ragoût. Terrine of agrumes, fromage frais sorbet.

Den Gyldene Freden, Österlånggatan 51, ✉ S-103 17, ☎ (08) 24 97 60, *info@gyldenefreden.se, Fax (08) 21 38 70* – ⇔. MC AE DC VISA JCB. ✗ AZ s
Meals (dinner only and Saturday lunch)/dinner 550 and a la carte 300/580 ♀.
◆ Restaurant in early 18C inn with fine vaulted cellars owned by Swedish Academy. Traditional, Swedish, robust cooking incorporating plenty of flavours and good local produce.

Brasserie by the Sea, Skeppsbrokajen, Tullhus 2, ✉ S-111 31, ☎ (08) 20 20 95, *bythesea@pontusfrithiof.com, Fax (08) 22 08 28,* ≤ Stockholm harbour and islands, – MC AE VISA AZ k
closed Bank Holidays, Sunday, Monday and lunch September-April – **Meals** a la carte 305/515 ♀.
◆ Quayside view of shipping, harbour and islands. Good value modern dishes, including shellfish. Dine on the attractive covered and heated terrace, followed by a game of boules.

Fem Små Hus, Nygränd 10, ✉ S-111 30, ☎ (08) 10 87 75, *fem.sma.hus@telia.com Fax (08) 14 96 95* – ⇔. MC AE DC VISA JCB AZ r
closed 25 December-1 January – **Meals** (dinner only) a la carte 375/535 ♀.
◆ Characterful restaurant located in 17C cellars of five adjacent houses and filled with antiques. Popular with tourists. Several menus available offering traditional cuisine.

at Djurgården :

Scandic H. Hasselbacken, Hazeliusbacken 20, ✉ S-100 55, ☎ (08) 517 343 00, *hasselbacken@scandic-hotels.com, Fax (08) 517 343 11,* , – , ⇔ rm, ▤ rm, TV ♿ – 250. MC AE DC VISA. ✗ rest DZ e
closed Sunday – ***Restaurang Hasselbacken*** : **Meals** *(closed Sunday dinner)* (booking essential) (dinner only and lunch Saturday and Sunday) 375 and a la carte – **111 rm** ☕ 1560/2670, 1 suite.
◆ Modern hotel situated on island in former Royal park, close to the Vasa Museum. Up-to-date bedrooms, some with views. Regular musical events. Restaurant with ornate mirrored ceilings, attractive terrace and pleasant outlook ; traditional Swedish cooking.

Ulla Winbladh, Rosendalsvägen 8, ✉ S-115 21, ☎ (08) 663 05 71, *ulla.winbladh@telia.com, Fax (08) 663 05 73,* – MC AE DC VISA. ✗ DY a
closed 24-25 December – **Meals** (booking essential) a la carte 163/465 ♀.
◆ Pleasant late 19C pavilion in former Royal hunting ground houses several welcoming dining rooms and extensive terraces in summer. Traditional Swedish cuisine.

at Södermalm :

Hilton Stockholm Slussen, Guldgränd 8, ✉ S-104 65, ☎ (08) 517 353 00, *stockholm-slussen@hilton.com, Fax (08) 517 353 11,* ≤, , , , – , ⇔ rm, ▤ TV ♿ – 300. MC AE DC VISA JCB. ✗ rest CZ e
Eken : **Meals** *(closed lunch Saturday and Sunday)* (buffet lunch) 160/445 and a la carte 415/570 ♀ – ☕ 135 – **281 rm** 2800/3000, 8 suites.
◆ Busy commercial hotel, overlooking Old Town and surrounding water, housed in three buildings with central lobby. Caters well for groups and conferences. Modern style restaurant with excellent view of Old Town and water. Traditional and modern Swedish cuisine.

Clarion, Ringvägen 98, ✉ S-104 60, South : by Götgatan ☎ (08) 462 10 00, *reservation.stockholm@clarion.choicehotels.se, Fax (08) 462 10 99,* – ▮, rest, – 500. AE VISA.
Gretas Kök : **Meals** (buffet lunch) 205/550 and dinner a la carte 295/465 – **522 rm** 1795/2495, 10 suites.
◆ Large modern glass-fronted building. Décor includes contemporary Swedish artwork ; also live music. Stylish bedrooms with wood floors ; good views to west and south. Contemporary style restaurant serving Swedish dishes with a modern influence.

The Rival, Mariatorget 3, ✉ S-118 91, ☎ (08) 545 789 00, *reservations@rival.se, Fax (08) 545 789 24,* – rm, – 700. AE VISA. CZ r
The Bistro : **Meals** a la carte 163/506 – 145 – **97 rm** 1690/3040, 2 suites.
◆ Modern boutique hotel and Art Deco cinema in 1930's building. Stylish bedroooms with cinema theme décor and high-tech facilities. First floor open plan bar and bistro/restaurant. Classic Swedish cooking in the bistro ; more modern dishes in the restaurant.

Eriks Gondolen, Stadsgården 6 (11th floor), ✉ S-104 56, ☎ (08) 641 70 90, *info@eriks.se, Fax (08) 641 11 40,* Stockholm and water, – . AE VISA.
closed Sunday – **Meals** 295/395 and a la carte 410/590 ♀. CZ a
◆ Glass enclosed suspended passageway, renowned for stunning panoramic view of city and water. Open-air dining and barbecue terraces on 12th floor. Traditional Swedish fare.

Gässlingen, Brännkyrkagatan 93, ✉ S-117 26, ☎ (08) 669 54 95, *gasslingen@telia.com, Fax (08) 84 89 90* – . AE VISA. BZ
closed 1 week Easter, 24 June-23 August, 19 December-6 January, Sunday, Monday and Saturday lunch – **Meals** (booking essential) 275/545 and a la carte 511/891 ♀.
◆ Personally-run neighbourhood restaurant with rustic beamed interior ; ceramic tiles, wood and paintings with ducks and geese motif. Classic and modern influenced dishes.

to the North :

Stallmästaregården, Norrtull, ✉ S-113 47, North : 2 km by Sveavägen (at beginning of E 4) ☎ (08) 610 13 00, *info@stallmastaregarden.se, Fax (08) 610 13 40,* , – , – 200. AE VISA JCB.
closed 20 December-7 January – **Meals** (see below) – **36 rm** 1995/2400, 13 suites.
◆ Attractive 17C inn with central courtyard and modern bedroom wing. Quieter rooms overlook waterside and park. 18C style rustic Swedish décor with modern comforts.

Stallmästaregården (at Stallmästaregården H.), Norrtull, ✉ S-113 47, North : 2 km by Sveavägen (at beginning of E 4) ☎ (08) 610 13 01, *info@stallmastaregarden.se, Fax (08) 610 13 40,* <, , –, . AE VISA.
Meals 425 (dinner) and a la carte approx 535 ♀.
◆ Part 17C inn with elegant 18C Swedish décor. Beautiful waterside terrace in summer. Open kitchen. Modern Swedish cuisine.

to the East :

at Ladugårdsgärdet :

Villa Källhagen with rm, Djurgårdsbrunnsvägen 10, ✉ S-115 27, East : 3 km by Strandvägen ☎ (08) 665 03 00, *villa@kallhagen.se, Fax (08) 665 03 99,* <, , , – , , rm, – 55. AE VISA.
closed 25-26 June and 21-28 December – **Meals** a la carte 309/525 ♀ – **18 rm** 1700/2200, 2 suites.
◆ Modern building in lovely waterside setting with contemporary bedrooms, all with view of water. Extensive open-air terraces amid trees. Traditional Scandinavian cuisine.

at Fjäderholmarna Island *25 mn by boat, departure every hour (½ hour in season) from Nybrokajen* CY :

Fjäderholmarnas Krog, Stora Fjäderholmen, ✉ S-100 05, ☎ (08) 718 33 55, *fjaderholmarna@atv.se, Fax (08) 716 39 89,* < neighbouring islands and sea, –, . AE VISA JCB.
May-September and December – **Meals** - Seafood - (booking essential) 195/560 and a la carte 335/520 ♀.
◆ Delightful waterside setting on archipelago island with fine view. Fresh produce, mainly fish, delivered daily by boat. Wide selection of traditional Swedish dishes.

to the Southeast :

at Nacka Strand *Southeast : 10 km by Stadsgården DZ or by boat from Nybrokajen :*

Hotel J , Ellensviksvägen 1, ✉ S-131 27, ☎ (08) 601 30 00, *nackastrand@hotelj.com, Fax (08) 601 30 09,* < sea, – , – 30. AE VISA. rest
restricted opening Christmas and New Year – **Meals** (see ***Restaurant J*** below) – **41 rm** 1495/3295, 4 suites.
◆ Former politician's early 20C summer residence in quiet waterside setting. 'Boutique' style hotel with maritime theme. Stylish spacious rooms, some with sea view.

X **Restaurant J,** Augustendalsvägen 52, ✉ S-131 27, ☎ (08) 601 30 25, *info@restaurantj.com, Fax (08) 601 30 09,* ≤ Sea, 斎 –, ⚓ MC AE D VISA. ⚔
closed Christmas and New Year – **Meals** 260/475 (dinner) and a la carte 275/575.
• Bright, informal restaurant with sleek maritime décor and attractive terrace beside marina. Selective menu of Swedish and international dishes.

to the South :

at Johanneshov (Globen City) :

Quality H. Globe, Arenaslingan 7, ✉ S-121 26, South : 1 ½ km by Rd 73 ☎ (08) 686 63 00, *info@globehotel.se, Fax (08) 686 63 01,* 斎, – |¦|, ⚔ rm, TV ♿ – 220. MC AE D VISA JCB. ⚔ rest
Tabac **: Meals** a la carte 280/370 – **287 rm** 1595/1795.
• Located in industrial office complex and well equipped for conferences. Functional rooms with good facilities. Friendly staff. Modern informal eatery in conservatory overlooking small lake and fountain. Swedish cuisine with popular international dishes.

to the West :

at Lilla Essingen *West : 5 ¼ km by Norr Mälarstrand* BY :

XX ✿ **Lux Stockholm** (Norström), Primusgatan 116, ✉ S-112 62, ☎ (08) 619 01 90, *info@luxstockholm.com, Fax (08) 619 04 47,* ≤, 斎 – ⚔ ▤. MC AE D VISA. ⚔
closed 24 December-1 January, Monday and lunch Saturday and Sunday – **Meals** a la carte 460/555 ♀.
• Converted brick warehouse overlooking waterways. Light and airy with green and white décor. Large window into kitchen ; innovative Swedish cooking with distinctive twists.
Spec. Oyster and mussel cocktail with lemon cucumber. Venison steak with spiced sausage, potato purée. Rhubarb jelly with yoghurt ice cream.

at Bromma *West : 5 ½ km by Norr Mälarstrand* BY *and Drottningholmsvägen :*

XX **Sjöpaviljongen,** Tranebergs Strand 4, Alvik, ✉ 167 40, East : 1 ½ km ☎ (08) 704 04 24, *info@paviljongen.se, Fax (08) 704 82 40,* ≤, 斎 –, ⚓ ⚔. MC AE D VISA JCB
closed 23 December-6 January – **Meals** (booking essential) 275/375 and a la carte 281/425 ♀.
• Modern pavilion in attractive lakeside setting. Swedish style décor. Good value classic Swedish cuisine at lunch ; more modern dishes at dinner.

to the Northwest :

XXX **Ulriksdals Wärdshus,** ✉ 170 79 Solna, Northwest : 8 km by Sveavägen and E 18 towards Norrtälje, taking first junction for Ulriksdals Slott ☎ (08) 85 08 15, *info@ulriksdalswardshus.se, Fax (08) 85 08 58,* ≤, 斎, – P. MC AE D VISA JCB. ⚔
closed 24-26 December, Monday January-15 May, Monday September-20 November and Sunday dinner – **Meals** (booking essential) 550 (dinner) and a la carte 460/625 ♀.
• 19C former inn in Royal Park with classic winter garden style décor. Wine cellar features in Guiness Book of Records. Extensive smorgasbord at weekends.

at Sollentuna *Northwest : 15 km by Sveavägen* BX *and E 4 (exit Sollentuna c) :*

XXXX ✿✿ **Edsbacka Krog** (Lingström), Sollentunavägen 220, ✉ 191 35, ☎ (08) 96 33 00, *info@edsbackakrog.se, Fax (08) 96 40 19,* – P. MC AE D VISA JCB. ⚔ rest
closed 10 July-6 August, 23 December-8 January, Good Friday, midsummer and Sunday and Monday except May, June and December – **Meals** 720 (dinner) and a la carte 660/900 ♀.
• Charming part 17C inn in small park with elegant rustic Swedish décor. Superb range of menus offering highly accomplished and original modern dishes.
Spec. Salmon with lemon biscuits and dill. Saddle of roe deer with blackcurrant sauce. Chocolate palette with fig and cardamon.

X **Bistro Edsbacka,** Sollentunavägen 223, ✉ 191 35, ☎ (08) 631 00 34, *info@svenskasmaker.se, Fax (08) 96 40 19,* 斎 – ⚔ ▤ P. MC AE D VISA JCB. ⚔
closed midsummer, 19-25 July and 24-26 December – **Meals** 325/395 and a la carte 265/529 ♀.
• Simple modern bistro, contrasting with hotel opposite, with black and white décor. Attractive rear terrace shielded from traffic. Good value menu of classic Swedish dishes.

at Arlanda Airport *Northwest : 40 km by Sveavägen* BX *and E 4* – ✉ *Arlanda :*

Radisson SAS Sky City, at Terminals 4-5, 2nd floor above street level, ✉ 190 45 Stockholm-Arlanda, Sky City ☎ (08) 506 740 00, *sales.skycity.stockholm@radissonsas.com, Fax (08) 506 740 01,* – |¦|, ⚔ rm, ▤ TV ♿. MC AE D VISA JCB. ⚔
Stockholm Fish **: Meals** - Seafood - *(closed Saturday, Sunday and Bank Holidays)* 98/299 and a la carte 202/463 ♀ – 135 – **229 rm** 2100, 1 suite.
• The perfect place not to miss your plane : modern, corporate airport hotel. Three décor styles : standard Scandinavian ; Art Deco or superior business style. Balcony restaurant overlooking airport terminal offering fish-based menu.

Radisson SAS Arlandia, Benstocksvägen, ✉ 190 45 Stockholm-Arlanda, Southeast : 1 km ☎ (08) 506 840 00, *sales.arlandia.stockholm@radissonsas.com, Fax (08) 506 840 01*, – rm, rest, – 240. rest *closed 23 December-3 January* – ***Cayenne*** : **Meals** a la carte approx 250 – **327 rm** 1400/1800, 8 suites.
◆ A short shuttle ride from the terminal. Bright and modern corporate hotel and congress hall. Ecological, maritime and Scandinavian themed bedrooms. Contemporary styled restaurant and adjacent bar for light snacks, pastas and traditional Scandinavian fare.

GOTHENBURG (GÖTEBORG) *Sverige* 711 O 8 – *pop. 437 313.*

See : *Art Gallery★★ (Göteborgs Konstmuseet)* CX **M1** – *Castle Park★★ (Slottsskogen)* AX – *Botanical Gardens★★ (Botaniska Trädgården)* AX – *East India House★★ (Ostindiska Huset : Göteborgs stadmuseum)* BU **M2** *Museum of Arts and Crafts★★ (Röhsska Konstlojdmuseet)* BV **M3** – *Liseberg Amusement Park★★ (Liseberg Nöjcspark)* DX *Horticultural Gardens★★ (Trädgårdsföreningen)* CU – *Natural History Museum★ (Naturhistoriska museet)* AX – *Maritime Museum★ (Sjöfartsmuseet)* AV – *Kungsportsavenyn★* BCVX **22** – *Götaplatsen (Carl Milles Poseidon★★)* CX – *Seaman's Tower (Sjömanstornet) (※★★)* AV *Göteborgs-Utkiken (※★★)* BT – *Masthugg Church (Masthuggskyrkan) (interior★)* AV.

Envir. : *Öckerö Archipelago★ by boat or by car : N : 17 km by E 6 and road 155 – New Älvsborg Fortress★ (Nya Älvsborgs Fästning)* AU – *Bohuslan★★ (The Golden Coast) N : - Halland coast to the south : Äskhult Open-Air Museum★ ; Tjolöholms Slott★* AX.

18 Albatross, Lillhagsvägen Hisings Backa ☎ (031) 55 19 01 – 18 Delsjö, Kallebäck ☎ (031) 40 69 59 – 18 Göteborgs, Golfbanevägen, Hovås ☎ (031) 28 24 44.

Scandinavian Airlines System : Reservations ☎ (770) 727727 Landvetter Airport : ☎ (031) 94 10 00.

To Denmark : contact Stena Line A/B ☎ (031) 775 00 00, Fax (031) 85 85 95 – To Continent : contact DFDS Seaways ☎ (031) 65 06 50, Fax (031) 53 23 09.

Kungsportplatsen 2 ☎ (031) 61 25 00, Fax (031) 61 25 01.

Copenhagen 279 – Oslo 322 – Stockholm 500.

Plans on following pages

Radisson SAS Scandinavia, Södra Hamngatan 59-65, ✉ S-401 24, ☎ (031) 758 50 00, *reservations.scandinavia.gothenburg@radissonsas.com, Fax (031) 758 50 01*, – rm, – 450. BU b
Atrium Bar & Restaurant : **Meals** (buffet lunch) 95/110 and a la carte 250/450 – 125 – **335 rm** 1850/1950, 14 suites.
◆ Grand commercial hotel with impressive atrium courtyard complete with water features and glass elevators. Spacious rooms with a choice of décor and good modern facilities. A range of international dishes offered in restaurant housed within the atrium.

Gothia Towers, Mässans Gata 24, ✉ S-402 26, ☎ (031) 750 88 00, *infomaster@gothiatowers.com, Fax (031) 750 88 82*, – rm, – 1500. rest DX k
Heaven 23 : **Meals** 263/510 and dinner a la carte 365/600 ♀ – ***Incontro*** : **Meals** *(closed 22 December-11 January, Sunday and Monday dinner)* (buffet lunch) 115/315 and dinner a la carte 285/395 ♀ – **693 rm** 1690/2590, 11 suites.
◆ Large twin tower hotel owned by Gothenburg Exhibition Centre, popular with conference delegates and business people. Elegant modern Scandinavian décor. Top floor restaurant, Heaven 23, for spectacular city views and modern cuisine. Buffet lunch in Incontro.

Elite Plaza, Västra Hamngatan 3, ✉ S-404 22, ☎ (031) 720 40 00, *info@gbgplaza.elite.se, Fax (031) 720 40 10*, – – 50. BU s
closed 24-26 December – **Meals** (see ***Swea Hof*** below) – **141 rm** 1665/2850, 2 suites.
◆ Discreet and stylishly converted late 19C building. Rooms embody understated luxury with those overlooking the atrium sharing its lively atmosphere. Smart cocktail bar.

Scandic H. Europa, Köpmansgatan 38, ✉ S-404 29, ☎ (031) 751 65 00, *europa@scandic-hotels.com, Fax (031) 751 65 11*, – rm, – 60. rest BU a
Meals (in bar Sunday) (buffet lunch) 158/250 and dinner a la carte 280/400 ♀ – **447 rm** 1550/2380, 3 suites.
◆ Large modern commercial hotel in one of Gothenburg's main shopping areas. Comfortable rooms with Scandinavian décor and good level of facilities. Ground floor bar and mall. Selection of Swedish and international dishes, more formal dinners.

Scandic H. Crown, Polhemsplatsen 3, ✉ S-411 11, ☎ (031) 751 51 00, *crown@scandic-hotels.com, Fax (031) 751 51 11*, – – 300. CU d
Meals *(closed Saturday lunch and Sunday)* (buffet lunch) 98/650 and a la carte 286/393 ♀ – **336 rm** 1595/2195, 2 suites.
◆ Modern group hotel in good location for transport connections. Fresh bright functional rooms with wood floors and colourful fabrics. Executive rooms with balconies. Pleasant atrium restaurant with a wide range of Swedish and international cuisine.

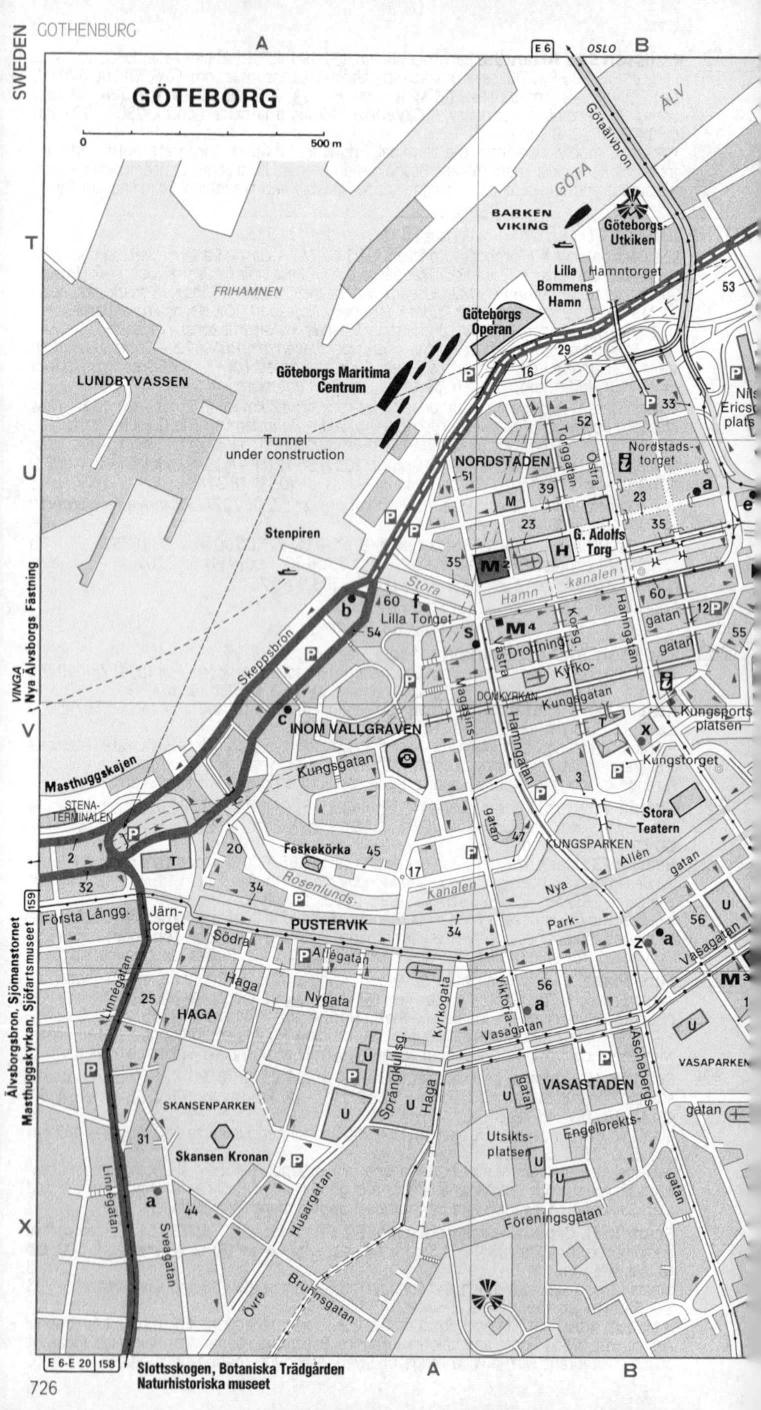
GÖTEBORG
0
500 m
A
B
T
U
V
X
E 6
OSLO
GÖTA
ÄLV
Götaälvbron
BARKEN
VIKING
Göteborgs-
Utkiken
Lilla
Bommens
Hamn
Hamntorget
53
FRIHAMNEN
Göteborgs
Operan
29
16
Göteborgs Maritima
Centrum
LUNDBYVASSEN
Tunnel
under construction
33
Nils
Erics
plats
52
Torggatan
Östra
Nordstads-
torget
NORDSTADEN
51
39
23
35
a
e
Stenpiren
23
G. Adolfs
Torg
35
Stora
Hamn
-kanalen
60
60
f
b
Lilla Torget
54
12
55
S
M4
Västra
Korsg.
Drottning
Kyrko-
gatan
gatan
Hamngatan
VINGA
Nya Älvsborgs Fästning
Skeppsbron
Magasins-
DOMKYRKAN
Kungsgatan
Kungsports
platsen
c
INOM VALLGRAVEN
X
Kungstorget
Masthuggskajen
Kungsgatan
Hamngatan
3
STENA-
TERMINALEN
Stora
Teatern
KUNGSPARKEN
Allén
2
20
Feskekörka
45
gatan
47
17
gatan
32
34
Rosenlunds-
kanalen
Nya
159
Första Långg.
Järn-
torget
PUSTERVIK
34
Park-
56
U
Södra
Allégatan
Z
a
Vasagatan
M3
Älvsborgsbron, Sjömanstornet
Masthuggskyrkan, Sjöfartsmuseet
Haga
Nygata
Linnégatan
25
HAGA
Viktoria-
56
a
Kyrkogata
Vasagatan
Sprängkullsg.
U
Aschebergs-
VASAPARKEN
Haga
VASASTADEN
gatan
gatan
SKANSENPARKEN
U
U
U
Utsikts-
platsen
Engelbrekts-
31
Skansen Kronan
U
U
a
44
Husargatan
gatan
Linnégatan
Sveagatan
Föreningsgatan
Övre
Brunnsgatan
E 6-E 20
158
Slottsskogen, Botaniska Trädgården
Naturhistoriska museet

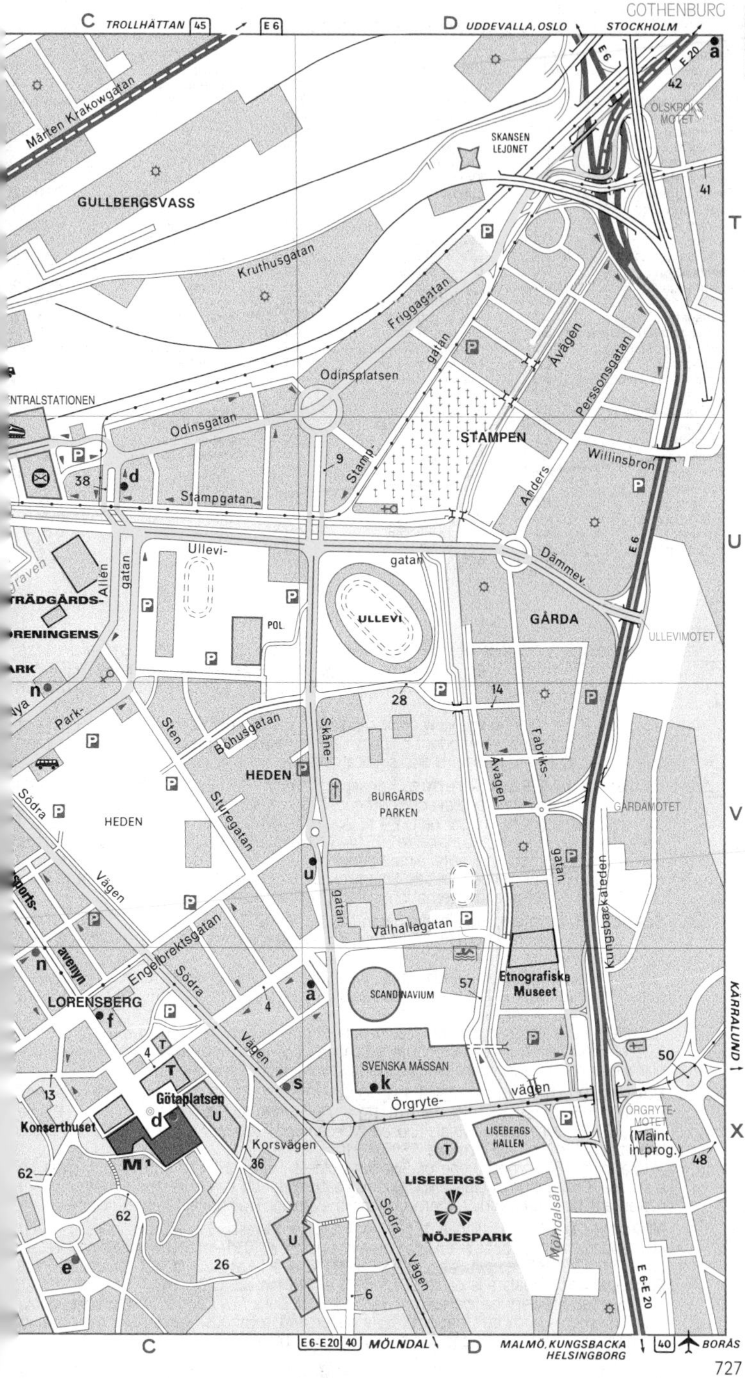

C TROLLHÄTTAN 45 E 6
D UDDEVALLA, OSLO
STOCKHOLM
E 6
E 20
42
OLSKROKSMOTET
41
Mårten Krakowgatan
GULLBERGSVASS
SKANSEN LEJONET
Kruthusgatan
Friggagatan
Odinsplatsen
CENTRALSTATIONEN
Odinsgatan
Stampgatan
Stampgatan
STAMPEN
Åvägen
Perssonsgatan
Willinsbron
Anders
Dämmev.
Ullevigatan
Allén
Vallgraven
TRÄDGÅRDSFÖRENINGENS PARK
POL.
ULLEVI
GÅRDA
ULLEVIMOTET
Nya Park-
Sten Sturegatan
Bohusgatan
Skånegatan
28
14
Fabriksgatan
Åvägen
HEDEN
HEDEN
BURGÅRDS PARKEN
GÅRDAMOTET
Kungsbackaleden
Södra Vägen
Engelbrektsgatan
Valhallagatan
Etnografiska Museet
57
SCANDINAVIUM
SVENSKA MÄSSAN
Avenyn
LORENSBERG
Götaplatsen
Konserthuset
Örgrytevägen
Korsvägen
ÖRGRYTEMOTET (Maint. in prog.)
50
48
LISEBERGSHALLEN
LISEBERGS NÖJESPARK
Mölndalsån
Södra Vägen
E 6-E 20
KÄRRALUND
T
U
V
X
C E6-E20 40 MÖLNDAL
D MALMÖ, KUNGSBACKA HELSINGBORG
40 BORÅS

STREET INDEX TO GÖTEBORG TOWN PLAN

Anders Perssonsgatan DTU
Andréegatan AV 2
Aschebergsgatan BX
Avägen DTV
Basargatan BV 3
Berzeliigatan CX 4
Bohusgatan CV
Brunnsgatan AX
Drottninggatan BU
Drottningtorget BU 5
Dämmevägen DU
Eklandagatan DX 6
Engelbrektsgatan BCVX
Fabriksgatan DV
Folkungagatan DU 9
Fredsgatan BU 12
Friggagatan DT
Föreningsgatan BX
Första Långgatan AV
Geijersgatan CX 13
Gustaf Adolfs Torg BU
Gårdavägen DV 14
Götabergsgatan BX 15
Götaleden BT 16
Götaplatsen CX
Götaälvbron BT
Haga Kyrkogata AX
Haga Nygata AX
Hamntorget BT
Hvitfeldtsplatsen AV 17
Järntorget AV
Järntorgsgatan AV 20
Köpmansgatan BU 23
Korsgatan BU
Korsvägen CDX
Kruthusgatan CDT
Kungsbackaleden DVX
Kungsgatan ABV
Kungsportsavenym BCVX
Kungsportsplatsen BV
Kungstorget BV
Kyrkogatan BU
Landsvägsgatan AX 25
Lennart Torstenssonsgatan CX 26
Levgrensvägen DV 28
Lilla Bommen BT 29
Lilla Risåsgatan AX 31
Lilla Torget AU
Linnégatan AVX
Magasinsgatan ABV
Masthamnsgatan AV 32
Mårten Krakowgatan CT
Nils Ericsonsgatan BT 33
Nils Ericsonsplatsen BT
Nordstadstorget BU
Norra Allégatan AV 34
Norra Hamngatan ABU 35
Nya Allén BCV
Odinsgatan CU
Odinsplatsen DT
Olof Wijksgatan CX 36
Övre Husargatan AX
Parkgatan BCV
Polhemsplatsen CU 38
Postgatan BU 39
Redbergsvägen DT 41
Riddaregatan DT 42
Risåsgatan AX 44
Rosenlundsgatan AV 45
Sahlgrensgatan BV 47
Sankt Sigfridsgatan DX 48
Sankt Sigfrids Plan DX 50
Skeppsbron AU
Skånegatan DV
Smedjegatan AU 51
Spannmålsgatan BTU 52
Stadstjänaregatan BT 53
Stampgatan CDU
Sten Sturegatan CV
Stora Badhusgatan AU 54
Stora Nygatan BU 55
Storgatan BVX 56
Sveagatan AX
Sven Rydells Gata DX 57
Södra Allégatan AV
Södra Hamngatan ABU 60
Södra Vägen CDX
Sprängkullsgatan AX
Torggatan BTU
Ullevigatan CDU
Utsiktsplatsen BX
Valhallagatan DV
Viktor Rydbergsgatan CX 62
Viktoriagatan BVX
Willinsbron DU
Vasagatan BVX
Västra Hamngatan BUV
Åvägen DTV
Örgrytevägen DX
Östra Hamngatan BU

Riverton, Stora Badhusgatan 26, ✉ S-411 21, ☎ (031) 750 10 00, *riverton@riverton.se, Fax (031) 750 10 01,* ←, – |‡| ⋟, rest, – 300. – **Meals** *(closed Sunday)* (dinner only) 225/495 and a la carte 365/475 ♀ – **187 rm** 1345/1845, 4 suites. AV c
◆ Modern hotel offering fine view of city and docks from upper floors. Sleek Swedish décor with wood floors and warm bright colours. Good business facilities. 12th floor restaurant, overlooking Göta Älv river and docks. Local and international cuisine.

Radisson SAS Park Avenue, Kungsportsavenyn 36-38, ✉ S-400 16, ☎ (031) 758 40 00, *reservations.parkavenue.gothenburg@radissonsas.com, Fax (031) 758 40 01,* – |‡|, rm, rest, – 550. CX f
Park **: Meals** 125 (lunch) and a la carte 295/445 1050/1895 – **301 rm** 1800/2100, 17 suites.
◆ Well located commercial hotel aimed principally at business clientele who appreciate its well organised conference facilities. Smart, executive bedrooms. Cosy restaurant in open plan format. Swedish and international dishes for all tastes.

Scandic H. Opalen, Engelbrektsgatan 73, ✉ S-402 23, ☎ (031) 751 53 00, *opalen@scandic-hotels.com, Fax (031) 751 53 11,* – |‡|, rest, – 180. rest DV u
closed Christmas, Easter, Sunday and lunch June and July – **Meals** (dancing Thursday-Saturday evenings except mid June-mid August) a la carte 256/442 – **238 rm** 1395/1695, 4 suites.
◆ Modern hotel catering for business people. Rooms vary in size, but all with same good level of facilities. Large restaurant, varied choice of Swedish and international dishes. Popular weekend entertainment, with dancing several nights a week.

Eggers, Drottningtorget, ✉ S-401 25, ☎ (031) 80 60 70, *hotel.eggers@telia.com, Fax (031) 15 42 43,* – |‡|, rm, – 55. BU e
closed 23-26 December – **Meals** *(closed 2 December-7 January and July)* 179/275 and a la carte 177/400 ♀ – **67 rm** 1395/1910.
◆ Charming 1850's hotel, one of Sweden's oldest : wrought iron and stained glass on staircase, Gothenburg's oldest lift. Rooms feature period furniture and fittings. Ornate restaurant busy during day, more elegant in evening. Traditional Swedish cuisine.

Novotel Göteborg, Klippan 1, ✉ S-414 51, Southwest : 3 ½ km by Andréeg taking Kiel-Klippan Ó exit, or boat from Lilla Bommens Hamn ☎ (031) 14 90 00, *info@novotel.se, Fax (031) 42 22 32,* ←, – |‡|, – 120. rest
Carnegie Kaj **: Meals** a la carte 267/432 ♀ – **143 rm** 1290/1430, 5 suites.
◆ Converted brewery on waterfront with view of Göta Älv. Central atrium style lobby. Spacious rooms with international style décor and sofabeds. Restaurant overlooking the harbour. International cooking to appeal to all tastes.

Mornington, Kungsportsavenyn 6, ✉ S-411 36, ☎ (031) 76 73 400, *goteborg@mornington.se, Fax (031) 711 34 39,* ... – ... rm, ... – 45. MC AE ... VISA. ... rest BV e
Brasserie Lipp : **Meals** *(closed Sunday October-April)* a la carte approx 400 – **92 rm** ... 1395/1895.
◆ Modern office block style façade conceals hotel on one of the city's most famous shopping streets. Rooms are compact with comfortable functional furniture and bright décor. Pleasant brasserie-style restaurant, hearty home cooking and international fare.

Quality H. Panorama, Eklandagatan 51-53, ✉ S-400 22, ☎ (031) 767 70 00, *info@panorama.se, Fax (031) 767 70 75,* ... – ... rm, ... – 100. MC AE ... VISA. ... rest DX
closed 22 December-8 January – **Meals** *(closed lunch Sunday and Bank Holidays)* a la carte 285/400 ♀ – **339 rm** ... 1350/2100.
◆ Commercial hotel popular with business people and conferences. Compact functional rooms, larger on top floors. First floor hotel restaurant in Scandinavian brasserie style. International menu.

Victors, Skeppsbroplatsen 1 (4th floor), ✉ S-411 18, ☎ (031) 17 41 80, *info@victors-hotel.com, Fax (031) 13 96 10,* ≤ Göta Älv river and harbour, ... – ... rm, ... – 40. MC AE ... VISA JCB. ... rest AU b
closed 22 December-2 January – **Meals** *(closed Friday-Sunday)* (dinner only) a la carte 315/385 – **27 rm** ... 1300/1700, 17 suites.
◆ Hotel occupies floors 4-6 of an office block on busy intersection but overlooking harbour. Compact reception and all-purpose dining/breakfast/coffee area. Functional rooms. Good view from restaurant. Choice of international cuisine.

Ramada Tidbloms, Olskroksgatan 23, ✉ S-416 66, Northeast : 2 ½ km by E 20 ☎ (031) 707 50 00, *info.tidbloms@swedenhotels.se, Fax (031) 707 50 99,* ... – ... rm, ... – 70 DT a
42 rm.
◆ Old red brick hotel in quiet residential area. Quaint turret and semi-circular veranda cum conservatory. Room décor in simple traditional style with standard comforts. Rustic circular restaurant. Hunting trophies adorn the walls. Simple steak-house style menu.

Poseidon without rest., Storgatan 33, ✉ S-411 38, ☎ (031) 10 05 50, *info@hotelposeidon.com, Fax (031) 13 83 91* – ... MC AE ... VISA JCB. ... BV a
49 rm ... 980/1250.
◆ Informal hotel in residential area not far from main shopping street. Comfortable neutral décor and functional furnishings in rooms. Accommodation for families available.

Onyxen without rest., Sten Sturegatan 23, ✉ S-412 52, ☎ (031) 81 08 45, *info@hotelonyxen.com, Fax (031) 16 56 72* – ... MC AE ... VISA DX a
Closed Christmas – **34 rm** ... 1290/1590.
◆ Small privately run hotel on outskirts of town in late 19C town house. Compact rooms on five floors. Quiet at rear. Convenient for Liseberg Park.

Sjömagasinet, Klippans Kulturreservat 5, ✉ S-414 51, Southwest : 3 ½ km by Andréeg taking Kiel-Klippan Ö exit, or boat from Lilla Bommens Hamn ☎ (031) 775 59 20, *info@sjomagasinet.se, Fax (031) 24 55 39,* ≤, ... – ... MC AE ... VISA. ...
closed Christmas and New Year, Saturday lunch and Sunday – **Meals** - Seafood - (booking essential) 395 (lunch) and a la carte 540/845 ♀.
◆ Delightful 18C former East India Company warehouse on waterfront. Forever busy restaurant spread over two floors with charming terraced. Accomplished seafood cooking.
Spec. Classic herring platter. Sole with lobster, truffles and asparagus. Haythorne soufflé.

Swea Hof (at Elite Plaza H.), Västra Hamngatan 3, ✉ S-404 22, ☎ (031) 720 40 40, *Fax (031) 720 40 10* – ... MC AE ... VISA. ... BU s
closed Sunday – **Meals** 395/795 and a la carte 485/625 ♀.
◆ Striking atrium style restaurant in heart of hotel with glass roof on metal framework and open plan kitchen. Dinner menu offers elaborate, modern cuisine.

Thörnströms Kök, Teknologgatan 3, ✉ S-411 32, ☎ (031) 16 20 66, *info@thornstromskok.com, Fax (031) 16 40 17* – ... MC AE ... VISA JCB. ... CX e
closed 20 June-12 August, 25 December-1 January, Sunday, Monday and Bank Holidays – **Meals** (booking essential) (dinner only) 385/650 and a la carte 395/585 ♀.
◆ Restaurant in quiet residential area near university. Stylish elegant ambience and décor. Formal service. Menu offers gourmet international dishes.

28 + (Lyxell), Götabergsgatan 28, ✉ S-411 34, ☎ (031) 20 21 61, *28plus@telia.com, Fax (031) 81 97 57* – MC AE ... VISA JCB. ... BX n
closed 24 June-20 August, 22-26 and 30 December, 1-3 January and Sunday – **Meals** (dinner only) a la carte 500/745 ♀.
◆ Characterful restaurant located in cellar down a steep flight of steps. Features fine wine cellar accessible to diners. Modern Swedish cuisine with emphasis on seafood.
Spec. Grilled scallops with caviar and pickled fennel. Rabbit with sweetbreads and artichoke purée. Chocolate pastry with Cognac jelly.

XX **Linnéa,** Södra Vägen 32, ✉ S-412 54, ☎ (031) 16 11 83, *restaurang.linnea@swipnet.se, Fax (031) 18 12 92* – MC AE D VISA JCB. rest CX s
closed Christmas-New Year, Saturday lunch, Sunday and Bank Holidays – **Meals** 245/395 and a la carte 515/625 ♀.
◆ Smart well run restaurant in classic building. Simpler lunch venue, more formal and elaborate for dinner with stylish place settings. Well prepared modern Swedish cuisine.

XX **Basement,** Götabergsgatan 28, ✉ S-411 34, ☎ (031) 28 27 29, *bokning@restbasement.com, Fax (031) 28 27 37* – MC AE D VISA. BX n
closed Sunday – **Meals** (dinner only) 480/690 and a la carte 330/450 ♀.
◆ Restaurant below street level with modern décor and white walls enlivened by contemporary paintings and lithographs. Imaginative modern cuisine using Swedish produce.

XX **Fiskekrogen,** Lilla Torget 1, ✉ S-411 18, ☎ (031) 10 10 05, *info@fiskekrogen.com, Fax (031) 10 10 06* – MC AE D VISA. AU f
closed July, 2 weeks Christmas and Sunday – **Meals** - Seafood - 195/595 and a la carte 418/685 ♀.
◆ Busy 1920's restaurant with reputation for its seafood. Striking rooms with high ceilings, wood panelling, columns and modern Scandinavian art.

XX **Kock & Vin,** Viktoriagatan 12, ✉ 411 25, ☎ (031) 701 79 79, *info@kockvin.se, Fax (031) 711 49 60* – MC AE D VISA BX a
closed 25 June-13 August, Sunday and Monday – **Meals** (dinner only) 395/465 and a la carte 315/695 ♀.
◆ Attractive candlelit neighbourhood restaurant. Modern paintings but 19C painted ceiling. A la carte or set menu with complementary wines ; best of Swedish ingredients.

X **Fond,** Götaplatsen, ✉ S-412 56, ☎ (031) 81 25 80, *fond@fondrestaurang.com, Fax (031) 18 37 90*, – MC AE D VISA. CX d
closed July, 2 weeks Christmas-New Year, Sunday, Saturday lunch and Bank Holidays – **Meals** a la carte 465/665 ♀.
◆ Bright semi-circular glass structure outside Art Museum houses contemporary colourful restaurant. Traditional Swedish fixed lunch and modern elaborate dinner menus.
Spec. Marinated herring, whitefish roe and pickled onions. Fillet of venison with roasted root vegetables and ceps. Berry crumble, strawberry vodka ice cream.

X **Hos Pelle,** Djupedalsgatan 2, ✉ S-413 07, ☎ (031) 12 10 31, *hos.pelle@swipnet.se, Fax (031) 775 38 32* – MC AE D VISA AX a
closed 6 weeks in summer, 24-25 and 31 December, 1 January and Sunday – **Meals** (dinner only) 500/545 and a la carte 485/768 ♀.
◆ Popular local restaurant with simple décor and comfortable atmosphere. Serves mixture of classic and modern Swedish cuisine prepared to high standard. Ground floor bistro.

X **Trädgår'n,** Nya Allén, ✉ S-411 38, ☎ (031) 10 20 80, *tradgarn@tradgarn.se, Fax (031) 10 20 89*, – MC AE D VISA. CV n
closed Sunday, Saturday lunch and Monday dinner – **Meals** 245/295 and a la carte ♀.
◆ A modern complex backing onto a charming park. Coolly decorated restaurant with large terrace with a lighter menu and a separate Cabaret/night club. International cooking.

BRASSERIE

X **Tvåkanten,** Kungsportsavenyn 27, ✉ S-411 36, ☎ (031) 18 21 15, *info@tvakanten.se, Fax (031) 20 13 93*, – MC AE D VISA. CX n
closed 25-26 June, 23-24 December and Sunday lunch – **Meals** 245/465 and a la carte 350/525 ♀.
◆ Busy characterful restaurant in city centre setting attracting varied clientele. Spacious dining rooms with oak floors and large bar. Swedish fare.

X **Herr Dahls,** Kungstorget 14, ✉ S-411 10, ☎ (031) 13 45 55, *info@herrdahls.nu, Fax (031) 13 45 59*, – MC AE D VISA JCB. BV x
closed July, 23 December-3 January and Sunday – **Meals** 215/475 and a la carte 269/491 ♀.
◆ Centrally located restaurant with terrace and adjoining shop. Large hatch giving view of kitchen. Set menu at lunch ; a la carte for dinner ; good quality Swedish produce.

X **Ivy Grill,** Vasaplatsen 2, ✉ -411 28, ☎ (031) 711 44 04, *info@ivygrill.com, Fax (031) 711 29 55*, – MC AE D VISA JCB. BV z
closed Monday – **Meals** (dinner only) 465 and a la carte 325/485 ♀.
◆ Step down from the lively bar to this trendy restaurant with its unusual décor. Menu specialises in grills ; simple lunch on the terrace in summer only.

at Eriksberg *West : 6 km by Götaälvbron BT and Lundbyleden, or boat from Lilla Bommens Hamn*

Quality Hotel 11, Maskingatan 11, ✉ S-417 64, ☎ (031) 779 11 11, *info.hotel11@quality.choicehotels.se, Fax (031) 779 11 10,* ≤ – |‡| ⇆ ▤ TV ☎ P – 🏛 1200. MC AE ⊕ VISA. ✻ rest
closed 17 December-10 January – ***Kök & Bar 67 :*** **Meals** *(closed lunch Saturday and Sunday)* 176/375 and dinner a la carte – **177 rm** ☕ 1345/1800, 7 suites.
◆ Striking former shipbuilding warehouse, part see-through there is so much glass ! Rooms feature stylish modern Scandinavian interior design with pale wood and bright fabrics. Upper floor restaurant, waterway views. International cooking.

Piren, Dockepiren, ✉ S-417 64, ☎ (031) 51 00 00, *piren@pirenbg.com, Fax (031) 51 00 01,* ≤ Göta Älv river and harbour traffic, 🏡 –, ⚓ ⇆ ▤. MC AE ⊕ VISA JCB. ✻
closed Saturday – **Meals** 250 (lunch) and a la carte 305/653 ♀.
◆ Uniquely sited restaurant at end of private pier, overlooking the busy harbour, with terraces on deck. Simpler ground floor dining room, more formal upstairs.

at Landvetter Airport *East : 30 km by Rd 40 DX – ✉ S-438 13 Landvetter :*

Landvetter Airport H., ✉ S-438 13, ☎ (031) 97 75 50, *info@landvetterairporthotel.se, Fax (031) 94 64 70,* 🏡, ≘s – |‡|, ⇆ rm, TV ☎ ♿ P. MC AE ⊕ VISA. ✻
Meals 198 (lunch) and a la carte 179/430 ♀ – **103 rm** ☕ 1245/1395, 1 suite.
◆ Airport hotel a short walk from the treminal. Rooms are bright and welcoming and feature typical Swedish décor in bright colours. Full modern and business facilities. Relaxed restaurant and terrace off the main lobby. Offers popular Swedish fare.

Switzerland

Suisse
Schweiz
Svizzera

BERN – BASLE – GENEVA – ZÜRICH

PRACTICAL INFORMATION

LOCAL CURRENCY – PRICES

Swiss Franc: *100 CHF = 64,22 euro (€) (December 2003)*

National Holiday in Switzerland: *1st August.*

LANGUAGES SPOKEN

German, French and Italian are usually spoken in all administrative departments, shops, hotels and restaurants.

AIRLINES

SWISS International Air Lines Ltd.: *Genève-Airport, 1215 Genève 15, ✆ 0848 852 000, unique zurich airport, 8058 Zürich 58, ✆ 0848 852 000.*

AIR FRANCE: *15 rte de l'Aéroport, 1215 Genève 15, ✆ 0228 278 787, Fax 0228 278 781.*
Kanalstr. 31, 8152 Glattbrugg, ✆ 014 391 818.

ALITALIA: *Genève-Airport, 1215 Genève 15, ✆ 0227 982 080, Fax 0227 885 630.*
Neugutstr. 66, 8600 Dübendorf, ✆ 018 244 550, Fax 018 244 510.

AMERICAN AIRLINES: *Hirschengraben 82, 8001 Zürich, ✆ 016 545 256, Fax 016 545 259.*

BRITISH AIRWAYS: *Chantepoulet 13, 1201 Genève, ✆ 0848 801 010, Fax 0229 061 223.*
Löwenstr. 29, 8001 Zürich, ✆ 0848 845 845, Fax 0848 845 849.

LUFTHANSA: *rte de Pré-Bois, 1215 Genève-Cointrin, ✆ 0229 295 151, Fax 0229 295 144.*
Gutenbergstr. 10, 8002 Zürich, ✆ 014 479 966, Fax 012 867 205.

POSTAL SERVICES

In large towns, post offices are open from 7.30am to noon and 1.45pm to 6pm, and Saturdays until 11am. The telephone system is fully automatic.
Many public phones are equipped with phone card or credit card facilities. Prepaid phone cards are available from post offices, railway stations and tobacconist's shops.

SHOPPING

Department stores are generally open from 8.30am to 6.30pm, except on Saturdays when they close at 4 or 5pm. They are closed on Monday mornings.
In the index of street names, those printed in red are where the principal shops are found.

TIPPING

In hotels, restaurants and cafés the service charge is generally included in the prices.

SPEED LIMITS – MOTORWAYS

The speed limit on motorways is 120 km/h - 74 mph, on other roads 80 km/h - 50 mph, and in built up areas 50 km/h - 31 mph.
Driving on Swiss motorways is subject to the purchase of a single rate annual road tax (vignette) obtainable from border posts, tourist offices and post offices.

SEAT BELTS

The wearing of seat belts is compulsory in all Swiss cantons for drivers and all passengers.

BERN

3000 Bern 729 G 5, 551 J 7 – *pop. 122 469 – alt. 548.*

Basle 100 – Lyons 315 – Munich 435 – Paris 556 – Strasbourg 235 – Turin 311.

Tourist Center, Railway Station ✆ 0313 281 212, info-res@bernetourism.ch, Fax 0313 281 277 – Tourist Center, at Bärengraben – T.C.S., Thunstr. 63, ✆ 0313 563 434, Fax 0313 563 435 – A.C.S., Theaterplatz 13, ✆ 0313 113 813, Fax 0313 112 637.

18 Blumisberg, ✉ 3184 Wünnewil (mid March-mid November), ✆ 0264 963 438, Fax 0264 963 523, Southwest : 18 km.
18 at Oberburg, ✉ 3414 (March-November), ✆ 0344 241 030, Fax 0344 241 034, Northeast : 20 km.
Bern-Belp, ✆ 0319 602 121, Fax 0319 602 128.

See: *Old Bern★★ : Marktgasse★* DZ ; *Clock Tower★* EZ **C** ; *Kramgasse★* EZ ; *views★ from the Nydegg Bridge* FY ; *Bear Pit★* FZ ; *Cathedral of St Vincent★* EZ : *tympanum★★, panorama★★ from the tower* EZ – *Rosengarden* FY : *view★ of the Old Bern – Botanical Garden★* DY – *Dählhölzli Zoo★ – Church of St Nicholas★.*

Museums: *Fine Arts Museum★★ : Paul Klee Collection★★* DY – *Natural History Museum★★* EZ – *Bernese Historical Museum★★* EZ – *Alpine Museum★★* EZ – *Communication Museum★* EZ.

Excursions: *The Gurten★★.*

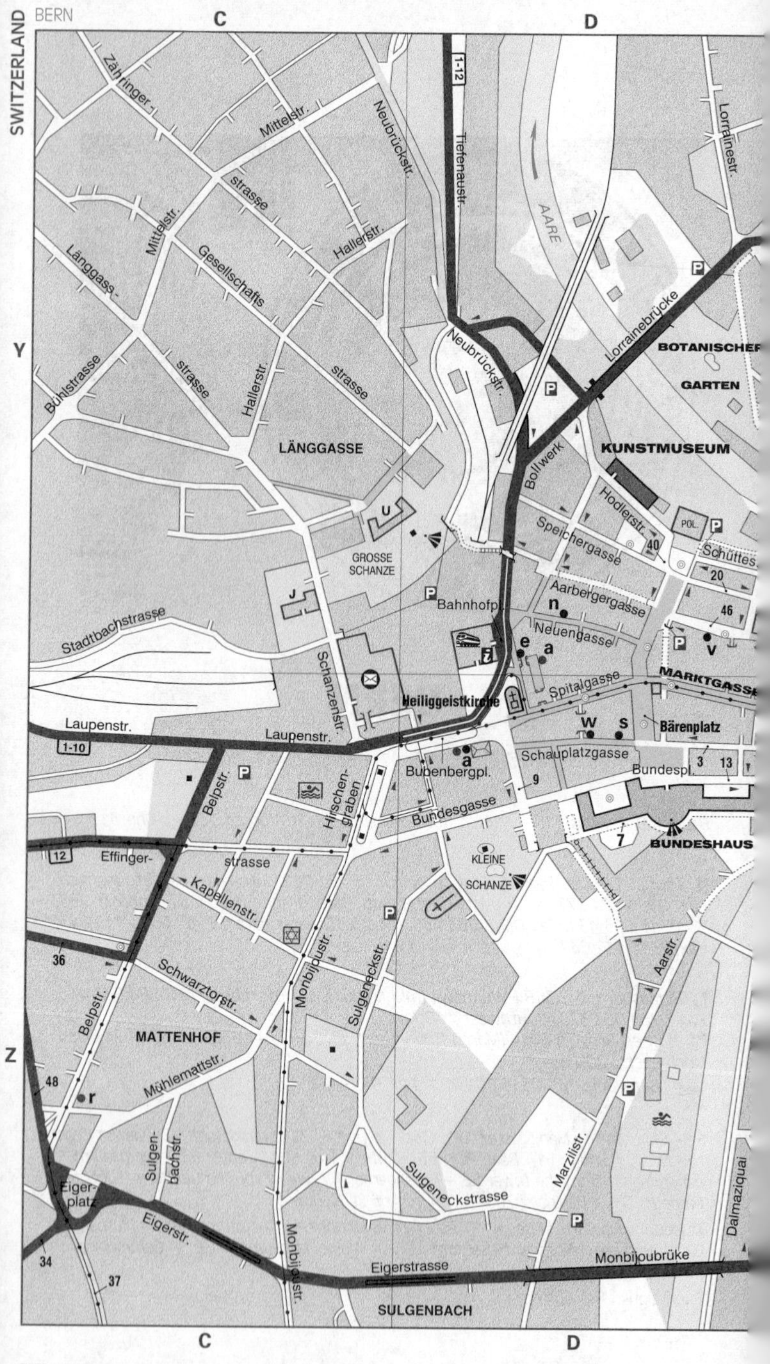
C
D
Y
Z
Zähringer-
Mittelstr.
Neubrückstr.
Tiefenaustr.
1-12
AARE
Lorrainestr.
strasse
Mittelstr.
Hallerstr.
Gesellschafts
Länggass-
strasse
Bühlstrasse
strasse
Hallerstr.
strasse
Neubrückstr.
Lorrainebrücke
BOTANISCHER
GARTEN
LÄNGGASSE
KUNSTMUSEUM
Bollwerk
Hodlerstr.
U
POL.
Speichergasse
GROSSE
SCHANZE
40
Schüttes
20
J
Bahnhofpl.
n
Aarbergergasse
46
Stadtbachstrasse
Neuengasse
e
a
v
MARKTGASSE
Schanzenstr.
Spitalgasse
Heiliggeistkirche
w
s
Bärenplatz
Laupenstr.
Laupenstr.
1-10
a
Schauplatzgasse
Bubenbergpl.
Bundespl.
3
13
Belpstr.
Hirschengraben
9
Bundesgasse
7
BUNDESHAUS
12
Effinger-
strasse
KLEINE
SCHANZE
Kapellenstr.
Aarstr.
36
Monbijoustr.
Sulgeneckstr.
Schwarztorstr.
Belpstr.
MATTENHOF
48
r
Mühlematstr.
Sulgenbachstr.
Marzilistr.
Dalmaziquai
Eigerplatz
Sulgeneckstrasse
Eigerstr.
Monbijoustr.
34
37
Eigerstrasse
Monbijoubrüke
SULGENBACH
C
D

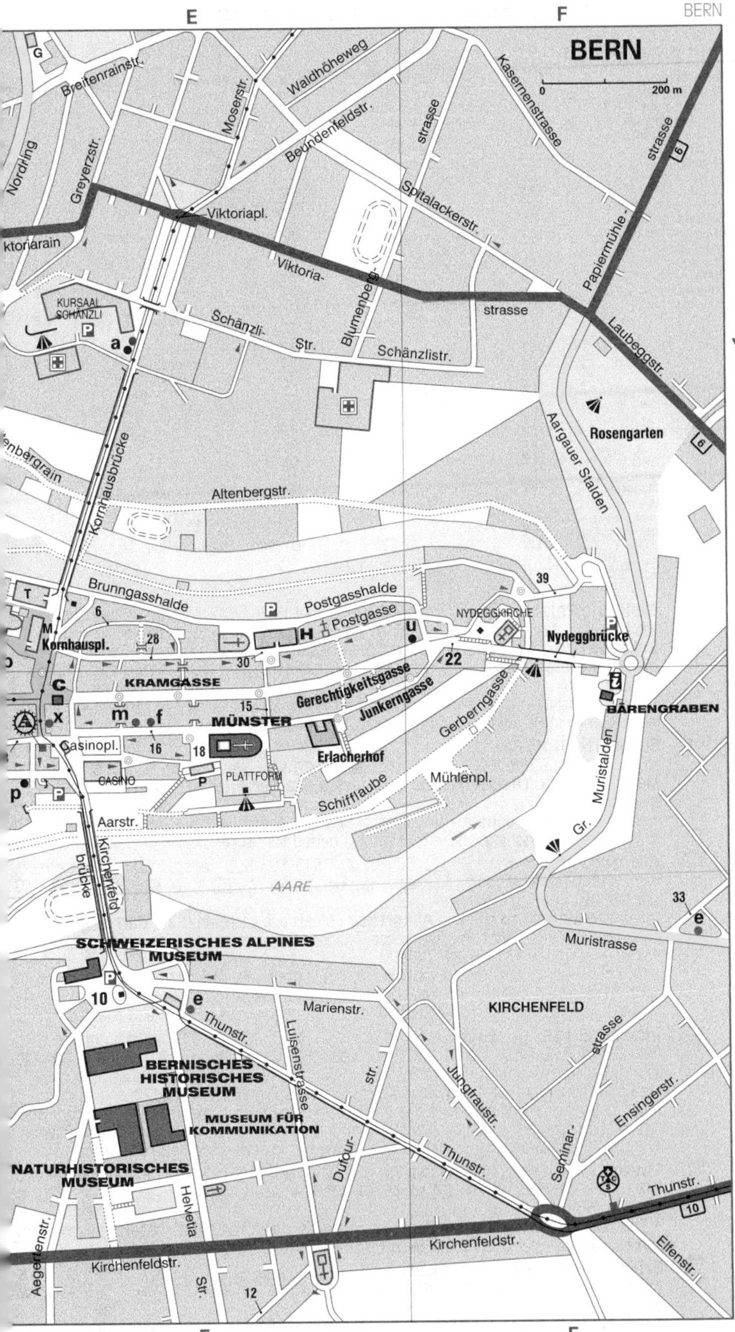

E
F
BERN
0
200 m
Y
Z
G
Breitenrainstr.
Waldhöheweg
Moserstr.
Beundenfeldstr.
strasse
Kasernenstrasse
strasse
6
Nordring
Greyerzstr.
Viktoriapl.
Spitalackerstr.
Papiermühle-
ktoriarain
Viktoria-
Blumenberg-
strasse
KURSAAL SCHÄNZLI
Schänzli-
Str.
Schänzlistr.
Laubeggstr.
a
Rosengarten
6
enbergrain
Kornhausbrücke
Aargauer Stalden
Altenbergstr.
T
Brunngasshalde
Postgasshalde
39
6
Postgasse
NYDEGGKIRCHE
M
H
u
Nydeggbrücke
Kornhauspl.
28
30
22
KRAMGASSE
Gerechtigkeitsgasse
C
Junkerngasse
BÄRENGRABEN
x
m
f
15
MÜNSTER
Gerberngasse
Casinopl.
16
18
Erlacherhof
Muristalden
CASINO
P
PLATTFORM
Mühlenpl.
p
Schifflaube
Aarstr.
Gr.
Kirchenfeld-
brücke
AARE
33
e
SCHWEIZERISCHES ALPINES MUSEUM
Muristrasse
10
e
Marienstr.
KIRCHENFELD
Thunstr.
Luisenstrasse
BERNISCHES HISTORISCHES MUSEUM
str.
Jungfraustr.
strasse
Ensingerstr.
MUSEUM FÜR KOMMUNIKATION
Dufour-
Thunstr.
Seminar-
NATURHISTORISCHES MUSEUM
Thunstr.
10
Helvetia
Kirchenfeldstr.
Elfenstr.
Aegertenstr.
Kirchenfeldstr.
Str.
12
E
F

STREET INDEX TO BERN TOWN PLAN

Street	Grid	No.
Aarbergergasse	DY	
Aargauer Stalden	FY	
Aarstrasse	DEZ	
Aegertenstrasse	EZ	
Altenbergrain	DEY	
Altenbergstrasse	EFY	
Amthausgasse	DEZ	3
Bahnhofplatz	DY	
Bärenplatz	DZ	
Belpstrasse	CZ	
Beundenfeldstrasse	EFY	
Blumenbergstrasse	EFY	
Bollwerk	DY	
Breitenrainstrasse	EY	
Brunngasse	EY	6
Brunngasshalde	EY	
Bubenbergplatz	DZ	
Bühlstrasse	CY	
Bundesgasse	DZ	
Bundesplatz	DZ	
Bundesterrasse	DZ	7
Casinoplatz	EZ	
Christoffelgasse	DZ	9
Dalmaziquai	DZ	
Dufourstrasse	EZ	
Effingerstrasse	CZ	
Eigerplatz	CZ	
Eigerstrasse	CDZ	
Elfenstrasse	FZ	
Ensingerstrasse	FZ	
Gerberngasse	FZ	
Gerechtigkeitsgasse	EYZ	
Gesellschafts strasse	CY	
Greyerstrasse	EY	
Hallerstrasse	CY	
Helvetiaplatz	EZ	10
Helvetiastrasse	EZ	
Hirschengraben	CZ	
Holderstrasse	DY	
Jubiläumsstrasse	EZ	12
Jungfraustrasse	FZ	
Junkerngasse	EFZ	
Kapellenstrasse	CZ	
Kasernenstrasse	FY	
Kirchenfeldbrücke	EZ	
Kirchenfeldstrasse	EFZ	
Kochergasse	DEZ	13
Kornhausbrücke	EY	
Kramgasse	EZ	
Kreuzgasse	EZ	15
Längassstrasse	CY	
Laubeggstrasse	FY	
Laupenstrasse	CZ	
Lorrainebrücke	DY	
Lorrainestrasse	DY	
Luisenstrasse	EZ	
Marienstrasse	EZ	
Marktgasse	DEZ	
Marzilistrasse	DZ	
Mittelstrasse	CY	
Monbijoubrücke	DZ	
Monbijou strasse	CZ	
Moserstrasse	EY	
Mühlemattstrasse	CZ	
Mühlenplatz	FZ	
Münstergasse	EZ	16
Münsterplatz	EZ	18
Muristalden	FZ	
Muristrasse	FZ	
Nägeligasse	DY	20
Neubrückstrasse	CDY	
Neuengasse	DY	
Nordring	EY	
Nydeggasse	FY	22
Papiermühlestrasse	FY	
Postgasse	EY	
Postgasshalde	EY	
Rathausgasse	EY	28
Rathausplatz	EY	30
Schanzenstrasse	CYZ	
Schänzlistrasse	EY	
Schauplatzgasse	DZ	
Schifflaube	EY	
Schosshaldenstrasse	FZ	33
Schüttestrasse	DEY	
Schwarzenburgstrasse	CZ	34
Schwarztorstrasse	CZ	36
Seftigenstrasse	CZ	37
Seminarstrasse	FZ	
Speichergasse	DY	
Spitalackerstrasse	EFY	
Spitalgasse	DZ	
Stadtbachstrasse	CY	
Sulgenbachstrasse	CZ	
Sulgeneckstrasse	CDZ	
Thunstrasse	EFZ	
Tiefenaustrasse	DY	
Untertorbrücke	FY	39
Viktoriaplatz	EY	
Viktoriarain	EY	
Viktoriastrasse	EFY	
Waisenhausplatz	DY	40
Waldhöheweg	EY	
Zähringerstrasse	CY	
Zeughausgasse	DY	46
Zieglerstrasse	CZ	48

Bellevue Palace, Kochergasse 3, ✉ 3001, ✆ 0313 204 545, *direktion@bellevue-palace.ch, Fax 0313 114 743,* ≤, 🍽 – |♦|, ▤ rm, TV ✆ ♿ – 🏛 15/350. AE ◑ ◎◎ VISA JCB. ✱ rest
Bellevue Grill / Bellevue Terrasse : *(Grill : closed lunch and in summer ; Terrasse : closed dinner in winter)* **Meals** 68 (lunch)/125 and a la carte 72/118 – **115 rm** ☕ 350/540, 15 suites. EZ p

◆ This recently renovated luxury hotel breathes an air of aristocratic refinement, effortlessly combining tradition and modernity. Beautiful views of the river from the terrace.

Schweizerhof, Bahnhofplatz 11, ✉ 3011, ✆ 0313 268 080, *info@schweizerhof-bern.ch, Fax 0313 268 090* – |♦|, ⇔ rm, ▤ rm, TV ✆ – 🏛 15/120. AE ◑ ◎◎ VISA JCB
Meals see ***Schultheissenstube*** and ***Jack's Brasserie*** below – **78 rm** ☕ 310/495, 6 suites. DY e

◆ In the Old Town opposite the station. Spacious rooms with varied décor, some with elegant, dark furnishings, others featuring period furniture.

Allegro, Kornhausstr. 3, ✉ 3013, ✆ 0313 395 500, *allegro@kursaal-bern.ch, Fax 0313 395 510,* ≤, 🍽, 🏋, ≘s – |♦|, ⇔ rm, ▤ rm, TV ✆ ♿ P – 🏛 15/350. AE ◑ ◎◎ VISA JCB EY a
Meals see ***Meridiano*** below – ***Allegretto :*** **Meals** a la carte 41/82 – ***Carrousel :*** **Meals** a la carte 38/94 – ***Wok-In :*** Asian rest. - *(closed Saturday and Sunday)* **Meals** a la carte 35/62 – ☕ 25 – **171 rm** 215/450.

◆ One of the city's newest and most fascinating hotels, in a variety of styles ranging from contemporary to trendy Japanese. The Allegretto has an open kitchen and pleasantly unfussy atmosphere ; the Carrousel has a terrace with views of Bern and the mountains.

Innere Enge 🐎, Engestr. 54, ✉ 3012, ✆ 0313 096 111, *info@zghotels.ch, Fax 0313 096 112,* 🍽 – |♦|, ⇔ rm, TV ✆ ♿ P – 🏛 20. AE ◑ ◎◎ VISA JCB by Tiefenaustrasse DY
Meals 50 (lunch)/68 and a la carte 49/100 – ☕ 20 – **26 rm** 220/420.

◆ Quiet establishment almost in the countryside. The rooms are fitted with elegant furniture and feature Provençal colour schemes. Breakfast is served in the historic Pavillon. The Jazz Cellar is a city institution. Welcoming bistro-style café and restaurant.

Savoy without rest, Neuengasse 26, ✉ 3011, ✆ 0313 114 405, *info@zghotels.ch, Fax 0313 121 978* – |♦| ⇔ TV ✆. AE ◑ ◎◎ VISA JCB DY n
☕ 20 – **56 rm** 195/260.

◆ This fine old town house is in Bern's pedestrianised centre. Bright, tastefully decorated, and reasonably spacious rooms, with up-to-the-minute technical facilities.

Bristol without rest, Schauplatzgasse 10, ✉ 3011, ✆ 0313 110 101, *reception@bristolbern.ch, Fax 0313 119 479,* ≘s – |♦| ⇔ TV ✆. AE ◑ ◎◎ VISA JCB DZ w
92 rm ☕ 190/300.

◆ This old town house has been completely refurbished and accommodates its guests in modern rooms with massive wooden furniture. Small sauna shared with the Hotel Bern.

Bären without rest, Schauplatzgasse 4, ✉ 3011, ✆ 0313 113 367, *reception@baerenbern.ch, Fax 0313 116 983* – |♦|, ⇆ TV ✆. AE ⓓ MC VISA JCB DZ s
57 rm ☕ 170/300.
• Just a stone's throw from the Bundesplatz, a hotel with rooms furnished in contemporary style with a good range of technical facilities for business travellers.

Belle Epoque, Gerechtigkeitsgasse 18, ✉ 3011, ✆ 0313 114 336, *info@belle-epoque.ch, Fax 0313 113 936* – |♦|, ⇆ rm, TV ✆. AE ⓓ MC VISA JCB FY u
Meals 62 (dinner) and a la carte 46/96 – ☕ 19 – **17 rm** 225/320.
• An establishment of great charm. From the lovely foyer to the tasteful rooms, there is an abundance of Art Nouveau details and fascinating original pieces. The restaurant serves light lunches and specialises in roasts in the evenings.

Bern, Zeughausgasse 9, ✉ 3011, ✆ 0313 292 222, *hotelbern@hotelbern.ch, Fax 0313 292 299,* – |♦|, ⇆ rm, TV ♿ – 🏛 15/120. AE ⓓ MC VISA JCB EY b
***Kurierstube** : (closed July and Sunday)* **Meals** 33 (lunch)/70 and a la carte 51/115 –
7 Stube : **Meals** a la carte 36/92 – **100 rm** ☕ 245/325.
• This establishment in the heart of the Old Town is proud to bear the name of city and canton. Rooms with functional furniture and fittings, plus good facilities for seminars. Classically elegant Kurierstube. Traditional cuisine in the 7-Stube.

City without rest, Bubenbergplatz 7, ✉ 3011, ✆ 0313 115 377, *city-ab@fhotels.ch, Fax 0313 110 636* – |♦| TV. AE ⓓ MC VISA JCB DZ a
☕ 18 – **58 rm** 135/205.
• This hotel is located right by the station. Contemporary rooms with decent, timeless furnishings and parquet floors throughout.

Kreuz, Zeughausgasse 41, ✉ 3011, ✆ 0313 299 595, *info@hotelkreuz-bern.ch, Fax 0313 299 596,* – |♦|, ⇆ rm, TV ✆ – 🏛 15/120. AE ⓓ MC VISA JCB DY v
Meals *(1st floor) (closed 5 July - 9 August, 19 December - 11 January, Saturday and Sunday)* a la carte 32/59 – **100 rm** ☕ 145/210.
• This hotel specialises in meetings and conferences. Most rooms are in contemporary style with dark wooden furniture. Seminar rooms of various types are available.

Schultheissenstube - Hotel Schweizerhof, Bahnhofplatz 11 (1st floor), ✉ 3011, ✆ 0313 268 080, *info@schweizerhof-bern.ch, Fax 0313 268 090* – AE ⓓ MC VISA JCB DY e
closed July - August, Saturday, Sunday and Bank Holidays – **Meals** 85 (lunch)/145 and a la carte 84/149.
• On the first floor of the Schweizerhof, a small restaurant with lovely place settings. Beyond is the cosy Simmertalerstube with its authentically rustic atmosphere.

Meridiano - Hotel Allegro, Kornhausstr. 3, ✉ 3013, ✆ 0313 395 245, *allegro@kursaal-bern.ch, Fax 0313 395 510,* ⩽ Bern and mountain, – ▤ P. AE ⓓ MC VISA JCB EY a
closed July, Saturday lunch, Sunday and Monday – **Meals** 48 (lunch)/135 and a la carte 78/136.
• The highlights of this restaurant on the fifth floor of the Hotel Allegro are the stylish modern ambience and the striking panorama of Bern and the mountains from the terrace.

Scala, Schweizerhofpassage 7, ✉ 3011, ✆ 0313 264 545, *antimo@ristorante-scala.ch, Fax 0313 264 546* – AE ⓓ MC VISA JCB DY a
closed mid July to 5 August, Monday (except December and Summer) and Sunday – **Meals** a la carte 53/95.
• Bright, modern restaurant in elegant Italian style on the first floor of one of Bern's shopping arcades. Parquet floors add to the congenial ambience.

Jack's Brasserie - Hotel Schweizerhof, Bahnhofplatz 11, ✉ 3011, ✆ 0313 268 080, *info@schweizerhof-bern.ch, Fax 0313 268 090* – ▤. AE ⓓ MC VISA JCB DY e
Meals 88 (dinner) and a la carte 59/114.
• On the ground floor of the Hotel Schweizerhof, this eating place is in refined brasserie style with nicely upholstered benches. Separate entrance, contemporary menu.

Mille Sens, in the market hall, Bubenbergplatz 9, ✉ 3011, ✆ 0313 292 929, *info@millesens.ch, Fax 0313 292 991* – AE ⓓ MC VISA DZ a
closed Sunday and Bank Holidays, from July - August also Monday and Saturday lunch – **Meals** 59 (lunch)/125 and a la carte 68/112 – ***Marktplatz*** : **Meals** a la carte 51/86.
• A modern restaurant in the midst of busy shops : black leather chairs, smart white tablecloths, parquet beneath your feet and air ducts along the ceiling. The no-nonsense Markthalle bistro serves a concise and well-priced menu.

Kirchenfeld, Thunstr. 5, ✉ 3005, ✆ 0313 510 278, *Fax 0313 518 416,* – AE ⓓ MC VISA EZ e
closed Sunday and Monday – **Meals** 47 (lunch)/62 and a la carte 50/91.
• This neo-Baroque edifice contains within its walls a garden café and a separate main room, both of which serve contemporary-style meals.

Wein und Sein (Blum), Münstergasse 50, ✉ 3011, ☎ 0313 119 844, *blum@weinundsein.ch* – ▤. MC VISA. ✗ EZ f
closed 18 July - 9 August, 21 to 29 December, Sunday and Monday – **Meals** *(dinner only)* (booking essential) (set menu only) 88.
• This is a typical Bern cellar restaurant, newly refurbished and with a wine bar. Gourmets come here in the evenings for a fascinating menu, changed daily
Spec. Berner Trüffel (October-November). Wild aus der Sommerjagd (May-July). Gebackene Desserts (Winter)

Frohsinn, Münstergasse 54, ✉ 3011, ☎ 0313 113 768, *frohsinn-bern@bluewin.ch, Fax 0313 112 052,* – AE ⓓ MC VISA JCB EZ m
closed 4 to 12 April, 18 July - 1 August, Sunday and Monday – **Meals** 78 and a la carte 40/91.
• This typical Old Town restaurant is called the "Good Cheer", and its rustic, homely interior and good food are sure to put a smile on your face.

Frohegg, Belpstr. 51, ✉ 3007, ☎ 0313 822 524, *Fax 0313 822 527,* – AE ⓓ MC VISA
closed Sunday – **Meals** (booking essential) 49 (lunch)/58 and a la carte 44/91. CZ r
• In an outer part of town, this is a local restaurant with an attractive, subdivided interior and a terrace off the rear courtyard. Sensibly-priced plain food.

Schosshalde, Kleiner Muristalden 40, ✉ 3006, ☎ 0313 524 523, *Fax 0313 521 091,* – P. AE ⓓ MC VISA FZ e
closed 19 July - 15 August, Saturday lunch and Sunday – **Meals** - Italian rest. - (booking essential) 60 and a la carte 53/96.
• Diners are made to feel welcome in this inviting little restaurant with its Italian decor. Wide range of dishes including fish specialities.

at Muri *Southeast : 3,5 km by Thunstrasse – alt. 560 – ✉ 3074 Muri bei Bern :*

Sternen, Thunstr. 80, ☎ 0319 507 111, *info@sternenmuri.ch, Fax 0319 507 100,* – |‡|, ✗ TV ☏ P. – 15/120. AE ⓓ MC VISA
Meals 40 (lunch) and a la carte 42/75 – **44 rm** ☕ 170/230.
• Village centre hotel in typical Bernese country style. Bright, functional rooms in the original house and annex. The "Läubli" and the lounge bar serve traditional dishes.

at Liebefeld *Southwest : 3 km direction Schwarzenburg – alt. 563 – ✉ 3097 Liebefeld :*

Landhaus, Schwarzenburgstr. 134, ☎ 0319 710 758, *landhausliebefeld@freesurf.ch, Fax 0319 720 249,* – P. AE ⓓ MC VISA
closed Sunday, Monday and Bank Holidays – **Meals** (booking essential) ***Rôtisserie :*** **Meals** 93 and a la carte 78/117 – ***Taverne Alsacienne :*** Meals 47 (dinner) and a la carte 49/85.
• This governor's residence of 1641 houses a bright and cheerful rotisserie serving modern cuisine. The former prison cells downstairs are now stocked with fine wines. The rustic Taverne Alsacienne offers regional specialities, including tartes flambées.

BASLE (BASEL) 729 G3 551 K3 316 J11 – *164 850 – alt. 277.*

See : *Old Town★ : Cathedral★★ (Münster) : ←★ "Pfalz" terrace* CY – *Fish Market Fountain★ (Fischmarktbrunnen)* BY – *Old Streets★* BY – *Zoological Garden★★★* AZ – *The Port (Hafen) ✳★, "From Basle to the High Seas"★ Exhibition – City Hall★* BY **H.**
Museums : *Fine Arts★★★ (Kunstmuseum)* CY – *Historical★★ (Historisches Museum)* BY – *Ethnographic★ (Museum der Kulturen)* BY **M¹** – *Antiquities★★ (Antikenmuseum)* CY – *Paper Museum★ (Basler Papiermühle)* DY **M⁶** – *Haus zum Kirschgarten★* BZ – *Jean Tinguely Museum★.*
Envir : *✳★ from Bruderholz Water Tower South : 3,5 km – Chapel of St.-Chrischona★ Northeast : 8 km – Augst Roman Ruins★★ Southeast : 11 km – Beyeler Foundation★★ Northwest : 6 km at Riehen.*

18 at Hagenthal-le-Bas, ✉ F-68220 (March - November), Southwest : 10 km, ☎ (0033) 389 68 50 91, Fax (0033) 389 68 55 66.

EuroAirport, ☎ 0613 253 111, Basle (Switzerland) by Flughafenstrasse 8 km and – at Saint-Louis (France), ☎ (0033) 389 90 25 11.

Tourist Office, in the casino, at Barfüsserplatz, ☎ 0612 686 868, info@baseltourismus.ch, Fax 0612 686 870 – T.C.S., Steinentorstr. 13, ☎ 0612 059 999, Fax 0612 059 970 – A.C.S., Birsigstr. 4, ☎ 0612 723 933, Fax 0612 813 657.

Bern 100 – Freiburg im Breisgau 72 – Lyons 401 – Mulhouse 35 – Paris 554 – Strasbourg 145.

Plans on following pages

Drei Könige, Blumenrain 8, ✉ 4001, ☎ 0612 605 050, *info@drei-koenige-basel.ch, Fax 0612 605 060,* ←, – |‡|, ✗ rm, ▤ rm, TV ☏ – 15/50. AE ⓓ MC VISA JCB
Rôtisserie des Rois : **Meals** 62 (lunch)/155 and a la carte 110/178 – ***Königsbrasserie :*** **Meals** 25 (lunch) and a la carte 49/108 – ☕ 32 – **82 rm** 285/700, 6 suites. BY a
• Historic old hotel on the banks of the Rhine, once frequented by luminaries like Theodor Herzl. Spacious rooms with genuine antique furniture. Lavish Rotisserie and terrace with legendary view of the Rhine. Less expensive Königsbrasserie.

Swissôtel Basel, Messeplatz 25, ✉ 4021, ℘ 0615 553 333, *reservations.basel@swissotel.com, Fax 0615 553 970,* rm, – 15/35. DX r
Meals *(closed Sunday)* a la carte 52/81 – 30 – **230 rm** 520/570, 8 suites.
◆ Right by the trade fair centre, this extensive establishment offers business travellers an up-to-the-minute level of comfort, particularly in the recently refurbished de-luxe rooms. Contemporary bistro-style restaurant.

Hilton, Aeschengraben 31, ✉ 4002, ℘ 0612 756 600, *info.basel@hilton.com, Fax 0612 756 650,* – 15/300.
Wettstein : **Meals** 39 and a la carte 62/111 – 30 – **204 rm** 460/660, 10 suites.
◆ This purpose-built establishment not far from the station harmonises well with the neighbouring buildings. Contemporary rooms designed with the needs of the business traveller in mind. Dine in the English-style Wettstein at basement level. CZ d

Radisson SAS, Steinentorstr. 25, ✉ 4001, ℘ 0612 272 727, *info.basel@radissonsas.com, Fax 0612 272 828,* rm, – 15/150. BZ b
Steinenpick : (Brasserie) **Meals** a la carte 47/92 – 29 – **205 rm** 460/600.
◆ In common with the majority of the rooms, the recently renovated foyer radiates a cool elegance. The inside rooms are quiet, the outside rooms well soundproofed. Welcoming ambience in the Steinenpick restaurant.

Victoria, Centralbahnplatz 3, ✉ 4002, ℘ 0612 707 070, *hotel-victoria@balehotels.ch, Fax 0612 707 077,* – – 15/80. BZ d
Le Train Bleu : **Meals** 45 (lunch)/75 and a la carte 54/90 – 23 – **107 rm** 340/450.
◆ This lovely hotel right by the station welcomes its guests with a splendidly spacious open-plan foyer. Rooms with up-to-the-minute comfort and tasteful décor. Le Train Bleu in elegant contemporary style, further enhanced with works of art.

Europe, Clarastr. 43, ✉ 4005, ℘ 0616 908 080, *hotel-europe@balehotels.ch, Fax 0616 908 880* – rm, – 15/120.
Meals see ***Les Quatre Saisons*** below – ***Bajazzo :*** (Brasserie) **Meals** 38 and a la carte 43/76 – 23 – **158 rm** 340/450. CX k
◆ This business hotel by the trade fair centre has air-conditioned, functionally designed rooms with contemporary furniture. Plenty of room for meetings and conferences. Brasserie Bajazzo with fresh, contemporary décor.

Basel, Münzgasse 12, Spalenberg, ✉ 4001, ℘ 0612 646 800, *reception@hotel-basel.ch, Fax 0612 646 811,* – rm, rm, – 25.
Brasserie Steiger : **Meals** a la carte 40/99 – 14 – **72 rm** 255/420. BY x
◆ In a tranquil location in the central pedestrian area with parking facilities and elegant, up-to-the-minute rooms. Admirably suited to both business travellers and other guests.

Euler und Central, Centralbahnplatz 14, ✉ 4051, ℘ 0612 758 000, *reservation@hoteleuler.ch, Fax 0612 758 050,* – rm, – 15/45.
Le Jardin : *(closed Saturday and Sunday)* **Meals** 42 (lunch) and a la carte 53/93 – 28 – **66 rm** 375/515. BZ m
◆ Right by the station, this city centre hotel has been a symbol of traditional hospitality for 135 years. Guests are accommodated in tasteful rooms and stylish suites. The elegant Le Jardin restaurant boasts lovely wall paintings.

Ramada Plaza Basel, Messeplatz 12, ✉ 4058, ℘ 0615 604 000, *basel.plaza@ramada-treff.ch, Fax 0615 605 555,* – rm, – 15/500. rest DX h
Filou : **Meals** 28 (lunch) and a la carte 48/108 – 28 – **230 rm** 240/270.
◆ A business hotel in the Trade Fair Tower : modern design, elegant glass and interesting light effects in the reception and the practical, warm-toned rooms. Stylish ambience in the Filou restaurant, its glass balcony giving views of the Messeplatz.

Palazzo without rest, Grenzacherstr. 6, ✉ 4058, ℘ 0616 906 464, *mail@hotel-palazzo.ch, Fax 0616 906 410,* – DY e
30 rm 220/320.
◆ Among the amenities of this modern hotel is an indoor golf-driving range. Air-conditioning in the rooms facing the street. Conservatory giving onto the little rear garden.

St. Gotthard without rest, Centralbahnstr. 13, ✉ 4002, ℘ 0612 251 313, *reception@st-gotthard.ch, Fax 0612 251 314* – BZ f
103 rm 220/360.
◆ Two adjoining hotels close to the station have been combined into one. The conversion has resulted in rooms with timeless, lightwood décor with good sound insulation.

Der Teufelhof, Leonhardsgraben 47, ✉ 4051, ℘ 0612 611 010, *info@teufelhof.com, Fax 0612 611 004* – – 20. BY g
closed Christmas – **Meals** see ***Der Teufelhof*** below – **29 rm** 180/365, 4 suites.
◆ Rooms in the "Art Hotel" are completely restyled every three years. The "Gallery Hotel" stages changing art exhibitions. Vinotheque in the foundations of the old city walls.

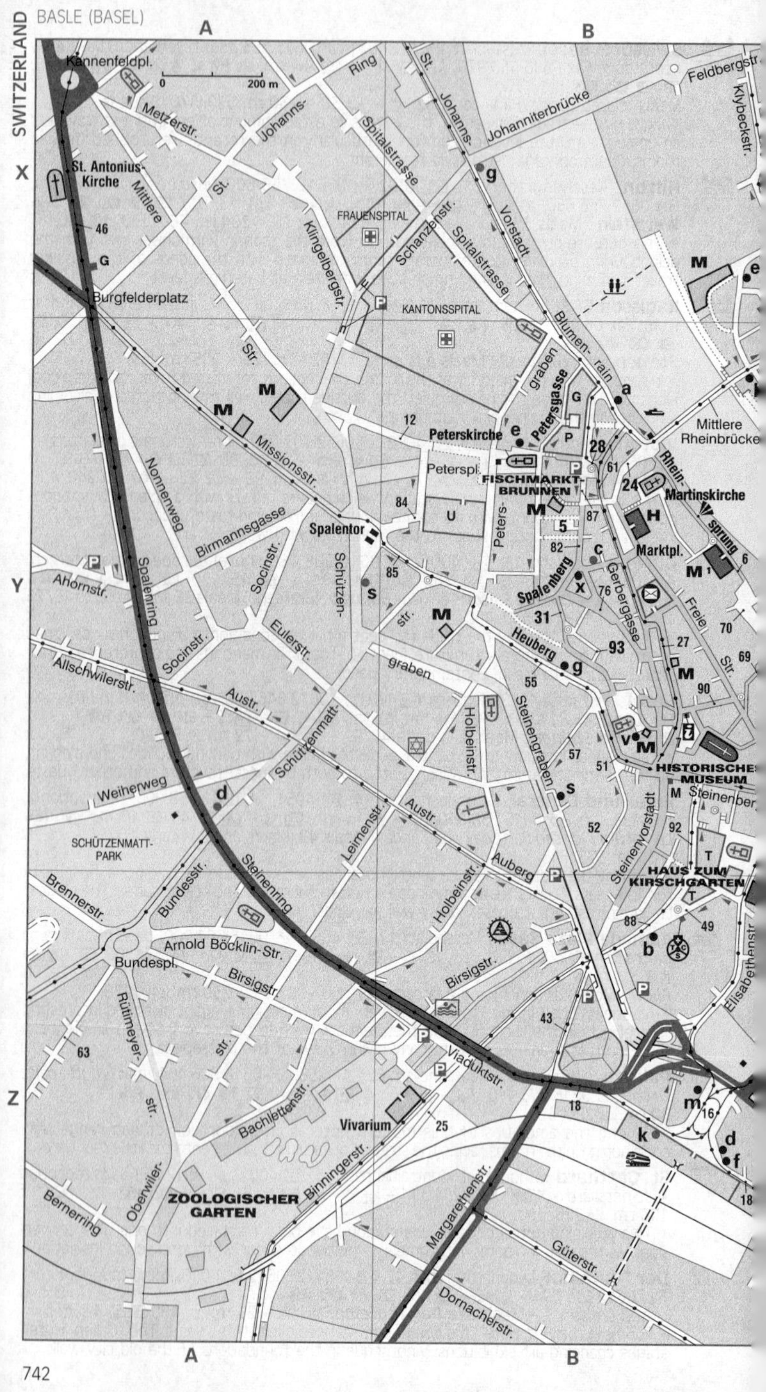
A
B
X
Y
Z
0
200 m
Kannenfeldpl.
Metzerstr.
St. Antonius-Kirche
Mittlere
St.
Johanns-
Ring
Spitalstrasse
St.
Johanns-
Vorstadt
Johanniterbrücke
Feldbergstr.
Klybeckstr.
FRAUENSPITAL
Klingelbergstr.
Schanzenstr.
Spitalstrasse
KANTONSSPITAL
Burgfelderplatz
Str.
Blumen-
rain
graben
Petersgasse
Mittlere
Rheinbrücke
Peterskirche
Rhein-
Martinskirche
sprung
Missionsstr.
Peterspl.
FISCHMARKT-
BRUNNEN
Marktpl.
Nonnenweg
Birmannsgasse
Spalentor
Peters-
Spalenberg
Gerbergasse
Freie
Str.
Ahornstr.
Socinstr.
Schützen-
str.
Spalenring
Socinstr.
Eulerstr.
Heuberg
graben
Allschwilerstr.
Austr.
Schützenmatt-
Holbeinstr.
Steinengraben
HISTORISCHES
MUSEUM
Steinenberg
Weiherweg
Austr.
Leimenstr.
Steinenvorstadt
SCHÜTZENMATT-
PARK
Auberg
HAUS ZUM
KIRSCHGARTEN
Brennerstr.
Bundesstr.
Steinenring
Holbeinstr.
Elisabethenstr.
Arnold Böcklin-Str.
Bundespl.
Birsigstr.
Birsigstr.
Rütimeyer-
str.
str.
Viaduktstr.
Bachlettenstr.
Vivarium
Binningerstr.
Margarethenstr.
ZOOLOGISCHER
GARTEN
Oberwiler-
Bernerring
Güterstr.
Dornacherstr.

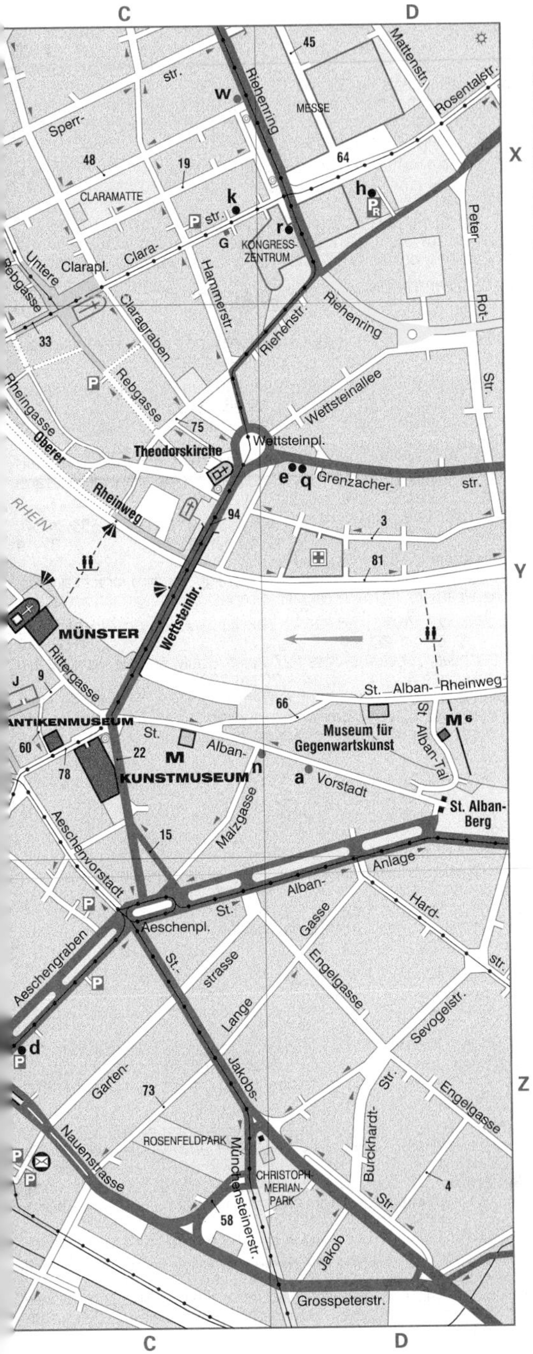

BASEL

Street	Grid	No.
Aeschenvorstadt	CYZ	
Alemannengasse	DY	3
Andreas-Heusler-Strasse	DZ	4
Andreasplatz	BY	5
Augustinergasse	BY	6
Barfüsserplatz	BY	7
Bäumleingasse	CY	9
Bernoullistrasse	ABY	12
Brunngässlein	CYZ	15
Centralbahnplatz	BZ	16
Centralbahnstrasse	BZ	18
Claraplatz	CX	
Drahtzugstrasse	CX	19
Dufourstrasse	CY	22
Eisengasse	BY	24
Erdbeergraben	BZ	25
Falknerstrasse	BY	27
Fischmarktplatz	BY	28
Freie Strasse	BY	
Gemsberg	BY	31
Gerbergasse	BY	
Greifengasse	BCY	33
Innere Margarethenstrasse	BZ	43
Isteinerstrasse	DX	45
Kannenfeldstrasse	AX	46
Klingentalstrasse	CX	48
Klosterberg	BZ	49
Kohlenberg	BY	51
Kohlenberggasse	BY	52
Leonhardsgraben	BY	55
Leonhardsstrasse	BY	57
Lindenhofstrasse	CZ	58
Luftgässlein	CY	60
Marktgasse	BY	61
Marktplatz	BY	
Marschalkenstrasse	AZ	63
Messeplatz	DX	64
Mühlenberg	CDY	66
Münsterberg	BY	69
Münsterplatz	BY	70
Peter Merian-Strasse	CZ	73
Riehentorstrasse	CY	75
Rümelingsplatz	BY	76
St.Alban-Graben	CY	78
Schaffhauserrheinweg	DY	81
Schneidergasse	BY	82
Spalengraben	BY	84
Spalenvorstadt	BY	85
Stadthausgasse	BY	87
Steinentorstrasse	BZ	88
Steinenvorstadt	BYZ	
Streitgasse	BY	90
Theaterstrasse	BY	92
Unterer Heuberg	BY	93
Wettsteinstrasse	CY	94

Merian, Rheingasse 2, 4005, 0616 851 111, *kontakt@merian-hotel.ch, Fax 0616 851 101,* – rm, – 15/80. BY b
Café Spitz : - Fish specialities - **Meals** 54/82 and a la carte 49/95 – **63 rm** 230/305.
• Historic establishment right on the Rhine. The rooms facing the river are quieter and have a wonderful view of the city's river frontage and the Minster. The Café Spitz tempts diners with fish dishes and with a sunny terrace overlooking the Rhine.

Dorint, Schönaustr. 10, 4058, 0616 957 000, *info.basbas@dorint.com, Fax 0616 957 100* – rm, – 15/80. rest in the North DX
Olive Tree : **Meals** 33 (lunch) and a la carte 42/90 – 22 – **171 rm** 270/405.
• An ideal hotel for business travellers, with modern, functional rooms with ample work desks and all technical facilities, proximity to trade fair grounds and congress centre.

Wettstein without rest, Grenzacherstr. 8, 4058, 0616 906 969, *mail@hotel-wettstein.ch, Fax 0616 910 545* – DY q
40 rm 200/190.
• Contemporary, functional bedrooms, bright breakfast room and a pretty little courtyard garden. Apartments in the adjoining buildings for long-stay guests.

Balade, Klingental 8, 4058, 0616 991 900, *info@hotel-balade.ch, Fax 0616 991 220,* – rm, BX e
Meals *(closed Saturday lunch and Sunday)* 48 (lunch) and a la carte 42/87 – 15 – **24 rm** 170/230.
• Close to the city museum and the museum of Basel Minster, the accommodation in this modern building with its red façade consists of simply-designed rooms with excellent facilities. The bistro-style restaurant opens out onto the foyer.

Steinenschanze without rest, Steinengraben 69, 4051, 0612 725 353, *info@steinenschanze.ch, Fax 0612 724 573,* – BY s
closed 24 December - 4 January – **54 rm** 180/250.
• Not far from the city centre, this establishment offers straightforward, practically furnished rooms. When the weather's warm, breakfast is served on the garden terrace.

Au Violon, Lohnhof 4, 4051, 0612 698 711, *auviolon@iprolink.ch, Fax 0612 698 712,* – BY v
closed 22 December - 8 January ; Rest also closed 27 June - 6 July, Sunday, Monday and Bank Holidays – **Meals** a la carte 45/84 – 14 – **20 rm** 100/180.
• The old remand prison is a most unusual but extremely convenient place to stay, right on the central Barfüsserplatz, from where guests are transported by lift straight up to the reception. The restaurant's offerings are more suitable for kings than convicts.

Bruderholz, Bruderholzallee 42, 4059, 0613 618 222, *bruderholz@bluewin.ch, Fax 0613 618 203,* –
closed 24 February - 8 March, Sunday and Monday (except fairs) – **Meals** 68 (lunch)/195 and a la carte 148/228. South by Margarethenstrasse BZ
• This imposing mansion high up above the city is furnished in classically comfortable style and boasts a lovely flower garden. Creative cuisine for the committed gourmet.
Spec. Soupe crémeuse aux truffes noires du Périgord et sa royale de volaille (Autumn - Winter). La queue de langoustine grillée au velours d'anchois citronné et émulsion de poivrons doux (Spring - Summer). La poularde de Bresse poêlée, jus de cuisson au foie gras, coussinets maigres aux épinards

Les Quatre Saisons - Hotel Europe, Clarastr. 43 (1st floor), 4005, 0616 908 720, *hotel-europe@balehotels.ch, Fax 0616 908 880* – CX k
closed 26 July - 23 August and Sunday (except fairs) – **Meals** 63 (lunch)/135 and a la carte 81/145.
• Contemporary-style restaurant on the first floor of the Europa, where diners are treated, by flawlessly trained staff, to international delicacies of the highest quality.
Spec. Périgord-Trüffel im Strudelteig. Gedeckte Kalbsmilken-Torte mit schwarzem Trüffel und Lauch. Pithiviers mit Sanglé und Tannenhonig

Rest. Der Teufelhof - Hotel Der Teufelhof, Leonhardsgraben 47, 4051, 0612 611 010, *info@teufelhof.com, Fax 0612 611 004,* – BY g
closed Christmas – ***Bel Etage*** : *(closed 1 to 6 January, July - August) (Saturday lunch, Sunday and Monday except fairs)* **Meals** 77 (lunch)/180 and a la carte 91/164 – ***Weinstube*** : **Meals** 70 and a la carte 66/102.
• Contemporary, strikingly creative cuisine served in tasteful rooms with lovely parquet floors. The dining experience is enhanced by a superb array of well-chosen wines. Beyond the courtyard, the congenial wine cellar offers a more straightforward menu.
Spec. Gänseleber-Tiramisù mit Quittengelée und Schalottenconfit. Gegrilltes Loup de Mer mit Olivennage, Orecchiette und Artischocken. Holunderblütenkaltschale mit Schokoladencannelloni und Erdbeereis

XXX **Zum Schützenhaus,** Schützenmattstr. 56, ✉ 4051, ☎ 0612 726 760, *restaurant@schuetzenhaus-basel.ch, Fax 0612 726 586,* – . AE MC VISA AY d
Gartensaal : **Meals** 59/75 and a la carte 75/138.
◆ The historic guilds building houses the country-style Gartensaal with wooden tables and cheerful décor as well as the straightforward Brasserie - both with a terrace.

XX **Chez Donati,** St. Johanns-Vorstadt 48, ✉ 4056, ☎ 0613 220 919, *Fax 0613 220 981,* BX g
closed 11 July - 9 August, 29 February - 8 March, Sunday and Monday – **Meals** - Italian rest. - a la carte 72/127.
◆ The interior of this old building is in classic late-19C style, with chandeliers, pictures, stucco and woodwork all helping to produce an ambience of great elegance.

XX **Charon,** Schützengraben 62, ✉ 4051, ☎ 0612 619 980, *Fax 0612 619 909* – . AE MC VISA JCB AY s
closed 8 to 12 April, 11 July - 8 August, 21 to 29 December, Monday from October - April, Saturday from May - September, Sunday and Bank Holidays – **Meals** 95 (dinner) and a la carte 62/120.
◆ Appealing little restaurant with a bistro-style ambience and beautifully decorated with plants. Ever-changing menu based on the choicest and freshest ingredients.

XX **Hong Kong,** Riehenring 91, ✉ 4058, ☎ 0616 918 814, *info@restaurant-hongkong.ch, Fax 0616 918 836,* – AE MC VISA JCB CX w
closed Easter, July and Christmas – **Meals** - Chinese rest. - 50 (lunch)/86 and a la carte 52/90.
◆ The offerings here cover the spectrum of Chinese cuisine from Canton to Szechwan, and are served up in a setting effectively evoking the Orient.

XX **St. Alban-Stübli,** St. Alban-Vorstadt 74, ✉ 4052, ☎ 0612 725 415, *Fax 0612 740 488,* – AE MC VISA DY a
closed 30 July - 8 August, 24 December - 5 January, Saturday (except dinner from September - June) and Sunday – **Meals** (booking essential) 48 (lunch)/90 and a la carte 59/112.
◆ Solid, traditional dishes served up in the cosy parlour or in the garden. Afterwards, it's up the staircase to the smoking room to savour a good cigar.

XX **Zur Schuhmachernzunft,** Hutgasse 6 (1st floor), ✉ 4001, ☎ 0612 612 091, *mschneiter@digi-com.ch, Fax 0612 612 591* – . AE MC VISA BY c
closed 26 June - 15 August, 24 to 28 December, Saturday (except November - December) and Sunday (except fairs and carnival) – **Meals** (booking essential) 87 and a la carte 64/116.
◆ This welcoming restaurant is on the first floor of an old city residence. Venerable wood panelling, lots of pictures, a grand piano and lovely place settings set the tone.

X **Sakura,** Centralbahnstr. 14, ✉ 4051, ☎ 0612 720 505, *info@bahnhofrestaurants.ch, Fax 0612 953 988* – . AE MC VISA BZ k
closed 5 July - 15 August, Saturday lunch, Sunday and Bank Holidays – **Meals** - Japanese rest. - ***Teppanyaki :*** **Meals** 64/114 and a la carte 37/93 – ***Yakitori :*** **Meals** 47/85 and a la carte 53/108.
◆ This establishment in the station building stands under the sign of the Rising Sun. It smilingly invites guests to savour its delicately presented teppan-yaki specialities. Japanese hospitality and the chance to see the chefs deploy their well-honed skills.

X **St. Alban-Eck,** St. Alban-Vorstadt 60, ✉ 4052, ☎ 0612 710 320, *pluess@st-alban-eck.ch, Fax 0612 738 609* – AE MC VISA CY n
closed 17 July - 9 August, Saturday lunch and Sunday – **Meals** 43 (lunch)/91 and a la carte 67/115.
◆ This old corner building with its half-timbered façade is located in a quiet residential area close to the Rhine. Congenial, rustic interior with lots of wood and panelling.

at Riehen *by ② : 5 km – alt. 288 – ✉ 4125 Riehen :*

XX ✿ **Schürmann's,** Äussere Baselstr. 159, ☎ 0616 431 210, *Fax 0616 431 211,* – AE MC VISA
closed 26 July - 7 August, 4 to 16 October, 1 to 7 March, Sunday and Monday (except major fairs) – **Meals** *(dinner only)* 95 and a la carte 74/137.
◆ A modern restaurant with changing picture exhibitions and a garden terrace on which to enjoy a creative, tasty menu fashioned from ultra-fresh ingredients.
Spec. Spezialitäten mit weissem Albatrüffel (Autumn - Winter). Badische Spargeln (Spring). Reh und Wildsau aus der Region (Summer - Autumn)

at Birsfelden *East by ④ : 3 km – alt. 260 – ✉ 4127 Birsfelden :*

Alfa, Hauptstr. 15, ☎ 0613 156 262, *alfa.birsfelden@bluewin.ch, Fax 0613 156 263* – 15/80. AE MC VISA
Meals *(closed Sunday)* 22 (lunch) and a la carte 36/110 – **51 rm** 105/200.
◆ Located only 15 minutes from the city centre by tram. Functional and sensibly-priced rooms offering a useful alternative to a stay in a city centre establishment.

at Muttenz *by ⑤ : 4,5 km – alt. 271 – ✉ 4132 Muttenz :*

Baslertor, St. Jakobs-Str. 1, ☎ 0614 655 555, *hotel-baslertor@balehotels.ch, Fax 0614 655 550,* – , – – 15/20. AE VISA
Meals *(closed Saturday and Sunday) (dinner only)* a la carte approx. 43 – ☕ 13 – **43 rm** 270/330, 4 suites.
◆ Spacious rooms in a large-scale complex that also includes a shopping centre. Also available are apartments with fully equipped kitchens.

at Binningen *South : 2 km by Oberwilerstrasse AZ – alt. 284 – ✉ 4102 Binningen :*

Schloss Binningen, Schlossgasse 5, ☎ 0614 212 055, *wdammann@schloss-binningen.ch, Fax 0614 210 635,* , – P. AE VISA JCB
closed 21 February - 8 March, Sunday and Monday (except fairs and Bank Holidays) – **Meals** 50 (lunch)/98 and a la carte 65/130.
◆ Dinner in the Empire Salon, an intimate tête-à-tête in the Castle Parlour - pleasurable experiences abound in this stylishly decorated manor house set in parkland.

The Castle, Hasenrainstr. 59, ☎ 0614 212 430, *welcome@thecastle.ch, Fax 0614 217 709,* ← – P. AE VISA
closed 2 weeks in August, Saturday lunch, Monday and Tuesday – **Meals** 55 (lunch)/138 and a la carte 89/132.
◆ Parquet floors, paintings and lovely place settings lend character to this elegant, English-style establishment divided up by arcades. Superb views over the city.

Gasthof Neubad with rm, Neubadrain 4, ☎ 0613 020 705, *gasthof.neubad@datacomm.ch, Fax 0613 028 116,* – rm, TV P. AE VISA
closed 21 February - 6 March and Wednesday – **Meals** 50 (lunch)/90 and a la carte 49/112 – **6 rm** ☕ 125/240.
◆ This lovely building of 1742 was originally an inn with a little spa attached. Good plain food is served here, as well as in the pretty garden restaurant.

GENEVA 729 C7 552 B11 – *175 998 – alt. 375.*

See : *The Shores of the lake★★ : ←★★★ FGY – Parks★★ : Mon Repos GX, La Perle du Lac and Villa Barton – Botanical Garden★ : alpine rock-garden★★ – Cathedral St-Pierre★ : north Tower ✳★★ FZ – Old Town★ : Reformation Monument★ FZ* **D** *; Archaeological Site★★ – Palais des Nations★★ – Parc de la Grange★ – Parc des Eaux-Vives★ – Nave★ of Church of Christ the King – Woodwork★ in the Historical Museum of the Swiss Abroad – Baur Collection★ (in 19C mansion) GZ – Maison Tavel★ FZ.*

Museums : *Ariana★★ – Art and History★★ GZ – Natural History★★ GZ – International Automobile Museum★ – Petit Palais : Modern Art★★ GZ – International Red Cross and Red Crescent Museum★★.*

Excursions: *by boat on the lake, Information : Cie Gén. de Nav., Jardin Anglais ☎ 0223 125 223, Fax 0223 125 225- Mouettes genevoises, 8 quai Mont-Blanc, ☎ 0227 322 944 - Swiss Boat, 4 quai Mont-Blanc, ☎ 0227 324 747.*

18 at Cologny ✉ 1223 (March - December), ☎ 0227 074 800, Fax 0227 074 820 ; 18 at Bossey ✉ F-74160 (March - December), ☎ (0033) 450 43 95 50, Fax (0033) 450 95 32 57 by road to Troinex ; 27 at Esery ✉ F-74930 Reignier (March - December), ☎ (0033) 450 36 58 70, Fax (0033) 450 36 57 62, Southeast : 15 km.

18 Maison Blanche at Echenevex-Gex ✉ F-01170 (March - mid December) ☎ (0033) 450 42 44 42, Fax (0033) 450 42 44 43, Northwest : 17 km.

✈ Genève-Cointrin, ☎ 0227 177 111.

Tourist Office, 18 r. du Mont Blanc, ☎ 0229 097 000, info@geneve-tourisme.ch, Fax 0229 097 011, GenèveAirport, Arrival, c/o Amdaco – T.C.S., 8 cours de Rive, 1204 Genève, 4 ch. de Blandonnet, 1214 Vernier, ☎ 0224 172 030, Fax 0224 172 042 – A.C.S., 8 r. de l'Arquebuse, ☎ 0223 422 233, Fax 0223 013 711.

Bern 164 – Bourg-en-B. 101 – Lausanne 60 – Lyons 151 – Paris 538 – Turin 252.

Plans on following pages

Right Bank (Cornavin Railway Station - Les Quais) :

Des Bergues, 33 quai des Bergues, ✉ 1201, ☎ 0229 087 000, *info@hoteldesbergues.com, Fax 0229 087 090,* – , rm, rm, TV – 15/190. AE VISA JCB. rest
FY k
Meals see ***Amphitryon*** below – ***Le Pavillon :*** **Meals** 49 and a la carte 67/118 – ☕ 45 – **110 rm** 595/1030, 12 suites.
◆ Close to the financial quarter, a large hotel much appreciated by high society. Rooms furnished in Louis Philippe or Directoire style, the most desirable overlooking the lake. De luxe brasserie with hot and cold luncheon buffet and classic evening menu.

Le Richemond, 8 - 10 r. Adhémar-Fabri, ✉ 1201, ☎ 0227 157 000, *reservation@richemond.ch, Fax 0227 157 001*, ≤, 余, Fø - 🛗 ▤ TV ☎ 🚗 - 🏋 15/200. AE ⓓ MC VISA JCB FY u

Le Gentilhomme : - Lebanese rest. *(closed Saturday lunch, Monday lunch and Sunday)* **Meals** a la carte 55/88 – ***Le Jardin :*** - Italian rest. **Meals** 55 and a la carte 79/121 – ☕ 48 – **86 rm** 560/890, 12 suites.

◆ Refined 19C grand hotel close to the lake. Personalised rooms with antique furnishings. The Gentilhomme brasserie has Lebanese cuisine. Sophisticated décor, candle-lit ambience, and a tempting traditional menu in Le Jardin restaurant.

Mandarin Oriental du Rhône, 1 quai Turrettini, ✉ 1201, ☎ 0229 090 000, *mogva-reservations@mohg.com, Fax 0229 090 010*, ≤, 余, Fø, ≘s - 🛗, ⇔ rm, ▤ TV ☎ ♿ 🚗 - 🏋 15/150. AE ⓓ MC VISA JCB. ⚘ FY r

Meals see ***Le Neptune*** below – ***Café Rafael :*** ☎ 0229 090 005 **Meals** 58 (lunch) and a la carte 74/109 – ☕ 39 – **180 rm** 510/930, 12 suites.

◆ Central location on the right bank of the Rhone. Sumptuous rooms with Art Deco furnishings and sparkling marble bathrooms. The Café Rafael offers light and highly diverse cuisine using local ingredients.

Noga Hilton, 19 quai du Mont-Blanc, ✉ 1201, ☎ 0229 089 081, *gvahitwfb@hilton.com, Fax 0229 089 090*, ≤, 余, Fø, ≘s, 🏊 - 🛗, ⇔ rm, ▤ TV ☎ ♿ - 🏋 15/800. AE ⓓ MC VISA JCB GY y

Meals see ***Le Cygne*** below – ***La Grignotière :*** **Meals** a la carte 52/102 – ☕ 39 – **401 rm** 475/790, 9 suites.

◆ Built on a grand scale by Lake Geneva. Spacious rooms in avant-garde style. Unwind in the casino, boutiques or swimming pool. Relax and enjoy a snack in the stylish but conservative brasserie-style dining room with its traditional menu. Panoramic terrace.

Président Wilson, 47 quai Wilson, ✉ 1201, ☎ 0229 066 666, *resa@hotelpwilson.com, Fax 0229 066 667*, ≤, 余, Fø, ≘s, 🏊 - 🛗, ⇔ rm, ▤ TV ☎ 🚗 - 🏋 15/600. AE ⓓ MC VISA JCB GX d

Spice's : **Meals** 55 (lunch)/115 and a la carte 96/141 – ***L'Arabesque :*** - Lebanese rest. *(closed 4 July - 22 August and Sunday)* **Meals** 55 (lunch)/95 and a la carte 52/78 – ***Pool Garden :*** *(May - September)* **Meals** 45 (lunch)/58 and a la carte 67/111 – ☕ 40 – **219 rm** 610/780, 11 suites.

◆ Wood and marble abound in this hotel whose finest rooms look onto the lake. Spice's Café has 3World Cuisine4 in a modern setting, while the Arabesque offers mouthwatering Lebanese delights. Try eating al fresco in the Pool Garden in summer.

Beau-Rivage, 13 quai du Mont-Blanc, ✉ 1201, ☎ 0227 166 666, *info@beau-rivage.ch, Fax 0227 166 060*, ≤, 余 - 🛗, ⇔ rm, ▤ TV ☎ - 🏋 15/120. AE ⓓ MC VISA JCB FY d

Le Chat Botté : **Meals** 60 (lunch)/145 and a la carte 89/146 – ***Le Patara :*** ☎ 0227 315 566 - Thai rest. - *(closed 9 to 12 April, 22 December - 4 January, Saturday lunch and Sunday lunch)* **Meals** 85 and a la carte 63/126 – ☕ 37 – **87 rm** 480/995, 6 suites.

◆ Facing the lake, this atmospheric establishment has been in the family since 1865. The bedrooms have a refined retro feel. Elegant atrium with fountain and colonnades. Experience the flavours of Thailand in the inviting atmosphere of the Patara restaurant.

Angleterre, 17 quai du Mont-Blanc, ✉ 1201, ☎ 0229 065 555, *angleterre@rchmail.com, Fax 0229 065 556*, ≤, Fø, ≘s - 🛗, ⇔ rm, ▤ TV video ☎ 🚗 - 🏋 15/35. AE ⓓ MC VISA FGY n

Windows : **Meals** 55/110 and a la carte 79/116 – ☕ 39 – **45 rm** 620/920.

◆ This languid lakeside establishment has an extremely distinguished atmosphere. Spacious, homely rooms, intimate bar-cum-library and pleasant service. Restaurant with snug conservatory looking out over the lake. Good modern food among the greenery.

Sofitel, 18-20 r. du Cendrier, ✉ 1201, ☎ 0229 088 080, *h1322@accor-hotels.com, Fax 0229 088 081*, 余 - 🛗, ⇔ rm, ▤ TV video ☎. AE ⓓ MC VISA JCB. ⚘ rest FY t

Meals 46 and a la carte 65/92 – ☕ 35 – **95 rm** 430/545.

◆ City-centre hotel, distinctive rooms with rustic or Louis XVI décor. The lounge with its open fireplace and pianist in the evening is a real gem. Classic/traditional fare in the restaurant, which has a terrace for those lazy summer days.

Bristol, 10 r. du Mont-Blanc, ✉ 1201, ☎ 0227 165 700, *bristol@bristol.ch, Fax 0227 389 039*, Fø, ≘s - 🛗, ⇔ rm, ▤ TV ☎ - 🏋 15/100. AE ⓓ MC VISA JCB FY w

Meals 49 (lunch)/85 and a la carte 63/104 – ☕ 32 – **95 rm** 385/580, 5 suites.

◆ Just a few steps from the lakeside, the Bristol has an elegant foyer and spacious, refurbished rooms. Fitness centre, sauna and a hamman to stay in shape. The bright and airy dining room with its Louis XV décor overlooks a little garden.

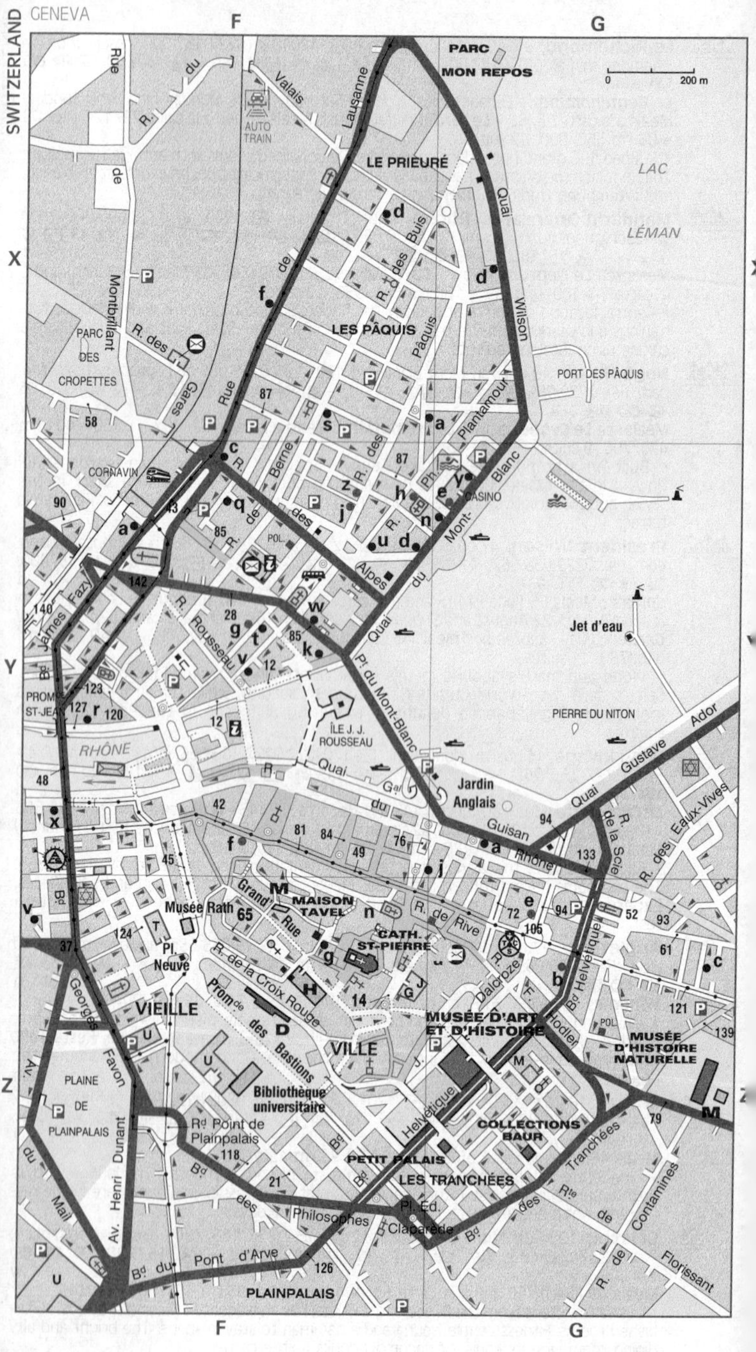

F
G
PARC
MON REPOS
0
200 m
AUTO TRAIN
LE PRIEURÉ
LAC
LÉMAN
X
LES PÂQUIS
PARC DES CROPETTES
PORT DES PÂQUIS
CORNAVIN
CASINO
POL.
Jet d'eau
Y
ÎLE J. J. ROUSSEAU
PIERRE DU NITON
RHÔNE
Jardin Anglais
MAISON TAVEL
Musée Rath
CATH. ST-PIERRE
Pl. Neuve
VIEILLE
VILLE
MUSÉE D'ART ET D'HISTOIRE
MUSÉE D'HISTOIRE NATURELLE
Z
PLAINE DE PLAINPALAIS
Bibliothèque universitaire
COLLECTIONS BAUR
Rd Point de Plainpalais
PETIT PALAIS
LES TRANCHÉES
Pl. Éd. Claparède
PLAINPALAIS
Quai Wilson
Quai du Mont-Blanc
Pt du Mont-Blanc
Quai Gustave Ador
Quai du Général Guisan
R. de Lausanne
R. de Montbrillant
R. des Gares
R. de Berne
R. des Alpes
R. de Rive
Grand' Rue
Bd Helvétique
Bd des Philosophes
Bd du Pont d'Arve
Av. Henri Dunant
Bd Georges Favon
Bd James Fazy
R. de la Croix Rouge
Prom. des Bastions
Rte de Florissant
R. de Contamines
Bd des Tranchées
R. des Eaux-Vives
R. de la Scie
R. Rousseau
R. des Pâquis
R. Plantamour
R. du Valais

STREET INDEX TO GENEVE TOWN PLAN

Warwick, 14 r. de Lausanne, ✉ 1201, ☎ 0227 168 000, *resa.geneva@warwickhotels.com, Fax 0227 168 001* – |♦|, ⇔ rm, ▤ TV video ☎ – 🏛 15/150. AE ⓓ MO VISA JCB FY c
Les 4 Saisons : (expected change of concept) – ***La Bonne Brasserie :*** **Meals** 29 and a la carte 42/86 – ☐ 29 – **167 rm** 345/545.
◆ Right in front of the station, ideal for tourists and conference guests worried about missing the train. Contemporary, functional rooms. The restaurant is about to undergo a complete makeover. The Bonne Brasserie has a Parisian bistro feel.

Epsom, 18 r. de Richemont, ✉ 1202, ☎ 0225 446 666, *epsom@manotel.com, Fax 0225 446 699,* 🏋 – |♦|, ⇔ rm, ▤ TV ☎ ♿ – 🏛 15/60. AE ⓓ MO VISA JCB FX d
Portobello : **Meals** 35/45 and a la carte 52/106 – ☐ 25 – **153 rm** 345/510.
◆ Very contemporary hotel on a quiet city-centre street. Relaxing atmosphere, homely rooms and high-tech conference facilities. Modern rotisserie with a glass roof.

Royal, 41 r. de Lausanne, ✉ 1201, ☎ 0229 061 414, *royal@manotel.com, Fax 0229 061 499,* 🏋, ≘s – |♦|, ⇔ rm, ▤ TV ☎ ♿ 🚗 – 🏛 15/30. AE ⓓ MO VISA JCB FX f
Rive Droite : **Meals** 55 and a la carte 46/106 – ☐ 25 – **165 rm** 345/600, 7 suites.
◆ Situated between the station and the lake, the Royal classically furnished rooms are elegant and plush ; it also has several luxury suites. Parisian brasserie-style restaurant offers a good value menu chalked up on the slate board.

Novotel Genève Centre, 19 r. de Zürich, ✉ 1201, ☎ 0229 099 000, *H3133@accor-hotels.com, Fax 0229 099 001* – |♦|, ⇔ rm, ▤ TV ☎ 🚗 – 🏛 15/80. AE ⓓ MO VISA JCB FX s
Meals 29 (lunch)/46 and a la carte 39/74 – ☐ 25 – **194 rm** 250/410, 12 suites.
◆ Chain hotel conveniently situated near the station and the lake, and hence much appreciated by business travellers. Well-equipped rooms are a good size.

Le Montbrillant, 2 r. de Montbrillant, ✉ 1201, ☎ 0227 337 784, *contact@montbrillant.ch, Fax 0227 332 511,* 🍴 – |♦|, ⇔ rm, TV ☎ ♿ P – 🏛 15/50. AE ⓓ MO VISA JCB FY b
gastro : **Meals** 48/98 and a la carte 66/112 – ***Café de la Gare :*** **Meals** a la carte 48/87 – **82 rm** ☐ 190/350.
◆ Invaluable accommodation for those who want to be near the station. Similar to a mountain retreat, with angular rooms and studios with kitchenette. The restaurant with its veranda feels like a bistro and offers contemporary fare.

Les Nations without rest, 62 r. du Grand-Pré, ✉ 1202, ☎ 0227 480 808, *info@hotel-les-nations.com, Fax 0227 343 884* – |♦| ⇔ TV video ☎. AE ⓓ MO VISA
71 rm ☐ 220/330. in the West FX
◆ Popular with business travellers and EU officials, Les Nations has been totally refurbished. The rooms, though on the small side, are as charming as they are smart.

du Midi, 4 pl. Chevelu, ✉ 1201, ☎ 0225 441 500, *info@hotel-du-midi.ch, Fax 0225 441 520,* 🍴 – |♦|, ▤ rm, TV ☎ ♿. AE ⓓ MO VISA FY v
Meals *(closed Saturday and Sunday)* 32 (lunch)/50 and a la carte 48/89 – ☐ 24 – **89 rm** 230/400.
◆ On a little square by the Rhône, this spacious hotel has great rooms. In the evenings, a pianist plays relaxing melodies in the lounge. Comfortable modern restaurant with summer terrace.

Edelweiss, 2 pl. Navigation, ✉ 1201, ☎ 0225 445 151, *edelweiss@manotel.com, Fax 0225 445 199* – |$|, rm, TV. AE VISA JCB. rest FX a
Meals *(closed 1 to 19 January and for lunch)* 55 and a la carte 43/89 – **42 rm** 234/315.
◆ The outside of this establishment gives a good idea of the pleasures within. It's a real Swiss chalet, with cosy bedrooms and a congenial galleried dining room where you can enjoy traditional fare and typical cheese dishes to the accompaniment of music.

Cornavin without rest, Cornavin Station, ✉ 1201, ☎ 0227 161 212, *cornavin@fhotels.ch, Fax 0227 161 200* – |$| TV – 60. AE VISA JCB FY a
18 – **162 rm** 358/474.
◆ Patronised by the famous boy detective Tintin (see "The Calculus Affair"), this hotel has sound-proofed and air-conditioned rooms and, in the foyer, the world's biggest clock.

Grand Pré without rest, 35 r. du Grand-Pré, ✉ 1202, ☎ 0229 181 111, *info@grandpre.ch, Fax 0227 347 691* – |$| TV – 25. AE VISA JCB
closed 20 December - 3 January – **89 rm** 266/371. by rue du Fort-Barreau FX
◆ In the part of town where the international organisations are located, this hotel has spacious rooms with contemporary furnishings. The rooms facing the courtyard are quieter.

Eden, 135 r. de Lausanne, ✉ 1202, ☎ 0227 163 700, *eden@eden.ch, Fax 0227 315 260* – |$| TV video – 20. AE VISA JCB in the North FX
Meals *(closed 19 July - 8 August, 24 December - 4 January, Saturday and Sunday)* 35 and a la carte 38/67 – **54 rm** 225/300.
◆ This establishment facing the Palais des Nations is regularly refurbished. Bright and functional classically furnished rooms. Traditional restaurant where local people rub shoulders with guests and passers-by.

Strasbourg - Univers without rest, 10 r. Pradier, ✉ 1201, ☎ 0229 065 800, *info@hotel-strasbourg-geneva.ch, Fax 0227 384 208* – |$| TV. AE VISA. FY q
51 rm 190/270.
◆ Close to the station and the Cornavin car park, this refurbished establishment has small, functional rooms with cosy public areas.

Ibis without rest, 10 r. Voltaire, ✉ 1201, ☎ 0223 382 020, *h2154@accor-hotels.com, Fax 0223 382 030* – |$| TV. AE VISA in the West FY
14 – **65 rm** 129.
◆ This completely refurbished establishment is typical of the new generation of Ibis hotels. Contemporary comfort in rooms with modern, no-nonsense furnishings.

Amphitryon - Hotel Des Bergues, 33 quai des Bergues, ✉ 1201, ☎ 0229 087 000, *info@hoteldesbergues.com, Fax 0229 087 090* – AE VISA JCB. FY k
closed 2 to 20 August, 22 December - 2 January, Saturday, Sunday and Bank Holidays – **Meals** 67 (lunch)/95 and a la carte 99/166.
◆ Gourmet restaurant in the Hotel Des Bergues. Plush ambience and glittering décor topped off by period furnishings are the setting for an up-to-date culinary selection.

Le Cygne - Hotel Noga Hilton, 19 quai du Mont-Blanc, ✉ 1201, ☎ 0229 089 085, *gvahitwfb@hilton.com, Fax 0229 089 090,* ← – . AE VISA JCB. GY y
closed 5 to 19 April, 8 to 30 August and 1 to 5 January – **Meals** 61 (lunch)/159 and a la carte 83/166.
◆ De luxe restaurant in the Noga Hilton. Geneva harbour is the backdrop for this cosy setting which serves great modern seasonal specialities.
Spec. Raviole de langoustines royales à la feuille de citronnier, fondant de jeunes poireaux. Rouget barbet en papillon rôti à la fleur de thym, concassé de tomates au gingembre. Petit macaron citron-safran et ses abricots flambés au limoncello. **Wines** Lully

Le Neptune - Hôtel Mandarin Oriental du Rhône, 1 quai Turrettini, ✉ 1201, ☎ 0229 090 006, *mogra-reservations@mohg.com, Fax 0229 090 010,* – . AE VISA JCB. FY r
closed 31 July - 22 August, 20 December - 4 January, Saturday, Sunday and Bank Holidays – **Meals** 72/130 and a la carte 96/156.
◆ Culinary artistry and modern cuisine from the Mandarin Oriental du Rhône Le Neptune restaurant 6 the god himself appears in the wall-paintings.
Spec. Foie gras frais de canard en croûte de tomate, réduction de Banuyls. Tronçon de turbot breton au lomo, jus à l'aceto balsamico. Biscuit Sicard, abricots rôtis aux amandes fraîches, jus de cuisson, sorbet verveine. **Wines** Dardagny, Lully

Tsé Yang, 19 quai du Mont-Blanc, ✉ 1201, ☎ 0227 325 081, *Fax 0227 310 582,* ← – . AE VISA JCB GY e
Meals - Chinese rest. - 45 (lunch)/135 and a la carte 71/162.
◆ Elegant restaurant with oriental décor and carved wooden partitions. Savour Chinese specialities while admiring the view over Lake Geneva.

XXX **La Perle du Lac,** 126 r. de Lausanne, ✉ 1202, ✆ 0229 091 020, *info@perledulac.ch, Fax 0229 091 030,* ≤ lake, 🏠, 🌳 – 🅿 – 🏊 15/60. AE ① MO VISA. ✂
closed 21 December - 19 January and Monday – **Meals** 58 (lunch)/115 and a la carte 84/140. in the North FX
◆ This venerable chalet has a fine location in a lakeside park and a spacious outdoor terrace. Bold colours distinguish the décor of the more modern of the two dining rooms.

XX **Mövenpick Cendrier,** 17 r. du Cendrier, ✉ 1201, ✆ 0227 325 030, *restaurant.cendrier@moevenpick.com, Fax 0227 319 341* – ▤. AE ① MO VISA JCB FY g
Meals a la carte 38/79.
◆ By the lake, this restaurant offers a wide range of dishes in appropriate settings. You can choose fish specialities, world cuisine, or the offerings of "Beef Corner".

XX **Thai Phuket,** 33 av. de France, ✉ 1202, ✆ 0227 344 100, *Fax 0227 344 240* – ▤. AE MO VISA JCB in the North FX
closed Saturday lunch – **Meals** - Thai rest. - 35 (lunch)/90 and a la carte 43/97.
◆ Authentic ambience and décor in this Thai restaurant where attentive waitresses in traditional costume wait on diners hand and foot.

XX **Le Vitti,** 5 r. Alfred Vincent, ✉ 1201, ✆ 0227 311 313, *Fax 0227 311 313* – AE ① MO VISA JCB FY h
closed 22 August - 12 September, 24 December - 6 January, Saturday lunch and Sunday – **Meals** 42 (lunch)/78 and a la carte 62/116.
◆ Italianate atmosphere, mouthwatering little modern menu with Mediterranean influences. Le Vitti is welcoming with pleasant service – all in all, highly recommended!

X **Bistrot du Bœuf Rouge,** 17 r. Alfred-Vincent, ✉ 1201, ✆ 0227 327 537, *Fax 0227 314 684* – AE ① MO VISA JCB FY z
closed 24 December - 5 January, Saturday and Sunday – **Meals** - Specialities of Lyons - 37 (lunch)/52 and a la carte 50/92.
◆ Typical Parisian-style brasserie with mirrors, zinc counter, and wall seating. Specialities from Lyons and dishes of the day. A real gourmet rendezvous.

X **L'Entrecôte Couronnée,** 5 r. des Pâquis, ✉ 1201, ✆ 0227 328 445, *Fax 0227 328 446* – AE ① MO VISA JCB FY j
closed Christmas, New Year, Saturday lunch and Sunday – **Meals** 55 and a la carte 54/85.
◆ This is the place to experience the real Geneva. Bistro-style ambience with contemporary food. Plenty of prints and paintings evoke the spirit of this old city.

X **Sagano,** 86 r. de Montbrillant, ✉ 1202, ✆ 0227 331 150, *Fax 0227 332 755,* 🏠 – ▤. AE MO VISA JCB in the North FX
closed Saturday lunch and Sunday – **Meals** - Japanese rest. - 29 (lunch)/90 and a la carte 46/119.
◆ Hungry for a taste of the exotic with a little zen? Head for this Japanese restaurant with its tatami mats and low tables. A culinary voyage from the Land of the Rising Sun.

Left Bank (Commercial Centre) :

🏨 **Swissôtel Genève Métropole,** 34 quai Général-Guisan, ✉ 1204, ✆ 0223 183 200, *reservations.geneva@swissotel.com, Fax 0223 183 300,* ≤, 🏠, 🏋 – 🛗, ⇆ rm, ▤ TV video ✆ – 🏊 15/90. AE ① MO VISA GY a
***Le Grand Quai* : Meals** a la carte 51/106 – ☕ 35 – **118 rm** 490/820, 9 suites.
◆ Hotel built in 1854 whose beautiful traditional rooms afford a view of Lake Geneva with its famous Jet d'Eau. Panoramic roof terrace and fitness centre. The Grand Quai with its trompe l'œil frescoes offers everything from traditional food to Asian delights.

🏨 **La Cigogne,** 17 pl. Longemalle, ✉ 1204, ✆ 0228 184 040, *cigogne@relaischateaux.com, Fax 0228 184 050* – 🛗 ▤ TV ✆. AE ① MO VISA. ✂ FGY j
Meals *(closed Sunday lunch and Saturday from July - August)* 59 (lunch)/105 and a la carte 74/105 – **46 rm** ☕ 360/570, 6 suites.
◆ Impressive turn-of-the-century façade in a square in the Old Town. Stylish rooms and luxury suites to suit every taste, with a sprinkling of objets d'art around the hotel. Art Deco-influenced restaurant serves modern dishes under a glass roof.

🏨 **Les Armures** 🐚, 1 r. du Puits-Saint-Pierre, ✉ 1204, ✆ 0223 109 172, *armures@span.ch, Fax 0223 109 846,* 🏠 – 🛗 ▤ TV video ✆. AE ① MO VISA JCB FZ g
Meals *(closed Easter, Christmas and New Year)* 52 and a la carte 40/91 – **28 rm** ☕ 340/530.
◆ Elegant 17C town mansion, tucked away in the heart of the Old Town. Antique furnishings and exposed beams in tastefully decorated rooms. Eat your fill of traditional dishes in a picturesque setting. Fondue served in the "carnotset" (drinking den).

Tiffany, 1 r. des Marbriers, ✉ 1204, ☏ 0227 081 616, *info@hotel-tiffany.ch, Fax 0227 081 617* – |‡|, ▤ rm, TV ✆. AE ⓓ ⓜⓒ VISA JCB FZ v
Meals *(closed Easter, Christmas and New Year)* 45 (lunch) and a la carte 52/95 – **46 rm** ☕ 230/370.
◆ This hotel built on the site of a late 19C monument has modern facilities and inviting rooms which show a Belle Époque influence. Snug lounge and bar. Interesting retro dining room which fits perfectly with the house style.

Sagitta without rest, 6 r. de la Flèche, ☏ 0227 863 361, *sagitta@span.ch, Fax 0228 498 110* – |‡| ▤ TV ✆ P. AE ⓓ ⓜⓒ VISA GZ c
42 rm ☕ 199/259.
◆ In the commercial district but secluded, this establishment has rooms, studios, apartments and numerous kitchenettes. The uninspiring façade belies renovated facilities.

Churchill without rest, 15 r. du Simplon, ✉ 1207, ☏ 0225 918 888, *hotelchurchill@bluewin.ch, Fax 0225 918 878* – |‡| ⇔ TV video ✆. AE ⓓ ⓜⓒ VISA
35 rm ☕ 169/264. by quai Gustave Ador GY
◆ This establishment is a practical option for anyone wanting to stay close to the lake. Functional rooms of various shapes and sizes. Check in beneath Churchill's haughty gaze.

Parc des Eaux-Vives with rm, 82 quai Gustave-Ador, ✉ 1207, ☏ 0228 497 575, *info@parcdeseauxvives.ch, Fax 0228 497 570*, ≤, ☂, – |‡|, ▤ rm, TV ✆ P. AE ⓓ ⓜⓒ VISA. ⚘ rest by quai Gustave-Ador GY
Meals (1st floor) *(closed 2 weeks January, Monday and Tuesday)* 160/210 and a la carte 179/220 – ***Brasserie* : Meals** 49 (lunch) and a la carte 61/99 – ☕ 29 – **7 rm** 750/850.
◆ This opulent restaurant with its lovely terrace is on the first floor of a sumptuous 18C house in a delightful public park. The rooms are exquisite. The luxurious modern brasserie serves contemporary dishes.
Spec. Le rouget de Méditerranée aux chipirons et aux artichauts violets. Le bœuf de Simmental aux fruits d'automne. Le chocolat noir ébène et blanc ivoire. **Wines** Dardagny

Le Béarn (Goddard), 4 quai de la Poste, ✉ 1204, ☏ 0223 210 028, *Fax 0227 813 115* – ▤. AE ⓓ ⓜⓒ VISA FY x
closed 12 July - 22 August, 16 to 22 February, Saturday (except dinner from October - May) and Sunday – **Meals** 65 (lunch)/190 and a la carte 105/178.
◆ Geneva's gourmets have been coming to this elegant eatery for more than 20 years to savour its fine cuisine. The menu is constantly updated.
Spec. Soufflé de truffes fraîches (December - February). Poêlée de langoustines à l'émulsion de petits pois et morilles (Spring). Oursin de Bretagne et coquilles St. Jacques à la coque (October - November). **Wines** Dardagny

Roberto, 10 r. Pierre-Fatio, ✉ 1204, ☏ 0223 118 033, *Fax 0223 118 466* – ▤. AE ⓜⓒ VISA GZ e
closed 25 December - 1 January, Saturday dinner and Sunday – **Meals** - Italian rest. - a la carte 65/125.
◆ Vast restaurant made to look even more spacious by the mirrors on the walls. Enjoy a candle-lit dinner in an intimate ambience. The menu features Italian specialities.

Le Patio, 19 bd Helvétique, ✉ 1207, ☏ 0227 366 675, *Fax 0227 864 074* – AE ⓓ ⓜⓒ VISA GZ b
closed 24 December - 5 January, Saturday and Sunday – **Meals** a la carte 63/103.
◆ This establishment has two modern dining rooms, one of them designed as a winter garden. A selection of seasonal recipes and Provençal specialities make easy bedfellows.

Buffet de la Gare des Eaux-Vives (Labrosse), 7 av. de la Gare des Eaux-Vives, ✉ 1207, ☏ 0228 404 430, *Fax 0228 404 431*, ☂ – AE ⓜⓒ VISA
closed 3 to 12 April, 31 July - 15 August, 20 December - 4 January, Saturday and Sunday – **Meals** 48 (lunch)/115 and a la carte 75/111. East direction Annemasse Z
◆ Not your ordinary station buffet, here is a boldly contemporary yet sober interior with a railway fresco, a waterside summer terrace and an inventive up-to-the-minute menu.
Spec. Bruschetta de homard et tomate confite, vinaigrette au piment doux, millefeuille de légumes. Dos de cabillaud en risotto tomate, réduction de vieux balsamique (Summer). Suprême de pintade de la Drôme rôti au beurre d'herbes, tartine persillée de girolles (Summer). **Wines** Dardagny, Peissy

Brasserie Lipp, 8 r. de la Confédération (2nd floor), ✉ 1204, ☏ 0223 111 011, *lipp@swissonline.ch, Fax 0223 120 104*, ☂ – ⇔ ▤. AE ⓓ ⓜⓒ VISA FY f
closed Christmas – **Meals** a la carte 44/93.
◆ On the second floor of a shopping arcade, this establishment in the style of a Parisian brasserie offers an excellent choice of seafood and stays open right up to 12.45am.

Environs to the North :

Palais des Nations : *by quai Wilson* FGX :

Intercontinental, 7-9 ch. du Petit-Saconnex, ✉ 1209, ✆ 0229 193 939, *geneva@interconti.com, Fax 0229 193 838,* ←, ☂, Fà, ≘s, ⛱ – |♦|, ⇆ rm, ▤ TV ✆ ♿ ⇔ P – 🔬 15/400. AE ⓓ ⓜ VISA JCB. ✂ rest
Meals see ***Les Continents*** below – ***La Pergola*** ✆ 0229 193 360 **Meals** 47 (lunch) and a la carte 64/101 – ☕ 28 – **264 rm** 415/800, 63 suites.
◆ Next door to the Palais des Nations and ideal for conferences, this hotel counts heads of state among its guests. Rooms regularly refurbished. Dine in comfort at La Pergola with its tempting buffet, or laze at a poolside table in summer.

Les Continents - Hotel Intercontinental, 7-9 ch. du Petit-Saconnex, ✉ 1209, ✆ 0229 193 350, *geneva@interconti.com, Fax 0229 193 838* – ▤ P. AE ⓓ ⓜ VISA JCB. ✂
closed Easter, Christmas - New Year, Saturday and Sunday – **Meals** 62 (lunch)/130 and a la carte 82/153.
◆ On the ground floor of the Intercontinental, this sumptuous restaurant with its panelling and crystal chandeliers is the perfect setting for excellent French cuisine.
Spec. Asperges lardées et cuites meunière, œuf de poule en brouillade aux truffes noires (Spring). Homard breton au lait d'amande fraîche et vinaigrette au curry rouge (Summer). Sablé breton au beurre demi-sel, pommes Golden caramélisées et crème glacée au cidre de Cornouaille (Winter). **Wines** Genève

at Chambésy *North : 5 km – alt. 389 – ✉ 1292 Chambésy :*

Relais de Chambésy, 8 pl. de Chambésy, ✆ 0227 581 105, *Fax 0227 580 230,* ☂ – AE ⓓ ⓜ VISA JCB
closed 20 December - 12 January, Saturday and Sunday – **Meals** 36 (lunch)/85 and a la carte 60/106 – ***Le Bistrot :*** **Meals** 39 (lunch) and a la carte 37/62.
◆ Authentic country inn on the village square. Three delightful dining rooms offers tasty, classic bourgeois dishes. The Bistrot more traditional fare is simpler and cheaper.

at Bellevue *by rte de Lausanne : 6 km – alt. 380 – ✉ 1293 Bellevue :*

La Réserve 🐦, 301 rte de Lausanne, ✆ 0229 595 959, *info@lareserve.ch, Fax 0229 595 960,* ←, ☂, ⊚, Fà, ≘s, ⛱, ⛱, ⛵, ✂, ⚘, ⚓ – |♦|, ⇆ rm, ▤ TV video ✆ ♿ ⚘ ⇔ P. AE ⓓ ⓜ VISA JCB
Tsé Fung : - Chinese rest. **Meals** a la carte 68/170 – ***Le Loti :*** **Meals** a la carte 62/134 – ☕ 35 – **85 rm** 550/990, 17 suites.
◆ Most of the modern rooms of this luxury hotel have a terrace overlooking the park with its swimming pool. Splendid Garcia décor. Sample fine Chinese cuisine at the Tsé Fung or contemporary food at the Loti.

to the East by road to Evian :

at Cologny *by Quai Gustave Ador* GY *: 3,5 km – alt. 432 – ✉ 1223 Cologny :*

Auberge du Lion d'Or (Byrne/Dupont), 5 pl. Pierre-Gautier, ✆ 0227 364 432, *Fax 0227 867 462,* ☂ – AE ⓓ ⓜ VISA JCB
closed 5 to 19 April, 20 December - 5 January, Saturday and Sunday – **Meals** 68 (lunch)/170 and a la carte 106/150 – **Meals** (see ***Le Bistro de Cologny*** below).
◆ This elegant restaurant with its Louis XVI chairs affords diners a superb view over lake and mountains. The menu offers an array of irresistible suggestions.
Spec. Poêlée de St. Jacques, gnocchi de pommes de terre et cèpes, jus à la ventrèche (Winter). Pavé de loup de mer aux artichauts poivrade et tomate mi-confite (Spring). Suprême de poularde, jardinet de saison, crémé d'estragon et jus réduit à la réglisse

Le Bistro de Cologny - Auberge du Lion d'Or, 5 pl. Pierre-Gautier, ✆ 0227 365 780, *Fax 0227 867 462,* ☂ – AE ⓓ ⓜ VISA JCB
closed 5 to 19 April, 20 December - 5 January, Saturday and Sunday – **Meals** 42 (lunch) and a la carte 58/103.
◆ Attached to the Lion d'Or, this recently refurbished bistro makes an attractive setting for a range of tempting dishes at what are more than reasonable prices.

at Anières *by road to Hermance : 7 km – alt. 410 – ✉ 1247 Anières :*

Auberge de Floris (Legras), 287 rte d'Hermance, ✆ 0227 512 020, *contact@auberge-de-floris.com, Fax 0227 512 250,* ← lake, ☂ – P. AE ⓓ ⓜ VISA
closed 11 to 19 April, 31 October - 16 November, 24 December - 4 January, Sunday and Monday – **Meals** 62 (lunch)/135 and a la carte 101/162 – **Meals** (see ***Le Bistrot*** below).
◆ This elegant and panoramic restaurant with its period furniture offers an up-to-date menu. Lovely view over the lake. Relax in the lofty, observatory-style summer restaurant.
Spec. Bouillabaisse à la façon du chef (October - May). Le pressé de poissons du Lac Léman et sa vinaigrette tiède aux écrevisses. Les langoustines de la Mer d'Irlande. **Wines** Anières

Le Bistrot - Auberge de Floris, 287 rte d'Hermance, ✆ 0227 512 020, *contact@auberge-de-floris.com, Fax 0227 512 250,* – P. AE ⓓ MC VISA
closed 11 to 19 April, 31 October - 16 November, 24 December - 4 January, Sunday and Monday – **Meals** (booking essential) 45 and a la carte 58/98.
◆ Banish hunger at the bistro of the Floris inn, which offers diners a wonderful menu of contemporary dishes. Interesting themed fortnights throughout the year.

to the East by road to Annemasse :

at Thônex *by rte de Chêne GZ : 5 km – alt. 414 – ✉ 1226 Thônex :*

Le Cigalon (Bessire), 39 rte d'Ambilly, at the customs border of Pierre-à-Bochet, ✆ 0223 499 733, *jmbessire@le-cigalon.ch, Fax 0223 499 739,* – P. AE ⓓ MC VISA
closed 18 July - 9 August, 24 December - 5 January, Sunday and Monday – **Meals** 44 (lunch)/99 and a la carte 72/129.
◆ Lovers of seafood should pause here before crossing the border and allow themselves a gastronomic interlude. Fish dishes have pride of place on the limited modern menu.
Spec. Paupiettes de thon rouge de Méditerranée aux huîtres de Marenne d'Oléron (Spring - Summer). Tartare de brochet du Lac Léman et son caviar (Winter). Loup de ligne rôti sur ses écailles, émulsion aux herbettes. **Wines** Satigny, Dardagny

to the South :

at Conches *Southeast : 5 km – alt. 419 – ✉ 1231 Conches :*

Le Vallon, 182 rte de Florissant, ✆ 0223 471 104, *Fax 0223 476 381,* – P. AE ⓓ MC VISA
closed 9 to 18 April, 21 June - 11 July, 24 December - 4 January, Saturday and Sunday – **Meals** 42 (lunch)/72 and a la carte 64/105.
◆ Charming bistro-style establishment where you can see into the kitchen as a range of dishes are prepared. Little easels propping up the menu, a nice touch. Secluded terrace.

at Vessy *by road to Veyrier : 4 km – alt. 419 – ✉ 1234 Vessy :*

Alain Lavergnat, 130 rte de Veyrier, ✆ 0227 842 626, *Fax 0227 841 334,* – P. AE ⓓ MC VISA
closed 25 July - 15 August, 21 December - 5 January, Sunday and Monday – **Meals** 50 (lunch)/96 and a la carte 75/133 – ***Le Bistrot de la Guinguette :*** **Meals** a la carte 53/97.
◆ Refined classic cuisine in the rustic dining room of this old Genevan villa with a winter garden. Cheaper, more traditional fare at lunchtime in the Bistrot de la Guingette.

at Carouge *by Av. Henri-Dunant FZ : 3 km – alt. 382 – ✉ 1227 Carouge :*

Ramada Encore, 12 rte des Jeunes, ✆ 0223 095 000, *geneve.encore@ramada-treff.ch, Fax 0223 095 005* – |♿|, ⇆ rm, ▤ TV video ✆ ♿ – 🅰 15/240. AE ⓓ MC VISA. ⚘ rest
Meals *(closed Saturday and Sunday)* 32 and a la carte 44/66 – ☕ 23 – **130 rm** 230/290.
◆ Modern building by a motorway exit, between a stadium and a shopping centre. Conference centre, neat and tidy rooms and good breakfasts. Meals are buffets or a concise international selection à la carte.

Auberge de Pinchat with rm, 33 ch. de Pinchat, ✆ 0223 423 077, *Fax 0223 002 219,* – TV P. AE MC VISA
closed 4 to 12 April, 14 August - 6 September, 23 December - 4 January – **Meals** *(closed Sunday and Monday)* 40 (lunch)/96 and a la carte 66/124 – **5 rm** ☕ 120/145.
◆ Sobriety and tradition are the watchwords of this homely inn with its charming outside terrace for summer dining. Limited number of bedrooms available.

L'Olivier de Provence, 13 r. Jacques-Dalphin, ✆ 0223 420 450, *Fax 0223 428 880,* – AE ⓓ MC VISA JCB
closed 24 December - 4 January, Saturday except dinner from September - 24 June, Sunday and Bank Holidays – **Meals** 46 (lunch)/98 and a la carte 76/110 – ***Le Bistrot :*** **Meals** 29 (lunch)/36 and a la carte 41/65.
◆ An open fireplace, exposed beams and stonework lend character to this residence dating in part from the 18C. The Bistrot has an appealing menu with Provençal specialities.

at Petit-Lancy *by Av. Henri-Dunant FZ : 3 km – alt. 426 – ✉ 1213 Petit-Lancy :*

Hostellerie de la Vendée, 28 ch. de la Vendée, ✆ 0227 920 411, *info@vendee.ch, Fax 0227 920 546,* – |♿| ▤ TV ✆ – 🅰 15/60. AE ⓓ MC VISA JCB
closed Easter, 20 - 31 May (except hotel) and 20 December - 4 January – **Meals** *(closed Saturday lunch, Sunday and Bank Holidays)* 54 (lunch)/150 and a la carte 67/156 – **Meals** (see ***Bistro*** below) – **34 rm** ☕ 180/340.
◆ In a quiet residential area, this hotel is just the place for a good night sleep. The elegant dining room of the gourmet restaurant is extended outwards in the form of a delightful winter garden-style conservatory. Classic French meals much loved by foodies.
Spec. Nougat de foie gras de canard et ris de veau aux morilles (Spring). Fricassée de homard du Maine à la citronnelle, fin ragoût de cébettes (Summer). Soufflé chaud aux fruits de la passion (Winter). **Wines** Satigny

Bistro - Hostellerie de la Vendée, 28 ch. de la Vendée, ☎ 0227 920 411, *info@vendee.ch*, *Fax 0227 920 546*, – . AE VISA
closed Easter, 20 - 31 May, 20 December - 4 January, Saturday lunch, Sunday and Bank Holidays – **Meals** 38/48 and a la carte 50/83.
◆ Fill up at this bistro with its reasonably priced classic dishes. The fixed-price meals with wine are a great success, as is the pretty summer terrace.

at Lully *South-West : 8 km by road to Bernex – alt. 430 – ✉ 1233 Bernex :*

La Colombière (Lonati), 122 rte de Soral, ☎ 0227 571 027, *Fax 0227 576 549*, – P. AE VISA
closed 20 August - 20 September, 19 December - 12 January, Saturday and Sunday – **Meals** (number of covers limited - booking essential) 48 (lunch)/135 and a la carte 79/118.
◆ This picturesque old farmhouse with its lovely country-style interior owes its success to its cuisine, which is both refined and innovative.
Spec. Pressé de thon rouge de la Méditerranée aux herbes aromatiques et gros sel. Filet de canette sauvagine au chou nouveau et foie gras. Crêpes soufflées citron vert, granité citron jaune, fraise et banane. **Wines** Lully

to the West :

at Peney-Dessus *by road to Satigny and private lane : 10 km – ✉ 1242 Satigny :*

Domaine de Châteauvieux (Chevrier) with rm, 16, ch. de Châteauvieux, ☎ 0227 531 511, *info@chateauvieux.ch*, *Fax 0227 531 924*, ←, – TV P – 15. AE VISA
closed 18 to 26 April, 1 July - 16 August and 21 December - 5 January – **Meals** *(closed Sunday and Monday)* 84 (lunch)/210 and a la carte 172/228 – **14 rm** 195/385.
◆ This old farmstead among the vineyards has been converted into a country hostelry. Luxurious dining room well-suited to the appreciation of exquisite dishes and fine wines.
Spec. Bar de ligne cuit au gros sel et au lemongras. Chausson aux truffes et foie gras (January - February). Bécasse rôtie à la broche (October - December). **Wines** Satigny

at Cointrin *by road to Lyons : 4 km – alt. 428 – ✉ 1216 Cointrin :*

Mövenpick Genève, 20 rte Pré-Bois, ☎ 0227 987 575, *hotel.geneva@moevenpick.com*, *Fax 0227 910 284*, , – , rm, TV – 15/400. AE VISA JCB
Kamome : - Japanese rest. *(closed 15 July - 15 August, Saturday lunch, Monday lunch and Sunday)* **Meals** 56 (lunch)/110 and a la carte 60/103 – ***La Brasserie :*** *(closed July - August and Sunday)* **Meals** 46 (lunch) and a la carte 45/104 – 31 – **344 rm** 440/560, 6 suites.
◆ Close to the airport, this chain hotel has lounges, bars, shops and meeting rooms. All bedrooms have been refurbished. As well as the Brasserie classic fare, there are Japanese specialities at the Kamome, including teppanyaki, sushi and sashimi.

Ramada Park Hotel, 75-77 av. Louis-Casaï, ☎ 0227 103 000, *resa@ramadaparkhotel.ch*, *Fax 0227 103 100*, , – , rm, TV – 15/550. AE VISA JCB. rest
La Récolte : **Meals** 32 and a la carte 43/109 – 30 – **302 rm** 195/440, 6 suites.
◆ Next door to the airport, a hotel with a wide range of amenities including a newspaper kiosk, a hairdresser's, a sauna and fitness centre, and meeting rooms. The bedrooms are modern. Some weeks the contemporary restaurant stages a themed menu.

Express by Holiday Inn without rest, 16 rte de Pré-Bois, ☎ 0229 393 939, *info@expressgeneva.com*, *Fax 0229 393 930* – TV video – 15/25. AE VISA
154 rm 225.
◆ Intended to be modern and practical, this new addition to the Holiday Inn chain is tailor-made for business travel. Good triple-glazed rooms.

Ibis, 10 ch. de la Violette, ☎ 0227 109 500, *H3535@accor-hotels.com*, *Fax 0227 109 595*, – , rm, TV . AE VISA
Meals 28 and a la carte approx. 35 – 14 – **109 rm** 129.
◆ Near the motorway and Geneva airport, you can find the whole range of the Ibis chain hotel services. Standard rooms with bathroom units. The restaurant has a slightly globe-trotting menu and a comfortable terrace.

Plein Ciel, 2nd floor at the airport, ☎ 0227 177 676, *restaurant@canonica.com*, *Fax 0227 987 768*, ← – . AE VISA
Meals *(closed Sunday lunch except mid September - mid June and Saturday lunch)* 55 (lunch) and a la carte 64/124 – ***Café Bréguet :*** *(closed dinner except weekends and Summer)* **Meals** 36 (lunch)/46 and a la carte 35/80.
◆ Restaurants set around a Bréguet Atlantic cabin on the second floor of the terminal, with a great view of airport activity. The café is nice for a stopover in fair weather.

at Meyrin *by road to Meyrin : 5 km – alt. 445 – ✉ 1217 Meyrin :*

NH Geneva Airport Hotel, 21 av. de Mategnin, ☎ 0229 899 000, *nhgeneva.airport@nh-hotels.ch, Fax 0229 899 999* – |‡|, ⇹ rm, ▤ TV ☎ 🚗 – 🏛 15/60. AE ⓓ ⓜ VISA
Meals 25 (lunch)/56 and a la carte 46/93 – ☕ 25 – **189 rm** 330/390.
• A circular red brick construction whose outer appearance is indicative of the modernity within. The functional rooms are all alike. There is a contemporary new restaurant whose menu aims for a Mediterranean feel.

at Palais des Expositions *by quai Wilson* FGX *: 5 km – alt. 452 – ✉ 1218 Grand-Saconnex :*

Crowne Plaza, 26 voie de Moëns, ☎ 0227 470 202, *sales@cpgeneva.ch, Fax 0227 470 303,* ⛹, ≘s, ▢ – |‡|, ⇹ rm, ▤ TV ☎ ♿ 🚗 – 🏛 15/180. AE ⓓ ⓜ VISA JCB
L'Olivo : **Meals** a la carte 50/117 – ☕ 32 – **500 rm** 470/680.
• By the airport, this American-style hotel has contemporary rooms, conference halls and a fitness centre among other things. The restaurant with its southern décor offers classic dishes.

Vufflens-le-Château *1134 Vaud* 729 D6, 552 D10 – *636 – alt. 471.*
Bern 118 – Geneva 53 – Lausanne 14 – Morges 3 – Pontarlier 72 – Yverdon-les-Bains 41.

XXXX ✿✿ **L'Ermitage** (Ravet) ⛵ with rm, 26 rte du village, ☎ 0218 046 868, *ermitage@ravet.ch, Fax 0218 022 240,* 🌳 – TV ☎ P. AE ⓓ ⓜ VISA
closed 9 to 25 August, 22 December - 14 January, Sunday and Monday – **Meals** 68 (lunch)/198 and a la carte 168/222 🍇 – **9 rm** ☕ 360/400.
• Food and pleasure in perfect harmony in this delightful residence with its garden and lake. Exquisite rooms, plus everything necessary for a superlative dining experience.
Spec. Dinette des quatre foies gras d'oie et de canard. Poissons du Lac Léman (March - September). Jarret de veau doré sur l'os à la broche. **Wines** Morges sur lie, La Côte

Cossonay *1304 Vaud* 729 D6 552 D9 – *2 487 – alt. 565.*
Bern 107 – Lausanne 16 – Fribourg 78 – Geneva 62 – Yverdon-les-Bains 28.

XXX ✿✿ **Cerf** (Crisci), 10 r. du Temple, ☎ 0218 612 608, *Fax 0218 612 627* – AE ⓜ VISA JCB
closed 10 July - 5 August, 20 December - 6 January, Sunday and Monday – **Meals** (see ***La Fleur de Sel*** below) 80 (lunch)/215 and a la carte 117/211.
• This 16C establishment offers a gorgeous blend of venerable décor (pillar room with Louis XIII chairs) and inventive cuisine. Visual delight allied to gastronomic pleasure.
Spec. Foie gras en duo de café et grue, gingembre confit au Porto. Effilochée de cabillaud en escabèche de coquillages et aubergine. Aiguillette de canard farcie de son confit aux senteurs de flouve. **Wines** Echichens

X ☺ **La Fleur de Sel** - Cerf, 10 r. du Temple, ☎ 0218 612 608, *Fax 0218 612 627* – ▤. AE ⓜ VISA JCB
closed 10 July - 5 August, 20 December - 6 January, Sunday and Monday – **Meals** 52 and a la carte 58/106.
• This tiny bistro shares an entrance with the Restaurant du Cerf. Simple but attractive interior. Tempting menu with a choice selection of local specialities.

Crissier *1023 Vaud* 729 D6 552 E9 – *5 756 – alt. 470.*
Bern 112 – Geneva 71 – Lausanne 6 – Montreux 40 – Nyon 50 – Pontarlier 64.

XXXX ✿✿✿ **Hôtel de Ville - Philippe Rochat,** 1 r. d'Yverdon, ☎ 0216 340 505, *Fax 0216 342 464* – 🏛 15. AE ⓓ ⓜ VISA
closed 25 July - 17 August, 21 December - 9 January, Sunday and Monday – **Meals** 155 (lunch)/260 and a la carte 136/240.
• Behind the venerable façade of this restaurant is an elegantly refurbished interior harmonising perfectly with the refinement and excellence of the cuisine.
Spec. Consommé de tomates en gelée, beignets de fleur de courgette aux pétales de thym (Summer). Queue de langoustine d'Ecosse croustillante au poivre de Sichuan, chutney d'abricot au jus de curry (Summer). Vapeur de filet mignon de veau au citron vert, artichaut barigoule aux olives (Summer). **Wines** Féchy, Villette

Cully *1096 Vaud* 729 E6 552 E10 – *1 748 – alt. 391.*
Bern 93 – Geneva 77 – Lausanne 8 – Montreux 15 – Pontarlier 77 – Yverdon-les-Bains 45.

XXX ✿✿ **Le Raisin** (Blokbergen) with rm, 1 pl. de l'Hôtel de Ville, ☎ 0217 992 131, *raisin@worldcom.ch, Fax 0217 992 501,* 🏖 – |‡|, ▤ rest, TV. AE ⓓ ⓜ VISA
Meals 89 (lunch)/198 and a la carte 101/198 – ***La Pinte :*** **Meals** 48/89 and a la carte 64/122 – **9 rm** ☕ 280/350.
• A choice of two dining rooms, one contemporary, the other country-style, inventive dishes with a local touch, personalised bedrooms - it all adds up to an establishment of great character. La Pinte offers good traditional cooking with no frills.
Spec. Omble chevalier, sauce au Dézaley blanc (Summer). Filet de truite du lac aux chanterelles (Summer). Côte de veau double du Simmental aux petits légumes. **Wines** Lavaux, Aigle

Brent *Vaud 729 E6 552 F10 – alt. 569.*
Bern 85 – Geneva 89 – Lausanne 25 – Martigny 47 – Montreux 5.

XXX ✿✿✿ **Le Pont de Brent** (Rabaey), 4 rte de Blonay, ✆ 0219 645 230, *rabaey@bluewin.ch, Fax 0219 645 530* – AE MC VISA
closed 18 July - 9 August, 21 December - 5 January, Sunday and Monday – **Meals** 90 (lunch)/240 and a la carte 128/213.
◆ Gracious building in local style with an elegant interior, a fine setting for a sumptuous cuisine abounding in exquisite flavours. A gastronomic experience to be savoured!
Spec. Marbré de cabillaud à la ratatouille, coulis de poivrons doux (Summer - Autumn). Saltimbocca et croustillant de ris de veau aux oignons confits (Autumn - Winter). Conversation aux fraises et à la rhubarbe (Spring). **Wines** Yvorne, Villette

Vevey *1800 Vaud 729 E6, 552 F10 – 15 420 – alt. 386.*
Bern 85 – Geneva 90 – Montreux 7 – Lausanne 16 – Yverdon-les-Bains 53.

XXX ✿✿ **Denis Martin,** 2 r. du Château, ✆ 0219 211 210, *chateau2@bluewin.ch, Fax 0219 214 552,* – AE MC VISA
closed 21 December - 15 January, Sunday and Monday – **Meals** 98 (lunch)/210 and a la carte 131/181.
◆ Charming old house belonging to the worshipful company of vintners. Cuisine reflecting current tastes in the two arched dining rooms or on the flowery terrace by the lake.
Spec. St. Jacques en émulsion de cacahuètes grillées (Spring). Les fèves en fraîcheur de citrons et Patta Negra (Summer). Le bar de ligne aux poivrons reconstitués et basilic (Autumn). **Wines** Lavaux, Chablais

---

ZÜRICH 729 J3 551 P5 – *340 873 – alt. 409.*

See : *The Quays★★ : ≤★ FZ ; Mythenquai : ≤★ CX – Fraumünster cloisters★ (Alter Kreuzgang des Fraumünsters), windows★ EZ – Church of SS. Felix and Regula★ – Cathedral★ (Grossmünster) FZ – Fine Arts Museum★★ (Kunsthaus) FZ – Zoological Gardens★ (Zoo Zürich) – Bührle Collection★★ (Sammlung Bührle).*

Museums : *Swiss National Museum★★★ (Schweizerisches Landesmuseum) EY – Rietberg Museum★★ CX* **M**[2].

Envir : *Uetliberg★★ South-West : by rail – Albis Pass Road★ Southwest by the Bederstrasse – Former Abbey of Kappel★ Southwest : 22 km – Eglisau : site★ North : 27 km.*

Excursions : *Boat Trips, Information : Zürichsee-Schiffahrtsgesellschaft, Mythenquai 333, ✆ 014 871 333, Fax 014 871 320.*

9 Dolder (late March-mid November), ✆ 012 615 045, Fax 012 615 302 ; 18 at Zumikon, ✉ 8126 (April-October), ✆ 019 180 050, Fax 019 180 037, SE : 9 km ; 18 at Hittnau, ✉ 8335 (April-October), ✆ 019 502 442, Fax 019 510 166 E : 33 km, 18 at Breitenloo, ✉ 8309 Nürensdorf (April-October), ✆ 018 364 080, Fax 018 371 085 N : 22 km.

unique zurich airport, ✆ 0438 162 211.

Tourist Office, in the main station, ✆ 012 154 000, info@zurichtourism.ch, Fax 012 154 044 – T.C.S., Alfred Escher-Str. 38, ✆ 012 868 686, Fax 012 868 687, Uraniastr. 14, ✆ 012 173 070, Fax 012 173 061 – A.C.S., Forchstr. 95, ✆ 013 877 500, Fax 013 877 509.

Bern 125 – Basle 109 – Geneva 278 – Innsbruck 288 – Milan 304.

Plans on following pages

On the right bank of the river Limmat (University, Fine Arts Museum) :

Dolder Grand Hotel, Kurhausstr. 65, ✉ 8032, ✆ 012 693 000, *info@doldergrand.ch, Fax 012 693 001,* ≤ Zurich lake, town and mountains, – 15/180. AE MC VISA JCB. rest by Gloriastrasse DV
***La Rotonde* : Meals** 74 (lunch)/115 and a la carte 78/153 – **152 rm** 420/620, 11 suites.
◆ This imposing edifice in its tranquil hilltop location offers a wonderful view over the city, the lake and the Alps. Rooms with classically elegant furnishings. La Rotonde is a superb restaurant with a panoramic terrace.

Zürich Marriott, Neumühlequai 42, ✉ 8006, ✆ 013 607 070, *marriott.zurich@marriotthotels.com, Fax 013 607 777,* ≤, – rm, – 15/250. AE MC VISA. rest EY c
***White Elephant* :** - Thai rest. *(closed Saturday and Sunday lunch)* **Meals** 38 (lunch)/85 and a la carte 58/112 – ***La Brasserie* : Meals** a la carte 46/108 – 31 – **251 rm** 295/360, 9 suites.
◆ This tall building with basement parking and riverside location offers comfortable, modern, recently renovated rooms varying in size and décor. The White Elephant restaurant transports diners to far-off Siam, while the Brasserie is somewhat less exotic.

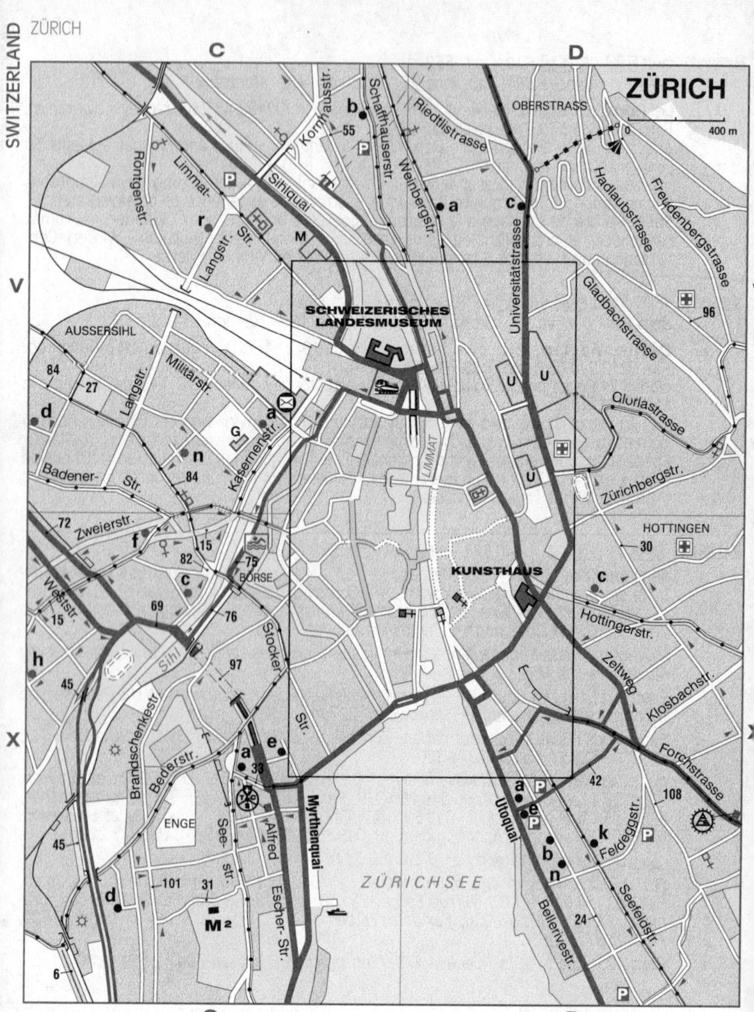

Street	Grid	No.
Allmendstrasse	CX	6
Augustinergasse	EZ	9
Bahnhofstrasse	EYZ	
Bärengasse	EZ	10
Beethovenstrasse	EZ	12
Bellevueplatz	FZ	
Birmensdorferstrasse	CX	15
Claridenstrasse	EZ	18
Clausiusstrasse	FY	19
Culmannstrasse	FY	21
Dufourstrasse	DX	24
Feldstrasse	CV	27
Fraumünsterstrasse	EZ	28
Freiestrasse	DVX	30
Gablerstrasse	CX	31
General Wille-Strasse	CX	33
Hafnerstrasse	EY	36
Kantonsschulstrasse	FZ	39
Konradstrasse	EY	40
Kreuzstrasse	DX	42
Limmatquai	FYZ	
Löwenstrasse	EY	
Manessestrasse	CX	45
Marktgasse	FZ	46
Münsterhof	EZ	48
Museumstrasse	EY	49
Nelkenstrasse	FY	52
Neumarkt	FZ	54
Nordstrasse	DV	55
Paradeplatz	EZ	
Peterstrasse	EZ	57
Poststrasse	EZ	58
Rathausbrücke	EFZ	60
Rennweg	EYZ	63
Rindermarkt	FZ	64
Schimmelstrasse	CX	69
Seebahnstrasse	CX	72
Selnaustrasse	CX	75
Sihlhölzlistrasse	CX	76
Stadelhoferstrasse	FZ	78
Stampfenbachplatz	FY	79
Stampfenbachstrasse	EFY	81
Stauffacherplatz	CX	82
Stauffacherstrasse	CVX	84
Storchengasse	EZ	85
Strehlgasse	EZ	87
Sumatrastrasse	FY	88
Talacker	EZ	90
Tannenstrasse	FY	91
Theaterstrasse	FZ	93
Toblerstrasse	DV	96
Tunnelstrasse	CX	97
Uraniastrasse	EYZ	
Usteristrasse	EY	100
Waffenplatzstrasse	CX	101
Weinbergfussweg	FY	103
Zollikerstrasse	DX	108

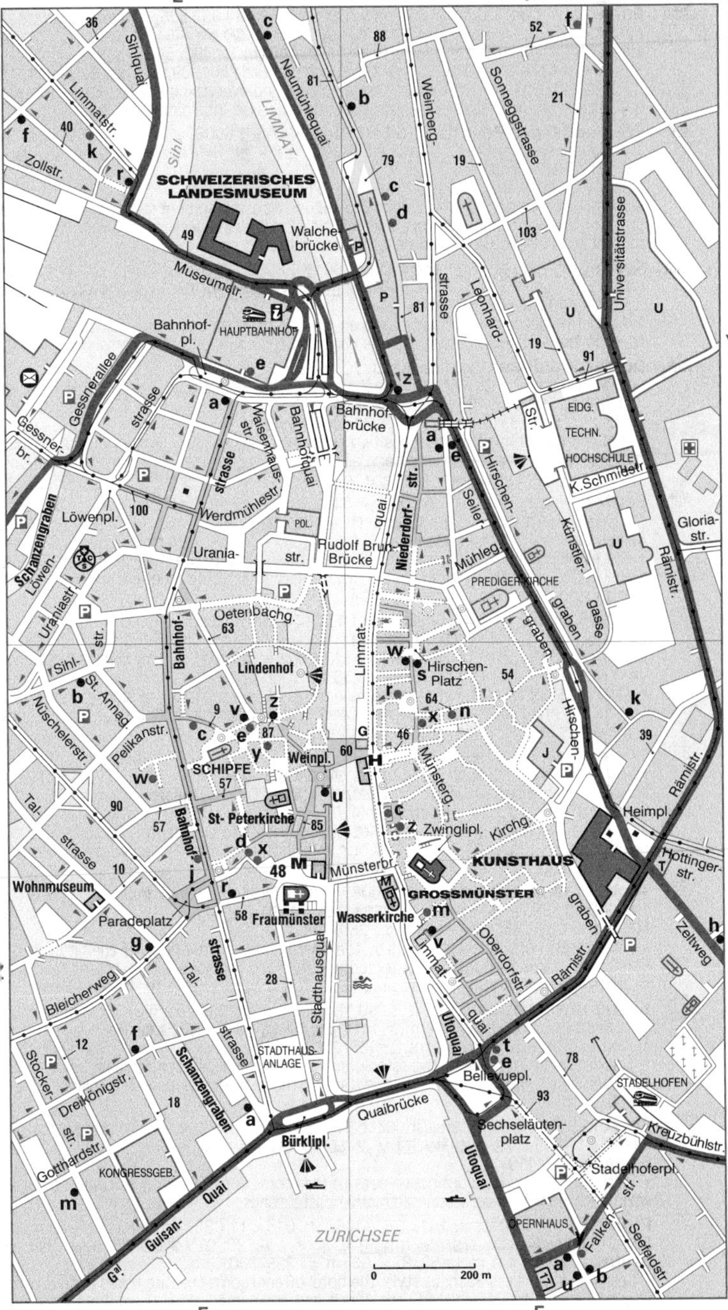

SCHWEIZERISCHES LANDESMUSEUM
HAUPTBAHNHOF
EIDG. TECHN. HOCHSCHULE
KUNSTHAUS
GROSSMÜNSTER
Fraumünster
Wasserkirche
St- Peterkirche
Lindenhof
SCHIPFE
Wohnmuseum
STADTHAUS-ANLAGE
KONGRESSGEB.
STADELHOFEN
OPERNHAUS
ZÜRICHSEE
PREDIGERKIRCHE
Bahnhofbrücke
Rudolf Brun-Brücke
Münsterbr.
Quaibrücke
Walchebrücke
Bahnhofpl.
Paradeplatz
Bürklipl.
Bellevuepl.
Sechseläutenplatz
Stadelhoferpl.
Hirschen-Platz
Zwinglipl.
Löwenpl.
Heimpl.
Weinpl.
Limmatquai
Utoquai
Bahnhofstrasse
Bahnhofquai
Stadthausquai
Neumühlequai
Gal Guisan-Quai
200 m

Eden au Lac, Utoquai 45, ✉ 8008, ✆ 012 662 525, *info@edenaulac.ch, Fax 012 662 500,* ≤, – AE MC VISA JCB. rest DX a
Meals 48 (lunch)/145 and a la carte 64/139 – **48 rm** 390/640, 5 suites.
◆ Having set the architectural tone for Zürich's lakeside in 1909, this neo-Baroque hotel is now a listed cultural monument. Inside you will find everything you expect from a luxury hotel. The menu sets out a fine selection of classic international cuisine.

Steigenberger Bellerive au Lac, Utoquai 47, ✉ 8008, ✆ 012 544 000, *bellerive@steigenberger.ch, Fax 012 544 001,* ≤, – rm, – 15/25. AE MC VISA DX e
Meals 49 (lunch) and a la carte 50/112 – **51 rm** 300/490.
◆ With its elegant décor in the style of the 1920s, this establishment stands on the lakeside. State-of-the-art design, comfort, and technical facilities in every room. Small, stylish restaurant with classic décor and beautifully upholstered seating.

Sofitel without rest, Stampfenbachstr. 60, ✉ 8006, ✆ 013 606 060, *h1196@accor-hotels.com, Fax 013 606 061* – – 15/40. AE MC VISA FY b
32 – **149 rm** 360/550, 4 suites.
◆ Attractive décor throughout, based on the use of wood and warm colours, from the foyer in the style of an elegant Swiss chalet to the soundproofed rooms.

Dolder Waldhaus , Kurhausstr. 20, ✉ 8030, ✆ 012 691 000, *reservations@dolderwaldhaus.ch, Fax 012 691 001,* ≤ Zurich and lake, , , , – , rm, rest, – 15/30. AE MC VISA JCB by Gloriastrasse DV
Meals a la carte 53/106 – 20 – **70 rm** 240/460.
◆ In a quiet location, this hotel has two types of room, modern with colourful wooden furnishings, and classic-contemporary, all with balcony and fine views over city and Alps. 1970s-style restaurant with a terrace to the front.

Central Plaza, Central 1, ✉ 8001, ✆ 012 515 555, *info@central.ch, Fax 012 518 535,* – , rm, rm, . AE MC VISA JCB FY z
King's Cave : - Grill room **Meals** a la carte 42/95 – 18 – **94 rm** 360/385, 6 suites.
◆ This establishment is right on the River Limmat directly opposite the main station. Rooms are all in the same modern and comfortable style, calculated to meet guests' every need. The vaulted cellars house the King's Cave grill.

Florhof, Florhofgasse 4, ✉ 8001, ✆ 012 614 470, *info@florhof.ch, Fax 012 614 611,* – , rm, . AE MC VISA FZ k
Meals *(closed 9 to 24 April, 20 December - 10 January, Saturday, Sunday and Bank Holidays)* 44 (lunch)/88 and a la carte 73/115 – **35 rm** 240/360.
◆ Tasteful décor characterises the rooms in this lovely old patrician mansion from the 16C. Careful attention to detail and excellent technical facilities throughout. Tempting dishes await diners in the elegant restaurant.

Tiefenau, Steinwiesstr. 8, ✉ 8032, ✆ 012 678 787, *info@claridge.ch, Fax 012 512 476,* – . AE MC VISA JCB FZ h
closed 19 December - 4 January – ***Orson's :*** *(closed Sunday)* **Meals** 37 (lunch)/75 and a la carte 45/96 – 24 – **31 rm** 280/420.
◆ This establishment enjoys a quiet location outside the city centre. Rooms based on diverse design concepts, some with Louis XV furnishings. Orson's serves contemporary cuisine with an Asian touch.

Ambassador, Falkenstr. 6, ✉ 8008, ✆ 012 589 898, *mail@ambassadorhotel.ch, Fax 012 589 800* – , rm, . AE MC VISA JCB FZ a
Meals a la carte 45/115 – **45 rm** 250/460.
◆ This stately hotel is located right by the opera house on the edge of the city centre. Rooms and suites furnished in contemporary style and provided with excellent technical facilities. Restaurant with fantastic murals depicting scenes from the opera.

Krone Unterstrass, Schaffhauserstr. 1, ✉ 8006, ✆ 013 605 656, *info@hotel-krone.ch, Fax 013 605 600* – , rm, rm, – 15/75. AE MC VISA CV b
Meals a la carte 38/92 – **57 rm** 185/280.
◆ Just above the city centre, this establishment offers classically comfortable, newly refitted rooms in a tasteful, modern style. One of the restaurants boasts a splendid open fireplace.

Seefeld without rest, Seefeldstr. 63, ✉ 8008, ✆ 013 874 141, *info@hotel-seefeld.ch, Fax 013 874 151,* – . AE MC VISA JCB DX k
64 rm 200/410.
◆ Black furniture lends a distinctive note to the rooms in this recently refurbished hotel, while each floor is decorated in attractive pastel tones.

Rigihof, Universitätstr. 101, ✉ 8006, ✆ 013 611 685, *info@hotel-rigihof.ch, Fax 013 611 617,* – , rm, – 20. AE MC VISA JCB DV c
Bauhaus : **Meals** a la carte 52/87 – **66 rm** 225/390.
◆ Designed in timeless Bauhaus style, the hotel offers rooms that are linked in an artistic way to personalities associated with Zürich and are named after them. Bold lines and colours distinguish the Bauhaus restaurant.

Opera without rest, Dufourstr. 5, ✉ 8008, ☎ 012 589 999, *mail@operahotel.ch, Fax 012 589 900* – FZ b
62 rm ☐ 260/360.
◆ Directly opposite the opera house to which this business hotel owes its name. Well-maintained rooms with contemporary comforts.

Europe, Dufourstr. 4, ✉ 8008, ☎ 012 611 030, *info@hoteleurope-zuerich.ch, Fax 012 510 367,* – rm, FZ u
Quaglinos : **Meals** a la carte 52/98 – ☐ 21 – **40 rm** 180/290.
◆ Not far from the opera on the edge of the city centre. The somewhat sober, beige-coloured rooms have period furnishings and a variety of nostalgic touches. Quaglinos is a fashionable place to eat.

Wellenberg without rest, Niederdorfstr. 10, ✉ 8001, ☎ 012 624 300, *reservation@hotel-wellenberg.ch, Fax 012 513 130* – FZ s
45 rm ☐ 295/410.
◆ This establishment is located right in the middle of the Old Town. Modern bedrooms, some in Art Deco style. Elegant breakfast room with a sun terrace.

Helmhaus without rest, Schifflände 30, ✉ 8001, ☎ 012 518 810, *hotel@helmhaus.ch, Fax 012 510 430* – FZ v
24 rm ☐ 233/342.
◆ In the very heart of the city, this hotel offers rooms most of which have bright and functional décor featuring white built-in furniture. Breakfast on the first floor.

Adler, Rosengasse 10, at Hirschenplatz, ✉ 8001, ☎ 012 669 696, *info@hotel-adler.ch, Fax 012 669 669,* – rm, FZ w
Swiss Chuchi : *(closed Christmas)* **Meals** a la carte 38/93 – **52 rm** ☐ 170/250.
◆ Rooms with bright, functional wooden furniture and up-to-the-minute technical facilities are also hung with pictures of Zürich as it was in the past. Country-style ambience in the rustic Swiss-Chuchi restaurant facing the street.

Lady's First without rest, Mainaustr. 24, ✉ 8008, ☎ 013 808 010, *info@ladysfirst.ch, Fax 013 808 020,* – DX n
28 rm ☐ 195/280.
◆ Especially for women travellers, this establishment boasts a sauna giving onto a spacious roof terrace. Guests sleep in contemporary style rooms with built-in furniture.

Seegarten, Seegartenstr. 14, ✉ 8008, ☎ 013 883 737, *seegarten@bluewin.ch, Fax 013 833 738,* – DX b
Latino : - Italian rest. - *(closed Saturday lunch and Sunday lunch)* **Meals** a la carte 51/93 – **28 rm** ☐ 179/299.
◆ A Mediterranean atmosphere pervades this establishment, from the luxuriantly planted foyer to the rooms with their parquet floors and cane or natural wood furnishings. The theme is continued in the restaurant with its terracotta floor and Southern decor.

Hirschen without rest, Niederdorfstr. 13, ✉ 8001, ☎ 0432 683 333, *info@hirschen-zuerich.ch, Fax 0432 683 334* – FY g
27 rm ☐ 130/190.
◆ Said to be the oldest hotel in town, the Hirschen offers practical, modern rooms, some with exposed brickwork. Wine bar in the vaulted cellars, which date back to the 16C.

Rütli without rest, Zähringerstr. 43, ✉ 8001, ☎ 012 545 800, *info@rutli.ch, Fax 012 545 801* – FY a
closed 23 December - 4 January – **62 rm** ☐ 195/290.
◆ Located at the entrance to the Old Town. Freshly refurbished rooms with parquet floors and straightforward wooden furnishings give a reasonable standard of comfort.

Rex, Weinbergstr. 92, ✉ 8006, ☎ 013 602 525, *hotelrex@swissonline.ch, Fax 013 602 552,* – rm, DV a
Blauer Apfel : *(closed Saturday and Sunday)* **Meals** a la carte 43/82 – **38 rm** ☐ 145/195.
◆ On the edge of the city centre, this hotel has functionally designed rooms in various sizes and styles with straightforward blue furnishings. The Blauer Apfel restaurant with cheerful, inviting décor.

Sonnenberg, Hitziweg 15, ✉ 8032, ☎ 012 669 797, *restaurant@sonnenberg-zh.ch, Fax 012 669 798,* ≤ Zürich and lake, – by Gloriastrasse DV
Meals - veal and beef specialities - (booking essential) a la carte 77/151.
◆ High up in the FIFA Building with a grandstand view of city, lake, and Alps. Contemporary dishes served in the half-moon-shaped panoramic restaurant.

Wirtschaft Flühgass, Zollikerstr. 214, ✉ 8008, ☎ 013 811 215, *Fax 014 227 532* – by Zollikerstrasse DX
closed 17 July - 15 August, 24 December - 4 January, Saturday (except dinner from November - December) and Sunday – **Meals** (booking essential) 60 (lunch)/130 and a la carte 64/122.
◆ The old 16C wine bar is now a congenial three-roomed restaurant serving cuisine with a traditional French flavour. Simpler menu in the rustic Gaststube.

XX **Kronenhalle,** Rämistr. 4, ✉ 8001, ☎ 012 516 669, *Fax 012 516 681* – ▤. AE ⓓ MC VISA FZ t
Meals (booking essential) a la carte 64/162.
◆ This rather unobtrusive building houses a Zürich institution, a restaurant with a remarkable art collection and a repertoire of classical dishes.

XX **Zunfthaus zur Schmiden,** Marktgasse 20, ✉ 8001, ☎ 012 505 848, *schmiden@dinner.ch, Fax 012 505 849* – ▤. AE ⓓ MC VISA. ✻ FZ x
closed mid July to mid August, New Year, Saturday, Sunday and Bank Holidays – **Meals** 42 (lunch)/90 and a la carte 50/108.
◆ The first floor restaurant in this 15C guild house serves dishes with a modern flavour. The character of the setting has been preserved despite new furnishings and fittings.

XX **Haus zum Rüden,** Limmatquai 42 (1st floor), ✉ 8001, ☎ 012 619 566, *info@hauszumrueden.ch, Fax 012 611 804* – |♦| ▤. AE ⓓ MC VISA JCB FZ c
closed Christmas, Saturday and Sunday – **Meals** 59 (lunch)/138 and a la carte 72/136.
◆ This restaurant, with an amazing wooden ceiling, is in a 13C guild house. The elegant, historical atmosphere in keeping with a classic menu.

XX **Zunfthaus zur Zimmerleuten,** Limmatquai 40, ✉ 8001, ☎ 012 505 363, *zimmerleuten-zurich@bluewin.ch, Fax 012 505 364,* 余 – |♦| ▤. AE ⓓ MC VISA FZ z
closed 25 July - 8 August, 25 to 26 December and 2 January – ***Restaurant :*** (1st floor) **Meals** a la carte 49/111 – ***Küferstube :*** **Meals** 57/87 and a la carte 46/79.
◆ Carved beams set a welcoming tone in the first floor restaurant ; with old barrels and dark wood fittings in the Coopers : perfect for an 18C carpenters hall.

XX **Riesbächli,** Zollikerstr. 157, ✉ 8008, ☎ 014 222 324, *Fax 014 222 941* – AE ⓓ MC VISA by Zollikerstrasse DX
closed 27 July - 12 August, 25 December - 6 January, Saturday (except dinner from November - March) and Sunday – **Meals** 110 and a la carte 73/146 ♣.
◆ This traditional restaurant is divided up into three visually separate dining areas. Remarkable choice of wines to go with a range of classic dishes.

XX **Conti-da Bianca,** Dufourstr. 1, ✉ 8008, ☎ 012 510 666, *Fax 012 510 686* – AE ⓓ MC VISA FZ y
closed 2 weeks July - August, Saturday lunch and Sunday – **Meals** - Italian rest. - a la carte 65/122.
◆ On the edge of the city centre. Tastefully decorated and elegantly lit, this establishment consists of a long dining room with a stucco ceiling. Classic Italian cuisine.

XX **Jacky's Stapferstube,** Culmannstr. 45, ✉ 8006, ☎ 013 613 748, *jackys@stapferstube.ch, Fax 013 640 060,* 余 – P. AE ⓓ MC VISA FY f
closed 15 July - 15 August, Sunday and Monday – **Meals** 38 and a la carte 65/161.
◆ Older style of edifice with green shutters. A welcoming place to eat, with lots of wood giving the interior an attractively rustic character. Pictures used as decoration.

XX **Vorderer Sternen,** Theaterstr. 22 (1st floor), ✉ 8001, ☎ 012 514 949, *info@vorderer-sternen.ch, Fax 012 529 063,* 余 – AE ⓓ MC VISA FZ e
Meals a la carte 40/102.
◆ Straightforward café on the ground floor, above it a homely restaurant with dark wood décor. Good modern dishes at reasonable prices.

XX **Casa Ferlin,** Stampfenbachstr. 38, ✉ 8006, ☎ 013 623 509, *casaferlin@swissonline.ch, Fax 013 623 534* – ▤. AE ⓓ MC VISA FY c
closed 17 July - 15 August, 20 December - 4 January, Saturday and Sunday – **Meals** - Italian rest. - (booking essential) 52 and a la carte 63/124.
◆ Traditional interior with open fireplace and rustic furnishings. The menu offers a choice of Italian dishes accompanied by the appropriate wines.

XX **Blue Monkey Cocostin,** Stüssihofstatt 3, ✉ 8001, ☎ 012 617 618, *koenigstuhl@bluewin.ch, Fax 012 627 123,* 余 – 🚹 15/40. AE ⓓ MC VISA FZ r
Meals - Thai rest. - 55 and a la carte 58/92.
◆ A Thai restaurant has been established on two floors of the historic guildhall called the Zunfthaus zur Schneidern. Ground floor bistro-style bar, fine dining above.

X **Blaue Ente,** Seefeldstr. 223 (mill Tiefenbrunnen), ✉ 8008, ☎ 013 886 840, *info@blaue-ente.ch, Fax 014 227 741,* 余 – AE ⓓ MC by Zollikerstrasse DX
closed 25 July - 16 August and 24 December - 4 January – **Meals** (booking essential) a la carte 52/101 ♣.
◆ This trendy establishment with lots of glass, pipework, and gigantic gearwheels is housed in an old mill. Cheerful atmosphere and good plain cooking in a modern style.

X **Oepfelchammer,** Rindermarkt 12 (1st floor), ✉ 8001, ☎ 012 512 336, *Fax 012 627 533,* 余 – AE ⓓ MC VISA FZ n
closed 19 July - 17 August and 24 December - 6 January – **Meals** 110 and a la carte 53/94.
◆ The famous 19C Swiss writer Gottfried Keller was a regular in the wine bar in this 14C establishment. Good solid fare in the restaurant including local specialities.

Rosaly's, Freieckgasse 7, ✉ 8001, ☎ 012 614 430, *info@rosalys.ch.ch, Fax 012 614 413,* – AE ⓓ MC VISA FZ e
closed Saturday lunch and Sunday lunch – **Meals** a la carte 42/80.
◆ Contemporary, simply furnished restaurant with relaxed atmosphere, offering interesting international dishes prepared in a refined traditional style.

Frieden, Stampfenbachstr. 32, ✉ 8006, ☎ 012 531 810, *Fax 012 531 812,* – AE ⓓ MC VISA FY d
closed 28 March - 13 April, 3 to 17 October, Saturday and Sunday – **Meals** a la carte 52/92.
◆ Housed in a municipal building, this is a bistro-style restaurant with plain wooden furnishings and parquet flooring. Friendly service.

Ban Song Thai, Kirchgasse 6, ✉ 8001, ☎ 012 523 331, *bansong@bluewin.ch, Fax 012 523 315* – AE MC VISA FZ m
closed 19 July - 8 August, 22 December - 5 January, Saturday lunch and Sunday – **Meals** - Thai rest. - (booking essential) 57 and a la carte 46/99.
◆ This restaurant is very close to Kunsthaus and Cathedral. Its name evokes its offerings - you are cordially invited by your hosts to take a gastronomic trip to Thailand.

On the left bank of the river Limmat (Main railway station, Business centre) :

Baur au Lac, Talstr. 1, ✉ 8001, ☎ 012 205 020, *info@bauraulac.ch, Fax 012 205 044,* – , rm, TV – 15/60. AE ⓓ MC VISA JCB. EZ a
Le Pavillon/Le Français : **Meals** 90 (lunch)/140 and a la carte 81/174 – ***Rive Gauche :*** *(closed 3 weeks July - August, Sunday and Bank Holidays)* **Meals** 90 (lunch)/140 and a la carte 81/174 – ☕ 38 – **103 rm** 470/680, 22 suites.
◆ A traditional hotel with a lovely garden and luxurious rooms. A roof-top fitness centre overlooks the lake. Diners are treated to classic culinary delights in the Pavillon in summer and in the Français in winter. The Rive Gauche has a touch of colonial style.

Savoy Baur en Ville, Paradeplatz, ✉ 8001, ☎ 012 152 525, *welcome@savoy-zurich.ch, Fax 012 152 500* – , rm, TV video – 15/70. AE ⓓ MC VISA JCB. EZ r
Savoy : (1st floor) **Meals** 64 (lunch) and a la carte 70/145 – ***Orsini :*** (in front of the cathedral) - Italian rest. - *(booking essential)* **Meals** 59 (lunch)/98 and a la carte 76/138 – **104 rm** ☕ 470/720, 8 suites.
◆ In the heart of town, the grandiose 19C architecture of this establishment offers guests the most stylish of settings. Exemplary service and an elegant, modern interior. The first-floor Savoy is classically elegant ; the Orsini provides an Italian alternative.

Widder, Rennweg 7, ✉ 8001, ☎ 012 242 526, *home@widderhotel.ch, Fax 012 242 424,* – , rest, TV – 15/100. AE ⓓ MC VISA. rest EZ v
Meals 88 (dinner) and a la carte 72/125 – **42 rm** ☕ 450/810, 7 suites.
◆ Ten historic Old Town houses have been renovated and combined to form this hotel. Distinguished interior, superlative comfort, contemporary architectural features. The two restaurants are full of charm and character.

Schweizerhof, Bahnhofplatz 7, ✉ 8001, ☎ 012 188 888, *info@hotelschweizerhof.com, Fax 012 188 181* – , rm, TV – 15/40. AE ⓓ MC VISA JCB. rest EY a
La Soupière : (1st floor) *(closed Saturday dinner, Sunday and Bank Holidays)* **Meals** 72 (lunch) and a la carte 79/135 – **115 rm** ☕ 420/680.
◆ This historic establishment stands in the very heart of town directly opposite the main station. Beyond the imposing façade is an interior of contemporary elegance and great comfort. The La Soupière restaurant has a classically tasteful ambience.

Ascot, Tessinerplatz 9, ✉ 8002, ☎ 012 081 414, *info@ascot.ch, Fax 012 081 420,* – , rm, TV – 15/50. AE ⓓ MC VISA JCB CX a
Lawrence : *(closed Saturday and Sunday)* **Meals** 58 (lunch) and a la carte 69/116 – ***Fujiya of Japan :*** ☎ 012 081 555 - Japanese rest. (Teppan-Yaki) - *(closed Saturday lunch, Sunday and Monday)* **Meals** 55 (lunch)/140 and a la carte 66/112 – **74 rm** ☕ 390/580.
◆ This stylishly decorated establishment offers rooms with furniture in either mahogany or limewashed oak. Up-to-the-minute technical facilities. The Lawrence is in Tudor style, while the Fujiya of Japan is a typical Teppan-yaki restaurant.

Zum Storchen, Weinplatz 2, ✉ 8001, ☎ 012 272 727, *info@storchen.ch, Fax 012 272 700,* – , rm, rm, TV – 15/20. AE ⓓ MC VISA JCB. rest EZ u
Rôtisserie : (1st floor) **Meals** 69/84 and a la carte 59/106 – **73 rm** ☕ 330/690.
◆ This traditional hotel - one of the city's oldest - is situated directly on the Limmat. The elegant, comfortable furnishings ensure a relaxing stay. The restaurant features a lovely riverside terrace offering a fine view across the Limmat to the Old Town.

ArabellaSheraton Neues Schloss, Stockerstr. 17, ✉ 8002, ☎ 012 869 400, *neuesschloss@arabellasheraton.com, Fax 012 869 445* – |♦|, ⇔ rm, ▤ TV ☎ 🚗 – 🏛 20. AE ⓓ MC VISA JCB EZ m

Le Jardin : *(closed Saturday lunch and Sunday except for residents)* **Meals** 57 (lunch)/85 and a la carte 67/103 – ☕ 30 – **60 rm** 420/520.

• Not far from the lakeside, this establishment makes an excellent base for your stay in Zürich. The recently renovated rooms have elegant wooden furnishings in contemporary style. The ground floor restaurant is lavishly decorated with indoor plants.

Alden Hotel Splügenschloss (Suitenhotel)**,** Splügenstr. 2 / Genferstrasse, ✉ 8002, ☎ 012 899 999, *welcome@alden.ch, Fax 012 899 998* – |♦|, ⇔ rm, ▤ TV ☎ P – 🏛 20. AE ⓓ MC VISA JCB. ⚹ rest CX e

closed December - March – **Meals** *(closed Saturday and Sunday)* a la carte 55/155 – **10 rm** ☕ 700/900, 22 suites.

• With its little tower, this hotel really does look like a castle from a distance. The rooms are basically similar in style, though with varying layouts and colour schemes. Dining in the tasteful ambience of the Schlossrestaurant is certainly a good idea.

Inter-Continental Zurich, Badenerstr. 420, ✉ 8004, ☎ 014 044 444, *zurich@interconti.com, Fax 014 044 440,* 🌂, Fб, ≘s, ▢ – |♦|, ⇔ rm, ▤ TV ☎ ♿ 🚗 – 🏛 15/400. AE ⓓ MC VISA JCB by Badenerstrasse CV

Relais des Arts : *(closed Bank Holidays)* **Meals** 45 (lunch)/85 and a la carte 61/105 – ☕ 30 – **364 rm** 300/370.

• Among the amenities of this hotel - as well as its comfortable and functional contemporary style rooms - is its accessibility to the airport and the motorway. Guests are invited to dine in the bright and elegant surroundings of the Relais des Arts.

Glärnischhof, Claridenstr. 30, ✉ 8002, ☎ 012 862 222, *info@glaernischhof.com, Fax 012 862 286* – |♦|, ⇔ rm, ▤ rest, TV ☎ P – 🏛 25. AE ⓓ MC VISA JCB EZ f

Le Poisson : - Fish specialities *(closed Saturday and Sunday)* **Meals** 59 (lunch)/95 and a la carte 72/113 – ***Vivace :*** - Italian rest. - **Meals** a la carte 44/92 – **62 rm** ☕ 340/490.

• This building on the edge of the city centre has functional rooms with fine wood furnishings and fresh and bright colour schemes. The restaurants' names spell out their wares : fish dishes in Le Poisson, Italian cuisine in Vivace.

Engimatt, Engimattstr. 14, ✉ 8002, ☎ 012 841 616, *info@engimatt.ch, Fax 012 012 516,* 🌂, ✂ – |♦| TV ☎ ♿ 🚗 P – 🏛 15/25. AE ⓓ MC VISA JCB CX d

Meals 45 (lunch)/85 and a la carte 42/97 – **80 rm** ☕ 210/330.

• Close to the city centre but nevertheless in an attractively leafy setting. Rooms solidly furnished in contemporary style, some with a tastefully rustic touch. The Orangerie restaurant is a modern interpretation of a winter garden in steel and glass.

Glockenhof, Sihlstr. 31, ✉ 8001, ☎ 012 259 191, *info@glockenhof.ch, Fax 012 259 292,* 🌂 – |♦|, ⇔ rm, ▤ rest, TV ☎ ♿ P – 🏛 15/40. AE ⓓ MC VISA JCB

Meals 29 (lunch) and a la carte 40/93 – **100 rm** ☕ 260/430.

• Its city centre location is only one of the many advantages of this well-run hotel. Amenities include rooms in contemporary style and excellent technical facilities. Enjoy the pleasantly relaxed ambience in the Glogge-Stube. EZ b

Mercure Hotel Stoller, Badenerstr. 357, ✉ 8003, ☎ 014 054 747, *info@stoller.ch, Fax 014 054 848,* 🌂 – |♦| ⇔ TV ☎ P – 🏛 15/25. AE ⓓ MC VISA JCB

Meals a la carte 46/95 – **79 rm** ☕ 215/250. by Badenerstrasse CV

• On the edge of the city centre close to a tram stop. Rooms in similar style with furnishings in grey veneer. Quieter rooms with balcony to the rear. The restaurant is divided into two rooms with dark wood furnishings. Street café in summer.

Greulich, Herman Greulich-Str. 56, ✉ 8004, ☎ 0432 434 243, *mail@greulich.ch, Fax 0432 434 200,* 🌂 – ⇔ rm, TV ☎ ♿ P – 🏛 20. AE ⓓ MC VISA EZ g

Meals 42 (lunch)/110 and a la carte 64/117 – ☕ 18 – **18 rm** 180/260.

• Trim, modern, practically equipped rooms and mini-suites face a courtyard garden shaded by birches. Simple styling, warm colours and parquet floors set the tone in the restaurant.

Novotel Zürich City-West, Schiffbaustr. 13, ✉ 8005, ☎ 012 762 222, *H2731@accor-hotels.com, Fax 012 762 323,* 🌂, Fб, ▢ – |♦|, ⇔ rm, TV ☎ ♿ 🚗 – 🏛 15/120. AE ⓓ MC VISA by Seebahn-, Hard- and Pfingstweidstrasse CV

Meals 39 (lunch) and a la carte 36/95 – ☕ 25 – **142 rm** 189/235.

• This newly-built hotel with its cladding of black glass offers identical, contemporary style and reasonably spacious rooms featuring white built-in furniture.

Walhalla without rest, Limmatstr. 5, ✉ 8005, ☎ 014 465 400, *walhalla-hotel@bluewin.ch, Fax 014 465 454* – |♦| ⇔ TV ☎ – 🏛 15/20. AE ⓓ MC VISA JCB EY r

☕ 15 – **48 rm** 170/220.

• Good public transport access, by a tram stop behind the main station. Rooms with dark wood furniture and paintings of gods indulging in pleasure.

Kindli, Pfalzgasse 1, ✉ 8001, ☎ 0438 887 676, *reservations@kindli.ch, Fax 0438 887 677,* – 🛗 TV 📞. AE ⓓ MC VISA EZ z
Meals *(closed Sunday and Bank Holidays)* 72 (dinner) and à la carte 46/103 – **20 rm** ☕ 230/360.
◆ This historic town house has an interior in English country-house style with rooms individually designed by Laura Ashley. Discreetly elegant restaurant offers classically inspired modern cooking.

Montana, Konradstr. 39, ✉ 8005, ☎ 0433 666 000, *reservation@hotelmontana.ch, Fax 0433 666 010* – 🛗, ⇄ rm, TV 📞 ♿ P. AE ⓓ MC VISA JCB EY f
Bistro Le Lyonnais : *(closed Sunday and Bank Holidays)* **Meals** 25 (lunch)/40 and a la carte 44/97 – **74 rm** ☕ 180/310.
◆ This establishment is located to the rear of the station. A glass lift rises through the covered courtyard to take guests to their rooms which feature plain but elegant, dark built-in furniture. Le Lyonnais bistro with own entrance and appropriate décor.

Ibis, Schiffbaustr. 11, ✉ 8005, ☎ 012 762 100, *h2942@accor-hotels.com, Fax 012 762 101,* – 🛗, ⇄ rm, TV 📞 ♿ 🚗. AE ⓓ MC VISA
Meals *(closed Sunday lunch)* a la carte 36/65 – ☕ 14 – **155 rm** 139.
◆ This new hotel has established itself in the old shipbuilding sheds : practical rooms provide a reasonable level of comfort for what is a very favourable price. The Swiss Park bistro offers specialities from all four of the country language communities. by Seebahn-, Hard- and Pfingstweidstrasse CV

Sukhothai, Erlachstr. 46, ✉ 8003, ☎ 014 626 622, *heymann@sukhothai.ch, Fax 014 626 654* – ▤. AE ⓓ MC VISA. ✗ CX h
closed 8 to 12 April, 25 July - 7 August, 24 December - 2 January, Sunday and Monday – **Meals** - Thai rest. - *(dinner only)* (booking essential) 149 and a la carte 81/147.
◆ A discreetly elegant and welcoming establishment ornamented with a number of Thai artworks and serving a wonderful range of culinary delights from the same country.

Kaiser's Reblaube, Glockengasse 7, ✉ 8001, ☎ 012 212 120, *rest.reblaube@bluewin.ch, Fax 012 212 155,* – AE ⓓ MC VISA. ✗ EZ y
closed 26 July - 15 August, Monday dinner from April - September, Saturday lunch and Sunday – ***Goethe-Stübli :*** (1st floor) (booking essential) **Meals** 58 (lunch)/138 and a la carte 67/110 – ***Weinstube :*** **Meals** a la carte 62/103.
◆ Historic townhouse hidden in a maze of streets. Modern cooking in the first floor Goethe-Stübli ; traditional favourites in the lively wine bar and bistro, which has a garden.

Zunfthaus zur Waag, Münsterhof 8 (1st floor), ✉ 8001, ☎ 012 169 966, *zunfthaus-zur-waag@bluewin.ch, Fax 012 169 967,* – AE ⓓ MC VISA JCB EZ x
Meals a la carte 62/120.
◆ The first floor of the hatters' and weavers' guildhall now houses a well-stocked restaurant with Biedermeier-style décor. Traditional offerings on the menu.

Accademia, Rotwandstr. 62, ✉ 8004, ☎ 012 414 202, *Fax 012 414 207* – 🚗. AE ⓓ MC VISA. ✗ CV n
closed Saturday (except dinner from November - December) and Sunday – **Meals** - Italian rest. - a la carte 61/123.
◆ This restaurant with its traditional décor is divided into two sections. As well as serving Italian dishes and appropriate wines it also offers grilled specialities.

Carlton, Bahnhofstr. 41, Nüschelerstr. 6, ✉ 8001, ☎ 012 271 919, *info@carlton-zuerich.ch, Fax 012 271 927,* – ▤. AE ⓓ MC VISA EZ w
closed 1 to 4 January, Sunday and Bank Holidays – **Meals** 46 (lunch) and a la carte 57/101.
◆ This spacious restaurant is elegantly decorated in Art Deco style. The kitchen produces contemporary interpretations of traditional recipes. Wine cellar open to visitors.

Casa Aurelio, Langstr. 209, ✉ 8005, ☎ 012 727 744, *Fax 012 727 724,* – AE ⓓ MC VISA. ✗ rest CV r
closed 3 weeks August, 23 December - 4 January and Sunday – **Meals** - Spanish rest. - 42 (lunch)/60 and a la carte 69/103.
◆ Frescoes decorate the walls of the visually separate rooms of this restaurant in old Spanish-villa style. Guests are served with dishes from the Iberian repertory.

Sala of Tokyo, Limmatstr. 29, ✉ 8005, ☎ 012 715 290, *sala@active.ch, Fax 012 717 807,* – AE ⓓ MC VISA JCB EY k
closed 9 to 12 April, 18 July - 9 August, 21 December - 5 January, Saturday lunch, Sunday and Monday – **Meals** - Japanese rest. - 67/120 and a la carte 50/117.
◆ Wood-panelled interior with sushi-bar and restaurant, to the rear a section in contemporary style with yakitori grills. The kitchen is sure to bring a smile to your lips.

Il Giglio, Weberstr. 14, ✉ 8004, ☎ 012 428 597, *Fax 012 910 183* – AE ⓓ MC VISA CX c
closed 24 July - 16 August, 24 December - 5 January, Saturday (except dinner from September - May), Sunday and Bank Holidays – **Meals** - Italian rest. - 47 (lunch)/95 and a la carte 62/106.
◆ The little white-ceilinged restaurant with walls covered in modern art is a short distance from the city centre. Choice of Italian dishes.

Cantinetta Antinori, Augustinergasse 25, ✉ 8001, ☎ 012 117 210, *cantinetta-antinori@bindella.ch, Fax 012 211 613,* – AE ⓓ MC VISA EZ c
Meals - Italian rest. - a la carte 52/114.
◆ Sophisticated dining room with original décor and lovely wainscoting on the first floor. Plainer fare served in the ground floor restaurant. Italian cuisine.

Strozzi's Più, Bahnhofstr. 25, ✉ 8001, ☎ 012 256 025, *strozzispiu@strozzis.ch, Fax 012 256 026,* – ▤. AE MC VISA EZ j
closed Sunday except lunch from October - May and Bank Holidays – **Meals** 74 (dinner) and a la carte 48/94.
◆ The long bar and lilac club chairs match the clean-lined interior of the Credit Suisse building. Trendy modern cuisine prepared in the old bank vaults.

Barometer, Glockengasse 16 / Widdergasse 5, ✉ 8001, ☎ 012 115 665, *info@barometer.ch, Fax 012 115 663,* – AE ⓓ MC VISA EZ e
closed 24 December - 4 January, Saturday and Sunday – **Meals** a la carte 52/82.
◆ Bistro with décor featuring yellow pastel colours. Light Mediterranean dishes served inside or on the terrace with its sturdy wooden benches and tables.

Heugümper, Waaggasse 4, ✉ 8001, ☎ 012 111 660, *info@restaurantheuguemper.ch, Fax 012 111 661* – 15/40. AE ⓓ MC VISA EZ d
closed 9 to 12 April, 10 July - 8 August, 24 December - 4 January, Saturday (except from October - February) and Sunday – **Meals** a la carte 58/116.
◆ In the part of the Old Town around the Fraumünster this restaurant consists of a smart bistro and an elegant dining room, both serving dishes with a modern twist.

Caduff's Wine Loft, Kanzleistr. 126, ✉ 8004, ☎ 012 402 255, *caduff@wineloft.ch, Fax 012 402 256* – AE ⓓ MC VISA CV d
closed 24 December - 5 January, Saturday lunch and Sunday – **Meals** (booking essential) 52 (lunch)/115 and a la carte 46/133.
◆ This former wholesale flower market now serves tasty morsels at the long bar and well-sourced dishes accompanied by a fine wine from the famous cellars.

Ciro, Militärstr. 16, ✉ 8004, ☎ 012 417 841, *ciro@swissonline.ch, Fax 012 911 424,* – AE ⓓ MC VISA CV a
closed Sunday and Bank Holidays – **Meals** - Italian rest. - a la carte 48/80.
◆ In the welcoming interiors of this restaurant close to the station guests are served with a variety of Italian dishes and the wines to accompany them.

at Zürich-Oerlikon *North : by Universitätstrasse* DV *: 5 km – alt. 442 – ✉ 8050 Zürich-Oerlikon :*

Swissôtel Zürich, Marktplatz, ☎ 013 173 111, *reservations.zurich@swissotel.com, Fax 013 124 468,* <, , , , – |‡|, ▤ rm, TV P – 15/400. AE ⓓ MC VISA.
Dialog : **Meals** 60 (lunch) and a la carte 52/114 – ***Szenario :*** **Meals** 55 and a la carte 40/92 – 30 – **337 rm** 250/310, 10 suites.
◆ Tall building on the market place in the centre of town. Rooms with timeless lightwood furnishings. Swimming-pool on the 32nd floor with view over the whole town. Open-plan dining area with two sections, one serving plain food, the other more refined dishes.

at Zürich-Seebach *North : by Schaffenhauserstrasse* CV *– alt. 442 – ✉ 8052 Zürich-Seebach :*

Landhus, Katzenbachstr. 10, ☎ 013 083 400, *info@landhus-zuerich.ch, Fax 013 083 451,* – |‡| TV P – 15/300. AE ⓓ MC VISA
Meals a la carte 43/81 – **28 rm** 130/150.
◆ On the edge of town, reached via the Schaffhausen road. Reasonably spacious rooms with contemporary furnishings in dark wood. Colourful, up-to-the-minute restaurant serving good plain food.

at Glattbrugg *North : by Universitätstrasse* DV *: 8 km – alt. 432 – ✉ 8152 Glattbrugg :*

Renaissance Zürich Hotel, Talackerstr. 1, ☎ 018 745 000, *renaissance.zurich@renaissancehotels.com, Fax 018 745 001,* , , – |‡| ▤ TV – 15/300. AE ⓓ MC VISA JCB
Asian Place : - Asian rest. *(closed July, August, Saturday lunch and Sunday)* **Meals** a la carte 53/112 – ***Brasserie :*** **Meals** a la carte 48/96 – 30 – **196 rm** 350/395, 8 suites.
◆ In a building complex with an extensive basement-level leisure area, this establishment offers rooms nearly all of which have tasteful, dark furnishings. To the rear of the foyer, the brasserie offers a range of contemporary cuisine.

Hilton, Hohenbühlstr. 10, ℰ 018 285 050, *zurich@hilton.ch, Fax 018 285 151,* – rm, – 15/280.
Horizon : *(closed Saturday lunch and Sunday lunch)* **Meals** 49 (buffet)/68 and a la carte 57/130 – ***Market Place :*** **Meals** 49 (buffet)/68 and a la carte 52/103 – 34 – **310 rm** 329/439, 13 suites.
◆ Close to the airport, this establishment offers freshly refurbished rooms with bright maplewood furnishings. New executive rooms have been provided on two floors. Modern design in the Horizon restaurant. Open kitchen in the Marketplace restaurant.

Mövenpick, Walter Mittelholzerstr. 8, ℰ 018 088 888, *hotel@movenpick-zurich-airport.ch, Fax 018 088 877* – rm, – 15/220.
Appenzeller Stube : *(closed mid July - mid August and Saturday lunch* **Meals** 45 (lunch)/85 and a la carte 56/117 – ***Mövenpick Rest. :*** **Meals** a la carte 39/107 – ***Dim Sum :*** - Chinese rest. *(closed mid July - mid August, Saturday lunch and Sunday lunch)* **Meals** a la carte 44/105 – 28 – **332 rm** 320/400.
◆ This hotel is right by the exit off the motorway. All of the rooms have been refurbished, some have exercise equipment. Enjoy the typically Swiss atmosphere in the Appenzeller Stube or try International dishes in the Mövenpick restaurant.

Novotel Zürich Airport Messe, Talackerstr. 21, ℰ 018 299 000, *h0884@accor-hotels.com, Fax 018 299 999,* – rm, – 15/150.
Meals a la carte 40/94 – 25 – **257 rm** 205/265.
◆ On the edge of the town centre and just a few minutes from the new trade fair centre, this hotel offers convenient parking and functional rooms with lightwood furnishings.

Airport, Oberhauserstr. 30, ℰ 018 094 747, *reservation@hotel-airport.ch, Fax 018 094 774,* – rm, rm, rest
Edo Garden : *(closed Saturday lunch)* **Meals** a la carte 51/117 – ***Fujiya of Japan :*** *(closed Monday, Tuesday and lunch from 15 July - 15 August)* **Meals** a la carte 60/117 – 20 – **44 rm** 175/250.
◆ This centrally located establishment has reasonably spacious rooms in identical style and layout with light built-in furniture. Modern bathrooms. European and Asian cuisine in the Edo Garden. Fujiya of Japan with food cooked at your table.

NH Zurich Airport, Schaffhauserstr. 101, ℰ 018 085 000, *nhzurich.airport@nh-hotels.ch, Fax 018 085 100,* – rm, – 15/45. rest
Meals a la carte approx. 65 – 26 – **140 rm** 180.
◆ The rooms of this airport hotel with their contemporary, functional décor and furnishings are above all suitable for business travellers. Shuttle service to the airport.

at Kloten *North : by Universitätstrasse DV : 12 km – alt. 447 – ✉ 8302 Kloten :*

Allegra, Hamelirainstr. 3, ℰ 018 044 444, *reservation@hotel-allegra.ch, Fax 018 044 141,* – – 15/30. rest
Meals a la carte 31/72 – **132 rm** 185/230.
◆ New business hotel offers spacious, well-soundproofed rooms with colourful built-in furniture. Free airport bus service. Modern restaurant : Swiss favourites and a salad bar.

Fly away Ⓜ, Marktgasse 19, ℰ 018 044 455, *reservation@hotel-flyaway.ch, Fax 018 044 450,* – rm, rm,
closed 24 December - 4 January (Hotel only) – ***Mercato :*** - Italian rest. **Meals** a la carte 31/81 – 15 – **42 rm** 155/202.
◆ Close to the station, this hotel has spacious rooms all similar in décor and layout and all with timeless, functional furnishings.The Mercato restaurant is Mediterranean in style with contemporary décor and wooden furnishings.

Rias, Gerbegasse 6, ℰ 018 142 652, *ria.richner@bluewin.ch, Fax 018 135 504,* –
closed Saturday dinner and Sunday – **Meals** 44 (lunch)/95 and a la carte 48/94.
◆ This contemporary style restaurant is tucked away rather unobtrusively down a little street. Separate bar and à la carte dining room offering reliable traditional fare.

at Küsnacht *Southeast : by Bellerivestrasse DX : 8 km – alt. 415 – ✉ 8700 Küsnacht :*

Ermitage am See with rm, Seestr. 80, ℰ 019 144 242, *info@ermitage.ch, Fax 019 144 243,* ≤ Zurich lake, – rest
Meals *(closed 27 December - 6 January)* 65 (lunch)/175 and a la carte 96/159 – **22 rm** 195/410, 4 suites.
◆ In a beautiful waterside location, this country house with its terrace, garden, and delightful interior, offers its guests a lovely view over Lake Zürich.
Spec. Sandre et écrevisses en salade de chou-fleur tiède aux pistaches. Chevreuil d'été mariné, omelette soufflée, champignons et roquette. Filet de bœuf du Simmental et culotte de veau, crème légère de raifort. **Wines** Regensberg, Feldbach

XXX ⊛⊛ **Petermann's Kunststuben,** Seestr. 160, ✆ 019 100 715, *petermannskunstuben@bluewin.ch, Fax 019 100 495,* ☂ – ▤ P. AE ⊙ MC VISA
closed 23 August - 12 September, 9 to 22 February, Sunday and Monday – **Meals** (booking essential for dinner) 78 (lunch)/195 and a la carte 127/206.
◆ Imaginatively created classic dishes, perfectly presented in elegant interiors or in the lovely little garden : there's no mistaking Petermann's prestigious restaurant.
Spec. Le dos de loup de mer de petit bateau en croûte de poivre de Jamaïque et jus de fruits de la passion. Le pigeon farci sous la peau aux abattis, feuilles et côtes de blette mijotées. La soupe au champagne et pêche pochée à la lavande, glace aux feuilles de citron.
Wines Freisamer, Meilener

at Gattikon *South by motorway A3 CX : 11 km – alt. 510 – ✉ 8136 Gattikon :*

XX ⊛ **Sihlhalde** (Smolinsky), Sihlhaldenstr. 70, ✆ 017 200 927, *Fax 017 200 925,* ☂ – P. AE MC VISA
closed 18 July - 8 August, 21 December - 5 January, Sunday and Monday – **Meals** (booking essential) 115 and a la carte 68/121.
◆ Tucked away on the edge of town, this establishment with its three individually styled dining rooms pampers clients with an array of delectable dishes from its classic menu.
Spec. Artischocken an Verveineschaum. Steinbutt in Variation. Gratin von Wollmispeln mit Sauerrahmeis

at Uetikon am See *Southeast by Bellerivestrasse : 18 km – alt. 414 – ✉ 8707 Uetikon am See :*

XX ⊛⊛ **Wirtschaft zum Wiesengrund** (Hussong), Kleindorfstr. 61, ✆ 019 206 360, *hussong@wiesengrund.ch, Fax 019 211 709,* ☂ – P. AE ⊙ MC VISA. ✗
closed 25 July - 16 August, 1 to 16 February, Sunday and Monday – **Meals** (booking essential) 68 (lunch)/160 and a la carte 90/184.
◆ An inconspicuous exterior hardly hints at the culinary masterpieces being served in the contemporary style restaurant or on the lovely little garden terrace.
Spec. Cassolette von Langustinen parfümiert mit Estragon. Kalbsfilet aus dem Emmental mit Gänseleber und Perigordtrüffel. Praliné von Ziegenkäse auf Gemüsesalat und Limone

United Kingdom

LONDON – BELFAST – BIRMINGHAM – EDINBURGH
GLASGOW – LEEDS – LIVERPOOL
MANCHESTER

PRACTICAL INFORMATION

LOCAL CURRENCY

Pound Sterling: *1 GBP = 1,42 euro (€) (Dec. 2003)*

TOURIST INFORMATION

Tourist information offices exist in each city included in the Guide. The telephone number and address is given in each text under ℹ

FOREIGN EXCHANGE

Banks are usually open between 9.00am and 4.30pm on weekdays only and some open on Saturdays. Most large hotels have exchange facilities. Heathrow and Gatwick Airports have 24-hour banking facilities.

SHOPPING

In London: *Oxford St/Regent St (department stores, exclusive shops) Bond St (exclusive shops, antiques)*
Knightsbridge area (department stores, exclusive shops, boutiques)
For other towns see the index of street names; those printed in red are where the principal shops are found.

THEATRE BOOKINGS IN LONDON

Your hotel porter will be able to make your arrangements or direct you to Theatre Booking Agents.
In addition there is a kiosk in Leicester Square selling tickets for the same day's performances at half price plus a booking fee. It is open 12 noon-6.30pm.

CAR HIRE

The international car hire companies have branches in each major city. Your hotel porter should be able to give details and help you with your arrangements.

TIPPING

Many hotels and restaurants include a service charge but where this is not the case an amount equivalent to between 10 and 15 per cent of the bill is customary. Additionally doormen, baggage porters and cloakroom attendants are generally given a gratuity.
Taxi drivers are customarily tipped between 10 and 15 per cent of the amount shown on the meter in addition to the fare.

SPEED LIMITS

The maximum permitted speed on motorways and dual carriageways is 70 mph (113 km/h.) and 60 mph (97 km/h.) on other roads except where a lower speed limit is indicated.

SEAT BELTS

The wearing of seat belts in the United Kingdom is compulsory for drivers, front seat passengers and rear seat passengers where seat belts are fitted. It is illegal for front seat passengers to carry children on their lap.

CONGESTION CHARGING

The congestion charge is £5 per day on all vehicles (except motor cycles And exempt vehicles) entering the central zone between 7.00 and 6.30pm Monday to Friday except on bank holidays.
Payment can be made in advance, on the day, by post, on the Internet, by telephone 0845 900 1234, or at retail outlets.
A charge of up to £80 will be made for non-payment.
Further information is available on the Transport for London website-www.cclondon.com

LONDON

504 *folds* ㊷ *to* ㊹ *– pop. 6 679 699*

Britain Visitor Centre, I Regent Street, WI, *(020) 8846 9000.*

Heathrow, *08700 000123 –* **Terminal** *: Airbus (A1) from Victoria, Airbus (A2) from Paddington – Underground (Piccadilly line) frequent service daily.*

Gatwick, *08700 002468, by A 23 and M 23 –* **Terminal** *: Coach service from Victoria Coach Station (Flightline 777, hourly service) – Railink (Gatwick Express) from Victoria (24 h service).*

London City Airport, *(020) 7646 0000.*

Stansted, at Bishop's Stortford, *08700 000303, NE : 34 m. by M 11 and A 120.*

British Airways, Ticket sales and reservations *: 213 Piccadilly W1,* *0845 606 0747.*

SIGHTS

HISTORIC BUILDINGS AND MONUMENTS

Palace of Westminster★★★ : House of Lords★★, Westminster Hall★★ (hammerbeam roof★★★), Robing Room★, Central Lobby★, House of Commons★, Big Ben★, Victoria Tower★ 39 ALX – *Tower of London★★★ (Crown Jewels★★★, White Tower or Key★★★, St-John's Chapel★★, Beauchamp Tower★, Tower Hill Pageant★)* 34 ASU – *British Airways London Eye (views★★★)* 32 AMV – *Banqueting House★★* 31 ALV – *Buckingham Palace★★ (Changing of the Guard★★, Royal Mews★★* 38 AIX – *Kensington Palace★★* 27 ABV – *Lincoln's Inn★★* 32 AMT – *London Bridge★* 34 ARV – *Royal Hospital Chelsea★★* 37 AGZ – *St. James's Palace★★* 30 AJV – *Somerset House★★* 32 AMU – *South Bank Arts Centre★★ (Royal Festival Hall★ National Theatre★, Country Hall★)* 32 AMV *The Temple★★ (Middle Temple Hall★)* 32 ANU – *Tower Bridge★★* 34 ASV – *Albert Memorial★* 36 ADX – *Apsley House★* 30 AHV – *Burlington House★*

30 AIV – *Charterhouse★* 19 UZD – *George Inn★, Southwark* 33 AQV – *Gray's Inn★* 32 AMV – *Guildhall★ (Lord Mayor's show★★)* 33 AQT – *International Shakespeare Globe Centre★* 33 APV – *Dr Johnson's House★* 32 ANT – *Lancaster House★* 30 AIV – *Leighton House★* 35 AAX – *Linley Sambourne House★* 35 AAX – *Lloyds Building★★* 34 ARU – *Mansion House★ (plate and insignia★★)* 33 AQV – *The Monument★ (✻★)* 34 ARU – *Old Admiralty★* 31 AKV – *Royal Albert Hall★* 36 ADX – *Royal Exchange★* 34 ARU – *Royal Opera Arcade★ (New Zealand Jouse)* 31 AKV – *Royal Opera House★ (Covent Garden)* 31 ALU – *Spencer House★★* 30 AIV – *Staple Inn★* 32 ANT – *Theatre Royal★ (Haymarket)* 31 AKV – *Westminster Bridge★* 39 ALX.

CHURCHES

The City Churches – *St. Paul's Cathedral★★★ (Dome ⋞★★★)* 33 APU – *St. Bartholomew the Great★★ (choir★)* 33 APT – *St. Dunstan-in-the-East★★* 34 ARU – *St. Mary-at-Hill★★ (woodwork★★, plan★)* 34 ARU – *Temple Church★★* 32 ANU – *All Hallows-by-the-Tower (font cover★★, brasses★)* 34 ARU – *Christ Church★* 33 APT – *St. Andrew Undershaft (monuments★)* 34 ARU – *St. Bride★ (steeple★★)* 32 ANU – *St. Clement Eastcheap (panelled interior★★)* 34 ARU – *St. Edmund the King and Martyr (tower and spire★)* 34 ARU **B** – *St. Giles Cripplegate★* 33 AQT – *St. Helen Bishopsgate★ (monuments★★)* 34 ART – *St. James Garlickhythe (tower and spire★, sword rests★)* 33 AQU – *St. Magnus the Martyr (tower★, sword rest★)* 34 ARU – *St. Margaret Lothbury★ (tower and spire★, woodwork★, screen★, font★)* 33 AQT – *St. Margaret Pattens (spire★, woodwork★)* 34 ARU *St. Martin-within-Ludgate (tower and spire★, door cases★)* 33 APU – *St. Mary Abchurch★ (reredos★★, tower and spire★, dome★)* 33 AQU – *St. Mary-le-Bow (tower and steeple★★)* 33 AQU – *St. Michael Paternoster Royal (tower and spire★)* 33 AQU **D** – *St. Nicholas Cole Abbey (tower and spire★)* 33 APU – *St. Olave★* 34 ARU – *St. Peter upon Cornhill (screen★)* 34 ARU **L** – *St. Stephen Walbrook★ (tower and steeple★, dome★),* 33 AQU – *St. Vedast (tower and spire★, ceiling★),* 33 APT.

Other Churches – *Westminster Abbey★★★ (Henry VII Chapel★★★, Chapel of Edward the Confessor★★, Chapter House★★, Poets' Corner★)* 39 ALX – *Southwark Cathedral★★* 33 AQV – *Queen's Chapel★* 30 AJV – *St. Clement Danes★* 32 AMU – *St. James's★* 30 AJV – *St. Margaret's★* 39 ALX – *St. Martin in-the-Fields★* 31 ALV – *St. Paul's★ (Covent Garden)* 31 ALU – *Westminster Roman Catholic Cathedral★* 39 ALX.

PARKS

Regent's Park★★★ (Terraces★★), Zoo★★ – *Hyde Park* 29 AFV – *Kensington Gardens★★* 28 ACV *(Orangery★)* 27 ABV – *St. James's Park★★* 31 AKV.

STREETS AND SQUARES

The City★★★ 33 AQT – *Bedford Square★★* 31 AKT – *Belgrave Square★★* 37 AGX – *Burlington Arcade★★* 30 AIV – *Covent Garden★★ (The Piazza★★)* 31 ALU – *The Mall★★* 31 AKV – *Piccadilly★* 30 AIV – *The Thames★★* 32 ANU – *Trafalgar Square★★* 31 AKV – *Whitehall★★ (Horse Guards★)* 31 ALV – *Barbican★* 33 AQT – *Bond Street★* 30 AIU *Canonbury Square★* – *Carlton House Terrace★* 31 AKV – *Cheyne Walk★* – *Fitzroy Square★* – *Jermyn Street★* 30 AJV – *Leicester Square★* 31 AKU *Merrick Square★* – *Montpelier Square★* 37 AFX – *Neal's Yard★* 31 ALU – *Piccadilly Arcade★* 30 AIV – *Portman Square★* 29 AGT – *Queen Anne's Gate★* 39 AKX – *Regent Street★* 30 AIU – *Piccadilly Circus★* 31 AKU – *St. James's Square★* 31 AJV – *St. James's Street★* 30 AIV – *Shepherd Market★* 30 AHV – *Soho★* 31 AKU – *Trinity Church Square★* – *Victoria Embankment gardens★* 31 ALV – *Waterloo Place★* 31 AKV.

MUSEUMS

British Museum★★★ 31 AKL – *National Gallery★★★* 31 AKV – *Science Museum★★★* 36 ADX – *Tate Britain★★★* 39 ALY – *Victoria and Albert Museum★★★* 36 ADY – *Wallace Collection★★★* 29 AGT – *Courtauld Institute Galleries★★ (Somerset House)* 32 AMU – *Gilbert Collection★★ (Somerset House)* 32 AMU – *Museum of London★★* 33 APT – *National Portrait Gallery★★* 31 AKU – *Natural History Museum★★* 36 ADY – *Sir John Soane's Museum★★* 32 AMT – *Tate Modern★★ (views★★★ from top floors)* 33 APV – *Clock Museum★ (Guildhall)* 33 AQT – *Imperial War Museum★* 40 ANY – *London's Transport Museum★* 31 ALU – *Madame Tussaud's★* 17 QZD – *Museum of Mankind★* 33 DM – *National Army Museum★* 37 AGZ – *Percival David Foundation of Chinese Art★* 18 SZD – *Planetarium★* 15 HV **L** – *Wellington Museum★ (Apsley House)* 30 AHV.

LONDON CENTRE

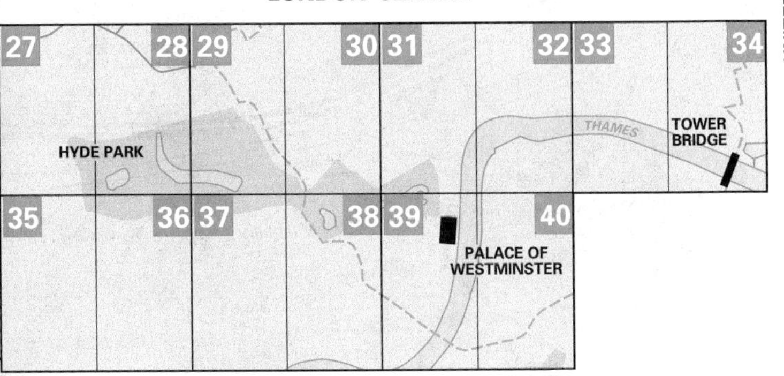

STREET INDEX TO LONDON CENTRE TOWN PLANS

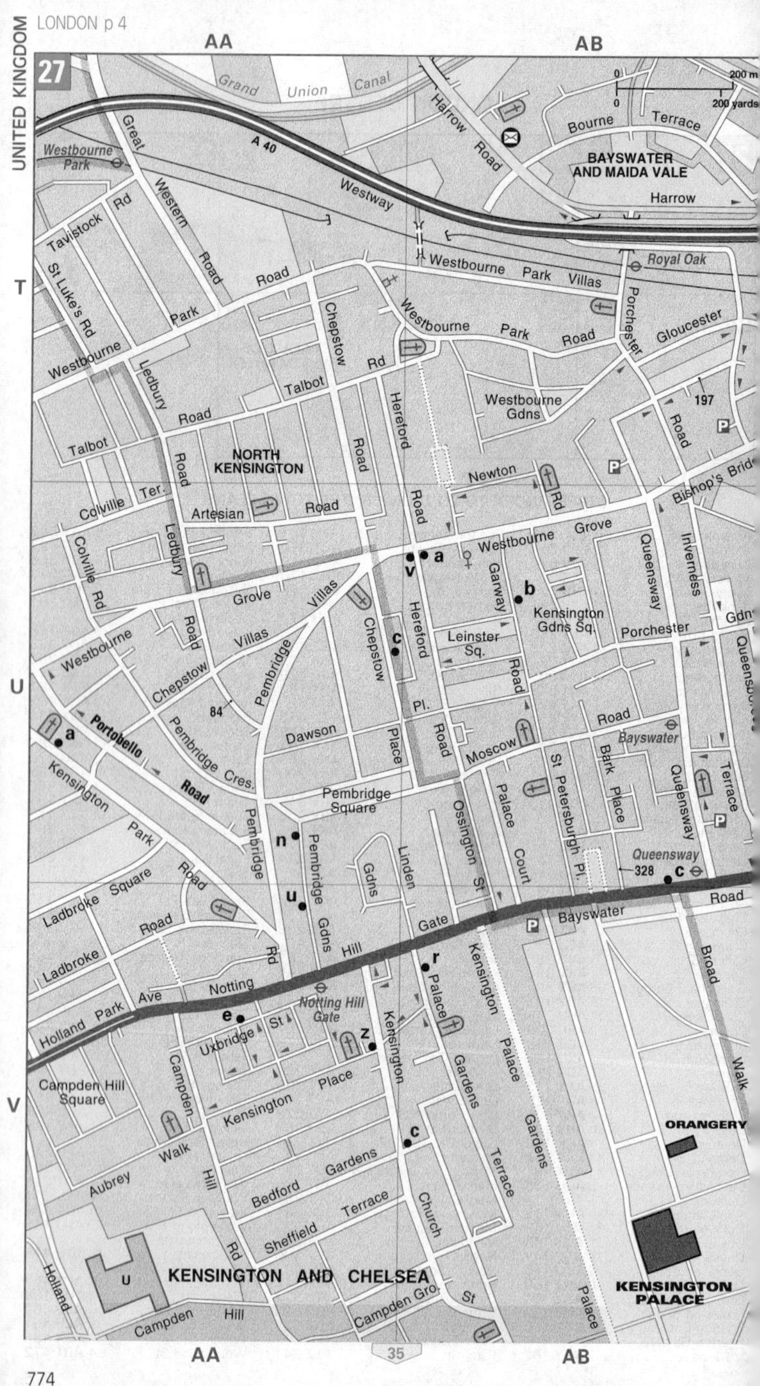
AA
AB
27
Grand Union Canal
A 40
Westway
Westbourne Park
Great Western Road
Harrow Road
BAYSWATER AND MAIDA VALE
Bourne Terrace
Harrow
Royal Oak
Westbourne Park Villas
Westbourne Park Road
Porchester Road
Gloucester
Tavistock Rd
St Luke's Rd
Westbourne Park Road
Ledbury Road
Chepstow Rd
Talbot Road
Hereford Road
Westbourne Gdns
197
NORTH KENSINGTON
Talbot
Colville Ter.
Artesian Road
Newton Rd
Bishop's Brid
Westbourne Grove
Queensway
Inverness
Colville Rd
Grove Villas
Garway Road
Kensington Gdns Sq.
Porchester Gdns
Leinster Sq.
Westbourne
Chepstow Villas
Pembridge
Chepstow Pl.
84
Dawson Place
Moscow Road
Bayswater
Portobello Road
Kensington Park Road
Pembridge Cres.
Pembridge Square
Ossington St
Palace Court
St Petersburgh Pl.
Bark Place
Terrace
Queensway
328
Pembridge Rd
Pembridge Gdns
Linden Gdns
Ladbroke Square
Ladbroke Road
Notting Hill Gate
Bayswater Road
Broad Walk
Holland Park Ave
Notting Hill Gate
Uxbridge St
Kensington Palace Gardens
Kensington Church
Palace Gardens Terrace
Campden Hill Square
Campden Hill Rd
Kensington Place
Aubrey Walk
Bedford Gardens
Sheffield Terrace
Church
ORANGERY
KENSINGTON PALACE
KENSINGTON AND CHELSEA
Holland
Campden Hill
Campden Gro.
St
Palace
T
U
V
a
v
a
b
c
c
n
u
r
e
z
c
a
U
0
200 m
0
200 yards
35

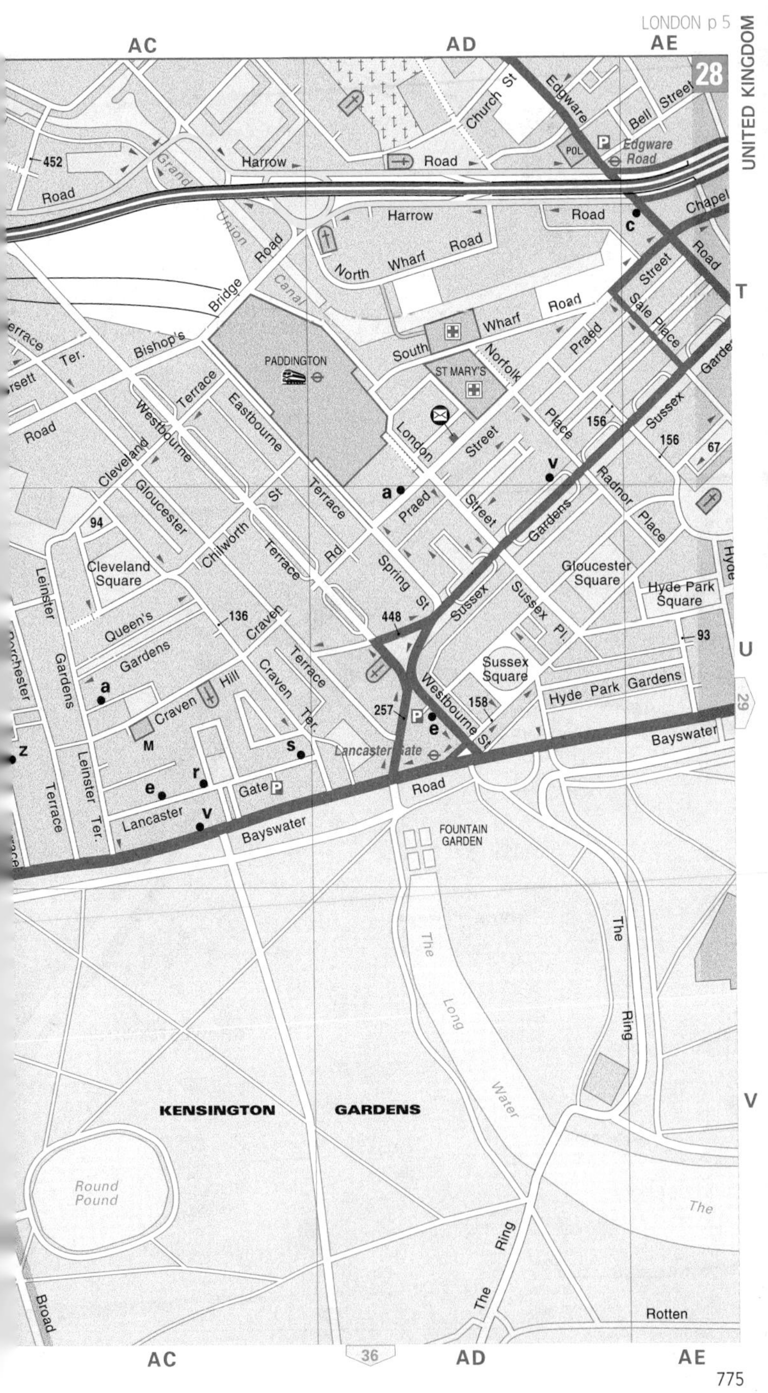
AC
AD
AE
28
Edgware
Bell Street
Church St
Harrow
Road
Edgware Road
POL
452
Road
Grand
Union
Canal
Harrow
Road
Chapel
Road
North Wharf Road
Street
Road
T
Bridge
Road
Bishop's
Wharf
Road
Praed
Sale Place
South
Norfolk
PADDINGTON
ST MARY'S
Terrace
Ter.
Road
Westbourne
Terrace
Eastbourne
London
Street
Place
156
Sussex
156
67
Gardens
Cleveland
Gloucester
Terrace
Praed
Street
Radnor
Place
94
St
Chilworth
Terrace
Rd
Spring St
Gardens
Gloucester Square
Hyde Park Square
Hyde
Cleveland Square
Leinster
Gardens
Queen's
Gardens
136
Craven
448
Sussex
Sussex Pl.
93
U
Dorchester
Craven
Terrace
Hill
Craven Ter.
Westbourne St
Sussex Square
Hyde Park Gardens
158
29
257
Lancaster Gate
Bayswater
Leinster Ter.
Terrace
Gate
Road
Lancaster
Bayswater
FOUNTAIN GARDEN
The Long Water
The Ring
V
KENSINGTON
GARDENS
Round Pound
The
The Ring
Rotten
Broad
36
AC
AD
AE

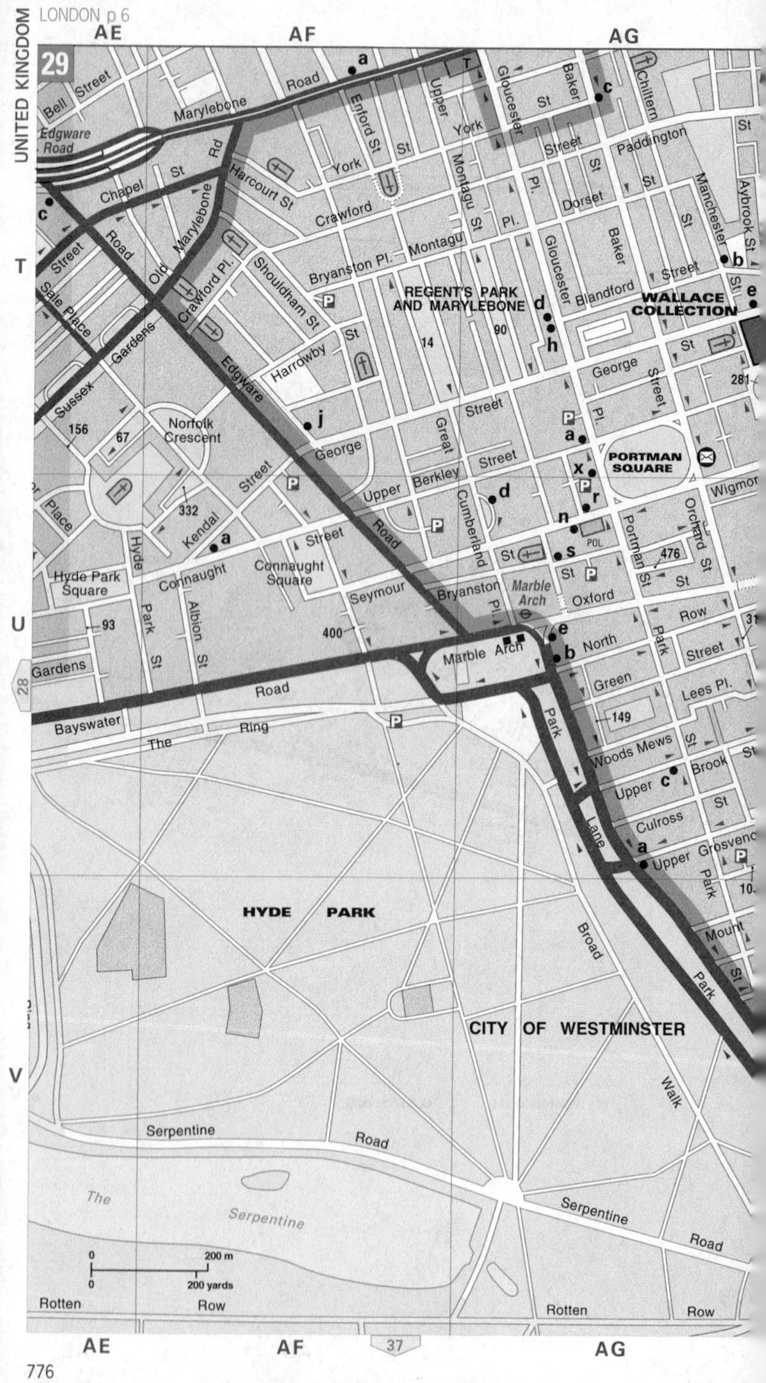
AE
AF
AG
29
Bell Street
Marylebone Road
Edgware Road
Chapel St
Harcourt St
Crawford
York St
Enford St
Upper York
Gloucester
Baker St
Chiltern
Paddington St
Montagu Sq
Dorset St
Manchester St
Aybrook St
Bryanston Pl.
Montagu Pl.
Shouldham St
REGENT'S PARK AND MARYLEBONE
Blandford Street
WALLACE COLLECTION
George St
Harrowby St
Old Marylebone Rd
Crawford Pl.
Sale Place
Sussex Gardens
Edgware Road
Great Cumberland Pl.
Norfolk Crescent
George Street
Upper Berkley Street
PORTMAN SQUARE
Wigmore
Portman St
Orchard St
Kendal St
Connaught Street
Connaught Square
Hyde Park Square
Hyde Park St
Albion St
Seymour St
Bryanston St
Marble Arch
Oxford St
North Row
Park Street
Green St
Lees Pl.
Woods Mews
Upper Brook St
Culross St
Upper Grosvenor St
Mount St
Gardens
Bayswater Road
The Ring
Park Lane
HYDE PARK
Broad Walk
Park
CITY OF WESTMINSTER
Serpentine Road
The Serpentine
Rotten Row
0 200 m
0 200 yards
T
U
V
28
37
POL.

AH
AI
AJ
30
MAYFAIR
Grosvenor Square
Berkeley Square
Cavendish Sq.
Hanover Sq.
Golden Sq.
Oxford Circus
BURLINGTON HOUSE
BURLINGTON ARCADE
PICCADILLY ARCADE
ST JAMES SQUARE
SHEPHERD MARKET
SPENCER HOUSE
QUEEN'S CHAPEL
ST JAMES PALACE
LANCASTER HOUSE
GREEN PARK
Green Park
Bond St
MIDDLESEX
BRITISH TELECOM TOWER
PICCADILLY
REGENT ST
NEW BOND ST
OLD BOND ST
JERMYN ST
ST JAMES'S ST
T
U
V
31
38
AH
AI
AJ

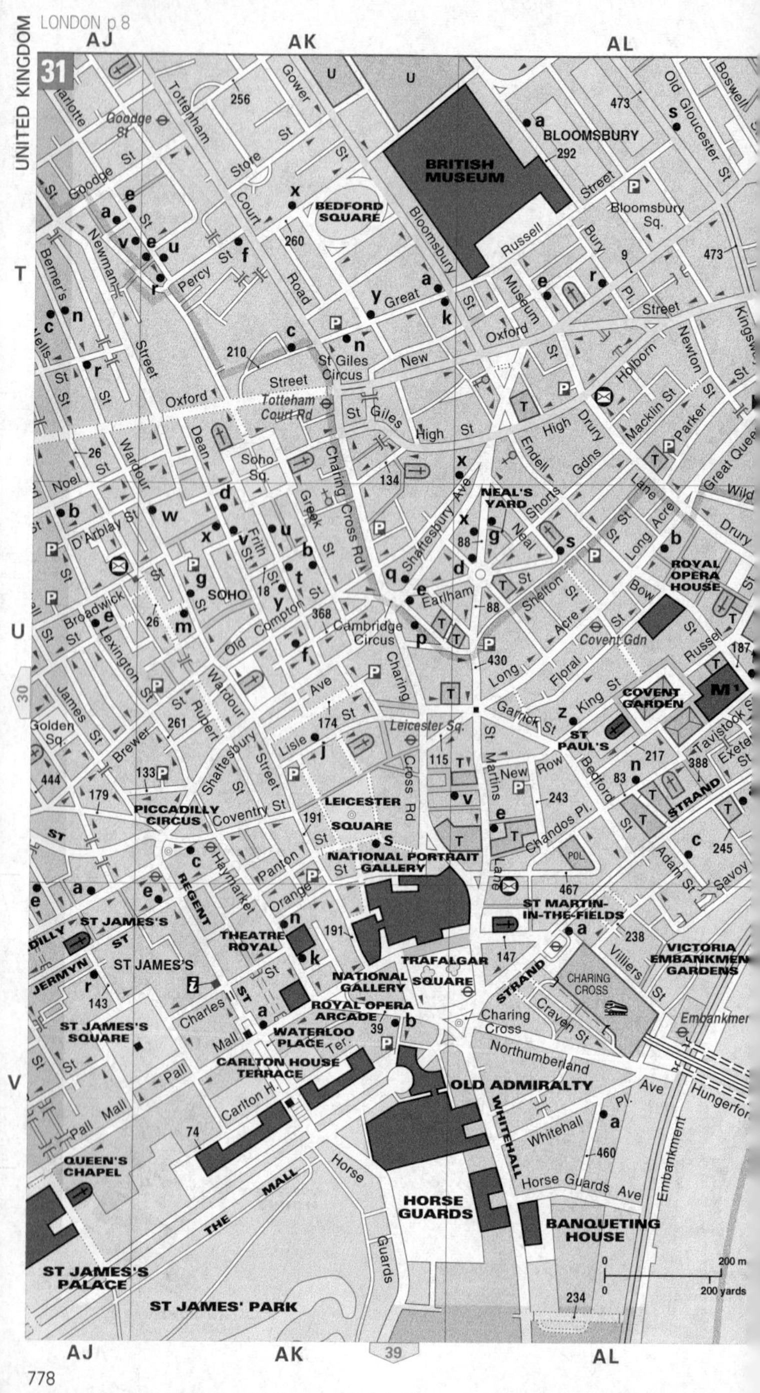

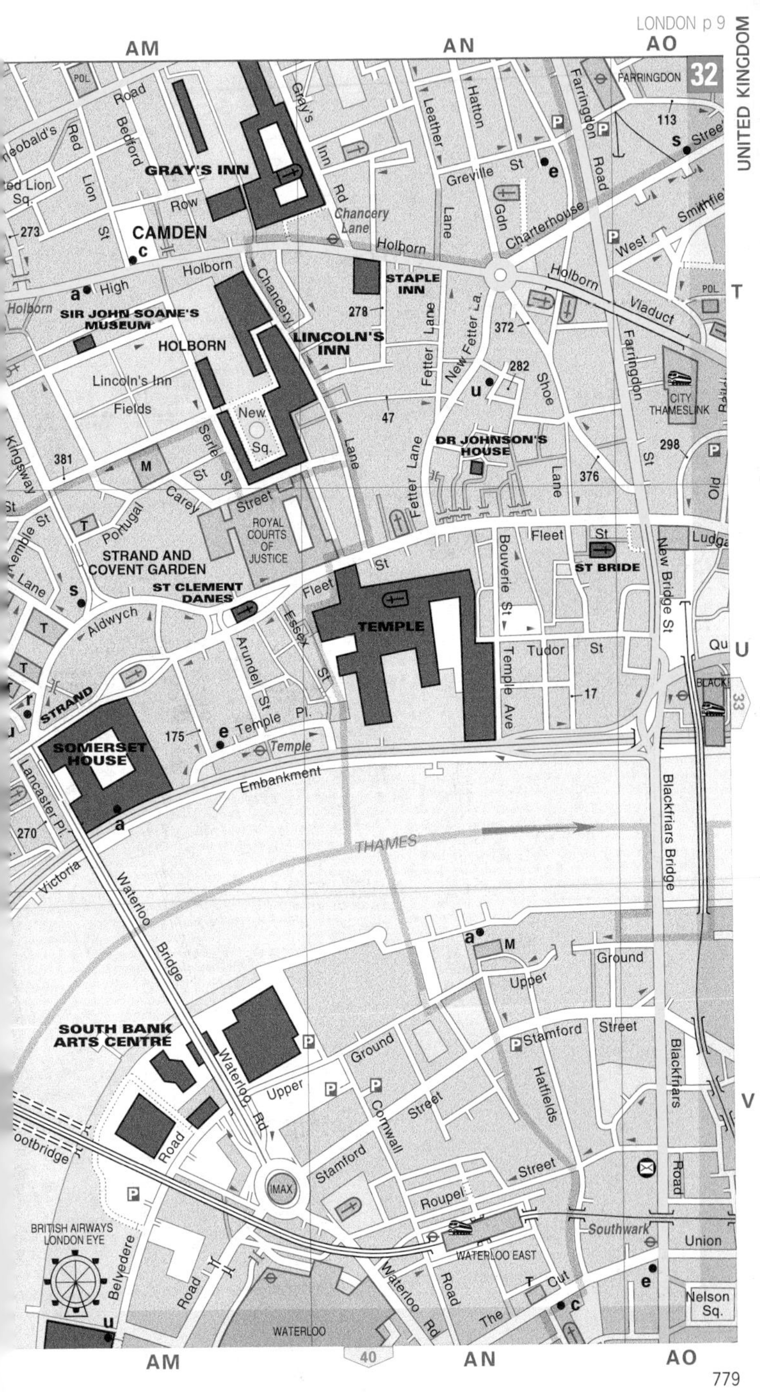
AM
AN
AO
32
FARRINGDON
GRAY'S INN
CAMDEN
STAPLE INN
SIR JOHN SOANE'S MUSEUM
HOLBORN
LINCOLN'S INN
Lincoln's Inn Fields
DR JOHNSON'S HOUSE
CITY THAMESLINK
ROYAL COURTS OF JUSTICE
STRAND AND COVENT GARDEN
ST CLEMENT DANES
ST BRIDE
TEMPLE
STRAND
SOMERSET HOUSE
Embankment
THAMES
Waterloo Bridge
Blackfriars Bridge
SOUTH BANK ARTS CENTRE
IMAX
BRITISH AIRWAYS LONDON EYE
WATERLOO EAST
WATERLOO
Southwark
Holborn Viaduct
Fleet St
Chancery Lane
Fetter Lane
Farringdon Road
Farringdon St
New Bridge St
Stamford Street
Upper Ground
Waterloo Rd
Blackfriars Road
The Cut
Union
Nelson Sq.
T
U
V
33
40

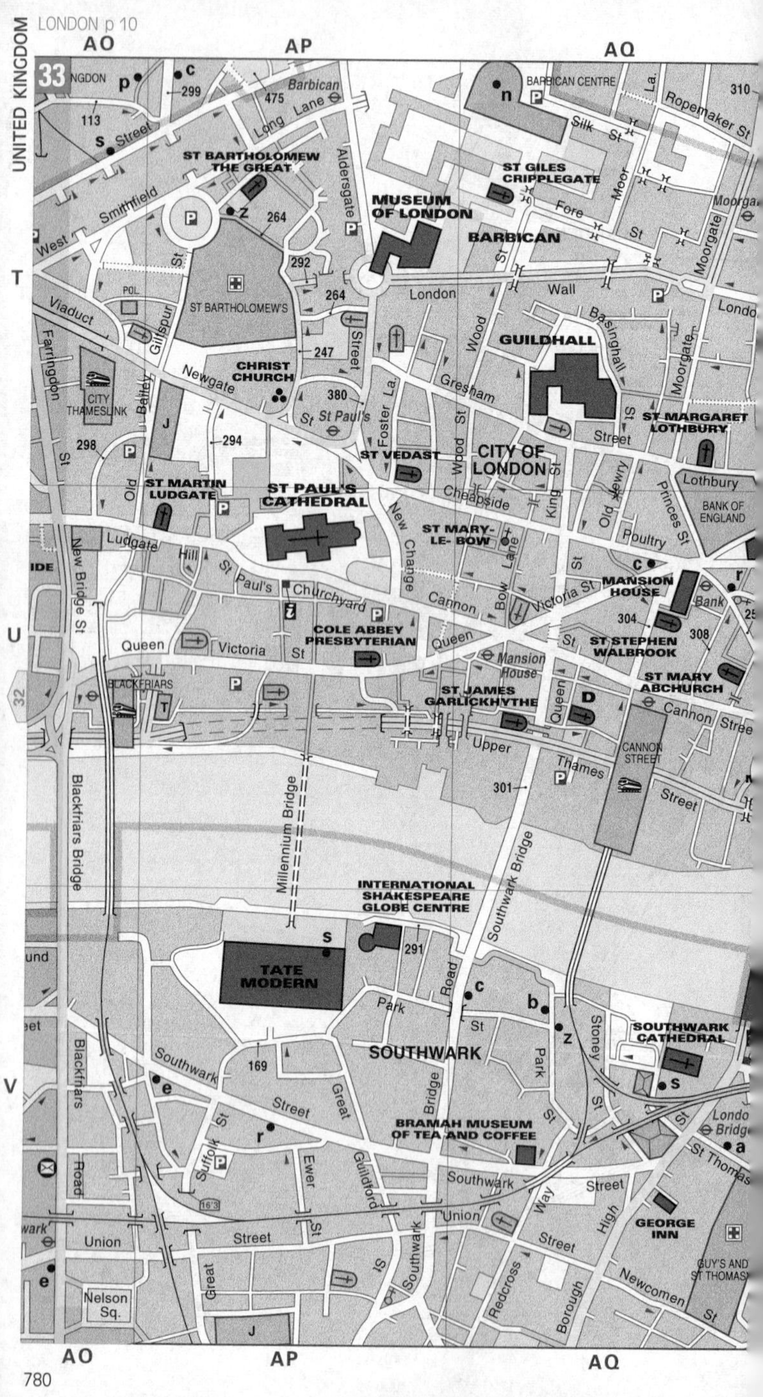
AO
AP
AQ
33
ST BARTHOLOMEW THE GREAT
MUSEUM OF LONDON
BARBICAN CENTRE
ST GILES CRIPPLEGATE
BARBICAN
ST BARTHOLOMEW'S
GUILDHALL
CHRIST CHURCH
CITY THAMESLINK
ST MARGARET LOTHBURY
ST VEDAST
CITY OF LONDON
ST MARTIN LUDGATE
ST PAUL'S CATHEDRAL
BANK OF ENGLAND
ST MARY-LE-BOW
MANSION HOUSE
COLE ABBEY PRESBYTERIAN
ST STEPHEN WALBROOK
ST MARY ABCHURCH
BLACKFRIARS
ST JAMES GARLICKHYTHE
CANNON STREET
Millennium Bridge
Blackfriars Bridge
Southwark Bridge
INTERNATIONAL SHAKESPEARE GLOBE CENTRE
TATE MODERN
SOUTHWARK
SOUTHWARK CATHEDRAL
BRAMAH MUSEUM OF TEA AND COFFEE
GEORGE INN
GUY'S AND ST THOMAS'
T
U
V

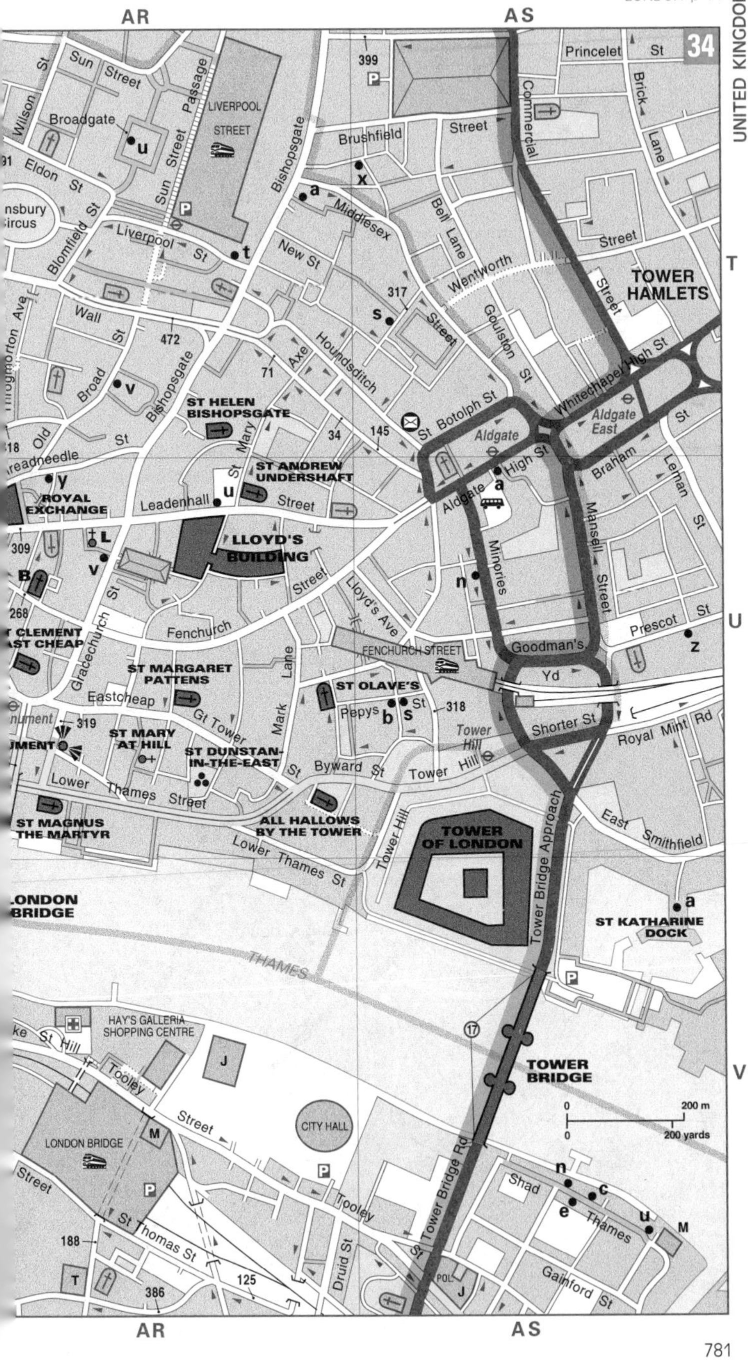
AR
AS
34
T
U
V
Sun Street
Wilson St
Broadgate
Eldon St
Finsbury Circus
Blomfield St
Liverpool St
Sun Street Passage
LIVERPOOL STREET
Bishopsgate
Brushfield Street
Commercial Street
Princelet St
Brick Lane
Middlesex Street
New St
Bell Lane
Wentworth Street
TOWER HAMLETS
Goulston St
Throgmorton Ave
Wall St
Broad St
Old Broad St
Threadneedle St
ROYAL EXCHANGE
ST HELEN BISHOPSGATE
St Mary Axe
Houndsditch
ST ANDREW UNDERSHAFT
Leadenhall Street
LLOYD'S BUILDING
St Botolph St
Aldgate
Aldgate High St
Whitechapel High St
Aldgate East
Braham St
Leman St
Mansell Street
Minories
Prescot St
Lloyd's Ave
FENCHURCH STREET
Fenchurch Street
Gracechurch St
ST CLEMENT EASTCHEAP
ST MARGARET PATTENS
Eastcheap
Lime St
Mark Lane
ST OLAVE'S
Pepys St
Goodman's Yd
Shorter St
Royal Mint Rd
Gt Tower St
ST MARY AT HILL
ST DUNSTAN-IN-THE-EAST
Byward St
Tower Hill
Lower Thames Street
ST MAGNUS THE MARTYR
ALL HALLOWS BY THE TOWER
Lower Thames St
TOWER OF LONDON
Tower Bridge Approach
East Smithfield
LONDON BRIDGE
ST KATHARINE DOCK
THAMES
HAY'S GALLERIA SHOPPING CENTRE
Duke St Hill
Tooley Street
CITY HALL
TOWER BRIDGE
0 200 m
0 200 yards
LONDON BRIDGE
Street
St Thomas St
Tooley St
Druid St
Tower Bridge Rd
POL
Shad Thames
Gainford St
399
317
472
71
34
145
309
268
319
318
188
386
125
17

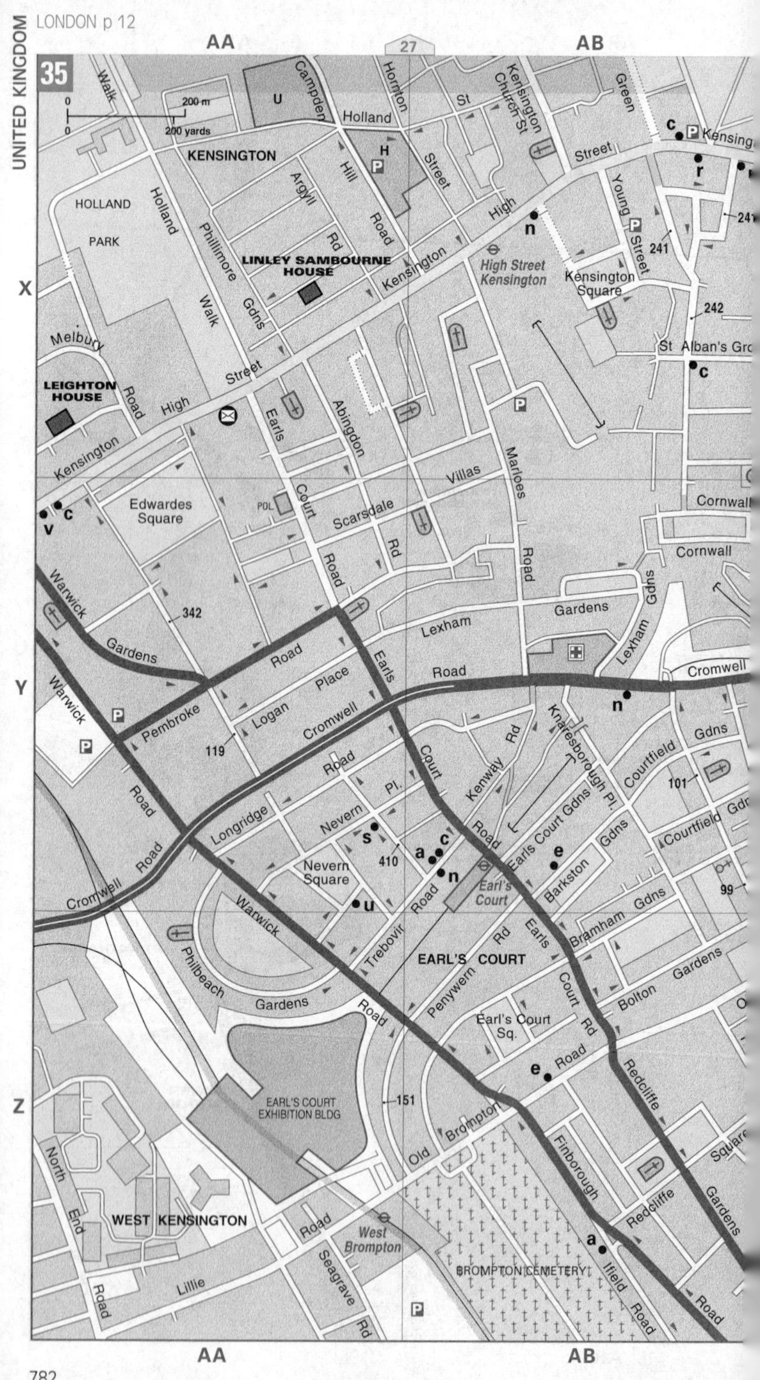
AA
27
AB
35
0
200 m
0
200 yards
X
Y
Z
KENSINGTON
HOLLAND PARK
LINLEY SAMBOURNE HOUSE
LEIGHTON HOUSE
High Street Kensington
Kensington Square
Edwardes Square
EARL'S COURT
Earl's Court
Nevern Square
WEST KENSINGTON
West Brompton
EARL'S COURT EXHIBITION BLDG
BROMPTON CEMETERY
Holland Walk
Campden Hill Road
Hornton Street
Holland St
Kensington Church St
Kensington High Street
Argyll Rd
Phillimore Gdns
Phillimore Walk
Melbury Road
Earls Court Road
Abingdon Road
Marloes Road
Scarsdale Villas
Young Street
Kensington Green
St Alban's Gro
Cornwall Gdns
Warwick Gardens
Warwick Road
Pembroke Road
Logan Place
Lexham Gardens
Lexham Gdns
Cromwell Road
Longridge Road
Nevern Pl.
Kenway Rd
Knaresborough Pl.
Courtfield Gdns
Earls Court Gdns
Barkston Gdns
Bramham Gdns
Bolton Gardens
Trebovir Road
Penywern Rd
Philbeach Gardens
Earl's Court Sq.
Old Brompton Road
Redcliffe Gardens
Redcliffe Square
Finborough Road
Ifield Road
North End Road
Lillie Road
Seagrave Rd
POL
U
H
c
r
n
v
s
a
e
u
241
242
342
119
410
101
99
151

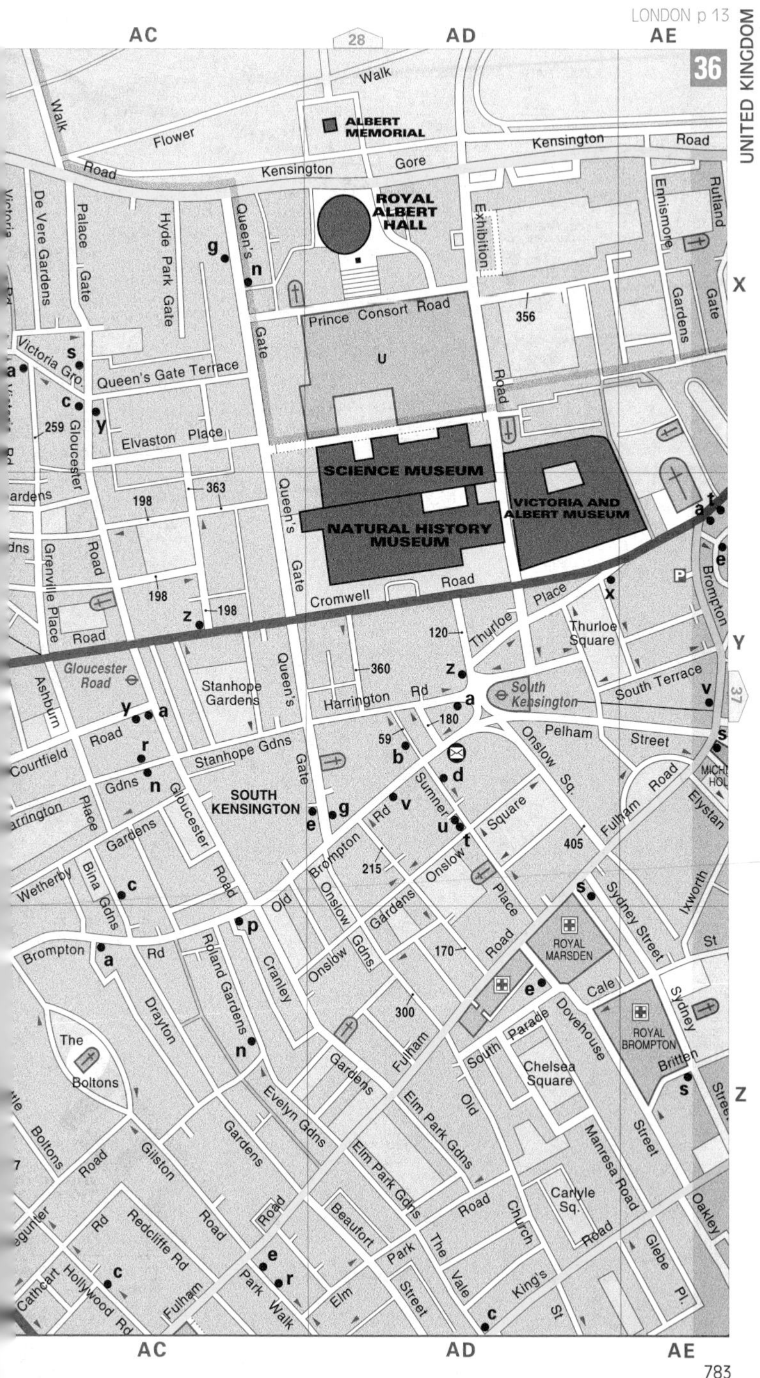
AC
AD
AE
28
36
UNITED KINGDOM
ALBERT MEMORIAL
ROYAL ALBERT HALL
SCIENCE MUSEUM
NATURAL HISTORY MUSEUM
VICTORIA AND ALBERT MUSEUM
ROYAL MARSDEN
ROYAL BROMPTON
SOUTH KENSINGTON
Kensington Gore
Kensington Road
Flower Walk
Prince Consort Road
Exhibition Road
Queen's Gate
Queen's Gate Terrace
Elvaston Place
Cromwell Road
Thurloe Place
Thurloe Square
South Terrace
Harrington Rd
Stanhope Gardens
Stanhope Gdns
Gloucester Road
Onslow Sq.
Onslow Square
Onslow Gardens
Onslow Gdns.
Pelham Street
Fulham Road
Sumner Place
Sydney Street
Old Brompton Rd
Cranley Gardens
Roland Gardens
Drayton Gardens
Evelyn Gdns
Elm Park Gdns
Elm Park Road
Old Church Street
Carlyle Sq.
Chelsea Square
Dovehouse Street
Manresa Road
The Boltons
Redcliffe Rd
Hollywood Rd
Park Walk
King's Rd
X
Y
Z
37
AC
AD
AE

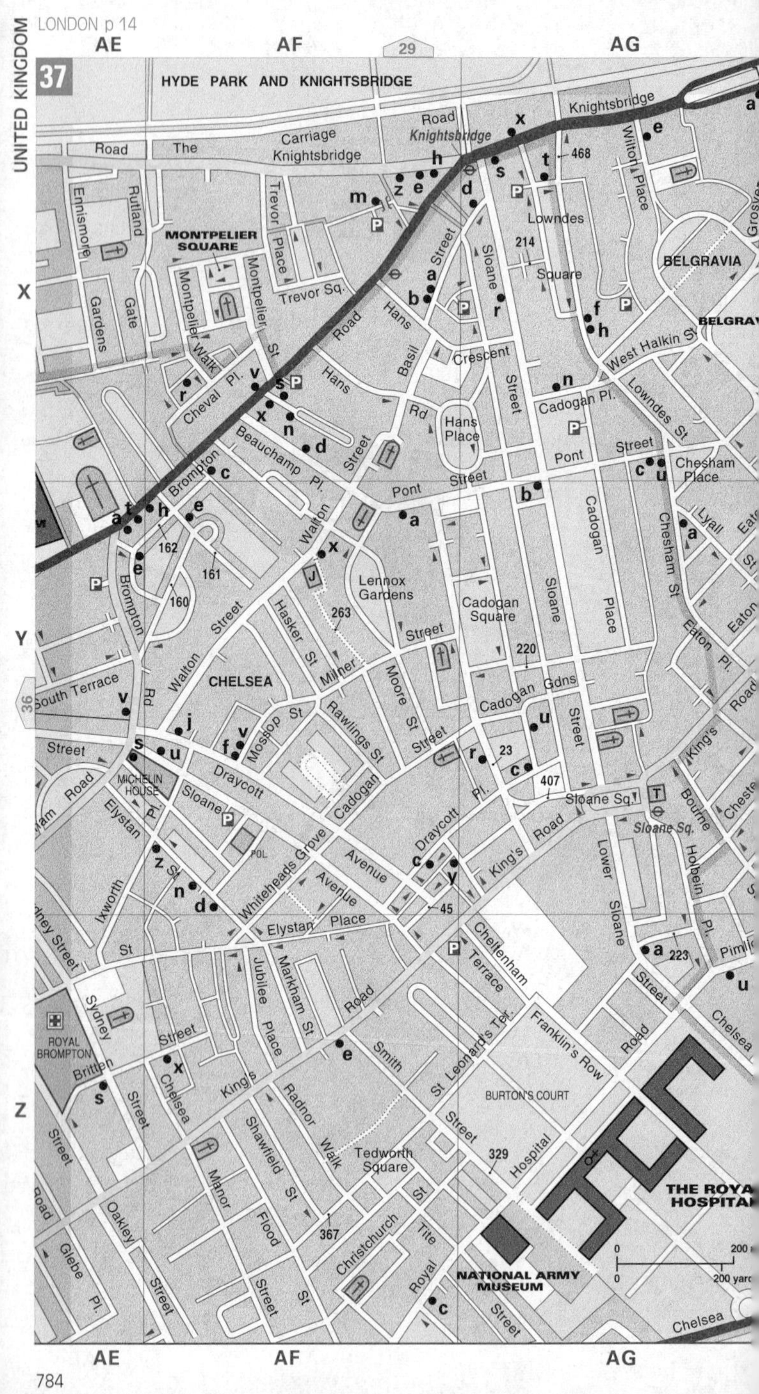
37
HYDE PARK AND KNIGHTSBRIDGE
MONTPELIER SQUARE
BELGRAVIA
CHELSEA
MICHELIN HOUSE
BURTON'S COURT
ROYAL BROMPTON
THE ROYAL HOSPITAL
NATIONAL ARMY MUSEUM
Knightsbridge
Sloane Sq.
Tedworth Square
Lennox Gardens
Cadogan Square
Hans Place

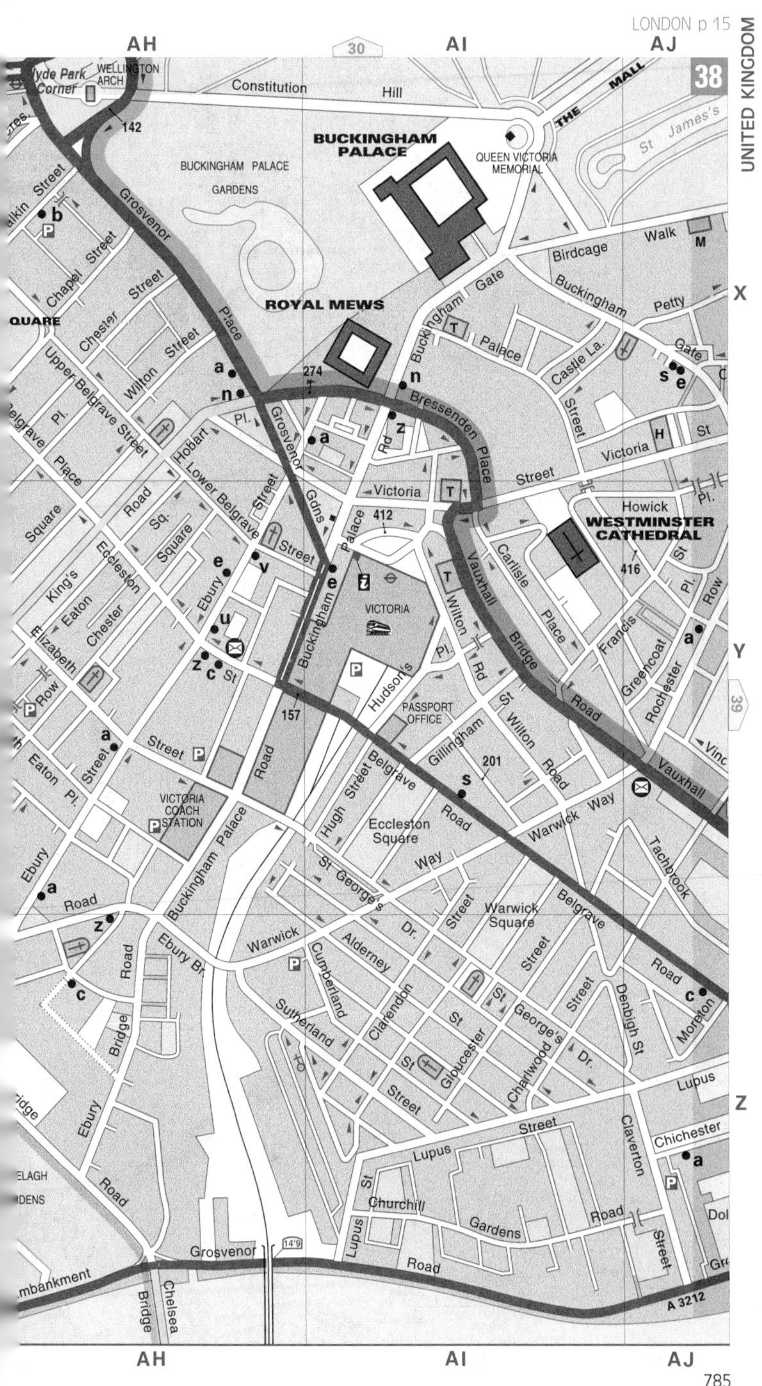

AH
AI
AJ
30
38
Hyde Park Corner
WELLINGTON ARCH
Constitution Hill
THE MALL
BUCKINGHAM PALACE
QUEEN VICTORIA MEMORIAL
BUCKINGHAM PALACE GARDENS
ROYAL MEWS
WESTMINSTER CATHEDRAL
VICTORIA
PASSPORT OFFICE
VICTORIA COACH STATION
Eccleston Square
Warwick Square
X
Y
Z
39

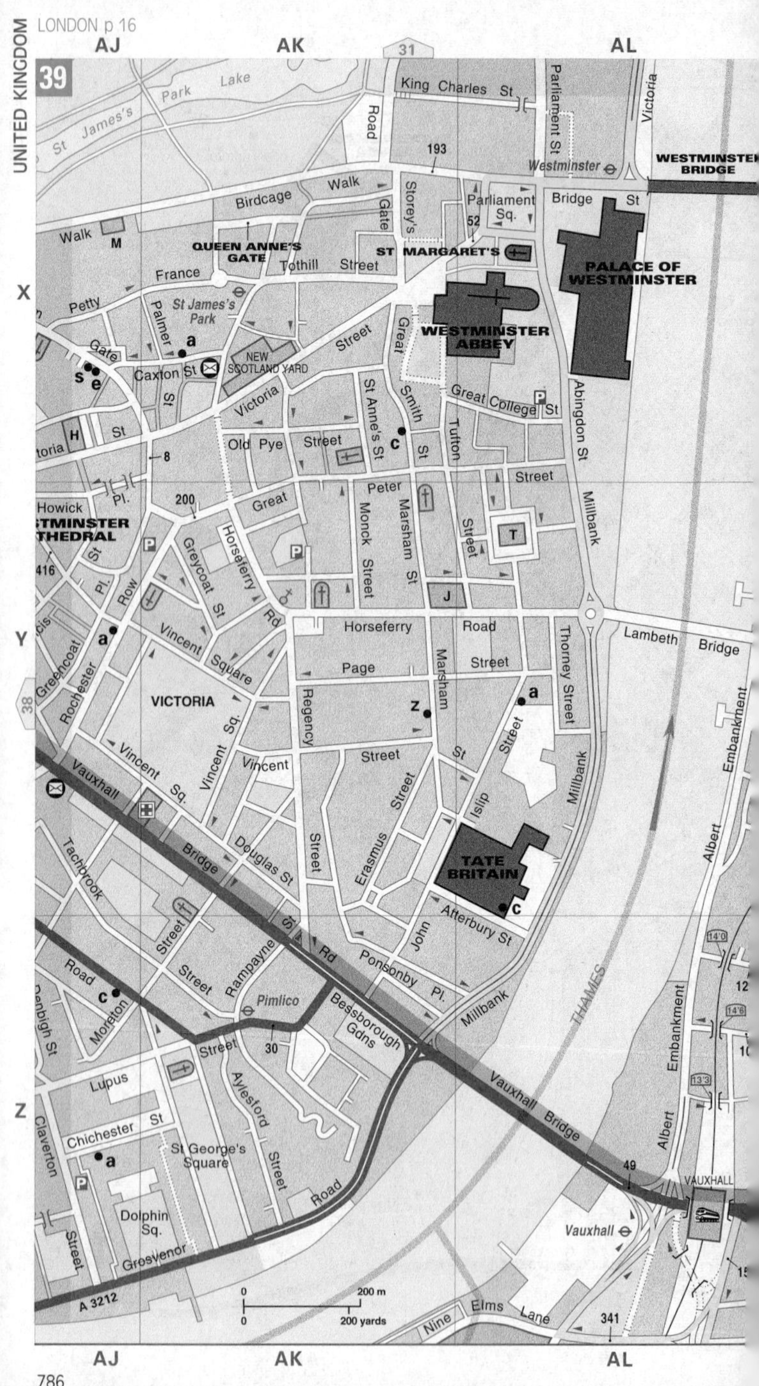
AJ
AK
AL
39
31
38
X
Y
Z
St James's Park Lake
King Charles St
Parliament St
Victoria
Westminster
WESTMINSTER BRIDGE
Road
193
Birdcage Walk
Gate
Storey's
Parliament Sq.
Bridge St
52
Walk
M
QUEEN ANNE'S GATE
ST MARGARET'S
PALACE OF WESTMINSTER
Tothill Street
France
Petty
St James's Park
Palmer
Great
WESTMINSTER ABBEY
Gate
Caxton St
NEW SCOTLAND YARD
Victoria Street
St Anne's St
Smith St
Great College St
Abingdon St
Tufton
H
St
Old Pye Street
Peter Street
8
Howick
Pl.
200
Great
Monck Street
Marsham St
Street
T
Millbank
Horseferry
Greycoat St
Row
Horseferry Rd
J
Vincent Square
Horseferry Road
Lambeth Bridge
Thorney Street
Page Street
Greencoat
Rochester
VICTORIA
Regency
Marsham St
Street
Vincent Sq.
Vincent
Street
Vincent Sq.
Vauxhall
Erasmus
Street
Islip
Millbank
Embankment
Bridge
Douglas St
Street
TATE BRITAIN
Albert
Tachbrook
Atterbury St
John
Street
Rampayne
Rd
Ponsonby Pl.
Road
Street
Pimlico
Bessborough Gdns
Millbank
THAMES
Moreton
Denbigh St
Street
30
Vauxhall Bridge
Embankment
Lupus
Aylesford
Albert
Chichester St
Claverton
St George's Square
Street
49
VAUXHALL
Road
Dolphin Sq.
Vauxhall
Grosvenor
Street
A 3212
0 200 m
0 200 yards
Nine Elms Lane
341

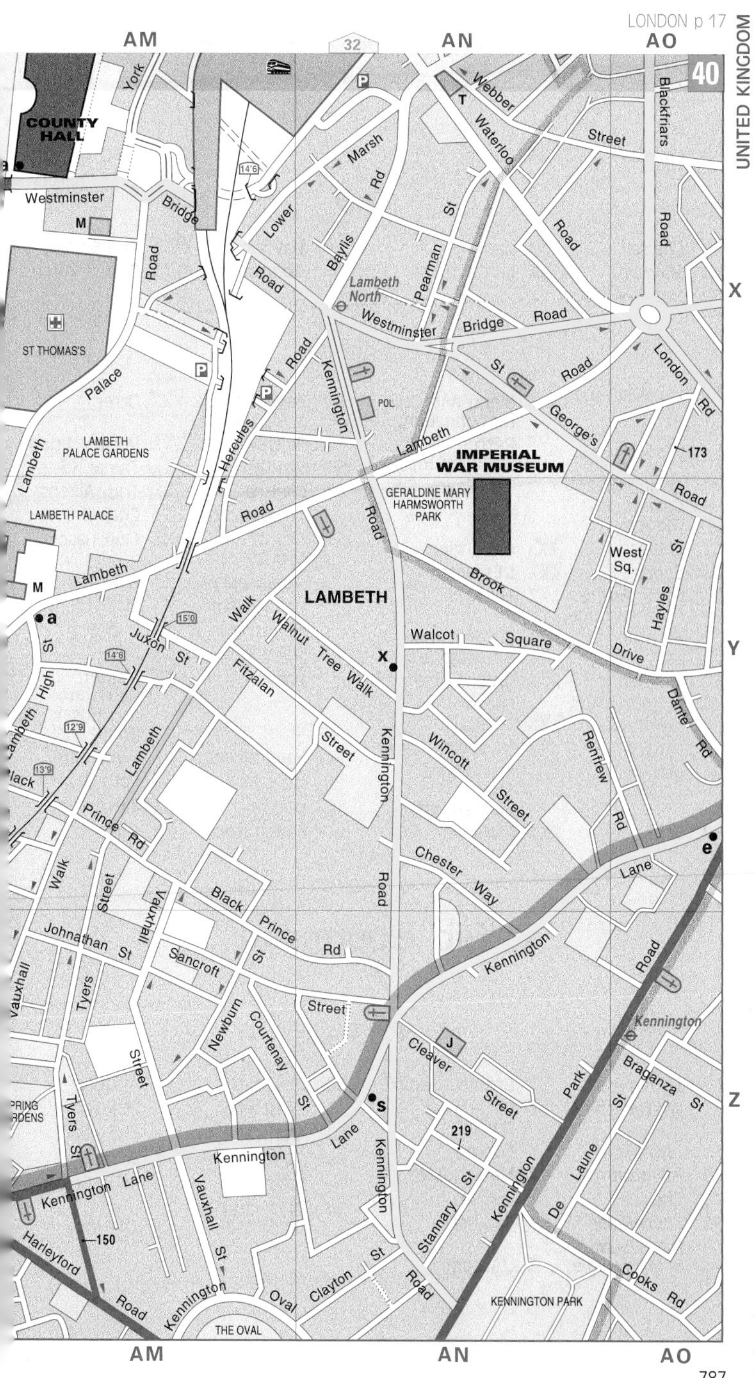
AM
32
AN
AO
COUNTY HALL
Westminster
Bridge
York
Road
Lower
Marsh
Rd
Baylis
Lambeth North
Westminster
Bridge
Road
Webber
Waterloo
Street
Blackfriars
Road
St
Pearman
ST THOMAS'S
Palace
LAMBETH PALACE GARDENS
Lambeth
LAMBETH PALACE
Hercules
Kennington
POL
Lambeth
IMPERIAL WAR MUSEUM
GERALDINE MARY HARMSWORTH PARK
St George's
Road
London
Rd
173
West Sq.
Hayles
Brook
Drive
LAMBETH
Walk
Walnut Tree Walk
Walcot
Square
Juxon
St
High
Fitzalan
Street
Wincott
Street
Renfrew
Rd
Dante
Lambeth
Black
Prince
Chester
Way
Lane
Johnathan St
Vauxhall
Sancroft
Tyers
Newburn
Courtenay
Cleaver
Street
Braganza
St
Park
Kennington
Harleyford
150
Oval
Clayton
Stannary
219
De Laune
Cooks Rd
KENNINGTON PARK
THE OVAL
X
Y
Z
AM
AN
AO

Starred establishments in London

✿✿✿

37	*Chelsea*	XXXX	Gordon Ramsay

✿✿

36	*Chelsea*	🏨	Capital
58	*Mayfair*	XXXX	Le Gavroche
59	*Mayfair*	XXXX	The Square
26	*Bloomsbury*	XXX	Pied à Terre

✿

59	*Mayfair*	XXXX	Menu and Grill (at Connaught H.)
55	*Belgravia*	XXXX	Pétrus (at The Berkeley H.)
70	*Strand and Covent Garden*	XXXX	The Savoy Grill
37	*Chelsea*	XXX	Aubergine
68	*Soho*	XXX	L'Escargot
56	*Hyde Park & Knightsbridge*	XXX	Foliage
59	*Mayfair*	XXX	Gordon Ramsay At Claridge's
59	*Mayfair*	XXX	Greenhouse
64	*Regent's Park & Marylebone*	XXX	Locanda Locatelli
59	*Mayfair*	XXX	Mirabelle
31	*City of London*	XXX	1 Lombard Street (Restaurant)
67	*St. James's*	XXX	L'Oranger
64	*Regent's Park & Marylebone*	XXX	Orrery
51	*Putney*	XXX	Putney Bridge
60	*Mayfair*	XXX	Tamarind
37	*Chelsea*	XXX	Tom Aikens
52	*Wandsworth*	XX	Chez Bruce
31	*City of London*	XX	Club Gascon
26	*Bloomsbury*	XX	Hakkasan
	Twickenham	XX	McClements
55	*Belgravia*	XX	Nahm
61	*Mayfair*	XX	Nobu
68	*Soho*	XX	Richard Corrigan at Lindsay House
32	*Hammersmith*	XX	River Café
73	*Victoria*	XX	Roussillon
55	*Belgravia*	XX	Zafferano
42	*Kensington*	XX	Zaika

"Bib Gourmand"

Good food at moderate prices

 Meals

67	*St James's*	XX	Brasserie Roux
51	*Whitechapel*	XX	Café Spice Namaste
33	*Olympia*	XX	Cotto
35	*Islington*	XX	Metrogusto
38	*Chelsea*	XX	Racine
52	*Southfields*	XX	Sarkhel's
54	*Bayswater & Maida Vale*	X	L'Accento
68	*St James's*	X	Al Duca
43	*Kensington*	X	Malabar
33	*Archway*	X	The Parsee
29	*Camden*	X	Samphire
69	*Soho*	X	Soho Spice
54	*Bayswater & Maida Vale*	X	The Vale

Restaurants classified according to type

Bangladeshi

Page	Area	Class	Restaurant
54	*Bayswater & Maida Vale*	X	Ginger

Chinese

Page	Area	Class	Restaurant
59	*Mayfair*	XXXXX	The Oriental
60	*Mayfair*	XXX	Kai
40	*Chelsea*	XX	Good Earth
26	*Bloomsbury*	XX	✿ Hakkasan
31	*City of London*	XX	Imperial City
39	*Chelsea*	XX	Mao Tai
32	*Fulham*	XX	Mao Tai
42	*Kensington*	XX	Memories of China
56	*Hyde Park & Knightsbridge*	XX	Mr Chow
28	*Hampstead*	XX	ZeNW3
69	*Soho*	X	Fung Shing

Danish

Page	Area	Class	Restaurant
45	*South Kensington*	XX	Lundum's

English

Page	Area	Class	Restaurant
59	*Mayfair*	XXXX	Grill Room (at Dorchester H.)
60	*Mayfair*	XXX	Brian Turner Mayfair
60	*Mayfair*	XXX	Scotts
73	*Victoria*	XXX	Shepherd's
70	*Strand & Covent Garden*	XX	Rules

French

Page	Area	Class	Restaurant
58	*Mayfair*	XXXX	✿✿ (Le) Gavroche
31	*City of London*	XXX	Coq d'Argent
5	*Islington*	XX	Almeida
6	*Regent's Park & Marylebone*	XX	(L')Aventure
7	*St James's*	XX	☺ Brasserie Roux
9	*Chelsea*	XX	Chez Max
3	*Shepherd's Bush*	XX	Chez Moi
1	*City of London*	XX	✿ Club Gascon
39	*Chelsea*	XX	(Le) Colombier
26	*Bloomsbury*	XX	Mon Plaisir
38	*Chelsea*	XX	Poissonnerie de l'Avenue (Seafood)
38	*Chelsea*	XX	☺ Racine
73	*Victoria*	XX	✿ Roussillon
46	*Kennington*	X	Lobster Pot (Seafood)
74	*Victoria*	X	(La) Poule au Pot
40	*Chelsea*	X	Thierry's
69	*Soho*	X	(La) Trouvaille

Indian & Pakistani

Page	Area	Class	Restaurant
0	*Mayfair*	XXX	Benares
5	*South Kensington*	XXX	Bombay Brasserie
8	*Chelsea*	XXX	Chutney Mary
3	*Victoria*	XXX	(The) Cinnamon Club
8	*Soho*	XXX	Red Fort
0	*Mayfair*	XXX	✿ Tamarind
3	*Victoria*	XXX	Quilon
8	*Bermondsey*	XX	Bengal Clipper
50	*Spitalfields*	XX	Bengal Trader
68	*Soho*	XX	Café Lazeez
51	*Whitechapel*	XX	☺ Café Spice Namaste
61	*Mayfair*	XX	Chor Bizarre
40	*Chelsea*	XX	Haandi
31	*City of London*	XX	Kasturi
45	*South Kensington*	XX	Khan's of Kensington
27	*Bloomsbury*	XX	Malabar Junction

Indian & Pakistani

Page	Area	Rating	Restaurant
46	*South Kensington*	XX	Memories of India
67	*St James's*	XX	Mint Leaf
39	*Chelsea*	XX	(The) Painted Heron
65	*Regent's Park & Marylebone*	XX	(La) Porte des Indes
65	*Regent's Park & Marylebone*	XX	Rasa Samudra (Vegetarian) (Seafood)
52	*Southfields*	XX	☺ Sarkhel's
41	*Earl's Court*	XX	Sticklebackpink
46	*Herne Hill*	XX	3 Monkeys
39	*Chelsea*	XX	Vama
62	*Mayfair*	XX	Yatra
42	*Kensington*	XX	✿ Zaika
52	*Wandsworth*	X	Bombay Bicycle Club
46	*South Kensington*	X	Café Lazeez
34	*Finsbury*	X	Café Lazeez City
52	*Tooting*	X	Kastoori (Vegetarian)
43	*Kensington*	X	☺ Malabar
27	*Bloomsbury*	X	Mela
33	*Archway*	X	☺ (The) Parsee
69	*Soho*	X	☺ Soho Spice
62	*Mayfair*	X	Veeraswamy

Italian

Page	Area	Rating	Restaurant
60	*Mayfair*	XXX	Cecconi's
38	*Chelsea*	XXX	Floriana
73	*Victoria*	XXX	(L') Incontro
56	*Hyde Park & Knightsbridge*	XXX	Isola
64	*Regent's Park & Marylebone*	XXX	✿ Locanda Locatelli
68	*Soho*	XXX	Quo Vadis
73	*Victoria*	XXX	Santini
60	*Mayfair*	XXX	Sartoria
38	*Chelsea*	XXX	Toto's
61	*Mayfair*	XX	Alloro
54	*Bayswater & Maida Vale*	XX	Al San Vincenzo
42	*Kensington*	XX	(The) Ark
65	*Regent's Park & Marylebone*	XX	Bertorelli
65	*Regent's Park & Marylebone*	XX	Caldesi
39	*Chelsea*	XX	Caraffini
73	*Victoria*	XX	(Il) Convivio
43	*North Kensington*	XX	Edera
51	*Putney*	XX	Enoteca Turi
65	*Regent's Park & Marylebone*	XX	Latium
35	*Islington*	XX	☺ Metrogusto
26	*Bloomsbury*	XX	Neal Street
39	*Chelsea*	XX	Pellicano
32	*Hammersmith*	XX	✿ River Café
65	*Regent's Park & Marylebone*	XX	Rosmarino
26	*Bloomsbury*	XX	Sardo
61	*Mayfair*	XX	Teca
48	*Bermondsey*	XX	Tentazioni
42	*Kensington*	XX	Timo
55	*Belgravia*	XX	✿ Zafferano
54	*Bayswater & Maida Vale*	X	☺ (L') Accento
68	*St James's*	X	☺ Al Duca
54	*Bayswater & Maida Vale*	X	Assaggi
69	*Soho*	X	Bertorelli
66	*Regent's Park & Marylebone*	X	Caffé Caldesi
48	*Bermondsey*	X	Cantina Del Ponte
43	*Kensington*	X	Cibo
54	*Bayswater & Maida Vale*	X	Green Olive
74	*Victoria*	X	Olivo
27	*Bloomsbury*	X	Paolo
27	*Bloomsbury*	X	Passione
69	*Soho*	X	Vasco and Piero's Pavillion

Japanese

Page	Area	Rating	Restaurant
31	*City of London*	XXX	Tatsuso
39	*Chelsea*	XX	Benihana
29	*Swiss Cottage*	XX	Benihana
29	*Holborn*	XX	Matsuri-High Holborn
68	*St James's*	XX	Matsuri
61	*Mayfair*	XX	✿ Nobu
61	*Mayfair*	XX	Sumosan
50	*Canary Wharf*	XX	Ubon by Nobu
56	*Hyde Park & Knightsbridge*	XX	Zuma
27	*Bloomsbury*	X	Abeno
40	*Chelsea*	X	Itsu
69	*Soho*	X	Itsu
46	*Clapham*	X	Tsunami

Kosher

65	*Regent's Park & Marylebone*	XX	Six 13

Lebanese

61	*Mayfair*	XX	Fakhreldine
65	*Regent's Park & Marylebone*	XX	Levant
55	*Belgravia*	XX	Noura Brasserie

Moroccan

62	*Mayfair*	XX	Momo
46	*South Kensington*	XX	Pasha

North African

32	*Hammersmith*	X	Azou

Polish

43	*Kensington*	X	Wódka

Pubs

40	*Chelsea*	Admiral Codrington
32	*Hammersmith*	Anglesea Arms
35	*Islington*	(The) Barnsbury
	Chiswick	(The) Bollo
40	*Chelsea*	Builders Arms
33	*Islington*	Centuria
40	*Chelsea*	Chelsea Ram
	Chiswick	(The) Devonshire House
35	*Islington*	Drapers Arms
29	*Primrose Hill*	(The) Engineer
47	*Wimbledon*	(The) Fire Stables
33	*Shepherd's Bush*	Havelock Tavern
41	*Earl's Court*	Hollywood Arms
29	*Tufnell Park*	Junction Tavern
40	*Chelsea*	Lots Road Pub & Dining Room
28	*Hampstead*	(The) Magdala
35	*Islington*	(The) Northgate
34	*Finsbury*	(The) Peasant
29	*Primrose Hill*	(The) Queens
33	*Archway*	St John's
32	*Hammersmith & Fulham*	(The) Salisbury Tavern
35	*Islington*	(The) Social
40	*Chelsea*	Swag and Tails
54	*Bayswater and Maida Vale*	(The) Waterway
28	*Hampstead*	(The) Wells

Scottish

74	*Victoria*	XX	Boisdale
31	*City of London*	XX	Boisdale of Bishopgate

Seafood

38	*Chelsea*	XXX	One-O-One
50	*St Katherine's Dock*	XX	(The) Aquarium
62	*Mayfair*	XX	Bentley's
31	*City of London*	XX	Chamberlain's
54	*Bayswater & Maida Vale*	XX	Jason's
70	*Strand & Covent Garden*	XX	J. Sheekey
38	*Chelsea*	XX	Poissonnerie de l'Avenue (French)
65	*Regent's Park & Marylebone*	XX	Rasa Samudra (Indian) (Vegetarian)
40	*Chelsea*	X	Bibendum Oyster Bar
50	*Southwark*	X	Fish!
49	*Southwark*	X	Livebait
71	*Strand & Covent Garden*	X	Livebait
46	*Kennington*	X	Lobster Pot (French)

South East Asian

39	*Chelsea*	XX	Eight over Eight
61	*Mayfair*	XX	Taman Gang
62	*Mayfair*	X	Khew

Spanish

46	*South Kensington*	XX	Cambio de Tercio
26	*Bloomsbury*	XX	Fino
27	*Bloomsbury*	X	Cigala

Thai

32	*Fulham*	XX	Blue Elephant
51	*Battersea*	XX	Chada
55	*Belgravia*	XX	Mango Tree
55	*Belgravia*	XX	✿ Nahm
54	*Bayswater & Maida Vale*	XX	Nipa
46	*South Kensington*	X	Bangkok
66	*Regent's Park & Marylebone*	X	Chada Chada
52	*Tooting*	X	Oh Boy

Turkish

65	*Regent's Park & Marylebone*	XX	Ozer

Vegetarian

65	*Regent's Park & Marylebone*	XX	Rasa Samudra (Indian) (Seafood)
52	*Tooting*	X	Kastoori (Indian)

Vietnamese

34	*Highbury*	X	Au Lac

***Greater London** is divided, for administrative purposes, into 32 boroughs plus the City; these sub-divide naturally into minor areas, usually grouped around former villages or quarters, which often maintain a distinctive character.*

of Greater London: ***020.***

LONDON AIRPORTS

Heathrow *Middx. West : 17 m. by A 4, M 4* **Underground** *Piccadilly line direct.*

(020) 8759 4321 – **Terminal :** Airbus (A 1) from Victoria, Airbus (A 2) from Paddington.

Terminals 1, 2 and 3, Underground Station Concourse, Heathrow Airport (0839) 123456.

Radisson Edwardian, 140 Bath Rd, Hayes, UB3 5AW, (020) 8759 6311, *resre@radisson.com, Fax (020) 8759 4559,* – rm, – 550.
Henleys : **Meals** *(closed Saturday-Sunday)* 25.00 and a la carte 33.00/41.00 **s.** – 15.00 – **442 rm** 233.80/276.10, 17 suites.
• Capacious group hotel with a huge atrium over the leisure facilities. Plenty of comfortable lounges, well-appointed bedrooms and attentive service. Henleys boasts oil paintings and cocktail bar. Informal, slim leather-chaired Brasserie.

Crowne Plaza London Heathrow, Stockley Rd, West Drayton, UB7 9NA, (01895) 445555, *reservations.cplhr@ichotelsgroup.com, Fax (01895) 445122,* – rm, – 200.
Concha Grill : **Meals** 18.50/25.50 **s.** and a la carte (see also ***Simply Nico Heathrow*** below) – 16.00 – **457 rm** 195.00, 1 suite.
• Extensive leisure, aromatherapy and beauty salons make this large hotel a popular stopover for travellers. Club bedrooms are particularly well-equipped. Bright, breezy Concha Grill with juice bar.

London Heathrow Marriott, Bath Rd, Hayes, UB3 5AN, (020) 8990 1100, *reservations.heathrow@marriotthotels.co.uk, Fax (020) 8990 1110,* – rm, – 540.
Tuscany : **Meals** - Italian -*(closed Sunday)* (dinner only) a la carte 22.90/40.95 – ***Allie's grille :*** **Meals** a la carte 22.75/33.50 – 16.45 – **388 rm** 149.20/223.25, 2 suites.
• Built at the end of 20C, this modern, comfortable hotel is centred around a large atrium, with comprehensive business facilities : there is an exclusive Executive floor. Tuscany's is bright and convivial.

Sheraton Skyline, Bath Rd, Hayes, UB3 5BP, (020) 8759 2535, *res268skyline@sheraton.com, Fax (020) 8750 9150,* – – 500.
Sage : **Meals** a la carte 23.50/41.00 – 17.00 – **348 rm** 199.00, 2 suites.
• Well known for its unique indoor swimming pool surrounded by a tropical garden which is overlooked by many of the bedrooms. Business centre available. Classically decorated dining room.

Hilton London Heathrow Airport, Terminal 4, TW6 3AF, (020) 8759 7755, *gmheathrow@hilton.com, Fax (020) 8759 7579,* – rm, – 250.
Brasserie : **Meals** a la carte 23.40/42.95 **s.** – ***Zen Oriental :*** **Meals** - Chinese - a la carte 14.40/59.80 **s.** – 18.50 – **390 rm** 229.12, 5 suites.
• Group hotel with a striking modern exterior and linked to Terminal 4 by a covered walkway. Good sized bedrooms, with contemporary styled suites. Spacious Brasserie in vast atrium. Zen Oriental offers formal Chinese experience.

Holiday Inn London Heathrow, Sipson Rd, West Drayton, UB7 0JU, (0870) 4008595, *rmheathrowm4@ichotelsgroup.com, Fax (020) 8897 8659,* – rm, – 140.
Sampans : **Meals** - Asian - *(closed Sunday dinner)* (dinner only) 18.95/29.95 and a la carte 22.90/35.45 – ***Rotisserie :*** **Meals** (buffet meals) 15.95/19.50 **s.** – 15.00 – **610 rm** 179.00, 4 suites.
• Busy group hotel where the Academy conference suite attracts the business community. Bedrooms come in a variety of styles. Popular Irish bar. Sampans offers regional Chinese dishes. Spacious Rotisserie with chef carving to order. Pizzas and pasta at Fresca.

Renaissance London Heathrow, Bath Rd, TW6 2AQ, ☎ (020) 8897 6363, *lhrrenaissance@aol.com, Fax (020) 8897 1113,* Fitness, Sauna – Lift, ⇔ rm, ▤ TV ☎ ♿ P – 🎓 520. MC AE D VISA. ✈
Meals 18.50/22.00 and a la carte 20.00/38.50 **s.** ♀ – ☐ 15.95 – **643 rm** 139.00, 6 suites.
◆ Low level façade belies the size of this easily accessible hotel. Large lounge and assorted shops in the lobby. Some of the soundproofed bedrooms have views of the runway. Open-plan restaurant with buffet or à la carte.

Holiday Inn Heathrow Ariel, 118 Bath Rd, Hayes, UB3 5AJ, ☎ (0870) 4009040, *reservations-heathrow@ichotelsgroup.com, Fax (020) 8564 9265* – Lift, ⇔ rm, ▤ rest, TV ☎ P – 🎓 55. MC AE D VISA
Meals (bar lunch Saturday) (buffet lunch) a la carte 17.15/29.15 **s.** – ☐ 14.95 – **186 rm** 159.00.
◆ Usefully located hotel in a cylindrical shape. Modern bedrooms with warm colours. Third floor executive rooms particularly impressive. Conference rooms available. Subtly-lit, relaxing restaurant.

Travel Inn Heathrow Capital, 15 Bath Rd, TW6 2AB, ☎ (0870) 6075075, *Fax (0870) 2419000* – Lift, ⇔ rm, ▤ TV ☎ ♿ P – 🎓 30. MC AE D VISA JCB. ✈
Meals (grill rest.) – **590 rm** 69.95.
◆ Well-priced Travel Inn with modern, wood-panelled exterior and huge atrium. Well-equipped meeting rooms. Bedrooms are of good quality with triple glazing. Bright, airy, informal grill restaurant.

Simply Nico Heathrow (at Crowne Plaza London Heathrow H.), Stockley Rd, West Drayton, UB7 9NA, ☎ (01895) 437564, *heathrow.simplynico@corushotels.com, Fax (01895) 437565* – ▤ P. MC AE D VISA
closed Saturday lunch and Sunday – **Meals** a la carte 25.00/42.90 ♀.
◆ Located within the hotel but with its own personality. Mixes modern with more classically French dishes. Professional service in comfortable surroundings.

Gatwick

Gatwick *W. Sussex South : 28 m. by A 23 and M 23* - **Train** *from Victoria : Gatwick Express* 504 T 30 – ✉ *Crawley.*
✈ ☎ *(0870) 0002468.*

Hilton London Gatwick Airport, South Terminal, RH6 0LL, ☎ (01293) 518080, *londongatwick@hilton.com, Fax (01293) 528980,* Fitness, Sauna, Pool – Lift, ⇔ rm, ▤ TV ☎ ♿ P – 🎓 500. MC AE D VISA JCB. ✈
Meals 21.95 and a la carte 27.15/40.45 ♀ – ☐ 14.50 – **791 rm** 164.50.
◆ Large, well-established hotel, popular with business travellers. Two ground floor bars, lounge and leisure facilities. Older rooms co-ordinated, newer in minimalist style. Restaurant enlivened by floral profusions.

Le Meridien London Gatwick, Gatwick Airport (North Terminal), RH6 0PH, ☎ (01293) 576070, *sales.gatwick@lemeridien-hotels.com, Fax (01293) 567739,* Fitness, Sauna, Pool – Lift, ⇔ rm, ▤ TV ☎ ♿ P – 🎓 300. MC AE D VISA JCB. ✈
***Gatwick Oriental* : Meals** - Asian - 17.00/35.00 ♀ – ***Brasserie* : Meals** (dinner only) 23.95 and a la carte 25.05/31.40 ♀ – ☐ 15.95 – **494 rm** 210.00, 6 suites.
◆ Modern hotel with short covered walkway into North Terminal. Comprehensive leisure facilities. Very comfortable rooms, with Le Royal Club members enjoying use of own lounge. Gatwick Oriental offers Far Eastern ambience. Informal modern brasserie.

Renaissance London Gatwick, Povey Cross Rd, RH6 0BE, ☎ (01293) 820169, *Fax (01293) 820259,* Fitness, Sauna, Pool, squash – Lift, ⇔ rm, ▤ TV ☎ ♿ P – 🎓 180. MC AE D VISA
Meals 18.50 and a la carte 23.50/34.50 **s.** ♀ – ☐ 12.50 – **252 rm** 119.00, 2 suites.
◆ Large red-brick hotel. Good recreational facilities including indoor pool, solarium. Bedrooms are spacious and decorated in smart, chintzy style. Small brasserie area open all day serving popular meals.

Travel Inn Metro, Longbridge Way, Gatwick Airport (North Terminal), RH6 0NX, ☎ (01293) 568158, *Fax (01293) 568278* – Lift, ⇔ rm, ▤ rest, TV ♿ P. MC AE D VISA. ✈
Meals (grill rest.) (dinner only) – **219 rm** 49.95.
◆ Consistent standard of trim, simply fitted accommodation in contemporary style. Family rooms with sofa beds. Ideal for corporate or leisure travel.

CAMDEN

Bloomsbury

Bloomsbury – ✉ *W1/WC1/WC2.*

Le Meridien Russell, Russell Sq, WC1B 5BE, ☎ (020) 7837 6470, *sales.russell@lemeridien.com, Fax (020) 7837 2857* – Lift, ⇔ rm, ▤ TV ☎ – 🎓 400. MC AE D VISA JCB. ✈
Meals 16.95/22.50 and dinner a la carte 20.90/32.00 ♀ – ☐ 19.50 – **369 rm** 182.10/211.50, 2 suites.
◆ An impressive Victorian building dominating Russell Square. Boasts many original features including the imposing marbled lobby and staircase. Traditional or modern rooms. Restaurant has noticeable feel of grandeur.

Holiday Inn Kings Cross, 1 Kings Cross Rd, WC1X 9HX, (020) 7833 3900, *reservations@holidayinnlondon.com, Fax (020) 7917 6163,* – , rm, – 220. VISA.
***Lahore* : Meals** - Indian - *(closed Saturday lunch)* a la carte 20.00/40.00 – ***Carriages* : Meals** a la carte 32.50/42.00 – 12.50 – **403 rm** 190.00, 2 suites.
• In a fast developing part of town and close to Kings Cross station. Comfortable bedrooms with all mod cons. Clubby lobby bar with deep leather armchairs and sofas. Lahore offers bold surroundings. Carriages is half lounge, half restaurant.

Marlborough, 9-14 Bloomsbury St, WC1B 3QD, (020) 7636 5601, *resmarl@radisson.com, Fax (020) 7636 0532* – , rm, rest, – 200. VISA JCB. 31 AKT k
***Glass* : Meals** *(closed Sunday)* 27.50 and a la carte 30.00/36.00 – 15.00 – **171 rm** 229.00/298.45, 2 suites.
• A Victorian building around the corner from the British Museum. The lobby has been restored to its original marbled splendour and the bedrooms offer good comforts. Bright, breezy restaurant with suitably modish cooking.

Mountbatten, 20 Monmouth St, WC2H 9HD, (020) 7836 4300, *Fax (020) 7240 3540,* – , rm, – 90. VISA JCB. 31 ALU d
***Dial* : Meals** 27.50 and a la carte 30.00/36.00 – 15.00 – **149 rm** 302.00/371.30, 2 suites.
• Photographs and memorabilia of the eponymous Lord Louis adorn the walls and corridors. Ideally located in the heart of Covent Garden. Compact but comfortable bedrooms. Bright, stylish restaurant.

Covent Garden, 10 Monmouth St, WC2H 9HB, (020) 7806 1000, *covent@firmdale.com, Fax (020) 7806 1100,* – – 50. VISA. 31 ALU x
***Brasserie Max* : Meals** (booking essential) a la carte 26.50/40.00 – 18.00 – **56 rm** 229.00/346.60, 2 suites.
• Individually designed and stylish bedrooms, with CDs and VCRs discreetly concealed. Boasts a very relaxing first floor oak-panelled drawing room with its own honesty bar. Informal restaurant.

Grafton, 130 Tottenham Court Rd, W1P 9HP, (020) 7388 4131, *resgraf@radisson.com, Fax (020) 7387 7394,* – , rm, – 100. VISA JCB.
***Aston's* : Meals** 27.50 and a la carte 30.00/36.00 – 12.00 – **326 rm** 229.10/298.50, 4 suites.
• Just yards from Warren Street tube. Discreet Edwardian charm that belies its location in one of London's busier streets. Bedrooms to becalm in soft beige tones. Open-plan restaurant and bar.

Kenilworth, 97 Great Russell St, WC1B 3BL, (020) 7637 3477, *resmarl@radisson.com, Fax (020) 7631 3133,* – , rm, – 100. VISA JCB. 31 AKT a
Meals - Asian - 27.50 and a la carte 30.00/36.00 – 15.00 – **186 rm** 229.00/298.50.
• Usefully placed for the shops of Oxford Street. Stylish interiors and modern designer hi-tech bedrooms, equipped to meet the needs of the corporate traveller. Smart dining room with a modern style.

Jurys Gt Russell St, 16-22 Gt Russell St, WC1B 3NN, (020) 7347 1000, *gtrussellstreet@jurysdoyle.com, Fax (020) 7347 1001* – , rm, – 220. VISA. 31 AKT n
***Lutyens* : Meals** a la carte approx. 29.00 – 16.00 – **168 rm** 225.00, 1 suite.
• Neo-Georgian building by Edward Lutyens, built for YMCA in 1929. Smart comfortable interior decoration from the lounge to the bedrooms. Facilities include a business centre. Restaurant has understated traditional style.

Montague on the Gardens, 15 Montague St, WC1B 5BJ, (020) 7637 1001, *bookmt@rchmail.com, Fax (020) 7637 2516,* , , , – , rm, – 120. VISA 31 ALT a
***Blue Door Bistro* : Meals** 13.50/19.00 and a la carte 27.95/36.00 – 16.50 – **98 rm** 205.60/229.10, 6 suites.
• A period townhouse with pretty hanging baskets outside. The hushed conservatory overlooks a secluded garden. The clubby bar has a Scottish golfing theme. Rich bedroom décor. Restaurant divided into two small, pretty rooms.

Holiday Inn Bloomsbury, Coram St, WC1N 1HT, (0870) 4009222, *bloomsbury@ichotelsgroup.com, Fax (020) 7837 5372* – , rm, – 300. VISA JCB.
Meals *(closed Saturday and Sunday lunch)* 15.00 and a la carte 19.65/28.85 **s.** – 14.95 – **313 rm** 179.00.
• Bright, modern bedrooms in warm, neutral tones. Have a drink in either the stylish bar with leather chairs or Callaghans Irish themed bar. Relaxed and contemporary dining.

Thistle Bloomsbury, Bloomsbury Way, WC1A 2SD, (020) 7242 5881, *bloomsbury@thistle.co.uk, Fax (020) 7831 0225* – rm, rest, – 80. 31 ALT r
Meals *(closed lunch Saturday, Sunday and Bank Holidays)* 23.95 – 14.95 – **138 rm** 215.00/246.75.
◆ Established over 100 years ago and retains much charm. Quiet and discreet lobby. An old fashioned lift leads up to the bedrooms that have a very English feel. Combined bar and dining room.

Myhotel, 11-13 Bayley St, Bedford Sq, WC1B 3HD, (020) 7667 6000, *bloomsbury@myhotels.co.uk, Fax (020) 7667 6001,* – – 40. 31 AKT x
Yo ! Sushi : **Meals** - Japanese - a la carte 16.00/22.00 – 16.00 – **78 rm** 223.25/258.50.
◆ The minimalist interior is designed on the principles of feng shui ; even the smaller bedrooms are stylish and uncluttered. Mybar is a fashionable meeting point. Diners can enjoy Japanese food from conveyor belt.

Bonnington in Bloomsbury, 92 Southampton Row, WC1B 4BH, (020) 7242 2828, *sales@bonnington.com, Fax (020) 7831 5758,* – , rm, – 250. 31 ALT s
Meals *(closed Sunday)* (bar lunch)/dinner 20.95 **s.** – **239 rm** 125.00/159.00, 8 suites.
◆ Built in 1911 and providing easy access to a number of tourist attractions. Functional, but well-kept, bedrooms offer traditional comforts with many modern extras. Classically decorated dining room.

Pied à Terre, 34 Charlotte St, W1T 2NH, (020) 7636 1178, *p-a-t@dircon.co.uk, Fax (020) 7916 1171* – . 31 AJT e
closed last week December, first week January, Sunday and lunch Monday and Saturday – **Meals** 24.00/49.00.
◆ Frosted glass front hints at the understated, cool interior. The kitchen offers an elaborate and adventurous, yet refined take on modern French cuisine. Well-chosen wine list.
Spec. Seared and poached foie gras in a Sauternes consommé. Saddle of rabbit with Pommery mustard sauce. Chocolate tart with stout ice cream.

Incognico, 117 Shaftesbury Ave, WC2H 8AD, (020) 7836 8866, *Fax (020) 7240 9525* – . 31 AKU q
closed 4 days Easter, 10 days Christmas, Sunday and Bank Holidays – **Meals** 12.50 (lunch) and a la carte 29.00/46.00.
◆ Opened in 2000 with its robust décor of wood panelling and brown leather chairs. Downstairs bar has a window into the kitchen, from where French and English classics derive.

Neal Street, 26 Neal St, WC2H 9QT, (020) 7836 8368, *Fax (020) 7240 3964* – 31 ALU s
closed 25 December-2 January and Sunday – **Meals** - Italian - 25.00 (lunch) and a la carte 27.50/39.50.
◆ Light, bright and airy ; tiled flooring and colourful pictures. Dishes range from the simple to the more complex. Mushrooms a speciality. Has its own shop next door.

Sardo, 45 Grafton Way, W1T 5DQ, (020) 7387 2521, *info@sardo-restaurant.com, Fax (020) 7387 2559.*
closed Saturday lunch, Sunday and Bank Holidays – **Meals** - Italian (Sardinian specialities) - a la carte 20.50/32.40.
◆ Simple, stylish interior run in a very warm and welcoming manner with very efficient service. Rustic Italian cooking with a Sardinian character and a modern tone.

Hakkasan, 8 Hanway Pl, W1T 1HD, (020) 7907 1888, *mail@hakkasan.com, Fax (020) 7907 1889* – . 31 AKT c
Meals - Chinese (Canton) - a la carte 28.80/79.00.
◆ A distinctive, modern interpretation of Cantonese cooking in an appropriately contemporary and cavernous basement. The lively, bustling bar is an equally popular nightspot.
Spec. Stir-fry scallop and prawn cake. Pan-fried rib-eye of beef, sweet soya and almonds. Jasmine tea smoked chicken.

Fino, 33 Charlotte St (entrance on Rathbone St), W1T 1RR, (020) 7813 8010, *info@finorestaurant.com, Fax (020) 7813 8011* – 31 AJT a
closed 25 December, Easter, Saturday lunch, Sunday and Bank Holidays – **Meals** - Spanish - a la carte 16.00/29.50.
◆ Spanish-run basement Tapas bar with modern style décor and banquette seating. Wide-ranging menu of authentic dishes ; 2 set-price selections offering an introduction to tapas.

Mon Plaisir, 21 Monmouth St, WC2H 9DD, (020) 7836 7243, *eatafrog@mail.com, Fax (020) 7240 4774* – 31 ALU g
closed 25-26 and 31 December, 1 January and lunch Saturday and Sunday – **Meals** - French - 15.95 (lunch) and a la carte 25.50/32.20.
◆ London's oldest French restaurant and family-run for over fifty years. Divided into four rooms, all with a different feel but all proudly Gallic in their decoration.

Archipelago, 110 Whitfield St, W1T 5ED, (020) 7383 3346, *Fax (020) 7383 7181* – MC AE DC VISA JCB
closed 25 December, Saturday lunch, Sunday and Bank Holiday Mondays – **Meals** 20.50/38.50.
◆ Eccentric in both menu and décor and not for the faint hearted. Crammed with knick-knacks from cages to Buddhas. Menu an eclectic mix of influences from around the world.

Malabar Junction, 107 Great Russell St, WC1B 3NA, (020) 7580 5230, *Fax (020) 7436 9942* – ▤. MC AE VISA 31 AKT y
Meals - South Indian - a la carte 20.50/31.00.
◆ Specialising in dishes from southern India. Bright restaurant with a small fountain in the centre of the room below a large skylight. Helpful and attentive service.

Passione, 10 Charlotte St, W1T 2LT, (020) 7636 2833, *Liz@passione.co.uk, Fax (020) 7636 2889* – MC AE DC VISA JCB 31 AKT u
closed 23 December-2 January, Saturday lunch, Sunday and Bank Holidays – **Meals** - Italian - (booking essential) a la carte 31.00/42.00.
◆ Compact but light and airy. Modern Italian cooking served in informal surroundings, with friendly and affable service. Particularly busy at lunchtime.

Cigala, 54 Lamb's Conduit St, WC1N 3LW, (020) 7405 1717, *tasty@cigala.co.uk, Fax (020) 7242 9949* – MC AE DC VISA JCB
closed 25 December – **Meals** - Spanish - 18.00 (lunch) and a la carte approx. 26.50 ♀.
◆ Spanish restaurant on the corner of attractive street. Simply furnished with large windows and open-plan kitchen. Robust Iberian cooking. Informal tapas bar downstairs.

Paolo, 16 Percy St, W1T 1DT, (020) 7637 9900, *info@paolorestaurant.com, Fax (020) 7637 9696* – ▤. MC AE DC VISA JCB 31 AKT f
closed 24-26 December and Sunday – **Meals** - Italian - 17.50 (lunch) and a la carte 24.00/35.00 ♀.
◆ Wood floored restaurant with intimate basement and brighter ground floor dining rooms. Authentic, rustic Italian dishes with a predominately Northern Italian style.

Mela, 152-156 Shaftesbury Ave, WC2H 6HL, (020) 7836 8635, *info@melarestaurant.co.uk, Fax (020) 7379 0527* – MC AE DC VISA JCB 31 AKU e
closed 25 December – **Meals** - Indian - 10.95/35.95 (dinner) and a la carte 11.35/26.85 **s.**
◆ Vibrantly decorated dining room with a simple style in a useful location close to Theatreland. Enjoy thoroughly tasty Indian food in a bustling, buzzy environment.

Abeno, 47 Museum St, WC1A 1LY, (020) 7405 3211, *okonomi@abeno.co.uk, Fax (020) 7405 3212* – ▤. MC AE DC VISA JCB 31 ALT e
closed 25-26 and 31 December and 1 January – **Meals** - Japanese (Okonomi-Yaki) - 6.50/16.50 (lunch) and a la carte 12.25/30.80.
◆ Specialises in Okonomi-yaki : little Japanese "pancakes" cooked on a hotplate on each table. Choose your own filling and the size of your pancake.

Euston – ✉ *NW1/WC1.*

Novotel London Euston, 100-110 Euston Rd, NW1 2AJ, (020) 7666 9000, *h5309@accor-hotels.com, Fax (020) 7666 9100*, – |♦|, ⇔ rm, ▤ TV ♿ – 450. MC AE DC VISA JCB.
Meals 16.00 (lunch) and a la carte 23.50/29.90 ♀ – 14.50 – **311 rm** 160.00/180.00, 1 suite.
◆ Extensive conference facilities that include the redeveloped Shaw theatre. Large marbled lobby. Modern bedrooms that offer views of London's rooftops from the higher floors. Lobby-based restaurant and bar look onto busy street.

Euston Plaza, 17-18 Upper Woburn Pl, WC1H 0HT, (020) 7943 4500, *info@euston-plaza-hotel.com, Fax (020) 7943 4501*, – |♦|, ⇔ rm, ▤ TV ♿ – 150. MC AE DC VISA JCB.
Three Crowns **: Meals** *(closed Saturday and Sunday lunch)* (dinner only) 19.95 and a la carte 23.40/32.50 **s.** ♀ – ***Terrace*** **: Meals** a la carte 15.40/18.40 **s.** ♀ – 12.95 – **150 rm** 153.00/238.50.
◆ Nearby transport links make this a useful location. Scandinavian owned, which is reflected in the style of the bedrooms. Executive rooms are particularly well-equipped. Three Crowns has smart basement location. Lighter fare in Terrace conservatory.

London Euston Travel Inn Capital, 141 Euston Rd, WC1H 9PJ, (0870) 2383301, *Fax (020) 7554 3419* – |♦|, ⇔ rm, ▤ rest, TV ♿. MC AE DC VISA.
Meals (grill rest.) (dinner only) – **220 rm** 79.95.
◆ Budget accommodation with clean and spacious bedrooms, all with a large workspace. Double glazed but still ask for a quieter room at the back.

UNITED KINGDOM

Hampstead – ✉ NW3.

Winnington Rd, Hampstead ☎ (020) 8455 0203.

Holiday Inn, 215 Haverstock Hill, NW3 4RB, ☎ (0870) 4009037, *reservations-hampstead@6c.com, Fax (020) 7435 5586,* – rm, MC AE VISA JCB
Meals 15.00 (lunch) and a la carte 16.95/22.00 **s.** – 14.95 – **140 rm** 165.00.
• A well-equipped group hotel adjacent to a petrol station. Convenient for the boutiques and cafés of Hampstead. Bright, modern bedrooms. Formula menus.

The House without rest., 2 Rosslyn Hill, NW3 1PH, ☎ (020) 7431 8000, *reception@thehousehotel.co.uk, Fax (020) 7433 1775* – MC AE
11.00 – **23 rm** 120.00/165.00.
• Large Victorian house close to the shops and not far from Hampstead Heath. Pleasant breakfast room/bar. Invidually styled, well appointed rooms, with smart marbled bathrooms.

Langorf without rest., 20 Frognal, NW3 6AG, ☎ (020) 7794 4483, *info@langorfhotel.com, Fax (020) 7435 9055* – MC AE VISA.
41 rm 82.00/110.00, 5 suites.
• Converted Edwardian house in a quiet residential area. Bright breakfast room overlooks secluded walled garden. Fresh bedrooms, many of which have high ceilings.

ZeNW3, 83-84 Hampstead High St, NW3 1RE, ☎ (020) 7794 7863, *Fax (020) 7794 6956* – MC VISA
closed 25 December – **Meals** - Chinese - 14.50/35.00 and a la carte approx. 22.50.
• Contemporary interior provided by the glass topped tables and small waterfall feature on the stairs. Professional service. Carefully prepared Chinese food.

Cucina, 45a South End Rd, NW3 2QB, ☎ (020) 7435 7814, *postmaster@cucinahampstead.co.uk, Fax (020) 7435 7815* – MC AE VISA
Meals a la carte 21.85/34.85 ♀.
• The small deli at the front gives few clues to the large room inside. Eclectic mix of artwork scattered around the room. Modern menu with influences from around the globe.

The Wells, 30 Well Walk, NW3 1BX, ☎ (020) 7794 3785, *Fax (020) 7794 6817,* – MC AE VISA
Meals a la carte 23.75/31.00 ♀.
• Attractive 18C inn with modern interior. Ground floor bar and a few tables next to open-plan kitchen ; upstairs more formal dining rooms. Classically-based French cooking.

The Magdala, 2A South Hill Park, NW3 2SB, ☎ (020) 7435 2503, *Fax (020) 7435 6167,* – MC VISA
closed 25 December – **Meals** a la carte 15.70/24.25 ♀.
• Located on the edge of the Heath. Two bars popular with locals, one with open-plan kitchen. Upstairs dining room, open at weekends, offers robust cooking. Simpler lunch menu.

Hatton Garden – ✉ EC1.

Bleeding Heart, Bleeding Heart Yard, EC1N 8SJ, off Greville St ☎ (020) 7242 8238, *bookings@bleedingheart.co.uk, Fax (020) 7831 1402,* – MC AE VISA
closed 24 December-5 January, Saturday, Sunday and Bank Holidays – **Meals** a la carte 21.40/35.85 ♀. 32 ANT e
• Wood panelling, candlelight and a heart motif ; a popular romantic dinner spot. By contrast, a busy City restaurant at lunchtime. French influenced menu. Weighty wine list.

Holborn – ✉ WC1/WC2.

Renaissance Chancery Court, 252 High Holborn, WC1V 7EN, ☎ (020) 7829 9888, *sales.chancerycourt@renaissancehotels.com, Fax (020) 7829 9889,* – rm, – 400. MC AE VISA JCB. 32AMT a
Meals (see **QC** below) – 17.95 – **354 rm** 311.35/346.60, 2 suites.
• Striking building built in 1914. converted to hotel in 2000. Impressive marbled lobby and grand central courtyard. Very large bedrooms with comprehensive modern facilities.

Kingsway Hall, Great Queen St, WC2B 5BX, ☎ (020) 7309 0909, *reservations@kingswayhall.co.uk, Fax (020) 7309 9129,* – rm, – 150. MC AE VISA. 31 ALT b
Harlequin : **Meals** *(closed lunch Saturday, Sunday and Bank Holidays)* 14.95/17.95 **s.** and dinner a la carte – 15.25 – **168 rm** 185.00, 2 suites.
• Large, corporate-minded hotel. Striking glass-framed and marbled lobby. Stylish ground floor bar. Well-appointed bedrooms with an extensive array of mod cons. Relaxing restaurant in warm pastel colours.

QC (at Renaissance Chancery Court H.), 252 High Holborn, WC1V 7EN, ☎ (020) 7829 7000, *Fax (020) 7829 9889* – MC AE VISA JCB 32AMT a
closed Saturday lunch and Sunday – **Meals** 21.50 (lunch) and a la carte 31.50/47.00 ♀.
• Impressive dining room with walls clad in Italian marble ; Corinthian columns. Waiters provide efficient service at well-spaced tables ; original menus.

Primrose Hill - NW1.

Matsuri - High Holborn, Mid City Pl, 71 High Holborn, WC1V 6EA, (020) 7430 1970, *eat@matsuri-restaurant.com, Fax (020) 7430 1971* - . MC AE VISA JCB
closed 24-26 and 31 December, 1-2 January, Sunday and Bank Holidays - **Meals** - Japanese - 22.00/25.00 and a la carte 23.50/43.00. 32AMT c
◆ Spacious, airy Japanese restaurant. Authentic menu served in main dining room, in basement teppan-yaki bar and at large sushi counter, where chefs demonstrate their skills.

Odette's, 130 Regent's Park Rd, NW1 8XL, (020) 7586 5486, *Fax (020) 7586 0508* - MC AE VISA
closed Saturday lunch and Sunday dinner - **Meals** 14.50 (lunch) and a la carte 35.00/45.00.
◆ Identified by the pretty hanging baskets outside. A charming interior with mirrors of various sizes covering the walls. Detailed service. Contemporary cuisine.

The Queens, 49 Regent's Park Rd, NW1 8XD, (020) 7586 0408, *Fax (020) 7586 5677*, - MC VISA
Meals a la carte 16.90/21.90.
◆ One of the original "gastropubs". Very popular balcony overlooking Primrose Hill and the high street. Robust and traditional cooking from the blackboard menu.

The Engineer, 65 Gloucester Ave, NW1 8JH, (020) 7722 0950, *info@the-eng.com, Fax (020) 7483 0592*, - MC VISA
closed 25-26 December and 1 January - **Meals** a la carte 25.25/29.25.
◆ Busy pub that boasts a warm, neighbourhood feel. Dining room, decorated with modern pictures, has modish appeal. Informal, chatty service. Modern cuisine.

Swiss Cottage - NW3.

Marriott Regents Park, 128 King Henry's Rd, NW3 3ST, (020) 7722 7711, *Fax (020) 7586 5822*, , , - , rm, - 300. MC AE VISA.
Meals (bar lunch)/dinner a la carte 18.00/31.50 **s.** - 16.45 - **298 rm** 143.75, 5 suites.
◆ Large writing desks and technological extras attract the corporate market to this purpose-built group hotel. The impressive leisure facilities appeal to weekend guests. Large, open-plan restaurant and bar.

Swiss Cottage without rest., 4 Adamson Rd, NW3 3HP, (020) 7722 2281, *reservations@swisscottagehotel.co.uk, Fax (020) 7483 4588* - - 35. MC AE VISA.
53 rm 66.00/120.00, 6 suites.
◆ Made up of four Victorian houses in a residential conservation area. Bedrooms vary in size and shape, reflecting the age of the house. Basement breakfast room.

Bradley's, 25 Winchester Rd, NW3 3NR, (020) 7722 3457, *Fax (020) 7435 1392* - . MC AE VISA JCB
closed 25 December-1 January and Saturday lunch - **Meals** 16.00 (lunch) and a la carte 25.50/36.50.
◆ Warm pastel colours and modern artwork add a Mediterranean touch to this neighbourhood restaurant. The theme is complemented by the cooking of the chef patron.

Benihana, 100 Avenue Rd, NW3 3HF, (020) 7586 9508, *benihana@dircon.co.uk, Fax (020) 7586 6740* - . MC AE VISA
closed 25 December - **Meals** - Japanese (Teppan-Yaki) - 19.25/25.50.
◆ An entertaining experience where Japanese chefs chop, juggle and cook in front of you. Be prepared to talk with strangers as guests are seated in groups around the counters.

Globe, 100 Avenue Rd, NW3 3HF, (020) 7722 7200, *globerella@aol.com, Fax (020) 7722 2772* - . MC VISA
closed Saturday lunch and Sunday dinner - **Meals** a la carte 19.00/25.50.
◆ Next to the Hampstead Theatre, which opened in 2003, so this airy, conservatory establishment tends to be busier earlier and later in the evening. Stylish upstairs bar.

Tufnell Park *Gtr London* - NW5.

Samphire, 135 Fortess Rd, NW5 2HR, (020) 7482 4855, *Fax (020) 7482 4856* - . MC VISA
closed 25-26 December and 1 January - **Meals** (dinner only and Sunday lunch) a la carte 19.40/24.85.
◆ Modern decor in grey and burgundy ; smoking upstairs. Well chosen menu of dishes made of good quality ingredients and served in generous portions by friendly staff. Good value.

Junction Tavern, 101 Fortess Rd, NW5 1AG, (020) 7485 9400, *Fax (020) 7485 9401*, - MC VISA JCB
closed 24-26 December - **Meals** a la carte 16.50/25.00.
◆ Typical Victorian pub with wood panelling. Eat in the bar or in view of the open plan kitchen. Robust cooking using good fresh ingredients, served in generous portions.

CITY OF LONDON – ✉ E1/EC2/EC3/EC4.

Great Eastern, Liverpool St, EC2M 7QN, ☎ (020) 7618 5000, *sales@great-eastern-hotel.co.uk, Fax (020) 7618 5011,* – rm, – 250. MC AE ⓓ VISA 34 ART t

Fishmarket* : Meals** - Seafood - *(closed Saturday, Sunday and Bank Holidays)* a la carte 24.55/47.00 ♀ – ***Miyabi* : Meals** - Japanese - *(closed Saturday, Sunday and Bank Holidays)* (booking essential) 23.50 (lunch) and a la carte 21.50/39.50 (see also ***Aurora below) – ☕ 22.00 – **264 rm** 264.30/370.10, 3 suites.

◆ A contemporary and stylish interior hides behind the classic Victorian façade of this railway hotel. Bright and spacious bedrooms with state-of-the-art facilities. Fishmarket based within original hotel lobby. Miyabi is compact Japanese restaurant.

Grange City, 8-10 Coopers Row, EC3N 2BD, ☎ (020) 7863 3700, *city@grangehotel.com, Fax (020) 7863 3701,* – rm, – 450. MC AE ⓓ VISA JCB 34 ASU s

***Forum* : Meals** - Italian - *(closed lunch Saturday and Sunday)* 25.00 and a la carte 18.20/32.00 **s.** ♀ – ***Koto II* : Meals** - Sushi - a la carte approx. 14.00 **s.** – ☕ 16.00 – **234 rm** 280.00, 5 suites.

◆ Smart commercial hotel with splendid view of the Tower of London. Well-appointed wood furnished rooms. Superb leisure centre with large pool. Striking and colourful Forum with Italian menus. Informal Koto II has Japanese theme and sushi conveyor belt.

Threadneedles, 5 Threadneedle St, EC2R 8AY, ☎ (020) 7657 8080, *resthreadneedles@etontownhouse.com, Fax (020) 7657 8100* – – 35. MC AE ⓓ VISA JCB. 34 ARU y

Meals (see ***Bonds*** below) – ☕ 17.95 – **69 rm** 311.40/364.25, 1 suite.

◆ A converted bank, dating from 1856, with a stunning stained-glass cupola in the lounge. Rooms are very stylish and individual featuring CD players and Egyptian cotton sheets.

The Chamberlain, 130-135 Minories, EC3 1NU, ☎ (020) 7680 1500, *thechamberlain@fullers.co.uk, Fax (020) 7702 2500* – rm, – 40. MC AE ⓓ VISA. 34 ASU n

closed 24 December-3 January – **Meals** (in bar Saturday and Sunday) a la carte 14.20/16.20 ♀ – ☕ 10.95 – **64 rm** 159.00.

◆ Modern hotel aimed at business traveller, two minutes from the Tower of London. Warmly decorated bedrooms with writing desks. All bathrooms have inbuilt plasma TVs.

Novotel London Tower Bridge, 10 Pepys St, EC3N 2NR, ☎ (020) 7265 6000, *h3107@accor-hotels.com, Fax (020) 7265 6060,* – rm, – 95. MC AE ⓓ VISA. 34 ASU b

***The Garden Brasserie* : Meals** 18.95 (lunch) and a la carte 20.00/28.00 **s.** ♀ – ☕ 12.95 – **199 rm** 155.00/175.00, 4 suites.

◆ Modern, purpose-built hotel with carefully planned, comfortable bedrooms. Useful City location and close to Tower of London which is visible from some of the higher rooms. Informally styled brasserie.

Travelodge without rest., 1 Harrow Pl, E1 7DB, ☎ (08700) 850950, *Fax (020) 7626 1105* – . MC AE ⓓ VISA JCB. 34 AST s

142 rm 79.95.

◆ Suitable for both corporate travellers and families alike. Spacious, carefully designed, bright and modern rooms with sofa beds and ample workspace.

Aurora (at Great Eastern H.), Liverpool St, EC2M 7QN, ☎ (020) 7618 7000, *restaurants@great-eastern-hotel.co.uk, Fax (020) 7618 7001* – . MC AE ⓓ VISA 34 ART t

closed Saturday, Sunday and Bank Holidays – **Meals** 28.00/45.00 and a la carte 32.50/52.50 ♀.

◆ Vast columns, ornate plasterwork and a striking glass dome feature in this imposing dining room. Polished and attentive service of an elaborate and modern menu.

Rhodes Twenty Four, 24th floor, Tower 42, 25 Old Broad St, EC2N 1HQ, ☎ (020) 7887 7703, *reservations@rhodes24.co.uk, Fax (020) 7877 7725,* London – . MC AE ⓓ VISA 34 ART v

closed Christmas-New Year, Saturday, Sunday and Bank Holidays – **Meals** a la carte 25.00/40.00 ♀.

◆ Modern restaurant on the 24th floor of the former Natwest building with panoramic views of the city. Extensive menu of classic British dishes. Attentive service.

Whites, 1 New Street Sq, EC4A 3BF, ☎ (020) 7583 1313, *sales@wslrestaurants.co.uk, Fax (020) 7353 1662* – . MC AE ⓓ VISA JCB 27 NU u

closed Saturday, Sunday and Bank Holidays – **Meals** 34.00 (dinner) and a la carte 34.00/42.50 ♀.

◆ Up a spiral staircase to this first floor open plan restaurant with linen-clad tables, chairs and banquettes. Very busy at lunch time. Good sized classical menu.

XXX **Coq d'Argent,** No.1 Poultry, EC2R 8EJ, ✆ (020) 7395 5000, *Fax (020) 7395 5050,* – |‡| ▤. MC AE ⓓ VISA 33AQU c
closed Saturday lunch and Sunday dinner – **Meals** - French - (booking essential) 25.00 (lunch) and a la carte 29.50/41.00 ♀.
◆ Take the dedicated lift to the top of this modern office block. Tables on the rooftop terrace have city views ; busy bar. Gallic menus highlighted by popular shellfish dishes.

XXX **Tatsuso,** 32 Broadgate Circle, EC2M 2QS, ✆ (020) 7638 5863, *Fax (020) 7638 5864* – ▤. MC AE ⓓ VISA JCB 34 ART u
closed Christmas-New Year, Saturday, Sunday and Bank Holidays – **Meals** - Japanese - (booking essential) 38.00/97.00 and a la carte 50.00/100.00 **s.**.
◆ Dine in the busy teppan-yaki bar or in the more formal restaurant. Approachable staff in traditional costume provide attentive service of authentic and precise dishes.

XXX ✿ **1 Lombard Street (Restaurant),** 1 Lombard St, EC3V 9AA, ✆ (020) 7929 6611, *hb@1lombardstreet.com, Fax (020) 7929 6622* – ▤. MC AE ⓓ VISA JCB
closed Saturday, Sunday and Bank Holidays – **Meals** (lunch booking essential) 32.00/34.00 and a la carte ♀. 33AQU r
◆ A haven of tranquillity behind the forever busy brasserie. Former bank provides the modern and very comfortable surroundings in which to savour the accomplished cuisine.
Spec. Carpaccio of tuna with Oriental spices, ginger and lime vinaigrette. Fillet of lamb, tomato and mint velouté. Strawberries in Sauternes with black pepper, crème fraîche sorbet.

XXX **Prism,** 147 Leadenhall, EC3V 4QT, ✆ (020) 7256 3875, *prism@harveynichols.co.uk, Fax (020) 7256 3876* – ▤. MC AE ⓓ VISA 34ARU u
closed 24 December-5 January, Saturday and Sunday – **Meals** 25.00 (dinner) and a la carte 34.00/41.00 ♀.
◆ Enormous Corinthian pillars and a busy bar feature in this capacious and modern restaurant. Efficient service of an eclectic menu. Quieter tables in covered courtyard.

XXX **Bonds** (at Threadneedles H.), 5 Threadneedle St, EC2R 8AY, ✆ (020) 7657 8088, *bonds@theetongroup.com, Fax (020) 7657 8089* – ▤. MC AE ⓓ VISA JCB 34ARU y
closed Saturday, Sunday and Bank Holidays – **Meals** a la carte 33.95/46.00 ♀.
◆ Modern interior juxtaposed with the grandeur of a listed city building. Vast dining room with high ceiling and tall pillars. Attentive service of hearty, contemporary food.

XX ✿ **Club Gascon** (Aussignac), 57 West Smithfield, EC1A 9DS, ✆ (020) 7796 0600, *Fax (020) 7796 0601* – ▤. MC AE VISA 33 APT z
closed 23 December-3 January, Saturday lunch, Sunday and Bank Holidays – **Meals** - French (Gascony specialities) - (booking essential) 35.00/55.00 and a la carte 27.00/45.50 ♀.
◆ Intimate and rustic restaurant on the edge of Smithfield Market. Specialises in both the food and wines of Southwest France. Renowned for the foie gras tasting dishes.
Spec. Variations of duck, creamed caviar and sardine sorbet. Glazed veal sweetbreads, rosemary and mousserons. Lamb fritto, spicy vegetables.

XX **Boisdale of Bishopgate,** Swedland Court, 202 Bishopgate, EC2M 4NR, ✆ (020) 7283 1763, *info@boisdale-city.co.uk, Fax (020) 7283 1664* – ▤. MC AE VISA
closed 25 December-2 January, Saturday, Sunday and Bank Holidays – **Meals** - Scottish - a la carte 22.95/40.00 ♀. 34 ART a
◆ Through ground floor bar, serving oysters and champagne, to brick vaulted basement with red and tartan décor. Menu featuring Scottish produce. Live jazz most evenings.

XX **Searcy's,** Barbican Centre, Level 2, Silk St, EC2Y 8DS, ✆ (020) 7588 3008, *searcys@barbican.org.uk, Fax (028) 7382 7247* – ▤. MC AE VISA 33 AQT n
closed Saturday lunch and Sunday – **Meals** 22.00/32.00 ♀.
◆ Stylish modern surroundings, smooth effective service and seasonal modern British cooking. Unique location ideal for visitors to Barbican's multi-arts events.

XX **Kasturi,** 57 Aldgate High St, EC3N 1AL, ✆ (020) 7480 7402, *reservation@kasturi-restaurant.co.uk, Fax (020) 7702 0256* – ▤. MC AE VISA 34ASU a
closed 24 December-1 January, Saturday lunch, Sunday and Bank Holidays – **Meals** - Indian - a la carte 17.65/23.90.
◆ Spacious wooden floored restaurant enhanced by mirrors ; modern art on walls. Good service. Varied menu with original and authentic dishes.

XX **Imperial City,** Royal Exchange, Cornhill, EC3V 3LL, ✆ (020) 7626 3437, *enquiries@orgplc.co.uk, Fax (020) 7338 0125* – ▤. MC AE ⓓ VISA 34ARU a
closed 25-26 December, Saturday, Sunday and Bank Holidays – **Meals** - Chinese - 17.00/32.95 and a la carte 18.00/29.50 ♀.
◆ Vaulted basement restaurant with large water feature ; originally Royal Exchange wine cellars. Smart, friendly service of an authentic menu covering all regions of China.

XX **Chamberlain's,** 23-25 Leadenhall Market, EC3V 1LR, ✆ (020) 7648 8690, *info@chamberlains.org, Fax (020) 7648 8691* – MC AE ⓓ VISA 34ARU v
closed Christmas, Saturday, Sunday and Bank Holidays – **Meals** - Seafood - 15.95 (dinner) and a la carte 25.95/39.45 ♀.
◆ Bright, modern restaurant in ornate Victorian indoor market. Top quality seafood from fish and chips to mousse of lobster. There's even a fish tank in the lavatories !

HAMMERSMITH AND FULHAM

Fulham – ✉ SW6.

London Putney Bridge Travel Inn Capital, 3 Putney Bridge Approach, SW6 3JD, ✆ (020) 7471 8300, *Fax (020) 7471 8315* – |$|, ⇔ rm, ▤ rest, TV ♿. MC AE ⓓ VISA.
Meals (grill rest.) (dinner only) – **154 rm** 74.95.
◆ A longer name for a larger lodge. Converted office block offering clean, well-priced accommodation. All rooms have sofa beds and large worktops.

Blue Elephant, 4-6 Fulham Broadway, SW6 1AA, ✆ (020) 7385 6595, *london@blueelephant.com, Fax (020) 7386 7665* – ▤. MC AE ⓓ VISA
closed 24-26 December, 1 January and Saturday lunch – **Meals** - Thai - (booking essential) 15.00/33.00 and a la carte 20.50/43.50.
◆ Elaborately ornate, unrestrained décor : fountains, bridges, orchids and ponds with carp. Authentic Thai food served by attentive staff in national costumes.

Mao Tai, 58 New Kings Rd, Parsons Green, SW6 4LS, ✆ (020) 7731 2520, *info@maotai.co.uk, Fax (020) 7471 8994* – ▤. MC AE ⓓ VISA
closed 25-26 December – **Meals** - Chinese (Szechuan) - 12.50/24.70 and a la carte 25.05/38.20 ♀.
◆ A light and modern interior with wood flooring and framed artwork with an eastern theme. Well organised service. Chinese cuisine with Szechuan specialities.

Zinc, Fulham Island, 1 Farm Lane, SW6 1BE, ✆ (020) 7386 2250, *Fax (020) 7386 2260*, – ▤. MC AE ⓓ VISA
closed 25-26 December – **Meals** 15.00 (lunch) and a la carte 23.50/30.50 ♀.
◆ Bright modern bar ; informal chic restaurant. Grills, seafood and modern international fare. No booking so arrive early for a table on the canopied and heated terrace.

The Salisbury Tavern, 21 Sherbrooke Rd, SW6 7HX, ✆ (020) 7381 4005, *thesalisburytavern@longshotplc.com, Fax (020) 7381 1002* – ▤. MC AE VISA JCB
closed 25 December – **Meals** (live jazz Monday evening) 17.50 (lunch) and a la carte 21.40/26.70 ♀.
◆ Its residential location attracts a local crowd to the stylish bar. Separate, and equally à la mode, dining room with pleasant young staff. Wide ranging traditional menu.

Hammersmith *Gtr London* – ✉ *W6.*

River Café (Ruth Rogers/Rose Gray), Thames Wharf, Rainville Rd, W6 9HA, ✆ (020) 7386 4200, *info@rivercafe.co.uk, Fax (020) 7386 4201*, – MC AE ⓓ VISA
closed Christmas-New Year, Sunday dinner and Bank Holidays – **Meals** - Italian - (booking essential) a la carte 41.00/54.00 ♀.
◆ Warehouse conversion with full length windows on one side, open plan kitchen the other. Canteen-style atmosphere. Accomplished rustic Italian cooking, uses the finest produce.
Spec. Pasta parcels with roast pigeon, pork and pancetta. Wood-roasted turbot with capers and marjoram. Lemon and pine nut cake.

Snows on the Green, 166 Shepherd's Bush Rd, Brook Green, W6 7PB, ✆ (020) 7603 2142, *sebastian@snowsonthegreen.freeserve.co.uk, Fax (020) 7602 7553* – ▤. MC AE ⓓ VISA
closed 24-28 December, last 2 weeks August, Saturday lunch, Sunday and Bank Holiday Mondays – **Meals** 12.50/16.50 (lunch) and a la carte 22.00/28.00 ♀.
◆ Name refers to the chef patron, not the inclement weather found in west London. Mediterranean influenced decoration matched by the style of the cooking.

The Brackenbury, 129-131 Brackenbury Rd, W6 0BQ, ✆ (020) 8748 0107, *Fax (020) 8741 0905*, – MC AE VISA
closed Easter, 25-26 December, 1 January, Saturday lunch and Sunday dinner – **Meals** 15.00 (lunch) and a la carte 21.00/27.50 **s.** ♀.
◆ The closely set wooden tables, pavement terrace and relaxed service add to the cosy, neighbourhood feel. Cooking is equally unfussy ; modern yet robust.

Azou, 375 King St, W6 9NJ, ✆ (020) 8536 7266, *azourestaurant@artserve.net, Fax (020) 8748 1009* – ▤. MC ⓓ VISA
closed lunch Saturday and Sunday and Bank Holidays – **Meals** - North African - (lunch booking essential) a la carte 16.40/23.50.
◆ The North African theme is not confined to the menu ; the room is decorated with hanging lanterns, screens and assorted knick-knacks. Friendly service and well priced dishes.

Anglesea Arms, 35 Wingate Rd, W6 0UR, ✆ (020) 8749 1291, *Fax (020) 8749 1254*, – MC VISA
closed 1 week Christmas and 1 January – **Meals** (bookings not accepted) 12.95 (lunch) and a la carte 14.95/21.95 ♀.
◆ The laid-back atmosphere and local feel make this pub a popular venue. Worth arriving early as bookings are not taken. Modern cooking from blackboard menu.

Olympia *Gtr London* - ✉ *W14.*

XX **Cotto,** 44 Blythe Rd, W14 0HA, ✆ (020) 7602 9333, *bookings@cottorestaurant.co.uk, Fax (020) 7602 5003* – ▤. MC AE VISA JCB
closed 1 week Christmas, Saturday lunch, Sunday and Bank Holidays – **Meals** 15.00/18.00 ♀.
◆ On two floors, with vivid abstract paintings on white walls, chrome-framed chairs and music. Efficient service from black-clad staff. Modern cooking with some originality.

Shepherd's Bush - ✉ *W14.*

K West, Richmond Way, W14 0AX, ✆ (020) 7674 1000, *Fax (020) 7674 1050,* – ▤ TV & – 60. MC AE VISA.
Meals a la carte 27.00/41.00 ♀ – 18.00 – **222 rm** 276.00/411.25.
◆ Former BBC offices, the interior now decorated in smart, contemporary style. Bedrooms in understated modern style, deluxe rooms with work desks and DVD and CD facilities.

XX **Chez Moi,** 23 Richmond Way, W14 0AS, ✆ (020) 7602 6004, *chezmoirest@hotmail.com, Fax (020) 7602 8147* – MC AE VISA
closed Saturday lunch, Sunday dinner and Bank Holidays – **Meals** - French - 12.50/17.50 (lunch) a la carte 22.50/31.50 ♀.
◆ Friendly neighbourhood restaurant with window onto garden. Red and black décor. Classic French menu of popular traditional dishes.

Havelock Tavern, 57 Masbro Rd, W14 0LS, ✆ (020) 7603 5374, *Fax (020) 7602 1163,* – ▤
closed 22-26 December – **Meals** (bookings not accepted) a la carte approx. 19.50/23.50 **s.** ♀.
◆ Typical new wave London pub where the kitchen produces generously portioned modern food. Pine tables and chairs, and a large central bar. Privately owned.

ISLINGTON *Gtr London.*

Archway - ✉ *N19.*

X **The Parsee,** 34 Highgate Hill, N19 5NL, ✆ (020) 7272 9091, *dining@theparsee.co.uk, Fax (020) 7687 1139* – ▤. MC AE VISA JCB
closed 25 December-1 January and Sunday – **Meals** - Indian (Parsee) - (dinner only) a la carte 19.40/22.70 ♀.
◆ Two brightly painted rooms, one non smoking and featuring a painting of a Parsee Angel. Good value, interesting, carefully spiced cuisine, Persian and Indian in inspiration.

St John's, 91 Junction Rd, N19 5QU, ✆ (020) 7272 1587, *stjohnsarchway@virgin.net, Fax (020) 7687 2247* – MC AE VISA
closed 25-26 December and Monday lunch – **Meals** a la carte 15.50/25.00 ♀.
◆ Busy front bar enjoys a lively atmosphere ; dining room in a large rear room. Log fire at one end, open hatch into kitchen the other. Blackboard menu ; rustic cooking.

Barnsbury - ✉ *N1.*

XX **Morgan M,** 489 Liverpool Rd, N7 8NS, ✆ (020) 7609 3560, *Fax (020) 8292 5699* – ▤. MC VISA
closed 24-30 December, Saturday lunch, Sunday dinner and Monday – **Meals** 19.50/27.50 ♀.
◆ Simple restaurant in a converted pub. Smartly-laid tables complemented by formal service. Modern dishes based on classical French combinations.

X **The Dining Room,** 169 Hemingford Rd, N1 1DA, ✆ (020) 7609 3009, – MC VISA
closed 1 week Christmas, last 2 weeks August, Sunday dinner and Monday – **Meals** (dinner only and Sunday lunch) a la carte 20.50/24.00 ♀.
◆ Simple, attractive and cosy neighbourhood restaurant with fawn colours and mirrors. Open hatch into kitchen. Asian-influenced cooking at a fair price.

Canonbury *Gtr London* - ✉ *N1.*

Centuria, 100 St Paul's Rd, N1 2QP, ✆ (020) 7704 2345, *Fax (020) 7704 2204* – MC VISA
closed lunch Monday-Friday – **Meals** a la carte 20.25/23.50 ♀.
◆ Large pub in a residential area, with the dining room separate from the busy bar. Open-plan kitchen produces a modern menu, with influences ranging from Italy to Morocco.

Clerkenwell - ✉ *EC1.*

The Rookery without rest., 12 Peters Lane, Cowcross St, EC1M 6DS, ✆ (020) 7336 0931, *reservations@rookery.co.uk, Fax (020) 7336 0932* – TV. MC AE VISA JCB.
closed 24-26 December – 9.75 **32 rm** 252.60/323.10, 1 suite.
◆ A row of charmingly restored 18C houses. Wood panelling, stone-flagged flooring, open fires and antique furniture. Highly individual bedrooms, with Victorian bathrooms.

XX **Smiths of Smithfield,** Top Floor, 67-77 Charterhouse St, EC1M 6HJ, ☎ (020) 7251 7950, *smiths@smithfield.co.uk, Fax (020) 7236 5666,* ←, 🏠 – |‡|, ▤. MC AE ⓞ VISA
closed 25-26 December and 1 January – **Meals** a la carte 19.25/24.25 ♀ – ***The Dining Room*** : **Meals** *(closed Saturday lunch, Sunday and Bank Holidays)* a la carte 20.75/25.25 ♀.
♦ On three floors where the higher you go the more formal it becomes. Busy, bustling atmosphere and modern menu. Good views of the market from the top floor terrace. The Dining Room with mirrors and dark blue walls. 33 AOT s

X **St John,** 26 St John St, EC1M 4AY, ☎ (020) 7251 0848, *reservations@stjohnrestaurant.com, Fax (020) 7251 4090* – ▤. MC AE ⓞ VISA JCB 33 APT c
closed Christmas-New Year, Easter, Saturday lunch and Sunday – **Meals** a la carte 24.90/28.00 ♀.
♦ Deservedly busy converted 19C former smokehouse. Popular bar, simple comforts. Menu specialises in offal and an original mix of traditional and rediscovered English dishes.

Finsbury – ✉ *EC1.*

XX **The Clerkenwell Dining Room,** 69-73 St John St, EC1M 4AN, ☎ (020) 7253 9000, *zak@theclerkenwell.com, Fax (020) 7253 3322* – ▤. MC AE ⓞ VISA JCB
closed 25-26 December, 1 January, Saturday lunch and Sunday – **Meals** 16.00 (lunch) and a la carte 26.75/30.75 ♀.
♦ Former pub, now a stylish modern restaurant with etched glass façade. Three adjoining dining areas with bar provide setting for contemporary British cooking.

X **Café Lazeez City,** 88 St John St, EC1M 4EH, ☎ (020) 7253 2224, *clerkenwell@cafelazeez.com, Fax (020) 7253 2112* – ▤. MC AE ⓞ VISA
closed Saturday lunch, Sunday and Bank Holidays – **Meals** - North Indian - a la carte approx. 18.00 ☺.
♦ Past the busy bar into this modern Indian restaurant. Has a certain warehouse feel, with a high ceiling and wood flooring. North Indian cooking from the open-plan kitchen.

X **Quality Chop House,** 94 Farringdon Rd, EC1R 3EA, ☎ (020) 7837 5093, *qualitychophouse@clara.co.uk, Fax (020) 7833 8748* – ⇌ ▤. MC AE VISA
closed 24 December-1 January and Saturday lunch – **Meals** a la carte 17.75/28.00.
♦ On the window is etched "Progressive working class caterers". This is borne out with the individual café-style booths and a menu ranging from jellied eels to caviar.

X **Moro,** 34-36 Exmouth Market, EC1R 4QE, ☎ (020) 7833 8336, *info@moro.co.uk, Fax (020) 7833 9338* – ▤. MC AE ⓞ VISA JCB
closed 2 weeks Christmas, Saturday lunch, Sunday and Bank Holidays – **Meals** (booking essential) a la carte 25.50/28.00 ☺ ♀.
♦ Daily changing menu an eclectic mix of Mediterranean, Moroccan and Spanish. Friendly T-shirted staff. Informal surroundings with bare tables and a large zinc bar.

🍺 **The Peasant,** 240 St John St, EC1V 4PH, ☎ (020) 7336 7726, *eat@thepeasant.co.uk, Fax (020) 7490 1089* – MC AE VISA
closed 1 week after Christmas, Saturday lunch and Sunday – **Meals** (booking essential) a la carte 21.00/27.00 ♀.
♦ Large, busy pub with half of the ground floor given over as a bar. Dining continues in the high-ceilinged room upstairs. Robust and rustic cooking with generous portions.

Highbury – ✉ *N5.*

X **Au Lac,** 82 Highbury Park, N5 2XE, ☎ (020) 7704 9187, *Fax (0207) 704 9187* – ▤. MC ⓞ VISA
closed lunch Saturday, Sunday and Bank Holidays – **Meals** - Vietnamese - 16.00 and a la carte 8.20/20.00.
♦ Cosy Vietnamese restaurant, with brightly coloured walls and painted fans. Large menus with authentic dishes usefully highlighted. Fresh flavours ; good value.

Islington *Gtr London* – ✉ *N1.*

🏨 **Hilton London Islington,** 53 Upper St, N1 0UY, ☎ (020) 7354 7700, *resislington@hilton.com, Fax (020) 7354 7711,* 🏠, Fa, ≘s – |‡|, ⇌ rm, ▤ TV ☎ ♿ – 🏛 35. MC AE ⓞ VISA JCB. ✂
Meals a la carte 22.90/31.65 **s.** ♀ – ☕ 16.00 – **178 rm** 186.80, 6 suites.
♦ Benefits from its location adjacent to the Business Design Centre. A purpose-built hotel with all bedrooms enjoying the appropriate creature comforts. Open-plan brasserie with small bar.

🏨 **Jurys Inn London,** 60 Pentonville Rd, N1 9LA, ☎ (020) 7282 5500, *jurysinnlondon@jurysdoyle.com, Fax (020) 7282 5511* – |‡|, ⇌ rm, ▤ TV ☎ ♿ – 🏛 55. MC AE ⓞ VISA. ✂
closed 24-26 December – **Meals** (bar lunch)/dinner 18.00 **s.** and a la carte – ☕ 8.50 – **229 rm** 104.00.
♦ A corporate group hotel with good local transport links. Large lobby leads off to the characterful Irish themed pub. Uniform-sized bedrooms, all well-equipped.

XX **Lola's,** The Mall, 359 Upper St, N1 0PD, ☎ (020) 7359 1932, *lolas@lolas.co.uk*, *Fax (020) 7359 2209* – ▤. MC AE ⓓ VISA
closed 25-26 December and 1 January – **Meals** 18.75 (lunch) and a la carte 27.75/37.00 ♀.
◆ On the first floor of a converted tram shed above the antique shops. Bright and airy, with glass ceiling and assorted artwork : an ideal setting to enjoy modern British dishes.

XX **Frederick's,** Camden Passage, N1 8EG, ☎ (020) 7359 2888, *eat@fredericks.co.uk*, *Fax (020) 7359 5173*, 🏡, 🌳 – ▤. MC AE VISA JCB
closed 24 December-2 January, Sunday and Bank Holidays – **Meals** 15.50 (lunch) and a la carte 23.50/34.50 ♀.
◆ Long-standing restaurant among the antique shops of Camden Passage. Attractive garden and al fresco dining ; main room with large, plant-filled conservatory.

XX **Almeida,** 30 Almeida St, N1 1AD, ☎ (020) 7354 4777, *oliviere@conran-restaurants.co.uk*, *Fax (020) 7354 2777* – ▤. MC AE ⓓ VISA JCB
closed 25-26 December and 1-2 January – **Meals** - French - 17.50 (lunch) and a la carte 19.50/37.50 ♀.
◆ Spacious, open plan restaurant with pleasant contemporary styling adjacent to Almeida Theatre. Large à la carte : a collection of classic French dishes.

XX **Metrogusto,** 13 Theberton St, N1 0QY, ☎ (020) 7226 9400, *Fax (020) 7226 9400* – ⅍ ▤. MC AE VISA JCB
closed Christmas, Bank Holidays and lunch Monday-Thursday – **Meals** - Italian - 18.50 (lunch) and a la carte 22.50/28.50 ♀.
◆ Stylish and smart with a contemporary feel. Dining in two rooms with striking modern art on the walls and a relaxed atmosphere. Modern, carefully prepared Italian food.

Drapers Arms, 44 Barnsbury St, N1 1ER, ☎ (020) 7619 0348, *Fax (020) 7619 0413*, 🏡 – MC VISA
closed 26-28 December, 1-2 January and Sunday dinner – **Meals** a la carte 18.50/29.00 ♀.
◆ Real presence to the the façade of this Georgian pub tucked away in a quiet residential area. Spacious modern interior where competent, contemporary dishes are served.

The Northgate, 113 Southgate Rd, N1 3JS, ☎ (020) 7359 7392, *Fax (020) 7359 7393*, 🏡 – MC VISA JCB
closed 24-26 December and 1 January – **Meals** (dinner only and lunch Saturday and Sunday) a la carte 20.00/25.00 ♀.
◆ Corner pub with wood flooring and modern art on display. Rear dining area with a large blackboard menu offering a cross section of internationally influenced modern dishes.

The Social, 33 Linton St, N1 7DU, ☎ (020) 7354 5809, *Fax (020) 7354 8087* – MC AE VISA JCB
closed 25-31 December and lunch Monday-Friday – **Meals** (booking essential) a la carte 15.50/25.00.
◆ The former Hanbury Arms has a youthful clientele attracted by the DJ and music in the bar. The open plan kitchen and restaurant serve from a modern, sensibly priced menu.

The Barnsbury, 209-211 Liverpool Rd, N1 1LX, ☎ (020) 7607 5519, *info@thebarnsbury.co.uk*, *Fax (020) 7607 3256*, 🏡 – MC VISA
closed 25-26 December and 1 January – **Meals** a la carte 17.50/26.45 ♀.
◆ Former public house with pine tables and chairs arranged round central counter bar ; art work for sale on the walls. Robust and hearty food in generous portions.

KENSINGTON and CHELSEA *(Royal Borough of)*.

Chelsea – ✉ *SW1/SW3/SW6/SW7/SW10.*

The Carlton Tower, Cadogan Pl, SW1X 9PY, ☎ (020) 7235 1234, *contact@carltontower.com*, *Fax (020) 7235 9129*, ≤, Ⅎ₆, ≘s, 🏊, 🌳, 🎾 – |♦|, ⅍ rm, ▤ TV ☎ ♿ 🚗 – 🎤 400. MC AE ⓓ VISA. ⅌ 37 AGX n
***Rib Room* : Meals** 26.00 (lunch) and a la carte 38.00/61.00 ♀ – ☕ 22.50 – **190 rm** 381.80, 30 suites.
◆ Imposing international hotel overlooking a leafy square. 'The Peak' health club is particularly well-equipped. Generously proportioned rooms have every conceivable facility. Rib Room restaurant has a clubby atmosphere.

Conrad London, Chelsea Harbour, SW10 0XG, ☎ (020) 7823 3000, *lonchrs@hilton.com*, *Fax (020) 7351 6525*, ≤, Ⅎ₆, ≘s, 🏊 – |♦|, ⅍ rm, ▤ TV ☎ ♿ 🚗 – 🎤 250. MC AE ⓓ VISA JCB
Meals (see ***Aquasia*** below) – ☕ 18.75, **160 suites** 229.00/259.00.
◆ Modern, all-suite hotel within an exclusive marina and retail development. Many of the spacious and well-appointed rooms have balconies and views across the Thames.

Sheraton Park Tower, 101 Knightsbridge, SW1X 7RN, (020) 7235 8050, *central.london.reservations@sheraton.com, Fax (020) 7235 8231*, ←, – |‡|, ✗ rm, ▤ TV ✆ & – 100. MC AE ◑ VISA JCB. 37 AGX t
Meals (see ***One-O-One*** below) – 20.75 – **258 rm** 446.50/470.00, 22 suites.
◆ Built in the 1970s in a unique cylindrical shape. Well-equipped bedrooms are all identical in size. Top floor executive rooms have commanding views of Hyde Park and City.

Capital, 22-24 Basil St, SW3 1AT, (020) 7589 5171, *reservations@capitalhotel.co.uk, Fax (020) 7225 0011* – |‡|, ✗ rm, ▤ TV ✆ – 25. MC AE ◑ VISA JCB 37 AFX a
Meals (booking essential) 28.50/55.00 ♀ – 16.50 – **48 rm** 223.25/440.00.
◆ Discreet and privately owned town house with distinct English charm. Individual, opulently decorated rooms with plenty of thoughtful touches. Elegant and intimate restaurant.
Spec. Seared tiger prawns, scallops and calamari. Pot-roast pigeon, potato and bacon galette, truffle jus. Apple consommé with liquorice ravioli and gingerbread.

The Cadogan, 75 Sloane St, SW1X 9SG, (020) 7235 7141, *info@cadogan.com, Fax (020) 7245 0994*, – |‡|, ✗ rm, ▤ rest, TV ✆ – 40. MC AE ◑ VISA JCB 37 AGY b
Meals *(closed Saturday lunch)* 18.90/29.50 **s.** ♀ – 16.50 – **61 rm** 170.30/346.60, 4 suites.
◆ A true English hotel retaining many Edwardian features : Oscar Wilde was arrested here ! Charming wood panelled drawing room. Smart bedrooms in a country house style. Discreet, cosy wood panelled restaurant.

Basil Street, 8 Basil St, SW3 1AH, (020) 7581 3311, *info@thebasil.com, Fax (020) 7581 3693* – |‡|, ✗ rm, TV ✆ – 30. MC AE ◑ VISA JCB.
Meals 22.00/27.00 **s.** – 16.50 – **80 rm** 170.30/240.80. 37 AGX d
◆ Classic English hotel in a pleasant residential road between Harrods and Harvey Nichols. Exclusive ladies only lounge. Traditionally furnished rooms with modern amenities. Dining room boasts rich style of a bygone era.

Draycott, 26 Cadogan Gdns, SW3 2RP, (020) 7730 6466, *reservations@draycotthotel.com, Fax (020) 7730 0236*, – |‡| ✗, ▤ rm, TV ✆. MC AE ◑ VISA
Meals (room service only) – 18.50 – **31 rm** 129.25/340.75, 4 suites. 37 AGY c
◆ Charming Victorian house in an exclusive residential area. Elegant sitting room overlooks the tranquil communal garden. Individually decorated rooms in a country house style.

Millennium Knightsbridge, 17-25 Sloane St, SW1X 9NU, (020) 7235 4377, *reservations.knightsbridge@mill-cop.com, Fax (020) 7235 3705* – |‡| ✗ ▤ TV ✆ & – 120. MC AE ◑ VISA JCB. 37 AGX r
Meals (see ***Mju*** below) – 19.00 – **218 rm** 270.25/329.00, 4 suites.
◆ Modern, corporate hotel in the heart of London's most fashionable shopping district. Executive bedrooms are well-appointed and equipped with the latest technology.

Franklin, 22-28 Egerton Gdns, SW3 2DB, (020) 7584 5533, *bookings@franklinhotel.co.uk, Fax (020) 7584 5449*, – |‡| ✗ ▤ TV ✆. MC AE ◑ VISA. 37 AEY e
Meals 29.50 (dinner) and a la carte 23.00/34.50 **s.** ♀ – 16.50 – **47 rm** 188.00/293.75.
◆ Attractive Victorian town house in an exclusive residential area. Charming drawing room overlooks a tranquil communal garden. Well-furnished rooms in a country house style.

Knightsbridge, 10 Beaufort Gdns, SW3 1PT, (020) 7584 6300, *knightsbridge@firmdale.com, Fax (020) 7584 6355* – |‡| ▤ TV ✆. MC AE VISA. 37 AFX s
Meals (room service only) – 14.50 – **44 rm** 170.30/300.00.
◆ Attractively furnished town house with a very stylish, discreet feel. Every bedroom is immaculately appointed and has an individuality of its own ; fine detailing throughout.

The London Outpost of the Carnegie Club without rest., 69 Cadogan Gdns, SW3 2RB, (020) 7589 7333, *info@londonoutpost.co.uk, Fax (020) 7581 4958*, – |‡| ✗ ▤ TV. MC AE ◑ VISA JCB 37 AGY r
16.95 – **11 rm** 188.00/317.25.
◆ Classic town house in a most fashionable area. Relaxed and comfy lounges full of English charm. Bedrooms, named after local artists and writers, full of thoughtful touches.

The Sloane, 29-31 Draycott Pl, SW3 2SH, (020) 7581 5757, *reservations@sloanehotel.com, Fax (020) 7584 1348* – |‡|, ✗ rm, ▤ TV ✆. MC AE ◑ VISA JCB. 37 AFY c
Meals (room service) – 12.00 – **22 rm** 193.80/293.70.
◆ Intimate and discreet Victorian town house with an attractive rooftop terrace. Individually styled and generally spacious rooms with antique furniture and rich fabrics.

Eleven Cadogan Gardens, 11 Cadogan Gdns, SW3 2RJ, (020) 7730 7000, *reservations@number-eleven.co.uk, Fax (020) 7730 5217*, , , – |‡| TV ✆. MC AE ◑ VISA JCB. 37 AGY u
Meals a la carte 21.50/31.50 – 13.00 – **55 rm** 145.00/295.00, 4 suites.
◆ Occupying four Victorian houses, one of London's first private town house hotels. Traditionally appointed bedrooms vary considerably in size. Genteel atmosphere.

Egerton House, 17-19 Egerton Terrace, SW3 2BX, (020) 7589 2412, *bookings@egertonhousehotel.co.uk, Fax (020) 7584 6540* – . MC AE VISA JCB. 37 AFY e
Meals (room service only) – 16.00 – **29 rm** 188.00/293.75.
◆ Stylish redbrick Victorian town house close to the exclusive shops. Relaxed drawing room popular for afternoon tea. Antique furnished and individually decorated rooms.

Beaufort without rest., 33 Beaufort Gdns, SW3 1PP, (020) 7584 5252, *enquiries@thebeaufort.co.uk, Fax (020) 7589 2834* – . MC AE VISA JCB. 37 AFX n
29 rm 182.00/305.50.
◆ English floral watercolours adorn the walls throughout this elegant Victorian town house. Modern and co-ordinated rooms. Tariff includes all drinks and continental breakfast.

Parkes without rest., 41 Beaufort Gdns, SW3 1PW, (020) 7581 9944, *reception@parkeshotel.com, Fax (020) 7581 1999* – . MC AE VISA JCB. 37 AFX x
10.00 – **19 rm** 229.00/282.00, 14 suites 381.00/487.00.
◆ Behind the portico entrance one finds a well-kept private hotel. The generally spacious and high ceilinged rooms are pleasantly decorated. Friendly and personally run.

Myhotel Chelsea, 35 Ixworth Pl, SW3 3QX, (020) 7225 7500, *mychelsea@myhotel.co.uk, Fax (020) 7225 7555,* – – 60. MC AE VISA JCB 37 AFY z
Meals a la carte 21.00/25.00 – 16.00 – **43 rm** 205.60/240.87, 2 suites.
◆ Restored Victorian property in a fairly quiet and smart side street. Conservatory breakfast room. Modern and well-equipped rooms are ideal for the corporate traveller.

Sydney House, 9-11 Sydney St, SW3 6PU, (020) 7376 7711, *info@sydneyhousechelsea.com, Fax (020) 7376 4233* – . MC AE VISA JCB. 36 ADY s
Meals (room service only) – 12.00 – **21 rm** 175.00/250.00.
◆ Two usefully located Victorian town houses. Basement breakfast room ; small lounge near entrance. Compact contemporary style bedrooms ; one on top floor with own roof terrace.

57 Pont Street without rest., 57 Pont St, SW1X 0BD, (020) 7590 1090, *no57@no57.com, Fax (020) 7590 1099* – – 30. MC AE VISA JCB. 37 AFY a
closed 24 December-1 January – 10.00 – **20 rm** 146.00/264.00.
◆ Small, friendly, modern townhouse with discreet plaque at the end of Pont Street. Basement breakfast room and sitting room with deep brown suede chairs. Snug, modern rooms.

L'Hotel, 28 Basil St, SW3 1AS, (020) 7589 6286, *reservations@lhotel.co.uk, Fax (020) 7823 7826* – , rest, . MC AE VISA JCB. 37 AFX b
Le Metro **: Meals** *(closed Sunday dinner)* a la carte 19.50/21.50 – **12 rm** 116.30/188.00.
◆ Discreet town house a short walk from Harrods. Wooden shutters, pine furniture and stencilled walls provide a subtle rural theme. Well-appointed, comfy and informally run. Basement café dining.

XXXX ✿✿✿ **Gordon Ramsay,** 68-69 Royal Hospital Rd, SW3 4HP, (020) 7352 4441, *Fax (020) 7352 3334* – . MC AE VISA JCB 37 AFZ c
closed 2 week Christmas, Saturday, Sunday and Bank Holidays – **Meals** (booking essential) 35.00/65.00 .
◆ Elegant and sophisticated room. The eponymous chef creates some of Britain's finest, classically inspired cooking. Detailed and attentive service. Book one month in advance.
Spec. Caramelised pig's trotter with veal sweetbreads and celeriac rémoulade. Fillet of sea bass, crushed new potatoes and sautéed langoustine. Chocolate and hazelnut soufflé, milk ice cream.

XXX ✿ **Aubergine,** 11 Park Walk, SW10 0AJ, (020) 7352 3449, *Fax (020) 7351 1770* – . MC AE VISA 36 ACZ r
closed 24 December-2 January, Saturday lunch, Sunday and Bank Holidays – **Meals** (booking essential) 32.00/50.00 .
◆ Intimate, refined restaurant where the keen staff provide well drilled service. French influenced menu uses top quality ingredients with skill and flair. Extensive wine list.
Spec. Galette of pig's head with langoustine. Veal sweetbread with artichoke, lemon and mustard cream. Warm cherries with beignet, vanilla ice cream.

XXX ✿ **Tom Aikens,** 43 Elystan St, SW3 3NT, (020) 7584 2003, *info@tomaikens.co.uk, Fax (020) 7584 2001* – . MC AE VISA JCB 37 AFY n
closed 2 weeks August, 2 weeks Christmas-New Year, Saturday, Sunday and Bank Holidays – **Meals** 24.50/49.00 .
◆ Smart restaurant ; minimalist style decor with chic tableware. Highly original menu of individual and inventive dishes ; smooth service. Book one month in advance.
Spec. Rabbit confit with carrot and Sauternes jelly. John Dory with langoustine beignet and apricot purée. Caramel parfait with almond mousse.

XXX **Drones,** 1 Pont St, SW1X 9EJ, ✆ (020) 7235 9555, *sales@whitestarline.org.uk, Fax (020) 7235 9566* – ▤. MC AE ⊕ VISA 37 AGX c
closed 1 January, dinner 25 December, Saturday lunch and Sunday dinner – **Meals** 17.95 (lunch) and a la carte 24.50/43.50 ♀.
◆ Smart exterior with etched plate-glass window. L-shaped interior with moody film star photos on walls. French and classically inspired tone to dishes.

XXX **Bibendum,** Michelin House, 81 Fulham Rd, SW3 6RD, ✆ (020) 7581 5817, *manager@bibendum.co.uk, Fax (020) 7823 7925* – ▤. MC AE ⊕ VISA 37 AEY s
closed 25-26 December – **Meals** 25.00 (lunch) and dinner a la carte 32.50/46.50 ♀.
◆ A fine example of Art Nouveau architecture ; a London landmark. 1st floor restaurant with striking stained glass 'Michelin Man'. Attentive service of modern British cooking.

XXX **Floriana,** 15 Beauchamp Pl, SW3 1NQ, ✆ (020) 7838 1500, *Fax (020) 7584 1464* – ▤. MC AE ⊕ VISA JCB 37 AFX d
closed 25-26 December, 1 January, Easter and Sunday – **Meals** - Italian - 19.50 (lunch) and a la carte 19.50/35.00 ♀.
◆ Behind the busy bar is a refined and contemporary restaurant. Approachable service of an elaborate, modern Italian menu. 1st floor room, with atrium roof, is more relaxing.

XXX **Fifth Floor** (at Harvey Nichols), Knightsbridge, SW1X 7RJ, ✆ (020) 7235 5250, *Fax (020) 7235 7856* – |‡| ▤. MC AE ⊕ VISA 37 AGX s
closed 25-26 December, 1 January and Sunday dinner – **Meals** 25.00 (lunch) and dinner a la carte 29.00/42.50 ♀.
◆ Wander through this famous store or take the lift straight to the top floor. Chic restaurant with comfy tub chairs overlooks a busy bar and the impressive delicatessen.

XXX **One-O-One** (at Sheraton Park Tower H.), William St, SW1X 7RN, ✆ (020) 7290 7101, *Fax (020) 7235 6196* – ▤. MC AE ⊕ VISA JCB 37 AGX t
Meals - Seafood - 25.00 (lunch) and a la carte 39.50/55.50 ♀.
◆ Modern and very comfortable restaurant overlooking Knightsbridge decorated in cool blue tones. Predominantly seafood menu offers traditional and more adventurous dishes.

XXX **Toto's,** Walton House, Walton St, SW3 2JH, ✆ (020) 7589 0075, *Fax (020) 7581 9668* – MC AE ⊕ VISA JCB 37 AFY x
closed 3 days Christmas – **Meals** - Italian - a la carte 26.50/46.00 ♀.
◆ Converted mews house in tucked away location. Ornately decorated and bright restaurant with additional balcony area. Professional service of an extensive Italian menu.

XXX **Chutney Mary,** 535 King's Rd, SW10 0SZ, ✆ (020) 7351 3113, *mw@realindianfood.com, Fax (020) 7351 7694* – ▤. MC AE ⊕ VISA
Meals - Indian - (dinner only and lunch Saturday and Sunday) 16.50 (lunch) and a la carte 23.00/44.50 ♀.
◆ Striking murals of British India adorn the walls of this forever popular restaurant. Extensive menu of specialities from all corners of India. Complementary wine list.

XX **Aquasia** (at Conrad London H.), Chelsea Harbour, SW10 0XG, ✆ (020) 7300 8443, *Fax (020) 7351 6525,* ≤, 🍽 – ▤ P. MC AE ⊕ VISA JCB
closed Saturday lunch and Sunday dinner – **Meals** a la carte 25.00/40.00 ♀.
◆ Modern restaurant located within Conrad International hotel. Views over Chelsea Harbour. Cuisine captures the essence of the Mediterranean and Asia.

XX **Bluebird,** 350 King's Rd, SW3 5UU, ✆ (020) 7559 1000, *Fax (020) 7559 1111* – |‡| ▤. MC AE ⊕ VISA
Meals a la carte 26.00/43.75 🎭 ♀.
◆ A foodstore, café and homeware shop also feature at this impressive skylit restaurant. Much of the modern British food is cooked in wood-fired ovens. Lively atmosphere.

XX **Poissonnerie de l'Avenue,** 82 Sloane Ave, SW3 3DZ, ✆ (020) 7589 2457, *info@poissonnerie.co.uk, Fax (020) 7581 3360* – ▤. MC AE ⊕ VISA 37 AFY u
closed dinner 24 December-3 January, Sunday and Bank Holidays – **Meals** - French Seafood - 22.00 (lunch) and a la carte 26.00/32.00.
◆ Long-established and under the same ownership since 1965. Spacious and traditional French restaurant offering an extensive seafood menu. An institution favoured by locals.

XX **English Garden,** 10 Lincoln St, SW3 2TS, ✆ (020) 7584 7272, *Fax (020) 7584 1961* – ▤. MC AE ⊕ VISA JCB 37 AFY y
closed Monday lunch – **Meals** 19.50/30.00 ♀.
◆ Attractive mid-19C house in a stylish residential area. Relaxed restaurant with British slate covered walls. Conservatory to the rear. Detailed service, modern cooking.

XX **Racine,** 239 Brompton Rd, SW3 2EP, ✆ (020) 7584 4477, *Fax (020) 7584 4900* – ▤. MC AE VISA 37 AEY t
closed 25-26 December – **Meals** - French - 16.50 (lunch) and a la carte 21.25/34.75 🎭 ♀.
◆ Dark leather banquettes, large mirrors and wood floors create the atmosphere of a genuine Parisienne brasserie. Good value, well crafted, regional French fare.

XX **Mao Tai,** 96 Draycott Ave, SW3 3AD, ℘ (020) 7225 2500, *info@maotai.co.uk, Fax (020) 7225 1965* – ▤. MC AE Diners VISA 37 AFY f
closed 24-25 December – **Meals** - Chinese (Szechuan) - 12.50/24.70 and a la carte 25.05/38.20 Ÿ.
◆ Spacious Chinese restaurant in the heart of Chelsea. Modern, stylish décor with distinctive Eastern feel. Unique Szechuan menus, boasting some highly original dishes.

XX **Chez Max,** 3 Yeoman's Row, SW3 2AL, ℘ (020) 7590 9999, *sales@whitestarline.org.uk, Fax (020) 7590 9900* – ▤. MC AE Diners VISA 37 AFX c
closed 25-26 December – **Meals** - French - 17.50 and a la carte 21.50/32.50 Ÿ.
◆ Warm welcome guaranteed : colourful posters and deep burgundy walls embrace diners. Competent Gallic staff serve well priced, assured dishes from the classic French repertoire.

XX **The Painted Heron,** 112 Cheyne Walk, SW10 0DJ, ℘ (020) 7351 5232, *Fax (020) 7351 5313* – ▤. MC VISA
closed 25-26 December and Saturday lunch – **Meals** - Indian - a la carte 23.00/26.50 Ÿ.
◆ Just off Cheyne Walk near the river. Contemporary in style, exemplified by oil paintings. Modern Indian dishes with eclectic ingredients drawn from around the sub-continent.

XX **Pellicano,** 19-21 Elystan St, SW3 3NT, ℘ (020) 7589 3718, *pellicanor@aol.com, Fax (020) 7584 1789,* (terrace) – ▤. MC AE Diners VISA JCB 37 AFY d
closed 24 December-2 January and 9-13 April – **Meals** - Italian - 15.00 (lunch) and a la carte 20.00/32.50 Ÿ.
◆ Attractive neighbourhood restaurant with dark blue canopy over pavement terrace. Contemporary interior with wood floors. Tasty and interesting modern Italian dishes.

XX **Mju** (at Millennium Knightsbridge H.), 17-25 Sloane St, SW1X 9NU, ℘ (020) 7201 6330, *mju@mill-cop.com, Fax (020) 7235 3705* – (private dining) ▤. MC AE Diners VISA JCB 37 AGX r
closed Sunday and Bank Holidays – **Meals** 24.95/40.00 and dinner a la carte 19.00/36.00 Ÿ.
◆ On the first floor of the Millennium Knightsbridge Hotel, a large glass ceiling provides plenty of light. Original mix of flavours underpinned by a classical French base.

XX **Brasserie St Quentin,** 243 Brompton Rd, SW3 2EP, ℘ (020) 7589 8005, *reservations@brasseriestquentin.co.uk, Fax (020) 7584 6064* – ▤. MC AE Diners VISA 37 AEY a
closed 1 week Christmas and 2 weeks August – **Meals** 16.50 (lunch) and a la carte 18.95/36.85 (wine) Ÿ.
◆ Authentic Parisien brasserie, with rows of closely set tables, banquettes and ornate chandeliers. Attentive service and a lively atmosphere. French classics aplenty.

XX **Benihana,** 77 King's Rd, SW3 4NX, ℘ (020) 7376 7799, *benihana@dircon.co.uk, Fax (020) 7376 7377* – ▤. MC AE Diners VISA 37 AFZ e
closed 25 December – **Meals** - Japanese (Teppan-Yaki) - 19.25/25.50.
◆ Vast basement restaurant. Be prepared to share your table with other guests ; teppanyakis sit up to eight. Theatrical preparation and service of modern Japanese cooking.

XX **Caraffini,** 61-63 Lower Sloane St, SW1W 8DH, ℘ (020) 7259 0235, *info@caraffini.co.uk, Fax (020) 7259 0236,* (terrace) – ▤. MC AE VISA 37 AGZ a
closed Sunday and Bank Holidays – **Meals** - Italian - a la carte 24.10/32.95.
◆ The omnipresent and ebullient owner oversees the friendly service in this attractive neighbourhood restaurant. Authentic and robust Italian cooking ; informal atmosphere.

XX **Vama,** 438 King's Rd, SW10 0LJ, ℘ (020) 7351 4118, *andy@vama.co.uk, Fax (020) 7565 8501* – MC AE Diners VISA JCB
closed 25-26 December and 1 January – **Meals** - Indian - (booking essential) 13.00/20.00 and a la carte 19.95/35.20 Ÿ.
◆ Adorned with traditional artefacts, a modern and bright restaurant. Keen and eager service of an elaborate and seasonally changing menu of Northwest Indian specialities.

XX **Le Colombier,** 145 Dovehouse St, SW3 6LB, ℘ (020) 7351 1155, *Fax (020) 7351 0077,* (terrace) – MC AE VISA 36 ADZ e
Meals - French - 17.50 (lunch) and a la carte 20.20/37.90 (wine) Ÿ.
◆ Proudly Gallic corner restaurant in an affluent residential area. Attractive enclosed terrace. Bright and cheerful surroundings and service of traditional French cooking.

XX **The Collection,** 264 Brompton Rd, SW3 2AS, ℘ (020) 7225 1212, *office@thecollection.co.uk, Fax (020) 7225 1050* – ▤. MC AE VISA 37 AEY v
closed 25 December and Bank Holidays – **Meals** (dinner only and lunch Saturday and Sunday) 35.00 and a la carte Ÿ.
◆ Beyond the impressive catwalk entrance one will find a chic bar and a vast split level, lively restaurant. The eclectic and global modern menu is enjoyed by the young crowd.

XX **Eight over Eight,** 392 King's Rd, SW3 5UZ, ℘ (020) 7349 9934, *Fax (020) 7351 5157* – ▤. MC AE Diners VISA JCB
closed Christmas – **Meals** - South East Asian - a la carte 22.00/26.50 Ÿ.
◆ Lively modern restaurant in converted theatre pub ; bar in front and dining room at rear. Enthusiastic service. Eclectic Asian menu : strong flavours and unusual combinations.

XX **Good Earth,** 233 Brompton Rd, SW3 2EP, ☎ (020) 7584 3658, *goodearthgroup@aol.com, Fax (020) 7823 8769* – ▤. MC AE VISA JCB 37 AFY h
Meals - Chinese - 25.00/35.00 (dinner) and a la carte 9.95/25.10 ♀.
◆ Ornately decorated, long-established and comfortable restaurant. Polite and efficient service. Extensive and traditional Chinese menu.

XX **Dan's,** 119 Sydney St, SW3 6NR, ☎ (020) 7352 2718, *Fax (020) 7352 3265,* – MC AE VISA 37 AEZ s
closed Sunday dinner – **Meals** 19.50 (lunch) and a la carte 25.50/33.40.
◆ The eponymous owner oversees the operation in this long established neighbourhood restaurant. Eclectic menu with global influences. Private dining available.

XX **Haandi,** 136 Brompton Rd, SW3 1HY, ☎ (020) 7823 7373, *haandirestaurant@btconnect.com, Fax (020) 7823 9696* – ▤. MC AE ① VISA JCB 37 AFX v
Meals - Indian - a la carte 16.82/35.40 ♀.
◆ Spacious basement restaurant, though with natural light in some sections. Live jazz in the bar and chefs very much on display. Flavoursome, succulent north Indian food.

X **Thierry's,** 342 King's Rd, SW3 5UR, ☎ (020) 7352 3365, *eat@thierrys-restaurant.co.uk, Fax (020) 7352 3365* – ▤. MC AE ① VISA 36 ADZ c
closed 24 December-3 January, last 2 weeks August, Sunday dinner and Monday – **Meals** - French - a la carte 17.70/35.95 ♀.
◆ Keen service at this cosy and friendly French bistro. Favoured by local residents, the traditional menu features many of the classics.

X **Bibendum Oyster Bar,** Michelin House, 81 Fulham Rd, SW3 6RD, ☎ (020) 7589 1480, *manager@bibendum.co.uk, Fax (020) 7823 7148* – MC AE ① VISA 37 AEY s
closed 25-26 December – **Meals** - Seafood specialities - (bookings not accepted) a la carte 19.00/29.00.
◆ Dine in either the busy bar, or in the light and relaxed foyer of this striking landmark. Concise menu of mainly cold dishes focusing on fresh seafood and shellfish.

X **itsu,** 118 Draycott Ave, SW3 3AE, ☎ (020) 7590 2400, *cebsonetcomuk.co.uk, Fax (020) 7590 2403* – ▤. MC AE VISA 37 AFY j
closed 25 December – **Meals** - Japanese - (bookings not accepted) a la carte 15.00/20.00 ♀.
◆ Sit at the conveyor belt and select your dishes from it. Cosmopolitan 'euro sushi' selection with Asian specialities. Fashionable and willing staff. Busy bar upstairs.

Admiral Codrington, 17 Mossop St, SW3 2LY, ☎ (020) 7581 0005, *theadmiralcodrington@longshotplc.com, Fax (020) 7589 2452* – ▤. MC AE VISA JCB 37 AFY v
closed 24-26 December – **Meals** a la carte 19.85/27.95 ♀.
◆ Aproned staff offer attentive, relaxed service in this busy gastropub. A retractable roof provides alfresco dining in the modern back room. Cosmopolitan menu of modern dishes.

Chelsea Ram, 32 Burnaby St, SW10 0PL, ☎ (020) 7351 4008, *pint@chelsearam.com, Fax (020) 7349 0885* – MC VISA JCB
closed 25 and 31 December – **Meals** a la carte 17.00/24.00 ♀.
◆ Wooden floors, modern artwork and books galore feature in this forever popular pub. Concise menu of modern British cooking with daily changing specials. Friendly atmosphere.

Swag and Tails, 10-11 Fairholt St, SW7 1EG, ☎ (020) 7584 6926, *swagandtails@mway.com, Fax (020) 7581 9935* – MC AE VISA JCB 37 AFX r
closed 10 days Christmas-New Year, Saturday, Sunday and Bank Holidays – **Meals** a la carte 17.90/28.00 ♀.
◆ Attractive Victorian pub close to Harrods and the fashionable Knightsbridge shops. Polite and approachable service of a blackboard menu of light snacks and seasonal dishes.

Builders Arms, 13 Britten St, SW3 3TY, ☎ (020) 7349 9040, *Fax (020) 7351 3181* – ▤. MC VISA 37 AFZ x
Meals (bookings not accepted) a la carte 18.40/25.00 ♀.
◆ Modern 'gastropub' favoured by the locals. Eclectic menu of contemporary dishes with blackboard specials. Polite service from a young and eager team.

Lots Road Pub & Dining Room, 114 Lots Rd, SW10 0RJ, ☎ (020) 7352 6645, *lotsroad@thespiritgroup.com, Fax (020) 7376 4975* – ▤. MC AE VISA
closed 25 December – **Meals** a la carte 16.00/25.00 ♀.
◆ Traditional corner pub with an open-plan kitchen, flowers at each table and large modern pictures on the walls. Contemporary menus change daily.

Earl's Court – ✉ SW5.

K + K George, 1-15 Templeton Pl, SW5 9NB, ☎ (020) 7598 8700, *hotelgeorge@kkhotels.co.uk, Fax (020) 7370 2285,* – ▤ TV P. MC AE ① VISA JCB. 35 AAY s
Meals (in bar) a la carte 14.10/22.20 ♀ – **154 rm** 175.00/210.00.
◆ Converted Victorian house overlooking its own large rear garden. Scandinavian style to the bedrooms with low beds, white walls and light wood furniture. Smart business centre. Informal dining in the bar.

Twenty Nevern Square, Nevern Sq, SW5 9PD, ☎ (020) 7565 9555, *hotel@twentynevernsquare.co.uk, Fax (020) 7565 9444* – ⎈ TV ☏ P. MC AE ◑ VISA JCB. ⚘
Meals *(closed Sunday)* (residents only) (dinner only) 16.00 and a la carte 15.95/19.45 s. ♀ – ☕ 9.00 – **19 rm** 110.00/140.00. 35 AAY u
◆ In an attractive Victorian garden square, an individually designed, privately owned town house. Original pieces of furniture and some rooms with their own terrace.

Mayflower without rest., 26-28 Trebovir Rd, SW5 9NJ, ☎ (020) 7370 0991, *mayflowerhotel@mayflower-group.co.uk, Fax (020) 7370 0994*, – ⎈ ⚘ TV ☏ MC AE VISA JCB
☕ 9.00 – **48 rm** 69.00/99.00. 35 ABY n
◆ Two white houses combined into a stylish establishment with secluded rear garden, juice bar and breakfast room. Highly individual bedrooms with Indian and Asian décor.

Henley House without rest., 30 Barkston Gdns, SW5 0EN, ☎ (020) 7370 4111, *reservations@henleyhousehotel.com, Fax (020) 7370 0026* – ⎈ TV. MC AE ◑ VISA JCB. ⚘
☕ 3.40 – **21 rm** 74.00/89.00. 35 ABY e
◆ Located in a pleasant redbricked square, just yards from the high street. Bedrooms all styled similarly, with floral designs and good extras. Conservatory breakfast room.

Amsterdam without rest., 7 and 9 Trebovir Rd, SW5 9LS, ☎ (020) 7370 2814, *reservations@amsterdam-hotel.com, Fax (020) 7244 7608*, – ⎈ ⚘ TV. MC AE ◑ VISA JCB. ⚘
19 rm ☕ 72.00/86.00, 8 suites. 35 ABY c
◆ Basement breakfast room and a small secluded garden. The boldly decorated bedrooms dazzle with vivid colour schemes ; some boast their own balcony.

Rushmore without rest., 11 Trebovir Rd, SW5 9LS, ☎ (020) 7370 3839, *rushmore-reservations@london.com, Fax (020) 7370 0274* – ⚘ TV. MC AE ◑ VISA JCB. ⚘
22 rm ☕ 59.00/79.00. 35 ABY a
◆ Behind its Victorian façade lies an hotel popular with tourists. Individually decorated bedrooms in a variety of shapes and sizes. Piazza-styled conservatory breakfast room.

Langan's Coq d'Or, 254-260 Old Brompton Rd, SW5 9HR, ☎ (020) 7259 2599, *admin@langansrestaurant.co.uk, Fax (020) 7370 7735*, – ▤. MC AE ◑ VISA JCB
closed Monday and Bank Holidays – **Meals** (dinner only and lunch Saturday and Sunday) 16.50. 35 ABZ e
◆ Formal reception area leads into a modern, open-plan restaurant. Walls adorned with photographs of assorted celebrities. Smooth service and traditional British food.

Sticklebackpink, 168 Ifield Rd, SW10 9AF, ☎ (020) 7835 0874, *info@stickleback-restaurant.com* – ▤. MC AE VISA 35 ABZ a
closed Monday – **Meals** - Indian - a la carte 20.00/41.00 ♀.
◆ Basement and conservatory restaurant reached by a spiral stair from the bar. Elegantly-laid tables and friendly service. Menu of modern Indian dishes.

Hollywood Arms, 45 Hollywood Rd, SW10 9HX, ☎ (020) 7349 7840, *Fax (020) 7349 7841* – ▤. MC AE ◑ VISA 36 ACZ c
closed 25 December – **Meals** a la carte 19.50/24.00 ♀.
◆ Period pub in smart residential area with stylish interior furnished in rich autumnal colours. Efficient service. Concise menu with Mediterranean influences and flavours.

Kensington – ✉ *W8/W11/W14.*

Royal Garden, 2-24 Kensington High St, W8 4PT, ☎ (020) 7937 8000, *sales@royalgarden.co.uk, Fax (020) 7361 1991*, ≤, ⅛, – ⎈, ⚘ rm, ▤ TV ☏ ♿ P – 🏛 600. MC AE ◑ VISA JCB. ⚘ 35 ABX c
Park Terrace : **Meals** 21.00 (lunch) and a la carte 26.75/47.75 (see also ***The Tenth*** below) – ☕ 18.00 – **376 rm** 287.80/393.60, 20 suites.
◆ A tall, modern hotel with many of its rooms enjoying enviable views over the adjacent Kensington Gardens. All the modern amenities and services, with well-drilled staff. Bright, spacious, large-windowed restaurant.

Hilton London Kensington, 179-199 Holland Park Ave, W11 4UL, ☎ (020) 7603 3355, *saleskensington@hilton.com, Fax (020) 7602 9397* – ⎈, ⚘ rm, ▤ TV ☏ ♿ P – 🏛 200. MC AE ◑ VISA JCB. ⚘
Imbue : **Meals** *(closed lunch Saturday and Sunday)* 20.00/22.00 and a la carte 25.00/29.00 ♀ – ***Zen Oriental :*** **Meals** - Chinese a la carte 12.50/24.00 – ☕ 15.00 – **602 rm** 210.30/233.80.
◆ The executive bedrooms and the nearby exhibition centres make this a popular business hotel. Equally useful spot for tourists ; it has all the necessary amenities. Warm, pastel coloured Market. Zen Oriental serving authentic classic Chinese cooking.

Hilton London Olympia, 380 Kensington High St, W14 8NL, ☎ (020) 7603 3333, *rmolympia@hilton.com, Fax (020) 7603 4846*, ⅛ – ⎈, ⚘ rm, ▤ TV ☏ ♿ P – 🏛 250. MC AE ◑ VISA JCB
Meals *(closed Saturday lunch)* 20.00 and a la carte 16.00/29.50 ♀ – ☕ 16.50 – **395 rm** 128.00, 10 suites.
◆ Busy, corporate hotel, benefiting from being within walking distance of Olympia. Bedrooms of a good size, with light wood furniture and fully tiled bathrooms. Bright dining room with large windows.

The Milestone, 1-2 Kensington Court, W8 5DL, ☎ (020) 7917 1000, *Fax (020) 7917 1010*, – rm, . *%*
Meals (booking essential to non-residents) 19.95 (lunch) and a la carte 35.00/55.00 ♀ – ☐ 17.00 – **52 rm** 340.75, 5 suites. 35 ABX u
◆ Elegant 'boutique' hotel with decorative Victorian façade and English feel. Charming oak panelled lounge and snug bar. Meticulously decorated bedrooms with period detail. Panelled dining room with charming little oratory for privacy seekers.

Holland Court without rest., 31-33 Holland Rd, W14 8HJ, ☎ (020) 7371 1133, *reservations@hollandcourt.com, Fax (020) 7602 9114*, – . *%*
22 rm ☐ 95.00/125.00.
◆ Privately owned and run terraced house. Pretty little garden next to the conservatory extension of the breakfast room. Well-kept bedrooms benefit from the large windows.

The Tenth (at Royal Garden H.), 2-24 Kensington High St, W8 4PT, ☎ (020) 7361 1910, *Fax (020) 7361 1921*, ≤ Kensington Palace and Gardens – .
closed last week December, first week January, last 2 weeks August, Saturday lunch, Sunday and Bank Holidays – **Meals** (live music Saturday) 21.00 (lunch) and a la carte 26.75/36.20 ♀. 35 ABX c
◆ Named after the hotel's top floor where this stylish yet relaxed room is situated. Commanding views of Kensington Palace and the Park. Well-structured service ; modern menu.

Belvedere, Holland House, off Abbotsbury Rd, W8 6LU, ☎ (020) 7602 1238, *sales@whitestarline.org.uk, Fax (020) 7610 4382*, , – .
closed Sunday dinner in winter – **Meals** 24.50/32.50 ♀.
◆ Former 19C orangery in a delightful position in the middle of the Park. On two floors with a bar and balcony terrace. Huge vases of flowers. Modern take on classic dishes.

Zaika, 1 Kensington High St, W8 5NP, ☎ (020) 7795 6533, *info@zaika-restaurant.co.uk, Fax (020) 7937 8854* – . 35 ABX r
closed 25-26 December, 1 January and Saturday lunch – **Meals** - Indian - 17.95 (lunch) and a la carte 30.25/46.25 ♀.
◆ A converted bank, sympathetically restored, with original features and Indian artefacts. Well organised service ; careful and accomplished modern Indian cooking.
Spec. Imli Bateyer (quail glazed with tamarind and cumin). Karara Kekda Khichdi (soft shell crab and scallops with lentils). Zaika chocolate platter.

Clarke's, 124 Kensington Church St, W8 4BH, ☎ (020) 7221 9225, *restaurant@sallyclarke.com, Fax (020) 7229 4564* – . 27 ABV c
closed 10 days Christmas-New Year, Sunday and Bank Holidays – **Meals** (set menu only at dinner) 28.50/40.00 ♀.
◆ Open-plan kitchen, personally overseen by the owner, provides modern British cooking. No choice, set menu at dinner. Comfortable and bright, with a neighbourhood feel.

Babylon (at The Roof Gardens), 99 Kensington High St (entrance on Derry St), W8 5SA, ☎ (020) 7368 3993, *babylon@roofgardens.virgin.co.uk, Fax (020) 7938 2774*, ≤, – . 35 ABX n
closed 25 December, 1 January, Saturday lunch and Sunday dinner – **Meals** 21.50 and a la carte 24.00/37.50 ♀.
◆ Situated on the roof of this pleasant London building affording attractive veiws of the London skyline. Stylish modern décor in keeping with the contemporary, British cooking.

Launceston Place, 1a Launceston Pl, W8 5RL, ☎ (020) 7937 6912, *LPR@place-restaurants.co.uk, Fax (020) 7938 2412* – . 35 ACX a
closed 24-26 December, 1 January and Saturday lunch – **Meals** 18.50 (lunch) and a la carte 27.00/38.00 ♀.
◆ Divided into a number of rooms, this corner restaurant is lent a bright feel by its large windows and gilded mirrors. Chatty service and contemporary cooking.

Memories of China, 353 Kensington High St, W8 6NW, ☎ (020) 7603 6951, *Fax (020) 7603 0848* – . 35 AAY v
closed 25 December and 1 January – **Meals** - Chinese - (booking essential) a la carte 23.50/40.00 ♀.
◆ Subtle lighting and brightly coloured high-back chairs add to the modern feel of this Chinese restaurant. Screens separate the tables. Plenty of choice from extensive menu.

Timo, 343 Kensington High St, W8 6NW, ☎ (020) 7603 3888, *Fax (020) 7603 8111* – . 35 AAY c
closed 25 December and 1 January – **Meals** - Italian - 19.50/31.50 ♀.
◆ Modern restaurant with unadorned lime green walls and comfortable seating in brown suede banquettes. Italian menus of contemporary dishes and daily changing specials.

The Ark, 122 Palace Gardens Terr, W8 4RT, ☎ (020) 7229 4024, *mail@thearkrestaurant.co.uk, Fax (020) 7792 8787*, – . 27 ABV r
closed 25-26 December, Sunday dinner and Monday lunch – **Meals** - Italian - 15.00 (lunch) and a la carte 27.00/31.50 ♀.
◆ The hut-like external appearance belies the contemporary interior of this Italian restaurant. Comfortable, bright feel with bar and lounge. Smoothly run, rustic cooking.

Kensington Place, 201 Kensington Church St, W8 7LX, ☎ (020) 7727 3184, *kpr@placerestaurants.co.uk, Fax (020) 7229 2025* – ▤. MC AE ① VISA 27 AAV z
closed 25-26 December – **Meals** (booking essential) 16.50/24.50 and a la carte 26.00/42.00 ♀.
◆ A cosmopolitan crowd still head for this establishment that set the trend for large, bustling and informal restaurants. Professionally run with skilled modern cooking.

Cibo, 3 Russell Gdns, W14 8EZ, ☎ (020) 7371 6271, *Fax (020) 7602 1371* – MC AE ① VISA
closed 10 days Christmas, Saturday lunch and Sunday dinner – **Meals** - Italian - a la carte 20.75/34.75.
◆ Smoothly run Italian restaurant that combines style with the atmosphere of a neighbourhood favourite. Unaffected service with robust and tasty food.

Malabar, 27 Uxbridge St, W8 7TQ, ☎ (020) 7727 8800, *feedback@malabar-restaurant.co.uk* – MC VISA 27 AAV e
Meals - Indian - (booking essential) (buffet lunch Sunday) 14.75/20.00 and a la carte 20.60/28.50.
◆ Indian restaurant in a residential street. Three rooms with individual personalities and informal service. Extensive range of good value dishes, particularly vegetarian.

Wódka, 12 St Albans Grove, W8 5PN, ☎ (020) 7937 6513, *john@wodka.demon.co.uk, Fax (020) 7937 8621* – MC AE ① VISA 35 ABX c
closed lunch Saturday and Sunday – **Meals** - Polish - 13.50 (lunch) and a la carte 18.00/30.00 ♀.
◆ Unpretentious Polish restaurant with rustic, authentic menu. Assorted blinis and flavoured vodkas a speciality. Simply decorated, with wooden tables and paper napkins.

North Kensington – ✉ W2/W11.

Pembridge Court without rest., 34 Pembridge Gdns, W2 4DX, ☎ (020) 7229 9977, *reservations@pemct.co.uk, Fax (020) 7727 4982* – |♦| ▤ TV ☎. MC AE ① VISA 27 AAU n
20 rm ☕ 125.00/195.00.
◆ Privately owned 19C town house ; very charmingly run, with comfortable sitting room, small lounge and flowery breakfast room. Bright, light bedrooms, some particularly large.

Abbey Court without rest., 20 Pembridge Gdns, W2 4DU, ☎ (020) 7221 7518, *info@abbeycourthotel.co.uk, Fax (020) 7792 0858* – ⇆ TV ☎. MC AE ① VISA JCB. ✻ 27 AAV u
22 rm 105.00/155.00.
◆ Five-storey Victorian town house with individually decorated bedrooms, with many thoughtful touches. Breakfast served in a pleasant conservatory. Friendly service.

Portobello without rest., 22 Stanley Gdns, W11 2NG, ☎ (020) 7727 2777, *info@portobello-hotel.co.uk, Fax (020) 7792 9641* – |♦| TV ☎. MC AE VISA
☕ 10.00 **24 rm** 120.00/275.00.
◆ An attractive Victorian town house in an elegant terrace. Original and theatrical décor. Circular beds, half-testers, Victorian baths : no two bedrooms are the same.

Notting Hill Brasserie, 92 Kensington Park Rd, W11 2PN, ☎ (020) 7229 4481, *enquiries@nottinghillbrasserie.com, Fax (020) 7221 1246* – ▤. MC AE VISA JCB 27 AAU a
closed Sunday – **Meals** 18.50 (lunch) and dinner a la carte 25.50/34.50 ♀.
◆ Modern, comfortable restaurant with quiet, formal atmosphere set over four small rooms. Authentic African artwork on walls. Contemporary dishes with European influence.

Edera, 148 Holland Park Ave, W11 4VE, ☎ (020) 7221 6090, *Fax (020) 7313 9700* – ▤. MC AE ① VISA
Meals - Italian - 19.50/22.50 ♀.
◆ Split level restaurant with 4 outdoor tables. Attentive service by all Italian staff. Set-price menus of modern Italian cooking with some unusual ingredients and combinations.

Manor, 6-8 All Saints Rd, W11 1HH, ☎ (020) 7243 6363, *mail@manorw11.com, Fax (020) 7243 6360* – ▤. MC AE VISA
Meals (dinner only and lunch Saturday and Sunday) a la carte 22.50/32.50 ♀.
◆ Bustling, vibrant restaurant in the heart of Notting Hill. Wood-floored with banquette seating. Good sized menus : the cuisine is modern with Spanish influences.

Notting Grill, 123A Clarendon Rd, W11 4JG, ☎ (020) 7229 1500, *nottinggrill@aol.com, Fax (020) 7229 8889,* 🏛 – MC AE ① VISA JCB
closed 25-26 December, Good Friday and August Bank Holiday – **Meals** - Steak specialities - (dinner only and lunch Saturday and Sunday) a la carte 29.50/40.00 ♀.
◆ Converted pub that retains a rustic feel, with bare brick walls and wooden tables. Specialises in well sourced, quality meats.

South Kensington - ✉ SW5/SW7.

Millennium Gloucester, 4-18 Harrington Gdns, SW7 4LH, ℘ (020) 7373 6030, *gloucester@mill-cop.com, Fax (020) 7373 0409,* – rm, – 650 36 ACY r
Bugis Street : **Meals** - Singaporean - 7.95/20.00 and a la carte 17.45/35.90 – 15.50 – **604 rm** 250.00, 6 suites.
◆ A large international group hotel. Busy marbled lobby and vast conference facilities. Smart and well-equipped bedrooms are generously sized, especially the 'Club' rooms. Informal, compact Bugis Street.

The Pelham, 15 Cromwell Pl, SW7 2LA, ℘ (020) 7589 8288, *pelham@firmdale.com, Fax (020) 7584 8444* – rm, 36 ADY z
Kemps : **Meals** a la carte 20.00/33.00 – 17.50 – **48 rm** 176.20/293.70, 3 suites.
◆ Attractive Victorian town house with a discreet and comfortable feel. Wood panelled drawing room and individually decorated bedrooms with marble bathrooms. Detailed service. Warm basement dining room.

Blakes, 33 Roland Gdns, SW7 3PF, ℘ (020) 7370 6701, *blakes@blakeshotels.com, Fax (020) 7373 0442,* – rest, 36 ACZ n
Meals a la carte 50.00/70.00 **s.** – 25.00 – **36 rm** 190.00/393.00, 5 suites.
◆ Behind the Victorian façade lies one of London's first 'boutique' hotels. Dramatic, bold and eclectic décor, with oriental influences and antiques from around the globe. Fashionable restaurant with bamboo and black walls.

Harrington Hall, 5-25 Harrington Gdns, SW7 4JW, ℘ (020) 7396 9696, *sales@harringtonhall.co.uk, Fax (020) 7396 9090,* – rm, – 260. 36 ACY n
Wetherby's : **Meals** 22.50/27.50 and a la carte 25.00/29.00 **s.** – 15.50 – **200 rm** 195.00/260.00.
◆ A series of adjoined terraced houses, with an attractive period façade that belies the size. Tastefully furnished bedrooms, with an extensive array of facilities. Classically decorated dining room.

Millennium Bailey's, 140 Gloucester Rd, SW7 4QH, ℘ (020) 7373 6000, *baileys@mill-cop.com, Fax (020) 7370 3760* – rm, – 460. 36 ACY a
Olives : **Meals** (bar lunch)/dinner 20.00 and a la carte approx. 25.00 – 15.50 – **211 rm** 135.00/250.00.
◆ Elegant lobby, restored to its origins dating from 1876, with elaborate plasterwork and a striking grand staircase. Victorian feel continues through into the bedrooms. Modern, pastel shaded restaurant.

Vanderbilt, 68-86 Cromwell Rd, SW7 5BT, ℘ (020) 7761 9013, *resvand@radisson.com, Fax (020) 7761 9003,* – rm, – 120. 36 ACY z
Meals 27.50 and a la carte 30.00/36.00 – 13.50 – **215 rm** 229.10/298.45.
◆ A Victorian town house, once home to the Vanderbilt family. Retains many original features such as stained glass windows and fireplaces. Now a modern, group hotel. Restaurant has unusual objets d'art and striking cracked glass bar.

Rembrandt, 11 Thurloe Pl, SW7 2RS, ℘ (020) 7589 8100, *rembrandt@sarova.co.uk, Fax (020) 7225 3476,* – rm, rest, – 200. 36 ADY x
Meals (carving lunch) 18.95 and a la carte 14.70/27.40 **s.** – **195 rm** 190.00/240.00.
◆ Built originally as apartments in the 19C, now a well-equipped hotel opposite the VA museum and a short walk from Harrods. Comfortable lounge, adjacent leisure club. Spacious dining room.

London Marriott Kensington, 147 Cromwell Rd, SW5 0TH, ℘ (020) 7973 1000, *events.kensington@marriotthotels.co.uk, Fax (020) 7370 1685,* – – 200. 35 ABY n
Fratelli : **Meals** - Italian - 18.00 (lunch) and a la carte 23.50/33.50 – 14.95 – **216 rm** 233.80.
◆ Modern seven-storey hotel around atrium with good leisure centre. Coffee bar and Spanish tapas bar. Spacious, comfortable, well-equipped bedrooms with many extras. Informal Italian restaurant with open kitchen and wide ranging menu.

Jurys Kensington, 109-113 Queen's Gate, SW7 5LR, ℘ (020) 7589 6300, *kensington@jurydoyle.com, Fax (020) 7581 1492* – rm, – 80. 36 ADY g
Meals (dinner only) 18.50 and a la carte 15.00/18.50 – 16.00 – **173 rm** 130.00/230.00.
◆ A row of 18C town houses that were converted into a hotel in the 1920s. Spacious lobby lounge and busy basement Irish pub. Well-equipped, comfortable bedrooms. Dining room exudes a traditional appeal.

Regency, 100 Queen's Gate, SW7 5AG, ✆ (020) 7373 7878, *info@regency-london.co.uk, Fax (020) 7370 5555,* – rm, – 100. 36 ADY e
Meals *(closed lunch Saturday and Sunday)* (carvery lunch)/dinner a la carte 11.00/24.00 **s.** – 15.00 – **199 rm** 187.00/234.00, 11 suites.
◆ Impressive Regency house in an elegant tree lined street and close to the museums. Bedrooms vary from rather compact singles to spacious duplex suites. Basement restaurant with cocktail bar.

Gore, 189 Queen's Gate, SW7 5EX, ✆ (020) 7584 6601, *reservations@gorehotel.co.uk, Fax (020) 7589 8127* – rm. 36 ACX n
closed 24-25 December – ***Bistrot 190 :*** **Meals** (booking essential) a la carte 23.00/48.50 – 15.95 – **53 rm** 182.10/228.25.
◆ Opened its doors in 1892 ; has retained its individual charm. Richly decorated with antiques, rugs and over 4,000 pictures that cover every inch of wall. Seafood menu with global twists at The Restaurant at One Ninety. Bistrot 190 boasts French-inspired décor.

John Howard, 4 Queen's Gate, SW7 5EH, ✆ (020) 7808 8400, *info@johnhowardhotel.co.uk, Fax (020) 7808 8402* – rm.
Meals *(closed Sunday)* (dinner only) 15.00 and a la carte 15.25/20.00 **s.** – 12.50 – **45 rm** 99.00/129.00, 7 suites. 36 ACX g
◆ Occupies the site of three mid-19C houses, just a short walk from Kensington Palace. Some rooms with floor to ceiling windows and balconies, others look onto a quiet mews. Candlelit basement dining room.

Number Sixteen without rest., 16 Sumner Pl, SW7 3EG, ✆ (020) 7589 5232, *sixteen@firmdale.com, Fax (020) 7584 8615,* – 36 ADY d
14.50 **41 rm** 111.60/264.30.
◆ Four Victorian town houses in a smart part of town. Discreet entrance, comfortable sitting room and charming breakfast terrace. Bedrooms in English country house style.

The Cranley, 10 Bina Gdns, SW5 0LA, ✆ (020) 7373 0123, *info@thecranley.com, Fax (020) 7373 9497* – rm. 36 ACY c
Meals (room service only) – 9.95 – **36 rm** 182.10/258.50, 3 suites.
◆ Attractive Regency town house that artfully combines charm and period details with modern comforts and technology. Individually styled bedrooms ; some with four-posters.

Five Sumner Place without rest., 5 Sumner Pl, SW7 3EE, ✆ (020) 7584 7586, *reservations@sumnerplace.com, Fax (020) 7823 9962* – 36 ADY u
13 rm 100.00/152.00.
◆ Part of a striking white terrace built in 1848 in this fashionable part of town. Breakfast served in bright conservatory. Good sized bedrooms.

Aster House without rest., 3 Sumner Pl, SW7 3EE, ✆ (020) 7581 5888, *asterhouse@btinternet.com, Fax (020) 7584 4925,* –
14 rm 100.00/190.00. 36 ADY t
◆ End of terrace Victorian house with a pretty little rear garden and first floor conservatory. Ground floor rooms available. A wholly non-smoking establishment.

Bombay Brasserie, Courtfield Rd, SW7 4QH, ✆ (020) 7370 4040, *bombay1brasserie@aol.com, Fax (020) 7835 1669* – 36 ACY y
closed 25-26 December – **Meals** - Indian - (buffet lunch) 18.95 and dinner a la carte 27.25/33.25.
◆ Something of a London institution : an ever busy Indian restaurant with Raj-style décor. Ask to sit in the brighter plant-filled conservatory. Popular lunchtime buffet.

Lundum's, 119 Old Brompton Rd, SW7 3RN, ✆ (020) 7373 7774, *Fax (020) 7373 4472,* – 36 ACZ p
closed 22 December-4 January and Sunday dinner – **Meals** - Danish - 15.50/21.50 and a la carte 23.00/36.50.
◆ A family run Danish restaurant offering an authentic, traditional lunch with a more expansive dinner menu. Comfortable room, with large windows. Charming service.

L'Etranger, 36 Gloucester Rd, SW7 4QT, ✆ (020) 7584 1118, *etranger36@aol.com, Fax (020) 7584 8886* – 35 ACX c
closed 25-26 December, Saturday lunch and Sunday dinner – **Meals** (booking essential) 16.50 (lunch) and a la carte 27.50/41.50.
◆ Corner restaurant with mosaic entrance floor and bay window. Modern décor. Tables extend into adjoining wine shop. French based cooking with Asian influences.

Khan's of Kensington, 3 Harrington Rd, SW7 3ES, ✆ (020) 7584 4114, *Fax (020) 7581 2900* – 36 ADY a
closed 25 December – **Meals** - Indian - a la carte 14.35/24.75.
◆ Bright room with wood flooring and a large mural depicting scenes from old India. Basement bar in a colonial style. Authentic Indian cooking with attentive service.

XX **Cambio de Tercio,** 163 Old Brompton Rd, SW5 0LJ, ✆ (020) 7244 8970, *restaurant@cambiodetercio.co.uk, Fax (020) 7373 8817* – MC AE VISA 36 ACZ a
closed 2 weeks Christmas – **Meals** - Spanish - a la carte 24.90/30.00 ♀.
◆ The keen young owners have created a vibrant room with rich red walls decorated with assorted bullfighting accessories. Sophisticated Spanish cooking.

XX **Pasha,** 1 Gloucester Rd, SW7 4PP, ✆ (020) 7589 7969, *Fax (020) 7581 9996* – ▤. MC AE ① VISA JCB 36 ACX y
closed 25-26 December, 1 January and Sunday lunch – **Meals** - Moroccan - a la carte 12.25/29.25 ♀.
◆ A marble fountain, lanterns, spice boxes and silk cushions help create a theatrical Moroccan atmosphere. Service is helpful and able : the menu is more extensive at dinner.

XX **Memories of India,** 18 Gloucester Rd, SW7 4RB, ✆ (020) 7589 6450, *Fax (020) 7584 4438* – ▤. MC AE ① VISA JCB 36 ACX s
closed 25 December – **Meals** - Indian - 16.95/34.95 and a la carte 11.85/21.85.
◆ A long-standing local favourite, decorated in traditional style with whicker chairs and pink linen tablecloths. Polite and able service. Authentic Indian cooking.

X **Café Lazeez,** 93-95 Old Brompton Rd, SW7 3LD, ✆ (020) 7581 9993, *southkensington@cafelazeez.com, Fax (020) 7581 8200* – ▤. MC AE ① VISA 36 ADY v
Meals - North Indian - a la carte 14.75/25.00 ♀.
◆ Glass-topped tables and tiled flooring add an air of modernity to this Indian restaurant ; reflected in the North Indian cooking. Willing service. Upstairs room more formal.

X **Bangkok,** 9 Bute St, SW7 3EY, ✆ (020) 7584 8529 – ▤. MC VISA 36 ADY b
closed Christmas-New Year and Sunday – **Meals** - Thai Bistro - a la carte 17.70/32.45.
◆ This simple Thai bistro has been a popular local haunt for many years. Guests can watch the chefs at work, preparing inexpensive dishes from the succinct menu.

LAMBETH

Clapham Common – ✉ *SW4.*

🏠 **Windmill on the Common,** Clapham Common South Side, SW4 9DE, ✆ (020) 8673 4578, *windmill@youngs.co.uk, Fax (020) 8675 1486* – ⇋ rm, ▤ TV 📞 ♿ P. MC AE VISA ✻
Meals a la carte 12.85/24.90 **s.** ♀ – **29 rm** ☕ 96.00/120.00.
◆ A former Victorian pub that has been sympathetically extended over the years. Pleasant spot on the Common. Well-kept and comfortable rooms of assorted sizes. Dining room and adjacent log-fired bar.

XX **Thyme,** 14 Clapham Park Rd, SW4 7BB, ✆ (020) 7627 2468, *adam@thymeandspace.com, Fax (020) 7627 2424* – MC AE VISA JCB
closed Sunday-Monday – **Meals** 12.50/40.00 and a la carte 21.50/29.00 ♀.
◆ Distinct neighbourhood feel with bustling but intimate ambience. Modern décor. Three set menus ; imaginative cooking.

X **Tsunami,** Unit 3, 1-7 Voltaire Rd, SW4 6DQ, ✆ (020) 7978 1610, *Fax (020) 7978 1591* – MC VISA
closed 25-27 December, 31 December-2 January and Sunday – **Meals** - Japanese - (dinner only and Saturday lunch) a la carte 12.90/35.40 ♀.
◆ Trendy, mininalist-style restaurant. Interesting Japanese menu with many dishes designed for sharing and plenty of original options. Good Sushi and Sashimi selection.

Herne Hill – ✉ *SE24.*

XX **3 Monkeys,** 136-140 Herne Hill, SE24 9QH, ✆ (020) 7738 5500, *jan@3monkeysrestaurant.com, Fax (020) 7738 5505* – ⇋ ▤. MC AE ① VISA JCB
closed 25-26 December and 1 January – **Meals** - Indian - (dinner only) a la carte 19.00/30.45 ♀.
◆ 'New wave' Indian restaurant in a converted bank. Dining room in bright white reached via a bridge over the bar and kitchen. Menu uses influences from all over India.

Kennington *Gtr London* – ✉ *SE11.*

XX **Kennington Lane,** 205-209 Kennington Lane, SE11 5QS, ✆ (020) 7793 8313, *Fax (020) 7793 8323*, ☂ – ▤. MC AE VISA JCB 40 ANZ s
Meals 13.75 (lunch) and a la carte 23.90/25.90 ♀.
◆ Green-hued entrance with large awning leads into the contemporary interior. Bare wooden tables and fresh white walls. Purposeful staff, modern menu with European influences.

X **Lobster Pot,** 3 Kennington Lane, SE11 4RG, ✆ (020) 7582 5556 – ▤. MC AE ① VISA JCB
closed 23 December-7 January, Sunday and Monday – **Meals** - French Seafood - 13.50/39.50 and a la carte 26.30/37.30. 40 AOY e
◆ A nautical theme so bold you'll need your sea legs : fishing nets, shells, aquariums, portholes, even the sound of seagulls. Classic French seafood menu is more restrained.

Lambeth *Gtr London* – ✉ *SE1.*

Novotel London Waterloo, 113 Lambeth Rd, SE1 7LS, ✆ (020) 7793 1010, *h1785@accor-hotels.com, Fax (020) 7793 0202,* Fö, ≘s – |‡|, ⇔ rm, ▤ TV ✆ ♿ ⇔ – 🏔 40. MO AE ① VISA JCB. ✈ 40AMY a
Meals (bar lunch Saturday and Sunday) 19.95 and a la carte 22.20/29.30 **s.** ♀ – ☐ 12.95 – **185 rm** 140.00/160.00, 2 suites.
• Modern, group owned purpose-built hotel, convenient for the station. Uniformly decorated bedrooms, with a good level of extras. Secure basement parking. All-day brasserie and buffet lunch option.

Waterloo *Gtr London* – ✉ *SE1.*

Channel Tunnel : Eurostar information and reservations ✆ (08705) 186186.

London Marriott H. County Hall, SE1 7PB, ✆ (020) 7928 5200, *salesadmin.countyhall@marriotthotels.co.uk, Fax (020) 7928 5300,* ≤, Fö, ≘s, ☐ – |‡|, ⇔ rm, ▤ TV ✆ ♿ – 🏔 70. MO AE ① VISA JCB. ✈ 40AMX a
County Hall : **Meals** 26.50 (lunch) and a la carte 25.50/43.00 **s.** ♀ – ☐ 18.95 – **195 rm** 292.50, 5 suites.
• Occupying the historic County Hall building. Many of the spacious and comfortable bedrooms enjoy river and Parliament outlook. Impressive leisure facilities. Famously impressive views from restaurant.

London County Hall Travel Inn Capital, Belvedere Rd, SE1 7PB, ✆ (0870) 2383300, *london.county.hall.mti.@whitbread.com, Fax (020) 7902 1619* – |‡| ⇔, ▤ rest, TV ✆ ♿. MO AE ① VISA. ✈ 32AMV u
Meals (grill rest.) (dinner only) – **313 rm** 82.95.
• Adjacent to the London Eye and within the County Hall building. Budget accommodation in a central London location that is the envy of many, more expensive, hotels.

Days without rest., 54 Kennington Rd, SE1 7BJ, ✆ (020) 7922 1331, Reservations (Freephone) 0800 0280400, *reservations.waterloo@dayshotel.co.uk, Fax (020) 7922 1441* – |‡| ⇔ TV ✆ ♿. MO AE ① VISA. ✈ 40ANY x
☐ 5.95 **162 rm** 84.00.
• Useful lodge accommodation, opposite the Imperial War Museum. Identical bedrooms are well-equipped and decorated in warm colours. Competitively priced.

MERTON

Colliers Wood – ✉ *SW19.*

Express by Holiday Inn without rest., 200 High St, SW19 2BH, on A 24 ✆ (020) 8545 7300, *Fax (020) 8545 7301* – |‡| ⇔ TV ✆ ♿ ⇔ – 🏔 50. MO AE ① VISA JCB. ✈
83 rm 92.00.
• Modern, corporate budget hotel. Spacious and well-equipped bedrooms ; power showers in en suite bathrooms. Ideal for the business traveller. Continental breakfast included.

Wimbledon – ✉ *SW19.*

Cannizaro House ✈, West Side, Wimbledon Common, SW19 4UE, ✆ (0870) 333 9124, *cannizarohouse@thistle.co.uk, Fax (0870) 3339224,* ≤, ⛱, ⛱ – |‡|, ⇔ rm, TV ✆ P – 🏔 120. MO AE ① VISA JCB. ✈
Meals a la carte 21.00/41.00 ♀ – ☐ 14.50 – **43 rm** 259.00, 2 suites.
• Part Georgian mansion in a charming spot on the Common. Appealing drawing room popular for afternoon tea. Rooms in original house are antique furnished, some with balconies. Refined restaurant overlooks splendid formal garden.

Light House, 75-77 Ridgway, SW19 4ST, ✆ (020) 8944 6338, *lightrest@aol.com, Fax (020) 8946 4440* – MO AE VISA
closed 4 days Christmas, 2 days Easter and Sunday dinner – **Meals** - Italian influences - 12.50 (lunch) and a la carte 22.00/32.70 ♀.
• Bright and modern neighbourhood restaurant with open plan kitchen. Informal service of a weekly changing and diverse menu of progressive Italian/fusion dishes.

The Fire Stables, 27-29 Church Rd, SW19 5DQ, ✆ (020) 8946 3197, *thefirestables@thespiritgroup.com, Fax (020) 8946 1101* – ▤. MO AE VISA
closed 25 December – **Meals** a la carte 18.25/29.00 ♀.
• Modern "gastropub" in village centre. Open-plan kitchen. Polished wood tables and banquettes. Varied modern British dishes. Expect fishcakes, duck confit salad or risotto.

SOUTHWARK

Bermondsey – ✉ SE1.

London Bridge, 8-18 London Bridge St, SE1 9SG, ☎ (020) 7855 2200, *sales@london-bridge-hotel.co.uk, Fax (020) 7855 2233,* – rm, – 100. AE VISA JCB. 33 AQV a
Georgetown : **Meals** 12.50/15.00 (lunch) and a la carte 17.50/21.75 **s.** – 13.95 – **135 rm** 150.00/190.00, 3 suites.
◆ In one of the oldest parts of London, independently owned with an ornate façade dating from 1915. Modern interior with classically decorated bedrooms and an impressive gym. Restaurant echoing the colonial style serving Malaysian dishes.

London Tower Bridge Travel Inn Capital, 159 Tower Bridge Rd, SE1 3LP, ☎ (020) 7940 3700, *Fax (020) 7940 3719* – rm, AE VISA.
Meals (grill rest.) (dinner only) – **195 rm** 74.95.
◆ Ideal for tourists by being next to a tube station and the famous bridge. Clean and spacious budget accommodation, with uniform-sized bedrooms.

Le Pont de la Tour, 36d Shad Thames, Butlers Wharf, SE1 2YE, ☎ (020) 7403 8403, *Fax (020) 7403 0267,* ≤, – AE VISA 34 ASV c
Meals 29.50 (lunch) and dinner a la carte 32.50/43.00 ♀.
◆ Elegant and stylish room commanding spectacular views of the Thames and Tower Bridge. Formal and detailed service. Modern menu with an informal bar attached.

Bengal Clipper, Cardamom Building, Shad Thames, Butlers Wharf, SE1 2YR, ☎ (020) 7357 9001, *clipper@bengalrestaurants.co.uk, Fax (020) 7357 9002* – . AE VISA
Meals - Indian - a la carte 12.25/17.25. 34 ASV e
◆ Housed in a Thames-side converted warehouse, a smart Indian restaurant with original brickwork and steel supports. Menu features Bengali and Goan dishes. Evening pianist.

Tentazioni, 2 Mill St, Lloyds Wharf, SE1 2BD, ☎ (020) 7237 1100, *tentazioni@aol.com, Fax (020) 7237 1100* – AE VISA JCB
closed 25 December, Sunday, lunch Saturday and Monday – **Meals** - Italian - 26.00 and a la carte 25.00/34.00 ♀.
◆ Former warehouse provides a bright and lively environment. Open staircase between the two floors. Keenly run, with a menu offering simple, carefully prepared Italian food.

Blueprint Café, Design Museum, Shad Thames, Butlers Wharf, SE1 2YD, ☎ (020) 7378 7031, *Fax (020) 7357 8810,* ≤ Tower Bridge – AE VISA 34 ASV u
Meals a la carte 22.50/39.50 ♀.
◆ Above the Design Museum, with impressive views of the river and bridge : handy binoculars on tables. Eager and energetic service, modern British menus : robust and rustic.

Cantina Del Ponte, 36c Shad Thames, Butlers Wharf, SE1 2YE, ☎ (020) 7403 5403, *Fax (020) 7403 4432,* ≤, – AE VISA 34 ASV c
Meals - Italian - 13.50 (lunch) and a la carte 16.20/27.40 ♀.
◆ Quayside setting with a large canopied terrace. Terracotta flooring ; modern rustic style décor, simple and unfussy. Tasty, refreshing Mediterranean-influenced cooking.

Butlers Wharf Chop House, 36e Shad Thames, Butlers Wharf, SE1 2YE, ☎ (020) 7403 3403, *Fax (020) 7403 3414,* ≤ Tower Bridge, – AE VISA 34 ASV n
closed Sunday dinner – **Meals** 23.75 (lunch) and dinner a la carte 23.00/33.75 ♀.
◆ Book the terrace in summer and dine in the shadow of Tower Bridge. Rustic feel to the interior, with obliging service. Menu focuses on traditional English dishes.

Dulwich – ✉ SE21.

Belair House, Gallery Rd, Dulwich Village, SE21 7AB, ☎ (020) 8299 9788, *info@belairhouse.co.uk, Fax (020) 8299 6793,* – AE VISA
closed Sunday dinner and Monday lunch – **Meals** 22.00/32.00 ♀.
◆ A striking Georgian summer house, floodlit at night, and surrounded by manicured lawns. By contrast, interior is bright and modern with summery colours. Eclectic menu.

Rotherhithe – ✉ SE16.

Hilton London Docklands, 265 Rotherhithe St, Nelson Dock, SE16 5HW, ☎ (020) 7231 1001, *Fax (020) 7231 0599,* ≤, – rm, – 350. AE VISA.
closed 23-29 December – ***Traders Bistro :*** **Meals** *(closed Sunday)* (dinner only) a la carte 20.00/30.00 ♀ – ***Terrace :*** **Meals** (dinner only) 25.00 **s.** ♀ – 15.00 – **361 rm** 125.00, 4 suites.
◆ Redbrick group hotel with glass façade. River-taxi from the hotel's own pier. Extensive leisure facilities. Standard size rooms with all mod cons. Eat on board Traders Bistro, a reconstructed galleon moored in dry dock. The Terrace for buffet style dining.

Southwark Gtr London – ✉ SE1.

Novotel London City South, 53-61 Southwark Bridge Rd, SE1 9HH, ☎ (020) 7089 0400, *h3269@accor-hotels.com, Fax (020) 7089 0410,* – rm, – 100. 34 AQV c
The Garden Brasserie : **Meals** 18.95 and a la carte 15.45/30.90 **s.** – 12.95 – **178 rm** 140.00/160.00, 4 suites.
◆ The new style of Novotel with good business facilities. Triple glazed bedrooms, furnished in the Scandinavian with keyboard and high speed internet. Brasserie style dining room with windows all down one side.

Mercure, 71-79 Southwark St, SE1 0JA, ☎ (020) 7902 0800, *h2814@accor-hotels.com, Fax (020) 7902 0810,* – , rm, – 60. 33 APV r
The Loft : **Meals** (bar lunch Saturday and Sunday) 14.50/18.00 and a la carte – 12.95 – **144 rm** 140.00/160.00.
◆ Newly converted office block, providing bright and spacious accommodation. Modern, open-plan lobby leads to well-equipped and comfortable bedrooms. Split-level dining room with tiled flooring.

Premier Lodge, Anchor, Bankside, 34 Park St, SE1 9EF, ☎ (0870) 7001456, *Fax (0870) 7001457* – , rm, . 33 AQV b
Meals (grill rest.) a la carte approx. 14.50 – **56 rm** 72.00.
◆ A good value lodge with modern, well-equipped bedrooms which include a spacious desk area, ideal for the corporate and leisure traveller.

Express by Holiday Inn without rest., 103-109 Southwark St, SE1 0JQ, ☎ (020) 7401 2525, *stay@expresssouthwark.co.uk, Fax (020) 7401 3322* – . 33 APV e
88 rm 98.00.
◆ Useful location, just ten minutes from Waterloo. Purpose-built hotel with modern bedrooms in warm pastel shades. Fully equipped business centre.

Southwark Rose without rest., 43-47 Southwark Bridge Rd, SE1 9HH, ☎ (020) 7015 1480, *info@southwarkrosehotel.co.uk, Fax (020) 7015 1481* – 34 AQV c
7.95 **78 rm** 105.00, 6 suites.
◆ Purpose built budget hotel south of the City, near the Globe Theatre. Top floor breakfast room with bar. Uniform style, reasonably spacious bedrooms with writing desks.

Oxo Tower, (8th floor), Oxo Tower Wharf, Barge House St, SE1 9PH, ☎ (020) 7803 3888, *oxo.reservations@harveynichols.co.uk, Fax (020) 7803 3838,* ≤ London skyline and River Thames, – . 32 ANV a
closed 25-26 December – **Meals** 28.50 (lunch) and dinner a la carte 27.50/43.50 (see also ***Oxo Tower Brasserie*** below).
◆ Top of a converted factory, providing stunning views of the Thames and beyond. Stylish, minimalist interior with huge windows. Smooth service of modern cuisine.

Baltic, 74 Blackfriars Rd, SE1 8HA, ☎ (020) 7928 1111, *info@balticrestaurant.co.uk, Fax (020) 7928 8487* – 33 AOV e
closed Saturday lunch – **Meals** - East European with Baltic influences - 13.50 (lunch) and a la carte 18.00/30.00.
◆ Set in a Grade II listed 18C former coach house. Enjoy authentic and hearty east European and Baltic influenced food. Interesting vodka selection and live jazz on Sundays.

Oxo Tower Brasserie, (8th floor), Oxo Tower Wharf, Barge House St, SE1 9PH, ☎ (020) 7803 3888, *Fax (020) 7803 3838,* ≤ London skyline and River Thames, – . 32 ANV a
closed 25-26 December – **Meals** 18.50 (lunch) and a la carte 21.50/31.50.
◆ Same views but less formal than the restaurant. Open-plan kitchen, relaxed service and the modern menu is slightly lighter. In summer, try to secure a table on the terrace.

Cantina Vinopolis, No.1 Bank End, SE1 9BU, ☎ (020) 7940 8333, *cantina@vinopolis.co.uk, Fax (020) 7940 8334* – . 33 AQV z
closed Christmas, New Year and Sunday dinner – **Meals** 26.95 and a la carte 20.95/33.70.
◆ Large, solid brick vaulted room under Victorian railway arches, with an adjacent wine museum. Modern menu with a huge selection of wines by the glass.

Livebait, 43 The Cut, SE1 8LF, ☎ (020) 7928 7211, *livebaitwaterloo@groupchezgerard.co.uk, Fax (020) 7928 2279* – 32 ANV c
closed 25-26 December, 1 January, Sunday and Bank Holidays – **Meals** - Seafood - 15.95 (lunch) and a la carte 30.00/40.00.
◆ Slight Victorian feel with wall tiles and booths. Lively atmosphere is distinctly modern. Helpful and obliging service. Comprehensive seafood menu from the on-view kitchen.

Tate Cafe (7th Floor), Tate Modern, Bankside, SE1 9TE, (020) 7401 5020, *Fax (020) 7401 5171,* London skyline and River Thames – . *closed 24-26 December* – **Meals** (lunch only and dinner Friday-Saturday) a la carte 19.75/26.50. 33 APV s
◆ Modernity to match the museum, with vast murals and huge windows affording stunning views. Canteen-style menu at a sensible price with obliging service.

Fish !, Cathedral St, Borough Market, SE1 9AL, (020) 7407 3803, *borough@fishdiner.couk, Fax (020) 7387 8636,* – . 33 AQV s
closed 25 December and 1 January – **Meals** - Seafood - a la carte 24.45/32.45.
◆ Under railway arches, an unusual structure made entirely of glass and metal. Seafood menu where diners choose the fish as well as the accompanying sauce.

TOWER HAMLETS

Blackwall – *E14.*

Ibis without rest., 1 Baffin Way, E14 9PE, (020) 7517 1100, *h2177@accor-hotels.com, Fax (020) 7987 5916* – rm, .
87 rm 71.95.
◆ Useful and sensibly priced accommodation, convenient for those visiting Canary Wharf. Bedrooms are all identically shaped, simply decorated and well-equipped.

Canary Wharf *Gtr London* – *E14.*

Four Seasons, Westferry Circus, E14 8RS, (020) 7510 1999, *Fax (020) 7510 1998,* – – 200. .
Meals (see ***Quadrato*** below) – 20.00 – **128 rm** 352.50/411.25, 14 suites.
◆ Stylish hotel opened in 2000, with striking river and city views. Atrium lobby leading to modern bedrooms boasting every conceivable extra. Detailed service.

Circus Apartments without rest., 39 Westferry Circus, E14 8RW, (020) 7719 7000, *res@circusapartments.co.uk, Fax (020) 7719 7001,* – . .
45 suites 293.75/346.60.
◆ Smart, contemporary, fully serviced appartment block close to Canary Wharf : rooms, comfortable and spacious, can be taken from one day to one year.

Ubon by Nobu, 34 Westferry Circus, E14 8RR, (020) 7719 7800, *ubon@nobures taurants.com, Fax (020) 7719 7801,* River Thames and city skyline – .
closed Christmas-New Year, Bank Holidays, Sunday and Saturday lunch – **Meals** - Japanese - a la carte approx 75.00 **s.**
◆ Light, airy, open-plan restaurant, with floor to ceiling glass and great Thames views. Informal atmosphere. Large menu with wide selection of modern Japanese dishes.

Quadrato (at Four Seasons H.), Westferry Circus, E14 8RS, (020) 7510 1999, *Fax (020) 7510 1998,* – .
Meals - Italian - 28.00/30.00.
◆ Striking, modern restaurant with terrace overlooking river. Sleek, stylish dining room with glass-fronted open-plan kitchen. Menu of northern Italian dishes ; swift service.

East India Docks – *E14.*

Travelodge, A 13 Coriander Ave, off East India Dock Rd, E14 2AA, off East India Dock Rd (08700) 850950, *Fax (020) 7515 9178,* – rm, rest, .
Meals (grill rest.) – **232 rm** 79.95.
◆ Overlooking the Millennium Dome, a larger than average lodge-style hotel with uniform sized bedrooms. Acres of parking and an informal café-bar on the ground floor.

St Katherine's Dock – *E1.*

The Aquarium, Ivory House, E1W 1AT, (020) 7480 6116, *info@theaquarium.co.uk, Fax (020) 7480 5973,* – 34 ASV a
closed 24-25 December, Monday dinner, Saturday lunch October-April, Sunday and Bank Holidays – **Meals** - Seafood - 20.50 and a la carte 24.25/60.50.
◆ Seafood restaurant in a pleasant marina setting with views of the boats from some tables. Simple, smart modern décor. Menu of market-fresh, seafood dishes.

Spitalfields – *E1.*

Bengal Trader, 44 Artillery Lane, E1 7NA, (020) 7375 0072, *trader@bengalresta urant.com, Fax (020) 7247 1002* – . 34 AST x
Meals - Indian - a la carte 12.00/15.70.
◆ Contemporary Indian paintings feature in this stylish basement room beneath a ground floor bar. Menu provides ample choice of Indian dishes.

Whitechapel - ✉ E1.

Cafe Spice Namaste, 16 Prescot St, E1 8AZ, ✆ (020) 7488 9242, *info@cafespice.co.uk*, *Fax (020) 7481 0508* – ▤. MC AE ⓓ VISA JCB 34 ASU z
closed 1 week Christmas, Sunday, Saturday lunch and Bank Holidays – **Meals** - Indian - 25.00 and a la carte 23.00/35.00 ♀.
◆ A riot of colour from the brightly painted walls to the flowing drapes. Sweet-natured service adds to the engaging feel. Fragrant and competitively priced Indian cooking.

Wapping - ✉ E1.

Wapping Food, Wapping Wall, E1W 3ST, ✆ (020) 7680 2080, *wappingfood@wapping-wpt.com*, *Fax (020) 7680 2081*, – P. MC AE ⓓ VISA
closed 24 December-3 January and Sunday dinner – **Meals** a la carte 22.50/34.00.
◆ Something a little unusual ; a combination of restaurant and gallery in a converted hydraulic power station. Enjoy the modern menu surrounded by turbines and TV screens.

WANDSWORTH

Battersea - ✉ SW8/SW11/SW18.

Express by Holiday Inn without rest., Smugglers Way, SW18 1EG, ✆ (020) 8877 5950, *wandsworth@oreil-leisure.co.uk*, *Fax (020) 8877 0631* – ▤ TV P – 35. MC AE ⓓ VISA.
148 rm 92.00.
◆ Modern, purpose-built hotel on major roundabout, very much designed for the cost-conscious business guest or traveller. Adjacent steak house. Sizeable, well-kept bedrooms.

Chada, 208-210 Battersea Park Rd, SW11 4ND, ✆ (020) 7622 2209, *enquiry@chadathai.com*, *Fax (020) 7924 2178* – ▤. MC AE ⓓ VISA JCB
closed Sunday and Bank Holidays – **Meals** - Thai - (dinner only) a la carte 17.20/26.65 ♀.
◆ Weather notwithstanding, the Thai ornaments and charming staff in traditional silk costumes transport you to Bangkok. Carefully prepared and authentic dishes.

The Stepping Stone, 123 Queenstown Rd, SW8 3RH, ✆ (020) 7622 0555, *thesteppingstone@aol.com*, *Fax (020) 7622 4230* – ▤. MC VISA
closed 5 days Christmas, Saturday lunch, Sunday and Bank Holidays – **Meals** a la carte 18.00/27.00.
◆ Big bold colours and thoughtful service make this pleasant contemporary restaurant a local favourite. Eclectic, modern menu. Small bar to the rear.

Ransome's Dock, 35-37 Parkgate Rd, SW11 4NP, ✆ (020) 7223 1611, *chef@ransomesdock.co.uk*, *Fax (020) 7924 2614*, – MC AE ⓓ VISA JCB
closed Christmas, August Bank Holiday and Sunday dinner – **Meals** a la carte 18.75/35.75 ♀.
◆ Secreted in a warehouse development, with a dock-side terrace in summer. Vivid blue interior, crowded with pictures. Chef patron produces reliable brasserie-style cuisine.

Putney - ✉ SW15.

Putney Bridge, Lower Richmond Rd, SW15 1LB, ✆ (020) 8780 1811, *Fax (020) 8780 1211*, ← – ▤. MC AE ⓓ VISA JCB
closed 25-26 December, 1 January and Sunday dinner – **Meals** 22.00 (lunch) and a la carte 31.50/55.50 ♀.
◆ Winner of architectural awards, this striking glass and steel structure enjoys a charming riverside location. Exacting service ; accomplished and detailed modern cooking.
Spec. Scallops with Jabugo ham and beurre noisette. Barbary duck with honey blossom and Szechuan pepper. Slow-roast lobster with orange and sweet spices.

Enoteca Turi, 28 Putney High St, SW15 1SQ, ✆ (020) 8785 4449, *Fax (020) 8780 5409* – ▤. MC AE ⓓ VISA
closed 25-26 December and Sunday – **Meals** - Italian - a la carte 21.75/31.75 ♀.
◆ A friendly neighbourhood Italian restaurant, overseen by the owner. Rustic cooking, with daily changing specials. Good selection of wine by the glass.

The Phoenix, Pentlow St, SW15 1LY, ✆ (020) 8780 3131, *phoenix@sonny's.co.uk*, *Fax (020) 8780 1114*, – ▤. MC AE ⓓ VISA
closed Bank Holidays – **Meals** - Italian influences - 19.50 (lunch) and a la carte 21.00/34.75 ♀.
◆ Light and bright interior with French windows leading out on to a spacious terrace. Unfussy and considerate service. An eclectic element to the modern Mediterranean menu.

Southfields - ✉ SW18.

Sarkhel's, 199 Replingham Rd, SW18 5LY, ✆ (020) 8870 1483, *veronica@sarkhels.co.uk, Fax (020) 8874 6603* – ▤. MC VISA
closed 25-26 December – **Meals** - Indian - 10.00 (lunch) and a la carte 18.00/27.35 ♀.
◆ Recently expanded Indian restaurant with a large local following. Authentic, carefully prepared and well-priced dishes from many different Indian regions. Obliging service.

Tooting - ✉ SW17.

Kastoori, 188 Upper Tooting Rd, SW17 7EJ, ✆ (020) 8767 7027 – ▤. MC VISA
closed 25-26 December and lunch Monday and Tuesday – **Meals** - Indian Vegetarian - a la carte 12.75/24.50.
◆ Specialising in Indian vegetarian cooking with a subtle East African influence. Family-run for many years, a warm and welcoming establishment with helpful service.

Oh Boy, 843 Garratt Lane, SW17 0PG, ✆ (020) 8947 9760, *Fax (020) 8879 7867* – ▤. MC AE D VISA JCB
closed 25-26 December, 1 January and Monday – **Meals** - Thai - (dinner only) 22.00 and a la carte 12.25/18.35.
◆ Long-standing neighbourhood Thai restaurant. Extensive menu offers authentic and carefully prepared dishes, in simple but friendly surroundings.

Wandsworth - ✉ SW12/SW17/SW18.

Chez Bruce (Poole), 2 Bellevue Rd, SW17 7EG, ✆ (020) 8672 0114, *chezbruce2@aol.com, Fax (020) 8767 6648* – ⇔ ▤. MC AE D VISA
closed 24-26 December and 1 January – **Meals** (booking essential) 23.50/30.00 ♀.
◆ An ever-popular restaurant, overlooking the Common. Simple yet considered modern British cooking. Convivial and informal, with enthusiastic service.
Spec. Red mullet with fennel, potato and olive salad. Grilled calf's kidney with balsamic vinegar. Strawberry and Champagne trifle.

Ditto, 55-57 East Hill, SW18 2QE, ✆ (020) 8877 0110, *christian-gilles@ditto1.fsnet.co.uk, Fax (020) 8875 0110* – MC VISA
closed 24-27 December, Sunday and Monday – **Meals** (bar lunch)/dinner 19.50 and a la carte 24.00/28.00 ♀.
◆ Relaxed bar on one side, informal restaurant on the other. Bright walls with modern pictures and a monthly changing modern menu. Personally run by the young owners.

Bombay Bicycle Club, 95 Nightingale Lane, SW12 8NX, ✆ (020) 8673 6217, *Fax (020) 8673 9100* – MC AE D VISA
closed 25-26 December, Easter Monday and Sunday – **Meals** - Indian - (dinner only) a la carte 17.25/21.50 ♀.
◆ Nestling in a residential area and decorated with plants and murals. Relaxed atmosphere with an authentic, rustic appeal. Sound Indian cooking.

WESTMINSTER (City of)

Bayswater and Maida Vale - ✉ NW6/W2/W9.

Hilton London Paddington, 146 Praed St, W2 1EE, ✆ (020) 7850 0500, *paddington@hilton.com, Fax (020) 7850 0600,* Fø, ≘s - |‡|, ⇔ rm, ▤ TV ✆ ♿ - 🏛 400. MC AE D VISA JCB. ✂ 28ADU a
***The Brasserie* :** Meals 20.00/33.00 ♀ - ☕ 18.50 - **335 rm** 229.10, 20 suites.
◆ Early Victorian railway hotel, sympathetically restored in contemporary style with Art Deco details. Co-ordinated bedrooms with high tech facilities continue the modern style. Contemporarily styled brasserie offering a modern menu.

Royal Lancaster, Lancaster Terr, W2 2TY, ✆ (020) 7262 6737, *sales@royallancaster.com, Fax (020) 7724 3191,* ≤ - |‡|, ⇔ rm, ▤ TV ✆ ♿ P - 🏛 1400. MC AE D VISA JCB. ✂ 28ADU e
Meals (see ***Nipa*** below) - ☕ 15.00 - **394 rm** 290.00/378.00, 22 suites.
◆ Imposing purpose-built hotel overlooking Hyde Park. Some of London's most extensive conference facilities. Well-equipped bedrooms are decorated in an Asian style. Park overlooks charming Italian Gardens. Pavement is a relaxed brasserie.

Hilton London Metropole, Edgware Rd, W2 1JU, ✆ (020) 7402 4141, *Fax (020) 7724 8866,* ≤, Fø, ≘s, 🏊 - |‡|, ⇔ rm, ▤ TV ✆ P - 🏛 2000. MC AE D VISA JCB. ✂ 28 AET c
Meals a la carte 22.50/29.85 ♀ - ☕ 17.50 - **1033 rm** 175.00/198.50, 25 suites.
◆ One of London's most popular convention venues by virtue of both its size and transport links. Well-appointed and modern rooms have state-of-the-art facilities. Vibrant restaurant and bar.

The Hempel, 31-35 Craven Hill Gdns, W2 3EA, (020) 7298 9000, *hotel@the-hempel.co.uk*, *Fax (020) 7402 4666*, – rm. 28ACU a
closed 25-26 December – ***I-Thai :*** **Meals** - Italian-Japanese-Thai - *(closed Sunday)* 60.00 and dinner a la carte – 21.00 – **40 rm** 346.60, 6 suites.
◆ A striking example of minimalist design. Individually appointed bedrooms are understated yet very comfortable. Relaxed ambience. Modern basement restaurant.

Marriott, Plaza Parade, NW6 5RP, (020) 7543 6000, *marriottmaidavale@btinternet.com*, *Fax (020) 7543 2100*, – rm, – 200.
Fratelli : **Meals** - Italian - *(closed Sunday)* (dinner only) a la carte 23.95/32.25 – 16.95 – **222 rm** 116.30, 16 suites.
◆ A capacious hotel, a short walk from Marble Arch and Oxford Street. Well-equipped with both business and leisure facilities including 12m pool. Suites have small kitchens. Informal restaurant and brasserie.

Thistle Hyde Park, Bayswater Rd, 90-92 Lancaster Gate, W2 3NR, (020) 7262 2711, *Fax (020) 7262 2147* – – 25. 28ACU v
Meals *(closed Sunday)* (bar lunch Saturday) 19.50 (lunch) and dinner a la carte 25.70/38.25 **s.** – 14.95 – **52 rm** 245.50/280.80, 2 suites.
◆ Behind the ornate pillared façade sits an attractively restored hotel. Appealing to the corporate and leisure traveller, the generally spacious rooms retain a period feel. Aperitifs in relaxed conservatory before formal dining.

Colonnade Town House, 2 Warrington Cres, W9 1ER, (020) 7286 1052, *colonnade@theetoncollection.com*, *Fax (020) 7286 1057*, – rm,
Enigma (*(020) 7432 8455* **: Meals** - Italian - *(closed Monday)* (light lunch)/dinner 20.00/30.00 and a la carte 15.00/25.00 – 12.50 – **43 rm** 148.00/270.00.
◆ Two Victorian townhouses with comfortable well-furnished communal rooms decorated with fresh flowers. Stylish and comfortable bedrooms with many extra touches. Enigma restaurant named after AlanTuring, the code-breaker who was born here.

Gresham Hyde Park, Lancaster Gate, W2 3NZ, (020) 7262 5090, *info@gresham-hydeparkhotel.com*, *Fax (020) 7723 1244*, – rm, – 25. 28ACU e
Meals 30.00 (dinner) and a la carte 18.00/29.50 **s.** – 15.00 – **188 rm** 185.00.
◆ A smart hotel in the modern style in a quiet street just off Hyde Park. Spacious brightly decorated rooms with every conceiveable facility including robes, slippers etc. Contemporary style restaurant with serving a very concise menu.

Mornington without rest., 12 Lancaster Gate, W2 3LG, (020) 7262 7361, *london@mornington.co.uk*, *Fax (020) 7706 1028* –
closed 24-27 December – **66 rm** 125.00/160.00. 28ACU s
◆ The classic portico facade belies the cool and modern Scandinavian influenced interior. Modern bedrooms are well-equipped and generally spacious. Duplex rooms available.

Commodore, 50 Lancaster Gate, Hyde Park, W2 3NA, (020) 7402 5291, *reservations@commodore-hotel.com*, *Fax (020) 7262 1088*, – rm, 28ACU r
Meals (dinner only) 15.00/45.00 – **81 rm** 105.00/145.00, 3 suites.
◆ Three converted Georgian town houses in a leafy residential area. Bedrooms vary considerably in size and style. Largest rooms decorated with a Victorian theme. Relaxed, casual bistro.

Hilton London Hyde Park, 129 Bayswater Rd, W2 4RJ, (020) 7221 2217, *reservationshydepark@hilton.com*, *Fax (020) 7229 0557* – , rest, – 100. 27ABU c
Meals (bar lunch)/dinner 21.95 and a la carte approx. 28.00 – 12.95 – **128 rm** 145.70/157.45, 1 suite.
◆ Classical Victorian hotel on busy main road. Well-appointed bedrooms enjoy up to date facilities. Rooms to front have Park views. Intimate dining room or relaxed bar for meals.

Delmere, 130 Sussex Gdns, W2 1UB, (020) 7706 3344, *delmerehotel@compuserve.com*, *Fax (020) 7262 1863* – rm, 28 ADT v
Meals *(closed Sunday)* (dinner only) 19.00 – 6.00 – **36 rm** 86.00/107.00.
◆ Attractive stucco fronted and porticoed Victorian property. Now a friendly private hotel. Compact bedrooms are both well-equipped and kept. Modest prices. Bright, relaxed restaurant and adjacent bar.

Miller's without rest., 111A Westbourne Grove, W2 4UW, (020) 7243 1024, *enquiries@millersuk.com*, *Fax (020) 7243 1064* – 27ABU a
8 rm 188.00/264.00.
◆ Victorian house brimming with antiques and knick-knacks. Charming sitting room provides the setting for a relaxed breakfast. Individual, theatrical rooms named after poets.

Byron without rest., 36-38 Queensborough Terr, W2 3SH, ☎ (020) 7243 0987, *byron@capricornhotels.co.uk, Fax (020) 7792 1957* – |♦| ▤ TV. MC AE ◑ VISA JCB. ✻
44 rm ☕ 75.00/120.00, 1 suite. 28ACU z
◆ Centrally located and refurbished in the late 1990's - an ideal base for tourists. Bright and modern bedrooms are generally spacious and all have showers ensuite.

Nipa (at Royal Lancaster H.), Lancaster Terr, W2 2TY, ☎ (020) 7262 6737, *Fax (020) 7724 3191* – ▤ P. MC AE ◑ VISA JCB 28ADU e
closed Saturday lunch, Sunday and Bank Holidays – **Meals** - Thai - 14.90/28.00 and a la carte 30.30/42.30 **s.**.
◆ On the 1st floor and overlooking Hyde Park. Authentic and ornately decorated restaurant offers subtly spiced Thai cuisine. Keen to please staff in traditional silk costumes.

Al San Vincenzo, 30 Connaught St, W2 2AF, ☎ (020) 7262 9623 – MC VISA JCB
closed Saturday lunch and Sunday – **Meals** - Italian - (booking essential) 34.50 ♀.
◆ A traditional Italian restaurant that continues to attract a loyal clientele. Rustic, authentic cooking and a wholly Italian wine list. Attentive service overseen by owner. 29 AFU a

Jason's, Blomfield Rd, Little Venice, W9 2PA, ☎ (020) 7286 6752, *enquiries@jasons.co.uk, Fax (020) 7266 2656,* ☂ – MC AE ◑ VISA
closed Sunday dinner and Monday lunch – **Meals** - Seafood - 15.00 (lunch) and a la carte 23.45/35.00.
◆ Hidden behind a wall, one finds this charming spot beside Regent's Canal. Seafood can be enjoyed in the bright dining room or on the busy terrace beside the boats for hire.

Green Olive, 5 Warwick Pl, W9 2PX, ☎ (020) 7289 2469, *Fax (020) 7266 5522* – ▤. MC AE VISA
closed Christmas-New Year – **Meals** - Italian - (booking essential) 18.00/30.00 ♀.
◆ Attractive neighbourhood restaurant in a smart residential area. Modern Italian food served in the bright street level room or the more intimate basement.

Assaggi, 39 Chepstow Pl, (above Chepstow pub), W2 4TS, ☎ (020) 7792 5501, *nipi@assaggi1.demon.co.uk* – ▤. MC ◑ VISA JCB 27 AAU c
closed 2 weeks Christmas, Sunday and Bank Holidays – **Meals** - Italian - a la carte 25.95/39.15.
◆ Polished wood flooring, tall windows and modern artwork provide the bright surroundings for this forever busy restaurant. Concise menu of robust Italian dishes.

The Vale, 99 Chippenham Rd, W9 2AB, ☎ (020) 7266 0990, *thevale@hotmail.com Fax (020) 7286 7224* – ▤. MC ◑ VISA JCB
closed 1 week Christmas, Easter, 25-31 August, Sunday dinner and lunch Monday and Saturday – **Meals** 12.00/15.00 and a la carte 19.00/25.00 ♀.
◆ Dine in either the light and spacious conservatory, or in the original bar of this converted pub. Modern British food with Mediterranean influences. Destination bar below.

Ginger, 115 Westbourne Grove, W2 4UP, ☎ (020) 7908 1990, *info@gingerrestaurant.co.uk, Fax (020) 7908 1991* – ▤. MC AE VISA JCB 27 ABU v
closed 25-26 December – **Meals** - Bangladeshi - a la carte 13.40/22.40.
◆ Bengali specialities served in contemporary styled dining room. True to its name, ginger is a key flavouring ; dishes range from mild to spicy and are graded accordingly.

L'Accento, 16 Garway Rd, W2 4NH, ☎ (020) 7243 2201, *laccentorest@aol.com, Fax (020) 7243 2201* – MC AE VISA JCB 27 ABU b
closed 25-26 December and Sunday – **Meals** - Italian - a la carte 22.00/28.00.
◆ Rustic surroundings and provincial, well priced, Italian cooking. Menu specialises in tasty pasta, made on the premises, and shellfish. Rear conservatory for the summer.

Formosa Dining Room (at Prince Alfred), 5A Formosa St, W9 1EE, ☎ (020) 7286 3287 *theprincealfred@thespiritgroup.com, Fax (020) 7286 3383* – ▤. MC AE VISA
closed 25 December – **Meals** a la carte 24.50/37.00 ♀.
◆ Traditional pub appearance and a relaxed dining experience on offer behind the elegant main bar. Contemporary style of cooking.

The Waterway, 54 Formosa St, W9 2JU, ☎ (020) 7266 3557, *Fax (020) 7266 3547* ☂ – ▤. MC AE VISA
closed 24-26 December – **Meals** 15.00 (lunch) and a la carte 23.00/34.50 ♀.
◆ Pub with a thoroughly modern, metropolitan ambience. Spacious bar and large decked terrace overlooking canal. Concise, well-balanced menu served in open plan dining room.

Belgravia – ✉ SW1.

The Lanesborough, Hyde Park Corner, SW1X 7TA, ☎ (020) 7259 5599, *info@lanesborough.com, Fax (020) 7259 5606,* 🏋 – |♦|, ⇔ rm, ▤ TV ☎ ♿ P – 🏛 90. MC AE ◑ VISA JCB. ✻ 37 AGX a
***The Conservatory* :** **Meals** 30.00/48.00 and a la carte 42.50/76.00 **s.** ♀ – ☕ 24.50 – **86 rm** 334.80/528.75, 9 suites.
◆ Converted in the 1990s from 18C St George's Hospital. A grand and traditional atmosphere prevails. Butler service offered. Regency-era decorated, lavishly appointed rooms. Ornate, glass-roofed dining room with palm trees and fountains.

The Berkeley, Wilton Pl, SW1X 7RL, ✆ (020) 7235 6000, *info@the-berkeley.co.uk, Fax (020) 7235 4330,* – rm, – 220. 37 AGX e

Boxwood Café *(✆ (020) 7235 1010)* **: Meals** a la carte 22.00/35.50 ♀ (see also ***Pétrus*** below) – ☕ 27.00 – **186 rm** 198.60/493.50, 28 suites.

• A gracious and discreet hotel. Relax in the ornately gilded and panelled Lutyens lounge or enjoy a swim in the roof-top pool with its retracting roof. Opulent bedrooms. Split-level basement restaurant, divided by bar, with modern stylish décor ; New York-style dining.

The Halkin, 5 Halkin St, SW1X 7DJ, ✆ (020) 7333 1000, *res@halkin.co.uk, Fax (020) 7333 1100* – 38 AHX b

Meals (see ***Nahm*** below) – ☕ 22.00 – **37 rm** 364.25/464.10, 4 suites.

• One of London's first minimalist hotels. The cool, marbled reception and bar have an understated charm. Spacious rooms have every conceivable facility.

Sheraton Belgravia, 20 Chesham Pl, SW1X 8HQ, ✆ (020) 7235 6040, *central.london.reservations@sheraton.com, Fax (020) 7201 1926* – rm, – 25. 37 AGX u

The Mulberry **: Meals** 22.00 (dinner) and a la carte 24.00/31.00 ♀ – ☕ 17.50 – **82 rm** 329.00, 7 suites.

• Modern corporate hotel overlooking Chesham Place. Comfortable and well-equipped for the tourist and business traveller alike. A few minutes' walk from Harrods.

The Lowndes, 21 Lowndes St, SW1X 9ES, ✆ (020) 7823 1234, *contact@lowndeshotel.com, Fax (020) 7235 1154,* – rm, – 25. 37 AGX h

Brasserie 21 **: Meals** 16.95 and a la carte 22.00/32.00 ♀ – ☕ 17.50 – **77 rm** 305.50, 1 suite.

• Compact yet friendly modern corporate hotel within this exclusive residential area. Good levels of personal service offered. Close to the famous shops of Knightsbridge. Modern restaurant opens onto street terrace.

Diplomat without rest., 2 Chesham St, SW1X 8DT, ✆ (020) 7235 1544, *diplomat.hotel@btinternet.co.uk, Fax (020) 7259 6153* – 37 AGY a

26 rm ☕ 95.00/170.00.

• Imposing Victorian corner house built in 1882 by Thomas Cubitt. Attractive glass-domed stairwell and sweeping staircase. Spacious and well-appointed bedrooms.

Pétrus (Wareing) (at The Berkeley H.), Wilton Pl, SW1X 7RL, ✆ (020) 7235 1200, *petrus@marcuswareing.com, Fax (020) 7235 1266* – 37 AGX e

closed 2 weeks Christmas, Saturday lunch and Sunday – **Meals** 26.00/70.00 ♀.

• Elegantly appointed restaurant named after one of the 40 Petrus vintages on the wine list. One table in the kitchen to watch the chefs at work. Accomplished modern cooking.

Spec. Lobster "Arnold Bennett". Braised hare, celeriac purée, Madeira sauce. Peanut parfait, chocolate mousse and candied peanuts.

Zafferano, 15 Lowndes St, SW1X 9EY, ✆ (020) 7235 5800, *Fax (020) 7235 1971* – 37 AGX f

closed 25 December and 1 January – **Meals** - Italian - 26.50/37.50 ♀.

• Forever busy and relaxed. No frills, robust and gutsy Italian cooking, where the quality of the produce shines through. Wholly Italian wine list has some hidden treasures.

Spec. Green beans, cuttlefish salad and black olives. Flat linguini with lobster and tomato. Tiramisu.

Nahm (at The Halkin H.), 5 Halkin St, SW1X 7DJ, ✆ (020) 7333 1234, *Fax (020) 7333 1100* – 38 AHX b

closed lunch Saturday and Sunday – **Meals** - Thai - (booking essential) 26.00/47.00 **s.** ♀.

• Wood floored restaurant with uncovered tables and understated decor. Menu offers the best of Thai cooking with some modern interpretation and original use of ingredients.

Spec. Crab and pomelo with roasted coconut, peanuts and caramel dressing. Salad of grilled duck with cashew nuts and Thai basil. Crispy fishcakes with pork and salted eggs.

Mango Tree, 46 Grosvenor Pl, SW1X 7EQ, ✆ (020) 7823 1888, *mangotree@mangotree.org.uk, Fax (020) 7838 9275* – 38 AHX a

closed 25-26 December and 1 January – **Meals** - Thai - 15.80/35.00 and a la carte 21.80/31.50 ♀.

• Thai staff in regional dress in contemporarily styled dining room of refined yet minimalist furnishings sums up the cuisine : authentic Thai dishes with modern presentation.

Noura Brasserie, 16 Hobart Pl, SW1W 0HH, ✆ (020) 7235 9444, *Fax (020) 7235 9244* – 38 AHX n

Meals - Lebanese - 14.50/31.00 and a la carte 23.00/30.00.

• Dine in either the bright bar or the comfortable, contemporary restaurant. Authentic, modern Lebanese cooking specialises in char-grilled meats and mezzes.

Hyde Park and Knightsbridge – ✉ *SW1/SW7.*

Mandarin Oriental Hyde Park, 66 Knightsbridge, SW1X 7LA, ✆ (020) 7235 2000 *molon-reservations@mohg.com, Fax (020) 7235 2001,* ≤, ₣ð, ≘ – |ǂ|, ⇹ rm, ▤ TV ✆ ♿ – 🏛 220. MC AE ⓓ VISA JCB. ✂ 37 AGX
The Park : **Meals** 27.00 (lunch) and a la carte 26.00/43.00 (see also ***Foliage*** below) – ☕ 22.00 – **177 rm** 299.00/640.00, 23 suites.
◆ Built in 1889 this classic hotel, with striking façade, remains one of London's grandest Many of the luxurious bedrooms enjoy Park views. Immaculate and detailed service.

Knightsbridge Green without rest., 159 Knightsbridge, SW1X 7PD, ✆ (020 7584 6274, *reservations@thekghotel.co.uk, Fax (020) 7225 1635* – |ǂ| ⇹ ▤ TV ✆. MC AE ⓓ VISA. ✂ 37 AFX
☕ 10.50 – **16 rm** 110.00/145.00, 12 suites 170.00.
◆ Privately owned hotel, boasting peaceful sitting room with writing desk. Breakfast sausage and bacon from Harrods ! - served in the generously proportioned bedrooms.

✿ **Foliage** (at Mandarin Oriental Hyde Park H.), 66 Knightsbridge, SW1X 7LA, ✆ (020 7201 3723, *Fax (020) 7235 4552* – ▤. MC AE ⓓ VISA JCB 37 AGX
Meals 27.00/42.50 ♀.
◆ Reached via a glass-enclosed walkway that houses the cellar. Hyde Park outside th window reflected in the foliage-themed décor. Gracious service, skilled moder cooking.
Spec. Duo of foie gras with caramelised endive Tarte Tatin. Ballottine of sole, roast tomat consommé and crab tortellini. Banana crème brûlée, caramel ice cream.

Isola, (basement) 145 Knightsbridge, SW1X 7PA, ✆ (020) 7838 1044 *Fax (020) 7838 1099* – ▤. MC AE VISA 37 AFX
closed 24-26 December, 1 January and Sunday – **Meals** - Italian - 18.50/38.00 and dinne a la carte 29.50/39.50 ♀.
◆ In a contemporary basement, the main restaurant offers clean Italian cooking and prim ingredients. Large selection of wines by the glass.

Zuma, 5 Raphael St, SW7 1DL, ✆ (020) 7584 1010, *info@zumarestaurant.com Fax (020) 7584 5005* – ▤. MC AE ⓓ VISA 37 AFX
closed 25-26 December – **Meals** - Japanese - a la carte 45.00/80.00 ♀.
◆ Strong modern feel with exposed pipes, modern lighting and granite flooring. A theatric atmosphere around the Sushi bar and a varied and interesting modern Japanes menu.

Mr Chow, 151 Knightsbridge, SW1X 7PA, ✆ (020) 7589 7347, *mrchow@aol.com Fax (020) 7584 5780* – ▤. MC AE ⓓ VISA JCB 37 AFX
closed 24-26 December, 1 January and Easter Monday – **Meals** - Chinese - 18.00 (lunc and a la carte 35.00/40.50 ♀.
◆ Cosmopolitan Chinese restaurant with branches in New York and L.A. Well establishe ambience. Walls covered with mirrors and modern art. House specialities worth optin for.

Mayfair – ✉ *W1.*

Dorchester, Park Lane, W1A 2HJ, ✆ (020) 7629 8888, *reservations@dorchesterhc el.com, Fax (020) 7409 0114,* ₣ð, ≘ – |ǂ|, ⇹ rm, ▤ TV ✆ ♿ 🚗 – 🏛 550. MC AE ⓓ VISA JCB. ✂ 30 AHV
Meals (see ***The Oriental*** and ***Grill Room*** below) – ☕ 24.50 – **201 rm** 317.25/387.7 49 suites 587.50/2,496.80.
◆ A sumptuously decorated, luxury hotel offering every possible facility. Impressiv marbled and pillared promenade. Rooms quintessentially English in style. Faultle service.

Claridge's, Brook St, W1A 2JQ, ✆ (020) 7629 8860, *info@claridges.co.u Fax (020) 7499 2210,* ₣ð – |ǂ|, ⇹ rm, ▤ TV ✆ ♿ – 🏛 200. MC AE ⓓ VI JCB. ✂ 30AHU
Meals 29.50 and a la carte 33.50/60.00 ♀ (see also ***Gordon Ramsay at Claridge's*** belov – ☕ 23.50 – **143 rm** 405.30/464.10, 60 suites.
◆ The epitome of English grandeur, celebrated for its Art Deco. Exceptionally we appointed and sumptuous bedrooms, all with butler service. Magnificently restore foyer.

Grosvenor House, Park Lane, W1K 7TN, ✆ (020) 7499 6363, *Fax (020) 7493 3341,* ₣ ≘, ▣ – |ǂ|, ⇹ rm, ▤ TV ✆ ♿ 🚗 – 🏛 2000. MC AE ⓓ V JCB. ✂ 29AGU
La Terrazza : **Meals** - Italian influences - *(closed Saturday lunch)* a la carte 24.00/38.0 ♀ – ☕ 21.50 – **378 rm** 352.50, 74 suites.
◆ Over 70 years old and occupying an enviable position by the Park. Edwardian style déc The Great Room, an ice rink in the 1920s, is Europe's largest banqueting room. Brig relaxing dining room with contemporary feel.

Four Seasons, Hamilton Pl, Park Lane, W1A 1AZ, (020) 7499 0888, *fsh.london@fourseasons.com, Fax (020) 7493 1895,* – rm, – 500. 30 AHV b
***Lanes* : Meals** 36.00/33.50 and a la carte 35.50/59.50 **s.** – 21.00 – **185 rm** 352.50/417.10, 35 suites.
◆ Set back from Park Lane so shielded from the traffic. Large, marbled lobby ; its lounge a popular spot for light meals. Spacious rooms, some with their own conservatory. Restaurant's vivid blue and stained glass give modern, yet relaxing, feel.

Le Meridien Piccadilly, 21 Piccadilly, W1J 0BH, (020) 7734 8000, *lmpiccres@lemeridien-hotels.com, Fax (020) 7437 3574,* , squash – rm, – 250. 31 AJV a
Meals (see ***Terrace*** below) – 22.50 – **248 rm** 170.30/217.30, 18 suites.
◆ Comfortable international hotel, in a central location. Boasts one of the finest leisure clubs in London. Individually decorated bedrooms, with first class facilities.

London Hilton, 22 Park Lane, W1K 4BE, (020) 7493 8000, *reservations@hilton.com, Fax (020) 7208 4146,* London, – rm, – 1000. 30 AHV e
Trader Vics *(* *(020) 7208 4113)* **: Meals** *(closed lunch Saturday, Sunday and Bank Holidays)* 18.00 and a la carte 28.00/49.00 – ***Park Brasserie* : Meals** 22.50 (lunch) and a la carte 30.00/42.50 (see also ***Windows*** below) – 21.00 – **396 rm** 382.00, 65 suites.
◆ This 28 storey tower is one of the city's tallest hotels, providing impressive views from the upper floors. Club floor bedrooms are particularly comfortable. Exotic Trader Vics with bamboo and plants. A harpist adds to the relaxed feel of Park Brasserie.

Connaught, 16 Carlos Pl, W1K 2AL, (020) 7499 7070, *info@the-connaught.co.uk, Fax (020) 7495 3262,* – 30AHU e
Terrace* : Meals** a la carte 21.00/38.00 (see also ***Menu and Grill below) – 26.50 – **68 rm** 352.50/499.00, 23 suites.
◆ 19C quintessentially English hotel, with country house ambience. The grand mahogany staircase leads up to antique furnished bedrooms. Smart indoor terrace restaurant with green metal furniture. Attentive service. Menu ranging from one dish to a 3-course meal.

Brown's, Albemarle St, W1S 4BP, (020) 7493 6020, *Fax (020) 7493 9381,* – – 70. 30 AIV m
Meals (see ***1837*** below) – 22.00 – **112 rm** 340.00/376.00, 6 suites.
◆ Opened in 1837, a classic English hotel, celebrated for its afternoon tea. Past guests include Alexander Graham Bell who made his successful telephone call from here.

Inter-Continental, 1 Hamilton Pl, Hyde Park Corner, W1J 7QY, (020) 7409 3131, *london@interconti.com, Fax (020) 7493 3476,* – rm, – 1000. 30 AHV s
Meals 26.00/30.00 and a la carte approx 38.00 – ***Le Souffle* : Meals** *(closed lunch Monday and Tuesday and Sunday dinner)* 29.50/40.00 and a la carte approx 46.00 – 20.50 – **418 rm** 376.00/434.75, 40 suites.
◆ A large, purpose-built, international group hotel that dominates Hyde Park Corner. Spacious marbled lobby and lounge. Well-equipped bedrooms, many of which have Park views. Informal café style dining or more intimate Soufflé.

Park Lane, Piccadilly, W1Y 8BX, (020) 7499 6321, *central.london.reservations@sheraton.com, Fax (020) 7499 1965,* – rm, – 500. 30 AHV x
Citrus *(* *(020) 7290 7364)* **: Meals** 19.00/22.00 **s.** and a la carte – 19.95 – **287 rm** 305.50, 20 suites.
◆ The history of the hotel is reflected in the elegant 'Palm Court' lounge and ballroom, both restored to their Art Deco origins. Bedrooms vary in shape and size. Summer pavement tables in restaurant opposite Hyde Park.

London Marriott Park Lane, 140 Park Lane, W1K 7AA, (020) 7493 7000, *mhrs.parklane@marriotthotels.com, Fax (020) 7493 8333,* – – 75. 29AGU b
***140 Park Lane* : Meals** a la carte 23.00/38.00 – 18.95 – **148 rm** 323.10, 9 suites.
◆ Superbly located 'boutique' style hotel at intersection of Park Lane and Oxford Street. Attractive basement health club. Spacious, well-equipped rooms with luxurious elements. Attractive restaurant overlooking Marble Arch.

Westbury, Bond St, W1S 2YF, (020) 7629 7755, *sales@westburymayfair.com, Fax (020) 7495 1163,* – rm, – 120. 30 AIU a
Meals *(closed lunch Saturday and Sunday)* 19.50/21.50 and a la carte – 17.75 – **233 rm** 282.00/305.50, 21 suites.
◆ Surrounded by London's most fashionable shops ; the renowned Polo bar and lounge provide soothing sanctuary. Some suites have their own terrace. Bright, fresh restaurant enhanced by modern art.

The Metropolitan, Old Park Lane, W1Y 4LB, (020) 7447 1000, *res@metropolitan.co.uk, Fax (020) 7447 1100,* ←, – , rm, . VISA JCB. 30 AHV c
Meals (see ***Nobu*** below) – 20.00 – **147 rm** 305.50/569.80, 3 suites.
◆ Minimalist interior and a voguish reputation make this the favoured hotel of pop stars and celebrities. Innovative design and fashionably attired staff set it apart.

Athenaeum, 116 Piccadilly, W1J 7BS, (020) 7499 3464, *info@athenaeumhotel.com, Fax (020) 7493 1860,* , – , rm, – 55. VISA
Bulloch's at 116 : Meals *(closed lunch Saturday and Sunday)* 18.00 (lunch) and a la carte approx. 35.35 **s.** – 21.00 – **124 rm** 311.00/370.00, 33 suites. 30 AHV g
◆ Built in 1925 as a luxury apartment block. Comfortable bedrooms with video and CD players. Individually designed suites are in an adjacent Edwardian townhouse. Conservatory roofed dining room renowned for its mosaics and malt whiskies.

London Marriott Grosvenor Square, Duke St, Grosvenor Sq, W1K 6JP, (020) 7493 1232, *Fax (020) 7491 3201,* – , rm, – 600. VISA JCB. 30AHU s
Diplomat : Meals *(closed lunch Saturday and Monday-Tuesday dinner)* 15.95 and a la carte 22.25/37.85 – 15.95 – **209 rm** 270.00, 12 suites.
◆ A well-appointed international group hotel that benefits from an excellent location. Many of the bedrooms specifically equipped for the business traveller. Formal dining room with its own cocktail bar.

Washington Mayfair, 5-7 Curzon St, W1J 5HE, (020) 7499 7000, *sales@washington-mayfair.co.uk, Fax (020) 7495 6172,* – , rm, – 90. VISA. 30 AHV c
Meals 17.95/33.85 **s.** and a la carte – 16.95 – **166 rm** 235.00, 5 suites.
◆ Successfully blends a classical style with modern amenities. Relaxing lounge with traditional English furniture and bedrooms with polished, burred oak. Piano bar annex to formal dining room.

Chesterfield, 35 Charles St, W1J 5EB, (020) 7491 2622, *bookch@chmail.com Fax (020) 7491 4793* – , rm, – 110. VISA JCB
Meals *(closed Saturday lunch)* 16.95/19.95 and a la carte 28.00/45.00 – 16.50 – **106 rm** 264.30/346.60, 4 suites. 30 AHV
◆ An assuredly English feel to this Georgian house. Discreet lobby leads to a clubby bar and wood panelled library. Individually decorated bedrooms, with some antique pieces. Classically decorated restaurant.

Flemings, Half Moon St, W1J 7BH, (020) 7499 2964, *sales@flemings-mayfair.co.uk Fax (020) 7491 8866* – , rm, – 55. VISA JCB.
Meals 25.00 – 18.00 – **111 rm** 198.60/233.85, 10 suites. 30 AIV
◆ A Georgian town house where the oil paintings and English furniture add to the charm. Apartments located in adjoining house, once home to noted polymath Henry Wagner. Candlelit basement restaurant with oil paintings.

No.5 Maddox St without rest., 5 Maddox St, W1S 2QD, (020) 7647 0200, *no5maddoxst@living-rooms.co.uk, Fax (020) 7647 0300* – . VISA JCB. 30 AIU
17.50, **12 suites** 287.80/705.00.
◆ No grand entrance or large foyer, just a discreet door bell and brass plaque. All rooms are stylish and contemporary suites, with kitchenettes and every conceivable mod con.

Hilton London Green Park, Half Moon St, W1J 7BN, (020) 7629 7522 *Fax (020) 7491 8971* – – 130. VISA JCB. 30 AIV
Meals 21.95/35.00 and a la carte 21.95/41.70 **s.** – 17.50 – **161 rm** 198.50/210.3
◆ A row of sympathetically adjoined townhouses, dating from the 1730s. Discreet marble lobby. Bedrooms share the same décor but vary in size and shape. Monet prints decorate light, airy dining room.

Hilton London Mews, 2 Stanhope Row, W1J 7BS, (020) 7493 7222 *Fax (020) 7629 9423* – – 50. VISA JCB. 30 AHV
closed 24-28 December – **Meals** (dinner only) 20.00/35.00 and a la carte 21.95/34.95 – 16.50 – **71 rm** 186.80/198.55.
◆ Tucked away in a discreet corner of Mayfair. This modern, group hotel manages to retain a cosy and intimate feel. Well-equipped bedrooms to meet corporate needs. Meals in cosy dining room or lounge.

Le Gavroche (Roux), 43 Upper Brook St, W1K 7QR, (020) 7408 0881, *bookings@le-gavroche.com, Fax (020) 7491 4387* – . VISA JCB 29AGU
closed Christmas-New Year, Sunday, Saturday lunch and Bank Holidays – **Meals** - French - (booking essential) 42.00 (lunch) and a la carte 57.40/101.40.
◆ Long standing renowned restaurant with a clubby, formal atmosphere. Accomplished classical French cuisine, served by smartly attired and well-drilled staff.
Spec. Foie gras chaud et pastilla de canard à la cannelle. Râble de lapin et galette au parmesan. Le palet au chocolat amer et praline croustillant.

XXXX **The Oriental** (at Dorchester H.), Park Lane, W1A 2HJ, ✆ (020) 7317 6328, *Fax (020) 7317 6464* – ▤. MC AE ⓓ VISA JCB 30 AHV a
closed Saturday lunch and Sunday – **Meals** - Chinese (Canton) - 17.00/48.00 and a la carte 27.00/67.50 **s.** ♀.
◆ London's grandest Chinese restaurant, decorated with sculptures, antique silks and gilded mirrors. Asian themed private dining rooms. A variety of menus available.

XXXX **Grill Room** (at Dorchester H.), Park Lane, W1A 2HJ, ✆ (020) 7317 6336, *Fax (020) 7317 6464* – ▤. MC AE ⓓ VISA JCB 30 AHV a
Meals - English - 22.00/39.50 and a la carte 35.00/55.00 **s.** ♀.
◆ Ornate Spanish influenced, baroque decoration with gilded ceiling, tapestries and highly polished oak tables. Formal and immaculate service. Traditional English cooking.

XXXX ✿ **Menu and Grill** (at Connaught H.), 16 Carlos Pl, W1K 2AL, ✆ (020) 7592 1222, *angelahartnett@the-connaught.co.uk, Fax (020) 7592 1223* – ⊁ ▤. MC AE ⓓ VISA JCB 30 AHU e
Meals (booking essential) 25.00/60.00 ♀.
◆ Refined Italian influenced cooking can be enjoyed in the elegant panelled 'Menu'. The more intimate 'Grill' offers a selection of traditional British favourites.
Spec. Spaghetti with roast lobster, parsley and garlic. Caramelised duck breast, balsamic onions and baby leeks. Lemon panna cotta with thyme syrup.

XXXX **1837** (at Brown's H.), Albemarle St, W1S 4BP, ✆ (020) 7408 1837, *brownshotel@ukbusiness.com, Fax (020) 7493 9381* – ▤. MC AE ⓓ VISA 30 AIV m
closed Sunday – **Meals** a la carte 37.00/47.50 ♀.
◆ The name refers to the date the hotel opened. An elegant and comfortable wood panelled room that evokes a bygone age. By contrast, the kitchen provides contemporary cooking.

XXXX ✿✿ **The Square** (Howard), 6-10 Bruton St, W1J 6PU, ✆ (020) 7495 7100, *info@squarerestaurant.com, Fax (020) 7495 7150* – ▤. MC AE ⓓ VISA JCB 30 AIU v
closed 25-26 December, 1 January and lunch Saturday, Sunday and Bank Holidays – **Meals** 30.00/55.00 ♀.
◆ Marble flooring and bold abstract canvasses add an air of modernity. Extensive menus offer French influenced cooking of the highest order. Prompt and efficient service.
Spec. Lasagne of crab with shellfish and basil cappuccino. Roast foie gras with late picked Muscat grapes. Saddle of lamb with herb crust, shallot purée and rosemary.

XXXX **Windows** (at London Hilton H.), 22 Park Lane, W1Y 4BE, ✆ (020) 7208 4021, *wow@hilton.com, Fax (020) 7208 4147,* ✳ London – ▤. MC AE ⓓ VISA JCB 30 AHV e
closed Saturday lunch and dinner Sunday and Bank Holidays – **Meals** 39.50/59.50 and dinner a la carte 47.50/62.00 ♀.
◆ Enjoys some of the city's best views. The lunchtime buffet provides a popular alternative to the international menu. Formal service and a busy adjoining piano bar.

XXX ✿ **Gordon Ramsay at Claridge's,** Brook St, W1A 2JQ, ✆ (020) 7499 0099, *reservations@gordonramsay.com, Fax (020) 7499 3099* – ▤. MC AE VISA JCB 30 AHU c
Meals (booking essential) 25.00/60.00 ♀.
◆ A thoroughly comfortable dining room with a charming and gracious atmosphere. Serves classically inspired food executed with a high degree of finesse.
Spec. Mosaïque of foie gras with smoked goose breast, baby spinach salad. Pigeon with caramelised parsnips and purée of dates. Baileys bread and butter pudding.

XXX ✿ **Mirabelle,** 56 Curzon St, W1J 8PA, ✆ (020) 7499 4636, *sales@whitestarline.org.uk, Fax (020) 7499 5449,* ☂ – ▤. MC AE ⓓ VISA 30 AIV x
Meals 19.95 (lunch) and a la carte 31.95/53.50 ♀.
◆ As celebrated now as it was in the 1950s. Stylish bar with screens and mirrors, leather banquettes and rows of windows. Modern interpretation of some classic dishes.
Spec. Ballottine of salmon Prunier. Tuna with aubergine caviar, sauce vierge. Bresse pigeon "en cocotte", confit of garlic.

XXX ✿ **The Greenhouse,** 27a Hay's Mews, W1X 7RJ, ✆ (020) 7499 3331, *reservations@greenhouserestaurant.co.uk, Fax (020) 7499 5368* – ▤. MC AE ⓓ VISA JCB
closed January-February, Saturday lunch, Sunday and Bank Holidays – **Meals** 28.00 (lunch) and a la carte 45.00 ☺ ♀. 30 AHV m
◆ A pleasant courtyard, off a quiet mews, leads to this well established restaurant. Original British cooking and inventive touches ensure an enjoyable dining experience.
Spec. Sweetcorn soup with roast langoustine, beans and liquorice. Cumin-roasted loin of lamb on smoked aubergine, samosa of braised shoulder. Iced caramel parfait, meringue and mango cream.

XXX **La Rascasse** (at Café Grand Prix), 50A Berkeley St, W1J 8HA, ✆ (020) 7629 0808, *reservations@cafegrandprix.com, Fax (020) 7409 4708* – ▤. MC AE VISA 30 AIV n
closed Saturday lunch, Sunday and Bank Holidays – **Meals** 15.00/20.00 and a la carte approx 33.00 ♀.
◆ A basement restaurant with an interior of striking, stark elegance. Sit in sumptuous banquettes or armchairs at tables clad in crisp linen. Modern menus.

XXX **Benares,** 12 Berkeley House, Berkeley Sq, W1X 5HG, ☎ (020) 7629 8886 *Fax (020) 7491 8883* – ▤. MC AE VISA 30 AIU
closed 24-30 December, lunch Saturday and Sunday and Bank Holidays – **Meals** - Indiai - 12.95 (lunch) and a la carte 25.50/29.50 ♀.
◆ Indian restaurant where pools of water scattered with petals and candles compensat for lack of natural light. Original Indian dishes ; particularly good value at lunch.

XXX **Embassy,** 29 Old Burlington St, W1X 3AN, ☎ (020) 7851 0956, *embassy@embassyl ndon.com, Fax (020) 7734 3224*, – ▤. MC AE VISA 30 AIU
closed 25-26 December, Saturday lunch, Sunday and Monday – **Meals** 19.95 (lunch) an a la carte 29.40/46.40 ♀.
◆ Marble floors, ornate cornicing and a long bar create a characterful, moody dining room Tables are smartly laid and menus offer accomplished, classic dishes.

XXX **Sartoria,** 20 Savile Row, W1X 1AE, ☎ (020) 7534 7000, *sartoriareservations@conra -restaurants.co.uk, Fax (020) 7534 7070* – ▤. MC AE ◐ VISA 30 AIU
closed Sunday lunch – **Meals** - Italian - 17.50/22.95 (lunch) and a la carte 29.90/44.5 ♀.
◆ In the street renowned for English tailoring, a coolly sophisticated restaurant to sui those looking for classic Italian cooking with modern touches.

XXX **Brian Turner Mayfair** (at Millennium Mayfair H.), 44 Grosvenor Sq, W1K 2HP, ☎ (020 7596 3444, *turner.mayfair@mill-cop.com, Fax (020) 7596 3443* – ▤. MC AE ◐ VISA JCB 30AHU
closed 24-29 December, Saturday lunch and Sunday – **Meals** - English - 21.50 (lunch) an a la carte 28.25/40.75 ♀.
◆ Located within the Millennium Mayfair overlooking Grosvenor Square. Restaurant o several levels with sharp modern décor. Good English dishes with modern twist.

XXX ✿ **Tamarind,** 20 Queen St, W1J 5PR, ☎ (020) 7629 3561, *tamarind.restaurant@virgin.ne Fax (020) 7499 5034* – ▤. MC AE ◐ VISA JCB 30 AHV
closed 25-27 December and lunch Saturday and Bank Holidays – **Meals** - Indian - 16.5 (lunch) and a la carte 25.75/42.50 ♀.
◆ Gold coloured pillars add to the opulence of this basement room. Windows allow diner the chance to watch the kitchen prepare original and accomplished Indian dishes.
Spec. Khumb chaat (tandoor-grilled mushrooms). Peshawari champen (lamb chops wit Indian spices). Achari jhinga (prawns with pickling spices).

XXX **Cecconi's,** 5a Burlington Gdns, W1S 3EP, ☎ (020) 7434 1500, *info@cecconis.co.u Fax (020) 7494 2440* – ▤. MC AE ◐ VISA 30 AIU
closed 25 December and Sunday lunch – **Meals** - Italian - a la carte 25.00/48.50 ♀.
◆ A chic bar and a stylish, modern dining venue, invariably busy ; the menus call on th Italian classics with unusual touches.

XXX **Terrace** (at Le Meridien Piccadilly H.), 21 Piccadilly, W1V 0BH, ☎ (020) 7851 3085 *Fax (020) 7851 3090*, – ▤. MC AE ◐ VISA JCB 31 AJV
Meals 16.00/40.00 and a la carte 24.00/38.00 **s.** ♀.
◆ On the second floor of the hotel, a bright and airy room. Large conservatory style glas ceiling and seating area by the balcony. Modern cooking with a subtle French bias.

XXX **Berkeley Square Café,** 7 Davies St, W1K 3DD, ☎ (020) 7629 6993, *info@berkele squarecafe.com, Fax (020) 7491 9719*, – MC AE VISA JCB 30AHU
closed Christmas, 2 weeks August, Saturday, Sunday and Bank Holidays – **Mea** 18.95/37.50 **s.** ♀.
◆ Despite its name, this is a fairly smart contemporary restaurant with pavement terrac and recordings of famous novels in the loos ! Modern British food with original touche

XXX **Scotts,** 20 Mount St, W1K 2HE, ☎ (020) 7629 5248, *bc@scottsrestaurant.co.u Fax (020) 7499 8246* – ▤. MC AE ◐ VISA JCB 30AHU
closed 25 December, Good Friday, Saturday lunch and Bank Holidays – **Meals** - English a la carte 31.00/50.75 ♀.
◆ Established in 1851 and a favoured haunt of Winston Churchill. Now a stylish and cor temporary restaurant specialising in seafood. Pianist in the smart downstairs bar.

XXX **Kai,** 65 South Audley St, W1K 2QU, ☎ (020) 7493 8988, *kai@kaimayfair.con Fax (020) 7493 1456* – ▤. MC AE ◐ VISA JCB 30 AHV
closed 25 December and 1 January – **Meals** - Chinese - 20.00/40.00 and a la cart 26.50/45.00 ♀.
◆ Marble flooring and mirrors add to the opulent feel of this smoothly run Chinese res taurant. Extensive menu offers dishes ranging from the luxury to the more familiar.

XX **Patterson's,** 4 Mill St, W1S 2AX, ☎ (020) 7499 1308, *enquiries@pattersonsrestaur nt.com, Fax (020) 7491 2122* – ▤. MC AE VISA 30 AIU
closed 25-26 December, 1 January, Saturday lunch, Sunday and Bank Holidays – **Mea** 16.00/30.00 ♀.
◆ Stylish modern interior in black and white. Elegant tables and attentive service. Moder British cooking with concise wine list and sensible prices.

XX **Deca,** 23 Conduit St, W1S 2XS, ✆ (020) 7493 7070, *Fax (020) 7493 7090* – ▤. MC AE ① VISA 30 AIU x
closed 10 days Christmas, 4 days Easter, Sunday and Bank Holiday Mondays – **Meals** 12.50 (lunch) a la carte 30.00/46.00 ♀.
◆ Attractively styled and comfortable, personally-run restaurant. Menu offers an appealing mix of modern French and traditional English dishes.

XX **Teca,** 54 Brooks Mews, W1Y 2NY, ✆ (020) 7495 4774, *Fax (020) 7491 3545* – ▤. MC AE ① VISA 30AHU f
closed 24 December-2 January, Sunday, Saturday lunch and Bank Holidays – **Meals** - Italian - 19.50/36.00 ♀.
◆ A glass-enclosed cellar is one of the features of this modern, slick Italian restaurant. Set price menu, with the emphasis on fresh, seasonal produce.

XX **Alloro,** 19-20 Dover St, W1S 4LU, ✆ (020) 7495 4768, *Fax (020) 7629 5348* – ▤. MC AE ① VISA 30 AIV r
closed 25 December-2 January, Saturday lunch, Sunday and Bank Holidays – **Meals** - Italian - 25.00/35.00 ♀.
◆ One of the new breed of stylish Italian restaurants, with contemporary art and leather seating. A separate, bustling bar. Smoothly run, with modern cooking.

XX **Hush,** 8 Lancashire Court, Brook St, W1S 1EY, ✆ (020) 7659 1500, *info@hush.co.uk, Fax (020) 7659 1501,* 🏠 – |‡| ▤. MC AE ① VISA JCB 30AHU v
hush down : **Meals** a la carte 28.50/43.50 ♀ – ***hush up :*** **Meals** *(closed Saturday lunch, Sunday and Bank Holidays)* (booking essential) 26.50 (lunch) and a la carte 35.50/53.00 ♀.
◆ Tucked away down a side street : spacious, informal hush down brasserie with a secluded courtyard terrace. Serves tasty modern classics. Join the fashionable set in the busy bar or settle down on the banquettes at hush up. Serves robust, satisfying dishes.

XX **Fakhreldine,** 85 Piccadilly, W1J 7NB, ✆ (020) 7493 3424, *info@fakhreldine.co.uk, Fax (020) 7495 1977* – ▤. MC AE ① VISA 30 AIV e
closed 25 December and 1 January – **Meals** - Lebanese - a la carte 25.00/36.00 ♀.
◆ Long standing Lebanese restaurant with great view of Green Park. Large selection of classic mezze dishes and more modern European styled menu of original Lebanese dishes.

XX **Noble Rot,** 3-5 Mill St, W1S 2AU, ✆ (020) 7629 8877, *reception@noblerot.com, Fax (020) 7629 8878* – ▤. MC AE ① VISA 30 AIU r
closed 25-26 December, 1 January, Saturday lunch, Sunday and Bank Holidays – **Meals** 15.95/19.50 (lunch) and a la carte 30.00/41.45 ♀.
◆ A modern room with framed photographs, tiled flooring and venetian blinds. Ambient lighting and music. Modern cooking with some French regional specialities.

XX ✿ **Nobu** (at The Metropolitan H.), 19 Old Park Lane, W1Y 4LB, ✆ (020) 7447 4747, *confirmations@noburestaurants.com, Fax (020) 7447 4749,* ⩽ – ▤. MC AE ① VISA JCB 30 AHV c
closed 25-26 December, 1 January and lunch Saturday-Sunday – **Meals** - Japanese with South American influences - (booking essential) 50.00/70.00 and a la carte approx. 75.00 **s** ♀.
◆ Its celebrity clientele has made this one of the most glamorous spots. Staff are fully conversant in the unique menu that adds South American influences to Japanese cooking.
Spec. White fish tiradito. Black cod with miso. Peruvian style spicy rib-eye steak.

XX **Taman Gang,** 140a Park Lane, W1K 7AA, ✆ (020) 7518 3160, *info@tamangang.com, Fax (020) 7518 3161* – ▤. MC AE VISA JCB 29AGU e
closed 25-26 and 31 December, Sunday dinner and lunch Bank Holidays – **Meals** - South East Asian - a la carte 35.00/75.00 ♀.
◆ Basement restaurant with largish bar and lounge area. Stylish but intimate décor. Informal and intelligent service. Pan-Asian dishes presented in exciting modern manner.

XX **Sumosan,** 26 Albemarle St, W1S 4HY, ✆ (020) 7495 5999, *info@sumosan.co.uk, Fax (020) 7355 1247* – ▤. MC AE ① VISA 30 AIU e
closed lunch Saturday, Sunday and Bank Holidays – **Meals** - Japanese - 25.00/65.00 and a la carte 33.50/69.00 ♀.
◆ A very smart interior in which diners sit in comfy banquettes and armchairs. Sushi bar to the rear with some semi-private booths. Extensive menus of Sushi and Sashimi.

XX **Chor Bizarre,** 16 Albemarle St, W1S 4HW, ✆ (020) 7629 9802, *chorbizarrelondon@oldworldhospitality.com, Fax (020) 7493 7756* – ▤. MC AE ① VISA JCB 30 AIV s
closed 25-26 and 31 December – **Meals** - Indian - 16.50 (lunch) and a la carte 24.50/33.50 **s.**.
◆ Translates as 'thieves market' and the décor is equally vibrant ; antiques, curios, carvings and ornaments abound. Cooking and recipes chiefly from north India and Kashmir.

Yatra, 34 Dover St, W1S 4NF, ✆ (020) 7493 0200, *yatra@lineone.net, Fax (020) 7493 4228* – ▤. MC AE VISA 30 AIV b
closed 25 December, Saturday lunch, Sunday dinner and Bank Holidays – **Meals** - Indian - a la carte 22.75/27.50 ♀.
◆ Behind the large bar, a richly decorated room with a choice of high or low level seating. Elaborate and ornate table setting. Indian cooking with an innovative twist.

Bentley's, 11-15 Swallow St, W1B 4DG, ✆ (020) 7734 4756, *Fax (020) 7287 2972* – ▤. MC AE D VISA JCB 30 AJV e
closed 25-26 December and 1 January – **Meals** - Seafood - a la carte 32.65/53.70 ♀.
◆ One of London's oldest restaurants. Ground floor oyster bar leads to the upstairs dining room. Booth seating and walls adorned with oil paintings. Specialises in seafood.

Momo, 25 Heddon St, W1B 4BH, ✆ (020) 7434 4040, *momoresto@aol.com, Fax (020) 7287 0404,* 余 – ▤. MC AE D VISA 30 AIU n
closed 25-26 December, 1 January and Sunday lunch – **Meals** - Moroccan - a la carte 23.00/35.50.
◆ Elaborate adornment of rugs, drapes and ornaments mixed with Arabic music lend an authentic feel to this busy Moroccan restaurant. Helpful service. Popular basement bar.

Khew, 43 South Molton St, W1K 5RS, ✆ (020) 7408 2236, *drew@khew.co.uk, Fax (020) 7629 7507,* 余 – ⊁ ▤. MC AE VISA 30AHU r
closed Sunday and Bank Holidays – **Meals** - South East Asian - 12.95 (lunch) and a la carte 19.50/29.75 ♀.
◆ Ground floor : a sushi counter ; downstairs : a wonderfully curvaceous restaurant offering varied Asian menus exuding much originality amongst the dim sum and tempura dishes.

The Cafe (at Sotheby's), 34-35 New Bond St, W1A 2AA, ✆ (020) 7293 5077, *Fax (020) 7293 5920* – ⊁. MC AE D VISA 30 AIU y
closed 23 December-6 January, 15 August-1 September, Saturday, Sunday and Bank Holidays – **Meals** (booking essential) (lunch only) a la carte 21.50/30.50 **s.** ♀.
◆ A velvet rope separates this simple room from the main lobby of this famous auction house. Pleasant service from staff in aprons. Menu is short but well-chosen and light.

Veeraswamy, Victory House, 99 Regent St, W1B 4RS, entrance on Swallow St ✆ (020) 7734 1401, *info@realindianfood.com, Fax (020) 7439 8434* – ▤. MC AE D VISA JCB
Meals - Indian - 14.75 (lunch) and a la carte 22.50/36.95 ♀. 30 AIU t
◆ The country's oldest Indian restaurant boasts a new look with vivid coloured walls and glass screens. The menu also combines the familiar with some modern twists.

Zinc Bar & Grill, 21 Heddon St, W1R 7LF, ✆ (020) 7255 8899, *Fax (020) 7255 8888* – MC AE D VISA 30 AIU f
closed Sunday – **Meals** 15.00 (lunch) and a la carte 18.75/35.95 ♀.
◆ The eponymous bar takes up half the room and is a popular after-work meeting place. Parquet flooring and laminated tabletops. Offers a wide selection of modern cooking.

Regent's Park and Marylebone – ✉ *NW1/NW8/W1.*

Landmark London, 222 Marylebone Rd, NW1 6JQ, ✆ (020) 7631 8000, *reservations@thelandmark.co.uk, Fax (020) 7631 8080,* Fð, ≘s, ▢ – |‡|, ⊁ rm, ▤ TV ✆ ♿ ⇔ – 🔬 350. MC AE D VISA. ✂ 29 AFT a
Winter Garden **:** **Meals** 26.00 (lunch) and dinner a la carte 26.00/45.00 ♀ – ☕ 21.00 – **290 rm** 229.10/417.10, 9 suites.
◆ Imposing Victorian Gothic building with a vast glass enclosed atrium, overlooked by many of the modern, well-equipped bedrooms. Winter Garden popular for afternoon tea.

Langham Hilton, 1c Portland Pl, Regent St, W1B 1JA, ✆ (020) 7636 1000, *langham@hilton.com, Fax (020) 7323 2340,* Fð, ≘s, ▢ – |‡|, ⊁ rm, ▤ TV ✆ ♿ – 🔬 250. MC AE D VISA JCB. ✂ 30 AIT e
Memories **:** **Meals** 19.00 (lunch) and a la carte 34.00/44.50 ♀ – ***Tsar's*** **:** **Meals** *(closed Saturday lunch and Sunday)* 17.00 (lunch) and a la carte approx 27.30 ♀ – ☕ 21.50 – **409 rm** 257.30, 20 suites.
◆ Opposite the BBC, with Colonial inspired décor. Polo themed bar and barrel vaulted Palm Court. Concierge Club rooms offer superior comfort and butler service. Memories is bright elegant dining room. Russian influenced Tsar's : hundreds of vodkas available.

Churchill Inter-Continental, 30 Portman Sq, W1A 4ZX, ✆ (020) 7486 5800, *churchill@interconti.com, Fax (020) 7486 1255,* Fð, ≘s, ⚘ – |‡|, ⊁ rm, ▤ TV ✆ ♿ – 🔬 300. MC AE D VISA JCB. ✂ 29 AGT x
Terrace on Portman Square **:** **Meals** a la carte 27.75/38.50 ♀ – ☕ 20.75 – **405 rm** 399.50, 40 suites.
◆ Modern property overlooking attractive square. Elegant marbled lobby.Cigar bar open until 2am for members. Well-appointed rooms have the international traveller in mind. Restaurant provides popular Sunday brunch entertainment.

Charlotte Street, 15 Charlotte St, W1T 1RJ, (020) 7806 2000, *charlotte@firmdale.com*, *Fax (020) 7806 2002*, – – 65. 31 AKT e
Meals (see ***Oscar*** below) – 18.00 – **44 rm** 229.10/364.20, 8 suites.
• Interior designed with a charming and understated English feel. Welcoming lobby laden with floral displays. Individually decorated rooms with CDs and mobile phones.

Sanderson, 50 Berners St, W1P 3NG, (020) 7300 1400, *sanderson@ianschragerhotels.com*, *Fax (020) 7300 1401*, , – , rm, .
Spoont : **Meals** a la carte 38.00/58.00 – 20.00 – **150 rm** 370.00/393.60.
• Designed by Philipe Starck : the height of contemporary design. Bar is the place to see and be seen. Bedrooms with minimalistic white décor have DVDs and striking bathrooms. Stylish Spoon+ allows diners to construct own dishes. 31 AJT c

The Leonard, 15 Seymour St, W1H 7JW, (020) 7935 2010, *theleonard@dial.pipex.com*, *Fax (020) 7935 6700*, – . 29AGU n
Meals (room service only) – 18.50 – **21 rm** 200.00/258.50, **20 suites** 329.00/646.00.
• Around the corner from Selfridges, an attractive Georgian townhouse : antiques and oil paintings abound. Informal, stylish café bar offers light snacks. Well-appointed rooms.

Radisson SAS Portman, 22 Portman Sq, W1H 7BG, (020) 7208 6000, *sales.london@radissonsas.com*, *Fax (020) 7208 6001*, , , – , rm, – 650. 29 AGT a
Talavera : **Meals** (buffet lunch)/dinner a la carte 37.50/55.00 **s.** – 19.50 – **265 rm** 229.10/235.00, 7 suites.
• This modern, corporate hotel offers check-in for both British Midland and SAS airlines. Rooms in attached towers decorated in Scandinavian, Chinese and Italian styles. Restaurant renowned for its elaborate buffet lunch.

Montcalm, Great Cumberland Pl, W1H 7TW, (020) 7402 4288, *montcalm@montcalm.co.uk*, *Fax (020) 7724 9180* – , rm, – 80.
Meals (see ***The Crescent*** below) – 17.95 – **110 rm** 270.25/293.75, 10 suites.
• Named after the 18C French general, the Marquis de Montcalm. In a charming crescent a short walk from Hyde Park. Spacious bedrooms with a subtle oriental feel. 29AGU d

Ramada Plaza, 18 Lodge Rd, NW8 7JT, (020) 7722 7722, *sales.plazalondon@ramadajarvis.co.uk*, *Fax (020) 7483 2408* – , rm, – 150.
Minsky's : **Meals** 19.50/20.95 and a la carte 18.50/35.00 – 15.50 – **376 rm** 199.00, 1 suite.
• Modern hotel offers extensive conference facilities. Some of the functional bedrooms either overlook Regent's Park or Lord's cricket ground. Minsky's is designed on a New York deli theme. Kashinoki has Oriental ambience.

Berners, 10 Berners St, W1A 3BE, (020) 7666 2000, *berners@berners.co.uk*, *Fax (020) 7666 2001* – , rm, rest, – 160.
Meals *(closed Saturday lunch)* (carving lunch) 17.95/19.95 and a la carte 26.95/40.15 – 15.95 – **213 rm** 190.00/260.00, 3 suites. 31 AJT r
• Series of five converted Georgian houses. Impressive lobby with ornately carved plasterwork ceiling. The floor of club rooms have their own lounge and compact gym. Art Deco themed restaurant..

Jurys Clifton Ford, 47 Welbeck St, W1M 8DN, (020) 7486 6600, *clifton@jurysdoyle.com*, *Fax (020) 7486 7492*, , , – , rm, – 230. 30 AHT a
Meals a la carte approx 22.95 – 16.00 – **253 rm** 225.00, 2 suites.
• A fairly quiet spot, despite being a short stroll away from the Oxford Street shops. Modern, corporate hotel benefits from an extensive leisure club. Spacious modern rooms. Subtly Irish influence to menu.

Holiday Inn Regent's Park, Carburton St, W1W 5EE, (0870) 4009111, *reservations-londonregentspark@ichotelsgroup.com*, *Fax (020) 7387 2806* – , rm, – 350.
Junction : **Meals** *(closed Saturday lunch)* 15.50 and a la carte 16.35/25.45 **s.** – 14.95 – **333 rm** 179.00.
• Modern corporate hotel and a forever busy conference destination. 1st floor lounges are particularly spacious. Bright bedrooms have a certain Scandinavian feel. International menus.

London Marriott Marble Arch, 134 George St, W1H 5DN, (0870) 400 7255, *salesadmin.marblearch@marriott.co.uk*, *Fax (020) 7402 0666*, , , – , rm, – 150. 29 AFT j
Mediterrano : **Meals** *(closed lunch Saturday and Sunday)* a la carte 19.85/29.85 – 16.45 – **240 rm** 198.50/233.80.
• Centrally located and modern. Offers comprehensive conference facilities. Leisure centre underground. An ideal base for both corporate and leisure guests. Mediterranean-influenced cooking.

Berkshire, 350 Oxford St, W1N 0BY, ✆ (020) 7629 7474, *resberk@radisson.com,* *Fax (020) 7629 8156* – rm, – 40. MC AE VISA JCB.
Ascots : **Meals** (dinner only) 27.50 and a la carte 30.00/36.00 – 15.00 – **145 rm** 290.20/370.10, 2 suites. 30AHU n
◆ Above the shops of Oxford St. Reception areas have a pleasant traditional charm. Comfortably appointed bedrooms have plenty of thoughtful touches. Personable staff. Stylish, relaxed dining room.

Durrants, 26-32 George St, W1H 5BJ, ✆ (020) 7935 8131, *enquiries@durrantshotel.co.uk, Fax (020) 7487 3510* – rest, – 55. MC AE VISA. 29 AGT e
Meals 17.50 (lunch) and a la carte 26.75/36.75 – 13.50 – **88 rm** 92.50/165.00, 4 suites.
◆ First opened in 1790 and family owned since 1921. Traditionally English feel with the charm of a bygone era. Cosy wood panelled bar. Attractive rooms vary somewhat in size. Semi-private booths in quintessentially British dining room.

Dorset Square, 39-40 Dorset Sq, NW1 6QN, ✆ (020) 7723 7874, *reservations@dorsetsquare.co.uk, Fax (020) 7724 3328,* – MC AE VISA.
The Potting Shed : **Meals** *(closed Saturday lunch and Sunday dinner)* (booking essential) (live music Tuesday and Saturday dinner) 19.50 and a la carte 23.50/29.00 – 15.75 – **37 rm** 147.00/211.50.
◆ Converted Regency townhouses in a charming square and the site of the original Lord's cricket ground. A relaxed country house in the city. Individually decorated rooms. The Potting Shed features live entertainment.

Sherlock Holmes, 108 Baker St, W1U 6LJ, ✆ (020) 7486 6161, *info@sherlockholmeshotel.com, Fax (020) 7958 5211,* – – 45. MC AE VISA JCB 29 AGT c
Meals 16.50 (lunch) and a la carte 28.00/42.00 – 12.75 – **116 rm** 252.60.
◆ A stylish building with a relaxed contemporary feel. Comfortable guests' lounge with Holmes pictures on the walls. Bedrooms welcoming and smart, some with wood floors. Brasserie style dining.

10 Manchester Street without rest., 10 Manchester St, W1U 4DG, ✆ (020) 7486 6669, *stay@10manchesterstreet.fsnet.co.uk, Fax (020) 7224 0348* – . MC AE VISA JCB. 29 AGT b
5.00 – **37 rm** 120.00/150.00, 9 suites.
◆ Redbrick hotel built in 1919 ; speciality shops and Wallace Collection are on the doorstep. Thoughtful extras such as mineral water, chocolates complement comfortable rooms.

Hart House without rest., 51 Gloucester Pl, W1U 8JF, ✆ (020) 7935 2288, *reservations@harthouse.co.uk, Fax (020) 7935 8516* – . MC AE VISA JCB.
15 rm 70.00/105.00. 29 AGT c
◆ Once home to French nobility escaping the 1789 Revolution. Now an attractive Georgian mid-terraced private hotel. Warm and welcoming service. Well kept bedrooms.

St George without rest., 49 Gloucester Pl, W1U 8JE, ✆ (020) 7486 8586, *reservations@stgeorge-hotel.net, Fax (020) 7486 6567* – . MC AE VISA.
19 rm 95.00/135.00. 29 AGT h
◆ Terraced house on a busy street, usefully located within walking distance of many attractions. Offers a warm welcome and comfortable bedrooms which are spotlessly maintained.

Orrery, 55 Marylebone High St, W1M 3AE, ✆ (020) 7616 8000, *Fax (020) 7616 8080* – . MC AE VISA JCB
closed 1-3 January and August Bank Holiday – **Meals** (booking essential) 23.50 (lunch) and a la carte 31.50/50.50.
◆ Contemporary elegance : a smoothly run 1st floor restaurant in converted 19C stables with a Conran shop below. Accomplished modern British cooking.
Spec. Ballottine of chicken, foie gras and celeriac, Muscat grapes. Whole roasted Barbury duck. Chocolate fondant, milk ice cream.

Locanda Locatelli, 8 Seymour St, W1H 7JZ, ✆ (020) 7935 9088, *info@locandalocatelli.com, Fax (020) 7935 1149* – . MC AE VISA 29AGU
closed Christmas, Easter, Sunday and Bank Holidays – **Meals** - Italian - a la carte 34.50/52.50.
◆ Very stylishly appointed restaurant with banquettes and cherry wood or glass dividers which contribute to an intimate and relaxing ambience. Accomplished Italian cooking.
Spec. Roast rabbit wrapped in ham with polenta. Linguini with chilli and crab. Nettle risotto.

The Crescent (at Montcalm H.), Great Cumberland Pl, W1H 7TW, ✆ (020) 7402 4288, *reservations@montcalm.co.uk, Fax (020) 7724 9180* – . MC AE VISA JCB
closed lunch Saturday, Sunday and Bank Holidays – **Meals** 25.00. 29AGU
◆ Discreetly appointed room favoured by local residents. Best tables overlook a pretty square. Frequently changing fixed price modern menu includes half bottle of house wine.

XX **Six13,** 19 Wigmore St, W1H 9UA, ✆ (020) 7629 6133, *info@six13.com, Fax (020) 7629 6135* – ▤. MC AE ① VISA 30 AHT n
closed 25 December, Friday, Saturday and Sunday – **Meals** - Kosher - 24.50 (lunch) and a la carte 31.75/37.75 ♀.
◆ Stylish and immaculate with banquette seating. Strictly kosher menu supervised by the Shama offering interesting cooking with a modern slant.

XX **Oscar** (at Charlotte Street H.), 15 Charlotte St, W1T 1RJ, ✆ (020) 7907 4005, *charlotte@firmdale.com, Fax (020) 7806 2002* – ▤. MC AE VISA 31 AKT e
closed Sunday lunch – **Meals** (booking essential) a la carte 32.50/47.50 ♀.
◆ Adjacent to hotel lobby and dominated by a large, vivid mural of contemporary London life. Sophisticated dishes served by attentive staff : oysters, wasabi and soya dressing.

XX **The Providores,** 109 Marylebone High St, W1U 4RX, ✆ (020) 7935 6175, *anyone@theprovidores.co.uk, Fax (020) 7935 6877* – ⅔. MC AE VISA JCB 30 AHT s
closed 25 December, 1 January and Bank Holidays – **Meals** a la carte 18.50/33.50 ♀.
◆ Swish, stylish restaurant on first floor ; unusual dishes with New World base and fusion of Asian, Mediterranean influences. Tapas and light meals in downstairs Tapa Room.

XX **La Porte des Indes,** 32 Bryanston St, W1H 7EG, ✆ (020) 7224 0055, *pilondon@aol.com, Fax (020) 7224 1144* – ▤. MC AE ① VISA JCB 29AGU s
closed 25-26 December, 1 January and Saturday lunch – **Meals** - Indian - 33.00/35.00 and a la carte 30.50/46.50 ♀.
◆ Don't be fooled by the discreet entrance : inside there is a spectacularly unrestrained display of palm trees, murals and waterfalls. French influenced Indian cuisine.

XX **Rosmarino,** 1 Blenheim Terr, NW8 0EH, ✆ (020) 7328 5014, *Fax (020) 7625 2639*,
– ▤. MC AE ① VISA
closed 25-27 December and 1-3 January – **Meals** - Italian - 19.50/35.00 ♀.
◆ Modern, understated and relaxed. Friendly and approachable service of robust and rustic Italian dishes. Set priced menu is carefully balanced.

XX **Ozer,** 4-5 Langham Pl, Regent St, W1B 3DG, ✆ (020) 7323 0505, *info@sofra.co.uk, Fax (020) 7323 0111* – ▤. MC AE ① VISA 30 AIT z
Meals - Turkish - 11.00 (lunch) and a la carte 14.75/21.80 ♀.
◆ Behind the busy and vibrantly decorated bar you'll find a smart modern restaurant. Lively atmosphere and efficient service of modern, light and aromatic Turkish cooking.

XX **Rasa Samudra,** 5 Charlotte St, W1T 1RE, ✆ (020) 7637 0222, *Fax (020) 7637 0224* – ⅔. MC AE ① VISA 31 AKT r
closed 24-30 December, 1 January and Sunday lunch – **Meals** - Indian Seafood and Vegetarian - 22.50/30.00 and a la carte 13.25/24.40.
◆ Comfortably appointed, richly decorated and modern Indian restaurant. Authentic Keralan (south Indian) cooking with seafood and vegetarian specialities.

XX **Levant,** Jason Court, 76 Wigmore St, W1H 9DQ, ✆ (020) 7224 1111, *Fax (020) 7486 1216* – ▤. MC AE ① VISA JCB 30 AHT c
Meals - Lebanese - 8.50/39.50 and a la carte ♀.
◆ The somewhat unpromising entrance leads down to a vibrantly decorated basement. Modern Lebanese cooking featuring subtly spiced dishes.

XX **Latium,** 21 Berners St, Fitzrovia, W1T 3LP, ✆ (020) 7323 9123, *info@latiumrestaurant.com, Fax (020) 7323 3205* – ▤. MC AE VISA 31 AJT n
closed Sunday – **Meals** - Italian - 18.00/23.50 ♀.
◆ Latium, the Latin for Lazio, reflects the patrons' interest in football. The minimalist décor is enlivened by colourful artwork. Italian country cooking ; daily specials.

XX **Caldesi,** 15-17 Marylebone Lane, W1U 2NE, ✆ (020) 7935 9226, *Fax (020) 7935 9228* – ▤. MC AE ① VISA JCB 30 AHT e
closed Saturday lunch, Sunday and Bank Holidays – **Meals** - Italian - a la carte 30.40/43.50.
◆ A traditional Italian restaurant that continues to attract a loyal clientele. Robust and authentic dishes with Tuscan specialities. Attentive service by established team.

XX **Bertorelli,** 19-23 Charlotte St, W1T 1RL, ✆ (020) 7636 4174, *bertorellisc@groupechezgerard.co.uk, Fax (020) 7467 8902* – ▤. MC AE ① VISA JCB 31 AJT v
closed 25-26 December, Saturday lunch, Sunday and Bank Holidays – **Meals** - Italian - 18.50 and a la carte 30.00/35.00 ♀.
◆ Above the informal and busy bar/café. Bright and airy room with vibrant décor and informal atmosphere. Extensive menu combines traditional and new wave Italian dishes.

XX **Blandford Street,** 5-7 Blandford St, W1U 3DB, ✆ (020) 7486 9696, *info@blandford-street.co.uk, Fax (020) 7486 5067* – ▤. MC AE ① VISA 30 AHT v
closed 25 December-4 January, Easter Saturday, Saturday lunch, Sunday and Bank Holidays – **Meals** 15.00 (lunch) and a la carte 21.50/31.50 ♀.
◆ Understated interior with plain walls hung with modern pictures and subtle spot-lighting. Contemporary menu with a notably European character.

XX **L'Aventure,** 3 Blenheim Terr, NW8 0EH, ☎ (020) 7624 6232, *Fax (020) 7625 5548*, – MC AE VISA
closed first 2 weeks January, Easter, Sunday, Saturday lunch and Bank Holidays – **Meals** - French - 18.50/32.50.
◆ Behind the pretty tree lined entrance you'll find a charming neighbourhood restaurant. Relaxed atmosphere and service by personable owner. Authentic French cuisine.

X **Villandry,** 170 Great Portland St, W1W 5QB, ☎ (020) 7631 3131, *Fax (020) 7631 3030* – ⇔ ▤. MC AE ⓓ VISA 30 AIT s
closed 25 December, 1 January and Sunday – **Meals** a la carte 19.00/35.45 ♀.
◆ The senses are heightened by passing through the well-stocked deli to the dining room behind. Bare walls, wooden tables and a menu offering simple, tasty dishes.

X **Union Café,** 96 Marylebone Lane, W1U 2QA, ☎ (020) 7486 4860, *unioncafe@brinkleys.com, Fax (020) 7486 4860* – MC AE VISA 30 AHT d
closed Sunday – **Meals** a la carte 25.50/29.00 ♀.
◆ No standing on ceremony at this bright, relaxed restaurant. The open kitchen at one end produces modern Mediterranean cuisine. Ideal for visitors to the Wallace Collection.

X **Caffè Caldesi,** 1st Floor, 118 Marylebone Lane, W1U 2QF, ☎ (020) 7935 1144, *people@caldesi.com, Fax (020) 7935 8832* – ▤. MC AE ⓓ VISA JCB 30 AHT s
closed Sunday and Bank Holidays – **Meals** - Italian - a la carte 20.00/30.50 ♀.
◆ Converted pub with a simple modern interior in which to enjoy tasty, uncomplicated Italian dishes. Downstairs is a lively bar with a deli counter serving pizzas and pastas.

X **Chada Chada,** 16-17 Picton Pl, W1M 5DE, ☎ (020) 7935 8212, *enquiry@chadathai.com, Fax (020) 7924 2178* – ▤. MC AE ⓓ VISA JCB 30AHU b
closed Sunday and Bank Holidays – **Meals** - Thai - a la carte 17.20/26.65 ♀.
◆ Authentic and fragrant Thai cooking ; the good value menu offers some interesting departures from the norm. Service is eager to please in the compact and cosy rooms.

X **No.6 George St,** 6 George St, W1U 3QX, ☎ (020) 7935 1910, *Fax (020) 7935 6036* – ⇔ ▤. MC VISA 30 AHT a
closed 2 weeks August, 2 weeks Christmas, Saturday and Sunday – **Meals** (lunch only) a la carte 25.40/32.95.
◆ To the front is a charming delicatessen offering fresh produce and behind is a simple, well-kept dining room. Daily changing menu with good use of fresh ingredients.

X **La Contenta,** 90-92 Wigmore St, W1H 9DR, ☎ (020) 7486 1912, *Fax (020) 7486 1913* – ▤. MC AE ⓓ VISA 30 AHT f
closed dinner 24 December-26 December and 1 January – **Meals** a la carte 17.00/26.50.
◆ Light and airy open dining room with simple columned décor and some banquette seating. Menu of modern dishes.

St James's – ✉ *W1/SW1.*

Ritz, 150 Piccadilly, W1J 9BR, ☎ (020) 7493 8181, *enquire@theritzlondon.com, Fax (020) 7493 2687*, Fø – |‡|, ⇔ rm, ▤ TV ☎ – 🏛 50. MC AE ⓓ VISA JCB. ✗ 30 AIV c
Meals (see ***The Restaurant*** below) – ☕ 26.00 – **116 rm** 352.50/428.80, 17 suites.
◆ Opened 1906, a fine example of Louis XVI architecture and decoration. Elegant Palm Court famed for afternoon tea. Many of the lavishly appointed rooms overlook the park.

Sofitel St James London, 6 Waterloo Pl, SW1Y 4AN, ☎ (020) 7747 2200, *h3144@accor-hotels.com, Fax (020) 7747 2210*, Fø – |‡|, ⇔ rm, ▤ TV ☎ ♿ – 🏛 180. MC AE ⓓ VISA JCB. ✗ 31 AKV a
Meals (see ***Brasserie Roux*** below) – ☕ 19.50 – **179 rm** 323.12/423.00, 7 suites.
◆ Grade II listed building in smart Pall Mall location. Classically English interiors include floral Rose Lounge and club-style St. James bar. Comfortable, well-fitted bedrooms.

Dukes 🐚, 35 St James's Pl, SW1A 1NY, ☎ (020) 7491 4840, *bookings@dukeshotel.com, Fax (020) 7493 1264*, Fø – |‡|, ⇔ rest, ▤ TV ☎ – 🏛 50. MC AE ⓓ VISA. ✗
Meals *(closed Saturday lunch)* (residents only) 19.50 (lunch) and a la carte 29.50/43.50 ♀ – ☕ 16.00 – **82 rm** 229.00/305.50, 7 suites. 30 AIV f
◆ Privately owned, discreet and quiet hotel. Traditional bar, famous for its martini's and Cognac collection. Well-kept spacious rooms in a country house style.

Hilton London Trafalgar, 2 Spring Gdns, SW1A 2TS, ☎ (020) 7870 2900, *lontshirm@hilton.com, Fax (020) 7870 2911* – |‡|, ⇔ rm, ▤ TV ☎ ♿ – 🏛 50. MC AE ⓓ VISA JCB. ✗ 31 AKV b
Jago : **Meals** *(closed Saturday lunch and Sunday)* a la carte 27.00/45.00 ♀ – ☕ 18.50 – **127 rm** 233.80, 2 suites.
◆ Enjoys a commanding position on the square of which the deluxe rooms, some split-level, have views. Bedrooms are in pastel shades with leather armchairs or stools ; mod cons. Low-lit restaurant with open-plan kitchen.

Stafford, 16-18 St James's Pl, SW1A 1NJ, (020) 7493 0111, *info@thestafforddhotel.co.uk, Fax (020) 7493 7121* – 40. 30 AIV u
Meals *(closed Saturday lunch)* 32.50 (lunch) and dinner a la carte 42.00/70.00 **s.** – 16.50 – **75 rm** 264.30/376.00, 6 suites.
◆ A genteel atmosphere prevails in this elegant and discreet country house in the city. Do not miss the famed American bar. Well-appointed rooms created from 18C stables. Refined, elegant, intimate dining room.

Cavendish, 81 Jermyn St, SW1Y 6JF, (020) 7930 2111, *cavendish.reservations@devere-hotels.com, Fax (020) 7839 2125* – rm, – 100. 30 AIV v
Meals *(closed lunch Saturday and Sunday)* a la carte 29.00/44.00 – 16.95 – **227 rm** 276.10/311.30, 3 suites.
◆ Modern hotel opposite Fortnum & Mason. Contemporary, minimalist style of rooms with moody prints of London; top five floors offer far-reaching views over and beyond the city. Classic styled restaurant overlooks Jermyn Street.

22 Jermyn Street, 22 Jermyn St, SW1Y 6HL, (020) 7734 2353, *office@22jermyn.com, Fax (020) 7734 0750* – 31 AKV e
Meals (room service only) – 12.65 – **5 rm** 246.75, **13 suites** 346.60/393.60.
◆ Discreet entrance amid famous shirt-makers' shops leads to this exclusive boutique hotel. Stylishly decorated bedrooms more than compensate for the lack of lounge space.

The Restaurant (at Ritz H.), 150 Piccadilly, W1V 9DG, (020) 7493 8181, *Fax (020) 7493 2687*, – 30 AIV c
Meals (dancing Friday and Saturday evenings) 37.00/43.00 and a la carte 46.50/103.00 **s.**
◆ The height of opulence: magnificent Louis XVI décor with trompe l'oeil and ornate gilding. Delightful terrace over Green Park. Refined service, classic and modern menu.

L'Oranger, 5 St James's St, SW1A 1EF, (020) 7839 3774, *Fax (020) 7839 4330* – 30 AIV d
closed 24 December-2 January, Saturday lunch, Sunday and Bank Holidays – **Meals** 26.00/45.00
◆ Behind the period façade lies a stylish, understated and comfortable restaurant. The refined and precise dishes are enjoyed by the regular clientele. Booking recommended.
Spec. Terrine of foie gras and artichoke. Roast fillet of John Dory with langoustine. Chocolate fondant, vanilla and nougatine ice cream.

Osia, 11 Haymarket, SW1Y 4BP, (020) 7976 1313, *Fax (020) 7976 1919* – 31 AKV n
closed 25 December, 1 January, Saturday lunch and Sunday – **Meals** 23.00 (lunch) and a la carte 27.50/34.50
◆ Converted bank with high ornate ceilings; dining hall separated by wine display case from long bar in leather boothed lounge. Interesting menus of Asian and Australian dishes.

Quaglino's, 16 Bury St, SW1Y 6AL, (020) 7930 6767, *Fax (020) 7839 2866* – 30 AIV j
Meals (booking essential) 18.50 (lunch) and a la carte 23.25/37.50
◆ Descend the sweeping staircase into the capacious room where a busy and buzzy atmosphere prevails. Watch the chefs prepare everything from osso bucco to fish and chips.

Mint Leaf, Suffolk Pl, SW1Y 4HX, (020) 7930 9020, *reservations@mintleafrestaurant.com, Fax (020) 7930 6205* – 31 AKV k
closed 25-26 December, 1 January and lunch Saturday and Sunday – **Meals** - Indian - 15.00 (lunch) and a la carte 23.00/35.00
◆ Basement restaurant in theatreland. Cavernous dining room incorporating busy, trendy bar with unique cocktail list and loud music. Helpful service. Contemporary Indian dishes.

Criterion Grill Marco Pierre White, 224 Piccadilly, W1J 9HP, (020) 7930 0488, *sales@whitestarline.org.uk, Fax (020) 7930 8380* – 31 AKU c
closed Sunday – **Meals** 17.95 (lunch) and a la carte 23.00/43.50
◆ A stunning modern brasserie behind the revolving doors. Ornate gilding, columns and mirrors aplenty. Bustling, characterful atmosphere, Pre and post-theatre menus.

Brasserie Roux, 8 Pall Mall, SW1Y 5NG, (020) 7968 2900, *h3144-fb4@accor-hotels.com, Fax (020) 7747 2242* – 31 AKV a
Meals - French - a la carte 18.50/33.50
◆ Informal, smart, classic brasserie style with large windows making the most of the location. Large menu of French classics with many daily specials; comprehensive wine list.

Le Caprice, Arlington House, Arlington St, SW1A 1RT, (020) 7629 2239, *Fax (020) 7493 9040* – 30 AIV h
closed 25-26 December, 1 January and August Bank Holiday – **Meals** (Sunday brunch) a la carte 26.75/61.25
◆ Still attracting a fashionable clientele and as busy as ever. Dine at the bar or in the smoothly run restaurant. Food combines timeless classics with modern dishes.

The Avenue, 7-9 St James's St, SW1A 1EE, ✆ (020) 7321 2111, *avenue@egami.co.uk, Fax (020) 7321 2500* – ▤. MC AE ⓓ VISA JCB 30 AIV y
closed 25-26 December and 1 January – **Meals** 17.95/19.95 and a la carte 19.95/29.75 ♀.
◆ The attractive and stylish bar is a local favourite. Behind is a striking, modern and busy restaurant. Appealing and contemporary food. Pre-theatre menu available.

Matsuri, 15 Bury St, SW1Y 6AL, ✆ (020) 7839 1101, *dine@matsuri-restaurant.com, Fax (020) 7930 7010* – ▤. MC AE ⓓ VISA JCB 30 AIV w
closed 25 December and Bank Holidays – **Meals** - Japanese (Teppan-Yaki, Sushi) - a la carte 24.00/45.50 ♀.
◆ Specialising in theatrical and precise teppan-yaki cooking. Separate restaurant offers sushi delicacies. Charming service by traditionally dressed staff.

Al Duca, 4-5 Duke of York St, SW1Y 6LA, ✆ (020) 7839 3090, *info@alduca-restaurants.co.uk, Fax (020) 7839 4050* – ▤. MC AE ⓓ VISA JCB 31 AJV r
closed 25-26 December, 1 January and Sunday – **Meals** - Italian - 20.50/24.00 ♀.
◆ Relaxed, modern, stylish restaurant. Friendly and approachable service of robust and rustic Italian dishes. Set priced menu is good value.

Soho – ✉ W1/WC2.

Hampshire, Leicester Sq, WC2H 7LH, ✆ (020) 7839 9399, *reshamp@radisson.com, Fax (020) 7930 8122,* , – |, ⇆ rm, ▤ TV ✆ – 100. MC AE ⓓ VISA JCB.
The Apex **:** **Meals** 27.50 and a la carte 30.00/36.00 – 16.00 – **119 rm** 386.50/507.60, 5 suites. 31 AKU s
◆ The bright lights of the city are literally outside and many rooms overlook the bustling Square. Inside, it is tranquil and comfortable, with well-appointed bedrooms.

Hazlitt's without rest., 6 Frith St, W1D 3JA, ✆ (020) 7434 1771, *reservations@hazlitts.co.uk, Fax (020) 7439 1524* – TV ✆. MC AE ⓓ VISA JCB 31 AKU u
22 rm 205.60/240.80, 1 suite.
◆ A row of three adjoining early 18c town houses and former home of the eponymous essayist. Individual and charming bedrooms, many with antique furniture and Victorian baths.

L'Escargot, 48 Greek St, W1D 5EF, ✆ (020) 7437 2679, *sales@whitestarline.org.uk, Fax (020) 7437 0790* – ▤. MC AE ⓓ VISA JCB 31 AKU b
Ground Floor **: Meals** *(closed 25-26 December, 1 January, Sunday and lunch Saturday)* 17.95 (lunch) and a la carte approx. 26.95 ♀ – ***Picasso Room*** **: Meals** *(closed 2 weeks Christmas-New Year, August, Sunday, Monday and Saturday lunch)* 25.50/42.00.
◆ Ground Floor is chic, vibrant brasserie with early-evening buzz of theatre-goers. Finely judged modern dishes. Intimate and more formal upstairs Picasso Room famed for its limited edition art.
Spec. Ravioli of langoustine, fennel bouillon. Squab pigeon "en vessie" with ravioli of wild mushroom, thyme jus. Millefeuille of Muscat grapes and liquorice.

Quo Vadis, 26-29 Dean St, W1D 3LL, ✆ (020) 7437 9585, *sales@whitestarline.org.uk, Fax (020) 7734 7593* – ▤. MC AE ⓓ VISA 31 AKU v
closed 25-26 December, 1 January, Sunday and Saturday lunch – **Meals** - Italian - 19.95 (lunch) and a la carte 28.00/38.00 ♀.
◆ Stained glass windows and a neon sign hint at the smooth modernity of the interior. Modern artwork abounds. Contemporary cooking and a serious wine list.

Red Fort, 77 Dean St, W1D 3SH, ✆ (020) 7437 2525, *info@redfort.co.uk, Fax (020) 7434 0721* – ▤. MC AE ⓓ VISA 31 AKU x
closed 23-29 December and Sunday – **Meals** - Indian - 12.00 (lunch) and a la carte 23.45/31.50 ♀.
◆ Smart, stylish restaurant with modern water feature and glass ceiling to rear. Seasonally changing menus of authentic dishes handed down over generations.

Richard Corrigan at Lindsay House, 21 Romilly St, W1D 5AF, ✆ (020) 7439 0450, *richardcorrigan@lindsayhouse.co.uk, Fax (020) 7437 7349* – ▤. MC AE ⓓ VISA
closed 1 week Christmas, 2 weeks summer, Sunday and Saturday lunch – **Meals** 23.00/48.00 ♀. 31 AKU f
◆ One rings the doorbell before being welcomed into this handsome 18C town house, retaining many original features. Skilled and individual cooking with a subtle Irish hint.
Spec. Organic hen's egg, leeks and lobster. Scallops with pork belly and spiced carrots. Granny Smith apple parfait with chocolate and mint.

Café Lazeez, 21 Dean St, W1V 5AH, ✆ (020) 7434 9393, *soho@cafelazeez.com, Fax (020) 7434 0022* – ▤. MC AE ⓓ VISA 31 AKU d
closed 25-26 December, 1 January, Sunday and Bank Holidays – **Meals** - North Indian - a la carte 16.55/23.15 ♀.
◆ In the same building as Soho Theatre ; the bar hums before shows, restaurant is popular for pre- and post-theatre meals of modern Indian fare. Refined décor ; private booths.

The Sugar Club, 21 Warwick St, W1R 5RB, ☎ (020) 7437 7776, *reservations@thesugarclub.co.uk, Fax (020) 7437 7778* – ⇔ ▤. MC AE ① VISA JCB 30 AIU h
closed lunch Saturday-Monday and restricted opening Christmas-New Year – **Meals** 19.50 (lunch) and a la carte 25.90/42.40 ♀.
◆ Light interior with a glass-fronted bar and additional basement seating. Asian and Oriental influenced cuisine with good use of diverse ingredients and combinations.

Mezzo, Lower Ground Floor, 100 Wardour St, W1F 0TN, ☎ (020) 7314 4000, *info@conran-restaurants.co.uk, Fax (020) 7314 4040* – ▤. MC AE ① VISA 31 AKU g
closed Sunday and lunch Monday, Tuesday and Saturday – **Meals** 16.50 (lunch) and a la carte 23.50/38.50 ♀.
◆ Through the vast bar and down the sweeping staircase to this enormous and sonorous basement. Well-drilled service. Windows into the kitchen which produces modern cooking.

Bertorelli, 11-13 Frith St, W1D 4RB, ☎ (020) 7494 3491, *bertorelli-soho@groupechezgerard.co.uk, Fax (020) 7439 9431,* ☂ – ▤. MC AE ① VISA 31 AKU t
closed 25-26 December, Saturday lunch, Sunday and Bank Holidays – **Meals** - Italian - 18.50 and a la carte 30.00/35.00 ♀.
◆ A haven of tranquilllity from the bustling street below. Discreet and professionally run first floor restaurant with Italian menu. Popular ground floor café.

La Trouvaille, 12A Newburgh St, W1F 7RR, ☎ (020) 7287 8488, *Fax (020) 7434 4170,* ☂ – MC AE ① VISA 30 AIU g
closed Sunday and Bank Holidays – **Meals** - French - 19.75 (lunch) and a la carte 23.00/32.45 ♀.
◆ Atmospheric restaurant located just off Carnaby Street. Hearty, robust French cooking with a rustic character. French wine list with the emphasis on southern regions.

Alastair Little, 49 Frith St, W1D 5SG, ☎ (020) 7734 5183, *Fax (020) 7734 5206* – ▤. MC AE ① VISA 31 AKU y
closed 25-26 December, 1 January, Sunday, Saturday lunch and Bank Holidays – **Meals** (booking essential) 29.00/35.00.
◆ The eponymous owner was at the vanguard of Soho's culinary renaissance. Tasty, daily changing British based cuisine ; the compact room is rustic and simple.

Vasco and Piero's Pavilion, 15 Poland St, W1F 8QE, ☎ (020) 7437 8774, *vascosfood@hotmail.com, Fax (020) 7437 0467* – ▤. MC AE ① VISA JCB 31 AJU b
closed Sunday, Saturday lunch and Bank Holidays – **Meals** - Italian - (lunch booking essential) 23.50 and lunch a la carte 27.00/31.00.
◆ A long standing, family run Italian restaurant with a loyal local following. Pleasant service under the owners' guidance. Warm décor and traditional cooking.

itsu, 103 Wardour St, W1V 3TD, ☎ (020) 7479 4790, *glenn.edwards@itsu.co.uk, Fax (020) 7479 4795* – ⇔ ▤. MC AE VISA 31 AKU m
closed 25 December and 1 January – **Meals** - Japanese - (bookings not accepted) a la carte 15.00/20.00.
◆ Japanese dishes of Sushi, Sashimi, handrolls and miso soup turn on a conveyor belt in a pleasingly hypnotic fashion. Hot bowls of chicken and coconut soup also appear.

Aurora, 49 Lexington St, W1F 9AJ, ☎ (020) 7494 0514, *Fax (020) 7494 4357,* ☂ – MC VISA
closed 24 December-5 January, Sunday and Bank Holidays – **Meals** (booking essential) a la carte 19.40/24.45. 31 AJU e
◆ An informal, no-nonsense, bohemian style bistro with a small, but pretty, walled garden terrace. Short but balanced menu ; simple fresh food. Pleasant, languid atmosphere.

Soho Spice, 124-126 Wardour St, W1F 0TY, ☎ (020) 7434 0808, *info@sohospice.co.uk, Fax (020) 7434 0799* – ⇔ ▤. MC AE ① VISA 31 AKU w
closed 25-26 December – **Meals** - Indian - (bookings not accepted) a la carte 15.40/20.40 ♀.
◆ Busy, buzzy, café-style Indian restaurant with basement cocktail bar. Vivid colours on the wall matched by the staff uniforms. Indian food with a contemporary twist.

Fung Shing, 15 Lisle St, WC2H 7BE, ☎ (020) 7437 1539, *Fax (020) 7734 0284* – ▤. MC AE ① VISA 31 AKU j
closed 24-26 December and lunch Bank Holidays – **Meals** - Chinese (Canton) - 17.00/30.00 and a la carte 14.10/23.10 ♀.
◆ A long-standing Chinese restaurant on the edge of Chinatown. Chatty and pleasant service. A mix of authentic, rustic dishes and the more adventurous chef's specials.

Strand and Covent Garden – ✉ *WC2.*

Savoy, Strand, WC2R 0EU, ☎ (020) 7836 4343, *info@the-savoy.co.uk, Fax (020) 7240 6040,* ⚇, ≘s, – |$|, ⇔ rm, ▤ TV ☎ ⇐ – 🏛 500. MC AE ① VISA. ✂
River : **Meals** (dancing Friday and Saturday dinner) 33.50/52.50 and a la carte ♀ (see also ***The Savoy Grill*** below) – ☕ 24.50 – **236 rm** 340.75/434.75, 27 suites. 31 ALU a
◆ Famous the world over, since 1889, as the epitome of English elegance and style. Celebrated for its Art Deco features and luxurious bedrooms. Immaculate service from classical menus at River.

Swissôtel London, The Howard, Temple Pl, WC2R 2PR, (020) 7836 3555, *reservations.london@swissotel.com, Fax (020) 7379 4547*, rm, – 150. VISA JCB. 32AMU e
Meals (see ***Jaan*** below) – 23.00 – **148 rm** 346.60, 41 suites.
• Cool elegance is the order of the order of the day at this handsomely appointed hotel. Many of the comfortable rooms enjoy balcony views of the Thames. Attentive service.

One Aldwych, 1 Aldwych, WC2B 4RH, (020) 7300 1000, *reservations@onealdwych.com, Fax (020) 7300 1001*, – rm, – 50. VISA JCB. 32AMU r
Indigo* : Meals** a la carte 25.55/36.40 (see also ***Axis below) – 19.25 – **96 rm** 346.00/446.50, 9 suites.
• Decorative Edwardian building, former home to the Morning Post newspaper. Now a stylish and contemporary address with modern artwork, a screening room and hi-tech bedrooms. All-day restaurant looks down on fashionable bar.

St Martins Lane, 45 St Martin's Lane, WC2N 4HX, (020) 7300 5500, *sml@ianschragerhotels.com, Fax (020) 7300 5501*, – rm, – 40. VISA. 31 ALU e
***Asia de Cuba* : Meals** - Asian - 25.00 and a la carte 50.00/71.00 – 20.00 – **200 rm** 311.30/334.80, 4 suites.
• The unmistakable hand of Philippe Starck evident at this most contemporary of hotels. Unique and stylish, from the starkly modern lobby to the state-of-the-art rooms. 350 varieties of rum at fashionable Asia de Cuba.

Thistle Charing Cross, Strand, WC2N 5HX, (020) 7839 7282, *charingcross@thistle.co.uk, Fax (020) 7839 3933* – rm, – 150. VISA JCB. 31 ALY a
***The Strand Terrace* : Meals** 15.95/17.95 and a la carte 26.40/31.35 – 16.95 – **239 rm** 293.75/329.00.
• Classic Victorian hotel built above the station. In keeping with its origins, rooms in the Buckingham wing are traditionally styled whilst others have contemporary décor. Watch the world go by from restaurant's pleasant vantage point.

The Savoy Grill (at Savoy H.), Strand, WC2R 0EU, (020) 7592 1600, *savoygrill@marcuswareing.com, Fax (020) 7592 1601* – VISA JCB 31 ALU a
Meals 25.00/55.00.
• Redesigned in 2003 to conserve its best traditions, the Grill buzzes at midday and in the evening. Formal service ; menu of modern European dishes and the Savoy classics.
Spec. King prawn tortellini with lime and chervil. Braised pork belly with Jerusalem artichoke and braised red onions. Sherry trifle.

Ivy, 1 West St, WC2H 9NQ, (020) 7836 4751, *Fax (020) 7240 9333* – VISA JCB 31 AKU p
closed dinner 24-26 and 31 December, 1 January and August Bank Holiday – **Meals** a la carte 23.50/51.50.
• Wood panelling and stained glass combine with an unpretentious menu to create a veritable institution. A favourite of 'celebrities', so securing a table can be challenging.

Axis, 1 Aldwych, WC2B 4RH, (020) 7300 0300, *sales@onealdwych.co.uk, Fax (020) 7300 0301* – VISA JCB 31AMU r
closed Saturday lunch and Sunday – **Meals** (live jazz at dinner Tuesday and Wednesday) 19.75 (lunch) and a la carte 23.15/39.95.
• Lower-level room overlooked by gallery bar. Muted tones, black leather chairs and vast futuristic mural appeal to the fashion cognoscenti. Globally-influenced menu.

Jaan (at Swissôtel London, The Howard), Temple Pl, WC2R 2PR, (020) 7300 1700, *jaan.london@swissotel.com, Fax (020) 7240 7816*, – VISA JCB
closed lunch Saturday and Sunday – **Meals** 19.50/22.00 and a la carte 25.00/35.00. 37 EX e
• Bright room on the ground floor of the hotel with large windows overlooking an attractive terrace. Original cooking - modern French with Cambodian flavours and ingredients.

J.Sheekey, 28-32 St Martin's Court, WC2N 4AL, (020) 7240 2565, *Fax (020) 7240 8114* – VISA JCB 31 ALU v
closed dinner 24-26 December, 1 January and August Bank Holidays – **Meals** - Seafood - (booking essential) a la carte 23.50/57.50.
• Festooned with photographs of actors and linked to the theatrical world since opening in 1890. Wood panels and alcove tables add famed intimacy. Traditional British cooking.

Rules, 35 Maiden Lane, WC2E 7LB, (020) 7836 5314, *info@rules.co.uk, Fax (020) 7497 1081* – VISA JCB 31 ALU n
closed 4 days Christmas and 1 January – **Meals** - English - (booking essential) a la carte 27.40/36.40.
• London's oldest restaurant boasts a fine collection of antique cartoons, drawings and paintings. Tradition continues in the menu, specialising in game from its own estate.

XX **Adam Street,** 9 Adam St, WC2N 6AA, ✆ (020) 7379 8000, *info@adamstreet.co.uk*, *Fax (020) 7379 1444* – ▤. MC AE VISA 31 ALU c
closed Christmas-New Year, Saturday, Sunday and Bank Holidays – **Meals** (lunch only) 17.95 and a la carte 19.50/35.00 ♀.
◆ Set in the striking vaults of a private members club just off the Strand. Sumptuous suede banquettes and elegantly laid tables. Well executed classic and modern English food.

XX **The Admiralty,** Somerset House, The Strand, WC2R 1LA, ✆ (020) 7845 4646, *Fax (020) 7845 4658* – ⇎. MC AE ① VISA JCB 32AMU a
closed 24-26 December and dinner Sunday and Bank Holidays – **Meals** 25.00/33.00 ♀.
◆ Interconnecting rooms with bold colours and informal service contrast with its setting within the restored Georgian splendour of Somerset House. 'Cuisine de terroir'.

XX **Bank,** 1 Kingsway, Aldwych, WC2B 6XF, ✆ (020) 7379 9797, *aldres@bankrestaurants.com*, *Fax (020) 7379 5070* – ▤. MC AE ① VISA 32AMU s
closed 25-26 December and 1 January – **Meals** 15.00 (lunch) and a la carte 22.75/35.95 ♀.
◆ Ceiling decoration of hanging glass shards creates a high level of interest in this bustling converted bank. Open-plan kitchen provides an extensive array of modern dishes.

XX **Le Deuxième,** 65a Long Acre, WC2E 9JH, ✆ (020) 7379 0033, *Fax (020) 7379 0066* – ▤. MC AE VISA 31 ALU b
closed 24-25 December – **Meals** 14.50 (lunch) and a la carte 22.00/28.50 ♀.
◆ Caters well for theatregoers : opens early, closes late. Buzzy eatery, quietly decorated in white with subtle lighting. Varied International menu : Japanese to Mediterranean.

XX **Maggiore's,** 33 King St, WC2 8JD, ✆ (020) 7379 9696, *enquiries@maggiores.uk.com*, *Fax (020) 7379 6767* – ▤. MC AE ① VISA JCB 31 ALU z
closed 24-26 December and 1 January – **Meals** - Bistro - 17.50 (lunch) and dinner a la carte 24.20/40.80 ♀.
◆ Narrow glass-roofed dining room with distinctive lighting and greenery creating a woodland atmosphère. Quick service and good value wide-ranging pre-theatre menu.

X **Le Café du Jardin,** 28 Wellington St, WC2E 7BD, ✆ (020) 7836 8769, *Fax (020) 7836 4123* – ▤. MC AE VISA 31 ALU f
closed 24-25 December – **Meals** 14.50 (lunch) and a la carte 21.50/26.50 ♀.
◆ Divided into two floors with the downstairs slightly more comfortable. Light and contemporary interior with European-influenced cooking. Ideally placed for the Opera House.

X **Livebait,** 21 Wellington St, WC2E 7DN, ✆ (020) 7836 7161, *lb-coventgdn@groupechezgerard.co.uk*, *Fax (020) 7836 7141* – MC AE ① VISA 32AMU u
closed 25-26 December, 1 January, Sunday and Bank Holidays – **Meals** - Seafood - 15.95 (lunch) and a la carte 30.00/40.00 ♀.
◆ Busy front bar and back restaurant both decorated with black and white tiles. Energetic service and a menu offering fresh seafood in relaxed surroundings.

Victoria – ✉ *SW1.*

ℹ *Victoria Station Forecourt.*

Royal Horseguards, 2 Whitehall Court, SW1A 2EJ, ✆ (0870) 333 9122, *royalhorseguards@thistle.co.uk*, *Fax (0870) 333 9222*, ☖, ⅃ – ▮, ⇎ rm, ▤ TV ✆ – 🏟 200. MC AE ① VISA. ✂ 31 ALV a
One Twenty One Two : **Meals** *(closed lunch Saturday, Sunday and Bank Holidays)* 19.50/25.50 and dinner a la carte 27.75/38.90 – ☕ 17.50 – **276 rm** 333.70/385.40, 4 suites.
◆ Imposing Grade I listed property in Whitehall overlooking the Thames and close to London Eye. Impressive meeting rooms. Some of the well-appointed bedrooms have river views. Stylish restaurant, sub-divided into intimate rooms.

Crowne Plaza London St James, 45 Buckingham Gate, SW1E 6AF, ✆ (020) 7834 6655, *sales@cplonsj.co.uk*, *Fax (020) 7630 7587*, ⅃, ≘s – ▮, ⇎ rm, ▤ TV ✆ ♿ – 🏟 180. MC AE ① VISA. ✂ 39 AJX e
Mediterranée : **Meals** 15.00 (lunch) and a la carte 21.45/47.00 ♀ (see also ***Quilon*** and ***Bank*** below) – ☕ 15.20 – **323 rm** 293.70, 19 suites.
◆ Built in 1897 as serviced accommodation for visiting aristocrats. Behind the impressive Edwardian façade lies an equally elegant interior. Quietest rooms overlook courtyard. Bright and informal café style restaurant.

51 Buckingham Gate, 51 Buckingham Gate, SW1E 6AF, ✆ (020) 7769 7766, *info@51-buckinghamgate.co.uk*, *Fax (020) 7828 5909*, ⅃, ≘s – ▮ ▤ TV ✆. MC AE ① VISA 39 AJX s
Meals (see ***Quilon*** and ***Bank*** below) – ☕ 17.50 –, **82 suites** 370.00/940.00.
◆ Canopied entrance leads to luxurious suites : every detail considered, every mod con provided. Colour schemes echoed in plants and paintings. Butler and nanny service.

The Goring, 15 Beeston Pl, Grosvenor Gdns, SW1W 0JW, (020) 7396 9000, *reception@goringhotel.co.uk, Fax (020) 7834 4393,* – 50. VISA.
Meals *(closed Saturday lunch)* 25.00/38.00 – 16.50 – **68 rm** 232.60/293.70, 6 suites.
◆ Opened in 1910 as a quintessentially English hotel. The fourth generation of Goring is now at the helm. Many of the attractive rooms overlook a peaceful garden. Elegantly appointed restaurant provides memorable dining experience. 38 AIX a

41 without rest., 41 Buckingham Palace Rd, SW1W 0PS, (020) 7300 0041, *book41@rchmail.com, Fax (020) 7300 0141* – VISA JCB 38 AIX n
17 rm 258.50/371.30, 1 suite.
◆ Take the lift to the 5th floor- London's first all-inclusive hotel. Relaxed and exclusive club-like lounge where meals and most drinks complimentary. State-of-the-art rooms.

The Rubens at The Palace, 39 Buckingham Palace Rd, SW1W 0PS, (020) 7834 6600, *bookrb@rchmail.com, Fax (020) 7828 5401* – – 90. VISA JCB 38 AIX n
Meals *(closed lunch Saturday and Sunday)* (carvery) 16.95 – ***The Library* : Meals** (dinner only) a la carte 26.50/35.00 – 15.00 – **170 rm** 235.00/264.30, 2 suites.
◆ Traditional hotel with an air of understated elegance. Tastefully furnished rooms : the Royal Wing, themed after British Kings and Queens, features TVs in the bathrooms. Intimate, richly decorated Library restaurant has sumptuous armchairs.

Dolphin Square, Dolphin Sq, Chichester St, SW1V 3LX, (020) 7834 3800, *reservations@dolphinsquarehotel.co.uk, Fax (020) 7798 8735,* , , , , , squash – , rest, – 85. VISA JCB. 39 AJZ a
The Brasserie* : Meals** 14.50 and a la carte (see also ***Allium below) – 13.50 – **30 rm** 205.00/229.00, **118 suites** 229.00/529.00.
◆ Built in 1935 and shared with residential apartments. Art Deco influence remains in the Clipper bar overlooking the leisure club. Spacious suites with contemporary styling. Brasserie overlooks the swimming pool.

Jolly St Ermin's, Caxton St, SW1H 0QW, (020) 7222 7888, *reservations@jollyhotels.co.uk, Fax (020) 7222 6914* – , rm, – 150. VISA.
***Cloisters Brasserie* : Meals** 22.50 – 11.95 – **282 rm** 205.00/229.00, 8 suites.
◆ Ornate plasterwork to both the lobby and the balconied former ballroom are particularly striking features. Club rooms have both air conditioning and a private lounge. Grand brasserie with ornate ceiling. 39 AKX a

Thistle Victoria, 101 Buckingham Palace Rd, SW1W 0SJ, (020) 7834 9494, *victoria@thistle.co.uk, Fax (020) 7630 1978* – , rm, – 200. VISA JCB.
Meals 18.00 – 13.50 – **361 rm** 245.50, 3 suites. 38 AIY e
◆ Former Victorian railway hotel with ornate front entrance and grand reception. Harvard bar particularly noteworthy. Well-appointed rooms are generally spacious.

Thistle Westminster, 49 Buckingham Palace Rd, SW1W 0QT, (0207) 834 1821, *westminster@thistle.co.uk, Fax (0207) 931 7542* – , rm, – 150. VISA JCB. 38 AIX z
Meals 20.00 and a la carte 18.50/23.50 – 13.95 – **134 rm** 242.05/337.20.
◆ Proximity to station and Palaces make this a popular destination for corporate and leisure guests. Comfortable and well-equipped bedrooms benefit from mini-bars and safes. Shelves with cook books for sale in restaurant.

City Inn, 30 John Isup St, SW1P 4DD, (020) 7932 4602, *westminster@cityinn.com, Fax (020) 7233 7575,* – – 100. VISA JCB.
***City Cafe* : Meals** 17.50 and a la carte 17.50/30.00 – 19.00 – **444 rm** 185.00, 16 suites. 31 ALY a
◆ Modern hotel five minutes' walk from Westminster Abbey and Tate Britain. Well-appointed rooms with high-tech equipment and some with pleasant views of London. Brasserie serving modern style food next to a glass covered terrace with artwork feature.

Tophams Belgravia, 28 Ebury St, SW1W 0LU, (020) 7730 8147, *tophamsbelgravia@compuserve.com, Fax (020) 7823 5966* – – 30. VISA JCB.
closed 24 December-2 January – **Meals** *(closed Saturday and Sunday)* (dinner only) a la carte 17.45/23.45 **s.** – **36 rm** 115.00/170.00. 38 AHY e
◆ Family owned and run since 1937, this hotel has a certain traditional charm. Cosy lounges, roaring fires and antique furniture aplenty. Individually decorated bedrooms. Homely basement dining room.

Winchester without rest., 17 Belgrave Rd, SW1V 1RB, (020) 7828 2972, *winchesterhotel17@hotmail.com, Fax (020) 7828 5191* – . 38 AIY s
closed 24-26 December – **18 rm** 85.00/100.00.
◆ Behind the portico entrance one finds a friendly, well-kept private hotel. The generally spacious rooms are pleasantly appointed. Comprehensive English breakfast offered.

Express by Holiday Inn without rest., 106-110 Belgrave Rd, SW1V 2BJ, (020) 7630 8888, *info@hiexpressvictoria.co.uk, Fax (020) 7828 0441* – . VISA JCB. – **52 rm** 105.00. 39 AJZ c
◆ Converted Georgian terraced houses a short walk from station. Despite property's age, all rooms are stylish and modern with good range of facilities including TV movies.

XXX **Allium** (at Dolphin Square H.), Dolphin Sq, Chichester St, SW1V 3LX, ✆ (020) 7798 6888, *info@allium.co.uk, Fax (020) 7798 5685* – ▤. MC AE ⓓ VISA 39 AJZ a
closed Saturday lunch, Sunday dinner and Monday – **Meals** 22.50/32.50 and a la carte 30.00/34.20 ♀.
◆ A calm atmosphere prevails in this richly decorated room. Raised tables to rear with sumptuous banquettes for more privacy. Interesting and assured modern British cooking.

XXX **The Cinnamon Club,** Great Smith St, SW1P 3BU, ✆ (020) 7222 2555, *info@cinnamonclub.com, Fax (020) 7222 1333* – ▤ P. MC AE ⓓ VISA 39 AKX c
closed 24-31 December, Saturday lunch and Sunday – **Meals** - Indian - 19.00/22.00 (lunch) and a la carte 30.93/57.38 **s.** 🎭 ♀.
◆ Housed in former Westminster Library : exterior has ornate detail, interior is stylish and modern. Walls are lined with books. New Wave Indian cooking with plenty of choice.

XXX **Quilon** (at Crowne Plaza London St James H.), 45 Buckingham Gate, SW1 6AF, ✆ (020) 7821 1899, *Fax (020) 7828 5802* – ▤. MC AE ⓓ VISA 39 AJX e
closed 1 week Christmas, Sunday, Saturday lunch and Bank Holidays – **Meals** - Indian - 15.95 (lunch) and dinner a la carte 17.50/28.95 🎭 ♀.
◆ A selection of Eastern pictures adorn the walls in this smart, modern and busy restaurant. Specialising in progressive south coastal Indian cooking.

XXX **L'Incontro,** 87 Pimlico Rd, SW1W 8PH, ✆ (020) 7730 6327, *cristiano@lincontro-restaurant.com, Fax (020) 7730 5062* – ▤. MC AE ⓓ VISA JCB 37 AGZ u
closed Easter, 25-26 December and lunch Saturday and Sunday – **Meals** - Italian - 19.50 (lunch) and a la carte 28.50/47.50.
◆ Cool, understated and comfortable with attentive service. Simple, unfussy, traditional Italian cooking ; set lunch good value. Private dining downstairs for 30 people.

XXX **Santini,** 29 Ebury St, SW1W 0NZ, ✆ (020) 7730 4094, *Fax (020) 7730 0544* – ▤. MC AE ⓓ VISA JCB 38 AHY v
closed 25-26 December, lunch Saturday, Sunday and Bank Holidays – **Meals** - Italian - 26.00 (lunch) and a la carte 29.00/51.00 ♀.
◆ Discreet, refined and elegant modern Italian restaurant. Assured and professional service. Extensive selection of modern dishes and a more affordable set lunch menu.

XXX **Shepherd's,** Marsham Court, Marsham St, SW1P 4LA, ✆ (020) 7834 9552, *admin@langansrestaurants.co.uk, Fax (020) 7233 6047* – ▤. MC AE ⓓ VISA JCB 39 AKY z
closed Saturday, Sunday and Bank Holidays – **Meals** - English - (booking essential) 28.00.
◆ A truly English restaurant where game and traditional puddings are a highlight. Popular with those from Westminster - the booths offer a degree of privacy.

XX ✿ **Roussillon,** 16 St Barnabas St, SW1W 8PE, ✆ (020) 7730 5550, *alexis@roussillon.co.uk, Fax (020) 7824 8617* – ▤. MC AE VISA JCB 38 AHZ c
closed Sunday and lunch Monday and Tuesday – **Meals** - French - 21.00/45.00 ♀.
◆ Tucked away in an smart residential area. Cooking clearly focuses on the quality of the ingredients. Seasonal menu with inventive elementsand a French base.
Spec. Late summer fruit and vegetables truffle broth. Venison with poached pear, celeriac and truffles. Spicy soufflé, gingerbread "soldiers" and maple syrup.

XX **The Ebury (Dining Room),** 1st Floor, 11 Pimlico Rd, SW1W 8NA, ✆ (020) 7730 6784, *info@theebury.co.uk, Fax (020) 7730 6149* – ▤. MC AE VISA 38 AHZ z
closed 24-26 December – **Meals** (lunch by arrangement Monday-Friday) 29.50 ♀.
◆ Mount the spiral stair to the formal restaurant with tall windows overlooking the street. Open-plan kitchen provides set gastronomic style menu using firstclass ingredients.

XX **Il Convivio,** 143 Ebury St, SW1W 9QN, ✆ (020) 7730 4099, *comments@etruscagroup.co.uk, Fax (020) 7730 4103,* 🏛 – ▤. MC AE ⓓ VISA 38 AHY a
closed 25 December, 1 January and Sunday – **Meals** - Italian - 19.50/32.50 and a la carte 20.25/30.50 ♀.
◆ A retractable roof provides alfresco dining to part of this comfortable and modern restaurant. Contemporary and traditional Italian menu, with home-made pasta specialities.

XX **Simply Nico,** 48a Rochester Row, SW1P 1JU, ✆ (020) 7630 8061, *westminster@simplynico.co.uk, Fax (020) 7828 8541* – MC AE ⓓ VISA 39 AJY a
closed Easter, 24-26 and 31 December, 1 January, Saturday lunch, Sunday and Bank Holidays – **Meals** (booking essential) a la carte 24.00/30.20 ♀.
◆ Relaxed and discreet restaurant with a certain bistro atmosphere. Lunch is especially busy. Short, Anglo-French menu. One of a small chain.

XX **Bank,** 45 Buckingham Gate, SW1E 6BS, ✆ (020) 7379 9797, *westres@bankrestaurants.com, Fax (020) 7379 5070,* 🏛 – ▤. MC AE ⓓ VISA JCB 39 AJX e
closed 25-26 December, 1 January, Saturday lunch, Sunday and Bank Holidays – **Meals** 15.00 (lunch) and a la carte 25.15/40.95 🎭 ♀.
◆ The understated entrance belies the vibrant contemporary interior. One of Europe's longest bars has a lively atmosphere. Conservatory restaurant, modern European cooking.

XX **Boisdale,** 15 Eccleston St, SW1W 9LX, ☎ (020) 7730 6922, *katarina@boisdale.co.uk, Fax (020) 7730 0548,* – ▤. MC AE ◑ VISA JCB 38 AHY c
closed Saturday lunch, Sunday and Bank Holidays – **Meals** - Scottish - (live jazz at dinner) 14.00/17.45 and a la carte 27.50/49.00 ♀.
◆ Popular haunt of politicians ; dark green, lacquer red panelled interior. Run by a Scot of Clanranald, hence modern British dishes with Scottish flavour : Crofter's pie.

XX **Tate Britain,** Tate Gallery, Millbank, SW1P 4RG, ☎ (020) 7887 8825, *tate.restaurant@tate.org.uk, Fax (020) 7887 8902* – ▤. MC AE ◑ VISA 39 ALZ c
Meals (booking essential) (lunch only) 21.50 and a la carte 24.75/31.75 ♀.
◆ Continue your appreciation of art when lunching in this basement room decorated with original Rex Whistler murals. Forever busy, it offers modern British fare.

XX **Memories of China,** 65-69 Ebury St, SW1W 0NZ, ☎ (020) 7730 7734, *Fax (020) 7730 2992* – ▤. MC AE ◑ VISA 39 AHY u
closed 25 December – **Meals** a la carte 20.50/45.15 ♀.
◆ An air of tranquillity pervades this traditionally furnished room. Lattice screens add extra privacy. Extensive Chinese menu : bold flavours with a clean, fresh style..

X **The Ebury (Brasserie),** Ground Floor, 11 Pimlico Rd, SW1W 8NA, ☎ (020) 7730 6784, *info@theebury.co.uk, Fax (020) 7730 6149* – ▤. MC AE VISA 38 AHZ z
closed 24-26 December – **Meals** a la carte 20.00/40.00 ♀.
◆ Victorian corner pub restaurant with walnut bar, tables and 267-seater seafood bar. Friendly service. Wide-ranging menu from snacks to full meals.

X **Olivo,** 21 Eccleston St, SW1W 9LX, ☎ (020) 7730 2505, *maurosanna@oliveto.fsnet.co.uk, Fax (020) 7823 5377* – ▤. MC AE VISA JCB 39 AHY z
closed lunch Saturday and Sunday and Bank Holidays – **Meals** - Italian - 18.00 (lunch) and dinner a la carte 23.25/27.50.
◆ Rustic, informal Italian restaurant. Relaxed atmosphere provided by the friendly staff. Simple, non-fussy cuisine with emphasis on best available fresh produce.

X **La Poule au Pot,** 231 Ebury St, SW1W 8UT, ☎ (020) 7730 7763, *Fax (020) 7259 9651,* – ▤. MC AE ◑ VISA JCB 38 AHY a
Meals - French - 16.00 (lunch) and a la carte 25.50/39.50.
◆ The subdued lighting and friendly informality make this one of London's more romantic restaurants. Classic French menu with extensive plats du jour.

Bray-on-Thames *Windsor & Maidenhead* 504 R 29 – *pop. 8 121* – ✉ *Maidenhead.*

London 34 – Reading 13.

XXXX ✿✿✿ **Waterside Inn** (Roux) with rm, Ferry Rd, SL6 2AT, ☎ (01628) 620691, *reservations@waterside-inn.co.uk, Fax (01628) 784710,* ≤ Thames-side setting –, ⚓ ▤ TV P. MC AE ◑ VISA JCB.
closed 26 December-29 January and 12-15 April – **Meals** - French - *(closed Tuesday except dinner June-August and Monday)* (booking essential) 39.50/80.00 and a la carte 72.50/106.00 – **8 rm** 150.00/190.00, 1 suite.
◆ Thames-side idyll still delights : opulent dining room, drinks in the summer houses, exquisite French cuisine and matchless service. Bedrooms are restful and classically chic.
Spec. Tronçonnettes de homard poêlées minute au Porto blanc. Filets de lapereau grillés aux marrons glacés. Soufflé chaud aux framboises.

XX ✿✿✿ **Fat Duck** (Blumenthal), High St, SL6 2AQ, ☎ (01628) 580333, *Fax (01628) 776188* – MC AE VISA
closed 2 weeks Christmas, Sunday dinner and Monday – **Meals** 29.75/60.00 ♀.
◆ History and science combine in an innovative alchemy of contrasting flavours and textures. Modern art, stylish, relaxing milieu, confident service.
Spec. Roast foie gras, almond purée and cherry. Salmon poached in liquorice gel with roast asparagus. Macerated Mara des Bois, purée of black olive, pistachio scrambled eggs.

Oxford *Oxon.* 503 504 Q 28 – *pop. 118 795.*

ℹ The Old School, Gloucester Green ☎ (01865) 726871.
London 59 – Birmingham 63 – Bristol 73.

✿✿ **Le Manoir aux Quat' Saisons** (Blanc), Church Rd, OX44 7PD, ☎ (01844) 278881, *lemanoir@blanc.co.uk, Fax (01844) 278847,* ≤, – rest, ▤ rest, TV P – 50. MC AE ◑ VISA JCB.
Meals - French - 45.00 (lunch weekdays) and a la carte 70.00/90.00 ♀ – ☕ 12.00 – **25 rm** ☕ 295.00/610.00, 7 suites 700.00/855.00.
◆ World famous and picture perfect, its beauty lies in its refinement. Sumptuous lounges and rooms, classic and modern, surrounded by Japanese, ornamental and kitchen gardens. Virtuoso classic French menu of precision and flair, inspired by the seasons.
Spec. Essence of tomato, its sorbet and pressed tomatoes. Red mullet and scallops, fricassé of squid, cod brandade, bouillabaise jus. Cassolette of apricots and poached meringue, Kirsch vanilla cream.

BELFAST *Antrim* 712 O 4 *Ireland G. – pop. 277 391.*

See : *City★ - Ulster Museum★★ (Spanish Armada Treasure★★, Shrine of St Patrick's Hand★) – City Hall★* BY – *Donegall Square★* BY **20** – *Botanic Gardens (Palm House★) – St Anne's Cathedral★* BX – *Crown Liquor Saloon★* BY – *Sinclair Seamen's Church★* BX – *St Malachy's Church★* BY.

Envir. : *Belfast Zoological Gardens★★ AC, N : 5 m. by A 6* BX.

Exc. : *Carrickfergus (Castle★★ AC, St Nicholas' Church★) NE : 9 ½ m. by A 2* BX – *Talnotry Cottage Bird Garden, Crumlin★ AC, W : 13 ½ m. by A 52* BX.

18 Balmoral, 518 Lisburn Rd ☎ (028) 9038 1514 – 18 Belvoir Park, Church rd, Newtonbreda ☎ (028) 9049 1693 – 18 Fortwilliam, Downview Ave ☎ (028) 9037 0770 – 18 The Knock Club, Summerfield, Dundonald ☎ (028) 9048 2249 – 18 Shandon Park, 73 Shandon Park ☎ (028) 9080 5030 – 9 Cliftonville, Westland Rd ☎ (028) 9074 4158 – 9 Ormeau, 50 Park Rd ☎ (028) 9064 1069.

Belfast International Airport, Aldergrove : ☎ (028) 9442 2888, W : 15 ½ m. by A 52 BX *Belfast City Airport : ☎ (028) 9045 7745* – **Terminal** : *Coach service (Ulsterbus Ltd) from Great Victoria Street Station (40 mn).*

to Liverpool (NorseMerchant Ferries Ltd) daily (11 h).

35 Donegal Pl ☎ (028) 9024 6609, info@nitic.com – Belfast International Airport, Information desk ☎ (028) 9442 2888 – Belfast City Airport, Sydenham Bypass ☎ (028) 9093 9093.

Dublin 103 – Londonderry 70.

Plans on following pages

Hilton Belfast, 4 Lanyon Pl, BT1 3LP, ☎ (028) 9027 7000, *hiltonbelfast@hilton.com, Fax (028) 9027 7277,* – rm, – 400. MC AE VISA BY s
Sonoma : Meals 16.95/22.50 and dinner a la carte 23.50/36.80 **s.** – ***Cables :*** Meals a la carte 24.95/35.00 – 17.25 – **189 rm** 150.00, 6 suites.
◆ Modern branded hotel overlooking river and close to concert hall. Spacious and brightly decorated rooms with all mod cons. Upper floors with good city views. Striking California-style décor and good city views from Sonora. Contemporary Cables bar-restaurant.

Europa, Great Victoria St, BT2 7AP, ☎ (028) 9027 1066, *res@eur.hastingshotels.com, Fax (028) 9032 7800* – rm, – 750. MC AE VISA BY e
Gallery : Meals *(closed Saturday lunch and Sunday)* 21.50/26.50 – ***The Brasserie :*** Meals a la carte 15.95/23.20 **s.** – 12.00 – **235 rm** 115.00/170.00, 5 suites.
◆ Busy hotel in the heart of the lively Golden Mile area. Extensive meeting facilities. Most executive rooms are well-equipped with hi-fis. Formal Gallery restaurant and immaculate bar. Pleasant feel suffuses Brasserie ; fish and chips a favourite here.

Stormont, Upper Newtownards Rd, BT4 3LP, East : 3 ½ m. on A 20 ☎ (028) 9065 1066, *res@stor.hastingshotels.com, Fax (028) 9048 0240* – rm, rest, – 400. MC AE VISA.
Shiraz : Meals *(closed Sunday)* (dinner only) a la carte 19.15/23.75 – ***La Scala Bistro :*** Meals a la carte 15.85/22.85 **s.** – 15.00 – **109 rm** 115.00/145.00.
◆ In a suburb opposite the gardens of Stormont castle ; an up-to-date conference and exhibition oriented hotel. Brightly decorated, modern bedrooms. Comfortable, split-level Shiraz. All-day La Scala has appealing ambience.

The McCausland, 34-38 Victoria St, BT1 3GH, ☎ (028) 9022 0200, *info@mccauslandhotel.com, Fax (028) 9022 0220* – rm, – 60. MC AE VISA.
closed 24-27 December – ***Merchants :*** Meals *(closed lunch Saturday and Sunday)* a la carte 14.40/24.70 **s.** – **60 rm** 140.00/180.00. BY v
◆ An unstuffy, centrally located hotel hides behind its intricate Victorian façade. Originally two warehouses, many original features remain. Modern, comfortable rooms. Vibrantly decorated restaurant offers an eclectic menu.

Ramada Belfast, Shaws Bridge, BT8 7XA, South : 3 ¾ m. on A 55 (by Malone rd) ☎ (028) 9092 3500, *mail@ramadabelfast.com, Fax (028) 9092 3600,* – rm, – 1000. MC AE VISA JCB.
Belfast Bar and Grill : Meals *(closed Saturday lunch)* 16.50/22.50 and a la carte 20.05/32.50 – 9.50 – **118 rm** 110.00, 2 suites.
◆ Good leisure, and Belfast's most extensive conference facilities ; situated on city bypass. Modern bedrooms are well equipped for business travellers. First floor restaurant offering modern-style classics.

Tensq, 10 Donegall Square South, BT1 5JD, ☎ (028) 9024 1001, *reservations@tensquare.co.uk, Fax (028) 9024 3210* – rm, MC AE VISA. BY x
Porcelain : Meals - Asian specialities - *(closed Sunday)* a la carte 22.50/34.50 – **23 rm** 160.00/240.00.
◆ Victorian mill building in heart of city renovated to a thoroughly contemporary standard. Notably spacious deluxe bedrooms. Access to private bar for guests. Restaurant décor maintains the modern style of the hotel.

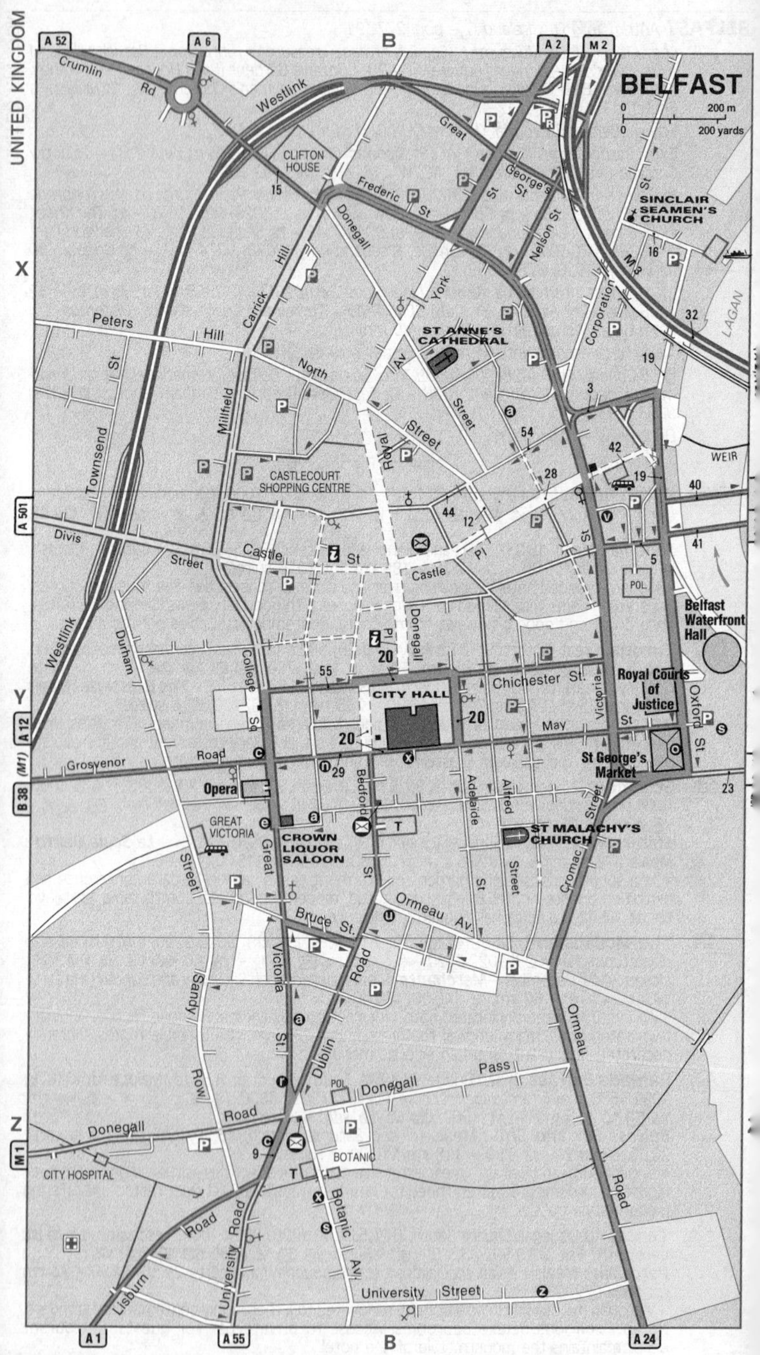
BELFAST
0
200 m
0
200 yards
A 52
A 6
B
A 2
M 2
Crumlin Rd
Westlink
CLIFTON HOUSE
15
Great George's St
Frederic St
Donegall St
York St
Nelson St
SINCLAIR SEAMEN'S CHURCH
16
M 3
Corporation St
LAGAN
32
19
X
Peters Hill
Carrick Hill
Millfield
North Street
Royal Av
ST ANNE'S CATHEDRAL
3
54
42
WEIR
28
19
40
Townsend St
CASTLECOURT SHOPPING CENTRE
44
12
A 501
Divis Street
Castle St
Castle Pl
Victoria St
5
41
POL.
Belfast Waterfront Hall
Westlink
Durham
College Sq
Donegall Pl
20
55
CITY HALL
20
Chichester St.
Royal Courts of Justice
Oxford St
May St
Y
A 12
(M1)
B 38
Grosvenor Road
29
Bedford St
Adelaide St
Alfred Street
St George's Market
23
Opera
GREAT VICTORIA
Great Victoria Street
CROWN LIQUOR SALOON
T
ST MALACHY'S CHURCH
Cromac Street
Bruce St.
Ormeau Av.
Sandy Row
Victoria St.
Dublin Road
Ormeau Road
POL.
Donegall Pass
Z
Donegall Road
M 1
9
CITY HOSPITAL
BOTANIC
Botanic Av.
Lisburn Road
University Road
University Street
A 1
A 55
A 24

INDEX OF STREET NAMES IN BELFAST CENTRE

In Northern Ireland traffic and parking are controlled in the town centres. No vehicle may be left unattended in a Control Zone.

Holiday Inn Belfast, 22 Ormeau Ave, BT2 8HS, ☎ (0870) 4009005, *belfast@ichotelsgroup.com, Fax (028) 9062 6546,* Fitness, sauna, pool – lift, no-smoking rm, air-conditioning, TV, telephone, disabled access – conference 140. MC AE DC VISA. no dogs BY u
The Junction **: Meals** *(closed 25-26 December and Sunday lunch)* 15.00/25.00 and dinner a la carte approx 24.15 **s.** ♀ – ☕ 13.95 – **168 rm** 155.00, 2 suites.
◆ Convenient city-centre location, up-to-date conference facilities and trim, well-equipped rooms in modern colours make this an good business choice. Plenty of choice from the menu of modern cooking.

Malone Lodge, 60 Eglantine Ave, BT9 6DY, ☎ (028) 9038 8000, *info@malonelodgehotel.com, Fax (028) 9038 8088,* Fitness, sauna – lift, no-smoking rm, air-conditioning rest, TV, telephone, disabled access, parking – conference 120. MC AE DC VISA. no dogs
The Green Door **: Meals** 11.50/39.50 and a la carte 17.45/28.15 **s.** – **50 rm** ☕ 85.00/120.00, 8 suites.
◆ Imposing hotel in Victorian terrace in quiet residential area. Elegant lobby lounge and smart bar. Conference facilities. Basement gym. Stylish, modern rooms with big beds. Restaurant provides a comfortable, contemporary environment.

The Crescent Townhouse, 13 Lower Cres, BT7 1NR, ☎ (028) 9032 3349, *info@crescenttownhouse.com, Fax (028) 9032 0646* – air-conditioning rest, TV. MC AE VISA. no dogs BZ x
closed 11-28 July, 25-26 December and 1 January – ***Metro Brasserie*** **: Meals** (dinner only) 13.50 and a la carte 18.20/26.75 ♀ – **11 rm** ☕ 80.00/125.00.
◆ Intimate Regency house that blends original features with modern amenities. Relaxed, discreet atmosphere. Spacious and luxurious rooms with interior designed period feel. Modern classic brasserie with a lively and relaxed ambience.

Madison's, 59-63 Botanic Ave, BT7 1JL, ☎ (028) 9050 9800, *info@madisonshotel.com, Fax (028) 9050 9808* – lift, no-smoking rm, air-conditioning rest, TV, disabled access. MC AE VISA. no dogs BZ s
The Restaurant **: Meals** a la carte 19.40/22.40 **s.** – **35 rm** ☕ 70.00/80.00.
◆ Contemporary hotel in a lively and fashionable area packed with bars and restaurants. Spacious bedrooms with up-to-date facilities. Brightly decorated with modern art. Vibrantly decorated bar and restaurant with a busy and buzzy atmosphere.

Benedict's, 7-21 Bradbury Pl, Shaftsbury Sq, BT7 1RQ, ☎ (028) 9059 1999, *info@benedictshotel.co.uk, Fax (028) 9059 1990* – lift, air-conditioning rest, TV, disabled access. MC AE DC VISA. no dogs BZ c
closed 11-12 July and 25 December – ***Benedicts Restaurant*** **: Meals** 18.00/22.00 (dinner) and a la carte 18.35/23.85 **s.** ♀ – **32 rm** ☕ 60.00/70.00.
◆ A lively, strikingly designed bar with nightly entertainment can be found at the heart of this busy commercial hotel. Well-appointed bedrooms above offer modern facilities. Relaxed, popular restaurant.

Jurys Inn Belfast, Fisherwick Pl, Great Victoria St, BT2 7AP, ☎ (028) 9053 3500, *jurysinnbelfast@jurysdoyle.com, Fax (028) 9053 3511* – lift, no-smoking rm, TV, telephone, disabled access – conference 30. MC AE DC VISA. no dogs BY c
closed 24-26 December – ***Arches*** **: Meals** (dinner only) a la carte approx 15.95 – ☕ 7.45 – **190 rm** 75.00.
◆ Beside the opera house and convenient for the shops. Modern and functional hotel suitable for both corporate and leisure travellers. Generously proportioned family rooms. Restaurant offers popular international menu with subtle Asian touches.

Express by Holiday Inn, 106A University St, BT7 1HP, ☎ (028) 9031 1909, *express@holidayinn/ireland.com, Fax (028) 9031 1910* – |‡|, ⇔ rm, TV ☎ ♿ P – 🏛 200. MC AE ① VISA. ✈ BZ z
Don's **:** **Meals** a la carte approx 18.70 – **114 rm** ☐ 62.95.
◆ Good value and ideal for business travellers. Spacious, bright and modern bedrooms with plenty of work space. Complimentary Continental breakfast. Traditional and busy buffet-style Don's restaurant.

Travelodge, 15 Brunswick St, BT2 7GE, ☎ (08700) 850950, *Fax (028) 9023 2999* – |‡|, ⇔ rm, ▤ rest, TV ♿. MC AE ① VISA. ✈ BY a
Meals (grill rest.) – **90 rm** 79.95.
◆ Modern lodge, with bright, spacious and generally well-kept bedrooms ; all with additional sofa beds. Meals can be taken in the first floor café-bar.

Ash Rowan Town House, 12 Windsor Ave, BT9 6EE, ☎ (028) 9066 1758, *ashrowan@hotmail.com, Fax (028) 9066 3227,* ⚘ – ⇔ TV P. MC VISA. ✈
closed 23 December-6 January – **Meals** (by arrangement) 35.00 – **5 rm** ☐ 52.00/96.00.
◆ Late 19C house in quiet tree-lined avenue. Personally run ; interestingly "cluttered" interior. Comfy conservatory sitting room. Well-judged bedrooms with thoughtful touches.

All Seasons without rest., 356 Lisburn Rd, BT9 6GJ, ☎ (028) 9068 2814, *allseasons@fsmail.net* – ⇔ TV P. MC VISA. ✈
6 rm ☐ 25.00/45.00.
◆ Close to Windsor Park stadium, a bay-windowed redbrick house offering good value accommodation, bright, modern and en suite : rear-facing rooms are quieter.

The Old Rectory without rest., 148 Malone Rd, BT9 5LH, ☎ (028) 9066 7882, *info@anoldrectory.co.uk, Fax (028) 9068 3759,* ⚘ – ⇔ TV P. ✈
closed 24 December-1 January and Easter – **6 rm** ☐ 36.00/60.00.
◆ Former Victorian rectory in residential area ; period charm retained. Attractive drawing room. Traditionally furnished rooms. Hot Irish whiskey served as guests retire to bed.

Roseleigh House, 19 Rosetta Park, BT6 0DL, South : 1 ½ m. by A 24 Ormeau Rd ☎ (028) 9064 4414, *info@roseleighhouse.co.uk, Fax (028) 9064 2983* – ⇔ TV P. MC VISA. ✈
closed 25 December – **Meals** (by arrangement) 17.50 – **9 rm** ☐ 38.50/60.00.
◆ Imposing Victorian house close to the Belvoir Park golf course and in a fairly quiet residential suburb. Brightly decorated and well-kept bedrooms with modern amenities. Honest, home-cooked dinner in a traditionally appointed dining room.

Restaurant Michael Deane, 36-40 Howard St, BT1 6PF, ☎ (028) 9033 1134, *michaeldeane@deanesbelfast.com, Fax (028) 9056 0001* – ▤. MC AE VISA BY n
closed 1 week July, Easter, Christmas, New Year and Sunday-Tuesday – **Meals** (dinner only) 40.50 ♀ (see also ***Deanes Brasserie*** below).
◆ Elegant 1st floor restaurant with rich, plush décor. Polished and professional service by approachable team. Concise menu of refined, classically based modern Irish dishes.
Spec. Pan-fried scallops, baby asparagus and young garlic. Local lamb with carrot, foie gras and cinnamon. Roulade of chocolate, vanilla and black cherry.

Aldens, 229 Upper Newtownards Rd, BT4 3JF, East : 2 m. on A 20 ☎ (028) 9065 0079, *info@aldensrestaurant.com, Fax (028) 9065 0032* – ▤. MC AE ① VISA
closed 2 weeks July, Saturday lunch, Sunday and Bank Holidays – **Meals** a la carte 17.00/26.00 ♀.
◆ Personally run, spacious and contemporary restaurant in "up-and-coming" suburb. Extensive selection of confident, modern dishes. Moderately priced midweek menu also offered.

Cayenne, 7 Ascot House, Shaftesbury Sq, BT2 7DB, ☎ (028) 9033 1532, *reservations@cayennerestaurant.com, Fax (028) 9026 1575* – ▤. MC AE ① VISA BZ r
closed 25-26 December, 1 January, 12 July and lunch Saturday – **Meals** (booking essential) 15.50 (lunch) and a la carte 18.75/35.00 ♀.
◆ Striking modern artwork and a lively atmosphere feature in this busy, relaxed and stylish restaurant. Carefully prepared selection of creative Asian influenced dishes.

Shu, 253 Lisburn Rd, BT9 7EN, ☎ (028) 9038 1655, *eat@shu-restaurant.com, Fax (028) 9068 1632* – ▤. MC ① VISA
closed 11-13 July, 24-26 December and Sunday – **Meals** 16.00/27.50 and a la carte 19.00/26.25 **s.** ♀.
◆ Trendy, modern restaurant on the Lisburn Road. Converted from terraced houses, it is spacious and uncluttered with neutral and black décor. Eclectic, contemporary dishes.

The Wok, 126 Great Victoria St, BT2 7BG, ☎ (028) 9023 3828 – ▤. MC VISA BZ a
closed 25-26 December and lunch Saturday and Sunday – **Meals** - Chinese - 10.00/20.00 and a la carte 11.00/24.80 **s.**.
◆ Smart, modern Chinese restaurant with pleasant ambience. Menus feature classic interpretations and less well-known authentic dishes : most regions of China are represented.

Oxford Exchange, First floor, St Georges Market, Oxford St, BT1 3NQ, ✆ (028) 9024 0014, *oxfordexchange@mountcharles.com, Fax (028) 9023 5675* – ▤. MC ⓓ VISA *closed 1 week July, 25 December, 1 January, Sunday and Saturday lunch* – **Meals** (grill rest.) a la carte 22.00/28.00 ♀. BY o
◆ Airy, glass-roofed restaurant atmospherically set just atop the Victorian St. George's market. Stresses the use of very seasonal and hearty ingredients.

Deanes Brasserie, 36-40 Howard St, BT1 6PF, ✆ (028) 9056 0000, *Fax (028) 9056 0001* – ▤. MC AE VISA BY n
closed Easter, 12-13 July, 25-26 December, Sunday and Bank Holidays – **Meals** a la carte 16.25/21.50 ♀.
◆ Ornately decorated, lively and modern street level brasserie continues to attract a loyal regular following. Robust and cosmopolitan cooking with a traditional Irish base.

Nick's Warehouse, 35-39 Hill St, BT1 2LB, ✆ (028) 9043 9690, *nicks@warehouse.dnet.co.uk, Fax (028) 9023 0514* – ▤. MC AE ⓓ VISA BX a
closed 2 days Easter, 17 March, 1 May, 12 July, 25-26 December, 1 January, Saturday lunch, Monday dinner and Sunday – **Meals** a la carte 21.90/29.20 ♀.
◆ Built in 1832 as a bonded whiskey store. On two floors, the ground floor Anix is relaxed and buzzy. Upstairs more formal. Well informed service of an eclectic menu.

at Belfast International Airport *West : 15 ½ m. by A 52* BX – ✉ *Belfast*

Fitzwilliam International, Aldergrove, BT29 4ZY, ✆ (028) 9445 7000, *reservations@fitzwilliaminternational.com, Fax (028) 9442 3500* – |♦|, ⇔ rm, ▤ TV ✆ ♿ P – 🏛 250. MC AE ⓓ VISA. ✂
***The Terrace* : Meals** (booking essential) (buffet lunch)/dinner 16.95 **s.** – ☐ 10.00 – **106 rm** 110.00/125.00, 2 suites.
◆ Imposingly up-to-date hotel with sun-filled lobby, 50 metres from terminal entrance. Terrace, secluded garden, cocktail bar ; conference facilities. Distinctively modern rooms. Formal restaurant with smart, cosmopolitan ambience.

BIRMINGHAM *W. Mids.* 503 504 O 26 *Great Britain G.* – *pop. 965 928.*

See : *City★ – Museum and Art Gallery★★* LZ **M2** – *Barber Institute of Fine Arts★★ (at Birmingham University)* EX – *Cathedral of St Philip (stained glass portrayals★)* KYZ – *Thinktank★, Millennium Point* FV. – **Envir.** : *Aston Hall★★* FV **M.**

Exc. : *Black Country Museum★, Dudley, NW : 10 m. by A 456 and A 4123 – Bourneville★, SW : 4 m. on A 38 and A 441.*

18 Edgbaston, Church Rd ✆ (0121) 454 1736 FX – *18 Hilltop, Park Lane, Handsworth ✆ (0121) 554 4463 – 18 Hatchford Brook, Coventry Rd, Sheldon (0121) 743 9821* HX – *18 Brand Hall, Heron Rd, Oldbury, Warley ✆ (0121) 552 2195 – 18 Harborne Church Farm, Vicarage Rd, Harborne (0121) 427 1204* EX.

✈ *Birmingham International Airport : ✆ (0121) 767 5511, E : 6 ½ m. by A 45.*

ℹ *Convention & Visitor Bureau, 2 City Arcade ✆ (0121) 643 2514, Fax (0121) 616 1038 – Convention & Visitor Bureau, National Exhibition Centre ✆ (0121) 780 4321 – Birmingham Airport, Information Desk ✆ (0121) 767 7145 Visitor Information Centre, 130 Colmore Row ✆ (0121) 693 6300.*

London 122 – Bristol 91 – Liverpool 103 – Manchester 86 – Nottingham 50.

Malmaison, Mailbox, 1 Wharfside St, B1 1RD, ✆ (0121) 246 5000, *birmingham@malmaison.com, Fax (0121) 246 5002,* ⅂₆, ≘s – |♦|, ⇔ rm, ▤ TV ✆ ♿ – 🏛 45. MC AE ⓓ VISA. ✂ LZ e
***Brasserie* : Meals** 12.95/13.95 and a la carte 19.85/29.45 ♀ – ☐ 11.95 – **186 rm** 125.00, 3 suites.
◆ Modern hotel near shops and nightlife. Ground floor leisure centre. Stylish bar. Spacious contemporary bedrooms with every modern facility ; good view from upper floors. First floor brasserie serving contemporary French influenced cooking at reasonable prices.

Hyatt Regency, 2 Bridge St, B1 2JZ, ✆ (0121) 643 1234, *birmingham@hyattintl.com, Fax (0121) 616 2323,* ≤, ⅂₆, ≘s, ▢ – |♦|, ⇔ rm, ▤ TV ✆ ♿ 🚗 – 🏛 240. MC AE ⓓ VISA JCB. ✂ KZ a
***Court Cafe* : Meals** 13.50 lunch and a la carte 22.00/41.00 **s.** ♀ – ☐ 13.25 – **315 rm** 180.00, 4 suites.
◆ Striking mirrored exterior. Glass enclosed lifts offer panoramic views. Sizeable rooms with floor to ceiling windows. Covered link with International Convention Centre. Large dining room with Impressionist prints.

Birmingham Marriott, 12 Hagley Rd, B16 8SJ, ✆ (0121) 452 1144, *Fax (0121) 456 3442,* ⅂₆, ▢ – |♦|, ⇔ rm, ▤ TV ✆ ♿ P – 🏛 30. MC AE VISA. ✂
***West 12* : Meals** (bar lunch Saturday) a la carte 20.00/31.00 **s.** ♀ – ☐ 13.95 – **100 rm** 149.00, 4 suites. JZ c
◆ Edwardian grand foyer with Italian marble and mahogany. Drawing room popular for afternoon tea. Egyptian theme fitness centre. Individually appointed, sizeable rooms. Stylish, modern restaurant.

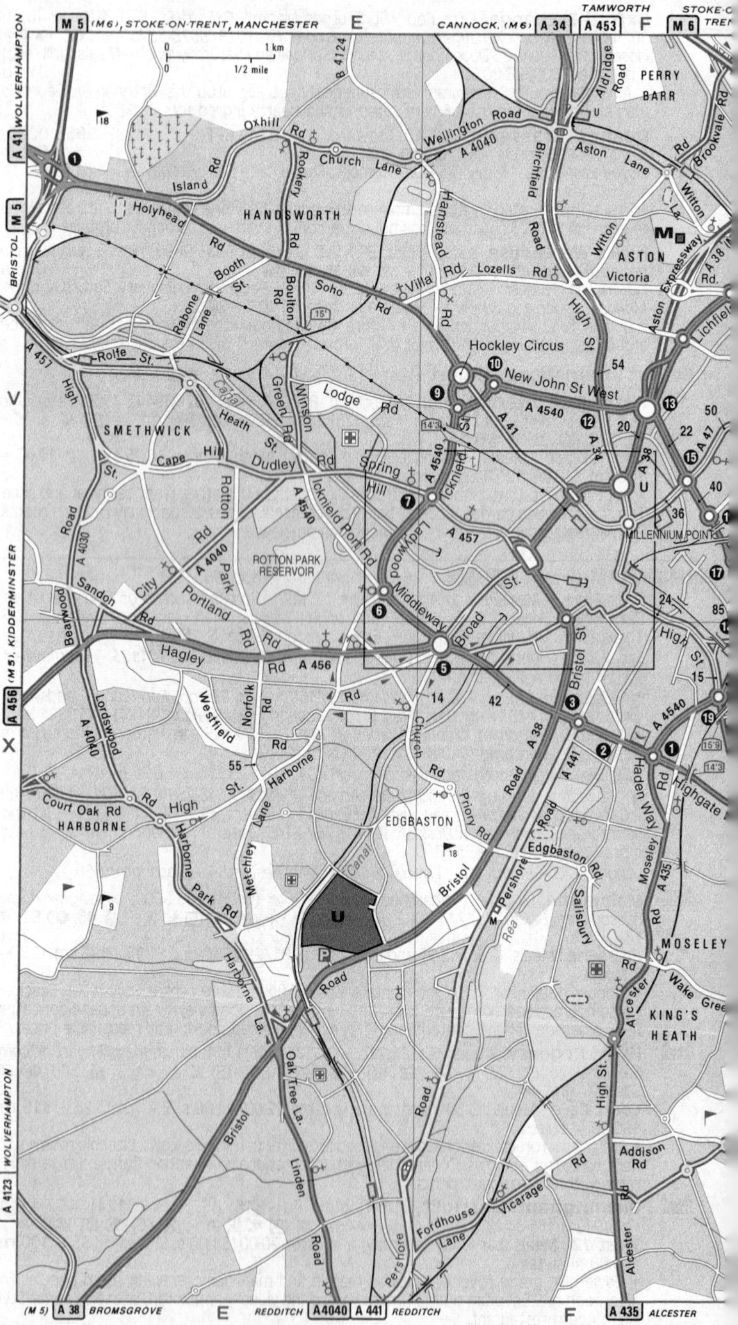

M 5 (M6), STOKE-ON-TRENT, MANCHESTER
E
CANNOCK, (M6) A 34 A 453 TAMWORTH
F
M 6 STOKE-ON-TRENT

A 41 WOLVERHAMPTON
M 5 BRISTOL
V
A 456 (M 5), KIDDERMINSTER
X
A 4123 WOLVERHAMPTON

0 1 km
0 1/2 mile

B 4124
Oxhill Rd
Wellington Road
A 4040
Aldridge Road
PERRY BARR
Brookvale Rd
Island Rd
Rookery Rd
Church Lane
Birchfield Road
Aston Lane
Witton La.
Holyhead Rd
HANDSWORTH
Hamstead Rd
Witton Rd
ASTON
Expressway
A 38 (M)
Booth St.
Boulton Rd
Soho Rd
Villa Rd
Lozells Rd
Victoria Rd.
Rabone Lane
High St
Aston
Lichfield
Rolfe St.
A 457
Canal
Hockley Circus
New John St West
54
High
Green Rd
Winson
Lodge Rd
A 4540
A 41
A 34
20
22
50
A 47
SMETHWICK
Heath St.
Icknield St
A 38
Cape Hill
Dudley Rd
Spring Hill
A 4540
U
40
St.
Rotton Park Rd
A 4540
Icknield Port Rd
Ladywood
A 457
36
MILLENNIUM POINT
Road
A 4030
City Rd
A 4040
ROTTON PARK RESERVOIR
St.
Sandon Rd
Portland Rd
Middleway
Broad St.
24
85
Bearwood
Hagley Rd A 456
High St
Bristol St
15
Lordswood
Westfield
Norfolk Rd
Rd
14
42
A 4040
A 38
A 4540
Rd
Church Rd
A 441
Haden Way
Rd
Highgate
55
Harborne
St.
Road
Court Oak Rd
High Rd
Priory Rd
HARBORNE
Lane
EDGBASTON
Road
Edgbaston Rd
Moseley Rd A 435
Harborne Park Rd
Metchley
Canal
Bristol
Pershore
Salisbury
Rea
MOSELEY
U
Road
Rd
P
Wake Green
Harborne La.
Alcester
KING'S HEATH
Oak Tree La.
High St.
Road
Bristol
Linden Road
Addison Rd
Rd
Rd
Vicarage
Fordhouse Lane
Pershore
Alcester

(M 5) A 38 BROMSGROVE
E
REDDITCH A4040 A 441 REDDITCH
F
A 435 ALCESTER

G
A 5127 LICHFIELD
CANNOCK A 452
H
A 38
A 4040
ERDINGTON
B 4148
Tyburn Rd
Chester
Rd
Wood End Rd
Hill
Bromford
Road
Kingsbury
Rd
GRAVELLY HILL JUNCTION
6
Gravelly
Tyburn
Canal
A 47
5
Lane
Newport Rd
CASTLE BROMWICH
B 4118
Road
M 6
Bromford
Road
Rd
Bradford
Rd
Aston
Church
Rd
Heath
Bromford
Coleshill
Lane
Cole
Washwood
Highfield
Rd
Road
Alum
Rock
Rd
Stechford
La.
Rd
V
31
SALTLEY
Rock
Rd
Alum
Bowyer
Rd
Station
Road
Bordesley Green
Rd
Bordesley
Green
Green
Bordesley
Cattell
Rd
Rd
Church
Sheldon
YARDLEY
Stoney La
Heath
Small
Heath
Rd
Coventry
Rd
Road
A 45
Highway
Road
Church
Rd
Coventry
SHELDON
Church Road
Hillock
Golden
Rd
X
Stoney
Lane
Warwick
M
Road
A 4040
Stockfield
Yardley
Lane
Wagon
Rd
Sheaf La.
A 45
COVENTRY AIRPORT
Stratford
A 34
Yardley
25
Road
87
Road
Hob's Moat
Rd
Shaftmoor
Lane
Rd
College Rd
Olton
Boulevard
East
Richmond
Road
Cole
Hollies
H
A 41 M 42, WARWICK
Wood
Rd
Road
Fox
Brook
Lane
Shirley
Road
Robin
Road
Highfield
Hood
Lane
74
G
STRATFORD-UPON-AVON A 34
BIRMINGHAM
BUILT UP AREA
Bordesley Middleway ...... FX 10
Calthorpe Rd ...... FX 14
Camp Hill .... FX 15
Corporation St ..... FV 20
Darmouth Middleway ...... FV 22
Digbeth .... FV 24
Dudley Park Rd .... GX 25
High St .... GV 31
Jennen's Rd....... FV 36
Lawley Street ..... FV 40
Lee Bank Middleway ..... FX 42
Nechell's Parkway .. FV 50
New Town Row ... FV 54
Nursery Rd .... EX 55
Saltley Rd .... GV 66
Solihull Lane ..... GX 74
Watery Lane ...... FV 85
Westley Rd ...... GX 87

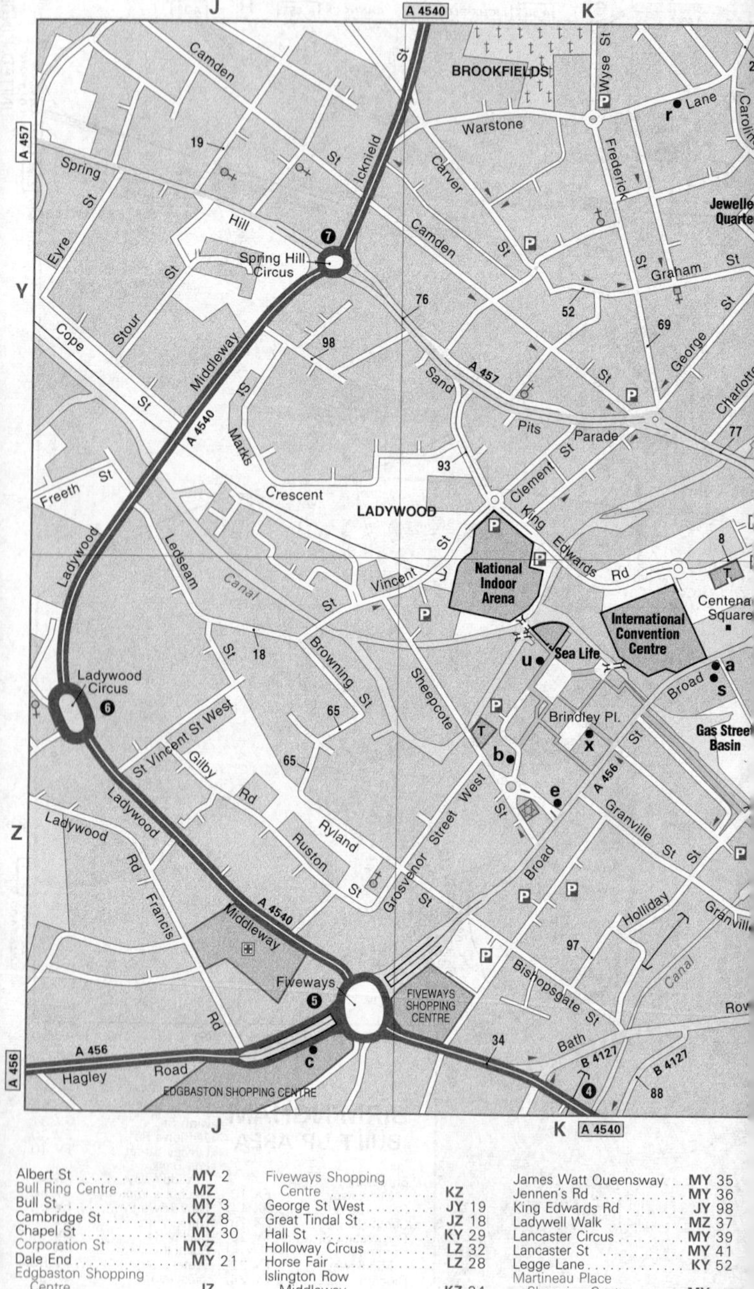

Albert St . . . . **MY** 2
Bull Ring Centre . . . . **MZ**
Bull St . . . . **MY** 3
Cambridge St . . . . **KYZ** 8
Chapel St . . . . **MY** 30
Corporation St . . . . **MYZ**
Dale End . . . . **MY** 21
Edgbaston Shopping
Centre . . . . **JZ**

Fiveways Shopping
Centre . . . . **KZ**
George St West . . . . **JY** 19
Great Tindal St . . . . **JZ** 18
Hall St . . . . **KY** 29
Holloway Circus . . . . **LZ** 32
Horse Fair . . . . **LZ** 28
Islington Row
Middleway . . . . **KZ** 34

James Watt Queensway . . **MY** 35
Jennen's Rd . . . . **MY** 36
King Edwards Rd . . . . **JY** 98
Ladywell Walk . . . . **MZ** 37
Lancaster Circus . . . . **MY** 39
Lancaster St . . . . **MY** 41
Legge Lane . . . . **KY** 52
Martineau Place
Shopping Centre . . . . **MY**

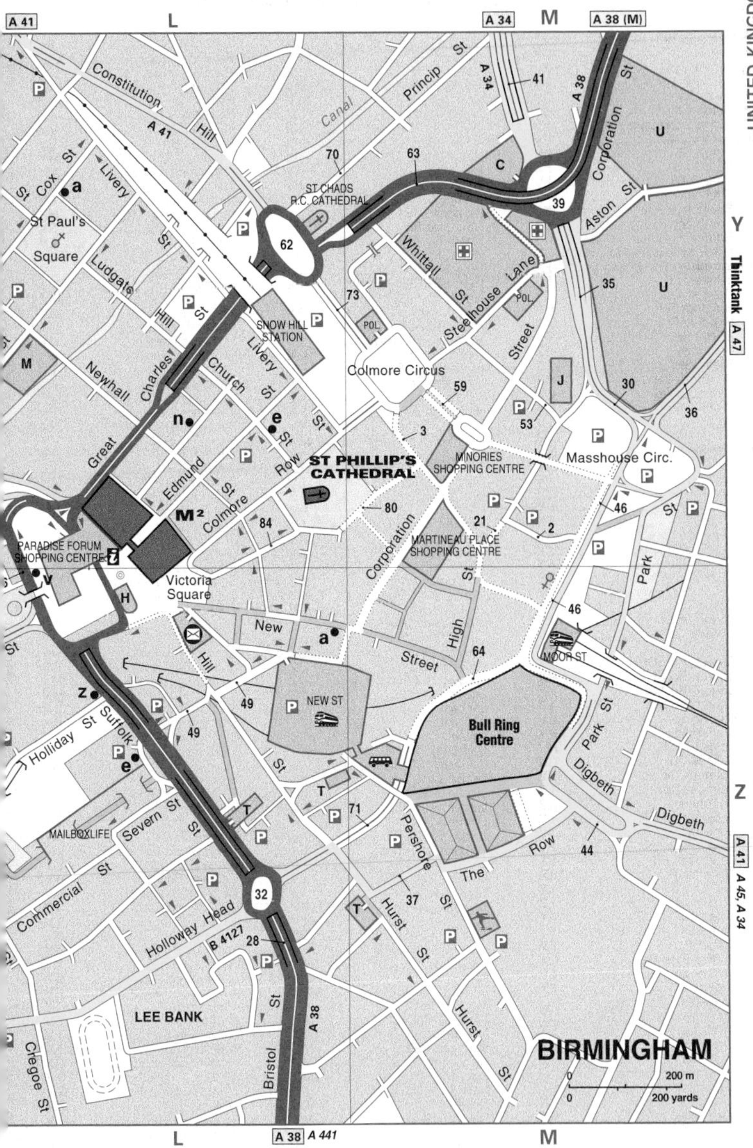
A 41
L
A 34
M
A 38 (M)
Constitution
Hill
A 41
Canal
Princip St
A 34
41
A 38
Corporation St
U
70
63
C
ST CHADS
R.C. CATHEDRAL
39
Aston St
St Paul's
Square
Cox St
Livery
St
62
Ludgate Hill
Whittall St
Steelhouse Lane
Y
Thinktank
A 47
35
U
SNOW HILL
STATION
73
POL.
POL.
Street
M
Newhall
Charles
Church
Livery
St
Colmore Circus
59
J
30
36
53
n
e
St
Great
Edmund
St
Row
3
MINORIES
SHOPPING CENTRE
Masshouse Circ.
ST PHILLIP'S
CATHEDRAL
M²
Colmore
84
80
Corporation
21
2
46
St
MARTINEAU PLACE
SHOPPING CENTRE
PARADISE FORUM
SHOPPING CENTRE
Victoria
Square
H
New
a
High
St
46
Park
St
Street
64
MOOR ST
Hill
49
NEW ST
Bull Ring
Centre
z
Suffolk
St
49
Holliday
Park St
e
Digbeth
Z
Digbeth
St
T
T
71
MAILBOXLIFE
Severn St
Pershore
A 41
A 45, A 34
Row
44
Commercial St
The
32
37
St
Holloway Head
T
Hurst
B 4127
28
St
LEE BANK
St
A 38
Hurst
Cregoe St
Bristol
St
BIRMINGHAM
200 m
200 yards
L
A 38
A 441
M

STREET INDEX TO BIRMINGHAM TOWN PLANS

Addison Rd ... FX
Albert St ... MY 2
Alcester Rd ... FX
Aldridge Rd ... FV
Alum Rock Rd ... GV
Aston Church Rd ... GV
Aston Expressway ... FV
Aston Lane ... FV
Aston St ... MY
Bath Row ... KZ
Bearwood Rd ... EV
Birchfield Rd ... FV
Bishopsgate St ... KZ
Booth St ... EV
Bordesley Green ... GV
Bordesley Green Rd ... GV
Bordesley Middleway ... FX 10
Boulton Rd ... EV
Bowyer Rd ... GV
Bradford Rd ... HV
Brindley Pl. ... KZ
Bristol Rd ... EFX
Bristol St ... LZ
Broad St ... KLZ
Bromford Lane ... GV
Bromford Rd ... HV
Brook Lane ... GX
Brookvale Rd ... FV
Browning St ... JZ
Bull Ring Centre ... MZ
Bull St ... MY 3
Calthorpe Rd ... FX 14
Cambridge St ... KYZ 8
Camden St ... JKY
Camp Hill ... FX 15
Cape Hill ... EV
Caroline St ... KLY
Carver St ... KY
Cattell Rd ... GV
Centenary Square ... KZ
Chapel St ... MY 30
Charlotte St ... KLY
Chester Rd ... HV
Church Lane ... EV
Church Rd EDGBASTON ... FX
Church Rd SHELDON ... HX
Church Rd YARDLEY ... HX
Church St ... LY
City Rd ... EV
Clement St ... KY
Coleshill Rd ... HV
College Rd ... GX
Colmore Circus ... MY
Colmore Row ... LY
Commercial St ... LZ
Constitution Hill ... LY
Cope St ... JY
Corporation St ... FV 20
Court Oak Rd ... EX
Coventry Rd ... GHX
Cox St ... LY
Cregoe St ... LZ
Dale End ... MY 21
Darmouth Middleway ... FV 22
Digbeth ... FV 24
Dudley Park Rd ... GX 25
Dudley Rd ... EV
Edgbaston Rd ... FX
Edgbaston Shopping Centre ... JZ
Edmund St ... LY
Eyre St ... JY
Fiveways ... JZ
Fiveways Shopping Centre ... KZ
Fordhouse Lane ... FX
Fox Hollies Rd ... GX
Francis Rd ... JZ
Frederick St ... KY
Freeth St ... JY
George St ... KY
George St West ... JY 19
Gilby Rd ... JZ
Golden Hillock Rd ... GX
Graham St ... KY
Granville St ... KLZ
Gravelly Hill ... GV
Great Charles St ... LY
Great Tindal St ... JZ 18
Grosvenor St West ... JKZ
Haden Way ... FX
Hagley Rd ... JZ
Hall St ... KY 29
Hampstead Rd ... FV
Harborne Lane ... EX
Harborne Park Rd ... EX
Harborne Rd ... EX
Heath St ... EV
High St ... MZ
High St ASTON ... FV
High St BORDESLEY ... FX
High St HARBORNE ... EX
High St KING'S HEATH ... FX
High St SALTLEY ... GV 31
High St SMETHWICK ... EV
Highfield Rd ... GX
Highfield Rd SALTLEY ... GV
Highgate Rd ... FX
Hill St ... LZ
Hob's Moat Rd ... HX
Hockley Circus ... FV
Holliday St ... KLZ
Holloway Circus ... LZ 32
Holloway Head ... LZ
Holyhead Rd ... EV
Horse Fair ... LZ 28
Hurst St ... MZ
Icknield Port Rd ... EV
Icknield St ... JKY
Island Rd ... EV
Islington Row Middleway ... KZ 34
James Watt Queensway ... MY 35
Jennen's Rd ... MY 36
King Edwards Rd ... JY 98
Kingsbury Rd ... HV
Ladywell Walk ... MZ 37
Ladywood Circus ... JZ
Ladywood Middleway ... JYZ
Ladywood Rd ... JZ
Lancaster Circus ... MY 39
Lancaster St ... MY 41
Lawley St ... FV 40
Ledseam St ... JYZ
Lee Bank Middleway ... FX 42
Legge Lane ... KY 52
Lichfield Rd ... FV
Linden Rd ... EX
Livery St ... LY
Lodge Rd ... EV
Lordswood Rd ... EX
Lozells Rd ... FV
Ludgate Hill ... LY
Martineau Place Shopping Centre ... MY
Masshouse Circus ... MY
Metchley Lane ... EX
Minories Shopping Centre ... MY
Moat Lane ... MZ 44
Moor St Queensway ... MYZ 46
Morville St ... JZ 65
Moseley Rd ... FX
Navigation St ... LZ 49
Nechell's Parkway ... FV 50
New John St West ... FV
New St ... LMZ
New Town Row ... FV 54
Newhall Hill ... KY 69
Newhall St ... MY
Newport Rd ... HV
Newton St ... MY 53
Norfolk Rd ... EX
Nursery Rd ... EX 55
Oak Tree Lane ... EX
Olton Bd East ... GX
Oxhill Rd ... EV
Paradise Circus ... LYZ 56
Paradise Forum Shopping Centre ... LYZ
Park St ... MYZ
Pershore Rd ... FX
Pershore St ... MZ
Portland Rd ... EV
Princip St ... MY
riory Queensway ... MY 59
Priory Rd ... FX
Rabone Lane ... EV
Richmond Rd ... HX
Robin Hood Lane ... GX
Rolfe St ... EV
Rookery Rd ... EV
Rotton Park Rd ... EV
Ruston St ... JZ
Ryland St ... JKZ
St Chads Circus ... LY 62
St Chads Ringway ... MY 63
St Marks Crescent ... JY
St Martin's Circus ... MZ 64
St Paul's Square ... LY
St Vincent St ... JKZ
St Vincent St West ... JZ
Salisbury Rd ... FX
Saltley Rd ... GV 66
Sand Pits Parade ... KY
Sandon Rd ... EV
Severn St ... LZ
Shadwell St ... LMY 70
Shaftmoor Lane ... GX
Sheaf Lane ... HX
Sheepcote St ... KZ
Sheldon Heath Rd ... HX
Shirley Rd ... GX
Small Heath Highway ... GX
Smallbrook Queensway ... LMZ 71
Snow Hill Queensway ... LMY 73
Soho Rd ... EV
Solihull Lane ... GX 74
Spring Hill ... JY
Spring Hill Circus ... JY
Station Rd ... HV
Stechford Lane ... HV
Steelhouse Lane ... MY
Stockfield Rd ... GX
Stoney La. MOSELEY ... GX
Stoney La. YARDLEY ... HX
Stour St ... JY
Stratford Rd ... GX
Suffolk St ... LZ
Summer Hill Rd ... JKY 76
Summer Hill St ... KY 93
Summer Row ... KY 77
Temple Row ... MY 80
The Row ... MZ
Tyburn Rd ... GHV
Vicarage Rd ... FX
Victoria Rd ... FV
Victoria Square ... LZ
illa Rd ... FV
Wagon Lane ... HX
Wake Green Rd ... FX
Warstone Lane ... KY
Warwick Rd ... GX
Washwood Heath Rd ... GV
Waterloo St ... LY 84
Watery Lane ... FV 85
Wellington Rd ... FV
Westfield Rd ... EX
Westley Rd ... GX 87
Wheeley's Lane ... KZ 88
Whittall St. ... MY
William St ... KZ 97
Winson Green Rd ... EV
Witton Lane ... FV
Witton Rd ... FV
Wood End Rd ... GV
Wyse St ... KY
Yardley Rd ... HX
Yardley Wood Rd ... GX

Hotel Du Vin, 25 Church St, B3 2NR, (0121) 200 0600, *info@birmingham.hoteldu vin.com, Fax (0121) 236 0889*, – rm, – 85. LY e

Bistro : **Meals** a la carte 29.90/31.90 – 13.50 – **66 rm** 100.00/195.00.

• Former Victorian eye hospital with striking, wine themed interiors. "Cave du Vin" for wine, cigar purchases. Low lighting in rooms of muted tones ; one has 8ft bed and gym. Champagne in "bubble lounge" ; Parisian style brasserie.

Crowne Plaza Birmingham, Central Sq, B1 1HH, (0121) 631 2000, *Fax (0121) 643 9018*, – rm, – 150. LZ z

closed 24-26 December – **Meals** *(closed lunch Saturday and Sunday)* 19.50 and dinner a la carte – 14.95 – **281 rm** 159.00, 3 suites.

• Ideal for both corporate and leisure guests. Extensive leisure facilities include children's pool. Well-equipped bedrooms with air-conditioning and triple glazing. Conservatory restaurant with views across city.

The Burlington, Burlington Arcade, 126 New St, B2 4JQ, (0121) 643 9191, *mail @burlingtonhotel.com, Fax (0121) 643 5075*, – rm, rest, – 400. LZ a

closed 25-26 December – ***Berlioz :*** **Meals** 19.95 (dinner) and a la carte 22.85/25.50 – 13.50 – **107 rm** 130.00/165.00, 5 suites.

• Approached by a period arcade. Restored Victorian former railway hotel retains much of its original charm. Period décor to bedrooms yet with fax, modem and voice mail. Elegant dining room : ornate ceiling, chandeliers and vast mirrors.

Copthorne, Paradise Circus, B3 3HJ, (0121) 200 2727, *sales.birmingham@mill-cop .com, Fax (0121) 200 1197*, – rm, rest, – 180. LYZ v

Goldsmiths : **Meals** (dinner only) 29.95 and a la carte 29.00/38.00 – ***Goldies :*** **Meals** *(closed 1 January and Saturday lunch)* 18.00 (dinner) and a la carte 25.00/34.00 – **209 rm** 155.00/175.00, 3 suites.

• Overlooking Centenary Square. Corporate hotel with extensive leisure club and cardio-vascular gym. Cricket themed bar. Connoisseur rooms offer additional comforts. Flambé dishes offered in intimate Goldsmiths. Goldies is all-day relaxed brasserie.

Jonathan's, 16-24 Wolverhampton Rd, Oldbury, B68 0LH, West : 4 m. by A 456 (0121) 429 3757, *bookings@jonathans.co.uk, Fax (0121) 434 3107* – , rest, – 100.

closed 1 January – ***Victorian Restaurant :*** **Meals** - English - (booking essential) 10.90 (lunch) and a la carte 25.00/45.00 – ***Secret Garden :*** **Meals** *(closed Monday)* (dinner only) 16.50 and a la carte – **43 rm** 98.00/125.00, 2 suites.

• Unique property decorated with Victorian furnishings and memorabilia. Country house ambience. Reconstructed Victorian street. Individual bedrooms with antiques. 19C artefacts in Victorian Restaurant. Secret Garden is verdant conservatory brasserie.

Asquith House without rest., 19 Portland Rd, Edgbaston, B16 9HN, (0121) 454 5282, *tina@totelapartment.co.uk, Fax (0121) 456 4668* – JX c

1 rm, 9 suites 60.00/95.00.

• 19C house converted into comfortable, spacious fully-serviced apartments, individually styled with modern facilities. Friendly service. Continental breakfast served in room.

City Inn, 1 Brunswick Sq, Brindley Pl, B1 2HW, (0121) 643 1003, *birmingham.reser vations@cityinn.com, Fax (0121) 643 1005*, – rm, – 80. KZ b

closed 25-26 December – ***City Café :*** **Meals** 12.50/16.50 and a la carte 19.95/30.50 **s.** – 11.50 – **238 rm** 129.00.

• Vast hotel ; the spacious atrium with its bright rugs and blond wood sets the tone for equally stylish rooms. Corporate friendly with many meeting rooms. Eat in restaurant, terrace or bar.

Novotel, 70 Broad St, B1 2HT, (0121) 643 2000, *hlo77@accor-hotels.com, Fax (0121) 643 9796*, – rm, rest, – 300. KZ e

Meals 16.00 and a la carte 12.40/28.60 **s.** – 11.00 – **148 rm** 115.00/125.00.

• Well located for the increasingly popular Brindleyplace development. Underground parking. Modern, well-kept, branded bedrooms suitable for families. Modern, open-plan restaurant.

Jessica's, 19 Portland Rd, B16 1HN, (0121) 455 0999, *Fax (0121) 455 8222* – EX c

closed 2 weeks early August, 1 week January, 25 December, Sunday and lunch Saturday and Monday – **Meals** 19.50/29.50.

• Restaurant with conservatory facing garden and fountain. Contemporary décor and furniture. Good value menu offering accomplished modern British cooking.

Bank, 4 Brindleyplace, B1 2JB, (0121) 633 4466, *birmes@bankrestaurants.com, Fax (0121) 633 4465,* – . KZ u
closed Sunday and 1 and 4 January – **Meals** 14.00 (lunch) and a la carte 20.55/33.40.
◆ Capacious, modern and busy bar-restaurant where chefs can be watched through a glass wall preparing the tasty modern dishes. Pleasant terrace area.

La Toque D'Or, 27 Warstone Lane, Hockley, B18 6JQ, (0121) 233 3655, *didier@latoquedor.co.uk, Fax (01562) 754957* – KY r
closed Easter, 2 weeks August, Christmas-New Year, Sunday, Monday, Tuesday after Bank Holidays and Saturday lunch – **Meals** - French - (booking essential) 18.50/24.50 **s.**
◆ A different type of gem in the Jewellery Quarter. Personally run former rolling mill : bare brick and stained glass. Well-judged seasonal menu bears classic French hallmarks.

Metro Bar and Grill, 73 Cornwall St, B3 2DF, (0121) 200 1911, *Fax (0121) 200 1611* – . LY n
closed 25-26 December, Sunday and Bank Holidays – **Meals** (booking essential) a la carte 18.85/29.85.
◆ Gleaming chrome and mirrors in a bright, contemporary basement restaurant. Modern cooking with rotisserie specialities. Spacious, ever-lively bar serves lighter meals.

Zinc Bar and Grill, Regency Wharf, Gas Street Basin, Broad St, B1 2DS, (0121) 200 0620, *Fax (0121) 200 0630,* – . KZ s
Meals 15.00 (lunch) and a la carte 16.50/27.50.
◆ Purpose-built restaurant in lively pub and club area of city. Spiral staircase leads to dining area, including terrace overlooking canal. Modern, classically toned, dishes.

Henry's, 27 St Paul's Sq, B3 1RB, (0121) 200 1136, *enquiries@henrysrestaurant.co.uk, Fax (0121) 200 1190* – . LY a
closed 25-26 December and 1 January – **Meals** - Chinese (Canton) - 16.50/38.00 and a la carte 8.00/40.50.
◆ An extensive range of Cantonese dishes offered in this well-established and personally run restaurant. Private dining rooms available for 40. Opposite the 18C square.

at Birmingham Airport *Southeast : 9 m. by A 45* HX – *Birmingham :*

Holiday Inn Birmingham Airport, Coventry Rd, B26 3QW, on A 45 (0870) 4009007, *reservations-birminghamairport@ichotelsgroup.com, Fax (0121) 782 2476* – , rm, – 130.
Meals *(closed Saturday, Sunday and Bank Holidays)* 15.00 and a la carte 15.35/27.35 – 14.95 – **141 rm** 149.00.
◆ Modern purpose-built hotel with bright, contemporary bedrooms. 30 % of rooms are Superior and have extra workspace, improved lighting and bathrobes as standard. Bright, popular restaurant.

Novotel, Passenger Terminal, B26 3QL, (0121) 782 7000, *H1158@accor-hotels.com, Fax (0121) 782 0445* – , rm, – 35.
Meals (bar lunch Saturday, Sunday and Bank Holidays) 12.95/20.50 and a la carte 13.60/29.25 – 12.50 – **195 rm** 115.00.
◆ Opposite main terminal building : modern hotel benefits from sound proofed doors and double glazing. Mini bars and power showers provided in spacious rooms with sofa beds. Open-plan garden brasserie.

at National Exhibition Centre *Southeast : 9 ½ m. on A 45* HX – *Birmingham :*

Hilton Birmingham Metropole, Bickenhill, B40 1PP, (0121) 780 4242, *Fax (0121) 780 3923,* , – , rm, rest, – 2000.
closed 24-29 December – **Meals** (carvery) 18.00/29.95 **s.** – ***Primavera :*** **Meals** - Italian - (booking essential) (dinner only) a la carte 25.20/39.20 **s.** – ***Millers :*** **Meals** - American grill - (dinner only) a la carte 17.15/27.80 **s.** – 13.50 – **787 rm** 180.00/225.00, 15 suites.
◆ Imposing, modern conference oriented hotel beside lake. NEC within walking distance. Spacious and well-equipped bedrooms, some with the benefit of a balcony. Conservatory restaurant. Bright, Mediterranean influenced Primavera.

Crowne Plaza, Pendigo Way, B40 1PS, (0870) 400 9160, *Fax (0121) 781 4321,* , – , rm, – 180.
Brian Turners : **Meals** (bar lunch Saturday) 24.50/37.95 – 14.50 – **242 rm** 225.00.
◆ Modern hotel adjacent to NEC. Small terrace area overlooks lake. Extensive conference facilities. State-of-the-art bedrooms with a host of extras. Basement dining room : food with a Yorkshire twist.

at West Bromwich *Northwest : 6 m. on A 41* EV – *Birmingham :*

Howard Johnson without rest., 144 High St, B70 6JJ, (0121) 525 8333, *howardjohnson@westbromwich.co.uk, Fax (0121) 525 8444,* , – – 250.
closed 24-26 December – **133 rm** 67.00/73.00.
◆ Good value lodge, an ideal stopping off point for the business traveller : gymnasium, conference facilities, and modern, well-equipped rooms, some with panoramic views.

Chagford *Devon* 503 *I 31 – pop. 1417.*
London 218 – Bath 102 – Birmingham 186.

Gidleigh Park, TQ13 8HH, Northwest : 2 m. by Gidleigh Rd (01647) 432367, *gidleighpark@gidleigh.co.uk, Fax (01647) 432574,* Teign Valley, woodland and Meldon Hill, – rest, TV P. MO AE VISA
Meals (booking essential) 35.00/77.50 – **12 rm** (dinner included) 275.00/550.00, 3 suites.
• Spectacular hotel of sensual delights. Outstanding rooms decorated in a flourish of style. Oak panelled lounge with watercolours. Water garden, herb beds and croquet lawn. Culinary specialities abound, full of exquisitely prepared local produce.
Spec. Wild salmon with courgette tagliatelle, sage and onion purée. Local beef fillet, roast shallots and red wine sauce. Poached cherries with cherry and Kirsch ice cream.

Cheltenham *Glos.* 503 504 *N 28 – pop. 91301.*
77 Promenade (01242) 522878.
London 99 – Birmingham 48 – Bristol 40 – Oxford 43.

Le Champignon Sauvage (Everitt-Matthias), 24-26 Suffolk Rd, GL50 2AQ, (01242) 573449, *Fax (01242) 254365* – MO AE VISA JCB
closed 3 weeks June, 10 days Christmas-New Year, Sunday and Monday – **Meals** 22.00/44.00.
• Cheerful restaurant with artwork on yellow walls ; intimate feel with nine well-spaced tables. Masterful cooking : ingredients combined with inventiveness to seduce the palette.
Spec. Pan-fried foie gras with walnuts and quince, Maury syrup. Roast local partridge with caramelised chicory. Bitter chocolate cheesecake, coffee ripple ice cream.

Ludlow *Shrops.* 503 *L 26 – pop. 9040.*
Castle St (01584) 875053.
London 162 – Birmingham 39 – Hereford 24 – Shrewsbury 29.

Hibiscus (Bosi), 17 Corve St, SY8 1DA, (01584) 872325, *Fax (01584) 874024* – P. MO VISA JCB
closed 22 December-15 January, last 2 weeks July, Sunday, Monday and lunch Tuesday – **Meals** (booking essential) 25.00/35.00.
• Two dining rooms, one with 17C oak panelling and the other with exposed stone walls. Precise cooking with some original and innovative touches ; attentive formal service.
Spec. Foie gras ice cream with emulsion of brioche and caramel. Carpaccio of scallops with leek and liquorice vinaigrette. Hazelnut millefeuille with butternut squash ice cream.

EDINBURGH *Edinburgh* 501 *K 16 Scotland G. – pop. 418914.*
See : *City★★★ Edinburgh International Festival★★★ (August) – Royal Museum of Scotland★★★ EZ* **M2** *National Gallery of Scotland★★ DY – The Castle★★ AC DYZ : Site★★★ Palace Block (Honours of Scotland★★★) St Margaret's Chapel (★★★) Great Hall (Hammerbeam Roof★★) – St Margaret's Chapel (★★★) Great Hall (Hammerbeam Roof★★) ★★ from Argyle and Mill's Mount DZ Abbey and Palace of Holyroodhouse★★ AC – (Plasterwork Ceilings★★★, ★★ from Arthur's Seat) BV Royal Mile★★ : St Giles' Cathedral★★ (Crown Spire★★★) EYZ – Gladstone's Land ★ AC 5EYZ* **A** *Canongate Talbooth★ EY* **B** *– New Town★★ (Charlotte Square★★★ CY* **14** *The Georgian House★ CY* **D** *– Scottish National Portrait Gallery★ EY* **M6** *Dundas House★ EY* **E***) – Scottish National Gallery of Modern Art★ Victoria Street★ EZ* **84** *Scott Monument★ (★) AC EY* **F** *– Craigmillar Castle★ AC, SE : 3 m. by A 7 BX Calton Hill (★★★ AC from Nelson's Monument) EY.*
Envir. : *Edinburgh Zoo★★ AC – Hill End Ski Centre (★★) AC, S : 5 ½ m. by A 702 – The Royal Observatory (West Tower ★) AC – Ingleston, Scottish Agricultural Museum★, W : 6 ½ m. by A 8.*
Exc. : *Rosslyn Chapel★★ AC (Apprentice Pillar★★★), S : 7 ½ m. by A 701 and B 7006 – Forth Bridges★★, NW : 9 ½ m. by A 90 – Hopetoun House★★ AC, NW : 11 ½ m. by A 90 and A 904 – Dalmeny★ Dalmeny House★ AC, St Cuthbert's Church★ (Norman South Doorway★★), NW : 7 m. by A 90 – Crichton Castle (Italianate courtyard range★) AC, SE : 10 m. by A 7 and B 6372.*
18, 18 Braid Hills, Braid Hills Rd (0131) 447 6666 – 18 Carrick Knowe, Glendevon Park (0131) 337 1096 – 18 Duddingston, Duddingston Road West (0131) 661 7688 – 18 Silverknowes, Parkway (0131) 336 3843 – 18 Liberton, 297 Gilmerton Rd (0131) 664 3009 – 18, 18 Marriott Dalmahoy H. & C.C., Kirknewton (0131) 335 8010.
Edinburgh Airport : (0131) 333 1000, W : 6 m. by A 8 – **Terminal :** *Waverley Bridge.*
Edinburgh & Scotland Information Centre, 3 Princes St (0131) 473 3800, info@visitscotland.co.uk – Edinburgh Airport, Tourist Information Desk (0131) 344 3213.
Glasgow 46 – Newcastle upon Tyne 105.

EDINBURGH

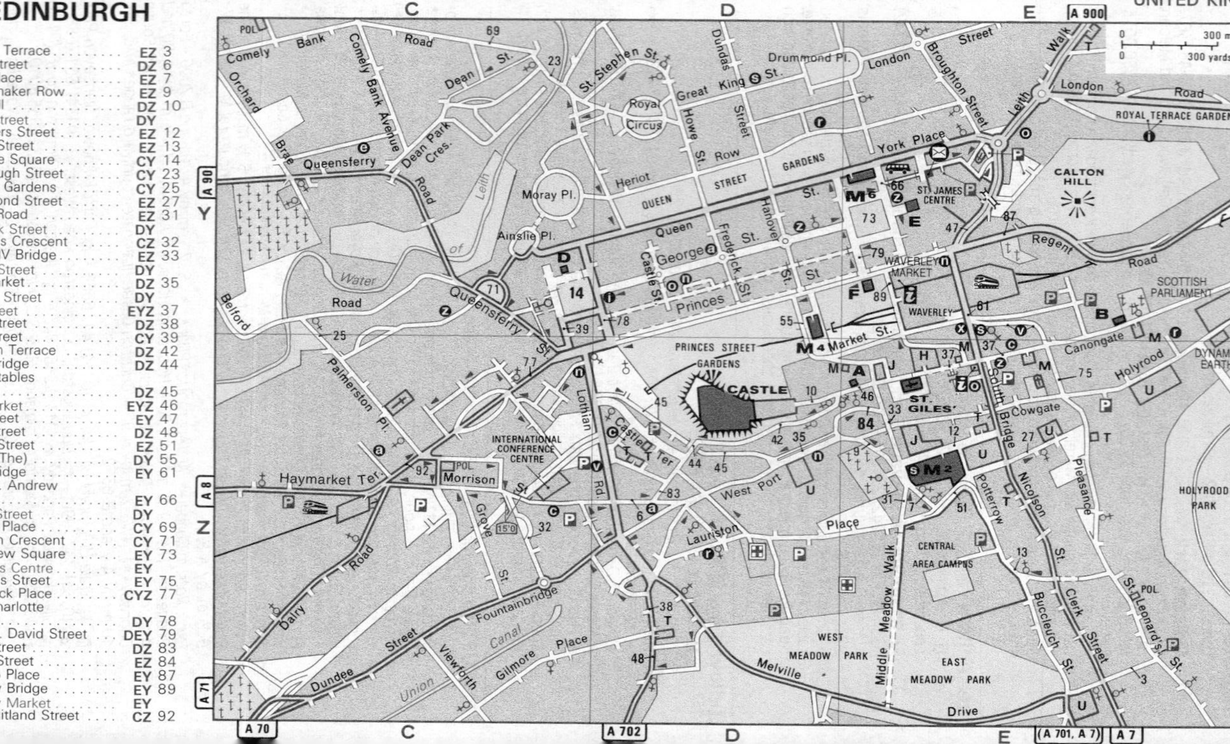

CASTLE
CALTON HILL
HOLYROOD PARK
SCOTTISH PARLIAMENT
DYNAMIC EARTH
ST. GILES'
PRINCES STREET GARDENS
INTERNATIONAL CONFERENCE CENTRE
WAVERLEY MARKET
ST. JAMES CENTRE
CENTRAL AREA CAMPUS
WEST MEADOW PARK
EAST MEADOW PARK
ROYAL TERRACE GARDENS
QUEEN STREET GARDENS
Princes St.
George St.
Queen St.
Canongate
Holyrood
Pleasance
Nicolson St.
Clerk Street
South Bridge
Cowgate
Lothian Rd.
Haymarket Ter.
Queensferry St.
Melville Drive
Lauriston Place
West Port
Fountainbridge
Dalry Road
Union Canal
Water of Leith
300 m
300 yards

Balmoral, 1 Princes St, EH2 2EQ, ☎ (0131) 556 2414, *reservations@thebalmoralhotel.com, Fax (0131) 557 8740,* – 350. VISA. EY n
Meals (see ***Number One*** and ***Hadrian's*** below) – 17.00 – **167 rm** 190.00/330.00, 21 suites.
◆ Richly furnished rooms in grand baronial style complemented by contemporary furnishings in the Palm Court exemplify this de luxe Edwardian railway hotel and city landmark.

Caledonian Hilton, Princes St, EH1 2AB, ☎ (0131) 222 8888, *ednchhirm@hilton.com, Fax (0131) 222 8889,* – rm, rest, – 250. VISA JCB. CY n
The Pompadour : Meals *(closed Saturday lunch, Sunday and Monday)* 19.50/21.50 and dinner a la carte 35.85/47.80 – ***Chisholms :*** Meals (dinner only and lunch Saturday-Monday) 17.50 and a la carte 21.80/32.40 – 15.50 – **238 rm** 225.00/280.00, 13 suites.
◆ Overlooked by the castle, with handsomely appointed rooms and wood panelled halls behind imposing 19C facade. Unfussy elegance in The Pompadour. Fine period stonework defines Chisholms brasserie.

Sheraton Grand, 1 Festival Sq, EH3 9SR, ☎ (0131) 229 9131, *grandedinburgh.sheraton@sheraton.com, Fax (0131) 229 6254,* – rm, – 500. VISA. CDZ v
Terrace : Meals (buffet only) 19.95/20.95 (see also ***Grill Room*** below) – 16.50 – **243 rm** 216.00/256.00, 17 suites.
◆ A modern, centrally located and smartly run hotel. A popular choice for the working traveller, as it boasts Europe's most advanced urban spa. Comfy, well-kept rooms. Glass expanse of Terrace restaurant overlooks Festival Square.

The George Intercontinental, 19-21 George St, EH2 2PB, ☎ (0131) 225 1251, *edinburgh@interconti.com, Fax (0131) 226 5644* – rm, – 200. VISA JCB. DY z
Le Chambertin *(☎ (0131) 240 7178)* **:** Meals a la carte 25.25/31.50 **s.** – ***Carvers*** *(☎ (0131) 459 2305)* **:** Meals 9.95/19.95 and a la carte 17.00/31.50 **s.** – 16.00 – **192 rm** 185.00/240.00, 3 suites.
◆ An established classic that makes the most of Robert Adam's listed 18C design. Welcoming marble-floored lobby, convivial Clans bar and well-proportioned bedrooms. Le Chambertin is light, spacious and stylish. Carvers is set in magnificent glass-domed room.

The Howard, 34 Great King St, EH3 6QH, ☎ (0131) 557 3500, *reserve@thehoward.com, Fax (0131) 557 6515* – – 30. VISA. DY s
The Atholl : Meals (dinner only) 32.00 – **13 rm** 145.00/295.00, 5 suites.
◆ Crystal chandeliers, antiques, richly furnished rooms and the relaxing opulence of the drawing room set off a fine Georgian interior. An inviting "boutique" hotel.

The Scotsman, 20 North Bridge, EH1 1YT, ☎ (0131) 556 5565, *reservations@thescotsmanhotel.co.uk, Fax (0131) 652 3652,* – rm, rest, – 80. EY x
accommodation closed 26 December – ***Vermilion :*** Meals (dinner only) a la carte approx 35.00 – ***North Bridge Brasserie :*** Meals 15.00 (lunch) and a la carte 18.00/30.00 **s.** – 16.50 – **56 rm** 180.00, 12 suites.
◆ Imposing former offices of "The Scotsman" newspaper, adjacent to Royal Mile. Marble reception hall and historic "Scotsman" prints. Well-equipped modern bedrooms. Restaurant with original marble pillars ; ornate staircase leads to balcony for intimate dinners.

The Glasshouse without rest., 2 Greenside Pl, EH1 3AA, ☎ (0131) 525 8200, *resglasshouse@theetongroup.com, Fax (0131) 525 8205,* – – 35. VISA JCB. EY o
16.50 – **65 rm** 195.00.
◆ Centrally located guesthouse with breakfast room at the rear. Individual contemporary styled bedroms with view of spacious roof garden or with balcony and city view.

Channings, 15 South Learmonth Gdns, EH4 1EZ, ☎ (0131) 315 2226, *reserve@channings.co.uk, Fax (0131) 332 9631* – – 35. VISA. CY e
Ochre Vita : Meals a la carte approx 21.85 (see also ***Channings*** below) – **43 rm** 140.00/230.00, 3 suites.
◆ Sensitively refurbished rooms and fire-lit lounges blend an easy country house elegance with original Edwardian character. Individually appointed bedrooms.

The Bonham, 35 Drumsheugh Gdns, EH3 7RN, ☎ (0131) 226 6050, *reserve@thebonham.com, Fax (0131) 226 6080* – – 50. VISA. CY z
Meals 15.00 (lunch) and dinner a la carte 28.50/40.40 – 8.50 – **46 rm** 145.00/245.00, 2 suites.
◆ A striking synthesis of Victorian architecture and the eclectic fittings and bold, rich colours of a contemporary décor. Numerous pictures by "up-and-coming" local artists. Chic dining room with massive mirrors and "catwalk" in spotlights.

The Roxburghe, 38 Charlotte Sq, EH2 4HG, (0131) 240 5500, *roxburghe@esmm.co.uk, Fax (0131) 240 5555,* , , – , , rest, – 400. DY i

***The Melrose* : Meals** a la carte 16.00/31.00 – 12.50 – **197 rm** 170.00/190.00, 1 suite.

• Attentive service, understated period-inspired charm and individuality in the British style. Part modern, part Georgian but roomy throughout ; fine 19C atrium. Restaurant subtly reflects the grandeur of Adam's exterior.

The Carlton, 19 North Bridge, EH1 1SD, (0131) 472 3000, *carlton@paramount-hotels.co.uk, Fax (0131) 556 2691,* , , , squash – , rm, rest, – 250. EY s

***Bridge* : Meals** a la carte 22.00/29.00 **s.** – **184 rm** 250.00, 5 suites.

• In a busy spot on North Bridge, a former department store with a period façade and contemporary interior. Large rooms with facilities for tourists and business travellers.

Crowne Plaza, 80 High St, EH1 1TH, (0131) 557 9797, *rescpedinburgh@allianceuk.com, Fax (0131) 557 9789,* , , – , rm, – 250. EY z

closed 24-26 December – **Meals** 18.95 and dinner a la carte 20.85/38.65 **s.** – 14.50 – **238 rm** 85.00/230.00, 10 suites.

• Recreates the look of a baronial Great House. Rooms are pleasantly spacious, some looking down on the Royal Mile. Compact leisure centre with jet stream swimming pool. Basement restaurant flaunts eye-catching suspended lighting.

Prestonfield , Priestfield Rd, EH16 5UT, (0131) 668 3346, *info@prestonfield.com, Fax (0131) 668 3976,* , 18, , – , rm, – 500. by A 7 EZ

Meals a la carte 22/37.50 – 8.95 – **29 rm** 195.00.

• Superbly preserved interior, tapestries and paintings in the main part of this elegant country house, built in 1687 with modern additions. Set in parkland below Arthur's Seat. Period-furnished 18C dining room with fine views of the grounds.

Point, 34 Bread St, EH3 9AF, (0131) 221 5555, *info@point-hotel.co.uk, Fax (0131) 221 9929* – , rm, – 100. DZ a

Meals *(closed lunch Saturday and Sunday)* 11.90/14.90 – 10.00 – **133 rm** 140.00/160.00, 4 suites.

• A Victorian office block converted in daring minimalist style. Boldly coloured lobby and light, clean-lined rooms. Castle views over the rooftops from the upper floors. Strikingly lit avant-garde restaurant.

Le Meridien Edinburgh, 18 Royal Terr, EH7 5AQ, (0131) 557 3222, *reservations.royalterrace@lemeridien.com, Fax (0131) 557 5334,* , , , – , rest, – 90. . EY i

***Conservatory* : Meals** 19.95 (dinner) and a la carte – 10.50 – **104 rm** 115.00/225.00, 4 suites.

• Attractively furnished accommodation in a peaceful terrace of Georgian town houses with an agreeably clubby cocktail bar. The rear garden is especially pleasant in summer. Cosy conservatory restaurant with verdant views..

Edinburgh Marriott, 111 Glasgow Rd, EH12 8NF, West : 4 ½ m. on A 8 (0870) 400 7293, *edinburgh@marriotthotels.co.uk, Fax (0870) 400 7393,* , , – , rm, rest, – 300. .

***Mediterrano* : Meals** 14.95/19.50 (lunch) and a la carte 17.50/26.00 – 13.95 – **241 rm** 150.00, 4 suites.

• Excellent road connections for the airport and Glasgow and well-equipped rooms make this large, group-operated hotel a practical choice for business travel. Modern restaurant with Mediterranean twist.

Hilton Edinburgh Grosvenor, Grosvenor St, EH12 5EF, (0131) 226 6001, *reservations@edinburgh.stakis.co.uk, Fax (0131) 220 2387* – , rm, – 500. . CZ a

Meals (bar lunch)/dinner 18.50 and a la carte 16.95/29.40 **s.** – 12.50 – **187 rm** 190.00, 2 suites.

• Company hotel in an attractive 19C row, with some rooms in the annex across the road. Relax in the welcoming lounge and bar after a day in the main shopping streets nearby. Scottish themed restaurant.

Holyrood Aparthotel without rest., 1 Nether Bakehouse (via Gentles entry), EH8 8PE, (0131) 524 3200, *mail@holyroodaparthotel.com, Fax (0131) 524 3210* – , . . EY r

41 suites 145.00/180.00.

• These two-bedroomed apartments are neat and up-to-date with well-stocked kitchens. Located in a booming area of the city, not far from the Palace of Holyrood.

Edinburgh City, 79 Lauriston Pl, EH3 9HZ, ℰ (0131) 622 7979, *reservations@bestwesternedinburghcity.co.uk, Fax (0131) 622 7900* – *closed 25-26 December* – **Meals** (bar lunch)/dinner a la carte 19.00/24.00 – **51 rm** 115.00/165.00, 1 suite. DZ r
◆ A tidily run hotel within easy walking distance of the centre. The good-sized rooms of this listed Victorian building have been converted in a bright, contemporary style.

Frederick House without rest., 42 Frederick St, EH2 1EX, ℰ (0131) 226 1999, *frederickhouse@ednet.co.uk, Fax (0131) 624 7064* – **44 rm** 65.00/90.00, 1 suite. DY a
◆ Just off George St., this warmly furnished and carefully maintained hotel retains a few of its 19C features and benefits from conscientious service. Distinctive, homely feel.

Ibis without rest., 6 Hunter Sq, EH1 1QW, ℰ (0131) 240 7000, *h2039@accor.hotels.com, Fax (0131) 240 7007* – EZ o
99 rm 69.95.
◆ Interior design reflects the group's ethos - compact and functional, yet comfortable. A super position just off the High Street will appeal to tourists throughout the year.

17 Abercromby Place without rest., 17 Abercromby Pl, EH3 6LB, ℰ (0131) 557 8036, *eirlys.lloyd@virgin.net, Fax (0131) 558 3453* – DY r
3 rm 70.00/100.00.
◆ Once home to architect William Playfair. Bedrooms - some overlooking wooded gardens - are furnished with character and attention to detail. Cosy library to rear.

Number One (at Balmoral H.), 1 Princes St, EH2 2EQ, ℰ (0131) 622 8831, *Fax (0131) 557 8740* – EY n
closed Saturday and Sunday lunch – **Meals** 18.50/41.00 and a la carte 40.50/50.25 ♀.
◆ Edinburgh's nonpareil for polished fine dining and immaculate service ; spacious basement setting. Original dishes with a well-balanced flair showcase Scottish produce.
Spec. Isle of Skye crab with onion purée and caviar. Trio of veal and beef with foie gras. Roast baby pineapple with sorbet and chocolate florentine.

Grill Room (at Sheraton Grand H.), 1 Festival Sq, EH3 9SR, ℰ (0131) 221 6422, *Fax (0131) 229 6254* – CDZ v
closed Saturday lunch, Sunday and Monday – **Meals** 24.00/45.00 and a la carte 35.50/45.50 ♀.
◆ Ornate ceilings, wood panels and modern glass make an ideal setting for imaginative, well presented cooking. Local ingredients with a few European and Pacific Rim elements.

Oloroso, 33 Castle St, EH2 3DN, ℰ (0131) 226 7614, *info@oloroso.co.uk, Fax (0131) 226 7608* – DY o
closed 1 January – **Meals** a la carte 30.00/62.00 ♀.
◆ Modish third floor restaurant in heart of city. Busy, atmospheric bar. Lovely terrace with good views to the west. Stylish, modern cooking with strong Asian influence.

Santini, 8 Conference Sq, EH3 8AN, ℰ (0131) 221 7788, *Fax (0131) 221 7789* – rest. CDZ v
closed 1-11 January, Saturday lunch and Sunday – **Meals** - Italian - 22.50 (lunch) and a la carte 24.00/40.00 **s.**
◆ The personal touch is predominant in this stylish restaurant appealingly situated under a superb spa. Charming service heightens the enjoyment of tasty, modern Italian food.

Forth Floor (at Harvey Nichols), 30-34 St Andrew Sq, EH2 2AD, ℰ (0131) 524 8350, *Fax (0131) 524 8351,* ≤ Castle and city skyline, – EY z
closed 1 January, Christmas and Sunday and Monday dinner except August – **Meals** a la carte 17.50/34.50 ♀.
◆ Stylish restaurant with delightful outside terrace affording views over the city. Half the room in informal brasserie-style and the other more formal. Modern, Scottish menus.

Atrium, 10 Cambridge St, EH1 2ED, ℰ (0131) 228 8882, *Fax (0131) 228 8808* – DZ c
closed 25-26 December, 1 January, Sunday and Saturday lunch except during Edinburgh Festival – **Meals** 18.00/25.00 and a la carte 28.00/37.50 ♀.
◆ Located inside the Traverse Theatre, an adventurous repertoire enjoyed on tables made of wooden railway sleepers. Twisted copper lamps subtly light the ultra-modern interior.

Off The Wall, 105 High St, EH1 1SG, ℰ (0131) 558 1497, *otwedinburgh@aol.com* – EY c
closed 25-26 December, 1-2 January and Sunday – **Meals** 14.95/18.95 (lunch) and dinner a la carte 28.85/38.90 ♀.
◆ Located on the Royal Mile, though hidden on first floor away from bustling crowds. Vividly coloured dining room. Modern menus underpinned by a seasonal Scottish base.

Duck's at Le Marche Noir, 2-4 Eyre Pl, EH3 5EP, ℰ (0131) 558 1608, *bookings@ducks.co.uk, Fax (0131) 556 0798* – by A 1 EY
closed 25-26 December, and lunch Saturday-Monday – **Meals** a la carte 21.65/35.60 ♀.
◆ Confident, inventive cuisine with a modern, discreetly French character, served with friendly efficiency in bistro-style surroundings - intimate and very personally run.

The Marque, 19-21 Causewayside, EH9 1QF, ✆ (0131) 466 6660, *Fax (0131) 466 6661* – ⇔. MC AE VISA by A 701 EZ
closed Christmas, first week January, Monday and Tuesday – **Meals** 11.50/17.00 and a la carte 22.00/31.00 ♀.
♦ Arresting yellow decor and modern art won't distract attention from an original menu and smart service. A good lunch or pre-theatre choice ; expect subtle Provençal touches.

Channings (at Channings H.), 12-16 South Learmonth Gdns, EH4 1EZ, ✆ (0131) 315 2225, *Fax (0131) 332 9631*, – ⇔. MC AE ⓓ VISA CY e
closed Sunday-Monday – **Meals** 16.00/19.00 (lunch) and dinner a la carte 22.00/46.00 ♀.
♦ Choose between rich traditional warmth or a chic, Scandinavian-inspired conservatory and enjoy a well thought-out range of characterful dishes, some with Italian overtones.

Martins, 70 Rose St, North Lane, EH2 3DX, ✆ (0131) 225 3106, *martinirons@fsbdial.co.uk* – ⇔. MC AE ⓓ VISA JCB DY n
closed 10 days June, 10 days October, 24 December-late January, Sunday and Monday except during Edinburgh Festival and Saturday lunch – **Meals** (booking essential) 19.00/25.00 and a la carte 29.50/37.00 ♀.
♦ A concise menu of tasty, well-prepared options from local, mostly organic produce behind an unprepossessing façade. An impressive cheeseboard.

Hadrian's (at Balmoral H.), 2 North Bridge, EH1 1TR, ✆ (0131) 557 5000, *Fax (0131) 557 3747* – ▤. MC AE ⓓ VISA JCB EY n
Meals 11.00 and a la carte 13.75/24.75 ♀.
♦ Drawing on light, clean-lined styling, reminiscent of Art Deco, and a "British new wave" approach ; an extensive range of contemporary brasserie classics and smart service.

Rogue, 67 Morrison St, EH3 8HH, ✆ (0131) 228 2700, *info@rogues-uk.com, Fax (0131) 228 3299* – MC AE ⓓ VISA CZ c
closed 25-26 December, 1-2 January and Sunday – **Meals** 13.50 (lunch) and a la carte 20.75/36.00.
♦ Stylish, bright venue with beautiful wooden stripped bar. Contemporary feel : chrome and leather chairs and covered tables. Modern international menu includes grill section.

Marque Central, 30b Grindley St, EH3 9AX, ✆ (0131) 229 9859, *Fax (0131) 221 9515* – MC AE VISA DZ i
closed first week September, Sunday and Monday – **Meals** 12.50/15.00 and a la carte 18.65/28.40 ♀.
♦ Generous, reasonably priced dishes which draw on contemporary Scottish and Italian traditions with equal facility. A popular modern restaurant near the Old Town.

Yumi, 2 West Coates, EH12 5JQ, ✆ (0131) 337 2173, *Fax (0131) 337 2818* – ⇔ P. MC ⓓ VISA JCB by A 8 CZ
closed 1 week spring, 2 weeks Christmas-New Year and Sunday – **Meals** - Japanese - (dinner only) 25.00/45.00.
♦ Comprehensive Japanese dining experience : authentically prepared cuisine comes into its own, thanks to charming, attentive staff and a number of well-structured set menus.

The Tower, Museum of Scotland (fifth floor), Chambers St, EH1 1JF, ✆ (0131) 225 3003, *mail@tower-restaurant.com, Fax (0131) 220 4392*, – ⇔ ▤. MC AE ⓓ VISA EZ s
closed 25 December – **Meals** a la carte 18.40/42.85 ♀.
♦ Game, grills and seafood feature in a popular, contemporary brasserie style menu. On the fifth floor of the Museum of Scotland - ask for a terrace table and admire the view.

La Garrigue, 31 Jeffrey St, EH1 1DH, ✆ (0131) 557 3032, *jeanmichel@lagarrigue.co.uk, Fax (0131) 5573032* – MC AE VISA JCB EY v
closed 26 December-1 January – **Meals** - French - 19.50/21.50 and a la carte 14.70/15.95.
♦ Very pleasant restaurant near main railway station : beautiful handmade wood tables add warmth to rustic décor. French regional cooking with classical touches.

Iggs, 15 Jeffrey St, EH1 1DR, ✆ (0131) 557 8184, *iggisbarioja@aol.com, Fax (0131) 652 3774* – MC AE ⓓ VISA JCB EY v
closed 1-2 January and Sunday – **Meals** 14.50 (lunch) and a la carte 23.50/31.25.
♦ Just off the Royal Mile, a comfortable, friendly restaurant overseen by the owner. Dishes are tasty, Spanish-influenced and of generous proportions.

Leith *Edinburgh.*

Malmaison, 1 Tower Pl, EH6 7DB, ✆ (0131) 468 5000, *edinburgh@malmaison.com, Fax (0131) 468 5002*, – ▤ TV P – 55. MC AE ⓓ VISA. by A 900 EY
Meals - Brasserie - 12.95/13.95 and a la carte 19.85/29.45 ♀ – ☕ 11.95 – **96 rm** 125.00/160.00, 5 suites.
♦ Imposing quayside sailors' mission converted in strikingly elegant modern style. Thoughtfully-appointed, good-sized rooms combine more traditional comfort with CD systems. Sophisticated brasserie with finely wrought iron.

Express by Holiday Inn without rest., Britannia Way, Ocean Drive, EH6 6JJ, ✆ (0131) 555 4422, *info@hiex-edinburgh.com, Fax (0131) 555 4646* – 30. by A 900 EY
145 rm 99.00.
◆ Modern, purpose-built hotel offering trim, bright, reasonably-priced accommodation. Convenient for Leith centre restaurants and a short walk from the Ocean Terminal.

Martin Wishart, 54 The Shore, Leith, EH6 6RA, ✆ (0131) 553 3557, *info@martin-wishart.co.uk, Fax (0131) 467 7091* – by A 900 EY
closed 25-26 December, 1 January, Sunday, Monday and Saturday lunch – **Meals** (booking essential) 18.50 (lunch) and a la carte 36.50/47.50.
◆ Dockside conversion, compact and simply decorated, with a growing reputation. Modern French-accented menus characterised by clear, intelligently combined flavours.
Spec. Roast halibut and braised pig's trotter with caramelised endive. Soufflé of lobster and smoked haddock. Tartare of scallop and foie gras, caviar sauce.

Zinc Bar and Grill, Ocean Terminal, Ocean Drive, EH6, ✆ (0131) 553 8070, *Fax (0131) 553 8080,* – by A 900 EY
Meals 15.00 (lunch) and a la carte 16.50/29.50.
◆ Fashionable contemporary styling within modern shopping complex. Enjoy a wide range of classic and modern dishes, dine on the terrace for a view of the Royal Yacht Britannia.

The Vintners Rooms, The Vaults, 87 Giles St, EH6 6BZ, ✆ (0131) 554 6767, *enquiries@thevintnersrooms.com, Fax (0131) 555 5653* – by A 900 EY
closed 1-15 January and Sunday – **Meals** 15.00 (lunch) and dinner a la carte 16.00/28.50.
◆ Atmospheric 18C bonded spirits warehouse with high ceilings, stone floor, rug-covered walls and candlelit side-room with ornate plasterwork. Modern British cooking.

at Bonnyrigg *(Midlothian) Southeast : 8 m. by A 70 EZ and A 7 on A 6094 – ✉ Edinburgh :*

Dalhousie Castle, EH19 3JB, Southeast : 1 ¼ m. on B 704 ✆ (01875) 820153, *enquiries@dalhousiecastle.co.uk, Fax (01875) 821936,* – 120.
Dungeon : **Meals** (booking essential to non-residents) (dinner only) 32.00 – ***The Orangery :*** **Meals** a la carte 16.00/23.65 **s.** – **33 rm** 130.00/185.00.
◆ 13C castle in woodland on the South Esk. Period-style furnishing in the spacious rooms, eclipsed by the library's 19C panelling and rococo ceiling. Meals served in the ancient barrel-vaulted stone chambers. Orangery restaurant overlooks the river and parkland.

at Kirknewton *Southwest : 7 m. on A 71 CZ – ✉ Edinburgh*

Marriott Dalmahoy H. & Country Club, EH27 8EB, ✆ (0131) 333 1845, *reservations.dalmahoy@marriotthotels.co.uk, Fax (0131) 333 1433,* – rest, – 220.
Pentland : **Meals** (buffet Saturday-Sunday) 22.50/35.00 – ***The Long Weekend :*** **Meals** (grill rest.) a la carte 14.50/24.50 – 13.95 – **212 rm** 150.00, 3 suites.
◆ Extended Georgian mansion in 1000 acres with 2 Championship golf courses. Comprehensive leisure club, smart rooms and a clubby cocktail lounge. Tranquil atmosphere with elegant comfort in Pentland restaurant. Informal modern dining at The Long Weekend.

at Edinburgh International Airport *West : 7 ½ m. by A 8 CZ – ✉ Edinburgh :*

Hilton Edinburgh Airport, 100 Eastfield Rd, EH28 8LL, ✆ (0131) 519 4400, *Fax (0131) 519 4422,* – rm, rest, – 240.
Meals *(closed Saturday lunch)* (carvery lunch)/dinner 19.50 **s.** – 13.50 – **150 rm** 195.00.
◆ Busy, purpose-built hotel offering large, well-equipped rooms designed with working travellers in mind. Shuttle service to the terminal and excellent road links to the city. A large modern restaurant, comfortable and informal.

Write to us...
If you have any comments on the contents of this Guide.
Your praise as well as your criticisms will receive careful consideration and, with your assistance, we will be able to add to our stock of information and, where necessary, amend our judgments.
Thank you in advance!

GLASGOW *Glasgow* 501 502 H 16 *Scotland G. – pop. 662 853.*

See : *City★★★ – Cathedral★★★ (<★) DZ The Burrell Collection★★★ – Hunterian Art Gallery★★ (Whistler Collection★★★ Mackintosh Wing★★★) AC CY* **M4** *– Museum of Transport★★ (Scottish Built Cars★★★, The Clyde Room of Ship Models★★★) – Art Gallery and Museum Kelvingrove★★ CY – Pollok House★ (The Paintings★★) – Tolbooth Steeple★ DZ Hunterian Museum (Coin and Medal Collection★) CY* **M5** *– City Chambers★ DZ* **C** *– Glasgow School of Art★ AC CY* **M3** *– Necropolis (<★ of Cathedral) DYZ – Gallery of Modern Art★ – Glasgow (National) Science Centre★, Pacific Quay.*

Envir. : *Paisley Museum and Art Gallery (Paisley Shawl Section★), W : 4 m. by M 8.*

Exc. : *The Trossachs★★★, N : 31 m. by A 879, A 81 and A 821 – Loch Lomond★★, NW : 19 m. by A 82 – New Lanark★★, SE : 20 m. by M 74 and A 72 BX.*

Littlehill, Auchinairn Rd ☎ (0141) 772 1916 – Rouken Glen, Stewarton Rd, Thornliebank ☎ (0141) 638 7044 – Linn Park, Simshill Rd ☎ (0141) 633 5871 – Lethamhill, Cumbernauld Rd ☎ (0141) 770 6220 – Alexandra Park, Dennistoun ☎ (0141) 556 1294 – King's Park, 150a Croftpark Ave, Croftfoot ☎ (0141) 630 1597 – Knightswood, Lincoln Ave ☎ (0141) 959 6358 Ruchill, Brassey St ☎ (0141) 946 7676.

Access to Oban by helicopter.

Erskine Bridge (toll).

Glasgow Airport : ☎ (0141) 887 1111, W : 8 m. by M 8 – **Terminal** : *Coach service from Glasgow Central and Queen Street main line Railway Stations and from Anderston Cross and Buchanan Bus Stations Prestwick International Airport : ☎ (01292) 479822* **Terminal** : *Buchanan Bus Station.*

11 George Sq ☎ (0141) 204 4400, enquiries@seeglasgow.com – Glasgow Airport, Tourist Information Desk, Paisley ☎ (0141) 848 4440.

Edinburgh 46 – Manchester 221.

Plans on following pages

Hilton Glasgow, 1 William St, G3 8HT, ☎ (0141) 204 5555, *glahitwgm@hilton.com, Fax (0141) 204 5004*, <, rm, – 1000. CZ s

Minsky's : **Meals** 16.00/25.95 and a la carte 20.70/29.85 **s.** (see also ***Camerons*** below) – 15.50 – **315 rm** 190.00, 4 suites.

◆ A city centre tower with impressive views on every side. Comfortable, comprehensively fitted rooms. Louvres and ceiling fans in Raffles bar - relaxing Colonial escapism. Spacious, modern brasserie in the style of a New York deli.

Radisson SAS, 301 Argyle St, G2 8DL, ☎ (0141) 204 3333, *reservations.glasgow@radisson.sas.com, Fax (0141) 204 3344*, rm, – 800. DZ o

Collage : **Meals** a la carte 13.95/29.85 **s.** – ***TaPaell'Ya*** : **Meals** - Tapas - *(closed Saturday lunch and Sunday)* a la carte 6.90/12.90 – 13.50 – **246 rm** 180.00, 1 suite.

◆ Curved glass entrance to city centre hotel with some period features. Large reception area. Basement leisure club. Smart, modern bedrooms in three styles. Collage is a bright modern restaurant. Ta Paell'Ya serves tapas.

Glasgow Moat House, Congress Rd, G3 8QT, ☎ (0141) 306 9988, *cbgla@queensmoat.co.uk, Fax (0141) 221 2022*, <, rm, – 800. CZ r

closed 23-28 December – ***The Mariner*** : **Meals** (dinner only) a la carte 18.50/31.50 – ***No.1 Dockside*** : **Meals** *(closed lunch Saturday and Sunday)* (buffet) 18.00 **s.** – 13.50 – **267 rm** 159.00/179.00, 16 suites.

◆ Modern business hotel between Science Museum and Scottish Exhibition Centre. Comfortable, well-proportioned rooms and a large open-plan lounge on a subtly nautical theme. Spacious, smartly-run Mariner restaurant. Clydeside informality in No 1 Dockside.

One Devonshire Gardens without rest., 1 Devonshire Gdns, G12 OUX, ☎ (0141) 339 2001, *reservations@onedevonshiregardens.com, Fax (0141) 337 1663* – – 40. by A 82 CY

15.00 – **35 rm** 185.00/275.00, 3 suites.

◆ Collection of adjoining 19C houses in terrace, comfortably furnished with attention to detail. Elegantly convivial drawing room, luxurious bedrooms and unobtrusive service.

Glasgow Marriott, 500 Argyle St, Anderston, G3 8RR, ☎ (0870) 4007230, *Fax (0870) 4007330*, <, rm, – 700. CZ a

Mediterrano : **Meals** a la carte 18.85/30.00 **s.** – 13.95 – **300 rm** 119.00.

◆ Neat, compact, city centre accommodation with every necessary convenience for working travellers and an extensive lounge and café-bar. Upper floors have views of the city. Strong Mediterranean feel infuses restaurant..

Thistle Glasgow, 36 Cambridge St, G2 3HN, ✆ (0141) 332 3311, *glasgow@thistle.co.uk, Fax (0141) 332 4050,* – rm, rest, – 1500. DY z

Gengis **: Meals** a la carte 18.70/27.45 – 12.95 – **297 rm** 194.00, 3 suites.

◆ Purpose-built hotel just north of the centre, geared to the corporate market. Smartly-appointed rooms and excellent inter-city road connections. Extensive meeting facilities. Grills meet tandoori in themed restaurant.

Malmaison, 278 West George St, G2 4LL, ✆ (0141) 572 1000, *glasgow@malmaison.com, Fax (0141) 572 1002,* – rm, – 30. CY c

The Brasserie *(✆ (0141) 572 1001)* **: Meals** 12.95/13.95 and a la carte 19.85/29.45 – 11.95 – **64 rm** 125.00, 8 suites.

◆ Visually arresting former Masonic chapel. Comfortable, well-proportioned rooms seem effortlessly stylish with bold patterns and colours and thoughtful extra attentions. Informal bistro in glass-roofed atrium.

Millennium Glasgow, 40 George Sq, G2 1DS, ✆ (0141) 332 6711, *reservations.glasgow@mill-cop.com, Fax (0141) 332 4264* – rm, – 40. DZ v

Brasserie on George Square **: Meals** *(closed Sunday lunch)* a la carte 12.50/35.00 **s.** – 15.25 – **112 rm** 175.00/235.00, 5 suites.

◆ Spacious, contemporary accommodation, intelligently planned and pleasingly unfussy, with a relaxing lounge and veranda. Central location, close to main railway station.

ArtHouse, 129 Bath St, G2 2SJ, ✆ (0141) 221 6789, *info@arthousehotel.com, Fax (0141) 221 6777* – rm, rest, – 70. DY v

Grill **: Meals** 12.00/25.00 and a la carte 18.40/32.25 – 9.25 – **63 rm** 110.00/150.00.

◆ Near Mackintosh's School of Art, an early 20C building decorated with a daring modern palette : striking colour schemes and lighting in the spacious, elegantly fitted rooms. Basement grill restaurant, plus seafood and sushi bar.

Carlton George, 44 West George St, G2 1DH, ✆ (0141) 353 6373, *salesgeorge@carltonhotels.co.uk, Fax (0141) 353 6263* – – 35. *closed 24-27 December and 1-3 January* – ***Windows*** **: Meals** 14.95 (lunch) and dinner a la carte 11.95/30.95 – 12.95 – **64 rm** 140.00. DZ a

◆ Modern hotel, perfectly located in the main shopping district. Very comfortable bedrooms, smartly furnished and meticulously kept throughout, and a 24-hour Business Lounge. Ask for brasserie table with view across city's rooftops.

Milton, 27 Washington St, G3 8AZ, ✆ (0141) 222 2929, *sales@miltonhotels.com, Fax (0141) 270 2301,* – – 200. CZ z

Medici Grill **: Meals** 19.95 – **129 rm** 89.00/139.00, 12 suites.

◆ Centrally located and well designed with corporate travellers in mind. Spacious, comfortable bedrooms and well-equipped suites and apartments for long lets. Leisure centre. Modern, grill restaurant.

Sherbrooke Castle, 11 Sherbrooke Ave, Pollokshields, G41 4PG, ✆ (0141) 427 4227, *mail@sherbrooke.co.uk, Fax (0141) 427 5685,* – , rest, – 250. by M 8 CZ

Morrisons **: Meals** 15.50/25.00 and dinner a la carte 25.00/35.00 – **20 rm** 68.00/88.00, 1 suite.

◆ Late 19C baronial Romanticism given free rein inside and out. The hall is richly furnished and imposing ; rooms in the old castle have a comfortable country house refinement. Panelled Victorian dining room with open fire.

Ewington, Balmoral Terr, 132 Queen's Drive, G42 8QW, ✆ (0141) 423 1152, *ewington.info@countryhotels.net, Fax (0141) 422 2030* – – 80.

Meals 10.95/17.50 – 10.50 – **42 rm** 79.00/119.00, 1 suite. by A 77 DZ

◆ Well-kept, spacious and attractively decorated accommodation in a Victorian town house overlooking Queens Park. A short drive to the Burrell Collection or the city centre. Mackintosh-inspired decor in candlelit restaurant.

Langs, 2 Port Dundas Pl, G2 3LD, ✆ (0141) 333 1500, *reservations@langshotel.co.uk, Fax (0141) 333 5700,* – rm, rest, . DY n

Las Brisas **: Meals** a la carte 19.45/38.75 **s.** – ***Oshi*** **: Meals** - Asian specialities - 11.00 (lunch) and dinner a la carte 14.50/26.50 **s.** – **100 rm** 150.00/185.00.

◆ Opposite the Royal Concert Hall. Themed loft suites and stylish Japanese or Californian inspired rooms, all with CD players and computer game systems. Cool and contemporary. Las Brisas is a soft-toned mezzanine eatery. Gently flowing waterfall in relaxed Oshi.

City Inn, Finnieston Quay, G3 8HN, ✆ (0141) 240 1002, *glasgow.reservations@cityinn.com, Fax (0141) 248 2754,* – rm, – 50. CZ u

closed 24-26 December – ***City Café*** **: Meals** 11.50/13.50 and a la carte 18.70/31.85 **s.** – 11.50 – **164 rm** 89.00.

◆ Quayside location and views of the Clyde. Well priced hotel with a "business-friendly" ethos ; neatly maintained modern rooms with sofas and en suite power showers. Restaurant fronts waterside terrace.

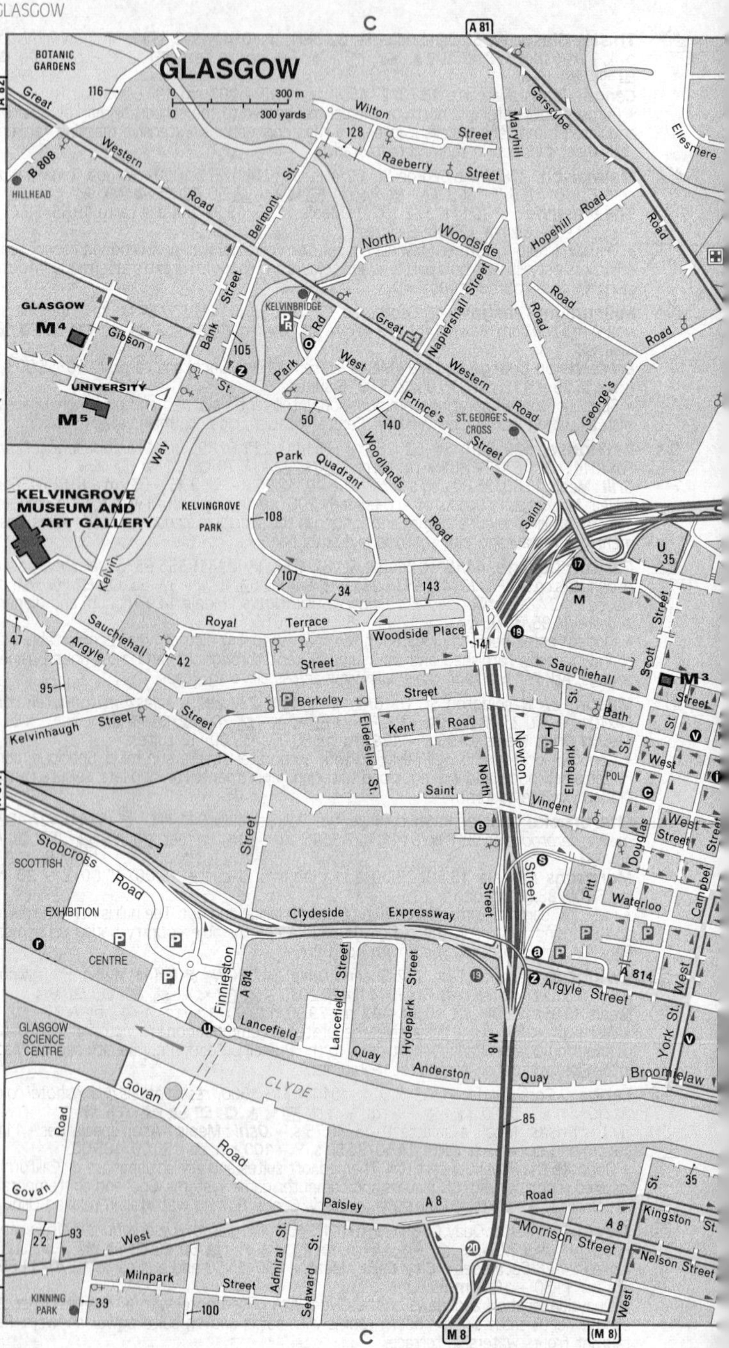

GLASGOW

0 300 m
0 300 yards

C
A 81
A 82
Y
Z
A 814
A 8
M 8
(M 8)

BOTANIC GARDENS
HILLHEAD
B 808
Great Western Road
116
Wilton Street
128
Raeberry Street
Belmont St.
Maryhill Road
Garscube Road
Ellesmere
Hopehill Road
North Woodside Road
Napiershall Street
KELVINBRIDGE
Park Rd
Bank Street
105
GLASGOW
M4
Gibson St.
UNIVERSITY
M5
West Prince's Street
140
50
ST. GEORGE'S CROSS
St. George's Road
Kelvin Way
KELVINGROVE MUSEUM AND ART GALLERY
KELVINGROVE PARK
Park Quadrant
108
107
34
143
Woodlands Road
Saint George's
U 35
M
Royal Terrace
Woodside Place
141
47
Sauchiehall Street
42
Argyle Street
95
Kelvinhaugh Street
Berkeley Street
Elderslie St.
Kent Road
North Street
Saint Vincent Street
Newton Street
Elmbank St.
Bath Street
Scott Street
M3
T
POL
West Street
Douglas Street
West Street
West Campbell Street
Pitt Street
Waterloo Street
Stobcross Road
SCOTTISH EXHIBITION CENTRE
Clydeside Expressway
Finnieston Street
A 814
Lancefield Street
Lancefield Quay
Hydepark Street
Argyle Street
A 814
York St.
GLASGOW SCIENCE CENTRE
CLYDE
Anderston Quay
Broomielaw
Govan Road
85
Govan Road
Paisley Road West
A 8
Kingston St.
35
Morrison Street
A 8
Nelson Street
93
22
Milnpark Street
Admiral St.
Seaward St.
KINNING PARK
39
100
West St.
19
20

Albert Bridge	DZ	2	Oswald St.	DZ	
Argyle Street	CZ		Otago Street	CY	105
Brand Street	CZ	22	Oxford Street	DZ	106
Bridegate	DZ	24	Park Gardens	CY	107
Bridge Street	DZ	25	Park Terrace	CY	108
Buchanan Galleries	DY		Port Dundas Rd	DY	110
Buchanan St.	DZ		Queen Margaret Dr.	CY	116
Cambridge Street	DY	32	Renfield St.	DYZ	
Claremont Terrace	CY	34	Robertson St.	CZ	120
Clyde Place	CZ	35	St. Enoch Shopping Centre	DZ	
Cochrane Street	DZ	36	St. Vincent St.	DZ	
Commerce Street	DZ	37	Sauchiehall St.	DY	
Cornwald Street	CZ	39	Stirling Road	DY	126
Derby Street	CY	42	Stockwell Street	DZ	127
Dumbarton Road	CY	47	Striven Gardens	CY	128
Eldon Street	CY	50	Trongate	DZ	
Glasgow Bridge	DZ	60	Union Street	DZ	
Gordon Street	DZ	65	Victoria Bridge	DZ	132
Jamaica Street	DZ	77	West Graham Street	CY	135
John Knox St.	DZ	80	West Nile Street	DYZ	139
Kingston Bridge	CZ	85	Woodlands Drive	CY	140
Kyle Street	DY	86	Woodside Crescent	CY	141
Lorne Street	CZ	93	Woodside Terrace	CY	143
Lymburn Street	CY	95			
Middlesex St.	CZ	100			
Moir Street	DZ	102			

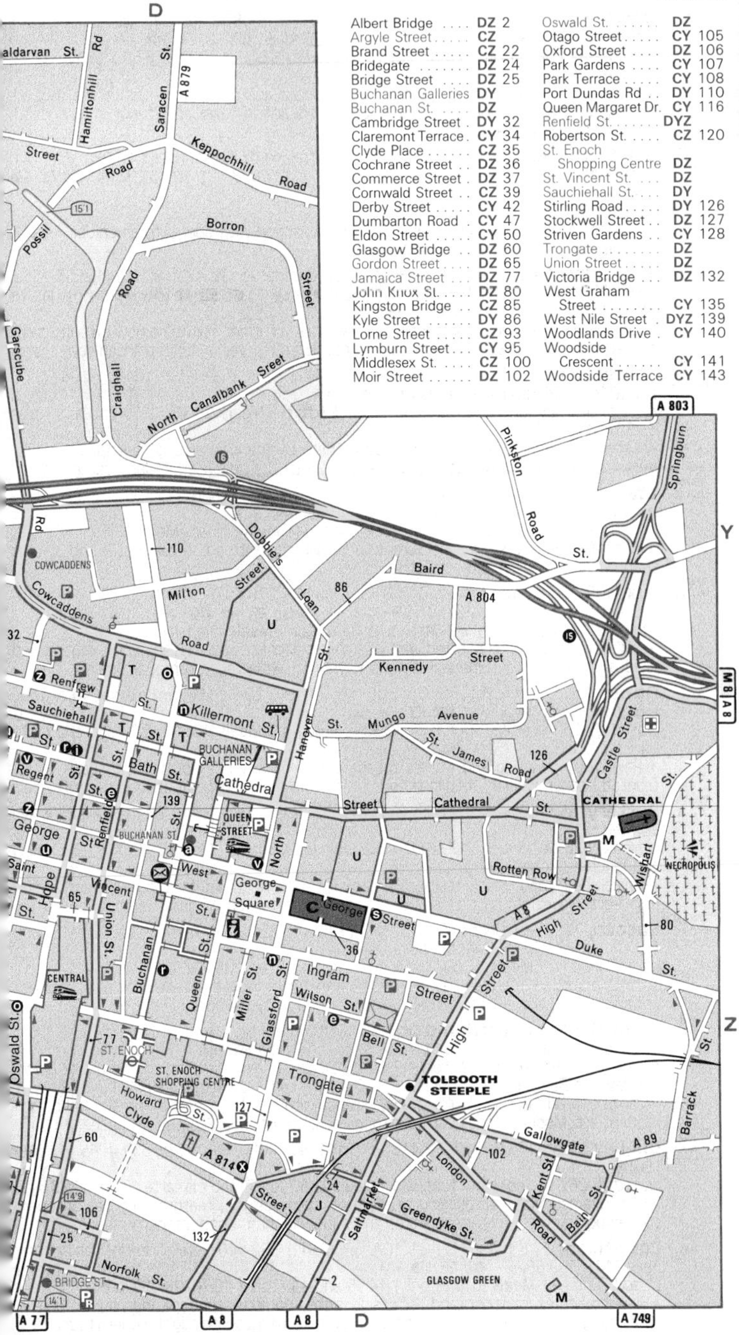

Bewley's, 110 Bath St, G2 2EN, ✆ (0141) 353 0800, *gla@bewleyshotels.com, Fax (0141) 353 0900* – lift, ⇔ rm, ▤ rest, TV ✆ ♿. MC AE ① VISA. ✈ DY i
closed 25-26 December – ***Loop :*** **Meals** a la carte 16.20/24.50 – ☕ 6.50 – **98 rm** 59.00, 5 suites.
◆ A well-run group hotel, relaxed but professional in approach, in the middle of Glasgow's shopping streets. Spacious, affordable accommodation with modern fittings. People-watch from glass-walled brasserie.

Express by Holiday Inn without rest., Theatreland, 165 West Nile St, G1 2RL, ✆ (0141) 331 6800, *express@higlasgow.com, Fax (0141) 331 6828* – lift ⇔ TV ✆ ♿. MC AE ① VISA JCB DY o
88 rm 69.00.
◆ Modern accommodation - simple and well arranged with adequate amenities. Equally suitable for business travel or short breaks.

Travel Inn Metro, Montrose House, 187 George St, G1 1YU, ✆ (0141) 553 2700, *Fax (0141) 553 2719* – lift ⇔, ▤ rest, TV ✆ ♿ P – 🏛 40. MC AE ① VISA. ✈ DZ s
Meals (dinner only) – **254 rm** 49.95.
◆ Close to George Square and the City Chambers, a former tax office now offering neat, modern rooms at a reasonable price. The restaurant serves a Mediterranean-style menu.

Camerons (at Hilton Glasgow H.), 1 William St, G3 8HT, ✆ (0141) 204 5511, *Fax (0141) 204 5004* – ▤ P. MC AE ① VISA CZ s
closed Saturday lunch, Sunday and Bank Holidays – **Meals** 20.50/39.50 and a la carte 33.50/48.50 **s.** ♀.
◆ Carefully prepared and full-flavoured modern cuisine with strong Scottish character. Very formal, neo-classical styling and smart staff have advanced its local reputation.

étain, The Glass House, Springfield Court, G13 3JN, ✆ (0141) 225 5630, *etian@conran.com, Fax (0141) 225 5640* – lift ▤. MC AE ① VISA JCB DZ r
closed 25 December, 1 January, Saturday lunch and Sunday dinner – **Meals** 18.50/28.00 **s.** ♀.
◆ Centrally located, stylish restaurant with linen-clad tables and banquette and leather seating. Very modern and attractive dishes.

Lux, 1051 Great Western Rd, G12 0XP, ✆ (0141) 576 7576, *lux-stazione@gtwestern-rd.fsnet.co.uk, Fax (0141) 576 0162* – ⇔ ▤ P. MC AE ① VISA JCB by A 82 CY
closed 25-26 December, 1-2 January and Sunday – **Meals** (dinner only) 28.50.
◆ 19C railway station converted with clean-lined elegance : dark wood, subtle lighting and vivid blue banquettes. Fine service and flavourful, well-prepared modern menus.

Opus, 150 St Vincent St, G2 5NE, ✆ (0141) 204 1150, *info@opusglasgow, Fax (0141) 204 1140* – ▤. MC AE ① VISA DZ u
closed 25-26 December, Sunday and Bank Holidays – **Meals** 12.50/26.00 and a la carte 24.50/34.00 ♀.
◆ Pale wood panelling and a glass façade create an airy open-plan dining space. Glass-fronted kitchen where Scottish produce is prepared with international herbs and spices.

Buttery, 652 Argyle St, G3 8UF, ✆ (0141) 221 8188, *Fax (0141) 204 4639* – ⇔ P. MC AE VISA CZ e
closed 25-26 December, 1-2 January, Sunday and Monday – **Meals** 34.00/41.00 (dinner) and lunch a la carte 34.00/41.00 ♀.
◆ Established, comfortable restaurant away from the bright lights ; red velour and ageing bric-a-brac reveal its past as a pub. Ambitiously composed modern Scottish repertoire.

Rococo, 202 West George St, G2 2NR, ✆ (0141) 221 5004, *res@rococoglasgow.com, Fax (0141) 221 5006* – ▤. MC AE ① VISA DYZ z
closed Sunday – **Meals** 18.00/36.50 and lunch a la carte 26.75/32.20 ☺ ♀.
◆ In style, more like studied avant-garde : stark, white-walled cellar with vibrant modern art and high-backed leather chairs. Accomplished, fully flavoured contemporary menu.

Brian Maule at Chardon d'Or, 176 West Regent St, G2 4RL, ✆ (0141) 248 3801, *info@brianmaule.com, Fax (0141) 248 3901* – ⇔. MC AE VISA CY i
closed 2 weeks January, 2 weeks July, 25-26 December, 1-2 January, Saturday lunch, Sunday and Bank Holidays – **Meals** 17.50 (lunch) and a la carte 24.50/37.00 ☺ ♀.
◆ Large pillared Georgian building. Airy interior with ornate carved ceiling and hung with modern art. Modern dishes with a strong French tone, fine Scottish produce.

Quigley's, 158-166 Bath St, G2 4TB, ✆ (0141) 331 4060, *Fax (0141) 331 4065* – ▤. MC AE VISA DY u
closed 25-26 December and 1 January – **Meals** 12.50 (lunch) and a la carte 19.50/31.50 ☺ ♀.
◆ A converted Victorian building that retains many original features and has an open, contemporary feel. Deep banquettes and subtle lighting. Good, modern menus.

Corinthian, 191 Ingram St, G1 1DA, ✆ (0141) 552 1101, *info@corinthian.uk.com, Fax (0141) 559 6826* – MC AE ① VISA DZ n
closed Sunday – **Meals** (dinner only) 14.95 and a la carte 19.70/26.15 ☺ ♀.
◆ Breathtaking example of grand 19C design : a glass-domed bar and spacious, supremely elegant dining room serving solid, competently prepared dishes with a light modern touch.

XX **Papingo,** 104 Bath St, G2 2EN, ✆ (0141) 332 6678, *info@papingo.co.uk, Fax (0141) 332 6549* – MC AE VISA DY r
closed 25-26 December, 1-2 January and Sunday lunch – **Meals** 10.00 (lunch) and a la carte 22.00/34.00 ☺ ♀.
◆ Parrot motifs recur everywhere, even on the door handles! Well-spaced tables and mirrored walls add a sense of space to the basement. A free-ranging fusion style prevails.

XX **Zinc Bar & Grill,** Princes Sq, G1 3JX, ✆ (0141) 225 5620, *zincglasgow@conran.com, Fax (0141) 225 5640* – ▤. MC AE ⓓ VISA JCB DZ r
closed 25 December and 1 January – **Meals** 14.00 (lunch) and a la carte 14.50/25.50 **s.** ♀.
◆ Modern city centre restaurant with the Conran touch revealed in the stylish décor and tableware. Modern menu offering popular dishes.

XX **Ho Wong,** 82 York St, G2 8LE, ✆ (0141) 221 3550, *Fax (0141) 248 5330* – ▤. MC AE ⓓ VISA CZ v
closed 3 days Chinese New Year and Sunday lunch – **Meals** - Chinese (Peking) - 27.00 (dinner) and a la carte 21.20/27.10.
◆ In an unfashionable part of town, a long-established, traditionally furnished restaurant with a large front bar. Authentic Chinese cuisine with the emphasis on Peking style.

XX **Amber Regent,** 50 West Regent St, G2 2QZ, ✆ (0141) 331 1655, *Fax (0141) 353 3398* – ▤. MC AE ⓓ VISA DY e
closed Chinese New Year and Sunday – **Meals** - Chinese - 9.95/38.95 and a la carte 22.25/42.90.
◆ Traditional Chinese dishes served by conscientious staff. Comfy, personally managed restaurant in a 19C office building in the heart of the city. Good value lunch.

XX **Shish Mahal,** 66-68 Park Rd, G4 9JF, ✆ (0141) 3398256, *reservations@shishmahal.co.uk, Fax (0141) 572 0800* – ⇷. MC AE VISA JCB CY o
Meals - Indian - 15.95/20.95 and a la carte 10.40/18.35.
◆ Tandoori specialities in a varied pan-Indian menu, attentive service and an evocative modern interior of etched glass, oak and Moorish tiles have won city-wide recognition.

X **The Ubiquitous Chip,** 12 Ashton Lane, G12 8SJ, off Byres Rd ✆ (0141) 334 5007, *mail@ubiquitouschip.co.uk, Fax (0141) 337 1302* – MC AE ⓓ VISA JCB by B 808 CY
closed 25 December and 1 January – **Meals** 21.50/37.50 and a la carte 12.95/24.45 ♀.
◆ A long standing favourite, "The Chip" mixes Scottish and fusion styles. Well known for its glass-roofed courtyard, with a more formal but equally lively warehouse interior.

X **No. Sixteen,** 16 Byres Rd, G11 5JY, ✆ (0141) 339 2544, *Fax (0141) 576 1505* – MC VISA by B 808 CY
closed 5-19 January, 25 December, 1 January and lunch 26 December, 2 January – **Meals** 12.50 (lunch) and a la carte 19.45/27.25 ☺.
◆ In the student quarter; small, friendly and personally run. Justly popular for modest prices and a regularly changing, confidently prepared menu: fresh, varied, unfussy.

X **Shimla Pinks,** 777 Pollokshaws Rd, G41 2AX, ✆ (0141) 423 4488, *Fax (0141) 423 2434* – ▤. MC AE ⓓ VISA by A 77 DZ
closed 1 January and lunch Saturday and Sunday – **Meals** - Indian - 6.95 (lunch) and a la carte 10.40/24.85.
◆ Simple, modern interior with white walls and contemporary lighting. Sound repertoire of Indian cuisine. A well-run restaurant to south of city. Good value set lunch menu.

X **Mao,** 84 Brunswick St, G1 1ZZ, ✆ (0141) 564 5161, *info@cafemao.com, Fax (0141) 564 5163* – ▤. MC AE VISA DZ e
closed 24-26 and 31 December and 1 January – **Meals** - Southeast Asian - 13.50/16.50 (dinner) and a la carte 15.00/22.00 **s.** ♀.
◆ Eatery located over two floors which are decorated in bright, funky style with vivid, modern colours - broadly themed on Chairman Mao. Thoroughly tasty South East Asian food.

LEEDS *W. Yorks.* 502 P 22 *Great Britain G.* – *pop. 424 194.*
See: *City★ - Royal Armouries Museum★★★* GZ *City Art Gallery★* AC GY **M.**
Envir.: *Kirkstall Abbey★* AC, *NW : 3 m. by A 65* FY – *Temple Newsam★ (decorative arts★)* AC, *E : 5 m. by A 64 and A 63.*
Exc.: *Harewood House★★ (The Gallery★)* AC, *N : 8 m. by A 61 – Nostell Priory★, SE : 18 m. by A 61 and A 638 – Yorkshire Sculpture Park★, S : 20 m. by M 1 to junction 38 and 1 m. north off A 637 – Brodsworth Hall★, SE : 25 m. by M 1 to junction 40, A 638 and minor rd (right) in Upton.*
18, 18 *Temple Newsam, Temple Newsam Rd, Halton* ✆ *(0113) 264 5624* – 18 *Gotts Park, Armley Ridge Rd* ✆ *(0113) 234 2019* – 18 *Middleton Park, Ring Rd, Beeston Park, Middleton* ✆ *(0113) 270 9506* – 18, 9 *Moor Allerton, Coal Rd, Wike* ✆ *(0113) 266 1154* – 18 *Howley Hall, Scotchman Lane, Morley* ✆ *(01924) 472432* – 9 *Roundhay, Park Lane* ✆ *(0113) 266 2695.*
✈ *Leeds - Bradford Airport :* ✆ *(0113) 250 9696, NW : 8 m. by A 65 and A 658.*
ℹ *The Arcade, City Station* ✆ *(0113) 242 5242, tourinfo@leeds.golf.uk.*
London 204 – Liverpool 75 – Manchester 43 – Newcastle upon Tyne 95 – Nottingham 74.

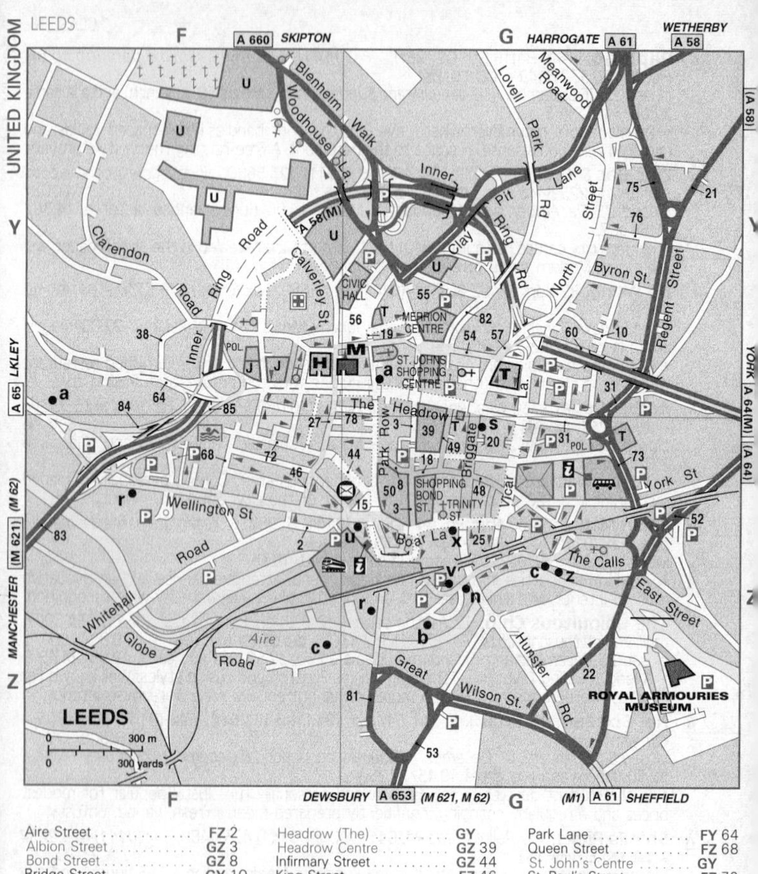

Aire Street . . . . FZ 2
Albion Street . . . . GZ 3
Bond Street . . . . GZ 8
Bridge Street . . . . GY 10
Briggate . . . . GZ
City Square . . . . GZ 15
Commercial Street . . . . . . GZ 18
Cookridge Street . . . . GY 19
County Arcade . . . . GZ 20
Cross Stamford St . . . . . . GY 21
Crown Point Road . . . . . . GZ 22
Duncan Street . . . . GZ 25
East Parade . . . . FGZ 27
Eastgate . . . . GZ 31
Hanover Way . . . . FY 38
Headrow (The) . . . . GY
Headrow Centre . . . . GZ 39
Infirmary Street . . . . GZ 44
King Street . . . . FZ 46
Kirkgate . . . . GZ 48
Lands Lane . . . . GZ 49
Leeds Shopping Plaza . . . . GZ 50
Marsh Lane . . . . GZ 52
Meadow Lane . . . . GZ 53
Merrion Centre . . . . GY
Merrion Street . . . . GY 54
Merrion Way . . . . GY 55
Millennium Square . . . . . . GY 56
New Briggate . . . . GY 57
New York Road . . . . GY 60
Park Lane . . . . FY 64
Queen Street . . . . FZ 68
St. John's Centre . . . . . . GY
St. Paul's Street . . . . FZ 72
St. Peter's Street . . . . . . GZ 73
Sheepscar St. South . . . . GY 75
Skinner Lane . . . . GY 76
South Parade . . . . FGZ 78
Trinity St. Shopping Centre . . . . GZ
Victoria Road . . . . GZ 81
Wade Lane . . . . GY 82
Wellington Road . . . . FZ 83
West Street . . . . FZ 84
Westgate . . . . FZ 85

Radisson SAS without rest., No.1 The Light, The Headrow, LS1 8TL, ✆ (0113) 236 6000, *Fax (0113) 236 6100* – |‡| ⅕ ▤ TV ✆ ♿ P – 🏛 50. MC AE ① VISA. ✕ GY a
☐ 12.95 – **146 rm** 130.00/175.00, 1 suite.
◆ Impressive new hotel in heart of city. Open atrium and individually styled furnishings throughout. State-of-art meeting rooms. Ultra modern, very well appointed bedrooms.

Devere Oulton Hall, Rothwell Lane, Oulton, LS26 8HN, Southeast : 5 ½ m. by A 61 and A 639 on A 654 ✆ (0113) 282 1000, *oulton.hall@devere-hotels.com*, *Fax (0113) 282 8066*, ⋖, ⅙, ≋s, ⛳, 18, 9, – |‡| ⅕, ▤ rest, TV ♿ ⚐ P – 🏛 330. MC AE ① VISA
Bronte **:** Meals 13.50 (lunch) and dinner a la carte 23.50/38.00 **s.** ♀ – ***Haworth*** **:** Meals (dinner only Tuesday-Saturday) a la carte approx. 38.00 – **150 rm** ☐ 150.00/170.00, 2 suites.
◆ Once home to Leeds' Calverley family ; neo-Classical mansion set in woodland with PGA standard golf course. The drawing room and main house bedrooms exemplify elegant style. Pictures of the famous sisters adorn walls of Bronte.

Thorpe Park H and Spa, 1150 Century Way, LS15 8ZB, East : 6 m. by A 64 and A 63 on B 6120 ☎ (0113) 264 1000, *thorpepark@shirehotels.co.uk, Fax (0113) 264 1010,* – – 200.
Meals *(closed Saturday lunch)* a la carte 25.00/45.00 **s.** – **119 rm** 140.00/160.00, 4 suites.
◆ Handily placed hotel, close to motorways. Open-fired reception and richly toned central atrium. Fully equipped leisure centre with spa. Immaculate rooms with host of extras. Spacious, modern restaurant.

Leeds Marriott, 4 Trevelyan Sq, Boar Lane, LS1 6ET, ☎ (0870) 400 7260, *reservations.leeds@marriotthotels.co.uk, Fax (0113) 236 6367,* – rm, – 320. GZ x
***John T's* : Meals** (dinner only) 24.00 and a la carte 24.50/26.50 – 14.00 – **243 rm** 125.00/145.00, 1 suite.
◆ Between Corn Exchange and station with smart, modern bedrooms behind its Victorian façade. Extensive business facilities and a good leisure centre. Relax in informal bar/bistro.

Crowne Plaza Leeds, Wellington St, LS1 4DL, ☎ (0113) 244 2200, *sales.cpleeds@ichotelsgroup.com, Fax (0113) 261 6809,* – rm, – 200. FZ r
***Boccagrande* : Meals** *(closed lunch Saturday and Sunday)* 14.00/18.00 and a la carte 18.15/30.95 – 12.95 – **132 rm** 145.00, 3 suites.
◆ Well-appointed rooms and a state-of-the-art health club. Close to station and ring road. Ideal for business or breaks. Reception foyer houses impressive gallery. Vibrant restaurant with modern 'buzz'.

Malmaison, Sovereign Quay, LS1 1DQ, ☎ (0113) 398 1000, *leeds@malmaison.com, Fax (0113) 398 1002* – rm, – 45. GZ n
Meals 12.95/13.95 and a la carte 19.85/29.45 – 10.95 – **100 rm** 95.00/125.00, 1 suite.
◆ Relaxed, contemporary hotel hides behind imposing Victorian exterior. Small spa. Vibrantly and individually decorated rooms are thoughtfully furnished with CD players. Dine in modern interpretation of a French brasserie.

Quebecs without rest., 9 Quebec St, LS1 2HA, ☎ (0113) 244 8989, *res-quebecs@etontownhouse.com, Fax (0113) 244 9090* – FZ a
closed 24-26 December – 13.50 **45 rm** 125.00/250.00.
◆ Ex-19C Liberal Club, now a stylish, intimate city centre hotel. Original features include oak staircase and stained glass window depicting Yorkshire cities. Very comfy rooms.

42 The Calls, 42 The Calls, LS2 7EW, ☎ (0113) 244 0099, *hotel@42thecalls.co.uk, Fax (0113) 234 4100,* – – 85. GZ z
closed 4 days Christmas – **Meals** (see ***Pool Court at 42*** and ***Brasserie Forty Four*** below) – 13.75 – **38 rm** 140.00/210.00, 3 suites.
◆ Stylish, contemporary converted quayside grain mill retaining many of the original workings. Rooms facing river have best views ; all have CD players and host of extras.

Le Meridien Queen's, City Sq, LS1 1PL, ☎ (0113) 243 1323, *queensreservations@paramount-hotels.co.uk, Fax (0113) 242 5154* – rm, – 600. GZ u
***No.1 City Square* : Meals** (carvery lunch) 16.50/21.00 and dinner a la carte 18.95/29.95 – 12.75 – **194 rm** 130.00/160.00, 5 suites.
◆ Imposing 30s landmark. Renowned for afternoon tea in the Palm Court, it maintains a style of yesteryear. Most rooms now have a contemporary feel. Pianist occasionally accompanies restaurant diners.

Weetwood Hall, Otley Rd, LS16 5PS, Northwest : 4 m. on A 660 ☎ (0113) 230 6000, *sales@weetwood.co.uk, Fax (0113) 230 6095,* squash – – 180.
***The Woodlands* : Meals** (bar lunch Monday-Saturday)/dinner 18.50 and a la carte 17.70/24.20 **s.** – 10.75 – **106 rm** 109.00/125.00.
◆ Extended 17C sandstone manor farm ; popular business venue as it boasts some of the region's finest meeting and leisure facilities. Well-appointed, comfortable bedrooms. Dining options : main restaurant or welcoming pub in former 16C stables.

Hilton Leeds City, Neville St, LS1 4BX, ☎ (0113) 244 2000, *leehnhngm@hilton.com, Fax (0113) 243 3577,* – rm, rm, – 400. GZ r
***New World* : Meals** (bar lunch)/dinner 18.95 and a la carte 21.85/29.85 – 12.95 – **186 rm** 125.00, 20 suites.
◆ Proximity to station, business and commercial districts make this 1970s tower block a favourite for the corporate traveller. Neat and spacious rooms have views of city. Blackboard menus or international cuisine.

Haley's, Shire Oak Rd, Headingley, LS6 2DE, Northwest : 2 m. by A 660 ☎ (0113) 278 4446, *info@haleys.co.uk, Fax (0113) 275 3342* – ⇔, ▤ rest, TV ☎ P – 🎪 25. MC AE VISA JCB. ⚘ *closed 26-30 December* – **Meals** *(closed Sunday dinner to non-residents)* (dinner only and Sunday lunch)/dinner 27.50 ♀ – **27 rm** ☕ 110.00/175.00, 1 suite.

♦ Named after a prominent stonemason, this part 19C country house in a quiet area is handy for cricket fans. Antique furnished public areas. Individually styled bedrooms. Elegant, relaxed dining room with collection of original local artwork.

Novotel, 4 Whitehall, Whitehall Quay, LS1 4HR, ☎ (0113) 242 6446, *h3270@accor-hotels.com, Fax (0113) 242 6445,* 🏋 – 🛗, ⇔ rm, ▤ TV ☎ ♿ P – 🎪 80. MC AE ⓓ VISA JCB FZ x

***The Garden Brasserie :* Meals** 16.50/16.95 and a la carte 15.05/27.70 **s.** ♀ – ☕ 11.50 – **194 rm** 105.00, 1 suite.

♦ Just a minute's walk from the main railway station. Ideally suited to the business traveller, with desk modems and meeting rooms. Compact exercise facility. Functional rooms. Informal brasserie adjacent to lobby.

No.3 York Place, 3 York Pl, LS1 2DR, ☎ (0113) 245 9922, *dine@no3yorkplace.co.uk, Fax (0113) 245 9965* – ▤. MC AE VISA FZ e

closed Christmas-New Year, Saturday lunch, Sunday and Bank Holidays – **Meals** 18.50 (lunch) and a la carte 24.85/44.85 🎭.

♦ Striking, stylish, minimalist interior keeps the spotlight on the accomplished cuisine. Classic flavours reinterpreted in an imaginative repertoire of seafood and game dishes.

Pool Court at 42 (at 42 The Calls H.), 44 The Calls, LS2 7EW, ☎ (0113) 244 4242, ✿ *poolcourt@onetel.net.uk, Fax (0113) 234 3332,* 🏠 – ⇔ ▤. MC VISA GZ z

closed Saturday lunch, Sunday and Bank Holidays – **Meals** 30.00/44.00.

♦ Book early for the small terrace overlooking the Aire. Sophisticated, modern menus with seasonal dishes and attentive service make for formal yet intimate armchair dining.

Spec. Roast foie gras with spiced pineapple, Muscat butter sauce. Fillet of beef, Tatin of caramelised onions, red wine sauce. Summer fruits and Champagne jelly.

Simply Heathcotes, Canal Wharf, Water Lane, LS11 5PS, ☎ (0113) 244 6611, *leeds@simplyheathcotes.co.uk, Fax (0113) 244 0736,* ⋖ – ▤. MC AE VISA FZ c

closed Bank Holidays except Good Friday – **Meals** 15.50 (lunch) and a la carte 17.75/26.00 ♀.

♦ Converted grain warehouse by the canal. Distinctive modern feel with rich black banquettes. Effective contemporary cooking with prominent "northern" slant.

Leodis, Victoria Mill, Sovereign St, LS1 4BJ, ☎ (0113) 242 1010, *Fax (0113) 243 0432,* 🏠 – MC AE ⓓ VISA GZ b

closed 26 December, Sunday and lunch on Saturday and Bank Holidays – **Meals** 16.95 (lunch) and a la carte 18.90/27.90 ♀.

♦ Appealing converted riverside storehouse offers hearty roasts, carving trolley and other generous British-style favourites in a bustling atmosphere. Friendly service.

Quantro, 62 Street Lane, LS8 2DQ, ☎ (0113) 288 8063, *Fax (0113) 288 8008,* 🏠 – ▤. MC AE VISA by A 58 GY

closed 25-26 December, 1 January and Sunday – **Meals** 12.95 (lunch) and a la carte 20.00/28.80 🎭 ♀.

♦ Modern restaurant in suburban parade. Stylish décor : the smart atmosphere is augmented by friendly service. Excellent value lunches ; modern dishes with international twists.

Brasserie Forty Four (at 42 The Calls H.), 44 The Calls, LS2 7EW, ☎ (0113) 234 3232, *brasserie44@onetel.net.uk, Fax (0113) 234 3332* – ▤. MC ⓓ VISA GZ z

closed Sunday, Saturday lunch and Bank Holidays – **Meals** a la carte 22.95/28.95 🎭.

♦ Former riverside warehouse with stylish bar ; exudes atmosphere of buzzy informality. Smokehouse and char-grilled options in an eclectic range of menu dishes.

Fourth Floor (at Harvey Nichols), 107-111 Briggate, LS1 6AZ, ☎ (0113) 204 8000, *Fax (0113) 204 8080,* 🏠 – ▤. MC AE ⓓ VISA GZ s

closed 25-26 and 31 December, 1 January, Easter Sunday and dinner Sunday-Wednesday – **Meals** (lunch bookings not accepted) 18.00 (lunch) and a la carte 18.00/25.00 🎭 ♀.

♦ Watch the chefs prepare the modern food with world-wide influences in these bright, stylish, buzzy, contemporary surroundings. Advisable to get here early at lunch.

Maxi's, 6 Bingley St, LS3 1LX, off Kirkstall Rd ☎ (0113) 244 0552, *info@maxi-s.co.uk, Fax (0113) 234 3902* – ▤ P. MC AE ⓓ VISA by Burley Rd FY a

closed 25-26 December – **Meals** - Chinese (Canton, Peking) - 17.80 and a la carte 12.30/45.20.

♦ Savour the taste of the Orient in this ornately decorated and busy pagoda style restaurant. Specialises in the rich flavours of Canton and hot and spicy Peking dishes.

The Calls Grill, Calls Landing, 38 The Calls, LS2 7EW, ☎ (0113) 245 3870, *Fax (0113) 243 9035* – ▤. MC AE ⓓ VISA JCB GZ c

closed 24 December-5 January and Sunday – **Meals** (dinner only) 12.50/18.50 and a la carte 17.50/33.50 🎭 ♀.

♦ Restored Aireside textile mill with rustic ambience : exposed brickwork and timbers. Well-priced modern British cooking ; bustling informality. Steaks a speciality.

at Garforth *East : 6 m. by A 64 GY and A 63 at junction with A 642 – ✉ Leeds :*

XX **Aagrah,** Aberford Rd, LS25 1BA, on A 642 (Garforth rd) ☎ (0113) 287 6606, *sabir@aagrah.com* – ▤ P. MO AE VISA
closed 25 December – **Meals** - Indian (Kashmiri) - (booking essential) (dinner only) 14.00/15.00 and a la carte 14.10/19.15 **s.**.
◆ Part of a family owned and personally run expanding group. Classic regional Indian cooking, specialising in the fragrant and subtly spiced dishes of the Kashmir region.

at Pudsey *West : 5 ¾ m. by M 621 FZ and A 647 – ✉ Leeds :*

XX **Aagrah,** 483 Bradford Rd, LS28 8ED, on A 647 ☎ (01274) 668818, *sabir@aagrah.com* – ▤ P. MO AE VISA
closed 25 December – **Meals** - Indian (Kashmiri) - (booking essential) (dinner only) 14.00/15.00 and a la carte 14.10/19.15 **s.**
◆ Advance booking most definitely required here ; a very busy and bustling traditional Indian restaurant. Offers an extensive range of carefully prepared authentic dishes.

at Horsforth *Northwest : 5 m. by A 65 FY off A 6120 – ✉ Leeds :*

X **Paris,** Calverley Bridge, Calverley Lane, Rodley, LS13 1NP, Southwest : 1 m. by A 6120 ☎ (0113) 258 1885, *Fax (0113) 239 0651* – ▤ P. MO AE O VISA JCB
closed 26 December, 1 January and Saturday lunch – **Meals** 13.95 and a la carte 16.50/28.30.
◆ Bistro styling in this converted railway hotel, just 10 minutes from city centre. Tables in the conservatory can be particularly pleasant. Carefully priced European dishes.

Winteringham *North Lincolnshire 502 S 22 – pop. 4 714 – ✉ Scunthorpe.*

London 176 – Leeds 62.

XXXX ✿✿ **Winteringham Fields** (Schwab) with rm, Silver St, DN15 9PF, ☎ (01724) 733096, *wintfields@aol.com, Fax (01724) 733898* – ⇔ TV P. MO VISA
closed 10 days Christmas, first 10 days August and last week March – **Meals** *(closed Sunday-Monday)* (booking essential to non-residents) 31.00/38.00 and a la carte 59.75/70.50 **s.** – ☕ 12.50 – **8 rm** 100.00/185.00, 2 suites.
◆ Cosy 16C house : beamed ceilings, narrow passages, original range with fire. Conservatory or lounges for drinks. Exceptional, original food superbly prepared. Elegant bedrooms.
Spec. Duckling with foie gras on brioche, apple and quince jelly. Bouillabaisse "modern", crispy vegetables à la Provençale. Liquorice soufflé with clementine sorbet.

LIVERPOOL *Mersey. 502 503 L 23 Great Britain G. – pop. 481 786.*

See : *City★ - The Walker★★* DY **M3** *– Liverpool Cathedral★★ (Lady Chapel★)* EZ *– Metropolitan Cathedral of Christ the King★★* EY *– Albert Dock★* CZ *(Merseyside Maritime Museum★ AC* **M2** *- Tate Gallery Liverpool★).*

Exc. : *Speke Hall★ AC, SE : 8 m. by A 561.*

18, 9 *Allerton Municipal, Allerton Rd ☎ (0151) 428 1046 –* 18 *Liverpool Municipal, Ingoe Lane, Kirkby ☎ (0151) 546 5435 –* 9 *Bowring, Bowring Park, Roby Rd, Huyton ☎ (0151) 489 1901.*

Mersey Tunnels (toll).

✈ *Liverpool Airport : ☎ (0870) 7508484, SE : 6 m. by A 561 –* **Terminal** : *Pier Head.*

⛴ *to Isle of Man (Douglas) (Isle of Man Steam Packet Co. Ltd) (2 h 30 mn/4 h) – to Northern Ireland (Belfast) (NorseMerchant Ferries Ltd) 1-2 daily (11 h) – to Dublin (NorseMerchant Ferries Ltd) 2 daily (approx 7 h 45 mn) – to Dublin (P & O Irish Sea) daily (8 h) – to Dublin (Seacat) daily February-November (3 h 45 mn).*

⛴ *to Birkenhead and Wallasey (Mersey Ferries) frequent services daily.*

ℹ *Queens Square ☎ (0906) 680 6886, askme@visitliverpool.com – Atlantic Pavilion, Albert Dock ☎ (0906) 680 6886.*

London 219 – Birmingham 103 – Leeds 75 – Manchester 35.

Plans on following pages

Crowne Plaza Liverpool, St Nicholas Pl, Princes Dock, Pier Head, L3 1QN, ☎ (0151) 243 8000, *sales@cpliverpool.co.uk, Fax (0151) 243 8111,* ≤, Lδ, ≘s, ▢ – |♦|, ⇔ rm, ▤ TV ☏ ♿ P – 🏛 700. MO AE O VISA. ✗ CY a
closed 24-26 December – ***Plaza Brasserie :*** **Meals** 15.95/22.95 and a la carte 22.15/32.20 **s.** ♀ – ☕ 13.95 – **155 rm** 115.00, 4 suites.
◆ A busy conference venue within the popular dockside development. Enjoys views of the Mersey and the Liver Building. Well-appointed and very comfortable rooms. Spacious, informal ground floor brasserie.

LIVERPOOL

Street	Grid	No.
Argyle St.	DZ	6
Blackburne Pl.	EZ	10
Bold St.	DZ	
Brunswick Rd	EY	19
Canada Boulevard	CYZ	22
Canning Pl.	CZ	23
Church St.	DY	
Churchill Way	DY	26
Clarence St.	EYZ	27
Clayton Square Shopping Centre	DY	
College Lane	DZ	28
Commutation Row	DY	30
Cook St.	CY	32
Crosshall St.	DY	36
Daulby St.	EY	40
Erskine St.	EY	45
Fontenoy St.	DY	48
Forrest St.	DZ	49
George's Dock Gate	CY	51
Grafton St.	DZ	53
Great Charlotte St.	DY	54
Great Howard St.	CY	56
Hatton Garden	DY	57
Haymarket	DY	58
Hood St.	DY	62
Houghton St.	DY	65
Huskisson St.	EZ	66
James St.	CY	68
King Edward St.	CY	69
Knight St.	EZ	72
Leece St.	EZ	73
Lime St.	DY	
Liver St.	CZ	76
London Rd	DEY	
Lord St.	CDY	
Mansfield St.	DEY	80
Mathew St.	CDY	81
Moss St.	EY	86
Mount St.	EZ	88
Myrtle St.	EZ	89
Newington	DZ	92
New Quay	CY	93
North John St.	CY	96
Norton St.	EY	97
Parker St.	DY	103
Prescot St.	EY	105
Prince's Rd	EZ	107
Queen Square	DY	
Ranelagh St.	DY	108
Renshaw St.	DEZ	
Richmond St.	DY	109
Roe St.	DY	114
St. James Pl.	EZ	117
St. Johns Centre	DY	
St. John's Lane	DY	118
School Lane	DYZ	122
Scotland Pl.	DY	123
Setton St.	DZ	129
Seymour St.	EY	130
Skelhorne St.	DY	133
Stanley St.	CDY	135
Suffolk St.	DZ	137
Tarleton St.	DY	139
Victoria St.	DY	143
Water St.	CY	150
William Brown St.	DY	156
York St.	DZ	157

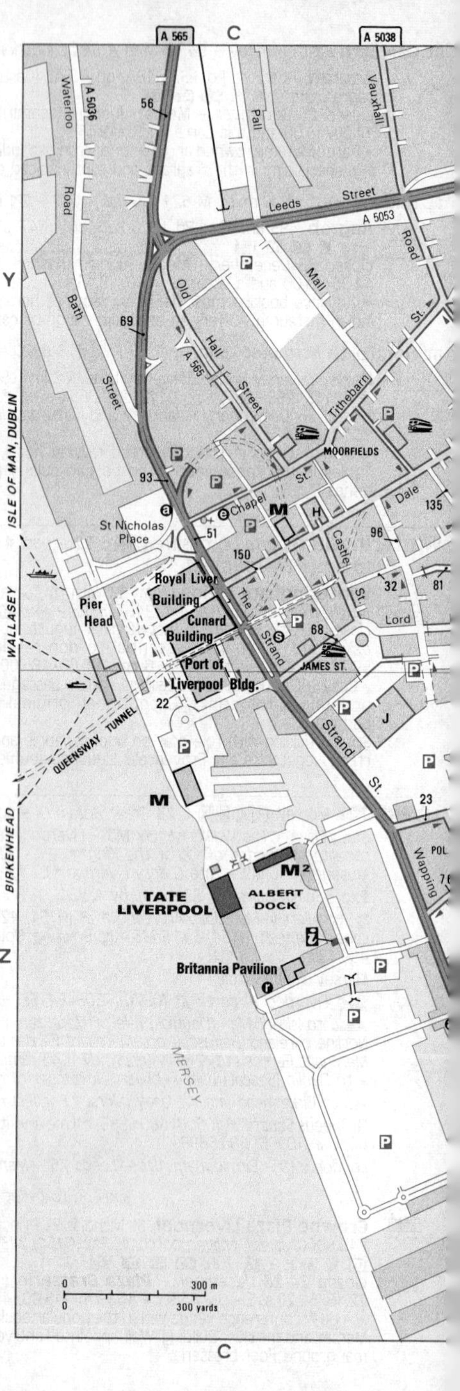

Great Britain and Ireland is now covered by an Atlas at a scale of 1 inch to 4.75 miles.

Three easy to use versions: Paperback, Spiralbound, Hardback.

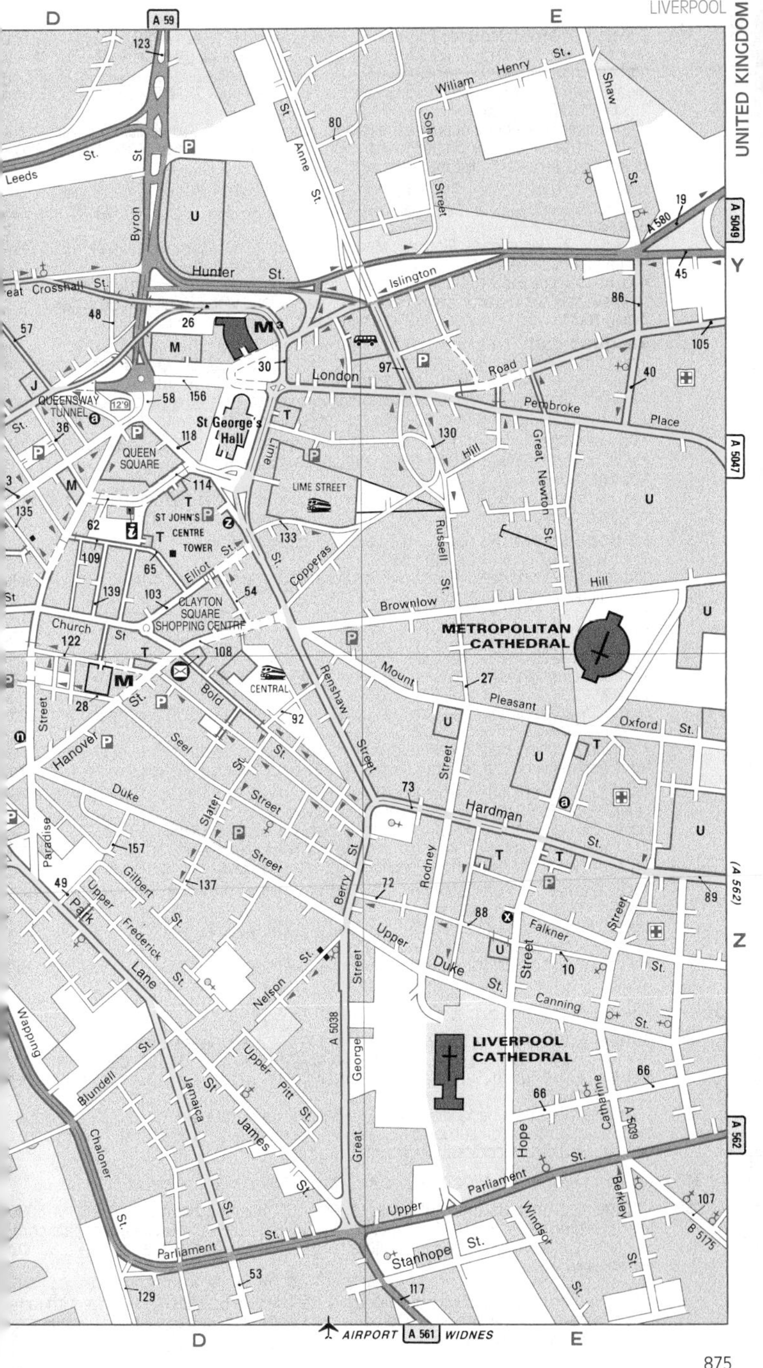
D
A 59
E
123
William
Henry
St.
Shaw
St.
Anne
St.
80
Soho
Street
Leeds
St.
Byron
St.
U
St.
19
A 580
A 5049
Y
Hunter
St.
Islington
45
Great Crosshall
St.
86
48
26
M³
57
M
105
30
London
97
Road
40
J
QUEENSWAY
TUNNEL
12'9
58
156
Pembroke
Place
St.
36
St George's
Hall
T
118
130
Hill
Great
Newton
St.
Lime
QUEEN
SQUARE
A 5047
LIME STREET
114
M
T
U
135
ST JOHN'S
CENTRE
TOWER
62
St.
133
Russell
St.
109
65
Elliot
St.
Copperas
139
103
54
Hill
St
CLAYTON
SQUARE
SHOPPING CENTRE
Brownlow
U
Church
St
METROPOLITAN
CATHEDRAL
122
108
T
Mount
M
27
Bold
CENTRAL
Pleasant
28
St.
Renshaw
Street
U
Oxford
St.
92
Hanover
Seel
St.
U
T
Slater
St.
Street
Hardman
73
Duke
Street
St.
U
Paradise
Street
157
St.
T
T
Berry
Street
Gilbert
(A 562)
Rodney
137
Upper
49
72
St.
89
Park
Frederick
88
Falkner
Upper
Z
Lane
Street
St.
St.
Duke
U
10
St.
Canning
Nelson
St.
St.
Wapping
A 5038
Street
LIVERPOOL
CATHEDRAL
Upper
Pitt
St.
George
Blundell
66
St.
66
Jamaica
St
Catharine
A 5039
St.
James
Chaloner
A 562
Great
Hope
St.
Parliament
Berkley
107
Windsor
Upper
St.
St.
St.
B 5175
St.
Stanhope
St.
Parliament
St.
53
St.
117
129
AIRPORT
A 561
WIDNES
D
E

Liverpool Moat House, Paradise St, L1 8JD, ℘ (0151) 471 9988, *gmliv@moathousehotels.com, Fax (0151) 709 2706,* ⅎ6, ≘s, ☒ – |♦| ⋟ ▤ TV ℭ P – ♗ 500. MC AE ① VISA JCB. ⅏ DZ n
Meals (buffet lunch)/dinner 16.95/25.95 and a la carte 21.00/28.00 ♀ – ☕ 11.50 – **261 rm** 109.00/129.00, 2 suites.
♦ Converted office block opposite the famous Albert Dock ; now a popular corporate hotel. Some of the generously proportioned, top floor rooms have views of the Mersey. Busy, relaxed brasserie with distant views of the river.

Holiday Inn, Lime St, L1 1NQ, ℘ (0151) 709 7090, *sales@cidc.co.uk, Fax (0151) 705 2800,* ⅎ6 – |♦|, ⋟ rm, ▤ TV ℭ ♿ – ♗ 350. MC AE ① VISA JCB. ⅏ DY z
closed 23-27 December – ***Signals :*** **Meals** *(closed lunch Saturday and Sunday)* 16.95 (dinner) and a la carte 12.70/25.20 **s.** – ☕ 13.95 – **138 rm** 140.00, 1 suite.
♦ Opposite Lime Street station and part of the shopping centre. Smartly furnished bedrooms in bold colours with large check bedspreads, blond wood furniture and stylish lamps. Dining room's wall of windows offers panoramic views of station.

Racquet Club, Hargreaves Buildings, 5 Chapel St, L3 9AA, ℘ (0151) 236 6676, *Fax (0151) 236 6870,* ⅎ6, ≘s, squash – |♦| ⋟ TV ℭ – ♗ 80. MC AE VISA CY e
closed 25 December – **Meals** (see ***Ziba*** below) – ☕ 10.00 – **8 rm** 95.00.
♦ Ornate Victorian city centre building converted into club offering unusual accommodation. Good leisure facilities open to residents. Simple rooms with good facilities.

Travelodge without rest., 25 Old Haymarket, L1 6ER, ℘ (08700) 850950, *Fax (0151) 227 5835* – |♦| ⋟ TV ♿. MC AE ① VISA JCB. ⅏ DY a
105 rm 79.95.
♦ Purpose-built hotel providing a handy central location for visitors to the city. Dependable standard of accommodation : compact and functional, yet comfortable.

60 Hope Street, 60 Hope St, L1 9BZ, ℘ (0151) 707 6060, *info@60hopestreet.com, Fax (0151) 707 6016* – ▤. MC VISA EZ x
closed 25-26 December, 1 January, Saturday lunch, Sunday and Bank Holidays – **Meals** 14.95 (lunch) and a la carte 28.40/40.85 ♀.
♦ Modern restaurant within an attractive Grade II Georgian house. Informal basement café-bar, brightly decorated dining room and private room above. Modern European cooking.

Simply Heathcotes, Beetham Plaza, 25 The Strand, L2 0XL, ℘ (0151) 236 3536, *liverpool@simplyheathcotes.co.uk, Fax (0151) 236 3534,* 余 – ⋟ ▤. MC AE VISA CY s
closed 25-26 December and Bank Holiday Mondays – **Meals** 15.50 (lunch) and a la carte 15.75/22.50 ♀.
♦ Behind a sloping glass façade is a modish dining room where staff in emblemed shirts serve variations on the classics : hash brown of black pudding. Views of water sculpture.

Ziba (at Racquet Club), Hargreaves Buildings, 5 Chapel St, L3 9AA, ℘ (0151) 236 6676, *Fax (0151) 236 6870* – ▤. MC AE VISA CY e
closed 25 December and Sunday dinner – **Meals** a la carte 18.85/29.95 ♀.
♦ Modern restaurant in old Victorian building with huge windows and artwork on walls. Small lunch menus, more extensive dinner menus, offering classic-based modern dishes.

The Other Place Bistro, 29a Hope St, L1 9BQ, ℘ (0151) 707 7888, *Fax (0151) 707 7888* – MC VISA JCB EZ a
closed 25-26 and 31 December, 1 January, Sunday, Monday, Saturday lunch and Bank Holidays – **Meals** a la carte 18.85/26.15 ♀.
♦ Victorian end of terrace ground floor and basement eatery with green painted brick and wood floors. Good value dishes are supplemented by a concise wine list.

at Knowsley Industrial Park *Northeast : 8 m. by A 59* DY *and A 580* – ✉ *Liverpool*

Suites H., Ribblers Lane, L34 9HA, ℘ (0151) 549 2222, *enquiries@suiteshotelgroup.com, Fax (0151) 549 1116,* ⅎ6, ≘s, ☒ – |♦| ⋟ ▤ TV ℭ ♿ P – ♗ 300. MC AE ① VISA
Meals *(closed lunch Saturday and Sunday)* a la carte 17.75/25.75 **s. 80 suites** ☕ 97.50/107.50.
♦ Adjoins a business park, with smartly designed work areas. A well-equipped, privately owned hotel, ideal for corporate clients. All rooms are comfortably furnished suites. Upbeat, vibrantly decorated dining room.

at Huyton *East : 8 ¼ m. by A5047* EY *and A 5080 on B 5199* – ✉ *Liverpool :*

Village H. and Leisure Club, Fallows Way, L35 1RZ, Southeast : 3 ¼ m. by A 5080 off Whiston rd ℘ (0151) 449 2341, *village.whiston@village-hotels.com, Fax (0151) 449 3832,* ⅎ6, ≘s, ☒, squash – |♦| ⋟, ▤ rest, TV ℭ ♿ P – ♗ 280. MC AE ① VISA. ⅏
Meals 17.50 and a la carte 14.35/24.45 **s.** ♀ – **62 rm** ☕ 98.00/145.00.
♦ Modern, corporate hotel with unrivalled high-tech leisure facilities. A favourite with families at weekends. The spacious bedrooms are comfy and well equipped. Spacious restaurant and conservatory.

at Grassendale *Southeast : 4 ½ m. on A 561 EZ – ✉ Liverpool :*

Gulshan, 544-548 Aigburth Rd, L19 3QG, on A 561 ☎ (0151) 427 2273, *Fax (0151) 427 2111* – . MC AE VISA

Meals - Indian - (dinner only) a la carte approx. 16.80.

◆ A richly decorated and comfortable traditional Indian restaurant within a parade of shops. Smart and efficient service of an extensive menu of authentic dishes.

at Woolton *Southeast : 6 m. by A 562 EZ, A 5058 and Woolton Rd – ✉ Liverpool :*

Woolton Redbourne, Acrefield Rd, L25 5JN, ☎ (0151) 421 1500, *reception@wooltonredbourne.fsnet.co.uk, Fax (0151) 421 1501,* – rest, TV P. MC AE VISA JCB

***Lady Catherine* : Meals** (dinner only and Sunday lunch)/dinner 22.95 and a la carte 22.15/40.90 **s.** – **17 rm** 68.00/99.00, 1 suite.

◆ Imposing Grade II listed Victorian mansion built by Sir Henry Tate in 1884. Period antiques throughout. Many of the spacious rooms overlook the attractive terraced gardens. Partly wood-panelled restaurant.

at Speke *Southeast : 8 ¾ m. by A 561 EZ – ✉ Liverpool*

Liverpool Marriott H. South, Speke Aerodrome, Speke Rd, L24 8QD, West : 1 ¾ m. on A 561 ☎ (0870) 4007269, *reservations.liverpoolsouth@marriotthotels.co.uk, Fax (0151) 494 5051,* , squash – TV P – 350. MC AE VISA.

***Starways* : Meals** *(closed Saturday lunch)* 25.00 (dinner) and a la carte 15.50/25.00 **s.** – 13.95 – **163 rm** 105.00, 1 suite.

◆ Converted Art Deco airport terminal building, built 1937. Aviation and 1930s era the prevailing themes throughout. The modern, well-equipped bedrooms have a stylish appeal. Smart brasserie within original airport terminal ; in keeping with hotel's style.

If you are held up on the road - from 6pm onwards -
confirm your hotel booking by telephone.
It is safer and quite an accepted practice.

MANCHESTER *Gtr Manchester* 502 503 504 N 23 *Great Britain G.* – *pop. 402 889.*

See : *City★ - Castlefield Heritage Park★ CZ – Town Hall★ CZ – Manchester Art Gallery★ CZ* **M2** – *Cathedral★ (stalls and canopies★) CY – Museum of Science and Industry★ CZ* **M** – *Urbis★ CY – National War Museum North★, Trafford Park.*

Envir. : *Whitworth Art Gallery★, S : 1 ½ m.*

Exc. : *Quarry Bank Mill★, S : 10 m. off B 5166, exit 5 from M 56 – Bramall Hall★, SE : 13 m. by A 6 and A 5102.*

Heaton Park, Prestwich ☎ (0161) 654 9899 – Houldsworth Park, Houldsworth St, Reddish, Stockport ☎ (0161) 442 9611 – Chorlton-cum-Hardy, Barlow Hall, Barlow Hall Rd ☎ (0161) 881 3139 – William Wroe, Pennybridge Lane, Flixton ☎ (0161) 748 8680.

Manchester International Airport : ☎ (0161) 489 3000, S : 10 m. by A 5103 and M 56 – **Terminal** : *Coach service from Victoria Station.*

Manchester Visitor Centre, Town Hall Extension, Lloyd St ☎ (0161) 234 3157, manchestervisitorcentre@notes.manchester.gov.uk – Manchester Airport, International Arrivals Hall, Terminal 1 ☎ (0161) 436 3344 – Manchester Airport, International Arrivals Hall, Terminal 2 ☎ (0161) 489 6412 Salford T.I.C., 1 The Quays, Salford ☎ (0161) 848 8601.

London 202 – Birmingham 86 – Glasgow 221 – Leeds 43 – Liverpool 35 – Nottingham 72.

Plan on next page

The Lowry, 50 Dearmans Pl, Chapel Wharf, Salford, M3 5LH, ☎ (0161) 827 4000, *enquiries@thelowryhotel.com, Fax (0161) 827 4001,* – TV P – 400. MC AE VISA CY n

Meals (see ***River Room Marco Pierre White*** below) – 16.50 – **158 rm** 209.00/239.00, 7 suites.

◆ Stylish contemporary design with a minimalist feel. Smart spacious bedrooms have high levels of comfort and facilities ; some overlook River Irwell. State-of-the-art spa.

Crowne Plaza Manchester-The Midland, Peter St, M60 2DS, ☎ (0161) 236 3333, *reservations.cpmanchester@ichotelsgroup.com, Fax (0161) 932 4100,* , squash – , rm, TV P – 450. MC AE VISA CZ x

Trafford Room* : Meals** *(closed Monday and Tuesday dinner and Saturday lunch)* (carving rest.) 16.95/26.95 (see also ***The French and ***Nico Central*** below) – 14.50 – **289 rm** 160.00, 14 suites.

◆ Edwardian splendour on a vast scale in the heart of the city. Period features and a huge open lobby combine with up-to-date facilities to create a thoroughly grand hotel. Classically proportioned restaurant with carvery based menu.

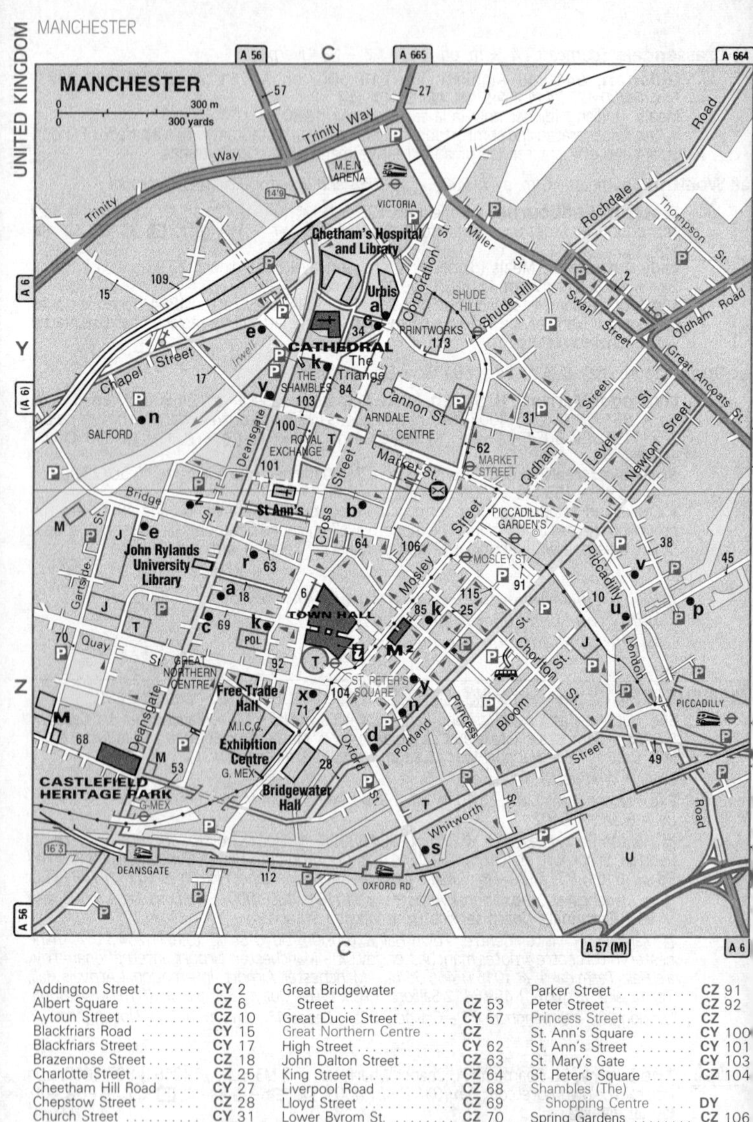

Addington Street	CY 2	Great Bridgewater Street	CZ 53	Parker Street	CZ 91
Albert Square	CZ 6	Great Ducie Street	CY 57	Peter Street	CZ 92
Aytoun Street	CZ 10	Great Northern Centre	CZ	Princess Street	CZ
Blackfriars Road	CY 15	High Street	CY 62	St. Ann's Square	CY 100
Blackfriars Street	CY 17	John Dalton Street	CZ 63	St. Ann's Street	CY 101
Brazennose Street	CZ 18	King Street	CZ 64	St. Mary's Gate	CY 103
Charlotte Street	CZ 25	Liverpool Road	CZ 68	St. Peter's Square	CZ 104
Cheetham Hill Road	CY 27	Lloyd Street	CZ 69	Shambles (The) Shopping Centre	DY
Chepstow Street	CZ 28	Lower Byrom St.	CZ 70	Spring Gardens	CZ 106
Church Street	CY 31	Lower Mosley Street	CZ 71	Viaduct Street	CY 109
Corn Exchange	CY 34	Mosley Street	CZ	Whitworth Street West	CZ 112
Dale Street	CZ 38	New Cathedral Street	CY 84	Withy Grove	CY 113
Deansgate	CYZ	Nicholas Street	CZ 85	York Street	CZ 115
Ducie Street	CZ 45				
Fairfield Street	CZ 49				

Le Meridien Victoria and Albert, Water St, M3 4JQ, ✆ (0161) 832 1188, *front office.manchester@hotels.com, Fax (0161) 834 2484* – |‡|, ⇔ rm, ▤ TV ✆ ♿ P – 🎪 250. MO AE ① VISA. ✻ by Quay St CZ
***Sherlock Holmes :* Meals** (bar lunch Monday-Saturday)/dinner 25.00 and a la carte 25.00/35.50 ♀ – ☕ 14.95 – **154 rm** 170.00, 4 suites.
◆ Restored 19C warehouses on the banks of the River Irwell, with exposed brick and original beams and columns. Bedrooms take their themes from Granada Television productions. Restaurant proud of its timbered warehouse origins.

Malmaison, Piccadilly, M1 3AQ, ✆ (0161) 278 1000, *manchester@malmaison.com, Fax (0161) 278 1002,* ⅼ₅, ⇌ – |‡|, ⇹ rm, ▤ TV ✆ ♿ – 🏃 75. MO AE ⓓ VISA. ✗ CZ u
Brasserie : **Meals** 12.95/13.95 and a la carte 19.85/29.45 ♀ – ☕ 11.95 – **154 rm** 125.00, 13 suites.
• A more modern brand of hotel that combines contemporary design and fresh décor with an informal and unstuffy atmosphere. Bedrooms are bright, stylish and hi-tech. Bright, characterful brasserie.

Renaissance, Blackfriars St, Deansgate, M3 2EQ, ✆ (0161) 831 6000, *manchester.sales@renaissancehotels.com, Fax (0161) 835 3077* – |‡| ⇹ ▤ TV ✆ P – 🏃 250. MO AE ⓓ VISA CY v
Robbies : **Meals** 15.50 (dinner) and a la carte 23.65/31.95 ♀ – ☕ 12.50 – **196 rm** 129.00, 4 suites.
• Converted 15-storey office block with large, marbled lobby well sited at top of Deansgate. Spacious, well-equipped bedrooms, most enjoying city skyline views. Airy dining room with adjacent bar.

Le Meridien Palace, Oxford St, M60 7HA, ✆ (0161) 288 1111, *Fax (0161) 288 2222* – |‡| ⇹ TV ✆ – 🏃 700. MO AE VISA. ✗ CZ s
Waterhouses : **Meals** (carvery lunch)/dinner 23.95 – ☕ 14.95 – **233 rm** 170.00, 19 suites.
• This former Refuge Assurance building boasts stunning Victorian Gothic architecture. Equally ornate interior with pillars and marble. Some particularly capacious bedrooms. A striking bar, comfortable lounge and restaurant with liveried staff.

The Place without rest., Ducie St, M1 2TP, ✆ (0161) 778 7500, *reservations@theplaceforliving.com, Fax (0161) 778 7507* – |‡| ⇹ TV ✆ P. MO AE ⓓ VISA JCB. ✗ CZ p
108 suites 99.00/295.00.
• Unique to the city : an impressive 19C former warehouse with stylish apartments or penthouses available for lets. All contain fully equipped kitchen and lounge with mod cons.

Rossetti, 107 Piccadilly, M1 2DB, ✆ (0161) 247 7744, *info@aliasrossetti.com, Fax (0161) 247 7747* – |‡| ⇹ TV ✆. MO AE VISA CZ v
Cafe Paradiso : **Meals** a la carte 17.15/26.20 **s.** ♀ – ☕ 10.95 – **57 rm** 105.00/145.00, 4 suites.
• Former 19C textile factory with original features : tiled staircases, cast iron pillars. Staff, by contrast, in casual attire. Chic basement bar. Rooms exude designer style. Informal restaurant with wood-burning stove and rotisserie dishes.

Novotel, 21 Dickinson St, M1 4LX, ✆ (0161) 235 2200, *h3145-gm@accor-hotels.com, Fax (0161) 235 2210,* ⅼ₅, ⇌ – |‡|, ⇹ rm, ▤ TV ✆ ♿ – 🏃 90. MO AE ⓓ VISA JCB
Meals 13.85/16.75 and a la carte 16.95/28.95 ♀ – ☕ 12.00 – **164 rm** 103.00. CZ n
• The open-plan lobby boasts a spacious, stylish bar and residents can take advantage of an exclusive exercise area. Decently equipped, tidily appointed bedrooms. Compact dining room with grill-style menus.

Premier Lodge, North Tower, Victoria Bridge St, Salford, M3 5AS, ✆ (0870) 7001488, *mpremierlodge1@snr.co.uk, Fax (0870) 7001489* – |‡| ⇹, ▤ rest, TV ✆ ♿ P – 🏃 35. MO AE ⓓ VISA. ✗ CY e
Meals (grill rest.) (dinner only) a la carte approx 14.50 – **170 rm** 50.00.
• Modern accommodation with bright, well-planned rooms. Convenient city centre location close to Deansgate and Victoria station. The higher the room the better the view.

Travel Inn Metro, 112-114 Portland St, M1 4WB, ✆ (0870) 2383315, *Fax (0161) 233 5299* – |‡| ⇹, ▤ rest, TV ✆ ♿ P. MO AE ⓓ VISA JCB. ✗ CZ d
Meals (grill rest.) – **225 rm** 49.95.
• Maintains the group's reputation for affordable accommodation and simple contemporary styling. Neat, bright rooms, spacious and carefully designed.

The French (at Crowne Plaza Manchester-The Midland H.), Peter St, M60 2DS, ✆ (0161) 236 3333 – ⇹ ▤ P. MO AE ⓓ VISA CZ x
closed Sunday – **Meals** (dinner only) 29.00 and a la carte 40.85/53.85 ♀.
• As grand as the hotel in which it is housed, with gilded paintings, large mirrors and heavy drapes. Attentively formal service, classically French-based cooking.

Le Mont, Urbis, Levels 5 and 6, Cathedral Gardens, M4 3BG, ✆ (0161) 605 8282, *robert@urbis.org.uk, Fax (0161) 605 8283,* ≤ – |‡| ⇹ ▤. MO AE VISA CY a
closed 24 December-7 January, Saturday lunch, Sunday and Bank Holidays – **Meals** a la carte 26.95/33.95 ♀.
• Set on top of the Urbis Museum, boasting spectacular views of the city : formal dining in dramatic surroundings. Imaginative modern cuisine based around a classic French style.

River Room Marco Pierre White (at The Lowry H.), 50 Dearmans Pl, Chapel Wharf, Salford, M3 5LH, ✆ (0161) 827 4003, *enquiries@thelowryhotel.com, Fax (0161) 827 4001,* 🍽 – ▤ P. MO AE ⓓ VISA CY n
Meals 18.00/35.00 and a la carte 18.25/36.00 **s.** ♀.
• Matching its surroundings, this is a stylish modern restaurant serving, in a precise manner, classic dishes that have stood the test of time. Irwell views, for good measure.

XX **Second Floor - Restaurant** (at Harvey Nichols), 21 New Cathedral St, M1 1AD, ☎ (0161) 828 8898, *Fax (0161) 828 8570* – ⇔ ▤. MC AE D VISA JCB CY k
closed 25-26 December, 1 January and Sunday dinner – **Meals** a la carte 20.00/33.00 ♀.
◆ Central location on second floor of a department store. Well-designed restaurant with immaculate linen-clad tables. Brasserie style cooking.

XX **Yang Sing,** 34 Princess St, M1 4JY, ☎ (0161) 236 2200, *info@yang-sing.com, Fax (0161) 236 5934* – ▤. MC AE VISA CZ y
closed 25 December – **Meals** - Chinese - a la carte 20.00/30.00 ☺.
◆ This most renowned of Chinese restaurants continues to provide some of the most authentic, carefully prepared and varied cooking of its kind to be found in the country.

XX **Nico Central** (at Crowne Plaza Manchester-The Midland H.), 2 Mount St, M60 2DS, ☎ (0161) 236 6488, *manchester@nicocentral.co.uk, Fax (0161) 236 8897* – ▤. MC AE D VISA CZ x
closed Saturday lunch, Sunday and Bank Holidays – **Meals** 13.95 (lunch) and a la carte 22.40/29.85 ☺ ♀.
◆ Contemporary in style with high ceilings, bold colours and an array of mirrors that add to the subtle Art Deco feel. Cooking has its roots in classic Continental techniques.

XX **Hurricane Bar & Grill,** King St, Spring Gardens, M2 4ST, ☎ (0161) 835 2785, *Fax (0161) 834 6364* – ⇔. MC AE D VISA JCB CZ n
closed 25-26 December, 1-2 January and Sunday – **Meals** a la carte 17.40/36.40 ♀.
◆ Former Victorian club in city centre with original fireplace and windows contrasting with elegant modern tables. Attractive menu of modern grill-based dishes ; very flexible.

XX **The Lincoln,** 1 Lincoln Sq, M2 5LN, ☎ (0161) 834 9000, *mail@thelincolnrestaurant.com, Fax (0161) 834 9555* – ▤. MC AE D VISA CZ a
closed 25-26 December, 1 January, Saturday lunch, Sunday dinner and Bank Holidays – **Meals** 14.50 (lunch) and a la carte 22.90/31.85 ☺ ♀.
◆ Tucked away in a central square, this modern restaurant proves popular with the business community. An interesting menu with original dishes in a contemporary style.

XX **Pacific,** 58-60 George St, M1 4HF, ☎ (0161) 228 6668, *enquiries@pacific-restaurant-manchester.co.uk, Fax (0161) 236 0191* – |♦| ▤. MC AE D VISA CZ k
Meals - Chinese and Thai - 9.50/38.50 and a la carte 21.00/34.00.
◆ Located in Chinatown : Chinese cuisine on first floor, Thai on the second ; modern décor incorporating subtle Asian influences. Large menus boast high levels of authenticity.

XX **Simply Heathcotes,** Jackson Row, M2 5WD, ☎ (0161) 835 3536, *manchester@simplyheathcotes.co.uk, Fax (0161) 835 3534* – |♦| ⇔ ▤. MC AE D VISA CZ c
closed 25-26 December, 1 January and Bank Holidays except Good Friday – **Meals** 15.50 (lunch) and a la carte 15.70/25.00 ☺ ♀.
◆ Contemporary interior, with live jazz in the wine bar, contrasts with the original oak panels of this Victorian former register office. Robust menu is equally à la mode.

XX **Koreana,** Kings House, 40a King St West, M3 2WY, ☎ (0161) 832 4330, *alexkoreana@aol.com, Fax (0161) 832 2293* – MC AE D VISA CZ z
closed 25-26 December, 1 January, 1 week August, Sunday, lunch Saturday and Bank Holidays – **Meals** - Korean - 12.40 and a la carte 11.50/26.50 ☺.
◆ Family run basement restaurant, bustling yet still relaxed, offers authentic, balanced Korean cuisine. Novices are guided gently through the menu by staff in national dress.

X **The Restaurant Bar and Grill,** 14 John Dalton St, M2 6JR, ☎ (0161) 839 1999, *Fax (0161) 835 1886* – ▤. MC AE D VISA CZ r
closed 25-26 December – **Meals** a la carte 12.30/27.95 ♀.
◆ Stylish ground floor lounge bar and lively first floor eatery. Extensive international repertoire from an open kitchen. Very busy with business community at lunch.

X **Second Floor - Brasserie** (at Harvey Nichols), 21 New Cathedral St, M1 1AH, ☎ (0161) 828 8898, *secondfloor.reservations@harveynichols.com, Fax (0161) 828 8815* – ⇔ ▤. MC AE D VISA CY k
closed Sunday dinner – **Meals** a la carte 17.00/24.50 ♀.
◆ Open and lively restaurant with minimalist décor. Wide range of cocktails available at the large bar. Attractive menu with a European eclectic mix of dishes.

X **Le Petit Blanc,** 55 King St, M2 4LQ, ☎ (0161) 832 1000, *Fax (0161) 832 1001* – ▤. MC AE VISA CZ b
closed 25 December – **Meals** 16.00 (lunch) and a la carte 18.75/30.70 ☺ ♀.
◆ Busy, group-owned brasserie with large bar and polished tables. Extensive menus of classic and modern British dishes as well as regional French options. Attentive service.

X **Palmiro,** 197 Upper Chorlton Rd, M16 0BH, South : 2 m. by A 56 off Chorlton Rd ☎ (0161) 860 7330, *bookings@palmiro.net, Fax (0161) 861 7464,* 🏠 – MC VISA JCB
Meals - Italian - (dinner only and Sunday lunch)/dinner a la carte 17.45/22.40 **s.**
◆ Spartan interior with grey mottled walls and halogen lighting : a highly regarded neighbourhood Italian eatery boasting good value rustic dishes cooked with maximum simplicity.

Livebait, 22 Lloyd St, Albert Sq, M2 5WA, (0161) 817 4110, *lbmanchester@groupechezgerard.co.uk, Fax (0161) 817 4111* – CZ k
closed 25-26 December, 1 January, Sunday and Bank Holiday Mondays – **Meals** - Seafood - 10.95/13.95 and a la carte 19.20/30.65
• A friendly atmosphere in which to dine at linen-clad tables amid Art Deco styling. Plenty of choice from seafood oriented menus ; indeed, crustacea are on display.

Shimla Pinks, Dolefield Crown Sq, M3 3EN, (0161) 831 7099, *Fax (0161) 832 2202* – CZ e
closed 25-27 December, 1-2 January and lunch Saturday and Sunday – **Meals** - Indian - 8.95/14.95 and a la carte 17.45/23.15.
• Centrally located Indian restaurant. Colourful artwork and murals and a bustling modern ambience. Extensive menus of authentic Indian dishes and regional specialities.

Zinc Bar & Grill, The Triangle, Hanging Ditch, M4 3ES, (0870) 3334333, *zinc@conran-restaurants.co.uk, Fax (0161) 827 4212,* – CY c
Meals 15.00 (lunch) and a la carte 16.00/26.50.
• Converted 19C corn exchange with bustling atmosphere, background jazz and a late-night bar. Tables available on pavement and in shopping centre. Modern international menu.

at Crumpsall *North : 3 ½ m. on A 56 CY and A 576 – Manchester*

Travel Inn, Middleton Rd, M8 4NB, (0161) 720 6171, *Fax (0161) 740 9142* – rm, rest,
Meals (grill rest.) – **45 rm** 44.95.
• Good value, group owned, purpose-built lodge set on a main road in the city's suburbs. Bedrooms decorated in a uniform fitted modern style. Rear rooms quietest.

at Didsbury *South : 5 ½ m. by A 5103 CZ on A 5145 – Manchester*

Didsbury House, Didsbury Park, M20 5LJ, South : 1 ½ m. on A 5145 (0161) 448 2200, *enquiries@didsburyhouse.co.uk, Fax (0161) 448 2525,* –
Meals (room service only) – 11.50 – **22 rm** 125.00, 4 suites.
• Grade II listed 19C house : grand wooden staircase, superb stained glass window. Otherwise, stylish and modern with roof-top hot tubs. Spacious, individually designed rooms.

Eleven Didsbury Park, 11 Didsbury Park, M20 5LH, South : ½ m. by A 5145 (0161) 448 7711, *enquiries@elevendidsburypark.com, Fax (0161) 448 8282,* –
Meals (room service only) – 11.50 – **14 rm** 125.00/160.00.
• The cool contemporary design in this Victorian town house creates a serene and relaxing atmosphere. Good-sized bedrooms decorated with flair and style. Personally run.

Cafe Jem &I, 1c School Lane, M20 6SA, (0161) 445 3996, *jemosullivan@aol.com* –
closed 25-26 December, lunch Monday and dinner Bank Holidays – **Meals** 11.95 and a la carte 17.95/26.70 **s.**
• Simple, unpretentious cream coloured building tucked away off the high street. Open-plan kitchen ; homely, bistro feel. Good value, tasty modern classics.

at Manchester Airport *South : 9 m. by Lower Mosley St. CZ and A 5103 off M 56 – Manchester :*

Radisson SAS Manchester Airport, Chicago Ave, M90 3RA, (0161) 490 5000, *sales.airport.manchester@radissonsas.com, Fax (0161) 490 5100,* – rm, – 250.
Phileas Fogg : **Meals** *(closed Saturday lunch)* (buffet lunch) 19.99/31.50 – ***Runway Brasserie :*** **Meals** a la carte 16.50/20.50 **s.** – 14.50 – **354 rm** 150.00, 6 suites.
• Vast, modern hotel linked to airport passenger walkway. Four room styles with many extras. Ideal for business clients or travellers. Phileas Fogg is curved restaurant with eclectic menus and runway views. All-day Runway with arrivals/departures info.

Hilton Manchester Airport, Outwood Lane (Terminal One), M90 4WP, (0161) 435 3000, *Fax (0161) 435 3040,* – rm, – 300.
Meals 21.00 and a la carte – ***Lowry's :*** **Meals** *(closed Saturday lunch)* 12.95/25.00 and dinner a la carte – 16.50 – **224 rm** 165.00, 1 suite.
• Popular with corporate travellers for its business centre and location 200 metres from the airport terminal. Comfortable, soundproofed bedrooms. Portico is fine dining room. Open-plan bar leads to informal Lowry's.

Etrop Grange, Thorley Lane, M90 4EG, (0161) 499 0500, *etropgrange@corushotels.com, Fax (0161) 499 0790* – – 80.
The Restaurant : **Meals** 15.00/36.95 and a la carte 19.70/31.90 **s.** – 13.50 – **62 rm** 129.00/149.00, 2 suites.
• Sympathetically extended Georgian house that retains a period feel. Rooms vary in size ; all are pleasantly decorated with some boasting four-posters, others cast-iron beds. Intimate, traditionally styled dining room.

Bewley's, Outwood Lane, (Terminal One), M90 4HL, ☎ (0161) 498 0333, *man@bewleyshotels.com, Fax (0161) 498 0222* – rm, rest, – 90.
Meals (bar lunch)/dinner 14.95 and a la carte 21.00/26.00 **s.** – 6.95 – **226 rm** 59.00/99.00.
♦ Good value, four-storey, purpose-built group hotel with modern, open lobby. Brightly decorated bedrooms that all have either one double bed and sofa or two double beds. Main restaurant or lobby café dining options.

Moss Nook, Ringway Rd, Moss Nook, M22 5WD, East : 1 ¼ m. on Cheadle rd ☎ (0161) 437 4778, *Fax (0161) 498 8089*, –
closed 2 weeks Christmas-New Year, Saturday lunch, Sunday and Monday – **Meals** 19.50/36.50 and a la carte 32.00/49.25.
♦ Decorated in a combination of Art Nouveau, lace and panelling. Long-standing owners provide polished and ceremonial service ; cooking is robust and classically based.

at Trafford Park *Southwest : 2 m. by A 56 CZ and A 5081 – ✉ Manchester*

Golden Tulip, Waters Reach, M17 1WS, ☎ (0161) 873 8899, *info@goldentulipmanchester.co.uk, Fax (0161) 872 6556* – – 180.
Meals (see ***Watersreach*** below) – 12.00 – **157 rm** 105.00, 3 suites.
♦ Manchester United fans will not only appreciate the proximity to the ground but also the football paraphernalia in the lobby. Uniformly decorated bedrooms are a good size.

Old Trafford Lodge without rest., Lancashire County Cricket Club, Talbot Rd, Old Trafford, M16 0PX, ☎ (0161) 874 3333, *lodge@lccc.co.uk, Fax (0161) 282 4068*, –
closed 1 week Christmas-New Year – **68 rm** 54.00/59.00.
♦ Purpose-built lodge within Lancashire County Cricket Club ; half the rooms have balconies overlooking the ground. Good value accommodation in smart, colourful bedrooms.

Watersreach, Waters Reach, M17 1WS, ☎ (0161) 868 1900, *watersreach@goldentulipmanchester.co.uk, Fax (0161) 868 1901* –
closed lunch Saturday, Sunday and Bank Holidays – **Meals** a la carte 18.85/27.95.
♦ Modern, stylish, David Collins designed restaurant, adjacent to Old Trafford. Smart bar area has comfortable seating. Good, eclectic mix of precisely cooked dishes.

at Salford Quays *Southwest : 2 ¼ m. by A 56 CZ off A 5063 – ✉ Manchester*

Copthorne Manchester, Clippers Quay, M50 3SN, ☎ (0161) 873 7321, *roomsales.manchester@mill-cop.com, Fax (0161) 873 7318* – rm, rest, – 150. by A 56 CZ
Chandlers : **Meals** *(closed Sunday)* (dinner only) a la carte 22.80/41.45 **s.** – ***Clippers :*** **Meals** (carving rest.) (bar lunch Saturday) a la carte 20.20/30.70 **s.** – 15.25 – **166 rm** 155.00/215.00.
♦ Part of the redeveloped Quays, overlooking the waterfront, with a Metrolink to the City. Connoisseur bedrooms are particularly well-appointed.

Express by Holiday Inn without rest., Waterfront Quay, M5 2XW, ☎ (0161) 868 1000, *managersalfordquays@expressholidayinn.co.uk, Fax (0161) 868 1068*, – – 25.
120 rm 75.00.
♦ Its pleasant quayside position and modern, well-equipped bedrooms make it a popular choice with both business and leisure travellers. Complimentary breakfast provided.

at Eccles *West : 4 m. by A 56 CZ, A 57 and M 602 – ✉ Manchester*

Highbury without rest., 113 Monton Rd, M30 9HQ, Northwest : 1 ¼ m. by A 576 on B 5229 ☎ (0161) 787 8545, *enquiries@highbury-hotel.co.uk, Fax (0161) 787 9023* –
16 rm 38.00/49.50.
♦ Located in a residential area and providing good value accommodation. Friendly, family run, part 19C house with a homely feel and comfortable rooms, quieter at the rear.

at Worsley *West : 7 ¼ m. by A 6 CY, A 5063, M 602 and M 62 (eastbound) on A 572 – ✉ Manchester :*

Marriott Worsley Park Hotel & Country Club, Worsley Park, M28 2QT, on A 575 ☎ (0870) 400 7270, *reservations@worsleypark@marriotthotels.co.uk, Fax (0870) 400 7370*, – rm, rest, – 250.
Brindley's : **Meals** *(closed Saturday lunch)* (carving lunch) 15.50/32.50 and dinner a la carte 26.45/36.30 **s.** – 13.95 – **153 rm** 115.00, 5 suites.
♦ Built around restored Victorian farm buildings in over 200 acres. Excellent leisure facilities including a championship standard golf course. Large, well-equipped bedrooms. Restaurant is former farm building with high beamed ceiling.

Calendar of main tradefairs and other international events in 2004

AUSTRIA

Vienna	*Wiener Festwochen*	*7 May to 12 June*
Salzburg	*Salzburg Festival (Festspiele)*	*3 to 12 April* *26 July to 31 August*

BENELUX

Amsterdam	*Holland Festival*	*17 to 22 February*
Bruges	*The Holy Blood Procession*	*Ascension*
Brussels	*Guild Procession (Ommegang)*	*first Thursday of July and the previous Tuesday*
	Holiday and Leisure Activities International Show	*18 to 22 March*
	Belgian Antique Dealers Fair	*6 to 15 February*
	Eurantica (Antiques Show)	*18 to 28 March*

CZECH REPUBLIC

Prague	*Spring International Music Festival*	*6 May to 15 May*
	International Book Fair	*6 to 9 May*

DENMARK

Copenhagen	*Fashion and Design Festival*	*April*
	Tivoli Gardens	*16 April to 19 Sept.*
	Jazz Festival	*2 to 11 July*
	International Ballet Festival	*August*
	Golden Days Festival	*3 to 26 Sept.*
	Night of Culture	*8 October*
	Tivoli Christmas Market	*mid Nov. to 23 Dec.*

FINLAND

Helsinki	*Finnish Boat Fair*	*6 to 15 February*
	Helsinki Festival	*20 August to 5 Sept.*
	Helsinki International Horse Show	*14 to 17 October*

FRANCE

Paris	*Paris Fair* *International Tourism Show* *Book Fair*	*29 April to 9 May* *11 to 14 March* *19 to 24 March*
Cannes	*International Film Festival*	*12 to 23 May*
Lyons	*Lyons Fair*	*12 to 22 March*
Marseilles	*Marseilles Christmas Fair*	*Last weekend November to 31 December*
Monaco	*Spring Art Festival*	*8 to 18 April*
Nice	*Carnival*	*13 to 25 February*
Strasbourg	*Christmas Market*	*End of November to Christmas*
	European Fair	*3 to 13 September*

GERMANY

Berlin	*Berlin Fair (Grüne Woche)*	*16 to 25 January*
Frankfurt	*International Fair*	*20 to 24 Feb. and 27 to 31 August*
	Frankfurt Book Fair	*6 to 11 October*
Hanover	*Hanover Fair*	*18 to 24 March*
Leipzig	*International Book Fair*	*25 to 28 March*
Munich	*Beer Festival (Oktoberfest)*	*18 Sept. to 3 Oct.*

GREECE

Athens	*Athens Festival*	*June to Oct.*

HUNGARY

Budapest	*Spring Festival* *Fashion Days* *11th International Wine and Champagne Festival* *Autumn Festival*	*19 March to 4 April* *25 to 27 August* *5 to 15 Sept.* *21 Oct. to 31 Nov.*

IRELAND

Dublin	*St Patrick's Festival*	*17 March*
	Dublin International Film Festival *Dublin Horse Show*	*12 to 22 February* *6 to 10 August*

ITALY

Milan	Bit (International Tourism Exchange)	14 to 18 February
	Fashion Fair (Moda Milano)	22 February to 1 March 26 September to 4 October
	SMAU (International Exhibition of Information and Communication Technology)	21 to 25 October
Florence	Pitti Bimbo	2 to 4 July
	Fashion Fair (Pitti Immagine Uomo)	24 to 27 June
Turin	International Book Fair	6 to 10 May
Venice	International Film Festival	last week August-first week September
	The Carnival	6 to 24 February

NORWAY

Oslo	World Cup Nordic Skiing and Ski Jumping	13 to 17 March
	International Jazz Festival	11 to 17 August
	Fashion Fair	last week August
	Horse Show	24 to 26 October
	International Film Festival	14 to 24 Nov.

POLAND

Warsaw	International Book Fair	20 to 23 May
	Mozart Festival	15 June to 26 July
	Jazz Jamboree	22 to 24 October

PORTUGAL

Lisbon	Contemporary Art Fair	18 to 22 November

SPAIN

Madrid	Fitur	26 to 30 January 2005
	Madrid International Auto Show	20 to 30 May
Barcelona	International Tourism Show in Catalonia	22 to 25 April
Seville	April Fair	27 April to 2 May
València	Fallas	15 to 19 March
	Automobile Trade Fair	27 November to 8 December

SWEDEN

Stockholm	International Furniture Fair	4 to 8 February
	International Antique Fair	13 to 15 February
	Restaurant Days	30 May to 2 June
	Festival of Steam Boats	2 June
	Jazz Festival	17 to 24 July
	International Film Festival	11 to 21 November
	Nobel Prize Day	10 December
Gothenburg	Boat Show	31 Jan to 8 Feb.
	Motor Show	19 to 22 Feb.
	International Horse Show	8 to 12 April
	Ice Hockey World Championship	26 April to 11 May
	International Book Fair	23 to 26 Sept.
	International Consumer Goods Fair	26 to 30 September

SWITZERLAND

Bern	BEA : Exhibition for Handicraft, Agriculture, Trade and Industry	23 April to 2 May
Basle	Baselworld European Watch, Clock and Jewellery Fair	15 to 22 April
Geneva	International Exhibition of inventions, new technologies and products	31 March to 4 April
	International Motor Show	3 to 13 March 2005
Zürich	Züspa : Zurich Autumn Show for Home and Living, Sport and Fashion	23 September to 3 October

UNITED KINGDOM

London	Book Fair	14 to 16 March
	Fine Art and Antiques Fair	3 to 13 June
	International Map Fair	5 to 6 June
	International Film Festival	2 weeks October
Birmingham	Motor Show	27 May to 6 June
	Antiques for Everyone	15 to 18 April
	International Motorcycle & Scooter Show	4 to 14 November
	Toy Collectors Fair	29 August
	Horse of the Year	6 to 10 Oct.
Edinburgh	Military Tattoo	6 to 28 August
	Fringe Festival	8 to 30 August
	International Book Festival	14 to 30 August
	International Film Festival	14 to 28 August
	International Festival	15 August to 4 Sept.
Glasgow	West End Festival	11 to 27 June
	International Jazz Festival	28 June to 7 July
	Antiques for Everyone	18 to 20 June
Leeds	International Film Festival	7 to 17 Oct.

International Dialling Codes

Note : when making an international call, do not dial the first "0" of the city codes (except for calls to Italy).

Indicatifs Téléphoniques Internationaux

Important : Pour les communications internationales, le zéro (0) initial de l'indicatif interurbain n'est pas à composer (excepté pour les appels vers l'Italie).

from \ to	A	B	CH	CZ	D	DK	E	FIN	F	GB	GR
A Austria		0032	0041	00420	0049	0045	0034	00358	0033	0044	0030
B Belgium	0043		0041	00420	0049	0045	0034	00358	0033	0044	0030
CH Switzerland	0043	0032		00420	0049	0045	0034	00358	0033	0044	0030
CZ Czech Republic	0043	0032	0041		0049	0045	0034	00358	0033	0044	0030
D Germany	0043	0032	0041	00420		0045	0034	00358	0033	0044	0030
DK Denmark	0043	0032	0041	00420	0049		0034	00358	0033	0044	0030
E Spain	0043	0032	0041	00420	0049	0045		00358	0033	0044	0030
FIN Finland	0043	0032	0041	00420	0049	0045	0034		0033	0044	0030
F France	0043	0032	0041	00420	0049	0045	0034	00358		0044	0030
GB United Kingdom	0043	0032	0041	00420	0049	0045	0034	00358	0033		0030
GR Greece	0043	0032	0041	00420	0049	0045	0034	00358	0033	0044	
H Hungary	0043	0032	0041	00420	0049	0045	0034	00358	0033	0044	0030
I Italy	0043	0032	0041	00420	0049	0045	0034	00358	0033	0044	0030
IRL Ireland	0043	0032	0041	00420	0049	0045	0034	00358	0033	0044	0030
J Japan	00143	00132	00141	001420	0149	00145	00134	001358	00133	00144	00130
L Luxembourg	0043	0032	0041	00420	0049	0045	0034	00358	0033	0044	0030
N Norway	0043	0032	0041	00420	0049	0045	0034	00358	0033	0044	0030
NL Netherlands	0043	0032	0041	00420	0049	0045	0034	00358	0033	0044	0030
PL Poland	0043	0032	0041	00420	0049	0045	0034	00358	0033	0044	0030
P Portugal	0043	0032	0041	00420	0049	0045	0034	00358	0033	0044	0030
RUS Russia	81043	81032	81041	810420	81049	81045	81034	810358	81033	81044	81030
S Sweden	0043	0032	0041	00420	0049	0045	0034	00358	0033	0044	0030
USA	01143	01132	01141	011420	01149	01145	01134	011358	01133	01144	01130

* *Direct dialing not possible** * *Pas de sélection automatique*

Internationale Telefon-Vorwahlnummern

Wichtig : bei Auslandsgesprächen darf die Null (0) der Ortsnetzkennzahl nicht gewählt werden (ausser bei Gesprächen nach Italien).

Indicativi Telefonici Internationali

Importante: per le comunicazioni internazionali, non bisogna comporre lo zero (0) iniziale dell'indicativo interurbano (escluse le chiamate per l'Italia).

Prefijos telefónicos internacionales

Importante: para las llamadas internacionales, no se debe marcar el cero (0) inicial del prefijo interurbano (excepto para llamar a Italia).

H	I	IRL	J	L	N	NL	PL	P	RUS	S	USA	
0036	0039	00353	0081	00352	0047	0031	0048	00351	007	0046	001	**Austria A**
0036	0039	00353	0081	00352	0047	0031	0048	00351	007	0046	001	**Belgium B**
0036	0039	00353	0081	00352	0047	0031	0048	00351	007	0046	001	**Switzerland CH**
0036	0039	00353	0081	00352	0047	0031	0048	00351	007	0046	001	**Czech Republic CZ**
0036	0039	00353	0081	00352	0047	0031	0048	00351	007	0046	001	**Germany D**
0036	0039	00353	0081	00352	0047	0031	0048	00351	007	0046	001	**Denmark DK**
0036	0039	00353	0081	00352	0047	0031	0048	00351	007	0046	001	**Spain E**
0036	0039	00353	0081	00352	0047	0031	0048	00351	007	0046	001	**Finland FIN**
0036	0039	00353	0081	00352	0047	0031	0048	00351	007	0046	001	**France F**
0036	0039	00353	0081	00352	0047	0031	0048	00351	007	0046	001	**United Kingdom GB**
0036	0039	00353	0081	00352	0047	0031	0048	00351	007	0046	001	**Greece GR**
	0039	00353	0081	00352	0047	0031	0048	00351	007	0046	001	**Hungary H**
0036		00353	0081	00352	0047	0031	0048	00351	*	0046	001	**Italy I**
0036	0039		0081	00352	0047	0031	0048	00351	007	0046	001	**Ireland IRL**
00136	00139	001353		001352	00147	00131	00148	001351	*	00146	0011	**Japan J**
0036	0039	00353	0081		0047	0031	0048	00351	007	0046	001	**Luxembourg L**
0036	0039	00353	0081	00352		0031	0048	00351	007	0046	001	**Norway N**
0036	0039	00353	0081	00352	0047		0048	00351	007	0046	001	**Netherlands NL**
0036	00390	00353	0081	00352	0047	0031		00351	007	0046	001	**Poland PL**
0036	0039	00353	0081	00352	0047	0031	0048		007	0046	001	**Portugal P**
81036	81039	810353	81081	810352	81047	81031	81048	810351		81046	8101	**Russia RUS**
0036	0039	00353	0081	00352	0047	0031	0048	00351	007		001	**Sweden S**
01136	01139	011353	01181	011352	01147	01131	01148	011351	*	01146		**USA**

** Automatische Vorwahl nicht möglich * Selezione automatica impossibile * No es posible la conexión automática*

Manufacture française des pneumatiques Michelin
Société en commandite par actions au capital de 304 000 000 EUR
Place des Carmes-Déchaux – 63 Clermont-Ferrand (France)
R.C.S. Clermont-Fd B 855 200 507

Michelin et Cie, propriétaires-éditeurs, 2004
Dépôt légal : mars 2004 – ISBN 2.06.710248-6

Printed in Belgium : 02-2004/1

Compogravure : Maury imprimeur S.A., Malesherbes

Impression : Casterman Printing, Tournai

Reliure : SIRC, Marigny-le-Châtel

Illustrations : Nathalie Benavides, Patricia Haubert, Cécile Imbert/MICHELIN
Narratif Systèmes/Genclo, Rodolphe Corbel.